EX
LIBRIS

Kevin P. McGrath

The Shell Guide to England

Cover picture: Kentish oast houses. From a painting by Rowland Hilder

End-papers: A view from the South Downs below Firle Beacon. *Photo by Noel Habgood*

The Shell Guide to
England

Edited by John Hadfield

Preface by J. B. Priestley

Introductory essays by

John Arlott
Phyllis Bentley
Ronald Blythe
Ivor Brown
Richard Church
Olive Cook
Phil Drabble
Peter Fleetwood-Hesketh
H. L. V. Fletcher
G. E. Fussell
Geoffrey Grigson
Miles Hadfield

Jacquetta Hawkes
Paul Jennings
Barbara Jones
James Lees-Milne
John Lewis
Jack Longland
Laurence W. Meynell
L. T. C. Rolt
Anne Scott-James
Thomas Sharp
Sir John Summerson
Maurice Wiggin

Gazetteer entries by

Therese Appleby · Gerald Barry · Nigel Batley
Euan Bowater · Sybil Burnaby · Judy Cowell
Frances Howell · Betty James · John and Anne Mason
Michael Webber · J. B. Willan · Ellen Wilson

Book Club Associates London

This edition published in 1973 by
Book Club Associates
by arrangement with Michael Joseph Ltd and Rainbird Reference Books Ltd

© Shell-Mex and B.P. Ltd 1970

This book was designed and produced by
Rainbird Reference Books Ltd
Marble Arch House, 44 Edgware Road, London W2

House Editor: George Speaight
Assistant Editors: Raymond Kaye, Gillian Robinson,
Gabrielle Wilson
Cartographer: John Flower
Picture Research: Patricia Vaughan, Frances Latty
Designer: Gwyn Lewis

It was printed by Jolly & Barber Ltd, Rugby
and bound by Dorstel Press Ltd, Harlow
Paper made by Wiggins Teape Mill Sales Ltd
and supplied by Gerald Judd Ltd

The maps on pages 921–36 are based on the Ordnance Survey
Map with the sanction of H.M. Stationery Office (Crown
Copyright reserved)

Contents

Colour Plates

Editor's Foreword

This book is the fourth in a series of Shell *Guides* to the British Isles. It differs in several respects from the earlier volumes on Scotland, Ireland and Wales. The area covered is much larger: England comprises more than 50,000 square miles, often densely populated, as against less than 30,000 sparsely populated square miles in Scotland, some 32,000 square miles in Eire and Northern Ireland, also thinly populated, and less than 7,500 square miles in Wales.

Although it was a herculean task, it was possible for one author to encompass Scotland, and for two pairs of authors to compile the volumes on Ireland and Wales. In view of its relative size and number of towns and villages it was too much to expect a single author, or even two, to tackle the whole of England.

Moreover, in each of the three countries already covered there are national characteristics – of racial origin, history, language, even of scenery and architecture – which make for a certain unity and comprehensibility. Despite conflicts of interest between Highlands and Lowlands, or between Eire and Ulster, a Scotsman is unmistakably a Scotsman, and an Irishman – from north or south – has the map of Ireland on his face and the sound of Synge in his voice. But what are the distinctively *English* characteristics of an Englishman? Apart from the use of the same basic language there is as much difference between a Yorkshireman and a Cockney, or between a Cornishman and a Geordie, as there is between a Welshman, an Irishman and a Scot. And their environments, their local landscapes and ways of life, are equally varied. Admass, standardized education and TV are breaking down the differences, but they are still there. A supporter of Everton or Liverpool football clubs is more conscious of being a man of Merseyside than of being English. The same sense of local identity goes for a Cornishman, a Fenman or an East Anglian.

This regional individuality, which is often related to variations of landscape, agricultural or industrial background, or the form and material of the houses which people live in, still survives sufficiently for us to have to call on local writers to sum up the characteristics of each region. It is not easy to find an all-round, representative, English author, except possibly that cosmopolitan but dyed-in-the-Bradford-wool Yorkshireman who writes the Preface to this book. For this reason, this Shell *Guide* is a symposium – a work to which several people have been invited to contribute, each according to his "roots".

The introductory chapters are written for the most part by specialists in their fields, and it is hoped that they provide a certain amount of solid historical, topographical, botanical and architectural information. But their aim is primarily to set the scene, to alert the reader, the traveller, the tourist, the weekend motorist, to standards of judgment, comparison and interest which he or she may apply to things observed. The purpose of this book is to enable England to be enjoyed – but enjoyed with reasonable discrimination, a due sense of the past, and an eye for what used to be called "the Picturesque" rather than the conventional "tourist's

attraction". As a further change from the conventional guide-book, these introductory chapters – and some of the regional essays – are illustrated not with colour
photographs but with paintings and watercolours by artists who have had a special
feeling for the English scene.

The area covered by the gazetteer includes the whole of the mainland of England.
The Scilly Isles and the Isle of Man are excluded. The country has been divided
into eleven regions, within each of which the places of interest are arranged in
alphabetical order.

After the name of the place in the gazetteer comes the name of the county in
italic type, and then a map reference within brackets. The map reference refers to
the map section at the end of the text. The first figure in the map reference refers
to the page in the map section; the following group of letters and figures indicates
the position of the place according to the National Grid reference system. Thus,
for example, the reference for Amberley is 6–TQ0313; this means that Amberley
will be found on page 6 of the map section, within the 100-kilometre square TQ, 3
kilometres east and 13 kilometres north of the south-west corner of the square.
As the National Grid is shown on the maps in the map section, it will in practice
be found a simple matter to identify on the map every entry in the gazetteer.

In London a different system has been employed. Places in Outer London will
be found on the appropriate area map of England by means of the system described
above. Places in London are numbered in a single numerical series, grouped in the
areas into which London is divided, and are shown on the special London map on
page 16 of the map section.

Cross references in the gazetteer to places which are themselves described in
other gazetteer entries are printed in small capitals. In some cases the description
of a place of comparatively minor importance is included under the gazetteer
entry of a larger or more important place in its vicinity. In these cases, the name of
the additional place thus described is printed in bold type, to give it emphasis.

Particulars are not given of times of opening of museums, country houses,
gardens, etc.; nor are prices of admission, or other details that are liable to change.
The traveller is advised to furnish himself with one of the annual guides to houses
and other properties open to the public as a complement to this book.

The Index lists in one alphabetical sequence all the entries and sub-entries in the
regional gazetteers.

As General Editor of the book I want to pay tribute to my colleague George
Speaight, who has organized and supervised the formidable task of compiling the
gazetteer, and to Raymond Kaye and Gillian Robinson, who have performed
wonders in checking, revising, correlating and arranging so vast an assemblage of
facts. Thanks are also due to the County Librarians of almost all the counties in
England, who have read and checked the entries relating to their areas. All the
contributors to the gazetteer owe a great debt to the pioneer work of Sir Nikolaus
Pevsner in recording the architectural heritage of individual counties in his
magnificent series, *The Buildings of England*. They also wish to acknowledge the
help and guidance they have derived from the many published volumes in the
series of *Shell County Guides*.

Like any other guide-book this must inevitably be far from perfect. Although
every effort has been made to provide accurate and up-to-date information, the
editor will welcome any corrections or suggestions for improvement for future
editions that readers may care to send.

J.H.

Preface

ON ENGLAND

J. B. PRIESTLEY

Out of a little stir of memories, from about forty years ago, that old German has returned to me. We were fellow passengers on a veteran tub out of San Francisco and bound for New Zealand. But she called at Papeete, Tahiti, where I was going. I cannot remember where the old German was going, but I know where he had been – and that was almost everywhere. Leisurely and not too expensive world travel was his way of life. (Does the type still exist? I doubt it.) Rolling easily down the Pacific, which day after day would look like moving dark-blue marble with thin foam its veins, the old German and I would talk for hours at a stretch. Finally I chanced to ask what was the most beautiful country he had ever seen. Very seriously, not trying to please me, he said "England".

You might say that even in those days I was getting around. Since then, perhaps anxious somewhere in the dark of my mind to out-travel that old German, I have got around more and more. A holiday painter, sketching in gouaches as other people take colour photographs, I have taken out tubes, brushes and (with any luck) Ingres paper in Marrakesh, Samarkand, Jaipur, Hong Kong, in Martha's Vineyard, New England, and Death Valley, California, in Cuernavaca, Yucatan and the dense jungle of northern Guatemala, along the desert coast of Peru and among the lakes and volcanoes of southern Chile, and have landed in the black howling night of the Aleutians and in the dazzling daylight of Alice Springs, Australia. But enough – though there is plenty more – or it will be all mere boast and brag!

The point is, I have now probably travelled at least as far as that old German, and I am ready to reply as he did – "England". But only, of course, what we have left of it. And between the England that German had seen and admired and the England we see now there stands, like a mountain of trash, the dreadful legacy of the 'thirties, surely the most determinedly tasteless of all our decades. I am staring now at a volume I found on one of the top shelves in my library. It is called *The Beauty of Britain*, was published bang in the middle of those 'thirties, and I wrote an Introduction to it. There, I have just discovered to my astonishment, I called attention to the Council for the Preservation of Rural England, that very C.P.R.E. (the name is the worst thing about it) for which I have made a public speech or two in the West Midlands. It was certainly not winning then. Is it winning now? Here and there I think it is, but what I like to call the "Evil Principle", which haunts planners and surveyors and inspires them to pull down only charming old houses or rows of cottages to make way for the motor road, is hard at work among us.

Mind you, we do not see everything as we did in 1935, when I wrote that other Introduction. For example, when I return now to my native West Riding it is not the old mills and the steep Victorian streets surrounding them that offend my eye. No, it is the occasional new factories and blocks of flats, all glass and glitter and California, that annoy me – so many swaggering invaders. The old familiar scene, belonging to my boyhood, begins to look so much industrial archaeology, and I feel that at any time now my wife and her colleagues will begin to explore it, removing samples to distant museums.

We may not have done our best to ruin our enchanting country, but we have undoubtedly had a devil of a good try. Any readers who question this should do what we did a few years ago, when we went by road from Brighton to Portsmouth Harbour, on our way back to the Isle of Wight. I do not think any other people in Europe would have done what we have done to that coastline. Ranging from the tasteless to the peculiarly horrible, it is one long monument to the Evil Principle. When we can afford to get round to it, the whole thing should be bulldozed back into the ground, like another Carthage. So please remember, before it is too late, the C.P.R.E.

But now let us – as that curious American song had it – "accentuate the positive". To begin with, I claim there is a magical element in England and the English (unruined) scene. And if I can believe this, after having lived here since 1894, then few others should doubt it. The magic starts in the astonishing difference between the geographical size of England and her *real size*. She is just pretending to be so small. Once you have made her acquaintance, letting her see that you find her attractive, then you discover there is more and more of her. I have already mentioned the Isle of Wight, and now I offer it as a perfect illustration of what I mean. Any man from America or Australia might take one glance at the island as something on a map, and then decide to give it a couple of hours. But you can spend days and days and days exploring the Isle of Wight, which, if you are really interested, begins magically enlarging itself for you.

England is like that, only of course on an immensely larger scale. There are whole regions I cannot pretend to know, even after living in this country so long. They remain in my imagination like mysterious provinces. I have passed through them, of course, but I do not really *know* them. So much of England is *round the corner*. (I shall return to this later.) I can offer the usual rational explanations. First, we have an astonishing variety of scene and landscape in comparatively small areas, packed like boxes of Japanese toys. Secondly, we have a lot of history on show. Here you wander not only along little winding roads, determined to slow you up, but also down through the centuries, even back to the Romans. (How many overseas tourists go north to see the Wall, the furthest outpost of the Roman Empire, and one of the most romantic sights in all Europe?) But even so, there remains something inexplicable here – the magical enlargement.

Take our mountains, up in the Lake District, where in the early 'twenties I spent much time, scrambling up and down every one of their peaks. On paper they are a joke, just so many hills. Go up there and you find they are real mountains, capable of killing you if you are too careless. A Swiss guide, taken there for the first time, allotted two days to climbing one of them, when in fact only two or three hours were needed. The magical element had deceived him. It deceives us, too. Just lately there has been a lot of archaeological digging to find King Arthur's Camelot. But it would not surprise me if somebody decided to follow some tiny overgrown lane and then found that at the end of it Camelot was still there, with nettles thick around a dusty Round Table.

In large countries you can go two hundred miles along one valley, three hundred miles across one monotonous plain. These are countries for which the jets were invented. Fly – and get done with them. Even the English should not fly over England. The magical element vanishes; the soul of the country does not reveal itself. Among so much that will be missed is the wonderful relationship here between Man and Nature. They are not in conflict as they tend to be in huge countries, where Nature is permanently hostile to Man and tries to drive him out with blizzards, dust storms, hurricanes and tornadoes. English weather is often abused, chiefly because it is changeable, does not offer sufficient sunlight, has too many grey days. So the foolish people rush abroad, to cook their bodies day after day. But it is this hazy weather, avoiding the glare of strong sunlight, that has given us the best watercolour painters in the world, trying to capture the delicate shades and the harmonious tones of this unique landscape. Why do I go away to try again to paint what I see? Because I know I am not good enough for the vague enchantments of the English scene, with its harmonious relationships, its tender variety.

I make one grand exception, faulty as I am. I keep returning to the Yorkshire Dales, which I believe to be the most rewarding, the most satisfying countryside in the world, from the bold and challenging uplands of the moors down to the fresh foliage, the sparkling trout streams, the white-washed old villages and their little bridges. And a man must linger here and not go tearing through it, thinking he is seeing everything when he is seeing nothing. Do not, I beg you – and now I am directly addressing overseas visitors – turn yourself into the victim of some ambitious itinerary that rushes you from one "high spot" to the next, doing six cathedral cities in a day. Better, far better, to take your car to one centre – it could be in the Cotswolds, East Anglia, the West Country, the Yorkshire Dales or the Lake District – and then do some leisurely exploring at twenty miles an hour. Only in this way can the magical element work for you, for ever enlarging and deepening your interest, taking you where you must not fail to go – *round the corner*.

The Beginnings

JACQUETTA HAWKES

Where can one begin the history of England? If one keeps to the name and looks no further back than the coming of the Anglo-Saxons, then millennia of creative history, scores of most visitable monuments, will be lost. If, on the other hand, one begins to follow the relationship between the people and the land on which they lived, then one will soon be travelling back through geological aeons towards the flames and particles of the birth of the solar system.

Plainly it is necessary to be practical. The most practical point at which to begin a guide-book would seem to be when men first left monuments worth being guided to. In England that time was rather over 5,000 years ago – unless one includes those few caves hallowed by having given shelter to Old Stone Age hunters.

Yet, before reaching men and monuments, some account of the countryside itself is justified. All landscape is, after all, historical: the creation first of the slow interplay of titanic natural forces, later modified, for better and for worse, by the hand of man. The geological foundations of the landscape have had an irresistible influence on where and how men have lived and on the character of their monuments.

In comparison with the rest of the United Kingdom, England is, of course, a soft and low-lying country, relatively young in terms of geological time. Within the last million years much of East Anglia and the Midlands was blanketed with clays, sands, gravels and loams left by ice-sheets and glaciers. Great stretches of these lands formerly supported oak and other deciduous forest, with such a formidable undergrowth of thorn and bramble that prehistoric man left them well alone. In the gravel terraces of the Thames and other river valleys of southern England lie the flint implements of the primitive hunters who lived during the warmer intervals of the Ice Age. There, too, lie the fossil bones of the elephants, rhinoceros and hippos that were their contemporaries. In a gravel pit by the lower Thames at Swanscombe fragments of a human skull were found. These are the earliest known human remains in Britain, dating back about a quarter of a million years. Swanscombe Man is recognized as one of the direct ancestors of *Homo sapiens* – as an examination of his famous skull (now in the Natural History Museum, South Kensington) will clearly show.

Away from the gently undulating Midland Plain there is no part of lowland England that is not agreeably broken by hills. Most characteristic, perhaps, are the chalk downs with their smooth, rounded polls. From the nodal point of Salisbury Plain and the hills of the White Horse, one line runs south-west into Dorset and another connects with the best known of all the chalk hills, the South Downs that end in the splendid cliffs of Beachy Head and the North Downs that give us the white cliffs of Dover. A third limb of the chalk stretches north-eastward as the Chilterns, the Gog Magog Hills of Cambridgeshire and the Norfolk Edge. Across the Wash it reappears in much greater bulk and beauty as the Lincolnshire and Yorkshire Wolds.

Running parallel with the chalk along its western side are the older, harder limestone hills. In Dorset the formation is broken up, but has created the beauty spot of Lulworth Cove as well as the Purbeck Hills and the Isle of Portland. In Portland it yields the finest building stone in Britain, much of it quarried to rebuild London after the Great Fire. The line of the limestone becomes clearly marked with the beginning of the Cotswold Hills near Bath. Here again is good building stone, already appreciated by the Romans when they made the original baths. The Cotswolds, extending north-eastward to within a few miles of Stratford-upon-Avon, show man and nature working together in sweetest harmony.

Beyond the Cotswolds the limestone can be followed along battle-renowned Edgehill, the miniature Dasset Hills, through Northamptonshire and Rutland to the spine of Lincoln Edge. This spine is hardly more than wide enough to carry Roman Ermine Street on its way to York. After this the limestone is almost buried by the chalk Wolds, but comes out again boldly, mixed with grittier sandstone, to reach 2,000 feet along the lovely western part of the North Yorkshire moors.

When seeing these downs and hills through car windows, much more when walking among them, it can add to one's pleasure to think of their substance being laid down in the days of the great reptiles.

In the oceans and lagoons where the limestone and later the chalk were forming, shoals of fish were preyed on from below by giant ichthyosaurs, from above by twenty-foot pterodactyls. On land dinosaurs of all shapes and sizes, some ferocious carnivores, others mild vegetarians, were the supreme form of life. In a rich vegetation of gingkos, archaic conifers, fern and maidenhair trees, flapped the first birds, still half reptilian. As the snowy chalk precipitated, it was probably sponges or some other simple form of marine life that produced those beds of flint nodules that so often show as black bands in cliffs and chalk-pits. Some hundred million years later they were to be mined by late Stone Age man as the finest raw material for his tools.

It will by now have become apparent that as one drives westward across England one is also driving further and further back into geological time. This ageing of the landscape is continued beyond the limestone belt by the New Red Sandstone that runs up the western side of England from Devon, through the west Midlands, to the far north of Cumberland. This rock was formed not on sea-beds but in arid heat. It is the red of desert sands that glows so warmly in Devon soil and which gives a ruddy complexion to so many buildings in the north-west.

In their day these desert sandstones formed against rock so ancient that some existed before life itself had taken any recognizable shape. The ancient moors and mountains comprise Wales and Scotland. England's share is smaller, yet in the south-west peninsula with its cliffs and moorland, in the Mendips, the Welsh border land, the Lakeland mountains and the great Pennine Chain, she has enough to provide her with some height, some rugged wildness, where old ways and peoples have held out against the sharpness of change.

While the forested lowlands were left to the wild beasts, the hills and the milder slopes of the ancient highlands were relatively more open and attractive for human settlement. Their lighter woodland could be cleared with axes of stone or bronze, helped out by burning. From the time when farming was first introduced it was these areas that were most populous – and it is therefore in these areas that the greatest concentrations of prehistoric remains are to be seen today.

It is not chance that three of the finest prehistoric monuments in Britain – and indeed in Europe – were raised in the heart of the chalk downlands of Wiltshire. Stonehenge, the Avebury circles and Silbury Hill are near the centre point of the

whole upland system. They would have been places of ready access for the tribesmen of all the radiating chalk and limestone ridges, and of the Mendips and the
South-west. Men and ideas moved freely on the upland trackways.

The earliest men to inhabit the country made little more impression upon it
than the animals they hunted. Swanscombe Man and his successors for an immensely long time are known to us only from their tools and their bones. During
the last glacial age, however, the hunters took to living in caves and these dwellings
do help to make their existence seem nearer and more real. Britain was bitterly
cold and could not support large or prosperous communities, such as those that
created the marvellous works of art found in France and Spain. There are, however,
two places in England where the Old Stone Age has some imaginative life in it –
Cheddar Gorge in the Mendips and Cresswell Crags in Derbyshire. The earliest
cave dwellers (at Cresswell only) were almost certainly of the low-browed
Neanderthal breed, but they were succeeded some 30,000 to 40,000 years ago by
men of modern type, skilled hunters with brains quite as good as our own. Among
the occupation rubbish in one of the Cresswell caves was a bone engraved with a
horse's head. Although this sketch is a poor thing if set beside the French and
Spanish treasures, it is good enough to suggest what the Cresswellians might have
accomplished in easier conditions.

At this time Britain was a promontory of north-western Europe. About 10,000
years ago, however, the ice-sheets and glaciers began to melt back towards their
present positions, and the release of enormous quantities of water raised the sea
level. By about 6000 B.C. the North Sea had been formed, and the landbridge with
France severed. Britain had become an island. The warmer climate allowed the
spread of trees and the hunters had to adapt to forest conditions. They became
skilled with bow and arrow, and as fishermen and carpenters. We can picture small
groups living in huts on river banks, by lakes, their dug-out canoes moored nearby.
Others hunted on the moors and others again took to a beachcombing life by the
seashore.

It is impossible to guess how long the islanders would have continued to live
in this quite efficient but mute and inglorious manner if they had not been roused
by the arrival of foreign immigrants. The first of these newcomers crossed from
northern France – their material culture had much in common with that of the
earliest Swiss Lake dwellers. A little later other settlers, probably hailing from
Brittany or still further south, settled up the western coasts of Britain all the way
from south-west England to the Orkneys. All these people are likely to have
crossed in oxhide boats akin to Irish curraghs. They certainly arrived, men, women
and children together, and brought with them breeding livestock and supplies of
seed corn. They also brought with them a knowledge of the art of potting.

These revolutionary events took place during the second half of the fourth
millennium B.C. They mark the beginning of the New Stone Age in Britain. Since
the beginning of human time mankind had been wholly dependent on what nature
had to offer. Now there was to be a fundamental change in the economic basis of
society. Although the men did not entirely give up hunting, nor women the culling
of wild fruits and vegetables, their main economic concerns were henceforward
to be with domestic flocks and herds and the cultivation of wheat and barley.

For those who want to visit prehistoric monuments, the most important result
of the revolution lies in the fact that it brought about a sudden increase in man's
creative activity. This was partly due to better food supplies supporting much
larger communities. But it must also have been due to a tradition derived, however

tenuously, from the higher civilizations now flourishing in the Eastern Mediterranean and beyond. These Stone Age farmers had already been imbued with the idea that they could enhance the power of their religious rites by providing them with monumental settings.

They did, it is true, put considerable labour into building for practical purposes. They made roughly circular embankments, probably mainly used for the management of cattle, of a type known to archaeologists as causewayed camps. Then on Dartmoor and elsewhere in the south-west "hut circles" of quite sizable stones represent dwellings with substantial foundations. Both labour and organization were needed to sink shafts and drive galleries into the chalk to obtain fresh flint for their axes. (The best known group of flint mines is at Grimes Graves in Norfolk, but there are several of them also in Sussex and the southern Chilterns.) Yet their greatest and most imaginative efforts went into sacred buildings and particularly into making monuments for the dead.

Everyone who is at all familiar with the downlands of England will have noticed the burial mounds that so often stand out conspicuously against the sky. The oldest of these were raised by the farmers of the New Stone Age. They are easily distinguished by their long, narrow form – originally often wedge-shaped, although the angles have been rounded by time. The largest are as much as 300 feet in length. The broader and higher end usually pointed eastward, and it was here that the burials were made. There was always more than one corpse, sometimes over twenty. Men, women and children were interred in them without discrimination, but it seems that such burial was probably reserved for the families of chiefs. Long barrows are commonest on the Wessex chalk – there is a beauty at the Winterbourne crossroads near Stonehenge. But they are also to be seen on the South and North Downs, the Lincolnshire and Yorkshire wolds and the North Yorkshire moors.

Although their sheer size makes these barrows impressive, they are far less spectacular than the megalithic tombs that were built by the settlers along the western coasts. In megalithic funerary architecture the burial chamber is formed of huge blocks of stone, the spaces between them often filled with drystone walling. In Britain the chambers are usually also roofed with big slabs, but occasionally with corbelled vaults. They were made dark and cave-like by a covering mound – either round or elongated. Like the family vaults of recent times, they could be reopened to admit a succession of burials. Perhaps the dead were consigned to these dark chambers in the hope of rebirth through the Mother Goddess.

England has not so many megalithic tombs as Wales, nor such splendid ones as Ireland and Scotland; yet in Cornwall and the Cotswolds – with a few notable outliers further east – there are plenty that are well worth seeing. Wind and rain have denuded most of the Cornish tombs so that the stones stand out starkly in the bare landscape. In the Cotswolds the chambers are hidden in long cairns. At Hetty Pegler's tump one can enter through the low portal to find the chamber just as it was when it was in use 4,000 years ago. Here is the earliest architecture in England.

While the immigrant farmers were spreading about the country, what was happening to the native population of hunters and fishers? At first they were dominated by the superior culture while at the same time learning from it. They were soon keeping domestic animals and making pots. They seem also to have played some part in flint-mining and the trade in flint and polished stone axes. Then, as the centuries went by, these old stocks began to reassert themselves, and

Victoria and Albert Museum

Stonehenge. Watercolour drawing by John Constable, c. 1835

in the end it was they rather than the immigrant population who made the greater contribution to the succeeding Bronze Age.

These native peoples were the originators of a type of monument, unique to Britain, that had a very splendid future before it. This is the "henge", a variety of sanctuary named after the genuine folk name of Stonehenge itself. The henges built towards the end of the New Stone Age were quite simple affairs. A bank and ditch, nearly always circular, enclosed a sacred area where there was some-times a ring of ritual pits, sometimes rings of standing stones or posts. The best known example is the enclosing bank and ditch with the Aubrey holes at Stone-henge. These represent the first stage of a monument that was to be elaborated over many centuries.

The further development of henge architecture was probably due to the conquest of Britain by the Beaker Folk. This name is something of a joke, but is too well established to be given up. Though they came in various groups with differing cultural traditions, they were on the whole a physically strong and warlike people, archers and wielders of shapely stone battle axes. The Beaker Folk began to arrive before bronze had come into use in Britain, but as their enterprise helped to stimulate its introduction it is convenient to relate their conquest with the beginning of the Bronze Age. This was in about 1800 B.C.

The Beaker Folk certainly played a major part in the building of what is in some ways the most fascinating prehistoric monument in Britain: the great henge of Avebury. The enclosing bank and ditch are enormous – most of the present-day village stands inside them – and the sarsen stones of the several internal circles and the long processional avenue are on a corresponding scale. (Nearby, as well as the huge mound of Silbury Hill, there is a causewayed camp, the West Kennet megalithic tomb and a variety of barrows. There is no better place for an excursion into prehistory.) At Stonehenge the Beaker Folk had a hand in the second main stage of construction. This was when the "blue-stones" were transported all the way from the Prescelly hills in Wales. The much larger sarsen circle and trilithons were added in about the fifteenth century B.C., when foreign trade and pastoralism had made Wessex very prosperous.

Although Avebury and Stonehenge dwarf the rest, there are several other henges in England that are well worth seeing. One is Arbor Low in Derbyshire; there are the fine though stoneless Knowlton circles in Dorset, while in Maumbury Rings near Dorchester, in the same county, there is the oddity of a henge converted by the Romans into an amphitheatre.

Circles of standing stones without embankments must be distinguished from the henges. It is true that they, too, must have been sacred places intended for ritual use, and that they date from the Bronze Age – although they probably outlasted the true henges. Their distribution, however, is quite different, so that they cannot have been raised by the same people. Most of them are to be seen on moors in the ancient highland country. There are a few on Exmoor, many on Dartmoor and Bodmin Moor in the south-west. In this region, but off the moorland, there is a remarkable group of circles and alignments at Stanton Drew, Somerset. Of those in the North-West the most appealing is Castlerigg near Keswick. Keats visited this circle and probably had it in mind when in *Hyperion* he wrote of a "dismal cirque of Druid stones, upon a forlorn moor . . .". The Rollright circle between Stratford-upon-Avon and Oxford is in distinguished isolation so far to the east.

Standing stones, or menhirs, are sometimes found associated with stone circles, sometimes in isolation or in small groups. Like the circles themselves, they are most numerous on the moorlands of the south-west and north. The finest examples are both in Yorkshire, the Devil's Arrows at Boroughbridge and the standing stone in the churchyard at Rudston, on the Wolds. It is over twenty-five feet high – taller than any upright at Stonehenge.

The Beaker Folk were certainly involved in the building of the complex English henges and probably to some extent with the raising of stone circles. They affected our prehistoric landscapes even more extensively by the monuments they raised for their dead. All over England the old practice of building long barrows or megalithic tombs for family or communal burial came to an end. The warrior Beaker Folk brought with them from northern Europe the custom of individual burial under a circular mound. The round barrow became the usual form of tomb for the whole of the Bronze Age and by far the commonest form of field monument. There are over 4,000 still to be seen in Wessex alone – and great numbers must have been destroyed.

On the chalk hills these barrows are shaped with extreme precision; on moors and in other stony country they have the looser form of piled cairns. The Beaker Folk themselves usually raised simple mounds shaped like soggy puddings (but known as bowl barrows) with a ditch immediately outside the mound. Later the same prosperous Wessex pastoralists who added the sarsens to Stonehenge devised more elaborate barrows. The most easily distinguished are the bell barrow, in which a level space was left between the mound and the ditch, and the disc barrow, in which the mound was very small, the main features being a ditch with a neat bank outside it. Round barrows of all types crowd round Stonehenge, for just as the great men of today may hope for a Westminster Abbey funeral, the great of the Bronze Age sought to be buried beside their noblest sanctuary. Several of these barrows covered richly furnished graves. One of the most princely was that of the Bush Barrow on Normanton Down, where a powerfully built warrior had been buried with his bronze weapons, gold ornaments and a sceptre.

Although there are some mounded Iron Age burials in Yorkshire, one can be reasonably sure that any round barrow on an upland site dates from the Bronze Age. On the other hand a rather steep-sided barrow on a low-lying site may possibly be Roman – Holborough Knob in Kent and the Six Hills at Stevenage, Hertfordshire, being good examples out of the hundred or so that are known. More rarely still the Anglo-Saxons and Vikings made burial mounds. Of these far and away the most famous is the group at Woodbridge, Suffolk, which included the treasure-filled Sutton Hoo ship burial.

The latter part of the Bronze Age saw great advances in both agriculture and metallurgy, but it was not a period that has left any conspicuous field monuments. They are not to be found again until well after the beginning of the Iron Age in the sixth century B.C. This was a time of stress on the Continent when various Celtic-speaking peoples migrated to Britain. The first to cross were still living within the native tradition of prehistoric Europe, but the culture of those who followed after 300 B.C. had been affected by their contacts with the Greek world. Then towards the very end of the second century there were several incursions by Belgic tribes who carved out kingdoms for themselves in south-eastern and southern England. It was the Belgae who first brought Britain into the light of history. Their powerful princes were in touch with Rome, they imported Roman luxuries, issued inscribed coin – and yet, when the time came, put up the fiercest resistance to the Roman legions.

The Celtic aristocracy was much given to inter-tribal warfare. If it were not already known from Roman history, their warlike ideals would be proved by the fact that the finest work of Celtic artists was lavished on splendid helmets, shields, weapons and accoutrements for war chariots. They are also manifest in the massive hill-forts which were their great contribution to the English landscape. Now for the first time most labour was given not to sacred buildings and tombs, but to military fortification.

Hill-forts come in endless variety. The older ones mostly had a single bank and ditch following the natural contours. Later the ramparts might be increased to two or three, and the entrances were strengthened by hornworks and other ingenious devices. Most of the larger hill-forts cover from 15 to 20 acres, but Wessex has larger ones – up to the 46 acres of Maiden Castle, Dorset, much the largest and most elaborate of them all. When looking at the earthen ramparts of today it should be remembered that they were originally faced with vertical walls of wood, chalk or turf, while the ditches were far deeper. In the highland country the ramparts were built of stone blocks – as can still be seen for example at the fort on towering Ingleborough in Yorkshire, or in the small but immensely strong Chun Castle above Land's End.

All these Iron Age strongholds were essentially defensive in purpose. They were intended as refuges for men and beasts in times of stress – whether due to invasion or inter-tribal fighting. For many of them, including Maiden Castle, their last defence was against the Roman legions.

This is no place to attempt an account of the Roman conquest or of Roman Britain. It is in all the history books. From the point of view of field monuments the most significant distinction is between the military zones in the west and north and the usually peaceful civilian lowlands. Many of the well-to-do Roman Britons lived on large agricultural estates in the comfortable country houses we have come to call Roman villas. There are so many across southern England that selection is difficult. Perhaps the best of all is at Fishbourne, near Chichester; then Bignor, also in Sussex, is an old favourite. Lullingstone in Kent is of great interest, and so too, away to the west, is Chedworth in the Cotswolds.

The introduction of Mediterranean-style town life was the most important of Roman innovations, and ruins of town walls and public buildings form the other main category of civilian monuments. They still stand in many existing cities – for instance in the City of London itself, in St Albans, Cirencester, Lincoln and York. Perhaps Colchester is even more remarkable, for there, as well as striking remains of the first capital of the Roman province, one can see the earthworks of the earlier Belgic capital, and what may be the tomb of its most famous ruler – King Cymbeline.

Lowland England has some fine though late military remains in the Forts of the Saxon Shore built against barbarian raiders. The best are at Burgh Castle near Yarmouth, Richborough in Kent, and Pevensey in Sussex. Nearly all the great military works, however, are in the west and north, where garrisons had to be maintained all through the four centuries of Roman rule. Remains of the legionary fortress that served as the base for holding down the Celtic tribes of Wales are to be found at Caerleon in Monmouthshire. England's finest Roman monument is, of course, Hadrian's Wall, the strongly manned frontier held against unconquered Scotland. It has a dozen sites worth visiting, but to understand and enjoy it one should walk its whole length from sea to sea. Up there on the frontier it is not hard to imagine the collapse of the Roman province before the barbarian attacks: Scots and Picts and their allies in the north, Angles, Saxons and Jutes in the south. But that is another story – the beginning of the story of medieval England.

The Agricultural Heritage

G. E. FUSSELL

The English rural scene as it exists today, with all its variations in different parts of the country, is the result of thousands of years of work. Farmers of former days have left their indelible mark upon the countryside, from the tiny hill farms of prehistoric man that can still be traced on Dartmoor and the Sussex Downs to the "factory farming" enterprises of today.

Nature, however, places severe restraint upon man's farming and indeed upon the appearance of the land. Climate, elevation, slope, dry uplands, wet and marshy lowlands, are elements in the fashioning of farm work, and consequently upon the appearance of the man-made, as opposed to the original, countryside. Today most of the landscape has been so much worked over by man that it is difficult to imagine what it looked like before this human interference. The scene has always been in a state of flux, even before man began to work upon it, but in historic times our land has been more modified by human activity than by natural forces, although coast erosion, with a trifle of compensating lift at some places, has made some changes.

The most marked changes were made by farmers, during the thousand years after A.D. 900. In the midland arable area which runs from the East Riding to Dorset, right across the country, these changes fall into three stages. Traces of the first can still be seen in some of these counties, as they can also in Gloucestershire. It was the laying out of the farm lands in the acre strips of the open fields, one example of which is being preserved by the Ministry of Agriculture at Laxton, Nottinghamshire. Other remnants of the system can be seen at Haxey and Epworth in the Isle of Axholme, and fragments at Braunton, in Devon. Each man's farm was made up of pieces of land scattered amongst those of his neighbours in two or three great fields, which were often several hundred acres in extent. The boundary between each piece was either a drainage furrow, a balk, a track or way giving access to the different pieces, or an occasional wider path forming an unmade road. The great stretches of arable were unfenced except for temporary obstacles to prevent grazing cattle from trespass. The villages of the Vale of White Horse and some of those in Lincolnshire had only two arable fields. These were on the lower slopes, and lay between the wet riparian meadows and the dry grazing of the upper downs; they were formed of intermixed semi-rectangular pieces. The farmed fields everywhere were surrounded by large areas of uncultivated land. The farm-houses and cottages were lined along a village street and grouped round the church and manor house.

This was the general appearance of the countryside where the major occupation was the production of cereal crops, although that main activity was usually combined with some stock breeding, horses, cattle, sheep, pigs and poultry. All this area remained in much the same state for many centuries, minor changes excepted. For example, some villages lost their entire population in the Black Death in the fourteenth century and became desolate. Others were depopulated by the lords for the sake of sheep grazing at a slightly later date. Occasionally a progressive and ambitious farmer got together a few adjacent pieces of land and fenced them to form a field within a field. In some places these changes were substantial but in others they took place very slowly.

The next stage was a major alteration in farm lay-out, made at a much more rapid rate between about 1760 and 1845, some six million acres being affected. This is only a fraction of the whole country, but the area most changed was the midland arable area, and consequently a most important part of the country's surface. As I have said, the enclosure and redistribution of the open fields and waste had been going on slowly in a limited way for a long time. Some great spaces of open field had been surveyed and re-arranged into hedged fields more or less square or rectangular in shape. This process was enormously accelerated as the so-called agricultural revolution gathered momentum, a revolution that provided the opportunity of growing fodder crops alternately with food crops and so enabled more and better livestock to be kept. The necessities of this new, or at least modified, system of farming caused new hedges to be planted, or, in the Cotswold country, dry-stone walls to be built so that the stock could be kept in the selected field to graze. Over much of the Midlands these fields are still in being. Some have been put down to grass, and in these traces of the old ridge and furrow can still be seen. This ridge and furrow is especially clear in some parts of Gloucestershire. A caveat must be issued here. Only where the old ridge and furrow crosses from one field to the next in spite of the relatively new hedges can it be assumed that once upon a time they were part of holdings dispersed about an open field. This is a part of England's agricultural heritage that is worth while looking for when travelling through the Midland counties and some others.

A good deal of the arable of the Midlands and indeed elsewhere was turned over to grass in the depression of the last twenty-five years of the nineteenth century. This did not change the shape of the fields, but developments during and after the two wars have done this on a large scale. First, the root break has given place to sugar beet, not completely, of course, but to a large degree. Potatoes, too, have been grown on a greater area. Second, the effective use of massive modern agricultural machinery demands large fields so a great many of the carefully created and main-tained hedgerows of the eighteenth century have been rooted out, ditches filled and covered drains substituted, and huge fields have once again come into being. Much of the countryside has become similar, though on a lesser scale, to the great wheat fields of the former prairie in Canada and the U.S.A.

Outside the belt of former open fields the possibilities were different, and in-genious landowners and farmers of former times made a quite dissimilar impression. Ever since Roman times efforts to drain the eastern Fens have been in progress. Where a waterlogged area of some 750,000 acres was inhabited by a semi-amphi-bious race who lived on wild game and fish and who pastured a few cattle on the dry spots there is now an area of rich and productive farms intensively worked. The former inhabitants walked through the pools and sluggish rivers on stilts and their cattle often had to swim to their grazing grounds. The drainage, the work of centuries, has dried out the land so that it has shrunk, and roads and canals are now well above the surrounding cultivated land. It is a flat black landscape, divided into fairly large fields, where such crops as celery, potatoes and carrots are grown.

At the opposite side of the country there was the large area of marshy land, known as King's Sedgemoor, in Somerset, where the Monmouth Rebellion came to defeat at the end of the seventeenth century. Only a century ago this land was

Farm Waggon. Painting by Tristram Hillier, 1943

still not effectively drained, although an Act for draining it had been passed in 1791. The contours here, as in the Fens, were an obstacle, but the land has now been laid comparatively dry, and is intersected by wide deep drains called rhines. The marshland has become rich grazing land given over to cattle and dairy produce. The county, like Devon and Cornwall, is very varied in elevation. Taunton Vale, for example, is rich arable. Exmoor, formerly almost uninhabited, as Blackmore's *Lorna Doone* demonstrates, was reclaimed and made into productive enclosed farms by the efforts of the Knight family and its successors. This transformation has so far proved impossible on Dartmoor, still a wild waste, or on Bodmin Moor, though on both there are some tiny scattered holdings where life is painfully isolated.

It seems that neither Devon nor Cornwall passed through the open-field arrangement of farm lands, or, where they did, the change to individual enclosed fields was made at a very early date. Devon has always been famous for its breeds of cattle and sheep, the Red Devons being bred in the north of the county and a large less individual breed in the south. The main industry is mixed farming, with some early vegetables in south Cornwall. The high banks, with hedges growing on the tops enclosing the fields, and the narrow lanes of some parts of Cornwall, are familiar to modern travellers.

Dorset is famous for its breed of sheep. Defoe said that over 600,000 were kept within a few miles of Dorchester in the early eighteenth century. The large, now enclosed downland farms devoted to corn growing were formerly in open fields. The west of the county has always been devoted to dairy farming. The blue vinney cheese is renowned. Hampshire is divided into two parts, north and south, the former being largely downland, at one time in open fields, but now in large enclosed farms of big fields, still under a system of mixed farming combining grain growing with cattle and sheep. Here are to be seen some great and extensive enterprises run on the most modern lines. The New Forest in the south is an unenclosed area given up to deer and ponies, and on its fringes the homes of many retired people. From Chichester to the Kent coast runs the line of the South Downs.

The South Downs are open, mainly unfenced, and covered with short, springy grass of a most nutritious kind. The Southdown sheep still flourish, but not in their former numbers, and much of this land has now been cultivated. Heavy crops of grain are grown, using up the accumulated fertility of the centuries during which the lonely shepherd and his flock were the sole inhabitants. The coastal belt south of the Downs is shrinking before the onslaughts of modern town expansion. North of the Downs is the Sussex and Kentish Weald, an area of heavy land and small hedged fields that were gradually reclaimed from the extensive forest. Oxen were used for ploughing and transport in this area until recently. Here, too, settlement is increasing, and the farming area shrinking, as it is more rapidly on the North Downs though there are still pleasant rural places there.

Sheep seem to flourish everywhere, from the mountain to the marshes. The Romney Marsh breed is an example. The Romans began the draining of this Marsh, and the work has gone on continuously ever since until the whole area is divided into larger and smaller plots by ditches and waterways. The rest of Kent is renowned for its hops, orchards and productive land. It is an umbrageous countryside, since many hedgerow trees are left to grow and the hedges them- selves are pretty well maintained. The agricultural heritage there has many com- ponents. In many parts an almost garden culture is given to remunerative crops.

Essex has some similarities to Kent. Many of its farms were made by felling the forest trees and opening up fields. Near London urban expansion is rubbing away at the farm land, and on the coast the same thing is happening; but much of the county remains under highly productive farming practice. There are still some smallish fields, mainly in the west. In the east and north the hedges, so carefully kept up in former times, are being eradicated, and large arable fields suited to modern farming machinery created – sometimes that is happening elsewhere in East Anglia.

Suffolk and Norfolk, and more particularly north-west Norfolk, were the site of the so-called agricultural revolution that slowly matured from the beginning of the seventeenth century, and was an example for the greater part of the kingdom. It formed the pattern for the productive mixed farming of the nineteenth century. This in turn was superseded as changes in equipment and science became possible and were adopted to meet the contingencies of the past half-century. There are, however, patches of unproductive land in both counties which are now being used for forestry.

William Cobbett in the 1820s remarked upon the fertile farms with large fields that had recently been made from the former wild waste of Lincoln Heath. In this huge county there are naturally differences in the way the land has been farmed. Some part of it was settled in long, rather narrow parishes, something like those on the north of the Berkshire Downs. There was grazing land on the saltings near the coast, arable on the slightly more elevated slopes, and grazing again on the upper hills.

The northern counties, from Yorkshire to Northumberland, and then west and south to Lancashire, have much in common, but also considerable differences. It is a countryside of wild hills and moors, but also productive farms. Some of it is thronged with the great populations of industrial cities and mining centres, but there are vast agricultural areas surrounding these centres. The Vale of York is a scene of enclosed fields and mixed farms. The Cleveland hills were the home of a famous breed of horses, the Cleveland Bay. The moorland of the East Riding, or at least a part of it, was enclosed and made into arable farms with large fields in the late eighteenth and early nineteenth century, largely by the efforts of the Legard family. There are still large areas of unreclaimed moorland in the West Riding, but there are also villages and farms, the latter necessarily small, with a trifle of cultivated land supported by hill grazing. There are also farms on some of the upland, which were made by enclosure; but most of the farms, and indeed villages, as elsewhere in these forbidding hills, are in the valleys. This is a county, too, where dry-stone walls, built of material from the fields themselves, take the place of hedges as boundaries. The same sort of walls confine the roads, many of them narrow and winding as the lie of the land makes necessary. Sheep graze the hills, and there are some dairy cows from whose milk famous cheeses, such as the Wensleydale, are made. Derbyshire hill farms and fields are enclosed in the same way, and so are those of Durham, the home of the famous Durham Shorthorn cattle. Northumberland, Westmorland, Cumberland and the hills of Lancashire present the same scene of dry-stone walled enclosures, and miles of these walls running across the slopes. Cobbett noticed the large grain and cattle farms about Hexham, and in the border country where the then most approved methods were practised. John Grey of Dilston had been one of the "improvers" here, and Ernle in his picturesque language described how Grey's father had "taken his axe (to cut the tall broom, etc.) and like a backwoodsman, cleared a space on which to begin his farming operations". Precisely a century ago his daughter, Josephine E. Butler, wrote a *Memoir of John Grey*, describing how some of these great farms had been made.

The farms of Cumberland and Westmorland were smaller, and were the homes of the owner-occupiers, the renowned "Statesmen". They were largely grazing farms. A large landowner, John Christian Curwen, made an example of his Schoose Farm to encourage improved farming about Whitehaven. The low-lying coastal land of Lancashire is used for dairy and arable. The southern borders of the county and across the river in Cheshire may be said to be the birthplace of potato culture on a large scale in England.

The flat Cheshire plain which stretches into Shropshire and parts of Stafford has been famous for dairy produce for a thousand years. It is a land of fields enclosed by hedges, many of them meadows where the cows find their pasture. These meadows have been carefully maintained through the centuries, first by treating them with marl, later with crushed bones to restore the phosphates extracted by the feeding animal, and today by combined fertilizers. The farmers were not slow to adopt the so-called artificial grasses to supplement the gifts of nature, and they also grow some arable crops. Southwards and eastward the hills rise again, and these are all used for cattle and sheep breeding. This is the part of the country where the "black neat" cattle were bred, the Longhorn breed to which Robert Bakewell mistakenly devoted his attempts to improve them.

Worcestershire and Herefordshire are both renowned for special crops. The former is fairly flat, the latter hilly in the west. The countryside of both is speckled with orchards containing all kinds of fruits. Soft fruits, too, are widely grown. Hop grounds flourish. It is a countryside with a flavour all its own. The hills towards Wales are the breeding ground of the renowned Hereford cattle.

This has been a brief tour of farming England, which could only be fully elaborated in much more space. Enough has perhaps been said to demonstrate the ever-changing character of rural England, where so many different facets of farming can be seen on the surface of a relatively small country. All these divergencies are indications, not only of the resourcefulness and industry of our forbears, but also of the adaptability and capacity of the present-day English farmer, who is doing his best to preserve England's agricultural heritage, whatever changes modern methods may force him to make in the superficial appearance of the rural scene.

Harvest in Suffolk – the classic farming scene. Detail from the background of the portrait of Mr and Mrs Andrews by Thomas Gainsborough, c. 1749   London, National Gallery

Trees and Woodlands

MILES HADFIELD

In the remote future, when Macaulay's traveller from New Zealand stands on a broken arch of London Bridge to sketch the ruins of St Paul's, he will probably hear in the midst of the "vast solitude" the sounds of those birds we hear today in any woodland ride. Until man arrived, our islands were woodland; and to woodland they will at last return should man decide to retire and leave nature to wreak its will. Indeed, most of our natural wild life today is substantially the relic of a forest world. And the speed with which trees re-assert their domination could be seen during and after the last war on many a bombed site.

The astonishing permanence of minute pollen grains, preserved, for instance, in layers of peat – the species from which each one came being still identifiable and countable – has made possible a history of the types of woodland as they varied with the changes in the English climate.

About 18000 B.C., as the climate improved after the ice age or ages which had virtually obliterated vegetation, trees spread northward (we were not then an island) from Europe. The birch came, then Scots pine, hazel, oak and elm and alder. In the Boreal climate of 7000 B.C., which was warm and dry in summer, it is believed that hazel formed masses of pioneering scrub round dense pinewoods; the birch became very common. Oak and wych-elm increased.

Over the next 2,500 years the climate became moister and warmer; the alder spread, and the pine receded northwards. And then the land began to fall, and immigration slowed down. The oak dominated the dense forests, in which wych-elm and lime formed an important part.

The linking of the Atlantic and the North Sea to make Britain an island enables us to define the commonly used term "native". This is applied to the trees that had arrived here before that happening. Once we were separated from the European continent other kinds could come only if brought by man – who began this activity at least as early as the Iron Age. We can say with certainty that only the following qualify as true natives of England: the hawthorns (*Crataegus monogyna*, common, and *C. oxyacanthoides*, rather rare), the rowan, whitebeam and wild service (*Sorbus aucuparia*, *S. aria* and *S. torminalis*), crab-apple (*Malus sylvestris*), holly (*Ilex aquifolium*), beech (*Fagus sylvatica*), the pedunculate oak, with short-stalked leaves and long-stalked acorns (*Quercus robur*), and the sessile or durmast oak, with its long-stalked leaves and acorn cups sitting on the shoots (*Q. petraea*), the white and crack willows (*Salix alba* and *S. fragilis*) and various shrubby willows which sometimes reach tree size, the aspen (*Populus tremula*), possibly the black and grey poplars (*P. nigra* and *P. canescens*), a number of elms, particularly the wych-elm (*Ulmus glabra*) and the hedgerow elm (*U. procera*), which is believed to have originated in the Severn Valley, the two very common birches (*Betula pubescens*, with softly downy twigs, and *B. verrucosa*, with harsh rough twigs), the field maple (*Acer campestre*), the hornbeam (*Carpinus betulus*), the small- and large-leaved limes (*Tilia cordata* and *T. platyphyllos*), the alder (*Alnus glutinosa*),

In early Spring. Painting by John William Inchbold (1830–88)   Oxford, Ashmolean Museum the wild cherry or gean (*Prunus avium*), the bird-cherry (*P. padus*), the yew (*Taxus baccata*), and the Scots pine (*Pinus sylvestris*).

No sweet or horse-chestnut, no sycamore, no larches, none of the "cedars" and "cypresses"; all of these, and indeed the vast majority of the 500 to 600 different kinds of tree which grow here now, had to be brought from overseas by man.

Probably the first tree introductions from the Continent were made in Neolithic times; but they were fruit trees, not affecting our forests except in so far as they would seed along their margins – much as we find them today. At that period, too, immigrants may well have introduced the elms we still see in East Anglia, not for their timber but for their foliage which was cut for winter fodder.

It is not difficult to imagine the landscape of England at the time of the Roman occupation. In places woodland was being gradually cleared, probably by burning, the wood ash adding fertility to the land. Since about 450 B.C. the Weald and Dean Forests had been producing iron; and this industry continued to use timber for fuel and for the charcoal required in the process until A.D. 1775, when coke came into use. In Roman times sheep grazing increased, and where sheep graze they destroy seedling trees. Yet these depredations still affected the forests but little; Roman Britain remained a country dominated by trees.

All the heavy, fertile, well-drained soils were covered with a dense growth of the English pedunculate oak, a hiding place for wild beasts and human enemies. On the lighter soils, and climbing up into the mountains (as it still does in Wales and the north), the durmast oak, able to thrive on a more meagre diet, was most conspicuous. There were ashes and limes on the limestone soils, and wych-elms in the north and west. Often, even in the dense shade, yews would be scattered. On the dry, heathy land oaks would again be scattered where the soil was thicker, but here would grow principally birches, thorns and hollies. In and around the many marshy places alders and willows would be found. The Scots pine had by then, by climatic changes, been driven from the south into Scotland. The beech was present only in southern England and South Wales, the hornbeam in an even more restricted area in south-east England. The Celts, like the Greeks, associated trees, particularly the oak, with gods, and had sacred groves in which their tribal deities were supposed to live.

Through this jungle, always on the firm, hard ground, the Romans ran their great roads. They successfully introduced the sweet chestnut (*Castanea sativa*) and the walnut (*Juglans regia*), both for their nuts (we only had the hazel) and the latter probably also for oil – we have no oil-bearing natives, such as the olive.

In the long Anglo-Saxon period that followed trees and forests played an important part in the making of the settlements. Trees abound in the Anglo-Saxon place names, and often marked boundaries. The more open areas of woodland in which deer lived were preserved for hunting, to become under the Normans royal forests, places under special laws, complex and severe, designed to preserve the deer and other sporting rights – the first woods preserved for "amenity".

The Normans produced the famous Domesday survey, which recorded the description and ownership of the land and, in a general way, its value. It is not concerned with boundary marks, and so, contrary to a popular belief, does not name a single tree. Nor is it much help in assessing the area or describing the type of woodland then existing. It gives no details of the royal forests (which contained much open land necessary for the health of the deer) as they were royal, not private, property, and it describes woodlands in terms of inconsistent measurements, more particularly the number of swine a wood could support on the acorns and beechmast – a figure that it is impossible to translate into any terms of area.

Norman and subsequent medieval agriculture, building, iron and glass production and ship-building made steady inroads on English trees, but there was still an over-abundance of timber. It is worth recalling that massive quantities were usually transported by water. Several of the great East Anglian ecclesiastical buildings were built of large timbers from the fertile soils of the Midlands taken eastwards down, for example, the River Trent. And it was the Church, not only by its great buildings, that made the first great assault on our trees. The Cistercians arrived in England during the reign of Henry I. By 1170 they had some forty houses. Unlike the other monastic orders they were entirely rural. Often settling in wild, woodland country besides a small river, as for example at Rievaulx, they farmed on a large scale, particularly with sheep. Nothing like this had been known before: Melrose Abbey eventually had about 12,000 breeding sheep. This phase lasted for some 200 years, devastating woodlands by the destruction of all young trees.

The next major assault on the forests was the increasing development of the iron industry, whose timber consumption leaped forward with the general introduction of the blast furnace at the time of Queen Elizabeth I. Ship-building, house-building, glass-making, leather-making (oak bark was used for tanning), brewing (for cask-making) – all expanded rapidly under the developing economy of Henry VIII. The lands owned by the monastic orders, with all their fine timber, came on to the market. Fortunes were made by the buyers. No replanting was done. For the first time, instead of having a superabundance of timber we were short.

The story of English woodlands subsequently is of devastation, with weak attempts to provide timbers for our ships, both naval and mercantile. With the use of iron and steel for these, and the removal of all import duty on imported timber in 1866, devastation turned to neglect. The rabbit had replaced the sheep as a devourer of young trees. Swine were no longer turned into the woods to fatten, and so, accidentally, to trample mast into the ground to assist its germination. At the beginning of the nineteenth century the introduced grey squirrel began to show a destructive fondness for trees. Generally, English woods produced little timber, though many were saved because of their sporting value. They became less healthy, if more picturesque. Only a handful of people realized that timber-producing forests might one day again be vital to the country.

While England's forests were, owing to neglect and reckless exploitation, losing their economic value as suppliers of timber, there was a growing interest in trees for other reasons, particularly in those kinds growing abroad which, it was found, would thrive when introduced into England.

The Romans, as I have said, had introduced the sweet chestnut and the walnut – unaware that the timber of the latter would in time be of great value for gun stocks and furniture. The sycamore (*Acer pseudoplatanus*) was brought to Scotland, where it is still called a plane, in medieval times. It has spread all over Britain, though it rarely grows to any extent in forests; it is a valuable tree for wind-swept situations, and the soft, white timber has long been valued for utensils and decorative work. In the sixteenth and early seventeenth centuries came the oriental plane (*Platanus orientalis*), still a rare tree and better known to us as a parent of the hybrid London plane (*P. hybrida* or *acerifolia*). The larch (*Larix decidua*) was brought over from the Continent at about that time, while the Scots pine (*Pinus sylvestris*), which had retreated to Scotland, was re-introduced to southern England and soon re-established itself. The common lime (*Tilia vulgaris* or *europaea*), a hybrid between our native large- and small-leaved limes, was an introduction also; we first read of it planted in avenues "both for shade and sweetness" in 1609. From Turkey, via France, came the horse-chestnut (*Aesculus hippocastanum*), first recorded in John Tradescant's garden in Lambeth in 1633.

The great nobles were largely responsible for the early collections for which these trees were acquired. Instances were the Lord Protector Somerset at Syon, whose adviser was William Turner (1515–68) the "father of English botany", the 1st Earl of Salisbury (1563–1612) at Theobalds, and Lord Burleigh (1520–98) at Hatfield.

In 1580 the shortage of oak was so serious that Burleigh ordered the sowing of acorns on thirteen acres of Windsor Park, the first recorded instance of forest planting. Little else was done until the Restoration. The brilliant court of Charles II, during their exile on the Continent, had seen something of the great gardens of Le Nôtre in which trees, planted to form dense bosquets or in long avenues, played a great part. Ornamental tree planting began here on a scale not hitherto known, and was to continue in formal style until the reign of Queen Anne. The Dutch are a nation of horticulturists, and the influence of William and Mary was considerable. Yet in spite of an increasing interest in trees, and their greatly increased use ornamentally, England's native woodlands continued to languish and our natural resources were exploited without any regard for the future.

After the return of Charles II the Royal Society was formed, and in September 1662 there was presented to it by the Commissioners for the Navy a paper on the desperate shortage of the rugged, angular, strong timber produced by the pedunculate oak, which was essential to build His Majesty's warships. The subject was referred to a committee, which body, as is not unusual, left it to one of its members, John Evelyn. On 15 October, 1662, Evelyn wrote in his diary: "I this day delivered my Discourse concerning Forest-trees to our Society upon the occasion of Certaine Queries sent us by the Commissioners of His Majesties Navy". This was the origin of his great work, *Sylva*, the first volume ever to be published by the Royal Society, and one of the most important. It was not only the first exhaustive study of our native trees and their uses, but the first to include introduced exotic trees that might be of value. It certainly resulted in many trees being planted. In the dedication to the King of his second edition in 1670 Evelyn claimed that his book had been the "sole occasion of furnishing your almost exhausted Dominions with more than two Millions of Timber Trees". Perhaps more important, his work may be said to mark the beginning of the remarkable British enthusiasm for arboriculture. A whole line of amateurs, from Henry Compton, Bishop of London, (1632–1713) down to the creators of such great collections as those at Dropmore and Westonbirt, on occasions supported by bodies such as the Royal Horticultural Society, have resulted in our small islands containing thriving specimens of more species from temperate climates than any comparable area in the world. The search for and experimental growing of exotic trees has had far-reaching effects on England's present forests and woodlands – indeed, upon the landscape as a whole.

The Norway spruce (*Picea abies*) has since ancient times been one of the most important timber trees in northern Europe, and in pre-glacial times it was present in England. When it was re-introduced is not known. Evelyn, however, describes it clearly and, except for the sweet chestnut, it was the first exotic to be grown for timber. Today, supplying when young the Christmas tree, it ranks as the fifth tree in numbers. The first use of an exotic on such a scale as to alter our forests entirely was in 1740. In that year the then Duke of Atholl began planting larches on high ground above Dunkeld, in Scotland. The trees succeeded. By 1826 he and his successors had planted over fourteen million; the first great change in Britain's treescape had begun.

Even more extensive changes were to follow. Between 1790 and 1795 Captain George Vancouver made his great voyage. Archibald Menzies was his surgeon and botanist. Menzies returned with an account of the great forests on the Pacific coast of North America. In 1824 David Douglas (1799–1834), a young Scot employed by what is now the Royal Horticultural Society, made his first visit to collect the trees Menzies had described. Between then and his early accidental death he introduced the Sitka spruce (*Picea sitchensis*), the Douglas fir (*Pseudotsuga menziesii*), the giant fir (*Abies grandis*) and the noble fir (*A. procera*). All these thrived in England. Two other exotic conifers have a similar power to produce good timber: the Corsican pine (*Pinus nigra maritima*), faster and taller growing than our native pine, introduced in 1795 from the Mediterranean, and the Japanese larch (*Larix leptolepis*) brought from Japan in 1861 (distinguished from the European kind by its red twigs in winter). These trees began to insinuate themselves into the woodlands of enterprising landowners during the latter part of Queen Victoria's reign; not until the present century did they begin to dominate them. They all produce valuable timber on poorer land than will support our native trees.

During the reigns of the Stuarts the planting of trees in formal designs had played an essential part in the development of the great estates. As I have said, the inspiration came from the huge French lay-outs which reached a climax in the reign of Louis XIV. The style was an international one. But as early as the late 1690s a reaction was developing among English men of letters against this rigidity of lay-out. It came into the open in Joseph Addison's *Remarks on Several Parts of Italy in the Years 1701, 1702, 1703*, in the writings of Alexander Pope and others, and later in the publications of philosophers such as Burke. Travellers on the Grand Tour returned in ecstasies not over the magnificent Renaissance gardens of Rome, but the irregular beauties of the Campagna, with its rough patches of woodland, its serpentine streams, and a scatter of classical remains.

The result was the creation of the English landscape garden, whose constituents were undulating grass, trees and water. A visit to Blenheim Palace will show what an important part trees played in its design. The exponents of this manner were Lancelot ("Capability") Brown (1716–83) and his successor, Humphry Repton (1752–1818). They were responsible for planting trees in immense numbers: 100,000 was not exceptional for a single Brown landscape. Even so, the impact that this school made on England's woodland is apt to be exaggerated. Brown and Repton between them landscaped only some 300 estates, most on land unsuited to agriculture, and largely in the Midlands and Home Counties. Though we may agree with the poet that their work

> . . . scoops in circling theatres the vale
> Calls in the country, catches opening glades,
> Joins willing woods, and varies shades from shades

we must not forget the less publicized but well-documented fact that the tree planting was frequently done eventually to increase the revenue from timber.

We cannot consider trees in the landscape without mentioning orchards. Though England grows some of the finest apples in the world the only native is a small, sour, inedible crab, which does not enter into the breeding of the kinds of apple we now grow. The gean is a native, and this does play a part in the breeding of "sweet" cherries. We cannot claim either pears or plums as native fruits, in the strict sense.

There is evidence that the Romans introduced some of the better kinds of fruit; but not until Tudor times did the English become serious fruit growers. The great period of development in fruit-cultivation began in the late eighteenth century. Immense progress in breeding was made by Thomas Andrew Knight (1759–1838) and others. Richard Cox (*c.* 1776–1845), a successful brewer who retired about 1820 to Colnbrook, near Slough, developed Cox's Orange Pippin sometime in the 1830s. Since then England has been in the forefront of fruit-growing. In the last two decades new methods have greatly altered the orchard scene – in Worcestershire, Herefordshire, Kent, Essex and Suffolk especially – by replacing spreading old trees with small, intensively grown bushes.

At the end of the nineteenth century many of England's woodlands were in a state of neglect, and of little economic significance. Much of the planting done in the early nineteenth century was of the type of oak suitable only for ship-building, of which the Napoleonic wars had shown we were desperately short. This was to be ready for use early in the twentieth century. But by that time, of course, steam, iron and steel had replaced our "wooden walls". The timber now required must be straight and strong for structural work or for producing veneer, not angular to provide crucks for ship-building.

A small number of landowners, however, had been experimenting with the new western American conifers, only too well aware that if there should be any interference with our huge imports of wood the economy of our islands would be badly hit. Governments ignored their warnings.

In 1914 came the dreaded climax of a century of neglect. Trees were felled indiscriminately. The need was for the moment: there was no time to consider the results. In 1919 the Forestry Commission was belatedly set up. It took over the few remaining royal forests, was given power to acquire land and plant trees – the larger areas they handled were called forests, now with a very different meaning from the old royal sporting reserves. Help was given to landowners.

The fact that the type of forestry practised was essential to twentieth-century needs aroused much hostility from a prejudiced public which still seemed to think on lines more applicable to the timber-framed houses of Shakespeare's day and the ships of Nelson's time. But by 1939 the gawky adolescence of our new forests was being outgrown, and a new type of forest, of great beauty, was being appreciated. Then war broke out again. Schemes of planting were calamitously disordered while improved methods of felling caused the destruction of old woodlands that had survived the First World War. Since 1945 the work has gone forward again. What was its purpose? Quite simply and brutally the key lies in the fact that we are now a debtor country and yet pay £500 million a year for wood and wood products that we could produce ourselves, if only on a limited scale.

What has to be recognized, when considering England's woodlands, is that since Tudor times the rate of destruction of trees has exceeded their natural power to replace themselves. As a result, virtually the whole of our treescape has become man-made, almost entirely for the provision of saleable, usable timber. There have been other very limited objectives, such as provision for sport. But seldom have our great woods been planted primarily for visual effect. Even the scenic ornamental planting of the eighteenth and nineteenth centuries did not ignore utilitarianism. Fortunately, good forestry results in good landscapes.

The English Village

PAUL JENNINGS

Let us imagine that in the twinkling dark cosiness of a village pub, among the regulars who have dropped in before lunch, there are two strangers. One is a young representative, who grew up in Manchester and is now buying a house in Croydon. He has spent almost all his life in an urban background, and neither he nor his wife have ever really had serious thoughts about living in the country. His company-provided new Cortina is parked outside.

Next to it is the fairly ancient Rover, smelling comfortably of old leather and wood, of the other visitor. He is one of those vague, scholarly men, with steel-rimmed glasses and some kind of old canvas shoulder-bag with many straps and buckles, who look as if they would be much happier walking than driving a car at all. He is in fact a leading authority on carved wooden screens, and has spent the morning examining the one in the church visible from the saloon-bar window (it is justly famous, although it is a matter of wonderful separate panels, the muntins as though carved of solid stone rather than wood, not fully integrated in an intricate whole design as in the full late Tudor glories, he is thinking).

For him this is a planned, prepared visit. For the other it is almost a casual stop. It is a matter of chance whether they fall into conversation; but the point is that the motives that made the first man stop are only a generalized and diffuse form of what appears in the other as a highly specialized enthusiasm. They are both attracted, in their different ways, by a village thing. The young representative may never have given two consecutive thoughts to "the English village" (although this would be unlikely – and foolish – in anyone with the opportunity of using a car intelligently); but even if he had only thought to himself, "Something attractive about this place; old church, grouping of buildings, air of peace, think I'll stop here for early lunch – besides, easier to park here," he would have been responding to an appeal which grows more and more irresistible as one's knowledge of the English village grows.

There are many now who dismiss the whole thing as Ford dismissed history; if they don't quite dare to go so far as to say it is bunk, they do say it is *sentimentalism*, an irrelevant attempt to opt out from the technological age into a vanished pastoral civilization. In actual fact, not only the quite substantial movement of settling-down young families to new estates in villages, and the new council housing, but even the disappearance of the ploughman from the old thatched cottages (sometimes to re-appear in a council house) and the modernization of those thatched cottages by the despised "sentimentalists", is part of a process which is still, after all these centuries, the distinguishing mark of the English village; the process of *organic growth*.

I do not think it is just one's natural chauvinism which makes one say that although everyone has a (doubtless romanticized) mental picture of "the English village", with thatched cottages and a church tower set among Rowland Hilder-type elms, our villages differ one from another much more than those on the

Village Scene. Charcoal drawing by Thomas Gainsborough (1727–88)

Continent. Of course a Provençal village looks different from those with one long street of varnished maroon bricks, mortar-lines picked out in white, and heavy stone lintels – more like Holland, really – which fill the first afternoon southwards from Calais; but neither France nor any other country offers, on the scale which England does, exploration in reverse, as it were. Exploration usually means a going outwards, a crossing of horizons; but here somehow the spiral goes the other way; one curls inwards, in a landscape where little low ridges, absent-minded lanes, spacious parks fitted into valleys or woods much too small for them by any rational arithmetic, culs-de-sac, glimpses of water, make one realize that over the centuries we have somehow created inner space.

It is the result of a national empiricism, a penchant for doing things by one and one, not according to any scheme, grafted on to a fortunate geological and geographical diversity. What a lot of sharply differentiated areas there are in England, each so definite in character that it gives the impression of being much bigger than it is. No Canadian prairie could give a greater impression of skyey immensity than the Fens. The Lake District, the Cotswolds, the Peak, the orcharded Severn valley, the bare Wiltshire downs – all these and many other countries-within-a-country each produce instantly recognizable types of village, absolutely in harmony with the landscape because built out of the material on which they stand. Incidentally, there is no need to say that modern transport has made such reliance on local materials another "sentimentalism" with no practical justification. But there is plenty of aesthetic justification, as may be seen when you drive out of the Peak National Park, where all new housing has to be of that beautiful sober stone; the first red-brick house on the road to Chesterfield hits you like an oath.

This is no place for trying to summarize Cox or Betjeman on churches (or Pevsner on everything, let alone the fantastically knowledgeable and entertaining authors of the Shell *County Guides*); but fundamentals are fundamentals, and a thousand years free from invasion have allowed our villages to develop in a uniquely local and individual way. And the church is indisputably the most obvious example in most villages.

Now and again you may find scars of old violence, such as the cannon-ball marks on the tower of St Mary the Virgin in Painswick, which was occupied by Parliamentary troops in 1644; and of course there were the image-breakers, like the man who pulled down some statues in Winchester Cathedral with ropes "and down came all ye golden godes with *heyho rumbelo*", or the appalling William Dowsing who went round East Anglia smashing things – at Southwold "we brake down 130 superstitious pictures . . . and 14 cherubims", and you can see angry mutilations scored on the delicious screen showing ARKEANGEL, SARAFYN (Seraphim), TRONEE (Thrones) and the rest. But the main impression is of peaceful continuity.

At Langford, hidden in Oxfordshire meadows, there is a Crucifixion and a Christ in Majesty that were there before William did his Conquering (and he might not have managed *that* if Harold had not had to rush down from beating Tostig and Harald Hardrada at Stamford Bridge). And every first-year art student draws (or used to draw) the great Anglo-Saxon church of Earls Barton in Northampton-shire, with its pilastered tower. Both these churches are in the central limestone belt that runs from Gloucester and Dorset to the Humber.

Whether built, like the houses surrounding them, of this stone, or of the flint which is all that was available in East Anglia or most of Sussex, or the Midland sandstone, or any other local material, many of the churches have, side by side, illustrations of succeeding styles. They may perhaps have started as aisleless build-ings; later a chapel will have been added, that will have been lengthened into a north aisle, followed perhaps by a south aisle in the fourteenth century, a tower in the fifteenth. At Southease in Sussex it is the other way round; in the fourteenth century it had a north and a south aisle; now it is aisleless. There are no *rules*.

Only development – in its proper sense, before it became a dirty word: develop-ment as organic growth, something uniquely local, never imposed – almost, you might say, the opposite of planning. Obviously there is an overall, general, wander-ing correspondence with the slow changes of time and style. The catastrophe of the Black Death in 1350 meant the end of Decorated Gothic, partly because there were no longer enough craftsmen, but also because the Perpendicular, the church as "a box of light" was invented, according to Dr Cox, at Gloucester; and it gave Gothic a new impetus which carried it to a last sophistication unknown on the Continent, where they were by that time on to Renaissance styles. Hence King's College, but also hence all those marvellous Perpendicular churches built well on in the fifteenth century, often with the endowment of a rich merchant or clothier – Thomas Spring at Lavenham, or Tame at Fairford with its unsurpassed glass. There is one in my own village of East Bergholt, where Cardinal Wolsey's seizure of monastic lands for his abortive college at Ipswich is traditionally connected with the abandonment of the church tower after only one stage; so our bells are rung on axles, in a wooden cage on the ground, to the endless delight of crowds of summer tourists.

That same Black Death loosened the tying of the villein to the land, and hastened the progress of consolidation from copyholder to yeoman farmer with hired labour; and of course the growth of the weaving-grazing complex into a big-money affair led to a hedging and boundary-making that reached its climax in the eigh-teenth century. But here again it happened in different ways in different villages. I used as a boy to walk from Coventry over fields, now built on, that still, as everywhere on the Midland clays, were ridged from medieval strip farming. Some villages still have huge commons, some have long since lost them. At Meriden one drives from Coventry to Birmingham past a little green on which the cross is said to mark the centre of England. At Eltisley, between Cambridge and Bedford, one drives across the hypotenuse of an enormous one; and not far away at Ickwell the green is half a mile across. In East Bergholt most of it was snapped up in the nineteenth century by what was later the house of Mr Randolph Churchill. At Aldborough, Yorkshire, the children dance round a maypole which turns out to date only from 1903.

And why not? Perhaps a real danger today is that of being self-conscious about self-consciousness. Granted that mechanized metropolitan audio-visual culture is everywhere, militating against the old "one and one" English variety, does it matter if old traditions are researched by historical-minded and sincere newcomers? Do not such discoveries enrich the lives of communities still evolving, round W.I.s where half the members were born in London, round pubs where the Saturday-night regulars may have come from twenty miles away? Where the smith not only welds farm equipment but shoes the ponies of little girls from suburban-looking estates and makes wrought-iron gates, weather-vanes and even ornamental tops for false wells?

In the face of the massive onslaught of the twentieth century the wonder is that so much *does* survive (and perhaps an awareness of the need for rural preservation, however self-conscious and, to your standard pragmatist, sentimental, has developed just in time). A friend of mine, a Londoner with one of the despised weekend cottages in Suffolk, demurred when the eighty-year-old man who looks after his garden suggested the garden tool shed were left unlocked, instead of the old man (who often went away) keeping the key. "We'll hang it up then," said the old man, "*in a shy place*."

My friend will now certainly speak of "a shy place" for the rest of his life. But will the old man's grandsons? Sometimes I think we underestimate the immensely strong life of the rooted local past. Children whizz on their bicycles down the hill past my open window shouting almost impenetrable dialect to one another, although they may have watched three hours of dreary mid-Atlantic television last night. In the Norfolk village of Hickling the field names are Home Fanny, Middle Fanny, Top Fanny, Garbage, Shales, Pott's Pightle, The Spong, Rushy Bottoms, Honey Pots, Puttocks, Weasels, Pasture Aldermans, Pig's Pightle, Large Pictures, Little Pictures.

In Warwickshire a mole-hill is an *oonty-tump*. In Dorset they talk about an ant-hill as an *emmet-butt* – and *nish* or *nesh* is soft, to *plim* is to swell up, *linny* is a lean-to shed, a *tunnegar* is a funnel. In Willoughby, Lincs., *bluther* means to weep, *goosen* is to act silly, *gallibaulk* is a chimney, *kelter* is rubbish, and the extremely expressive way of saying "shut the door" is "*put wood i'th'wal*".

English villages, sited from the requirements of Anglo-Saxon agriculture on good soil by a stream ("the hill-top village, a frequent Continental feature, is here something of a rarity – there was never the same need for defence" says Charles Bradley Ford), have gradually replaced the forest, cleared or burnt (which is all *Brentwood* means), and in so doing they have all become as it were watertight pockets well able to maintain individuality.

Obviously there *is* a sense in which the village as an ideal place, a pastoral invented by metropolitan poets who do not know one end of a plough from the other, is something that has to be put in the past. But the not too remote past.

Probably most people, whether English or not, asked to write twenty words describing our countryside, would mention the hedges. Now it is true that some hedges are quite old. In fact, at a recent conference arranged by the Botanical Association and the Standing Conference of Local Historians, under the title "Hedges and Local History", Mr D. E. Allen of the Linnean Society read a paper called *Bramble Dating: A Promising Approach*, in which it appeared that since wild species take a definite number of years to die out, you can date a hedge simply by counting the number of species in it. (In the Isle of Man, where there are forty different species, he had found the oldest hedges to be the ones lining the road to the ancient Manx Parliament, the Tynwald.)

But of course there is nothing immemorial about our chessboard hedgerow landscape, most of which dates merely from the eighteenth century (and a lot of it resulted from enclosures which meant appalling dispossessions and hardships for agricultural labourers). And really it calls for a constantly intelligent and inquiring interest (and therefore increased joy) in the countryside not to have this merely "pastoral" interest in (for example) hedgerows. To preserve them as windbreaks, conservers of top-soil and wild life – good. To make prairies – bad. But to amalgamate two fields really too tiny for tractor working, on part of a rational well-run farm – good. And picturesque hedges on an all-meadow, stockbroker's tax-loss farm – bad. One can say this of abstract cases; perhaps only God or a computer could say it of actual ones.

So it is no use being romantically against big concrete barns or silos (quite nice shapes, actually, when you are used to them; they have tiny shiny domes, like little Baroque towers in Bavaria) or against any new housing being built anywhere in villages. With all its new inhabitants, the village is still the place that offers most chance of a sense of community. Possibly the period from the Elizabethan development of parish administration to the immediately pre-motor age was one of a now irrecoverable local identity. It is noticeable how many village histories tell of a much greater self-sufficiency fifty or a hundred years ago, with a cobbler, a baker, a watchmaker in places of any size. Kimcote, Leicestershire, in 1965 had only one shop; since 1846 the baker's, butcher's, tailor's and other shops had disappeared one by one.

You could almost say that the village went on becoming *more* itself during the railway age. Such "sentimental" newcomers as the railway brought, either to new Mr Franching-of-Peckham-style villas behind gloomy hedges or to genuine Georgian or earlier houses, in the Home Counties or the unspoilt bits of Cheshire, were indeed a separate element, the precursors of those in anyone-for-tennis plays who have a comic char from the village who comes in through the French window wearing a turban and smoking. (There is a ridiculous and highly controvertible generalization. Village life is for *anyone* who loves it.) And it is curious how in many villages the post-Beeching railway line already looks as irrelevant, as archaeological, as a Roman road. Stations I myself have seen are used now (*a*) as a factory for making scientific glassware, (*b*) for painting Oxford Playhouse scenery, and (*c*) for rearing pigs.

Yet those grass-grown tracks, sprouting willow herb and marguerite daises, represent the first stage on the road to what now amounts practically to the total accessibility of all villages. It is only necessary to get out of the car in any of them, and look at the church, or the pub, or the green, or to speak to someone, to count the species in the hedge, to see when the Methodist chapel or the station was built, to find the manor house or the stream, to know in what way it is still a unique place.

English Townscape

JOHN SUMMERSON

In every English town much conforms with the norm of modernity. All traffic signs are the same everywhere. The fascias and window-dressing of the chain stores are the same. Advertisements are the same. The brands in the shops are the same. The citizens are also very much the same. Most of them being strangers to each other, they are in no wise strange to the stranger. All this is very convenient; all urban life flows together into one continuous urban life and the approach to an unfamiliar town offers no problems. It might be added that all modern buildings are very nearly the same, or if they are not they very soon will be. What matters about them is not so much what form they take as where they are put.

No English town would be better worth visiting than any other English town were it not for the enormous, obstinate and overwhelming legacy of the past. There is so much of it that even the most affluent and rapidly developing town cannot entirely wipe its old self out. The buildings remain so long as there is no sharp economic incentive to replace them; or, more rarely, because the laws protecting historic buildings and urban amenities have come into action. It is this great hinterland of architectural lumber which gives each separate town its "character". The "character" of a town today is necessarily "historic character". But perhaps, after all, it is the same with people; "character" is a function of biography.

So, for the curious visitor, the town has to be unwrapped, layer by layer, horizontal and vertical, to reveal its true character: a complicated process because the layers interpenetrate; they never come away in continuous strips. Take the main shopping street of almost any town. What is it made of? One half of it (the lower half) is made of shops. The other (upper) half is made of semi- or demi-semi-houses. Their lower parts have been sheared away by the shop-keepers. But these scraps of houses themselves protrude from different layers of the town's growth. Some may still have fifteenth- or sixteenth-century timbering in them; this may have been exposed and fussed over (and spoilt) for prestige sake, or it may stay, suspect only, behind a coat of Georgian stucco. Other scraps may be substantial eighteenth-century work, the chamber floors of aldermen and attorneys, now riding on steel bressumers over plate glass. Others again may be the sometime residences of Victorian shop-keepers whose elaborate and demonstrative shop-windows were found inconvenient and ugly in the 'twenties and 'thirties of this century.

One can go further into the past life of a main street. What, for instance, happens behind the houses? What shapes are the sites and how far back do they go? We can probably discover this by slipping through a passage between buildings or into a tradesman's yard. The backs of buildings are sometimes less disturbed than the fronts. In scraps of forgotten garden, in a Georgian summer-house used for storing ironmongery or perhaps even in a Gothic gable or two which nobody has bothered either to destroy or restore we can see more strips of time fall away.

This is perhaps moving too far towards a specialized investigation of urban "character", but the point needs to be made that a town more than two centuries old (and most English towns go back, at least in name, five times as far) is a very complex sort of artifact: most complicated in the many-layered centre, less complicated in the fringes where the buildings, built not so long ago, have never been rebuilt or overlaid or, indeed, notably changed in their function.

In nearly all towns are three typical elements which may be sought and found even without the help of a guide-book. First there is the medieval centre, then the Georgian outgrowth, and lastly the Victorian perimeter. The relative positions of the first two are never quite the same, but half an hour's judicious driving round the town should discover them all. The Victorian perimeter is likely to be discovered first, and although perhaps it should be explored last it should not be dismissed. It subdivides. Somewhere there will be the favoured streets of Victorian success, with houses by *the* local architect (who probably lived in one of them). Some of the houses will be of stone or brown brick-and-stone in that curious mixture of Gothic and Italian Romanesque which a Victorian critic shrewdly labelled "latitudinarian"; others, after 1870, will have gone over to "Queen Anne", a brown-and-red brick style about which the first thing to be said is that it is almost everything which the architecture of Queen Anne's England was not. Elsewhere in the Victorian perimeter we shall find the inevitable rows of bay-windowed houses with cocky roofs and ferny panels, appropriate to the clerks and managers and piano teachers and widows with small means. And elsewhere again the stiff harsh regiments, in the commonest brick, of the houses suited to the workers on the railway or in whatever industry the railway brought to the town or fostered within it. In passing, it may be observed that the railway station is a key monument in any town.

Signs of affluence in the Victorian perimeter may well predict what we shall find in the medieval centre. Affluence will have produced an Italian Corn Exchange in the 1860s, an Anglo-Venetian town hall in the 1870s, some blocks of "business premises" in London style in the 'eighties, a school of art, perhaps, and a public library in the 'nineties. And affluence will certainly have restored the church.

The church is the great repository of the town's memories. An English town is inconceivable without a church – so much so that in designs for new towns, made in an age of galloping decline in church attendance, there is sometimes proposed some abstract "vertical feature", some object of superstitious non-worship to symbolize the steeple of the church which, were it built, would serve, but so much more expensively, the ancient inarticulate need.

Churches may be cathedrals, in being which they contract out of the rôle of being "the church". Even in cathedral cities there is always a principal parish church though it loses, in the cathedral aura, the dignity of the definite article. In middling towns "the church" is the object by which all distances and directions are estimated. Its silhouette, if it is at all striking, is accepted and cherished as the symbol of the town. It is impossible to utter such names as Grantham, Coventry, Newark or Boston without a silhouette crossing the mind; while to speak of Chesterfield is to allude, however obscurely, to the thing that happened there in the fourteenth century, when the newly built spire contorted itself irrevocably into a nameless and horrible shape.

Town churches have usually suffered from affluence. Rarely can one feel in them that deep penetration into the past which belongs to the poor country church. Often they have been rebuilt in whole or in part in the eighteenth century; or, if a medieval fabric has come through to the nineteenth, it will have been so expensively scraped and renewed as to have lost all the bloom of antiquity. The churchyard, too, will have been scraped and tidied, the head-stones laid flat to make a pavement or massed against the churchyard wall. Nothing will repay the visitor so well as the memorials within. They are a directory to what the town has been and who made it so.

The church will necessarily belong to the town's medieval pattern, its ancient self, and that pattern can sometimes be traced without more guidance than the sense of restriction and irregularity which the central streets afford. Not always, however. Sometimes the church stands apart, linked to the urban centre by a Church Street; sometimes the centre itself has shifted away from the church and the original centre been distorted or erased.

After the close of the Middle Ages towns grew ribbon-wise: new houses lengthened the main streets, they also grew in density; lesser houses were built behind and in the grounds of greater ones. But very rarely did any great increase or any formal novelty arrive before the eighteenth century. Under the Georges every town which had its share of agricultural and industrial prosperity acquired a suburb of mansions. In a small town this suburb may be simply one short street. In a larger town it may be a geometrical area of streets and squares. It is always there, and it is wonderful how often its integrity has survived. Its source is metropolitan; it is a piece of London attached, not without pride, to a country town.

These three elements – medieval centre, Georgian outgrowth and Victorian fringe – are constants in all towns with a deep past. Having said that, it may appear that there is something like a standard English town. There is not. There is perhaps a hypothetical standard which is useful. But if our three elements are constant in appearance their disposition and their ratio one to the other are not. Sometimes one, sometimes another of the elements dominates. It depends much on the geographical mould in which the town was cast and on which of the centuries saw its most energetic growth. The balance or imbalance of the three elements is what most notably gives towns their character.

Take first the cathedral cities. The presence of the cathedral, the space around it and its attendant buildings, at once dismiss the typical. The effects vary, however. At York, with its walls still standing, the medieval centre *is* the city; the Georgian outgrowth (the noble street called Bootham) is outside the walls. At Salisbury, on the other hand, the chosen Georgian area is around the cathedral and its close. At Exeter the city had before the war and still partly has a planned Georgian wing, like a piece of Bloomsbury. No two cathedral cities have developed alike, and their functions have, after all, not been wholly ecclesiastical. York, Norwich, Exeter, Salisbury, Chester and Bristol have always been regional capitals, a distinction independent of their rôle as the seat of a bishop.

The regional capital which is also the seat of a bishop is the grandest kind of English town. It can be seen as a miniature London. Bristol is still, despite the bombs, a wonderful likeness of what London was a century ago. The medieval centre is the "city" quarter with "city churches", a Guildhall and an Exchange. The Georgian outgrowth is the equivalent of London's "west end" and stretches into Clifton as London stretches into Bayswater but more gracefully and with continuously exciting contours. To compensate for having no "St Paul's" there is a stately if inconspicuous medieval cathedral and there is the spire of St Mary Redcliffe, a marvel which medieval London itself might have envied.

The regional capital has something of everything. In sharp contrast are those towns where the Georgian outgrowth has run away with the situation. They are towns which at a certain moment became irrevocably dedicated to health and pleasure. Bath is the queen of them. Bath is a medieval city, and the medieval pattern,

King's Parade, Cambridge. Painting by Thomas Malton (1748–1804)

the constriction of the long vanished walls, can still be felt in the streets around the cathedral. But beyond where the walls stood the Georgian outgrowth, begun under Queen Anne, gathered such momentum that by the end of the eighteenth century Bath was a very large Georgian city with a very small ancestral appendage. The hot springs were the cause of this. Elsewhere it was the sea. At Brighton the discovery that sea-bathing and sea-air were beneficial converted, within fifty years, a small fishing town with a small medieval church, and a few streets running down to the sea, into a metropolitan pleasure-centre. For two reasons Brighton is a special case. First, because of its early patronage by Royalty (and, consequently, the building of the Royal Pavilion). Second, because of its relative proximity to London. But the same elements are there, even if the "medieval centre" is almost nothing, the Georgian outgrowth regal, and the Victorian perimeter vast. This, incidentally, is a Victorian perimeter which contains, among other things, the finest collection of nineteenth-century Gothic churches of any town in the kingdom.

The health resorts mostly had Georgian seed-times and in some of them is a double Georgian harvest – first the formal pattern of streets, squares and crescents which Bath invented, and later the informal "picturesque", with villas disposed in calculated disorder. In Calverley Park at Tunbridge Wells, and at St Leonard's-on-Sea, the "picturesque" is most purposefully promoted by a single architect. Elsewhere, as at Cheltenham and Leamington, it grew more casually. Bournemouth started in this way as an early Victorian adventure in estate development, and became in effect one great Victorian perimeter with (how rare!) no medieval centre at all and not a solitary Georgian street.

Cathedral cities, regional capitals and health resorts are the English towns which by tradition and convention may be visited for the pure pleasure of visiting them. To them must be added that celebrated pair, Oxford and Cambridge. Of these it must be said that the only difference between them and dozens of other county towns, up and down the country, is that they have accidentally attached to themselves, in their very centres, institutions of world fame with buildings often venerable and sometimes sublime. But county towns they remain, as they go about

their county business and their thriving industries. Oxford bus-conductors still
do not know one college from another.

All these towns have "something to show". There remain the towns to which
tradition and convention almost forbid a visit unless for a hard and positive
reason. They are supposed to have nothing to show. This is sometimes but not
always true. It cannot be said that Liverpool or Manchester or Birmingham have
nothing to show. It is true that they are black. It is true that they have long ago
ceased to be articulate and have merged with lesser towns into limitless "conur-
bations". But still if one seeks one finds the old elements as before – the ancient
but dreadfully modernized church, the modest brick streets and stucco villas
built before the industrial deluge and – one need hardly add – Victorian perimeters
of the most tremendous proportions. But one finds also things special to these
places. At Liverpool the proudest Classical building in Britain, after St Paul's
Cathedral and the royal palaces, is the first thing the railway traveller sees as he
emerges from Lime Street Station: St George's Hall. In the hinterland the greatest
of modern Anglican cathedrals rises on one eminence, the most original of modern
Catholic cathedrals on another. Down in the dock area is a miscellany of Georgian,
Victorian and Edwardian architecture more extravagant than anything in London.

How can one or how should one evaluate towns? Each traveller must decide
for himself. There is the hedonist evaluation on the score of sheer physical pleasure
– the pleasure of walking through serene, quiet streets and in the shadow of ancient
masterpieces whose performance seems, even in the late twentieth century,
colossal. This experience is being shattered by modern traffic but where it is still
to be had it is golden. A "beautiful" town is coming to mean a town in which it is a
pleasure to walk. There is another, more rigorous, kind of evaluation which judges
a town by the intricacy and strangeness of its growth and by the human invention
to which its fabric bears witness, even if it is a grim fabric. The sense of curiosity
rather than the sense of beauty is satisfied. Whoever favours the first kind of
evaluation may find his goal in Ludlow or King's Lynn; whoever favours the
second, in Halifax or Hull. But has the town ever been built which is of interest to
nobody? If it has it is surely a very rare piece.

Some towns are more easily remembered than others and the main factor in the
memory equation is wholeness. The town which can, today, be seen and felt as a
whole is necessarily rare. Town walls, the best guarantee of wholeness, disappeared
early in England. The walls of York and Chester are famous, but Berwick-upon-
Tweed still has walls: walls built by Elizabeth I to keep the Scots at bay and still
enclosing, uselessly but splendidly, a quietly beautiful market town. Intensity of
function has been another effective promoter of wholeness. St Ives, in Cornwall,
grew round its granite church as a granite settlement of fisher folk, hard and
clustered against the sea. Today it is a holiday town, but the intensity is still visibly
there. Of other towns it could be said that they have derived a certain wholeness
from disaster. Warwick suffered a conflagration in the seventeenth century, the
little Dorset town of Blandford in the eighteenth century. Both rebuilt themselves
with a new sophistication and in the architecture of both it may still be felt. But
when all is said and done it must be admitted that only a fairly small town – one
that has not been particularly successful in the urban rat-race – is likely to have
preserved this enviable and charming quality of being an imaginable whole. Towns
grow and go on growing and not often do they unfold all their mysteries to the
newcomer without some learning and perception on his part – some exercise of
the rôle, humbly undertaken, of urban anatomist.

The English Country House

JAMES LEES-MILNE

At the turn of this century a traveller along the English lanes would observe from the saddle of his push-bicycle or the seat of his dog-cart one "big house" standing at an average interval of two miles from another. The "big house" might be a palace at the end of a long, impressive avenue. It might be a manor house little larger than a farmstead, and close to the dusty highway. Whatever its size and pretension the appurtenances, lawns and herbaceous borders would certainly present a trim and well-groomed air. It would not be a commuter's weekend retreat, for such places did not then exist. On the contrary, it was the nucleus of a large or small agricultural kingdom. It was a living, hierarchical community of indoor servants, outdoor coachmen, gardeners and labourers, revolving round an owner who "belonged" to the district.

Until 1888, when county and rural district councils were established, England was governed by the squires, regionally as well as nationally. After this date their authority waned; but until the outbreak of the last war their influence was still paramount. A glance at Burke's *Landed Gentry* confirms that their ranks were being recruited by new families throughout the 1930s. The ambition of the *nouveaux riches*, as the old families used to call them, was to acquire estates and country houses – occasionally to build new ones – in which to establish dynasties of their own. Since the last war this process has for obvious reasons slowed down, if not ceased altogether. Prosperous business men today prefer to live in the suburbs of industrial towns, known as "dormitories", in modest-looking villas equipped with every labour-saving device, to adorn their wives with mink, and cram their garages with smart cars. This change of social pattern has virtually doomed the squirearchy.

We must discriminate between the rôles played in past social history by the great and the lesser country houses, or rather by their inmates. Let us take the small squire first. Until a hundred years ago he was very much a countryman, spending most of his time on the hunting field and his own broad acres, active on the Bench, consequential in the church pew, and merry in the village taproom. His manor house, teeming with offspring, was no shrine of virtu, but a family home, architecturally robust or prim, and usually comely. The great lord, on the other hand, played little part in county politics, being too preoccupied by affairs of court or state at St James's or Westminster. Nonetheless, the land was very dear to him for ancestral, financial and prestige reasons. He sprang from it. It provided him with his wherewithal. He visited it as often as his metropolitan duties allowed. He returned to die upon it. Ever since the Reformation the great lord's interest had been to amass more and more acres. And the immense wealth of the sixteenth-century families like the Cecils, Russells and Cavendishes had derived from the expropriation of monastic lands. The great lord's wealth and station were commensurate with his acreage. His rent roll was assessable by the magnitude of his country seat. The two were interdependent. Even today a big house divorced from its estate seems anomalous, if not uneconomic.

From the sixteenth to the nineteenth century the great lord held himself conspicuously aloof from the common herd. His tenantry may have found him grasping and forbidding. His neighbours among the lesser gentry must have found him unapproachable. They were seldom, if ever, invited within his unwelcoming portals. Indeed, until 1945 some great houses like Woburn and Longleat had not for centuries been entered by anyone outside the family and a restricted circle of intimates. The public's extraordinary interest in them today may partly be explained by curiosity to see for themselves what sort of exclusive life was lived by dukes and marquesses until comparatively recent times.

It follows that the owners of large country houses in the past were not always popular. On the other hand they were often creative. By no means all were amateur architects of the calibre of Sir Roger Pratt (Coleshill), Lord Burlington (Chiswick) or Lord Sudeley (Toddington). Yet the majority had the taste to engage and the learning to direct the foremost architects and craftsmen of their day. Many, too, were remarkably discerning patrons of artists, like the 4th Earl of Pembroke (Wilton), the 1st Earl of Leicester (Holkham), the 3rd Earl of Egremont (Petworth), and – to descend the social scale – Sir Justinian Isham (Lamport), Sir Andrew Fountaine (Narford) and Sir George Beaumont (Coleorton). These earls and baronets filled their houses with paintings and rare manuscripts, sculpture, tapestry, furniture and porcelain, which they collected on the Continent, or commissioned from their contemporaries at home. Their halls and courts, which at one time were accessible to the few, are today open to the many. Not only in the country houses, but also in their contents, we can enjoy the greatest contribution which our nation has made to the visual arts.

Not satisfied with embellishing his house, a landowner endeavoured to fashion his estate into a concerted work of art. The whole domain became, as it were, an integral extension of the house. First the pleasure grounds, secondly the park, and thirdly the woods and fields beyond, were laid out with an expert's eye for picturesque grouping. It was as though the connoisseur owner had employed Claude Lorrain or Richard Wilson to transpose from canvas upon the smiling face of England idyllic and bucolic scenes of ancient Greece and Rome.

Between 1700 and 1800 the whole country was tamed into one gigantic parkscape. Rivers and streams were changed overnight into serpentine lakes. Unsightly villages were razed to the ground. Hillocks were moved from one horizon to another. By the early twentieth century, when our Edwardian traveller was bicycling or driving along the highways, the woods and hedgerows of the Georgian planters had reached their prime. England was the most picturesque, no, the most beautiful country in the world. Today we can enjoy the residue of this rapidly dwindling capital of natural beauty – but only just. We should make the most of it – since we are doing nothing to replenish it – for as long as it may last.

It is nowadays fashionable to deride the aristocrats of the past ages. Recent publications have made much play with their selfishness, exploitation of the oppressed, and their frivolity. One might just as well revile for their religious bigotry the bishops and abbots under the Plantagenets. These prelates sponsored the cathedrals and minsters which are now the lasting witness of their age. Likewise the patricians built the country houses which are the witness of theirs. We should not be deflected from admiring the visual sensibility of these men, however much we may choose to ignore some other virtues which, according to the standards of their day, they indubitably possessed. We should not, I suggest, withhold from them our profound gratitude. We should likewise feel beholden to the country houses for the numbers of great Englishmen they in their turn have given birth to and nurtured – statesmen, agriculturists, philanthropists, theologians, scientists and poets.

Until the Reformation English country houses, judged by cultural and social standards, were secondary to the monasteries, which were the seats of learning and healing, and the founts of charity. But like them they were, as dwellings, stark and uncomfortable. Oakham Castle (1180) consists of one vaulted, pillared hall like a church, in which a whole household and retinue of retainers dossed down on straw-strewn mud at nights, and lived and fed by day little better than beasts in a pen. At Boothby Pagnell, Lincs., the late-Norman manor house resembles a noncon-formist chapel in being approached from outside by stone steps, and having tiny twin-light windows in the thick walls, without glass but with rough, wooden shutters. The squat peel-tower residences, like Longthorpe in Northampton-shire (late thirteenth century) and Yanwath in Westmorland (fourteenth century) were unashamedly utilitarian. Fourteenth-century Bodiam and fifteenth-century Tattershall castles were still designed for defence, not delight. Gradually a con-geries of annexes would grow up round the nuclear peel. Compton Wynyates in Warwickshire is such a place. To a modest Henry VI core was added in the en-suing centuries a hotchpotch of towers, turrets, crenellated wings, black and white gables, twisted chimneystacks, and every variety of window, pointed, mullioned, arched, flat-headed, cusped, and even sashed. The result is the most lovable, picturesque jumble of a house imaginable. But it cannot be called conscious architecture. Its beauty is accidental, approximating to the beauty of the oaks and elms which have grown laboriously out of the English soil. Like these rugged, shaggy trees it becomes increasingly venerable with the passage of time.

After the Reformation the nobility, enriched by the spoils of the Church, were more sophisticated and art-loving than their predecessors, the uncouth barons who waged the Wars of the Roses. Patronage rapidly shifted from churchmen to laymen; and masons and craftsmen concentrated upon secular building. As the medieval churches had been raised for the glory of God the Renaissance houses were raised for – I was going to say, the sake of art – but I fear it was sometimes self-glorification. With the disintegration of Catholic England a crop of domestic palaces and manor houses sprang up in the shires. At first they were comparatively simple in plan and decoration. Sutton Place, Surrey (1520), is of this sort. Of modest dimensions, its plain brick surfaces are only enlivened by a few panels of terracotta. Within a decade country houses began to be ambitious and ornate. Hengrave Hall, Suffolk (finished 1538), and Dingley Hall, Northants (1558), indulged in polygonal turrets and finials, and jazzy skylines. By Queen Elizabeth I's reign country houses had ceased to be defensive, and became domestic. The largest were often ostentatious, even vulgar like Burghley and Wollaton, both of which conformed to the character of their newly risen owners. The Elizabethan and Jacobean raisers of palaces were as often as not unscrupulous adventurers. Yet, strangely enough, some of these wholly inestimable persons created the most alluring houses in existence. Among them may be included Hardwick Hall, Blickling Hall, Montacute House and Chastleton House. All these houses are distinguished by vertical lines, uncongested surfaces, and huge casement windows; and above all by extremely sympathetic materials. They are still Gothic, colourful and intensely romantic.

It goes without saying that the Tudor and Jacobean mansions have none of the pretensions to scholarship of the contemporary villas of the Brenta. Nevertheless, in variety of materials and inventiveness of patterns they have no equals. We have merely to consider some materials with which the different regions of England abundantly supplied the native builders: claret brick in the Home Counties, honey stone in the Cotswolds, silvery oak in the Midlands, icy blue flint in East Anglia, not to mention cob, clunch, thatch, parge and wattle and daub almost everywhere. Yet it is a fallacy to assume that the medieval, Tudor and Jacobean builders were deliberately "olde worlde". Nothing is further from the truth. They were un-deviatingly functional. For example, the master carpenters of the half-timbered houses, who have been specially subjected to the charge of "quaintness", worked with hard-headed precision. They usually prefabricated the outer walls on the ground. Consequently they were obliged to measure and cut each beam and strut accurately to the fraction of an inch before they could raise and tenon the finished skeleton together. It is time and the seasons which have given the "black and white" buildings the weathered and warped look which the twentieth century finds appealing.

With the Caroline century came the recognition that what mattered in building was classical propriety. Adherence to Vitruvian rules assumed a vital importance. Inigo Jones was the first to introduce the rules from Italy. Wren, after profound study of French architecture, reaffirmed them. Meanwhile the native builders tried desperately to keep abreast with the foreign textbooks of Serlio, Fréart and Le Pautre. Often they failed signally to translate the new precepts into their work. Yet their first strivings towards classical regularity rendered houses like Ramsbury Manor (1675), Belton House (1694) and Hanbury Hall (1700) no less sympathetic to live in than the more correct achievements of their successors. For Caroline and Queen Anne houses, large or small, have the quality of homeliness and warmth.

Georgian houses, on the other hand, reach the ultimate excellence of art and craftsmanship. The golden age of enlightened patron and professional builder spanned the reigns of the four Georges. The partners, working together within strictly imposed limits and mastering the classical formulae, seldom put a foot wrong. The houses they created were as gracious and outwardly conforming as themselves. Their ostensible hallmark was manners. Architectural manners had to be as irreproachable as the expensive and elaborate clothes worn by the people who lived in these houses. The country-house way of life likewise became an art in itself. It persisted throughout the nineteenth and lasted even into the twentieth century. No one who did not experience it during its more relaxed years between the wars can conceive how civilizing were the amenities it offered.

The opening of the eighteenth century coincided with the building of vast country palaces in the Baroque style. The Chatsworths, Castle Howards and Blenheims were a triumphal expression of the aristocratic ascendancy over the monarchy, resulting from the Glorious Revolution of 1688. After the accession of George I the predominant architectural style was the Palladian. It was outwardly more staid, more glacial and less flamboyant than the Baroque, just as the Hanoverians were outwardly dull and respectable compared with the fabulous Stuarts. Holkham, Badminton and Wentworth Woodhouse come within the Palladian category. They are grandiose, not cosy houses. The Palladian style endured until the accession of George III in 1760. It was succeeded by the Adam-Wyatt style, which was more delicate, at times a trifle effeminate. Osterley, Syon and Shugborough are representative of this style. The rooms of these houses are so elegant that only the most refined furniture made by Chippendale, Sheraton or the *ébénistes* of Louis XVI looks well in them. Furniture of earlier or later date seems gross and out of place. Towards the end of George III's reign the Regency style was in the ascendant. Introduced by the Prince Regent, Holland and Nash, it has distinct Gallic and academic undertones. Regency decoration and furniture echo Napoleonic tastes and reflect Greek and Egyptian archaeological discoveries. Southill in Bedfordshire, Ickworth in Suffolk and Dodington in Gloucestershire attain an economy of line in architecture and furnishing which verges on the austere and pedantic. Inevitably the Regency gave way to the eclectic and often hectic over-ornamentation of the Victorian style.

The growth of our country houses has coincided with the evolution of the English race and language. It is impossible for anyone who professes to love the poetry of Shakespeare, Milton, Pope and Tennyson to be unmoved by them. Here we touch upon their peculiarly literary quality. By strict Italian standards they are sometimes amateurish, illogical and haphazard in design and composition. Yet they resemble rich pages of history which make compulsive reading. Their mellow walls, lichen-covered roofs, their family portraits, treasures and bric-à-brac, and their long continuity of ownership render them intrinsically poetic. You cannot tinker with poetry. The moment you start emending, correcting or bowdlerizing a Shakespearean sonnet or Tennysonian elegy you drive the magic out of it. Similarly, if you were to take a characteristic Cotswold manor house, cover the outside with fire escapes, rip out the panelling of the gallery, distemper the drawing-room a healthy hospital green, lino the oak floors, asphalt the garden paths and litter the lawns with classrooms, you might get a much needed reformatory for maladjusted teenagers. You would also have totally destroyed the ethos of the building. You would do better to raze it to the ground and cherish its memory.

Although taxation and the disappearance into thin air of the domestic servant have doomed the English country house as a single family unit, there are alternative ways of preserving some, if not most, of these national monuments. A few local authorities, the Ministry of Public Buildings, the National Trust and the Mutual Households Association provide praiseworthy compromises. Belgrave Hall, outside Leicester, has been filled with furniture and pictures that belonged to local families, and so beautifully arranged that the visitor may stroll through the rooms and garden under the happy illusion that he is the possessor of this medium-sized dwelling. Saltram in Devon, Dyrham in Gloucestershire, Danny in Sussex and Aynhoe in Northamptonshire still retain the splendid decoration and the principal contents which have always belonged to them. In these and in many other houses flats have been carved out of the bedroom floors and service wings, whereas the state rooms are regularly open to the public. Often the state rooms are used for concerts, exhibitions and various cultural activities. At Croft Castle, Herefordshire, different members of the Croft family live in separate corners of the house and share the ground-floor rooms with the public.

By these means historic country houses can still be kept alive; and, what is so important, their special character as homes is more or less maintained. After all, they were not built merely to be looked at and admired; they were meant to be lived in and loved as well.

Cathedrals and Churches

OLIVE COOK

For a large part of our population the symbolic meaning of our churches and cathedrals has become almost as remote as that of the Parthenon or the temples at Paestum. Already the fate of those pagan shrines threatens to overtake the sanctuaries of the Christian faith. Some have fallen into total disuse and have become derelict; others have even been pulled down in the interests of commerce; while many are in such bad repair that they could not endure without the splendid work of bodies such as the Historic Churches Preservation Trust and The Friends of Friendless Churches. But the vulnerability of these impressive monuments in a materialistic age heightens our appreciation of them as works of art and as the most eloquent of witnesses to the historic past. The visual scene in England is still dominated by our parish and greater churches. Their power simply as images, their magnificent variety, their enchanting detail, compel attention.

Cathedral and parish churches came into being for different purposes, and their design and evolution can only be understood if these differences are borne in mind. The cathedral was the focal point of a whole region while the parish church was the centre of both the religious and the social life of a local community. Its secular uses were varied: it became a place of refuge and defence in troubled times; the nave was the setting for miracle plays and for the feast of the patron saint; the porch (on the south side of the building) was used until the mid-sixteenth century for the rite of Holy Matrimony; and there tradesmen assembled to bargain and barter, lawyers interviewed their clients, and wool merchants stored their bales.

Churches which started their lives as the pivots of the parochial system (inaugurated in Anglo-Saxon times) were served originally by a single priest, whose sole concern was the spiritual care of the parishioners. The basic requirement was therefore no more than a two-celled structure, such as emerged in the north under Celtic influence, and the simplest form of which can still be seen at Escomb in Durham. Though a group of early churches in the south-east, inspired by the Augustinian and Roman missions, show a cruciform plan with an apsidal chancel, as at Worth in Sussex, these had little general effect on parish church design. The severe northern plan became the prototype of most parish churches, despite the fact that it was the Roman rite connected with the south-eastern foundations which eventually supplanted that of the Celtic church. The cruciform plan, on the other hand, was universally adopted for monastic and cathedral churches. And all cathedrals, except Exeter, were furnished with a central tower as well as two western towers, whereas the parish church normally had but a single western tower. Cathedral designers shared with the builders of parish churches a preference for the square-ended chancel. The apsidal terminations of Westminster Abbey, Tewkesbury, Canterbury and some Norman parish churches reflect Continental influence, and are exceptions.

The peculiarly English square end, like the strict adherence to an east–west orientation in both parish church and cathedral architecture (which significantly does not obtain in Italy), may perpetuate a pagan tradition which demanded that altar and celebrant should be bathed in the full light of the morning sun.

Parish church plans developed sporadically in accordance with ritual requirements and the growth, piety and wealth of the population; they were lengthened and they acquired aisles and chapels, built by trade guilds, or founded by wealthy merchants and nobles for the welfare of their souls. Thus the parish church embraces structures as touchingly small and plain as Strethall in Essex, and as complex and ornate as St Mary Redcliffe, Bristol. The plans of cathedrals and the greater non-cathedral churches were affected by different factors. In the Middle Ages there was no important distinction, except for the presence of the *cathedra* or bishop's throne, between a cathedral, a monastic church and a collegiate church (a church attached to a foundation prescribing a life in common for resident canons or chaplains). None was primarily directed to the requirements of a lay congregation, even though some Augustinian and Benedictine monasteries granted the laity the use of part of the abbey church. These great buildings were expressly designed to meet the doctrinal needs of the clergy, and to provide pathways for the Sunday processions.

The line of demarcation between the parish and the greater church has often been blurred by later developments. The present cathedrals of England include abbey churches like St Albans, converted to cathedral use in 1878, parochial churches such as those of Newcastle and Chelmsford, recently erected into cathedrals, and collegiate foundations like Ripon and Southwell. Westminster Abbey plays an exceptional rôle. Founded as a Benedictine monastery, perhaps as early as the seventh century, it became a cathedral for a decade only, from 1540 until 1550, and now, neither cathedral nor parish church, it owes its continued existence to its unique connection with the monarch and the state. It is the coronation as well as the burial church of England's kings and queens, and its chapter house was already referred to by Langland in the fourteenth century as the parliament.

Most abbey and collegiate churches, however, which were not reduced to ruins by the Dissolution became parochial. Among them were Binham and Wymondham in Norfolk, Blyth in Nottinghamshire, Romsey and Christchurch in Hampshire, Sherborne in Dorset, Tewkesbury in Gloucestershire, Abbey Dore in Herefordshire, and Malmesbury in Wiltshire. Unusual details in the plan of a parish church and unusually elaborate masonry such as the possession of a stone vault instead of the timber roof, which is among the most typical features of the normal parish church, can often be explained by its previous history as a monastic or collegiate building. Visitors to Fotheringhay in Northamptonshire, for example, will be struck by the fact that the spectacular tower, a massively square structure surmounted by an octagonal lantern, battlemented and pinnacled, rises at the east instead of at the west end of the church. The reason for this oddity is that the tower was formerly central, with beyond it a collegiate chancel which was demolished after the Act of Suppression of 1547. Again, anyone entering the church of Thorney, Cambridgeshire, for the first time must surely stand amazed at the aspect of the interior. Norman piers of giant girth protrude from the walls of the aisleless nave and soar to the low roof. The entire design, with its two stories of round-headed arches, is strangely cramped and altogether lacking in the sense of rhythm which informs most medieval churches. The mystery is solved when it is realized that the present parish church was once part of Thorney Abbey and that the arches represent the nave arcade and the triforium gallery of the huge monastic church.

Our cathedrals and parish churches are the highest expression of the art of architecture in the Middle Ages. They testify as much to the overriding enthusiasm for this art as to the piety of their founders and patrons. Their very size, the difficulties their builders confronted so boldly, problems such as that of supporting the central tower, and the inclusion of complicated and costly structures which were purely ornamental adjuncts, such as the cloisters attached to cathedrals like Salisbury and Wells, which were not originally monastic, are all eloquent of a passion for building for its own sake. The architects who so brilliantly sustained this passion, and of whose identities and activities more and more is being revealed by modern research, include Henry Yevele, Stephen Lote, John Wastell, Walter of Coventry, William Wynford, Thomas Witney, John Meppushal, John and William Ramsay, Nicholas of Ely and Christopher Scune.

The work of these and many other masters shows a progressive understanding of construction and materials, an advance from the massive, heavy compositions of the Normans, such as the naves of Peterborough, Selby or Waltham Abbey, towards ever lighter, airier and more harmonious organizations, culminating in the conception of the church body as a stone framework for long ranges of majestic windows filled with rectilinear tracery and, above all, as a unified design in which space is no longer divided longitudinally by bays and vertically by the three stages of arcade, triforium and clerestory, which are so emphatically differentiated in such works as the Early English nave of Wells or the late Norman nave of Malmesbury. In the most perfect examples of the last of the Gothic styles, the exquisitely clear-cut chapel of King's College, Cambridge, Bath Abbey and the stirring choir of Gloucester, these elements are all fused in an insistently vertical and totally coherent work of art. In each of these interiors the eye is led directly upwards to the fan vault, the feature which, although it cannot be separated from the constructional planning of the Perpendicular church, the shape of its arches and mouldings and the panelling of the walls, may be regarded as the apotheosis of our medieval period, an English development which owed nothing to foreign example.

Triumphant as was this last florescence of the Gothic spirit, there is not a stage in the whole architectural evolution which does not offer overwhelming experiences. Who that has seen them can ever forget the Norman nave of Durham, where the immense pillars, deeply channelled with spirals, flutes and zigzags, are as broad as the openings; the superb transepts of Hexham Priory, where a rippling band of Early English trefoil arcading is surmounted by two tiers of excessively tall, narrow arches; the enchanting stellar vault of the choir at Tewkesbury; the soaring spire of Salisbury – the tallest in England; the glorious western Norman tower of Ely crowned by its Gothic lantern; the famous central octagon of the same cathedral, designed to replace the Norman central tower which fell in 1322, a unique work, probably by John Ramsay, conceived in the shape of the popular octagonal chapter house of the period and raised up on high with incredible ingenuity and audacity; the chapter house at Wells where the vault ribs spring out from the central pier like jets from a fountain; the broad, bold angel choir of Lincoln; or the peerless nave of Canterbury, the great work of Yevele in his old age and of his successors, Lote and Mapilton?

English parish churches repeat this great progression in miniature; and whereas the cathedrals and greater churches are monuments of the best and most advanced art of their period, these humbler buildings are the memorials of local craftsmanship. In their case the interest of the development is enhanced by the existence of pre-Conquest work. For it is in our parish churches, and in them alone, that the

Salisbury Cathedral from the Bishop's garden.
Detail from an oil sketch by John Constable, c. 1822

building art of the Anglo-Saxons is displayed. The general impression made by such square, unbuttressed towers, delicately and flatly patterned with irregular arcading and pilaster strips, as that of Barton-on-Humber, and by such tall, narrow interiors as that of the nave at Bradford-on-Avon is of an architecture as distinctly linear and vertical as that of the Perpendicular period.

With very few exceptions, among them Salisbury Cathedral, built entirely in the Early English style, the cruciform church of Patrington in Yorkshire, a noble example of the Decorated mode, and a number of great Perpendicular churches including St Mary Redcliffe, Bristol, Salle in Norfolk, Lavenham in Suffolk and Saffron Walden in Essex, no English medieval church, either cathedral or parochial, exhibits a uniform style. Norman and Early English are juxtaposed at Chichester; Norman is combined with Decorated at Ely, Hereford, St Albans and Southwell; Perpendicular cloaks and joins with earlier styles at Worcester, Gloucester, Winchester and Ripon. At Cley in Norfolk a Perpendicular tower soars over a Decorated nave and chancel; at Edington in Wiltshire the wonderfully battlemented, rambling exterior fuses the Decorated and the Perpendicular; at Eaton Bray, Bedfordshire, a fifteenth-century shell and a modern tower leave the visitor quite unprepared for the thirteenth-century door with its graceful, flowing ironwork and the pure Early English interior; at Monkwearmouth, Durham, a north aisle of 1874 dwarfs the Anglo-Saxon nave. This patchwork character, depending on economic factors as well as upon the desire to preserve the relics of earlier buildings, is typically English.

All medieval buildings are to some extent marked by regional characteristics. The individuality of the great arcaded front of Lincoln derives in part from the local yellow ironstone of which it is fashioned; the grey-green Purbeck piers of the nave of Exeter relate this cathedral to the south-west even if not to its immediate environment; and the chalky white clunch of the Ely Lady Chapel at once evokes the Cambridgeshire landscape. But the materials for such great churches were often brought from considerable distances. Thus King's College Chapel was built of stone from Weldon in Northamptonshire; the stone for Norwich came largely from Barnack, the quarry which also supplied material for Rochester Cathedral and for the Abbey at Bury St Edmunds; Clipsham limestone makes its appearance in cathedrals as far apart as Canterbury and York; and the stone for Beverley Minster was brought from the Thevesdale quarries near Tadcaster.

Parish churches are much more intimately connected with their local geological formation. In Norfolk and Suffolk, where there is little or no good building stone for quoins, rounds towers are common. In this same area flint is the conspicuous building material, and knapped flint appears as a wall-facing in conjunction with stone tracery. The intractable granite of which most Cornish churches are constructed accounts for the simplicity of their window tracery and the severity of piers and capitals, while the high quality of Cotswold stone encouraged the designers of Norman doorways to fill the tympana with sculpture, and masons of all periods to excel in refined decorative work such as that which distinguishes the pinnacled, traceried porch of Northleach, with its ogee-framed door, canopied niches and statues. The former densely wooded character of Essex is expressed in the use of timber for towers which vary from simple bellcots to structures of several stages, like that at Blackmore. In Hertfordshire and south Cambridgeshire the lack of stone led to the invention of small, acutely pointed lead-sheathed spirelets, as at Anstey, Knebworth and Duxford, which, known as "Hertfordshire spikes", rise from the centre of broad flint rubble towers. Splendid stone spires occur in districts where good material lay close to hand. These spires are almost always octagonal, and are poised on a square tower by filling in the bases of the canted sides with semi-pyramids, called broaches. The home regions of the broach spire are Lincolnshire, Northamptonshire and Rutland.

The diversity of parish church architecture is not only the product of geology; it is also the expression of the preferences and particular skills of local masons and carpenters and of social conditions. Thus Devon towers are often furnished with a huge stair turret oddly placed along one of the tower walls instead of at an angle; and Somerset towers can be recognized by their tall pinnacles and elaborately worked open parapets, the pairs of buttresses each side of every angle, and especially by the windows in the belfry stage which are filled with perforated tracery. East Anglia is noted for the brilliant development of timber roof design, which ranges from the simple tie-beam type, as seen at Outwell in Norfolk, to magnificent and ingenious double hammer-beam structures like those at Needham Market, Suffolk, and Knapton, Norfolk, the latter adorned at the end of every hammer-beam and along the ridge-piece by angels, fluttering like giant moths against the dark woodwork. In Cornwall, Somerset and Devon, on the other hand, carpenters evolved a roof with a curved brace to every rafter, thus forming a series of closely set arches, which are usually boarded or plastered over to form a barrel or waggon vault. Cornwall and Devon are also remarkable for a distinctive local parish church plan. A strong wave of piety in the fifteenth century resulted in the re-building of many churches in the region, and in these churches the usual arrangement of a nave with aisles and clerestory was replaced by a structure with three aisles of equal length, height and breadth, each crowned with its own roof, so that the east end presented a range of three separate gables, as at Launceston, Bodmin, St Keverne and St Erth in Cornwall, and at Haberton, Berry Pomeroy and Staverton in Devon.

Local style is as much evident in the furnishings of medieval parish churches as in the fabric. The spreading fan vaults and bands of carved foliage in screens of the south-west, which usually run right across the church, contrast with the shorter, lighter screens of East Anglia, which are seldom vaulted. The square-headed bench-ends of West Country churches, carved with figure reliefs, differ from the trefoil-shaped finial terminations common elsewhere, and so inventively treated in the eastern counties. The latter region is further distinguished for a splendid series of fifteenth-century fonts whose octagonal sides are sculptured with figures illustrating the Seven Sacraments. There are sixteen examples in Norfolk and twelve in Suffolk.

Considering the terrible losses due to iconoclasm, and considering the wear and tear of the centuries, it is astonishing what immense quantities of woodwork, of sculpture in stone and even of painted glass survive in both parish church and cathedral. These arts are usually to be seen at their aristocratic best in the cathedrals. Canterbury and York are pre-eminent for their glass; St Albans and Chichester contain important wall paintings; while the canopied stalls of Winchester and Chichester, the 400 bosses in the nave and cloisters of Norwich, the thirteenth-century sculpture at Lincoln, Worcester and Westminster Abbey, all represent the highest flights of genius. Fine sepulchral sculpture, however, is just as likely to be found in the most obscure parish church as in the cathedral. It is only necessary to mention Rysbrack's half-reclining likeness of Sir Edward Ward at Stoke Doyle, Northamptonshire, J. F. Moore's monument to Earl Ferrers at Ettington, Warwickshire, or Nicholas Stone's memorial to Sir Thomas Lucy at Charlecote in the same county. All this imagery is as richly rewarding to the historian as to the connoisseur of art. Tombs and the heraldry decorating them reveal whole family stories. Furthermore, sepulchral effigies, including the flat brasses set in the floor of the church, mirror every change in fashion from the early Middle Ages to the end of the eighteenth century. And in buildings which were so closely connected with the lives of the people all the manifold activities of medieval man, of kings, nobles, knights and commoners, are vividly recorded in the sculptured and painted imagery. Misericords show tumblers, acrobats, itinerant musicians and clowns; hawking and hunting the stag, boar and hare with dogs; tournaments and ship-building. A boss at Ugborough pictures a blacksmith at work; sculpture at Lincoln and Malvern is concerned with seasonal work in the fields; a man on a capital at Winchester carries a chequerboard, and a capital at Manchester is carved with two men playing backgammon.

For the student of local history the parish church is an invaluable source. The registers of baptisms, marriages and deaths, dating, if they are complete, from 1538, provide essential information for the study of population changes, as well as of the state of public health over the last 400 years. The dedications and changes in dedication are also revealing. Unique dedications to rare saints probably represent actual foundations by the saints themselves. Such are St Gonand of the Rock and St Non, Altarnun, both in Cornwall. The richness or poverty of the church fabric will also furnish the historian with important clues. He will, for example, draw obvious conclusions about the state of the Fenland in the Middle Ages from the fact that a series of magnificent churches arose from the twelfth century onwards to the west and to the south of the Wash; and he will relate the fine Perpendicular churches of Wiltshire, such as those of Trowbridge, Calne, Lacock and Steeple Ashton, to a period of unusual prosperity in the fifteenth and sixteenth centuries.

A great gulf divides the churches of the Middle Ages from those of Renaissance and modern England. The events of the sixteenth century destroyed a living tradition of architecture by substituting Italianate, horizontal forms for the native Gothic, vertical mode; and the rejection of Catholicism meant that one of the chief incentives to building, the belief in the spiritual benefit of pious works, such as endowing a chantry or making a donation to the church fabric fund, no longer obtained. It is significant that although some of the most spectacular great houses were erected during the reign of Elizabeth probably less church building was carried out in that period than at any other time before the present century.

The break in tradition was, however, bridged for a brief moment by the genius of Wren, who created a brilliant synthesis between the Gothic and Classic styles in the churches he designed expressly for Protestant worship. Some of Wren's buildings were actually composed in the late Perpendicular manner, such as St Mary Aldermary; but it is in his original steeples that his great power of synthesis is most dazzlingly displayed. Infinitely versatile, they retain all the flickering, soaring character of Gothic architecture, even though they exhibit exclusively Classical motifs; and, like traditional Gothic towers, they all rise over a square plan. St Paul's, one of the supreme masterpieces of Classical art, unites Renaissance forms with a plan which, with its well-marked transepts, its long eastern and western arms and its twin-towered west front, continues the English medieval cathedral tradition, while the central feature – the eight great piers and the four counter-thrusts supporting the dome – alludes directly to the octagon at Ely.

Wren's followers, with but few exceptions, among them Nicholas Hawksmoor, author of the monumental and aspiring composition of Christchurch, Spitalfields, lacked his sense of tradition and became ever more "correctly" Classical. The west end of the church was transformed into the pillared portico of a latter-day Roman temple, behind which the tower degenerated into a superfluous accretion sitting on the nave roof, as at Mereworth in Kent and at James Gibbs's St Martin-in-the-Fields, London.

Victorian Gothic churches are interesting as attempts to revive the native tradition and as full-flavoured expressions of a discordant period. They were the work of men who believed that the vertical mode embodied the spirit of Christianity more fitly than the horizontal, Classical style, and who also were (mistakenly) convinced that good morals could produce good architecture and would enable them to foist the style of a truly religious age on to one that was eminently materialistic. But the church was no longer bound up with the lives of the people and the sharp dividing line between sacred and secular could not be erased. Architects of talent produced some original interpretations of medieval Gothic themes. The slate-hung lantern supported on tall, clustered cast-iron shafts at St James, Teignmouth, by Andrew Patey, repeats the Gothic idiom in a surprisingly new medium. Burges's weighty, ornate east end at Waltham Abbey is comparable in vitality and strength to the Norman work beside it, and Sedding's stone version of a Devon timber roof at St Peter's, Sheldon, is as arresting as his patterning of the arcades with giant rustications. But all too often Victorian interiors which were intended to inspire awe and devotion merely exude a crushing air of respectability, and this is as true of a meanly conceived building such as St Saviour, St George's Square, Westminster, as of the compellingly ugly but boldly planned red-and-black brick bulk of Street's St James the Less, in the same district.

Nevertheless, Gothic has persisted as the dominant style for church building until the present day. The gleaming, elegant church of St Mary, Wellingborough, by Sir Ninian Comper, completed in 1930, combines a late-Gothic framework and an elaborate plaster vault of fans, pendants and star patterns with a mixture of furnishing styles. And despite its grid walls of concrete and glass and its clear affinities with twentieth-century commercial building, Sir Basil Spence's Coventry Cathedral, consecrated in 1962, is basically Gothic. The proportions of the interior, the division of the space into nave and aisles, and the suggestion of a ribbed vault, all derive from medieval example even if they are utterly remote from any medieval church in feeling and execution.

Follies

BARBARA JONES

The English love to break down the natural scene. In the seventeenth and eighteenth centuries the areas of natural heath and scrub left untouched by medieval
husbandry were vigorously taken in hand and built upon, gardened, afforested and
landscaped; most of England was arranged by man. In the nineteenth century the
whole country was netted over with railways, and the cities grew; but, in fact, the
scene was not altered very much. In this century we have come to accept that
scene as natural, as "the country". We in our turn are trying to break it down, with
motorways, industrial sites and new cities.

At all times since the end of the Tudor wars there have been English landowners,
with anything from a ducal estate to a suburban front garden, who have not been
content with other people's ideas of breakdown, with the ordinary thing. Even if
they have been able to commission idiosyncratic houses from great architects,
they have still wanted something more, something wilder. The results of these
impulses are scattered all over the country, and are called – by the other English
– "follies".

Follies take many forms. We may discount at once the follies in name alone –
houses of which neighbours disapproved, or houses built too far from water, or
with too little money to finish them, and also various clumps and belts of trees (the
word was corrupted from *feuillée*). And the ordinary garden house, temple or
gazebo does not qualify either. The element of eccentricity is essential; follies are
fantastic, a little crazy in desire or design. Architecture is building for shelter;
follies are building for building, a purer art. Towers and obelisks build upwards;
labyrinths and tunnels build down. Other follies are aggregates of unlikely
materials, abstractions of shells and minerals, bark and branches, nearer sculpture
than architecture, the desire to amass solids in space.

The earliest folly I have found is Freston Tower in Suffolk, built in the middle of
the sixteenth century, a brick tower on the banks of the River Orwell, near Ipswich.
At the end of the century Rushton Triangular Lodge was built in Northamptonshire by Sir Thomas Tresham. Everything is in threes: the plan is triangular; each
wall three times three times three feet, three sets of three-by-three triangles on top
of the walls; three floors; three windows each side on each floor; trefoils and triangular pinnacles. Ten miles away at Lyveden is the shell of Tresham's house,
extending the arithmetic of three to five, seven and nine.

More follies and conceits, and some tunnels, were built in the next century,
mostly surviving only in visitors' accounts of them, though there is a sinister
temple of bark nailed over wood at Exton Park in Rutland, and there are fine
grotto rooms of stone and shells at Skipton in Yorkshire and at Woburn Abbey
in Bedfordshire.

In the eighteenth century follies became fashionable as well as eccentric; a
nobleman's estate positively needed one. Towers, tunnels, and grottoes continued
in production, and all sorts of new follies were invented – sham castles and

ruins, hermitages, labyrinths, obelisks, and eye-catchers. In the nineteenth century fewer follies were built, and those more by the rich than the noble; but Druids' Circles were invented, and some superb folly gardens were laid out, with a curiosity round every corner. Late in the century fantastic gardening with broken china, slag, shells, flint, glass, coal, and coral became fashionable for the poor as well as for the rich. Only two or three dozen follies have been built in the twentieth century, but the little gardens continue, with gnomes added to the older materials.

The commonest sort of folly, and the easiest to find, is that which is built upwards. There are a great many ordinary little ones, but there are also some magnificent towers, built to commemorate great happenings or to command great prospects. There is a nice triangular one in London, in Castlewood Park at Shooters Hill, 64 feet high, built in 1784 to the memory of Sir William James and to "Record the Conquest of the CASTLE OF SEVERNDROGG on the COAST of MALABAR which fell to his Superior Valour and able Conduct on the 2nd Day of April MDCCLV". In the nineteenth century it was used for select parties, and now it is a teashop.

Another triangular folly is Haldon Belvedere, near Exeter, built by an ex-Governor of Madras, with a floor made of marble from Hyderabad, and really exquisite plaster work. At Wentworth Woodhouse in Yorkshire is Hoober Stand, 1748, a superb 100-foot soot-stained golden tower on a triangular plan, its sides tapering to a hexagonal lantern. It was built by Thomas, Marquis of Rockingham, in honour of George II. Nearby is Keppel's Pillar, built by the 2nd Marquis in 1782 to commemorate the British Fleet at Ushant. It soars up, supporting nothing, an amazing 150 feet. Also nearby is the Needle's Eye, a tall stone pyramid pierced by an ogival arch and crowned by a lovely urn, built, the story goes, for a crack whip to drive through after he had boasted that he could drive a coach and horses through the eye of a needle. At Wentworth Castle there are more conceits.

Many follies have good stories attached: you may be told that the builder is buried under the floor because he quarrelled with the parson, or is there standing on his head, or with his favourite horse under him. One man seems to have deserved all the stories: Mad Jack Fuller, who built a Needle, a Mausoleum, a Tower, a Rotunda, and an Observatory at Brightling in Sussex, and at Dallington a neat cone called the Sugar Loaf, to justify a night-time statement that he could see Dallington church spire from his dining-room window. In daylight this statement proved wrong, but he made a sham spire just over the skyline, to be right for his next dinner-party. Attached to his pyramid tomb is the most persistent of all the legends: that he is sitting at table inside, with a bottle and a bird before him.

At Tong in Shropshire are some pyramids with no legends at all, perhaps because the builder George Durant said exactly what everything was for – and imagination could invent nothing stranger. "Quaint buildings, monuments with hieroglyphs, and inscriptions alike to deceased friends, eternity, and favourite animals – were then to be found on every path of the demesne", says an old local guidebook. Pyramidal gate-piers are carved as though bound with heavy ropes, and such objects as lamps and snails are carved in panels on the walls. A gazebo called The Pulpit has animals and snakes. On a nearby farm there is also an Egyptian Aviary, a pyramidal hen-house labelled AB OVO. Durant was one of the few gentlemen of his time who not only longed to have a hermit in the grounds to show to visitors, but achieved a very contented one, for a gentleman who had fallen on hard times lived in a cave at Tong until he died in 1822.

The contemporary terms for the employment of hermits were usually much alike; a cave (or a rustic hermitage of roots, branches and knotty wood) was provided, and a hermit was advertised for, to serve a period of seven years, living secluded, with hair long, and nails unclipped, never speaking, with good food sent down from the house daily. But it seems that few people are even mock hermits by nature, or few people know how to employ one kindly. One gentleman was forced to use a wax image; and there are many records of early failure – the hermit went away, or he was found drinking in the village and dismissed. One known success, however, was the Hermit Finch, whose Sanctuary lies down in the woods of the park at Burley on the Hill in Rutland, preserved with most remarkable and imaginative rustic architecture and furniture, a pebble-and-knuckle-bone floor, and even the hermit's sacking bed.

The desire to dig downwards is rarer than the desire to build up. It is also much more expensive; so the tunnellers had to be very rich or very determined. The 5th Duke of Portland's underground rooms at Welbeck are the most famous mole-works. The Duke was said to speak willingly only to the men who dug the tunnels.

Most excavations have an air of sadness. Many have walls of bare earth, or lined with cement, or strung along with a handful of cockle shells. But they were highly esteemed in the last century, for the Catacombs at High Beech in Epping Forest were a pleasure resort. They are a wild descent into the dark earth of huge blocks of masonry said to have come from Chelmsford gaol, hidden under the garden.

As well as the plain tunnels of compulsive digging, there are excavations of great beauty in the form of grottoes, where the surface has been decorated with glittering minerals, exotic shells, fossils, tufa – all the natural objects that became commonly wonderful in the eighteenth century. I have referred to the shell rooms at Skipton and Woburn; in both of these there is contemporary architecture with an overlay of shells. In the eighteenth century this style continued in fashion, greatly refined, culminating in the exquisite Shell House made by the 2nd Duchess of Richmond at Goodwood in Sussex. True grottoes, though not always under-ground, look like caves under the sea, spar and shells arranged in waves and stalactites. We have the name of Josiah Lane as builder, with his son, of a series of superb grottoes – at St Giles House, Cranborne, in Dorset, Fonthill in Wiltshire, St Anne's Hill and Pain's Hill in Surrey, amongst others. The two-roomed grotto at Wimborne St Giles is in the park and is shown with the house; it has been restored and is probably the finest shellwork of this sort that we have, a wonderful composition of surfaces and colours, the insides of shells gleaming against the duller backs, small shells offsetting large.

At Stourhead in Wiltshire the National Trust owns a famous grotto, large and formal, built round one of the headwaters of the Stour, with fine statues of a nymph and a river-god. The walk round the lake runs through the grotto, a green, cool melancholy contrast to the splendid Capability Brown landscaping. Another remarkable grotto was built by Thomas Goldney in his garden on top of Clifton gorge at Bristol, with a cascade leaping from an urn held by Neptune, echoes from the wild water, a Lions' Den and fine shells.

All these grottoes are professional work, and look it, but by the beginning of the nineteenth century only amateur grotto-builders remained. The fashion spread wide; most towns, especially those by the seaside, have a bit of shellwork some-where. There is a big one at Margate, probably made by two brothers called Bowles in an existing excavation. It was lost to sight for about thirty years, and found again in 1834 or 1835 by a schoolmaster's son digging a duckpond. There is almost no fantastic origin that has not been claimed for it – Cretans, Druids, even

Tibetans, are supposed to have built it, and the simple amateur shellwork has been interpreted in a hundred gnostic symbols: we are a romantic-minded race. Druids were very fashionable in the first quarter of the century; there is a good sham Circle on the Yorkshire moors near Masham, a real prehistoric temple moved from Jersey to a back garden in Henley-on-Thames, and a Druids' Table among the bone grottoes and bone-lined caves at Banwell on Mendip in Somerset, elaborated during the years after 1824 by the Bishop of Bath and Wells over and down some mine-shafts and two natural caves with stalactites and stalagmites. Ancient animal bones were ready on the floor, and the Bishop made the most of them.

Back to the eighteenth century, and back above ground. The Middle Ages and the Barons' Wars became very modish, and Gothic architecture was admired again, not often for gentlemen's houses, in spite of Walpole at Strawberry Hill, but certainly for follies. Suddenly hundreds of gentlemen wanted to see the ruins of a Gothic castle crumbling at a suitable distance from the house. A few of them had real ones; the others plunged into the fun of building fakes. Some of the sham castles were ruinous in design, like that at Wimpole in Cambridgeshire; some rapidly became so through being knocked up in a hurry or on the cheap; and some were built very crisp and new like Sanderson Miller's Sham Castle outside Bath, a façade rising about forty feet on a hill-top, flat as a piece of scenery, which indeed it is, a wall without a room.

Some castles were in fact made of painted canvas on wooden frames, so great was the scramble to get them up. Some were rich with Gothic detail, trefoils and quatrefoils, and castellations and arrowslits, but often reproduced on an absurdly large scale as there was no need to consider the strength of the wall, and defence could become decoration. Others were so ungothic that they could not be called castles; they were curious spiky constructions, often of flint, that were given names used for no other architecture, like eye-catcher, terminal, conceit, or vista-closer. Many of them were undoubtedly designed by eager amateurs of the arts, and put up by the estate workers; but a timid amateur could find plenty of help in the dozens of books on the Picturesque or the Grotesque that were published, with illustrations, plans, elevations and dimensions of every variety of hut, retreat, cascade, bath-house, mosque and pagoda, from trifles made with Rude Branches to enormous Mauresque Pavilions beyond the Do-It-Yourself of all but the greatest estates.

Some people, having built one folly, went on. Hawkstone in Shropshire was an estate with many fine follies. The hermitage, with mock hermit, and an ornamental windmill have disappeared; but half a dozen survive, including a marvellous labyrinth that rises to the sunlight on top of a rocky bluff. Stourhead has a Rustic Convent, St Peter's Pump, and Alfred's Tower, as well as the grotto; and West Wycombe in Buckinghamshire has a Mausoleum, St Crispin's Cottages – built to look like a church from the house – a Sham Lodge, and caves, now with *son et lumière*.

Today, the folly impulse is concentrated in the small gardens, the miniature model villages that have succeeded the real ones of the rich, and a continuing tradition of topiary; we still have such gardens as the breath-taking solid geometry clipped from yew at Levens in Westmorland, that has been clipped since 1689. And there is a new one in Wolverhampton that has privet topiary of sixteen Scotch terriers, two cats and a rat.

The Industrial Heritage

L. T. C. ROLT

Other countries have their characteristic landscape beauties, their prehistoric and Roman antiquities, their great Gothic churches and splendid Renaissance architecture, but England's industrial monuments are unique. They are unique because it was here that the Industrial Revolution began. Because that Revolution, in a mere three hundred years, has changed man's way of life on this planet more profoundly than in the previous two millennia, even those who think life would have been better if it had never happened must agree that the physical traces of its beginnings have become monuments.worthy of preservation and study. Yet, strangely enough, it is only in the last few years that we have become aware of the importance of England's industrial heritage. Only twenty years ago who would have thought that the National Trust could become responsible for such things as an early textile mill, a canal, or a Cornish beam engine? Or that government departments, hitherto preoccupied with prehistoric sites and medieval buildings, would be not only listing and scheduling such monuments but assisting both financially and practically in their preservation?

Today, when the bulldozer has become a symbol of our vastly enhanced power of rapid destruction, this belated recognition comes only just in time; it amounts to a last-minute rescue operation. This work of rescue is often peculiarly difficult. Pressure for demolition is particularly great because, by their very nature, industrial monuments often occupy valuable sites. Again, it is difficult to justify the preservation of an early industrial building which has ceased to serve its original purpose unless some alternative use for it can be found. However, the use of the Snape Maltings as a concert hall, the use as a theatre of the original London & Birmingham Railway locomotive round-house at Chalk Farm, or the recent proposal to convert Philip Hardwick's splendid range of warehouses at Telford's St Katherine's Dock into an Arts Centre are examples of what can, or might be, done in this direction.

One of the reasons why our industrial monuments have been so neglected until recently is that to most lovers of landscape or architecture "industrial" has become a loaded word, carrying a weight of ugliness. It has become so because we equate it with modern industrialism which, by its large scale and dreary uniformity, spells death to landscape beauty. In the eighteenth and early nineteenth centuries, however, industrial man had not acquired the power to ruin a landscape. His works were at best comely and at their worst dramatic or idiosyncratic. Only very seldom were they bleakly utilitarian or downright ugly. Consequently they are not only eloquent as evidence of bygone activity and aspiration, but often strangely beautiful. The artists of the Romantic Movement, with which the first momentous phase of the Industrial Revolution coincided, recognized this, whereas it is only just becoming evident to us. For this failure of vision the divorce of science and technology from the arts is mainly responsible.

That this divorce is a reality and not just an abstract theory was demonstrated when that fascinating exhibition "Art and the Industrial Revolution" opened at the Manchester City Art Gallery in 1968. At first it was poorly attended because the technologists felt it would be too "arty" to interest them while the artists thought it would be too technical. Eventually, however, the message got around that the exhibition was of equal interest to both sides, and for the last few weeks the gallery was crowded. What was true of this exhibition is also true of our industrial monuments; their appeal is to both sides, and we are belatedly becoming aware of this fact.

It was fortuitous that the beginnings of our Industrial Revolution coincided with a more conscious appreciation of natural beauty that enabled the artists of the Romantic Movement to record for us the landscape of a pre-industrial England whose unsullied loveliness now seems to us almost paradisial. It was in such an idyllic pastoral setting that the first manifestations of the new world appeared: a great steam-powered textile mill, an ironworks plumed with smoke and flame, a many-arched canal aqueduct or railway viaduct. Such striking contrasts appealed strongly to the imagination of the Romantic artist, who called them "sublime" or "awful" – using that word in its old sense. They regarded them with the same fascinated ambivalence that John Milton reveals in his attitude to Satan in *Paradise Lost*, an attitude that undoubtedly influenced William Blake and led him to coin the phrase "dark satanic mills". This is the vision we should try to recapture when we visit England's industrial monuments. It should not be too difficult because, whereas the contemporary artist could only grasp their significance intuitively through the exercise of his imagination, we, in the knowledge of all that has happened since, are only too well aware of it.

Most people regard the cotton industry of Lancashire as the precursor. It was certainly the first industry of modern type, organized on the factory system and producing for a world export market. But those textile mills of Lancashire and the Pennine Valleys to which Blake referred were already highly mechanized, with steam power driving their spinning frames, carding engines and looms. An industry organized on so intensive a scale could not have existed without three things: a plentiful supply of iron, mechanical power and an economical means of transporting goods in bulk.

It was Abraham Darby who provided a solution to the problem of England's iron industry by successfully smelting iron with coke in 1709, while Thomas Newcomen built the first successful steam engine in 1712, and the construction of England's canal system began in 1760 on the initiative of the Duke of Bridgewater and his engineer, James Brindley. These were the three key developments, and the Industrial Revolution rapidly gained momentum by the vigorous interaction between them. More coal produced more iron; more iron made possible larger and more powerful steam engines which enabled more coal to be won from deeper levels; canals were the essential arteries through which coal and iron flowed.

If any place in England deserves to be called the cradle of the Industrial Revolution it is that small industrial district of Shropshire in the vicinity of the Severn gorge where, at his Coalbrookdale Ironworks, Abraham Darby first smelted iron successfully with coke. Hitherto, English ironmasters had used charcoal in their furnaces and had to compete with other industries, notably ship-building, for the country's dwindling supplies of timber. So acute was the timber shortage that the ironmasters had to build their furnaces in remote and inaccessible parts of the country where timber was still plentiful – Wales, Cumberland and Scotland. Consequently the best preserved example of a charcoal blast furnace today is in the Scottish Highlands at Bonawe, near Taynuilt, Argyll. Slowly at first, but surely, Darby's discovery changed all this. For the fifty years before the coming of canals the Darby family in particular and the Shropshire ironmasters in general enjoyed a unique reputation which attracted enterprising men, civil and mechanical engineers and architects, from all over England. This success was due not only to their enterprise and skill but also to the fact that they had chosen one of the very few districts where natural supplies of coal and iron ore were situated conveniently close to a great navigable river – the Severn – which provided cheap bulk transport.

No wonder that this Shropshire district scored a succession of historic "firsts". In 1723 Coalbrookdale began producing the first large iron steam-engine cylinders, of which more anon. In 1767, to improve internal transport, the Coalbrookdale Company laid the first iron railways in the world, and in 1779 the ribs of the world's first iron bridge were cast at Coalbrookdale. This bridge, which has given a name to a place – Ironbridge, still spans the Severn with its single iron arch of 100 feet and is now England's finest industrial monument. It was within sight of this bridge that the famous ironmaster John Wilkinson, who owned the nearby New Willey Furnaces at Broseley, launched the first iron boat into the Severn in 1787. The assembled crowd fully expected it to sink, but were disappointed. It was this same John Wilkinson, incidentally, who perfected a machine which could bore a cylinder with sufficient accuracy to make James Watt's improved steam engine practicable. The cylinders for all Watt's early engines were cast and bored by him.

In 1797 the iron work for the world's first metal-framed building was cast at Coalbrookdale. This building, erected at Shrewsbury by Charles Bage, still stands, and is known today as Jones's Maltings. It was the first of many early iron-framed buildings in England, some of which still stand, most notably the Boat Shed at Sheerness. The latter building, although built in 1860, looks extraordinarily modern and is the true ancestor of every skyscraper.

Among the famous men associated with the Shropshire ironmasters were Thomas Telford, Richard Trevithick, and the Regency architect John Nash. Telford, when surveyor of Shropshire, was so inspired by their achievements that he became the first great master in the structural use of iron. He built his first iron bridge over the Severn at Buildwas. Although this bridge no longer exists, other Telford iron bridges survive, such as that over the Severn at the Mythe, Tewkesbury, which was cast by the Shropshire ironmaster William Hazledine. Telford was also responsible for the world's first iron trough aqueduct which carries the Shrewsbury Canal over the Severn's tributary, the Tern, at Longdon-upon-Tern, near Wellington. Its trough was cast at Ketley Ironworks by William Reynolds, who was closely associated with the Darby family. This aqueduct, too, survives. It was the prototype of Telford's famous aqueduct at Pont Cysyllte in the valley of the Dee just over the Welsh border.

Richard Trevithick was the great Cornish pioneer of the use of high-pressure steam who, by its aid, transformed the steam engine into a relatively small, light and compact power unit which, as he was the first to realize, possessed infinite possibilities in the field of mechanical transport, on rail, road and water. Recognizing the unique practical expertise of the Coalbrookdale Ironworks, Trevithick carried out many of his historic experiments there. One of the results was that the first steam locomotive in the world first ran on Coalbrookdale rails in 1802 before the more spectacular and better known trial on the Penydaren tramway in South Wales.

In a very different field John Nash recognized the possibilities of iron in architecture. In 1805 he designed for Lord Berwick at Attingham Park near Shrewsbury the oldest surviving roof-lit picture gallery. The slender, curving iron frames in which its glass rooflights are held were cast at Coalbrookdale.

The coming of canals enabled richer coal and iron districts, notably the Black Country of Staffordshire, to be tapped, and the Severn ceased to be a unique transport asset. Consequently the Black Country became the greatest iron-producing district in Europe, while the Coalbrookdale area declined. Although this was unfortunate for the Shropshire ironmasters it is fortunate for us because it meant that the scene of their activities became "frozen" at an early stage of industrial development, with the effect that this Shropshire birthplace of the new iron age has now become a vitally significant part of our industrial heritage. It retains an indefinable but strongly evocative atmosphere which few other places associated with early industry possess. Anyone with a spark of imagination who descends the steep hill from Madeley down into the Severn gorge at Ironbridge can hardly fail to be aware of this, particularly when dusk is falling, when lights are beginning to glimmer from the little brick cottages that spill down its steep slopes under the hanging woods but the graceful black arc of Darby's iron bridge is still visible against the sky-reflecting surface of the Severn.

Although this bridge is now the only substantial reminder of bygone achievement, at such a time it is easy to imagine the valley as it was when it was filled with the flare and fume of the iron furnaces and echoed with the thud of forge hammers. No wonder such dramatic activity, practised in an equally dramatic landscape setting, attracted contemporary artists like a magnet. Cotman, Turner and de Loutherbourg were three of the many who fell under its spell.

On the bank of the Severn downstream of the iron bridge stand some broken walls of blackened brickwork, heavily overgrown with wild creepers. This is all that remains of Bedlam Furnace, which Cotman painted in 1802 from the opposite bank of the river, its fierce glare – reflected in the night sky – lighting up the water and the landscape foreground. Turner used furnace light to similar effect in his *Lime Kiln at Coalbrookdale* (*c.* 1797) except that here stunted trees are sharply silhouetted as though against some unnatural sunset.

Thomas Newcomen, a blacksmith and ironmonger of Dartmouth, was responsible for building the world's first successful steam beam engine. It was the ancestor of the later Watt engine and the nineteenth-century Cornish beam engine, of which a number of good examples are now preserved in the Duchy by the National Trust in association with a local society. Until recently, magnificent beam engines of Cornish type were widely used throughout England for waterworks pumping. They are now disappearing fast, though efforts are being made to preserve a few of them. Of the earliest Newcomen type engines only a very few survive – two only outside museums. One of these is at a colliery at Elsecar near Sheffield, while the other stood near Coventry but was re-erected recently at Dartmouth as a permanent memorial to its inventor. The latter is almost certainly the oldest piston engine still in existence. Although it has been modified in later years its iron cylinder was most probably cast at Coalbrookdale in 1725. The cylinders of the earliest Newcomen engines were of brass, laboriously hand-finished. They were very costly, and necessarily of relatively small size. It was the ability of the Coalbrookdale Ironworks to cast and bore iron cylinders up to six feet in diameter that made possible the much larger and more powerful pumping engines that enabled deep coal seams to be exploited, particularly in the Tyneside area. It was James

Coalbrookdale. Engraving by G. Perry and T. Smith, 1758

Watt who, by making a more economical, double-acting rotative engine, suitable for driving machinery, made possible a vast extension of the factory system. Hitherto the water-wheel had been the only practicable source of power. Many water-wheels, some of great size and power, still survive in England, but only in locations where a copious and unfailing source of water was assured.

The third of the essential prerequisites of the Industrial Revolution – cheap goods transport – was first provided by the canal system. Today this system represents our greatest single heritage of eighteenth- and early nineteenth-century civil engineering. Much of it is now disused commercially but has recently acquired a new lease of life as a pleasure-cruising ground. At many strategic points on the networks of canals covering the English Midlands it is now possible to hire a comfortable cruiser and set off on a voyage of exploration. There is no better way of appreciating just how rapidly English civil engineering developed during the great period of canal construction between 1760 and 1836. The best idea of its eighteenth-century beginnings can be obtained by travelling northwards from Banbury by the Oxford Canal, for this section of canal has remained virtually unchanged since it was built in 1778, when, to avoid earthworks as far as possible, engineers followed the natural contours. For this reason it is extremely tortuous, taking eleven miles to cover a point-to-point distance of only four miles.

To appreciate to the full the progress made, travel northwards from Wolverhampton towards Nantwich along the Shropshire Union Canal. Laid out under the direction of Thomas Telford, this was the last major line of canal to be built in England (completed 1836) and it cuts straight through the rolling countryside by a series of deep cuttings and lofty embankments. To experience the dramatic contrast between these two canals is to understand how the experience gained during the canal-building age paved the way for the railway builders.

Whereas we did not pioneer canals, steam railways were England's particular contribution to world communications. Completed by 1842 and still in use today, the first of our great main lines linking London with the north-west, with Bristol and Southampton, were engineered on a heroic scale by Robert Stephenson, I. K. Brunel and Joseph Locke, setting an example which the rest of the world soon copied but never surpassed.

Although the earlier builders of roads and canals made excellent pioneering use of cast-iron the railway builders found it too brittle and treacherous to serve their greater purposes. The only surviving example of a major railway bridge in which cast-iron was used is Stephenson's celebrated high-level bridge over the Tyne at Newcastle. It was opened in June 1849 and has been carrying increasingly heavy road and rail traffic on its two decks ever since.

An increasing output of wrought-iron from the nineteenth-century ironmasters enabled the railway engineers to perform feats of construction the like of which the world had never seen. Unfortunately, many early examples of wrought-iron railway bridges have been demolished in recent years, but happily two of the most outstanding historically are still in use. These are Stephenson's great Menai tubular bridge (1850), the first in the world, and Brunel's magnificent bridge over the Tamar at Saltash. In a different context Brunel's famous wrought-iron suspension bridge across the Avon Gorge at Clifton is the finest surviving example of its kind and makes an instructive contrast with the new Severn suspension bridge only a few miles away.

Just as the great Gothic cathedral epitomizes the Age of Faith, so, just as certainly, does the great Victorian railway station express the material aspirations of the Age of Steam. In such secular temples stone gives place to iron – cast-iron columns supporting huge vaults of wrought-iron and glass. Newcastle Central was the prototype. It was the work of a versatile local architect named John Dobson, who not only designed the station building but also the special machines with which the curving iron roof ribs were rolled. Some of his original work still survives in the present station. His work was the precursor of other great station roofs: York, Manchester Central, Bristol Temple Meads, Paddington and St Pancras. These were the most daring architectural adventures of their day, exploiting to the utmost the possibilities of what was then a novel structural material; yet how few of the hurrying crowds they shelter ever pause to give them a second glance.

England's Industrial Revolution was pre-eminently a new Iron Age, but it was not only in iron that a pioneer generation of engineers could express themselves. To study the classical grandeur and symmetry of Rennie's canal aqueduct at Limpley Stoke near Bath, or Brunel's towering tunnel portal at nearby Box, both in Bath stone, is to realize that these engineers, like the artists of the period, understood very well the significance of what they were doing. They were changing the world and they recorded that momentous fact in monumental masonry. So shameful an act of vandalism as the destruction of the Euston Arch must never occur again; for we owe it to posterity to cherish this eloquent heritage that the engineers of the past have bequeathed to us.

Mountain, Hill and Moorland

JACK LONGLAND

The English do not live in a land of great mountains. For those you must travel elsewhere, to the 2,000-mile belt of Himalaya, Karakoram and Hindu Kush which guards the Indian peninsula; or to the Andes, the high and lop-sided back-bone that runs the 5,000-mile length of South America. Look, nevertheless, at a small-scale physical map of England, and note how much of it is coloured brown. The high ground runs almost continuously, shaped like a capital L turned back to front, from the Cheviots on the Scottish border, down the long Pennine chain from Cross Fell to Kinder Scout, getting considerably less bumpy through Leicestershire and Warwickshire, at the turn of the L, and then picking up splendidly with the Cotswolds. Mendips, Quantocks and Salisbury Plain (which should be called Salisbury Plateau) then give on to the flatter parts of Somerset and Hampshire, but the hill-line is carried on, charmingly, through Dorset, and achieves a real wildness again, not seen since the tail-end of the Pennines, over Exmoor and Dartmoor. Beyond that, the eye of faith, or better still a pair of legs, can find some high ground all the way to the granite cliffs of Land's End. And east of this long line, the flatter half of England is delightfully variegated with hills and moors of a lesser kind, the North York moors, the Yorkshire and Lincolnshire Wolds, the Suffolk uplands. In the south-east corner come the long lines of the Downs, which Hilaire Belloc's forgivable patriotism elevated into "the great hills of the South Country".

England is so small that you are never very far from hill country. Indeed, you have to cross over into Scotland to find a mountain-top or patch of moor which is more than five miles away from a motorable road. Cross Fell, the highest point of the Pennines, can make you feel remote and lonely, as when my wife and I climbed it one Coronation night, to see the bonfire that wasn't there, because the men from two outlying villages couldn't agree which of them should carry up the fuel. Yet we steered our way down by compass to a car which a friend had driven on a moor-land track to within four miles of the summit. Or you could set out from Gilsland on the Roman Wall, and walk the hard way to Falstone on the North Tyne. Easy to start with, along the Roman road to Bewcastle with its fort and Saxon cross, but over Bewcastle Waste you would find only wild duck and wild goats, no sheep even, and it would be mostly stiff heather-hopping up to Sighty Crag and Black Knowe, before the long descent to Falstone. Here again, though you might feel splendidly cut off from the life of the towns, you are in fact never very far from a road, and nowadays, with the growth of the great Kielder Forest, there must be forestry roads all over the place.

This brings in another virtue of English hills and mountains. They are not only easy to reach by road, but nearly all of them can be walked over. This is true in the technical sense, that you can in theory climb any English peak with your hands in your pockets, though there are a few exceptions like Chrome Hill and Parkhouse Hill in upper Dovedale and two of the tops of Harter Fell in the Lakes, where you would have to be pretty expert to avoid using hands as well. It is true too that most of our hills can be walked over with fair ease, thanks to the efficiency of the grazing sheep in keeping thick vegetation down, and the past activities of man, in felling trees and clearing scrub.

Even if you are a climber and want to take your mountains the hard way, it is another fortunate accident of geology and weathering that so much of our English rock is sound and climbable. So we can climb at will on the volcanic ash of the Lake District, or the gritstone and dolerite and limestone of the Pennines, on the little sandstone edges in Kent, or on the good granite of Dartmoor and the cliffs of Cornwall. And technical improvements in climbing ability, in safeguarding devices and in the load of ironmongery that the modern climber carries round with him, have brought within his reach steep or overhanging cliffs which another generation thought impossible, and types of rock, such as limestone, which less well-equipped climbers had considered unsafely loose. But even the bravest young climber avoids the villainous chalk of Beachy Head, and, except when they are frosted into temporary firmness by a hard winter, the crumbling shales of Mam Tor in Derbyshire. Elsewhere, and leaving alone many of our less stable sea cliffs, it is becoming true that wherever rock is found, it can be, and is being, climbed.

It is again lucky for another reason that, in a small country without big mountains, there is so much rock that can be climbed. Mountaineering and rock-climbing began as a sport not much more than a hundred years ago. They were pursued by a very small number of enthusiasts, who were regarded as amiable lunatics. But since the last war climbing has undergone a population explosion, caused partly by giving a substantial fraction of young people some kind of mountain training to help them win the war – though the Mountain Division was in fact used on the island of Walcheren, which is mostly below sea-level – partly because climbing has come to share the popularity of those sports, such as sailing, canoeing, sub-aqua swimming, and horse-riding, which give the greatest possible contrast to the regimented life of cities, and indeed to the organized rules without which you cannot play team-games.

When I was at university, long years ago, to go and climb in the Lakes was a serious expedition, demanding the co-operation of the rare friend who owned a car, or a very difficult rail journey which could hardly be fitted into a term-time *exeat*. So we had to make do with college walls and roofs, or with the alarming chalk quarries at Cherry Hinton, just outside Cambridge. The current and growing demand for such an individual and adventurous sport as climbing could only have been satisfied by the concurrently enormous growth in the number of cars, to be owned, borrowed, sometimes stolen. It is not only Adventurous Man, but specifically Mobile Man (and of course Mobile Woman, as the opera sings) who crowds the cliff-faces and the climbing pubs. That is why it is today specially fortunate that we have so much rock around in England. The rocks must be accessible, and they are. There must also be enough unclimbed rock to challenge the skill of the young climbers who keep the sport in a state of continuous development.

There are obstacles, of course, to access to moor and mountain. For example, they are all owned by someone, private individual, shooting syndicate, the Crown, or such bodies as the National Trust. Even in the National Parks of England the land is not owned by the nation, as it is in America's national parks. Whole areas of Dartmoor are closed, because used as firing ranges by the Services. Afforestation has covered in trees open hills where once we walked freely. I found recently, over the Border in New Galloway, that it was almost impossible to get on to that fine range, the Rhinns of Kells, at any point, so close ringed was it with new plantations. But the Forestry Commission are beginning to open up many of their forests, with roads and picnic-sites, and in general access to our hill country is slowly being extended. In the Peak District it has been a fifty-year battle, sometimes literally fought out between walkers and gamekeepers, but after years of patient work by the Peak Park Planning Board, access agreements now cover most of the best and wildest moorland, and the most popular of the gritstone crags there. It took nearly as many years to open up the Pennine Way, which gives 250 miles of incomparably wild and rough walking from its starting point at Edale, in the High Peak, to the village of Kirk Yetholm across the Scottish Border. Bogey for the course is between 14 and 17 days, though it has been done in less. But the virtue of the Pennine Way for most walkers is that you can pick a section of it, mild or savage, long or short, genuine mountain or less arduous middleground, according to taste and the length of your legs.

Continued access to some of the hills where in the past we have been free to walk or climb, but which are privately owned, or which you must walk through farmland to reach, is beginning to be in doubt. The post-war flood of climbers is large, and contains many people who have never been disciplined in good mountain behaviour. Whether some mountains may be closed to us in future will largely depend on all of them learning to live, as well as to read, the Country Code.

I have so far dodged the question of when it is a hill, and when it is a mountain. There is no accepted formula based on height above sea-level, and I think it really depends on the *local* scale or scene. Scafell Pike, at 3,210 feet our highest English mountain, would be unnoticed if you dumped it in the middle of the Swiss Alps. But if you stand on top of Helvellyn, and look eastwards to the dark, long, menacing line of the Pennines, you have not the slightest doubt that these are real mountains, although there are few peaks, and those not spiky ones, and although that part of the Pennines is mainly high moorland, too. And the paradox about Derbyshire's High Peak is that there isn't one. If you walk across Kinder Scout or Bleaklow in winter, particularly when the cloud is down, you must navigate across a largely featureless tableland – with an excessively rumpled tablecloth on top of it. You scramble continuously down into and up out of deep twisting channels in the peat ("Groughs" is the local name), and you can lose your sense of direction completely in fifty yards, and wish instead you were on some nice sharp Lakeland ridge that *led* somewhere. So for all their unmountainy shape these are serious mountains. They are lonely in winter, blizzard or cloud can make it a fight to survive, and the walking is very rough indeed. Bleaklow lives up to its name, especially if you remember that the "low" part of it is the same as the Scottish "Law" and means hill.

Even smaller hills, in friendlier places, seem sometimes to deserve the title of mountain. There is of course no doubt that the humped whale-back of Bredon, patched with woodland and squares of arable, is just a hill, though my favourite hill in all England, as it was of the novelist John Moore. But the Malverns pose a more difficult question – certainly not mountainous in height, but the splendidly abrupt way in which they break out from the Worcestershire plain, the long chain of steepish peaks, and the bareness of sheep-cropped flank and top all help to make me see the Malverns as mountains, not hills. I do not think it is just a question of size. There is an old rhyme that goes:

> The highest hills betwixt Tweed and Trent
> Are Ingleborough, Whernside and Penyghent.

It's not true, of course, though early Yorkshire observers, unacquainted with trigonometry, gave them heights that varied between 4,000 and 6,000 feet, whereas Whernside, the highest, is only 2,415. But the instinct was right. Each of these, and particularly Ingleborough, is a distinctive peak, rising sharply and separately from the lower ground. And even if they're not, they *look* very high.

But I must not carry the upgrading of hill into mountain too far. If I did, I should put in a bid for the delightful little Gog Magog hills near Cambridge, where, they say, if you look towards a certain easterly point of the compass, you will find no ground higher than that on which you stand until you reach the Urals! Which goes to show that one reason why England has so many good hills and mountains is that she hasn't any wide plains or steppes.

What then are our English hills, to motorist, townsman, walker, climber? If you stand on the top, it is a simple and self-evident bit of achievement. But a hill is also earth set a little skew-wise, a glimpse of our geological history, a rapid passage through different zones of climate and of vegetation which it would take a thousand miles of journey northward on flatland to match. It is a perpetually surprising change of view, it is a reminder of the precariousness of our survival against wind, cold, snow or thunderstorm. Above all, a hill is *different* – non-human in scale, dwarfing even modern technological man, and telling him how small he is, and how short are his legs.

Ours is a lucky landscape, shaped by the lucky climate that surrounds us in this moment of geological time, 10,000 years away from the last Ice Age, and perhaps 10,000 on to the next one. It has given us hillscapes of infinitely varying charm and nature. You see how blest we are, in comparison, when you fly over Spain and those barren parallel ridges, looking like ribs which have come through the starved skin, or over the Persian rock desert, which really does look like the abomination of desolation.

I believe we have hills "in our bones" because our ancestors lived in an England where the valleys were choked with forest and swamp, and with rivers crossed only by hazardous fords. The trackways of primitive peoples ran along the high bare watersheds, and there you will find the remains of their settlements, like the great fortified camp of Maiden Castle, looking down on what is now Dorchester. And our new-found mobility is taking us back to those hills. I believe too that we need to go there, and that the more our population grows, and the bigger our cities become, the more we shall feel this need.

Let me take you back again, on a clear, rain-washed Cotswold day, to Bredon Hill, with the Herefords chewing a drowsy cud in the fields below. With luck you will see the little slate-blue triangle of the Wrekin to the far north-west, and the edge of the Brecon Beacons standing sharp over Wales, beyond the familiar Malvern Hills. South is the line of the Cotswold scarp, and you remember walking down the convex valley slopes there, and only at the last moment discovering the hidden limestone village, built alongside its quiet stream. Yes, we need valleys and villages, too, and towns, I suppose, but the poet who wrote, "There is much comfort in high hills" knew what he was talking about.

Seascape

JOHN LEWIS

The British Isles have over 7,000 miles of coastline. England must have something like 1,350 miles, excluding inlets. No wonder we have always been a maritime nation. Ours is a coast of much variety, offering disconcerting hazards to the yachtsman and often havens of peace to the motorist or the walker. However, the proper way to see a coastline is from the sea. Let us take a mythical cruise, starting at Berwick-on-Tweed.

The Northumbrian coast consists of low-lying sand dunes and limitless hard, sandy beaches. A few miles off this coast lie the Farne Islands, a string of bare rocks which are a nature reserve and the home of thousands of seabirds. On one of these rocks St Cuthbert established himself in a little cell in sight of his Abbey at Lindisfarne. Behind Lindisfarne (or Holy Island) there is a little natural harbour where a small vessel can lie protected from wind and sea. There could be no better introduction to seeing the coastline of England than to begin here, for much of English history starts at this point. The abbeys of Lindisfarne and of Jarrow and Wearmouth, some forty-five miles down the coast, provided one of the main spring-boards for the Carolingian renaissance. Today the abbey of Lindisfarne stands isolated and in ruins, brooding over the wastes of the North Sea, yet still retaining an atmosphere of peace and serenity. As the tide ebbs one can cross the causeway to the mainland and walk the few miles to Bamburgh – to see one of the greatest castles in England.

Sailing south from Lindisfarne one is soon in sight of the pit-heads of the Northumbrian coalfields. The coal port of Blyth offers protection for the night, and for entertainment the most important yacht club of the area. Few yachtsmen would be tempted into the industrial ports of the Tyne, and the twenty-five-mile coast of Durham has little of interest, with its low cliffs and even less protection. The Yorkshire coast is not much more hospitable, though Staithes is a fascinating little fishing village and Whitby has an abbey high on the cliffs and a harbour with a difficult entrance. Whitby is a seaside resort of some interest and is the birthplace of Captain James Cook, who trusted to Whitby workmanship to carry him round the world in the *Endeavour Bark*, a former Whitby collier. Robin Hood's Bay, another picturesque fishing port, is just south of Whitby. Sailing on down the coast, one passes the resorts of Scarborough and Filey. After rounding Flamborough Head one comes to Bridlington, where the coast is suffering constant erosion. The forty miles or so of coastline, from Flamborough Head to Spurn Head at the mouth of the Humber, are often spectacular but devoid of harbours and have nothing to offer the mariner. At Spurn, where there is a nature reserve, the shingle and sand that has been washed away from Bridlington Bay is helping to build up the spit that curves in opposite Grimsby, to provide most conveniently a safe anchorage for small craft. And they need it, for the Humber has fast tides, and a nasty sea can build up at the entrance to the estuary.

Hull and Grimsby are both important fishing ports, and are the main bases for the trawlers that fish the most distant fishing grounds. About half the fish netted by British fishermen is landed at these Humber ports. The Lincolnshire coast runs from the Humber to the Wash. It is a coastline without harbours and has only one important resort – Skegness, which is reputed to be "so bracing".

The Wash, a rectangular indentation about fourteen miles square, is an area of sandbanks and narrow channels. At low water, these banks rise up like miniature mountains. The common seal lies basking in the sun or swims lazily round one's boat. On the Long Sands fishing boats are stranded high and dry with their masts pointing in all directions. Between them there is a frieze of contorted figures. These are the fishermen digging for cockles. The Wash is reminiscent of the great Dutch estuaries, with the Lincolnshire coast revealed by a shimmering line of poplars and in the distance the tower of the great Boston church, the Boston Stump. It is possible to enter the inland navigable waterways at Boston and to travel by water all the way over the Pennines to Liverpool (providing your boat is shallow enough), or up the Welland to Stamford or the Nene to Wisbech and on to Birmingham (if your boat is narrow enough), or through King's Lynn, one of the most beautiful towns in England, to Cambridge and Bedford.

The coast of Norfolk is low-lying and there is no reputable harbour between the Wash and Great Yarmouth, a distance of seventy miles. However, there is Wells and there is Blakeney, whose harbours only those with much local knowledge would dream of entering. Once inside they are very rewarding. There is a bird sanctuary here, and Blakeney harbour is a large expanse of sandbanks and narrow channels that dry out at low water. Both villages and nearby Cley are all charming if wind-swept villages, where dinghy sailors and bird-watchers congregate. Sheringham and Cromer are both flourishing seaside resorts. Great Yarmouth is the Black-pool of the East Coast, and with Lowestoft is the main centre for the East Anglian trawling and drift-net fishing. The Scroby Sands lie off Yarmouth, forming the Yarmouth Roads and providing shelter for coasters in easterly winds, and also harbouring colonies of the grey seal, about which there has been so much con-troversy. Yarmouth and Lowestoft both provide access to the Norfolk Broads, and coasters can continue up the River Yare to Norwich. The Norfolk coast is a wreck-strewn coast; in the winter of 1865–6 a series of north-easterly gales sank over 500 collier brigs, billyboys and other vessels, many of them on these sands.

The next harbour southwards is Southwold, which with shifting shingle banks has an entrance that can change overnight. Once inside the jetties the harbour becomes the River Blyth. Across the marshes one can see Blythburgh church, and in a dinghy one can sail right up to it. As to whether Blythburgh or Southwold has the finer of these two magnificent knapped-flint churches, the traveller can decide for himself. Southwold lies on the north bank of the Blyth and is faced by Walbers-wick on the south. Wilson Steer used to paint his limpid watercolours here. A little further down the coast is what remains of Dunwich (most of it is under the sea) and then one comes to Minsmere. This is a great bird sanctuary, with rare visitors like the spoonbill and the avocet, which it shares with Havergate Island on the Orford River. There are bearded tits as well. The next landmark is the Sizewell Power Station, and then one comes to Aldeburgh, which has an R.N.L.I. lifeboat (it used to have two) and fishing boats drawn up on the beach. It has a music festival, a golf club and a yacht club, but to enter the Aldeburgh River one has to sail a dozen miles and round Orford Ness to reach Orford Haven (a miniature Spurn Head) for Aldeburgh once had a harbour with access to the sea. The Suffolk coastline is as low and featureless as Norfolk's, but to provide a little relief there is a succcssion of Martello towers erected against Napoleon's threatened invasion.

The Orford River is the northern limit of what is known as "East Coast sailing". The rivers southwards from here are the Deben, with an entrance as difficult as the Ore, the Orwell and the Stour at Harwich, the Walton backwaters behind the Naze, the Colne and the Blackwater, the Crouch and the Roach, and finally the Thames. For the East Coast sailor these are sailing grounds of infinite variety in spite of the featureless coastline. To reach the Thames one has to round the Maplin Sands, which may one day become a great airport. The Thames can at the moment hardly be called a yachtsman's paradise, though many sail out of Southend and Leigh-on-Sea, the home of the cocklers.

Over on the Kentish shore there is the Medway. In a suitable boat one can sail right up to Maidstone. The Medway towns of Rochester and Chatham still have a Dickensian flavour, and the marshes on the Isle of Grain are just as Dickens described them in *Great Expectations*. The Swale divides Sheppey from the mainland, and in the various creeks that run up to Faversham, Upnor and Sittingbourne many small boats are kept. Sailing along the north coast of Kent, if the tide is high and there is an "R" in the month, one might drop anchor off Whitstable to buy some Whitstable natives. Continuing on one's way one passes the twin towers of Reculver's Anglo-Saxon church, once a Trinity House guide for shipping, and then, sailing inside the Goodwins, one makes for Margate with its fun-fairs and other jollifications before rounding the North Foreland. If the weather looks unpromising, one can lock into Ramsgate's Inner Harbour. The outer harbour is no place to lie in if a north-easterly wind is blowing, for the shallow shelf that extends out from Pegwell Bay can cause a sea that only Turner could paint.

Once past Deal and Walmer Castle and through the Downs, where sailing ships used to anchor waiting for a fair wind to take them down Channel, we can round the South Foreland, and the Channel opens up before us. Those vaunted but not so very white cliffs of Dover are surmounted by Dover Castle, one of the earliest (Norman) and least restored of English castles. As for Dover harbour, it is no place for a yacht. In fact it is no place for a harbour at all; but that is by the way. Harbours for small craft are once again far apart. Folkestone, which must be lovely for retired colonels, is no use for sailors, and there is nothing at Hythe. The still mysterious Romney Marsh lurks behind the low coastline, looking as if it ought to be somewhere in East Anglia. The Varne Light Vessel, in contrast to the plethora of lightships in the Thames Estuary, keeps solitary guard on the entrance to the Channel. One has to round Dungeness, featureless except for its power station, before coming to Rye Bay, where in fair weather and with some local knowledge one can make the entrance to the narrow cut that leads up to the old town of Rye. It is not much of a harbour and dangerous to enter, but Rye still has many charms, perched on a hill above the surrounding marshes. Hastings has a small fishing harbour; Bexhill and Eastbourne have plenty for the holidaymaker but nothing for the sailor, who will probably give them and Pevensey Bay a wide berth, sailing outside the Royal Sovereign Light Vessel to clear Beachy Head, a high cliff famous for the number of people who throw themselves off it each year. Newhaven not only has packet steamers but offers much better harbourage for yachtsmen than Dover. The coastline west from here is ribbon development all the way to Selsey Bill. This ranges from the shacks and bungalows of Peacehaven and Kemp Town to the Regency elegance of Brighton and Hove. At Brighton apple-bowed, clench-built fishing boats are drawn up on the beach, looking much the same as when John Constable painted them.

Rounding Selsey Bill, Chichester harbour is on the starboard hand, with a creek leading up to the old town of Bosham, where King Cnut's daughter is said to be buried in the little churchyard. The creeks are crowded with sailing craft. We have arrived at the heart of English yachting. Cowes, set at the mouth of the Medina River, is the yachting world's equivalent to Ascot or Longchamps. Osborne House, Queen Victoria's beloved "little home" is a mile from East Cowes. It is now a convalescent home for service officers and senior civil servants and is open to the public. In every creek and every river on both sides of the Solent and Spithead there are yachts. The River Hamble which runs off Southampton Water has a waiting list for moorings which won't be met in five years, and the other rivers are almost as crowded, though the pretty wooded shores of the Beaulieu River have at least been spared ribbon development. One leaves the Solent through the Hurst Narrows, with Hurst Castle on the starboard hand at the end of a long shingle spit. The Needles mark the westerly end of the Isle of Wight and the point where, as far as yachtsmen go, you can begin to separate the men from the boys. Behind the island lies relatively sheltered water, ahead the open channel, the Portland Race, the Chesil Bank and the wide spaces of Lyme Bay, which from Portland Bill to Start Point is nearly sixty miles across.

Lyme Bay has some spectacular coastal scenery, of great geological interest. It also has Lyme Regis and Sidmouth, both charming and unspoilt resorts – Sidmouth particularly, with its Regency architecture and gentle climate much loved by retired people – but they offer no protection to the yachtsman. The coastline is changing from shingle banks to rocky cliffs. The River Exe, however, is much like an East Anglian estuary, with low banks and shoal water. Halfway up the estuary on the west bank boats can lock into the canal that goes up to Exeter or they can sail up to Topsham with its strand of pretty Dutch-gabled houses.

From Exmouth to Land's End there is an abundance of seaside resorts, grand and expensive like Torquay, or minute like Mullion and Portloe. For sailors it provides a perfect sailing ground, with long Atlantic seas and clear green water. It is warmed by the Atlantic Drift and is the home of the lobster, the crab and prawns in their millions. Brixham and Newlyn are the main fishing ports, though there are plenty of inshore fishing boats, whose owners take time off in the summer to give tourists a taste for the water at places like Looe, Mevagissey and Polperro. The choice of rivers and estuaries for the yachtsmen seems unlimited. Whilst still on the red-cliffed Devon coast there is the Dart with high green banks; there is Salcombe, which is almost sub-tropical and is a good launching-off point for boats making a passage across West Bay; there is the Yealm, with Newton Ferrers just inside the entrance; and finally Plymouth Sound conjuring up memories of Frobisher and Drake, with one of the greatest natural harbours in the country. Plymouth is a large naval station and a commercial port. It is perhaps not ideal for yachtsmen, but with the Cornish rivers lying ahead who would want to linger in Plymouth? Fowey is only eighteen miles along the coast. It is a pretty river, and Fowey itself is an interesting old town with historical associations at least dating back to Edward III, when the town provided nearly fifty ships for the siege of Calais. Leaving Fowey, one can see the man-made mountains of white china clay behind St Austell. Mevagissey lies across St Austell Bay. It is a miniature Brixham, with, like Brixham, an inner harbour that dries out.

Falmouth Harbour and the Carrick Roads evoke memories of the last of the great square-rigged sailing ships, which would lie here awaiting orders to sail for Australia for their annual cargo of grain. These waters and the adjacent Helford

The Needles. Watercolour drawing by John Sell Cotman (1782–1842)

River provide perfect sailing grounds. There are miles of sheltered water and winding creeks. St Mawes in the pretty Roseland Peninsula is probably the warmest place in England. From Falmouth westwards it is advisable to get clear of the coast, for it is a coastline cluttered with reefs and rocks. The dreaded Manacles are the first obstacle. Hundreds of deep-sea ships, coasters and fishing vessels have been lost on this rock-bound peninsula. Rounding the Lizard, Mounts Bay lies between the point and Land's End. The sea floor shoals rapidly towards Marazion and the 250-feet-high St Michael's Mount, which is joined to the shore by a three-quarter-mile causeway, covered at high tide. This counterpart of Mont Saint Michel in Brittany has a castle and fourteenth-century chapel which are open to the public. Newlyn has fishing boats and artists. Penzance is the port for the Scilly Islands. The steamer sails the forty miles to St Mary's and passes the solitary Wolf Rock Light House on the way. There are over 100 islands in this archipelago, once thought to be part of the legendary Lyonesse of King Arthur. The Scillies enjoy the full benefit of the warm Atlantic Drift and have an even milder climate than Cornwall. They grow spring flowers, and on St Agnes there is a bird sanctuary. The only disadvantage these islands have for the yachtsman is that there is no anchorage that is protected from every direction. If the winds shift, the boats have to move also. Off the south-western end of the islands is Bishop's Rock, where Sir Cloudsley Shovell's flagship came to grief in 1707.

Land's End, with its ice-cream vendors and shacks selling rubbish to tourists, is better and more impressively seen from the sea. One has to pick one's weather, for the Longships are not something to trifle with in a strong south-westerly wind.

Once round Land's End, St Ives is the first possible harbour. It has, like Newlyn, both fishing boats and artists.

The north coasts of Devon and Cornwall are quite unlike the south of the peninsula. It is an unfriendly shore, with few harbours, and some of those little more than clefts in the rocks. However, its sandy beaches and roaring breakers provide magnificent surf-bathing at places like Newquay and Perranporth. Padstow, on the Camel estuary, has a harbour, and that is about the sum total of resting places for the yachtsman until he has sailed past Tintagel Head, across Bude Bay and rounded the fearsome cliffs of Hartland Point, to come to anchor in Bideford Bay or to cross the bar and to drop the hook off the little fishing village of Appledore, or even to sail up the Torridge to Bideford.

Lundy Island lies about twelve miles north of Hartland Point. It is an isolated pinnacle of granite, which provided the stone for the Victoria Embankment in London. The coast of Lundy is cliff bound, but there is a landing place at the south-east end behind Rat Island. Lundy is now a bird sanctuary and all through the summer nights one can hear the unearthly screams of the Manx shearwater. We are now in the Bristol Channel. Sailing eastwards, under the shadow of Exmoor, the Welsh mountains can be seen to the north. Steep Holme and Flat Holm lie ahead and the shallows of Bridgwater Bay are on the starboard hand. Weston-super-Mare has mud, jollity, a pier and steamers that cross to Cardiff. Tides are fierce and this is not an ideal place for small yachts. Our journey might well come to a stop at Avonmouth, or we might sail up the Avon Gorge under Brunel's Suspension Bridge past Clifton and come to rest in Bristol, a town still full of maritime history.

As this is a book about England we must miss the coasts of Wales and pick up the thread of our journey in the estuary of the Dee. The sands of the Dee are more suitable for "driving home the cattle" or for cockling than for sailing. Rounding the flat levels of the Wirral peninsula, one comes into Liverpool Bay and the mouth of the Mersey. Liverpool, that gutsy, brash place with its Liver Building and incomparable waterside, deserves a chapter to itself. However, we have no time to stop here and have to sail northward past Southport to the Ribble estuary. We might pick up a mooring off Lytham and St Annes, a resort famous for its championship golf course. But if the wind is blowing from the west, a vicious sea can be kicked up off Lytham so one would be well advised to sail up the river some five miles and lock into the Rufford Branch of the Leeds and Liverpool Canal. Travelling north past Blackpool, with its Golden Mile, Wakes' Week crowds and surprisingly expensive luxury hotels, the next port is Fleetwood. This is the north-west coast's equivalent of Grimsby or Hull, and is the main base for the deep-sea trawlers. The mountains of the Lake District, the Furness Fells and the Old Man of Coniston can be seen, if it is not raining, across the muddy wastes of Morecambe Bay. Morecambe Bay used to be a great centre for trawling. The fishing boats were pretty little counter-sterned cutters. The prawns are still to be found out in the Irish Sea, but cockling is the main activity of the Morecambe Bay fishermen now. There is a bird sanctuary at Leighton Moss and a Nature Reserve at Grange-over-Sands.

Our coastal tour is nearly over. Ahead lies the west coast of Scotland, which is indeed a yachtsman's paradise. All we can do is to round St Bees Head and take a northerly course for the Solway Firth, finally dropping anchor off the Roman fort at the western end of the Roman Wall at Bowness-on-Solway. We began our coastline tour with the seventh-century Northumbrian saints; we end with Hadrian's attempt to defend what is now England from the Picts in the second century A.D.

Yachts off Lytham St Anne's. Detail of painting by L. S. Lowry, 1955   *Beaverbrook Art Gallery Foundation*
                                                                                                     Frederickton,

Rivers

MAURICE WIGGIN

To the river fancier, dry land is a necessary pre-condition which determines the direction, scope and gradient of streams. It guides them, separates them, and intermittently contains them. It modifies them and is itself modified by them. Though it would be an unpardonable licence to speak of symbiosis, yet it is true that they cannot leave one another alone. The river fancier, especially if he has some sense of history, sees the land almost wholly in terms of watersheds, which remain constant; valleys, which occasionally alter; and estuaries, which change continually. Rivers nourish his historical sense, delight his aesthetic sense, and, if he be an angler, ravish and enslave him – though not all equally.

Some of the best English rivers are of Welsh descent. The two noblest of them rise, not far apart, on the lonely wastes of Plynlimon – *Pumlumon Fawr*.

> Happy the eye
> 'Twixt Severn and Wye

sang the poet; and indeed it would be a baleful eye and a curmudgeonly heart which failed to respond to the enchantment of that gracious and haunted land, a land of creamy curd-cropping pastures, crooked little cwms and valleys, star-spangled orchards, cottages clinging to hillsides and sending up blue smoke under pearly skies. I begin with Severn and Wye for the simple reason that I came to love them first, and most. I would not seriously try to erect some inflated structure of theory in defence of their "supremacy": the Severn can be really dull at times. It simply happens that to me, and to many, Severn and Wye are primely numinous.

The Severn, especially, has moved impressionable people to all sorts of extravagance. Belloc, of course, in his inimitable mixture of good fancy and good sense, dubious insight and indubitable observation, put it thus:

> The men that live in West England,
> They see the Severn strong
> A-rolling on rough water brown
> Light aspen leaves along.
> They have the secret of the Rocks,
> And the oldest kind of song.

"The secret of the Rocks . . .", "The oldest kind of song . . .", what rubbish it is, really. Yet Severnside does trick otherwise quite rational people into that sort of mysticism. The Romans came up short against Sabrina Fair; they stood a long time pondering its "rough water brown". Belloc had the essence of it, after all: rough water indeed, brown beyond question, and a-rolling, a-rolling ceaselessly, a very strong and formidable river. Not far from Newtown, and in other parts of its early or Montgomeryshire life, and again in its lower reaches, it is not very interesting; but between, say, Shrewsbury and Stourport, or even perhaps as far as Worcester and beyond to Upton, it is the very model of what a river may be. If you

On the River Greta. Watercolour drawing by John Sell Cotman, 1805   *Leeds, City Art Gallery*

observe the Severn upstream and downstream of the enchanting (now seriously threatened) eighteenth-century town of Bewdley, you see what a river may be when its gradient and width and flow are just right, and when they are complemented by exactly the right degree of steepness and woodedness in the banks or shoulders of the valley. A steep and deep-cut valley, suggesting the earlier immensity of the flood, and essentially green, embowered with trees – this suggests the antiquity of the river, occludes it from the casual vulgar eye, makes it an adventure. One does not want exactly a gorge, such as the Avon inhabits at Clifton: a gorge proper is too awesome. But neither does a river really come into its own when flowing through a valley so wide and gentle and flat that you are not conscious of the river until you practically fall into it. It may well be an extremely rewarding river – the Ouse and others of the East Anglian rivers are delightful in their own way, and the Hampshire rivers have their own perfection. But without the preparation and drama of the steep valley, somehow a river is robbed of some of its proper power.

There should, too, be a lot of *nature* left in a river. One that has been too assiduously tamed is too tame for full delight: I can never feel really at home in the Thames Valley. It is a pretty river, of course, and must once have been as numinous as the Severn. But people can rarely leave well alone. Anywhere downstream of Port Meadow the Thames is too well-regulated for my austere or anachronistic taste. Hardly an inch of the bank is original: the flow is directed, where it is not diverted, the locks come thick and fast, civilization is never far away, and the people on the banks and in the boats very nearly outnumber the fish within. I must concede that if you want to spend time *on* the river, there's none to match the Thames. It is the great beast of burden; it seems made to carry human traffic, and there are many less delightful ways of spending a holiday than in a punt on the Thames. There is no river from which it is more exhilarating to set sail for foreign parts; to set off in a trading steamer from Pool of London bound for Hamburg, say, used to be a bracing experience. Even to toddle jollily from Tower Bridge to Southend and back, on the *Golden Daffodil*, has been worth doing. One regrets nothing, not a minute, that was spent on or in or by the water. . . .

However, it is undeniable that the Thames is *used*, a bit too much used, overmodified: friendly though it is upstream of the Trout Inn at Godstow, pleasant then all the way to Lechlade, with its gentle tributaries, like Windrush and Evenlode, beloved of the fly fisher. But these do not, I think, bear comparison with Severn's splendid brood. Prime among those I name the Teme, also a river of Welsh descent, of course, which in stature and gradient is exactly what the fly fisher desires in his heart. Like the Usk above Abergavenny, a river unfortunately outside the scope of this essay, the Teme matches you blow for blow, it has the nature and the stature of a medium-sized man's medium-sized adventure river. It is virtually not navigable, in any serious sense, though one can, in imagination, quite see it strewn with coracles, like the incomparable Teify, princess of them all. No, it is the wader's dangerous river, rift with flaws, perilous to the unwary sliding in ever another yard for that unmanageable cast which will just cover the far fish's lie. . . . And it is embowered with trees, girt with greenery, suddenly come-upon. Anywhere from Tenbury Wells upstream, or almost anywhere, and even for a very few miles downstream, the Teme is the river of my dreams.

There is a clutch of Celtic rivers, some more or less mildly anglicized, which feed the Severn and the Wye, all beautiful, all seductive; they all have the Celtic grace. Clun, Arrow, Onny, Corve, Rea, Vyrnwy – even the thick Lugg which bears its load of Herefordshire loam. The rivers of the March drain a haunted land.

Different in character but similar in scope and magnitude is the veining of slower streams which drain the eastern parts of England. I hasten to acknowledge that these Anglian rivers also have an unearthly beauty, flowing as they do for the most part under wide pearly skies, through creamy loams that nourish an even richer greenery than the pastures of the March, which become attenuated when the rocks begin to rise. The Great Ouse is too mechanical and regulated for my wild taste, but it and its companion the Little Ouse have their own tranquillity. The rivers of the Broads, Bure and Waveney, are a float fisherman's delight, but prettier and comelier are streams like the Brett that feed the quiet Stour. I guess the quintessence of pastoral tranquillity is to be found, in the riparian sense, in Constable Country.

Further north the tranquillity is repeated, but less snugly, with an undertone of awe created by the greater range and vastness of the slightly harsher spaces, in the valleys of the Witham and the Ancholme. Lincolnshire has a curious quality: it is large and often louring, it is bracing but often dour. The river systems offer some consolation. Many the happy hour I have spent watching a float, by Ancholme and Witham: hours snatched from the ardours of airfields, always the most lowering environment created by man. Of course, one must never forget the two other river systems which drain into the Wash, filling the gap between the Ouse-Stour duality and the Lincolnshire rivers to the north: I mean the Welland and the Nene. Where else does the float fisherman's satisfaction find such perfect expression? Rivers of slow but perceptible flow, draining good land, peaceful and accessible . . . these are river valleys that induce peace. Whereas the rain-fed Celtic rivers which rise and fall, race and dwindle, in my heavenly March-land, go naturally with the fly fisher's energetic and optimistic pursuit, so these gentler and richer rivers of the east are perfectly suited to the float fisher's meditative and statuesque immobility.

It is odd to have written so many words about our rivers without even using the word which of all words means river, the British *avon* or *afon*. A lovely word it is. There are so many Avons it is hard to know where to begin. The Bard's Avon, that flows turgidly through Stratford? Yes, historically it must take precedence, and it can be a pretty little river, and certainly is a river rich in literary associations. But the fishing is very undistinguished, and it is vulgarized and put out of countenance by a multitude of pleasure boats and hemmed in by all too many caravans, right down from Stratford to Tewkesbury, where John Halifax, Gentleman, would wonder what had happened to his rural stream.

Little better is the equally turgid Avon that drains the Somerset marshes and debouches through Bristol into the affronted Severn. Its chief if not its only claim to fame is that gorge, that marvellous Clifton Suspension Bridge – and the fact that adventurers innumerable have started and ended their voyages upon its murky water.

Much the most distinguished Avon is that which enters the English Channel at Christchurch. It rises near Devizes and flows through Salisbury, Downton, Fordingbridge and Ringwood to that strange conclusion, an estuary almost without a peer in mystery. This Hampshire Avon, as it is naturally known, is the most celebrated coarse fishery in England – not necessarily the best, but the legendary one. It is also a river of great disappointment to many, for anglers coming to it from the slow streams of the Midlands and the east and north-east are sometimes cast down by its swift and remorseless flow, which imposes upon them stout tackle and heavy weights and methods wholly at variance with the "toothpick float" gossamer-web subtlety of their native waters. It is a river that yields up specimen roach, barbel and chub, excellent dace, some fine trout, and salmon which are infrequent but immense.

The keypoint about the Hampshire Avon, the quality which distinguishes it from other Avons and, indeed, from most other rivers, the component which allies it to a very rare and special group of streams, is that it is a chalk stream. What is a chalk stream? There are very few of them. They issue from underground reservoirs, vast storage reservoirs unseen by man, which lie below the chalk strata of downland country. The rain percolates through the chalk, the rivers run out from the points where the water-table is appropriate. It follows (*a*) that chalk streams are filtered, pure and clear, and (*b*) that they are not much affected by rainfall, in the short term. Whereas a rain-fed river, in the sense that most of the March-rising rivers and indeed all mountain-born streams are rain-fed, rises and falls in a direct and variably quick response to the rain falling in its upper valley, a chalk stream is little affected by either drought or flood. True, it has its ups and downs, but they are gentle and marginal – whereas a true "spate river", one that has a relatively short and relatively steep gradient and a bed mainly of rock or gravel, rises and falls almost like a lift. True, there are innumerable rivers that are neither spate rivers nor chalk streams – rivers which flow down a more or less gentle gradient, through rich alluvial land; these rise and fall in relation to rainfall, of course, but less suddenly than spate rivers, and vastly more abruptly than chalk streams, which to the casual eye seem not to vary at all.

Coming to a chalk stream is an experience which your Midland angler, for example, never quite gets over. I shall never forget my first sight of the Kennet. Leaning over a bridge and looking down, my favourite pursuit, I simply could not believe that water could be so pellucid. Rapid water I was familiar with, but even that had been dark and turbid in comparison. To see yards and yards away, the weeds and the fishes, as in a mirror – it was akin to the day when I walked out of the optician's wearing my first glasses, and really *saw*.

The Kennet, important only as a marvellous angling stream, rises on the north side of the chalk watershed of downland and flows, actually, into the old Thames – by a biscuit factory at Reading. But the great chalk streams of Hampshire flow south from this divide. The Avon, as aforementioned, empties itself into the sea at Christchurch. The Test and the Itchen flow into Southampton Water. The Bourne joins the Avon at that heavenly spot "where the bright waters meet". These are the pellucid and infinitely beguiling streams of the dry fly trout fisher, the real haven waters to which, in imagination, all dry fly fishermen retire. I have fished them rarely enough, in all conscience; they are fearfully expensive and exclusive. But no one who has cast a fly upon these waters ever forgets that experience.

Actually, the chalk stream is not confined to Hampshire. Chalk streams may rise elsewhere: the Driffield Beck and Foston Beck in Yorkshire – tributaries of the Hull! – are such; truly chalk streams, truly enchanting. Yet one thinks generally of the chalk stream as a glory of the south.

There is a whole group of related rivers of the West Country, not perhaps magnificent, but all with tremendous character, which one thinks of with affection undiminished throughout the years. The rivers of Devon take a hold of one's heart; they, like the Teme, are of just the right gradient and scope, they run through beautiful valleys, just steep enough and sufficiently well-wooded – oh, those endless stands of scrubby hanging oaks! – and they, too, offer treacherous wading, all sorts of chances of mishap, an infinite variety of pools and runs and glides – altogether the most beguiling, adventurous-on-a-small-scale, satisfying fishing. I suppose the Two Rivers, Taw and Torridge, the heavenly twins that enter the Bristol Channel via Barnstaple and Bideford at Appledore, are just about as attractive as smallish rivers can be. But the Dart has enormous charm and grace, the Teign is distinctive and delicious, the Tamar that divides Devon from Cornwall (and England from Abroad, some would say) is full of character if less strong on charm, the Exe and Axe and the Fowey all have their proper devotees. Yet another Avon, the Devonshire Avon, is most peculiar. It is for the most part of its inconsiderable length a mere bit of a bushed-over, tricky little trout stream; then suddenly and inexplicably, at Aveton Gifford, which is the head of the tide, it widens out into an immense lagoon – and the vast quantities of tidal water in this lake have to enter and drain away, twice daily, rushing through a tiny narrow mouth into the twisting estuary proper, which enters the sea near Thurlestone (Bantham Sands). Once fished, never forgotten. I love that river.

Rather strangely, the West Country group of westward-running rivers are counterparted north of the Mersey, where some quite Devonian rivers flow into the Irish Sea. The Eden and the Lune are for the most part both beautiful and productive; the Border Esk is celebrated, and the much smaller Esk that enters the sea near Ravenglass – name to conjure with! – is deeply attractive to those who have discovered it and return to fish Hugh Falkus's water year by year. I imagine that much the same was once true of the north-east coast rivers which feed the North Sea from the other side of the great divide; but industrial pollution, water abstractions, and sheer pressure of building and population have scarcely improved Tyne and Wear and Tees. The Aln and the Coquet remain to remind us what glories once were there.

The rivers of Surrey and Middlesex, which once were on a par with, say, the unsensational little rivers of Dorset and Somerset – Frome and Parret, Piddle and Brue – are now much reduced in value. One is thankful that the Mole and Wey are still there, on the grounds that any river is better than none; but they are poor things. The little rivers of Essex, almost all estuary, are the yachtsman's friend rather than the fisherman's; the rivers of Kent are inconsiderable; but the rivers of Sussex still wring a sort of rueful poetry out of sundry impressionable souls. Belloc raved about the Arun in his romantic way, and heaven knows I am indebted to Arun for many placid hours fishing for pike, and also for several colds and chills of unusual malignancy; it is a vaporous valley which can strike dankly chill to the unwary, its water is dark and glum. The Adur is a jolly little stream, and a funny one. The Sussex Ouse, which flows through Lewes and enters the Channel at the grim port of Newhaven, carries more sea trout than strangers are encouraged to think by the uncommunicative inhabitants of suspicious Sussex.

I have said too little about the heavenly streams of Yorkshire – Swale, Wharfe, Nidd, Aire, Greta, and the rest. They have their own sort of upland charm. They are in fact very good company. A river is the best of company for a man who can get his mind off money. If he can't, it will do the job for him.

The English Garden

ANNE SCOTT-JAMES

Of all forms of sightseeing, visiting gardens is the least historical. Churches, houses, pictures, furniture, tapestries, can often be seen in their original condition, or, if they have been altered, every step in their growth or restoration is probably on record. But a garden changes with time and with every new plantsman. A garden is a living, growing, progressing, backsliding thing, never the same for more than twenty or thirty years. However perfectly a garden is planned, later generations with new tastes, new knowledge and a wider range of plants to play with will seek to improve it. It may even go backwards, if it falls into the hands of a tactless plantsman or takes a knock from the weather.

So when one visits a historic garden one may speculate enjoyably on the men who planted it, and on the sort of life people lived in the Great House in the sixteenth, seventeenth, eighteenth or nineteenth centuries; but what one is seeing is an object of contemporary, not historic beauty. Every garden is alive.

There are almost no traces left of the earliest English gardens, though there are a few conscientious reconstructions. The medieval English garden was a utilitarian patch rather than a pleasure ground, with fruit trees, vegetables, vines, herbs, medicinal plants and a few flowers. Regrettably, we were poor gardeners compared with Continental countries, particularly Italy.

The first gardens with any aesthetic pretensions were Tudor. In 1520 Sir Thomas More, surely one of the most civilized men in English history, made a pleasure garden in Chelsea, with rosemary hedges, blossoming trees and flowers, and a view of the Thames. A few years earlier, Cardinal Wolsey had begun to lay out the gardens at Hampton Court in the formal Italianate manner which was to be the inspiration for the next two hundred years. After Wolsey's death these were extended and elaborated by Henry VIII in a complicated geometric arrangement of terraces, fountains, box hedges and alleys, embellished with topiary, mazes, carved heraldic animals and "knots" – elaborate patterns of clipped shrubs or herbs, filled in with coloured earth or flowers. It must all have looked very fussy.

Throughout the sixteenth century horticultural skill developed fast. Travellers brought home exotic plants; the first herbals were published; scented flowers were cultivated; waterworks and fountains were constructed (they didn't always work); and, as in the other arts, refugees from France and Flanders arrived and taught the inelegant English their more sophisticated Continental skills.

When great new houses were built, like Haddon Hall, Hardwick and Montacute, they were graced with spacious pleasure gardens, and, though no original plantings are left, some of these gardens (as at Haddon Hall and Montacute) still retain something of their Elizabethan shape and style. The formal style continued into the Jacobean period, the decorations becoming even more ornate. The garden of Hatfield House, built for the 1st Earl of Salisbury, had terraces, fountains, a crowd of statues and ornaments, an artificial stream, fish-ponds, trained fruit-trees and oranges (which were protected in winter) and a wide range of plants. Traces of the original garden are still to be seen, though there has been much restoration.

The Restoration saw the climax of the formal garden, and English gardeners turned to a new master, the Frenchman, Le Nôtre, who was designing grandiose gardens for the palaces of Louis XIV. A Le Nôtre garden was an exercise in mathematics. Always a central vista stretched from the house to the horizon; on either side of it were elaborate parterres, formal lakes and canals, and groves of trees planted at exact intervals, the whole arranged on a geometric plan of axes, circles and squares.

Overlapping with the Le Nôtre period, the Dutch style was an influence in England, especially after the accession of William and Mary. This, too, was formal, but more intimate and inward-looking (a Le Nôtre garden, however vast, could be absorbed in one glance from the windows of the house), with many plantings of clipped evergreens and bulbs. But neither the French nor the Dutch style gardens laid out in England in the second half of the seventeenth century and during the reign of Queen Anne were ideally suited to the rounded contours of the English landscape, and most were later redesigned completely, but not all. At Chatsworth, the seventeenth-century cascade and the temple from which the waters flow (1703) are still to be seen in all their magnificence; and the gardens of Bramham Park, Yorkshire, and of Melbourne Hall, Derbyshire, retain their Queen Anne structure and the mood of Versailles.

Then the pendulum swung. It had to. Gardens had become so intellectual as to be absurd. The poet Pope was one of the first to laugh at man's distortion of nature and at the pretentiousness of all the topiary and statuary and parterres. In 1719 he designed a much simpler kind of garden for his own house at Twickenham. The landscape gardens which we admire so much today came into fashion; the first of a series of great exponents was William Kent, who was followed by Lancelot (Capability) Brown and Humphry Repton. In their hands, the garden ceased to be an enclosure; the house, its garden and the open country beyond were designed like a landscape painting; the whole picture was to be "natural", with a perfection which, of course, required consummate art.

In these growing, living landscapes, trees were gracefully grouped (many avenues fell to the axe), streams meandered, lakes were re-modelled in natural curves, there was often an artificial ruin or two, and the new device of the ha-ha, uniting the garden with the open country beyond, often replaced the old boundary hedge or fence. Flowers were not important – the scale of the landscapes was too large. Many of these eighteenth-century landscape plantings can be seen today; three notable examples are at Rousham House, a charming, cool, green garden with a classical arcade and perfectly placed statues by Kent; the park and lake of Blenheim Palace, by Capability Brown; and Sheringham Hall, by Repton.

The landscape style continued to be admired until the death of Repton in 1818, when a new style of garden came in with a new society. Industrialization, the rise of the middle class, the birth of many smaller estates, improved greenhouses, cheap labour and inventions like the lawn-mower, combined to produce a more mechanical style of garden which one can call neo-Italianate, or simply Victorian. The important elements were neat lawns, gravel paths, formal beds and carpet bedding. At the same time there was a wonderful increase in plant material, and exotics, like orchids, and strange trees, like the monkey puzzle, became Victorian status plants.

This return to formality was demolished for the second time towards the end of the nineteenth century when William Robinson and the redoubtable Miss

Jekyll introduced the "natural" or "wild" garden. Fiery characters both, they abominated bedding plants, topiary and Victorian knick-knackery, and extolled herbaceous plants, naturalized plantings, stream and woodland gardening, mixtures of exotics with simple native flowers, climbing and rambling plants, ground cover and a seemingly haphazard beauty. This is the style which is still dominant today.

But one does not visit a garden primarily to dig into history, although this can be a bonus pleasure. Most of us are not antiquarians, and we go partly for the visual delight and partly to learn something for our own gardens. There is nothing like a fine piece of planting to fire the humbler gardener to go home and do likewise – it is impossible to calculate the number of roses which are climbing up old apple trees as a result of visits to Sissinghurst.

There are something like two thousand gardens in England which are open to the public, either for charity or to earn money for the estate, and one can class them loosely in three categories: landscape gardens, country-house gardens, and cottage gardens.

The landscape gardens are those which surround the great houses of the eighteenth century, and they are not true gardens so much as pleasure grounds or parks; the important features are trees, lakes, vistas and small classical temples and follies. One visits these grand park-gardens, humbly, to admire rather than learn. Gardens like Stourhead, Blenheim, or Longleat are spectacularly beautiful, but as remote from one's own life as the court of Versailles.

If a foreign visitor had a single day for seeing one of the grand gardens, I think Stourhead, in Wiltshire, is the one he should choose. Stourhead is a landscape garden on the finest scale, designed in the middle of the eighteenth century by the owner of the house himself, Henry Hoare the younger, and developed and elaborated by his successors. The focus of the landscape is a serpentine lake which lies in a deep basin surrounded by hills which are richly planted with beeches and conifers. The visitor takes a long and winding walk round the lake, and at every turn his eyes fall upon some fresh and exquisite vista – there is a view to the bridge, the grotto, the rock arch, the Pantheon, the Temple of the Sun. The landscape at Stourhead is a masterpiece, but spoilt for some eyes, including mine, in the months of May and June, when modern plantings of rhododendrons come into fiery blossom and outrage the cool, classical landscape of water and trees and stone.

There are park-gardens on this splendid scale in nearly every region of England, from Heveningham Hall, Suffolk, which has a wooded landscape by Capability Brown and an orangery by James Wyatt, to Blenheim, Oxfordshire; from Castle Howard, Yorkshire, a Vanbrugh mansion with grounds and a Temple of the Four Winds by Vanbrugh, to Luton Hoo, Bedfordshire, with a park by Brown. These landscapes are perhaps the most important contribution to the visual arts that England has ever made – pay no attention to jealous mutterers who pretend that we cribbed them from the Chinese.

The second category is of country-house gardens, which are true gardens rather than landscapes, plantsmanship of flowers and shrubs being more important than trees. Though the site may be historic, the planting nearly always belongs to this century – I am thinking of such country-house gardens as Sissinghurst, Hidcote, Haseley Court, Great Dixter, Nymans, Sutton Courtenay, Charleston Manor, Bampton Manor and Highdown. However different the size and the site, there are characteristics common to nearly every modern garden, of which the first is an informality which descends from William Robinson, though judging, perhaps unfairly, from what is left of his own garden at Gravetye, many of the creators of these gardens were better artists than he.

Even if the garden near the house is formal (as at Haseley Court, with its pleached lime trees and topiary chessmen on the lawn) the newer plantings are nearly always in the cottage style; soft shrub roses are preferred to stiff hybrid teas; foliage plants carpet the ground; clumps of flowers spill over on to paths; planting is lavish and mixed, with climbers intertwining, roses spraying out between flowering shrubs, mixed herbaceous borders, bulbs naturalized in grass. The variety of plants is enormous, for the modern country-house gardener is increasingly a connoisseur. Rare, strange and species plants will be seen in these gardens, as will ferns, water plants, winter-flowering plants and green-flowered plants, like euphorbias and hellebores. The visitor to such gardens should take a notebook, for there are many mixtures, colour schemes and unfamiliar names he will want to remember.

The second principle which governs such gardens is the need for economy of labour. Therefore, shrubs and permanent planting have replaced in-and-out bedding schemes, and few gardeners, having seen the restful beauty of permanent gardening, regret the change. Unhappily, the vegetable garden, too, has had to go into decline; totting up the awful cost of home-grown vegetables, most garden owners limit themselves to a few choice varieties.

Of all country-house gardens, my personal favourite is Sissinghurst, in Kent, which was created largely since the last war by Sir Harold Nicolson and his wife, Vita Sackville-West, he designing and she planting in a supremely happy partnership.

The principle of the garden is "separate rooms" – a series of intimate enclosures leading one into another, each planted with a different theme: there is a rose garden, a herb garden, a spring garden, a white-and-grey garden, and so on. The plantsmanship is charming, so informal and free as to be almost cottagey, although the size of the garden, and the massing of plants in groups, make Sissinghurst an idealized rather than a literal cottage garden. The choice of highly scented climbing and old-fashioned shrub roses make it a paradise in June, while the white garden (conceived on a snowy day in January) is cool even in midsummer, with its white statue, white irises, white pansies, paeonies and lilies.

A perhaps even greater garden designed as "separate rooms" is Hidcote Manor, in the Cotswolds, which I put second only because I know it less well. It is an earlier garden than Sissinghurst – Miss Sackville-West drew much inspiration from it and wrote a graceful essay in tribute to its beauty – and was created at the beginning of this century from rough, untilled fields by an architect-botanist-plantsman, the late Major Lawrence Johnston.

Hidcote consists of a series of separate, secret gardens, enclosed by high hedges, opening (unlike Sissinghurst) off one long main vista. The gardens are of wondrous variety and delight – there are waterfalls, gazebos, pools, topiary, pleached avenues, winding steps, gateways of yew, a stream – but all have one common quality, that they are planted with extraordinary profusion. "What I should like to impress upon the reader is the luxuriance everywhere; a kind of haphazard luxuriance, which of course comes neither by hap nor hazard at all", wrote Miss Sackville-West. Trees, flowering shrubs, water plants, climbers, roses, tender plants, foliage plants, all are there in lavish masses, planted with a botanist's skill and an artist's eye.

Lastly, there are the cottage gardens; and, though the country-house gardens may claim to be "cottagey", they are not true cottage gardens. They are on too large a scale to be totally informal – there is always some group planting of trees, always some massed flowers or shrubs – and they need a gardening staff to work them. The true cottage garden is planted and worked by the owner, with a minimum of staff, is highly personal and informal throughout.

All over England there are old rectories, small manor houses, farms, mills and cottages with small, personal gardens which are opened to the public for one or two days every summer for charity.

The most interesting of all is the garden at East Lambrook Manor, Somerset, created by the late and much mourned Mrs Margery Fish. It is the paragon of cottage gardening. Mrs Fish was above all a plantswoman. She crammed her small garden with a spectacular variety of plants, trying form after form of each species because she thought it dull gardening to duplicate – she grew no less than seven forms of the lesser periwinkle.

Her garden is, therefore, a glorious jumble. Structurally it is a patchwork, with narrow beds and zigzag paths, and in the beds is the ultimate in cottage mixtures, the commonest lilies growing cheek by jowl with the rarest euphorbias. Some consider this garden too quaint, but to me it expresses such a love of flowers that it is pure joy to visit. It is a generous garden, with all the climbing, rambling things (there are wonderful clematis) spilling over the outer walls to give pleasure to passers-by.

There are many cottage gardens not unlike East Lambrook, of which notable features are always shrub roses, clematis, variegated plants, a great variety of ground-cover plants, winter-flowering plants, like hellebores, old-fashioned plants, like columbines and pansies. I confess that, since they are within my range, and I wouldn't want Blenheim even if I were offered it, I love these gardens best.

Finally, there are many gardens which do not fit neatly into any category, but are of interest to the specialist. The Royal Horticultural Society's 150-acre garden at Wisley, Surrey, has something exciting every month of the year, with exceptional wild and alpine sections. The Pleasure Garden at Westonbirt School, Gloucestershire, planted by a great arboriculturist exactly a hundred years ago, has one of the finest collections of trees and shrubs in the world. Highdown, Goring-on-Sea, Sussex, is a true country-house garden, of special interest because it was made in a chalkpit and shows what a wealth of plants can be grown on an alkaline soil. And Mr Roy Elliott's Alpine garden in Birmingham (seen by appointment only) has over four thousand alpine varieties growing in the heart of an industrial city.

Once you start visiting gardens, there is always another you feel compelled to see, and then another, and another. It becomes the most delightful of obsessions.

The "cottage" garden at Sissinghurst   Edwin Smith

London

London Postal Districts   Middlesex

IVOR BROWN

London is a clay-saucer with a surrounding rim of hills which are promoted by estate agents to offer "most desirable properties on the Northern (or Southern) Heights". There is nothing mountainous to climb, but there are quite steep slopes once favoured by a few Georgians, then more thickly covered by the Victorians in search of an eminence, and now happily populated by families who value the nearby heaths and parks as well as the fresher air. In Hampstead or Highgate one can be housed 400 feet above the sea, and since the old nuisance of smoking chimneys has been drastically reduced the occupants of these ridges can look across the bowl on a clear day to the uplands of Kent and Surrey, to Greenwich Park or Epsom Downs.

Within the saucer rise the new, many-storied and many-windowed concrete piles of the new architecture. On a fine evening they catch the sunlight from the west, which makes these pallid monsters of day-time become surprisingly radiant and even roseate for an hour or so. If there is a clear sky or only a film of cloud one splendid antique, undefeated by the soaring office-blocks, can be seen standing staunchly for the old faith amid the clustered and domineering premises of the new commerce. From the steps of my front door in Hampstead I have the view which, when seen from the modest hummock of Primrose Hill near Regent's Park, moved an otherwise sad and sceptical minor poet John Davidson, to a memorable tribute:

> Dissolving, dimly reappearing,
> Afloat upon ethereal tides
> St Paul's above the city rides.

The German bombers failed to sink it. Still it floats. Below it Davidson felt "the heart of London beating warm". There is still that cardiac and cordial murmur, and still that majestic dome. Despite all its modern nuisances of noise, size and congestion, London has its pleasing prospects. The visitor who goes to a ridgeway suburb to meet friends or to see the local sites and pleasaunces should stop to gaze into and across the bowl.

London can be seen from the top in several places, from Wren's Monument in the City, from the far higher Post Office Tower near the Tottenham Court Road, or from the roof of a sky-scraping office block, most notably at the Millbank Tower on the Westminster riverside. To climb or to be lifted to any of them is useless unless the weather is fine. From the last of these I have looked out on a day which fortunately happened to be cloudless. Below me the devious and serpentine Thames was meandering on its way from Windsor Castle, just visible in the distant west, to the Port of London. It is the old, abiding lifeline, always in service since the Romans waded and then bridged it. A myriad merchants down the centuries throve on its banks, sometimes fouled the water, and sometimes beautified its shores. Viewed from a height the Thames cuts through the urban browns and greys which are pleasantly relieved by the green of many parks. Inevitably one gets the sense of an undisciplined sprawl, since London grew casually, first edging its way in a narrow strip along the ribbon of the river and later pushing backwards to the ridges as a container for the ever-multiplying population. Not even in the centre was it deliberately planned or grandly developed as a capital with broad avenues radiating from an imposing centre where palatial pomp was on display and there was august accommodation for the statesmen and the civil powers.

To enjoy the essence of the town it is necessary to nose one's way into it instead of peeping down from the sky. For that kind of penetration the river is the best of guides. One can traverse it by steam-boat from Hampton Court to Greenwich. One can follow it by car or on foot. That the Thames is "liquid history" is a statement so often quoted as to have become a cliché. But a cliché can be true. The familiar phrase sums up the chronicles of social change. The rich Elizabethans had their riparian mansions with their lawns leading to the water-gates. Royal, seigneurial, and ecclesiastical splendour was there established while the Commoners set their Houses of Parliament by the stream and crowded increasingly along the docks and factories.

It is a compliment to London that it should have been so magnetic, draining the country and the other towns of its talented and ambitious families. Now the attraction of being "with it" by being in it has become so powerful as to create a problem, the excessive overspill of population into South-East England. There are efforts to decant the flood but the eagerness to get in is stronger than the willingness to get out into the New Towns planned as a relief. London is people-jammed and traffic-jammed but the jam has not turned to vinegar and is sweet enough to defeat the designs for dispersion.

Those who wisely do their sight-seeing by or near the water should try to envisage the London of the Elizabethans. Their monarch was indeed a River Queen whose history was as liquid as illustrious. She was born at Greenwich, reigned at Whitehall, and died at Richmond. The Thames was then broader and shallower. The embankments are only a century old. But it was clean, even sweet and silvery to the poets, with salmon leaping among the swans and the stately, sumptuous barges of the great as they travelled about their business and their pleasures from Westminster to the City. That was the comfortable transport since La Straunde, which became the Strand, was then a rough and ill-kept road. On the southern shore of London Bridge is Southwark where there must be the most eminent of ghosts for those who can feel them in the air.

For a leisurely walk there can be few better than a stroll southward over Blackfriars Bridge with a left turn past the eighteenth-century almshouses to take the waterside way to the east. Across the river the spires of Wren's City churches, gleaming round Tower Hill, are like stone set to music. The entry to Shakespeare's Bankside may evoke the protest that there is nothing of that now. Yet there is Southwark Cathedral, the old parish-church of the players, with its tombs of poets and playwrights. It contains a Harvard Chapel since the great John of American university fame was christened here in 1607. To this end of London Bridge came the travellers from the Channel, and there were many inns to receive them.

From one of them, the Tabard, Chaucer sent his pilgrims on the road to Canterbury. In another Dickens made Mr Pickwick meet Sam Weller. The novelist stayed as a boy in little-altered Lant Street while his father was imprisoned for debt in the neighbouring Marshalsea gaol. A notable survivor in the High Street is the

J. Allan Cash

The Vale of Health on Hampstead Heath

seventeenth-century George Inn, with its galleried courtyard. The coaches drew in there and still do, with different traction. Horses will not be seen. London on the Thames has become London on petrol. But, for me at least, the busy new Southwark is a place where the past unforgettably defies and so enriches the present. Its Hop Market serves the brewers and the beer-drinkers where the Elizabethan actors took their wine and the coach-and-four passengers in winter came off the chilly roof for revival by steaming tots of spirits.

Since it was seldom deliberately planned London can be fairly described as a "round-the-corner" city. The fine approach frequently misses the fine sight which is round the corner. The view down Whitehall does not include the splendours of Westminster. The Strand should have been a broad and notable conduit to the majesty of St Paul's on Ludgate Hill. It has not happened thus. Dispersal of theatres is convenient because it lessens the traffic-jam when audiences are coming and going. But the concealment is excessive in the case of the two great "Royals", Drury Lane and Covent Garden. They began their varied and intermittently lost and renewed lives in 1662 and 1732, when entertainment was sought further east than it is now. So they must be sought in narrow streets where there are market-lorries instead of buses for passengers. The main road in Chelsea is now valuable for the turnings off it. Make for the river and there is much of quality and history to see. And so it is with Fleet Street. The lawyers' riverside Inns are to be found by deviating into a narrow lane or down a passage. Legal, like political, power has its corridors.

I thought that I knew the buried treasure of the London lanes and alleys fairly well but the detailed guidance so well provided in this book has proved my ignorance. There is much in the following pages about some nooks and niches which deserve discreet penetration. In London the good pedestrian, like the good motorist, must learn to take his corners.

The desire to live in a once neglected portion of the saucer or, better still, on one of the rims has produced some odd migrations, especially of the professional

A. F. Kersting

The Nash Terraces on the edge of Regent's Park

classes and the followers of the arts. The high cost of central housing makes for dispersion. Camden Town was little thought of not long ago: it was a low-price, low-life area through which the bus carried me when I was a boy in Hampstead. I knew it only as the home of a famous murderer, Dr Crippen. Now the sad Victorian streets have their gloom dispelled by occupiers with stage, radio, television and gossip-column reputations. Mouldering façades have been brightened by new paint and colourful doorways. The same thing has happened on the slopes of Islington, where the Elizabethans went to shoot wild-fowl and the Georgians drank much more than water in the pleasure-ground of Sadler's Wells. There they took their coaches for the northward roads while Charles Lamb was happy with tongue, pen, and tobacco beside the canal. Then came decline. Now to be an Islingtonian is to be in the fashion. And so it is to live by a canal.

A home by the Thames is naturally prized where it looks over a great sweep of the river with its varied traffic of sail, steam, and racing oarsmen. That is the special attraction of Hammersmith and Chiswick. The vogue is less understandable when the view is of a static and murky "inland water-way". But the taste for such an outlook is strong and growing. In Maida Vale an old basin for barges has become known as "Little Venice", a title more complimentary than exact. It has culture in the air. Robert Browning was a Victorian resident and there are titled folk as well as authors and artists living round the pool. Out of it past Regent's Park and its Zoo, through Camden Town and under and into Islington wanders the old canal, sombre but alluring to those who prefer a liquid to a pavement view. To be on the bank is now to be fashionably in the swim. The promotion of once common-place suburbs has some excellent results. The new money coming in brings the ability to restore and re-decorate. A once grubby terrace begins to display a butterfly gaiety. There is a flutter of new tints, a pride in appearance, and life at a new tempo. There are many drab districts which are being taken over and given a face-lift. The London of tomorrow will be on the move upwards, and sensibly so.

Many strangers to London will bring memories of Charles Dickens whose

J. Allan Cash

Houseboats at Little Venice

reading public is so widespread and so constant. If they expect to find it as dark as he drew it their fears are groundless. He was haunted by the smelly suffocating fogs which were aggravated by the smoke from coal-fires in every house. "Give the people light, give them air" was one of his most urgent pleas. He would have rejoiced in today's multitude of windows and the spectacle of London floodlit. Among the many discomforts of noise and crowding imposed by recent conditions there has been one remarkable and insufficiently praised benefit. The compulsion to use smokeless fuel in many areas has effectively cleared the air and cleaned the surface of the town. The inevitable mists of winter are no longer loaded with soot and turned into the sticky mess which clogged the throat and menaced the lungs. Paint is not immediately smudged as soon as it is laid on. Not long ago it was impossible to see across the saucer from the ridges. Now there is no blanket of fumes over London. One can go about the streets without dreading the immediate smear of dirt on face, hands, and linen which our predecessors had to endure. With the diesel trains pouring in and out of the central railway termini there is an end to the nuisance caused by steam-engines belching thick smoke by day and night. If London strives to be colourful it is no longer frustrated by the winter "smog" and by the soot which even in summer blackened the grass in the gardens. London has washed its face.

What London has lost in civic calm it has gained in colour. In streets which not long ago were dingy one can see bright paint laid on to the previously scruffy doors and window-sills. These frontages are like a button-hole nosegay worn on a shabby coat. In the neighbourhood of the parks the mansions are kept in better trim. The stucco façades which make a sad spectacle if neglected and flaking away are now gleaming, most notably where Portland Place leads on to the Nash Terraces inspired by the Prince Regent. Overlooking the well-kept lawns and flower-beds of the pleasaunce which he ordered they have survived war-time disaster and their maintenance in splendour is a joy to the eye. Inside the parks there are more blossoming trees to make April earn the Shakespearian adjective, proud-pied. The flowering cherry showers its richness on the suburbs when the almond-trees are wilting. Front gardens are given a light golden gaiety with forsythia. Much more than in my boyhood does spring come "bursting out all over". It is the right time for a visit.

The skill of the gardeners, whether working for the Crown in the Royal Parks or for the Greater London Council in its numerous demesnes, deserves the public gratitude. They are not grudged money to spend and they have the craft to use it admirably. From the coming of the crocuses and the daffodils to the pomp of tulip-time and on to the autumn consolation of the chrysanthemums there is replacement and renewal in the flower-beds. "Never a dull moment" is the policy. Those who go in midsummer to the Open Air Theatre in Regent's Park pass the splendid array of roses in Queen Mary's Garden, a superb approach to the Shakespearian flowers of speech. The aeroplanes may sometimes drown the words first heard on Southwark's Bankside and lingering in the minds of men for ever. But many a traveller has been air-borne to London. He has had the advantage of speed before he finds amenity interrupted. He cannot have it both ways.

Britain has few opponents of the monarchy. If a stern Republican is using his freedom of speech to pour scorn on royalty from a dais at Speakers' Corner in Hyde Park he should remember that the Park was a royal gift to the people made by Charles I and that Cromwell wanted to hire it out for private exploitation.

The parklands and public gardens, of which Richmond and Kew are spacious examples, were not originally designed for public recreation. But to that good end these and others have come by gradual stages. Frequently there was royal initiative in their creation. St James's Park began as the site of a King's menagerie. Presented with camels, James I pastured them beside his palace. Now, gay with water-fowl, it is the perfect back-garden of Whitehall. The lawns of Kensington Palace became Kensington Gardens. Regent's Park would not be there unless the Prince had thought of saving its expanse from building and then of building magnificently on its rim. The monarchy has paid some handsome dividends in return for its inheritance of power and privilege. It helped to make London a landscape as well as a city.

Timber is plentiful and keenly guarded. If an elderly and ailing trunk is cut down there is immediate protest. There are vandals who misuse the common property, but there are also devotees who zealously resist any invasion or diminution of this legacy. They want their London to be as rural as may be. They proudly retain the name of Village for the oldest parts of their favourite suburbs. To be considered a Villager in Hampstead or Highgate, Dulwich or Wimbledon, delights the inhabitants.

The Dickensian demand for light and air is variously met. The street-lamps in some areas are criticized as inadequate, since the standards and methods change awkwardly from one district to another. Just before lighting-up time there are, especially in autumn, sunsets of rare beauty: to look west is to find in the sky that delicate texture of pink and grey which adorns the necks of the town's super-abundant pigeons. It is the hour of release for myriads and of plans for the evening's entertainment. The windows of the soaring offices begin to twinkle. Then comes the adroitly contrived floodlighting of the principal buildings, best seen along the river. It is a fascinating panorama with the contrast of the dark water and the brilliance overhead. The parks are London's paint-box by day. The city wears jewellery at night.

NOTE Car parks in London are scattered and often full by mid-morning; parking meters are operative almost everywhere except on Saturday afternoons and Sundays. We advise the motorized sightseer to leave his car on the outskirts of London and use public transport or taxis: the underground is fast and easy for strangers to use; the top of a bus provides the best view of the streets; and cruising taxis can be picked up at most times of the day.

London: Gazetteer

FRANCIS HOWELL

THE CITY, EAST END AND SOUTHWARK

This is where London began, and where visitors to London should also begin, but seldom do. When the Emperor Claudius and his elephants arrived here in A.D. 43 he recognized the military and commercial desirability of the site and 20 years later Tacitus was able to record that the city was already crowded with merchants.

The Romans called it Londinium, turned it into a port, built a bridge to the south bank – it remained the sole London crossing point of the Thames until 1750 – gave it style, opulence and order, and withdrew 367 years later, having suffered in the meantime a notable but soon avenged defeat at the hands of Queen Boadicea. For their future security they encircled the city with a stone wall with watch towers and six gates. This, for a long time, was the extent of London: 330 acres, with the whole of the south side a waterfront.

Between the departure of the Romans and the arrival of the Normans, London had capitulated to Christianity and variously endured or repulsed the Danes. St Paul's Cathedral, which had been built, twice destroyed and rebuilt, became a symbol of resistance and solidarity to the people, who in 1066 voluntarily acknowledged William the Conqueror instead of being defeated by him. Nevertheless, he founded the Tower of London when he built the White Tower to keep the populace in their place as much as invaders out of it. He did, however, confirm the rights which the citizens had exercised under Edward the Confessor, which led eventually to the City acquiring the status and privileges of a county. In the Middle Ages the political and financial interdependence of the Crown and the City was established. Trades and crafts flourished, and the guilds which they formed founded such architectural riches as the Guildhall and several halls of liveried companies. Since members of the trades tended to congregate, we are left with descriptive street names such as Fish and Bread streets, Garlick Hill and Pudding Lane.

This 600-year consolidating period must have been one of great wealth, possibly of piety, certainly of manifold development, because by 1666 the City's tiny area boasted something over 100 churches, a bridge which outshone the Florentine Ponte Vecchio, and a mass of appalling slums. Then came the Great Fire. The plague had decimated the poorer population the previous year – the rich escaped to Westminster, Knights-bridge, Highgate and other villages – but the fire knew no social barriers. During the four days of the conflagration it consumed 13,200 houses, 84 churches and St Paul's itself.

It is said that within a week Sir Christopher Wren submitted a plan for rebuilding, and John Evelyn and others later, but none was carried out. Wren eventually built 51 churches and spent the rest of his life fighting for "his" St Paul's. He also built the Monument which still stands at the meeting of five streets, not far from London Bridge.

From then on London grew. The City boundaries crept outwards to embrace The Temple, Fleet Street, Holborn and beyond Aldersgate and Moorgate, while suburbs engulfed the surrounding villages. But the City remains a commercial centre. When 164 of its 460 built-up acres were devastated during the war, it scarcely faltered. St Paul's was hit twice and everything around it was flattened. Once again there was a plan. It could be said that the new buildings have developed in spite of it rather than because of it, but they do, to some eyes, form an imposing background of anonymous planes against which the elegant spires and façades of remaining 17th-, 18th- and early-19th-cent. London are displayed.

While the City was stretching out greedily towards the W. and N., the area to the N. and E., the East End, was also developing. Its prosperity remains dependent on the Docks which are in Stepney, Poplar and Canning Town; except for the colourful Sunday street markets, the Whitechapel Art Gallery and the Bethnal Green Museum, there is little for the tourist. Architectural delights, like a terrace of Georgian houses in south Hackney, can be found only by the diligent walker.

Southwark, or more modernly the South Bank, is a faceless area, although it is nearly as old as the City; but such features as it has are of considerable note. Close to the south side of London Bridge stands Southwark Cathedral built in the 13th cent.; nearby is the 17th-cent. George Inn, the only galleried inn left in London. Near here, too, is the site of Shakespeare's Globe Theatre, now marked only by a plaque in the wall of a brewery. Further to the W. is the Old Vic Theatre, and then to the S. – the river curves right round here – are the Festival Hall and Lambeth Palace, London residence of the Archbishop of Canterbury, in continuous use since

Aerofilms

The City of London. St Paul's Cathedral stands at its heart, now encircled by modern office blocks

the 13th cent. A last landmark is THE OVAL, Surrey's cricket ground. For the rest, this is a district of railway stations, warehouses and rather dingy streets of identical houses, now giving way more and more to skyscraper blocks of flats. Here again are delightful examples of earlier domestic architecture, but, as in the East End, they must be sought out.

ALL HALLOWS BY THE TOWER, *Tower Hill* (16–32), also known as All Hallows Barking, was bombed twice in December 1940 which left some of its walls standing, most of the tower and little else. In the rebuilding more of its history was discovered. In the undercroft a piece of tessellated Roman pavement can be seen *in situ*, ashes of Boadicea's sacked London were found 7 ft below the building, an Anglo-Saxon archway was discovered, and pieces of two Anglo-Saxon crosses which had been used by later builders as hardcore. In the rebuilding of the church by Lord Mottistone concrete was cleverly used to produce galleries and a barrel roof, and the very big, clear east window makes the church exceptionally light, the better to see the interesting things it contains, many of which emphasize its connection with seafaring men. The pulpit, about 1670, comes from the Church of St Swithin, and outside the lovely spire of St Dunstan-in-the-East near BILLINGSGATE – all that survived the bombing of that church – can be seen some 100 yds to the W. All Hallows' own spire is a post-war addition, deliberately placed to fill a skyline gap.

A great deal can be learned about London in All Hallows, not least from its enthusiastic guardians. The register states that John Quincy Adams, 6th U.S. President, was married here, and William Penn was baptized here in 1644.

AMEN COURT (16–10). A very small and utterly delightful 17th-cent. oasis set quietly in the heart of London. Said to have been built by Wren, these flat-faced, dark-red-brick houses have plain iron lamps arched over the doorsteps, and an uncluttered elegance set off by the trees that shade the courtyard. They are residences of the enviable canons of ST PAUL'S. Amen Court is reached from Ave Maria Lane; the STATIONERS' HALL separates it from ST MARTIN LUDGATE. It stands on the line which the Roman wall took towards the river, and a remnant of it forms the base of a modern wall in the court. Another small section is in the basement of offices in Warwick Lane, just N. of Amen Court.

BANK OF ENGLAND, THE, *Threadneedle Street* (16–21), is an island surrounded on all four sides by streets. It stands very solidly indeed upon some three acres, and from the Lothbury side looks faintly oriental. After operating initially in Grocers' Hall, the Bank's first home was built by George Sampson, 1732–4. Only 50 years later Sir John Soane built the great, windowless structure with its clever columns and an interior which has been described as his masterpiece. Nevertheless, in 1921–37 it was rebuilt by Sir Herbert Baker, retaining only Soane's screen wall and adding seven stories above it and three below. Only the entrance hall is open to the public, a stolidly rich, rather complacent ante-room to power, upheld in one sense by 18-ft 6-in. high Belgian granite one-piece columns in pairs, and in another by the dignified liveried gate-keepers in pink tails, scarlet waistcoats and top-hats.

The senior gate-keeper, during certain hours of the day and providing the inside temperature is below 70 °F., dons an upswept tricorne hat and red robe.

BARBICAN, THE (16–15). This huge scheme for building on the destruction wrought by the War in the N. of the City area, just W. of Moorgate, was conceived soon after the War and is as yet unfinished. The centre-piece is St Giles, Cripplegate, which has been there for 600 years. It received a direct hit in the very first air raid on the City, further damage by fire later, and was restored in 1960. Now its gravestones have been set in raised paving on its north side, which makes a promenade decorated with old street lamps for the inhabitants of one of the many blocks of flats; nearby will be a lake. Here are gravestones to John Milton, map-maker John Speed, and Frobisher.

All round the Barbican is a raised walkway. Sections of Roman wall found on the site have been imaginatively treated, one stretch being incorporated into St Alphage garden, beside the tiny, partly fenced-in remains of this ancient church. The Museum of London, incorporating the Guildhall Museum and the LONDON MUSEUM, will be established here, as will a London theatre for the use of the Royal Shakespeare Company.

BETHNAL GREEN MUSEUM, *Cambridge Heath Road* (16–2), is part of the VICTORIA AND ALBERT MUSEUM, and is known for its collection of early toys, dolls and dollshouses. There is also a good collection of ceramics and silver, and in the upper galleries a history of costume, with exquisite examples of work of the famous, once local, Spitalfields silk weavers.

BILLINGSGATE MARKET, *Lower Thames Street* (16–30). This market must be visited early in the morning to catch it in action. It was built in 1875 of yellow brick, with Britannia sitting more or less on the roof supported by dolphins standing on their heads. Fish has probably been sold here since Anglo-Saxon times, but now, although the market backs on to the river, the fish arrives by lorry. It is handled by men wearing special hats made of wood and leather. The market unofficially extends up the narrow lanes towards East Cheap – Lovat Lane, St Dunstan's Hill and St Mary At Hill, which goes past the church of that name. It is the fishermen's church, and cobbled lanes around make it seem like a small port. Pudding Lane, where the Great Fire started, and the MONUMENT, which perpetuates its memory, are to the W. Along Lower Thames Street is ST MAGNUS THE MARTYR, another Wren building.

DOCKS, THE (16–37). The London Docks proper, and St Katherine's, which was built by Telford in 1825, are immediately E. of Tower Bridge; hard by the Port of London Authority has its main office near THE TOWER and administers the docks from TOWER BRIDGE to Tilbury. These are grouped into five main systems – on

The Docks: the stretch between London Bridge and Tower Bridge is called the Pool of London

the North bank London and St Katherine; India and Millwall; Royal Victoria & Albert and King George V; and TILBURY. On the south side there is just the Surrey Commercial, which handles for the most part timber. Each dock specializes in its own merchandise: spices, wines, quicksilver and dried fruits go to London; Millwall has pneumatic equipment to deal with grain. **St Katherine's Dock** is no longer used for commerce, and there are plans for converting the warehouses into an arts centre. In all, the Port of London handles nearly a third of the country's trade and more than 260,000 passengers a year use Tilbury for their travels.

GEFFRYE MUSEUM, TI E, *Kingsland Road* (16–1). With a bequest from Sir Robert Geffrye, master of the Ironmongers' Company and Lord Mayor of London in 1685, a group of one-story almshouses were built round a leafy courtyard in the country quiet of Shoreditch in 1715. It was then, and is, the centre of the cabinet-making industry. When London had overwhelmed this rural retreat the L.C.C. turned the property into a museum of furniture and domestic equipment arranged in a series of period rooms. Every detail is correct, and behind each window is painted a contemporary period view. Children are encouraged to come to the museum to draw and learn handicrafts, and even act historical scenes in appropriate costume in the rooms. There is a library, and students can get technical help from the staff.

GEORGE INN, *Borough High Street* (16–41), is the last galleried inn left in London; it used to be twice its present size. It is entered through an uninviting archway and overshadowed by a hideous chimney. You can still buy the landlord's "ordinary" and a pint such as Dr Johnson often

enjoyed, and from the gallery it is easier to ignore the inn's surroundings and imagine Shakespeare acting in his own play in the courtyard below. The inn now has a restaurant.

A little further S. down the street is the site of Chaucer's Tabard Inn, which survived as The Talbot until 1876. Across the road in Park Street a tablet on a brewery marks the supposed site of Shakespeare's famous Globe Theatre; at the bottom of Park Street is **Bankside,** a fascinating strip of no-man's-land with splendid views across the river to ST PAUL'S, and on the corner is a historic 17th-cent. inn, The Anchor, again with a restaurant.

GOLDSMITHS' HALL, *Gresham Street* (16–14). Tucked away in narrow Foster Lane which runs between Cheapside and Gresham Street is the imposing façade of the Goldsmiths' palatial hall, built for them by Philip Hardwick in 1835, with six great columns and four armorial shields in bold relief. From the street there is a glimpse of panelled interior opulence; admission will normally be granted on previous application. It contains a collection of plate and some portraits. It is the duty of the Goldsmiths' Company, incorporated in 1327, to assay and stamp silver and gold with the leopard's-head hallmark.

In this area, lying between ST PAUL'S and the BANK OF ENGLAND, are to be found the guild halls of the Saddlers – whose guild is said to date back to the Anglo-Saxons – Wax Chandlers, Haberdashers, Coach-makers, Parish Clerks, Pewterers, Cordwainers, Coopers, Mercers, Grocers, Armourers, Brasiers, Brewers, Girdlers and the GUILDHALL itself.

GUILDHALL, *Gresham Street* (16–16). This building, destroyed by fire in 1666 and to some extent by bombs in 1940, remains the oldest lay

J. Allan Cash

Lambeth Palace is the London home of the Archbishop of Canterbury

building in the City and the centre of its civic life. The present façade, scrubbed clean, with four pinnacles and gay coats of arms, leads into a genuine 15th-cent. vaulted porch from which a dignified way leads on to the great hall. This is 15th-cent. but the famous wooden figures Gog and Magog were victims of the war, and have been replaced by new versions carved by David Evans. This hall is the setting for City ceremonial, the Lord Mayor's banquet, the election of the Sheriffs on Midsummer Day, the giving of freedoms and receiving of royalty. It was the setting for the trial of Lady Jane Grey and her husband; of Anne Askew, Protestant and martyr burned in 1546; of Henry Garnet, Jesuit, in 1606; and Henry Howard, Earl of Surrey. The hall contains memorials to national heroes, including Nelson, Wellington, the Younger Pitt, and Churchill by Oscar Newman.

There is an impressively vaulted crypt below, and to the E. are the gallery, displaying its own or loaned pictures, and the library, containing an ever growing collection of reference books dealing with the history of London, and the libraries of the Worshipful Companies of Gardeners and Clockmakers. Extensive restoration of the library and picture gallery was undertaken in 1969–70.

IMPERIAL WAR MUSEUM, THE, *Lambeth Road* (16–46), established 1920, is in the Geraldine Mary Harmsworth Park. It has a pair of huge naval guns in front of the porch. The building once formed part of Bethlehem Hospital

for the insane, better known as Bedlam, and many upstairs windows are still barred. It was severely damaged during the war, and again recently by fire. It is both a record and a memorial, displaying the devices of defence, guerilla and "home front" war, of both world wars and the Korean war. Apart from the large collection of model ships and instruments of war there is a library of war documents, books and photographs available for reference.

LAMBETH PALACE, *South Embankment* (16–47), is the London residence of the Archbishops of Canterbury, and has been for 700 years. It is medieval with Tudor brick and white stone facings, and a castellated gatehouse; the main entrance is by Morton's Tower. Its great hall has a 70-ft-high hammer-beam roof resembling that of WESTMINSTER HALL, and now houses the library which is based on books bequeathed by Archbishop Bancroft in 1610. Among nearly 1,500 manuscripts are some by Caxton, a letter of Francis Bacon, diaries of Gladstone, and Elizabeth I's prayer book. The guard chamber contains a collection of portraits of archbishops by many famous artists. There is a crypt, probably dating from 1200, and a chapel about 20 years younger. Here Wycliffe was tried for the second time in 1378, and the 15th-cent. Kentish ragstone Lollard's Tower was so named on account of having had Wycliffe's followers imprisoned in it. Near the gatehouse is St Mary's, the parish church of Lambeth. The palace garden has fig trees in it said to have been planted by Cardinal Pole. Originally the palace was nearer the water, and the archbishops made their way to WESTMINSTER by private barge; others crossed by the old horse ferry which was surplanted by Lambeth Bridge. Admission is only by previous arrangement and mostly on Saturdays.

LONDON BRIDGE (16–39), which has so long, according to the old song, been "falling down", has now been taken down and packed off to America. The new London Bridge, a beautiful flying design by the city engineer, Harold Knox King, will cost £3¼ million and take three years to complete. It will be 100 ft wide with six traffic lanes and two footways. The previous bridge, by John Rennie, took six years to build, from 1825, and cost £815,000.

No one quite knows when the first London Bridge was built, but it was probably early on in the Roman occupation of Britain. Certainly there was one in the time of Ethelred because it is known he extracted tolls from ships passing it. Thereafter it was frequently destroyed and rebuilt. In 1176 "old London Bridge" was begun, the first stone one, with 19 arches, but it was made into a street when houses and a chapel were added later. It became one of the sights of Europe, but began to sag and eventually the houses were demolished, though the bridge itself lasted until 1825.

LONDON STONE, *Cannon Street* (16–24). It is suggested that this stone was the *milliarium* of Roman London, the centre point of their great network of roads. Jack Cade struck it and proclaimed himself lord of London, according to Shakespeare. In 1188 Henry, son of Eylwin de Londenstane, was connected with it. It was moved from one side of Cannon Street to the other in 1742, and back again in 1798, when it was embedded in the wall of St Swithin's Church. When St Swithin's was bombed out of existence the stone was housed in the wall of the Bank of China, which arose on the site.

MANSION HOUSE, THE, *Mansion House Street* (16–22). The Lord Mayor's residence faces one corner of the Bank of England at the heart of the City, where eight important roads converge, where once a stream ran – the Walbrook – and where the streets bear such evocative names as Poultry, Cornhill, Lombard and Threadneedle. The Mansion House stands four square; its front door is on first-floor level approached by steps at either end of a balcony. It was erected by George Dance the Elder in 1739–53 in Palladian style with an imposing Corinthian portico. Inside – admission by written application to the Lord Mayor's secretary – are a series of sumptuous 18th-cent. state rooms, of which the 90-ft Egyptian hall is regarded as the greatest. Here banquets and balls are held in great pomp. This hall has no connection with Egypt; Dance modelled it on Vitruvius' Egyptian hall, also without Egyptian connections.

MERMAID THEATRE, THE, *Puddle Dock* (16–9). The City and public subscription supplied the money, Sir Bernard Miles and his wife the inspiration. The location was a blitzed warehouse between Blackfriar's Underground station and the river. This unlikely combination has resulted in the Mermaid Theatre, the first for 300 years to be built in the City.

A Statute of 1572 had stigmatized Common Players as "rogues and vagabonds". They could only perform under the protection of the Crown or a nobleman. The puritanical City fathers continued to keep them out but they could legally play in areas known as "liberties". Blackfriars provided one of these. Close to the historic site of the new Mermaid there was a fheatre from 1576 until 1653. First it was occupied by the Children's Companies, whose popularity is mentioned in *Hamlet*. Later it was taken over by Shakespeare's company, the King's Men. Shakespeare was a shareholder in this venture, which prospered. Sir Bernard Miles built on traditional ground.

His theatre is a success. It is not decorative, but strictly functional. The stage has no proscenium or orchestra pit, but a 20-ft revolve and a splendid battery of floodlights. The sloping auditorium guarantees uninterrupted vision for its 498 seats. With its unadorned walls it is the prototype for many new theatres being built or modified throughout the country. There is also an 80-seat restaurant overlooking the Thames.

MONUMENT, THE, *Fish Street Hill* (16–27). This fluted Doric column of Portland stone was designed by Wren to commemorate the Great Fire of London. Its 202 ft are alleged to represent the distance from its site to the baker's shop in Pudding Lane where the fire originated. A spiral staircase of 311 steps leads to a caged-in public gallery, from which it was possible to get a splendid view of the City, but modern buildings have lessened its impact. There is an amusing view of the Monument down King William Street from beside the Bank, where the people at the top look curiously large.

OLD BAILEY, THE, *Newgate* (16–7). Officially the Central Criminal Court, it stands on the site of the old Newgate Prison, which was demolished in 1903. The 12-ft-high bronze figure of Justice by F. W. Pomeroy is a London landmark, standing on the roof with its 8-ft arm-span; figures over the entrance represent Truth, the Recording Angel and Patience. The exterior of the building is rugged Cornish granite and Portland stone; inside it is Edwardian baroque. There is often a long queue of spectators hoping to get into court. When executions were carried out in front of the prison, space was allowed for spectators, which is why Old Bailey, meaning the street of that name, is wider opposite the court.

OLD VIC THEATRE, THE, *Waterloo Road* (16–44). Many theatre-loving visitors to London will wish to see a performance here since it is, and probably till 1973 will remain, the headquarters of the excellent National Theatre Company headed by Sir Laurence Olivier. Originally called Royal Coburg Theatre because a prince and princess headed the subscription list, it was opened in 1818 with spectacular plays and ballets. It failed to draw a fashionable public because the district was then thought rough and a journey to it dangerous. Renamed the Victoria, it offered crude melodrama. Later on it became a music-hall with a bad reputation. In 1880 it was taken over for serious purposes by Miss Emma Cons and named the Royal Victoria Hall and Coffee Tavern. Music and lectures replaced comic songs and alcohol. Miss Lilian Baylis, niece of Emma Cons, expanded its work and in 1914 introduced Shakespeare's plays for which she found young stars in the making. John Gielgud was one of them. Badly bombed in the Second World War it was restored and offered the fine and now widely inclusive repertory, which has continued with increasing renown. A completely new National Theatre is planned for a site just E. of Waterloo Bridge on the South Bank.

OVAL, THE, *Kennington Oval* (16–48), is the Surrey County Cricket Club ground, and the final Test match every season is played there. It was opened in 1846. Kennington was a royal manor with a palace, given by Edward III to the Black Prince.

PATERNOSTER SQUARE (16–12) is part of the modern complex about ST PAUL's which has given rise to such angry controversy. The public can use the viewing gallery on the seventh floor of Juxon House, level with the top gallery of St Paul's and with Justice on top of the OLD BAILEY; behind Wren's delicate lead spire of ST MARTIN is ST BRIDES, Fleet Street.

These large, glass-faced buildings form an irregular semi-circle about the cathedral, with steps leading up to Paternoster Square and thence to Cathedral Place, two flagged courts decorated with flowers, young trees, seats, all dominated by the bulk of Sudbury House, on stilts. The cathedral is beautifully framed at the top of the steps. The booksellers (breviaries and rosaries) and publishers, last remnants of Paternoster Row, devastated by fire in 1940, have now completely disappeared from this site.

ROYAL EXCHANGE, THE, *Cornhill* (16–26), stands in line with, but a few paces behind, the BANK OF ENGLAND. Their entrances are at right angles. The first Exchange, built at the behest of Sir Thomas Gresham, was burned down in 1666; likewise the second in 1838. The present building by Sir William Tite has a range of columns over which a tympanum depicts a series of city dignitaries, merchants of all races and Commerce. There is also a campanile with a grasshopper as vane and a carillon.

Inside is a large, glass-covered courtyard with wall arcades and a floor of Turkish honestone, in which the great merchants used to operate. Today the hard wooden benches beneath the huge historical pictures, are occupied by recumbent figures and middle-aged couples, and the whole place echoes with whispers. The entrance to this arena is by the centre door. The flanking doors lead to insurance offices. In the entrance hall on the right is an 18th-cent., six-man, hand-operated fire engine, with its leather hose. There is also one of the oval wall plaques issued by the early insurance companies to make clear which houses were insured and therefore worth saving.

ROYAL FESTIVAL HALL, *South Bank* (16–42). This is one of only two buildings surviving from the 1951 Festival of Britain, the other being the National Film Theatre, which is actually beneath WATERLOO BRIDGE, but still a part of this South Bank cultural complex. The Festival Hall, designed by Robert Matthew and J. L. Martin, was completed in 1964–5 with an auditorium seating 3,000, claimed by some musicians to be acoustically the best in the world. It has two restaurants; linked to it are the Queen Elizabeth Hall, the Purcell Room and the Hayward Art Gallery, the whole interplay of grey planes supported on mushroom columns. There is an embankment walk in front of the group and a pier with summer steamer services to BATTERSEA PARK.

ROYAL MINT, *Tower Hill* (16–34). To visit this money factory it is necessary to write in for permission to the Deputy Master at least six weeks in advance – longer in summer. Most of the processes of coin-making are shown to the visitor. The Mint makes not only our coin of the realm, but also that of several other countries, besides medals and the state seals. There is a museum. The building was designed by Sir Robert Smirke in 1810, enlarged later, and bomb-damaged in 1941. From 1699 to 1727 the office of Master of the Mint was held by Sir Isaac Newton. When, in 1870, this office was absorbed by the Chancellor of the Exchequer, the Deputy Master became responsible for the actual running of the Mint.

In 1972 the Mint will move from London to amalgamate with its subsidiary in Wales.

ST BARTHOLOMEW-THE-GREAT, *Smithfield* (16–6), is the City's oldest church. The priory was founded in 1123 by Henry I's courtier, Rahere, who was ordered to do so in a vision, and became its first prior. The Order's concern was mostly for the poor and sick, which led to the founding of the adjacent hospital, best known as Barts.

This church has been greatly altered and misused; although shortened it is still big enough to be a cathedral; but it is dark and the initial impression is gloomy. The entrance from west Smithfield is through a 13th-cent. gate, to which the church once extended, with an Elizabethan half-timbered gatehouse above, and then across a small churchyard. Inside are huge Norman columns and arches, repeated on a smaller scale in the gallery. On the south side is an oriel window,

Woburn Walk this quiet row of houses preserves the atmosphere of the 18th cent.   Picturepoint

which Prior Bolton is thought to have put there in order to attend services without leaving his lodgings. The Lady Chapel of 1330 looks deceptively new. There is also a vaulted crypt and much-restored cloisters. For a long time a fringe factory was supported on iron pillars above the high altar, and the Lady Chapel was a printing works, where Benjamin Franklin was employed. The few early furnishings left are of great interest.

North of the church is a tiny street called **Cloth Fair** – the name dates from the early purpose of SMITHFIELD; in it is a 17th-cent. house, with wooden bay windows which are probably earlier; Barley Mow Passage is beside it. In the grounds of the hospital is St Bartholomew-the-Less, dating from the 15th cent. but completely rebuilt in 1823-5 and restored in 1950. In contrast to its great neighbour it is octagonal, painted in two-tone grey, with clerestoried windows by Hugh Easton, and many wall memorials, mostly to doctors.

ST GEORGE'S CATHEDRAL, *St George's Road* (16–45). Near the IMPERIAL WAR MUSEUM on the triangular site where, in 1780, the "No Popery" rioters assembled, stands the Roman Catholic cathedral of the diocese of Southwark. It was built in 1840-8 by Augustus Pugin, and rebuilt by Romilly Croze from the original designs after having been bombed in 1941. It is extremely chaste and unemotional, with a stone interior in a mixture of styles, and red-brick exterior. The tower, planned by Pugin, has not yet been built.

ST LAWRENCE JEWRY, *Gresham Street* (16–17), is an extremely sumptuous rebuilding by Cecil Brown after destruction by bombing in 1941. It was a Wren church of suitable magnificence for worship by the City Corporation, and so it is again. Its very heavy woodwork, sparkling white paint, shining brass and coloured heraldic arms form fierce contrasts; you feel this is more an extension of the GUILDHALL than a church in its own right. There are lunch-time concerts. It forms a very attractive part of Guildhall Square, with a paved walk about it, an old tree and an ornate drinking fountain. Its position causes Gresham Street to bend slightly and there is an interesting view of it from the W. The name "Jewry" commemorates the Jewish community that lived in this area up to 1290 when they were driven out.

ST MAGNUS THE MARTYR, *Lower Thames Street* (16–29), is encircled at the time of writing by road-widening operations; from 1176 to 1831 what is now its churchyard was part of the roadway approach to LONDON BRIDGE. The inside has been immortalized by T. S. Eliot: ". . . inexplicable splendour of Ionian white and gold". It is the more breath-taking for its contrast with nearby BILLINGSGATE. The 1712 organ is original. Miles Coverdale, responsible for the first English Bible, was rector here, and Henry Yevele, who built the WESTMINSTER ABBEY nave, was buried here in 1400.

ST MARTIN LUDGATE, *Ludgate Hill* (16–8). It would be very easy to miss the unassuming entrance of this neighbour of the great ST PAUL'S. It is wedged in between shop fronts, and its plate-glass doors are misleading. Within there is a feeling of aged withdrawal, due doubtless to the double doors and screen designed to defeat the noise of Ludgate Hill traffic. It is tall, cruciform and with a great deal of fine dark panelling. A chandelier immediately catches the eye in a rather dim interior and in contrast to the sombre 17th-cent. furniture. The bell of St Martin, a gift of 1693, stands on an old chest in one corner, victim of the last war. Wren rebuilt this church 1677-87 with a slender spire, which he placed in particular relationship to the dome of St Paul's.

ST MARY ABCHURCH, *King William Street* (16–25), is found in a little, triangular backwater behind the MANSION HOUSE. Between King William Street and Cannon Street runs Abchurch Lane, a romantically bleak area of high finance, in which the small churchyard with its patterned cobbles, seats and tub plants offers a welcome respite. The church, 17th-cent. red brick and very beautiful within, is by Wren, and was tenderly restored after war damage. It is rich in everything – a painted dome, dark wood, stone floor, panelled pews, two sword rests, clustered lights and Grinling Gibbons carving. The shape, square with a large, domed ceiling, is unusual, and because of the clear, post-war glass, it is attractively light. There are many sumptuous urns and monuments, yet the atmosphere is intimate, welcoming, much-used.

ST MARY ALDERMARY, *Cannon Street* (16–19). This Wren-Gothic church stands at one of the busier City traffic intersections, where Queen Victoria Street crosses Cannon Street diagonally, while Garlick Hill goes off to the S. and Bow Lane, one of the very few narrow, old shopping alleys left in the City, goes northwards by the west front of the church. The glory of this building is in its fan vaulting, extraordinarily light and delicate. Wren's use of the Perpendicular is seen again in the nave columns, uncommon in City churches, but as a whole the church has suffered from late-19th-cent. modifications, particularly in crude, varnished wood.

ST MARY-AT-HILL, *Billingsgate* (16–28). The building is mostly Wren, with high box pews, sword rests, a mass of splendid woodwork, and an ornate pulpit with a long, curving staircase. Much of the woodwork was redone by W. Gibbs Rogers in the mid-19th-cent., so well that it nearly deceives experts. Entrance to the church is in Lovat Lane; it is not always open.

ST MARY-LE-BOW, *Cheapside* (16–18), or Bow Church, has a special significance in the life of the City because it was Bow Bells that recalled Whittington to be four times lord mayor of London. True cockneys must be born within earshot of these same bells. The original Bow bells

St Mary-le-Bow houses the famous Bow Bells

was buried on the north side of the high altar. After its first destruction it was rebuilt in 1686–94 by Wren's master mason, Edward Strong, and the elaborate tower was completed in 1713. After its second destruction, official argument as to whether it should or should not be restored lasted for 20 years.

It now forms the north side of Whittington Gardens, a new, imaginatively laid out, small garden with seats, and the Innholders' Hall with its engraved windows provides a worthy east side. Inside the simple rectangular church is an inspired mixture of the old and new, with a bright blue ceiling and the palest of pink walls setting off the beautiful stained-glass windows by John Hayward and the carved pulpit, font and 17th-cent. brass candelabra which survived. The panelling and pews are all new in natural wood.

ST OLAVE'S, *Hart Street* (16–31), is much more a parish church than many of its City neighbours, and looks rather like a country church. It is probable that a wooden church stood on the site in 1055; certainly a church was founded here in 1109. The present building dates from 1450, escaped the Great Fire, but was badly damaged in the war. It has Norwegian associations, and when it was restored in 1951 the late King Haakon VII laid the "King's Stone" in front of the sanctuary, a stone which in fact came from Trondheim Cathedral. The Wine and Spirit Trades hold their Vintage Harvest Festival here.

ST PAUL'S CATHEDRAL, *Ludgate Hill* (16–13). There is a difference of expert opinion concerning the age of this site as a place of Christian worship, but there seems some degree of acceptance that in A.D. 604 a wooden church was built for Bishop Mellitus and endowed by King Ethelbert. This was burnt down, rebuilt in stone in 675–85; laid waste by the Vikings and rebuilt again in 962, then destroyed by fire in 1087. The next church was bigger and was completed in 1220. Later in the Middle Ages physical and spiritual decay set in, and the cathedral was used for business and as a thoroughfare, even for horses. At last in 1634 Inigo Jones was asked to restore it, but the Civil War intervened and in 1666 the cathedral was completely destroyed in the Great Fire. In 1675 Wren's third plan was accepted, and the building of today's cathedral began. It was completed after many difficulties in 1708; the final block of Portland stone was put in place by Wren's son. Just before the last war the dome supports were strengthened, and the dome itself encircled by a steel chain, which possibly saved it from collapse when a bomb demolished the high altar and another damaged the crypt. Many windows were destroyed, and were replaced with the clear glass Wren had always wanted. In 1964 the exterior was cleaned to uncover the true golden colour of the stone. Post-war building has allowed views of the cathedral, and the churchyard has become a public garden. The new choir school is a sturdy but sensitive piece of modern architecture.

were lost in the Great Fire, and their replacements crashed to the ground during the 1941 blitz. The new bells were made from their remains. Before the Wren church built in 1670, there was St Marie de Arcubus, said to be the first in the City to be built on arches – or bows – of stone, and discoveries suggest that before the Norman crypt was built around 1090 there was an Anglo-Saxon church on the site.

From Bow Lane it looks much as it must have always, but that is the result of careful restoration. The interior has not been restored but redesigned by Laurence King with windows by John Hayward. It is sumptuous, white and gold, with a turquoise ceiling, a highly coloured suspended rood and a bold black-and-white floor. It has as yet little feeling of a place of worship.

ST MICHAEL PATERNOSTER ROYAL, *College Street* (16–20). In July 1944 a flying bomb landed on this church, leaving only the tower and badly scarred exterior walls standing. This was the second time it had been destroyed, since it had previously fallen victim to the Great Fire of 1666. Records suggest that the church existed in the mid-13th cent. Certainly it was there and in need of restoration at the time of Dick Whittington, who had a house just above it in College Hill (there is a plaque). He undertook to rebuild it at his own expense, and when he died in 1423 he

The dome dominates inside. There is rich ornamentation of every kind, including a great deal of Grinling Gibbons carving. The frescoes in the dome are by Sir James Thornhill. In the crypt, believed to be the biggest in Europe, many great names are enshrined: chief among them is the massive tomb of the Duke of Wellington; Nelson is in the sarcophagus originally intended for Cardinal Wolsey; there is a simple marble slab covering Sir Christopher Wren, above which are the words of his son: "*Si monumentum requiris, circumspice.*"

ST STEPHEN'S WALBROOK (16–23). Wren made the dome for this small church a rehearsal for ST PAUL'S, and broke the church's rectangular shape with a clever arrangement of 16 columns which appear to be slightly out of true. Old pews have been replaced by bent-wood chairs, and the Victorians retiled the floor. The church is an ingenious technical exercise in combining in one building the need of a Reformation congregation to be able to see and hear with the traditional form of nave and aisles.

SHELL CENTRE, *South Bank* (16–43). Standing just across Belvedere Road from the ROYAL FESTIVAL HALL are the two new (1957–62) monster blocks of the Shell Centre with a connecting tunnel. Covering $7\frac{1}{2}$ acres, it is said to be the biggest office building in Europe, and houses 5,000 workers. Its observation gallery on the 25th floor, 317 ft up, is reached at a speed of 800 ft per minute in the public lift; it gives a superb view.

A. F. Kersting

St Paul's Cathedral: (above) *the choir from the nave;* (below) *Nelson's tomb in the crypt*

St Stephen's Walbrook

A. F. Kersting

SMITHFIELD MARKET, *Charterhouse Street* (16–5). It is difficult to believe that this very busy, noisy area was ever outside the City walls and a place of leisure. Smithfield used to be Smoothfield, where for 700 years the great Bartholomew Fair, England's most important cloth fair, took place each summer; costers gathered to buy and sell donkeys; executions were performed here, too.

Its correct name is London Central Markets. It is a huge, largely glass and iron building which was opened with a banquet in 1868, and added to in 1875, 1898 and 1899. In 1958 it was badly damaged by fire, and in 1964 a new, domed poultry market was opened. The market is at its most Hogarthian between 5 and 9 in the morning.

Adjacent is the church of ST BARTHOLOMEW THE GREAT, said to be the oldest church in London after the chapel in the TOWER. It was founded in 1123, as was St Bartholomew's Hospital, also adjacent, and London's oldest hospital, with a fine gatehouse.

SOUTH LONDON ART GALLERY, *Peckham Road* (16–49), has a permanent collection of paintings, some with local Camberwell associations, and puts on loan exhibitions, mostly for short periods. It displays the work of modern artists, and pictures are sometimes for sale.

SOUTHWARK CATHEDRAL, *Borough High Street* (16–40), must surely rank first in London for awful surroundings. When it was first built in 1106 immediately S. of LONDON BRIDGE it looked on the river on one side and a peaceful Norman England on the other; today it suffers from London Bridge traffic and a fruit and vegetable market; the river is hidden by warehouses and cranes, and trains lumber almost overhead on a viaduct carrying traffic from three stations.

It is basically 13th cent. but after many vicissitudes was largely rebuilt in 1890–6. A few arches of the original church are in the south-west corner of the nave, and an original canon's door is in the north side. Behind the high altar is a screen, given to the church in 1520 by Chancellor Bishop Fox, who also beautified his own cathedral of WINCHESTER. The gilding and statues are 19th-cent. additions. The cathedral is very rich in monuments, including a modern one to Shakespeare, and the Harvard Chapel commemorates John Harvard, founder of the great American university, who was born in the parish in 1607. Shakespeare's brother is buried here, with the two dramatists, John Fletcher and Philip Massinger. The Globe Theatre stood a few yards away, and the GEORGE INN still stands nearby.

STATIONERS' HALL, *Ave Maria Lane* (16–11), stands in a courtyard off Ave Maria Lane. It was originally built soon after London's Great Fire as the guild house of the Stationers' Company which, in existence since 1402, had received the royal charter in 1557, and contrived to hold a monopoly on almanack printing until 1771. Copyrights were registered here up to 1911, and in the courtyard seditious books were burnt. The building, with its tiny lantern roof, was stone-faced in 1880 and enlarged in 1887. Badly damaged during the war, it has now been restored and contains some interesting 17th-cent. work, which visitors who have made written application may see.

STREET MARKETS (16–3) are to be found in Club Row and Petticoat Lane, Bethnal Green; and the Old Kent Road, Lambeth Walk and Bermondsey Square, S. of the river, best reached via Westminster or Lambeth bridges. The Caledonian Market, which originated on the Caledonian Market site near King's Cross, has now moved to Bermondsey but retains its old name. Many of these markets are open on Sundays, and they all sell an enormous range of astonishing merchandise. Some specialize, for instance Club Row, which goes in for pets and small livestock; the Caledonian is particularly good for furniture. Lambeth Walk is the centre of a nest of lanes in which markets flourish, and so is the Old Kent Road. The new-found popularity of these markets has put up prices; all of them are battlegrounds of wits.

TOWER BRIDGE (16–36) was built 1886–94. Its Gothic towers are a stone skin clothing the steel structure which carries the bridge mechanism. It has never failed to open the two 1,000-ton bascules in 90 secs. and road traffic must give way. The high pedestrian walk was permanently closed 50 years ago because it was much used by suicides. Written application to be shown the works has to be made to the GUILDHALL and permission is not inevitable.

TOWER HILL (16–33) is the way down to the TOWER steps and the Thames boats; it is a car park and a place where buskers try to catch the tourist on his way to queue for a ticket to the Tower. N. of this noisy, bedraggled area is Trinity Square, where a small, quiet garden with stone wind-breaks lies behind a simple arch. This is a double memorial to the men of the Merchant Navy and Fishing Fleets who lost their lives in two wars, 36,000 all told, whose names are engraved on the bronze plaques that line the walls. The arch is by Sir Edwin Lutyens, and the extension about its sundial is by Sir Edward Maufe; to one side of the arch is the site of the scaffold. Behind, to the right, is the decorous Trinity House, typical of 18th-cent. restraint, and on its left the monstrous 1922 P.L.A. building.

TOWER OF LONDON, THE, (16–35), looks very impressive when floodlit; the rest of the time its blood-soaked history inspires awe if not respect. William the Conqueror built the White Tower because he did not trust his new people, and Henry I's bishop of Durham completed it in time to head the list of famous prisoners. It was a garrison, armoury and royal palace. Cromwell did away with the palace; the Victorians

The Tower of London, Tower Hill, Tower Bridge, and Wapping with the Docks stretching beyond

moved the zoo, which had been there since the 14th cent.; the ROYAL MINT moved out in 1810; the Observatory went to GREENWICH in 1675; it ceased to be a prison in 1820. Among well-known heads that rolled or languished in the Tower were kings of Scotland, France, England; Lady Jane Grey and her sister; Sir Thomas More; James, Duke of Monmouth; Princess, later Queen, Elizabeth for six months; Sir Walter Raleigh; William Seymour, who came out, but whose wife, Arabella Stuart, was then imprisoned. Their names, carved on the walls of the Bell Tower and St Thomas's Tower, are a Debrett in stone.

The entrance to the Tower from the river was through the grim Traitor's Gate and into the moat, now drained. Recently another watergate, probably pre-Traitor's Gate, has been discovered beneath St Thomas's Tower, believed to have been used by Henry III as an unpublicized route to his private oratory. Tower Green is a pleasant contrast with its half-timbered Queen's House (now the governor's residence), ravens and yeoman warders. Opposite the Queen's House is the Jewel House, with the site of the execution block for political prisoners between. Other prisoners went to TOWER HILL, except Lord Lovat, whose axe and block are two of many gruesome relics in the crypt of the Norman chapel of St John, on the first floor of the White Tower.

WAPPING (16–38). Down St Katherine's Way to the left of Tower Hill is Wapping High Street, a place with a history of official and unofficial violence, not steeped in tranquillity even today. Before the inshore docks were built gangs of thieves used to attack the ships moored on the river, sometimes taking not only the cargoes but also the ships, which is doubtless why the architect of the first dock to be built in 1800 was Asher Alexander, who had already built DARTMOOR prison. Wapping Old Stairs still exists but is little used; in a pub nearby the infamous Judge Jeffreys was trapped, disguised as a sailor, in 1688 and went to the TOWER.

Near Tunnel Pier there is a warehouse with the letter E on one wall. This stands on the site of Execution Dock, where the hanged bodies of rebellious and otherwise violent sailors dangled in chains, in and out of the tides. The most notorious of these was Captain Kidd, 1701. Close by is the Prospect of Whitby, once a smugglers' pub and now a tourists', with a fascinating riverside view.

WHITECHAPEL ART GALLERY, *Whitechapel High Street* (16–4). Built in 1901 by Harrison Townsend, it has no permanent exhibition, but has recently acquired a reputation for putting on really exciting international modern exhibitions. On the upper floor special art exhibitions for children are arranged.

In Commercial Street, running to the north, is **Toynbee Hall**, a pioneer settlement founded in 1884 where Oxford university men lived among the poor of the East End, breaking down the barriers of class segregation and introducing many valuable educational and cultural activities.

Further north, along the same road, is the superb **Christchurch, Spitalfields**, a monumental church exterior by Nicholas Hawksmoor, Wren's pupil. The interior is at present closed.

WESTMINSTER AND WHITEHALL

In 1050 Edward the Confessor founded the ABBEY and monastic buildings 2 m. away from the City on the Island of Thorns, which was not so much an island as a strip of firm land in a riverside bog. The Romans had been there and so had the early Christians, with a church or monastery associated with Sebert, King of the East Saxons, but the abbey as we know it was the inspiration of the Confessor.

After a while he built a residence nearby from which to watch the abbey's progress. By doing this he established two traditions: he coupled Church and State geographically and he separated the rulers from the money-makers in the City. He established Westminster and laid the foundation of Whitehall.

Today in a triangle cornered by WESTMINSTER ABBEY, TRAFALGAR SQUARE and BUCKINGHAM PALACE, measuring no more than 1½ sq. m., is to be found the nucleus of England's pomp: the place where the Guards perform their ceremonial; the buildings to which all informed visitors must flock; the seat of government; historic street names – Buckingham, Caxton, Queen Anne, King Charles. Ninety-three of these important and expensive acres are a park, with a lake, and on it the world's most pampered ducks.

Buckingham Palace did not become the royal London residence until the time of George III. Before, there was ST JAMES'S PALACE, and before that WHITEHALL PALACE, which covered most of the land from Westminster to CHARING CROSS along the river, and back to ST JAMES'S PARK. Today nothing is left except the BANQUETING HOUSE; the gigantic, faceless Ministry of Defence stands on layers of Victorian and 18th-cent. mansions, a Tudor palace and YORK HOUSE, acquired by the Archbishop of York in 1208. Modern Whitehall is a wide street, a splendid backcloth for ceremonial occasions, attractive when floodlit.

On the west side of Whitehall are government buildings for its whole length, including DOWNING STREET, the Admiralty and the Foreign Office, concealing St James's Park. Parliament Square, given to the public in 1950, is now a simple, turfed garden with seats and statues of Abraham Lincoln (a copy of one in Chicago), Lord Beacons-field, and a dubiously successful Epstein of Field Marshal Smuts.

The HOUSES OF PARLIAMENT, with WESTMINSTER HALL partially masking them, form the whole of the east side of the square. To the S. are ST MARGARET'S CHURCH, WESTMINSTER ABBEY and Dean's Yard. Slightly left of the BIG BEN tower is County Hall on the far side of WESTMINSTER BRIDGE; at the other end of the Houses of Parliament are Victoria Tower Gardens with fine views of the river and SOUTH BANK, and memorials to Mrs Pankhurst and her daughter, Dame Christabel. There is also a reproduction of Rodin's *Burghers of Calais surrendering to Edward III.* There are a number of attractive streets and small squares off the south and west sides of Parliament Square.

St James's Park could probably be counted the most beautiful of London's parks, which are the envy of most other capitals. Along the south side is Birdcage Walk, so named because of an aviary belonging to James I, and on the north side is THE MALL, a procession route between Buckingham Palace and the Admiralty Arch, an impressive vista either way between a double row of plane trees; views across St James's Park from anywhere on this avenue are entrancing. The north side of The Mall is flanked by royal palace gardens and the impressive line of Carlton House Terrace.

Admiralty Arch, which leads greyly into TRAFALGAR SQUARE, was designed by Sir Aston Webb as part of the nation's memorial to Queen Victoria. The obtrusive bunker on the right, familiarly known as The Citadel, was built for the Admiralty during the last war, and has a mown lawn on its roof. Shortly before the arch is an Adrian Jones memorial to the Royal Marines on one side, and on the other a statue of Captain Cook erected 135 years after his death. A little further on, at a focal point, is the Le Sueur bronze of Charles I sitting elegantly on his horse and looking down Whitehall, towards the place only a few hundred yards away where he died so tragically with so much dignity. This statue stands on the original site of Charing Cross, the hub of London, the City-Whitehall axis, and the spot from which road mileages from London are measured.

BANQUETING HOUSE, THE, *Whitehall* (16–70), was the first Palladian architecture in London, and a very early use of Portland stone. The architect was Inigo Jones and it is called his masterpiece. It was built on the site of an earlier banqueting hall burnt down in 1619, and was intended to be the first of many such beautiful buildings which would turn WHITEHALL Palace into a truly royal estate; but in 1698 the rest of the palace buildings were destroyed by fire, and the monarch never returned to Whitehall. The weathervane on the Banqueting House roof was put there by James II to inform him when the Prince of Orange might be blown across Channel.

There is a lead bust of Charles I above the entrance, put there in 1800; it was from one of the windows of the banqueting hall that he stepped out to his execution.

For years the Banqueting House was misused, but in 1963 it again became a centre for occasions. The main hall, 115 ft long and 60 ft wide, has an allegorical ceiling, painted by Rubens for Charles I in 1629–34, depicting the apotheosis of the Stuart dynasty in nine panels which should be viewed from the far end of the room. The ceiling has been cleaned and restored, and the exterior has also been cleaned. It is open to the public when not in use.

A. F. Kersting   *Picturepoint*

The Banqueting House, designed by Inigo Jones   *Buckingham Palace: the Guards' Band*

BIG BEN, *Westminster* (16–76). It is a common mistake to suppose that Big Ben is the name of the HOUSES OF PARLIAMENT clock in its 320-ft tower in the north face of the building. "He" is in fact its bell. Weighing 13½ tons, it was cast in Whitechapel in 1858 – or rather recast because it was fashioned out of the original bell of the old Palace of Westminster clock, given by William III to the Dean of ST PAUL'S. It is named after Sir Benjamin Hall, who was First Commissioner of Works in the year when the bell was hung. The four dials of the clock are 23 ft square; the minute hand 14 ft long, and the figures 2 ft high. The clock is a good timekeeper and has hardly ever stopped. The chime was first broadcast on 31 December 1923; a microphone in the turret connects directly with Broadcasting House. Although the House of Commons was nearly destroyed by bombs one night in May 1941 Big Ben continued to strike the hours right through the war, and the broadcast chimes at the beginning of the 9 o'clock news assumed a significance which was felt by people all over the world. A light above the clock shines at night whenever Parliament is sitting.

BUCKINGHAM PALACE, *The Mall* (16–61). This palace was built as a house for the Duke of Buckingham in 1703. In 1762 George III bought it, and his Queen Charlotte resided there. It was then called the Queen's House. Extensive alterations were made to it by Nash for George IV who, however, never lived in it. Queen Victoria had its huge, arched gateway moved to Tyburn, where it has remained under the name of MARBLE ARCH. Since the beginning of Victoria's reign it has been the regular royal residence; the standard flies when the monarch is in London. The true front of the house faces on to the 40-acre garden. What is presented to THE MALL is a façade,

originally put there in 1847 and replaced by a Sir Aston Webb design in 1913. The palace was damaged by bombs, mostly in the area of the private chapel. The Changing of the Guard is at 11.30 every morning on the forecourt, and for a while traffic is at a standstill. The sentries have now retreated behind the railings which protect them from over-enthusiastic sightseers.

CATHERINE PLACE (16–64) is a charming, right-angled street preserved only slightly blemished from Queen Anne's London on the edge of a huge new office complex of steel, glass and concrete. Buckingham Place, built slightly later and also very attractive, leads out, but is overshadowed by the new Watney and Portland Houses. No. 10 Buckingham Place has a coroneted crest over the door which, at the request of the College of Heralds, is painted in incorrect colours. The house once belonged to the Leicester family.

DOWNING STREET (16–73) is named after its builder, Sir George Downing, who was a Cromwellian civil servant. No. 10 has been the official residence for the Prime Minister since 1735 when Sir Robert Walpole first occupied it, but the street astonishes visitors by its pettiness, and even by 1744 Smollett, a Scottish surgeon seeking work, felt it humble enough for him. There is a good deal more to No. 10 than appears from its unassuming, much-photographed front door, and the interior has recently been rebuilt at great cost. The Cabinet Room is on the ground floor; the Prime Minister's family occupies a flat on an upper floor. No. 11 next door is the official residence of the Chancellor of the Exchequer.

GUARDS' CHAPEL, *Birdcage Walk* (16–66), or the Royal Military Chapel, is at Wellington

Barracks and is reached through a memorial cloister built in 1954–6. The entrance is near Queen Anne's Gate, in Birdcage Walk. The original chapel, built in 1838, was the result of the Rev. W. W. Dakins's importuning for a better religious environment for the Brigade of Guards, to which he was then chaplain. Neither the Duke of Wellington nor Queen Victoria attended the dedication service and Dakins lies in an unmarked grave near the south cloister of the Abbey. In 1875–8 his chapel was completely redesigned by G. E. Street, but in June 1944 a flying bomb fell on it during morning service, killing 121 people including the chaplain. The beautifully austere chapel by George, Trew and Dunn incorporates the earlier ornate apse – almost all that survived the bomb – most effectively, and there are wrought-aluminium screens by Geoffrey Clarke. Six south chapels are dedicated to the Household Cavalry and the five regiments of Foot Guards. The chapel is open to the public for some hours morning and afternoon, and for early and evening services on Sundays. Tickets must be obtained from the chaplain to attend morning service, when the singing is beautifully and most movingly accompanied by a Guards' band.

HORSE GUARDS, THE, *Whitehall* (16–69). The Horse Guards are a very impressive and colourful sight, immobile on their beautifully groomed mounts on hour-long stints between 10 and 4 o'clock. Where they do sentry duty under two small arches on either side of the low clock tower, beneath which no cars may drive except those of royalty and a few privileged persons, was once the guard-house of Whitehall Palace, but it was redesigned by Kent and completed by Vardy, 1750–60. Today it is the office of the Commander in Chief of the Home Forces. There are also two dismounted troopers on sentry duty the other side of the archway, leading on to Horse Guards Parade. They come from the Life Guards (red tunics and white plumes), who formed a bodyguard for Charles I, or the Royal Horse Guards (blue with red plumes), who grew out of a regiment serving Cromwell. George IV fitted them out in breast-plates. Together they now form the Household Cavalry, which provides the Queen's bodyguard on all state occasions.

The Horse Guards Parade is a large, gravelled area on which privileged civil servants park their cars; the public may use it at Christmas time. The space is used for the ceremony of Trooping the Colour on the Queen's official birthday in June, a splendid ceremony which no visitor to London at that time should miss.

HOUSES OF PARLIAMENT, THE (16–78). Still technically the Palace of Westminster, the name dates from the time of Edward the Confessor, who rebuilt the minster, now the Abbey, W. of the City of London and inserted a palace for himself between it and the river. This remained the royal residence until Henry VIII moved into Whitehall Palace. During its history it acquired WESTMINSTER HALL and ST STEPHEN'S

CHAPEL, which were virtually the only parts to survive in a fire in 1834. In 1840 Sir Charles Barry with the help of his eccentric assistant, Pugin, began building the neo-Gothic new House which still graces Parliament Square, although it was badly bombed in 1941. The Commons Chamber was completely destroyed; the new one designed by Sir Giles Gilbert Scott was opened in 1950. From the outside there is no trace of this damage; nor of the Victoria Tower's recent gutting to double the number of stories to make extra space for parliamentary documents.

As you look at the Houses of Parliament from Parliament Square, the Commons on the left, the Lords on the right. Standing a little to the W. of the building is Westminster Hall, and outside this is Thornycroft's large, bluff, thigh-booted statue of Oliver Cromwell with a rather embarrassed-looking lion at his feet. Outside the Lords is Richard Cœur-de-Lion by Marochetti, mounted, waving his sword at the sky and clad in such well-fitting chain mail that it looks like knitwear. Behind him is St Stephen's Entrance where the public queues for admission. The Houses are open to the public on Saturdays 10–4.30 and on most public holidays providing Parliament is not sitting. When it is a flag flies on the Victoria Tower by day and a light shines above BIG BEN at night. The interior of the House is sumptuous: rich in pictures, staircases, furniture and the trappings of tradition. Circulation is only in guided parties or with a Member.

LAMBETH BRIDGE (16–82). At one time there was a horse ferry across the Thames at this point, hence Horseferry Road. Then there was a 19th-cent. suspension bridge, and the present one was put up in 1932. At the west end of it are the pleasant little Victoria Tower Gardens in front of the massive Imperial Chemical House and Thames House, and not far away Millbank Tower rears 387 ft into the sky. On the east side of Lambeth Bridge is LAMBETH PALACE, London residence of the Archbishop of Canterbury, in continual use for 700 years, and up Lambeth Palace Road is St Thomas' Hospital, where Somerset Maugham trained and worked, hence his first novel, *Liza of Lambeth*. From the Albert Embankment and Lambeth Palace Road, which respectively run right and left from the bridge roundabout on the east side, is the best view of the HOUSES OF PARLIAMENT.

On the Westminster side of the bridge there are pleasing Georgian streets and squares between Horseferry Road and the Abbey. One of them is Smith Square, where both the Conservatives and the Labour Party have their headquarters. In the centre are the remains of the bombed church of **St John the Evangelist**, which has a tower at each corner and was criticized by Dickens, who thought it looked like a petrified monster with its legs in the air. There are plans to convert it into a concert hall. In Gayfere Street there is a row of little, Dickensian cottages. Dickens' friend, Angela Burdett-Coutts, heiress of her banker grandfather, built **St Stephen's** Church in Roch-

Picturepoint

The Horse Guards: the Changing of the Guard

ester Row and used her money to such good purpose that she was raised to the peerage.

LANCASTER HOUSE (16–57), originally Stafford House, occupies one side of Stable Yard in the St James's royal complex. Partly built by Benjamin Wyatt in 1825–7 for the Duke of York, it was continued by Barry and Smirke from 1841 for the 1st Duke of Sutherland. Lord Leverhulme renamed it and gave it to the nation. It housed the LONDON MUSEUM until 1939, was badly war damaged, redecorated in Louis Quinze style, and is now used for official functions, but is open to the public at weekends. It has a sumptuous Victorian interior with a staircase by Barry.

MALL, THE (16–58), runs, tree-lined, from BUCKINGHAM PALACE to Admiralty Arch, with ST JAMES'S PARK on the right, and on the left royal residences and Carlton House Terrace. This simple background to ceremony is slashed by the sweep of steps leading to WATERLOO PLACE, over which the Duke of York presides on his column. Opposite the steps a carriageway peels off to encircle St James's Park.

MARLBOROUGH HOUSE, *Pall Mall* (16–55), forms a corner of the west end of Pall Mall with Marlborough Road, which leads into THE MALL. The Wren design of 1710 has been added to since. It has an unassuming entry to its large garden, a sumptuous hall and stairway, some frescoes depicting Marlborough's victories, and an allegorical ceiling painted by an Italian protégé of Charles I's, intended for the Queen's House at GREENWICH. Marlborough House, which was the home of Edward VII and George V, is associated with two very different ladies – Sarah, Duchess of Marlborough, and the late Queen Mary. It was also the residence of Queen Alexandra, and is now the Commonwealth Conference Centre. In the grounds of Marlborough House, entry from Marlborough Road, is the Queen's Chapel, designed by Inigo Jones in 1623 for the Infanta Maria of Spain, who was to marry Charles I, and completed for Henrietta Maria, who did. It is possible to see this interesting chapel on guided tours.

MIDDLESEX GUILDHALL (16–74). Immediately outside the west entrance of WEST-

MINSTER ABBEY the road widens. This is Broad Sanctuary, so named because the old belfry of the Abbey, which stood where the Middlesex Guildhall now stands, marked the boundary of the Abbey's privileged area wherein fugitives could seek sanctuary. Middlesex Guildhall was built in the years 1906–13 and served as the legal tribunal until the union of Middlesex with London in 1965. During the last war the military and maritime courts of allied powers in Britain were held here, hence the panels in the entrance hall signed by Queen Wilhelmina of the Netherlands, King George of Greece and King Haakon of Norway.

On the opposite corner of Broad Sanctuary stands **Central Hall**, headquarters of the Methodist Church, built in 1912 to a design expressly intended not to compete with the Abbey. Near here once stood the Almonry, where William Caxton had his press.

NATIONAL GALLERY, *Trafalgar Square* (16–51), occupies the north side of TRAFALGAR SQUARE, with a raised entrance giving a splendid view across the square and down WHITEHALL. It was built 1832–8 on the site of the original royal mews to dominate the square. It is a William Wilkins design, which beat a Nash design in open competition, and cost £96,000. On the west slip lawn flanking the gallery there is a startling statue of James II wearing Roman dress, by Grinling Gibbons, and on the east one of George Washington, which is a reproduction of a Houdon work in Richmond, Virginia.

In 1824 Parliament accepted the idea of a national collection of pictures and voted £60,000 with which to buy 38 of Mr John Angerstein's collection. Thirty years later it was decided to make a regular grant for buying pictures, since when an almost, if not quite, unrivalled collection, from the 13th cent. to the 20th covering the whole of western European art has been built up. It is particularly strong in Italian and 17th-cent. Dutch, Flemish and French art.

NATIONAL PORTRAIT GALLERY, *St Martin's Place* (16–50), is a rather inconspicuous building hidden behind the NATIONAL GALLERY. The collection starts on the top floor, to which there is a lift, and descends in chronological order. Early coins provide portraits of the Anglo-Saxon kings, and Henry VII is the subject of the earliest painting from life, after which portraiture is launched on the riches of the Tudors. There are no portraits of anyone living except members of the royal family but dead statesmen, churchmen, men of all the Services and women, too, musicians and artists are there. Ear-plug transistors are for hire in the Tudor Room with tape-recorded guides to the pictures.

NELSON'S COLUMN, *Trafalgar Square* (16–54). Although all authorities agree that Nelson himself is 17 ft tall, possibly plus 2 or 4 in., the given height of the column on which he stands varies from 150 to 186 ft. The Ministry of Public Building and Works settled for 170 ft 2 in.

with Nelson standing 17 ft 4 in. The fluted column is made of granite quarried in Devon and the statue is carved in Granton granite, but opinion differs as to whether it consists of two pieces or three. The story goes that before the scaffolding came down, 14 men dined on the pedestal platform. It was designed by William Railton, after a Corinthian column in Rome; Nelson was carved by E. H. Baily and set up in 1849; the lions *couchant* by Landseer were added in 1867. Around the base of the column are four huge bronze reliefs, depicting the battles of St Vincent, Copenhagen and the Nile, and Nelson's death in the *Victory*, all allegedly cast from captured French cannon. The column was completed 62 years after the victory that it commemorates.

NEW SCOTLAND YARD, *Broadway* (16–68). Contrary to a fairly popular misconception, sometimes committed to print, the public cannot visit this massive police establishment that stands on Broadway, off Victoria Street. The building is new, and looks impressively efficient; entry is only permitted in pursuance of business.

QUEEN ANNE'S GATE (16–67), formerly Queen Square, although it can never have been a proper square, was built by William Paterson and is a complete street of early-18th-cent. houses. They are all offices, but retain 18th-cent. porches, torch extinguishers, railings, and along one side a line of keystone heads, and a faded little statue of Queen Anne by some unknown artist. Where the street bends slightly and becomes Old Queen Street, there is a narrow way down to Birdcage Walk, known as Cockpit Steps. Westwards, Queen Anne's Gate meets Petty France, for centuries a fashionable residential street where at one time Milton lived. Today it is drear; Queen Anne's Mansions, 1884, one of the first blocks of flats to be put up in London, remains one of the dullest and now belongs to the Ministry of Defence.

QUEEN'S GALLERY, THE, *Buckingham Gate* (16–62), dates from 1963, when at the suggestion of the Queen part of the war-damaged private chapel was made into this small public gallery. Exhibitions of selections from the royal collection last for the best part of a year and are pleasantly and effectively displayed. In the passageway leading from the turnstile to the gallery there is an interesting series of prints showing the evolution of BUCKINGHAM PALACE.

ROYAL MEWS, THE, *Buckingham Palace Road* (16–63), are open to the public once weekly throughout the year and twice weekly in summer. They contain various forms of royal transport, including the Balmoral sociable, the four-horse French charabanc, Edward VII's 1903 Daimler and the current Rolls Royce Phantom Vs. Eight or ten carriage horses are in the stables, the rest of the 35 being out at HAMPTON COURT, and there are also harness, liveries, racing colours and gifts from abroad, such as a droshky harness,

Oliver Cromwell

Lord Nelson

Charlotte Yonge

John Ruskin

NATIONAL PORTRAIT GALLERY

given to Queen Victoria by the Tsar. The gold state coach was made from designs selected by Sir William Chambers in 1762 with panels by Cipriani. Everything on the coach is symbolic of England, including a reference to the just completed Seven Years War, and the pious hope of *Peace Burning the Implements of War*. It was made for George III, weighs 4 tons, and requires eight horses to pull it.

ST JAMES'S PALACE, *Pall Mall* (16–56), may be viewed only from the outside, which provides an opportunity to notice the sweeping bracket-lamp holders; the savage arrangement of spikes; the formality of the sentry duty; the ancient look of Henry VIII's splendid gate tower, with its two little doors flanking the big one. This is all that is left of the original fabric. After Henry VIII used the site of an early hospital for his palace, it grew more or less as the result of royal whim: Friary Court commemorates a Capuchin Friary established by Henrietta Maria, which stood where MARLBOROUGH HOUSE now stands; YORK HOUSE joins the palace on the W., and on another corner is Clarence House, one-time home of Princess Elizabeth and the Duke of Edinburgh, now that of the Queen Mother.

St James's Palace became the official royal residence in 1698, after WHITEHALL PALACE was burnt down, and remained so until 1861. The British court is still known as the court of St James's, to which ambassadors are accredited, although it now functions in BUCKINGHAM PALACE, just down THE MALL. St James's Palace has seen births and deaths of many English monarchs; Charles I spent his last days here, leaving to walk across the park to Whitehall and his execution. The Lord Chamberlain has his offices here now.

ST JAMES'S PARK (16–59). This is the only London park which has always been royal, and the only park land which has never been used for anything else. Before Henry VIII drained it to make a deer park it was marshland. By the early Stuarts it had become a proper park – more formal than it is now – and a favourite promenade for the court and its privileged hangers-on. Charles II beautified it and used it a great deal, going for fast walks surrounded by dogs and courtiers. By that time the public was allowed in, and so were the cows, whose milk was sold plain or as a syllabub until after the death of Queen Victoria. Charles II swam in the lake, a pleasure no longer permitted; THE MALL was then an alley with trees where the king played pall-mall – or pell-mell – a game not unlike croquet.

Nash informalized the park and gave the 5-acre lake its present shape. From it the view of WHITEHALL and BUCKINGHAM PALACE are famous. The lake birds are very much a feature of the park. The pelicans are known to have been there in 1665, when Evelyn saw them, and are said to have been a diplomatic gift from Russia. The park today covers 93 acres, slightly less than before the building of The Mall.

ST MARGARET'S, WESTMINSTER (16–81), just outside WESTMINSTER ABBEY, is much as it was when completed in 1523. It is attractively simple, with crude walls which look almost modern, and west windows with a stained-glass pattern resembling rain. The famous east window was made in Holland around 1505. It depicts the betrothal of Catherine of Aragon to Prince Arthur, brother of Henry VIII. Since 1614 St Margaret's has been the parish church of the House of Commons, and has become the church for fashionable weddings. Pepys was married here in 1655, followed a year later by Milton, and 242 years later by Winston Churchill. Sir Walter Raleigh, who was executed just across the road, lies in the chancel.

ST MARTIN-IN-THE-FIELDS, *Trafalgar Square* (16–52). From as early as the 11th cent., when TRAFALGAR SQUARE was marshland, there was a church on this site. The first was a cruciform chapel used by the monks of WESTMINSTER ABBEY when they came out to work in the convent garden. In the mid-16th cent. this building was replaced with a larger one. In 1720 it was rebuilt again; the task of designing the new church was given to James Gibbs, pupil of Sir Christopher Wren. The foundation stone of this very large church was laid in 1721 and it was completed by 1726. The famous Italians, Artari and Bagutti, were responsible for the gold embellishments on the beautiful, elliptical ceiling of the nave, which partially collapsed in 1960, probably from bomb-damage. Restoration took 15 months and cost £18,000. In 1940 a bomb had removed the Duncannon Street wall, blasting out the windows. The replacement tinted glass with a simple blue cross above the altar results in the nave being exceptionally light, allowing a better appreciation of this Grecian-style church, considered by some people the finest in England. Notable are the font, which came from the second church; a high pulpit attributed to Grinling Gibbons, and the elegant, semi-circular soffits to the ceiling below the south gallery.

The crypt of St Martin's is famous. Its vaults received the dead up to 1853, including Nell Gwynn, but after an outbreak of cholera they were cleared. In 1914 Canon "Dick" Sheppard kept the church constantly open for the soldiers; it remained open for the homeless; during the Second World War it served as an air-raid shelter. Now it is the meeting place of 50 organizations, several of which are concerned with music and drama, and is much used for memorial services for authors and actors of renown. Concerts are frequently held in the church, and its chamber-music, the Academy of St Martin-in-the-Fields, has an international reputation. The Dick Sheppard and the Sunday School chapels are both in the crypt, besides numerous wall memorials and two relics from the past – a 16th-cent. whipping post, and one of the plaques depicting the story of St Martin and the beggar, which adorned all the parish lamp standards until the introduction of modern lighting.

ST STEPHEN'S CRYPT, *Houses of Parliament* (16–79), known as St Stephen's Chapel, the Church of St Mary Undercroft, or the Commons Crypt, is reached from WESTMINSTER HALL, where a door in the south-east corner guarded by a wrought-iron cage leads to a flight of worn steps, and so to the crypt, which is in fact the lower half of a two-story chapel – the top for kings, the bottom for courtiers. It was built by Edward I between 1292 and 1297 and served by a college of canons who worked in the cloisters beside the chapel. The chapel roofing is said to be the earliest example of lierne vaulting known, intricate and presenting fascinating perspectives. After the Dissolution in 1547 the upper part of the chapel was used for parliamentary meetings and the lower as a stable, and later as a state dining-room for the Speaker. When most of the Palace of Westminster was destroyed by fire in 1834, the crypt survived with Westminster Hall and was later cleverly integrated with the new Parliament building by the addition of Pugin's elaborate decoration; the gold and reds have now faded. In the chapel there is some beautiful, 600-year-old, Sussex wrought iron, a tiny, ornate baptistry and, at the bottom of the stairs, an ancient window designed with an utterly modern simplicity. The chapel escaped with only the slightest bomb damage; it is used by Members for marriages, baptisms and Communion.

TATE GALLERY, THE, *Millbank* (16–83). This imposing Edwardian building with Portland stone pillars by Sidney R. J. Smith rose by the Thames in 1899 on the site of a huge prison, demolished in 1890. It has been enlarged three times, and currently there are plans for further enlargement; war damage repairs were completed in 1949. In 1965–7 the pictures were reorganized and the dominant background which overwhelmed them was subdued. Since there is only room to display a quarter of the collection at any time pictures are frequently changed. The gallery is in three parts: British painting from 1500 to the present day; modern foreign painting, from French Impressionism onward; and sculpture, including work by Rodin, Eric Gill, Epstein, Henry Moore and Barbara Hepworth. There is a gallery for loan exhibitions, where the Young Contemporaries was first exhibited in 1967. The restaurant was decorated by Rex Whistler.

TRAFALGAR SQUARE (16–53) was laid out from 1829 to 1841 in belated gratitude for Nelson's victory, and not completed with Landseer's lions until 1867. Previously the site, which Sir Robert Peel described as "the finest in Europe", had been occupied by the royal mews. The best view is from the terrace of the NATIONAL GALLERY, from which the square has a pleasing symmetry, although the full impact of Nelson's colossal column is better appreciated from the S. On either side of the column are statues of Sir Henry Havelock and Sir Charles James Napier; in the north-east corner stands an equestrian statue of George IV, commissioned by himself; in

the opposite corner is an empty pedestal.

South Africa House on the E. and Canada House on the W. form solid wings to set off the gaiety of the fountains and the kaleidoscopic movements of the crowds within the encircling streams of traffic. In December the giant Christmas tree from Norway points at a dark sky, surrounded by carol-singers. On 21 October there is a ceremony to commemorate the battle of Trafalgar. Some weekends the square is a centre for marchers and demonstrations, but during the week it is given over to tourists and pigeons.

VICTORIA MEMORIAL, *The Mall* (16–60). This much maligned memorial serves as an excellent free grandstand on ceremonal occasions. Designed by Sir Aston Webb and Sir Thomas Brock, it was put up in 1911. It is basically a white marble pyramid, with a 13-ft Queen Victoria looking down The Mall, attended by Truth, Motherhood and Justice on the other three sides. The scheme of the memorial provided an abundance of ledges and minor plinths on which to stand Peace and Progress, Science and Art, Industry and Agriculture, Naval and Military Power, Courage and Constancy, with a Winged Victory at the top. It is, after all, a memorial to a queen who concerned herself with these things for 60 years.

WESTMINSTER ABBEY (16–80). Possibly the established association of the crown with the abbey saved it from the Reformation. It was built by Edward the Confessor in the 11th cent., and rebuilt by Henry III in 1245 as an act of homage to his canonized forebear. It is this pure and excellent example of Early English architecture which stands today. In 1269 the Confessor's body was moved to the still uncompleted church, and intermittent building culminated in the wonder of King Henry VII's chapel, finished in 1519. Since King Harold, all our monarchs except Edward V and VIII have been crowned at Westminster, and from the second half of the 13th cent. until George III it was also used for royal burials. Many of the greatest Englishmen are buried here.

Enter by the great west door: the impressive length of the stone-flagged nave repeats the diminishing line of the vaulted roof, clean and touched with gold, the grave of the Unknown Soldier edged with poppies a sharp contrast in the foreground. The choir, looked at from the E., repeats this theme in miniature and even more richly. The east end of the abbey is filled with tombs and memorials, through which sightseers must shuffle in single file, and Poets' Corner to which Byron's name was belatedly added. Behind the altar is Edward the Confessor's tomb in a raised chapel, shared with the Coronation Chair, and immediately ahead of it is the Henry VII Chapel, with Queen Elizabeth's startling tomb in its north aisle. This chapel, a triumph of 16th-cent. architecture, was originally designed as a shrine for the saintly King Henry VI.

Beyond the abbey are cloisters, the chapter house, the museum, with its fascinating display

Westminster Abbey: the head of Richard II from the effigy on his tomb

richly dark marble from all over the world, rise in unfaced, almost black brick into arches of splendid purity. The simplicity and contrast of these textures is arresting, but it will be lost if the cathedral is finished according to plan, for all this lovely rude material, right up into the domes, is scheduled to be covered with twinkling mosaics, of which there are examples in some of the side chapels. You should notice Eric Gill's stations of the cross on the piers and the attractive hanging lights. A lift takes visitors to the top of the 284-ft campanile.

The cathedral, the seat of the Archbishop of Westminster, the senior Roman Catholic see in England and Wales, was started by Archbishop Vaughan in 1895 on the foundations of a prison and the structure took only eight years to complete, although its architect, J. F. Bentley, died in 1902. Among the objects of interest is Cardinal Hinsley's tomb with his red hat hanging above it, and a shrine of Blessed John Southworth, whose body lies in red vestments within a glass casket. For ministering to the Catholics in the reign of James I he was hanged, drawn and quartered, after which his remains were secreted in France by the Howards of Norfolk, until they could be returned and enshrined, in 1929. There is also a medieval alabaster statue of Our Lady.

of wax funerary effigies at one time carried in the funeral processions of persons buried here, the chapel of the Pyx, the abbey treasures, and eventually Dean's Yard, passing Dean's Court, still in use, with its cobbles, gas lamp and secretive archway.

WESTMINSTER BRIDGE (16–75), built 1750, was the next bridge to span the London Thames after the Roman LONDON BRIDGE. Here Wordsworth was inspired in 1802 to write his much-quoted sonnet on the view. Sixty years later it was replaced by the present bridge, designed by Thomas Page. At its west end is an enormous statue of Boadicea in her chariot by Thomas Thornycroft, put there in 1902. Westminster Bridge overlooks the House of Commons terrace, and diagonally across the river is County Hall. Nearby, on the VICTORIA EMBANKMENT, is Westminster Pier, from which the pleasure boats leave in summer to go down to GREENWICH or up to HAMPTON COURT and points in between.

WESTMINSTER CATHEDRAL, *Ashley Gardens* (16–65). This huge, red-and-white striped, early-Christian, Byzantine-style exterior does not prepare the visitor for the austere beauty of its interior. Until the eyes grow accustomed to the dark within, they are focused some 300 ft away on the one point of light, the pale red and gold rood hanging against a black background. The nave, including the aisles and side chapels, is 149 ft wide; the main arches are 90 ft and the domes 112 ft high. At the west end are two huge red Norwegian granite columns, and the solid, square piers, covered to about a third of their height with

WESTMINSTER HALL, *Parliament Square* (16–77). This beautiful, ancient hall, a little to the W. of and yet part of the HOUSES OF PARLIAMENT, is reached through New Palace Yard. It is 290 ft long, 68 ft wide and 92 ft high. It was built in 1097 by William II and modernized, particularly its roof, by Richard II in 1399. Here Charles I was condemned to death in 1649; Edward II abdicated in 1327; Oliver Cromwell was installed as Lord Protector; William Wallace, Sir Thomas More, Bishop Fisher, Sir Thomas Wyatt, the Earl of Essex and Guy Fawkes all in their time received sentence of death. Here the trial of Warren Hastings, a great and fashionable public spectacle until people became bored, dragged on for seven years before his acquittal. Many of these grim occasions are commemorated on the floor with brass tablets, as well as other happier occasions. Richard II put in a superb hammer-beam roof of Sussex oak. The hall is adorned with simple, full-sized statues of kings. For centuries it served as a meeting place of the Courts of Law, Chancery, King's Bench and Common Pleas, each with its appointed position; the rest of the wall space was shops and stalls. It was a centre of London life, a very public place in which to have sentence passed; it remains lofty, beautiful, impressive and empty, the oldest part of the Palace of Westminster and the most lovely. It is open to the public every day until an hour before the House sits.

WHITEHALL (16–72). Up to the 18th cent. the Palace of Whitehall covered the area between WESTMINSTER BRIDGE and CHARING CROSS, from the river to ST JAMES'S PARK. Modern

Whitehall is a collection of government offices on that same ground, but only the wide thoroughfare that runs from TRAFALGAR SQUARE to Parliament Square is strictly Whitehall, and the last few southerly yards of that is Parliament Street on the east side. In 1245 the nucleus of Whitehall was York House, which was the London residence of the archbishops of York. Wolsey greatly enlarged it, then Henry VIII, ridding himself of everything to do with York, took it for his own and renamed it Whitehall. Later the BANQUETING HOUSE was built, and there were grandiose plans to turn the whole place into a sort of English *Palais du Louvre*, but Whitehall Palace was burnt down in 1698.

Modern Whitehall is a jungle of architectural styles forming a nondescript background for its highlights – the HORSE GUARDS, the BANQUETING HOUSE and the Cenotaph. As you come from Trafalgar Square, the Horse Guards are on the right about a third of the way down Whitehall. Opposite them is the Banqueting House, and back again on the same side, the first turning on the

right is DOWNING STREET. A little further S. in the middle of the street stands Sir Edwin Lutyens' Cenotaph, plain, simple, perhaps a little blank, with flags fixed to its sides.

YORK HOUSE, *Whitehall* (16–71). The wine cellar of York House is one of the few bits of Whitehall Palace still remaining. It is always known as King Henry VIII's Wine Cellar, but was in fact one of the many additions Cardinal Wolsey made to York House, London residence of the archbishops of York. The Church bought the original mansion in 1298; enriched, embellished and enlarged it over 230 years; Henry VIII seized it in 1529 and renamed it, and as Whitehall Palace it housed the monarchy for 150 years until it was destroyed by fire. When the Ministry of Defence was built over a period of 20 years beginning in 1935, the 70-ft-long cellar was found to be an obstruction, so it was moved in its entirety 43 ft to one side, lowered 20 ft, and then moved along again. It may be viewed on written application to the Ministry of Public Building and Works.

HOLBORN AND THE STRAND

The first move of any significance from the City was to Westminster in the 11th cent. The area between, Holborn, filled in later, particularly after the plague and the Great Fire. Today it has a great deal of individualistic commercial architecture; insurance companies have done their best to enliven the scene, especially the Prudential with its pale-red-brick Gothic, and there are some austerely interesting new buildings, in particular State House, like an accentuated charcoal drawing, with a Barbara Hepworth sculpture in the courtyard, which went up in 1961, and another huge block, National Westminster House, opposite Grays Inn Road, which cleverly picks up the line of STAPLE INN frontage and appears to lean a little over its courtyard.

Staple Inn, a former Inn of Chancery, stands between Holborn and Chancery Lane, on the far side of which is LINCOLN'S INN. Southwards are the LAW COURTS, which abut on to the Strand; further S. is the TEMPLE, then the river. The order of the Knights Templar, who operated in England from this Temple site, was dissolved in 1312; there is mention of the Temple as an Inn of Court in 1449.

The VICTORIA EMBANKMENT immediately below the Temple is attractive because the river makes an almost right-angle turn S., giving a double view – from near Blackfriars to WATERLOO BRIDGE and on towards Westminster, where the slightly absurd baronial Norman Shaw North Building, once New Scotland Yard, stands just short of the seat of government. The Embankment as a whole is delightful. There are gardens (with seats); a view of the Festival Hall group, the only buildings besides County Hall on the south side visible from the north worth looking at; four old ships moored, *Discovery, President, Welling-*

ton and *Chrysanthemum*; and numerous memorials including CLEOPATRA'S NEEDLE.

Much of the area so far mentioned is technically part of the City of London, but it is unlikely that anyone working in FLEET STREET would regard himself as a City worker. Nevertheless, TEMPLE BAR, where ceremonial entries to the City are made, stands at the west end of Fleet Street and the most westerly point of the City boundary is marked in Holborn.

The Strand runs W. to CHARING CROSS, a nebulous street. Evocatively named streets come up from the river – Essex, Arundel, Norfolk, Buckingham, Villiers, and just short of Charing Cross is the exclusive ADELPHI, by the brothers Adam. The Strand has two churches, ST MARY-LE-STRAND and ST CLEMENT DANES, which are encircled by traffic. The view of Nelson over the roof tops as you go W. is never better than with a watery sun behind it.

Aldwych curves on to the east end of the Strand, and Kingsway runs N. from the centre. N. of the Strand is the confusion of COVENT GARDEN, scruffy, atmospheric, traffic-choked by lorries banging over its cobbles. It is to be redeveloped, but is an amazing example of old London contriving to do a job its planners could never have imagined. Solid among the chaos stand the ROYAL OPERA HOUSE and the Theatre Royal, Drury Lane.

N. of Covent Garden is a nondescript rectangle, but across Oxford Street is Bloomsbury, spacious, solidly academic, with lovely squares such as Tavistock and Woburn (though part has been ruthlessly demolished), surrounded by 18th-cent. houses, and the BRITISH MUSEUM. W. of this the new POST OFFICE TOWER with its revolving restaurant dominates London.

ADELPHI, THE (16–118), is next door to CHARING CROSS. Originally Durham House, town residence of the Bishops of Durham, occupied the site; it then belonged to Sir Walter Raleigh; in 1768 the Scottish brothers John, Robert and William Adam acquired it and put into effect their grandiose composition which included a first attempt at an Embankment. They built streets with some houses on arches which became rather insalubrious, but what little is left of their buildings shows how gracious their ideas were. Adelphi Terrace, based on the Diocletian Palace at Split, was the centre-piece, now replaced by an office block. Garrick, Hardy, Shaw, Sir James Barrie, Galsworthy, Rowlandson and Dickens lived or worked in these streets, in which the names Adam, John Adam and Robert survive, though William Street is now Durham House Street.

In the same block, once the estate of George Villiers, Duke of Buckingham, some older streets remain – Buckingham Street, with its old houses and watergate, where Pepys lived; Villiers Street, George Street and York Place, which is really Of Alley.

BEDFORD SQUARE (16–89). In the 18th cent. almost the whole of the land which has become Bloomsbury belonged to the Russell family, the dukes of Bedford. Bedford Square, like Russell Square but unlike most others in Bloomsbury, is square, with roads entering only at its corners, and a very good garden in the centre. Unfortunately buses now enter the square and so it is difficult to appreciate the architecture, of splendid doors set in rounded recesses, sash windows and dark brick façades. The Adam brothers were responsible for several of the houses. At one time the square was grandly fashionable, housing the Lord Chancellors Loughborough and Eldon; Henry Cavendish, philosopher; the actor, Sir Johnston Forbes Robertson; the Earl of Oxford, who, as Henry Asquith, was prime minister from 1908 to 1916, and his second wife, Margot Tennant by birth, the vivacious and witty social figure. Today the square is largely occupied by publishers, the offices of the Architectural Association, and the French Consulate, but still belongs to the Duke of Bedford.

BRITISH MUSEUM (16–90). The world's largest museum was built by Robert and Sydney Smirke, 1823–47, and is awe-inspiring inside and out. Apart from the library it is said to contain eight million exhibits. It began when Sir Hans Sloane "bequeathed", for a down payment of £20,000, his collection, mainly of natural history, in 1753. To this was immediately added the Cottonian Library and much of that formed by the Harleys, Earls of Oxford. In 1757 George II presented the royal library, and this was followed by George III's similar gift in 1823; the royal gift conferred on the museum the right to a copy of every book printed. This has now produced a super-abundance of books, which has caused some controversy about the future of the British

Museum building. Originally entry to the Pugin building on this site was by ticket only, and tickets went to gentlemen. Now anyone can be a visitor, but those wishing to see objects not ordinarily displayed, to visit the Reading Room, the Department of Prints and Drawings, and the Manuscript Room must have tickets.

The official guide gives a helpful list of "musts"; exhibits range from Egyptian dead to the Magna Carta, the Elgin Marbles to a ticking roomful of clocks and watches. The Edward VII Gallery has made a selection from the other departments and provides a museum within a museum.

CHARING CROSS (16–119). Charing Cross proper is a central point in the meeting of WHITE-HALL and TRAFALGAR SQUARE, on which Edward I erected in 1291 the thirteenth cross that marked the funeral stages of his Queen Eleanor from Nottinghamshire to WESTMINSTER ABBEY. This was the centre of London, from which mileages were measured. In 1647 it was removed, and replaced in 1675 by the Le Sueur statue of Charles I. Charing Cross station, at the south-east corner of Trafalgar Square, was built in 1863 in 19th-cent. Gothic on what was once Hungerford Market, which had been Sir Edward Hungerford's town house, burnt down in 1669. The complicated cross in the station yard is a memorial to Eleanor's Cross, and in no way a copy. It was done by E. M. Barry in 1865. Old Scotland Yard, once the police headquarters, was here, and in Dickens's time the Yard was a dock for coal-boats. The name derived from a mansion occupied in the Middle Ages by Scottish kings visiting London.

CHESHIRE CHEESE, THE, *Fleet Street* (16–101). On the north side of FLEET STREET, just W. of Ludgate Circus, is the famous Cheshire Cheese (entrance in Wine Office Court), rebuilt in 1667, where you may drink, and eat steak and kidney pudding in cramped conditions of carefully preserved, smoke-blackened antiquity, believing that Dr Johnson, Boswell and Goldsmith did so too. A chair there is alleged to have been Dr Johnson's favourite. Goldsmith is said to have written *The Vicar of Wakefield* in No. 6 Wine Office Court, and behind it is an area packed with literary associations: The Royal Society operated from Crane Court when Sir Isaac Newton was president, and Coleridge lectured here on Shakespeare. Dr Johnson lived for a time in Johnson's Court, and also in Bolt Court, both houses demolished, and in Gough Square which remains. There are still some 17th-cent. houses in Red Lion Court.

CLEOPATRA'S NEEDLE, *Victoria Embankment* (16–121). This eye-catching monument is not a needle and has nothing to do with Cleopatra. It is a pink granite monolith 68½ ft tall, presented to Britain by Mohammed Ali, Viceroy of Egypt, in 1819, and erected 59 years later. The monolith was one of those set up by Thotmes at Heliopolis around 1500 B.C. and there is another in Central Park, New York, and a third in the Place de la Concorde, Paris. Hieroglyphics on

Gold and silver goat, Ur c. 2500 B.C.   *The Demeter of Knidos, Greek c. 350 B.C.*

Lindisfarne Gospels, Northumbrian c. 700   *Royal Gold Cup, French c. 1400*

THE BRITISH MUSEUM

the pedestal record either the vicissitudes of the monolith itself or the history of Thotmes III and Rameses II. The bronze sphinxes which support it are by G. Vulliamy, and it was damaged by bombs in 1917. The Needle was ship-wrecked on its way from Egypt in 1877. When it was erected on the Embankment mementoes of the age were put inside it, which included a Bradshaw, contemporary cigars and pipes, and "photographs of a dozen pretty English women". All the way along the Embankment the iron seats continue the Egyptian motif, with kneeling and heavily loaded camels as side supports. The lamp-posts are ornamented with dolphins.

COURTAULD INSTITUTE GALLERIES, *Woburn Square* (16–87). In these galleries are brought together several collections bequeathed to London University, the greatest of which is the Courtauld Collection of Impressionist and early Post-Impressionist paintings. Samuel Courtauld, whose life spanned more than the last quarter of the 19th cent. and half of this one, was one of the last of the great English collectors, with a flair for buying masterpieces, among which are Manet's *Bar at the Folies-Bergère*, and paintings by Cézanne, Seurat, van Gogh and Gauguin. Van Gogh's well-known *Portrait of the Artist with His Ear Cut Off* is there. Other collections are Lord Lee's (1869–1947) of primitive to Renaissance painters, with some English portraits, and Roger Fry's, which consists mostly of work done by his own Bloomsbury contemporaries. The latest addition is the great Gambier-Parry collection, of work by Degas, Botticelli, Bellini, Renoir and Rubens.

COVENT GARDEN (16–107) is believed to have been the convent garden of St Peter's, Westminster, which stretched to Long Acre, from which the monks sold surplus vegetables. After the Reformation the property passed to the 1st Duke of Somerset, subsequently beheaded, and then to John Russell, 1st Duke of Bedford, who commissioned Inigo Jones to develop it as a residential area. His design was based on the Piazza d'Arme at Livorno, with arcaded walks, and the south side open to glimpse the Thames across the STRAND, still visible down one slit in Southampton Street. Traces of the Inigo Jones splendour are still to be found, and surrounding street names – Bedford, Tavistock, Russell – tell their own story. The building was finished in 1638. In 1671, by right of charter, it became a small market which gradually filled the piazza. In 1830 the 6th Duke of Bedford rebuilt it in its present form, the largest fruit, vegetable and flower market in the country, but now it is scheduled to be moved S. of the Thames.

Voltaire lodged in Maiden Lane, 1726–9; Turner was born there; Jane Austen stayed sometimes with her brother in Henrietta Street; King Street, where there is the residue of the building which was once Evans's Supper Rooms, also housed Coleridge; the Garrick Club, established in 1831, gave its name to the street; in No. 4 York Street, now Tavistock Street, de Quincey wrote *Confessions of an Opium Eater*. Bernard Shaw's *Pygmalion* opens under the portico of ST PAUL'S Church, and an inscription on the wall records that Punch's puppet show was first performed nearby in 1662.

DR JOHNSON'S HOUSE, *Gough Square* (16–99). As you approach Gough Square through the alleyways leading from FLEET STREET through Johnson's Court, No. 17 is the first house to come into sight, pretty in dark brick and white, with a tiny courtyard garden. It is a 17th-cent. house, with minor war damage restored in 1948, and here the great doctor lived from 1748 to 1758. Visitors can wander through each room, in which the contents are described on hand-readers, and the descriptions of pictures and personal belongings contain a good deal of biography. The Dictionary was compiled in the attic, with five clerks standing at a high table like draughtsmen.

DOUGHTY STREET (16–88). Sidney Smith, canon of St Paul's, founder of the *Edinburgh Review* and most pungent wit, lived at No. 14 from 1803 to 1806. Charles Dickens lived at No. 48 for 2½ years from spring 1837, but moved on account of his increasing family to Devonshire Terrace, where he remained for 12 years in a house now unfortunately demolished. Dickens's house belongs to the Dickens Fellowship and has been reconstructed as exactly as possible, but is really a museum since it was not acquired until 1924. It contains letters, portraits, illustrations, personal relics and a Dickens library. There is a "Dingley Dell" kitchen in the basement.

FLEET STREET (16–100). When the western extremity of the City wall was Ludgate, halfway up what is now Ludgate Hill, the Fleet River (which had its source in HAMPSTEAD) passed just W. of Ludgate to join the Thames at Blackfriars. The opposite side of the Fleet sloped up to TEMPLE BAR, which was the boundary with Westminster. This slope is now Fleet Street and the Fleet is a sewer beneath Farringdon Street. When Holborn Viaduct was completed in 1869, the Fleet was still above ground. Modern Fleet Street is the only street within the City boundaries which is as alive at night as it is in the day: lights blaze from the newspaper offices, and the courts and alleyways off The Street throb with printing presses. The activity subsides briefly at around 3.0 a.m. when the late editions of the dailies have gone on their way, but soon starts up again with the evening papers.

Fleet Street is a jumble of styles from the 17th-cent. CHESHIRE CHEESE to the 20th-cent. *Daily Express* glass-faced pile. Near Temple Bar is Child's Bank, founded in 1671, with such names as Pepys, Nell Gwynn, Oliver Cromwell and Dryden on its books. No. 22 is the Cock Inn, with a sign, preserved inside, carved by Grinling Gibbons. In St Dunstan's-in-the-West are statues of King Lud and his sons that came from Ludgate, demolished in 1760. DR JOHNSON'S HOUSE is just

Paul Cézanne, "The Card Players"

Edouard Manet, Sketch for "Le Déjeuner sur l'Herbe"

Edouard Manet, "Charles Baudelaire"

Honoré Daumier, "Don Quixote and Sancho Panza"

COURTAULD INSTITUTE GALLERIES

off Fleet Street to the N. in Gough Square, and ST BRIDE'S CHURCH is just off to the S. It was excellently reconstructed after war damage, and W. E. Henley called its graceful steeple, which survived the damage, "a madrigal in stone".

GRAYS INN (16–91), the last of the four Inns of Court – Inner, Middle, Lincoln and Grays – was badly damaged during the war, but has now been restored. The public are allowed to walk through its gardens, providing they behave properly, which includes not making a noise. This liberty is with-held on Ascension Day. It is not easy to find the way in from Holborn through a narrow, undistinguished archway.

The site is known to have been occupied in 1370 by lawyers who lived in buildings which had formed part of Lord Grey de Wilton's manor of Portpool. There have been many famous members of Grays Inn, from Thomas Cromwell to F. E. Smith, later Lord Birkenhead, but perhaps the greatest was Francis Bacon, who had chambers there from 1597 to 1626 when he died. He was Treasurer of the Inn and a bronze statue of him by F. W. Pomeroy stands on the lawn of South Square, with the catalpa tree which he is alleged to have planted. After the war the hall and library were completely rebuilt, but the 16th-cent. screen survived. The North Court chapel was also rebuilt, but the whole retains a tranquillity from another age. At one time the walk through Grays Inn was fashionable and accordingly was taken by Pepys and his wife. Today W. of Grays Inn there are a number of 18th-cent. streets that are worth walking in, notably Bedford Row, Great James Street and John Street, leading to DOUGHTY STREET.

HATTON GARDEN (16–92). In this dreary, even seedy, street, once a garden, much of the world's trade in diamonds is done. Much, too, goes on in the withdrawn-looking triangular building of the Diamond Corporation, which presents a politely unwelcoming exterior towards HOLBORN CIRCUS, with sides in Charterhouse Street and Holborn Viaduct.

E. of Hatton Garden is **Ely Place**, built in 1772 on the site of the London house of the bishops of Ely, which is still sanctuary. The police may not enter, not even the old Mitre Inn, and in Ely Court, a slit connecting Ely Place with Hatton Garden, no one can be arrested. When the bishops held Ely Place, where John of Gaunt died in 1399, the garden was famous and the right to walk there and gather roses in perpetuity remained with the bishops after they were forced to cede the land to Sir Christopher Hatton. There is still a lodge gateway to Ely Place, and until the war a beadle used to make hourly announcements throughout the night that all was well. Ely Chapel, or **St Etheldreda's**, dating from 1290 but with Roman foundations, is the only pre-Reformation church in England to return to the Catholics. In 1874 the Welsh congregation who owned it sold it to the Rosminian Fathers. The upper church has interesting modern stained glass.

HOLBORN CIRCUS (16–93). Looking E. down Holborn, the Wren-modified, 15th-cent. tower of St Andrew's, which withstood the blitz although the rest of the church was ruined, catches the eye. Cleaned in 1969, it appears floodlit even by day. The rebuilt interior is functional. In this church the 12-year-old Benjamin Disraeli was received into the Christian faith.

Immediately behind St Andrew's is the Congregational City Temple, built in 1874 for a Congregation founded in 1640, and now rebuilt after being destroyed by fire in 1941. Atlantic House, opposite, is the monster headquarters of H.M. Stationery Office. The blue and terracotta slab towering over the Circus as you look back is the *Daily Mirror* building.

Between St Andrew's and the City Temple a typical City bridge of maroon-painted iron carries the road over the crevasse of Shoe Lane. It is a small version of the 1,400-ft-long Holborn Viaduct, erected 1867–9 to span the Hole-bourne (now Farringdon Road), which is also maroon iron, with statues depicting Agriculture, Science, Art and Commerce, in the same mood as the ALBERT MEMORIAL.

JEWISH MUSEUM, *Upper Woburn Place* (16–85). This little museum is one room on the first floor of Woburn House, the Jewish Communal Centre, on the corner of Tavistock Square, and must be of great interest to Jewish visitors, though it assumes a knowledge probably not possessed by most gentiles. A labyrinth of ritual antiquities are here displayed, although owing to a history of persecution there is little earlier than the 16th cent. The focal point of the collection is an early Venetian ark in walnut with Spanish lettering, probably made for the use of the Spanish and Portuguese Jews who fled the Inquisition in 1584, which contains a number of handwritten scrolls.

Nearly opposite Woburn House is the Lutyens home of the **British Medical Association**; a tablet incongruously states it is near the site of the house where Charles Dickens wrote *Bleak House* and *Little Dorrit*. In the gardens of Tavistock Square there is a robust statue of Gandhi seated cross-legged.

LAW COURTS (ROYAL COURTS OF JUSTICE), *Strand* (16–103). This 13th-cent.-style building was designed in 1874 by G. E. Street. Outside are little towers and pointed doors; inside the main feature is its enormous mosaic-paved central hall, 238 ft long by 38 ft wide with a ceiling 80 ft above. There is a public way between the buildings to LINCOLN'S INN FIELDS.

At Michaelmas the Quit Rents ceremony, said to be the oldest London ceremony, dating from 1235, is held in public at the Law Courts. The Corporation of London pays a bill-hook and a hatchet for a piece of land supposedly in Shropshire, and six horse-shoes and sixty-one nails for a forge at ST CLEMENT DANES, both accepted on behalf of the Crown by the Queen's Remembrancer. No one can now remember where exactly these properties were.

LINCOLN'S INN (16–98). There is doubt about which Earl of Lincoln gave his name to this Inn of Chancery; one authority is in favour of Henry de Lacy, who died in 1311, and is convinced that lawyers worked on this site from 1292, although records go back only to 1424. The Inn consists of buildings set about courtyards. Old Buildings, just inside the Gatehouse from Chancery Lane (built by Sir Thomas Lovell in 1518), was recently declared unsafe and entirely rebuilt. The stone lintels and wood doors are original, but the bricks are copies. Few would know.

Old Buildings embraces Old Hall, 1490–2, and the chapel, and has sinister stairways leading to chambers above. The chapel has an open undercroft, used once for business, more recently as an air-raid shelter. Old Hall was built in 1492, with the south bay added in 1624, and restored in 1926–8. From 1733 to 1873 it served as the Court of Chancery, where Dickens was briefly a solicitor's office boy acquiring a marked distaste for the Law.

N. of Old Buildings is Sir Robert Taylor's classical Stone Buildings, and to the W. New Square, with its smooth lawns and famous plane trees, about which walk smooth and famous gentlemen of the Law. 17th-cent. offices flank the square and in the NE., standing a little apart, is New Hall and Library, 19th-cent. Tudor red brick and yet successful. Many of these buildings are open to the public on request to a porter; the gardens are free to anyone who deports himself suitably. One of the pleasantest entries to New Square is under the house arch from Carey Street.

LINCOLN'S INN FIELDS (16–97). The largest square in London, separated from LINCOLN'S INN only by a brick wall, seems part of it. The central gardens, like a small park, have a bandstand, tennis and netball courts, a café, flower-beds, shrubs and some splendid trees. James I appointed Francis Bacon to lead a committee of gentlemen preservationists in 1613, and they secured the square from development and had it laid out by Inigo Jones in 1618. It was decreed a public space by Oliver Cromwell in 1656. These gardens, where office workers spend their lunch hours, were once the haunt of thieves, a favourite duelling ground and the scene of many executions.

Since the last war the north walk has been called Canada Walk, to commemorate the Royal Canadian Air Force, who had their headquarters in the square. The north side of the square has Sir JOHN SOANE'S MUSEUM in it; the south is largely the Royal College of Surgeons, whose Hunterian Museum is open, on application to the secretary in advance; it has some interesting lay pictures and cartoons. On the west side, among a number of pleasingly elegant houses, is Lindsey House, Nos. 59–60, said to be by Inigo Jones, a fine example of his restrained style.

LONDON SILVER VAULTS, *Chancery Lane* (16–95), also have an entrance in Southampton Buildings, in the basement of which the vaults are situated. The market, for such it is, was established in 1882, and some 50 silver merchants gathered here offer the largest collection of silver in the world. There is a bazaar atmosphere, with little but a convention marking off one merchant's territory from his neighbour's, and silver heaped about them so that they have to pick their way among their stock, keeping up a knowledgeable sales patter as they go.

OLD CURIOSITY SHOP, *Portsmouth Street* (16–104). This crooked, blackened old shop is popularly believed to be the original of Dickens's story, though experts claim that the Dickens shop was in Charing Cross Road. Nevertheless, it is an interesting 17th-cent. survival of London village-type building in a one-time slum area, which also contains Clare Market, with Dick Turpin and Jack Sheppard associations.

ROYAL OPERA HOUSE, THE, *Covent Garden* (16–106). The present opera house, with 2,320 seats, was built by E. M. Barry in 1858. He also built the market near it, into which it blends. It has a Corinthian colonnade with a sculptured frieze by Flaxman. This came from the previous building of 1809 which had been burnt down and had itself replaced the burnt-out building of 1792. The recently redecorated interior is a rich but unobtrusive background for its fine audiences. This theatre is also the home of the Royal Ballet.

Opposite the opera house is Bow Street Police Station, the chief of the 14 Metropolitan Police courts, and the first, established in 1739. Among famous past residents of this street are Wycherley, Fielding, Peg Woffington and Grinling Gibbons.

SADLER'S WELLS, *Rosebery Avenue* (16–84). A well was found in the garden of the Clerkenwell house of Mr Thomas Sadler and was developed as a popular spa. London's first proper water supply, piped in from the N., was created by Sir Thomas Myddelton in 1613, and here still is the headquarters of the Metropolitan Water Board. Mr Sadler converted his house into a theatre, and by the 18th cent. though the well was forgotten, the theatre was well-known. In 1931 it was rebuilt and came under the control of Lilian Baylis of the OLD VIC, who made it the home of national ballet and opera. The ballet company, under Ninette de Valois, became world famous and was eventually merged with the Royal Ballet. The opera company has now moved to the London Coliseum in St Martin's Lane, but retains its Sadler's Wells title. The theatre continues with normal productions.

ST BRIDE'S CHURCH, *Fleet Street* (16–102). The excavation that followed war-time bombing added 1,000 years to this church's history. The Romans dug a ditch and put up a building; the first stone church was 6th-cent.; there were two more before the first one with a tower in the late 12th cent., which was used by King John for his parliament house; the sixth arose during the 15th cent., had seven altars and forged the first links between St Bride's and FLEET STREET. Wynkyn de Worde, apprentice and follower of Caxton, set up his press near St Bride's where the literate but poor clergy lived. This sixth church lasted until the Great Fire, and was one of the first burnt-out churches to be rebuilt, by Wren, with a spire which has been described as "a madrigal in stone"; only the spire and outer walls remained after 1940. Seventeen years later it was rebuilt and rededicated.

Today Wren's gallery, the stained-glass east window, and the huge later organ which concealed his minstrels' gallery have gone. Instead there is a large, heavily ornate, free-standing reredos, a *trompe l'œil* apse, and the west doors are plate glass, so that from the Press Association tunnel from Salisbury Court it is possible to see through the old porch below the spire right down the nave, with its journalist-named pews, to the altar. St Bride's is known as the cathedral of Fleet Street. The crypt is a very important part of the church, with a medieval chapel and John Lansell's re-creation of 2,000 years of Church and Community in Fleet Street. Outside, the paved gardens form a buffer of quiet between the church and the Press.

ST CLEMENT DANES, *Strand* (16–111), just a few yards E. of ST MARY-LE-STRAND, is much used and cherished. A church has been on this site, just outside the City boundary, since the 9th cent., and it is said that when King Alfred expelled the Danes from London those who had English wives were permitted to stay in this area, hence St Clement (of the) Danes. It was rebuilt by William the Conqueror; again in the Middle Ages; was not burnt in the Great Fire, but became unsafe in 1680, so was rebuilt by Christopher Wren; about 250 years later the Germans reduced it to a heap of rubble inside pitted walls, and in 1955 reconstruction began. The R.A.F. adopted it. W. A. S. Lloyd, the architect, produced an ingenious design based on the Wren concept but cleverly modernized: for instance the wide aisle, which contributes so much to the impression of space, is achieved by having telescopic pews which can be pulled out to provide extra seating when necessary; in the paved floor are 750 squadron and unit badges of the R.A.F.; the famous bells were recast in Whitechapel, whence they originally came; 800 hassocks were embroidered and presented by people throughout the world; the beautiful, movable wrought-iron lectern was a gift from Australia; and the original Grinling Gibbons pulpit is back.

ST MARY-LE-STRAND, *Strand* (16–110). The original church to stand on what is now an island site in the middle of the STRAND S. of Aldwych, was pulled down in 1547 by the Duke of Somerset, who wanted the stone to build SOMERSET HOUSE. Queen Anne levied a tax on coal to pay for 50 new churches, and the present St Mary by James Gibbs, 1714–17, is one of eight which were in fact built. The famous maypole used to stand on the space before the church;

when it was removed in 1718 Sir Isaac Newton bought it to be a rest for his telescope. Charles Dickens's parents were married here and Thomas à Becket is said to have been a rector.

It has a soaring spire and a delightful, rounded Ionic portico from which there is a splendid view of the Strand to the W. Inside, it smells slightly of incense. It is small, quiet, with bright blue windows over the altar and a wedding-cake ceiling of cherubs' heads, flowers and foliage.

ST PAUL'S, *Covent Garden* (16–108). When the 1st Duke of Bedford was developing COVENT GARDEN he acknowledged the need for a church, but suggested to his architect that something in the nature of an inexpensive barn would serve. Inigo Jones gave him just that, a squat, solid, but expensive, structure with a large roof, built back-to-front; the portico overlooks the market at the east end and the main entrance is at the west end. It was finished in 1638 and rebuilt after a fire in 1795. The interior is theatrical, although Inigo Jones could not have known that it would become the actors' church. More famous people are buried here than in any other church except St Paul's Cathedral and the Abbey: Samuel Butler, Wycherley, Dr Arne and Grinling Gibbons; and the ashes of Dame Ellen Terry are in a silver casket. Most of the tombstones were moved out of the graveyard to make it a very charming and restful little garden.

SAVOY CHAPEL, *Savoy Street* (16–116), more properly the Queen's Chapel of the Savoy and the Chapel of the Royal Victorian Order, is compressed behind the Savoy Theatre and the Savoy Hotel, and is the private property of the reigning monarch, through the Duchy of Lancaster inheritance. The chapel was at one time part of the Savoy Palace built in 1245 and later the property of John of Gaunt, Duke of Lancaster. After it was fired by Wat Tyler in 1381 it was rebuilt by Henry VII as a hospital. The present chapel was rebuilt by Queen Victoria in 1864 after another fire, in the late-Perpendicular style of the first, and is a single chamber with an air of restrained opulence. The two royal pews, like thrones, are at the west end, and the stalls of the Knights of the Royal Victorian Order are each marked with a copper plate bearing the arms of the holder. When the National Anthem is sung here the words "Long Live our noble Duke" replace the usual second line. It is believed that Geoffrey Chaucer presented the picture over the altar, because he was married in the palace.

SHELL-MEX HOUSE, *Strand* (16–117), a sensation in 1933, is one of the largest office blocks, with a vast number of windows. From the river it dominates the VICTORIA EMBANKMENT with its 200-ft-high tower, and its great square clock is still the biggest in London. It is the headquarters of Shell-Mex and B.P. Ltd.

SIR JOHN SOANE'S MUSEUM, *Lincoln's Inn Fields* (16–96). As with the WALLACE COL-

LECTION, the founder of this museum stipulated that nothing was to be added or altered, so that to all intents and purposes this is an early-19th-cent. house and collection. Soane was the architect of the clever version of the BANK OF ENGLAND, largely destroyed, so the ingenious arrangement of these rooms, using mirrors for effect, is perhaps not surprising. Surprising is the vast range of objects displayed, collected from all periods and much of the world, including America: the sarcophagus of Seti I, 1370 B.C.; Greek vases; bronzes; architectural models; books; furniture; Napoleon's pistol; Christopher Wren's watch; and a grotesque tomb dedicated to Mrs Siddon's favourite dog, "poor Fanny".

Most important are the pictures, especially the twelve paintings of Hogarth's *Rake's Progress*. There are other works by Hogarth and by Canaletto, Watteau, Reynolds and Turner, a large collection of pictures by less well-known painters, and more than 20,000 architectural drawings. The museum is not open on Mondays or in August.

SOMERSET HOUSE, *Strand* (16–115). In 1547 the Duke of Somerset, Protector of the infant King Edward VI, took stone from ST MARY-LE-STRAND to build himself a palace here. It was never finished because he was executed in 1552, but Queen Elizabeth I lived there while Mary reigned; James I, Charles I and Charles II all housed their queens here, and here Oliver Cromwell lay in state. The present building was erected by Sir William Chambers, 1776–86, for the purpose it now serves – to house administrative offices. It is entered by an imposing courtyard from the STRAND, and has a 600-ft frontage to the river; its basement arcade rose out of the river, the centre arch being a watergate. The east wing, built some 40 years later by Sir Robert Smirke, now houses King's College of London University. The west wing, by Sir James Pennethorne, was put up in 1856. The south front was intended for the Royal Academy, but that went to BURLINGTON HOUSE. Somerset House is the headquarters of the Board of Inland Revenue, the Probate Registry and the Registrar General. Wills stored here date from 1382; among them are those of Shakespeare, Dickens, Nelson, Wellington, Dr Johnson, Florence Nightingale and Van Dyck.

STAPLE INN, *Holborn* (16–94). The entrance to Staple Inn from HOLBORN, among the flat, giant buildings of commerce, is a little, leaning, black-and-white affair of overhangs and oriels, plaster and wood, and small doorways dating from 1586, although its legal history as an Inn of Chancery goes back to Henry V, and before that it is believed to have been a wool-staplers' hostel. Dickens knew it well and describes it in *Edwin Drood* as the home of Mr Grewgious. Today it is a row of shops and an archway leading into the quiet of Staple Inn itself – two little quadrangles. There are still one or two 18th-cent. houses there, but a flying bomb in 1944 demolished the 16th-cent. hall and much that stood round it. It has been rebuilt with the old material, but has to regain the patina of age. On the W. the courtyards are overlooked by a modern building, cleverly designed but overwhelming; the very good gates which give on to the second courtyard from beside Staple Inn Buildings are dwarfed.

STRAND, THE (16–109). The Strand was at one time the way along the river bank from TEMPLE BAR to the village of Charing. The position of the river then is marked by the YORK HOUSE watergate at the bottom of Buckingham Street; the Thames was a much-used thoroughfare in those days, for private as well as public transport. Because it joined the CITY OF LONDON to the PALACE OF WESTMINSTER it became a favourite site for rich mansions, of which remain only SOMERSET HOUSE and evocative street names. Today the Strand has little of architectural significance except ST CLEMENT DANES and ST MARY-LE-STRAND – Somerset House stands back within a courtyard, and Aldwych is interesting only because it is huge, comparatively new and contains Australia, India and Bush Houses. Coutts's Bank, founded in 1622, with whom the Royal Family has banked for 200 years, moved to these premises from across the street in 1904. Otherwise the Strand is made up of two hotels, three theatres, a hospital and shops.

TEMPLE, THE (16–112). The collective name "Temple" covers two of the four Inns of Court, Inner and Middle. It occupies a large area S. of FLEET STREET stretching down to the EMBANKMENT, with one entrance through Wren's gatehouse in Middle Temple Lane, a few yards E. of TEMPLE BAR. There is a way in on the south side from the Embankment, and in the E. via Tudor Street, but it is not a thoroughfare for cars. There are many courtyards, passages, steps; ancient trees, gas lights, fountains, gardens; the buildings are 17th-cent., except those which were destroyed in the war and have been rebuilt.

Originally the land was the property of the militant crusading Knights Templar, who were involuntarily disbanded in 1312. The property was taken over by the Knights Hospitaller of St John, who leased it to the lawyers, probably during the reign of Edward III, although the first record of an Inn of Court was 1449. Since then it has always been the most important part of legal London.

As you look N. the Temple is divided roughly in half by Middle Temple Lane, with Middle Temple, bearing the lamb and flag insignia, on the left, and the flying horse of the Inner Temple on the right, nearer to the City. Middle Temple consists of four courts – Fountain, New, Brick and Essex – with a regrettable Victorian corner, and the Middle Temple Hall, dating from 1570 and faithfully restored after serious war damage. Many authorities state it as fact that Shakespeare played a part in *Twelfth Night* in this hall in 1601. Inner Temple has fewer courts but a larger garden, the Temple Church, which serves both

Temples, its own hall and library and 14th-cent. crypt, and the delightful King's Bench Walk with 17th-cent. houses, some of which are attributed to Wren. Since Shakespeare said the original red and white emblems of the Wars of the Roses were picked in the Temple gardens such roses have always been grown there.

TEMPLE BAR, *Strand* (16–112). A few strides W. from Chancery Lane in the middle of the traffic stands the Temple Bar Memorial, put up in 1880 to mark the position of the old Temple Bar, and publicly described as "feeble". On it are statues of Queen Victoria and the Prince of Wales, later Edward VII, by Boehm, topped by a griffin by C. B. Birch. The Temple Bar removed in 1878 because the traffic had outgrown it was a Portland stone gateway designed by Wren with statues of James I and his Queen Anne, Charles I and Charles II, with a row of spikes for head display. In 1502 there had been a wooden boundary marking where Westminster ended and the City began, and prior to that probably a chain, although the west entry to the City was really through Ludgate. Nevertheless, Temple Bar became the accepted spot on which a monarch calling on the City from Westminster must stop to ask permission of the Lord Mayor to enter. This is done with the usual traditional trappings of fanfares and the giving and returning of a sword, after which ceremonial niceties will be deemed to have been observed. Wren's gate, after a period on Plumstead marshes, was erected at the entrance of Theobald's Park, Waltham Cross.

TEMPLE CHURCH, THE *The Temple* (16–114). Serving both the Inner and Middle Temples, this Church of St Mary the Virgin is one of only five remaining round churches in England, and is a "peculiar", i.e. it is exempt from episcopal jurisdiction. It is modelled on the Holy Sepulchre of Jerusalem, and was consecrated in 1185 when the Order of Knights Templar had their English headquarters on the Temple site. The square porch is sunk in the hillside, with a carved Norman doorway. In 1240 an oblong chancel in very beautiful Early English style was added to the round church, greatly increasing its size. The oblong is carried by green Purbeck stone piers. The reredos by Wren was banished during 19th-cent. restoration, and so missed the very severe war damage suffered by the rest of the church, but it and the various monuments are now restored. In the round part are nine effigies of 12th- and 13th-cent. Knights set in the paved floor; there are also two striking coloured monuments of Richard Martin and Edmund Plowden, "repaired and beautified 1687". The whole way round are niches, empty now except for the names of war dead, but enlivened by a circle of laughably familiar little faces. At one time the round section was used for law business.

Immediately NE. of the church is the Master's House, charming home of the incumbent, rebuilt after the Great Fire, and rebuilt again after destruction in the war.

THEATRE ROYAL, THE, *Drury Lane* (16–105), referred to as Drury Lane, is the fourth theatre on the site, the previous ones having burnt down. The first was put up in 1672, and the last, a huge theatre with 3,000 seats, in 1812; a prologue for the opening was written by Byron. It has been subject to all sorts of troubles including riots – in 1668 on account of the pit audience being rained on, and in 1754 as a demonstration against papists and Frenchmen in the cast; and in 1800 an attempt was made to assassinate George III. It was managed by Garrick and by Sheridan, and most leading actors have played there. The dignified interior is studded with busts, statues and reliefs commemorating famous players, and also Samuel Whitbread, whose money rebuilt the theatre after its last fire in 1809. Once famous for its pantomimes, today it is the house of spectacular musicals, usually American.

VICTORIA EMBANKMENT, THE (16–120). The idea for this 1-m. stretch between Blackfriars and WESTMINSTER bridges was originally Wren's, but it was not built until 1862–70

The Temple Church: effigies of knights

A. F. Kersting

under Sir Joseph Bazalgette (in order to lay some much-needed sewers) on land reclaimed from the river; YORK HOUSE Watergate, erected by mastermason Nicholas Stone, marks the position of the water's edge in 1625. Today it is a gate to the Embankment Gardens, which contain an uncommon number of memorials, including a tiny bronze to the Imperial Camel Corps. Burns, Fawcett, General Lord Cheylesmore, Sir Joseph Bazalgette, Gilbert and Sullivan, Lawson, Lord Trenchard, General Gordon, Tyndale, Plimsoll, Mill, the R.A.F., the submarines of the First World War and Belgium's gratitude to Britain are all remembered in bronze or stone. There is also CLEOPATRA'S NEEDLE.

Outside the Gardens steps lead to Hungerford footbridge, which crosses the road and river next to Charing Cross Railway Bridge. The only view, citywards, is not as good as that from WATERLOO BRIDGE, but includes the Waterloo spans. Towards Westminster the Embankment is less enjoyable, though there is a view of the HORSE GUARDS down the Avenue. The City's entrance is marked by two rampant dragons, and beyond, the gracious gardens of THE TEMPLE – as opposed to the unimaginative Temple Gardens – can be admired between the thick railings; the two training ships, *Chrysanthemum* and *President*, both open to the public, and *Wellington*, the floating livery hall of the Master Mariners' Company, are moored here. Near Waterloo Bridge is S.S. *Discovery*, now a recruiting vessel, and open to the public, and close by is the floating headquarters of the river police.

WATERLOO BRIDGE (16–122) first spanned the river in 1817. It was built by John Rennie to be a monument as well as part of the road system, and lasted well until 1923. Eleven years later it was demolished, and its 70,000 tons of fine stone were dumped in a field. The new bridge, by Sir Giles Gilbert Scott, was officially completed in 1945, though it was in use earlier. It is very beautiful from every angle – in profile slender and serene, with the City's skyline above it eastwards, and Parliament's pinnacles to the S. It has the best views of the river, and a convenient low parapet. To the N. is the splendid terrace of SOMERSET HOUSE and its watergate. Opposite is the ROYAL FESTIVAL HALL and its associated buildings. The road continues S. to the Elephant and Castle.

WOBURN SQUARE (16–86) has on its north-west corner the newly built Warburg Institute, and beside it the COURTAULD INSTITUTE of Fine Art holding Samuel Courtauld's bequeathed collection of French Impressionists and Post-Impressionists. Across the square, narrow and green, stands Christ Church, in which Burne-Jones's paintings commemorate Rossetti. One side of this attractive square of Georgian houses, owned by the University of London, has been pulled down and rebuilt, despite many protests.

A few minutes' walk to the N., and on the other side of Woburn Place, is **Woburn Walk**, a charming fragment of 18th-cent. London that has survived the extensive rebuilding in this area.

WEST END, SOHO AND REGENT'S PARK

Up to the end of the 1920s the area bounded by PICCADILLY, Oxford Street, Park Lane and Bond Street, known as Mayfair, was forbidden to commerce. For two and a half centuries it was of great social significance; the Duke of Westminster, greatest of the landlords, would permit no trade plates to appear in its dignified streets. Now there is hardly a house without one, and if it were not for the modern merchants many more of the fine houses of London's West End would have fallen victims to the developers.

Beside the big stores and more exclusive shops the West End contains most of the large hotels, cinemas, restaurants and theatres. The latter three are clustered in Shaftesbury Avenue, Haymarket, LEICESTER SQUARE and Charing Cross Road, though the restaurants spread into Soho, Mayfair and St James's.

St James's is the area bounded by Piccadilly, GREEN PARK, PALL MALL and the Haymarket. ST JAMES'S STREET is the home of that singular instution, the man's club, and contains the Carlton Club, founded by the Duke of Wellington in 1832 and today the premier Conservative club; the Constitutional; Brooks's, the Whig club founded in 1764; Boodle's, and White's. White's is the oldest London club, and was the leading Conservative establishment in the 18th cent. The

Devonshire Club occupies the house which was once famous as Crockford's gaming hell. The Reform, Travellers' and Athenaeum are just round the corner in Pall Mall. Most of these clubs have very beautiful premises. St James's, still dignified in spite of today's traffic, has been associated with many famous men; Byron acquired overnight fame at No. 8 St James's Street, now replaced by Byron House; Louis Napoleon lived for two years in King Street; Haydn lodged for a year in Bury Street; the rich Samuel Rogers entertained literary gentlemen of standing to breakfast at No. 22 St James's Place; Sir John Moore and the Duchess of Richmond, who modelled for Britannia, are associated with St James's Square, and Nell Gwynn lived in Pall Mall. Christie's world-famous auction rooms are still in King Street after over 200 years, and Lock's the Hatters in St James's Street have records back to 1700; among them are the head measurements of Nelson and the 1st Duke of Wellington.

Soho is a congestion of narrow, tatty, late-17th-cent. streets. It is roughly bounded by REGENT STREET, Oxford Street, Charing Cross Road and Leicester Square, though Leicester Square is really more West End, with its idling crowds, bright lights, and cinemas on three sides. The arrival of thousands of French refugees in 1685, followed throughout the years by people from all over Western Europe, particularly Spain, Italy and Malta, have given it a Continental atmosphere – Italian shops, French smells, crowded street markets of many nations. It has excellent foreign restaurants, and is famed for its strip clubs and bill-boards advertising masseuses and French lessons.

A wilderness of blind-eyed wholesale establishments and the rear elevations of Oxford Street stores gradually merges into the medical belt, the lovely Harley, Devonshire, Cavendish, Wimpole, Welbeck and Weymouth streets, all named after members of titled families, including Robert Harley, Earl of Oxford and Mortimer, who at one time owned the manor of Marylebone and made his mark in no uncertain manner, and all full of medical practitioners. Marylebone is one of the many places in London with a village atmosphere.

Further N. is REGENT'S PARK, with the ZOO, an open-air theatre, a large area of turf and some beautifully kept flower gardens. It was designed by Nash for the Prince Regent – to our considerable advantage, particularly the Regency terraces gracing the southern and eastern sides of the Park.

ALBANY, *Piccadilly* (16–137), is an exclusive covered walk of residential chambers, reached through a courtyard and portered mansion at the PICCADILLY end, or two discreet lodges in Burlington Gardens – between which a glimpse of the place is possible. Entry is by invitation of a resident only. It was built in 1770 and converted to its present layout in 1812. Among past and present residents are Byron, Macaulay, Gladstone, Bulwer Lytton, "Monk" Lewis, Canning, Clifford Bax, Compton Mackenzie, J. B. Priestley, Harold Nicolson, Graham Greene – all men of letters; at one time many novels and plays featured a character with rooms in Albany. It was originally limited to bachelors, but married couples (though not children) and suitable single women are now accepted as tenants.

APSLEY HOUSE, *Piccadilly* (16–150). "No. 1, London", on the north side of HYDE PARK CORNER (of which there is a good view from the second floor) was opened to the public as the Wellington Museum in 1952. Built of red brick, 1771–8, by Adam, it was bought by the 1st Duke of Wellington in 1817 and some years later faced with stone and a portico and the Waterloo gallery added. Until the Duke's death in 1852 the gallery was the setting for the annual Waterloo banquet; the ornate 9-yd centre-piece and service used for these occasions are on show. Indeed, the house contains many dinner services given to the Duke by grateful crowned heads. There are also a number of personal mementoes, decorations, and pictures by Velazquez, Goya, Rubens and Correggio. Some of the Adam decorations remain, and the house has a very impressive staircase, beside which stands a much more than life-size nude statue of Napoleon holding a small Winged Victory. This startling manifestation of approval came from the Iron Duke's monarch.

BERKELEY SQUARE (16–136), the heart of Mayfair, remains one of London's most attractive squares, chiefly on account of its proportions. It is in fact a rectangle, and its great plane trees give depth and beauty, but there is much post-war building. The elegant Queen Anne houses on the west side show what Mayfair has lost. The square was built early in the 18th cent. on the grounds of Berkeley House, and was from the first a haunt of the aristocracy. Horace Walpole, Lord Rosebery, Lord Clive, William Pitt and Lord Brougham have been associated with it and Queen Elizabeth II was born in No. 17 Bruton Street, now demolished but then the house of the Earl of Strathmore.

BURLINGTON ARCADE, *Piccadilly* (16–138). Built by Lord George Cavendish in 1819 in order "to give employment to industrious females", this covered way of exquisite shops with little bow-fronted upper floors is unique in London. The PICCADILLY entrance was redesigned in 1931, the other rebuilt after bombing in 1941. There are strict rules regarding behaviour in the arcade – no whistling, singing, running, opening of umbrellas or playing of musical instruments – enforced by the uniformed beadles who by tradition are ex-N.C.O.s of the 10th Hussars. They ring a handbell each afternoon to empty the arcade before locking the gates at 5.30. D. H. Lord, hosier and glover, is the only name to remain out of the original 47 leaseholders. In Victorian times the arcade had a reputation that made it unsuitable for ladies to shop there.

BURLINGTON HOUSE, *Piccadilly* (16–139). Next door to BURLINGTON ARCADE three high archways in an Italianate façade lead into a sober quadrangle, in the middle of which is a statue of Sir Joshua Reynolds by Alfred Drury. Burlington House is the home of the Royal Academy of Arts, which has its summer exhibition of new work from May to August, and special exhibitions in the winter. Burlington House was built in 1664 and witnessed a period of splendour under the 3rd Earl of Burlington, 1695–1753, a great patron of the arts. Plans for an academy of arts were first put up by Hogarth's father-in-law in 1724, but George III founded the present Royal Academy in 1768, with Sir Joshua Reynolds as the first president. The wings on the E. and W. of the quadrangle house several learned societies and are not open to the public. Old Burlington House, which is in the centre, has permanent collections on the upper floors, which mostly consist of Academicians' own work presented on their election. They include paintings by Reynolds and Gainsborough.

CARNABY STREET (16–133) is a short, narrow Soho street, which preceded the KING'S

Camera Press

Carnaby Street

ROAD as the home of modern gear with some men's boutiques. It is now mostly frequented by tourists, whom it entertains with pop records blaring from the shops, and (once) a nude live window display.

DESIGN CENTRE, THE, *Haymarket* (16–141). A small, constantly changing exhibition of the best in British design in products ranging from seat belts to tableware, lawn mowers to saucepans. Besides the items on show there is a comprehensive photographic file of other products, but nothing is sold here. Hours of opening are extended on Wednesdays and Thursdays. A few doors away is a bow-fronted shop which has survived for some 200 years.

GREEN PARK (16–149). This park forms the south side of PICCADILLY. It is well named, being truly green except for daffodils in March; no flower-beds divert the eye from the artistically sculptured naturalness created in 1660. Down the east side of Green Park is Queen's Walk, linking Piccadilly and THE MALL, with a spur off into the purlieus of ST JAMES'S PALACE. Almost every Sunday there is an exhibition of pictures on the park railings on the Piccadilly side.

GROSVENOR SQUARE (16–130) was conceived originally by Sir Richard Grosvenor on the site of Oliver's Mount, an anti-Charles I earthwork thrown up by the frightened citizenry at the beginning of the Civil War. It was completed in 1725. The garden, designed by Kent, was circular, with a statue of George I, whose mistress, the Duchess of Kendall, occupied No. 43. It is also associated with Lord Chesterfield, who moved out in 1750; the Earl of Shaftesbury, Lord Beatty; and John Adams, later president of the United States, began Little America when he chose to reside at No. 9 in 1785. Today the opulent and impressive square is almost totally occupied by American administration. The west side is the embassy, designed by the Finn, Eero Saarinen, and completed in 1958, topped by a giant eagle. In the gardens, now square, there is a tranquil statue of F. D. Roosevelt by Reid Dick.

HANOVER SQUARE (16–132). This once quiet square is now edged with several modern office blocks, and there are probably no private houses left. A large bronze statue of William Pitt stands in the centre of the garden. In Hanover Street the dark-pillared portico of St George's Church pushes out across the pavement. The interior, Wren-influenced, disappoints. The register records the marriage of many famous people, including Disraeli, Shelley, George Eliot and Emma Hamilton, and the church was a favourite for society weddings until the late 1920s.

HYDE PARK CORNER (16–151) was considerably enlarged when the E.–W. underpass was built. This extended the circuit for the rest of the traffic and enhanced the Wellington, or GREEN PARK, Arch which used to form the entrance to Constitution Hill, but now serves no purpose. Decimus Burton designed it in 1848 to stand opposite the HYDE PARK entrance. It was topped by the Adrian Jones quadriga in 1912. The Decimus Burton triple archway into Hyde Park is also now unused. Inside the park is the huge Achilles statue which is in fact a Roman horse tamer, put there for Wellington and his soldiers by their admiring countrywomen, while his official statue sits astride the horse that carried him at Waterloo, on the island opposite APSLEY HOUSE. Here he is guarded by a Grenadier, a Royal Highlander, a Welch Fusilier and an Inniskilling Dragoon. A Machine Gun Corps War Memorial stands nearby and also the splendid Royal Artillery First World War memorial.

LEICESTER SQUARE (16–140). Leicester Square was built towards the end of the 17th cent. on Leicester Fields, named after the house of the earls of Leicester, descendants of Sir Philip Sidney. The gardens in the centre, set out in 1720, still carry some indication of their Dutch design. They contain a copy of the WESTMINSTER ABBEY Shakespeare statue, and in the four corners busts of famous residents. Today the square is devoted to mass entertainment and mass feeding, and the entire west side is the sombre A.A. head office.

Lord's: the premier cricket ground in the world

LORD'S CRICKET GROUND, *St John's Wood Road* (16–125), is the property of the Marylebone Cricket Club, known as the M.C.C., and the premier cricket ground in the world. It is the ambition of every overseas cricketer to play at Lord's. The Middlesex County Cricket Club also have their headquarters at Lord's, which they rent from the M.C.C.

In 1786 the White Conduit Cricket Club played at Islington, and when they asked their groundsman, Thomas Lord, to find them new premises he selected the field which is now Dorset Square, and the first match was played there in 1787. In 1811 Whites became the M.C.C., and in 1814 moved to their present ground, technically in Marylebone. The Club has a very fine collection of cricket pictures, some of which are on display in a small museum.

MADAME TUSSAUD'S, *Marylebone Road* (16–126). This exhibition was first opened in the STRAND at the time of George III, then moved to Marylebone Road, where it was burnt down in 1925, and reopened two years later. The original Marie Tussaud, friend of Louis XVI's sister, fled to England from the Revolution bringing with her a collection of death masks of guillotined titled heads which she had been forced to make. These formed the basis of her exhibition, and she added English murderers and body snatchers. Today the display has a much wider appeal, and includes sportsmen, politicians, pop idols, Prince Charles and Snow White, with suitable smells and noises. Almost everything displayed, except the actual bodies, is authentic, including the guillotine.

The Planetarium now forms part of Madame Tussaud's.

MARBLE ARCH (16–129). This arch was designed by Nash to commemorate the Napoleonic wars and erected as an entrance to BUCKING-HAM PALACE in 1828. Queen Victoria had it moved in 1851 to a position where it could form an entrance to HYDE PARK. By 1908 it could no longer take the traffic, so was by-passed, and in recent traffic flow alterations has become quite isolated. The iron gates are worth looking at.

Previously called Tyburn, this place was the scene of many public hangings on its permanent, three-legged gallows in the 17th and 18th cents. The condemned were brought in a cart from Newgate in the City, along what is now Oxford Street. It was also the location for public flogging and torture. A stone slab marks the spot where many religious martyrs, as well as highwaymen and other criminals met their deaths.

NEW ZEALAND HOUSE, *Haymarket* (16–142), forms the massive south-east corner of this street, which was originally paved by a tax levied on any load of hay or straw passing along it. New Zealand House, opened in 1963, has a good roof view over TRAFALGAR SQUARE and South London, and any New Zealand visitor is welcome to take the lift up.

Next to New Zealand House on the N. is **Her Majesty's Theatre**, with a baroque copper dome; across the street is the **Haymarket Theatre**, built by Nash in 1820. Its beautifully proportioned Corinthian façade is best viewed from Charles II Street.

PICCADILLY (16–144) sweeps gently uphill, with handsome houses on one side and GREEN PARK on the other, from HYDE PARK CORNER to Piccadilly Circus, where hoardings and bright lights surround the charming statue of Eros. Erected in 1893 to the 7th Earl of Shaftesbury, it was the first monument in London to be made of aluminium. Sir Alfred Gilbert was paid £3,000 for designing it, which caused him to emigrate in a rage.

particularly that of the Prince Regent, and was not opened to the public until 1838. Its conception was much grander than appears now, but there is enough left to make it unusual and delightful. The Inner Circle, with the imposingly rich Nash terraces, now largely government offices, and Queen Mary's Gardens, which in rose time are lovely, has also an attractive, irregular lake with several types of waterfowl. There are other well-kept gardens at the south end of the Broad Walk, which drives beneath trees straight across the park towards the Zoo.

REGENT STREET (16–134) was conceived by Nash in 1810 as a *grande route* connecting the administrative area of WHITEHALL with REGENT'S PARK. It had great beauty, but was rebuilt in 1925–6 with 20th-cent. Tudor incongruously inserted at the top.

ST JAMES'S CHURCH, *Piccadilly* (16–143), is set back on the south side, with a courtyard and a small attractive Garden of Remembrance, given by the late Lord Southwood to commemorate the fortitude of Londoners during the last war.

The church dates from 1674, when Henry Jermyn, Earl of St Albans, who had obtained from Charles II permission to develop the neighbourhood, set aside a site at the top of York Street for the church which would be the parish church of his new ST JAMES'S SQUARE. Christopher Wren was the architect; the foundation stone was laid in 1676 and the building consecrated in 1684. For almost 300 years the church was supported by fashionable congregations, a great many eminent men were its rectors, and various embellishments were added. In October 1940 the church was bombed. Little was left, but the next year services were held in the south aisle, which remained the one usable piece of the building for thirteen years. Rebuilding began under Sir Albert Richardson and was completed in 1954, except for the tower and spire, which were finished in 1968. The clock face, spire and weathervane, which look like lead, are actually fibre glass.

Inside, the gallery is supported by six Corinthian columns on each side of the nave; the ceiling is attractively squared by plaster ribs; the embellishments are exact reproductions of the originals, made from drawings, casts and photographs of the bombed fragments. The reredos and font, which is a marble sculpture by Grinling Gibbons, were removed before the bombing and are now back in position.

ST JAMES'S SQUARE (16–145). One of the early London squares. Although nothing remains of its 1660 original, enough of the 18th cent. survives to give the square grace, though there are some modern intrusions. The garden in the centre, rich in spring-flowering trees, is private, with an equestrian statue of William III. Probably no other square has quite such a record of aristocratic tenants. At one time there were six dukes and seven earls living there; Queen Caroline lived there during her trial; the Duchess of

Picturepoint

The Post Office Tower

POST OFFICE TOWER, *Howland Street* (16–127). London's highest building is 580 ft with a 40-ft mast on top. It was opened to the public in 1966. It has the highest, first and only revolving restaurant in the country. There are three viewing galleries but the high parapet makes it unsuitable for small children.

Round the corner, on Scala Street, is **Pollock's Toy Museum**, a delightful collection of toy theatres, early cinema toys and dolls, with traditional gingerbread men to eat if you like.

REGENT'S PARK (16–124) contains Bedford College; the American embassy residence; the former St Katherine's Hospital, now only St Katherine's Chapel, church of the Danish community in London; an open-air theatre; THE ZOO; and rowing boats can be hired on its lake. This royal park, which began as part of Henry VIII's hunting forest, was planned for private leisure,

Richmond, who modelled Britannia on the coin of the realm, had a house there; three prime ministers, Pitt the Elder, Derby and Gladstone, lived in Chatham House, now the Royal Institute of International Affairs; Nos. 14 and 4 house the London Library.

Duke of York Street, which enters the square from the N., has in it one of the best preserved Victorian pubs – the Red Lion; the north side of King Street, which leaves the square to the W., is typical of St James's architecture (the south side has been developed) and houses purveyors of art, cigars, wine, boots and rare antiques. Christie's auction rooms are here.

ST JAMES'S STREET (16–147) contains Boodle's, White's, Brooks's and the Carlton Club. Only a few such houses remain, but they catch the eye. There are also the successful new *Economist* building and the 14th-cent. gatehouse of ST JAMES'S PALACE, curiously one-dimensional, at the bottom, between Norman Shaw's banded red-brick Alliance Assurance office on the corner of PALL MALL, and his post office on the opposite side. On the east side the three stories of Lock's have history in hats lined up in the window, and nearly next door Berry Bros. & Rudd have been supplying wine as long. Beside this shop, with its dark external panelling, is a narrow passage leading to Pickering Place, a tiny square of four charming 18th-cent. houses, paved and containing a sundial. This was where the last duel was fought in London. On the left in the passageway leading to St James's Street is an easily overlooked door which carries an iron plaque announcing that here, in 1842–5, was housed the Legation to the Court of St James of the Republic of Texas.

On the other side of St James's Street, St James's Place, narrowly opulent, contains Spencer House, by Vardy, 1758–65, and one of the most chastely expensive blocks of flats in London. To the N. is Blue Bell Yard, with an entry resembling that to a public baths and within, a cobbled mews, and a row of one-time stables, with living accommodation above reached by stairs leading to either end of a wooden balcony. Further up St James's Street on the west side is the Royal Overseas League in Park Place, where Messrs Carhill Ltd are still purveying cigars to the successors of many 19th-cent. royalty.

SAVILE ROW (16–135) has become synonymous with good quality tailoring. Most fashionable tailors have their premises in this street. It was named after the wife of the 3rd Earl of Burlington, who was a Savile. His own titles, Boyle, Clifford and Cork went to other solid streets round about. Savile Row has modern government buildings and a multi-story car park, but there are old houses left, including No. 14, which bears a tablet to Sheridan, who lived there; he died at No. 17.

SHEPHERD MARKET (16–148) is a rectangle of 200-year-old London, an oasis of narrow streets, some only pavements, reached from PICCADILLY along gloomy little Whitehorse Street, or from Curzon Street through an archway, beneath which is the entrance to the Steering Wheel Club, haunt of racing drivers, rally men, motoring journalists. In the 1920s it was much favoured by smart young professional people; today, with its tiny shops selling cut-price drink and tourist trinkets, and its cafés, it is like a bazaar.

SOHO SQUARE (16–131), just S. of Oxford Street, is unusual in that the five streets entering it do so on the sides, leaving four attractive and undisturbed corners. This gives interesting views, particularly from Soho Street southwards to the south-east corner, with the red Roman Catholic church of St Patrick and its campanile on the left. A French Protestant church stands on the north side. On the corner of Greek Street is the house of St Barnabas (open to the public), once the home of William Beckford, now housing a charity but preserving many features from Soho's early days, including a chapel.

A weather-beaten statue by Cibber of Charles II stands in the square's small garden, once part of Soho's village green and site of the Duke of Monmouth's house. The name Soho is said to derive from the password of his army used at Edgemoor, itself adopted from the rousing cry of the hunt, once seen in the St Giles area close by. In the 18th cent. Soho Square was socially desirable; its reputation slipped as the result of fashionable excesses, then returned to respectability when it became a meeting place for scientists. Today it is largely modern offices.

WALLACE COLLECTION, THE, *Manchester Square* (16–128), is in Hertford House, which forms the north side of Manchester Square. It is the largest and most valuable ever to be bequeathed to a nation by one person. Its French 18th-cent. art is so comprehensive, varied and expert that French art students come to study it. Many Dutch painters are represented, and there is a large collection of armour. The 3rd Marquess of Hertford, who specialized in Dutch cabinet pictures, was greatly aided in his buying by his wife's two fortunes, which were left to her by George Selwyn and the Duke of Queensberry, who both claimed to be her father; his son, a dedicated francophile, added the French *objets d'art*; his son, the illegitimate Sir Richard Wallace, amassed medieval and Renaissance items, and armour. After his death his French wife gave the collection to the nation. In accordance with the terms of the bequest the collection is unalterable; nor can it be loaned.

WATERLOO PLACE (16–146) is the repository of a number of memorials placed with tidy-minded symmetry. In the northern half Lord Herbert of Lea (1810–61) and Florence Nightingale (1820–1910) flank a group commemorating the Crimean War. In the southern half Edward VII rides between Captain Scott (Antarctic),

J. Allan Cash

The Zoo: the elephant house

Lord Clyde (Lucknow), Lord Lawrence (India), Sir John Franklin (Arctic) and Sir John Burgoyne (Crimea). Carlton House Terrace crosses Waterloo Place just before it terminates in the Duke of York's steps, from which there is a splendid view over ST JAMES'S PARK towards WHITEHALL. At the top of the steps a bronze statue of the Duke of York, second son of George III, is mounted on a 124-ft column erected in 1833. He was the one who "marched them up to the top of the hill. And he marched them down again".

ZOO, THE, *Regent's Park* (16–123), properly the gardens of the Zoological Society of London, has been there since the first quarter of the last century. A grand development plan by Sir Hugh Casson to stave off anachronism is not expected to be complete until the 1970s; meanwhile there is a lack of cohesion about its 36 acres. This zoo aims to be the greatest in the world, and must nearly have achieved that object. The informative illustrated guide is a great help, and contains a coloured plan.

CHELSEA AND KENSINGTON

In the N. of the area are KENSINGTON PALACE, the only one besides BUCKINGHAM PALACE fully active with royalty, and KENSINGTON GARDENS, last stronghold of the uniformed nanny, which have never, in spite of being joined to HYDE PARK, really relinquished the original formality of royal design. Chelsea has for long been unconventional, if not bizarre; Carlyle, writing of it with affection and with the firm intention of making it his home, described it as very dirty.

In 1520 Sir Thomas More built a house in Chelsea, in which he entertained Holbein and Erasmus, and doubtless drew the attention of his ungrateful monarch to the delights of the village. Sixteen years later, after More was beheaded, Henry VIII built a new palace there, where Queen Elizabeth I lived for 11 years prior to his death, and where Anne of Cleves died. Under Charles II Chelsea became gay. The Duke of Beaufort sumptuously rebuilt More's old house; Wren put up Chelsea Hospital for the king; a few years later the Earl of Ranelagh acquired part of the grounds and set up Ranelagh Gardens. Nothing is left except the Hospital and Beaufort

Street. From the 18th cent. Addison, Steele, Swift, Leigh Hunt, Smollett, Rossetti, Whistler, Wilde, George Eliot, Augustus John, Ellen Terry lived in Chelsea, but Kensington was respectable from the beginning: John Stuart Mill, Fox, Macaulay, Gladstone are associated with it, though Addison formed a link between the two places when he married the Countess of Warwick. Kensington squares, and such wide ways as Queens Gate are pleasing. In the space bounded by Exhibition Road and Queens Gate, with Kensington Gore in the N. and Cromwell Road in the S., is Prince Albert's academic complex surrounding the ALBERT HALL, over which he watches from his ornate memorial. In South Kensington Baden-Powell House collects many young in its international hostel; almost opposite is the French Lycée; further out along the Cromwell Road is the West London Air Terminal. At the east end Cromwell Road passes into Brompton Road, which leads through Knightsbridge to Harrods.

Battersea, although on the other side of the river, is being absorbed by Chelsea, and is certainly already part of it visually.

ALBERT BRIDGE (16–178) is a delicate and pretty looking suspension bridge, coloured milk chocolate, cream and blue. It was put up in 1873; a notice at either end requests troops to break step when marching across in case it starts to sway.

On the north end of the bridge there is a "Boy David" figure by Derwent Wood, to whom it is a memorial. In the gardens immediately left of the bridge is a pensive statue of Carlyle with his back towards Cheyne Row, where he lived, and close by there is a seated statue of Sir Thomas More, with his back to the OLD CHURCH. On Oakley Street, facing Albert Bridge, a tablet marks the house where Captain R. F. Scott lived.

ALBERT HALL, THE, *Kensington Road* (16–159), is across Kensington Gore from the ALBERT MEMORIAL, on the site of Lady Blessington's Gore House. It holds 8,000 people and is a competent piece of engineering. It is interesting as the first piece of Albert's vision of a huge complex of learning and culture to arise on land bought out of the proceeds of the Great Exhibition. Clustered near are the Royal College of Music, with a collection of musical instruments open to the public; the Royal Geographical Society, with a little museum; the Royal College of Organists; the Royal College of Art, with periodical exhibitions; the Imperial College of Science and Technology; the Royal School of Mines – and in the centre of it all another memorial to Albert, smaller, and standing in Prince Consort Road. On the Cromwell Road, at the southern edge of the Blessington estate, are the VICTORIA AND ALBERT MUSEUM and the NATURAL HISTORY MUSEUM.

ALBERT MEMORIAL, THE, *Kensington Gardens* (16–158), was designed by Sir George Gilbert Scott and dedicated by Queen Victoria "and Her People" to Prince Albert of Saxe-Coburg-Gotha, her consort. The statue of the prince, seated and holding a catalogue of the Great Exhibition of 1851, is by Foley. On the steps are four marble groups representing Europe, Asia, Africa and America, while at the angles of the plinth are further groups depicting Commerce, Manufacturing, Engineering and Agriculture. The plinth itself carries marble reliefs of the world's architects of history. Above this is an extremely ornate Gothic canopy, depicting everything suitable to a memorial.

BATTERSEA BRIDGE (16–177). The wooden, piered structure of 1771 that stirred Whistler, Turner and de Wint was declared unsafe and demolished in 1885 and was replaced in 1890 in Victorian functional style. At the Chelsea end it debouches on to CHEYNE WALK, still struggling to preserve something of its earlier exclusive attraction in the face of increasing heavy traffic. The first turning right on the south side is Battersea Church Road, which leads between featureless new blocks spaced in a sort of wilderness to the old Parish Church of **St Mary, Battersea**, rebuilt 1776, attractively sited on a tiny

Picturepoint

The Albert Hall

The Albert Memorial

A. F. Kersting

promontory overlooking the river, which contains several older monuments. Nearby in Vicarage Crescent stands **Old Battersea House** containing William De Morgan's collection of pottery and paintings. (Viewing by arrangement.)

BATTERSEA PARK (16–179) forms a green box on the south bank of the river in a grey area of light industry and terrace houses. It stretches between Chelsea and Battersea bridges and was laid out in 1852–8, chiefly as a result of dumping earth excavated from the Royal Victoria Dock on what had been a swamp, on which the Duke of Wellington had fought a duel with the Earl of Winchelsea in 1829. It is today a very pleasing park. The fun fair, left over from the Festival of Britain, fronts the river. There is a boating lake, rowing and motor boats for hire, a fishing lake stocked with roach and tench, and a sub-tropical garden. Its lawns are adorned with modern sculpture and its flower-beds are superb. There are a number of facilities for eating, including a furnished picnic area, and there is also a small children's zoo.

BEAUCHAMP PLACE (16–165). This narrow street with neat step-up shops is painted white from end to end. It is lined with expensive boutiques in the front rooms of what recently were private houses, and contains antique shops, the most up-to-date men's hairdresser and exclusive speciality shops for such luxurious items and silks and china.

BROMPTON ORATORY, *Brompton Road* (16–164), was built in 1884 by H. Gribble. It stands massively with its dome and statue at the junction of Cromwell Road and Brompton Road. Inside it is large, sombre, Italianate, with huge marble apostles by Mazzuoli taken from Siena Cathedral. The nave, 51 ft, is exceptionally wide.

Behind the Oratory, down a tree-lined walk, is the Victorian Gothic **Holy Trinity** church and gardens. Cottage Place, a row of bright, pigmy houses, leads to Ennismore Gardens Mews, and close by is the narrow, exclusive, treed Brompton Square, which opens on to Brompton Road.

CAMPDEN HILL (16–152) is a short street where John Galsworthy once lived, though the name covers the area round, popular since the 17th cent., which still has some fine houses standing in their own grounds. It is a place to wander on foot and discover curious backwaters such as Kensington Church Walk, the gardens of Gordon Place, the remnants of expansive living in Duchess of Bedford's Walk, and Campden Hill Square, which is charming, and has a tradition of putting lighted candles in its windows on Christmas Eve.

One wing of the intellectually famous **Holland House** survived the air raids, and forms part of a quadrangle with a well-built modern youth hostel. The gardens, **Holland Park**, are open to the public, have a café and a restaurant, and are much used.

CARLYLE'S HOUSE *Cheyne Row* (16–173). In 1834 Thomas Carlyle moved with his wife Jane to London where he settled in Chelsea, to live there until his death. In the house today the chair in which he died is still preserved, also the desk at which he wrote – at the top of the house in the so-called sound-proof attic – and even his dressing-gown laid in a drawer. This is the small museum par excellence. Over the fireplace in the front dining-room is a painting of the room with the Carlyles in residence, and the National Trust has seen to it that the room today repeats the painting, with identical wallpaper and Mrs Carlyle's favourite armchair upholstered in much the same material as the artist gave it. In the study a framed letter from Disraeli should be noted as a model of tact, courtesy and charm from No. 10 Downing Street. Among other interesting pieces of furniture are Mrs Carlyle's piano, on which Chopin played to her, and the sofa she bought, after haggling, for one pound.

CHELSEA BRIDGE (16–171) was opened in 1858 and rebuilt nearly 80 years later. It marks the eastern extremity of the mile-long CHELSEA EMBANKMENT, and in Chelsea Bridge Road, which leads to it from the N., entertainment is frequently provided by the Guards drilling in the newly rebuilt Duke of York barracks. On the other side of the same road was the old Ranelagh Gardens, now returned to the pensioners of the ROYAL HOSPITAL, to whom it belonged. It is open to the public.

On the south side of the bridge is **Battersea Power Station**, in pink brick with four enormously high chimneys, often emitting plumes of especially treated, inoffensive smoke. At night it is an impressive sight and features in all the programmes of London tour operators.

CHELSEA EMBANKMENT (16–172) stretches for over a mile between CHELSEA and BATTERSEA BRIDGES, tree lined, and particularly attractive in late evening. Starting from Chelsea Bridge in the E., there is an entrance to ROYAL HOSPITAL on the right, and a little further on is Paradise Walk, the first of the delightful 18th-cent. streets. Then comes the famous CHEYNE WALK with large houses behind tall railings, and CHELSEA OLD CHURCH backing on to it. Immediately beyond, a small, modern block of flats, Roper's Orchard, faces its small, sunken Roper's Garden – both named after Sir Thomas More's son-in-law – with newly planted mulberry trees and a simple, attractive bronze of a nude girl by Gilbert Ledward. Next is CROSBY HALL in Danvers Street. On the waterside here is a houseboat colony, and W. of Battersea Bridge a pavement exhibition of Chelsea artists is held on Sundays.

CHELSEA OLD CHURCH, *Cheyne Walk* (16–174). Correctly titled All Saints, this church beautifully situated on the corner of Cheyne Walk and Old Church Street, dates from the 12th cent. but was almost totally destroyed by a landmine in 1941. A great many of the memorials were spared, and have been replaced in their former positions, and the More Chapel, the only part of the old fabric not destroyed, has been incorporated into the new red brick. Sir Thomas More, who then lived nearby, rebuilt this chapel in 1528 as his own; next to it is the tomb of his first wife, which was to receive him and his second wife, but he was executed and his body disappeared. A statue of the saintly Lord Chancellor is nearby.

The church has a square nave with medieval chancel and chapels and, in the entrance of the Lawrence Chapel, a free-standing triumphal arch of 1563 commemorating Richard Jervoise. There are an astonishing number of memorials of all sorts, including one of Sara Colville rising from the tomb in her shroud, and a Baroque piece for Lady Jane Cheyne. Here are reminders of that remarkable 16th-cent. Chelsea set, and of a span of social history from the 16th to the 18th cents. There are also some chained books, the only ones in any London church, given by Sir Hans Sloane, for whom a commemorative urn stands unscathed in the churchyard. His statue is in the Physic Gardens down the road. He once owned the Manor of Chelsea and died aged 92 in 1753. His collection formed the basis of the BRITISH MUSEUM.

CHEYNE WALK (16–176) stretches from the hideousness of Lot's Road in the W. to E. of the bridge, where its elegant mansions slide behind vestigial gardens to merge with Royal Hospital Road. Lindsey House (National Trust), Nos. 96–100, is the only 17th-cent. mansion in Chelsea. It was once, in 1770, the headquarters of the Moravian sect in England, and later one of Whistler's many Chelsea homes. Father and son Brunel lived on the west side, and Mrs Gaskell was born there. To the east side CROSBY HALL stands on the corner of Danvers Street, with CHELSEA OLD CHURCH on the next corner, and CARLYLE'S HOUSE a block away. Where Cheyne Walk joins Royal Hospital Road are the **Physic Gardens**, established by the Apothecaries Society on land presented by Sir Hans Sloane, of whom there is a statue.

CROSBY HALL, *Cheyne Walk* (16–175), stands on the corner of CHEYNE WALK and Danvers Street. Part dates from 1926, but the ancient part began life in Bishopsgate in 1466 as a mansion built by Sir John Crosby, a wool merchant, friend of Edward IV. It was at one time occupied by the Duke of Gloucester, later Richard III, then by William Roper, son-in-law of Sir Thomas More, who bought it in 1523. In the 16th cent. it housed ambassadors; in the 17th it survived a fire that destroyed the rest of Crosby Place, and it became many things including a restaurant before, in 1910, it was bought by the University and City Association of London, transported, and re-erected on ground next to the site of Sir Thomas More's Chelsea house. It is now the dining hall of the British Federation of University Women's hostel. It has a good hammer-beam roof, with the smoke vent of the medieval fireplace preserved. The furniture is Jacobean and Cromwellian, and one of the three copies of Holbein's picture of the More family is there.

EARL'S COURT (16–167). In the whole large, tightly packed acreage between Kensington and Earl's Court Road and one block beyond to the W., there is a hardly a house occupied solely by one family. It is a district of squares and oblong gardens, small hotels, prosperously middle class and unmemorable, known best for its Exhibition building, which can be reached by covered way from Earl's Court underground station or direct from Warwick Road. Covering nearly 19 acres, it was rebuilt in 1936–7 and is the home of the Motor Show and other large exhibitions.

HYDE PARK (16–154) has been considerably altered during the past years by incorporating the eastern side of the ring road into the one-way Park Lane traffic scheme. The triple archway designed by Decimus Burton in 1828 to be the main entrance to Hyde Park from Constitution Hill (across HYDE PARK CORNER) is now abandoned; MARBLE ARCH is marooned by the traffic, and a short section of road in KENSINGTON GARDENS which passes the ALBERT MEMORIAL is no longer used.

From the Conquest to the Dissolution the monks of Westminster owned the 361-acre manor of Hyde, which Henry VIII acquired in 1536 for hunting; James I opened it to the public; Charles I built the ring, which became a highly fashionable carriageway; under Cromwell the park was sold to speculators, but was retrieved with the return to monarchy. At this time deer were still hunted there, and during the reigns of William and Mary and Queen Anne the paths were infested with footpads. It became a favourite place for duels, and suicides in the Serpentine. The **Serpentine**, which occupies 41 acres in depths ranging from $4\frac{1}{2}$ to 14 ft has bathing from the lido and boating. Bands perform on the bandstands at advertised times and there are putting and bowling greens nearby. There is a restaurant and bar beside Rennie's bridge over the Serpentine, and another at the opposite end of the lake near the Knightsbridge exit. Rotten Row leads from the west ring road to Hyde Park Corner and Achilles' Statue, raised for the Duke of Wellington by his grateful countrywomen; close by is a statue of Byron by Belt; at Stanhope Gate is the 1914-18 Cavalry War Memorial by Adrian Jones; at Marble Arch **Speakers' Corner** provides an unmolested platform for controversial speeches.

KENSINGTON GARDENS (16–153) were once the private gardens of KENSINGTON PALACE. These 275 acres join HYDE PARK, but they are quite different; the formal boundary still divides the two parks. The gardens were laid out in 1728–31 under the direction of George II's wife, Caroline, with emphasis on avenues, though today the great elms of the Broad Walk have unfor-

Camera Press

Cheyne Walk: Whistler's house

Camera Press

King's Road displays every freak of fashion

tunately been felled, and the replacement limes are still young. There is a well-planned garden bordering the long Flower Walk, which runs between the west end of Rotten Row and the Broad Walk.

The Serpentine is here called the Long Water. A path along the west side leads to the Peter Pan statue by Frampton; close by is Watts's horse and rider statue to Physical Energy, put up in 1907. The Long Water terminates in a paved garden with fountains, a statue of Edward Jenner and a little pavilion, once a pumping station, said to have been designed by the Prince Consort. Beyond is Queen Anne's Alcove, built like a porter's chair, by William Kent. On the west side of the gardens, near the Broad Walk, is the Round Pond, used for sailing model boats, and the open space round it is much used by kite fliers.

KENSINGTON PALACE, *Kensington Gardens* (16–155), which, with its grounds, lies on the west boundary of KENSINGTON GARDENS, was the royal residence from 1689 to 1760. Queen Victoria was born there, and lived there until she came to the throne in 1837. Among the State Apartments open to the public is the room in which she received the news of her accession from the Archbishop of Canterbury. Many of the rooms are furnished with royal mementoes, including a delightful selection of the young Princess Victoria's own dolls.

Outside there is a very attractive sunken garden with a pleached lime walk on three sides. Nearby is a pale, young Queen Victoria romantically sculpted by her daughter Princess Louise; on the south front is a flamboyant statue of William III, who acquired the palace from the 2nd Earl of Nottingham. W. of the palace is Kensington Palace Gardens, known also as

millionaires' row, a private road of opulent houses in their own gardens, built on the kitchen gardens of the palace, which includes a house designed by Thackeray for himself. Many embassies, including those of France and of the U.S.S.R., are situated here.

The LONDON MUSEUM is at present housed in part of the Palace.

KENSINGTON SQUARE (16–157). This delightful square was fashionable at the beginning of the 18th cent. when KENSINGTON PALACE was much used by the court. Thackeray featured it in *Esmond*. The flamboyant actress, Mrs Patrick Campbell, lived at No. 33, J. S. Mill at No. 18, and Burne-Jones at No. 41.

KING'S ROAD (16–169) stretches from E. of SLOANE SQUARE to Putney Bridge, nearly 3 m., though for most people its attractions are in the first mile W. of Sloane Square. This is mainly full of boutiques of men's and women's up-to-date clothes, but there are also many restaurants, antique shops, art galleries, modern furniture shops and pubs. On Saturdays visitors from the suburbs and abroad combine with local shoppers to take over the road from cars, so that traffic is halted by brilliantly-dressed strolling groups of young people.

On either side of King's Road are a number of pleasant squares and short, tree-lined streets, which make it possible to believe that King's Road was once the private route of Charles II out to the great mansions of Chelsea, edged by fields and gardens with the unembankmented river nearly always in sight.

LONDON MUSEUM, *Kensington Gardens* (16–156). This intimately housed collection, illustrating the history of London from before the

Romans to the present day is displayed in part of KENSINGTON PALACE. There are interesting models of Old London Bridge, Old St Paul's, and the Fire of London; a splendid fire engine; a fascinating display of toys sold for a penny on the streets of London at the beginning of this century; coronation robes; theatrical relics; reconstructed shop fronts; and much good furniture, glassware and costumes.

MORMON CHAPEL, THE, *Exhibition Road* (16–161). The Hyde Park Chapel of Jesus Christ of the Latter-Day Saints stands midway on the east side of Exhibition Road, a modern Perpendicular building with a thin, tapering, gold leaf spire. Inside the large chapel hall has virtually no horizontal lines and nearly everything, including the inset of the windows, is angled. It was designed by Sir Thomas Bennett, and built in 1959–61. The organ, the second biggest to be built in this country since the war, is the dominant feature of the chapel. There are free organ recitals at lunch-time on alternate weekdays.

NATURAL HISTORY MUSEUM, *Cromwell Road* (16–162). This huge building by Alfred Waterhouse is a museum and a research centre, and there is a children's section where for a small fee drawing blocks and pencils may be borrowed.

It is divided into five departments: Zoology, Entomology, Palaeontology, Mineralogy and Botany, which means that the exhibits range from the minutiae of fossils to the 84-ft 9-in reconstruction of a dinosaur. There are coral from the Great Barrier Reef; a quarter of a million butterflies; remains of extinct birds, reptiles and mammals; stuffed specimens of many living species; reconstructions of early *Homo sapiens*; and the unedifying story of the Piltdown Man.

OLYMPIA, *Hammersmith Road* (16–166), was *the* exhibition hall until the EARL'S COURT Exhibition was built. When Olympia was opened in 1866 it stood a little back from Hammersmith Road, but was extended up to it in 1929. There is a District Line station beside it and the terminus for the motor-rail services to Wales and the SW. Olympia is divided into two exhibition halls, and houses small exhibitions. W. on Hammersmith Road stood the red-brick building which was St Paul's School from 1884 to 1968; the school had previously been situated by St Paul's churchyard from 1509. Many famous pupils include Milton, Marlborough, Pepys, Judge Jeffreys and Lord Montgomery, who used the buildings as his headquarters before the D-Day Invasion of 1944.

ROYAL HOSPITAL, THE, *Royal Hospital Road* (16–170). Charles II founded the Royal Hospital in 1682. Wren designed the hospital, which stands elegantly in grounds much reduced from their original size. A large part of the property was made over to the Hospital Treasurer, the Earl of Ranelagh, at the time of William III, and it was here that the famous Ranelagh Gardens flourished.

"Persons admitted to the Hospital Grounds are expected to conduct themselves in an orderly manner." They are allowed to look at the chapel, magnificently carved and decorated, and the Great Hall, now restored to use as the pensioners' dining-room. There is an imposing array of royal portraits, the royal arms of William III, and an interesting clock by Jacob Odell of St Albans. Round the walls battles from 1662 to Korea are commemorated, with the names of pensioners who took part listed in the panels. Three great leather jugs – black jacks – stand on a table. They were once used to carry beer from the cellars and hold five gallons. The building was damaged during the blitz and has been restored in its original style.

SCIENCE MUSEUM, *Exhibition Road* (16–160) shows the application of science to our lives directly and through industry. There is a full-size replica of Stephenson's *Rocket*; a section devoted to the evolution of the pedal cycle, and the car; superannuated locomotives and Continental rolling stock stand proudly in their national colours; Amy Johnson's Gipsy Moth and a V2 rocket are in the aeronautical collection, and so are Montgolfier's balloon and Professor Piccard's stratosphere gondola. There is a children's gallery with dioramas and working models.

SLOANE SQUARE (16–168) has a central paved area with trees, a fountain and the smartest public lavatories in the metropolis, painted blue for the Gents and pink for the Ladies. On the east side of the square is the **Royal Court Theatre,** which always performs controversial productions; on the west Peter Jones's excellent 1930s building.

VICTORIA AND ALBERT MUSEUM, *Cromwell Road* (16–163), originated in the Marlborough House Museum of Ornamental Art, which was established in 1852, which itself partly stemmed from the Great Exhibition the previous year, and was moved to South Kensington in 1857. The present Renaissance-style building was designed by Sir Aston Webb and opened in 1909 as the Victoria and Albert Museum of Fine and Applied Arts. The object was the "improvement of public taste in design". Today it constitutes the greatest collection of fine and decorative art in the world. The Primary Collection is described as "masterpieces of all the arts brought together by style, period or nationality", which takes in armour, carpets, clocks, costume, fabrics, jewellery, gold, silver, iron and wood work, tapestry and glass. The Study Collections, which are on the top floors, are objects gathered together in kind, so that studies in depth can be conveniently pursued. Among so much richness, the galleries of model stage designs and of musical instruments may too easily be missed.

Besides these two categories, there is a special collection of John Constable paintings and drawings given by the Constable family, Raphael cartoons done for Pope Leo X, and usually an important loan exhibition.

Chinese sculpture, Sung dynasty

Chinese vase, Sung dynasty

Byzantine ivory panel, 12th cent.

Romanesque Spanish relief, 12th cent.

VICTORIA AND ALBERT MUSEUM

MIDDLESEX AND THE PERIMETER VILLAGES

One of the earliest settlements in the London area was at Heath Row where, in the course of excavating for airport runways, the remains of an Iron Age village were unearthed, complete with temple. Experts date it between 500 and 300 B.C. The villages of HARLINGTON and HARMONDSWORTH by London Airport had Norman churches. At GREENWICH the Danes fought hard when they overran Kent, and killed St Alfege when he refused to be ransomed. After the early 15th cent. the monarchy and Greenwich were linked until William III moved his residence to KENSINGTON PALACE; the palace at Greenwich eventually became a naval college.

By the beginning of the 16th cent. London started to expand. Henry VIII accepted HAMPTON COURT as a present from Wolsey; Protector Somerset started to build SYON HOUSE (when he was also building SOMERSET HOUSE in the Strand). He had no time to finish either because he was executed for treason. Late in the same century Sir Thomas Gresham realized the potential of Brentford and built OSTERLEY PARK. He was the first landowner in outer London not to build on the Thames, but Lord Burlington reverted to it when he built CHISWICK House 150 years later. DULWICH grew up in the 19th cent., well S. of the Thames. HIGHGATE and HAMPSTEAD existed in the mid-17th cent., but became fashionable in the 18th cent. Hampstead had its spa and also attracted a smart set of revellers. The reputation as a colony of artists came later. The Heath was always popular with the Cockney out for the day, and Karl Marx was also a constant visitor.

BLACKHEATH (7 inset–TQ3977). This high and windy common has been named and in use at least since 1381, when Wat Tyler's rebels gathered there before attacking London, and Jack Cade's followed suit in 1405. Early in the 17th cent. golf was introduced to England by James I on the course laid out on Blackheath. The club still exists but has moved. In the 18th cent. The Paragon, a fine Georgian crescent, was built on the south-east corner of the heath, and other Georgian houses are to be found in Dartmouth and Montpelier Rows. Near The Paragon is Morden College, which was built by Wren around 1700 at the behest of Sir John Morden, who was a rich merchant of Aleppo. It is and always has been not a college but an almshouse; it stands in its own grounds and has some Lely portraits. This handsome portion of a once-neglected suburb has recently become fashionable, and the old houses are expensive.

On the north side of the heath where it joins GREENWICH Park, Ranger's House also stands in its own grounds and is now a public tea-room. It is a pleasant, early-18th-cent. building with splendid rose gardens, and was once owned by the Earl of Chesterfield. Blackheath church has a spire of such refined height that it is sometimes called the "Needle of Kent". Regrettably the A2, the Dover road, cleaves a line right across the middle of Blackheath.

Blackheath: Morden College is an almshouse, designed by Sir Christopher Wren

A. F. Kersting

CHISWICK (7 inset–TQ2077). Apart from its flyover, Chiswick is notable for its Mall, William Hogarth's house, and Chiswick House. **Chiswick Mall** is a delightful stretch of riverside houses with balconies, railings and flowers and a feeling of privacy. St Nicholas Church stands at its west end, in which are the tombs of the 3rd Earl of Burlington, William Kent and Hogarth. The entrance to **Hogarth's House** is on the busy Great West Road; it has been preserved against all pressure of development.

Chiswick House, a little further W., was designed by Lord Burlington and embellished by William Kent, with a rotunda as the centre-piece and exterior stairways. It was intended as a meeting place, gallery, villa, not a home; that was the function of the Jacobean mansion long vanished. The house fell on hard times but was saved from demolition by the Ministry of Works. What stands now is the inspired result of 10 years' work of top craftsmen – wedding-cake cornices, velvet-covered walls, gilt decoration of fabulous intricacy make the place an architect's and designer's dream. On the ground floor, where Lord Burlington had his library and admitted only a favoured few, there is an excellent display of drawings showing the development of the villa.

The gardens, which were laid out to Kent's design, are now a public park, but lack the finish they deserve. The illustrated guide book is an elegant memento of a collector's piece.

CRYSTAL PALACE, THE, *Sydenham* (7 inset–TQ3470). A monster conservatory was opened at Upper Norwood in 1854, a rebuilding of Paxton's large hall for the 1851 Great Exhibition held in HYDE PARK. In 1936 it was destroyed by fire except for its two great water towers, which were demolished in 1940. The site is now a recreation centre and has facilities for a number of sports including motor racing.

DULWICH (7 inset–TQ3373). About 5 m. S. of the City, this is a most interesting example of London's early perimeter settlements. The core of it is actually called Dulwich Village. Basically one well-shaped street, it contains a pub and an eating-house and a number of delightful Georgian houses. A little way outside the village is **Dulwich College Picture Gallery** in Gallery Road. It was designed by Sir John Soane in 1814 and was the first public art gallery London could claim. Partially destroyed by a flying bomb in 1944, it was reopened 9 years later. It contains paintings from the French, Dutch, Italian, Spanish and British schools, but is strongest in Dutch. The original portraits of Elizabethan actors, often reproduced in books about Shakespeare and his period, are here.

Dulwich College, first called "The College of God's Gift", was founded by Edward Alleyn, 1566–1626. He was a leading Elizabethan actor and the rival of Shakespeare's leading player, Burbage. He became rich through his share in the Bear Garden in Southwark, where the savage spectacle of baiting bulls and bears was immensely popular. He spent his profits well on his bountiful foundations in Dulwich. These include a charming public park, which has a carriageway making a great uneven loop round a lake, and is full of rhododendrons and azaleas. Near the swimming-pool of the present College buildings,

Chiswick House was closely modelled on the Rotunda by Palladio at Vicenza

A. F. Kersting

Greenwich: the Royal Naval College

built in 1866, is the boat Shackleton used to make his rescue voyage over the Antarctic Sea. College Road, which leads to the CRYSTAL PALACE, has on it the last operative tollgate in London.

GREENWICH (7 inset–TQ4077) is nearly 6 m. down river. The boat trip through the Port of London is fascinating and much the best way to approach this ancient seafaring town. Royal Greenwich dates from the early 15th cent., when it was the Manor of Humphrey, Duke of Gloucester, who collected a great library; Margaret of Anjou lived there; Henry VII loved it; Henry VIII was born there, and so were his daughters, Mary and Elizabeth. He married twice there, and there signed Anne Boleyn's death warrant. Under Cromwell the palace decayed, but rebuilding was begun by Webb for Charles II. It was completed by Wren for William III, but Greenwich was no place for a man with asthma, so the four splendid quadrangles with their twin domes became the Greenwich Hospital, for disabled and aged naval pensioners. In 1873 the pensioners were moved and the building became the **Royal Naval College**. In it is the sumptuous Painted Hall, used now, as originally intended, as a dining-hall. Here the body of Nelson lay in state. There is also a chapel.

Between the two halves of the college there is a way, closed by two pairs of splendid wrought-iron gates, to the Queen's House, an elegant, economical little palace of 29 rooms designed by Inigo Jones. It was meant for Anne of Denmark, wife of James I, but she died and it was completed for Charles I's Henrietta Maria. Today it is part of the **National Maritime Museum**, and is linked to it by an open, colonnaded walk. Greenwich Park rises

behind to the old Royal Observatory, on the Greenwich Meridian, which now only keeps the time.

On the way back from the Observatory is the church of **St Alfege**, by Hawksmoor. Here General Wolfe and Thomas Tallis were buried, and Henry VIII was baptized. Alfege was an archbishop of Canterbury whom the Danes took prisoner and beat to death on the spot where the church now stands.

The old *Cutty Sark*, with her lovely tracery of rigging, and Sir Francis Chichester's valiant little *Gipsy Moth IV* are both permanently on view.

HAMPSTEAD AND HIGHGATE (7 inset– TQ785). These two are often associated, partly because they are linked on the map by the high-pitched road between them with wonderful views over London and the Home Counties, but more because they have similar personalities. Highgate is older. Rich people who fled the plague in 1665 settled in Highgate, but long before that Dick Whittington, who became Sir Richard and Lord Mayor of London, sat on Highgate Hill and listened to Bow Bells. There is a monument to him and his cat, put up in 1964. Francis Bacon died there in 1626. The poet Andrew Marvell (1621–78) had a house there. The best part of Highgate is an 18th-cent. village. It is full of unexpected corners and delightful Georgian residential roads, most notably the Grove at the top of the hill where several famous writers, including Coleridge, have lived. It also has the huge, hill-side cemetery with the tombs of Karl Marx and many other famous people. The vast Victorian mausolea are a wonderful example of the taste of

Hampton Court: a fine wrought-iron screen in the grounds

their time. **Waterlow Park**, which was the garden of Lauderdale House, now a refreshment room, once belonged to Charles II's notorious minister, the Duke of Lauderdale, who lent it to Nell Gwynn to the annoyance of the neighbours. The connecting road with Hampstead passes two famous inns, Jack Straw's Castle and the Spaniards. Both have gardens for refreshment in summer. Dickens liked to walk or ride out to Hampstead and take a chop at the former. The latter is mentioned in *The Pickwick Papers*.

Old Hampstead on the hilltop is also largely 18th-cent. It became fashionable on account of its wells, hence Flask Walk and Well Walk, where Keats and Constable lived. Keats spent more time in a house now called Lawn Bank, which used to be Wentworth Place when the present Keats Grove was called John Street. Lawn Bank has become the **Keats Memorial House** and contains many personal relics of the poet. **Fenton House**, built about 1693, is also open to the public and has a charming garden and a fine collection of furniture, porcelain and musical instruments. The public is admitted to **Kenwood**, halfway between Hampstead and Highgate. It was the seat of the Earl of Mansfield in the reign of George III, reconstructed by Robert Adam in 1767, given to the nation by Lord Iveagh in 1927, and houses a fine collection of paintings and furniture. In its magnificent grounds with their woods and a lake open-air concerts are given on summer evenings. The music comes across the water to crowds sitting on the hillside. No one visiting Hampstead should fail to see Church Row with its 18th-cent. church. The steep road from it to the summit of the Heath passes through the fascinating cluster of streets and old houses known as Hampstead Village. Famous residents were the great tragic actress, Sarah Siddons, the Victorian author and artist George du Maurier, and John Galsworthy.

HAMPTON COURT (7 inset–TQ1568). Henry VIII's image is stamped on Hampton Court and ambitious Cardinal Wolsey, who planned and built this great palace for himself, is chiefly acknowledged in a sign of a public house nearby. From the gatehouse the palace is magnificent; inside it is overwhelming. There is a vast amount to see, from the weapons arranged on the wall of the king's guardroom, to the marble washbasins in the queen's private chamber; from the enormous tapestries, to a Renaissance ceiling said to be the most perfect in the country. The wear and tear of sightseeing has left its mark: the interior is a little shabby, and the lighting far from adequate for viewing the remarkable collection of paintings. However, the recently restored Cumberland Suite is a model of lightness and brightness.

The gardens are renowned for their splendour. They are beautifully cared for and seen to advantage from the first floor of the palace. Here are a knot garden, a wilderness, a sunk garden and the fountain garden; tiltyard, orangery, great vine and maze have all to be seen. The royal stables are separated from the Palace by a busy road, but they are finely built in the same red brick as the palace. The chilly, lamp-lit passages leading to the kitchens and the cellar, where the servitors of the great led a life unimagined by those above stairs, convey a vivid sense of the past.

The river trip from Westminster takes about 4 hours.

Crown copyright

Osterley Park: the tapestry room

Strand-on-the-Green

Noel Habgood

HARLINGTON (7 inset–TQ0978) is immediately N. of LONDON AIRPORT reached from there on the A437 passing over the M4. It is the residue of a village, cut off from the open country to the S. by the motorway, hemmed in by new buildings and the railway on the N. It possesses, however, the Parish Church of SS. Peter and Paul with a much praised, much decorated Norman doorway. The rest of the church is not particularly impressive, although it has a number of interesting details.

HARMONDSWORTH (7 inset–TQ0678). Immediately adjacent to LONDON AIRPORT on the north-west corner, Harmondsworth village remains curiously calm, and unspoilt except for the noise. Its 13th-cent. church of St Mary has a Norman doorway, which is classed as top among the monuments of Middlesex. There is also a tithe barn, probably dating from the late 14th cent., when the manor belonged to William of Wykeham, who included it in his endowment of WINCHESTER College.

LONDON AIRPORT, *Heathrow* (7 inset–TQ 0777). The magic of Heathrow is not in its huge buildings by Frederick Gibberd. Aeroplanes can be watched from the roof garden of the Queen's Building, or through the windows of the observation lounge. For either place there is a small charge, varying according to season and the day of the week. The summer months offer the best value, but with 50 airlines operating through London, there is no dearth of entertainment. On this ground devoted to advanced technology, the remains of an Iron Age village were unearthed when the airport was built.

London Transport provides a 4½-hour afternoon trip from Victoria Coach Station, which tours the airfields, hangars and maintenance shops.

OSTERLEY PARK (7 inset–TQ1578). Built by Sir Thomas Gresham in the late 16th cent., Osterley was embellished by a later owner employing Robert Adam. The house stands in fine grounds, now a public park, with two conservatories and a long lake. Osterley still displays its Tudor origins in its red brick and corner towers. The most remarkable feature of the front elevation, however, is the work of Adam: an immense, pillared portico stands above wide, shallow steps. The inner courtyard is raised and the continuation into the entrance hall gives lightness and a Classical austerity. This is most effectively broken by the intricate decoration of the ceiling and cornices, and by the sharpness of the key-patterned floor tiles. Adam furniture and an Adam-designed carpet make the rooms magnificently uniform, except for the Long Gallery, which is earlier.

STRAND-ON-THE-GREEN (7 inset–TQ 2177), more correctly Strand-on-Green, by Kew Bridge, is a remnant of a waterside way of life with 18th- and 19th-cent. cottages and small houses

A. F. Kersting

Syon House: the Long Gallery designed by Robert Adam

now greatly coveted as period dwellings. Porches and walls are covered with trailing plants, clematis, passion flower and wistaria. Stepped-up doors remind that flood water needs to be kept at bay. There is a boat-builder's yard and such rewarding names as Magnolia Wharf, and Post Office Alley; at The City Barge you can sit at tables on the tow-path and enjoy everything but the planes passing overhead to and from LONDON AIRPORT.

SYON HOUSE, *Brentford* (7 inset–TQ1877). The name Syon was originally given to a monastery founded by Henry V. It was one of his attempts to expiate his father's sins. The original foundation was near Twickenham Bridge but later moved to the present site. At the Dissolution Syon became Crown property and in 1547 the Duke of Somerset, Protector of the young Edward VI, acquired it and began to build himself a house. He was presently accused of treason by John Dudley and executed. His accuser acquired Syon, and was created Earl of Northumberland. When the earldom became a dukedom in 1750, the 1st Duke employed Robert Adam to renovate and adorn the house. He was given a free hand: not only was the architecture adapted – one of the most delightful features is a vista obtained from one end of the house to the other and on into the gardens by Capability Brown – but

Adam was also responsible for all the decoration, the furniture, and a carpet in which the colour persists to this day. In the 19th cent. Syon suffered a Duke who refaced the Tudor brick, encasing the house in Bath stone. The general elevation is daunting, but makes the surprise of the interior the more enjoyable.

Syon has a Garden Centre selling plants and gardening equipment, and a rose garden, which is lovely, laid out by noted commercial growers.

In a disused church in Brentford High Street is the **Piano Museum,** an unusual collection of pianolas and other forms of automatic music. Concert demonstrations are given at weekends during the summer.

WIMBLEDON (7 inset–TQ2470). It could be claimed that Wimbledon is the longest established of London's suburban villages, because Caesar's Camp is marked on the Ordnance Survey maps in the south-west corner of the 1,045-acre Common. It is a pleasant area of silver-birch woods and heathland, with two ponds, a golf course and an 1817 windmill; in the High Street at the top of Wimbledon Hill, Eagle House is dated 1613. Wimbledon is synonymous with tennis, since the All England Lawn Tennis and Croquet Club holds its annual championships in June in Wimbledon Park.

The South-East

Surrey   Kent   Sussex

RICHARD CHURCH

South-East England covers a wider range than the three counties explored in the section of this book which it is my privilege to introduce. The Weathermen at the B.B.C. use a larger envelope when they discuss the weather daily, as it affects what they call the "south-east of the country". They include all that lies on the Continental side of a line from the Wash to Southampton. But for our purposes that is too vague and general. Each of the Home Counties has a personality of its own, even bits of Middlesex and Hertfordshire, as other sections of this *Guide* demonstrate. As for East Anglia; that is really a small nation unto itself, with a metropolis of its own, as every native of Norwich believes.

This local patriotism ensures a concise sense of pride and responsibility, something substantial and immediate. It need not be hostile; indeed, it can be benevolent and hospitable, based on the assurance of a place of one's own. It gives civic pride a touch of religious mystery. To hold that state of mind about a vast and ill-defined mass of the earth's surface is impossible. That is why empires fall apart, after much ill-feeling and injustice. It is not so with small communities, conditioned by their local geography, weather, natural advantages and difficulties.

That is why I see Surrey, Sussex and Kent as a complex which is also a simplicity. That simplicity is a matter of contours. Of course, a geologist would object that these contours held in common by the three counties are in fact extremely involved, because they present stratum upon stratum of sub-structure turned up like the edges of a saucer, thus exposing horizontally along the northern and southern edges of the counties a sort of geological synopsis of the evolution of the earth's crust. So many different kinds of soil are exposed, each with its unique flora and fauna.

Ages ago this east-west horizontality was an alpine range. Time has eroded the mountain tops, decaying those great molars. The long cavity left (what we now call the Weald) became one vast forest, called by our forefathers the Forest of Anderida. It stretched westward from the fall behind the turn of the Downs behind Dover and Folkestone, for a hundred and forty miles or more, into Hampshire. Bits of it remain, relics of the royal hunting lands commandeered by the Norman kings who introduced the feudal system.

The differences between the three counties were less in the Middle Ages, when that almost unbroken forest gave them a sylvan uniformity. The New Forest in Hampshire is a ghostly survival of that era, and even in patches of Surrey commons, and in the Ashdown Forest in mid-Sussex, as well as in still smaller fragments dotted about the Kentish Weald, the primeval sameness can still be found, like tiny shards of pottery on an archaeological site. Yet, even as late as the reign of Edward III we learn that when he made one of his Royal Progresses he had to employ no less than twenty-two guides to lead the way southward through the Forest from London to Rye. It is impossible to conceive today what the solitude must have meant, in an England of little more than two million souls in all. Nature still predominated; the fox, the wild-cat, maybe the wolf, were still formidable rivals to man, who was settling here and there, gradually cutting out "denes" in the Forest, where he could maintain a few domestic animals, mainly the pig, and expand a primitive agriculture. In such a country and in such social circumstances, outlaws could elude justice indefinitely. Also, honest men, and those with energy and enterprise towards more massive territorial exploitation, needed to surround themselves with their own defences: moats, castles, larger settlements which became communities under the dominance of an overlord. Relics of that way of life survive today through the three counties. Most of them can be visited with some intimacy, because their owners can no longer maintain them as private property served by dozens or even hundreds of retainers. The National Trust now maintains most of the great country houses and castles originally established on the natural wealth of the three counties. Many of them are world famous: Knole, Polesden Lacey, Sissinghurst Castle, Penshurst Place.

It is, however, the anonymous folk who have left the most pervasive mark. The farmers, the quarrymen, the smiths and the carpenters have gradually moulded nature into the pattern of civilization which still exercises a shaping authority over acres into which time and continued social practice sub-divided that wilderness on which Julius Caesar stared so acquisitively. Celt, Roman, Saxon and Jute, Frank and Norman, all played their part in taming this wilderness. Their closely intermingled descendants today are continuing the process, not altogether wisely or reverently, as the numbers grow and in that growth become less closely rooted and more mobile, making greater and greedier demands upon the natural resources of this small south-east corner of the island, its waters, its woods, its aesthetic attractions.

Those demands have gone on for a long time. The soil beneath the medieval Forest has always been rich in iron. East Kent is also veined at a great depth with coal that runs out under the sea-bed. For centuries the Weald was therefore the Black Country of England. The indigenous oaks of the Forests were cut down and roasted into charcoal, to be used to smelt the ore. Foundries were small, primitive, but they supplied the iron for the armour and the weapons which were the tools of so much famous, and infamous, conquest as English blood was spilt to make English history and tradition. The oaks, too, supplied the timber that built the wooden ships, until in the early nineteenth century the Royal Navy and most of the merchant navy became ironclad. Queen Elizabeth I, no doubt advised by her shrewd economist Cecil, had to make a law rationing the felling of oaks in the Wealden forests, which were already fragmented among the agricultural clearings and the growth of towns and villages.

This industry of iron-founding in the Weald has vanished, leaving only place names and craft names, such as Hammer-pond and Furnace Mill. The last iron-foundry to close down was the Gloucester Forge at Lamberhurst, an exquisite village that stands on the frontier between Kent and Sussex, on the A21 road to Hastings. The forge ceased work in 1765. The railings round Christopher Wren's St Paul's Cathedral were forged there: a massive job that weighed two hundred tons and cost eleven thousand pounds. After that, the iron-founding industry followed the coal-mines of the Midlands and the North, and the only evidence of iron today is to be seen in the tiny trickles of rust-coloured water staining the ditches beneath the hedgerows canopied by wild rose, honeysuckle and bramble. But the iron still lies in the sub-soil, giving vitality to the fruit, hops and cereals whose quality and abundance have made Kent "the Garden of England".

Great fortunes were made in the past by the ironmasters; and the houses built by them in village, town and open country from the fifteenth to the eighteenth centuries survive today, rivals in beauty and dignity to those other symbols of affluence, the mansions of the weavers. Edward III invited master craftsmen from Flanders to settle in England during the fourteenth century, and they brought with them not only their superior skill in the weaving industry, but other sophistications domestic and civic, in building and furnishing. They settled in Cranbrook first, and began by rebuilding the church, which is still called "the Cathedral of the Weald".

In the Medici palace in Florence there is a map-room, with the maps done in tempera on the walls. That of England shows Kent. The towns named on it are Canterbury, Dover, Rochester and – Cranbrook. The Medicis financed most of the woollen industry of Europe, and the "florins" flowed into Kent, enriching not only Cranbrook but smaller villages strung along the Weald: Tenterden, Biddenden, Smarden, Goudhurst, all of which can show today one or more noble houses, with the weaving hall, built by the Flemish masters of the craft. The activity flowed westward into Sussex, as also did the iron-founding. At Burwash, well over the border on the road to Lewes from Lamberhurst, magnificent examples of both ironmasters' and weavers' houses are to be seen. One of them, called Bateman's, was the home of Rudyard Kipling. The Hussey family made its wealth in Burwash, and built a noble mansion at the opening of the High Street. The present representative of that family, the architect Christopher Hussey, lives at Scotney Castle, near Lamberhurst. This is worth a visit, because the fourteenth-century castle stands in a moat fed by the stream which marks the boundary between Kent and Sussex. Old maps show the whole castle as being in Sussex, but today Kent claims it. Indeed, from that point southward, down to the Romney Marsh and the coast, the boundary line becomes convulsive. I suspect it of changing overnight, and in all my explorations down there in what I would call the uplands rising from the Marsh I have never been sure from one mile to another in which county I stood.

I have said that geographically the three counties are similarly structured, each carrying its part of the North Downs, the Weald with its middle ridge, and the South Downs that form the sea-board rim of the great east-west stretch of the Weald, which has always been one of the richest parts of England. Their situation close to the Continent has meant cultural and commercial contact. Their rich variety of soils is due to the up-turning of the sub-strata: chalk, various kinds of clay, and that fruit-loving stuff called "Hastings Bed". All these advantages have been common to the three counties since the beginning of our history.

Yet the natives are in some indefinable way distinct from each other, county by county. They maintain a certain rivalry, about nothing in particular. It is merely that a native of Surrey does not want to be mistaken for a native of Sussex, or for either a Kentish Man or a Man of Kent. That last reference suggests that even within Kent itself there is a division. It is real enough, because there is a Society of Kentish Men and Men of Kent. We are not very precise about the cleavage, but roughly speaking Kentish Men are native west of the River Medway, and Men of Kent east of that famous tributary of the Thames. Maidstone, the capital, stands on the Medway, and does much to pollute it. Above Maidstone the river with its several sub-tributaries is idyllic, from its springs near Edenbridge, through Tonbridge, where it meanders through meadows as serenely as Izaak Walton's prose wanders through *The Compleat Angler*. But after leaving Maidstone the Medway

Oast houses and apple blossom in Kent   Jane J. Miller loses its rural peace and becomes commercial; and later, at Rochester and Chatham, it is merged into the semi-marine estuary of the Thames, amid a confusion of channels round the Isle of Sheppey.

East Kent, thus given a riparian definition, is a world unto itself, as also is Romney Marsh. Its people are said to be descendants of the Jutes who came at a later date than the Anglo-Saxons. Part of their land was once an island, Thanet, on the seaward side of the North Downs where they turn downward across the county to end at Dover and Folkestone cliffs, whose white bastions at the gateway into England gave us our name of Albion. There is a great gap in the Downs at Ashford, which leads into Thanet, where one can meet these Jutish colonists. They are uncommonly hospitable folk, with just that shade of difference in approach to distinguish them from the Kentish Men, and still more, of course, from the natives and settlers of Surrey and Sussex, about whom I could offer infinite psychological sub-divisions due to their incessant inhuming of blood not only from London but also from the rest of Great Britain. For Surrey and Sussex are counties beloved of people towards the retiring age. Both offer amenities, natural and social.

Surrey, even though much of it has been swallowed into suburban London, is by the grace of nature an exquisite countryside. It may be troublesome to the farmer, because of its tendency to laze into sandy commonland. But what a playground for townsfolk that commonland can be. The North Downs reach their highest point at Leith Hill, and Box Hill is not much inferior. Under the shadow of the latter lived George Meredith, and in an inn nearby the poet John Keats, in 1816, finished his boyish epic poem *Endymion*.

Nowadays, the elaborate network of motorways around Leatherhead has driven the furtive River Mole still further underground, and somewhat isolated Box Hill from its southern slope. Even so, this is a countryside characteristic of the almost dainty prettiness of Surrey, with its silver birches, its commons golden with broom and gorse, its pine trees set as wind-breaks, its wide panoramas which throughout the county invite the townsman to an uplift of heart and involuntary deep-breathing, greedy for the fragrant air combined of sea-drift and pine-sap.

One of the most inspiring of these vistas is at the Kentish border of the county, above the lovely village of Limpsfield, looking from the top of Titsey Hill southward to the bare Downs which are its sea-wall. There was a Roman villa at Titsey, besides a spring. It is interesting to note that in the Black Forest, in Germany, near Freiburg, there is a mountain lake called Titisee. It means "fairy water". The slopes of Titsey Park justify that derivation.

I have said nothing about the Thames shore of Surrey, with its string of riverside towns and relics, the last of the Elizabethan palaces at Richmond, with the Royal Park, and the scene immortalized by Turner, from a spot where the Scottish poet James Thomson in the eighteenth century wrote *The Seasons*. Up the southern slopes of the Thames valley, through pine woods and over sandy commons, the scene towards Sussex and the felted South Downs, whose flora fits them like a glove, is a heartening sight, especially to the town-dweller. Even one's lungs exult.

Guildford is somewhat puzzled by its traffic problem, but the new cathedral stands aloof on its hill outside the town, and soon the university will be its neighbour, and let us hope, its consort in a world reviving from the deathly sickness of go-getting and materialism. There is going but not go-getting in the spacious landscape seen from the Hog's Back, and along the further ridge into Hampshire. That sight gives us a sense of escape from our own affairs and ambitions. It offers a perspective line, not only in fact but in the human spirit. We feel the same exhilaration as we go southward into Sussex, either from that end of Surrey into West Sussex, or from the Kentish frontier into East Sussex, which is of a different character from its other half-county.

West Sussex is close, intimate, lush and opulent, with its hills steep and huddled, closing in on its narrow valleys or "hangers". Round about Midhurst, Petersfield (again where county boundaries are confused), the Hartings – all this area shuts the traveller into "a green thought in a green shade". But travelling eastward from there, along mid-county, the landscape opens out and the Ashdown Forest spreads like moorland, an up-rising from the Weald; to the north the uplands of the wooded Downs, to the south the South Downs which I have rightly described as "felted", though, since the needs of the last war required more ploughing, much of that gloved surface has been broken into by agriculture.

Even so, the general character of the Downs, sung by Hilaire Belloc, Richard Jefferies, W. H. Hudson and Kipling, survives as something primeval, close-cropped by the centuries. That skin of the South Downs smells of timelessness. It is all in miniature, inch by inch, as it flows in vast folds, swirling round Chancton-bury Ring and other landmarks. Examine it, and see it in all its open secrecy, another of nature's paradoxes: the tiny herbs that utter perfume as you tread on them, thyme, mints, stunted heather and dwarfed fennel. The harebell (which is the "bluebell of Scotland") trembles there as the sea-breeze whiffles through the turf. You can leave the car at any road-end against the northern slopes, and walk as freely as in the Peak or the Pennines, with the advantage of a greater fragrance.

I have said nothing about one outstanding feature of the three counties – their coastline. Surrey's is limited to a fresh-water one, the banks of the Thames. But this has its glories and a tiny literature of its own, notably Jerome's *Three Men in a Boat*. Sussex coastline has much to boast of: Brighton, Bexhill, Eastbourne, Hastings; and I would even include Newhaven, which has a sleazy quality of its own. But the Lanes of Brighton and its Royal Pavilion, as well as the old fishing-sheds on the unfashionable end of the front of Hastings, are worth collecting by the connoisseur, except that they are not transportable. Both Brighton and Hastings, too, have a tonic quality in the air that braces up the visitor even after an afternoon's visit. It was this halogenic touch in the air, the ozone, the iodine, that persuaded Mrs Fitzherbert to bring her Royal morganatic consort here for the betterment of his gout.

Hastings, with Battle behind it, dated 1066, lies eastward, and further still we come to the complex of the Marshes of Walland and Romney, and into Kent again, with its seaside towns in profusion, notably Folkestone, which in another book I have called the Nice of the North, because of its magnificent sea-front, the Leas. And Dover? But Dover is the doorway, inward and outward, to Britain and the rest of the world, even in this age of air-travel. Its Castle claims that office, and I wish I could stand on its ramparts, above the cliff, and blow my Introduction like a trumpet, heralding the three counties that stand nearest to the rest of the inhabited world that begins, and ends, at Calais.

The South-East: Gazetteer

JOHN AND ANNE MASON

ABINGER HAMMER, *Surrey* (6–TQ0947), with the neighbouring village of Abinger Common, lies in some of the most delightful wooded land in the county. It is notable for the clock which juts out over the DORKING–GUILDFORD Road, and on which the figure of a blacksmith strikes the hours on a bell; it bears the inscription, "By me you know how fast to go".

The "hammer" in the name is a reminder that the village was in the Sussex iron-forging district.

In the neighbourhood are the remains of a Roman villa, and in a lonely spot is a granite cross where Bishop Wilberforce, son of the great reformer William Wilberforce, was killed in a riding accident in 1873.

ALFRISTON, *Sussex* (6–TQ5103). An ancient town which has among its treasures the first building to be acquired by the National Trust: the 14th-cent. Priests', or Clergy, House, an example of a pre-Reformation vicarage. It is a half-timbered and wattle-and-daub building which had fallen into decay at the turn of this century, but judicious restoration has left it much as it was originally, including a clay floor and soot-blackened timbers. These are original, although re-roofing was necessary when the house came into the keeping of the National Trust. It is open throughout the year.

The parish church stands on an ancient Anglo-Saxon mound, and is often referred to as the "Cathedral of the Downs". It dates mostly from the 14th cent. and has a central shingle spire in the form of a Greek cross. Internally it is of fine proportions, with lofty 14th-cent. arches and piers, triple sedilia, three piscinas and a fine sculptured reredos.

The Star Inn is one of the oldest in England, dating from the 15th cent. An outstanding feature of this hostelry is its magnificently carved woodwork. The village also has the stump of a medieval market cross and a number of picturesque old buildings.

Not far from the village an Anglo-Saxon burial place was discovered during a building operation. More than 100 graves were excavated and skeletons and a variety of objects uncovered; many of these are now to be seen in the Barbican House Museum in LEWES.

ALLHALLOWS, *Kent* (7–TQ8377). A small holiday resort on the Thames Estuary. Here, at the mouth of the Yantlet Creek, stands a stone obelisk marking the limit of the authority of

the Port of London over the River Thames. Nearby is an iron beacon erected in Elizabethan times, one of the many set up to warn of threatened invasion. The former railway station (it was of very modern design when built in 1932) is now the unusual site of a shop. The line was closed down when the expected tourist traffic failed to materialize. Parts of the church date from the 12th cent.

AMBERLEY, *Sussex* (6–TQ0313). Another of the many Sussex villages that have kept their character, with many old cottages, some thatched. Amberley Castle was originally built in the Norman period. It became the residence of the Bishops of Chichester and was dismantled by the Parliamentarians during the Civil War. The towered gatehouse dates from the 14th cent.

The church retains some Norman features, but dates mainly from the 13th and 14th cents.

ANGMERING-ON-SEA, *Sussex* (6–TQ 0704). A pleasant seaside place with a good beach and the well-known country club of Ham Manor, with an excellent golf course. The village of Angmering, about 2 m. W., preserves something of its old character. It has many old houses. One of these is Pigeon House, a medieval yeoman's homestead, now under the care of the Sussex Archaeological Trust.

The parish church was rebuilt in 1852, but part of the chancel, including the arch, remains from the 12th cent.

ARDINGLY, *Sussex* (6–TQ3429). Near here is Wakehurst Place, a 462-acre estate which has been a branch of KEW GARDENS since 1965. This estate has been used to relieve the congestion at the Royal Botanic Gardens and to provide an environment with purer air than the original establishment. About 100 acres are now cultivated gardens, and the remainder is woodland. Although, like Kew, these gardens are primarily for scientific and experimental work, they are open to the public daily throughout the year.

The property was originally held by the Wakehurst family from the early 12th cent. to the mid-15th cent. It then passed to the powerful Culpeper family who held it until the end of the 17th cent. This family built the mansion (not open to the public) in 1590. After the Culpepers the property passed through several hands until it was bought by Gerald Loder, later Lord Wakehurst, at the turn of the century. He spent a great part of his life developing and improving its natural beauty.

G. Douglas Bolton

Abinger Hammer: the clock on which the figure
of a blacksmith strikes the hours

Noel Habgood

Alfriston church stands on an ancient Anglo-Saxon
site with its central shingle spire

ARUNDEL, *Sussex* (6–TQ0107). A pleasant
town on the River Arun, dominated by the great
bulk of Arundel Castle. The town is an ancient
one and was prominent in pre-Conquest times,
but its buildings are now generally of the Victorian
era, although some much older ones remain,
including a coaching inn in the High Street. There
is a fine park covering more than 1,000 acres, and
the river offers excellent fishing. There has been a
bridge over the river here since ancient times, but
the present stone bridge was built in 1935.

Arundel Castle is picturesque, much restored,
rebuilt and altered; in its present form, said to
approach its medieval magnificence, it is often
described as a smaller edition of Windsor Castle.
It has for more than 500 years been the home of
the Fitzalan family, Earls of Arundel, and through
female descent the Howard family, Dukes of
Norfolk (the names were combined in 1842),
premier peers and hereditary Earls Marshal of
England. A castle stood on this site before the
Conquest, but the oldest parts of the present
building date from Norman times. The castle
underwent several sieges and was extensively
damaged during the Civil War, when it was
bombarded by the Parliamentary forces, and
during their subsequent occupation of it. Afterwards it fell into a dilapidated state until it was
largely rebuilt in the 18th cent. Late in the 19th
cent. it was again restored and rebuilt and two
towers added by the 15th Duke, father of the
Earl Marshal who was responsible for organizing
the coronation of Elizabeth II.

The rebuilding was carried out in magnificent
style. Particularly is this notable in the Baron's
Hall, a splendid reproduction of a medieval hall.
Throughout there is much fine carving and
Victorian reconstruction of the early English
Gothic. The library, built early in the 19th cent.,
is 117 ft long by 35 ft wide and constructed entirely
of Honduras mahogany, one of the first usages of
that timber in this country. Around the room are
a number of chairs dating from the William and
Mary to the Regency periods. There are many
fine examples of period furniture and furnishings
throughout the castle, some dating from the 15th
cent. One sumptuous Victorian room contains a
bed and matching furniture specially designed
and made for the visit of Queen Victoria and
Prince Albert in 1846.

The castle is also rich in art treasures, and
contains a collection which includes works by
Van Dyck, Gainsborough and Reynolds. In the
long art gallery are hung the portraits of Earls of
Arundel and Dukes of Norfolk arranged in
chronological order. The domestic chapel was
built at the turn of this century in Early English
Gothic style. The slender pillars are of Purbeck
marble and carry beautiful leaf-carving; the
stained glass is modern. The Fitzalan chapel is
part of the parish church (see below).

The castle is open to the public at advertised
times in the summer season.

The Parish Church of St Nicholas was pulled
down some time after 1349 and the Black Death
and rebuilt in 1380; it is a fairly complete example
of Early English architecture. On the walls are
traces of medieval murals, including the Coronation of Our Lady, the Seven Works of Mercy and
the Seven Deadly Sins.

An unusual feature of the church is that though
it is the Anglican parish church, one end of it is
the Fitzalan Chapel, where Roman Catholic
services are held, the Fitzalan-Howard family
being Catholic. The chapel fell into disrepair
after the Dissolution of the Monasteries by
Henry VIII, and was further damaged and desecrated by the Parliamentary soldiers during the

Civil War. It was restored to its original beauty and purpose in 1886 by the 15th Duke. Here can be seen many of the tombs of the Earls of Arundel and Dukes of Norfolk, and a bronze monument to the 15th Duke.

Until recently the two sections were separated by a brick wall which was erected in 1880 following an unfortunate law-suit. The then vicar of St Nicholas claimed the chapel as part of his church; he lost the case and the duke caused the wall to be built. This wall has now been removed and replaced by a clear partition. This chapel can be entered from the castle and is included in the castle tour.

Up the street from the parish church stands the Roman Catholic Cathedral of Our Lady and St Philip Neri. It was built in grandiose French Gothic style between 1869 and 1873, and was dedicated to St Philip Neri. It seemed very large for a parish church for a town of this size. However, when the bishopric of Arundel and Brighton was created in 1965, Arundel was chosen as the seat and the church became a cathedral in fact as well as dimension. The cathedral gives an impression of spaciousness and light, with some fine modern stained-glass windows. Six splendid pointed arches divide the aisles from the nave, which has a length of 97 ft and a width of 33 ft, each of the aisles being 12 ft wide. The groined vaulted ceiling of the nave is composed of bands of chalk and stone, and decorated with carved foliage.

ASHBURNHAM, *Sussex* (7–TQ6914). The last place where the centuries-old Sussex iron industry flourished; its iron-foundry closed in the early 1800s. It is notable for the beauty of its countryside and the great park of Ashburnham, laid out by Capability Brown and more than 1,000 acres in area, with dense woods of oak and beech, and pastureland broken up by clumps of tall trees. Two lakes adorn the front of Ashburnham Place, for many years the seat of the Earls of Ashburnham; it was inherited by the Rev. John Bickersteth and now houses the Ashburnham Christian Trust, partly in new buildings.

The Parish Church of St Peter dates mainly from the 17th cent. when it was rebuilt, but there are parts dating from the two previous centuries. The tower is Perpendicular. The font, pulpit and box pews are 17th-cent., as are the iron screens and the panelled waggon roof.

ASHFORD, *Kent* (7–TR0142). A village that became a major railway junction with important workshops and so grew into a busy commercial centre.

The town is noted for its regular cattle auctions and the Cattle Show, one of the oldest in the country; perhaps as important as the cattle are the Romney Marsh sheep.

AYLESFORD, *Kent* (7–TQ7359). On the MEDWAY, 3 m. from MAIDSTONE, this village has kept much of its old character although so close to the county town. It has a number of old houses

and a restored medieval stone bridge spans the river. Aylesford has large paper-mills.

On the outskirts of the village is the Carmelite Friary. The monastery was dissolved by Henry VIII but the Carmelites returned in 1949, the first of the dissolved orders to come back to their own home and find portions of it still under the same roof as when they left. During their 400-year absence some of the buildings had been pulled down and others allowed to decay; extensive repairs were needed on their return. However, much of the old fabric remains from the 14th and 15th cents., with some traces of 13th-cent. work still visible. Although restored and re-roofed the 15th-cent. Pilgrims' Hall, where medieval guests received hospitality, is structurally little altered, and is today, appropriately, the guests' dining-hall. The modern furniture was made by the brothers and lay-craftsmen in the friary's own workshop. They also make excellent pottery ware and statuary for sale.

Notable is the modern piazza which can hold a congregation of 2,000 pilgrims. Modern mosaics have been beautifully used at the back of the altar. The monastery guest-house can accommodate 80 guests and is open to all, regardless of denomination.

The triumphant return of the Order to its ancient home is expressed by the inscription over the entrance to the main courtyard: "The flower of Carmel once cut down now flourishes more luxuriantly than ever."

About 1 m. N. on a low hill is the spectacular megalithic monument known as **Kit's Coty House**. This is the exposed burial chamber of a Neolithic long barrow and is probably at least 5,000 years old. The burial mound has long since disappeared but the dolmens remain, one great stone forming the roof, with three mighty supports. It is the finest prehistoric monument of its type in Kent.

BARFRESTON, *Kent* (7–TR2650). A small village notable for its Norman church. Built in the 12th cent. its chief distinction is the richness and quantity of carving and moulding, similar in style to that of CANTERBURY and ROCHESTER Cathedrals. It was probably by the craftsmen who worked on those cathedrals, or others of the same school. The carvings include a king's head, St Thomas à Becket in full regalia, and numerous animals. Many of the figures illustrate customs and habits of the day.

Why so much skilled work should have been put into a small church in a remote area has never been explained, but Barfreston repays a visit for this alone.

BATTLE, *Sussex* (7–TQ7416). A town built on the site of one of the most momentous events in British history, the Battle of HASTINGS, when William the Norman defeated Harold II and thus became the Conqueror and King of England. The thriving town is dominated by the massive gatehouse of the Abbey which stands on a rise at the head of the High Street. Battle contains many old buildings, some dating back to the 13th and 14th cents., but the main interest centres around the Abbey and the historic events of 1066.

The origins of the Abbey date back to the day of the battle when William vowed that he would build a church on the site if God gave him victory. This he did, having the high altar set up on the spot where Harold fell. Subsequently Benedictine monks built an abbey close by. With the dissolution of the monasteries by Henry VIII, Battle Abbey was granted to his Master of Horse, Sir Anthony Browne, who pulled down much of the existing buildings and converted the abbot's lodgings into a private house. The house, much restored, is now a girls' school, but the grounds and buildings, except the school, are open to the public all the year.

Of the church built by William nothing remains above ground, but some traces have been excavated and the plan of its foundations is quite clear. On the site of the high altar stands Harold's Stone, erected by members of the Souvenir Normande who visited Battle in 1903. The refectory built by the Benedictines still stands, roofless, but otherwise well preserved. The impressive gateway has survived largely in its original state.

Those interested in the battle itself can easily form an idea of how the opposing armies were disposed. The details are well known: William marched from Hastings and took up a position on a hill about 400 yds S. of the English army, drawn up on a higher hill. After unsuccessful uphill charges on the English shield-wall, the Normans retreated. The English pursued them, abandoning their good defensive position. Seeing this, William rallied his men, who turned and destroyed the English forces. Harold, already wounded, was despatched by Norman knights.

The terrace of the abbey is, perhaps, the best vantage point; this was the Senlac Hill on which the English took up their positions, their lines running for about 800 yds E. to W. The terrace overlooks a deep gully, where there is now a farm, between the two positions, and about 400 yds S. is the lower hillock on which the Norman forces were drawn up. It can be seen from the terrain why the early charges of the Norman knights in their heavy armour were unsuccessful. Beyond the site of the Norman line is a higher hill, Telham Hill, where William established an advance post, and from where his scouts first reported the approach of Harold and his English army.

From the top of the abbey wall near the Harold Stone there is a good view over the town and a deep gully beyond, the scene of the English retreat after the Normans had broken through their positions. Along the Hastings Road, which skirts

Barfreston: Norman carving over the church doorway

Bodiam Castle stands in a lake-like moat

the abbey wall, there is a railway bridge which marks the approximate position from where William commanded his forces. From about 100 yds W. of this is a good view over the intervening ground and the English positions, now partly obscured by trees and buildings.

The Battle Historical Society's Museum, in Langton House, contains a wide variety of exhibits dealing with Sussex history from the Neolithic Age to the present day; especially comprehensive is the fine collection of examples of the Sussex iron industry which flourished for more than 1,000 years. There are mementoes of the Conquest period including a half-scale reproduction of the Bayeux Tapestry made in 1821.

The parish church, St Mary's, dates in part from the 14th and 15th cents. It was tastefully restored in 1869.

Another important event, the Gunpowder Plot, is annually celebrated in Battle. The firework displays and processions on 5 November are most spectacular.

BENTLEY WILDFOWL COLLECTION, Sussex (6–TQ4817).

This consists of over 700 wildfowl representing more than 100 species, kept in a 23-acre park near Halland. The collection was started with the object of helping to preserve many types of birds and has proved a great attraction to ornithologists and nature lovers. Here the birds can be seen in natural surroundings under conditions as near as possible to their native habitat: the park contains a variety of suitable trees and shrubs, as well as small lakes, pools and pens.

Included here are birds from Asia, Britain and Europe, North and South America, Iceland, Australia and New Zealand.

In the Pump House are paintings of the park's denizens; these make interesting pictures and help visitors identify the birds they see in the park.

The collection is open to view at advertised times in the summer season.

BEXHILL-ON-SEA, Sussex (7–TQ7407).

A popular seaside resort, with good sand beaches. It has the usual resort amenities and all kinds of recreation and sport: bowls, golf, riding and yachting. There is an excellent yacht club, and first-class angling in the sea, the River Rother, and in local reservoirs. A feature is the De la Warr Pavilion, designed in 1935–6 by the former Bauhaus architects Mendelsohn and Chermayeff. It contains a theatre which seats 1,200, also a ballroom, banqueting suite, restaurant and sun terrace.

A popular annual event is the summer Festival of Music, which includes morning lectures on music.

BIDDENDEN, Kent (7–TQ8538).

On the corner of the High Street and the A262 is a tiny green with a sign showing the figures of two women apparently joined together. These are the Biddenden Maids, who, legend says, were Siamese twins named Chulkhurst, born here in 1100 (only the date is rather unlikely and may have been a misreading for 1400 or 1500 in an early document), joined at the shoulder and hip. On their death 34 years later they left the income from their property to provide bread and cheese for the poor. Their benefaction is remembered in the Chulkhurst Charity: every Easter Monday old age pensioners who present themselves at the Old Workhouse receive a gift of bread and cheese, and any visitor to the town on that day may receive a special commemorative biscuit.

The charity was originally distributed from the parish church at the end of the High Street and it was not until late in the 19th cent. that the ceremony was moved to the Old Workhouse. The parish church dates in part from the 13th cent. It has a late 14th- or early 15th-cent. tower and the roof is 16th-cent. There is a 13th-cent. font.

A few minutes' walk from the church is the Old Workhouse, or Bread and Cheese House as it is called locally. It was built in the 15th cent. and rebuilt in the 16th. Late in the 18th cent. it was remodelled and converted into the present almshouses.

On the main road is the 15th-cent. Woolhouse. Although much restored, it preserves its ancient character.

The High Street, which leads off the main road, is lined with 15th-cent. houses and shops, originally the homes of Flemish weavers who set up here some 500 years ago. The buildings received new fronts in the 18th and 19th cents.; as they have been declared Ancient Monuments, these houses will keep their original structural form, and the High Street its beauty, enhanced by the original pavements of Bethersden marble.

BIGGIN HILL, *Kent* (6–TQ4159). The interest of Biggin Hill lies in the fact that it was one of the main, and perhaps the best known, of the R.A.F. fighter stations in the Battle of Britain. Today it is the scene of one of the most spectacular air shows in the country.

BIGNOR ROMAN VILLA, *Sussex* (6–SU 9814). This Roman villa, discovered near the hamlet of Bignor in 1811, is one of the largest in Britain, and contains mosaics which are among the finest yet uncovered in this country. It consisted of 70 buildings in a walled enclosure of about 4½ acres, and is thought to have been the house of an estate of some 2,000 acres, certainly the home of a very prosperous person. The building of the villa (following earlier wooden buildings) is believed to have been started about the end of the 2nd cent. A.D., with numerous later additions, and it is thought to have been occupied until the end of the 4th cent. and perhaps the beginning of the 5th cent. Unlike most Roman villas uncovered in Britain it does not appear to have been burnt or sacked by raiders, but more likely just fell into decay.

After the excavation most of the rooms were covered up again, and others were given hutted structures for protection. The walls of most of them were excavated up to 2 ft above the original ground-level; these were restored and built up to full height, the original Roman materials being largely used for this. They were then roofed over. Today, at first glance, the whole ensemble has the appearance of a group of farm buildings, but inside there is laid out a vivid impression of the splendour of the home of a well-to-do Roman or Romano-Briton.

In some instances the mosaics are much as they were found, but others which were in a poorer condition have been skilfully restored, mainly with the same materials as the originals. The mosaics are made up of tesserae ranging from cubes of about 1 in. to tiny pieces no more than 1/5 and 1/6 of an in. The designs depict the usual subjects popular with the Romans: legends, heads of goddesses – that in the Venus room is a particularly striking example – geometric designs. One mosaic shows the various stages in a contest of gladiators rather in the manner of a strip cartoon.

A tour of the villa shows the home comforts enjoyed by the Romans, but not to be known again for more than 1,000 years after the fall of their empire. One room clearly shows their efficient central heating: there is a flue enclosed in the base of the original wall which would have been part of a complete system of ducts carrying hot air from a furnace beneath the floor all through the house. In another room is a piscina about 18 in. deep, and while there is no evidence of how the water was fed into it, there is a lead outlet pipe which has been traced underground, ending some distance away from the building and emptying the waste water into some kind of repository. Many other refinements that were unknown through medieval times and much later periods are also evident here.

One of the excavated rooms is maintained as a museum, and here are displayed many of the finds from the excavations: household items; coins ranging in date from the 1st cent. A.D. to the second half of the 4th cent.; and some animal bones and skulls found on the site. There is also a model showing the villa as experts consider it would have looked at the height of its prosperity.

BILLINGSHURST, *Sussex* (6–TQ0825). This pleasantly situated village is chiefly notable for groups of old cottages in its two main streets. The parish church is Norman in origin but the oldest parts still existing are the tower and Lady Chapel, both dating from the 13th cent. The 15th-cent. nave roof has more than 100 carved bosses.

Five m. SE. of the village is **Shipley** where stands the only remaining working smock mill in West Sussex. Built in 1879, it was the property of novelist Hilaire Belloc and was restored in 1957 as a memorial to him. It is now owned by his daughter and is open to the public on certain weekends, but parties may arrange to visit it by written appointment.

BISLEY, *Surrey* (6–SU9559). Famous as the home of the National Rifle Association, and for its finely appointed rifle ranges. Here are held the annual rifle shooting competitions of which the most important is the King's Prize; this draws first-class shots from all over the Commonwealth. The small village church dates from the 13th cent. but it was much restored in the 19th cent.

BODIAM CASTLE, *Sussex* (7–TQ7826). Few castles are so beautifully set as Bodiam, 10 m. NW. of WINCHELSEA. It stands in a lake-like moat covered with water lilies, and almost seems to float on the water. The last of the military

Noel Habgood

Bosham harbour

castles to be built in England, it was constructed in 1385 by licence of Richard II as a measure against possible invasion from France. The castle was not put to the test at that time, though it did see military action twice – and quickly surrendered on each occasion. The second of these was when General Waller's Parliamentary army besieged it during the Civil War. Waller "slighted" the castle, since when it has never been inhabited, and it fell into decay. It was rescued and preserved by Lord Curzon of Kedleston who bequeathed it to the nation in 1925.

Seen from the outside the castle looks to be just as it was originally, complete and habitable – but inside it is a roofless, though well-preserved ruin. The courtyard is now a lawn, but it is easy to visualize the castle as it must have been in its heyday – the lord's private apartments, the servants' quarters, the garrison's quarters, kitchens and dungeons. It had many amenities far in advance of its time; ducts were let into the walls to carry away smoke from the fireplaces and were so devised as to provide rudimentary central heating.

There is a small museum attached to the castle where objects found during excavations are kept, and this is worth visiting.

BOGNOR REGIS, *Sussex* (6–SZ9399), was one of the early watering-places by the sea. It became fashionable with royalty and the aristocracy in the late 18th cent., and to Queen Victoria it was her "dear little Bognor"; there is much architecture here dating from those days. Sand and shingle beaches provide ideal bathing. It is well supplied with gardens; it has a delightful children's zoo, and also a large holiday camp.

Felpham, only 1 m. distant, is a little village that has kept some of its country charm and a number of thatched-roof cottages. The church is a mixture

of architectural styles and still shows traces of its Norman origins.

The poet and painter William Blake lived here in 1801–4.

BOSHAM, *Sussex* (6–SU8004). The most westerly town in Sussex, where, so legend has it, King Cnut demonstrated that even he, King of England, Norway and Denmark, had not the power to order the sea to turn back, which his courtiers, acting strangely unlike their usual Anglo-Saxon or Viking selves, had claimed for him.

It was from here in 1064 that Harold set sail on the journey that led to his meeting with William of Normandy – the occasion on which he is said to have been tricked into sacred promises that were to prove so fateful for the English at Hastings. His departure for Normandy is depicted in the Bayeux Tapestry.

The Church of the Holy Trinity was originally Anglo-Saxon and shows traces of pre-Norman work, including a chancel arch. Note a magnificent octagonal font, Norman columns and much from the 13th and 14th cents. Among the tombs is one that contains the remains of a daughter of King Cnut, and another that was long believed to be that of Herbert of Bosham, secretary to St Thomas à Becket, who saw the murder of the archbishop; but this is now doubted.

Yachtsmen and artists like Bosham.

BOUGHTON MONCHELSEA, *Kent* (7–TQ7749). The centre of Kentish ragstone quarrying, this pleasant village is, naturally, largely built of this durable material. The quarries, on the edge of the village, have been worked almost continuously for seven centuries, but it is believed they were in use long before: both the Romans and the Anglo-Saxons quarried the stone. Re-

Kenneth Scowen

Box Hill: stepping stones over the River Mole

mains of a Roman bath-house have been excavated. Stone from these quarries was used in the building of Westminster Abbey, and Henry III ordered a large quantity of cannon-balls to be made from the stone. Much of the village stands on the old quarries, for as they were worked out they were filled and roads and new houses built over them – good, solid foundations.

Both the manor house, Boughton Monchelsea Place, and St Peter's Church are ragstone buildings. The church tower is Norman but the rest is of later date; the lych-gate, erected in 1470, was built entirely without nails, and is believed to be the oldest in England.

Boughton Monchelsea Place was once the home of Sir Thomas Wyatt who led the Men of Kent in revolt against Mary I and was executed in 1554. The present manor house dates from shortly after this, but it was extensively altered during the second half of the 18th cent. and early in the 19th. However, much of the original remains. A feature of the house is the unusual pattern of the stained-glass windows by the main staircase, the result of two accidents. The windows were originally in the church and were smashed by Parliamentary forces who occupied the village during the Civil War; afterwards the pieces were gathered, reassembled and put in their present position. During the Second World War the windows were blown out by a bomb blast – and again they had to be pieced together. The result is most interesting. View the windows from both inside and outside the house.

The large gardens give magnificent views over the Weald, and a herd of fallow deer with one white doe can be seen among the trees. Legend has it that there must be just one white doe for luck.

The house, which has interesting furniture and tapestries, is open on stated days.

BOXGROVE, *Sussex* (6–SU9007). The Church of SS. Mary and Blaise retains much of its original Norman work, and also has some of the finest Early English architecture extant, especially notable in the chancel built about the middle of the 13th cent. Notable also are the Norman pillars and graceful Early English shafts, and the use of Purbeck marble. A fine piece of work is the chantry, a mixture of Gothic and early Renaissance, built in 1532 for his tomb by the 9th Earl de la Warr. The church is all that remains of a Benedictine priory founded early in the 12th cent.

BOX HILL, *Surrey* (6–TQ1751). One of the best-known beauty-spots of the South-East, Box Hill rises to nearly 700 ft above sea-level. Much of the land, as at LEITH HILL, is under the care of the National Trust. Walk up any of the tracks or footpaths that lead to the summit and enjoy the fine views over the valley of the Mole and large expanses of the surrounding countryside.

BRAMBER, *Sussex* (6–TQ1810). One of the prettiest Sussex villages, it has, while experiencing modern development, kept much of its old charm. Here is found an unusual little museum, the privately owned Potter's Museum and Exhibition of Humorous Taxidermy. It was established by a taxidermist, William Potter, about 100 years ago, and during his life he assembled a large collection of animals and arranged a number of tableaux with them. These include such studies as "The Kitten's Wedding", "The Rabbit's School", "Death and Burial of Cock Robin" and "The Rat's Den". The museum is open to the public throughout the year, although closed on some days during the winter months.

The Norman castle, built on older earthworks, has little more than its ancient gateway remaining, although the old walls may be easily traced. It was one of the many dismantled after the Civil War and allowed to fall into decay. Now in the keeping of the National Trust, it is open throughout the year.

Of the older buildings the house known as St Mary's is outstanding, a fine example of 15th-cent. timber fronting. It was reduced in size in the 17th cent. but restored to its former dimensions and general appearance in the 19th. It has interesting panelling and a fine collection of antique furniture, tapestries, lace and fabrics. It is open to the public.

The Parish Church of St Nicholas was originally built in the 11th cent. and there are still traces of the Norman work. The nave and tower were rebuilt after damage in the Civil War.

There is a pleasant walk to neighbouring **Botolphs**, once a thriving village but now only a handful of scattered houses and a church, of which the chancel arch and wall have Anglo-Saxon origins. The bells date from the 16th cent. and the pulpit is Jacobean.

Coombs, further down the valley, has a tiny church where wall paintings have been discovered.

BRAND'S HATCH, *Kent* (7–TQ5665). This motor-racing circuit is located in rolling country-side 20 m. from London, just off the A20. It is set in a natural amphitheatre between two hills, with the public stands on the slopes of one, and one of the car parks on the steeper slopes of the other. From both sides spectators can see most of the track.

The circuit was established in the early 1920s when club motorcycle events were held on grass tracks. After the Second World War a hard surface was laid, motor-racing was introduced, and in 1964 it was the venue for the European Grand Prix. Important races held at Brand's Hatch include the B.O.A.C. International 500 for sports cars, and the *Daily Mail* Race of Champions. The club circuit is 1·24 m. in length, but the Grand Prix Circuit for major races is extended to 2·65 m.

The circuit is open to the public on advertised days for trial laps in their own cars at advertised charges.

BRIGHTLING, *Sussex* (7–TQ6821), stands on a hill with a commanding view over some of the most heavily wooded land in the county. A handful of old houses cluster around a school and the Parish Church of St Thomas à Becket. This was built in Norman times, on the site of an earlier Anglo-Saxon church, and preserves a Norman doorway and part of the walls of that period. It contains 13th-cent. glass in an Early English window, a 14th-cent. chapel of St Nicholas, and some interesting medieval tombs.

Well remembered here is that eccentric M.P. of the late 18th and early 19th cents., Squire Jack Fuller, and many of the monuments he erected remain. Brightling Needle, a great stone obelisk, stands on the highest point in the district (657 ft) and commands a magnificent view. Sugar Loaf is an odd building near Wood's Corner. The story goes that Fuller stated he could see the spire of Dallington Church from his grounds. A friend realized this was impossible and wagered that he could not. So Fuller had the Sugar Loaf built, with a spire to resemble that of Dallington Church, and which could be seen from his park. The story does not relate if he won the bet.

In the grounds of Brightling Park, surrounded by trees, is a domed building which Fuller erected as his private observatory, astronomy being one of his hobbies. It is now a private home. His tomb in the churchyard is marked, in the same grandiose Fuller manner, by a 60-ft high pyramid.

BRIGHTON, *Sussex* (6–TQ3105). This is the largest town in Sussex and the largest seaside resort in the South-East. An amalgam of "the raucous and the refined" as one writer put it, it combines gracious 18th-cent. architecture with modern swimming pools and places of amusement.

Although evidence of occupation by Neolithic tribes and later by the Romans has been found here, Brighton today has only a few buildings older than the Regency period. The old name was Brighthelmstone. A fishing village, long ago buried under the sea, preceded modern Brighton. The Tudor town was built behind walls as a defence against French raiders, but this did not save it from being burnt down at least twice in the 16th cent.

In 1754 a Dr Richard Russell arrived at the seaside village from LEWES, and prescribed sea-bathing and the drinking of sea-water as a cure for most ills. So persuasive were his methods that wealthy invalids flocked to the village to take the new cure, soon transforming it virtually into a spa.

In 1783 the Prince of Wales, later King George IV, arrived on a visit. He liked the place and his patronage made the town fashionable. His friends shared his enthusiasm, building the lovely Regency terraces for which Brighton is famed. In 1787 the Prince commissioned Henry Holland to build him a marine residence on the site of a farmhouse he had rented in the Steyne. A large building in Classical style was erected and the interior decorated in the "Chinese taste" popular at that time. Between 1815 and 1822 this Royal Pavilion was rebuilt to the plans of John Nash in its present Indian Moghul style, with onion-shaped domes, spires and minarets, but still generally keeping the Chinese décor inside.

After becoming king he still occupied it regularly until 1827. His brother, William IV, also spent much time there, and later Queen Victoria stayed at the Pavilion, but abandoned it in 1845 for she considered it did not offer enough privacy; with her went most of the furnishings. Later the Brighton authorities bought the Pavilion and in the following years many of the furnishings were returned from Buckingham Palace and Windsor Castle. Further items were permanently loaned by Queen Elizabeth II. Other contemporary items have been given or loaned so that the Pavilion appears much as it did when a royal residence.

The Pavilion is open daily throughout the year.

During the summer season there is a special Regency Exhibition with additional items and longer opening hours.

The interior of the Pavilion is as fantastic as its exterior. This is immediately apparent in the entrance hall: light green walls and ceiling, with a lantern hanging in the centre, and columns painted with Chinese mythological figures. A 162-ft corridor, with its chandelier in the shape of a water lily and several Chinese lanterns, leads into the Banqueting Hall. Here the domed ceiling is 45 ft high, painted to represent an Eastern sky framed in palms; below hangs a silvered dragon and from its claws hangs a chandelier weighing nearly a ton. There are four other chandeliers in the shape of water lilies; much of the wall decoration is of a later date. During the summer exhibition the long table is laid as if for a banquet in the time of the Prince Regent, using the superb Londonderry silver, much of it made by Paul Storr. This is on loan.

The Great Kitchen will delight all those interested in cooking equipment, for among the pots are 550 pieces of copperware, most of which belonged to the Duke of Wellington. The menu of one banquet served from this kitchen in 1817 lists 116 dishes.

The Music Room is only set up during the summer exhibition, and shows the instruments popular in private musical evenings of the time. The King's Apartments contain many of George IV's personal items. The Queen's Bedroom was Victoria's private apartment and is furnished as it was when she occupied it, showing that the Chinoiserie decorations continued into the early years of her reign.

Across the roadway from the Pavilion stands the Dome, originally the Royal stables, built in 1806. The dome itself is 80 ft high and 65 ft in diameter, and was modelled on the Halle au Blé in Paris. The building was remodelled in 1935 and is now a concert hall seating 2,100. Well known orchestras and solo artists often perform here.

At the entrance to the Pavilion in Church Street are the Museum and Art Gallery, housed in rooms that were originally intended as an in-door tennis court for the Prince Regent. Here are a number of paintings by English and Continental masters; the Willett Collection of English pottery; Chelsea and Worcester porcelain; exhibits of ethnological, archaeological and historical interest; and a collection of wax busts of Georgian personalities.

The Booth Bird Museum in Dyke Road, about 1½ m. from the town centre, contains a comprehensive collection of stuffed birds. There are about 3,000 exhibits covering many hundreds of British species. The main collection was assembled between 1865 and 1890: some of the species displayed are now becoming rare. A good butterfly collection is also shown. The museum is open daily throughout the year.

Brighton is one of the most popular holiday resorts in the country and offers all kinds of entertainment, from the usual seaside amusements to concerts and plays of the highest quality. It enjoys city amenities as well, for, with its less extrovert neighbour **Hove**, it has a population of around a quarter of a million.

The beach is mainly shingle. A long promenade follows the whole of the front. It was extended in the 1930s by an undercliff walk between Black Rock and ROTTINGDEAN (since extended to Salt-dean) which protects the chalk cliffs from erosion. It was largely built by unemployed Welsh miners. The Palace Pier and the West Pier have the customary amusements; the latter also has a concert hall where first-class programmes are presented in the season. The famous Chain Pier was destroyed in a storm in 1896.

Close to the Palace Pier is the Aquarium, open daily. It was established more than 100 years ago and has fish from all over the world. A Dolphinarium has been added. It seats 1,000 and contains seals and sea-lions besides the four dolphins that give displays at advertised times daily. Also near the Palace Pier is a waxworks, devised by a great-grandson of Madame Tussaud on similar lines to the London original.

Volk's Electric Railway, owned by the Corporation, runs between the Aquarium and Black Rock. The original was one of the earliest electric railways.

The area known as The Lanes retains aspects of old Brighton. Here small houses, some attractively bow-windowed, which used to be fishermen's homes, have been converted into antique and curio shops. Adjoining the old Lanes is a modern square with fashion and novelty shops and a licensed restaurant with tables outdoors under gay umbrellas.

St Nicholas Church, although rebuilt in 1853, has parts dating from the 14th cent. It has a Norman font and a notable 15th-cent. chancel screen. St Peter's Church, which replaced St Nicholas as the parish church of Brighton in 1873, was built in 1825 in Gothic style by Charles Barry. It has a mass of pinnacles and inside there is much late 19th-cent glass.

Brighton has about 1,200 acres of parks and gardens. Stanmer Park, on the LEWES Road, is an area of undulating lawns and woodland walks covering 537 acres, and there is also a fine plant nursery in one corner. Moulescoombe Wild Park, also on Lewes Road, comprises 143 acres of natural downland.

Adjoining Stanmer Park are the modern buildings of the University of Sussex designed by Sir Basil Spence. Plainly visible from the Lewes Road, these are interesting and functional pink-brick buildings set among trees. Permission to view can be obtained from the porter at Falmer House, the main block fronting the Brighton–Lewes Road.

Sportsmen are well catered for with bowling greens, tennis courts and some excellent golf courses in and around the town. About 1 m. from the centre is a well-appointed race-course with an average of 14 meetings a year. For children there are playgrounds, paddling pools and other facilities.

The Brighton year includes the Veteran Car

Kenneth Scowen

Brighton: the Royal Pavilion built for the Prince Regent

Run, from LONDON to Brighton, held in November. This race for veteran and vintage cars finishes at Madeira Parade – and the town is somewhat *en fête* on that night.

An annual Brighton Festival takes place in May, when world-famous musicians are invited to perform in a series of concerts ranging from jazz to classical music. Operas and plays are also staged.

Preston Manor, $2\frac{1}{2}$ m. N. of the sea-front, is a Georgian mansion built in 1738 on 13th-cent. foundations. It houses the Thomas-Stanford Museum. This family occupied the house for nearly 200 years and bequeathed it to the Brighton Corporation in 1932. Set in Preston Park, it is preserved as a typical country home, with its period furniture and fittings much as when the family lived here. The furniture is mainly Georgian, but there are pieces from the 16th and 17th cents., including a cabinet that once belonged to Queen Anne. There is also a fine collection of silver and 17th-cent. Chinese figures. The house is open at advertised times all through the year. Across the Brighton–London road is a rock garden laid out in Willow Plate design, which is illuminated at night.

BROADSTAIRS, *Kent* (7–TR3967). A popular seaside resort in the NE. corner of the county, inescapably linked with Charles Dickens. The town lies between MARGATE and RAMSGATE; a somewhat quieter place, with less of a funfair atmosphere than its neighbours, it nevertheless possesses all that makes a modern resort. There are a number of bays and inlets with sandy beaches, giving first-class, safe swimming. There is also good angling from boat, beach or the little harbour and pier, which date from the time of Henry VIII.

But it is Dickens who provides the major attraction. His name appears everywhere, as do those of his novels, and the characters and places in them. Bleak House, where he summered for many years during the 1850s and 1860s, stands on a rise above the harbour; he called it his "airy nest", and here he wrote his most famous work, *David Copperfield*, and did much other writing and planning. In his day it was called Fort House, having originally been the residence of the captains of one of the two small forts guarding the harbour. It was dubbed Bleak House following the publication of the novel of that name, but was not officially so called until the beginning of this century. The house is now a private residence and is in two distinct parts: the original house in which Dickens lived and which is kept as it was in his day, as a museum to his memory, and a new wing added in 1901, where the owners live.

In the house, a crenellated structure of austere appearance, there are a number of Dickens's own pieces of furniture, including a chair in his study (a room with a good view over the sea and from which the French coast is visible on a clear day), some original editions of his works, letters, drawings and photographs. Some other items are contemporary, and include a bed in which he slept at the Bull Inn in ROCHESTER. The garden is also maintained much as it was in Dickens's time.

Bleak House is open daily at specified times from March to November.

Dickens also stayed in a number of other places in Broadstairs before he occupied Bleak House. Among them was the Albion Hotel in Albion Street.

Across the bay from the harbour is Dickens House. A private residence, it is identified with Betsy Trotwood's house in *David Copperfield*. It also has a commanding view, and is occasionally open to the public.

The Dickens Festival, the principal event of the Broadstairs year, lasts a week and is generally held during June, when many people wear the dress of the Dickensian period. The festival programme includes a presentation of one of his works at Bleak House.

Only a couple of hundred yards away from Bleak House, at the harbour end of Albion Street, is the Parish Room of Holy Trinity Church, formerly Old St Mary's, built in 1601. It stands on the site of a shrine to Our Lady of Bradstow, to which passing ships dipped their topsails. Of other old buildings there is St Peter's Church in St Peter's, which dates, in part, from the 11th cent. There are also an excellent park and sports ground in this area.

BURWASH, *Sussex* (7–TQ6724). A village of old houses, many from the Tudor and Stuart periods (and a few even earlier), and some of the old ironmasters' residences. The houses are largely in the one main street, long and wide, which follows a high ridge. One of the old ironmasters' houses is Bateman's, which was the home of Rudyard Kipling from 1902 until his death in 1936. It is now a museum and contains many of his possessions. His study is maintained exactly as it was when he used it, including the huge 10-ft-long desk, untidily crowded with the things he kept on it. There is a fine staircase and some excellent Jacobean panelling. The house is set in pleasant gardens, with ancient yews and other trees, largely as the Kiplings laid them out. Bateman's is open at advertised times.

The Parish Church of St Bartholemew has a Norman tower and some Norman windows, some fine lancet windows, and a 15th-cent. octagonal font. On a wall near the south door is a small, oval bronze plaque to the memory of Kipling's only son, John, killed at the age of 18 at the Battle of Loos in 1915; it was the first commissioned work of Sir Charles Wheeler.

CANTERBURY, *Kent* (7–TR1557). A very ancient city with more than 2,000 years of history, and the site of Canterbury Cathedral, Mother Church of the Anglican communion. There were Belgic settlements here in pre-Roman times. Julius Caesar took the area by storm in 54 B.C. After their conquest of Britain in A.D. 43 the Romans established a regional centre here (Durovernum), and were followed by the Anglo-Saxons. In 597 St Augustine arrived on his mission to spread Christianity in England, and built his first cathedral, and a few years later Canterbury became the Metropolitan City of the English Church. In the 10th and 11th cents. it suffered repeatedly from Danish raids.

In the Civil War the city was damaged during the struggle for its possession, and at the hands of the Parliamentary forces after they gained control. The Industrial Revolution largely passed it by, but during the Second World War it was severely damaged in bombing raids. However, for nearly 14 centuries, through all its vicissitudes, Canterbury has remained the centre of Christianity in England, dominated by the cathedral which escaped almost unscathed, except for some windows, in the bombings of the last war.

Park your car in one of the central car parks and wander round the old part of the city on foot to get the best views of the ancient architecture of this fascinating place.

Something like one half of the medieval walls which encircled the old city remain, on the eastern side, and run in a continuous line from near Wincheape to Radigund's Street. They date, in the main, from the 13th and 14th cents. and have been excellently maintained. They were partly built on Roman foundations, remnants of which have been discovered during restorations. There are a number of bastions also well preserved. Of the seven original gates only one remains as it was, the West Gate (the old walls have disappeared in this area) which straddles picturesquely but inconveniently the entrance to the main thoroughfare, St Peter's Street. An imposing structure of the late 14th cent., it guarded the entrance to the city from the direction of London. It subsequently became a gaol, and now houses a museum devoted mainly to the history of Canterbury. There is a fine view over the city from the battlemented top of the gate.

Of the castle only the keep remains. It was built during the 11th and 12th cents. but seems to have been ineffective, quickly surrendering every time it was attacked. The castle was demolished over the centuries, but attempts to break up the keep were defeated by the very solidity of its structure.

In addition to the cathedral, Canterbury has a number of very interesting churches. St Martin's, which is about $\frac{1}{2}$ m. outside the city walls to the E., is said to be the oldest church in England still in use. It is believed there was a church dedicated to St Martin on this site in pre-Anglo-Saxon days. Some experts say the chancel dates, basically,

Canterbury Cathedral: the Bell Harry Tower

from before the arrival of St Augustine in 597, and the nave from shortly after. The tower was built in the Middle Ages and there are other additions of this era. To many, this is the cradle of Christianity in England.

St Dunstan's is another old church in which masonry of the 11th cent. survives. A chapel by the porch dates from the 14th cent. but there was considerable restoration in the 19th cent. It was this church, in 1174, that Henry II entered to remove his ordinary clothes before walking barefoot to the cathedral to do penance for his part in the murder of Thomas à Becket.

St Mildred's Church was reconstructed in the middle of the 13th cent. but some of the older fabric remains. St Peter's and St Alphege's are of similar date and retain their medieval atmosphere.

St George's Church, where Christopher Marlowe was baptized, was destroyed in the bombing except for its tower, which still stands, preserved as a central landmark in the new shopping section which has been built around it.

Beneath the Longmarket, a modern pedestrian precinct replacing the old covered market which was destroyed in the 1942 bombing, are Roman remains with a tessellated pavement and mosaic panels. These can be seen in the basement beneath the shops.

The ruins of St Augustine's Abbey are one of the most important ecclesiastical sites in England. An abbey was first built here in the time of St Augustine, but was subsequently torn down more than once. Much of the material was used to build St Augustine's College, originally a missionary college, but now part of King's College, London. The impressive Fyndon Gate, facing Lady Wootton's Green, is the entrance to the college grounds, which may be visited on application to the Warden. Excavations of the old ruins, which are

open to the public, give some idea of their construction over the centuries; the re-use of Roman bricks indicates that the Romans may have had a building here at some time. The adjacent modern buildings of Christ Church Teachers' Training College make an interesting contrast.

On Tyler Hill, overlooking the old city and the cathedral, is the complex of buildings of the University of Kent. These express the old collegiate tradition in modern architectural forms. It is usually possible to see over parts of the university and those wishing to do so should apply to the Porter.

Among the many interesting old buildings which can be seen in the city is the Poor Priests' Hospital in Stour Street, originally established by the Black Friars, the oldest part of which dates from the 14th cent.; it now houses the Regimental Museum of the Buffs. Greyfriars, built over the river on a series of arches, with parts dating from the late 13th cent., was remodelled in 1920. It is all that is left of the first Franciscan house in England. St Thomas's or Eastbridge Hospital is mostly medieval, with an interesting crypt. All these are open to the public. Nearby, overlooking the River Stour, is The Weavers, made up of a group of Tudor houses, now a restaurant and gift shop. The upper story still houses some of the old looms brought over to Canterbury by Flemish and Huguenot refugees, and exhibitions of weaving are open to the public.

In the pleasant Dane John Gardens is a prehistoric mound topped by a 19th-cent. column; here also is a monument to Christopher Marlowe, the local writer and contemporary of Shakespeare. The Marlowe Theatre in Castle Street is a modern building with a pseudo-Tudor front. Near the entrance to the Dane John Gardens is displayed the steam engine, *Invicta*, which worked one of the first regular railway passenger routes in the world (1830)—the Canterbury–Whitstable line.

One of the most delightful cricket grounds in England is the St Lawrence Ground where the Kent County Cricket Club play. Here the Kent Cricket Week is held in July.

Just across the city boundary on the London road is the charming old village of Harbledown. On the left is the Hospital of St Nicholas, established by Lanfranc about 1084 as a leper hospital. Victorian cottages for old people replaced the old living quarters, but the ancient church remains and is worth visiting.

THE CATHEDRAL

The cathedral dominates the city and its history. It was a centre of pilgrimage for many centuries – and still is in a sense, although most of the visitors today are tourists as well as pilgrims.

Of the original cathedral built by St Augustine on the site of a former church, nothing remains; nor, in fact, does anything of pre-Conquest buildings, destroyed more than once by the Danes. Shortly after the Conquest the cathedral burnt down and was entirely rebuilt by Lanfranc, the 35th primate and the first Norman archbishop. Since then there have been many additions and alterations. The crypt is the oldest part, dating from 1100. The last of Lanfranc's work disappeared when the north-west tower was rebuilt, in Gothic form, in 1840, after standing for nearly eight centuries.

Within the cathedral there is much more to see than can be properly appreciated in the 1½ hours or so of the guided tours. There are the tombs of more than half the archbishops since St Augustine, some of them most impressive. That of Henry Chichele, founder of All Souls' College, Oxford, and archbishop from 1414 to 1443, shows him in full regalia, and below as a cadaver, emphasizing the transitory nature of human glory; the tomb is restored every 50 years by the college he founded.

Only one English monarch is buried in the cathedral, Henry IV, who lies beside his queen, Joan of Navarre, in a tomb in Trinity Chapel. Also interred here is Edward, the Black Prince, son of Edward III and Prince of Wales, who died before his father. Above his tomb are replicas of his knightly accoutrements: helmet, crest, coat of arms, gauntlets, shield, sword-sheath and part of a belt; the originals, because of their delicate condition (they are 600 years old), are kept in glass cases close by. The tomb is one of the most magnificent in England.

Here also in Trinity Chapel is the site of the Shrine of St Thomas à Becket, archbishop from 1162 to 1170 when he was murdered by four knights of Henry II after his long and bitter feud with the king. His shrine was a scene of pilgrimage for more than 300 years, until it was dismantled and plundered of its jewels by Henry VIII. Just behind the high altar is a roped-off space, worn and uneven from the multitude of pilgrims who knelt there. A circular projection of the chapel, called the corona, contains St Augustine's Chair; of Purbeck marble it dates from about the 13th cent. and has been used for centuries for the enthronement of successive archbishops. The throne used by the archbishop when attending service is in the 12th-cent choir; it dates from 1840. The raised choir stalls are notable for their rich and superb carvings.

The nave, completed early in the 15th cent., is 187 ft long, 71 ft wide and 79 ft high from pavement to vaulting. The font dates from the Restoration. Beyond the nave is the south-west transept off which is St Michael's Chapel, better known as the Warriors' Chapel, because of the number of memorials to famous soldiers. It is now the Memorial Chapel of the Buffs, the Royal East Kent Regiment, one of the oldest regiments in the British Army. Every morning at 11 o'clock a soldier sounds a bell that formerly belonged to H.M.S. *Canterbury*, now hanging just outside the door of the chapel, and turns over a page of the Book of Memory, recording the names of men who died in battle.

The tall central Bell Harry Tower, the dominating external feature of the cathedral, dates from 1498 and is one of the earliest large brick structures in England; the exterior is stone, but within it is of brick, and in an excellent state of preservation. Viewed from the floor it is breathtaking; the whole of the interior to within 50 ft of the top is visible and high above, 130 ft above floor level, is the magnificent fan-vaulted ceiling.

The cathedral is rich in stained glass, despite destruction during the Civil War and Commonwealth period, damage caused in the last war, and injudicious restorations. Much of it is medieval, and there are a number of good modern windows, including some by the world-famous Hungarian-born artist, Bossanyi. The South Window with its 24 genealogical figures is a splendid example of 12th-cent. art, and the Miracle Windows in the ambulatory of Trinity Chapel are of particular interest.

The splendid crypt has Norman pillars and a fine vaulted roof and is the largest of its kind in the country. When Huguenot refugees settled here in great numbers in the days of Elizabeth I, permission was given for them to hold services in the body of the crypt, which they did for many years. These services are still held in French, but in a chapel on the south side of the crypt, as congregations are now smaller.

The cloisters of the Benedictine monastery adjoining the cathedral date from the early 15th cent.; they replaced 13th-cent. cloisters, traces of which can still be seen. Forming an interesting heraldic commentary of the period are the colourful decorations of the vaulting above, consisting of some 800 coats of arms; they are thought to be those of noble families from all over England who contributed to the cost of building the cloisters. Adjoining is the Chapter House of the 16th cent. The glass here is modern, but the tracery of the windows is original. Beyond the Chapter House is an octagonal structure jutting out into the lawn; this is the Water Tower, dating from 1160, which housed a wash-place for the monks. Water was led through leaden pipes to the tower, and from here to all parts of the monastery, giving a water supply and system of sanitation far in advance of the times.

Crossing the Green Court, approximating to the Great Court of the monastery, the visitor comes to what were the stables, brewhouses and workshops, now much altered and reconstructed to form parts of King's School. In the north-western corner of the court is a much restored gateway of the ancient walls, near which are roofed steps known as the Norman Staircase, one of the best-known examples of Norman domestic architecture surviving in England. These once led to a large hall established for poorer pilgrims, but which has long since disappeared.

CHALDON, *Surrey* (6–TQ3155). Notable for its ancient and unusual little church which contains one of the finest medieval wall paintings in the country. The building is short and wide, with a very high-pitched roof. The main structure dates from Norman times and still contains some of the masonry of that period. The south aisle and chapel are 13th-cent. and the north aisle 15th-cent. The pulpit dates from the Commonwealth, one of the few to be erected in England during that period. The bell is believed to be at least 700 years old, the oldest in the county and one of the oldest in the country.

The wall painting was discovered hidden under a coat of whitewash during restoration in 1869. It measures 17 ft by 11 ft, dates from the 12th cent. and is one of the most complete examples of Norman mural work in any church in England. Called the Ladder of Salvation, it depicts groups of little men and women either ascending to heaven or descending to hell. An angel is waiting to assist souls into heaven, while below fearsome demons and terrible torments await. St Michael is shown weighing the souls, and in a corner the Devil and his attendants try to tip the scales in their favour.

CHANCTONBURY RING, *Sussex* (6–TQ 1311). Near the village of **Washington** is an Iron Age camp on a rise nearly 800 ft above sea-level, the highest point in this area. Here prehistoric barrows have been discovered, and the remains of two Roman buildings, one a temple: they are listed as Ancient Monuments. A hoard of Anglo-Saxon coins was also found nearby. The site of the encampment is ringed by beech trees which were planted in 1760: many people mistakenly think this ring of trees is what gives the rise its name.

CHARING, *Kent* (7–TQ9549). A delightful village; although there are a lot of modern dwellings on the main Ashford road, a number of old houses are tucked away behind this highway, many dating from the 15th and 16th cents., some of them with overhanging stories. Here was once a palace of the Archbishops of Canterbury which, typically, was seized by Henry VIII; then, as was also his wont, allowed to fall into decay. The remains were later turned into a farm-house.

The embattled tower of the Parish Church of SS. Peter and Paul is nearly 600 years old, but the remainder of the church was rebuilt at the end of the 16th cent. after a disastrous fire. It has a fine timbered roof with painted beams and a medieval pulpit. Among its treasures is a vamp horn, one of the very few extant, an instrument formerly played in church orchestras.

In the nearby hamlet of **Newlands Farm** stands a disused Norman chapel with a good 12th-cent. doorway; there are also ancient chapels at **Burleigh** and **Pett Place**.

Chanctonbury Ring is a familiar landmark on the South Downs

Kenneth Scowen

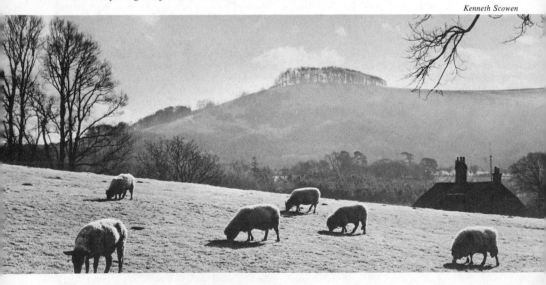

CHARTWELL, *Kent* (6–TQ4652). For more than 40 years the home of Sir Winston Churchill, Chartwell is set in hilly, wooded country 2 m. S. of WESTERHAM. This house is now dedicated to his memory and is maintained largely as it was when he lived and worked there.

The property was first mentioned about the middle of the 13th cent. and there was a small house here in the early 17th cent. which was to form the nucleus of the Victorian house which Churchill bought in 1922; some of the brickwork of the earlier house, which was probably only one room deep, can still be seen. Churchill made considerable alterations and additions, building one complete new wing. The house is now in the keeping of the National Trust and is open to the public in the summer.

The rooms are arranged almost as though they were still lived in. In the drawing-room is a card table set up for a game of bezique which Sir Winston often played with Lady Churchill, or with his guests; here there are a number of oil paintings including some, as in all parts of the house, by Sir Winston himself. The library contains his great collection of books; and inset in a bookcase is a model of the Mulberry Harbour at Arromanches, France, used in the Normandy landings.

In the room with its barrel-vaulted ceiling that was Lady Churchill's bedroom are more personal family mementoes, including two sketches by their daughter, Sarah. In the adjoining anteroom is a collection of Sir Winston's medallions, and white and gold china that was once the property of Napoleon III. This was bought by Clara Jerome, Churchill's American grandmother, when the Paris Communards auctioned the contents of the Tuileries Palace before burning the building in 1871.

Perhaps the most interesting room is Sir Winston's study which he used constantly, except during the war years, and where he did most of his writing. Here he wrote *A History of the English Speaking Peoples*, *The World Crisis*, *Marlborough*, *The Second World War*, and others of his works. This room is exactly as it was when he was last in it in 1964. The large writing desk was his father's, Lord Randolph Churchill; the small one is a copy of a rough unvarnished desk he used for many years – his favourite work desk. Above the fireplace hangs the first Allied flag flown in a European capital after its liberation during the Second World War: it was raised by the Fifth Army in Rome on 5 June 1944. In the rafters is a replica of his Garter banner.

A part of the house that has been altered are the museum rooms with their varied collection of Churchilliana. Around the walls are enlarged photographs illustrating phases of his eventful life from childhood to retirement. Here are displayed a number of the gifts he received from important people and leaders the world over – from de Gaulle, Stalin, the Belgian Government and many others. And three of his most prized possessions: the documents proclaiming him an honorary citizen of the United States; the Nobel Prize; and the volume of appreciation presented to him by the House of Commons on his 80th birthday.

Adjoining is the Uniform Room where can be seen a number of the uniforms which Churchill wore during his career, including that of the Lord Warden of the Cinque Ports, which office he held from 1941, and that of a Captain of Trinity House, as well as those of his days as a school cadet and as a young army officer (he was commissioned in 1894) and the well-known war-time "siren suit". There are also a number of his hats.

The gardens surrounding the house are delightful and cover an extensive area, including part of two lakes on which swim black swans from Perth, a gift of the Australian Government. Off one end is the old vegetable garden surrounded by the brick wall which Churchill himself built; working on the project as a relaxation, he took five years to complete it. The garden today comprises green lawns and flowering shrubs and plants. The gardens are open in the summer months.

At the foot of the gardens are a number of cottages that he had a share in building; one is the studio where he painted. There are a number of works here, all except three being his own – landscapes, seascapes, buildings and other studies, as well as some portraits. Displayed are some of the brushes and materials he used.

CHATHAM, *Kent* (7–TQ7567). Chatham is one of the Medway Towns and famous for its naval depot and dockyards. Although a settlement existed here in Anglo-Saxon times, the place was of little importance until early in the 16th cent. when Henry VIII established a dockyard. The name Chatham was associated with the dockyard about 100 years later. Over the years it continued to expand and the naval depot was established in 1890. Many famous ships were built here, perhaps the most notable being Nelson's *Victory*, launched in 1765, and a scale model can be seen in the Council Chamber of the Town Hall.

Charles Dickens spent some of his boyhood and schooldays here: his father, John Dickens, was attached to the Navy Pay Office.

Today Chatham is a busy commercial town, of no particular visual attraction but of some interest, although unfortunately the dockyards are not open to the public except on one day a year. The splendid gate of the dockyards, surmounted with the royal coat of arms, is worth seeing.

There are some good parks and gardens, one of which is behind the Town Hall (built at the end of the last century) and extends up a hill with a good view; here also are the remains of a fort from the Napoleonic Wars. Another park is Riverside, which is being developed on land that was until 1959 the War Department's Gun Wharf.

Of the churches there is very little that is really old. In the porch of St Mary's, which was rebuilt at the turn of the century, is a tablet found in the wall of the 12th-cent. Norman chapel; it is engraved with the figure of a Greek nymph.

Chatham was probably the site of the first voluntary hospital for the sick and poor in this country, St Bartholomew's Hospital, established in 1078. Of this, only the chapel remains, a Norman structure completely restored a century ago.

CHESSINGTON ZOO, *Surrey* (6–TQ1863). Set in spacious grounds on the outskirts of Chessington, this zoo has applied many modern ideas to the keeping of birds, animals and reptiles in captivity with as much freedom as the safety of visitors will allow.

Among the attractions is a pets' corner, of particular interest to children. Here are many domestic animals, including types rarely to be found in any British home, which children can safely handle. The zoo also has a model village designed to represent a typically rural community; and during the summer months a circus gives daily performances under the big top.

The zoo was founded in 1931 by Reginald Stuart Goddard in the grounds of Burnt Stub Manor, and shortly after the Second World War it came under the control of a private company. The original 14th-cent. manor house was burnt by Cromwellian troops in 1648 and rebuilt after the Restoration. It was then given the name of Burnt Stub as this was what it had been rebuilt from. It was severely damaged by fire in 1919, and was restored. Further damage was done in the Second World War, and afterwards it was again restored to its original form. Now a restaurant and the administrative offices of the zoo, the house contains some fine carving and panelling.

The zoo is open daily throughout the year.

CHICHESTER, *Sussex* (6–SU8605). The county town of West Sussex, Chichester is also a cathedral city. It is an ancient place. The Romans, to whom it was known as Noviomagus, established an important base here on their landing in A.D. 43. There is much evidence of their presence, especially in the substantial remains of their defensive walls and one bastion; also at FISH-BOURNE, where a palace, the largest Roman building yet uncovered in Britain, was discovered in 1960. The Saxons subsequently established themselves here. Aella, the first king of the South Saxons, gave the *ceaster*, as they called Roman towns, to Cissa – according to tradition his son. Cissa's Ceaster (both words pronounced with a "ch") eventually became Chichester. The city's history has been generally peaceful and prosperous. All trace of its only castle, demolished in the 13th cent., has disappeared, except for the mound on which it stood. The only serious disturbances were the two sieges of the Civil War, both comparatively short.

There are some old buildings in the city, but it is chiefly notable for its Georgian architecture, especially in a delightful street called Little London. The area known as the Pallants is graced by excellent town houses. It is quite easy for visitors to find their way around Chichester. It is divided into four parts by four major

Edwin Smith

Chichester Cathedral: a detail from the triforium of the retro-choir

thoroughfares, East, West, North and South Streets, all meeting at a point dominated by the Market Cross, an ideal centre from which to tour on foot.

The Market Cross is imposing and complex, and described as the finest structure of its type in the country. Built at the end of the 15th cent., it was a gift to the city by Edward Story, Bishop of Chichester from 1478 to 1503; it is sometimes called Bishop Story's Cross. It has undergone alteration over the centuries and has now been restored, but it largely retains its original form and character. It is an open-arcaded octagonal structure of Caen stone, with a massive central pillar from which spring flying buttresses. The whole is topped by an octagonal stone cupola rising to a height of 50 ft. It has fine stonework and makes a Chichester landmark.

The Hospital of the Blessed Mary (more commonly known as St Mary's Hospital) was built in the 13th cent. and combined a hospital for the aged and sick and a chapel in one long, single-roofed building, the usual pattern of medieval infirmaries. The inmates had their beds along the wall and were attended by the members of the order to which the establishment belonged. There were changes after the Dissolution, and following the Restoration of Charles II eight flats were built in the nave, four along each wall. These have been renovated and given modern comforts. Windows in the nave walls let in ample light. Old ladies occupy the flats. Despite this conversion into an almshouse, the building has in the main kept its 13th-cent. character under its high, tie-beamed roof. The hospital (or almshouse) part occupies about two-thirds of the structure, and the chapel the remainder; the two are separated by a finely carved medieval wooden screen. The 24 stalls and their misericords are of similar date. The side windows, piscina and canopied sedilia are of the early Decorated period. The east window is a modern reconstruction: long ago it fell into ruin and was blocked up by pieces of its stone mixed with mortar, but in 1880 this material was knocked out, the stonework carefully re-assembled and the new window built up much as it had been originally. St Mary's Hospital is open to the public at advertised times.

Another refuge for old people was the Cawley Almshouses, founded as the Hospital of St Bartholomew by William Cawley, the regicide, in 1625. These eventually became the city work-house, and are now used by the local hospital board.

Chichester has several museums. The new City Museum in Little London is an 18th-cent. building that was formerly a corn store and was converted in 1964. It contains collections devoted to local history and archaeology, 17th-cent. furniture, and exhibits telling the story of the Royal Sussex Regiment from its establishment in 1701.

Further collections are housed in a 13th-cent. building in Priory Park that was originally the choir of the Greyfriars.

Another museum is at the Military Police depot. It portrays the exploits and history of the provost-marshals (the first was created in the 14th cent.) and of the corps and contains a variety of equipment, uniforms, medals and flags.

The Festival Theatre in Oaklands Park is an arresting modern building. It has a hexagonal auditorium and arena stage. The seats are tiered steeply, rather as in a Roman amphitheatre, with no seat being more than 66 ft (the length of a cricket pitch as the directors explain) from the stage, and with no intervening obstruction. Acoustics are excellent. The theatre was opened in 1962, its first director being Sir Laurence Olivier. It ranks among England's leading theatres.

Chichester Cathedral is substantially the church erected by Ralph Luffa, who was bishop from 1091 to 1123, although there have been many alterations and additions since then. The see was originally at SELSEY, but was transferred to Chichester in 1075. The cathedral was built of stone from the Isle of Wight instead of stone imported from Caen, as was the practice in Norman times.

The first of the major alterations came in the late 12th cent. when much rebuilding was necessary after disastrous fires. Their effects are still being felt: weaknesses caused by the use of fire-damaged stone in the rebuilding of eight centuries ago are now having to be made good.

The 277-ft spire was added in the late 13th or early 14th cent., but it collapsed with the tower in a storm in 1861. The storm blew for several days while teams of men strove to avert the disaster. This episode is recorded in some surprisingly good photographs displayed in the south transept. Sir Gilbert Scott built a new spire, a replica of the original, in 1866.

The nave has fine pillars and a high vaulted ceiling; it is separated from the choir by the impressive arched, carved stone Bell-Arundel screen, erected beneath the tower by Bishop Arundel in 1475. Happily it was taken down not long before the collapse of the tower and so escaped possible destruction or damage. It was restored in 1960 in memory of Bishop Bell (bishop from 1929 to 1958) and his name was added to that of Arundel.

The new pulpit was installed in 1966. It is a dignified piece of modern work of stone-faced reinforced concrete with a cast-aluminium upper part lined with leather-covered wood.

At the east end of the choir is the modern altar backed by John Piper's modern tapestry in vivid colouring, hanging from a 16th-cent. oak screen. The choir stalls are finely carved and the misericords are noteworthy; the bishop's throne is an imposing piece of workmanship. On the south side of the choir are two beautiful 12th-cent. stone carvings believed to have been part of a stone choir screen of that period. They were found behind some choir stalls and erected in their present position in 1829. They depict Christ on his way to raise Lazarus from the dead and, secondly, the miracle performed. An 18th-cent. chandelier hangs over the centre of the choir.

The Lady Chapel contains some of the oldest

work in the cathedral, the first three bays dating from before the fire of 1187, the two eastern-most bays from about 1300. There are several good stained-glass windows in this chapel. In the north-west bay is the reputed coffin lid of Bishop Luffa. On both sides of the nave are a series of chapels. One of these, the 13th-cent. Chapel of St George, is set aside as the chapel of the Royal Sussex Regiment. The names of those who fell in the two World Wars are recorded here. In the north-west tower is the Sailors' Chapel, a memorial to Sussex men who died at sea between 1939 and 1945 and have no known grave. The lower part of this tower dates from the 12th cent. but the upper parts are later.

In the south transept is Bishop Langton's great window, of the early 14th cent. The tracery is of that period but the stained glass is late 19th-cent., richly coloured, but not enough to thwart the bishop's original purpose of letting in more light. Below is Langton's tomb. Here also is a 16th-cent. painting on wood by Lambert Barnard depicting Bishop Sherburne receiving from Henry VIII an assurance of the rights of the cathedral. Below are painted medallions of kings of England, with some blank spaces where there had been portraits damaged beyond restoration by Crom-wellian soldiers.

Other items of interest to look for in the cathedral include the fine Arundel tomb with effigies of Richard Fitzalan, Earl of Arundel, and his countess; also Graham Sutherland's painting *Noli me tangere* in the Chapel of St Mary Magdalene.

The late 14th- or early 15th-cent. bell-tower stands about 30 ft from the north-east entrance to the cathedral. It is the only bell-tower in England detached from its cathedral. The upper portion was refaced in 1964. Two of its peal of eight bells date from the 16th cent., the others from the 17th and 18th cents. There is a good view from the top, but permission to go up must be obtained from the verger. The cloisters were built soon after 1400; the roof timbers remind the viewer of an upturned boat and are of Irish oak. The Bishop's Palace is private, but the gardens may be visited at advertised times in the summer. An early 14th-cent. gateway at the end of Canon Lane leads to the palace. From Canon Lane can be seen the charming group of cottages in Vicar's Close which influenced Keats when he wrote "The Eve of Saint Agnes".

Chichester harbour has good yachting facilities. For racegoers, GOODWOOD is 3 m. N.

CHIDDINGFOLD, *Surrey* (6–SU9635). A large village in beautiful undulating country. Nearby is a State Forest where the English oak is being rehabilitated in an area of about 2,000 acres. Some 80,000 young oaks have been planted, and several other varieties of trees grow in the forest.

The Crown Inn has the oldest licence in Surrey and one of the oldest in England. An inn was established here in 1285. The earliest recorded reference is in the 14th-cent. title-deed, a copy of

which is displayed in the lounge of the Crown.

The Parish Church of St Mary contains some fine glass, some of it produced locally when Chiddingfold was the centre of a glassmaking industry in medieval times. There are also examples of modern Continental glass. One of the peal of eight bells is over 500 years old. The church faces a green and some attractive Georgian tile-hung cottages.

CHIDDINGSTONE, *Kent* (6–TQ5045). A village that is in the keeping of the National Trust. Its single street is lined with half-timbered 16th- and 17th-cent. houses built when the Wealden iron industry throve; they have been maintained in their original condition and make a peerless group. The church is 13th-cent. with later additions; the tower is Perpendicular, and there are some fine carvings and a Jacobean font and pulpit.

At the head of the street stands Chiddingstone Castle, the rebuilding, in mock Gothic, of an older manor house, home of the Streatfeild family. It contains a collection of Stuart furnishings and pictures, as well as Ancient Egyptian and Oriental exhibits. It is open to the public most of the year at advertised times.

Along a footpath behind the street is a large sandstone rock, the Chiding Stone, to which, so the story goes, nagging wives used to be taken to be nagged at retributively by the assembled village.

CHILHAM, *Kent* (7–TR0753). One of the least spoilt villages of the county. The houses are largely Tudor and Jacobean, dormer-windowed and with projecting gables and undulating roofs. The village rises to the spacious square, where architecture of different periods blends almost perfectly.

Of the Norman castle only the keep remains. Near the keep is a fine Jacobean mansion, and although neither the mansion nor the keep is open to the public, details of their architecture can be clearly seen from the grounds which are open at advertised times in the summer months.

The Church of St Mary is mainly Perpendicular with a good stone and flint tower. It contains a number of monuments, several of them from the 17th cent.

Chilham Park, of some 500 acres, merges into Godmersham Park, and these offer walks through woodland. **Godmersham,** 2 m. S. of Chilham, was frequently visited by Jane Austen, whose brother, Edward Knight, then owned Godmersham Park. The village church, St Laurence's, has a detached unbuttressed tower, and a semi-circular apse with Norman windows; the chapel is Early English and has a triple lancet window.

The tithe barn is one of the finest in the country.

CHISLEHURST, *Kent* (6–TQ4469). The attraction here is a labyrinth of caves and tunnels which may have a total length of some 15 m.; all but the 1½ m. open to the public has been sealed off. The origins of the caves are something of a

Chiddingfold: the parish church and Georgian houses on the green

mystery. Some claim that they date back to pre-historic times and, inevitably, that they were used by the Druids; others say they are of much more recent origin and were excavated to exploit the chalk and flints. That they may have provided shelter for primitive people against their human and animal enemies has not been proved, but they did make excellent air-raid shelters during the Second World War, accommodating about 15,000 people. Today they provide the subject for tours conducted by guides daily throughout the year. The house on the nearby golf course was the last home of ex-Empress Eugénie of France.

CISSBURY RING, *Sussex* (6–TQ1408). An Iron Age hill-fort between Worthing and Findon, occupied in the 5th cent. B.C. and lasting until the middle of the 1st cent. B.C. Flint was mined in this area during those times and perhaps before, and a number of the shafts have been discovered. The site was also later occupied by the Romans, and a Romano-British circular shrine has been un-covered, together with a quantity of pottery belonging to periods between the 1st and 3rd cents. A.D.

This vantage point gives fine views over the South Downs.

COBHAM, *Kent* (7–TQ6768). A village rich in history and old buildings, with traces of the Roman occupation.

The church, dedicated to St Mary Magdalene, was built in the 13th cent. and enlarged in the 14th. On the floor of the chancel are more than 18 brasses, the best in England and among the finest in the world. Stretching from wall to wall they are dedicated to members of the Cobham family over a period of two centuries of the later Middle Ages; they illustrate vividly the costumes of their time. Above them is a large and elaborate tomb, that of George, Lord Cobham, who died in 1558.

Behind the church are almshouses which incorporate a 14th-cent. hall and kitchen. These formed part of the Old College built by the 3rd Lord Cobham (who was responsible for the enlargement of the church) and which he endowed as living quarters for five priests whose duty it was to pray for his soul, and for those of his family. The college was suppressed in 1537 and it was altered to its present form for use as almshouses in the 17th cent.

Another very old building is Stone House, believed to have been erected as living quarters for the five priests while the college was being completed.

G. Douglas Bolton

Cobham Hall

Cobham Hall, one of the largest old houses in Kent, was built during the last 20 years of Elizabeth I's reign. The central hall was pulled down about 100 years later and rebuilt, and there were additions at the end of the 18th cent. and the beginning of the 19th. It contains some fine work by Inigo Jones and the Adam brothers. It was purchased in 1960 by the Ministry of Public Building and Works and two years later became a girls' school, an experimental establishment for pupils of many races. It is open to the public at advertised times during the school holidays.

A popular inn is the Leather Bottle, which featured in Dickens's *Pickwick Papers*. It has preserved its medieval timber front and the bars contain a good collection of Dickens prints and pictures. The Darnley Arms dates from the Middle Ages, and the Ship Inn is said to have been built from the timbers of a ship wrecked off Sheerness.

The house Owletts was built by a Cobham farmer late in the 17th cent. It has a splendid staircase but its appeal lies in its modest character and attractive garden. It was the home of the architect Baker who collaborated with Lutyens in the designing of New Delhi. Both houses are open to the public at advertised times.

At nearby **Sole Street** is the Yeoman's House, a typical yeoman's home of the 15th and 16th cents.

COMPTON, *Surrey* (6–SU9547). A village less than 3 m. from the centre of GUILDFORD and just off the A3, Compton possesses the fine little Watts Gallery, devoted chiefly to the works of the Victorian portraitist, allegorical painter and sculptor, George Frederic Watts. Here on exhibit are about 200 of his works, including *Love* and *Death*, and others on loan from the TATE GALLERY. The gallery opened in 1903, the year before Watts's death, but was enlarged and

planned on its present scale by his widow, the painter Mary Fraser-Tytler, who also endowed it and devoted the rest of her life to the preservation of his work.

The gallery is open at advertised times throughout the year.

About 200 yds away on the top of a hillock is the Watts Mortuary Chapel built on land donated by Mrs Watts for a second village burial ground, the churchyard having become full. The chapel, outwardly, is a not particularly attractive red-brick structure. It was built by the villagers with bricks made from local clay. The rich interior decoration of distinctive intaglio and relief work was executed in locally made gesso by Mrs Watts, who also designed the chapel. It is open at all times.

The Norman Parish Church of St Nicholas possesses some very early work, and a unique feature is its two-story chancel. The lower chamber of the chancel, which dates from the 11th cent., has a vaulted timber ceiling and contains an aumbry and piscina. The upper chamber, dating from about a century later, is above a Norman wood screen, the wood of which is so hard that it has been found almost impossible to drive ordinary nails into it. It was restored in 1953.

The tower probably dates from Anglo-Saxon times, as do parts of the nave walls. There is a half-buried Norman doorway, while the north and south aisles with their pillars and arches, entrance arches to tower and chancel, timber nave roof, and aumbry in the Lady Chapel are all 12th-cent., as is the font. The spire, re-shingled in 1950, is 13th-cent. and there are a number of other features of pre-Reformation date. The carved pulpit and canopy, altar rails and oak screen at the west end are 17th-cent.

CRANBROOK, *Kent* (7–TQ7735). An old town which came into prominence in the 15th cent. when it became a centre of the weaving industry. A number of old buildings date back to the days of its greatest prosperity. Dominating the town is the Union Mill, a three-storied windmill built in 1816; standing 72 ft high, it is the second highest in England. It is now in the care of the Kent County Council and is kept in full working order with all its gear intact.

The parish church, St Dunstan's, dating from the 15th cent., is well worth a visit. It is known as "the Cathedral of the Weald".

Cranbrook School was founded in 1574, and was granted a Royal Charter by Queen Elizabeth I. She also laid the foundation stone of School House, now the headmaster's house.

W. of Cranbrook on the B2085 is Glassenbury Park, a moated house mainly dating from the 15th cent. Only the gardens are open at stated times; there is a very fine avenue of lime trees, at one end of which lies buried the horse Napoleon rode at the Battle of Waterloo.

CRANLEIGH, *Surrey* (6–TQ0638). Cranleigh can lay claim to the first cottage hospital. It was founded in 1859 by a local surgeon named Napper, and Archdeacon Sapte, Rector of Cranleigh, and was set up in a cottage that had formerly been the vicarage. This building served the hospital needs for about 40 years, but since then several additions have been required.

A feature of Cranleigh are the Canadian maples lining the main street. These were planted by Canadian soldiers who were camped nearby during the First World War. They make a fine and unusual display in an English country town.

CRAWLEY, *Sussex* (6–TQ2636). A town with many old buildings, some dating back to the 15th cent. The church is mainly 14th- and 15th-cent., with a 14th-cent. font and some unusual carvings.

But the main interest here is in Crawley New Town, one of several modern towns developed since the war to take the overspill population from London, and the only one to be built S. of the capital. The town has been planned to cover 6,000 acres, and has been designed for the best of modern living conditions. There are some fine examples of modern architecture, especially the secondary school.

In the centre of Queen's Square is an unusual 25-ft clock-tower. Its theme is the annual London–Brighton veteran-car run which passes through the town; when the hour is struck models of old cars emerge on all four faces of the tower, and circle to the theme music for the film *Genevieve*, which was based on the veteran-car run.

CROWHURST, *Surrey* (6–TQ3947). In the churchyard is a yew tree famed for its size and great age; and there is a little mystery concerning a cannon-ball. The tree, which is said to be about 1,000 years old or more, has a circumference of some 30 ft; in the 19th cent. the trunk was hollowed out and a cannon-ball from the Civil War placed inside. During the Second World War the cannon-ball was found to be missing one morning, but nobody could imagine why it should have been taken. Some time after the war a cannon-ball was discovered when a former Canadian camp site was being cleared. The ball was returned to the church authorities and replaced in the hole, but it did not fit as snugly as formerly. Had the hole been enlarged when the ball was removed? Or, is this the same cannon-ball?

The Parish Church of St George has been restored several times since the 17th cent. but there are still traces of Norman work, and the south aisle is 13th-cent., the octagonal font dates from the same period, and there is good 15th-cent. glass.

CROYDON, *Surrey* (6–TQ3365). In less than 150 years Croydon has grown from little more than a large village into a bustling borough with a population of some 350,000. For two decades its growth has been exceptionally fast and it boasts many tall modern buildings.

Fairfield Hall, one of the most ambitious cultural centres in the country, was completed and opened in 1962. It comprises a main concert hall, a smaller theatre, an art gallery, and a general purposes lounge, which also serves as a second art gallery.

The main hall was planned primarily for orchestral concerts, but can be adapted for stage performances, arena events, cinema shows or lectures. It has a capacity of from 1,800 to 1,900 in tiered seats and a balcony.

The theatre, called the Ashcroft Theatre in honour of Dame Peggy Ashcroft, is smaller and more intimate, with a seating capacity of 734, and is also ideal for smaller concerts and chamber music recitals. The Arnhem Gallery has a wall space of more than 6,000 sq. ft, and is primarily designed for painting exhibitions, but also serves as a banqueting hall.

The Fairfield Hall building is one of several modern edifices forming a pleasant square centred with flowering shrubs and a fountain, a breathing space in a busy centre.

Nearby is the modern 20-story town hall, not far from its predecessor which now houses the Municipal Library, the Information Office, and sections of the police administration.

The Whitgift Centre is a well-designed, traffic-free shopping precinct.

The most historic building in Croydon was the Palace, summer residence of the archbishops of Canterbury from Norman times until the middle of the 18th cent. Much of this has now been demolished, but some has been preserved and is now incorporated in the Old Palace School, a direct-grant school for girls under the control of the Community of the Sisters of the Church. Of the medieval palace only the Norman undercroft, the 15th-cent. banqueting hall, the entrance porch from the churchyard, the solar or retiring room, and the guardroom remain, but there are considerable remains from the Tudor period. These include the chapel with seven windows with typical Tudor arches; the dining-room built at the end of the 15th cent.; the long gallery which still contains some 16th-cent. panelling; and the library with a Tudor ceiling and oaken staircase. There is also a room known as Queen Elizabeth's Bedroom – she really did stay here, for it is recorded that she made several visits on matters of state.

The palace was originally built by Archbishop Lanfranc in the 11th cent., and was considerably altered and added to over the centuries. It was last used by Archbishop Hutton in 1757. After that it fell into decay and was used for a time as a factory for printing linen. In 1887 the Duke of Newcastle bought it and handed it over to the Community of Sisters who established the school later in the same year, and in course of time had restorations and rebuilding carried out.

The Norman undercroft, guardroom, banqueting hall, Tudor chapel and Queen Elizabeth's bedroom are open to the public on advertised days, and at other times by prior arrangement with the school authorities.

Next to the school is the Church of St John the Evangelist, the largest parish church in Surrey. It was largely destroyed by fire in 1867 and the present structure dates from the late 1880s. The rebuilding followed the original Perpendicular church as far as possible. The tower dates from the 15th cent. and was completely restored after the fire, although its original interior work is almost intact. Also surviving from the fire is the 15th-cent. brass eagle lectern. In the church are the tombs of six archbishops of Canterbury.

In 1596 Archbishop Whitgift founded the hospital or almshouse that bears his name and still stands in the centre of Croydon. He also founded a grammar school.

At **Addington**, within the borough, is Addington Palace, built in 1772. It became a residence of the archbishops of Canterbury after they abandoned their former palace. It is now the Royal School of Church Music. Here also stands St Mary's Church, which retains a Norman chancel and some Norman windows; the south arches of the nave are 13th-cent.

Beside the village green at **Old Coulsdon** is the Church of St John the Evangelist, largely 13th-cent., but the stone and flint tower, nave arches and windows date from the 15th cent. All Saints' Church, **Sanderstead**, within the same urban district to the S. of Croydon, has a 13th-cent. nave and 14th-cent. chancel.

DARTFORD, *Kent* (7–TQ5474), has become an industrial town with crowded streets, and motorists bound for the Dartford Tunnel. This, opened in 1963, is nearly 1 m. long, boring beneath the Thames to connect the A2 in Kent with the A13 in Essex. The parish church, Holy Trinity, was originally built late in the 11th cent.; the tower is Norman, and there is Early English work, and a Jacobean pulpit. The church was restored and added to during the 19th cent., when an interesting 11th-cent. wall painting came to light. Of other old buildings the Bull Inn, with its galleried courtyard, is an interesting relic of coaching days.

DEAL, *Kent* (7–TR3752). Coastal town and popular holiday resort. The town is mainly modern, but Middle Street, which runs parallel to the Promenade, is lined with old houses and narrow lanes run off it. This old quarter is said to have been the haunt of smugglers.

The main historical monument is Deal Castle, one of the line of defensive forts built along the Channel coast in the 1530s when there was fear of invasion from France. It was a formidable fort with 145 gun embrasures and was constantly manned by a captain, lieutenant and a company of gunners which could be supplemented by local militia when required. However, its only taste of combat was during the Civil War. The castle was for the Royalists and it fell to Parliamentary forces after a siege of several weeks.

It is unique in design: circular in form, with two rings of semi-circular bastions surrounding a central keep. This symmetrical plan was meant to provide defence from all directions, while the rounded bastions and keep were designed to deflect shot. In later years the fort was altered considerably to make it a residence for the Captain of Deal Castle, a post which became honorary in the middle of the 18th cent. It has been vacant since 1951 and the castle, which was hit by a bomb during the Second World War, has been stripped and returned to its original architectural form, so that the visitor can easily visualize its life as a Tudor fort.

A room off the entrance hall is a small but interesting museum devoted to finds excavated in Deal and the surrounding district.

The castle parapets make an ideal setting for band concerts and military tattoos, especially those held at night by searchlight.

Here at Deal is the famous Walmer Lifeboat Station and lifeboat; both are on view to the public. There is usually one member on duty to show visitors around and explain how the service works. Past exploits are listed on plaques on walls of the station; Walmer lifeboatmen have attended more than 2,000 distress calls since the station was established in 1856. There are now between 20 and 30 calls on an average a year, many of them caused by the shifting Goodwin Sands which lie about 5½ m. offshore. These sandbanks are said once to have been an island that belonged to Earl Godwin, King Harold's father. There are pleasure cruises to the Sands during the summer months.

Between the pier and the lifeboat station is a plaque marking the spot where Julius Caesar is said to have landed in 55 B.C.

There is good swimming from the pebble beach. Anglers will find plenty of sport, with good fishing from the pier as well as from the beach, and fishing boats may be hired by the hour or by the day; big fish have been caught in these waters.

DORKING, *Surrey* (6–TQ1649). An ancient market town, and a good centre for walking, delightfully set between Box Hill and the Downs rising to the N. It is notable for the number of fine modern dwellings that are being

J. Allan Cash

Dover: the white cliffs, which provide the first glimpse of England to the traveller crossing the Channel, at St Margaret's Bay

built in the district; Dorking has an increasing population of residents who travel to work in London. There are also a number of old buildings but the Parish Church of St Martin dates only from the latter part of the 19th cent.; its 210-ft-high spire is a monument to Bishop Wilberforce. Two of the older inns are the White Horse, with a 400-year-old exterior, and the Red Lion, perhaps even older, which was known as the Cardinal's Hat in medieval times.

The poet and novelist George Meredith lived in a house at the foot of Box Hill, and John Keats finished writing his *Endymion* while staying at the Burford Bridge Hotel in 1817.

DOVER, *Kent* (7–TR3141), has played a major rôle in British history for more than 2,000 years. Since the coming of the Romans it has been one of the most important entries to the country, was one of the Cinque Ports, and is now the busiest passenger port in England. It has survived enemy assaults, threats of invasion and the bombard-

ments of two world wars when it was in the aerial and artillery front line.

Pre-eminent of its monuments is the mighty Dover Castle, standing on a high hill and dominating the town and harbour and the approach by sea from all directions.

The hill site was first utilized by the Ancient Britons who threw up earthworks. The oldest edifice now here is the ruin of the Roman pharos, or lighthouse, built in A.D. 43. Nearby mounds may have been part of earthworks put up by Harold II. Of other structures built up to the time of the Norman Conquest there is little or no trace.

The oldest part of the castle itself is Peverell's Tower, constructed shortly after the Conquest. The keep, the strongest in England, was erected in the second half of the 12th cent. and the outer walls in the 13th cent. when an unsuccessful French attack in 1216 demonstrated that the existing walls might not withstand a sustained battering by siege engines. Further additions and strengthening were carried out in the face of threatened attack during the Napoleonic Wars, and again during the Second World War. Throughout this long history, until the 1960s, the castle has been a military headquarters and garrisoned continuously.

In a tour of the castle (open daily throughout the year) the visitor sees the lower chapel; the well, which is 289 ft deep and is considerably older than the castle; the splendid banqueting hall with a display of armour; the main hall with plaques listing the names of all the Constables of the Castle; St Thomas's Chapel, dedicated to Thomas à Becket, and its little sacristy (still in use); two bed-chambers, one probably a royal bedroom (for this was a royal castle), with here some Tudor additions. In these rooms, and some above, are a number of carvings and inscriptions scratched into the stone by French prisoners-of-war lodged here in the 18th cent.

From the battlemented roof can be seen the gun emplacements set up during the Napoleonic Wars to meet the invasion that never came; the Channel and its shipping; and on a clear day the French coast.

In the basement were the huge kitchens, and in the ceilings can be seen the trapdoors through which the prepared food was hoisted to the rooms above. A visit to the tunnel system beneath the castle completes the tour. These tunnels were originally dug in 1216 at the time of the French attack. They were extended during the Napoleonic Wars. Some of the tunnels come out right at the cliff-face, others in the surrounding meadowland. They still had their uses in the Second World War as air-raid shelters.

The Church of St Mary-in-Castra was originally Anglo-Saxon and cruciform in plan. Despite additions and heavy restoration and rebuilding in the middle of the 19th cent., it has essentially retained its original form, with traces of the Anglo-Saxon work. Next to the church stands the pharos, which, although restored in part, retains much of its ancient Roman brickwork. It is not known when it ceased to be used as a lighthouse, but it served as the bell-tower of the church for many years.

The central core of the Town Hall, in Biggin Street, is the remains of a 13th-cent. guest-house, the Maison Dieu, shamefully treated in the 19th cent. when only part of the outer walls were left standing. The rebuilt interior contains some historic armour and a series of fine 19th-cent. stained-glass windows depicting important events in the town's history. On the end wall is a painting by Bernard Hailstone of Sir Winston Churchill in the uniform of the Lord Warden of the Cinque Ports. In the basement is a small, overcrowded museum. Exhibits include some concerning the town's history; noteworthy is the 12th-cent. Burgmote Horn.

Next to the Town Hall is the Dutch-gabled Maison Dieu House, built in 1665 and now the Municipal Library.

Close by is the 13th-cent. St Edmund's Chapel which was originally attached to the Maison Dieu. Measuring only 27 ft by 14 ft, it is claimed to be the smallest chapel in England in regular use, and is one of the few surviving 13th-cent. wayside chapels. It was converted to secular use when the Maison Dieu was dissolved in 1544 and was lastly a forge. It was scheduled for demolition in 1965 when it was realized what it had been originally. Restored and reconsecrated, it is a chapel again. It is a solid little building, plain inside, with an unadorned altar.

The parish church, St Mary's, is the oldest church in the town with parts dating back to the Norman period, but largely rebuilt in the 19th cent. The west door, the window above it and the vestibule are Norman. St James's Church in Woolchamber Street was almost as old but suffered extensive bomb damage in the war and later collapsed, leaving only one wall standing.

The port handles more than 3,000,000 passengers annually and hundreds of thousands of cars. The ordinary steamers leave from Admiralty Pier which forms the west arm of the harbour, and the car ferries from the Eastern docks. There are regular services to Calais, Ostend and Dunkirk. Hovercraft, taking only 40' minutes to skim to Calais, carry motorists and their cars as well as foot passengers.

There are all types of sports to be had in Dover. There is a wide variety of fish for the angler; also lobsters, crabs and prawns to catch with baited nets. There are a number of public gardens, and walking along the tops of the famous White Cliffs is exhilarating. There are good walks to FOLKE-STONE in one direction and to WALMER, passing St Margaret's Bay, in the other.

Dover has been the scene of many "firsts". Blériot is commemorated by a concrete slab, the size and shape of his monoplane, on the spot NE. of the castle where he landed from the first cross-Channel flight by a heavier-than-air machine (1909). Then there was the Hon. Charles S. Rolls who took off from here on the first two-way Channel flight in 1910, and in 1875 Captain Matthew Webb was the first person to swim the Channel; both are commemorated on the East Cliff Promenade.

DOWNE, *Kent* (6–TQ4361). A quiet village where Downe House stands, Charles Darwin's home for 40 years until his death in 1882, where he wrote *The Origin of Species* and many other scientific works. The house was built mainly in the 18th cent. but it was altered and considerably enlarged by Darwin to give space for his work and his family of 10 children.

The house, now administered by the Royal College of Surgeons, is maintained as a museum to his memory and work, and remains much as he left it. His study is as it was, and the modest equipment he used in his scientific experiments is on view, as well as letters, papers and other documents, and many of his own works. The house is open throughout the year at advertised times,

Also in the village is Downe Court, a Queen Anne manor house, built in 1690, which has been restored.

DUNGENESS, *Kent* (7–TR0917), is a great expanse of shingle jutting out to sea on the edge of Romney Marsh. It is chiefly notable today for its pair of atomic power stations, forming a new seamark. Also new is a slender lighthouse of modern lines and automated working. The old lighthouse still stands here and is lived in; built in 1904, it replaced a late-18th-cent. one left inland by the seaward growth of the shingle. The beach at Dungeness drops far too steeply for safe bathing, but the sea angling is good. Denge Marsh, behind Dungeness, is a bird sanctuary.

DYMCHURCH, *Kent* (7–TR1029). Fast becoming a favourite resort, Dymchurch has a good beach. For centuries it was the headquarters of the Lords of the Level, the local government of this area of Romney Marsh, who met in the New Hall, so named because it was built to replace the old one in 1590. Still retained in the building is the old lock-up, not used since 1866, when the Romney Marsh constables were replaced by the county police.

Today Dymchurch is probably best known because of the fame of its fictional parson, the notorious Dr Syn, brain-child of the Kentish author, Russell Thorndike. This reverend smuggler has inspired a regular festival at Dymchurch, when the townspeople dress up in period costume and enact some of the tales from his life.

The Parish Church of SS. Peter and Paul dates from the 12th cent. and there are still traces of medieval work to be seen. Nearby stand two of the Martello towers erected in 1804 during the Napoleonic Wars.

EASTBOURNE, *Sussex* (7–TV6199), can produce records to support its claim to pre-eminence among the resorts of England in the matter of sunshine. It is another of those watering-places which became popular at the turn of the 19th cent. and during the Victorian era; it still is. Although an old settlement, the town received a charter only in 1883.

A feature is the coastline to the W., dominated by some miles of chalk cliffs rising to 600 ft above the sea at Beachy Head, below which is the Beachy Head lighthouse, surrounded by the waters of the English Channel. Also prominent are the Seven Sisters, seven chalk cliffs. Walks along the top of the cliffs are exhilarating.

One of Eastbourne's oldest buildings, called Pilgrims, dates back to the early 12th cent. Underground passages, said to be of monastic origin, link it to the late-12th-cent. parish church, St Mary's, and to the Lamb Inn (1240).

Many fortifications were built along this coastline during the Napoleonic Wars, and two have been put to good use in the town. The present-day Redoubt is one such fort and it now houses a delightful model village, an aquarium, a grotto called the Blue Temple, and a sun lounge. The Wish Tower incorporates an old Martello tower, and here is housed the museum of the Royal National Lifeboat Institution, the first of its kind in England. Until 1937 this was the lifeboat station. Also in the Wish Tower is a café and sun lounge which give fine views over the coast.

Outstanding among the parks and gardens of the town are Motcombe Gardens and the colourful Carpet Gardens, near the pier.

The excellent Towner Gallery is established in a handsome 18th-cent. manor house. It features the works of 19th- and 20th-cent. British painters, as well as original prints by contemporary artists, and sculptures by Elizabeth Frink and Henry Moore. There are also a number of Georgian caricatures. Besides the permanent collection frequent temporary exhibitions are held.

Four m. N. of Eastbourne stands Polegate Windmill, built in 1817 and restored in 1967. It houses a collection of milling bygones and the sweeps turn in suitable weather. It is open at advertised times in the summer.

EAST CLANDON, *Surrey* (6–TQ0651). A village near GUILDFORD which has some old houses clustered round a basically Norman church. This church, St Thomas's, has a shingle spire; was restored in the 13th cent. and again, extensively, at the turn of the last century.

To the E. of the village is Hatchlands, a Georgian house with fine work by Robert Adam, said to be his first in England. The fine plaster ceilings are especially notable.

At neighbouring **West Clandon** is Clandon Park, built in the Palladian style in the 1730s, and with some excellent plasterwork; it is set in a park and gardens laid out by Capability Brown. Both houses are open to the public.

EAST GRINSTEAD, *Sussex* (6–TQ3938), is chiefly notable today for its famous Queen Victoria Hospital where such remarkable plastic surgery for badly burned servicemen was done in the Second World War. The hospital, with its fine modern buildings, is set in delightful grounds about 1 m. from the town.

In the High Street is Sackville College, founded in 1609 by Robert Sackville, Earl of Dorset, son of Thomas Sackville, the first of that family to own KNOLE. It was set up to house 21 men and 10 unmarried women from among his old servants, and is still a home for old people. It has been modernized, but retains its ancient character. It is open daily.

In Moat Road is St Margaret's Convent, Mother House of the Society of St Margaret, built in 1865. Here is located the School of Embroidery which produces fine vestments and needlework for the decorations of cathedrals and churches throughout the world. Visitors may be shown around by arrangement.

EFFINGHAM, *Surrey* (6–TQ1153). An old town that was prominent in Elizabethan times as the home of the Howards of Effingham, one of whom was the Commander-in-Chief of the English fleet which defeated the Spanish Armada in 1588; his house was Effingham Court Place, the last remnants of which are now known as Lower Place Farm.

What were two other important old manors here are the moated grange in Great Lee Wood, once the manor of Effingham la Leigh, and East Court, a property of the Earls of Gloucester in medieval times, now incorporated in a boarding school, St Theresa's Convent.

The Parish Church of St Lawrence was originally held by Merton Priory. Although restored several times it still has parts dating from the Middle Ages, including the 14th-cent. chancel.

EGHAM, *Surrey* (6–TQ0171). A historic town skirted by the River Thames and the fields of RUNNYMEDE, scene of the signing of Magna Carta in 1215. A not particularly impressive looking town, it is, however, a rewarding one to visit and its setting is pleasant.

On the outskirts of the town stands Royal Holloway College, since 1890 part of London University. The building, constructed between 1879 and 1886, is modelled on the Château de Chambord in France. It is a huge and ornate structure in the form of a double quadrangle, measuring 550 ft in length with a breadth of 376 ft. Thomas Holloway, a Victorian businessman and philanthropist, built it as a college for women (men students were admitted in 1965) where they might study for degrees at any university, and which might one day confer its own. His ideas of accommodation – two rooms to each student – dictated the size of the building.

The College has an excellent little art gallery containing works collected by Thomas Holloway and his brother-in-law, Sir George Martin-Holloway.

The college and gallery may be viewed by prior arrangement with the Residence Officer.

In the centre of the town is the Red Lion, a busy coaching inn during the 18th and 19th cents. with stabling for 70 horses; the inn has many relics of its past. Another former coaching inn is the Barley Mow at Englefield Green, more than 250 years old. About 1½ m. on the road to VIRGINIA WATER is Great Fosters County Hotel, originally a Tudor manor house; restored to its original form, it has mullioned windows, some fine plasterwork ceilings and a handsome fireplace.

At Englefield Green, which, like several villages incorporated in Egham, retains something of its rustic atmosphere, was fought the last recorded fatal duel in England: in a field on Priest's Hill, between two exiled Frenchmen (1845). One of the duellists, a man named Cournet, was fatally wounded and was carried to the Barley Mow Inn, where he died. He is buried in Egham churchyard. The victor stood trial for murder but was freed.

The Parish Church of St John the Baptist was built in the 17th cent. on the site of a former Norman church. It contains a fine Georgian pulpit and some Georgian sculptures. There is also a Magna Carta corner which includes replicas of the Surety Barons' coats of arms.

Historic is St Mary's Church in Thorpe, another former village. The church was originally connected with the Benedictine abbey at Chertsey and still has evidence of its Norman origins, including the causeway connecting the church with the abbey (of which no trace remains) and a Norman chancel arch. The church is mainly Early English with a brick Tudor tower.

St Paul's Church, Thorpe Road, is another interesting old church with a modern font, the gift of the children of Egham; next door are the modern buildings of the Magna Carta County Secondary School.

EPSOM, *Surrey* (6–TQ2160), has one of the world's best-known race-courses, Epsom Downs, where is run what is probably the most famed of all horse races, the English Derby. There has been racing here since the days of James I, who often stayed at Nonsuch Palace nearby, and the sport became firmly established in the 18th cent. The first Derby was run in 1780, the race being named after the Earl of Derby; the previous year had seen the introduction of another famous race, the Oaks, named after Lord Derby's ancestral home.

There are many famous old homes here, among them the 17th-cent. Waterloo House, and the 18th-cent. Durdans, home of the Earls of Rosebery. Epsom College, famed as the school for the sons of medical men, has a superb position.

Three m. from Epsom is **Woodcote Park**, the R.A.C. country club, set in grounds of 338 acres. It is residential with the usual club amenities; there is also an excellent 18-hole golf course. The club was founded in 1913, and the buildings are modern, the original premises, a 17th-cent. mansion, having been destroyed by fire in 1934.

ESHER, *Surrey* (6–TQ1464). A residential town on the River Mole. Claremont, a mansion built for Clive of India in 1772, lies ½ m. S. It is set in fine gardens laid out by Capability Brown, and has some good interior work by Holland. It was later presented to Princess Charlotte,. daughter of the Prince Regent, and her husband, Prince Leopold, who became King of the Belgians; she died there in childbirth. The young Victoria often stayed at the house both before and after she came to the throne. Louis-Philippe occupied it for a time after being deposed. Now a girls' school run by Christian Scientists, it is open at advertised times in the summer season.

Esher Mansion, built by Bishop William Waynflete in the 15th cent., was the most important of the town's early buildings; all that remains is the massive gatehouse and a tower.

ETCHINGHAM, *Sussex* (7–TQ7126). A pleasant village at the confluence of the Rivers Rother and Dudwell. The Parish Church of SS. Mary and Nicholas is a fine example of a 14th-cent. church in the Decorated style, much of the original fabric still being in evidence. Most of the glass is modern, but there are some fragments dating from medieval times, as well as original tiles. Four brasses include one, unfortunately mutilated, to Sir William de

Echyngham, who built the church. This is the oldest dated brass in Sussex.

Just outside the village is Haremere Hall, an early 17th-cent. manor house with a panelled great hall and some excellent carving; the house contains good examples of period furniture and an interesting collection of rugs. It is open on stated days in the summer; but parties can view on any day by prior arrangement.

EWELL, *Surrey* (6–TQ2262). A town which has many memories of the past. Nonsuch Park recalls that here was the palace of the same name, begun by Henry VIII and intended to be the finest in all Christendom. It was never finished, and what was built has long since disappeared. However, the fine park remains and is open to the public. There is an old spring, discovered early in the 17th cent., also the 18th-cent. Watch House, once the village lock-up. The castle, now a school, dates only from the last century. So does Ewell Court, now Council premises, but with gardens open to the public.

The church is also relatively modern, having been built in 1847, but the tower in the churchyard is old.

EWHURST, *Surrey* (6–TQ0940), is notable for its mill, about 150 years old, which has not worked for nearly 100 years. It seems that the mill served smugglers as well as millers, although so far from the sea; apparently it was an ideal place in which to cache contraband on its journey to its destined markets.

The Parish Church of SS. Peter and Paul possesses a fine 14th-cent. font.

Rising behind the village is Pitch Hill, a climbers' venue.

Ewhurst in springtime

Kenneth Scowen

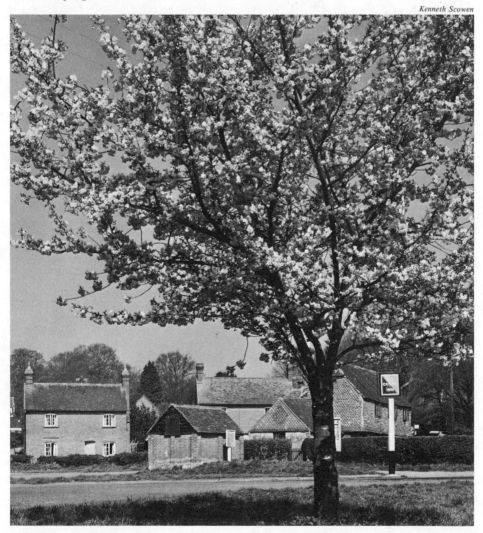

EYNSFORD, *Kent* (7–TQ5365), in the Darent valley, was once an important town, but is now a tranquil village with a group of neat half-timbered cottages. It also has LULLINGSTONE ROMAN VILLA, about ½ m. to the S.; Lullingstone Castle; Eynsford Castle; and a parish church worthy of note.

Lullingstone Castle was never a castle in a military sense. It is in fact a fine Tudor manor house, with additions and remodelling dating from early in the 18th cent. Much of the Tudor work is still in evidence, particularly in the gateway, which shows its original brickwork. The small Church of St Botolph in the castle grounds has a rich Tudor rood-screen. The castle is open on certain days in summer.

Eynsford Castle is a 12th-cent. ruin, but the curtain wall, of flint and mortar, still stands higher than might be expected. Inside are the ruins of the great hall.

The parish church was originally Norman and the present building, with its tall slender spire, dates largely from the 13th cent. It has an elaborate west door and a wide and impressive arch.

FARNHAM, *Surrey* (6–SU8446), is noted for its Georgian houses, as well as architecture of other periods; some of the best can be seen in Castle and West Streets. Willmer House, built in 1718, has a façade of cut and moulded brick, and there is much fine carving and panelling in the interior. It now houses a museum exhibiting finds from the district from earliest times, as well as 17th- and 18th-cent. furniture, clocks and costumes, and items connected with the work of local artists, craftsmen and inventors.

The castle, dating from the second half of the 12th cent., replaced one by Henry of Blois, Bishop of WINCHESTER, destroyed at the order of Henry II. It has the distinction of having been occupied almost continuously until recent times; as a seat of the Bishops of Winchester until 1925, then of the Bishop of GUILDFORD until 1956.

The present buildings are mainly from the 15th to 17th cents. but the court and wall date from the 12th and 13th cents., though much extended and altered over the years; the keep is the most impressive part. The castle is now a training college. The keep is open daily throughout the year, but the rest of the castle only on certain days.

William Cobbett, the essayist and Radical politician best known for his *Rural Rides*, was born in Farnham in 1762, in the house now the Jolly Farmer inn.

FAVERSHAM, *Kent* (7–TR0161), a historic town, which, after a period of apparent neglect, realized its heritage. Timely preservation has enabled the town to boast of a fine collection of memorials of its past. There were settlements here in prehistoric times and the Romans and Anglo-Saxons both established villages, and Faversham enjoyed considerable importance in medieval times. The town claims one of the largest collec-

tions of municipal charters of any city or town in Britain, some dating back more than 700 years; one bears the date 1252. A number are kept in the town archives in the Municipal Council chambers and may be seen by those interested.

For more than a quarter of a mile, from the Guildhall, both sides of Abbey Street are lined with buildings largely of the Tudor and Stuart periods, though many of them have Georgian fronts. However, the original architecture of most of them is evident, making this a somewhat unusual street, with its more than 50 "listed buildings", for so large a town, which is a port and primarily commercial. A historic house is No. 80, which was the home of Thomas Arden, who was mayor in 1547 and who was murdered by his wife and her lover during his term of office. The incident became the basis of an anonymous play, *Arden of Faversham* (*c.* 1586), described by many as the forerunner of the popular domestic drama of the English stage.

At the head of Abbey Street is Market Place, a small square with the Guildhall in the centre. The original Tudor guildhall was demolished early in the 19th cent. but the pillars and arches which supported it were retained, and the new hall of 1814 was built over them. On all sides of the Market Place are old buildings, mostly dating from Tudor or Stuart times. One was formerly an inn, the Queen's Arms, and here James II was held prisoner for several days after his capture by Faversham fishermen when he tried to flee the country in 1688.

The parish church, St Mary of Charity, is a cruciform building which contains some Norman arches and windows, much Early English work, good 15th-cent. stalls, as well as intricately carved misericords which are among the finest in the country. A coloured octagonal pillar is adorned with early 14th-cent. frescoes. The steeple, built in 1797, is a copy of Wren's St Dunstan's-in-the-East.

About 100 yds away, along a footpath, is the Masonic Hall, a Tudor building which was formerly the Grammar School. The school is now housed in modern buildings opposite.

Close by the town is Judd's Folly Hill, believed to have been the site of the Roman town and fort of Durolevum. Finds made in King's Field, now a part of the town playing fields, indicate that this was the site of the Anglo-Saxon village. Roman and Anglo-Saxon finds, and other exhibits relating to Faversham history are in a museum in the half-timbered Maison Dieu at Ospringe, a village now part of the town. Ospringe church dates from early Norman times and has two Norman doorways, and 13th-cent. arches; the tower is modern. The massive font is also Norman.

At **Davington** the parish church was formerly the 12th-cent. nave of Davington Priory, dissolved in 1535. It has several Norman features, including the tower and west doorway. The house called Davington Priory is a private residence which incorporates parts of the cloisters and frater of the original priory, founded in 1153 for Benedictine nuns. Another old church is St Catherine's at

Preston, which has been restored and enlarged twice, but retains Early English and 14th-cent. work.

FISHBOURNE, *Sussex* (6–SU8304). About 1 m. W. of CHICHESTER, the Roman Palace at Fishbourne is the largest Roman building yet discovered in Britain, and one of the largest anywhere. When first discovered it was thought to be a villa, but it was soon evident by its size, the quality of the materials and workmanship found on the site that it was more likely the palace of a very high official or even a king.

Although it is not known for certain for whom the palace was built, the experts believe a likely candidate is Cogidubnus, a Briton and king of the Regni tribe, a friend and supporter of the Romans who visited Rome and was made a senator. The building of the palace was started about A.D. 75 and although it lost its regal status about the end of the 1st cent. with the death of Cogidubnus, it remained a sumptuous dwelling until destroyed by fire about A.D. 280.

Nearly 17 centuries were to pass between the fire and the rediscovery of the palace: in 1960 a workman digging a trench turned up some small pieces of coloured stone. Archaeologists have since uncovered buildings that show the original palace to have covered an area of more than six acres, as well as evidence beneath the palace of earlier wooden structures, probably erected as early as A.D. 43, the year the Roman legions arrived. The palace was in four wings enclosing a courtyard, in which was evidence of the garden, the only complete Roman example to have been discovered. Not all has yet been excavated as part lies beneath Fishbourne village and part under the main road. Some excavated sections have been re-covered for their protection. However, the whole of the north wing has been enclosed in a protective building, and together with a site museum was opened to the public in 1968.

The palace was nearly discovered long ago – probably in the Middle Ages: this was established when a wide plough furrow was found to have been cut right across the mosaic floor of one room. Fortunately, the ploughman was not interested in what he turned up and it was left to more enlightened times for the discovery of the palace to be made and properly appreciated.

A walk round the area of the palace now on view gives a vivid picture of the splendour in which its occupants lived, and of the great skill of the men who built and decorated it. The early mosaics are superb pieces of artistry and workmanship, pieced together from hundreds of thousands of tesserae, some measuring less than ¼ in. across. The design with a centrepiece of a boy on a dolphin forms the finest mosaic floor yet uncovered in Britain.

Designs on other floors include some of the geometric forms so popular with the Romans. In one room there are two layers of mosaic; apparently one floor had become damaged, or the occupants had grown tired of it, and another mosaic was laid over it. Both mosaics are damaged, but show their fine workmanship.

Among other things to see are sections of the original partition walls; a perfectly preserved hypocaust, part of the palace heating system; and a warm plunge bath with a water-proofing course between floor and wall. There are some tiles here bearing what may have been the manufacturer's trade-mark. A skeleton was found in a hollow of one of the floors, probably one of several people believed to have perished in the fire of 280.

In the museum are exhibited finds made during the excavations, including another skeleton. In addition there are exhibits concerning life in Roman Britain, as well as in other places occupied by the Romans.

Outside, a section of the garden has been laid out as experts imagine it would have been when the palace was occupied. When excavated the garden as it was originally planned could be clearly seen, with the bedding and trenching, and remains of the water pipes that fed fountains and basins, and perhaps watered the gardens.

Fishbourne: a detail from the Roman mosaic

Topix

J. Allan Cash

Folkestone: the old fishermen's harbour provides a good anchorage for yachts and cruisers

FOLKESTONE, *Kent* (7–TR2336), a popular seaside resort which was developed in the middle of the last century; Victorian hotels and guest-houses line the front. Folkestone is also an important cross-Channel port.

A fine promenade, the Leas, runs for over a mile along the cliff-top 200 ft above the beach. From anywhere along the Leas there is a fine view over the busy Channel, and across to the French coast on a clear day. On the promenade is the Leas Cliff Hall, seemingly suspended on the cliff, where excellent orchestral concerts and other entertainments are presented. At the W. extremity is the East Kent and Folkestone Art Centre, a private gallery which holds first-class exhibitions. The cliffside has terraced gardens which offer a pleasant route from the beach to the Leas. There is also a funicular.

Of the churches the most interesting is the Church of SS. Mary and Eanswythe, the latter saint being a grand-daughter of Ethelbert, the first Christian king of Kent. She established the first nunnery in England in A.D. 630, just E. of the present church which dates from the 13th cent. Despite a complete restoration during the last century, much of the fabric of the 13th and 15th cents. remains. The relics of St Eanswythe are kept in a casket in her chapel. The font is 15th cent. but a 13th-cent. font, now broken, may also be seen. The glass is modern, the old windows having been destroyed during the Second World War.

Just off the Leas in a small park stands a solitary tower, all that remains of Christ Church, which was built in 1850 and destroyed in an air raid in 1942. The tower was restored as a memorial. There is a fine view from the top.

Old, narrow streets wind down to the original fishermen's quarter near the harbour. Folkestone has few really old buildings, but some of the oldest stand here. Close by are the amusement parlours and bingo clubs which have replaced a large section of the old quarter.

Of the modern buildings the Civic Centre is outstanding. It is of striking design and faces a broad tree-lined avenue; the Information Office is here.

There are many fine walks in and around the town: along the East Cliff towards DOVER, for example, with an extensive view of the White Cliffs. Here are great green areas, good for picnics. Above the town on the edge of the North Downs is the hill known as Caesar's Camp; this is excellent rambling country, and offers views over the town, the cliffs and the Channel.

A number of race meetings are held every year at the Folkestone Race-course at **Westenhanger,** about 5 m. distant on the main road to London.

FORDWICH, *Kent* (7–TR1859). A little village on the Stour, about 2½ m. E. of CANTERBURY. It was once the port of that city, when the river was wider and deeper, and ships smaller, and a sizable borough. The borough was eventually abolished, but the Town Hall was retained, a delightful, red-roofed, half-timbered Tudor building beside the quay with a ducking-stool crane. The Church of St Mary is in part Norman. A number of old houses, some of them quite large, remain from busier days. There are two attractive inns.

FRENSHAM, *Surrey* (6–SU8441). An outstanding beauty-spot, whose chief feature is the common, covering more than 1 sq. m., in which there is the Great Pond extending over more than 100 acres, and the much smaller Little Pond, which in the season is covered with water lilies. The sailing, swimming and fishing here are good.

On the common, which is a fine place for walks, are a group of prehistoric bowl barrows. The area is also rich in bird life: there are reputed to be more than 200 species there to watch and enjoy.

The parish church was largely rebuilt in the middle of the last century, but has a late 14th-cent. tower with massive buttresses and some timbers of the same period. The font is Norman. Of greater interest, however, is a copper cauldron, 9 ft in diameter and 1 ft deep, which stands on a tripod and is believed to be about 400 years old. Its origins are a mystery, but one story claims it was the property of a witch, Mother Ludlam, who used it in her witch's cave at Moore Park, near FARNHAM.

FRIMLEY, *Surrey* (6–SU8758). A very old village in a district where there have been numerous prehistoric and Roman finds; these are exhibited in the museum at **Camberley.** The manor was held by the monks of Chertsey from Anglo-Saxon times until the Dissolution in 1537. There was a church consecrated in 1606, but the present Parish Church of St Peter dates only from 1825. In the churchyard are buried many famous people, including the American novelist, Francis Bret Harte, who after a wandering and adventurous life settled in England. Woodlands ideal for rambling surround the village.

Camberley is important for the Royal Staff College and the nearby Royal Military Academy, Sandhurst, where the National Army Museum is open to the public.

GATWICK, *Surrey* (6–TQ2839). London's second airport is on the direct route by road and rail between LONDON and BRIGHTON. When it opened as a full-scale international airport in 1958 it was the most modern in Europe, the first to combine air, main road and rail facilities under one roof. It was also the first airport in Europe to adopt the pier system.

Originally opened in 1936, Gatwick was taken over by the Air Ministry who set up an R.A.F. flying training school in the following year. It became an important war-time R.A.F. station, expanding to include an adjoining race-course. It passed to commercial use after the war and was closed in 1956 for its modernization. Now more than 100 companies operate from here and there are up to 300 aircraft movements daily during the peak periods.

The general public is also well catered for: one spacious "finger" provides a platform for plane-spotting, or simply for watching the arrival and departure of aircraft of many nations, their loading and unloading.

GILLINGHAM, *Kent* (7–TQ7768). The largest of the Medway Towns, it merges into its neighbour, CHATHAM, with which it shares the naval dockyards and depot. Gillingham has prehistoric and Roman traces and the Anglo-Saxons gave the place its name. Later it became a Norman manor but, like Chatham, it did not come into prominence until late in the Middle Ages, principally for its docks and ship-building. Buildings are mostly comparatively modern, but two of its churches have origins dating back to Norman times.

The Parish Church of St Mary is on The Green, the heart of the oldest part of the town. It has some Norman work, including two pillars in the chancel, while the font, large enough for total immersion, is of the same period. The rood-screen and the arch from which it hangs are 14th-cent. and there is much work of the 15th and 16th cents. remaining. The building was thoroughly restored in the middle of the last century.

The Parish Church of St Margaret in Rainham, formerly a village but now part of the borough, dates mainly from the 14th and 15th cents. with some traces of Norman work. Remains of six medieval consecration crosses and some faint traces of a medieval mural may be seen.

The barracks of the Royal Engineers are generally referred to as being in Chatham but are actually at Brompton, in Gillingham. In the barracks is housed a most interesting military museum open to the public at advertised times throughout the year.

The museum was formed in 1912 and traces the history of the corps from its formation in 1716, although there are exhibits concerning military engineering in much earlier periods. There is a manual dealing with the subject which was printed in Latin in Verona in 1472, and among several other old handbooks is one used in Marlborough's time. Also here are exhibits relating to the early days of military aviation for, before the Royal Flying Corps was founded in 1912, flying was the province of the Royal Engineers. One room is devoted to General Gordon and deals mainly with his activities in China nearly a century ago.

An interesting exhibit is a complete model of the Mulberry Harbour that was prefabricated in England and towed across the Channel for the Normandy landings in 1944. Nearby is the first remote-controlled torpedo, a device invented in 1877 by an Australian, Louis Brennan, and named after him.

GLYNDEBOURNE, *Sussex* (6–TQ4510), has become renowned for its music and opera festivals, instituted by the late John Christie in 1934. Christie, a former science master at Eton and a lover of opera, devised the idea of having presentations of first-class opera at his ancestral home, and had built on to it an opera house harmonizing perfectly with the existing house. World-famous singers and conductors appear here every summer. The season lasts from May until August and performances begin early, about 5.30 to 6 p.m. and finish about 10 p.m. Evening dress is obligatory.

A feature is the supper interval, which usually lasts for 75 minutes, when patrons take supper on the wide lawns, picnic-style; this they can bring themselves or obtain from a buffet. A full dinner is also obtainable from the dining-room.

The gardens are magnificent. A wide variety of trees and shrubs grow, including yews and some fine oaks. Two oaks grow through the roof of the restaurant, and other trees rise up from the floor like pillars; they were carefully preserved when the restaurant was built.

GODALMING, *Surrey* (6–SU9743), has been, since 1872, the home of Charterhouse School, located on the outskirts of the town. The school for boys, and the Charterhouse Hospital for aged men, was founded in London in 1611 by a wealthy coal merchant, Thomas Sutton. In 1872 the school moved to Godalming (the hospital remained in London) into buildings constructed in Gothic style to give something of the character of the former London premises. The 150-ft Founder's Tower dominates the school. The imposing chapel was built in 1925 as a memorial to Old Carthusians who lost their lives in the First World War.

The museum, housed in two buildings erected in 1890, contains a collection of local antiquities, ancient pottery, and exhibits relating to the school and its history.

Both the school and the museum are open to the public during school terms; application to view should be made to the School Sergeant.

An old town, Godalming suffers from congested streets, which contain a number of old buildings, some dating back three centuries. There are a number of old coaching inns. One, the King's Arms, bears the date 1753, but this apparently refers only to rebuilding, for parts of the interior retain work of a much earlier period – and in 1689 it is recorded that Peter the Great ate sumptuously here. Another Tsar, Alexander I, was a guest in 1816.

The Old Town Hall belies its name; it dates only from 1814, and was rebuilt on the site of its predecessor. Here is housed the Borough Museum with exhibits illustrating the history of the town, and the Godalming Hundred, from prehistoric times. It is open at stated times throughout the year, but it may be visited at other times by prior appointment with the Librarian and Curator.

The Parish Church of SS. Peter and Paul was drastically restored in the mid-19th cent. but some of its old Norman and later medieval work remains. The panelled roof is early 16th-cent., the pulpit Elizabethan, and the altar in the south chapel is Jacobean.

About 3 m. S. of the town is **Winkworth Arboretum,** a 95-acre beauty-spot where a number of rare trees and shrubs grow. There are well-defined footpaths through the park, which contains a lake with some good fishing. The arboretum was founded by Dr William Fox, who, during the Second World War years, cleared this land of scrub and planted it with carefully chosen trees and shrubs, and in 1952 presented it to the National Trust. It is open throughout the year.

GOODWOOD RACE-COURSE, *Sussex* (6–SU8808). "Glorious Goodwood" in the Sussex downland has one of the loveliest settings of any race-course. It is also noted for the excellent condition of the track at all times: hundreds of tons of tan were used to give springiness to the turf, which never becomes too dry or too hard.

The course was first used in 1801 when the 3rd Duke of Richmond gave part of his estate to construct a track where members of the Goodwood Hunt Club and officers of the Sussex Militia (of which he was Colonel) could hold meetings. In the early days the meetings were informal, but were subsequently regularized until this became one of the foremost courses in the country.

Goodwood House, the seat of the Dukes of Richmond and Gordon, was built between 1780 and 1800. It is a fine example of Sussex flint work. It contains a superb collection of paintings, French and English period furniture, tapestries and magnificent Sèvres porcelain. The parkland surrounding the house has fine trees, including some very old cedars. The Shell House, built in 1739 by Sarah, Duchess of Richmond, is a small pavilion on a hill covered entirely with shells arranged in intricate patterns.

House and park are open during the summer at advertised times.

Near the race-course is an excellent 18-hole golf course.

GOUDHURST, *Kent* (7–TQ7337). A village on a hill with fine views of the countryside of orchards and hopfields around, and especially over the Weald to the N. Old houses grace the streets of Goudhurst, which achieved prosperity through the introduction of the weaving industry in the Middle Ages.

The church is mainly of the 15th cent. The 17th-cent. tower, in an odd mixture of Gothic and Renaissance styles, is usually open to the public; the top makes an excellent viewing point. Notable in the church is a table tomb, beneath a beautiful oriel window, with life-size painted wooden figures of Sir Alexander Culpeper, who died in 1537, and his wife. The Culpepers were among the most powerful landowners in Kentish history and this tomb is one of the finest of their many memorials in the county.

Bedgebury National Pinetum lies 2½ m. S. of Goudhurst. It is at once a scientific nursery, a museum of trees and a delightful parkland. An offshoot of Kew Gardens, it was founded in 1924 to grow experimentally various types of foreign trees, chiefly conifers, which did not thrive in the smoke-laden air of the London area. Here come scientists as well as all sorts of people seeking advice about trees, or a pleasant day's outing.

The 75-acre Pinetum contains a wide variety of pines and firs besides cypresses, cedars, larches, hemlock spruce and Californian redwoods. Broad-leaved trees include oak and birch. Many kinds of shrubs grow: rhododendrons abound and also line much of the winding road from Goudhurst to the Pinetum. There are three lakes, fed by small streams and covered with water lilies, where visitors may fish.

The Pinetum has two capacious car parks and there are footpaths to all parts. It is open to the public throughout the year.

Noel Habgood

Gravesend: tugs and fishing boats at the mouth of the Thames

The adjoining mansion, now a girls' school, was the home of the Beresford-Hope family.

GRAVESEND, *Kent* (7–TQ6473). An industrial town where the Thames pilots have their station. There is a great deal of Thames bustle, and the river front has some fascination.

This is where Pocahontas, the daughter of a Red Indian chieftain, is buried. Pocahontas saved the life of Captain John Smith, and, possibly, of all the settlers in the colony of Chesapeake, Virginia, when she interceded with her father on Smith's behalf when he was about to be put to death. She later married another settler, John Rolfe, and came to England with him. She became ill and decided to return, but was taken, dying, off the ship at Gravesend and was buried in the little Church of St George by the river in 1617. That building has since disappeared but the present Georgian church stands on the same site.

GREAT BOOKHAM, *Surrey* (6–TQ1454) Here is Polesden Lacey, a magnificent Regency house built in 1824 on the site of a house once owned by the 18th-cent. playwright and actor, Richard Brinsley Sheridan. The interior was considerably altered in 1906 and a cupola and clock tower added, but the Regency character was not spoilt. Opposite a superb staircase is a finely carved 17th-cent. reredos from St Matthew's Church, Cheapside, London. The drawing-room has a richly gilded ceiling from which hangs an enormous chandelier, and the room has gilded panelling. The house has some fine Flemish and Mortlake tapestries, several collections of china and porcelain, and paintings by famous masters.

The grounds cover 140 acres, laid out in delightful gardens bordered by imaginatively trimmed yew hedges.

The house is open at advertised times; the gardens daily throughout the year. It is now the headquarters of the South Eastern District of the National Trust.

The Bookhams – two adjoining villages with the prefixes Great and Little – have a number of attractive old houses. Great Bookham has a 12th-cent. church, with a chancel rebuilt in the mid-14th cent.

It is one of the most complete medieval buildings in the county.

GROOMBRIDGE, *Kent* (7–TQ5337), lies half in Kent and half in Sussex. Sussex has the newer, larger part, but there is more interest in the smaller, older Kentish section. The boundary between the two counties here is Kent Water, which feeds the MEDWAY. It is a post-medieval village; however, there are many old buildings and a green, lined with tile-hung cottages. The church was built in 1623 in Gothic style; it has a Jacobean pulpit and some heavy Victorian glass.

Groombridge Place is a handsome house built in the Wren manner. The lovely garden is open at times during the summer; the Jacobean diarist John Evelyn designed it.

About 1 m. S. are Harrison's Rocks, an outcrop that provides fine rock-climbing.

GUILDFORD, *Surrey* (6–TQ0049). The capital of Surrey, Guildford is an old town, although its history is neither turbulent nor spectacular. There may have been pre-Saxon settlements here, but it is first mentioned in the time of Alfred the Great. In medieval times the town became a favourite of a number of monarchs who had palaces and a castle here; the palaces have disappeared and little remains of the castle. It was at a friary near Guildford that Henry VIII signed the order dissolving the lesser religious orders.

The medieval **Pilgrim's Way** that led from WINCHESTER to CANTERBURY and the shrine of St Thomas à Becket, following a prehistoric track along the downs for part of its route, crossed the River Wey just S. of Guildford.

During the Middle Ages the town was a prosperous centre of the wool industry until its decline in the reign of Elizabeth I, and although this was followed by difficult times its strategic position ensured prosperity. Today it is a bustling town with many historic monuments.

The original Anglo-Saxon fortification was built on a partly artificial mound. The Normans built a keep on this mound and the castle grew up around it. In medieval times the castle was a favourite royal residence and was regarded as a royal nursery; a number of young princes spent their early years here. Today, only the keep remains, a square solid structure about 60 ft high. The interior is a bare ruin but the top is easily reached, and from here there is a fine view over the town. Surrounding the keep are pleasant

Guildford: the Guildhall, with its great gilded clock, in the High Street

Kenneth Scowen

gardens, in the corner of which is the remnant of a building which may once have been part of the Anglo-Saxon fort; adjoining is another small garden – the Garden of Remembrance containing the War Memorial.

Below Castle Hill in Quarry Street is the Norman Arch, all that remains of the entrance of the old castle; beside this is the headquarters of the Surrey Archaeological Society, which also houses the Guildford Museum. Here are exhibits concerning local archaeology and history, also items connected with Lewis Carroll, author of *The Adventures of Alice in Wonderland*. Carroll, whose real name was Charles Lutwidge Dodgson, was the son of a Yorkshire clergyman, and never actually resided in Guildford, but he spent much time with his six unmarried sisters who lived in a rented house called The Chestnuts. This house, where he died in 1898, is about 100 yds inside the Norman Arch; it is marked by a plaque, but is a private residence and not open to the public. Carroll is buried in the Mount Cemetery.

In the centre of the High Street is the Guildhall, a handsome but quite modest building with a turreted roof. A large, gilded clock, bearing the date 1683, juts out right over the street – a famous Guildford landmark. The Guildhall also dates from 1683, and it replaced a former medieval guildhall on the same site. Both the court room and council chamber are elegantly panelled, and above the bench hangs a great two-handed sword of 16th-cent. German make, which is carried before the mayor in formal processions. The Corporation plate (which is shown by special arrangement) includes a silver-gilt mace presented by Henry VII; it is one of the few 15th-cent. maces in the country. There are also a number of fine 16th- and 17th-cent. pieces. The Council no longer meets in the Guildhall except for the mayor-making ceremonies and the annual meetings. New municipal buildings were erected in the early 1930s.

Further along the High Street, on the same side, stands the Abbot's Hospital, or Hospital of the Blessed Trinity, founded by George Abbot, a Guildford man and Archbishop of Canterbury under James I. Built in 1619 as a home for 12 old men and 8 widows or spinsters, it still accommodates 23 old people of the town. The brick building is much as it was originally, and particularly interesting is the chapel with splendid 17th-cent. stained-glass windows depicting the story of Jacob in eight panels. Short services are held every morning for the members, who attend in Tudor hats and gowns. The Hospital is open to the public daily at advertised hours; the guide of the day wears the traditional cap and gown.

Also in the High Street is the Royal Grammar School; on one side of the street is the old school built in the latter half of the 16th cent. and facing on the other side are the new buildings. The old school buildings were damaged by fire in 1962, but were carefully restored and are still in use. Permission to inspect the old school may be granted on written application to the headmaster.

Guildford House was built in 1660 and has been carefully restored. It is now used for art exhibitions and as a meeting place for cultural organizations. A timber-framed building, it has a fine oak and elm staircase, and some beautifully moulded ceilings. Another kind of cultural centre is the modern Yvonne Arnaud Theatre, built in delightful surroundings by the River Wey in memory of the actress, Yvonne Arnaud, who died in 1958.

Oldest building in the town is St Mary's Church in Quarry Street near the castle, with which it was closely associated for centuries. The church was originally built in Anglo-Saxon times and the tower dates, basically, from the days of Edward the Confessor, although the castellated top is modern. Constructed mainly during the 11th to 13th cents., the church was carefully restored in this century and much of the original work has been retained. The central apse facing on to the street was shortened and the curve taken out in 1825, at the request, so it is said, of George IV because his coach could not comfortably negotiate the narrow street.

Holy Trinity Church was rebuilt in the mid-18th cent. after being ruined by the collapse of the tower. Of the original building only a chantry remains, and it is now used as a vestry; a number of tombs escaped, including that of George Abbot, a fine piece of sculpture now in the south chapel.

Both the Congregational and Methodist churches are noteworthy modern buildings which have won architectural awards.

The town has several interesting old hostelries. The Angel Inn, formerly a coaching inn, still incorporates the old courtyard from where the coaches left; it has been carefully restored.

Guildford is rich in parks, gardens and open spaces. Close to the town centre is Rack's Close, which forms a natural amphitheatre and is used for the presentation of amateur open-air drama. A little further out, but less than a mile from the centre, is Stoke Park, where is held the one-day Surrey Agricultural Show, one of the largest of its kind in the country. Also held here, in September, is the two-day Guildford Town Show.

S. of the town bridge the riverside is attractive. The River Wey, which was one of the first English rivers to be converted to a navigable waterway, and still has locks and tumbling bays built in the 17th cent., is the property of the National Trust from Godalming to the Thames. It was given by the navigation companies, whose barges used it until the 1950s. Boating and punting can be enjoyed on the river in summer.

Guildford was part of the diocese of WIN-CHESTER until this was divided in 1927, two new dioceses being formed, Guildford in the NE. and PORTSMOUTH in the S., in addition to the existing one of Winchester. The first bishop of the diocese, Dr J. H. Greig, was enthroned in Holy Trinity Parish Church, but this was too small to make a cathedral and it was decided to build one.

The Cathedral of the Holy Spirit stands on Stag Hill, about 1 m. outside the town, the first cathedral to be built on an entirely new site in the South of England since the Reformation. Contributions from all over the county and country financed its building. It is an exceptional piece of modern cathedral architecture, designed by Sir Edward Maufe in a simplified Gothic style. It includes work by some of the foremost contemporary artists and craftsmen.

The foundation stone was laid in 1936, but building was halted in 1939 by the outbreak of the Second World War, and it was not until 1952 that work could start again. This was completed in 1961 and the cathedral was consecrated on 17 May of that year. The building is cruciform and has seating for 1,750 people. The exterior is of bricks hand-made from local clay; the roof is copper, and the tower is 160 ft high and surmounted by a gilded angel. The foundation stone rests on stones from the fabric of Canterbury and Winchester Cathedrals.

There is little stained glass in the cathedral; almost all the glass is of the clear, Remy Amber type, giving a light, bright interior, heightened by the newness of the light-coloured stone and plasterwork. The piers of the nave and aisles are of brick covered with plaster and Doulting stone; the roof concrete with a very effective acoustic plaster. There is a clear view down the great vaulted nave, crossing and choir right through to the high altar with its golden dorsal reaching up to a fine rose window.

Guildford: the Yvonne Arnaud Theatre, delightfully situated by the River Wey

Kenneth Scowen

The chancel and sanctuary are paved with Purbeck marble, and the bishop's throne with its two chaplain's stalls, one on either side, is gilded oak, a fine piece of modern workmanship. It was made by one craftsman who assembled it on the spot himself. The stalls are of lime oak.

The crypt was used for services and was the local parish church until the cathedral was consecrated; it now provides accommodation for the choir. At the top of the steps leading from the south ambulatory is the Jerusalem Stone, quarried in Jerusalem, on which the story of the crypt is inscribed. The baptistry has a blue vaulted ceiling; the seven-sided font was made from a single block of Travertine marble, and is adorned with fine carvings.

Also modern are the buildings of the University of Surrey, set on the north slope of Stag Hill, close to the cathedral. The university was granted its charter by Queen Elizabeth II in September 1966.

Three m. SW. of Guildford is **Loseley House**, an Elizabethan mansion built by Sir William More, a kinsman of Sir Thomas More, and it has been in the family ever since. The house was built from stone from Waverley Abbey. Inside is panelling from Henry VIII's Nonsuch Palace, some fine ceilings, an interesting chimney-piece carved from local chalk, and old furniture and tapestries; some of the furniture dates from the early days of the house.

Shalford, a small village, has a picturesque 18th-cent. watermill beside the River Tillingbourne which is open to the public on application. The church is comparatively modern, having been built in the mid-19th cent. but it contains some appointments from a previous church on this site.

Four m. NE. off the A3 is **Sutton Place**, a Tudor red-brick house, now the property of the American multi-millionaire, Paul Getty. The gardens are open on certain days during the spring for local charities.

HADLOW, *Kent* (7–TQ6349), a growing village which now possesses little that is old, and is chiefly interesting for a 170-ft tower. Known as "May's Folly", it is all that remains, with the gatehouse, of Hadlow Castle, a 19th-cent. mansion. It was built by the owner, Walter May, in order, so it is said, that he could have an uninterrupted view over the Weald as far as the Channel coast. The tower was reprieved when the rest of the mansion was demolished. It is not open to the public, but remains as a spectacular landmark and a memorial to one man's eccentricity.

Near the Folly is Hadlow Church, dating in part from the 12th cent. and possessing an interesting pyramidal spire. It was for centuries the property of the Knights Hospitallers of St John of Jerusalem, and there are a number of Crusaders' crosses cut into the door, which is believed to be of Anglo-Saxon origin.

HAILSHAM, *Sussex* (7–TQ5909), was an important market town as far back as Norman times, and still has one of the largest markets in Sussex; on the south side of the town the present-day market-place covers more than 3 acres.

The church is 15th-cent. and replaced one built in 1200.

Two m. W. of the town, at Upper Dicker, is Michelham Priory, an Augustinian house founded in 1229. It was dissolved in 1536 and partially destroyed, but the remnants formed the nucleus of a Tudor house built late in the 16th cent. In the following centuries the building was used mainly as a farm-house, and in 1959 it was presented to the Sussex Archaeological Society. One of the largest moats in the country surrounds it: about 1 m. in circumference and originally 12 ft deep, but now only half that depth through silting over the years. It is spanned by an ancient bridge. The priory has a splendid 14th-cent. gatehouse, and there is still much medieval work in the main building, although there has been extensive rebuilding and restoration during this century.

The house contains exhibits of furniture, tapestries, ancient stained glass, Sussex ironwork, musical instruments and a doll's house. In the 7-acre grounds are the great barn, old waggons and ploughs, a typical old Sussex wheelwright's shop and forge, and a Sussex craft shop.

Art exhibitions and musical festivals are regularly held here. The house and grounds are open daily in the summer.

HANDCROSS, *Sussex* (6–TQ2630). One m. SE. of the village are the beautiful Nymans Gardens. Covering 30 acres, they have been carefully built up and continuously improved since they were established at the beginning of this century. Trees, shrubs and plants growing here have come from all over the world. There is a pinetum and a heather garden. A solitary old wistaria is famous.

The gardens are open at advertised times from April to October.

HASLEMERE, *Surrey* (6–SU9032). A town set in hilly, wooded country, much of it in the keeping of the National Trust, and fine for walking. The town itself has some old buildings, but its outstanding attractions are its Educational Museum, the Dolmetsch Workshop and the annual festival which features medieval music and instruments.

The Educational Museum has been described not only as a "living museum", but as a "lively museum". It was founded in 1888 by a prominent Victorian surgeon, Sir Jonathan Hutchinson, who spent much time walking around the countryside picking up fossils, plants and anything else that interested him, and in talking to children. From their reactions he got his idea of establishing a museum that would be not merely a place where things were preserved and exhibited, but where they would be linked with instructive and interesting talks in which the visitors would be active participants. This began in his own home, then in wooden buildings in the town (now the offices of the Urban District Council) and finally it was moved to its present premises in the High Street.

The museum is divided into Botany, Geology, Zoology, Archaeological and History sections, each containing a wide variety of exhibits, largely concerned with Sussex, including its natural history, and the Wealden glass and iron industries, but embracing all countries. A special feature is British bird life: the collection of several hundred specimens is claimed to be second only to the Bird Museum at BRIGHTON. A hive enables study of the life of a colony of bees.

The Educational Museum is open daily throughout the year.

The Dolmetsch Workshops were founded shortly after the First World War by Arnold Dolmetsch, a musician of Swiss descent who settled in the town in 1917. He specialized in ancient music and musical instruments, and today the Dolmetsch family devote themselves to the manufacture of recorders, lutes, spinets, virginals, viols, harpsichords and forte-pianos. Visitors are welcome and may not only see many of these instruments but watch them being made. However, it is a workshop and factory, and intending visitors should telephone for an appointment. Viewing times are in normal working hours.

The Haslemere Festival, largely the idea of the Dolmetsch family, is usually held during July. It is devoted to music from early times to the early 18th cent., played chiefly on ancient instruments, not only those reproduced in the Dolmetsch workshops, but also on several original old instruments.

HASTINGS, *Sussex* (7–TQ8009). An ancient town that became famous as the base from which William the Conqueror set out to fight the Battle of Hastings – although battle was not joined here, but at BATTLE, 6 m. NW. William landed at PEVENSEY, a few miles to the W., marched to Hastings and made his preparations. The town later became one of the Cinque Ports and prospered for a period in the Middle Ages, although suffering heavily, like other south-eastern coastal towns, from French raids during the Hundred Years' War. After the harbour had silted up its prosperity waned, but during the 19th cent. it became a popular watering-place and is now a leading resort.

Hastings has an extensive shingle beach and a long pier supplying the usual seaside amusements. A wide promenade follows the beach line and below it is a covered, all-weather promenade called Bottle Alley: its walls are ornamented with thousands of pieces of coloured glass.

The most interesting part is the Old Town, the fishermen's quarter. Fishing has been for centuries the main industry here, carried on in the typical beach boats of this part of the coast. For lack of a harbour, these craft are still hauled up on to the shingle, nowadays by motor rather than muscle-power. Several attempts have been made to build a new harbour, but have failed. The last was in 1893 when one arm was constructed which now acts as a breakwater.

High on the beach stand the net-lofts, usually three-storied and built on concrete bases about 8 ft square. Thrift ordained this tall, narrow shape: the fishermen had to pay ground rent and so built on the smallest possible area; they needed room for big nets and other gear and built high. Use of these tarred towers began in the mid-16th cent. and some of those standing today are quite old. Fire destroyed a number in 1961, but these have been replaced. Fishermen can often be seen mending their nets outside the lofts.

The Fishermen's Museum close by was originally their chapel, built in 1854 but never consecrated; it served as a military store during the Second World War and was converted to a museum in 1956. In it are exhibited a clinker-built lugger, the *Enterprise*, the last fishing vessel to be built in Hastings before the shipyards closed down in 1909, and many items concerned with the Hastings fishing industry. The font has been retained, and there is a pulpit on the *Enterprise*. Children of seafaring people are baptized here, and there is a harvest festival in September; the public are welcome at these services. The museum is open in the summer season.

Just above this stretch of sea-front, known as Rock-a-Nore, is a lift to the top of the East Cliff, which gives a splendid view. Nearer the town another, longer lift goes to the top of Castle Hill, where the ruins of Hastings Castle stand, overlooking the town and beaches. Little remains of this structure, built on the site of an earlier Norman castle, probably of wood, and said to have been brought from Normandy by William, ready to erect; nothing remains of it today. On the West Hill, an extension of Castle Hill, are St Clement's Caves, a series of sandstone caves which penetrate to 60 ft below the surface. Both castle and caves are open to the public; guides are required for tours of the caves.

For those who like walks in the salt wind, the cliff-tops here are ideal. They stretch for several miles and present some fine views of the steep rock faces.

Housed in a special room in the White Rock Pavilion is the Hastings Embroidery. Inspired by the Bayeux Tapestry, it was made for the celebrations of the 900th anniversary of the Battle of Hastings. The Embroidery, the work of the Royal School of Needlework, measures 243 ft long by 3 ft high, and consists of 27 panels and 81 pictures depicting major events in English history since the Battle of Hastings.

Another reminder of 1066 is the Conqueror's Stone, by the promenade near the pier. William breakfasted in Hastings, using, it is said, a great stone as a table. This is the stone, it is claimed, at which he sat.

There is good angling at Hastings, either deep-water or from the pier or harbour arm; also freshwater fishing in nearby streams. The annual sea-angling festival, usually held early in the autumn, is one of the biggest events of its kind in England.

Another annual event is the Town Criers' contest held in August. Stentorian-voiced competitors, dressed in Georgian costume, give out resounding cries of "Oyez! Oyez!" and read out short proclamations as of old.

HAYWARDS HEATH, Sussex (6–TQ3324).

A large market town, many of whose residents travel to work in London. It is still an important agricultural centre and presents both a town and a rural aspect. On Muster Green was fought the Civil War battle of Hayward's Heath when a Royalist force was routed with the loss of more than 200 men. A rough granite memorial commemorates the local men who lost their lives in the First and Second World Wars.

Two houses in the district are noted for their beautiful gardens. **Borde Hill**, $2\frac{1}{2}$ m. N. of the town, has rare trees and shrubs, herbaceous borders, magnolias and camellias; and **Heaslands**, $1\frac{1}{2}$ m. SW., a delightful water garden in undulating terrain, with a collection of waterfowl, as well as a walled garden and many roses. Both these gardens are open, infrequently, at advertised times.

Sheffield Park Gardens, a few miles E. of Haywards Heath and just E. of the A275, are open at advertised times. Rhododendrons in early summer and maples and a variety of shrubs in autumn make a colourful display. There are five lakes at different levels. Sheffield Park Station is on the popular privately-run Bluebell Railway.

HEATHFIELD, Sussex (6–TQ5821),

is divided into two sections: the modern housing development which is rapidly growing; and Old Heathfield, a pretty village which was one of the major centres of the Sussex iron industry. One of its most momentous occasions was in 1450 when Jack Cade, the rebel leader, was killed there by Alexander Iden, Sheriff of Kent. The occasion is marked by a plaque on the Jack Cade Stone in Cade Street.

Another monument is the sandstone Gibraltar Tower, 60 ft high, erected in honour of General George Elliot, the heroic defender of the Rock in the siege of 1779 to 1783, who was later created Baron Heathfield; he had purchased Heathfield Park some years before with his share of prize money after the victory of Havana. The Tower, which has been allowed to fall into a state of disrepair, was erected in 1793. Standing in the north-west corner of Heathfield Park, it bears the simple inscription "Calpes Defensori".

The Parish Church of All Saints is mainly 13th-cent. The tower is of chalk construction faced with local sandstone; the spire surmounting it is somewhat out of alignment, built deliberately that way, so it is said, to allow for the prevailing winds. Inside the tower is the date 1445, in Arabic figures, one of the earliest dates to be so written in England.

In 1607 the Vicar of Heathfield, Roger Hunt, accompanied the colonists who went to Chesapeake Bay, Virginia, to establish the first permanent English settlement in North America. A window in the church depicts him administering Holy Communion to the colonists, with a group of Red Indians looking on. Nearby is a tablet set up in 1957 by the American and British Commonwealth Association to commemorate the 350th anniversary of the event.

The village has two old windmills; one may sometimes be seen with sails turning.

HERNE BAY, Kent (7–TR1768),

popular seaside resort on the north shore of the county, notable for its pier. Nearly three-quarters of a mile long, it is the second longest in England. Dominating the sea-front is the Clock Tower, built in 1837.

The beach is shingle and pebble, and the town makes the usual provisions for holidaymakers and trippers. Behind the sea-front much of the architecture of the Victorian era remains; in those days it was a popular watering place.

One m. inland is the parent village of Herne, which has kept something of its rural character, the centre with its cluster of old buildings and church being unspoiled. Notable is the Parish Church of St Martin, of 13th-cent. origin, altered and extended in the 14th cent. In 1538 Nicholas Ridley was appointed vicar and he caused the Te Deum to be sung in English here, the first time this was done in England, and aroused the fury of the Church authorities. It was of this church and parish that he said, "Farewell Herne, thou worshipful and wealthy parish" when he was burnt at the stake in Oxford.

HERSTMONCEUX, Sussex (7–TQ6410).

Herstmonceux Castle is now the home of the Royal Greenwich Observatory. Built in the mid-15th cent. it stands surrounded by a wide moat and is reminiscent of BODIAM CASTLE, erected 55 years earlier. Built of brick with thin, lofty walls, slender turrets and a massive gatehouse, it was a fortified manor house constructed more as a private residence than as a fort. It was dismantled in the 18th cent. and restored in the 1930s. In 1948 the Royal Greenwich Observatory moved there. The Isaac Newton Telescope Building (1967) is open at advertised times.

The castle is an attractive building, especially when its graceful lines are reflected clearly in the moat. It is not open to the public, but the extensive grounds and gardens in which it is set can be visited at advertised times in the summer.

The parish church dates from the 12th to the 15th cents. with Perpendicular windows and a splendid canopied tomb of the 16th cent.; there are some good table tombs in the churchyard. Nearby is. a fine example of a 14th-cent. tithe barn. The village is noted for its woodcrafts, traditional in this part of the Sussex countryside.

HEVER CASTLE, Kent (6–TQ4744),

in Tudor times the home of the Boleyn family, and of Anne, who became mistress to Henry VIII and then his tragic queen. Originally a fortified farm-house built in the 13th cent., it was transformed into a crenellated manor house early in the 15th cent. After the fall of the Boleyn family the house sank into obscurity and early in the present century was simply a farm-house. Then it was bought by a

Herstmonceux Castle is a fine example of the fortified manor house

wealthy American, William Waldorf Astor, who applied a fortune and an army of workmen to modernizing it, building a village in Tudor style as extensions to the main house (which meant diverting a river some 200 yds from its course) and laying out gardens. But he did not touch the exterior and the restoration work was carried out so expertly that the whole is in perfect harmony.

The gardens are magnificent. There is a 35-acre lake excavated during the restoration work; extensive flower beds laid out in Tudor fashion; a half-mile avenue of chestnuts, and another of similar length of limes; a maze with more than 1,000 yew trees and a set of chessmen shaped from more such yews; and an Italian garden and loggia containing a large number of statues, columns and busts which the first Lord Astor had collected in Rome.

The castle and gardens are open to the public at stated times.

HINDHEAD, *Surrey* (6–SU8736), is high up among woodland and heath, much of it belonging to the National Trust. This is one of Surrey's best-known beauty-spots and a splendid place for views over Sussex and the Weald. Gibbet Hill (894 ft) overlooks the hollow called the Devil's Punchbowl.

HOG'S BACK, *Surrey* (6–SU9348), is the name given to the road between GUILDFORD and FARNHAM, following the ridge which rises high above the surrounding countryside. It is one of the most scenic drives in the South-East, and the grass verges on either side allow for motorists to stop and admire the fine views. There are also many good places along this stretch of road where motorists can stop and picnic.

HOLMWOOD, *Surrey* (6–TQ1743). North and South Holmwood are two villages set in forest land, with a common of about 600 acres. Hilly and wooded, this is ideal country for walking and for horse-riding.

Just N. of the village on the Horsham Road is a memorial to Alfred Gwynne Vanderbilt, a member of the American family of millionaires, who was drowned in the sinking of the *Titanic*. He sacrificed himself by giving his life-jacket to a woman passenger. He had fallen in love with this part of Surrey, and spent much of the last 20 years of his life in Holmwood.

HORSHAM, *Sussex* (6–TQ1730). A busy town where modern development has not altered too much of the old character, and fascinating little corners remain. Leading from the railway station to the town centre, North Street is a wide and pleasant garden-lined thoroughfare in which are the modern buildings of the Rural District Council, and, opposite, the mellowed offices of the Urban District Council behind trees and hedges. North Street leads into the Carfax, from which seven streets radiate.

One of these, Pump Alley, is a short street with old buildings, many now shops, on either side. Many retain their original, if restored, fronts. Facing the Carfax is the Old Town Hall, built about 300 years ago, but somewhat altered and restored in the beginning of the 19th cent. It has a crenellated front with a clock and is flanked by two turreted towers. At the bottom of the east and west walls can be seen the barred windows of the cells used when this was an assize town. In a wall in the street a box is let into the stonework with the inscription: "Ye Olde Post Box of Horsham". Do not post letters there; it is a relic of the old coaching days.

Pump Alley leads into the Causeway where most of the houses originate from 300 years or more ago; some are basically 15th- and 16th-cent. with walls that bulge and roofs that undulate. Some bear plaques giving brief details of their history and occupants. One of these buildings is Causeway House, home of the Horsham Museum, devoted chiefly to the history of Horsham and the agricultural life of the county. Among the exhibits are a variety of ploughs and other farm implements dating from the late 18th cent., and harnesses and more than 1,000 items of horse brasses and bits, the collection of William Albury, a Horsham saddler for more than 60 years until the 1940s. The museum also has a completely equipped saddler's shop based on the one run by Albury; there are also replicas of the shops of a wheelwright and a blacksmith whose family was in the business in Horsham for more than 200 years until the 1960s. Other exhibits relate to the natural history of the county; a toy museum features a mainly Victorian collection.

The house retains much of its 16th-cent. work, including a fine old oak staircase.

The Causeway is a cul-de-sac. At the end stands the Parish Church of St Mary, parts of which date back to the 12th cent., for example the 800-year-old sandstone tower, tall and heavily buttressed. Frescoes on the tower arch reproduce 15th-cent. frescoes on this spot, remnants of the original being incorporated. In the west end of the north wall is a Norman doorway and deeply splayed window. The Trinity Chapel is 14th-cent. and the octagonal font 15th-cent.

St Mark's Church in North Street was built in 1839. However, it was rebuilt and restored only 30 years after its original building, being considerably changed in the process; this is demonstrated by a print in the west porch showing the church before restoration. The church is well proportioned internally and has a fine oak rood-screen.

One m. SW. of the town is Christ's Hospital, the Bluecoat boys' school, where the pupils still wear the ankle-length blue coats which have been the uniform since the school was founded in London by Edward VI in 1552 on the site of the Greyfriars Convent, dissolved by Henry VIII. The school moved to Horsham in 1902 and into extensive red-brick premises built in Tudor Gothic in grounds covering about 1,200 acres, the largest school site in England. The buildings incorporate features from the London premises, which were demolished after the move: the main gate; the Grecians' Arch, which was adapted and built into the cloisters; and a wall built by Christopher Wren in 1666. Also in the new school are statues and paintings from the old premises, and the original 15th-cent. font.

The school is open on certain advertised days, called Verrio Days, during the summer term; application to view should be made to the headmaster's principal secretary.

HORSLEYS, THE, *Surrey* (6–TQ0952 and TQ0753). The villages of East and West Horsley are often referred to locally simply as The Horsleys. They lie in a well-wooded area, which includes the spacious Netley Heath. There are a number of old manors and mansions in the district. One of them, the Jacobean mansion of West Horsley Place, was the home of Sir Walter Raleigh's son, Carew. Following his father's execution, Carew obtained possession of the head, which had been exhibited on London Bridge, and had it buried in West Horsley church.

HURSTPIERPOINT, *Sussex* (6–TQ2816). Here is **Danny**, the Elizabethan manor house built by George Goring in the form of a letter E in honour of Queen Elizabeth I who granted him the estate; it later became the home of the Campion family, who added a new wing in the reign of Queen Anne. In 1918 the War Cabinet, one of whose members was Winston Churchill, held meetings here presided over by the Prime Minister, Lloyd George, and drew up the terms of the armistice with Germany. A plaque in the great hall commemorates these meetings. The house contains many interesting exhibits, mainly concerned with its history and that of the Campion family. It is open at advertised times.

HYTHE, *Kent* (7–TR1635). Once a port, and one of the Cinque Ports, the town today stands a little back from the sea, though it is virtually a seaside resort; the beach is mainly shingle. The Royal Military Canal, constructed in the days of the Napoleonic Wars, is here flanked by gardens and provides an attractive and popular recreational feature. The gardens and canal are the scene of an annual summer pageant, called the Water Festival or Venetian Carnival, the highlight of which is a procession of decorated floats along the canal, followed by a fireworks display on, and over, the water.

Numbers of buildings 200 years old or more can be found in the back streets of the town, and on the sea-front is an interesting round house, converted from a Martello tower.

The Church of St Leonard stands in a commanding position on the steep side of a hill. The soaring 13th-cent chancel rises 13 steps above the nave of the original Norman church; it was built in this fashion because of lack of space. Below the church is a crypt containing thousands of human bones, the origin of which is not definitely known. The church has some fine mouldings, and the east window, of modern glass, is an excellent piece of work.

About ½ m. N. is the village of **Saltwood**, notable for Saltwood Castle. Originally a Norman castle, it was rebuilt in 1160. One winter evening 10 years later four knights, Fitzurze, de Tracy, de Moreville and le Bret, rode out from the castle for Canterbury, there to assassinate Thomas à Becket. The castle was granted to the archbishops of Canterbury by King John, but it became a royal possession, being a "gift" from Cranmer to Henry VIII. It fell into a ruinous state, but was restored in Victorian times and is now a private home, the impressive 14th-cent. gatehouse being the main residential part. The castle and grounds are open on certain advertised dates during the summer.

IGHTHAM, *Kent* (7–TQ5956), is a delightful village. There are a number of Tudor houses and shops in the main street, and a tea-room in a building which dates from the 13th cent., set in a pleasant garden.

A few hundred yds from the centre of the village on a little hill stands St Peter's Church, dating from the 14th and 15th cents. with later additions, and containing excellent glass. The churchyard has several curious headstones carved in the shape of a head and shoulders and with incised faces; they are fine examples of a type peculiar to parts of Kent and Sussex. The oldest of these decipherable here is dated 1673.

Two m. from the village is Ightham Mote, one of the few moated manor houses remaining in England. The house was originally built more than 600 years ago, and derives its name, not from the fact that it has a moat, but from the moot, or council, which met here in medieval times. Despite alterations and additions, and some interior modernization for comfort, much of the early fabric remains, and a sense of the past. Especially is this noticeable in the inner courtyard, on one side of which is the oldest part of the house, the Great Hall, Crypt and Solar Room, much as they were originally.

A lived-in ancient home, surrounded by its moat on which swans are often seen, Ightham Mote is open to the public at stated times during the season.

KEW GARDENS, *Surrey* (6–TQ1877). The Royal Botanic Gardens at Kew are the world's most famous gardens, and one of the world's most pleasant parks. However, these gardens are primarily a scientific institution for the accurate identification and classification of plants and plant materials, and for the distribution of these plants and materials and of botanical information

A. F. Kersting

Kew Gardens: the Chinese Pagoda

to all parts of the world. Kew is also a quarantine station for plants being sent from one country to another. The training of botanists and gardeners is a further important function. Many hundreds who have trained here have served in gardens and botanical institutions all over the world. In the course of this work more than 25,000 specimen plants have been assembled, and these have also supplied the great variety of material used for its secondary function – public enjoyment of the gardens.

For more than 100 years the royal family had several houses here, and it was a favourite country residence during the reigns of the first three Hanoverian kings. Augusta, widow of Frederick, Prince of Wales, and mother of George III, who lived in Kew House (long since vanished), was greatly interested in botany and in 1759 had a garden of 9 acres planted here. The gardens expanded and became famous under their unofficial director, Sir Joseph Banks, who introduced many new and exotic plants, and a head gardener (later curator), William Aiton, who spent 34 years here. This garden was acquired by the State in 1841 and soon was greatly expanded; in 1898 Queen Victoria presented more of the property to the country, and by 1904 the whole 300 acres of the present Kew Gardens became the property of the State to fulfil both its scientific and popular functions.

The gardens can be divided roughly into two sections, the W. part being largely woodland and arboretum and E. part more formally laid out in lawns and gardens, with various houses for the specimens that need special climatic conditions or care: there are tropical houses for growing plants rarely to be seen in these islands, a temperate house, Australia house and so on. Of particular interest is Decimus Burton's Palm House, an early example of glass and wrought iron used to splendid effect, built between 1844 and 1848. In this great building the temperature and humidity is maintained at a level suitable for palms from all over the world.

Two interesting museums are housed in the gardens, the General Museum and the Wood Museum. The first-named houses the main collection, which includes a large range of plants and plant materials collected over more than a century. One odd exhibit is a boomerang – not from Australia, but from Egypt, and more than 4,000 years old.

In addition to the botanical glories of Kew Gardens there are a number of structures of interest. Perhaps the one which attracts most attention is the Chinese Pagoda, a Kew landmark. It is octagonal in shape and stands 163 ft high in 10 stories, the bottom one being 26 ft in diameter and 18 ft high; in each successive story both diameter and height are decreased by 1 ft. Inside there is only a staircase. At one time each of the 8 corners of each roof was decorated by a coloured dragon, and the roofs at each story were covered with iron plates of varying colours, but these have long since disappeared.

The pagoda was purely for decoration, and

was designed by Sir William Chambers who was responsible for much of the building in the gardens. He had spent some time in China. The Chinese Pagoda does serve one useful purpose these days, for it helps visitors get their bearings as they wander round the large expanse of the gardens.

Another landmark is the 225-ft flagpole on a mound called Victory Hill. It is made of a single Douglas fir presented to the gardens by the Government of British Columbia; it has been shaped to be 2 ft 9 in. square for 16 ft from the base, tapered octagonally for 140 ft and then circular with a diameter of 1 ft at the top. When felled in 1959 the tree was about 370 years old. Near the flagpole two young specimens of Douglas fir are growing.

Of several royal buildings originally built in this district, only three remain: the Dutch House, which is generally called Kew Palace; the Queen's Cottage; and the Orangery. The Dutch House was built in 1631 in Dutch style, and was used by the royal family from 1727 to 1818. It was shut up from 1818 until 1890 when the service wing was demolished, then in 1899 Queen Victoria opened it to the public, and it is this portion, the former royal living quarters, that can be seen today.

Kept and furnished much as it was when George III and his family lived here, it demonstrates the comparatively quiet living the family enjoyed in this country residence; the life that has been described as that of country gentlefolk. The house contains old panelling, including some from the 16th-cent. house which previously stood on this site. There are some family paintings and a tapestry portrait of George III, furniture and personal items. Kew Palace is open daily in the summer season. Behind it a 17th-cent. garden has been re-created.

The Orangery was built at the order of Princess Augusta in 1761 and was designed by Sir William Chambers. A pleasant building, it later became a museum, but has now been restored to its original purpose.

Queen Charlotte's Cottage was built in 1772 for the queen and was used by the family as a summer house and a place to take tea. It is a two-story building of brick with timber facing and is typical of the rustic edifices built by the gentry in those days. The interior décor, said to have been designed by Princess Elizabeth, third daughter of George III, was designed to give the impression of a tent. It is open to the public at weekends during the summer.

There are a number of other structures from the royal period to be found in the gardens. These include the Temples of Bellona, Aeolus and Arethusa, all built as rest alcoves; and King William's Temple built in the reign of William IV, which once contained a number of plaster busts of the royal family, but these have since been removed to Windsor. The walls are now decorated with tablets bearing the dates and names of battles fought by British units between 1760 and 1815.

KINGSTON-UPON-THAMES, *Surrey* (6–TQ1869). The name probably means that this was an estate belonging to the king, and not that Anglo-Saxon kings were crowned here on the stone that now stands on a site adjoining the modern Guildhall.

Certainly this is an old town that was prosperous in Anglo-Saxon times, and probably before that in Roman days, for the Thames was fordable here. The river has been bridged at Kingston since medieval times, and the present stone bridge was built in 1825. There has been a regular street market for centuries and today the market stalls are among the best and most attractive in the country.

The parish church was completely reconstructed in the Perpendicular style early in the 18th cent. but retains some of its ancient monuments. In London Road is the 14th-cent. Chapel of St Mary Magdalene.

KNOLE, *Kent* (7–TQ5354), 1½ m. SE. of SEVEN-OAKS, is one of the largest and most famous homes in England. There was a house here in the Middle Ages but the present building really dates from 1456 when it came into the possession of Thomas Bouchier, Archbishop of Canterbury, who gave it as a palace for future archbishops. They held it until the time of Cranmer, when Henry VIII took a liking to it and grabbed it for himself. So it came into the possession of Elizabeth I who, in 1566, presented it to her cousin, Thomas Sackville, who was later created Earl of Dorset by James I. The earldom became a dukedom but the title died out for lack of male heirs. Marriage with the de la Warr family joined two names to make Sackville-West, and the Barony of Sackville was created in 1876. During their more than 400 years of ownership the Sackville family have improved the great house and vast estate, keeping its old treasures and adding new ones. In 1946 the 4th Lord Sackville handed it over to the National Trust with an endowment for its upkeep, ensuring the preservation of this historic house for the nation. Victoria Sackville-West was born here in 1892. She wrote a history of Knole, and her poem *The Land* sums up the character of the county.

The house has 365 rooms, 52 stairways and seven courtyards, leading some to refer to it as the "Calendar House". The first of the courts after entering the main gate is the Green Court, the whole façade of which was built by Archbishop Bouchier. This leads to the Stone Court, of stone flags, where some idea of the growth of the house can be gauged: there is work here dating from the time of Bouchier to the Georgian period. From here the visitor passes into the Great Hall to start a tour that has few equals in stately homes.

There are many interesting rooms open to the public and they contain a large number of portraits by many great artists, among them two Van Dycks. There are many magnificent tapestries.

Much fine silverwork is displayed including several sets of fire-irons, an unusual material for this purpose. In a room called the King's Bedroom, said to have been prepared at great cost for James I (but it is not certain that he, or any other king, ever occupied it), is a magnificent solid silver table, silver mirror, silver jars and other silver ornaments, and a complete dressing-table set, including even a little silver eye-bath, made in 1673. The splendid bed, with stump work of silver and gold, and hangings embroidered in the same metals, is said to have cost about £40,000 at present-day values.

Among the most prized possessions of Knole are its furnishings, many items of which date from Elizabethan times. Exceptional are those in the Brown Gallery, where coverings of brocade, velvet, silk or damask on chairs and settees are original, some more than 400 years old. The bed hangings and covers are also very fine.

Knole is open to the public at advertised times throughout the year.

The magnificent park is open to the public every day of the year. It covers 1,000 acres of pleasant undulating country with a flatter central area, and well wooded mainly with oak, chestnut and beech. Deer roam freely and are tame enough to come up to visitors, in or out of their cars; however, visitors are requested not to feed them. Bird life is also plentiful in the park.

LAMBERHURST, *Kent* (7–TQ6735), is on the TUNBRIDGE WELLS–HASTINGS road. Its long village street passes over the Teise and has retained much of its ancient character. The interior of the parish church, which dates originally from the 14th cent., has been remodelled to accommodate a smaller congregation than in the past when Lamberhurst was a much larger place, but carefully done so as not to spoil the original design. It has a 17th-cent. pulpit.

The Owl House is a small tile-hung, half-timbered, 16th-cent. house, a former haunt of wool smugglers. It has a garden of fine spring flowers, azaleas, roses, rhododendrons and rare shrubs, and woodland lakes, open to the public at stated times.

Scotney Old Castle, 1 m. SE. of the village, is a massive rust-stained tower built in 1378 and the ruins of a Tudor manor house which nestle in a wooded valley, surrounded by a moat of water lilies and set in magnificent gardens.

These contain a wealth of trees, flowers and shrubs, some of them grown on the sides of an old quarry to give the effect of an Alpine garden. Open to the public at advertised times – but not the new castle built in 1837 and a private residence.

LANCING, *Sussex* (6–TQ1804). A dominating feature of the district is Lancing College chapel. The school was founded in 1848; the buildings are neo-Gothic and playing fields and grounds of about 500 acres surround them. Built on high ground, the school chapel is of cathedral-like proportions and has a vaulted roof of stone and chalk rising to a height of 90 ft; the windows are clear making it very light inside. There are fine tapestries and rich carving, including some canopies formerly at Eton College. The chapel is open daily to the public.

Leith Hill: the view across the Weald to the South Downs

The Parish Church of St James the Less is at North Lancing in a setting of cedars, limes and other trees. It contains some 13th- and 14th-cent. work with later additions.

LEATHERHEAD, *Surrey* (6–TQ1656).

An old town where the Parish Church of SS. Mary and Nicholas existed in Anglo-Saxon times. The present structure on the same site has nave arcades and a chancel arch dating from the 12th cent. The chancel and transepts are 14th-cent. and the tower, which dominates the valley, is 15th-cent. Handel is reputed to have played on the organ keyboard.

The Royal School for the Blind, established in 1799, is one of the largest in the world; at Kingston House, John Wesley preached his last sermon a few days before he died in 1791 at the age of 88; and in the Council offices are two cannon made in Seville in 1747 and captured at the Battle of Havana in 1762.

LEITH HILL, *Surrey* (6–TQ1342).

A famous beauty-spot which rises beyond Wotton Common to 960 ft. The eminence is crowned by a 64-ft tower from which there is a view over a wide area; on a clear day you can see the wooded Weald, the Downs beyond, and in the distance the waters of the English Channel and the Kentish hills. The tower was built by Richard Hill of Leith Hill Place in 1766. Originally it contained furnished rooms but was allowed to fall into decay; more recently new stairs to the top have been put in, and bronze direction plates point out what can be seen.

About 1 m. from the summit is Leith Hill Place, a 17th-cent. mansion surrounded by woods and with splendid azaleas and rhododendrons. It is noted for its collection of early Wedgwood ware and portraits of the Wedgwood family by Romney, Stubbs and Reynolds. Now owned by a member of

the family, it is open to the public at stated times during the summer months.

LEWES, *Sussex* (6–TQ4110).

The county town of East Sussex, and the county town of all Sussex when it had only one administration. This is a rewarding town in which to walk, but not to drive, for the streets are mainly steep and narrow. The High Street has many Georgian buildings, and a number much older. The hilly streets afford good views and unexpected and interesting little corners delight the eye.

Lewes is an old town and came into prominence soon after the Conquest when a fort was erected here, one of the many built in the South for keeping the conquered English under control.

In 1264 was fought the Battle of Lewes on the Downs just outside the town, between Simon de Montfort and his barons and Henry III. The king was defeated and the ensuing terms of peace are regarded by many as the beginnings of parliamentary government in England. Later Lewes was a stronghold of Protestantism and its people suffered many martyrdoms in the reign of Mary I.

The castle keep, built on high ground near the centre of Lewes, has a commanding position and a good view over the whole town and surrounding countryside. The castle was built on two artificial mounds instead of the customary one. The original fort was built of wood, but there were stone constructions before the end of the 11th cent. In the mid-14th cent. it was left uninhabited and over the years suffered from decay and spoliation by the townspeople, until the Sussex Archaeological Society stepped in to save it in the last century; it is now in their care. What can be seen today are the remains of the keep dating from Norman days and the 13th cent., but with much 19th-cent. restoration and addition, also the massive 14th-cent. barbican and fragments of the connecting walls. In the castle grounds are a number of exhibits of historical interest.

Opposite the castle gates is Barbican House, a 16th-cent. timber-framed building, enlarged and re-fronted in the 18th cent.; now a museum of the Sussex Archaeological Society with a wide range of exhibits of local and general interest from prehistoric times, Sussex watercolours, and some excellent tapestries.

Both the Castle and the Barbican House Museum are open on weekdays the year round.

Another museum also run by the Society is the Sussex Folk Museum in Anne of Cleves House in Southover High Street. (Southover was once a separate village, but is now part of Lewes.) No less interesting is the house, which was built in the early 16th cent.; it was part of the Priory of Lewes and when this was dissolved by Henry VIII he gave it to his divorced wife, Anne of Cleves. The front of the house is much the same as it was originally, with the addition of a porch built about 100 years later. Inside, the house has retained much of the original structure, with the Tudor timbers and the upstairs rooms open to the heavily beamed roofs. Ten rooms are given over to exhibits mainly concerned with Sussex arts and crafts, agricultural and industrial life, items of historical importance, as well as some aspects of wild life. Of particular interest is a large room devoted to a collection of Sussex ironwork. Much of it is intricately patterned and some of it is beautifully embossed; here are examples of practically every type of iron appliance used in an old English home. Also worthy of attention are some embossed firebacks of the 16th and 17th cents. The museum is open on weekdays.

Of the old buildings in the High Street one of the most interesting is the Old Bull, once an inn, then a store and now a popular restaurant. Dating partly from the 15th cent. it was the home of the revolutionary pamphleteer, Thomas Paine, author of *The Rights of Man* and *The Age of Reason*. Here Paine lodged from 1768 to 1774 when he was an excise officer (Lewes was then a river port). It might be said that it was here he started his pamphleteering, for he was dismissed after writing one demanding a better deal for excise officers (although the authorities gave other reasons for his dismissal). Paine married the daughter of the landlord, a snuffmaker, and on his death Paine joined the business. The marriage later broke up and Paine went to America to join the revolutionaries there. His rooms have been restored to much the same condition as when he occupied them, and are on show to the public on certain weekdays.

Another old house is the 16th-cent. Southover Grange, for a time the home of John Evelyn, the diarist contemporary of Samuel Pepys. The house is largely used by government departments and for meetings, but parts are open to the public (apply to the Town Clerk's department). Worth noticing is a timber 16th-cent. fireplace. The house is set in delightful public gardens.

St Michael's Church, which abuts right on to the High Street, was rebuilt in the middle of the 18th cent. It has a round tower dating from the 13th cent. and an arcade of the 14th. There is some excellent stained glass in the windows. St Anne's Church has 12th-cent. parts. The font is 12th-cent. with basket-work carving, and there is a 17th-cent. carved oak pulpit and altar rails. Another old and interesting church is St John the Baptist, of varying dates from the 12th to 18th cents.; there is some attractive stained glass.

One of the principal events in the Lewes year is the 5 November celebration. There are torch-light processions through the town, with many of the participants wearing period costume, and bonfires blaze spectacularly.

Four m. SE. of Lewes stands **Firle Place**, in the possession of the Gage family since the late 15th cent. Most of the original house was pulled down in the 18th cent. but the ancient Caen building stone and the Horsham stone roof were re-used. The house contains items brought back from America by General Thomas Gage who was Commander-in-Chief of the British Army in the early part of the American War of Independence. There is also a fine collection of paintings by celebrated masters; china and porcelain; furniture by Chippendale and William Kent as well as Louis Quinze items. Firle Place is open to the public at stated times.

Also about 4 m. SE. of the town is **Glynde Place**, a 16th-cent. mansion largely rebuilt in the mid-18th cent. The Long Gallery has 17th-cent. panelling and contains a good collection of bronzes and paintings, also fine needlework and pottery. The house is open at stated times in the summer months.

LIMPSFIELD, *Surrey* (6–TQ4152). Set in fine walking country near the Surrey and Kent borders, Limpsfield has a main street with many old buildings. To the N. the Downs rise to nearly 900 ft above the village, and afford superb views from the top of **Titsey Hill**, where there was once a Roman villa; to the E. is a superb area of woodland known as the High Chart.

The Parish Church of St Peter is of Norman origin. The Norman tower is unusually placed, standing in the south wall of the east end of the church. Nave and chancel aisle are 12th-cent. and the chancel is 13th-cent. There is other 13th-cent. work in evidence, and some of the stained glass dates from the 16th cent.

LINGFIELD, *Surrey* (6–TQ3943). This ancient village has a number of old buildings from the 15th cent. and Tudor, Jacobean and Georgian times; most are scheduled as Ancient Monuments.

An unusual structure is St Peter's Cross and Cage. Built of local stone and dating from the 18th cent. its original use is unknown, though it is thought it may have been a look-out – or perhaps a lock-up. It is now the village museum.

The parish church dates, in the main, from the 15th cent., with later additions. Round pillars support Perpendicular arches surmounted by a fine oaken roof. The font is Tudor and the pulpit is Jacobean, and there are three finely carved

15th-cent. screens. There are notable brasses, especially those of the Cobham family who built the original church.

LITTLEHAMPTON, *Sussex* (6–TQ0302), is a place for relaxation and holiday. It has pleasant beaches and good, safe swimming. Sailing is excellent; with two active clubs, the Littlehampton Sailing and Motor Club, and the Arun Yacht Club. For golfers there is an 18-hole course across the River Arun from the town. Sea and river offer good fishing.

The hinterland is made up of open down country and woodlands, suitable for horse-riding and rambling.

LULLINGSTONE ROMAN VILLA, *Kent* (7–TQ5265). One of the most important archaeological finds in Britain, this villa, near EYNSFORD, has revealed much of the way of life of wealthy country families in Roman Britain, and of their domestic architecture. Although not uncovered until 1949, its existence was known in the 18th cent. when farm labourers sinking fence posts dug up pieces of a mosaic that had been pierced by two of their posts. The pieces were examined, but, fortunately, nothing was done about them, and it was left to a more scientific age to carry out excavations.

Although not large, the remains of the villa are more complete and preserved than most other Roman relics uncovered in this country, and it has been possible to trace much of its history and the mode of living of the families who occupied it from its original building late in the 1st cent. A.D. to its destruction by fire in the 5th cent. Now the villa has been almost completely excavated, a glass and timber pavilion protects it from the weather and allows it to be open to the public throughout the year.

The plan of the building is easily followed: the main living rooms, the deep room, the original bath-house with its warm room and cool room, etc. There are traces of pagan worship in the deep room, and a Christian chapel has also been revealed, used when the occupants were converted to Christianity, probably late in the 4th cent. It is unique in that this is the only case in which a chapel has been found within the walls of a private Roman villa in Britain. Another striking feature is the height of the walls, some of those of the lower rooms reaching 8 ft, and in good order – also unusual, for in most Roman buildings that have been discovered in Britain only the foundations have remained. Also outstanding is the mosaic flooring; it is in excellent condition, the only damage being two holes in it, made by those 18th-cent. labourers. A number of ancient legends are pictured in the mosaics. There are also some vivid murals.

A number of objects dug up during the excavations are kept in a small museum in the pavilion.

LYDD, *Kent* (7–TR0421). Important for its airport, Ferryfield, which is an air car-ferry terminal with frequent flights to continental Europe.

A notable landmark in Lydd is the pinnacled tower of the parish church; from the top there is a good view. The church, dating from the 13th to 15th cents., incorporates remains of a former Anglo-Saxon church and a Norman structure. It was severely damaged in the Second World War, necessitating rebuilding and restoration, but its essential character has been retained.

LYMPNE, *Kent* (7–TR1235). This village on the edge of Romney Marsh was once on the sea. The Romans called it Portus Lemanis and built a fort here in the 3rd cent. A.D. Soil subsidence and neglect have taken their toll of the fort, but the remains, called Studfall Castle, are still worth a visit. About 300 yds from the Roman fort on a prominent hill stands Lympne Castle, a fortified manor house originally built in the 14th cent. Early in the present century it was largely rebuilt and restored, but retains much of its former character. From the castle there are views over the Military Canal, dug as part of the coastal defences in the Napoleonic Wars, Romney Marsh and the Channel. The house is open at advertised times in the summer months.

The parish church, St Stephen's, dates from the Norman period but has undergone much rebuilding and restoration. It has an old square font of Bethersden marble.

The airport here was the place from which distances were calculated in the days of the pioneer flights to establish routes to Australia, New Zealand, southern Africa and other far-off destinations. Renamed Ashford Airport in 1969, it is now a minor international airport with frequent daily services to the Continent.

MAIDSTONE, *Kent* (7–TQ7656). The busy county town of Kent on the MEDWAY has many interesting features and is an excellent centre for excursions. There was a settlement here in Anglo-Saxon times (and probably before that in Roman) but it did not come into prominence until around the 14th cent., then mainly as a centre of revolt and support of lost causes. John Ball, the "mad priest", was imprisoned here; Wat Tyler, the leader of the tragic Peasants' Revolt, came from Maidstone; Sir Thomas Wyatt, who led the rebellion of the Men of Kent against Mary I, was a landowner in the district; the town supported the Royalist cause in the Civil War, and lost an engagement with the Parliamentary forces at nearby Farleigh Bridge. But for all this, Maidstone prospers, as it has always done. It is the centre of the hop-growing country and has a flourishing brewing industry, as well as cement, engineering and confectionery manufacture.

Many industrial buildings front the river, but there is also a fine group of 14th-cent. structures: the Archbishop's Palace, All Saints Church and the College buildings. All of them are better seen from the river banks than from the road.

All Saints is built in Kentish ragstone in Decorated and Perpendicular style. It is the widest and one of the largest parish churches in the country. It has a magnificent oaken vaulted

Arundel Castle, as seen from the town   Picturepoint

roof, and there are some good 18th-cent. stained-glass windows. There is a fine carved marble reredos representing the Te Deum, but this, unfortunately, hides a splendid window from direct view. The font is Jacobean. At one time there were no seats in the church except those along the walls, reserved for the aged and infirm; it was in this arrangement that the seemingly harsh saying "the weakest go to the wall" originated.

A mural tablet near the tower door commemorates Laurence Washington, a great-uncle of George Washington; it is surmounted by the family crest with the stars and stripes that were to be perpetuated in the United States flag. Laurence Washington, whose grave is in the churchyard, lived in a mansion in Knightrider Street little more than 100 yds from the church. Unfortunately the house has been demolished and the site is now a car park.

The Archbishop's Palace antedates the church by more than half a century. It was built as a residence for the archbishops of Canterbury and as a place for them to rest on journeys between CANTERBURY and London. The central part is original, the wings Tudor. It has been restored by the Maidstone Corporation and contains a beautifully panelled banqueting hall. It is now used for public and private functions and receptions.

Across the road from the palace is another 14th-cent. building known as the Tithe Barn, although it was more likely the palace stables. It now houses the Tyrwhitt-Drake carriage museum, largest of its kind in England, and includes several exhibits loaned by H.M. the Queen. Here are horse vehicles from the late 17th cent. to after the First World War: royal coaches and street cabs, mail vans and delivery carts, and many privately owned vehicles, some the property of famous people.

Flanking the church on the south side are the remains of the 14th-cent. collegiate buildings. These are now the Rural College of Music. Beyond are a row of almshouses built about the same time.

Probably the oldest building in Maidstone is the small 13th-cent. St Peter's Chapel in St Peters Street, a gem surrounded by industrial buildings. It was originally the chapel of a hospital for travellers and pilgrims which has long since disappeared. After several centuries of secular use the chapel was restored and re-decorated in the 1830s.

Chillington Manor is a Tudor mansion which now houses the Museum and Art Gallery. Here is kept a large collection of exhibits with the accent on Kentish history from early days. A vivid model of LULLINGSTONE ROMAN VILLA as experts imagine it looked originally can be seen here. A recent addition is a section devoted to Kentish industry, especially hop-growing and brewing.

Among the more modern buildings are the imposing County Hall, with broad flanking wings, which stands in front of Maidstone Prison; and the 12-story Kent County Council Library on the outskirts. The skyline of this county town has changed as many new buildings have gone up.

Maidstone is well served with parks and gardens. Outstanding is Mote Park covering 558 acres, including a 40-acre lake. Here are sports grounds, a large area of meadowland, and wooded walks. The lake is colourful at weekends when enthusiasts sail their craft there. The 18th-cent. manor, Mote House, standing on a secluded hill, is now a Cheshire Home.

Then there are Brenchley Gardens behind the Museum; a small park on the river front backed by the Church of All Saints and the Palace; and also the large South Park 1 m. from the town centre, with tennis courts, bowling greens, midget golf, and football and cricket pitches.

The village of **Loose** is just over 2 m. from the centre of Maidstone. Although it is now really a suburb, it has kept its rural aspect, and possesses a number of old buildings, best of which is the Woolhouse. Loose was once a milling centre, and the little river which drove the mills flows through the village. The women of the village prefer its name to be pronounced as in "lose".

About 2 m. NE. of the town is **Allington Castle**, now owned by the Carmelite Friary at AYLESFORD. It is beautifully set in dense woodlands, and its walls and turrets rise from a green surround in spring and summer. The present building was constructed in the late 13th cent. on the site of a former manor house and earlier castle, and although extensively restored during the first quarter of this century much of the original fabric has been retained without great structural alterations. The castle once belonged to the Wyatt family, but they lost it after Sir Thomas Wyatt led his unsuccessful rising against Queen Mary. Later its owners hid refugee priests during a period of persecution in the reign of Elizabeth I. Today the Carmelites show visitors the priests' hole in the entrance to the chapel.

The castle contains a number of excellent, and valuable, religious paintings and a fine collection of ikons. There are interesting sculptures in the chapel.

Allington Castle is a retreat house with accommodation for 20 guests, and is open to persons of any denomination who may, or may not, take part in the religious life of the community as they wish. It is open to public inspection at regular stated times.

MARGATE, *Kent* (7–TR3670). Pre-eminently a pleasure resort, the oldest and most famous in Kent, and one of the best-known in England; it is sometimes called the Blackpool of the South. It caters for a wide variety of tastes. Dreamland, a 20-acre amusement park, is not only a funfair, but also contains an old-time music hall and a luxurious modern cinema, a ballroom, a restaurant, a bar and a cafeteria. The Winter Gardens, a concert hall, has room for an audience of 2,000; it stands on Fort Hill, formerly the site of a gun battery.

Scotney Old Castle, near Lamberhurst, dates from the 14th cent.   Picturepoint

Margate may be said to have given birth to the idea of seaside holidays. It was here, some 200 years ago, that bathing machines were first used, the invention of a local Quaker, Benjamin Beale. These were like little caravans in which the bather changed, was drawn into the water, then emerged to swim, more or less concealed from the vulgar gaze. The idea of sea-bathing caught on with the gentry and became a favourite pastime of George III and other members of the royal family.

Today Margate caters for more than two million visitors annually.

MEDWAY, RIVER, Kent. This river is the boundary which separates the Men of Kent (to the E.) from the Kentish Men (to the W.).

It is navigable from TONBRIDGE to its mouth in the Thames Estuary, and flows through a delightful countryside of apple, pear and cherry orchards, and mile after mile of hopfields. It is also spanned by attractive bridges, notably the medieval stone-arched bridges at AYLESFORD and East Farleigh. A fine modern bridge carries the M2 over the river near ROCHESTER.

There are pleasure trips along the Medway in summer, or boats may be hired for private cruising. Altogether there are seven locks between Tonbridge and Aylesford, where the river becomes tidal to its mouth 10 m. away. Along it are a number of delightful inns, and no parking problems. The river also provides excellent coarse fishing, especially around Wateringbury,. where two tributaries, the Beult and the Teise, meet the Medway in a welter.

MEREWORTH, Kent (7–TQ6553). This village 8 m. W. of MAIDSTONE, has two outstanding attractions: its church and Mereworth Castle 1 m. E., both built in the Palladian style.

The church was built in the early 18th cent. and is one of the few remaining in England of Palladian design, with a rounded and pillared front and entrance. Another unusual feature is its steeple, a dominating landmark, the size of which seems out of place on the parish church of such a small village. In its churchyard is the grave of the first winner of the Victoria Cross, Rear-Admiral Charles Davis Lucas. He won the award in 1854 for outstanding bravery in naval battle in the Baltic during the Crimean War; he received the decoration shortly after its inauguration in 1856.

Mereworth Castle was built in the early 18th cent. and is one of the purest forms of the Palladian style extant in Britain. It was designed by Colin Campbell, foremost exponent of the style at that time, and is almost an exact copy of the famous villa, La Rotunda, near Vicenza, Italy.

Seen from the long drive it has the appearance of an ancient temple, for it is a squared, pillared building designed around a circular, domed hall, and without chimneys. Although there are a number of fireplaces in the building, the flues are built into the ribs of the dome and have a common outlet at the apex, which not only does away with chimneys, but provides a form of central heating

as well. The hall is a complete circle surmounted by a 60-ft dome, and adorned with rich stucco work. The Italian Amigoni painted fine ceiling panels which are framed by elaborate stucco designs. There is also furniture of the period designed by William Kent.

MIDHURST, Sussex (6–SU8821). On the outskirts of the town are the ruins of Cowdray Park, a substantial, fortified mansion built in the first half of the 16th cent. by the Earl of Southampton, and destroyed by fire in 1793. For several generations it was the home of the Viscounts Montague, descendants of Sir Anthony Browne who was Master of the Horse to Henry VIII, from whom he received BATTLE Abbey. Early this century Cowdray was purchased by the first Viscount Cowdray of Midhurst, who saved the ruins from total decay, and saw to their preservation.

The Cowdray Museum contains a number of paintings and other exhibits relating to the mansion and its owners, and to the district and its history.

The ruins are open all the year, but the museum only at stated times. Enquire of the caretaker.

The famous Cowdray Park polo grounds, where Prince Philip frequently plays, form part of the estate in which the ruins stand, and the public may watch the matches. Polo is also played on Ambersham Common about 2 m. distant.

The area abounds in delightful country with many picnic spots, such as Benbow Ponds, St Anne's Hill, where the foundations of ancient Bohun Castle may be seen, and at Blackdown, between Midhurst and Petworth, which is nearly 1,000 ft above sea-level.

The town of Midhurst possesses some attractive domestic architecture of the 16th and 17th cents. and two old inns.

MINSTER-IN-THANET, Kent (7–TR3163). Parent town of Thanet, also called the Isle of Thanet; it was formerly separated from the mainland by the Wantsum channel. There were probably settlements in pre-Roman times. The Romans established themselves here and traditionally this is where the Anglo-Saxons first landed. There are many ancient buildings, some dating from medieval times; the Old House was erected in 1350, and the Old Oak House is nearly as old.

Here was established one of the first nunneries in England, being built in the 7th cent. The land was granted to Princess Ermenburga, better known by her religious name of Domneva, by her uncle King Egbert, as wergild (compensation) for the murder of her two brothers by his thane, Thunor, for which Egbert felt responsible. The princess demanded such land as could be encompassed by her pet hind at a single run. Thunor, so legend has it, was alarmed at the amount of ground the hind was covering and in attempting to halt it, he and his horse fell into a ditch or well and were drowned; a chalkpit is pointed out as the spot where this happened. The hind completed its run and the princess received more than 1,000

G. Douglas Bolton

The Medway River at Maidstone, with the 14th-cent. Archbishop's Palace

The Medway River is spanned by a medieval stone bridge at East Farleigh

Kenneth Scowen

acres. The story is illustrated in the windows in the Parish Church of St Mary.

The nunnery was sacked by the Danes late in the 9th cent. It eventually came into the possession of the monks of St Augustine's, CANTERBURY. They rebuilt it and added a grange, now called Minster Abbey. Much of the Norman and Early English work is still to be seen in the cloisters and other parts of the ruins (open to the public) and the abbey, which is private. It was repossessed by Benedictine nuns in 1937.

St Mary's is also old. The massive tower is early Norman, and Roman bricks from an earlier building can be seen in the tower and nave. The transepts with their lancet windows and stone-groined roofs are 13th-cent. The richly carved oaken stalls are early 15th-cent. and the carved oaken lectern is 17th-cent.

NEWHAVEN, *Sussex* (6–TQ4401). A town of no particular interest in itself, but certainly important to motorists, as it is the terminal of a car-ferry service to Dieppe in France. The service operates throughout the year, with more frequent crossings in the summer.

NEW ROMNEY, *Kent* (7–TR0624). The capital of Romney Marsh, this was one of the original Cinque Ports, although now about a mile from the sea. In its heyday the town had five churches; only one of these remains, the Parish Church of St Nicholas, the churchyard of which was once lapped by the sea. It is in Norman and Decorated styles, and some of the work of these periods is still in evidence. The tower is 32 ft square, and 100 ft high; there are some excellent stained-glass windows.

Though no longer on the sea, the town has its close neighbour **Littlestone**. This is on the sea and fast developing as a popular resort.

NORTHIAM, *Sussex* (7–TQ8324). A village of old houses with a green, Northiam looks down the Rother valley where a number of little streams flow down the northern slopes to join the river. Chief attraction is Great Dixter, a 15th-cent. manor house with a half-timbered and plastered front and a Tudor porch; the great hall is notable. Beside it is another old house which was brought from Benenden, Kent, and re-erected. Both stand in a famous garden, open to the public.

Part of the Parish Church of St Mary dates from the 12th cent., and there is also 14th- and 15th-cent. work; most of the chancel is modern.

Northiam was the home of Sheila Kaye Smith, who built a beautiful little Roman Catholic church at Doucegrove, a converted oasthouse. The house has burnt down. It stood just S. of the hamlet of Horn's Cross.

OTHAM, *Kent* (7–TQ7954). A village 5 m. SE. of MAIDSTONE delightfully set in orchard country, and possessing some old yeoman houses. Stoneacre, a fine example of this type of dwelling built towards the end of the 15th cent., is open to the public at stated times throughout the year.

PATRIXBOURNE, *Kent* (7–TR1855), is notable for its church, similar in style to that at BARFRESTON. It is small, mainly in the Perpendicular style, with a Norman door under the tower and a Norman window. There are some rich carvings: especially notable is the priest's door with a rather disfigured saint's head above it. There is some good early glass, and 16th- and 17th-cent. Swiss windows.

PENHURST, *Sussex* (7–TQ6916). This one-time busy iron town is today a hamlet lying by ASHBURNHAM Park. Its old church has largely escaped the sometimes heavy hand of the restorer. The fabric is in the Perpendicular style, and has a 14th-cent. nave with king-post roof, and 15th-cent. chancel with a waggon roof. The fine rood-screen is 14th-cent. and the lectern and pulpit date from the 17th cent. There are some fragments of medieval glass.

PENSHURST, *Kent* (7–TQ5243). A village in a hilly wooded setting, Penshurst has retained much of its Tudor aspect. Within its small compass there is much of visual interest, for most of the houses belong to periods of from 200 to 400 years ago, each with its own individuality. The lanes and paths of the surrounding countryside make pleasant walks.

The Parish Church of St John the Baptist is reached through an ancient lych-gate around which was built a two-storied Tudor house, now with bulging walls and bent, weathered timbers. The church was originally built in the 12th cent. and there is much work remaining from the 13th, 14th and 15th cents. The tower is 17th-cent. and its window, formerly in Penshurst Place, dates from 1627. The ornamented font is 15th-cent. There was considerable rebuilding and restoration in the middle of the last century. The chapel of the Sidney family was built in 1820, but it was the third such chapel; it contains many monuments and relics of this historic family. Notice the fine painted ceiling.

Penshurst Place, the ancestral home of the Sidney family since 1552, is the centre of the village, but does not dominate it, being hidden behind tall trees. This was the home of Sir Philip Sidney, the Elizabethan poet, diplomat and courtier. He was also author of the romance *Arcadia*, his own home being the inspiration for the Arcadian house he describes.

The Sidneys became Earls of Leicester, the male line dying out in the mid-18th cent. A descendant through the female line, John Shelley, a kinsman of the poet Percy Bysshe Shelley, took the name of Sidney on succeeding to the property. Later the family became Barons de l'Isle and Dudley and carried out much restoration work.

The original manor house was built in 1340 for Sir John de Pulteney, a prosperous wool merchant and four times Lord Mayor of London. Much of what he built still remains and is incorporated within the much more extensive home that was constructed 200 years later. The Baron's Hall is generally considered to be the finest 14th-

cent. domestic hall to survive in England. It is of noble proportions with a remarkably high and wide roof of chestnut; around the top of the wall are carved wooden figures, believed to represent retainers of the medieval owners. Also in the hall are two trestle tables of the same period, thought to be the only two in existence today. Here can be seen the helmet worn by Sir Philip Sidney.

The state dining-room was formerly the solar or withdrawing room of the original house; it is one of the rooms open to the public but is still used by the family on special occasions. The great table is set with a beautiful Rockingham dinner service that was made for William IV, and bears the Royal Arms. A splendid 17th-cent. silver wine fountain and its companion cistern stand at the end of the table.

Throughout the part of the house open to the public are relics of the family during their long occupation, including some excellent paintings and tapestries, one being French Gothic of the early 16th cent. and two Brussels tapestries of the 17th cent. In the crypt beneath the Baron's Hall is a collection of arms and armour, and, as a contrast, the Buttery houses a collection of 18th- and 19th-cent. toys.

The house stands in delightful grounds with a formal Italian garden, and a lake in the park with water lilies.

House and gardens are open at advertised times in the summer season.

PETWORTH, *Sussex* (6–SU9721), has been described as the town which stands at the gates of Petworth House, the great mansion built by the Duke of Somerset towards the end of the 17th cent. The house, which has a west front of 320 ft, stands in a magnificent park of some 2,000 acres, surrounded by a wall 13 m. long.

The estate came into the possession of the Percy family, the Earls of Northumberland, in Norman times, and has remained in the possession of their descendants ever since. Parts of an earlier manor house were incorporated by Somerset (who married the Percy heiress) and there were reconstructions carried out in the 19th cent. The house, together with about 750 acres of parkland, came into the keeping of the National Trust in 1947.

Outstanding is the Carved Room with its rich carvings by Grinling Gibbons, and said to be his finest work. The State Rooms contain a fine gallery of paintings with such masters as Van Dyck, Holbein, Rembrandt and Reynolds (who stayed some time at Petworth House). There is a magnificent Grand Staircase, with some fine frescoes.

The house and park are open in the summer season.

The town has a number of very old houses, some timber-framed and many of them in a knot of narrow streets around the little market square, which dates from early Tudor to Georgian times. A typical 16th-cent. residence is Tudor House. Somerset Lodge, a mid-17th-cent. stone house with mullioned windows and oak staircase, is worthy of note, as is New Grove House, built early in the same century. Gibbons is said to have stayed there when working at Petworth House. The town hall in the market square is an unpretentious arcaded building of the late 18th cent. considerably restored.

The parish church was built in the 14th cent. but almost completely rebuilt in 1827; a little of the ancient masonry remains, also some excellent glass, a 14th-cent. font and a number of impressive tombs and memorials to the owners of Petworth House.

PEVENSEY CASTLE, *Sussex* (7–TQ6405). A Norman castle built within the Roman fort of Anderida; fort and castle have played their part in British history for more than 17 centuries. The Roman fort was built as part of the defences of the Saxon Shore. It was not ready to oppose William the Conqueror when he landed at Pevensey Bay in 1066, for he found it unmanned and was able to consolidate his position immediately. He realized its strategic importance and gave it to his half-brother, Robert, Count of Mortain, who built the Norman castle. Improvement and rebuilding continued until the 14th cent. Later it was equipped to meet the threats from the Spanish Armada, from Napoleon, and from Hitler in 1940, when several pill-boxes were built into its walls, so cleverly that they have to be pointed out: one is in a pile of rubble where the Roman wall has collapsed.

More than half the stone walls of the Roman fort are still standing, and in some parts have been excavated to the original ground level and have heights of up to 10 ft; there are also two rounded Roman bastions, restored in the 11th cent. The castle is mostly in a ruinous state, but some parts, including the dungeons and the lower part of the keep, have been well preserved. The small detachments of troops garrisoned here during the Second World War quite possibly occupied rooms that were soldiers' quarters in medieval days.

Tudor houses and shops adorn the little village of Pevensey.

PLAXTOL, *Kent* (7–TQ6053), possesses a rarity in Old Soar, a Georgian mansion which has attached to it the remains of the fortified home of a 13th-cent. knight. Preserved here is the original solar room, or the knight's private quarters, and the remains of the great hall. This is open at advertised times in the summer months, but the mansion is private and is not open.

There are a number of other old buildings, some with origins dating back about 600 years. The former village forge is now a restaurant.

The church is unusual in that it was built during the Civil War, and has no dedication; it was enlarged in 1894. It has a splendid 17th-cent. hammer-beam roof, a beautiful carved reredos and an old pulpit.

Also at Plaxtol is the 17th-cent Fairlawne

Penshurst: the village and the parish church

Noel Habgood

House, once the home of Sir Harry Vane, the famous governor of Massachusetts. It now includes an establishment where horses owned by the Queen and the Queen Mother are trained.

PULBOROUGH, *Sussex* (6–TQ0418). Here stands Parham Park, an Elizabethan mansion which, after various later alterations, has been carefully restored to give it much of its original form. From the beginning of the 17th cent. to the early 1920s it was in the ownership of the Bysshops, and a number of portraits of this family are among the collection of paintings on show. Features of the house are the great hall, with unusually tall mullioned windows and a fine plastered ceiling, and the long gallery, 158 ft long and 18 ft wide. In addition to the more than 300 paintings displayed, there is period furniture, china, carpets, tapestries and fine needlework. The house is open at advertised times.

In the grounds stands the Church of St Peter, a basically Perpendicular structure, restored and redecorated in the Gothic style in the 19th cent. The lead font is 14th-cent.

RAMSGATE, *Kent* (7–TR3865), gained importance as a port after SANDWICH silted up. It became a fashionable resort after George IV spent a season there in 1827. It is now a very popular holiday resort, and like many others on the SE. coast features Victorian architecture, especially along the front. There are good sand beaches.

About 1 m. W. of the town at Pegwell Bay is a novel monument to an important event in early English history: the replica of a Viking longship which commemorates the landing at Ebbsfleet (now some distance from the sea) of the legendary Anglo-Saxon leaders Hengist and Horsa in A.D. 449. This ship, the *Hugin*, was sailed across from Denmark by a party of Danes in 1949 in an anachronistic representation of the craft and warriors of 1,500 years before (5th-cent. Anglo-Saxon war boats probably had no sails; and the Danish onslaught on England did not begin until more than three centuries later). After being shown in London and several other places, it was presented to Ramsgate. Today it rests in a concrete cradle, and in the season is decked out with colourful Viking shields and oars.

Not far away is the base for a much more modern craft, the Ramsgate Hoverport, opened in 1969. From here hovercraft skim across the Channel, reaching Calais in 40 minutes. The hovercraft carry both motorists and their cars, as well as other passengers.

Some distance inland is a memorial of another important landfall – that of St Augustine with 40 monks in A.D. 597 to bring Christianity to the Anglo-Saxons. The spot where the saint is supposed to have met King Ethelbert is near some lavender gardens on the Minster Road, and is marked by a Celtic cross.

Ramsgate is not rich in ancient buildings. St Lawrence's Church, with a massive square tower, stands on a prominent hill; it attained its present

J. Allan Cash

Ramsgate harbour

form early in the 13th cent. and much of it dates from Norman times. St George's, the parish church, dates only from 1827, and is built in the florid Gothic Revival style of the period. The tower, similar to that of Ely, is 137 ft high; the Trinity House authorities helped towards its cost so that a lantern could be placed on it to guide shipping. There are some fine stained-glass windows commemorating the Dunkirk evacuation. The Roman Catholic St Augustine's Abbey and Church, dedicated in 1851, is considered Pugin's finest work. Its interior furnishings, especially the oak screens, stained glass and metalwork, are good examples of early Victorian design.

Another example of craftsmanship with a historical flavour is the Model Village on the top promenade not far from St Augustine's Abbey. It is an attractive miniature Tudor village.

RECULVER, *Kent* (7–TR2269). About 3 m. NE. of HERNE BAY. Reculver is the site of Roman Regulbium, one of the forts built about the middle of the 3rd cent. A.D. to defend the Saxon Shore. Although in a good condition until early in the 18th cent. erosion has eaten away the cliff on which it stands, causing much of the walls to slide into the sea, and there are now only partial remains.

An Anglo-Saxon church was built on the site in the 7th cent. and its plan can easily be traced. The church was later enlarged and in the 12th cent. the Normans added two mighty towers and a west front, and these remain almost intact.

The church remained in regular use until early in the 19th cent. when the vicar decided it was too remote and put it to his parishioners that it be demolished and the materials used to build another, more accessible church. The proposal was carried by one vote and the vicar started the demolition work. Only the intervention of Trinity House officials stopped the completion of the tragedy. They took over the west front and the great towers, which had been a seamark for hundreds of years; thus preserved they continued to guide Thames-bound ships. There is a good view from the top. The site is open to the public throughout the year.

The new church, built out of the old, is at Hillborough, about 1 m. inland from Reculver. Here can be seen fragmentary remains of the original.

REIGATE, *Surrey* (6–TQ2550). Although not mentioned under this name until the 12th cent., Reigate is an old town. It was a manor of the powerful de Warenne, Earl of Surrey in the reign of William the Conqueror. He built a strongly fortified castle here. Nothing of it remains above ground except the mound on which it stood, now in the pleasant gardens called Castle Grounds, with traces of the moat and the dry fosse. But below is the Barons' Cave, a central underground court off which led a number of medieval tunnels, some penetrating for long distances beneath the town and reaching to the priory on Reigate Heath, and even, so it is said, as far as Bletchingley Castle some miles distant. It was in the Barons' Cave, according to local tradition, that the barons deliberated before their meeting with King John at RUNNYMEDE and the signing of Magna Carta.

During the Second World War the cave and the tunnels were put to good use, serving as stores and air-raid shelters.

Most of the tunnels have now been sealed off, but the main cave, the more modern chamber, and part of the old tunnel system are open to the public; application to view should be made to the Head Gardener of the Castle grounds.

The gateway to the grounds is a reproduction of the medieval structure, and was erected in the 18th cent.

The Church of St Mary Magdalene, one of the largest parish churches in Surrey, is built of local stone, except for the tower, which was rebuilt in 1874. The oldest part, the nave, dates from the late 12th cent. Externally the church is mainly in Perpendicular style; the interior is of various earlier periods. The chancel is 14th- and 15th-cent. and contains a fine stone reredos and sedilia. In the ancient vaults is buried Lord Howard of Effingham, the admiral who led the English fleet to defeat the Spanish Armada.

In the vestry is one of the oldest public libraries in England; it was founded in 1701 by the vicar, and now contains about 2,000 volumes, mainly on theological subjects, and is open to the public on advertised weekdays.

Just outside the town on Reigate Heath stands an old windmill which has been converted into a church. It is a subsidiary to St Mary Magdalene, and regular monthly services are held here. The interior retains much of its old form and has a heavy beamed ceiling. It has been given a new set of sails and restored to its original appearance, but not to working order. It is open to the public and application to view should be made to the caretaker in an adjoining cottage. Another mill, on Wray Common, 2 m. from the town, has been preserved externally much as it was; it is now a private residence.

On Reigate Heath, which covers 130 acres and includes a 9-hole golf course, have been found Iron Age barrows and remnants of a settlement of that period.

Redhill, 2 m. W. of Reigate, is part of the borough of Reigate and almost a railway creation. It quickly grew in importance until it outstripped its parent to become virtually the commercial centre of the borough, a rôle that was further increased by the creation of GATWICK Airport, 3 m. to the S.

RICHBOROUGH CASTLE, *Kent* (7–TR 3259). 1½ m. NW. of SANDWICH are the ruins of the Roman Richborough Castle which defended Rutupiae, the base the Romans established with their invasion of A.D. 43. Rutupiae was for many years the chief port of entry for the legions sent to Britain, and the key fort in the Saxon Shore defences. It guarded the entrance to the Wantsum Channel and stood at the beginning of Watling Street, the great road that led to London and on to CHESTER. The fort, which covered an area of about six acres, was largely rebuilt in the 3rd cent. There are substantial remains of the walls, with thicknesses of 12 ft and heights of up to 24 ft. These are among the best preserved examples of Roman walls in England. There was an extensive series of defensive ditches surrounding the fortifications; these were excavated in 1926 and are clearly defined.

Inside the fortifications the remains of several buildings have been excavated, including a 1st-cent. cellar, various structures of the 2nd and 3rd cents., one of which was a 3rd-cent. bath-house, and the foundations of a chapel. There is also a cruciform platform, the foundations of what must have been a large edifice, possibly a monument.

On the site is a museum containing a collection of Roman pottery, coins, bronze weapons and ornaments, lamps, amphorae and other items found during the excavations. Both fort and museum are open throughout the year.

RICHMOND, *Surrey* (6–TQ1874). Situated on a delightful stretch of the River Thames, Richmond is a royal manor of which the Lord of the Manor is the sovereign, and it has long been popular with royalty. Edward I built a palace here in the 13th cent. and it was rebuilt and enlarged by Henry VII, the first of the Tudor monarchs, who was Earl of Richmond before he became king. Later, successive monarchs resided in Richmond, until this century, and the royal connection continues with the Thatched Cottage, residence of Princess Alexandra and her husband, Mr Angus Ogilvy.

Little remains of the old palace, which was pulled down in the 18th cent. An archway bearing the arms of Henry VII leads into a courtyard, on the left of which are Wardrobe Court and the Gate House, now containing a number of fine apartments. But there are many reminders of regal days, especially around the Green, formerly part of the palace grounds. Here are many picturesque houses, some dating from the time of Queen Anne and the Georges, where lived members of the court. Facing the Green on the west side is Maids of Honour Row, erected in the reign of George I to accommodate ladies of the court when his son, the Prince of Wales, and his wife resided here.

Built on the slopes of a hill, Richmond has good views of the Thames; many artists, notably Turner, have painted them, and Reynolds enthused over them and made them a subject of one of his rare landscapes. The river here is dominated to the N. by graceful Richmond Bridge, built in 1777, and sweeps in a generous curve to the W. Boating here is excellent. Craft of all sorts can be hired, and there are trips up or down river in larger boats.

Richmond is rich in parks and gardens. Foremost is Richmond Park, covering an area of 2,358 acres, with 11 entrance gates. This park was created and enclosed in the reign of Charles I for hunting. It now includes great stretches of rough pasture where wild deer can be seen, woodlands, and the Pen Ponds – two artificial lakes with good fishing. The Isabella Plantation is a delightful water garden.

In the park stands White Lodge, originally built as a royal residence in 1727. The central part, of that date, is built of Portland stone in Palladian style; early in the 19th cent. two pavilions were added and joined to the main building by circular corridors. Queen Victoria spent some time here as did Edward VII, and George V and Queen Mary in the early days of their marriage. The Duke of Windsor was born here. Later, George VI and Queen Elizabeth spent their honeymoon here when Duke and Duchess of York. Some of the rooms of White Lodge, which is now part of the Royal Ballet School, are open to the public at advertised times during August. These include the grand salon with its coved ceiling and original fireplace; the Nelson Room where Nelson is said to have planned his tactics for the Battle of Trafalgar; and the Library, which contains some fine paintings.

Other parks include the Terrace Gardens, on the upper lawns of which the Richmond Shakespeare Society present Shakespearean plays. Above the Terrace Gardens is The Terrace, a favourite promenade giving the famous view over the Thames – and over six counties and sometimes, on very clear days, to Windsor Castle. James Thomson and the painter Reynolds lived in houses near the Richmond Gate entrance.

The Parish Church of St Mary Magdalene was built in the reign of Henry VII, and the tower dates from that period; there are many later additions, and the whole church was restored in the mid-18th cent. and a new chancel, chancel aisle and chapel were built at the beginning of this century.

The 17th-cent. **Ham House** lies near the attractive village of **Petersham**. Impressive but somewhat plain and austere from the outside, it contains some of the richest decoration and furnishings of any house in England. It was built as a modest manor house by Sir Thomas Vavasour early in the 17th cent. and later came into the possession of the 1st Earl of Dysart. He bequeathed it to his daughter, who also later succeeded him in her right to the title. She married the Duke of Lauderdale, member of Charles II's Cabal cabinet, and they greatly extended the house and re-decorated it in flamboyant baroque style, installing a wealth of fine paintings and tapestries. Much of the furnishings and other items with which they filled the house have been retained and are on display today, although there were some alterations and additions both to the house and its contents by the 4th Earl.

The house is set in extensive grounds. Both house and gardens are open to the public at advertised times throughout the year.

ROBERTSBRIDGE, *Sussex* (7–TQ7323). This little town lies in well-wooded country near the River Rother. It contains a number of old houses, and some distance down the valley is Abbey Farm, built from the ruins of a nearby medieval Cistercian abbey. In the neighbouring village of Salehurst the Parish Church of St Mary's dates mostly from the 13th cent. and is in the Decorated style; the font is 12th-cent.

An important local industry is the making of cricket bats by the firm of Gray-Nicolls, who have been in the business since 1876. A cricketing ancestor started making bats for friends and the demand became so heavy that he turned his hobby into a business. One of his early clients was W. G. Grace, who scored more than 2,000 runs with the first bat. A photograph of Grace and a letter of congratulation concerning the bat are displayed on a wall of the factory. Interested persons may see over the factory, but by previous appointment.

ROCHESTER, *Kent* (7–TQ7467). Although far from beautiful, this port and commercial centre has a wealth of interesting features. It has a long history. There were probably prehistoric, and certainly Celtic, settlements. The Romans established an important base which they called Durobrivae, here where their road crossed the MEDWAY; after the Romans came the Anglo-Saxons who called it Hrofesceaster, from which the present name derives. William the Conqueror, realizing its strategic importance, decreed that a castle be maintained permanently there. Rochester Castle was one of the most important strong-points in the realm during medieval times. It was originally built shortly after the Conquest; today much of its walls remain in good condition,

Rochester: "Jasper's Gate", featured by Dickens in Edwin Drood

Peter Baker

including a bastion, but of the castle itself there is only the mighty keep, built in Henry I's reign. It makes a prominent landmark, standing 113 ft above ground level and 70 ft square at the base, with walls averaging from 11 to 13 ft thick, in which passages and a circular stairway lead up to the battlements. On the way up can be seen the site of the banqueting hall, a Norman chapel and mural galleries. From the top the view over the city, the surrounding countryside and the River Medway, the docks, and, further off, the Thames, rewards the climb. The castle grounds make a pleasant green park. The castle and grounds are open to the public.

Near the castle stands the cathedral, pleasantly set in a close. The bishopric of Rochester is the second oldest in England, having been established at the beginning of the 7th cent. The present cathedral stands on the site of the original Anglo-Saxon church and was largely built in the latter part of the 12th cent. There were con-siderable alterations after severe damage by Parliamentary troops during the Civil War, and heavy restoration in the 19th cent. There is much Norman, Perpendicular and 15th-cent. work still in evidence. Worthy of note are the Norman west doorway, the 13th-cent. transepts and a 13th-cent. crypt with heavy ribbed vault below. A fine series of bishops' tombs dates from more than seven centuries ago.

Around the cathedral are the remains of the former monastic buildings, the ruined chapter house and the cloisters. There are three ancient gates: Priors Gate, Deanery Gate and Chertsey's Gate leading into the High Street. The last of these is popularly known as Jasper's Gate, under which name it appeared in Dickens's last novel, the unfinished *Mystery of Edwin Drood*. Also nearby is St Nicholas Church, originally built in the 15th cent. and rebuilt in the 17th. It has been converted for use as diocesan offices, but the central part is retained as a parish church – small, simple, but dignified.

In the High Street stands the Guildhall. Built in 1687, it is of red brick on Doric columns, and above its tiled roof is a cupola surmounted by a weathervane in the shape of a full-rigged ship. Designed in 1780, this vane is of copper, and 5 ft long. The council room is finely panelled and has a beautifully moulded ceiling, the gift of Sir Cloudsley Shovell, an admiral in Queen Anne's navy and an M.P. for the city. He went down off the Scilly Isles with his ship, which was eventually to become the object of a deep-water treasure hunt. Close by is the Corn Exchange, the modern part of which was built about 100 years ago, and the older, now called Prince's Hall, early in the 18th cent. at Shovell's expense. From the front projects a huge clock on an ornamental bracket bearing the admiral's coat of arms; this was the "moon-faced clock" of Dickens's *Uncommercial Traveller*.

In the High Street are two interesting old hotels, the Bull and the George. The latter, originally built about 1600 and remodelled as a coaching inn in the 18th cent., stands on the site of a former church, and beneath is a vault dating from 1325. It retains its ancient pillars and archways, and there are a number of monks' heads sculptured on the ceiling. From it three passageways (now blocked up) led, it is believed, to the cathedral, the castle and the river. The licensee will show the vault to anyone interested. The Bull (or to give it its full name, the Royal Victoria and Bull) was originally built about 400 years ago. Dickens stayed there and it featured in *Pickwick Papers*, and was the "Blue Boar" of *Great Expectations*. Queen Victoria once stayed there (hence the extended name) and much of the hotel décor is in Victorian style.

A neat, gabled building in the High Street bears an inscription over the doorway to the effect that it was for "six poor travellers". It was erected in 1771 on the site of an original home founded in 1579 by Sir Richard Watts, a wealthy citizen, in which six poor travellers were entitled to stay one night, receive dinner, and, before departing the following morning, the sum of fourpence in lieu of breakfast. The present building, which Dickens used in *Seven Poor Travellers*, is now occupied, but is open to visitors at certain times.

In Maidstone Road is Restoration House, where Charles II spent the night of 28 May 1660 on his way to London to reclaim his throne; it is open to the public at certain times. Twenty-eight years later James II was held for a week in the city on his flight to France in 1688. He was detained in the home of Sir Richard Head which is now the premises of Lloyd's Bank in the High Street.

Eastgate House, at the eastern end of the High Street, is a fine example of late Tudor domestic architecture and yet another favourite Dickens locale: it was Westgate House in *Pickwick Papers*, and the Nun's House in *Edwin Drood*. Today it is a museum with exhibits of local history, as well as those of general archaeological, geological and ethnological interest. Included in the museum's Dickensiana is the chalet from his garden at Gad's Hill Place where he wrote the unfinished *Edwin Drood*. It was acquired by the Corporation in 1961, restored and re-erected in the grounds of Eastgate House.

Those interested in shipping will find much of interest in the busy dockyards.

ROMNEY, HYTHE AND DYMCHURCH LIGHT RAILWAY, Kent.

This little railway claims to be the smallest public railway in the world, and with a track of 15-in. gauge it may well be so. The nine steam locomotives, which weigh about 9¼ tons laden, can haul a dozen or more fully loaded coaches, and speeds of over 20 m.p.h. are attained; they are good copies of actual engines which once ran on main lines, and they have been given famous names. One is called the *Winston Churchill*; another *Dr Syn*, the name of the fictional clergyman-smuggler associated with the Romney Marsh area.

The railway, between HYTHE and DUNGE-NESS, was founded in 1927 by Captain Jack Howey, a noted motor-racing driver of the day and a miniature railway enthusiast. Although primarily for carrying holidaymakers, it is a complete railway in miniature and has fulfilled much more serious transport rôles, not least in the Second World War; during that period it was taken over by the army, and, with anti-aircraft guns mounted on some of its rolling stock, it patrolled along this part of the potential invasion coast. The war over, it later reverted to its original rôle.

A ride on this train is great fun, and even exhilarating; a taste, even if in miniature, of the days before British Rail ran out of steam.

The little Romney, Hythe and Dymchurch Railway operates in the summer months with a number of services every day in each direction.

ROTTINGDEAN, *Sussex* (6–TQ3702). Although only 3½ m. from BRIGHTON and within that borough, its residents like to think of it as an independent village. In fact, it has kept that air although so near the big town. The main road, the A259, skirts but does not enter Rottingdean.

The High Street is a quiet thoroughfare along which stand a number of old buildings dating back 200 years or more. Just off the High Street is a little green and the village pond, usually graced by swans. Famous people have been captivated by this rustic scene, among them Rudyard Kipling, who lived here for several years in The Elms, a house which faces the green, and where he wrote several of his most famous works before moving on to BURWASH. The house is a private residence and not open to the public.

Of great interest is the Toy Museum in The Grange, a Georgian house that was originally the Vicarage; it was given its present name by the famous painter, Sir William Nicholson, who lived here just before the First World War. The museum contains many hundreds of toys which have been popular over the past 150 years or so. These are mainly British, but there are also exhibits from all over the world. They range from magnificent rocking horses to tiny lead soldiers. There are a large assortment of dolls, inanimate toys and toys worked by mechanical means; toys to amuse and toys educational; model theatres and many other aspects of everyday life in miniature. It is a most comprehensive collection to delight children and adults alike.

One room is devoted to Kipling and contains letters and papers, photographs and drawings, some of his first editions, reproductions of some of the illustrations for *The Jungle Book*, and other items closely connected with the famous author.

Another room contains a small collection of exhibits concerning the history of the village and the locality; another room is used as a small art gallery for one-man shows, as well as for the Victoria and Albert Museum travelling exhibitions.

The Parish Church of St Margaret was restored and largely rebuilt in the middle of the 19th cent.

but it retains much of its original work, including the substantial 13th-cent. tower and some Norman windows uncovered during later restoration work, as well as some 14th-cent. windows. The stained glass is mainly modern, the work of Sir Edward Burne-Jones. The font is a modern reproduction of the original Norman font, which can also be seen in the church. Some years ago an American offer was made for the church, with the idea of pulling it down and re-erecting it in the Forest Lawns cemetery in Los Angeles. This offer was not accepted, but by agreement the would-be purchasers made a careful study of the church and then built an exact replica at Forest Lawns, calling it the Church of the Recessional, after Kipling's poem which he wrote while living in Rottingdean.

On a hill just outside the village stands a fine old hooded windmill, restored in 1922. It was long a seamark, and was the model used by Sir William Nicholson for the imprint of a well-known publishing firm.

RUNNYMEDE, *Surrey* (6–TQ0072). The green expanse of Runnymede, outside EGHAM, is a historic spot for Englishmen; in these meadows on 15 June 1215 Magna Carta was signed. Although it was the outcome of a struggle for power between King John and the barons, without much regard to the rights of the people, the charter signed by the two factions became the basis of the rights that eventually extended to all.

King John had his headquarters at Windsor Castle, across the Thames. The barons, already in possession of London, marched to Staines, crossed the bridge and established themselves on the fields of Runnymede and Long Mede, where the king met them in parley, and after several days of negotiations, reluctantly signed the charter. Opinions differ as to the exact location of the signing; some point to it as the mede, or meadow, lying below the wide bend in the Thames NW. of Egham; others to a small islet in the river. There is now a memorial to mark the approximate spot.

There was no memorial until modern times: the American Bar Association set it up in 1957. It is a simple pillar of English granite on a base beneath a star-spangled dome resting on eight octagonal stone pillars. The inscription on the column reads: "To commemorate Magna Carta, symbol of freedom under law". The memorial is surrounded by venerable English oaks.

A little distance away is a memorial to John F. Kennedy, the president of the United States assassinated in 1963. Three acres of land opposite Magna Carta Island were presented to the United States and on this land the memorial was erected. This is a simple block of Portland stone weighing 7 tons, and bearing an inscription taken from the address Kennedy gave at his inauguration on 20 January 1961, famous words that accord well with the ideals the English-speaking world links with Magna Carta.

These fields, or meadows as they are described in the documents, beside the Thames are as pleasant as they are historic. On Cooper's Hill to the S. there is further cause for remembrance, the Commonwealth Air Forces Memorial.

It was designed by Sir Edward Maufe, the architect of GUILDFORD Cathedral, and was consecrated in 1953. Austere and impressive, it is built to follow the semi-circular contour of the hill on which it stands. In the arcaded galleries which surround the green quadrangle are columns designed to suggest the successive pages of stone "books", by which term they are known. On them are recorded the names of 20,455 airmen from Commonwealth countries who lost their lives over Britain or Europe and who have no known grave. On the ceiling above the "books" are the arms of the Commonwealth countries.

In the 18th cent. Egham race-course was on Runnymede and regular meetings were held there. For a period the meetings were fashionable, then suffered a setback until George IV attended in 1828. Thus revived, they continued until 1886, when the London police refused to supply the men needed to keep order – and no more were held.

RYE, *Sussex* (7–TQ9220). One of the most picturesque towns in England, which, while catering in a modern way for an ever-growing inflow of tourists, has managed to keep its ancient character. It is a town for strolling in, with hilly streets, many of them cobbled, and a wealth of medieval, Tudor, Stuart and Georgian houses. All have been well kept up, and necessary restoration and rebuilding have not spoilt them.

Today Rye stands near the mouth of the Rother, nearly 2 m. inland, yet it was once a flourishing port, the sea at its walls. It was one of the original Cinque Ports, and suffered many naval attacks and raids. At least four times the French landed here and in 1377 they burnt Rye to the ground, except for a handful of stone buildings. Its prosperity declined with the silting up of the harbour in the second half of the 16th cent. Since then it has had ups and downs and smuggling was for long an important part of its economy.

There is much to see in Rye; perhaps it is best first to visit the museum, housed in one of the most historic monuments, Ypres Tower, restored for this purpose in 1928. This was the old town fort built in the 13th cent. and then called Badding Tower; it survived the burning of 1377. But less than 100 years later it was considered to be of no further use and was sold to a John de Ypres, from whom it took its name. It was re-acquired by the authorities in 1518 and served various purposes, including nearly three centuries as a prison. The building is square with three-quarter round towers and a detached tower of the 19th cent. The exhibits in the museum relate to the history of the Cinque Ports, ships and ship-building and the various local industries, including pottery. (There are a number of potteries in Rye where visitors can see potters at work, and their products.)

Below the tower is Gun Garden, so called because a battery of cannon were once kept here. Now it is a terraced garden with a view over the river and yacht anchorage. Another of the pre-1377 structures is the Land Gate, built some decades earlier. It is the only gate left of four that gave access to the walled town. The Augustinian Friary also dates from this era; it is now used as a pottery.

The Parish Church of St Mary was first built during the 12th cent. Despite severe damage done by the French in 1377 and by time, some of the original fabric remains. There have been several additions over the centuries and a major restoration in the 19th cent. The church escaped severe damage in the Second World War; post-war restorations were occasioned by old age. Today it is a mixture of Norman, Transitional, Early English, Decorated, and modern.

The altar is magnificently carved mahogany dating from the early 18th cent.; the fine candelabrum hanging in the chancel is dated 1759; the font, of Caen stone, is 19th-cent. The windows are mainly of the late 19th and 20th cents.

A major point of interest is the clock, claimed to be the oldest church turret clock in England still functioning with its original works. It was made in Winchelsea in 1560. The giant pendulum swings inside the church where the original weights used to hang. The distinctive painted clock-face is flanked by the figures of two boys who strike the bell on the quarter hours but not the hours; hence the name Quarter Boys. The tower is open to the public (weather permitting). There is a fine view from the top over the town and the surrounding country, much of which was once sea.

Mermaid Street is, perhaps, the best-known of Rye streets: steep, cobbled, it is lined by houses which are mostly of the 15th to 17th cents. Although generally much restored, they have kept their original form. Here stands the Mermaid Inn, the most notorious of the smugglers' haunts in the 18th cent. At one time it was a headquarters of the Hawkhurst desperadoes, greatly feared and seldom opposed. Much of the rear of this hotel is as it was in those days.

Across the street is The House Opposite, so called, it is said, because of the number of people who came looking for the Mermaid Inn; the occupants became so wearied with these enquiries that they adopted this name, inferring that they were opposite the popular inn. Just around the corner from Mermaid Street, in West Street, also largely of buildings of the same periods, stands The Other House. This was occupied by a carpenter who bore the same name as another family in the street. The latter were constantly receiving callers seeking his services who were informed that the carpenter was "at the other house" – and so it became named.

In a quiet spot good for bird-watching, about 1 m. from the town, are the ruins of Camber Castle, built in Henry VIII's reign as part of the defences against possible invasion from France. Originally sea-lapped, by the mid-17th cent. it was high and dry and some distance from the water. Further on is **Camber**, noted for its fine sandy beaches.

SANDWICH, *Kent* (7–TR3358). A delightful old town, now some 2 m. from the sea, Sandwich was once one of the most important naval bases in England, and one of the original Cinque Ports. The town dates from Anglo-Saxon times and 1½ m. to the NW. are the remains of the Roman RICHBOROUGH CASTLE.

Sandwich is best toured on foot, starting, perhaps, with a circuit of the ramparts, which follow the line of the old town walls. This 2-m. walk skirts for a while the River Stour, and for a considerable part the old moat, generally called the Ditch, where cows now graze. The more elevated parts of the walk give a good view over the town and many of its important landmarks.

On the tiny central square, called Cattle Market, is the Guildhall, a 16th-cent. building which has been little altered inside or out. The façade has been retained, as has the old oak flooring and heavy beams and other Tudor features inside. One room has been set aside as a museum of the history of Sandwich.

Across the square a retired saddler displays in his windows a large collection of horse-brasses covering the past 200 years. None of the items is for sale, but the owner welcomes all enthusiasts to come in and discuss his collection.

Sandwich is rich in 16th- and 17th-cent. architecture, and there are a number of houses with the overhanging upper stories typical of this period. Strand Street has many such buildings, of which the Elizabethan Weaver's House is a good example.

A fine medieval monument is the Barbican, once the main gateway to the town; although much restored it retains its ancient character. It is now a toll-gate to a bridge over the Stour; also an excellent starting point for the ramparts walk. A little lower down the river is the Fishergate, another medieval gateway.

St Clement's, the parish church, has a fine Norman tower, and much else of the original Norman fabric remains. The finely carved stone font is early 15th-cent. St Peter's, which dominates the centre of the town, was formerly the parish church, and originally dates from the 13th cent. but has many later alterations and additions. It is now the chapel of the Sir Roger Manwood's Grammar School which is housed in three mansions on the Sandown Road, just outside the town. The Church of St Mary the Virgin also dates from the Norman period, and although little used now, contains much of interest.

Golfers will find several excellent courses in the Sandwich area, including the famous Royal St George, one of the finest in England. Others are Prince's, with an 18-hole course, as well as a 9-hole, and the Royal Cinque Ports. Adjoining the Royal St George links is a long sandy beach 2 m. long, still comparatively uncrowded in summer.

SEDLESCOMBE, *Sussex* (7–TQ7818). The parish of Sedlescombe lies in a pleasant district, with a charming village strung along the main street, which broadens out into the green where stands an old pump under a gable-roofed shelter. A large hoard of Anglo-Saxon coins found here in 1867 is popularly supposed to have been buried by Harold's paymaster after the Battle of HASTINGS. Some 16th- and 17th-cent. houses enclose the green, and the Queen's Head Inn, although much restored, dates from the 15th cent.

The Parish Church of St John the Baptist has been rebuilt several times during the last two centuries, but the tower remains much as it was in the early 15th cent.

Just outside the village is a large old mansion surrounded by 174 acres of woods and farmland. This is the headquarters of the Pestalozzi Children's Village, where refugee children from many different countries are being educated not only in the British way of life but also in their own traditions and languages. The village was established in August 1959. The children are separated into nationalities under the care of house-parents from their own countries, but attend the local schools.

An open day is held in the lovely gardens once a year, but interested visitors can see the village on certain days by appointment.

SELSEY, *Sussex* (6–SZ8593), was an island in ancient times and is still almost completely surrounded by water: the English Channel on two sides, the inlet that was Pagham Harbour, now an inland lake, and the Brook, known as Broad Rife, on the other sides. There is little of pre-Norman Selsey, including the cathedral, to be seen, for the sea swallowed it long ago. However, Roman and Anglo-Saxon coins and other objects have been dug up in the area. The Romans called their settlement Regnum.

The Selsey peninsula has a good sunshine record and the climate is clear and bracing, making outdoor activities pleasant. There are many good yachting anchorages, and three beaches for swimmers: one of sand with long shallows, another steeper and of shingle, and the third the fishermen's beach complete with boats. On this beach is the famous Selsey Lifeboat Station.

The peninsula abounds in bird life and part of Pagham Harbour is a wild-life sanctuary. There is also a variety of plant life. Here is country for the naturalist and nature lover.

The Parish Church of St Peter was put on its present site just over 100 years ago, but is much older, for it was moved from Church Norton, on Pagham Harbour, where it was originally built in the 12th cent. The pillars are Norman, as is the Purbeck marble font. The roof of the nave and the wooden lectern are both pre-Reformation. On the former site at Church Norton stands the Chapel, a 13th-cent. structure which was previously the chancel of the parish church. The Roman Catholic Church of Our Lady of Mt Carmel and St Wilfred is modern, completed in 1962.

SEVENOAKS, *Kent* (7–TQ5355). Set in pleasant wooded country, Sevenoaks has developed into a popular residential area particularly favoured by businessmen, but has preserved its rural atmosphere.

It is believed there was a settlement here in ancient times, but it is not mentioned until A.D. 1114. Local tradition says that the name came from a clump of seven oaks which once grew here, long since gone but replaced by seven trees taken from Knole Park and ceremoniously planted on the common on the outskirts of the town in 1955.

The town achieved prosperity and became fashionable in the 15th cent. when the property of KNOLE, on the outskirts, came into the possession of Archbishop Bouchier, and the manor was rebuilt as a palace for the archbishops of CANTERBURY.

There are few buildings in the town of any great age, but the Parish Church of St Nicholas retains some stonework believed to date from Anglo-Saxon times. The church is basically of the 13th to 15th cents. but has been altered several times and drastically restored in the middle of last century. The font is 14th-cent. and there is some old stained glass, but most of it is of the 19th cent.

Sevenoaks School is one of the oldest and most famous boys' schools in the country; it was established in the 15th cent. by Sir William Sevenoke (a foundling who took his name from the town, and who later became Lord Mayor of London).

Cricket has been popular here for more than two and a half centuries; it was played on The Vine, still the main recreational grounds, early in the 18th cent. The game gave its name to a neighbouring village – Bat and Ball – where the making of cricket bats was a flourishing industry.

The A21 Sevenoaks bypass is an outstanding example of road landscaping. The terrain makes the minor roads cross at varying heights and angles; the result is a series of beautiful bridges.

SHEPPEY, ISLE OF, *Kent* (7–TQ9669). A Thames Estuary island just E. of the mouth of the MEDWAY, 10 m. long and 5 m. wide. Since 1959 it has been linked to the mainland by a bridge over the Swale. The reclaimed land beside this channel has long been famed for its sheep: Sheppey, Anglo-Saxon in origin, meant "sheep island". Sheerness at the NW. tip of Sheppey has a shingle bathing beach and was formerly a naval base. The establishment is notable for its Victorian Boat Shed, a superb piece of forthright, unadorned building in a florid age.

SHOREHAM-BY-SEA, *Sussex* (6–TQ2105). A popular seaside resort and an ancient town, the original part, called Old Shoreham and lying to the N. of the main centre, was established by the South Saxons in the 5th cent. The modern town is separated from the sea by the River Adur, the harbour, and a long spit of land known as Shoreham Beach. The extensive beach is mainly shingle, but there is good swimming. The harbour provides a safe yacht anchorage and the river some excellent fishing.

The Marlipins Museum contains a wide variety of exhibits relating to the history of the town and district, including archaeological finds and later local relics, and a fine collection of photographs and prints of old ships and other maritime subjects, and of the town. It is housed in a building of flint and stone dating basically from the 12th cent.

The Parish Church of St Nicholas, located near the old wooden toll-bridge in Old Shoreham, has some work dating from Anglo-Saxon and Norman times; the building was much restored in 1840. The Kingston Buci church, dating from the 12th and 13th cents. has traces of pre-Norman work; also notable is the two-decker Jacobean pulpit.

SISSINGHURST, *Kent* (7–TQ7937). A long village with many of the old Kentish white-painted weather-board houses, Sissinghurst achieved prosperity with the growth of the weaving industry introduced here in Edward III's reign. This industry continued until the 16th cent. but nothing survives of it today except some of the houses built by wealthy weavers.

Best known of the old houses in the district is Sissinghurst Castle. This manor house was built in the late 15th cent., with additions in the 16th cent. Little remains of the original building except the long entrance range which includes the present gatehouse and arch. It suffered from neglect and misuse. During the Seven Years' War it was used as a prison for captured French seamen; they left it a wreck and the only part still intact was used as a workhouse, then as farm buildings, until, in a derelict state, it was rescued in 1930 by Sir Harold Nicolson and his wife, the writer Victoria Sackville-West.

They restored what was left of the once-great manor house and established one of the finest gardens in the country in its grounds. Much of the gardens is laid out in Elizabethan style: of special interest is the White Garden planted entirely with silver-leaved white flowering species, separated by box hedges. The Priest's House (1560) stands in it. Parts of the house are open to the public, including the restored 16th-cent. tower which V. Sackville-West used as her work-room. The rest of the house, and the Priest's House, are private. Now under the care of the National Trust, the gardens are open daily in the summer season.

Sissinghurst Court is a charming 16th-cent. house, much added to and restored, with a delightful garden of about 3 acres, with lily ponds and fountains, which is open for charity at advertised times in summer. The house is not open. Another garden open to the public every day in the summer months is Sissinghurst Place; the house here was built on the site of an old weaver's dwelling and a fulling mill.

SMALLHYTHE, *Kent* (7–TQ8930). It is hard to visualize this little hamlet on the road between TENTERDEN and HYTHE, among fields and far from the sea, as the thriving port and ship-building centre it was in medieval times, when the River Rother flowed past wide and deep enough for the ships of those days. Among craft built here was a warship ordered by Henry VIII. Today there are only a few houses and the river is a trickle. However, the bus stop for Smallhythe is named the Ferry, recalling days when a ferry probably plied here.

Although small enough to escape the motorist's notice, this place is well worth a stop, especially for those interested in the theatre. For here lived the actress, Ellen Terry, for more than a quarter of a century, and her old home, Smallhythe Place, is now a museum devoted to her memory and to the theatre. The house itself is an interesting building of the late 15th cent. It was originally the Port House and later the home of a yeoman farmer. Although much altered over the centuries it has largely kept its original character with the post-and-pan timbering typical of the period; much of the timber and the solid oaken floors is original.

Exhibited in the museum are costumes worn by Ellen Terry in many of the rôles of her long stage career, and also some worn by Sir Henry Irving with whom she was associated in the theatre for more than 25 years. There are also many reminders of her private and family life, as well as mementoes of other stage personalities back to David Garrick and Sarah Siddons. The museum is open to the public.

The Parish Church of St John, where Ellen Terry worshipped and in which her private funeral service was conducted, is largely 16th-cent. but the glass is modern, the original having been blown out by a bomb during the Second World War. The font is 15th-cent. and is set in an ancient millstone presented by Ellen Terry.

Next door is the Priest's House of about the same period. Of some architectural interest, it is now a private house.

SMARDEN, *Kent* (7–TQ8842). A pretty village with a number of old, well-preserved buildings. Smarden Church has long been known as the "Barn of Kent" because of the great height (36 ft) and structure of its wooden roof, and the great width of its nave; it dates from the 15th cent. Other old buildings are the Penthouse and a fine example of a cloth hall.

SOMPTING, *Sussex* (6–TQ1605), has one of the oldest churches in the country, the Parish Church of St Mary. It is mainly Norman, but there is considerable Anglo-Saxon work in evidence, especially the tower, which is early 11th-cent. The chancel is mainly Norman, with some Anglo-Saxon work, and the north transept is divided by 12th-cent. arches. The chapel is 14th-cent. The 100-ft high tower is unique in England, the pyramid cap of shingle having a steep gable rising into it from each wall face; known as a "Rhenish helm", this type of tower is common in villages along the Rhine.

Another building of architectural interest is the manor house, Sompting Abbots, now a preparatory school.

Kenneth Scowen

Tenterden: Georgian shops in the High Street

STONE, *Kent* (7–TQ5774). A village near DARTFORD in the industrial and commercial centre of the county. The Church of St Mary, according to tradition, was built by masons who worked on Westminster Abbey, a belief which is borne out by its interior appearance.

The church is one of the finest examples of Gothic architecture in Kent. The nave is lofty with a double arcade of piers, a splendid tower arch, a fine choir and a superb vaulted roof. The rich carving throughout is magnificent.

STOPHAM, *Sussex* (6–TQ0119), stands where the Rivers Rother and Arun meet, with a medieval seven-arch stone bridge over the latter. This was built early in the 14th cent., replacing a former Anglo-Saxon wooden structure; it was restored in the 16th cent. and again in 1865. The three arches on either side are of the same height, with a taller and wider central arch to allow the passage of small craft in the main channel.

The parish church dates from Norman times and retains much of the original work, with an Elizabethan parish chest and a 15th-cent. font.

STROOD, *Kent* (7–TQ7369). One of the Medway Towns on the opposite side of the river facing ROCHESTER. It is chiefly notable for Temple Manor which was originally built by the Knights Templars in the first quarter of the 13th cent. It later became a nunnery until the suppression of the religious orders by Henry VIII and following that was a farm-house for centuries. In a ruinous state after the Second World War, it has been restored and is open to the public throughout the year. The building contains a 13th-cent. hall on a vaulted undercroft of three bays, and 17th-cent. brick extensions. Much was rebuilt, but the original form was retained.

TENTERDEN, *Kent* (7–TQ8833). One of the most charming towns of the South, it has a broad High Street lined with shops and dwellings, nearly all with their original façades dating from Elizabethan to Georgian times. The Georgian predominates, most of the houses being built between 1720 and 1760. This is one of the most delightful streets in Kent for shopping, or just browsing. The private dwellings beyond the shopping area have also largely retained their old appearance, and the parks and greens which surround the town enhance its beauty. The town has fine old inns, one of the most attractive being the William Caxton, named after the man who brought printing to England and who may have been born in Tenterden in 1422.

The tower of the Parish Church of St Mildred dominates the town. Built in the 15th cent., it rises more than 100 ft above the ground and from the top there is a clear view across the Weald to the Channel coast. It is possible at times to see shipping in the Channel, and even the French coast. At the base of the tower are the twin west doors of which there is only one other example in Kent (at LYDD) and four others outside the county. The main fabric of the church was built between the 12th and 15th cents. but there have been considerable alterations and restorations since.

TONBRIDGE, *Kent* (7–TQ5845). An ancient town: there was a settlement here in Anglo-Saxon and, perhaps, Roman times. Built on the navigable extremity of the MEDWAY, it has a long history of commercial importance, and is still a thriving town.

Its most important ancient landmark, on a rise in the centre of the town, is the ruined Norman castle of which there are substantial remains. The massive gatehouse with its flanking drum-towers is early 14th cent., as is the shell of the keep. The remains of the wall date from the 12th cent. Inside the wall is a tremendous mound which may have been the site of an earlier Anglo-Saxon fort, but of which no trace remains. In later years the castle passed through many hands and 18th-cent. builders pillaged it for materials. However, one owner used stone from the castle to build a pleasant Georgian house now used as council offices (it adjoins the castle). An Ancient Monument under the care of Tonbridge Council, the castle is open to the public throughout the year.

The Parish Church of SS. Peter and Paul is substantially Early English, but there is evidence of earlier work. There are a number of later additions, and the church was enlarged and restored in the 1870s.

The town is the home of the famous Tonbridge School founded in 1553 by Sir Andrew Judd, Master of the Skinners' Company and a former Lord Mayor of London. On his death in 1558 he left the administration in trust to the Skinners' Company and they have remained its governors ever since. It is now housed in mainly 19th-cent. buildings in the High Street.

There are numerous walks around the district, a favourite one being along River Walk, following the banks of the Medway, with good views of the castle; also through the low-water meadows, criss-crossed by paths and channels, and well shaded by willows.

TROTTISCLIFFE, *Kent* (7–TQ6460). One of a number of unhelpful Kentish spellings; the name of this village is pronounced "Trosley". It contains some pleasant old houses.

The chief attraction is the Coldrum Stones, near the village, a long barrow which rivals Kit's Coty House in interest. The great stones of the central burial chamber are in more or less their original position, and around the mound are the fallen uprights of a stone circle. It is believed to have been a royal tomb, and the bones of some 20 people of the Neolithic Age have been excavated. This collection is housed in Trottiscliffe Church, a small and ancient building of no great architectural merit, but which possesses a huge carved pulpit out of keeping with its size: it stood originally in Westminster Abbey.

TUNBRIDGE WELLS, *Kent* (7–TQ5838), is a "new" town in that there is nothing medieval here, or even Tudor, for this was only forest until Lord North discovered the chalybeate springs in 1606. He took the news of his discovery back to court and soon members of the royal family and the nobility were going to the springs to take the waters. But for the first 30 years there were no buildings, and royalty and courtiers alike camped out or lodged in the nearest towns. In the 1630s building began in earnest and by the end of the century Tunbridge Wells was a flourishing and fashionable spa, and remained so throughout the 18th and 19th cents. In 1735 came the famous Beau Nash from Bath, who, as Master of Cere-

monies, virtually ran the social life of the town for many years.

Today Tunbridge Wells still thrives, but is in no way aggressively commercial; it retains much of the charm and taste for which it was so famous. The tranquillity of former years prevails in the best known of its areas, the Pantiles, a delightful, shaded walk lined with elegant shops, and with an 18th-cent. "musick" balcony.

The Pantiles was originally grassed and known as The Walks, and from early days was the fashionable promenade. In 1699 Princess (later Queen) Anne visited the spa with her son, the Duke of Gloucester; the young duke slipped and hurt himself walking there. The Princess complained and the town authorities promised to lay a paved walk, but this had not been done when she came the following year, and she left in a huff, vowing never to return. The town fathers quickly repaired their omission and paved The Walks with square pantiles. The Pantiles has been the name ever since. Only 15 of the original pantiles remain, near the springs in Bath Square.

But it did the town fathers no good as far as Queen Anne was concerned. She never returned. Visitors to The Pantiles may still drink the medicinal waters from the springs.

Many gracious houses of the Georgian and Victorian periods remain, some set in magnificent gardens. Some are hotels; the Calverley Hotel was formerly Calverley House where the young Princess Victoria used to stay with her mother, the Duchess of Kent; she continued to visit Tunbridge Wells for some time after becoming queen.

The oldest church is that of St Charles the Martyr, built in 1678 and attaining its present form in 1696. Dedicated to Charles I, it is a plain, square building, but has a beautiful ornamental ceiling. There is a tablet let into the front of the north gallery marking the pew occupied by Princess Victoria between the years 1827 and 1834. Holy Trinity Church, consecrated in 1829, was the work of Decimus Burton, the noted architect of the period, who designed many of the houses of the town, including Calverley Park.

Tunbridge Wells is rich in parks and gardens, foremost being the Common which reaches into the town. Some 250 acres in extent, it has grassy slopes and many curiously weathered rocks. It is excellent for walks and as a playground for children. Another park is Dunorlan, formerly the grounds of a mansion; it has an area of 30 acres with a six-acre lake where boating can be enjoyed. There are several other small parks in and around the town. Tunbridge Wells is also a good centre for walks to such places as Rusthall with its strange sandstone rocks, including Toad Rock, a large outcrop shaped as its name suggests; and Happy Valley, also with unusual rock formations. High Rocks, 2 m. distant, is the headquarters of the Sandstone Climbing Club of Great Britain. Permission to climb may be obtained from the proprietor on payment of a fee.

Although essentially a residential town, light

Tunbridge Wells: The Pantiles   Noel Habgood

industry has been neatly provided for. Fifteen factories stand in a 28-acre estate pleasantly laid out in rural surroundings, well furnished with approach roads and essential services – and in no way intruding on the town.

UPNOR, *Kent* (7–TQ7470). On the MED-WAY and backed by wooded hills, Upnor has become a resort for the people of the Medway Towns. It is an excellent yachting base and has a flourishing club.

The main attraction is the castle which is like a fortified manor house, crenellated and turreted. It was built in 1561 as one of a number of block-houses to protect the Medway and the approaches to Chatham. When tested, it did not prove equal to the task. It made only a feeble effort to stop a Dutch fleet under de Ruyter making its way up the Medway in 1667 and destroying a number of English men-of-war before sailing away again, virtually unmolested; an ignominious defeat sportingly celebrated on the 3rd centenary in 1967 by a Dutch Week in the Medway Towns. One of the guns fired ineffectively at the Dutch fleet has been salvaged from the river and now stands silent guard outside the entrance to the fort, which is still an attractive, if not noble monument.

Here also is one of the last of the old sailing vessels, the *Arethusa* (formerly the *Peking*), sister ship to the luckless *Pamir* and now a training ship.

Upnor Church was built in 1878; it contains a fine stained-glass window by Burne-Jones.

VIRGINIA WATER, *Surrey* (6–SU9967), em-braces a considerable area of the part of Windsor Great Park which lies in Surrey, in the south-eastern corner of which is Virginia Water Lake, covering about 160 acres. Overflow waters from the lake form a cascade which is visible from the Great South-West main road. The park was laid out in 1746 by the Duke of Cumberland, victor of the battle of Culloden. On the south side is a colonnade of pillars, a number of them broken, brought from Leptis Magna and set up here on the orders of George IV. On the opposite side of the A30 is a tower, a rebuilt version of an observa-tory which was destroyed by fire in the late 18th cent.

The grounds round the lake have many excel-lent picnic spots, and the lake offers fine boating. The surrounding park and country are good for rambling.

WALMER CASTLE, *Kent* (7–TR3750). About 1½ m. S. of DEAL, and the official residence of the Lord Warden of the Cinque Ports. The castle was built as one of a line of coastal forts by Henry VIII as a protection against possible French invasion. It became the residence of the Lord Warden in 1708, and was to be the home of many famous men. When appointed Lord Warden in 1941, Sir Winston Churchill stated he would not take up residence there as it was in range of enemy guns and would inevitably become a target and be destroyed; he handed it over to the nation.

However, the castle is again lived in for at least part of the year: the present Lord Warden, the former Prime Minister of Australia, Sir Robert Menzies, stays there on his official visits to England. The castle is open daily to the public except during the brief periods of the Lord Warden's residence.

Over the years many alterations and modifica-tions have been made to the castle, so that much of the original atmosphere has gone; it is now more a stately home than a fort. The castle is also something of a museum of its former residents, especially Pitt and the Iron Duke. Pitt's tenure of office (1792–1806) is remembered in the Pitt Room where many items of his personal property are preserved. The magnificent gardens were mostly laid out during this period and were designed by his niece, the eccentric Lady Hester Stanhope who was later to gain fame for her wanderings in the Middle East. Wellington held the post from 1829 until 1852, and many of the pieces of furniture he used have been preserved, as well as items of uniform and clothing – and his telescope through which he often scanned the coast of France, for he always maintained that the old enemy might attack one day, the contingency against which the castle had been built three centuries before. The duke entertained many famous people here, including Queen Victoria and Prince Albert, and the rooms they occupied are maintained much as they were during their visit.

WALTON-ON-THE-HILL, *Surrey* (6–TQ 2255). Not far from the village have been found the sites of two Roman villas. Anglo-Saxons settled here, and it was an important manor in Norman times.

The Parish Church of St Peter was rebuilt in 1895, but is notable for a rare leaden Norman font. Around the bowl is a series of arches; be-neath each one is a seated figure either reading or with hand upraised in blessing. There is also some fine 16th-cent. Flemish glass from Woburn Abbey.

WARLINGHAM, *Surrey* (6–TQ3658). A plea-sant and growing town separated by the Green Belt from the more built-up areas to the N. Its parish church is notable for two important ecclesiastical "firsts". Here the new English prayer-book authorized by Edward VI was first used, its compiler, Archbishop Cranmer, attend-ing the service. Four centuries later a service from the church was televised, the first ever to be seen on television in Britain. Although the church was restored and enlarged in 1894, it is basically 13th-cent. and contains much that is old, including a 15th-cent. wall painting of St Christo-pher. The octagonal font is 15th-cent. and three piscinas are medieval. Most of the glass is modern but there is one window from the 15th cent.

WESTDEAN, *Sussex* (7–TV5299). This ham-let lies in a valley in Friston Forest, some distance off the main road.

The forest sweeps up to the N. and 1 m. to the

SE. are the Seven Sisters, chalk cliffs abruptly descending to the sea. The church has a gabled tower and some good 17th-cent. monuments; nearby stands the rectory, dating from the 13th cent. Just to the N. is Charleston Manor, a pleasing mixture of Tudor and Georgian architecture set in delightful gardens with ancient dovecots. The gardens are open daily in the summer, but the house only by appointment.

WESTERHAM, *Kent* (6–TQ4454). In the main street and around the tiny green of this village stand a number of old buildings, including two coaching inns. The village is notable as the birthplace of General James Wolfe, victor of the decisive battle between the English and French at Quebec in 1759, in which he lost his life. Standing at the head of the green and dominating the main street is a bronze statue of him wielding his sword.

Quebec House, where he lived as a boy, is a 16th-cent. mansion largely rebuilt in the 17th cent. It is now maintained by the National Trust as a museum to his memory, and contains a collection of relics of his life and career. It is open to the public at advertised times in the summer.

Squerryes Court, a mansion of the late 17th cent., also has Wolfe connections. He was a friend of the Warde family whose descendants still own the house, and it was in their garden that he received his commission in 1741; a monument marks the spot. The house has a collection of Dutch paintings, a number of portraits, and period furniture and tapestries; there is also a room set aside for Wolfe exhibits. The house is open on regular days each week in the summer months.

A more recent famous person with close connections with the town is Sir Winston Churchill, who lived at CHARTWELL, 2½ m. S., for over 40 years. There is a bronze statue of Sir Winston by Oscar Nemon on Westerham green. The white marble plinth was given by Marshal Tito and the people of Yugoslavia.

The parish church dates from the 13th to 15th cents. with a three-gabled east end and a squat tower. It has a rare spiral staircase leading up the tower, and painted on wood are the arms of Edward VI, also a rarity. There are some fine stained-glass windows, including a memorial window to Wolfe by Burne-Jones. The font is 14th-cent. and here Wolfe was baptized, as were two of Sir Winston Churchill's grandchildren.

WEST MALLING, *Kent* (7–TQ6857). West Malling became prominent in Norman times when an abbey was established here. The abbey was destroyed by fire, along with the village, in the 12th cent. It was re-established for the Benedictine nuns, then had an eventful history after the Dissolution under numerous owners. The abbey has been partly restored and is again occupied by Benedictine nuns.

Most of the buildings in West Malling's High Street have been scheduled as places of architectural interest under the Town and Country Planning acts. Ford House, in the High Street, is

600 years old, and the Swan Hotel is substantially Tudor; it was a prominent coaching inn and favoured by Dr Johnson on his visits to this district. The parish church has a massive Norman tower, and an Early English chancel with triple lancet east window; the nave was rebuilt early in this century.

The administrative building of the **East Malling** Research Station is a fine brick Queen Anne mansion, with a panelled great hall. The station can be visited by appointment by people with a professional interest in horticulture and fruit-growing.

WEYBRIDGE, *Surrey* (6–TQ0764). An old town on the site where, according to tradition, Julius Caesar crossed the Thames in 55 B.C., presumably near where the modern bridge stands.

During the Tudor period there was great royal activity here. Henry VIII built one residence, Oatlands, and purchased another, Ashley Park; both mansions are gone but the estates remain as entities, now residential areas. The old Manor House was the home of John Bradshaw, president of the judges who tried Charles I, and he is said to have signed the king's death warrant there.

The museum contains exhibits concerned with the archaeology of north-west Surrey, local customs, costumes and handicrafts.

The Church of St Mary is of Norman origin; the present tower dates from the 15th cent.

Close by is Brookwood Cemetery, one of the most extensive in the world; several London parishes and communities have their own burial grounds here, and there is a special military graves section and war memorials to the fallen of both World Wars. There is also a simple but impressive memorial to the Commonwealth soldiers who died in the Second World War and who have no known graves.

Brooklands Motor Course was from 1907 to 1939 the scene of international and national races, record attempts, and test runs. It was the world's first banked motor-racing circuit. A section of the banking remains and a plaque commemorates past glories. The course is now an airfield belonging to the British Aircraft Corporation.

WHITSTABLE, *Kent* (7–TR1166), a seaside resort on Kent's north shore, long renowned for its oysters. The beach is shingle and there are the usual seaside amenities and entertainments.

The Urban District Council offices are in a pretentious, crenellated building known as The Castle. The tower, of brick, is 15th-cent. and was originally used as a look-out post to keep watch for invaders. The rest of the castle is pseudo, built in the middle of the last century. The Castle is set in parkland that is open to the public. The excellent greenhouses may also be inspected by request.

Whitstable is a popular yachting centre, and there are three clubs offering first-class facilities to visiting yachtsmen.

A feature of the shoreline is a finger of land jutting out about 1½ m. into the sea, affording an unusual and pleasant promenade at low tide.

At **Chestfield**, on the outskirts, are an excellent example of a Kentish oasthouse, and a 16th-cent. tithe barn. Here also is the golf course, the clubhouse of which is claimed to be the oldest in England.

WILMINGTON, *Sussex* (7–TQ5404), is renowned for the Long Man of Wilmington, a great figure cut out of the turf of Windover Hill overlooking the village. The figure holds two long staves upright on either side of him. Its origins are a mystery, and there is no written record of it before the 18th cent. However, some archaeologists think it may have much earlier origins, dating back to Anglo-Saxon times, and may be the work of Viking raiders. A similar device appears on a Danish silver cauldron from the 1st cent. B.C., and another on a 7th-cent. Swedish plaque. Ancient barrows and flint mines surround the figure.

The ruins of Wilmington Priory date from Norman and Tudor times, with a Tudor crypt. Housed here is an excellent agricultural museum, showing the farming implements used 150 years ago and more. The priory is under the care of the Sussex Archaeological Trust and is open to the public.

WINCHELSEA, *Sussex* (7–TQ9017). A quiet little town on a prominent hill about 2 m. from RYE. Now more than 1 m. from the sea, it was once a flourishing sea-port, and a later member of the Cinque Ports. The Winchelsea of today is not the original town; that was submerged by the sea in the late 13th cent. As the sea encroached, the inhabitants built new houses on the higher ground, and had moved into their new town before final disaster overtook the old. Winchelsea remained a thriving port for some years, although it suffered heavy damage in repeated French raids. Finally the sea, whose encroachment had played such havoc, receded and took away its means of prosperity.

The new town was built on a grid plan, still evident today. It has a number of old buildings, but is largely of the last 100 years.

One of the oldest buildings is the Court Hall, parts of which date back to the earliest days of the town; it was drastically restored in the 16th cent. and at later dates. It now houses a museum devoted to the history of the town and district; there is an interesting model of the town as it was centuries ago, and a series of models showing the changes in the coastline. Below are the ancient prison cells and dungeons.

St Thomas's Church consists of only the 14th-cent. chancel of the original building. There are monuments and a wall painting from the 14th cent., and some 15th-cent. carved stone seats and stained glass. Most of the glass is modern. Here also is the tomb of England's first admiral, Gervase Alard.

The town walls have disappeared, but three of the ancient gates remain: the Strand Gate; New Gate; and Pipewell, or Land Gate. The two former are 13th-cent. and the latter an early 15th-cent. replacement.

Scattered around the town are a number of wells which once provided the townsfolk with a good water supply.

Although so few of the ancient buildings remain, Winchelsea has a number of medieval vaulted cellars; a typical example is to be seen in the Manna Plat restaurant.

WISLEY GARDENS, *Surrey* (6–TQ0658). These are the experimental gardens and laboratories of the Royal Horticultural Society and surround Wisley village.

The gardens were established in 1904 with a gift of 60 acres to replace the Society's research station which had been in use at CHISWICK for over 80 years. The property now covers over 300 acres; 150 acres are garden, 6 acres are used for vegetable trials, and the rest is farm and woodland. The gardens contain a wide variety of trees, shrubs and plants, many of them rare in this country, and look particularly magnificent in spring and late autumn. Horticultural enthusiasts, and anyone who enjoys parks and gardens, will find much to interest them, and much cultivated and natural beauty.

The gardens are open to the public daily (except Sundays) throughout the year.

WITLEY, *Surrey* (6–SU9439). Set in wooded country, Witley has a common of more than 500 acres, in the care of the National Trust. An outstanding beauty-spot is Sweet Water.

In the Parish Church of All Saints are traces of Anglo-Saxon work, including portions of the nave walls, and in the west gable there is a window with an oaken framework believed to be more than 1,000 years old. The tower, transepts and chancel date from the 12th cent.

WOKING, *Surrey* (6–TQ0058). One of the largest towns in Surrey, Woking is comparatively new, only really developing with the advent of the railway in the late 1830s. However, Old Woking, 2 m. from the centre of the modern town, is an old settlement dating from Anglo-Saxon times and mentioned in the Domesday Book. It was fortunate: listed as a personal possession of the king, it did not pay taxes.

The Parish Church of St Peter stands in Old Woking. Its origins lie in the 11th cent. but it was twice restored, in 1878 and again in 1888. Two of the walls still stand much as they were in Norman times, with a Norman doorway on the site of what is believed to have been the original west entrance. The present entrance is 13th-cent., like the chancel and several of its lancet lights. The pulpit and gallery are 17th-cent.

Woking has the biggest mosque in England, founded by Dr Leitner, an accomplished linguist and Orientalist. In 1885 he founded an Oriental institute in a building which had previously been a drama school. A few years later he erected a mosque in the grounds. After the doctor's death the institute ceased to function but the mosque continued to fulfil its rôle and has become a centre of Islamic religion and life in this country.

WORTHING, *Sussex* (6–TQ1402). Worthing has all the amenities of a large town, including the Connaught Theatre, as well as the attractions of an increasingly popular seaside resort, and extensive sand and shingle beaches. Sea fishing is excellent, from the beaches or from boats.

At the Museum are displayed local finds from prehistoric times, flint tools from CISSBURY RING and later civilizations – Roman, Romano-British and Anglo-Saxon (there is some interesting glass from this period), and relics of the more recent life of the county, including 19th-cent. toys, and 18th- to 20th-cent. costumes. The Art Gallery features English art, especially early watercolours.

At **Highdown Hill**, 3 m. NW. of Worthing, a 50-acre archaeological site has yielded evidence of a late Bronze Age settlement beneath an Iron Age hill-fort. Pagan Saxons later buried their dead within the ramparts. At Highdown, a garden has been arranged in a chalkpit. It is open to the public at advertised times.

WYE, *Kent* (7–TR0546), is notable chiefly for its agricultural and horticultural college. The first foundation was a college of priests, by John Kempe, Archbishop of Canterbury in 1447. This was dissolved by Henry VIII and a few years later was made into a grammar school. In 1893 it became an agricultural college, and in 1900 a school of the University of London giving degree courses in agriculture and horticulture. Part of the original college still exists, a small building with mullioned windows at the west end and cloisters; additions have been made in the style of the original.

The Parish Church of SS. Martin and Gregory was built in the 15th cent. and largely rebuilt in the 17th, when the tower collapsed, demolishing the nave.

There is an excellent race-course where several meetings are held every year.

There are a number of interesting old houses here. Olantigh House is mostly modern, having been largely rebuilt after a fire in the early 1900s. However, it incorporates many features of the original, including an imposing front portico. It is part of the setting for the Stour Music Festival, held annually in June.

About 1 m. to the W. are the villages of **Boughton Aluph** and **Boughton Lees**, set in parklands. Boughton Aluph actually lies in the 2,000-acre Eastwell Park, which with other surrounding park and woodlands makes good rambling country. The spacious square church is the centre of the music festival.

Wilmington: a view along the line of the Downs

Noel Habgood

The South Country

Berkshire   Hampshire   Isle of Wight
Wiltshire   Dorset

JOHN ARLOTT

This region of southern England – Berkshire, Wiltshire, Dorset, Hampshire and the Isle of Wight – approximates to the kingdom of Wessex of both Alfred the Great and Thomas Hardy, whose boundaries, in the first case, varied and, in the second, were never strictly defined; nevertheless, it is – and used to be even more definitely – a unity.

It may be said of the region in general that the districts furthest from London preserved their identity longer: but, in face of modern development, the areas remote not only from London but also from any of the other major towns have retained most of the character they possessed for centuries but which has, in many cases, been destroyed within the last couple of decades.

The south of England is essentially an agricultural area. Its largest towns – Portsmouth, Southampton, Bournemouth, Swindon and Reading – have little of the sympathy with the rest of the area that, for instance, Bristol has with the West, Nottingham or Leicester with the Midlands, Norwich with East Anglia or Leeds with the West Riding. In fact, these towns – now becoming centres of such large built-up areas as to have lost much even of their own original identity – are, to varying extents, artificial growths. Portsmouth is less a Hampshire city than a naval centre, peopled, at its active core, by sailors from all over the country who have no roots there. The Aldershot-Farnborough district is equally services territory. Southampton is the liner base created a little more than a century ago out of the fact that an early railway happened to link London with an anchorage which had the freak advantage of four high tides a day. Swindon was arbitrarily selected to become a railway workshop centre, while Bournemouth is simply a cosmopolitan seaside resort which might be anywhere where sand, sea and pine trees occur together. (In contrast, its neighbour, Poole, is an integral part of the area.) Reading represents the attempt to introduce industry into an agricultural district. Unlike every other place on the banks of the Thames, it seems quite oddly uninvolved with the river: the visitor to the town may easily be more aware of the Kennet than of the Thames.

There is far more of the quality of these counties in the country towns such as Salisbury, Dorchester, Winchester, Christchurch, Abingdon, Newbury, Marlborough, Lymington, Devizes, Sherborne, Wareham or Blandford: or in many smaller towns, like Beaminster, Wickham, Wantage, Alresford, Botley, Wootton Bassett, Romsey, Bridport or Lyme Regis: and in countless villages, some of them miraculously, if only temporarily, preserved, which still hold the simple truth of the social form which grew up around church, manor house, vicarage, manor and church farms, and the village green.

This is, too, a region of great houses, with their steadily changing significance. Some have become schools or hostels: others still exert a feudally dominant influence over a district. Nowadays, too, some are commercial "stately homes" attracting tourists in such numbers as to create a fresh country industry. These

G, Douglas Bolton

The Pantheon in the beautiful grounds of Stourhead in Wiltshire

great houses – Wilton House, The Vyne, Forde Abbey, Beaulieu, Stourhead, Wardour Castle, Bramshill House, Stratfield Saye, Broadlands – and their parks and land are a major factor in the shaping of landscape.

It is an area of immense variety, from the heathy, Surrey-type scrubland, through the great chalk hills, the New Forest bogs, the Wiltshire fringe of limestone, the greensand and clay country, to the rich pastures of the Vale of Blackmore and the intensive horticulture of Botley and parts of the Isle of Wight. All its districts, however, have in common the rivers. When Drayton wrote the view of England which he titled *Polyolbion*, he constructed it round the rivers which are the arteries – once of communications and industry, now of sport, pleasure and scenery – of the country. The south of England contains the two classic chalk streams of the trout fisherman, the Itchen and the Test. They are, though, more than that. Both are fine salmon rivers and, like many other nearby fishing rivers – the Meon, which Izaak Walton fished, the Wylye, the Frome, the Kennet, the Bourne, the Wiltshire Avon and the Stour – they are the main factors in some characteristically southern English scenery.

Wessex, partly because of its chalk hills, is the country of the hill figures, especially the White Horses. Apart from one in Sussex, one in Yorkshire and one in Scotland, there are, I believe, no other White Horses in Britain. There are other chalk hill-figures in the south, notably the Cerne Giant, which, with the Uffington Horse, is of unquestionable antiquity and considerable linear interest. There are nineteenth-century Horses at Broad Town, Alton Barnes, Hackpen and Marlborough: eighteenth-century examples at Westbury – though that has been several times remodelled and lately filled with concrete – and a little one at Woolbury in Hampshire. The "New" Pewsey Horse – its predecessor became overgrown – was cut in 1937. The Osmington Horse, a few miles outside Weymouth, is an equestrian figure of George III, while the Kiwi at Bulford and the regimental badges at Fovant, Compton Chamberlayne and Sutton Mandeville – on the Plain about ten miles outside Salisbury – were cut by soldiers stationed in the area during the First World War.

Little else about the counties is uniform. Although Windsor – apart from its western edges – and Windsor Great Park are visually striking and rare pieces of preservation, east Berkshire and north-east Hampshire have been virtually swallowed by London as dormitory, overflow and regular motorized occupation which began, so far as Maidenhead was concerned, as long ago as the 1920s. Reading has been bled by London. Basingstoke and, soon, Andover will be so occupied – at the wish of their people – and made into London overspill territory as to lose completely their former character. The area on the London side of Basingstoke has long been commuter territory and in part "stockbroker belt".

West and north-west Berkshire are altogether different from the east of the county, although the Atomic Research Establishment has altered the balance and economy of the west. Faringdon is almost a tiny capital; many of the villages have kept their old identity, as in the Vale of the White Horse: and the downs, although many of them have been ploughed up, are a magnificently dignified, even majestic, march to the west.

The Thames forms the northern boundary of Berkshire almost to Oxford, with some characteristic riverside towns, notably Wallingford, several bridges of distinction and, above all, spectacular stretches of scenery. The Thames, however, is cosmopolitan, of no county, and Berkshire occupies only one of its banks, though the flat orchard country by the river is part of the heart of the county, and Pangbourne is an interesting study in Edwardian riverside architecture.

Hampshire has been so heavily built upon since 1945 as to have lost much of its independent personality. Southampton, Portsmouth and Bournemouth have all spread out hungrily over the surrounding country, and so much of the coastal belt has been used for residential – "retirement" – development that most of the coast consists of a deep swathe of modern housing. The central part of the county, around Winchester, has also been much built upon, but the watermeadows and the villages of the Itchen and Test valleys, like Easton, Avington, Ovington, Wherwell and Longparish, still possess much of their freshness. Indeed, many of the villages never looked so attractive as they do now, since their cottages were taken over, improved and smartened by a higher-income group than the earlier villagers. Unfortunately a number of villages have suffered from what the planners call "infilling" so that in the case of, for instance, Old Basing, the visitor finds it difficult to trace the original village among the speculative building.

Few English cities so much repay unhurried study as Winchester, with its different seams of interest, its concentration of so much history of so many centuries

H.M.S. Victory *in Portsmouth harbour*   Pix Photo

within such a small and assimilable compass: and it is no museum piece, but alive. Stoner Hill is a splendid surprise of scenery and, if the village of Selborne is not itself impressive, the hangers and most of the surrounding country are exactly as Gilbert White knew them, giving visual bones to his great *Natural History*. Hampshire is at its best away from the main roads; in fact, over 75 per cent of the county's traffic is carried on less than 10 per cent of its roads: and it is too often the main-road aspect of a town that the visitor sees. Alton, for instance, behind its main street which is also the main road, is a genuine and pleasing country town. One of the happiest features of Hampshire's small towns and villages is the wide main street – wide enough for a coach and horses to turn in – such as you find in Odiham, perhaps the most architecturally distinguished place in the county, Botley, Alresford, Wickham and Stockbridge.

The New Forest is a separate entity, even within Hampshire, with customs, a Court and an attitude of mind solely its own. Although it is invaded by trippers, picnickers and campers, they merely scratch its edges along the main-road routes. There remain huge stretches of the Forest penetrable only to those prepared to leave their cars and walk. The Forest towns and villages, apart from Lymington and Bucklers Hard, have no great distinction, but those who know it, and their subject, can still discover there rare flowers, moths and birds, some of them not to be found anywhere else.

The Isle of Wight has particular charms and particular problems. Its coastline impressed the eighteenth-century topographers as "picturesque": its miniature – almost doll's-house – quality seemed to the Victorians "quaint", and it still appeals to many today on a sentimental level. It is remarkable in the variety of scenery within its small area, and it is inherently neat and clean. The island's main source of income has long been the hotel trade, but the holiday crowds are anathema to many people from other parts of the country who have come to the Isle of Wight in their retirement. The hotel and boarding-house trade is seasonal; the winter sea passage is not reliable enough to guarantee regular employment for islanders on the mainland and, for many years now, the average age of the island population has been increasing, as children born there find work on the mainland after they leave school.

The Isle of Wight remains one of the most popular of seaside areas, especially for what are called family holidays, though improved mainland rail timings and the hovercraft service have brought a marked increase in the number of day trippers. The visitors usually make for the sea beaches, the spectacular chines, the rustic prettiness of Winkle Street or the historic and well-presented Carisbrooke Castle. In doing so they overlook such worthwhile places as Brighstone, Mottistone, the smaller Yaverland and the dignified, miniature perfection of Kingston. The real time to enjoy the Isle of Wight, however, is out of the holiday season, when in many parts it can be seen for what it originally was – a part of rural southern England with a coastline of rich variety.

The Wiltshire of Salisbury Plain is a place of space and of loneliness and most of it has escaped the ravages of "development" which have urbanized so much of Hampshire. No one who has visited it in recent years will ever forget Imber, the always isolated, and now inaccessible, village which has been emptied of its inhabitants and turned into a War Office battle area. Its silence, the loneliness, the vast stretch of Salisbury Plain running away from it, and just a single skylark hovering high over it, is an unforgettable scene. Salisbury Plain, although the Army has scarred it, remains a bold and generous landscape, simple yet – even

The Dorset landscape of plain and downs, looking towards Askerswell   Noel Habgood

Jane J. Miller

New Forest ponies

apart from Stonehenge, Silbury and Avebury – in some indefinable way wearing the look of its long history since the Icknield Way was the high road of primitive civilization.

Yet it is a mistake to think of Wiltshire as the Plain. Salisbury is a city of dignity and intimacy, and its spire, rising from the watermeadows, is one of the most moving sights in Britain, while Old Sarum is memorable in quite a different way. Marlborough, with its fine main street, its canal scenery, and Savernake at its doorstep, has a separate and distinct ethos; so have the Vale of Pewsey, the valley of the Wylye, the two Avons, Downton, Wilton and Lacock; while Bradford-on-Avon, climbing up its hill, is one of the most absorbing small towns in Britain.

Dorset has the advantage, so far as preservation of its character and quality is concerned, of having no more than a single, brief contact with one of the major trunk roads, and that only in one corner. For those who have read Thomas Hardy, Dorset is inextricably interwoven with memories of his novels and poems, which add richness and understanding to a county of great interest and beauty. Although Weymouth and Swanage have suffered from suburban sprawl, they and Lyme Regis are seaside resorts of unusual distinction; but the true county lies inland. Dorchester still wears many aspects of the county market town of Hardy's youth, full of activity but strictly local – Dorset – activity. The roads, and more particularly the lanes, give the same impression of distance as Hardy conveys when he describes one of his characters walking, or travelling by horse-cart, along them.

G. Douglas Bolton

Thomas Hardy's birthplace at Higher Bockhampton in Dorset

The villages are far enough apart to have different characters, yet all unmistakably Dorset. Places like Sherborne, Blandford, Corfe, Cerne Abbas, Milton Abbas, Tolpuddle, the quite unique Portland – Hardy's "Isle of Slingers" – Wareham with its striking riverside, seem to have little in common yet they fit into a pattern of country and county life not yet so profoundly disturbed as in Berkshire and Hampshire, even though the Winfrith Atomic Power Station stands on Hardy's "Egdon Heath", theme of the majestic opening to *The Return of the Native*.

Modern communications and the independence and mobility of industry have blurred many county boundaries. There have been moves to transfer Lyme Regis from Dorset to Devon, and Emsworth – a small seaport of absorbing interest – from Hampshire to Sussex: the planned expansion of Newbury will spill over into Hampshire. If the Maud report is accepted the traditional county boundaries will be swept away altogether, or retained only for matters which will at once seem unimportant because they are shaped by outmoded conditions. For the moment, however, these four counties and one island command deep loyalties and they are without doubt separate and distinct entities. Uffington is an essence of Berkshire, Beaminster of Dorset, Romsey of Hampshire, Tilshead of Wiltshire, Shalfleet of the Isle of Wight. None of them could be anywhere but in the south of England. In their different ways they contain the spirit of the south of England, of the counties that Alfred welded into a kingdom more than a thousand years ago and which, within the last century, Hardy could still see clearly as a unity.

The South Country: Gazetteer

SYBIL BURNABY, EUAN BOWATER, JUDY COWELL

ABBOTSBURY, *Dorset* (4–SY5785), is a long village with yellow-stone and thatched or slated cottages.

It has a famous swannery which has existed since 1393 at least. It is about $\frac{1}{2}$ m. S. of the village, on the lagoon formed by the CHESIL BANK, and was created by the monastery which, practically vanished except for the tithe barn, stood just S. of the village church. It now has some 560 swans and also a few wild geese and variety of duck. Visiting duck are lured into a decoy to be ringed and for other research purposes.

St Catherine's Chapel, a 15th-cent. seamen's chapel standing on a hilltop, has a particularly fine vaulted stone ceiling. It is best reached from a turning close to the Ilchester Arms in the village. The terraces on the hillside were caused by the Anglo-Saxon strip and earlier "lynchet" cultivation system. The parish church, mainly 15th- and 16th-cent., has an excellent early-17th-cent. canopied pulpit, in which bullet holes bear witness to fierce Civil War strife locally, an unusual plastered chancel ceiling (1638), and in its porch an effigy (*c.* 1200) of an abbot of the monastery. Fragments only of the monastery, founded *c.* 1040 by one Orc, King Cnut's chief steward, to whom the King had given the manor, can be seen immediately S. of the churchyard.

The beautiful sub-tropical gardens, about $1\frac{1}{2}$ m. W., have peacocks, magnificent magnolias, camellias, lily-ponds and numerous rare plants. The road past them leads to a place on the Chesil Bank popular with seine-net mackerel fishermen, where, occasionally, giant sharks, and once even a whale, have been landed.

About 1 m. NW. (just N. of the B3167) is an Iron Age fort called Abbotsbury Castle which has good views. And the road WNW. to BRIDPORT also provides glorious views, over low-hedged windy fields to the sea; SE. to PORTLAND and W. to the great cliffs around Lyme Bay.

ABINGDON, *Berkshire* (5–SU5297), is one of the oldest and most important towns in the area, and lies near the lush green watermeadows of the River Thames, just where it is joined by the little Ock. From the 15th-cent. bridge, rebuilt in the 19th cent., there are splendid views of the town with the spire of St Helen's soaring above it.

Abingdon originally grew up round its abbey, which was founded in 676, ravaged by the Danes and later re-founded in 955. It became very prosperous and kings came and went. But later the abbey was dissolved under Henry VIII and the town sank into relative decline.

The abbey church and much else has long disappeared, but down by the river some interesting buildings remain. First is a two-storied stone and timber-framed house, containing a long gallery. Nearby stands a 13th-cent. stone building with a groined undercroft below. The upper story is remarkable for the fire-place and particularly for its rare chimney, best seen against the skyline from the lane. Another group of buildings, which was probably the granary, now contain an Elizabethan theatre in which performances are given during the summer; they are open to the public.

The abbey gateway also still stands, and nearby are the abbey house grounds, where various architectural fragments are on display. The gateway is 15th-cent., with three archways, one on the south being 19th-cent. and it is now linked to municipal buildings. The former St John's Hospital Chapel is now the borough court, while above it is a splendid 18th-cent. council chamber decorated with portraits, including those of Charles II and of George III and his queen by Gainsborough. The Corporation plate is kept there, and includes some splendid 18th-cent. pieces; linked to the building is part of the old Roysses Grammar School, founded in 1563.

The rest of the town has some good Georgian building, and some earlier timber-framed houses. But of all these the 17th-cent. Town Hall is by far the most elegant. It has been attributed, though without any evidence, to Sir Christopher Wren and to Christopher Kempster; it stands on tall pilasters, the arcades on the ground floor leaving room for market stalls. Above, one room contains the Borough Museum, which has a collection of fossils and archaeological remains as well as charters and documents.

The Church of St Nicholas faces the Market Place and dates back to Norman times, though much restored and altered later. However, St Helen's is more remarkable and dates mostly from the 14th, 15th and 16th cents. It not only has five aisles, making the church broader than it is long, but also boasts a remarkable late-14th-cent. painted roof, showing kings, prophets, Christ Crucified, the Annunciation and the Tree of Jesse. There are also interesting monuments, some late Georgian and 19th-cent. stained glass and a 17th-cent. font cover and pulpit.

The church is set amongst picturesque almshouses; Long Alley Almshouses, 1446, face the west front, while Brick Alley and Twitty's Almshouses both date from the early 18th cent.

A. F. Kersting

Abingdon: the painted roof of the Lady Chapel in St Helen's Church

ALDBOURNE, *Wiltshire* (5–SU2675), pronounced Auburn, is beautifully set on the downs near Berkshire. The village is large, with modern additions, but attractive, and used to be famous both for its bell foundry and willow and straw plaiting industry.

Near the green stand an old cross and the church, built in the 12th cent., which is now mostly Perpendicular in style. Inside is the magnificent alabaster tomb of John Stone, vicar here in the 15th cent., and a splendid memorial to the Walrond brothers. Also in the church is a 16th-cent. monument to the Goddard family and two 18th-cent. fire engines.

Nearby, a man-made protective trough is set in the downs. King John is supposed to have hunted at Aldbourne Chase and John of Gaunt is supposed to have had a hunting lodge nearby, perhaps even at **Upper Upham House**, now a stone manor house, some 3 m. from Aldbourne. From here the view is splendid, as indeed it is from **Baydon**, a neighbouring village set on an old Roman road. It stands 764 ft above sea-level and is the highest village in Wiltshire.

ALDERMASTON, *Berkshire* (5–SU5965), is one of the prettiest villages in the area. Above are thick woods, and below the River Kennet, while the village street rises from the Hind's Head – an old 18th-cent. inn – at one end to the splendid 17th-cent. lodges leading to Aldermaston Court at the other. The church is nearby, among more magnificent trees, including cedars, yew and limes.

The original Aldermaston Court was burnt down in the 19th cent., but the magnificent

17th-cent. carved staircase has been built into the new 19th-cent. Tudor-style building. Now under commercial ownership, the house at one time belonged to the Forsters, whom both Henry VIII and Queen Elizabeth I visited.

Many of the family lie in the church. Originally a 12th-cent. building, with a 13th-cent. chancel, but showing later work, the church is immensely long. In the south transept there is an early-14th-cent. painting of St Christopher fording the stream carrying the infant Christ. Nearby a mermaid and fish disport themselves under a great canopy. The 16th-cent. triptych showing the Adoration is Flemish, and there is also some 13th-cent. glass depicting the Annunciation and Coronation of the Virgin. But one of the chief beauties of the church is the splendid alabaster tomb to Sir George Forster, who died in 1526. He lies clad in armour with a hind at his feet; beside him lies his wife with her pet dog while below are carvings of their quite enormous family.

Aldermaston has other claims to fame. In 1770 the village schoolmaster produced the famous William pear. The old mill – though no longer used as such – has an attractive setting; and down on the Kennet and Avon Canal the old wharf has great charm.

The district has obviously been important since early times, for there are still a good many remains of ancient boundary earthworks, probably made by 5th-cent. Britons in order to keep intruding Saxons out. **Grim's Bank**, for example, starts 1 m. SE. of the village, and in part still reaches a height of 8 ft, as does another earthwork set in Old Park, and running for just under a mile.

The presence of the Atomic Weapons Research

Establishment brings a more dreadful mode of warfare to mind.

ALDWORTH, *Berkshire* (5–SU5579). From STREATLEY the road rises steeply to Aldworth, a lonely village on chalk downs. There is a covered well descending 372 ft, one of the deepest in England; an enormous yew in the churchyard is extremely old, perhaps 1,000 years, and in the church lie nine huge effigies of the de la Beche family. No one knows their individual names, owing to the Earl of Leicester's carelessness in not replacing the table of names he showed to Queen Elizabeth I when she visited the church. No one knows either quite when they were carved, but it was probably in the 14th cent.

There they lie, nine great figures, though some were sadly mutilated in Puritan times. Under their intricately decorated canopies, one knight and his lady lie turned on their sides, and another knight is semi-recumbent, leaning on one elbow, a position rarely seen on tombs.

ALRESFORD, *Hampshire* (5–SU5832). Old and New Alresford are separated by less than a mile, and between them lies all that is left of Bishop Godfrey de Lucy's splendid reservoir, Alresford Pond, which was built in the 12th cent. to make the River Itchen navigable from SOUTH-AMPTON to Bishops Sutton just near here. It is crossed by a causeway, and was reputed in the 18th cent. to be a good place for eels. There are extensive watercress beds here.

New Alresford is a pleasant market town, which before the Conquest belonged to the Bishops of Winchester. There has been new development, and there are few very old houses since a succession of fires swept through in the 17th and 18th cents. The most pleasing architecture is to be found in and near Broad Street, which is as wide as its name implies. Here, as a plaque states, Mary Russell Mitford, author of *Our Village*, was born, and at the bottom of the street there is an old medieval bridge. Alresford church is 19th-cent., in Perpendicular style, and contains two Anglo-Saxon roods. The gravestones include some to Napoleonic prisoners of war.

Old Alresford is smaller, a pleasant village with a stream running through the green. The church, on the way to New Alresford, was rebuilt in the 18th cent. and transepts added in the 19th.

Northington is 1 m. to the N., and the church on the hill here is a splendid example of the 19th-cent. Gothic revival. The flint and stone chequer-work is attractive, and the whole church, built by Thomas Jackson for Lord Ashburton in 1889, is impressive. The Grange, a mansion with a superb neo-classical exterior, is threatened with demolition.

ALTON, *Hampshire* (5–SU7139). In summer the fields hereabouts are green with trailing hops to supply Alton's breweries. But the town used also to be famous for the manufacture and sale of such clothes as bombasine and barragon, names you hardly hear nowadays. Long before that Alton, which stood on the Pilgrim's Way, sent

two members to Parliament under Edward I.

It is a pleasant old market town, with some attractive Georgian building at the centre. Parts of the red-brick grammar school date back to the 17th cent., and the Curtis Museum is also interesting. Named after the famous 18th-cent. botanist William Curtis, the museum has a good collection of pottery, porcelain, archaeological finds and some interesting old farming tools.

The Church of St Laurence is mainly Perpendicular and has two naves and two chancels. The old central Norman tower remains, complete with arches, the capitals lively with crude 11th-cent. carvings of dragons, birds and the like. On the north face of one pillar are three interesting wall paintings of saints dating from the 15th cent.

Other parts of the church show bullet marks, for in 1643 Captain Boles, together with 80 Royalists, held out here until finally overwhelmed by Parliamentarians. There is a brass to the captain in the church and another monument to him in WINCHESTER Cathedral.

ANDOVER, *Hampshire* (5–SU3645). Although the town seems new, it is in fact very long established, and was already a municipal borough under King John, and later achieved importance for its wool trade. At present Andover is expanding rapidly and has some interesting modern development.

The 19th-cent. Church of St Mary, built by a former headmaster of Winchester, is fine. In Early English style and set on a hill, it stands out well from its surroundings. Also worth a visit is the Museum, which contains geological and archaeological remains.

Andover is a good centre, ringed by places of interest. 1 m. SW. of the town is an early Iron Age camp, named **Bury Hill**, which gives good views over the countryside.

Of the pretty villages in the area, **Abbots Ann** has charm and is linked to an interesting custom. In the church, rebuilt in 1716, hang white paper garlands. Right up to this century they were carried at the funerals of maidens and bachelors who were "reputed to have died virgins", as Gilbert White of SELBORNE delicately phrases it.

Amport lies nearby, and has thatched cottages, a green, and a stream trickling through it. Amport House is a 19th-cent. Elizabethan house belonging to the Marquess of Winchester.

A little further W. is **Quarley**, almost on the border with Wiltshire. Nearby Quarley Hill soars to over 560 ft and gives marvellous views. It is a well-known landmark and has an old Iron Age hill-fort, excavated in 1938, and Bronze Age boundary ditches can also be seen.

Longparish, just SE. of Andover, has a long main street, as its name would indicate. It is set on the Test and has attractive thatched cottages. To the NW. is **Hiarwood Forest**, with a beech avenue leading from the Andover road to Deadman's Plack, which commemorates the murder of Ethelwulf by King Edgar, 959–76. Edgar sent Ethelwulf to seek out a beauty named Elfrida. Unfortunately Ethelwulf fell for her charm and married her himself. When Edgar found out he killed Ethelwulf and subsequently made Elfrida his queen.

To the NE. of Andover is **St Mary Bourne**, a charming village set on the River Bourne. The church here is particularly remarkable for its enormous black marble carved font brought from Tournai. A similar one can be seen at WIN-CHESTER Cathedral.

APPULDURCOMBE HOUSE, *Isle of Wight* (5–SZ5480). The remains of a Baroque house near **Wroxall** that for 300 years was the seat of the Worsley family and is now in the care of the Ministry of Public Building and Works. It is set in gardens originally laid out by Capability Brown. On the nearby down stands an obelisk in memory of Sir Robert Worsley, dated 1774. Wroxall is a good point from which to explore the downs.

ASHBURY, *Berkshire* (5–SU2685). Set on rising chalk downs, the manor, now a farm, dates from the 15th cent. The church, which has a good roof, has work from many periods; the south door, for example, decorated with chevrons is Norman and the nave arcades are Perpendicular.

Ashdown House, set in a valley among pretty gardens, is only 2 m. away. It looks just like a square little dolls' house, and four avenues lead directly from the house to the N., S., E. and W. The architect was probably William Winde, who also built the original house at CLIVEDEN. It was designed for Lord Craven, a lifelong admirer of Elizabeth of Bohemia, Charles I's sister. He not only dedicated the house to her – though she never visited it – but also sent £30,000 to her son Prince Rupert to equip an army to fight for her husband's throne. When she died she left him her pictures and papers.

Standing three stories high and crowned by a golden cupola, the house dates from *c.* 1665, and now together with about 40 acres belongs to the National Trust. It is open to the public at certain times, and inside, the remarkable staircase takes up a quarter of the interior.

Alfred's Castle is on Swinley Down, W. of Ashdown Woods. Here a very small earthwork lies inside a larger one. Iron Age, Romano-British and Anglo-Saxon remains have been found, and the camp probably has nothing to do with Alfred though he did win a battle in 871 against the Danes somewhere on these downs. Not far away are the remains of a Romano-British settlement, and traces of Celtic fields, and since the area is near Wiltshire, sarsen stones also scatter the district.

ASHMORE, *Dorset* (4–ST9117). The highest village in Dorset, 700 ft up in the chalk hills of CRANBORNE CHASE, it has a duck pond surrounded by flint, brick, stone and colour-washed cottages, Georgian houses, a church and a cedar tree. In extreme winters it has occasionally been snow-bound for weeks. The church was rebuilt in 1874 and furnished accordingly, though it has a Norman font.

AVEBURY, *Wiltshire* (5–SU0969), though larger than STONEHENGE and in some ways more impressive, has never caught public imagination in quite the same way. John Aubrey, writing in the 17th cent., thought it exceeded Stonehenge as a cathedral does a parish church, and persuaded Charles II to visit it. But Avebury only became better known after William Stukely published his book a century later.

The best introduction is by way of an impressive avenue of great stones set parallel to the road from West Kennet. The site itself covers some 29 acres and is surrounded by a bank some 15 ft high, which probably seems less high than it was originally, as the surrounding outer ditch has gradually silted up. This bank, which also encloses the village, is intersected by four roads, three of which – and probably the fourth, though this has not yet been excavated – were ancient causeways.

Originally there was a circle consisting of some 100 sarsen stones, brought from the Marlborough Downs. But unlike those at Stonehenge none of these stones was worked. Instead they seem to have been chosen for their natural shape, some being tall uprights and others like diamonds, perhaps representing the male and female figure. Of the particularly large stones which stood at the circle's entrances two survive at the south and one at the north entrance.

Inside this great outer circle were two smaller formations. The Central Circle was made up of about 30 stones, though today, sadly, only about four survive. Inside stood three stones, of which two still stand, called a cove.

The other small formation, known as the South Circle, originally consisted of some 32 stones, of which five now stand, but the position of some others is marked. There was also a large stone at the centre. Inside the South Circle stones were set roughly in the shape of a huge D, the upright line of smaller stones being known as Z stones. Standing separate was one single stone, pierced by a natural hole.

Avebury was probably built during the late Neolithic period, between *c.* 2000 and 1600 B.C., by the Beaker Folk. Some of the pottery after which these people were named has been found nearby. But although Avebury probably had a religious significance no one knows quite why it was constructed.

Unfortunately, the site has suffered great desecration. Even in the 14th cent. stones were being toppled and broken, as a skeleton discovered in 1938 proves. The man had been crushed by a stone falling on him. Silver from the reign of Edward I was found in his pouch, while a pair of scissors hung at his belt.

Later, in the 18th cent., as Stukely has indignantly described, many of the stones were heated and subsequently broken up in order to clear the ground. Fragments can still be seen built into the manor, the church and village houses. Since that date excavations had been made, culminating in the great work undertaken by Alexander Keiller before the second World War.

The National Trust owns over 900 acres in the area, but Avebury itself is under the care of the Ministry of Public Building and Works and is open to the public. Much of what has been excavated hereabouts can be seen in the museum in the village.

S. of the Bath Road, and at the end of the Kennet Stone Avenue, lies the **Sanctuary**, a series of concentric circles, with the holes marked which were dug to take wooden posts and stones. The site is open to visitors.

Silbury Hill – a curious cone which juts out from the landscape – is only 1 m. from Avebury, built on a natural chalk ridge. About three-quarters of the hill, which covers 5½ acres at the base and reaches a height of 130 ft, is artificial. No one quite knows why, or even when, it was built. But it was certainly there before the Roman road, since this runs round it.

Various efforts to excavate have been made, the latest in 1967 when the B.B.C. sank a shaft. But not much of interest has been discovered. Silbury Hill is under the care of the Ministry of Public Building and Works, and can easily be seen from the road, or indeed from Avebury.

Nearby, and approached by a footpath from the Bath Road, is the **West Kennet Long Barrow**. It is a mound about 350 ft long and was used as a tomb over a period of years. Made up of a long passage and five burial chambers, it was probably built *c.* 2700 B.C.

Windmill Hill is a rounded hill 1½ m. NW. of Avebury, the top of which shows the remains of three concentric lines of earthwork built *c.* 2500 B.C., though the reason for it is not known. The hill gave its name to the Neolithic farmers who arrived from the Continent in *c.* 3000 B.C. and colonized southern England.

Avebury village is both pretty and interesting, and boasts a fine church and a manor house. Avebury Manor stands on a site once given to Sir William Sharington, the owner of LACOCK, at the Dissolution. But it was taken away again after he had been convicted of clipping the coinage at the BRISTOL Mint.

The house itself dates back to Elizabethan times, and is open to the public. It contains interesting panelling and plasterwork, and is also famous for its gardens and topiary, and a magnificent circular dovecot dating back centuries.

The Church of St James lies just outside the grassy bank of Avebury. It is mentioned in the Domesday Book, some of the nave and windows dating back to Anglo-Saxon times. The Norman aisles were built in the 12th cent., and there is also an early Norman font. The tower and rood-screen are 15th-cent., but the arcades and chancel date from the 19th cent., when the church was restored.

AVINGTON, *Berkshire* (5–SU3767), is hidden quietly away just N. of the River Kennet, and the rectory, the neighbouring house, and the church make a delightful group set amongst trees.

The church is almost entirely Norman and is unspoiled by restoration. Inside it is dark and full of mystery. There is no tower, no aisles, and nearly all the windows, mostly small and round-headed, are original.

The church is rich in Norman carving, the south porch and chancel arch being decorated with chevrons and beak-heads, while the columns have carved capitals. There are more scalloped capitals in the chancel, which was once intended to be vaulted. There is a Norman sedilia and a tub-shaped Norman font with 11 arches, carved with 13 figures, including a bishop and devils.

AVINGTON, *Hampshire* (5–SU5332), has pretty cottages and is set amidst meadows and woods on the River Itchen. The view from the downland on to Avington Park, lying in a slight hollow below, is magnificent and the County Council have bought a stretch of these grassy slopes so that you may park with ease and enjoy the scene.

Avington church is a perfect 18th-cent. church, which seems to have been completely untouched since first built by the Marchioness of Caernarvon, and the rich mahogany fittings, pulpit and tester, gallery, pews and a fine reredos, stand out against the simple interior. There are also some splendid marble monuments, including one to the Marchioness of Caernarvon, 1768, and one to George Bridges, 1751. Another commemorates John Shelley, 1866, brother of the poet.

Both the Shelleys and the Bridges at one time owned Avington Park, a magnificent house, which is open to the public. Charles II also stayed here with Nell Gwynn. Facing on to a lake, the house is primarily a red-brick 18th-cent. building, with an immense portico, but some parts date from much earlier. Inside there is rich decoration. The paintings in the hall and the trellis-work are late 18th-cent. The gilding in the ballroom is also 18th-cent., while the ceiling painting is 17th-cent. The Library is decorated by a wall painting, and those in the drawing-room date from the 19th cent.

Easton, the next village to the W., has much thatch and a church that dates from about 1200. It was restored in its original style in the 19th cent., and the waterleaf capitals to the chancel arch are outstanding.

BADBURY RINGS, *Dorset* (4–ST9602). An ancient Iron Age fortification, circular in shape, it has three concentric rings of massive chalk trenches and banks rising to, and tightly enclosing, a dark wood. Two important Roman roads – from BATH to POOLE Harbour, and from DORCHESTER to OLD SARUM – intersected at Badbury. Some say it was the site of a great battle between Britons, commanded by their legendary Arthur, and the invading Anglo-Saxons. An old legend said that King Arthur still lived in its wood, in the guise of a raven. Now the ravens have gone and the banks, fragmented, are scarred white by the feet of picnickers. It is approached by a magnificent beech avenue, along the B3082, which was planted *c.* 1875.

About 1½ m. SE., in a beautiful park, is

Kingston Lacey, home of the Bankes family (*see* CORFE CASTLE) since it was built for them by Sir Roger Pratt, 1663–5. It is among the finest houses of its period in Dorset and contains an outstanding collection of paintings by artists including Velazquez, Murillo, Giorgione, Zurbaran, Rubens, Van Dyck, Titian and Raphael.

BARBURY CAMP, *Wiltshire* (5–SU1476), is between SWINDON and MARLBOROUGH. It lies high on the chalk downs on Hackpen Hill with views right across to the Vale of the White Horse.

Sometimes called Barbury Castle, the site has interesting historical associations spanning the centuries. Built originally as a hill-fort, covering some 12 acres, it is encircled by two ditches and a rampart. Although never excavated, some interesting remains – jewellery, coins, arrowheads and so forth, dating from the 3rd and 2nd cents. B.C. – have been found here. They can now be seen in MARLBOROUGH Museum.

Centuries later the West Saxons are said to have inflicted a stinging defeat on the Britons here in the Battle of Beran Byrig in A.D. 556. In the 19th cent. the whole region was a favourite haunt of Richard Jefferies, the writer. He lived at Coate, about an hour's walk away, and often wandered in these hills. A large sarsen stone now stands here, carrying a memorial both to him and to Alfred Williams, the 19th-cent. railwayman and poet.

Barbury Castle is reached by walking over the downs following the Ridgeway, an ancient track. The effort is worth while for the views, especially over to LIDDINGTON, 4 m. away.

BASING, *Hampshire* (5–SU6652), lies on the River Loddon, and is surrounded by meadows and wooded hills; while in the village itself old brick cottages are prettily grouped round the church and old Basing House.

A Norman castle once stood here, but was replaced in the 16th cent. by a splendid crenellated Tudor mansion, built by Sir William Paulet, first Marquess of Winchester. A most remarkable man, he not only left 103 descendants, but also held high office under all monarchs from Henry VIII to Elizabeth, who came to stay here. During the Civil War, Basing House, together with DONNINGTON CASTLE, near NEWBURY, held the key to the west. The house was besieged, and at one time some 7,000 Roundheads were at its gates, while at another the besiegers tried to starve the castle into surrender. But the inmates, including Inigo Jones, held out for over two years, until eventually the house was stormed and captured by Oliver Cromwell in person in 1645. He looted the place and burnt it down, so that little remains today.

The site is open to the public at certain times of the year, and the remains of the boundary walls and two octagonal towers, one a summer-house, the other a dovecot, can still be seen. Recently a great deal of excavation has been done and Iron Age pottery, Roman coins and a great many finds from later centuries can be seen at the New Museum. The Old Museum contains Tudor and Elizabethan remains, including some sculpture.

The outer gatehouse of Basing House is in the village street, and the splendid brick barn at nearby Grange Farm should not be missed.

The Perpendicular Church of St Mary, which stands near the house, was also damaged during the Civil War, but was later rebuilt and then heavily restored by T. H. Wyatt in the 19th cent. There is a beautiful 16th-cent. statue of the Virgin and Child, somehow overlooked by the destructive Parliamentarians, several 15th- and 16th-cent. tombs to the Paulet family, and monuments to the six Dukes of Bolton. The 6th Duke has a fine white marble tomb, 1794, by Flaxman.

Hackwood House, nearby, has one of the few gardens in this country laid out in French style.

BASINGSTOKE, *Hampshire* (5–SU6351), is not in itself a beautiful town, but it has some interesting modern development.

The Parish Church of St Michael is mostly Perpendicular but much restored. Inside can be seen the Royal Arms of Elizabeth, James I and William III, and some early 16th-cent. glass in the south aisle and the south chapel. This originally came from the old Chapel of the Holy Ghost, which lies in a cemetery near the station. Founded in 1525 by Bishop Fox and Lord Sandys, who also built The Vyne near SHERBORNE ST JOHN, parts still survive.

The Willis Museum in New Street contains geological and archaeological finds and much else concerning the history of Hampshire.

Round about there is much to see. **Herriard Park Gardens** lie only 4 m. S. on the A339, with 5 acres of beautiful gardens, including a walled rose garden, open to the public.

Wincklebury camp, 1½ m. NW. of Basingstoke, is an ancient earthwork covering nearly 20 acres. Signs of both rampart and ditch can still be seen.

Some of the surrounding villages are charming. **Dummer**, 5 m. SW., has pretty cottages, some thatched, and an interesting church. The nave is Perpendicular and chancel Early English, and it has an interesting 15th-cent. rood canopy and a very early pulpit. In the 19th cent., cremation urns dating from prehistoric times were found in this area, but are now in READING and SOUTHAMPTON museums. Dummer lies near **Farleigh Hill**, which gives fine views over four counties. And only 1 m. away is **Deane**, an attractive old village with less than 100 inhabitants.

Preston Candover, 8 m. S. of Basingstoke, also has charm, and the area must have been inhabited since earliest times, for ancient barrows lie hereabouts, Roman and Bronze Age remains have been discovered, and the Droveway – probably an ancient track for driving sheep – is nearby.

Upton Grey, about 4 m. SE. from Basingstoke, is also an attractive village, with a pond, willow trees and some 17th-cent. cottages. Finally there is **Steventon**, a pleasantly secluded village about 5 m. SW. It is famous as the birthplace of Jane Austen. The church where her father preached dates mostly from the 13th cent., and in it can be seen monuments to the Austen family.

BEAMINSTER, *Dorset* (4–ST4801), is one of the most appealing towns of its size (population about 2,000) in the South-West and is set in beautiful country of steep hills dividing deep cups of farmland. Undulating itself and centred on a square and a 1906 market cross, it is largely of yellow-golden stone, from Ham Hill for most of its major buildings, from local quarries for the rest. Virtually destroyed by a great fire when Royalist troops were quartered in it during the Civil War and much damaged by other fires in 1684 and 1781, it was rebuilt with almost the same consistency as BLANDFORD, though in a very different, less urban style. Fortunately all these conflagrations missed the church, for it has possibly the most splendid tower – early 16th-cent. and magnificently pinnacled and figure-sculptured – in the county. Its interior was mainly restored in the 19th cent., though there is a mighty monument (1753) to George Strode and his wife dressed as Romans. Just NW. of the churchyard are pretty almshouses of 1603.

The Strodes lived at **Parnham,** 1 m. SSW., which is among the best Tudor houses in Dorset and is frequently open or, if not, can be seen by appointment. It is now owned by the National Association for Mental Health.

Two m. SE. is another fine, basically Tudor house, **Mapperton,** the gardens of which are occasionally open. The population of the village that surrounded it was wiped out by the Great Plague in 1660.

Netherbury, 1½ m. SW., and **Stoke Abbot,** 2 m. W., are pretty villages, the latter particularly so, reached by tunnel-like lanes and with, in its middle, a particularly attractive 18th-cent. farmhouse. Netherbury has a notable 14th- to 15th-cent. church.

About 2¼ m. S., **Melpash Court,** another Tudor building, is well seen from the A3066 to BRIDPORT. Very occasionally its gardens are open.

The road from Beaminster W. to AXMINSTER is beautiful and comparatively traffic free, following a high ridge and affording numerous fine views.

BEAULIEU, *Hampshire* (5–SU3801). The village is charming and quite unspoilt. The Cistercian abbey was founded here in 1204 by King John, who also richly endowed it. When Henry III came for the dedication in 1246, such was the rejoicing that he forgave the abbot a fine imposed for poaching in the New Forest. Beaulieu is beautifully situated among woods and hills on the Beaulieu River, and was for many years important, providing sanctuary for the Lancastrian Margaret of Anjou, Perkin Warbeck, pretender to the throne at the time of Henry VII, and others. Later, at the Dissolution, much was destroyed and the stones from the church were carried off to build such places as Hurst Castle.

Today the abbey is a beautiful ruin, with the foundations carefully marked out. The outer gatehouse has excellently preserved 13th-cent. work. The 14th-cent. great gatehouse has become Palace House. In the grounds is the Montagu Motor Museum, opened in 1952 by Lord Montagu in memory of his father, an early car enthusiast. It contains a unique collection of vintage cars, bicycles, motorcycles, and even a Spitfire.

The outer wall and four towers were added in the 18th cent. as a protection against French privateers. The lay brothers' dormitory, an enormous room some 100 ft long, has now been restored. Their old refectory has become a museum, containing headstones, tiles and a model of the abbey as it was, and the cellar below has been turned into a restaurant. Nearby is the ancient washroom.

The three arches that were part of the cloisters and chapter house are beautiful, and the abbey refectory – which faces N. to S. instead of the usual E. to W. – has become the church. It is a spacious room, with lancet windows, and is chiefly remarkable for its stone pulpit, from which a monk used to read to his brothers during meals.

Outside, the old wine press still remains, and to the NW. is the 13th-cent. Conduit House, which supplied the water.

The abbey, including Palace House and the Motor Museum, is open to the public.

One m. W. of Beaulieu is **Hatchet Pond,** one of the few inland lakes that exist in Hampshire. It lies in moorland on Beaulieu Heath. **Bucklers Hard** is about 2 m. S. and consists of just one broad street flanked by charming terraced 18th-cent. houses. There was once an attempt to make Bucklers Hard into a port. Later in the 18th-cent., it became a ship-building centre, and the great New Forest oaks were felled to build some of the ships that fought at Trafalgar. There is a Maritime Museum here.

At **St Leonards,** a little S. of Bucklers Hard along a pretty road, there are the remains of the great abbey barn. Since the lower part of the north wall remains intact, as does a gable in the east wall, it is possible to gain some idea of its massive size. The ruined Chapel of St Leonard, built about 1300, also lies here.

BEMBRIDGE, *Isle of Wight* (5–SZ6488), with its harbour and bay, lies below Bembridge Down and is the most easterly village on the island. To the N. lie St Helen's marshes. Yachting gives the place its character and the Bembridge Sailing Club, on the Toll Road with a fine clubhouse, is one of the most important in southern England. At Lane End is the lifeboat station, open to the public on Thursdays. Beyond is a holiday camp, a growing industry on the island, but not allowed to make the areas chosen unsightly.

Whitecliff Bay and the **Culver,** favoured by picnickers, are where the glistening white chalk cliff meets other formations of interest to the geologist. On the Down is the Yarborough Obelisk, a monument to the 1st earl of the name, who was also the first commodore of the Royal

Bisham: the tombs of Sir Thomas and Sir Philip Hoby

Yacht Squadron. The road to SANDOWN, 5½ m. away, offers splendid views.

Bembridge Windmill (National Trust) has 18th-cent. wooden machinery and may be visited.

BERE REGIS, *Dorset* (4–SY8494). This water-cress-growing village situated on a road junction was in the Middle Ages famed for its fairs and a resort of kings on their way to the South-West; its former splendour is well commemorated by its medieval church. Strong towered, big and impressive, it has a nave roof of much renown. From a complication of massive curved and straight beams, large statues of the 12 Apostles, brightly painted and dressed as Tudor gentlemen, project face downwards over the congregation. Perhaps not beautiful, but certainly magnificent and probably unique, this roof is thought to have been given *c.* 1475 by Cardinal Morton, Lord Chancellor to Henry VII, who was born locally. There is much else of interest: finely carved and entertaining late Norman capitals on the pillars, a few good 15th-cent. carved bench-ends and the ravaged tombs of the Turbervilles, the family whose story inspired Thomas Hardy's *Tess of the D'Urbervilles*. In that novel Bere Regis was Kingsbere. It is said that King John had a palace in the field immediately E. of the church.

BISHAM, *Berkshire* (5–SU8585). Bisham Abbey and church lie quietly in an idyllic setting between the Thames and wooded hills.

The Church of All Saints has been much restored apart from the Norman tower and 16th-cent. Hoby Chapel with its remarkable monuments. The most beautiful shows an obelisk surmounted by a heart and protected by four

swans. Dated 1605, it commemorates Margaret Hoby, *née* Carey – a family whose crest featured a swan – the widow of Sir Edward. Elizabeth Hoby – later Lady Russell – took great pains with her own splendid tomb, 1609, and also built tombs to her husband Sir Thomas Hoby, 1566, and his half-brother Sir Philip, 1558. Both lie in full armour.

Bisham Abbey is perhaps a misnomer since it only served as such for a very few years when it was both established and disestablished by Henry VIII in quick succession. Originally a preceptory of the Knights Templar, it passed after their suppression to William Montecute, Earl of Salisbury. In the 14th cent. he built an Augustinian priory. Four of the Earls of Salisbury were buried here, and so too is Richard Neville, Earl of Warwick, the King-maker. In 1557, after the Dissolution, Sir Philip Hoby started building a house, later finished by his hälf-brother, which incorporates parts of the abbey. This today belongs to the Central Council of Physical Recreation.

Of the priory, the front door, the decorated porch, part of the chapel wall and the great hall remain. Several rooms, including two that are panelled and one with an oriel window, belong to the 16th cent.

BISHOP'S CANNINGS, *Wiltshire* (5-SU 0364), is made charming by its thatch and is famous for many reasons. In the 17th cent. the village had a musical vicar and entertained James I and his queen to a masque. On one occasion, when caught raking the pond for smuggled liquor casks, some of the locals fooled the ex-cisemen into thinking they were catching the moon's reflection – or moon-raking. Because of this story people born in Wiltshire are called Moonrakers.

But most of all today Bishop's Cannings is famous for its beautiful cruciform 13th-cent. church. The tall spire and clerestory are 15th-cent., the vaulted south porch 14th-cent. The triple lancet windows are Early English 13th-cent. The Ernle Chapel contains some good monuments, and the church has a curious carrel, painted with a large hand and inscribed with Latin texts. Perhaps this was once a monk's meditation chair. Money for the organ was given by William Bayley of this parish, who sailed with Captain Cook.

Nearby on the downs can be seen early cultivation terraces, or lynchets, and the **Wansdyke**, a curious bank and ditch, which stretches some 80 m. There are superb views from this area, and there is a nine-hole golf course near the village.

BISHOPSTONE, *Wiltshire* (5–SU0625), lies SW. of SALISBURY. The cruciform church is remarkable and might, it is said, have been designed by William of EDINGTON. Almost all in Decorated style, the chancel and south transept have magnificent stone vaulting and superb windows. The roof bosses are interesting and one of the monuments dates back to medieval times. Another, by Pugin (19th-cent.) is in the south transept. The pulpit may have come from Spain, and the woodwork in the stalls is also probably foreign.

BISHOP'S WALTHAM, *Hampshire* (5–SU 5517). The streets of this old town set in chalk downs are narrow. The Church of St Peter has been much restored and altered over the centuries, but the chancel is mostly 15th-cent., and it contains a magnificent pulpit complete with tester, given by Bishop Andrewes in 1600.

Bishop's Waltham was at the peak of its importance during the medieval period and much earlier when it was the seat of the Bishops of Winchester. The palace once stood in an enormous park of some 10,000 acres. Henry de Blois, brother of King Stephen, started the building in the 12th cent. Much was added later, especially by Bishop Langton, 1493–1501, and probably also by the great William of Wykeham, who died here in 1404. During Henry II's reign the town raised large sums for a crusade and Richard I came here after his coronation. In 1644 the bishop and some 200 Royalist troops were besieged here by Roundheads. The bishop escaped in a dung cart and the castle was ruined and never rebuilt. The ruins are now under the care of the Ministry of Public Building and Works and are open to the public.

The palace was surrounded by a moat, some of which remains. In the west side of the inner courtyard remains the west wall of the great hall, some 65 ft long, with windows still showing. To the east of this hall once stood a chapel, and nearby much remains of the ruined 12th-cent. tower, with fire-places and 15th-cent. windows. To the NE., set apart at the end of the courtyard,

is the Great Barn, so called when it was incorporated into farm buildings, but originally used to house retainers. It is early 14th-cent., with later alterations, and still stands, as does a neighbouring brick and stone building, with traces of medieval timberwork. Even today the red-brick wall built by Bishop Langton still partly surrounds the palace, and nearby can be seen the Abbot's fish pond.

BLANDFORD FORUM, *Dorset* (4–ST8806), has the most handsome and uniform Georgian red-brick-and-stone town centre in the South-West. The first cause of this was a great fire in 1731; the second, the wave of public sympathy and financial help that followed (its being the home town of the Archbishop of Canterbury, William Wake, doubtless helped); the third, the talent of two local architects, John and William Bastard, who did much of the rebuilding. The church (1739) is among the largest and grandest of its period outside London. A classical portico by the churchyard commemorates "God's dreadful visitation by Fire".

The fire began in a tallow chandler's on the site of the present King's Arms (about 100 yds NW. of the Market Place) and with the wind from the N., virtually everything S. of it went. Within an hour all available fire engines were burned, soon all ladders and in the end some 400 houses; the church bells according to an eye-witness "dissolved and ran down in streams". The only major pre-1731 buildings left today are Ryves Almshouses (1682) and Dale House (1689, with an exceptional tulip tree in its garden), both in Salisbury Street, and the Old House (the doctor's at the time of the fire) in The Close, NE. of the church. Outside the fine Market Place, one of the best Georgian buildings is that of the British Legion in Church Lane.

The town is the hub of a rich farming area – dairying, arable and, more distinctively, watercress growing. Formerly it was famous for its lace, stained glass and buttons (of which the SHAFTESBURY Museum has examples). Now beer is its main product. The large long-established Army Camp, 2 m. NE., where Wolfe and Wellington both reviewed troops, boosts its trade.

Just S. of the town the bridge over the beautiful, slow, weed-dappled River Stour bears the plaque common on Dorset bridges to the effect that anyone "injuring" it is "liable to be transported for life".

The town is proud of being the birthplace, in 1818, of Alfred Stevens, the sculptor and painter, who was called by Orpen "the most thoroughly educated artist the county has seen". One of his best known works is the Wellington monument in ST PAUL'S. Blandford was Thomas Hardy's "Shottesford Forum".

About ½ m. NW., **Bryanston School** is housed in a mansion built *c.* 1890 for the Portman family within a fine park. It has two churches, one Georgian, one contemporary with the house. They may be visited, but it is advisable to have a word with the Lodge Keeper first.

BLEWBURY, *Berkshire* (5–SU5385), used once to be far more important than it is now. But it is a charming village, with the downs rising round it, plenty of trees, timber-built houses and old inns.

The church is a large, light cruciform structure, which shows both Norman and later work, Perpendicular predominating. The south porch is timbered, the chancel and crossing rib-vaulted, a delightful Perpendicular door leads to the remains of rood stairs, and the piscina was once a rood-loft altar. There are various brasses of the 15th and 16th cents. and, much more unusual, one from the 19th cent.

E. of the village stands **Blewburton Hill,** topped by a magnificent prehistoric camp, and travelling E. of the hill you come to **Aston Tirrold** – a village which is as pretty as its name.

BOCKHAMPTON, *Dorset* (4–SY7392). There are two hamlets here. At **Higher Bockhampton,** on the edge of the great heath he called Egdon, Thomas Hardy, the novelist, was born in 1840. The relevant thatched house, National Trust owned and frequently open, is at its north-east end in a wood at the end of a narrow lane. Nearby is an obelisk erected by "a few American admirers" in 1931. At **Lower Bockhampton,** the larger and prettier of the two hamlets, Hardy first went to school. When he died (1928) his heart was buried in the churchyard at **Stinsford,** 2 m. SW. (Mellstock in *Under the Greenwood Tree*) and his ashes in WESTMINSTER ABBEY.

About ½ m. E. of Stinsford is the grand house of Kingston Maurward, now the Dorset Farm Institute, built *c.* 1720. Nearby, the Elizabethan manor house which it replaced has recently been restored, but is not open to the public.

BONCHURCH, *Isle of Wight* (5–SZ5778), is a small village in a beautiful setting, below St Boniface Down, the island's highest point. On the cliffside are neat Victorian marine villas. Below the village is a little cove, known as Monks Bay. The Old Church is Norman, built on the site of an 8th-cent. Anglo-Saxon structure. It is recorded in the Domesday Book and is dedicated to St Boniface.

Not far from the Old Church is the site of a Roman Camp, and the tumbled rock of the Upper and Lower Landslips. This whole southern part of the island is well signposted and has good roads, but exploring the winding footpaths of the area will provide many extra rewards in terms of beauty, history and pleasure.

The poet Swinbourne is buried in the churchyard of the New Church.

BOSCOMBE, *Wiltshire* (5–SU2038). Isaac – son of Izaak Walton of *Compleat Angler* fame – was once the vicar of this unspoilt village church. So, too, was the 16th-cent. theologian, Richard Hooker. Inside there are box pews dating back to Jacobean and Georgian times and a Jacobean three-decker pulpit with tester dated 1633. The church has a 14th-cent. nave and chancel and a 16th-cent. transept.

Not far away, 4 m. NE. of SALISBURY and ½ m. off the London road, is an Iron Age hill-fort called **Figsbury Ring.** Some 27 acres hereabouts belong to the National Trust, and since the fort is 478 ft above sea-level, views, especially over Salisbury, are magnificent.

BOURNEMOUTH, *Hampshire* (5–SZ0991). Although a late starter compared with BRIGHTON, Bournemouth is a queen of resorts. Until the early 19th cent., the land hereabouts was still wild moorland. In 1810 Lewis Tregonwell built a holiday house here – part of which is still incorporated into the Royal Exeter Hotel. By 1840 a marine village had been laid out, and the first pines – now so prolific – were planted. By 1890 the population was 37,000; now it is the centre of a vast "conurbation" stretching far inland.

The situation has enormous natural advantages. The town faces S., the climate is mild and the beach has 6 m. of golden sand. Pines still scatter the landscape and even line some streets, and the steeply rising cliffs provide a magnificent background to the Esplanade. From the road above there are spectacular views over to the Isle of Wight.

As the years went by parks and gardens were added. Meyrick Park covers some 194 acres of heathland, half of which is a golf course. It lies on the west end of Bournemouth, near **Talbot** village, which consists of farms, cottages, almshouses, a church and a school, all founded by Miss Georgina Charlotte Talbot. East of Meyrick Park is Queens Park, covering some 175 acres, and from here there are good views over the New Forest. In the centre of town the River Bourne runs through the Lower, Centre, and Upper Gardens, near the Pavilion.

Bournemouth has wide streets, a pier, a pavilion, a theatre and its own symphony orchestra, but it has few buildings dating back a century, and today new luxury blocks are springing up.

Of the churches, St Stephen's, built by J. L. Pearson between 1881 and 1908, is the most beautiful. Built in Early English style, with an impressive, spacious nave, it has good screens and reredos and stained glass by Clayton and Bell. At the Church of St Peter the heart of the poet Shelley lies buried.

The city has two museums. The Rothesay Museum has a varied collection of porcelain, pottery, butterflies and moths, and also a marine room. The Russell-Cotes Museum has a collection of porcelain, furniture and Japanese and Burmese art collected and given by Sir Merton Russell-Cotes, a former Lord Mayor. The picture collection includes such artists as Landseer, Cox and Fragonard. On the geological terrace there are specimens from quarries in all parts of Britain.

BOVINGTON, *Dorset* (4–SY8288). An excellent tank museum is the Army's peace-offering for mutilating miles of surrounding heath which Thomas Hardy called Egdon. It is in the camp and includes over 130 vehicles, both British and foreign, built from 1900 onwards.

"One mile north Bovington camp", as T. E. Lawrence said in a telegram to Henry Williamson only minutes before his mortal motorcycle crash in May 1935, is his home, Clouds Hill, now looked after by the National Trust. A woodsman's or gamekeeper's cottage, he found it derelict during his time in the Army, stationed at Bovington, 1923–5, rented it and renovated it. It remains very much as it was when he lived in it and is fascinating. The Greek inscription over the door means "nothing matters".

Just N. of **Wool**, 2 m. SE. of the camp, the attractive Woolbridge Manor, now a hotel, was once the home of the Turbervilles, where Hardy imagined his Tess coming for her honeymoon. Basically Elizabethan, its front was rebuilt *c.* 1652. The old bridge over the River Frome close to it is also Elizabethan.

About ½ m. E. of Wool, set in a lovely garden, are the ruins of Bindon Abbey, founded for Cistercians in 1172. Head-high walls, dark fish-ponds, the open abbot's coffin in which Hardy's Angel Clare walking in his sleep laid his Tess, all in the shade of huge beech and sycamore trees.

Round its church, Wool is old, thatched and pretty. Some 1½ m. W., the hefty buildings near Winfrith are used for atomic energy research.

BRADFIELD, *Berkshire* (5–SU6072), is chiefly famous for its college, the foundation of which came about in a curious way. The vicar and the squire, the Reverend Thomas Stevens, having spent enormous sums on restoring the church, decided that he needed a choir to sing in it. He thereupon started Bradfield College in 1850, which after various financial difficulties became famous under Dr Herbert Gray.

Originally the school was fashioned from the old manor house, but not much remains and the buildings are mostly 19th-cent., with some splendid windows by Burne-Jones – designed when he was only 24 – in the dining hall. Nearby is the chalk pit fashioned into a classical open-air theatre where the famous Greek plays are performed.

Although dominated by the school, Bradfield has some attractive houses, Georgian and earlier, and lies in the Pang valley just before it joins the Thames.

A few miles W. along the banks of the Pang you come to the village of **Bucklebury** – a lively place when Swift, Gay, Pope and others used to stay with Viscount Bolingbroke in the manor house, now destroyed. The village has some pretty cottages, a splendid oak avenue and a large common. The church has a curious feature: on the chancel window a 17th-cent. artist has painted a fly – body and legs on one side of the glass, wings on the other. It is so lifelike that you long to brush it off.

BRADFORD ABBAS, *Dorset* (4–ST5814), has a beautiful 15th-cent. church at the end of a

Bradford-on-Avon: the old stone bridge with its domed lock-up

Jane J. Miller

pretty Ham stone village street. The church tower is of Somerset excellence and is particularly good when viewed from the W. Inside are many good carved bench-ends, those near the chancel entrance being particularly fine, a panelled roof, stone screen and an unusual elaborately figured font, all of which are 15th-cent., and a Jacobean pulpit. All the woodwork has been kept light coloured, which enhances it. In the churchyard is a fine cross. The Rose and Crown pub, built possibly as a monks' rest-house in the late 15th cent. and afterwards used as a malt house, has a grand stone fire-place with good panelling above it. Till the Dissolution the village was owned by the abbots of SHERBOURNE, whose moated manor house was Wyke Farm, ½ m. E.

BRADFORD-ON-AVON, *Wiltshire* (4–ST 8260), is a place in which to linger. Once there it is hard to leave, for the streets are so narrow and twisted that every turn shows a new delight.

Already important in the 10th cent., as time passed Bradford grew rich from the manufacture of cloth – which accounts for the proliferation of fine mellow stone buildings of many centuries. They huddle together against a backdrop of hills, and the town rises so steeply from the river that in parts it has to be stepped. An old stone bridge crosses the river, with two arches dating back to the 14th cent., the rest being 17th-cent. In the middle is a small lock-up, fashioned from a chapel.

The Anglo-Saxon church is one of the only ones in the country almost complete. For years it was lost in a jumble of later buildings, its original function unknown. It was only discovered in 1856 when the vicar happened to look down over the roofs and saw an unknown cross. Later St Laurence became a church once again. A plain building, as high as it is long, it is unadorned inside. Over the narrow chancel arch two 10th-cent. sculptured angels fly towards one another.

The parish church, Holy Trinity, was originally 12th-cent. though it was added to later and restored in the 19th cent. Inside are some noble monuments. The painting of the Virgin with St Anne on the east chancel wall is 14th-cent., the painted Flemish glass in the nave mostly 17th-cent. On the north wall of the aisle is a delightful fragment, the head of a 14th-cent. woman wearing a wimple.

Church House and the Old Priory are 15th-cent. The Chantry is 16th to 17th cent., with a fine classical front. But one of the most important buildings is the Hall built by John Hall, a clothier, in 1610. With mullioned windows and an attractive porch, it shows the transition between Tudor and Palladian architecture.

As time passed so Bradford-on-Avon continued to flourish, adding some very fine Georgian architecture. Westbury House is a large early Georgian building near the bridge.

On the other side of the bridge at Barton Farm is one of the biggest tithe barns in England, which is exactly in tune with this busy, beautiful and successful town. Dating back to the 14th cent., 168 ft long, and with great timbers spanning the roof, it

is now under the care of the Ministry of Public Building and Works and can be visited.

Within striking distance of the town there is much to see. **Great Chalfield Manor** is 2½ m. NW. Surrounded by a moat, the house, church and buildings give an impression of life as it must have been in the 15th cent. They were built about 1480 by Thomas Tropenell; a contemporary mural showing his portrait can still be seen in the great hall. The house has been carefully restored.

Westwood Manor is 1½ m. SW. Built in stone, some parts date back to the 15th cent., but much was added later. The Jacobean plaster ceilings and modern topiary gardens are particularly interesting. Both these houses belong to the National Trust and can be visited.

BRADING, *Isle of Wight* (5–SZ6087), was once a harbour. As recently as the 1870s, small ships sailed up the Yar at high tide. Since 1880 a mile-long causeway has cut off the sea from the town, adding some 650 acres of flat, marshy land to the area, rich in bird life. St Mary's Church is the oldest on the island, with Norman work. The tower is Early English, and is fretted with arches, so that processions circling the church could remain on consecrated ground. Skeletons of prehistoric men 7 ft tall were once unearthed on the site. The church has monuments of the Oglander family, part of the island's history for 800 years. In the reign of Henry I they owned Nunwell Manor which is still in their possession. Charles I was their guest here.

Edward VI gave Brading its definitive charter and administration today is in the hands of eight members of the Parish Council and a Town Trust. It is no longer a borough.

In the centre of the town is evidence of the old bull ring, and there are stocks under the old town hall. Brading has another claim on the visitor's time, for at Morton Farm near **Yarbridge** is a well-preserved Roman villa considered the best of the eight discovered on the island. The mosaics are of special interest.

BRAY, *Berkshire* (5–SU9079). "Whatsoever King shall reign, I will be the Vicar of Bray, Sir!" So ran the old song about the 17th-cent. vicar, who kept changing his religion in order to keep his living.

The village is set on a bend of the Thames, spanned by a magnificent red-brick bridge designed by Brunel. The irregular streets with timber-framed and Georgian houses are delightful, and the large church contains much of interest. The earliest brass, of Sir John de Foxley and his wives, dates from 1378, and one of the monuments shows William Goddard, while his statue also stands at the entrance of Jesus Hospital which he founded. Here charming 17th-cent. gabled almshouses surround a quadrangle, and the chapel shows an old carved screen.

In the parish churchyard there stand both the Chantry Chapel of St Mary, which became a school in the 17th cent., and a delightful 15th-cent. timber-framed gatehouse.

Under 2 m. SW. lies Ockwells Manor, built between 1446 and 1466 for Sir John Norreys, an almost perfect example of a timber-framed manor house of its period. It belongs to the National Trust and is not open.

BREAMORE, *Hampshire* (5–SU1517), pronounced Bremmer locally, is on the edge of the New Forest, and boasts one of the few almost complete Anglo-Saxon churches in Hampshire. It lies in parkland, beside splendid cedars and a yew of great age, near the red-brick Elizabethan manor house.

The church dates back to about 1000 and was originally cruciform, but the north transept has disappeared. Some 32 yds long, the walls, except for the porch, are Anglo-Saxon. Over the south door there is a defaced Saxon rood, with the Virgin Mary and St John, which was originally painted and is now protected by the porch. Over the arch in the south transept in 6-in.-high letters is an Anglo-Saxon inscription, which being translated says, "Here is Manifested the Covenant to Thee."

Breamore House, the Elizabethan manor, was completed in 1583, and suffered a fire in 1857, which luckily did not affect the outside structure. The house, which is open to the public, has belonged to the Hulse family for over 200 years, and they have gradually built up a splendid collection of pictures, furniture and works of art. NW. of the village on Breamore Down, there is a curious medieval maze, The Miz Maze, set in a wood. It is cut in turf and measures about 30 yds across. The grass paths, cambered at the corners, gradually lead on to a central hillock. There is another maze at St Catherine's Hill near WINCHESTER, but no one knows quite why it was built though it may have religious significance. To the S. lies a long barrow, and NW. is **Grims Dyke**, a prehistoric earthwork, on the border with Wiltshire. **Castle Hill** is about 1 m. SE. of the village and gives splendid views over the Avon.

BRIDPORT, *Dorset* (4–SY4692). At one time a "Bridport dagger" meant a hangman's noose. The town makes less actual rope now, but remains, as it has been since the Middle Ages, England's principal producer of netting twines and cord, and claims, indeed, to be the biggest in Europe. These traditional industries made use of the great width of its predominantly Georgian main streets, the pavements of which were once wider than the road itself and were used for the twisting, drying and general handling of nets and ropes. The streets converge at the handsome arcaded town hall (1785–6). Opposite it the chemist's shop is on the site of the inn where Charles II, after the Battle of WORCESTER in 1651, disguised and searching for transport to France, had a meal after having been let down by a CHARMOUTH boatman. A popular stopping place in coaching days, the town has several old and handsome pubs. The local history museum, in a restored Tudor house in South Street, has finds from a Roman army camp near Stoke Abbot, 5 m. N., and a

natural history section. Further down this street, the basically 13th to early-15th-cent. parish church was greatly altered in the 19th cent. It contains a fine knight-in-armour effigy.

West Bay, 1½ m. S., the town's small port, has been annexed by the tourist industry, though it is still quiet in the evenings. There are plenty of commercial fishing boats in its harbour, and the sandstone cliffs rise vertically from its shingle beach. The harbour entrance is very narrow and in rough weather incoming tides pound through it excitingly. West Bay exports gravel and sand and imports timber.

BRIGHSTONE, *Isle of Wight* (5–SZ4282), an excellent centre for holiday visitors of a quiet turn of mind, with **Calbourne** 2¾ m. to the N. offering good places for picnics. The sea at Chilton Chine has safe bathing at high tide.

BRITFORD, *Wiltshire* (5–SU1528). The village is small with some pretty cottages, and lies on the banks of the Avon. The cruciform church was built on Anglo-Saxon foundations and still shows traces of work from this period in the nave. Most of the church is in Decorated style, and the tower dates from 1764.

When Street restored the church in 1873, several recesses were discovered, and two at the east end of the nave were thought to have led at one time to side chapels. One is carved with a pattern of vine scrolls, while the other has less intricate decoration. They may date back either to the 9th or to the 11th cent., or even to Roman times.

BROCKENHURST, *Hampshire* (5–SU2902), may mean "Badgers Wood". A residential village with plenty of life and some attractive thatched cottages, it is excellently placed for visiting the New Forest. The church, like so many in these parts, is built on a mound and is mainly Norman and Early English. In the churchyard there is an enormous yew that may well date back 1,000 years. "Brusher" Mills, a famous snake catcher who died at the start of the century, lies buried here.

There are plenty of attractive villages to visit nearby. **Boldre** is about 3 m. to the S. and there are pretty views of the river from the bridge. The church, a white plastered building, is set away from the village on top of a hill. The nave and south aisle date back to Norman times, while the north aisle is Early English and the chancel is in Decorated style. Not far away, at **Pilley,** there is an old thatched inn, called the Fleur de Lys.

Sway lies on the south-west edge of the forest, and it was somewhere near here that Captain Marryat set his famous *Children of the New Forest.* Not far away is Peterson's Folly, a concrete tower that soars to 220 ft. It dates from the 1870s, and was put up by a retired Indian judge to show the excellence of local concrete. However, the lights at the top so confused shipping that they had swiftly to be removed. **Burley** is almost due W. of Brockenhurst and

Jane J. Miller

Bridport: the harbour at West Bay

is a pretty residential village. There is an ancient earthwork on Castle Hill nearby, and since the hill is over 300 ft high it gives good views over the neighbourhood.

BROWNSEA ISLAND, *Dorset* (4–SZ0190), is the largest island in POOLE Harbour, about 1 m. long by ¾ m. broad, predominantly wooded but with some open spaces and a very nice beach which, being a fair walk from the quay, is seldom crowded. National Trust owned, Brownsea is partly a nature reserve, around which there are guided tours. Outside the reserve are peacocks, various exotic species of pheasant, some shy red squirrels and, on the shore, wild geese. There is also a daffodil field and rhododendrons. The main buildings are the castle, rebuilt after a fire in 1896, a church and some cottages and a restaurant by the quay. The church, in a beautiful setting and with a splendid 16th-cent. Italian well-head in its yard, was built in 1853 by Colonel William Waugh, who bought the island confident he would make his fortune from its china clay. Unfortunately he went bankrupt. In 1907 it was the site of Baden-Powell's first experimental Boy Scout Camp.

The boat trip from Poole Quay takes from 10 to 20 minutes and there is a charge for landing.

BURGHCLERE, *Hampshire* (5–SU4658). The chief interest of this village, apart from the countryside around, is in the Sandham Memorial Chapel. Built by Mr and Mrs J. L. Behrend in 1926 to commemorate a relation who died in the First World War, it now belongs to the National Trust and keys can be obtained from the nearby almshouses. It is decorated with frescoes by Stanley Spencer, who was greatly influenced by experiences first as a Red Cross orderly and later as a soldier in the First World War. The 19 pictures show the ordinary – not the heroic – life of a soldier in war time. At the east end is an enormous

Resurrection, with a tumble of wooden crosses in the foreground, each one handed in by a soldier.

Near the village a climb to **Beacon Hill,** an ancient Iron Age camp at 858 ft, gives remarkable views over the country. **The Chase,** at Woolton Hill, 3 m. SW. of NEWBURY, belongs to the National Trust, and over 130 acres of land, including woods and a stream, have now become a nature reserve.

BUSCOT, *Berkshire* (5–SU2297). The Thames, barely more than a stream and bordered by willows, runs by the village; nearby the old rectory and the church add to the charm. The church has a Norman chancel arch, a 17th-cent. Spanish wooden lectern, two windows by Burne-Jones and monuments to the Loveden family who once owned Buscot Park.

The house, which is open to the public, was built in the Adam style by Edward Loveden Townsend just before 1780. It was later altered, but the Victorian additions have been removed and the interior restored to its original state by Lord Faringdon. It has elegant ceilings, some splendid furniture, mostly Regency, and outstanding pictures. The collection includes pictures by Italian, Flemish, Dutch and Spanish painters, and also representatives of the English schools, including Gainsborough, Lawrence and many others. There is a remarkable series by Burne-Jones illustrating the legend of the Sleeping Princess, still in their original ornate frames.

The park, with its lake, was landscaped in the 18th cent., and in the 20th cent. Harold Peto designed the Italianate water gardens, with fountains, cascades and statuary. But now all this, including the house, Buscot village, and some 3,863 acres of farm and woodland belong to the National Trust, as does Buscot Old Parsonage. It was built about 1703 in stone, and can sometimes be visited if application is made in writing.

Castle Combe is considered one of the prettiest villages in England

CALNE, *Wiltshire* (5–ST9971). The wool trade was once the principal industry here, now it is bacon. After a history of some 1,000 years Calne remains a market town and still holds weekly markets. There are some good Georgian buildings and the church, in Perpendicular style, is impressive. It has an imposing 12th-cent. nave, and a fine 17th-cent. Gothic tower which replaced the one that fell in 1638.

Neighbouring villages are attractive. **Compton Bassett**, some 3 m. E., has delightful chalkstone cottages and an attractive 12th- and 13th-cent. church, well restored. **Bremhill**, 3 m. NW. of Calne, is charming. Nearby is a column in remembrance of Maud Heath who, in 1474, left all her money to build a causeway from Wick Hall to CHIPPENHAM. In the 19th cent. Canon Bowles, vicar and poet, was in the habit of keeping sheep, with their bells tuned in thirds and fifths. Bowles was a great favourite at **Bowood House**, 2 m. SW. of Calne, seat of the Marquess of Lansdown. It lies in 1,000 acres of magnificent parkland and woods, and a wing, still remaining, was copied from Diocletian's palace in Yugoslavia by Robert Adam in the 18th cent. The gardens were laid out by Capability Brown in 1763. Though these grounds are private, you may walk the main drives of the estate.

In the 19th cent. the 3rd Marquess of Lansdowne erected a column to commemorate an ancestor. It soars 125 ft above **Cherhill**, an attractive village some 2½ m. E. of Calne. Just S. is **Oldbury Camp,** an ancient Iron Age camp, set high, with a white horse carved in 1780 just below. While the land hereabouts is privately owned, there are several old public paths which give access.

CARISBROOKE CASTLE, *Isle of Wight* (5–SZ4888), and its village, for centuries the capital of the island, lies about 1 m. from NEW-

PORT, the present capital. The castle is set on a plateau 150 ft high and its architecture embodies Norman, Elizabethan and Jacobean work. The keep is Norman, *c.* 12th-cent., and is built on an artificial mound 58 ft high overlooking the Tudor buildings. Its ramparts afford a panoramic view of this fort which was built for Elizabeth I as a defence against the Armada by Gianbelli, an Italian, who with local labour completed the work within 245 days. The Well House is a restored 16th-cent. building, the well itself being sunk in 1150. Water is still raised in buckets by the original method of donkey labour, a great attraction for the children who visit it today.

In 1647 Charles I took refuge with Colonel Robert Hammond, governor of the castle. His exile soon became imprisonment, and Charles made two abortive attempts to escape. A museum collection records the island's history from earliest times with artifacts and antiquities. It also includes the oldest church organ in Britain. In the village of Carisbrooke, St Mary's Church with a Norman nave, Early English aisle and 15th-cent. west tower, is considered the most important and most beautiful in the island.

CASTLE COMBE, *Wiltshire* (4–ST8477), has been rated Britain's most beautiful village. Set in a wooded valley, the charming stone cottages, the 17th-cent. Dower House, the arched bridge over the Bye brook and the ancient market cross all have picture-book prettiness. The 17th-cent. manor house, beautifully set, is now a hotel, and a visit to the church helps you trace the history of the village. Mainly Perpendicular, it was built with the help of rich clothiers – theirs being an important local industry. Inside is an effigy, dated 1270, to Walter de Dunstanville, who built the original castle which gave Castle Combe its name. There is also an interesting 13th-cent. font, and fan vaulting.

The ancient Fosse Way passes near Castle Combe, and a Roman villa and cemetery have been found nearby.

CERNE ABBAS, *Dorset* (4–ST6601). The Cerne Abbas Giant, best seen from the A352 just N. of the village, was cut in the turf of a chalk hillside during the Roman occupation or earlier. It is 180 ft tall and was associated with ancient fertility rites. The site is looked after by the National Trust.

Till the 19th cent. the village, one of Dorset's most attractive, had a famous leather industry, and from 987 to 1539, a Benedictine abbey. The remains of this – a gatehouse with fine oriel window and a guest-house – are behind Abbey House at the head of the street past the church. From here you can walk to the Giant. The abbey's 14th-cent. tithe barn, now partly a house, is at the southern end of the village. The church is mainly 15th-cent., though the chancel is *c.* 1300 and the tall brown-yellow tower *c.* 1500. The interior is beautiful and was admirably restored in the 1960s. It has light, height and space with stone screen, exceptional Jacobean pulpit and 14th-cent. wall paintings. The grand east window with 15th-cent. glass is thought to have come from the abbey. In the churchyard is a wishing-well.

Three m. NW., **High Stoy Hill** is a splendid viewpoint. This was the country of Thomas Hardy's *The Woodlanders*.

One m. NNW., **Up Cerne** is an attractive hamlet with an excellent *c.* 1600 manor house and tiny church.

Two m. N., the fine gardens of **Minterne House**, 1904, are periodically open.

CHALE, *Isle of Wight* (5–SZ4877), NW. of St Catherine's Point, overlooks Chale Bay. This part of the coast has always been dangerous to shipping and was much used by wreckers. The village of Chale is unremarkable apart from the church with its great Perpendicular tower, once a beacon for shipping, but the manor house, now the Abbey Farm, dates from the 14th cent. and there is a fine 15th-cent. barn. About ½ m. to the S. lies **Blackgang Chine**; its name derives from the old smuggling gangs. There is no way down to the beach from this stream-cut chine, whose sides of dark-blue clay interlarded with yellow sandstone rise 400 ft. The clay is a manifestation of the "blue slipper", liable to slide the layers above it off high points carrying buildings and topsoil with them into the sea. It explains the Landslip, and the Upper and Lower Slips that are features of this coast.

The Observation Post gives good views of the area and has, besides a car park and restaurant, a children's maze, a water garden and a museum. The museum displays many objects from wrecked ships, including two Armada deck cannon, and the skeleton of an 82-ft whale.

CHARLTON MARSHALL, *Dorset* (4–ST 8903), has a considerable amount of modern building. Its church was, save for the 15th-cent.

tower, built in the reign of Queen Anne and is well-kept and full of light, a rare and pretty example of that period. It was probably the work of the builder-architects, John and William Bastard (*see* BLANDFORD FORUM), or of their father, and was paid for by the rector, Dr Charles Sloper. The canopied pulpit is particularly fine and the wall monuments pleasant.

CHARMOUTH, *Dorset* (4–SY3693). Jane Austen found it a nice place for "sitting in unwearied contemplation", but that was before the motor-car, when it was a fashionable coach-stop. Its hillside street is still lined with thatched houses and some Regency bow windows. It is situated in one of the few gaps in the hills that break into the cliffs overlooking the wide sweep of Lyme Bay. Its most historical building is the Queen's Armes. Built, it is thought, as a house for an abbot of FORDE, it was stayed in by Catherine of Aragon soon after her arrival in England in 1501, and also, when later an inn, by the fugitive Prince Charles in 1651, after he had come disguised from his TRENT hiding-place looking for a boat to take him to France.

The beautiful beach, sandless at high tide, is about ½ m. S. It is good for fossil hunting and there are good walks over the cliffs. At **Black Ven**, about ½ m. W. of the car park, a 12-year-old girl in 1811 found the famous fossilized ichthyosaurus now in the NATURAL HISTORY MUSEUM, London. The sandstone-scarred cliff-top to the E. called **Golden Cap** is most easily reached from CHIDEOCK.

CHAWTON, *Hampshire* (5–SU7037), is a village with some thatch, set in pretty country 1 m. S. of ALTON. The Victorian church was designed by Sir Arthur Blomfield and contains a fine monument to Sir Richard Knight, 1679. The Knights owned Chawton House, which has a 17th-cent. south front and stables dating from 1591. It was left to Jane Austen's brother.

She herself lived from 1809 to 1817 in an unpretentious brick house near the main WINCHESTER to GOSPORT road, and wrote *Mansfield Park*, *Emma* and *Persuasion* while here. Jane Austen belonged to Hampshire, for except for a few years at BATH she spent her whole life in the county, first at Steventon, near BASINGSTOKE, then in SOUTHAMPTON and finally in Chawton. Her house contains a museum with various of her personal effects and those of her family. It is open to the public. She is buried in WINCHESTER Cathedral.

CHESIL BANK, *Dorset* (4–SY5882). The huge bank of shingle which connects PORTLAND with the mainland and extends NW. along West Bay almost to BRIDPORT. Some 18 m. long and up to 45 ft high near Portland, it is said to be unique in Europe both geologically and in extent. As to where the sea brings its pebbles from, there have been generations of learned dispute. From its west to east end they increase in size so consistently that, tradition says, a smuggler could reckon his whereabouts in the dark by fingering them and fishermen by listening to the sound of the surf. Moreover, to the W. they are mainly varying shades of brown-yellow, near Portland predominantly grey. No land lies between the bank and the Atlantic, and not only numerous sailing ships but great sea creatures have been cast up – sharks, rays and even whales. After storms beachcombers' loot has included Roman coins, gold ingots, bits of Spanish galleons and plants from South America. The greatest recorded storm was in 1824 when an East Indiaman went down with all hands and another ship ended up over the bank in the long lagoon called The Fleet which it encloses and which stretches from WEYMOUTH to the ABBOTSBURY Swannery.

Beautiful from above – notably from Portland and the road W. from Abbotsbury – it is laborious to walk on, dangerous to bathe from.

"Chesil" comes from an Old English word for shingle.

CHIDEOCK, *Dorset* (4–SY4292), is the principal village of a small, richly fertile vale, hilllocked on three sides, sloping gently to the sea and scattered with farm-buildings and cottages of the yellow sandstone (yellower than Ham stone) that is locally exposed in every scarred bank or cliff. The village itself is largely of this stone and darkly thatched. It is especially pretty S. of the A35, which runs through it. The otherwise unexceptional parish church, mainly of the 15th cent., contains a remarkable mother-of-pearl cross formerly carried by monks in processions in and around Jerusalem and put in the care of the vicar, the Rev. Dr. W. D. Omand, in 1962. It also has a good Purbeck marble effigy (*c.* 1515) to a member of the Arundel family. The odd building just N. of the church is a Roman Catholic mortuary chapel, and ½ m. N., beside the early-19th-cent. manor house, is an extraordinarily ornate Roman Catholic church (*c.* 1870) with many murals. Both manor and church were built – and some of the murals painted – by the same Weld family responsible for the first legal post-Reformation Roman Catholic church in England (*see* DURDLE DOOR); and the family continues to lead a strong local Catholic community.

Seatown, ½ m. S., is a hamlet with a shingle (and therefore seldom crowded) beach, attractive with drawn-up fishing boats and grand cliff views. It is probably the best place from which to approach the 619-ft domed **Golden Cap** (National Trust), the highest cliff on England's South Coast: about ¾ m. of steep walking. Till as late as the mid-19th cent., this seems to have been a keen smuggling area, brandy being the main import; the clumps of trees that strangely top local hills were planted, some say, as landmarks for illicit traders.

CHILCOMB, *Hampshire* (5–SU5028). Although this small village is only 2 m. from WINCHESTER it has all the charm of a rural setting, with timbered cottages nestling around a green. It is set under the downs, but from here

there are splendid views over the city of Winchester.

The church, set away from the village, is plain and Norman, with primitive zigzag patterns on the chancel arch. There is an attractive 17th-cent. screen, made locally, and some splendid 15th-cent. tiles in the chancel, showing lions, griffins and fleurs de lis. Above the altar is an old hook for hanging the pyx – a vessel in which consecrated bread was kept – and in the south-east corner of the nave a mass dial.

CHIPPENHAM, *Wiltshire* (4–ST9173). A market town for centuries, King Alfred spent much time here and used to hunt in the nearby forests. Now a new concrete bridge, built in 1966, spans the Avon and leads to the town. Although industrial, it has a 15th-cent. Town Hall, as well as some attractive half-timbered houses and others in stone dating from the 18th cent. St Andrew's Church was rebuilt in the 19th cent., but the Hungerford Chapel is 15th-cent. and contains some interesting monuments.

Hardenhuish, pronounced Harnish, is now almost a suburb of Chippenham. On a green hill stands the church designed in 1779 by John Wood of BATH, a delightful example of Georgian church architecture, with two Venetian windows of particular charm.

Kingston St Michael is 6 m. NW. of Chippenham and has attractive 17th-cent. gabled stone almshouses. In the church is a window in memory of John Aubrey, writer, gossip and antiquarian, born here in 1626. An authority on Wiltshire, he persuaded Charles II to visit AVEBURY and at STONEHENGE the Aubrey Holes were named after him. At Priory Farm, close by, some remnants of a 12th-cent. Benedictine nunnery that once stood here have been built into the walls.

CHOLSEY, *Berkshire* (5–SU5886), is only a mile from the River Thames near WALLINGFORD, and has some interesting historical associations. Ethelred the Unready founded an abbey here in 986, probably in expiation of the murder of his brother Edward. This was destroyed by the Danes who ravaged the area, and later the abbey was attached to that of Reading. Of all these buildings nothing remains, but it is thought that part of the cruciform church, namely the central tower, may date back to Anglo-Saxon times. However, St Mary's today is mostly Norman, though the chancel was lengthened in the 13th cent. and the tower raised some time later. Amongst the monuments there is a brass to John Mere, vicar, dated 1471.

CHRISTCHURCH, *Hampshire* (5–SZ1593). This tranquil town lies between the Avon and the Stour, the two rivers meeting before they flow out into Christchurch harbour. First mentioned in about 900, at the time of the Domesday Book there were already 21 houses here and 24 canons attached to the church. In the old days the town was named Twynham, a name which tradition says was changed when the church was built.

Reece Winstone

Christchurch Priory: the Norman turret

Legend has it that a site for the church was originally chosen on St Catherine's Hill, some 165 ft high with wonderful views over the town. But every day the building work was undone and materials were mysteriously moved to another site. When a beam cut short in error was miraculously lengthened by a stranger, it was decided that he must be Christ in person, and both the site and the name of the town were changed. The beam can still be seen built high in the wall above the choir.

The church was first started in the 11th cent. by Flambard, who rose from being superintendent of the King's kitchen to Bishop. Later the town was given to Richard de Redvers by his cousin, Henry I. Christchurch became an Augustinian priory in about 1150, and the main building was finally finished about a century later. At the Dis-

solution the priory buildings were destroyed, but the church was retained to serve the parish.

The nave is 118 ft long and seven massive Norman arcades still remain. The crypt, too, is Norman, but the finest work from this period is undoubtedly the turret in the north transept. The impressive north porch, approached by an elm avenue, is 13th-cent. The magnificently carved stone reredos is 14th-cent., and some of the wood carving in the choir is 13th-cent., some 15th-cent. The chantries are perhaps the church's chief glory, and of these the Salisbury Chantry is the most beautiful. It is built of Caen stone, which is so hard that even today every detail of the carving is sharp. It has a sad story attached to it, for Margaret, Countess of Salisbury and niece of Edward IV, lost brother, son, father and grandfather either in battle or to the axe, and when over 70 was herself beheaded by Henry VIII. Burial here was refused and she lies near the TOWER of London.

Of the castle, not much remains except the walls of the keep, but in the gardens of the King's Arms Hotel close by there are the remains of the Norman Castle Hall, or the constable's house. The roof has disappeared, but the massive walls remain, as does part of the old Norman staircase. On the first floor there is a hall, still with its original windows and round chimney. Down below the windows are looped for defence. Nearby are the remains of a medieval garderobe, and also a small thatched house, with plasterwork front and low eaves, where the courts leet were once held. The two-arched bridge over the Avon is Norman, and the old priory mill still stands.

There is much of interest nearby. The Red House Museum and Art Gallery is housed in a Georgian building and has natural history exhibits and antiquities. At **Hengistbury Head**, which belongs to BOURNEMOUTH Corporation and lies between that town and Christchurch, there is an old earthwork with double ditch. N. of the harbour are the **Stanpit Marshes**, a nature reserve and the home of rare wildfowl, from which there are good views. **Mudeford**, once separate but now joined to Christchurch, has some pretty thatch and retains the atmosphere of an old fishing village.

CODFORD ST PETER, *Wiltshire* (4–ST 9640), is memorable for part of a 9th-cent. cross which can be seen in the church. The church itself shows traces of Early English and later work, but was restored in the 19th cent. Inside is the stone, which stands about 4 ft high, tapering from a base of about 12 in. to about 6 in. at the top. It is a most remarkable and beautiful piece of work. A man stands, with his head well back, apparently either grasping fruit or holding up the branch of a tree. In his other hand he holds a hammer.

Codford St Mary is linked to Codford St Peter and from here a walk on the downs gives a remarkable view of the valley. It was a view much admired by Cobbett for its churches, sheep and watermeadows, and for its air of peaceful serenity.

COMBE, *Berkshire* (5–SU3760), lies in a great amphitheatre of chalk hills near INKPEN. It is not only isolated and the highest village in Berkshire, but only became part of the county in the late 19th cent. The church, still part of WINCHESTER diocese, is a simple building dating mostly from the 13th cent. In the old days the manorial courts used to be held at Combe Manor, just beside the church, and it is thought that Charles II, accompanied by Nell Gwynn, used to spend happy days here.

Nearby, three hills soar majestically, and the greatest of these is **Walbury Hill**, which at 974 ft is the highest for many miles. It is topped by a prehistoric camp covering over 80 acres, the largest in the county, and built on a prehistoric track called the Old Way. Nearby Sheepless Hill rises to 876 ft, and Combe Hill to·over 900.

Between Inkpen and Walbury Hill is **Combe Gibbet**, an old Neolithic barrow some 200 ft long and complete with ditches. It takes its name from an eerie gibbet where a man and a woman were hanged in the 17th cent., and it is to this day the duty of the tenant of a local farm to keep the gibbet in repair.

COOKHAM, *Berkshire* (5–SU8985). With its green surrounded by the pretty houses and pleasant high street, Cookham draws many visitors. The river here also has great charm, enhanced by the hanging woods of CLIVEDEN.

In the village stands an old sarsen stone. Sir Stanley Spencer (1891–1959) was born and lived here, and the Stanley Spencer Gallery, King's Hall, shows some of his works, many of them inspired by his native village. He combined religious themes with everyday settings, and one of his major paintings, *Resurrection* (TATE GALLERY) shows Christ at the doorway of Cookham church. The Queen's Swan Keeper also lives here and at certain seasons can be seen wearing his ancient costume. The church, of the Norman, Early English and Perpendicular periods, has several brasses and monuments, including one to Sir Isaac Pocock by Flaxman, 1810.

There are four bowl barrows at Cock Marsh. Here 132 acres, and 78 more including Cookham Dean Common, belong to the National Trust, as does Widbrook Common, 1 m. S. of Cookham.

CORFE CASTLE, *Dorset* (4–SY9681). From almost any direction it is one of the most spectacular ruined castles in Britain, but perhaps most romantic view of it is from the road N. to ARNE. Another superb view is from KINGSTON, 1¾ m. S. The ruins are best approached from the car park beside the road W. towards Church Knowle.

The existing buildings (of Purbeck stone) date from the time of William the Conqueror to the 14th cent. But the West Saxon kings, probably from Alfred onwards, fortified the site against the Danes and had a hunting lodge nearby; and here in 978, the 18-year-old King Edward, later called the Martyr, was murdered at the instigation of his stepmother who coveted the throne for her son,

Ethelred the Unready. He called for a drink at the lodge where she was living and was given wine and a dagger in the back. It saw further foul deeds under King John. He made it his periodic residence, treasure-house and state prison. In its dungeons he starved to death 22 French nobles who had supported his nephew Arthur's claim to the throne. He also locked up the hermit, Peter of Pomfret, who had been unwise enough to forecast the King's downfall, before having him dragged to WAREHAM and back on a hurdle and then strung up. The Civil War brought the castle's destruction. Then owned by Sir John Bankes, Charles I's Chief Justice, it proved quite impregnable to the Roundhead forces, mines, cannon and two walking "tanks" called "the boar" and "the sow" all proving ineffectual, until Colonel Pitman, a member of the garrison, turned traitor and let in the enemy. It fell, long after most Royalist strongholds, in February 1646. Sir John Bankes had died in 1643, but throughout the siege Lady Bankes and her family had remained most spiritedly in residence, and were reasonably treated afterwards. Like so many, the castle was slighted after the war, much of its stone going to build houses in the village.

The village in the Middle Ages had a considerable marble-carving industry, and the engraved stones over some doorways are usually the work of the Purbeck Marblers. The church, much illtreated by Roundheads, was, except for the 15thcent. tower, which has good gargoyles, rebuilt in 1859. In West Street, the Town Hall, which is 18th-cent. with some earlier parts, contains a small museum, and off the same street is a model of the castle as it is thought to have once looked.

CORHAMPTON, *Hampshire* (5–SU6120). Two pleasing villages, Corhampton and **Meonstoke**, face one another across the banks of the peaceful Meon River, but Corhampton has the added attraction of a small Anglo-Saxon church. Pilaster strips and the long and short stones typical of Anglo-Saxon work can clearly be seen. The church is mainly 11th-cent., although the east end of the chancel is later. The old stone chair may be Anglo-Saxon, and the fascinating wall paintings are 13th-cent. All that remains is the picture of a seated bishop with a woman standing nearby. Below are stylized designs of drapery, circles and squares decorated with birds. Outside, near the porch, is an Anglo-Saxon sundial and close by an enormous old yew.

Meonstoke is attractive, though it was greatly damaged by fire in the 18th cent., and modern bungalows have appeared. **Winchester Hill** is only 2½ m. NW., and is sometimes called the Roman Camp. Rising to 650 ft, the summit is crowned by an ancient Iron Age hill-fort. Roman remains have also been uncovered, and there are bowl barrows nearby. There are wonderful views over to the Isle of Wight from this area, now declared a nature reserve.

The next village downstream is **Droxford**, quite large and with plenty of Georgian building about. In the Second World War the railway station – no longer in use – was the headquarters of Sir Winston Churchill and others for the invasion of Europe. Izaak Walton ended his days with his son at the 18th-cent. rectory. It now belongs to the National Trust, as does some meadow land and a beech avenue.

Exton, the next village upstream from Corhampton, has tranquil charm, and its neighbour **Warnford** is set in delightful country. The church, says the 12th-cent. Latin inscription, was founded by Wilfrid of York, an early Christian missionary to the Jutes in this area, and renovated by Adam de Port in Norman times. It now also shows later work. Nearby is a house named King John's House, which, although not his, dates from the early 13th cent. It consisted of a great hall with kitchens attached, probably with a second story above. One of the pillars, 25 ft tall, still remains in the hall.

CORSHAM, *Wiltshire* (4–ST8669). The town of Corsham has grown considerably in recent years, and there is a lot of modern development. But the centre retains its old character with 17th- and 18th-cent. golden-stone houses, old weavers' cottages and the Hungerford Almshouses.

The Church of St Bartholomew dates back to the 12th and 15th cents., but suffered greatly at the hands of the Victorian restorers. However, the 15th-cent. screen is interesting, and in the churchyard lies Sarah Jones who died in 1753 aged 107. "Some time before her death she had fresh teeth", adds the headstone.

Nearby stands **Corsham Court**, its history stretching back to Anglo-Saxon times. The estate belonged to the Royal family, and then later traditionally became part of the dower of the queens of England. In 1582 it was sold to Thomas Smythe – or Customer Smythe as Aubrey calls him, because he grew rich from customs dues collected in London. He built an attractive Cotswold house with gables and mullioned windows, much of which remains today. In 1777 the house was bought by Paul Methuen, in the expectation of inheriting a collection of pictures from his cousin, Sir Paul Methuen. Capability Brown, known more as a landscape gardener than as an architect, was commissioned to make alterations and add a picture gallery to the existing house. Later, in 1800, John Nash added another gallery, but much that he built in Strawberry Hill Gothic style suffered from damp, and was later altered by Bellamy.

The house contains some fine furniture by Chippendale, Adam, Johnson and Cobb, and has a garden laid out by Humphry Repton. But it is chiefly to see the magnificent paintings by old masters that visitors come. Correggio, Van Dyck, Rubens and many others are represented, and the collection includes portraits by Reynolds and George Romney. Part of the house is now occupied by the BATH Academy of Arts, but both house and gardens are open to the public.

COWES, *Isle of Wight* (5–SZ4995). Cowes Week in August is one of the great events of the yachts-

man's year. The headquarters of the Royal Yacht Squadron on Victoria Parade below Cowes Castle, the main boatyards and moorings, and most features of interest to the visitor lie W. of the River Medina which divides the town. During the Second World War the castle was the chief operations centre for the Normandy landings. Northwood House has fine gardens and rare trees.

Cowes is the entry port to the island from SOUTHAMPTON and regular ferry services cross the Solent.

The first English settlers for Maryland sailed from Cowes in 1633 and Dr Arnold of RUGBY fame was born here.

CRANBORNE, *Dorset* (4–SU0513). Once the town of the hunting forest of CRANBORNE CHASE, seat of the Chase Court and with a market, grammar school and Benedictine abbey (980–1102), it is now only a village but an attractive one, an example of how pleasant modern red brick can be made to look. Its manor house, mainly Jacobean, is visible from the village green. It is one of Dorset's finest and its gardens are occasionally open. Since the early 17th cent. it has been in the Cecil family (Marquesses of Salisbury) who still own the whole village. To persuade the County Council a speed limit was needed, the Parish Council Chairman once pretended the High Street was a Grand Prix track with a county official as his passenger. The large church is rare in having an entirely 13th-cent. nave. Victorian chancel and furniture dull it, but there are remains of medieval wall paintings, a fine pulpit dating from the early 15th cent., and some 17th-cent. monuments of interest, including one to a boy aged seven.

About ½ m. SE. is a strikingly chalk-capped earthwork called **Castle Hill**, about which the only thing known for sure is that a Mr Tregonwell buried his horse on it. Possibly it is Anglo-Saxon.

Some 2 m. E., the Dorset-Hampshire border is still formed by **Bokerly Dyke**, the great defensive bank thought to have been built by the Romano-British in the 4th and 5th cents., first against insurrection, then against Anglo-Saxons.

CRANBORNE CHASE, *Dorset* (4–ST9114 around). Strictly the Chase, covering over 100 sq. m., was the long southern slope of the chalk massif which, between SHAFTESBURY and SALISBURY, straddles the Wiltshire-Dorset border. The creatures hunted were mainly fallow deer; red deer were introduced but did not like the chalk lands.

In the Middle Ages the hunting rights passed from the Earls of Gloucester to King John and were held by most monarchs between him and James I, from whom they passed to the Earls of Salisbury, to the Earls of Shaftesbury and finally to the Pitt-Rivers family. In 1830 an Act of Parliament ended a system which had sterilized this vast tract, causing it to become a refuge of smugglers and criminals generally. Confrontations, often bloody, between poachers and gamekeepers had been frequent. At that time mostly forest, it is now rolling grassland scattered with fine beech woods. The road from SHAFTESBURY to SIXPENNY HANDLEY provides a representative and beautiful view of it. The Ackling Dyke, one of the finest Roman roads in Britain, crosses it, leading from BADBURY RINGS to OLD SARUM. This can be well seen where, about ¼ m. S. of the A354, it crosses the Sixpenny Handley–CRANBORNE road. Near here, too, with an Ordnance Survey map, you can trace the Dorset Cursus. It is some 6 m. long, roughly parallel with the A354, and is conjectured to have been a Neolithic processional way.

In the village of **Chettle**, 4½ m. SW., is Chettle House, built c. 1710–15 by Vanbrugh's pupil, Thomas Archer. It is now occupied by flats but is still fine from the outside and has an elaborate double staircase within.

CRAWLEY, *Hampshire* (5–SU4234), between the valleys of the Test and the Itchen, shows all the charm of an English village, and may have been Thackeray's model for Queen's Crawley in *Vanity Fair*.

A small place, it consists of not much more than one street, flanked with houses from all periods and sprinkled with thatched timber-framed cottages. The village was planned as a whole and until 1931 belonged to Crawley Court, which was rebuilt in the 19th cent. in Elizabethan style. There are a school, an inn and a village hall, once a barn and built of chalk. Other buildings also have chalk walls, but most cottages are of brick and flint.

The flint and rubble church is in Early English style, the chancel being rebuilt in 1887. However, the wooden arcades in the nave are perhaps 13th-cent., the chancel arch Early English and the pillars of this arch Norman.

CRICKLADE, *Wiltshire* (5–SU0993), lies on a Roman road running from CIRENCESTER to Seend, and was given its name by the Anglo-Saxons. Later 9th-cent. fortifications were added. A pleasant little town, with some 17th- and 18th-cent. building, it was described centuries ago as being "in lovely surroundings, abounding in all kinds of riches". Cricklade is near the source of the Thames and its real glory is the magnificent Church of St Sampson. The great central Tudor tower, richly adorned, soars above the rest of the town. Work inside spans time from the 12th to the 16th cents., and includes some rich heraldic work and a delightful late-15th-cent. south chapel. In 1930 Martin Travers added new windows and decoration.

From Cricklade you can walk to see the junction of the North Wilts with the Thames and Severn Canal. Four m. W. of the town is the pretty village of **Ashton Keynes**, where numerous little bridges span the upper Thames.

CRONDALL, *Hampshire* (5–SU7948), is admired for its prettiness. The Court is a fine Georgian building, and the Church of All Saints, approached by a lime avenue, is magnificent.

Originally Norman, it was later restored in the same style. At least three doorways are 12th-cent., and the interior, with clerestoried nave and vaulted chancel, is grand. The red-brick tower was added in 1658 for the sum of £428, and on the chancel floor is an ancient brass to Nicholas Caerwent, who died in 1381.

Round about, the country is varied, with woods, farms, and downs, along which runs the prehistoric Harrow Way. **Caesar's Camp** is just NE. of the village; but this earthwork, with double ditch and rampart, dates back to far earlier times, although the rich treasure of gold coins – found here in 1828 are now in the Ashmolean Museum at OXFORD – dates from c. A.D. 600. There are two Norman motte-and-bailey camps on the FARNHAM road, and Powderham Castle and Bailey Pound Copse are now scheduled as Ancient Monuments.

CROWTHORNE, *Berkshire* (5–SU8464), is a pleasant village set amongst heathery fir-scattered country. One m. S. is **Wellington College**, founded in the 19th cent. as a memorial to the Duke of Wellington.

This part of the country is remarkable for the splendid views it affords. One m. W. of Crowthorne the National Trust owns 60 acres of land at **Finchampstead Ridges**. From here the views over Berkshire, Hampshire and Surrey, over heath, heather, woodland and the valley of the Blackwater are magnificent. Nearby, the Devil's Highway, an old Roman Road, takes you to Heath pool, a further 12 acres of National Trust woodland, and there is more at Simons Wood nearby.

Down below lies the village of **Finchampstead**. Together with EASTHAMPSTEAD it is one of the oldest villages of the great WINDSOR Forest, which in the early 19th cent. covered some 59,000 acres. Finchampstead church, which sits on a platform and is enclosed by an old earthwork, is another good vantage point.

CUMNOR, *Berkshire* (5–SP4604), is connected with one of the most intriguing puzzles in history. In 1560 Amy Robsart, wife of Robert Dudley, Queen Elizabeth's favourite, was found dead at the foot of the stairs at Cumnor Place. Did she fall? Was she pushed? No one will ever know, although it seemed at the time that Dudley wanted her out of the way in order to be free to sue for the Queen's hand. Old Cumnor Place is no more, but memories of the old story are still kept alive by the monuments in the old church. It shows work from many periods: originally Transitional, it has many features in the Decorated style. The tower is late 12th- or early 13th-cent. and the north arcade is Early English. Inside are a statue of Queen Elizabeth and some of Amy Robsart's letters. At the time of her death she was staying with Anthony Forster, a Dudley retainer, who owned Cumnor Place. He kneels by a magnificent canopied tomb, 1572, with his children and wife about him. There is also a good two-decker Jacobean pulpit and a 17th-cent. spiral staircase leading to the belfry.

The village with its stone houses has a Cotswold, rather than Berkshire, atmosphere, and if you climb the hills to over 500 ft there are magnificent panoramic views of the spires of OXFORD and of the Cotswold country.

DEVIZES, *Wiltshire* (5–SU0061). An old market town situated on the edge of the downs, Devizes is an attractive place to spend time, and a good centre. The town first grew in importance after the old Norman castle was built, but this was later destroyed – or "slighted" as he liked to put it – by Cromwell, and a 19th-cent. crenellated edifice has been built on the same site.

Although there are 16th-cent. buildings in Devizes, as, for example, the Elm Tree Inn, the town is particularly rich in 18th-cent. building. Brownstone House dates from this time, as do the Wool Hall and Greystone House. The Bear Hotel is particularly interesting. During the 18th cent. Thomas Lawrence, who put posts to guide travellers across the plain from SALISBURY, was the landlord here. It became a fashionable hotel and Mrs Siddons, Mrs Thrale and Fanny Burney all admired the landlord's charming small son, who later became Thomas Lawrence the painter.

In the large Market Place the cross erected in 1814 is interesting for the moral story it tells. Ruth Pierce asked Heaven to strike her dead if she lied during a quarrel over money. Heaven obliged: "She instantly fell and expired", reads the inscription.

Devizes has three extraordinarily attractive churches. St John's dates back to the 12th cent. with a Norman tower. In the 15th cent. the nave was rebuilt and aisles added. There are also 16th- and 19th-cent. additions. The Beauchamp Chapel is particularly lovely and holds many monuments. The Norman stone vaulting to the chancel is interesting. St Mary's boasts a stone-vaulted 12th-cent. chancel, but the nave, aisles and tower were rebuilt in 1436. St James's has a handsome late-Perpendicular tower, but the church was mainly rebuilt in 1832.

For a longsighted view of the area visit the Museum of the Wiltshire Archaeological and Natural History Society. Much that has been excavated from the Wiltshire barrows is here. So also are a collection of fossils and some 19th-cent. watercolours of the county.

There are some agreeable walks round the town, either down the Kennet and Avon Canal, which has 29 locks between Devizes and Caen Hill, or to Roundway Down, where the Roundheads were beaten in a battle in 1643. **Oliver's Castle,** an ancient camp on a small hill, is ¾ m. away.

For the more energetic, **Bromham,** 3½ m. NW. of Devizes, is attractive. Old Bromham House, a Tudor mansion famous for being as large as Whitehall, once stood here, but was mostly destroyed in the Civil War. The remaining wing is built into a farm, and some material was used to build the gateway into **Spye Park.** There a 19th-cent. house stands now, set in 600 acres of lovely wooded country. Thomas Moore, the poet, lies buried near a Celtic cross in the Church of St Nicholas at Bromham.

Urchfont, 5 m. SW., is a delightful village set on a green, with a William and Mary manor house, once owned by Pitt the Elder. The church, mostly 14th-cent. with a 15th-cent. tower and porch, is notable. It has 14th-cent. glass, fine stone vaulting and a 13th-cent. font.

DIDCOT, *Berkshire* (5–SU5290). Before the railway came to Didcot it was simply a tiny village set in unspectacular country, but in spite of the expansion this brought about, the old village has managed to remain relatively untouched. It still retains an atmosphere of thatch and charm, in contrast to the somewhat drab building elsewhere in the town.

The Church of All Saints is mostly from the Decorated period, though altered and renovated later. It has a wooden bell turret and a shingled spire, and inside a splendid Purbeck marble effigy of a mitred bishop dating from about 1293. This may commemorate Ralph de Dudecot.

DINTON, *Wiltshire* (5–SU0131), is beautifully set in the Nadder Valley and is chiefly remarkable for four houses belonging to the National Trust. First is Philipps House, a splendid residence, designed in 1816 in Neo-Grecian style by Sir Jeffry Wyatville, the nephew of Wyatt, the Gothic restorer, who had designed some beautiful houses in classical style himself. The house, once the home of the Wyndham family, has a splendid Ionic portico and a beautiful staircase. It stands in Dinton Park, which consists of about 205 acres and includes a farm, some cottages and Wick Camp, an old Iron Age hill-fort encircled by a single ditch. The house is let to the Y.W.C.A. but can be visited at certain times, or on application.

Near the church, which has a pleasing chancel in Decorated style and an interesting early Purbeck marble font, is Hyde's House. Edward Hyde, Chancellor of England, whose daughter married James II, is said to have been born here. It is a late Tudor house, originally built in the 16th cent. and remodelled in the style of Wren in 1725. By the side of the house stands a large medieval dovecot. Hyde's House is not open to the public.

Little Clarendon and Lawes Cottage are also quite near the church, and stand in about 29 acres. Little Clarendon is a late-15th-cent. Tudor stone house, while Lawes Cottage dates from the 17th cent. William Lawes, a composer friend of John Milton, lived here. In spring the garden is a mass of daffodils. Little Clarendon and Lawes Cottage are both open to the public on written application.

Near Dinton at **Fovant,** huge regimental badges are cut into the chalk downs and can be seen from the road. These were originally cut by regiments stationed here in the First World War.

DONNINGTON, *Berkshire* (5–SU4668). There is no doubt that the gatehouse of Donnington Castle is one of the most romantic ruins in a county which, WINDSOR apart, seems short of good castles. For set on a spur it is not only a

A. F. Kersting

Donnington: the castle gatehouse

Louis & Daphne Peek

Dorchester, a market town and county capital

wonderful landmark but also gives excellent views of the surrounding countryside.

The history of Donnington goes back at least to the 11th cent. but after passing through various hands it came to Richard de Abberbury, a knight attached to the Black Prince. He was made guardian of the prince's small son, who, as Richard II, gave permission to crenellate the castle in 1386. Later it belonged to Thomas Chaucer, supposed to be the son of the poet. It was later the property of Queen Elizabeth I, who certainly stayed at Donnington, as did Henry VIII and Edward VI. But its finest hour was during the Civil War. Strategically placed on the BATH road it was of great importance to the Royalists, who under Sir John Boys held out for 20 months in spite of immense pressure. Finally, the King's cause being unquestionably lost, they were allowed an honourable surrender.

The castle was originally oblong with round towers at each of the four corners, square towers in two walls, and a gatehouse on the third. But today little more than the gatehouse remains. It is a splendid oblong structure flanked by two circular towers and soaring to some 65 ft. Built about 1386, it is three-storied and the views from the top are splendid.

The castle is now under the care of the Ministry of Public Building and Works, and is open to the public. Apart from the gatehouse, the outline of the castle can be seen, as well as the remains of the earthworks built during the Civil War at the great cost of £1,000. Also on display are some relics of the war.

The village of Donnington has almost been

eaten up by NEWBURY. Donnington Hospital is, however, delightful. Built 1602, restored in the 19th cent., these houses belong to a far older foundation.

DORCHESTER, *Dorset* (4–SY6990). The county's capital makes a fine first impression if approached from E. to W., its main street climbing from the River Frome. Its buildings, of pale-grey Portland stone, are architecturally disappointing, partly because they were damaged by a series of fires in the 17th and 18th cents. and consequently rebuilt without the uniformity or inspiration of BLANDFORD. Nevertheless, of ancient foundation, it has much that is of interest.

Romans seem to have founded it shortly after capturing MAIDEN CASTLE, 1½ m. SW., in *c.* A.D. 43, walled it and made it one of their main towns in the South-West. The Normans gave it a castle, thought to have been one of the hunt-loving King John's numerous temporary residences, and a friary, both since vanished. In the Middle Ages, it manufactured cloth and was famous for its ales. In the 17th cent. it became very Puritan, a shipload of its citizens founding New Dorchester in New England *c.* 1628, and keenly supporting the Roundheads in the Civil War. In 1685, after the Monmouth rebellion, Judge Jeffreys presided at a "bloody assize" in the town, having 74 men hanged, chopped up and bits of them exemplarily distributed about the country. The house in the High Street where he lodged is now a restaurant named after him, and a room in the Antelope Hotel in South Street is thought to have been his court room. In 1834, the old Shire Hall in the High

Street was the scene of another famous trial: that of the TOLPUDDLE Martyrs. The court room is now owned by the T.U.C. as a memorial and is open to the public.

These days Dorchester is a livestock marketing and farmers' shopping centre with a big brewery and other light industries. It has been made famous by the novels of Thomas Hardy (1840–1928), whose posthumous fame it has eagerly cultivated. He was born at Higher BOCKHAMPTON nearby and lived his last years on the town's eastern outskirts at Max Gate.

The County Museum about halfway up the High Street, is easily Dorset's best museum, with many excellent Roman and pre-Roman finds, remarkable fossils, traps for catching poachers, and Hardy relics including a reconstruction of his study. Next to it, St Peter's Church is mainly 15th-cent., restored by a local architect with the young Thomas Hardy as assistant; it has an effigy of Denzil, Lord Holles, one of the five "the birds are flown" M.P.s whom Charles I went to the House of Commons to arrest. Just outside is a statue of William Barnes, the 19th-cent. dialect poet who, like Scotland's Burns, tends locally to be more honoured than read. The Shire Hall is a few doors up, and a little further on is a statue of Hardy by Eric Kennington. Some 200 yds N., in Colliton Park near the new County Hall, is an excellent example of the foundations and tessellated pavements of a Roman villa.

At the head of the High Street, the keep, at the former army depot barracks, has a museum.

Abçut ⅔ m. S. beside the WEYMOUTH road is a Roman amphitheatre, built on the site of a Bronze Age stone circle known as **Maumbury Rings**. It was used till the Middle Ages for beast-baiting and till the 18th cent. for public, and well-attended, executions. On the way to it, in South Street nearly opposite the Post Office, is one of the town's oldest buildings, Napier's Almshouses (1610), now shops. The most attractive church is St George's, Fordington, reached by turning S. off the High Street immediately W. of the river. It has an extremely fine Norman tympanum showing St George piercing Saracens with his sword on the behalf of the Crusaders. The Walks, avenues of limes, chestnuts and sycamores which girdle three sides of the town, are said to follow the line of the Roman walls.

Some 1¾ m. SSE. at **Winterborne Came** is the small church where William Barnes, the poet, was rector from 1862 until his death in 1886, and the thatched rectory where he lived, all in open parkland dotted with oak trees. Here also is one of the best-looking Palladian houses in Dorset, which was built in 1754 by the architect-builder Francis Cartwright for John Damer, one-time M.P. for Dorchester, younger brother of the creator of MILTON ABBAS. It is well seen from the road and open by appointment.

Near **Charminster**, 1½ m. N., is Wolfeton House, 15th-cent. ancestral home of the Trenchard family, which can be seen by appointment. Charminster church has a 13th-cent. porch and a dominating 15th-cent. tower.

DOWNTON, *Wiltshire* (5–SU1721), has a wide main street and was once a market town. The village lies in the Avon Valley and was of great importance in Anglo-Saxon times. At The Moot there is stepped seating cut in the grass and also an inner double horseshoe ring, surrounded by an outer ditch, dating from early times.

The church is a fine cruciform, in flint and stone, with features dating from the 12th to the 15th cent. The central tower and the glass are both of the later period, and the chancel, in 14th-cent. Decorated style, is particularly fine. Margaret Lady Feversham leans over an urn in an elegant manner, and there are other monuments to the same family.

Trafalgar House, an impressive Georgian brick and stone building, is near Downton. It was given to Lord Nelson, the Admiral's brother, by the nation. Recently it has been the home of Lord Chandos.

Two m. N. of Downton is an ancient Iron Age Camp called **Clearbury Ring**.

DRAYTON, *Berkshire* (5–SU4794), lies in flat countryside about 2½ m. S. of ABINGDON. Before the First World War it used to be an entirely agricultural village, but there has now been some development. Nevertheless, the High Street still has some pleasant buildings, and a Georgian manor house, and the village has both a church-yard and village cross. The church itself shows work from many periods and was restored in the 19th cent. The doorway to the chancel is early 13th-cent. Most of the windows are Perpendicular as is the north arcade. But the most remarkable feature is an alabaster reredos with six panels, showing the life of Christ. This was discovered buried in the churchyard where it had lain for years.

DURDLE DOOR, *Dorset* (4–SY8080), is the most beautiful constantly accessible place on this county's magnificent coast. Backed by an untarnished sweep of that downland unique to Dorset, two wide bays beneath vertical chalk-cliffs are divided by a headland out of which the great "door" has been cut by the sea. A reef and the headland enclose a sheltered bathing lagoon. The fake suicide in *Far from the Madding Crowd* was filmed here. It is approached through a large caravan park, but once through this soon disappears from view.

One m. E., the more vaunted, lake-like **Lulworth Cove** has been tourist-industrialized, and rowing boats can be hired on it. Geologically it is spectacular, and in winter still beautiful. A derelict red-brick coastguard station and adjoining shanties still stand on the cliff top. Over the cliffs to the E. is a "fossil forest" – tree stumps fossilized.

About 2¼ m. NE., **East Lulworth** is pretty and near it is the grand ruin of **Lulworth Castle** in a wooded park. Begun in 1588 and completed in the 17th cent., it was largely destroyed by fire in 1929. The nearby chapel (1786) was the first Roman Catholic church built legally in England after the Reformation, by special permission of George III to Thomas Weld, owner of the castle.

E. of here, some 7,000 acres of beautiful country, including over 4 m. of superb coast, are used by the Army as artillery ranges and, more often than not, forbidden to the public. The Army took over the area in 1943, ostensibly till the war was over. Roads across it are periodically open, but un-exploded shells make straying unwise. A notice left on the church door of the ruined village of Tyneham reads "Please treat the church and houses with care; we have given up our homes where we have lived for generations to help with the war to keep men free. We shall return one day and thank you for treating the village kindly."

Worbarrow Bay, 1 m. S. of East Lulworth, with, towering above it, a great pyramid of extra-ordinary rock strata and colour known as the Tout, is well worth a visit, but it is regularly accessible only in August.

EAST HAGBOURNE, *Berkshire* (5–SU5388), with its timber-framed cottages with thatch, gables, zigzag brick patterns and neat little gardens, is a picture-postcard village. Perhaps the prettiest group of buildings is by the old village cross, near the church.

The church itself is impressive, with an old porch. It is mostly 14th- and 15th-cent., and has noteworthy roof beams and carved bosses. There are also 15th- and 17th-cent. brasses and some beautiful 14th-cent. glass showing the Nativity and the Virgin Mary in the north window.

West Hagbourne is only 1 m. W., and with the same half-timbered thatched houses and a pond is a small version of its neighbour.

EASTHAMPSTEAD, *Berkshire* (5–SU8566). The long arm of modern development has reached out from Bracknell to Easthampstead. However, the core of the village remains as it was, though it is now quite hard to imagine that this was a forest village, set in rural seclusion.

However, interesting historical associations take you right through the centuries. Richard II and Catherine of Aragon visited Easthampstead Park – 1¼ m. W. of the village, rebuilt in the 19th cent. and now a college. The Church of SS. Michael and Mary Magdalene is Victorian, but has a 15th-cent. brass to Thomas Berwyck, an epitaph to Elijah Fenton by Alexander Pope, and some fine windows by Burne-Jones. But to come up to date you must go into **Bracknell**, Berkshire's only New Town, which has seen much develop-ment since the war. Point Royal, a 17-storied hexagonal building by Arup Associates stands out impressively.

This is an excellent area for both golf and for walking, and the heath, forest or pine woods also have their own long history.

Caesar's Camp, 1 m. S. of Easthampstead, although probably occupied by the Romans, was originally an Iron Age camp, covering some 20 acres. It gives some fine views, and now part is incorporated into a recreation ground.

A track runs from Caesar's Camp to join the **Devil's Highway,** under 1 m. S. The road was built by the Romans and runs from London to SILCHESTER, entering Berkshire near Bagshot. Parallel to this and N. of Caesar's Camp, Nine Mile Ride, another possibly Roman road, runs from E. to W. of the forest.

Of the towns and villages around, two are par-ticularly interesting. **Binfield**, about 3 m. N., has associations with Alexander Pope, who came to live here as a boy of 12 when his father, a linen draper, retired in 1700. There are also several good Georgian houses in the neighbourhood, and the church contains a 17th-cent. hour-glass.

Ascot – which again has been much developed at North Ascot – is, of course, famous for its race-course. Started by Queen Anne in 1711, racing was given great encouragement by the Duke of Cumberland in the 18th cent., and it was during the same century that the Royal Family started to attend regularly. The Ascot Gold Cup was first presented in 1807. Few of the original buildings remain today; the 19th-cent. grandstands have been demolished and the Queen Elizabeth II Grandstand and Tattersalls enclosure were erected in 1964.

EAST HENDRED, *Berkshire* (5–SU4588), is a pretty village under the downs, scattered with thatched and timber-built houses, some of which date back to the time when East Hendred was famous for cloth and held not only an annual fair, but also a revel as a welcome to May.

Carthusian monks built Champs Chapel in the Perpendicular style. But it is now no longer used as such, and the monks' houses have been turned into cottages. Hendred Manor also has its own 13th-cent. chapel. The Eystons have owned the house since the 15th cent. and were related to Sir Thomas More, of whom they still have memen-toes.

There is also a chapel dedicated to the same family in the parish church. Although heavily restored, the church has 13th-cent. arcades, 14th-cent. chancel, and much good woodwork, includ-ing a 17th-cent. pulpit complete with hour-glass.

West Hendred is under a mile to the W. and though smaller is also pretty. Here the church, set beside a brook, is mostly 15th-cent. Perpendicular. It has a pleasing interior with good woodwork, including the font cover, reading desk and pulpit, and some old glass.

Two round barrows lie near the village; one at Scutchamer Knob is just S. of **The Ridgeway**, and the other, on East Hendred Down, is N. of this ancient track. The Ridgeway itself is probably pre-Roman and in places rises to about 750 ft. In Berkshire it runs from above Ashbury to a point near Streatley, and is a wonderful place for views and walking. Up here the turf is springy, the flowers bloom, and groups of beech trees, known locally as follies, break the skyline. Below nestle the villages, and from above the Hendreds one can walk all the way into WANTAGE.

EAST MEON, *Hampshire* (5–SU6822), is set in one of the prettiest river valleys in Hampshire,

Kenneth Scowen

East Meon: the Norman church at springtime

with quiet lanes leading over the downs. In the hills to the S., the River Meon rises and gradually gathers strength on its way down to the Solent some 20 m. away.

The village is unspoilt and has some delightful cottages and two other remarkable buildings. The first is the church, a magnificent cruciform building, with an enriched Norman tower topped by a lead spire. The nave and transepts are mostly Norman and the church may have been built by Bishop Walkelyn, who built the first WINCHESTER Cathedral. Its chief glory is a magnificent black marble font from Tournai, with lively carvings of grapes, doves and dragons, and scenes from the life of Adam and Eve. On the outside of the church at the east end are the arms of Prior Hinton of St Swithun's Monastery, which also has a black Tournai font. He rebuilt the east part in the late 15th cent.

Opposite, the Court House has thick walls similar to those of the church, and was built in the 15th cent. The Bishops of Winchester used to hold their courts here. The house consists of a hall with offices at the north end, the south end having disappeared. Above this were living quarters. For many years incorporated into a farm, the house has now been restored into a private home.

West Meon, only 8 m. downstream, is another pretty village. Charming gabled plaster and timbered cottages, many of them thatched, are grouped together at the base of the downs. In the centre of the village is a stone cross, erected in memory of a doctor by the last of his 16 children. Lord, of Lord's cricket ground, is buried here.

To the N., 1½ m. SE. of the Pig and Whistle and just off the ALTON and West Meon road, is Coles in the village of **Privett**. Here a magnificent garden, with brilliant herbaceous borders and rose and water gardens, is sometimes open to the public.

EDINGTON, *Wiltshire* (5–ST9252). The priory church is magnificent. A cruciform, perfectly proportioned, with a central tower and splendid battlements, it soars from its setting.

In 1352, William of Edington, Bishop of Winchester but a native of this parish, founded a college for priests here. Later, at the behest of the Black Prince, this became a monastery for the Augustinian Order of Bonshommes. There was only one other foundation of this particular order in Britain, and that was at Ashridge (*see* LITTLE GADDESDEN).

The entire church, except for the porch, was built between 1352 and 1361. It is a superb illustration of the transition from the flowing Decorated style to the stiffer Perpendicular.

The porch is three-storied, the oak door massive, and inside the nave stretches for some 75 ft, with six arches each side. The beautiful pink and white plasterwork was added in the 17th cent. and the pulpit is of the same date. This part was for the use of the parish, while the chancel was reserved for the monks. A screen, 1500 but restored, divides the two and leads into the chancel, which has some extremely fine 14th-cent. carving.

The magnificent stained glass in the Lady Chapel is the same date as the church. There are some fine tombs, including some brought from IMBER. The splendid monument to Sir Ralph Cheney is 15th-cent.

Both inside and outside the church are the consecration crosses for which it is also famous. It is interesting to note that some of the masons' marks here are the same as those in WINCHESTER, which was rebuilt by William of Edington. Sadly little remains of the monastery, except the great stone walls and the fishponds, and there is not much to the village of Edington besides this great church.

EMSWORTH, *Hampshire* (5–SU7405), lies between two small creeks on the extreme SE. corner of the county, on CHICHESTER harbour.

It is an old port, which had its heyday in the 18th cent. and then fell on less prosperous times, until it became a yachting centre and took on a new lease of life. Yacht building is Emsworth's chief industry, and the harbour is usually bright with the masts of small boats.

There are some good Georgian corners in the town, and two splendid old tide mills, which obtained their power from the inflow of tidal water. One stands out against the jetty down on the quayside, and the other is not far away to the W. of the town.

At **Warblington**, 1½ m. W., the church has a Saxon core, and, in the churchyard, huts for watchmen against body-snatchers who crept up from the nearby creek at the dead of night.

EVERSHOT, *Dorset* (4–ST5704). A small village in the hills with a main street that appears oddly urban, with raised pavements and rows of bow shop-windows built on much older house faces of yellow and grey stone. Equally odd is the shape of its church with a spike of a spire. Rebuilt in 1853, it has a high handsome chancel and a good 16th-cent. brass memorial to a rector. The River Frome rises here to flow to POOLE Harbour. The country around has long contours and great trees, and is little defaced.

About 2 m. W., **West Chelborough**, at the end of a road, is just a few houses and a farm set around a tiny golden church of great charm. Behind it is an old orchard and a pastoral view over a tree-speckled plain.

FARINGDON, *Berkshire* (5–SU2895), lying on low hills between the Thames and the Vale of the White Horse, looks almost like a Cotswold town, since many of the buildings are of stone.

Strategically placed, Faringdon has had a very long history. The Anglo-Saxon kings probably once had a palace here. During the 12th-cent. civil wars there were disturbances here, and during the 17th cent. Radcote Bridge – 2½ m. N. and the oldest bridge over the Thames – was fortified against encroaching Parliamentarians. The town was much damaged during this period. The church steeple was knocked off by a cannon-ball, and the unfortunate Sir Robert Pye, who was married to Hampden's sister, was forced to besiege his own father's home, Faringdon House, on Cromwell's behalf.

However, Faringdon House has survived and the present building dates back to 1780. The Market Hall – for Faringdon has always been an important market town – is 17th-cent. and stands on pillars. The cruciform Church of All Saints is mostly 13th-cent. in Transitional style, with fine carving on the nave capitals. There are some fine monuments both to the Pye family and to the Untons who lived at Wadley House, 1 m. E., which still has some old woodwork.

To the N. of the town, 266 acres of field and woodland belong to the National Trust. To the E. Lord Berner's Folly – probably the last built in this country, in the 1930s – tops Faringdon Hill and gives marvellous views over the Thames valley.

Coleshill, W. of Badbury Hill (*see* GREAT COXWELL), is also set high at 400 ft, giving good views. There are some attractive buildings, and Pratt's splendid Coleshill Park burnt down in 1955, once stood here. **Shellingford**, 3 m. SE., has a limestone church which has been well restored, and contains 17th- and 18th-cent. monuments as well as some old glass in the east window.

FARNBOROUGH, *Hampshire* (5–SU8753), has developed enormously owing to its proximity to Aldershot. It is the home of the Royal Aircraft Establishment and the site of the Air Show, usually held every other year.

In 1881 the Empress Eugénie of France came here to Farnborough Hill, a gabled, turreted house built in 1862, now a convent. There she lived until her death in 1920. She added to the house and built an abbey for the Benedictines and the Church of St Michael, in splendid flamboyant French Gothic style, with a marbled floor and a dome. In the crypt she built a mausoleum with three magnificent granite tombs, for herself, Napoleon III and the Prince Imperial. The tombs, in the shape of a crucifix, each weigh 5 tons, and are reached by a fine stairway.

Nearby, the Church of St Peter has a 12th-cent. painting, depicting three saints, Agnes, Mary Magdalene and, appropriately, Eugenia. The church has a Norman nave and a 17th-cent. weather-boarded tower.

Two m. to the S. lies **Aldershot**, the home of the British Army, with its army museums and the Prince Consort Military Library.

FLEET, *Dorset* (4–SY6380). Suddenly the WEYMOUTH suburbs give way to an area in contrast extraordinarily quiet, its few houses almost invisible for trees, with fields sloping to the long lagoon called the Fleet which is flapped by ABBOTSBURY swans and rich in eels and bass. There is no village now. Most of East Fleet, round which Meade Falkner set his novel *Moonfleet*, was destroyed in the great storm of 1824 which sent at least one ship hurtling over the 30-ft top of the CHESIL BANK, and fire in 1938 virtually finished it off. Just a few cottages remain and the chancel of the old church containing 17th-cent. brasses to the Mohuns. The new church (1827–9), about ½ m. W. of the old, standing red-lichen clothed in a beech wood, is inside pleasantly unconventional with an apsidal chancel. You are likely to feel more welcome in this district if you park and walk, rather than drive to the limit of possibility.

FONTHILL, *Wiltshire* (5–ST9330). Near Fonthill Gifford and Fonthill Bishop once stood Fonthill Abbey – a Gothic dream translated into reality by William Beckford, an imaginative, but spoilt son of a London lord mayor.

At 21 he came into a million pounds sterling, and later achieved some reputation as a writer. Returning to England after travelling abroad, he commissioned Wyatt – the architect who destroyed much at SALISBURY Cathedral and elsewhere – to build him an abbey, half to be ruined, half perfect.

Work on this fantastic building started in 1796 and continued for some years, its progress followed by a fascinated public. The abbey was built in the form of a cross, with a huge Gothic tower some 275 ft high at the centre. The whole was considered by William Hazlitt to be "a glittering waste of industrious idleness".

In 1800 Nelson and Lady Hamilton paid a visit, amidst great pomp and splendour, to a still unfinished abbey. But in 1823 Beckford retired to BATH and sold the estate to John Farquhar for the immense sum of £330,000, warning him that the tower was unsafe. So it proved, as in 1825 it subsided and the whole abbey fell into ruins.

A. F. Kersting

Forde Abbey: the south porch

However, in 1859, the Marquess of Westminster built another house close by – this time in Scottish Baronial style.

Though little remains of the abbey, there is still a splendid gateway to the park at Fonthill Bishop – a village with some thatched cottages and a Victorian church. The best way to gain an idea of the attractive wooded country is to approach **Hindon**, drive on to Fonthill Gifford, and turn off to Fonthill Bishop in order to drive past the lake.

FORDE ABBEY, *Dorset* (4–ST3504), is now a large private house, a magnificent, but not always harmonious, Ham-stone mixture of Tudor and mid-17th-cent. embracing parts that are medieval. It has beautiful informal gardens and the view on a bright day of its south front from across its lily-lake to the SW. is superb. Its most famous contents are the large tapestry copies of Raphael's cartoons of scenes from the Acts of the Apostles, the work of Brussels weavers brought to England by Charles I.

The original abbey for 12 Cistercian monks was built in 1142–8 and by 1200 had achieved great wealth and scholastic reputation, which (unlike many monasteries) it retained till dissolved in 1539. It was much enlarged and embellished by its last abbot, Thomas Chard. Thereafter it seems to have been left to decay until bought as his residence, *c.* 1649, by Sir Edmund Prideaux, shortly to become Oliver Cromwell's Attorney-General, who had it extended to its present proportions. The next Prideaux in 1685 backed

the Duke of Monmouth, and paid a £15,000 fine in consequence. In 1702 the estate came by marriage to Sir Francis Gwyn, Secretary of War to Queen Anne who, for services rendered, presented him with the celebrated tapestries. From 1814 to 1817 the house was rented by Jeremy Bentham, the philosopher, among whose regular guests was James Mill. It came to its present owners at the end of the 19th cent.

It is frequently open to the public and, though there are no conducted tours, a good guide book is available.

FORDINGBRIDGE, *Hampshire* (5–SU1413). A medieval bridge, much restored and widened, crosses the Avon at Fordingbridge and gave the town its name. The views from here are attractive.

Fordingbridge is on the NW. of the New Forest and at one time provided the only exit at this point. Formerly known for the manufacture of canvas and sail cloth, it is now a market town, much favoured by holidaymakers, especially those who like fishing, walking and exploring generally.

A fine avenue of limes and sugar loaf yews leads to the church, which shows Early English, Decorated and Perpendicular work. The beautifully carved 15th-cent. roof in the north chancel chapel is remarkable, and outside, on the north wall of the north chapel, is a "Miracle Stone", said to have special properties.

At **Hale Purlieu** and **Millersford Plantation**, 3 m. NE. of Fordingbridge, 512 acres of moor and woodland belong to the National Trust, and Bronze Age remains have been found in the three barrows here.

Hale Park, also on the River Avon, lies a little way N. A Georgian mansion with fine contents, it was built by the architect Thomas Archer as his own home in 1715, and was partly remodelled by Henry Holland in 1770. Both house and gardens are open to the public.

FRESHWATER, *Isle of Wight* (5–SZ3486), near the Freshwater Bay to **Alum Bay** road, is chiefly associated with Tennyson, who lived in the village for 30 years. Across a rustic bridge named after him, a footpath leads to the High Down or Tennyson's Down, his daily haunt. A 38-ft monument, visible for miles, commemorates the poet. His house is now a hotel.

FROYLE, *Hampshire* (5–SU7542). Within easy reach of both ALTON and ODIHAM, Froyle is remarkable for its church, although there are also some interesting old houses in the village.

The red-brick Church of the Assumption of the Blessed Virgin Mary was rebuilt in 1722 and restored in the 19th cent. The chancel is in early Decorated style, and the east window has reticulated tracery with painted heraldic glass of the same period. Here can be seen the arms of Edward the Confessor, Edward I, Margaret of France, and Edward II as Prince of Wales. There is more 14th-cent. glass in the nave. The altar rails are Jacobean, and the brass chandelier 18th-cent.

GOSPORT, *Hampshire* (5–SZ6199), was for a long time merely a fishing hamlet, but it then became famous for yacht and boat building and also as a victualling station for the Navy. One of its most famous citizens was Henry Cort of LANCASTER. In the 18th cent. he set up his forge for iron puddling here, and the resultant discoveries eventually gave a huge fillip to the pig-iron industry.

The town was greatly damaged during the war and huge new buildings now line the seashore. Nearby is the Church of the Holy Trinity, originally late 17th-cent. but rebuilt in the 19th cent. Inside is an organ which once belonged to the Duke of Chandos and on which Handel composed some of his music.

Gosport Railway Station was designed by Sir William Tite, and between 1842, when it was built, and 1847 it also served PORTSMOUTH. Although badly damaged by fire and not used now, part remains, including the south façade with its splendid colonnades. Queen Victoria used to come here on her way to COWES on the Isle of Wight, and a special line ran from Gosport Station to the former Royal Railway Station, which now lies in the Royal Clarence Victualling Yard belonging to the Navy. Although some buildings remain, both platform and tracks have disappeared.

GREAT BEDWYN, *Wiltshire* (5–SU2764). Both the Kennet and Avon Canal and an old Roman road cross the village, which is on the edge of SAVERNAKE FOREST. The great avenue of beeches which starts almost at MARLBOROUGH eventually leads to Tottenham House, just S. of Great Bedwyn. Tottenham is a splendid mansion, in Corinthian style, and was formerly the home of the Marquess of Ailesbury, hereditary Warden of Savernake, but it now houses a school.

Although important as far back as the 7th cent., Great Bedwyn in Tudor times was "but a poore thing to syght", thought Leland. However, there is an old square and a flint church with a 14th-cent. tower and 13th-cent. chancel. The arcades, with their richly carved capitals in the nave, date back to late Norman times. Among the monuments is one to Sir John Seymour, also hereditary Warden of Savernake, and father of Jane Seymour.

Little Bedwyn is only 1½ m. SW. and also on the canal. Between the two is **Chisbury Camp**, an old Iron Age camp covering some 15 acres. Since it is 576 ft above sea-level, the views are fine. Just near, almost on the side of the camp, is a 14th-cent. chapel to St Martin. Built in flint, in Decorated style, it is now scheduled as an Ancient Monument.

GREAT COXWELL, *Berkshire* (5–SU2693). The enormous 13th-cent tithe barn, now belonging to the National Trust, is as magnificent today as it was when built by the Cistercian monks of BEAULIEU Abbey, to whom King John gave this manor. It is 152 ft long, 44 ft wide, and nearly 50 ft high, and is built in stone, with a stone-tiled

roof, in the shape of a cross. The east and west doors are original and the porch over the west door is particularly attractive. The thick walls are supported by buttresses, and inside, the splendidly timbered roof rests on beams and oak pillars.

The village church is mostly 13th-cent. with a Perpendicular top to its tower. The tracery on the north doorway should be noted.

From outside there are superb views of the White Horse and of **Badbury Hill**, an ancient earthwork set on a 500-ft hill, only 1 m. N.

HAMBLE, *Hampshire* (5–SU4806). Boat building, fishing, oysters, crabs and lobsters have all, in their time, brought fame to Hamble. Oyster shells found at SILCHESTER probably came from here. About 20,000 oysters a year were supplied by the priory to WINCHESTER, and the Hamble river supplied several ships for the Siege of Calais in 1346.

Set almost at the mouth of the Hamble river, this was once just a quiet fishing village, and although aircraft and other industries are now established here, the old village and the wharf remain as pretty as ever. From the wharf a steep street leads eventually to a square, one side of which has been made into a car park. The buildings around are pleasant, and from there the road leads on to the peaceful green.

There was once a Benedictine priory here. Founded in 1109, it was eventually bought by William of Wykeham. Of the buildings little remains, but the chancel of the Church of St Andrew – now in Early English style – served the monks, while the Norman nave was for parish use. The old trussed roof rafters with tie-beams are interesting, and the fine east window of the chancel is 13th-cent.

Hamble is famous as a yachting centre. Activities reach a high point in July at the time of the regatta, but at most times there is plenty to watch in the harbour. Alternatively, from Hamble Common you can either look back over the New Forest, or watch the big liners gliding sedately down SOUTHAMPTON Water.

Bursledon, 4 m. upstream, is well worth a visit, not only for attractive views over the river, but also for the quay and the old village, dotted with pretty cottages. This part remains relatively untouched in spite of new building.

Botley, at the head of the tidal reach of the Hamble, is busy, but there are some pleasing houses of the 16th and 17th cents. and later. One m. below Botley the National Trust acquired some 74 acres of land to preserve the beauties of the river.

HAMBLEDON, *Hampshire* (5–SU6414). To enthusiasts Hambledon means cricket. To others it is a pretty place, lying in a valley surrounded by wooded downland. It was at one time fairly isolated, which perhaps helped to preserve its charm, for there is plenty of Georgian and some timber-framed building in evidence.

The church, which impressed William Cobbett

by its size, is a mixture of many architectural styles. The nave still shows signs of Anglo-Saxon work. It was enlarged in Norman times, added to later, and finally restored in the 19th cent. A huge yew stands in the churchyard, which has good 17th- and 18th-cent. headstones and the graves of some famous cricketers. Nearby is the rectory, mainly of the 17th cent. Manor Farm is 13th-cent.

As to cricket, it was the Hambledon Club that gave the game its first proper rules, and the famous pitch where they played lies about 2 m. NE., at **Broadhalfpenny Down**. The club was most important between about 1772 and 1787, when, with its help, the M.C.C. was founded. Nearby is the old Bat and Ball Inn, which has recently been enlarged but still retains its old façade and narrow bar. Opposite is an imposing granite monument to commemorate cricket played here between 1750 and 1787.

Since those times there has been a new development, for today about 3,000 bottles of white wine are produced annually from local grapes. At certain times the vineyards and the new press-house may be visited.

HAMBLEDON HILL, *Dorset* (4–ST8512). A lonely, grass-covered chalk hill, it is worth climbing for more than just its mighty earthworks, raised for defence at various times between the Stone Age and the Roman conquest. Its sides being too steep both for the plough and the masses, it is a natural sanctuary for butterflies, including the beautiful marbled-white, and for small birds, and, though only 623 ft high, the view from the top is tremendous. The easiest approach is from about ½ m. SE. of Child Okeford. The path is a few yards N. of a lay-by and leads through fine beeches. Another, longer way is from ½ m. further SE., through a magnificent, dark, yew wood.

Hod Hill, its slightly lower neighbour to the SW., has earthworks of a similar vintage and also traces of a Roman camp, *c.* A.D. 45–63, in the north-west corner.

On the eastern slopes of Hambledon General Wolfe trained his troops before embarking to take Quebec. And here, too, around Shroton, in 1645 the Dorset Clubmen, some 4,000 men concerned less with who won the Civil War than that both sides should stop plundering, gathered to make their point. They were routed by Cromwell's army.

HAMMOON, *Dorset* (4–ST8114). A road flanked by willows and "liable to flooding" leads across the River Stour to this glowing garden hamlet. Almost side by side and in happy contrast are the tiny, towerless church with red-tiled roof and the early 16th-cent. manor house with dark-thatched roof and whitish stone façade. The church, cleanly restored, has a fine 15th-cent. stone reredos found in a London scrapyard, beautiful 1635 pulpit, superb oak door *c.* 1400 and unconventional 18th-cent. roof. In the Middle Ages the manor was held by the Norman baron family, the de Mohuns, from whom the hamlet

derived its name, Hammoon meaning "river-land of the Mohuns".

HARTLEY WINTNEY, *Hampshire* (5–SU 7756). There used to be a priory here, but it has disappeared. However, on the site stand two large barns dating back to pre-Dissolution times.

The country around this large village, bisected by the main road and partly set round a large green, is attractive heath, common and woodland.

West Green House is just over 1 m. W. A charming house dating mostly from the early 18th cent., it now belongs to the National Trust and is open to the public. Built in red brick, the house is square and has a half octagonal porch on the north front and an attractively enclosed forecourt. The furniture is mostly Regency, and much of the west front is taken up by a beautiful panelled room. At one time the house belonged to General Hawley, thought to have been the natural son of George I. He took part in unpleasant repressions after the 1745 Rebellion, which earned him the name of "Hangman" Hawley.

Interesting villages are scattered in the area. **Greywell**, 4 m. SW., has attractive cottages and a church with a rare late-15th-cent. screen complete with rood-loft and stairway. Greywell Moor, nearby, has been made into a sanctuary for wildlife.

Eversley, 4 m. NE., is famous for having Charles Kingsley as its rector from 1842 to 1875. The church at which he preached was rebuilt in the 18th cent. and restored in the 19th, and Kingsley lies buried in the churchyard.

Bramshill, 4 m. N., has a famous Jacobean house, Bramshill House, which was built between 1605 and 1612 for Lord Zouche, who meant to give it to Charles I's eldest brother, but as he died it was never finished. It is now used as a police college. The park contains Scotch firs, said to have been planted in the 17th cent.

HARWELL, *Berkshire* (5–SU4989). Set among orchards and fruit trees, in contrast to the bare chalk hills to the S., the village retains its charm in spite of development.

About 1½ m. SW. the Atomic Energy Research Establishment spreads over hundreds of acres and its enormous reactors and generator stand out as landmarks for miles around. But in the village itself all is peace, with some 15th-cent. buildings, 18th-cent. almshouses, and Middle Farm, most of which is 14th-cent.

St Matthew's Church is interesting and parts probably date from the 12th cent. Most of the present cruciform building is Early English, with a chancel in the Decorated style. Particularly noteworthy are the carved figures, two of which are by the chancel arch.

HAVANT, *Hampshire* (5–SU7106). Havant was once a market town, famous for the making of parchment, but it now takes the overspill from PORTSMOUTH. In the centre of the old town the Church of St Faith stands where four streets meet. It is mainly Early English in style, though much restored. It has an old foundation, since some of the piers rest on Roman concrete. The chancel is 13th-cent., the vestry 14th-cent., and there is a brass to William Aylward, 1413, rector here and private secretary to William of Wykeham.

One m. S. of Havant is the pretty village of **Langstone**, from which a road leads to HAYLING ISLAND.

HAYLING ISLAND, *Hampshire* (5–SU7201), is situated between Langstone and CHICHESTER harbours, and is joined to the mainland by road from Langstone. It is a very small island, only 10 sq. m. and about 4 m. long, but its history, as the old earthwork shows, stretches back centuries.

William the Conqueror gave Hayling Island to the Abbey of Jumièges, in Normandy, but the priory then built was destroyed by storms in the 14th cent. Although later rebuilt, it was suppressed in the 15th cent.

The island, ringed by sandy beaches, is completely flat, with woods to the centre and the north which are the quieter parts. Hayling North was completely burnt down in the 18th cent. except for the Early English church, which also escaped renovation in the 19th cent. The timber-front porch is 15th-cent., the font 13th-cent., and the poppyhead pews 14th-cent. The churchyard is full of late-18th-cent. and early-19th-cent. tombstones. One shows a wheatsheaf, another a sorrowing couple, and a third has this sad little rhyme:

Ye Virgins fair, your fading charms survey
She was what'er your tender hearts can say,
Let opening roses, drooping lilies, tell,
Like these she bloomed, and ah!, like these she fell.

Hayling South is the busier village, and bungalows radiate outwards to Mengham and West Town. There was some development here in the 19th cent., and part of a grandly planned crescent remains. The church, which is large and beautiful, is one of the best examples of Early English style in this district. The east chancel window has good 19th-cent. glass, and there is an Anglo-Saxon basin on show.

HEADBOURNE WORTHY, *Hampshire* (5–SU4831), is only 1½ m. N. of WINCHESTER, and is attractively set·on chalk downs. The church lies among woods a little away from the village, near a stream and the main Winchester road. It is mainly Anglo-Saxon, with later additions. There is an attractive 15th-cent. brass to a Winchester schoolboy. But it is the remains of the 11th-cent. rood, set against the west wall of the original Anglo-Saxon church, that are supremely important. The rood shows Christ, the Virgin Mary and St John, with the Hand of God above.

From the neighbouring village of **Kingsworthy**, 1½ m. N., there are attractive walks along the River Itchen. One footpath, the Nuns Walk, leads to Winchester. The village also boasts a 16th-cent. inn, the Coach and Horses.

HEYTESBURY, *Wiltshire* (4–ST9242). Heytesbury, on the River Wylye, is the place to go for magnificent views over the downs. To the S. lies the ancient **Corton Barrow**.

The village has delightful almshouses belonging to the Hospital of St John and St Katherine, restored in the original 17th-cent. style. The church is mostly of the 12th, 13th and 15th cents., and has attractive glass by Gibbs. One m. away lies **Knook**, also on the Wylye. At the church, which is Norman but much restored, there is a handsome carved tympanum at the south doorway. It shows animals feeding on trees and is said to date back to the 11th cent.

HIGHWORTH, *Wiltshire* (5–SU2092). Set 400 ft above sea-level, the town commands magnificent views over three counties. Some of the buildings are attractive and date from the 17th and 18th cents. The church tower still bears the mark of a cannon-ball which struck it during the Civil War. Inside is an interesting and curious memento. For there, on display, is the tattered tunic worn by some medieval knight long ago. Of the villages nearby, perhaps **Castle Eaton** on the River Thames is the most attractive.

HILTON, *Dorset* (4–ST7802). A hamlet of grey flint and dark thatched cottages situated in a combe hugged by wooded spurs of Bulbarrow Hill. Its church, mainly 15th-cent., has fragments taken from MILTON ABBEY at the Dissolution which include a set of early-16th-cent. panel paintings under the tower, north aisle windows (not glass), and porch fan vaulting.

Two m. N. **Bulbarrow**'s summit (902 ft) is the county's second highest, and has a fine view N. over Blackmoor Vale. There is an orientation stone in the car park.

About ¾ m. W. of here is an Iron Age fort, **Rawlsbury**, from which there is another good view. And over the hill SW. of Hilton, in the valley of the Devil's Brook (about 2 m. round by road), **Bingham's Melcombe** is one of the most praised manor houses in the area. The gatehouse is 13th-cent., the house basically mid-16th-cent. with sensitive additions. It was built for the Binghams and retained by them till 1895. It is not normally open, but the small restored 14th-cent. church in its grounds is. It contains fragments of medieval glass, a 17th-cent. chapel screen and the history of the Binghams in monuments.

Some 1½ m. NE. of Bulbarrow, **Ibberton** has one of the most attractively situated churches in the county, with 50 steps leading up to it. It is mainly 15th-cent. with some old glass.

HORTON, *Dorset* (5–SU0307). A faintly mysterious place, in a landscape of big, sweeping fields. Beside the rather battered-looking church, grass growing from the brim of its tower, was once a nunnery of turbulent history, then a priory. A ghostly shrouded lady is intermittently seen about the parish. The church, rebuilt in 1722, possibly to a design by Vanbrugh, has a

Kenneth Scowen

Hurley church

bright interior: an 18th-cent. reredos with gold and cherubs, a blue and gold painted staircase to the pulpit, and a shining brass lectern. There are two extraordinarily fine effigy-tombs to the Norman Sir Giles de Braose and his wife. Another monument is to one Henry Hastings, who hunted stags and ladies here both with equal zeal until he was over 80, and who always dressed in green. When in 1697 Humphrey Sturt acquired the lordship of the manor he apparently stripped the church of all monuments to his immediate predecessors save that to a girl aged six. He also built the fantastic 120-ft tower on the hill to the S. for spotting deer herds. He used ladders rather than a staircase for getting to the top. In 1685, the Duke of Monmouth fleeing from SEDGEMOOR was captured in the "Monmouth Ash" on Horton Heath, some 2 m. E., betrayed by a woman who afterwards committed suicide.

One m. SW., high on a hill with views to the Isle of Wight, is the quaint little **Chalbury** church. It is red-tiled and white-washed without, with modern grey gloss paint over Georgian box pews within.

And 2¾ m. SW., **Witchampton** is a smart, pretty village at the gates of Crichel House, possibly the grandest of all Dorset's 18th-cent. houses but not open and only very distantly visible from any public place.

HUNGERFORD, *Berkshire* (5–SU3368). Near this old town, set on the Roman road to BATH, are chalk downs, wooded hills and a charming river valley. For Hungerford lies not only on the Kennet and Avon Canal, but also on the River Kennet, which has always been famous for both trout and crayfish. "A fayre river", it was said, "which yieldeth store of fishes and especiallie trowtes".

John of Gaunt, Duke of Lancaster, first gave the town its fishing rights in the 14th cent., and they have been jealously guarded ever since. He also gave the town a horn, which is now kept in the Town Hall. For many years, on the Tuesday after Easter, all those who held fishing rights were summoned to attend the court by horn, while two tuttimen (tithe-men), carrying decorated poles, went round the houses extracting kisses in return for an orange, and even today, although much of the pageantry has disappeared, this particular day is celebrated.

Pepys did not think much of the town, but Hungerford has a pleasant, wide High Street and is not industrialized. The Bear Hotel was given both to Anne of Cleves and Catherine Howard, and amongst other monarchs, William III stayed here in 1688. Even today Hungerford continues the old tradition of presenting any sovereign passing through with the red rose of Lancaster.

HURLEY, *Berkshire* (5–SU8283). The river at Hurley splits to form islands, which together with some charming backwaters make this stretch of the Thames very attractive.

The village itself has some delightful half-timbered cottages, the Old Bell inn – said to be one of the oldest inns in the county – and the ruins of an old mansion and a monastery.

Edith, sister of Edward the Confessor, is thought to be buried here, and a church stood here since Anglo-Saxon times, but later a Benedictine monastery was formed, and consecrated in 1086 by St Osmund, Bishop of Sarum.

The ruins of the old buildings can still be seen in a quadrangle charmingly named Paradise. The nave of the parish church is part of the old monastery, and all windows, except one, are Norman, as are most of the doorways. The church, which was restored in the 19th cent., also shows traces of Anglo-Saxon work, and contains monuments to the Lovelaces.

Of the monastery parts remain, including a section of the old refectory now built into a house. At the time of the Dissolution, the monastery passed to the Lovelace family. They built Ladye Place, a Tudor mansion, destroyed in 1837, but traces of which, set among beautiful gardens, can still be seen. In the vaults of the house – originally part of the monastery – John, Lord Lovelace and his friends met when plotting the overthrow of James II in the 17th cent. Nearby are two 14th-cent. barns, and a circular dovecot of much the same date.

HURSLEY, *Hampshire* (5–SU4225). Set at over 500 ft on the downs W. of WINCHESTER, Hursley has pretty cottages, some of them Tudor. The great man of the village was its vicar, John Keble, poet, essayist and leader of the Oxford Movement. Keble College, OXFORD was named after him. He had the parish church entirely rebuilt in about 1848, except for the tower, and lies in the churchyard, as does Richard Cromwell, son of Oliver. Richard Cromwell once lived at Hursley Park. In the grounds, on the site of an Iron Age fort, are the remains of Merdon Castle, built by Henry de Blois, Bishop of Winchester, in the 12th cent. All that remain are mounds and the old well which is said to be 300 ft deep.

One m. from Hursley there are several ancient barrows and the remains of a camp. This was, it is thought, the site of a battle between the Anglo-Saxons and the Danes. For good views of the district go to **Farley Down** nearby, which has a monument to a racehorse.

HURSTBOURNE TARRANT, *Hampshire* (5–SU3853), set in the upper Test valley, is one of the prettiest villages in the county. It was greatly admired by William Cobbett, and acquired the last half of its name when it belonged to a nunnery in Dorset in the 13th cent. One of the best places for a view of the village roofs below is from the steep bank on the south side of the valley.

The flint church is of interest. Although the south door is late Norman, the rest of the church dates from many periods. Inside are some remarkable early 14th-cent. paintings. One shows the Three Quick and the Three Dead, and nearby, rather fainter, are traces of a wheel of the Seven Deadly Sins.

IDSWORTH, *Hampshire* (5–SU7414). There is no village here, just an avenue of lime trees and a church in a field, with a cottage – part of the

stables of the former big house – below.

The church was originally 12th-cent., but widened in the 16th cent., and carefully restored in 1912 to give an 18th-cent. atmosphere. It contains some remarkable 14th-cent. wall paintings. The upper frieze shows men, one with a bow and a horn, with dogs sweeping through the forest to meet a strange wolf-like creature. This may be the story of St Hubert, who cured a man from thinking himself a wolf. The paintings below show scenes from the life of St John the Baptist. His prison, a crenellated tower, is there, so too is St John with his fearsome executioner. Also shown are the tables laid for Herod's feast, while Salome dances and St John's head appears on a charger. The paintings show great vitality and are mostly in reds and yellows. On the jambs of the east window in the chancel are two portraits of St Peter and St Paul.

IMBER, *Wiltshire* (4–ST9648). "Imber on the Down, Four miles from any town", runs the old couplet, and it paints a fairly accurate picture. For Imber lies in the chalk emptiness of Salisbury Plain – a plain measuring some 20 m. by 23 m., which used to be just grassland. Nowadays some parts are cultivated and the army has also brought changes. Imber is a slightly desolate place, but interesting as it is a forgotten village, which has always been somewhat cut off. It has for a long time been in the Army Training Area, and is now half destroyed. The small Decorated and Perpendicular church is fenced off by barbed wire, but is open at least once a year. (For the specific date check with H.Q. Strategic Command, Wilton, Salisbury, Wilts.)

INGLESHAM, *Wiltshire* (5–SU2098), lies in the north of the county, in the green valley of the Thames, just above the last lock. More hamlet than village, it consists of a few honey-coloured stone buildings, an ancient village cross, and the church. It is for this towerless church, mostly Transitional and Early English, that the village is famous. Some of the windows are Perpendicular. Through the efforts of William Morris who lived nearby, it is one of the few churches to have escaped restoration. The ancient roof beams, old screens, Jacobean box pews and uneven floor are completely unaltered. Traces of medieval wall painting even remain, and there is a much weathered sculpture of the Virgin and Child with the hand of God reaching down, dating back to the 11th cent. Fragments of early glass brighten some windows, but most are clear. Outside in the churchyard are attractively carved Georgian tombstones.

INKPEN, *Berkshire* (5–SU3564). No one can miss Inkpen, for the great beacon soars out from the landscape. The village itself has a church dating from the 13th cent., but much restored later. Inside lies a Crusader knight somewhat mutilated. But Inkpen has other claims to fame, especially in the horticultural field. Le Nôtre who planned the gardens at Versailles stayed in the late-17th-cent. rectory, and may have had something to do with the design of the garden. It is also thought that the tulips, lilies and other flowers that here grow wild were first introduced from Asia Minor by the Knights Templar.

Just S., Inkpen Beacon rises to a height of 954 ft and is a landmark for miles around. The area must have been important since earliest times, for a prehistoric beaker and bowl have been found on the hill, and the Wansdyke, an ancient defensive earthwork, runs from near here all the way to Somerset.

The views from the flat summit of Inkpen are spectacular, the bare chalk ridges contrasting with the richness of the Kennet valley.

ITCHEN STOKE, *Hampshire* (5–SU5532). The River Itchen rises at Hinton Ampner, flows past Itchen Stoke and Itchen Abbas on its way to WINCHESTER, and then finally joins the sea at SOUTHAMPTON. It is a charming river, with rich watermeadows and clear waters full of trout.

At one time it was far more crowded with boats than today, and as far back as the 12th cent. Bishop de Lucy, Bishop of Winchester, constructed an artificial lake and dam at ALRESFORD to improve navigation. Even as late as the second half of the 19th cent., barges were sailing peacefully up the Itchen Navigation, but as with many canals in England it is no longer navigable today.

You can still follow the same paths that have been used for centuries. The one which runs from the Bush Inn at **Ovington** to Itchen Stoke church is part of the old Pilgrims Way and makes a delightful walk. Today these two parishes are united and face each other across the river. Itchen Stoke has the traditional attractions of an English village, with thatched and half-timbered cottages grouped round a green. At Ovington there are pretty little cottages and an old mill. For some fine views of the district take the road from Itchen Stoke to **Abbotston** a village 2 m. NW. with an old mill.

Itchen Abbas, the next village downstream, is set in beautiful scenery. Within the last 100 years an old Roman villa was found nearby. Today there are signs of modern development. The church was rebuilt in Victorian times, but in the churchyard is the grave of John Hughes, said to be the last man hanged for sheep stealing in England. This was in 1825.

KIMMERIDGE, *Dorset* (4–SY9179). Its bay is geologically famous. A type of soft rock known as Kimmeridge Clay, which preserves fossils remarkably, is more deeply exposed in these cliffs than anywhere else in the world. It makes them dark, shaly and crumbling. A band of bituminous oil shale in them was mined by Britons during the Roman occupation. They polished the coal-like lumps till they looked like jet and made them into ornaments and furniture popular with the Romans; examples of these, and fossils found in the clay, can be seen in the DORCHESTER Museum. Now an oil well, sunk in 1959 and producing some 10,000 tons a year,

stands above the cliffs. Tramway tracks and broken piers, ruins of 18th- and 19th-cent. attempts to exploit the bituminous shale for solid fuel, can be traced. They failed because it smelt sulphur-foul. A row of cottages built in the mid-19th cent. for miners remains, but they were never so occupied because the company failed first. The bay is sandless and seaweedy, and is mildly popular for surfing and skin-diving. The tower about ⅓ m. E. on the cliff-top, built *c.* 1800 for uncertain purposes, is unsafe, but there are good views from round it. Army territory begins ¾ m. W. (*see* DURDLE DOOR).

One m. SE. of the thatched village (through which you pass to reach the bay) is **Smedmore House**, mainly 18th-cent., partly earlier, periodically open. Among its attractions is a collection of antique dolls.

KING'S SOMBORNE, *Hampshire* (5–SU 3631). A branch of the River Test runs through this little village with a green. King John is said to have spent time here, while hunting nearby. John of Gaunt also came, and the remains of a palace can still be seen.

The church was restored in 1886, but contains a 14th-cent. stone effigy of a priest in vestments and two 14th-cent. brasses of men with short swords and cloaks in the chancel. The large Purbeck marble font is probably 13th-cent. Nearby is Marsh Court, set above the River Test. Built in chalk, it was designed by Lutyens at the start of the century.

At **Little Somborne**, a small village nearby, there is an Anglo-Saxon nave to the church.

KINGSTON, *Dorset* (4–SY9578). Here, dominating a small, grey, hill-top village, is the finest 19th-cent. church in the area. It was built 1874–80 of local stone by local craftsmen and cost some £60,000. The pillars are of black Purbeck marble, the arches white outlined in black, the pulpit and screen of wrought iron and the chancel stone-vaulted. The architect was G. E. Street, the sponsor, the 3rd Earl of Eldon, whose family still owns the grand 18th-cent. house of **Encombe**, 1 m. SW. which is set in a marvellous amphitheatre-vale locally known as the **Golden Bowl**. The gardens of Encombe are sometimes open.

From just E. of the village there is a tremendous view of CORFE CASTLE, and from Swyre Head, about 1¾ m. SW. (the last ¾ m. being on rough track) a superb aerial view into the Golden Bowl and, in the other direction, over farmland and coppices to the sea. The conspicuous obelisk was erected by the 1st Lord Eldon, Lord Chancellor at the beginning of the 19th cent., to his brother.

KINGSTON BAGPUIZE, *Berkshire* (5–SU 4098). To the south flows the River Ock, and to the north the Thames, which is crossed by a beautiful bridge called Newbridge, leading into Oxfordshire. Certainly one of the most picturesque bridges on the river, it is probably also one of the oldest.

The River Lambourn winds through peaceful Berkshire countryside

The curious name of Bagpuize was added by a Norman of that name who acquired the manor after the Conquest. The church with its domed belfry supported by eight oak pillars was built in 1699. Nearby, a pair of beautiful wrought-iron gates lead to Kingston House, a splendid brick building dating from about 1720. At certain times of the year the gardens are open to the public and you can wander among roses, shrubs, bulbs and herbaceous borders, admiring a little chequer-brick summer-house and the house, which backs straight on to a terrace.

KINGSTON LISLE, *Berkshire* (5–SU3287). The downs rise to a height of 750 ft near this small village which lies on the edge of the Vale of the White Horse. The manor house is 18th-cent., and the church has a mainly 14th-cent. chancel and a nave which dates back to about 1200. But it is the medieval wall paintings that are principally interesting. St Peter and St Paul are painted on the jambs of the east window. On the north wall Herod's Feast with Salome dancing on her hands still stands out clearly.

But it is the blowing stone that most people come to see. It was brought down from White Horse hill, is about 3 ft high, and made of red sarsen. In *Tom Brown's Schooldays* the stone is described as being perforated by "two or three queer rat holes". If blown correctly they produce an eerie sound, and this, it is said, is how King Alfred summoned his armies.

Legends apart, this portion of the old West Saxon kingdom has many historical associations with Alfred. He was born at Wantage a few miles E. and fought some of his battles against Guthrum's Danes on the downs.

LACOCK, *Wiltshire* (4–ST9168). The village with its twisted streets, gabled roofs and timber buildings is one of the prettiest in England. The houses span the centuries, dating from medieval times to the 18th cent., but none is later than about 1800. There is a 14th-cent. barn opposite the Red Lion Hotel, an old village cross much restored and the magnificent Church of St Cyriac. Especially fine is the Perpendicular roof of the nave and the chapel north of the chancel. Fan-vaulted and beautifully decorated, here lies the tomb of Sir William Sharington. Also noteworthy are the 16th-cent. brass to the Talbots in the south transept, and the strange grotesques both inside and outside the church, including one in the north clerestory showing a man smoking a pipe.

Lacock Abbey was originally founded by Ela, Countess of Salisbury in 1229, after the death of her husband, a son of Henry II. She was a remarkable woman. Not only was she abbess for 17 years, but she became the only woman Sheriff of Wiltshire. This accounts for the fact that Lacock formerly housed one of the original copies of the Magna Carta, though today it has only a photostat copy.

In 1539, long after Ela's death, Lacock was the last religious house in England to be suppressed – perhaps because no fault could be found with its management. It was bought by Sir William Sharington, a profiteer of those days, but one with great taste. Though the abbey church was destroyed, he kept much of the original building, including the cloister, sacristy, chapter house and warming room, and he adapted them into a house for everyday living. His additions include the large courtyard, with its timber-framed building, and the large octagonal tower.

In the 17th cent. the abbey passed to the Talbots under romantic circumstances. Olive, locked up by her father for recalcitrance, leapt from the abbey into her lover's arms, thereby nearly killing him. She was fortunately saved by her petticoats billowing to break her fall, and as a result of her courage, permission to marry a Talbot was granted.

Later, in the 18th cent., John Ivory Talbot had the great hall built in Gothic style by Sanderson Miller. But the whole building at Lacock is a jumble of styles which blend into a delightful whole. Inside there is much to see, including the Mechlin Pot, dated 1500, a great cauldron said to be the nuns' cooking vessel. There is also a photograph by Henry Fox Talbot, the pioneer of photography. Dating back to 1835, the negative is now in the SCIENCE MUSEUM in London. Fox Talbot also planted some interesting rare trees in the garden, including black walnuts.

Lacock Abbey and Lacock village were both given to the National Trust in 1944 by Miss Matilda Talbot, and the abbey is open to the public. For a magnificent view of Lacock nestling below, go to **Bowden Hill** nearby, an area from which the abbey originally drew its water. **Bewley Common**, on either side of Bowden Hill, belongs to the National Trust, and there are parking facilities.

LAMBOURN, *Berkshire* (5–SU3278), on the River Lambourn, lies in a hollow between downs that are ideal for exercising horses. Today Lambourn is famous for its racing stables, but past centuries are recalled by Roman pottery found in the neighbourhood, and it is thought that a resounding defeat was inflicted on the Danes nearby in 871.

Lambourn featured as Maryland in Thomas Hardy's *Jude the Obscure*. It is a pleasant village, with some 19th-cent. almshouses built round a courtyard, and an old cross with the original shaft and steps standing near the church. This impressive cruciform building shows many styles, the earliest being late Norman, with 15th- and 16th-cent. chapels added later. Inside there is much to see, including good brasses of the 14th, 16th and 17th cents. and a delightful carving of hounds hunting a hare in an arch in the south transept. Another alabaster relief carving shows Charles I flanked by two angels, and in the north chapel the old village stocks have found their last curious resting place.

Two m. N. is an area called **The Seven Barrows**, where in fact more than 20 barrows lie grouped together in a hollow of the downs. Membury Camp, covering some 30 acres, is also nearby, though this is mostly in Wiltshire.

Away from the hills, travelling down the Lambourn River is a great pleasure, since the waters are clear, and open frequently into a series of deep transparent pools. **Eastbury** is only 2 m. SE. downstream, and here the little bridges leading to cottages have distinct charm, while the King of Mercia used to have a palace at **East Shefford**.

LAVERSTOKE, *Hampshire* (5–SU4948), on the River Test gives the impression of being set in a park, and has a group of attractive thatched cottages, built this century, nestling near the Church of St Mary. The church itself dates from 1896 and has a fine reredos copied from a medieval painting. Laverstoke House was built by Joseph Bonomi in the 18th cent. in Classical Revival style.

Behind high walls in the village lie the famous paper mills. There is a romantic story attached to their founding by Henry de Portal. When small he was concealed in an oven while soldiers searched the house for Huguenots after Louis XIV revoked the Edict of Nantes. He then fled to England, learned to make paper and founded Bere Mill near Whitchurch. Eventually, in 1724, he rose to making notes for the Bank of England.

Laverstoke is now joined to Freefolk, and in the latter is the small Church of St Nicholas, which contains a 17th-cent. monument to Sir Richard Powlett.

About 1 m. E. and also on the Test lies **Overton**, which used to be much more important than it is now. Coaches passed through and there was a market, sheep fair and silk mills. But since those glories disappeared it has become a slightly sad place. The main street is wide, and most of the town is on one side of the Test, facing the church and manor on the opposite bank.

Whitchurch is about 1 m. W. of Laverstoke and used to be a busy place in coaching days. Charles I chose to spend the night here before the second battle of Newbury in 1644. The church, which was restored in Victorian times, contains some outstanding treasures. There is an Anglo-Saxon gravestone here, which was used for years as a convenient stand by the bell ringers. Probably 9th-cent., the Latin inscription reads: "Here lies the body of Frithburga, buried in peace." Above is the bust of Christ. Frithburga may have been a nun from WHERWELL. There is also a 17th-cent. panel showing the Commandments and biblical scenes, and a remarkable set of steps leading to the belfry. Each step is a single block and the surrounding walls are of wood.

Just outside the town is **Hurstbourne Park**. Kingsley once said that he considered the park here to be the finest in England.

LETCOMBE BASSETT, *Berkshire* (5–SU 3785), in a beautiful setting below the downs, is famous for its watercress beds. Swift spent the summer here in 1714, and Thomas Hardy chose this village as his model for Cresscombe in *Jude the Obscure*. It was mentioned in the Domesday Book and the church still retains much Norman work, particularly in the chancel, but also shows traces of later styles.

On Segsbury Down, N. of the Ridgeway, the Iron Age fort is known either as **Segsbury Camp,** or Letcombe Castle. It covers about 26 acres, and it seems that the rampart was once faced with sarsen blocks, some of which can still just be seen.

W. of the village is a deep depression in the land known as the Devil's Punch Bowl.

LIDDINGTON, *Wiltshire* (5–SU2081). The village boasts attractive thatched cottages, a 17th-cent. manor house, and a church that dates back to the 13th cent. but was later restored.

High above the village, about 1 m. S., stands Liddington Castle. An ancient Iron Age earthwork, it consists of a ditch and a 40-ft-high rampart. Like BARBURY CAMP, this, too, was a favourite haunt of both Richard Jefferies – naturalist and writer – and Alfred Williams – poet – in the 19th cent. There is a plaque commemorating both men here, and there are magnificent views over three counties.

LITTLE BREDY, *Dorset* (4–SY5888). A marvellously pastoral, peaceful place, deep in a green valley beneath downs. From its church, paths under huge beeches and elms radiate to a scattering of old cottages: through the lych-gate to the thatched rectory; past splendid aged farmbuildings to a great house called Bridehead, *c.* 1830. Its church, mostly rebuilt *c.* 1850, is unexceptional within but very pretty without. Stone gateposts flanking the road to the outside world complete a sense of sanctuary.

About 1½ m. W. at **Long Bredy,** the grand house of Kingston Russell, medieval seat of the Duke of Bedford's ancestors, is not open, but from its entrance gate its almost white west front (*c.* 1730) looks very fine.

And 3 m. further to the SW., **Puncknowle** is a neat village of stone and thatch under big trees. It has a small, partly Norman and partly rebuilt church containing an intriguingly ghoulish 17th-cent. wall monument. Just SW. of the church is a 16th- and 17th-cent. manor house.

LITTLECOTE, *Wiltshire* (5–SU3070), a magnificent and romantic manor house, built between 1490 and 1520, is beautifully situated in the chalk valley of the River Kennet near the Berkshire border. In spring and summer the rich watermeadows are brilliant with wild flowers and full of birds.

The house itself is typically Tudor, the south side being of attractively mellowed brick and stonework, while the north, and some of the rest, is built in flint. But Littlecote has tragic associations.

Today it belongs to the Wills family, but previously it was the home of the Darells. A gruesome story is told of a local midwife brought secretly one night to the house to deliver a baby. Later "Wild" Darell, the last of the family, brutally murdered the child by casting it into the fire. The house then passed to Sir John Popham, a judge, perhaps given as a bribe to save Darell's life. "Wild" Darell was killed in 1598 while hunting in the park, at a spot still called Darell's Style.

It is said that the room where the baby is supposed to have been killed is haunted, and that the ghost of Darell and his hounds have been seen in the park. However, other stories connected with Littlecote are less bloodthirsty. Henry VIII is said to have courted Jane Seymour here, an event that is commemorated by their entwined initials in a stained-glass window in the magnificent great hall. Later, during the 1688 revolution, William of Orange paused here to consider the propositions put forward by James II's commissioners.

The house contains much of interest and is open to the public. There is a splendid long gallery and some magnificent armour, but perhaps most interesting of all is the Cromwellian Chapel, considered one of the finest examples of this period.

LONGFORD, *Wiltshire* (5–SU1626), seat of the Earl of Radnor, is a romantic castle and was taken by Sir Philip Sidney as a model for his castle in *Arcadia.* It was built by Sir Thomas Gorges, who bought the estate in 1573 and now lies, with his wife, in a magnificent tomb in SALISBURY Cathedral.

His wife, Helena, a Dane and former lady-in-waiting to Queen Elizabeth, wanted to base the design both on the shield of the Holy Trinity seen on an old coat of arms and on the castle at Uranienberg. John Thorpe, who also built Holland House, was called in to build the triangular house, with triangular moat and thick round towers at the corners. It almost ruined Sir Thomas financially, as piles had to be sunk to hold the foundations. However, when a Spanish galleon was wrecked while Sir Thomas was Governor of Hurst Castle, his wife begged the hull from the Queen. The ship was later discovered to be full of silver bars, and with this fortune Longford was completed in 1591.

Cromwell besieged Longford during the Civil War, but it escaped damage and in 1717 was bought by the Bouveries, who have been there ever since. Alterations and additions were made in the 18th and 19th cents., when Anthony Salvin was called in to restore the house.

Set in gardens designed originally by Capability Brown, Longford is a fascinating house. It has beautiful furniture, mainly 18th-cent., designed by Kent, Goodison and others, and some pieces have special rounded backs to fit against the circular walls. Longford also boasts a magnificent steel chair, which was presented to Emperor Rudolf II in the 16th cent. but was later looted at Prague and then sold to the Bouveries. It contains about 130 compartments depicting historical scenes stretching back to antiquity.

There is also a wonderful collection of pictures, occasionally open to the public; Velazquez, Van Dyck, Holbein and many other Continental masters are represented, as well as some from the English school, including Kneller, Gainsborough and Reynolds.

LONGLEAT, *Wiltshire* (4–ST8142). The seat of the Marquess of Bath, and one of the first of the great houses to be opened to the public, Longleat has for some time been a remarkable show-piece. Nowadays there is the added attraction of the lion park, where these great beasts roam almost in their natural state, plus monkeys, zebra, giraffe and other attractions on land and lake.

The history of the house dates back to the 13th

Longleat houses a lion park which visitors may enter in safety provided they do not leave their cars

cent. when an Augustinian priory stood here. However, little remains from that era except the fishponds SW. of the house. In 1540, after the Dissolution of the Monasteries, the house was bought by Sir John Thynne, a friend of the Protector Somerset, for £53. It has remained in the same family ever since.

Longleat is one of the finest Elizabethan houses in England, and was one of the first to be designed uniformly on all four sides. Robert Smythson was among the architects who worked on the house, which took 12 years to build, and cost £8,086 13s. 8¼d. Since that time there have been alterations and additions, but Longleat remains essentially as it was, a magnificent building with great mullioned windows, classic pillars, turrets and balustrades softening the outline.

Many people helped with the construction. Some of the first workmen were brought down from Scotland in the 16th cent., and were permitted to build one of the earliest Presbyterian chapels at **Horningsham**, the local village. It can still be seen.

In the 18th cent. Capability Brown laid out the magnificent gardens, and at the same time an orangery and terrace were added. In the 19th cent. Wyattville added stables and remodelled much of the interior, which included re-placing the original Wren staircase.

Also in the 19th cent. the 4th Marquess of Bath, influenced by all he had seen on his Grand Tour, brought Italians over to embellish the doors with marquetry, to add marble fire-places and to paint and gild the ceilings of the state rooms. The same marquess also decorated the bedrooms with charming Chinese wallpapers, which can still be seen today. Indeed there is a great deal to see at Longleat. The splendid wood roof, old panelling and fire-place in the hall are interesting, as are the magnificent tapestries, velvet hangings and some good pictures.

Over the centuries many famous people have stayed here – among them Elizabeth I, Charles II and George II. But of all visitors Bishop Ken has left the greatest impression. As Bishop of Winchester he once refused to allow Nell Gwynn to stay in the Cathedral Close. However, Charles II bore no malice and Ken became Bishop of Bath and Wells. Later on, refusing to take the oath of allegiance to William and Mary, he was offered a home at Longleat. The old library at the top of the house, where he spent much of his time, has hardly altered since the 17th cent.

New Heavens Gate – where Bishop Ken is said often to have sat – is on the WARMINSTER road. From here there is a magnificent view of the grounds and the house, situated in parkland 400 ft below in the valley.

LONG WITTENHAM, *Berkshire* (5–SU 5493), lies parallel to the Thames. It seems as long as its name suggests, and is dotted with half-timbered houses, including the Plough Inn and another house with an overhanging upper story near the church. There is also a fine village cross.

The interesting church is mainly 13th- and 14th-cent., but the carved chancel arch, the lead font and other details are Norman; some of the fine woodwork, which includes Jacobean poppyhead stalls, pulpit, screen and font-cover, was brought from Exeter College, Oxford, into whose care the church passed in 1322. The timber porch is attractive, but more interesting is the piscina, where two angels form a canopy to protect a very small sculptured knight below.

Many interesting remains have been found in the area, including an Anglo-Saxon cemetery, probably Christian, which was uncovered at Freeacre, S. of the village.

The road through the hamlet of Little Wittenham leads to **Wittenham Clumps**, two hills giving marvellous views, and the site of an Iron Age fort. (*See also* WALLINGFORD.)

LYDIARD TREGOZE, *Wiltshire* (5–SU 1084), consists of Lydiard House and the church close by. There is no village, and the curious sounding name, Tregoze, was adapted from Trois-gots in Normandy, original home of the family who once owned the estate. From the 15th to the 20th cent. the property belonged to the St John family. Then in 1943 it was bought by SWINDON Corporation, who restored the house, opened it to the public and adapted part as conference rooms.

It was remodelled in 1743, and there is splendid wood and plasterwork to be found in the state rooms. The ballroom has a Rococo ceiling. Although the original contents have all been sold, the corporation has gradually refurnished, mostly with Georgian furniture. They have also bought back some family portraits.

If Lydiard House is interesting, the church is overwhelming. Set in the park, it has always served more as a private family, rather than a parish, church, and is richly embellished with memorials to the St John family. The church itself is 15th-cent. and the naves and aisles are plain, but there is some rich 15th-cent. Flemish glass, a most moving mural of the risen Christ, and some beautiful 17th-cent. wrought-iron work.

But it is the monuments that are remarkable. For these, said John Aubrey in the 17th cent., "It exceeds all churches in this countie." In his days there were also pennants and heraldic devices. These have disappeared, but the unique triptych, erected in 1615, remains. It shows members of the St John family in Elizabethan days, and their family tree, for they were proud of sharing ancestors with the Tudor kings.

The Golden Cavalier – the lifesize figure in golden armour topped by a marble canopy – is striking. It is a monument to Edward St John who died fighting at the second Battle of Newbury in 1645. There is also a great canopied tomb to Sir John St John, who did so much to embellish this church. He died in 1648 and lies with his two wives. Among the other monuments is a charming conversation piece to Katherine St John, who married Giles Mompesson, and another carved by Rysbrack. The church is generally kept locked, but will be opened on application to the custodian.

LYFORD, *Berkshire* (5–SU3994), hidden away in the valley of the Ock, has a 17th-cent. manor house, an ancient timber-framed farm-house, and some attractive almshouses. Founded in 1611, though rebuilt later, they occupy three sides of a quadrangle and would seem well able to supply the wants of this small village. The church is in Early English style, except for the clerestory which is Perpendicular, and later restoration work. The pulpit is Jacobean.

It was at Lyford that Edmund Campion, the Jesuit martyr, was captured in July 1581. Though destined for a brilliant career, he became a Roman Catholic priest at a time when this was dangerous. A spy heard him celebrating mass at Lyford and sent for the constables to make an arrest. He was tortured and then executed at Tyburn.

LYME REGIS, *Dorset* (4–SY3492). A busy medieval port and cloth town with a part in

Kenneth Scowen

Lyndhurst: a scene in the New Forest

several of history's dramas, it became, in the mid-18th cent., one of the first seaside resorts in the South-West, beloved of Jane Austen and the society of BATH. And it remains a small resort, exceptionally beautifully situated, sloping to its wide, hill-cliffed bay, the beaches of which have more shingle than sand.

There were three outstanding moments in its history: in 1588 when the first skirmish between Drake's fleet (including five local ships) and the Armada took place in its bay; in 1644 when, strongly supporting Parliament, it withstood a two-month-long Royalist siege; and 1685 when the Duke of Monmouth and his followers landed on its beach before raising the rebellion. Another of a different sort was in 1811, when the 12-year-old Mary Anning found the famous fossilized ichthyosaurus in the rocks at Black Ven, 1 m. E. along the shore.

Perhaps its most attractive place is the old harbour called the Cobb, a little W. of the town centre, first built c. 1300 for fishermen, now thick with pleasure boats. Monmouth landed a few yards to the W. and subsequently 12 of his local supporters were hanged there. You can walk to it along the sea-front or drive from beside the A3052 car park up the hill.

In the town, the mainly 15th-cent. church, said to be sliding gradually down the hill, is interesting and quite handsome. It is built on three levels, its west porch being the nave of a Norman church on the site. It has a good 17th-cent. pulpit and gallery and, on the north wall, a probably 16th-cent. tapestry which may depict Henry VIII's marriage. The nearby Town Hall (1887–8) contains a museum of local history including good fossils. The River Lym, which drove the town's medieval cloth mills, still surges powerfully through it, and the narrow Coombe Street (best walked) leads pleasantly to an area of converted mills. In Pound Street, the way out to the W., the Peek Memorial Chapel, made from a stable in 1844, is colourfully Victorian. There is an aquarium at the Cobb.

All around Lyme Bay bits of the sandstone-topped blue lias cliffs periodically flake away, and occasionally there are mighty landslips. The greatest of these was on Christmas Day 1839 when, about 3 m. W. of the town, some 40 acres collapsed opening a chasm a mile long and up to 400 ft wide. At various times since, virtually the whole coast to the mouth of the River Axe has drastically changed face. Most of "the landslip" is now a National Nature Reserve. A path from the A3052 car park leads to it. The walk is rewarding but often muddy and overgrown and definitely not for the weak-hearted. Keep well clear of cliff-edges.

LYMINGTON, *Hampshire* (5–SZ3295), lies almost on the edge of the New Forest on the Boldre or Lymington river. Most people rush through on their way to catch the ferry to YARMOUTH on the Isle of Wight, so they miss a pleasant small town, with bright cottages and attractive Georgian and 19th-cent. houses in the broad High Street.

The church has a strangely shaped 18th-cent. cupola. The nave and galleries are Georgian, and the north chapel 13th-cent. The church contains a bust by Rysbrack of Charles Colborne, 1747, and another of Captain Rogers, 1795, by John Bacon, R.A. The poet Coventry Patmore is buried in the churchyard, and another famous writer, Edward Gibbon, once represented Lymington in Parliament.

The town once grew rich from its saltworks, known as "salterns", which were closed in the 19th cent., and in the 14th cent. it supplied far more ships for the invasion of France than PORTSMOUTH. Nowadays boat-building is confined to yachts.

Round and about there is a pleasant heath and woodland, and 1 m. N. an ancient Iron Age earthwork with triple rampart called **Buckland Rings**. In 1744 2 cwt of Roman coins were dug up here.

Milford-on-Sea, about 4½ m. W. of Lymington, has been a resort since Victorian times. Here the air is clear, the shingle beach and bathing good, and the country around pleasant. Views of ships crossing the skyline and of the Isle of Wight are attractive, and Milford also boasts a parish church mentioned in the Domesday Book, but now mostly Early English.

Hurst Castle, nearby, was built for defence by Henry VIII. At one time Charles I was held prisoner here, but today the castle is in the care of the Ministry of Public Building and Works and is open to the public.

Keyhaven, between Milford and Lymington, is a quiet little place with its own river and two sailing clubs. Nearby, the marshes which stretch to Pennington are now a bird sanctuary.

LYNDHURST, *Hampshire* (5–SU2907, known as the "capital" of the **New Forest**, is a busy tourist centre, and consists mainly of one street, dominated by the Victorian Gothic style church. The spire soars to a height of 160 ft, and inside is some splendid pre-Raphaelite glass and a fresco by Lord Leighton. Alice Liddell, the original Alice in Wonderland, is buried here.

Queen's House, an attractive 17th-cent. building, used to be the home of the Lord Warden of the forest, and the Verderers, who administer the forest, still meet here. Their Court Room, a panelled room hung with antlers, is open to the public. In it is the old dock, which has obviously been shaped with an axe, and an old stirrup, measuring about 10½ in. by 7½ in., which according to legend, once belonged to William Rufus. In reality it is much later, and in the old days only dogs which could pass through it were allowed in the forest.

The forest lies all around, and once stretched from the Wiltshire border to the coast and from the River Avon to SOUTHAMPTON. Today it covers over 92,000 acres. It was thought once to have been "full of habitations and thick set with churches", until destroyed by William the Conqueror. However, this is not true, and William was the first monarch to order more afforestation. Over the centuries, however, more and more timber was illegally felled and the forest shrank, until in the 17th cent. Charles II and William III both ordered more planting. Even so abuses continued until a commission was appointed in 1848. In the 20th cent. the forest passed into the care of the Forestry Commission.

The New Forest is not just a dense wood stretching for miles; it consists of immensely varied countryside of woods, glades, streams, ponds, heath and moorland, with villages dotting the clearings. Old earthworks and barrows are scattered in the district. Trees of many varieties – oak, chestnut, ash and beech among them – grow in the woods, where the paths are clearly marked. Many kinds of wild animals, including deer, make their home here, but the ponies should not be fed. There are also rare birds and insects and a rich variety of flowers.

Lyndhurst is surrounded by delightful villages. **Cadnam**, $3\frac{1}{2}$ m. N., has some attractive cottages and an inn. **Minstead**, the "Place where Mint grew", is about 3 m. NW., a completely unspoilt village. The church looks almost like cottages, and has a 13th-cent. nave and chancel with Georgian additions. There are box pews, galleries and family pews with their own fire-places. Not very far away is the stone which marks the place where William Rufus was killed by an arrow in 1100.

For a good view of the whole area go to **Bramble Hill**, 414 ft high, to the NW. of Lyndhurst, and to see the biggest oak in the whole of the New Forest go to Knightwood, just SW. of the town.

MAIDEN CASTLE, *Dorset* (4–SY6688). The most famous pre-Roman fortress in Britain, thrilling even if your interest in history in minimal. A maze of miniature wild-grass ravines, their sides up to 90 ft high and gracefully curved, enclose a flattish hill-top some 100 acres in area.

Though inhabited much earlier, most of the now-visible ramparts were, it seems, dug by invaders from Brittany in the 1st cent. B.C. They lived in wooden huts on the plateau and kept dogs, sheep and cattle. In *c.* A.D. 43 the eastern entrance was stormed by the Romans, the Britons' slingstones bouncing off their leather shields. Thereafter it was gradually abandoned, though in the 4th cent. a pagan temple, of which the foundations are traceable, was built by the Romano-British near its eastern end. In 1937 a mass grave of casualties to swords and arrows was found near the eastern entrance.

The conventional well-signposted approach is from DORCHESTER. Alternatively, if you make for its south-west corner, park by a gate and walk $\frac{1}{3}$ m., you may well have the whole western end to yourself. The Ministry of Public Building and Works preserves it. Finds from it can be seen in the County Museum, Dorchester.

MAIDENHEAD, *Berkshire* (5–SU8881), owes much of its growth to its position, and as far back as the 13th cent. its bridge brought prosperity. It was an important strategic point in the Civil War,

the 1688 Revolution and earlier affrays. In the 18th cent. the bridge was replaced by another, and in the 19th cent. a railway bridge with two wide spanning arches designed by Brunel was added, and later painted by Turner in his picture, *Rain, Steam and Speed.*

Maidenhead is a pleasant residential town and popular for boating. Bridge Road still has some Georgian building, and two sets of almshouses dating from 1659 and 1895, while the Henry Reitlinger Bequest Museum has interesting glass, ceramics, pictures, sculpture and other items.

Maidenhead was an important stage post on the London–Bath route and many people chose to pause here so as to cross Maidenhead Thicket – a notorious haunt of highwaymen – in daylight. As a result the main street used to be full of posting houses, at one of which Charles I while captive was allowed to meet his children. Today 530 acres of wooded countryside belong to the National Trust, and Robin Hood's Arbour, a 1st-cent. Belgic farm enclosure, has been found here.

Walks along the towpath are rewarding and **Boulter's Lock**, a famous beauty-spot, is $\frac{1}{2}$ m. away.

MALMESBURY, *Wiltshire* (4–ST9387). High on a hill between the Avon and a lesser river, Malmesbury was well situated for defence. Perhaps that is why its history stretches back for centuries, and an abbey was founded here in the 7th cent.

One of the oldest boroughs in England, this attractive small town, built mostly in stone, originally grew rich from weaving. The town's history may be traced through the architecture.

The Old Bell Inn has a 13th-cent. window, and was probably part of the old castle. The White Lion may originally have been one of the abbey buildings. In the high street stands a fine octagonal Gothic market cross dating back to the start of the 16th cent. "Right faire", commented Leland. There is also attractive 17th- and 18th-cent. building, and a 13th-cent. window in the St John's Almshouses.

The abbey, soaring above the town, is Malmesbury's chief glory. Once it was a vast cruciform building. Today the porch and nave, divided into three stories, remain and are used as a parish church. The abbey was originally Norman, with 14th-cent. additions, and the south porch has some of the best Romanesque sculpture in this country. The 12th-cent. arches are magnificent, as are the later clerestory, and the projecting box-like watch-tower. Sections of the 15th-cent. rood-screen remain, and, although empty, there is a 15th-cent. tomb to King Athelstan, grandson of Alfred the Great. A visit to the Porch Room to see the illuminated MS. is also memorable.

After the Dissolution of the Monasteries the abbey was handed over, at a price, to one Master Stumpe, a rich clothier, who set up his looms here. However, it is thanks to him that the abbey was turned into a most noble parish church. The last restoration was made in 1928.

Thomas Hobbes, who wrote *Leviathan*, was born in Malmesbury. So, too, was Oliver, an 11th-cent. monk, who fixed wings to his hands and feet and jumped from the abbey tower. Sadly such initiative left him lame for life. In the churchyard lies one Hannah Twynoy, who met her end by a "Tyger fierce" in 1703.

Some pleasing villages lie within easy reach of Malmesbury. **Charlton**, 2½ m. NE., boasts Braydon Pond, the largest lake in Wiltshire, some pretty cottages and Charlton Park which is 17th-cent. **Crudwell**, 4 m. N., has a green and a stream which feeds the source of the Thames. **Easton Grey**, 3½ m. W., is another village on a river and has old houses and a splendid 16th-cent. bridge.

MARLBOROUGH, *Wiltshire* (5–SU1869). The history of Marlborough stretches back centuries. It is even said that Merlin is buried at the Castle Mound, the oldest part of the town and now part of Marlborough College. Situated in the valley of the Kennet and on the main road, Marlborough was always well placed, especially in coaching times.

The town had some turbulent moments. During the Civil War, there was fierce fighting here and marks can still be seen on the north face of St Mary's Church tower. In 1653 a great fire broke out and destroyed at least 250 buildings. Subscriptions for rebuilding were raised all over the country, but fires again broke out in 1679 and 1690, until it was specifically forbidden to thatch.

As Marlborough suffered so greatly from fire, most of the older half-timbered houses are hidden in the small back lanes off the High Street, an impressively wide road that sweeps down the centre of the town. The effect here is Georgian, but houses built at various times make up a harmonious whole. On the north side are particularly pleasing colonnades.

At either end of the main street stands a church. St Peter's is a mainly Perpendicular stone building, restored in the 19th cent. St Mary's is also mainly Perpendicular and has been restored at various times. During this restoration work, a Roman statue of the goddess Fortuna was found.

Marlborough College, standing on the site of the old castle, was founded in 1843. One of the houses of this famous public school has an interesting history. Originally built by John Webb, it belonged to the Seymours until rebuilt by the Duke of Somerset in 1700. There, Frances, Lady Hertford, held sway over a court of poets and painters. In the mid-18th cent. the house became famous as the busy coaching Castle Inn. At one time Lord Chatham stayed here while unwell.

The White Horse near Marlborough was cut by some schoolboys in 1804. **Mildenhall** is 1 m. E. of Marlborough and was once a Roman station. It contains a curious 19th-cent. Gothic octagonal building, which forms part of a school. The church is also interesting, since it was entirely refitted in 1816 and today the box pews, the pulpit reading desk and gallery, all in oak, are just as they were. The church itself dates from Norman times, with 13th- and 15th-cent. additions.

Fyfield is 2 m. W. About 610 acres of the chalk downs hereabouts have been declared a nature reserve. Some of the great sarsen stones called "grey wethers", and like those used to build STONEHENGE, can be seen here.

MELBURY BUBB, *Dorset* (4–ST5906), is a beautifully sited large farm-hamlet with one of the most rewarding small churches in Dorset. Protected from the W. by a wooded hill, a row of red-brick and yellow-stone houses face E. down long sloping fields to the chalk downs. The church was, except for its 15th-cent. tower, rebuilt in the mid-19th cent., but most sensibly, using much original material. It has good roofs (rare in Dorset churches), some exquisite, graphic, medieval stained glass and an exceptional Anglo-Saxon font carved with wrestling animals, all upside down. A notice suggests that the reason for this is that it was once part of a cross.

Some 3½ m. E. by devious route, the tiny church at **Hillfield** is worth visiting for its profusion of unusual carved bench-ends. No one seems sure who did them and when: Flemish early 17th-cent. seems the most likely answer. The church is ministered by Franciscans, whose friary is about ⅓ m. SW.

Immediately S. is **Batcombe Down**. The drive along its crest from Dogberry Gate on the A352 W. to Holywell gives beautiful views.

MELKSHAM, *Wiltshire* (4–ST9063). In medieval times Melksham was rather cut off by the surrounding forest. But since then it has developed into a busy industrial town set on the Avon. Mostly stone-built, some 17th- and 18th-cent. houses are gathered near the church, W. of which there is a 14th-cent. tithe barn, now used as a school. At one time Melksham tried to become a spa, but all that is left of that short-lived experiment is the now converted pump-room and a fine crescent of houses on the DEVIZES road.

There are several interesting old houses just outside the town. At **Beanacre** on the outskirts of Melksham an Elizabethan manor still stands. Gifford Hall, 2¼ m. to the W., is pleasantly set on the green at **Broughton Gifford**. A village house, dated 1688, its plasterwork and panelled rooms are particularly attractive, and may be visited.

Holt, 3 m. W., was for a short time a spa, and has some attractive houses clustered about the green. Set in lovely gardens is The Courts, a splendid example of Gothic architecture with an ornate and exuberant façade. It was so called as it was where weavers used to bring their disputes for arbitration. Given to the National Trust by Major T. C. E. Goff, the house is open to the public. Some of the contents once belonged to his great-grandfather, King William IV.

MERE, *Wiltshire* (4–ST8132). This old stone town lies near both the Dorset and Somerset borders, and near both open downland and wooded hills. It used once to have a castle at Castle Hill. Today nothing remains, but from here there are fine views of the pretty town below.

The inns are interesting, the old Ship Inn for its beautiful wrought-iron sign, made in the first half of the 18th cent. by Kingston Avery, who also made the church clock. Charles II, heavily disguised during his flight after the Battle of WORCESTER, once stayed at the George Hotel, now modernized.

Attractive small houses belonging to Georgian times nestle round the church. Nearby is the 15th-cent. Chantry House, once a school kept by the Dorset poet William Barnes. The church itself is both splendid and spacious, and is mainly Perpendicular but shows signs of earlier work. The two chantry chapels are 14th-cent., and the 15th-cent. screens are particularly fine, as are the 14th- and 15th-cent. brasses. There is some 15th-cent. glass, 17th-cent. pews, and an interesting old alabaster carving of the Adoration of the Magi, which was dug up nearby. The room above the porch is now a small museum.

STOURHEAD is only 3 m. W. of Mere, and just to the N. at **White Sheet Hill**, there is an Iron Age hill-fort. This area is now a nature reserve.

MILTON, *Berkshire* (5–SU4892), is near STEVENTON, 1½ m. away, and it is pleasant to walk from one to the other, mostly along the valley of the little River Ginge.

Some extremely ancient jewellery has been found at Milton. Near rising chalk downs, it has timber-framed cottages and also Milton Manor House, a 17th-cent. building with 18th-cent. wings, which was traditionally said to be designed by Inigo Jones.

The house is open to the public, as is the pretty walled garden. William III stayed here after arriving in England in 1688. Inside is a splendid plaster ceiling and chimney-piece, and the telescope of the gallant Admiral Benbow is on display. The most interesting features are the library and chapel, both in Strawberry Hill Gothic style; the latter contains some late-14th- and 16th-cent. glass.

MILTON ABBAS and MILTON ABBEY, *Dorset* (4–ST8001). A place of exceptional interest. Huge 18th-cent. Gothic mansion and abbey church stand side by side in a sumptuous bowl of woods and farmland, while, just far enough away to be hidden from them, is what is considered by some to be the first example of an integrally planned village in Britain. A monastery was founded here in 938 by King Athelstan and made an abbey by King Edgar in 964. The existing large and splendid church, built 14th–15th cent., is but a fraction of what would have been an enormous one, but the Dissolution came with the nave still to be added. The property was then given by Henry VIII to the lawyer, Sir John Tregonwell, who had arranged his divorce from Catherine of Aragon. In 1771 it was bought by Joseph Damer, later Earl of Dorchester, and the mansion was built for him, partly by Sir William Chambers, architect of Somerset House, London, partly by James Wyatt. In it they incorporated the old Abbot's Hall (1498) which retains a fine

Reece Winstone

Milton Abbey: the Damer monument

hammer-beam roof. The other abbey domestic buildings were obliterated. And likewise, astonishingly, Damer razed the considerable village that had grown up round the abbey, save for one thatched house that still stands to the SE., replacing it with the planned village out of his view. This consists of a single hillside street of almost identical thatched cottages well separated, the uniformity only broken in its ½-m. length by a set of red-brick and flint almshouses (1779) and a red-stone church (1786), all behind wide, scrupulously mown verges and rowan trees.

The mansion is now a boys' public school, the abbey church its chapel. The latter is always accessible, and the mansion is open in the school holidays. Perhaps the finest part of the church is the glowing Ham-stone vaulted crossing, on which you enter from the W. with south window by Pugin (1847) and white marble monument to Joseph Damer's wife by Carlini (*c.* 1775). The intricately carved 15th-cent. "hanging tabernacle" suspended from the chancel north wall is a rare possession. Due E. of the church a flight of some 111 grass steps leads to the little, mainly Norman, St Catherine's Chapel. Tradition says it was founded by King Athelstan on the spot where, on his way to battle with rebels, he was told in a vision he would win: as he did.

An excellent view of the church and mansion is from a little along the road NW. towards HILTON.

MORETON, *Dorset* (4–SY8089). Beside the River Frome, just S. of the conifer forests and moor of Thomas Hardy's Egdon Heath, Moreton has an unusual and cheerful little church. Full of daylight with pale-blue and white apsidal chancel, the church with its excellent stonework was built in the mid-1700s and altered somewhat in the mid-18th cent. In 1940 it lost its north wall when a stray bomb dropped in its churchyard, and was restored to look, as far as possible, as before. In 1958 it was given remarkable engraved glass chancel windows by Laurence Whistler. From beside the church can be seen well the 1744 manor house of the Framptons, who also built the church. About 200 yds SW., beside the Wool road, is the cemetery where T. E. Lawrence (*see* BOVINGTON) was buried.

MOTTISFONT, *Hampshire* (5–SU3226). The hamlet of Mottisfont, near the River Test, has a church with a fine Norman chancel arch and some excellent stained glass. That in the east window is 15th-cent. The nave of the church is Norman, and the chancel Perpendicular.

At **Brook,** close by, a stream named the Farburn was converted into one of the earliest known reservoirs by means of an artificial dam some 25 ft high. The lake has been partially restored, and its gleaming waters cover some 15 acres.

Mottisfont Abbey is beautifully set on green lawns, amidst vast old trees, and is bound on one side by the rich watermeadows of the Test.

The original priory of the Austin Canons was founded here at the start of the 13th cent. In the 14th and 15th cents., it suffered from lack of money, until in 1536 the priory was suppressed. In return for the villages of Chelsea and Paddington, it was given to William, Lord Sandys, Lord Chamberlain to Henry VIII, who already owned The Vyne near SHERBORNE ST JOHN.

Lord Sandys pulled down most of the priory living quarters and made his home out of the nave of the church with wings over the old cellarium and chapter house, thus building in the shape of an E without the middle bar. Today the north side, apart from such details as windows, remains much as it was when converted in Tudor times. The south side is almost entirely Georgian, dating from the 1740s, and in 1836 a stable block was added.

Of the old priory, various details, dating from the 12th and 13th cents., can be seen in the ground-floor offices. The old pulpit, adorned with eight stone shields, is remarkable, but even more interesting is the undercroft of the monks' cellarium, where the graceful 13th-cent. circular stone columns remain quite unaltered.

In 1938 Rex Whistler transformed one of the rooms in the house with a *trompe l'œil*. It is a charming Gothic fantasy, with ceiling, walls and even the curtain pelmets all delicately painted.

The house, which is open to the public, was, together with some 2,028 acres (including the village and woodland), given to the National Trust in 1957 by Mrs Gilbert Russell, who still lives at Mottisfont.

MOTTISTONE, *Isle of Wight* (5–SZ4083), 1¾ m. along the main road W. from BRIGHSTONE, belonged to the Cheke family, one of whose members tutored Edward VI. It has an unspoilt example of a Tudor manor house.

Behind the manor is the island's only megalith, an iron sandstone pillar 13 ft high, with a second stone lying at its feet, dating from the 3rd millennium B.C. Mottistone church is of 12th- and 14th-cent. origin with a Jacobean font and pulpit. The 18th-cent. organ is by John England.

NETLEY ABBEY, *Hampshire* (5–SU4508), on the east bank of Southampton Water, is now a romantic ruin, set in green lawns against a background of trees.

The abbey was founded in the 13th cent. by Cistercian monks from BEAULIEU led by Peter des Roches. He was at one time tutor to Henry III, who endowed the abbey and attended the dedication with his queen.

At the Dissolution Netley passed to William Paulet, 1st Marquess of Winchester and Comptroller of the Royal Household, and he made a house from the nave and south transept of the church and part of the abbey buildings, as some of the brickwork still seen today indicates. In the 18th cent., Netley was sold to a builder from SOUTHAMPTON, but before he could demolish much, part of the tracery of the west window fell and killed him. So once again, the abbey, which had suffered less than most at the Dissolution, survived. It is now under the care of the Ministry of Public Building and Works and is open to the public.

The shell of the abbey church remains, a graceful compliment to Early English architecture, since it is almost all built in this style. It measured over 210 ft in length, and the nave and chancel aisle walls still stand, with a spectacular east window gracefully etched against the skyline. The bases of four pillars which supported the tower are still to be seen, and although the north transept was demolished to provide a sham ruin at Cranbury Park near OTTERBOURNE, much of the south transept remains, and two chapels retain their vaulting.

Not much remains of the cloister on the south side of the church, or of the cloister walls, but the north-east corner of the cloister leads to the vaulted vestry, which has a tile display. S. of this is the chapter house, which although without a roof still shows the springers of the vaulting. A passage leads S. to the dormitory undercroft, and nearby is the infirmary, a vaulted room with a large fire-place and a kitchen at the W. SE. of the church and apart from it, is the two-storied abbot's lodging, which has two wings, and a vaulted chapel to the S. From here the view over the site is particularly good.

Nearby stands the 19th-cent. Church of St Edward the Confessor. Under the tower can be seen part of the tomb of a knight, with crossed legs, which originally came from the abbey.

Between the abbey and the shore, Henry VIII converted the gatehouse of the abbey into a Tudor fort, and this in the 19th cent. was again converted into Netley Castle, a Gothic building.

The other great building in the vicinity was the 19th-cent. Military Hospital, which was ¼ m. in length, but is now demolished except for the royal chapel with its dome.

NEWBURY, *Berkshire* (5–SU4666), is an important town whose history stretches back to prehistoric times. The Anglo-Saxons were here, as were the Normans who built a castle, now no more. It was the scene of two battles in the Civil War, in 1643 and 1644. The 19th-cent. Falkland Memorial on the Andover Road commemorates Lord Falkland, who, despairing of peace, fell in the first of these battles. On Wash Common several mounds very like ancient burial barrows probably contain the graves of those who fell in the Civil War.

Strategically placed on the road to the west, Newbury grew rich from cloth; its most famous son is Jack of Newbury, alias John Smallwood or John Winchcombe. He arrived here with nothing, to become such a successful clothier that he probably had 200 looms. He entertained Henry VIII and later, when asked to raise six men to fight the Scots, he led 100 of his men to fight at Flodden in 1513.

Jack of Newbury started to build the Church of St Nicholas, completed by his son in 1532. Almost entirely in Perpendicular style, it is airy and spacious, with a beautiful pulpit, 1607, and a brass to Jack of Newbury dated 1519.

His home can also still be seen in Northbrook Street, beside the hotel of his name. Although the façade seems later, parts of the old house remain in Marsh Lane. Northbrook Street contains many 18th-cent. houses, others in the town date from much earlier, including the Cloth Hall built in the 17th cent. as a workshop to give employment to the poor. With its overhang resting on oak pillars it now contains the museum, which displays antiquities and much that concerns the history of the town and district.

Other buildings of interest include Shaw House, an Elizabethan mansion built by a rich clothier and now a school. There are several almshouses, including St Bartholomew's Hospital which dates from the 17th cent.

Many places can be reached by footpaths, including DONNINGTON CASTLE, and Sandleford Priory which is approached over Wash Common. Founded in the 12th cent. the remains have been incorporated into a school. In the 18th cent. Mrs Montagu, a friend of Dr Johnson's, built a house here in which she used to hold literary court.

Pretty villages are easily accessible. **Boxford**, NW. in the Lambourn valley, is particularly charming. **Enborne**, 8 m. W., has a church, much of which is Norman. The chancel is Early English and contains a beautiful 14th-cent. painting of the Annunciation.

NEWPORT, *Isle of Wight* (5–SZ4981), the commercial capital, is on the River Medina which cuts the island into East Wight and West Wight, from N. to S. Quite large vessels sail up into the busy harbour, a distance of some 5 m. from COWES on the north coast. The French sacked the town in 1377, and Charles I held talks with the Cromwellian commissioners, which resulted in the abortive Treaty of Newport, 1648. The town sent representatives to Westminster for nearly 300 years, among them the Duke of Wellington, Lord Palmerston and George Canning. The town has many historic buildings. The Old Grammar School (1619) was the lodging for King Charles. Other old houses are God's Providence House (1701), the Chantry House (1612), and the Castle Inn. The present Parish Church of St Thomas the Apostle has a fine Jacobean oak pulpit and a splendid peal of eight bells, both saved from the original church. Here can be seen the monument by Marochetti, in Carrara marble, to Princess Elizabeth, Charles I's second daughter, who at the age of 15 died in captivity at CARISBROOKE CASTLE. The Guildhall designed by John Nash is now used for legal business and Quarter and other Sessions.

The Roman villa in Avondale Road is open at certain times to the public.

NORTH MORETON, *Berkshire* (5–SU5689), is just W. of WALLINGFORD, and its old houses, timber-framed cottages and ancient barn make it an attractive place to visit.

The church is set amongst trees and although Norman in origin is mostly 13th-cent., and has a splendid 14th-cent. chantry chapel dedicated to the Stapleton family. The east window – note especially the tracery – has beautiful glass showing 15 scenes from the Life of Christ, the Virgin Mary, St Peter, St Paul and St Nicholas. More fragments of 14th-cent. glass are to be found in other windows.

Just to the N. of the village are the **Wittenham Clumps**, part of the Sinodun hills.

ODIHAM, *Hampshire* (5–SU7350), is an old town, as the prehistoric trade route, Harrow Way, and excavations have shown. It is also an attractive one, particularly when approached by way of a magnificent oak avenue from FARNHAM.

Buildings of all centuries, often low and colourwashed, mingle happily together in the wide high street of this market town. Some houses are Georgian, some half-timbered, and others, such as the George Hotel, are a mixture of styles. Although first licensed in 1540, this hotel is now mainly Georgian and has an old oak panelled room which was formerly a court room. Both the Priory and Palace Gate Farm are of interest, since both incorporate parts of the old Tudor palace.

King Street has some charming Tudor cottages, but the Bury is the true centre of town. Here old cottages nestle near the church; almshouses fringe three sides of a courtyard; and one small cottage with an exceedingly large chimney was the old Pest House, for unfortunate plague victims.

The church is large and impressive. Originally Norman it is now mostly 14th-cent., with part of the tower added in 1647. The 17th-cent. gallery staircase and balustrades and the pulpit are interesting, and there is a 13th-cent. chalk font. Of all the 15th-, 16th- and 17th-cent. brasses the most pathetic is to Margaret Pie. She is in swaddling clothes, for she died a baby in 1636. Near the north side of the churchyard are stocks and a whipping post, and inside lie the graves of two French prisoners of war from Napoleonic times.

Some of these prisoners were housed in cottages, which still stand near the vast chalk pit at the S. of the town. This pit may have been used since Iron Age times.

Under 1 m. from Odiham, **North Warnborough** has its own quota of pretty cottages and also Odiham Castle, which is just near the tow-path of the old Basingstoke Canal. King John set out from here in 1215 to sign the Magna Carta. The barons, not trusting him, called in the French to help them, and the Dauphin besieged this castle. It later passed to Simon de Montfort's wife, the Duchess of Pembroke, and then David, King of Scotland, was held here in the 14th cent. Now all that remains is a ruin of a fine 13th-cent. octagonal keep – the only one of its shape in this country.

Just near the road to Alton, there is **Odiham Firs**, or **Beacon Hill**, rising to 400 ft and belonging to the town. This was once used as a signalling post during the Armada invasion scare, and it gives magnificent views in all directions.

OLD SARUM, *Wiltshire* (5–SU1332). The story of Old Sarum stretches back to prehistory. The site covers 56 acres, on which once stood an Iron Age camp. The Romans were here, so too were the Anglo-Saxons, and the Danes, who pillaged the place in 1003. Later William the Conqueror reviewed his victorious troops on the plains below in 1070. Shortly afterwards the Episcopal See was transferred to Old Sarum from SHERBORNE, and a splendid Norman cathedral and castle were erected. But gradually the squabbles between the castle soldiers and the clergy grew so acrimonious, and water so short, that in 1220 it was decided to build a new cathedral in New Sarum – or SALISBURY. Stones from the old cathedral, which lay between the castle and the outer wall, were used for the new, and the castle also fell gradually into ruins. The town, which used to be a thriving community of houses crowded between the outer defences and the castle, built high above in a central enclosure, was gradually abandoned. However, until the Reform Bill of 1832, 10 voters only continued to return two members to Parliament, including, at one time, Pitt the Elder.

The best way to find out what Old Sarum looked like in its heyday is to inspect the model in Salisbury museum. This clearly shows the conical hill, protected by an outer wall and ditch, and all the buildings that once stood there. Today little remains except the excavated foundation of the cathedral and a few remnants of the castle. The site is under the care of the Ministry of Public Building and Works and is open to the public.

OSBORNE HOUSE, *Isle of Wight* (5–SZ 5194), is a monument to the "high noon" of the Victorian Age. The whole carries the imprint of Queen Victoria's mind and personality. Designed by Thomas Cubitt and the Prince Consort in 1845–8, it is an Italianate place overlooking the waters of the Solent near COWES. The state and private apartments are open to the public, as are most of the 2,000 acres of grounds and gardens, where every kind of English tree has been planted, including a great evergreen English oak. The Ministry of Public Building and Works preserves the house for the nation. Rooms remain much as in the Queen's lifetime: the Durbar Room with its plumed exoticism and Indian plaster decoration, by John Lockwood Kipling, father of Rudyard Kipling; the Dining Room with a brass plate marking the place where the lying-in-state was held, and miniature chairs for the Royal children with embroidered initials of each owner; the Gothic gloom of the Antler Room; and the pillared pomposity of the Billiard Room. In the grounds a life-size dolls' house, an imported Swiss chalet, houses the royal utilitarian toys, gardening tools, kitchen equipment, etc.; the Albert Barracks, a miniature fort, is made of bricks fired by the princes themselves. Over 400 works of art, pictures and furniture pieces are catalogued in Osborne's treasures. On the terraces are tombstones to many favourite dogs and other animals. Breakfast was often taken here to the accompaniment of bagpipes. Whippingham Church nearby, with its Royal and Battenberg chapels, was regularly attended by Queen Victoria, latterly in a small chaise pulled by a white donkey. In the churchyard are the graves of the parents of Earl Mountbatten, the present Governor of the Island.

OTTERBOURNE, *Hampshire* (5–SU4522), lies in the pretty Itchen valley, on the main road from SOUTHAMPTON to WINCHESTER. Above the village there is an attractive common, now somewhat reduced in area by bypass construction, and in Otterbourne itself there is a church erected by the father of Charlotte M. Yonge the novelist. It contains 17th-cent. Flemish altar rails, and in the churchyard a cross to John Keble, who once had the living here. All that remains of the old church is the ruined 13th-cent. chancel nearby.

Cranbury Park, a splendid 18th-cent. house designed by Sir George Dance, is just S. of Otterbourne. Once an old priory stood here, and there are still the remains of a Roman encampment in the garden, as well as a mock ruin built from some of the material from NETLEY ABBEY.

PADWORTH, *Berkshire* (5–SU6166). Set among pine trees near ALDERMASTON, the River Kennet and the border of Hampshire, Padworth has a memorable church.

Perched on a slope, together with the 18th-cent. manor house, the Church of St John the

Baptist, except for five Perpendicular windows, is almost pure Norman. The outside is plastered, and it has a dignified interior. The decorated north and south doors and the chancel arch with its carved capitals are all impressive. There is a timber bell-turret, and a vaulted apse, and on the east wall of the nave are traces of an old wall painting showing St Nicholas with the three boys he restored to life after their murder, while another figure lies beneath. There are two 18th-cent. monuments.

PAMBER END, *Hampshire* (5–SU6158). The village is part old, part new, and somewhat scattered. Round about is Pamber Forest, which, though still in existence, used to be very much larger.

W. of the village, set in peaceful fields and approached by a magnificent oak avenue, is Pamber Priory Church. As its name implies, it incorporates the remains of a priory, once attached to a Normandy Benedictine abbey. Founded in the 12th cent., it was suppressed in the 15th cent. and today belongs to Queen's College, OXFORD. The Norman central tower and beautiful Early English choir were part of the old priory. The piscina is Early English, and there are various coffin slabs, one of the 12th cent. inscribed with Gothic lettering. Even more interesting is the carved wooden effigy of a knight, 13th- or 14th-cent. He lies dressed in chain mail, his crossed legs resting on a lion.

The priory also gave its name to the neighbouring village of **Monk Sherborne**. It lies a little S., and has some pretty 17th-cent. cottages and a peaceful atmosphere. To the W., in a pretty downland setting, lies the village of **Kingsclere** (6 m.); the restored Norman church contains notable family monuments.

PANGBOURNE, *Berkshire* (5–SU6376). The Pang joins the Thames at Pangbourne and one of the prettiest views is looking over the river and weir to Pangbourne meadow.

Although somewhat developed today, Pangbourne has some pleasant 17th- and 18th-cent. houses, and the Nautical College, founded in 1917, is on top of the hill. Bere Court, which once belonged to the abbots of Reading, is early Georgian.

Apart from the 18th-cent. brick tower, the church was rebuilt in the 19th cent., but inside are a Jacobean pulpit, and a monument to Sir John Davis in armour, 1625, surrounded by his family, including a daughter-in-law who was sister to Sir John Suckling, the poet. This stretch must encourage writers, for Kenneth Grahame, author of *The Wind in the Willows*, lived here, and Jerome K. Jerome's *Three Men in a Boat* paused at the Swan Inn.

PETERSFIELD, *Hampshire* (5–SU7423). The town's first charter was granted in the 12th cent. It grew prosperous from the wool trade and later became famous as a coaching centre. There were once as many as nine inns here and about 27 coaches a day came through.

Today much of the bustle has gone and the atmosphere in the streets of this market and agricultural town is peaceful. There is plenty of elegant Georgian building in evidence.

The once gilded figure of William III, mounted and slightly incongruous in Roman dress, surveys the square. Nearby is the Church of St Peter, much of which dates back to the 12th cent. The top of the tower is Perpendicular, as are the north windows, and the church was much restored in the 19th cent. The Norman chancel arch is outstanding, and there are 18th-cent. monuments

Poole: the Fisherman's Harbour

J. Allan Cash

inside, and interesting headstones outside in the churchyard.

Street names in Petersfield tell their own story. The Spain is thought to have gained its name from the Spanish wool merchants who bought at the market here. The origin of Sheep Street is obvious, and Music Hill dates back to the time when 18th-cent. military bands played there.

There is great interest in the surrounding country. Petersfield is set in a wide valley. To the N. the hills are fringed with beech and to the S. they open into wide spacious downland. Less than 1 m. SE., **Petersfield Heath** has a lake and 21 ancient barrows, mostly of the bowl variety, scattered over its 80 odd acres.

Butser Hill, less than 3 m. SW., soars to 889 ft, and gives magnificent views as far as the Isle of Wight. The land here is open and dotted with gorse. There is plenty of evidence of previous occupation, with two round barrows on the hill itself and three more bowl barrows on Ramsdean Down nearby. There is also evidence of ramparts and ditches and an ancient Celtic cultivation system.

Nearby **Buriton** is beautifully situated in the shadow of the downs. It is a charming village with a pond, pretty cottages and a Georgian manor which once belonged to the father of Edward Gibbon, the historian.

NE. of Petersfield on the road to Haslemere is **Liphook** with the Royal Anchor Hotel, a famous late-17th-cent. posting inn, patronized by the famous, among them General Blücher and Queen Victoria.

Just N. of Liphook about 40 acres of **Bramshott Chase** belong to the National Trust, as do a further 645 acres nearby, including **Ludshott Common** and **Waggoners Wells** – a string of ponds first constructed for use in the iron industry.

PEWSEY, *Wiltshire* (5–SU1659). Between Salisbury Plain and the barren Marlborough Downs lies the rich fertile Vale of Pewsey, dividing the N. of Wiltshire from the S.

A white horse is cut in chalk near Pewsey, an attractive agricultural town, where some shops are still thatched and the statue of Alfred the Great stands gazing over the River Avon. The 12th- to 15th-cent. church is chiefly interesting because the exterior of the south aisle rests on sarsen, similar to the huge blocks of stone used for STONEHENGE. Inside are carvings by the one-time vicar, Canon Bouverie, and mahogany altar rails taken from a ship captured by Nelson off Cape St Vincent in 1797.

Pewsey is surrounded by pretty villages. Amongst them, **Manningford Bruce**, 2 m. away has charming cottages and a memorial in the church to Mary Nicholas who helped Charles II escape after the Battle of Worcester. Near **Woodborough**, $3\frac{1}{2}$ m. away, are the remains of prehistoric cultivation terraces.

PIDDLETRENTHIDE, *Dorset* (4–SY7099), has yellow-stone houses scattered for nearly a mile along the narrow base of the deep and beautiful Piddle valley. Its pubs look inviting. Halfway along to the E. is the fine 18th-cent. manor house framed by beech trees. The church, at the very northern end, has one of Dorset's best towers (15th-cent.), which is graphically gargoyled; inside it is unexceptional but has some pleasant wall monuments. There are nice views of the stream and houses from the numerous bridges spanning the Piddle.

The chalk ridges lie N. to S. here, and the switchback route W. to CERNE ABBAS, SYDLING ST NICHOLAS and Maiden Newton combines some of the best and most distinctive Dorset scenery and villages.

PILSDON PEN, *Dorset* (4–ST4101). The highest hill in Dorset (909 ft). The view S. from it over the great bowl of Marshwood Vale is marvellous. There is a big lay-by opposite the quite short path leading to its top, which is ringed by an Iron Age earthwork, and scattered with heath and gorse. At Racedown House, about $\frac{3}{4}$ m. W. of the summit and visible from the road, Wordsworth and his sister Dorothy lived for a while in the 1790s.

The B3705 SW. from here to Hunters Lodge Inn crossroads is continuously beautiful, partly beech avenued, with a fine view N. So is the one E. to Broadwindsor, $2\frac{1}{4}$ m., where the fugitive Prince Charles spent a night on his way to CHARMOUTH in 1651. There is a plaque commemorating this on a cottage in its centre. Its church, not otherwise special, has an extremely fine 16th-cent. pulpit.

POOLE, *Dorset* (4–SZ0190). This is easily Dorset's largest town. On the map it and BOURNE-MOUTH look one vast seaside conurbation and their suburbs do indeed merge, but their characters are very different. Poole's has been largely shaped by its tremendous natural harbour, over 100 m. round, much of its shore still undeveloped, with inlets and islands splendid to explore by boat (hirable at Sandbanks on the east side). From the town's quay right round to Sandbanks, it is an immense park of yachts and other pleasure boats. Its luck in having twice the normal number of high tides means it is seldom muddy. A car ferry plies from Sandbanks to Shell Bay.

Not surprisingly with such a site the town, as distinct from its buildings, is old. In the early Middle Ages it superseded WAREHAM as the county's chief port. From then till the 19th cent. its history was adventurous. Buccaneers, in particular one Harry Page, found it a snug base from which to rob the ships of France and Spain. In 1586, Queen Elizabeth made it "a county", a status it retained till 1888. Smugglers appreciated the surrounding creeks and in 1747 even made so bold as to raid the Customs House, departing with a rich cargo of tea. During the Civil War it was a Roundhead stronghold; in the 18th and 19th cents. it became one of the main ports for the Newfoundland trade and provided some of that former colony's first settlers. Today it remains energetic, far from content to rest on tourism, with a wide variety of light industries.

Geographically it is confusing and a wise first call is the Information Bureau at the Civic Centre, built in 1932. This is on the Bournemouth road, some way from the quay area which is the town's heart. You can usually park on the quay, close to the Customs House (1813). Behind it and the Harbour Office (1820) is, pleasantly free from heavy traffic, the rest of what remains of an older Poole: St James's Church (1820), big and smart inside, rather like a town hall; a little E., the former Guildhall (1761) with nice twin stair-cases to its door; and, SE. in High Street, the original Town House (15th-cent. and parts earlier) now open as a museum with the largest Bronze Age canoe found in Britain among its exhibits. Further up this street another museum, of local and natural history, adjoins the Public Library. The brand-new pedestrian shopping precinct almost opposite has a sports centre with facilities for almost every indoor sport imaginable.

Back on the quay, the famous Poole Pottery shows visitors how the pottery is made; and frequent boats go to and round the harbour's biggest island, BROWNSEA, and go shark fishing. Over the bridge just W., the huge power station invites people to see inside it.

Of the numerous good parks and gardens, Poole Park has the most entertainments: a big boating lake, miniature railway, zoo and plenty of others. But purely as gardens, Compton Acres (private but open), in the affluent eastern suburbs, surpass all others here. In seven styles, including Italian, with fountains, statues and lily-ponds, and Japanese, built by Japanese, they are set on a pine-tree hill with a superb view over the harbour to CORFE CASTLE. They cost nearly £250,000 to make in the 1920s: Poole would be worth visiting for them alone. Of the nearby Poole Bay beaches, reached by cuttings called chines, BRANKSOME is perhaps the best, but all are admirably sandy. In addition Branksome has one of Dorset's best early-20th-cent. churches: St Aldhelm's by G. F. Bodley. A nice drive is round the Sand-banks headland, and Evening Hill is a popular viewpoint. There are two good golf courses nearby: the **Broadstone** (4 m. N.) and Parkstone (below Compton Acres). At Broadstone, too, Yaffle Hill's garden, with rare trees and shrubs, is sometimes open. About 1 m. further N. are the **Merley Bird Gardens**, which have exotic birds in aviaries big enough for them to fly about.

PORTCHESTER, *Hampshire* (5–SU6105), lies on the edge of PORTSMOUTH Harbour, and from the seashore the cranes in Portsmouth dockyard and H.M.S. *Victory* are quite easily seen. Al-though there has been much development in the town, a few 18th-cent. buildings remain, but the chief glory of Portchester is its castle.

Set on a spit of land it is lapped on three sides by the sea. In the late 3rd cent. the Romans built a fort here, probably one of a string put around the southern and eastern coasts of England. The fortress covered 9 acres bounded by a magnificent 20-ft-high wall. It still stands today, as do 14 of the original 20 fat round bastions. The fort was probably occupied until A.D. 370, and then again for a time by the Anglo-Saxons. During the first third of the 12th cent. Henry I added the keep – still impressive today – and walled off a small courtyard which he protected by a moat in the north-west corner.

In 1133 the priory was also founded, though about 15 years later the Augustinians moved to SOUTHWICK, probably because of the difficulties of living in a fort used for military purposes. The priory and its church were outside the inner court-yard, and of the general buildings little remains. The church, however, apart from the south tran-sept, is more or less intact and unaltered. The west front is particularly fine, as is the 12th-cent. carved font, resting on a 19th-cent. base.

The next major building phase started in the 14th cent. Between 1376 and 1381 Sir Robert Assheton, Constable of the Castle, built a great tower. The shell still stands today and it is known as Assheton's Tower. Towards the end of the 14th cent. Richard II built a palace within the inner courtyard, and was in such a hurry about it that building was continued at night time. It is still possible to see the shell of the porch leading to the great hall, which had kitchens and so on on the east side. On the west side there were an enormous room, the Queen's chamber, and the Exchequer set against the keep. Later Sir Thomas Cornwallis, Governor until 1618, made further alterations and traces of Tudor building remain.

Originally the Romans built two large gates and two small posterns. Of these not much remains, but nearby are the Landgate, originally 12th-cent. but added to in the 14th, and the Watergate, which dates from the 12th and 14th cents. and is less preserved.

Portchester Castle was popular with its royal residents, and kings usually stayed here when visiting Portsmouth. John certainly came here and once ordered the castle to be destroyed, an order later rescinded. Henry V stayed here before Agincourt and Henry VIII came with Anne Boleyn. The castle belonged to the Crown till 1632, but fell gradually into disrepair. It had, however, been used as a prison from early times. Dutch and French prisoners – the latter during the Napoleonic wars – have been kept here, as have others. But today the castle is under the care of the Ministry of Public Building and Works and is open to the public.

PORTESHAM, *Dorset* (4–SY6085). A wel-coming village with a green and full of flowers and trees at the foot of the 777-ft chalk hill called Black Down. Its 15th-cent. church of attractively pale limestone, spoilt inside by Puritans and restorers in turn, has managed to preserve a good Jacobean pulpit. Portesham House at the south end of the village was the home of Admiral Sir Thomas Hardy, who was beside Nelson at his death at the Battle of Trafalgar in 1805, and about 1½ m. NE., on the hill-top, is a tower memorial to him. It is quite ugly but the views from it are tremendous. The area is scattered with prehistoric remains, most notably a rebuilt, but impressive, cromlech called the Hell Stone, about ½ m. N. of the village and 200 yds E. of the road.

One m. E. is **Waddon Manor**, the late 17th-cent. wing of a vanished Tudor mansion, standing amid trees above fine farm buildings and drystone garden walls, with a superb long view to the sea.

PORTLAND, *Dorset* (4–SY6972). All but an island geographically, it is certainly one in character. On the whole it is ugly, but unique. About 4½ m. long by 1¾ m. wide, it is almost treeless, quite densely populated (about 12,150 people) in a scattering of merging austere villages, littered with the appurtenances of the military and prison services, and with the Portland stone quarries from which has come the material for so many of England's great buildings. The highest point (496 ft) at its northern centre affords immense views NW. along the CHESIL BANK and NE. to the white cliffs of DURDLE DOOR and far beyond. From here it slopes S. till, at Portland Bill, the cliffs are only about 20 ft. It becomes relatively gentle only at Church Ope Cove, half-way along the east coast, where there is a bathing and boating beach and even a few trees. To the N. is the huge naval harbour, almost as big as the "island", enclosed by massive breakwaters built mainly by convict labour between 1849 and 1905.

In the Middle Ages Portland lived remote from the mainland, interbreeding, smuggling, fishing, using dung or the timbers of wrecked ships for fuel, and grazing an unusual breed of sheep which has since died out. The villages were clustered round wells, as their names witness. The people were famously adept with the sling, for which Chesil Bank provided the ammunition, and their origin, though unknown, is thought to differ from the mainlanders. According to Thomas Hardy in *The Well-Beloved*, they cherished "strange beliefs and singular customs". Portland claims its women were the first in England to have the same property rights as men. Its fame began to grow when, in *c*. 1520, Henry VIII gave it one of his numerous South Coast castles, continued in the next century with the recognition, mostly by Inigo Jones (BANQUETING HOUSE, Whitehall) and later by Wren (ST PAUL'S), of the excellence of its stone, and was confirmed in 1847 by the Government decision to build the naval base and a prison to house the project's labour force. Till the early 20th cent., however, it was still smuggling, and it remains a royal manor, as it has been since 1066, still paying a token rent to the Queen.

Today its former prison is a Borstal, its former army citadel a prison of milder type. In the Grove Road, near the former, St Peter's Church was built in 1872 by convicts: the pulpit by Irish Fenians (note the shamrocks), the chancel mosaics by Constance Kent. Above Church Ope Cove, the Pennsylvania Hotel was built (*c*. 1800) by James Wyatt as the house of the Governor at the time, John Penn, grandson of the founder of Pennsylvania state. Beside the gates is the museum in an old cottage which Hardy made the home of his Avice. Exhibits include fearsome fossils and pictures of famous Portland stone buildings. From the cove there are good cliff walks to the N., and undercliff walks to the S. Above it are the dangerous remains of a Norman castle, vaguely known as Rufus. At the Bill, a rather elegant red and white lighthouse (1906) can be visited. Close to it the old lighthouse is a now a bird observatory. The waves breaking on Pulpit Rock are spectacular and the meeting of tides, called the Race, frenzied even on a calm day. Easily the "island's" best church is St George's (1777) in Weston Road. It is big, with box pews and with twin pulpits, but it is now disused and lamentably decaying. A Friends' Society is trying to find the money to restore it. The parish church in Easton village was built in 1916. Henry VIII's castle is formidably preserved by the Ministry of Public Building and Works, but is rather lost among modern naval buildings on the northern shore.

PORTSMOUTH, *Hampshire* (5–SU6500), has been important in the history of the Navy since early times. Richard I built the first dock here as far back as 1194, and in 1495 the first dry dock in the world was built here. There was further development in the 17th cent., with Pepys much concerned, and from then on Portsmouth has gone from strength to strength until today the dockyards spread over about 300 acres, compared with the 8 acres they covered in the time of Henry VIII.

Charles Dickens was born here, and his modest house in Commercial Road is full of mementoes of his life and is open to the public. Jonas Hanway, the inventor of the umbrella in the 18th cent., came from Portsmouth, and the town also has associations with many of the great men in naval history, including the unfortunate Admiral Byng who was brought here to be shot in 1775.

Portsmouth is a town that grew up by itself rather than to plan. It suffered greatly during the Second World War, so there has been much new building. The old part is near the Round Tower, part of an old fortification now open to the public. The square Tower was added later by Henry VII and it is near here in Broad Street and High Street that the old houses are to be found. One is named after the Duke of Buckingham, one-time Lord High Admiral, who was murdered in 1628.

In the dockyard is Nelson's flagship, H.M.S. *Victory*, which remains more or less as it was at Trafalgar. The Victory Museum shows relics of Admiral Nelson and his navy, as well as model ships, figure-heads and so on. Also in the dockyard are some splendid 18th-cent. houses. The Navigation School is particularly attractive, as is a terraced row built as offices.

The cathedral was originally founded as a church in the 12th cent. in honour of St Thomas à Becket. The nave and tower were rebuilt after being damaged in the Civil War, and in this century, when the church was promoted to Cathedral, extensive alterations and additions were made.

The Garrison church is mostly 13th-cent., but

restored in the 19th cent. and then bombed during the war. It was formerly part of an old hospital built to welcome the sick and travellers. Later part of these buildings became the Governor's house. Catherine of Braganza was married to Charles II from here. She brought Tangier as part of her dowry, and plate from there can still be seen at the cathedral.

Southsea, joined to Portsmouth on the E., has grown up as a resort. At the Cumberland House Museum and Art Gallery there are some interesting natural history exhibits.

POTTERNE, *Wiltshire* (5–ST9958). A magnificent cruciform church dominates the village. It is almost pure Early English, though the tower, front porch and battlements were added later. Inside the proportions are noble and there is little adornment. There is a 15th-cent. pulpit, and particularly interesting is an ancient bucket-shaped font. Not used today and only discovered in the 19th cent., it may be pre-Norman.

Potterne has several charming half-timbered houses, amongst them the 15th-cent. Porch House, which may once have been either a church house, or an inn, or even both. The dining hall is spacious and has a fine oriel window. Upstairs there are spy holes through which you can gaze down to see what is happening below. The Porch House is open to the public.

POWERSTOCK, *Dorset* (4–SY5196). A yellow-stone village straggling with pleasant indiscipline up a combe into the chalk downs. The B.B.C. decided in 1968 that it was the village least changed by the 20th cent. they could find – still with a blacksmith, and the vicar riding to visit his parishioners, etc. – and made a documentary about it. The church, though partly rebuilt in 1859, has a fine, ornamented Norman chancel arch and 15th-cent. south doorway. Just down the hill, the church school was built in 1848, mainly of bits from a demolished medieval chapel; for instance its doorway is 12th-cent. The "castle", about ¼ m. E., is now merely a moated grass mound said to mark the site of one of King John's numerous hunting lodges. The hill called **Eggardon**, towering over 800 ft high to the SE., bears what is perhaps, after MAIDEN CASTLE, the most impressive Iron Age fort in Dorset, commanding an outstanding view. To reach it by decent road, leave the village to the NE. and turn S. at the first crossroads: about 5 m. in all. A little further S. is the small village of **Askerswell**, beautifully situated in typically English countryside.

PUDDLETOWN, *Dorset* (4–SY7594). Off the trunk roads that quarter it, this village is one of Dorset's most attractive. It has an excellent church, mainly 15th-cent., which is beautifully light, largely Jacobean furnished, with box pews, canopied pulpit and gallery. It also has a fine, unusual, 15th-cent. panelled roof, a late Norman font and a chapel of splendid 16th-cent. effigy-tombs to the Martyns, formerly of ATHEL-HAMPTON and Waterston.

The village was Hardy's "Weatherby" in *Far from the Madding Crowd*. Officially, till the early 1950s it was Piddletown; above it, in the Piddle valley, the villages still begin with "piddle" while below it they have long ended "puddle".

Starting 1 m. SW. of the A35 is Rhododendron Mile, with bushes, at their best in May and June, planted both sides of the road through Puddletown Forest. Also in the forest, a nature trail walk has been laid out.

Waterston House, 2 m. NW., Hardy made the home of his Bathsheba. Not open to the public but visible from the B3142, it was badly damaged by fire in 1863 but restored to look convincingly Jacobean, as it was.

Three m. NE., **Dewlish House**, 1700–2, in a fine park, is open sometimes. On a nearby hillside bones of pre-Ice Age elephants were discovered.

PURTON, *Wiltshire* (5–SU0887). Purton, in the N. of the county, is set high and there are good views from here, especially into the Cotswolds. It has an attractive old part and an Elizabethan manor house and tithe barn. Nearby, the Church of St Mary the Virgin is remarkable for having two towers, one, with a spire, rising from the centre, the other from the west end. Built between the 13th and 15th cents., but mostly Perpendicular, there are traces of wall paintings. One shows the Virgin Mary, another the daughter of Jairus. There is also some fine medieval glass.

An Anglo-Saxon burial ground has been found nearby, and 3 m. SW. of the village is **Ringsbury Camp**. It was probably an old Iron Age camp.

QUARR ABBEY, *Isle of Wight* (5–SZ5693). These ruins lie off the main NEWPORT to RYDE route near **Binstead**, where there is a small Shell museum. The abbey, built from the now worked-out quarries, was founded by Cistercian monks in 1132. It suffered many changes: the monks were dispersed; it was used as a defensive blockhouse; and finally it became a farm. Today, ½ m. distant, stands the new abbey, maintained by the Benedictines. Built of warm-coloured Flemish brick, it is a thriving place of worship with a renowned choir.

RADLEY, *Berkshire* (5–SU5398), was once a hunting estate for the monks at ABINGDON. At the Dissolution it passed to the Lord Seymour who married Catherine Parr, widow of Henry VIII, and after his execution, went to Mary Tudor.

The village, by the Thames, has some thatched half-timbered houses and an attractive old rectory. In 1847 Dr Sewell started Radley College in the 18th-cent. manor house, considering that beautiful surroundings were beneficial to boys.

The church is mainly Perpendicular and is interesting for its woodwork, particularly the arches and pillars in the south arcade. The canopy of the pulpit is Perpendicular and the stalls 17th-cent. There is some interesting heraldic and other 16th-cent. glass, a Norman font, and a splendid tomb to Sir William Stonehouse, 1631. Elizabeth Stonehouse who also lies here is believed to have rebuilt the chancel.

RAMSBURY, *Wiltshire* (5–SU2771), used to be an important place, when, between 908 and 1058, it was a bishopric. Today it is a pleasing village on the Kennet, with thatch, Georgian and Jacobean houses. The 17th-cent. manor house was designed by John Webb, son-in-law of Inigo Jones, and nearby, at **Axford**, there is a picturesque old watermill on a farm. The 14th-cent. chapel, with lancet windows, has been turned into living quarters.

Built of flint and stone, on early Anglo-Saxon foundations, Ramsbury church is mostly Early English and Decorated. There are 18th-cent. chandeliers, which – says the record – cost £22 16s. 6d. to buy. In the church are monuments from the 17th, 18th and 19th cents., and a 15th-cent. chapel where some of the Darells of LITTLE-COTE lie buried.

But it is the Anglo-Saxon stone fragments that are of special interest. They include parts of shafts of crosses and a grave cover, and probably date back to the 9th cent. Some are decorated with vine scrolls and interlacing patterns and another shows the curved body of some animal biting its own tail. These stones all stand on the west side of the north aisle.

READING, *Berkshire* (5–SU7272). Henry I lies buried in this county town where John of Gaunt was married. Archbishop Laud was born in Reading, Jane Austen went to school here and Oscar Wilde was imprisoned in Reading Gaol.

Strategically placed on the Thames, occupied by the Danes in 871 and sacked again later, Reading has always been important; it was known at one time for its cloth, but now for its University and various industries. Henry I founded an abbey planned for 100 monks here in 1121. It was consecrated by Thomas à Becket in 1164 in the presence of Henry II and was for many years an important centre. Sovereigns came, Parliament met here, and the abbey was rich enough for Henry VIII to cast covetous eyes upon it at the Dissolution. The last abbot was hanged at the gates on an apparently trumped-up charge and Henry built a palace which was last used by Charles I. However, almost as little remains as of the previous Reading castle.

The Inner Gatehouse, or Abbey Gate, now a museum, was built in the 13th cent., restored in the 19th and still stands. The shell of some of the chapter house is now covered with ivy, and the west wall of the dormitory and south wall of the refectory still remain. Of great interest are the beautiful capitals, *c.* 1130, to be found in Reading Museum in Blagrave Street. The museum also has Delft ware, old metalwork and Roman antiquities dug up at SILCHESTER.

Forbury Gardens, where the monks used to walk, now contains a massive lion erected in memory of the 19th-cent. Afghan campaigns. The Church of St Laurence, originally built by order, of Henry I in the 12th cent., is now mostly 15th-cent. Greyfriars Church – at one time Guildhall, poor-house and town gaol – was built in 1285 by the Franciscans. What remains is mostly 14th-

cent. and it was restored in the 19th. St Mary's, the original parish church, occupies a central position in the town.

Reading boasts some Georgian buildings, for instance in London Street, a few earlier houses, and the splendid 19th-cent. Royal Berkshire Hospital. There are several interesting museums. The Museum of English Rural Life at White-knights Park was founded by the University of Reading in 1951 and has a collection covering all aspects of past village and country life. The Cole Museum of Zoology is mostly for students and exhibits dissections, skeletons and models, while the Museum of Greek Archaeology has a display of antiquities. Both are part of Reading University.

RINGWOOD, *Hampshire* (5–SU1405), a market town and a favourite place for retirement, is situated by the River Avon. Houses date from all periods and include pretty thatch. The church, which is particularly attractive when viewed from the bridge, was built in Early English style in the 19th cent., but contains a 15th-cent. brass to John Prophete.

Monmouth stayed here during his abortive rebellion, at a house still named after him. Later, after the disastrous Battle of Sedgemoor in 1685, he was brought back to the White Hart, and from there wrote abject letters to his uncle James II, but these did nothing to save his head. The original White Hart Inn is so named because Henry VII is said to have spared the life of a white hart while hunting nearby, giving it a fine gold collar and taking it off to WINDSOR.

Ringwood is just outside the New Forest, but with heath and woodland near at hand, it is a good centre for riding and golf and for exploring. **Hightown Common**, 2 m. E., also lies just on the edge of the forest. From here there are wonderful views, not only over the woods, but also to Dorset and down to CHRISTCHURCH, 9 m. to the S.

Just over 2 m. N. the road leads to **Ellingham** and St Mary's Church, lying on the banks of the Avon. The church has a 15th-cent. screen, a barrel roof and an hour-glass, and an almost unique tympanum, with the Lord's Prayer, the Commandments and texts all written out in a beautiful hand. The Royal Arms are dated 1671. The reredos is said to be by Grinling Gibbons, and the church has a fine picture of the Last Judgment, which was brought back from the sack of Cadiz in 1702. Dame Alicia Lisle of Moyles Court nearby lies in the churchyard. She was one of the first victims of the infamous Judge Jeffreys' Bloody Assizes. Aged about 70, she was beheaded for harbouring rebels after the Battle of Sedgemoor. The conviction was annulled four years later by special Act of Parliament on petition by her two daughters.

ROCKBOURNE, *Hampshire* (5–SU1118). Set in a hollow in the downs, complete with clear running stream, this little village is one of the prettiest in the county.

The church, restored at the end of the 19th cent., still shows traces of an earlier Norman building, particularly in the arch to the vestry. The south aisle is 13th-cent., and some lancet windows are ancient. There is an early 16th-cent. triptych, and various members of the Coote family, who used to live in the village, lie buried here. Below Rockbourne there is a column to Sir Eyre Coote, who fought with Clive in India and died in 1783.

The manor house is a fascinating building. It once belonged to the father of the Earl of Shaftesbury, who featured in Dryden's *Absalom and Achitophel*. Part is Elizabethan, the chapel 13th-cent., the splendid barn 14th-cent., and there have been 19th-cent. additions.

The country around is worth exploring. **Martin**, a charming old village with thatch, lies 2 m. W., hidden away in a corner that once was part of Wiltshire. N. of this village runs **Grims Ditch**, an old earthwork, which also runs N. of Rockbourne and BREAMORE, partly following the county boundary.

One m. SE. of Rockbourne are the interesting remains of a Roman villa. It consisted of some 46 rooms, and was discovered in 1942.

Up on the downs near the village are some splendid barrows. Grans Barrow and Knap Barrow, about 320 ft long, are both on Toyd Down. Duck's Nest Long Barrow on Rockbourne Down is particularly fine, though smaller, and here the ditches can still be seen.

ROMSEY, *Hampshire* (5–SU3521), like CHRISTCHURCH, grew up around the abbey. It lies on the banks of the River Test and the statue of Lord Palmerston gazes out over the market square. His former home, Broadlands, lies just over the bridge. A splendid porticoed house, built by Capability Brown and John Holland, it now belongs to Lord Mountbatten of Burma. Also in the market place is the former Swann Inn, where, as an old story has it, a soldier was hung from the bracket which can still be seen outside.

King John's Hunting Box was built at the beginning of the 13th cent. and later suffered various vicissitudes, becoming, in turn, abbey guest house, cottages and even a workhouse, and was only rediscovered during this century. It is a flint and stone house with dogtooth moulding. In 1306 Edward I probably visited with attendant nobles, for scratched on the plaster walls of an upper room are the heads, shields and mottoes of various nobles, as well as a lifesize drawing of the King, complete with crown. A century before, King John had sent his daughter here to be educated, paying the governess just 2d. a day.

The abbey dates back to the start of the 10th cent. During restoration work Anglo-Saxon foundations were discovered and can still be seen by lifting a trapdoor in the church. But the main body of the building as it stands today was built by Henry de Blois, Bishop of Winchester, in the 12th cent. Later, in spite of the fact that it had all its Royal charters confirmed during the time of the Dissolution, the convent buildings were ruthlessly swept away, and the abbey itself was sold to the town as a church for £100. Except for the west front, the abbey is almost entirely 12th-cent. The

Kenneth Scowen

Salisbury: the High Street Gate

Norman nave is over 250 ft long and soars to a height of some 70 ft. There are wonderful treasures to be seen. At the back of the altar in the south choir aisle is a small Anglo-Saxon rood, showing Christ with angels and soldiers. A Crucifixion, with the hand of God reaching down, hangs on the west wall of the south transept, and dates back to Anglo-Saxon times. It was found facing into the wall, which is probably why it has survived. An early-16th-cent. painted reredos shows the Resurrection, and there is also a portion of an ancient cope and an old chest, about 1500, on display. Among the monuments, the 13th-cent. effigy of a woman in Purbeck marble and the monument to Sir William Petty, who helped found the Royal Society, are outstanding. The vestry contains the Romsey Psalter, an illuminated manuscript of the 15th cent., and the deed of sale of the abbey to the townspeople, signed by Henry VIII.

East Wellow lies a little W. of Romsey and is mainly remarkable for its church. Florence Nightingale, who lived at Embley Park nearby, lies buried in the churchyard. Inside are some remarkable 13th-cent. wall paintings. A woman carrying a spindle gazes at a knight nearby, while crowned figures watch the scene. Part of St Christopher holding a child remains, and there is a very faint painting of the murder of St Thomas à Becket.

RYDE, *Isle of Wight* (5–SZ5992), the island's chief entry port, is 4½ m. across the roadstead of

Spithead from PORTSMOUTH on the mainland, with which it is connected by British Rail ferries and hovercraft. The town stands on steep hills and the area is well wooded. The parish church, All Saints', has the tallest spire of the Ryde skyline and it is visible for miles around.

Ryde is the island's largest holiday resort and its population of 20,000 can be more than doubled in the season. The pier, nearly ½ m. long, the Esplanade and the Parade Gardens edge a sandy beach that stretches for 7 m. round to Seaview at Nettlestone Point. Seaview, which has good prawn and lobster fishing, is very much a family resort; children like Puckpool Park. Ryde has an array of social and sporting clubs, and a special feature is the yearly carnival and fair held at the beginning of September.

ST CATHERINE'S POINT, *Isle of Wight* (5–SZ4975). This is the most southerly point on the island. The River Medina rises in the northern part of **St Catherine's Down**, and here, too, is the Alexandrian Pillar, by Michael Hoy, commemorating the visit to Great Britain of the Emperor of all the Russias. Ironically, the pillar also bears a tablet honouring the British dead of the Crimean War. The St Catherine lighthouse stands 136 ft above the sea, and flashes its light over a radius of 18 m. Below the main light is a fixed red light, and in bad weather a foghorn sounds at intervals. Because of landslides the main road round St Catherine's Point from VENTNOR now goes through **Niton** and over the Upper Cliff to join the old road again W. of **Blackgang**.

SALISBURY, *Wiltshire* (5–SU1429), is a delight, a town where there is no need to go looking for interests in dark corners. It is everywhere in the streets, flanked by gabled houses and buildings of all periods set in happy juxtaposition. Although architecture gracefully spans the centuries, it is all part of an original plan. Unlike WINCHESTER, which grew up as a medieval medley, Salisbury was built on a grid or chequer system, which left space between the blocks.

Ancient medieval bridges span the river, for the city is built on the junction of the Avon and Nadder. Constable painted one of his famous pictures here. Inns date from all periods. Pepys once stayed at The Old George, sleeping in a silken bed. It was built in 1320, with later additions; the ground floor has now been removed to form the entrance to a pedestrian shopping precinct. The restaurant next door contains a splendid Jacobean staircase. Fielding lived in the Cathedral Close, though it is doubtful whether he wrote *Tom Jones* while there. Nell Gwynn bought a pair of scissors here for 100 guineas, and all through the ages kings, queens and the famous have visited this city. Perhaps the unhappiest was the Duke of Buckingham, beheaded as a traitor by Richard III in 1485. But most of the city's history is less gory, since it managed to escape most disturbances.

Salisbury's history dates back to the 13th cent.

when it was decided to move the bishop's see from OLD SARUM, where it had been made uncomfortable by too much wind, too little water and squabbles with the military. The site of the cathedral, or so the old story goes, was chosen by the fall of an arrow from a bow drawn at venture. The foundations were laid in 1220, and the main part of the building was complete by about 1258. It is said to have been built on woolpacks for a total sum of £27,000.

The first sight of the cathedral is particularly impressive when approached through St Ann's Gate. It soars, an elegant example of Early English architecture, built as a whole in one single style, though the magnificent spire, 404 ft tall and the highest in England, was added in the 14th cent., and the cloisters and chapter house were also added later.

The west front has tier upon tier of niches, most of which stand empty. The nave, measuring 198 ft, has a clear, uncluttered beauty, little changed since it was first built. However, at the end of the 18th cent. James Wyatt, who enjoyed the unflattering title of "destroyer", swept away screens, tombs, chantries, campanile and more, as if on some gigantic spring-clean. He is actually said to have thrown the ancient stained glass down a drain. He also rearranged the nave tombs into nice tidy lines, thus, for example, divorcing the ancient Altar of Relicks, with the niches for the sick to creep into, from the tomb of St Osmund, the patron saint of the cathedral.

However, many beautiful tombs do lie in Salisbury Cathedral, and in the north transept there is the oldest clock in England, dating back to 1386. Made in wrought iron and with no dial, it struck only the hours.

The choir has a beautiful 13th-cent. roof painting, covered by Wyatt, but later restored. In the octagonal chapter house the stone vaulting flies away from one single pillar, and a series of beautiful sculptures decorate a stone plinth around the walls. The library is particularly interesting for it contains many old manuscripts and documents, including a closely written copy of the Magna Carta. The medieval glass in the cloister should also be noted.

The Cathedral Close is one of the most beautiful in all England. Graves were ruthlessly swept away at the end of the 18th cent., and the whole was smoothed and levelled. There has always been a tradition of good building here, and houses from various centuries harmonize gracefully. Mompesson House dates from the start of the 18th cent. Built for a rich merchant, the panelling, plasterwork and superb staircase are particularly outstanding. The house belongs to the National Trust and can be visited, as, sometimes, can The Old Deanery, which is now part of Sarum St Michael Teachers' Training College. Originally built in the 13th cent., the timber roof is unique, since it still shows the hole through which smoke from a central fire escaped. The former Bishop's Palace, now Choristers' School, should not be missed, and may be visited by appointment with the headmaster.

Salisbury churches, too, are of interest. St Martin's, in the SE., is the oldest, dating back before the Early English period, but with later additions. St Thomas of Canterbury in the centre of town boasts a remarkable Doom painting over the chancel arch. It is mostly Perpendicular, as is St Edmund's, though the tower here is later.

The list of buildings with interest is unending. The façade of the Joiners' Hall in St Ann Street is 16th-cent., the Shoemakers' Guildhall 17th, and the Guildhall 18th-cent. The Poultry Cross in Silver Street is much earlier – c. 15th cent. Of the many charitable buildings Frowd's Almshouses in Bedwin Street have particular charm, as has Trinity Hospital, now mostly 18th-cent. The Banqueting Hall of John Halle – a bad-tempered 15th-cent. mayor – should not be missed. It is at the entrance to the Odeon Cinema and was restored by Pugin in 1834.

The Council House, an attractive red-brick building rebuilt in the 18th cent., now belongs to the town, and in the tree-studded grounds are the remains of the city's ramparts. But for an overall picture of the region visit the museum. Exhibits date back to prehistory. There are some charming interiors and a delightful collection of pottery and porcelain.

SANDFORD ORCAS, Dorset (4–ST6220).
Along the hills to the W. of this village ran a pre-Roman ridgeway, probably part of the route from MAIDEN CASTLE to CADBURY CASTLE. At the north end of the village beside the church is a fine manor house, open to the public. Mainly Elizabethan, on much earlier foundations, it is lived in and has some good period furniture and an attractive garden with peacocks. The church, 13th- to 15th-cent., though the interior was much restored in the 19th cent., has a section of a 15th-cent. screen across its tower arch and an interesting alabaster monument (1607) to William Knoyle, of the manorial family, in the chapel off its south porch.

SANDHURST, Berkshire (5–SU8361).
Although the straggling village could not be called beautiful, the country round it is attractive, for Sandhurst lies near the River Blackwater, surrounded by moor, firs and magnificent beechwoods.

Development came with the removal here from Great Marlow of the Royal Military Academy in 1807, to be built on land bought by William Pitt from his niece in 1801. (See CAMBERLEY.)

SANDOWN, Isle of Wight (5–SZ5984), lies 2
m. N. from its twin town SHANKLIN. The 6-m. sweep of Sandown Bay, known for safe bathing, is probably the finest stretch of coast-line on the island. It curves round from fort-crowned BEMBRIDGE Down to Culver and Red Cliffe, past the Chine and Luccombe on to the bluff of Dunnose. The 1,000-ft pier has a pavilion and sun terrace, the Esplanade a mile of amusements, bars, eating places and gardens. The Museum of Geology displays a unique collection of fossils.

SAVERNAKE FOREST, Wiltshire (5–SU
2266), covers some 2,300 acres, and dates back to before the Norman Conquest. The trees – oak, elm and beech – are magnificent. Deer roam here, and rare birds and plants can be found in some of the less popular glades.

Jane Seymour's father was once the hereditary Warden of Savernake, and she is said to have danced in the great barn at Wolfhall near Burbage to celebrate her wedding to Henry VIII. Today the Warden is the Marquess of Ailesbury, and Tottenham House, his former seat but now a school, is at the SE. of the forest. From there, through the trees, you can see the Ailesbury Column, erected to commemorate the recovery of George III from his madness.

Savernake has grown more beautiful over the centuries. Many of the splendid beech avenues were planted in the 18th cent. The greatest of the stately rows is the Grand Avenue which runs from the NW. to the SE., right through the heart of the forest. From the centre of this avenue radiate eight riding and walking paths. Cars must be left on the metalled roads, and although picnickers are allowed in the forest, there is also a special picnic site, ¾ m. S. of MARLBOROUGH on the ANDOVER road.

SELBORNE, Hampshire (5–SU7433), is one
of the most famous villages in Hampshire and it was Gilbert White who made it so. Born in 1720, he was a don and sometime vicar of Selborne, and will always be remembered for his classic book, *The Natural History of Selborne*, published 1788.

The village is gathered around the green, named the Plestor, which was once a market place. Here, too, is the church, with its Norman arcades, Perpendicular tower arch, and later work added by William White, nephew of Gilbert. The church contains a 16th-cent. Flemish triptych showing the Adoration of the Magi winged by SS. Andrew and George, and a Flemish sculpture of much the same date showing the Descent from the Cross. There is also a window to Gilbert White showing St Francis feeding birds, and in the churchyard an enormous yew tree. Graves in the churchyard were built with brick vaults to counter body-snatching.

Gilbert White's House, the Wakes, is nearby and contains a museum. Part is devoted to this remarkable man, and other parts show mementoes of Captain Oates who accompanied Scott to the South Pole, and died so gallantly there.

One m. NE., at Priory Farm, the remains of a large church, part of the Augustinian priory founded in 1233, were recently excavated.

Behind the village is a steep hill covered with beech, called The Hanger. It is topped by a boulder called the Wishing Stone and was a favourite haunt of Gilbert White. Over 250 acres of common, including Selborne Hill and the woods around here, belong to the National Trust.

SHAFTESBURY, Dorset (4–ST8622). The
county's only hill-top town, it has a long history. It was a West Saxon fortified town; King Alfred

gave it a nunnery in *c.* 880, with his daughter, Ethelgiva, its first abbess, and an Anglo-Saxon town grew round it. To the abbey in 981 Edward the Martyr (*see* CORFE CASTLE) was brought for burial. It became one of the richest in the area, with an immense church, but after the Dissolution was destroyed. Its foundations can be inspected W. of the Market Place.

In its buildings the town is now disappointing, but, falling steeply S. from St Peter's Church, the ancient, wide, curved and cobbled Gold Hill is probably the most photographed street in Dorset. At its top is an excellent, small museum containing a collection of the buttons for the manufacture of which this town and BLANDFORD FORUM were till the 19th cent. famous. St Peter's Church, early 15th-cent., has an elaborately carved north parapet, some 15th-cent. glass and a crypt which was for long the next-door pub's cellar. Two other remarkable things: in the Grosvenor Hotel the Chevy Chase Sideboard, lavishly carved from a single piece of oak, and, in the Town Hall, the Byzant which was used till 1830 in rites connected with the town's need at that time to cart all its water up from the foot of the hill.

SHANKLIN, *Isle of Wight* (5–SZ5881). This busy and popular seaside town is set on a 150-ft cliff, but gentle slopes lead down to the beach, pier, esplanade and marine gardens and the many eating places, bars and amusements. The bathing is judged to be extremely safe. The wooded **Chine,** 180 ft wide and nearly 300 ft deep, is a noted beauty-spot where French raiders were defeated in an engagement in 1545. Keats wrote part of *Endymion* in the shade of its tall trees. A small stream, rising from the Chalybeate Spring, flows through the cleft to the beach. At the inland end of the Chine lies the **Old Village** and its thatched cottages with roses and honeysuckle round the doors. The fountain has the British and American flags emblazoned in the stonework, and a verse by Longfellow who stayed here in 1868. The Church of St Blasius, of 14th-cent. origin, has Shanklin Down for a backdrop.

SHERBORNE, *Dorset* (4–ST6316). A mainly yellow-stone town, with BLANDFORD FORUM the most architecturally consistent in Dorset, it also has the greatest wealth of medieval buildings. From 705, when the Anglo-Saxon King Ine of Wessex decided to divide the vast diocese of WINCHESTER, till 1075 when the see was transferred to OLD SARUM, it was a cathedral city, with St Aldhelm its first bishop. From 864 to 1539 it had a monastery, the monks taking over the cathedral as their abbey church, rebuilding it in the 12th cent. and again, to its present proportions, in the 15th. Ever since its monastic days, education has been its most famous business: it has major boys' and girls' public schools and several others, both private and state. Since 1740 it has made silk, and since 1871 gloves, and now has mineral water, soft drinks, printing, dairying, fibreglass and other industries. None of these is obtrusive: its centre remains compact and unindustrialized.

The supreme thing in the abbey is the 15th-cent. vaulted Ham-stone roof covering its entire length. By putting money in a slot (attached to a pillar in the south aisle) you can floodlight the choir. In the Lady Chapel behind the choir is an engraved glass reredos (1968) by Laurence Whistler, and a brass in the abbey says two kings, Ethelbald (860) and Ethelbert (866), were buried in it. In the west wall is an Anglo-Saxon doorway.

Just SW. of the abbey the almshouses, founded in 1437 and extended in the 19th cent., have an attractive chapel with an exceptional triptych painted on oak (*c.* 1475), probably Flemish or German. Nearby is the museum devoted to local history. E. of the Abbey, beside Cheap Street, the main shopping one, the conduit was the monks' wash-house, dating from the 14th or 15th cent. and not much restored. Sherborne School for boys is immediately N. of the Abbey. Founded in 1550, it took over many of the dissolved monastery's buildings. The chapel was the Abbot's Hall. Also worth hunting out are the 17th-cent. schoolhouse, now a dining hall, the Library and the Abbot's Kitchen. Long Street, Hound Street, Newland and the Green all have rows of pretty houses. Lord Digby's School, built *c.* 1720, towers grandly above a wall N. of Newland. The building contains paintings by Sir James Thornhill. William Macready, the actor, once lived here.

Just E. of the town are its two castles, locally known as the Old and New, the one very ruinous, the other a stately home and open to the public. The Old was built *c.* 1107–39 by Bishop Roger, Henry I's Chancellor; was twice besieged and taken by Cromwell's forces in the Civil War and was afterwards destroyed by them. The core of the ugly but interesting New was built by Sir Walter Raleigh in *c.* 1594. In 1592 he had rented the Old with the intention of modernizing it as his home, but soon decided to build a new house instead. It was here, it is said, that, while smoking tobacco he had brought back from Virginia, he was doused with beer by his servant who thought he was on fire. Four wings were added to the building in 1625. In it William of Orange is believed to have printed his Proclamation to the English People (1688). The artificial lake between the two castles and the grounds of the New were designed by Capability Brown in the 18th cent.

The town has an annual week-long carnival, its climax being the first Saturday in September.

SHERBORNE ST JOHN, *Hampshire* (5–SU 6155), lies close to BASINGSTOKE, so there has been much new building in this village, but there is still an old part. The old church is mostly Perpendicular, and the south door dates back to the middle of the 12th cent. Inside, the king-post roof is impressive, as are the Norman font and the 17th-cent. desk and pulpit. There are also some interesting brasses, dating mostly from the 15th cent., in the Brocas chapel. This family has owned Beaurepaire Park, an old moated house near the village, for many years, but unfortunately it suffered a severe fire some years ago and was badly damaged.

The Vyne, a mellow Tudor brick house facing on to a great artificial lake on the north side, lies in a hollow about 1 m. NW. of Sherborne St John. It was built between about 1500 and 1520 by William Sandys, who rose to be Lord Chamberlain under Henry VIII and entertained that monarch here at least three times. In 1653, the house passed to the Chute family and many additions and alterations were made in that century and the following. The house now belongs to the National Trust and is open to the public.

One of the most remarkable parts of this beautiful house is the chapel, which was probably built between 1518 and 1527 and was once described by Horace Walpole as the "most heavenly chapel in the world". The ceiling is vaulted, and the two tiered stalls with canopies are particularly beautiful. The 16th-cent. Flemish glass in the windows shows portraits of Henry VIII, Catherine of Aragon and Margaret of Scotland with attendant patron saints. Pet dogs nestle by the two queens.

The remarkable oak gallery, which runs along the whole west front of the house, also dates from this period. It must have been built sometime before 1528, since that is the date of Cardinal Wolsey's fall, and his device is shown among others that decorate the walls above and below the fine linen-fold panelling which stretches almost from floor to ceiling. The carved marble chimney with its cascade of fruits is by John Webb, the son-in-law of Inigo Jones.

He also designed the pretty domed Garden House, and in 1654 built the Classical portico on the north side – the first one to be added to an English country house.

About a century later John Chute, a friend of Horace Walpole, made further alterations. He designed the magnificent staircase, one of the glories of the house, enhanced by the moulded ceiling, and beautifully fluted pillars. The staircase had to be fitted into a limited space, which was narrow but long, and this was achieved by a single narrow flight, which branches and then sweeps round to form galleries.

SHOTTESBROOKE, *Berkshire* (5–SU8377). In 1337 Sir William Trussell founded a college here, and the church thus became collegiate, one of only three in Berkshire. Although college and church were destroyed by fire in the 14th cent., they were rebuilt, only to be suppressed in 1548.

Nothing remains of the college buildings, but the remarkable flint cruciform Church of St John the Baptist is preserved in its entirety in the Decorated style. It has a particularly graceful ribbed spire, flowing tracery round the windows, a fine south porch, and a sedilia and piscina in the chancel. There is also a fine canopied tomb to Sir William Trussell and his wife, and a carved figure, 1535, of William Throckmorton, the last warden of the college. The church also contains interesting brasses, and some of the original glass.

In the churchyard lies Francis Cherry, a squire with such strong Jacobite sympathies that he led William III over dangerous jumps in the hunting field, with the idea of disposing of him.

The church stands in Shottesbrooke Park, next to a mostly 18th-cent. mansion, incorporating Tudor brickwork.

SILCHESTER, *Hampshire* (5–SU6462), is near the Berkshire border, and to approach from the direction of Mortimer gives you an idea of how lonely and empty the location must have looked to the Roman inhabitants.

However, long before the Romans arrived the site was important, since there was a great Celtic earthwork here. Later the Roman walls followed the line of the earthwork, which is a curious octagonal shape.

Though the land today is now mostly arable, the remains of the Roman wall, built of flint, can still be seen. In parts it must have reached 20 ft high, and it enclosed an area of about 100 acres. The wall was broken in four places by main gates, probably set to join Roman roads, and also by two smaller gates.

Silchester, or Calleva Atrebatum as it was then called, was built on the usual Roman block system, with a central square containing the forum. The remains of three temples, of not very high standard, have been found, so also have baths, houses, shops and an unusually large basilica, which may have been as much as 60 ft high. The main trade was probably dyeing, and from bone remains shops such as poulterers and a butcher have been identified. But Silchester was not a particularly large place and probably only contained between about 70 and 80 houses of any size.

Inside the walls there stood one remarkable building: a tiny Christian church dating back to the 4th cent., and the only one known to have been built during the Roman occupation. Just outside the east gate are the remains of an oval amphitheatre, one of the few that were built in Britain.

However, the only buildings that can be seen today are an old farm and the parish church, which is mainly Early English, with additions in Decorated and Perpendicular style and with a 15th-cent. screen, medieval wall painting and the 14th-cent. effigy of a woman.

For when the Romans left, Calleva Atrebatum simply decayed. It was not razed, indeed it was probably inhabited. But the town faded away, and stayed quite forgotten until excavations were started in the mid-19th cent. and continued into the 20th.

There is a small Calleva Museum on the site which shows casts of some of the finds. For instance, a head of the god Serapis, a bronze eagle, and an inscription from one of the temples can be seen here, and there are also models of houses, the old church and the west gate, just as they must have been. But to see most of what was excavated here you must go to READING Museum.

Four m. E. is **Stratfield Saye House**, rebuilt in 1795 and presented to the 1st Duke of Wellington by the British Parliament.

SIXPENNY HANDLEY, *Dorset* (5–ST9917). An attractive rural village, this was the home of the county's most infamous smuggler, Isaac Gulliver. In 1768 he married a local landlord's daughter and made the pub the headquarters of his operations which extended from POOLE to LYME REGIS. In the days when CRANBORNE CHASE was a royal hunting forest, the village was the home of keen deer poachers. An inscription on a tombstone by the north-west gate of the churchyard tells how carcasses were hidden under it. In 1892 a great fire destroyed the village. It was rebuilt without the help of great architects or rich patrons. The 19th-cent. restored church still has its 15th-cent. tower and some fierce-looking gargoyles.

The road NW. over Cranborne Chase to SHAFTESBURY is beautiful.

SONNING, Berkshire (5–SU7575), is only just over 3 m. from READING, yet is still secluded and one of the prettiest of all the riverside villages, with thatched timber-framed cottages and hotel, mellowed red-brick houses and an old mill.

The river is spanned by an 11-arched bridge, one of the oldest crossing the Thames. Two m. away it is joined by the Kennet, but at Sonning it splits into several channels. The woods of Holme Park, the site of Reading's Blue Coat School, overhang the water.

In the 16th cent. Leland described the Bishop's House here as a "fair old house of stone". Sonning was once part of the diocese of RAMSBURY in Wiltshire and the Bishop's Palace stood here till the 16th cent. Now there is only a mound, beside the path from the church to the tow-path.

The church, heavily restored in Victorian times, shows work from many periods, including an Anglo-Saxon coffin lid built into a north-aisle buttress. There is an oak screen, some splendid monuments, and many brasses, the earliest dating from 1434.

SOPLEY, Hampshire (5–SZ1596), is beautifully set by the watermeadows of the River Avon, a few miles from CHRISTCHURCH. On the opposite bank of the river is St Catherine's Hill, 160 ft high, which gives fine views over the country.

The cruciform church is built on an artificial mound, which may date back centuries. Mostly 13th-cent., it has a good Jacobean pulpit and some attractive linen-fold panelling. Two figures, the man in tunic and hood, and the woman with a wimple, are carved in Purbeck marble and might be the church's founders.

Two m. N. is **Tyrrell's Ford.** It is said that Sir Walter Tyrrell fled across here after he had killed William Rufus, though according to him the killing was an accident. Bisterne House can just be seen from the road, 2 m. N. Edward IV once conferred a knighthood on its owner for killing a fearsome dragon.

SOUTHAMPTON, Hampshire (5–SU4212). The story of a great seaport must, in broad outline, tell the history of a seafaring nation. So it is with Southampton. Today it is a spreading city, commercially important as well as a seaport, but its history stretches back centuries. The Romans had a station nearby at Bitterne. The Danes plundered on several occasions and in 1016 Cnut was offered the crown of England here. It is said that he rebuked his courtiers by commanding the waves to recede at Southampton, although BOSHAM in Sussex also claims this odd tale.

Armies embarked for the Crusades from here, as they did to win the battles of Crécy and Agincourt. Philip II of Spain landed here on his way to marry Queen Mary, and the Emperor Charles V also visited. Southampton has played an important part in all matters connected with the sea, and in 1620 the Mayflower set out from here to America, a fact which is now commemorated by a column.

Southampton was the main English port of call for Venetian ships till the 16th cent., after which its trade declined. In the 18th cent. it became a fashionable resort with the assembly rooms and theatre associated with this development in Georgian times. Pope, Swift, Horace Walpole and Jane Austen all came on visits. It was an embarkation port in the Napoleonic wars and began to develop again as a trading port after the opening of the first dock in 1842. Thereafter Southampton developed into the great passenger port of today.

Southampton suffered heavy devastation during the Second World War and much of the building is new. Although the old castle has long since disappeared, much that is old has miraculously survived.

Situated on a peninsula, the town was often attacked and needed fortifications. The south and west walls of these defences faced the River Test, and the east and north walls were moated. Bargate is one of the finest town gates surviving. It dates back to Norman times, though altered and restored later, and a statue of George III in a toga stands near. On the first floor the old Guildhall has now been turned into a museum and can be visited.

The 15th-cent. Catch Cold and the round 14th-cent. Arundel towers are close by, while God's House Tower has now become a museum for local archaeological exhibits. There is also a fine series of arches with houses above.

Some interesting houses have also survived. The Wool House, now the Maritime Museum, is early 14th-cent. and in the 18th cent. was used for Spanish prisoners of war. One 12th-cent. house is called Canute's House, and another Norman two-storied building, with a fire-place and chimney, is named King John's Palace. In Simnel Street is some 14th-cent. vaulting, but perhaps the most interesting house of all is the Tudor House. Henry VIII and Anne Boleyn, it is said, stayed here, and there is still a panelled banqueting room and minstrels' gallery to be seen. Now a museum showing local antiquities, Tudor House has an attractive Elizabethan garden.

Of the churches, St Michael's is the oldest, with tower arches dating back to Norman times, though the rest has been much restored. Inside is an early black font, one of the few in this country, imported from Tournai. The Southampton Art

Gallery, which specializes mostly in contemporary British painting, can be found at the Civic Centre.

To the NE. (4½ m.) lies **Eastleigh**, an important railway centre that was laid out in the 19th cent. with its streets on a grid pattern.

SOUTHWICK, *Hampshire* (5–SU6208). Southwick, though only 3 m. N. of PORTSMOUTH, retains its peaceful charm. There has been development, but this is separate, and in the unspoilt part there are timber-framed houses, some thatch and 18th-cent. buildings.

The church is mostly in Perpendicular style, but shows work from other periods. It possesses a splendid 18th-cent. painted altar-piece, showing joyful cherubs and doves, and a 17th-cent. gallery and pulpit. Here lies John Whyte, 1567, and his wife, with brasses of the whole family on top of the tomb. Whyte acquired the Augustinian priory here at the Dissolution. The house, founded in 1133 at PORTCHESTER, moved here 15 years or so later. Whyte razed most of the buildings, including the church, and fashioned a house from the prior's lodging. This and a subsequent house were destroyed by fire, and now Southwick House dates from the 19th cent. and is occupied by the Navy. It was used as Eisenhower's Headquarters for the Normandy invasion. In the grounds are small remains, including an ancient undercroft, perhaps of the priory refectory.

Just S. of Southwick there are some fine views from **Boarhunt**. The main fabric of the church here is late Anglo-Saxon, though much restored in the 19th cent.

Fareham, a short distance SW., is well worth a visit if only to see the High Street. Naval officers used to retire here, and since the busy centre of the town has moved, this road has again become peaceful. It is lined with Georgian buildings of many styles, some with bow windows, and in the characteristic red brick of the district.

SOUTH WRAXALL, *Wiltshire* (4–ST8364). Near the Somerset borders and only 2½ m. N. of BRADFORD-ON-AVON, South Wraxall has much of interest. The 17th-cent. Longs Arms Inn stands near the church, which is 15th-cent. but much restored. The tower dates back to the 13th cent. and has a saddleback roof, unusual in these parts. Inside are some splendid tombs to the Long family, dating from medieval to present times.

But the glory of this village is South Wraxall Manor – one of the most lovely stone medieval houses to be found anywhere and started by Robert Long in the early 15th cent.; the gatehouse, with oriel window, and the hall belong to this period. The house is built round three sides of a court and has been added to over the years. The drawing-room, for example, which has beautiful plasterwork, is 17th-cent. The manor belongs to the Long family, and it is said that together with Sir Walter Raleigh, Sir Walter Long was one of the earliest tobacco smokers in England.

Nearby are the remains of a 14th-cent. hospice, which used to receive travellers. The hall and chapel still exist, and are part of a farm.

SPARSHOLT, *Berkshire* (5–SU3487), is a pleasant village with thatched half-timbered cottages, and a Georgian manor house. It lies under the downs on the edge of the Vale of the White Horse.

The large church is of great interest. The north doorway is late 12th-cent., the chalk chancel early 14th-cent. and contains a chalk sedilia and Easter Sepulchre. The Decorated windows have delightful tracery, the wooden nave roof is impressive, and the north nave window has medieval glass. As well as about nine brasses, the earliest dated 1353, there are some interesting monuments. An early-14th-cent. effigy of a knight with crossed legs rests in the chancel and there are three rare and beautiful 14th-cent. oak effigies showing a knight and his two wives.

On Sparsholt Down nearby there are two ancient bowl barrows.

STALBRIDGE, *Dorset* (4–ST7317). A small town which, as well as serving the farmers of Blackmoor Vale, has for generations made high-quality gloves. Its centre is mainly old, of cream-grey stone and pleasantly disorganized. Beside its main street is the finest market cross in Dorset, 14th-cent., some 30 ft tall and sculptured, gloriously brown-gold. It is restored, but faithfully. The church, up a steep lane at the north end of the town, was rebuilt in 1878. It has a nice north chapel, which was restored in 1965, containing a curious skeletal effigy of a woman. The splendid 5-m. wall just W. encloses Stalbridge Park. The great house, built in 1638, was the home of Robert Boyle, the scientist, but it has long since gone.

Three m. W., **Purse Caundle Manor** (*c.* 1470), in the middle of its village, is frequently open and is attractive. Some years ago its ghost became so worrying that a staircase had to be removed.

About 3½ m. E., **Marnhull** – Thomas Hardy's "Marlott", birthplace of Tess – has a fine church with a grey 15th-cent. tower patched up with white stones. It has an outstanding nave ceiling of carved panels and an alabaster tomb with effigies of John Carent and his two wives (*c.* 1470). The east window is by Burne-Jones. Scattered around are numerous attractive houses; for instance, in Carraway Lane off the main road about ¼ m. S.

STEEPLE, *Dorset* (4–SY9080), in the wooded, sheltered central vale of the Isle of Purbeck, Steeple is just a strong, modest grey church on a hillock above a farm and manor house. Over the east doorway of the church's north transept (and elsewhere) the arms of the Lawrence family, medieval lords of the manor, are blended with the stars and stripes commemorating the Washington family who produced the first President of the United States. The families intermarried in the 14th cent.

Over the ridge, 1 m. N. of Steeple, is **Creech Grange**, an old house and garden of wistful beauty, frequently open. Tudor basically, it was largely rebuilt in the 17th, 18th and 19th cents.,

Southampton docks

but in Tudor style. Perhaps the nicest thing at Creech Grange, long the home of the Bonds, related to Thomas Bond who built BOND STREET, is the little formal garden falling to a still, dark lake. There are peacocks, and, on the wooded hillside to the S., a folly-arch of *c.* 1740.

From ½ m. E., at Creech Barrow, there are views for miles N., E. and W.

Some 1¼ m. NE., the famous **Blue Pool, Furzebrook** is a pretty lake, a flooded clay pit, amid pine trees, its surrounds worn threadbare by countless feet, its extreme blue-greenness an effect of the clay.

STEEPLE ASHTON, *Wiltshire* (4–ST9056), used to be known as Staple Ashton, on account of the wool market established by charter in 1387. Today a market cross – said to date back to 1071 but several times repaired since then – still stands in the centre of the village. Although there is some fairly uninteresting new building, there are some attractive old houses.

But most impressive of all is the magnificent Perpendicular Church of St Mary, built between 1480 and 1500. The tower is even earlier, but it lost its stone spire when struck by lightning in 1670.

A late-medieval church in its full glory, the oak and plaster nave roof, the stone-vaulted aisles and the carving are all particularly beautiful. On the north wall is a two-sided brass to Deborah Marks, who died aged 99 in 1730, having lived under Cromwell and seven monarchs.

The neighbouring village of **Keevil**, about 3 m. NE., is pretty with cottages, Talboys, a 15th-cent. half-timbered house, and a stone manor house dating from 1580. Cruelly imprisoned here for two years by her father for falling in love with the curate, Anne Beach scratched her name on the window pane. Eventually, faced with the choice of her fortune or her curate, she chose marriage, but sadly died soon after.

STEVENTON, *Berkshire* (5–SU4691), a large village on the slopes of the downs, has some picturesque half-timbered houses and a large green fringed with trees. More trees line the

ancient causeway which runs from the church to the green. Originally built by monks, it was designed to protect people from getting their feet wet in bad weather, and dates back to the days when there was an alien priory at Steventon. Little remains of this, except Priory Cottages, which used once to be part of the old buildings, and still contain the great hall of the priory. Today they belong to the National Trust, as does the Causeway, a medieval timber-framed building, with parts dating from the 13th and 15th cents.

STOCKBRIDGE, *Hampshire* (5–SU3535). Permission to hold a weekly market here was granted as far back as the reign of Richard I. Stockbridge was also, until the 1832 Reform Bill, the most corrupt of all rotten boroughs, and it is said that Sir Richard Steele, when canvassing, promised an apple stuck full of guineas to the first couple to have a child after he was elected. However, he did not get in and was therefore not obliged to keep his promise.

It is set in the Test valley, which has some of the best, and most expensive, fishing in England, and Stockbridge is therefore a great fishing centre. Fishermen forgather in particular at the Grosvenor Hotel, which has an enormous overhanging porch with a room above and is in the main street opposite the 19th-cent. town hall.

The wide, irregular street, made bright with houses of all styles but predominantly Tudor and Georgian, crosses a low bridge, which gives delightful views, and rises to a hill at each end. It gives the impression that Stockbridge is a big town, but hardly any side streets back the main one.

Of the old church only the chancel – mostly 13th-cent. – still stands, and the original door ring and traces of wall paintings also remain. A new 19th-cent. church has been built.

Nearby is some beautiful country. Some 223 acres roundabout, together with the lordship of the manor, belong to the National Trust, and the manorial courts still meet every March, when a 17th-cent. mace is exhibited.

One m. E. of the village, Stockbridge Down, a chalk down dotted with about 15 ancient barrows and showing traces of old earthworks, also belongs to the National Trust. Up here, among the juniper bushes and fir trees, is **Woolbury Camp**, an old Iron Age hill-fort, covering about 20 acres and giving marvellous views as far as the Isle of Wight. Another camp, **Danebury Ring**, dates from the same period and lies NW. of the village; it has been acquired by the County Council as a public amenity and nature trail.

STOCKTON, *Wiltshire* (5–ST9738). The boundaries of this small village remain much the same as they were in the Domesday Book. Set on the River Wylye, with pretty thatch and a fine Elizabethan farm-house complete with great barn, there is much to recommend Stockton.

Stockton House, a beautiful building, was first started by John Topp, in Elizabethan times, and he also built the charming almshouses. Approached by an archway, they cluster round a courtyard.

The church, mainly 14th-cent., has many fine monuments. John Topp (1640) lies here, together with his wife and children, in a tomb with a canopied top. Nearby is the tomb of Jerome Poticary (1596) who built the farm-house. A wall, solid apart from a doorway and two squints, cuts off the chancel. There is a Norman font.

STONEHENGE, *Wiltshire* (5–SU1141). There is nothing quite like this awe-inspiring monument anywhere else in the world, yet at first sight it is curiously disappointing, probably because it is set on a plain so vast that in comparison the stones at first seem insignificant. It is only when man stands close to the stones that he seems so puny in comparison and it is hard to imagine how centuries ago, with only primitive tools to help them, men could possibly have placed these huge boulders into position.

First to be seen are a bank and a ditch some 100 ft from the stones. Inside this earthwork is a circle of some 56 holes, some of them marked with chalk. These were discovered by John Aubrey in the 17th cent. and named after him, but at no time did the holes contain stones.

The ancient doorway to this site was formed by the so-called Slaughter Stone, now fallen, at the entrance to the earthwork. About 100 ft outside the entrance is a large stone known as the Heel Stone. Both are sarsens, a type of sandstone boulder.

All this work belongs to Stonehenge I, or the first phase of building, which took place in the late Neolithic period somewhere around 2000 B.C., but little is known of its purpose.

Between about 1700 and 1600 B.C., during Stonehenge II, about 80 blue stones, brought over by sea from the Prescelly Mountains in Pembrokeshire, were placed in two concentric circles with the entrance at the NE. This work was never quite finished, but the stone avenue, leading from the entrance to the Avon and enclosing the Heel Stone, also belongs to this period. It probably marks the route by which these stones were brought on to the site. This was all the work of the Beaker Folk, agricultural invaders from the Continent. They settled peacefully here and were given their names from the pottery vessels they used.

Stonehenge III started soon after 1600 B.C., during the Bronze Age – a rich and successful time for those who lived then. At this time the blue stones were moved and about 80 enormous sarsen stones were dragged here from the MARLBOROUGH Downs. These were formed into the outer ring of large uprights, linked together by capping lintels, some curved. Others were made into an inner horseshoe shape, consisting of five trilithons – a trilithon consisting of two upright stones topped by a lintel.

During the second phase of Stonehenge III, from about 1550 to 1400 B.C., an oval of blue stones was placed inside the horseshoe of sarsens and included two small blue-stone trilithons. A sandstone block, named the Altar Stone, was brought over from Milford Haven, dressed, and then placed in the centre. Outside the sarsen circle two circles of holes were dug but never filled, since for some reason the whole project was then abandoned.

The third phase of Stonehenge III took place in about 1300 B.C., the oval of blue stones being then arranged into a horseshoe shape, consisting of some 19 stones which still stand. Meanwhile, a circle of blue stones was also placed between the sarsen horseshoe and the outer sarsen circle.

The whole history of Stonehenge covers a period from about 2200 B.C. to 1300 B.C., but exactly why it was built remains something of a mystery. A great many theories have been advanced. But one fact is certain. The axis of Stonehenge was carefully aligned with the sunrise on 21 June, the longest day in the year. Lately it has been discovered to be an extremely sophisticated arrangement; but, to oversimplify, it seems that, among other purposes, Stonehenge was built in order to calculate the annual calendar and seasons. It was, in spite of popular belief, nothing whatever to do with the Druids, since they arrived in Britain long after Stonehenge was completed. Nor is there any proof that the Altar or Slaughter stones had anything to do with human sacrifice.

Whatever its use, to build Stonehenge must have required an enormous and disciplined labour-force, working over a long period and using primitive tools for such exact work as curving the lintels and carving tenons in the uprights to slot exactly into the holes made in the lintels to receive them.

For a long time it was thought that the Bronze Age builders of the later period must have had connections with the Mediterranean civilizations. This has been confirmed by the discovery of carvings of axe heads and of a dagger on sarsen stones. The axes were of a kind exported from Ireland to the Mediterranean between about 1600 and 1400 B.C. and the dagger's counterpart has been discovered in the graves at Mycenae in southern Greece.

The site is under the care of the Ministry of

Public Building and Works and is open to the public, while some 1,200 acres hereabouts have been acquired by the National Trust in order to preserve the setting of this monument.

Near Stonehenge are prehistoric barrows of various shapes. About 2 m. NE. is **Woodhenge**. It consists of a large circular bank with a ditch inside. Inside this ditch are six concentric rings for holes. Remnants of wood were found in these holes, which led to the theory that this was once a roofed building supported on wooden posts. However, little remains today.

STOURHEAD, *Wiltshire* (4–ST7733). The village of Stourton is a charming introduction to the great house of Stourhead, the church being attractively set against a heavily wooded hillside. Inside are interesting memorials, including one to a 16th-cent. Lord Stourton, whose family owned this estate from before the Conquest. In the 18th cent. it passed to the Hoares, but today belongs to the National Trust and is open to the public.

Just inside the gates to the park is an ancient stone cross dating back to 1373. It once stood at a crossroads in BRISTOL, and the lower niches hold statues of King John, Henry III, Edward III and Edward IV. These are original. The statues of Henry VI, Elizabeth I, James I and Charles I on the upper part were added in 1663.

Stourhead was one of the first great houses to be built in the Georgian style. A magnificent Palladian mansion, it was designed by Colen Campbell and completed in 1722.

It is said that Edward Gibbon, browsing through the library here when only 14, was inspired to write his *Decline and Fall of the Roman Empire*. Unfortunately in 1902 a fire gutted the library and the inside of the centre wing. But all was rebuilt. The façade remains much as it was, though the two wings are later additions.

Stourhead has some magnificent pictures, statues by Rysbrack and a collection of furniture of quite astonishing beauty and variety by Thomas Chippendale.

When the house was handed over to the National Trust, over 2,000 acres of farmland and garden were included with the gift. It is the gardens that are Stourhead's chief delight.

A walk of just over 1 m. around the lake is delightful, as it leads past grottoes, a Temple of Flora, a Pantheon copied from Rome, and a Temple of the Sun copied from one at Baalbek. All this was designed and laid out in the 18th cent. by Henry Hoare, and every turn, past rustic cottages, bridges and statues, is carefully placed to provide a new vista. Spring, when the azaleas and rhododendrons bloom, is particularly beautiful, but all seasons are pleasurable, since the trees have been carefully chosen to harmonize.

To the NW. of the estate, some 1,000 ft above sea-level, **Alfred's Tower**, 160 ft high, makes a magnificent landmark. It was built in 1772, to mark the point where, it is said, Alfred raised his standard in 878 to repel the invading Danes. Views from here look over three counties, but

access to the tower itself is no longer permitted, owing to the poor state of the structure.

STRATFIELD MORTIMER, *Berkshire* (5–SU6764), set among beautiful fir groves near SILCHESTER and the Hampshire border, has an ancient Anglo-Saxon tomb cover which only came to light by chance when the Church of St Mary was rebuilt in 1869. The Latin inscription reads: "On the eighth before the Kalends of October Aegelward son of Kypping was laid in this place. Blessed be the man who prays for his soul. Toki wrote me."

Aegelward was probably the ealdorman (governor of a district) and historian mentioned in the Anglo-Saxon Chronicle in 994; Kypping was the lord of this manor, and Toki one of King Cnut's courtiers.

Behind the organ is a mosaic of glass, which includes a portrait of William of Wykeham, founder of WINCHESTER College, and New College, OXFORD.

It is interesting to note that two flourishing farms hereabouts, Great Park and Little Park, were given away five times by Henry VIII as parts of a marriage portion to his various wives.

STRATFORD TONY, *Wiltshire* (5–SU0926). The Ebble crossed here and there by small bridges and some stepping stones, winds its way through this pretty village, which derives its name from the Strete Ford, where the old Roman road from OLD SARUM crossed the river, and from Ralph Toni – William the Conqueror's standard-bearer at the Battle of Hastings – who was granted land here. The church is set just above the river and has a Perpendicular tower. Of special interest are the 14th-cent. chancel and the vestry, which was added in the 18th cent. The original stone altar slab is still used today.

STREATLEY, *Berkshire* (5–SU5980), is linked to its neighbour Goring in Oxfordshire by an attractive bridge over the Thames. But Streatley is the prettier of the two, with its delightful Georgian houses and cottages, and its old 19th-cent. gabled malthouse.

It is for the views over the countryside that Streatley is justly famous, for it lies in a gorge-like gap which divides the Chilterns from the Berkshire Downs. Streatley Hill, a steep chalk bluff, scattered with juniper bushes, rises directly behind the village. From here you can see over the Goring Gap to the landscape rising then falling to the flat watermeadows of the Thames. Thirty-eight acres of Larden Chase here belong to the National Trust, as do 28 acres of Lough Down.

STUDLAND, *Dorset* (4–SZ0382). The village is mainly of red brick and is set on a beautifully soft bit of coast, with trees and combes, dunes and beaches. Essentially it is a place for walking: the sea is not even visible from the road. The church is the finest Norman one in the county, built on Anglo-Saxon foundations with superb rounded arches and vaulting. The outside north

wall is wondrously red with lichen, and a nearby
yew cannot be much younger than the church.

N. from the village to the mouth of POOLE
harbour is a National Nature Reserve with nature
trail and observation post.

About 1 m. NW., in the great moor which
stretches unbroken almost to WAREHAM, is the
Agglestone, a single rock some 17 ft high and
reckoned to weigh 400 tons. You have to walk to it.

STURMINSTER NEWTON, *Dorset* (4–
ST7813). Sturminster has a nice variety of house-
styles – red-brick, thatch, whitened cob, stone
and even some exposed Tudor-type timbering.
Each Monday this small town holds the most
important livestock market in the southern half
of the Blackmoor Vale, which was Hardy's "vale
of little dairies". William Barnes, the dialect
poet, was born here and went to the school near
the church. The latter, down a pretty street SE.
from the square, was dulled in the 19th cent. but
has a good 15th-cent. waggon roof with carved
bosses and stars, one entertaining 1921 window
by the Irishman, Harry Clarke, and plenty of
Victorian drama in others.

Just S., leading to Newton over the beautiful
Stour, is one of Dorset's finest medieval bridges.
Like several others in the county, it bears a
plaque saying anyone "injuring" it will be
deported: the anticipated weapon, apparently,
was an over-laden cart. Nearby is a still-busy
mill. The local coarse-fishing is celebrated.

About 1½ m. E. at **Fiddleford** is another working
mill attached to a 14th- and 15th-cent. house.

SULHAMSTEAD, *Berkshire* (5–SU6368), is
a scattered village in wooded country by the River
Kennet. It used once to be divided into Sulhamstead Abbots – so called since it was in the care of
the Abbot of Reading – and Sulhamstead
Bannister, but now the two are joined. The
church is a restored flint building, with a wooden
bell turret and Norman font, and a brass to
Ralph Eyer 1524, warning against the terrible
blandishments of Eve.

Folly Farm is an impressive house mostly
built by Lutyens in this century.

SUTTON COURTENAY, *Berkshire* (5–SU
5093), is a pretty village with cottages and old
timbered houses scattered through lanes and
about the green. The Thames, bordered by willow
and elm, runs through the village.

This was once for a long time a royal manor,
until given to the Courtenays by Henry II, but in
part also belonged to Abingdon Abbey, the monks
of which built a country retreat in the village.

Of three important buildings in the village, the
oldest is the Norman Hall, or Court House,
dating from the 12th cent. A plain stone building,
it has carved Norman doors, lancet windows and
inside a great open timber roof. The larger
Manor House with gables and barge-boarding
lies S. of Norman Hall. Inside is a 13th-cent. hall
and a magnificent banqueting hall with a minstrels'
gallery. The third of the trio is just S. of the church

Jane J. Miller

Swanage: the Mill Pond

and named the Abbey, which it never was. This,
too, has a 14th-cent. great hall, with an oak roof
and some Decorated windows.

The Church of All Saints to the N. has work
from the 12th to the 16th cents. The tower is
Norman, the wide nave mostly 14th-cent. and the
chancel 13th-cent. There is a rood-screen, three
Perpendicular tomb-chests, an effigy of a priest,
box pews and a Jacobean pulpit.

SUTTON POYNTZ, *Dorset* (4–SY7084). An
attractive grey-stone village snuggled into a cleft
in the chalk down, round a willow-bordered duck
and goldfish pond. The road N. from it leads into
a fine downland valley and ½ m. W. to below the
Iron Age fort of Chalbury. An avenue of pollarded
willows softens the entry to WEYMOUTH suburbs
at Preston, ½ m. S. of which and E. of the main
road is the floor of a Roman temple protected
by the Ministry of Public Building and Works.

Some 1½ m. NE. of here, the horseman cut in
chalk on the downs is George III, Weymouth's
benefactor. It measures 108 yds high by 93 across.

Osmington, just E. of it, is a smart, well-preserved, floriferous, grey village, Its church contains a monument bearing a Latin inscription
which appealed to Thomas Hardy. Constable
spent his honeymoon here, during which time he
painted his *Weymouth Bay*, now in the NATIONAL
GALLERY.

About 3½ m. NE. of Osmington, **Moignes Court**
at Owermoigne is one of Dorset's oldest houses,
partly 13th-cent. with at least one exceedingly
macabre episode in its history. It is open by
appointment.

SWALLOWFIELD, *Berkshire* (5–SU7264),
set near the meeting of the Loddon and the Blackwater rivers, is memorable both for Swallowfield
Park and as the village where Mary Mitford (*see*
THREE MILE CROSS) spent her last years. In

1851 she came here to be near the Russells of Swallowfield Park. Four years later she died and lies in the churchyard near the park gates. The little church is of flint, with a Norman nave and a Decorated chancel.

Swallowfield Park, a fine mansion, is open to the public. It was rebuilt in 1678 for the 2nd Earl of Clarendon by Talman. A magnificent gateway decorated with garlands and drapes now stands in the garden.

In 1820 the house was remodelled by William Atkinson for Sir Henry Russell, as you can see from the enormous porch with Tuscan columns.

Many famous people have stayed there. When Charles II came, 11s. 8d. was paid to the bell-ringers for ringing a welcome. Queen Anne used to visit her uncle, the 2nd Earl of Clarendon, and in the 17th cent. John Evelyn described the gardens as "So beset with all manner of sweete shrubs that it perfumes the aire". In 1719 the house passed to Thomas Pitt, grandfather of William Pitt, 1st Earl of Chatham. He was an East India merchant trading in diamonds; the Pitt diamond, as big as a plum, which he used to hide in his boot, became part of the State jewels of France.

SWANAGE, *Dorset* (4–SZ0278), is a cosy, not-too-big resort on a marvellous bay of yellow sands and white cliffs, flanked by downs grand for walking and views. It is about the only place between POOLE and WEYMOUTH where you can get a car right next to a really good beach.

It seems to have begun life as an Anglo-Saxon port often raided by Danes. A column on the sea-front, curiously topped by cannon-balls, commemorates King Alfred's rout of a Danish fleet in the bay in 877, many of the enemy being wrecked on Peveril Point, just beyond the pier. Later its main business became quarrying and shipping Purbeck marble from the hills and cliffs immediately S. and W. The arrival of the railways in the 19th cent. opened the way to resorthood. Big local attractions are the Great Globe, a 40-ton Portland stone model of the world at Durlston Head, about 1 m. S., and the Tilly Whim Caves, an old cliff quarry, smugglers' hide and source of remarkable fossils, ¼ m. further on, near the Anvil Point lighthouse which can also often be visited. The cliffs here are particularly grand, too, and it is well worth walking on W. about 1¾ m. to the strange rock platform called the Dancing Ledge. Another equally good walk is from the other end of the town N., past the Elizabethan Whitecliffe Farm, over Ballard Down to above where the chalk spires known as Old Harry Rocks jut from the sea (about 2 m. each way from the nearest road point).

Of the town itself, the oldest and most attractive part is about ¼ m. inland off the High Street, round the Mill Pond and St Mary's Church, which is mainly Victorian, but whose tower was perhaps originally a fort, begun by Anglo-Saxons. Nearby, the Town Hall is remarkable for having a façade designed, though not for it, by Wren in 1670. This came in 1883 from the predecessor to the present Mercers' Hall in London

and was one of several remarkable gifts to the town in the 19th cent. by the Burt and Mowlem families, whose contracting business gave them the chance of such acquisitions. Another was the Clock Tower, near the pier, which was moved from the southern end of London Bridge in 1867, another the Great Globe. They also built, in 1876, the substantial Purbeck House, now a convent, almost opposite the Town Hall, behind which is a little lock-up built in 1803 "for the prevention of vice and immorality".

Near **Peveril Point**, the lifeboat, modern and of frequent service, can often be inspected. Examples of marble quarries, now worked only on a very small scale, and of grey quarrymen's cottages can be well seen about 2 m. W. between Langton and WORTH MATRAVERS.

SWINDON, *Wiltshire* (5–SU1484), the largest town in the county, developed in three stages. First came the old town, of which some part remains. Then Swindon expanded greatly with the coming of the railways. Finally there has been much post-war development. Of the modern buildings, the Princess Margaret Hospital is perhaps the finest example.

The town has two museums. At the Railway Museum there is a permanent exhibition of historic locomotives, while the town museum contains an interesting collection of shells, archaeological and geological exhibits and others.

Nearby, 1½ m. towards Marlborough, lies **Coate**, where Richard Jefferies, the writer and naturalist, was born. His house, which is open to the public, contains mostly manuscripts and personal items, arranged as a museum. Close by, part of Coate Water, a former reservoir, has been turned into a bird sanctuary.

About 3½ m. S. of Swindon lies **Burderop Park**. Open to the public by appointment, the house has been the home of the Calley family for over 200 years. While the interior of the house is Elizabethan, dating from the 17th cent., the façade is early Georgian.

SYDLING ST NICHOLAS, *Dorset* (4–SY 6399), has some 5 m. of chalk-stream valley to itself and lies deep but open between downs, an attractive and still rustic, though quite large village of yellow stone and flint and often thatch. Every approach to it is beautiful, whether over the hills from CERNE ABBAS or Maiden Newton, or up the Sydling water from the S. Its church, beside the manor house and tithe barn amid tall trees, has been fairly humbly restored. It is 15th-cent., except for an 18th-cent. chancel, with many 18th- and 19th-cent. monuments and good tower gargoyles. The manor house is late 18th- and 19th-cent., incorporating bits of a Tudor one which was owned by Queen Elizabeth I's Sir Francis Walsingham in 1590. In the village, some 200 yds NE. of the church, is part of a medieval wayside cross. The vicarage near it is 17th-cent. with some stone-mullioned windows. In numerous places on the hillsides around are terraced traces of the old Celtic "lynchet" cultivation system.

SYMONDSBURY, *Dorset* (4–SY4493). The perfect escape from A35 traffic jams: a quiet village almost entirely of the local brown-yellow sandstone and thatched – indeed, noted for its thatchers. It is one of Dorset's villages least changed by the 20th cent. Its church is basically 15th-cent., attractively restored inside.

TARRANT CRAWFORD, *Dorset* (4–ST92 03). There is no village, merely a rather special little church in a field at the end of a drive through a farm. It is mainly 12th-cent., beautifully restored, its walls almost entirely covered with 14th-cent. (and in one case 13th-cent.) murals, de-plastered properly only in 1948, faint but still eloquent. Beside the church was once the abbey of nuns for whom was written the famous 13th-cent. rule book, *Ancren Riwle,* by, it is thought, Bishop Richard Poore who instituted the building of SALISBURY Cathedral *c.* 1220. Poore was buried in the abbey, and so, at about the same time, was King John's daughter Joan, Queen of Scotland, who, weary of the world, had retired to the abbey. Now the tombs are lost, but their lids are on either side of the altar in the church.

TEFFONT EVIAS, *Wiltshire* (4–ST9831), is beautifully set in the wooded valley of the Nadder. Little bridges lead to stone cottages and span the clear waters of the river. The Tudor rectory was later embellished with sham Gothic towers, and on the green lawn of the stone manor house stands the impressive church, protected by an enormous yew tree. Rebuilt in the 19th cent. it has an imposing tower and spire. The interior is spacious, with some Flemish glass and a 16th-cent. tomb to Henry Ley and his two sons.

Teffont Magna, nearby, is smaller but just as attractive. Thatched cottages nestle round the church. Again there are bridges, crossing the stream that eventually flows into the Nadder. The church is Early English. Very plain, it has a 14th-cent. chancel screen, an attractive plaster ceiling and a medieval font. There is also part of an Anglo-Saxon cross dating back to the 9th cent. to be seen.

THATCHAM, *Berkshire* (5–SU5167), may well be the oldest village in Berkshire, since traces of a Mesolithic settlement dating from about 6000 to 4000 B.C. have been found here.

However, there is little suggestion of the distant past in this busy little place in the Kennet valley. It spreads out from the old part centred on the large open square where markets have been held since the reign of Henry I.

Thatcham church is large with a Norman south doorway but was heavily restored in 1852. The Fuller Chapel is Perpendicular and contains monuments to Sir William Danvers, a judge in Tudor times, and to Nicholas Fuller and his large family, dated 1620.

Also in the town is a 14th-cent. chapel bought in the 18th by Lady Frances Winchcombe to be converted into a Blue Coat School, which survived until this century.

THEALE, *Berkshire* (5–SU6371). Some interesting remains from the Romano-British and Anglo-Saxon eras have been found here. Today Theale is somewhat industrialized, and the traffic is heavier and noisier than when it was a stage-post, but there are still old coaching inns to be seen.

There are some pleasant Georgian buildings in the main street, but the most interesting feature is the 19th-cent. church towering above the village. Modelled on Salisbury Cathedral, it was paid for by Mrs Sophia Sheppard, who lies protected by Bishop Waynflete's 15th-cent. stone chantry. It was brought here from Magdalen College, OXFORD, by her brother, the college president.

Two m. SE. **Burghfield** is interesting for the effigies in the church. The church itself is in neo-Norman style, built in 1843; the two alabaster figures, somewhat damaged, portray Richard Neville, 1st Earl of Salisbury, born *c.* 1400, and his wife. Their son was Warwick the Kingmaker, and the effigies were probably brought from BISHAM Abbey, where Warwick was buried. The 14th-cent. wooden effigy of Roger de Burghfield is also damaged.

THREE MILE CROSS, *Berkshire* (5–SU 7167). Although READING has almost reached out to touch this village lying 5 m. S., it will always maintain its identity, because of Mary Russell Mitford (1787–1855), authoress of *Our Village.*

This, her most famous book, was based on this village where she spent much of her life. "A long straggling street of pretty cottages", is how she described it, and although much has changed there is still a group of pleasant buildings, including a village hall, a library and Mary Mitford's cottage next to the Swan Public House. The family moved here soon after her extravagant father had run through both his wife's fortune and £20,000 won by Mary from a lottery ticket when she was ten. She then contrived to support the family by her writing, and moved to SWALLOWFIELD nearby, where she lies buried, only after the death of her parents.

TICHBORNE, *Hampshire* (5–SU5730), in the Itchen valley, is quite delightful. With 16th- and 17th-cent. houses and much thatch, it has all the charm of an unspoilt village. The church, too, is interesting and set a little apart. The chancel is 11th-cent., and the box pews and communion rail Jacobean. In the Tichborne Chapel, among other family monuments, there is a splendid alabaster effigy of Sir Benjamin Tichborne, 1621, who lies with his wife, while his children kneel below.

Tichborne House was rebuilt at the start of the 19th cent., but the family have owned it since Anglo-Saxon times and are especially famous for the Tichborne Dole. It all started in 1150 when Sir Roger de Tichborne agreed to his wife's request for a dole for the village, provided she would mark out land to support that charity. Though dying, she managed to do this, at the same time uttering a curse should her dole ever be discontinued. In the 19th cent. Tichborne again burst into the news when Arthur Orton claimed to be Sir Roger Tichborne, the heir presumed drowned at sea. The case cost £90,000 and lasted 100 days in a blaze of publicity.

Round and about are some attractive villages. **Cheriton**, 1 m. S., was the scene of a great battle in 1644, when 10,000 Royalists met an equal number of Parliamentarians. The mounds of the graves can still be seen today. **Bramdean**, about 3 m. away, has a good common and some fine large houses: Woodcote Manor is Jacobean, Bramdean Manor Queen Anne, and Brockwood Park Georgian. At **Beauworth**, 3 m. away, there is an old tread-wheel at the Fox and Hounds Inn, which donkeys once trod to draw water. And at **Kilmeston**, 1 m. from Beauworth, there is a 17th-cent. manor house which was improved in Georgian style when the Prince Regent stayed there.

TILSHEAD, *Wiltshire* (4–SU0347). Centuries ago Tilshead was as important as CALNE, but no longer. It is a village set on Salisbury Plain, which gives it a wonderful open feeling. There are charming chequered flint and stone cottages, attractively thatched, and a church that seems almost too big for the village. It is Norman with a central tower and an Early English chancel, and was well restored in 1846.

The plain hereabouts is dotted with various prehistoric remains and tumuli, among which is the Old Ditch, which runs for some miles and is just what its name implies. The **White Barrow** now belongs to the National Trust. A Neolithic earth long barrow, it measures some 255 ft in length and is 8 ft high with ditches on either side.

TISBURY, *Wiltshire* (4–ST9429). More a town than a village. The history of Tisbury stretches back to the 7th cent. when an Anglo-Saxon track ran through the village. Later the manor belonged to Shaftesbury Abbey, and at Place Farm, formerly an abbey grange, there is a wonderful group of 15th-cent. medieval domestic buildings. Through an old archway lie the farm-house originally a hall room, the farm buildings and one of the largest barns in England, about 200 ft long.

Tisbury has some attractive old buildings, but the most magnificent is the important cruciform church, dating back to the 12th cent., with 14th- and 15th-cent. additions. There is a splendid timbered porch, and the panelled ceilings inside are a particular feature. There are several memorials to the Arundell family. Lady Blanche who so bravely defended WARDOUR during the Civil War lies here, so also does Catherine Howard's sister. In 1762 when the stone spire fell it was replaced.

In the churchyard there is an enormous yew, some 36 ft in circumference, said to be 1,000 years old. Rudyard Kipling and his parents are buried here. **Pyt House**, 2½ m. W., is a handsome late-Georgian house in Palladian style, and is open to the public.

TITCHFIELD, *Hampshire* (5–SU5305). Arrowheads and Roman coins found in the area show that it must have been inhabited from early times. Titchfield today is a delightful small town, with Georgian and 17th-cent. houses lining the peaceful streets. Some, such as the old Bugle Hotel, even show Dutch roof tiles. For Titchfield was once a seaport, until in the 18th cent. the Delmé family built a wall across the River Meon to drain the marshes and called in Dutch engineers to help.

Many buildings are individually interesting. The Queen's Head is Georgian, and the Market Hall, a timber-framed building, dates from the early 17th cent. Part of St Peter's Church dates back as early as the 9th cent., but the church as a whole is a jumble of architectural styles, showing Norman, Decorated and Perpendicular work. The south chapel is its most splendid possession. The 2nd Earl of Southampton left the enormous sum of £1,000 for tombs for himself and his parents, but only one magnificent 16th-cent. monument was built. Here, too, is a charming effigy of little Mary Wriothesley, who died in 1615 aged only four.

Titchfield Abbey is only ½ m. N. of the town. It was founded in 1232 and all that remains of the actual abbey dates from that century. After the Dissolution it passed to Thomas Wriothesley, 1st Earl of Southampton, who converted part into Place House, a building finished in 1542 and inhabited till it was demolished in 1781.

Now a ruin, the remains are magnificent. The three-storied Tudor gatehouse is particularly imposing, with its large turrets, crenellated roof, gargoyles on the parapets and mock arrow-slit windows. The original doors also remain. The wings were fashioned from the old nave with mullioned windows, superb chimneys and crenellation added. Other parts remaining include the entrance to the old chapter house, some of the cloister with its superb 13th-cent. tiles, and the old fish pond, which once overflowed nearly drowning Richard II. That is only one of the stories connected with the house. Later, when Margaret of Anjou married Henry VI at the abbey, she was given the curious present of a live lion. Charles I spent his last night of freedom in the house, and it has connections with Shakespeare, since the 3rd Earl of Southampton was his patron.

Open to the public, the site is now under the care of the Ministry of Public Building and Works, who have marked out the lines of the original abbey.

TOLLARD ROYAL, *Wiltshire* (4–ST9417), lies in romantic country with historical associations. It won the right to add Royal to its name from King John who, between about 1200 and 1213, spent much time hereabouts. He lived, it is said, in a house named simply King John's House. A charming stone and wood building now on the site was excavated and restored in 1889 by the famous archaeologist, General Pitt-Rivers, who found traces of 13th-cent. work in a much later building. Also in the village is the church, which is particularly interesting for an effigy of Sir William Payne, who died in 1388. He lies with sword drawn and feet resting on a lion, and is clad in banded mail, examples of which are rarely seen.

Larmer Gardens are about 1 m. above the village and were given their name from the larmer tree – an old wych elm – under which King John is said to have met his huntsmen and Tollard court leets were held. The tree finally blew down in 1894 and was replaced by an oak. In the same century, General Pitt-Rivers turned Larmer into delightful pleasure grounds, with statues, temples and a small wood open-air theatre. The gardens are open for all to visit.

King John, it is said, often hunted in CRANBOURNE CHASE nearby. Views are spectacular from **Win Green Hill**, the highest point of Cranbourne Chase. Crowned by a circle of trees, 38 acres now belong to the National Trust. From **Winklebury Camp**, near Berwick St John, an ancient earthwork with ditch and 40-ft-high rampart, there are views right over Dorset and Hampshire.

TOLPUDDLE, *Dorset* (4–SY7994). A tiny village with a firm place in trade-union history. In 1831, under a sycamore in the village centre, six farm labourers decided to go together to ask for an increase in wages. Three years later, after numerous meetings between themselves and with their employers from which they had gained nothing, they were abruptly arrested under an obscure law, marched the 7 m. to DORCHESTER, and sentenced to seven years transportation. There followed a public outcry. Free pardon was granted, though not before the men were in Australia. The right to bargain collectively had, painfully, been established. The men have become known as the Tolpuddle Martyrs.

The old sycamore, propped up by the National Trust, still stands. Across and above the main road are six cottages built in 1934 by the T.U.C. as a memorial, and a cottage on the road, a former home of one of the men, and the Methodist chapel (their leader was a Methodist) bear memorial plaques. Annually in July there is a memorial service and parade attended by trade unionists from far and wide.

About 1½ m. W., **Athelhampton** is the most beautiful Tudor house open to the public in Dorset. It is mainly *c.* 1485 and is magnificently furnished, immaculately kept and lived-in. The lovely gardens alone make a visit worthwhile.

On **Affpuddle Heath**, about 1 m. S. of Tolpuddle, are a series of strange hollows known as swallet-holes; the largest, called Cull-peppers Dish, is about 100 yds across by 40 ft deep. It is roughly ½ m. SW. of the pretty village of **Bryants Puddle**.

TRENT, *Dorset* (4–ST5918). A beautiful, sequestered village, its air in summer heavy with the scent of shrubs like *Philadelphus.* Ham-stone houses of unfailing elegance, amid trees of rare luxuriance and variety, are scattered about an interesting church. In the manor house just NW. of the churchyard Charles II was hidden for a fortnight after the Battle of WORCESTER (1651)

by his host Colonel Francis Wyndham, and listened to the villagers cheering rumours of his capture. The church, mainly 13th–15th cent. with fine 14th-cent. tower and spire, has – most unusual for this area where church interiors suffered so much Puritan destruction – an excellent wooden rood-screen (15th-cent.) and carved bench-ends (early 16th-cent.); also – and even more unusual – a lavishly carved Dutch pulpit (*c.* 1600) and in its east window a splendid jumble of 16th- and 17th-cent. Swiss and German glass. The pulpit and glass were collected by a former rector of the parish.

TROWBRIDGE, *Wiltshire* (4–ST8557), is the administrative centre of Wiltshire. "It flourishith by drapery", remarked Leland in the 16th cent. In those days there was a castle here, and Fore Street still follows the curves of the old ditch and rampart. If the castle has disappeared, cloth mills have not, and other industries have also come to this attractive stone town which grew rich by weaving.

In The Parade is a magnificent series of stone 18th-cent. merchants' houses, and there are others in Fore Street and Roundstone Street.

The Church of St James is splendid with a fine spire. It was much restored in Victorian times. George Crabbe, the poet, was rector here from 1814 to 1832. There is a monument to his memory by E. H. Baily, and another one in the churchyard to Thomas Helliker, who was thought to be the leader of riots which broke out with the coming of the power loom and was executed in 1803, aged only 19.

UFFINGTON, *Berkshire* (5–SU3089), is in the Vale of the White Horse, and the horse itself is only a short distance away. The whole area has been made famous by Thomas Hughes in his book *Tom Brown's Schooldays*.

The large cruciform Church of St Mary, with its unusual octagonal tower once topped by a spire, is almost entirely 13th-cent. Early English. There is an impressive rib-vaulted south porch with a door fastened by elaborate hinges. Each of the three chapels has its own piscina, and is lit by unusual lancet windows. There are a sedilia and two monuments, one dated 1638 showing the semi-reclining effigy of John Saunders. The chalk building close by dates from 1617.

The hills round about are fascinating for their legends and ancient monuments. **White Horse Hill** at 856 ft is the highest point on the Berkshire Downs. It lies near the village and can also be climbed by the Portway, an old Roman road. On the way up you see a separate round hill, named Dragon Hill; it is here that St George killed the dragon, according to fictitious tradition.

Higher up, the great chalk white horse seems to be galloping across the grass. It is about 360 ft long, about 130 ft high, and although tradition says that it was cut by King Alfred, it is far older and may originally date from the Iron Age. The hill is crowned by **Uffington Castle**, a prehistoric fort which gives superb views in many directions.

Aerofilms

Uffington: the White Horse

be seen. There was much activity here during the 12th-cent. disorders, but finally the Treaty of Wallingford gave Henry II the throne and in 1155 he gave the town its first charter.

There were also some 14 churches here, but by the 16th cent. Wallingford had fallen on evil days. However, during the Civil War the castle again assumed importance, the town being the last Royalist stronghold to surrender. But it was finally razed to such effect by Parliamentary forces that only fragments remain in the gardens of Castle House, a private residence occasionally open to the public.

There are many fine Georgian and timber-framed buildings. The Town Hall is 17th-cent. and contains portraits by Gainsborough and others. The White Hart is early 16th-cent. and the George Inn probably 17th-cent., as are a group of almshouses. The Lamb Hotel is Georgian.

Of the churches St Leonard's, though much restored, is Norman as the herringbone work, the north door and arches east of the nave show; and St Peter's, rebuilt in the 18th cent., has a needle-like spire.

About 1½ m. SW. and now, like all this area under the care of the Ministry of Public Building and Works, is **Wayland's Smithy**, a megalithic long barrow. The smith was a figure of Anglo-Saxon and Scandinavian myth who made invincible swords and armour. He re-shod the horses which travellers left here overnight with a coin, never appearing in person. The Ridgeway, a prehistoric track, runs close by.

VENTNOR, *Isle of Wight* (5–SZ5677), owes its reputation as a winter holiday and health resort to its sheltered southerly aspect which ensures a mild climate and encourages luxuriant vegetation. The town lies at the foot of an 800-ft hill. The steep descent to sea-level is made by gradients of 1 in 4, and walking through the winding streets can be arduous. There are three distinct tiers from the shore with flights of steps in places to ease the way up. A thoughtful Town Council has put seats at appropriate intervals.

Ventnor has a pier built in 1955 and a small esplanade. The sea-front is bisected by a cascade which runs down past the Winter Garden Pavilion, with its glass-encased stairs to the roof and sun terrace. These give wide views over the coast, from **Luccombe** to the N. and St Catherine's Point, **Blackgang** and Chale to the W. and S.

WALLINGFORD, *Berkshire* (5–SU6089). Since early times the site of a ford over the Thames, now spanned by a many-arched bridge, which was of supreme importance. Romans probably settled here, and Anglo-Saxons certainly did and it was probably they who fortified the town, traces of the ramparts still being visible today. In 1006 the Danes destroyed Wallingford.

There was once a priory and a great castle here; of the priory made over to Wolsey in 1525 nothing remains, but a little of the castle can still

WALTHAM ST LAWRENCE, *Berkshire* (5–SU8276). A village with picturesque half-timbered cottages and an old pound carefully marked out by four trees. The pretty half-timbered Bell Inn dates back to the 14th cent., and was given to the village by Ralph Newbery in the 17th cent. The church has work of many periods, and a small part is Norman. There are traces of early 14th-cent. paintings on a north pier, and among other monuments is one to Sir Henry Neville, 1593, the owner of a great house nearby, who lies with his two wives and one daughter.

The churchyard has a fine 300-year-old yew, and here lies John Newbery (1713–67), publisher to many of the great writers of his time, including Dr Johnson.

White Waltham is nearby, beyond SHOTTES-BROOKE, with timber-framed cottages and two great barns. The farm-house near the church was once lived in by Prince Arthur who died in 1502, leaving the way clear for his younger brother to ascend the throne as Henry VIII. Though much restored, the church shows some Norman work and has a fine 13th-cent. chancel. Near it you can still see the old stocks and whipping post.

WANTAGE, *Berkshire* (5–SU4087), is a market town, situated in the Vale of the White Horse. King Alfred was born here in 849 and there is a statue to him by Count Gleichen in the market place, where you can also find some 18th-cent. houses.

The Church of SS. Peter and Paul is a large cruciform building, mostly 13th-cent., but incorporating Perpendicular and later work. A silver plate owned by the church is said to have belonged to Peter the Great. The stalls have both misericords and poppyheads, and there are several fine 14th-, 15th- and 16th-cent. brasses as well as an alabaster tomb to Sir William Fitzwarren and his wife Alicia, dated 1361.

East Lockinge, 3 m. SE., preserves much of a model estate village built in the 19th cent.

To the W. of Wantage lies **Childrey**, an attractive village set under the downs. The cruciform church is mostly Perpendicular and Decorated, and has a 12th-cent. lead font with figures of bishops, and 15th-cent. chancel stalls and screen. There is also a remarkable collection of brasses.

WARDOUR, *Wiltshire* (4–ST9226). Old Wardour Castle is a unique hexagonal castle. Two great square towers flank the main entrance, and there is a hexagonal courtyard in the centre. Originally built in 1392 on the authority of Richard II, it was planned at a time when castles were beginning to be designed for living and entertainment rather than primarily for defence.

During the Civil War it was twice besieged. In 1643, Lord Arundell being absent, his 60-year-old wife Blanche, with the help of only 25 fighting men, held out against a Parliamentary army of 1,300. She only surrendered when mines were used and petards threatened, whereupon – quite contrary to agreement – the Roundhead army inflicted immense and wanton destruction on both the castle and its contents.

Later Wardour was again besieged, this time by Royalists. Among them was Lord Arundell, who had inherited when his father died from wounds. Although the Parliamentary army eventually surrendered, a great deal of damage was done, and the castle was never entirely rebuilt. Instead, in the 18th cent., gardens were laid out and the ground landscaped.

Today the castle is a romantic ruin, standing against a background of wooded hills, overlooking a lake. But the walls still soar to their original 60 ft height, and much that remains is interesting.

Old Wardour House was built in the late 17th cent. and stands within sight of the castle, on the lake. Unlike the ruin, which is in the care of the Ministry of Public Building and Works and open to the public, it cannot be visited.

New Wardour Castle is about 1 m. away, and was designed for Lord Arundell by James Paine in 1769. A magnificent Palladian mansion, it has many treasures, among them a superb circular staircase and a splendidly decorated chapel. It now houses Cranborne Chase School, and is open to the public during the summer holidays.

WAREHAM, *Dorset* (4–SY9287). This tidy, quietly attractive small town, like BLANDFORD FORUM, had a great fire (1762), and is, as a result, similarly, though less grandly, Georgian red-brick, but of ancient origin and turbulent beginnings. Well-sited on a low ridge between the rivers Frome and Piddle, it was an important Anglo-Saxon town and river port, protected by massive earthen ramparts. During the troubled period from the 9th to 11th cent. it frequently took the brunt of Danish invasion, and suffered further ravage from various parties in the Stephen-Matilda wars of the mid-12th cent. Then gradually, during the Middle Ages, the Frome silted up,

spoiling its port, till today it is a shopping centre of friendly pubs and some light industry, its quay sleepily pretty with fishermen and pleasure motorboats offering trips, and its old granary now a restaurant.

The walls survive as a bank best seen on the west side of the town. St Martin's Church, mainly Anglo-Saxon, *c*. 1030, the oldest church extant in Dorset, stands actually on it to the N., and contains Eric Kennington's effigy of T. E. Lawrence (1939) (*see* BOVINGTON). Between it and the town centre a small museum contains T. E. Lawrence relics, including photographs. The town's other, and principal, church, Lady St Mary's, NE. of the quay, is also worth visiting. It was mainly rebuilt in 1842, but is very pleasant inside with much medieval detail, including a lead-bowled font, *c*. 1200, said to be unique, two exceptional 13th-cent. effigies of knights in armour, and, off the chancel, a fine vaulted chapel. It stands where a priory is thought to have once stood, and the Tudor house just S. of it is called the Priory of Lady St Mary. Its gardens are sometimes open.

SE. for some 7 m. to STUDLAND is mainly heath, with heather, birch scrub and young conifer forest, much of it nature reserve. Across this, **Arne**, about 3½ m. E. by road, is an ash-tree shaded hamlet from which you can walk for about 1 m. to the shore of POOLE Harbour. The drive SW. from here to CORFE CASTLE gives a tremendous view of the ruined castle.

One m. SE. of Wareham, **Ridge** was once a busy river port, possibly where King Alfred built his fleet to fight the Danes.

WARFIELD, *Berkshire* (5–SU8872), famous for brick and tile works, is set in one of the three ancient clearings of Windsor Forest which once supported 100 pigs and several ploughs. At the time of Edward the Confessor, Warfield was held by Queen Edith, and later passed to William the Conqueror.

The surrounding country is still well-wooded and pleasantly undulating, and the village itself contains one of the most interesting medieval churches in the county. Surrounded by green leafy limes and elms, set above the small river, it stands near the medieval half-timbered school, which still retains its enormous old bread oven.

St Michael's Church is mostly 14th-cent. Inside it is light and airy, and the north aisle and nave roofs are beautifully timbered. The east window has elegant tracery and some early-14th-cent. stained glass of angels swinging censers. There is a 15th-cent. wooden screen and a rare surviving section of the rood loft. There are several 17th-, 18th- and 19th-cent. monuments, and the whole church was well restored by Street in the 19th cent.

WARGRAVE, *Berkshire* (5–SU7878). With its narrow roads, its trees, and riverside houses, Wargrave is a most attractive village with Georgian and timber-framed buildings. Just near here the Thames meets the River Loddon and this particular stretch of river is both charming and relatively quiet, except during summer weekends when the boats are out in full force.

The church, except for the 17th-cent. tower, was burnt down in 1914 and has been rebuilt. Looking back further, Wargrave has had some interesting inhabitants, among them Thomas Day (1748–89), who wrote *Sandford and Merton*, an instructive book about a poor and a rich boy which was once widely read. Day died trying to ride an unbroken horse, attempting to prove his theory that animals are obedient in response to kindness.

WARMINSTER, *Wiltshire* (4–ST8644), is situated 400 ft above sea-level, above the valley of the Wylye. It grew rich from the manufacture of cloth and the sale of wheat. At the heyday of the great market as many as 300 sacks of wheat changed hands in a single morning.

Warminster has dignity and grace. It was, thought Cobbett, "A very nice town; everything belonging to it is solid and good." The main street runs almost the length of the town. There are Georgian houses and cottages and some splendid inns, the 18th-cent. Bath Arms and the Old Bell among them. The school, too, is interesting, founded in 1707 by Lord Weymouth. Dr Arnold of RUGBY was at one time a pupil. The parish church was heavily restored in the 19th cent. by Sir Arthur Blomfield, but has an organ, beautifully encased, originally given by George III to SALISBURY Cathedral.

The ancient Iron Age hill-fort at **Cleyhill** is about 3 m. W. of the town. Standing on chalk, at some 800 ft, about 85 acres hereabouts belong to the National Trust.

WELFORD, *Berkshire* (5–SU4073), offers a pretty view from the two bridges of the River Lambourn, and of thatched roofs and the manor house and church set in a deer park. The church is much restored, though the Norman tower and 13th-cent. spire have been rebuilt in their original style. The font is truly Norman, and there are brasses and monuments.

Wickham, which lies only 1½ m. SW., also has thatch, and here the Church of St Swithin has a massive Anglo-Saxon tower. The rest of the church has ornate Victorian decoration, with much carving. Two angels hold up the nave roof, and the north aisle roof appears to be supported by eight spectacular papier-mâché elephants' heads, brought over from the 1862 Paris exhibition.

WESTBURY, *Wiltshire* (4–ST8751). Once, it is thought, the palace of the kings of Wessex stood on the moated site at Palace Green. Later Westbury became known for its wool trade and glove-making – still local industries. It is a charming small town. Georgian houses are grouped round the Market Place and more are to be found near the church, which is mainly Perpendicular and was restored in 1847. Inside are an interesting modern rood-screen, 17th- and 18th-cent. monuments, and a chained copy of the Paraphrase of the New Testament by Erasmus.

High above Westbury stands the oldest White Horse in Wiltshire, said originally to have commemorated King Alfred's victory over the Danes in the 9th cent. It was a carthorse, until "a wretch by the name of Gee", steward to Lord Abingdon, remodelled it in 1778, as he thought, more elegantly. The horse measured some 180 ft in length and 107 ft in height to the shoulder.

The small hamlet of **Dilton** is close to Westbury and well worth visiting to see the Church of St Mary. Probably built in the 14th or 15th cent. and now painted white, the interior is delightful. The church remains just as it was in the 18th cent., with box pews, some allotted to particular families, a three-tier pulpit and small galleries all completely unchanged. As the church is seldom used now, it may be locked. Ask at neighbouring houses for the key.

WEST DEAN, *Wiltshire* (5–SU2526), lies on a river and is a pretty place with some thatch and a green. The remains of Roman villas were found nearby, and some of what was excavated is now housed in SALISBURY museum.

There are two churches. The parish church was built in 1866, incorporating earlier medieval fragments. Just near a 16th-cent. barn is the other church, that of St Mary. Only the 14th-cent. chantry in Decorated style remains, embellished with some remarkable monuments to the Evelyn family. Sir John Evelyn, uncle of the famous diarist, bought an estate here in the 17th cent. The earliest tomb is to John Evelyn and his wife, who kneel facing each other. There are others, but the most outstanding is to Robert Pierrepont erected in 1669 by his wife (*née* Evelyn). It consists of a lifesize figure with flowing hair at prayer, swathed in a sheet and attended by a cherub. Not to every taste, it shows Italian Baroque influence.

From **Dean Hill,** rising to 500 ft near the village, there are remarkable views over the country, as there are from **Pepperbox Hill** nearby. This hill owes its name to the shape of a curious tower, known as Eyre's Folly. This 17th-cent. folly stands in 73 acres of open land, scattered with juniper bushes, and belongs to the National Trust. Just N. of this hill two woods at **Grimstead Beeches** also belong to the National Trust and can be visited. There is a car park.

WEST STAFFORD, *Dorset* (4–SY7289). Its thatched roofs almost black, its business farming, the oaks in the Frome valley fields about it fat and old, this village has changed very little in a long time. Its church was rebuilt in 1640 and remains admirably Jacobean: screen, canopied pulpit, pews nicely shaded with carving under a wide barrel roof. Hardy seems to have considered it the place of Tess's wedding. The village pub contains entertaining things. About ⅓ m. W., Stafford House, 16th-cent., looks splendid from the road. Some 2½ m. NE. is **Woodsford Castle,** a fortified house, basically 14th-cent., said to be one of the largest thatched buildings in England.

WEYMOUTH, *Dorset* (4–SY6778). Here in 1763, it is said, the first bathing machine was used, and in 1789 came King George III to try out the new invention while the band played "God save the King". He returned frequently, staying in what is now the Gloucester Hotel; and, thus honoured, the port which had sent 20 ships to help Edward III besiege Calais and six to resist the Armada, grew rapidly into one of the most handsome resorts in the South-West. The king is commemorated by his equestrian figure cut in the chalk at **Osmington**, 3½ m. NE. of the town. Today Weymouth is Dorset's second largest town, and sprawling with predictably boring suburbs, it retains a remarkably good-looking sea-front, where long, tall, late-Georgian terraces back the wide Esplanade and sand-beach. The brightly painted Queen Victoria Jubilee Clock Tower fits in happily. To the S. down St Thomas Street – the main and quite metropolitan shopping one – the river-harbour, shut between pubs and warehouses, is busy and affluent with big yachts and motor cruisers and cargo ships that bring fruit and vegetables from the Channel Islands.

Nearby, No. 3 Trinity Street (often open) is converted from two early 17th-cent. cottages and has 17th-cent. furnishings. The narrow streets on either side of St Thomas Street are worth exploring. St Mary's Church (1817) is pleasant Georgian and contains a Last Supper painting by Sir James Thornhill (1675–1734), whose most famous works are the paintings in the dome of ST PAUL'S CATHEDRAL. A good walk for views, especially over the naval base of PORTLAND Harbour, is round the Nothe headland, from the end of the road on the south side of the harbour.

Immediately W. of the Town Bridge the river bends N. and widens as **Radipole Lake**, on which the Romans had a port and where there is now a swannery and, at its upper end, a bird sanctuary. On the east bank are gardens, including public tennis courts and a children's paddling pool. Boats of all kinds can be hired on the sea-front or at the harbour, and there are frequent sailing races in the bay, particularly in August. The sea angling, whether from boat, shore or the pier, is said to be unusually good. There are water-polo matches off the pier. Pop stars perform at the Pavilion. The Information Bureau is at the south end of the Esplanade, near the statue (1809) of George III.

WHERWELL, *Hampshire* (5–SU3840), is a delightful village, with thatched and timbered cottages and a tributary of the River Test trickling through. The 19th-cent. church stands beside a bridge, and here can be seen part of an Anglo-Saxon cross, decorated with an interlacing pattern, two remarkable small 14th-cent. reliefs and some monuments. One to a nun dates from the early 15th cent.

On a wall near the gate leading to the big house is an inscription recording the destruction of the priory at the Dissolution, through the "zeal or avarice of King Henry". It was founded in 986 by Queen Elfrida, widow of King Edgar, in expiation of the murder of her stepson King Edward, and fragments of the remains can still just be seen in the gardens of the Priory, a 19th-cent. house.

WHITCHURCH CANONICORUM, *Dorset* (4–SY3995). The drive to it from the A35 over the western shoulder of Hardown Hill is beautiful and gives magnificent views over the rich Marshwood Vale renowned for its oak-trees. There are attractive roadside cottages of a varied nature: yellow-stone, white-washed or old red-brick, and mainly thatched. The village has a fine church of several periods from the 12th to early 15th cent., with a *c.* 1400 tower. It is specially interesting as the only parish church in England with a shrine containing bones agreed to be those of its patron saint. The shrine of St Wite is in the north transept. Tradition says she was an Anglo-Saxon woman murdered by Danes who landed near CHARMOUTH. Other theories are described in the church's booklet. Her bones were found in a lead casket long in the church but opened only in 1900. In the chancel is a notable 1611 monument to Sir John Jeffery, different from most of that era, its ornamentation so well carved from limestone as to look almost like plasterwork.

WILTON, *Wiltshire* (5–SU0931). Formerly a county town, once a bishopric and a royal residence, Wilton is one of the oldest boroughs in England. Wiltshire is derived from "Wiltonshire". In 871 King Alfred founded an abbey here – where Wilton House today stands – and there were once 12 churches in this flourishing small town, though nothing much remains of these. The chantry of the old parish church was restored by the former American Ambassador, Robert Bingham, in honour of his ancestor Bishop Bingham, but its place has been taken by the new parish church, built by T. H. Wyatt for Sidney Herbert in 1844. An Italian basilica in flamboyant Lombardic style, it has mosaics, marble and twisted columns and also contains some magnificent medieval foreign glass and tombs of the Herberts, Earls of Pembroke. The town also has remnants of the Hospitals of St Giles and St John.

Wilton is famous for carpets – perhaps the first place in England to manufacture them. This industry was encouraged by the Pembrokes, one earl going so far as secretly to import skilled French weavers hidden away in a wine barrel. The Royal Wilton Factory can be visited and is attractively housed.

In 1544 the Abbey of Wilton was finally dissolved and the lands were given to William Herbert, 1st Earl of Pembroke, by Henry VIII. Soon afterwards Wilton House was finished, perhaps based on designs of Hans Holbein the painter. From that era the delightful entrance porch, no longer attached to the main building, remains.

After a fire in 1647 the house was redesigned by Inigo Jones and his son-in-law John Webb. The east front still shows their work, as do the seven magnificent state rooms. Most remarkable of these are the double and the single cube rooms. The cube is exactly 30 ft long, wide and high. In 1800 James Wyatt made other alterations, particularly to the north and west fronts, and more changes have been made since.

Poets and writers have always been made welcome at Wilton, perhaps particularly when the 2nd Earl married Sir Philip Sidney's sister. Shakespeare may have played here. Edmund Spenser, Ben Jonson and Marlowe certainly visited, as did the Royal family. Charles I began coming every summer, he liked it so much.

Wilton contains some splendid furniture and a superb collection of pictures – Rubens, Van Dyck and Tintoretto all being represented. The gardens are delightful and are especially remarkable for the old cedar trees and a Palladian bridge over the Nadder. An imposing triumphal arch, topped with a statue of Marcus Aurelius, stands at the entrance to the north side of the house.

WIMBORNE MINSTER, *Dorset* (4–SZ 0199), is a friendly little town, almost like a miniature cathedral city, so centred is it on its church and so distinctive and fine is this building.

Romans settled the site; Anglo-Saxons developed it. In the 8th cent., Cuthberga, to whom the Minster is dedicated, sister of the Wessex king, Ine, founded its ecclesiastical importance by giving it a nunnery. During the 9th and 10th cents. the district was frequently ravaged by Danes from their favourite beach-head in POOLE Harbour, and in 871 King Ethelred, slain by them in a nearby battle, was brought to the town and buried by his younger brother and successor, Alfred. Later the Danes destroyed the nunnery; but Edward the Confessor replaced it with a college of secular canons which survived till 1547. In the Middle Ages the town prospered on the wool trade and as a market, with a noted school founded "to teach grammar to all comers", which continues as Queen Elizabeth's Grammar School, with 19th-cent. buildings, just S. of the minster. Today Wimborne Minster remains a market town, and market-gardens on quite a major scale. It also has some manufacturing industry.

The minster, with its chequered dark-red and almost white stone exterior and crown-like central tower, is like no other church. It is of all periods from Norman to 15th-cent., a good deal of it Norman. Its central tower bore a spire until one day in 1600 when it was "strangely cast down" in a "mist". On the north face of the west tower a wooden "quarter Jack" (1613), once a monk, now a Grenadier, strikes the quarter hours. Inside, despite 19th-cent. restoration, it retains much grandeur and a wealth of excellent detail that makes purchase of its admirable guide book essential. Particularly not to be missed are two 16th-cent. effigy tombs, the Norman Purbeck marble font, the enormous clock (*c.* 1320), and, above the vestry, the chained library, including churchwardens' accounts from 1403, a 14th-cent. manuscript on vellum and 17th-cent. sermons.

E. of the minster, the 16th-cent. Priest's House Museum specializes in local history. A little W., through Cornmarket, is displayed a model of the entire town reduced by nine-tenths. The road N. from the Square has some good Georgian buildings, and on the north-west edge of the town, beside the BLANDFORD road, St Margaret's Leper Hospital, now almshouses, has a medieval chapel

with remains of 15th-cent. murals.

One m. S. are the Merley Bird Gardens (*see* POOLE). Merley House was built *c.* 1760.

About 1½ m. SE. at **Canford Magna** is the gigantic 19th-cent. Gothic mansion that is now Canford School. It contains an elaborately carved staircase and grandiose hall ceiling. It is not open, but in the school holidays you might be sympathetically received. Always open is the nearby part-Norman church. Both are beside the River Stour at its most beautiful.

WIMBORNE ST GILES, *Dorset* (4–SU 0212). This pretty village, with flint-and-brick thatched cottages among tall trees at the southern foot of CRANBORNE CHASE, grew up round the great house. St Giles House was built mainly in the 1650s by Anthony Ashley-Cooper, 1st Earl of Shaftesbury, in the style of, and maybe to a design by, Inigo Jones. It has been the property of the Earls of Shaftesbury ever since. It was once visited by kings and cabinet ministers, philosophers like Locke and musicians like Handel. A curiosity in its grounds is the Shell Grotto, made by an Italian in 1751, grotesque but fascinating. The church, built in 1732, was semi-destroyed by fire in 1908. By 1910 the Scottish architect, Sir Ninian Comper, had given it a beautiful new interior. The fine almshouses next to it were built in 1624.

Some 1½ m. SW., visible from afar in a vast sweep of arable land backed by dark woods, a ruined church stands tightly circled by a Bronze Age bank of probably religious significance called the **Knowlton Rings**. No one knows the meaning of it.

WINCHESTER, *Hampshire* (5–SU4829). The story of Winchester runs like a golden thread through the country's history. Already an important town in Roman times, it became the capital under the Anglo-Saxons, and in Alfred's time (871–901) was a great centre of learning. William the Conqueror kept Winchester as his capital, though by this time London was almost of equal importance. As late as the 17th cent. Charles II planned a palace here.

Since it is closely linked with history, buildings of interest are not hard to find. The city's focal point is the High Street, ornamented by a 15th-cent. cross, restored in the 19th cent., and a statue to King Alfred. Nearby is the 19th-cent. Guildhall, and not far away a Plague monument, commemorating 1666 but erected in 1759. There are many little alleyways decorated by houses of all centuries and each is worth exploration.

At one end of the High Street is Westgate which, together with Kingsgate near the cathedral, is one of the original five city gates. Mainly 13th-cent., it has magnificent views from the top. Once a prison, it is now a museum tracing the history of the city, and showing a unique collection of ancient weights and measures. For more of the city's history, plus prehistoric and other finds from all over Hampshire, visit the City Museum near the cathedral. Two other museums are of

J. Allan Cash

Winchester: the chantry chapel of the College

Noel Habgood

Windsor: a corner of the town

more specialist interest. The Royal Green Jackets Museum is concerned with regimental history, as also is the Royal Hampshire Regimental Museum, housed in Serle's House, a splendid 18th-cent. building.

Winchester is rich in important buildings. Of William the Conqueror's castle, from which the Empress Matilda escaped hidden in a coffin in the 12th cent., not much remains, since it was demolished by Parliament during the Civil War in return for declaring for the King. But at Castle Hall, near Westgate, the great Hall can still be seen. Completed in 1235, it is a magnificent example of 13th-cent. domestic architecture and can be visited. It is now an assize court. Walter Raleigh was condemned to death here in 1603 and the notorious Judge Jeffreys held court here in 1685. On the wall hangs what is called King Arthur's Round Table, marked out and inscribed for his knights. It was refurbished in Tudor times to honour the visiting emperor, Charles V.

Wolvesey, another castle, was originally built in 1138 by Bishop Henry de Blois, half-brother to King Stephen. Mary Tudor spent her honeymoon here, but later the castle was slighted by Cromwellian forces. However, romantic ruins have survived, and in 1684 a new palace was built, completing the west wing, which is still the bishop's palace. Nearby are parts of the old city walls.

Of the many churches, St John the Baptist's is the most interesting. Mainly in Transitional Norman style, there is a splendid geometrical Decorated window in the south wall, and some outstanding 13th-cent. wall paintings.

But no church can compete with the mag-

nificence of the cathedral. One stood here in Anglo-Saxon times, but after the Conquest the new building was started in 1079 by Bishop Walkelyn and consecrated in 1093. Work from this period can still be seen in the crypt, transepts and east part of the cloister. Between 1189 and 1204 Bishop de Lucy extended the choir and built the Lady Chapel. During the 14th cent. William of Edington, who also built EDINGTON Priory, started to refashion the west front and nave in Perpendicular style and this work was completed by his successor William of Wykeham.

Thus the cathedral shows architectural styles from massive Norman to graceful Perpendicular. It is the second longest in Europe. Among the cathedral treasures are a magnificent 12th-cent. black marble font from Tournai with vigorous carvings depicting legends from the life of St Nicholas – a boy saved from drowning and decapitated heads restored; and the great Winchester Bible also dating from the 12th cent.

Many kings lie here, as do the famous, among them Jane Austen and Izaak Walton, but unfortunately St Swithun's tomb, though marked, has been destroyed. There is much else of beauty, including the paintings in the part 13th-cent. Lady Chapel, the Chapel of the Guardian Angels and the beautiful chantry chapels to William of Wykeham, Bishop Langton and others.

Outside, in the close, the Old Deanery has a 13th-cent. entrance and 15th-cent. windows. Dome Alley has 17th-cent. houses, and Cheyney Court is attractively half-timbered. Nearby is the Pilgrims' School, and at its side the 14th-cent. Pilgrims' Hall has a magnificent hammer-beam roof and is open to the public.

In 1382 William of Wykeham founded Winchester College. Many of the old buildings, which can be visited, retain their original atmosphere and the chapel has its original wooden vaulting.

In 1136 Bishop Henry de Blois founded the Hospital of St Cross for the benefit of 13 poor men. Today they still wear black gowns decorated with a silver cross and a medieval cap, while those from the Almshouses of the Noble Poverty, founded in 1445 by Cardinal Beaufort, wear mulberry gowns and cardinal's hats with swinging tassels. The old buildings here are mellow and peaceful, and the vaulted Chapel of St Cross is quite outstanding. It has a 12th-cent. choir and transepts, a 14th-cent. tower, 15th-cent. glass and beautiful old wall paintings and woodwork. Anyone visiting this foundation may still be given the Wayfarer's Dole – bread and beer served in a horn – which has been dispensed since the 12th cent.

Winchester lies in a hollow so you do not see much on approach, but there are magnificent views from both St Giles Hill, E. of the city and now a park, and from St Catherine's Hill to the SE. There is a mizmaze, or old labyrinth, here, as at BREAMORE, and an ancient Iron Age fort.

WINDSOR, *Berkshire* (5–SU9676), is dominated, both in spirit and in fact, by its magnificent castle. Yet the town itself is very attractive, with Georgian and Victorian buildings, and Church Street is one of its prettiest areas.

The Parish Church of St John, rebuilt in the 19th cent., stands in the High Street and has interesting contents. The chapel railings are by Grinling Gibbons; a painting of the last supper by de Cleyn was given by George III; and among the monuments are two from the 18th cent. by Scheemakers. Nearby, the Guildhall was designed at the end of the 17th cent. by Sir Thomas Fitch and completed by Sir Christopher Wren. Statues of Queen Anne and her husband decorate the façade. It is open to the public, and various charters, documents and exhibits concerning local history are on display, while portraits of the kings and queens line the walls.

However, it is the castle, the largest inhabited castle in the world and covering 13 acres, that draws all eyes. Its story starts with William the Conqueror who quickly grasped its strategic position and the advantage of a forest for hunting close by. Since then practically every sovereign has had a hand in the building. Henry II put up the first stone buildings, including the Round Tower, and the defences are still mainly those built by Henry III. Edward III was born at Windsor and loved it. He enlarged the royal apartments, and founded the Order of the Knights of the Garter, making Windsor a centre for chivalry.

Almost all succeeding monarchs made alterations, including the two queens, Mary and Elizabeth I. A great deal of work was done under Charles II and again during the reign of George III, while later Sir Jeffry Wyatville made enormous changes for George IV, giving the castle the unforgettable skyline we see today.

The castle is made up of three parts: the Lower Ward, which includes St George's Chapel; the Upper Ward in which lie the State Apartments; and the Middle Ward where the enormous Round Tower, open to the public, gives wonderful views of 12 counties, especially over the Thames.

Walking through Henry VIII's Gateway, you arrive first at St George's Chapel, a sumptuous and impressive building which yet gives an effect of light and spaciousness. The Perpendicular chapel was begun by Edward IV in 1475, and completed in the reigns of Henry VII and VIII. Many sovereigns and famous men and women lie buried here, including Charles I, Henry VIII and Jane Seymour. Here the 19th-cent. monument to Princess Charlotte and the Albert Memorial Chapel stand out in bold contrast. It is almost impossible to appreciate all at once the magnificent fan vaulting, the chantries, paintings, delicate ironwork and the rich carvings of the choir stalls. Each stall shows the arms of every Knight of the Garter who has sat there, while the banner and crested helm of the present holder flutter above.

The state apartments are in the upper ward. Quite apart from their fascinating historical associations these 16 rooms contain a quite remarkable collection of furniture, porcelain, armour, Grinling Gibbons carvings, Verrio ceilings, and above all paintings. The collection, which is particularly strong in the works of Van Dyck and Rembrandt, changes constantly, as pictures are often on loan, or removed to another Royal residence. Subject to the requirements of the Court, these apartments are open to the public. So too are St George's Chapel, the castle precincts, collections of old master drawings, and Queen Mary's dolls' house. Designed by Sir Edward Lutyens in the 1920s it is a 20th-cent. house in exquisite miniature, with every detail perfect.

Home Park lies near the castle, enclosed by the Thames. Stretching over some 400 acres, it is in part open to the public. Near the 18th-cent. Frogmore House is the Royal Mausoleum, shaped like a Greek cross with a copper dome, where Queen Victoria and Prince Albert lie buried. It is on rare occasions open to the public. Close by is another mausoleum to Queen Victoria's mother, the Duchess of Kent.

Windsor Great Park is S., covering an enormous acreage of wooded park, and contains some magnificent gardens. Charles II created the Long Walk, which stretches 3 m. and ends at the colossal statue of George III, erected in 1831 at Snowhill. In the 18th cent. Queen Anne added another 3-m. ride, leading to Ascot, and in the same century the Duke of Cumberland called in Thomas Sandby and his brother to create VIRGINIA WATER, a beautiful lake covering 150 acres. In 1816 the Prince Regent donated some Roman ruins from Leptis Magna in Tripoli to add to the effect.

Windsor Great Park has remarkable gardens. The Savill Garden, with every conceivable flower from roses to rock plants, magnolias to rhododendrons, is open to the public and covers some

20 acres. The Valley Garden is near Virginia Water, and in the south-east corner the Kurume Punch Bowl is ablaze with Japanese azaleas.

Flowers apart, Windsor Great Park and forest are in effect a vast nature reserve, where animals of all kinds including deer, and waterfowl at Virginia Water, can be studied.

WINTERBORNE CLENSTON, *Dorset* (4–ST8302). A hamlet in a wide chalk valley, it has a grand late-15th- to early-16th-cent. manor house and, close by, a tithe barn with one of the finest hammer-beam roofs in Dorset, which may have come from MILTON ABBEY. The house, attractive from the outside, can be seen over by appointment. It has an unusual turret staircase. A little down the valley, the church looks faintly as if it should be in Switzerland. It was built in 1840, neatly spired, and inside is cheerful with a blue-starred chancel ceiling.

WINTERBORNE STEEPLETON, *Dorset* (4–SY6289). The east end of the village is in a forest of cypresses and hardwoods. The west end, beside a poplar-lined, slab-bridged stream, is sunny and open. The church, a grey building with a medieval spire, stands in a glade near which the trees are thickest. It has, built into the exterior of its south wall, a sculptured angel which, if the dating of it to *c.* 950 is correct, is one of the oldest pieces of church sculpture in England. It also has a fine Anglo-Saxon font. Across the road the manor house, now a private hotel, is 19th-cent., but the nearby church hall was built *c.* 1407 and is still in use.

The Winterborne chalk streams, of which there are two in Dorset, are so called because they are apt to retire underground in summer. But, here at any rate, this one ripples all the year round.

About 1¼ m. NW., close to the A35, **Nine Stones** is a prehistoric stone circle of uncertain origin, looked after by the Ministry of Public Building and Works.

WINTERBORNE TOMSON, *Dorset* (4–SY8997). A simple and memorable tiny, towerless, 12th-cent. church at the end of a road through a field. From the outside it could almost be mistaken for a barn, and as such it was being used by pigs and hens till between 1929 and 1931, when it was restored by A. R. Powys, Secretary to the Society for the Protection of Ancient Buildings, on the proceeds of the sale of some Thomas Hardy architectural manuscripts. It has box pews, Georgian canopied pulpit, small gallery and apsidal chancel of delicately curved and carved roof timbers, a plaque to Powys being virtually its only embellishment. It is now immaculately kept.

WOKINGHAM, *Berkshire* (5–SU8068), near Windsor Forest has been for centuries a pleasant market town, also known for its bell foundry, and silk industry, indicated by some mulberry trees.

But although the town has expanded enormously it still has some half-timbered houses with overhanging gables, particularly in Rose Street.

Molly Mog, the landlord's daughter of the Rose Inn, now demolished, is said to have inspired John Gay to verse, when he, Swift and Pope spent a wet afternoon here.

All Saints' Church is much restored, but five bays with carved capitals in the nave are medieval, and there is a beautifully carved Perpendicular font. The Lucas Hospital at Luckley, 1 m. S., is a most interesting building, where low brick buildings dated 1665 flank three sides of a neat garden.

Bearwood, lying 3 m. W. in forested country, has a spectacular rhododendron drive, and a large artificial lake. Near the church at **Hurst**, 4 m. N., are some 17th-cent. red-brick almshouses, and timber-framed houses are scattered through the village. The Castle Inn is of 16th-cent. origin and has a very old bowling green. The church, part of which dates back to Norman times, has a quaint hour-glass, some good 17th-cent. woodwork, and several fine monuments of the 16th, 17th and 18th cents.

WOOTTON BASSETT, *Wiltshire* (5–SU 0682), set high on a hill, was used, before the 1832 Reform Bill, to return two Members of Parliament, one of whom was Edward Hyde, Lord Clarendon. Today it is a most attractive small town, consisting, more or less, of one street. Here various styles of architecture spanning more than three centuries blend most happily together.

In 1700 the 1st Earl of Rochester built the half-timbered town hall. Restored in 1889, it still stands today, while the traffic swirls round it. The upper room, approached by a handsome oak staircase, is now a public library, while down below, under a stone colonnade, still stand the old stocks and a ducking stool. There is also an old fire engine with wooden wheels.

The church dates back to the 13th cent. It has an old panelled roof to the nave sprinkled with stars, and before it was enlarged by Street in 1870 it had a double nave. Both the priest's room above the vaulted south porch and the splendid Elizabethan painted pulpit are noteworthy.

Not far away on the north-west ridge of the Marlborough Downs, **Hackpen Hill** gives wonderful views of the area. On the lower slopes one of the white horses of Wiltshire is cut.

WORTH MATRAVERS, *Dorset* (5–SY9777), is situated on the long mound of country W. from SWANAGE to KIMMERIDGE, which is unlike anywhere else in Dorset, intricately drystone-walled, and almost treeless. It is where the famous Purbeck marble came (and to some extent still comes) from, and this attractive grey-stone village in a sun-trap nook in the hillside was once an important quarrying centre. The church is basically Norman, incorporating some Anglo-Saxon work, and is well restored. Some of the quarries which scatter the area can be well seen about 1 m. NE., close to the road.

From a farm ½ m. W. of the village, 1½ m. of track leads to **St Aldhelm's Head**, with coastguard station and a sturdy, square Norman chapel in remarkably good order. From the head, above cliffs nearly 400 ft high, the views along the coast are magnificent.

From the same farm another track descends a beautiful winding valley to **Chapman's Pool**, a cove good for fossil-hunting and seeing cormorants, but less good for bathing.

WYLYE, *Wiltshire* (5–SU0037), lies on the banks of the River Wylye, in a peaceful green valley. At one time William Cobbett counted about 30 villages between OLD SARUM and WARMINSTER, along this river. Wylye is one of the most attractive of these villages, for it is set against a wooded hill and has delightful 17th-cent. chequer workhouses and some attractive Georgian buildings. The church has a Perpendicular tower, but was much restored in the 19th cent. The east window with its triple lancet is beautiful. The splendid 17th-cent. wooden pulpit, heavily carved and complete with canopy, was brought from WILTON together with the fine candelabra.

YARMOUTH, *Isle of Wight* (5–SZ3598). Yarmouth is a small and historic port on the Solent in the W. of the island. In the harbour the ruins of a Henry VIII castle are of interest as the construction differs from those he built at COWES and SANDOWN: square and with the first arrow-headed bastion in England. In St James's Church there is a white marble statue of Sir Robert Holmes, who was Governor of the island in the 17th cent. The head is of Sir Robert, but the rest was a statue of Louis XIV captured from the French. Sir Robert plundered the Dutch in the East, and from the gold he brought back from Guinea the first coins of that name were minted. He took New Amsterdam, now New York, in 1665.

A causeway, gained by a drawbridge over the Yar, links the port to the FRESHWATER peninsula. Yarmouth is a good starting point from which to explore the island along good roads in all directions. **Totland Bay** is only 3 m. away, with **Alum Bay** just beyond on the seaward face of the 377-ft Headon Hill. Alum Bay is renowned for its sands of many colours; as many as 12 different shades have been recorded. Further to the W. are the chalk pinnacles of the Needles, and the Needles lighthouse; the highest was 120 ft high but fell in 1764. A good car park and other amenities are provided here for those wishing to view these famous geological features. But a walk in the air of the downs was according to Tennyson "worth 6*d*. a pint". Off the main road to Totland from Yarmouth's **Colwell Bay** is a 2-m. curving stretch of sand. In the opposite direction, to the E., lie the typical villages of **Shalfleet**, with its fine Norman church, and **Newtown**, whose 18th-cent. town hall is the last relic of perhaps the oldest borough on the island.

YATTENDON, *Berkshire* (5–SU5474). A Bronze Age cache discovered in the neighbourhood shows how long it has been inhabited. Yattendon was also once a market town, but today it is visited for the charm of a peaceful village, with thatch and timber, standing in wooded country above the River Penge.

The rectory is Georgian, as is the stone malthouse and the stately brick manor built by a Florentine who gained fame as a dancer in London. It once belonged to the Norreys family, and Sir John, who entertained Henry VIII here lavishly, was later beheaded, accused of being too intimate with Anne Boleyn.

There is a tablet to his son, who sailed with Drake under Elizabeth, in the church, built by another John Norreys in 1450. The present structure is mostly Victorian. Robert Bridges (1844–1930), Poet Laureate, lies in the churchyard and once made the choir one of the best in England.

YAVERLAND, *Isle of Wight* (5–SZ6185), reached by a winding road some 5½ m. from BEMBRIDGE, can boast of a fine Jacobean Manor House, adjoining the small 12th-cent. church. Nearby, on the SANDOWN road, is **Yarbridge**, set inland a mile from the sea. Good angling can be had in the River Yar, with a licence obtained from the Fishery Officer. Within easy distance are Alverstone Watermill and the hamlet of Queen's Bower, so named after Isabella de Fortibus, Lady of the Wight, chatelaine of Carisbrooke Castle, who kept a hunting lodge here. She died aged 56 in 1293. Not far away is Borthwood Copse, a sanctuary of flowered beauty administered by the National Trust.

YETMINSTER, *Dorset* (4–ST5910), is a handsome large village, its houses of yellow stone, in many cases 17th-cent. and earlier and with stone-mullioned windows. Its big 15th-cent. church has a 13th-cent. chancel and some quite good monuments and brasses and several beautiful tombs and headstones in its yard. The outstanding house is Upbury Farm (15th-cent. with 16th- and 17th-cent. additions) just SW. of the churchyard; and the Manor House (16th- and 17th-cent.) and Gable Court (*c*. 1600) in the main street are worth looking for.

Two m. SW., **Melbury Osmond** is a pleasant village at the entrance to the large estate of **Melbury Sampford**. The great house, mainly built by Sir Giles Strangways, *c*. 1540, and extended in the 17th cent., can be distantly seen from the A37. Its gardens are occasionally open and there are fortnightly Sunday services in the church in the grounds.

ZEALS, *Wiltshire* (4–ST7731), lies in hilly country, right on the border with Somerset and Dorset. The village is pretty with thatch, and from here there are spectacular views, especially looking southwards into Dorset. The church dates from 1848 and was designed by Scott.

On the road towards MERE is **Zeals House**, some of which dates back to medieval times, though some parts were added in the 19th cent. Inside there is an interesting carved ceiling. During the Civil War, Charles II stayed here for one night, during his flight towards the coast after the Battle of Worcester had been lost.

The West Country

Somerset   Devon   Cornwall

GEOFFREY GRIGSON

Somerset, Devon and Cornwall – these three western counties each preserve a distinct character, derived from the interaction of man and basic landscape, history and geography. Each at the same time affords that variety within a small space (small at any rate compared with the wide, often monotonous divisions of other European countries, such as France and Germany) which is the charm and mark of England.

Of the three, Somerset is the most urbane. Its Old English name seems to mean (the land of) the "summer-farm dwellers", the land of strong pasture to which the West Saxon farmers brought their cattle in the summer, thirteen centuries ago. In Somerset, as in the other two counties, the record of settlement goes back far beyond the arrival of the English. Twelve thousand years have passed since hunters of the Old Stone Age found temporary quarters in the mouths of the caves and under the rock shelters of the Mendip limestone. The standing stones and stone circles of Stanton Drew, in deep meadow country immediately south of Bristol, and the chambered long barrow at Stoney Littleton, near Radstock, are Neolithic evidences exciting enough to visit. Hill after hill in Somerset – where a population of hills stand up bare and sharp, and green – is crowned with a "hill camp", a fortified farmstead, of the quarrelsome Celtic centuries which preceded the Roman occupation of Britain. Then before the English, or rather West Saxon, "summer dwellers" began to take permanent hold of Somerset in the seventh century, it had been Romanized.

The Fosse Way, the military highway which the Roman engineers laid across England from Lincoln, or the North Sea, to the Channel, enters Somerset just outside the once Roman city of Bath, and bisects the county, subsidiary roads running east and west from the Fosse Way into the Romanized *villa* country – the country of Roman farm or ranch estates.

There are exhibits in the excellent County Museum at Taunton which show how life changed in Somerset from "native" to Roman. From one of the crannogs or "lake-villages" of the first and second centuries B.C. which have been found in the Somerset marsh land near Glastonbury there are decorated bowls from which the British drank their gruel; and from a *villa* house a few miles west of the Fosse Way you can see in the Museum a fourth-century mosaic pavement of scenes from the story of Dido and Aeneas, from Virgil's *Aeneid*.

Bath, by European standards the supreme exhibit, the extreme attraction of the county, proves the strength of its Roman tradition. The city grew up around the supposedly healing and supposedly divine properties of its hot springs. In the sag of a valley bastioned by great hills, these springs were, for the Romans and the Romanized Britons, the *Aquae Sulis*, the waters of the local god Sulis, a deity with attributes like those of Minerva. The waters of Sulis were fed into the faintly steaming baths one can see today, they became the centre of a Roman pleasure town; and when the architect John Wood, followed by his son, set about refurbishing and reshaping the pleasure town of the eighteenth century his desire was to create, once more, a "Roman" city of square and crescent and circus. No one can realize the achievement of English eighteenth-century urbanism, indeed of English eighteenth-century culture, without walking through the Circus at Bath, and crossing the wide sweep of turf embraced by the Royal Crescent; without sitting there, and looking up at the Crescent and absorbing the scale, the dignity, the high thought of this architectural victory.

Stone in large part has created the courteous quality of Somerset – limestone which drains well and provides both a cheerful habitat and healthy pasture, which again produced, in cattle, sheep, wool and cloth, the wealth by which the stone was quarried and the buildings were erected. Bath is limestone, mined inside the hills nearby. Wells Cathedral and Glastonbury Abbey are limestone, of a better kind, which was quarried at Doulting, on the road from Wells to Frome. It is this Doulting stone which gives a whitish grey tone to houses and villages in the northern part of Somerset; whereas south Somerset, nearer the border with Dorset, has buildings warm with brown and gold, derived from the quarries in Hamdon Hill, which stands up between Yeovil and Taunton, close to the old Roman Fosse Way. Tinted with iron oxide "Ham Hill stone" was used for medieval churches, Tudor manor houses, seventeenth- and eighteenth-century mansions, whole villages, whole market towns.

Hamdon Hill is in the parish of East Stoke. The next-door parish is Montacute (a name, by the way, epitomizing much of Somerset – monkish medieval Latin *mons acutus*, sharp mount, sharp hill), and in the National Trust's Montacute House, with its garden plaisances, its balustrading and obelisks, Ham Hill stone can be seen employed with outstanding virtuosity. Another Ham Hill building, or group of buildings, in the same neighbourhood near Yeovil, is Brympton d'Evercy, less known and reached only by teasing a way into a park along a dead-end road. Here this lichen-colonized stone gives warm unity in variety to a medieval church, a late medieval dower house, a mansion part Tudor, part eighteenth-century, and stables of the late seventeenth century.

Yet the outstanding, upstanding speciality of Somerset is its church towers, the climax of Somerset's ecclesiastical continuity. Glastonbury, richest monastery in England after Westminster Abbey, flourished for six centuries from its refoundation in 943. Wells, just south of the bulky range of the Mendips dividing most of Somerset from Bristol and Bath, had its first cathedral in the sixth century. For more than Somerset alone they were centres of art and architecture, centres of a tradition which at last raised the tall square towers of parish church after parish church throughout the county. Among towers by the dozen, which often stand in happy relationship to sharp hill slopes, my choice of three – none of them a great way from Montacute, where the mansion succeeded a wealthy priory – would be the towers of St Mary's, Taunton (1488–1514), of the Isle Abbots (*c.* 1480), a church on a Sedgemoor "island" which belonged to the wealthy Benedictines of Muchelney Abbey, and of Huish Episcopi (*c.* 1505), a church which belonged to the bishops of Wells. Sir Nikolaus Pevsner analyses the style and rhythm of these Perpendicular towers of Somerset in his two Penguin guides to the buildings of the county.

Looking back to Glastonbury and Wells, it is a major loss that the grand thirteenth- and fourteenth-century abbey church of Glastonbury should have been reduced to fragments – splendid as the site may be, accented with tower-crowned St Michael's Tor, on top of which the last abbot of Glastonbury was hanged in 1539 – and it is a major happiness that we should have in Wells, in the cathedral, the

Vicar's Close, the Deanery, the gateways and the moated palace of the bishops, a surviving assembly of medieval buildings without parallel.

Moving westward across the hill ranges, the Quantocks, the Brendon Hills, to Exmoor gives a foretaste of the more savage landscape which defines much of Devon and Cornwall. One comes to a high brackeny Somerset of less fertile sandstone, a land of ochre (at any rate autumnal ochre) rather than vivid green, breaking off to a sullen shore, shelving out to sea, and often noisy with the grinding of pebbles like solid skulls.

If Somerset seems English in spirit, here on the west side of the marshes were the outlying hilly lands of the British – of the British kingdom of Dumnonia – into which the English of Somerset, of Wessex, made no headway until the seventh century.

According to mood or temperament one may prefer this north-western Somerset, its steep-hilled roads, its cleft valleys, its brows raised over the peculiar Severn Sea. This is the country of those three connoisseurs of landscape, William Wordsworth, Dorothy Wordsworth and Coleridge, who walked and talked along its ridges, delighted in its mountain ashes, and sheltered among its bright-leaved holly woods. For this part of the world, reflected also in Coleridge's *Kubla Khan*, which was written down in a farm-house above the cleft of Culbone, the essential document is Dorothy Wordsworth's *Alfoxden Journal*, January to May 1798, kept while she and her brother were tenants of Alfoxden House, on the seaward slope of the Quantocks: it varies the Somerset theme of walking along the hill-tops.

Devon, across the border, soon divides into granite and combe, into the great water-soaked water-shedding boss of Dartmoor, where the granite obtrudes in castellated tors, and the deep combes enclosing rivers which make a rough journey southward to the Channel. Barren as Dartmoor may be, Devon was on the whole worth possessing. The Romans had gone little further west than Exeter, *Isca Dumnoniorum*, Isca of the Dumnonii, which was their westernmost town. The West Saxons had gone eastward beyond Exeter to the Tamar, the "dark river", dividing Devon and Cornwall, by 682. Part of their prize was the Devon "Red Lands", the Devon portion of a band of soil of extreme fertility which stretches from north-west Somerset down to Tor Bay. Coleridge, who came from east Devon, from Ottery St Mary, where his father was parson and schoolmaster, talked of the heaped-up richness of Devon. North or south, round Lynton and Lynmouth or at the back of Torquay, the exploring motorist who is used to tamer country will be surprised by the gradients he has to tackle.

The greater hills were, and are still, sheep country; and that Devon became well-to-do, in spite of its barren interior lands, was due largely to the export of serges woven on its cottage looms and fulled in little tucking mills on the rapid streams off the Moor. Less urbane than Somerset, yet with many abbeys and priories, with its great cathedral at Exeter (founded in 1050), the see of which extended across the Tamar to Land's End, and with its busy ports, Devon flourished from the Middle Ages to the end of the eighteenth century, its cloth prosperity reflected and recorded in churches often boldly proportioned, if rather more provincial than the churches of Somerset.

The speciality of these Devon churches is wood-carving, a richness of intricately, exquisitely carved rood-screens, of the fifteenth or early sixteenth century. Some churches to visit for this craft at its most surprising are, in North Devon, Atherington church, on the road from South Molton to Great Torrington; in South Devon, Harberton church near Totnes, and a group of three churches a

Photo Warburg Institute

Evidence of Roman occupation is provided by this mosaic of Dido and Aeneas from a villa in Somerset. Somerset County Museum, Taunton

little way south of Exeter – Kenton, Ashton and Bovey Tracey. The white-washed or colour-washed villages, largely built of "cob" (mud, straw and horsehair) not stone, contrast with tall church towers. They look as if they might have been a kind of mushroom growth from the up-and-down landscape, and they are a reminder that, comfortable as it may have been, Devon remained a culturally remote conservative part of England.

In Devon the major contrasts are between heathery upland and green lane, Dartmoor and the coloured luxuriance of the Channel coast. Staying at Bovey Tracey, then at Teignmouth, the poet Gerard Manley Hopkins caught the peculiar colours and contrasts of South Devon scenery. He walked home off the Moor "by starlight and Jupiter, stumbling down steep dark lanes", he remarked a liquidness in the growth of trees, admired the "soft maroon or rosy-cocoa-dust-coloured handkerchiefs of ploughed fields". Staying at Teignmouth, he remarked on what he called "the bole, the burling and roundness of the world". He looked down at Babbacombe Bay to a sea like blue silk, under red cliffs, to "white ashy shingle", and "green inshore water"; big clouds rose against the blue of the bay "as if they were great white roses sunk in a blue dye."

Turn away from this colour and luxuriance and from the sea; and, perhaps through rain, the Moor ascends the sky, grey and disturbing. The scenic attractions of Dartmoor, grey or purple or egg-yolk-coloured with gorse, may have been overrated. But it amounts to a queer museum of past eras and activities. Less boggy in the drier Bronze Age, it was settled by farming and pastoral communities, who have left granite-built pounds, circles, hutments, alignments and burial mounds for our inspection. A wetter phase thinned out or drove out the population of the

Dartmoor ponies seem to be descended from animals turned out on to the Moor in Anglo-Saxon times

Moor, until a sparse English reoccupation took place in the Middle Ages, between the twelfth and fourteenth centuries. Farmers pushed to the upland, tinners came to work the valleys over to find the black dust of tin. So extra monuments in the durable "moorstone" or surface granite were added to the moorstone monuments of prehistoric antiquity, including the blowing-houses (smelting houses) of the tinners, the long houses of farmers (which sheltered, with a passage in between them, both the family and their cattle), and the clapper bridges (there is neither evidence nor likelihood that these slab bridges were prehistoric) by which man and packhorse crossed the quick-flooding streams. Dartmoor ponies seem to be descendants of animals turned out on to the Moor in Anglo-Saxon times earlier than this medieval reoccupation. The official guide to the Dartmoor National Park, edited by Professor W. G. Hoskins, is the indispensable brief introduction to all these peculiarities of the Moor.

Then Cornwall. Unfair perhaps to ask, exactly how Cornish is Cornwall? – since the true answer in such an ethnic matter is that today's Cornish are precisely as Cornish as they may feel. Certainly the Tamar in its wide and then narrow trough remained the boundary between Cornish and English until the beginning of the ninth century. Then, in 838, just across the Tamar, above Gunnislake, Egbert of Wessex defeated a united army of Cornish and Vikings.

Certainly "Cornwall" was a name which meant first of all the foreigners of the land of *Corn*, the land pushing out like a *corn*, or horn, into the sea. Cornwall had become the last remnant of the Dumnonia of the British. But if you cross the Tamar by the road bridge over its tidal waters at Saltash or by the bridge upstream at Gunnislake, you very soon come near Cornish-named villages or farms – Landulph, Trewin, Trevollard near Saltash; Pencrebar, Menheniot, Trevigro not far beyond Gunnislake. Names with Tre- (*tref*) in Cornish are equivalent to names with -*ton* (*tūn*) in English, *tref* and *tūn* meaning farmstead. Look round in East Cornwall, indeed look some way into the county, and names with -*ton* and *tre*- quickly reveal themselves side by side. Callington, the name of the first town on the Cornish side along the A390, the Gunnislake road, mixes Cornish and English. In Cornish it was *Celliwic*, the Wood. The English added -*tūn*, making it the wood farm. The second town along this road into Cornwall is Liskeard, pure Cornish, the *lis*, the court, of a king or chieftain named Cerruyt.

Or follow the names as you cross from Devon into Cornwall further upstream along the A30(T), which then runs down the granitic backbone of Cornwall. You leave English names behind you in Devon – Okehampton, Bridestone, Lifton – you climb from the Tamar to Launceston, another Cornish name (? Stephen's church) to which the English -*tūn* was added. The road crosses the moors till you reach Bodmin, Cornish again, the "house of the monks". Cornish names thicken as you push towards Penzance and Land's End; but it is clear that in the east Cornish and English had lived side by side; and from the old form of the eastern Cornish names philologists have concluded that the Cornish language died out in that part of the county a thousand years ago.

So the Cornish are mixed. A difference in Cornwall there certainly is, but if some of its elements derive from a British past, more have to do with land and sea, with the mineralization of the rocky substructure of Cornwall, with the high Atlantic cliffs of the north coast, and the lower profile of the south coast, where valleys have been invaded or "drowned" by the sea; with the county or country's position on prehistoric trade routes between France and the Irish Sea; then with isolation and poverty in later centuries; and with its gentleness of climate.

Cornwall is to be visited, not for that architectural excellence and urbanity of English Somerset, but for crude hamlet churches tucked into rough hills and valleys, not for parklike hills and parklike farmlands but for "pills" or creeks, wriggling secretively in from the sea, and packhorse lanes squeezed between high earthen hedges which grow a profusion of primroses and foxgloves, and perhaps struggle down to a cove or a beach of fine sand in which a water-mint stream loses itself on the edge of the sea.

Dolmens, stone circles, hill-forts, fogous (artificial caves or storerooms attached to hill-forts), parishes and holy wells named after British saints, the patchwork-quilt system of small solid-hedged fields, roofless engine houses of abandoned tin mines or copper mines, coloured mine adits driven into cliffs which are buffeted by the Atlantic, even the modern white hills of waste from china-clay works – these, and other features I have mentioned, combine into a something – however touched by England – which lies outside the norm of English scene and settlement. Therein, whether one labels it "Celtic" or not, lies the speciality of Cornwall.

The West Country: Gazetteer

EUAN BOWATER

ALTARNUN, *Cornwall* (2–SX2281), is in many ways a refreshing village. It is wonderfully soft looking after (or before) the bare greyness of Bodmin Moor, sheltered by hills and tall trees, with simple yet cared-for cottages beside a fast river and old packhorse bridge, and it has a superb church that is manifestly still very much alive. The name of the village means "the altar of St Non", who (6th cent.) is said to have been the mother of Wales' St David. The church, built between 1470 and 1536 on the site of a Norman one, is big – as befits the county's largest parish (15,018 acres) – and spacious in attractive light grey stone. Its ancient bench-ends are very fine indeed, both abstract and figurative, and for once the artist is named: Robert Daye created them between 1510 and 1530. Its Norman font, with bearded, staring faces at the corners, is one of the best. There are better waggon roofs, but this one, timbers all exposed, is nevertheless lofty and grand. On either side of the altar are interesting paintings on wood (1620).

In the village, over the door of the old Methodist chapel, is a head of John Wesley by the sculptor Nevill Burnard (1818–78), one of whose major works is the Lander statue in TRURO. He was born in Altarnun.

Three m. E. is **Polyphant**. From its quarries came stone found in old churches throughout Cornwall, liked especially by the Normans because it is easy to work. This pleasantly dishevelled hamlet has several pretty old quarryman's cottages, all massively shaded by horse-chestnuts, sycamores, oak and beech trees. The quarries still operate.

At **Trewint**, $\frac{3}{4}$ m. SW. on the A30, is a cottage where Wesley once stayed and several times called. It contains a little chapel and some relics.

APPLEDORE, *Devon* (3–SS4630). No narrow streets even in Cornwall are prettier than those sloping dead-straight down to Appledore's quay. They are of simple, similar, flat-faced, mainly Georgian cottages in a variety of pastel colours. The streets crossing the slope, which have rainwater gutters down their centres and occasional Elizabethan bow-fronts, are pretty, too, but not so distinctive. Where there are extra large upstairs' windows there were once sail-makers' lofts.

Ship-building, fishing – both deep-sea and salmon netting inshore – and, till about a century ago, smuggling have been the livelihood of this small town throughout its history. Appledore Ship Builders Ltd show visitors round. Ship-building has revived remarkably here, as a large covered dry dock demonstrates. The replica of the Hudson's Bay Company's first ship, *Nonsuch* (1688), was built in 1968 by the firm of Hinks and Son just W. of the town. The Appledore lifeboat is famous, the bar at the mouth of the Taw and Torridge estuaries notorious. Nevertheless, sailing is very popular here, and the view at low tide over a vast spread of sandbanks to distant breakers is particularly beautiful.

ARLINGTON COURT, *Devon* (3–SS6140). There is more than just a fine house to see here. In the stables is a riveting display of 19th-cent. vehicles, including a town coach (like a Royal one), a coach deemed suitable for Continental travel, broughams, victorias, gigs, pony-drawn bath chairs, plus a few of the very first motor-cars. Down by the lake is a heronry and duck sanctuary and in the park are Shetland ponies and Jacob's sheep. The house itself was designed by Thomas Lee of BARNSTAPLE, commissioned by a branch of the Chichester family, owners of the estate since the 14th cent., and built 1820–3. It is neither very big nor, from the outside, very grand. Inside, all doors open on to its central hall, which has a fine sweeping staircase and is, peculiarly, its largest room, the others being comparatively small. There is a fascinating collection, of almost museum proportions, of furniture, model ships, snuff-boxes, shells, books, paintings, pewter, porcelain, etc., gathered together by Miss Rosalie Chichester who lived here alone, except for retainers, from 1908 to her death in 1949. She left the house and the 3,471-acre estate to the National Trust. She made the grounds into a nature reserve. Peacocks still threaten to wander in the front door.

ASHBURTON, *Devon* (3–SX7569). Serves with shops, schools and builders the south-east corner, which is the softest yet most spectacular one of DARTMOOR. An animated little town, it was once an important place. From the 12th cent., when the moor was the richest source of tin in Europe, till that mining finally petered out in the 19th cent., it was one of the four stannary towns (TAVISTOCK, Plympton and later CHAGFORD were the others), to which all tin was brought to be assessed and taxed. It also, in medieval times, had nine cloth mills, and was a popular coach-stop on the EXETER–PLYMOUTH road. This road now by-passes it, enabling it to remain tightly, medievally urban with many pleasant slate-hung build-

Ashton: the medieval paintings on the church screen

ings (though Devon's slate-hanging never has Cornwall's attractiveness) and projecting first stories. Its big 15th-cent. church has a splendid tower, tall and slender, framed by evergreens. The interior was restored by G. E. Street, but its medieval roofs – both waggon and flat – are fine. There is a small museum in the Little House, West Street. The ironmonger's at No. 4 North Street was formerly the Mermaid Inn, a headquarters of Fairfax during the Civil War.

Holne, 3 m. W., and **Buckland-in-the-Moor**, 3 m. NW., both have attractive small churches, both 13th-cent. enlarged in the 15th, both with medieval screens bearing more than usually interesting panel paintings. Charles Kingsley was born at Holne vicarage. The drive between them, through deep woods beside the River Webburn, is very beautiful. Holne Woods, ¼ m. N. of the village and sloping to the Dart, are National Trust.

ASHPRINGTON, *Devon* (3–SX8157). A village 350 ft up on one of the numerous wooded undulations of the Dart's west bank. The church, with a curiously thin tower of *c*. 1350, is, in the tradition of this area, tall and light, its white pillars looking good against pale-brown woodwork. It is basically 15th-cent., though restored.

From here it is worth driving on S. to **Tuckenhay**, ½ m., where beside a long, silent creek there are old wharfs and a famous paper-mill which was started in *c*. 1830 and produces material for banknotes. Road-stone was shipped from the wharfs to London, and in the mid-19th cent. there was a corn mill, a sailcloth mill and a cider factory here. Still to be seen is the gas house, which gave Tuckenhay gas-lights in *c*. 1806, before parts of London.

Cornworthy, 1 m. further S., has a mainly 15th-cent. church with an attractively light Georgian

interior: box pews, canopied pulpit, rather battered 15th-cent. screen in pale wood offset by granite pillars. About ½ m. W. of the village is the ivy-covered 14th-cent. gatehouse of an Augustinian nunnery, founded in *c*. 1231–8.

Dittisham, 3 m. SE., is a pretty village with thatched cottages and views of the river. Its church has an exceptional 15th-cent. carved stone and painted pulpit, similar to that at St Saviour's DARTMOUTH but much more appealing. A car ferry crosses from here to Greenway at irregular intervals. There, though not in the existing house, Sir Humphrey Gilbert (*see* Compton Castle, TORQUAY) was born.

ASHTON, *Devon* (3–SX8584). In the church on a knoll among trees above the main street of **Higher Ashton** are possibly the finest medieval screen paintings in the West Country. The most interesting of all are on the back of the splendidly carved screen which spans the church. Altogether it is an exceptional village church, restored in 1905 with the minimum removal of old furnishings. These include 15th-cent. bench-ends, font, studded oak doors, some heraldic stained glass and an Elizabethan pulpit with tester and iron hourglass stand beside it. An odd thing about the building is that the apex of the east window is not in line with the roof apex.

In the churchyard will be found a gravestone to a Mr Stooke, a farmer, who, tradition says, found the King's Purse discarded by its Keeper when he was fleeing from Roundheads, and years later, driven by his conscience, founded local charities which still survive.

Lower Ashton, about 1 m. W., has a nice street of cob and thatched cottages and looks pretty from its early-17th-cent. bridge, with angled pedestrian refuges, over the Teign.

From there it is worth driving the 2 m. N. to

Doddiscombsleigh. The way is beautiful through steep farming country and oak and hazel woods, the contours sharp enough to counter the high hedges that so often spoil things for the motorist in Devon. Doddiscombsleigh church is made special by its possession of easily the largest amount of medieval (15th-cent.) stained glass in any church in Devon. Five large windows remain almost intact, their gentle colours and shapes quite different from the Victorian glass so often seen in churches. The church is down a pedestrian lane past the farm of Town Barton, the former manor house, probably 15th-cent.

For another equally exceptional piece of church furniture, go to **Bridford**, 2 m. NW., past an old station on the disused Teign Valley railway line, excellently converted into a house. Here again it is a screen, but very different from Ashton's. Dating from about 1508, it is covered with exquisitely carved figures and still bears much of its ancient blue, red and gold colouring. The pulpit, similarly carved, and the ceiling are fine, too. This side of the Teign is the edge of DARTMOOR. Immediately W. of the village the landscape becomes bleaker with areas of gorse, granite boulders piled like ramparts along the hedges, and horizons topped by tors as massive as most on the moor itself. The mightiest of these, Blackingstone Rock, towers mightily above the road W. to Moretonhampstead (*see* CHAGFORD).

ATHERINGTON and HIGH BICKINGTON, *Devon* (3–SS5923). Neither the country around, nor these two villages (1¾ m. apart), nor their churches are, as a whole, special; but both churches contain quite exceptional and beautiful things. The rood-loft (*c.* 1530–40) in Atherington church is the only original one left in the West Country. Moreover, both loft and screen, the work of two CHITTLEHAMPTON men, are an extremely fine example of intricate wood-carving. In the loft are the remains of some Elizabethan panel paintings.

From just N. of the village is a good view over the Taw Valley to EXMOOR.

High Bickington's glory is in its early-16th-cent. bench-ends. There are about 70 of them (the largest collection in North Devon) and they are deeply and passionately carved, proving the extent to which bench-end carving was a genuine art-form. The processions of animals carved in 1904 on the choir pews are pleasant but not comparable.

AXBRIDGE, *Somerset* (3–ST4255). The base from which Anglo-Saxon and Norman kings hunted stags on the MENDIPS, it was made a borough by Edward the Confessor and remains one of the most ancient-looking small towns and one of the few with exposed-timber Tudor buildings in the county. From the Middle Ages to the Industrial Revolution it was a wool town specializing in knitting stockings. That Hannah More, the pioneer social worker, found it in the late 18th cent. "a wretched beggarly town . . . all anarchy and malice" does not mean its merchants were not rich. Now, happily by-passed by the main road, it is famous for its strawberries.

The town is mainly one long winding street bulging at one point into a square. From this, steps lead up to its handsome, mainly 15th-cent. cruciform church containing an unusual decorated-plaster nave ceiling (1636), an outstanding sculptured font (*c.* 1460) and fine vaulting under the tower. The connection between the obviously Elizabethan building called King John's Hunting Lodge and that king is obscure, but he seems undoubtedly to have frequented the town as a hunter. Bull-baiting took place in the square as late as the 19th cent., and instruments of this torture and others are in the museum in the Town Hall (1833); also records of the town's history. The domed 17th-cent. manor house, a little W. of the square, is sometimes open.

AXMINSTER, *Devon* (3–SY2998). Famous for its carpets, Axminster was one of the first West Saxon settlements in Devon (late 7th cent.) and is now a small market town. It has an attractive centre, with a green shaded by elms, cedars and yews, an outwardly handsome church and good coaching pubs, like the 18th-cent. George. The carpet industry was founded in 1755, in the building immediately NE. of the church, by Thomas Whitty who had carefully studied Turkish methods. In 1835 the business was sold to a WILTON weaver, and no more carpets were made in the town till a new factory was opened in 1937. This is near the station and can be visited.

Two m. SW., **Ashe House**, open to the public, was the home from the 15th to the 18th cent. of the Drake family, cousins of Sir Francis. It is claimed that a son was born here in 1650 (though there are other claimants) to Elizabeth Drake and her husband, Winston Churchill. This boy was later to become the famous general, the Duke of Marlborough. The house, though part medieval, today has few pretensions. The gardens are a pure-bred poultry reserve and hens and ducks of enormous variety wander everywhere. Visitors are given a tin of food for them.

BABINGTON, *Somerset* (4–ST6951). A small Georgian church (1750) and late 18th-cent. house stand side by side in a garden reached by a beech and elm avenue. The church was probably not, as has been suggested, designed by Wren, but is nevertheless interesting and attractive with domed chancel, box pews, two-decker pulpit and decoratively plastered east wall.

About ¾ m. N., **Kilmersdon** is an excellent, strong stone village with a square lock-up and a church with a good, gargoyled tower.

One mile NE. of it, the Lutyens-designed yew gardens of Ammerdown Park are periodically open. The house was built in 1788, designed by James Wyatt. Some 2½ m. NE., **Radstock** is a small coal-mining town with one colliery still working.

BANWELL, *Somerset* (3–ST3959). A large, ancient, now mainly ugly, village with an extremely fine, late-14th- and 15th-cent. church. This is renowned for its screen (*c.* 1520), but its high waggon-roofed nave and slender pillars, carved stone medieval pulpit and the medieval glass in the east windows of its aisles all contribute to a general effect of great beauty.

In the wood to the S. of the main road is a large mysterious cross drawn on the ground with mounded turf. No one knows who made it or when or why, but it is deemed an Ancient Monument. A gateway opposite the entrance to Banwell Castle (19th-cent. and private) leads to it.

Two m. SW., **Christon** has an excellent little Norman church and is an attractive small village.

BARNSTAPLE, *Devon* (3–SS5533), was minting its own coins in the 10th cent. and is one of the oldest boroughs in Britain, Till the rapid growth of the Torbay area in the 19th cent. it was Devon's third largest town. During the Middle and Elizabethan Ages it was a major textile and ship-building centre and port. It also made beautiful tiles, seen on some church floors, for example at Launcells. Its textile industry declined in the 17th cent. Ship-building continued till 1880. By about that time silting up of the Taw estuary had taken all importance from its port. It remains, however, North Devon's largest town, an important agricultural centre and, increasingly, an industrial one.

The town has a fine estuary setting, with a 16-arch bridge, originally built *c.* 1437 but much widened and renewed. Not in general outstandingly picturesque, it has, however, several attractive small areas. Of these perhaps the nicest is between the south-east end of the narrow High Street and Boutport Street. Here, behind the Guildhall (1826), is the big, covered Pannier Market (still lively with stalls on Fridays), with beside it Butchers Row, an extremely pretty and unusual mid-19th-cent. street of small identical shops, many still used by butchers. A gap between these leads to a retreat of grass and trees, flanked by the parish church with its 17th-cent. lead spire, the early-14th-cent. St Anne's Chapel (now a museum) and, facing a lane off it, a row of 17th-cent. almshouses. Opposite the Guildhall, the Three Tuns, though considerably altered, is still recognizably 15th-cent. A little SW., the Royal Fortescue Hotel and the Westminster Bank (formerly a hotel, too) are excellent 17th-cent. buildings, and the latter has a very fine decorated plaster ceiling.

Probably the town's most famous structure is Queen Anne's Walk (originally 1609, rebuilt *c.* 1708), a little arcade, much carved and topped with a statue of Queen Anne. Situated between the Strand and the old quay, it was where merchants and ship-owners did business. A little NW., towards the new multi-story Civic Centre, a mound in a park marks the site of the town's castle, which was probably early 12th-cent. Beside it is the Cattle Market which, like the shopping one, functions on Fridays.

Back in the main square by the bridge, the dark-red Athenaeum (1888) houses a library and museum which contains spoons made from silver from the COMBE MARTIN mines. In Litchdon Street, which runs off the square, is a courtyard of very pretty 17th-cent. almshouses; also a famous pottery that can be visited. Holy Trinity Church (*c.* 1847) has a grand tower.

Barnstaple's heroes include John Gay (b. 1685), author of *The Beggar's Opera*; James Wilson, a sea-captain taken prisoner by the Spaniards, who was offered freedom in return for piloting the Armada, and refused; and Sir Francis Chichester.

Pilton, now a suburb to the N., is of older foundation than Barnstaple, existing in King Alfred's day to protect the estuary from Danes. Its church, in an area of attractive old houses, has a mid-15th-cent. screen of unusual type and two stately monuments to Chichesters.

Marwood church, 3 m. N., has a beautiful screen, though only part of it remains.

BARRINGTON COURT, *Somerset* (3–ST 3918). A fascinating, big, spiral-chimneyed, Tudor house in almost equally interesting surroundings. Built *c.* 1520 of yellow Ham-stone, it is one of the earliest Elizabethan-style houses in Britain. In it, in 1680, the Duke of Monmouth was entertained to dinner. When, in 1907, the National Trust bought it, most of its interior had been abandoned to cobwebs and gutted of furniture, its farming inhabitants living in the kitchen. It was given new life in the 1920s by Colonel A. A. Lyle of the sugar company acting as the Trust's tenant. For some time he had been collecting panelling and other wooden fittings from dying houses and here seemed just the place to put them. The house's interior is, therefore, a sort of wooden monument to him: vast areas of linen-fold panelling; massive carved beams from Italy; a 16th-cent. KING'S LYNN shop-front converted into a screen and elaborate ribbed ceiling from the same source; huge staircase, part early 17th-cent., part reproduction; exquisite applewood table; 18-ft-long refectory table (*c.* 1600); and much else, including new panelling for a ladies' exercise gallery which runs the length of the house. At the same time Colonel Lyle re-created surroundings appropriate to such a house: a park of horse-chestnuts ringed by Tudor-style estate employees' houses and dairy farm buildings, and a beautiful garden. There is a ten-faced sundial of unusual design in the grounds. The house and garden are frequently open to the public.

The village and church of Barrington are of admirable Ham-stone.

BATH, *Somerset* (4–ST7464), is the county's largest town and the most celebrated of English spas. The Roman city, called Aquae Sulis, grew up around the baths establishment, one of the foremost of its kind in the western empire. Its remains form an impressive monument to Roman Britain. The main pool is below the modern street level and open to the sky. Its lead floor and some of the paving around are original. Parts of the hypocaust remain in another section and a Roman outflow pipe is still in use. Judicious

J. Allan Cash

Bath: the Pulteney Bridge

reconstruction gives a good idea of how it all looked in Roman days, and a museum displays finds from the site and elsewhere in the district.

The Roman baths were only rediscovered in 1879. They fell into ruins or were destroyed at some date between the departure of the legions and the capture of the place by the West Saxons in 577. The latter gave the city its present name, but knowledge of the Roman baths seems to have been lost during the medieval period and they were built over. In about 800 a monastery was founded; Edgar, of the house of Wessex, was crowned King of all England in its church in 973.

The Norman abbey on this site was replaced by the present structure, begun in 1499. Restoration work in about 1603 made good the damage suffered at the Dissolution. Further restoration in 1860–83 included the stone vaulting of the nave. The original vaulting of the choir is notable and the church has the fine large windows characteristic of Perpendicular building.

The mineral waters have continued in use for much of the city's history; Bath is still a centre for the treatment of rheumatic diseases. Conditions in medieval, Tudor and Stuart times were squalid, but this changed in the 18th cent. when Bath became a resort for fashionable society, presided over by Beau Nash. (The Information Bureau near the abbey supplies, among other things, a list of the famous people associated with Bath, and the places where they lived.) The work of providing a suitably elegant environment began, notably under the patronage of Ralph Allen who owned the quarries at Combe Down, whence came the warm-toned Bath stone for the new schemes. John Wood the Elder designed Queen Square (1728) and the Circus (begun in 1754) as architectural entities. He also built Prior Park on a hill overlooking the city for his patron in 1735. This Palladian house, now a Roman Catholic school, is opened to the public at times. John Wood the Younger was responsible for Royal Crescent, an open design of 30 houses in a sweep-

ing semi-ellipse facing a sloping lawn. The next great improver was William Pulteney. Robert Adams designed the Florentine and shop-lined Pulteney Bridge (*c.* 1777) for him, and Thomas Baldwin built the Guildhall (1775), with its fine banqueting hall, and the colonnaded Bath Street. Baldwin was also responsible for Pulteney Street (1785), held by some to be the loveliest street in Europe. The Pump Room, near the Abbey, rebuilt in 1795, is still a favoured meeting place where the waters can still be taken; a visit here can be combined with a tour of the Roman baths.

These men, and others, gave the central area the character it has largely kept: a planned town of Georgian terraces, crescents and squares with subtly varying architectural detail, the whole unified by 18th-cent. canons of proportion and taste and by the use of Bath stone, and in harmony with the Avon valley setting. Later building has been mainly plain and in keeping; only a large Victorian hotel near the abbey, occupied by the Admiralty, might be wished elsewhere. The approach of the railway to Bath from the E. – Brunel's old Great Western – is worth looking at for its excellent landscaping.

An abundance of parks and gardens sets off the formality of the Georgian architecture. Victoria Park W. of Royal Crescent has good trees, a children's playground, parking space and a notable botanical garden. A pavilion built for Sydney Gardens in 1796–7, called the Holbourne of Menstrie, now contains a good collection of china, glass and paintings. The Assembly Rooms, built in 1771 and bombed in 1942, have now been admirably restored with interior decoration by Oliver Messel. They house what must be one of the world's finest costume museums; the collection is well presented, partly against period backgrounds. The Art Gallery displays, besides its paintings, pre-Conquest coins from the local mint. Claverton Manor, 2½ m. E. of the city, is now the American Museum in Britain, concerned with American domestic life from the 17th to 19th cents. which it illustrates with furniture, furnishings, household equipment and period rooms. Paintings by American primitives complete a well-thought-out exhibition, open in the summer.

Bath streets deserve to be toured on foot. For a general view over the city walk or drive to Beechen Cliff (turn E. off the A367 just S. of the river) or climb to the Sham Castle, a folly on a hill to the E. The tow-path of the Kennet and Avon Canal, which starts on the eastern edge of the city, is good for walks.

The Bath Festival is held in June. It is particularly associated with Yehudi Menuhin, who directed it until 1968. The emphasis is on music, but there are also plays, exhibitions, lectures, ballets and other events.

BEAFORD, *Devon* (3–SS5514). The Beaford Centre, established in 1966, is a major off-shoot of DARTINGTON Hall and is as enterprising: an arts centre for Mid- and North Devon in a big Georgian house near the church. It has its own resident group of actors, and sponsors plays, concerts, films, etc., throughout the region. It also holds evening classes and residential courses in subjects like pottery, painting, printing, dyeing, gardening, dress-making and music appreciation. Most relevant for the casual visitor, it has a theatre and exhibition gallery.

Two m. SW., **Dolton** church has a famous font made from elaborately carved pieces of an Anglo-Saxon cross. And 2½ m. S. of it, **Iddesleigh** is a village of considerable unsophisticated charm.

BEDRUTHAN STEPS, *Cornwall* (2–SW85 70). A grass and gorse field suddenly becomes, at one's feet, a sheer drop of 300 ft to a beach out of which a line of black, gnarled crags rises some 200 ft. Since there is no way down except for the acrobatic or suicidal, sea birds have the beach to themselves, so it is useful to have binoculars. Here in 1846 the brig *Samaritan*, laden with cargo from the Orient, was wrecked, with the result that surprisingly exotic wares appeared in many humble Cornish cottages.

The spectacle is best on a sunny evening. Payment for parking your car beside the café is merely requested, not demanded, which is pleasant, as the road is kept up for tourists only.

BEER, *Devon* (3–SY2289). Beer Head, 426 ft high, is an isolated chalk cliff (the most westerly in England), spectacularly white against its red neighbours. The numerous caves in the cliffs were cherished by smugglers and one of Devon's most famous, Jack Rattenbury, lived locally. Gout forced him to give up smuggling and so he wrote a book about his exploits in 1837. Fishing boats operate from the beach and the catch can be bought as it is landed. One m. NW., Bovey House, now a hotel, is mainly Tudor. It was formerly a smugglers' lair, with appropriate hiding places and a great water-wheel. About ¾ m. W. are the quarries which produced the magnificent white stone for the pillars in so many Devon churches and for much of EXETER

Cathedral. Those S. of the road were first worked by Romans. Permission is necessary and a guide advisable before exploring.

Some 2½ m. W., the village of **Branscombe**, sprawling up a shallow valley, has a quite interesting church. Basically Norman on Anglo-Saxon foundations, cruciform with 13th-cent. transepts, it has a grand three-tier Georgian pulpit and good 16th-cent. gallery. On either side of where the road runs down to a seaside car park, the National Trust owns some 300 acres, including two medieval farm-houses, thatched cottages, a forge and an old-style bakery. The cliffs to the E. rise to 400 ft.

Two m. NE., at **Axmouth**, is England's first concrete bridge (1877), which spans the rather beautiful, muddy, boat-scattered mouth of the River Axe. The village has some fine and pretty houses. Its church is basically Norman.

Almost immediately E. along the coast begins the evidence of the great landslip of Christmas Day, 1839 (*see* LYME REGIS).

BERE FERRERS, *Devon* (3–SX4563). A marvellously situated village, right beside the broad last reach of the River Tavy, at the end of a road which goes nowhere else. Too far off-route for most tourists, it is very quiet. It has an extremely interesting and attractive church. Surprisingly big for so tiny a place, the church is earlier than most in Devon (mainly *c.* 1300–30) and is bright and spacious. It contains Devon's oldest stained glass (14th-cent.) after EXETER Cathedral; two rather beautiful medieval effigy-tombs, one of William de Ferrers, who built it, and his wife; fine, massive, battered 12th-cent. font; traces of medieval paintings on the remains of its screen. It is still warmed by an open fire in winter.

Two m. NW. at **Weir Quay** are two lead and tin smelting works, closed towards the end of the 19th cent. Permission to visit can be obtained.

BERRY POMEROY CASTLE, *Devon* (3–SX8261). It is unusual that the moment of supreme crisis in a great house's history should be completely unrecorded, but so it is with this mysterious and spectacular ruin which stands on a shelf above a ravine amid huge oaks and beeches. The Norman family de la Pomerai (later Pomeroy) built the castle in the late 13th and 14th cents. In 1548, they sold it to Edward Seymour, the Lord Protector Somerset. At the end of that century and beginning of the next, his descendants spent a fortune on building within the castle walls a mansion of extreme splendour, full of fittings and ornaments in alabaster and marble. Today this mansion stands skull-like. In 1688 William of Orange, on his way from BRIXHAM to become king, was received here. Yet in 1701 John Prince, the local vicar, wrote in his *Worthies of Devon*: "all this Glory lieth in the Dust, buried in its own Ruines". Why, no one knows, not even the Seymours who still own it. Tradition speaks of fire and lightning.

About ¾ m. SW., Berry Pomeroy's 15th-cent. church has a good coloured screen and Pomeroy and Seymour monuments.

BICTON GARDENS, *Devon* (3–SY0785). Magnificent Italian gardens laid out *c.* 1735 by Henry (later Lord) Rolle, who was probably Devon's richest landowner at the time, to designs by the same André le Nôtre responsible for the gardens at Versailles. Bicton also has one of the finest collections of coniferous trees in Britain (the Pinetum, 1840), American Gardens, conservatories, Countryside Museum covering many aspects of rural life and industry, and railways, both steam and diesel, to take visitors to the outlying regions. A 1928 Austin "toast-rack" bus runs to the most distant point, the Hermitage, a 19th-cent. summer-house with its own pretty lake and garden. Tea is available in a classical "temple". Altogether an admirable place for all ages on a fine afternoon. The great house just N., built in 1730, is now an agricultural college. The unremarkable church (1851) in the grounds has beside it the remarkable Rolle mausoleum by A. W. Pugin, with the 1638 marble tomb of Denys Rolle: well worth the walk.

BIDEFORD, *Devon* (3–SS4526). Once a considerable port, it now looks for its trade mainly to a farming hinterland, some light industry and tourists.

Its greatest years as a port were the 200 starting from *c.* 1550. The Grenville family patronized it and gained it its charter of incorporation in 1573. The defiant little *Revenge*, of Sir Richard's epic fight with 15 Spanish ships off the Azores in 1591, was crewed by Bideford men. Its shipbuilding yards were renowned. It both manufactured and exported cloth, and imported wool from Spain and Ireland to supply the famous weavers of Devon. From Newfoundland, it shipped salted cod; from America more tobacco between 1700 and 1755 than any other port in Britain (an American Indian is buried in its churchyard). Amid all this mercantile affluence, it was the home of Devon's last three executed witches (1682).

For various reasons its traditional overseas trades declined in the late 18th cent., and its port's business gradually dwindled thereafter. Yet its broad, tree-shaded quay remains lively with coasters and occasionally small ships from the Baltic; and its best street, Bridgeland, W. of the Quay, laid out with rich merchants' houses *c.* 1690, still has some good façades of that period. The bridge, replacing a timber one, was built in *c.* 1460, widened in 1925. It is curious in that each of its 24 arches is of different width. In 1968 it began to fall down and was closed to traffic for three months, causing much unexpected business for local boatmen. It was subsequently widened as well as repaired. At its head, the Municipal Buildings contain a local history museum. The nearby St Mary's Church, mainly rebuilt in 1865, has a fine Norman font but little else exciting. Beside Victoria Park, near the north end of the Quay, is a pleasant small art gallery. The cannons round the bandstand in this park are said to have come from Armada galleons. Across the river in the Royal Hotel, which was originally a merchant's house (1688), Charles Kingsley wrote part of *Westward Ho!* There is a zoo on the south-west edge of the town.

Rowing is popular locally, with a regatta usually held in early September, and the estuary is good for sailing. Lime-burning for fertilizer was formerly quite a big local industry, and about 2 m. upstream, beside the Torridge's tributary, the Yeo, is a grand old lime-kiln looking rather like a castle, best seen from the river.

Westward Ho!, about 2 m. NW., has one of the oldest and most famous golf courses in Britain, and an excellent beach.

Two m. NE., near Instow (which also has a good beach), are **Tapeley Park Gardens**, laid out in Italian style by the mother of John Christie, creator of the Glyndebourne Opera. They are often open.

About 2½ m. SW., **Littleham** has an unusual and fascinating small church with a bright, gilded, late-19th-cent. rood-screen and loft, medieval wall painting of St Swithin, and a few superbly carved bench-ends. Though not easy to find, it is well worth the effort.

A little further SW., Orleigh Mill is a four-story grist mill still in commercial use, its wheel still turned by water.

BISHOPS LYDEARD, *Somerset* (3–ST1629). Its old centre, round the church, is red in colour and attractive. Its fine 15th-cent. church tower, also red, is similar, though inferior, to that of St Mary Magdalene, TAUNTON, and has yellow Ham-stone windows. Inside, the church has a good screen and bench-ends of the 16th cent., good Jacobean pulpit and 15th-cent. font. In the south-west corner of its churchyard of splendid yew trees, is an exceptionally fine weathered 14th-cent. cross mounted on an octagonal, stepped base looking faintly Buddhist. To the NW. there is a good view of a nice Georgian house.

During the Civil War, the church tower was used by John Stawell (*see* COTHELSTONE) to store his army's weapons. Close to the village his enterprise was crushed by Robert Blake, Parliamentarian general and later scourge of the Dutch as a sailor. Nearby are busy quarries and all around is rich farmland.

BLACKAWTON, *Devon* (3–SX8050). The narrowness of the lanes about it ensures that this village suffers very little through-traffic. Farmyards stand hard against smart little houses. Its church has parts of the 12th, 14th and 15th cents., and is beautifully wide, light and spacious. It has an outstanding, deeply carved, 12th-cent font of red sandstone; exquisite, almost black, Jacobean pulpit; a 15th-cent. screen with intriguing panel paintings; and a good 16th-cent. brass. Blue carpeting down the nave adds to the friendly, drawing-room atmosphere; as does a grand piano.

BLISLAND, *Cornwall* (2–SX0973). Its little church is celebrated for its very gaily coloured, intricately carved screen, the restoration work of F. C. Eden *c.* 1896: this, the experts say, is how most of the West Country's medieval church screens would have looked in their youth. The church is part Norman, mainly 15th- and 16th-cent. and has finely carved roof timbers, crooked with age, and a grand Jacobean pulpit restored in 1894 when cherubs and flowers carved from lime-wood were added to it.

The village is one of the Cornish few centred on a green and this, too, is attractive with fine old ash and sycamore trees and some good stone cottages around it. On 22 September, or the first Sunday after, the Feast of St Pratt's is celebrated with a procession, and the following day is held a sheep fair of some renown.

At **Bradford**, 3 m. NE., is one of the best pre-served ancient clapper bridges in Cornwall.

BODMIN, *Cornwall* (2–SX0767), is officially the county capital. The Assizes are held here, though the Council Offices are at TRURO. The guilty mostly go to gaol in EXETER, and Bodmin's old prison now houses a night-club. Today rather straggling and architecturally undistinguished, it was throughout the Middle Ages Cornwall's largest town. A monastery is said to have been founded here by the Welshman, St Petroc, *c.* 550. He was also the patron saint of the Augustinian priory founded here, *c.* 1124, on the site of which now stand the Municipal Offices.

The Dissolution and the town's rebellious nature were the reasons why it never really expanded. In 1496 two of its men led to London and massacre the great Cornish protest march against excessive taxes. The next year Bodmin rose for Perkin Warbeck, the pretender, and followed him to defeat at Exeter. In 1549 it was, with HELSTON, the main Cornish source of revolt against Edward VI's Prayer Book in English, with the macabre sequel that its mayor was hanged after dinner on the gallows he had been asked during the meal by his guest, the Provost-Marshal, to have erected for "an execution". The railway between Bodmin and WADEBRIDGE, opened in 1834, was among the first in Britain; but not till 1887 was it linked to the main railway system. Bodmin became the county town in 1835, re-placing LAUNCESTON. Recently it has gained some manufacturing industry.

Its best building is St Petroc's Church, the largest parish church in the county, built 1469–91. It originally had a spire, which was felled by lightning in 1699. The things particularly to note in it are the groined roof of the porch, the fine late-Norman font, the grandly carved catacleuse-slate monument to Prior Vyvyan, the fine roof timbers over the Lady Chapel, and the 12th-cent. ivory reliquary of Moorish-Spanish style in a cabinet in the south wall. The latter is thought once to have contained the relics of St Petroc and to have been stolen away to Brittany by a delinquent monk in 1177, and recovered only after Henry II had taken a hand in the hunt.

Of the rest, the Assize Courts date from 1837. On application at No. 24 Fore Street (the main street) an exceptionally large granite fire-place, recently found buried can be inspected. This long narrow street widens into an area of stone workmen's cottages.

The former barracks of the Duke of Cornwall's Light Infantry, beside the B3268 S., contains a museum of the regiment's history. The town is proud of its new public indoor swimming-pool, and there is an admirable little one for children in a park just across the road S. from St Petroc's, next to a large car park. The obelisk, 144 ft high, on the hill to the SW., was erected in 1856 in memory of Sir Walter Raleigh Gilbert, a soldier of worthy service in India. The local rivers Camel and Fowey provide good fishing.

BODMIN MOOR, *Cornwall* (2–SX1674), is a plateau mainly over 800 ft high. Its highest peak, Brown Willy, is 1,375 ft, and it is roughly 12 m. across both N. to S. and E. to W. Not a National Park, bad weather and infertility protect its wild-ness fairly successfully. Rough Tor has been given to the Wessex Regiment and there is a regimental memorial at the top.

It is rather drab, with rough grass instead of heather, and indecisive contours. Yet Brown Willy and its second peak, Rough Tor (formerly Rowtor), 1,311 ft, look from a distance more like Scots mountains than hills in southern England, and from close to Rough Tor is as impressive as any tor on Dartmoor. A road SE. from Camel-ford ends about 3 m. from the latter. Brown Willy can be reached from Codda Farm, ¾ m. N. of Bolventor.

The moor's other most spectacular places are on its west edge: the Hanter Gantick Valley, grandly rocky with a cascading stream just E. of the famous De Lank granite quarries, and the Hannon Valley some 3 m. N. where two sentinel crags called the Devil's Jump flank a ravine. Dozmary Pool, considered bottomless until it dried up in 1869, and still held by some to have been the recipient of King Arthur's sword, Excalibur, is a big, bleak pond. A road S. from Bolventor, where Jamaica Inn, on which Daphne de Maurier based her novel, is intriguing from without but fairly normal within, passes close to it.

Of the prehistoric remains that dot the moor, probably the most impressive is Stripple Stones, a circle of standing stones on the south-east slopes of Hawkstor, just N. of the china-clay mine beside the A30. The enclosure called King Arthur's Hall, about 1¾ m. NE. of St Breward, is thought to have been built *c.* 2000 B.C. as a shelter for live-stock. In the Middle Ages the Knights Templar had a chapel at Temple, a short detour off the A30 S. of the clay works.

To appreciate the moor at all you must leave the A30 and walk. Some interesting villages round its edge are ALTARNUN, BLISLAND, ST NEOT, ST CLEER, ST CLETHER and Laneast.

BOSCASTLE, *Cornwall* (2–SX0990). A classic beauty-spot. The Valency and Jordan pour out of oak woods to converge in a rock-topped moorland glen. Halfway along this glen, where the joint rivers meet the tide, is a strong-walled harbour. Beyond it, with a narrow, S-shaped, slate-cliffed bend, the glen becomes the sea. When the river in spate meets a strong tide the collision is dramatic. Even on a normal roughish day when the incoming tide surges through a blow-hole near the mole which extra-protects the harbour, spray is thrown high, explosively.

You have to leave your car at least 300 yds short of the harbour and walk. One of the last buildings on the right is a Witches Museum.

Until the 1890s when the railway came to Camelford, Boscastle was quite a busy little port and is said to have had a minor sealing industry, the seals being caught in the caves in the cliffs.

The main part of the village is in the steep woods behind the harbour, off the main road: a surprisingly unsophisticated place with some very old houses and an unusual long, broad street climbing straight and steeply up the hill.

The stocky-towered grey church crouching above the cliffs to the W. of the harbour is that of **Forrabury**. Parts of it are Norman and over the north hedge of its churchyard you can see, on Forrabury Common, one of the few extant examples of the ancient agricultural system of cultivation in strips. The strips are known as "stitches", each about 20 yds wide by $\frac{1}{2}$ m. long, and are so arranged that each contained some good and some poorer land.

One m. E. of the village by foot and about 3 m. by car (go out on the Bude road and take the second turning right) is St Juliot Church, isolated and peaceful. Its main interest is that its restoration in 1870 was supervised by Thomas Hardy, the novelist, then aged 30 and a practising architect. On a wall are two sketches by him and one by his first wife, Emma, and also a newspaper article of 1928 headlined "Duchy's Link with Hardy". Outside, close to the south door, is a finely carved slate-topped tomb.

BRAUNTON BURROWS, *Devon* (3–SS45 36).

This is one of the grandest sand-dune areas in Britain, over 1,000 acres in extent, backing Saunton Sands, one of the West Country's finest beaches, some 3 m. long. It is botanically important as part of the dunes is a National Nature Reserve and nature trails have been laid over them by the Nature Conservancy. A joy of the place is that it is virtually free of all buildings, the sands wonderfully wild in winter and even in summer not crowded. However, the Army rather spoilt it during the Second World War and still use it (watch for red flags). Jet fighter planes from nearby Chivenor roar over frequently, with the result that there are fewer species of rare birds than of old. Saunton Golf Course, at the northern end of the dunes, is among the two or three best in Devon; used for major tournaments. Braunton Great Field, just SW. of Braunton village, is one of the few remaining examples of the ancient strip system of farm land tenure (*see* BOSCASTLE).

Braunton, population about 4,000, claims to be Britain's largest village (having no corporation, merely a parish council). Its main-road face on the A361 is thoroughly modern; its more attractive part is round the church at its north-east end.

The church is interesting more than attractive, with a massive Norman tower topped by a 15th-cent. lead-shingled spire, good carved bench-ends and a waggon roof.

To the NW., **Croyde** and **Georgeham** are pretty villages with thatched cottages. The latter has a *c.* 1300 carving of the Crucifixion in its 19th-cent. church.

Baggy Point, W. from Croyde, has fine cliffs and is wonderful for watching birds and, sometimes, seals. A rock garden is open to the public.

About $\frac{1}{4}$ m. E. of Georgeham is the Chapel Wood Nature Reserve, under the care of the Royal Society for the Protection of Birds, from whose representative, Mr Cyril Manning, Sherracombe, Raleigh Park, BARNSTAPLE, a permit can be obtained to visit it. There are ravens, buzzards, green woodpeckers and many smaller species.

BREAGE, *Cornwall* (2–SW6128).

In its 15th-cent. church are some fine medieval murals; the clearest is of St Christopher carrying the child Christ. The basic colour is terracotta but there are also strong blues.

Germoe, a tiny village 2 m. W., has a very different church, compact, in a dip beside a stream, lichen making its tower a beautiful grey-green in the sun. Parts of the south and east walls date from 1100; most of the rest of the structure is 14th-cent. Note the stone animal figures on either side of the porch door; they may have represented evil. NE. in the churchyard is a stone seat with a roof over it, called St Germoe's Chair: one theory is that in the Middle Ages on Palm Sundays the priest read the lesson from it to a procession of his flock, but its purpose and date are open to speculation.

About $\frac{3}{4}$ m. S. of Germoe is **Pengersick Castle**. Only the tower remains of this fine, *c.* 1530 fortified house, but it is in good condition and has recently been restored inside. It was said that Millaton, a murderer, built it as a refuge; the story may be grossly unfair to Millaton, but its history remains mysterious.

Some $1\frac{1}{4}$ m. SW. (but about 3 m. round by road) is Prussia Cove from which John Carter, the Al Capone of Cornish smugglers, operated from 1770 to 1807. Close to it the battleship *Warspite* ran aground on her way to be scrapped in 1947.

From Tregonning Hill, 1 m. NW. of Breage, is a good view of this whole area.

BRENT KNOLL, *Somerset* (3–ST3350).

From the Iron Age fort on the summit of this isolated little round hill, 457 ft high, can be appreciated better, perhaps, than from anywhere else the vast flatness of the Somerset fen-lands and how very nearly they are still sea. As late as 1607 it became briefly an island when about 100 sq. m. of the area was flooded. It is best reached from the SW. via a farm at the top of Hill Lane. The fort was used by the Romans and by Anglo-Saxons as a refuge from raiding Danes. The base of the hill is ringed by smart housing, some of it attractive. Brent Knoll church (Norman, 14th- and 15th-cent.) is famous for three bench-ends (probably

J. Allan Cash

Brixham harbour

15th-cent.) showing the descent from dignity to hanging of a fox dressed as an abbot: the Abbot of GLASTONBURY lived locally. It has also a fine tie-beam roof, good Jacobean pulpit, a 1663 monument flamboyant even for that period, and more than usually grotesque tower gargoyles.

BRENTOR, *Devon* (3–SX4781), is an isolated peak topped by a little church, a landmark for miles, even from the sea some 18 m. away, and quite dominating the view from the western edge of the DARTMOOR plateau before TAVISTOCK. Its origin is volcanic, its summit 1,100 ft above sea-level. An earthwork circling it may have enclosed a hill-fort, possibly late Iron Age.

The first church on the site seems to have been built *c.* 1130 at the behest of Robert Giffard, a member of a powerful Devon land-owning family of Norman origin, possibly to expiate a sin. Tradition, however, talks of a rich merchant who, fearful in a storm at sea, promised to build St Michael a church on the first land spotted if he survived.

About 1300 the church was apparently rebuilt and there have been later additions, including the tower in the 15th cent. It is one of the smallest parish churches in England. The path up to it is ill-defined, slippery and steep, but over 20,000 visitors manage it annually and regular services are held for five months of the year.

BRIDGWATER, *Somerset* (3–ST3037), grew in the Middle Ages from a village to a major river-port. It proclaimed Monmouth king, and here, in July 1685, he and his followers spent their last night before being routed on Sedgemoor (battle site 3 m. SE.). From long decline following the death of the cloth industry in the area, it has

emerged in the 20th cent. as an enterprising industrial town with more buildings both old and modern. Its port now does little business.

The best part of it is W. of the River Parrett. Castle Street, running down to the West Quay, is all *c.* 1720 and is perhaps the finest street of this period in the West Country. King's Square, at the top of this street, is on the site of the 13th-cent. castle destroyed by Roundheads after the Civil War, during which it was held by Royalists, though the townspeople were for Parliament. St Mary's Church (13th- to 15th-cent.) has some magnificent features: a slender 175-ft spire of Ham-stone, one of the finest in the West Country; exceptional black oak pulpit (1490); Jacobean screen fronting an unusual side area of pews intended for members of the Corporation; and an unusually good late Renaissance altar painting, acquired in a sale of naval prizes at Plymouth in the 18th cent. Monmouth climbed the tower to survey the evening, and you can, too.

Of the modern buildings among the most notable are the Somerset River Authority's (1965) by R. Nicholls in Chandos Street, off the West Quay, the Congregational Church (1964) in West Street, and the Technical College.

The town's most honoured son is Robert Blake, the Cromwellian admiral (1598–1657). The house where he is said to have been born is now the museum and behind it is a pretty public garden. His statue is in Cornhill, which was the medieval market place, in front of the successfully amateur-designed Market Hall (*c.* 1834).

Twice a day the tidal bore comes up the River Parrett. Times are posted on the bridge. There is an Arts Centre, including a theatre, in Castle Street, and splendid swimming baths built in 1959 just off the Broadway.

Some 5 m. N. begins the Bridgwater Bay National Nature Reserve, comprising the mouth of the Parrett and the coast's foreshore from Lilstock nearly to BURNHAM. Among the birds sometimes seen in this great area of mud-flats and salt marshes are white-fronted geese (in winter), and many types of duck and wader. There are also rare plants.

BRIXHAM, *Devon* (3–SX9255). The pictur-esque fishing port of Brixham lies on the broad sweep of Tor Bay, together with the resorts of TORQUAY and PAIGNTON. In 1850 the port of Brixham had nearly 300 trawlers. The establish-ment of a cooperative has revitalized the fishing industry here, and an increasing number of boats work out of the port. Not many of its houses are individually pretty but they make a decidedly pretty general effect, rising in tiers around the harbour. Here in 1688 William of Orange first set foot on English soil and is said to have stated boldly, "Mine goot people, I mean you goot, I am here for your goot, for all your goots"; there is a statue of him. The fish market is fun. Opposite it is an aquarium with baby sharks and octopuses. Off Mount Pleasant Road is a floodlit stalagmite and stalactite cave which, when discovered in 1858, contained bones of prehistoric humans, bears, hyenas, rhinoceros and other beasts. In Middle Street is a good museum with maritime emphasis. The Rev. Henry Lyle, early-19th-cent. vicar of All Saints' Church in Higher Street, wrote several well-known hymns, including "Abide with Me", and the church's fine carillon does him regular honour. A nice short walk from the spacious car park W. of the harbour is over a bushy cliff-top hill called Battery, which gives grand views of the bay and of the prettiest of the nearby beaches, Fishcombe. Even better views are from Berry Head, 1 m. E., where there is a lighthouse (sometimes visitable), Napoleonic War forts and a quay. The cliffs are unfenced, so care should be taken. A vanished earthwork may have marked the site of a Celtic-Roman trading port.

BROADCLYST, *Devon* (3–SX9897). Its church has a beautiful 16th-cent. red and grey church tower with exquisite window tracery. Inside, the church, tall and expensive, with stone angels flying from white pillar capitals, has one of the most lavish Jacobean monuments in Devon (to Sir John Acland) and, across the chancel, another more modest but just as fine. Around the church and the yew-ringed churchyard the village is thatched and pretty. Much of it is owned by the National Trust, including a well-preserved mill on the River Clyst.

A Domesday farm called Churchill in Broadclyst parish is thought to have been the original home of the Churchill family.

Two m. N., **Killerton Park** (300 acres) and Gardens are owned by the National Trust, and even in the late evening visitors can put their money in the box, stroll on a hillside scented by an infinite variety of trees and shrubs, and look far S. over a great plain and W. to DARTMOOR. On the top of the hill is a heronry of 20–30 nests; on the east side of the park a chapel built 1841. The house, late Georgian, is not open. All was created by the Acland family (*see* DULVERTON).

BROADHEMBURY, *Devon* (3–ST1004), is perhaps the best example of a thatched village in the West Country. It is almost all thatched, with houses as well as cottages, amid a fine variety of trees. The standard of thatching is superb. The church, of the 14th and 15th cents., has a Perpendicular font with figure sculptures. The Rev. Augustus Toplady (*see* BURRINGTON COMBE) was its vicar, 1768–78. The Priest's House, just W. of the churchyard, is 15th-cent. or earlier. The village pub was probably the Church House.

One m. SE., high above the village, **Hembury Fort** was inhabited from *c.* 200 BC to *c.* A.D. 75. The view from it to the HALDON BELVEDERE (*see* DUNCHIDEOK), over 20 m. SW., and DARTMOOR, is staggering. A lay-by on a crest of the A373 is the start of the short, steep walk to the viewpoint. Bracken rather hides the earthworks in summer. To appreciate them you must walk about ⅔ m. to the north end. The main entrance was from the W. and the best way to this is up a lane just W. of the lay-by.

N. from here begins a great tract – nearly 100 sq. m. – of upland country uncrossed by main road and little visited, culminating in the Blackdown Hills to the N.

About 3½ m. SW., **Plymtree**'s 14th- to 15th-cent. church has a magnificent 15th-cent. roodscreen with panel paintings.

BRUTON, *Somerset* (4–ST6834), is an ancient-rooted, friendly little town of grey stone and weathered red-tiled, and in some cases slabbed, roofs in a groove of land on either side of a small river. The view W. from its churchyard is one of the most fascinatingly medieval in the county. Its fine church is basically 15th-cent. with a splendid tower and tie-beam nave roof, and an 18th-cent. chancel sprucely painted in attractive contrast. An unusually narrow packhorse bridge crosses the river. A nice walk leads over it, via lanes and arches, to, at the west end of the High Street, the courtyard of Hugh Sexey's Hospital, founded in 1638, now old people's houses, with a pretty oak-panelled chapel on its south side.

Before the Norman Conquest, the town was a borough with a mint. In 1142 it was given a priory which, in 1510, became an abbey, of which the remains are the long, buttressed wall close to the packhorse bridge, and the dovecot in the field behind. From *c.* 1300 to *c.* 1800 it had a thriving wool industry. This was replaced by silk manufacture, later by brewing and lace, bacon and furniture-making, and sawmills. Of these industries, however, only the sawmills remain and its population has declined steadily since 1831. Now its main products are farm-animal foods. It has two old and respected boys' schools.

About 1½ m. W. at **Wyke Champflower** is an attractive and interesting tiny church attached to a manor house. It was built in 1623 and contains box pews and a fine carved-stone pulpit.

Three m. N., **Batcombe** is worth visiting for its splendid 15th-cent. church tower and for the countryside around.

BUCKFAST ABBEY, *Devon* (3–SX7367). Perhaps the most remarkable thing about this vast building is that it was built almost entirely by amateurs; basically between 1906 and 1932, by French Benedictine monks. They had a professional architect, Frederick Walters, and one monk who had been sent to learn stone-masonship in 18 months. Never more than six monks worked on it at a time, "the oldest not yet twenty-five". It would be unreasonable, therefore, to expect too much, but there is much fine detail and the chapel, *c.* 1966, at the building's eastern end may, in particular, be found beautiful. Its windows were both designed and made by monks; the large wood collage by David Weeks with monk assistants. The abbey stands on the site of a medieval Cistercian monastery which was pulled down after the Dissolution and replaced in 1806 by a Gothic mansion and woollen mill. The Benedictines acquired it in 1882. The mansion is incorporated in the abbey buildings. The mill, with slated face, is now used by a metal plate company. Next to it a Cooperative woollen factory can be seen over by appointment; and across the road is a Shell Museum, which has the same owner.

Some ¾ m. S. **Buckfastleigh** Station is the northern terminal of the Dart Valley Railway. The line from here to TOTNES was closed by British Rail in 1962 and bought by steam-engine enthusiasts in 1967. The trip to Totnes takes 30 minutes; the return journey 63 minutes. You can also stop off halfway at Staverton Bridge (*see* DARTINGTON). There is no better way of seeing an exceptional bit of country.

BUCKLAND ABBEY, *Devon* (3–SX4966). Monks' dwellings become laymen's are not uncommon; abbey churches converted into stately homes are. Here is an instance of the latter; founded for Cistercians in 1278, converted after the Dissolution by Sir Richard Grenville, later of the *Revenge* (*see* BIDEFORD), and Sir Francis Drake who, returning rich and famous from his adventures, bought it in 1581. The old church tower still tops it, the hall has good plasterwork, and there is a drawing-room panelled to Drake's wishes. The rest is now naked, a museum of various sections: Drake relics, Folk (farm implements, cooking utensils, HONITON lace, etc.), and Naval (excellent model ships). Most splendid by far is the early-14th-cent. monastic tithe barn next door, over 160 ft long by 30 ft across and 40 ft high under a marvellous timber roof. It has larger museum exhibits: a cider press, farm waggons, fire engines and PLYMOUTH's first ambulance. The gardens are beautiful with grand cedars, magnolias, camellias and rhododendrons round a wide lawn. The National Trust acquired it from the Drakes in 1947 and lease it to the Plymouth Corporation. It is open throughout the year, slightly less frequently in winter.

One m. N. **Buckland Monachorum** church contains Drake monuments, and nearby the terraced gardens of the Garden House are sometimes open.

About ½ m. S. **Milton Combe** has a pub called The Who'd Have Thought It, and at Lopwell Dam, 1 m. further SW., salmon can sometimes be seen leaping the weir or being netted.

BUDLEIGH SALTERTON, *Devon* (3–SY 0682). Originally (from the 13th cent. or so) a salt-panning village, hence the name, Budleigh grew during the Napoleonic Wars, not as elegantly as SIDMOUTH, but cosily. Almost anything grows here, including tobacco. There is plenty of scope for outdoor recreations, including the best golf course in South Devon. Between the red cliffs is a big beach with unusually large pebbles (no sand) and lobster fishermen not short of local custom. There are occasional pretty late Georgian houses, as in East Terrace. Near the sea-front, in Fore Street, is the small but enterprising Fairlynch Arts Centre and Museum in an 18th-cent. thatched house with a look-out. There is a nice walk from the easternmost sea-front car park to the mouth of the River Otter, just across which are the remains of a fine garden laid out for a grand house which was never built. About 1¾ m. W., West Down Beacon above 500-ft cliffs is a tremendous viewpoint. Three m. NE., **Ladram**, where red sandstone crags rear off-shore, is one of the more spectacular Devon bays.

Two m. N., **East Budleigh** church was attended by the parents of Sir Walter Raleigh (the front two pews on the left were theirs). It has a fine collection of carved bench-ends (mainly 16th-cent.) and round it are pleasant cob-and-thatched cottages. The farm where Raleigh was born in 1552, Hayes Barton, 1 m. W. of the village, is often open to the public.

One m. further N. are BICTON GARDENS, and 2½ m. NW., Woodbury Common is a surprisingly Surrey-like heath and pine-tree hill, good for walking and views.

Four m. W. of Budleigh Salterton, **Exmouth** (population about 20,000) is almost unimaginably different from it. The oldest yet most architecturally disappointing of Devon resorts, it has all the conventional seaside amenities including a zoo and excellent sands. Some people admire Holy Trinity Church, which is mostly 1905–7. About 2 m. N. of the sea-front, E. off the EXETER road, a house called A la Ronde (1798), is unique and entertaining with a collection of exotic shells. It is open in the summer. Nearby is a quaint complex of almshouses and a tiny chapel called Point in View; all built by two imaginative spinsters.

BURNHAM-ON-SEA, *Somerset* (3–ST3048). This small, but fast growing, mainly red-brick and gabled resort with huge sands, has, most enterprisingly, a summer-long Amateur Dramatic festival in its Town Hall, with societies from all over the county taking part and performances twice weekly. From the sea-front the view SW. over Hinkley Point nuclear power station to the QUANTOCKS is splendid. Stert Island, just SW., is part of the BRIDGWATER Bay Nature Reserve (*see* Bridgwater). One of the town's very few old buildings is its 15th-cent. church, curious for its leaning tower (the result of sand foundations), in which high winds make fierce noises, and remarkable for its early-17th-cent. marble reredos designed by Inigo Jones and made by Grinling Gibbons. This was made for Whitehall Chapel; saved when that building was burned; passed on to WESTMINSTER ABBEY; and saved from the junk heap for Burnham. The Roman Catholic church, built 1966, at the south end of the town is interestingly modern.

The golf course at **Berrow**, 1 m. N., preserves an area of dunes from the development which stretches N. of it unbroken for nearly 4 m. to Brean Down peninsula. Berrow's little church is beautifully situated in the middle of the course.

A walk over Brean Down, National Trust protected, good for birds and with a small Iron Age fort, makes worthwhile the dreary drive to it. From it, in 1897, Marconi wireless messages were successfully transmitted to Lavernock Point on the Welsh coast, 9 m. away – at that time the longest distance over water that a wireless message had been sent.

BURRINGTON COMBE, *Somerset* (3–ST 4759), is nothing like so spectacular as the CHEDDAR GORGE but is similar and not so commercialized: a nice place to explore and picnic. An inscription on one of its great rocks tells how the Rev. Augustus Toplady, while sheltering under it from a storm, was inspired to write the hymn "Rock of Ages" (*c.* 1762). There are several caves.

Burrington village, a little NE., has the peacefulness of a place reached by lanes which go nowhere else. The church is not outstanding but pleasant, with an unusual spired staircase turret and very fine tie-beam roofs to its aisles.

The drive 1½ m. E. to **Blagdon** is particularly beautiful, through deep woods past a small waterfall and lake.

CADBURY CASTLE, *Somerset* (3–ST6225). This round-table of a hill, rising steep-sided from lowlands just S. of the A303, is believed by some to be the most likely site of King Arthur's Camelot. It was excavated in 1913 but not thoroughly, and work was restarted on the site in the summer of 1966. Evidence has been discovered that the site was defended during the Neolithic and Iron Ages and by Romans, Britons (5th–6th cent. A.D.) and Anglo-Saxons (*c.* 1010 and, after a lapse, subsequently). King Arthur is supposed to have lived in the late 5th cent. and traces of a timber hall of that period have been found. Visitors are welcomed and, in July and August if the excavations are on, guides will show you round. Without their help, a layman will not gather much. The view is tremendous, over the broad tree-scattered milkvales typical of Somerset. To the NE. is the beautiful Elizabethan Cadbury House.

The approach is up a lane from South Cadbury village in whose church are displayed a few of the finds and an account of the excavations.

CAMBORNE-REDRUTH, *Cornwall* (2–SW 6440). These towns together comprise the largest sprawl of population in Cornwall: the centre of what was 100 years ago the world's most productive copper-mining area and one of its major sources of tin. In the 1850s two-thirds of the world's copper came from Cornwall. In 1856, the peak, 209,000 tons of copper ore were produced and fetched £2 million. Some of the mines were an amazing depth: the old Dolcoath Mine E. of Camborne was, at 3,000 feet, in its day the deepest in the world. The industry's decline, mainly due to foreign competition, began in about 1866. In 1900 only 500 tons of copper were produced. Tin mining declined less swiftly, both World Wars bringing revival. But in 1969 there were just two mines operating in Cornwall: the South Crofty, S. of the A30 about mid-way between Camborne and Redruth, and the Geevor mine at Boscaswell (*see* ST JUST IN PENWITH).

The district now has plenty of light industry, including the biggest manufacturer of pneumatic equipment (drills, etc.) in the Commonwealth; Camborne's School of Metalliferous Mining remains one of the most respected of its kind in the world; and, with the rise in world tin prices, there is hope of another tin-mining revival.

For anyone remotely interested in engineering, probably the most interesting things to see are National Trust preserved winding engine (1887) and pumping engine (1892) at Pool, on the A30 between the towns, and the excellent Holman Museum in Camborne. Two-story brown-grey buildings predominate, but a surprisingly splendid eastern head to Camborne's main street is provided by the Centenary Wesleyan Church, and, near Pool, the Cornwall Technical College has some notable modern buildings designed by the County Architect, A. J. Groves.

Mining problems encouraged engineering invention. Richard Trevithick, who in 1801 completed the first steam vehicle to carry passengers, was born in Camborne in 1771 and there is a statue of him outside its Public Library. In 1792 William Murdoch, a Scotsman, became, in Redruth, the first person to gas-light a house.

On Carn Brea, the grey, monument-topped hill to the SW. of Redruth, are traces of a major Iron Age fort, also older hut circles and a semi-ruined castle, basically old but mainly folly. The monument was raised in 1836 to Lord Dunstanville of the local landowning Basset family. From it on a clear day you can see the sea to both N. and S.

About 2 m. E. of Redruth is Gwennap Pit. Since its domestication in 1805 it has been a symmetrical grass-covered amphitheatre, about 100 yds in diameter at the top, with 12 terraces falling to a circle about 5 yds in diameter. Originally caused, possibly, by a mine falling in, it was, if the old prints in the little Methodist chapel beside it are true, an irregular, steep-sided chasm when John Wesley preached in it in 1762 and several times subsequently. Wesley gained many followers in the mining areas. Every Whitsun Methodists hold a service in the pit.

Near Camborne was the most westerly Roman settlement so far discovered in England.

Five m. SW. of Camborne, the Hayle Estuary was one of the original sea-gateways to Cornwall. It was on the Bronze Age trade route between Ireland and Europe and from the 6th cent. A.D. was the landing place of Irish missionaries. The town of **Hayle** is not distinguished but has massive sands. Just N., the Towans is fine sand-dune country.

CAMELEY, *Somerset* (4–ST6157), is just beautiful grey-stone and red-tiled farms and their outbuildings, a pretty garden or two, and a peculiar and fascinating little red-towered church among yew trees. Most of its structure is 12th-cent., much of its interior Jacobean. The 15th-cent. pews here are not carved like most surviving from that period, and since not more than 50 people could be squeezed into them, galleries were installed, one in 1711, another in 1819. The Jacobean pulpit with tester is beautiful. Over the arch of an exquisitely simple chancel, are 13th-cent. red-painted scrolls and 17th-cent. Ten Commandments. There are also traces of early-14th-cent. wall paintings. "Although visitors are most cordially welcomed to the church, treasure hunts are forbidden in its precincts", says a mysterious notice at the churchyard gate. Most of its congregation comes from Temple Cloud, ¾ m. E.

Immediately NW. of here the country becomes beautiful with views over the reservoir called Chew Lake.

CASTLE CARY, *Somerset* (4–ST6332). On entering this small town it seems as if it will be all of perfect golden Ham-stone, but it becomes, at its centre, round the pretty horse-pond turned duck-pond, mainly pebble-dashed and painted. Nevertheless, it has rows of attractive old houses, and a rare round lock-up, just 7 ft in diameter inside, built in 1779. This is in a square up a street, in which is the local artists' gallery, opposite the basically 16th-cent. George Inn. Behind it the Post Office has possession of a fine Georgian House. The big, pillared building is the Town Hall (1855) on top of the earlier Market Hall. The church is worth visiting for its exceptional 15th-cent. pulpit, which somehow escaped when the Roundheads broke up the rest of its interior, and for the enterprise of the mosaic, under the west window, made by secondary school children.

The castle stood on the hillside above the horse-pond, but seems to have survived only from about the 11th to the 12th cent. It is now invisible. In 1651 Charles II, fleeing disguised as a servant after the Battle of WORCESTER, spent a night in a local manor, long since demolished. From the Middle Ages to the Industrial Revolution wool spinning and weaving were the town's industries. Now it makes ropes, horse-hair products and wooden crates, and supplies farmers.

CAWSAND and KINGSAND, *Cornwall* (3–SX4350). These beautiful coast villages are situated off the main routes and are therefore not much visited by tourists. They have narrow streets of colour-washed and sometimes red-stone cottages, falling to a quay and beaches and a sun-trap bay. In the early 19th cent. particularly they were notorious for smuggling. Until the 1830s the boundary of Devon and Cornwall ran between them.

Rame, ¾ m. SW., has an interesting, basically Norman, little church. W. of it, Whitsand Bay has a majesty that even the odd shanty suburbia on its slopes and the Army with its concrete and red flags can only mildly mar. Bathing from its tempting beaches is, however, dangerous.

Two m. NE., **Mount Edgcumbe Park** is frequently open and attractive with follies and fine views over PLYMOUTH Sound. The 16th-cent. great house, home of the Edgcumbes (*see* COTEHELE) was bombed in 1941 and restored in 1960, but is not open.

Four m. N. is **Antony House** (National Trust), built in 1710–21 for Sir William Carew, great-grandson of Richard Carew who was responsible for the invaluable *Survey of Cornwall* (1602). It is one of the finest houses of its period in the West Country, well furnished and with a number of good and interesting portraits.

CHAGFORD, *Devon* (3–SX7087), is a popular, affluent, friendly small town with smart shops. It is admirably situated in the soft lea of DARTMOOR with the beautiful River Teign at its feet and is attractive – if seldom architecturally distinguished – round its square. In the last century it was the first of the towns on the edge of the moor to gain a tourist trade. Its best looking buildings date from the Middle Ages when, from 1305, it was a stannary town (*see* ASHBURTON) and span wool. They include a nearly faultless 15th-cent. granite church (note the 16th-cent. Whyddon monument) and, side by side, the former Church House and Three Crowns. In the porch of the latter during the Civil War the poet Godolphin was shot. He is said to haunt it. Another shooting incident, in the churchyard, is said to have given Blackmore the idea for the wounding of Lorna in his *Lorna Doone*. A local guide-book details numerous excellent walks, also old farm-houses worth seeing. There is a fine view from Meldon Hill, just S. The way to Kestor Rock, 2½ m. SW., passes good examples of prehistoric hut circles, and Fernworthy Reservoir, in a fir forest 3 m. SW., is a nice place. At **Gidleigh**, 2 m. W., is a fragment of a Norman castle. The Chagford Pony Fair is held in October.

About 3½ m. SE., **Moretonhampstead** is very different in character from Chagford, considerably less sophisticated but no less attractive or cheerful. It, too, has a fine 15th-cent. granite church and a famous row of 1637 almshouses (beside the road out to EXETER). Its carnival in late August is one of Devon's most enterprising. In the public library is a small museum.

CHARD, *Somerset* (3–ST3208). At 400 ft up it is the highest town in the county. Its mile-long main street, possibly Roman, has, from the stately pillared Guildhall W. especially, lots of attractive buildings. Almost opposite the Guildhall, the fine Ham-stone three-story façade is Elizabethan, formerly of a manor house: an alley leads from the street to its first-floor court-room, which can be visited, with splendid windows, fireplace and well-restored plasterwork ceiling. Further up the street are good almshouses, founded in 1663 and well rebuilt in 1861; also the basically Elizabethan Choughs pub; and at the top on either side many fine cottages, one bearing a plaque to John Stringfellow who in 1848 became the first person to make a power-driven aeroplane (a model one) fly. At the bottom of the street part of the Grammar School buildings date from 1671.

Away from this street red-brick and dreariness takes over. The mainly 15th-cent. parish church is about ¼ m. S.: rather sombre but with some grand Ham-stone tombs in its yard.

The town grew first as a tanning centre in the 13th cent., then as a weaving centre in the 15th cent. When the latter industry declined, c. 1800, it made lace. Today it has various industries and is trying to attract more. Its products include artificial limbs, bearings, air blowers, shaving brushes, hydraulic jacks and animal feeds. Surrounded by rich farmland, it also has an important dairy. In the past strongly nonconformist, it backed Cromwell in the Civil War and Monmouth in 1685. Margaret Bondfield, the first woman cabinet minister, was born in it in 1873.

Pretty villages nearby are **Wambrook**, 2 m. SW., **Whitestaunton**, 2½ m. NW., **Winsham**, with an interesting church and Elizabethan manor house, and CRICKET ST THOMAS.

CHEDDAR GORGE, *Somerset* (3–ST4553). For the best part of a mile pale-grey limestone cliffs rise up vertically, or nearly so, to 450 ft and more on either side of the road. A hundred years ago it must have been tremendously wild and exciting. Now it is the most commercialized natural phenomenon in the West Country. It looks best approached from the N., and in the daytime probably the most spectacular view is from the top of the cliffs, most simply reached by "Jacob's Ladder" at the north end. The two main caves, Cox's and Gough's, contain fine stalagmites and stalactites. Bones of possibly cannibalistic prehistoric men have been found in them, and also Roman coins. Everything costs money except driving straight through or finding, from the north end of the gorge, a path to the top of the cliffs.

At the south end is a good motor-car museum. Past it is the relatively old village of Cheddar, which has a good market cross and rather grand 14th- to 15th-cent. church with fine tower, tie-beam roof and excellent 15th-cent. carved-stone pulpit. Behind Manor Farm are the ruins of a medieval chapel near which there have been recent excavations in search of Cheddar's one-time Anglo-Saxon palace.

Cheddar cheese was made in local farm-houses from the 12th cent. at the latest. As a cottage industry it still exists, but only just. The factory product of various other parts of Somerset is different. Apart from tourism, Cheddar's main industries now are market gardening (especially strawberries), limestone quarrying and cheese-straw making. In the late 18th cent. its squalor was the inspiration for Hannah Moore's pioneer social work. Her cottage headquarters in Venn's Close are now used by the Red Cross and as an old people's centre.

CHEWTON MENDIP, *Somerset* (3–ST5952). This rather grey, former lead-mining (*see* MENDIPS) village has an exceptionally interesting (if not all that beautiful) church with one of the best towers (126 ft) in the county. A mixture of Norman, 13th- and 15th-cent. architecture, it has in its chancel one of the very few frid, or sanctuary, seats extant. It has also a first edition of the Authorized Version of the Bible (1611), a good Jacobean lectern, and a splendidly carved 15th-cent. effigy-tomb. In the churchyard is a fine medieval canopied cross – a rare feature.

The lead mines were at **Torhole**, 1¾ m. SW.

CHINA CLAY COUNTRY, THE, *Cornwall* (2–SW9860). Of all the world's industrial landscapes, this is one of the most beautiful and weird.

Peter Baker

Clovelly retains its cobbled streets and is surrounded by woods

It stretches from Indian Queens in the W. to Treverbyn in the E., and from the A3058 N. almost to ROCHE: some 24 sq. m. of man-serrated plateau, ranging from 400 to 1,000 ft in height. Within this area are over 30 working and some 60 disused pits, with spoil heaps like gigantic white mole-hills and chasms sometimes 300 ft deep and covering up to 50 acres. There are also outlying pits, but this is where Cornwall's greatest industry (*see* ST AUSTELL) is concentrated. On a hot day it is a blinding, burning shadeless place: all white and pale-green, dust and lorries. "Danger" notices discourage looking into the working pits; but the disused ones are approachable and, when used as reservoirs for water needed in clay refining, often contain almost magically blue lakes. Good examples of these are to the W. of the A391 on either side of Carthew, about 2 m. N. of St Austell.

The two largest villages of the area are **St Dennis** and **St Stephen-in-Brannel**, the latter possessing a fine church with splendid tower and restored but attractive interior with an excellent five-legged Norman font and good 1920 east window. At **Bugle** a major bandsmen's festival is held in June. The beacon on Hensbarrow Downs (1,027 ft), about ½ m. SW. of it, is a good viewpoint.

CHITTLEHAMPTON, *Devon* (3–SS6325). Its church tower (early 16th-cent.) is probably the most elegant in Devon. Professor W. G. Hoskins, the county's premier local historian, says it is "unquestionably the finest". In the Middle Ages the church was a place of pilgrimage, to the shrine (on the north side of the sanctuary) of St Urith or Hieritha, to whom it is dedicated. She is said to have been a Celtic martyr.

In good farmland, the village was one of the first important West Saxon settlements in the area (8th cent.); from the early 16th cent. it enjoyed the patronage of the powerful Giffards (*see* BRENTOR). The church and churchyard occupy grandly the highest side of a large tarmac central square, which has thatched cottages on the others. The church's interior, mainly rebuilt 1871–2, is elegant, too: tall, light and unusually smart with a chancel arch that frames beautifully its chancel and a particularly fine carved stone pulpit, *c.* 1500.

High hedges make the immediate vicinity boring for the motorist, but the drive from Clapworthy, 1½ m. SE., down the valley of the River Bray is beautiful.

CHYSAUSTER, Cornwall (2–SW4735). Here is the oldest identifiable village street in England. The houses lack inhabitants, roofs and the top halves of their walls, but their shape is clear. They were lived in from about 100 B.C. to the 3rd cent. A.D. by people who farmed and probably streamed and smelted tin, who kept small terraced gardens, who had no need of fortifications for defence but built their house walls up to 15 ft thick against the elements. The hillside site they chose, now sheltered only by a few twisted hawthorns, may seem crazily exposed above lush valleys; but the valleys were then less habitable. To the SW. is a fogou (artificial cave) of uncertain purpose but possibly for storage. The houses may have been thatched or stone "beehive" like those on the Dingle peninsula in western Ireland. You walk about ½ m. uphill from the road to it over several stone stiles.

The remains of the Iron Age fort called **Castle-an-Dinas** on the same hill's summit are most easily reached by turning off the B3311, then walking about ½ m.: the best thing for the layman is the view from it.

CLEEVE ABBEY, Somerset (3–ST0739). Here are some of the finest surviving monastic buildings in the West Country. The monastery was Cistercian, inhabited from 1198 to 1538 by 30 monks at its maximum, by about 15 when dissolved. The church, except for its foundations, is gone, but most of the living quarters remain in remarkably good order – in particular the great 13th-cent. dormitory and the 15th-cent. refectory hall with magnificent timber roof – and the monkish existence can be clearly pictured. They were not always good monks, running into debt and, in 1339, committing apostasy. But today it seems a friendly place, fun to explore. It was used as a farm for many years. In 1951 it was taken over by the Ministry of Public Building and Works and, like all that ministry's ancient charges, is excellently kept and open at all reasonable times.

CLEVEDON, Somerset (3–ST4071). This resort has long been fashionable owing to its nearness to BRISTOL and remains more Victorian than most both in aspect and manner. Seventy-four years before the opening of its pier confirmed its resorthood in 1869, the poet Coleridge came to it for his honeymoon and stayed two months. The Elton family regularly entertained the famous at their great house of Clevedon Court. This beautiful house (on the eastern outskirts), now owned by the National Trust, is Clevedon's outstanding building. Basically 12th-cent. with major additions, principally in the 14th, the 16th and 17th cents., it has a fine great hall, an exceptional 14th-cent. window, and contains a collection of Elton Ware pottery and Nailsea glass. While a guest in it, Thackeray wrote parts of *Henry Esmond* and *Vanity Fair*.

The Pottery, across the road, in Court Lane, invites visitors to see pots being made. After that the student of Victoriana might find interest in Linden, Victoria, and Prince's roads, the Six Ways and the G.P.O., all near the town centre. Otherwise there is the sea-front with most of the usual amenities; or, beside an unspoilt headland at the south-west end of the town, St Andrew's Church, which is partly Norman and in which Arthur Hallam, whose sudden death inspired Tennyson's "In Memoriam", was buried. The experts say Coleridge's honeymoon home was near here, although a cottage some way E. in Old Church Road bears a plaque claiming it was there. To the NE. of the town is a golf course, in the centre of which the probably early-17th-cent. ruined folly called Walton Castle is highly dangerous and private. Also to the N. Ladye Bay is, unusual for this coast, a rocky cove, and the downs beyond it make pleasant walking.

CLOVELLY, Devon (3–SS3124), is unique in England in that no traffic can enter the village; cars must be parked at the top of the steep hill above it. As a result its streets are still cobbled. Few fishing villages are so luxuriantly surrounded by woods, or stop, as it does, not at the sea but at the edge of a precipice down which steps zigzag to its harbour. The place remains exceptionally pretty and, architecturally, virtually undefiled since its "discovery" on the recommendation of Kingsley and Dickens in the mid-19th cent. Although it faces due N., its roses and fuchsias bloom as early as those on South Devon's coast.

The most attractive approach is via the Hobby Drive, the entrance to which is about ½ m. W. of Bucks Cross on the A39. A good walk (apart from the obvious ones) is W. from just above the harbour to Gallantry Bower, 2 m. away, where cliffs are nearly 400 ft high.

The church, mainly 15th-cent., is well above the village, down a path of shrubs and a yew avenue. The dominant things in it are the ornate 17th-cent. memorials to the Cary family, then lords of the manor, on the walls of the narrow chancel. Clovelly Court, the late-18th-cent. manor house beside the church, has been described as "Cockney Gothic".

Clovelly Dykes. about ½ m. S. near Clovelly Cross, is an Iron Age fort, possibly later used by Romans.

About 2½ m. E., **Bucks Mills** is a tiny, much quieter, but no less attractive place. It was formerly entirely inhabited by a single family of redoubtable seamen, the Braunds. There are several recently restored lime-kilns.

Six m. SE., **West Putford** has a rare feature in that its medieval church is completely unrestored. It is 14th-cent., with a 15th-cent. tower.

COLYTON, *Devon* (3–SY2493). A neat, busy small town supplying a rich farming vale. West Saxons settled it as early as the 7th cent. Its church is remarkable for the octagonal lantern top, built on 15th-cent. wool profits, to its tower, and its exceptionally large west window. It contains an Anglo-Saxon cross and numerous monuments, notably those of the Courtenays and the Poles, and is pleasantly high and light with slender white pillars, though it is perhaps too complicated to be a complete success. Other buildings worth looking for are the Great House in South Street, the Vicarage in Queen Square and the Church House.

Some 2¼ m. N., **Shute Barton** (National Trust) is the surviving two wings of an embattled medieval manor house behind an attractive 16th-cent. gatehouse. It has a fine hall roof with collar-beams and wind-braces, and is generally interesting. In the 16th cent. it was owned by the father of Lady Jane Grey who, like her, lost his head. The house can be visited on application to the tenant.

The church just E. contains a marble statue of Sir William Pole (d. 1741), Master of Queen Anne's Household.

COMPTON MARTIN, *Somerset* (3–ST5456). Its church contains some of the best Norman architecture surviving in the West Country. The nave and vaulted chancel are entirely Norman. In the 15th cent. it was apparently intended to alter the building drastically, as was the fashion. However, when work began the foundations slipped (note the strangely flattened chancel arch) and the builders apparently decided to leave well alone, contenting themselves with adding two aisles and extending the tower. They also carved one of the Norman pillars with spiral fluting.

One m. E., **West Harptree** is a prettier village, of red stone, with two fine 17th-cent. former manor houses on either side of the main road.

The two big BRISTOL reservoirs, Chew and Blagdon (Yeo), a little N. and W. respectively, both offer excellent trout fishing and fit quite attractively into this tree-scattered landscape. Fishing permits can be obtained from Woodford Lodge, Chew Stoke and the Anglers' Hut on the south-west bank of Blagdon.

COMBE MARTIN, *Devon* (3–SS5846), is a straggling small town, stretching for over a mile down its combe to the sea. It scarcely enhances its glorious coast, but is an excellent base for walking, and has a unique building in its Pack of Cards pub, and a fine one in its church. The

former, looking like a card house with numerous chimneys, is said to have been built by a gambler. The church, mainly 15th-cent., has the only rood-screen in North Devon still with its original panel paintings (15th-cent.). It is about ⅔ m. up the street and off to the right. In the Middle Ages it was a village famous for its silver mines, some of the shafts running under the street. Scanty remains can be seen up a lane E. almost opposite the church. Now it market-gardens prosperously and is a minor resort with a small beach which has sand at low tide only. From immediately E. of it to LYNMOUTH is perhaps the most continuously beautiful stretch of unspoilt coast in Devon. One of the best short walks is to the hill called Little Hangman's Point above the cliffs to the E. Another is to the wooded valley hamlet of Berry-narbor, about 1½ m. W. (also driveable).

About 1½ m. E. of Coombe Martin, **Watermouth Castle**, built in 1825, overlooking a beautiful bay, caters enthusiastically for the public.

COTEHELE HOUSE, *Cornwall* (2–SX4268), is one of the best examples in England of an early Tudor manor house: no exterior timbering and white-wash, just brownish-grey stone, very solid, yet anything but austere, with a beautiful garden sloping down a combe to the Tamar.

The earliest parts of it, represented mainly by the small-stone areas of the outer wall, are late 13th- and early 14th-cent. Most of it was built between 1485 and 1539 by Richard Edgcumbe, who led local rebellion against Richard III, fought for Henry VII on Bosworth Field and became one of that king's most trusted ambassadors. Only the north-west tower (1627) and east front (1862) were added later.

The tremendously rich furnishings, mostly 16th- and 17th-cent., all belong to the house: all were collected by the Edgcumbe family. Almost every room shown to the public, apart from the great hall, is lined with tapestries. The great hall, with its superb roof and grand array of armour, weapons and hunting trophies, including (dangerously you might think) the head of an albatross, perhaps best gives a feel of the spirit of its former owners and its history.

The little-restored chapel in the garden was built by Richard Edgcumbe to mark the spot where in 1483 he hid from Richard III's henchmen after cunningly hurling his cap and a stone into the Tamar to make them think he was there.

The house and garden are now owned by the National Trust, presented by the Edgcumbes in part lieu of death duties in 1947.

About 3 m. W. and 1 m. S. of the A390 (turn off S. about ½ m. E. of Callington) is Dupath Well. It is an early-16th-cent. holy well chapel through which flows a spring; is built of exceptionally large blocks of granite and has a most curious crown-like affair on its top. Among the farm buildings beside it is a very splendidly-walled old barn.

COTHELSTONE, *Somerset* (3–ST1831), is an exquisite hamlet: Jacobean manor house, little church, prosperous farm buildings, matching cottages all tightly packed together on the wine-red soil of the last south-western slope of THE QUANTOCKS. The house was originally much bigger. In the Civil War its owner, Sir John Stawell, raised a private army for the King and the Roundheads, having defeated him, partially smashed his home in retribution. From the road up the hill through grand beech woods the view is superb.

COVERACK, *Cornwall* (2–SW7818). After the race-track road over GOONHILLY DOWNS it is surprising to find this fishing, and formerly smuggling, village so unsophisticated. New and middle-aged building is mainly unobtrusive on top of the hill. Its harbour is classically shaped and there is quite good fishing from its wall. As it faces east, away from the prevailing west wind, few of its houses are slate-hung but several are thatched (you seldom find thatch in Cornish villages exposed to the west).

The village has a tradition of lifeboat heroism, many rescues having been made off the dreaded Manacles 3 m. NE. These rocks accounted in 1809 for two troop-ships from the Peninsular War with the loss of 200 men; in 1855 for an immigrant ship bound for Canada (196 drowned); and in 1898 for the steam ship *Mohegan* (106 lost); and have caused many lesser wrecks. The richest fishing grounds in the area are around them.

At Lowland Point, about 1½ m. NE. of Coverack, is a good example of a "raised beach", caused by the Ice Age. You can walk to it: ask directions locally. Between Coverack and **St Keverne**, 2 m. N., is a narrow belt of, for this district, particularly fertile soil. St Keverne has a large square; unusual for a Cornish village. Its big, steepled church contains a beautiful Jacobean pulpit and other good woodwork.

CREDITON, *Devon* (3–SS8300), is the main town of that tongue of sometimes almost fantastically red soil which stretches W. from the Exe to HATHERLEIGH. Like so many other towns in lush vales in the West Country, Crediton was an early Anglo-Saxon settlement. It was said to be the birthplace in *c.* 680 of St Boniface, "the apostle of Germany", destined, as Archbishop of Mainz, to crown Pepin, Charlemagne's father. Then in 909 it actually became Devon's cathedral "city" and so remained till the see went to EXETER in 1050. In the 15th cent. it became one of the most prosperous of the county's wool towns.

Today about the only clue to that past (and the main reason for visiting it) is its splendid red sandstone medieval collegiate church of almost cathedral proportions.

Four m. NE., **Cheriton Fitzpaine** is a large, excellent cob-and-thatched village with a good 15th-cent. church. From the wooded crest of the B3214 about 2 m. E. of it, there is a grand view over the red-soil vale to the tors of DARTMOOR.

Three m. W. **Colebrooke** also has a good church, of the 14th and 15th cents., with some fine rustically carved bench-ends.

CREWKERNE, *Somerset* (3–ST4409), is a rugged small town of ancient foundation. It minted Anglo-Saxon coins and was formerly famous for its sailcloth; made the sails for Nelson's *Victory* and for Americas Cup competitors, and much parachute harness in the Second World War. Recently, like its neighbours CHARD and ILMINSTER in this area of dairy farms and pleasantly hilly but unexceptional country, it has been busy attracting new industry, and produces shirts and pyjamas, chrome castings for the motor and ship-building industries, webbing, twine and plastic deck-chair covers. In the Civil War armies passed to and fro through it rather as the holiday traffic does now. In 1685 it supported Monmouth and suffered King James's vengeance. In 1688, to happier result, it entertained William of Orange on his way from Torbay to London.

The rugged 15th-cent. Ham-stone church is its best building. It has a west front of almost cathedral splendour, a fine nave roof of unusual type, and a south porch with good gargoyles. Unique and unexplained is a seated recess in the outside wall of the south transept; one theory says it was a hermit's home. Just N., in Abbey Street, the 17th-cent. Church Hall was formerly the Grammar School where Captain Hardy, in whose arms Nelson died (*see* PORTESHAM), was educated. It contains a memorial to him.

A two-day fair, mainly modern in form but ancient in origin, takes place during the first seven days in September.

Two m. NE. is **Haselbury Plucknett**, where lived and died (1154) the remarkable Wulfric, who renounced squirehood to become a hermit, dressed permanently in chain mail and whose counsel was sought by kings. It is a pretty village with a fine medieval bridge; and so, 1 m. S. of it, is **North Perrott**.

CRICKET ST THOMAS, *Somerset* (3–ST 3708), is an ancient and beautiful 1,000-acre estate, part of which has, since 1966, been stocked with exotic animals and birds and opened to the public. S. of the great beech avenue that is the A30 (originally a Roman road), over Windwhistle Ridge, parkland sweeps down to a fine Ham-stone house (1804) and on, via gardens and terraces, to a river dammed to make lakes and waterfalls. Here creatures like llamas, camels, bison, wapiti, wallabies, flamingoes, rheas, black swans, storks, cranes and many type of duck co-exist apparently happily and attractively. There is also a zoo and aviary and a tea-room; and in the afternoon (about 3 pm) visitors are invited to watch part of the estate's dairy herd being milked and make friends with the calves. From 1757 to 1897, the estate was owned by the famous naval Hood family.

About 2 m. N. **Cricket Malherbie** is a pretty yellow farm-hamlet, where cheese from the estate's dairy herd is made. It consists of a grand *c.* 1820 house, with a majestic staircase to its front door, an outwardly unusual and appealing 19th-cent. spired Ham-stone church, and farm buildings.

CROSCOMBE, *Somerset* (3–ST5844). An elongated yet neat, stone and tiled, formerly wool-rich village, in which the church is the most opulently Jacobean furnished in the county. The lords of the manor, the Fortescues, instead of following the gentry fashion and spending their money on vast monuments to themselves, gave the church most (though not all) of a quite re-markable display of woodwork: box pews, waggon-roof bosses, a screen of unusual design, and a superb canopied pulpit, all lavishly carved. The nearby Baptist church is in part of what was a Fortescue manor house. A cause of village pride is that when, in the 19th cent., their 14th-cent. cross (by the main road) was scheduled for demolition, they, with oaths and staves, success-fully defended it.

Dinder, 1 m. W. and just N. of the main road, is a pleasant village and its church and fine Georgian house together make a good picture.

CROWCOMBE, *Somerset* (3–ST1336). This village under THE QUANTOCKS has probably the best preserved (with the help of restoration) church house (1515) in the county. The church itself has some extremely well-carved and interest-ing bench-ends of *c.* 1534, seemingly pagan in their imagery, symbolizing fertility. Next door and clearly seen is the big Georgian house, Crow-combe Court (*c.* 1725). A little S. in the centre of the village, is a 13th-cent. market cross.

CULBONE, *Somerset* (3–SS8448). Of the claimants to the title of "smallest complete parish church in England" the church here is the most likely. It is also very pretty and fascinatingly situ-ated : ½ m. from the nearest place accessible by car, in a combe-glade beside a stream on a steep wooded hillside above wooded cliffs. Inside it is 33 ft 10 in. long, its nave 12 ft 4 in. wide, its chancel 10 ft. Basically Norman, it probably replaced an Anglo-Saxon church. One of its windows may be Anglo-Saxon, cut from a single stone slab. A legend is attached to its tiny slated spire which dates from the early 19th cent. This says POR-LOCK'S, which was knocked off by lightning, was confiscated by St Michael as a punishment for sins and given to Culbone.

The normal approach is either from Porlock Weir or from the Toll Gate on the Toll Road to-wards LYNMOUTH (a very pretty walk but some 2 m. each way). Otherwise, with the farmer's per-mission, you can shorten the walk to ½ m. by turning off the main Lynmouth road at Culbone Stables Inn, an old coaching stop. A cottage near the church provides refreshment.

In one of the farm-houses above the church Coleridge wrote *Kubla Khan.*

CULLOMPTON, *Devon* (3–ST0207), has one of the finest and most interesting churches in Devon. Now a small market town, in the 16th and 17th cents. it had a woollen (especially kersey) industry almost as prosperous as TIVERTON's and this accounts for its church's splendour: lavish waggon-roof, brightly coloured but not gaudy;

huge coloured screen, not as intricate as some but larger than most; finely carved Jacobean gallery; and whole extra aisle with splendid fan-vaulted stone roof paid for by a wool stapler, John Lane, in *c.* 1526. The town suffered a great fire in 1839 and has a fair number of ugly buildings, but opens out pleasantly in its centre, as do so many coaching-towns, with cobbled pavements behind lime trees. The Manor House Hotel is basically *c.* 1603, enlarged in the 18th cent., and near it Walronds, a private house, was built 1603–5. Higher Kingsmill, on the north-east edge of the town, is the oldest paper mill (1757) still operating in Devon.

Two m. ENE **Kentisbeare** church has a fine screen (late 15th-cent.), much more intricate than Cullompton's, and Priesthill, the medieval old church-house nearby, is well preserved with good panelling and minstrels' gallery. It can be visited on application to its owner (Tel: Kentisbeare 338).

DARTINGTON HALL, *Devon* (3–SX7862), a medieval estate and house turned into a centre both for new ideas in education and the arts and for thoroughly practical research into the scienti-fic development of rural industries. The estate dates from the early 9th cent. at the latest. The Hall itself, among the finest surviving medieval domestic buildings in the West Country, was built between 1388 and 1400 by John Holland, half-brother of Richard II, soon to become Duke of Exeter. The place was set on its present intellectual and highly successful course by Dr and Mrs Leonard K. Elmhirst – she American, idealistic and just come into a fortune, he influenced (among others) by Gandhi. In 1925 they bought the buildings plus 820 acres. The trust they set up to fulfil their dreams now owns some 4,000 acres. The educational side comprises one of Britain's most progressive schools and a College of Arts, plus adult education and young people's centres. The business and experimental side has farms (about 1,000 acres), forests (about 2,000 acres in various places), sawmills, a textile mill, shops and civil engineering, contracting, electrical, plant hire and glass-making companies. There is plenty of communication between the two. Visitors are no longer shown the inner workings (excessive demand caused this reluctantly to be discon-tinued). But you can drive through the estate (fine avenue from the south entrance); stroll into the great quadrangle that is its heart; go into the Hall if it is not in use; wander through the gardens where there is a Henry Moore master-piece and where the terraces were originally for a tiltyard in the 15th cent.; and, if you can get in, go in the evening to the Barn Theatre which is one of the three in Devon (the Northcott, EXETER and BEAFORD centre are the others) where intelligent plays and films are the rule. It is all very pleasant, the atmosphere essentially friendly and university-like, windows emitting the strains of practising oboists and choirs. About ½ m. SW. at Shinners Bridge, beautiful under trees beside the A384, is the mill, shop, other educational buildings and two well-preserved lime-kilns. The church, ¼ m. N. along this road, was built 1878–80 using old fittings, including an excellent screen. These came from its predecessor which stood close to the quadrangle entrance, where its 15th-cent. tower remains.

About ¾ m. N., Staverton Bridge, built in *c.* 1413, with seven arches spanning the Dart, is one of the oldest in the country.

DARTMOOR, *Devon* (3–SX6880). Here you can get further from habitation than anywhere else in Southern England. It is a plateau, mainly over 1,000 ft high, mainly treeless and uncultivated, made entirely of granite overlaid with peat, punctuated with tors. The highest, though far from the most spectacular, of these peaks is High Willhays, 2,039 ft. The plateau extends, at maximum, about 23 m. from N. to S. and about 13 m. from E. to W. Hoskins calls it "the great source", for from it come most of Devon's rivers, careering off its edge through the wooded gorges that are among its splendours, and the granite, which built not only many of Devon's churches but, all round it, some of the best medieval farm-houses extant. Till about the time of Christ, when the surrounding lowlands were often disease-ridden swamps, it was, compared to now, densely inhabited, and few places in England have so many prehistoric remains. In the 12th cent. it was found to be the richest source of tin in Europe. Freelance miners rushed upon it from all directions to scrape and sift. They became so powerful as to be almost autonomous, with their own laws, courts and prison (*see* LYDFORD) and even their own "parliament" which met on the misty height of Crockern Tor (½ m. NE. of Two Bridges). Stannary towns were designated where the tin was assessed and taxed (*see* ASHBURTON). Exhaustion of the surface tin, combined with the Black Death in 1349 which hit the moorland settlements as hard as any, ended this boom. But tin mining dwindled on till the early 20th cent., and in the 19th cent. copper mining prospered round Mary Tavy (*see* TAVISTOCK). Old tin workings can best be seen between the Warren House Inn on the B3212 and Grimspound, which is the most impressive of the prehistoric settlements (*see* WIDECOMBE-IN-THE-MOOR).

Dartmoor Prison at **Princetown** was the inspiration of Sir Thomas Tyrwhitt, Lord Warden of the Stannaries and friend of the Prince Regent. He dreamed of making the moor's bleakest centre bloom, built himself a grand house – Tor Royal (1785–98) ½ m. SE. of Princetown – and, when he found it hard to recruit labour for his scheme, had the idea of putting French prisoners from the Napoleonic Wars to work. The prison was built to house them in 1806–13, and was first used for criminals and enlarged in 1850. Princetown also has a television mast today and is altogether Dartmoor's ugliest part, but sadly not its only ugliness. Although a National Park, the moor is becoming scattered with conifer forests and the Water Boards demand increasingly to flood parts of it to form reservoirs. Moreover, the Army uses

some 40 sq. m. of its northern half for shooting.

The main roads bisecting the moor – the A384 and B3212 – provide a good view of it but, because on the whole so fast and busy, only a mild feeling of its atmosphere. The road leading nearest to its heart is the one S. from OKEHAMPTON. Otherwise it is best to walk, but in selected areas. Indiscriminate walking often leads to nowhere except bleakness and bogs. An Ordnance Survey map is essential, the excellent *Dartmoor: National Park* booklet (H.M. Stationery Office) very useful. Good walks are: from the track SW. from Belstone to Belstone Tor and Cullever Steps; from Kestor (*see* CHAGFORD) NW. to the River Teign and up to one of the best prehistoric stone circles, Scorhill; from the end of the Okehampton loop road to Hangingstone Hill (1,983 ft); from the same road via a track to High Willhays and Yes Tor; from Two Bridges, or a gateway about 1¼ m. NE., to the extraordinary wood of antique dwarf-oaks called Wistman's (nature reserve: respect enclosed areas); up the East Dart from Postbridge; from near the active Merrivale granite quarries either N. to Great Mis Tor or SE. to Vixen Tor; from past Horndon, with its early-19th-cent. miners' cottages, to the splendid Tavy Cleave (you can drive almost to the ancient frontier farmstead of Nat Tor); from Hound Tor (*see* NORTH BOVEY) SE. to the ruins of a medieval village, possibly Black Death decimated, recently excavated; and up the gorge of the River Dart through Holne Woods (National Trust). For others see SHEEPSTOR, LYDFORD, DREWSTEIGNTON and, for the Yarner Wood Nature Reserve, NEWTON ABBOT. The most famous hike is to Cranmere Pool, the bog-pond at the northern half of the moor's centre. Remember always to ask at a Post Office if the Army is shooting or to watch for red flags.

The east side of the moor is the gentler, most heathery, yet has many of the finest tors. Beside the road about ½ m. NE. of the Warren House Inn is a survivor of the crosses which marked the medieval trans-moor tracks. At Postbridge is a probably 13th-cent. slab bridge, and 2½ m. SW. behind Powder Mills Farm is the old chimney of a mill which, from 1844 to 1890, made gunpowder for quarry blasting.

There is an Information Centre at Two Bridges in the summer and a permanent one at County Hall, Topsham Road, EXETER.

DARTMOUTH, *Devon* (3–SX8751). The hillsides on the west side of this once so adventurous and prosperous port are covered in new housing, but within an easy walk of the Quay are several of the best Elizabethan house fronts and one of the most richly furnished old churches, St Saviour's, in Devon; while from the ruins of its main castle guarding the estuary mouth to the S., the town looks beautiful, even if the Royal Naval College, built in 1905, dominates it rather weightily.

The latter, since it originated aboard the H.M.S. *Britannia* in 1863, plus the charms of the Dart river, have largely kept the town alive. For it is short of industry and of all Devon's great ports

Dartmouth's has declined the most. In the early Middle Ages it was one of Devon's, and one of England's, greatest. The fleets for the Second and Third Crusades were assembled in its estuary, and in 1346 it sent 31 ships, less only than FOWEY and YARMOUTH, to besiege Calais. It exported wool and cloth, and brought home wine from Bordeaux. It was later a leader in the Newfoundland fish trade. It then suffered, as did other Devon ports, from dying trade, and by 1900 had become no more than a yachtsman's paradise and a coaling station; and is now not even the latter. During the Second World War it was, however, briefly reminded of its former glory as a port when 485 American ships assembled off it before D-Day.

A convenient car park is by Coronation Park on the river front. In a shed by its entrance is the first-ever effective steam-engine invented by the locally born Thomas Newcomen (1663–1729) to pump water from mines; and just SW. in Duke Street is the renowned and extremely pretty arcade called The Butterwalk, built c. 1635 when dairy produce was sold in its shelter. Much superior to TOTNES's, it contains a museum and good decorated plasterwork in one of its shops (a chemist's) and in the restaurant upstairs. A short walk further SW. via Anzac Street (in which is another museum) is St Saviour's Church, with a magnificent 14th-cent. ironwork door, 17th-cent. gallery, 15th-cent. screen and painted stone pulpit, several good brasses, and, most unusual, an altar with large, carved and coloured evangelists (1588). All the flat part of the town was reclaimed from the river, mostly in c. 1600; water lapped, till 1567, against the churchyard's north wall. S. from the church, steps lead up to particularly attractive old houses in Higher Street which was original dry land. About ¼ m. S. of the Quay, Bayards Cove is the least altered part of the waterfront. It has a good group of 17th-cent. houses, and the remains of one of the castles built by Henry VIII along the Channel coast for defence against possible French invasion. Both this castle and the one mentioned earlier (built 1488–94) can be visited; as, near Bayards Cove, can the 15th-cent. but much restored Agincourt House.

A regatta of some fame is held annually in late August, a carnival in early July. Well worth the time – about an hour and a half each way – is the motor-launch trip up the estuary to Totnes. About 3 m. SW. Blackpool Sands is the nearest good beach and often not too crowded. From about ¾ m. further on there is a beautiful view over SLAPTON Ley and beach.

A car ferry connects Dartmouth with Kingswear and the Torbay area.

DAWLISH, *Devon* (3–SX9676). An unstrident seaside town of similar kind to LYME REGIS (Jane Austen loved both), but of humbler history, less splendid situation and greater architectural honesty. Its outstanding feature is its Lawn: a sort of magnified toy garden in its centre laid out in 1803 round the stream which flows through the town, with tiny waterfalls and black swans from Australia which were given in 1937.

Until the late 18th cent. Dawlish was just a small fishing village lying back from the sea, but then, as to so many places, the Napoleonic Wars, which restricted travel to the Continent, brought resorthood; it grew modestly with much neat, rather than grandiose, Regency housing, curious in that most of it turns its back on the sea, which is faced by deep-red cliffs and good safe beaches. Dickens made it Nicholas Nickleby's birthplace. Between town and beach runs Brunel's railway, originally atmospheric (*see* KENTON), with an "Egyptian-style" viaduct spanning the pedestrian way to the sea, and the little station is also by Brunel. The journey by it from EXETER to NEWTON ABBOT (it remains part of the main London–PENZANCE line) is among the most scenic in Britain. Further inland the stream is again lawn-banked and, this time, shaded by Lebanese cedars in the grounds (open) of the Manor House (1800), which is now the offices of the Urban District Council off Old Town Street. And still further along this road, Stonelands, built in 1817 by John Nash for the distinguished engineer Sir John Rennie, with gardens by Capability Brown, is fairly frequently open. Lea Mount, overlooking the sea just S., is nice for views; and below it Coryton Cove is grand for children, with trains popping in and out of cliff tunnels behind. In the combes of the surrounding hills is a considerable flower-growing industry. The town has amateur dramatics at the Shaftesbury Theatre and a small Arts Festival in June and July.

About 1½ m. NE., Dawlish Warren is a sand-dune peninsula with golf course, and is noted for its birds and wild plants.

DELABOLE, *Cornwall* (2–SX0884). The Delabole slate quarry, one of the largest in England, has been worked continuously since Henry VII and may be older. It has provided roofs for most of Cornwall and many other places, too. In 1910 the quarry employed 500 men, now only 80, the decline being due to the availability of so many cheaper roofing materials.

Some 2¼ m. NW. is Trebarwith, a cove of slate, with a grand, almost unspoilt beach at low tide. A natural causeway of slate leads to the sea. A hump of an island called Gull Rock stands tall, dark and mysterious ahead.

DOWNSIDE ABBEY CHURCH, *Somerset* (4–ST6551). Beside the famous Roman Catholic boys' school, it is a huge building, with an immensely high, comparatively narrow nave, all white stone pillars and vaulting and black-robed meditating priests. Its warmth lies in its chapels.

Downside monastery was founded in 1814 by English Benedictine monks who had settled in France but were driven from there by the French Revolution. In 1899 it became an abbey. The church was completed in its present form in 1935; minor extensions are planned. The choir (1905) is by Thomas Garner, much of the rest (added later), including the nave and top 30 ft or so of the tower, by Giles Gilbert Scott. The windows are

Jane J. Miller

Dulverton: the River Barle is renowned for fishing of many kinds

fine examples of their period. The Madonna over the Lady Chapel entrance has a singularly beautiful face.

The approved approach is from a lane to the N.

DREWSTEIGNTON, *Devon* (3–SX7391). Perhaps the most beautifully shaped of Devon villages, it wears scarcely a touch of make-up and has very little in common with its smart neighbour, CHAGFORD. It stands on the crest of a steep-sided ridge, thatched (mainly) round a square, at the head of which is a neat, yellow-lichened 15th-cent. church tower. Every night this tower is floodlit and is worth a journey to see then. The square looks at its best, however, on Trinity Saturday when it is the scene of an annual charity fair: modest but very appealing.

The village is on the edge of the DARTMOOR National Park and immediately S. and SW. of it the country becomes spectacular. About ¾ m. SE., **Fingle Bridge** is a beauty-spot; but to appreciate fully this exceptional stretch of the Teign Valley you should walk up it about 1½ m. to where it opens to fields: up by the high Hunters' path, back by the low Fisherman's. There is a pool thick with eel and salmon. Ravens and swifts nest in the crags on the north side. On the hill-top to the S. is the Iron Age **Cranbrook Castle**, of which the ramparts are visible. The valley looks thrilling from it. With luck fallow deer can be seen. Immediately S. above Fingle Bridge is another Iron Age castle, **Prestonbury**.

About 1 m. SW. of the village, Castle Drogo

(*c*. 1911–30), built by Sir Edward Lutyens entirely of granite, is marvellously sited amid trees high above the Teign. This last castle built in England is not open.

Some 2½ m. W., Spinsters Rock, in a field, is Devon's only cap-stoned cromlech: it is Bronze Age.

DULVERTON, *Somerset* (3–SS9127), is the shopping centre and general headquarters for the south-east quarter of EXMOOR, and has probably had this kind of importance since the 13th cent. A jumble architecturally, it nevertheless has character, superbly situated in a cup of densely wooded steep hillsides near the junction, 2 m. SE., of Exmoor's two main rivers, the Barle and Exe. The River Barle, which flows through it, is particularly beautiful just above the town – a broad rapid banked by tall trees. Both rivers are famous hereabouts for salmon and trout fishing. A massive sycamore some 250 years old (very old for a sycamore) almost obscures the 13th-cent. church tower, and there is a nice view of the town from beside it. Sadly the church's interior was spoilt in the 19th cent. In summer local painters exhibit in Exmoor House by the bridge.

Pixton, ¾ m. SE., was the home in the 18th cent. of Sir Thomas Acland, owner of Exmoor's first resident pack of stag-hounds.

About 1½ m. NE., on the W. of the MINEHEAD road, are the ruins of Barlinch Priory.

Some 4½ m. SE., **Bampton**, a neat, unpretentious small town, is famous for its fair (late October) when the herds of rounded-up Exmoor ponies are brought to it for sale. It has a restored 14th- and 15th-cent. church.

DUNCHIDEOCK, *Devon* (3–SX8787). The tower on the top of the Haldon Hills above this scattered village is known as Lawrence Castle or Haldon Belvedere. The nearer you get to it the more weird it seems. Pony-cropped grass grows up to its doors; it looks forsaken, yet is inhabited by two farmer brothers and is periodically open.

It was built in 1788 by Sir Robert Palk, who had risen from humble origins to become Governor of Madras and then owner of Haldon House and estate, as a memorial to General Stringer Lawrence who had commanded the British forces in India from 1747 to 1767 and left Palk his fortune. The tower stands 829 ft above sea-level. A spiral staircase climbs 70 ft to its roof. From there on a clear day it is possible to see about 60 m. In the centre of the main, round, ground-floor room is a huge statue of Lawrence.

Of Haldon House itself, about 1 m. E., only one wing now remains. Built in the 1730s, it was mainly demolished for want of a buyer in 1925. Illustrations show that it was once splendid. However, part of the estate gardens, now known as Haldon Grange Gardens, are beautifully maintained, open to the public and well worth a visit.

Dunchideock church is about ½ m. N. (take a turning N. just up the hill from the thatched old Post Office with a veranda). Basically late 14th-cent., it is small, of red sandstone and pretty, isolated from the rest of the village in the company of fine old farm buildings and two good houses. Inside it has a very beautifully carved screen and a monument to Stringer Lawrence.

About 1 m. S. of Lawrence Castle, through quite an attractive conifer plantation, is Haldon Race Course where there are steeplechase meetings.

DUNSTER, *Somerset* (3–SS9943). Its castle tops classically a wooded pyramid-shaped hill. In the park between it and the A39 archery contests are frequently held. Dunster is in appearance medieval and feudal, and has many attractive and interesting ancient buildings.

The castle was founded in 1070 and has been continuously inhabited ever since; from 1375 by the Luttrell family. It is often open in the summer. It is mainly 16th- to 19th-cent. and has many splendid features, in particular a magnificently carved staircase (1681), each panel from a solid block of elm, a 1681 plaster ceiling in the dining-room, and a remarkable set of 17th-cent. Spanish or Portuguese painted leather panels. During the Civil War the Luttrells were for Parliament, but the Royalists took the castle and it was their last stronghold to fall in Somerset, after a siege of five and a half months (1646).

The yarn-market in the centre of the High Street was built in *c.* 1589 when the town was an important cloth centre. The Luttrell Arms was originally a house of the Abbot of CLEEVE and still has medieval parts, including the porch. The extraordinary, slate-hung building on the sharp corner at the south end of the High Street may have been a guest-house for the priory which, from the 12th to the 16th cent., existed just N. of the church which it shared with the laity. The 15th-cent. church is much the finest in this area, with magnificent wide waggon roof (*c.* 1500), equally good flat roof to the south aisle (*c.* 1450) and a rood-screen claimed to be the longest in England. Of the monuments, one to Elizabeth Luttrell (1493) at the east end of the south aisle is worth noting. The north door leads into an exquisite walled garden, once the Prior's. At the far end is the dovecot and a medieval tithe barn.

An attractive street, more modest than the High Street, runs SW. from the church. The first turning S. off it leads to an old mill, the second to a packhorse bridge over the River Avill and thatched cottages.

The conspicuous tower on the hill to the N. was built in *c.* 1770 for landscaping purposes. A nice, quite short, walk for a view is to Grabbist Hill to the W.: the path starts past the school.

EAST COKER, *Somerset* (3–ST5312).

In my beginning is my end. Now the light falls
Across the open field, leaving the deep lane
Shuttered with branches, dark in the afternoon,
Where you lean against a bank while a van passes,
And the deep lane insists on the direction
Into the village, in the electric heat
Hypnotised.
                    "East Coker", T. S. Eliot

And on 4 January 1965 in the church of this beautiful Ham-stone village, whence in the 17th cent. his ancestors went to New England, the poet was buried. The almshouses at the foot of the path to the church are mid-17th-cent.; the manor house beside it is basically Tudor. William Dampier, one of the first men from Britain to set eyes on Australia, was born in the village in 1651. A brass plaque in the church tells more about him. Parts of the mosaic floors of Roman villas in the valley are in the TAUNTON Museum.

EXETER, *Devon* (3–SX9292). One of Britain's oldest towns, a cathedral and university city, administrative capital of Devon, with a population of about 92,550. In May 1942 German bombs flattened much of its centre; subsequent rebuilding has been worthy rather than artistic, with an over-enthusiasm for red brick. But a fair amount that is fine and/or old survives, above all its tremendous cathedral, spared in the same miraculous way as was ST PAUL'S.

In barest outline the city's lively history is as follows. It was founded in *c.* A.D. 50 by the Romans, who surrounded it in *c.* 200 with a great red-stone wall much of which, strengthened in Norman times but Roman at base, still stands and can be well seen in the car parks off Paul Street and Southernhay and where the lower ring road cuts through it. Exeter became an important town under the Anglo-Saxons. Twice the Danes ravaged it: in 876, occupying it for three years, and in 1003. Not till 1068 and after an 18-day siege did William the Conqueror capture it. The town became an important cloth manufacturing and trading centre, and so remained till the late 18th cent. It was also a busy port, except for the period from *c.* 1285, when the Countess of Devon, out of spite, built a weir across the River Exe (hence Countess Weir on the by-pass), till 1563 when its ship canal, the first in England, was opened. But the price of importance was painful involvement in most of the insurrections and calamities of history from 1350 to 1700, as is made admirably clear in the official guide to Exeter available at the Information Bureau in Queen Street. After the 1549 Prayer Book Rebellion, for instance, one of its vicars hung for four years from the top of his church tower.

A cathedral was established at Exeter in 1050 but it was rebuilt by the Normans between 1107 and 1137. In about 1260, however, the building was demolished except for the two towers, which were incorporated in the present cathedral, built between then and *c.* 1394. The 14th-cent. west front is adorned with fine stone figures. The interior has magnificent rib-vaulting, and among its most notable features are the minstrels' gallery, the chantry chapels and the finely carved bishop's throne.

The city's most attractive areas are the Cathedral Close; just E. of it the excellent Georgian (*c.* 1805 red-brick terraces of Southernhay round pretty municipal gardens, and a little NE. Barnfield Crescent of the same period; and the Quay district E. of the two road bridges. The Close's best buildings are along its north-east side; several are medieval. The art shop on the corner was formerly Mol's Coffee House in the first-floor room of which, it is said, Drake, Hawkins and others used to meet. You can inspect the room without being a customer. The Bishop's Palace, SE. of the cathedral, is not open but the Cathedral Library sometimes is and contains some of the most valuable Anglo-Saxon manuscripts extant. The porticoed Guildhall in the High Street is nice inside with excellent 15th-cent. roof and panelling and some good portraits. The portico dates from 1595. Of the little red-stone churches scattered among modern shops all over this area, the best is St Mary Arches, the most completely Norman church in Devon. St Mary's Steps has an entertaining clock, and the steep and cobbled Stepcote Lane beside it retains an ancient atmosphere. Nearby are some 16th-cent. buildings, close to where the city's west gate was and the lower ring road is. Halfway up Fore Street, Tucker's Hall, built for the Guild of Weavers, Fullers and Shearmen in 1471, has a fine timbered roof. The underground passages, which provided medieval Exeter with, unlike most medieval cities, a constant supply of pure spring water, can sometimes be inspected; apply to the Information Bureau, close to which is the Museum and Art Gallery. There is another museum, good for Roman remains, in Castle Street near the restored red gate-tower of the otherwise demolished Norman Rougemont Castle. Also nearby are the County Courts (1774) and the very pleasant Rougemont Gardens. The Ship, the White Hart and the Turk's Head (where Dickens found his Fat Boy) are all basically medieval pubs.

All these things are within walking range of the several central car parks. And so, really, is the Quay. This area has a splendid, tall, early-19th-cent. warehouse, 1681 Customs House, good pubs and night-club overlooked by the exceptionally pretty late-18th-cent. Colleton Crescent, and a 13th-cent. bridge has been excavated. An added attraction is the outstanding Maritime Museum, opened in 1969, which exhibits vessels (not models) ranging from an Arab dhow to a sprit-sail barge to a Fijian outrigger. On the whole, like so many English towns, Exeter wastes its river, and the local popularity of this small well-used part stresses the pity of it. Smallish ships still bring timber and oil up the 5-m. canal. Its tow-path is attractive to walk along.

The spired church, even more conspicuous than the cathedral, is St Michael's, built 1867–8.

The University campus is on the northern edge of the town, superbly sited in an estate presented to it in 1922 with an arboretum containing 150 varieties. The university buildings, dating from 1925 to 1964, are, with PLYMOUTH's town centre, the most ambitious modern group in the West Country. The Northcott Theatre (1967), also in this group of buildings though independent of the university, is the region's only full-time professional theatre company and stages original productions of a high quality.

The Exeter livestock market is, with TAUNTON's, the most important in the West Country, handling some 285,500 beasts per annum. It takes place on Mondays and Fridays, with a horse-sale on the first Tuesday of every month.

In the western outskirts, beside the A30, Bowhill is a good restored manor house with a very fine timbered hall roof. From the top of the hill past it is one of the best views of the city.

EXMOOR, *Somerset* and *Devon* (3–SS7440). DARTMOOR for wildness, Exmoor for beauty. For grace of contour, glowing richness and variety of summer colour and delicacy of winter bleakness, it is without English moorland rival. It is line upon unflinching line of undecorated dark horizons. It is heather and secret valleys of lonely thorn trees and oak coppices. It is clear day views across blue sea to Wales and down to the fertile patchwork of Porlock Vale with its shingle crescent bay. It is wild ponies, circling, mewing buzzards, and red deer. It is humble, isolated little churches like Stoke Pero, Trentishoe and CULBONE. It is altogether wonderfully romantic, and was associated with Blackmore's *Lorna Doone*, but it has a major drawback: it has the worst weather in southern England and can be for days on end a swirl of driving rain.

The National Park takes in the **Brendon Hills**, beginning W. of the Wiveliscombe–WATCHET road at Elworthy, but the real moor does not start till W. of the A396 between DULVERTON and DUNSTER. It is roughly 21 m. from E. to W. and 12 m. from N. to S. at maximum, its peak Dunkery Beacon (1,706 ft). Within it are considerable and increasing areas of cultivation. These and beech hedges make comparatively dull the B3358 road from Wheddon Cross to Simonsbath. Among the most beautiful drives are: from Wheddon Cross via Dunkery Gate and Webber's Post to Luccombe (*see* SELWORTHY) and PORLOCK; from Webber's Post via Cloutsham to Exford; from Exford via Hawkcombe Head to Porlock; from Exford via Winsford Hill to DULVERTON; from Exford via Withypool to Sportsman's Inn, then left via Molland Common to MOLLAND; from LYNTON via Simonsbath as far as Yard Down on the SOUTH MOLTON road. For others see under OARE, Lynton and COMBE MARTIN. For one of the best walks see under Oare as well. Others are: from Dunkery Gate over the hill's summit to the woods and waters below Cloutsham, about 2 m.; up or down Exmoor's finest river, the Barle, starting from Landacre Bridge, Tarr Steps, Withypool, or (down best) Simonsbath; from the Dunkery road lay-by to Hanny Combe; and, to see in what bleakness farmers lived, to Larkbarrow, used for target practice in the Second World War, and on, by unusual route, to Badgworthy (*see* Oare).

The moor's wildest part is W. from Brendon Two Gates on the B3223 where, on the distant high ridge, are those bogs dreaded by horsemen, The Chains. Its outstanding and famous antiquity is **Tarr Steps**, an ancient packhorse bridge, some

180 ft long with 17 spans. It has probably been rebuilt many times; certainly twice in the last 30 years, in 1942 and 1952. No one knows where its massive stone slabs came from; they are not local. It crosses the Barle below Winsford Hill to the W., and opposite the turning to it, a few yards from the road, is the inscribed Caratacus Stone, about 5 ft high, reckoned to be 5th-cent. Celtic. Bronze Age earthworks are numerous.

From Anglo-Saxon times till 1818 an area varying from 3 to 4 m. in radius round Simonsbath (and till *c*. 1300 a much larger area) was a royal forest for hunting, though in fact it was seldom hunted by kings. "Free Suitors" from Withypool and Hawkridge villages were, in feudal manner, allowed to graze their beasts on it in return for services. Simonsbath House was built *c*. 1654 by one of the forest wardens, James Boevey. By 1820 most of the royal forest had been acquired by John Knight, of a family of Worcestershire ironmasters, who, living at Simonsbath, sought to turn it into a profitable estate, surrounding it with a mighty wall, introducing new breeds of sheep and horses. He also built the eerie Pink-worthy Pond, 1 m. N. of the county boundary between Simonsbath and Challacombe. By 1900 the Knights had sold out to Earl Fortescue (*see* SWIMBRIDGE). The estate is now fragmented.

Of the highland villages, **Exford** is the largest and most vital. It is the unofficial headquarters of stag-hunting and the kennels are here. It has cheerful pubs, a nice green and a modest little church with a remarkably fine 15th-cent. screen. **Withypool** is quite pretty. **Wheddon Cross** and **Blackmoor Gate** have important livestock markets. **North Molton** (*see* SOUTH MOLTON) was in the 19th cent. a copper-mining centre. The moor's farmers mainly go in for beef cattle – Devons (*see* MOLLAND) and cross-breeds – and sheep – Exmoor Horns and Closewools.

The hunting seasons are mid-August to mid-September and mid-April to the end of May for stags, and mid-September to mid-April for hinds. Any Post Office or local paper will say where the meet is. The famous sale of moor ponies at Bampton Fair is in late October.

There is an Exmoor Information Centre in the Market House, the Parade, MINEHEAD.

FALMOUTH, *Cornwall* (2–SW8032). Suddenly the stillness of the wooded creeks turns into a fairly typical, fairly ugly resort. Its setting is magnificent; its harbour is claimed to be the third largest natural one in the world; it also claims the most temperate climate of any resort in Britain. Its port, though less busy than once, remains Cornwall's largest, occasionally welcoming tankers of up to 90,000 tons, and, with some 17,500 residents, it is the county's largest single town.

Its development was late and rapid. When Sir Walter Raleigh landed here in *c*. 1590, it was a hamlet with a manor house and **Pendennis Castle**, built *c*. 1543 to protect (with ST MAWES Castle across the strait) the existing ports of the Fal estuary. TRURO and Penryn; and although

Kenneth Scowen

Exmoor: the Tarr Steps are a medieval packhorse bridge

Raleigh advocated its potential in high places, not till 1664 did it become a parish or till 1670 have a quay. Yet in 1688 it was chosen as a Mail Packet Station, and by 1827, 39 ships were delivering letters all over the world from it. This heyday ended in 1852 when its mail duties were transferred to SOUTHAMPTON and LIVERPOOL. Like PLYMOUTH's its port's usefulness declined with the coming of steamships, to which the westerly winds beating down the English Channel were small problem. However, soon after the railway reached it in 1863 the first tourists came.

The town still presents two very different aspects. On the south side of its peninsula are the beaches and public gardens overlooked by large 19th- and early-20th-cent. hotels and villas. On the north side are the harbours and docks backed by the mainly 18th- and 19th-cent. buildings of its shopping centre and narrow streets on a hillside. The long main street, running parallel to the river and one row backs, contains most that is historically interesting. The 1662–5 Parish Church of King Charles the Martyr is one of the few so dedicated anywhere and also one of the few of that period in the West Country. In the Georgian Polytechnic Hall, home of an enthusiastic arts society, is a small museum, containing excellent model sailing ships and an art gallery. In Upton's Slip, one of the alleys to the quay, two fine old ships' figureheads are displayed. Near the Customs House, towards the south-west end of the street, is an old brick chimney called the King's Pipe where contraband tobacco used to be burned. A little further on is the 17th-cent. manor, Arwenack, built on the site of the Tudor original. Leading from the main square, are 111 steps known as Jacob's Ladder.

Pendennis Castle can be approached by Castle Drive, which circles the headland. The castle's main action was in the Civil War when, under the command of the 70-year-old Sir John Arundell of Trerice and Lanherne (*see* NEWQUAY and MAWGAN-IN-PYDAR), it for five months withstood a Roundhead siege. It is open to the public.

Off Melville Road is the very pretty and well-kept Fox Rosehill public garden, with exotic shrubs like tree ferns and in spring glowing with pieris, magnolias and embothriums. All Saints' Church in Killigrew Road, built mainly 1887–90, is a large and interesting example of the work of the architect R. D. Sedding.

Penryn, 2 m. NW., was a prosperous little town before Falmouth was conceived. Some 1½ m. W. at **Mabe** are important granite quarries, and granite processing remains one of Penryn's main industries. It tends to be ignored by visitors, unjustly, and has a compact, attractive centre with good granite, slate-hung houses. About ½ m. W., the grounds of Tremough, a convent school, contain one of the most representative collections of rhododendrons in England, but are, unfortunately, not normally open.

One of the shortest of many worthwhile boat trips from Falmouth is to **Flushing** across the river. Said to have been founded by Dutch families before Falmouth existed, it is extremely pretty, with rows of coloured and white cottages that seem, in their simplicity and uniformity, quite Dutch. It is popular with yachtsmen. Some 1½ m. NE. of it, **Mylor** church is beautifully sited close to the shore of a creek that was once a royal dockyard, now a yacht anchorage. It has a strange, thin tower, splendidly coloured east window and Elizabethan pulpit.

Two m. N., on Restronguet Creek, is the Pandora Inn, one of the oldest pubs in Cornwall. Built as a friary in the 11th cent., it has been a pub since the 14th cent. It is said Captain Bligh of *Bounty* fame was once its landlord.

In August there are numerous regattas on the Fal estuary.

FARLEIGH HUNGERFORD CASTLE,

Somerset (4–ST7957). Its ruins rise beside a main road, attractive among trees. The principal buildings remaining are the 14th-cent. chapel and the tower in which a Hungerford kept his wife locked up for about four years; he was executed in 1540 for treason and unnatural vice. The chapel contains much of interest, including armour and weapons, a 15th-cent. wall painting, some pretty Flemish or Dutch 17th- or 18th-cent. stained glass and enormous effigy tombs.

The core of the castle was built, as a safe house, *c*. 1370–80 by Sir Thomas Hungerford, first Speaker of the House of Commons, and enlarged by his son, Sir Walter, who returned richer than

ever from the Battle of Agincourt. At one time the Hungerfords could, it is said, ride the 30 m. or so to SALISBURY entirely on their own land. The castle remained in the family – except briefly in the 15th cent. – till 1689. It is now looked after by the Ministry of Public Building and Works.

At **Rode**, 2¼ m. S., a pretty, little-visited village, are Tropical Bird Gardens, with some 170 species, including flamingoes, pelicans, cranes, vultures and cockatoos, both in aviaries and flying free.

FOWEY, *Cornwall* (2–SX1251), is a popular town with delightfully narrow streets. In the days of the Crusades, Fowey was, with DARTMOUTH, EXETER and BARNSTAPLE, one of the four most important ports W. of BRISTOL. In 1346 it is said to have produced 47 ships and 770 men for Edward III's blockade of Calais. It remains, though its population is only 2,300, a thriving port, 10,000-ton ships being loaded with china clay looking enormous in the narrows of the river just above the town.

During the 14th and 15th cents. few French north-coast towns were without the constant fear of a raid by the "Fowey Gallants". When Edward IV agreed with the French to stop harrying them, the Fowey men failed to comply, with the result that Edward conspired successfully with the Dartmouth men to steal Fowey's ships.

Relics of its swaggering days are the ruined forts at the river mouth, which formerly had a chain between them to slice off enemy masts. Its church (1336), in the town centre, was, till 1684, also used as the town hall. Its 16th-cent. tower is one of the highest in Cornwall and is beautifully banded with carving; inside is a particularly fine Norman font of catacleuse slate. Place House dates from the early 15th cent. with later alterations and additions. When Frenchmen, retaliating to the raids of the "Gallants", invaded the town in 1457, it was the population's refuge. In the 19th cent. it was the home of Joseph Treffry, one of Cornwall's most energetic industrial developers, who built its tower, and it is still the home of the Treffry family. Its grounds are open occasionally.

The best view of the town is from Polruan, which can be reached by a pedestrian ferry.

There is an annual sailing regatta in August.

Polridmouth, 1¾ m. SW., and **Polkerris**, 1¾ m. W., are pretty coves. Between them, shut in by woodlands, is Menabilly, from the 16th cent. the home of the Rasleigh family and lately of Daphne du Maurier. Gribbin Head provides good views and cliffs. **Par**, 3 m. NW., purpose-built as a china-clay port, has vast sands.

Castle Dore, about 2½ m. N., is an Iron Age earthwork which has been connected with the medieval romance of King Mark, Tristram and Iseult. The 6th-cent. Castle Dore stone, on the Fowey–LOSTWITHIEL road, formerly stood near Castle Dore and is inscribed to the son of a Cunomorus, who may have been King Mark.

FROME, *Somerset* (4–ST7747). Holiday-bound traffic battling through this road-junction town is often unaware that it has one of the most attractive, old, narrow-streeted areas in Somerset. This is just SW. of its Market Place centre: Catherine Hill, Stony Street, Palmer Street; while at the E., Cheap Street, the most famous, is cobbled and has a water-course down its centre. All should be walked rather than driven. On the hillside above Cheap Street, the parish church, St John the Baptist's, is most remarkable for the elaborateness of its Victorian-restored interior, cause of much expert indignation, but, built in stages between *c.* 1150 and *c.* 1450, it also has plenty of good detail including Anglo-Saxon carvings, Norman doorways, well-carved medieval pillar-capitals, and quite pleasant 1924 glass in its Lady Chapel and side windows. In the churchyard is the tomb of the famous and outspoken 17th-cent. Bishop Ken, and nearby a museum specializes in local history and lore.

Till the Industrial Revolution a cloth-manufacturing town, Frome today has numerous industries, including printing, metal-casting, carpeting, dairying and light engineering. In 1685 Monmouth and his followers spent a night here, with the result that 12 men were later strung up in the Market Place by the King's servants. Frome's Amateur Operatic Society is of great local repute. One m. NW., the wooded Vallis Vale is both beautiful and of geological interest.

The town's name is pronounced Froom.

Jane J. Miller

Frome: Cheap Street with its central water-course

GLASTONBURY, *Somerset* (3–ST4938).

Many people still believe that under the waters of a spring on the slopes of its Tor, which is topped by a basically 14th-cent. church tower, Joseph of Arimathea buried the chalice used at the Last Supper; that when, on a nearby hill, he thrust his thorn staff into the ground it took root to produce the distinctive Glastonbury winter-flowering thorn-tree; and that, on what was later to be the site of the great abbey round which the town grew, he built a church of daub and wattle and there made the first conversions to Christianity in Britain. This, briefly, is the Legend of Glastonbury, still the cause of pilgrimages.

At the time of the Crucifixion the place would have been an island amid marshes and lakes, surrounded by lake-villages. In *c.* 688, King Ine of Wessex gave it a monastery. This was rather larger than WELLS Cathedral and became one of the richest and most beautiful in the land, as is still clear from the ruins of its church. A later legend says King Arthur and Queen Guinevere were re-buried in the abbey; and the spot, like everything else in the now excellently maintained precinct, is informatively sign-boarded. Two of the buildings remain intact: the kitchens containing a minor museum, and the 14th-cent. Abbot's Barn.

The other best buildings are in the High Street. St John's Church, with an exceptionally fine tower (1475), contains a tomb which legend once held to be Joseph of Arimathea's and some 15th-cent. stained glass. It is tall, slender-pillared and splendid, and there is a Glastonbury thorn in the churchyard. The 15th-cent. tribunal abbey court-house is now the museum specializing in finds from the lake-villages including a dug-out canoe. The splendidly stone-faced George Inn was built in the 15th cent. to lodge pilgrims. The handsome Market Cross is 19th-cent.

The walk to the Tor, which the superb view makes almost compulsory, is from the junction of Chilkwell Street and Wellhouse Lane (SHEPTON MALLET road); very near here is Chalice Well. The waters were formerly considered to be curative. Weary-All Hill, where St Joseph's staff is supposed to have taken root, is to the SW. The original thorn-tree was hacked down by a Roundhead who, it is said, also hacked off his leg in the process.

The town was a wool centre from the 13th to the 19th cent. It now goes in for sheepskin products and has a livestock market.

One of the lake-villages where archaeologists made major finds was about 1 m. NW. but has little to show the layman. Another was at MEARE.

GLENDURGAN GARDENS, *Cornwall* (2–SW7528),

are among the finest open to the public in Cornwall. So are **Penjerrick's**, 2½ m. N. Both excel in shrubs, rhododendrons, camellias, magnolias and embothriums, and also many others that can in England be grown only in South Cornwall, like tree ferns, banana trees and some cypress species. Both gardens flank a valley, falling towards the sea, and both, like the Fox Rosehill gardens at FALMOUTH, were created by the Fox family. Glendurgan, started by Alfred Fox, a Falmouth shipping agent, in 1823, was given to the National Trust in 1962. Penjerrick remains private.

You can walk down through Glendurgan to the pretty Helford river hamlet of **Durgan**. And about 2 m. W., the road to it winding past secret, silent creeks, is Porth Navas, headquarters of the famous Duchy of Cornwall Oyster Fisheries.

GODOLPHIN HOUSE, *Cornwall* (2–SW60 31). Begun *c.* 1475, it was from then till the family died out in the late 18th cent. the home of one of Cornwall's most enterprising families. Francis Godolphin (1534–1608) was among the first landlords to patronize tin-mining; the poems of Sidney Godolphin, killed in the Civil War, appear in anthologies; a later Sidney was Queen Anne's Lord High Treasurer.

Framed by cypresses as you approach, its very unusual, long, colonnaded front (1635) looks old, mysterious and grand. Woods all round keep it warm and secret. Inside, much fine furniture includes a splendid early-Jacobean carved-oak entablature.

It remains a family home, lovingly kept, since 1937 the home of Mr S. E. Schofield and his family.

GOONHILLY DOWNS, *Cornwall* (2–SW 7120), is a moor, almost flat, mainly of dull-coloured grass, gorse and heather, about 7 sq. m. in area, with its centre an earth-satellite radio station. The serpentine rock (*see* K YNANCE COVE) is, with the wind, the cause of most of the Lizard peninsula's lack of vegetation. But some plants like it for its magnesium content, including the Cornish Heath, sold in nurseries all over England.

Via the radio station, with its two rotatable saucers on steel legs, came the first live television broadcast from America in 1962, and from Japan in 1969. There is a public car park close beside it.

The Downs are said once to have borne oak forests (*see* MULLION) and to have been the home of a renowned breed of pony.

GUNWALLOE, *Cornwall* (2–SW6520). Perhaps, understandably, the Cornish want to keep it to themselves: their Official Guide does not mention it. Its coast has, thanks to the National Trust, been spared development. Off Church Cove in 1526 a treasure ship of the King of Portugal sank, and a famous pirate is said to have buried a treasure chest nearby at about the same time. In 1770 John Knill of ST IVES searched elaborately, for no reward. In 1785 another ship, laden with coins, was wrecked off the cove. Nothing but the odd coin on the beach has ever been found.

A little, grey, basically 15th-cent. church, its tower peculiarly detached from its body, nestles against a grass headland beside this cove, so close to the sea that spray sometimes soaks it. It is said to have been built there as an oblation, in the hope that its parishioners would be kept safe from the sea. The roof of its south aisle is fine, and there is good carving on the screen and some bench-ends.

The steep path up the headland leads to a

Courtauld Institute

Halberton church: the screen and pulpit

plateau of wild flowers edged by cliffs, and, to the N., a bay, grander and less frequented than the cove. Only the hotel on Polden Point (*see* MULLION) mars a wild and beautiful scene. But watch children, for the brink of vertical cliffs comes without warning; and local advice should be taken about when and where it is safe to bathe.

HALBERTON, *Devon* (3–ST0113), has a mysterious pond. It has never frozen within living memory. Hot springs are the obvious explanation, but no one is positive. A lane called Pound Hill leads down to it from the A373 which runs through the long village. Mallard sleep on its edge, and willows and sycamores overhang it pleasantly. The lane goes on between red walls and old houses to a well-proportioned reddish church, which is mainly 14th-cent. It contains a fine, early-15th-cent. screen and an exceptionally striking pulpit which could be 14th-cent.

The Grand Western Canal (*see* TIVERTON) passes through the village just N. of the main road. To the S. is a fertile, tree-speckled plain more typical of Somerset than Devon.

HARTLAND, *Devon* (3–SS2624). This is the most sparsely populated farming (as distinct from moorland) area of the West Country, a great cul-de-sac of an 18,000-acre parish. Though it is mainly flat and bleak, its every suspicion of a valley is fern-filled and the oaks grow strong, if stocky. It has an outstanding church and its sea cliffs are tremendous.

The little town called Hartland which supplies it is pleasant but contains nothing special. The 14th-cent. church dedicated to the Celtic St Nectan is 1½ m. W. Its superb, multi-buttressed 128-ft tower (15th-cent.) is among the highest in Devon. Its rood-screen is one of the finest and largest in Devon and is, remarkably, unrestored, bearing traces of its original colouring. The waggon roof (exceptional over the Lady Chapel) is unusually high, partially painted with large stars, rather prettily. In the chancel is a fine altar tomb (15th-cent, or earlier). Altogether it is splendidly light and almost arrogantly unadorned.

The tower may be climbed; neither the spiral staircase nor the exit to the roof are easy, but the view is good, particularly of the 18th-cent. house to the NE. that stands on the site of the long-demolished Hartland Abbey, founded in the 12th cent., and of the empty combe that leads from it to the sea.

One m. further W. is Hartland Quay (the quay long since washed away) and perhaps the most exciting cliffs and rocks on the whole north coast of Devon and Cornwall; fantastic not so much for their height as for their grey shapes, some sliced clean as with a knife, some like sleeping monsters, all rising from a base of innumerable parallel ridges. One m. over the cliffs is the very beautiful Speke's Waterfall.

Strangely, between here and Hartland Point (about 3 m. N.) the cliffs' colour changes from grey to red. The Point itself is fenced off, but the little white lighthouse hidden below it may be visited. In early summer the earth-ledges on the cliffs above it are covered with yellow flowers.

HATHERLEIGH, *Devon* (3–SS5404), is a small town at the western extremity of the mid-Devon fertile red-soil belt. Immediately W. of it begins the dreaded "cold clay", stretching to Holsworthy and beyond, on which the farms have to be big to prosper and population is, accordingly, sparse. Basically it exists for farmers to buy their groceries, have their vehicles mended and get a drink in, and it has a cattle market. Its charm is that it is off the main tourist routes and far more attractive to outsiders than it suspects.

Few of the many thatched cottages with bulging walls in its main street climbing a hill have been titivated. Odd chimneys sprout from them. The George Hotel is 15th-cent. and may have begun life as a court-house. The church, glimpsed from the main street through alleys, though violently restored, has 15th-cent. barrel-roof timbers.

In the local rivers there is good trout and salmon fishing. And the country around, particularly to the N., is of classical English long landscapes of rolling farmland.

HELFORD, *Cornwall* (2–SW7526), is one of England's exquisite villages, with abundant flowers and palms. Rows of cottages, white-walled and thatched or slated, face each other across a creek no wider than a main road, with slow, green water and swans as well as boats. Hills rise steeply on either side. Wherever there is not a house or garden there are trees.

A pedestrian ferry crosses the Helford River from here to Helford Passage.

About ½ m. W. is **Frenchman's Creek**, best reached by boat.

HELSTON, *Cornwall* (2–SW6527). Be here on 8 May, the day of the Furry Dance. It is a holiday; at 7.0 a.m. the church bells ring and the town band begins to play; and from then till the pubs close there is dancing up and down the hilly streets and in and out of the houses, most of the population taking part (some in top hats) or watching. The dance's origin is ancient. It may well be a pre-Christian survival. Legend says a dragon dropped a rock on the town and that the inhabitants danced wildly from relief that it had done so little damage.

On other days Helston is a fairly ordinary town. Until the Loe Bar formed across the mouth of its Cober River in the 13th cent. it was quite an important port. In Elizabethan times it was, with LISKEARD, LOSTWITHIEL and TRURO, one of Cornwall's four stannary or coinage towns, where all smelted tin had to be brought to be tested for quality and taxed. In 1549 it was one of the main Cornish sources of recruits for the rebellion against the imposition of Edward VI's new Prayer Book. Now it supplies farmers and the Navy's big air station at Culdrose (just S.), has a little light industry and one of the county's most important cattle markets (at the west end of the town).

Its best streets are the main one, Coinagehall (Angel Hotel was the enterprising Godolphin family's town house), and Cross Street, near St Michael's Church, which is well-preserved Regency. Its most honoured sons are Henry Trengrousse (1772–1854), who invented rocket life-saving apparatus, and Bob Fitzsimmons, the heavy-weight boxer. Charles Kingsley went to its grammar school. Behind the rather ponderous early Victorian guildhall (almost opposite you at the lights as you come in from the E.) is a good little museum containing a magnificent cider press, grist-mill and old implements of all sorts.

Loe Pool, 1 m. S., is Cornwall's biggest lake, rich in fish, bordered by woods. The bar separating it from the sea is of gravel and a type of flint not, for some unexplained reason, found elsewhere in the vicinity; it is like a miniature CHESIL BEACH. A culvert takes the overflow from the lake to the sea, and after heavy rains the waters meet in turmoil. Before the culvert was built, people with lakeside homes liable to be flooded would go ceremonially to the lord of the manor at Penrose on the west shore to ask permission to make a cut in the bar. You have to walk to the lake from a path off the road to Porthleven or from the E. from a lane off the road to GUNWALLOE, a quicker route.

Porthleven, 2 m. SW. of Helston, is a thriving fishing port with shell-fish deep-freeze plants and a boat-building and net-making industries. SE. for 2 m. runs a great beach made not of sand but of minute round stones, much smaller than shingle and very pretty.

HINTON ST GEORGE, *Somerset* (3–ST 4212). Within a belt of county roughly 6 m. deep on either side of the A303/A308 between YEOVIL and ILMINSTER virtually every village is predominantly of that attractive stone quarried from Ham Hill (*see* STOKE-SUB-HAMDON), matching the colour of the Jersey and Guernsey cows that graze its lush pastures. Hinton St George is perhaps the nearest to perfect of these villages, with a broad main street almost entirely Tudor, Jacobean or Georgian, and a fine 15th-cent. church. This has a splendidly gargoyled tower and contains monuments to the Pouletts who, from the 15th cent. till recently, owned the great house (of various periods) and vast estate just to the W.

On the last Thursday of October the village children parade through the streets with lanterns made from turnips and mangolds for the Punkie Night celebration, unique to Hinton St George but similar to Halloween.

HOLBETON, *Devon* (3–SX6150). A compact, stone village with slate or thatched roofs more concerned with farming than tourism in this least visited part of South Devon. Its church, central and dominating, with a fine *c.* 1300 spire, has a sumptuous interior with a splendid *c.* 1900 chancel screen and carved bench-ends, and 16th-cent. chapel screens.

Mothercombe, 2. S., is a hamlet of thatch-and-cob cottages and an excellent Queen Anne house; and close to it on the wooded shores of the Erme estuary is a very pretty sandy beach, private but often accessible.

About 1½ m. NE., Flete House, a splendidly sited, basically Elizabethan mansion, greatly enlarged in 1878, is frequently open in summer.

HOLCOMBE ROGUS, *Devon* (3–ST0519). Holcombe Court is probably the finest Tudor house in the county. It dates basically from the early 16th cent. with later additions and alterations, built for the Bluett family, who remained the local squires till 1858. Its fine south front can be well seen through its entrance arch; the interior by written appointment. The 15th-cent. church beside it contains a Jacobean family pew used by the Bluetts, which is square with 5-ft-high walls. There are two vast 17th-cent. Bluett monuments.

The village is demurely pretty, far off the tourist routes.

HOLFORD, *Somerset* (3–ST1541). The poet Wordsworth and his sister Dorothy found its surroundings idyllic when for a year (1797–8) in their twenties they lived at Alfoxden House (now a hotel), just W. The village is at the foot of one of the Quantocks' most beautiful wooded combes.

At **Dodington,** 1 m. SE., a fine Elizabethan house faces the road. During the Civil War its resident alarmed even Royalists by the readiness with which he slaughtered anyone who might have Roundhead sympathies.

In **Nether Stowey,** 1¼ m. further E., a large,

prosperous and architecturally homogenous village, the cottage where Coleridge lived from 1796 to 1799 and wrote the *Ancient Mariner*, is preserved by the National Trust (west end of the village). He, too, was in his twenties and a friend of the Wordsworths. They were regarded with suspicion locally on account of their sympathy with the ideals of the French revolutionaries, particularly as Britain and France were at war. At the east end of the village is a neat 17th-cent. gazebo. Stowey Court, behind it, is Elizabethan but hard to see for walls. The church, largely rebuilt in the 19th cent., is, for a village one, remarkably plush.

HONITON, *Devon* (3–ST1600). The splendid by-pass has entirely changed its stature. Instead of being suffocated by motorists, it is revealed as it was to horse and coach travellers: an unusually attractive small town with a long, Georgian main street. Among older buildings are Marwood House, now an antique shop, at the east end, and St Margaret's Hospital, a group of partly 16th-cent. thatched cottages at the west end. The lace for which Honiton was famous from the 16th to the 19th cent. can be seen in a shop and also, together with mammoth bones dug up in the making of the by-pass, in the museum in an old chapel beside the parish church. Lace-making survives, just. Visitors can see pots made in a pottery. The town is an antiques trade centre, and, in lush milking-cow country, has recently gained a £500,000 dairy. There is a livestock market on Tuesdays. The most popular building with children is the embattled toll-house called the Copper Castle by the road out to AXMINSTER.

ILFRACOMBE, *Devon* (3–SS5147). A holiday and retirement resort annexing a chunk of superb country, it is curious as being almost without rival, even among fellow resorts, for the variety and immodesty of its Victorian architecture. The beauty and restrictedness of the site between cliffs and hills accentuates the size and dominance of the huge hotels and boarding houses. From the restraint of the Tunnel Baths (1836) to the grandiosity of the Holiday Inn (1870), to the confused efforts of the early 20th cent., the changes in taste of a hundred years are, within a very short walk, most entertainingly displayed. And behind, farmed hills rise high before folding into deep valleys of big trees and shrubs like fuchsias which, although this is a north coast, are not cut down by frost.

Like most of the larger West Country resorts, Ilfracombe became popular during the Napoleonic Wars. Before that it was a small fishing port and, from the 14th to the 16th cent., quite an important trading port. Its harbour remains attractive, full of small boats. It is a departure-point for LUNDY and for cruises along the coast and across to Wales. On a peninsular hill beside the harbour is the basically 14th-cent. St Nicholas Chapel, since the 18th cent. a lighthouse. The climb to it, and also to Hillsborough (447 ft) to the E., is worthwhile for the view. There is no

Ilfracombe harbour

main beach, rather a series of coves, both rocky and sandy, extra good for shell hunting.

The numerous public gardens are mostly above average both in their setting and in their quality. On the Torrs, a semi-moorland hill just to the W., pony rides are offered. At Comyn Hill is a zoo; near the Holiday Inn, a museum. The parish church, Holy Trinity, though in general much restored, has ancient waggon-roof timbers.

About 1½ m. SE. of the harbour, **Chambercombe** is a small, mainly 16th- and 17th-cent. manor house of considerable quaintness and charm round courtyards with fuchsias. It contains a fine Elizabethan tester-bed, and boasts, inevitably perhaps, a ghost. It is open to the public.

At **Lee**, about 3 m. W., a lush valley leads down to an exciting rocky bay. Unfortunately, the big brown, gabled buildings, rather than the thatched cottages, dominate the scene.

Some 2½ m. E. of Ilfracombe is Watermouth Castle (*see* COMBE MARTIN).

ILMINSTER, *Somerset* (3–ST3614), is an industrially-expanding small town on the A303. The most beautiful parts, however, are off this road: first a row of thatched and white-washed cottages like those often seen in Devon; then a mainly yellow Ham-stone square round a pillared market house; finally, on a perfect central site, a splendid Ham-stone church, floodlit in the evening. Mainly 15th-cent., this church has perhaps the finest tower in southern Somerset, modelled on WELLS Cathedral's central one, and, inside, a particularly beautiful south transept chapel. All light, high and simple under a tie-beam roof, this contains the fine tombs with outstanding brasses of Sir William Wadham (d. 1452), whose money built much of the church, and Nicholas and Dorothy Wadham (d. 1609 and 1618), who founded Wadham College, OXFORD. Immediately N. of the church, the old grammar school is basically Elizabethan. The lane past it, called Court Barton, leads to a pretty residential square. A plaque on the George Hotel says it was the first hotel Queen Victoria stayed in – she was aged seven months at the time.

A wool centre from the Middle Ages to the early 19th cent., and till 1201 controlled by the monks of MUCHELNEY, Ilminster now makes, among other things, shirts, collars, gloves, plastics, agricultural machinery and quartz crystals, and has a large dairy.

About ½ m. N. (2 m. round by road, turn off at **Whitelackington** 1¼ m. E.), is **Dillington House,** a grand Tudor house enlarged in the 19th cent., now a college for adult education and an arts centre run by the county education committee. Plays, films, recitals and lectures, all open to the public, are given in a theatre created out of the former stately stables, and an excellent art gallery has recently been built on. For information about courses write to the Warden. The house was the home of Lord North when he was Prime Minister, 1770–82.

All round Ilminster are exquisite Ham-stone villages, particularly **Stocklinch**, 2¼ m. NE., **Dowlish Wake**, 1½ m. SE., and **Donyatt**, 1¼ m. W. (2¾ m. by road); and Whitelackington's church is worth a stop. About 4 m. N., the church at **Isle Abbots** has one of the finest Perpendicular towers in the county.

Six m. W., **Castle Neroche** is an impressive Norman earthwork amid fine beech trees 900 ft up in the Blackdown Hills, commanding wide views of willow plains to the N. And nearby, **Staple Fitzpaine** is a pretty village with a grand 15th-cent. church tower.

ISLE OF ATHELNEY, THE, *Somerset* (3–ST3428). Here in 878 or 879 King Alfred is said to have burnt the cakes and rallied the Anglo-Saxons before the Battle of Ethandune against the Danes. If it is an island still it is made one only by ditches. It lies in Somerset fen-farmland, to the S. of the A361 between Lyng and Burrow Bridge, the source of osiers for these villages' basket industries. Not a trace of anything Alfred built remains, but the hill called the Mump above Burrow Bridge may be the site of an Anglo-Saxon fort. A ruined church now stands on the hill, from which there are good views.

Just off the main road is a memorial erected in 1801. **Lyng**'s pretty church, containing an excellent Elizabethan or Jacobean pulpit and good 16th-cent. bench-ends, is said to have been founded as a chapel of an abbey which Alfred, after his victory, built in Athelney. It is not certain where Ethandune was, but it was probably about two days' march eastwards from Athelney.

KENTON, *Devon* (3–SX9583). A large village in the lushest of red-soil farmland with an outstanding red church (*c.* 1360–70) containing one of the county's most famous rood-screens which dates from *c.* 1480.

About ½ m. E. is **Powderham Castle**, seat of the Courtenay family (Earls of Devon) since *c.* 1390, frequently open in summer. Mainly 18th- and 19th-cent. and scarcely beautiful from without, it is splendidly and tastefully furnished and decorated. The very pretty chapel with excellent carved bench-ends should not be missed. There are deer among the fine cedars in the park. Till the 18th cent. the River Exe came right up to its walls and nearby was the small harbour of Kenton. The 15th-cent. church, ½ m. NE., has several Courtenay monuments.

Starcross, 1½ m. SE., has rather an appealing, faded, early-19th-cent. dignity. It never became popular as a resort, and the red tower of the pumping house for Brunel's atmospheric railway adds to the air of gallant failure. Atmospheric trains (on the vacuum principle) were reaching 70 m.p.h. between EXETER and NEWTON ABBOT in *c.* 1818; but they failed because, in those pre-rubber days, the leather valves leaked. Starcross has a pretty harbour and at **Cockwood**, a hamlet just S., there is another, faced by pleasant pubs.

KILKHAMPTON, *Cornwall* (2–SS2511). The church is renowned for its 157 carved bench-ends *c.* 1570. Other churches may have better individual examples, but few, if any, so many. It is a big and generally fine church, with a late-Norman doorway elaborately carved with zigzags and strange, snouted faces, and a splendid barrel roof with timbers exposed and carved. The Grenvilles (*see* MORWENSTOW) have always been its patrons and here Sir Bevil Grenville, a famous Cornish Royalist leader in the Civil War (*see* STRATTON) was buried.

KINGSBRIDGE, *Devon* (3–SX7344). Shopping centre for an exceedingly fertile farming district known as the South Hams, it is at its best after dark when its steep, narrow main street is made glamorous by its shape and the quality in its lit-up shop windows. The magic fades rather with daylight; but there is plenty of pleasant – and some curious – slate-hanging in this street, a quaint arcaded building called the Shambles (1796), and a good, terse, early Socialist epitaph just inside the churchyard on the right. And it is nice down by its estuary-head where, amid lots of other boats, you can have tea on an old pleasure-steamer.

From the 14th to the 19th cent. it was a port, shipping – in the Middle Ages – wool and sharp tools from its foundry, and building ships, and

running – in the 19th cent. – a steamer service to PLYMOUTH. It also had flour, cider, textile and brewing industries. These businesses have all gone, but it continues to prosper. Local artists have a summer exhibition in a gallery in Church Street (TOTNES road). **Dodbrook** church, further up this road, has a good 15th-cent. screen. William Cookworthy, discoverer of china clay in England, was born in the town in 1705.

KYNANCE COVE, *Cornwall* (2–SW6813). This famous cove, NW. of LIZARD POINT, is well worth visiting. It is not just the shape of the rocks rising in pillars and pyramids and making caves round a floor of glistening hard sand, but also their colour. The soft serpentine stone is in delicate shades of all rainbow colours except yellow, and lichen provides that. Much of the Lizard peninsula is made of it; this is where you can see it best.

Be there within 2½ hours either side of low tide. If you want to escape the masses, branch away from the path where it crosses the stream and head for the crest opposite. Here are untrampled wild flowers, a grand view, a wild combe of gorse and rock and a stream falling in tiny waterfalls to the cove.

Steps which anyone with reasonable heart, lungs and legs should manage lead down to it.

About ⅓ m. N. of the cove an ancient settlement, inhabited *c.* 1130–1100 B.C. and again from *c.* 500 B.C. to *c.* A.D. 100, has recently been excavated.

LAND'S END, *Cornwall* (2–SW3425). England ends with a cream-coloured hotel, souvenir

Land's End and the Longships lighthouse

Kenneth Scowen

shops, snack bars, hawker-photographers, thread-bare grass networked with paths, and cliffs. The good road surface ceases about ¼ m. short. The cliffs, of brownish, clean-cut granite slabs divided by vertical crevices, are fine, but less so than many others locally. Visible are the Longships light-house (1795, present building 1883), about 1 m. offshore, and the Wolf lighthouse (1869), 8 m. away.

Sennen Cove, 1 m. N., has a good beach but not much of a village, though the round, tarred wind-lass house at the west end is entertaining.

LANGPORT, *Somerset* (3–ST4226). Much the best part of this little town, which has a long-established glove industry and was formerly celebrated for its eels (gleaned from the ditches of SEDGEMOOR), is on its hill-top from which through traffic is discouraged. Here is the so-called "hanging chapel" spanning the road, built in the 15th cent. as a tradesmen's guildhouse, and the fine church, with an east window of medieval stained glass (of which there is very little in Somerset), a 12th-cent. Norman tympanum and splendid tie-beam chancel roof. From the church-yard there is a great view over the plain to the S.; across the road rather a pretty whitened Roman Catholic church. And only ¼ m. E. along this road is the church of **Huish Episcopi**, which has one of the finest towers in Somerset and a Norman door-way remarkable for its terracotta colour caused accidentally by fire.

Langport dates from the Anglo-Saxons and grew up round a fordable place on the River Parrett. It was the scene of a decisive battle in the Civil War.

LANHYDROCK HOUSE, *Cornwall* (2–SX 0864). An attractive great house of warm brown stone and simple lines, with long wings and a big three-sided court, *Magnolia grandiflora* softening the walls. In front and on one side are formal gardens of lawns, rose-beds and toy-like clipped cypresses; behind it, a fine shrub garden; and through the park that slopes gently away from it, a ½-m. avenue of beeches and a few older syca-mores leads E. to the main road at Respryn Bridge.

Inside are some fine portraits, but the outstand-ing feature is the plaster ceiling (*c.* 1650) of the gallery. Some 116 ft long, it vividly illustrates the early part of the Old Testament. It is in the north wing which, with a bit of the west wing, was the only part of the original house (1620–42) to sur-vive a fire in 1881. Its builders were the Robartes family, TRURO merchants and bankers, who were, in the Civil War, Parliamentarians. Originally the house completely enclosed its court, but the east wing was demolished in 1780. Externally the post-1881 part blends well with the old. The church behind is much restored but pretty. The gatehouse dates from 1636 to 1658.

LANTEGLOS-BY-FOWEY, *Cornwall* (2–SX1451). A beautiful 14th-cent. church alone on a hill by a farm in beautiful, deep-valleyed country. Its tower is perfectly proportioned with sharp

corners, and is stained by yellow lichen. The interior is simple, with a wide, open-timbered waggon roof. There is a brass to the Mohuns, husband and wife, who died of sweating sickness.

Much of the area is National Trust protected. Especially pretty is Pont Pill, a creek of ducks and swans: the road to the church from the E. passes it.

About ½ m. S. Lantic Bay is wild and splendid, and, because it is hard to get to, comparatively uncrowded.

LANYON QUOIT, *Cornwall* (2–SW4333), is the most accessible of the four cromlechs (*see* ZENNOR) in this moorland area thick with pre-historic remains: it is about 20 yds from the road. In 1815 its 18 ft by 9 ft capstone fell, struck, it is locally said, by lightning. In 1824 the Navy, fresh from replacing the logan stone at Treen (*see* PORTHCURNO), came with a crane to raise it, but succeeded only after reducing the height of the three upright stones by half.

About 1½ m. NW. and ⅓ m. from the nearest road is Chun Quoit, the smallest of the area's cromlechs, but the only one never dislodged. Near it is Chun Castle, said to be an exceptionally fine Iron Age fort but not much to look at.

More exciting is the Men-an-Tol (about ¾ m. up a track to the E. off the road just N. of Lanyon Quoit). It is a wheel-shaped stone with a hole in the middle, standing on its rim between two semi-upright stones. Once children were passed through it to cure them of disease.

LAUNCESTON, *Cornwall* (2–SX3384), stands on a hill crowned by the ruins of its castle; it is impressive at first sight from E. and N. Till 1838 it was the county's capital. Its fine site gained a settlement early, Celtic, then West Saxon. The pre-sent town is an agricultural centre with a weekly market (Tuesdays) and little other industry. It is attractive in an ancient way with narrow streets, many interesting, and a few beautiful, buildings; it produces good rugby players, and is surrounded by good trout rivers.

Most interesting features are within a short walk of the main square (car park). Outstanding is St Mary Magdalene's Church, unique in that, except for the 14th-cent. tower, its outside walls are entirely covered with carvings.

It was built 1511–24, and contains a fine pulpit, probably early 16th-cent.

What exists of the castle probably dates from the early 13th cent., replacing an earlier Norman castle. Its main action seems to have been fought during the Civil War when, surprisingly, for it looks to have been almost impregnable, it four times changed hands. The view from the top is quite good. In a room close to its north gate George Fox, the Quaker leader, was shut up for eight months in 1656 for distributing "sub-versive" literature. On the greensward below, people were publicly hanged till 1821.

Just NE. of the castle, in Castle Street, is one of the best rows of Georgian red-brick houses in Cornwall. One, Lawrence House, was a rendez-vous for French officer-prisoners on parole during the Napoleonic Wars. Now it is the borough museum.

The grand South Gate, spanning a main street, is almost all that remains of the wall built round the town during Henry VIII's reign. The cattle and sheep market is about 100 yds outside it; just inside a plaque marks the birth-house of the Governor of New South Wales from 1800 to 1806, who caused Launceston in Tasmania to be so named.

In the Square, the wriggly building on the south corner was the home of the town's mayor in 1555, and the White Hart Hotel incorporates a doorway from the Augustinian priory that existed at the village of St Thomas from 1127 to 1538.

The 15th-cent. St Thomas's Church has an exceptionally large and fine example of a Norman font. A medieval footbridge crosses the river and leads to the village of **St Stephen**, thought older than Launceston itself. Its church tower is conspicuous from the castle top.

About 4 m. S. is **Trecarrel**, the manor house of Henry Trecarrel, which has a 16th-cent. hall and chapel of great charm. It can be visited by appointment.

And about 4½ m. NE. is **Wortham Manor**, 15th-cent. with earlier parts.

LERRYN, _Cornwall_ (2–SX1556), is a marvellously pretty hamlet at the highest place navigable by yacht on this tidal creek, with gentle grass banks, stone cottages half-screened by trees, and old warehouses half-covered with creeper.

Some 1½ m. W. (2¾ m. by road) St Winnow's Church is beautifully situated with just a farm on one side, on the other the River Fowey, ¼ m. broad here and becoming a great plain of mud at low tide. This church is very attractive (mainly 15th-cent.) with a fine, mainly early-16th-cent. east window, an early-16th-cent. rood-screen (restored), an Elizabethan pulpit, and boldly carved bench-ends of the 16th and early 17th cents. Below the churchyard is a landing stage for people coming to church by boat.

Boconnoc Park, 3 m. NE., was landscaped in the 18th cent. by Thomas Pitt, Lord Camelford. William Pitt the Elder (Prime Minister 1757–61) spent some of his boyhood at the rather dull Boconnoc House in the park. Neither it nor the grounds are normally open to the public.

LISKEARD, _Cornwall_ (2–SX2564), is one of the county's most progressive small towns: lively in atmosphere and pleasant to look at. It lacks priceless possessions, but has some good Georgian and Victorian architecture. Chartered in the 13th cent. and a stannary town (_see_ HELSTON) soon afterwards, it was, for several centuries till the late 19th, made prosperous by the Caradon Hill copper mines (_see_ ST CLEER). Now it has probably the busiest livestock market (Mondays and Thursdays) in East Cornwall and, helped by its position on the railway and an important road junction, is increasingly attracting light industry to a new industrial estate.

Some of its best Georgian buildings are where the A390 widens by the War Memorial. Nearby, in Pike Street, its Victorian guildhall is finely dark and strong with a grand clock-tower. Running S. from this its narrow-streeted shopping centre in a valley has some pretty slate-hung houses and an ancient Pipe Well, formerly considered curative.

St Martin's Church, basically 15th-cent., up the hill to the E., is the largest parish church in the county after BODMIN's. Given a new tower in 1902 and mainly Victorian furnished, it is, however, quite handsome with fine slender granite columns. The town's oldest part is round it. The Lake Lane housing estate just NE. won a Civic Trust Award in 1962.

Among the town's M.P.s was, in 1774, Edward Gibbon, the historian, though he seems to have had little else to do with Liskeard or Cornwall. In the slate-covered house beside the A390 Charles I spent seven nights in 1644.

In spring and early summer the embothriums in private gardens on the south side of the town are glorious.

LIZARD POINT, _Cornwall_ (2–SW6911). The most southerly tip of England is grand for ship spotting, and its 180-ft cliffs are like a huge, wild rock garden. On a calm day it at first seems innocent, but the jagged rocks offshore are dangerous, and in Pistol Meadow, a little W. of the point, were buried some 200 bodies found on the rocks below at one low tide in the mid-18th cent.

The lighthouse can be visited. The first on the site was built in 1619. The present one dates from 1752 and has not been much altered except that it was given a more powerful lighting system about 1900. Its beam cuts the horizon at 23 m. but its reflection is said to be visible 100 m. away.

A short walk E. of the lighthouse is a funnel in the cliff-top, known as the Lion's Den, formed when a cave's roof collapsed in 1847.

The industries of the unlovely settlement called Lizard Town are tourism, and souvenir-making out of serpentine rock. The road E. out of it, to Church Cove, leads suddenly to trees and farmyards, the church of **Landewednack** and thatched cottages, all in soothing contrast to the surrounding bleakness. The last sermon in Cornish is supposed to have been delivered in this church in about 1660. It has a pulpit of serpentine, a fine lectern made of old bench-ends and an unusual rib-vaulted south porch. Basically Norman, its dedication is to a 6th-cent. Breton saint, and fishermen from Brittany still occasionally visit it.

The road peters out before Church Cove. A path to the right and then steps lead to Kilcobben Cove, where one of Cornwall's newest lifeboats is stationed. The crew reach it by lift but this is not for the public.

The best bathing beaches locally are Housel Bay, near the lighthouse, and Kynance (_see_ KYNANCE COVE).

Cadgwith, 2 m. NE., is a genuine fishing hamlet (shell-fish mainly) with a shingle beach at the foot of a steep-wooded combe, enclosed by rock headlands and stone houses, several thatched. Just S. is

another and bigger cliff-top chasm, the Devil's
Frying-Pan.

LONG ASHTON, *Somerset* (3–ST5470). Just
N. of this village is the enormous mansion of
Ashton Court. It is not open to the public but by
driving through its park you get a good view of
its south front. The left of this (as you look at it)
dates from *c.* 1633, the right and the gatehouse
are early 19th-cent.; behind there is more of
various periods from the 16th cent. onwards.
Owned by the Smyths, originally a merchant
family from BRISTOL, for over 400 years, it was
bought in 1960, in ill-repair, by the Bristol
Corporation.

Long Ashton church, in a peaceful retreat from
the main road and prevailing suburbia, has a
fairly good screen and a fine effigy-tomb of Lord
Chief Justice Choke (1486). The Research Station
just SW. is concerned with fruit-growing and
preservation, and cider-making.

Backwell, 4 m. SW., an affluent Bristol commuter village, has a fine church with a good tower,
15th-cent. screen, and beautiful 1360 north-east
chapel. From its churchyard there is a grand view
N. over **Nailsea**, which in the 19th cent. made
famous glass, to the hills, and W. over the tree-
scattered plain of Kenn to the sea.

About 1½ m. SW. from here a turning E. off the
A370 leads to the beautiful, wooded Brockley
Combe.

LOOE, *Cornwall* (2–SX2753), is the most
efficiently tourist-commercialized fishing port in
the West Country, possibly in England. The "seaside resort" and "quaint fishing village" offers its
attractions, plus sailing and motor-boat trips
along the coast or to its offshore island, and of
course its shark fishing, for which it is the main
British centre. It is also, in general if not in detail,
exceptionally beautiful.

In summer it is appallingly crowded. Park your
car just SE. of the bridge: to press on is pointless.
The walk to the beach, either via the quay or the
main street, is short and attractive.

Until 1883 East and West Looe were separate
towns facing each other across the river. The new
guildhall (1877) in Fore Street was the symbol of
their amalgamation. Their joint population is
now about 4,050. East Looe is the elder. In 1346
it was contributing 20 ships and 315 men to
Edward III's fleet besieging Calais, only five ships
less than London. But unlike their neighbour,
FOWEY, in the main the twin towns minded their
own business: fishing and that second industry,
smuggling, which tourism has now so happily
replaced.

Of the old buildings, the Guildhall, possibly
16th-cent., in a street running E. off Fore Street, is
pretty. It now houses a small museum. The most
attractive church is that of St Nicholas in West
Looe, which was for much of the period *c.* 1650 to
1851 West Looe's guildhall. At one stage its
tower was used as "a cage for scolding women . . .
and a most effective one" (Rev. E. Seymour, vicar
in 1851). In 1852 it was restored, a new roof, more

like an old barn's than a church's, being made
from the timbers of the Spanish ship, *San Josef*,
said to have been captured by Nelson.

On East Looe quay are some fine Victorian
warehouses; close to them are an aquarium that
includes a stuffed shark and an old boat-building
shed with meticulously cobbled floor turned into
a gallery for local painters. In Lower Street is an
extremely entertaining Cornish museum. In Fore
Street, the house of Thomas Bond, town clerk in
the 18th cent., contains good Jacobean panelling;
it is now a café. To the NW. of the bridge, which
replaced its predecessor in 1855, the old millpond
is now a boating lake for children.

The British International Sea Angling Festival
is held annually from Looe in late September or
early October. Some 55,000 sharks have been
caught for fun since the sport became organized
here in 1953. These are cut up for crab and lobster
bait. They are not normally found alive within
12 m. of the shore.

About 3 m. E. of Looe is the **Murrayton
Monkey Sanctuary**. Here woolly monkeys, an
unusually attractive variety from the Amazon
jungle, do tricks and romp around among
spectators in a beautiful setting.

LOSTWITHIEL, *Cornwall* (2–SX1059), is far
smaller than you might expect from the map and
from its history. In the 13th cent. it was the
capital of the Duchy, under the aegis of Edmund,
Earl of Cornwall, in his castle, Restormel, and
throughout the Middle Ages a stannary town (*see*
HELSTON). Now it has little but the trappings of
borough status. It is compact (having been built
to a medieval grid plan) with several interesting
old buildings and few ugly ones, and slopes to the
River Fowey, which is here deep enough for
small boats yet fast enough for trout and crossed
by an old bridge. One of its least lovely buildings,
the Methodist Church (1900), dominates its
main-road aspect.

Outstanding are the 13th-cent. lantern spire of
its parish church, the finest of its kind in Cornwall: the same church's celebrated 14th-cent. font,
which is most entertainingly carved, and the
linen-fold panelling in its guildhall (1740). The
church, which also contains quite an attractive
1886 east window by the well-known firm of
Clayton and Bell, was treated even more sac-
rilegiously than most by Parliamentarian soldiers
in the Civil War. At the font they christened a
horse Charles, used the building as a prison, and
tried to blow up two prisoners who escaped to the
tower. The old brown buildings in Quay Street
are the remains of a great hall built *c.* 1280 as the
county treasury, and the former stannary offices:
beneath the granite slabs that floor an arch at the
south end a stream flows. In North Street a wall
plaque tells you that Walter Kendall has a 3,000-
year lease, starting 1652, on the house.

Restormel, 1 m. W., commanding the Fowey
Valley, is the best preserved castle of its period in
the county. Parts of it may date from *c.* 1100, but
most of what now exists is late 13th-cent. By the
16th cent. it was abandoned. Parliamentarian

Peter Baker

Looe: the harbour

forces used it in the Civil War till driven out by Sir Richard Grenville's men in 1644.

LUNDY ISLAND, *Devon* (2–SS1345), lies about 11 m. NW. of HARTLAND Point and 21 m. W. of ILFRACOMBE whence ships of about 600 tons run visitors to it. The trip takes 1½ hours. It can also be reached by smaller vessels from BIDEFORD and CLOVELLY.

The island is 3 m. long by about ¾ m. at its widest; is of an exceptionally hard granite (used for the Thames Embankment); is mainly plateau (highest point 471 ft) above high – and on its west side particularly exciting – cliffs; grows grass, heather and a fine variety of wild flowers. The wind forbids trees or shrubs, except in sheltered pockets, as round the house of its former owner. It is a bird sanctuary, particularly the haunt of puffins and peregrines. St Patrick, it is said, rid the island of its snakes as he did Ireland's. Seals bask on its rocks, and there are deer and goats. Rat Island, near the landing stage, is one of the last British retreats of the indigenous black rat and a rare species of spider. Near the south-west point is a chasm called the Devil's Limekiln, some 300 ft deep. Buildings consist of the ruins of a probably 13th-cent. castle, an hotel, a pub (always open when ships arrive), a church (1889) and a few cottages. The population is about 20.

Throughout the Middle Ages the island was a pirate stronghold. In the late 17th cent. it was ravaged by the crew of a French ship, who pretended they wanted to bury a sailor in the church (since replaced). They came ashore in force to the funeral with a coffin full of weapons, made prisoners and removed the clothes of the unsuspecting inhabitants, tossed over the cliffs all the animals they could lay hands on, and departed. In the mid-19th cent. the island passed into more honourable, though still private, ownership. It remained a private domain until sold to the National Trust in 1969.

LUSTLEIGH, *Devon* (3–SX7881). Its thatchers are renowned. The path from the stone cross in the village centre past the village cricket ground leads to one of the prettiest communities of thatched granite cottages in Devon. The principal and oldest is Wreyland Manor, built as a court house in 1389, converted to a manor house in 1680.

Elsewhere Lustleigh has many rather obtrusive 20th-cent. houses, but the church is good, with a fine 15th-cent. tower, lavishly carved mid-15th-cent. screen and in its porch a stone bearing an ancient inscription.

From the hill to the W. of the village you can look upon Lustleigh Cleave, one of Devon's great romantic views. A steep hillside, bare except for granite boulders, falls titanically to the River Bovey and then sweeps widely up again through oak, beech, birch and hazel woods till the crags of Hound Tor break a DARTMOOR horizon.

LUXULYAN VALLEY, *Cornwall* (2–SX 0458), is among the most beautiful of these Cornish valleys so deep between wooded hillsides as to seem almost underground, and the stream beside this one is often milk-like with china clay. The best entry is from St Blazey (take care to follow signs to "Luxulyan Valley" not just "Luxulyan") or, if you are coming from the N., head for Luxulyan and then St Blazey. The road passes under the grand granite viaduct built by Joseph Treffry (*see* FOWEY) in 1839 to carry a railway from his quarries. It also carried water beneath the huge slabs on which the lines lay. The railway has long since gone, but the aqueduct is still used by the china-clay industry.

Luxulyan village is small and quite pretty on the valley side, its basically 15th-cent. and pleasantly plain church built of unusually large blocks of granite.

LYDFORD, *Devon* (3–SX5084). The prime Devon example of a town that became redundant: now a small grey village. Anglo-Saxons fortified it against the Danes and it was one of the four places in the county where they minted coins. Though already declining in the Middle Ages, it remained a headquarters of the tin-miners who virtually ruled DARTMOOR. It contained their prison. This, called a castle, built in 1195 and still grimly standing, was officially described in 1512 as "one of the most heinuous, contagious and detestable places in the realm". Among its inmates at about that time was Richard Strode, M.P., flung in by the tinners for introducing a bill to which they objected. His protest contributed to the establishment of parliamentary privilege. Lydford parish, over 78 sq. m., still covers roughly half the moor, and an ancient "lych way", by which the dead were brought to its graveyard, can still be followed, with the help of an Ordnance Survey map, from near Lydford Tor in the moor's centre. The church is worth a look for its excellent modern (1904) screen and carved bench-ends; and in the churchyard is a famous, lengthy epitaph to George Routleigh, watchmaker.

But the main visual reason for coming here is the Gorge (National Trust) just SW. Great trees almost roof it; wild garlic carpets its sides; the river, with its boulders, dark pools, cascades and long rapids, is endlessly changing, always beautiful. The descent from the Lydford end is steep; the length of the gorge about a mile. In the 17th cent. it was, tradition says, inhabited by the Gubbinses, a family of outlaws both fearsome and "lewd", who made off with "two strumpets" and multiplied accordingly – see Kingsley's *Westward Ho!*.

Sydenham, 5½ m. W. near Marystow, is one of the best Jacobean houses in Devon. It can be well seen from the road and is open by appointment. It contains a fine Renaissance carved staircase.

LYNTON and LYNMOUTH, *Devon* (3–SS 7149). Round these two villages, the one by the sea, the other almost vertically above is concentrated a sample of almost every facet of the scenery that makes EXMOOR superlative: ravine sides that seem too steep for trees yet are covered with them; moorland rivers meeting and together cascading through boulders to the sea; cliffs nearly 1,000 ft high yet strangely not savage, streaked red so they glow gloriously in the evening sun, their tops rounded with grass and bracken. The place's unique contribution is the Valley of the Rocks where you can walk a ridge of shaly pinnacles amid semi-wild, but amiable, mountain goats and look down one side 800 ft to the sea and down the other to what must be the most spectacularly situated village cricket field in England. There is, however, much insensitive 1850–1940 building.

Lynmouth, through which the river pours (and caused the 1952 "Lynmouth disaster" when, in one night of deluge, it brought its boulders with it), was a disconsolate fishing village when the Napoleonic Wars brought it popularity as a resort. Till *c.* 1607 it had a prosperous herring industry. Then, quite suddenly it seems, the herring shoals went elsewhere. In 1812 Shelley came to stay here, far from family disapproval, with his 16-year-old bride, and extolled the place. So did Southey.

Lynton, on the hill-top, until then a few cottages round a church, received its first hotel in 1807. Later it was loved and patronized by George Newnes, the publisher, who put up the money for its town hall (1900) and the Cliff Railway (1890) which still carries people between the villages. This works like kitchen scales: the car to go down is weighted with water and pulls the other one up. Newnes also backed the Lynton–BARNSTAPLE railway, opened in 1898, but closed in 1936 as uneconomic; said to have been one of the prettiest, and slowest, railways in Britain.

Beside Lynmouth harbour is a classic row of thatched cottages. Lynton's Roman Catholic church in Lee Road has a font and sanctuary wall of rather rare and beautiful marble. In one of Lynton's prettier cottages, St Vincent's, is the Lyn and Exmoor Museum which is worth visiting.

The Valley of the Rocks is just to the W. Beyond it, Lee Abbey (*c.* 1850) is not monastic, but a rest, conference and study centre for people involved with the Anglican Church. A farm-house previously on the site was owned by the De Wichehalses, about whom there are conflicting dramatic tales and who feature (fictitiously) in *Lorna Doone*. The drive on W. to COMBE MARTIN is exceedingly beautiful. At Lee Bay there is some sand and you can bathe, though none too safely. Lynmouth itself has no sand, and, in fact, there is not a proper children's beach between MINEHEAD and ILFRACOMBE.

Watersmeet, where the East and West Lyn rivers converge in splendour, is 1½ m. inland from Lynton, just off the Simonsbath road.

The view of Lynmouth's bay from the road up to Countisbury to the E. is supreme. From the top of the hill, the land collapses to the right into a perfect Exmoor valley. Hereabouts a Danish incursion is said (though Northam, near BIDEFORD, claims the same battle) to have been repulsed in 878. There are vestiges of an ancient fort.

MARTOCK, *Somerset* (3–ST4619). The interior of its Ham-stone church is perhaps the grandest in Somerset, the effect of the golden stone against probably the finest – certainly the most lavishly decorated – of the county's great tie-beam roofs overwhelming. The building is mainly late 15th-cent. but incorporates a good deal of earlier masonry (identified usually by bigger stones); the roof is dated 1513. Outside, near the north porch, can be seen traces of a buttress, which was used in the 18th cent. as a fives court (this seems to have been a keen fives-playing district), with cemented-up footholds cut for climbing to the roof to retrieve balls.

The street past the church is full of fine Ham-stone buildings. The Treasurer's House (so called because the local vicar was formerly Treasurer of WELLS Cathedral) is partly 13th-cent., but mainly 14th- and 15th-cent. The Market House, at the head of the street, is good Georgian, and the manor house, close to it, 17th-cent. The particularly attractive, low, tall-chimneyed building S. of the church began life as the Court House in the early 17th cent. or earlier, became the Grammar School and is now the Church House.

The little town makes, among other things, tarpaulins, tents and poultry houses, and is famous for the quality of its beans.

Two m. W., at **East Lambrook**, the Manor, a small, pretty, basically Tudor house with a beautiful cottage-style garden, is frequently open.

MEARE, *Somerset* (3–ST4541). In a strange, utterly flat landscape, this straggling village lay, till the 18th cent., beside a marshy lake some 5 m.

in circumference. Round and on the lake from *c.* 300 B.C. to *c.* A.D. 100 was a village of huts built on wooden stilts and heaps of brushwood. Of this scarcely a trace is visible (excavated finds are in the TAUNTON Museum). But E. of the church still stands the early-14th-cent. building where the fishermen employed to supply the monks of GLASTONBURY lived and salted and stored their catch. It can be visited (key from nearest farm). A field away is the manor house which was the summer residence in *c.* 1340 of the Glastonbury abbots. The church's tower and chancel are of the same period, its fine roofs and stone pulpit 15th-cent. The medieval wrought-iron work on its south door is among the finest in the West Country.

Wedmore, 4½ m. NNW., a small stone town raised on an "isle" in the great flatness, is the place associated with King Alfred's peace treaty with the Danes. It has a big dominant cruciform church of great local repute. It is mainly 15th-cent. with a *c.* 1200 south door under a three-story porch, particularly impressive west front, good chapel ceilings, fine Jacobean pulpit and, above it, several murals of St Christopher carrying Christ painted on top of each other, the earliest *c.* 1520.

MELLS, *Somerset* (4–ST7249). One of Somerset's prettiest villages. Coal was mined nearby until the 19th cent. Mells is unspoilt, with grey and yellow stone cottages, a good church (1460–70) in a lawn-like churchyard, and an Elizabethan manor house. The latter was for some years owned by a family by the name of Horner. The house is just W. of the church. Mells Park House, a little further W., is the work of Sir Edwin Lutyens. The church has fine stone-vaulting to its porch roof and under its tower, and a beautiful timber roof (1520) to the Horner Chapel.

Leigh-on-Mendip, 3 m. SW., has a fine church with a splendid tower and particularly good bench-ends.

MENDIPS, THE, *Somerset* (3–ST5055). This range of hills, some 25 m. long by about 5 m. wide at its centre, effectively cuts in half north-western Somerset's body and character. It has very little in common with the county's other major hills like EXMOOR and the QUANTOCKS, and is almost like those of Derbyshire, so austere (though mostly cultivated) and pale-coloured is its central plateau. It is basically of limestone over old red sandstone. Its highest part and heart are to the N. of the WELLS–AXBRIDGE road, its summit Black Down (1,068 ft) on its north-western edge. On its steep southern side are great gorges and caves, notably at CHEDDAR and WOOKEY HOLE. To the E., round Radstock and Midsomer Norton, coal has been mined since 1305, if not longer. It was settled by prehistoric man and the Romans mined it for lead. Anglo-Saxon and Norman kings hunted it for stags (*see* Axbridge). Lead mining was revived in the Middle Ages and, though practically finished by 1850, struggled on till about 1900. Mining rights were divided between four Lords

Royal. Anyone who wanted to mine bought a licence and set off to dig his trench or "scruff" (for the lead lay very close to the surface). In the 19th cent. calamine was mined round Shipham and Rowberrow. Today the main industries are farming and quarrying.

The Roman mining area was just N. of **Charterhouse** village, and just NW. a depression rather doubtfully called an amphitheatre can be seen. The later mining centre was **Priddy**. The ruins of St Cuthbert's lead mines, closed in 1908, are NW. of the crossroads at Hunter's Lodge Inn. A good place to see "scruff" diggings is Lamb Bottom, E. of the road about 1¼ m. N. of Castle Comfort Inn. Most of the isolated inns and those at Priddy date from the mining period. Outstanding viewpoints are Crook's Peak (W. of Axbridge), the top of the hill on the road N. from Westbury to Priddy, and the hill to the N. of the Roman "amphitheatre". Just SW. of East Harptree are the ruins of the Norman **Richmont Castle**, once besieged and taken by King Stephen from the supporters of Matilda. There is not much of the building to see but the site is beautiful. A curiosity beside the A39 about ½ m. S. of Green Ore is a group of four pillars bearing a slab on which is a wolf suckling Romulus and Remus; it was built by an Italian Second World War prisoner. The grandest building, though hardly a product of the Mendips, is DOWNSIDE ABBEY. The villages of CHEWTON MENDIP, COMPTON MARTIN, CROSCOMBE and Leigh-on-Mendip have particularly good churches. For centuries an annual sheep fair has been held at Priddy on the nearest Wednesday to 21 August.

MEVAGISSEY, *Cornwall* (2–SX0144). Walk up the path among the cottages on the north side of the harbour and you could almost be on a Greek Island. Fishermen and their wives sit on their doorsteps talking quietly, with children playing about them. The cottages are often three-story, the top two faced with slate or planks. They are nothing from a distance: you have to go among them.

Otherwise Mevagissey lacks the magic that overrides commercialization in LOOE or POLPERRO. In the 18th and 19th cent. it grew rich on pilchard fishing and, like so many Cornish coast villages, smuggling. Vast quantities of pilchards were exported: 4,000 tons in 1724. Italy was the biggest customer. Now the little town's main industry is tourism, but fishing is thriving again after a decline earlier in the present century.

At the far end of the north quay an attractive small museum in an 18th-cent. boat-builder's shed includes fishing gear, china-clay industry implements and a cider press. The old lifeboat shed on the other side of the harbour now houses an aquarium. After Looe this is the main centre for shark fishing.

The nearest beaches are **Polstreath** to the N. and **Portmellon** to the S. To the former you have to walk, steeply; to the latter you can drive.

Goran Haven, 2 m. S., was Mevagissey's rival in the great pilchard days. Tiny, it has one pretty street containing a supreme example of a slate-hung house, and a small beach. In Goran church, 1 m. inland, are good 16th-cent. bench-ends.

A further 2 m. S. is Dodman Point, a gorse-covered headland rising some 370 ft above the sea. You have to walk the last ½ m. to it, but on a sunny day either in spring or late summer the yellow gorse against the blue sea is stunning.

MILVERTON, *Somerset* (3–ST1225). Rich as it is in fine churches, Somerset has fewer of those splendid, rugged, graphic, carved bench-ends possessed by many Devonian and Cornish churches. Milverton's, however, has a big and fine collection of them, *c.* 1540. Moreover, the small town is attractive, much of it Georgian, North Street being particularly good.

About 4 m. SE. **Cothay Manor** is one of the finest small 15th-cent. manor houses in Britain, frequently open, but a private home and friendly, looking on to a lake with ducks and beautiful yew-hedged garden. There have been later additions but its core dates from 1481. It contains exceptional 15th-cent. wall paintings, found under several layers of plaster and wall-paper, and much else typical of the period and fascinating. Some way from a main road, it is not easy to find. Make for Greenham or Kittisford and then ask. Opposite the T-junction at **Greenham** is another attractive manor house of the same period, but it is not open.

The obelisk on the hill above **Wellington**, 3 m. E. of Cothay, is to the Duke of Wellington, erected 1817–8.

MINEHEAD, *Somerset* (3–SS9746). Hidden within this resort of much gabled Victoriana and 20th-cent. Tudor and sands so broad at low tide that the sea seems to disappear, is an exquisite village. It is on the face of the hill at the town's western end. A wide flight of tiled and cobbled steps leads up between red-stone or yellow-coloured cottages, which are mainly thatched with tall chimneys, to the big 14th- to 15th-cent. church. This contains much of interest, including an excellent screen (*c.* 1500), figured font (15th-cent.), early-17th-cent. pulpit, good modern wrought-iron and brass lectern, and a beautiful illuminated missal (*c.* 1400) in a glass case. The harbour area is also attractive: a row of former fishermen's cottages facing Quay Street with among them the little St Peter's Chapel which was originally a salt store. In Market House Lane, near the town centre, are some 1630 almshouses. The statue of Queen Anne (*c.* 1719) in Wellington Square is the work of Francis Bird. St Andrew's Church (late 19th-cent.) beside it was designed by G. E. Street.

During the Middle Ages and till the late 18th cent., Minehead was an important port, both for fishing (herrings mainly) and trade (particularly with Wales and Ireland – wool, hides, cattle and coal especially). Great fires in 1791 and 1815, the disappearance of herrings from the area, and the silting up of its harbour brought slump. But early in the 19th cent. tourists began to arrive and in 1874 came the railway.

The town has an excellent climate. On May Day it has a Hobby Horse Festival of rather less fame than PADSTOW's. The top of North Hill to the W. is moorland and affords fine walks and views over the sea and to Exmoor. Day-cruises along the coast or to Wales are offered.

Bratton Court, 1 m. W., is a fine medieval manor house, visible through its gatehouse.

MOLLAND, *Devon* (3–SS8028). The interior of the church of this small village on EXMOOR's southern slopes is exceptional in that it was restored a hundred years or so before the heyday of the Victorian improvers from whom so many churches suffered. It is, therefore, almost entirely Georgian, with box-pews nearly 5 ft high, a three-decker pulpit with heavy canopy, white walls, and a Royal coat of arms over the chancel entrance.

Near Molland during the 18th cent. the indigenous red cattle of Exmoor were transformed by selective breeding into the famous red Devons of today by the Quartly brothers, Henry and James. Devons were then valued as draught oxen as much as for beef. The Quartly's farms were West Molland Barton and Molland Chamson, both just W. of the village. They also were pioneers of the now typical hill-farm irrigation system by which moorland streams were channelled horizontally across steep fields.

In the days when Exmoor was a Royal hunting forest, Molland men were keen deer poachers. Molland Common, the first open moorland to the N., is one of the more likely places on Exmoor to see stags.

MONTACUTE, *Somerset* (3–ST4916). An almost entirely Ham-stone village with beside it one of the finest Elizabethan houses in Britain, also of Ham stone. Montacute House (frequently open to the public) was basically built 1588–1601 for Edward Phelips probably by the mason-architect William Arnold, also responsible for Wadham College, OXFORD and the remodelling of DUNSTER Castle. The Phelipses were a lawyer-politician family: Edward became Speaker of the House of Commons in 1604 and prosecuted at the trial of Guy Fawkes in 1606. The house remained in the family till 1931 when it was bought for the National Trust. From 1915 to his death in 1925 it was rented as his country home by Lord Curzon and redecorated for him by Elinor Glyn.

Its east front is beautiful; so are the gardens, still immaculately kept, with big lawns and clipped yew trees. The heavier west front was, apart from the wings, added later but is in style about 50 years earlier. It was brought stone by stone in 1786 from Clifton Maybank House, about 6 m. SE. at BRADFORD ABBAS, then being partially demolished. Until this was added Montacute had, like most Tudor houses, no corridors. The contents include good plasterwork, panelling, tapestries, paintings and furniture.

The village church contains fine 15th- and 16th-cent. effigies of Phelipses. Its chancel arch is Norman, transepts and north porch *c.* 1300, and the rest mainly 15th-cent. Just SW. of it, the embattled building, now a private residence, was the 15th-cent. gatehouse of a priory (originally Cluniac) founded in 1102, nothing else of which remains. The village's name derives from the wooded hill above – *mons acutus*: the pointed hill – on which in the 11th cent. a vision caused to be dug up the Holy Cross of WALTHAM ABBEY, Essex. The summit tower is a 1760 folly on the site of a vanished Norman castle.

At **Tintinhull**, 1½ m. N., is another, but very different, National Trust house, frequently open, with an exquisite garden and lily-pond. It is mainly *c*. 1600 with fine early-18th-cent. west front, pediment and hipped roof, and contains excellent, unpretentious furniture.

The very attractive Tintinhull Court, well seen from the road near the church, is mostly Jacobean.

MORWENSTOW, *Cornwall* (2–SS2015). A

walk of ¼ m. from the church, down and across a gorse-sided combe, brings you to the highest cliffs in Cornwall, 450 ft sheer, called Hennacliffe. In sail days this coast was among the most notorious in England: if a ship heading NE drifted SE. of a line with Hartland Point and the wind was onshore, it was practically doomed. Many bodies of drowned sailors were brought up and buried in Morwenstow churchyard.

From 1834 to 1875 the church's vicar was Robert Stephen Hawker, poet, eccentric, author of the poem "And shall Trelawney die". The vicarage he had built, with chimneys in the form of miniatures of church towers, is just NE. of the churchyard. The hut on the cliff-top to the S. of the combe was his retreat. The church itself is remarkable for the zigzag Norman work over the south porch – called by Hawker "the ripple of the lake of Gennesareth, the spirit breathing upon the waters of baptism" – and for the three western arches of the north arcade and the splendid stone carving over them, all Norman. The south window is a memorial to Hawker.

The village, well away from the church, was described by a mid-19th-cent. traveller as "a wretched hamlet". There is not much of it now.

About ½ m. SW., **Tonacombe**, a 15th- to 16th-cent. manor house can be visited by written appointment.

Two m. S. **Coombe Valley** is beautiful. The way to it passes a satellite communication station begun in 1969. At its cove, called Duckpool, rocks stretch out from the cliffs' feet in a great, exciting jagged wilderness, as at HARTLAND Quay; and there is a good beach. At the head of the valley is a pretty, restored mill. About ¼ m. S. up the hill is the wall of what was formerly an estate of the Grenvilles (Sir Richard of the *Revenge*, Sir Bevil of the Civil War battle of Stamford Hill, *see* STRATTON). The original house has gone and so has its Palladian successor, parts of which are now incorporated in SOUTH MOLTON's Town Hall. But through the gate you can glimpse a fine Georgian farm-house.

MOUSEHOLE, *Cornwall* (2–SW4626). An

architecturally consistent village with few frills. Its tiers of mainly brown-grey stone houses, slate roofs often cement-sealed against lifting winds, semi-circle a harbour once busy with pilchards.

In 1595 NEWLYN and PENZANCE were the victims of a violent episode. From four galleys that had evaded the Elizabethan admirals, 200 Spaniards landed, burned Mousehole and raped women. Four hundred more did the same at Newlyn, then, altogether, they set upon Penzance, before, in the face of a force rallied by Sir Francis Godolphin (*see* GODOLPHIN HALL), they decided they had had enough and went home. In Mousehole about the only building to survive was the 15th-cent. Keigwin Arms, in the village centre.

Now only three professional fishing boats operate from the harbour: small ones catching mackerel. But it is becoming popular with artists. John Wesley had much success here, and it still has only one pub.

On its south side is an R.S.P.C.A. Bird Sanctuary, very busy after the *Torrey Canyon* went aground in 1967.

The parish church, ½ m. NW. at Paul, contains an epitaph in Cornish, which is unusual, dated 1709. The area is said to have been one of the last strongholds of that language. Its Male Voice Choir is famous.

MUCHELNEY, *Somerset* (3–ST4224). Here,

on what was in Anglo-Saxon times an island in the marshes (the name means great island) are the remains of the second oldest monastery in the county (after GLASTONBURY's). It was founded *c*. 697, traditionally by King Ine of Wessex, and dissolved in 1538. It had a maximum of 20 resident monks. The surviving buildings are early 16th-cent.: the Abbot's House, which has a particularly good stone staircase, and the monks' barn-like wash-room, called a reredorter. The most remarkable thing in the admirable 15th-cent. church is its unusual painted ceiling (*c*. 1600) of robustly contoured lady angels in Tudor dress. Also unusual are the 13th-cent. sanctuary floor tiles which came from the abbey. Around the church are two magnificent cedars and other fine trees and shrubs. Stone snaffling from the abbey is said to account for the village's many stone-mullioned windows.

The medieval thatched priest's house is National Trust and is open by appointment.

MULLION, *Cornwall* (2–SW6719). The village

is unexciting, but its church has one of the finest sets of bench-ends in the West Country; *c*. 1535, carved in oak, their images very varied. The tower (*c*. 1500) is partly serpentine, the basic multi-coloured stone of the LIZARD peninsula.

Mullion Cove, 1 m. SW., is splendidly cliff-walled, and has a cave that may have been used by smugglers, accessible when the tide is out.

One m. SW. at **Poldhu Point**, behind a massive Victorian hotel, is a memorial marking the site of the Marconi radio station, where, in 1901, the first-ever transatlantic morse signals were transmitted and received.

NEWLYN, *Cornwall* (2–SW4628). Now a suburb of PENZANCE. It is the main fish-landing port in Cornwall, its harbour lively and colourful with deep-sea, as well as inshore, boats. Although the rest of it is rather drear, brown-grey without its neighbour MOUSEHOLE's redeeming pattern and consistency, it has some good cottages, particularly just N. of the harbour; and the Royal National Deep Sea Fishermen's Mission building is a fine one.

In the 19th and early 20th cent., it had a famous artists' colony, now moved to ST IVES. But Newlyn still has its painters and a gallery, the Passmore Edwards, by the main Penzance road.

Like Penzance and Mousehole it was ravaged by Spaniards in 1595.

NEWQUAY, *Cornwall* (2–SW8161), has the most magnificent beaches and probably ugliest town in Cornwall, and is the county's most popular seaside resort. There are vast stretches of sand, and it is probably the best place for surfing in England. Behind are tall cliffs with exciting caves, the best being in front of the north-east end of the town round Porth Island on which was Newquay's original settlement.

That settlement was Iron Age. Its remains are just visible. Virtually the only other thing visible built on this town's site before the railway reached it in 1875 is the Huer's House on the headland just W. of the harbour. Murray's 1856 *Handbook for Travellers* called Newquay "a small watering place where the pilchard industry is pursued on a considerable scale". The pilchards came abundantly, but periodically. The huer's job was to watch for the shoals reddening the water and with a great shout waken the village when he saw them.

The railway was intended to bring china clay and tin to Newquay's port. But the port was not really up to it, the water too shallow, and increasingly the trains brought mainly tourists.

The most attractive places are on the town's perimeter: the harbour, where are preserved several of the old pilot gigs which, in the 19th cent., used to escort in the cargo schooners and ketches; Trenance Gardens, in a valley to the E., containing a new zoo, Cornwall's only one; and Towan and East Pentire heads to the W. for views.

The nearest attractive church and old cottages are at **St Columb Minor,** about 2 m. E., Newquay's mother parish, now one of its suburbs. The church's 15th-cent. tower, 115 ft high, finely pinnacled and lichen-coloured, is one of Cornwall's best.

Four m. SW. is the village of **Crantock,** once famous for its smugglers. Its church is worth seeing, a show-piece of Edwardian restoration. It has an elaborate rood-screen which is mainly a reproduction, and a disproportionately large, highly decorated chancel. In the churchyard, as by many Cornish churches, the old stocks are displayed. A plaque tells the story of the last man put in them, c. 1817, "a smuggler's son and a vagabond". A road leads to splendid dunes beside the narrow, steep-sided creek of the Gannel estuary, and vast sands at low tide.

About 3 m. SE., among narrow lanes and elm trees, is **Trerice,** an Elizabethan manor house, now owned by the National Trust. It has beautiful east and south façades and fine plaster ceilings. The plasterwork, probably by an Italian, is very similar to that at BUCKLAND ABBEY and Collacombe (*see* TAVISTOCK), and the theory is that Sir John Arundell, who built Trerice, passed on his craftsman to his friends, Sir Richard Grenville and Edmund Tremayne respectively. The best route to it is via Lane and Trevilly, passing through a ford.

NEWTON ABBOT, *Devon* (3–SX8671). A purposeful, busy and unpretentious town with, on Wednesdays, the most entertaining market in South Devon. From the arrival of the railway in 1846 it grew at great pace; first as a rail junction, then increasingly as a market town and as a centre for the clay mines between **Kingsteignton,** 1¼ m. N., and **Bovey Tracey,** 5 m. NW. These mines produce some of the best quality ball-clay in the world. As a result there are several good potteries locally which can be visited: the New Devon in the Industrial Estate just E. of the station; Candy & Co. (glazed tiles) beside the A38 towards EXETER, 3½ m. NW., and, outstanding perhaps, that of David Leach, son of Bernard Leach (*see* ST IVES), called Lowerdown on the Haytor road out of Bovey Tracey.

The most interesting housing in Newton Abbot is between Courtenay Park and Devon Square, just W. of the station. Forde House, now an antique shop near the Industrial Estate entrance, was built for Sir Richard Reynell in 1610, stayed in by Charles I in 1625 and by William of Orange on his way to London (*see* BRIXHAM). It has some very good decorated plaster ceilings. Off the TOTNES road, Bradley Manor is basically 15th-cent., National Trust owned and sometimes open.

Up a road almost opposite, St Mary's Church, **Wolborough** (15th- and early 16th-cent.), has a fine early-16th-cent. screen with a great number of panel paintings. Its brass eagle lectern is 15th-cent.

Frequent National Hunt meetings are held at Newton Abbot Race-course.

Some 1½ m. E. at **Netherton,** the Teign Cider Company welcomes visitors.

Bovey Tracey (*see above*) is a pleasant, small, hillside town. Its church, which has a 14th-cent. tower but is otherwise mostly 15th-cent., had a good screen, lavishly carved and coloured stone pulpit (both early 15th-cent.), two above average 17th-cent. monuments and other good detail.

The Heath immediately S., a source of the precious clay, saw a great rout of Royalists in 1646 by forces led by Cromwell himself.

Immediately W. rises DARTMOOR, and at **Haytor,** about 3½ m. W., is one of the moor's most spectacular crags. From its old quarries came granite for the BRITISH MUSEUM and the NATIONAL GALLERY, and there was a tramway to carry the stone some 6 m. SE. to a canal wharf at Teigngrace. It operated from 1820 to 1858 when the quarries closed; can be best seen

Peter Baker

Newlyn is Cornwall's main fishing port

near where it crosses the Manaton road ⅓ m. NW. of the Rock Inn, Haytor Vale, which was built in 1825 as a quarrymen's hostelry.

About ¾ m. N. of Haytor Vale, is the **Yarner Wood National Nature Reserve**. Trees – mainly oak, rowan, holly and birch – are its main interest, but it is also rich in birds. A nature trail is marked out. Permits are necessary to visit it; these are available at the lodge at its entrance off the B3344. Bovey Tracey–Manaton road.

NEWTON FERRERS, *Devon* (3–SX5447). The approach to it leads through much holiday suburbia, but along the waterfront it is exceptionally attractive. It has a beautiful yacht anchorage in the Yealm estuary, enclosed by steep oak-wooded hillsides, the water a deep green, the yachts elegant, with a pretty group of buildings by the quay on the further shore. The majority of the cottages lining the narrow reach above the anchorage and facing Noss Mayo were built long before the village became fashionable, though few are now occupied by fishermen.

The whole estuary is beautiful and as good for walking as for boating. The slate-slab cliffs of Stoke Point, 1½ m. S., are dramatic. Close to them are the ruins of the mainly 14th-cent. Church of St Peter, built probably as a seamark.

Some 2 m. N., beside the most direct road to PLYMOUTH and well seen from the road, is Puslinch House, early Georgian in date, Queen Anne in style, a fine example of its period.

NORTH BOVEY, *Devon* (3–SX7483). A tiny thatched village of famous and considerable prettiness, round an oak-tree green. The standard of thatching is excellent. The 15th-cent. church has a screen, a waggon roof with carved bosses and bench-ends all of the same period.

One m. N., in the grounds of the vast Manor House Hotel, which was built for Viscount Hambledon of the W. H. Smith family *c.* 1907, is an immaculately kept, highly entertaining and scenically beautiful golf course.

W. from North Bovey a switchback road leads after about 2 m. to **Manaton** via a particularly exciting view of the moor. Manaton is a scattered village with dreary modern parts, but it is nice round its church, which has a good 15th-cent. screen. Just S. **Becky Falls** are spectacular after heavy rain.

Bowerman's Nose, ½ m. W., is a natural freak: a 25-ft column of rocks that looks as if a puff of wind could blow it down. Some ½ m. further on **Hound Tor** is perhaps the grandest – and certainly one of the most accessible – of the tors.

All over this area on the edge of the moor N. to CHAGFORD are fine, basically medieval farm-houses built of moorstone (surface granite).

NORTH CADBURY, *Somerset* (3–ST6327). A big Elizabethan house and 15th-cent. church, both of glowing Ham stone, stand grandly side by side at the head of a beech avenue. An out-building of the house gives the churchyard a wall for shrubs like clematis and ceanothus. The church, high and light, has a regal chancel and an exceptionally large east window, graphic 16th-cent. bench-ends (one shows a cat catching a mouse and a Tudor mouse-trap), and a fine tie-beam roof. Cadbury Court, well seen through its entrance arch and from the south side of the churchyard, was built by the 3rd Earl of Hunting-don. The village is mainly of Ham stone with pretty gardens.

NORTON ST PHILIP, *Somerset* (4–ST7755). A former wool village made famous by one of England's best-preserved and most interesting medieval inns, The George. This began life, *c.* 1230, as a guest-house for Hinton Priory, 2 m. N. (*see* WELLOW), accommodating especially, since the monks ran the wool market, merchants and staplers. Its fine half-timbered and oriel-windowed upper two stories were probably added in the 15th cent. At the Dissolution (1539) it became an inn. The Duke of Monmouth stayed here with his advisers in 1685, after his decision not to attack BRISTOL. His troops skirmished successfully with the King's nearby. In 1668 Samuel Pepys and wife "dined very well 10 shillings" in it. The room where the wool merchants bargained may be seen on request.

The church has an odd tower, with bits from the destroyed priory possibly used in it, and contains a tomb-effigy, *c.* 1460, also curious, and a plaque to "twin ladies" who had, Pepys reported, only one stomach between them.

NUNNEY, *Somerset* (4–ST7345). The tall, grey shell of a castle stands in the middle of this grey-stone, red-tiled village.

Strictly the castle is a fortified house with a moat. It was built as his home in 1373 by Sir John de la Mare, who had just returned from the war in France with, it is said, much booty. His effigy is in the church. In the Civil War the King's troops held it and were besieged. To show the enemy how well supplied they were, the garrison daily tortured their only pig to sound as if it was being slaughtered. In due course, however, Roundhead cannon broke the walls, and afterwards Cromwell ordered this castle, like so many others, to be slighted.

Beside the castle a fine Queen Anne house has a lively farmyard including peacocks, white doves, racing-pigeons and mallard. Footbridges over the moat and village stream lead to the church.

OARE, *Somerset* (3–SS8047). This village made famous by Blackmore's *Lorna Doone*, is in one of EXMOOR's most beautiful valleys, which can best be seen by turning off the A39 in Culbone Wood and driving to Brendon. Badgworthy Water (walkable only) runs N. from MALMSMEAD ($\frac{3}{4}$ m. W. of Oare), where there is a nice old bridge and ford. Two stream-valleys opening into Badgworthy from the W. – Lank Combe about $1\frac{1}{2}$ m. up and Hoccombe Combe 2 m. – have between them most of the characteristics of Blackmore's *Lorna Doone* stronghold, and both are beautiful.

OKEHAMPTON, *Devon* (3–SX5895). A splendid situation in the shadow of DARTMOOR's highest part has failed to inspire this small town to beauty. But there are things worth seeing around it.

About $\frac{1}{2}$ m. W., picturesque on a knoll above the river close to the A30, are the ruins of what was one of the largest and most important castles in Devon. Mainly 13th-cent., it was the home of the Courtenays (Earls of Devon) before they moved to Powderham (*see* KENTON). It looks especially good from the golf course on the hillside opposite. From the Army camp on the hill-top ($1\frac{1}{4}$ m. S.) a road, usable when there is no firing (watch for red flags or ask at the town Post Office), makes a loop $3\frac{1}{2}$ m. long into the wild heart of the moor, where tiny valleys make good picnic spots.

About 2 m. NE. of Folly Gate, is the **Pine Valley Wild Life Park** which was begun in 1969.

OTTERY ST MARY, *Devon* (3–SY0995). An unexciting small town, it has a large church of great age, fame and interest, if not, perhaps, beauty. Mainly 14th-cent. it is said to have been modelled on EXETER Cathedral, but close comparison would be invidious. It has stone-vaulted ceilings, a choir with a corridor round it and a Lady Chapel to the E. as in a cathedral, a clock showing the phases of the moon said to be 14th-cent., and interesting medieval effigy-tombs. Its interest is in its detail and complex history, explained at length in the guide book on sale inside. From 1061 to 1335 the manor was owned by Rouen Cathedral in France, from whom the Bishop of Exeter then bought it and greatly extended the church.

Peter Baker

Oare: an old bridge in the river valley

The poet Coleridge was born and grew up in the town and wrote a "Sonnet to the River Otter". From 1760 to 1781 his father was the local vicar. Thackeray set his *Pendennis* here. In the Chanters House (18th-cent. front) at the end of a lane N. of the church, Cromwell in 1645 convened a meeting to demand money for his Civil War cause, and Fairfax for a time made the town his headquarters. A wool centre in the Middle Ages, it turned to lace and milk in the 19th cent. The old serge mill (1788), a fine four-story brick building near the railway station, is now used by an electrical switchgear firm. Other present industries include mushroom growing, brickworks and garden nurseries. The "rolling of the tar barrels" is still enthusiastically a part of the annual carnival on 5 November.

Cadhay, 1 m. NW., is one of the finest Tudor houses in Devon, built *c.* 1550 by a lawyer, John Haydon. It is periodically open.

The Otter is a good – and pretty – trout stream.

PADSTOW, *Cornwall* (2–SW9175). "One of those antiquated, unsavoury fishing-towns which are viewed most agreeably from a distance." (Murray's *Handbook*, 1856.) It remains antiquated but not unsavoury. With ST IVES and PORT ISAAC it is one of the three most attractive towns of the Cornish north coast, with narrow, mainly unspoilt streets converging on its harbour and an unusually pretty semi-circle of buildings round the quay. The good stonework in the older buildings is notable.

It was already a village when in the 6th cent.

St Petroc came from Ireland in his coracle to give it a monastery. From then until the West Saxons came in the 9th cent. it was Cornwall's ecclesiastical capital. In the Middle Ages it was much visited by Irish pilgrims *en route* to Santiago de Compostela in Spain. Till the mid-19th cent. it was important for building war, cargo and fishing boats, but the gradual sanding up of its harbour caused this and its fishing industry to decline. However, its estuary remains a cherished place of shelter for trawlers in rough weather. In the 19th cent. the sand from the bar across the estuary's mouth, The Doom Bar, was widely valued as fertilizer owing to its high carbonate of lime content. Till 1952 its lifeboat, formerly at Rock across the estuary, was Britain's largest, and the amount it was used can be seen from the shipwreck chart on a wall in the North Quay.

Its most interesting buildings are Prideaux Place, a fine, castellated Elizabethan house, built on what may have been the site of St Petroc's monastery, not normally open to the public but visible from the road; Abbey House on the North Quay, 15th-cent., built possibly as an assembly house for merchants; Raleigh's Court House, 16th-cent., on the South Quay, where Sir Walter presided when he was Warden of Cornwall; and St Petroc's Church. The latter, mainly 15th-cent., has a fine, strong tower (with odd bulges round the windows), excellent stonework, a particularly good Elizabethan pulpit and aisle roof, and an elaborate Prideaux memorial.

Padstow's great annual event is the Hobby Horse dance festival on May Day. It is claimed to be the oldest dance festival in Europe, and is proudly and keenly kept going.

The two-pronged peninsula to the NW. of the town is ringed by splendid sea places: **Constantine Bay** has the greatest stretch of sand, **Treyarnon** has one of the best surfing beaches in England. Near **Harlyn**, the dullest beach, an Iron Age cemetery was discovered in 1900. A museum beside the lower Polmark Hotel contains finds from it. Virtually all carved slate to be seen in Cornish churches came from cliff quarries just W. of Harlyn; called catacleuse, it was the only type of slate that could be carved with any ease.

The peninsula's eastern prong is the least developed; the cliffs round Day Mark Beacon (you have to walk) are good for seeing sea-birds.

PENFOUND MANOR, Cornwall (2–SX21 99). About 1 m. E. of the A39 at Poundstock, is one of the oldest inhabited manor houses in Britain, once owned by the wife of Edward the Confessor, and with one Anglo-Saxon wall 6 ft thick. Most of what you can see is Elizabethan, but it has much charm. The timbers of the staircase and one of the beds, found washed up on an Irish shore, came from Spanish Armada galleons. The tester bed is fine; so are the Florentine early-18th-cent. wrought-iron gates. A stream from the well used to run through the house via an indoor pool.

The house is privately owned, government subsidized and can be visited.

PENZANCE, Cornwall (2–SW4731), was the first Cornish town to become a resort. It is the only Cornish resort with a promenade; rather a grand one, backed by Victorian and some Regency terraces, looking to a fine bay and ST MICHAEL'S MOUNT. It is the western end of the railway and receives flowers from the Scillies, and recently its own market gardening has become quite prosperous. With a population of about 14,500 it is the county's third largest single town.

It grew on the tin trade and, perhaps, smuggling. In 1595 Spaniards burned what little there was of it (*see* MOUSEHOLE). It rebuilt itself energetically, and though ravaged by both sides in the Civil War became in the 19th cent. a stannary town (*see* HELSTON). In 1769 its mayor was well known to be a smuggler. In it, as in CAMBORNE and REDRUTH, mining problems stimulated science; of the several notable scientists and engineers it has produced, the greatest was Humphry Davy (1778–1829), world-famous chemist as well as inventor of the miner's safety lamp for which he is generally known.

The town has few outstanding buildings – the 1836 pillared market hall (now Lloyds bank) in the main street behind a statue of Humphry Davy is the most impressive. The Morrab municipal gardens are admirable, containing a modern recreation room for people over 60. There are three museums: the Geological (its Royal Geological Society was founded in 1814) in the Municipal Buildings opposite the Information Bureau; the Penlee containing local archaeological finds a model of CHYSAUSTER; and at No. 52 Chapel Street is a new one containing finds brought up by frogmen from the ship *Association*, sunk in 1707.

Two m. W. **Trengwainton Gardens** contain *Embothrium coccineum lanceolatum, Eucryphia × nymansensis, Magnolia campbellii* and, among the rhododendrons, several from Assam and Burma, which flowered here for the first time in Britain. They were given to the National Trust by Sir Edward Bolitho in 1961.

Just N. of **Madron** (1½ m. NW.), and about ⅓ m. down a footpath to the E. is what was once perhaps the most famed of Cornwall's holy wells; now not very impressive.

About 1½ m. NE. of Penzance town centre, **Gulval**'s churchyard is thick with sub-tropical plants; the embothriums are outstanding, particularly in a May evening sun. Gulval is an interesting example of a moneyed Victorian attempt to make a "pretty" village.

PERRANPORTH, Cornwall (2–SW7554). St Piran's "lost church" is one of the oldest in Britain. Built between the 7th and the 10th cents., it had by the 11th cent. been abandoned under drifting sand. It was cleared again in the 19th cent. Periodically the sands have also revealed bones from its cemetery. In 1910 it was encased for protection in a hideous concrete building and after wet weather is often flooded. But it is extraordinary and the walk to it (about 1 m. over easy ground) from a turning off the

NEWQUAY road about 1 m. N. of Perranporth, is into grand sand-dune country. About 400 yds NE. of it, clear on the skyline, stands a fine Celtic cross, 8 ft 10 in. high, close to where, in *c.* 11th cent., a second church (now demolished) was built to replace the lost one, only in its turn to be made unusable by sand in 1803.

The **Piran Round,** beside the Newquay road, about 1¾ m. NE. of Perranporth, is an Iron Age hill-camp, later used as a place for games. In 1969 students from the BRISTOL University Drama Department gave performances there of a Cornish trilogy of *c.* 1350.

Perranporth itself, once a tin-mining village (peak year 1874), is now an architecturally typical small resort with fine sands and a good seaside golf course. At Droskyn Point, just S., cliffs are carved into arches, some by nature, some by mining.

St Piran was a 5th-cent. saint, supposedly from Ireland. He was the patron saint of tinners.

PLYMOUTH, *Devon* (3–SX4755). With a population of 247,000, nearly three times that of any other town in the South-West apart from BRISTOL, Plymouth is a city (since 1928, embracing the formerly separate towns of Devonport and Stonehouse) without a cathedral. Because it was the base of Elizabethans like Drake, Raleigh, Hawkins and Gilbert, rather than by official choice, it became, during the 16th-cent. Spanish Wars, the base of the English Navy. On the Hoe, so tradition says, Drake finished his game of bowls before dealing with the Armada. Then in 1689, with William of Orange's decision to build the Royal Dockyard on the marshes that were to become Devonport, about a mile W. (at that time) of the town, it gained the Navy officially; and has kept it. As late as 1952, Nikolaus Pevsner could write, "it is the only British city whose existence appears to be centred on war". Now it is having to change. Since the Second World War at least 25 industries have been established about the city, but it needs more. The Navy still employs nearly a third of its employable men, but it will not always need so many.

It is a city of distinct parts, two of them well worth wandering through: its modern central area and the Barbican. German bombs, 1940–3, smashed its centre even more comprehensively than Exeter's; Plymouth's rebuilding has been much the more ambitious. For a tremendous view, to get your bearings, and to appreciate the extent of the bomb damage, a good first move is, by lift, to the top of the skyscraper Civic Centre (1962). On the ground floor, which is an exhibition gallery, the Information Bureau will supply a map. Of the new buildings the Council Chambers, in the two-story block adjoining the Civic Centre, and the Law Courts, with a perforated concrete screen over its doorway, are especially worth considering; as, not only for its architecture, is the multi-domed Market a little to the NW. No other West Country market has such almost oriental vitality and concern for appearance in its stall dressing. Slightly less of a

success is the Guildhall (opposite the Civic Centre), partly – including its tower – 1870–4, rebuilt. The windows of its main hall are quite interesting. Far better, however and indeed the best modern windows in Devon, are those by John Piper in the Parish Church of St Andrew's next door, which was bombed and has now been restored. Immediately SE. of this church, the 15th-cent. Prysten House is the city's oldest building, probably built for the monks of Plympton Priory (4 m. NE.) who till 1439 ruled the place.

Then the Barbican. This, perhaps the most attractive small urban area in Devon, is the site of the original town as Drake knew it, beside the harbour of Sutton Pool around which, in the 12th cent. when Exeter was a major city, was merely "a mene thing as an inhabitation for fishers". Its streets are narrow and sloping; the harbour packed with boats both for pleasure and commercial fishing. Two or three new housing blocks blend excellently with the old – notably Hanover Court. Several genuine Elizabethan merchants' houses survive, and No. 32 New Street is period furnished and open to inspection, as is in Southside Street, the 16th-cent. refectory of a Dominican friary incorporated in a gin distillery. On the Quay the Old and New Customs Houses were built in 1586 and 1810 respectively. At the Mayflower Steps, plaques commemorate that and other famous sailings. And there are good pubs about.

After these two areas there is, of course, the Hoe, with one of Britain's great harbour-views, and the outstanding Aquarium of the Marine Biological Association beside the Citadel. The best thing about this otherwise dreary barracks, founded in 1670 by Charles II to keep in order the town which had for two years resisted his father's forces, is its Baroque main gateway. Smeaton's Tower was from 1759 to 1882 the lighthouse on Eddystone Rock (14 m. S.). It was replaced because the rock began to give way and was re-erected as a decoration on the Hoe. Drake's Island in the Sound, one-time fortress, then a prison, is now an "adventure centre" running courses for youth organizations and schools.

Other attractions are scattered. Perhaps the grandest building in the city is the Royal William Victualling Yard (naval supply centre) built 1826–35 by Sir John Rennie. It is in Stonehouse, about 1 m. W. of the Hoe; not open but well seen from the Cremyll Ferry or the end of the pier at low tide. Further W. in Devonport, H.M. Dockyard, containing much of naval, architectural, and also macabre interest, can at times be visited if you are British. Back in Plymouth, in the middle of a roundabout, the shell of Charles Church (1664) – said to be the only church built in Devon in that century – is kept as a memorial to the 1,172 people killed, and thousands more hurt, by German bombs. Near it, in Tavistock Road, the Museum and Art Gallery is a highly enterprising one with a particularly good section on prehistoric DARTMOOR, several portraits by Sir Joshua Reynolds, a room of good contem-

Plymouth Hoe: Smeaton's Tower was the original lighthouse on Eddystone Rock

porary paintings and two Epstein busts. In Central Park is, among other amusements, a zoo.

Finally the work of John Foulston. In the early 19th cent. this London emigrant architect gave parts of the conurbation (as it was then) a splendour exceeded in the West Country only by BATH. Bombs accounted for most of his work in Plymouth, but till recently much of his Devonport Civic Centre and his terraces in Ker Street survived. Now most of these, too, have gone, leaving his Town Hall (1823), modelled on the Parthenon, "Egyptian-style" Odd Fellows' Hall, and column, all looking very dejected in one of the city's slummiest districts. Probably his happiest surviving work – very pretty still and smart – is Albermarle Villas, off Paradise Road, Devonport, built 1828–30 for retired sea captains.

Just outside the city are two of Devon's finest houses open to the public. About 3 m. NE. of the Civic Centre, **Saltram** (National Trust) is mainly mid- to late 18th-cent. round a Tudor core and with 19th-cent. additions by Foulston. It was built for the Parker family, chiefly for John Parker, M.P. for Devon 1762–84. It is ornately, but exquisitely, furnished and decorated, with several rooms by Robert Adam, probably the finest collection of paintings in Devon including many by Reynolds, who was a friend of the family, and is set in fine grounds containing an orangery.

For **Antony House**, just across the Tamar W., *see* CAWSAND.

At **Plympton St Maurice**, which was an important stannary (*see* ASHBURTON), market and industrial town, but is now quietly residential, are the ruins of a 12th-cent. castle (from which there is a nice view), and the 17th-cent. (restored) Guildhall is open. Sir Joshua Reynolds was born here and went to the local grammar school.

POLPERRO, *Cornwall* (2–SX2051). Although tourism has replaced smuggling (the Preventive Service was created in the early 1800s for Polperro's particular benefit), this remains one of the most magical of Cornish coastal villages. The commercialization is not too ugly, and the ban on cars in its heart, enforced by local attitude rather than law, admirable.

It lies in not so much a combe as a ravine; its harbour mouth is so narrow that in rough weather it can be closed by stout, metal-tipped timbers fitted into slots. The least titivated old cottages are round the west end of the quay. In the Warren, on the quay's east side, a house's front has been embossed all over with shells in various patterns by a retired fisherman. Close to it is an entertaining smugglers' museum. The house, probably Elizabethan, lived in for 60 years in the 19th cent. by Dr Jonathan Couch, village doctor, naturalist and collector of fossils, can be visited.

Not surprisingly, perhaps, the village is some distance from its two churches; **Talland,** 1½ m. E., and **Lansallos,** 2½ m. W. Both contain good wood-carving; below both are good bathing beaches. It is a pleasant walk to both, and rare wild flowers can be found in the cliffs.

PORLOCK, *Somerset* (3–SS8846), is a large, lively village, marvellously situated between EXMOOR and the sea at the head of a beautiful vale stretching E. to MINEHEAD. Porlock is popular with riders and has a famous riding school. It is also an ideal base for Exmoor, and Anglo-Saxon kings may have had a hunting lodge here.

Its buildings are a medley, some pretty, some far from it. Some are thatched, including a good group opposite the church. The best is Doveray Court at the east end, a 15th-cent. manor, now partly reading rooms. The church, mainly 13th-cent., contains the tomb of John Harrington, who is said to have fought at Agincourt and who died in 1418. It is topped by an almost lifesize alabaster effigy of him and his wife.

Though the village is under 1 m. from the sea, private fields separate them, and to reach the shore you must go to **Porlock Weir,** 1½ m. W., or down a lane from Bossington, 1 m. NE. And then there is no sand, just pebble banks. Porlock Weir is pretty, with a small harbour, pubs and cottages. From it you can walk to CULBONE.

Porlock Hill, the start of the road to LYNTON, is one of the steepest in Britain, the view back from its top one of the most beautiful. The Toll Road is attractive and less steep, but misses this view.

PORTHCURNO, *Cornwall* (2–SW3822), has an exceptional beach of almost white sand, and would be worth visiting just to see the open-air Minack theatre, even if you cannot attend a performance. The Minack is the nearest thing in Britain to an ancient Greek theatre and probably even the Greeks never managed a grander site, hewn from the face of granite-slab cliffs, some 200 ft above the waves. Its creation was the inspiration of Miss Rowena Cade, whose little terrace rock garden, older than the theatre, is also cut out of the cliffs beside it, and was largely built by her and two men in six months in 1932. In that year the theatre staged *The Tempest.* Its summer season productions since have ranged from *King Lear,* to *The Hostage,* to *West Side Story.* Some later, concrete additions to the theatre have been made, but so well has it been cut and weathered that it is often hard to distinguish from stone. All box-office takings and sixpences in the box provided go to maintenance and expenses.

The village is a terminal for underwater transoceanic telegraph and telephone lines, which accounts for the Cable and Wireless Station.

About ½ m. W. of the Minack, the parish church, St Levan's, is pretty, with some finely carved 15th-cent. bench-ends and lower half of a rood-screen, and several crosses in its churchyard made beautiful by grey-green lichen.

Porthgwarra, ½ m. further W. but about 2¾ m. round by car, is as undefaced as any cove accessible by car on the Penwith peninsula. A tunnel through the cliffs leads from its few and attractive cottages to the base of a steep hard, up which small boats are winched. About ¼ m. W. is a great crater in the cliff-top about 100 yds across and 80 ft deep.

From **Treen,** a nice hamlet about 1½ m. E. of Porthcurno, a walk of about 1 m. leads to a famous logan stone on the cliffs. In 1824 a boisterous naval lieutenant unperched it and was made to replace it at his own expense. It now takes some moving; but the cliffs make the walk worthwhile.

Two m. NE. of Treen, **St Buryan** has a grand big granite church, dominating not only its grey village but the tree-scarce miles around, and containing a well-restored, late 15th- or early 16th-cent. screen, unusually lavishly carved for Cornwall.

One m. N. of St Buryan is the **Boscawen-un,** the most famous of Cornish prehistoric stone circles, with 19 stones standing round a leaning pillar. It is where the Gorsedd of the Bards of Cornwall is sometimes held. A footpath S. from the A30 leads in about ¼ m. to it.

Near Drift, 1½ m. NW. of here, is **Carn Euny,** an ancient ruined settlement and fine fogou (*see* St Just-in-Penwith).

PORT ISAAC, *Cornwall* (2–SW9980), is the most Mediterranean of the Cornish north-coast villages, all its old part compressed into an exceedingly steep combe with white-washed walls bulging precariously, staircases up to front doors, alleys bridged by first stories, crooked slate and cement-grouted roofs. All converges on the harbour, which is the whole narrow inlet formed by cliffs on two sides, the beach on a third, with a man-made breakwater across the mouth. You do not immediately feel the place lives on tourists. A long, finely stoned warehouse by the harbour is the headquarters of the local shell fishermen.

To the motorist it is tantalizing. It does not provide anywhere to stop, let alone park, below the new village on top of the hill.

About 2 m. W. at the head of a tiny, curved, secret inlet is **Portquin,** a fishing hamlet till the occasion when in the last century many of its men were drowned. Now it consists of about four old-grey-brown stone cottages, intelligently done up, and about the same number in ruins. It is beautiful, with no new building near it. On the headland W. of it is a folly, a sort of dwarf castle built in about 1830, called Doyden Castle. The National Trust owns it and lets it for holidays.

PROBUS, *Cornwall* (2–SW8947), has, it is generally agreed, the county's finest tower; beautifully carved yet streamlined, seeming French in the elaborate carving which yet avoids over-ornate effect; attractively green-coloured by lichen; 125 ft high. It was built between *c.* 1523 and *c.* 1560; the granite for it is said to have been carried by the villagers from quarries near St Stephens, about 5 m. NE. The interior is an anticlimax.

Trewithen, a 17th-cent. and Georgian house about 1½ m. E., has famous gardens.

Ladock, 2½ m. N., has a small folk museum at Bissick Manor.

At **Tresillian Bridge,** about 1¼ m. W., Cornish Royalist resistance ended with surrender to Fairfax in 1646.

QUANTOCKS, THE, *Somerset* (3–ST1537). This ridge of hills – about 12 m. long by some 3 m. wide and 1,261 ft at its highest – looks best from the S. and W., and particularly splendid from just E. of Elworthy on the B3188. In some ways it is similar to Exmoor, with heather, whortleberries and bracken on its top and fine views to the sea, and it is one of the very few places in England with wild red deer (introduced from Exmoor in *c.* 1861) and stag hunting. It lacks, however, Exmoor's romantic bare horizons, as it is much more heavily wooded. It also has far more fine houses about its lower slopes. One reason for this is that the surrounding lowlands are much more fertile than Exmoor's (apart, notably, from the latter's Vale of Porlock); another that it was never frozen by being a royal hunting forest. Soon after the Conquest it was parcelled out to Norman barons and its estates have changed families less than in most areas.

Among its grand houses well seen from the road are **Halswell,** near Goathurst (1689, now flats and far from its former splendour but still beautiful), **Durleigh Manor** (15th-cent.), overlooking the reservoir 1 m. W. of Bridgwater, Dodington, Crowcombe Court (Georgian) and Cothelstone. Its best villages include **Spaxton, Enmore,**

East **Quantoxhead** and CROWCOMBE. The one road crossing the moorland part of the ridge is a beautiful drive from Over Stowey to Crowcombe. Near **Aisholt** is a new reservoir on which sailing is allowed. Cockercombe, Seven Wells Combe and Hoddens Combe (HOLFORD) are outstandingly wooded valleys on the north-east side. The west side is much the steeper. The stag-hunting seasons are spring and late summer, and winter for hinds. Some of the regular places for meets are the Traveller's Rest pub, Cothelstone, Plainsfield, Holford and Triscombe Stone. A walkers' track runs the length of the ridge's top and is worth using. Quietness may be rewarded by the sight of a deer, fox, or, at dusk, a badger. There are plenty of ponies, and birds that may be seen include buzzards, kestrels, meadow pipits and, if you are lucky, both green and spotted woodpeckers.

QUEEN CAMEL, *Somerset* (3–ST5924), displays the ability, typical of Somerset villages, to avoid being corrupted by a main through road. The immediate approach from the W. to its church, via a cobbled lane of grey-stone cottages, is exceptionally pretty. The church's interior is also beautiful. Yellow 14th-cent. arcades harmonize superbly with *c.* 1500 deep-brown tie-beam roof, pulpit and extra good screen: all very simple without elaborate decoration or huge monuments. The bells are said to be the heaviest six in the world. In the 16th cent. the village was "famous for its fine peel of bells and for the fine sort of brown thread called nun's thread".

Beside the road N. to Sparkford is the 17th-cent. entrance arch for what was intended to be the world's most splendid house, but never built. It was to have been at Low Ham, near LANGPORT, whence the arch was brought. Behind it now is Hazelgrove House, which was built in 1732 by J. and W. Bastard, the BLANDFORD FORUM architects, and is now a preparatory school.

ROCHE, *Cornwall* (2–SW9860). A group of crags, the tallest about 100 ft and topped by the ruined Chapel of St Michael (saint of high hills), rise out of a drear plain on this northern edge of the china-clay country. They are known as Roche Rocks and still make a dramatic picture even if, these days, rather dwarfed by the clay mountains to the S. The chapel was built in 1409 as part of a hermitage. From it there is a fine view of the village cricket pitch and the church's 15th-cent. tower which, with its Norman font, is its best feature.

The Rocks are just SE. of the village.

The village laments the closing of its railway which used to take china clay to FOWEY and Par.

ST ANTHONY IN MENEAGE, *Cornwall* (2–SW7725). This is one of Cornwall's most dulcet, luxuriant corners, and the change is dramatic as you come to it, quite suddenly, from the bleak plateau, 200 ft to 300 ft high, and fierce coasts that constitute most of the Lizard peninsula. The road from Manaccan, which has a famous fig tree growing from its church's south wall, clings to Gillan Creek, canopied by mighty pines. The church stands no more than 30 yds from where sailing boats are pulled up from a waveless sea. On one side of it is a farmyard, on another the Georgian rectory, and behind, among its gravestones, a holy well. It is said to have been built by Normans who were shipwrecked nearby and vowed to build St Anthony a church if he would save them. The chancel and parts of the south wall are Norman. It contains nothing marvellous, is just extremely pretty and idyllically situated.

ST AUSTELL, *Cornwall* (2–SX0152). The china-clay capital: the spoil heaps like white mountains behind the town when approached from the E. The industry employs nearly 35 per cent of the working population of the St Austell area. The clay, used in making paper, face-cream, paint, some medicines and numerous other products as well as for porcelain, is one of Britain's major exports and apart from China, Britain is the world's main producer of it. William Cookworthy discovered it in Cornwall in 1755. The first pits opened soon afterwards, and St Austell grew steadily from a tin-mining village into a town with a population of about 20,000. Yet its centre has more the air of a market town than an industrial one.

Its church built of stone from Pentewan, some 4 m. S., is exceptional. Its 15th-cent. tower is decorated, finely and unusually for a Cornish church, with sculptured figures. Inside, a curious thing is a pronounced bend in the axis of the church at the entrance to the chancel. Whether this was for dramatic effect, or due to a building difficulty, or accidental, or to symbolize the droop of Christ's head as he died on the Cross, no one is sure. There is a fine late-Norman font and a good waggon roof.

Just S. of the main street (Fore Street) is a pedestrian precinct with overhead walkways and the like. Of the other modern buildings locally the biggest of the china-clay driers is impressive. It is on the outskirts of the town, well-seen from Trewoon, 1 m. W. on the NEWQUAY road.

But after the church the important thing not to miss is **Menacuddle Well**, about ¼ m. out, on the left of the BODMIN road. It is an enchanting place, with rhododendrons, one at least 30 ft high, growing among great beeches, a stream, made milk-like by china clay, pouring over small waterfalls; a bridge over it leading to a tiny granite shrine over a Holy Well, the waters of which, it was believed, strengthened weakling children; nearby, a granite chair.

On the top of a hill about 1¼ m. NE. of the town centre is the tremendous Carclaze mine. Originally an open-cast tin-mine, then worked for china clay, it is now used for purifying the latter.

Two of the nicest seaside places locally are **Porthpean** and **Ropehaven**, about 1½ m. and 3 m. S. respectively. **Charlestown**, about 1 m. SE., is a small china-clay port, surprisingly pretty with late-Georgian houses and a good beach close by. There is good bathing here in the shelter of Carlyon Bay.

ST CLEER, *Cornwall* (2–SX2468). This village is the core of an area of ancient monuments, strange natural phenomena, ruined mine buildings and hill-farms, and a scattering of hamlets that once housed miners and quarrymen. Its church has a splendid, tall, dark tower, as you approach from the S. its top, with yellow-lichened pinnacles looking oddly like a crown sitting on top of the hill. The Holy Well, beside the road about 200 yds NE. of it, was a healing well. Caradon Hill to the NE., with an I.T.V. transmitter, had perhaps the greatest of Cornish copper mines, employing some 4,000 men in the mid-19th cent.

Trethevy Quoit, ¾ m. NE., is, with LANYON QUOIT, the most easily accessible of Cornwall's prehistoric chambered tombs, and, of the two, perhaps the more imposing because it is taller. It is about 20 yards from the road.

About 3 m. N. is a famous natural pile of rocks known as the **Cheesewring,** owing to its similarity to a cheese press. You are locally advised to sit in a natural stone chair beside it and have a word with the Devil. Close to it are several slightly smaller formations. The views from here are tremendous.

Just W. of Minions, some 200 yds from the road, are three stone circles called The Hurlers because, says tradition, the stones are men petrified for playing hurling on the Sabbath.

Two m. further SW. King's Doniert's Stone has faint carvings on it, which have been deciphered as "Doniert ordered . . . for . . . his soul". It is suggested he may have been otherwise known as King Dungarth of Cornwall, drowned in 875. Siblyback Lake, beside which East Cornwall Water Board signs invite you to picnic, is a new reservoir 1 m. N. of here, field-banked, treeless, like a gigantic puddle.

Continuing SW. the hard country drops to the River Fowey. From Draynes Bridge is a beautiful, if rather popular, ½-m. walk downstream to Golitha Falls.

ST CLETHER, *Cornwall* (2–SX2084). Here, in hill-farm land on the northern edge of Bodmin Moor, is the largest of Cornwall's numerous holy well chapels. Built in the 15th cent. on a site sacred since the 5th, it was restored by that enormously energetic man, the Rev. Sabine Baring-Gould, prolific author and hymn writer ("Onward Christian Soldiers"), in 1895. It is very simple, an altar consisting of a slab of granite resting on two others being the only furnishing, fresh aired, and well looked after, and is sited on the hillside below granite crags which shelter it from three sides.

You can park by the church, which is not special; collect the key from the church porch; head W. by SW. keeping below the crags and after about ⅓ m. reach it.

About 2 m. E. is the extremely beautiful little church of **Laneast.** Its interior has tremendous rustic integrity, and is mostly ancient, containing 38 bench-ends, all different, carved between 1450 and 1500, fascinating both for their execution and subject matter; a waggon roof with finely carved bosses and cornices; an early-16th-cent.

pulpit; fragments of 15th-cent. glass in the east window; a somewhat later but attractive screen. Outside the south porch is a fine Celtic wheel-cross found while digging a grave not long ago. John Wesley preached in the church.

There is a holy well at the bottom of the field across the road, the water of which is still used for baptisms.

ST COLUMB MAJOR, *Cornwall* (2–SW 9163), feels darkly ancient. Its narrow main street is now the A39, but the traffic seem to bruise rather than influence it. It has fascinating slate-hung houses, but many need repair. It produced a champion wrestler, James Polkinghorne (later landlord of the Red Lion), and is a stronghold of the wild Cornish version of hurling (played every Shrove Tuesday and the second Saturday after). "Agriculture and its associated rural undertakings" are, it states, the main industries of its population of about 3,250. Its back streets are full of interest.

The church is clearly important, looking unexpectedly grand in a big, treeless churchyard. The tower is oddly semi-detached, acting as a porch for the next door. Inside are some of the best 16th- and 17th-cent brasses in Cornwall, to the Arundells of Lanherne (*see* ST MAWGAN IN PYDAR), long its patrons; also many well-carved, 16th-cent. bench-ends and exposed barrel-roof timbers. In 1676 it was accidentally partially blown up. Like the rest of the town, it makes little attempt to charm. Close to the lych-gate the Glebe House (1638) is excellently slate-hung.

In the valley N. of the church the former rectory (now a hotel), rebuilt in 1855, is, for some uncertain medieval reason, moated.

On **Castle-an-Dinas** (700 ft), 2¼ m. E. and ½-m. climb from the road, is the most elaborate prehistoric fort in Cornwall; three rings of earthworks are visible.

ST CUBERT, *Cornwall* (2–SW7857). In a windswept landscape just inland from the dunes, the church has a curious tower with spire looking rather like a bishop's hat, and windows so placed to look like eyes. The interior was well restored by G. E. Street in 1852, and has a low roof with extremely fine medieval roof bosses. The pulpit, made up of old bench-ends, is good, too; so is the Norman font and slate floor. Close to the ground in the tower's outside west wall is a stone bearing an inscription, which, translated, reads: "Conectocius, son of Tegerno, a sad loss". It is said to have been carved by an Anglo-Saxon mason in the 7th cent.

In a cave at the hamlet of **Holywell,** 2 m. NW., is the Holy Well of St Cubert (about whom little is known), accessible only at low tide. The water was particularly renowned for the cure of children's skin diseases, though modern science deems it unextraordinary. Steps lead down to the largest of a series of small natural rock basins.

ST ENDELLION, *Cornwall* (2–SW9978). St Endellion was a virgin saint, daughter of a 6th-cent. Welsh king, who lived as a hermit feeding on nothing but the milk of her cow. Before she died – killed by a landlord on whose property her cow trespassed – she had asked that her body be put on a cart pulled by young cattle, that they be allowed to run free and that she should be buried where they stopped: St Endellion Church marks the spot. It is beautiful, compact and sturdy, built of LUNDY ISLAND granite in a windswept landscape. Inside it is spacious and uncluttered, with a fine barrel roof and, at the south-east end, a magnificently carved slate altar-tomb dated *c.* 1400. In the churchyard are several Georgian headstones bearing entertaining inscriptions.

At **St Minver**, about 2½ m. SW., is another church worth visiting, outwardly very different in character, with a 120-ft spire and altogether softer surroundings. The way into the churchyard from the E. is pretty, between a bay-windowed cottage and its paved garden. The north lych-gate has a granite cattle-grid. Inside, the church has some good 16th-cent. benches, a fine memorial brass (1517) in the floor of the south aisle, and a "Vinegar Bible" dated 1717. It was restored, but not too fiercely, in the 19th cent., by St Aubyn.

St Enodoc, about 1½ m. further W., has probably the finest golf course in Cornwall. And surrounded by its fairways, beside the 9th green, is the little, basically Norman Church of St Enodoc. For centuries, till 1863, it was buried in drifted sand, only its stubbed spire visible. To prove he had a job to do the clergyman used once a year to descend through a hole in the roof to hold a service. The best way to it is from Daymer, down a path past affluent houses amid cedars. On Brea Hill, just to the W. of the church, was a Roman settlement.

The best beaches in the locality are at **Polzeath**, 1 m. N., and at **Rock**, 1½ m. S., which is good for sailing and water-skiing, too.

ST GERMANS, *Cornwall* (2–SX3557). This is one of the prettiest of the county's villages, its cottages beautifully consistent and simple, dappled with the rust-coloured stone characteristic of the area.

Athelstan set up a bishopric here for Devon and Cornwall *c.* 936. In 1043 it moved to CREDI-TON and in *c.* 1162 a priory of Augustinian canons was established at St Germans. It is the priory church which remains. Its west face is Norman with in its centre a magnificent, cathedral-like doorway. The tops of the two interestingly different towers were built on the bases of Norman ones, the north in the early 13th cent., the south in the 15th. The body of the church has at various times been much altered (a north aisle was demolished in 1802). However, recent restoration has been with a fine sense of the dramatic, and the interior retains a grandly baronial air, its 13th-cent. font of Purbeck stone looking particularly splendid. The east window is by the painter, Burne-Jones. Below the north tower is an outstanding monument by Rysbrack, 1722, to Edward Eliot, showing him in Roman dress. The Eliots live in Port Eliot, next to the church on the site of the old priory. It is a fine house, largely rebuilt in the early 19th cent. with parts by Sir John Soane.

At the west end of the village is an interesting row of 17th-cent. almshouses. To the E., a little out of the village, is the quay, no longer used commercially, with a railway viaduct looming over it. At its entrance a board gives the old tariffs. Stone used to be shipped from it. Cornwall has many prettier places, but it is peaceful and nostalgic.

ST IVES, *Cornwall* (2–SW5140), is a magnet for artists, of which it has probably the most per head of population of any town in Britain, and for tourists. Its shape and situation are marvellous and, thanks partly to the artists who have fought hard to stop it becoming like NEWQUAY, its old part remains mostly unspoilt.

In the last century it was among the most prosperous of Cornwall's many pilchard ports – 75 million fish, it is said, being taken in one day in 1864 – and copper and tin were shipped from it. Then, in the 1880s, just as these industries were declining, painters came and delighted in its clear light; others followed.

St Ives seems always to have been fairly anti-establishment. When, in 1497, the pretender Perkin Warbeck landed nearby, it proclaimed him King. In the Civil War it was for Parliament amid mainly Royalist neighbours. John Wesley found it a good source of converts, his effect reflected in street names like Teetotal and Salubrious Place.

The best part of the town is on the neck of land between the harbour and the grand surfing beach of Porthmeor. The streets here are narrow and steep, but there are good big car parks all round. Among the prettiest streets are Fore Street, the main street, which has excellent shops, Digey and Bethesda Hill, which are steep alleys, and Back Street East. Near the east end of the latter is the museum, which includes a good section of the town's history and former industries, and paintings by the founders of the artists' colony. Also in Back Street East is the excellent Penwith Gallery, the main one for contemporary abstract paintings. In Norway Square is the St Ives Society of Arts Gallery, the main figurative one, in a former Victorian-built church.

The church, mainly 15th-cent., is of unusual brown Zennor granite. It is fine, if not outstanding, with excellent waggon roof and, in the Lady Chapel, a Madonna and Child by Barbara Hepworth, the sculptress, who lives in the town and was in 1968 awarded its freedom. Another of its distinguished artist residents is Bernard Leach, whose potteries are in the Stennack. Until recently it was the home of Ben Nicholson and Peter Lanyon, who was killed in his glider. Patrick Heron lives at Zennor, 4½ m. W. Roger Hilton, Bryan Winter and Alan Davie frequent it.

A nice walk, particularly in the evening, is to the headland called Island topped by the little fishermen's Chapel of St Nicholas. There are grand, lonely views. The harbour beach has good sand.

The obtrusive monument on a hill behind the town was raised in 1782 at the expense of one John Knill, Mayor of St Ives, smuggler, and later a GRAY'S INN bencher. He made it a condition of a bequest that once every five years on 25 July, ten little girls and two widows should dance round his monument to the music of the fiddle. This still happens.

Near **Lelant**, which is a pretty village, there is a good golf course.

From Trencrom Hill, 3 m. S., are splendid views over the Hayle estuary, S. to ST MICHAEL'S MOUNT and NEWLYN, W. to the high haunts of prehistoric man and tinners. On a good day it is said that 20 church towers are visible. An early Iron Age rampart surrounds the hill and is visible in places.

ST JUST-IN-PENWITH, *Cornwall* (2–SW 3632). About ¾ m. NW. of the town begins the greatest concentration of abandoned, ruined, mining engine-houses in Cornwall. A very rough but negotiable road bumps through a positive town of them. Virtually dead by 1900 and completely so soon afterwards, now just weeds and ruins against the sea, it is a strange, evocative landscape. The most famous mine, Botallack, is the W. of the end of the road, close to the shore. It was over 1,000 ft deep and extended nearly 150 yds under the sea. During storms the noise of the waves above was, apparently, tremendous. Care should be taken when walking not to fall down a semi-hidden mine shaft. In the old Count House, the last before you come to the mines, a folk-singing group performs in summer. Nearby is a fine small basically 15th-cent. manor house.

Both St Just's former prosperity and philosophy are suggested by its two unusually expensive and externally handsome Methodist chapels. In 1866 its population was about 9,000; a century later it had dropped to less than 4,000. Its buildings are mostly grey and Victorian. It contains the remains of a "round", like the Piran Round (*see* PERRAN-PORTH), used for games. The church is basically 15th-cent. but not exceptional.

Some 2½ m. N. **Boscaswell** is still a mining village. The rich Geevor Tin Mine is here.

The views from round the lighthouse at **Pendeen Watch** are as good as from any of the west-coast headlands. And nearby, in the grounds of Manor Farm, Pendeen, is one of the most interesting of Cornwall's fogous (underground, stone-lined prehistoric chambers). Ask at the farm for permission to see it.

ST JUST-IN-ROSELAND, *Cornwall* (2–SW 8435). The churchyard is extremely beautiful; it is Cornwall at its most sub-tropical. The church is near the shore of a creek full of yachts and old abandoned barges off the Fal estuary. The churchyard, sloping steeply down from the road, is luxuriant with trees and shrubs, some rare in Britain, like the African strawberry tree and Chilean myrtle, as well as camellias, rhododendrons, hydrangeas and palms. The tree-planting was begun in the mid-19th cent. by the rector at

that time, the Rev. C. W. Carlyon; most of the shrubs have been introduced since 1950 by one of his successors. The path down is lined with granite blocks inscribed with verses and quotations from the Bible. The prettiest picture of it is that framed by the lych-gate on the road, which is higher than the church tower. SE. of the church is a second lych-gate, interesting for its granite cattle-grid.

The church itself is pleasant but not exceptional; the earliest part is the chancel (1261), the tower is 14th-cent.; the 15th-cent. font and ewer are notable. Across the road the rectory and the cottage beside it are finely slate-hung.

St Just is thought to have been a 6th-cent. Celtic saint.

ST KEW, *Cornwall* (2–SX0276). This village's church has, with St Neot's, the finest ancient stained glass in the county. It has less than St Neot's but the quality is as good. The north-east window, dated 1469, is of the Passion and almost complete; the south-east window, *c.* 1350, depicting the Tree of Jesse, is damaged, but still beautiful. Perhaps because its nave is unusually high the church feels less intimate than some but contains many fine things: carved slate memorials on north and south walls dated 1601 and 1602; an Elizabethan pulpit; waggon roof with carved bosses; carved capitals to its granite arcade; and, beside a miniature museum in the south-west corner, a 15th-cent. lantern cross.

ST KEYNE, *Cornwall* (2–SX2460). Mr Paul Corin's collection of musical instruments (not little ones but gigantic ones, like the 27 ft by 20 ft Mortier organ and the Hoogluys fairground organ, most of which play by themselves) is worth going miles to see. It is about ½ m. E. of St Keyne village, just off the most direct road from LISKEARD to LOOE.

About ¼ m. S. is the famous St Keyne Holy Well. Keyne, a Welsh saint of the 5th cent., is supposed to have cast a spell on the well to the effect that whichever of two newly-weds drinks first from it "the mastery gains". The water is now stagnant. It is almost hidden in the hedge beside a road junction.

About 1¾ m. SW., **Duloe** church has an odd, squat, pyramid-capped, 13th-cent. tower and, in a chapel in its north-east corner enclosed by a fine black oak screen, a number of carved slate monuments including one to Sir John Colshill (1483), remembered as a rich man. He lies on his back, somewhat knocked about, on a slate altar which is rather better carved than he is.

In a field E. of the main street in Duloe is a stone circle, 30 ft in diameter. On the road to Sandplace is the Holy Well of St Cuby.

To the W. the road plunges down into the lush and beautiful depths of the West Looe valley.

ST MAWES, *Cornwall* (2–SW8433), is beautifully situated, but is among the least tourist in-dustrialized of the Cornish south coast's small towns. The quality of its shops suggests local

St Ives: the old town and the beach

affluence; so does the smartness of the old houses along its waterfront. Several are thatched as they are sheltered from the west, looking E. to a bay splendid for sailing. Behind the quay the hill rises exceptionally steeply with narrow streets. Beside the road just up from the Victory Inn is an ancient Holy Well restored and re-dedicated in 1939, its waters formerly of repute for curing worms. Apparently St Mawe, a Welsh saint and hermit of the Dark Ages, used to spend a good deal of time sitting beside it contemplating the sun.

But the main thing to see is the fortress known as St Mawes Castle, built by Henry VIII in the early 1540s at roughly the same time as FAL-MOUTH's Pendennis Castle. Together they were to guard the mouth of the Fal estuary. In fact neither saw action except in the Civil War when St Mawes's Royalist commander, claiming the fortress was indefensible to land attack, surrendered to the Roundheads as soon as confronted, whereas Pendennis was besieged for about five months. Both are excellently preserved. The St Mawes one is considered a particularly fine example of military architecture. It is also a grand place for young children, exciting and not, comparatively, dangerous.

During the Middle Ages, the town had some importance as a port and, in the 16th cent., two M.P.s.

ST MAWGAN IN PYDAR, *Cornwall* (2–SW 8765), lies in the vale of Lanherne, one of the most beautiful of those Cornish groves of luxuriance into which you drop from the predominant, comparatively bleak uplands. From the 13th to the end of the 16th cent. it was the seat of the Arundells, among the noblest of the county's families, whose heroic-tragic history was of conflict between ardent loyalty to the Pope and England's monarch; and it retains an air of benevolent feudalism.

Lanherne, the Arundells' house (they also built Trerice some 8 m. S. – *see* NEWQUAY), and the church are side by side, just above the centre of the scattered village. The main male line of the family having died out in 1701, the house was given in 1794 to English Carmelite nuns from Antwerp, refugees from the French Revolution, and it remains a nunnery. However, its chapel, which

contains a Rubens and a Van Dyck, can be visited, and to reach this you pass the front and earliest (1580) part of the house.

In the churchyard is perhaps the finest lantern cross in Cornwall (*c.* 1420). The church has an impressive, granite-buttressed, pinnacled and turreted tower (14th–15th cent.), and feels used, with local children's paintings stuck up on a wall.

Carnanton Woods (entrance near Falcon Inn) may be walked in: they are beautiful.

Man has disfigured **Mawgan Porth**, 1½ m. NW., but it has a good beach, cliffs and surfing.

ST MERRYN, *Cornwall* (2–SW8874). In this affluent "cottage-in-Cornwall" area, the little, basically 15th-cent. church, isolated from the new hub of the village that bears its name with a few old cottages like a bodyguard about its feet, is defiantly one of the most attractive and best cared for in Cornwall. The pillars of its arcade are dark blue-grey, in the local catacleuse slate, which is unusual and looks fine; as does the carved font of the same material. It has a barrel roof; well-carved, if modern, choir pews; and a Charles II coat of arms showing it was for the King in the Civil War.

ST MICHAEL PENKEVIL, *Cornwall* (2–SW 8742). It takes some finding but when you succeed it seems a retreat from the world. It is hemmed in by woods, feudal outside the gates of the great mansion of **Tregothnan**, whose park abounds with deer; formal round a classic green. Its church was rebuilt in the 19th cent. by G. E. Street and feels more like a family's than a congregation's, with monuments to the Boscawens (Lord Falmouth) one by Rysbrack and two by Nollekens – Victorian restored with pre-Raphaelite windows.

Two m. E. the wild marshes of the Fal River round Ruan Lanihorn are loud with wildfowl.

ST MICHAEL'S MOUNT, *Cornwall* (2–SW 5130), looks at its best when, just short of Marazion as you head W., it suddenly appears like a fairy castle on the left. At high tide it must be reached by boat, but at low tide it is possible to walk across the causeway and up the steep cobbled pathway to its battlements. There are

St Michael's Mount is completely isolated at high tide

guided tours, the only way to see the castle.

In prehistory it seems to have been joined to the mainland permanently, tree stumps having been found under the sea about it. In 1044 a Benedictine monastery was founded on it, owned by the monks of Mont St Michel off Brittany, to which it bears a striking resemblance. From the 12th cent. onwards, however, its potential as a fortress attracted both English kings and their rebellious nobles, and in 1425 the Crown annexed it and ejected the monks. From then until the Civil War control of it passed, either by royal consent or by force, from noble to noble. In 1657 the St Aubyn family bought it and still live in the castle, though since 1954 the island has been owned by the National Trust. The present population is 48.

Particularly attractive is the church, basically 14th-cent., with fine north door, 15th-cent. west window, good roof, and brass chandelier which is probably 15th-cent. Flemish. The fine lantern cross outside it is probably 13th-cent.

ST NEOT, *Cornwall* (2–SX1867). Its church contains much the finest collection of ancient stained-glass windows in Cornwall. About half the glass in twelve of the windows is late 15th- or early 16th-cent.; they are well described in the booklet available in the church. St Neot seems to have been an extraordinary person, and a window in the north aisle is all about him. Legend says he was only 15 in. high, made crows obey him, and, when a thief stole his oxen, ploughed with stags (apparently the area was rich in red deer till at least the 16th cent.). It also says he was related to King Alfred. At some medieval time his remains were taken to a Benedictine monastery in Huntingdonshire, the monks of which named the town St Neots after him.

The church is altogether a fine one: note especially the granite vaulted porch roof, the carved roof timbers inside, and a grand early-17th-cent. tomb-chest. It has had death-watch beetle and the whole roof was restored in 1969 with minimum loss of old timbers. An oak branch bearing oak-apples permanently crowns the tower. It commemorates Charles IIs escape by hiding in an oak tree at the Battle of Worcester; it is changed ceremonially each year on 29 May by the bell-ringers using bell ropes.

Just up a lane beside the garage in the village centre is St Neot's holy well; its waters were formerly believed to strengthen delicate children. A pipe leads from it to a tap by the road.

The village is pretty, in a last pocket of luxuriance before the bleakness of the moor begins.

SALCOMBE, *Devon* (3–SX7338). No car ferry across the estuary: the only approach is from the E. And from KINGSBRIDGE the road is boringly high-hedged and, in summer, slow. But when, quite suddenly, the land vanishes to your right, becomes a precipice of houses and, far below you, a yacht-lake sea, all is forgiven. Salcombe is one of the most beautifully situated seaside towns in England: everywhere wooded hillsides above creeks, tiny sandy bays and cliffs. Yet till the late 19th cent. its main business was building schooners. In 1856 it had only two inns "both of very humble description" (Murray's *Handbook*) and the shores about it were "almost as unknown as those of Kamschatka". Even today it has only about 2,500 residents, though now hotels have grown up, their sites often almost Mediterranean in appearance, among lemon, orange, myrtle and other such un-English trees.

The town itself is narrow-streeted with craft shops and local artists' shows and one or two good restaurants. Fort Charles, just S., which saw Royalist heroism in the Civil War, is all but gone. A pedestrian ferry goes to **East Portlemouth** and is worth taking for the views from there of the estuary, right up to Kingsbridge. Dinghies can be hired, all manner of fish caught. S. from the town the road follows the coast past good bathing bays, as far as Overbecks Museum (antiques, model boats, excellent butterflies) and **Sharpitor Gardens** (all National Trust). Beyond these begins the beautiful walk to Bolt Head, about 1 m., which is well worth continuing along the cliffs to Bolt Tail and Hope Cove, about 6 m. in all. It is a completely unexploited area, splendid for birds and wild flowers, the black cliffs – over 400 ft high at Bolt Head – the most spectacular on the South Devon coast.

Thurlestone, about 6 m. NW., is a small resort with the best golf course in the area, a good beach and thatched cottages. It takes its name from a wave-cut arch at the south end of its bay. The gardens of the Old Rectory are open most summer days.

Bantham, about ¾ m. N. of it, has a good, but none too safe, surfing beach.

SALTASH, *Cornwall* (3–SX4259). The Royal Albert Bridge over the Tamar was one of the engineering wonders of Victorian England and the final masterpiece of that astonishing engineer, Isambard Brunel. Completed in the year he died, 1859, it remains the main rail link between Devon and Cornwall. Brunel's problems were made exceptional by the Admiralty's insistence on clearance of at least 100 ft between it and the water level at high tide. The central pier, which was built within a vast cylinder, had to go down 80 ft below high-water level to reach solid rock. The cast-iron, sausage-like trusses were floated into position, then jacked up, one end at a time, while the piers were built under them. The first truss was so raised in 1857, the infinitely precise floating operation watched by a great silent crowd and conducted by Brunel himself from a platform on the truss, by means of flag signals. He was too ill to direct the raising of the second.

The best place from which to compare this bridge with the road one (opened 1961) is Saltash Quay, just S. a place of pubs and plenty of life. The town's other most pleasant part is on the crest of the steep hill above. Here, in Alexandra Square, the council offices are characteristically slate-hung. Next door almost, the little, mainly Norman parish church has carved medieval roof timbers and a very fine early Tudor chalice. Beside it the cheerfully painted Guildhall is basically 17th-cent. A house nearby was the home of Sir Francis Drake's bride. Far older than PLYMOUTH (it was incorporated in the 12th cent.), and formerly a prosperous fishing port, apparently noted especially for its strong oarswomen, the town is becoming increasingly, and rather sadly, a Plymouth suburb.

One m. W. on a hill-top, St Stephen's, basically 15th-cent., was the parish church till the mid-19th cent. Beside it a pretty row of cottages – slate-hung, colour-washed and cement-rendered – forms one side of a nice square of what is now a separate and still unsullied little village.

About ¾ m. SW. of it is **Trematon Castle**, home of Lord Caradon. Only its Norman keep can be seen from the road.

Ince Castle, about 1 m. W. but about 4 m. by road, is a towered 16th-cent. manor house. Its gardens are open occasionally.

The **Tamar**, rising some 50 m. N. of Saltash in the bleak lands of the HARTLAND peninsula, is perhaps the grandest of all the West Country's rivers and marks much of the boundary between Devon and Cornwall. Beautiful, exceptionally rich in bird life – one of the few places frequented by the avocet – it was in the 19th cent. the artery of great mining activity, the relics of which remain plentiful along the shores of its 8-m.-long, many-armed estuary (*see* TAVISTOCK and BERE FERRERS). In summer regular "study cruises" up the river go from Saltash Pier and others less studious from Phoenix Wharf, PLYMOUTH.

SAMPFORD COURTENAY, *Devon* (3–SS 6301). The area between the fringes of its two great moors is visually Devon's dullest. But it has its attractive parts, mainly on the rich red soil which, between meaner land, stretches W. from CREDITON to HATHERLEIGH. And in one of them is this village of white-washed cob, thatched roofs, tidy gardens, and fine 15th-cent. church, which in 1549 gained a niche in national history.

That was the year when Edward VI introduced his new Prayer Book in English. When, on Whit Sunday the new Prayer Book was first used, objections to it were vehement. Local gentry came to reason with the peasants, one, evidently, too arrogantly. As he descended the church-house steps a farmer chopped him in the neck with a bill-hook, whereupon others, disregarding his "pitiful requests and lamentations . . . cut him into small pieces". Thus committed, the villagers joined forces with a much larger band of Cornish Catholics in the hopeless Prayer Book Rebellion and marched on EXETER, which they besieged for five weeks. They were then shattered on Clyst Heath (*see* TOPSHAM), and finished off back in the streets of their village with subsequent mass hangings.

The New Inn contains a collection of bric-à-brac remarkable even for a Devon pub. And 1 m. N., at **Honeychurch** is perhaps the prettiest of Devon's tiny churches: little restored, basically 12th-cent., with a tower and porch of the late 15th or early 16th cent.

SEDGEMOOR, *Somerset* (3–ST4233), is a beautiful great expanse of fenland, broken by a few isolated low hills, some 120 sq. m. in area, its approximate centre the village of **Othery**. In prehistory much of it was sea-covered. Now it is prosperously cattle-grazed, scattered with red-brick farms, and its pollarded willows provide the raw material for village basket industries.

One fine view of it is from beside the A39 along the ridge of the Polden Hills, but there are others as good and very different from lower down, for instance from Moorlinch churchyard. It looks best of all, perhaps, when, as frequently in winter, it is semi-flooded.

At Aller (2 m. NW. of LANGPORT) the Danish leader Guthrum was baptized at the insistence of his captor, King Alfred, in 879. The Battle of Sedgemoor (1685) was fought near WESTON ZOYLAND.

Many of the villages are now thickly ringed by new houses for commuters to the surrounding towns. **Stawell**, marvellously red and compact as you look down on it from the Poldens, is one that has been largely spared this. **Chedzoy** and **Middlezoy**, both much involved in the 1685 battle, have fine churches. On the buttress on the south wall of Chedzoy's are marks where, it is said, Monmouth's men sharpened their weapons. Other churches of interest are at Othery, Stoke Gregory, Low Ham, North Curry and North Petherton.

SELWORTHY, *Somerset* (3–SS9146). All the villages of the beautiful Vale of Porlock are pretty, but Selworthy is perhaps the most famous and has the best view. It is on a luxuriantly wooded hillside, facing S. across the vale to the heather-peak of Dunkery, sheltered on all other sides. Its houses are almost all thatched. Its church, which is mainly 16th cent. with a 14th-cent. tower, is externally unusual in being white, and has a particularly fine south aisle. In the car park is a telescope for deer spotting. The walk of about ¾ m. up past the church to Selworthy Beacon (1,013 ft) is well worthwhile.

Luccombe, about 1½ m. S., snuggling under EXMOOR, has red, rose-covered walls, red soil, and cottages with old bread ovens; and a good church.

Horner, 1 m. NW. of Luccombe, is a hamlet with a packhorse bridge at the foot of one of Exmoor's most beautiful wooded clefts. In its water and woods many a stag has come to the end of the hunt.

Allerford, 1 m. N. of Horner, has a high-arched packhorse bridge beside a ford shaded by a walnut tree, in a setting of variegated red-stone and thatched cottages.

Bossington, ¾ m. NW. of Allerford, also mainly thatched, has fine walnut trees and, at its south-east end, superb farm buildings with among them a 16th-cent. manorial chapel. (There is another, thatched but more restored, at **Tivington**, 1½ m. SE. of Selworthy.) A lane NW. from the village leads to the shingle of **Porlock Bay**, good for sea fishing though not for bathing. The hillside to the N. is steep, but the view is worth the climb.

Most of the vale is National Trust protected and remains unspoilt.

SHEEPSTOR, *Devon* (3–SX5668). A hamlet with a strangely appealing little grey moorstone (*see* NORTH BOVEY) church, in a particularly varied and harshly beautiful margin of the moor; above it, almost mountainous, the grey eminence of the same name; just NW. the pleasant Burrator reservoir (1891–8); just SW. the steep, deeply wooded River Meavy valley. The church has a screen which was well copied in 1914, from a 15th-cent. one; also bench-ends of the same period and an attractive small 17th-cent. wall monument. Sir James Brooke, who in the 19th cent. made the whole of Sarawak, Borneo, his estate retired to Burrator House and died there in 1868. His tomb and that of his successor, Sir Charles Brooke, are in the churchyard.

Meavy, 1½ m. W., has in its centre the propped-up wreck of an very ancient oak, and about ½ m. W. of the village, near a pretty cattle ford, is a fine medieval wayside cross.

One m. S. of Sheepstor on Lynch Common is an isolated, bleak and thrilling beech wood. Three m. SSW. are the Lee Moor china-clay mines, their white mountains dramatic, especially from the SE.; and about 2¼ m. W. (about 1¾ m. of walking) Eylesbarrow Mines were the last place (mid-19th cent.) where tin was smelted on the moor. Another, very different, but equally beautiful walk is about ½ m. up the bouldered River Plym from Shaugh Bridge (about 3 m. SW.) to the Dewerstone, a sheer cliff, 100 or so feet high, of ghostly legend and popular with climbers. Above it, in an oak forest, is a mighty tor. **Shaugh Prior** church has a remarkable 15th-cent. font cover.

About 2 m. SW. of Sheepstor, the area of **Trowlesworthy Warren**, and NE. from it for some 2 m. on either side of the Plym, is one of the moor's richest in prehistoric (mainly Bronze Age) remains – hut circles, enclosures, etc. You can conveniently park near Cadover Bridge, ⅓ m. NE. of which **Brisworthy** was in the 12th cent. one of the first settlements in the early tin-mining days.

Yelverton, 2¼ m. W., an odd, ugly settlement, has ponies wandering all over its flat common and Second World War gun emplacements; and it has, just S., the best inland golf course in Devon.

SHEPTON MALLET, *Somerset* (4–ST6143). Its church has the finest, most intricately carved barrel ceiling in the West Country and a carved stone pulpit which is less spectacular but just as good. Both date from the 15th cent. when the town was an important wool centre. It is now an agricultural town, the permanent site of the Bath and West Show, and its industries include cider-making and brewing, glove and shoe making from the hides of cattle, and agricultural machinery. Few towns gave a rougher reception to John Wesley and to the "spinning Jenny". Wives used to be sold in the square, round the fine market cross which was mainly rebuilt in 1841. The museum in the square contains finds from MENDIP caves (*see* WOOKEY HOLE), Roman remains and minerals.

About 2½ m. E., the quarries at **Doulting** produced the stone for GLASTONBURY Abbey and WELLS Cathedral.

Two m. SW., **Pilton**, a grey-stone village round a natural amphitheatre, has a good church and fine tithe barn on the hill opposite.

Some 3½ m. SE., **Evercreech** has one of the most spectacular even of Somerset church towers.

SIDMOUTH, *Devon* (3–SY1287), was in the 19th cent. one of the most select seaside resorts in Britain. As a result it presents, once you have battled through the suburbs, a possibly unique display of the fashionable Regency style of seaside architecture known as cottage orné: mostly in cream and white, a mass of wrought-iron balconies (and wooden ones made to look like wrought iron) and all sorts of entertainingly shaped windows. Forbidden Europe by the Napoleonic Wars the elegant and the elderly discovered this, then, fishing village superbly situated in a gap in the grandest of Devon's red cliffs (500 ft) with the white bastion of Beer Head in brilliant and beautiful contrast to the E. Here, aged seven months, Queen Victoria first saw the sea.

Armed with a map, it is worth, after strolling the Esplanade, looking in particular for Fortfield Terrace, York Terrace, Elysian Fields and Sidlands. Off Heydons Lane a curiosity is the Old Chancel, a house built of medieval parts of the parish church, discarded when it was being rebuilt in 1860. The museum is in one of the oldest buildings, just E. of the main street and halfway up. The cricket ground is said to be among the earliest in England (1820) and is enthusiastically used. In August there is an international Folk Song and Dance Festival. The town looks especially attractive from the hill to the W., and High Peak, 2 m. W., is a splendid viewpoint.

About 1 m. E. on the Salcombe Regis road, the Norman Lockyer Observatory (astronomical and geophysical) is occasionally open. A minor road to it (S. of the main one) from the town centre passes through a wide and pretty ford. From Salcombe Regis there is a nice walk to the beach, then E. along it and up the beautiful Weston Mouth Combe: a round walk of about 2½ m.

Three m. N., **Sidbury**'s church is quite interesting: Norman, with an Anglo-Saxon crypt which can be seen on application to the vicar.

The country around here is the most beautiful in East Devon.

SLAPTON, *Devon* (3–SX8244). For some 2½ m. the road is a causeway between a freshwater lake and the sea, protected from the latter by an immense pebble-beach. It is one of the few places on the South Devon coast that can seem wild in August: no buildings, just a memorial column presented by the U.S. Army to the people of surrounding villages who were evacuated from December 1943 to September 1944 when the beach was used for D-Day landing practice. The beach is good for pretty shells and pebbles, but steep shelves make bathing dangerous for non-swimmers. The lake, which in some lights can be extraordinarily, mistily beautiful, is a Nature Reserve, rich in duck, reed warblers, water-rail, coots, moorhens, pike, roach and perch. The reeds are used for thatching.

Slapton village is ½ m. inland. The conspicuous tower is the remains of a chantry founded in 1373 by Edward III's standard-bearer. The church, 14th- to 15th-cent., has a spire and restored screen of that date. Torcross, at the south end of the great beach, was, in the pilchard-fishing days, the most easterly pilchard port.

Further S., 1 m. and 2½ m. respectively via a maze of high-hedged lanes, are **Beesands** and **Hallsands**, both small fishing places, the latter rebuilt after being washed away in storms in 1903 and 1917 following ill-advised dredging of protective shingle. And about 1 m. beyond it is **Start Point**, craggy and grand, excellent for watching sea-birds (gannets nose-diving if you are lucky), and with a lighthouse that can be visited though it is a fair walk.

SOMERTON, *Somerset* (3–ST4828). Under the West Saxons it was the main settlement and capital of Somerset. Today it is almost the model grey-stone and red-roofed small town, architecturally remarkably uniform, compact round its square, with a wide street and very interesting church.

The church's curious octagonal-topped tower was probably built in stages, from the 12th to the 15th cent. Inside, it has one of the finest tie-beam roofs (15th-cent.) even in Somerset, splendidly set off by its yellow Ham-stone arcades, and a beautifully simple altar – just two brass candles

on an oak table (1626) with oak panelling for a reredos. In the square the arcaded market cross is 17th-cent. and the Town Hall is *c.* 1700, enhanced by Ham-stone windows, as are the Hext Almshouses (1626) at the west end of the town. Other buildings to note are the Unicorn Hotel, and the Old Parsonage at the south-east end. The White Hart is believed to be on the site of the Anglo-Saxon castle and to incorporate some of its masonry.

About 3 m. SE. is **Lytes Cary**, a good manor house, mainly of the 14th, 15th and 16th cents., with a chapel of *c.* 1343. It is owned by the National Trust and is sometimes open.

SOUTH MOLTON, *Devon* (3–SS7125). It grew as an Anglo-Saxon colony *c.* 700; was prosperous from the early Middle Ages to the mid-19th cent. with a woollen industry, as a coach stop on the route to BARNSTAPLE and BIDEFORD, and as the nearest town to the iron and copper mines round North Molton. Then the wool industry declined, the railway (1854) spoilt the coach trade, and soon the mines closed. Since 1850 its population has decreased by nearly a half. It is now a pleasantly modest, lively small town, serving a large farming area including south-west EXMOOR, with, since 1961, a livestock market. Its attractive, mainly Georgian, square is given grandeur by the Guildhall (1740–3) and Assembly Rooms (1863), which are also interesting inside. Opposite them a pollarded lime avenue leads to a big church with a fine 15th-cent. tower and excellent carved stone pulpit. Behind the Guildhall is a museum, the contents of which include good pewter, a 1736 fire engine and an old cider-press.

North Molton, 2¾ m. NE., is a largish, hillside village with attractively simple houses round a big tarmac square, and an excellent church. The latter has an exceptionally beautiful medieval pulpit and a rather splendid vast alabaster monument (*c.* 1626) to Sir Amyas Bamfylde, his wife and many children. The Bamfyldes were local mining landlords. The main copper mines were at Heasley Mill, about 1½ m. N. At **Flitton Barton**, 1½ m. NW. of the village, is a hollow oak of great age, possibly 1,000 years or more.

SOUTH POOL, *Devon* (3–SX7740). At the head of one of the easterly and most beautiful tree-dark, sandy-shored creeks of the KINGSBRIDGE estuary, it is a pretty village with thatch and a mainly 15th-cent. church with a big strong slate tower, excellent screen and Easter Sepulchre of some renown. Far less visited than the other, this side of the estuary affords much the best views of it, and the one from **East Portlemouth**, about 2 m. SW., looking right back up to Kingsbridge, is sensational. East Portlemouth church also has a screen in the best Devon tradition. Prawle Point, 2¾ m. SE., is the climax of a fierce, undesecrated cliff coast where there is a Lloyds' signal station and a tiny, wild beach.

STANTON DREW, *Somerset* (3–ST5963). In a field just E. of this village are three circles of massive upright stones, the highest of which is about 10 ft, thought to have been put there for religious reasons at roughly the same time as AVEBURY's, c. 1800 B.C. The entrance is from a farm where you pay to enter the field. And a little SW., beside the churchyard, is a group of three huge stones called "the core", of even more uncertain prehistoric purpose. The rectory, near the bridge over the River Chew, is basically medieval. The curious building a little further N. is an old toll-house.

About 1½ m. N. the hill called Maesknoll is a good place to see the **Wansdyke**, the great earth wall which once stretched from Portishead, on the Bristol Channel, to Salisbury Plain. It, also, is of uncertain origin, but the Romano-British certainly used it against the West Saxons and probably strengthened it.

Three m. W. of here, **Dundry**'s extraordinary pinnacle-heavy church tower was built by the Merchant Adventurers in 1484 as a seamark.

Some 1½ m. W. of Stanton Drew, **Chew Magna** church has a very fine 15th-cent. tower and contains a monument to Sir John Hantville, who is supposed to have possessed super-human strength. His effigy's feet rest on a lion which contrives to look like a grief-stricken dog.

STICKLEPATH, SOUTH ZEAL and SOUTH TAWTON, Devon (3–SX6394). Suddenly, after some 16 dreary miles on the A30 W. from EXETER, there is a burst of habitation in the form of these three merging, but very different, villages. John Wesley often stopped here to preach. Each village has something to see. South Tawton has an excellent 15th-cent. granite church framed by thatched cottages, a very fine 16th-cent. Church House and an elm-centred square. In South Zeal – a lively ex-copper-mining village (the waste heaps tower above a sharp bend on the A30) – is a splendid, early-16th-cent. manor house turned pub said to be haunted. In Sticklepath the Museum of Rural Industry at the Finch Brothers foundry is unique in the West Country. From 1814 to 1960 the foundry, powered by water-wheels, produced virtually every type of sharp tool used by Devon miners and farmers, and was also the village blacksmith's. Since 1966 a trust has restored the machinery to working order and established a museum. Also open in Sticklepath is the exquisite tiny garden of Mrs Mary Lees who a few years ago bought from a Welsh-speaking lady in the Welsh mountains some bulbs of a lily thought to be extinct. She propagated it, and has had it named after her by the Royal Horticultural Society.

Belstone, 1½ m. W., is the entrance to one of the most beautiful parts of DARTMOOR, which provides, moreover, unusually easy walking.

STOGURSEY, Somerset (3–ST2042). The east end of its church was built c. 1180 as an extension to a Norman church built on Anglo-Saxon foundations. It remains entirely medieval architecturally, with round Norman arches and vaulting, echoing flagstones and wide stone steps leading to a plain yet dominating altar. It contains two grand 14th- and 15th-cent. tombs and an unusual, fine font that is certainly not later than Norman. The Norman nave was rebuilt, probably in the 15th cent. Some of the stones in the walls were tooled by Anglo-Saxons, perhaps even by Romans. The tower is Norman.

Of a priory which stood beside the church till the 15th cent., only the rebuilt dovecot remains, now used as a barn by a nearby farm. To the SW., reached by a path to the right 100 yds down Castle Street, are the ruins of a Norman castle, which was destroyed in the Wars of the Roses.

Two m. N., on the coast, is Hinkley Point nuclear power station.

STOKE GABRIEL, Devon (3–SX8457). The only village on the Dart estuary apart from DARTMOUTH's annexe, Kingswear, and a very pretty one with cobbles, orchards and anchored boats. Salmon net-fishing was formerly one of its main trades; it is still done but less earnestly. In the churchyard is a vast propped-up yew, between 1,000 and 1,500 years old. The church contains a well-restored 15th-cent. screen with panel paintings, some of them good, and a coloured pulpit of the same date. The north chapel was provided as penance by a local knight because "upon some controversy between him and the parson, the knight in his fury slew the parson". John Davis, the Elizabethan searcher for the North-West Passage, was born in the house at Sandridge, 1 m. SE., replaced by the present one built by John Nash in 1805. About ¾ m. E. of it, Waddeton Court is mid-19th-cent. Elizabethan.

STOKE-SUB-HAMDON, Somerset (3–ST 4717). From Hamdon Hill immediately to the S. of this village came, and still comes, the yellow Ham Hill stone which makes beautiful the villages and grand houses of this area. The Britons fortified the hill. The Romans quarried it and made it one of their main military strongholds in Somerset. The line of their ramparts can be well appreciated from the A303, a little NE. of its junction with the A3083. Today the grass-covered mounds and pits of old quarryings and fortifications on its top make sheltered and popular picnic places with good views.

Stoke-sub-Hamdon church (actually at **East Stoke** about ¾ m. E. of the main village) is basically Norman, of Ham stone and attractive. Its porch (1325), with Norman carvings over the church door, is exceptional. The village itself is virtually all of Ham stone, mainly old and amazingly unspoilt by the main road. Beside the road N. from its centre is a magnificent set of Tudor and earlier buildings called the Priory, now owned by the National Trust. The great hall can be visited. Behind the nearby Fleur-de-Lis Inn is a fives court, built c. 1756 to discourage the playing of the game against the church walls. The inn is basically c. 1540.

STRATTON, Cornwall (2–SS2206). Mother to the resort of Bude, it is the most attractive small town of this region, on a hillside with narrow streets and nice old houses, some thatched. The Tree Inn was formerly a manor house of the Grenville family. In 1643 it was Sir Bevil Grenville's headquarters before he led the Royalists to victory at Stamford Hill ($\frac{1}{2}$ m. NW.). A plaque on the inn's wall commemorates the battle. It was also the birth and death place of the famous giant of over 7 ft, Anthony Payne, a Grenville retainer, who fought beside Sir Bevil at Stamford Hill and soon afterwards carried home his master's dead body from another battlefield, Lansdown Hill near BATH. The church contains an excellent brass (1561) to Sir John Arundell, Henry VIII's Vice-Admiral, a Burne-Jones east window, and a finely carved waggon roof.

Two other churches nearby are well worth a visit. **Poughill**'s, 1 m. NW., is basically 15th-cent. and has two big 15th-cent. wall paintings, restored in 1894 but still splendid, and excellent 16th-cent. carved bench-ends. **Launcells**, $1\frac{1}{4}$ m. SE., is mainly 14th-cent. and stands in a wooded hollow, its yellow-lichened tower looking grand from a distance. It is exceptional for two reasons. Firstly, its interior has hardly been restored at all and is therefore much as it was in the 15th cent. Secondly, its big windows are quite without coloured glass, making it beautifully light: a great help in appreciating its complete set of original carved bench-ends and fine 15th-cent. Barnstaple tiles on its sanctuary floor.

Bude, $1\frac{1}{2}$ m. W. of Stratton, is an unusual little resort in that it stands well back from its abundant sands. Between the two is a vast grass playground containing cricket pitch and golf courses. All around are ugly hotels, churches and houses. The canal through the town was built 1819–26 for £128,000 and extended some 30 m. to LAUNCESTON. One of its main cargoes was beach-sand, like PADSTOW's valued as fertilizer because of its high lime content. The railways made the canal redundant and now only about 2 m. of it are navigable. The quaint castle on a grass promontory just S. of the canal was built in 1850 by Sir Goldsworthy Gurney, the inventor who experimented with steam and lighting, and introduced steam stage coaches between London and BATH. It now houses the Urban District Council. In Bude was formed the first Surf Life Saving Club.

STREET, *Somerset* (3–ST4836). Here is Millfield School and a village industrial-success story. In the early 1820s young James Clark, an apprentice in his brother's sheepskin rug firm, had an idea that waste bits of sheepskin would make good slipper linings. In his spare time he cut them out and got local shoemakers to make the slippers. In 1825 he and his brother founded what is now the largest shoe company in Britain, and Street, then a village, has grown to a town of 7,200 people, of whom some 2,500 are in the shoe industry. The factory can be visited. Close to the church, at the town's north-east end, is an admirable group of modern buildings including a secondary school, technical college and the enterprising Strode Theatre.

Ivythorn Hill (National Trust), 1 m. S., has beautiful woods and there are fine views from it over SEDGEMOOR to the QUANTOCKS and N. past Glastonbury Tor to the MENDIPS. On this hill, at Marshall's Elm, 30 of Monmouth's followers were hanged in 1685. On its southern slopes is a fine Tudor manor house, once the country house of the Abbot of GLASTONBURY. The monument on the hill to the E. was erected in the 19th cent. to Admiral Hood, who died in 1814.

Sharpham Park Farm, 1 m. NW. of Street, was for a time in the 18th cent. the house of Henry Fielding, author of *Tom Jones*.

SWIMBRIDGE, *Devon* (3–SS6230). This otherwise fairly ordinary main-road village has a church which, made externally unusual only by its 14th-cent. lead-shingled spire, contains many splendid things: a screen (*c.* 1490) across the nave and both aisles, as lavishly carved as any in Devon; a stone pulpit of the same date, carved with beautifully serene figures; and, most unusual, a font enclosed in a tall, octagonal, elaborately carved wooden cupboard, topped by an equally elaborate canopy, of various periods from the 16th to the 18th cent. The carved barrel-roof timbers are also above average.

At **Filleigh**, 3 m. E., a grand, yellow, basically 1684 house is well seen to the N. It is Castle Hill, the seat of the Fortescues, for centuries one of the largest land-owning and publicly active families in North Devon. The main road runs through its grounds. On the hill to the S. is a triumphal arch; on the hill behind the house a folly.

TAUNTON, *Somerset* (3–ST2324). The county capital (population about 37,500), it is a prosperous town, situated in the centre of one of Britain's most fertile plains. Its exceptional feature is the beautiful tower of its Church of St Mary Magdalene: 163 ft high and slender, of red sandstone from the QUANTOCKS, with yellow Ham-stone windows and pinnacles which in the evening sun might be of gold. Built in the late 15th cent., it was deemed unsafe in 1858 and taken down, but was rebuilt to look precisely as before. It is perfectly framed by the town's best street, which is all Georgian, mainly deep-red brick and white porticoed, laid out by the local M.P., Sir Benjamin Hammet in 1788. Though Taunton has no more buildings in this class, it has much else of interest.

Tradition holds that King Ine, an early king of the West Saxons, gave the site a castle and thus its first importance in *c.* 710. The castle was rebuilt by the Normans. King Stephen, anxious to win its support against his cousin Matilda, gave the town its first charter, and the privileges written into this opened the way to prosperity. In 1219 the town had the first cloth-fulling mill in the West Country; and for the next 550 or so years it was a major wool centre (wool money built its great church tower). It was, however, with its merchant population, far from politically or religiously conformist. In 1497 it proclaimed Perkin Warbeck King. In the Civil War it was for Parliament.

Royalist forces occupied it, while its castle, commanded by Blake (*see* BRIDGWATER), withstood a siege. In 1685 many of its people backed Monmouth and suffered ghastly vengeance after his defeat at SEDGEMOOR.

The decline of the wool industry brought it comparatively little pain, for it was already a considerable agricultural marketing and servicing centre and a principal road (and soon rail) junction. Today, it has, with EXETER, the most important livestock market in the West Country (Saturdays and Tuesdays off Priory Bridge Road NE. of its centre), and is increasingly gaining manufacturing industry as well.

The castle, at various times altered, added to and made domestic, houses the exceptionally well-presented County Museum. Part of this is in the great hall where, in 1685, Judge Jeffreys held one of his bloodiest assizes. It includes finds from one of the lake-villages that once existed near GLASTONBURY, and a superb Roman floor mosaic (*c.* 350) discovered in 1938 at Low Ham near LANGPORT. The tower of St James's Church pales by comparison with that of St Mary's, to which it is similar in style, but would be outstanding anywhere else. It is actually the older of the two but was likewise rebuilt in the 19th cent. The red-brick pub in the middle of the main traffic junction was the Market House (1770). The Tudor House restaurant across the road from it is basically *c.* 1578. It was, during the Monmouth rebellion, a home of the M.P., Sir William Portman; he entertained Judge Jeffreys to dinner there.

The Municipal Offices, on the corner of High Street and Corporation Street, include the old 16th-cent. Grammar School buildings. The High Street, wide and pleasant and off the main traffic routes, is mainly Georgian and leads to the gates of Vivary Park. Parallel with it to the W., the Crescent is Georgian in contrast to the new glass-and-steel County Offices opposite.

The thatched building amid lawns, ahead as you enter the town from the E., was built as a leper hospital, is mainly Tudor, now used as offices. Further in along East Street are Gray's Almshouses (1635), and there are more 17th-cent. almshouses in the street S. of St Mary Magdalene's – an attractive area generally. John Wesley is said to have supervised the building of the Octagon in Middle Street in 1776.

The town has three well-known public schools, Queen's and King's Colleges and Taunton School. The Somerset College of Art in Corporation Street has an appearance reminiscent of the TATE GALLERY. The County Cricket Ground is between St James's Church and the River Tone. The Racecourse is to the SE. of the town.

The Information Bureau is in the Public Library opposite the Municipal Buildings.

TAVISTOCK, *Devon* (3–SX4774). A greyish but pleasant town of long and varied industrial history which has possibly Devon's most entertaining annual fair, the Goose Fair, held in the second week in October. The town grew round a Benedictine abbey founded in the 10th cent. which was the wealthiest in the county by the Dissolution. THE DARTMOOR tin-rush brought it stannary (*see* ASHBURTON) status in 1305. After tin-mining declined *c.* 1500, it thrived as a cloth centre. Then, just as this industry was dying *c.* 1800, mining revived, this time for lead, zinc, iron, silver and, above all, copper, especially near Mary Tavy, 3½ m. NE., and Blanchdown, 3 m. W., where, in the mid-19th cent., the Great Consols Mine was one of the biggest and richest in the world. By *c.* 1902 most of the mines were abandoned but the district still holds much haunting evidence of them. The town now has a cattle market (Wednesdays) and a pannier market (Fridays), light engineering and timber-working firms.

Of the abbey mere fragments remain, some exposed, some incorporated in 19th-cent. buildings. It occupied the area round the Bedford Hotel (*c.* 1820), bounded, roughly, by the River Tavy, the Parish Church of St Eustachius and the Guildhall. The big church (mainly 15th-cent.) lacks marvellous contents but is strangely memorable with its simplicity, its high, narrow aisles, its finely carved pink alabaster monument (1600) to the lawyer, Sir John Glanville, and its east window of the north aisle by William Morris. Much of the town dates from the second mining boom, sponsored by the Russell family (Dukes of Bedford) who owned the place from 1539 to 1911. On the southern edge of the town beside the PLYMOUTH road is an estate of workers' cottages built *c.* 1850 for £22 each. Near it (in the middle of the road junction) is an 1883 statue of Sir Francis Drake with reliefs of scenes from his life round its base. He was born about 1 m. SW. but the house has now vanished.

The Tavistock Canal can be followed on foot along its tow-path until it disappears into a tunnel. Dug 1803–17, closed in the 1880s, it connected the town with the Tamar, and carried mineral ore from the Mary Tavy mines one way, coal and fertilizer the other. It went as far as the now-dead port of **Morwellham,** 3½ m. SW., which was 240 ft above the quay, the barges being hauled up and lowered down an inclined plane by a water-wheel powered windlass. Morwellham is one of the most industrial-nostalgic places in Devon: in the mid-19th cent. an important port, now with as many of its cottages abandoned as occupied, round a wasteland crossed by unsurfaced road. However, it is good for exploring, and beautiful, with the Morwell Rocks rising dramatically from the Tamar's tree-wrapped banks nearby.

About 5 m. NE., just E. of the A386 on the side of a bare hill named Gibbet, the roofless engine-house and chimney of the Wheal Betsy mine (lead, silver and zinc) is now cared for by the National Trust. Legend says medieval criminals were shut in cages on Gibbet Hill (1,158 ft) and left there to die. There are splendid contrasting views from its summit. On the north edge of Mary Tavy, Wheal Friendship was an immensely productive mine, mainly for copper, operated till 1925. Four m. NW. of Mary Tavy is one of the moor's most

Exeter Cathedral   Picturepoint

spectacular valleys, Tavy Cleave (*see* Dartmoor).

About 3½ m. NW. of Tavistock, **Collacombe Manor** is a fine Elizabethan house with exceptional transomed window, open by appointment.

At **Gunnislake**, 3½ m. W., a medieval bridge spans the Tamar on the boundary between Devon and Cornwall.

TAWSTOCK, *Devon* (3–SS5529). In the 19th cent. it was said that here at one glance could be seen the most valuable manor, the best mansion, the finest church, and the richest rectory in the county. Now the mansion (used as a school), built in 1787 to replace one that was burnt, looks rather unkempt. For some 500 years from the 15th cent. either the Bouchier family (Earls of Bath) or the related Wreys lived here and there are many huge monuments to them in the church, which Nikolaus Pevsner found "one of the most architecturally interesting" in North Devon. Probably the biggest of these monuments is to the 5th Earl of Bath (d. 1680): four marble dogs crouching on one marble tomb carrying another on their shoulders. But it is closely rivalled by the 3rd Earl's: he and his wife recumbent with kneeling children in attendance, all red, black and blue. Perhaps the most attractive is the 14th-cent. wooden effigy of a woman in a recess in the north wall. Some of the inscriptions are quite witty.

TEIGNMOUTH and SHALDON, *Devon* (3–SX9473). Of South Devon's beautiful estuaries, the Teign is the most easily appreciated from the road, the least secluded by trees, and the only one, apart from the Tamar, crossed by a road bridge. Nor is it devious with creeks like the others, but broad and straightforward, brimming with boats when the tide is in, displaying mollusc-encrusted mud-banks at low tide. It looks particularly good from the bridge, and never better than from the club-house of the admirable Teignmouth golf course on the hill-top to the N., from near which the view is also splendid to the DARTMOOR peaks of Hound Tor and Haytor, especially in the evening. About 3 m. W. of Shaldon, **Coombe Cellars** is an attractive place with an inn formerly used by smugglers.

The two towns are very different: Shaldon, in its area E. from the end of the bridge, very daintily pretty with narrow streets of well-cared for late Georgian and Regency cottages; Teignmouth much bigger and busier but, on the whole, ugly. The nicest part of the latter is certainly The Den, which is on the sea-front. The Church of St James (dating from 1820 except for its tower) is curious. With Exmouth, Teignmouth is said to be Devon's oldest resort, popular since the mid-18th cent. It was a port that Frenchmen considered worth ravaging in 1340. In 1821 it shipped the Dartmoor granite for LONDON BRIDGE and nowadays the ball-clay of world-renowned quality found near **Kingsteignton** (4½ m. W.). It also builds good boats. E. of Shaldon, the Ness Headland is popular, council developed, with a "smugglers" tunnel leading to a beach. A little S. Labrador, of smuggling fame, is a pleasant cove.

THORVERTON, *Devon* (3–SS9202). Far from the holiday crowds yet within easy range of EXETER and in hilly and sheltered red-soil country, Thorverton is a genteel but extremely attractive large village with colonnaded butcher's shop (18th-cent.), much smart cob and thatch, the bridge over its stream draped with flowers in summer. It is also interesting for having an unusually well-recorded history, published by the local branch of the British Legion.

About 6 m. E., **Bradninch** is an example of an ancient and once important town, well sited on an orchard hillside, which never found adequate replacement for its medieval woollen industry.

Brampford Speke, 2½ m. S., was considered by a 1891 traveller "the most perfect [village] I have ever seen". He may have slightly overrated it, but it is still pretty.

TINTAGEL, *Cornwall* (2–SX0588). An undistinguished village usually full of tourists, but the ruin-strewn headland is wonderfully romantic and legend connects the site with King Arthur. The peninsula known as "the Island" is the best place from which to see the great black slate caverns on the north side of Tintagel Cove, the stream that from the vale forms a waterfall as it drops to the cove, and the cliffs with great slate peaks rising from them.

A monastery was founded on this peninsula in *c.* A.D. 500 and abandoned by 1086. It must have been in its setting a sort of Celtic Mount Athos. A Norman castle was built here in *c.* 1145 by Reginald, Earl of Cornwall, bastard son of Henry I. The ruins can be seen.

A Land Rover bus service runs from the café above the cove back to the village.

Beside one of the car parks is a museum of coins. The crinkly roofed old building on the south-west side of the village street, known as the Old Post Office, should be visited. Built in the 14th cent. as a minor manor house, it is one of the few fairly humble ancient residences open to the public. The National Trust preserves it. King Arthur's Hall on the other side of the street is the headquarters of the Fellowship of the Round Table.

Tintagel church, on the headland to the SW., is basically very old, most of its shell being Norman, parts even Anglo-Saxon. Inside it has several interesting things, including a curious five-legged Norman font.

Bossiney, ½ m. NE. of Tintagel village, has a good bathing beach. Sir Francis Drake was, in his later years, one of its two M.P.s.

There are beautiful walks in the richly wooded Rocky Valley about ½ m. further NE., at right angles to the road to BOSCASTLE: either up it about 1 m. to St Nectan's (or St Knighton's) Kieve, a 40-ft waterfall, or down it to the sea. The "kieve" is the rock basin into which the water falls, and St Nectan, a Celtic hermit saint, is said to have had an oratory beside it.

At **Slaughter Bridge**, about 5 m. inland and 1 m. N. of Camelford, was fought in 823 a decisive battle between Celts and Anglo-Saxons and also a legendary combat between Arthur and Mordred.

Bedruthan Steps: a striking rock formation on the Cornish coast Noel Habgood

TIVERTON, *Devon* (3–SS9512), is a prosperous industrial and agricultural town on the River Exe and its tributary, the Lowman, with a livestock market on Tuesdays. One of the first Anglo-Saxon settlements after their 7th-cent. conquest of the South-West, it was, during the heyday of the Devonian cloth industry in the 17th and 18th cents., the county's principal industrial centre, famous for its kersey. And then, just as the cloth industry was dying in the early 19th cent., John Heathcoat, a lace manufacturer, came from Leicestershire, where Luddites had smashed his machines, to try his luck and was rewarded. Today the Heathcoat organization is the town's dynamo, its products ranging from artificial fibres to agricultural machinery, embracing iron foundries and sawmills, employing about 2,000 people. Its main factory is on the west bank of the Exe just N. of the bridge. Viscount Amory, the former Chancellor of the Exchequer, is a member of the Heathcoat family, and was the local M.P. from 1945 to 1960. Lord Palmerston was the town's M.P. from 1835 to 1865.

Architecturally a fairly dignified medley of styles and materials, it has some good buildings bequeathed by its rich wool merchants, notably a big church, St Peter's, the old buildings of Blundells School and three sets of almshouses. The outstanding features of St Peter's Church, at the northern end of the town, are its sculptured south porch and chapel and its organ. It is said that on the latter, claimed to be one of the finest in England, Mendelssohn's "Midsummer Night's Dream" march was first played for a wedding (1847). Flanking the sanctuary are fine tombs of the merchants Waldron and Slee who were responsible for two of the sets of almshouses, in Wellbrook Street (E. of the Exe) and St Peter's Street respectively. The third set, in Gold Street, was endowed by another merchant, John Greenway, who also paid for the church's south porch and chapel. The Greenway and Waldron almshouses are both Tudor and have attractive chapels attached. Opposite the Slee ones (1610) is the pretty dark-red stone Chilcott School (1611). Gold Street leads from the town centre to the River Lowman, and just over this is "Old Blundell's" (1604). The new buildings of this famous school, whose pupils have included R. D. Blackmore, author of *Lorna Doone*, and Frederick Temple, Archbishop of Canterbury from 1896 to 1902, are beside the A373 on the eastern outskirts. Beside St Peter's are the remains of a 14th-cent. castle now incorporated in a private house but recognizable from the road.

A great fire in 1731 resulted in some good Georgian building in the town centre, and St George's – next to the fantastic, Victorian-Baroque Town Hall – is possibly the best Georgian church in Devon. St Andrew Street beside it leads to the museum in an old school which has a particularly good section on farm implements.

At the south-east edge of the town begins the Grand Western Canal, built 1811–14, 11 m. long, intended as a branch of the canal linking the Bristol and English channels which was, however, never built. Its tow-path is pleasant for walking.

The gardens of Knightshayes Court (1869), 2 m. N., the home of the Heathcoat Amorys, are sometimes open to the public.

Bickleigh, 4 m. S. on the main road to EXETER, is a much photographed riverside village, with thatched cottages by a five-arched bridge. Nearby stands Bickleigh Castle, for generations the home of the Carews, with a Norman chapel and an impressive gatehouse.

TOPSHAM; *Devon* (3–SX9788). From Roman times to the 19th cent. Topsham was EXETER's port. From 1282, when the spiteful Countess built her weir (*see* Exeter), till the Exeter ship canal was opened in 1567, it boomed. At other times some trade by-passed it. Although now part of Exeter, it has never become a suburb, always keeping its own character and life, in the past building ships, sending more ships than any other port to catch cod off Newfoundland, catching herring locally and salmon in the estuary. Its ports, like so many, died because it was too shallow for big steamships, but the remnants can be seen at the waterfront: derelict warehouses and shipyards; rotting hulls in the mud. The Strand is extraordinarily attractive with it row of "Dutch" houses built *c.* 1700–25 by merchants who sold cloth to Holland. It ends at a small slipway and a place where local children sail model yachts. Parking is generally difficult and there is no real tourist commercialization. There are, however, many pubs worth inspecting and, at No. 25 The Strand, a small museum.

Some 1½ m. NE., on what was then heath round **Clyst St Mary,** the 1549 Prayer Book rebels (*see* SAMPFORD COURTENAY) suffered their decisive defeat at the hands of Lord Russell, principal recipient of dissolved monastic lands in the West Country.

TORBRYAN, *Devon* (3–SX8266), has one of Devon's best village churches, *c.* 1440, spared both the Puritans and 19th-cent. restoration. It is beautifully light and simple, with box pews, a coloured screen with panel paintings and a coloured pulpit, very finely carved altar and fan-vaulted porch, and fragments (though these are less special) of medieval glass. It has an unusual gaunt grey tower. Apparently the vicar during the Civil War hid its treasures and white-washed the screen.

The tiny village is situated in a pastoral bowl sheltered by tree-bristled limestone tors from which, with the Norman de Bryan who owned the manor, it takes its name. The Church House (*c.* 1500) is now an attractive pub. Nearby (ask directions locally) are caves where the bones of prehistoric animals have been found.

TORQUAY, *Devon* (3–SX9164). In 1790 it was a fishing village "discovered" only by a select few. During the Napoleonic Wars it became the home of wives of officers from the warships anchored for long periods in Torbay. In 1815 Napoleon, a prisoner waiting to hear his fate, gazed at the site from the deck of the *Bellerophon* and pronounced it *"beau"*. By 1850 it was calling itself "the Queen of Watering Places". Napoleon III came, as did Russian Royalty, and its fame gained a further boost from the discovery in Kent's Cavern of human bones with those of Ice Age beasts, proving that man had existed far earlier than had hitherto been thought. It grew fast – from a population of about 6,000 in 1840 to 54,000 in 1969 – and it is today the most glamorous, grandly sited and well planned of West Country resorts.

It has some ambitious modern buildings, if mainly blocks of flats, mingled with the great trees and sub-tropical shrubs to the SE. of the harbour on what is possibly England's most opulent headland. A drive round this – Marine Drive – is a good first move in order to taste the ethos and for the views over Thatcher Rock, with its clouds of sea-birds, and over Tor Bay to Berry Head (*see* BRIXHAM) and over **Babbacombe Bay** to the red cliffs of DAWLISH. Kent's Cavern, now a floodlit extravaganza of stalagmites and stalactites, with a few bones still to be seen, is at the east end of this drive close to Anstey's Cove, which is pretty when not too crowded. At the west end is the splendid cream façade of Hesketh Crescent (*c.* 1846), now the Osborne Hotel. Above it, Lincombe Drive is also worth following; then comes the harbour bright with boats on which – rather than on the long beach W. of it – the town converges. The sea-front continues excellent, past hillside gardens floodlit in many colours at night and the Princess Theatre (1961), to the now public grounds of the buildings collectively called Torre Abbey. These are the town's oldest buildings of consequence: a mainly 18th-cent. house containing the Corporation Art Gallery and Museum and, periodically, contemporary art exhibitions; a gatehouse (*c.* 1320); and a well-preserved tithe barn from the abbey founded for Premonstratensians in 1196. It is known as the Spanish Barn because prisoners from the Armada were locked up in it. Of the churches, the most notable is St John's (1861–71) by G. E. Street with Burne-Jones windows and murals. It is in Montpelier Terrace, off Union Street behind the harbour, and a little E. of it is the Natural History Museum specializing in finds from Kent's Cavern. The aquarium above the harbour's south pier has reptiles and tropical, as well as local, fish. In the suburb of Babbacombe, 1½ m. N. of the harbour, there is a model village, beautifully made and maintained; it even has wedding bells in its churches. Nearby is a cliff railway to Oddicombe beach which is also fun.

Paignton, about 3 m. SW., also has some splendid features. Oldway Mansion, the entrance to which is beside the A379, is the most sumptuous house in Devon; built *c.* 1874, with Versailles in mind, by Isaac Merritt Singer, American founder of the sewing-machine company; altered 1904–7, when the south colonnade was added by his son, Paris, among whose long-term guests was Isadora Duncan. It is now the Civic Centre, open at most times. The Zoo, off the A385 TOTNES road, is an outstanding one, said to have the largest collection of animals in England outside London, spread over 75 acres with peacocks, lake islands of gibbons, and a children's miniature railway through the "jungle". Kirkham House in Kirkham Street (about ¼ m. NW. of Oldway) is a medieval house restored by the Ministry of Public Building and Works to show what life was like in the 16th cent. The red-sandstone St John's Church (about 200 yds W.) is mainly 15th-cent. and has a distinguished south transept chapel built by the Kirkham family with lavishly sculptured stone screen tombs, damaged by Puritans but still fine, and an excellent ceiling. The Festival Hall on the sea-front was built in 1967. The harbour is picturesque and there is an aquarium by it. Before it became a resort, Paignton was famed for its cabbages and cider.

From the Torquay sea-front you can ride 2 m. to **Cockington** by landau. It is a thatched village popular with tourists, with a pub (1934) by Sir Edward Lutyens. The grounds of Cockington Court, with a perfect village cricket square, are nice to wander through to see the pretty little 14th- and 15th-cent. church. The Court itself is basically Elizabethan with a 17th-cent. front. It was formerly the home of the Carys, then of the Mallocks, two of the three families (the Palks were the third) who guided Torquay's development.

About 1¾ m. W. of Cockington, near Marldon, is **Compton Castle**, the best surviving example of a medieval fortified manor house in Devon, home in the 16th cent. of Sir Humphrey Gilbert, the explorer. It dates from the 14th, 15th and 16th cents., with a restored great hall. It is all in excellent condition, cared for by the National Trust.

TOTNES, *Devon* (3–SX8060), has terrible suburbs even for South Devon which has, by and large, the dreariest in South-West England. But steep up its middle runs an attractive narrow old main street, which is spanned by a room marking its medieval East Gate and with one of Devon's finest churches. Moreover, well situated at the highest navigable point on the Dart, it is the starting point for steamer trips down that stretch of river whose beauty is almost completely denied the car-bound.

Ancient legend claimed that the town was founded by one Brutus, grandson of the Trojan Aeneas. More certainly it was an Anglo-Saxon town with a mint, and in the 15th and 16th cents., with a cloth industry and a port, was second in the county only to EXETER in merchant affluence. Slow, however, to respond to the fashion for the Flemish-originated "new draperies", it thereafter declined rapidly, till, in the 19th cent. retired *bourgeoisie* began to appreciate the charms of its hinterland. Manifestly recovered today it is a centre for rich farming (livestock market Tuesdays) and retirement country with some of the smartest antique shops and boutiques in Devon, and quite a colony of neo-craftsmen (potters, silversmiths, etc.). Its industries include bacon-curing, small-boat buildings, dairying and sweet-making, and its port still does some business.

Its great red church was built *c.* 1400–68, a great many people taking a hand, the local bishop having promised indulgence to all who helped. Its outstanding feature is a superb stone screen (1460), rivalled in the West County only by EXETER Cathedral's, but much else is splendid, notably its ceilings, pulpit, beautifully carved Corporation pew-fronts (16th-cent.) and monument to Christopher Blackhall (d. 1633). Immediately N. of the church, the 16th-cent. Guildhall has a court-room of 1553, council chambers of 1624 and various museum pieces. It is open when not in use. It stands on the site of the priory. Below the building spanning the High Street is an Elizabethan merchant's house which is now the museum.

At the top of the street is the arcaded Butterwalk, not comparable with DARTMOUTH's but pleasant; and near it, in contrast, is the new Civic Hall, outside which there is a market on Fridays and in which, periodically, the local craftsmen exhibit. Some of the latter can be watched in their workshops (ask locally). About 50 yds N. of the Butterwalk are the ruins of a 12th-cent. castle, architecturally unexciting but good for views, and close to its entrance is the arch of the town's former North Gate and some pretty, well-restored cottages. A tree-shaded island just below the fine three-arched bridge (1826) over the river is a nice place to watch boats go by. And from the station a privately owned train carries passengers up the valley to Buckfastleigh (*see* ASHBURTON).

About 2 m. SW. of Totnes, **Harberton** church has a finely carved rood-screen and stone pulpit.

TREVAUNANCE COVE, *Cornwall* (2–SW 7251), is one of the prettiest coves on the Cornish north coast. It has a safe (comparatively) beach, good for surfing. Like a fortress guarding a pass, a ruined tin-mining engine-house stands above the wooded combe by which you approach, and mineral ore stains its cliffs reddish brown. The area produced some of the best-quality Cornish tin and in 1794 a pier was built to make the cove a port. But the pier was washed away.

The buildings in the cove are modern and ugly, but fortunately few. There is a seal sanctuary, where sick or orphaned seals swim in a pool and sunbathe St Agnes Head, about 1 m. W., is a grand place to walk to. The off-shore rock islands are called the Man and his Man.

For hundreds of years till late in the 19th cent. the little town of **St Agnes** thrived on mining. Now it is a pleasant, unsophisticated place with cottages on steep slopes.

TRURO, *Cornwall* (2–SW8244). The county's cathedral city and in all but name its capital. On one of the many arms of the Fal estuary, it was in the Middle Ages an important port for the export of mineral ore, long before FALMOUTH was of any importance, and, from the early 13th cent. until 1752, a stannary town (*see* HELSTON). It is still a port but minor, mainly a market town and

Peter Baker

Truro Cathedral

administrative centre with some light industry. In the 18th cent. it became fashionable with rich merchants who found Falmouth, though their place of business, a less wholesome residence, and, at about the same time, it was a hub of county society. As a result, it has some of the best Georgian terraces W. of BATH. From *c.* 1859 it became an important rail junction. In 1890 its cathedral was begun and in 1912 came the County Council. During the Civil War it stood strongly for the King; otherwise its history seems to have contained little public drama.

The main things to see are the cathedral, the museum, Lemon Street and Walsingham Place. The cathedral, incorporating the old Church of St Mary, was finished in 1910. Its architect was J. L. Pearson; the style he chose Early English. Though without the spacious precinct given to most provincial English cathedrals, it dominates the city, its spire 250 ft high. It is best entered via the south rather than the west door, because from the west the yellow stonework of its nave may seem dull; it is much more impressive looking back from the chancel entrance, and from there, too, the carved Bath stone reredos makes a splendid first impact. The attractive baptistry should not be missed. On the wall of the north choir aisle a terracotta relief of Christ, Romans and crowd on the way to Calvary, presented as a thanksgiving for two sons returned safe from the Boer War, is conventional yet fascinating. Close to it is a hefty restored Jacobean monument. Full architectural details are given in a leaflet available in the building. The chapter house extending into the small lawn to the N. was completed in 1967 and won a Civic Trust award.

Near the cathedral's west door, the old theatre and assembly rooms, which was a favoured rendezvous for 18th- and 19th-cent. Truro society, has a most excellent Georgian façade (1772). The museum, in River Street, is Cornwall's best. It contains a number of old masters, paintings and drawings and is notable particularly for its examples of Cornish minerals, but good on Cornish history, too, and all excellently laid out, diagrammed and captioned. Lemon Street, laid out c. 1795 and still mainly of that period, curves southwards from the city centre. Walsingham Place, about 20 years later, is an exquisite crescent, tucked away off Victoria Place, SW. of the cathedral. Strangeways Terrace, off Lemon Street, is fairly good Regency and from it you get one of the best views of the cathedral. The Victorian City Hall in Boscawen Street is worth a look: grand, dark-grey granite. About 50 yds N. in St Nicholas Street over a shoe-filled window is a remarkable florid Victorian facade. One of the city's most famed buildings, the former Red Lion Inn, which stood almost opposite the City Hall, had to be demolished after being lashed beyond repair by a lorry in 1967. In the 18th cent. it was the home of the parents of Samuel Foote, the actor. Near the top of Lemon Street is a monument to two other men of the city, Richard and John Lander, explorers of the River Niger 1825–30.

At Lake's Pottery in Chapel Street, one of Cornwall's oldest and most famous, visitors can see pots being made.

The launch-trip down the river to Falmouth is highly recommended, though the double journey takes the best part of a day.

The National-Trust-owned gardens of **Trelissick**, 4 m. S., contain many shrubs that cannot be grown in England outside South Cornwall. The house (not open to the public) has an elegant, porticoed façade of the 1820s.

At **Come-to-Good**, a little E. of Devoran, 4½ m. SW. of Truro, is one of the oldest Quaker meeting houses in England, c. 1710.

One m. SW. of Devoran, just off the A39, **Tullimaar House**, home of Princess Marthe Bibesco, contains a remarkable collection of Napoleonic relics, including a plaster head of him by David D'Angers and the cockade he wore at the Battle of Austerlitz. It is open to the public most summer afternoons.

VERYAN, *Cornwall* (2–SW9240). Veryan is made unique by five old round houses each with a cross on top, two at each end of the village, one in the centre.

The village marks the entrance to **Roseland**. The name seems appropriate to the soft, lush landscape, but in fact derives from the Cornish word *ros* meaning hill, spur or heath. A strange avenue of twisted elms leads into the village of **St Anthony-in-Roseland**. Behind a lawn and sheltered sandy cove is a Victorian mansion turned hotel incorporating in its kitchen part of the refectory of a monastery formerly on the site. And hidden behind and adjoining it (key from the hotel) is the Church of St Anthony, mainly 13th-cent. with a possibly Norman south doorway, heavily but pleasantly restored in c. 1850, unusual in having a central belfry.

The peninsula's tip is surrounded by pretty bays and woods and is mostly National Trust land. St Anthony Head is good for views, and the lighthouse below it can sometimes be visited.

WADEBRIDGE, *Cornwall* (2–SW9972), has one of the finest medieval bridges in Britain. It dates from c. 1485. The money to build it was raised by Thomas Lovibond, vicar of Egloshayle (¼ m. E.), who considered the ferry too dangerous. It is said that packs of wool were used to make a firm base for the piers on the deeply-sanded river bed. Now just over 100 yds long, it has been widened twice and reduced from 17 to 14 arches, but most of the east side is original. A little riverside park just N. of its east end is an excellent place from which to look at it.

The Wadebridge–Bodmin railway was the first opened in Cornwall (1834) and in the 1960s was one of the first to be closed.

The Iron Age hill-camp of Kelly Rounds or Castle Killibury, 2 m. NE. then ½ m. down a track from a crossroads, has been suggested as a possible site for a fort of King Arthur: all you can see, however, is a couple of banks and ditches.

Two m. N., between Chapel Amble and Trewornan Bridge on an arm of the Camel Estuary, is the **Walmsley Bird Sanctuary** noted for geese and waders.

WATCHET, *Somerset* (3–ST0743), is a busy little commercial port with an attractive harbour. Wood pulp, timber, fertilizers, potatoes and tinned fruit are among its imports, paper its main export. Paper-making is its main industry, a local mill employing some 600 people. A port since Anglo-Saxon times and much raided by Vikings, it was made prosperous in the 19th cent. by iron mines in the Brendon Hills to the S. The closure of the mines and the wrecking of its harbour by a great storm in 1900 brought decline till the paper industry came. Coleridge is said to have thought of it as the port of departure for his Ancient Mariner. It has little architectural merit, yet is not unattractive. Its church, on the hill behind, contains good 16th- and 17th-cent. brasses.

Blue Anchor, 2½ m. W., has a good beach and, but for its caravan site, would be pretty, with various coloured cliffs and long views (painted by Turner) to MINEHEAD's north hill.

WEARE GIFFARD HALL, *Devon* (3–SS 4526). Built c. 1462 by the Fortescues (*see* SWIMBRIDGE) it contains a hammer-beam roof without rival in Devon, and is altogether one of the county's most fascinating houses, with whole rooms of beautiful panelling. In 1967 it was in sad repair when bought by two enterprising ladies who restored it at their own expense. It is now a private hotel. There is a fine panoramic view of the house and the church next door from the main BIDEFORD–Torrington road. The village is famous for its strawberry teas.

Beside the church at **Frithelstock**, about 2 m. SW., are the ruins of an Augustinian priory which was founded in 1220, dissolved in 1536. The west wall remains intact, though some of the masonry has been renewed in order to preserve it.

WELLOW, *Somerset* (4–ST7358). This attractive village, 6 m. from BATH, looks as if it should be in the Cotswolds. Its church (mainly *c.* 1372) is beautifully light, high and uncluttered, with fine undarkened carved-timber roofs, flagstone floor and some good bench-ends. Its original patron was Sir Thomas Hungerford, first Speaker of the House of Commons. The gabled 17th-cent. farmhouse opposite the school was formerly the Hungerford manor (*see also* FARLEIGH HUNGERFORD). Remains of a Roman villa were found near the village but there is now virtually nothing to see. There is a theory, encouraged by the church's dedication to St Julian, that Romans may have been converted to Christianity here. St Julian's Well, in the valley a little E. of the church, has a ghost story attached to it.

About 2 m. SW., Stoney Littleton Long Barrow is a prehistoric stone burial chamber. You can go inside. Apply at Long Barrow Farm for key and candle.

About 2½ m. E., and about ¾ m. NW. of Hinton Charterhouse village, are the ruins of the Carthusian **Hinton Priory**, founded in 1232. A three-story gabled building with vaulted rooms and stone staircase survives; also the refectory. They are privately owned and sometimes open.

WELLS, *Somerset* (3–ST5445), is a cathedral city and for centuries its contribution to history was purely architectural and ecclesiastical, national drama impinging on it only rarely, as when Monmouth's followers stabled their horses in the cathedral. In the 13th cent. its population was about 4,000, and has less than doubled since. Today it is important for its cheese and has other light industries. But the town still seems to hang humbly about the gates of what is the largest and best preserved medieval ecclesiastical precinct in the county. Taken as a whole the cathedral itself is one of the finest buildings (as well as the oldest of anything like its size) in Somerset. The best road approaches are from the E. and N.; the view of it from round **Dulcote**, 1 m. SE., probably the finest of all. The city's streets are one-way, and to save driving in circles it is wise to make at once for a car park: the nearest is in the Market Place just NW. of the cathedral.

Begun in *c.* 1180, the cathedral was built in stages: the east end of the nave is the earliest part, the astonishing west front and the nave west of the north porch *c.* 1235, the central tower 1318, and at roughly the same time the Lady Chapel was added and the choir reconstructed. The two western towers were the last additions, the south one *c.* 1384, the north *c.* 1424. Across the nave a brilliant swirl of arches was put up shortly after the central tower to stop it falling. Particularly beautiful are the 12th-cent. north porch, the nave, the Lady Chapel and its windows, and the choir's 14th-cent. east window. In the north transept is a remarkable 14th-cent. clock, across the face of which knights joust on the hour. Close to it a superb stone staircase leads to the Chapter House (*c.* 1300) which has a fine fan-vaulted ceiling emanating from a central column. The cathedral's south door leads to beautiful 15th- and 16th-cent. cloisters.

Of the precinct's other buildings, the Vicar's Close, an outwardly little-altered street just N. of the Chapter House, has similar 14th-cent. houses. It houses the "vicars choral" – clerical assistants with special reference to singing. Above the entrance to it is their fine dining-hall with much of its original furniture. Just W. of this, beside the 15th-cent. Deanery, is the museum which has a collection of samplers and specializes in WOOKEY HOLE finds and local history. S. across the green, the moated Bishop's Palace (basically 13th-cent.) is not normally open, but the episcopal swans entertain by ringing a bell near the drawbridge when hungry.

The city's civic – as distinct from ecclesiastical – centre has traditionally been a few hundred yards to the W., beyond the shopping centre. Here is the 15th-cent. Church of St Cuthbert, which is tall and light inside with a tie-beam roof and, just to the N. 15th-cent. almshouses and the ancient Guildhall.

Almost all the numerous pubs between these two areas are in some respect ancient and attractive; in particular the City Arms, near St Cuthbert's Church, which was the city gaol till the 19th cent., and in the courtyard of the 17th-cent. Crown, William Penn, the Quaker, is said to have preached to an audience of 2,000 and been arrested. The new Public Library received a Civic Trust award.

WEMBURY, *Devon* (3–SX5148). The village has been developed as a seaside resort, but it has a medieval church which confronts the sea more boldly than any other in Devon, a landmark to shipping for some 600 years, superbly sited on a cliff above a rocky cove and a lush watermeadow. Moreover, it has a good 14th-cent. tower and several quaint monuments. From the field above its cemetery are fine views down the coast to the mouth of the Yealm to the E., to Rame Head to the W., and ahead to the Mew Stone.

Return through the village and turn E. and you pass a pretty row of houses dated 1682 and reach an attractive hamlet. Where, after a short distance, this road ends, National Trust land begins. Over it there are good walks to the Yealm estuary.

WESTON-SUPER-MARE, *Somerset* (3–ST 3261). Easily the county's largest seaside resort, it is also the biggest town on the West Country's north coast and the second biggest in Somerset. Though few resorts have grown so quickly – population under 100 in 1800, about 19,000 in 1900, today roughly 44,200 – it is to some extent planned, with splendidly wide sea-front roads,

A. F. Kersting

Wells Cathedral: the astronomical clock

Wells Cathedral: the Chapter House steps

A. F. Kersting

pavements and gardens. At low tide the sea retreats far, exposing mud, but this, it is said, gives off the ozone which is claimed to make its air so salubrious. It entertains lavishly: two theatres, two cinemas, a model village, aquarium, small zoo, ten-pin bowling, a dance-hall also used for concerts, variety shows and wrestling, three swimming-pools two of which are indoor and heated, two piers, donkey rides on the beach, marine lake where children can boat happily, motor-boat and yacht races, county cricket in early August, tennis courts, two golf courses nearby, and medicinal baths for a great variety of

ailments. Moreover, its public gardens, in particular the Winter Gardens, are excellent.

Though architecturally seldom distinguished, its Church of All Saints, just E. of Grove Park, is an outstanding example of its period. It was built 1898–1902 by G. F. Bodley, with later additions by F. C. Eden. The museum, in the Boulevard, includes finds from the Iron Age fort on Worlebury Hill, at the north end of the town, where there are earthworks and nice woodland walks. Immediately N. again, **Kewstoke** has a good Norman to 15th-cent. church and a long, very ancient flight of steps called Monks Steps which provide a good viewpoint.

About 3 m. NNE., is **Woodspring Priory** founded in 1210 by William Courtenay, grandson of one of Thomas à Becket's murderers. An extremely attractive group of 15th-cent. (or in some cases perhaps 14th-cent.) buildings remain – church, chantry, court-room and barn – recently acquired by the National Trust after long use as part of a farm.

Two m. S., **Uphill,** the ruined Norman Church of St Nicholas has been roofless since 1864, and was replaced because it was inconvenient to get to. It stands on the last western hillock of the MENDIPS, overlooking the mouth of the River Axe where, it is thought, Phoenicians traded, Romans had a port, and, if you like, that Joseph of Arimathea arrived from Palestine (*see* GLASTONBURY). It is worth the climb.

The tiny islands of **Flat Holm** and **Steep Holme** are, respectively, about 6 and 5 m. offshore. There are regular motor-boat trips to the former, which has a lighthouse and an occasionally occupied farm-house. The latter, more barren and rocky but growing rare plants, is privately owned, leased to naturalists and archaeological societies. Special permission is needed to visit it.

WESTON ZOYLAND, *Somerset* (3–ST35 34), was the headquarters of King James II's army before the Battle of Sedgemoor (6 July 1685) – England's last major ground battle – in which they defeated the untrained and primitively armed forces of Charles II's illegitimate son, the Duke of Monmouth, claimant to the throne. The battle took place about ½ m. NW of the church. It began between 1 and 2 am and was all over in one and a half hours. Sixteen of the King's men were killed, some 300 rebels. A number of prisoners were shot or hanged on the spot. About 500 were locked up in the church till daybreak, many of them wounded. Five died in the church. The survivors were then herded to BRIDG-WATER, some being hanged *en route*.

The church's superb yellow-grey tower is a landmark in a flat, fen landscape. The building is mainly 14th- and 15th-cent. Inside, it is high, light and uncluttered, with a tremendous tie-beam roof and great expanses of flagstone floor. The village is now a dormitory for Bridgwater's factories and has much new housing.

A memorial marking the battle site is down a track beside a rhine (ditch-canal) at the village's edge.

WIDECOMBE-IN-THE-MOOR, *Devon* (3–SX7176). Here headed Uncle Tom Cobbleigh and All in the well-known song. The village, as its name suggests, is situated high up on DART-MOOR. Its church has one of the finest towers (*c.* 1500) in Devon, 120 ft high and pinnacled, paid for by tin-miners keen to manifest their newly acquired wealth. It has a story attached to it: in 1638 in the middle of a Sunday service and during a thunderstorm, a "bolt of fire" hit the church, knocking down a tower pinnacle, killing four people, injuring 62, and generally causing great confusion. At once a survivor remembered seeing a mysterious traveller exposing, in an unguarded moment, a cloven hoof. You can read more about it inside the church. The Church House (National Trust) and Glebe House, both built *c.* 1600, are in a nice tiny square by the church gate. The fair takes place in early September.

About 3 m. NW., is **Grimspound**, probably the most impressive of the moor's numerous pre-historic settlements. It is Bronze Age; a village of at least 24 huts surrounded – for protection against wild animals rather than man – by a wall 10 ft thick and now about waist high. There is a magnificent granite-slabbed entrance on the south side and much else to see. It looks across a valley to good examples of old tin workings.

WOOKEY HOLE, *Somerset* (3–ST5347). Here, in the southern limestone slopes of the MENDIPS, is one of the major cave complexes in Britain. The floodlit Great Cave contains remark-able formations of stalagmites and stalactites. Through it, slow and blue-green, flows the cause of it, the River Axe. During the Iron Age and as late as the Roman occupation it was inhabited, and the implements found (serious excavation did not begin till 1912) have greatly increased know-ledge of that period. Many of them can be seen in the local museum and that at WELLS. Its inner recesses are still being explored with the help of aqualungs. Of other nearby caves, one was a hyenas' den, probably towards the end of the Ice Age. Their bones and those of the animals they fed on, including mammoth and wild horse, were found in it, also traces of Stone Age human habitation. On the hillside above are ancient cultivation terraces. Visitors to the Great Cave should wear strong shoes and warm clothes, as the temperature is permanently low and it is damp.

Close to the path to it is one of the oldest paper mills in Britain (1610). It specializes in high-grade writing paper.

In a building beside the car park, Titania's Palace is probably the world's most intricate, lavish and fantastic dolls' house. It is a work of astonishing imagination, labour and ingenuity, begun in 1907 by Sir Nevile Wilkinson at his home in Ireland for his three-year-old daughter. It was finished in 1922 and has been exhibited all over the world.

Ebbor Gorge, ¾ m. NW., is a smaller, much more wooded version of CHEDDAR GORGE, with the advantages that no road goes through it and that it is a National Nature Reserve. It is most easily reached from the W., from the Priddy road where there is a car park, or you can walk from Wookey Hole.

WOOLACOMBE and MORTEHOE, *Devon* (3–SS4545). The former has, with SAUNTON, the finest sand and surf beach on this north-west coast N. of BUDE. The sea does not expose miles of mud at low tide as at many places on the Bristol Channel. It is enclosed by steep, moorland slopes rather than by cliffs, and its houses climb pleas-antly up the gorse-covered hillsides behind. Be-yond the houses are romantic bare combes, grand for walking or riding.

Mortehoe is older and has some pretty cottages. Its church, founded in Norman times, enlarged *c.* 1300 and subsequently, is small and quite interesting but not especially beautiful. From beside it a path leads to Morte Point where the slate cliffs are thrilling. The Morte Stone, the furthest point, claimed five ships in the winter of 1852. To the N. the lighthouse (1879) at Bull Point can be visited, but it is advisable to make an appointment.

YATTON, *Somerset* (3–ST4265). Within an old nucleus, thickly coated with modern housing for BRISTOL commuters, it has a grandly austere high-naved church, famous for its beautifully panelled and vaulted 15th-cent. porch and, dis-played in a frame, an exceptional piece of 15th-cent. embroidery. The church also contains two unusually fine 15th-cent. effigy-tombs. With a population of over 4,000, factories making furniture and bird food and a large tannery, the village is well on the way to small township. It has a livestock market on Mondays.

Cadbury Hill (not the Camelot one), just to the E., is a good place for views and pictures. Excava-tions of an earthwork on it have produced interesting Iron-Age, Roman and Dark-Age finds.

Some 1¾ m. SE., **Congresbury**, too, has an attractive centre, an interesting basically 15th-cent. vicarage, and one of the best church spires in Somerset.

YEOVIL, *Somerset* (3–ST5515). An exceed-ingly busy town with more new glass-and-metal buildings springing up than in any other place within a wide radius. The headquarters of West-land Aircraft, Europe's largest helicopter com-pany, it also has major, long-established glove, leather and dairying industries, numerous smaller ones, and two important livestock markets (Mondays and Fridays, the former specializing in pedigree cattle). With leather-working rather than wool traditionally its main living, it was spared the slump caused to many other Somerset small towns by the growth of the North's textile indus-tries in the 18th and 19th cents. Since it became a borough in 1846, its population has nearly quad-rupled. The Romans clearly liked its site in rolling fertile land beside the River Yeo.

Its older centre, which suffered greatly from fires in 1499, 1623 and 1640, and from Second

World War bombs, is congested but worth visiting mainly for its Ham-stone church. Scarcely beautiful, it is, however, big and ruggedly impressive. Moreover, built *c.* 1380–90, it is older than most of its size. It contains an outstanding 15th-cent. brass lectern, and the War Memorial window in the north aisle is intriguing.

About ¼ m. SW. of the church, the museum in Henford Manor has a good collection of firearms and local Roman finds; and the walk to it, via George Street past the municipal buildings (1926) and matching Post Office, shows quite a handsome bit of the town.

Other buildings worth seeing: Abbey Farm with medieval Ham-stone tithe barn, on the western edge of the town, beside the ILMINSTER road; Newton Surmaville, an early-17th-cent. manor house, just SE. of the main railway station; the Roman Catholic church in Higher Kingston (about ¼ m. N. of the parish church), which is pleasant neo-Gothic (1897–9). Babylon Hill, just E. of the town, is a good viewpoint and was the scene of a Civil War skirmish.

Two m. W., **Brympton d'Evercy**, now a school, is one of the most attractive places in Somerset: a fine mainly 16th- and 17th-cent. house claiming the longest straight staircase in England; beside it a good church, chiefly 14th-cent. The house is open one day a week.

YEOVILTON, *Somerset* (3–ST5422). Within the Royal Naval Air Station, which here straddles the A303, is the excellent Fleet Air Arm Museum. It includes most of the planes – Swordfish, Sea Fury, Sea Vampire and many others – used by the service since its formation in 1914, and scale models, many photographs, documents and equipment. There is also an enclosure where you can watch the planes of today taking off and landing.

Two m. SW., **Ilchester** was an important Roman military station on the Fosse Way. The main roads SW. and NE. follow for some way this great highway which they created between Lincolnshire and EXETER, and there are Roman bricks in the church tower walls. Roger Bacon, the remarkable monk-scientist, was born here in 1214.

ZENNOR, *Cornwall* (2–SW4538), is the most compact of the grey villages in the northern half of the gale-swept Penwith peninsula, its houses seeming to hug their church in a landscape of boulders, dry-stone-walled fields and almost no trees. On the side of a chair in the church's chancel is carved a mermaid. Legend says she came from the sea to hear the wonderful singing of the squire's son and lured him back there with her, never to be seen again.

The Wayside Museum has an excellent collection of relics of old Cornish crafts and industries.

The cliffs round Zennor Head, ½ m. N., are tremendous.

About ½ m. SE. is Zennor Quoit. A quoit was a chambered tomb formed by raising oblong boulders on end to support a vast slab for a roof and then walling it all in with small stones or turf. They date from *c.* 2500–1500 B.C. In all known cases the walls have long since gone. The slab of the Zennor one is the largest known in England, 18 ft by 9½ ft, fallen at one end. There are three others in the vicinity (*see* LANYON QUOIT).

Some 2¼ m. SW. – and about ⅓-m. walk from the road – is **Bosporthennis**, the site of an Iron Age "beehive" settlement, like those of western Ireland but much less well preserved.

Woolacombe sands

Jane J. Miller

East Anglia

Essex   Cambridgeshire   Suffolk   Norfolk

RONALD BLYTHE

In an age of new boundaries the old concise limits of East Anglia – Suffolk, Norfolk and the Isle of Ely – the South Folk, the North Folk and the Isle of Eels – have been stretched alarmingly in order to accommodate weather forecasts, regional develop-ment schemes and TV programme planning. While not allowing, as these authori-ties sometimes do, that the area reaches upwards to Hull and across to Birmingham, it is possible to see that Essex – the East Saxons – and Cambridgeshire do share an affinity with the chief characteristics of the region, though for the East Anglian proper his country begins in the Stour Valley, rides steadily out to the chilly North Sea in a fine parabola of heath, shingle and marsh, until it reaches the Wash, and concludes in the geometrical sluices and peat of the Fens. This was the kingdom ruled by the Wuffingas, whose burial ground at Sutton Hoo has thrown a very civilized light upon the Dark Ages. And before both the Roman and Anglo-Saxon conquests it was the highly populated kingdom of the Iceni.

Some logical as well as tribal instinct kept East Anglia's identity intact right up until the railway age. Its off-centre geography helped, too. Unless some specific business drew a man along the road to Norwich the entire plateau of little clay fields and huge forests was by-passed by centuries of travellers. The earliest travellers followed a low chalk ridge which sweeps up from the North Downs, crosses southern Cambridgeshire, and once joined the Lincolnshire wold. This was the track which became the Icknield Way. Marsh and forest dominated the eastern counties until comparatively modern times, and it is startling in the context of today's prairie-like conditions in many parts of the area that when Queen Elizabeth I made her extravagant progresses into Suffolk she rode through almost continuous woodland, and that the memory which the many emigrants from this part of England to the New World took with them was that of a still rather secluded place.

"Oaken" East Anglia disappeared because there was no forest law to protect the trees, and the wheat for which the "Whitelands", as the chalk-based farms of Cambridgeshire were called right up until the First World War, were so famous, spread across the Suffolk and Norfolk clays. In the eighteenth century Norfolk played a large part in the agricultural revolution, particularly in a respect to the famous sowing rotation called "Norfolk four-course" – wheat, roots, barley, seeds.

One of the most attractive features of East Anglia is the way in which intensively cultivated or inhabited districts alternate with patches of heath and solitude, so that history and prehistory have equal evidence. There is no better place to ex-perience the latter than Wandlebury, the Iron Age fort on the crest of the Gog Magog Hills at Cambridge. The approach to it is a pale stretch of unmetalled Roman road, part of the great Via Devana; and to stroll along it on a hot blue June day, with beech and wild mignonette filling the hollows from which the light earth was dug to make the camber of this classic country lane, is one of those rare travel experiences. From the height one can view the prototype East Anglian scene, the brilliant arable plain which was eventually to become the landscape of the eastern kingdom. A mile or two below lies Stourbridge Common, where for centuries was held the most important fair in Europe, and on which Bunyan based his Vanity Fair. Sir Isaac Newton bought his prisms here. West lies King's College Chapel. Thus, as in a compact airiness, can be seen from this modest hill those components which make up the character of the whole area: intense religion, leading to an equally intense questioning, and manufacturing giving way to farming.

The ancient Breckland further along on the chalk ridge shows a kind of East Anglian progress in reverse, for until the 1920s the moor here remained much as the prehistoric "dwellers of the field" had left it. Now its huge coniferous plantations have transformed it into a fragment of Schleswig-Holstein. A last-minute look at this unique region as it was before the forest hid it is described in that little masterpiece of naturalist writing, R. R. Clarke's *In Breckland Wilds*.

The celebrated architecture of East Anglia sprang from three more or less inexhaustible local materials, chalk, clay and wood. From the chalk came the flints used with such prodigious skill and fantasy to make decorative facings for the churches. It also supplied clunch for such exquisite ornaments as the Lady Chapel at Ely and the Gate of Honour for Caius College. The clays produced bricks of great colour variation. During the revival of brick-building in the fifteenth century and for centuries afterwards the glowing red bricks such as those found in Charsfield (Suffolk) church and the gatehouse at Layer Marney, Essex, were favoured, but Georgian architects later made elegant use of "Suffolk white-brick" in many a country house. Snape Maltings, one of the most beautiful industrial buildings in rural England, displays a whole spectrum of local clay hues in its walls. The glaring gault bricks with which so much of modern Cambridge is built are less attractive. Local clays, too, were used in and after the eighteenth century for the pantiles which, when they are not blue-glazed, as in Norfolk, give many an East Anglian village a faintly Tuscan look.

But *the* building material throughout the area is wood. For generations of forest-born carpenter-artists its uses were virtually limitless. There was wooden engineering (the whole oaks on which Ely's lantern is balanced), wooden visions of paradise (the church roofs at March, Blythburgh and in many other places), wooden lace to screen chancels, wooden houses and barns, and, all along the river estuaries, the unceasing construction of wooden ships. It seemed that the East Anglian, everywhere confronted by something so vitally enduring as oak, felt obliged to use it for his needs, to the limits of his strength and imagination. The most moving example of this forest art is not such a miracle of craftsmanship as the font cover at Ufford in Suffolk but the simple church at Greensted in Essex, made of split oaks which chemical tests have dated to A.D. 850. The Anglo-Saxon carpenters' adze marks are still plainly visible. Something of the sacredness of trees to a woodland community remains here. One thinks of the "gospel" oaks at Great Yeldham in Essex and Polstead in Suffolk, and then of the woodwoses – the old forest gods – which stand subjected by the weight of many an East Anglian font.

As might be expected, scientific farming is drastically altering the natural history of the area. Small farms are amalgamated into larger units as their tenancies lapse. Villages which fifty years ago had a dozen farms are now likely to have only three or four. Hedges fall and ditches are filled in to make big fields. The weedless crops present a bland gloriousness in the summer and there is something potent and splendid about a road sunk in tall unhedged wheat. But botanists and ornithologists must mourn the price paid for such efficiency, and the long-term effects of the new farming on the ecology of East Anglia remain unknown. Yet this is a country-side which is still full of wild patches and secret places, and one of the best corners of Britain for plant exploration and bird-watching. Pasch flowers and shimmering cotillions of Adonis Blue butterflies – as well as a silence which overwhelms – can be found on those gigantic defences near Newmarket known as Fleam and Devil's dykes, and at Framsden in Suffolk there are acres of fritillaries. Saltings, meres, marshes and estuaries all the way from the Blackwater to the Ouse make the East Anglian coast a thrilling bird territory, and avocets breed on Havergate Island. But those superb beasts the Percheron and Punch horses, which held monumental rank in the local animal kingdom almost up until the last war, have quite disappeared.

East Anglia has often in its long history accepted industrial change. The Little Domesday of 1086 shows it to have been the most densely populated part of Britain. During the late Middle Ages, after the manufacturing revolution created by the Flemish weavers, the whole region entered upon a period of wealthy trading. A handsome part of its profits went into the building of the great wool churches, the subsidizing of learning at Cambridge, and, incidentally, into creating conditions which bred a self-assurance and a dissenting frame of mind. Modern changes which have profoundly affected the area include North Sea gas, nuclear power stations at Sizewell and Bradwell – the latter poetically adjacent to the chapel built by St Cedd in the seventh century to generate "the true Light which lighteth every man" – the post-war foundation of the Universities of Essex and East Anglia, as well as Churchill College, Cambridge, the co-existence between groups of villages and the United States aerodromes which dominate them, the international standing of the Aldeburgh Festival, the revitalization of many a sleepy market town by emigrant London firms, and the drastic reorganization of the ancient parish-centred religious life. Yet visitors will, for a long time yet, find an open country with close secrets, a land where the peculiar extremes of the English character, a hard-headed rationality and great imagination, exist side by side.

Essex, the first part of the region, is grossly undervalued as a county to explore. At first glance this neat fifty or so miles stretching between the Thames and the Stour might appear to have been concreted out of existence. London surges into it, and over a million of its inhabitants – its growth-rate over the past century has been the fastest county population expansion in Britain – live in streets which seem a very long way from East Anglia. In the 1840s William Morris could stand in the fields of Walthamstow and see London far off with "the sun shining down in one flood of peaceful light over the long distance". Shortly after this the confines broke, and the towns and villages east of the Thames were overrun. During the inter-war years the more prosperous of these new Londoners extricated themselves from Victorian terraces and tried to get back into some kind of country life by building along the edges of the main roads. Ribbon-development, with its pebble-dash, appliquéd Tudor beams and sunburst gates, soon linked one piece of Essex–London with its neighbour. Specialists in urban sprawl will find much to interest them in this part of Greater London and may even find something touching in these diverse Jazz-age homes. Fill-in has, in most cases, destroyed their brief freedom. The fields behind them are now covered by estates. Tower blocks soar in the meadows. The roads in front which, not so long ago, were cheerful with Baby Austins and charabancs on the way to Southend, are now a solid welter of traffic. To many a motorist it must seem that this desert of supermarkets and garages strangely called Essex can never be crossed. Yet suddenly he finds himself in rich farmland or arriving at a remote clapboarded pub – which happens to be twenty miles from Marble Arch. So, far from being crushed out of existence by London, Essex is in fact attractively alive and flourishing.

It is a dipping, rolling, ambling kind of country, crossed by regularly spaced-out rivers and edged by undramatic but very individual islands: Canvey, Foulness, Wallasea, Havengore, Northey, Mersea, Horsey, etc., their very names carrying across the centuries a sense of the cries of the Viking invaders. The rivers themselves at first glance seem dull enough, yet if Britain had an Iliad its heroes might well have lived on their banks. This is the country of King Cunobelin (Shakespeare's Cymbeline or Old King Cole), Boadicea, Caractacus, and, above all, of Brithnoth, whose exploits are so superbly described in *The Battle of Maldon*.

The most Romanized part of Britain, because of the conquerors' decision to make Colchester their capital, Essex has had excellent roads from the very earliest times; and the traffic of today still uses great stretches of the ancient routes: Stane Street, Icknield Street and the Via Devana. For a road, like a river, divides and rules, bilaterally keeping the laws of the past and the present. And in Essex it is fair to say that all roads lead to Colchester, rather than to London. One cannot help feeling that if Colchester had been in southern Europe or Asia Minor it would have the literature and the draw of a Trebizond. When Tacitus described it in his *Annals* – the first time a British city had received a written record – it was already very old. Capital of the Icenic kingdom, sacked by Queen Boadicea at the time when St Paul was sending his Epistles to the new churches, possessing a complete second-century wall and the biggest Norman keep in Europe on foundations made by men who were contemporary with Christ, it is an enthralling place. There is no other town in the country in which the national myths and realities so overlay each other, making such an eloquent humus of over two thousand years of civilization.

To discover the best of Essex one should travel through the villages centred on Halstead, Dunmow and Thaxted. These range from Finchingfield (the most photographed) to Borley (the most haunted) and include the artistic Bardfields and the mysterious Belchamps. The Dunmow–Thaxted area has a special fascination, for it is here that a kind of Shavian version of art-cum-socialism took place under the direction of Lady Warwick. This is the country in which Holst composed "The Planets", Conrad Noel flew red flags from his church tower at Thaxted, and H. G. Wells wrote that best-seller of the First World War, *Mr Britling Sees It Through*.

The traditional products of Essex verge on the exotic – Colchester "natives" from the celebrated oyster beds at Brightlingsea, roses, Tiptree jam, Maldon salt and, not so very long ago, saffron from Saffron Walden, venison from the vast Waltham Forest – of which Epping is the remaining fragment – and candied eringo root. Its chief assets, however, still stem from its farms. The great industrial complexes, including Courtauld's, Crittall's, Ford's and the Thames docks, have so far not been able to obscure its essentially agricultural identity. Yet for the visitor the particular flavour of this county must always lie in the extraordinary contrasts it can present in so small an area. In Southend and Frinton one has the poles of the English seaside ideal. Everywhere one goes the suburban tide looks as if it must engulf all, yet "all" turns out to be astonishingly large and quite capable of looking after itself – *vide* the great Stansted victory. Essex, one feels, after its drab savaging by the developers, is now calling the tune.

Suffolk, the most eastern county in England, begins amidst pastoral scenes of overwhelming familiarity. Here, along the banks of the border river, John Constable painted his great series of Stour pictures – his "six-footers", as he called them, and here the churches, lanes, meadows, mills and farms, the originals of these paintings, remain in startling reality. At Sudbury, further along the same river, is the home of Thomas Gainsborough. Prospect Hill, the road along which he must have walked as a young man to paint his masterpiece *Cornard Wood*, after winding its way through a housing estate, slips back in time to produce the famous view. Constable's rich uncle owned this picture and it became an early influence on the Flatford miller's son. Two miles from Gainsborough's house in Sudbury is a country-house park in which the artist's school friend and his new wife sat for their likenesses, thus creating what has been described as the quintessence of the English portrait. *Mr and Mrs Andrews*, now in the National Gallery, reflects a moment in the East Anglian countryside which agricultural historians have called the golden age of English country life. A journey along the valley towns and hamlets from East Bergholt to Sudbury is thus one of the most remarkable that can be made, for it leads one to a great moment in art and a recognition of what is meant by "Englishness".

At Long Melford the West Suffolk parks become very grand, mounting in degrees of splendour until they reach the last word in Georgian rural magnificence – Ickworth. Nearby lies Bury St Edmunds which, twice in its history, has been the centre of a far greater world than it knows today. First when, as one of the most important shrines in Christendom, its semi-regal abbots inherited most of the remaining privileges of the ancient East Anglian kingdom, and again when, in Georgian times, the town became Suffolk's Bath. So the beginning of exploration on this side of the county is dramatic and extraordinary. Yet, take any lane east of the Stour and one is back on the high, lonely ground where the medieval clothiers lived and worked. Paced out over this central Suffolk cornland stand their churches, the towers still showing a kind of strategic munificence. Although one successful merchant's tomb shows a confident belief in heaven's not judging a man by his money – "This day a Sudbury camel passed through the eye of a needle" – the beautiful wool churches are saved from being merely great architectural displays by the deep and complex spiritual qualities still to be felt in them. The question they seem to ask is, profit – and lose? Lavenham church is the greatest surety paid by the Suffolk clothiers. Their names were Spring and Branch. The heart of the trade was in this corner of the county and hundreds of fine wood and plaster houses, some isolated in the fields, others lining the streets of Hadleigh, Bildeston, Boxford, Sudbury and Kersey, still contain the large rooms where the looms clicked, making what Shakespeare called "Lindsey-Kersey stuff".

Suffolk's wool empire collapsed in the seventeenth century, never to revive – though many of its skills were retained and have found an outlet in the silk-weaving industry at Sudbury and Braintree. The collapse coincided with an English traveller's thoughtful observation in Belgium of how the different fields on each farm were sown in a certain rotation. . . . Arable East Anglia as it is today took a long time in the making and endured agricultural disasters every bit as terrible as that of the wool trade. The latest – and worst – was movingly documented by that excellent Norfolk farmer (and novelist) Sir Henry Rider Haggard in his *Rural England*. The food needs of the nation, plus science, broke the curse in 1940. The prosperity visible today does not conceal the uncertainties of a farming society still in the full swing of a second agricultural revolution.

Ipswich, the county town, is prosaic but not negative. It takes its name from the upper reaches of the Orwell which are called the Gipping – Gipeswic. Thomas Tusser thought it "like Paradise", but this hasn't been the general opinion for quite a long time. There are many antiquities, but the most attractive sight is the docks at night, full of foreign ships, sentinelled by massive grain wharfs and profoundly silent.

The A12 runs up into Norfolk from here, dividing the claylands from the coastal heaths which are Edward FitzGerald's and George Crabbe's Suffolk. The rivers Deben, Butley, Alde and Blythe are tidal all along this coastal strip, the mysterious centre of which is Dunwich, once a splendid city, now scarcely a place at all; the sea has devoured it. The inland towns of East Suffolk maintain a great calm. Framlingham, for centuries the home of the different families who have possessed the dukedom of Norfolk, is pure Froissart. But it is Blythburgh church, which many people believe is the most wonderful building in a county full of fine architecture, that sums up the character of Suffolk. Its mixture of creative and destructive forces, its brightness and its darkness, are all unforgettably combined here.

Norfolk is the biggest and least populated county in the East Anglian group. Off-centre, and spread out before the best viewing-point in the county – Mousehold Heath – lies Norwich itself, a rare and extraordinary city. Norfolk is hard to know and has therefore been much generalized over. "Flat and cold" is the usual verdict. The first is more a hallucination than a libel because the scenery here carries undulation to the most subtle limits. Many of the loveliest villages are curiously reticent in their shallow valleys and behind artfully screening elms. The impression is often one of desertion, the little brick-and-flint cottages rigid with secrecy. Every church seems to contain the kind of treasure which would have made it famous were it in any other county, but which here is taken for granted. As for the climate, it is bracing – a word which means that one won't feel the chill if one keeps moving. Certainly, the notorious east wind is inexorable. But also the summers are really hot and the effect of the weather generally is one of Spartan well-being.

Almost a peninsular land, with a great semi-circle of variegated waters – marshes, broads, dykes, the Wash and the rivers Yare, Waveney and Little Ouse – isolating it, Norfolk has always been a place which men have visited for itself alone. One does not pass through Norfolk on the way to somewhere else. Norwich itself is not the usual cathedral city, but East Anglia's cultural and metropolitan centre. The controlling factor has been the calm and manageable growth of its population: 15,000 in the reign of Elizabeth I to only 120,000 in that of Elizabeth II. It has never allowed the short-term requirements of history either to deface it or to swamp it, and today it remains a lesson in urban expansion. Basically a medieval city based on Bishop Losinga's superb monastic cathedral, and crowded with churches, guilds, old inns and ancient squares which it calls "plains", it has never succumbed to the picturesque but has remained intellectually alive. London must have always been a second city for the Pastons, Nelson, Coke, Townshend, Sir Thomas Browne, the Frys and the Gurneys – even Sir Robert Walpole.

The religious life of the county, before the Reformation, was vivid and inimitable, its summit being the establishment of the *casa sancta* legend at Walsingham. Whether the angels carried the Virgin's house to Norfolk or to Loreto, Walsingham soon developed into one of the greatest pilgrimage centres in the Christian world. A twentieth-century Anglican revival of these devotions has given this interesting little town an extraordinary atmosphere.

But to most people Norfolk means the Broads, those wide expanses of water which have become obligingly trapped in centuries of peat workings. They lie between Oulton and Stalham on a flat, lush plateau across which the small, lethargic rivers Bure, Thurne and Ant creep towards them, creating a brack at the fringe of the lakes in which thrive the reeds for the famous local thatching. The Broads are a world of their own, a mixture of decoys, nature reserves and a nice kind of pottering indolence. They have a charming surrealism: sails glide through farms and apparently over fields. In the winter, the level monotonous sweep of land from Yarmouth and Blundeston has a violent and bitter feeling which is most impressive. It is the subject of one of Dickens's greatest descriptive passages as the coach carrying David Copperfield fights its way through a gale to the sea.

Broadland is complemented on the other side of the county by Marshland, through which the Fen waters drain to the coast. The names of the villages all around here – Walpole, Walsoken, West Walton – remind one of the endless preoccupation of the Marshland people with their flood walls. A flood board in West Walton church sums up the wasted effort:

> Surely our sins were tinctured in grain,
> May we not say the labour was in vain,
> So many washings, still the spots remain. . . .

In the seventeenth century the complex of dykes, cuts and sluices made by the Dutch engineer Vermuyden and the Lord Chief Justice Sir John Popham began a process of reclamation which has turned all the country between Burwell and Terrington into a district which seems to have become detached from the Zuyder Zee. This Dutch feeling also touches King's Lynn, a town which still emanates all the virtues of the old self-sufficiency in its handsome mixture of first-class religious, mercantile, public and private buildings.

North Norfolk includes the great hoop of the coast, along which lie the small and intimate seaside resorts of Hunstanton, Wells-next-the-Sea, Blakeney, Salthouse, Sheringham, Cromer (a Regency watering-place), Happisburgh (pronounced Hazeborough), Caister (with a fine castle) and Great Yarmouth itself, East Anglia's own favourite beach. Yarmouth is also, with Lowestoft, the major centre of the East Anglian fishing industry. This, and the fact that it is the focus of a thousand village outings, creates a cheerful confusion of riot and work.

Norfolk is a place which makes little or no effort to present or explain itself. It is a province full of slumbering parishes and containing one great wide-awake city.

Cambridgeshire, including the Isle of Ely, has a dual geographical atmosphere, that created by the Uplands, which is fresh and optimistic, and that ordained by the Fens, which carries with it many generations of prejudice, for this dramatic grid of dead-straight roads and water, inland wharfs, black soil and pale bleached windmills and churches is often very beautiful, and always intriguing. Cambridge itself stands at the point where Upland and Lowland meet, the University a jewel of the best English architecture of the last seven hundred years or so. The perfection of the grouping of the colleges cannot be exaggerated. The presence of nearby watermeadows, streams and pools, as at Ely, lightens the density of such great masses of stone.

A similar river-domination affects the whole county. Once the watery landscape provided conditions for famous local industries such as basket- and paper-making but, although the latter is still carried on at the famous mill at Sawston, it is modern drainage which decrees today's economy. Smallholdings on scraps of manageable

The arable agriculture of East Anglia required many windmills to grind the corn: the post-mill at Saxstead Green in Suffolk

land have given way to broad acres of cereals on the upland and potatoes in the Fens. But the sparse villages of Cambridgeshire still have a quiet islanded quality, and for so small a county there is a surprising sense of distance. Nearly all the villages lie in the south-west, so that the north, with its flimsy farms and solitary causeways, wind-pumps and feeling of man-versus-the-elements, seems empty and strange. Ely itself is surrounded by some fourteen villages, each standing on its own island. It is curious how few miles separate this place, where men have found it difficult to exist because of the wet, and that part of the county in the south-east where men have never lived because it is an arid plain. Most evocative of all the Cambridgeshire river villages is, of course, Grantchester – Chaucer, Byron, Brooke – but a mixture of watermanship and ordinary farming, plus contacts with the University, have made many another village in this county unusually interesting.

The epithets generally applied to the 860 square miles of Cambridgeshire are "gentle" and "charming", which could be a kinder way of saying "dull". But a close investigation – particularly that part of it made on foot – will reveal an absorbing scene which is a mixture of the tough and the lyrical.

East Anglia: Gazeteer

MICHAEL WEBBER

ACRES, THE, *Norfolk* (11–TF8115). The most important of these villages is **Castle Acre** which has the remains of a Norman castle, the ruins of an 11th-cent. priory and an outstanding parish church. Of the great castle the main survivals are the earthworks, which have been described as "perhaps the finest castle earthworks in England". Of stone buildings little remains except the 13th-cent. gateway at the east end of the village. The castle was built for William de Warenne, 1st Earl of Surrey, on the line of the Peddars' Way, which was the work of the Romans. The road running N. from here to the coast still follows its line. Nearby is the River Nar and 4 m. to the S., on the A1065, is SWAFFHAM.

William de Warenne, the son of the founder of the castle, founded the priory *c.* 1090 for the Cluniac brethren. Though there was never a large number of monks the size of the building is remarkable, and the ruins are still extremely impressive. Once past the gatehouse the visitor will be struck by the beauty of the west front with its magnificent arcading of the 12th cent. Over the main Norman doorway is a large and, certainly at one time, beautiful window of later date. Attached to this west front are some of the priory buildings, notably the prior's house with its flushwork in chequer patterning. Within the area of the priory are the picturesque ruins of the old buildings.

Near the priory is the Church of St James, mainly Perpendicular. Inside are piers of earlier date which were used by the men who later added to the church. There is a noble font cover which is 26 ft high. There are traces of the original painting and gilding. Hardly less excellent is the hexagonal 15th-cent. pulpit with its painted panels, showing the four Latin Fathers of the Church.

One m. to the S. is **South Acre**, on the other side of the river. Here, in the Church of St George, are some important monuments: firstly some excellent brasses, one to Sir John Harsick and his wife, d. 1384, and another to Thomas Leman, d. 1534; then a strange wooden effigy, in a very poor state of preservation but almost certainly medieval, and another of a crusader of Norman times. A large alabaster monument in the Lady Chapel commemorates Sir Edward Barkham and his wife, d. *c.* 1623. Barkham was once a Lord Mayor of London. The screen under the tower arch is 14th cent.

To the W. is **West Acre**, once the site of an Augustinian priory founded *c.* 1100. It must have been a comparable institution to that at Castle Acre and the gatehouse is 14th-cent. and built of flint. The ruins which remain include parts of the church and the chapter house.

All Saints' Church next to the gatehouse is mainly Perpendicular with some parts of earlier date and has been restored. In the north porch is a small sculpture probably from the keystone of an arch and representing a seated figure (perhaps a Madonna), probably 13th-cent.

ALDEBURGH, *Suffolk* (11–TM4656), has become famous as the centre of the Aldeburgh Festival which was started by the great English composer Benjamin Britten in 1948, and which is held each year in June. The little town was, like its northern neighbours, DUNWICH, WALBERSWICK and SOUTHWOLD, at one time a prosperous port. This was in the 16th cent. Then came the sea and the storms which Britten captured so unforgettably in his opera, *Peter Grimes*. The quaint little Moot Hall, now almost on the sea-wall, was at one time in the centre of the town, which shows just how much has been eroded in the course of four centuries.

The Church of SS. Peter and Paul stands on a hill overlooking the town and the sea. Mostly of the 16th cent., it has a tower some 200 years older. There is an elaborate pulpit made in 1632 and several Elizabethan brasses. In the north aisle is a memorial by T. Thurlow to the Rev. George Crabbe (1847). Crabbe was born at Aldeburgh in 1754 and after leaving school became an errand-boy. He returned to his home town and studied medicine and in 1780 went to London to try to make a living by writing. He was ordained in Mayfair and became chaplain at BELVOIR CASTLE. He went back to East Anglia to GREAT GLEMHAM, in 1796, before finally settling in the West Country where he died in 1832 and was buried at Trowbridge. One of his most famous works is *The Borough*, published in 1810, which became the inspiration for Britten's opera.

The Moot Hall, *c.* 1520–40, is a timber-framed building, with end walls of brick, built over an arched ground floor which was at one time used as an open market. The tall chimneys to the S. date from the 16th cent., but most of the building was restored in 1855.

N. of the Moot Hall is the White Lion Hotel, and a terrace of typical 19th-cent. seafront houses ending with the Sundial House of the 1920s, a fanciful design by Oliver Hill.

S. of the Moot Hall, two roads run parallel:

Kenneth Scowen

Noel Habgood

Aldeburgh: the Moot Hall

Audley End, a magnificent Jacobean mansion

one is the High Street, the other runs nearer the seafront. The High Street contains a number of excellent shops and the Union Chapel of 1822. The seafront has many quaint cottages and several houses which date from around the time of the First World War. Above the High Street along the cliff top are a number of larger houses and lodges.

Along the seafront is a look-out tower, a tall square building with a spiral iron staircase running up the outside. The Martello Tower, Slaughden, is one of those built along the East Anglian coast in 1810–12 as a defence against Napoleonic invasion. The name comes from a "Torre della Martella" in Corsica seen by the British in 1794. Nearer to the Moot Hall is the site of the famous Aldeburgh lifeboat.

Alde House was the home of two famous sisters. Elizabeth Garrett Anderson, as she became by marriage, was born in 1836. She managed to enter the medical profession, at that time closed to women, and opened the hospital in London which still bears her name. She was at one time the Mayor of Aldeburgh, the first woman mayor in England. Her younger sister, Millicent, was a pioneer of women's suffrage and married the blind professor Henry Fawcett, who became Postmaster-General.

ASHINGDON, *Essex* (7–TQ8693). Near here Cnut defeated Edmund Ironside in October 1016, to succeed him as King of England when Edmund died just one month later. The Church of St Andrew has a long history, its first priest, Stigand, becoming the Bishop of Winchester in 1047. In

1052 he was uncanonically appointed Archbishop of Canterbury, an appointment which was finally ratified by Benedict X in 1058. In this capacity he crowned William the Conqueror. A few years later his fortunes changed yet again and he was deprived of his see, to die imprisoned two years later. In the church is a replica of a silver coin of Cnut found nearby.

AUDLEY END, *Essex* (11–TL5139). As splendid as this magnificent Jacobean mansion is today, it is but a part of the house built by the first Earl of Suffolk, Lord Howard de Walden. He inherited the estate of Audley End in 1603, on which site the Abbey of Walden had stood, given to Sir Thomas Audley by Henry VIII after the Dissolution. There is some resemblance to Hatfield House, but here the building is faced with stone, not brick. Sir John Vanbrugh was called in to work on the house early in the 18th cent. and demolished some of the building and more was destroyed later in the century, when it passed to the ninth Baron Howard de Walden, created Lord Braybrooke in 1788. The visitor is immediately impressed by the façade with its beautiful arrangement of windows, its many turrets with their delicate caps and the richly elaborate porches, making a striking composition as seen from across the park.

The Great Hall of the house features a massive screen carved with a Baroque profusion of detail. Facing it there is a stone screen of simple, classical design, in striking contrast to its partner. Behind is a dual staircase and above a flat ceiling enriched with timbering and panels of plaster.

East Barsham Manor is a fine example of Early Tudor architecture

One of the most interesting sections of the house is the chapel completed in 1786, an exquisite example of the Georgian Gothic style.

Apart from Vanbrugh some of the other great artists and architects who worked on the house were Robert Adam, Biagio Rebecca and Hobcraft. The grounds of Audley End were landscaped by Capability Brown and among the architectural fantasies they contain are the circular temple and bridge both by Adam, the Springwood Column (1774) and an icehouse lodge (1827). The house is owned by the Ministry of Public Building and Works and is open to the public. Audley End village lies outside the gates and the road leads to the College of St Mark (originally built as Elizabethan almshouses) and to the town of SAFFRON WALDEN.

AYLSHAM, *Norfolk* (11–TG1927). A small town on the River Bure with an attractive market place to the N. of which is the Church of St Michael, Decorated and Perpendicular. There is a two-story porch built in 1488, with good flush panelling. The font is 15th-cent. and has the arms of John of Gaunt on the shaft. The pulpit dates from 1637. There is a fine west gallery supported by posts and beams, some interesting stained glass and a number of monuments, including those to Humphry Repton, the famous landscape gardener and associate of Nash who died in 1818 and whose grave is in the churchyard, his body giving, as his own epitaph puts it, "form and colour to the Rose".

Around the market place are several good buildings among which is the Black Boy Inn of the Queen Anne period. Close to the market place are several fine houses, The Knoll, *c.* 1700, Aylsham Old Hall, 1689, The Manor House, 1608 and many others. Half a m. to the SW. are the remains of a windmill and not far away the former workhouse built in 1849 in Victorian Tudor style. Abbot's Hall, $1\frac{1}{2}$ m. to the NE., is contemporary with the manor house and is on the site of the house which belonged to the abbots of BURY ST EDMUNDS. A similar distance to the NW. stands BLICKLING Hall (National Trust).

BARHAM, *Suffolk* (11–TM1451). St Mary's Church has parts dating from the early 14th cent. and a fine window in the vestry made early in the 16th cent. in the Early Renaissance style. Inside the church on the chancel floor is a brass to Robert Southwell and his wife (1514). In the chancel is a large 17th-cent. monument to Sir Richard Southwell and his wife.

Opposite the church is the gateway and wall of the former Barham Hall and $\frac{1}{2}$ m. to the E. is Barham Manor, a good example of Tudor brickwork with octagonal chimneys.

A mile or so the the N. is **Shrubland Park** which contains the spectacular Shrubland Hall, now a health hydro. The original house, designed by James Paine in 1770–2, forms the centre-piece of the Italianate building designed by Sir Charles Barry in 1848–52. The gardens, also designed by

Barry, are terraced in the style of the Villa d'Este at Tivoli and fall in a remarkable display of steps, cascades and urns. The gardens were further developed by William Robinson in 1888.

The Old Hall in the grounds has two windows made of terracotta similar in style to that already noted in Barham church.

BARSHAMS, THE, *Norfolk* (11–TF9234). Changing the normal order of the compass you should first consider **East Barsham**, famous for the splendid Early Tudor manor house built by Sir Henry Fermor in 1520–30. Whether you first notice the battlemented top, the magnificent chimneys or the superb two-storied gatehouse, its warm brickwork is most attractive. The vertical buttresses and the bands of ornament in moulded brick, the patterning of the windows and the group of ten chimneys, each one carved differently from its neighbours, are all features which add richness to this architectural feast. Restorations done in the present century have not (as yet) affected the character of this enchanting building.

All Saints' Church, much affected by time, has a Norman south doorway and two pieces of sculpture worth noting: an alabaster group of St Anne teaching the Virgin to read and a splendid memorial to Mrs Calthorpe, whose family lived in the Manor House and who died in 1640. She is shown rising from her grave wrapped in her shroud in this monument made by John and Matthias Christmas, local sculptors whose work may also be seen in St Stephen's, IPSWICH.

North Barsham, by the River Stiffkey, has All Saints' Church with a 13th-cent. Purbeck marble font, a Stuart table and a Victorian pulpit.

West Barsham, making a triangle with its neighbours, has the restored Church of the Assumption of the Virgin. There is an early-13th-cent. doorway and the nave has pre-Conquest work, including two double-splayed windows.

BARTON BROAD, *Norfolk* (11–TG3421). This is one of the largest of the Broads and is now a broadening of the River Ant which flows directly through it. At one time the river was artificially led into and out of the broad, which like most of the others was once by-passed by the river. It is situated in the triangle of WROXHAM, Stalham and POTTER HEIGHAM. The basin reaches a depth of about 9 ft and reedswamp and alder fen may be seen growing at the ends of the peat ridges. Coypu have destroyed much of this plant growth in recent years, so much so that the character of the vegetation has changed considerably in the past decades. Mostly this has happened at the south end of the broad; the fen area at the north end has been allowed to grow more extensively and is more resistant to attack by these voracious rodents. The broad is freely open to boats.

BASILDON, *Essex* (7–TQ7189). The new town of Basildon is one of the eight planned after the last war which would encircle London and take over some of its surplus industry and population. It overlooks the estuary of the River Thames and is placed upon undulating country, containing seven parishes and an indigenous population of some 25,000. Placed as it was along the railway and the main A127 road from London to SOUTHEND it has been planned as a rectangle some 6 m. from W. to E., and 3 m. from N. to S. The number of people it will accommodate has increased from the original 50,000 and it seems likely that it will ultimately reach between 110,000 and 140,000.

Though the new buildings will attract immediate attention the visitor should not forget that the churches of the original seven parishes are worth noting. Holy Cross, Basildon, has a 14th-cent. nave, a brick chancel of 1597, and a weathervane dated 1702. At Laindon, St Nicholas has a timber belfry, weather-boarded and with a broach spire, with typical Essex timber framing inside. St Mary's at Langdon Hills is 16th- and 17th-cent., with a chapel rebuilt in the 19th. A feature is a royal coat of arms on the wall over the nave which is dated 1660. At Vange is All Saints, a church of Norman times, restored in 1837 when the west gallery was added. Nevendon has in St Peter's, a church showing work of the 13th, 14th and 15th cents., while there are two Victorian churches at Langdon Hills (St Mary's – 1876) and at Pitsea (St Michael's – 1871) with a tower dating back to the early 16th cent.

However, to see the buildings of the New Basildon you should start at the town centre, which really is right in the middle of the town. It lies just N. of the railway and over 1 m. S. of the A127 at the junction with the CHELMSFORD road. Sir Basil Spence was consultant to the architect of the Development Corporation, Mr A. B. Davis. The main feature is a traffic-free pedestrian concourse with the 14-story Brooke House which stands on eight reinforced concrete V-shaped supports, as its main vertical accent. The surrounding buildings are still in course of development.

Surrounding the town centre are a number of new areas which include much residential building of varying degrees of success and to the NE. major industrial areas.

BECCLES, *Suffolk* (11–TM4290). The town is nicely placed on the River Waveney. In Norman times the sea reached into the town which is now some 7 or 8 m. from the coast. Many of the Georgian houses have Dutch gables which remind the visitor of the many connections there once were between East Anglia and the Netherlands.

The 14th-cent. St Michael's Church has its tower standing separate from the main body of the church. Stone-faced and 97 ft tall it contains a peal of ten bells. The Old Town Hall, close by, was built in 1726. On the west side of the Old Market is St Peter's House built of brick in the 18th cent. and containing a remarkable Gothic fire-place of the same date. It is but one of a large number of attractive Georgian buildings.

Much earlier is Roos Hall, dated 1583, on the

Bungay road, its step gables again betraying Dutch influence.

The Church of St Benet (Roman Catholic) in St Mary's Road was built in 1889 in the Romanesque style for the Benedictine Order.

In the season the staithe (quay) by the river presents a busy picture with holiday vessels of all types at their moorings. There is an annual regatta which has often provided a subject for painters.

BELCHAMPS, THE, *Essex* (11–TL8041), is the name given to a group of three villages in the N. of the county near the border with Suffolk, and thus to the S. of the River Stour. **Belchamp Otton's** Church of St Ethelbert and All Saints was dedicated to the ancient king of East Anglia, and has a Norman nave, and a finely carved Norman south doorway. Each of the following centuries has added something to the church, one of the most attractive items being the belfry of the 19th. Just to the N. is **Belchamp St Paul**, so called because it was given to St Paul's Cathedral 1,000 years ago by Athelstan, King of England. The Church of St Andrew is mainly 15th-cent. with a fine west tower. It is especially famous for the carved misericords in the chancel stalls, which are among the very few in all Essex. Brasses to the Golding family (1587 and 1591) are reminders of Arthur Golding who was well known in the 16th cent. for his translations of Caesar, Ovid and Seneca, and whose work provided William Shakespeare with themes for many of his plays. A window in the church was given by one of his American descendants.

Belchamp Walter is the most southerly of the villages and above the stream which is a tributary of the Stour stands the Church of St Mary, mainly 14th- and 15th-cent. The nave is from the former, the tower, and the timbered porch from the latter. The interior features a number of paintings which include a *Wheel of Fortune*, and a 14th-cent. *Virgin suckling the Child*. The font is 12th-cent., the elaborate monument to Sir John Boutetort, d. *c.* 1324, is like *Hamlet* without the Prince, in that the tomb-chest and the effigy are missing. A later monument by Robert Taylor commemorates John Raymond, d. 1720, whose family built the very fine Hall in that same year. Additions were made in the 19th cent. and the Hall was restored in 1966.

BILDESTON, *Suffolk* (11–TL9949). At one time an important town for cloth. The 15th-cent. Church of St Mary is on a hill at the edge of the village. The south door is splendidly carved and the roof alternates tie-beams with hammer-beams. In the village are many timber-framed cottages with fine plastering and projecting upper stories. The market place has houses of the early 19th cent. and a Victorian clock tower. The King's Head and the Crown Inn are both of architectural interest. The Baptist chapel was founded in 1731, though rebuilt in the mid 19th-cent.

Garrod's Farmhouse S. of the market place dates from the 15th and 16th cents. and has many attractive and unusual features including much decorative carving.

BILLERICAY, *Essex* (7–TQ6794). Here in Mayflower Hall, opposite the church, the Pilgrim Fathers met before they set off on their voyage to America in 1620. Christopher Martin, the ship's purser, together with his wife Marie and her brother-in-law Solomon Prower were among the band who left England to seek freedom across the Atlantic. Not one of the group from Billericay survived the epidemic which accounted for so many of the *Mayflower*'s passengers as she lay off Plymouth, Massachusetts.

Apart from the 16th-cent. Hall, there are many other buildings of note in this town, placed on the main SOUTHEND to BRENTWOOD road, the A129. Between it, and the neighbouring developing town of BASILDON, is the village of **Great Burstead**, with its Church of St Mary Magdalen. Billericay itself has its own church of the same name which stands at the junction of Chapel Street and High Street. Though the tower is early 16th-cent. and made of brick, the rest of the church is later, with three interior galleries supported on delicate cast-iron columns.

Close by are several attractive buildings: the Chequers Inn, the Nook and St Aubyns are all 16th- or 17th-cent. From the 18th cent. come a number of houses in both Chapel and High Streets, while the early 19th cent. is represented by St Andrew's Hospital (1840), one of the earlier designs of G. G. Scott and originally the Poor Law institution. Quite apart from its importance as the meeting place of the Pilgrim Fathers, Billericay has its place in the history books as the scene of the peasants' revolt of 1381, when the followers of Jack Straw were captured during the many protests which followed the imposition of the poll tax in 1379.

BINHAM, *Norfolk* (11–TF9740). This small village was once a great Benedictine centre, and the priory founded *c.* 1100 by Peter de Valoines as an offshoot of ST ALBAN'S Abbey is still, even though no longer complete, an impressive sight. The Norman nave of this priory now forms part of St Mary's Church. However, the first thing to be seen is the west front which is one of the first examples of Early English architecture in the country, built before 1244. Even with its great window bricked up it is a noble composition of arches and columns whose refined proportions make a strong contrast with the sturdy Norman work of the nave. Three tiers of semi-circular arches line each side and of the original nine bays seven still stand.

The seven-sacrament font is built on steps. The ruins of the earlier priory may be seen around the church. In the village is the remains of an ancient cross.

BLAKENEY, *Norfolk* (11–TG0243), is a picturesque small town on the north coast of Norfolk on the estuary of the River Glaven. It is much favoured by yachtsmen and in the season its

A. F. Kersting

Blickling Hall, a surperb 17th-century house

quays present a lively scene. Though once a port of some importance it is now almost completely devoted to pleasure-boating. The other sport particularly associated with Blakeney and its near neighbour, CLEY, is wild-fowling. The Church of St Nicholas in Blakeney is curious in having two towers: the west tower is Perpendicular and over 120 ft high, the other tower at the north-east corner is only 8 ft wide and was used as a beacon to guide mariners. Another rather unusual feature is the low, finely arched chancel which has a chamber above it with its own window. The height of the nave is enhanced by this contrast. Inside is an Easter Sepulchre, stalls with good misericords and a Stuart table.

Contrasting with the many flint cottages is a red-brick house at the west end of the quay. The Guildhall stands on a brick vaulted undercroft and dates from the 15th cent., and just to the N. of the church is a house which includes some of the remains of the Carmelite friary founded in 1296.

Blakeney's chief feature is perhaps the great expanse of marshy creeks which extend towards Blakeney Point. From the Far Point to Cley is almost 4 m. and like Scolt Head (*see* BRANCASTER) is National Trust property and a paradise for naturalists. As at Scolt, barrier beaches enclose a vast area of marshy flats and the range of plant and bird life is immense. Much of what

has been said of Scolt applies to Blakeney but additional factors may be mentioned. One of these must be the hybrid grass *Spartina* which spreads so fast that it presents a great control problem. Another is the huge depth of shingle which is able to support a wide variety of vegetation, and a third the dunes which are formed beyond the reach of the normal high tides (though the exceptional conditions of 1953 are remembered by a mark which shows the abnormal level of water reached at that time).

Among the rarer plants here are some which are normally found far away. The *Limonium bellidifolium* is mainly Mediterranean, the *Suaeda fruticosa* is another which comes from the South and which has established itself in the unusual conditions prevailing here. Entomologists, too, have much to observe, as a wealth of insect life may be found at all seasons. Mammals such as rabbits, rats and shrews are numerous, and seals appear from time to time. The birds include those mentioned in the note on Scolt Island.

BLICKLING, *Norfolk* (11–TG1728). Here is one of the county's greatest show-pieces, a superb Jacobean house built between 1616 and 1627 for Sir Henry Hobart. The architect was Robert Lyminge and visitors who are familiar with Hatfield House will recognize his hand. Blickling Hall stands on land which is itself full of history. Once the property of King Harold, it was given by William the Conqueror to Herbert de Losinga, the Bishop of NORWICH and the builder of its great cathedral. Later it came into the possession of Sir John Fastolf, the builder of CAISTER Castle, and later still into the Boleyn family, though there is no evidence that Anne was born in the house. The present house was built within the existing moated area and it was altered in 1767–79 by Thomas, William, and John Ivory, a family of Norwich architects. As late as 1725 it was open to the N.

The façade, with gables, turrets with ogee tops and bay windows, is capped by a turret with an open-topped lantern. The interior is no less splendid with a great carved staircase, a magnificent dining-room, anteroom and drawing-room, and perhaps most beautiful of all, the gallery with its carved plaster ceiling. The gardens were attributed to Humphry Repton, buried nearby at AYLSHAM, and include a parterre designed in 1930 by Mrs Lindsay. One m. to the NW. of the house is the remarkable mausoleum designed by Joseph Bonomi in 1793 for the Earl and Countess of Buckinghamshire. It stands on a 45 ft square and is a perfect pyramid, a concept executed elsewhere in Europe at that time.

The Church of St Andrew must take second place, and though parts are Early English and Perpendicular, much was restored by Butterfield and Street in 1851 and 1876. The octagonal font (Perpendicular) is typically East Anglian and there are many monuments and brasses. One of the latter is to Anna Boleyne, d. 1479, and one of the former, to the 8th Marquess of Lothian, is by G. F. Watts, 1878.

BLUNDESTON, *Suffolk* (11–TM5197). The church has the tallest and thinnest round tower in East Anglia. The south door is 11th-cent. and the plate includes a chalice of the Civil War period. Blundeston House was one of Sir John Soane's earliest designs, 1785. A prison has been built in the grounds.

Readers of *David Copperfield* will remember that the hero of Dickens's novel was born at Blundeston and spent several holidays with Peggotty's family between here and GREAT YARMOUTH.

BLYTHBURGH, *Suffolk* (11–TM4575). Approached from the London to LOWESTOFT road the magnificent Church of the Holy Trinity rises from the marshy estuary of the River Blyth as majestically as does the Cathedral of ELY from its surrounding fens. There are few sights in Suffolk more splendid than this great church, whether standing out clearly in the crisp East Anglian light, or whether veiled in the mists that can hang over the marsh. It sails the horizon like some great liner, an impression enhanced should you see the church at night, when with windows alight it sparkles in the darkness.

Holy Trinity's size (it is 127 ft long and 54 ft wide), indicates the importance of Blythburgh in the 15th cent. when it had two annual fairs, its own mint and gaol and busy quays crowded with craft from home and overseas. Yet even before the century ended the town had begun the sad decline so typical of East Coast towns and due this time to the shallow channels which could no longer float the larger vessels. As the town decayed so did the church, described by Suckling in 1847 as "mouldering into ruin". In 1931, however, extensive restorations were begun which have continued to this day.

Now all is light and airy, the vast wooden roof no longer bearing the scars of the spire which crashed through it in the great storm of 1577, and decorated with carved angels and coloured patterns of painted flowers. Note the bookrests of the pews and the bench near the south porch door, made from the post of the old mill at **Westleton**, also the bench-ends showing the seven deadly sins: Greed with swollen stomach, Slander with protruding tongue and Avarice on his money chest. Apostles and saints may be seen in the carvings on the choir benches and a wooden "Jack-o'-the-Clock" is one of the few remaining in England.

Little remains of the busy town of long ago, which is now a through route for the holiday tourist, but still remains unsurpassed for the beauty of its site.

BOCKING, *Essex* (11–TL7623). A town which almost imperceptibly leads into BRAINTREE. It was to Bocking that George Courtauld came almost 100 years after his family had come from France as Huguenot refugees. Thus having been one of the great centres of the wool trade, East Anglia was to gain a new prosperity founded on another fabric – artificial silk. So the Paycockes (*see* COGGESHALL) of one era were replaced by the Courtaulds of another. When George moved from **Pebmarsh** (to the NE. of HALSTEAD) to Bocking in 1809 he began an industry which was to bring not only trade to Essex but was, through the wisdom and generosity of his descendant Samuel Courtauld (1876–1947), to give England a wonderful collection of French paintings, the Courtauld Institute and his Robert Adam house in Portman Square. Through the famous Courtauld-Sargent concerts the musical life of the capital and the development of generations of young people was also enriched.

The 17th-cent. post-mill at Bocking is deservedly famous and with the Church of St Mary and the vast factories is among the more obvious architectural features. The church is 15th-cent., except for the chancel which is 14th-cent. The tower has buttresses and a corner stair-turret. Nearby are the factory buildings close to the river which played so important a part in the early days of the mill. In the town a number of buildings of great interest include Doreward's Hall, timber-framed, with a brick façade dated 1572, the Deanery and Bocking Hall, both timber-framed and, in Church Lane, Tabor House (16th-cent.), Wentworth House (17th) and Boleyns (18th). Leading to Braintree, Bocking End contains more buildings of note, including The White Hart, 17th-cent., with later alterations.

BOREHAM, *Essex* (11–TL7509). There are three buildings of great interest to be seen in this village just off the main CHELMSFORD to COLCHESTER road, the A12. Many motorists must have admired the beautiful façade of Boreham House set back from the main road, and now the training centre for Ford's Tractor Division. The house was built by James Gibbs for Benjamin Hoare in 1728 and its simple, yet impressive, façade is enhanced by the straight lake which calls to mind the Canal Pond at Chatsworth. The wings of the house were added in 1812 by Thomas Hopper. Inside are some superb rooms, notably the entrance hall and the salon which date from the building of the original part of the house.

New Hall is a splendid house, now a convent, which dates from the original Hall built by Henry VIII, *c*. 1520. The magnificent south façade which you see today gives some idea of the great richness of the original mansion. Seven superbly simple bay windows, the central one containing the entrance, are topped by a plain parapet. Since 1798 the house has been run by the canonesses of the Holy Sepulchre from Liège. In the chapel is a very fine carved coat of arms of Henry VIII, similar to that at CAMBRIDGE.

In the centre of the village is the Church of St Andrew, which has a central Norman tower topped by a pyramid roof. The nave and aisles are unusual in shape and the chancel is narrow, with the 16th-cent. Sussex Chapel which contains the triple monument to the three Earls of Sussex, d. 1542, 1567 and 1583. On the opposite side of the church is the Tufnell Chapel of *c.* 1800.

Salle: the Church of SS. Peter and Paul. Painting by Edward Bawden, 1968   London, Fine Art Society

BOTTISHAM, *Cambridgeshire* (11–TL5460). The Church of the Holy Trinity contains some interesting work of the 13th and 14th cents. The west or Galilee porch by the tower is perhaps derived from that at ELY. Inside there are two 14th-cent. parclose screens worth noting. Among the several monuments are those to Sir Roger Jenyns and his wife and to the two young Allington children, Lionel and Dorothe.

The village is also the site of one of the village colleges built in the 1930s.

Some 1½ m. to the NW is **Anglesey Abbey,** now in the care of the National Trust. Anglesey was an Augustinian priory founded in the 12th cent. Some time after 1591 the priory was converted into a house by the Fokes family. In the present century it was bought and altered by the late Lord Fairhaven and since that time the extensive gardens of over 100 acres have been created. Inside the house is an outstanding collection of paintings, sculpture and *objets d'art.*

BOURN, *Cambridgeshire* (10–TL3256). Bourn Hall, Jacobean but much restored, is on the site of an old Norman castle. St Mary's Church dates from Norman times with subsequent additions right up to the last century. The tower, probably dating from the middle of the 13th cent., is surmounted by a noteworthy spire.

The windmill at Bourn was recorded as far back as 1636 and has claim to being the oldest surviving windmill in the country. It is a post-mill, which means that the body of the mill which contained the machinery and carried the sails was kept turned to face the wind by being mounted on an upright central post.

BRADENHAMS, THE, *Norfolk* (11–TF 9308). **West Bradenham** is famous for its association with two men and two women. The men were Lord Nelson and Rider Haggard and the women were Nelson's sister and Lady Hamilton. Nelson's sister, Mrs Bolton, lived in the Hall which had been built *c.* 1760 and it was to this house that Lady Hamilton often came.

The Hall came into the possession of the Haggard family and it was here on 22 June 1856 that Sir Henry Rider Haggard was born. Before he was 20 he went to South Africa and at the age of 32 became Master of the High Court of the Transvaal. He returned to Norfolk to marry in 1880 and took a great interest in agricultural matters. *Dawn,* his first novel, was published in 1884, to be followed by *King Solomon's Mines,* 1886, and many other popular books.

St Andrew's Church, 13th- to 14th-cent., has an Easter Sepulchre and monuments to the Haggard family.

East Bradenham with its fine village green has the Church of St Mary (Decorated and Perpendicular). Some interesting monuments include those to John Greene, d. 1684, and Gibson Lucas, d. 1758, which are particularly attractive.

BRADWELL-JUXTA-COGGESHALL, *Essex* (11–TL8122), is situated on the A120 COL-CHESTER to BRAINTREE road some 2 m. W. of COGGESHALL, and should not be confused with the village of similar name on the estuary of the Blackwater. The Church of the Holy Trinity has many portions of Norman date with later additions in the Decorated and Perpendicular styles. It contains a series of wall paintings which date from *c.* 1320. Among the subjects are *Doubting Thomas, The Trinity,* and *Christ Rising from the Tomb.* There are almost certainly many other paintings underneath the plastering of the church but those that remain visible are distinguished by their artistic quality.

Beyond the traceried 15th-cent. screen, behind the altar, are particularly interesting monuments to Anthony Maxey, d. 1592 and his wife and to their son, Sir Henry Maxey, d. 1624, and his wife

BRADWELL-ON-SEA, *Essex* (7–TM 0006), also known as Bradwell-juxta-Mare, lies near the Blackwater almost opposite MERSEA ISLAND. Its neighbour Bradwell Waterside is on the estuary. About 3 m. from the two villages, by the sea-wall and reached by a footpath, are the foundations of the Roman fort of Othona, similar in style to that at BURGH CASTLE, near GREAT YARMOUTH. Here also is one of the most ancient of all England's churches, St Peter's-on-the-Wall, which, as its name suggests, is built on the very walls of the Roman fort. It is almost certainly the church which was built by the priest St Cedd in about A.D. 654. All that remains is the nave, built mainly of Roman materials, and for many years this historic place of worship served as a humble barn, some 50 ft by 20 ft in area and with walls rather over 20 ft tall, until an observant visitor saw in it the outlines of the original Anglo-Saxon church.

Inland is the Parish Church of St Thomas which has a west tower added in 1706 to an earlier structure. Bradwell Lodge is a delightful Georgian house, which overlooks the river. Originally Tudor, it was rebuilt in 1781–6 for the Rev. Sir Henry Bate Dudley, friend of Thomas Gainsborough. The internal decorations are almost certainly by Robert Adam, and include paintings by Angelica Kauffmann, and beautiful fireplaces. On top is a belvedere of unusual size and charm, while within is a vaulted entrance hall and oval library.

Between the church and the Lodge is the village green surrounded by cottages. In striking contrast with the ancient Church of St Peter and indeed the district as a whole is the nuclear power station which was begun in 1957.

BRAINTREE, *Essex* (11–TL7622), grew up as a town placed at the junction of important Roman roads, Stane Street running E.–W. and, crossing it from SW. to NE. the CHELMSFORD to SUDBURY road, and also on the River Blackwater. Like its neighbour BOCKING, into which it gradually merges, it has derived its prosperity from the silk trade founded by the Courtaulds, which followed on the wool trade of an earlier age. Its other great industry is the making of metal

Sudbury: Cornard Wood, known as "Gainsborough's Forest".
Detail of painting by Thomas Gainsborough, 1748

windows which was established by Francis Crittal in 1884 and which has since developed into a very important international enterprise. Another famous Braintree character was Nicholas Udall (1505–56) who, after being dismissed from his post as headmaster of Eton, became vicar of Braintree in 1537. It was possibly at about the time he became headmaster of Westminster School (1554) that he wrote the first known English comedy, *Ralph Roister Doister*.

The Church of St Michael the Archangel has a good 13th-cent. tower with a shingled broach spire, but the rest of the exterior is mainly 19th-cent. Inside is a chapel built by Udall. Braintree itself has a town hall built 1926–8 and among several buildings of earlier date should be noticed the corn exchange of 1839, the 18th-cent. Horns Hotel, the Georgian Constitutional Club and the 16th-cent. Old Manor House. Near the White Hart (*see* Bocking) is another fine inn, The Swan, with good timbering.

BRANCASTER, *Norfolk* (11–TF7743). Almost 2,000 years ago this was the site of Branodunum, a Roman fort, of which little now remains. The village, which is close to the north coast on the A149, has a 14th-cent. church, St Mary's. There is a 14th-cent. font with a particularly remarkable cover, Perpendicular in style and telescopic in its action. Three Italian lanterns on poles are now operated by electricity.

One m. to the N. across the reeded, marshy flats is Brancaster Bay and 1 m. to the E. is Brancaster Staithe, a popular boating centre. From here you may go by boat to **Scolt Head Island**.

The island is about 4 m. long and one of the best known features of the coast. Bathing can be particularly dangerous due to the tidal currents. Scolt is a shingle ridge resting on sand flats, partly covered by dunes and enclosing marshes. (*See also* BLAKENEY.) Marram grass may be seen on the dunes, as well as many other types of vegetation. Behind the beaches the marshes support plant and insect life in abundance. The entire area is in the care of the National Trust and naturalists will find numerous things to interest them. Among the many birds to be seen are various species of gull (some rare), terns, even including an occasional arctic tern, gannets and arctic skuas. Cormorants, redshanks and greenshanks, oystercatchers, ducks and geese in many varieties are only a few of the birds to be seen on this part of the coast which has one of the longest lists of birds in the British Isles.

BRANDON, *Suffolk* (11–TL7886). Brandon is situated in the NW. corner of the county almost on the Norfolk border and is part of the area known as Breckland. It is in that tiny portion of Suffolk which lies to the W. of the A11. Flints have provided its main industry for centuries. It is on the Little Ouse near the new State Forest of THETFORD Chase. St Peter's Church is some way from the town which grew up along the main road. The village displays the local building materials, flint of course, chalk, plaster and brick. The school in the Gothic style dates from 1878. The old stone five-arched bridge links Suffolk with Norfolk.

Extensive Roman remains have been found here at Fenhouse Farm. Brandon Hall is 18th-cent. Simon Eyre, the shoemaker who became Lord Mayor of London in Thomas Dekker's *The Shoemaker's Holiday* (1600), was based on the Simon Eyre, native of Brandon, who became Lord Mayor of London in 1445.

BRECKLAND, *Norfolk* (11–TL8590). This is the name given to that part of East Anglia which surrounds THETFORD and through which runs the Little Ouse. For many years it was a barren region of heathland but now the work of the Forestry Commission and the immense tree-planting programme which they have undertaken has changed the character of a once empty area. Meres make for variety and provide the fisherman with sport and the bird-watcher with a chance to observe some of the many species which make Norfolk their home.

Breckland leads into the fens, and includes areas where cultivation has made agriculture a source of livelihood. There are still traces of droves along which the nomadic tribes of ancient days travelled with their flocks across the width of England, and the flints which provided their tools were found at GRIME'S GRAVES and may be seen in many of the buildings of Thetford and in a number of the museums in the counties of Norfolk, Suffolk and Cambridgeshire.

BREDFIELD, *Suffolk* (11–TM2653). The birthplace of the famous writer Edward FitzGerald who was born at Bredfield House on 31 March 1809. The building was damaged during the last war and has since been demolished. All that remains are the stables and some minor outbuildings. FitzGerald married Lucy, daughter of Bernard Barton, one of the WOODBRIDGE Wits and is best remembered for his translation of *The Rubaiyat of Omar Khayyam* and his letters, many of them written from the rectory in 1853–60, where he often stayed with the rector, George Crabbe, son of the poet. He died on 14 June 1883 and is buried at Boulge, 1 m. from Bredfield. A rose grown from a Persian seed, said to be from Omar's tomb, flowers on his grave.

The Church of St Andrew has Tudor brick battlements and flushwork decoration on the tower. Near the village is the village pump, with an elaborate wrought-iron crown dating from the 18th cent.

BRENT ELEIGH, *Suffolk* (11–TL9547). St Mary's Church contains much Jacobean woodwork (pulpit and box pews, etc.) and a south door (14th-cent.), also finely carved. There is a monument by Thomas Dunn to Edward Colman (1743), a Fellow of Trinity College, CAMBRIDGE, who built the library which once stood in the churchyard (since rebuilt). A series of wall paintings of the 14th cent. has recently been discovered in the church.

Brent Eleigh Hall is basically Elizabethan in plan but with additions from later centuries. The ceiling over the staircase has fine plastering surrounding a painted oval centre-piece. In the 1930s the Hall was added to by Sir Edwin Lutyens. Colman is commemorated again in the almshouses of 1731.

BRENTWOOD, *Essex* (7–TQ5993), lies off the main London to CHELMSFORD road, the A12, on the original roadway, the crossing point of the roads which run diagonally across the county. Its White Hart Hotel is a famous old coaching inn dating back to the late 15th cent. Also in the High Street are the ruins of the 14th-cent. St Thomas's Chapel. The present churches are modern, the new St Thomas's being built in the 1880s in the Gothic style, and the Roman Catholic cathedral dating from 1861. Rather earlier is the Congregational chapel of 1847.

Brentwood School was founded in 1557. Remains of old buildings in Ingrave Road include School House, a fine Georgian building dated 1773. Many additional buildings were added both here and in Shenfield Road in later centuries.

To the SW. Great Warley church (1904) should be seen for its elaborate display of Art Nouveau.

BRESSINGHAM, *Norfolk* (11–TM0780). Bressingham Hall, open to the public on certain days throughout the summer, contains an outstanding collection of steam locomotives, tractors and other engines, fairground roundabouts and a miniature railway. The owner, Mr Alan Bloom, is one of the country's leading horticulturists and the gardens, almost 6 acres in extent, will delight all lovers of hardy plants and Alpines. Among the collection of more than 20 different engines is the famous Britannia Class Pacific No. 70013 *Oliver Cromwell*.

The village is 2½ m. W. of DISS on the A1066 to THETFORD. The church of St John the Baptist was rebuilt in 1527 by Sir Roger Pilkington, though much of it was, of course, earlier in date. Its particular feature is its magnificently carved bench-ends, some of which show figures, while others have various combinations of grotesques and designs based on twining plant forms. There are also three collecting shoes dated 1631. These relics of the 17th cent. were used in churches to collect offerings before being replaced by bags and plates. They are not in fact shoes, but look rather like a modern dustpan.

BREYDON WATER, *Norfolk* (11–TG4907). This is not a broad in the true sense of the word. It is really an extension of the estuary of the River Yare which is almost closed off from the sea by the sandbanks upon which GREAT YARMOUTH is built. Along its banks may be found the yellow Flag Iris, *Iris pseudacorus*. Due to its proximity to the sea, river prawns, common to Holland as well as to Norfolk, may be found, and are locally known as Jack shrimps. Brown shrimps also abound but these only exist in salt water.

Breydon Water made an ideal natural harbour at the time of the Romans and it is on the high ground of its south-west end that the fortress of Gariannonum, now known as BURGH CASTLE, was built at the end of the 3rd cent.

Breydon is the site of a big electrically-powered water-pumping station opened in 1948 and capable of drawing 100 tons of water a minute.

BRIGHTLINGSEA, *Essex* (11–TM0816). Reached from the B1027 road from COLCHESTER to CLACTON-ON-SEA, Brightlingsea is almost an island on the River Colne. As such it is not only a centre for yachting and boat building but also for the cultivation of the oysters which are found at so many points along the Essex coast. Roman remains testify to its ancient origin, and Roman brickwork may be seen in the Church of All Saints which dates from Norman times, though it is now mainly in the Perpendicular style. The tower, the flint and flushwork are excellent examples of their kind. Inside the church is a rich collection of brasses and monuments. The former date from 1496 (to John Beryf and his wife) and the latter includes an important memorial to Nicholas Magens, d. 1764, made by N. Read.

In the High Street is an ancient timbered house, Jacobs, which was bought by the Beriffe family from the Jacobs in the early 15th cent. The house itself was mentioned as far back as 1315. There is an early 16th-cent. brick stair-turret and an interesting roof. Surrounding the house is an attractive pattern of narrow streets, Victorian cottages and Georgian houses.

BROADS, THE, *Norfolk* (around 11–TG 4020). That unique combination of lakes, rivers and cuts which is to be found in the triangle bounded by NORWICH, LOWESTOFT and HAPPISBURGH. Famous for the magnificent boating they provide, they are also the home of a multitude of birds, flowers, insects and plants.

Largely man-made, the broads are the water-filled pits left by the turf cutters of long ago. Each is different and while some are fresh water, others are salt. If it were not for the coastal defence system, the entire region might well be flooded as it was in older times. While the main industry is now the tourist traffic, there is still evidence of the ancient crafts of thatching and basket-making, and many areas are managed as Nature Reserves.

It should be emphasized that while the area is excellent touring ground for the motorist, with its many picturesque villages, its fine churches and delightful countryside, it is not possible to gain a real idea of the true nature of the broads from the road. There are relatively few good viewpoints owing to the general flatness of the countryside, and to gain such a picture you must take to the water. Where good roadside views *are* obtainable they will be mentioned in the notes on individual broads. In this respect RANWORTH, ORMESBY and ROLLESBY are exceptional.

In recent years many of the broads have continued that silting up which began many years ago, and constant efforts have to be made to keep the waterways free for the traffic which is at its peak in the summer months. Boats may be bought or hired from the many yards and staithes. However, there are restrictions on entry to certain broads and a copy of the Navigation Map should be in the possession of anyone who intends to do any serious touring. Sailing requires much more skill and experience than the driving of a motor cruiser. Fishing, too, is a popular broadland sport with a wide range of fish including bream, perch, pike, roach, rudd and tench. Some areas are set aside for the use of anglers.

The main broads are as follows (notes on each will be found separately): Barton, Breydon, Hickling, Horsey, Hoveton, Ormesby, Ranworth, Rollesby, Salhouse, South Walsham and Wroxham. The Rivers Bure, Thurne, Ant, Yare and Waveney all flow into the North Sea at GORLESTON and GREAT YARMOUTH.

BUNGAY, *Suffolk* (11–TM3389). In the 12th cent. Bungay, which is now a market town and yachting centre on the River Waveney, saw the building of a great castle by Roger Bigod. Little now remains of the 70 ft square keep which includes in the south-west corner a mining gallery. This defensive feature was a tunnel supported by timbers which could be removed when attack threatened, thus causing the entire corner of the building to collapse on the invaders! The main headquarters of the Bigods was at FRAMLINGHAM though they retained a house in the town.

The Church of St Mary was once the church of the Benedictine nunnery founded in the 12th cent. by Gundreda. Like many other buildings in the town, it suffered considerable destruction in the Great Fire of 1688. Its tower, built at the end of the 15th cent., is one of the most remarkable in the county, with its polygonal buttresses and turrets.

The Church of Holy Trinity contains a fine pulpit of 1558 and a monument to Thomas Wilson by Thomas Scheemakers.

In the market place stands the Butter Cross erected in 1689 after the fire. The statue of Justice which surmounts the dome was added in 1754. There are a number of Georgian houses in the market place and its immediate neighbourhood and that at No. 6 St Mary's Street should be noticed. Also note the oriel windows of Nos. 14–18 with the arms of the Drapers Company, the Maids Head of the Mercers Company, and a merchant's mark.

In the middle of the 18th cent. John King, a local chemist, established some baths here. As in so many East Anglian towns of similar size there was a theatre which at one time became a corn exchange and is now in commercial use. Bungay's chief activity since the 18th cent. has been printing.

BURGH CASTLE, *Suffolk* (11–TG5104). Situated in the north-east corner of the county, almost on the Norfolk borders, this was the Gariannonum of the Romans. By the end of the occupation it was one of a chain of fortresses guarding the East Coast. The massive walls and the round bastions still give the spectator some idea of the strength of the original building, probably erected c. A.D. 290. With the departure of the Romans the castle saw the coming in c. 640 of the Irish missionary St Fursey who founded a monastery within its walls. The pendulum of change saw the site used by the Normans as a castle once again and in later ages many of its stones were used to build houses for the villagers.

History again comes to life in the great beam in the Village Institute with its inscription carved in 1548. The Church of SS. Peter and Paul has a Norman round tower and has been much restored. The font (Perpendicular) is finely carved.

BURNHAM-ON-CROUCH, *Essex* (7–TQ 9496). Like so many of the Essex estuary towns Burnham-on-Crouch is noted as a yachting and boat-building centre and also for its oyster beds. Along the quay is a terrace of houses with, as its centre-piece, the White Hart Hotel. Nearer the sea is the headquarters of the Royal Corinthian Yacht Club built in 1931. The High Street has a mixture of buildings including weather-boarded cottages, Georgian houses and examples of the Victorian period. Among the latter is the Clock Tower of 1877. Where the High Street broadens out was doubtless the site of the old market.

One m. N. of the town itself is the Church of St Mary which overlooks the coast from its slightly elevated position. The exterior features battlements which may also be seen on the south porch, decorated with four stone coats of arms. The north porch is 16th-cent. and has a stepped gable. Inside the church the lack of divisions between the nave, chancel and aisles gives it an unusual appearance. The font is Norman and made of Purbeck marble, and a wall tablet reminds us of the Rev. Alexander Scott who was chaplain on H.M.S. *Victory* when Nelson was killed in battle.

BURNHAMS, THE, *Norfolk* (11–TF8243), are a group which once numbered seven parishes. It was at **Burnham Thorpe**, in the now demolished Parsonage House, that Horatio Nelson was born on 29 September 1758, the fifth son of the 11 children of the Rev. Edmund Nelson. As such it is one of our most historic sites. When he was nine his mother died and at the age of 12 the young Nelson was sent to sea. The puny-looking lad soon achieved rank and was a captain (on the frigate *Hinchingbroke*) at the age of 20. His marriage, his rapid promotions and his relationship with Lady Hamilton are part of our history, and his death on the *Victory* on 21 October 1805 is one of the unforgettable episodes in the chronicles of the British people. After lying in state in the Painted Hall of Greenwich Hospital, Nelson was buried in St Paul's Cathedral on 9 January 1806.

Though the house is no more, its site is marked by a plaque close to the road. The Church of All Saints (Decorated and Perpendicular) has a Purbeck marble font and many memorials of the great sailor, and a lectern made from the timbers of Nelson's ship *Victory*. There is hardly need to

Kenneth Scowen

The Broads: a typical scene on the River Bure

state the name of the village inn! **Burnham Market** is the central village of the group with a fine main street and at its west end St Mary's Church. On top of its tower is a battlemented parapet with unusual carvings of Biblical scenes from the Old and New Testaments. Behind the church is Westgate Hall, built to the design of Sir John Soane in 1783.

Just NE. of Burnham Market is **Burnham Overy**, and on the way is a fine windmill of 1814 (National Trust). Where the road crosses the River Burn stands a watermill and a charming group of cottages. St Clement's Church with its Norman central tower, which was later lowered to receive a cupola of the 17th cent., has a tiny painting of St Christopher, a Stuart table and tables of the Commandments. One m. to the N. is Overy Staithe with a small harbour for light craft.

Two other Burnhams include **Burnham Norton** where St Margaret's has a round Norman tower. Inside is a large square Norman font and a Jacobean pulpit of exquisitely delicate hexagonal design. The panels are painted and there is a backboard and canopy.

Burnham Norton was the site of a Carmelite Friary founded in 1241. The gatehouse is Decorated in style and has excellent flush panelling.

Burnham Deepdale, near the coast on the A149, has a tower dating from before the Conquest and a magnificent Norman font. Around it are 12 carved panels representing each of the months, all surmounted by a frieze of lions and foliage.

BURWELL, *Cambridgeshire* (11–TL5866). One of the largest villages in Cambridgeshire and the centre of barge-building, turf and other industries. The rebel Geoffrey de Mandeville was killed here in 1144. It is the site of a 12th-cent. castle, of which all that remains is the moat. The Church of St Mary is a fine example of the spaciousness and brightness of the Perpendicular style. The interior is mainly built of clunch, hard East Anglian chalk. Over the chancel arch may be seen some beautifully carved tracery enclosing a "wheel" window which is unusual in that the spokes are replaced by whirl-like arms known as mouchettes.

The village contains a number of very attractive buildings as well as two windmills, only one of which is in working order.

Two m. SW. is **Swaffham Prior** famous for having two churches in one churchyard. St Mary's, with its octagonal tower on a sturdy Norman base, will remind the visitor of the great octagon at ELY. St Cyriac's also has an octagonal tower, but the rest of the building has become derelict.

Swaffham Prior House was built in 1753 but even more interesting is Baldwin Manor, a beautiful half-timbered building from the first half of the 16th cent.

Two windmills, one preserved and one derelict, echo the two churches. Windmill Hill gives wonderful views of the chalk heights above the Icknield Way.

BURY ST EDMUNDS, *Suffolk* (11–TL8564). The cathedral town, and the county town of West Suffolk. Its motto, "Shrine of a King, Cradle of the Law" commemorates two of the outstanding episodes in its history. Edmund, last king of the East Angles, was killed in 869 by the Danes at "Haegelisdun" (possibly Hellesdon, near NORWICH). The English held his death to be a martyrdom; for many years he was patron saint of England. His remains were later taken to Beodricesworth and from the early 11th cent. this town was known as St Edmundsbury. In 1020 Cnut, having become king of England on the death of his rival, another Edmund, and no doubt glad to make a gesture that might help resolve discord between the English and Danish communities of his new kingdom, gave the monastery where the saint was buried the status of abbey.

At the time of the Conquest the abbot was Baldwin, a Frenchman and a Norman sympathizer, and town and abbey were spared disturbance.

The second historic episode took place on 20 November 1215 when the barons "Swore at St Edmund's altar that they would obtain from King John the ratification of Magna Carta".

Bury St Edmunds today still retains the complete rectangular plan set out by Abbot Baldwin in the 11th cent. It is essentially Georgian in appearance though many buildings and houses are of earlier date than their façades would suggest.

The famous abbey was over 500 ft long with a west front nearly 250 ft wide which made it one of the greatest churches in the country. What remains of it today, though but a small fragment of the original buildings, is sufficient to give some idea of its former splendour. The Norman Gate, *c*. 1120–50 stands squarely and firmly like some religious keep. It presents an interesting contrast to the Abbey Gate *c*. 1430–40 which, no less sturdy in appearance, has an altogether more refined pattern of decoration.

The remains of the abbey church are mostly those of the west front and into them have been built dwelling houses, a fact which still excites fierce controversy among those who would wish them to remain and those who press for their removal. Other parts of this once great abbey may be traced in the grounds which lead down towards the River Lark.

The cathedral church since 1914 has been St James's immediately S. of the Norman Gate. It is 16th-cent. with 19th-cent. additions by Gilbert Scott. There are plans to enlarge it to a size more in keeping with its status as the only cathedral in the county. St Mary's Church has a magnificent Perpendicular exterior and its interior is no less perfect. The stone pendant in the roof of the Notyngham Porch, the splendid roof of the nave as well as that of the chancel are among the finest examples of their kind.

Another outstanding religious building is the Unitarian (originally Presbyterian) chapel in Churchgate Street, 1711–12, comparable to that at IPSWICH. Its double-decker pulpit is noteworthy.

Bury, as it is locally known, abounds in fine examples of civic and domestic buildings. The Town Hall, originally designed in the 1770s by Robert Adam as a theatre, is a classically symmetrical composition of considerable charm.

Moyse's Hall, now an outstandingly interesting museum, dates from the 12th cent. (it may be East Anglia's oldest domestic building) and houses prehistoric, Roman and medieval exhibits. Only a little later in date is the famous Abbot's Bridge across the River Lark, near where Mustow Street meets Eastgate Street.

Bury is a town to walk in. Angel Hill, for example, with its spacious feeling of earlier days leads you into the central complex of the city with its many beautiful buildings of the 17th and 18th cents. Near the General Post Office is Cupola House built in 1693 and featuring above its steeply pitched roof the cupola or turret, from which pleasing views could be obtained.

Not far away is the Athenaeum with its ballroom, the work of Francis Sandys. At the far end of Crown Street is the Theatre Royal, built in 1819 by William Wilkins, architect of the National Gallery, and of Downing College, CAMBRIDGE. It has been restored as one of Britain's finest Regency theatres.

The Guildhall, built in the 13th cent., was remodelled in the 19th. Near St James's churchyard is the Provost's House, built in 1730, as an asylum at the bequest of Dr Clopton. Angel Corner (National Trust), a Queen Anne house, contains a memorable collection of clocks, watches and time-pieces of many kinds. Open on occasion is the Suffolk Regimental Museum, full of items connected with the famous regiment.

Among the famous literary figures associated with the town was "Ouida", Louise de la Ramée (1840–1908). Born at Bury, the daughter of a French teacher, for some years she lived in London but about 1874 went to Italy where she died after having written over 40 novels, including a book of stories for children, *Bimbi*. Edward Fitz-Gerald, the translator of *The Rubaiyat of Omar Khayyam* came here to school and Dickens wrote of the Angel Inn in his works. A tablet on a house in St Mary's Square commemorates Thomas Clarkson, the fighter against slavery (*see* WISBECH).

CAISTER-ON-SEA, *Norfolk* (11–TG5211), a seaside resort separated from GREAT YARMOUTH by the links of the Great Yarmouth and Caister Golf Club (18 holes) which are on the main A149 coast road. Excavations have shown the extent of the Roman town to the N. of the Caister–Acle road. In later centuries it was also an Anglo-Saxon town of some importance.

The Church of Holy Trinity dates from the 13th cent. though it has been much restored. Inside is a huge font almost 5 ft high and $3\frac{1}{2}$ ft across. A

Commandment board has the familiar figures of Moses and Aaron and the Royal coat of arms shows some interesting changes to the dates which were originally painted on it.

Just over 1 m. inland is **Caister Castle**, one of the best of its period (15th-cent.) in the country. It was built in 1432–5 for the same Sir John Fastolf who appeared in Shakespeare's *Henry VI*. After his death in 1459 the castle came into the possession of the Paston family and it was here that many of the famous Paston Letters were written. Indeed it is a picturesque ruin, with one large tower at its north-west corner and its moat which indicates its original rectangular plan. At the opposite corner is the present Caister Hall with Georgian dressings to the original walls.

A motor museum is open to the public.

CAISTOR ST EDMUND, *Norfolk* (11–TG 2303), which lies 4 m. S. of NORWICH by the River Tas, was the site of the Roman town of Venta Icenorum which suggests that it was probably here that the Iceni settled after Boadicea's revolt of A.D. 70. Some of the walls are still well preserved and excavations have revealed the porter's lodge at the south gate.

The Church of St Edmund is reached by crossing the moat of the old Roman city. It is a simple building with a chancel, c. 1300 and a later tower and nave. Its most remarkable feature is the font dating from c. 1410, octagonal in shape with many interesting carvings, among them angels, lions and the signs of the Evangelists. The nave has a large painting of St Christopher.

Caistor Old Hall, N. of the church, dates from 1647, but parts are earlier. The entrance, for example, is dated 1612.

CAMBRIDGE, *Cambridgeshire* (11–TL4658). Cambridge is one of the most important and beautiful towns not only in East Anglia, but also in Britain and even Europe. The quality of its buildings, in particular those belonging to the University, and the particular atmosphere caused by the felicitous combination of river and gardens have given the city a place in the itinerary of every visitor to this country.

The old phrase "Town and Gown" suggests the ancient division, culminating in riots in 1381 during Wat Tyler's revolt, between that part of the city which is devoted to the University and the remainder which is residential and commercial – the city of everyday life in fact. The University has influenced not only the architecture of the town but also its character: its bookshops are among the finest in the country, and the adventurous programmes of the two theatres and several cinemas, the frequency of excellent concerts and the wide range of restaurants reflect the tastes and interests of the academic population. The history of Cambridge began many hundreds of years before the first college, Peterhouse, was founded in 1284 by Hugh de Balsham, Bishop of ELY. In the century preceding the Roman Conquest a Celtic settlement had arisen on what is known as Castle Hill, lying between Castle Street and Chesterton Road to the N. of the town. At the foot of the hill was a ford across the River Cam, and successive Roman developments probably included the building of a bridge at this point. This bridge became the only one to have given its name to an English county. Its location was of great importance as marking the place where the Roman roads, in particular the *Via Devana* from COLCHESTER to CHESTER, converged with the system of rivers and canals. As the northernmost point before reaching the fens such a site was of great strategic and commercial importance.

With the departure of the Romans the town continued to spread to its present position on the East Anglian side of the river. The Normans, however, rebuilt the castle and moved over to the opposite bank of the Cam. Nothing remains of the castle today but the mound. The 13th cent. saw the founding of the first Cambridge college and the consequent increase in the importance of the city as a seat of learning and a centre of communal life.

As the visitor will undoubtedly begin his tour with the University buildings, it is those which will be described first. A word on the possible origins of the University may not be out of place. In the 12th cent. students were still attached to the schools of the monasteries and cathedrals and the gradual development of universities in Italy and France was followed by the migration of scholars moving from one centre to another. Thus some went from Paris to OXFORD in 1167, and in 1209 further groups went from Oxford to Cambridge. Several religious orders settled in Cambridge in the 12th cent., and their houses attracted sufficient numbers of students for it to be recognized as a seat of learning by a writ for its governance made by Henry III in 1231.

In its early days the University used whatever accommodation was available, sometimes churches and on other occasions houses. The normal master's course was of seven years' duration and might sometimes be followed by a further ten years of study for a doctorate in theology. Students started earlier than now at the age of about 14 and generally completed their studies to become schoolmasters. The students at this time lived in lodgings in the town and due to the unsatisfactory conditions under which they had to exist, hostels in the care of one of the masters came into being. Such were the origins of the college system which prevails today.

Many of the colleges are on the main street (Trumpington Street, becoming King's Parade and then St John's Street) which runs parallel to the river between it and Market Hill. The "backs", peaceful green lawns running down to the river where it is crossed by bridges and shaded by willows, are in summer the essence of the Cambridge idyll of punting and May Balls.

Christ's College: Originally founded in 1439 as "God's House" and re-established under its present name in 1505 by Lady Margaret Beaufort. Imposing Gateway to St Andrew's Street. Fellows' Building added after 1640, important building of three stories plus dormers. 20th-cent.

Cambridge: the "Bridge of Sighs" links two of the buildings of St John's College

additions by Albert Richardson, P.R.A. Fine collection of plate, particularly Tudor, including Foundress's Cup pre-1440. Its most famous son was Milton.

Clare College: Founded as University Hall in 1326 by Richard de Baddow. Refounded by Elizabeth de Burgh of Clare, taking its present name since 1346. The court has, like Christ's, three stories plus dormers. The bridge, *c.* 1640, was built by Thomas Grumbold in the classical style, the first of its kind in Cambridge. New Court across the river was designed by Sir G. G. Scott and built 1924–35. Collection of candlesticks and foreign silver from Flanders, Germany, etc.

Corpus Christi: Founded by the town's merchants in 1352. Old Court still retains original appearance of the 14th cent. even though restored and added to. New Court built by W. Wilkins, 1823–7. The college has the best collection of silver plate in Cambridge. The Drinking Horn, *c.* 1347, may be the earliest piece of plate in Cambridge (*see* Trinity Hall). Christopher Marlowe studied here.

Downing College: A late addition, designed by William Wilkins in 1807, seven years after its foundation. Classic Grecian style and spacious grounds create admirable feeling of open-plan college. Additions in 1873, 1929, etc., and most imaginatively in 1969.

Emmanuel College: Founded 1584 by Sir Walter Mildmay on site of the Dominican or Black Friars house. In 1666 Sir Christopher Wren designed the chapel in the new classical style. Other additions in 18th and 19th cents., and in 20th cent. by Leonard Stokes. Fine collection of plate, both English and foreign. John Harvard, founder of the American college, was an alumnus.

Gonville and Caius College: Founded by Edmund Gonville 1348, re-established by Dr Caius 1557. Caius had studied at Gonville and determined to found a new college which would include his own. The three gateways, the Gate of Humility, the Gate of Virtue and Wisdom, 1567, a particularly impressive structure, and the Gate of Honour symbolize a student's progress. Monument in the chapel to Dr Caius by Theodore Haveus. Additions in 18th and 19th cents. and across Trinity Street in 20th. The plate includes two of the three "coco-nut cups" in Cambridge and the sceptre presented by Dr Caius first to the Royal College of Physicians and then to his own college.

Jesus College: Founded by Bishop Alcock of Ely in 1496. The number of students is not as great as in some of the colleges, and it is larger than many, which gives it a feeling of spaciousness. The chapel contains Norman portions dating from the nunnery which Bishop Alcock took over. It has decoration by Pugin, William Morris, Ford Madox Brown and Burne-Jones, and contains a memorial to Constable's son. Among its scholars were Coleridge, Laurence Sterne and Malthus.

King's College: Founded by Henry VI in 1441 at the same time as he established the school at ETON. Fellows' Building was designed by James Gibbs, 1723, in a simple classical style. A hundred

Cambridge: New Hall is a modern college for women

years later added to by William Wilkins, with further additions into the present century. The bridge, artfully sited, dates from 1818. The chief glory of King's College and of Cambridge itself is the chapel, considered by some the most outstanding building in Britain and the finest Gothic building in Europe. It was begun in 1446. Its unusual dimensions, almost 300 ft long, 80 ft high and 40 ft wide, prepare the spectator for its extraordinary system of spatial relationships. The effect of the interior is breathtaking. The shafts on either side of the chapel lead the eye up into the roof where the profusion of delicate fan-vaulting appears as if made of lace rather than stone. The placing of the organ case (1606) with its curves echoing those of the ceiling, and the superb quality of the woodwork of the screen and the choir stalls (1536) act as a perfect foil to the splendours above. No less important is the stained glass, dating from 1515, the year the chapel was completed. The windows tell stories from the Old and New Testaments. Note the *Adoration of the Magi* by Rubens, c. 1634, and the 20th-cent. bronze candlestick by Benno Elkan.

Magdalene College: Founded in 1542 incorporating the original monks' hostel which had been established in 1428 by the prior of the Benedictines at Cambridge, and which was the only early college on the west bank of the river. The first court and the chapel date from the mid-15th cent. and were named Buckingham College. After the Dissolution it came into the hands of Lord Audley

of AUDLEY END and was re-founded under its present name. Additions were gradually made to the original buildings including Pepys Building, which includes the Pepysian Library housed in his own bookcases together with his own desk. His diaries are on exhibition. A more recent building, Mallory Court, commemorates the famous mountaineer.

Pembroke College: Founded in 1347 by Mary, Countess of Pembroke. A notable addition was made by Sir Christopher Wren who designed the chapel, a gift to the college from his uncle, the Bishop of Ely. It was consecrated in 1664, the earliest classical building in the city. The famous Anathema Cup (1481–2) and the Foundress's Cup, perhaps even earlier, are among the fine collection of plate. Edmund Spenser, Archbishop Whitgift, Nicholas Ridley, William Pitt the Younger and the poet Gray were all Pembroke men.

Peterhouse College: This was the earliest of the colleges to be founded, established by the Bishop of Ely in 1281 and moving to its own hostels in 1284. The original hall is part of the south side of the Main Court but little remains due to the 19th-cent. restoration. The chapel, dating from 1632, seems to combine some of the features of the earlier chapel at King's, the corner turrets for example, with an awareness of some of the classical motifs which were to be fully realized by Wren in the next generation.

Queens' College: Whereas some of the colleges

were founded twice, Queens' was founded no less than three times. First in 1446, by Andrew Docket, under the name of St Bernard's College, then in 1448 by Margaret of Anjou, under the name of Queen's College, and finally about 1465 by Elizabeth Woodville, Queen of Edward IV. Thus it is not Queen's but Queens' College. Perhaps its most famous feature is the President's Lodge c. 1540, a picturesque timbered building over the north cloisters. Inside, the panelling, part carved and part linenfold, is particularly worthy of attention. The famous Mathematical Bridge was constructed in 1749 without the use of any nails. The chapel contains some interesting brasses, and a fine 15th-cent. painting. Erasmus resided here in 1510.

St Catharine's College: Founded in 1473 by Robert Wodelarke though none of its buildings of that time remain, most of them having been reconstructed at the end of the 17th cent.

St John's College: Founded by Lady Margaret Beaufort, mother of Henry VII, in 1511, again at the instigation of John Fisher. The First Court still manages to give a good idea of its original appearance. An elaborate gatehouse shows a fine display of heraldic carvings. The hall contains the original hammer-beam roof of the 16th cent. The Combination Room, with its patterned plaster ceiling and the library, c. 1623–4, are important additions, and the bridge built by Grumbold c. 1710 was based on designs by Wren. New Court, built on the other side of the Cam, 1825–31, was at the time the largest building of any college. The famous Bridge of Sighs which connects it with the old buildings was designed by Hutchinson in 1831. Later came the chapel by Scott and additional buildings in the present century. The Hercule's Cup is among its collection of plate. Roger Ascham, Herrick, Wordsworth and Palmerston were John's men.

Sidney Sussex College: Founded in 1596 by Lady Frances Sidney, Countess of Sussex, on the site of the Franciscan house. Much worked on by Sir Jeffry Wyatville early in the 19th cent. The chapel rebuilt in 1912 by T. H. Lyon is a fine building in the classic style. The painting over the altar is by Pittoni. The plate includes good examples from the 17th cent. to the present day. Oliver Cromwell entered as a fellow commoner in 1616.

Trinity College: King's Hall, founded 1336 by Edward III, was re-founded by Henry VIII as Trinity College, in 1546. At the same time another college, Michaelhouse, founded 1323, was also incorporated. A number of the original buildings including King Edward's Tower and King's Hall were utilized and considerable extensions commenced in the 16th cent. The Great Gate, 1519, was included in the Great Court, much of which was built under the direction of Dr Thomas Nevile, a court larger than any at Cambridge or Oxford. The Renaissance Fountain dates from 1602 and the magnificent library, the work of Sir Christopher Wren, was commenced in 1676. The carving is by Grinling Gibbons. Fine sculptures include busts of Newton, by Roubiliac, and of Byron, and there is also an exceptional

collection of plate from the 17th cent. onwards.

Trinity Hall: Founded in 1350 by the Bishop of NORWICH. The 16th-cent. library is the best remaining of its date. It is the only college still known as a Hall, to distinguish it from Trinity College, and is famous for the number of Chief Justices it has produced. An outstanding collection of plate includes a Founder's Cup, pre-1350, one of the two earliest pieces of plate in the whole of the University (*see* Corpus Christi).

1869 saw the founding of the first college for women, *Girton,* which moved from Hitchin to its present site in 1873. In 1871 Miss Anne Clough had founded *Newnham* which moved into its present buildings in 1875. *Selwyn College,* for men, was founded in 1881 to be followed by *Ridley Hall, Westcott House* and *Westminster College,* all theological institutions.

Though considerable building had taken place between the wars it was 1954 before another college was founded. This was *New Hall,* a third women's college. It is a striking modern design by Peter Chamberlin, with a remarkable dome as one of its central features. *Fitzwilliam Hall* (formerly House) is another completely new building by Denys Lasdum (1960). In the same year *Churchill College* was founded to designs by Richard Sheppard, again in an uncompromisingly modern idiom. The University buildings apart from the colleges include the *Old Schools,* commenced in 1350. Many additions were made in succeeding years including the Palladian part by Stephen Wright, 1754–8.

Senate House by James Gibbs, 1722–30, handsomely adapts the tradition of Wren to the Palladian style. Among the plate is the Essex Cup after the Earl of Essex, installed as Chancellor in 1598. The *Old Library* was built by Cockerell in 1836–42 and the *New Library* by Sir G. G. Scott in 1931–4. The many laboratories, etc., include the world-famous *Cavendish Laboratory* where Rutherford was Professor.

The *Botanic Gardens* in Bateman Street were opened in 1846, and the *Scott Polar Research Centre* in Lensfield Road dates from 1933–4.

The Fitzwilliam Museum was founded by the 7th Viscount in 1816 and was built to the design of George Basevi. It is an impressive classical building and contains a magnificent collection of works of art of all kinds. Antiquities from Egypt, Greece and Rome; works from medieval times, drawings, paintings and sculptures of all schools, and large collections of coins, ceramics, glass and armour make it one of the most important collections in the country. The city contains many churches of great interest, particularly *St Benet's,* the oldest church in the county. The tower is Anglo-Saxon, probably c. 1000, and the interior arch is exceptionally well preserved. *St Mary-the-Great,* the University Church, stands in the centre of town; basically 15th-cent., it has a 17th-cent. tower and 14th-cent. details. University sermons are given here. Other churches worth exploring are *St Andrew the Less; St Botolph's; St Edward's; St Mary the Less; St Mary Magdalene,* originally the chapel of the leper hospital at Stourbridge; *St*

Michael's and of course *Holy Sepulchre*, Bridge Street. This last is the oldest (*c.* 1130), of the four remaining round churches in England and though drastically restored in the 19th cent. it still conveys the strong character of early Norman architecture. There are no civic buildings of outstanding architectural importance.

Hobson's Conduit (1614), in Brookside, is a reminder of the one-time carrier who became Mayor of the city. It was from his insistence that customers took the first horse offered, that the expression "Hobson's choice" derives.

The Gog Magog (or Grogingog) "Hills" just outside the town are popular for walking and have a golf course; on the crest of the hills is Wandlebury, an Iron Age fort. Below it lies Stourbridge Common, where an important fair was held for many years.

CANEWDON, *Essex* (7–TQ8994). Here the Church of St Nicholas, with its large tower, stands in a fine position on a hill above the River Crouch. Like many an East Anglian tower, it may well have done duty as lighthouse and vantage point. The pulpit came from a City church (St Christopher's) and the font from the demolished church at Shopland. The vicarage was commenced in 1758, and has been much added to; Canewdon Hall, a simple but attractive building, dates from 1807.

Near the church is the lock-up of 1775, which contains the old stocks.

The village of the 1960s contrasts with the timber-framed Lambourne Hall, 1 m. to the E.

CANVEY ISLAND, *Essex* (7–TQ7783). Though mentioned as far back as Norman times the island, situated in the Thames estuary, to the W. of SOUTHEND-ON-SEA, was subject to flooding until it was walled by the Dutch engineer Joos Croppenburgh in 1622. Its associations with Holland are brought to mind by the two Dutch cottages, 1618 and 1621, one of which is now a little museum. Octagonal and thatched, they are reminiscent of the Round House near the village of FINCHINGFIELD, though they are, of course, earlier. Though the island is now almost one vast spread of bungalows and caravan sites, the Church of St Nicholas, 1960, is most interesting and there is a modern War Memorial Hall, opened in 1953.

That year is remembered in Canvey for the dreadful night when great storms whipped across the East Coast causing such terrible loss of life and property.

CASTLE HEDINGHAM, *Essex* (11–TL78 35). Built on a hill overlooking the River Colne is the great castle which gives the village its name. It was constructed by the de Vere family in about 1140 and remains one of the most impressive keeps in England. Reached by a bridge (*c.* 1500) over the protecting ditch the tower, almost 100 ft high, is dominated by the two corner turrets. The richness of the carved decoration and the strength of the heavy stone walls add to the effect

of grandeur. The Church of St Nicholas was begun some 50 years after the building of the castle, and the interior is a perfect example of the late Norman style, with fine arcades and a magnificent south door; in the churchyard the War Memorial, a re-erected 12th-cent. cross. The tower was rebuilt in the 16th cent. and was renovated again in 1616 and this, together with the general impression of the exterior, makes the interior of the church rather a surprise. A particularly impressive monument is that to the 15th Earl of Oxford, d. 1539, and his wife, which was probably carved by Cornelius Harman (*see* SAFFRON WALDEN).

Apart from the castle and the church the town has a number of domestic buildings of charm and merit. Near the church is an old inn, and in Queen Street are two excellent houses of Georgian date: The Rectory and Trinity Hall. In 1191 a Benedictine nunnery was founded to the W. of the village, near the Colne, but nothing now remains of its buildings.

CASTLE RISING, *Norfolk* (11–TF6624), has the remains of the castle built in the middle of the 12th cent. by William de Albini, perhaps on the site of Roman earthworks. The great keep, one of the largest in England, reminds one of that at NORWICH. Its great breadth contrasts with its height of some 50 ft. The exterior walls are richly decorated with arcading. The castle is entered through a fore-building and a strong, dramatic staircase; there are only two stories, the upper containing the great hall. Kitchens, a gallery and a small domestic chapel were included in the structure.

The Church of St Lawrence is famous for its Norman west front with a fine Norman doorway on the lower level, and an even finer window above, on either side of which is a group of intersecting arcades. Above this is a round window flanked by further arcading. This latter window may have been added when the church was much restored in the 19th cent. The font, which has a richly carved square bowl standing on a short circular shaft, is especially noteworthy.

On the green to the W. of the church is a large 15th-cent. cross. On the other side of the church is the Howard Hospital founded by Henry Howard, d. 1614. It is now an almshouse for old ladies, and visitors may still see the rooms with their original Jacobean furniture. Its inhabitants attend church on Sundays wearing red cloaks bearing the badge of the Howard family.

CAVENDISH, *Suffolk* (11–TL8046). One of Suffolk's most attractive villages and former ancestral village of the Dukes of Devonshire. Around the village green are thatched cottages and the Church of St Mary – a typically English traditional scene. The church has flushwork panelling and a clerestory. The 14th-cent. tower contains a room with a fire-place and shuttered windows. There are two lecterns, one a brass eagle and the other of wood, and two interesting statues, one Flemish and the other Italian. Other buildings include the mill, part of a mainly 18th-cent. group; Cavendish Hall to the W., early 19th-cent. in classic style; and Nether Hall Farmhouse, near the church, a 16th-cent. timber-framed building of two stories.

The 16th-cent. Old Rectory is now owned by Sue Ryder, and is one of the many homes she has established for refugees from all parts of the world.

CAWSTON, *Norfolk* (11–TG1324). A village about 12 m. NW. of NORWICH on the B1149 which has one of the finest churches in the county. This Church of St Agnes in the Perpendicular style was much patronized by Michael de la Pole, Earl of Suffolk, d. 1414. The west tower, 120 ft high, is starkly impressive, its simplicity relieved by the combination of window and doorway. Inside the church, the nave of which was probably built after the tower, there is a magnificent roof with great hammer-beams and numerous carved angels. The screen still has its doors and the original paintings, while the 15th-cent. pulpit is delicately poised on a stone base. Some of the stalls and benches have carvings.

Off the AYLSHAM road S. of the Woodrow Inn is the Duel Stone which commemorates a duel fought between Sir Henry Hobart and Oliver Le Neve in 1698.

CHELMSFORD, *Essex* (7–TL7006). The county town of Essex, though in terms of historical, architectural and archaeological interest it cannot be compared with COLCHESTER more to the NE. corner of the county. However, its position on the main road from London to Colchester and IPSWICH and on the cross routes from the SE. to the NW. of the county as well as its placing on the River Chelmer and the River Can has made it an important thoroughfare town since Roman times.

The Parish Church of St Mary was raised to the status of a cathedral just before the First World War and with its fine 15th-cent. tower topped by an open lantern and spire added in 1749, is a prominent feature of the city. In particular the south porch with elaborate Perpendicular flush-work patterning demands attention. Restorations took place early in the 19th cent. and again early in the 20th. Many of the interior fitments such as the pulpit, the altar, the provost's stall and the bishop's throne are comparatively recent, but there are a number of interesting monuments from the 16th cent. and later.

The Shire Hall was built by John Johnson (who was later to work on the church) in 1789–91. Though not large it is finely proportioned and suited to the dignity of a small town. The County Hall was built in 1935. As an important market and thoroughfare town traffic came to Chelmsford by water and rail as well as by road and its continued development in the 18th and 19th cents. has left a number of good domestic buildings, inns and, in particular, mills of which those at Springfield, Barnes and Moulsham are the best examples.

Later industrial development came when Marconi developed his electronic industry here and at WRITTLE. Civic buildings of the 19th cent. include a number of chapels and meeting houses and the conduit of 1814. The main public library, municipal offices and civic theatre are at the top end of Duke Street, while the excellent Chelmsford and Essex Museum is in Oaklands Park near the junction of Moulsham Street and the Chelmsford bypass.

The town is well provided with sporting facilities, the County Cricket team play here and there is an excellent football team.

CHIPPING ONGAR, *Essex* (7–TL5502). A small town which derives its name from the old word "chipping" or market, which grew in the shadow of the castle built by the Normans in the 11th cent. and of which little remains but the mound some 50 ft high. The Church of St Martin of Tours is very much Norman with a belfry of the 15th cent. and dormer windows of the 18th. Inside is an attractive west gallery supported on columns. The pulpit is early 17th-cent. with strapwork decoration and there is a monument by the well-known sculptor, Nollekens.

Where the old market met, the High Street widens and close by are some interesting houses, one at the corner of the lane to the church is dated 1642, with opposite, the King's Head (1697). It was in the Congregational church (1833) that the famous missionary and explorer David Livingstone was trained. In the same church one of the pastors was Isaac Taylor, one of a famous family of writers, artists and craftsmen. It was the daughters of one of the Taylors who wrote *Twinkle, twinkle, little star* at LAVENHAM at the end of the 18th cent.

CLACTON-ON-SEA, *Essex* (11–TM1715), has for a long time been one of the most popular of holiday resorts, with behind it the two villages of **Great** and **Little Clacton**. The former has a much restored Norman church (St John the Baptist), the Mansion House (Georgian), the Ship Inn and the bow-windowed Queen's Head. The latter has St James's, another church of Norman origin with a Purbeck marble font.

Clacton-on-Sea developed in the 1870s and followed the pattern of the other resorts on the East Coast, such as FRINTON and WALTON. There are three Martello towers, a feature of much of the coast-line. The Royal Hotel was built in 1872, the Grand in 1897 and the other buildings associated with a resort soon followed. St James's Church in Tower Road was built in 1913, presenting an odd contrast in styles; the Roman Catholic church in Church Road was a little earlier (1902).

The pier has been rebuilt several times since it was first erected in 1873, to be followed in 1890 by the pavilion. The giant scenic railway, one of the most striking features of the front, was added in the 1930s at about the same time as the Town Hall.

Despite its name the Moot Hall is a private

Noel Habgood

Cley-next-the-Sea: the 18th-century windmill

house, built from timbers taken from an old barn at Hawstead, not far from BURY ST EDMUNDS. The rash of holiday camps which have spread along the coast provides excellent holiday facilities, if not adding anything to the visual appeal of the town. To the S. is **Jaywick Sands**, a caravan and chalet centre.

The beach is sandy, there is every possible holiday amenity and entertainment and there is golf at the Clacton-on-Sea Golf Course (18 holes) at West Road, on the A133.

CLARE, *Suffolk* (11–TL7645). It was here that William Dowsing, the infamous iconoclastic Parliamentary visitor of Suffolk churches, "brake down 1,000 superstitious pictures" and as a result there is little of the original stained glass left in the Church of SS. Peter and Paul. Though some parts, e.g. the tower, are earlier, the church is mainly 15th-cent. and contains some notable wood-carving, especially the delicate work of the chancel door.

The town was the site of a castle first mentioned in 1090, and on the mound stand some impressive remains. It was also the site chosen by the Austin Friars in 1248 for the first house of the order in the country. The prior's house, cellar and infirmary are still in use.

Clare is another of the beautiful towns along the LONG MELFORD–HAVERHILL road and many of the houses display that pargetry work (ornamental plaster coating) which is one of the specialities of the region. The Ancient House which has the date 1473 on some of its later parts, belonged at one time to the priest. The Grove is of similar date with additions from the 19th cent. The Swan Inn in the High Street has fine carving, and along Nethergate Street The Cliftons has

clustered chimneys of the 16th cent. On the Chilton road is Chapel Cottage with an original doorway of the 12th cent.

CLEY-NEXT-THE-SEA, *Norfolk* (11–TG 0444). Cley is situated on the North Coast Road (A149) some way inland from the sea and on the east bank of the River Glaven. At one time it was a busy and prosperous little port but embankments built in the 17th cent. led to its decline. The village itself has many small flint-built houses along narrow streets. The Church of St Margaret S. of the village is large and impressive with a remarkable clerestory composed of alternate circular and arched windows. The Perpendicular south porch is finely proportioned with a traceried parapet. The south transept which has been in ruins for centuries has a beautifully traceried window and inside the Galilee porch west of the tower is an equally beautiful doorway. Inside the church is some fine woodwork and brasses, while the churchyard contains, as at BLAKENEY, some carved 18th-cent. tombstones.

Perhaps the most picturesque sight in Cley is the windmill which dates from 1713 and stands like a sentinel over the great expanse of marshes which lie between it and the sea. The shingle beach is at the end of a long road across these flats. The front of the Post Office is apparently built with the ground-up bones of horses and cattle.

CODDENHAM, *Suffolk* (11–TM1354), was Combretonium in Roman times. The site was thought to be by the ford across the River Gipping, but modern research has located it more exactly in the Baylham House area, where many finds of archaeological interest have been yielded.

St Mary's Church was recorded in Norman

times and has many Perpendicular additions. There is a large Italianate painting of Christ and a rare 15th-cent. alabaster carving of the Crucifixion which escaped destruction by Dowsing (*see* CLARE), by being hidden in a village home. On the east gable of the nave is a stone sanctus bell turret. A double hammer-beam roof with angels and monuments to Captain Philip Bacon and the Puritan statesman Nathaniel Bacon are to be seen.

In the village street is the Post Office, once an inn, dating from *c.* 1500, and in a park is the 18th-cent. vicarage. One m. N. is an early 15th cent. building, Choppings Hill Farmhouse.

COGGESHALL, *Essex* (11–TL8522). The Roman road from COLCHESTER to the W., now the A120 passes through the village in which is one of the most famous Tudor houses in the country, Paycocke's House (National Trust), a superb example of a half-timbered building *c.* 1500. From the street the façade, even though restored, presents an ideal picture of the home of a wealthy Tudor merchant. Five bays composed of oriel windows above, and entrance door, windows and gateway below are divided vertically by timber studs and horizontally by an elaborate beam. On either side of the gateway are carved figures, and between the timbers are bricks.

Inside, there is a wealth of carving: on the beams of the hall, in the linenfold panelling of the dining-room and in the carved bressumer which supports the brickwork over the fireplace. There are equally fine ceilings in the upstairs rooms where some of the original Tudor flooring still remains. There is a handsome garden from which the house presents a very different appearance as it is completely plastered.

Next door, in what is now the Fleece Inn, lived some of the descendants of the Paycocke family. The Church of St Peter has been carefully rebuilt after considerable destruction in 1940. Inside are a number of brasses to the Paycocke family and another to the remarkable Mary Honywood, d. 1620, who left 367 surviving descendants.

The village itself contains a large number of excellent houses, many displaying the traditional pargeting of the region, and in the Woolpack Inn one of the most picturesque hostelries in the country.

Not far from the village is Houchin's Farm, a beautiful timber-framed building dating from the early 17th cent.

Little Coggeshall just to the S. was the site of an abbey founded by King Stephen in the middle of the 12th cent. The foundations of the abbey have been traced and excavations have revealed many interesting features. Though the church itself has vanished, some of the ancillary buildings have survived, including a two-storied corridor and an early-13th-cent. gate chapel. The monastic priest-house contains possibly the earliest medieval brickwork in England. Not far from the chapel is an exceptionally interesting group of farm buildings with an early-16th-cent. barn.

COLCHESTER, *Essex* (11–TM0025). Colchester calls itself "Britain's oldest recorded town" and in fact, though in the 1st cent. B.C. it has been settled by the Trinovantes and named Camulodunum, the area has traces of settlements going back as far as the Bronze Age, *c.* 1000 B.C. In the early years of the Christian era it was the capital city of Cunobelin who reigned over South East England. In A.D. 43 the Romans invaded and it was here that Claudius received the surrender of the British kings. The first Roman city in this island was founded here, but it fell to Queen Boadicea despite its strengthened defences when she made her historic challenge to the might of the Romans. Though her armies had slain 70,000 people she was in the end defeated and the Roman city rose again to become a walled city and one of the most important Roman centres in Britain.

Parts of the walls of this ancient town still stand and within them have been found the remains of almost 100 buildings and relics. From this wall the Balkerne Gateway still survives as a ruined arch next door to an inn in Balkerne Lane where it was originally the main exit from the town to London and the west. When the Romans left, the town inevitably decayed and was the scene of invasions by the Anglo-Saxons, the Danes and finally the Normans.

The Normans found in Colchester a flourishing town of some 2,000 persons and its position made it an obvious site for a major fortress. Though the precise date of the commencement of building is not known for certain it is usually put at *c.* 1085. Though only the keep survives, its massive proportions convey an idea of the size of the original building. It was the largest keep built in Europe, almost 100 ft high and 150 ft in length by 110 ft in width. At the base the walls are more than 12 ft thick. Its great size is no doubt due to the fact that it was built upon the vaults of the great Roman Temple of Claudius. The castle is now a museum containing a fine collection of Roman and other antiquities.

Shortly after the castle was built St John's Abbey was founded just S. of the original Roman walls. All that remains now is the 15th-cent. gatehouse with its pinnacled towers on either side. Not far from St John's is St Botolph's Priory founded shortly after St John's as the first English Augustinian house. The remains of the priory are no less splendid than the castle itself. The great doorway with its rich carvings leads into the open nave bounded by the massive columns supporting tiers of Norman arches. Though the building itself is almost 900 years old the bricks with which it is made are more than twice that age, being made by the Romans themselves. Destroyed during the siege of 1648, until which time it was the principal church of the town, the priory has as neighbour a new church built in 1837.

Earlier than the priory is the tower of Holy Trinity Church with its Anglo-Saxon west door close by Trinity Street. It is in an unknown grave here that one of the greatest of Elizabethan composers lies buried. William Wilbye lived in a house close to the church for the last ten years of his life and was buried there in 1638. His madrigals have been sung for the past 300 years or more. Inside the church is the alabaster carving in memory of William Gilbert, Elizabeth I's physician, the first man to use the word electricity and who used to amuse her with his electrical experiments. Tymperleys, the house in which he lived, may be seen through the archway facing the church in Trinity Street.

Facing the castle is the Church of All Saints, now used as a Natural History museum. Almost opposite All Saints towards East Hill is Hollytrees, the best 18th-cent. house in the town, now a museum. Across the road is the Minories which dates from 1776 and which is now the town's art gallery holding frequently changing exhibitions of national as well as local interest.

Turning back to walk along the High Street, at the far end may be seen the red-brick water tower built in 1882 and locally known as "Jumbo". But before this extraordinary construction is reached you would pass the Red Lion Hotel, a timber-framed building of the late 15th cent. The earliest part, now the Grill Room, still has the moulded beams. On the right of the High Street is the Town Hall, built at the beginning of this century. The 162-ft-high tower supports the figure of St Helena and the façade contains a number of statues, including that of Boadicea.

During the Middle Ages the chief trade was that of making cloth, and the industry owed much to the help of the Flemish refugees who came in the 17th and 18th cents. Nowadays Colchester is famous principally for its oysters, which have been highly esteemed since Roman times, and for engineering and the growing of roses. The original Cant Nurseries were established in 1766 and the family is still one of the best-known growers in the country.

One of the sights of Colchester is undoubtedly Bourne Mill in Bourne Road in the south-east corner of the town. This was built in 1591, probably for use as a fishing lodge. At each end of the single-storied stone building are two gables which ascend in concave and convex curves. At some time the house was used as a water mill and the weather-boarded hoist-loft was added. A little further down the stream, Cannock Mill, another water mill, is still in working order.

On the outskirts of the town along the estuary of the River Colne is the University of Essex, one of the newest of the post-war universities. Set in Wivenhoe Park, made famous in a number of paintings by John Constable, the four huge residential towers, the library centre and the other university buildings are already becoming a familiar feature of the neighbourhood.

Before leaving Colchester the motorist can forge a link with ancient times by touring the area of the dykes. Leaving on the Lexden Road, there is near St Clare Road a tumulus, perhaps that of Cunobelin. First comes Triple Dyke then Grymes Dyke and once back at Lexden Straight Road leave the car near the Mormon Temple and walk up to Half Moon Dyke. These dykes formed

a huge fortified enclosure almost 12 square m. in area and have yielded many treasures, including that found in the Lexden Tumulus now on view in the Colchester and Essex Museum.

Colchester has one of the best small zoos in the country, at Stanway.

COLTISHALL, *Norfolk* (11–TG2619). Though nowadays known particularly for the R.A.F. Station 2 m. N. of the village, Coltishall, which is situated on the River Bure, is itself an attractive village with many pleasant 18th-cent. brick houses.

Rather earlier, and dated 1692, is The Limes, perhaps the best house in the village.

The Church of St John the Baptist, which is thatched, has two small Anglo-Saxon windows in the north wall and a Perpendicular west tower.

Between the village and the R.A.F. Station stands the church of Great Hautbois, now mostly in ruins but with a round Norman tower and a chancel which is still roofed.

A little to the SW. the village of **Horstead** has, in addition to the Church of All Saints with its 13th-cent. west tower, a famous mill by the River Bure which formerly stood on six arches, but has recently been partly destroyed by fire.

CONSTABLE COUNTRY, *Suffolk* (11–TM 0734). Constable, perhaps the most natural of all landscape painters, and one of the greatest English artists, was born in EAST BERGHOLT on 11 June 1776. His father was a well-to-do miller and though he hoped the boy would enter the Church, or at least take over the family mills, the call of art was to prove too strong. Such was the power of John Constable as a painter that through his eyes millions have been taught to see the countryside about which he himself cared so passionately.

Late in life he was on a coach journey from London when one of his travelling companions used the phrase "Constable country", a name which has ever since been used to describe the villages which the artist painted so many times. Each will be dealt with more fully but the places which, as Constable himself said "made me a painter", group themselves along the River Stour, whose reaches the artist loved to draw and paint. East Bergholt no longer boasts his place of birth which may be seen on some of his canvasses but the church still stands. It was at the rectory that Constable met Maria, the grand-daughter of the rector, Dr Rhudde, the girl he married. FLATFORD MILL, now a field studies centre, DEDHAM, Langham, Stratford St Mary, and the other villages of NAYLAND, STOKE-BY-NAYLAND, Brantham, Bures, POLSTEAD stretch towards COLCHESTER and form part of the country which time has caused to be given the name of the great painter.

COPFORD, *Essex* (11–TL9222). Just off the ever-busy A12 road from London to COLCHESTER, near the junction at Marks Tey, is the little village of Copford whose Church of St Mary the Virgin

Cromer: the old town and the beach

is one of the finest examples of Norman work in the county. Much of the original Norman work still remains: the nave, chancel and apse, though the barrel-vaulted roof was replaced with a wooden structure in the 15th cent. In this Norman work may be seen many Roman bricks and, in one of the arches of the south aisle, some of the earliest of English-made bricks. Though the architectural qualities of the church are so interesting, and though the font is solid Purbeck marble, the chief treasure is the marvellous series of wall paintings.

They date from the time of the construction of the church in the middle of the 12th cent. and although they have been restored they can still remind us of how the interior of this, and many other churches in East Anglia used to look. Over the altar Christ sits in glory, supported by angels, the arch which spans the apse shows the signs of the zodiac and among the other subjects to be seen are the Virtues.

Near the church is Copford Hall, a red-brick mansion of Georgian date, which is beautifully set in a fine wooded park. On this site, though not in this house, lived the bishops of London, and it is thought that Bishop Bonner, who died in 1569, may be buried in the church.

COVEHITHE, *Suffolk* (11–TM5281). Approached from WRENTHAM on the A12, Covehithe is a completely unspoilt village with a fine stretch of sandy beach. On the left stand the majestic remains of the church which was dismantled in 1672 when the town began to decline. Among many artists who have captured the spirit of these ruins was John Sell Cotman. The road continues past the church until a barrier prevents all but pedestrians passing through on to the cliff top. From the top of the cliff the coast sweeps N. towards LOWESTOFT and S. to SOUTHWOLD. The energetic can gain access to the

beach by clambering down the face of the cliff, not as hazardous an adventure as it might sound. Those with a little more time can walk along the cliff top to the left where it gradually slopes down to the beach.

Those who prefer to bathe in almost complete isolation will find Covehithe much to their liking. They would be advised, however, to avoid weekends and Bank Holidays, the only times when any considerable number of people are to be seen.

CREAKES, THE, *Norfolk* (11–TF8538; North Creake), situated midway between **Burnham Market** and FAKENHAM these two villages have interesting churches and in the case of **North Creake**, the ruins of an abbey founded for the Augustinians in 1206. Though not extensive the ruins are impressive. St Mary's Church (14th- and 15th-cent.) has a good hammer-beam roof and a fine brass to Sir William Calthorpe, d. *c.* 1500, who did much for the church.

South Creake's church, St Mary's, is a mixture of the Decorated and Perpendicular styles, large in scale and with a hammer-beam roof over the lofty arcading of the nave. The 15th-cent. pulpit is another of those which tapers gently towards its base. The screen and font are also worthy of attention. Brasses include one to a priest, *c.* 1400, and another to John Norton, *d.* 1509.

Just to the S. of the village is the site of an ancient encampment of Iron Age origin.

CRESSING, *Essex* (11–TL7920). The Church of All Saints, though with much work of Norman date, must give way in interest to the two magnificent barns which are all that remains of the Temple of the Knights Templars and Hospitallers. There is a third barn, dated 1623, which is much later than the Wheat Barn and Barley Barn which stand near it. Tests have shown that the timbers of the Barley Barn date from the 11th cent. Those of the Wheat Barn are some two centuries younger, and with its length of 140 ft it is the largest of the three. The exteriors of the two barns differ: the Barley Barn is weather-boarded, the Wheat Barn has brick fillings in between the timbers.

CROMER, *Norfolk* (11–TG2142). A delightful seaside resort dominated by the splendid tower of SS. Peter and Paul, which, 160 ft high, is the tallest in the county. Originally a small fishing village, Cromer rose to popularity in the 19th cent. The cottages of the original village are picturesquely grouped around the church on top of the cliffs, and the later developments are along the terraces and cliffs.

The church is mainly Perpendicular and the tower with its decorated battlements and pinnacles very impressive. The interior with lofty arcades and tower arch includes a chancel rebuilt in 1887–9 by Sir Arthur Blomfield.

From the cliff gardens pathways lead to the generally sandy beach which provides excellent bathing. The storm of 1953 damaged the pier, which has since been rebuilt. From the pier is launched the famous Cromer lifeboat, the *Henry Blogg*, named after the remarkable coxswain who saved so many lives in the period 1909–47. Before his death in 1954 he had been awarded 3 gold and 3 silver medals, the B.E.M. and the G.C.

Also to the E. is the lighthouse, open to the public on occasions. The rather grand Victorian hotels and the Town Hall typify the respect of the 19th cent. for wealth and solidity.

The cliffs are a favourite haunt of geologists and fossil hunters, and cliff top walks with fine views may be taken to N. and S.

Not far away is a zoo and an aviary, and the Royal Cromer Golf Club (18 holes and a six-hole practice course) is a famous seaside links at Overstrand Road, 1 m. E. of the town on the A149.

DAGENHAM, *Essex* (7–TQ5084). On the River Thames and the site of the Ford car factory, one of the largest in Europe. In consequence there is much utilitarian urban building of little distinction. However, the Church of SS. Peter and Paul is not only early but interesting, though its later additions such as the tower and the west porch are not really in keeping. The vicarage has parts dating from the 17th cent., and the Cross Keys Inn is even earlier.

The Civic Centre is at Becontree and was built in 1936 near the vast sprawl of the housing estates. The South East Essex Technical College in Longbridge Road was built at the same time.

DALHAM, *Suffolk* (11–TL7261). Dalham Hall belonged to the Rhodes family and though the more famous brother, Cecil, rests far from Suffolk, Francis is buried in the Church of St Mary where he was brought after his death in Capetown in 1905.

The village is by the River Kennet and contains many thatched cottages. The Hall was built

c. 1704–5 by the then Bishop of ELY, and has several tree-lined avenues including one which leads directly to the church.

St Mary's is remarkable for its monuments and for the great inscription which describes how the steeple was erected in 1625. Its spire was said to have fallen in the gale which swept England on the night that Oliver Cromwell died (1658). The monuments include those to Thomas Stutevyle (1571); Sir Martin Stutevyle, who voyaged with Sir Francis Drake (1631); and in the churchyard an obelisk to General Sir James Affleck (1833).

DANBURY, *Essex* (7–TL7805), set on a hill on the A414, CHELMSFORD to MALDON road, with some attractive houses, a green and a church set within an earthwork which may date back to Danish times. Inside the Church of St John the Baptist are the finely carved wooden figures of three knights, dating from *c.* 1300. Though the three figures all lie with legs crossed, each has a different attitude and expression, showing individual craftsmanship. The church is mainly 14th-cent. with a gallery of *c.* 1600 and a south chancel chapel rebuilt by Scott in 1866. On top of the battlemented tower is a spire which is a local landmark, rising as it does from the hill which is over 350 ft high.

Among the 16th-cent. buildings in the village are the Griffin Inn and Frettons. Hill House and Millington are 18th-cent. and Danbury Place, a large brick house in the Tudor style, was built by Hopper in 1832. Less than 1 m. NW. of the village are two interesting houses, Old Riffhams (early 18th-cent.) and New Riffhams (early 19th-cent.) while 2 m. to the SE. is Slough House, a timber-framed building of the early 16th cent.

DEBENHAM, *Suffolk* (11–TM1763), is at the source of the River Deben. The straggling village street, tree-lined and attractive, rises to the Church of St Mary with its superb west porch and 15th-cent. nave arcade with hammer-beam and tie-beam roof. Parts of the tower are pre-Norman and there are some interesting monuments. Many old buildings remain despite the fire of 1744.

Six m. SW. is Earl Stonham with its interesting church. Note the exceptionally fine hammer-beam roof and the 17th-cent. pulpit with its four hour-glasses.

At Mendlesham N. along the A140 there is in St Mary's Church a collection of armour of the 15th to 17th cents. This is kept in the chamber over the south porch which has been used as the parish armoury since 1593. Note, too, the pulpit, reading desk and font cover all made by John Turner in 1630, the fine west tower and the notable north porch with its perfectly preserved carving.

North again off the B1077 is **Bedingfield** where the family of this name lived at the magnificent Fleming's Hall from *c.* 1309. It was rebuilt *c.* 1586 with a moat, brick porch and timber-framed walls, clusters of chimneys and Dutch gables; it is one of Suffolk's most striking houses.

DEDHAM, *Essex* (11–TM0533). The village with its pinnacled church has been immortalized in the paintings of John Constable, who attended the local grammar school in the late 18th cent. The Church of St Mary, built about 1500, appears in so many of Constable's paintings that its silhouette has become familiar to many who have never set foot in the county, much less the village. There are some splendid timbers in the roof and a great many interestings monuments and furnishings. In the window above the Webbe tomb some fragments of old glass show the initials E.S. These refer to Edmund Sherman who was the direct ancestor of General Sherman, the hero of the American Civil War. Edmund's cousin, Samuel, left Dedham for Massachussetts in 1634 to settle in Contentment, 20 m. from Boston, a town which was later renamed Dedham. A modern addition is the Gallery Tower Door designed by the East Anglian architect, Raymond Erith, R.A.

Another famous East Anglian artist, Sir Alfred Munnings, lived at Castle House, Dedham. Munnings was born in 1878 and though he lost the sight of one eye early in his career he achieved remarkable success. In 1920 he moved to Castle House and married. The year before he had been elected an Associate of the Royal Academy and he became a full R.A. in 1925. In 1944 he received a knighthood and in the same year became President of the Royal Academy, the first East Anglian artist to be given that office, and one of its most outspoken and controversial holders. In 1949 Munnings retired from the presidency and he died on 17 July 1959. Castle House was opened to the public by Lady Munnings in 1961 as a tribute to her husband's memory. The building is partly Tudor and partly Georgian and contains the studios used by the artist and a collection of over 100 of his drawings and paintings.

Other buildings to note in the village include the Grammar School, part of it dating from 1732, Sherman's house with its elaborate Georgian façade, Southfields, a timber-framed house and the neo-Georgian Great House.

DENNINGTON, *Suffolk* (11–TM2866). Its chief attraction is the Church of St Mary, the resting place of Lord Bardolph who fought under Henry V at Agincourt and was probably the original of the Lord Bardolph in Shakespeare's *Henry IV, Part II.* He was buried here in the mid-15th cent. Especially noteworthy are the 15th-cent. parclose screens, complete with lofts and traceried parapets, and the fine 14th-cent. carved chancel windows, all creating an impression of lightness and elegance. The numerous benches contain some of the best carvings in Suffolk, representing birds and beasts both real and mythological. Note the sixth on the right in the central aisle with its "Sciapod", a fabulous creature said to live in the desert, shown lying on his back using his enormous foot as a shade against the sun. This is the only such representation in England.

In the north aisle is a sand-table used to teach sums to children in the mid-19th cent. Note, too, the tower clock in use from 1675 to 1948, and the very rare hanging pyx-canopy suspended in front of the altar.

DENVER, *Norfolk* (11–TF6101). A village just S. of DOWNHAM MARKET and on the edge of the FENS. St Mary's Church has a 13th-cent. tower made of carstone; the rest of the church is of flint. Denver Hall is 16th-cent. with a very fine stepped gable and a little gatehouse dated 1570. To the SW. is a fine windmill of the smock type (in which the cap only, and not the body, revolves), once used for grinding corn.

To the W. are the Sluices, with the road crossing them. Vermuyden, the Dutchman who had done much to drain the Fens, built the first sluice using mills as water-pumps in 1652. Later centuries saw a continuous programme of water control which has continued right up to the present time. The work of the Great Ouse Flood Protection Scheme was completed in 1964.

This is good sailing territory, and fishermen will find it much to their liking, too.

DEREHAM, *Norfolk* (11–TF9812). When people say Dereham, it is East Dereham that they mean rather than West, which can be confusing as the two places are very different in size and some two dozen miles apart. East Dereham is famous for its association with the poet William Cowper (1731–1800) whose unhappy life at last ended in this Norfolk town. Here also lived Bishop Bonner, 1500(?)–1569, chaplain to Cardinal Wolsey, and former Bishop of London. The cottages in which he lived are now the home of the Dereham Archaeological Society, and are dated 1502.

St Nicholas' Church, joined to the Market Place by Church Street, is noteworthy for having two towers, one central, the other, the belltower, detached, and both in the same sturdy, uncompromising style. The church itself shows a mixture of styles from Norman (south doorway) to Perpendicular (the south porch, etc.). The seven-sacrament font, which it is of interest to note cost £12 13s 9d in 1468, is one of the county's loveliest, with finely carved panels and vaulted top. The lectern is East Anglian brass, c. 1500 and there is a monument to Cowper by the great sculptor, Flaxman. A well in the churchyard reminds the visitor of St Withburga, who founded a nunnery here and died in A.D. 654.

Around the charming market place are many notable buildings, including the Assembly Rooms, 1756; the George and King's Arms Hotels; the Corn Hall of 1857 and the many Georgian redbrick houses. Near the Bishop's cottages is the Guildhall, late 18th-cent.

Spanning the road near the Market Place is an ornate gallows sign, erected to commemorate the town's 1,300th anniversary in 1954.

Less than 2 m. to the S. is the village of **Dumpling Green** where the writer George Borrow was born in 1803.

About 11 m. to the NW. is **Raynham Hall,**

built in the 17th cent. for Sir Roger Townshend, by William Edge. The interior was remodelled for the famous agricultural reformer "Turnip" Townshend, the second viscount, in the 18th cent. by William Kent.

DISS, *Norfolk* (11–TM1179). Right in the S. of the county almost on the Suffolk border, Diss is a small town built around a very large lake called The Mere. The market place is the centre of the town and contains a number of excellent buildings. The Shambles (Victorian shops), the King's Head and the former Dolphin Inn are all fine of their kind, especially the last with its half-timbering, over-sailing and impressive gable. At the head of the triangular market place is St Mary's Church with a tower built right up to the street and processional arches N. and S. The west doors are finely carved and inside are 14th-cent. arcades and a Commandment board with the figures of Moses and Aaron.

The streets which lead off the Market Place have many interesting buildings of Georgian and earlier date. On the right of Market Hill is the timber-framed Greyhound Inn, and opposite a house with a carved corner-post. A little further on is the Corn Exchange, 1854. The road leads to Lacon's Maltings, 1788, with its huge arches.

It was at Diss that John Skelton, the poet and tutor to Henry VIII, was rector. Skelton, b. 1460, took orders in 1498 and was given the living of Diss. He died in 1529.

DITCHINGHAM, *Norfolk* (11–TM3391). Rider Haggard (*see* THE BRADENHAMS) lived here in Ditchingham House, to the S. of St Mary's Church. This is a Perpendicular building with an elaborate tower, and containing, in the chancel, the Haggard family tomb. Ditchingham Hall dates from the first years of the 18th cent. and its grounds were landscaped by Capability Brown. S. of the church the gatehouse is dated 1613 and close by are a number of attractive mansions – Alma House, Waveney and Ditchingham Lodges, etc.

To the E. is the Community of All Hallows, 1858, which has been much added to in later years. The modern housing estate of Windmill Green is said to be the first in England (1947) to revert to terraced houses as opposed to the almost universal "semis" or "double-dwellers", as they are called in East Anglia.

DOWNHAM MARKET, *Norfolk* (11–TF 6003), stands above the surrounding fens, 12 m. S. of KING'S LYNN, on the River Ouse. Rich finds of Romano-British pottery show that the district was an important early centre, and the position of the crossroad at the junction of the A1122 and the A10 substantiates this.

The Church of St Edmund has a spire on top of its Early English tower; the rest of the building is Perpendicular. The west gallery is wooden and 18th-cent., and over the chancel door is an ancient Gothic crucifix.

Buildings worth seeking out include Howdale

Home, the former workhouse built in 1836 in the Elizabethan style; Mount Tabor Chapel in Bridge Street, 1809; and the cast-iron neo-Gothic Clock Tower of 1878.

DUNMOWS, THE, *Essex* (11–TL6221). **Great Dunmow** is on the main Roman road (Stane Street), now the A120 from Bishop's Stortford to BRAINTREE. **Little Dunmow** is 2½ m. to the E. on the side road which leads to FELSTED. The River Chelmer passes through the former and not far from the latter. It was at Great Dunmow that the fine amateur artist Sir George Beaumont was brought up. He became the first patron of John Constable and one of the two co-founders of the National Gallery. He lived at Clock House, a timber-framed house of the mid-16th cent., which owes its name to the clock turret dated *c.* 1651. The Church of St Mary, outside the town, has been much restored. Inside is a 15th-cent. wooden balcony and some stained glass of the same period. There are monuments to the Beaumont family.

In the town near the square is Doctor's Pond where the first lifeboat was tested in 1785 by Lionel Lukin. An early work of G. G. Scott was the Workhouse of 1840 on the CHELMSFORD road.

The famous flitch of bacon which the name of Dunmow brings to mind is presented at Little Dunmow to any couple able to swear, and prove, that they have never regretted their marriage for a "year and a day"! The ancient ceremony goes back to the time of Robert Fitzwalter, the marshal of the group which forced the Magna Carta on the King. One of his family, Walter (d. 1432), is commemorated in a beautiful tomb in the Church of St Mary.

The church is part of the priory of Augustinian canons founded in 1106 and long since destroyed except for its Lady Chapel, which forms the village church, and to which was added a turret in 1872. The present north wall was thus the south arcade of the original chapel and is notable for its superb piers, *c.* 1200. In the middle of the 14th cent. five windows were added, of which four have Decorated tracery, while the fifth is Perpendicular in style. In the chancel is the chair in which sits the winner of the flitch. The monument to Walter Fitzwalter, already mentioned, is one of the finest 15th-cent. English sculptures.

DUNWICH, *Suffolk* (11–TM4770). Lonely and desolate, apart from a few holidaymakers who appreciate the isolation of its shingle beach, Dunwich is one of the most evocative of East Anglia's villages. Little is left now of the once thriving town, apart from the ruins of the chapel of the leper hospital, the priory and its 19th-cent. church, and yet this is a historic site which has the power to move the traveller in a manner out of all proportion to its visible remains.

The Romans almost certainly were here, and were followed by Sigebert who came from Gaul to claim the throne of East Anglia and to convert the inhabitants to Christianity. Felix of Burgundy came here to become Bishop, and perhaps, too, the Irish monk, Furseus, who is said to have established the first recorded school in England. By the time of the Conquest the town was of considerable size, and at the beginning of the 13th cent. the town was granted its first charter by King John. No less than nine churches were needed to serve its population, many of whom earned their living from that same sea which was gradually to destroy their township.

Storms had already begun to eat their way into the town and the great storm of January 1326 caused such severe flooding that three more churches were washed away. The continuous erosion of the cliffs and the floodings of the storms have reduced one of the East Coast's busiest towns to a handful of cottages, an inn and a general store. The little museum tells the tragic tale and the fallen stones and the still-crumbling cliffs spell out the story of ruin and decline.

Dunwich has long been the haunt of artists and writers. Edward FitzGerald, the translator of *The Rubaiyat of Omar Khayyam*, one of the so-called "WOODBRIDGE Wits", a group which included the poet Bernard Barton and the artist Thomas Churchyard, stayed here; so did Henry James, Charles Keene, who drew it, Swinburne, whose poem "By the North Sea" it inspired, Jerome K. Jerome, and many others. During the Second World War the marshes were blockaded with squat cubes of concrete, the beach mined and the cliffs at Minsmere, now a bird sanctuary, became one of the first radar sites in England.

The houses with their lattice windows and Elizabethan chimneys were built by Frederick Barne, one of a line which had held the land since 1552 when Sir George Barne, Lord Mayor of London, came here; hence the three leopard's heads on the family crest, these being the assay mark for London. This long association ended when the estate was sold in 1947. The inn, the beach café and the fishermen's hut where you will be able to buy the freshest of fresh fish as soon as the local fishermen have berthed their vessels on the beach; the vast expanses of the heaths and the cliff-top walks, these are the pleasures of Dunwich today.

EARL SOHAM, *Suffolk* (11–TM2263). The long village street has a row of cottages and Georgian houses on one side and allotments on the other. St Mary's Church has a fine late-15th-cent. tower, and inscriptions on the buttresses of the church commemorate some of its builders. An octagonal font and a number of monuments to the Hindes family are interesting.

Earl Soham Lodge overlooks a moat and was at one time the home of the owner of FRAMLING-HAM.

A couple of miles to the NW. is **Monk Soham**, where the monks from BURY ST EDMUNDS came in earlier days. The Church of St Peter has a particularly wide five-light window in the chancel, a 15th-cent. seven-sacrament font which, though defaced, is full of admirable detail, and a 14th-cent.

iron-banded chest over 8 ft long. Among the excellent woodwork is a Stuart Holy Table.

In the last century Archdeacon Robert Hindes Groome, who became rector in 1845, did much to restore the church and four yews by its gates were given to him by his friend, the writer and poet Edward FitzGerald.

EAST BERGHOLT, *Suffolk* (11–TM0734). Here was born John Constable, one of the two greatest artists of East Anglia, on 11 June 1776. He was the son of a miller and his talent for painting was encouraged by the local amateur John Dunthorne whose son was a great friend of Constable. In 1799 he entered the Royal Academy Schools in London and exhibited there for the first time in 1802. Constable presents the greatest possible contrast to his great contemporary, J. M. W. Turner. Whereas the latter artist travelled continuously Constable loved his home landscape; "These scenes made me a painter", he said, and he never left England. Suffolk, SALISBURY, HAMPSTEAD, BRIGHTON, these are the places he loved to paint. A journey to the LAKE DISTRICT did not arouse his enthusiasm. Moving to London he lived in Charlotte Street and in Well Walk, Hampstead; both houses still stand. The death of his wife, to whom he was deeply attached, affected his life and work and did not compensate for his belated election to the Royal Academy in 1829. A perceptive lecturer on art as well as a superb painter of landscapes, he died suddenly on 31 March 1837.

His birthplace no longer stands but many of the scenes he loved to paint may still be seen (*see* FLATFORD MILL).

The Church of St Mary is remarkable for its unfinished tower which was begun in 1525. In the churchyard is the even more remarkable bell-house, a timber building of the 16th cent. which contains the bells which are hung upside down and are rung by hand. Inside the church is a 15th-cent. wall painting; a monument to Maria, the wife of the painter; and in the south window, a memorial glass to the artist by Constable of Cambridge (1897). The graves of his parents, of both the Dunthornes and of Willy Lott can be seen in the churchyard. North of the church is The Gables, a good timber-framed house of the 16th cent. There are also a number of good 18th- and 19th- cent. houses.

Until his death, Randolph Churchill, the son and biographer of Sir Winston, lived at Stour, his house in the village, where he created a famous garden.

EAST HARLING, *Norfolk* (11–TL9986), near the River Thet and some 10 m. to the E. of THETFORD. Though the village is attractive the great glory is the Church of SS. Peter and Paul, a magnificent building in the Perpendicular style. The tower is well buttressed and has a miniature spire which itself rises like a fountain out of a cascade of flying buttresses. The porch is flush-work and panelled and the interior is beautifully proportioned with an excellent hammer-beam roof. The base of the screen has very interesting carved panels which include a Crucifixion. The south aisle has an even finer screen, with doors, erected for Sir Robert Harling and his wife whose tomb (1435) is nearby. Another magnificent tomb is that to the Chamberlain family of 1462 with its richly carved canopy. Yet more treasures are to be seen in the stained glass in the east window. These panels are late 15th-cent. and their preservation today is due to their removal in earlier, more dangerous, times.

EASTONS, THE, *Essex* (11–TL6125). Two villages on either side of the River Chelmer close to the A130 road between THAXTED and GREAT DUNMOW. **Great Easton** has the remains of an ancient motte and bailey castle close to the church of SS. John and Giles with its Norman nave and 19th-cent. belfry. **Little Easton** has some spectacular treasures in the Church of St Mary. There are some outstanding paintings of a seated prophet, *c.* 1175, and a series of episodes from the Passion of Christ, early 15th-cent.; an 18th-cent. wrought-iron screen for the Maynard Chapel, at one time one of the gates for the now demolished Easton Lodge; and 17th-cent. stained glass from Germany in the south windows and a memorable group of brasses and monuments. These monuments are to various members of the Bourchier and Maynard families, and include those to Lord Maynard, elegantly posed leaning against an urn, surrounded by busts of his family and a portrait of his wife; to Sir William Maynard and his wife, a large wall-standing monument with figures in Roman costume; to Sir Henry Maynard and his wife shown as reclining figures; and tomb-chests to Lady Bourchier, *c.* 1400, and Viscount Bourchier and his wife, d. 1483.

ELVEDEN, *Suffolk* (11–TL8279). Elveden is another of those small Suffolk villages where you are suddenly reminded of the existence of famous men. In this village, surrounded by heathland and with its glorious park, lived Admiral Keppel and Maharajah Duleep Singh. The Admiral was a subject of one of the finest portraits painted by Sir Joshua Reynolds (Tate Gallery) and died at Elveden, after a remarkable career, in 1786. The house in which he had lived was purchased by the Maharajah in the 1860s and he was responsible for its conversion into a fantastic oriental palace. A profusion of marble carved on the spot by Italian workmen, eastern architectural devices and richly elaborate Indian detail were crowned with a vast dome of beaten copper. It appears that it took 150 men four years to complete the work and the house as it now stands surrounded by parkland, lakes and forests is one of the most striking sights in the county.

At the turn of the century the house was yet further enlarged by the 1st Lord Iveagh. In the neighbourhood are the estate houses and almshouses of red brick.

The Church of SS. Andrew and Patrick has been lavishly restored by both the Maharajah and, in the early years of the century, by Lord Iveagh. It is as elaborate in its Gothic fantasy as is the house in its oriental mannerisms.

ELY, *Cambridgeshire* (11–TL5380), stands above the River Ouse on a bluff which was formerly an island, accessible only by boat or causeways until THE FENS were drained in the 17th and 18th cents. It was the scene of Hereward's resistance to William the Conqueror. Just as the flat horizon of the fens is dominated by Ely's great cathedral so in its turn is the cathedral dominated by its magnificent west tower and the unique octagonal lantern. Ely itself contains, apart from its cathedral and two or three other buildings of merit, little of interest compared to some other East Anglian towns of similar size. Yet such is the splendour of the cathedral founded by St Etheldreda in A.D. 673 that the town cannot be omitted from any itinerary.

On entering the cathedral through the Galilee Porch you are passing through the first addition to the original Norman structure. At once the length of the nave is apparent; only those of CANTERBURY, ST ALBANS and WINCHESTER are longer than Ely's 537 ft. Passing the rows of Norman columns, you will see above you the painted wooden ceiling 72 ft from the ground followed at once by the octagon and lantern, a unique medieval inspiration. Conceived by Alan of Walsingham over 600 years ago, the extraordinary effect of its design with its beautiful fan vaulting and delicate tracery makes it one of the highlights of English architecture. A model on show in the transept illustrates the problem facing the medieval craftsmen who had not only to design a structure capable of supporting over 400 tons of wood and lead, but, with only simple equipment at their command, to get the great timbers into position.

Entering the choir with its admirably carved choir stalls you soon reach the point where the original Norman building was damaged when the central tower fell in 1322. The extension of the cathedral to the east is clearly seen in the line of delicately pointed arches leading up into the lierne vaulting of the roof. Here the relics of St Etheldreda were placed in their new resting place in 1252.

The chapels which surround this extension contain some of the most elaborate and extraordinary carvings to be seen in England, and the transepts on either side of the octagon are no less remarkable for their highly decorated roofs with angels as hammer bearers. At the north-east corner of the north transept is the Lady Chapel, the building of which was supervised by John of Wisbech and which was completed in 1349. Now the windows are plain and the whiteness of the walls gives the chapel a remarkable lightness. Once again the ceiling is important and each of the many bosses is a work of art in itself. Around the walls are stone stalls with fine carvings each of which has lost its head at the hands of some zealous reformer.

Around the precincts of the cathedral are the houses of the King's School founded by Henry

Ely cathedral with its commanding west tower and unique octagonal lantern

VIII. Nearby is the Bishop's Palace and St Mary's Church, in the vicarage of which lived Cromwell and his family from 1636 to 1647.

Looking back to the west front of the cathedral from the converted Fire Engine House at the end of the green you may speculate on the appearance of the cathedral had not the north-west transept disappeared in the 14th cent. Leaving Ely on the NEWMARKET Road to the SE. gives us perhaps the finest view with the east end, the lantern and the tower forming a noble composition. The village of **Stuntney** 1 m. to the SE. is where Cromwell once owned a farm; its hill commands a famous view of Ely.

EPPING, *Essex* (6–TL4602). What HAMP-STEAD Heath is to the North and West Londoner, Epping Forest is to those who live on its east side. Now some 6,000 acres, it was ten times this area 200 years ago. And 200 years before that it was probably as big again. In 1882 the forest was purchased for the public and it has inspired countless artists, among them the painter and sculptor, Sir Jacob Epstein. Its hornbeams are especially famous, and it was at **High Beach** that the poet Tennyson used to live in his early days. The Catacombs are an underground grotto built of huge blocks of stone in the 19th cent.

Despite its nearness to the ever outward sprawl of London, Epping retains its identity as a small market town. Its Church of St John the Baptist is Victorian, built in 1889 with the tower added 20 years later, by Bodley and Garner. The medieval Church of All Saints is at **Epping Upland**, to the NW. and is 13th-cent., with a 16th-cent. brick tower.

Not far from Epping are two houses designed by Kempe, Wood House, which is based on the marvellous Sparrowe's House at IPSWICH, and Copped Hall, both of the 1890s. Evidence of much earlier occupation may be found in the forest at Loughton Camp and Ambresbury Banks, Iron Age earthworks marking the site of encampments of long ago.

EYE, *Suffolk* (11–TM1473). On the mound overlooking this pleasant little town there stood the castle first built by the Malets, a leading Norman baronial family. It is the noble church of SS. Peter and Paul which attracts the visitor today. Its west tower, late 15th-cent., just over 100 ft high, is panelled in Suffolk flushwork from ground to parapet and the south porch has, like the tower, the arms of the de la Pole family incorporated in the structure. No less important is the elaborate rood-screen which has been finely restored in this century by Sir Ninian Comper, who was also responsible for the font-cover. The paintings in the lower panels portray the saints and some of our kings.

N. of the church is the Guildhall, a timber-framed building of the early 16th cent. On one of the angle-posts is a carving of the Archangel Gabriel. Further on, the Tudor House leads to the ruins of the castle and on the opposite side of Castle Street, Stayer House, with timber-framed back and a Georgian front, and Stanley House, with its Georgian doorway and some timber framing, are appealing examples of domestic architecture.

Linden House in Lambseth Street is *c*. 1750 and there are two cottages which have, like the

Guildhall, carved animals on the sills of some oriel windows.

The artist William Hoare was born in Eye, and was one of the first Members of the Royal Academy, being elected in their second year (1769) at the age of 63. Like his greater contemporary Gainsborough he left his native Suffolk for the fashionable town of BATH, where he died in 1792.

FELBRIGG, *Norfolk* (11–TG2038). A village 2 m. S. of CROMER, which must have moved from its former position near the Church of St Margaret (Perpendicular), 1 m. away in the grounds of Felbrigg Hall. Though difficult to reach, the church is worth discovering for its west tower and its brasses and monuments. The brasses commemorate Simon de Felbrigg and Roger Felbrigg and their wives, with inscriptions in Norman French, a great rarity. They date from 1351 and 1380. Other brasses are to the Windham family. Among the many monuments is a fine example of the work of that talented and eccentric sculptor, Joseph Nollekens (1813), and another carved by Grinling Gibbons.

Felbrigg Hall, through the grounds of which you may drive on Tuesdays and Fridays, is associated with two families – the Felbrigges and the Wymondhams, or Wyndhams. The present house was erected for the latter family in 1620, was enlarged in 1674-87 and then again in 1750. Though not a large mansion it is a most beautiful example of the Jacobean style, the south front being particularly attractive. On its parapet are traceried the words Gloria Deo in Excelsis. There are three sets of chimneys, each with three shafts. The later ranges have a similar charm, and inside are some outstanding examples of the art of stucco plastering, notably in the drawing-room of 1687. Other stucco work may be seen in the dining-room which also has a fine fire-place. James Paine designed the library and the stair-case when he worked on the house in 1750. The grounds were laid out by Humphry Repton at the beginning of the 19th cent. and include an orangery (a century earlier), an octagonal dovecot and stables.

FELIXSTOWE, *Suffolk* (11–TM3034). One of the seaside resorts which developed at the end of the last century. As with some others it is also a port of some importance and in fact in recent years has handled an ever-increasing amount of freight and traffic.

Felixstowe was the site of a Roman fort which now lies in ruins beneath the sea. The Church of SS. Peter and Paul, much rebuilt, stands on what was possibly the site of the Benedictine priory of St Felix, founded in the late 11th cent.

The Landguard Fort which guards the entrance to the harbour at HARWICH, which is linked with Felixstowe by ferry, was first constructed in the middle of the 16th cent. and rebuilt in the 17th cent. and again in the 18th cent. It was painted by Thomas Gainsborough when he was a young unknown painter, at the request of his friend, Philip Thicknesse, at that time the fort's governor.

The Martello tower, S. of the Beach Station is comparable to that at ALDEBURGH and also dates from *c*. 1810–12. The pier which at one time was ½ m. in length was drastically shortened after the last war and some of the larger hotels have become offices, but the Amusement Park and 2 m. of concrete promenade as well as the shingle beach with its safe bathing ensure the popularity of Felixstowe as a holiday resort.

A number of boarding schools have developed in the town, which contains many large and typically Edwardian seaside houses. St Andrew's Church in St Andrews road is an interesting modern (1930s) design by Hilda Mason and the well-known East Anglian Member of the Royal Academy, Raymond Erith.

FELSTED, *Essex* (11–TL6720), sometimes spelt Felstead, lies to the S. of the Great DUNMOW to BRAINTREE road, the A120, not far from the River Chelmer. It is famous for its public school, founded in 1564 by Lord Rich. In fact you pass through part of the original school to reach the Church of the Holy Cross, with its Norman west tower topped by an 18th-cent. cupola. A 15th-cent south porch leads to the 12th-cent. doorway and inside the architecture shows a similar range of period. Its most splendid feature is the monument to Chancellor Lord Rich, d. 1568. This large wall tomb is probably by Epiphanius Evesham, one of the best known sculptors of his time (*see* the monument to John Troughton at INGATESTONE).

The Old School House through which you enter the church was part of the late medieval Guildhall; opposite stands a cottage with its beam proudly carved – "George Boote made this house 1596". Further along the main street to the E. are the Victorian buildings of the present school, dating from 1860 with additions at subsequent dates. From the days when Oliver Cromwell's sons were among its pupils it has had a fine record of academic and sporting success. It has a beautiful cricket ground nearby.

The unattractive factory used by the sugar-beet industry is something of a contrast, but its great expanse is to some extent relieved by the cottages and farm-houses to be found in and around the village.

FENS, THE, *Cambridgeshire* (11–TL5380). For thousands of years before the Roman occupation the area known as the fens had slowly evolved from ancient forests to a lonely expanse of marsh. The continual action of inundation by the sea and consequent flooding of land was followed by an emptying process caused by the rivers which found their way down to the sea along the East Coast.

The Romans, with their genius for civil and military engineering, set to work to drain many of the areas affected by tidal waters. They built great dykes to hold back the sea and causeways to enable them to travel from one part of the fen to another. With their departure the work of reclamation ceased and by the time of the Norman

Barnaby/Mustograph

Flatford: the bridge leading to Willy Lott's cottage and the mill

Conquest the fens were once again extensive areas of sea and marsh with occasional islands such as that at ELY rising above the surrounding level of the water.

The isolation of the fens made the district a natural area of resistance and also a refuge for holy men, robbers or anyone seeking isolation. The coming of the Norman Church and the re-establishment of religious communities at such places as Ely and THORNEY (where the original Anglo-Saxon foundations had been sacked by the Danes) led to renewed efforts to drain the region and reclaim the land. The local population tended their narrow strips of soil and caught the eels which gave Ely its Anglo-Saxon name. One of the first successful steps was the cutting of the 3-m. channel to Rebeck on the Ouse. Then in 1490 Bishop Morton cut the channel which still bears his name. Early in the 17th cent. an Act of Parliament was passed "For the recovering of many hundred thousand acres of marshes" and when the great Dutch engineer Cornelius Vermuyden was commissioned to tackle the problem the first real steps towards the reclamation of the fens had begun.

It is estimated that in the 17th and 18th cents. almost 700 windmills were at work draining the fens. The coming of the steam pump, first installed at BOTTISHAM in 1820, gradually led to the disappearance of the more picturesque windmill, and today diesel and electric power have in turn taken over from steam. A typical mill of the old type may be seen at WICKEN FEN where it still serves its original function.

This region of between 800 and 1,000 square m., covering an area extending from LINCOLN in the N. almost to CAMBRIDGE in the S., from HUNT-

INGDON and SPALDING in the W. to Ely and WISBECH in the E. has, due to the accumulations of decayed vegetable matter, become the finest agricultural land in the country. The growing of fruit and flowers has been carried on for many years with much success on the rich, black, peaty soil.

FINCHINGFIELD, *Essex* (11–TL6832). There can be few more photographed scenes than Finchingfield's pond and green backed with its cottages and church in its perfect setting close by the River Pant. This great popularity has not at all affected its charm which owes a great deal to its irregularity and unplanned appearance.

The Church of St John stands on a hill where its Norman tower, surmounted by a pretty 18th-cent. cupola, dominates the village. The nave, aisles and chancel show the work of later cen-centuries and the last-mentioned has a clerestory, an unusual feature. Inside are some exceptional screens, that for the rood being particularly complicated in its design. Among the monuments and brasses of interest is a sculpture by Westmacott (1811).

Near the church is the former Guildhall, a timber-framed building, *c.* 1500, and opposite the church on the other side of the green is Hill House whose five barge-boarded gables present a striking face to the general view of the village. To the N. is a fine windmill of the post variety and near it a hexagonal cottage, known as The Round House, built in the late 18th cent. by the owners of Spains Hall, the major mansion of the area, situated about 1 m. to the NW.

This is an Elizabethan mansion of red brick whose irregularities of shape echo those of the village itself. At one time it was inhabited by William Kempe, d. 1628 (whose monument is in the church). It was he who made, and kept, a vow of seven years' silence, because he had wrongly accused his wife. While silent he apparently dug ponds in the vast grounds of his mansion; its present lake was made from two of the eight original ponds. Later the house passed to the Ruggles-Brise family, who still own it.

FINGRINGHOE, *Essex* (11–TM0220), is on the south banks of the River Colne, SW. of WIVENHOE. The Church of St Andrew is beautifully situated and has a Norman nave, the banded tower, south aisle and chancel being added in the 14th cent. The porch, too, is later, with fine flint flushwork and a lively carving of St Michael and the Dragon. Inside the church are some wall paintings depicting, among other subjects, St Christopher, St Michael and Christ. There is also a good brass and a monument to one George Frere, d. 1655.

The Hall has a brick front with three large gables, *c.* 1650, later rebuilt in the Georgian style. The Tide Mill, now no longer used, was one of the few in the county which were driven by the tidal waters of the river. From the quay there is a very pleasant view of Wivenhoe on the opposite bank.

FLATFORD MILL, *Suffolk* (11–TM0834). For ever associated with the great landscape painter John Constable and pictured in so many of his paintings, the mill now belongs to the National Trust. Standing beside the River Stour with its wooden bridge, timbered houses and Willy Lott's white cottage it presents a scene which has attracted innumerable artists since Constable first painted it at the beginning of the 19th cent. It was in this mill that Constable spent much of his boyhood, and the years that have passed have seen remarkably little change since his day. The mill itself is now used by the Council for the Promotion of Field Studies and though its students are not necessarily artists it is appropriate that they study those aspects of nature which Constable loved.

FOULNESS, *Essex* (7–TR0192). Foulness is the largest island in the Thames estuary and has recently come into prominence as the possible site of London's third airport in place of the original choice of STANSTED. Foulness is a tiny community with a church dating from 1850. It is reached from the mainland by way of **Great** and **Little Wakering**, both of which have interesting churches.

FRAMLINGHAM, *Suffolk* (11–TM2863). A pleasant old market town with some attractive domestic architecture around Market Hill. Its most interesting features are the Church of St Michael and in particular the castle, the site of which was given by Henry I to Roger Bigod in 1100 or 1101.

Beginning as a fortified dwelling-house and developed as a military castle by Hugh Bigod, the

Framlingham: the monument to Sir Robert Hitcham

1st Earl of Norfolk, the existing walls and towers seem to have been reconstructed by the latter's son, Roger, before 1213 when he entertained King John within its walls. The vicissitudes of the Bigod family caused the castle to come under the direct control of the King who administered it through a constable. As king followed king so the castle changed hands, coming into the possession of the Mowbray family; in the last years of Elizabeth's reign the castle was used as a prison but it was restored to the Howards by James I in 1613. In 1655 it was sold to Sir Robert Hitcham who bequeathed it the following year to Pembroke Hall in CAMBRIDGE. The great hall was converted into a poorhouse and all except the walls, gatehouse and towers gradually demolished. The Ministry of Works took over the upkeep of the castle in 1913.

Around the massive walls are 13 towers, and a spiral stairway in the eleventh leads up to the wall-walk along which, if you have a head for heights, you may walk at least part of the way round the castle before you have to retrace your steps at the ninth tower. Though Framlingham Castle is, in the words of the WOODBRIDGE poet Bernard Barton, "a fall'n dismantled pile" it is one of the most impressive of such remains. It was the site of the Proclamation in 1553 of Mary as Queen and the home of some of the great families of East Anglia.

The late Perpendicular Church of St Michael would be remarkable if it contained nothing else than the tombs of the Howard family, including that of the Duke of Richmond, brought to Framlingham from THETFORD Priory. He was the bastard of Henry VIII and son-in-law of the 3rd Duke, whose poet son, the Earl of Surrey, is also buried here. A hammer-beam roof enclosed in false wooden fan vaulting, the magnificent organ case (1674) by Thamar of Peterborough brought to Framlingham from Pembroke College in 1708, and the monument to Jane Kerridge by the great 18th-cent. sculptor Roubiliac are among its features.

Two sets of almshouses are worth noting as are a number of fine shop fronts on Market Hill and along Castle Street. Framlingham College in the Gothic Revival style is on the DENNINGTON road and was paid for out of the balance left after the building of the Royal Albert Hall.

FRESSINGFIELD, *Suffolk* (11–TM2677). The Church of SS. Peter and Paul has the best example of a stone sanctus bell turret in the county and a 15th-cent. south porch probably built by Catherine de la Pole. A magnificent hammer-beam roof and even finer woodwork may be found on the set of nave benches each beautifully carved with buttressed arm-rests and poppyheads. One bench-end has the initials A.P., possibly for Alice de la Pole, Duchess of Suffolk and grand-daughter of Chaucer. Outside the south wall of the church is the tomb of William Sancroft, Archbishop of Canterbury, who was forced to return to his boyhood home, **Ufford Hall** (2 m. SE.), as an old man of 72 when he refused to take the Oath of Allegiance to William and Mary.

S. of the church is the timber-framed Fox and Goose Inn, at one time the Guild House of the village. The figure of St Margaret is carved on one of its corner-posts.

FRINTON, *Essex* (11–TM2319). A select seaside resort developed at the end of the last century by Sir Richard Cooker, and famous for its sand and its fishing. Its appearance has been changed recently by the construction of blocks of flats. Here may be seen one of the most famous examples of English domestic architecture of this century, The Homestead, built in 1905 by C. F. Voysey at the corner of Second Avenue and Holland Road. It is an unusual building with subtle differentiation of levels and fenestration, which, though modern in concept, are in the main tradition of English country building.

In the Church of Old St Mary are some panels of Morris stained glass designed by Burne-Jones and only recently presented to the church.

Frinton Golf Course (18 and 9 holes) is a famous seaside course.

GESTINGTHORPE, *Essex* (11–TL8138). This village has a place in our history as the birthplace of Captain Lawrence Oates, who in 1912 walked out into the snow so that his comrades in the Scott Antarctic Expedition might have a better chance of survival. His home, Over Hall, dates from 1735 in its facing, though it was built a century earlier for a wealthy clothier. The highlight of the mansion is the drawing-room with its plaster ceiling and elaborate fire-place.

In the Church of St Mary is a plaque which commemorates Oates's selfless deed. The large

tower was added at the end of the 15th cent., and the main body of the church has work of all three previous centuries. It is remarkable for its fine double hammer-beam roof, *c.* 1500, there not being many outstanding examples of roof timbering in Essex, in comparison with the numerous examples in the other three East Anglian counties. There is a good octagonal Perpendicular font and the screen, too, is worthy of note.

GLANDFORD, *Norfolk* (11–TG0441). A model village of flint and brick houses built like the church by Sir Alfred Jodrell of Bayfield Hall 1 m. to the S. The village is on the River Glaven 2 m. S. of BLAKENEY. In the village is the famous Shell Museum with its collection commenced by Sir Alfred, a collection which also includes pottery, jewellery, relics of Pompeii and a sugar bowl which once belonged to Queen Elizabeth I. The museum is open daily throughout the summer (except Sundays).

The Church of St Martin was in ruins until it was rebuilt in 1899–1906 in memory of Sir Alfred's mother, commemorated by a white marble angel of Florentine workmanship. The church is a Perpendicular restoration of the original and includes a copy of a typical East Anglian seven-sacrament font, stained glass by Kempe and his pupil Bryan, and a carillon.

GORLESTON, *Norfolk* (11–TG5204). The continuation of GREAT YARMOUTH, from which it is divided by the River Yare. It is a popular seaside resort with a long, sandy beach backed by the cliffs which are a familiar part of the coast from here to the N. The pavilion built in 1898, the lighthouse built a little earlier and the swimming-pool are part of its more obvious seaside attractions.

Fishermen and sailors are both well catered for, and concert parties and other shows are part of the holiday scene.

The Church of St Andrew in Church Lane is chiefly remarkable for the interior with two aisles which run the complete length of the church. There is one of Britain's earliest brasses, *c.* 1320, representing a knight, one of the Bacon family. The 19th-cent. stained glass has been variously described as "terrible" and "dreadful". Not to be missed is the Roman Catholic Church of St Peter the Apostle by Eric Gill, 1938–9. All is based on the pointed arch, which is used without vertical members.

GOSFIELD, *Essex* (11–TL7829). A tidy village with some houses built by the Courtaulds in the last century (*see* HALSTEAD). The Hall (now belonging to the Mutual Households Association, but open to the public) is basically a Tudor building, though it has been much restored in later years. The west front preserves its original appearance, made of red bricks with some diaper patterns in blue. The Hall contains a very fine Tudor long gallery, and the almost inevitable secret room.

The Church of St Katherine dates from the 15th and 16th cents. An unusual addition, made in

1735–6 was the room to the W. of the north chapel for the local squire and his family. Here they might worship backed by a grand monument to John Knight, d. 1733, by the sculptor Rysbrack. The whole thing is very un-English and theatrical in concept.

GRANTCHESTER, *Cambridgeshire* (10–TL 4355). Two m. to the S. of CAMBRIDGE, Grantchester was immortalized in the famous poem by Rupert Brooke (1887–1915). Brooke settled at the Old Vicarage on leaving King's College, Cambridge. In 1911 he was made a Fellow of King's and published a small volume of poems. Extensive foreign travels were interrupted by the First World War. He served with the Royal Naval Division at Antwerp and in 1915 was sent to the Dardanelles and died in Scyros.

The Church of SS. Andrew and Mary is noted for its Decorated chancel, the design of which shows similarities to the Lady Chapel at ELY.

GREAT BARDFIELD, *Essex* (11–TL6730). Almost the Chelsea of Essex, so many famous artists having made their homes in this attractive little town. The Church of St Mary the Virgin is at the south-east end of the village and is mainly 14th-cent. with much fine tracery in both the windows and the stone screen which stands between nave and chancel. There is a brass to the wife of William Bendlowes, d. 1584, who built Place House, now the home of one of East Anglia's several Royal Academicians, John Aldridge. This is a timber-framed building with brick fillings, and has a bracket dated 1564.

Not far from the church, on a hill, above the River Pant, is the Hall, another timber-framed building of the 16th to 17th cents. On the green in the centre of the village and along the High Street stand the most important houses. The Town Hall built in 1859 is set back from it; the Friends' Meeting House of 1804 and the Cottage Museum are worth noting. The brick tower-mill is prominent from many parts of the village.

GREAT GLEMHAM, *Suffolk* (11–TM3562). The Church of All Saints is well worth a visit for it contains a fine seven-sacrament font with many interesting details in the carvings, all of which appear against a "rayed" background. Above is an arch-braced roof with carvings and bosses at the main intersections. Three of the bells have inscriptions in Latin (15th-cent.).

Glemham House was built in 1814 with gardens which were originally laid out by Humphry Repton. The stables and octagonal dovecot are on the west edge of the grounds.

Crabbe lived in Great Glemham from 1796 to 1801.

GREAT SAXHAM, *Suffolk* (11–TL8061). St Andrew's Church was rebuilt in the 18th cent. but contains a Perpendicular font, a Stuart pulpit and some Flemish and German stained glass in the east window. A monumental brass commemorates the merchant traveller, John Eldred, d. 1632,

the first man to bring nutmegs to this country. He built a great house named Nutmeg Hall which was burnt out in 1779.

Saxham Hall was commenced by its owner Hutchison Mure, abandoning earlier designs by Robert Adam, in 1779 and completed for his successor, Thomas Mills from Mansby, by Joseph Patience in 1798. In the centre is an octagonal room with a painted ceiling. The grounds were originally laid out by Capability Brown.

One m. to the NE. is **Little Saxham** where the Church of St Nicholas is famous for its circular Norman tower. Round the top of the tower runs a band of arches. Many other parts of the church date from Norman times. There is a monument to Thomas Fitzlucas and this was altered in the 17th cent. so that a grand memorial for William Crofts could be constructed. Crofts, the 1st and only Baron, entertained Charles II and Pepys, too; his tomb by Storey shows him with his wife, Ann. Note the Stuart bier with sliding handles – a rare example.

GREAT YARMOUTH, *Norfolk* (11–TG 5207). Yarmouth, or Yaremouth, owes its unique plan to its position where the three rivers, the Bure, the Waveney and the Yare converge to find their way into the North Sea. It lies on a spit of land which has the sea on the E. side and the river on the W. and this water-surrounded environment gives it a character which is very much reminiscent of some of the Dutch and Flemish cities. As a busy harbour, whose magnificent herring fleet is regrettably dwindling, a market town and a popular seaside resort it has a great deal to offer both the casual visitor and the long-term holidaymaker.

It was a town of some importance in Norman times and was granted its charter by King John in 1208. There are still remains of the walls of the medieval town which established a plan which has been rightly compared to a miniature Manhattan. Within its walls the various orders, Benedictines, Carmelites, Dominicans and Franciscans set up houses, and a complex pattern of narrow streets, The Rows, was created, which was preserved almost to this day. The 18th cent. saw the rise of Yarmouth as a seaside resort and the 19th saw its full development, which has made Yarmouth into one of the most popular resorts on the English coast, with 5 m. of sea front and every possible holiday amenity.

The River Yare divides Yarmouth from its neighbour, GORLESTON, which may be reached by passenger ferry. Cars and other vehicles have to cross the river by the bridge at the north end of the town. From this bridge just to the S. of BREYDON WATER, the two main quays extend N. and S. Just before South Quay is Hall Quay, with the Town Hall (1882), Barclay's Bank (by Salvin in 1854) and the Duke's Head Hotel (dating from 1609).

Its continuation, on the other side of Regent Street, is South Quay, which has been called the finest quay in England and provides a visual experience which may be compared with such famous Continental cities as Ghent. Here were the homes of the wealthy merchants of the town. The Elizabethan House (National Trust) is 16th-cent. with a façade dating from the early 19th. Inside is some splendid panelling and a remarkable plaster ceiling. Further along is the Customs House which was built about 1720 as the home of John Andrews, said to be the greatest herring merchant in Europe.

Behind the South Quay were The Rows. At one time there were 145 of these narrow alleys which were numbered as an aid to recognition. In some of the Rows lived the fisher-folk and other humble people of the town and in others lived some of those merchants who were not quite able to own properties fronting the Quay. The Old Merchant's House, now a museum, is a good example.

Returning to the bridge you reach North Quay which contains the north-west tower of the old walls of the town. It leads to Bure Bridge and the road to NORWICH.

The market place in the centre of the town is large and open and from it King Street, one of the main shopping centres of the town, leads down to the river. At the north-east corner of the market place is Church Plain with the Fishermen's Hospital, founded in 1702, one of the most attractive buildings in the town. Next to the hospital is Sewell House (1646), the birthplace in 1820 of Anna Sewell whose novel *Black Beauty* has remained a favourite. Close by is the vicarage which dates from 1718, with alterations made in 1781. The Church of St Nicholas, which was completely refashioned with a neo-Gothic interior, after its war-time destruction in 1942, is generally held to be the largest parish church in England. The original Norman church was successively enlarged so that at the present time the enormously wide aisles are broader than the nave which they enclose.

At the opposite end of St George's Plain is the Church of St George with its probably unique design by John Price. Built in 1714–16, it features a west tower enclosed within the body of the church by two quadrant bays on either side, with a lantern of two stages topping the tower.

Along the peninsula which separates the River Yare from the sea is the great Nelson Column designed by William Wilkins (*see* CAMBRIDGE), and built in 1817. At 144 ft high it is just 1 ft less than that in Trafalgar Square and was built, of course, much earlier. Though when it was erected it was in a lonely isolated position it is now surrounded by factories. It is particularly interesting that the figure of Britannia turns inland to the W. and not seawards to the E., a fact which shows that even at that date Yarmouth still centred itself on the river rather than on the North Sea.

As a seaside resort Yarmouth naturally turns towards its magnificent beaches. At the north end of the town the North Denes are the site of the famous race-course. Along the promenade which runs the full length of the town towards the S., there are many attractions for tourists: bowling greens, tennis courts, a boating lake, a swimming-pool and theatre, all of which at night during the holiday season are brilliantly illuminated to pro-vide a gay spectacle. Britannia Pier with its theatre and Wellington Pier with its pavilion originally date from the 1850s, though with much rebuilding right up to recent times.

To the S. past the Royal Naval Hospital and the Nelson Column the factories give way to fun-fairs and caravan sites. During the season Yarmouth's many theatres and pavilions present a range of holiday entertainment which vies with that of its Lancashire rival.

GREENSTED-JUXTA-ONGAR, *Essex* (7–TL5404), contains one of England's architectural treasures, the Church of St Andrew. Here is the only surviving example of a wooden church made in Saxon times, with walls of solid oak. It has always been known to date from at least 1013, when the body of King Edmund rested here on its way to BURY ST EDMUNDS in Suffolk. Recent tests have shown that it may well be 150 years older. The nave is built of oak logs split into sections and fixed to a wooden sill. The present sill and plinth of brick dates from a restoration of 1848. The dormer windows, the porch and the chancel added in the 16th cent. make a charming composition. The wooden tower with its small, shingled spire was perhaps added at the same time. The lectern was made from a Greensted oak in our own time by a local craftsman.

GRIMES GRAVES, *Norfolk* (11–TL8290). These remarkable Stone Age flint workings are to be found 3½ m. NE. of BRANDON in the neighbouring county of Suffolk. They were first excavated in 1870 and of the over 300 pits which have been discovered two are open to the public. The first is some 30 ft deep with seven radiating galleries which connect with five other pits. The second pit contains a mound of levers or pick-axes made from antlers which have seen 4,000 years of history. Over 200 such picks have been found in these two pits alone.

The site covers about 35 acres and it became the centre of an industry which still continues in the little town of Brandon where flints are still "knapped" (broken) as in ancient times. Then as now it provided a flourishing export trade, though the masses of trees planted by the Forestry Commission in recent years would have perhaps surprised the Neolithic men who once worked these darkly mysterious mines.

HADLEIGH, *Essex* (7–TQ8087), should not be confused with the town of the same name in Suffolk. It was here that the great landscape painter John Constable sketched the ruins of the medieval castle which he later made into one of his most powerful compositions. (One version is in the Tate Gallery, another, more finished, in the collection of Mr and Mrs Paul Mellon, U.S.A.) The ruins still remain after a landslide in earlier times, which destroyed much of what must have been a most impressive 13th- to 14th-cent. building. From it you can see the River Thames as it makes its way to the North Sea.

The tiny Church of St James the Less stands on

the busy SOUTHEND road. It is a remarkably unspoilt Norman building, with nave and chancel and, much rarer, a Norman apse. The little belfry was added in the 15th cent. Inside are some valuable remains of early glass paintings, including one of an angel and another of St Thomas of Canterbury, both late 13th-cent.

HADLEIGH, *Suffolk* (11–TM0242). Not to be confused with its namesake in the neighbouring county of Essex, Hadleigh, formerly a wool town, lies on a tributary of the Stour. The Church of St Mary stands among a remarkable cluster of medieval buildings. Here you first notice the lead-covered spire, 72 ft tall, on top of the 64-ft tower. The tower is 14th-cent., the rest of the church mainly 15th-cent. Outside the tower is a 13th-cent. clock bell, perhaps the oldest in the county. Inside the church is an octagonal 14th-cent. font, delicately carved with angels at each corner. A bench-end in the south chapel dates from the 14th cent. and depicts the legend which tells how a wolf found and guarded the head of St Edmund. There is an unusual brass engraved on both sides commemorating the martyr Rowland Taylor who was burnt at the stake in 1555 after the accession of Mary Tudor. An obelisk marks the spot where he was put to death. Legend has it that near a tomb in the south aisle lies the body of the Danish king, Guthrum, who was buried in A.D. 889.

W. of the church is the Deanery Tower, the red-brick gatehouse of which is the only surviving feature of the palace built by Archdeacon Pykenham in 1495. Multi-sided turrets stand either side of an arched centre section which is three stories in height in contrast to the towers which are six.

Nearby is the timber-framed 15th-cent. Guildhall, which has been at various times a school and an almshouse.

Hadleigh contains an unusually large number of excellent houses dating from the 17th to the 19th cents. Close to the market place is the former Town Hall of 1851, the Corn Exchange and the Congregational church. In the High Street, with its exceptional variety of fine buildings, is the White Lion Inn, and in George Street the Baptist chapel of 1830 and the Pykenham Almshouses of 1807. The station is early Victorian and there is a particularly good 17th-cent. house at Nos. 62–66 High Street. Toppesfield Bridge spans the river with its three arches of medieval date.

One of East Anglia's finest sculptors, Thomas Woolner R.A., was born at Hadleigh in 1825. He was for some time a member of the Pre-Raphaelite Brotherhood, and became a full member of the Royal Academy in 1874. Among his most famous monuments are those to Thomas Carlyle and Alfred Lord Tennyson in Westminster Abbey. He died in 1892.

Fr Hugh James Rose (1795–1838) was rector of Hadleigh from 1830 to 1833. A meeting held in the rectory in July 1833 was an important landmark in the beginning of the Oxford Movement.

HALESWORTH, *Suffolk* (11–TM3877). A small market town which expanded in the 18th cent. with navigation on the Blyth and in the 19th cent. with the coming of the railways.

The church is basically Perpendicular, with many Victorian additions, although it is on the site of the original Anglo-Saxon church. Beneath the piscina on the south wall are the famous "Danestones" discovered during the alterations of 1889. They have been dated as 9th-cent. and probably formed part of the original Anglo-Saxon building. On the wall by the north door a tablet commemorates the association with Halesworth of Sir William and Sir Joseph Hooker, Directors of KEW Gardens, and their Wedgwood portraits may be seen in the vestry.

Opposite the church you will find the Halesworth Gallery, open from May to September and set in a beautiful old 14th-cent. building. The house is mentioned in 15th-cent. archives and at one time housed the Flemish workers who were employed to drain the marshes in these parts. Later it was altered and was used as almshouses. Besides the gallery it also houses the public library.

Georgian and Victorian maltings and a number of interesting shop-fronts add to the charm of this unpretentious market town.

HALSTEAD, *Essex* (11–TL8130). A small town situated in the Colne valley, with the Church of St Andrew in the centre of the town. Mainly of flint, it has a tower built in 1850 and contains a number of monuments to the Bourchier family. Two churches by G. G. Scott are Holy Trinity (1843) and St James's (1845). An ecclesiastical remain of a very different kind is to be found in the chapel in Fremlin's Brewery, where may be seen the font cover, reredos and other items from All Hallows, London. In 1826 the Courtauld family set up a factory here (*see* BOCKING) and the magnificent weather-boarded mill is reflected in the water, reached by the causeway.

N. of St Andrew's is what is left of an old smock-mill, while 1 m. to the E. is Blue Bridge House. This was the home of England's most remarkable butcher, John Morley, known as "merchant Morley", born in 1655 and buried in the churchyard in 1732. The house came into his hands in 1700 and shortly after that the front was rebuilt, though the estate dates back to at least the reign of Edward III. Morley was the friend of lords, poets and men of letters, and a man of some consequence.

Great Yeldham, 6 m. NW., has a famous gospel oak.

HAPPISBURGH, *Norfolk* (11–TG3731), will never be found unless its correct pronunciation is used – Haysborough. A coastal village which extends from the red-and-white striped lighthouse to the Church of St Mary. The tower is over 100 ft high with a fine west window. Mostly Perpendicular in style, it has earlier features. Standing on three large steps is a very remarkable font, 15th-cent. octagonal, with a shaft which has carvings of seated lions and "Wild Men" known as "wood-woses" or "woodhouses".

G. Douglas Bolton

Harwich: fishing boats in the harbour

The lighthouse was built in 1791 and that its beam is vitally necessary is proved by the many graves of shipwrecked seamen in the churchyard, whose numbers would have no doubt been increased but for the sight of its striped tower and flashing light.

The village itself is rather a jumble of old buildings including Monastery Cottage in Church Lane, and more recent houses and cottages. Happisburgh Manor, built in 1900, of local materials, is an important house of its period.

HARLESTON, *Norfolk* (11–TM2483), which is on the River Waveney, is an attractive small town close to the Suffolk border, with two market places, of which the older has many good Georgian houses. Not far from the disused station (1855) is Candler's House, an outstanding example of an early Georgian town house with seven bays and two stories. The Swan Hotel has parts which pre-date the Georgian period and a very decorative scroll-work sign, which projects from the façade. In the new market place is a Victorian clock tower (1873) and not far away the Corn Exchange, built in 1849. The Church of St John the Baptist dates from 1872 and is of no great interest.

HARLOW, *Essex* (11–TL4711), like BASILDON, was one of the eight new towns planned to orbit London and relieve the capital of some of its excess population and industry. However, unlike Basildon it was planned so that it should develop alongside, rather than round, the existing old town. It lies therefore to the W. of the main road from London to NEWPORT, CAMBRIDGE and NEWMARKET roads, and just to the S. of the River Stort and the A414 road which links Hertford with CHELMSFORD.

The old town has the site of a Romano-Celtic temple and theatre, but now the principal building is the Church of St Mary the Virgin, with its central crossing tower, which was much restored towards the end of the 19th cent. The most interesting interior feature is the large number of brasses in the north transept (early 15th- to 17th-cent.). With the church on the east side of the main road are several good buildings: from the 18th cent. – many around Mulberry Green; from the 17th cent. – the Stafford almshouses; and from the 16th cent. – The Gables and The Chantry.

The new town was conceived in 1947, with Sir Frederick Gibberd as the chief planner. The aim is a population of some 80,000. The Town Centre was the first to have a pedestrian precinct, and its size makes it the dominant feature of the surroundings. To the N. is the market square, which, with its gay striped awnings, is reminiscent of that at NORWICH. To the S. is the main area of the civic buildings, all by Gibberd, and others including St Paul's, the College of Further Education, etc. A road to the N. leads to the railway station, one of the outstanding examples of railway architecture in the country – clean and sharp to match the feel of modern travel. Apart from the residential developments close to the town centre, known as The High, there are three main population areas.

The north-east cluster was the first to be built and is grouped round The Stow. Like the other clusters there are, in addition to the residential buildings, shopping precincts, community centres, sports facilities, schools and places of worship. The south-east cluster centres round Bush Fair, and the most recent to be built, the south-west, is grouped round Staple Tye and shows an increase in density of population compared with the earlier groupings. All these areas feature many novel and attractive schemes, which attempt to make the town a coherent whole.

HARWICH, *Essex* (11–TM2332), shares the fate of many ports of departure in that it is neglected by those who visit it only to leave. Dovercourt, its extension to the S., is the more popular resort, but it is Harwich which has more of interest and character. It is placed where the River Orwell (from IPSWICH) and the River Stour (from MANNINGTREE) join to enter the North Sea and is protected by the peninsula which stretches S. from FELIXSTOWE. On this small wedge of land old Harwich grew up, a tightly planned medieval town with one of the earliest lighthouses in Britain, and the Church of St Nicholas added in later centuries. The church, dating from 1821, is of yellow brick with a tall tower and spire visible from far at sea. Inside is a Purbeck marble font and a painting of Moses giving the Commandments (early 18th-cent.). The tall lighthouse, built of white brick, dates from 1818.

Another notable building is the Guildhall of 1769 built of red brick with a surprising Gothic doorway. The Low Lighthouse, painted on more than one occasion by John Constable, has the look of some Eastern pagoda, while there is an odd reminder of the discipline of earlier days in the Naval Treadmill Crane, S. of the church. The Town Hall was originally built as the Great Eastern Hotel in 1864; other hotels of note are the Pier, the Angel and the Three Cups.

Parkeston, where the Continental ferries tie up, lies round the bay on the north side of the peninsula; Dovercourt is on the south side facing out across Mill Bay, 106 m. from the Hook of Holland and 90 m. from Flushing. Like many of the East Anglian coastal resorts it was developed in the 1850s, when the local M.P., Mr John Bagshaw, decided to promote it as a seaside resort. Along the front with its sandy beach stretches the Marine Parade, and behind it the main road runs to Ipswich and COLCHESTER. There is an Undercliff Walk and all the usual amenities of a successful holiday resort. The two lighthouses by the pier date from 1862. The parish church is All Saints, with a Norman nave and a chancel of the 14th cent. The west tower is Perpendicular and battlemented.

From such seafaring places local men have set off on many expeditions. Christopher Newport sailed with Raleigh, Christopher Jones with the *Mayflower* of which he was the master, and here, too, in the Three Cups Lord Nelson stayed. Captain Fryatt, who operated out of Harwich during the First World War, is commemorated in an impressive memorial.

HAVERHILL, *Suffolk* (11–TL6745) – pronounced Hayverill – is a town which, as it forms part of the population overspill plans of the Greater London Council, will see considerable development in the coming decades. A fire in 1665 destroyed much of the Church of St Mary, which has been much restored in later centuries. There is an interesting Elizabethan monument to one John Ward.

The town is predominantly Victorian, exhibiting some of the worst, as well as some of the better, types of buildings of that era. The Gurteen coarse-clothing factory of the mid-19th cent. gave employment to large numbers, and a dozen houses in Weavers' Row should be noted. One of the major industrial buildings of the "new" Haverhill is the factory at Duddery Hill, 1956.

HEACHAM, *Norfolk* (11–TF6737). On the village sign appears the portrait of the Red Indian princess, Pocahontas, who married John Rolfe of Heacham Hall in 1614. (The hall no longer stands.) Though she died at the age of only 22, the princess left a son who settled in Virginia, U.S.A., and founded a line which was to include the wife of President Woodrow Wilson. St Mary's Church has a modern memorial to her, and a monument to Robert Redemayne, d. 1625, the step-father of John Rolfe.

Not far away is **Caley Mill**, the centre of the main local industry, lavender growing. It is Victorian, but may well stand on the site of a mill mentioned in the Domesday Book. Though inland, on the A149, a road leads to the Wash where there is a beach of pebbles, with sand at low tide.

HELMINGHAM, *Suffolk* (11–TM1857). Helmingham Hall, set within a moat, is owned by the Tollemache family who moved from Bentley at the beginning of the 16th cent., having acquired it by marriage. It is basically a square, half-timbered Tudor house, with Georgian and later additions, including crenellation by Nash. Standing on its moated platform with its stepped gables, tall chimneys and drawbridge, it presents a unique picture, almost as if a French château had to come to rest in the English countryside. Constable's great landscape *Helmingham Dell* was painted in the deer park.

The interior of the house, which the family has occupied again since 1953, is no less splendid. The boudoir, once the library, with Venetian woodwork and carvings, and the present library, once the drawing-room, are two of the best rooms. Above the library is the room in which Queen Elizabeth I is supposed to have stayed. There is a fine collection of family portraits and other paintings and treasures.

The Church of St Mary is also much associated with the Tollemache family, one of whom built the fine west tower *c.* 1543. Many monuments commemorate the family and there are statues to the Countess of Dysart and her husband, Lionel Tollemache, by Nollekens. The 15th-cent. font has lions supporting the shaft which stand on human heads.

HENGRAVE, *Suffolk* (11–TL8268). A minute church and a magnificent mansion make this little village well worthy of a visit. The 15th-cent. Church of St John Lateran has a tower less than 13 ft in internal diameter and possibly pre-Conquest in date. The remainder of the building is of later date. An astonishing collection of monuments includes the pillared and canopied memorial to Margaret, Countess of Bath, *c.* 1561;

her second husband, Sir Thomas Kitson, lies beneath, and her first and third husbands also rest here! There is another six-posted monument to a later Thomas Kitson and a very fine alabaster wall memorial to the 22-year-old Thomas Darcy. Another monument is that to Sir Edmund Gage, d. 1707, one of whose descendants introduced the greengage to this country.

The famous Hengrave Hall, next to the church, may be seen by appointment, and is now a Convent School for girls. Here the great madrigalist John Wilbye (1574–1638) lived for some 30 years and was in charge of the music in the great country house, which was visited by Queen Elizabeth and the entire court in 1578. Wilbye died in 1638 and is buried in COLCHESTER. The Hall itself is one of the show-pieces of the county. Commissioned by the merchant Kytson from John Eastawe, it was commenced in 1525 and took some 13 years to complete. Over the doorway is a wonderfully elaborate oriel window, triple-shafted and with superb detail in the carving; supporting the window are Italianate cherubs holding shields in the Renaissance style, the only exception to the predominantly late Gothic style of the house. The doorway leads to the courtyard with battlements and more oriel windows.

Inside, the Hall has been much restored but it still contains much fine workmanship, and in the chapel stained glass of the early 16th cent. shows scenes from the book of Genesis and the life of Christ.

HERRINGFLEET, *Suffolk* (11–TM4797). Right in the north-east corner of the county where the River Waveney winds on its way to the coast at GREAT YARMOUTH. The round tower of St Margaret's Church is early Norman and there are several other Norman features. Interesting stained glass assembled in the 19th cent. from pieces of English and foreign glass of the 15th cent. are in the thatched church.

There is an octagonal smock-mill which was used for drainage and which has been restored to working order. The Priory Mill which was built in the present century is also used for drainage.

Some 1½ m. NW. of Herringfleet is St Olave's Priory, founded in the early years of the 13th cent. for the Augustinians. At that time it was on an island site. The foundations and the space occupied by the cloisters are still visible and some rare early vaulting still survives.

Back in the village, Manor House Farm, dated 1655, has Dutch-influenced gables and one of the largest barns in Suffolk.

HEVENINGHAM HALL, *Suffolk* (11–TM 3372). One of the finest Georgian mansions in the county, the Hall was commissioned in 1777. Sir Gerard Vanneck, who had become the Member for DUNWICH, engaged Sir Robert Taylor, Court Architect to George III, to enlarge the family's Queen Anne house at Heveningham. Taylor screened the north front with Corinthian columns, added wings on either side and created an impressive building in the Palladian tradition.

The talented young architect James Wyatt took over from Taylor and became responsible for the interior design. The task of painting decorations was given to Biagio Rebecca, an Italian artist of the time.

Within the last few years the Hall, which has continuously belonged to the Vanneck family, has been open to the public. Highlights include a superb entrance hall, with a semi-circular vaulted ceiling, the large dining-room, the Etruscan room which may be compared with the Pompeian room at ICKWORTH and the gardens, laid out by Lancelot (Capability) Brown in 1781. The walled garden contains some of the finest serpentine or "crinkle-crankle" walls to be found in East Anglia. The beautifully proportioned Orangery is the work of Wyatt.

Among the rooms open to the public are those containing some of the Vanneck collection of paintings, and others with exhibitions of designs and plans by James Wyatt and Capability Brown.

HEYDON, *Norfolk* (11–TG1127), a small village of great charm centred around one of the county's prettiest village greens. Heydon Hall was commenced in 1581 and was subsequently enlarged. The façade is planned as a shallow E with gabled bays and, above the roof, fine groups of chimneys. Its three stories of brick give a delightful effect. In the grounds, to the N., is an icehouse and to the SE., a look-out tower.

The Church of SS. Peter and Paul is in the Decorated and Perpendicular styles and the tower, the west doors and south porch are all 15th-cent. The interior arcades belong to the previous century, however, and there are some good furnishings including a 13th-cent. font, a Perpendicular pulpit, a screen, family pews and iron railings.

HICKLING BROAD, *Norfolk* (11–TG4122). Situated between the coast and the A149 GREAT YARMOUTH to STALHAM road. Associated with this, one of the most large and popular of all the broads, are Whiteslea and Heigham Sounds. Though very large in area they are the shallowest of the broads; except where specially dredged for sailing, they are rarely more than 6 ft deep. A century ago the area was even larger, though the three sections were still separate. The complex is part of the Thurne Valley and there is free access to the usual river craft.

This is a region particularly noted for birds. In the summer spoonbills may be seen, diving ducks are especially characteristic and in the spring and autumn the many species of waders are evident. Due to its proximity to the sea Hickling sees the passage of many thousands of migrants on their way to or from our shores, and in the evenings of late summer flocks of starlings spend their nights in the reed beds.

The Pleasure Boat Inn at the staithe is a famous Broadland rendezvous.

HINGHAM, *Norfolk* (11–TG0202). It was from this Hingham that Robert Peck set off in the early

A. F. Kersting

Holkham Hall: the entrance hall

HINTLESHAM, *Suffolk* (11–TM0843), is the scene of yet another festival which takes place each July. Hintlesham Hall, based like so many others on an Elizabethan house, built by Thomas Timperley, has an early Georgian façade and forms the centre of the annual festival. A filigreed plaster ceiling in the drawing-room is one of the finest in the county, and probably dates from the end of the 17th cent. The Hall is open during festival times and on other occasions by appointment.

The Church of St Nicholas has associations with the Timperley family and contains monuments to Thomas Timperley, d. 1593 and to Captain John Timperley, d. 1629 – a fine armoured figure engraved on a large slate. A fragment of a St Christopher wall painting remains opposite the south entrance in the nave.

Here in 1939 died Henry Havelock Ellis, the writer on sex and psychology who was born at Croydon in 1859. He was also the editor of a series on the English dramatists and published several volumes of art criticism.

HOLKHAM HALL, *Norfolk* (11–TF8944). A magnificent mansion in the Palladian style and one of the architectural show-pieces of the county. The Hall is the seat of the Earl of Leicester and on the return of the 1st Earl from the customary Grand Tour in 1718 he decided to rebuild the family home, the foundation stone being laid in 1734. The design was entrusted to William Kent who also designed much of the furniture. The basic plan is an H – a centre section with four wings, an arrangement which gives Holkham an extraordinarily elaborate interior. The entrance by way of the ground floor into the wonderful stone hall shows Kent's genius at its peak, and its effectiveness is intensified by contrast with the severe classical portico which is at the centre of the south side.

The hall is of alabaster, used not only on the walls but also on the columns which support a coffered ceiling of rich and splendid design. Around the gallery is an outstanding collection of sculptured panels. To mention all the rooms is impossible but the Saloon cannot be omitted. Beneath another coffered ceiling of great splendour is the original Kent furniture. The state bedrooms with their fascinating use of ceiling panelling and the lavish use of tapestries, fabrics and furniture show a masterly hand. There is a magnificent collection of pictures, and the long library has a fine collection of 18th-cent. books.

The grounds were laid out by Capability Brown in 1762, and contain a large lake W. of the Hall. To the N. is a monument to the son of the 1st Earl, Thomas Coke, who is better known as Coke of Norfolk. His work as an agricultural reformer is commemorated in a column 120 ft high designed by Donthorne and commissioned by his tenants at a cost of £4,000 in 1845. The gardens also contain an obelisk (1729), a temple of the same date and statuary by Boehm and Charles Smith. The south gates and the triumphal arch and the north gates are *c.* 1850.

17th cent. to found Hingham in Massachusetts, there to find the religious freedom denied to him and his associates at home. Connections are still maintained between the two towns. Peck was joined by Samuel Lincoln (*see* SWANTON MORLEY) in 1637, and it was from this Samuel that the great Abraham Lincoln was descended. (*See also* HEACHAM for other American associations.)

The town is most attractive, with Georgian houses grouped around an irregularly shaped market place to the W. of which is the green. St Andrew's Church has a fine 14th-cent. tower with a west doorway and window above. It is unusually consistent in its Decorated style. The interior has fine arcades with clustered columns and the east window (seven-light) is large and was considerably altered to fit the early-16th-cent. German stained glass purchased for the church in 1813. However, pride of place must go to the great monument to Lord Morley against the north wall of the chancel, described as one of the most impressive of its date (mid-15th-cent.) in the country. Standing the full height of the chancel wall, it has at its base the tomb-chest with shields and in the deep recess elaborate tracery which includes ten kneeling figures. The main arch of the tomb is enclosed within a magnificent framework which rises up to a veritable crescendo of fine carving.

In the park is the Church of St Withburga which was commenced in Anglo-Saxon times and was much restored in 1870. It is well placed on a slight rise and contains monuments by Nicholas Stone and Boehm. The Hall and park are open to the public in summer.

HOLLESLEY, *Suffolk* (11–TM3544), pronounced Hozely, is a tiny village close to what is perhaps the quietest of all Suffolk's quiet seaside places, **Shingle Street**. The Church of All Saints has been much restored, though its west tower is mid-15th-cent. This tower, like so many others built along the coast, served sailors as well as parishioners. From the sea it provided a welcome landmark which must have guided home many fishermen.

Here, too, is one of the Martello towers (*see* ALDEBURGH and LOWESTOFT) which were built at the beginning of the 19th cent. as part of our defence system. The Hollesley Bay Labour Colony was established in 1905 and became a Borstal institution for delinquents.

HOLT, *Norfolk* (11–TG0738), the site of the famous Gresham's School founded by Sir Thomas Gresham who was born here in 1519, and who also founded the Royal Exchange in London. The school was founded in 1555 and one of its former buildings stands on the site of his manor house in the market place, where it was built in 1858 in Tudor style. The school moved out to Cromer Road in 1900 and the "Big School", the chapel and the various houses form an interesting group.

The town itself has some pleasant buildings and a milestone recording the distances to many of the famous halls and houses of Norfolk. Attention should be drawn to the large and elaborate Home Place (1903–5) on the CROMER road, one of the most extraordinary private buildings in the county, now a convalescent home.

St Andrew's Church was destroyed by the fire which also destroyed much of the town centre in 1708. It was much restored by the Victorian architect Butterfield in 1864.

HOLTON, *Suffolk* (11–TM4077). An attractive village not far from HALESWORTH. You may just as easily see first the great mill as the Church of St Peter. The church has a round Norman tower and a Norman doorway, also a 15th-cent. octagonal font and a 16th-cent linenfold pulpit.

The post-mill dates from 1752 and has been carefully restored. It is beautifully situated on a hill among pine trees. The house close by has interesting pargeting of recent date.

Gavelcroft Farm has gables of Dutch design and there are Norman ruins at St Margaret's Chapel ¾ m. to the S.

HONINGTON, *Suffolk* (11–TL9174). Here was born one of East Anglia's most famous literary sons, the writer and poet, Robert Bloomfield. The cottage in which he was born in 1766 still stands close to the church. His father died when he was

one year old and he was brought up by his mother who kept the village school. He worked as a shoemaker in London, living in great poverty, and composed his first major poem *The Farmer's Boy* while he worked at the bench. It was published, with illustrations by Bewick, with the help of a local squire, Capel Lofft, in 1800. No less than 26,000 copies were sold within three years. Other works followed but Bloomfield died in poverty in 1823 at SHEFFORD in Bedfordshire.

The Church of All Saints has a good Norman doorway with typical decoration. The font is 14th-cent. with delicate tracery and a carved Crucifixion which shows the sun and the moon above the arms of the cross. Remains of wall paintings showing St Nicholas and St Thomas of Canterbury are above the south door of the nave.

HORNING, *Norfolk* (11–TG3517). A well known Broadland centre on the River Bure, with many picturesque cottages and occasional and attractive glimpses of the river from the main street. The Church of St Benedict has pinnacles representing the four Evangelists, and is mainly 13th- and 14th-cent. It has some carved benchends, with fantastic imagery. The Priest's Doorway is 13th-cent. and has carved dogtooth ornament.

One m. E. of the church on the road to St Benet's Abbey (*see* LUDHAM) was St James's Hospital. All that remains is the chapel which is now a barn in Horning Hall.

HORSEY MERE, *Norfolk* (11–TG4523). Only a barrier of sand dunes separates this broad from the North Sea. The seepage of sea water makes this the most brackish of all the broads and the water level stands 2 or 3 ft above the general level of the surrounding land. The basin is shallow, being only some 6 ft deep, and in comparison with many of the broads its size has changed little in the past century due to regular clearing of the vegetation which would otherwise have covered its surface. Due to the brackish water the plant, bird and insect life is rather special. A grey shrimp known as the opossum may often be found and some of the copepods are only to be found here and at nearby HICKLING. Bitterns also tend to favour the saline waters of the broad.

HOUGHTON HALL, *Norfolk* (11–TF7828). This was the mansion built by Sir Robert Walpole in 1721. The architect was Colin Campbell, assisted by Thomas Ripley, and much of the interior was the work of William Kent (*see* HOLKHAM). One of the most striking modifications to the original plan is the idea of the domes on the four corners – a conceit of James Gibbs. The façade has a classical portico and the vaulted entrance hall sets the tone of the building. Above it are the stone hall and the saloon, the first being a perfect cube of 40 ft dimensions. The effect of the carving is almost overwhelming, from the bustle of the ceiling to the fire-place carved by Rysbrack, whose work again appears over the fire-place in the dining-room.

Ickworth House has an impressive domed rotunda and a landscaped park

In a house noted for the brilliance of its ceilings and carvings the overmantels in the parlour should be noted as the work of the great Grinling Gibbons. The house at one time contained a collection of paintings which matched in magnificence the Hall itself, but unfortunately these had to be sold to the Empress of Russia in 1779 for the then high price of £40,000. The grounds of the house contain the stables and a water house, and S. of the gates is the village commenced shortly after the Hall itself. The house may only be seen by private arrangement. Among those who declined it when it was offered to them were the Duke of Wellington, who preferred Strathfieldsaye in Hampshire and Edward VII, who, when Prince of Wales, preferred the more intimate charms of SANDRINGHAM.

HOVETON BROADS, *Norfolk* (11–TG3118), comprises two broads known as Great and Little. The larger broad has changed considerably in size in the past 100 years, due to the continued encroachment of vegetation which has not only reduced its size but has also overgrown the various channels which linked it to the main curve of the River Bure. Only one such channel now remains, at the E. of the broad.

Whereas the large broad is inside the curve of the river, the Little Broad is on the outside of a curve further downstream. It tends to divide into two sections, an inner and an outer, linked by a channel cut through the peat and clay. In 1840 both sections were linked with the river, but now only the east section is linked by a channel by a dyke. This outer broad is open to the public but the inner one is private.

HOXNE, *Suffolk* (11–TM1877). Pronounced Hoxen, the village has for centuries been held to be where St Edmund was martyred, although Hellesdon agrees better with the "Haegelisdun" of the Anglo-Saxon Chronicle. This was in 869 after he had attempted to repel the invading Danes.

His body was taken to BURY ST EDMUNDS. Here, too, was one of East Anglia's two cathedrals until 1078 when the bishop moved to THETFORD.

The church of SS. Peter and Paul has a fine west tower and, inside, some very interesting wall paintings showing St Christopher, the Seven Deadly Sins and the Seven Works of Mercy, all dating from the 15th cent.

HUNSTANTON, *Norfolk* (11–TF6842). A resort, or almost two resorts, on the west coast of Norfolk, facing into the Wash. One of its features is the vast beach, shingle and sand, backed by cliffs. Old Hunstanton was the home of the le Strange family for 900 years and their hall was a moated mansion which has suffered in two severe fires, one in 1853 and the other in recent times. The Church of St Mary was extensively restored in the 19th cent. but has an interesting porch, traceried as if it were a window, and an east window of five lights with unusual tracery. There is a simple Norman font and a 16th-cent. screen. Among the good collection of brasses is that to Sir Henry le Strange, d. 1506, and the even earlier one to Edmund Greene and his wife, *c.* 1480.

Just to the S. is Hunstanton proper, sometimes known as St Edmund's after the church of that name, built in 1865. A window shows the saint landing on the coast, a site supposedly marked by a chapel near the lighthouse. On the green is the shaft of the village cross which once stood in the old village. Much of the town is, like the church, Victorian as it was built at the same time as the extension of the railway line from KING'S LYNN. Perhaps the most famous feature is natural, the striped cliffs to the N. of the pier.

ICKWORTH, *Suffolk* (11–TL8161). Near the church in the village of Horringer are the gates of Ickworth House which was conceived by Frederick Hervey, 4th Earl of Bristol and Bishop of Derry, in 1792. His family had owned the land since the

15th cent. and the bishop, whose income was considerable, was able to indulge his interest in architecture. One of the several houses he had had built in Ireland had a domed rotunda inspired by that on the mansion on Belle Isle on Lake Windermere. This domed rotunda became the central feature of his new fancy at Ickworth. The architect was Francis Sandys, who based his design on plans by Asprucci, the Italian architect. The bishop liked tall rooms and his original idea was that the elliptical rotunda would contain the living accommodation, with one wing to house his collection of pictures and the other for his sculpture. The collection was confiscated, however, when Napoleon invaded Italy, and the earl bishop died in 1803 before the building was complete.

Work on the house was finally resumed in 1826 by the 5th Earl. In 1907 further changes were made on the accession of the 4th Marquess who ordered the reconstruction of the main staircase. In 1956, after his death, the house and almost 2,000 acres of the estate, together with many of the works of art it contained, were handed over to the National Trust.

The park, landscaped by Capability Brown, effectively screens the house behind magnificent oaks and cedars, even though the building is over 600 ft in length and the dome 104 ft high. The entrance hall contains a noble marble group by Flaxman, whose illustrations to Homer formed the basis of the designs for the frieze in terracotta relief round the cupola. The library contains important pictures by Hogarth and Gravelot, the teacher of Thomas Gainsborough, three of whose finest portraits hang in the great drawing-room. A superb collection of silver, partly Bristol, *objets d'art* and miniatures are among the treasures to be seen by the visitor.

INGATESTONE, *Essex* (7–TQ6499), now bypassed by the A12, lies on the Roman road between BRENTWOOD and CHELMSFORD, and is closely linked with **Fryerning**. The tall west tower of the Church of SS. Edmund and Mary (an unusual combination of saints) is built of red brick with typical diaper patterning in black bricks. The west window has Perpendicular tracery and in the nave the north wall, built by the Normans, makes use of Roman bricks. The south chapel was added by the Petre family in 1556 and the church has a number of monuments to them, that to Sir William (d. 1572) and his wife being of especially high quality. They are seen resting, hands clasped in prayer, on rolled mats. Robert Petre, who died 21 years later, rests in the south chapel and John and his wife lie beneath a major wall monument in the north chapel. There is a elegant portrait bust set in an oval recess of John Troughton, d. 1621.

The Petre family lived at Ingatestone Hall, the former manor of the Barking nunnery. The house is of brick and dates from the mid-16th cent. The gateway was rebuilt at the end of the 18th cent. at which time the bell turret was added. The big stepped gables are echoed by those of the nearby barn. The house is now shared between the Essex County Council, whose admirable Record Office use it for exhibitions of local interest, and the Petre family, who occupy the south wing. It is open only at exhibition times.

The pleasant High Street has a number of 18th-cent and earlier buildings. Larger buildings include the Spread Eagle, the almshouses of 1840 and the Congregational church of the same date. Towards the end of the last century a development of Victorian-Tudor houses was built by the local architect, George Sherrin. A more recent development features a number of houses of adventurous design.

The owner of the Hyde, now destroyed, was the Rev. John Disney, whose collection of classical marbles now forms part of the Fitzwilliam Museum, CAMBRIDGE. Nearby Fryerning has a church (St Mary's) with a Perpendicular tower, again diapered in brick, and a Norman nave which again makes use of Roman bricks. The font is early (c. 1200) and there is a brass with figures on both sides. Not far N. is a post-mill which has been carefully restored.

IPSWICH, *Suffolk* (11–TM1744). The county town of East Suffolk, Ipswich is less immediately glamorous than its rival NORWICH. For one thing it has no castle and for another, no cathedral. Yet there is something about its cluster of narrow streets, its open parks and the dockland area by the River Orwell which makes Ipswich, though an unspectacular town, by no means unmemorable.

In its upper reaches the Orwell is called the Gipping. From the Anglo-Saxon name Gipeswic (the "g" being pronounced as a "y") comes the present name of the town. It is a place with a long history, a borough even before the Norman Conquest and with a charter granted by King John in 1199. Its fortunes fluctuated after it had reached a peak of importance in the 16th cent. but then in the 19th it began to rise again and is now not only a major port and market town but also the county town of East Suffolk, with a population of over 100,000 people.

Ipswich was the birthplace of Cardinal Wolsey and the home for some years of the rising star of English painting, Thomas Gainsborough. Many more will perhaps remember it for its association with Mr Pickwick, and with Margaret Catchpole, the adventuress who was deported to Australia for horse-stealing in 1801.

Northgate Street, Westgate Street and Tower Rampart help establish the medieval walls of old Ipswich, and Priory Street reminds us that the Augustinians, Franciscans, Dominicans and the Carmelites all set up houses in the town. In 1527 Wolsey founded the Cardinal College of St Mary. It was to remain unfinished, all that is left is the red-brick gateway, with its royal coat of arms, in College Street close to St Peter's Church.

Perhaps the most spectacular of all the buildings of Ipswich is the Ancient House in Butter Market. The house was built in 1567 and is also known as Sparrowe's House after the family who lived in it for a long period. The main front of the

Ipswich: pargeting on the Ancient House in Butter Market

house is an outstanding example of the East Anglian art of pargeting, the carving of plaster-work into decorative features and patterns. Underneath its oriel windows are panels repre-senting the then known continents of the world. Inside there is magnificent oak panelling and ceilings with heavy carved beams. The house is now one of East Anglia's most important book-shops.

Not far away at the corner of Tavern Street and Northgate Street is the Great White Horse Hotel where Mr Pickwick had his adventures, com-memorated in the murals which line the dining-room.

In Christchurch Park on the other side of Crown Street is Christchurch Mansion which stands on the site of the Priory of the Holy Trinity founded by the Augustinians. It was in 1548 that Edmund Withipoll began building his new house which was twice visited by Queen Elizabeth I, most appropriately as it had been designed on the Elizabethan E plan. In the 17th cent. it was apparently damaged by fire, and much rebuilding took place. At the end of the last century it was proposed that the house and land be cleared to make a housing estate, but this scheme was thwarted by the generosity of the Cobbold family who presented the house to the town on condition that the grounds were purchased and made into a park. Thus came into existence what has been called the finest park in any provincial town and a museum which contains a fine collection of furniture and pictures as well as an art gallery, a memorial to Wolsey, with works by Gains-borough, Constable, Munnings and many other famous Suffolk artists.

The Ipswich Museum of Archaeology and Natural History is in the High Street and contains an impressive collection of birds and animals, geological specimens and many other things which would delight adults as well as children. Among many exhibits which relate to Suffolk are some from the Anglo-Saxon cemetery at Ipswich and replicas of the treasures, now in the BRITISH MUSEUM, which were found at SUTTON HOO and MILDENHALL.

On the quayside is the Old Custom House built in the Palladian style in 1844, an otherwise symmetrical composition except for the Clock Tower at the north-west corner.

The civic church is St Mary-le-Tower, in Tower Street, rebuilt in the 19th cent. but with many interesting brasses. Among the other churches in the town must be mentioned St Margaret's close to Christchurch Mansion; St Matthew's with its outstanding 15th-cent. font; and St Peter's with its Tournai font, one of seven similar fonts in England made of black marble imported from Belgium at the end of the 12th cent. In contrast is the Congregational church in Dryden Road built in 1957-8 in contemporary style. Again not to be missed is the Unitarian Meeting House in Friars Street, 1699-1700, a building of simple dignity with a fine pulpit and brass chandelier.

The developments which made Ipswich essen-tially a town of the 19th cent. have in recent years been accelerated, so that a new Ipswich is rising, particularly on the west side of the town round Civic Drive where the tall blocks of modern flats and offices present a skyline very different from the medieval city which is at the heart of the town.

Just off the A45 to the SE. is Ipswich Airport adding a further dimension to the network of roads, railway and river which have served Ipswich for so long. Two m. to the S. of the town is Freston Tower, a red brick mid-16th-cent. folly containing six rooms one above another, in a park beside the River Orwell.

IXWORTH, *Suffolk* (11–TL9370). Not far from the village, in Stow Lane, are the remains of a Roman building, part of what might have been a large settlement near the camp of the Iceni.

Then in 1170 an Augustinian priory was founded here. The remains form part of **Ixworth Abbey**, on the site of the old priory.

The Church of St Mary has an elaborate canopied tomb to the memory of Richard Coddington, d. 1567, and his wife. They may be seen, with their children, in portrait brasses.

A couple of m. NW. is **Ixworth Thorpe**. The little Church of All Saints is thatched with a weather-boarded bell turret. The Norman doorway is less than 3 ft wide and only 5 ft high to the springing of the arch. Inside are a number of bench-ends showing more than two dozen animals, birds, humans and even a mermaid. A copy of a "Degree of Marriage", printed in 1771, is believed to be the best preserved in Suffolk.

KEDINGTON, *Suffolk* (11–TL7046). This small village contains one of Suffolk's most interesting churches. SS. Peter and Paul has been built over Roman remains, has an Anglo-Saxon cross and was recorded in Norman times. Inside, the number of important monuments has caused the church to be known as "The Westminster Abbey of Suffolk" (Cautley). Though there are no early clerestory lights the interior is bright due to the skylights added in the 19th cent. in the 16th-cent. roof.

Most of the monuments are to members of the Barnardiston family. The earliest seems to be that to Thomas Barnardiston who died in 1503; one dated *c.* 1610 shows another Sir Thomas with his two wives, the lid of the coffin protruding below. Next to it is another to his daughter Grissell, shown kneeling on a cushion.

The woodwork is exceptionally fine with many rare features: an alms-box made from a hollow tree trunk, a three-decker pulpit of Jacobean period, and special pews for children with seats for their school-teachers so that they might supervise their charges.

KELVEDON, *Essex* (11–TL8618), like its neighbour, WITHAM, has recently been bypassed by the main A12 road from London to COLCHESTER. As a result, its 18th-cent. character may well be preserved. There is much of earlier date, timber-framed cottages and the 17th-cent. Ormonde House, for example. The village runs along the old Roman road and is crossed by the River Blackwater and it was here that the famous preacher Charles Spurgeon was born in 1834. Joining the Baptists in 1850 he soon went to London where his sermons were so popular that the congregation invariably overflowed his church. His own church, the Tabernacle, was opened in 1861 and his sermons were printed and sold by the thousand. He died in 1892 and is buried at Norwood.

The Church of St Mary the Virgin has arcading of the 13th cent. and a 14th-cent. tower. It was restored in the 1870s. It contains an unusual carving of Esther and Ahasuerus which came from a local house and was probably originally brought from Flanders where it had been carved in the 17th cent.

Tourist Photo Library

Kersey village

King's Lynn: Customs House

A. F. Kersting

There is much to see in the High Street, good houses and shop-fronts of the 18th and 19th cents., the chapel of 1853 and the Friends' Evangelistic House, a century earlier. Just under 1 m. N. of the church is Felix Hall which was built *c.* 1760 and much altered later. There is a large and impressive classical portico, added *c.* 1830 by Lord Western and based on the Temple of Fortuna Virilis in Rome.

Nearby there is evidence of the Roman settlement of Canonium, and near the Freemasons' Hall excavations have resulted in important discoveries of Belgic and Roman material.

KERSEY, *Suffolk* (11–TM0044). Perhaps the most photographed of all Suffolk's villages and certainly one of the most picturesque. Set in a V-shaped valley, the centre-piece is the water-splash across the stream which runs through the village. On one side the road up the hill leads to the Church of St Mary and the vista is one of unforgettable loveliness. The church is mentioned in the Domesday Book but was much added to in the 14th and 15th cents. The roof of the south porch, though small, is of great beauty, being divided into 16 panels, filled with, and surrounded by, elaborate tracery. Look at the carving in the arcade of the north aisle and you are reminded of the Black Death which caused the cessation of the work in 1348. An unusual lectern has delicate buttresses attached to its hexagonal shaft.

The village was famous in earlier days for cloth. "Kersey" in fact was mentioned by Shakespeare in *Measure for Measure* and *Love's Labour's Lost* where a character speaks of "honest Kersey noes", and it is not difficult, even in the present century to imagine oneself back in the late Middle Ages while walking among the half-timbered cottages with their projecting upper stories and little steps which jut out on to the pavements.

Priory Farm has the remains of an Augustinian priory founded in the late 12th cent.

KESSINGLAND, *Suffolk* (11–TM5286). Another seaside village whose church tower has served as a landmark to generations of sailors. There are too many caravans and the holiday-maker seeking peace would be advised to go on to DUNWICH or COVEHITHE. However, it is not without some charm. The tower of the Church of St Edmund was built by Richard Russell of Dunwich who had also designed that at WALBERSWICK. Inside, there is a 14th-cent. font, one of Suffolk's finest, with excellent carvings on both the shaft and the bowl (both octagonal).

The heroes of Kessingland have been its lifeboatmen who saved 144 lives in the period 1869–1936.

Close by there is the Suffolk Wild Life and Country Park with several acres of woods and parkland and a large collection of animals, birds and children's pets.

KETTERINGHAM, *Norfolk* (11–TG1503), is a small village some 6 m. from NORWICH. The Church of St Peter, though it has a good west tower rebuilt in 1609, is mostly of interest for its monuments and brasses. It also has an octagonal font and a three-decker pulpit. The earliest brass appears to be dated *c.* 1470; there is another to Sir Thomas Hevenyngham and his wife, d. 1499; and one to a baby who died in 1530. Among the monuments are those to Sir William and Lady Heveningham, d. 1678 and Edward Atkyns, d. 1750. Others are by the well-known sculptors Westmacott (Edward Atkyns, 1807) and Flaxman (Harriet Peach, 1825).

The church and the adjacent thatched and timbered cottages stand in the grounds of Ketteringham Hall, now a school, but originally built in Tudor times. It was much altered in 1840–50 in the Victorian Gothic style.

KING'S LYNN, *Norfolk* (11–TF6220), before it became Royal property was called Bishop's Lynn. Nowadays the town is usually known simply as Lynn. It combines the attractions of a busy town, seaport and agricultural centre. Once it was a walled city of considerable importance; traces of the walls still remain. Its two great churches, two market places and two Guildhalls tell of its former size and there are many reminders of the Grey, Black, Austin and White Friars, all of whom had houses in the town. It had long been a port handling large quantities of wool, cloth and agricultural products and its position 2 m. S. of the mouth of the Great Ouse made it a natural site for a harbour. Most of the development is on the east bank. **West Lynn**, connected by ferry, is famous for the views it provides of Lynn proper.

The town centred round the Saturday Market and Tuesday Market, the former with its Church of St Margaret and the latter with that of St Nicholas. Its first charter was received from King John in 1204. Soon after the Conquest Bishop Losinga of NORWICH founded a priory here and commenced St Margaret's, a huge church, 235 ft long, made of white limestone. In keeping with its size it has two towers at the west end, a very rare feature for any parish church. There are many impressive features including the chancel with multiple columns and finely carved caps, the west window of the nave (between the towers) which has seven lights, and the Perpendicular shafts of the chapel attached to the north-west tower. The early Georgian pulpit, the brass lectern and above all two brasses, perhaps the largest, and certainly among the most famous, in the country, are immensely fine pieces.

St Nicholas' in St Anne's Street, is almost as long, and its west front has an even more magnificent window. There is a superb Perpendicular south porch *c.* 1410, not dissimilar to those at WALPOLE ST PETER and PULHAM ST MARY. The font was given to the church in 1627, but an earlier one is still in the church. One of the bench-ends has a medallion with a remarkable carving of a bishop.

Saturday Market and Tuesday Market both have interesting houses. Greyfriars in St James's

Street was founded in the mid-13th cent. and enlarged at the beginning of the 14th cent. Its tall octagonal tower survives. All Saints' has the remains of a Norman chapel. The most remarkable ecclesiastical building is probably Red Mount Chapel, built on a mound, octagonal in shape and dated c. 1485. It served as a wayside chapel on the Pilgrim's Way to WALSINGHAM, and is situated in a park called The Walks. Slightly later in date, c. 1520, is the South Gate, the last surviving gate of the town walls, through which traffic still passes on the main London Road.

The Guildhall and Town Hall in Queen Street are both built in a striking chequer design in flint. The Guildhall was built in 1421 for the Guild of Holy Trinity and the façade features a tall Perpendicular window of seven lights. Next to the Guildhall is a decorative porch, patterned in flint to match its neighbour and added in Elizabethan times. Inside the Guildhall is a remarkable collection of regalia including King John's Cup, a beautiful piece of medieval plate, gilded and decorated with translucent enamels showing hawking and hunting scenes, and the King John Sword, another medieval piece. The Town Hall close by dates from 1895.

One of the most photographed and famous of King's Lynn's many outstanding buildings is the Customs House built in 1683 by Henry Bell. Bell was a local architect who achieved far more than local reputation. The roof is surmounted by a lantern tower, and a niche contains a statue of Charles II.

Facing the Guildhall is Thoresby College, founded in 1500. Mostly 17th-cent. it includes a Perpendicular archway. Nearby in Nelson Street is Hampton Court, timber-framed and now converted into flats. Opposite is the Hanseatic Warehouse (1428) which served as both home and warehouse for Hansa merchants. Other merchant buildings of great interest include Clifton House, restored and rebuilt in 1708, and the Greenland Fishery House in Bridge Street (1605), again timber-framed and now a museum. St George's Guildhall in King Street dates from 1406 and was adapted as a theatre in the 1950s. The Museum and Art Gallery in Market Street contains items of natural history and archaeology, displays concerned with domestic life and the sea and a collection of paintings, glass and pottery.

The King's Lynn Festival of Music and the Arts takes place in July and features some of the world's leading orchestras and soloists. The Sailing Club has its headquarters in Ferry Lane, and the King's Lynn Golf Club (18 holes) is at Leziate, 4½ m. from the town on the B1145.

KNAPTON, *Norfolk* (11–TG3034). This is a church which is visited for the beauty of its roof, one of the finest in the county, and its font, not that the rest of the church, which is Decorated and Perpendicular, is of poor quality. The lover of the artists of the Norwich School will want to see the weathervane which is said to have been designed by the great John Sell Cotman, when he was giving drawing lessons in the neighbouring

house. But the roof is its most remarkable feature – a grand affair spanning a width of over 30 ft. It can be dated with reasonable accuracy to 1504 and, like so many East Anglian roofs, boasts a host of angels who perch like pigeons on every conceivable vantage point.

The font itself is 13th-cent. Purbeck marble, and now stands on three steps. Its cover, dated 1704, is a decorative piece of work with a palindrome (in Greek) which reads "Wash my sins and not my face only". The pulpit is said to be Victorian but all authorities agree that it looks much earlier.

LAKENHEATH, *Suffolk* (11–TL7182). Situated in the north-west tip of Suffolk and one of its few villages W. of the A11. It overlooks the fens and is the site of one of the largest United States Air Force bases in this country. No doubt due to its position away from the centre of the county its magnificent Church of St Mary is less well known than it should be. Its great number of interesting features make it one of the finest in a county famed for its churches.

The chancel arch is Norman and above is a splendid wooden roof carved with angels. More fine carving is to be seen on the benches in the nave and in the 15th-cent. octagonal pulpit. Every authority agrees that the font is the best 13th-cent. example in the county. Octagonal in shape it has deeply moulded arches and is supported by slender columns clustered around the main shaft. The many wall paintings include St Edmund, St John and scenes from the life of Christ. Brasses and monuments add to the interest of the interior.

Not far to the E. of the village there is evidence of Neolithic and Iron Age settlements and of later Roman occupation.

LAVENHAM, *Suffolk* (11–TL9149). This beautiful small town developed through the rise of the cloth trade before and after the 15th cent.

The Church of SS. Peter and Paul is, if not quite as remarkable as that of LONG MELFORD a splendid building. The great square-buttressed tower of flint, 141 ft high, tends to dwarf the main body of the church, but details compensate for any lack of proportion, for example, the superb porch, with its carvings and fan vaulting, the gift of John de Vere, 13th Earl of Oxford.

On entering the church the visitor is impressed by the air of spaciousness. Note the parclose screen round the tomb of Thomas Spring, a wealthy Lavenham clothier who endowed the steeple, and his wife, Alice. This is a fine piece of carving, possibly by Flemish craftsmen early in the 16th cent. More good woodwork may be studied in the chancel, which has misericords decorated with fantastic medieval imagery. The Spring and Branch Chapels are surrounded by beautiful screenwork.

The bells of Lavenham are so famous that they were broadcast on the death of H.M. Queen Mary and each year on 21 June a special peal is rung to celebrate the "birthday" of the tenor

Layer Marney: the gatehouse

All Saints has an excellent flint panelled tower. Inside is a tremendous seven-sacrament font standing on steps, the upper one of which is in the shape of a Maltese cross. The Stuart reading desk with its grotesque supporters, the pulpit and the benches of similar date are all well worth noting.

Opposite the church is the Guildhall, a small timbered building, and there is also a restored smock-mill, now power-driven.

LAYER MARNEY, *Essex* (11–TL9217). The most westerly of three villages, and without doubt the most rewarding. Some 7 m. SW. of COLCHESTER it may be found off the B1022 road. In the reign of Henry II the Marney family settled here and it was Sir Henry, in the reign of Henry VIII, who decided to build a grand hall in keeping with the family's position. His death in 1523, shortly after inheriting the title, followed two years later by that of his son, forestalled his plans and only the gatehouse and west wing were finished. The gatehouse was, however, one of the great buildings of its age. Larger than that at OXBURGH, and those of the CAMBRIDGE colleges, it was grander even than those of the Royal Palaces.

The magnificent towers flank an archway surmounted by two stories, each with an elaborate window. The exterior pair of towers have eight stories, the interior pair, seven, with a much flatter gateway in between. The red brickwork is diaper-patterned in blue, and there is much use of terracotta.

Close to the Hall (in private hands but open on Sunday afternoons in the summer or by arrangement) is the Church of St Mary the Virgin, again of brick, with diaper patterns in blue bricks. Its battlemented appearance and many-faceted tower owes much to the rebuildings of the Marney family in the 16th cent. Inside are many items of interest. A wall painting of St Christopher of the 15th to 16th cents., an iron-bound chest, bequeathed by Lord Marney in 1524, but almost certainly much older, and some stained glass must all give place to the tombs of the Marney family. These, in the Marney Chapel, remind the visitor of the line that ended as far back as 1525, with the death of John, Lord Marney.

Layer Breton, to the E., has a church of recent date (1923) with some interesting old sculptures – Italian, and English. Most easterly is **Layer-de-la-Haye** where the church now overlooks the reservoir. Mostly 14th-cent., there are parts dating from Norman times.

bell, made in 1625 by Miles Graye of COLCHESTER, reputed to be the finest toned bell in England, if not the world.

The domestic architecture of Lavenham includes a Guildhall, erected shortly after the founding of the Guild of Corpus Christi in 1529. A superb timber-framed building, one of its corner posts carries a full-length figure of the founder of the Guild, the 15th Lord de Vere. The Old Wool Hall, Tudor Shops, the de Vere House and several of the houses in Church Street, in particular Nos. 11, 12, 13 and 15 are all worthy of note. The pargeting on the façades, the timbering, the whole atmosphere of Lavenham is unique.

LAXFIELD, *Suffolk* (11–TM2972). Here was born the man whose name has become hated by all who love our heritage of church ornament. William Dowsing was appointed by the Puritans to destroy all manner of "superstitious things" in the country's churches, and guide-book after guide-book tells just how well he carried out his task. Like a man possessed he travelled the county smashing the stained-glass windows which formed an irreplaceable part of our cultural heritage. He once destroyed 1,000 pictures in a day, not to mention carvings; when the Restoration came he returned to his native village, where, by a master-stroke of irony, a tablet in the Church of All Saints commemorates his name!

LEISTON, *Suffolk* (11–TM4462). There can hardly be a greater contrast than that between the monastic discipline which prevailed in the abbey, now the principal monastic monument to be seen in Suffolk, and Summerhill the experimental school founded close at hand by the educationalist A. S. Neill. The abbey, originally established on the Minsmere Marshes in 1182, was moved to its present site by Robert de Ufford in 1363. As one of the smaller religious houses it was bestowed by the King on his brother-in-law, the Duke of Suffolk, in 1537. For hundreds of years the church was used as a barn and the abbey precincts as a farm, until in 1918 it was restored as a House of Prayer by Ellen Wrightson. The Ministry of Public Building and Works assumed custody of the ruins in 1964. Built into the nave and north side of the cloister is a dwelling used as a retreat for the local diocese.

Leiston itself is a busy industrial town which stands near the coast. One of the Garretts who ran the Iron Works produced a famous portable steam engine and threshing machine. His bust may be seen in the church (fine 13th-cent. font), and three of his stove-pipe hats in the council chamber.

Nearby is **Sizewell**, a small seaside village chosen in 1958 as the site of a new atomic power station.

LITTLE GLEMHAM, *Suffolk* (11–TM3459). On the main road from SAXMUNDHAM to WICKHAM MARKET. The Church of St Andrew has a Norman door to the nave and a white marble statue made by John Gibson in 1833 to the memory of Dudley North. Little Glemham Hall is a large brick mansion of the early 18th cent. which was built on the site of a still earlier house. Two projecting wings are, like the central section, three stories in height and the house contains a fine staircase, panelled rooms and Queen Anne furniture. There is a notable walled garden which, like the house, is open on occasions to the public.

LITTLE WENHAM, *Suffolk* (11–TM0738). Here is Little Wenham Hall, the oldest house in Suffolk, a miniature castle built *c.* 1270–80. Not only was it built as a house and not, despite its battlemented appearance, as a keep, it also represents a very early post-Roman use of brick for domestic building. The tiny chapel is rib-vaulted with a boss representing St Petronilla, a reminder that the house was inherited by Petronilla of Nerford in 1287.

The Church of All Saints is largely of the same date as the Hall, though the tower is later and the south porch 15th-cent. There are a number of wall paintings and a fine double-canopied brass with the figures of Thomas Brewse and his wife, d. 1514.

One m. SW. is **Great Wenham**. The Church of St John has a Perpendicular west tower and in the chancel unglazed patterned tiles, probably 15th-cent. The East family arms, complete with sword and helmet, are inside the church, and one of the 15th-cent. bench-ends is now in the collection of the VICTORIA AND ALBERT MUSEUM, London.

LODDON, *Norfolk* (11–TM3698), is a small town on the BECCLES to NORWICH road and divided by the River Chet from its sister village of **Chedgrave**. The village is built around a square on one side of which is the large Church of the Holy Trinity, late 15th-cent. Over the west door is a group representing the Holy Trinity. The interior is spacious and lit by 15 clerestory windows. Among the very interesting contents is the seven-sacrament font, on three traceried steps, the top one of which is shaped like a Maltese cross. There is a fine screen painted with scenes from the life of Christ, and less usual, the martyrdom of William of Norwich, and in the south aisle a painting of Sir James Hobart and his wife. Hobart was Attorney General to Henry VII and the background of the painting shows the church and a bridge. The Jacobean pulpit and large poor-box are worthy of note. Some excellent brasses (to the Hobarts) and an outstanding marble sarcophagus to Lady Williamson, d. 1684, who gave so much to the building of City churches after the Fire of London.

The square has some good buildings and close by is Loddon House, *c.* 1711, the best in the town. Around Loddon are several successfully planned modern estates by the local architects Tayler and Green.

Across the river, Chedgrave should be seen for its Church of All Saints, with a tower north of the chancel and a richly decorated Norman doorway.

LONG MELFORD, *Suffolk* (11–TL8646). One of Suffolk's loveliest villages, remarkable for the length of its main street, hence the epithet. To walk along the High Street, passing its fine houses and hotel, then progressing by way of the green to the magnificent church is a memorable experience.

Though the Church of Holy Trinity, considered the finest in Suffolk, comes almost last in the walk along the High Street, such is its size and splendour that it dominates the view and forms an almost symphonic climax to the progression. It was almost entirely rebuilt towards the end of the 15th cent., and its great length and enormous area of glass and flushwork are immediately striking. The well-proportioned tower is more recent, being built in 1903 around the earlier brick tower of the 18th cent. Its pinnacles emphasize the vertical lines of the Perpendicular style of the rest of the church.

From inside the church, the nave and chancel, over 150 ft in length, almost disappear in perspective and the arches of the arcade contrast with the timbering of the roof. The Lady Chapel built at the end of the 15th cent. is surrounded by its own ambulatory. In the Clopton Chantry the carved monument to John Clopton, d. 1497, a tomb without an effigy. Many brasses of the greatest interest show the styles in clothing and hair-dressing of the early and late 15th cent. In the chancel is the noble monument to Sir William Cordell, d. 1580, the builder of Melford Hall, Speaker of Parliament and the Master of the Rolls to Queen Elizabeth.

The stained glass is late 15th-cent., and the church still contains a great deal that has either escaped destruction or has been carefully restored and replaced.

By the church, Melford Green is large and triangular and slopes down towards the village. At the upper end is the Hospital and Melford Hall. The former building dates from 1573 but was much restored in 1847. The Hall is one of the best early Elizabethan houses left to us and is now owned by the National Trust. A superb brick house of three sides surrounding a courtyard and facing a garden, it is open to the public and contains a collection of pictures, furniture and porcelain.

A little to the N. of the village is Kentwell Hall, built *c.* 1563 by the Cloptons, also in brick and approached through a long avenue of lime trees. Returning to the high street on the right is Mill House, on the left the timber-framed Bull Inn and Brooke House. Georgian brick and timbered houses follow and finally Melford Place, the old home of the Martyn family, where the chapel has been made into the entrance hall.

LOPHAMS, THE, *Norfolk* (11–TM0381; South Lopham). Two villages near DISS, **South Lopham** on the main A1066 and **North Lopham** on the B1113. South Lopham should be seen first for its Church of St Andrew which has a marvellous central Norman tower. The arcading is simple but effective, and the parapet is Perpendicular. In the tower is an Anglo-Saxon window and later styles may be seen in the Decorated chancel and Perpendicular clerestory. The octagonal font has sensitive tracery and there is a great dug-out chest in the tower which is 8 ft long and may be of similar age.

Just to the S. of the village is the border with Suffolk and, on either side of the B1113, the sources of the Ouse and the Waveney.

North Lopham's Church of St Nicholas (Decorated and Perpendicular) is passed as you enter the village from the S. The west tower is Perpendicular, and the font has the same delicate tracery as that at South Lopham.

LOWESTOFT, *Suffolk* (11–TM5493). A seaside town of some character which pivots around the Swing Bridge, an area of, at times, intense traffic congestion. The Ness is the most easterly point in England. The area around the bridge across the estuary of the Lothing contains the harbour which makes the town into one of our most important fishing ports. This was where Joseph Conrad served when he arrived in England in 1878 to go to sea on the *Skimmer of the Seas.* The trawlers and other vessels, and the constant bustle of traffic, make Lowestoft a place of fascinating activity, with its still picturesque fishing quarter.

The site of the first recorded lighthouse in England, the town's North Light, is open to the public on weekdays. This north side of the town is noted for the Scores, narrow lanes which connected the road to the beach below. The area is now monopolized by a huge frozen-food factory, though one or two of the old houses for smoking the herrings remain. Just past the Light is the Royal Memorial in Belle Vue Park and the Sparrow's Nest close to the park in which summer concert parties perform. Further still, the road leads to Corton or GREAT YARMOUTH and GORLESTON.

South of the bridge lies the bathing and holiday section of the town with several hotels of note and Claremont Pier. Kensington Gardens, a little further on, is pleasantly laid out, with electric boats in addition to the usual amenities. Should the bridge be out of action, the road would follow the west limits of the town to OULTON Broad, the scene of more holiday activities and a busy boating centre.

St Margaret's Church is on the Oulton Road on the north side of the town, and is a fine 15th-cent. building which contains glazing in the south window of the chancel, by Robert Allen (1819) of the famous Lowestoft china factory. While you may well try to find pieces of Lowestoft ware while in Suffolk, do not be surprised if the prices they fetch are at least as high as those obtained in the capital. The wares of this small, but appreciated factory, which functioned from 1756 to 1803, are now much sought after.

Perhaps Lowestoft's most famous son is the composer Benjamin Britten, born here in 1913 on the anniversary of St Cecilia, the patron saint of musicians. Thomas Nashe, 1567–1601, the satirist, critic and playwright, was also born in Lowestoft.

Places of interest near Lowestoft must include **Pakefield** to the S., with two churches sharing not merely the same churchyard, but even the same building. Nowadays Pakefield is very much a residential and holiday suburb of Lowestoft. To the N. of the town lies **Gunton** with its ancient church, **Corton** and **Hopton**, now given over to holiday camps, BLUNDESTON and SOMERLEYTON.

Fritton with its small church and long wooded decoy for trapping wildfowl is some 6 m. to the NW. of the town on the A143 and is well worth an afternoon's drive.

LUDHAM, *Norfolk* (11–TG3818). A pleasant Broadland village on the B1354 which links WROXHAM with POTTER HEIGHAM. South of the village the Rivers Bure and Thurne wend their quiet ways and to the W. the River Ant runs into BARTON BROAD. Womack Broad is just by the village and the Staithe is at the end of a lane to the SE. The village centre has some very attractive Georgian houses and the Church of St Catherine, mainly 15th-cent., is outstanding. The wheel which is the emblem of that saint may be seen in the spandrels of the nave roof and the interior is impressive with the painted tympanum as one of the main features. This is a 15th-cent. painting of the Crucifixion, with, on the reverse, the Royal coat of arms of Queen Elizabeth I.

More important still as an example of early painting is the beautiful screen dated 1493. The tracery is most delicate and the paintings are of rare quality, showing saints and kings. Between the panels, are detached buttresses, another rare feature. Also to be noticed is a large iron-bound poor-box and the octagonal font.

Ludham Hall has a Georgian front covering an earlier Jacobean building. The brick chapel is 17th-cent. and the house at one time belonged to the bishops of NORWICH. The Bishop of Norwich is still Abbot of **St Benet's**, the ruins of which are almost 2 m. SW. near the junction of the Bure and the Ant. The first Sunday in August sees a visitation by the Abbot, made by water. Around the village are several ruined windmills.

MALDON, *Essex* (7–TL8506). A picturesque town set above the River Blackwater (and also the River Chelmer), it possesses a feature unique in England – the triangular tower of All Saints' Church. The town's commanding position made it the site of a fortress built early in the 10th cent. The Old English poem *The Battle of Maldon* tells of the fearsome struggle between a Danish and an English army in 991. All Saints' dates from the 13th cent. and apart from the tower is particularly renowned for the elaborate decoration of the south aisle built early in the 14th cent.

Of the Church of St Peter, only the tower remains, the building having been converted into a library by Dr Plume in 1704, rather than rebuilt as a church. St Mary the Virgin's Church has a shingled spire on top of a heavy tower, and though much restored still reveals traces of its Norman origin.

The 15th cent. saw a number of interesting buildings, of which the Moot Hall, once known as D'Arcy's Tower after its builder, the Blue Boar Hotel, with additions from the early 19th cent., the Swan Hotel and the vicarage are the best examples. Even earlier are the remains of the St Giles Hospital, founded for lepers in the 12th cent. Georgian buildings of some distinction are numerous and a stroll along the High Street, Silver Street and Market Hill will reveal much of interest.

Once down by the river the atmosphere of a fishing harbour and small resort is strengthened by riverside inns, the marine parade and the marine lake leading to the estuary and the marshes as the river makes its way slowly to the sea. About 1 m. to the N. is **Heybridge**, with a Norman church – St Andrew's – and the 17th-cent. Heybridge Hall and 19th-cent. The Towers. There is an attractive mill, W. of the church, and impressive ironworks, 1863.

Just over 1 m. to the W. are the remains of the 12th-cent. **Beeleigh Abbey**, which were incorporated in a picturesque house of the 16th cent.

MANNINGTREE, *Essex* (11–TM1031), stands, like MISTLEY, on the estuary of the River Stour, and has many Georgian and Victorian buildings of character. The Strand attracts swans in great numbers. The Roman Catholic church was converted from the old Corn Exchange.

The village centre is at the crossing of High Street and South Street; there are some pleasant buildings here, and in South Hill. Prominent is the Methodist church, 1807, with its cupola.

MAPLESTEADS, THE, *Essex* (11–TL8034; Great Maplestead). Of the five round churches built by the Knights Templars and Hospitallers, St John the Baptist in **Little Maplestead**, was the last to be built, *c.* 1335. The others at London,

LUDLOW, NORTHAMPTON and CAMBRIDGE were all Norman. Though the church was drastically restored after 1851 it is still possible to appreciate its design where, as in the Church of the Holy Sepulchre in Jerusalem, the nave is in the form of a circular rotunda. Here, though, there is a chancel complete with apse. The font is quite possibly older than the church itself.

The Church of St Giles at **Great Maplestead** has a strong Norman tower at one end and a Norman apse at the other. In between is an Early English chancel. The Perpendicular font was at one time brightly painted. Now, the most striking features are the monuments, especially that by William Wright of Charing Cross to Lady Deane, built in 1634 by her son behind whom she stands enshrouded, a very spectral concept. That to her husband, Sir John Deane, d. 1625, shows him resting on his arm, with the figures of his sorrowing wife and children kneeling above.

The Deane family lived at Dynes Hall, 1 m. to the S., which is mainly late 17th-cent. but with parts dating back to the previous century.

MARCH, *Cambridgeshire* (10–TL4197). At the centre of the network of railways linking the FENS to the surrounding counties, the town is particularly famous for its church, St Wendreda's, at the south end of the town in Church Street. The most spectacular feature of the church is the roof, one of the most quoted and photographed of all East Anglian church interiors. It is of double hammer-beam construction with, on every conceivable vantage point, finely carved angels spreading their wings.

There are few other buildings of interest in the town but a small, former Guild Hall, rebuilt as a school in 1827, now a store, should be noted.

MARGARETTING, *Essex* (7–TL6601). The tower of St Margaret's should not be missed, for it is built, like that of St Lawrence's, **Blackmore**, on ten wooden posts of immense dignity and strength, which are braced with additional beams. More timber-work of the same period, 15th-cent., may be seen in the north porch. Inside the church the east window boasts a complete "Stem of Jesse" window of 15th-cent. glass. The tree winds its way round medallions showing Abraham, Jacob, Joseph, King David and King Solomon, and finally the Madonna and Child. A brass of a knight and his lady reminds us of their connection with Killigrews, a moated house of Tudor date, but with additions from the 18th cent. (the east front) and later.

MELTON CONSTABLE, *Norfolk* (11–TG 0433). Melton Hall, built 300 years ago, is a perfect example of the country mansion in the Wren style, impressive yet not oppressive. It was built by Sir Jacob Astley in the second half of the 17th cent., and the minor additions do not affect the beauty of the house. The interior boasts some superb plastering on the ceiling of the Red Drawing Room, which is dated 1687 and which may well be by the same master craftsman who worked at

FELBRIGG and at HINTLESHAM at about the same time.

The small Church of St Peter is in the grounds of the Hall, at the north-east edge. It is basically Norman, with a central tower, but the visitor is warned that the doorway in the west wall is a 19th-cent. imitation. Most unusual is the opening above the west tower arch with a sturdy Norman pier dividing the opening into two sections. There are, of course, many monuments to the Astley family in the same modest taste as the house.

MERSEA ISLAND, *Essex* (11–TM0314), lies between the estuaries of the River Colne and the River Blackwater, separated from the mainland by the Pyefleet and linked to COLCHESTER by the B1025, known as the "Strood". **East Mersea**'s Church of St Edmund, King and Martyr, commands attention because of its large Perpendicular west tower complete with buttresses and battlements. Inside is an octagonal 15th-cent. font. Sabine Baring-Gould's novel *Mehalah* is set here.

West Mersea was a settlement in Roman times and when the burial mound, a mile or so to the NE. of the church, was excavated, the remains of a cremated body were found in a tiled burial chamber of the 1st cent. Now there are caravans and a large summer holiday population, but still the village retains much of its old charm. Weatherboarded and Georgian brick cottages tell of its earlier days as a small fishing, oyster and sailing centre.

SS. Peter and Paul's is in the old village and dates from Norman times. The tower has 14th-cent. additions and the nave was raised in the 19th cent. The font is 13th-cent. Purbeck marble and there is a sculptured lunette by, or in the style of, della Robbia.

MILDENHALL, *Suffolk* (11–TL7074). Lying just off the A11 at the Barton Mills junction, Mildenhall is in the north-west corner of the county. It has one of the finest churches for miles around, large in scale and with many superb features. Of all these perhaps the most famous is the roof, elaborately carved with biblical scenes, fantastic beasts and other designs and with a host of the angels for which so many Suffolk churches are renowned. This wonderful roof was peppered with shot by the zealous iconoclasts of the 17th cent. Fortunately, however, their action had little effect.

Over 160 ft in length with a tower over 110 ft in height this Church of St Mary has a particularly lovely north porch, over which is a Lady Chapel. The east window is of rare design with seven lights and like the chapel to the north of the aisle is of ELY design.

Pleasantly situated on the River Lark, Mildenhall was the site of the Mildenhall Treasure found in 1946. Now on display in the British Museum, this splendid hoard of more than 30 pieces of silver table-ware included the great dish showing Bacchus and Hercules. Some of this 4th-cent. Roman ware may well have originated in Rome itself.

The Royal Worlington and Newmarket Golf Club close to the town has been described as the best nine-hole course in the world.

MISTLEY, *Essex* (11–TM1231). On the estuary of the River Stour and noted for the swans which frequent its banks in large numbers, Mistley was drastically altered when Richard Rigby decided to turn it into a spa in the 18th cent. The original Church of St Mary survives only in its flushwork porch on Mistley Heath. When the village was given its "face-lift" a new church was built by Robert Adam. He had been called in by Digby, who had made extensive alterations to the Hall and its grounds, in about 1774. His first project, which came to nothing, was to design a bathing station by the river. Next came the church. Adam made use of the earlier church of 1735 and added to it two square classic towers, topped with drums and domes, and supported by free-standing columns. All that remains of Adam's part in these schemes are the two towers and the lodges built in 1782 for the Hall. The nave of the church was pulled down when yet another church was built in 1870, and the Hall itself no longer stands. The final St Mary's is Victorian Gothic.

Much of the village survives, however. Near the square stands the fountain, with its swan, which was to have symbolized the spa. The maltings and the quays remind us of the town's grander days.

MUNDESLEY, *Norfolk* (11–TG3136). A small seaside resort with a superb sandy beach and excellent bathing. Though at one time it was planned to develop the resort it has fortunately remained unspoilt. The larger hotels, the Continental (1892) and the Manor (1900) rival those at CROMER, 7 m. to the NW. In the village is Rookery House of the Queen Anne period, but rebuilt in the present century, and Cowper House, at which the poet stayed.

All Saints' Church was almost completely rebuilt just before the First World War. Just S. of the village is a smock windmill complete with cap and sails.

NAYLAND, *Suffolk* (11–TL9734). A village set in beautiful country by the River Stour, and at one time a busy cloth town. The bridge over the Stour into Essex was erected by William Abell who also made considerable additions to the Church of St James in the early 16th cent. Perhaps one of the most interesting features of the church is the altar-piece painted by John Constable, who was born nearby in EAST BERGHOLT. The subject is *Christ blessing the bread and wine* and it was painted early in his career in 1809. It may be compared with his still earlier painting of *Christ and the Children* painted in 1804, and now in the Church of St Michael at Brantham.

At the south end of Church Street is Alston Court, which dates from the 15th cent. and has magnificently carved timbering, especially the barge-boards. Various additions were made to the building in the following centuries. Inside, the finest rooms are the hall, dining-room and solar, all of which have fine beams and notable carving.

In the market place may be seen an obelisk milestone and a number of attractive cottages and inns.

NEEDHAM MARKET, *Suffolk* (11–TM 0855). A thoroughfare town on the IPSWICH to BURY ST EDMUNDS road (A45). There is much of interest, including Georgian houses in the High Street, the Bull Hotel with carved corner-post, the Friends' Meeting House and Graveyard and the 17th-cent. timber-framed Grammar School. The Church of St John the Baptist, while not especially remarkable outside, contains a unique timber roof. It is remarkably complex in structure and dates originally from the latter half of the 15th cent., although much of it had to be restored in the 1880s.

One of the Ministers of the Congregational Church was Joseph Priestley (1733–1804), famous as a chemist and for "discovering" oxygen when he settled in Pennsylvania in 1794.

NEWPORT, *Essex* (11–TL5234), stands by the River Cam on the main CAMBRIDGE to BISHOP'S STORTFORD road, the A11, at the junction with the B1038. The village is one of the county's most attractive and has a number of timbered houses, two of which are of particular interest and beauty. These are Crown House, which was faced with magnificent pargeting (decorative moulded plasterwork) in 1692, and Monks Barn, 15th-cent., timbered and with brick nogging. The Church of St Mary the Virgin is a big flint building with parts dating from the 13th cent., with many later additions, including the tower of 1858. While the 13th-cent. octagonal font is a good example, the great rarity is the 13th-cent. chest, which contains early paintings and must have been used as a portable altar-piece.

Less than 1 m. NE. is Shortgrove, a 17th-cent. H-shaped house, which was rebuilt in the 18th cent. and burnt down in the 20th.

NEWMARKET, *Suffolk* (11–TL6463). Though it contains little of overt architectural or archaeological interest Newmarket is a memorable town, due to its magnificent situation on the downs and heaths which straddle the main road from London to NORWICH, and for its historical associations as the centre of the English horse-racing world.

It is perhaps seen at its finest approached from the A11 across the Devil's Dyke (Anglo-Saxon earthworks), when against a background of blue sky the heath stretches as far as the eye can see. On the left as you enter the town is the racecourse, the scene of so many great classic meetings since the first recorded race in 1619, and the headquarters of the turf. Signs warn the driver of the dangers of meeting the string of horses which are taken for exercise on the heath and should it be the day of a race meeting you may well find yourself in a queue of traffic extending for 2 m. from one end of the town to the other. Just before the town proper is the Cooper Memorial Fountain of 1909 and then you pass the first of many fine houses and hotels which line the main road as it continues to the N.

On the right may be seen the Headquarters of the Jockey Club built in 1772 and restored and enlarged by the late P.R.A., Sir Albert Richardson. Further on is the Rutland Arms Hotel, a historic building with Georgian red-brick front, and even older interior walls. Next is the Jubilee clock tower, now a traffic roundabout, and, as you leave the town, many fine houses, the homes of trainers, owners and leading jockeys. Shortly afterwards the road divides, the Norwich and THETFORD roads straight ahead and, branching to the right, the road to BURY ST EDMUNDS and IPSWICH.

Newmarket is the home of more studs than any other town in England, among them the National Stud, which moved to its especially built home in 1964. The stud is open to visitors on Sunday afternoons and on the mornings of race days, and its fine design, by Peter Burrell, C.B.E., and its magnificent collection of stallions make it a must for all those interested in horses.

Horse-racing has taken place here for over three centuries and the heath has been the subject of innumerable paintings by the masters of English sporting pictures – Stubbs, Marshall and many others. Horse sales take place here every year.

NORTH ELMHAM, *Norfolk* (11–TF9821). Before the Normans came to Britain this was the site of an Anglo-Saxon cathedral, the centre of the See of Norfolk until it was moved to HOXNE, finally transferring to NORWICH itself in 1095. The ruins which remain are dated by the Ministry of Works as early 11th-cent. After the See moved to Norwich the cathedral was turned into a house by Bishop Henry le Despencer in 1370, who began the task of moating the dwelling. What remains is, though small, of much interest.

The present Church of St Mary has an imposing tower containing a west porch. The north doorway is also surprising, as it has a hood of leaved capitals, perhaps part of some other section of the church. Inside are tall 13th-cent. arcades which must have been added to an earlier, Norman, building. The pulpit dates from 1626, and was made by the parish clerk, who received £5 3s 4d for his labours! The rood-screen has painted figures of the saints and there is an altar-table of 1622.

NORWICH, *Norfolk* (11–TG2308). "Norwich has everything", says Sir Nikolaus Pevsner, and what greater compliment could be paid to this beautiful city, the capital of Norfolk? Norwich developed by a large double bend in the River Wensum, and within its medieval walls it was second only to London. By the time of the Conquest it was already a town of importance and the castle which was built, together with the cathedral which soon followed, gave the city the two focal points that remain to this day.

The great stone keep of the castle dates from *c.* 1160, and is perhaps the most splendid of all

A. F. Kersting

Norwich cathedral

surviving examples of Norman military architecture apart from the TOWER OF LONDON. However, in its external decorative scheme it yields to none, only CASTLE RISING approaching it in style. It is approximately 90 ft square by 70 ft high and the elaborate patterns of blank arcading which cover the walls were carefully refaced in 1833–9. After serving as the city prison it was adapted as a museum in 1894 and contains an outstanding collection of works by the artists of the Norwich School, headed by John Crome and John Sell Cotman. In addition, there are displays of archaeological interest and a fascinating collection of natural history, with many tableaux of birds in their natural surroundings. Important touring exhibitions are shown here at various times during the year. A new central rotunda has been added.

Norwich Cathedral, the Church of the Holy and Undivided Trinity, is one of the country's finest examples of Norman cathedral architecture, and lying in a depression, it is its superb spire which at first commands attention. The See of East Anglia set up at DUNWICH in A.D. 630, moved to NORTH ELMHAM, HOXNE, and on to

THETFORD. In accordance with the Normans' policy of having their cathedral in the largest town, the See moved to Norwich in 1095 under the great Bishop de Losinga, as by that time Norwich with its original castle and market place had already established itself as the foremost town in East Anglia. Losinga commenced his new cathedral a year later and when he died in 1119, to be buried in the chancel, the work continued under his successors. The cathedral was finally consecrated in 1278, but was substantially complete well before that date.

The Norman plan, the only one to survive in this country, featured a bishop's throne at the east end, in an apse behind the altar. The throne may be 1,000 years old, which would make it the oldest bishop's throne in any English cathedral.

The arcading of the nave is covered with a magnificent roof which contains many of the 800 roof-bosses in the cathedral. Those in the nave tell the story of the Old and New Testaments, and "read" from E. to W. The chancel is taller than the nave, with a clerestory added *c.* 1360 and the roof is, if anything, even more splendid than that of the nave. From outside the cathedral you will be able to see the astonishing array of flying buttresses which enabled the Norman walls to support this huge additional burden. Within the church, the stalls feature some of the finest English carving; Bishop Goldwell, who added the chancel roof in 1490, is buried beneath his masterpiece.

The spire which dominates the close and the city was added in the late 15th cent. by Goldwell, and at 315 ft high it is second only to SALISBURY. The cloisters are the largest in Britain, and though originally Norman were rebuilt in the 13th to 15th cents. Here again are many roof-bosses, easier to study because of the lower height of the vault.

Within the precincts is Norwich School, once Carnary College, founded in 1316. Its most famous pupil was Horatio Nelson, another was the writer George Borrow. Two gates lead from the town into the close. One is Ethelbert Gate which was built in 1316 by the townspeople to make amends for the riots of the previous century. It was restored by Wilkins (*see* CAMBRIDGE and GREAT YARMOUTH) on the basis of the original designs. Erpingham Gate, built in 1420 by Sir Thomas Erpingham, is exceptionally fine and contains a statue of its builder. By the river is the 15th-cent. Water Gate, now forming part of Pull's Ferry. It is one of the most picturesque and often painted Norwich scenes.

Inner Norwich may be traced in the city walls which follow a route encompassing an area N. of the river as well as the major portion to the S. of it. Carrow Hill, Queen's Road, Chapelfield Road, Station Road, Bakers Road and Bullclose Road surround an ear-shaped area as big as the City of London. In this congested centre are no less than 32 surviving churches, though 400 years ago there were many more. All the churches are medieval and many are of exceptional interest. Close by the great market place is the beautiful St Peter Mancroft, commenced in 1430, with a great west tower and a length of 180 ft, and entirely Perpendicular in style. Facing the church is the Guildhall built 1407–13, with a gable end of gaily patterned flint flushwork completed in 1535. It was in use as the seat of the City Council until the new City Hall, on the west side of the market place, was completed in 1938. This has been called the most impressive public building in England of its period. Its 200-ft tower makes a strong vertical accent, a foil to that of the cathedral.

Other notable buildings include St Andrew's Hall by St Andrew's Plain. Here it may be remarked that the term "plain" is in common use in Norwich and Norfolk and echoes the Dutch *plein* used of squares in Holland and Flanders. St Andrew's was the Black or Dominican Friary of the city and has been converted for use as a public hall. The Assembly House in Theatre Street dates from 1754 and has now been restored to its former function. Strangers' Hall is mid-15th-cent., with a façade of 1621 and is now a museum with rooms representing various periods. The Bridewell Museum in Bridewell Alley was first built about 1370 and became the gaol 213 years later. In 1925 it became a museum which specializes in local industries. Another museum not to be missed is that in the Church of St Peter Hungate, in Elm Hill. The church was built by the Paston family (*see* PASTON) in the 15th cent. and now houses a collection of ecclesiastical art, mostly East Anglian.

Elm Hill itself is one of the most attractive and frequently photographed and painted of all Norwich's streets. Its cobbled road and its irregularly placed houses gives it a medieval feeling, yet a century ago it was derelict and its present charm is due to the Corporation who restored it. It is the centre of the Norwich antique trade and as such it is irresistible to lovers of art and antiques. At the bottom of Elm Hill is Wensum Street, leading to the cathedral and Tombland. This name has nothing to do with tombs, but comes from an ancient word for market. Here is commemorated Nurse Edith Cavell, who was executed in the Great War and is buried in the cathedral precincts. Nearby is the Samson and Hercules House, now a ballroom, with the two figures who act as supporters for its porch. Across the river we are reminded of two famous women and the founder of the Norwich School. Elizabeth Fry, the famous prison reformer, was born in 1780, in Gurney Court and in the same house in 1802 was born the writer: Harriet Martineau. St Michael's Church in Coslany boasts a wonderful façade, which shows the East Anglian art of flushwork at its best. Of interest to art lovers is the fact that the tracery of the west door was drawn by Cotman, whose house at Palace Plain may still be seen. Cotman's great contemporary John Crome is buried in St George's Church nearby, the only one of East Anglia's four greatest artists to rest in his home county. Crome was born in 1768 in a Norwich ale-house, and after a brief education the young boy became errand boy to a local doctor. Two

years later he was apprenticed to a sign painter and thus developed his taste for painting. Helped by Thomas Harvey of Catton, a local collector and banker, Crome was able to study the Dutch painters and also the work of Wilson and Gainsborough (*see* SUDBURY). He thus developed his style of landscape painting in oils and water-colour. Only once did he go abroad, to France in 1814 – the results may be seen in some paintings of Paris and Boulogne. He died in April 1821.

Medieval Norwich had one of the largest Jewish communities in England and like similar cities, traces remain in cemeteries and in the houses which were built for the wealthier Jewish merchants and money-lenders. The Old Music House in King Street was built for such a man in the 12th cent. and was much added to in subsequent centuries. It is now a club. The monument of another faith is seen in the remarkable Roman Catholic Church of St John the Baptist, built in the Early English style in 1884–1910 by Sir George Gilbert Scott and J. O. Scott. It is a huge building 275 ft long and over 80 ft high inside the chancel. The tower is yet higher. As an exercise in architectural scholarship and unity of style it is an astonishing performance.

Modern entertainment takes place in the Maddermarket Theatre, rebuilt in the Elizabethan style, and in the television studios in the old Agricultural Hall (1882) in Prince of Wales Road, near the old G.P.O., converted from a bank of 1866. The municipal Theatre Royal has a coherent programme of music and drama and there are orchestral concerts in the St Andrew's Hall. There are many facilities for sport – the football fan is catered for by the Norwich City F.C. who play at Carrow Road. There are several golf courses, including the Royal Norwich at Drayton Road, Hellesdon, on the A1067 to FAKENHAM which has 18 holes.

Earlham Hall on the western edge of the city is now the home of the University of East Anglia, one of our most architecturally adventurous universities, whose unusual buildings are now an accepted part of the Norwich scene. The architect was Denys Lasdun.

The new buildings of the University typify the forward-looking attitude of the city which, famous for so many different things, from mustard to insurance, is at once a great treasury of medieval Britain and an expanding industrial centre.

ORFORD, *Suffolk* (11–TM4250). Once a populous small town, Orford, like so many similar places along the Suffolk coast, fell into a decline from which it only recovers during the holiday season. It is famous for its castle, the earliest in the kingdom for which documentary evidence survives in the form of the pipe rolls of the medieval exchequer. Its great tower or keep, which is now all that survives above ground level, was in earlier days the final strongpoint of a considerable military complex. The keep dates from 1165 when Henry II attempted to re-establish the royal power in East Anglia. Of unique design, the tower is cylindrical within but multi-sided on the exterior, and is buttressed by three rectangular projecting turrets whose tops with their battlements rise above the main body of the keep. It stands 90 ft high and the walls of the central tower are almost 10 ft thick – little wonder that it has withstood the buffetings of the past 800 years. Legend tells us of a merman who was caught by the local fishermen shortly after the building of the castle, but escaping from his captors he returned to the sea and has never been seen since.

Orford Church saw the first performance of some of Benjamin Britten's compositions, including *Noye's Fludde* in 1958 and *Curlew River* in 1964. There has been a light on the ness for over 300 years and radar experiments were carried out on the spit in the mid-1930s.

Famous today for its "Orford Butleys", a variety of smoked herring, and for other smoked fish, the village also boasts an amusing shop-sign, that of one Edward Pipe licensed to sell tobacco.

There is an Atomic Weapons Research Establishment on Orford Ness.

ORMESBY BROAD, *Norfolk* (11–TG4615), forms part of a complex of no less than five broads, of which the others are ROLLESBY (to the S.), Lily (to the SE.), and to the S., **Filby** and **Little Broads**. Due to the main road (the A149) which cuts across between Ormesby and Rollesby and also to the A1064 which crosses to the S. at Filby Bridge, the motorist can obtain superb views of the broads from the seat of his car, (rarely possible in this region). To diminish the risk of flooding, this group of broads has had its once-navigable dykes closed by sluices; this affects not only their use by pleasure craft but also the ecology of the area.

These are deep broads, and this factor also affects the nature of insect, plant and bird life which they can support. Thus in summer the water is often thick and green with algae, and all three known species of mud-dwelling water-fleas can be found on the bottom.

OULTON, *Suffolk* (11–TM5292). Oulton, the village to the W. of LOWESTOFT, is also the most southerly of the BROADS. It is the centre of a very lively boating industry and in the holiday season presents a colourful scene.

The church overlooks the River Waveney into neighbouring Norfolk. George Borrow once lived here in a house beside the broad, but no trace now remains. The North Landing of the Broad is one of the imaginative pieces of modern architecture to be found in this part of East Suffolk and East Norfolk.

The broad presents a remarkable sight at the time of the carnival which usually terminates with a grand firework display, the water reflecting the myriad colours of the set pieces and rockets.

OXBURGH, *Norfolk* (11–TF7401). The Hall, one of the most romantic and picturesque buildings of its period in the country, was begun in 1482 by Sir Edward Bedingfeld. It was built to a square plan and surrounded by a moat, crossed by a drawbridge and entered by a magnificent gatehouse. Though the drawbridge was replaced by a stone bridge in 1710 the great gatehouse remains, one of the most outstanding brick examples in the country and similar to those in such other East Anglian places as LAYER MARNEY. Through its mighty archway passed Henry VII when he came to visit the Bedingfeld family in 1497. Its octagonal turrets rise 80 ft from the surface of the moat, and though it cannot have been designed as a pure fortress, the effect is splendid.

The square plan was wrecked when Sir Richard decided to pull down the south side in 1776–8, but sensible rebuilding by another Bedingfeld, Sir Henry, at the beginning of the Victorian era, made amends with a fine south-east tower and careful restoration of the windows, etc. Inside the house, which is now owned by the National Trust, are excellent rooms containing many relics of the Bedingfeld family and tapestries worked by Mary Queen of Scots and Bess of Hardwick.

The chapel was built for the family in 1835 by Pugin and contains a number of items of Flemish origin, such as the Antwerp Altar of 1525, the communion rails, c. 1700 and some 16th-cent. stained glass. The Chapel of Our Lady and St Margaret is Roman Catholic, the faith of the Bedingfeld family.

The Parish Church of St John the Evangelist had at one time one of the tallest (150 ft) steeples in Norfolk, but in 1948 it collapsed, destroying much of the nave and south aisle. The chancel and the Bedingfeld Chapel were fortunately spared and the terracotta monuments to the family survive. They are extraordinarily vivacious, in the Italian Early Renaissance style.

PARHAM, *Suffolk* (11–TM3060), is set in the valley of the upper Alde. Parham Hall is a picturesque 16th-cent. moated house, timber-framed brick with much diaper patterning.

The Church of St Mary is mainly Decorated in style, with bells still hanging in their 14th-cent. frame. Little remains of Parham House, built at the beginning of the 17th cent. It was at Parham that Crabbe lived after he married Sarah Elmy, though his house, Ducking Hall, no longer stands.

A number of the buildings in the village display carvings representing animals as well as human beings.

PASTON, *Norfolk* (11–TG3234), is a village famous for its associations with the Paston family who lived here from the 15th cent. Letters written by John Paston and other members of the family cover the period 1422–1509 and are one of the most important surviving sources of our knowledge of life and manners in the 15th cent. In addition they give much information on the Wars of the Roses and on the members of this remarkable family. A very complete collection was published in 1904 by James Gairdner, and in 1956 a fictional study by Barbara Jefferis appeared entitled *Beloved Lady*.

The mansion of the Pastons has long vanished but a great barn, 163 ft long, constructed of flint is one of the county's finest. The title, too, is no more, the line having died out in 1732. The Church of St Margaret is 14th-cent. and is thatched. Some interesting wall paintings and memorials to the family include two by Nicholas Stone, dated 1628 and 1632.

POLSTEAD, *Suffolk* (11–TL9938). Near the Church of St Mary, Maria Marten met her doom in 1827 in the famous Red Barn which was to provide the Victorian stage with one of its most famous melodramas. The church itself still retains a considerable amount of Norman work and may indeed contain some of the earliest bricks made in England. The tower is 14th-cent. and is the only one in Suffolk which still has its original spire.

Polstead Hall was rebuilt in the Georgian style *c.* 1819, but still has some timbering from the 16th cent. More old woodwork is to be found in Pond Farm House which was re-fronted in 1760. The gospel oak, between the church and the hall, is said to be over 1,000 years old.

POTTER HEIGHAM, *Norfolk* (11–TG4119). One of the most popular of the Broadland centres and well known on account of its bridge and its boatyard. Situated on the River Thurne the old village is close to the 13th-cent. bridge with its three arches. The Church of St Nicholas has a thatched nave and chancel, and a round tower of Norman date with an octagonal top added in the 14th cent. A great rarity is the octagonal font made of brick. There are a number of paintings in the church, including in the south aisle, *The Works of Mercy*, and the screen has painted panels of many of the saints.

Also over the river is the railway bridge – a structure about which it is possible to have mixed feelings. Around the boatyard a new village has developed to cater for the large numbers of holidaymakers, who visit this busy little yachting centre both by road and water.

PULHAMS, THE, *Norfolk* (11–TM2185). The first thing to see here is the south porch of the Church of St Mary the Virgin in **Pulham St Mary**. This is a wonderful piece of 15th-cent. architecture, full of beautifully carved detail on the façade and with flushwork panelling at the sides. In the spandrels of the arch the Annunciation is depicted, and above this are the figures of some music-making angels. The west tower is also fine, but the second most interesting feature is the 13th-cent. piscina which is elegantly designed with three delicate columns within a square frame and surmounted by interleaved arches of considerable refinement. There are some well-carved bench-ends and some stained glass of the 14th and 15th cents.

The village school incorporates the schoolroom built by William Pennoyer in 1670, which in turn included the remains of a Guild Chapel of 1401.

Pulham Market, about 1 m. to the NW. is a very attractive village whose colour-washed cottages surround the village green. The Church of St Mary Magdalen is mainly Perpendicular with a large west tower in four stages. Across the disused railway tracks is the hangar in which were built the great airships R.33 and R.34. Almost 2 m. NE. is the Manor Farm, originally 16th-cent., but which has been restored leaving many of the interior features intact.

RANWORTH, *Norfolk* (11–TG3514), lies between two broads, with a church containing some of the country's finest treasures. St Helen's is mainly Perpendicular; its west tower may be climbed (quite safely) to yield some wonderful views over the surrounding Broads. The first thing to see is the 15th-cent. painted screen which has been described as "probably the finest coloured screen in the country". The central portion has eight "windows" and below them are panels with paintings of the 12 Apostles. Projecting wings with delicately carved buttresses show St George and St Michael and are flanked by small chapels on either side. These also have paintings of the saints.

Next you should see the lectern, *c.* 1500, just a little later in date than the screen. On one face is an eagle and part of the Gospel of St John and on the other, a medieval versicle in plain-song. This is not all that Ranworth has to offer, however, for locked away, but shown on request, is the Sarum Antiphoner containing verses of the Psalms arranged for part singing. It dates from *c.* 1400 and is beautifully illuminated.

Ranworth Broad is the largest in the Bure Valley even though now much smaller than it was a century ago. The dyke which leads from the River Bure links the smaller, inner broad with the outer section, sometimes known as Malthouse Broad. This latter is open to pleasure craft but the smaller section is a Nature Reserve and is only available to rowing boats and then only in summer and with permission. Some of the derelict marshes in the area have been flooded to provide shallow reedswamps for breeding duck. Archaeologists have discovered traces of iron-workers who worked in the area in the first century A.D. Now this tree-surrounded broad provides the motorist with some attractive views as the road descends almost to the level of the water.

REDENHALL, *Norfolk* (11–TM2684). A mile or so to the E. of HARLESTON on the main A143 road is the village of Redenhall, where the Church of St Mary has one of the finest Perpendicular church towers in the country. Superb flushwork panelling is contained between the impressive polygonal buttressing. The north porch is no less beautiful. Inside is an octagonal font and an unusual double-headed brass lectern. Of East Anglian manufacture, it dates from *c.* 1500. There is another eagle lectern in wood and later in date, and also a wooden chest from Gawdy Hall (now demolished), carved outside and with paintings inside the lid.

REDGRAVE, *Suffolk* (11–TM0478). Situated near the River Waveney close to the Suffolk/Norfolk border. It was here that the young Wolsey was rector of the Church of St Mary. Among its many interesting features is a 14th-cent. font, and 18th-cent. paintings of Moses and Aaron with the Commandments, and a particularly fine brass of 1609 to the memory of Anne Butts, who, with her husband Sir Nicholas Bacon, older brother of Francis, is seen in the outstanding monument by Nicholas Stone. Another work by Stone is the tablet to Lady Gawdy, d. 1621. The elaborate memorial to Sir John Holt, the Chief Justice, d. 1710, was made by Thomas Green of Camberwell.

Of the Bacon family home, only the ruined Tudor kitchen survives.

REEDHAM, *Norfolk* (11–TG4201). Situated on the River Yare, crossed by a chain ferry, which takes cars as well as passengers and makes a vast difference to the length of journeys around the county. Its gentle clanking, together with the sounds of the birds and cattle, are pleasant on a hot summer's day.

The Church of St John Baptist has a large Perpendicular west tower, and is thatched. It is unusual in that the nave and aisle have been made into one, with the two arches still remaining. The Berney Chapel contains monuments to the family and some interesting brasses. It has some stained glass worth noting, probably from the Netherlands.

Several windmills in various states of decay have been replaced by pumps driven by oil or electricity. But the famous **Berney Arms Mill,** 3 m. to the NE., is in full working order and at 70 ft high is the most splendid in the county, if not in East Anglia. It is open to visitors (Ministry of Public Building and Works).

REEPHAM, *Norfolk* (11–TG1023). There have been many towns in East Anglia where two churches have shared a common churchyard, but Reepham goes one better, for though only one ruined wall now remains of Hackford Church (1543) the other two churches still stand. The parish church is St Mary's and contains the fine tomb of Sir Roger de Kerdiston, d. 1337. The knight lies on a bed of stones or pebbles and the side of the tomb-chest is carved with the figures of eight mourners in various attitudes. Over the chest rises a canopy of two arches arranged so that a delicate pendant hangs between.

Close by is St Michael's, the parish church of Whitwell. It has a tall Perpendicular west tower and inside is a Jacobean pulpit with sounding-board.

Facing St Michael's is the attractive market place, with on the north side Dial House *c.* 1700, a good town house of some size. Hackford Hall, 1½ m. away to the W., is a further reminder of the now ruined church.

RODINGS, THE, *Essex* (11–TL5813), is the name given to a group of villages which lie between GREAT DUNMOW and CHIPPING ONGAR along or near the B184 in the valley of the River Roding. There are eight altogether and the name is often pronounced Roothings. Alphabetically they are:

Abbess – with St Edmund's Church, rebuilt 1867 and with some attractive monuments;

Aythorpe – with St Mary's Church and a fine post-mill, ½ m. to the SE.;

Beauchamp – with the tall tower of St Edmund's Church;

Berners – (pronounced Barnish) where the church, a simple structure with a weather-boarded belfry, is in the grounds of the Hall;

High – with a large barn at New Hall (the house no longer exists) and All Saints' Church, with a 19th-cent. bellcot and a north door with 13th-cent. ironwork;

Leaden – St Michael's Church has a weather-boarded belfry and a Norman nave and chancel;

Margaret – has a church of the same name, with a Norman doorway, Norman windows and a 19th-cent. bellcot. The doors here also have ironwork of the 13th cent.;

White – where St Martin's Church has a Norman nave, using Roman bricks, a south door with more 13th-cent. ironwork and a square Norman font of Purbeck marble, with incised decoration. About ½ m. to the W. of the church is Colville Hall, basically 15th-cent. with later additions. There is a Tudor gateway and a large barn with timber and brick nogging.

ROLLESBY BROAD, *Norfolk* (11–TG4415). Part of the ORMESBY BROAD complex (*q.v.*) and well seen from the A149 which runs between the two broads to give some of the best views in Broadland. As both share similar conditions much of what has been said concerning the one concerns the other. Archaeological excavations have shown the existence here of communities of the men known as Beaker Folk after the wares which they made in the period about 2000 B.C.

SAFFRON WALDEN, *Essex* (11–TL5438). Though it lies just to the E. of the main A11 LONDON to CAMBRIDGE and NEWMARKET roads, the town, which is one of the most delightful in the county, has a long history. There are remains of an Iron Age fort at Ring Hill, 1½ m. W. of the town; evidence of Roman occupation and the remains of a 12th-cent. castle. Most impressive of all is the great Church of St Mary the Virgin, perhaps the only rival to that at THAXTED, 7 m. to the S. Almost 200 ft long, the church has a spire which reaches to not far short of the same height. Its style reflects the traditions of neighbouring Cambridgeshire and Suffolk as well as those of its native Essex. Apart from a crypt and some of the arcades the church was rebuilt in the Perpendicular style between 1450 and 1550. The splendid stone spire was added in 1831. Windows, battlements and buttresses make the exterior full of interest and beauty. Inside the church are superb carvings and roofs magnificent in their variety and quality. The brasses date from the

15th to the 17th cents. and there is a black marble tomb-chest to Thomas, Lord Audley, the Lord Chancellor, d. 1544 (by Cornelius Harman).

Near the church are numerous buildings of merit. The former Sun Inn is famous for its pargeting, nowhere better to be seen than on the façade of this building. Close by is the Cross Keys and the Rose and Crown. While these buildings are 15th- and 16th-cent., those nearer to the Market Place are from the 19th – the corn exchange and the altered Town Hall (originally 18th-cent.).

Like all the towns in this region, Saffron Walden derived its prosperity from the cloth trade, but as its name indicates its other great trade came from the growing of saffron, formerly used as a dye and as a medicine. The Youth Hostel in Bridge Street with its timbering and courtyard survives from this period. Even older in its origins is the maze which is on the common at the E. of the town, one of the few surviving town mazes in the country. Close to the castle is the town museum, which is one of the most interesting in the county, especially for local material.

Much could be said of the surroundings of the town. Some 5 m. to the E., on the B1053, is **Hempstead.** Here was born the infamous Dick Turpin, a butcher's apprentice who became a robber and a murderer. The newly rebuilt tower of the church commemorates William Harvey (1578–1657), the discoverer of the circulation of the blood who lies buried here and whose image may be seen in the Church of St Andrew, a fine sculpture by Edward Marshall. Three m. to the NE. on the Ashdon road is **Hales Wood**, now a nature reserve, and most important of all, 1 m. to the W. is the great mansion of AUDLEY END.

ST OSYTH, *Essex* (11–TM1215). Here off the B1027, by one of the little creeks which run into the River Colne, are the remains of the 12th-cent. abbey which includes a gatehouse with beautiful flint and stone flushwork. St Osyth was the daughter of the first Christian king of East Anglia and near the site of the priory she established a nunnery before she met her death as a martyr in A.D. 653. A priory was established for the Augustinian canons by the Bishop of London, *c.* 1127. Later it became an abbey, which was eventually dissolved in 1539, to come into private hands. The gardens are open to the public throughout the summer, and the gatehouse during August (afternoons only).

While some of the early parts of the priory, to use the name by which it is generally known, may still be seen, it is the splendid gatehouse which is the most significant and impressive feature. In the richness and intricacy of its patterning it reminds the visitor of the gatehouse of St John's Abbey at COLCHESTER, built at about the same time in the 15th cent. Though lacking the latter's turrets and pinnacles, its battlemented top makes a satisfying conclusion to its façade. In the 16th cent. Abbot Vintoner added a mansion of brick with its own imposing gateway. When the building came into the possession of Lord Darcy in 1558 he made further additions to the structure, including the surviving south gable and clock tower, now with an 18th-cent. lantern. At the outbreak of the Civil War in 1642 the mansion was sacked.

The Church of SS. Peter and Paul is just to the SE. of the priory church. Though the mainly Perpendicular exterior with its 14th-cent. west tower is not without interest, it is the interior with its brick-built piers and arches which is most memorable. The Darcys are commemorated in two large wall monuments, *c.* 1580.

About ½ m. to the SE. is St Clair's Hall, a 14th-cent. H-shaped house with a central hall of unusual timbered construction. There are three Martello towers, a feature of the East Anglian coast, on the beach and on Beacon Hill.

St Osyth's priory gatehouse

A. F. Kersting

SALHOUSE BROAD, *Norfolk* (11–TG2714). Situated on the opposite (south) side of the River Bure to HOVETON BROADS, and therefore not far from WROXHAM. Discoveries in recent years have indicated that the nomadic settlers of the Middle Stone Age rested here. At the present time the area of reed-swamps provide the materials for the thatching of houses and ricks and a small local industry has developed.

Situated above the tree-fringed broad is the village of Salhouse; All Saints Church has a thatched roof and a 14th-cent. arcade. Salhouse Hall (1860–70) is a brick-built castellated mansion, symmetrical in design.

SALLE, *Norfolk* (11–TG1024), should be pronounced Saul and is famous for the Church of SS. Peter and Paul, considered by some the finest in the county. Its great size is out of all proportion to the size of the village as it now is, and it was built in the 15th cent., mainly by three local families, the Briggs, the Fountaynes and the Boleyns, though there is no proof that the body of Anne, wife of Henry VIII, is buried here. One wonders whether such a magnificent building would ever have been built to the glory of God in such a place at any other time.

The tower is 126 ft high and this sets the pattern of the church which is 171 ft long, with nave, aisles and transepts in proportion. The entire building dates from the 15th cent. and is in the Perpendicular style. There are two porches, of which the north is perhaps the finer with its intricate detailing. The interior is lofty and impressive. The chancel roofing is embellished with bosses, and the font is unique in having below the panels of the seven sacraments emblems of each of them. The font cover is a 12-ft tall canopy with 16 radial buttresses.

Another remarkable feature is the 15th-cent. pulpit complete with backboard and Jacobean canopy. More fine woodwork is to be seen in the carvings of the stalls and benches, with poppyheads and misericords. There are many brasses and monuments to the families chiefly associated with the church.

SANDRINGHAM, *Norfolk* (11–TF6928). Famous above all for Sandringham House, the residence of the Royal Family. The Royal Estate includes the 19th-cent. house, the park and the church, and the park is open to visitors when the Royal Family is not in residence. The house was purchased by Edward, Prince of Wales in 1861, in preference to HOUGHTON HALL, no doubt due to its more intimate atmosphere. It was much added to in the 1870s and again later in the century. The Norwich Gates, so called because they were made in NORWICH as a wedding present to the Prince from the County of Norfolk, were shown at the Great Exhibition of 1862.

The estates are extensive and include several parishes and farms, woodlands and other agricultural activities which are managed on behalf of the Royal Family. By tradition it is to this quiet spot the family comes each Christmas. It was here that King George V and King George VI died, the former in 1936 and the latter in 1952. King George VI was also born and baptized at Sandringham.

The Church of St Mary Magdalene is, of course, as the Royal Parish Church, of exceptional interest and attracts large numbers of visitors. The church was extensively restored in 1857 and has since been greatly enriched with many gifts, many from the Royal family themselves and others from their admirers. The organ was the last gift of King Edward VII and the roof of the nave, of English oak, was the gift of King George V. The unusual folding lectern was given by King George VI.

One of its most generous benefactors was the American Mr Rodman Wanamaker, among whose many gifts were the solid silver altar and reredos, presented to Queen Alexandra in 1911; the jewelled bible in the Sanctuary, presented in 1915; the silver processional cross, given in 1920 to commemorate the men from the estate who had died in the First World War; and the solid gold and richly jewelled set of communion plate presented to King George V in 1927.

The church contains many other items of exceptional interest. There are medallions in memory of King Edward VII, Queen Alexandra, King George V and Queen Mary, a richly panelled pulpit built of oak and covered in solid silver, a great deal of stained glass depicting many of the saints and at the foot of the tower a small baptistry which contains an exquisite Florentine marble font, presented by King Edward VII.

The chancel is richly decorated, both walls and ceiling being painted. It thus presents a striking contrast to the nave where the treatment is restrained and plain. Set into the floor of the chancel is a brass cross above which the coffins of members of the Royal Family have rested before being taken to WINDSOR. There is a tradition that no one may walk on this cross and even members of the choir divide as they pass it.

Outside the tower at the west end of the church is a remarkable Greek font over 1,000 years old and made from one solid block of marble.

SAWSTON, *Cambridgeshire* (11–TL4849). Among Sawston's claims to fame is the first village college built in 1930. The colleges were the idea of Mr Henry Morris and were intended to be regional centres serving a wide range of educational, social and cultural needs.

St Mary's Church is partly Norman and contains several interesting brasses.

Sawston Hall is the only Elizabethan mansion in the country to be built of clunch, the hard chalk which underlies the whole of the East Anglian outcrop at various places along its western edge. It was the material used in the Lady Chapel at ELY as well as in many of the cottages and farmbuildings along the Cambridgeshire and Norfolk borders. The Hall was probably built between 1557 and 1584. Queen Mary had spent a night in the original house in 1553 before it was burnt by a mob. The Hall, which has been occupied by the same family, the Huddlestones, for the past 400 years, is open to the public at various times during the year.

SAXMUNDHAM, *Suffolk* (11–TM3863). The town straddles the main IPSWICH to LOWESTOFT road and is some 6 m. from the coast. Its main street begins at the south end with cottages and Georgian houses and ends with the Post Office built in the 1950s. Along the way you will pass the Angel, the Bell Inn (1842) with Tuscan porch, and the former Town Hall of 1846. Just off the main road is the station and a level-crossing.

The Church of St John the Baptist, at the south end of the town, has been much restored, and under its hammer-beam roof are a number of good monuments by Nollekens, Westmacott and Thurlow who was himself buried in the churchyard. Near the church is Hurts Hall, built in 1893 in the Elizabethan style to replace an earlier mansion by Wyatt. The grounds contain the largest dovecot in Suffolk.

SAXTEAD GREEN, *Suffolk* (11–TM2664). Now an ancient Monument and in the care of the Ministry of Public Building and Works since 1951, Saxtead Green Mill is one of the finest examples of a traditional Suffolk post-mill. A windmill was recorded at Saxtead as long ago as 1309 and the present mill was certainly in existence in 1796, the miller at that time being one Amos Webber. Since that date the mill changed hands many times and was altered or rebuilt on a number of occasions.

The "buck" or body of the mill is set on a painted brick "roundhouse" and is rotated to face the sails into the wind by the "fantail" at the rear. Those who can climb the steep staircase into the buck will find the millstones and other machinery in perfect order and the entire mill is so well balanced that it may be revolved on its trackway at a touch.

The total height of the mill is 46 ft and the span of the sails almost 55 ft. Until the First World War the mill produced flour but then was given over to grinding foodstuffs for animals. It continued to work until 1947.

SCOLE, *Norfolk* (11–TM1579). As befits its position halfway between IPSWICH and NORWICH (on the A140), the village boasts a magnificent coaching inn, The White Hart, which dates from 1655. Built of brick with five Dutch gables along the facade and additional gables at the ends, the inn unfortunately lost its gallows sign which at one time stretched right across the main road. Despite modern traffic it is not too difficult to imagine yourself back in the great coaching days captured by Pollard and some of the other sporting painters of the times.

St Andrew's Church was damaged by fire in 1963 but has since been reconstructed with a modern interior and glass by Patrick Reyntiens, of COVENTRY and LIVERPOOL Cathedral fame.

SHELTON, *Norfolk* (11–TM2192). In this small village is one of the finest Perpendicular churches in Norfolk. It was built by the order of Sir Ralph Shelton who died in 1487 leaving instructions that it be completed as it had been begun. Thus the west tower is of flint in the Decorated style and the rest of red brick with stone dressings. The resulting effect is both novel and highly decorative, the magnificent windows of the aisles contrasting with those in the clerestory. Inside the church the tall arcading and the Perpendicular design of the panelling create an effect of airy spaciousness. A beautiful set of the the Royal Arms of William III may be seen above the tower arch, and monuments to the Shelton family are worth noting. There is an interesting memorial with a number of seated figures to Sir Robert Houghton, d. 1623, in the south aisle. The aisle windows have 15th-cent. stained glass.

SHERINGHAM, *Norfolk* (11–TG1543). Another in the chain of pleasant seaside resorts around the Norfolk coast. It faces N. and has a shingly beach with sand at low tide. Really there are two Sheringhams: Lower Sheringham is the resort and Upper Sheringham is the village built on the hillside above the coastal strip. As with CROMER and the other resorts Lower Sheringham developed at the end of the last century and the beginning of this. The hotels are typical of their time, but much newer is the cliff-top terrace dating from 1936, by which time the Roman Catholic Church of St Joseph was completed. This was an early work of Sir Giles Gilbert Scott and was commenced in 1910. St Peter's is a Victorian church, built in 1895 in the Early English style.

At the west end of the beach is the lifeboat, another in the series which ring the North Sea coast. One of the old boats is still on view close by.

Upper Sheringham's All Saints Church is mainly Perpendicular in style and has a fine 15th-cent. screen with an interesting overhang. Among the carved bench-ends is one representing a woman in a shroud. There are good brasses and a fine wall monument to Abbot Upcher by Bacon and Manning.

Sheringham Hall was built to the design of Humphry Repton, 1812–17. The grounds are certainly planned by him, although authorities think the house is more likely to be by his son. It may be seen by appointment on application in writing.

SHOTLEY, *Suffolk* (11–TM2533). On the peninsula formed by the Orwell and the Stour as they meet the sea between HARWICH and FELIXSTOWE. Such a place has always attracted mariners and it is appropriate that it is the site of H.M.S. *Ganges*, the Naval Training Centre where boys are prepared for a life at sea. The spectacular ceremony at which one lone cadet climbs to the top of the highest mast as "button-boy" is a famous occasion.

St Mary's Church, the nave of which is 14th-cent., was given a new chancel in 1745, elegantly

Georgian. From this time dates the panelling which includes paintings of Moses and Aaron, as well as the communion table. The churchyard has a cenotaph to those who fell in the World Wars with an inscription by Rudyard Kipling.

SIBLE HEDINGHAM, *Essex* (11–TL7734). The Black Prince, Paolo Uccello and the city of Florence are all brought to mind in this most unlikely place. Here was born Sir John Hawkwood, one of the most famous mercenaries of his time. He fought with the Black Prince at Poitiers, then moved on to Italy where he formed his own army which became so sought after that he was almost constantly fighting for one or other of the city states. Eventually Hawkwood became commander of the Florentine armies and when he died in 1394 he received a triumphant burial in that city's cathedral, where a fresco by Uccello shows Hawkwood mounted proudly in a great procession. Legend tells that his body was returned to England and he is commemorated by the monument in the south aisle of the village church (St Peter's, 14th-cent.)

Near the church is the White Horse Inn, 15th-cent., and the rectory, 18th-cent. Further along the main (Roman) road is Hawkwoods, the home of the Hawkwood family.

SNAPE, *Suffolk* (11–TM3959). Whoever has been delighted by Britten's *The Little Sweep* will have sung of Snape, up-river from ALDEBURGH and one of the homes of the June Festival. The magnificent concert hall built on the site of the old Maltings was the pride of Suffolk until the first night of the 1969 Festival when it was cruelly destroyed by fire. However, that it will rise again is certain. The Maltings themselves are a group of early industrial buildings whose appeal lies in their diversity. On the banks of the Alde, they were for many years the centre of a thriving trade and vessels from these quays plied the North Sea routes loaded with their cargoes of barley.

The Benedictines founded a priory here in 1155 and the village grew in importance even though it was some way from the sea. The decline of the Maltings Quay came with the development of road transport and the consequent lack of trade for the barges which were for many years a feature of the East Anglian coastal run. In 1966 the Aldeburgh Festival directors signed a 50-year lease to enable them to build the concert hall inside the shell of one of the great brick buildings.

As well as the June Festival the hall is used for concerts at other times and is the scene of a major Antiques Fair each September, one of the many which have proliferated in Suffolk's towns in recent years.

The Church of St John the Baptist contains a richly carved 15th-cent font. It was at the barrow on the S. of the road to Aldeburgh that Anglo-Saxon remains were found in the 19th cent. These were of similar date to those at SUTTON Hoo, not far away to the SW. Some of these items are now in the BRITISH MUSEUM.

SNETTISHAM, *Norfolk* (11–TF6834). On the KING'S LYNN to HUNSTANTON road, the A149, the village has a superb Decorated church, St Mary's. Originally cruciform, the demolition of the chancel has left the once central tower at the east end. The west end is very fine with a six-light window of exquisitely ornate design. At the corners are huge octagonal buttresses complete with miniature spires which are echoed in the pinnacles standing at each corner of the tower and supported by lighter flying buttresses.

Just to the W. of the church is the Old Hall made of carrstone and brick in the 17th cent. This is a distinguished-looking house with Dutch gables over the two bays. The village itself has an attractive sign, and there is another in the neighbouring village of **Shernborne**, 2 m. to the E., which commemorates the Coronation of King George V.

SNORINGS, THE, *Norfolk* (11–TF9533). The two villages of **Great** and **Little Snoring** share one of the most delightful of the many quaint names in which East Anglia abounds. They are on the by-road which joins the A1067 and the A148 to Little WALSINGHAM. Great Snoring's Church of St Mary shows a mixture of styles from Early English to Perpendicular. The entrance door (15th-cent.) has good tracery and inside the church is a large 17th-cent. Commandment Board with representations of Death, Heaven, Hell and Judgment, and a good set of Royal Arms dated 1688 but probably earlier.

The Rectory is rather remarkable: an elaborate building of 1525 which at one time belonged to the Sheltons, and was used as their manor house.

Little Snoring has in the Church of St Andrew an architectural curiosity. The present church must have replaced an earlier one, and made use of some of its fabric. The builders left the pre-Norman tower and commenced the new church several feet from it, re-assembling the south doorway of the old church in the newer "pointed" style. Inside is a circular Norman font with carved medallions, of a sturdy nobility.

SOHAM, *Cambridgeshire* (11–TL5973). Here in the early 7th cent. St Felix of Burgundy established an abbey a few years before Etheldreda founded ELY 5 m. to the NW. across the causeway.

Soham Abbey, however, unlike Ely, was not rebuilt after it had been destroyed by the Danes. St Andrew's, a great cruciform church of unusual interest, has some Norman work but also much from the succeeding centuries. The fine tower is Perpendicular, *c.* 1500, and the roof of the nave is interestingly constructed of hammer-beams alternating with tie-beams and queen posts.

SOMERLEYTON HALL, *Suffolk* (11–TM .4897). Somerleyton Hall was reconstructed in 1844 on the basis of an Elizabethan house owned by the Jernyngham family. It had been purchased by Sir Samuel Peto who created not only the Hall but an entire village with school, chapel and *cottages ornés*. The result was a building in the

Anglo-Italian style designed by John Thomas, a pupil of Barry whose work may be seen at **Shrubland.**

The Oak Parlour contains carvings by Grinling Gibbons and the beautiful dining-room has pictures by Wright of Derby, Ferdinand Bol (one of Rembrandt's pupils) and Clarkson Stanfield. In the house there are many big-game trophies testifying to the sporting interests of the Somerleyton family who have lived in the house since Sir Francis Crossley, Bt came there in 1861.

The gardens contain a large number of magnificent trees and shrubs, a number of walks and a maze of clipped yews.

SOUTHEND-ON-SEA, *Essex* (7–TQ8885). Though the great days of Southend as *the* holiday resort for Londoners have perhaps receded into the past with the coming of cheap Continental holidays, it still retains a unique place as the nearest resort to the capital. To this is due its popularity with the armies of day-trippers who invade the town in their coaches and trains, as well as with those who are able to sample its almost limitless tourist attractions for rather longer. Faster travel has also made it into a London "dormitory" for the thousands of commuters who make the journey each day.

Southend's history as a holiday resort dates from the early years of the last century when the villages of **Leigh** and **Prittlewell** commenced that expansion which now stretches along the mouth of the Thames estuary for some 7 m. The mention of the name Southend evokes an almost automatic response – "The Pier", and with its length of almost 1½ m. it is in fact the longest in the world – a far cry from the small wooden jetty erected in the 1830s. The pier with its railway, its amusements and its arcades caters for the fun-seeking tripper as well as serving as a port of call for the ships which make the voyage to London and the French ports. Excitement may be found, too, at the famous Kursaal, where every possible fairground device makes the season one long Bank Holiday fair.

The quieter side of life may be found at the resorts along the coast – at **Westcliff**, with its Edwardian bandstand, and at **Thorpe Bay** on the other side of the pier. As it has grown, so Southend has swallowed the villages which were once its neighbours. **Eastwood**, Leigh, Prittlewell, **Shoebury** and **Southchurch** once had separate identities, and each still retains something of its old character. Of the old churches and buildings which remain, the oldest are the ruins of Prittlewell Priory, founded *c.* 1110 in Priory Park by the Benedictines. The churches of Prittlewell, Southchurch, Eastwood and South Shoebury have Norman work and those of North Shoebury and Leigh are interesting though later.

Porters in Southchurch Road, Southend, is the Mayor's Parlour and is early 17th-cent. Southchurch Hall, now a library, was a moated manor house of the 14th cent., while Thorpe Hall along the boulevard is dated 1668. As might be expected in a town that is still growing, there are a number

of recent buildings, some worth noting: the bowling centre by the pier, the new Keddie's store in Warrior Square and some of the 20th-cent. churches in the various parishes for example.

All sports are catered for, angling and yachting, of course, and the Essex County cricket team plays in the town, as does the Southend soccer team. There is an airport of ever-increasing importance as a cross-Channel take-off point.

SOUTH WALSHAM BROAD, *Norfolk* (11–TG3813). An elongated broad which like that at RANWORTH now consists of an inner and outer section joined by a narrow channel. The outer broad is open to the public but the inner one is private. South Walsham is one of the likely centres of the Norfolk salt-making industry. Before the Norman Conquest salt helped the inhabitants preserve meat for the winter and in medieval times was used to preserve the herrings caught in the North Sea.

South Walsham village, not to be confused with the town of North Walsham, some 15 m. to the N., is famous for having two churches in adjoining churchyards. The Church of St Mary, Decorated, has an unusual font and a screen with an inscription commemorating John Gate, a serf who had been freed in 1437. A stained-glass window in the south aisle represents Astronomy and was made by R. O. Pearson in 1907.

There is an engraved slab to Richard de South Walsham, d. 1439, Abbot of St Benet's Abbey, which has a strange history. The slab has been used as the doorstep of a house in NORWICH and when the house was demolished it eventually found its way to its present position. The adjoining Church of St Lawrence is partly in ruins as a result of a fire in 1827.

SOUTHWOLD, *Suffolk* (11–TM5076). Southwold is a pleasant and dignified seaside town built on the cliffs overlooking the North Sea. With its triangular market square, its contrast between narrow streets and spacious greens around which are set cottages in flint, brick and colour wash, and the lighthouse which stands gleaming white in the very heart of the town in Stradbroke Road, Southwold presents vistas of quaint attractiveness. The greens came as the result of the fire of 1659 which caused the almost complete destruction of the town and led to more spacious planning when rebuilding was commenced, and the influence of the Dutch on the architecture may still be seen in the gables of the museum and in some of the cottages along Church Street.

From Norman times Southwold was a busy fishing port and the town developed in competition with its neighbours, WALBERSWICK and DUNWICH. With its beach of sand and shingle and its harbour, the town is now a lively little seaside resort with a small pier, competent local theatre company and the atmosphere of a rather more refined gaiety than may be found in its larger competitors.

Perhaps the chief pride of the town is the Parish Church of St Edmund built between 1430 and

Kenneth Scowen

Stansted Mountfitchet: a corner of the village

Reading Room on the cliff-top has a further collection of relics and models. From the cliffs there is an extensive view N. to KESSINGLAND and LOWESTOFT and S. to DUNWICH and ALDEBURGH and beyond to ORFORD Ness.

STANSTED MOUNTFITCHET, *Essex* (11–TL5124), will remain famous as the proposed site of London's third airport, but which launched a campaign so vigorous that the plan was abandoned (*see* FOULNESS). Nine hundred years ago it was the home of the Norman family from whom it derives its unusual full name. The origins of St Mary the Virgin's Church may be seen in the Norman arch of the chancel, and in the north and south doorways. The brick tower is 17th-cent. and carries a small spire. There are many monuments, including those to Hester Salusbury, d. 1614 and Sir Thomas Middleton, d. 1631, late Lord Mayor of London.

Traces of the Norman castle may be found near the 19th-cent. Church of St John the Evangelist. The tower mill is in exceptional condition. Stansted Hall (1871) is now a college and at Norman House is a popular wildlife park.

STEEPLE BUMPSTEAD, *Essex* (11–TL 6741). Another of the many East Anglian villages with delightful names. St Mary's Church has a Norman west tower with a brick top added later. There was a major restoration in 1880. The wall monument to Sir Henry Bendyshe, d. 1717, shows the knight in an elegant pose, framed by "barley-sugar" columns and an elaborate pediment. In the village which runs past the church is the restored Guildhall – an attractive half-timbered building dating from *c.* 1592. Moyns Park, to the SE., is a moated Elizabethan house with the remains of the Tudor south-west wing, half-timbered with three gables. To the SE. of the village is another house with Tudor remains – Latchleys.

STIFFKEY, *Norfolk* (11–TF9743). Whether it is pronounced as it is spelt, or as is often said, "Stewkey", is still a subject for argument. Famous for its cockles, it is a brick and flint village on the edge of the marshes between WELLS and BLAKENEY, and follows the course of the river of the same name. St John the Baptist's Church is mainly Perpendicular with a 13th-cent. chancel which was restored in 1848. A monument to Nathaniel Bacon, who owned the Hall, was erected before his death in 1615, and consequently does not include the date.

Stiffkey Hall was built by the Bacons and work commenced by 1578. Of the original large flint building only the west wing remains, together with some of the ruins of earlier sections destroyed by fire in the 18th cent., and a gatehouse dated 1604.

STOKE-BY-NAYLAND, *Suffolk* (11–TL 9836). A picturesque village with a fine group of half-timbered cottages near the Church of St Mary, the tower of which was one of Constable's

1460. With that of BLYTHBURGH this is the greatest of the churches of East Suffolk. It has a beautiful south porch, built of flint and stone arranged in the decorative patterns typical of the region, now empty of the statues which once stood there, and impressive carved entrance doors. The tower is 100 ft in height and on the roof should be noticed the *flèche*, a reproduction of the original Sanctus bell turret.

Careful restoration has given the interior of the church an unforgettable appearance of light and colour created by the large windows and the painted and gilded woodwork. The painted screen, dating from about 1500, is one of the most beautiful to be found in England. It runs across the full width of the church with magnificent figure paintings on the panels representing the Angels, Apostles and Prophets. The faces of Isaiah and David, were repainted by George. Richmond, R.A. who often stayed in the town. More fine painting and carving is to be seen in the pre-Reformation pulpit of the 15th cent. It was repainted in 1930 with money provided by the people of Southwold, Long Island, U.S.A., the settlement founded by travellers from Southwold in the 17th cent. The stalls and return stalls in the choir are finely carved with many grotesque heads including a jester, a monkey and strange bearded and winged figures. High above them all, are a lofty clerestory and a hammer-beam roof.

The museum which was founded in 1932, has a good collection of local interest, and the Sailors' favourite subjects. It is 120 ft high, built largely of brick with stone dressings, with four pinnacles that dominate the local landscape. The magnificently carved south doors, over 10 ft high, still have their figures intact. Many outstanding brasses include those to an anonymous lady of *c.* 1400; Sir William Tendring, 1408; Dame Katherine Howard, 1452; and some of the Mannock family of the 17th cent.

The Mannock home was Giffords Hall, a Tudor brick-built mansion with brick towers and a gateway bearing the family crest.

Nearer the church in School Street are the Guildhall and the Maltings, timber-framed buildings of the 16th cent. All that survives of Tendring Hall, designed by Sir John Soane in 1784, is a fishing lodge overlooking the lake.

STONDON MASSEY, *Essex* (7–TL5800). It was here that the great Elizabethan composer William Byrd (1543–1623) spent the last 30 years of his life. His home, Stondon Place, has been rebuilt at least twice since he settled here in about 1590. It is of interest to music lovers that two Elizabethan composers lived in Essex, the other being William Wilbye (*see* COLCHESTER). Though it is not known for certain where Byrd is buried he almost certainly rests in Stondon in accordance with his wish to be buried next to his wife.

The Church of SS. Peter and Paul has a Norman nave and chancel and a belfry, near the west end of the church. The pulpit is dated 1630 and has strapwork decoration.

STOW BARDOLPH, *Norfolk* (11–TF6205). A village associated with the Hare family whose home, Stow Hall was built in Tudor style in 1873. Holy Trinity Church contains an odd curiosity in the wax figure of Sarah Hare who died in 1744, like the Sleeping Beauty, from the prick of a needle. She is seen dressed in the clothes which she herself desired to wear, and being life-size she presents an almost horrific appearance. Other monuments in the church which has Norman work in the mainly Perpendicular tower, and was much rebuilt in 1848–9, include those to other members of the Hare family: Sir Ralph, d. 1623; Sir Thomas, d. 1693; and also to Susanna and Mary Hare.

STOWMARKET, *Suffolk* (11–TM0458), is a small market town with some light industry almost halfway between IPSWICH and BURY ST EDMUNDS on the A45 road, at the junction with the east–west road from FRAMLINGHAM to SUDBURY. The Church of SS. Peter and Paul contains a number of monuments to the Tyrell family, some grotesque carvings on the bench-ends and a rare wrought-iron wig stand dated 1675.

The railway station, built in 1849, is in the Victorian mock-Elizabethan style. The area around the market place has many buildings of the early 19th cent. and late Georgian periods while Stow Lodge Hospital in Onehouse Road was built as a workhouse *c.* 1777.

It was to Stowmarket that John Milton came to visit his tutor Thomas Young, who lived in the vicarage and is buried in the church near the lectern; here, too, George Crabbe spent some of his schooldays. The Tyrell family lived at Lynton House between the church and the site of the railway station.

The Abbot's Hall Museum of Rural Life in East Anglia is an admirable and essential collection, a visit to which will take you back to the days when farming was a simple family affair and when individual craftsmanship was of a high order.

STRADBROKE, *Suffolk* (11–TM2373). Possibly the birthplace of Robert Grosseteste. Though of humble family he was educated at OXFORD and Paris and in 1235 became the Bishop of Lincoln. Before this he had been rector of the Franciscans at Oxford where his beliefs led him into conflict with the Pope, the King and the monks of CANTERBURY and of LINCOLN itself. A prodigious writer of books on theology, philosophy, mathematics, agriculture and other subjects, he was a Greek and Latin scholar whose influence was felt for many years after his death in 1253.

The Church of All Saints has been much restored but its west tower is 15th-cent. and its turret stairs are higher than the main part of the tower itself. A screen with paintings of two kings is of excellent quality.

Hepwood Lodge Farm has features of Gothic Revival style and there is a well-designed modern school.

SUDBURY, *Suffolk* (11–TL8741). Sudbury on the River Stour is a very ancient borough, mentioned in the Anglo-Saxon Chronicle, and formerly an important cloth and market town. The "Eatanswill" of *Pickwick Papers*, the town is also famous as the birthplace of Thomas Gainsborough (1727–88). On Market Hill stands a bronze statue to the great painter, whose house nearby has been adapted to serve partly as a memorial and partly as a local art centre. The house was originally Tudor but the fine Georgian front was added by the painter's father, a local cloth merchant, shortly before Thomas was born. After studying in London the artist married and returned to Sudbury, shortly afterwards settling at IPSWICH. Success as a portrait painter led him to move to BATH where he very soon established himself in the first rank. In 1768 he was invited to become one of the founder members of the new Royal Academy in London, the President of which was his great rival Sir Joshua Reynolds. Though a portrait painter by profession, Gainsborough was by inclination a painter of landscapes and also a musician of considerable talent. His nephew, Gainsborough Dupont, was his only recorded pupil, some of whose best works have been attributed to the master himself. Gainsborough House contains a number of pictures by the artist, and many relics of his period. He died in 1788 and is buried in KEW Churchyard.

St Gregory's, at the west end of the town, was rebuilt *c.* 1365 on a very ancient foundation by

Archbishop Simon of Sudbury, the Archbishop of Canterbury who was murdered in 1381 at the time of the Peasants' Revolt. His head is preserved in the vestry. The telescopic font-cover is one of the finest in the country.

The Parish Church of St Peter, mainly late 15th-cent., on Market Hill was the chapel of ease of St Gregory's and an important wool church; it contains an interesting painting of Moses and Aaron c. 1730 by Robert Cardinall, a local painter; and a 15th-cent. embroidered velvet funeral pall. All Saints', another 15th-cent. wool church, has a painting showing the family tree of the Eden and Waldegrave families.

The Corn Exchange on Market Hill is an excellent example of early Victorian civic building.

Past Gainsborough House at No. 46 Gainsborough Street, you come to Stour Street with The Chantry and Salter's Hall, a merchant's house, both 15th-cent. Note the half-timbering and corner posts of the former and the fine carving on the latter.

SUTTON, *Suffolk* (11–TM3046). High on the heathland, this was the site of the Sutton Hoo ship burial, the great archaeological discovery made in 1939. Eleven mounds had stood on this spot for 1,300 years and the fourth mound to be opened revealed the impression in the sand of a ship and a priceless collection of relics of the Wuffinga dynasty of East Anglian kings. The ship was a rowing boat 89 ft long, the cenotaph to a great king, and the treasures it contained may now be seen in the BRITISH MUSEUM, London, including magnificent golden jewellery, Merovingian coins, Swedish armour and Byzantine silverware. Together they form what has been described by Norman Scarfe as "probably the most momentous single revelation of the Dark Ages ever made".

All Saints' Church once had a tower, but it fell in 1642. The early-15th-cent. font is octagonal, with an unusual narrow top.

Not far away is the American air base, R.A.F. Bentwaters, whose powerful jets contrast violently with the peace in which the Anglo-Saxon vessel lay for centuries beneath the earth.

SWAFFHAM, *Norfolk* (11–TF8109), a busy market town situated at the junction of the A47 and A1065 roads. Legend tells of the "Pedlar of Swaffham" who dreamed that if he travelled to London he would find treasure. Travel he did, and met a man who told him that he, in his turn, had had a dream that if he went to a village called Swaffham he would find treasure beneath a certain tree. The pedlar returned home, dug away and found riches which enabled him to build the north aisle of the great Church of SS. Peter and Paul. The pedlar is to be seen in the village sign, in a monument in the market place and in several carvings in the church.

The little town has a triangular market place with a "market cross" – in this case not a cross but a domed rotunda built in 1783 by the Earl of Oxford. A number of good Georgian houses may

be seen, including School House and the neighbouring Headmaster's House, the Assembly Room and several others. The Methodist Church dates from the early 19th-cent., the Shire Hall from 1839.

The Church of SS. Peter and Paul is 15th-cent. with a grand tower completed in 1510. On the roof is a graceful *flèche*. The west doorway is deeply recessed with a great window above and the south porch has its own hammer-beam roof. Inside the church the eye is held by the fine arcading and in particular by the great double hammer-beam roof with angels, open-winged, at the ends of the brackets. The Swaffham Pedlar, together with his dog, may be seen at the end of the prayer desk, a reminder of the north aisle which he had caused to be built at about the same time that the tower was completed (1510). The church possesses a large library of ancient books which may be seen on application.

SWANTON MORLEY, *Norfolk* 11–TG 0117). Beside the East DEREHAM road (the B1147) is a plot of land (National Trust) with the remains of the cottage in which lived the ancestors of Abraham Lincoln (*see* HINGHAM). The house belonging to Richard Lincoln, one of the family, has been converted into the Angel Inn. All Saints Church was begun sometime before 1378 and appears to have been completed about 50 years later. At once the attention is taken by the west tower, which has large bell-openings at the top and small rectangular sound holes below. Beneath is a fine doorway and at the sides the aisles of the church extend from the base, each having tall west windows with delicate tracery.

THAXTED, *Essex* (11–TL6131). The lofty spire of the church and the tower windmill are perhaps the first things the visitor notices as he arrives at this small town on the A130 between GREAT DUNMOW and SAFFRON WALDEN. The Church of St John the Baptist is one of the largest and grandest of all the Essex churches and its great size (183 ft long with a spire of almost exactly the same height), indicates the importance of the town in earlier days. It was in fact one of the centres of the cloth trade, and before that an important centre for cutlery.

St John's is an uncommonly fine example of a church which later restoration has dealt with kindly. The exterior is full of interesting detail: architectural, as in the battlements, buttresses and pinnacles; and sculptural, as in the carvings on the north porch and the north transept, etc. The interior of the church, due to the clear glass and use of white paint, is full of light and air. The tall arcades (*c.* 1340) were followed by various additions made in the following centuries and it may be noted that all the roofs are original. The font is unusual in that it is completely encased. The pulpit dates from the late 17th cent., the same period as the screens of the north and south chapels. Though the greater part of the glass in the church is clear there are some notable pieces of 14th- to 16th-cent. stained glass.

Though Thaxted has many attractive smaller houses and cottages, most of them traditionally timber-framed with plaster covering and pargeting, the most memorable building apart from the church itself is the 15th-cent. Guildhall. This is a three-storied building, each story overhanging the one below, the ground floor being open on three sides. Its restoration in the present century has hardly affected its medieval appearance. Near the Guildhall are some of the town's most picturesque houses, notably the Recorder's House.

S. of the church is a tower windmill built in 1805, on a site occupied by mills for centuries past.

Horham Hall, to the SW., is a Tudor brick mansion with a remarkable large bay window in its great hall.

THETFORD, *Norfolk* (11–TL8783). It hardly seems possible that this small market town on the River Thet and centrally placed at the junctions of no less than eight main roads was at one time the cathedral city of East Anglia. In the 11th cent. there were already 13 churches; by the time of Edward III there were 20. In addition there were at least four monastic houses and other buildings of some importance. Yet of all this splendour only three churches remain today and any number of attractive and worthwhile buildings of later date.

With the Dissolution Thetford seemed to come to a halt. The seat of the early Kings of East Anglia, it was the site of important Anglo-Saxon settlements. The castle Mound, still prominent, was the site of the Castle, demolished in 1173. Just 100 years before, the See of East Anglia had moved to Thetford from NORTH ELMHAM before it finally settled at NORWICH in 1095. Suddenly expansion stopped and Thetford lay dormant until around 1820 an attempt was made to make it a spa. But it soon slipped back into obscurity, and Thetford has remained a quiet little town, though recent years have seen an expansion of industrial and shopping facilities.

Perhaps its most famous citizen was Thomas Paine, the author of the *Rights of Man*. Paine was born in White Hart Street in 1737, son of a Quaker farmer. He left his wife in 1774 to settle in America where in 1776 he published *Common Sense*, a plea for American Independence. It was shortly after his return to England that he published the *Rights of Man* (1790–2), his most famous work, which sold 1½ million copies in England alone. Its notoriety made it necessary for him to flee to France where he wrote *The Age of Reason*. 1802 saw his return to America where seven years later he died in New York.

Thetford's churches are St Cuthbert's, St Mary-the-Less and St Peter's, all of which have been much restored and rebuilt. The Roman Catholic Church of St Mary and the Congregational church both date from the early 19th cent. Though the churches are not of great architectural interest the monastic remains are, and include those of the Cluniac Priory of Our Lady, founded in 1103, where at one time the Howard tombs were, later to be transferred to FRAMLINGHAM in Suffolk. Among the other scattered but impressive ruins are those of the Augustinian Priory of St Sepulchre and the Nunnery of St George. The Grammar School in London Road occupies the first site of the Cluniac priory.

In a town full of interesting streets and buildings space should be found for the timber-framed Ancient House, now a museum. Its main room has a fine ceiling of moulded and decorated Tudor beams. The early-16th-cent. Bell Hotel is also half-timbered and shows the early wattle and daub construction in a section which has been allowed to remain on view. The Dolphin Inn is dated 1694 and is of brick and flint. Behind the Guildhall, rebuilt in 1900, is the former lock-up and in Old Market Street stands the Old Gaol, a flint building dated 1816. King's House in King Street carries the Royal Arms as a token of the fact that an earlier house on the same site was used by King James I.

A statue to Thomas Paine stands opposite the Bell.

THEYDONS, THE, *Essex* (7–TQ4598; Theydon Bois). **Theydon Bois,** once a Norman forest, is now being eroded by the spread of the capital city. To the NE. **Theydon Garnon** has a church of particular interest. The tower is dated 1520 and the aisle 1644. The interior is attractive and contains a fine pulpit, some good brasses and monuments to the various members of the Archer family. The third village, to the E. of Garnon, is **Theydon Mount,** with a brick church of 1611–14 built on the hill by the Smith family, who are commemorated in a series of monuments and who owned the local mansion. Hill Hall has been described as one of the most important earlier Elizabethan houses in England. It was built by Sir Thomas Smith, a lecturer at CAMBRIDGE, who died in 1578. Inside the house, which is now run as an open prison for women, is a series of wall paintings of exceptional interest on the theme of Cupid and Psyche.

THORNEY, *Cambridgeshire* (10–TF2804). The most northerly of the Fenland islands, it was the site of a monastery founded at the end of the 7th cent. and destroyed by the Danes. Here Hereward the Wake made one of his last stands against William the Conqueror whose victory saw the rebuilding of the abbey. Much of it was removed at the Dissolution to provide building material for Corpus Christi College, CAMBRIDGE. All that remains is the tall west front and the nave incorporated in the Parish Church of SS. Mary and Botolph which was restored by Inigo Jones.

Many of the buildings in the village as well as the terraced houses were built to the order of the Dukes of Bedford, who owned the village and the abbey lands and were also responsible for much of the drainage of the surrounding fens.

THORNHAM MAGNA, *Suffolk* (11–TM 1072). Charles II stayed in this village with the Killigrews, subject of one of Van Dyck's portraits. Later it came into the hands of Lord Henniker (d. 1821), whose magnificent tomb by Kendrick may be seen in the Church of St Mary. The church itself was much restored in the last century.

About 1 m. away is the village of **Thornham Parva** with a small thatched church dating from Norman times. Its most interesting feature is the painted retable of *c.* 1300. The painting is in its original frame and contains a Crucifixion and eight saints, four to the left and four to the right. The figures are elegant in design and have a gesso background worked in various patterns. The painting was discovered in Lord Henniker's stables in 1927.

THORPENESS, *Suffolk* (11–TM4759). Thorpeness was planned as a seaside resort, a kind of garden city of the coast, by Stuart Ogilvie at the beginning of the present century. In 1910 a 65-acre lake known as the Mere was made, to be followed by the country club and the various houses which make up the estate. An inn and a small shopping centre are, like all the other buildings, built in a mock-Tudor style. One of its most fantastic creations is "The House in the Clouds", a water tower disguised as a house. Close to the tower is a fine early-19th-cent. windmill which was brought from **Aldringham**. Aldringham itself has in the Church of St Andrew an excellent 15th-cent. font and a Stuart Holy Table.

TILBURY, *Essex* (7–TQ6376), is an important port opposite GRAVESEND, the first of the Port of London docks on the Thames estuary. It was here that the first mission to the East Saxons was arranged by Bishop Cedd, and it was at Tilbury that Queen Elizabeth I came to address her troops as they prepared to face the Spaniards. Tilbury Fort, with its classically columned gateway, was built *c.* 1670 as a defence against other attackers, the Dutch and French, and ironically was designed by a Dutchman in 17th-cent. French style. It was in fact built *after* the Dutch had landed at **East Tilbury** in 1667. The huge docks have been steadily developed since the first installations were built in the 1880s.

At East Tilbury is St Catherine's Church, situated above the Coal House Fort of 1866. The church dates from Norman times; the fort was built by Gordon of Khartoum. The Bata shoe factory (1932) is in the style of the company's factories in Czechoslovakia. Recent additions include its recreation centre (1957) and near the docks a very advanced British Rail signal box.

TOLLESBURY, *Essex* (11–TL9510). On the estuary of the River Blackwater, Tollesbury is a fishing village popular with wildfowlers. It is also a centre of the Essex oyster trade. There is a charming square with old houses and a lock-up, placed in the corner of the churchyard. St Mary's has a tower and nave of Norman date, though the tower was buttressed in *c.* 1600. The 18th-cent. octagonal font has a strange carved inscription to

remind visitors of a fine imposed on its builder. Kempe stained glass, a good brass and a cartouche monument add to its interest.

Tollesbury Hall is timber-framed and dates from the 15th cent. One m. away is Bourchier's Hall, the home of the holders of the manor for over 240 years (1329–1570). The house is beautifully plastered and has a particularly interesting interior. To its W. is Guisnes Court, now a country club, which contains a fireplace taken from Bourchiers.

TOLLESHUNTS, THE, *Essex* (11–TL9011; Tolleshunt Major). A group of three villages around the B1026, MALDON to COLCHESTER road. **Tolleshunt Knights** is now associated with the Orthodox church which uses the old parish church of All Saints, which does in fact contain a much damaged figure of a knight holding his heart in his hands.

Tolleshunt Major is so in name but not in size. The name comes from the tenant at the time of Domesday. The Church of St Nicholas is remarkable for the large brick west tower added in the middle of the 16th cent. by the owner of nearby Beckingham Hall. It shows that beautiful diaper patterning typical of the county. The Hall itself is not especially important, but to its 16th-cent. structure was added a brick wall to the N. which contains an interesting gatehouse. It can be dated because there is a piece of the panelling of the house in the VICTORIA AND ALBERT MUSEUM, London, and is marked 1546, shortly after Stephen Beckingham obtained the manor from Henry VIII.

Tolleshunt D'Arcy is the largest of the three villages and its Hall dates from 1500, with additions from the following centuries. The Hall is surrounded by a moat crossed by an Elizabethan bridge dated 1585. D'Arcy House has a fine Georgian front. The Church of St Nicholas is Perpendicular in style with a battlemented west tower. Once inside, the visitor will not fail to admire the coved ceiling of the nave painted in 1897 by the Rev. E. Geldart, and also the excellent collection of brasses dating from the late 14th cent. The owners of the manor, Sir Thomas D'Arcy (d. 1593) and his wife may be seen as kneeling figures in a monument.

TRIMLEY, *Suffolk* (11–TM2736). Another case of two churches sharing the same churchyard. The church of Trimley St Martin is now mostly 19th-cent. That of St Mary has a ruined 14th-cent. west tower with a fine medieval doorway. Inside is a cartoon by an Italian artist showing the Madonna with the Infant Christ and John the Baptist.

The villages themselves are on the main road from IPSWICH to FELIXSTOWE and subject to ever-increasing traffic between the two towns, both of which are ports dealing with heavy freight.

Not far away is Grimston Hall, a farm-house where was once the home of Thomas Cavendish (1560–92), the second Englishman to circumnavigate the globe. Cavendish sailed with Raleigh,

Grenville and then set off from PLYMOUTH in July 1586 and returned two years and two months later with a ship full of treasures. Three years later he set out again but died off Ascension Island, leaving his ship to return home in 1593.

TRUMPINGTON, *Cambridgeshire* (10–TL 4455). The Church of SS. Mary and Michael contains a memorial brass to Sir Roger de Trumpington dated 1289 which is thus the second oldest brass in the country. The earliest recorded brass is that to Sir John Daubernoun in the Church of Stoke d'Abernon, Surrey, which is dated 1277. The church itself is elaborate and was much restored by Butterfield in 1876. Another monument of importance, though much more recent, is an inscribed tablet, an early work by Eric Gill dated 1914. Four reliefs by the same artist may be seen at the foot of the village cross, erected to commemorate the First World War.

Anstey Hall, built *c.* 1700, and Trumpington Hall slightly later in date, are among other attractions in the village which also boasts a 16th-cent. inn, The Green Man.

TRUNCH, *Norfolk* (11–TG2834). The Church of St Botolph is Perpendicular and is famous for one thing above all, its hexagonal font canopy. However, it is but one remarkable feature in a very interesting church. The nave roof has hammer-beams with spandrels filled with elaborately carved tracery, the priest's door porch is remarkable for having a buttress right in the middle of its roof and the beautiful carving of the screen, even though the paintings are rather faded, is a delight.

But it is to the font that the visitor will return, for here is one of the only four font canopies in England. Norfolk has another, at St Peter Mancroft, NORWICH. It may best be described as a crown set upon a hexagonal shaft which is in turn supported by six columns. The columns are full of intricately woven carvings which twine up to the second stage; this has six panels which were at one time probably painted. Finally comes the canopied top, richly crocketed (i.e. with a repeating pattern of twisting leaves), and with a finial on the top. The font which is enclosed by this astonishing construction is itself quite unremarkable.

The Manor House is ½ m. to the E. – a farm of Elizabethan or Jacobean date with interesting chimneys.

UFFORD, *Suffolk* (11–TM2953). A village by the ford of Uffa, an Anglo-Saxon chieftain. Its greatest treasure is the spectacular font-cover in the Church of St Mary. Incredibly elaborate, with a profusion of intricately carved detail it is 18 ft high above the font. Even Dowsing, whose sorry record of destruction has often been mentioned, remarked in 1643: "There is a glorious cover over the font . . . all gilt over with gold." Little now remains of the original gilding and coloured gesso-work. The roof of the church has alternate hammer-beams and tie-beams and many finely carved bench-ends.

A. F. Kersting

Waltham Abbey

Contrasting with the almshouses built in 1690 and some houses of similar and slightly later date is an estate of well-designed modern houses on the site of Ufford Place.

WALBERSWICK, *Suffolk* (11–TM4974). You may come to Walberswick by road from BLYTH-BURGH or on the ferry which plies across the estuary of the Blyth from SOUTHWOLD. Once one of the prosperous towns of the East Coast, its decline followed an all too familiar pattern. The ruins of St Andrew's, of which the west tower and the south aisle remain, are an indication of its former importance. Now it is a select resort, famous for sailing, with fine walks across the heaths and along the coast.

It was much painted by Wilson Steer early in this century. The estuary is untidy, but the sight of the ferry, a simple rowing boat, as it crosses to and fro takes you right back to the paintings of the great Dutchmen, van Goyen and van der Velde.

WALPOLE ST PETER, *Norfolk* (11–TF 5016), a marshland village which lies between the A17 and A47 roads, near the county boundary and the River Nene. The great Church of St Peter has been known as the "Queen of the Marshes" and in this respect it is worthy to be compared with those of ELY and BLYTHBURGH. Its quality is at once apparent in the lovely south porch with its fine doorway surrounded by panelling, buttresses, niches and window. The church is battlemented throughout and it is evident that the chancel was added to make the church over 160 ft long and even grander in design. It is in the Early Perpendicular style throughout, and though the west tower is less elaborate than the rest of the church it is none the less impressive. Elsewhere there is a profusion of sensitive detail, even in the pinnacles at the east end of the nave.

Under the east end of the chancel is a passage used for church processions as the chancel extends right to the church boundaries. The inside of the church is noted for the screen, c. 1610, which extends the full width of the church. It contains a rare example of a "hudd" or "hood". This was a movable shelter, like a sentry box, which was used for funerals held in inclement weather. In a church full of interest the chandelier (1701), the octagonal font (16th-cent.), the tall Jacobean font cover, the Jacobean pulpit, the brass eagle lectern and the carvings on the stalls are all of high quality.

WALSINGHAM, *Norfolk* (11–TF9336). Of the two Walsinghams it is Little Walsingham which is the more important because of its long history as a centre of pilgrimage. It was in 1061 that the Lady Richeld saw a vision which commanded her to build a replica of the House of Nazareth in which Gabriel appeared to the Virgin Mary. Accordingly a simple hut was built which contained a wooden statue of the Virgin and Child and to this shrine came pilgrims in their thousands, from simple people to the kings and noblemen of the land. On their journey they would stop at wayside shrines and the last of these to be reached before Walsingham itself was at **Houghton St Giles** where the Slipper Chapel (now Roman Catholic) was the spot where many of the more devout pilgrims would remove their shoes, to walk the final mile barefoot. During the next century a priory of Augustinian (or Black) Canons was founded and incorporated the shrine in its church. Henry III and Edward I were among the visitors and by the 15th cent. the priory had become the richest in the county, except for that at NORWICH itself. At the time of the Reformation the shrine, the priory and an additional friary founded by the Franciscans were all destroyed.

In 1897 the cult was revived and the New Shrine was built between 1931 and 1937. The remains of earlier buildings include the east wall of the church, which now is a very handsome archway with elaborate buttresses and turrets, and the south wall of the refectory. One room of the priory, which is open to visitors, is intact. The gatehouse led from the church into the town.

The friary ruins are by the FAKENHAM road and are now private property. Some of its buildings still remain. Of the shrine itself nothing, of course, remains today. It is almost certain that it stood to

the N. of the north aisle of the priory church.

The village itself is charming, with many picturesque buildings of the 16th cent. and later. The High Street runs N.–S. and at its foot is the market place, or Friday Market with St Hugh's House, a prominent red-brick Georgian building. N. of the gatehouse is the square or Common Place containing a 16th-cent. conduit, or pumphouse, made of brick and octagonal.

The Church of St Mary, restored after damage by fire in 1961, is in the Decorated and Perpendicular styles. The font is deservedly famous as one of the most perfect in the entire county. It stands on three steps, the topmost of which is in the shape of a Maltese cross, a not uncommon feature. The stem is finely carved and the bowl of the font shows the seven sacraments and the Crucifixion. There is a second font in the church, which is less fine and lacks the Jacobean cover of the other. There are some good brasses and monuments, including a famous modern sculpture, *The Risen Christ* by Sir Jacob Epstein.

Great Walsingham, 1 m. to the N. contains St Peter's, a fine church with a set of magnificently carved benches. To the N. of the church is Berry Hall, an Early Tudor house, and other domestic buildings of merit.

WALTHAM ABBEY, *Essex* (6–TL3800). Here, only 16 m. from London, is one of the finest surviving examples of Norman architecture in the country, worthy to be ranked with DURHAM and NORWICH, even though on a smaller scale. In fact, though the great nave, or rather what remains of it, is 12th-cent., the abbey was actually begun before the Conquest, by Earl Harold, an admirer of the Norman manner. It had been founded as a collegiate church in 1030 and was consecrated by Harold on 3 May 1060, some years earlier than the great abbey at Westminster, built by his brother-in-law, Edward the Confessor.

The present church of The Holy Cross and St Lawrence is less than one half of the original buildings much of which were destroyed after the Dissolution. What has survived is a magnificent Norman nave, whose sturdy columns support a gallery and a clerestory. The circular piers are, like those in the cathedrals mentioned earlier, patterned with deeply cut spiral or zigzag grooves while the arches above the heavy Norman caps all have zigzag ornaments.

The present tower was added c. 1556–68 to replace the original crossing tower which had collapsed. It features chequer-work in flint and stone and strong diagonal buttresses. The present church ends with the east wall which was rebuilt in 1859 by W. Burges. The windows have stained glass by Sir Edward Burne-Jones while the reredos was sculpted by T. Nicholls after 1876. Like the altar which is carved from American black walnut it was presented by Mrs Edenborough.

In the Lady Chapel may be seen the remains of a 14th-cent. painting on the east wall over the altar. The brilliantly designed ceiling of the nave was painted by Sir Edward Poynter in 1860.

Among the tombs contained in the church is that to Sir Edward Denny (d. 1600) and his wife and an elaborately carved alabaster monument to Captain Sir Robert Smith, d. 1697. One of the two slabs of Purbeck marble in the north aisle is from a tomb of an abbot, and the other has been held to be from the tomb of King Harold himself.

Little remains of the abbey buildings which were to the north of the nave. Some say that Harold was buried in what would have been the chancel and the spot is marked on the grass. A small section of the vaulted cloister is all that remains of the convent buildings.

Until 1540 the church organist was the great composer, Thomas Tallis (1505–85). In addition to Tallis, Essex was the home of two other of our greatest English composers, William Byrd (*see* STONDON MASSEY) and John Wilbye (*see* COL-CHESTER).

WALTON-ON-THE-NAZE, *Essex* (11–TM2421).

A seaside resort with fine sands and excellent sea-bathing due in part to its situation on the Ness which stretches into the North Sea. The red crag cliffs contain many fossils of interest to the geologist.

The resort itself was developed at the beginning of the 19th cent., and Marine Parade, then the Crescent, was built in 1832. Hotels, villas and cottages soon followed. There is a pier, the Naze Tower, originally built as a beacon in 1720, and a Martello tower.

WELLS-NEXT-THE-SEA, *Norfolk* (11–TF9143),

is a village, a small port and a seaside resort, on the North Coast road, the A149. There are three focal points, the church, the Buttlands and the quay. St Nicholas' Church is the Victorian (1880s) rebuilding of the original church destroyed by fire in 1879, and stands just S. of the large green known as the Buttlands, an attractive green lined by trees and surrounded by Georgian houses. The upper end of the green leads to the quay through narrow streets like the "rows" at GREAT YARMOUTH and the "scores" at LOWESTOFT.

The quay still sees activity with local boats as well as some pleasure craft, but the beach to its W. is perhaps more popular nowadays. The little bathing area is about 1 m. from the village and is locally known as Abraham's Bosom, a name which may owe something to its earlier use as a harbour. Only 2 m. to the W. is HOLKHAM HALL with the National Trust reserves at Scolt Head and BLAKENEY some 6 to 8 m. on either side of the village.

WENDENS AMBO, *Essex* (11–TL5136).

Its unusual name is only part of its charm, and comes from the joining of the two parishes of Great and Little Wenden in the 17th cent. It lies almost on the western boundary of the county, not far from AUDLEY END and SAFFRON WALDEN. St Mary the Virgin's Church is finely placed, and its sturdy Norman tower, surmounted by a later spire, has a Norman doorway made with Roman bricks

which shows how the conquerors of one era made use of the material left by the conquerors of another. There is a 15th-cent. pulpit and a 16th-cent. domed font-cover. Perhaps the most interesting feature is the cycle of medieval paintings discovered in 1934 on the theme of the life of St Margaret.

WESTHALL, *Suffolk* (11–TM4280).

A small village off the HALESWORTH to BECCLES road which has a church of more than usual interest. It is that of St Andrew and it shows continuous development from Norman times through to later centuries. The present south aisle was once the Norman nave, and until the 13th cent. when the west tower was added there was a fine Norman west façade. Similar discoveries may be made in many other parts of this fascinating church. There is a fine seven-sacrament font, which still retains traces of its original colouring and gesso decoration. An elaborately carved screen shows paintings of a number of saints and biblical characters. A tomb in the south-east corner of the south aisle commemorates the late Nicholas Bohun, d. 1602, and over it is an unusual brass with a genealogical table of the Bohun family.

Westhall Hall, which was rebuilt in the 1870s, has typical Dutch/Flemish gables.

WESTHORPE, *Suffolk* (11–TM0469).

The Church of St Margaret has a long history, but what survives is mainly in 14th- and 15th-cent. styles. There is a 14th-cent. parclose screen with intriguing patterns in the arches. The Barrow Chapel contains a white marble monument to Maurice Barrow who left £500 to be spent on a tomb in 1666.

Westhorpe Hall, a Georgian farm-house, still has a Tudor bridge over the moat. It was the residence of Henry VII's daughter, Mary Tudor. Her early marriage to Louis XII of France was short-lived and she then became the wife of Charles Brandon, the Duke of Suffolk. She is buried in St Mary's Church, BURY ST EDMUNDS.

WEST STOW, *Suffolk* (11–TL8170).

Though there is nothing particularly special about the Church of St Mary, some of the panels which formed part of its painted screen are now in London's VICTORIA AND ALBERT MUSEUM.

West Stow Hall, between the A1101 and B1106, is remarkable for its red-brick gatehouse dating from the 1520s and reminiscent of others in Suffolk, Essex and Cambridgeshire. Rather severe turrets flank a centre section with a stepped gable, which includes the arms of Mary Tudor, sister of Henry VIII, who died in 1533 (*see* WESTHORPE and BURY ST EDMUNDS). Little survives of the original house but in the room above the gateway there are some famous Elizabethan wall paintings representing the four ages of man, together with a hunting scene.

WICKEN FEN, *Cambridgeshire* (11–TL5770).

Wicken Fen is a Nature Reserve which belongs to the National Trust. It consists of three main areas:

Sedge Fen, Adventurers' Fen and St Edmund's Fen. Sedge Fen is open to the public and the visitor, having left his car in the car park, is advised to obtain the excellent guide book from the Keeper's Cottage. Once you cross the foot-bridge over Wicken Lode and start to follow the recommended route round the fen you enter an-other world in which only the cries of birds and busyings of insect life disturb the silence. The "lodes", or waterways are the ancient canals which served not only to irrigate the land but also acted as the highways through the flat fenland landscape. The fens themselves were crossed on foot through the "droves" and in ancient times the inhabitants cut the sedge for thatching and animal litter and dug into the ground for the abundant supplies of peat. Changing ways of life altered the original pattern of vegetation and in recent years the National Trust has tried to re-establish the old sedge fields without at the same time losing the rich variety of flora and fauna which had grown up.

There is thus a great variety of vegetation not only on the banks but also in the water of the lodes. A tower hide enables the visitor to study the rich bird life of the fen and the brick pits dug deep into the clay sub-soil have become pools containing numerous plants, insects and animals. A once derelict windmill has been restored and once again is used to pump water into the dykes. It stands as a symbol of the hundreds of mills which were once used to drain the fens. The complete walk of a little over 2 m. is full of scenes of strange

natural beauty and interest and the visitor cannot fail to be captivated by the spell of this unique Nature Reserve with its echoes of the past and its peaceful balance of the elements of land, water and sky.

WIMPOLE, *Cambridgeshire* (10–TL3350). Placed at the end of a 2 m. long avenue of elms is Wimpole Hall, almost certainly the finest mansion in the county. The original central block was built *c.* 1640 for Sir Thomas Chicheley. Later owners added to the property and when the house was taken over by the Earl of Hardwick, the Lord Chancellor, in 1740 major alterations were made, giving the building much as we see it today.

Perhaps the most impressive room is the chapel with its outstanding painted decorations in the Italian style by Sir James Thornhill, the father-in-law of William Hogarth. The wrought-iron altar rails *c.* 1730–5 and the pulpit are also worthy of attention. The library and gallery precede the Yellow Drawing Room, the work of Sir John Soane, *c.* 1793, an ingenious design with its dome, lantern and semicircular apses.

Originally formal in design, the gardens contain an important reminder of the English vogue for the Picturesque in the form of an artificial ruin built by Sanderson Miller. Shortly after the 1st Earl died the garden was landscaped by Capability Brown and then again in 1801 by Humphry Repton.

To the E. of the house is St Andrew's Church, much changed in the rebuilding of 1887. It

Wicken Fen Nature Reserve

G. Douglas Bolton

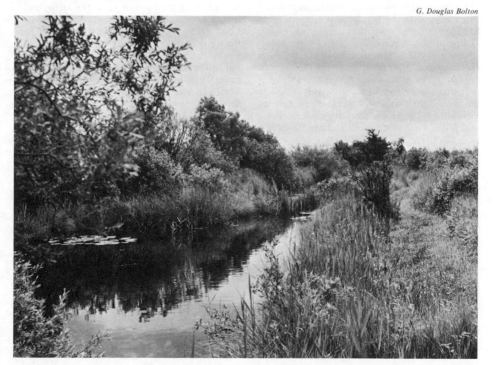

contains an outstanding collection of monuments by some of the most notable sculptors working in England – Scheemakers, Westmacott and Flaxman among others.

WINGFIELD, *Suffolk* 11–TM2276). Here is the only inhabited castle in the county and an unusually impressive church. The castle is picturesque and romantic, a four-sided moated building with gatehouse and angle-towers. A drawbridge remains over the moat and on the west side part of the original structure was replaced by a Tudor house. It was built by Michael de la Pole, in and after 1384. The original door still stands.

St Andrew's Church is connected with the founding of a medieval college here by Sir John Wingfield on his death in 1360. The tower is 14th-cent. and the north chancel contains a monument in memory of Sir John. Between the chancel and the south chapel is the monument to Michael de la Pole who died in 1415, a rare example of the use of wooden figures. The chapel itself is exceptionally elaborate. A further monument to John and Elizabeth de la Pole, *c.* 1491, has their effigies in alabaster under a canopied altar tomb. Elizabeth was the sister of Edward IV and Richard III.

WISBECH, *Cambridgeshire* (11–TF4609). Wisbech stands on the River Nene almost 12 m. from the sea. At one time it was only 4 m. away but changes in the river patterns have altered its position in relation to the Wash. Unlike MARCH whose church is perhaps the main reason for a visit to the town, the architectural beauties of Wisbech lie in its domestic buildings.

As you stand on the bridge over the Nene North Brink extends to the W. The impression is of an anglicized Delft with the terrace of mainly Georgian houses providing variety without sacrificing unity. The most famous of the buildings on the bank of the river is Peckover House, built in the 1720s and an important example of domestic architecture of the period. It is now in the care of the National Trust and you may see inside fine examples of decorative work in plaster and wood. The garden contains a number of rare trees, including one of the largest Maidenhair trees in the country and a glasshouse containing orange trees.

After the Friends Meeting House and a group of gabled houses a number of smaller houses lead to the buildings of the North Brink Brewery. Though North Brink is the more photographed and famous side, South Brink on the opposite bank is hardly less charming. Close to the bridge stands the monument designed by Sir George Gilbert Scott to Thomas Clarkson, one of the fighters for the abolition of the slave trade.

Still active as a port Wisbech is the centre of the agricultural and flower-growing industries of fenland. In the late spring of each year, usually at the end of May, the town is the centre of various routes through surrounding orchards. These routes, which are usually signposted, enable the motorist to see as much as possible of the beauties of the spring blossoms and at the same time avoid the heavy traffic on the main roads.

The large Church of SS. Peter and Paul has the unusual feature of twin naves and aisles. The tower built in the 16th cent. contains a host of sculptural detail and within the church is the monumental brass to Sir Thomas de Braunstone, an armoured figure some 7 ft long.

WISSINGTON, *Suffolk* (11–TL9534). On the Stour close to NAYLAND and one of the southernmost villages in the county. The Church of St Mary is Norman with several well-preserved original features. The south doorway to the nave is richly decorated with Norman carving and the two shafts have different patterns, alternate spirals on the left and horizontal zigzags on the right. The nave arch also has fine carving, with three recessions, two of which are patterned. The famous series of wall paintings dating from the 13th cent. give some idea as to the appearance of country churches at that time. On the south wall of the nave are representations which include the Magi asleep in bed, the presentation in the temple and the Nativity and on the end wall women gossiping encouraged by devils, and St Francis preaching to the birds.

Considerable restoration was undertaken in the 1850s when many additional features in a Victorian-Norman style were incorporated.

Wiston Hall stands close to the church and was built for the Admiral of the Fleet, Sir George Creasey, and enlarged by Sir John Soane in 1791 for Samuel Beechcroft of the Bank of England.

WITHAM, *Essex* (11–TL8114). It was only recently that the by-pass took the traffic away from this delightful town placed on the main A12 CHELMSFORD to COLCHESTER road, just where the River Brain crosses it. The town still retains its Georgian character, though its actual history goes back to the days when King Alfred's son, Edward, built the huge mound as a defence against the Danes, a mound later cut through by very different invaders, the railway engineers of the early Victorian age. Near the site of the mound, at Chippinghill, is the Church of St Nicholas, 14th-cent. Decorated style in flint, with a Norman south doorway and excellent carved mouldings and columns.

The High Street follows the ancient Roman road and is continued at either end by Bridge Street, and Newland Street, the three sections containing many pleasing houses of the 16th cent. and later. Prominent is the Spread Eagle, timber-framed and bow-windowed, a famous Essex inn. Two others are the White Hart and the Red Lion. Near the church, once the site of an old market place, are more attractive houses, many timber-framed, with a little distance away, Powers Hall, 16th-cent. with a large barn, and Howbridge Hall, also 16th-cent. On the River Blackwater is the weather-boarded Blue Mills, part of a picturesque group which includes Mathyns, a Georgian house of red brick.

Plans to expand the town have resulted in an

increase in industrial development, but the by-pass will deflect heavy traffic.

Tiptree, 4½ m. E., is famous for its fruit-preserving and jam-making industries.

WIVENHOE, *Essex* (11–TM0321), is on the River Colne, 5 m. from COLCHESTER. On the other side of the river once linked by a ferry, is **Rowhedge**. Wivenhoe park was painted by Constable and is now the site of the University of Essex (*see* Colchester) whose tall tower blocks are already a prominent feature of the landscape. The original house was built in 1758–61 but was much altered and enlarged in the 1850s. The University has been planned by Kenneth Capon and it is expected that it will ultimately accept some 3,000 students.

The attractive quay is still as it was long ago, a centre for boat building. The Church of St Mary the Virgin is mainly 19th-cent., though the west tower dates from 1500 and is surmounted by a wooden cupola of later date. Inside is a majestic brass to William, Viscount Beaumont, d. 1507. In East Street, S. of the church, is a house with one of the finest displays of pargeting in East Anglia.

Gourmets will appreciate the local oysters, an important industry.

WOODBRIDGE, *Suffolk* (11–TM2749). The River Deben which flows through Woodbridge to the North Sea made the town a busy seaport. Now it is mainly a sailing centre with a winding channel which finally emerges on the coast between Bawdsey and FELIXSTOWE. It is a most attractive small town, with its shire hall dominating the market square, its quays and river frontage and its many fine houses and cottages.

The high gables in the Dutch style were added to the shire hall about 1700, and the lower floor was at one time a covered market. Around the square are houses and shops dating from the 16th cent., many with Georgian fronts. The town has always been associated with the arts, and two art galleries continue this interest today. The artist Thomas Churchyard lived here; so, too, did Fitz-Gerald, and Tennyson was among those who stayed in the town. He stayed in the Bull, in the stable of which is the resting place of one George Carlow, who desired to be buried there rather than in the church in 1738.

SW. of Market Hill is the Church of St Mary, a stately building with an imposing tower, standing apart from, and above, the town. To the N., Theatre Street is so called after the Georgian building which is now a sale-room. Seckford Street leads to the library, a rich source of local information, housed in a 16th-cent. grammar school and then the red-brick almshouses, 1835–40, and the site of the old cattle market. New Street brings us to St John's Church (1842) with its *flèche* on the roof and also to the thoroughfare with fine houses and good shopping.

Thomas Seckford, a well-known Elizabethan public benefactor, did much to mould the character of the town and his name is commemorated in

Seckford Hall, a Tudor mansion of distinctive character, now a country-house hotel. The list of local buildings of architectural merit is lengthy; it must include the Bell, Angel and King's Head Inns, the Georgian houses of Thoroughfare and Cumberland Street and as an industrial curiosity, the old steelyard, or lever weighing machine, which may be seen at the Bell, used for weighing wool, hay and hides. The tide mills along the estuary, the barns and Kyson Hill, parkland owned by the National Trust, are other unique features which the visitor may enjoy.

The nearby air bases give the town a character which in some way echoes its days as a busy maritime port, when strange accents and foreign tongues must have been commonplace. The ships have been replaced by modern jets, and the carriages and horses of the past by American cars so huge that you wonder how their drivers can navigate them through the narrow streets and country lanes which surround this remarkably unspoilt little town.

Five m. N. of Woodbridge is **Charsfield**, whose church is worth visiting to see its glowing red bricks.

WOOLPIT, *Suffolk* (11–TL9762). One's expectations on entering the Church of St Mary through its magnificent stone south porch are fulfilled by the sight of the interior of this beautiful church. The elaborately carved porch dates from the mid-15th cent. and is big enough to contain the chamber above and the lierne vaulted roof. The nave has a superb double hammer-beam roof, renowned for the carved angels that grace it, and a beautiful screen high up over the chancel arch below the east window of the nave. The tiny aisles are less than 9 ft wide and again have beautifully timbered roofs. The brass eagle lectern is 16th-cent. and is said to have been the gift of Queen Elizabeth I. The tower and spire were rebuilt in the middle of the last century to replace the original tower which had collapsed after a storm.

In the village are some attractive timber-framed Tudor and Georgian houses as well as the Swan Inn, some parts of which are dated 1759 and others 1826.

WRENTHAM, *Suffolk* (11–TM4982). A large village which has grown up along the main A12, with side roads leading to COVEHITHE and SOUTHWOLD. The local garage has a display of carriage and vehicle lights and you might be fortunate enough to see the beautifully restored traction engine should there be a fête or rally in the neighbourhood.

The Brewster family built a Hall here in the 16th cent., demolished in the 19th. They were prominent as propagators of Puritanism. The Old Meeting House Farm is on the site of a chapel built in 1710. The brass effigy of Humphrye Brewster, 1593, may be seen in the church.

WRITTLE, *Essex* (7–TL6706). Now almost part of CHELMSFORD; it was from the village of

Writtle that Marconi sent out his first broadcasts. He had come to England from Bologna, and his radio factory, the first in the world, led to the subsequent developments in telegraphic and broadcasting techniques. Here, too, is one of the most famous village greens in the county, framed by some fine houses and to the S., the Church of All Saints. The west tower was rebuilt in 1802 and the 13th-cent. body of the church in 1879. Among the monuments is one by Nicholas Stone to Sir Edward Pinchon (1629) – a remarkable work, with harvest symbols crowned by an angel standing on a rock. There are brasses in plenty, many of them 16th-cent., and fine carving on stalls and benches.

On either side of the church stand beautiful houses: Aubyns, a half-timbered house dating from the early 16th cent., and Mundays, a plastered 17th-cent. house. Excavations at King John's Castle brought to light traces of buildings of the 13th to 15th cents., perhaps a link with the fabled palace of King John, and Robert Bruce of Scotland, who, legend has it, was born in these parts.

WROXHAM, *Norfolk* (11–TG2917). A yachting centre which has grown up on either side of the River Bure, which is spanned by a bridge first built in 1614 and later widened in 1897. It carries the A1151 from NORWICH, 6 m. to the SW.

Wroxham itself is a busy place which even out of season has the atmosphere of a yachting centre. All seems to converge on one crossroads with one general store which caters for every possible need. Wroxham Broad itself, while not large, is very popular for sailing, and the headquarters of the Norfolk Broads Yacht Club is on its west bank.

The Church of St Mary has a famous north doorway, with seven orders and three shafts. The churchyard contains the Trafford Mausoleum built in 1831 although medieval in appearance. Just to the SE. of the church is the manor house, in which is a panel dated 1623. The stepped gables betray Dutch influence.

In addition to boat-building, local light industry includes the canning of soft fruits.

WYMONDHAM, *Norfolk* (11–TG1101), lies on the main LONDON to NORWICH road, the A11, at the junction with the B1135. It is consequently a busy market town subject to heavy traffic. Its name is pronounced Windham, and its centre is still the market place with the market cross, a charming octagonal building dating from 1617 and raised on wooden arcading. Nearby are some timbered houses, including the Bridewell with the goal attached (1787). Among the many fascinating local inns are the King's Head, the Crossed Keys, and especially the Green Dragon, half-timbered and most attractive. However, the pre-eminent building is, of course, the great Abbey Church of St Mary and St Thomas of Canterbury.

The priory was founded in 1107 by William de Albini for the Benedictine order. In 1448 it became an abbey and its remains are dominated by the two fine towers, unusually placed one at either end of the church. The octagonal one was originally a central crossing tower, for at one time the church continued well beyond its present position. Differences of opinion between monks and villagers caused the church to be not only spiritually but physically divided and when the abbey section was destroyed it was the part belonging to the parishioners which was saved. Even so it is incomplete, for the west tower never received its parapet and battlements.

From the outside the church appears to be Perpendicular in style, as are its windows and panelling. Within is a magnificent Norman nave; this, however, has a superb 15th-cent. hammer-beam roof, decorated with angels and huge star bosses. The east end is still shut off by the wall built as the result of the disputes centuries ago and is now faced with an elaborate reredos made in 1935 by Sir Ninian Comper. Near the altar is a terracotta monument to Abbott Ferrers, similar to that at OXBURGH, and therefore probably of the same date, *c.* 1525.

There are the remains of the 13th-cent. font of Purbeck marble, and another typical East Anglian font complete with the Four Lions and Four Wild Men. The association of the church with the St Thomas whose name it bears is brought to mind in the Chapel of St Thomas à Becket, in Church Street. It was begun shortly after his murder and rebuilt in the 14th cent. It is 84 ft by 40 ft and is now a library.

The fire of 1615 caused considerable rebuilding in the town and as a result there are some fine houses; among later Georgian houses is Caius House, and others near it in Middleton Street.

The dissolution of the abbey in the 16th cent. resulted indirectly in the conflict between Robert Kett and John Flowerdew which led to the famous Kett Revolt of 1549. Kett's Oak associated with this is some 3 m. NE. of the town on the A11. Kett himself was put to death shortly after his short-lived success.

YOXFORD, *Suffolk* (11–TM3968). A deceptive village, because unlike so many on the main London to GREAT YARMOUTH route it developed not parallel to what has become an increasingly busy highway, but at right angles to it along the river. The result has been a community which has kept much of its original character.

The Church of St Peter contains some interesting brasses but more interesting is Cockfield Hall, originally built by Sir Arthur Hopton during the reign of Henry VIII. Catherine, a sister of Lady Jane Grey, was kept here at the orders of Queen Elizabeth I. The central block was rebuilt early in the 17th cent. and other alterations have taken place since, including, in 1896, the building of the "Stuart" great hall. The village is surrounded in addition to the parklands of Cockfield Hall by those of Grove Park and Rookery Park and this, together with the main street with its timbered, bow-windowed and balconied houses, gives the village its unique character.

Wymondham Abbey   Edwin Smith

The South-East Midlands

Hertfordshire   Buckinghamshire   Bedfordshire
Huntingdonshire   Northamptonshire

LAURENCE W. MEYNELL

"South-East Midlands" is a somewhat arbitrary grouping, a portmanteau word; and a portmanteau may be full of treasures, or it may be disappointingly empty. Happily there is no question of emptiness where the five English counties which are the subject of this section of the book are concerned. Buckinghamshire, Hertfordshire, Bedfordshire, Huntingdonshire and Northamptonshire make a compact block stretching from the urbanity of the Thames valley on its south-west to the comparative wildness of the still mysterious Fens on the north-east.

Scenery and structure are inescapably connected, and nowhere is this more evident than in the territory we are considering. The water which once covered the whole of Britain left on its recession a belt of limestone and clay which, starting at Portland Bill on the south coast, runs north-eastwards all through the Cotswold country, takes in the high parts of Northamptonshire and so eventually leaves our area towards the Wash. There is no better building material than limestone, and where iron has added a warm touch of colour to the coldness of the stone the effect is wholly pleasing.

Higham Ferrers, Oundle with its lofty spire, and Apethorpe are – at least as far as the old parts of them are concerned – splendid examples of how "right" local architecture using local materials can be. Turvey, on the Bedfordshire Ouse, was almost entirely rebuilt of native stone in the mid-nineteenth century; its long street of substantial houses dotted with good trees is most effective. The wide High Street of Brackley, lined with buildings of local stone, remains dignified despite the traffic.

All along this limestone belt you get churches with splendid spires – "a country of spires and squires" the old saying goes. Oundle's lofty crocheted one is notable; and, although off the limestone belt, the lofty broach spires of Huntingdonshire – Warboys and Alconbury particularly – are impressive.

Such an abundance of magnificent building material called into being a number of individual quarries which have been famous for centuries. We know that the Romans won stone from the quarries at Barnack, which continued to supply material all through medieval times. The church at Boston, the cathedral at Peterborough, and many churches in the Fen district (where water transport was easy) were hewed out of Barnack; and at one period the Abbot of Ramsey in Huntingdonshire paid the Abbot of Peterborough a fee of 4,000 eels for the right of quarrying Barnack stone. The Totternhoe (Beds) quarry was one of the gifts which Henry I bestowed on the Priory of Dunstable at its foundation in 1130, and a good deal of Windsor Castle and the interior of Westminster Abbey came from there. In contrast, the stones for old Saint Paul's were almost entirely quarried at Weldon (Northants).

Many of these good stone buildings are roofed with "Collyweston slates", thin layers of stone which weather to a delightful greeny-brown.

Parallel to the limestone ridge, and immediately to the south-east of it, there runs a belt of chalk and flint, and if, in Hertfordshire and Bedfordshire for instance, this does not give us lovely stone buildings harmonious with their surroundings it makes itself felt in other ways.

In Hertfordshire the underlying structure of things is more apparent in agriculture than in architecture. It has always been a great area for wheat and barley. As far back as 1586 Camden commented on "the incredible number of corn merchants, maltsters and dealers in grain". In the valley of the River Lea the fertile soil has given rise to the existence of the vast "glass-house" activities of Waltham, Cheshunt and Broxbourne. Not only is the valley soil naturally fertile, but the district was near enough to the Great Wen to get the benefit both of an insatiable market on the doorstep and of soil from earth closets, manure from stables and soot from innumerable Cockney chimneys to help keep that market supplied.

It is the clay – a deep stratum of Oxford clay near the surface, and thus easily workable – which gives rise to one of Bedfordshire's most interesting industrial features – the great brick works at Stewartby, where a single kiln holds more than nine million bricks. Stewartby works and the adjacent model village are a striking testimony to the imagination and energy of the late Sir Malcolm Stewart.

Where the Oxford clay mingles with the Lower Greensand belt a soil of great fertility results, and so we get what is sometimes rather unkindly referred to as the "brussels-sprouts" country of Sandy, Potton, Shefford and Biggleswade. Market gardening repeats itself in the Ramsey area of Huntingdonshire; and at Fletton close to Peterborough we have clay and therefore bricks again.

The third great structural influence literally underlying the area is the chalk of the Chiltern massif which, running in a fifty-mile curve from the Thames to the north-east, is strikingly displayed on Luton and Dunstable downs. The chalk gives us beautiful things. Blue flowers, blue butterflies, the hornbeam and the oak all flourish on it; but its greatest glory is the beech.

Hornbeam and oak you will see in plenty in the woods near Ashridge (the house has long since ceased to be in private occupation and is now a political college); indeed this whole south-east area was once very extensively wooded. Rockingham Forest (Northants) was once vast, and, although ruthlessly despoiled by Charles I in order to raise ready cash, and eroded by all sorts of changes since, it still remains pretty substantial, and the flat and fenny lands of Huntingdonshire still show round Kimbolton and north of Alconbury substantial remains of what were originally huge forests.

There are some notable and historic individual oak trees in the area, including what remains of that one at Hatfield House under which on 17 November, 1558, Elizabeth was told of the death of her half-sister Mary and so of her own accession to the throne. Better preserved is Waller's Oak at Coleshill (Bucks) under which Edmund Waller wrote some of his poems, and which is probably a thousand years old. But it is the beech which is the peculiar glory of the chalk, the beech which is lovely and colourful in all weathers. The very name Buckinghamshire proclaims this fact if the derivation from buccan (beech) is correct. "Leafy Bucks" it is indeed, and nowhere more gloriously so than at Burnham Beeches.

If geology has determined how things look it has also largely determined the way – literally – that they have gone: the lines of communication of the area. The first primitive footpaths were almost invariably on the hills; height meant safety and good going since you avoided the denser undergrowth and the swamps of the low-lying land. Tentative footpaths hardened into recognized trackways, and so the Icknield Way came into being.

In prehistoric England the most important inhabited region was Salisbury

Plain, and there was always the need of a highway from that religious and civic centre to the great cornlands of East Anglia. The Icknield Way was ancient when the Romans came, but they adapted very little of it; by their time the centre of gravity of the island had shifted from Salisbury Plain to the south-east, and the need was for a south-east to north-west link. Hence the Watling Street, of which the modern equivalent, running roughly parallel to it, is the M1.

Even today, notwithstanding traffic lights, chromium shop fronts and other belittling modernities, I always feel the authentic thrill of history in the very middle of Dunstable, at Dunstable Cross, where that primitive track, the Icknield Way, crosses the majestic authentic artery of Rome, the Watling Street. This nodal point was always important, especially when the adjacent scrub and woodland was infested with bandits; so much so that the town of Dunstable was founded by Henry I for the express purpose of guarding the safety of the ways. There used to be an Eleanor Cross here, one of a sequence built to mark the nightly resting places of Queen Eleanor's body on its journey from Leicestershire to London.

Of the Watling Street it may be interesting to recall that the legions normally reckoned to march eleven Roman miles (the equivalent roughly of twelve modern miles) in a day, so the Watling Street itinerary hereabouts reads Verulamium (St Albans) to Durocobrivae (Dunstable) 12 miles; Durocobrivae to Magisvinium (Little Brickhill, Bucks) 12 miles. The need for a London link with the north-east (to connect with the highly important Colonia at Lincoln) was met by the Ermine Street on which Godmanchester (Hunts) was one of the principal stations.

Man had to make roads; nature made rivers for him. Perhaps it was out of gratitude for this bounty that he gave them such delightful names – the Ivel, the Flitt, the Hiz, the Ouse and the Ousel in Bedfordshire; in Hertfordshire the Mimram, the Bean, the Rib, the Stort and the Lea; Northamptonshire's Nene; in Huntingdonshire the Nene again and the little Kym; then Buckinghamshire's Ray, Thame, Chess (with its watercress beds), Wye, Lovat, Lyde, and the disappearing Misbourne. The Thames – "Liquid History", the term is surely justified – only skirts our territory; the Ouse is central to it, the Ouse of quiet meadows, of straight-backed cattle lifting dripping muzzles, and of wind-bent willows with silver undersides. Chaucer knew the Lea, the "sedgy Lea" he called it; Izaak Walton loved and immortalized it.

Perhaps the most publicized river in the area is in fact really a canal; this is the New River constructed in 1609 by Sir Hugh Myddleton for the vital necessity of giving London a water supply. It is interesting to note that Royalty took a hand in trade with this enterprise, for James I shrewdly paid half the cost of the undertaking in exchange for half the profit. Starting at Amwell – where the church has a delightful Norman apse – the New River has brought water to London for three hundred years. When it first did so the water mains of the capital were hollowed-out elm trunks, and within the last five years I have seen specimens of these hollowed elm boles brought to light by road excavations and lying on the ground in Lincolns Inn.

Of canals proper the area has a splendid example in the Grand Junction, built in 1793 to connect London (via the Thames) with the Midlands. It was the natural successor to the highly successful canals built slightly earlier in the North by Brindley and his patron, the Duke of Bridgewater. Since canals must be fed it brought into being the great Tring reservoirs, now famous for black tern, crested grebe and many other wildfowl.

Along the roads and the rivers ran history. There are few parts of England where the story of man has been more continuously and intensively made than in the South-East Midlands. In the flat marsh-lands of Huntingdonshire the bones of wolf, hippopotamus and earlier mammals tell us of the very earliest things. Henlow (Beds) is now as modern as possible, with its R.A.F. flying establishment, but Stone Age implements discovered there speak of more primitive matters. At Maiden Bower near Sewell (Beds) you may see the great earthworks, ten acres in extent, thrown up in the Late Stone Age and occupied later by men of the Bronze Age. Dunstable Downs, hard by, are now much used for gliding; so does the past merge into the present and the present into the future.

Grim's Dyke, which is in some ways the most impressive prehistoric survival in the area, can be traced at many spots: near Berkhamsted and Wheathampstead in Hertfordshire, and in Buckinghamshire near Monks Risborough, in the woods of Lacey Green and at Bradenham, where later Isaac Disraeli was to live in the Great House (his better known, but not better read, son Benjamin came ultimately to Hughenden in the same county). The exact origin and purpose of the Dyke are both uncertain; but it seems more likely to have been a boundary mark than a defence. High above Hitchin (Herts) is Ravensburgh Castle, a prehistoric hill-fort of which now only the site remains.

Roman remains have been found at a score of places in the region. Biggleswade and Welwyn come to mind for coins and toilet articles; Shefford has the remains of a Roman cemetery; and farther north three important Roman roads met at Godmanchester. Roman pottery made at Castor (Northants) was famous all over Europe. Nowhere was the hand of Rome more clearly seen than at St Albans. Here, or hereabouts, was the headquarters of Cassivelaunus, the strongest chieftain in the island at the time of the first Roman invasion, and it was here 116 years later, in A.D. 61, that Boadicea, rebelling against the Roman establishment, attacked, captured and sacked Verulamium. Having dealt, after considerable difficulty, with Boadicea, Imperial Rome rebuilt the town on an imposing scale, giving it the enormous amphitheatre which has lately been excavated.

On the whole the Roman influence on the region was constructive; those great colonizers were by preference builders, not demolition contractors. The Vikings, to whose raids this part of England was particularly liable, were another matter. They brought their boats as far inland as Hertford, and at Willington (Beds) you can see the nausts or docks they used. Huntingdonshire shows us many villages – one thinks of the Sawtry and Woodwalton area – built a little away from the road so as to avoid if possible attracting the attention of the marauding Danes. They were beaten at Luton in 817, and again at Tempsford; but it was not until Alfred's peace of Wedmore in 878 that the Danish trouble was finally contained, and then only by granting them a very considerable slice of England – the Danelaw – which included the whole of Huntingdonshire, although oddly enough Huntingdonshire place-names show very little trace of Danish influence.

The Saxons left a fine 80-foot high tower at Clapham (Beds), and the Mass Dial on St Mary's church at Stevington in the same county may well be Saxon, too. Certainly a great deal of Wing church in Buckinghamshire is Saxon work and if there are few or no Saxon remains in Hertfordshire this is probably because there was no local stone available there. At Kimbolton (Hunts) the present castle, put up by Sir John Vanbrugh, is but the parvenu successor to the Saxon one which at one time stood on the same site and which belonged to Earl Harold.

The ever-increasing predominance of London inevitably affected the five counties of the South-East Midlands. They were always near enough to the capital to provide hunting grounds for Royalty; and Ampthill, where Queen Catherine of Aragon was imprisoned, Hatfield and Enfield Chase were the favourite spots. Northamptonshire, that "county of squires", is still great hunting country: Fitzwilliam, Grafton and Pytchley are bugle calls to many stout hearts.

Castles will be looked for almost in vain. Only the mound exists at Huntingdon, the building itself having been destroyed in the time of Henry II. Fotheringhay, which saw the execution of Mary Queen of Scots in 1587, has vanished. Of Bletsoe, where Margaret Beaufort, great-grand-daughter of John of Gaunt and grand-mother of Henry VIII, was born, only some slight remnants can be traced in a farm-house.

Civil Wars luckily touched this area but little; the opening engagement was fought at St Albans in 1455, there was a second battle half-way between that town and Harpenden six years later, and almost the last encounter of the war took place at Barnet in 1471. Perhaps the attitude of the district in the matter could be summed up by the action of William, 5th Earl of Bedford, who fought with deter-mination for Cromwell at Edgehill and later with equal gallantry for the King at Newbury.

Of the great houses Hatfield must surely be put first. It is the most impressive Jacobean house in England; even if one ignored the amount of English history which has been forged here there would still be the superb gardens, with their hornbeams and their great mulberry trees so loved by John Evelyn. Woburn is ducal, has been great, and is now a sort of superior fun fair. Althorp, with its gallery of fine pictures, is a splendid example of successful late-eighteenth-century remodelling, and some two miles south-east of Stamford stands the splendid Elizabethan mansion of Burghley House, where Grinling Gibbons's "heavenly room" is to be seen. In opulent Edwardian days the Rothschilds invaded Bucking-hamshire and at one time owned seven large establishments within an eight-mile radius of Aylesbury. Of these Halton is now an R.A.F. training centre, but Waddesdon may still be seen in its fullness of French Baroque, so unexpected in that homely setting. The manor house at Mackery End (Herts) has been immortal-ized in one of Elia's best known essays, and probably no one needs to be reminded that George Washington's forebears came from Sulgrave (Northants).

But there are more homely things than castles and great houses to be seen. The inns of England are magnificently represented here: the Roebuck at Knebworth, the George & Dragon at Buntingford, Much Hadham's Red Lion, Disraeli's famous Red Lion at High Wycombe, the Saracen's Head at Ware, which used to house the Great Bed, and the other Saracen's Head at Towcester, where Sam Weller ate "a very good dinner" though perhaps no better than the meal which Nicholas Nickleby and Mr Squeers ate at the White Horse at Eaton Socon (Beds) while "five little boys were put to thaw by the fire". St Albans claims that its Fighting Cocks is the oldest inn in England; and no less an authority than Professor Sir Albert Richardson of Ampthill stated categorically that the Swan at Bedford was "architecturally the finest in the country".

Nonconformity has always been a prominent thread in the tapestry of local history. John Bunyan was born at Elstow in 1628, and, as all the world knows, was imprisoned in a Bedford gaol. Jordans among the Chiltern Hills has long been a stronghold of the Quakers. Nearly every village in the area can show its little chapel, sometimes admittedly quite hideous, but occasionally splendidly satisfying in its whitewashed simplicity.

So, with the necessities of geology underneath and the accidents of history on the surface, we see the five counties of the South-East Midlands as they are today. Fast electric train services (Amersham, remember, is on the London underground system), arterial roads and motorways have inevitably made their impression. Once sleepy little towns with a marked individual flavour, like Bedford or High Wycombe, have felt in full the impact of immigration and the levelling effect of over-easy transport. At one time straw-plaiting, with its delightful terms – maiden's choice, fire strand, lovely lady and speckled – was a widespread cottage industry essential to the rural economy, as was shoemaking with leather tanned by the oak bark from Rockingham Forest. There is no cottage lace-making now, and boots and shoes are machine-made by the hundreds of thousands in the factories of Northampton. The blast furnaces and steelworks at Corby, the huge brickworks at Stewartby and Fletton, the industries of Luton and Northampton, are the marks of modernity.

Even so, the area still remains largely rural; a great deal of it, as in the north of Bedfordshire and much of Huntingdonshire, is still homely and pastoral. Standing on the bridge over the Ouse by the Woolpack Inn between Huntingdon and Godmanchester Cobbett called what he saw "the most beautiful scene and by far the most beautiful meadows that I ever saw in my life". The outspoken old Radical would not have to alter his opinion much today.

Delightfully improbable English names are still scattered through the country-side – Puddephats, Gubblecote, Potters Crouch, Raisins End, Hinton in the Hedges, Christmas Common, Lacey Green, Maids Moreton. The peculiar English sense of humour still declares itself from the signboards of inns: the Cold Bath at Hertford, the Labour In Vain at Much Hadham, the Tom in Bedlam at Red-bourn, the Rats Castle at St Albans, the Three Cranes at Turvey, the Jumps at Marston Moreteyn. The old sayings and the homely expressions of wisdom have not entirely vanished: your Hertfordshire man "stolches" through the mud; the harassed housewife of Bedfordshire claims she is "urged"; but she is "aggled" in Bucks. On the Chiltern Hills they talk of the "bud and the brown" meaning spring and autumn.

Aldbury, Little Missenden, the toy-like Old Warden, and Aynho with the peaches trained against the cottage walls, remind us that many of the old ways and things were beautiful; but the area can show imaginative modern development too, it boasts those two bold idealistic efforts, the garden cities of Welwyn and Letchworth, and much more recently the new towns of Hemel Hempstead and Stevenage.

Buckinghamshire, Bedfordshire, Huntingdonshire, Hertfordshire and North-amptonshire – in these five counties the traveller will look in vain for startling and dramatic scenic effects; but if he is looking for a quiet and gentle countryside, with a great deal of natural and man-made beauty in it, and impregnated with the continuous story of English history, he will be amply rewarded.

The South-East Midlands: Gazetteer

THERESE APPLEBY

ABBOTS LANGLEY, *Hertfordshire* (10–TL 0902). It was in this village that the only English pope was born, 800 years ago. Nicholas Breakspear by name, he became Hadrian IV. He was the son of a poor man who entered ST ALBANS monastery and left him to his own resources.

Langley House, now Breakspear Roman Catholic College, was built in commemoration of him in 1770.

The large, square vicarage, also Georgian, lies behind the church, and the manor house, gabled and cemented, is to the SW. of it.

St Lawrence's Church is of great architectural interest, with Norman arcades and a low west tower with diagonal buttresses which are of the 13th cent. as can be seen from the small lancet windows. The nave, of two bays, is short and the chancel lower than the nave. There are Perpendicular windows and the south chancel is very fine, its exterior of flint and stone mixed with brick, whereas the rest of the church is of flint with stone dressings. The chancel has interesting frescoes and the octagonal font is Perpendicular with quatrefoil embodying shields. There are many monuments of note, one in the south chapel to Dame Anne Raymond, a dignified and elegant figure; against one of the aisle walls is the semi-reclining figure of Lord Raymond, dated 1732.

Between the village and the Victorian Leavesden Mental Hospital are the Model Cottages, erected in 1896 at Prince Albert's request, in his efforts to improve the conditions of the working classes. They were first seen at the Great Exhibition in 1851 and were meant to be models for improved flats.

ALCONBURY, *Huntingdonshire* (10–TL1875). This small village has a brook on either side of it, Ellington and Alconbury, which flow into the River Ouse. Its hump-backed bridge with four arches is medieval and beside one brook is the long village green and old cottages. Manor Farm, of the 17th cent., has a handsome chimney stack with a barn standing beside it, built a century later. The manor house still retains much of its original Elizabethan timber-frame construction.

The Church of SS. Peter and Paul is Early English. The tower has a good 13th-cent. broach spire and the chancel is of the same period, with rich shafting and, on the north and south walls, high blank arcading on shafts. The clerestory has plain Y-tracery and the nave buttresses are chamfered.

To the NE. is Monks Wood, 375 acres of woodland acquired by the Nature Conservancy in 1953. It is notable for its rare plants and insects.

ALDBURY, *Hertfordshire* (10–SP9612). This village on the edge of the Chilterns is one of the most attractive in the county. Standing on the brow of Moneybury Hill in a ridge of beeches is a massive monument to the 3rd Duke of Bridgewater, in commemoration of his pioneering of English canals. The views and scenery are of outstanding beauty.

Life in the valley below centres around the large triangular village green with a pond overlooked by the church. On the green are the old stocks and the whipping post, and, surrounding it, many thatched cottages, with the tiny 300-year-old black-beamed, yellow almshouses a little further on. The timbered manor house is of the same period, its lattice windows looking on to the pond, and there are other lovely houses to be seen.

St John the Baptist's Church has a tall, slender tower, a long, low nave and a low chancel. The oldest part of the church is the masonry in which there is a tiny 13th-cent. lancet window. The arcades of the nave have octagonal piers with moulded capitals typical of the 14th cent. The timber lectern is of the 16th cent. and the church's most impressive feature, the Pendley Chapel, is divided from the aisle and chancel by a medieval stone screen in which is a monument to Sir Robert Whittington, 1471, showing him with his wife on a tomb-chest on which are carved family shields. There are other monuments and brasses in this beautiful church.

ALDENHAM, *Hertfordshire* (6–TQ1198). This little village centres around its green and ancient church, and from the hillside are magnificent views across the Colne Valley to ST ALBANS.

Aldenham House, 2 m. SE., is a brick building of the early 18th cent., with magnificent gardens of rare trees and flowering shrubs planned by the Hon. Vicary Gibbs in the latter part of the last century. He was a banker who specialized in horticulture and did little to disturb the beauty of the house he inherited. The house is now the home of Haberdashers' Aske's public school. Another public school which originated here is Aldenham School, on a hilltop, founded in 1597 by Richard Platt, a London brewer, for "children of poore people inhabitinge the parish of Aldenham and for children of the freemen of the company of Brewers London". Its original articles laid down that neither the Master nor Usher should take

Noel Habgood

Aldbury: the manor house

part in games or visit alehouses or taverns. It has been greatly enlarged in recent years and has extensive modern buildings. On the hillside is the little pond of Hill Slough, which is said to be the place where the body of William Weare, the victim of a brutal murder, was discovered.

St John the Baptist's Church, in the village, is full of beauty and interest. It is of flint with stone dressings and is long and well-proportioned. It has a complex history, with a Norman window in the south aisle, a 14th- and 15th-cent. nave, a Tudor vestry and a 13th-cent. font. The screen between the south aisle and south chancel chapel has been much renewed. There are many brasses of interest, for they show the changes in custom throughout the centuries. The most important one is in the south chancel chapel of two ladies of the Crowmer family with identical tomb-chests, forming one composition, with canopies above the four-centred arches. In the churchyard is a pedestal with a large urn to Lt-Gen. R. Burne, showing the places where he fought all over the world.

Edge Grove, a late-18th-cent. house with a four-column Ionic porch, is N. of the church, and further N. is Wall Hall, a cemented house, castellated and turreted, with a large Gothic conservatory and in the grounds an ice house. A short distance further on is Bricket Wood Common, reached by a narrow lane in richly wooded countryside, with rare flowers and trees of many types.

ALWALTON, *Huntingdonshire* (10–TL1395), is just off the A1 with the River Nene to the N. of it. It is a pretty, peaceful village with a cottage with mullioned windows dated 1645 and, NE. of the

church, the rebuilt porch of a house originally in CHESTERTON where Dryden lived. This has a round-arched doorway, two storied Tuscan columns and a patterned gable. It dates from about 1625. Manor House, nearby, is of the same period with wooden casements and a Venetian window. Alwalton was the birthplace of H. Royce of Rolls Royce cars and his ashes are buried in the parish church.

St Andrew's is a cruciform church with a late 13th-cent. tower and a chancel of the same period which was originally vaulted in two bays. Its oldest feature externally is the south doorway which has a Norman motif. The nave has three arches on one side and four on the other, all Norman. The font has been here since the 15th cent., and the altar table, in post-Reformation style, from the 17th cent.

Lynch Farm, which is 1 m. NE. of the village, is an L-shaped building with mullioned windows, a small gable and a round corner turret.

AMERSHAM, *Buckinghamshire* (6–SU9597). This old town stretches along the A413 in the valley of the River Misbourne. At the foot of the steep Gore's Hill is Bury Farm, once the home of Guilielma Springett who became the wife of William Penn. The broad High Street is a mixture of fine old buildings of many periods with timbered and gabled cottages and inns opening on to the road.

In the middle of the road stands the Market Hall, built by Sir William Drake in 1682. It is supported by arches above an open piazza with an old twin lock-up. Nearby is the old timbered grammar school and, behind four lime trees, a group of almshouses with a cobbled courtyard.

The Martyrs' Memorial, a monument to the many religious persecutions which took place in Amersham, lies just off the main road up a short hill.

The Crown Hotel is named in records of 1620 but wall paintings are judged to be Elizabethan and in the lounge a Tudor coat of arms, with the quarterings of England and France and the lion and dragon supporters, is thought to commemorate a visit by Queen Elizabeth to Shardeloes, the 16th-cent. mansion standing in parkland about ¾ m. from the town.

The King's Arms Hotel is 16th-cent. and the old gables are still in evidence at the back of the building. The Swan Inn has gable wings with the date 1671 on a chimney. The Elephant and Castle has an interesting sign, a gabled front and an old brick chimney. In 61 High Street, believed to have been once part of an inn, are wall paintings of great antiquarian interest. One depicts Julius Caesar wearing a scarlet cloak and blue helmet, another Duke Joshua in 16th-cent. armour. King David, shown with a harp, Hector of Troy, Charlemagne and Godfrey de Bouillon adorn the walls in panels.

The village church is 14th- to 15th-cent. The roof of the nave is supported on stone corbels of angels and grotesque figures. A spacious building, it was externally renewed in 1890. The vaulted porch, north chapel and tower are all 15th-cent. and the east window has 17th-cent. painted glass of foreign provenance, with Apostles and Evangelists, added in 1760. There are many large, heavy monuments to the Drakes. John Knox preached in this church.

In the 18th-cent. rectory garden is a timbered well-house with a well which was worked, within living memory, by a horse, and watermills stand at each end of the old street.

Amersham is a growing town with an extensive parish and several newer, residential areas. The traditional furniture, bricks, and craft wood products are still manufactured but many other industries have grown up, including that at the Radio-Chemical Centre which supplies radioactive materials for hospitals and research stations.

AMPTHILL, *Bedfordshire* (10–TL0337), is slightly on a hill with fine, wooded views below and is reached by winding roads in attractive countryside. It is a well-preserved little town of historical interest, for which Henry VIII had a great love and where Catherine of Aragon stayed during the period of her divorce.

It was originally a coaching town and at its crossroads is an obelisk pump, dated 1784, with distances and directions engraved on it. Nearby is the Victorian brick Moot Hall, with shaped gables and a cupola. There are many picturesque cottages and gracious Georgian houses and in Dunstable Street is the 18th-cent. White Hart Hotel, three stories high with seven bays and a doorway with an open pediment. A little further along is the large, red-brick Victorian workhouse with an octagonal centre. The modern offices of the Rural District Council are neo-Georgian with a cupola. Two Victorian Nonconformist chapels are in the same street, one Baptist and the other Methodist.

Avenue House, in Church Street, is probably the town's finest building and was built about 1780 for the brewer John Morris.

The Church of St Andrew's is in a small square, surrounded by pretty and gracious buildings. The Feoffee Almshouses, with a timbered front, were founded in 1690. Dynevor House, dated 1725, of chequer brick, with seven bays and a parapet, has a doorway with fluted pilasters and in the upper windows are frilly lintel bricks. Brandreth House is opposite, with curious corbels on its door-hood, and at the end of the square is the church.

It is of ironstone, rather small, with 14th-cent. arcades and chancel. Angels decorate the Perpendicular nave roof, and in the east of the south aisle is the sculptured head of a lantern cross. In the roof of the west tower is a wooden angel. On the west wall of the nave are interesting brasses and in the north aisle a fine standing monument to Richard Nicholls, 1672, with the cannon ball which killed him at Sole Bay. He became the first Governor of Long Island after fighting the Dutch in America.

In Woburn Street are thickly thatched cottages and the new Court House, a piece of simple, pleasant, modern architecture. Behind the parking space is Catherine's Cross, erected in 1773 in memory of Catherine of Aragon and bearing the arms of Castile and Aragon with verses on its base by Horace Walpole. A little further out are the Oxford Hospital Almshouses, erected by Wren and founded by John Cross of the university for old servants of OXFORD colleges. It is a handsome building of chequer brick, with three bay wings and a hipped roof. Below the pediment in the middle is a small chapel. Along a footpath off Park Hill is a very unusual pavilion added to Russett's Lodge, a 17th-cent. cottage.

Ampthill Park is now a Cheshire Home, but it originally belonged to the first Lord Ashburnham who built it in 1694 on land given to his family by Charles II. It has a hipped roof and is of blue brick with red dressings.

The remains of Houghton Conquest House – the "House Beautiful" of *The Pilgrim's Progress* – are nearby. The house is believed to have been built about 1615 by Inigo Jones, or a pupil, for Mary, Countess of Pembroke.

ASHWELL, *Hertfordshire* (10–TL2639), is a large attractive village with the River Rhee below it. There are many trees of interest but the ash is predominant.

The buildings of the village are well-preserved, mainly timber-framed or gable-bricked. Halfway along the High Street is St John's Guild Hall, a long building of the 17th cent. with closely spaced timber uprights and adjoining cottages, dated 1681, with bold rustic pargeting. Near the end of the High Street is Chantry House, opposite which is Westbury Farm, a plastered building with symmetrical gables. The Town House, which is the village museum, shows the history of Ashwell from prehistoric days to the present time, with Roman coins, straw-plaiting tools, a metal harvest horn, implements of the Stone and Bronze Ages and tools used by farmers, shepherds, blacksmiths, coach-builders and wheelwrights. It is now an Ancient Monument.

St Mary's Church is a magnificent 14th-cent. building, very light inside, with a high tower crowned by a lantern with leaded spike, in which clunch has been used as a facing material as well as elegant timber. The chancel is without aisles but has large windows; there is a screen in the Lady Chapel with 15th-cent. tracery, and the pulpit, dated 1627, has panels of diamond-cut pieces. The tower has two interesting *graffiti*, one inscription in Latin saying "Miserable, wild and distracted, the dregs of the people alone survive to witness . . .", a reference to the Black Death in England which killed one man in three. The lychgate at the entrance to the church is of the 15th cent.

ASPLEY GUISE, *Bedfordshire* (10–SP9337), is an old village lying below pine woods which cover the sandy hills. It centres around the cross-roads and has holly hedges 30 ft high and bracken growing out of the sand.

Aspley House is of chequer brick, two stories high with seven bays. It is dated 1695 and its doorway has an open pediment with cherubs' heads on corbels. The garden side of the house, added 50 years later, has two doorways with Doric pilasters and, in the middle bay, Venetian windows.

Guise House is early 18th-cent. with five-bayed front, and its doorway has a hood on carved brackets. The oldest house in the village is Old House, about 1575, a timber-framed building with good panelling.

St Botolph's Church, which is of ironstone, is externally almost completely Victorian, but the tower is Perpendicular and the north aisle and nave are also old. The font is drum-shaped and the screen Perpendicular. There is a brass to a priest, *c*. 1410, showing him kneeling with John the Baptist, and one to a knight, *c*. 1500.

AYLESBURY, *Buckinghamshire* (10–SP8213). Built on a hill in the heart of Buckinghamshire, at the junction of six main roads, this ancient town gives its name to the broad vale which it overlooks, stretching from the borders of Bedfordshire to those of Oxfordshire, a rich pastureland with many dairy farms.

Despite the modern industries and new buildings which it now contains – the County Council offices are a fine symbol of modern architecture – this busy county town with its narrow meandering streets is still a place of great historic interest.

In the cobbled Market Square, once the cattle market and now a car park, stands a Victorian clock-tower and three massive monuments: to John Hampden, at the top of the slope; Disraeli; and at the end of the square, Lord Chesham. John Hampden, the great parliamentarian whose home was nearby, is renowned for his stand against

King Charles I in 1635 when he refused to pay Ship Money, since he believed the tax was for the King's own pocket and not for the Navy. Although he lost the suit against him, the judgment was eventually cancelled and his protest in the name of freedom had been made.

Reached through arches under the Victorian Town Hall at the foot of the square is the Cattle Market which is still in use today and where farmers from miles around hold sales of cattle, sheep and pigs.

A noteworthy inn stands in the square, the King's Head which has been given to the National Trust. Dating from the 15th cent. and once a monastery guesthouse, it is entered through a medieval gateway to a cobbled courtyard. The lounge has a magnificent leaded window with the arms of Henry VI and his Queen, Margaret of Anjou, and those of Prince Edward who died at the Battle of TEWKESBURY. "Cromwell's Chair" rests in a corner of the lounge for it is here he is believed to have stayed on his journey back to Worcester. In the Civil War the town was a base for both the King and Parliament, according to the way the battle went. Holman's Bridge, on the BUCKINGHAM road, was the site of a crushing defeat for Prince Rupert and his Royalists. In one of the little alleys on the west side of the square will be found the Dark Lantern Inn.

The County Museum in Church Street, housed in a delightful Georgian building, has much of interest and is open to the public. One section of it tells the history of the county from prehistoric times. There is a splendid art gallery. Louis XVIII dwelt at Hartwell House, near Aylesbury, for five years of his exile and in the museum are many things used by him including a bed and confessional chair. The 15th-cent. roof of the museum was only discovered a few years ago.

Down Parson's Fee, a cobbled lane, will be found Prebendal House, an 18th-cent. building, now a girls' school, which was formerly the house of John Wilkes, the satirist and Member of Parliament for Aylesbury until he was expelled for insolence and libel. There are many 17th-cent. houses as well as old almshouses to be found.

Away from the bustle of the town is St Mary's Square, old terraced houses lining three of its sides, with the Parish Church of St Mary beyond the churchyard on the fourth side. Substantially 13th-cent., it is a large, handsome, cruciform building. Considerably restored by Sir Gilbert Scott in 1848, it still holds many of its former features. The 13th-cent. tower, on which rests a lead clock-tower and spire added in the 17th cent., is impressive. The font, late 12th-cent., is bordered with foliage and fluting, its cup-shaped bowl resting on a square base. From this font came the style known as the "Aylesbury Font" of which other examples are to be seen in the county.

An exquisite alabaster monument to Lady Lee of Quarrendon is of the Elizabethan period, showing Lady Lee with her three children and an inscription pleading that red flowers should always be left by her tomb, a request that is still observed.

F. Jewell-Harrison

Aylesbury: the County Council Offices and Library

With the Grand Union Canal adjoining it, Aylesbury is becoming a cruising centre and at the canal basin cabin cruisers may be hired to explore the beautiful, unspoilt scenery.

One of the town's great claims to fame was its ducks which were exported all over the world. Although they are still bred, the output has considerably declined since the war.

A house which can sometimes be visited is **Nether Winchenden House**, 6 m. SW. of Aylesbury. A Tudor manor with 18th-cent. additions, it was once the home of Sir Francis Bernard, the last Governor of New Jersey and Massachusetts in 1761. Formerly the property of Notley Abbey it then housed the monks who served in the churches and worked on the farms. The riverside grounds of the house are attractive.

Also for public viewing is **Wotton House** in Wotton Underwood, built in 1704 on the same plan as Buckingham House, which later became Buckingham Palace. Its park contains a lake and was laid out by Capability Brown.

AYNHO, *Northamptonshire* (10–SP5133). This is the county's southernmost village and one of its most attractive. It stands on the top of a hill from which can be seen the beautiful countryside of

Northamptonshire and Oxfordshire. The wide road running through it twists and turns on its way to London or BANBURY.

On the Banbury side is **Aynhoe Park**, a 17th-cent. mansion open to the public, which was the residence of the Cartwright family for nearly 350 years. It now belongs to the National Trust.

During the Civil War the house was burned by the Royalists, for the family were Cromwellians, but it was rebuilt shortly afterwards.

On many of the ancient stone cottages, which line the roadside with their pretty unfenced gardens, are climbing apricot trees, which provided the fruit with which the cottagers used to pay the Lord of the Manor's toll.

The Church of St Michael is reached by a no-through road leading to the village square, where stand its few shops and a row of thatched cottages. The church has a rich 15th-cent. tower but the body of it was altered in 1723. The simple interior has a gallery, box-pews and a Georgian pulpit, as well as an old carved wooden chair showing the Baptism. The majority of the monuments are to the Cartwrights, the best of them being a Victorian marble cross to Lady Elizabeth of Newbottle Manor.

The Rectory is 17th-cent., as is the Old Grammar School, now a private house. Although some new buildings have been added to the village, they are all in keeping with its character and are of light stone, similar to the older buildings.

AYOT ST LAWRENCE, *Hertfordshire* (10–TL1916). This is a picturesque, rural village with black-and-white timbered cottages and buildings of several centuries. It is reached through Priors Wood and a wooded dell.

George Bernard Shaw, the playwright, lived here for 44 years until his death in 1950, and his house, Shaw's Corner, a late Victorian building now National Trust property, is open to the public. His ashes were scattered in the garden.

In the village are the ruins of the old church, partly demolished by Sir Lionel Lyte until the bishop prevented further destruction. The new St Lawrence's Church, designed in 1778–9 by Nicholas Revett, is externally of Grecian style, while internally it has the classicism of Rome. It has a Greek temple portico with fluted columns. A columned screen separates the rectangular nave from the vestibule. The nave, flanked by two arched recesses, has a coffered ceiling.

Ayot House, of Georgian origin, was the seat of Sir Lionel Lyte. Its main front has three stories with the middle of the five bays slightly projected. Bride Hall, 1 m. S. of the church, is a Jacobean manor house, still retaining, in the hall, its original fireplace and ceiling beams.

Silk for royal vestments is produced at Lady Hart Dyke's Lullington Silk Farm, open to the public in the summer months.

BALDOCK, *Hertfordshire* (10–TL2434). is centred on four main streets which meet and form a cross, and was probably a coaching town in former days. Its architecture is mainly Georgian with little of earlier periods. Its main street is lined with trees and grass banks. At Quickswood Farm is a clock which has told the time since the reign of Charles I. The Wynne's Almshouses, dated 1621, are one-storied brick buildings, with a raised gateway in the wall which separates them from the street.

Simpson's Brewery, in the same street, is Georgian with a chequer-brick house. The brewery has seven bays and a centre of yellow brick. The Bull's Head, at the far end of Church Street, has close vertical timbers.

By the crossroads are the late Victorian Fire Station Buildings, of red brick with a tower on one corner.

St Mary's Church is spacious. Most of the interior is early 14th-cent. with 15th-cent. screens and roofs. It is mostly of flint, although the lower part of the chancel is in stone. There is a double piscina, part of which is 13th-cent., and a turret in the north-west section. The octagonal font, on nine shafts, is 13th-cent. and there are many early monuments.

BARLEY, *Hertfordshire* (10–TL4038). At the entrance to this village are pretty overhanging cottages and, at the top of the hill, a 300-year-old inn, the Fox and Hounds; its sign spans the road.

Town House, an original Tudor building with great oak beams, has a jutting-out porch at each end with an exterior staircase to the upper floor, which is one long room, once used "for the keeping of maides' marriages". The rooms on the ground floor were originally almshouses.

At Shaftenhoe End is the Big House, the doorways of which have hoods on carved brackets. The upper story projects on the south porch, dated 1624, and there is a large outer chimney and diagonal chimney stacks.

The foundations of St Margaret's Church were laid in Norman times but only the tower, a deep splayed ground-floor window and the round-headed upper windows are original. Most of the rest of the church is Victorian, although the screen is 15th-cent. The date of the pulpit, with its fine back and tester, is 1626. A brass of Andrew Willett, rector here for 23 years, shows him praying. Two other vicars of Barley became archbishops of Canterbury and one of them crowned Henry VIII.

BARNACK, *Huntingdonshire* (10–TF0705), is a village famous for its stone from which PETER-BOROUGH Cathedral, and many other abbeys, churches and houses, were built. The quarries were used from Roman times until the 18th cent. when they were exhausted and large mounds and hollows, known as the Hills and the Holes, mark their site.

There are many interesting houses in the village. Kingsley House, the former rectory, incorporates the remains of a medieval house, and Littlefield has a canted bay window, a small arched Anglo-Saxon window and a 13th-cent. fragment. In Millstone Lane are the 15th-cent. Feoffee Cottages with arched doorways, cross-slit windows and a traceried gable-end. There are several other attractive cottages and a derelict windmill.

St John the Baptist Church is of several periods. It has an Anglo-Saxon tower of two stages with long-and-short Saxon work and narrow stone pilaster strips. An octagonal belfry and spire were added in the 13th cent., and there are two large bell openings. The large, beautifully moulded nave arcades date from 1180 and 1220. The chancel is about 1300 and its east window has fine tracery. The Walcot Chapel is Perpendicular with richly decorated battlements and parapets. There is a late Anglo-Saxon sculpture of Christ in Majesty, and many interesting monuments.

Walcot Hall, ¾ m. SE. of the village, is a fine 17th-cent. house with a hipped roof and four square chimneys. It has a delightful garden with large trees, and in it are two temples and a rotunda.

BARNWELL, *Northamptonshire* (10–TL0485), was originally two villages with separate churches. Now the two villages have grown into one; joined by an old bridge and three fords that cross the stream running through it.

The original Barnwell Castle was built by Berengar le Moine in 1266. Its remains consist of a quadrangular court with towers at each corner and a large gateway flanked by two towers. It stands in the grounds of what is now called Barnwell Castle, an Elizabethan manor, the home of the Duke of Gloucester, and is open to the public once a year.

There are pretty stone cottages on either side of the stream, and almshouses founded by Nicholas Latham, a Jacobean benefactor who was for 51 years parson of the Church of St Andrew's which contains a bust of him. This church has a lovely spire rising from the 13th-cent. tower with its west doorway, circular window and belfry lights. Although the chancel is the oldest part of the church it has a large 15th-cent. east window. Both the altars in the east walls are ancient and the oak pulpit is Jacobean.

All that remains of the other church, All Saints, which is some distance along the stream, is the chancel with its large 15th-cent. windows. The church is filled with the memorials of the Montagus, who originally owned the present Barnwell Castle; one of special interest is a rather sad figure of a little boy who was drowned aged three, in 1625. He stands under a canopy in a gown of red and gold with ten painted shields above him and a shield and eagle beneath. Part of the inscription describes him as "a witty and hopeful child".

BEACONSFIELD, *Buckinghamshire* (6–SU 9490). The old town of Beaconsfield is separated from the new by over a quarter of a mile of wooded country. It is developed around what must have been two main highways, from London to OXFORD and from WINDSOR to AYLESBURY. There are coaching inns on opposite corners of the cross-roads.

Along the roads centred by a green are houses of the Queen Anne and Georgian periods. The main inns where the coaches halted in the 18th cent. are the Royal Saracen's Head, a large building of half-timbered construction, and the Royal White Hart at which Queen Elizabeth I stayed and where Oliver Cromwell stationed his troops in the grounds.

The old town retains much of the charm of former days with the buildings standing back from the roadside, allowing ample parking space.

The Old Rectory, overlooking the churchyard, is of the 16th cent., half-timbered with a panelled room and spiral staircase, and is now the parish meeting place. Edmund Burke, the great parliamentarian, lived in this village and was buried here in 1797, and G. K. Chesterton was resident here for many years.

Hall Barn House, a 17th-cent. brick mansion, is S. of the main road. It is ornately decorated and has stone pilasters and a garden filled with obelisks and temples.

St Mary's Church, on the corner of the crossroads, is of medieval origin, although mainly rebuilt in the last century. It has a fine flint tower rising above the trees, and between the chapel and the chancel is a section of a 15th-cent. screen. There are many monuments of interest and an exquisite tapestry. Of note is an iron-bound chest covered in paintings of ships by a quayside. Opposite the church is a Victorian building in which the police station is housed.

The new town of Beaconsfield, which began to form in 1909, is a pleasant residential area. Of particular interest is Bekonscot Miniature Village in Warwick Road, laid out with tiny cottages, farms and meadows, churches, a railway, a lake, streams and an airport. The village is modelled on the scale of 1 in. to 1 ft, and is a children's paradise.

Close by are the Chiltern beechwoods at **Coleshill** and just E. of the town is the golf course, adjacent to **Wilton Park**, a historic estate, from which can be seen the beauty of the countryside around.

BEDFORD, *Bedfordshire* (10–TL0449). This is the county town and, although a centre of industry, it has a great deal of interest both in its buildings and in the history connected with it. It has been a trading place for nearly 1,000 years and its position on the River Ouse, which divides the town in two, has added to its prosperity, as many of its manufactured agricultural implements were transported by barges. Its main industries now, however, are engineering and metallics.

The River Ouse has also given the town much of beauty, for around it has grown the Embankment, a fine street with public gardens on either side of the river. There are two bridges of note: one is Georgian, designed by Wing, with five segmental arches and stone balustrades; and the other, a suspension bridge for pedestrians only, is late Victorian.

Among the many old inns, the most notable is the Swan Hotel, at the northern end of the stone bridge. Built in 1794 for the Duke of Bedford, it is a gracious building, with a staircase believed to have been designed by Wren, with twisted balusters and a string, and taken from the dismantled Houghton Conquest House at AMPTHILL. Opposite the Swan Hotel on the south bank of the Ouse stands the tower block of the County Hotel.

The town's centre is St Paul's Square and the High Street, with the massive Church of St Paul, considerably restored in the last two centuries. The doorway of the church is Early English, but much of the rest seems to be 14th- and 15th-cent. with embattled clerestory and aisles and, on the upper floor, statue niches. Most of the interior was also restored in Victorian days but its most interesting feature is that the aisles are the same height as the nave with clerestory windows. The font has a decorated base and the ornate pulpit is 16th-cent. The rood-screen is by Bodley. Monuments of particular interest include one to the S. of the altar to Simon de Beauchamp, 1208, and to Sir William Harpur and his wife.

Bedford has always been one of the foremost centres for education, due mainly to Sir William Harpur, who eventually became Lord Mayor of London. Born in Bedford in 1496, he purchased land in London for a nominal sum and from the profits which accrued built the Bedford Grammar School. Just over 200 years later the value of the property had increased to £30,000 and the trust which administered it founded other schools, until, in 1866, 1,860 children were being educated from it. Part of a school house, built in 1756, is now the Town Hall, with Sir William's statue in the doorway. It is ashlar-faced and part of it was added in 1859. Behind the Town Hall are the new municipal offices, seven floors high.

The present Bedford School in De Parys Avenue is late Victorian, Gothic-styled with a turret, and in Harpur Street is Bedford Modern School. The 19th-cent. Public Library has a Greek Doric temple front. Bedford High School for Girls, of the same period, is one of the finest of the school buildings. In Tudor style, with giant pilasters in the centre, its corners have attractive half-domed bow-windows.

In Dame Alice Street is a long range of late Georgian, dark red-bricked almshouses (one range was demolished in 1968) and in the High Street is the Lion Hotel, of about the same time, stuccoed with large pilasters and first-floor balconies.

In Mill Street are buildings commemorating two of the town's most famous people, John Howard and John Bunyan. The stuccoed Congregational chapel is in memory of John Howard, born 1726, who spent his youth at CARDINGTON, travelled the world widely and became High Sheriff of Bedfordshire. He learnt of the appalling conditions in Bedford prisons, which were due mainly to the fact that the gaoler was not paid a fixed wage but extorted money from prisoners before allowing them to go free. Howard's discoveries and complaints led to two bills being passed in the House of Commons reforming goals. A statue of John Howard stands in St Paul's Square.

Bunyan Meeting House with its fine bronze doors commemorates the man who, born a tinker, was a Cromwellian soldier and eventually acquired deep religious convictions, preaching all over the country. At the time of the Restoration, this was illegal for one not ordained, and as a result he spent many years in prison, where it is believed he wrote *Pilgrim's Progress* and other notable works. The Bunyan Museum, adjoining the Meeting House, is filled with articles of interest, including his iron fiddle and other musical instruments, and the Public Library has a valuable Bunyan collection. A statue of him stands on St Peter's Green and the town has several plaques to his memory, including one on the County Gaol. In the surrounding countryside people still refer proudly to the fact that it is "Bunyan country".

In Kempston Road are the Victorian Britannia Ironworks, fine buildings with an interesting gateway.

Facing the river, close by Market Square, which has open markets twice a week, is Shire Hall, a late Victorian building of red brick and terracotta, with a Gothic porch and Elizabethan windows. Across the river is the new County Hall complex with council chamber, library and record office. Nearby is the Corn Exchange with an attic upon which are four massive chimneys. The mid-Georgian prison, with three pavilions and an archway in the middle, was designed by Wing and has been twice extended. The north wing of the Bedford General Hospital, in Kimbolton Road, incorporates the former 18th-cent. workhouse and has a hipped roof and an 11-bay brick front.

There are numerous medieval, Victorian and modern churches, St Peter's being the largest. St Merton de Merton shows evidence of Anglo-Saxon workmanship. It has a central Norman tower with twin bell-openings, and a Norman south doorway. The present chancel was the nave of the Anglo-Saxon church. The octagonal font is large with quatrefoils and motifs. St Mary's Church, in St Mary's Square, is also partly Norman, with a crossing tower containing large twin bell-openings. It has a simple but charming plaster and whitewash interior with plain Georgian benches and a sculptured Norman head.

The Cecil Higgins Art Gallery has a superb collection of paintings and prints, sculpture, including works by Epstein and Henry Moore, 18th-cent. furniture and old lace and embroidery. There is also a fine collection of English and Continental porcelain.

Bedford Museum tells the county's history, with Iron Age and Roman archaeological finds, works from Anglo-Saxon times, local animals and birds, and specimens of lace-making and straw-plaiting.

BENINGTON, *Hertfordshire* (10–TL3023). This enchanting village, slightly modernized on the outskirts, is reached through a wooded country lane winding upwards to the village green, with a pond overhung by willows. By the green are picturesque 16th-cent. cottages of timber and plaster and the old Bell Inn.

St Peter's Church, a simple village church of the 13th to 15th cents., has a lovely north chancel chapel, with flowing tracery in the windows and under one of its two arches a monument with two fine portraits of a knight and his lady. The workmanship is early 14th-cent. The chancel has much-restored sedilia decorated with crocket capitals. The octagonal font is 15th-cent. and the benches are of the same period.

The 17th-cent. Old Rectory has altered during the years but of particular interest are the windows in the gables. The Lordship is a Georgian house, converted to match the remains of the keep of Benington Castle, hiding behind the church. The kings of Mercia lived in the castle, and on the hill Berthulf is said to have held a council in A.D. 850.

BERKHAMSTED, *Hertfordshire* (10–SP 9907). This small town, of ancient origin, was the birthplace of Bishop Ken in 1637 and has much to interest the visitor, with its old churches, inns and other buildings. The rolling countryside adjoining it is attractive and the 1,200-acre common, with its beech and birch trees, gorse and bracken, is pleasant to walk and picnic in.

The town is set on a hill-top and although little remains today of its castle, except the motte and bailey and a unique double moat, it was once one of the most important castles in the country. William the Conqueror made a gift of it to his half-brother, Robert of Mortain, and Thomas à Becket spent 10 years there during his period as Chancellor. Besieged by King Louis of France in 1216, it eventually became an appendage of the Dukes of Cornwall. In 1376 the Black Prince spent the last days of his life there. Earthworks in the grounds are impressive and it is open to the public.

St Peter's Church is a large, handsome, cruciform building of flint with the outstanding feature of a blue and gold clock on a timber belfry. Five periods can be distinguished in the building, although it was heavily restored in 1871. Of 13th-cent. origin, it retains its original chancel, nave, transepts and central tower. It was added to during the centuries, and of particular interest are St Catherine's Chapel, of the 14th cent., its porch which was added later, St John the Baptist's Chapel and the 15th-cent. clerestory in the nave. The top story of the 13th-cent. tower was added 400 years ago. The screen in the west tower arch is of the 15th cent. and is adorned with many figures of importance. A carved chest is 300 years old and the pulpit, decorated with angels, is of 19th-cent. origin. The church contains many fine monuments and a medieval coffin with a floral cross. There are numerous brasses of interest.

The High Street, centred around the church, runs parallel with the River Bulbourne. Court House, a 16th-cent. timbered building with a projecting upper story, is SW. of the church and nearby, S. of the church, is Berkhamsted's finest building, Incent's House, also of the 16th cent. Half-timbered, with an overhanging upper story, it has been carefully restored in recent years. It is believed to have been the residence of John Incent, Dean of St Paul's, who founded Berkhamsted Grammar School in the 17th cent. The school, to the N. of the churchyard, its red brickwork mellowed with the years, has stone mullioned windows and a fine timber entrance. Its chapel has an altar reached from the nave by 19 steps.

The town has four inns of importance. There is the red-bricked King's Arms, with three bay windows on the first floor, and, by the War Memorial in the narrow part of the High Street, is the plastered and gabled Bell Inn. Swan Inn, of the 17th cent., has two gables, and near it are 18th-cent. houses with quoins and dressings. The Red House Hotel, also of the 18th cent., is ornate; its handsome porch of seven bays and Ionic columns and pediments has a large Venetian window above.

Also in the High Street are the Friends' Meeting House, dated 1818, and the Victorian Baptist church, a building of red and yellow brick, typical of its period.

The gabled Elizabethan house, Berkhamsted Place, the remains of a courtyard house built about 1580 and twice altered in the following century, has a central hall and entrance, an original oriel window and large fireplace, the latter altered in the 17th cent. On the first floor is an interesting ceiling. On the north-west side of the building the stone and flint chequer design is of the 16th cent.

The Sayer Almshouses, 1684, a row of six brick houses of one story centred by a large pediment, are close by Boxwell House, which was built in the early 18th cent. with three wide bays and a cemented front decorated with quoins.

One m. S. of Berkhamsted is Ashlyns, a large house built on the top of a slope in about 1800, with a charming bow-front centre and an iron veranda.

BIGGLESWADE, *Bedfordshire* (10–TL1944), is on the River Ivel and it is the river which gave the town its past prosperity, for within the memory of some of its oldest inhabitants the Ivel was navigable from the sea to just W. of the town. When the Romans built a major road, they made a ford over the river here and this ford formed the basis of what is now the town itself. The bridge which spans the river has three pointed arches and is of the 14th cent. Two great flour mills stand on the river's bank.

It has for long been a busy market-gardening area and recently light engineering has become its second largest industry. Market Place is the centre of the town, where a general market is held each week. The Old Market House is timber-framed with a timber roof, and the former Victorian Town Hall has a five-bayed stuccoed front with massive Roman Doric columns. The White Hart Inn is also timber-framed and the late-18th-cent. Crown Hotel has pleasant Art Nouveau lettering.

In London Road is the Limes, the former workhouse, of yellow brick with an octagonal centre and wings, dated 1835.

Berkhamsted is situated on the Grand Union Canal on its route from London to Birmingham

Raymond Lea/Spectrum

St Andrew's Church is large and, although externally renewed, is mainly Perpendicular. The tower is 18th-cent. and has round-arched bell-openings. Towards the nave is a high tower arch of the 14th cent. The font has a Perpendicular shaft, and the 15th-cent. south door a full traceried head. There is a brass to William Halsted and his wife dated 1449.

In St John's Street is the church of the same name, a yellow-brick, Victorian building with red-brick decoration. On the east gable of the nave is a big bellcot and there are several long lancets.

To the S. of the town, on the HITCHIN road, is a windmill, and to the N., Shorthand House, of yellow brick with a large Tuscan porch, built in the 18th cent.

BISHOP'S STORTFORD, *Hertfordshire* (11–TL4821). This hilly town, although greatly modernized, is of medieval origin with numerous old buildings and many of the Victorian era.

The George Hotel, at the corner of High Street and North Street, is two-storied and pargeted in the old part, with an early Victorian addition of three stories. In Bridge Street is the 16th-cent. Black Lion, a picturesque building, with exposed timbers, gables and an overhanging upper story. Nearby is the equally attractive Boar's Head, and across the bridge over the River Stort are the ruins of Waytemore Castle, with a narrow 40-ft-high mount. At the top of a hill is the 17th-cent. Cock Inn and in the same street are handsome 17th-cent. houses and one which is late Georgian. Hockerill Training College, of red brick, is Victorian with diaper work with stone edgings.

The Corn Exchange, in the Victorian part of the town, was built in 1828 in a neo-Grecian style. The ground floor has Tuscan piers and in its upper floors is a giant Ionic portico. Bishop's Stortford College is in the Gothic style with a memorial hall of the present century which is elegantly neo-Georgian.

The Congregational church in Water Lane is an elongated building of stock-brick with two towers and Italian-style edgings.

Windmill Hill has houses and cottages of several centuries with a 17th-cent. malthouse and granary attached to one group of cottages. Down Northgate End, amid large suburban houses and old cottages, is Brooke House, a fine building of white brick in three stories with lower wings and a Roman Doric doorcase.

Bishop's Stortford was the birthplace of Cecil Rhodes and in the Old Vicarage, which is now a museum, are preserved many of his possessions. These include the bed in which he was born, his bible, a watercolour he painted and his ceremonial uniforms.

There are two churches of interest. All Saints in Hockerill is of modern origin and overlooks the town, its large square tower supported by a hipped roof and with long, lancet windows. St Michael's is a large 15th-cent. church with a tall, prominent spire added to the tower in 1812. The only other later additions are the tall south vestry and the north chancel chapel, both 19th-cent. The chancel stalls have poppy heads in the front seats and misericords in the back. The large screen is richly carved with two tall four-light sections on each side of the entrance. The square 12th-cent. font is of Purbeck marble.

Wickham Hall, 1¾ m. NW. of the town, and Stortford Park, 1½ m. W., are particularly handsome farm-houses.

BLEDLOW RIDGE, *Buckinghamshire* (6–SU 7898). One of the finest beauty-spots in the county, Bledlow Ridge is reached by a steep hill with a road running across it. It is part of the Chilterns, with the village of its name deep in the valley below. The historic **Icknield Way** runs at its foot and the woods are thick with trees of many varieties: beeches and cherries, yellow limes and bronzed hornbeams. The green fields below have indents of white showing the chalk beneath the soil. To the W. of the ridge top lie the long, uneven lines of the hedgerows. Down the curving road, lined with yew trees and elms, is Wain Hill, on which, with the turf cut away and the white chalk beneath revealing the shape, is a great Greek cross, one of the only two turf-cut crosses in the county.

BLETSOE, *Bedfordshire* (10–TL0258). Set back from the main road, this little village has the remains of what was once a castle. It is now a farm-house, with a long Elizabethan front and a Jacobean staircase. Henry VII's mother, the Lady Margaret, was born here and it was visited by Queen Elizabeth I.

St Mary's Church, down a small turning off the main road, is mostly 14th-cent. with a 13th-cent. doorway and some Victorian restoration. The nave has traceried windows and the Perpendicular font is of octagonal shape with arched panels. In the north transept is a large alabaster monument to Sir John St John, 1559, with his family. That to Frances, Countess Bolingbroke, 1678, is a fine tablet with two urns.

The old Falcon Inn, by the river, was a favourite haunt of Edward FitzGerald, the translator of *The Rubaiyat of Omar Khayyam*, and his friend Thackeray.

BOUGHTON, *Northamptonshire* (10–SP7565), is a tiny, attractive village, on the outskirts of which are some prosperous houses. It has picturesque cottages, some of ironstone and some thatched. For 500 years a village fair was held on the green, which lies beside the ruins of the old church. In the village is the Church of St John, with a battlemented 15th-cent. tower. It has a simple interior, without aisles, and its nave and chancel have been rebuilt.

Boughton Park, nearby, with falconry towers which were used when hawking was fashionable, was rebuilt in Tudor style in 1844. The lodges and follies surrounding it, however, are Georgian.

BRACKLEY, *Northamptonshire* (10–SP5837). Negotiations on the Magna Carta took place at

Brackley Castle (no longer in existence) in 1215. It is a charming, residential town which was once a large wool centre. Its wide main street, over a mile long, is flanked by trees and there are good parking facilities. It is dominated by the 18th-cent. Town Hall which was built by the Duke of Bridgewater and has high roofs and a cupola. The streets running off the main one are very narrow, with old cottages. The oldest building is the Hospital of St James and St John, a monastery that became a school at the time of the Dissolution and it is still used for the same purpose. It is known as Magdalen College School, because in the 15th cent. the OXFORD college of that name purchased it and when the Plague raged its Fellows took refuge there. It has one of the oldest school chapels in the country, for although greatly restored it still retains many original features, with a Norman doorway and Norman font and a 13th-cent. tower.

Nearby is the manor house, also a school, with the old manor cottage adjoining it. There are several old inns, one of interest being the Plough, with its circular brick wall and large archway leading to what were once the stables. The Fire Station is Victorian and the long row of old almshouses has recently been modernized. On the outskirts are modern buildings and industries as well as the Brackley Saw Mills.

St Peter's Church is behind the main street. It has a 13th-cent. tower, the west front of which is enriched by arcades and corbels and a tiny lancet window. It has a Norman south doorway and has been much restored, but the spacious crypt has 700-year-old vaulting and over the west door are worn statues of St Peter and St Hugh. The windows are very fine and there are several monuments.

The National Trust Park covers three acres, a public park as well as a children's playground. From it can be seen fine views of the Ouse Valley.

BRADENHAM, *Buckinghamshire* (6–SU8297). This village, among wooded hillsides NW. of HIGH WYCOMBE, was the home of one of Britain's most renowned prime ministers, Benjamin Disraeli. He lived at Bradenham Manor with his father, Isaac Disraeli, who was a writer of repute and whose works include *Curiosities of Literature*.

Queen Elizabeth I was entertained at the manor during one of her many travels. The churchyard in which Isaac Disraeli is buried lies on one side of the house and the other side overlooks the large green which is now the village cricket ground. Around the green stand old cottages.

St Botolph's Church, by the side of the manor, has a 15th-cent. tower with a pyramid roof holding two of England's oldest bells. The nave and the doorway were both built about 1100; the latter has a modern porch. The richly carved lintel and pillars hold a simple tympanum within which is the figure of St Botolph adorned with flying swans and a model of a church. Almost overpowering the small building is a massive wall monument to Charles West, with life-sized 17th-cent. figures and a cherub's head at each

corner of the tomb. The modern rood-loft, with its attractive screen, stretches from wall to wall.

BRAMPTON, *Huntingdonshire* (10–TL2170), is on the loop of the River Ouse, with Alconbury Brook on its north side, over which stretches Nuns Bridge. New houses have been built here recently, but it still retains its village green, on which stands an 18th-cent. obelisk, a signpost for HUNTINGDON and London.

There are many picturesque old cottages and an ancient watermill, as well as the Black Bull Inn which is 300 years old. Samuel Pepys spent much of his time in Pepys House, a farm-house on the Huntingdon road. Brampton Park and the manor house have both been rebuilt.

St Mary's Church is mostly Perpendicular, but the chancel and the piscina are both late 13th-cent. The tower, with the date 1635 over the door, appears to be Decorated. The octagonal font has pointed quatrefoils and the Decorated rood-screen, with its one-light divisions, has doors with ogee arches. Three medieval stalls have finely carved *misereres* and the altar rails are 17th-cent. There are several monuments, one of particular interest, dated 1689, is to Mrs Jackson, sister of Pepys and the last member of the family to live in the parish.

BRILL, *Buckinghamshire* (10–SP6513), is one of the county's loveliest villages, reached by a climb of 600 ft. It commands magnificent views both of the Vale of Aylesbury and into Oxfordshire. The 17th-cent. red-brick windmill on the hill has been restored by the National Trust. One of its beams is carved with figures and letters.

The cottages and almshouses of this interesting village are set around two delightful greens. A royal palace existed here in Anglo-Saxon and Norman times. In 1664 it was the winter quarters for Oliver Cromwell's troops. There is a timber-framed Tudor manor house with red-brick gateposts.

The 12th-cent. parish church has been added to in later years. The low 15th-cent. tower has a small lead spire. Entered by two narrow Norman doorways, it has a Norman window above the pointed tower arch. The Jacobean chancel roof with its ornamental arches resting on a tie-beam and its five-pierced central arch is of special interest. The chancel and the font are both 14th-cent.

A short distance away, reached through a wooded valley down a steep hill, is Boarstall Tower belonging to the National Trust. The gateway to Boarstall House, it is now all that remains of this once massive building. It has a moat spanned by an 18th-cent. bridge.

During the Civil War this area formed the dividing line between the King at OXFORD and Cromwell at AYLESBURY and was held first by one side and then by the other until after two years the King surrendered.

BRIXWORTH, *Northamptonshire* (10–SP74 70), is situated about 6 m. N. of NORTHAMPTON and has one of the most remarkable structures in the county: the Church of All Saints, which was built about the 7th cent. by the monks of PETER-BOROUGH, when the district had only just been converted to Christianity. Most of the exterior is of stone rubble but the abaci and the arches have Roman tiles. In the 10th or early 11th cent. part of the present sanctuary and the circular staircase turret were added and the two-storied porch transformed into a tower, the top of which together with the spire, is medieval. In the tower is an upper chamber, reached by the staircase, with a window looking into the nave. The apse was restored on its old foundation in the mid-19th cent. Built into the side of the south doorway is an Anglo-Saxon carving of an eagle. The 17th-cent. south chapel is separated from the choir by 13th-cent. arches, in one of which is a 15th-cent. screen. The font is medieval, with a small bowl on a tall round shaft. In a recess in the south chapel is the 13th-cent. tomb of Sir John de Verdun, on which he lies in chain mail and a surcoat. Around the church, outside the apse, is the ambulatory or sunken passage, entered from the inside, for pilgrims viewing relics housed in recesses in the outer walls.

The church stands back from the village, in which there are old stone houses and an early 19th-cent. Methodist chapel. There is also part of the 14th-cent. market cross. Brixworth and the surrounding district have been a centre for hunting for as long as can be recalled and the Pytchley Hunt kennels are good neo-Georgian buildings.

BROMHAM, *Bedfordshire* (10–TL0051). One of the features of this residential village is its bridge with 26 archways which crosses the River Ouse. Although restored in the last century, it dates back to the 13th cent.

Charles I stayed at Bromham Hall, which was the home of Sir Lewis Dyve, a Royalist, who escaped during the Civil War by swimming the River Ouse. The house has a large 14th-cent. doorway.

St Owen's Church, set high in parklands with views of the valley below, appears to be originally 13th-cent. The interior of the church is of varying periods and has a high stair-turret attached to the tower, an octagonal Perpendicular font with tracery, a lectern with poppyheads and an hour-glass stand. Interesting monuments include a brass with 4-ft-long figures of Thomas Wideville and his two wives, 1435, and an alabaster five-poster with the reclining figure of Sir Lewis Dyve on a half-rolled-up mat, dated 1603. An early Victorian monument to twelve-year-old Eva Trevor shows her floating to heaven.

BROUGHTON, *Huntingdonshire* (10–TL 2878), nestles in a deep, secluded valley among delightful scenery, with only the top of the church spire indicating its existence. It was originally the chief administrative headquarters of the Abbots of RAMSEY, but only a moat marks the site of the mansion.

On the village green is an oblong-shaped brick lock-up of the 19th cent., and there are several outstanding Jacobean and Georgian farm-houses and a 17th-cent. house, SW. of the church, with a square porch, shaped end-gables and a frill cut into the bricks of the doorway.

Most of the Church of All Saints is Perpendicular, with its stone tower and broach spire. The chancel, with its double piscina, however, is Early English and the south doorways of the nave about 1300. The square font is Norman and has blank arcading, and the communion rail is 18th-cent. There are several paintings, including Doom, over the chancel arch, which is 15th-cent., and Expulsion, with Adam delving and Eve spinning. Only part of a brass to Laurence Marton and his wife, about 1490, is preserved.

BUCKDEN, *Huntingdonshire* (10–TL1967. This pretty village, once a posting station, was originally the site of the palace of the Bishops of LINCOLN. Only a little remains of what was, in the 13th cent., a very large building. There are still the outer gateway and walling, the inner gatehouse and the Great Tower, which is three stories high and oblong in shape, of red brick with dark blue bricks in the diapers. There is a basement entrance and a ground-floor entrance. The inner gatehouse is also three-storied. Buckden Palace, which incorporates the remains, has been restored and is now a Roman Catholic school. It is open to the public on Sundays.

In the High Street are several attractive brick houses, the best of which is Jessamine House, N. of the palace. The timber-framed Lion Hotel was built about 1500 and its entrance hall has moulded beams and a large boss with the Agnus Dei. The George Hotel, opposite, part 17th- and part 18th-cent. is a long, three-story brick building. The vicarage is in Church Street, as is the timber-framed Manor House, of the 16th and 17th cents. Bridge House is Georgian, and opposite it are yellow-brick Victorian almshouses.

St Mary's Church has a Perpendicular tower with a graceful steeple. The nave, dated 1436–9, is divided from the aisles by five-bay arcades. There are 16th-cent. Flemish Passion scenes on the readers' desks. The many interesting monuments include a lovely large white Gothic triptych to Robert Whitworth, dated 1831. The octagonal font is Perpendicular and the pulpit Jacobean.

BUCKINGHAM, *Buckinghamshire* (10–SP69 33). In the north of the county, reached through unspoilt countryside, is this town with its many historical associations. Situated on a hill-top and once the county town, made so by King Alfred in 886, it is now a place of great antiquity and is delightful to wander through with its steep narrow streets.

A typical market town, its main street is lined with old buildings which, although mostly converted into shops, have not been changed in structure from the times in which they were built.

In former days Buckingham was an important area for wool but because of its inaccessibility this industry declined and was lost. Perhaps

Burnham Beeches

because of its lack of any main industry, the town retains much of its original character.

Catherine of Aragon rested in Buckingham in 1513 and Charles I held a council of war in the old banqueting rooms of Castle House, still in existence, the fireplace and carved mantelpiece bearing the date of 1619.

The red-brick Georgian Town Hall holds much of historical interest, its clock-tower surmounted by the gilded swan of Buckingham. In the plain 14th-cent. Manor House Queen Elizabeth I dined in 1578; its fascinating twisted chimney is Tudor. The Old Gaol in the centre of the Market Square is 18th-cent. and was built on the assumption that the assizes would again be held there. The Old Latin School, of 16th-cent. origin and a National Trust property, is built on the site of a 13th-cent. chantry chapel and has a carved Norman doorway. Edward VI and Dame Isabel Denton gave monies to support the school.

The town has many old almshouses and inns, two of the most notable being the Swan and Castle Inn and the White Hart Hotel, the latter built in the 18th cent. after an earlier inn on the same site had been destroyed in a disastrous fire which swept the town in 1725. The portico and sign were added in Victorian times.

The Parish Church of SS. Peter and Paul, twice rebuilt in 1777 and 1862, and prominent on a hill-top, is believed to be on the site of an Anglo-Saxon fortification. The chancel is Victorian but the carved bench-ends, with shields and quarterings, bear the date 1619. A great shield, carved with a swan, rests over the west door. The Buckingham Needle and Thread Society have donated many things which give the church its lovely interior. In 1890 its east window, representing the *Te Deum*, was given by the Society, as well as the delightful altar cloth and the reredos depicting the Nativity. Presented in 1471 by John Rudying, a Latin manuscript Bible is preserved under glass now as it was once stolen and only recovered in the 18th cent.

BURNHAM, *Buckinghamshire* (6–SU9382). This fairly large residential village is of ancient origin, its greatest claim to fame being the forest of Burnham Beeches with huge pollarded beeches, glades and winding lanes. It stretches for nearly 600 acres. Centuries ago it was part of the Chiltern forests and is bordered by Dorneywood, a National Trust property. It is one of the country's finest beauty-spots.

On the slopes by an orchard still exists a fair that was famous in medieval days.

Although the village has modern shops and residential roads the old charm remains and there are many 15th- and 16th-cent. houses and a fine 13th-cent. church. The church has a tower with an oak-shingled spire. The great altar rails dated 1663 have five beautifully carved oak panels. At the end of the nave are many interesting brasses and by the south door a white marble wall monument sculptured by John Bacon.

To the S. of the centre of the village can be seen the remains of Burnham Abbey, founded in 1266, and although much rebuilt, still retaining segments from Norman times.

BUSHEY, *Hertfordshire* (6–TQ1395). This once small village has extended greatly in the past two decades, turning into a rambling commuter centre for London, but still retaining much of interest for the visitor, mainly around the old church.

St James's Church, in the High Street, enlarged in the last century, has a high 15th-cent. nave and west tower with a stair-turret. Built of flint, its chancel is of the 13th cent. and the windows to the N. and S. are original. An unusual feature, a tympanum with the royal arms of Queen Anne, rests on a large beam and divides the nave from the chancel. The Jacobean pulpit has strapwork motifs and the original sounding board above.

The Rectory, E. of the church, although altered in the 19th cent., still has many of its original 17th-cent. features, including two interesting fireplaces.

Around the church is a pretty group of cottages and, higher up the street, Bushey House, with a Greek-Doric portico built at the beginning of the 19th cent. Bourne Hall, opposite, is Georgian, three stories high with eight bays. There are a number of pleasant 19th-cent. Gothic villas but the Cloisters is mid-Victorian. Both the Congregational and the Methodist churches were built in 1904, the former in a style typical of the period.

In Aldenham Road, a little further out, is Bushey Hall, a large Victorian brick and stone mansion, its tower on the left standing away from the main structure.

There is an interesting 18th-cent. house, once known as Sly's Castle and now called Hilfield, in Hilfield Lane. It is a cemented building, castellated and turreted and has a gatehouse with porticullis.

CARDINGTON, *Bedfordshire* (10–TL0847). This attractive village, with much history attached to it, has an R.A.F. station, and has long been connected with aviation, as will be seen by the large sheds rebuilt for the two airships R100 and R101. The latter crashed on its maiden flight in 1930, killing all but eight of the people on board and the ensign that survived the disaster is now in Cardington church; there is a monument in the churchyard.

John Howard, the philanthropist, spent most of his life here and his house, Howard Villa, an 18th-cent. building with three bays, is by the village green. Many pleasant old houses surround the green, as well as several estate cottages built by John Howard, dated 1763, 1764.

Cardington Bridge, with its five brick arches, was built for Samuel Whitbread, the brewer, by John Smeaton in 1778. Samuel Whitbread also built the mill.

St Mary's Church is large and mainly of 1900, but the chancel, south doorways of the nave and south chapel are Perpendicular. The rare font, a gift of Harriet Whitbread in 1783, is of black Wedgwood basalt. The carved lectern dates from 1955. There are many splendid monuments, several of which are to the Whitbread family. Two tomb-chest brasses of special note are of Sir William Gascoigne, and his two wives, 1540, who was comptroller of Cardinal Wolsey's household, and of Sir Jarrate Harvye and his wife, 1638.

CASTLE ASHBY, *Northamptonshire* (10–SP8659). There are two places of interest here: Castle Ashby House and its church. The house is set in grounds covering over a square mile, which were landscaped by Capability Brown, although its avenues were planted after a visit of William III. There are seven ornamental lakes and lovely views. The house was started by the 1st Lord Compton, who eventually was created Earl of Northampton, in 1574, and is still owned by the same family. It was originally built in the shape of an E, but in the 17th cent. the openings were joined by a screen by Inigo Jones. It has numerous windows and two octagonal towers. In the parapet of the east wing is a carved Latin inscription. The great hall has a timber roof of 1770, as well as an organ and a minstrels' gallery, and the 17th-cent. wooden staircase is carved with animals, snakes, trees and cherubs as well as hunting scenes. There is a valuable collection of paintings and furniture, a collection of Greek vases and a pair of bellows by Benvenuto Cellini. House and gardens are open to the public.

The church, in the grounds, has a large yew standing by the gate and the building is much restored. It is 14th- and 15th-cent., with an attractive tower topped by a pyramid roof. A screen with Jacobean panels is at the end of the south aisle and the 17th-cent. pulpit has an ornate sounding-board. There are many monuments to the Comptons, but of particular interest is a brass in the chancel floor of the rector William Ermyn, 1401, his cope elaborately decorated with 10 saints all standing under traceried canopies.

CASTOR, *Huntingdonshire* (10–TL1298), is of Roman origin, standing on the banks of the River Nene, in beautiful countryside with grey stone farms and thatched cottages. At the west end of the village is Village Farmhouse, which has an Anglo-Saxon window in the side entrance. Castor House, at the east end, is a Georgian building of two stories with five bays. A mile further on, opposite PETERBOROUGH golf course, are two standing stones named Robin Hood and Little John, believed to date from the Bronze Age.

Milton Hall, the seat of the Fitzwilliam family, is in a vast park. The north front is Elizabethan and the south side 18th-cent. Sir William Fitzwilliam was the custodian of Mary Queen of Scots during the period of her imprisonment at FOTHERINGHAY. Nearby is Milton Ferry with its three-arched bridge, built in 1716.

The cruciform Church of St Kyneburgha is the only one in the country dedicated to this saint, who was the daughter of the pagan King Peada of Mercia, who eventually became a Christian and founded Peterborough Abbey. It has a fine Norman tower with a richly decorated steeple with an inscription 1124 recording the consecration of the church. The tower is in four stages, its walls panelled in Romanesque detail. There are fragments of older carvings and additions of the 14th cent. The pretty transept was once used as a village school. Three wall paintings depict the life of St Catherine, and a small stone statue of a man stands in the chancel and is believed to be 9th-cent.

Near the church are Roman remains excavated in 1822. Pavements, temples, villas and baths were found and covered up again.

A half m. SE. of the village at **Mill Hill** is the site of a Roman villa. It was a two-winged house with a small building nearby which was possibly the bath house.

CHALFONT ST GILES, *Buckinghamshire* (6–SU9993). A pretty village, lying in the valley of the Misbourne on the A413 to AYLESBURY, is renowned for its connections with John Milton the poet.

Milton came here during the plague year of 1665 to find peace and write. Growing old in loneliness and blindness it was here he wrote *Paradise Lost* and it was from here that his friend Ellwood the Quaker suggested he should write *Paradise Regained. Paradise Lost* brought him the princely sum of £5. Milton's cottage is now a museum open to the public.

The Church of St Giles is very much a family church. Built of flint, part of it is 12th-cent. Reached by a gateway, the doorway of the medieval church is decorated with 600-year-old ball-flowers, and the interior is a rich array of 14th-cent. paintings and 15th-cent. angels displayed on the roof. The tower was built in the 15th cent. when the church was refashioned.

In the churchyard lies a man of modern times, Bertram Mills, who will ever be remembered for his circuses. He was greatly beloved for his widespread charity.

The old Chalfont mill is on the River Misbourne, which is but a trickle now, and nearby is The Vache, the handsome 16th-cent. manor house often visited by Captain Cook who gave its name to a South Sea Island. A monument to him is in the grounds.

CHEQUERS, *Buckinghamshire* (10–SP8506). Near to Kimble, with ELLESBOROUGH as its parish church, stands the country home of the Prime Minister, hidden away from the road in hundreds of acres of parkland.

Chequers Court was given to the nation for the benefit of the prime ministers of Britain in perpetuity as a thank-offering for the ending of the First World War.

The 13th-cent. manor house was rebuilt by Sir William Hawtrey in the 15th cent. and in one of the great fireplaces are entwined the initials A.H. and W.H. The sister of Lady Jane Grey,

Lady Mary, was confined there in disgrace by Elizabeth I after her secret marriage to Thomas Keys who died in prison.

CHESHUNT, *Hertfordshire* (10–TL3502), is an old rambling village with its High Street stretching for over a mile. Much of this thoroughfare and the surrounding streets has been drastically modernized.

In Turner's Hill is a group of old houses with, of particular interest, the yellow-brick early-19th-cent. Grange and the 18th-cent. Manor House, three stories high with two-bay lower wings and a doorcase with rusticated pilasters. The Dewhurst Almshouses, 10 one-storied brick cottages in a line, were founded in 1642. The 18th-cent. red-brick Clock House, with seven bays and two stories is in Blind Man's Lane, and in College Road will be found the large houses of Cheshunt Cottage, early 19th-cent. with hood-moulds over the windows and bargeboard gables, and Brookside House, of the same period.

Cheshunt Great House, ½ m. NW. of the church, was originally a large moated house. All that remains is one wing of a courtyard house, but this is impressive with its late-15th-cent. great hall, 40 ft long with an original timber roof. The house was converted at the beginning of the 18th cent. and added to in the following century.

Near to the church in Churchgate and Churchfield can be seen some of the old character of the village, of particular note the brick-built Dewhurst Charity School, dated 1640, with three gables and mullioned brick windows.

St Mary's Church, built in the 15th cent., has an embattled west tower of ashlar stone and a south-east stair-turret. There are a number of brasses of interest.

CHESTERTON, *Huntingdonshire* (10–TL12 95), is not really a village, for there are no shops or main centre, but it has two features of interest, the church and the Roman ruins on the outskirts.

The entrance to the Church of St Michael is down a narrow path off a road running past spacious, modern houses. The church is of the 18th cent., a period of which there are few examples in the county, but it has a fine Early English tower with long lancets and twin bell-openings under a pointed arch. There is much Georgian work in the interior, including the chancel, a wooden screen in Roman Doric style and a broad reredos. The altar table, communion rail and font are also of this period. There is a monument to William Beville, 1483, and a Jacobean one to Sir Robert Beville and his family, showing two kneeling couples with their children facing them. There is also a memorial to John Dryden, cousin of the poet.

On the A1, a mile or so past Chesterton, are the extensive earthworks of **Durobrivae**, a Roman town enclosed in 40 acres, scheduled as an Ancient Monument.

CHILTON, *Buckinghamshire* (10–SP6811), stands on a hill with magnificent views all around it. It is a simple, unspoilt village with many old cottages, some timbered, others of wattle and daub. Roofs are both thatched and tiled.

St Mary's Church is sited on a rise and its foundations are Norman. The 14th-cent. tower has grotesquely carved gargoyles; the 16th-cent. roof of the nave is supported by corbels adorned with angels; and between the 13th-cent. chancel and the chapel is an oak screen with carved balusters. Within the chapel is the elaborate Jacobean tomb of the Croke family, with Sir John, his wife and 11 children. One of the red-robed sons was Speaker of the House of Commons during the reign of Elizabeth I.

Adjoining the church is Chilton House, the home of the Croke family for many generations. It is a handsome 18th-cent. building, said to be modelled on Buckingham Palace.

Claydon House: a door in the Chinese Room

Edwin Smith

CHORLEY WOOD, *Hertfordshire* (6–TQ 0396), is a pleasant little Victorian village surrounded by extensive gorse commons and magnificent views over the Chess valley.

C. F. A. Voysey was the architect of some of the houses of interest. His own, The Orchard, in Shire Lane, has identical gables and well-balanced centre. The hall of the house, together with its staircase and fireplace, are some of Voysey's best work, and the metalwork is typical of his direct style. Hill Cottage, further along the lane, has an addition on the right-hand side by Voysey, and Hollybank, which is most attractive, is also his work.

Christ Church, situated by the great common, was built in 1870 by George Street. It is of flint with a low-shingled spire. Inside there is a triple traceried opening connecting the chancel with the south chapel and in the churchyard are massive cedars.

CLAPHAM, *Bedfordshire* (10–TL0252). This residential village has attractive old buildings as well as many modern ones, for it is so near to BEDFORD that it is almost a dormitory. A picturesque thatched cottage stands on a ford of the Ouse on the outskirts of the town.

Two features are of interest here, the most important being St Thomas of Canterbury Church with its enormous Anglo-Saxon look-out tower, added to in Norman times, and over 80 ft high. There is a triangle-headed doorway to the simple Norman tower arch, Jacobean balusters on the ladder of the tower's ringing floor and a monument to Thomas Taylor, 1689, with an inscription with drapery and an urn at the top.

Clapham Park was built in 1872 for James Howard, founder of the Bedford Britannia Ironworks. In Tudor Gothic style, it is red-bricked and gabled, and in 1965 was added a chapel, designed by Desmond Williams, circular in shape with an octagonal roof and abstract stained glass, for the Society of Daughters of the Holy Ghost.

CLAYDON VILLAGES, *Buckinghamshire* (10–SP7126). The four villages of **Botolph Claydon, East Claydon, Middle Claydon** and **Steeple Claydon** are set apart from the rest of the county in wooded countryside, a few miles from each other, down lonely, winding lanes reached by the main road from AYLESBURY to BUCKINGHAM. Very small, they are dominated by the thatched roofs of timbered houses with gleaming-white stonework.

Claydon House, a National Trust property, was transformed in 1752 by the 2nd Earl of Verney to further his political ambitions and outdo the great house of Stowe, the home of one of his rivals. The foundations of the house, however, are several hundred years older. Situated in the village of **Middle Claydon**, the house is reached through lodge gates and the immediate impression is one of simplicity, with cattle grazing in the park. Although the transformation was never completed, through lack of money, the building contains magnificent state rooms with rococo decoration carved by Lightfoot, reputed to be the only known work by this craftsman.

On the walls of the house are many portraits of the Verney family, who still occupy it. The doorways and ceilings, long-shuttered windows and fine fireplaces in the hall, the drawing-room and the picture gallery are all delightful. The grand stairway inlaid with ebony and ivory has balusters with scrolls, ribbons and cornstalks of iron. In the Chinese Room, with its rococo alcove carved in wood, is a carving of a Chinese family at a picnic table complete with crockery and fringed tablecloth.

A suite of rooms once occupied by Florence Nightingale, sister of Parthenope, Lady Verney, and editor of the Verney papers, is now a museum to her. The tall cedar and cypress trees in the park are said to have been grown from seeds Florence Nightingale brought back from the Crimea.

Reached across a small lawn is Middle Claydon church, with its 15th-cent. tower. Inside the church door is a tomb to Margaret Giffard, a Verney ancestor who died in 1539. The chancel is 16th-cent. and the oak pulpit 17th-cent. Four of the windows and the south doorway of the nave have been here for 700 years. The church was restored by Sir Harry Verney, brother-in-law of Florence Nightingale and an M.P. for some 50 years. It was due to his interest that the 16th-cent. chancel screen, with panels of delicate tracery and a wide doorway with leaves in the spandrels, is in existence. One of the newest memorials in the church is a bronze relief of Sir Harry by Harry Pegram. The church holds many other memorials to the Verneys, the most important having been erected after Sir Ralph's wife, Mary, died at Blois. It was designed and made in Rome in 1652. Made of many-coloured marbles, with the Verney arms portrayed on it and the phoenix at the top, it has portrait busts of the family.

Despite the domination of Claydon House, the other villages are worth a visit. **East Claydon**, in agricultural country, has pretty black-and-white cottages near the church with its demon-faced angels on the chancel arch and, high up on the inside of the tower, a woman's head craning forward.

Steeple Claydon, a village of wayside cottages, has a church with one of the few steeples in the county. The manor was given to a great scholar, Sir Thomas Chaloner, by Mary Tudor; he is mentioned in Hakluyt's *Voyages*. His son was tutor to Prince Henry, the brother of Charles I. Thomas Chaloner built the school and created a trust for the schoolmaster. He was one of Charles I's judges and signed the death-warrant. The old school was restored by Sir Harry Verney in the last century and his son Edward opened the red-brick building which is the Chaloner library. A cheque for £50 from Florence Nightingale towards the cost of the books is still exhibited in the library.

The house of the Verneys can be seen from the churchyard and by the roadside is the Camp Barn where Cromwell's soldiers once stayed.

Botolph Claydon, with its old manor house now a farm-house, is attractive for its rural atmosphere, its black-and-white thatched cottages and its delightful scenery.

CLIVEDEN, *Buckinghamshire* (6–SU9185). Standing in magnificent wooded countryside is the great house of Cliveden. To discover it you turn off the A4 from London to MAIDENHEAD. On the left is Taplow Court, now the offices of British Telecommunications Research, with a Victorian lodge house at its gates. Along the Cliveden road is a superb avenue of Lombardy populars and on the left is the Canadian Red Cross Hospital.

Cliveden is now the property of the National Trust and is open to the public. The wooded area surrounding the house includes one on the most beautiful reaches of the River Thames. Built in 1851 this was the former home of the Astor family and was the third house of its name of this site. Standing above terraces, the impressive building contains many treasures, with fine tapestry and period furniture. In the large grounds are temples designed by Giacomo Leoni and among the trees and avenues of shrubs are sculptures and statues set in niches.

The road from the house winds steeply down in beautiful countryside as it follows the bends of the Thames.

COLLYWESTON, *Northamptonshire* (10–SK 9903), is a charming stone-built village, the home of the famous Collyweston tiles that cover the roofs of the houses here and in many other parts of the county. The tiles are still manufactured in the traditional way in the village. There is a manor dated 1696 and, W. of the church, an Elizabethan dovecot.

The church was built by Ralph Cromwell, who fought at Agincourt. It has a fine pinnacled tower and a 15th-cent. south doorway, the arch of which has a pinnacle on each side and moulding with carved flowers. The pews are carved with open tracery and the bench-ends have poppy-heads of fruit and foliage. The choir stalls are decorated with carvings of pelicans, the Christian symbol of sacrifice.

CONINGTON, *Huntingdonshire* (10–TL1785), is on the edge of the Fens, from which can be seen the Isle of Ely. It has moated enclosures, including those at Bruce's Castle Farm and at Round Hill, the latter being five-sided and covering 17½ acres. Holme Fen, just to the N., is a reserve of the Nature Conservancy.

Conington Castle, which was owned by the Cotton family from 1460, one of whose members started draining the fens in 1639, has recently been demolished.

All Saints Church is large and mainly Perpendicular. The massive tower is ashlar-faced, in four stages, with panelled polygonal buttresses, a recessed doorway with a pointed tunnel vault, bell-openings under four-centred arches and large pinnacles. The remainder of the church,

Daventry lies in typical rolling Northamptonshire country

with its embattled nave and aisles, is of cobbles, as is its higher rood stair turret. The chancel chapels are of only one bay, and the sedilia in the chancel have three small hanging vaults. There is a shelf in the piscina and the octagonal Norman font has intersecting pointed arches. Several screens are of interest. The stately wooden chair, resembling a throne, its armrests adorned with angels, swans and doves, is said to have been used by Mary Queen of Scots at FOTHERINGHAY while she was awaiting execution.

DAVENTRY, *Northamptonshire* (10–SP5762). This ancient town, whose major industry in the 18th cent. was whip-making, has expanded greatly in recent years, with large car factories and light engineering works, modern houses and new schools.

It still retains some of its past, however, with pleasant Georgian houses, the Roman Catholic church which was once the old grammar school of 1600, two inns of note, the Saracen's Head and the Wheatsheaf, and the tall, ironstone 18th-cent. Moot Hall, now council offices.

Daventry was an important coaching town in the 18th cent., for it lies on four main roads. It has been a market town since 1255 and dates back to the Iron Age, as is evidenced by the camp on Borough Hill, N. of the town. Borough Hill is 650 ft above sea-level and from its highest point may be seen seven counties. Nearby are the giant masts of the B.B.C.'s overseas transmitting station, near the spot where Charles I's army camped during the Civil War, before the Battle of NASEBY. The King spent several nights at the Wheatsheaf Inn, which has barely changed since those days.

The Church of the Holy Cross is mid-18th-cent., made of ironstone with a bulky tower and a solid steeple. In each of its aisles is a gallery, hidden behind Tuscan columns. The roof is groined, and the richly-coloured Resurrection reredos shows the Archangels Raphael and Gabriel.

DEENE, *Northamptonshire* (10–SP9492). In this tiny, unspoilt, limestone village, hiding among trees on the edge of Willow Brook, is Deene Park, the home of the Brudenells since 1514. It is imposing, with some of its original structure and additions and alterations made in the Elizabethan, Jacobean and Georgian periods. Built of pale Weldon stone, it has a large battlemented tower and the Georgian rooms overlook lakes formed from the Willow Brook. The ballroom has superb stained glass and a heavy marble fireplace built in memory of the 7th Earl of Cardigan who commanded the Light Brigade in their famous charge in the Crimea in 1854. His uniforms are still there. The house has many features of architectural and historical interest and in the spacious well-wooded grounds are rare trees and shrubs. It is open to the public.

DENHAM, *Buckinghamshire* (6–TQ0487). This picturesque village in wooded countryside off the A40 has many houses and brick and timbered cottages of interest. One of these, Old Cottage, a half-timbered Tudor building, has a fascinating unevenly-shaped front. There are several old inns and a tiny 1820 Wesleyan chapel.

The River Colne flows through the grounds of Denham Place which is at the end of the street, behind a high brick wall. It was built in Restoration times and beneath its high-pitched roof can be seen dormer windows. Captain Cook stayed here, as did Lucien and Joseph Bonaparte.

The Parish Church of St Mary, surrounded by limes, beeches and cypress trees, is of the 15th cent. A 500-year-old wall painting of Judgment Day adorns the walls in which can be seen the figure of an archangel sounding the Last Trump. Mounted on slender round pillars is the 13th-cent. font, the church's oldest possession. On each of the eight sides of the bowl are two pointed arches. There are many brasses of interest on the floor before the altar. The table tomb shows the figures of Sir Edmund Peckham and his wife. Sir Edmund was Master of the Mint to Henry VIII.

Set apart from the village, N. of the railway, are the famous film studios.

DINTON, *Buckinghamshire* (10–SP7610). This pleasant, unspoilt village, in rural countryside, was once the scene of a great historical occasion, for it was to Dinton Hall that Cromwell rode triumphantly after the Battle of NASEBY. His sword is still preserved in the Hall, a large light red-brick manor with an imposing porch and a large number of Tudor chimneys towering above the trees. One side of the house has eight gables, and there are lovely dormer windows and a 600-year-old cellar. It was once the home of Simon Mayne who fought with Cromwell in the Civil War and who was one of the signatories of the king's death-warrant. Although sentenced to death at the Restoration, he died in the Tower before the execution could take place and his body was brought to Dinton for burial.

In a field by the roadside stand the ruins of Dinton Castle, an 18th-cent. folly containing many ammonites embedded in its walls.

The varied farm buildings are gabled and timbered with lichened roofs and on the lawn by the church are the village stocks and the whipping post.

Next to the manor house is the Church of SS. Peter and Paul with its Norman door bearing an inscribed lintel. The great turreted tower is of the 15th cent., the font is 600 years old and in front of the 13th-cent. chancel is a finely carved Jacobean pulpit. In the churchyard is the shaft of an old cross.

DORNEY, *Buckinghamshire* (6–SU9379). The Palmer Arms, though modernized at the front, is an old coaching inn and was at one time the public house for the estate workers who were employed by the lords of the manor, the Palmer family, who have occupied this position for several hundred years.

The village itself is mentioned in the Domesday Book. Among the many historical buildings is an attractive flintstone cottage by Dorney Reach.

On the outskirts of Dorney is ancient BURNHAM Abbey, some distance from the road and completely hidden away by old outbuildings.

Down the High Street are many brick and timbered cottages with beech trees overhanging the road, and on the right is a dilapidated Victorian schoolhouse.

The little Church of St James is of Norman origin, and is reached down a tree-lined lane, close to Dorney Court, which dates from the 15th cent. The red-bricked roof of the church is Tudor and the box-pews of the 17th and 18th cents. The nave and the font are Norman and at the west end, reached by a short flight of stairs, is the music gallery with its oak seats and oak balusters, built in 1634. An unusual feature is a Jacobean monument to Sir William Gerrard and his wife, with their 15 children below them, some holding skulls to show that they died in infancy.

The first pineapple to be grown in England was produced at Dorney and given to King Charles II.

DUNSTABLE, *Bedfordshire* (10–TL0221), is a modern town, still retaining a few ancient and some Victorian buildings. It was originally a royal market town established by Henry I when he founded the Augustinian priory here in 1131. Until the Dissolution it was of some consequence and at the priory the annulment of Henry VIII's marriage to Catherine of Aragon was pronounced. Between 1742 and the coming of the railway it was a coaching town but is now mainly manufacturing, with the motor-vehicle industry as one of its largest trades.

There is a Victorian town hall, with three bays and a turret, and the white Municipal Offices in the High Street are early-19th-cent. with two pairs of Tuscan columns to the porch. Dunstable School, late Victorian, is of plum brick with a slender spire above it. Composed of two parts, it is linked with a square tower.

Most of the older buildings of interest are centred round the crossroads which are part of the ancient **Icknield Way** and **Watling Street**. Several have been preserved in West Street, the most important of which is the Windmill. In the High Street is the Sugar Loaf Hotel, dated 1717, of blue brick with red dressings, two and a half stories high with nine bays. The priory house has a fine early Georgian exterior with arched windows, a pedimented doorway and quoins and, on the ground floor, a long rib-vaulted room. The gardens are open to the public. Further S. are the Cart Almshouses of 1723, a row of blue and red brick houses; and Chew Grammar School, 1719, founded by Jane Cart, has two attractive figures of schoolboys over the doorway. It has a fine front with an unusual turret cupola.

Also near the crossroads are the new civic centre and shopping precinct.

A modern building of note is the Fire Station at the northern end of the town.

St Peter's has substantial parts of the old priory church. The original nave, which is very wide, still remains. Massive wall-shafts separate the bays, and the interior, richly decorated, has been restored through the centuries. The font is large, circular and Norman, and the rood-screen has five bays and is elaborately carved. The square pulpit, of red marble, is Victorian, but the pulpit cloth was donated in 1732. The Fayrey Pall was a gift of Henry Fayrey, a wealthy

A. F. Kersting

Earls Barton: the Anglo-Saxon tower

merchant, for use as a coffin covering at funerals. It is of red brocade with figures embroidered on the borders and is believed to be Flemish. There are many interesting monuments dating from the 13th cent. One, by Thomas Green of Camberwell, is of William Chew with two figures of naked boys and a death's head between them. The arch at the centre is draped and garlands decorate the top.

On the road towards IVINGHOE and Tring are fine views of Dunstable Downs.

Five Knolls is the finest prehistoric burial ground in the county, with eight sites consisting of two pond, three bell and three bowl barrows. It dates from the Early Bronze Age, but has earlier traces. In the largest and smallest mounds were found fragments of Neolithic and Beaker pottery when they were opened up. Two thousand years later pagan Anglo-Saxons were buried here.

EARITH, *Huntingdonshire* (10–TL3875), is a large riverside village to which, at one time, barges brought wood from Scandinavia. It is on the border of Cambridgeshire and was of vital importance at the beginning of the 17th cent. when the draining of the Fens began and impressive artificial waterways, 20 m. long, were constructed. These formed the Old Bedford River and the New Bedford River or Hundred Foots River, and they run to Salter's Lode Sluice and DENVER Sluice in Norfolk. The Ouse flows slowly past the village on its way to the great sluices.

Woodlands stands in the main street, of yellow brick with red-brick dressings, Doric pilasters, a pediment to its doorway and a Venetian window.

Near the bridge, which is comparatively new, is a field of 4¾ acres with earthworks probably

from the Civil War, in which are four arrow-shaped angle bastions. It is known as the Bulwark.

EARLS BARTON, *Northamptonshire* (10–SP8563). There is one feature of this large, over-grown village which justifies a visit, for its Church of All Saints has an outstanding Anglo-Saxon tower, one of the finest in England. Built of plaster, it is in four stages with pilaster strips from the ground to the belfry, round arches in the second stage, pointed arches in the third, and narrow window openings in the belfry. On the first floor are doorways which are inaccessible. There is a Norman entrance door on which are carved animal faces, and almost every century up to the 19th is represented. The clock is dated 1655. The chancel screen, of the 15th cent., is striking, and by it stands the Jacobean pulpit.

To the N., beyond the churchyard wall, is a mound which marks the site of the old castle.

EATON SOCON, *Bedfordshire* (10–TL1658), on the A1, borders on Huntingdonshire. It has a green with a Victorian lock-up in which there are two cells. The White Horse is a red-brick Georgian building with a panelled parapet. Charles Dickens is said to have stayed at the low, timber-framed Old Plough Inn. The Methodist chapel and the workhouse are both Victorian, the latter of yellow brick with an octagonal centre.

In Duloe Hill, 1 m. N., is a tower windmill without sails, with a cottage attached.

St Mary's Church, which borders on the River Ouse, was almost completely gutted by fire in 1930 and only the south arcades of five bays, the south clerestory and the west tower remain. The tower is high, with transomed two-light bell openings. The square font, of Purbeck marble, is Norman, and there is a large Flemish tapestry of the 17th cent. and a brass of a civilian and his wife, about 1450.

Close to the river bank and E. of the church are the Hillings, earthworks of a castle built in the 11th and 12th cents. Bushmead Priory, 4 m. NW., has some remains of the former conventual buildings.

EDLESBOROUGH, *Buckinghamshire* (10–SP9719). This tiny village, set on the edge of the Chilterns, has as its landmark the Church of St Mary the Virgin. At its foot, in a 16th-cent. barn stands a dovecot, and WHIPSNADE Zoo is on the outskirts of the village.

The tower of the church, with its high turret, is 14th-cent. The low 15th-cent. roof is supported by corbels, decorated with picturesque carvings. The fine woodwork justifies the church's claim to fame. The exquisite oak screen, in red, blue and gold, was carved to resemble a fine lace canopy in 1450. The pulpit is graced with a three-tiered carved canopy of great beauty. The *misereres* are adorned with fine, intricate carvings, a mermaid suckling a beast, dragons, frogs, owls and eagles.

Many brasses decorate the aisles and a small 15th-cent. stained-glass window shows a pilgrim in a red cloak and bright yellow hat carrying his bible and staff. In an iron bracket, near the pulpit, is an hour-glass, which the priest once used to time his sermon.

ELLESBOROUGH, *Buckinghamshire* (10–SP8306). The undulating road from WENDOVER to Ellesborough follows the tracks of the Icknield Way. From the high ground can be seen Wellwick Farm, down in the valley, a building of rose brick and flint, which is reputed to have been the house of the notorious Judge Jeffreys. The chimneys bear the date 1616 and the 17th-cent. barns have open timber roofs. Further along the road stands the old thatched Rose and Crown Inn.

The Church of SS. Peter and Paul, reached by a steep hill, is the parish church for CHEQUERS, the Prime Minister's country residence. This 15th-cent. building has a Norman tower and from the churchyard, which contains a sculpture of the Crucifixion, can be seen in the distance the vast expanse of the Vale of Aylesbury. Fragments of old stained glass cover the vestry windows, one showing the head of Christ crowned with thorns. The piscina in the 15th-cent. chancel is carved with flowers. The reredos with its charming triptych was designed by Sir Ninian Comper. On an imposing tomb lies a statue of Bridget Croke who was a member of the Hawtrey family, the original owners of Chequers. Four black pillars support the roof of her resting-place, under which she lies in Stuart dress, one hand holding a book.

Near the church are small 18th-cent. almshouses, the gift of Dame Dodd in 1746.

Towards Kimble, on the hillside, is **Cymbeline's Mount**, its Roman ramparts having commanding views of the valley below.

ELSTOW, *Bedfordshire* (10–TL0547). This attractive village, with many thatched cottages and houses, was the birthplace of John Bunyan, and the Moot Hall, *c*. 1500, a medieval market hall which is open to the public, houses a collection illustrating his life and times. The hall is of timber and has an overhanging upper floor which contains the main room.

The sister of William the Conqueror founded a nunnery here which had its own gallows, pillory and ducking pond. Remains of the nunnery's church are incorporated in the Church of SS. Mary and Helen. This was begun as a 13th-cent. building and, although much restored, still has fine Norman work. The vestry was once a small vaulted room, and its most unusual feature is a detached bell-tower of the 15th cent., with a spike on top and on each side transomed bell-openings. The octagonal font, Perpendicular and large, is decorated with quatrefoils on the bowl and figures on the base. The wooden pulpit is of the same period, with tracery panels. There are several interesting monuments.

Behind the church are the remains of Hillersdon Hall, built in 1616 from stone from the old abbey.

ELTON, *Huntingdonshire* (10–TL0893). This well-preserved, attractive and rather sprawling village is situated on the border with Northamptonshire, with the River Nene flowing past it. It has two main streets of stone-built houses and cottages with finely thatched roofs.

Cooper's Hospital is an almshouse founded in 1663 by the Rev. John Cooper, and the Methodist church, dated 1864, has arched windows. The 16th-cent. parsonage is gabled and there are many old houses around the green, some of the 17th cent., some Georgian. The Black Horse Inn is also Georgian with five bays on one side and a battlemented one on the other.

All Saints Church has no spire but an ashlar-faced lofty tower, which is Perpendicular, with a doorway with traceried spandrels. Much of the interior dates from around 1300. There are many windows of interest and an arch in the chancel appears to be pre-1300, with triple shafts and a nailhead. The simple octagonal font is about the same period. There are many monuments, including some to the Sapcote family who were owners of Elton Hall in the 15th cent. Two wheel-head crosses in the churchyard are Anglo-Danish.

Elton Hall, on the road towards OUNDLE, is set in a park of 200 acres. Parts of it are 15th-cent., including the gatehouse with a four-centred arch and a vaulted crypt. The house was mainly ruined during the Commonwealth, then rebuilt by Sir Thomas Proby later in the 17th cent., with alterations continuing for 200 years. It has been the seat of the Proby family for 300 years. It is open to the public and has fine pictures, 18th-cent. furniture and valuable books, including Caxton volumes, Henry VIII's bible with his signature, prayer books and early manuscripts.

ETON, *Buckinghamshire* (6–SU9678). This little town, known the world over because of its association with the famous school of this name, is of ancient origin. During the 11th cent. it was the residence of Queen Edith, wife of Edward the Confessor.

Eton College, the second oldest public school in the country, was founded by royal charter by King Henry VI in 1440. Originally it had 70 scholars who were fed and educated free of charge. Today, among its 1,100 pupils, there are still 70 who pay very low, or sometimes no, fees.

In the narrow streets of Eton, life focuses round the college, and the small shops have catered for the school for decades.

The school itself occupies a large part of the town and its extensive buildings are all of different architectural periods. The Lower School, dating from 1443 and still in use, was for 200 years the only schoolroom. The Upper School was built in 1694 and on the desks and panelling will be found the carved names of Walpole, Shelley, Gladstone, Macmillan and Eden. The chapel nearby is the finest Perpendicular building in the county, noted for its exquisite fan-vaulted roof of Clipsham stone. There are many features of interest in the college, including Lupton's tower, built in 1571, the beautiful cloisters and the 18th-cent. college library. Both the Natural History Museum – a modern building – and the college are open to the public.

A short stroll will bring you to the 15th-cent. Cockpit, once used for cock-fighting, and beside it are the parish stock and whipping post. If you visit the town during term-time everywhere will be seen the boys of the school, distinguishable by their coats and stiff Eton collars.

By the river, where there have been common lands since the 7th cent., there is a fine view of WINDSOR Castle. The famous boathouses by the bridge are a popular summer meeting place.

EYE, *Huntingdonshire* (10–TF2202), was built on an island before the Fens were drained and is now one of the largest villages in the north of the county, with brick-making as its major industry.

It has a straight village street of yellow-brick houses, with a tower windmill 80 ft high and of eight stories dominating the flat countryside. It is now power driven and used for producing animal foods. Eyebury Farm, of the late 17th cent., has a hipped roof, a Classical doorway and windows with mullions and transoms.

St Matthew's Church is early Victorian, a cruciform building with a broach spire on the tower and lancet windows. The octagonal font with eight supports is 14th-cent. and came from the church which previously stood on the site.

Three Bronze Age barrows lie on the S. of the parish, in one of which a food vessel was found.

FINEDON, *Northamptonshire* (10–SP9272), is a fairly large village with most of the newer buildings on one side and the older ones on the other. Scattered around are curiously decorated ironstone Victorian houses and cottages, built by the last squire of the village, Mr Mackworth Dolben, whose three sons all died tragically.

The Bell Inn is claimed to be the oldest licensed house in England, for it is on a site where an inn has been since 1042. On the road to Thrapston is the Round Tower, commemorating the Battle of Waterloo.

Near the church, which is at the far end of the village on a steep slope, is Thingdon Cottage, a curious building of several different heights. The Hall, the stone Vicarage and the schools are all of the same period. Finedon Hall has a courtyard with embattled walls, and the house has fine ornamental gables, on the walls of which are the two shields of the families of Mackworth and Dolben.

Reached through a lych-gate is the Church of St Mary, standing in a churchyard with hollies and yews. It is of dark ironstone, built in the 14th cent., with a large tower and a graceful spire rising to about 133 ft. There are lancets in the belfry, which has gargoyles at each corner, and inside, across the nave in front of the chancel, is an unusual strainer arch. The font is Norman and the 18th-cent. organ-case is by Shrider. The pews, which are original, have traceried panelling. In a room over the porch is an 18th-cent. theological library.

FINGEST, *Buckinghamshire* (6–SU7791). Along a narrow byway, lying in a deep hollow

of the Chilterns, is this lonely village, set among beechwoods, with one of the country's finest churches, the Church of St Bartholomew. It has a rare Norman tower, topped by twin gables. A high ancient roof covers the long narrow nave, the low seats giving height to the church. It is said that the nave was once the chancel, in which case the Norman arch spanning the width of the tower must have been the chancel arch. The four-ft thick walls have narrow slit windows and in the chancel are two slim lancets. The 15th-cent. font still has the staples which locked the cover to prevent water being stolen.

In the large churchyard are two 17th-cent. wishing gates which are part of the boundary wall, guarded by an avenue of limes.

Ruins of the palace of the bishops of LINCOLN are nearby and The Chequers inn is 300 years old.

FLAMSTEAD, *Hertfordshire* (10–TL0814). This little village lies above the River Ver and has many old cottages. Saunders Almshouses, dated 1669, are one-storied brick buildings with round-headed entrances and two-light windows. To the E. of them is Vine Cottage, an elegant, timber-framed house with brick infilling.

The Church of St Leonard, surrounded by giant sycamores, lilacs and red and white chestnuts, has the best wall paintings in the county after those in ST ALBANS Cathedral. Its low west tower is of flint, random stone, brick and Roman brick with a thin spike. Most of the structure is of the 14th cent., although there are traces of Norman work. The nave roof, on carved stone corbels, is a century later, and the pulpit later still. The screen is particularly interesting with tall arcades, the central mullion running to the apex of the arch and Perpendicular tracery. The wall paintings, not revealed until 1930, are between the spandrels of the nave arches and show, among others, St Christopher, Christ in Glory, and the Last Supper. Two monuments of note include one by Stanton of Saunders children, 1670, which is a large altar tomb with the figures of five young children praying, with the sixth kneeling on the floor. It is said to have cost £1,500. The other by Flaxman, 1762, is of Sir Edward Sedbright, with Hope and Faith, reclining on a slender fluted urn.

There are particularly fine views around the village.

FLETTON, *Huntingdonshire* (10–TL1997), is an industrialized town with only one building of note but that, St Margaret's Church, is of national interest.

The town itself is the centre of the largest brick-manufacturing area in the country and Fletton bricks have a world-wide reputation. Tall round brickyard chimneys dotted all over the horizon have replaced the trees that were here less than a century ago.

The church has Anglo-Saxon remains in the east buttresses dating from the first half of the 9th cent., before Alfred's time. They came from PETERBOROUGH Abbey after it was burned down in 1116 and are discoloured pink from the fire. They probably belonged to a frieze: one has human figures and the others are decorated with little birds and quadrupeds. The chancel arch, north chapel arcade and north arcade date from about 1160. Two panels of saints are also of the same period. The Norman chancel has a corbel table and buttressing. The tower has Y-traceried bell-openings, a broach spire and two tiers of lucarnes. The octagonal font, with plan panels, is about 1661.

In the churchyard is an Anglo-Saxon cross with a shaft of two handles and a wheel-type cross-head. It has an inscription in Norman lettering.

FLITWICK, *Bedfordshire* (10–TL0335), is a growing residential village with thatched cottages round its green and the River Flitt running through it. By the river lies the boggy Flitwick Moor in which can be found rare plants.

The Manor House, much modernized, is of three periods, 17th-cent., 1736 and mid-Georgian. It is of brick with a panelled parapet and in the garden is a grotto.

SS. Peter and Paul Church, though mainly Victorian, has an Early English south doorway and in the north wall a massive moulding from a Norman doorway with beakhead-like faces. The chancel arch is original and the west tower Perpendicular. The font has a fluted trough and is 12th-cent.

NW. of the church is the Mount, the remains of a small motte and bailey castle.

FLORE, *Northamptonshire* (10–SP6460), is on a gentle slope above the Nene valley, with modern buildings added to the old village, which appears in the Domesday Book as Flora.

In a small thatched house named Adams' Cottage are said to have lived the ancestors of John Adams, President of the United States after George Washington. The 17th-cent. Old Manor, standing next to the church on the edge of the village, is gabled with pinnacles and is surrounded by fine trees. Nearby is the village school which has the names of May Queens since 1890, for the festival it holds on May Day is the important local event.

The church, amid sycamores, cypresses, cedars, limes and yews, is partly 13th-cent. All the doors are medieval and richly carved. The massive tower is 14th-cent. The interior is graceful, its tower opening on to the nave through three arches, and the screen, with open tracery, is 15th-cent. There are Tudor panels on the priest's desk and the choir stalls. The font, which is 16th-cent. and is barrel-shaped, was for a time used as a cattle trough. There are several interesting brasses.

Brockhall, reached by a road N. of Flore, is an Elizabethan manor house with an Adam wing and a fine staircase of the same period. It can be viewed at any time, by appointment.

FOTHERINGHAY, *Northamptonshire* (10–TL0593). The road to this village runs through beautiful countryside and crosses the 18th-cent. bridge spanning the River Nene, over which hang tall willows.

There are many old cottages with small doors in the historic village, where Mary Queen of Scots was beheaded in 1587, and parts of the old inns still remain. The site of the old castle is down a narrow lane on the bend of the road opposite a row of thatched cottages, and it is necessary to park the car and walk to the site. The castle is now only a mound, but it was built by Simon de St Liz in the 12th cent. and enlarged

Fotheringhay: the view from the site of the castle where Mary Queen of Scots was beheaded

in the reign of Edward III. Richard III was born in the castle, in the hall in which Mary was executed. In the grounds are Scotch thistles which the Queen is said to have planted during her imprisonment.

The tower of the Church of St Mary and All Saints rises in stages and the whole building has a profusion of windows. On the corners of the first stage are four small turrets and crowning them, in place of a spire, is a superb octagonal lantern with two sets of lancet windows in each side adorned with tracery. Above are eight pinnacles surmounted by the badge of the House of York, a falcon and a fetterlock. The lower part of the tower opens three ways into the body of the church and is fan-vaulted. Behind the altar is an 18th-cent. reredos with three arches in which are set, in fine gold letters, the Lord's Prayer, the Commandments and the Creed. The pulpit, a gift from Edward IV, is one of the church's most attractive features, with its double canopy and much fine carving. The stone font, with heads of lions and foliage on its base, is 15th-cent. In the sanctuary are stone monuments in memory of Richard of York, Cecily Neville and their son Edmund, which were put there on the instructions of Queen Elizabeth I when she visited the village.

FURNEAUX PELHAM, *Hertfordshire* (10–TL 4327), is a little village, its main street lying in a hollow, at the end of which stands the Hall, a 16th-cent. brick manor house with shaped gables covered in creeper and a delightful garden.

St Mary's Church, mid-13th-cent., has an inscription painted round the clock on the tower: "Time Flies – mind your business". In the low-pitched nave roof are figures of angels with bright yellow hair and leopards with lolling red tongues. The windows are Late Perpendicular and the chapel was built in the early 16th cent. There is an octagonal font of Purbeck marble, and a splendid monument in the south aisle, a tomb-chest with quatrefoils and shields. Under a cusped canopy lie the exquisite brass figures of a man and a woman.

GAYHURST, *Buckinghamshire* (10–SP8446). A small hamlet on the River Ouse, Gayhurst is renowned for its part in the Guy Fawkes Gunpowder Plot. Its Elizabethan manor was given to Sir Francis Drake by Queen Elizabeth I as a reward for his travels round the world. But Drake did not want it and sold it the next day to William Mulsho, who refashioned it and turned it into the beautiful building that exists today. Mary Mulsho married Everard Digby who became involved in the Gunpowder Plot and it was from here that he was taken to the Tower.

The house is now partly a school. It has mullioned and transomed windows and pinnacles, and old stone stables and coach-houses.

The church, built in 1728, has a low square tower with a cupola and the chancel has carved wooden coping. There is a three-decker pulpit with a magnificent canopy and a monument to Sir Nathan Wrighte with a dragon's head crest. The Royal arms are at the east end of the church.

GEDDINGTON, *Northamptonshire* (10–SP 8983). This is a lovely, sprawling village, in wooded countryside, with many old cottages, most of them thatched. It is centred round the Eleanor Cross in the square, believed to be the finest of the remaining crosses erected by Edward I to mark the places where the coffin of his queen had lain for the night on its long journey to WESTMINSTER ABBEY in 1290. Square-shaped, of stone, it is finely and intricately worked, the small statues of the Queen showing her veiled.

The Church of St Mary Magdalene is medieval with some Anglo-Saxon and Norman work. The tower has an octagonal spire and gargoyles similar to those on the nave and chancel walls. The entrance is by a narrow 13th-cent. doorway and the nave is filled with light. The chancel has a double clerestory and a large window with five lancets. There are several lovely screens: one of the 14th cent. between the chancel and the south aisle is in richly carved woodwork.

Around the church are old cottages and nearby is a Victorian infants' school with a weather-vane.

Leading out of the square is the medieval bridge over the River Ise, beyond which are more thatched cottages and a larger thatched house, now the Post Office. The Congregational church is Victorian.

GODMANCHESTER, *Huntingdonshire* (10–TL2470), is an ancient Roman town, pentagonal in shape, with charters dating back to 1214, when it became a self-governing manor, a form of government which made the inhabitants free tenants, for which the town paid King John £120 a year. It became a borough in 1604.

Godmanchester adjoins HUNTINGDON by the ancient bridge crossing the River Ouse. It is said that the bridge, described in Huntingdon, was partly built by Godmanchester and partly by Huntingdon, that the two ends were started at the same time, without any co-ordinated plan and that by luck the workmen met in the middle, which accounts for the awkward curve in the bridge.

The town has many old thatched brick and timber cottages, ancient farm-houses on the outskirts and a wide common. In the centre is the Victorian town hall. Queen Elizabeth's Grammar School was founded in 1560 and parts of the original building are still in use. Near these two buildings is the delightful Chinese Bridge, constructed in 1827, which leads to the islands in the River Ouse.

The Causeway, which opens on to the river, is medieval, and on its east side is a timber-framed house dated 1597 and a yellow-brick late-Georgian building. In Earning Street is a two-gabled house dated 1625. Plantagenet House has gables and an oriel window with bargeboards, and Tudor House, built 1600–3, is timber-framed with gabled wings and overhanging upper stories. In London Road is Porch Farm and the former Shepherd and Dog Inn, and in Post Street is the 17th-cent. Island Cottage with overhanging stories and, lying back from the street, Island Hall, a large, red-brick building, two and a half stories high with lower two-bay wings. Farm Hall, in West Street, was built in 1746 of red and rubbed brick with a Tuscan porch and cast-iron railings. There is an avenue of limes in the garden and another leading towards the river.

The Parish Church of St Mary, one of the largest in the county, is mainly 13th- to 15th-cent., with a tower added in 1623. The church is of brown cobbles and the tower ashlar-faced. The chancel is Early English and has a rare 13th-cent. mass dial on one of the buttresses. The roodscreen is 1901, but the misericords on the stalls are late 15th-cent. and show a variety of finely carved animals. There is a 16th-cent. brass with a figure of a civilian.

The Roman town can be defined by the present roads which encircle it and recent discoveries are the south and west gates and a suite of baths, near Pinfold Lane, which were built about the 2nd cent. Traces of another building of the same date have been uncovered.

GOLDINGTON, *Bedfordshire* (10–TL0750), is now a suburb of BEDFORD, with one of the largest village greens in the county.

It possesses a modern power station with a cooling tower 165 ft high and a church which is over 500 years old. St Mary's has a Perpendicular tower and chancel. The round font is early 14th-cent., decorated on the underside. In the porch is an upright effigy of a lady, also of the early 14th cent., and there is a detailed black-and-white marble tablet to Benjamin Haselden, 1676.

Two m. E. are the 700-year-old ruins of Newnham Priory, known as **Risinghoe Castle**, with a 20-ft-high motte. Nearby is a small bridge known as "Bloody Battle Bridge" which is believed to have been an outpost for the Danes.

GRAFHAM, *Huntingdonshire* (10–TL1669), is a small village with a tiny, whitewashed church and an old rectory, part of a 16th-cent. house, adjoining it. All Saints Church has a west tower and three ancient bells. The chancel and double piscina are 13th-cent. The octagonal font is Decorated and there is a 14th-cent. effigy of a priest in the south porch.

Recently a new reservoir has been constructed which is said to be the largest man-made sheet of inland water in the country, 1,570 acres. It has become a favourite spot for fishing and sailing and there is also a bird sanctuary. Grafham Water Sailing Club is a three-story building of outstanding sculptural quality and won an award from the Civic Trust for a building which paid particular respect to the character of its surroundings. The reservoir also won an award as a landscaping project making an outstanding contribution to the surrounding scene.

GREAT GRANSDEN, *Huntingdonshire* (10–TL2755). This is a charming village, quite large yet unspoilt. It has many thatched cottages with pink or white plaster walls and two particularly pretty ones opposite the church, timber-framed,

one with russet tiles and one thatched. The almshouses, still in use, were built in 1679 by the Rev. Barnabas Oley, an ardent Royalist, who was vicar here for 53 years except during the Civil War when he went into hiding.

Although Rippington Manor House is Elizabethan, built on an H-shaped plan with a vast stone chimneybreast, the first Lord of the Manor was Alfar, brother of Hereward the Wake. A church is named here in the Domesday Book, but it was rebuilt in the 14th cent. Great Gransden Hall, a moated mansion, stands in a large park. It is 17th-cent., part early and part middle. In the centre is a panelled parapet curving to a higher centre part and the side-pieces of the front are two-bayed with massive Dutch gables. The College Farmhouse was also built at separate times in the same period. The vicarage, with its hipped roof, is Jacobean and was built by Barnabas Oley. Half a m. E. of the village is a wooden postmill.

St Bartholomew's Church is of brown cobbles and completely Perpendicular, embattled throughout. Its tower, in four stages, has two-light bell openings and a spike. The fine roof is decorated with figures and in the chancel is a crocketed piscina. The screen has 15th-cent. tracery and the pulpit, with carvings of fruit and foliage, was a gift of Barnabas Oley. The carillon and chimes of the church clock were added to celebrate the jubilee of the Rev. Barnabas Oley. There is a large stone slab monument to Thomas de Museum, parish priest, 1350.

GREAT LINFORD, *Buckinghamshire* (10–SP 8542). This small town on the Grand Union Canal was once a place of great commercial interest.

Its Church of St Andrew is a pleasant blend of 18th-cent. workmanship and Decorated Gothic. The 12th-cent. building has a 13th-cent. tower, a beautiful arcade and many fine windows. There are two porches, one with a winged figure of pre-Tudor period and the other with a vaulted roof. A brass of Roger Hunt and his wife relates how he paved the church during the years of the Wars of the Roses. The aisle has a 16th-cent. brass to Thomas Malyn, with his wife and child, and the chancel contains 17th-cent. brass portraits of John Uvedall, his wife and their eight children. There are box pews and a monument to Sir William Pritchard who lived in the manor and was at one time Lord Mayor of London.

It was Sir William who built the delightful red-roofed almshouses. The village has a Tudor rectory, a barn of the same period and a dovecot which houses 400 pairs of nesting birds.

GREAT MISSENDEN, *Buckinghamshire* (10–SP8901). Lying in the valley of the Chilterns with woods around it, this roadside town has many old houses and inns in the narrow High Street. The George Inn is 15th-cent. and the gateway has original timbers and a room over it.

On a plateau standing back from the village is the 14th-cent. Church of SS. Peter and Paul. This spacious church is filled with light from windows added 500 years ago. Stone angels with shields support the nave roof and the chancel wall has an exquisite arcade of seven bays with finials and pinnacles ending in small carved heads. The Norman font is an octagonal basin, the sides of which were re-cut in the 15th cent. Its stem has chevrons and its base is finely carved. In the transept pews are many 15th-cent. traceried panels. An interesting monument over the south doorway is that to William Blois, a scholar who lived in Stuart times.

Incorporated in the Abbey Mansion are the ruins of the Augustinian abbey which was founded in 1133 for the Black Canons. In earlier times it was used as a stopping place for English sovereigns travelling from their palace at BRILL to that at ST ALBANS. The abbey grounds are on steep slopes, covered by beechwoods.

Prehistoric flints and Roman coins have been discovered in the neighbourhood, and the moated earthworks at Redding Wick and Grim's Ditch near Woodlands Park have been scheduled for preservation as Ancient Monuments. In Rook Wood is a prehistoric earthwork.

GREAT PAXTON, *Huntingdonshire* (10–TL 2164), has large thatched cottages and the views from Paxton Hill are probably the most beautiful in the county. On one side are rolling downs and on the other thick woods. The River Ouse is clearly visible from the road with boats passing by.

Holy Trinity Church is Anglo-Saxon, very grandiose, a true cruciform church with its crossing as wide as the nave, chancel and transepts. Although the stubby steeple at the west end is 14th-cent., most of the cemented interior is original. The nave is striking, with proper compound piers, and the sedilia in the chancel are original. The responds are of long and short stones and under the tower arch is a Perpendicular screen. The south door has 13th-cent. ironwork.

GRENDON UNDERWOOD, *Buckinghamshire* (10–SP6720). This is a long straggling village, with many 17th-cent. cottages and Shakespeare Farm, of 16th-cent. origin, where, according to tradition, Shakespeare gained his inspiration for *A Midsummer Night's Dream.* In his time this farm was an inn, the sign of which – the Ship Inn – hangs in AYLESBURY Museum. The farm-house, with its lovely timbered and brick framework, is gabled and has windows containing the original lattice and leaded glass.

The River Ray runs through the village and in the Church of St Leonard Shakespeare is reputed to have lain in his drunken slumbers. The carved doorway is very beautiful and just inside it is a 15th-cent. stoup. The thick walls of the nave are evidence of their Norman origin but the tower is of the 15th cent., the hexagonal pulpit Jacobean. In the stair turret is a 15th-cent. door. The three bells in the church were made by Robert Atton and Richard Chandler in the 17th cent.

GRETTON, *Northamptonshire* (10–SP8994), is an old country village, standing on a hill-top, reached by a winding street. Magnificent views of the Welland valley are visible from the village green, on which still remain the old stocks and the whipping post.

The houses are all of stone, some spacious, others thatched cottages. On one old chimney is a sundial, and the inn sign is of oak leaves wrought in iron.

The Church of St James the Great is a medieval building with a brown stone 15th-cent. tower contrasting with the grey of the chancel and nave. There are Norman pillars in the nave which has Decorated aisles and fine carving. In the 17th cent. the chancel was raised to incorporate the Hatton family vault. The panelling and altar rails are of Queen Anne period, as is the pulpit, and the font is 15th-cent.

Two m. SE. of Gretton is **Kirby Hall,** which is open to the public and is now an Ancient Monument. It was begun in 1570 by Humphrey Stafford who owned the estate, in which there was then a village and church. Christopher Hatton, a favourite of Queen Elizabeth, bought it shortly afterwards but it was his descendants who lived there, entertained James I and his queen there, and commissioned the architect Inigo Jones to transform it into the beautiful house it became in the 17th cent. The long west front is Elizabethan, of Weldon stone with many gables, obelisks and chimneys. The north front is the work of Inigo Jones and resembles a Renaissance palace. The outer courtyard has three gateways, and across a large open space is the inner court, in which is a range of two-storied rooms, with a magnificent loggia by Inigo Jones at one end and the great hall at the other, 30 ft high with its original roof and a minstrels' gallery. The gardens, which have been restored, are also lovely.

HAMBLEDEN, *Buckinghamshire* (6–SU7886). This attractive village in the valley of the Chilterns is approached by a narrow road sheltered by beeches.

In the centre of the square under tall chestnut trees is the village pump, still in use. There are Georgian houses, including the Rectory surrounding it, and old cottages have been transformed into village shops. The Manor House was built in 1604.

On the River Thames, reached by a road used by the Romans, is the white-timbered Hambleden Mill, named in 1338, with a weathervane resting on its turret. Nearby is a lock and the river can be crossed by a narrow bridge from Hambleden to the Berkshire bank.

The archaeological museum houses a model of a Roman farm, discovered in the fields behind Yewden, complete with implements in use in Roman times.

St Mary the Virgin Church dates from the 14th cent., although much of it has been restored. Its size and beauty dominate its surroundings. In the tower, which was rebuilt in 1721, is a fascinating 16th-cent. panel, believed to have been the bedhead of Cardinal Wolsey and bearing the cardinal's hat and the Wolsey arms. The Norman font, simply carved, is believed to be that in which

Noel Habgood

Hambleden Mill on the River Thames

Thomas Cantelupe, who was canonized, was baptized.

The chancel contains beautiful carving and a decorated sedilia and piscina. On the walls are many interesting brasses and in the north transept the lovely monument showing Sir Cope Doyley with his wife Martha and their 10 children. The epitaph on the tomb was written by Lady Doyley's brother, Francis Quarles, the poet.

HARROLD, *Bedfordshire* (10–SP9456). This old village, in pleasant countryside, with its narrow bridge and causeway with 11 pointed and rounded arches dating back to the 14th cent., has now added modern houses which do not in any way spoil its character or its older buildings.

On the small village green, with its handsome trees, remain the old circular stone lock-up with a conical roof and the graceful octagonal Market House. Nearby are pretty thatched cottages and in the High Street is the Old Manor, *c.* 1600, in which is a fine wooden mantelpiece.

St Peter's Church was originally of the early 13th cent. and still retains one lancet window indicating, by its position, that the chancel has since been shortened. Some 50 years later the south arcade, with its octagonal pier, was built. In the Decorated north chapel is a tall arch and the west tower, of the same period, has a Perpendicular spire. The Jacobean screen has original woodwork. A monument in the church to Dame Anne Jolliffe, who lies buried in the chancel, is of

interest. In 1732 she founded almshouses and later married Dr Richard Mead, physician to Queen Anne and other members of the royal family, who established the practice of inoculation and spent much time and vast sums of money in seeking remedies to eradicate the plague.

HARTWELL, *Buckinghamshire* (10–SP8012). This quiet village two m. W. of AYLESBURY, with its now ruined 18th-cent. church, built to resemble YORK Minster, is famous for the house that bears its name.

It was in Hartwell House that Louis XVIII stayed with his court during the Napoleonic wars. The Queen of France died here during their exile and her coffin was taken from here to Sardinia. Standing in a walled park, it is a splendid Jacobean building with an 18th-cent. front and decorations. The entrance to the house is by a porch, flanked by carved pillars of stone, and a carved doorway. Above is a magnificent round oriel window sitting on embroidered stone corbels. The splendid staircase has carved newels supporting historical and mythical figures. The stone of the house and of the walls surrounding the garden came from a nearby quarry. Superb trees abound in the park, some of them bearing carvings by the Frenchmen who spent nearly a decade here. One of the park's splendours is its long lake fed from the springs nearby, with a stone bridge decorated by an ornamental parapet and containing an arch brought from Kew Bridge, Surrey. The house is now a school. In the old rectory is a moulded beam bearing the date 1552.

Hartwell has many charming cottages and its walls contain ammonites discovered in the local clay pits.

By Weir Lane are to be found the Egyptian springs which run into the lake at Hartwell House. Among the thickly overhanging trees and the clear spring water is a stone seat built in the Egyptian style and bearing an Egyptian inscription.

HATFIELD, *Hertfordshire* (10–TL2309). This is a town divided into the old and the new, the latter being an industrialized area of pleasant modern construction, the former retaining many of its characteristics of earlier times.

Its most famous and prized possession is the illustrious Hatfield House, built by Robert Cecil, the 1st Earl of Salisbury, between 1608 and 1612. The Cecil family still live there. It is exceptionally large, about 300 ft by 150 ft, with domes and towers and magnificent windows. A clock tower rises from the roof of the great hall, surmounted by an octagonal dome. The hall extends over two floors of the building and contains a spectacular screen of Jacobean carving. On the first floor is the long gallery, and the great staircase, with its elaborate tapering banisters and carved decorations, is a superb piece of workmanship. The house has its own chapel and every room holds much of beauty and interest. In the gardens, re-fashioned in the 19th cent., are original fountains, a large relief of Queen Elizabeth I and a maze. The park is the largest in the county and the remains of the oak tree, under which Princess Elizabeth was sitting when news was brought of her accession to the throne after the death of Mary Tudor, are still preserved. At the entrance to the park, opposite the railway station, is a large monument to the 3rd Marquis of Salisbury, Prime Minister in the last century. The house and grounds are open to the public.

Near Hatfield House is the Old Palace, which was built in 1480–90 and was the residence of Cardinal Morton. Over the archway of the gatehouse are ancient beams and a mullioned window. The west front of the palace is heavily buttressed with a square tower, and at the end a stepped gable is surmounted by a twisted chimney. The great hall is still there, with a few other rooms. It was in this palace that Queen Elizabeth I and Mary Tudor spent many years of their childhood, in virtual imprisonment.

Old Hatfield has many houses of interest, some half-timbered of the 16th cent., others Georgian. On the corner of Fore Street and Park Street is the low-roofed, timber-framed and gabled Eight Bells Inn which has barely altered since it was built in the 17th cent. Dickens referred to this inn as having been visited by Bill Sykes in *Oliver Twist*.

Fore Street, a fairly steep hill with some fine Georgian houses, leads to the churchyard with its ironwork gates made about 1710 and taken from St Paul's Cathedral.

The Parish Church of St Etheldreda dates from the 13th cent., but the exterior of the broad nave was rebuilt in 1872. The Salisbury Chapel holds the tomb of the 1st Earl of Salisbury: entirely in the Dutch tradition, it is ornate with figures surrounding that of the earl. There is a lovely 18th-cent. screen which was brought from Amiens by the 3rd Marquis and many other monuments of interest.

HELPSTON, *Huntingdonshire* (10–TF1205), is a large, pleasant, stone-built village, once the site of a Roman settlement, and ¾ m. S. of the village will be found Roman remains that were excavated in 1827.

The peasant poet, John Clare, was born here in 1793 and was buried in the parish church 70 years later. A rather odd memorial to him stands at the crossroads on the village green. The attractive village cross, which dates from about 1300, has a tall polygonal base with gables and battlements and four circular steps.

There are several fine houses, including College House, which is S. of the church, with two buttresses, a slit window and a four-centred archway, and Helpston House, up the hill from the village green, which has a canted bay window, gables and dormers.

St Botolph's Church has a Norman tower which was partly rebuilt in 1865. The tower becomes octagonal when it reaches the level of the clerestory and has 14th-cent. bell openings and a short spire of the same period with a tier of lucarnes. The chancel, with its arch of filleted shafts, is about 1300 and the sedilia and piscina are original. The porch entrance is early 14th-cent. On one wall is a large painting of the Royal Arms of James I.

Woodhall Manor, which dates back to 1146 and is one of the oldest houses in the county, has recently been remodelled and it received a commendation under the Civic Trust Awards as a work of restoration which paid particular respect to the character of its surroundings.

HEMEL HEMPSTEAD, *Hertfordshire* (10–TL0506). The Domesday Book mentions the mills of this attractive market town stretching along the River Gade. Like other towns in the county it has its old and new sections, with many recently developed industries as well as paper mills which were of importance in the 19th cent.

The High Street is delightful, rising in a gentle curve towards the church and churchyard. The 18th-cent. houses are of purple brick and red dressings and the Sun Inn is dated 1726. There are rambling cottages and the half-timbered King's Arms which retreats into a side alley, one of several alleys off the High Street. The neo-Jacobean town hall is of red brick with dressings and was added to in the 19th cent.

Off the High Street is the Friends' Meeting House in St Mary's Road, an early 19th-cent. building of purple and red brick with a burial ground at its side.

Lockers House, on Bury Hill, has an Elizabethan wing and elaborately decorated ceilings, and Lockers Cottage is an attractive timber-framed brick and plaster building. In the Marlowes, a street running parallel to Bury Road, are Little Marlowes House and Old Marlowes House, two-story cottages of the late 18th cent. with some early Georgian workmanship. Corner House, near the end of the street, is of the 15th or 16th cent., timber-framed with overhanging stories.

Near the church is Henry's Banqueting Hall, two brick and timber cottages built 300 years ago, their overmantels a mixture of Tudor roses, crowns and fleurs-de-lis.

The Church of St Mary's, a large 12th-cent. church standing at the far end of the town, is reputed to be one of the finest in the country. It has a 14th-cent. timber spire nearly 200 ft high. Most of its workmanship is Norman, with a nave of six bays, a clerestory, a crossing tower on the lower stage and a circular staircase turret in the upper. The roofs of the transepts are 15th-cent. with arched braces decorated with traceried spandrels. There is a fine brass to Robert Albyn and his wife.

On the road to **Piccotts End** is Marchmont House, an early 19th-cent. building with a Greek Doric doorway, and off Gadebridge Lane is Gadebridge, standing in its own grounds, the front 11 bays wide with a portico of massive Ionic pilasters.

Half a m. N. of Hemel Hempstead, on the B486, is Piccotts End, with a remarkable house with 14th-cent. wall paintings only discovered in 1953.

HEMINGFORD GREY, *Huntingdonshire* (10–TL2970), was the home of Dendy Sadler, the artist, and although a new housing estate has risen on its outskirts it still retains its old-world charm, with thatched cottages and timbered houses. The views from the banks of the River Ouse, on which it stands, are delightful.

N. of the church is Hemingford Grey House, built of red brick in 1697. It has a hipped roof, segment-headed windows and two stories. By the river's edge is one of the biggest plane trees in England, planted in 1702. River House, in the High Street, is late 18th-cent., of yellow brick with a handsome doorway, and Broom Lodge, at the corner of Braggs Lane, is another five-bay house with shaped end-gables. Further E. is the timber-framed Glebe Cottage, with thatched roof and closely set studs, dated 1583.

But of major interest is the manor house with its garden stretching to the river and a moat surrounding the house on the other three sides. Built of stone, it is one of the oldest inhabited houses in England, for much of it is 12th-cent. It is two stories high, with a first-floor entrance door, now a window, and its hall is on the first floor. There are Norman two-light windows in the west, south and east walls. Inside, the splendid Norman chimneypiece has two columns with scalloped capitals. The central chimney stack was added in the 16th cent.

St James's Church, on the river bank, has a Perpendicular tower with ball finials of the 18th cent. on the buttresses, and a truncated spire with eight ball finials. The remainder of the spire was destroyed by a hurricane in 1741. Of the north arcade, part is about 1180, with the east bay 13th-cent. and the west bay 14th-cent. The chancel is 13th-cent. with a lovely double piscina, its intersecting arches standing on Purbeck shafts. There are two inscribed panels, dated 1682 and 1715, one inside and the other outside the church.

HERTFORD, *Hertfordshire* (10–TL3212). This rural town is the county town of Hertfordshire. It centres around Parliament Square, which was formed as an open space in 1821, and is filled with many features of interest. In its picturesque streets stand houses and cottages of varying periods, with three rivers, the Lea, Beane and Rib, meeting at its centre.

Only a little remains of the ancient castle, built by the second son of King Alfred – Prince Edward – to protect London against the Danes. Today it is a modernized 15th-cent. gatehouse, now used as offices by the council, with walls 22 ft high. It stands in a charming park stretching down to the river and has four towers. The Gothic-style windows and one wing were added at the beginning of the 19th cent., and over the doorway is the coat of arms of England and France, for many kings stayed here, and Elizabeth I lived in the castle during her childhood. In the grounds, which are open to the public, is a boundary mark, a monument in the form of a pebble stone dated 1621. Near to the pebble stone is a beautiful tulip tree, one of the finest in England.

In Fore Street, leading off Parliament Square, will be found Christ's Hospital School for Girls, founded in 1683 for younger children by the governors of Christ's Hospital in London, the famous Bluecoat School. In the gateway and on the walls are figures of the Bluecoat boys and girls. The building has been enlarged in the last two centuries and in 1935 a new library was added.

The Victorian Corn Exchange and Public Hall has a stone-faced front, three bays with large Corinthian pilasters and a Cinquecento-style window. The Salisbury Arms, at the corner of Church Street and Fore Street, although much restored since the early 17th cent., still retains its Jacobean staircase and projecting upper floor.

Shire Hall, in the middle of the town, is of the 18th cent. and, although designed by the Adam brothers, it is not as graceful as might be expected. It is a simple large yellow-brick building and its rear arcades originally gave access to a covered market. In the centre of its upper floor is a splendid rotunda and in the hall are portraits of famous personalities including a painting by Sir Joshua Reynolds of Charles James Fox.

The old Hale's Grammar School, by the churchyard, is a 17th-cent. building of red brick with an interesting chimney and small dome. It is gabled and under its hood moulds are brick windows. The new Richard Hale Grammar School still retains the door from the old school.

Near Salisbury Square, on Bull Plain, is Lombard House, facing the River Lea, with its original 17th-cent. brick, timber and plasterwork intact. This was the home of the Hertfordshire historian and judge, Sir Henry Chauncy, who conducted one of the last witchcraft trials to be held in England, on Jane Wenham. Queen Anne reprieved her after she was sentenced to death and the case led to the abolition of the witchcraft laws.

Of modern interest, but fitting well in this ancient town, is County Hall, built in 1939, a large group of buildings fashioned in Scandinavian style with a slim cupola, fluted portico and ornamental motifs.

At Hertford Heath, 2½ m. to the SE., is **Hailey-bury College**, the boys' public school. Originally founded in 1806 as the East India College for the sons of Englishmen serving with the East India Company, it took its present status in 1862. The older school buildings are grouped round a spacious quadrangle.

HEXTON, *Hertfordshire* (10–TL1030), is set in beautiful countryside surrounded by the Barton Hills, part of the Chilterns, with an avenue of laburnam trees in the street and large yews surrounding the church.

St Faith's Church is early 19th-cent., except for parts of the nave and tower which seem to be 15th-cent. The piers of the nave on the south side are circular and on the north side quatrefoil. The south chancel chapel has a vault and Commandment Boards. There is a plain monument, 1601, to Peter Taverner and his wife.

One m. SW. on the Barton Hills is **Ravensburgh Castle**, an Iron Age hill-fort. It is oval-shaped, 22 acres in size, and has a large ditch surrounding it and high banks. The west side has a double ditch and there is an entrance in the north-west corner.

HIGHAM FERRERS, *Northamptonshire* (10–SP9669). On the outskirts of this delightful town, which is a borough and appears in the Domesday Book, are many new buildings, but once you turn into the High Street you will be greeted by much that is ancient and beautiful. The High Street is a long main road with many of the houses, of local limestone with Collyweston tiles, raised above street level.

In the Market Square in the centre is a 13th-cent. cross carved with oak leaves and ballflowers, with a Crucifixion on one side and a Madonna on the other. All around are buildings of interest, including the Regency Town Hall, the Elizabethan manor house, the Ivy House (1633) and the Green Dragon which has a dovecot. On one corner of the street is an old thatched cottage which is the local barber's shop.

67 High Street is on the site of the birthplace of Henry Chichele, who eventually became Archbishop of Canterbury. Beside the church, reached by a short lane (no cars allowed), is the striped stone Bede House which he built for 12 poor old men, with an open hall with an oak roof, a chapel and a vaulted crypt. He was also responsible for the Chantry Chapel, a lovely piece of architecture, which is separate from the church and was used for some time as a school until it was reconsecrated.

The beautiful spire of St Mary's Church, 170 ft high, dominates the skyline for miles around. The richly crocketed steeple has a pierced parapet, flying buttresses and Early English mouldings. The 13th-cent. tower has a carved doorway similar to the style of WESTMINSTER ABBEY. The interior is a double building with two naves, the south being 13th-cent. and the north 14th-cent. The carved woodwork, both old and modern, is very good. The stalls with misericords carved with animals, birds, kings, angels and grotesque figures, were given by Henry Chichele, as was the choir screen. In all, the church has seven screens. There are many interesting and elaborate brasses.

HIGH WYCOMBE, *Buckinghamshire* (6–SU 8593), stretches along the Wye Valley from WEST WYCOMBE in the W. to Loudwater and Wooburn in the E. It is the county's second largest town and has been a place of importance since Roman times. It has been notable throughout its history for its dissenters – Anabaptists, Independents and Quakers – and Cromwell also had a strong following here during the Civil War, although he treated the town so harshly during his rule that on the restoration of Charles II it became strongly Royalist.

At that time it was an important wool centre, having its own guild of craftsmen, but in time that trade gave way to lace-making and straw-plaiting which were its main industries until the 19th cent. In the 17th cent. the furniture industry, for which High Wycombe is now world-renowned, started in the simple form of chair-making. Among its other important modern industries are paper manufacture and engineering.

On the hills of the town are prehistoric buildings and ancient earthworks.

Standing in the Market Place, scheduled as an Ancient Monument, is the Guildhall, dating from 1757. In the upper story, supported on stone columns, is the large Council Chamber and ante-room, and beneath it, on market days, are gaily decked stalls. Facing the Guildhall is the Little Market House, or Shambles as it is called, also scheduled as an Ancient Monument. It was built in 1761 by the Adam brothers and is of a curious octagonal shape. On a wall above one of the stalls is a panel giving the toll prices for the privilege of holding a stall there.

The Museum, at Castle Hill, which is open to the public, shows many examples of craftsmanship of the 17th and 18th cents. Chairs made through the reigns of James I to Queen Anne are exhibited and there are examples of Chippendale, Hepplewhite, Sheraton and Windsor furniture.

The imposing Town Hall, in Queen Victoria Road, was erected in 1904 and is in the late Renaissance style. Its main hall, with a fine organ, seats over 1,000 people. The Oak Room, with its lovely windows, was panelled by local craftsmen.

Adjoining the Town Hall and of modern construction are the public library and the Art Gallery, which is open to the public.

Wycombe Abbey, now a girls' public school, stands in 250 acres of grounds. Built in 1795, it was originally the house of Loakes Manor, designed by James Wyatt for the first Lord Carrington.

Still standing in the High Street are two old inns, the White Lion and the Red Lion. It was from the balcony of the latter that Disraeli made his first speech and he is said to have had a special affection for the town.

Although the town is greatly modernized there are still many old buildings of interest, including the Elizabethan almshouses in Easton Street and others in Bowerdean Road.

The Parish Church of All Saints is a large town church, the biggest in the county, with a 13th-cent. exterior and a 15th-cent. interior. In its tower, rising 100 ft above the street, is a peal of 12 bells. There is much fine woodwork to be seen on screens and stalls. In the south chancel is a screen erected by Richard Redehole and dated 1468. Through the centuries much has been added to give the church its present beauty. A reredos, designed as a screen and stretching across the chancel behind the high altar, was erected as a war memorial in 1922. A large stained-glass window is particularly noteworthy. This was a gift of Dame Francis Dove in 1933 in memory of famous women, and depicts 17 of them, including Queen Victoria, St Hilda, St Bridget, Emily Brontë, Elizabeth Fry and Florence Nightingale. In the north chancel aisle is a monument by Peter Scheemakers to the Earl of Sherburne.

The town has many good examples of modern architecture, including the General Hospital and the College of Technology, and surrounding it are large areas of natural beauty.

HITCHIN, *Hertfordshire* (10–TL1829), is one of the most interesting of the county's towns.

Down by the River Hiz, which flows through the town, are the early-17th-cent. Biggin Almshouses, built round a narrow courtyard with a Tuscan colonnade. In Sun Street, off Market Square, are many buildings of quality. The Sun Inn, a well-preserved building of blue brick with rubbed-brick dressings and a central carriageway, has a low, half-timbered range in the courtyard and an assembly room which was added in 1770.

In Tilehurst Street is the Victorian Baptist church with giant angle pilasters and Tuscan columns. In the church is a chair given by John Bunyan. No. 35 Tilehurst Street is a late Georgian house of brick; on this site stood the house of George Chapman, the Elizabethan poet and playwright. Other houses in the street range from the 15th to the 19th cent.

On the west side of Market Square is the Victorian Corn Exchange, fashioned in the Italian style with a large Venetian window and a lantern turret. Around the square are ancient and interesting buildings interspersed with modern ones, and on its east side is Queen Street, mostly of Victorian buildings, with the Lister House Hotel at the end, a Victorian house in Georgian tradition.

Bancroft, a continuation of the High Street with houses of several centuries, is very fine and at its end range the Skynner Almshouses, dated 1670 and 1698.

In Brand Street off the High Street is the early Victorian old town hall by Bellamy, adjoining the library of the same period with a closed Tuscan porch and a temple front. The new town hall is opposite.

A house of particular interest is the Priory, built in 1770. Surrounded by a moat, it is in stone with a Palladian south front incorporating a semi-circular porch and two projecting wings with Venetian windows. The County Council owns it.

St Mary's Church, in the Market Place, has woodwork that is without equal in the county. It is representative of a wealthy late medieval town, for when the church was built the town had a thriving wool industry. It is embattled all around and its most outstanding feature is the south porch with a staircase turret, window openings, a lierne-vault and the arms of the Staple of Calais on the wall. The nave is of flint, the chancel of stone. There is a fine series of roofs with cusped panels and principals on stone angels.

The 15th-cent. screens, of which there are several, are rich and beautiful. Of the same period, the stone font has mutilated figures under arched canopies, and the pulpit has angle buttresses and restored panels. The painting of the Adoration of the Magi is Flemish. There are many interesting monuments but none of outstanding importance.

HOUGHTON, *Huntingdonshire* (10–TL2871), is a delightful riverside village with many picturesque cottages. There are pleasant walks along the tree-shaded paths and it is a popular yachting and boating centre.

On the village green is an elaborate Gothic-style pump in cast-iron, the only one of its kind in the county. Nearby is a bust of Potto Brown, a wealthy miller who worked the mill which still remains here. He was the village philanthropist and a devout Nonconformist. The watermill, believed to be the oldest remaining one on the River Ouse, is a massive timbered building of the 17th cent. It is the property of the National Trust and is used as a Youth Hostel.

The yellow-brick Union Chapel is early Victorian with an arched doorway and windows. Houghton House, late Victorian, is fashioned in the Elizabethan style with a large segmental pediment above the porch and a square bay window of 11 lights.

St Mary's Church, partly Decorated and partly Perpendicular, is of brown cobbles. The double piscina appears to be earlier, however, and the tower is an unusual shape, with buttresses finishing beneath the bell-openings, above which the tower becomes octagonal and has a stone spire with two tiers of lucarnes. The pulpit was made from a tree from Houghton Park.

HUGHENDEN, *Buckinghamshire* (6–SU8695). N. of HIGH WYCOMBE is Hughenden Manor, a large mansion modernized in Victorian times by Benjamin Disraeli, Earl of Beaconsfield and Prime Minister of Britain. He lived here with his wife from 1847 until his death in 1881 and the house holds many relics of his youth. It stands on the

Barnaby/Mustograph

Houghton watermill is believed to be the oldest one remaining on the River Ouse

slope of a hill with woods at its rear running down to a lovely stream in the valley below, and a parkland, with great trees, in front of it.

Disraeli's study is still as it was at the time of his death and there are manuscripts of his novels and letters from Queen Victoria.

The church on the estate, where Disraeli is buried, shows the work of Sir Arthur Blomfield; it still contains a medieval chancel and chapel and a bell of the pre-Reformation period. Outside the church and cut square is a yew, planted in 1690.

The house and gardens, which are National Trust property, are open to the public.

HUNTINGDON, *Huntingdonshire* (10–TL 2371). This is the county town, attractive with much of interest. The official name of the county is now Huntingdon and Peterborough. The town's narrow main street stretches for nearly 1½ m., but many of the places to visit are off this thoroughfare.

It has ancient origins, for Roman coins and pottery have been found here. The Anglo-Saxons created it a burgh, the Danes invaded it from the river and in 921 Edward the Elder repaired the damage they had made. At the end of that century a market and a mint were established, both indications of prosperity. In the 13th cent. there were 16 churches, of which only two remain, for the Black Death in 1348 caused devastation and the town lost its prosperity and became a backwater, except for the short period during the Civil War when first Cromwell and then Charles I made their headquarters here. Agriculture has always been its main industry.

Oliver Cromwell was born in the town; the grammar school which he, and Pepys, attended, founded about 1565, is now a museum of Cromwelliana. This building was originally the Hospital of St John the Baptist, founded about 1160, and considerable parts of the old structure remain. Cromwell House, in the High Street, is on the site of the Austin Friary.

All Saints' Church, in Market Place, is part of a previous building and is mainly 15th-cent. The upper stages of the tower were rebuilt after the Civil War and the top is Victorian. The organ chamber is attractive and the Perpendicular chancel roof has carved bosses. The bowl of the font is 13th-cent.

Nearby is the stately town hall, built in 1745 of red brick with three stories. Around the walls of the ballroom are interesting paintings, one by Gainsborough.

There are two interesting inns, the George, which still has two sides of its 17th-cent. courtyard, in one of which is an open gallery and external staircase, and the Falcon, with oriel windows and a massive door, which is believed to have been the headquarters of Cromwell during the Civil War.

At the end of the town, separating it from GOD-MANCHESTER, is the early-14th-cent. bridge, with cutwaters on both sides. It is said to be one of the finest medieval bridges in the country. Nearby, in a public open space, are the extensive earthworks of a castle founded by William the Conqueror.

The town is composed mainly of Georgian buildings, but there are a number of the 16th and 17th cents. Walden House, now council offices, is of red brick with a hipped roof and giant Ionic pilasters. The County Hospital in Brampton Road is of yellow brick and Victorian, as is Petersfield Hospital, a former workhouse, in St Peter's Road. In the same road is the former county gaol, built in 1828 of yellow brick. Cowper House, where the poet lived in 1765, has a steep three-bay pediment and window lintels with brick frills on the first floor. In George Street are rather humble yellow-brick almshouses of the Victorian period and in the High Street is Whitwell House, 1727, with three stories, segment-headed first-floor windows and pretty garden railings. Montague House, also Georgian, has an attractive doorway below its Venetian window. In Hartford Road is the Roman Catholic Church of St Michael, of brick and stone with a round arch.

St Mary's Church, in the High Street, has the remains of Norman buttresses in the corners of the nave and south aisle, the chancel is early 13th-cent. with a priest's doorway, and the solid ornate tower is Perpendicular. The arches have fine mouldings and there are several 17th-cent. inscriptions. Under the tower are a number of tablets, the largest to the Carcassonnett family, dated 1749.

About ½ m. away, on the road to BRAMPTON, is **Hinchingbrooke**, the seat of the Cromwell family, now a school, where Queen Elizabeth I was entertained in 1564. It has a gatehouse which is thought to have come from RAMSEY Abbey.

Along the river banks are pleasant walks, good fishing and yachting, and nearby is Portholme, a large meadow where rare wild flowers can be found.

HUSBORNE CRAWLEY, *Bedfordshire* (10–SP9535). This tiny village, with many old cottages, stands on the road to AMPTHILL, on the edge of Woburn Park.

Its Manor House, in front of the church, is a timber-framed building of the late 16th cent., and nearby is Crawley Park, a late-18th-cent. building of red brick.

St Mary's Church has a tower built of rare green sandstone and is in a wooded, hilly setting. The Perpendicular west tower has a higher stair-turret, and near the south doorway is a large stoup. The tower arch is pleasantly decorated with capitals and there is a large alabaster monument to John Thompson, 1597, with five columns and a studded ceiling. Another monument is to Talbot Williamson, 1765, with an urn before an obelisk.

ICKFORD, *Buckinghamshire* (10–SP6407), is a tiny village lying in some of England's best grazing land. The River Thames flows past it and is crossed by a 17th-cent. bridge with three attractive arches.

The Rectory, which is partly 16th-cent., was occupied by Archbishop Sheldon who was rector here for many years. He was imprisoned as a Royalist during Cromwell's rule and, after he became Archbishop of Canterbury, helped to rebuild St Paul's Cathedral.

The Church of St Nicholas was built in the 13th cent. and its saddleback tower, gabled walls and font are all of this period. The sanctuary has a modern window showing striking figures of Edward the Martyr and Edward I, but it still contains some 14th-cent. glass.

A strange Tudor tomb, the oldest monument in the church, is of Thomas Tippin with his wife and nine children. It is said that he had the tomb built in his lifetime.

ICKWELL, *Bedfordshire* (10–TL1445), is one of the county's most beautiful villages, its vast green surrounded by low thatched houses with dormer windows. On the green stand a gaily striped maypole and the smithy where Thomas Tompion, the clock-maker, once worked. At the northern end is a more formal house of the 18th cent.

Ickwell Bury, once a priory, was rebuilt after a fire in 1937. The new building, of a free neo-Georgian style, stands in a richly wooded park, and near a long avenue of limes and chestnuts is the octagonal dovecot of the 17th cent., with a revolving post and projecting beam. The stables adjoining the house are original, built in 1683 with 10 bays and a square cupola.

IVER, *Buckinghamshire* (6–TQ0381), is a delightful village in a scattered parish with shady lanes and Iver Heath nearby. There are modern film studios close by, but it has many 16th- and 17th-cent. houses, mostly built around the church, which is a mixture of styles. The 500-year-old tower has an ancient bell-chamber and the nave is Anglo-Saxon. The church's most beautiful feature is the 12th-cent. chancel with a wide pointed arch and a double piscina and triple sedilia. The pulpit, carved with cherubs, is 200 years old and the Norman font is a square marble bowl standing on round pillars. A brass inscription on the floor is to Ralph Aubrey, Clerk of the Kitchen to Prince Arthur, the first husband of Catherine of Aragon. There are many brasses and monuments of interest.

A house of particular note is the 18th-cent. Bridgefoot House, a clever blending of brick and glass.

In this village the family of the Dukes of Kent have resided for many years.

IVINGHOE, *Buckinghamshire* (10–SP9416). Ivinghoe Beacon belongs to the National Trust and is reached by a narrow road just outside the village. From the top of this hill, nearly 800 ft high, can be surveyed the extensive line of the Chilterns, the Quainton Hills and the Dunstable Downs. Only walking will take you to the summit but the scenery well justifies the climb.

This agricultural village, from which Sir Walter Scott took the name of his novel *Ivanhoe*, holds much of interest. An ancient windmill still remains in a field. The King's Head, a 15th-cent. inn rebuilt 200 years later, retains its oak beams and broad fireplaces.

The Church of St Mary the Virgin is very beautiful. Of 13th-cent. origin, it was greatly altered in the following two centuries. The roof is of great grandeur, with the outspread wings of angels reaching to the timbers, on which rest heads of people and animals, carved in stone corbels. The timbers are adorned with flowers. The chancel is graced with roses and leaves as well as angels. The pulpit is Jacobean and the lectern Elizabethan. Of amusing interest are the ends of the 38 pews, for within the poppyheads are distorted faces, typical of the work of medieval craftsmen.

JORDANS, *Buckinghamshire* (6–SU9791). Down a quiet country road, about 2 m. W. of CHALFONT ST GILES, lies this secluded village built around its green. A few minutes' walk take you to some of the most enchanting scenery in the county, among the Chiltern beechwoods.

History has made Jordans famous, for it is the burial place of William Penn, the Quaker, founder of Pennsylvania, U.S.A. The little brick Friends' Meeting House, just outside the village, was built in 1687, and the unvarnished deal benches standing on a plain brick floor still remain. Erected immediately after James II issued the Declaration of Indulgence, the building is a constant reminder of the days when men were beginning to want to think freely, since, although William Penn was the friend of kings, he was many times imprisoned for his outspoken Quaker beliefs. The walls of the Meeting House are decorated with portraits, autographs and other reminders of the pioneers of the period.

In the graveyard nearby are simple headstones recording the names of the Friends buried there. These include William Penn and his two wives, Mary and Isaac Penington, who supplied money for the Meeting House, and Joseph Rule, known as the White Quaker, a Thames waterman who wore undyed clothing.

Old Jordans Farm, the home of a yeoman in the days of Charles II, was where the Friends met and is now a hostel. The Mayflower Barn, set on walls of brick, has timbers which are reputed to have been taken from a ship, and one of the beams has on it the letters R HAR I, believed to stand for Mayflower, Harwich.

KETTERING, *Northamptonshire* (10–SP8778), is an industrial town set in pleasant countryside, with footwear as its main industry, for which it has its own Boot and Shoe College. It is an ancient town, dating back to 956, and in 1227 Henry III granted it market rights.

Its places of architectural interest are mostly near the church, which is reached by a narrow twisting High Street, round the bend of which is the large market place where open markets are held three times a week. There are many Victorian and Edwardian public buildings, including the Alfred East Gallery which has a good collection of paintings, with many by the artist who gave his name to the gallery, himself a native of the town. The Museum has local Roman and Anglo-Saxon remains, and the Corn Exchange and public library are typically Victorian. In Sheep Street are the 17th-cent. Sawyer's Almshouses

and beside the church is the old Georgian manor, now the Town Health Department. There are two earlier buildings: one in Gold Street is the Toller Chapel, which has records of early persecuted Nonconformists, and in Lower Street is the Mission House, where the Baptist Missionary Society was founded in 1792.

The steeple of the Church of SS. Peter and Paul, behind the market place, soars above the busy town. It is of Barnack limestone with lead roofs. Although much restored, it was originally Perpendicular and parts still remain of this period. The body is long and low.

About 1 m. from the town, towards Barton Seagrave, is Wicksteed Park which covers 100 acres of ground and was purchased by Charles Wicksteed at the turn of the century to create a pleasure park for the people of Kettering. It has many amenities, including a lake, miniature railway, ponies, and pools for model yachting, bathing and paddling.

Three m. N. on the road to Corby, set in flat, lush countryside, is **Boughton House**, resembling a miniature Versailles, for the Duke of Montagu, who lived there, had been Ambassador to the Court of Louis XIV. He brought back with him a fine collection of French furniture and china, which the house still contains. Many royal visitors have stayed there, for it is one of the seats of the Duke and Duchess of Buccleuch. The superb avenues of elm which surround the house were planted by the 2nd Duke of Montagu with the idea of linking the house with his London residence, 70 m. away. It can be viewed by appointment.

KIMBOLTON, *Huntingdonshire* (10–TL0967), is a small, beautiful town in a valley, with the River Kim running through it. It has a wide High Street, with several interesting houses, and this runs parallel with East Street, in which the buildings are also attractive. Narrow lanes connect the main streets.

There is a Moravian church, the only one in the county, erected in 1823.

The town is historically important because Kimbolton Castle, now a school and open to the public, was the last home of Catherine of Aragon, who died there. The castle stands in a large park. It was bought and remodelled in 1620 by the 1st Earl of Manchester, whose successor again remodelled it from a design by Sir John Vanbrugh. The portico in the north front is the largest feature of the house, with two giant Tuscan columns. Inside are many superb paintings on walls and ceilings by the Venetian Giovanni Pellegrini. The square gatehouse was designed by Robert Adam.

St Andrew's Church has a 14th-cent. tower with a broach spire, and at the top of the tower are carvings of small heads. The arcades of the church are early 13th-cent. The nave roof is original and the large, rather ugly font is about 12th-cent. In the south chapel is a fine screen of c. 1500 with paintings of kings and angels on four of the panels of the dado. There are several interesting monuments to the Manchester family.

KNEBWORTH, *Hertfordshire* (10–TL2520). Old and New Knebworth are separated from each other by about a mile of delightful countryside. Deard's End, at the top of a hill near the railway station, is a large farm with fine brick and timber barns.

In New Knebworth, on a hillside, is St Martin's Church, built by Lutyens. It is of red brick with stone dressings, without a tower but with extensively projecting roof eaves. Arches on Tuscan columns separate the aisle from the nave, and dividing the crossing from the transepts are two massive Tuscan columns.

Two buildings by Lutyens in the old village are the Golf Club House and Homewood, with its cottage windows on the low ground floor and its five weather-boarded gables.

The Church of SS. Mary and Thomas, surrounded by acres of green fields, is entered by a lych-gate covered with wild roses. The nave, chancel and tower are of the 15th cent. as are the plain benches. In the low Norman chancel is a blocked Norman window. The 18th-cent. pulpit has carved Flemish panels. The font is of the 15th cent. and a fine iron screen of a later period crosses the tower arch.

The Lytton Chapel was added at the beginning of the 18th cent. to contain lavish monuments to the family who have lived at Knebworth for over four centuries. There are three marble tombs as well as other memorials and brasses. The names of Strode and Robinson appearing in the chapel are all part of the Lytton family name.

From the church can be seen Knebworth House which, with its vast park, is open to the public. It started as a Tudor mansion in 1492 and the body of the house still remains. The plastered ceiling in the great hall and the detailed screen are both Jacobean, and the superb panelling in the hall, ending in the reredos which stretches the width of the room, is 17th-cent. The house was largely rebuilt in 1843 by Sir Edward Bulwer-Lytton, the 1st Lord Lytton, statesman and author of *The Last Days of Pompeii*. It contains some of his manuscripts, and has fine furnishings, relics and portraits. Many people of literary note stayed here, including Dickens and Disraeli. The grounds are lovely to wander in.

Not far away is the Victorian Lytton Arms built for employees of the big house.

LEIGHTON BUZZARD AND LINS-LADE, *Bedfordshire* (10–SP9125). The two towns, divided by the River Ouse, were only recently made into one. On the Linslade side, which is more industrialized, is the Grand Union Canal.

Leighton Buzzard, a fairly large, pleasant market town with narrow streets, is mentioned in the Domesday Book. There are still thatched brick and timber cottages, and the pentagonal Market Cross, dating from about 1400, is very fine, rising in two tiers of arches and topped by a pinnacle 20 ft high. In the upper story are five statues: of Christ, the Madonna and Child, a bishop, a king and St John the Baptist. In 1650,

during the Commonwealth period, it was repaired and a fourpenny rate was levied on the townspeople to pay for it.

By the Post Office is the Golden Bells Inn of the 14th cent., originally built as two cottages and still retaining its old oak fireplace and oak beams.

The majority of buildings of interest are near the Market Place. Opposite the cross is the Swan Hotel, an early Victorian white building, in a Classical style. In North Street is the town's most impressive house, Holly Lodge, built in the late 17th cent. of blue and red brick with two cross gables. Just past it is the Friends' Meeting House, 1789, with wooden cross-windows and a simple exterior. Nearby are the Wilkes Almshouses, of yellow brick with gables, to which an interesting ceremony is attached, for on Rogation Monday parts of the founder's will are read aloud while a choir boy stands on his head.

In Lake Street is a 17th-cent. inn, the Unicorn, three stories high and nine bays long. The County Branch Library, a Grecian-style building with four unfluted Ionic columns, is Victorian.

The Church of All Saints, a large, ironstone building, dates from the 13th cent. It has a crossing steeple and a high spire with large broaches on which are tiny pinnacles. Additions were made to the church two centuries later and it has a complete collegiate chancel with its original seating and screens still intact. The ironwork on the west door is that of Thomas of Leighton and the Kempe windows are very fine. There are medieval *graffiti* on piers and walls, the Early English font is cauldron shaped, and on the lectern is a finely carved wooden eagle of the 14th cent.

In Linslade, close to the canal, will be found St Mary's Church, of yellow limestone and ironstone, with its early-12th-cent. nave masonry and its unmoulded chancel arch. The west tower is 15th-cent. and the chancel 16th cent. The nave is embattled and there are no aisles. The circular font of the 12th cent. has a band of scrolls and beasts and there are the remains of a 15th-cent. screen.

E. of the church is Manor Farmhouse, an interesting 18th-cent. building of vitreous and red brick, its centre bay flanked by giant pilasters.

LITTLE GADDESDEN, *Hertfordshire* (10–SP9913). This is an ancient village verging on superb scenery of magnificent beechwoods, commons covered with bracken, massive oaks and wild cherry trees, all part of the National Trust and a sanctuary for wildlife.

The house of John of Gaddesden, near the Post Office, is a large timber-framed 15th-cent. building with an overhanging upper floor and a timber roof, and was named after the famous royal physician. The manor house, a century older, is of stone, with stepped gables to its two turrets and mullioned and transomed windows. It has interesting Elizabethan wall paintings and a collection of early keyboard instruments. Its beautiful gardens which, together with the house, are open to the public, have unusual ornamental yew hedges.

Ashridge House was built in 1276 and stands in a vast park on the ridge of the Chilterns. It was originally erected as a College of Bonshommes in Norman days and is now the Bonar Law College. During Mary's reign, Princess Elizabeth stayed here. The house of Totternhoe stone was restored by James Wyatt in 1808, but it still retains its former beauty. Its chapel has a twice stepped back tower and a tall slender spire. The main building has a three-arched loggia, tall entrance-hall windows and a staircase tower. In the grounds, facing the rose garden, is the barn which has much of the original monastic work.

The Church of SS. Peter and Paul is outside the village. The tower is of flint with diagonal buttresses and the remainder cement-rendered. The 15th-cent. screen is much renewed and some of the benches have poppyheads. Its main interest is its monuments. The kneeling figure of Elizabeth Dutton was removed from ST MARTIN'S-IN-THE FIELDS, London. There is a large Classical monument to Elizabeth, Viscountess Brackley, with an epitaph in script; one to Elizabeth, Countess of Bridgewater; and one to Francis Henry, 8th Earl of Bridgewater, with an inscription saying he bequeathed £8,000 to literary men who wrote religious essays.

LITTLE HADHAM, *Hertfordshire* (10–TL44 22). On the outskirts of this little village are many timber-framed cottages and farm-houses and on the ground rising above it stands a delightful windmill.

Hadham Hall was built for the Capel family in the 16th cent. Although parts of the building were destroyed by fire, it still retains much of its Elizabethan structure with entrance turrets, octagonal chimneys and a gallery nearly 140 ft long. Its brick outbuildings, with a gatehouse and a large brick barn, appear to be older than the house itself.

The small Church of St Cecilia lies N. of the village street. Its 14th-cent. tower with diagonal buttresses has a fine arch and the nave has Perpendicular windows. There is an interesting timbered south porch, the sides of which are trefoil-cusped along the tops. The transept opens in a four-centred arch and the three-decker pulpit, decorated with a big tester, is dated 1633. The screen is of the 15th cent. and there are two brasses of the same period.

LITTLE MARLOW, *Buckinghamshire* (6–SU8788). This tiny village lies on the Thames at the end of a no through road. It still holds the fragments of a 14th-cent. Benedictine nunnery and in its centre is a gabled Jacobean manor house with its original staircase.

Adjoining the manor is the Church of St John the Baptist, of Norman origin with a fine 14th-cent. tower. The chancel is divided from a chapel by a Norman arch; the font is of the same period and a Norman piscina can be found on a window-sill. The double-swinging lych-gate is worked by a pulley and the attractive churchyard was the burial place of Edgar Wallace.

LITTLE MISSENDEN, *Buckinghamshire* (6–SU9298). This is an unspoilt village containing many old houses and cottages centred round an Elizabethan manor house and a grey church, that of St John Baptist. The River Misbourne flows through the fields nearby and the Chiltern Hills which flank the village are thick with beechwoods. The manor house, with its numerous windows, has an interesting collection of outhouses and stables. The garden and terrace were designed by Angelica Kaufmann.

The church, which dates back to Norman times, is principally renowned for its series of wall paintings discovered in the 1930s. Those of St Christopher, St Catherine and the Crucifixion are all 14th-cent., and there are numerous fragments dating from the 12th to the 18th cent. A Norman font still remains and a key 15 in. long hangs on the wall. There is an interesting series of modern stained-glass windows.

LITTLE WYMONDLEY, *Hertfordshire* (10–TL2127). This little country village, with its attractive main street, has several buildings of interest.

S. of the church is the 16th-cent. Wymondley Bury, a gabled brick building with a moat surrounding it and a gabled dovecot in its grounds. Wymondley Hall is a handsome, early-17th-cent. timber-framed house with a six-gabled front and an interesting group of chimneys. It has a large attractive barn with elaborate medieval timbers supporting the tiled roof. The late Georgian Wymondley House is near the west end of the village. It is two and a half stories high, with five bays, and has a cemented front and a porch with Ionic columns.

Half a m. N. of the village is Wymondley Priory, originally a 13th-cent. Augustinian house and now a farm-house with a few remains of the original arches.

St Mary's Church, set on a small hill, has a 15th-cent. nave and small tower with an Elizabethan bell, but the rest of the church was added in 1875.

LONDON COLNEY, *Hertfordshire* (10–TL 1603). This little village stands on the River Colne and has several interesting old houses and inns.

Of particular note is All Saints Convent, an attractive late-Victorian building of red and purple brick and stone with a neo-Tudor front with a turret. The lower refectory has a big dais window and the gatehouse has a figure frieze above its door.

St Peter's Church is slim with a cemented façade and is in the Norman Revival style dated 1825. The interior is without aisles and the columns of the west gallery have Norman capitals. The stained glass, representing the Ascension, is in a slightly Raphaelesque style.

One m. E. of the village is Tyttenhanger, a large brick house built in the middle of the 17th cent., with brick quoins and window frames, a hipped roof and a squat cupola. It has a magnificent staircase and rather unusual doorcases in the staircase hall. There is a chapel on the second

Barnaby/Mustograph

Long Crendon: the Court House was given to Queen Catherine of Aragon by Henry VIII

floor with a two-decker pulpit and the Ten Commandments over the fireplace. A long gallery runs the length of the house and there is a great deal of Elizabethan panelling.

LONG CRENDON. *Buckinghamshire* (10–SP6908). This attractive village, with its many 16th- and 17th-cent. thatched cottages, was once an important lace-making centre.

The 15th-cent. Court House, now a National Trust property, was given to Catherine of Aragon by Henry VIII. Long and low with timber frames, the upper story overhangs the lower in five bays, four of which form one large room with a timbered roof. At the end of the house is a massive fireplace, with a 16th-cent. wood lintel, as well as a round brick oven.

There are two other interesting houses in the village, the 15th-cent. manor house, with tall Tudor chimneys and a dovecot, and the lovely Long Crendon Manor.

St Mary's Church is of medieval origin. The roof to the nave is of 16th-cent. oak and the three porches are each of different centuries. The 14th-cent. font is surrounded by lions, with angels with outstretched wings adorning its brim. The Dormer tomb is a richly decorated monument with Sir John Dormer in complete armour and his wife in a long dress of blue and white, her head resting on a cushion. The lace for the altar and communion cloth was made by village lace-makers.

One m. E. of the village is **Notley Abbey**, founded in 1162 by Augustinian monks and now a private residence.

LUTON, *Bedfordshire* (10–TL0821), is the largest town in the county. It is very prosperous, famed for its straw-plaiting and straw-hat-making which began in the 17th cent. Other industries have, to a great extent, replaced this trade, although 5 per cent of the town's industry is still hat-making. There is light engineering and a large motor-vehicle trade. It has its own airport.

In the centre of the town is Wardown Park with many amenities, including a large boating lake and a county cricket ground. The Victorian mansion, Wardown, is an art gallery and museum, housing many exhibits of local interest from the Stone Age to the present day.

The Town Hall, built in 1934 of Portland stone, with a clock tower rising to 144 ft, is a fine building. Water Tower, in West Hill Road, is one of the most pleasing buildings in Luton. In Moat Lane at Biscot is Moat House, the one remaining medieval house in the town, with a fine roof of *c.* 1500 and embattled collars and purlins. By way of Copt Hall will be found the ruins of Someries Castle, built by Lord Wenlock in the 15th cent. It still has a brick gatehouse, a brick chapel and other features of interest.

Dray's Ditches, near the South Bedfordshire golf course, have a linear dyke about half a mile long. In the excavations have been discovered Bronze Age urns and Iron Age pottery and ditches. Half a m. N. of Leagrave station is

Marlow: the River Thames is here the scene of lively activity

Waulud's Bank, an earthwork abutting on the River Lea. Inside a broad flat-bottomed ditch have been found Neolithic Rinyo-Clacton pottery fragments. Long Barrow is in the recreation ground of Sundown Park and stands over 7 ft high.

The town has many Victorian and modern churches. The chapels include the Union Chapel in Castle Street, early Victorian and one of the best buildings in Luton, with three bays and giant Greek Doric columns at the entrance.

St Mary's Church is the town's link with the past and one of the largest churches in England. It is a magnificent building begun in the 13th cent. and enlarged in the 14th and 15th cents. The exterior is of flint and stone chequer-work. The tower has a stair-turret. The elaborate Wenlock Chapel is very high and in two tiers, and opposite is the little chantry chapel of Richard Barnard, vicar in 1477, with an ornate vault. The octagonal font is of Purbeck marble c. 1330–40 with a majestic font canopy which contains a vault. There are several fine screens and the stalls in the chancel have carved heads on the arm-rests. There is a wealth of monuments, all of interest.

LUTON HOO, *Bedfordshire* (10–TL1018). In richly wooded countryside on the A6 to LUTON is the magnificent house of Luton Hoo, open to the public and situated in a park of 1,500 acres, landscaped by Capability Brown a year after Robert Adam started plans for the house itself. It has been the home of the Wernher family since 1903 when it was remodelled for Sir Julius, a diamond magnate. It originally belonged to the Earl of Bute, then Prime Minister.

The building is of ashlar stone, mainly of three stories, and has its own chapel. In the grounds are two lovely lakes, and the stables are by Adam. About 1¾ m. S. of the house is Lady Bute's Lodge, mid-Victorian but with a Norman doorway.

The house contains the Wernher collection, with paintings by Titian and Rembrandt, a fine collection of porcelain and china, magnificent tapestries and furniture, 16th- and 17th-cent. jewels and, in the Russian Room, robes worn at the court of the Tsars and mementoes of the Russian Imperial Family.

MARLOW, *Buckinghamshire* (6–SU8587). This fascinating little town, which has much to interest the traveller in its mixture of the old and the new, is planned in such a way that none of the new buildings in any way detract from the charm of the older ones.

In the High Street are many old houses, but its most famous feature is the suspension bridge, built in 1831 to the design of William Tierney Clark who constructed several similar bridges, including one linking Buda and Pest in Hungary. The one in Marlow, however, is the only remaining example of his work. From its centre are panoramic views of the river where swans are often to be seen and pretty gardens and handsome beech trees reach down to the water's edge. It is the dividing line of Berkshire and Buckinghamshire and on the opposite side, adjacent to the bridge, is the "Compleat Angler" Inn with its reminders of Izaak Walton's book. Adjoining the bridge, in the town itself, is All Saints Church, which contains a monument to Sir Miles Hobart, set up by Parliament to commemorate the parliamentary rebel, who in 1628 locked the door of the House of Commons until certain taxation resolutions were passed.

A short distance from the church is the obelisk milestone in the Market Place, erected in 1822, an indication that in the early 19th cent. the town was an important stopping-place for travellers. It is closely connected with the Cecil family of HATFIELD House, Hertfordshire, who were great sufferers from gout and used Marlow as a short cut to take the waters at BATH.

The Crown Hotel, originally called Remnantz, was reputedly a place where the famous highwayman Dick Turpin took hospitality and, probably, purses.

In West Street is Albion House which was once the home of Shelley, where he lived in 1817 with Mary Godwin whom he married. The 17th-cent. grammar school, which Shelley frequently visited, is nearby. West Street is familiarly known as Poets Row.

The Parsonage, in St Peter's Street, is believed to be the oldest house in the town, dating from the 14th cent.

MEDMENHAM, *Buckinghamshire* (6–SU80 84).

The road from MARLOW to Medmenham is lovely with its woods, hills, green verges, farmhouses and views of the river. It lies in a hollow of the Thames Valley under chalk cliffs, with flowers and brambles.

An inn of great interest is the Dog and Badger, built about 1390. This area was strongly Royalist during the Civil War and it is interesting to note that a cannon-ball was dug out of the wall of the Dog and Badger when the only reconstruction that has taken place in the inn since it was built was being carried out.

Nine Lombardy poplars line the roadside in this rambling village with its flint-stone cottages and its yew topiary. Down by the bottom of the village road, by the church, is the River Thames and the motorist should take care here for the tarmac road ends abruptly at the water's edge. It is a place to sit for a while with the water, overhung by willow trees, flowing by.

The Normans built an abbey here which fell into disuse and was later rebuilt by Sir Francis Dashwood to become a home for the Hell Fire Club.

The little church with its Norman doorways and 15th-cent. tower is flanked by chestnuts. The chancel of the same period is of oak with king-post tie-beams.

On a steep hill, above the crossroads, is Lodge Farm, a gabled property now belonging to the National Trust. A short walk to reach it will give good views of the countryside below.

MELCHBOURNE, *Bedfordshire* (10–TL 0365),

has a street of 18th-cent. thatched cottages which leads to St Mary Magdalene Church and Melchbourne Park. It was once the home of the Knights Hospitallers who used to hold a weekly market here.

The church is a Georgian building with a medieval tower and medieval masonry included in the Georgian chancel. The nave is wide with large arched windows, and there is a family pew with an unusual open fireplace.

Melchbourne Park, built of red brick about 1610, was previously the family seat of Lord St John of Bletsoe. It was fashioned in an H-plan with a big chimneybreast and was remodelled in 1741 when the two projecting wings and low parapet were added. The porch has two pairs of Tuscan columns and, inside, the staircase hall has a dainty plasterwork ceiling and a fine gallery.

MEPPERSHALL, *Bedfordshire* (10–TL1336),

was originally in two counties but in 1888 it lost its association with Hertfordshire. Outside the village, SW. of the church, are the Hills, the remains of a motte and bailey castle, probably a stronghold in the 12th cent.

The Manor House, standing just by the church, is early 17th-cent. and one of the most outstanding timber-framed buildings in the county. It has two big gables with timber decorations, between which are smaller gables. On the front of the middle one is a single pargeted thistle and crown.

St Mary's Church has a Norman crossing tower and is of ironstone. The crossing arches have all been restored at different times. In the south transept is a Perpendicular reredos with tracery and panels. The nave and north aisle, dated 1875, are by Sir Arthur Blomfield, but the chancel is 13th-cent. The aisle has a steep lean-to roof. There is an ancient parish chest and monuments to John Meptyshall and his wife, 1440, and to John Boteler and his wife, 1441.

St Thomas's Chapel, Chapel Farm, has a late Norman north doorway, lozenges in the arches and decorated capitals. It was probably built in the early 12th cent.

MONKEN HADLEY, *Hertfordshire* (6–TQ 2497).

This rare village combining Hadley Common and Hadley Green has a centre of Georgian buildings, the green and the triangular common separated by the church.

The common, with Hadley Wood in the background, has on the north side the 17th-cent. brick Church House and Mount House, probably the best house in the village, a red-bricked, five-bayed building with a pediment and a pedimented doorcase. On the south side it has Gladsmuir House, of red brick with a Victorian front, Hurst Cottage, of two stories and five bays, and Hadley House, a large 18th-cent. building with stables and a fine cedar tree in the front.

Hadley Green has on its west side Old Ford Manor House and Old Ford Manor Golf Club House. The latter, which was originally two cottages, has a 19th-cent. gateway, its parapet bearing on engraved ornament in the Sloane style. On the south-east side of the green are

Ossulton House, with a Gibbs-style surround to the arched doors, Hadley House, the biggest on the green with a Roman Doric porch and large stables, Fairholt, Monkenhold and the six Wilbraham Almshouses, dated 1612, of red brick with one story and interesting windows. On the edge of the green is Battle Obelisk, of Portland stone, recording the Battle of Barnet in 1471. In Drury Road to the S., is a ·Victorian brewery, which is rather out of keeping with its surroundings.

St Mary's Church has a date on the tower of 1494. The tower has diagonal buttresses and a higher turret. It is of flint and ironstone with white stone dressings and a rare copper beacon surmounting it. There are squints in the chancel chapels. The plate is old and very fine. The church has many brasses. In front of the altar is one of a lady, and another, of Sir Roger Wilbraham, 1616, is by Nicholas Stone.

N. of the church is the Priory, mainly early 19th-cent., but with some 16th-cent. remains, and just by the church is White Lodge with an early Georgian doorcase.

MONKS RISBOROUGH, *Buckinghamshire* (10–SP8104). Rising above this village on the slopes of the Chilterns can be seen the Cross of Whiteleaf cut out of the turf. The white chalk of the cross is visible many miles away for it is 80 ft in length and a similar distance in width.

In the village itself, hidden away amid glorious countryside thick with trees, are many thatched and timbered cottages and houses of distinction. It is said to have belonged to the monks of Christ Church, CANTERBURY until the Dissolution of the Monasteries.

St Dunstan's Church stands in a pleasant churchyard with high hedges and many trees, with the rectory close by. Its main structure is 15th-cent. but much of the interior is of earlier periods. The 12th-cent. font is fluted and exquisitely carved with foliage. The 14th-cent. tower has six inscribed bells, and the attractive roodscreen, of the 16th cent., is carved with flowers and has six brightly painted pictures of the Apostles.

MUCH HADHAM, *Hertfordshire* (10–TL 4319). This well-preserved village is perhaps the most attractive in the county. Its long main street is filled with buildings of fine quality.

There are gabled 17th-cent. houses such as North Leys, built in chequered brick, its canopy above the straight door supported by carved brackets. From the windows of the old Red Lion Inn can be seen meadows edged with lime trees. The Lordship, mid-18th-cent., is a large country gentleman's house with its own stables. It has two stories with nine bays, a Tuscan porch and, at the rear, a wing of what was probably part of a Tudor mansion.

The New Manor House is a Victorian building, picturesque but architecturally rather dull. Overhanging cottages adjoin Woodham House, of the 17th cent., with its fine exposed timbers, symmetrical gables and doorcase of a later period. Old House and Green Shutters also have fine timbers.

Much Hadham Hall is the most splendid mansion in the village. Standing beside a massive tree, the house, built in 1735, has a central Venetian window, a sloping roof and, beside the stables, an arched carriageway with four windows on each side. Camden Cottage and Castle House are both delightful, the latter in white with a 19th-cent. front and Gothic porch. Morris Cottage, also with exposed timbers, is probably of the 16th cent., and nearby is the 18th-cent. Moor Place, set in large grounds. It has blank arches on the entrance side of the ground floor and a fine interior with good fireplaces. The south wing was added in 1907.

St Andrew's Church is large with a complicated history. Although originally a 12th-cent. church, apparently nothing remains of that period. Rebuilding began with the chancel c. 1220, with its blocked north lancet window, then the south aisle, c. 1250, and the north aisle, c. 1300. The tower was added in 1382–1404 and has three stages and a tall spire. The clerestory, roofs and south porch were added in the 15th cent., when many windows were renewed. The screen has panel tracery and is also of the 15th cent., as are the stalls with poppyheads. There are two large rare c. 1400 chairs. Several brasses are interesting, in particular one of Judith Aylmer, wife of the Bishop of London.

Standing near the church is the Palace, for 800 years the country residence of the Bishops of London, and the birthplace of Edmund Tudor, father of Henry VII. It is a long brick house in which the old tie-beams are visible. The magnificent staircase and panelling are Jacobean.

The Rectory, S. of the churchyard, is early-17th-cent.

NASEBY, *Northamptonshire* (10–SP6878), is famous for the battle which decided the outcome of the Civil War. In June 1645 the opposing sides met in the fields outside the village. Cromwell defeated the Royalists, and King Charles I lost most of his army but managed to escape. Naseby Field has been enclosed since the battle and in it can be seen a dip in the ground where most of the fighting took place. There are two monuments: an obelisk dated 1823, which does not actually mark the site of the battle, and a more recent memorial on the field itself.

NEWPORT PAGNELL, *Buckinghamshire* (10–SP8743). An ancient town referred to in the Domesday Book as Newport, Pagnell being the name of the owners of the manor; it is situated on two rivers, the Ouse and the Lovat, the latter dividing the town. Once the greatest of all lacemaking towns, it is now a busy industrial centre.

Built of iron in c. 1810, now an Ancient Monument, Tickford Bridge crosses the Lovat; the stone North Bridge crosses the Ouse. Near to the Ouse and close to the church is Tickford Abbey, now modernized but still on the site of the priory founded in Norman times and in use until Cardinal Wolsey appropriated its funds for the construction of a college at Oxford. Remains of the old building are preserved within the newer version.

The 14th-cent. church oversees the whole town from the centre where it stands. It has two fine porches, one with a vaulted roof and a priest's room over it, the other with a 15th-cent. roof, beneath which are decorated corbels. The interior has many arcades typical of the period and a 14th-cent. piscina. A brass monument of a man in the dress of the times is on the turret doorway, next to the chancel porch. The finely carved screens are worth closer inspection.

Despite the numerous modern buildings, the town still has many Georgian houses and the late Victorian building of Queen Anne's Hospital, on the site of an earlier one built for the poor of the town by Queen Anne of Denmark, wife of James I, which has a 17th-cent. beam bearing the words of an appeal for money for those less fortunate who were treated in the hospital.

NORMAN CROSS, *Huntingdonshire* (10–TL1691). About ¾ m. N. of this little village is a monument of a bronze eagle on a column, erected in memory of the 1,800 French soldiers and sailors who died here as prisoners during the Napoleonic Wars.

On the road to YAXLEY is a three-storied house with parapet walls and three bays, which is believed to be the house of the commandant of the former prison built for French prisoners-of-war in 1796.

NORTHAMPTON, *Northamptonshire* (10–SP7561). This is the county town and a county borough in its own right. Its entrance from the S. is unprepossessing and slightly confusing, but leaving it on the other side, past large modern houses on the road to WELLINGBOROUGH, it slowly merges into the countryside.

It is an ancient Anglo-Saxon town, and during the Wars of the Roses the Yorkists captured Henry VI here at the Battle of Northampton in 1460. The Lancastrians were defeated through treachery, and as a result Edward IV seized the throne. During the Civil War the trade for which it is now famous, boot and shoe making, became important, since Northampton shod most of Cromwell's army.

In the centre of the town is All Saints' Church, occupying a whole square. Most of the building was destroyed in a fire, but the medieval tower survives. Charles II gave 1,000 tons of timber for the rebuilding and his gift is commemorated by a statue of the king on the wide portico. The west doors of the nave are richly carved and the nave is handsome, with timber and plaster ceilings. The font and pulpit are about 1680, and the crossing dome stands on Ionic columns. The medieval crypt is below the chancel.

By the church, in George Row, is the Sessions House, built in 1676, a small attractive building with cherubs perched on its balustrade and a

hipped roof. Opposite is the Victorian Town Hall, an ornate building in the Venetian Gothic style, with a gable flanked by two turrets and a clock tower.

St John's Church, in Bridge Street, was a hostel for travellers in the 12th cent. and an almshouse at the time of the Reformation. It is now a Roman Catholic church with medieval windows and parts of the original roof. Opposite is the old Charity School. Hazlerigg Mansion, in Marefair which leads from Gold Street, was built just prior to the fire and survived it. Its original owner was Sir Arthur Hesilrigg, a Cromwellian who died in the TOWER. Further along is another church which also survived the fire: St Peter's, one of the county's most impressive churches. It is large and predominantly Norman in style, with massive buttresses on the exterior and a 17th-cent. squat tower. Inside there is no chancel arch but an array of Norman carvings which run from east to west. There are many varied capitals and a 14th-cent. font with tracery and pinnacles.

Only 5,000 people inhabited this town in the 18th cent. During the Napoleonic wars they poured in to make army boots, increasing the numbers to 15,000, and now the population is over 120,000, which is more than a third of the whole county. It is surprising, for what was once a small town, how many churches of note there are in Northampton

In Sheep Street, which has several Georgian houses, is the interesting and unusual Church of the Holy Sepulchre, one of the four surviving round churches in England, built from the time of the Crusaders. It is of ironstone with a tall tower and spire. The original nave, dating from the 12th cent., is round, and 50 years later another nave was added to form the choir. The clerestory is 15th-cent., with old Norman columns supporting it, and the chancel, which is rich in design, is mid-Victorian. In Campbell Square, on the far side of the church, is one of the town's earliest industrial buildings, Manfield Warehouse, in ornate Italian style with a tall tower and many windows. It was built in the 1850s.

St Giles' Church, in St Giles Street, is a big, golden, ironstone medieval church with a central tower and the only peal of 10 bells in the county. Inside, where the clerestory is of paler stone than the rest of the building, there is a 17th-cent. pulpit and finely carved oak chair, a 15th-cent. Gobion tomb, chained books and Victorian glass of note in the east window.

The museum has many interesting exhibits, including a cobbler's shop and Queen Victoria's wedding shoes, as well as the ballet shoes of Fonteyn, Ulanova and Nijinsky. There are also archaeological finds dating from the Iron Age, medieval pottery, and paintings and furniture. Opposite stands the Victorian Repertory Theatre with an ornate painted ceiling and a gilt and red-plush auditorium.

The Market Square, believed to be the largest in England, is reached by a narrow street off Mercer's Row, which is on one side of All Saints' Church. It still has many Georgian and Victorian buildings and in one corner is Welsh House, which also survived the fire and dates back to 1595, with obelisks and heraldic shields on the front. It belongs to the days when the Welsh brought their cattle to the market. There is a large car park in the square and at the far end is a vast ornamented Victorian building called the Emporium Arcade, a covered market with little shops leading off the street inside. On the second floor, with a wooden balcony, are shops and offices, and in the ends and centre is an additional floor.

The railway station is on the site of the old medieval castle. It has a water garden, a statue of St Christopher and a wall decorated with features describing the history of the town's footwear industry.

Along the KETTERING road is a large recreation ground, the former race-course, and on the far side, in St George's Avenue, is the College of Technology, a pleasant modern building specializing in the theory and practice of leather and footwear. The county cricket ground is on the Wellingborough Road and just past it is Abingdon Park Museum, set in large grounds. The house dates from the 15th to the 18th cent. and contains a collection of English and Chinese porcelain, Northamptonshire lace, children's toys and agricultural and domestic exhibits of former days. In the beautiful grounds, now a public park, is a mulberry tree planted by David Garrick, and nearby is the old village church, originally Norman but rebuilt in the last century after damage by a storm. On the Billing road, to the SE., is Billing Aquadrome with five lakes, including one with exotic birds, and outdoor amusements of every description, as well as a folk museum in Billing Mill.

About 1½ m. S. of Northampton on the A508 at **Hardingstone**, is one of the Eleanor Crosses, now an Ancient Monument, which Edward I had erected to mark the resting place of the coffin containing his queen as it made its way from HARBY in Nottinghamshire to London.

To the S. of the town on the A43 is another Ancient Monument, Danes Camp on Hunsbury Hill, really an Iron Age earthwork. Six m. to the NW. is **Althorp**, the residence of the Earl Spencer, a 16th-cent. house much altered in later restorations, with a magnificent collection of portraits, furniture and china.

NORTH MIMMS, *Hertfordshire* (10–TL2304) is a tiny village in glorious wooded countryside.

North Mimms House, standing in 1,000 acres of parkland, is a magnificent building surpassed in the county only by HATFIELD House. It is fashioned on the H-plan in the late Elizabethan style, and is two stories high, with large windows, projecting gabled wings and a central porch behind which is a small cupola. The doorway is flanked by Tuscan columns with a triglyph frieze. The entrance hall has a French chimneypiece dated 1515. There are many outstanding paintings in the house, and in the grounds a renowned rose garden.

The Church of St Mary standing in the park is still almost all 14th-cent., although the panelled pulpit is Elizabethan. There are many fine monuments of interest including a brass to a priest, *c.* 1360, showing God the Father holding the soul of the priest in a cloth and the head of the priest in the canopy above. In the chancel is a large upright wall monument of John Somers, lawyer and parliamentarian, who framed the Declaration of Rights and became Lord Chancellor. Near the church is the late-17th-cent. vicarage.

SE. of the village is the park of **Gobions**, where the ancestral home of Sir Thomas More once stood. An 18th-cent. "folly" arch survives from the former mansion.

OAKLEY, *Bedfordshire* (10–TL0153). Wide views of the Ouse valley can be had from the hills surrounding this residential village, which is of ancient origin, its bridge still having arches of medieval stonework.

Oakley House, for long a seat of the Dukes of Bedford, is 17th-cent. although remodelled, and has a hipped roof and verandas on three sides. The Bedford Arms is a modernized but unspoilt old inn.

St Mary's Church has small slit-windows in its 12th-cent. tower, and the rest of the battlemented exterior is of the same time or a little later. The screen in the north chapel has paintings on the coving of Christ seated on a rainbow and that in the south chapel has rib-vaulted coving. The Perpendicular octagonal font has tracery motifs. Of the monuments, one has a coffin lid with a foliated cross growing from an animal, and another, early-14th-cent., is an effigy of a lady in a low tomb recess.

ODELL, *Bedfordshire* (10–SP9658). This winding, attractive country village, on a bend of the River Ouse, has many pretty thatched cottages of stone and a thatched pub. Odell Great Wood is a fascinating place for rare flowers, butterflies and birds.

There was formerly a castle here in Norman days and the mound of it still remains. The outbuildings of a 17th-cent. house can still be seen.

All Saints Church, set on the slopes of a hill, is a fine example of a 15th-cent. church built all at one time. The massive west tower is in four stages with clasping buttresses. The lovely interior has tall arcades, an original rood-screen under the tower arch and attractive diamond-pattern flooring in the nave and aisles. In the east window of the south aisle is a remnant of stained glass of rare and simple beauty showing a group of seraphs. A richly adorned monument of the 17th cent. is to the Alston family.

OLD WARDEN, *Bedfordshire* (10–TL1343). This little country village on a steep-banked lane is a pretty place with honey-coloured thatched cottages. The Church of St Leonard is late-12th-cent., its tower a little older, and is of brown cobbles. It has much good woodwork and was restored and renewed by Lord Ongley in 1841,

with a strong Continental influence. The large font originally had 12 shafts and is of the 14th cent. There is stained glass from Warden Abbey, and there are several monuments, including one, of particular interest, to Sir Samuel Ongley, dated 1726 and signed by Scheemakers, and Delvaux.

Old Warden Park was built for Joseph Shuttleworth in Jacobean style in 1872. It is of yellow brick with a large tower and a clock surrounded by an unusual openwork stone grille.

One m. WSW. is Warden Abbey, originally founded by Walter Espec in 1135. All that remains now is part of the early Tudor brick house of the Gostwicks, which was probably built about 1537. It has a chimney breast and a decorated stack and in the rear is a stair-turret.

N. of the church are the earthworks of Quint's Hill which are probably early Iron Age, although the site is unexcavated.

Of more modern interest is the aerodrome of the **Shuttleworth Trust**, with a unique collection of aircraft ranging from Blériot to the Spitfire. It is open to the public and there are regular flying displays.

OLNEY, *Buckinghamshire* (10–SP8851). Famous for its long-standing connections with William Cowper, Olney is the main town of north Buckinghamshire. It was once a lace-making centre but since the decline of that industry other trades have taken its place.

Its buildings are a mixture of new and old and in the market square is the red-bricked Cowper Memorial Museum, where William Cowper lived with his friend Mary Unwin, who cared for him during his bouts of insanity. It was here he wrote his poems and hymns. In glass cases round the walls are editions and illustrations of his work, and Mary Unwin's room holds her workbox and lace bobbins.

The broach spire of the Church of SS. Peter and Paul dominates the countryside, for it rises to 185 ft. Dating from the 14th cent., it is one of the county's finest churches. The tower is in four tiers, each containing a gabled window. Grotesque heads decorate the pinnacles and others peep out beneath the parapet of the chancel. John Newton was curate here during the time Cowper resided in Olney and became his close friend, writing together with him many of the Olney Hymns, such as "Hark my soul it is the Lord", "God moves in a mysterious way His wonders to perform", "How sweet the name of Jesus sounds" and "Glorious things of thee are spoken".

The splendour of this magnificent church can be seen from the small bridge which passes over the narrow strip of the River Ouse adjacent to the church at the end of the long main street of the town.

Olney's claim to world renown is its pancake race, which takes place every Shrove Tuesday and has survived since the middle of the 15th cent. In the town of Liberal in the United States a similar race is held annually. In Olney it is run between the market place and the church and the

first housewife to complete the course is rewarded by a kiss from the bellringer and a silver cup.

OUNDLE, *Northamptonshire* (10–TL0488), is an old country town, dating back at least to 972 when its markets and tolls were confirmed by King Edgar. Although its narrow main street carries heavy traffic, very little has changed in recent years.

The buildings, of stone and Collyweston tiles, are of three centuries, some tall and dignified with steeply pitched roofs, others gabled with oriels. There are fascinating alleyways and narrow yards; old almshouses in North Street, Church Lane and West Street; many ancient inns, the most notable being Talbot Inn, a gabled 17th-cent. building with a fine oak staircase; and numerous tiny old cottages with minute windows. The Town Hall is Victorian, as is the large Police Station.

The famous Oundle Public School and Laxton Grammar School were founded by the same man, William Laxton, a grocer who was born here in the 16th cent. and eventually became Lord Mayor of London. The two schools were separated in the last century, but Oundle is still owned by the Grocers' Company. Many of its buildings date from the 30 years during which Frederick Sanderson, who became headmaster in 1892, transformed it into the type of school it is today. It covers a large part of the town and houses over 600 boys. Both schools still remain under one headmaster and the boys of Laxton School join those of Oundle when they reach fifth-form level.

There are several churches in the town, with two of some note. Jesus Church was built in 1879 by Arthur Blomfield, who was also responsible for the improvements in the school. It is in the form of a cross, in Gothic style, with lancet windows in the nave, transept and chancel. It has an unusual central lantern, a turret which starts as a square and finishes as an octagon, with a dome-shaped ceiling. The other interesting church is St Peter's, large and opulent with a magnificent steeple and large surfaces of the tower panelled vertically towards the spire. The 15th-cent. south porch is richly decorated with battlements, pinnacles and gargoyles. The pulpit, painted with stars, dates from before the Reformation. There are two fonts, one of the 18th cent. and one dated 1909, several Perpendicular screens and a great many memorials and brasses.

Around the town flows the River Nene, making it a great sailing centre, and the views from the river are delightful, as is the countryside which greets you as you leave the town.

Cotterstock Hall is 1½ m. N. of Oundle and open to the public. It is a 17th-cent. grey stone manor house, built in an E-shape with good stone chimneypieces and Dutch gables. In the attic room Dryden wrote his *Fables*. It stands in a large garden with an avenue of elms leading down to the River Nene. Five m. to the N. lies the pretty village of **Apethorpe**, built in the local stone, with a Perpendicular church.

Olney: the spire of the 14th-cent. church dominates the countryside Noel Habgood

PEAKIRK, *Huntingdonshire* (10–TF1606), is an ancient stone village on the edge of the Fens, completely unspoilt. Close by are the Waterfowl Gardens, property of the Wildfowl Trust, with a variety of aquatic birds in the various waterways. The gardens are open to the public and there are good parking facilities.

In 716 St Pega, sister of St Guthlac, founded a cell here. On the site of the original cell is the Hermitage, E. of the church. After being in ruins for many years it was drastically restored, but the chancel dates from about 1280, its east window of three lights. There is also a fragment of an Anglo-Saxon cross-shaft with foliage.

St Pega's Church is the only one dedicated to her in the country. The west wall is part of a Norman building and the bellcot is also Norman. In the south doorway is an elaborate Norman tympanum and most of the interior is also Norman. The 14th-cent. lectern, with its wooden stem and slender attached shafts, is a rarity. The octagonal font is medieval. There are many wall paintings, mostly of the 14th cent., including Christ washing St Peter's feet, the Last Supper, the Crucifixion and the Resurrection, and also one of St Christopher of a later date. The north aisle has a rather unpleasant painting of the Three Quick and the Three Dead and another of two women whispering to each other with a devil pressing their heads together.

PENN, *Buckinghamshire* (6–SU9193). This is a long straggling village, on the remote edge of the Chilterns, rather typical of other villages in the county with 17th-cent. cottages of wood and brick and of wood and flintstone.

The Crown Inn and the village church are adjacent to each other by the village green, around which there are many Georgian houses. On the top of the hill is the Knoll, which was for a time the home of Princess Anne during the reign of William of Orange. A small belvedere in the roof of the house is called Princess Anne's window.

Holy Trinity Church has a medieval structure, the roof – one of the finest in the county – being 15th-cent. It was greatly altered by the Penns and the Curzons during the 18th cent. when many of its treasures were installed. Discovered in 1938 is the magnificent wall painting of "The Doom" of the Last Judgment. It was painted in the 15th cent. and hangs on the south wall. There are many brasses to the Penn family and although William Penn of Pennsylvania is buried at JORDANS, many of his descendants rest here under the floor of the south chapel.

From the churchyard, on this high ridge, can be seen about a dozen different counties and Penn Woods, nearby, is one of Buckinghamshire's many beauty-spots.

PETERBOROUGH, *Huntingdonshire* (10–TL 1999), is a prosperous city with an outstanding cathedral and is the biggest town in the county. As well as being a market town, it has many industries, including the processing of sugar beet grown in the surrounding countryside, and engineering.

In its centre is the Market Place where the old guildhall, built in 1671, predominates. This was once used as a butter market and above its open ground floor on Tuscan columns is the chamber, reached by a tiny spiral staircase. It was built to commemorate the Restoration of Charles II, and has a hipped roof and a steep gable. Nearby is St John the Baptist's Church, built in 1402 and containing the nave of a church that was in the precincts of the cathedral. In its tower, of rubble and ashlar, are 16th-cent. embroidered pictures of the Crucifixion. The octagonal font is large with quatrefoil panels, of about the same period as the church. Of the many monuments, an interesting one is by Flaxman, 1826, showing a mourning Grecian beside a tall pedestal and a medallion with the heads of Mr and Mrs Squire.

In Cumbergate are the Feoffee Almshouses, dated 1903, and the 17th-cent. old workhouse, of rubble on the ground floor with an overhanging timber-framed upper floor. Through a passage in the Causeway is Peterscourt, formerly St Peter's Training College, built in 1856 in Gothic style, and in St Mary's Street are new council flats which received a commendation in the Civic Trust Awards for the high-density development scheme of 139 flats with an underground garage on a site of 3¼ acres, one of the objectives being to secure minimum interference with views of the cathedral. In Westgate is the Bull Hotel, an early-18th-cent. low two-storied building. The Georgian Royal Hotel is plain and handsome and the Wortley's Almshouses are early Victorian in a Tudor style, with an inscription above the entrance from a previous building of 1744. In Lincoln Road are Victorian cottages.

The best Georgian houses are in Priestgate, on the corner of which is the three-storied Angel Hotel with its original staircase.

The town hall, in Bridge Street, built in the 1930s in a neo-Georgian style, has an imposing façade with Corinthian columns, a turret and cupola. The entrance hall and staircase are spacious and the whole building is in keeping with the architecture of the city. The gaol, in Thorpe Road, is Victorian but of Norman style with a gatehouse in the middle, and the Victorian St John's Close, formerly a workhouse, is now a hospital.

In Priestgate is the museum and art gallery, which was built in 1816 and has served as a private house, an infirmary and now a museum. It contains a fine collection of local exhibits, including the carved bone and marquetry work made by prisoners-of-war who were detained at Norman Cross Camp during the Napoleonic wars. There are archaeological finds from Romano-British and Anglo-Saxon times, and the natural history section has fossils from the local clay. The Mary Queen of Scots Room contains her own needlework and tiles and fragments from the castle at FOTHERINGHAY where she was executed. The art gallery has interesting paintings.

The bridge which crosses the River Nene was built in 1934 to replace a Victorian iron structure. By its side stands the former customs house, built

Hemingford Grey church: the spire was partly destroyed in the 18th cent.

about 1700, of rubble with a hipped roof and cupola. From here can be seen delightful views of the river which has good fishing and boating.

Peterborough Cathedral is a breathtaking sight. It was founded as a monastery in 655 by King Peada of Mercia, soon after he was converted to Christianity. It was destroyed by the Danes in 870 and refounded 100 years later by King Edgar. Hereward the Wake attacked and plundered it in about 1070 and 46 years later it was destroyed by fire. In 1118 the rebuilding of the present church started. After 80 years the nave was completed, and in 1238 the church was dedicated. Apart from restoration work, the only new building which has taken place since that date is the Retrochoir or New Building at the east end, about 1500.

The cathedral is of Barnack stone, and is 481 ft long, 206 ft wide and 81 ft high. Its tower reaches to 143 ft. It stands in a garden and the precincts are entered by a large gateway with the King's Lodging and Abbott's Prison on one side and St Thomas's Chapel on the other. A few yards past the chapel on the left-hand side is a large detailed map showing places of interest in both the interior of the cathedral and its surrounding buildings. The interior of the west doorway is of finely carved woodwork. The wooden nave ceiling is superbly decorated with saints, kings and grotesque monsters, and in the south aisle is heavy quadripartite ribbed vaulting. The carved wooden choir stalls, pulpit and bishop's throne are all Victorian, but the brass eagle lectern is 14th-cent. In the Retrochoir beyond the apse the ceiling has magnificent fan vaulting, and the Hedda Stone, an important piece of Anglo-Saxon sculpture, dates from about 800. The font, a decorated marble bowl, is 13th-cent. with modern pillars.

Just in front of the Retrochoir are two important burial places. On the left is that of Catherine of Aragon, whose ex-husband Henry VIII established the church as a cathedral in 1541, two years after the Dissolution, and on the right is that of Mary Queen of Scots. Her son, James I, instructed that the body should be removed to WESTMINSTER ABBEY, where it now rests. During the Civil War and Commonwealth the contents of the cathedral as well as carved stonework were savagely destroyed by soldiers, but after King Charles II came to the throne services were resumed in the building, which has been gradually restored through the centuries.

The city has been incorporated in the new county of Huntingdon and Peterborough.

PRINCES RISBOROUGH, *Buckinghamshire* (10–SP8003). This old-world town, with its growing residential population, has many 16th-cent. cottages and delightful houses.

In its centre is its brick Market House with open arcades where in former days a weekly market was held. Crowning the roof is a turret with a clock and bell. Vine House, a Tudor building very close to Market House, is gabled with herringbone brickwork and has a vine tree growing up it.

The Manor House, with its pilastered front, is of 18th-cent. origin. It has a beautiful Jacobean oak staircase and 18th-cent. wainscoting.

The Norman Church of St Mary's, which was heavily restored in the 13th and 14th cents., has a modern spire. It still possesses a Norman window and in the south aisle is a lovely triple lancet window. The pulpit was carved in the time of the Restoration.

RAMSEY, *Huntingdonshire* (10–TL2885), lies in cultivated fenland and is the agricultural centre for the large district surrounding it. Its long, wide street, the Great Whyte, was constructed in 1852 and covers the culverted Bury Brook which ran through the centre of the town.

Ramsey Abbey was founded in 969 and was one of the most important monastic houses until the Dissolution. Only the 13th-cent. Lady Chapel, the porter's lodge and a fragment of the 15th-cent. gatehouse remain. The new house, built about 1660, is now a school and has been greatly added to. The gatehouse, which is now National Trust property and open to the public, is ornate. It has a small doorway and panelled buttresses. Inside, on the ground floor, is a marble monument to Ethelwine, or Ailwin, the founder of the abbey.

Beside the gatehouse is Abbey Green, on which stands a former Victorian school and gabled stone almshouses of the same period. In the middle of Great Whyte is a Victorian clock on a cast-iron column, and there are several yellow-brick houses of the early 19th cent. The Methodist chapel and the Baptist chapel are both late Victorian.

St Thomas of Canterbury Church was originally built as a guest house for visitors to the abbey, in about 1180. The chancel is Norman, distinguished by a heavy rib-vault. The west doorway is in the ashlar-faced tower of 1672. The plain hexagonal font is of dark marble, probably 13th-cent. There is a faded painting of a man and an angel above the north arcade of the nave and there are several monuments.

Bodsey House, 1½ m. to the N., is moated and was originally a hermitage of the abbey. It was converted into a house after the Dissolution and has a fine 17th-cent. chimney stack and an unusual coved and panelled ceiling.

Not far from Ramsey is **Woodwalton Fen**, scheduled as a National Nature Reserve and occupying 514 acres. The large copper butterfly has been introduced here, and there are many rare birds, insects and aquatic plants.

RENHOLD, *Bedfordshire* (10–TL0953), is a straggling village, stretching down to the River Ouse, in attractive countryside reached by narrow twisting roads. The Danes occupied this part of the county at one period.

The Church of All Saints has brown cobbled walls and a Perpendicular tower with a lead spire. The Norman font, which is drum-shaped, has unfinished carvings on an ornamental band. The pulpit, with detailed panels, is of the 17th cent., but of special interest is the high altar tomb-chest, richly carved, with the figures in brass on the lid of Edmund Wayte and his wife, dated 1518.

Beechwoods in Ashridge Park, near Little Gaddesden   Picturepoint

Howbury Hall, 1¾ m. SE., although built in 1849, is in a pre-Victorian style with a five-bayed front and angle bay windows with cast-iron balconies. There is a top balustrade and a staircase with rustic columns.

One m. through the village, at Salph End, is Abbey Farmhouse, a large and delightful 17th-cent. house of brick and timber, with projecting gables either side of the centre and a small baking oven protruding unexpectedly from the wall.

RICKMANSWORTH, *Hertfordshire* (6–TQ 0594). This lovely old town, where three rivers meet, has lakes and water-meadows and one of the finest bathing lakes near to London, the Aquadrome.

In the long, winding High Street is the seven-bayed Hasing House, where William Penn lived with his wife after their marriage. Close by is St Joan of Arc's Convent School, a red-brick Georgian house with a central pedimented door. The 18th-cent. stables of a brewery are now used as offices, and further along is the Swan Hotel with its original Jacobean panelling, fireplaces and staircase. The Victorian Baptist church is simply designed with lancet windows.

In Rectory Road, set in rural surroundings, is Parsonage Farm, and in Uxbridge Road is York House School, a two-storied red-brick Georgian building with five bays. Further along still is Longland Farm, of yellow-washed brick with timber-framing and weather-boarded barns.

St Mary's Church, originally built in 1630, was twice almost completely rebuilt in the last century. The tower and the yellow-brick aisles and early Gothic windows are all that remain of the old church. There is a brass monument to Thomas Day and wives, and a tomb-chest of Henry Cary, Earl of Monmouth.

Near the church in Church Street is the Vicarage, a half-timbered medieval building with later alterations. It has enchanting gables, a bay window on the ground floor, and an overhanging oriel on the first floor. Around the church are two buildings of interest: the Bury, with brick and timber framework, an original staircase and carved overmantels; and the Priory of brick and timber.

Moor Park Mansion House is 1 m. SE. of Rickmansworth. Reconstructed in 1727 by Sir James Thornhill and Giacomo Leoni, it is a baroque house with superb interior decorations. Originally built in the 15th cent. for the Archbishop of York, it eventually became Cardinal Wolsey's country seat. The gardens were the work of Capability Brown. Both house and grounds are open to the public.

ROCKINGHAM, *Northamptonshire* (10–SP 8691). This pleasant village, with the River Welland below, is on a steep hill lined with many old thatched cottages, as well as new buildings of flintstone, which harmonize with the surroundings.

On the summit of a hill, from which can be seen five counties, stands Rockingham Castle. The original castle was built on the instructions of William the Conqueror, and although the site of the keep is now a rose garden surrounded by yew hedges, the moat remains, as well as foundations of the Norman hall and the twin towers of the old gatehouse. King John used it as a hunting lodge for Rockingham Forest, which once covered a vast area of the northern section of the county. The present building is mainly Elizabethan.

Rockingham is a pleasant village in which old and new buildings blend harmoniously

J. Allan Cash

James I was entertained there in 1603, and Dickens spent much time at the house and dedicated *David Copperfield* to the owners, Mr and Mrs Watson, whose descendants still reside there. In the house is an interesting collection of pictures as well as fine furniture and it is open to the public.

St Leonard's Church, by the castle, was rebuilt in the 19th cent. from the 13th-cent. building which was severely damaged during the Civil War. It has a Jacobean pulpit and many 17th- and 18th-cent. monuments to the Watson family.

ROTHWELL, *Northamptonshire* (10–SP8181). This small and interesting old industrial town makes footwear and has engineering works. It is reached by a slight hill and on the outskirts is a large thatched cottage with steep stone steps leading to an old door dated 1660. In the centre of the town is an Ancient Monument: Rothwell Market House, an elegant square building built in 1577 by Thomas Tresham, father of the betrayer of the Gunpowder Plot. Around its cornice are 90 coats of arms of county families. Nearby is a little old Sunday school, and further on is another small building, Rothwell Free Grammar School for boys and girls, founded in 1538. There are many Victorian buildings mixed with some more modern and some older ones, indicating Rothwell's continued importance through the centuries.

There is an annual Charter Fair which, started in 1204, lasts a week and is officially declared open by the reading of the Charter on Trinity Sunday. It was formerly an important trade fair.

The almshouses, known as Jesus Hospital, were built by Owen Ragsdale, who endowed the grammar school. They are grouped round a courtyard and were originally for old men who were allowed a room each and a hall for every four. They have recently been modernized and now house four married couples and six single people. In 1655 the county's first Nonconformist church was established here, in a barn, and the present Congregational church is dated 1735.

Holy Trinity Church is a large cruciform building, mainly 13th-cent. It is reached by a path past the Queen Anne manor house, now council offices, and is said to be the longest parish church in the county. The spire collapsed in the 17th cent., but its top was saved and reset on the turret beside the tower. The interior of the church is very light. Above the nave arcades are 14 clerestory windows and there are larger ones in the aisles of the chancel, all 15th-cent. The stalls have carved misereres. There are four old brasses, one of Owen Ragsdale which hangs above his altar tomb in the south chapel. The elaborate font is 13th-cent. Beneath the south aisle is the charnel, a vaulted crypt containing thousands of old bones, which were discovered in the 18th cent. by a sexton while digging a grave.

Leaving the town on the road to RUSHTON, there are magnificent views of the surrounding countryside.

ROXTON, *Bedfordshire* (10–TL1554), lies between the main road and the River Ouse, with thatched cottages and barns dotted about.

Of special interest is Roxton Chapel, a Congregational church of a most attractive and unusual design with a thatched roof and a tree-trunk veranda. It was founded in 1808 by Charles Metcalfe, the lord of the manor, who converted it from a barn into a chapel and later added two wings.

St Mary's Church, lying behind a row of pines, has brown cobble walls and a short west tower. A doorway in the south aisle is *c.* 1300, as are the three-bay arcade and the nave. There is a Perpendicular screen with painted saints on the dado, an early-15th-cent. Italian rood painting and, in the chancel, a tomb-chest to Roger Hunt, 1438, who was Speaker of the House of Commons and Baron of the Exchequer.

Earthworks will be found in Yarwood in a solitary mound 40 ft in diameter.

ROYSTON, *Hertfordshire* (10–TL3541). This small town, with its narrow streets and old inns and houses, lies at the crossing of Ermine Street and the old Icknield Way.

Below this crossroads is a strange monument, the bottle-shaped Royston Cave, discovered in 1742. Cut out of chalk, it is about 28 ft deep and 17 ft across. On the walls are crude carvings of, among others, St Christopher and the Crucifixion, but the date of their origin is in dispute. The cave, reached by a winding passage, is below the ground.

The remains of James I's palace are in Kneesworth Street, with two large original chimneys, the rest of the building having been rebuilt in the 18th cent. In the same street are Georgian houses, the white-bricked Rookery and the red-bricked Yew Tree House, with segment-headed windows.

W. of the crossroads is a large Victorian workhouse and in Melbourne Street are several interesting red- and purple-brick houses, and the white-brick Banyers Hotel, part 17th- and part 18th-cent. with massive Ionic pilasters and mullioned windows in two gables. Then comes the Victorian Town Hall in yellow brick.

In the High Street are many buildings of character including the early Victorian Bull Hotel of yellow brick, and in John Street a small Victorian Court House in Italian style. Next is the Priory, an enlarged Georgian building, on a site which was probably originally part of the monastery.

SS. John's and Thomas's Church, which lies on the corner of the old and new roads of the town, was originally 13th-cent. and later, but was greatly changed in the Victorian era. The west wall is of the old monastic church. There is oak panelling of the 14th cent., a 13th-cent. font bowl on a base of a later period, and the piscina is genuine 13th-cent. The exact dates of much of the rest of the church seem to be in dispute. Of the monuments, an effigy of a knight with angels at the head is 14th-cent. and a thin brass cross in the chancel is 15th-cent.

To the W. of the town is Therfield Heath on which are five round barrows and one long one, the only one of its kind in the county.

Sandon Mount at Notley Green is covered by a clump of trees. It is 87 ft in diameter, surrounded by a wide ditch in which there is an entrance. It was probably used as a look-out in the 13th cent.

RUSHTON, *Northamptonshire* (10–SP8483), is set amid lovely countryside and is reached by a narrow humped bridge. The buildings are old and of golden ironstone. Rushton Urban District Board School, 1892, is of red brick with iron railings and tiny windows high up.

Rushton Hall, now a school for the Royal Institute for the Blind, was built about 1500 and is open to the public. It was the home of the Tresham family, and Sir Thomas, who built many unusual structures expressing religious themes in the surrounding districts, was a Roman Catholic convert and was many times imprisoned for his beliefs. His son Francis was the betrayer of the Gunpowder Plot. The house has 17th-cent. plaster ceilings, a hammer-beam in the roof of the great hall, and a painted relief of the Crucifixion dated 1577. Screened by cedars, in a remote corner of the grounds of the house, is one of Sir Thomas's curiosities, Triangular Lodge, now an Ancient Monument. It has three sides, three floors, trefoil windows and three gables on each side; in fact everything plays on the number three, as an emblem of the Trinity.

The River Ise runs by the churchyard, separated only by a row of chestnuts. The church has a 13th-cent. tower, with a weather-vane on each of its four corners rising from the 15th-cent. battlements. The Norman nave is divided from the north aisle by three 13th-cent. arches. In the north chapel is a monument to William de Goldingham, a knight, 1296, and between the chapel and the chancel is the altar tomb of Sir Thomas Tresham, grandfather of the recusant Sir Thomas, showing him in the robes of a Grand Prior of the Knights Hospitallers, of which he was the last.

ST ALBANS, *Hertfordshire* (10–TL1507). This ancient city, with its narrow, twisting, hilly streets, was once one of the largest and most important Roman towns ever established in the country. The abbey is visible from miles around, and the town is a fascinating place to visit, with a wealth of features dating from Roman times to the present day.

The remains of Verulamium, open to the public, were only excavated in the present century. When the Romans occupied this part of the country a British settlement already existed here, according to Julius Caesar, since he refers to it in his *De Bello Gallico*, when he tells of his invasions in 54 B.C. By the middle of the 1st cent. A.D. it had become so important that it was elevated to the status of a *municipium*, the only British city to attain such an honour, which accorded the inhabitants the right of Roman citizenship. In A.D. 61 the town was sacked by Boadicea, but after her defeat and death it was rebuilt and re-

covered its prominence. Remains of the walls, some reaching to 12 ft, can still be seen. The theatre, the only Roman one in Britain, has been excavated and restored. Semi-circular in shape, it is 180 ft across and provided for 1,600 spectators. Among the other remains to be seen are a temple, to the S. of the theatre, and a mosaic floor, with the Roman form of central heating still intact.

In the museum are displayed jewellery, pottery, a Mithraic token, household implements and many other exhibits discovered during the excavations.

The cathedral, St Albans Abbey, was built on the site where the first British martyr, Alban, was beheaded in the 4th cent., after being converted to Christianity and assisting a persecuted priest to escape. Constructed largely from brick and flint taken from Roman remains, its nave is nearly 300 ft long. The crossing tower, of great breadth, appears squat because of its massive size. The abbey dates from the 11th cent., but every century has seen additions and alterations to it. The Lady Chapel, completed in the 14th cent., was made into a grammar school at the Dissolution, the nave was lengthened in the 13th cent., and the reredos erected in the 15th cent. The rood-screen, separating the monastic choir from the nave, is of stone. The large circular stone pulpit in the nave has 13th-cent. diaper patterning and was given by Lord Grimthorpe, who in 1879 personally paid for the restoration of the cathedral, which had deteriorated greatly in the 19th cent. The restoration is believed to have cost £130,000. The choir stalls were added in 1905, the font and cover in 1933. The watching loft of timber with a narrow staircase opens on to the Shrine of St Alban which was erected in the 14th cent., later destroyed and rebuilt in the 19th cent. after its several thousand pieces were found. Because the construction was of Purbeck marble it was possible to identify the pieces and they were pieced together by Sir Gilbert Scott. On the south side, the upper part shows the figure of King Offa. A scene of the martyrdom is at the west end and in the base are several holes, supposed to be healing holes, since miraculous cures are said to have occurred at the shrine. The medieval paintings are said to be unique in England, and there are many monuments of importance, three of particular interest being the chantry chapels to the Duke of Gloucester, 1447, Abbot Wheathamstead, 1465, and Abbot Ramryge, 1519. There is also a large collection of brasses.

The early-15th-cent. clock tower, facing the High Street, has a bell which still strikes on the hour and is older than the tower itself. From the tower, which is open to the public, can be seen a splendid view of the abbey and the surrounding countryside. Nearby, the Victorian fountain replaced a market cross which was erected after the famous Eleanor Cross, commemorating Queen Eleanor's brief resting place as her coffin was conveyed to its burial, was pulled down.

Beside the clock tower is the narrow Market Place, in which stands the 19th-cent. Town Hall,

G. Douglas Bolton

St Albans Abbey

facing St Peter's Street, its pillared front with a massive portico resting on fluted Ionic columns. It was here that two fierce battles took place during the Wars of the Roses. French Row, W. of the tower, is a reminder of French occupation in the early 13th cent. In the Fleur de Lys Inn, considerably restored but with much of its original timber framework, King John of France was imprisoned after the battle of Poitiers in 1356. Several of the buildings in this street date back to the 14th cent.

A few of the houses in the High Street are of medieval construction, although partially modernized. From the crossroads runs Holywell Hill, with the River Ver at its end. In the upper part of the street are Georgian buildings, several with massive angled pilasters and attic stories. The White Hart is a 15th-cent. restored building, and just off Holywell Hill, by Sumpter Yard, is the 18th-cent. Old Rectory, two stories high with five bays and Venetian windows.

Further down the hill, Sopwell Lane, with interesting small houses, runs parallel to the river. The ruins of Sopwell Nunnery are covered in ivy.

St Stephen's Hill crosses the river and leads to the 17th-cent. Vicarage, two and a half stories high with five bays and quoins. St Stephen's Church has many facets of Norman times: a window, chancel masonry and a blocked arch. There are other features of varying centuries: a 15th-cent. font heavily carved, an eagle lectern in brass of the early 16th cent; and stained glass mainly of the 19th cent. A brass monument to William Robbins and his wife is dated 1482, and in the churchyard is a Roman milestone.

In St Peter's Street is St Peter's Church, re-stored by Lord Grimthorpe into a Victorian building. Inside is a monument to Edward Strong, chief master mason of ST PAUL'S CATHEDRAL. He built Ivy House, further up the street, a three-storied building with four bays, giant pilasters and an interesting doorcase. Opposite the church is the Grange, a Georgian country-style house.

Nearby are the 16th-cent. Pemberton Almshouses and in Hatfield Road the Marlborough Almshouses, erected by the Duchess of Marlborough in 1736, with an open courtyard in which stands a large cedar tree.

George Street, which begins at the clock tower, has a number of medieval buildings with protruding upper stories, and off it is Romeland, with a green fronting the cathedral. By the side of the green, in Abbey Mill Lane, is one of the oldest inns in England, Fighting Cocks Inn, an octagonal, timber-framed building. Opposite it is an 18th-cent. silk mill, three stories high and nine bays long.

Romeland House, in Romeland Hill, a continuation of George Street, is of purple and red brick with seven bays, a large pedimented doorcase on Tuscan columns and a Venetian window.

Before crossing the river, in Fishpool Street is St Michael's Manor House with nine bays and an impressive entrance. Over the river in St Michael's Street are timber-framed houses. St Michael's Church, within the boundary of the Roman city, has an Anglo-Saxon nave, chancel walls of the 10th cent. and aisles of the 12th cent. The nave roof, on carved stone corbels, and the octagonal Perpendicular font are 15th-cent., and the pulpit with finely carved bookrests is 17th-cent. There are many monuments, but the most famous is that of Sir Francis Bacon showing him sleeping comfortably in a chair.

Gorhambury House and Park, 2½ m. N. of St Albans near the A5, is open to the public and was the home of Sir Nicholas Bacon, father of Sir Francis. Built in 1568, the original masonry of the hall, the porch and a projecting wing still survive. The porch has Tuscan attached columns on the ground floor and Ionic columns on either side of the two-light upper windows. The house was rebuilt in 1777 and the interior has magnificent fireplaces, many portraits of value and 16th-cent. enamelled glass. Numerous famous oaks, including one associated with Queen Elizabeth I, are in Gorhambury Park.

ST IVES, *Huntingdonshire* (10–TL3171). The town, which is a borough, presumably because of its important cattle market, traces its origin back to a village called Slepe, which was on the north bank of the River Ouse and meant slippery landing place. It was a manor of RAMSEY Abbey in 969 and eventually became a priory of the abbey, dedicated to St Ivo, a Persian bishop, and has been called St Ives ever since.

Henry I granted it the rights of an annual fair in 1110 and the town grew up around the fairground, to which people came from all over the country and abroad. The Black Death of 1349 caused its temporary closure and the town declined in importance.

St Ives is picturesque, with delightful riverside views. It has a narrow six-arched bridge built about 1415 with a bridge chapel, one of only three of its kind in England. There is single-line traffic across the bridge, controlled by traffic lights. On the far side is Bridge House, of the 18th cent., with a round arched window overlooking the river. Oliver Cromwell had a farm here and his statue stands in the Market Place.

Only a ruined wall remains of the priory, by the side of the modern council offices. There are many Georgian and Victorian houses in the Broadway, where a monument commemorates Queen Vic-

toria's Jubilee, and in Bridge Street, including the manor house dated about 1600 with three gables on the river side and four on the street and ornamental bargeboards.

The Corn Exchange and the Post Office are both Victorian and the Cattle Market was opened in 1886. The Free Church in Market Hill is dated 1642 and has a steeple 156 ft tall. In the twisting roads are many brick and timber houses.

All Saints Church, reached by a footpath through the Waits, overlooks the River Ouse. Built about 1450 it is large with an exceptionally fine steeple. The west door is ornate, with two niches, and in the south aisle is a double piscina which is early 13th-cent. The octagonal font is Norman and the pulpit, with elongated blank arches, is Elizabethan. The richly painted roodscreen, which fills the chancel arch, is modern, as is the loft and organ-case. Both are by Comper.

In Ramsey Road is Clare Court, a new housing development which received a Civic Trust Award for its outstanding contribution to the surrounding scene.

ST NEOTS, *Huntingdonshire* (10–TL1860). This pleasant, ancient market town on the River Ouse owes its origin to a priory founded in the 10th cent. by Benedictine monks. The Danes invaded it, and after the Conquest it was refounded and given to the Abbey of Bec in Normandy in 1081. The monastery was dissolved in 1539 and disappeared, but excavations have recently taken place and some of the foundations have been uncovered.

The town centres around Market Place, which is long and spacious. The Bridge Hotel, beside the modern bridge, dates from 1685 and has wall panelling that is even earlier. The Cross Keys Inn, of the same period, is low with two-bay windows, and the King's Head in South Street has a curious doorway. In Church Street is the Victorian vicarage with ivy-covered walls and gabled Tudor enlargements. To the left of it are walls and gatepiers with fine wrought-iron gates of the 18th

St Ives: the 15th-cent. bridge with its bridge chapel

Noel Habgood

cent. W. of the church is Brook House, built about 1700, with a hipped roof, seven bays and three stories. The Sun Inn was built about 1680 and apart from the fact that its thatched roof has been replaced by tiles, little has changed since that date. The oak beams still remain in the low ceilings and so do the open fires and many brasses.

St Mary's Church is one of the largest medieval churches in the county and very beautiful. It is tucked away from the town centre in a large churchyard. Of ironstone and pebbles with ashlar dressings, it has a fine tower, and the roof is almost completely flat. The tower is 130 ft high with high solid pinnacles. The windows are all large. The nave is separated from the aisles by high-bay arches. The nave, aisles and chapels have ornately decorated roofs. The pulpit and stalls are Victorian but a few of the latter are late 15th-cent. There are several Perpendicular screens. In the chancel is an unusual monument to Mr Rowley and his wife, which rises almost to the roof, with a gilded iron screen in the lower part.

Five m. to the E., the little village of **Eltisley** has an exceptionally large village green.

ST PAUL'S WALDEN, *Hertfordshire* (10–TL 1922), is a small, rural village, of particular interest because it was the birthplace of Queen Elizabeth, the Queen Mother. Her home was the Bury, a grand red-brick house, partly by Robert Adam, with polygonal bay windows, a hall with a vault and apses at each end screened by columns. On three sides of the drawing-room are bay windows, and in the grounds is Garden House, with Gothic-pointed windows.

Reached through the park of Walden Bury, with its avenue of fine trees, is the Church of All Saints. It is a low, flint church, its tower giving a majestic effect. It has a south-east stair-turret and the thickness of the nave wall suggests that it is older than the 14th-cent. windows. Other windows are Perpendicular, as is the nave clerestory. The chancel was remodelled in 1727 and is separated from the nave by a beautiful screen. The Queen Mother was baptized in the 15th-cent. font. In the tower window is a lovely 14th-cent. figure of the Virgin, clad in brown and olive green, with the Child in red. There are six bells in the tower, one subscribed by the villagers at the time of the coronation.

Stagenhoe, which was rebuilt after 1737, has an 11-bay front, its outer wings two-storied, the others three-storied. It stands in a magnificent park with avenues of limes and chestnuts and a great lake.

The Strathmore Arms, deep in the valley, is a delightful old country pub, its name a reminder of the close connection of the village with the Earls of Strathmore.

SANDY, *Bedfordshire* (10–TL1649). This is a small, but growing town, in pleasant countryside. It is mentioned in the Domesday Book and lay on a Roman road between GODMANCHESTER and Verulamium. The River Ivel runs through it and joins the River Ouse at the north boundary.

Although some light industries have recently developed, it is basically a market-gardening town.

St Swithun's Church, built in the 14th cent., was considerably restored in the 19th cent. It is a large, cruciform building of ironstone. Both the octagonal south piers and the west tower are medieval. The font is believed to be older than the original church. There is a fragment of a 15th-cent. alabaster panel in the chancel and several monuments. Of particular interest is a statue in white marble of the son of Prime Minister Sir Robert Peel, Captain William Peel, who was one of the first recipients of the Victoria Cross.

S. of the church is Sandy Place, once the home of the industrialist Sir Malcolm Stewart who built the model village at STEWARTBY. It is 18th-cent., of red brick with five bays.

Just outside the town on the Cambridge road is the Victorian Sandy Lodge rebuilt in a Tudor style of yellow brick with an unusual cupola over the stables. It is now the headquarters of the Royal Society for the Protection of Birds. There is a nature trail to the bird sanctuary, which is open to the public, and it is one of the most beautiful areas in the county.

NE. of the railway station, on a hill-top overlooking the Ivel, is Hillfort, enclosing 7 acres, where Roman remains have been found.

On Sandy Heath stands the ITV aerial.

SARRATT, *Hertfordshire* (6–TQ0499), is a tiny village in wooded countryside with a long village green and 17th-cent. farm-houses.

The small Church of the Holy Cross is of flint, with a short nave, and of particular interest are the arches in the chancel which are 12th-cent. The tower, of a later period, has a brick top with an unusual saddleback roof, its ridge at right angles to the line of the nave. On the wall of the south transept are some faded paintings and there is a monument to William Kingsley and his wife, dated 1611, with five sons and a daughter, all wearing ruffs.

Opposite the church are the pre-Victorian almshouses, with pointed windows and doors, and nearby is the tiny Cock Inn.

SAWTRY, *Huntingdonshire* (10–TL1683), is a large village near the A1 and overlooking the Fens. It has a triangular village green, on which stands the old lock-up. There are 17th-cent. cottages; the Manor Farm of the same period, with a flat framework of pilaster strips and large shaped end-gables; the moated Grange Farm and Abbey Farm with some monastic stonework.

William Sawtry was born in this village in the 13th cent. He became a priest and a follower of Wycliffe, was unfrocked because of his attitude to the faith, and was burnt in chains at Smithfield in 1401. He was the first Christian martyr to be burnt in England after the Conquest.

SE. of Sawtrey is the village college, a structure of progressive modern design and a cultural centre for the district.

There were two ancient parish churches here

until the last century when they were destroyed. All Saints Church, built in 1880 by Sir Arthur Blomfield, incorporates some material of older workmanship, including the north chapel with its two-bay arcade. The west window of the north aisle is 13th-cent., with bar tracery and a straight-headed window. One bell is believed to be 14th-cent. and there are tiles of the 13th and 14th cents. A 15th-cent. brass shows the figures of Sir William le Moyne in armour, with a lion at his feet, and his wife in a veiled head-dress, with a dog at her feet.

About 2½ m. SSE. of Sawtry is the excavated site of Sawtry Abbey, founded in 1147 for Cistercians. The foundations of the building can still be traced and the four fish ponds remain.

SHARNBROOK, *Bedfordshire* (10–SP9959). Amid lovely countryside is this attractive village with many old cottages, one of which, in the High Street, is now a bank. The Post Office is Victorian.

There is a Victorian Baptist chapel, its yellow-brick front trimmed with red, arched windows with Venetian tracery in the bays and a low gable stretching the length of the front.

Part of the 1613 structure of Tofte Manor, which originally belonged to Newnham Priory in BEDFORD, still remains, but an additional higher castellated section was added this century. The Grange is 17th-cent. and Colworth House, now the property of a commercial firm, is early Georgian, built of ashlar by Mark Antonie for the Magniac family.

St Peter's Church is an elegant building, the Perpendicular spire connected by thin flying buttresses. The south doorway is 13th-cent. but the remainder of the exterior is Perpendicular. The arcades of the interior are Early English, as is the chancel arch. The octagonal font is Perpendicular with fleurons on the underside. There are two interesting screens and several monuments of note, including one in French style to Hollingworth Magniac, dated 1867. The Magniac Mausoleum in the churchyard is also unusual and has wrought-iron gates dating from the 18th cent.

A short distance away, to the S., is an Iron Age settlement. Pieces of pottery of the 1st cent. A.D. were found in the floor of an hut, which was probably the home of a Belgic craftsman.

SHENLEY, *Hertfordshire* (10–TL1900), is a long, rambling village, reached through wooded countryside.

A small round hut on the village green with a beehive roof was once the lock-up. Of 18th-cent. origin, with an inscription: "Do well, be vigilant and fear not", it is of brick and plaster with a pointed door and small barred windows.

St Botolph's Church, 1 m. N. of the village, has only the remains of its former building, built from monies left by Maud, Countess of Salisbury, in 1424. The walls are of squared flint with brick dressings, and the windows, with two-centred arches, have simple Perpendicular tracery. There are the remains of a Georgian gallery with Tuscan

columns, and under the yews in the churchyard lies Nicholas Hawksmoor, the great architect and friend of Christopher Wren.

The most interesting house in the village is Salisbury Hall, 1 m. NE. of the church. It is a brick building, surrounded by a moat, with splendid fireplaces, fine staircase and panelling. It was built by the treasurer of Henry VIII and partially modernized in the 17th cent. In the interior its most important features are the medallions, purported to have come from Sopwell Nunnery, ST ALBANS.

One m. SE. of the village is High Canons, built in 1773, a five-bayed, two-story house in large grounds.

SHILLINGTON, *Bedfordshire* (10–TL1234), is on the borders of Hertfordshire, a sloping village street on the edge of a chalk-pit. The ancient Church of All Saints dominates the scenery. It is of ironstone, very long, with two square east turrets. Built about 1300, it has hardly been altered since. The chancel is divided from the nave by three fine arches and a screen of exceptional wealth, very high with one-light divisions. There are several other attractive screens in the church. Under the chancel is a fine vaulted crypt, part of which is built into the slope of a hill.

In nearby **Pegsdon**, 3 m. S., is a round barrow, 4 ft high and 20 ft in diameter. Knocking Knoll Long Barrow, 1 m. SSW. of Pirton, is 100 ft long and 10 ft high. The site was excavated in the 19th cent. and the mound now resembles two round barrows.

SIBSON CUM STIBBINGTON, *Huntingdonshire* (10–TL0997), is a double village on the banks of the River Nene and just off the A1. It is small, attractive and prosperous, with 17th-cent. buildings mostly of stone and a few thatched cottages. Its Hall has a fine façade, E-shaped with gables and mullioned and transomed windows and a long gallery. The gateway into the garden has strapwork with ogee curves on top. On either side of the church are the rectory, with a mulberry tree and sycamore in the garden, and Stibbington Lodge Farm House, with flat fronts and mullioned windows. Sibson Manor House, ¾ m. SSE. on the A1, is also of the 17th cent.

The Church of St John the Baptist is mainly Victorian, although the chancel is medieval and a little of the west doorway is Norman. The chancel arch, however, is 12th-cent. and inside are several structures of the same period. The octagonal font is also of the same time. In the chancel is a defaced, 14th-cent. effigy of a priest.

Just outside the village, on the A1 towards STAMFORD is an old inn, the Haycock, built as a posting house about the middle of the 17th cent. with the bedrooms centring round the courtyard and many outhouses. The exterior appears to be original and the interior is pleasantly and simply decorated with many old oak beams still remaining. A plaque in the courtyard states that Queen Victoria spent the night there in the early part of her reign.

Wansford Bridge, which is just past the hotel, dates from three periods, 1577, 1672 and 1795, and has 10 fine arches of varying shapes.

SLOUGH, *Buckinghamshire* (6–SU9779). This is the largest town and industrial centre in the county. It is a place of multiple trades with 800 factories on the Slough Trading Estate employing over 28,000 people. The estate was one of the first of its kind and has been copied in other parts of the country.

The town has many amenities for its large population, including a greyhound track, a golf course, cricket and football grounds and over 400 acres of parks and open spaces.

But despite its modernity the town still has links with the past. Its ancient roots are in the outskirts of Upton, around which the life of the village once evolved. Sir William Herschel the astronomer lived here and from the giant telescope in his garden he discovered the planet Uranus.

The Norman Church of St Lawrence can be reached by way of the Windsor road in the Upton section of the town. Although restored in 1850 the church still retains much Norman work. It is entered through a Norman doorway, adorned by chevron moulding and with carved capitals. The nave and the tower are 12th-cent., as is the chancel. The roof, in four bays, is 15th-cent. and the font was created by Norman craftsmen, who probably carved the pillar piscina. One of the church's treasures is a fascinating 16th-cent. almsbox with three locks. In the churchyard, reputed to be the inspiration of Gray's *Elegy*, are many ancient yews. Next to the church is the park of the 15th-cent. Upton Court, the property of Merton Abbey before the Reformation.

A short distance from the centre of Slough, on the same road as St Lawrence's Church, is Montem Mound, near Salt Hill. At this ancient spot an unusual ceremony was held by pupils from Eton College for the collection of "salt". A procession from the collage to the mound was led by twelve resplendent "salt-bearers", followed by the rest of the school. On reaching the mound the leader ascended it and waved a royal standard. After a short ceremony came the collection of "salt", which was, in fact, money, and Queen Victoria, who rarely missed the ceremony, was always stopped by the words, "Salt, Your Majesty, salt." The money so collected was given to the head boy of the school for payment of his expenses at King's College, Cambridge.

SPALDWICK, *Huntingdonshire* (10–TL1272), is a delightful country village beside Ellington Brook, with a 15th-cent. bridge of three arches. On the village green, shaded by chestnuts, is a fragment of a medieval cross.

The large Victorian Free Church has three arched windows, and the George Inn, dating from the 17th cent., has wall paintings on its upper floor. Manor Farm, Beech House and the Limes are Georgian, and Ivy House, with its flat bay front and giant angle pilasters, is dated 1688.

St James's Church has a fascinating 14th-cent. tower which is 152 ft high, and the stair-turret has a stone vault. The Norman north doorway is the oldest part of the church, and the chancery, with fine tracery windows, is 13th-cent. There is a Perpendicular screen in the south aisle and an Early English font.

STAGSDEN, *Bedfordshire* (10–SP9849). This is a tiny village, with thatched cottages and an old church, St Leonard's, standing on high ground with a 13th-cent. tower and a short lead spire. In the old Stacheden Chapel, named after the church's first vicar in 1220, is a lovely piscina and sedilia and the remains of a stone altar. The font is richly decorated with carvings of two praying figures, and the screen, with its four-light divisions, is Perpendicular. The tower has six bells.

Stagsden Bird Gardens are a breeding establishment for rare species of wild life. There are over 1,500 specimens, with a collection of shrub roses. The gardens are open to the public and are reached by turning N. at the church.

STAMFORD BARON, *Northamptonshire* (10–TF0305). Otherwise known as Stamford St Martin Without, this is part of STAMFORD, in Lincolnshire, which lies S. of the River Welland.

Apart from an almshouse near the bridge, built and endowed by Lord Burghley in 1597, it has but one building of interest which more than justifies a visit.

Burghley House is one of the largest Elizabethan mansions in the country. It is oblong, 240 ft by 125 ft, with short square towers, turrets, frilled balustrades and tall chimney-shafts. Built mainly of Barnack stone, the style is uniform throughout. William Cecil, who spent his childhood in an earlier house on the same site, built this mansion, which took nearly 30 years to complete, during the time that he was Secretary of State, Chancellor of the Gate and, during Elizabeth I's reign, Chief Secretary of State, when he became Lord Burghley. The house has belonged to the Cecil family since that time. It is built round a courtyard and the lofty kitchen was completed first. Then came the great hall with its steep, double hammer-beam roof and its huge fireplace. Next Scagliola Hall, the Marble Hall and the Andromeda Hall were built. The house has many beautiful rooms with painted ceilings, silver fireplaces and over 700 works of art, tapestries and furniture. The grounds were landscaped by Capability Brown, with an orangery, stables with a hipped roof, a bath-house overlooking the lake, a boathouse and a superb rose garden. Both house and grounds are open to the public.

STANDON, *Hertfordshire* (10–TL3922). To this tiny village came the first traveller from the skies, Vincenza Lunardi, a young Italian, who arrived by balloon in autumn 1784. A stone commemorates his landing 2 m. NE. of the village.

Half a m. away is the Lordship, now modernized but still including the remains of an early Tudor house, the home of Sir Ralph Sadler who looked after Mary Queen of Scots in Edinburgh. It retains its old carriageway with a four-centred arch and flanking turrets.

St Mary's Church has two features which are unique in the county: a big west porch and a detached tower. The church is on a hill so that the chancel is reached by raised steps. It is early 13th-cent. The arch of the chancel is rich with carving and from it can be seen three lancets over the altar. There is a tomb in the chancel to Sir Ralph Sadler, with his seven children and a pole that once bore the Royal Standard of Scotland.

S. of the church is the Endowed School, a long, two-storied, timber-framed building of the 16th cent.

Nearby is Upp Hall, a 17th-cent. manor house, and a spectacular barn, 140 ft long with original pointed-arched openings.

STANSTEAD ABBOTS, *Hertfordshire* (10–TL3811). This old village lies on the slopes of the Stort Valley, amidst cedar and pine trees.

The six Elizabethan Baesche Almshouses are two-storied brick buildings with three gables. In the village street will be found the 17th-cent. old Clockhouse School with quoins and a tiny cupola, a Victorian mill, now a factory, with a Greek temple roof, and the Red Lion Inn of the early 17th cent. with overhanging stories and gables. One house in the street is dated 1752 and is an unusual red-brick building, its circular stair-turret bearing an embattled top.

The centre block of Briggen was built in the early 18th cent., the bow windows added a century later, and extensions made in 1908.

Near to the church is Stanstead Bury, a picturesque manor built in the 15th cent. and altered during each successive century. It has a half-timbered stair-turret and seven bays in the garden front and is reminiscent of a large villa.

St James Church has a completely unspoilt interior with 18th-cent. box-pews and a three-decked pulpit. It is mainly of the 15th cent. with an open timber porch and Perpendicular windows. The tall, solid tower screen is of the 17th cent., but the nave is 12th-cent and the chancel 13th-cent. There are a number of monuments, including two of particular interest by Manning in the 19th cent. of Mrs Booth and Sir Felix Booth.

STEVENAGE, *Hertfordshire* (10–TL2325), is a fascinating place to visit for it has achieved the unexpected: a completely new town, spacious, well-planned and attractively modern, yet retaining in Old Stevenage its ancient charm and much of historical interest.

The new town has a number of varied industries as well as large office blocks and two modern buildings of particular interest. Barclay Co-educational Secondary Modern School in Walkern Road, has a variety of blocks and materials, good details and fixtures, and its main staircase is on a concrete spine not attached to the wall. There is a curved screen in the front entrance by Henry Moore. The new church is an unusual

building with a semi-circular roof and the upper half of the structure almost completely of glass.

In the old town, which is centred round the broad main street with its avenues of horse chest-nuts and limes and good parking facilities, are old cottages and houses, mostly used as shops, but still retaining their original features. At the end of the street is the grammar school, greatly extended now but with one room built in 1562 as Alleyn's Grammar School still with its original brickwork and open timber roof. The Grange, an early Georgian house, with a broad 12-bay front and large carriageway was formerly a coaching inn. Nearby is the Yorkshire Grey, another old inn with its original exterior of widely spread windows and the Tuscan pilasters of the door, but its interior is greatly modernized. Running off the High Street are narrow little streets with 17th-cent. cottages.

About ¾ m. S. are the Barrows of Six Hills, believed to have been built in Roman times for burial purposes.

Standing nearly a mile from the centre of the town is the Church of St Nicholas, dating from the 12th cent. It is of flint and its low Norman tower has a leaded spire. The roof, screens and stalls are 15th-cent., but the font is 13th-cent. There are screens between the aisles and chapels, chancel and chapels, and nave and chancel. The choir seats are decorated with misericords. There are two monuments of note: a brass to a 15th-cent. priest, Stephen Hillard, and an effigy of a woman with a wimple, accompanied by an angel and a priest, *c.* 1300.

The Roebuck Inn, 1 m. along the A1, is 400 years old and although the original building is still there, it has been extended greatly and is now called the Roebuck Motor Hotel.

STEVINGTON, *Bedfordshire* (10–SP9853). This village, with its rather grey buildings typical of old Bedfordshire, is on a narrow crossroads centred by the village cross, which is decorated with capitals and a large finial.

The Church of St Mary, on a terrace above the River Ouse, is reached by a cul-de-sac off the crossroads, down Church Road. It is a place of ancient pilgrimage for it is said that in medieval days people visited its holy well, which springs out of a rock on which the church stands and the waters of which are reputed never to have dried up. The church has a pre-Conquest tower and windows and a high screen under the tower. The arcade, with high quatrefoil piers, has deep hollows in the diagonals. Much of the workmanship is Decorated and Perpendicular. There are interesting poppyheads on the benches and a brass to Thomas Salle, 1422.

At either end of the street are old drinking fountains, Opposite one, in Church Road, are the church rooms, dated 1897.

On the other side of the crossroads, leading from the church, are ancient almshouses amidst many old cottages.

The windmill, built in the 18th cent., can be seen from the main road to BROMHAM, but to reach it turn up a narrow country lane. The keys for it may be obtained from a thatched cottage nearby. A wooden post-mill, it has recently had new sails attached, putting it back in working order.

STEWARTBY, *Bedfordshire* (10–TL0241), is believed to have the largest brickworks in the world, turning out about 650 million bricks a year. The kiln, which took a year to re-heat after the Second World War, holds 9 million bricks. The peculiarity of the clay from which the bricks are made is its high oil content. `

The model village, built for the employees, is attractive and well laid out, with its own village hall, club, secondary modern school and old people's homes, as well as an open-air swimming-pool.

Sir Malcolm Stewart built the village and named it after his father.

STOKENCHURCH, *Buckinghamshire* (6–SU 7596). On the top of the Chilterns is this little chair-making village with its magnificent beech-woods. The small factory was once a Sunday school, established in 1769 by Hannah Ball, one of the original founders of these schools. She was a close friend of John Wesley and prepared the plans of the Wesleyan chapel, which still holds her writing table and her diary, as well as the clock which timed the services.

In the village is a 17th-cent. coaching inn and an attractive 12th-cent. church with Norman columns and a Norman nave. The five-bayed roof has tie-beams and carved spandrels. In the rebuilt transept is a canopied piscina. There is an ancient font and there are brass monuments to Robert Morle, dated 1410 and 1415, and to Bartholomew Tipping and his lady.

STOKE POGES, *Buckinghamshire* (6–SU 9882). In the heart of the countryside, N. of SLOUGH, this out-of-the-way village is of interest for its connections with Thomas Gray, for it is here that he is said to have written his famous *Elegy*. St Giles Church, built about the 13th cent., stands back from the roadside and is reached by a short lane. In the large field at the side of the church is a simple 18th-cent. monument which is a National Trust property.

An altar tomb in the church, close to the walls, is the grave of Thomas Gray and his mother. The church is entered by two lych-gates and a long pathway edged with rose-trees. There is a fine timber porch and a massive nave roof, both of which are 14th-cent. An unusual feature in a stained-glass window is a kind of medieval "bicycle".

The Garden of Remembrance, close to the church, covers 30 acres. It is a garden graveyard, without stones, set in an avenue of trees and wild flowers leading to a delightful lake with a fountain and rose garden. Here one can, indeed, feel oneself "Far from the madding crowd's ignoble strife".

Behind the church is the Elizabethan manor house where Queen Elizabeth I was entertained and where Charles I was held prisoner. It is now the residence of Lord Grantley. Stoke Park, one of the great houses of the district, is now a golf club-house, while Stoke Court, once known as West End Cottage, the home of Thomas Gray and his mother, now forms the offices of a nationally famous research concern.

To the E. are Black Park and Langley Park comprising 1,060 acres, which are preserved as part of the green belt around London. Delightful walks can be taken in Black Park, which has a lake, and in Langley Park are the famous rhododendron gardens.

Stoke Poges: the unusual "bicycle window" in the famous church

Jane J. Miller

STOWE, *Buckinghamshire* (10–SP6736). Three m. N. of BUCKINGHAM, reached by an avenue of elms and beeches, is the historic house of Stowe, which was formerly the seat of the dukes of Buckingham and Chandos. The noble Corinthian Arch spans the road leading to the 800 acres of parkland which are dotted with Classical buildings.

The grounds and garden buildings are open to the public, but the magnificent house, the front of which is 900 ft long, is now one of the youngest of England's great public schools. Robert Adam, Vanbrugh, William Kent and Grinling Gibbons all took part in the construction of the buildings and the grounds in the 17th and 18th cents.

In the extensive grounds, laid out by Kent and Capability Brown, are many ornamental temples. In the Temple of Worthies can be seen busts of Drake, King Alfred, Inigo Jones and Shakespeare. The Congreve Monument was built by Kent in 1736. There is a temple containing armoury, and another, for music, has a Roman pavement. Across one of the delightful lakes is an ornamental bridge.

In the corner of the grounds can be seen the remains of Stowe Castle, built in the early 19th cent.

Also in the grounds of Stowe is the humble little medieval Church of the Assumption of the Blessed Mary. Notable for its general atmosphere rather than the building, it has interesting 17th-cent. monuments. The tower and a crucifix over the doorway are both 14th-cent. Nearby is an obelisk to the memory of General Wolfe.

SULGRAVE, *Northamptonshire* (10–SP5545). This tiny village, 7 m. from BRACKLEY, is dominated by its associations with the ancestors of George Washington who lived here for a century, over 300 years ago. The north wing of the house where they lived, Sulgrave Manor, is of the Queen Anne period but the other part was added in this century when the building regained its former glory after having been a farm for some considerable time. The house, a popular place of pilgrimage for Americans, contains many George Washington relics, including his black velvet coat and a fragment of the wedding dress of his bride Martha. The interior of the house, which has been restored, has great fireplaces complete with medieval implements, and there is a child's tea-set of 63 pieces. In the parlour is a spinet, and the great bed chamber, with its original oak mullioned windows, has a four-poster bed with a carved cradle at its foot, all hung with Elizabethan needlework. Over the porch is carved the original of the American flag, three stars and two stripes, and also Queen Elizabeth I's arms. A relief on the lid of a snuff-box, dated 1777, shows the President in uniform.

The 14th-cent Church of St James has three doorways of different periods, the west door in the tower suggesting that it was the site of an Anglo-Saxon church. On the chancel are heads of Edward III and Queen Philippa. The south porch bears the date 1564 with the initials E.R. and the fleur-de-lis. There are monuments to the Washingtons, including a pew and a chest in their name.

SUTTON, *Bedfordshire* (10–TL2247), has an unusual feature, a packhorse bridge, with two pointed 14th-cent. arches, which carries foot and horse traffic over the tributary of the Ivel. It is in the centre of the village.

In Sutton Park, with avenues of great limes, is a broad, deep moat marking the site of John of Gaunt's Hall, a mansion given to the Burgoyne family in perpetuity by John of Gaunt.

In the 13th-cent. All Saints Church are many monuments to the Burgoynes. In the south aisle is a Decorated piscina, and the ironstone tower is Perpendicular. There is a tall arch to the nave and, except for the chancel, all the church is castellated. The pulpit, 1628, has a sounding board, and the communion rail is 17th-cent., as are some of the box pews. A stone monument to John Burgoyne, 1608, is large and ornate, with a reclining effigy. A curiosity of the church is its barrel organ, which is still in use.

TAPLOW, *Buckinghamshire* (6–SU9182). This is a riverside resort with smooth grassy slopes leading down to the Thames where yachts are moored and fishing is a favourite sport.

CLIVEDEN can be seen in the distance from the cliffs high above the river, and in the woods near the water is Taplow Court, a Victorian mansion fashioned in Norman style, the residence of Lord and Lady Desborough. On the lawns of the house is an Anglo-Saxon tumulus.

There are many old cottages in the village as well as an Elizabethan farm-house and a modern 20th-cent. church with a copper spire reaching above the trees. In the chancel is a stone screen with a rood incorporated and the Norman font came from the old church which stood on the site. Many fine brasses of the 15th and 16th cents. are among its attractions.

TEMPSFORD, *Bedfordshire* (10–TL1653), is on the A1 where the Ouse and the Ivel meet. It is historically important for in 921 the Danes fortified it as a base against the Saxons, until it was captured by the son of King Alfred, Edward the Elder, who slew every man, woman and child there. Ninety years later the Danish army burnt down the town.

The bridge crossing the river has three round arches, and near the river is Gannock's Castle, earthworks 115 ft by 85 ft, probably of the 12th cent.

Across the A1 is Tempsford Hall, a large Victorian gabled building of red brick, built in the Elizabethan style, to which a new section has recently been added.

St Peter's Church, originally 12th-cent., has been much restored, but the tower is Decorated as are the windows of the aisle. The rest is mainly Perpendicular, but the nave is Victorian. The wooden pulpit, with traceried panels, is Perpendicular and old parts of the screen are in the dado.

N. of the church is Gannock House, a well-preserved, timber-framed house of the 15th cent. with large bracing and ogee members.

TEWIN, *Hertfordshire* (10–TL2714). This tiny scattered village, only an hour from London, is attractively situated above the River Mimram in wooded countryside with narrow lanes, sloping fields and winding paths.

The small Church of St Peter is still partly of the 11th cent. Its chancel was remodelled in the 13th cent. and the south aisle with lancet windows is of the same period. Changes have been made in the intervening centuries and a monument to the Governor of Gibraltar, General Joseph Sabine, is of *c.* 1739. The font is a fluted 18th-cent. bowl.

Close to the church is the Rectory, a Georgian house of two stories with five bays and timber-framed barn and stable.

There is a superb lake at Tewin Water, 1 m. WNW. of the village, which has a house built in 1819 in the neo-Grecian style, with seven bays, a recessed centre adorned by giant Ionic columns, shallow box windows and a tiny curved balcony.

About ¾ m. SW. of Tewin is Marden Hill, a house built in the 18th cent. of yellow brick. Later additions have turned it into a beautiful building with its Ionic porch, entrance hall and dining-room. The staircase is of special interest.

Queen Hoo Hall, beyond the upper green of Tewin, is a tiny, well-preserved, early Elizabethan house of brick. It has an unusual half-E plan, the projections having corbelled gables with honey-comb decorated finials. The brick windows are mullioned and there are Tudor arches and, in an upper room, Elizabethan mural paintings.

THORNHAUGH, *Huntingdonshire* (10–TF 0600), is a tiny, secluded village in a deep valley just off the A1. The rectory, although enlarged dates from about 1680, and the nearby manor house is also of the 17th cent. The large area of plantations between the UPPINGHAM and Kings-cliffe roads is known as the Bedford Purlieus. In Sibberton Lodge are the remains of a 14th-cent. building with a vaulted undercroft of two bays.

The 13th-cent. church was damaged when the spire fell at the beginning of the 16th cent. Its tower and chancel are original but the nave and chancel roof timbers are 15th-cent. In the south chapel, which is Perpendicular, is the tomb of William, Lord Russell of Thornhaugh, the 1st Duke of Bedford.

TODDINGTON, *Bedfordshire* (10–TL0129). The village is on a hill above the River Flitt and around the spacious village green are attractive houses and cottages, many of them Georgian. The best is Old Wentworth House, of chequer brick and built about 1700. Of its seven bays the three centre ones lie slightly back. Its doorway has fluted pilasters and there is a top parapet.

There is an old town hall and a village pond, as well as a new school of pleasant modern architecture.

The manor house was originally built about 1570, a quadrangular building with a large inner court. All that remains today, however, is a small oblong building with a hipped roof, believed to have been the Elizabethan kitchen, and a round tower.

St George's Church is a superb cruciform building of Totternhoe stone, built in the 13th and 15th cents., with the unique feature of a separate three-storied priest's house. The church has a central tower and is embattled. Beneath the battlements is a frieze of animals, a fish and a mermaid. The tower has bell-openings. In the transept is a double piscina. The crossing arches are low and the roof of the nave is decorated with angels and bosses. In the aisle are fascinating paintings and there are many monuments of interest.

E. of the church is Conger Hill with a motte and the remains of earthworks. One m. NW. of the village is Toddington Park.

TOSELAND, *Huntingdonshire* (10–TL2362), is mentioned in the Domesday Book. It was a meeting place of one of the four hundreds of the county and has a Moot stone in the churchyard where the Toseland Hundred met. It still gives its name to the Petty Sessional Division. An old Roman road passes near the village and in a wood to the N. are remains of an ancient camp.

Of great interest is its manor house, Toseland Hall, built towards the end of Queen Elizabeth's reign, with the original thatched barn, with tie-beams on braces and collar-beams, farm buildings and stabling. The house is of two stories with attics in the gables. In the main front are mullioned windows, a central porch and three gables. The clustered chimney stacks are octagonal. Its exterior is of mellow red brick.

The little pebble-built St Michael's Church, almost hidden in a field, with the Blue Ball Inn in front of it, was considerably restored in the latter part of the last cent. It was originally Norman and the masonry is mostly of that time, as is the south doorway. The chancel arch is also Norman and the capitals have volutes. The chalice is Eliza-bethan and a 17th-cent. oak table has twisted legs.

TOTTERNHOE, *Bedfordshire* (10–SP9921), has famous stone quarries, tunnelled into the Chilterns, which have supplied the stone for many of the county's churches. The stone is a soft limestone called clunch.

The ancient castle was once one of the strongest in the county, and its oldest building is NW. of the motte.

About ¾ m. E. of the castle remains is a site of chalk quarrying in which traces of Bronze and Iron Age settlements have been found, including fragments of vessels and an enclosure ditch in which was discovered a bronze, vase-headed pin dated back to the 6th cent. B.C.

The Cross Keys Inn, which is a thatched, half-timbered building, has a fireplace dated 1433.

St Giles Church is built from the quarries in the village and has a fine exterior. The gable of the nave has rich flint flushwork decoration. The building was begun in the 14th cent. and

Jeffery W. Whitelaw/Camera Press

Turvey: most of the houses in this village were rebuilt of local stone in the last century

completed in the 16th. The church is embattled and the north vestry pretty. Under the low tower arch is a screen in single-light divisions. There is a brass in the chancel floor to John Warwekhyll, vicar, 1524.

N. of the church is Lancotbury, a fine manor house with timber frames and closely set studs. It is probably 16th-cent.

TOWCESTER, *Northamptonshire* (10–SP69 48). This ancient town, once a coaching stop, stands on the site of the Roman settlement Lactodorum, with Watling Street running through it. The Anglo-Saxons fortified it and the Danes attacked it. Benedetto Gaetano, who eventually became Pope, held the living here in the 13th cent., and the Archdeacon Sponne, who was rector here in the 15th cent., founded the school and chantry and left a sum of money to pave the town.

The Town Hall, like many other buildings here, is Victorian. There are a number of Georgian houses including the Post Office dated 1799, and many old cottages. A number of old inns remain, including the Talbot, 1440, and the Saracen's Head which Dickens made famous in his *Pickwick Papers*.

By the side of the Town Hall is Chantry House and gateway, built of stone in the 15th cent., with an oak doorway and oak beams.

St Laurence's Church, reached by a narrow lane by the side of the Town Hall, has a tall, ironstone, Perpendicular tower. There are two ancient mass dials, one outside and one inside. In the modern chancel arch are two Norman pillars, and traces of Norman carving can be seen above the south arcade. The crypt is 13th-cent., and on the south chapel arch a jester's head is carved. The clerestory and font are 500 years old.

The chancel roof bears the date 1640 and other beams are of the 17th and 18th cents. In a long stall, with carved panels, are valuable black-letter books attached by chains. One of these is the Treacle Bible: "Is there not triacle [balm] in Giliad?" The exotic organ came from FONTHILL Abbey. There are wall paintings of interest and a sculptured head of William Sponne, the bene-factor, with a skeleton beneath it.

Dame Edith Sitwell is buried in the churchyard at **Weedon Lois,** about 6 m. W., and on her grave is a monument by Henry Moore.

Gayton Manor, about 2½ m. E. on the A5, is an Elizabethan house, of cruciform shape with unusual gables, and is open to the public. On the outskirts of the town is Easton Neston House, late 17th-cent., and in the park is Towcester race-course. Stoke Park Pavilions, 3 m. off the A508, with pavilions by Inigo Jones, a linking colonnade and beautiful gardens, are open to the public.

Although the centre of the town maintains its old atmosphere, there are new buildings on the outskirts and its industries include the manu-facture of electrical engineering components and compound cattle food. There are also wool warehouses which serve the surrounding districts. On the road to NORTHAMPTON is a hump-backed bridge and lovely countryside.

TURVEY, *Bedfordshire* (10–SP9452). Although historically ancient, the village was mainly rebuilt of local stone in the 19th cent. It is on the border of two counties, Buckinghamshire being reached by the long bridge and causeway with 16 arches, some of which are believed to be 13th-cent. On a tiny island, midway across the River Ouse, are two statues, one of recent origin, the other of Jonah, which was originally in the monastery of Bonshommes at Ashridge.

There are old cottages here, an old inn and ancient almshouses, as well as two stately houses.

Turvey Abbey is a gabled, irregular Jacobean house, made interesting by balustrades and pinnacles brought from Easton Maudit in Northamptonshire. The chimney-pieces are of particular interest and there is a medieval oblong dovecot and Georgian stables.

Turvey House, built nearly 200 years later, has giant Corinthian pilasters, the exterior much decorated. There is a cast-iron staircase in the house which came from the Crystal Palace.

The Church of All Saints tells the history of the countryside, for it is of Anglo-Saxon origin, although much restored. The 12th-cent. font has carved capitals at the corners, and the nave and tower are Anglo-Danish. The sedilia and piscina have 13th-cent. carvings and the fine ironwork is by Thomas of Leighton, a Bedfordshire man. Of special interest is the 14th-cent. painting of the Crucifixion in the south aisle. There are many monuments of interest, including several of the family of Mordaunts who lived for many centuries at the Old Hall.

UPWOOD, *Huntingdonshire* (10–TL2582), is a tiny village of old cottages and haystacks, with Cross Keys Inn and Carlton House both dating from the 17th cent.

Upwood House, W. of the church, is also 17th-cent., with two projecting wings on its red-brick front and two large flat chimney breasts which are probably older than the house. The beautiful grounds are open to the public under the National Gardens Scheme.

St Peter's Church has much Norman workmanship, including the font. In the nave is a Norman north arcade and a Norman chancel arch. There are simple screens of one-light divisions in the chancel and north chapel. A tablet to Peter Phesaunt dated 1649 has a Latin inscription, and one to Sir Richard and Lady Bickerton, 1811, has an urn with an inscription above.

WADDESDON, *Buckinghamshire* (10–SP74 16). W. of AYLESBURY on the road to BICESTER, this large village is famed to art lovers. There are many charming houses and an old inn with whimsically shaped yews.

The church, part Norman, part Perpendicular, is reached by an avenue of chestnuts. The tower is 15th-cent. and above the Norman doorway is a porch with a 14th-cent. recess holding a little statue of St Michael. The splendid nave, dominating the church, is in three arches renewed 600 years ago from the original materials of the old church. There are pretty heads between two of the arches. An oak screen decorates the Lady Chapel in which is a 14th-cent. piscina. The font is 600 years old. At the entrance to the chancel lies a statue, nearly 7 ft long, of a knight in armour with his hands on a sword and lion at his feet. It is believed to be Sir Roger Dynham.

Waddesdon Manor, resembling a French *château*, was built in the years 1880–9 by the architect Hippolyte Destailleur for Baron Ferdinand de Rothschild and is now National Trust property. It stands on a hill encircled by woods and parkland and is reached from the west end of the village. Its great state rooms contain exquisite oak panelling in rococo style brought from 18th-cent. Parisian houses. Important English, Dutch, Flemish and Italian paintings adorn the walls, and there are fine collections of French furniture, Savonnerie carpets and Sèvres porcelain. The Bachelor's Wing also contains a display of small-arms. A magnificently painted ceiling by De Witt is in the Red Room. The manor is open to the public.

WADENHOE, *Northamptonshire* (10–TL 0083), is a delightful agricultural village with picturesque scenery. At the end of the village, with its stone cottages and thatched and tiled roofs, the River Nene broadens and ripples over the ford beside the old mill, and the farms have limestone barns. To the W. is an enclosure called Castle Close in which are earthwork foundations, and on the Pilton road is a farm with a dovecot.

George Ward Hunt, a member of the notable Wadenhoe family, lived here. He was Chancellor of the Exchequer under Disraeli and it is said that the village had the first rural telegraph office in Britain installed so that he could keep in touch with Whitehall.

Above the river, up a steep, winding footpath, is the church. It has a rare saddleback tower, little Norman windows and dates back to the 13th cent. Large, amusing heads support the chancel arch. The bench-ends of the pews are 14th-cent., but the font is crudely carved with a medieval head. There are several monuments, including one to Joan Bridges Genersh showing two weeping cherubs and dated 1792. The keys for the church should be obtained before mounting the hill.

WALTHAM CROSS, *Hertfordshire* (10–TL 3600), lies on the New River on the borders with Middlesex. Not far from London, it is now mainly suburban.

About ¼ m. from the border stands one of the few remaining Eleanor Cross monuments erected by Edward I to commemorate the resting-places of the coffin of his queen, Eleanor of Castile, on its way to WESTMINSTER ABBEY. The cross was begun in 1291 and has been heavily restored. It is hexagonal, an unusual shape, and has three figures standing in niches under canopies. It is profusely decorated.

In the High Street, S. of the cross, is Harold House, a yellow-brick building with Ionic door-case and a decorated pediment.

Nearby is **Theobalds Park**, built by William Cecil, Queen Elizabeth's leading statesman. James I found the palace so attractive that he persuaded Robert Cecil, the Prime Minister, to exchange it with HATFIELD. It was dismantled shortly afterwards and four small houses were built in its place. Of these one remains, Old Palace House. Of the original palace only a high brick wall remains, which is part of the gardener's cottage.

At the entrance to Theobald's Park is a massive construction which was Temple Bar, erected in 1672 in FLEET STREET, London, by Sir Christopher Wren and removed to its present site in 1887. Below the house is an ornamental lake formed from New River.

WARBOYS, *Huntingdonshire* (10–TL3080), is a large, fenland village with, in its centre, a Victorian clock tower of yellow and red brick with a pyramid roof.

The Old Rectory, also of yellow brick, is early 19th-cent., and in its garden is a section of a large pier believed to have come from RAMSEY Abbey.

A strange tale is attached to the village, where the trial of the Witches of Warboys took place in 1593. An old lady in her eighties by the name of Samuel visited the sick child of her next-door neighbour with a black cap on her head. The child called her a witch, and when she became worse the doctor said witchcraft was responsible. The child's sisters also became ill and Mother Samuel's reputation as a witch grew. Eventually she, her husband and her child were all tried and executed.

In Ramsey Road is a Georgian house named the Chestnuts, with gates of Grecian design in cast-iron. The brick manor house, N. of the church, with Dutch-shaped gables, is mid-17th-cent., and an inn in the High Street is of the same period.

St Mary Magdelene Church is of brown cobbles with a 13th-cent. steeple and a broach spire. It is a stately building with a high tower and broad flat buttresses, lancet windows, bell-openings and three tiers of lucarnes. The chancel arch is Norman with scalloped capitals, the two arcades each with four bays are different, one having round and octagonal piers and arches, and the other with round piers, round capitals and round arches. The north doorway is of about 1300 and in the chancel is a 12th-cent. door knocker with a lion's head, the ring showing two dragons fighting.

WARE, *Hertfordshire* (10–TL3614), is where Lady Jane Grey was proclaimed Queen in 1553, and where John Gilpin ended his famous ride in Cowper's poem.

Two rivers cross the town, the Lea and New River. Along the Lea towpath, which is lined with trees, are houses with picturesque gazebos. Running parallel with the river is the High Street, with a mixture of gabled and straight-fronted houses dating from the 16th cent. In West Street is the old town hall, a simple Regency building with a heavy unfluted Ionic column. In Bluecoat Yard is Bluecoat House, the town's former manor house, a 15th-cent. timber-framed building which for nearly a century was the home of the famous Bluecoat School until it moved to HERTFORD in 1761. Opposite the house is a terrace of timber-framed cottages built in 1968 for nurses and children. The Corn Stores in Star Street include a 17th-cent. quadrangle of storehouses, with open-timber lean-to roofs. Outer ladders give access to the upper floor.

Baldock Street has many timber-framed and gabled as well as red-brick houses, the best one of the earlier period being the Bull Inn with overhanging stories and first-floor oriel windows. At the north end of the street is Thunder Hall, a tall red-brick Jacobean house, with a central porch and gable. A gatehouse and cloisters were added in the 19th cent. Canons Hotel, opposite, is of yellow brick and has a Greek Doric porch. Nearby are Canons Maltings, red-brick malthouses of *c.* 1600, with a row of buttresses on one side and a three-light brick window on the other.

The famous Great Bed of Ware, mentioned in the plays of Shakespeare and others, came from the Saracen's Head Inn, but is now in The VICTORIA AND ALBERT MUSEUM, London. The inn is now demolished.

The Priory, now council offices, has the remains of a house of Franciscan monks built in the 14th cent. It was refashioned after the Dissolution but still contains the old cloisters with three lancet lights and a four-centre arch.

Facing the bridges, across the river, is Amwell House, once the home of John Scott, the Quaker poet. It is a noble red-bricked building dating from about 1730. The Grotto, which was formerly in the gardens of the house, is now in Scott's Road. It is a delightful building with a confusion of passages and chambers lined with quartz, flint, bits of glass and shells. The biggest rooms are only about 12 ft by 6 ft.

The Church of St Mary is large and handsome although externally considerably restored. It lies in the centre of the town and is of flint, all embattled. The unusual feature of the church is the transepts which are carried to full nave height, with clerestories. The 14th-cent. octagonal font is probably the most elaborate in the county, with quatrefoil panels on the stem and figures of the Virgin and saints on the large bowl. The pulpit, with raised panels, is 17th-cent. There are several attractive monuments, one with a row of books at the foot of the obelisk.

About 1¼ m. NE. of the town is Fanhams Hall, a Queen Anne building with an interesting staircase and gallery 107 ft long.

WATFORD, *Hertfordshire* (6–TQ1196), is the county's biggest town, much modernized, with many industries including brewing and printing. It is, however, an ancient town, and there are still many buildings of interest to be seen.

The long narrow High Street leads down to the River Colne, which skirts the hill on which the town stands. A 16th-cent. half-timbered house, with an overhanging upper story, is on the corner of Church Street and High Street and to the S. are several houses of character. Lower down is the imposing 18th-cent. dwelling house of Benskin's Brewery, two and a half stories high with five bays and a lower outer wing, and behind it are the tall, yellow-brick Victorian brewing premises with 1836 maltings on the opposite side of the road. At the end of High Street is Frogmore House, three stories high, built about 1700. Its rusticated doorcase has Roman Doric columns topped by carved metopes.

In Church Road will be found the Victorian Salter's Company Almshouses, a long central line of houses of red-brick Tudor style with a tower and a stepped gable. Around the buildings are fine cedar trees and the gates to the street are of ornate iron.

About 1½ m. NW. of the centre of the town are two first-class farm-houses, Grove Mill House and Heath Farm House, and also the Grove, a red-brick house with stone quoins, which was built in 1756 and twice enlarged. It has two principal fronts accentuated by angle pilasters. The lodges, towards the Hemel Hempstead road, are late 18th-cent. stuccoed.

There is a modern town hall in the centre of the town with a "Scandinavian" lantern but it is generally fashioned in neo-Georgian style. It forms the nucleus of Watford's civic centre.

Cassiobury Park, once the home of the Earls of Essex, is now a golf course and part of it forms an attractive public park running down to the River Gade, where the banks are overhung by lovely willows.

There are several churches in the town but two are of particular interest, Holy Rood and St Mary's.

Holy Rood, a Roman Catholic church in Market Street, is Victorian with fine examples of the Gothic Revival style. The exterior, with its vestries and outer rooms encompassed in a square plan, is of flint, and its main feature is a square north-west tower and two turrets with copper spires.

St Mary's Church, standing in the large church-yard, is basically 13th-cent. with additions of the the 15th cent. It is long, broad and low, made of flint with a large tower which has diagonal buttresses, a stair-turret and a spike. In the chancel is a beautiful double piscina. The Essex Chapel (1595) is its most important feature. It is separated from the chancel by a Tuscan arcade and holds the tombs of the Morrisons of Cassiobury, both showing reclining life-sized figures under rich canopies with kneeling mourners. Many other lesser monuments are of interest.

Around St Mary's churchyard are pleasant low cottages and Mrs Elizabeth Fuller Free School, a charming brick building dated 1704, with a central cupola, a door with segmental pediment and arched windows. The Bedford Almshouses of 1580 have a five-gabled plastered front with outer gables.

WATTON-AT-STONE, *Hertfordshire* (10–TL3019). The River Beane flows through this straggling little village and becomes a wide lake in Woodhall Park nearby. Near the little bridge crossing the river is a slate-roofed mill, a successor to that mentioned in the Domesday Book.

Watton Hall is a plastered house with timber frames, three overhanging gables and three trefoil brick arches, and picturesque twisted chimneys. Inside is a beam dated 1636 on which are inscribed the words Watton Hall alias Watkins Hall. Nearby is a fascinating cast-iron 19th-cent. pump of baluster shape.

SS. Andrew and Mary Church is 15th-cent., of flint and embattled. It has a castellated porch, stair-turrets and a tower. Although most of the windows have been renewed, the east window is original. In the interior is a four-bay arcade with Perpendicular piers. A north chapel, added in 1851, has a tunnel-vault. There are many early monuments and brasses of interest, including one to John Botelier of Woodhall on a 15th-cent. slab with the inscription upside down.

About ¾ m. W. of the village is Broom Hall, a 16th-cent. brick house with a central chimney and porch and brick mullioned windows in the upper floor.

Two m. NE. is Aston Bury, a fine house with particularly good chimneys.

WELLINGBOROUGH, *Northamptonshire* (10–SP8968), is a residential as well as a manufacturing town, standing at the junction of the Rivers Ise and Nene. It is mentioned in the Domesday Book, was granted market rights by King John in 1201, and for a short while became a spa when it was visited by Charles I and Queen Henrietta in 1628. Its industries include footwear and clothing.

In Sheep Street and High Street are many old buildings and a 15th-cent. stone-built tithe barn. There are two old inns: the Hind and the Golden Lion, which has a minstrels' gallery. Cromwell stayed at the Hind on his way to NASEBY during the Civil War.

The Georgian Swanspool House, in Swanspool Gardens, now council offices, has gardens of 10 acres which are used by the public, and the Swanspool brook flows through the town. There is a private zoo, which is open to the public, in the grounds of Croyland House in Croyland Road.

The newly built Technical College is a fine piece of modern architecture with numerous windows.

At the end of High Street, by Broad Green, are the Manor and Hatton House, and fine avenues of trees line the roads.

Wellingborough has a public school, founded in the reign of Richard II as a grammar school. Some of its old buildings remain near the church, and the present one is built in Queen Anne style of brick and stone.

There are two churches of note: All Hallows and St Mary's. All Hallows stands back from the street in a tree-shaded churchyard. Parts of it are 600 years old and it has a tower and a broach spire. The chancel, with its outstanding east window, is Decorated. The roof, screens and stalls with misericords, are all 15th-cent. There are good, modern stained-glass windows by Piper, Home and Reyntiens.

The Victorian St Mary's Church was built by Sir Ninian Comper. It is very large and plain outside, but the interior is brilliantly coloured with a fine screen and, suspended above the nave, a large blue and gold painting of Christ in Majesty. The north chapel is attractive and the general impression is of light and spaciousness.

Sywell Aerodrome, off the main road to NORTHAMPTON, is the county Aero Club.

WELWYN, *Hertfordshire* (10–TL2316). This little old town still retains its charm, despite its proximity to WELWYN GARDEN CITY.

Most of the houses are Georgian, including Lockleys, ½ m. W. of the village, a nine-bay brick house now a school, which was built early in the period. The pediment of the doorway is on Roman Doric pillars and the windows are segment-headed. The dressings are of rubbed brick. A Roman villa has been excavated in the grounds and a plan of it is shown in turf and brick, indicating a rectangular five-roomed house of timber and mud, built in the 1st cent. A.D. The house and grounds are open to the public.

The village has two inns, the White Hart and the White Horse in Mill Lane. In School Lane is New Place, a Victorian building built by Philip Webb for his brother. It is L-shaped, of brick, with a steep-pitched roof, buttresses and sash-windows.

The River Mimram runs through the village and across the bridge, towards the church, is Bridge Cottage, with an iron veranda and a monkey puzzle in the garden, then Bridge House, and W. of the church the Wellington Hotel which, although Georgian, has some old half-timbering.

St Mary's Church is greatly restored externally so that it has lost its original character. Much of the interior was built in 1910 but the double piscina, with trefoil heads, is 700 years old and there is a long lancet window in the chancel. Edward Young, author of *Night Thoughts* and *On Original Composition*, was vicar of Welwyn from 1730 to 1765 and there is a monument to him in the church.

WELWYN GARDEN CITY, *Hertfordshire* (10–TL2412), was begun in 1919 as an artificially planned town in accordance with the ideas of Ebenezer Howard. Although the planning was wasteful of ground space by later standards, this "garden city" marked a significant development in 20th-cent. town planning. Originally developed by a private company with idealistic rather than commercial aims, the town was taken over in 1948 by the Ministry of Town and Country Planning as a "new town" to be linked with HATFIELD.

WENDOVER, *Buckinghamshire* (10–SP8708), is an old town on the edge of the Chilterns with many claims to history. The Icknield Way meets the main London to AYLESBURY road. There are many timbered cottages with dormer windows and at the junction stands a little Victorian building with a clock tower and a drinking fountain. It has a small, ivy-covered, red-brick room which was once the lock-up, and above the steep four-sided roof, green with moss, are a clock, an open lantern and a weathervane.

Among Wendover's many interests are its old inns. Of particular note is the Red Lion Hotel, a half-timbered building with brick nogging. Its old fireplace with chimney corners in the lounge still remains and the sturdy stairway leads to the room where Oliver Cromwell slept in 1642 while his soldiers packed the street below. Robert Louis Stevenson also visited the house on his walk through the Chilterns and wrote about it.

17th-cent. Bosworth House, in the village street, is an old timbered building now divided into three: a post office with panelled walls and doors, a cottage with a room over the open gateway, and a house. In the wall of the gateway is a 15th-cent. pillar piscina. When alterations were made to the building, many 16th- and 17th-cent. wall paintings were discovered of which two remain in the house, the others having been transferred to the Aylesbury Museum and the VICTORIA AND ALBERT MUSEUM in London.

There is a windmill, now a house, and a water-mill by the side of the stream running through Wendover has been transformed into a white-and-green timbered dwelling.

The church and manor house, lying side by side, are reached by a short walk down a pretty lane beside the stream, just outside the town.

The manor house was owned by John Hampden and his family. Hampden represented Wendover in five Parliaments and was the cousin of Oliver Cromwell.

Wendover church is mainly 14th-cent., although much restored. A tall 14th-cent. tower rises over the church and the manor and the churchyard path is flanked with limes, sycamores, chestnuts and two great yews. There are amusing carved heads on the arches of the chancel. The capitals of the pillars are beautifully carved with fruit, flowers and animals.

Along the village street and the **Icknield Way** is found some of the most breathtaking scenery in the county. Boddington Hill is on one side, Backham Hill on another and, crowning them both, Coombe Hill, one of the highest points in the Chilterns, over 850 ft. At the summit is a monument dedicated to the men of Buckinghamshire who fought and died in the South African War. On fine days it is claimed that from this viewpoint can be seen ST PAUL'S CATHEDRAL.

WEST WYCOMBE, *Buckinghamshire* (6–SU 8394). W. of HIGH WYCOMBE is this fascinating village where every house is National Trust property. The main street has been carefully repaired to retain the architecture of buildings ranging from the 15th to the 19th cent. which are of half-timbered construction and have mellowed tiles with red brick and stucco overhanging gables.

Of particular interest is Church Loft House, its upper story projecting over the pavement and forming a long room with a roof of 15th-cent. beams. In a corner of the roof is a 17th-cent. bell-turret and an unusual clock overhangs the pavement.

Adjoining the village is West Wycombe Park, its great house built by Repton in the Adam style with fine collections of paintings, tapestries and antique furniture. In its wooded park is a pillared Temple of Music. It was built for Sir Francis Dashwood, Chancellor of the Exchequer in 1762 and founder of the Hell Fire Club, and the family are still closely connected with the village.

On the hill opposite West Wycombe Park, over 600 ft above sea-level, can be seen the great golden ball on top of the tower of St Lawrence's Church which was also built for Sir Francis Dashwood.

In the church tower is a room seating ten people where the members of the Hell Fire Club, who also met at MEDMENHAM Abbey, are said to have foregathered to practise black magic. In the caves beneath are many curiosities of interest and these are open to the public.

The church is placed within an Iron Age flint earthwork. There are fine oak carvings behind the altar and cherubs by Grinling Gibbons on the east windows. The font, of silver gilt, is adorned with four doves, the stand encircled by a serpent gripping an escaping dove. It is a strange, but interesting, church.

The mausoleum, of flint with plastered columns, adjoins the church. It is a massive building open to the skies and contains the tomb of Lady Despencer, an ancestor of the Dashwoods.

WHEATHAMPSTEAD, *Hertfordshire* (10–TL1713), has grown in recent years and developed some modern industries, but it still retains its picturesque charm, and although the little cottages are now mainly shops they are interesting

and pleasing to look at. On a corner near the church is an unusual building, octagonal in shape, which houses a chemist's shop.

Hills look down on the village and the River Lea flows through it. The path by the river is overhung with trees.

On the north side of the road from ST ALBANS, are Roman remains, and two stretches of earthworks can be found on the heath of the slopes above the river: the Devil's Dyke and the Slad, both National Trust property. The Dyke is 1,400 ft long and the Slad is almost the same length but narrower and not so deep.

St Helen's Church was begun in the 13th cent. It is a large flint building with the nave the same length as the chancel and a crossing tower with a lead spire dominating the scenery. Both the north window in the north transept and the south window in the south transept have ogee tracery. The church is richly designed and contains a fine reredos and, in the chancel, a canopied piscina. The octagonal font is early 14th-cent., its carved leaves bearing quatrefoil circles. The pulpit is Jacobean and, like two benches in the north transept, was taken from a chapel at Lamer House. In the same transept is a Jacobean screen. There are many monuments showing the history of the village. One in the north transept, dating from about 1436, shows the figures of Hugh Bostok and his wife, parents of Abbot Wheat-

Wheathampstead: the ford over the River Lea at Water End

Barnaby/Mustograph

hampstead of St Albans. Also in the north transept is the Garrard Monument, the largest in the church, probably early 17th-cent., with big surrounds and columns and semi-reclining alabaster figures. There are many Garrard tablets here, for the Garrard family came from Lamer Park. One of particular interest shows Sir John, who was one of the earliest baronets, dressed in armour, with his wife and six sons and eight daughters. In the north transept is a rare stone reredos with seven canopied niches.

Water End Farm, 1¾ m. E. of the village, is a charming house by a ford. It was originally the manor of the Jennings family and was built of brick in about 1610; it has large decorated chimney stacks.

Mackery End, 1½ m. NE. of the village, is where Charles Lamb often visited and about which he wrote some delightful essays. He describes it as a gentle walk from Wheathampstead. It is a brick-fronted building with Dutch gables and a brick-plastered central porch.

The mill in the village is mentioned in the Domesday Book, and close by is Bricket Hill, a fine mansion of c. 1790.

WHIPSNADE, *Bedfordshire* (10–TL0117), famous for its zoo, is a small village on the edge of the Dunstable Downs and the Chilterns.

It has a delightful church, St Mary Magdalene's, with a 16th-cent. tower and an 18th-cent. nave, with arched windows and a Jacobean pulpit. The communion rail, with its slim twisted balusters, dates from about 1700. Green Cathedral, although not laid out as such, is a plantation of trees with 25 different species and services are held there.

The zoo, high on the Chilterns, is set in lovely countryside with the animals kept in natural and spacious enclosures. It has over 2,000 animals and is famous for its breeding record. It is open to the public and you may walk or drive round it.

WHISTON, *Northamptonshire* (10–SP8560), is a tiny limestone village, behind which is the lovely 16th-cent. Church of St Mary the Virgin, on a wooded hillside. Its tower, in two stages, is of ironstone and ashlar with delightful gargoyles and four pinnacles, and it is decorated with many separate stone carvings of humans, angels and animals. Richly carved wall-plates are in the roofs of the nave and aisles, and there is no chancel arch. In the reredos, carved in oak, is a copy of Leonardo's *Last Supper*. There are several monuments, including two sculptures by Nollekens, one showing a figure of a woman leaning on a torch and the other of a cherub wiping away a tear with his little hand.

WILLINGTON, *Bedfordshire* (10–TL1150), is of interest for its dovecot, an oblong structure with two nesting chambers and several stepped gables, and its stables, both of which are National Trust property and open to the public. They form part of the Manor House, of which only two minor buildings survive, where Sir John Gostwick,

Master of the Horse to Cardinal Wolsey, entertained Henry VII in 1541.

St Lawrence's Church is mainly late Perpendicular. It is of bluff stone with a fine north chapel of the early 16th cent. It was built by Sir John Gostwick and there is a large plain monument to him in the form of a tomb-chest dated 1541, as well as two other monuments to the Gostwicks which are also of interest. A bell bears the inscription: "Thomas Tompion fecit".

WING, *Buckinghamshire* (10–SP8822). To the NE. of Aylesbury, reached through delightful rolling countryside, this growing village, with its many modern buildings, contains the Anglo-Saxon Church of All Saints, the most important of that period in the county. The walls of the nave are Anglo-Saxon, as is the crypt, surrounded by a gallery, and one of only eight crypts surviving from this period in England. Seen from the churchyard, the apse, on narrow pilasters, is unusual; only four of these Anglo-Saxon apses remain in the country.

There is much of interest of later date. The roof of the large nave reached through a 14th-cent. doorway is decorated with carved bosses, angels, kings and saints. The screen, beautifully decorated, is 16th-cent. and the pulpit 17th-cent. Brass memorials are from the time of the Wars of the Roses and the series of Dormer monuments are splendid in design.

The village itself, the centre of a hundred in Norman times, still has many 17th- and 18th-cent. cottages, as well as the Dormer hospital built in 1569.

Half a m. E. of Wing is the house of **Ascott,** now a National Trust property and open to the public. Once the home of the de Rothschilds, it houses a fine collection of pictures, French and Chippendale furniture and outstanding Oriental porcelain with examples of Ming, K'ang Hsi, and Chun pieces of the Sung dynasty. The house, incorporating medieval timberwork and Jacobean work, is surrounded by 12 acres of grounds, and unusual trees grow in the gardens.

WOBURN, *Bedfordshire* (10–SP9433), is an old village, situated in picturesque, wooded countryside, with thatched red and white brick cottages. The yellow-brick almshouses have fine Jacobean stepped gables and are mid-Victorian. The village is attractive with several old inns. The Bedford Arms was formerly a famous posting-house and has extensive stabling at the back.

In the centre of the village is the Market House, red-bricked with an oriel, dated 1830. The mid-18th-cent. Old Rectory is a stately building with several columns, an attic over the centrepiece and the side of the house overlooking the cemetery.

The chapel is Victorian and beside it are the remains of the tower of Woburn's medieval church. It has an open octagonal stage and a crocketed spirelet. In it is a monument to Sir Francis Staunton and his wife, dated 1630.

Next to the chapel is the old school, of ironstone with mullioned windows.

Of major interest is Woburn Abbey, the residence of the Duke of Bedford. It is open to the public. There are paintings by Canaletto, Rembrandt, Van Dyck, Gainsborough and many others of renown, and a collection of 18th-cent. French and English furniture. There are 14 state apartments. Its 3,000-acre park contains 11 varieties of deer and many rare animals, as well as a bird sanctuary. The Antique Market is a great attraction.

St Mary's Church, in the village, is a large, solidly built, Victorian building, an estate church in late-12th-cent. style.

YAXLEY, *Huntingdonshire* (10–TL1892). On first appearance from the main road, this large and highly productive village has little to offer, but on turning down a side street you reach its centre and discover many buildings of interest. There are several 17th- and 18th-cent. houses, many attractive black-and-white thatched cottages, a thatched inn, a village green and an old pump. The village school is dated 1812 and has large trees in its playground. The Congregational church and the Methodist church are both early Victorian, as are a number of the houses.

St Peter's Church is on the top of a hill. It is large, cruciformed and its elegant steeple has flying buttresses. It is mostly 13th-cent. with some Perpendicular workmanship, and the chancel and transepts are of different roof levels. The font is original and the fine oak chancel screen is of the 15th cent. Above the screen is a large organ gallery and case by Temple Moore, 1904, who restored the church. The Perpendicular stalls are kneeling-desks with poppyheads on the ends and

panels in front. The pulpit with a sounding board is dated 1631. In the north transept is a monument showing two arms holding a heart, representing a heart burial and attributed to William de Yaxley, Abbot of Thorney.

On the outskirts of the village are several old farms.

YELDEN, *Bedfordshire* (10–TL0366), has some of the most interesting earthworks in the county. On the mounds above the River Till are the remains of a castle mentioned in the Domesday Book. The oblong motte is about 130 ft by 90 ft, and there are two large baileys and stone foundations, including the bases of two round towers in a corner of the principal bailey. On a smaller mound nearby is also a round tower base. It is reputed that there was battle on the site between the Romans and the Iceni.

St Mary the Virgin Church was built in the 14th cent., but has certain features which are Early English, such as south aisle and chancel doorways and the south arcade. The Decorated tower has bell-openings with flowing tracery and a corbel-frieze with flowers, animals and heads. Old timbers still remain in the roof of the nave, on one of which are carved the arms of Trailly. From the wooden Perpendicular pulpit John Bunyan preached one Christmas Day, but for permitting this the vicar William Dell was ejected from his living. On the walls are interesting paintings, one of St Christopher. In a carved recess in the north wall of the nave is a figure holding his heart, and in the south aisle a large and splendid tomb recess with spandrels and crockets on the gable.

Woburn Abbey: this 18th-cent. mansion was remodelled by Henry Holland in 1802

The West Midlands

Oxfordshire   Gloucestershire   Warwickshire
Worcestershire   Herefordshire

H. L. V. FLETCHER

If you approach the West Midlands from the east the change in the countryside is so gradual as to be imperceptible. It is undramatic, and you can cross from Buckinghamshire into Oxfordshire or from Northamptonshire into Warwickshire with nothing more than a roadside label to tell you where you are. Coming from the west it is a different story. The actual transition from Wales to England is not noticeable at first because when you leave the central plateau of Brecon, Radnor and Montgomery there are further lines of low hills; but once you cross the foothills the world opens out to reveal as wonderful a view as you are likely to see anywhere in England.

The best time to see it is in the evening, with the sun in the west, and it is never so striking as when rain is due. Before rain everything will be crystal clear and you can view the land plainly as far as the eye can see.

There are many places from which to look over this incomparable bit of England. One of my own favourite spots is Kingswood Common on the little ridge beyond Kington. The valley of the Wye lies below, and the level part of the central plain stretches for mile after mile after mile. It looks flat. After the crumpled hills of Brecon and Radnor it is bound to appear so. But it is not flat, not level at all; the portions of hard rock stick up like knuckles on a hand and if you have to walk up them, or even motor up such places as the ridge between the Wye and the Golden Valley, you will find there are some notable hills.

But the view seems to stretch without interruption from this last outpost of the Welsh mountains, and a man could stare at all this a long, long time and not have his fill. I was told once that from here one could see a fifth of England. These local legends grow and are repeated and sometimes are believed. Yet they do not have to be wholly true to hold the essence of truth. I have heard the same story about the Malverns, and from them it could be that the view is even finer than the one you see coming out of Radnorshire.

If you dawdle at Kingswood or on the Malverns you are looking on what was once part of the kingdom of Mercia. When boundaries swung to and fro as they often did in those days strange things could happen, and they left their effects. For instance, in Herefordshire long ago the Welsh got pushed away from the Wye up to their cold hills and they left a whole area full of their own people, like an island in a turbulent sea. And what did these castaways do but make peace with their neighbours and stay where they were? In return for being allowed to live in their own Welsh ways and keep their own Welsh laws and customs they allied themselves to the Anglo-Saxons and even fought with them in their wars. It was no forced service. This was an alliance of friends, and to the Men of Archenfield – that was the name of the colony – belonged the posts of honour in war. Camden, the historian, who wrote in Latin, left an account of them: *Viri de Archenfield, cum exercitus in hostem pergit, per consuetudinem faciunt Avantward, et in reversione Rereward.* "They marched in front of the army as it advanced, and held the rear as it retreated." An old story; all gone now except the name – yet not gone either, for the effects are in names and ways of people still part of the countryside.

All over this land there were, often still are, strange and individual customs and laws. There is the Forest of Dean, that almost unvisited tract between the Wye and the Severn, where coal and iron have been mined since pre-Roman times under almost rural conditions. There are a few small industrial towns, like Coleford, yet you could wander right across the Forest without a sight of industry. The Forest of Dean has so many private laws that they demand a volume of their own to do them justice. At Speech House (now a hotel) near Cinderford the Verderers' Court still meets to adminster them. High above the Wye at St Briavels there is the Castle that was once the headquarters of the Warden of the Forest, and if you visit it, remember those early English kings, from despised John downwards, who loved this spot.

The Forest of Dean is a fairy-tale forest, a forest in the Grimm tradition, where witches live and poor foresters purposely lose their children, and where robbers share out their gains under spreading oaks. What of other forests in the area? Well, Hereford no longer has any forest worthy the name, only sylvan woods where the wild daffodils bloom in their tens of thousands in spring. But in Warwickshire there is still something left of the Forest of Arden, and this you can learn of in *A Midsummer Night's Dream*. A wood near Athens, forsooth! Shakespeare discovered that wood in his native county, and he peopled it with village labourers from Bidford and Aston Cantlow and Snitterfield. I met a descendant of Bottom the Weaver myself in a pub not a hundred miles from Stratford, a nice, harmless, bragging, ignorant fellow who could set you right on everything, and knew everything, and could do everything: "Let me play the lion too: I will roar, that I will do any man's heart good to hear me."

Warwickshire is haunted by Shakespeare. How he loved this part of England! At every turn quotations come crowding into the memory. "Sweet lovers love the spring." It was a Warwickshire spring. Nowhere does it come more happily than in the Warwick lanes. "A day in April never came so sweet to show how costly summer was at hand." *Costly* summer: what could it be but an English one. Such richness the poet found nowhere as fully as he had at home in his youth. In the tragedies his powers towered to their greatest height, but in the early plays his country upbringing brought out the full, youthful, singing joyousness of life.

Warwick itself has one of the finest castles of England, second only to Windsor, yet the place it dominates still has some of the atmosphere of a country town. But the county is not all fields and woods. North is industry and the cities, absorbed in manufactures, noisy, dirty, crowded – everything the quiet villages in the south are not. Coventry, rebuilt after the bombing, has its notable cathedral that seems to set it apart, but Birmingham is typical and representative of the group. It is not the place you would choose for your summer holidays. Yet in Domesday Survey the place was as rural as Barton-on-the-Heath. "Richard holds of William four hides in Bremingeham. The arable employs six ploughs; one is in the demesne. There are five villeins and four bordars with two ploughs. Wood half a mile long and four furlongs broad. It was and is worth 20 s." I know it is sentimental and quite unrealistic, but stuck on a Birmingham pavement edge waiting for the mechanical flood to halt so that I can dart across a street I remember "wood half a mile long and four furlongs broad." It really *was* like that where we dodge and scurry, and somehow I like Birmingham the better for it.

From Bristol to Bromwich, from Henley to Hereford, this is a region for which the word peaceful seems specially coined. There are the few cities: Hereford and Gloucester, Worcester, Warwick and Oxford; but they have, especially to those who have known them for a long period of time, still something of the atmosphere of market towns. Over the region as a whole quietness reigns. It was not always so. This, especially in pre-Conquest days, was a cockpit for the whole country. On the whole the Romans avoided trouble. Not that there was never fighting or bloodshed, but generally the natives and colonists managed amicably, whether it was iron-working near Ross, or holding an outpost against the unruly Welsh at Kentchester outside Hereford. But after the Romans left successive waves of invaders passed through. The Danes came, burning what they could not take with them. Other Scandinavians appeared, ravishing and destroying. Some wanted to settle, and if you are going to settle you must, sooner or later, come to some sort of terms with your neighbours. It was those who came seeking what they could devour who despoiled the country; those who wanted to get back to their long ships, and get their long ships back in their home waters.

Not all raiders were from the east. Over the Severn and the Wye the Welshmen waited and watched.

> The mountain sheep are sweeter,
> But the valley sheep are fatter;
> We therefore deemed it meeter
> To carry off the latter.

When the time was ripe they swooped, stole flocks, killed and destroyed. Leominster went up in flames more than once, while Hereford was practically wiped off the map for a time. An uneasy truce must have existed some of the time on the border, but the Welsh did not stay. They took what they could; then went back to their cold hillsides.

Much has been made of the sufferings along the Marches under the Norman barons, but it is possible that it was not as bad a time as many have believed. The Marcher lords had power of life and death, so at times there was oppression. But the Normans came to settle. They were land-hungry, and they wanted rich acres, a prosperous countryside, land cropped and harvested, valleys thick with corn. You don't get valleys thick with corn if you bully the men who grow the corn, or burn their houses. The Marcher Barons used their brains, and after some inevitable tyranny the West Midlands developed into as rich an agricultural area as you could find in most of Europe. On the foundations laid then Cotswold wool became one of the richest commodities in the world and the six "W"'s of Herefordshire – Wool, Water, Wood, Wheat, Wine and Women – became the envy of the rest of England.

Occasionally the fighting was resumed, chiefly during the Wars of the Roses. The battle of Mortimer's Cross was as disastrous to the western counties as any battle could be. The final but less cruel conflicts came with the Civil War. Naseby is just outside our area, but the stupid mix-up of Edgehill was inside. So is Worcester, while Hereford and Gloucester as well as many other places were besieged, some more than once. The great castle at Kenilworth was taken and left in ruins by Cromwell. Minor skirmishes, like the one in Ledbury streets, went on everywhere, and there is difficulty in remembering who was chasing whom. But often battles were mainly for the gentry and the layabouts; sensible folk kept out of the way, and when the warriors had chased each other off the map they came out and got on with carrying in the corn.

There are differences between our five counties, but it is difficult to say exactly

Kenilworth Castle. Detail from a watercolour drawing
by David Cox, 1804–6

Birmingham, City Art Gallery

what the differences are. They are so subtle as to defy accurate description. Not every visitor could say whether he was in Oxfordshire or Worcestershire, but there is a variety in the roll of the land, the gradients of the hills, the wild flowers, the trees and the crops.

If I were pressed to differentiate my five counties I suppose I would point to the Wye and the orchards and hops of Herefordshire; the Severn, the Forest of Dean and the Cotswolds in Gloucestershire; the mixture of Shakespearean rurality and intense industrialism of Warwickshire; the Malvern-dominated fruit and market gardens of Worcestershire; and the willowy banks of the upper Thames in Oxfordshire, pointing out that relics of Roman and pre-Roman remains lie everywhere, while Dorchester-on-Thames might well have become the capital of England.

In this portion of what was Mercia there are half a dozen lovely, quiet country towns like Cheltenham and Cirencester, Stratford and Ross, Fairford and Faringdon, and the multi-syllabled Stow-on-the-Wold, Moreton-in-Marsh and Bourton-on-the-Water. The names trip off the tongue like a poem. The villages between stand as thick as stooks in a cornfield. On the wide rolling Cotswolds there is one in every valley. You can find churches within a few miles of each other as different as Norman Kilpeck is from cathedral-like Abbey Dore. In the Cotswolds the medieval wool merchants erected some of the finest churches in the country, great buildings like Northleach or gems like Fairford. Cirencester has the oldest parish church in the kingdom. From Stratford town you can pay a visit to the house of Mary Arden, Shakespeare's mother, in Wilmcote village, and there you will find one of the best museums of farm implements in the country.

The churches of Oxfordshire are noted for their spires, and, in spite of industrial envelopment, the best are in Oxford itself. There, too, is concentrated in a few square miles some of the best-preserved architectural treasures of England – the colleges.

The domestic building varies enormously. There are country houses of great charm and centuries of historical association. You find an Oxfordshire house such as Chastleton with its memories of the Gunpowder Plot (many of the conspirators met there) and its great treasure, the Bible Charles I at his execution gave to Bishop Juxon. Chastleton is stately, while Minster Lovell has its legends and its ghosts. What are we to say of Blenheim? Either you like it very much or you dislike it very much. Vanbrugh, its builder, was blamed for the load he laid on Mother Earth, but Sarah, Duchess of Marlborough, was probably to blame – or to be praised – for that weight. At quiet Bladon, nearby, Sir Winston Churchill is buried.

The houses of humbler folk vary as widely. There are timbered houses everywhere. Besford Court and Salwarpe Court are notable Worcestershire favourites. I do not know of a finer example than The Ley at Weobley, though Staick House at Eardisland in a different style runs it close. But then Weobley itself is notable for its black-and-white buildings. Perhaps it was because John Abel, the Hereford builder, King's Carpenter and restorer of churches, came from neighbouring Sarnesfield. To see the style of the period (though John Abel did not build it) there is the Old House in the centre of Hereford. It was natural to build timber-framed houses in a district so rich in sturdy oak and elm. There are fine trees on the Cotswolds, too, but stone is abundant and stone was used for the typical dry walls as well as for building. The old grey houses, with their heavy stone tile roofs, are beautiful, as everyone knows. But that is beside the point. They were built by local men in local methods and from local materials for local men to live in. The beauty evolved from the good taste and proportions that are a part of good craftsmanship.

Oxford: Merton College Gateway. Watercolour and black chalk drawing by Sir William Nicholson, 1904   Collection, A. W. Bacon Esq.

The West Midlands: Gazetteer

GERALD BARRY

ADDERBURY, *Oxfordshire* (5–SP4635), is a hilly village of ancient sun-soaked stone houses, some Georgian, some much earlier, 3 m. S. of BANBURY off the A423 OXFORD road. The 17th-cent. gabled Adderbury House was once the home of the profligate Earl of Rochester who was nevertheless a splendid Stuart poet. It is now a home for the elderly. The sturdy church with its unusually good Decorated and Perpendicular features is set off by a superb spire which no doubt inspired the local tag "BLOXHAM for length, Adderbury for strength and Kings Sutton for beauty". The interior of the church was mostly restored in the 19th cent. The 15th-cent. screen, however, retains much of its original beauty.

ALCESTER, *Warwickshire* (9–SP0857). This small town lies 8 m. W. of STRATFORD-UPON-AVON at the confluence of the Rivers Arrow and Alne and the junction of the A422, originally a Roman road, and Ryknild Street (the A435). These routes and the town's name (pronounced Olster) suggest Roman occupation and excavations have confirmed this.

Particularly attractive is the narrow Butter Street, off the High Street, with its jumble of ancient roofs. Just at the top is the 17th-cent., three-bayed, brick Churchill House with some fascinating carved friezes. Henley Street has among its features a timber-framed house with an overhang on carved supports. Church Street has remarkably unspoilt Georgian houses. Two of them at one time formed a single coaching inn which lost its clientele with the coming of the railways. Lovers of Victoriana will like The Priory, once the site of a Benedictine Abbey, where there is a house with a perfectly proportioned Doric porch, to which has been added a fantastic Victorian neo-Gothic folly. The oldest Alcester house stands in Malt Hill Lane off Church Street. This is a two-gabled, half-timbered building called the Old Malt House, built in 1500. The Classical Town Hall was built in 1618, a gift of Sir Fulke Greville.

Only the late 13th-cent. tower and 15th-cent. door witness to the early foundation of the Church of St Nicholas. The exterior is mostly restored Victorian Gothic, though the simple Classical interior designed by Thomas and Edward Woodward in 1729 is relieved by the rather grand altar-tomb of Sir Fulke Greville.

ALDERMINSTER, *Warwickshire* (9–SP 2248), just 3 m. S. of STRATFORD-UPON-AVON

on the A34 to OXFORD is a delightful village with an unusual row of old cottages spaced out along the main road. Its parish church has a good 13th-cent. tower with lancet windows looking across the Stour valley to Meon Hill and the Cotswolds. It has a Norman nave, with the rest of the church unfortunately much restored. Records show that the church was for some reason reconsecrated in 1286. Note the curious carved faces between the arches and the altar table standing on an altar stone with the original consecration crosses still showing. On the west bank of the Stour stands the little church of Whitchurch: also Norman and enlarged in the 15th cent. when a good east light was built. Just over the door inside is a medieval Agnus Dei carved in bas relief. It means leaving your car and walking across fields to see this mostly 11th-cent. gem.

Also just off the A34, ½ m. NE. of **Preston-on-Stour**, is a good Gothic Revival building, Alscot House. Started in 1750, it was built by James West, a secretary to the Treasury. Most of the present house was completed in 1764. The porch was added in 1825 by Thomas Hopper. The house is well planned and there is much good Victorian wrought-iron work inside. The river flows through a fine deer park to complete a typically late 18th-cent. ensemble. James West lies buried in the nearby parish church of Preston-on-Stour. It contains an unusual amount of 16th-cent. Continental stained glass which West presented to the church. The village of Preston is worth strolling through. It differs from the usual Cotswold villages but remains astonishingly unspoilt.

ALFRICK, *Worcestershire* (8–SO7453), is a pleasant little village, deep in the countryside towards the Herefordshire border. It is most easily reached by turning W. off the A4103 about 3 m. from WORCESTER and following an unclassified road through Leigh. Set in the shelter of the Suckley Hills among cherry orchards, it has an unchanging air. There is an old inn called the Wobbly Wheel, scattered cottages and a long low church with good 17th-cent. stained glass. There is a 15th-cent. panel portraying St Bernard of Clairvaux. It has two Norman windows and a wood-shingled bell-turret. Lewis Carroll was a frequent visitor to the nearby tall red-brick Georgian house, where his brother lived when he was the curate here.

ARBURY HALL, *Warwickshire* (9–SP3389), lies 3 m. SW. of NUNEATON, off the B4012. Its

Arbury Hall is a fine example of Gothic Revival

A little W. of Arbury Hall lies the village of **Astley**. This was once the home of the family of Lady Jane Grey. Not a great deal remains of the 16th-cent. Astley Castle, though the outer walls and moat date from before the 12th cent. In 1343 Sir Thomas Astley built a great collegiate church of which the former chancel is now the nave. Most unusual are the choir stalls with their painted backs of Apostles and Prophets. There are remains of what must have been very fine stained glass. Still discernible are a bear, human faces and birds and animals. The triptych over the altar is a 16th-cent. painting of the Flemish School of The Descent from the Cross.

ATHERSTONE, *Warwickshire* (9–SP3097), is a small market town on the A5 and owes its relative importance to its position on the Roman Watling Street. It has several attractive 18th-cent. houses. Its Grammar School boasts a 16th-cent. charter. Outside the gabled coaching inn, the Red Lion, with its unusual Gothic windows stands an old milestone incised "100 MILES LONDON". Though much of the parish church is modern restoration, it was originally the church of an Augustinian friary. Here Henry of Lancaster took the sacrament on the morning of the Battle of Bosworth. It has a good 15th-cent. stained-glass east window. The Old Swan is a fine timber-framed house with an overhang supported by diagonal braces. It was once the centre of the felt hat industry. A curious game of football is still played on the streets on Shrove Tuesday, a custom dating back to the 13th cent.

The ruins of **Merevale Abbey** are a little way W. of the town, near a minor turning off the A5. They are worth the short, signposted walk across a field.

BAGINTON, *Warwickshire* (9–SP3474), lies S. of the A45 near COVENTRY Airport. This village has the ruins of the 14th-cent. castle built by Sir William Bagot, characterized in Shakespeare's *Richard II*. In 1398 Henry Bolingbroke rode out from here to challenge the Duke of Norfolk in the lists before Richard II, both noblemen being banished for their pains. Although little remains of the castle, excavations have made a visit worth while.

The Church of St John the Baptist is Early English and tiny. It has a particularly fine brass of Sir William Bagot above the Priests' Door which brings the visitor straight into the chancel with its unusually good triple arch in Early English style. Sconces of candles and oil lamps still light the church. It possesses some good examples of late 17th- and early 18th-cent. silver plate.

The Old Mill, now a restaurant, was mentioned in Domesday Book and valued at ten shillings and eightpence per annum plus ninepence for the two ploughs. For 900 years the mill throve and then became a private residence for a few years before the Second World War. Gardens and willows make a pleasant setting for it by the River Sowe.

A Roman fort overlooking the river is being

claim to fame lies in the fact that most experts consider it the finest example of the Gothic Revival in England. It was originally a Tudor house which had been built on the ruins of an Augustinian monastery suppressed under Henry VIII and demolished in the reign of Queen Elizabeth I. Lord Chief Justice Anderson bought it and later exchanged houses with the Newdegate family who have owned it ever since. Sir Roger Newdigate (who spelt his name with an "i") set about Gothicizing the house at the same time that Horace Walpole began at Strawberry Hill, which in turn gave its name to this peculiarly English 18th-cent. revival.

Set in 300 acres of parkland with lakes and streams, the Hall remains a tribute to Sanderson Miller, Henry Keene and Henry Couchman of WARWICK who all had a hand in the exterior work and the unrivalled period décor within.

The plasterwork and fan vaultings seem to lighten the rather heavy Gothic chimney-pieces. The house is open at advertised times and the visitor has an opportunity of seeing much of the family collection of furniture, china and glass, and fascinating documents of the Newdegate history.

About ½ m. S. of the Hall is South Farm, where Mary Ann Evans was born in 1819. She was known to posterity as George Eliot the great novelist. *Adam Bede*, *The Mill on the Floss* and *Silas Marner* are all impregnated with this Warwickshire countryside where her father was agent for the estate.

excavated and restored to its original condition, with reconstructed defences and barrack blocks.

BAMPTON, *Oxfordshire* (5–SP3103). This quiet little market town was once known as Bampton-in-the-Bush owing to its difficulty of access in the 17th cent. Although it is on the busy A4095 S. of WITNEY towards FARINGDON, it lies in flat sleepy country, on the upper reaches of the Thames Valley. It comes to life at least twice a year. The Horse Fair on 26 August dates from Edward I's time and though there is little horse dealing done today, the merriment is maintained. At the Whit Monday Fête the spectator may see genuine English Morris dancing at its best and in its most classical form. There is a traditional fool known as "The Squire", and a "Sword-bearer" who holds a cake on his sword and distributes it to bystanders. A piece of cake is considered lucky, and recipients are expected to contribute to the "Squire's treasury". The little town hall stands in the centre of the market place surrounded by some good Georgian-fronted shops. The parish church is surmounted by a 13th-cent. buttressed spire rising 170 ft from its massive part-Norman tower. Each buttress is pinnacled at its base by an apostle in flowing drapery. The remarkable steeple was once the only way the traveller could find his way into Bampton. In the early Middle Ages it must have had quite an importance. The Empress Matilda built a fortress here and Aymer de Valence, Earl of Pembroke, erected an impressive castle of which only a doorway remains, now incorporated into an old farm-house, Ham Court. Just W. of the church is a fine Tudor manor considerably restored in Georgian times, known as the Deanery, which was once the summer residence of the Deans of EXETER, who still hold the living. The Grammar School is one of the oldest in the county. This Bampton should not be confused with its namesake in Devon, which also has a famous horse fair.

BANBURY, *Oxfordshire* (5–SP4540), at once evokes the well-known nursery rhyme. The original cross was destroyed by the Puritans in 1602 and the present one is a Victorian replacement. It is believed that the "fine lady" of the rhyme, was a member of the Fiennes (pronounced Fines) family who still live at and own BROUGHTON Castle. Its other distinction is the making of Banbury cakes to a 300-year-old recipe for flaky pastry lined with currants. Although many fine old houses remain, as well as twisted little medieval streets which retain their atmosphere, Banbury appears to have had a flair for destroying its own history. The citizens blew up with gunpowder their beautiful part-Norman, part-Decorated and Perpendicular parish church in 1792. They then commissioned S. P. Cockerell to build a neo-Classical church in 1793. The somewhat cold exterior is remedied by the use of bright colour in its inside. At least the old gabled and mullioned vicarage of 1649 was saved. The town once possessed a fine collection of municipal silver, but nearly all of this was sold in the early 19th cent. Two fine maces have come back into the town's possession, however. Banbury has two splendid old inns, richly timbered, gabled and mullioned. The most famous, the Reindeer Inn in Parsons Street, was responsible for another loss to the town: in 1912 it pulled out, dismantled and sold its priceless Globe Room with a superb plaster ceiling, panelled walls and 16th-cent. mullioned windows to a buyer in the United States.

Yet it remains a flourishing progressive community with one of the oldest breweries in the country, an important aluminium works and an agricultural implements factory all contributing to its growing wealth as a rising Midland industrial town.

Chacombe Priory, in the little village of Chacombe, is just 5 m. NE. from Banbury off the A422. Its Caroline façade belies its antiquity. The first priory was built before 1066 and was occupied by the Anglo-Saxon, Lord Bardi, until William the Conqueror bestowed it on a Norman knight. It has been lived in ever since. A disastrous fire destroyed the old priory in 1600 and the restorations date from this period. Eleven of the many rooms of this historic house are open to the public except during the winter. The fine early furniture, the paintings in the picture gallery and the Silver Room all form an impressive collection. The restored chapel is also on view. The owner of the house keeps rare ornamental fowl in the grounds.

BARFORD, *Warwickshire* (9–SP2660). On a loop of the River Avon with a splendid three-arched bridge across it, Barford lies 3 m. from WARWICK and 7 m. from STRATFORD-UPON-AVON. The village has many mellow brick cottages and Barford House, a white Regency house of nine bays with monumental Ionic columns, stands just to the SW. But it owes its fame to being the birthplace of Joseph Arch who revolutionized attitudes to the working conditions of farm labourers. From their ranks, he succeeded in getting into Parliament and became a friend of the Prince of Wales; he lived in the tiny cottage by the church and died there in 1919.

The Church of St Peter was entirely restored in 1844. Ancient yews line the path to the porch. The street leading to the church has some remarkably good early 18th-cent. houses.

BARNSLEY, *Gloucestershire* (5–SP0705), 3 m. SW. from BIBURY on the A433 is a perfect Cotswold village. Apart from the fine stone cottages, there is also the Palladian Barnsley Park with its magnificent plaster ceilings. It was here that Sir Isaac Newton's library of nearly 1,000 volumes was discovered after it had been moved from Thame Park. It is now in the possession of the Royal Society. The church has some good Norman arches, carvings and a corbel table with grotesque heads. The tower was built at the beginning of the 17th cent. and the church suffered some over-enthusiastic restoration in the mid-19th cent. There is Victorian glass by Wailes.

BERKELEY, *Gloucestershire* (4–ST6899), in a pleasant valley of the Severn Estuary is about halfway between BRISTOL and GLOUCESTER, just W. of the main road. The little Georgian town is dominated by its formidable castle, surrounded by 14-ft-thick buttressed walls. Most of what can be seen from the fields dates from the 14th cent., including the great hall, 60 ft long. Within the courtyard, however, still stands the solid Norman keep built in the reign of Henry II for the Fitzhardinges, whose family became Earls of Berkeley and still own and live in the castle. In its early history it had more than its share of gruesomeness. This was the scene of the frightful murder in 1327 of Edward II, instigated by his wife and the Earl Mortimer. The castle is open at certain advertised times to the public.

The fine Early English parish church with some original Norman features has a tranquil setting and some excellent Berkeley family monuments. By the chancel is the grave of Edward Jenner, discoverer of vaccination, who was born here in 1749 and came back to his home where he died in 1823. Today the town is famous for its manufacture of Double Gloucester cheese and for the great nuclear power station near the Severn.

BERKSWELL, *Warwickshire* (9–SP2479). Six m. W. of COVENTRY and S. of MERIDEN lies one of the most attractive villages in the county. It has red-roofed white cottages with weathered timbers and a most curious set of stocks. Legend says that their holes were to hold a recalcitrant villager with a peg leg and his two inseparable companions. One of the most delightful buildings in the village is the 16th-cent. Bear Inn, formerly the Bear and Ragged Staff. It has Cromwellian associations. Its great open fire-place is original.

The Church of St John the Baptist is one of the best of many good Norman churches extant in Warwickshire. The earliest part of the present church dates from 1150. The east end of the chancel is Norman. There is an unusual two-storied gabled and timbered porch dating from the 16th cent. The doorway is pure Norman but was moved to its present position in the 14th cent. The church's remarkable feature is, however, its Norman crypt, early enough to have given rise to a belief that part of it is Anglo-Saxon. It has a magnificent arch spanning the centre with vaulting on each side and lit from seven lancet windows.

A few steps away outside the churchyard gate is a 16-ft-sq. tank walled with stone with clear water running inside. This is the well of the village name. The two-gabled Old Rectory is 17th-cent. with some interesting moulded window surrounds. Berkswell Hall is notable for its rhododendrons. It is well worth the short walk, so too is Ram Hall about ½ m. SSE., built in the early 1600s.

BEWDLEY, *Worcestershire* (8–SO7875), is one of the pleasantest towns in Worcestershire and can best be appreciated by coming into it from the W., on the A456 which skirts the once mighty **Wyre Forest** and crosses Telford's beautiful three-arched stone bridge. This was completed in 1801; its unique approach is fenced by elegant cast-iron pillars. This leads on to the main thoroughfare, the wide and elegant Load Street. The Town Hall built in 1808 has a Classical self-assurance derived from its massive Doric pilasters. The Post Office is housed in a timber-framed, 16th-cent. building with a delightful recessed centre gable. The Angel Inn sheltered Charles I in 1645. In the Assembly Rooms, the famous actress Mrs Siddons laid the foundations of her successful career. The George Hotel, an old posting house with bay windows has authentic charm. The 17th and 18th cents. determined the whole character of the town. Its main church, St Anne's (1746), situated at the upper end of Load Street, has a pleasing exterior.

Bewdley was the birthplace of Stanley Baldwin, three times Prime Minister between 1923 and 1937. His family home was at Astley Hall 5 m. S. of the town. Nearby on a hillside to the W. is **Tickenhill Manor**, first given to that Roger Mortimer whose descendant became King Edward IV. It was a privileged royal palace and it was here in 1499 that Prince Arthur, Henry VIII's elder brother, was married by proxy to Catherine of Aragon. The house, now fronted with Georgian brickwork, has much of the earlier building surviving. The great hall has considerable Tudor work left and many of the beams date from the 13th cent. The Folk Museum formerly here has been removed to **Hartlebury Castle** just SE. of STOURPORT.

One m. S. of Bewdley on the banks of the Severn is the little village of **Ribbesford**, latterly much spoiled. Turreted and gabled Ribbesford House, once the home of the Beauchamps and the Actons, became the training centre for officers in General de Gaulle's Free French Forces between 1942 and 1944. The little village church was much restored in late Victorian times. It has, however, a trenchant Norman tympanum with a carving of a knight transfixing a fish with his sword. Members of the Quaker family of William Penn are buried near the east window. Although Ribbesford has been so suburbanized there are still lovely river and forest walks all around.

BIBURY, *Gloucestershire* (5–SP1106). This Cotswold village attracts many visitors and stands on the busy A433, so it is perhaps best seen late on a summer evening. William Morris described it as "the most beautiful village in England". The houses are of golden stone. Many cottage gardens face the little River Coln. The early 17th-cent. cottages of Arlington Row fronting the river are now owned by the National Trust. The old coaching inn the Swan at the end of the river-fronted street, opposite the bridge, leads on to a water garden where the Bibury Spring gushes 2½ million gallons of water every 24 hours. Over the bridge is one of the best known trout farms in England.

Bibury church has considerable remains of its Anglo-Saxon original, with Norman and Early English work harmoniously added. Splendid tombs in the churchyard are an indication of

J. Allan Cash

Bibury is built throughout of the local stone

Bibury's former wool-based wealth. Just behind the churchyard is the Jacobean Bibury Court with a 1639 wing reputed to be by Inigo Jones.

A little NW. of Bibury, and also on the River Coln, is the hamlet of **Ablington**. The old Manor House dates from 1590 and has a curiously inscribed gabled porch. The manor farm possesses a fine barn. Nearby is a prehistoric long barrow with a beehive chamber.

BICESTER, *Oxfordshire* (5–SP5822). Although there are no Roman remains to justify the "castra" ending of its name, the fact that it is only 1 m. N. of the site of the Roman town of Alchester on the present A421, itself following a Roman road, would suggest that there had been a military settlement here. Today it has one of the largest army depots in the country, in spite of which it is a curiously unspoilt little market town. The three-cornered Square has an interesting building once the Town Hall. There are several old gabled houses, mostly 16th-cent., in Sheep Street, where, from the many sadlers' shops you will smell the tang of good leather and saddle soap. Bicester is the centre of the Bicester Hunt, established in the late 18th cent. The roads surrounding and coming into the town have broad green verges on both sides and the hedges and ditches are trimmed, dug and maintained by a community proud of its hunting tradition.

The street going towards the church has some old stone houses. St Edburg's, the parish church, has some interesting 12th- and 13th-cent. features. One of the arches with a triangular head may well be Anglo-Saxon. It is joined by three Norman arches, one of which is now the chancel arch, the others having once formed part of a central tower. It possesses many fine monuments and some exceptional roof beams as well as some curious medieval carvings placed in unexpected parts of the church.

BIDFORD-ON-AVON, *Warwickshire* (9–SP 1051), lies 7 m. SW. of STRATFORD-UPON-AVON on the A439 and has Shakespearean connections. Accredited to the Bard is the famous doggerel

Piping Pebworth, dancing Marston
Haunted Hillborough, hungry Grafton
Dodging Exhall, Papist Wixford
Beggarly Broom and drunken Bidford

composed after a drinking bout at the Falcon Inn. This house has not been a tavern for generations. It has mullioned windows in a good 16th-cent. Cotswold exterior, but there are unfortunate signs of dereliction. The red telephone box outside the house obtrudes.

Bidford has a fine ancient bridge. It is mostly 15th-cent., but some of its eight irregular arches are of a much earlier period.

The Church of St Laurence has a fine medieval tower but was completely and badly restored about 1835 and again in 1889 when the chancel was rebuilt.

The Roman road crossed the river by the ford near to the church and here in 1922 an Anglo-Saxon burial ground was discovered with the graves of some 200 fully accoutred warriors and their women.

The main street has some good 15th- and 16th-cent. houses and is worthy rather of a market town than a small village.

BIRMINGHAM, *Warwickshire* (9–SP0787). With a population of well over one million, Birmingham is Britain's second largest city. The municipal boundaries enclose an area of 80 sq. m. Although mentioned in the Domesday Book, it developed slowly until the middle of the 16th cent., when it had already established its reputation as a small industrial town. Even then the Bull Ring was the centre of its many activities. Birmingham's metal industry had already advanced to such a state that it tempered over 16,000 sword blades for Cromwell's forces during the Civil War. Its Roundhead allegiance led in 1643 to a clash of arms in the Bull Ring area with Prince Rupert's forces. He had been ordered to clear a communications route for the Royalists between OXFORD and YORK after the citizens of Birmingham had seized King Charles I's plate and coin while the king was *en route* to relieve the besieged

BANBURY Castle. Some 90 houses were destroyed and 400 people made homeless. The town was fined £30,000, about £1 million in terms of today's values.

There is a great concentration of industry in the city, with factories, workshops, and head offices of international concerns. While metals remain a high priority, jewelry, toys, chemicals, brass, plastics and rubber products are manufactured. The chocolate and cocoa capital at Bourneville is within a few minutes of the city centre. The motor industry has a place to itself. Although some of the largest factories in Europe are established here, the individualistic character of Birmingham is maintained: the city still has over 1,500 separate firms of all types and sizes in production.

It was the Industrial Revolution that produced Birmingham's expansion – so rapid that in 1889 Queen Victoria declared it a city. Eleven years later it had its own university and in 1909 gave England its first official Town Planning Act.

Birmingham's new Bull Ring Centre is dominated by wide roads, banked by large buildings of concrete and glass with the shopping centre, terraced underneath the flyovers. This area is completely traffic free and is linked by subways with the older shopping streets where many of the department stores are. There are most kinds of retail shop, an open and a covered market, banks, restaurants and offices moulded into a whole that is dominated by the multi-storied Rotunda on its highest rise.

Among Birmingham's remarkable buildings is the Town Hall which is modelled on the Jupiter Stator in Rome. Here some of the world's leading orchestras may be heard. The City Museum and Art Gallery with its magnificent staircase and Joseph Southall's frescoes, a remarkable example of Edwardian painting, are striking. Here can be found some of the best examples of the pre-Raphaelite period of painting, including important works by Burne-Jones (who was a native of the city) and William Morris. The Science Museum houses the earliest English locomotive actually built (1784) among its vast collection of mechanical apparatus which placed England in the forefront of 19th-cent. technical development.

The city's most famous church is St Martin's. This forms a counterpoint to the architectural patterns of the new Bull Ring. The most ancient part of the present church dates from the 13th cent. Restoration has left only the interior of the lower part of its tower intact.

The fine 18th-cent. Cathedral Church of St Philip with its Baroque tower is notable for its inspired Burne-Jones windows.

A. W. N. Pugin designed the red-brick Roman Catholic cathedral in 14th-cent. Gothic style. It contains some fine works of art, mostly gifts of local industrialists.

The Reference Library in Ratcliff Place is one of the most comprehensive in the country and contains the Shakespeare Memorial Library with 40,000 books in some 30 different languages.

The Birmingham Repertory Theatre in Station Street has, through the energy and drive of its founder, the late Sir Barry Jackson, created a tradition of forward-looking theatre second to none.

In the new planning for Birmingham, it has not been forgotten that this is one of the few great cities in the world not built upon the banks of a river. So, incorporated in the plans is a decision to retain some of the attractive, yet mostly hidden, canals that criss-cross the city. In 1769 Samuel Simcock under the direction of James Brindley built a waterway from the coalfields of WEDNESBURY right into Birmingham's Paradise Street. With the intersections of the Birmingham Canal, the WORCESTER–Birmingham Canal and the Birmingham–Fazeley Canal being tidied up to form the eastern gateway to the Birmingham Canal Navigation system, Birmingham was left with more miles of waterway than Venice. There are pleasant walks along the canal right in the City Centre, and there are good vistas from Summer Row to Kingston Row where 18th-cent. cottages have been restored. Gas Street Basin will have moorings for the traditional narrow painted boats which have preserved their true folk-craft colourings as well as for modern pleasure cruisers. Restaurants and pleasant cafés all form part of this exciting experiment in the city's development.

BIRMINGHAM (SUBURBS) (9–SP0787). Most famous of the Birmingham suburbs is **Edgbaston**, about a six-minute car drive from the city centre. Here in hidden places are wedded good late Georgian, Regency and Victorian houses. In busy Hagley Road is Cardinal Newman's Classical church, the Oratory, with its typical Roman narthex and wealth of marble. Edgbaston boasts a fine Botanical Garden. Laid out by Loudon in 1831, it has the greatest varieties of trees and shrubs, Alpine plants, a rock garden, a rose garden and abundant cacti. Besides the plants there are cockatoos, bush babies and monkeys.

Edgbaston produced the Chamberlain family who made an indelible mark on England's political history.

Most remarkable, in a city of industrial expansion and change, is the fact that a great Jacobean House, **Aston Hall**, still stands among it all. Its building was begun in 1618 by Sir Thomas Holt, who took up residence in a house of truly palatial proportions 13 years later. The house seen today is in all major respects exactly as it was in 1635 when it was finished.

Its balustraded staircase sweeps right up to a second story of the house. The panelled long gallery is one of the best in the country. A treasure house of paintings, marbles and valuable furniture, it is set in fine parkland. It is open to the public at advertised times throughout the year.

Bournville is an unusually agreeable suburb just 4 m. SW. of the city centre. Inspired by Quaker idealism, the chocolate manufacturers George and Richard Cadbury started a new housing estate around their factory, to provide pleasant and hygienic surroundings for their workers. This grew rapidly into the Bournville Estate which was

Birmingham: the garden city estate at Bournville incorporates factories and houses in a model setting

to provide a model for many garden cities of England and today numbers some 4,000 houses. They are set in tree-shaded avenues with enviable amenities.

In the parish church of **Handsworth** is a fine statue of James Watt, who produced his steam engine at the Soho works in partnership with Matthew Boulton, the silversmith.

Longbridge is the centre of the Austin Morris Division of British Leyland Motor Corporation. The first factory rose on a small site here in 1905 and grew rapidly into one of the biggest automobile works in Europe. It is possible to watch the whole assembly line at work from the arrival of the steel to the finished motorcar. Particularly impressive is the Car Assembly Hangar designed by one of America's foremost industrial architects, C. Howard Crane. It should be mentioned that it is also possible to arrange to see over the Standard Car Works and those of the Rootes Industries.

Perry Barr, about 3¾ m. N. of the city, contains within its boundaries Oscott Roman Catholic Theological College, set in parkland. Permission can be obtained to visit this treasure-store of ecclesiastical art which is contained within the buildings built mostly by Pugin and Joseph Potter between 1835 and 1838.

Selly Oak, 3 m. SW. of the city, is chiefly renowned for its Quaker Woodbrooke College which possesses one of the most famous glass chalices in the world. It was originally found in the Crimea and is believed to be a 1st-cent. liturgical cup, with a Greek inscription. Here, too, is a priceless collection of ancient manuscripts.

Solihull, home of the Rover car works, is a county borough and not strictly a suburb of Birmingham. It has its own modern shopping centre – but also Tudor houses, some of them in the High Street. Its parish church has a 168-ft tower and a splendid peal of bells. From here came John Peckenham to be chaplain to Mary Tudor and finally to be the last Benedictine Abbot of Westminster. Just S. of Solihull stands the late 16th-cent. Malvern Park Farm, an excellent example of Warwickshire domestic architecture, which is now a school.

Just 1¼ m. E. of Solihull is another finely moated 16th-cent. house, Berry Hall, well worth seeing, since it has not suffered in any way from ill-conceived restoration.

BLENHEIM PALACE, *Oxfordshire* (5–SP 4416). John Churchill, 1st Duke of Marlborough (1650–1722), was responsible, both as soldier and as statesman, more than any other one man, for checking Louis XIV's imperialist ambition in Europe. He inflicted a crushing defeat on the French at Blenheim on 13 August 1704 and though he followed this up with many other victories, Queen Anne decided that his reward must match the importance of his achievements. In gratitude she conferred the Royal Manor of Woodstock with the hundred of Wootton on the Duke of Marlborough and his heirs forever, and a sum of £500,000 was voted by Parliament for the building of Blenheim Palace. Sarah Jennings who married John Churchill at the age of 18 was Anne's favourite companion before she became Queen in 1702. She had great influence over her and enjoyed royal patronage for many years until eventually it was dissolved with bitter recriminations. During the first period she obtained a dukedom for her husband. She was the real architect not only of her husband's fortunes but also of the great palace, whose foundation stone was laid in 1705. It was she who rejected Sir Christopher Wren's plans and chose those of Sir John Vanbrugh. He built this vast edifice covering 3 acres of ground (which can compare in magnitude with the largest palaces in Europe) between 1705 and 1722. Its park was first laid out by Henry Wise, gardener to Queen Anne, and his formal designs were later modified by Capability Brown in conformity with the task for the "natural" which was then popular. It covers some 2,500 acres and it is said that Brown planned the avenues and trees on a sketch of the actual campaign of the Battle of Blenheim. The vast lake was achieved by damming the River Glyme; it is spanned with a 390-ft-long bridge from which beautiful vistas may be seen in all seasons. In the distance is the enormous Column of Victory surmounted by the Duke swathed in a Roman toga. Everywhere are

A. F. Kersting

Blenheim Palace was built for the 1st Duke of Marlborough; it covers 3 acres of ground

charming walks through beechwoods, while winding paths skirt the shore-line of the lake. The late Duke had the terraced gardens on the south side redesigned, to follow Wise's original lay-out. The tremendous Triumphal Way, designed by Sir William Chambers and flooded by Brown, is one of the finest examples of landscape gardening in Europe. The sunken Italian Garden merits similar praise. The Water Gardens were designed by Duchêne in the early part of this century and are reminiscent of Versailles. The house's vastness defies description; perhaps it is best summed up by Pope's epigram:

> "Thanks, sir" cried I, "'tis very fine,
> But where d'ye sleep or where d'ye dine?
> I find by all you have been telling
> That 'tis a house and not a dwelling."

There is too much to appreciate in one visit: the magnificent tapestries, for which Queen Anne's ambassadors combed Europe; the splendid State Rooms; the Long Library with its statue of Queen Anne and its great organ; the priceless paintings and *objets d'art*; the doorcases carved by Grinling Gibbons and the flamboyant ceiling painted by Sir James Thornhill in 1716 depicting the Battle of Blenheim; the chapel with its marble tombs. In complete contrast is the small room on the ground floor where Sir Winston Churchill was born. It is simply furnished with a plain brass bed, some framed cartoons on the wall, a chest of drawers and a small marble fire-place and is somehow in keeping with the unassuming side of the great leader's character. Blenheim Palace and gardens are generally open to the public in spring, summer and autumn, though arrangements can sometimes be made for parties during the winter.

BLOXHAM, *Oxfordshire* (5–SP4235), is a largish village 3 m. SW. of BANBURY on the A361. Its stone houses rise on each side of a valley, one hill surmounted by a mid-Victorian public school and the other by a 14th-cent. church with a 190-ft-tall spire which is an outstanding landmark. While the building, originally Norman, is mostly 13th-cent., it was considerably enlarged

and improved in the 14th and 15th cents., and Street carried out restorations in the 19th cent. The circular arched west door has rich moulding and carvings of flowers and birds, and canopied steps, each set with an apostle before Christ in Judgment at the apex, are an unusual feature. The Milcombe Chapel has a much restored 14th-cent. reredos, as well as some 15th-cent. murals. The chancel screen is 15th-cent., again restored, but with some of the original colouring still showing. The glass in the great east windows is by William Morris and Burne-Jones. When the school is in residence, the choir music can be quite outstanding.

BODENHAM, *Herefordshire* (8–SO5251), is an attractive village with old timbered cottages, good stone houses and an interesting church. It can be reached by turning E. off the A49 HEREFORD–LEOMINSTER road on either side of Dinmore Hill. The River Lugg makes a loop and flows under an old bridge at the end of the village, where stand an octagonal 18th-cent. dovecot and close by a mid-Georgian brick house of considerable architectural originality. The black-and-white cottages are sheltered by a well-wooded hill. The parish church, set among riverside orchards, is remarkable for its lofty 14th-cent. arcades and its massive and impressive tower surmounted by a curiously small spire. Restrained restoration work was carried out in the last century when the church acquired a new chancel arch; this did not detract from its atmosphere, derived from good light and a sense of spaciousness. On the north wall is an interesting 14th-cent. monument of a wimpled mother with her baby.

There are some good medieval houses in the area. Outstanding is the 14th-cent. stone and timber building of Maund Farm, which has a fine 15th-cent. ceiling of moulded beams and an appearance that was somewhat radically changed by an extra wing added in the 17th cent. Bodenham's most impressive house is Broadfield Court, dating originally from the 14th cent. but much enlarged in the 16th. It has all the appearance of a Cotswold manor: gabled, with a good stone porch arched with ball-flower decoration. It seems to have every type of window from traceried Gothic and mullioned Tudor to Victorian bays, and gives the impression of a much loved and lived-in home. The stone-walled terrace and garden are well cared for.

BOURTON-ON-THE-HILL, *Gloucestershire* (5–SP1831), is built at the top of a steep hill W. of MORETON-IN-MARSH. St Lawrence's Church at the summit of the hill has a fine Norman south arcade with good scalloped capitals. At the bottom of the hill is the splendid 18th-cent. Bourton House. It has one of the most remarkable 16th-cent. tithe barns in the county, strongly buttressed and with a tall gabled porch. The cottages in the village with terraced gardens have attractive bow windows. A little to the S. of Bourton-on-the-Hill lies **Sezincote** at the head of the River Evenlode. In pleasant parkland is an extraordinary house built in the opening years of the 19th cent. for Sir Charles Cockerell. This was the early period of British ascendancy in India and Samuel Pepys Cockerell, Charles's brother, and Thomas Daniell collaborated in building a house that was English in plan but included such features as Oriental arches and onion domes. Humphry Repton landscaped the gardens in Indian terms. The total result was the inspiration for the Prince Regent's Pavilion at BRIGHTON. The house is extremely effective and gains much from the pinnacled north wing and greenhouse pavilion. The water garden, with lotus pools and stepped shrines to Indian gods, was completed by about 1803. There is a snake-headed fountain and the whole garden abounds with fine trees and rare plants. It is occasionally open to the public and is worth seeing.

BOURTON-ON-THE-WATER, *Gloucestershire* (5–SP1620), lies 4 m. SW. of STOW-ON-THE-WOLD. The Windrush flows beside the lawn-bordered main street under low-arched bridges and good Cotswold stone houses abound. Behind the New Inn there is a stone model of the village which is a popular attraction for tourists. At the other end of the village is an old mill. The chancel of the parish church dates from 1328 but the church suffered badly from restoration at the end of the last century. The roof, however, has some good modern heraldic painting. W. of the A429 unclassified roads lead to two pretty villages, **Lower Slaughter** and **Upper Slaughter**. The first village has a stream flowing under little stone bridges, a much painted scene. Both church and manor have charm; the former retains its 12th-cent. arcade but was much restored in the 1860s. The second village also has a tributary of the Windrush running through it. There are the usual picturesque Cotswold stone cottages and a good 17th-cent. parsonage. On a rise above the village is an Elizabethan manor house, perhaps one of the most visually satisfying in the Cotswold countryside. The church has many good Norman features and an unusual 14th-cent. sanctus bellcot. This church, too, suffered from

19th-cent. restoration, though the 15th-cent. chancel was left intact.

A short distance N. along the same unclassified road are two more famous villages, **Lower Swell** and **Upper Swell**. Sheltered in the green hills the little River Dikler flows through both villages. When restoration work was being done on Lower Swell church during the last century considerable finds of Roman jewels and coins were made. The church has some of the finest Norman carving in this part of the county. Upper Swell is particularly appealing, partly because of the fine trees which line the course of the Dikler. By the bridge it still turns a great millwheel and the pool beyond has many waterfowl. The small manor house above the little river has a fine Renaissance doorway. The church has something of all periods to offer with a good Norman doorway and an untouched 15th-cent. porch. All these villages can best be enjoyed by leaving the car and strolling by the riverside.

BRAMPTON BRYAN, *Herefordshire* (8–SO 3672). The story of this little village, to the W. of Leintwardine on the A4113 KNIGHTON–LUDLOW road, is really the story of a famous family, the Harleys. It derives its name from Bryan de Brampton who built a fortress here in the 13th cent. His daughter married Robert Harley who commenced building the castle, the substantial ruins of which can be appreciated in the massive two round towers leading to the inner gatehouse and the hall. All this is set in the great park of the Georgian brick mansion to the W. of the castle. The castle was irretrievably destroyed in spite of Sir Robert Harley's wife Brilliana, who, while her husband was away fighting for Parliament, bravely withstood a siege by the Royalists. After a short respite the Royalists again attacked and burnt down the castle, and only what is described above remained. The church was destroyed but rebuilt after the Civil War in its charming village setting of black-and-white cottages. It has a fine original hammer-beam roof and a 14th-cent. monument which survived the war and may be that of Margaret Harley who founded the line of this redoubtable family. In spite of continuing political and religious change they survived in power throughout the centuries. Harley Street in London is named after perhaps the most famous of them all: Robert, Earl of Oxford. Just to the N. of Brampton is **Coxwall Knoll**, some 400 ft up in the hills, a prehistoric camp half of which lies in Herefordshire and half in Shropshire. It is claimed locally to have been the site of the last battle between Caractacus and the Romans when the defiant Celt was finally taken prisoner and led to Rome.

BREDON, *Worcestershire* (8–SO9236), one of the loveliest river villages in the county, at the foot of the 991-ft Bredon Hill. Beside the Avon are well-weathered old cottages, timbered houses and a 14th-cent. tithe barn which is 132-ft long, with five porches, one with unusual stone cowling. The National Trust owns it. The village street is enhanced by the one-storied stone Reed Alms-houses built in 1696. St Giles's is a cruciform Norman church with a graceful 14th-cent. spire, 160 ft high. One doorway is sheltered by a two-storied Norman porch, sturdily vaulted. Two other Norman doorways have chevron-mould heads. The Mitton Chapel is Early English, with an array of trefoiled lancets. There is a vast alabaster and stone canopied monument to Giles Reed, whose grandchildren built the Alms-houses. In the 14th-cent. chancel are some in-comparably rare heraldic tiles on the altar steps. The four chancel windows are filled with good 14th-cent. stained glass. There is a modest memorial to the much loved Bishop Prideaux, of WORCESTER, who died during the Common-wealth; he had to sell all his possessions during the Civil War and was left with only a few shillings to eke out his last days. On the top of Bredon Hill is a notable south Worcestershire landmark: a re-markable Iron Age camp. The inner rampart covers 11 acres and was built at the end of the last century B.C. Since the encampment was excavated, more than 50 bodies have been dis-covered, all brutally hacked to pieces, near the entrance, apparently massacred when the fort was breached. Just inside the fort is a curious 18th-cent. tower known as Parson's Folly.

Great Comberton lies at the northern foot of Bredon Hill and has half-timbered farm-houses and thatched cottages. The walls of the extra-ordinary round dovecot in the village are over 3 ft thick and have more than 500 holes. Another dovecot, square, red-bricked and four-gabled, has no less than 1,425 nesting holes and is reputed to be one of the biggest in England. The church, which has a squat, square tower, appears to be early Norman. Nearby **Little Comberton** has Nash's Farm, a 17th-cent. black-and-white farm-house with circular stone dovecot, believed to be medieval. The church is Norman with many alterations over the centuries. The north doorway has its fine oak waggon roof over both the nave and chancel.

Off the road between EVESHAM and PERSHORE is a pretty village of black-and-white cottages facing the Avon called **Cropthorne**, and well worth visiting. In the old Norman church was discovered one of the finest Anglo-Saxon crosses in the country. Its intricate carving portrays birds and beasts in starkly bold trails and the sides are decorated with a Greek-key design. Local lore says that the cedar growing in the village was planted before the Conquest. On the opposite side of the river, past Charlton Hall, is another delightful village, **Fladbury**. Grouped behind its landing stage is an old inn, a watermill and a Norman church with much later addition and a chancel completely and unfortunately restored by the Victorians. The fine brasses on the large tomb-chest under the tower where John Throck-morton and his wife are buried are dated 1445.

BREDWARDINE, *Herefordshire* (8–SO3344), lies just off the B4352 road between HEREFORD and 7-m. distant Hay-on-Wye. It is one of the most beautiful spots on the banks of the Wye, sheltered by wooded hills. The 1,045-ft **Merbach Hill**, with its famous Neolithic long barrow called Arthur's Stone, rises behind and the summit can be reached as easily from here as from **Dorstone**. A mellow 18th-cent. brick bridge crosses the river and encourages the visitor to enjoy the view. The village also has an early 18th-cent. red-brick inn called the Red Lion and a long, curiously shaped Norman church, partly built of tufa. The west end is completely Norman but the elongation work curving slightly to the N. was completed in the 14th cent. The tower is 18th-cent. The plain interior is relieved by the effigies of two medieval knights, the later one carved in alabaster and almost certainly the figure of Sir Roger Vaughan, who was with Henry V at Agincourt. The Vaughans then lived at the castle, of which only the earthworks remain on a spur of land overlooking the river to the SE. of the church-yard. The diarist Francis Kilvert was the vicar here in the 1870s.

BRINSOP, *Herefordshire* (8–SO4344), lies 5½ m. NW from HEREFORD just N. of the A480 Hereford–KINGTON road on an unclassified road and near the woods of Credenhill and Merry-hill. In a valley stands a famous old 14th-cent. moated manor house, Brinsop Court, once the home of the Tirrels and the Danseys. It is a lovely rambling old house with its original great hall. Much of the house is Tudor in style with Jacobean and Georgian additions. A new wing was built early in this century, but all periods seem to have blended harmoniously into a whole. Wordsworth was a frequent visitor when his brother-in-law lived in the house and understandably had a deep feeling for a building so rooted in the soil of the county. The little St George's Church set in orchard land allows its unprepossessing exterior to hide a gem of a church inside. The 12th-cent. tympanum has flowing lines. The church itself is mostly early 14th-cent. In the chancel is a much defaced wall painting of the Annunciation. There are two beautiful pieces of 14th-cent. glass and some modern glass portraying the Nativity, in memory of Wordsworth and his family. The gilded oak chancel screen with gilded angels holding tapers dates from the 14th cent., as does the magnificent Christ in Majesty reigning from the Cross. Even the modern additions like the alabaster reredos or the windows portraying St Francis and St Hubert, erected to the memory of Hubert Astley, have all been achieved with a sensitive taste that has never allowed old and new to clash. Near the church are some earth-works believed to be Roman as some years ago a Roman well was discovered. Brinsop lies just off Stone Street and not far from Roman Kenchester, so this seems quite likely.

BRISTOL (4–ST5872). This thriving ancient city-port with its growing population of nearly half a million inhabitants has long been impor-tant to English trade and commerce. Three years before the death of Edward III in 1376, it was separated from neighbouring Gloucestershire and Somerset and made a county with its own sheriff. One hundred and fifty years previously the city installed its own mayor, and its first known royal charter was granted 28 years before this. The earliest proof of its commercial activity goes back to the time of Ethelred II in the 10th cent. when silver coins were minted here. All this was due to the fact that the Rivers Avon and Severn were navigable and to the natural basin, once fed by the little River Frome, which is now known as the Floating Harbour. Today this is dominated by the statue of Neptune. Bristol has several focal points; the Floating Harbour is the pivot of the city's life. From here Edward I's writ was sent up to the Constable of the already 100-year-old Bristol Castle, demanding the king's due: a considerable quantity of eels, hake, haddock, plaice and skate from every Bristol fishing-boat coming into port. From here, too, during the Hundred Years War, Bristol sent 22 ships and 600 men to France. A tablet nearby records that from this port John Cabot of Genoa and his Bristol-born son Sebastian set sail in 1497 in the 100-ton *Matthew* and with 18 sailors reached the mainland of North America, in Newfoundland.

The year A.D. 1552 saw the incorporation of the Merchant Venturers and from then on the fame of Bristol-based ships reached every port of the known world. They gave the English language the expression "all ship-shape and Bristol fashion". Wines and particularly tobaccos and chocolate gradually replaced wool as the main cargoes and the wealth of the city grew – not least on the slave trade – making it one of the most important towns of Britain. Over the last two centuries with the increased size of ships the docks, too, have increased in size. From Prince Street Bridge can be seen Prince's Wharf and Wapping Wharf where Baltic timber and Dutch merchandise are discharged. On Prince's Wharf is a tablet recording the launching in 1838 of Brunel's first steamship, *The Great Western*. Edging Wapping Road is the New Cut made in the last century channelling the Avon. From Mardyke Wharf opposite, the dockside bustle is seen to advantage. From nearby Hotwells Road can be seen the Albion Dockyards and Cumberland Basin where ocean-going vessels come in from the Avon. It is possible to visit the Avonmouth Docks by application to the Port of Bristol Authority in Queen Square.

For convenience, Bristol may be divided into seven main centres of interest. The old city is the area from Bristol Bridge, across Corn Street, up Broad Street to St John's Church. The first Bristol Bridge was built in the 13th cent. It was the entry to the walled town of the period. Over the bridge are the remains of the Church of St Nicholas and its Norman crypt. A traditional curfew is still rung every night at nine o'clock from its re-hung bells. The tower of St Mary-le-Port adjoining is the oldest part of the city. All Saints is a Norman foundation, much restored in the 18th cent. when the present cupola was added.

In nearby Corn Street is the splendid Classical building designed by BATH's famous John Wood, the Exchange. The four bronze pillars outside are known as "The Bristol Nails" where the city merchants completed their financial dealings – "paying on the nail". The Old Council House, rebuilt in 1828 by Sir Robert Smirke (who designed the BRITISH MUSEUM façade) on the site of a 16th-cent. building, has an unusual enamel and brass staircase. Beyond the recently restored Guildhall is the tranquil little 17th-cent. Taylors Court; its buildings once housed the Merchant Taylors' Guild. In the angle of Broad Street and Wine Street stands Christ Church where the poet Southey was baptized. The remarkable figures (the Quarter Jacks) striking the old bells on either side of the galleried and canopied clock are leased to the church by the Bristol Corporation for half a crown a year. St John's Church is built over an original (and the last) of the city's gates. There is some fine Jacobean woodwork inside this originally 14th-cent. church. The two famous figures niched in the arch outside are Brennus and Belinus, the reputed founders of Bristol.

King Street, which has many good 17th- and 18th-cent. buildings, leads off from the Centre, another area of interest, and has the renowned Theatre Royal, first opened to the public in 1766 and therefore even older than the 18th-cent. theatre at RICHMOND, Yorkshire. It preserves its Georgian lay-out and original décor. The Victorians gave this delightful theatre a pleasing façade. In 1943, when its future was in doubt, an Old Vic company took over the theatre; since 1962 it has been administered by a Civic Theatre Trust, and a high standard of performance is maintained. Nearby is the 18th-cent. Coopers Hall and the earlier St Nicholas Almshouses on the corner. Llandoger Trow, built in 1664, is one of the city's oldest inns. Nearby is a beautiful example of very early 18th-cent. town planning in Queen Square, built to commemorate the visit of Queen Anne in 1702. Parts were destroyed in riots in 1831 and later rebuilt. The first American Consulate in Europe opened in 1792 at No. 37.

Although a whole rebuilding scheme has been completed in the Redcliffe area since the Second World War, it has done no more than give an added vitality to one of the most historically rewarding parts of Bristol. It is dominated by a graceful 19th-cent. spire rising 285 ft from street level, resting on the fine 13th-cent. tower of St Mary Redcliffe. This is the church described by Queen Elizabeth I on her visit to Bristol as "the fairest, goodliest and most famous parish church in the kingdom". It has the breadth, width and height of a cathedral and has been cherished by the city these 600 years. The hexagonal north porch is exquisitely beautiful and all its carvings of men and beasts have survived every restoration or extension to the building. The church, with its 240-ft-long nave, its open parapets, immense areas of glass and superb flying buttresses, owes its first reconstruction to William Canynge in the 14th cent. His son, also William and one of the greatest of all Bristol's merchant princes, con-

The Temple Mead area, around the main railway station, has two interesting churches. One with a leaning tower is the old Temple Church which was much damaged during Bristol's air raids but is now preserved by the Ministry of Public Building and Works. The other is the fine 18th-cent. Classical Church of St Thomas built on Norman foundations. The Organ Gallery built in 1728 is one of the finest in the country.

The Broadmead area stretches from Old Market Street up to St James's. The modern shops and supermarkets which have sprung up since the Second World War, skirting the edge of St James's Park, are in the main a dull tale of missed opportunities. Among them are a number of historical buildings which survived both blitz and development. Just off Horsefair is the New Room, the first Methodist chapel in the world. John Wesley preached his first sermon here in 1739. On the other side of the Broadmead Circle are the cloisters of a Dominican friary which, having passed through various vicissitudes after the Dissolution, were acquired by the Society of Friends: hence their strange name of Quaker Friars. Further up, just off Haymarket, is St James's Church, reputed to be the oldest building in Bristol. Built by Robert, Earl of Gloucester, in the early part of the 12th cent., it is said that every tenth stone acquired for the building of the great keep, was set aside to build this church. The Romanesque wheel window surmounting the interlaced arcades of the west front was described in a manuscript of A.D. 1150. The Stag and Hounds in Old Market Street is one of the most ancient inns and centre of a medieval fair where the Court of Pie Poudre (the dusty feet) is still ceremoniously opened every 30 September.

The University of Bristol is growing rapidly and marks another of the city's areas of interest. This was the first British university to offer a faculty in drama. Its high tower is in a carefully reproduced Perpendicular style and was opened in 1925. The Great George bell which strikes the hour commemorates the visit of George V. Nearby in Park Row is the Red Lodge built for the Elizabethan merchant Sir John Young. Now a museum and cultural centre, it was once a girls' reformatory financed by Lord Byron's widow. The richly carved oak room is a particularly splendid example of period panelling. The City Museum and Art Gallery has one of the most interesting geological and archaeological collections in the provinces. In the Art Gallery is a fine Hogarth triptych from St Mary Redcliffe and some good early Lawrences. Sir Thomas Lawrence was born in Bristol. The nearby 16th-cent. Grammar School, though founded on the present site, was entirely rebuilt in late Victorian times. More interesting· is the neighbouring Royal Fort, a house built by a rich Bristolian merchant in 1761. The interior plasterwork and sweeping staircase are elegant.

The last of the areas lies around College Green. Across the way from Cabot Tower on Brandon Hill is the 12th-cent. Augustinian abbey, now Bristol Cathedral. Commenced in 1142, it retains much of its Norman solidity, particularly its

Bristol Cathedral: bosses in the roof

A. F. Kersting

Bristol: the Clifton Suspension Bridge

Noel Habgood

siderably enlarged and enriched his father's work on the church, all of which can be seen in the stone, timber and glass of its interior. This younger Canynge, who was twice member of parliament and mayor five times, renounced his wealth in 1467 and became a collegiate priest of the church he had so generously endowed. He sang his first Mass in the church on Whit-Sunday 1467. This is still commemorated every Whit-Sunday when the chancel is strewn with fresh rushes and the Lord Mayor and Corporation of Bristol attend the service. Admiral Penn, father of Pennsylvania's founder, is commemorated here. Nearby is the house where Thomas Chatterton, the tragic poet, was born in 1752. It is now a Chatterton Museum. In Colston Parade on the other side of the church is Plimsoll House where the inventor of the safety loading line, Samuel Plimsoll, was born in 1824. Across Redcliffe Hill is the famous Shot Tower where in the 18th cent. William Watts experimented by dropping tiny quantities of molten lead into water from the top of the tower to make perfectly spherical shot. He thus made his fortune and his tower is still used for this same purpose.

fine chapter house. From the 13th to the 15th cent. new chapels, transepts, choir and aisles were built. In the 16th-cent. choir stalls can be seen some of the most imaginative of carving. In a later age, Grinling Gibbons created his superb organ case for this not too well known cathedral. The east Jesse window has 14th-cent. glass. The fine bosses in the roof of the north transept can now be seen to advantage since all the dirt has been removed by modern processes. Further up, in a turning off Park Street, stands a perfectly preserved house of the late 18th cent., built by John Pinney, who made a fortune in the West Indies. Called the Georgian House, this, too, is now a museum. All its décor, furniture and fittings are Georgian. The New Council House is neo-Georgian; not everybody likes it, but it sweeps in a graceful curve about College Green. Queen Elizabeth II opened it in 1956. On the other side of the Cabot Tower is the Queen Elizabeth Hospital School, founded in 1590. As at Christ's Hospital, boarders wear the ceremonial blue cassocked coat with yellow stockings and buckled shoes.

Two other places of interest deserve mention. The first is St Stephen's Church in the centre with its hundreds of gilded bosses in the roof of the nave and its monument to Martin Pring, a sea captain who sailed with Sir Walter Raleigh and discovered Plymouth Harbour, where the *Mayflower* docked. The other is the famous Christmas Steps at the top of Colston Street, which is named after one of Bristol's many 17th-cent. benefactors, Edward Colston. The Steps lie just behind Quay Street and were built about 1669. Good antiques, old books and silver can still be discovered. At the top of the steps is the Chapel of the Three Kings of Cologne, a curious and ancient connection with the Rhineland city.

About 4 m. N. of the city, out over Durdham Downs, going out by Westbury Road, is Henbury. Here are 400 acres of woodlands, now owned by Bristol Corporation. This is **Blaise Castle Estate**. The castle is a folly with four castellated towers, built by Thomas Farr, Master of the Society of Merchant Venturers, in 1771. There are foundations of an ancient chapel to St Blaise nearby and caves. The Folk Museum is contained in a Georgian house by Nash and Paty. The reconstructed farm-house kitchen gives an idea of the old rural way of living. An 18th-cent. corn-mill and John Nash's early 19th-cent. thatched dairy have been preserved. The Blaise hamlet comprises nine thatched cottages on Hallen Road, also designed by John Nash for estate pensioners and grouped round a contrived village green, complete with a pillared sundial on a stone village pump.

Bristol Airport Terminal lies S. on the A38 at Lulsgate and is important and busy. It has a 6,600-ft runway and has been extensively modernized to handle the new large freight and passenger aircraft and continues Bristol's traditional rôle.

As the prosperity of Bristol increased in the late 18th cent. the wealthy began to move out to

Clifton. The elegant Windsor Terrace and Cornwallis Crescent date from this time: Royal York Crescent and the Paragon were built a few years later. Many famous civic houses and institutions have their setting in this pleasant area. It also has a famous Victorian public school. Clifton is best known for its Suspension Bridge, built by Brunel in 1864. It spans the Avon Gorge, separating Gloucestershire from Somerset, at a height of 245 ft above the river's high-water level. **Leigh Woods** at the Somerset end are National Trust property and open to the public. Above the Suspension Bridge is the Observatory with its camera obscura. It is open to the public in the summer months. Bristol Zoo also has its home in Clifton; it has a fine collection of animals, well displayed.

The Avon Gorge has some of the finest panoramic views any city can offer. The famous Scarlet Lychnis, known as the Flower of Bristowe (this was an earlier form of the name; the present "l" is a quirk of Bristol speech that also turns ideas into ideals and bananas into bananals) and almost indigenous to this city, grows on the rocky slopes of the Bristol side of the Gorge.

About 4 m. NE. of the city centre on the A38 is **Filton**, once a village. Now it is a huge centre of a giant aircraft industry. The British Concorde prototype was built here. Hidden away is the parish church, mostly modern but still possessing its fine medieval tower with its 12 curious gargoyles.

BROADWAY, *Worcestershire* (9–SP0937), lies 6 m. SE. of EVESHAM where the A46 crosses the A44. The view of its long and broad Main Street, grass-verged, climbing up towards **Fish Hill**, epitomizes the perfect Cotswold village. In spite of its popularity with tourists from all over the world (it is said to be the most publicized "show village" in England) it has retained its character and nothing has been allowed to impair its beauty. On both sides are lovely old cottages and fine gabled houses, nearly all built of golden Cotswold stone. Notable is the Abbot's Grange, which once belonged to the Abbots of Evesham and dates from the 14th cent. It has Elizabethan additions and two well-planned wings built in this century. It has its original chapel, hall, solar and abbot's study. The next house facing the green is the late 17th-cent. Farnham House. The Broadway Hotel in contrast is mostly timber-framed, with only one wing built of stone. Perhaps the best known building is an inn now called the Lygon Arms but originally known as the White Hart. At an even earlier date it was probably an important manor house. The Torrington Diaries of 1742–1813 record that the walls were very thick, "door oaken and wide, with a profusion of timber and remains of much tapistery for carpetting". The writer then went on to record that he was lodged in "the grand bedchamber of an old family seat". All of which, in spite of the additions of 20th-cent. plumbing and heating, is true today. During the troubled years of 1645–51 the house sheltered at different times both Charles I and Cromwell. With its recessed centre and projecting wings, its gables and dormer windows, its mullions and transoms and the beautiful preservation of its stone, it is still the most exciting of the many beautiful houses in the village. The Tudor House is often considered a rival, but its very formal symmetry may relegate it to second place for some people. Another beautiful old gabled house restored with care is now St Patrick's Tea Room.

There is another delightful little manor house called Hunters Lodge, built during the Commonwealth towards the top of the hill. This is now a hotel. Fish Inn was once a summer-house or gazebo on Sir John Cotterell's estate and has a curious rusticated Venetian window and frieze. A little to the S. of the inn is the Beacon Tower (sometimes called Fish Hill Tower) built by Lady Coventry and completed as a folly at the end of the 18th cent. It stands over 1,000 ft up and commands a view over several counties. On a fine day TEWKESBURY Abbey, WORCESTER Cathedral and WARWICK Castle can all be made out.

The old Parish Church of St Eadbury is hidden away at the other end of the village. A cruciform church with a central tower, it contains much of architectural merit from the 12th to the 17th cents. It is little used now. The present parish church was built in the 19th cent. Spring Hill House, 3 m. to the SE., was Lord Coventry's mansion. He commissioned Capability Brown to build it in 1763. Some 70 years later it was sold to General Lygon who added to it. Much of the landscaping has been altered over the years.

BROMSGROVE, *Worcestershire* (8–SO9570), is an ancient and sizeable market town, still famed for its manufacture of nails. Although an industrial town, its situation on the Lickey Hills is surrounded by lush orchard country. On the summit of a hill stands the fine red sandstone Church of St John the Baptist. It is reached by a long flight of easy steps. The lime trees surrounding the church were planted in 1790. The 14th-cent. tower and spire soar 200 ft into the sky. Little remains of the original Norman church. The 13th-cent. chancel has a restored priests' doorway but the old chancel arch with its nail-head capitals is original. Chained to a 17th-cent. lectern is a copy of Jewel's *Apology*, once an obligatory accessory in all Anglican churches. There are two monuments, in alabaster, one with the effigies of Sir Humphrey and Lady Stafford dated 1450, the other of Sir John Talbot dated 1550. The churchyard has some fascinating early 18th-cent. tombstones but none more interesting than two commemorating a railway accident which befell two engine drivers on 11 November 1840. The inscription on each reads:

My engine now is cold and still,
No water does my boiler fill:
My coke affords its flames no more;
My days of usefulness are o'er!

Not far from the church is an old timbered house with a floodmark 4 ft up the wall commemorating a disastrous rise in the water in 1792. The Golden Lion at No. 7 Worcester Road is an enchanting 18th-cent. house with Gothic Venetian windows. The old Hop Pole Inn was previously in the High Street and was taken down, removed and rebuilt with some considerable restoration, in New Road. However, most of the 1572 decoration has been left unimpaired. Bromsgrove School, also on the Worcester Road, is an excellent late 17th-cent., two-storied, five-bayed house with a splendid doorway, pedimented on carved brackets. The school was considerably enlarged in Victorian times, but these buildings are not visible from the road. Sir Giles Scott built the New Chapel during the 1930s and completed his work in 1958. The poet A. E. Housman was at school here. The views from the 1,000-ft Beacon Hill, the highest point of the Lickey Hills, rewards the climb. Just outside Bromsgrove is the little village of **Barnt Green** with a gabled, timber-framed mansion, Barnt Green House, of early 17th-cent. date and considerable charm.

BROMYARD, *Herefordshire* (8–SO6554), stands on a plateau 400 ft above sea-level, surrounded by orchards and hopfields that rise to gorse-covered hills with splendid views in every direction. The Frome flows through this smallest of Hereford's market towns, about halfway between WORCESTER and LEOMINSTER on the A44. It has a solid Norman church with a low central tower and flanking aisles. On the south side is a Norman doorway with a curious figure of St Peter carrying huge keys above some rich carvings. The interior has some high arcades of five bays. The slenderness of the piers is accentuated by their having been further heightened at the beginning of the 19th cent. There is an interesting tub-shaped Norman font with interlaced and zigzag decoration. The church has an extraordinary number of tomb recesses both inside and outside, all dating from the 14th cent. There are a number of interesting black-and-white houses in the town. Outstanding is the Tower Hill House built in 1630, where Charles I sheltered on the night of 3 September 1644. Just behind the little Market Place in Rowberry Street is a 16th-cent. house. It is a timber-framed building with good diagonal bracing and well worth visiting. At the other end was the Elizabethan Grammar School now part of the modern secondary school.

Lower Brockhampton, 2 m. E., has a timber-framed manor house of about 1400, owned by the National Trust and open at advertised times.

BROUGHTON, *Oxfordshire* (5–SP4238), lies 2½ m. SW. of BANBURY on the B4035 road to SHIPSTON-ON-STOUR. The village is an ingress for its historic church and castle. To reach the church, turn left before the Saye and Sele Arms, an inn on the left-hand side of the village. From the church, the mass of Broughton Castle can best be seen for the first time.

The castle is a splendid example of English 14th-, 15th- and 16th-cent. imaginative yet utilitarian building. It was first erected by Sir John de Broughton above Sor Brook as a fortified stone manor house in 1306. Some 70 years later on the death of his sister, it passed into the possession of William de Wykeham, founder of WINCHESTER School and New College, OXFORD. In 1405 Thomas Wykeham converted the manor house into a castle, adding the battlements and gatehouse, the latter as it stands today across the moat. The grand-daughter of Sir William's sister married Sir William Fiennes, 2nd Lord Saye and Sele, in 1451. The castle, which is open to the public in the summer and by arrangement at other times of the year, is still owned and lived in by the Fiennes (pronounced Fines) family.

By the end of the 1500s, the Fiennes were enjoying a period of affluence and built on two stories, inserted huge mullioned and leaded windows, removed the battlements and gabled and re-roofed the house, to complete the pleasant Tudor building seen today. No less ambitious were the interior decorations carried out at the same time, adding a beautiful plaster ceiling with hanging bosses to the Great Hall. The house is filled with romantic vaulted passages and curious stairways. One of these is very ancient and leads to the private chapel with adjoining priest's room, one of the oldest rooms in the castle. It contains many historical treasures, paintings, and carved chimney-pieces. Celia Fiennes, the 17th-cent. traveller and diarist, was a member of the family.

During and after the Civil War the family showed considerable political astuteness and in this period William Fiennes, Lord Saye and Sele, promoted with Lord Brook a Puritan settlement in Connecticut. The name remains in Saybrook and Saybrook Point on the Connecticut River.

The nearby church has a fine stone screen of the Decorated period and the tower, spire and tracery are of the same date. The coloured tomb of the original Sir Thomas Broughton is in a good state of preservation and so are the monuments of the Wykehams and the 1st Viscount Saye and Sele who died in 1662. There are traces of early wall paintings on the north wall of the chancel and interesting, ancient glass roundels with heraldic devices. At the right time of year, the water lilies in the moat surrounding the mellowed brickwork of Broughton Castle are particularly beautiful.

BURFORD, *Oxfordshire* (5–SP2512), is situated 20 m. W. of OXFORD on the A40 road to NORTH-LEACH. It can rightfully claim to be one of the most beautiful of the Cotswold towns. Its wide High Street slopes not too steeply down to the sparkling little River Windrush crossed by a narrow three-arched bridge, and on the way down every variety of golden Cotswold stone house can be seen. Some remain unaltered in appearance since the 15th cent. The Bear Inn, the Grammar School and the Crown Inn all date from this period. So, too, does the Bull, but like many Burford houses it was later given a Georgian façade. The Great House in Witney Street is a

typical example of this practice. Halfway down is the twin-gabled 15th-cent. Tolsey where once the wealthy wool merchants of Burford held their meetings. It now houses a museum which contains among its many interesting collections some ancient maces and charters as well as a perfect dolls' house with 18th-cent. rooms and costumes. Down by the river is the four-gabled 16th-cent. house built by Symon Wysdom and which he gave to the Grammar School. The ancient almshouses nearby were rebuilt in 1828. The Priory was another famous Elizabethan house, which was rebuilt in the early 1800s. It still has its Tudor gables, and the heraldic arms over the doorway are a reminder that the famous William Lenthall, Speaker to the Long Parliament, once owned the house.

The fine church with its slender steeple is one of the largest churches in Oxfordshire. It lies at the bottom of the High Street on the east side in pleasant meadows with the River Windrush beyond it. The west doorway is pure Norman and so is the central part of the tower, to which another stage was added in the 15th cent. as a base for the spire. Most of what is seen in the church today dates from this period. The fine south porch has dual stories above the doorway, with pinnacled niches enshrining its ancient saints. The ceiling is fan vaulted and there are no less than five medieval screens dividing various chapels. The North Chapel houses the ornate tomb of the religiously divided Tanfield family. By contrast Speaker Lenthall at his own request has no monument, though he is buried in the church. Considering that Cromwell suppressed the Levellers' Rising in the churchyard in 1649, surprisingly little damage was done.

In A.D. 752 the Anglo-Saxons defeated the Mercians at Battle Edge, now a playing field near to the church. Even earlier a council was convened at Burford in A.D. 683 attended by the King of Mercia at which the date of Easter was fixed for the English Church, to conform with the rest of Western Christendom.

The sheep country which was the source of Burford's great wealth in the Middle Ages rises beyond the church fields to a plateau separating the Windrush and Evenlode Valleys; a rural scene of ever-changing beauty.

CASSINGTON, *Oxfordshire* (5–SP4510), is a short distance out of OXFORD between **Yarnton** and **Eynsham** just off the B4449. A pretty village with stone-built thatch-roofed cottages surrounding the green, it has a fine Norman church with a splendid Decorated spire visible to boaters on the upper reaches of the river a mile away. Norman doorways, arches and font are set in a Norman tripartite building, whose peaceful atmosphere is partly derived from the muted colour from roundels of old foreign glass set in the windows. The oak pews or benches are among the oldest in use in the country. The Jacobean canopied stalls came from Oxford Cathedral. The coloured screen and wall paintings are also of interest. The shroud brass on the walls is of a

16th-cent. Hebrew scholar, Thomas Nele.

Just beyond the village, turn right for Yarnton which is 4 m. NNW. of Oxford. Another old village with stone cottages, its early 17th-cent. Manor House was built by Sir Thomas Spencer. After much Civil War damage it declined into a farm-house but was restored towards the end of the 19th cent. and gardens, walks and terraced lawns were laid out.

The 13th-cent. church was considerably restored by Sir Thomas Spencer who built on a chapel which has two excellent English Baroque family tombs; the latter was erected in 1684 and shows the development of this style from the earlier font of 1609. It has a good Jacobean screen which contrasts favourably with the 15th-cent. alabaster reredos behind the high altar. This was found in extraordinary circumstances as part of the floor of a house. The glass is mostly old English and Flemish and was presented by an antiquarian benefactor at the end of the 18th cent.

South of the Yarnton–Cassington road at a junction of the A4141 is Eynsham, a typical Oxfordshire village or very small market town. Approached from the attractive Swinford Bridge, an 18th-cent. parapeted construction, a toll must be paid at the stone-shingled toll-house. The village square surrounded by stone houses has an old arcaded Market Hall which has served in turn as prison, Roman Catholic chapel and public library. The 14th-cent. church with its two-storied porch has been spoilt by much restoration.

CHALFORD, *Gloucestershire* (4–SO8902). In the Golden Valley SE. of STROUD where the Frome offers good fishing is the steep village of Chalford. On wooded slopes stand the handsome houses of the master-weavers whose broadcloth brought fortune to Stroud. On Chalford Hill is a 17th-cent. cottage where Huguenot weavers once lived. There are still some of the original mills dating from the 18th-cent. heyday of prosperity. The church was built in 1724 but was refashioned in the mid-19th cent. The sculpture over the south door was executed by John Thomas who also worked on Sir Charles Barry's HOUSES OF PARLIAMENT. There is some good modern carving inside. One of the most impressive houses in the area is the sternly Classical St Mary's Mill House with its balustraded roof line hiding a quaint dormer window. Skaiteshill House, which was built at the beginning of the 19th cent., has considerable charm; so, too, has Springfield House with its unusual Regency staircase. Most of the streets on this hillside are too steep and too narrow to admit cars. Grand views down the valley reward those who explore the little streets on foot.

CHALGROVE, *Oxfordshire* (5–SU6695), has a stream flowing each side of its charming village street in which the front doors of thatched cottages are reached by little bridges. Its Transitional parish church with unusually good 14th-cent. wall frescoes is found in the middle of a modern estate housing an overflow from OXFORD.

The Battle of Chalgrove Field saw the mortal wounding of John Hampden, whose opposition to Charles I's Ship Tax was one of the original factors which sparked off the Civil War. Prince Rupert coming from nearby **Chislehampton** led his troops to victory over the Parliamentary forces in June 1643. An obelisk ½ m. from the village marks the site of the battle, which covered a wide flat area that was easily converted into an airfield during the Second World War.

CHASTLETON, *Oxfordshire* (5–SP2429). On a wooded sloping ridge of the Cotswolds, protruding into Warwickshire, is the little village of Chastleton about 4 m. SE. of MORETON-IN-MARSH and 5 m. NW. of CHIPPING NORTON. It possesses a superb Jacobean house (open to the public) and a small church of considerable interest, much of it Norman. A hill-fort once stood here, strategically situated on the meeting point of the Gloucester, Worcester, Warwick and Oxford shires. An older house on the site was owned by Robert Catesby who had been obliged to sell his property to pay the colossal fine imposed by Queen Elizabeth for his adherence to the cause of the Earl of Essex. It was bought by an affluent Cotswold wool merchant, Walter Jones, who built the present lovely symmetric house with its five gables and two towers. The house, still in possession of the descendants of Walter Jones, contains most of the original furniture. The secret room where one of King Charles's supporters, Arthur Jones, hid after WORCESTER and escaped due to the ingenuity of his wife in drugging the wine drunk by his pursuers, can still be seen. The Long Gallery on the top floor and the state rooms are perfectly preserved, avoiding a museum atmosphere. There are many historical treasures to be seen, among them a Bible given by Charles I to Bishop Juxon, who ministered to the King on the day of his execution. There are also some interesting miniatures of the King's head made specially for Queen Henrietta Maria.

Much of the 17th-cent. garden still remains with some excellent examples of imaginative topiary. The dovecot built on arches dates from 1751.

CHEDWORTH, *Gloucestershire* (5–SP0511), is a stone village W. of the Fosse Way (A429) in the hills around the little stream that flows down to the River Coln. The countryside is breathtakingly beautiful. It has a handsome church; the five splendid windows lighting the tall nave give it a mainly Perpendicular aspect, but the north side has a good Norman arcade and aisle. The tower is Norman with a 13th-cent. belfry added. Inside, the church has a wealth of good carving and a 15th-cent. wine-glass pulpit as well as a Norman interlaced font. A little to the N. is Chedworth Roman Villa near **Yanworth**; the remains are perhaps the most comprehensive of their type in England. Set in 6½ acres of woodland owned by the National Trust, it is open to the public. Here you can learn something of life as it was lived between the years A.D. 180 and 350 during the

A. F. Kersting

Cheltenham: the Promenade

Roman occupation of Britain. It was first discovered in 1864. The mosaic pavements and bathhouse are remarkable. There is a museum housing the smaller finds from almost continuous excavations. In the hamlet of Yanworth, standing in a field among farm buildings, is a small Norman church with fine zigzag carving almost untouched by time or weather.

CHELTENHAM, *Gloucestershire* (4–SO9422), 10 m. from GLOUCESTER is intersected by the A40 and five radiating major routes, making it easily accessible from all major towns within a radius of a hundred miles or so. Set on a sheltered ridge between the high Cotswolds and the Severn Vale the town enjoys a pleasant and equable climate. Cheltenham is one of the finest spa towns in Europe, with a wealth of Regency houses bordering elegant squares, crescents, terraces and open spaces. Two hundred and fifty years ago it was a typical Cotswold stone village, but its fortune was made when a mineral spring was discovered in 1715 by means of watching the habits of some extremely healthy pigeons, according to tradition. Today the pigeon is incorporated in the city's crest standing on a roundel with bars of silver and blue symbolizing the waters. In 1738 the first pump room was built and 50 years later the spa was founded. George III, an inveterate frequenter of spas, visited the town in that year and set his seal of approval by staying at Bayshill Lodge. In this period of imperial expansion it was rapidly discovered that the mineral waters were extremely beneficial to the military officers and colonial administrators returning from the tropics with liver complaints. The medicinal reputation of the spa grew so rapidly that a small number of brilliant architects were entrusted with plans to lay out an entirely

new town. Here elegance and good taste were to provide a setting in which people steeped in classical culture and with ample means for enjoying their period of retirement could live in comfort. Cheltenham was thus rebuilt as a residential town with wide streets and tree-shaded open spaces between 1800 and 1840 in the Grecian idiom, with occasional Gothic or Italianate variations. In spite of war damage and certain modern desecrations it has, on the whole, retained its unique character.

J. B. Papworth was responsible for much of the best architecture: Lansdown Place and Montpellier Parade, among similar thoroughfares, and the Rotunda, the design for its dome being based on the Pantheon in Rome. Montpellier Walk with its shops separated by caryatids must be one of the most unusual shopping precincts in the world. Many of the houses and villas still have their splendid Regency ironwork balconies and verandas. All this careful planning culminated in the Promenade which was finished about 1825. The Municipal Offices dating from this period are probably best seen floodlit at night when their detail shows to advantage. The Promenade is dominated at the far end by the Queens Hotel built in 1838 with Classical colonnades by another renowned Cheltenham architect, W. Jearrad. The Imperial Gardens opposite have colourful flower displays all the year round. Outstanding in a town with so many fine examples of Regency architecture is the Pittville Pump Room built in 1825 by J. B. Forbes in a parkland setting as an assembly hall suited to the growing social life of the spa. The interior of the dome, which has been restored since the Second World War, is particularly beautiful. Out on the BATH road are two of Cheltenham's famous schools. Cheltenham College for Boys was originally built between 1841 and 1843 by J. Wilson in early Gothic Revival style. As the college grew in importance, particularly as a public school for sons of Indian Army officers, considerable extensions to the building were made. Nearby is Cheltenham Ladies' College, founded by Miss Beale, the ardent Victorian champion of good education for girls.

Although rightly concerned with preserving its invaluable heritage, the town is none the less a lively modern community. Its industries include the design and assembly of jet aircraft; the manufacture of watches and clocks and small high-precision instruments. It manufactures air-venting equipment and houses the world's largest makers of thermostatic mixing valves. On the cultural side it has established the Cheltenham Festival of Music as one of the most important in the country. While providing a platform for modern British composers is one of the Festival's main concerns, it is equally possible to hear a superb Bach choir, listen to jazz or enjoy folk-singing in the Shaftsbury Hall. The Festival, with many "fringe" attractions, begins in the first half of July. In October there is a Festival of Literature which each year grows in popularity. Racing and cricket are the predominant sports. The Cheltenham Gold Cup is one of the main features of the English racing year. The attractive race-course is out at Prestbury Park to the N. of the town.

CHINNOR, *Oxfordshire* (5–SP7500), lies under the shelter of the Chiltern woods, just off the A40, a few minutes' drive out of THAME. It would be easy to be put off by the unsightly cement works, yet it possesses a moated manor house and a Decorated church which contains two beautiful 14th-cent. stained-glass windows, their greens, yellows and browns still brilliant, superbly leaded and depicting among other subjects St Lawrence and the proto-martyr St Alban. The early brasses are among the best in the country. Particularly fine is that of Reginald de Malyns, 1385, and some depicting vested priests are among the earliest extant. The carvings on the mouldings are also outstanding.

CHIPPING CAMPDEN, *Gloucestershire* (5–SP1539), near the Worcestershire border is 4 m. E. of BROADWAY. It is one of the most typical towns of the affluent wool merchants of the 14th and 15th cents. There are many gabled stone houses with oriel, dormer and mullioned windows with medieval monastic-looking doorways giving a good impression of how many of the richer market towns looked during the late Middle Ages, for instance the arched and timber-roofed Market Hall and the house in the main street of William Grevel, ancestor of the Warwick family, which has a beautiful upthrusting two-storied gabled bay window built about 1380. Many of the houses date from the 17th cent., among them the attractive group of almshouses built in 1624, raised above street level. At the end of the town stands a magnificent Perpendicular church, with an elegant 15th-cent. pinnacled

tower. There are some Norman traces and 13th-cent. stone work; the porch with scratch dials and north aisle and chancel all date from the 14th cent. The tall nave arcades with their soaring columns, the clerestory and chancel arch, were all built at the peak of Chipping Campden's prosperity in the 15th cent. The unusual window above the chancel arch portraying the Last Judgment was inserted during the 19th cent. with commendable care so as not to disturb the superb proportions. Among the excellent brasses are those of William Grevel and his wife set into the chancel floor before the high altar. One side chapel is leased perpetually to the Noel family who were linked in marriage with Sir Baptist Hicks, a philanthropist of considerable standing with Charles I, who did not hesitate to borrow very considerable funds from his friend. Sir Baptist Hicks built Campden House, a beautiful country residence, but ordered it to be burnt to the ground rather than let it fall into the hands of the Parliamentarians. The ruins, comprising a habitable lodge, two pavilions and an almonry, can be seen a stone's throw from the church. In the Noel Chapel is a fine 17th-cent. bust of his daughter Penelope and her sister-in-law Anne Noel, and an imposing monument to Sir Baptist, who became 1st Viscount Campden, and his wife. There is a rare collection of fine English embroidery, some dating back to the time of Richard II. Altar frontals, dorsals (one with angels' wings lined with peacock feathers), orphreys and a beautifully preserved medieval cope are displayed under glass on the west wall of the church.

A little way out of the town on the top of Broadway Hill is Broadway Tower, a gazebo built in 1797; a Gothic Revival fantasy, it has machicolations and three circular towers.

CHIPPING NORTON, *Oxfordshire* (5–SP 3127), is the highest Cotswold town in the county. One of the old wool towns, its prefix "Chipping" comes from an Old English word for market, and it was prosperous as early as the 13th cent. The typical Victorian pinnacled and turreted tweed mill built in the 19th cent. brought much-needed employment to the town which was gradually decaying. Once a great Norman castle stood on the mounds above the beautiful wool church which still dominates the town. The usual wide Cotswold market place contains many good examples of the 16th- and 17th-cent. stone-masons' craft. Outstanding are Henry Cornishe's Almshouses built in 1640. There are several well-built inns, particularly the 17th-cent. White Hart.

The Parish Church of St Mary is mainly of 14th- to 15th-cent. construction, though it incorporates much earlier features. The polygonal porch with a room above it has fascinating bosses of strange creatures tying the ribs of the vaulting. The Perpendicular clerestory fills the church with light from its vast expanse of glass. A lot of the medieval stonework has been restored. The font is 15th-cent. and its intricate tracery has a pleasing delicacy.

The Market Hall was built in 1842 to blend with the Cotswold atmosphere of the town and is an outstanding example of the work of the architect George Stanley Repton.

A brewery and a glove factory continue to ensure prosperity to the town.

CHIPPING SODBURY, *Gloucestershire* (4–ST7282), is an attractive little market town on the A432 just off the A46 from Old Sodbury. It has a typical wide Cotswold main street, with several good Georgian brick as well as some rather severe Cotswold stone houses. At the top of the street stands a 16th-cent. market-cross. Although its Town Hall is 15th-cent., it is masked by a Victorian Tudor façade built on to it in 1858. The fine 15th-cent. Church of St John the Baptist with its lofty pinnacled tower was considerably restored in 1869 by Street who built London's LAW COURTS. There is a 14th-cent. doorway with an enthroned Christus and a 13th-cent. chancel arch with a curious carving of a master clothworker and his wife. The unusual pulpit with its pinnacled canopy is reached through a hole in one of the nave pillars supporting the barrelled roof of the church. It had been completely lost and was rediscovered by Street when he was restoring the church.

Two m. SE. of Chipping Sodbury lies **Dodington Park**, landscaped by Capability Brown. Many generations of Codringtons have lived in the splendid early Regency Dodington House built by James Wyatt in 1796–1817. He gave the beautifully proportioned house a façade of six Corinthian columns surmounted by an imposing pediment. Inside is one of Wyatt's most elegant staircases, which must have been seen at its best during balls given to celebrate the victory of Trafalgar where one of the Codringtons fought with Lord Nelson. The imposing stables are well worth a visit. Wyatt built the little Classical church about six years after the house. The lakes and lodges in the park make for an interesting drive. Dodington is open to the public during the summer months.

CHURCHILL, *Oxfordshire* (5–SP2824). Two m. SW. of CHIPPING NORTON is the little hill village of Churchill. It is of historical interest as the birthplace in 1732 of Warren Hastings, the first Governor-General of India. He was impeached on charges of corruption and cruelty during one of the longest trials in English history, which ended with his acquittal and a handsome annuity from the East India Company. The house where he was born still stands in the village. So does the house of William Smith, born here in 1769, who first mapped the rock structure of England and was the founder of modern geological science. The Georgian Gothic church was copied from various OXFORD sources, its tower being a ⅔ scale reproduction of Magdalen Tower.

CIRENCESTER, *Gloucestershire* (5–SP0201), claims with some justification the title of Capital of the Cotswolds. It was certainly the capital of

the Dobuni when as Corinium Dobunorum in A.D. 43 it became one of the chief Roman administrative centres for South-West England. By the 4th cent. its situation at the hub of a network of Roman roads, the Icknield Way, Ermine Street and Fosse Way, made it the second most important town in Britain. With the withdrawal of the legions, it went into a complete decline until a later Anglo-Saxon town was built. It slowly regained its prosperity with the development of sheep rearing on the rich Cotswold meadowlands surrounding the town. This was due to the industry of the monks who completed a great abbey church in the reign of Henry II. Dissolved by Henry VIII, nothing remains of this vast abbey other than the Spital Gateway, a late Norman construction which stands on the site of the northern end of the abbey precincts. Such was the tremendous wealth of the wool merchants in the 15th cent. that they were able to build one of the greatest "wool churches" in the kingdom. The Parish Church of St John the Baptist with its superb tower and three-storied fan-vaulted porch which faces the market place has been judged one of the most beautiful Perpendicular churches in England. The lofty nave is supported by six great arches on either side, and above these a tall clerestory with fine glass reaches to the richly bossed and panelled roof, sending down a flood of light. Both the east and west windows have rich medieval glass which reflects glowing colours on to the stone and woodwork below. The painted and gilded wine-glass pulpit is a very rare pre-Reformation example of this unusual design. There are many fine brasses of wool and wine merchants to be seen, particularly in the Lady Chapel. It is worth walking some distance from the church to appreciate the parapeting, embattlements and crocketed pinnacles which distinguish the skyline of Cirencester. The church possesses some priceless silver plate which is occasionally on view to the public.

Apart from some old houses in Coxwell Street, most of the interesting buildings date from the 18th cent. The Palladian building housing Lloyds Bank in Castle Street is a particularly good example. The Corinium Museum in Park Street is a treasure-house of Roman finds. Excavations have established the complete lay-out of the Roman town, and some well-preserved and vivid mosaic pavements can be seen in the museum, together with other Roman relics. The Roman amphitheatre is just outside the town at the Querns earthworks.

Cirencester House, seat of the Earl of Bathurst, has a 3,000-acre park, complete with a charming folly built in 1721 by the 1st Earl of Bathurst aided by Alexander Pope. It is called Alfred's Hall, a buttressed, castellated false ruin satirizing every possible quirk of medieval building. Pope stayed here to recover from the ardours of translating the Iliad. A roofed rusticated stone seat on the edge of the avenues called the Seven Rides is named after him. Although the house is not open to the public, the park, with its superb 5-m.-long avenue of chestnut trees can be enjoyed freely by everyone. It is an important centre for polo and matches take place from May to September on most Sundays, in which some of the country's best players participate.

The Royal Agricultural College to the SW. of the town is housed in a huge mansion designed in Gothic style by Daukes.

At **Daglingworth**, to the NW. of Cirencester, the Church of the Holy Rood retains features of its Anglo-Saxon predecessor. On the walls of the nave and aisle are three Anglo-Saxon carvings discovered on the site of the priory nearby. They are a Christ in Majesty, a Crucifixion, and a burly St Peter, brandishing a key.

CLENT HILLS, THE, *Worcestershire* (8–SO 9380), lie 3 m. SE. of STOURBRIDGE and are largely in the care of the National Trust. They rise N. and E. of the village of Clent to a height of 1,035 ft. The area covers the two main heights of the Clent and Walton Hills and all the common-land, farmland and woods of the Clatterbach Valley. On the east side of Clent Hill is St Kenelm's Chapel, said to mark the site where this Anglo-Saxon saint was buried; according to legend, he was murdered while still a boy. The chapel has a Norman doorway. Nothing remains of a town which once stood on the hillside. These lovely hills draw hikers from all over the industrial Mid-lands. The village church has a well-restored late 12th-cent. arcade and a good waggon roof. Much restoration took place in the 1860s. **Walton Hall** is a red-brick Georgian mansion. Of Clent House only the stables with a fine cupola, dated 1709, remain.

CLIFTON HAMPDEN, *Oxfordshire* (5–SU 5495), is a Thamesside village 7 m. S. of OXFORD on the A415 from ABINGDON to DORCHESTER. The river is crossed by Sir Gilbert Scott's six-ribbed arched brick bridge, which takes the traveller into Berkshire. This popular weekend spot was chosen by Jerome K. Jerome as a setting for one of the riotous incidents in his *Three Men in a Boat*. There are several attractive Elizabethan cottages. The Plough Inn has an ancient crutched foundation and the church, situated on a cliff along the river, has some very early features remaining in Scott's almost complete restoration of the building in 1844.

COLWALL, *Herefordshire* (8–SO7542), on the west side of the Malvern Hills has two major claims on the visitor's attention. It was where Elizabeth Barrett Browning spent her youth, at a house called Hope End which no longer exists. It is only 3 m. NW. of the famous **Hereford Beacon**, one of the most dramatic of the summits of the Malvern range. Situated on the Herefordshire-Worcestershire border at 1,114 ft above sea-level, it is the site of a remarkable Iron Age camp cover-ing 44 acres and with a citadel formed of a thick stone wall, and some 50 yds in circumference, 60 ft above the fosse. The intricate network of ditches and earthworks cut into the hillside must have made it a formidable stronghold to attack. Besides

the ramparts an earthwork extends to N. and S., $1\frac{1}{2}$ m. in circumference and enclosing 20 acres. Very early pottery has identified the Celtic people who first fortified the camp; it seems probable that the Normans also took advantage of its strategic position and strengthened the citadel. As late as 1405 Owen Glendower is said to have rallied forces here in the struggle between England and Wales. On the south side below the camp is a rock with a cave cut into it, known as Hermits or Clutters Cave. Nearby is a spring called Walm's Well for which medicinal claims are made. The 13th-cent. Colwall church has a good south arcade and entrancing carvings of medieval men and women peering from behind the leaves of the capitals. A good walk along the crest of the hills leads 4 m. N. to the **Worcestershire Beacon**.

Not far away to the W., about 5 m. NNW. of LEDBURY on the A4154, is **Bosbury**, one of the county's most important hop-growing centres. Its grand late Norman red-stone church contains two splendid Elizabethan tombs of 1573. There are attractive black-and-white houses in its short street and the hop kilns characteristic of this borderland. The Crown Inn has a fine panelled room of 1571. N. of Colwall and also on the A4145 is **Cradley**, a sizable village sprawled out on the plain at the foot of the Malvern Hills with good groups of black-and-white houses. The most remarkable of these is the 15th-cent. parish hall with an overhanging story on brackets with exceptionally attractive timberwork. The church with its sturdy Norman tower has been much restored. It is believed by some that the 20-ft timbers supporting the interior of the tower were taken from an earlier Anglo-Saxon church. It has an amusing panel dated 1795 of admonitions to bell-ringers.

Ye Gentlemen Ringers both far and near,
That are disposed for to Ring here;
Observe this law and mark it well.
The Man that Overthrow his Bell;
Six-pence he to the Clerk must pay,
Before that he go hence away,
If he Ring with Glove, Spur or Hat,
Six-pence he must pay for that.
If he either Curse or Swear,
Six-pence must pay while you are here,
This is not a place to Quarrel in,
To Curse and Swear it is a Sin.

COMPTON VERNEY, *Warwickshire* (9–SP 3052), is a fine Classical mansion with its West Range built in 1714 (reputedly by Vanbrugh) in a sternly Palladian style. It was created for George Verney, 12th Lord Willoughby de Broke, who was Dean of WINDSOR. The Verneys lived in this wooded valley from 1440 to 1921. Before then Alice Perrers, Edward III's mistress, had owned the estate, and before her the Norman Murdaks. The house lies just off the Fosse Way on the B4086 between Kineton and Wellesbourne Hastings on the WARWICK to Kineton road. By 1780 Robert Adam began his work at Compton Verney. He gave the windows more importance and spaced them more widely. On the ground floor he put in a splendid Venetian window of a type he often used. Although the interior work is not particularly notable, the setting of the house is beautifully landscaped. Its cedar-bordered lake is crossed by a three-arched bridge, also attributed to Robert Adam. The grounds are reputed to have been laid out by Capability Brown, who certainly designed the chapel in 1772. This has some interesting 16th-cent. brasses of Verney forebears as well as alabaster tombs and sarcophagi. The 16th-cent. stained-glass windows for which the chapel was famed were sold and removed to America.

COMPTON WYNYATES, *Warwickshire* (9–SP3341), is one of the most visually satisfying houses in England. It lies in a hollow of hills stretching from Brailes to Tysoe and Edge Hill, just 8 m. W. of BANBURY and 11 m. SE. of STRATFORD-UPON-AVON. It is a composition of early Tudor pink brick, weathered wood and mellow stone. It was built from 1480 over a period of about 40 years. The earliest records show that in 1204 Philip de Compton, direct ancestor of the present owner, the Marquess of Northampton, was in possession of the late Norman manor house. The present house was begun when Edmund de Compton pulled down the old Norman house and built four diapered brick wings enclosing the courtyard, exactly as they stand today. The house passed to Edmund's son William who in 1493 was a young page to Prince Henry, afterwards Henry VIII. Some 19 years later, William distinguished himself at the Battle of Tournai and was knighted. Among his other royal rewards was the vast but ruined Fulbrook Castle near WARWICK. From here, he brought much of the material to build his battlemented towers and the great porch which still stands and has the arms of Henry VIII and Catherine of Aragon above the original door with its curiously contrived locks. From Fulbrook, too, came material to build the great hall; its four-bayed timbered roof was brought over intact and re-erected. The elegant oriel window likewise came from that castle. The minstrel gallery and carved panels depicting the Battle of Tournai all date from this period. The carved friezes in the hall are of later date. The two fine Early English portraits painted on wood are of John Talbot, 1st Earl of Shrewsbury who led the English against Joan of Arc, and Margaret his wife who was a daughter of Richard Beauchamp, Earl of Warwick. The 16th-cent. tapestry of Cupid picking grapes is believed to have been designed by Raphael's pupil Giulio Romano. The dining-room, hung with portraits of Compton ancestors, has a fine Elizabethan or perhaps early Jacobean ceiling. So, too, has the drawing-room, with its Giorgione painting. The house is filled with secret passages, stairways, sliding panels and hidden rooms. It is said that there are nearly 100 rooms and about 300 windows. Henry VIII did sleep here, in a room that has an unusual ceiling with curious bands and squares in its design.

In 1644, during the Civil War, the house was besieged and finally captured. Four hundred Parliamentary troops were billeted here in what are still called the barracks. The church was completely demolished at this time. The house was finally returned to the Comptons on condition that the moat was filled in and a fine of £20,000 paid. The gardens are remarkable for the imaginatively sculptured yews.

Compton Pike, a spire not quite ½ m. SW. of the house, is a beacon believed to have been built at the time of the Armada; it is also said to have indicated the position of Compton-in-the-Hole, a one-time alternative name to Compton Wynyates.

The church constructed from materials salvaged from its predecessor wrecked in the Civil War period is a perfect Restoration example of its kind. There is no chancel, just a central arcade which still has its original box pews. The plaster ceiling has two paintings of the firmaments, one by day and one by night. There are 17 hatchments or family arms hung on its walls. Many of the Compton effigies which were thrown into the moat by the Parliamentary forces were recovered, and can be seen at the east end of the chapel. A bronze plaque to John Berrill reminds posterity that it was a good steward who saved Compton Wynyates from destruction. Reckless gambling and a disastrously costly election made the Lord Northampton of the time decide to pull the house down. The contents were sold in 1774 but Berrill merely bricked up the windows. Sixty years later the 2nd Marquess and his son were thus able to restore the house to its full Tudor glory, without any material alterations to the original 15th- and 16th-cent. buildings.

CORNWELL, *Oxfordshire* (5–SP2727). Within easy walking distance of CHIPPING NORTON on the A44 to MORETON-IN-MARSH, the first lane to the left is signposted to Cornwell. A sharp turn leads to one of the prettiest villages in this area, nestling in a fold of hills with a stream running through it. It has a fine Georgian house with formal gardens, which, like the rest of the village, has had restoration work done by Clough Williams-Ellis of Portmeirion fame. The little Norman church has two good doorways and a round 12th-cent. font set on four lions. The church, which suffered poor Victorian restoration, is somewhat dark and the little chancel arch with beautifully scalloped corbels might well be missed.

COVENTRY, *Warwickshire* (9–SP3379), is a thriving city, with a growing population of 350,000. It probably owes its origin to the erection in the 7th cent. of an Anglo-Saxon convent. However, it was the later Benedictine abbey founded by Leofric, Earl of Mercia in the 11th cent. that gave the town its first impetus to growth. No account of Coventry can ignore the legend of Godiva, who, it is said, in order to obtain relief for the town from the taxes levied by her husband Leofric, rode naked through the city, modestly

Kenneth Scowen

British Travel Association

Compton Wynyates in its beautiful setting in a fold of the Warwickshire hills

Coventry Cathedral: the Graham Sutherland tapestry

preserved only by the length of her hair. The first recorded instance of the story only dates back to 1235; with the embellishment of a "Peeping Tom" not added until a century later. In A.D. 1553 it was granted its first charter.

Coventry, centrally situated, has always owed much to its communications but never more than today, when it is well-served by the motorway network and an electrified and modernized railway. From the Middle Ages, wool, needles and leather all contributed to its prosperity. The mechanization of the 19th cent. brought the manufacture of sewing-machines and bicycles right into the city. The Daimler Company produced the first English motorcar in 1898 and the car industry increased rapidly, giving rise in its turn to aircraft production. Workers not only from every part of Britain but from all over the world have been drawn here. The city has multiplied its population six times since the turn of the century.

In November 1940, much of the city was wiped out by a devastating air raid which almost completely destroyed the Cathedral Church of St Michael (it had only been raised to this dignity in 1918, the church previously being within the diocese of LICHFIELD), leaving only the magnificent medieval tower and spire standing.

In 1951 an open architectural competition for a new cathedral was won by Basil Spence, since knighted. The new cathedral, which draws thousands of visitors from all over the world, has been acclaimed as one of the most striking examples of modern architecture. The first impression of a long cliff of rosy sandstone with vertical lines suggesting Gothic buttresses is unforgettable, especially

for visitors who have not seen this delicately coloured stone before; the canopied link between the entrance to the new church and the charred walls of the old is a gesture of genius. Going in through John Hutton's engraved glass doors, the eye is at once held by a suggestion of great length. Yet the nave is only 270 ft long and 80 ft wide. The interior is coloured by deep greens, golden yellows, rose and vivid reds, blues and sombre purples from the splendid glass, mostly stretching from floor to ceiling. These glass windows, conceived and executed by Laurance Lee, Geoffrey Clarke and Keith New, with the Great Baptistry window by John Piper, have done much to give back to England her medieval fame for stained glass. Everything seems to culminate, as Sir Basil Spence intended it should, on the massive block of the altar stone surmounted by Geoffrey Clarke's metal abstraction of Cross and Crucified. The final focal point is the 75-ft-high tapestry designed by Graham Sutherland and woven in France, representing in almost Byzantine terms the Redeeming Saviour of the World. The green background sets off the muted whites, reds and purples woven into Christ's robes and the four medallions of Evangelists. Between the feet of Christ stands Man, diminutive, yet thrust against the background with dynamic force. The chapels are all designed to have the same sense of immediacy and involvement in modern life. Notable is the Chapel of Christ the Servant, with its maps giving the names and positions of all the industrial plants of Coventry. The Chapel of Unity has for its theme understanding among all races and religions. Finally, the visitor is likely to be impressed by the rugged Epstein bronzes of St

Michael and the force of Evil, two separate figures, outside the cathedral, against the walls immediately to the right of the flight of steps leading up to the entrance to the cathedral.

Few buildings remain from the medieval city. Most important of these is the Church of Holy Trinity, facing the new Precinct and thus immediately behind the cathedral. The proximity of two such important churches as the old destroyed St Michael's and Holy Trinity is a reflection of a medieval feud when the townspeople were roughly divided between the prior and the earl and were continually at loggerheads. Particularly splendid are the timbered ceilings, the 15th-cent. brass eagle lectern and pulpit of the same period. The other historic place of worship deserving mention is the Collegiate Church of St John the Baptist first built by the wife of Edward II. Nearby stand two black-and-white gabled houses. Bond's Hospital is the more important, facing the north side of St John's. Founded by a Coventry draper, Thomas Bond, in 1506 for the care of 12 elderly poor men, it still possesses some excellent period furniture. The other house is Bablake School alongside Hill Street and has a history much antedating its conversion to a school for boys. The only other medieval buildings of consequence, apart from two well-preserved city gates, is St Mary's Hall in Bayley Lane. It was built in 1340 as the hall of the Merchant's Guild. It possesses, as well as some fine early stained glass, a superb tapestry of the late 15th cent. depicting the Assumption of the Blessed Virgin with the kneeling figure of Henry VII and his wife. There is also a minstrel gallery.

The city has been in the throes of rebuilding ever since the Second World War. All this springs from forward-looking post-war planning. The Precinct in the city centre was the first stage. It started with what is now the Leofric Hotel facing Holy Trinity. The traffic-free shopping area has provided a prototype for all the new town centres of Britain. The architecture is undistinguished in the main, but the scale is more human and the place easier to use than some more pretentious centres.

The University of Warwick, whose first building took shape in 1964, has perhaps the finest campus in the country, covering an area of about 400 acres. Its white-tiled residential, tutorial and laboratory blocks are attractive against the foliaged green background. It houses 800 of its present 1,600 roll of students but is to cater for more than 15,000 in the foreseeable future. A £300,000 Arts and Sports Centre is planned. The university is situated 4 m. out of Coventry on the A46 WARWICK road at Gibbet Hill.

Arrangements can always be made to visit the great Coventry motorcar factories by prior application.

CRASWALL, *Herefordshire* (8–SO2836), is in wild, beautifully wooded country on the Herefordshire side of the Black Mountains, some 1,000 ft up with splendid views down the valley. It can be best reached by taking the road W. out of Vow-church in the GOLDEN VALLEY to the upland village of **Michaelchurch Escley** with its stream rushing down to meet the River Monnow and the secluded 17th-cent. Michaelchurch Court. The village church has on its north wall a very rare painting of Christ of the Trades surrounded by shears, axes, ploughs and flails. The road crosses the Monnow by an inn and follows the west bank of the river until it crosses back again into Craswall. The scenery is as impressive as any in the Black Mountain country and the search for the ancient Craswall Priory is now made easy by the new road into Hay. It was once a small Benedictine priory founded in 1222 by Roger de Lacy as an affiliation of the Norman Grandmont congregation which had only three houses in England. It was suppressed in the reign of Edward VI and its revenues diverted to Christ College, CAMBRIDGE. It is in the care of the Royal Commission for Historic Monuments. Many interesting fragments of painted glass, excellent encaustic tiles and a leaden altar casket for relics have been discovered. It is said that the present chancel window in the little parish church a mile away was originally brought from the priory. Many of the secluded farm-houses hereabouts are Tudor and in default of roads can only be reached on horseback; this is a paradise for romantics and escapists.

CROFT CASTLE, *Herefordshire* (8–SO4565), is 5 m. from LEOMINSTER and 9 m. from LUDLOW, and reached by turning right at Cock Gate just past the hamlet of Bircher on the B4362. The 1,363-acre parkland of Croft Castle is a remarkable property, now owned by the National Trust, which has been in the Croft family since the time of the Conquest, with one break of some 170 years from about 1750 when it was sold. The Crofts bought it back in 1923 and it passed to the National Trust in 1957. The castle as seen today retains its 14th- and 15th-cent. walls and pink-stone round towers. Its castellated front and interior was much modified during the 16th and 17th cents. The Gothicized bays on each side of the gabled front and the fine Gothic staircase and ceilings were added by the family of Thomas Johnes of Hafod between 1750 and 1760. The Blue and Gold Room with a splendid chimney is impressive. The porch was added as late as 1914. The park has some of the finest Spanish chestnut, oak and beech avenues in the county. It is open at advertised times in the summer months. The attractive little church nestled right up to the house contains the splendid tomb of Sir Richard Croft and his wife, who was a widow of one of the Mortimers. The effigy of Sir Richard is resplendent in finely carved armour copied from that he wore at the Battle of TEWKESBURY. Also on the estate N. of the park is the nearly 1,000-ft-high edge of Leinthall Common with an Iron Age camp. The fortification covered an area of about 24 acres and was occupied from 400 B.C. to A.D. 50. It is worth the climb as apart from its antiquarian interest it is said that more than a dozen counties can be seen from the summit.

CROOME D'ABITOT, *Worcestershire* (8–SO8944), lies mid-way between PERSHORE and GREAT MALVERN, with the M5 motorway actually intersecting the estate. Although now a school, Croome Court is one of the most impressive mansions in the county. It was built in 1751 by Capability Brown for the 6th Earl of Coventry. Some 10 years later Robert Adam was commissioned to complete the interior decorating. Much of this has been dismantled and sold; one of the ceilings was shipped intact to the United States. The house retains its correct Palladian exterior, built of Bath stone, and the library its fine Venetian window and the elegant bookcase specially designed by Adam. The gate piers with the Coade stone urn can still be seen as well as the rotunda, but many of the 18th-cent. structures in the park are becoming derelict. Quite outstanding is the Panorama Tower built by Adam in 1766, looking towards Severn Stoke. Beyond the lawn is a fine temple façade also by Adam. Still further away towards **Earls Croome** is a magnificent "eye-catcher" called **Dunstall Castle.** It stands on the western edge of Dunstall Common. The church, one of the earliest examples of the Gothic Revival, was intended principally as a mausoleum for the Coventry family and its interior elegance is typified by the black-and-white marble late Renaissance tomb of Thomas, 1st Lord Coventry. The wooden font is exquisite.

CROPREDY, *Oxfordshire* (5–SP4646). Six m. N. of BANBURY at Cropredy Bridge was fought one of the fiercest battles of the Civil War in 1644. The Royalists under the leadership of Charles I were encamped on the east bank of the Cherwell. The Parliamentary forces led by Waller believed they could pierce the defences of their opponents and Waller gave orders for the attack across the bridge. During the mêlée the villagers, fearing for their church and its treasures, withdrew a beautiful eagle lectern from the building and dropped it in the river. However, the fighting reached such a pitch that much of the artillery of the Parliamentarians was lost and the Royalists, seizing their advantage, pushed back Waller's troops. After his victory the King spent the night at nearby Williamscote, a fine house built by Walter Calcott in 1568 and still standing. In the ensuing confusion the villagers forgot the spot where they had dropped their precious lectern and it was not until many years later that it was recovered from the mud and restored to the parish church. This 14th-cent. building with part of its "Doom" fresco over the chancel arch still discernible, possesses many relics of the battle.

The walks along the river and canal with their many locks and bridges are rewarding for connoisseurs of canal engineering.

CUDDESDON, *Oxfordshire* (5–SP5902), is one of the many lovely little villages just outside OXFORD. Only 5 m. out of the city, it is within walking distance of Cowley. Two other villages, **Denton** and **Garsington,** are almost linked together in the pleasant undulating countryside

which rises to 400 ft in places. This village saw much of the terror of the Civil War in 1644 and the Manor House and old palace of the Bishops of Oxford were burnt down to prevent them falling into the hands of the Parliamentarians. The palace was rebuilt by Dr Fell. The Theological College founded by Bishop Wilberforce was designed by G. E. Street who built London's LAW COURTS.

The cruciform parish church is set on a green slope and is partly Norman, with a particularly good door of this period. The late Transitional builders achieved an effect of lightness in the tower arches springing from the massive 13th-cent. piers. The village slopes down to the river which is crossed by a bridge. Nearby is an 18th-cent. watermill still in working order.

DITCHLEY PARK, *Oxfordshire* (5–SP3821), 5 m. SE. of CHIPPING NORTON, 1½ m. off the A34 beyond **Kiddington,** is one of the greatest 18th-cent. Classical houses in the county. Designed by Gibbs (who built the Radcliffe Camera in OXFORD) for the 2nd Earl of Lichfield, it stands on the site of an earlier building owned by the Lee family, ancestors of the famous Confederate general of the American Civil War, Robert E. Lee. Here James I made his headquarters when hunting in WYCHWOOD FOREST. The Lees were ennobled by Charles II when Edward, the 1st Earl, married the king's daughter by the Duchess of Cleveland. Capability Brown laid out the lovely gardens and William Kent was responsible for most of the elegant interiors, including the splendid Great Hall. It is open to the public for three months during the summer. It is of recent historical interest as the weekend headquarters of Sir Winston Churchill, who directed operations here during the Second World War. The house is now used mainly as an Anglo-American Conference Centre under the Ditchley Foundation.

DORCHESTER, *Oxfordshire* (5–SU5794), is an ancient settlement of great importance, its history going back to the Bronze Age. It is a village of great charm easily reached from OXFORD, 8 m. away, and ½ m. above the meeting of the waters of the Rivers Thame and Thames. Its earliest communities built ditches, some as much as 36 ft wide, discovered by aerial photographs taken over the Dyke Hills. The Romans founded the town of Dorocina between the present village and the River Thames. An altar to Jupiter and Augustus has been discovered here, as well as tessellated pavements, Roman coins and other remains. The town was at this time well situated on the road linking Silchester with Alchester. In A.D. 634, the Milanese missionary Birinus came to preach to the West Saxons and here he baptized Cynegils, King of Wessex, and founded a bishopric whose territory reached up to the borders of Northumbria. Some years later, the see was transferred to WINCHESTER. The Venerable Bede tells the story at some length. Nothing remains of the old Anglo-Saxon cathedral, but the remarkable abbey built by the late Norman

Augustinian canons remains. It was enlarged in
the 13th and 14th cents. Although much restored
by Butterfield and Scott in the 19th cent., nothing
could diminish the beauty of this 200-ft-long
church. Its three outstanding treasures are the
superb Norman lead font, arched and foliated
with graceful sitting figures; its Jesse window with
tree branches of stone enshrining the original
carved figures and richly coloured glass telling
the story of Mary's genealogy; and its beautiful
14th-cent. three-seated sedilia under the south
window with its piscina. The finely traceried
canopies have curious triangular windows with
very old glass depicting the life of St Birinus.

To see the village to the best advantage the
motorist should leave his car and go on foot. There
is a variety of interesting old houses, particularly
the gabled George Hotel, which stands almost
opposite the abbey gates. The old School House
contains some remains of the priory which was
pulled down at the Dissolution. The bridge was
constructed in 1815. A short way beyond the
bridge is the fascinating hamlet of Overy with old
thatched cottages, one of them with the intriguing
name of Mollymops.

DOWN AMPNEY, *Gloucestershire* (5–SU
1097), 5½ m. SSE. on the A419 from CIREN-
CESTER going towards SWINDON the fourth unclassified road to the left leads to Down Ampney,
the most charming of all the many Cotswold
Ampneys in the Upper Thames countryside.
Surrounded by pleasant old cottages is an ancient
village cross which was restored with a canopied
Calvary in the 19th cent. by the owners of the
beautiful gabled Tudor manor house. The manor
is separated from the mostly Early English parish
church by a large yew hedge. The fine church
tower is surmounted by its original spire with a
gilded weathercock. The buttressed porch is 15th-
cent., while the north arcade is early 13th-cent.
The pointed arches rest on late Norman pillars
with varied capitals. There is a painted Jacobean
oak screen which embodies parts of a gallery from
the great church at Cirencester. In the panelled
transept is the tomb of Sir Anthony Hungerford,
dated 1653. The chapel in the south transept has
two 14th-cent. recumbent effigies of Sir Nicholas
Villiers, who fought in the Last Crusade, and his
daughter Margaret. The chancel has been much
restored, but with taste and sensitivity.

DROITWICH, *Worcestershire* (8–SO9063), is
an old town. The Romans called it Salinae as its
natural brine springs were already known. The
Anglo-Saxons called it Wic (pronounced with a
"ch") and to this the first element of the name,
meaning customary right or perquisite, was
added in Norman times. The radioactive springs
rising from beneath the town are said to be 10
times saltier than ordinary sea-water and even
saltier than the waters of the Dead Sea. Droitwich
was perfectly sited for its development as a spa
in the early part of the 19th cent. because of its
position in an undulating plain, sheltered by the
Malvern and Lickey Hills. This development

Edwin Smith

Dorchester Abbey: the Jesse window

was due to a far-seeing businessman, John Corbett, who by 1828 realized its tremendous possibilities, taking the waters being then fashionable. He not only built St Andrew's Brine Baths, which were rebuilt twice during the present century, but he remodelled the ancient timbered Raven Hotel, then a 16th-cent. house, and established other luxurious hotels. He may have been influenced in all this by his French wife. For her, just outside the town at Dodderhill, he built an imposing French château in the style of Francis I. Set in a well-wooded, 70-acre estate, it is now transformed into a hotel.

Droitwich is not large and a tour on foot is the best way of discovering its 16th-, 17th- and 18th-cent. houses. St Andrew's Church, in St Andrew's Street, has some good 13th-cent. features. St Peter's, 1 m. S. of the town, has a good Norman chancel and chancel arch with a Perpendicular timber-framed clerestory. In the south transept is some early 14th-cent. stained glass in the typical yellows and dark greens of the period. Nearby is St Peter's Manor, a 300-year-old timbered building which has been considerably restored. It has an old dovecot with 750 holes. The Roman Catholic church on the Worcester Road attracts a large number of visitors by its splendid series of mosaics depicting the life of Droitwich-born St Richard, who became a much-loved Bishop of Chichester in the reign of Henry III. The mosaics by Gabriel Pippet are in the manner of Ravenna but are inclined to harshness, perhaps because of their newness. The town has a number of fine parks, one of which has a swimming-pool filled with natural brine and water to reproduce the salinity of the Mediterranean. Droitwich still functions as a spa.

Just a little way S. of the town the Droitwich–Worcester Canal is cut through the little village of Salwarpe between the 16th-cent. half-timbered Salwarpe Court and the sandstone Norman church. It is a tranquil place, its valley watered by both the canal and the River Salwarpe. The gabled court with tall chimneys was once the home of the famous Talbot family. There are a number of memorials to this family in the church, which has a fine Transitional arcade but was much spoilt in the mid-Victorian restoration. However, there is some good 15th-cent. stone carving in the screens, and the richly chasubled effigy of a priest in the sanctuary marks the tomb of William Richepot, rector here between 1367 and 1401. The rectory is a good Georgian building. The Old Mill House reflected in the canal completes the peaceful scene.

DUDLEY, *Worcestershire* (8–SO9390), is called the "Capital of the Black Country", with some justification, as it was here in the 17th cent. that coal was first used for smelting iron, and its vast ironworks have prospered ever since. It lies 9 m. W. of BIRMINGHAM and is almost surrounded by Staffordshire, in which county its newer districts lie. From the keep of its Norman castle, the only important ruin of its kind in Worcestershire, the panorama extends over seven counties, often

smoke-hazed. There is an interesting 14th-cent. barbican to be seen and two drum towers. Its courtyard is surrounded by a 14th-cent. wall, over 8 ft thick in places, which has defied time and attack. Within the grounds is an excellent zoo with over 450 species, including rare fish. A chairlift brings visitors up the 200-ft slopes on which the castle stands. Below the castle are great limestone caverns which have not been quarried since the early 1920s. **Wren's Nest** is in fact sited in both Worcestershire and Staffordshire and is the only geological nature reserve in the country. It is the classical source of fossils from the Upper Silurian Dudley limestone. Over 300 species of fossil fauna are represented and they are at least 330 million years old. They were first studied here in 1686. Just across the county line is the excellent early 19th-cent. Church of St Thomas dominating the town from the heights and well worth visiting.

DURSLEY, *Gloucestershire* (4–ST7597). Some good Georgian houses remain among much new building in Dursley, a reminder of the town's 18th-cent. prosperity. The 18th-cent. Market Hall stands elegantly on 12 arches, enhanced by the fine statue of Queen Anne. The parish church has a good 15th-cent. chapel raised by one of the town's wool merchants and a Gothic tower which was built by Thomas Sumsion in the early 1700s. Although modern industry is bringing back a new surge of life to the town, nearby **Woodmancote** seems to escape suburbanization and has an interesting main street with good houses, among which Ferney Hill House and the Georgian Gothic Rangers are typical. A little further along the B4066 to the E. in wooded hills is the long village of **Uley**. It is a weaving village of great antiquity with some of the best 17th- and 18th-cent. houses in the county. At Wresdon Farm lived John Eyles who built the house in 1687. He won renown in Uley as being the first inhabitant to weave Spanish cloth. The house has some of the original furniture, including his four-poster bed. About 1 m. outside the village is a 14th-cent. house called Owlpen Manor which used to be famous for its yews. N. of Uley is the famous Stone Age barrow known as Hetty Pegler's Tump. It is one of the best preserved of these Cotswold barrows and is some 120 ft long and 90 ft wide with burial chambers enclosed within its stone walls. The views from the heights of the Tump extend right across the Severn to the Welsh mountains. On nearby Uley Bury about 800 ft above sea-level was a huge Iron Age camp later used by the Romans, whose hoards of coin and pottery have been discovered here.

EARDISLAND, *Herefordshire* (8–SO4158), lies 5 m. W. of LEOMINSTER on the A44. It is a lovely village, with a wealth of timber-framed cottages set on the banks of the River Arrow. A fisherman's paradise, it always attracts anglers in the mayfly season. The river widens just beyond the bridge and the tree-lined banks focus the eye on the beautiful Staick House, built about 1300 as a comfortable yeoman's hall. Although excellently restored in the early part of this century, it retains most of its original timberwork, doorways, windows and very early fire-places. An east wing was added in the 17th cent. The gabled outlines of the house are most satisfying and the low line of the roof of the recessed hall range is practically all the work of the original builder.

By the bridge stands the old village whipping post. On the south side is the old Schoolhouse and opposite is a 17th-cent. manor house with Queen Anne additions. It has a rare type of tall brick four-gabled dovecot which always arouses admiration. The church, which has a few interesting features, was mostly restored about 1864. One m. S. of Eardisland is an 18th-cent. house, Burton Court, with an excellent example of architect Clough Williams-Ellis's concept of the picturesque in the neo-Tudor frontage he gave the house some little time before the First World War.

ELKSTONE, *Gloucestershire* (5–SO9612). This small high windswept Cotswold village possesses one of the most rewarding Norman churches in a county in which so many are preserved. It lies less than 1 m. E. of the A417 which follows the Roman Ermine Street linking CIRENCESTER with GLOUCESTER. On the other side of the road is **Syde**, a little village which also has an old Norman church and an ancient stone-buttressed barn well worth visiting. Elkstone is first mentioned in the Domesday Book, deriving its name from Ealac's Stone which many believe is the curious pagan stone against the wall of the vestry. The church dates from about 1160 and has a sturdy Perpendicular tower at the west end with thick stone walls. This replaced the old central Norman tower which collapsed when Gloucester Cathedral was being built. The arches which supported the Norman tower separate the little choir and sanctuary from the tall nave. Although the porch is 14th-cent., the south door has preserved its beautiful romanesque tympanum with Christ in Majesty on a cushioned judgment seat with the symbols of the four Evangelists below. Above the finger of God points down and the surrounds have remarkable ornamentation deserving of close study, as the zigzags of the 12th-cent. arches and the little east window. The solid oak roof of the nave dates from the 15th cent., as do the font and the windows in the nave and the chancel. An almost unique dovecot above the chancel is reached by a stairway near the pulpit. There are a number of interesting monuments to various local yeoman families on the north side of the nave as well as two 17th-cent. table tombs which are both fine examples of their kind.

In the south-east corner of the churchyard, the little stone house with 15th-cent. windows was once the Priest's House and is now divided into two cottages. The Rectory, which has been well restored, has Stuart foundations, a Queen Anne façade and Georgian additions at the back. An interesting walk of about 2 m. is to the neighbouring villages of Syde and Winstone, through the Frome Valley.

ETTINGTON, *Warwickshire* (9–SP2447), is a village 5 m. SE. of STRATFORD-UPON-AVON on the A422 BANBURY road. Its chief claim to fame lies 1½ m. SW. of the village, towards Newbold-on-Stour where in Ettington Park stands one of the most impressive High Victorian houses in Warwickshire. It was the seat of the Shirley family, whose lineage went back to earliest Norman times. They tore down the old house in 1858 and commissioned two architects, John Prichard and J. P. Seddon, to remodel it completely in 13th-cent. Gothic style. The house, now a hotel, has an interior incapable of matching the skill shown in its exterior. However, the staircase hall is a good piece of Victorian inventiveness, producing an Henri IV atmosphere which catches some semblance of authenticity from the Elizabethan chimney-piece in the entrance hall. The Shirley motto "*Loyal je suis*" is much displayed.

Just behind the house stands a 17th-cent. summer-house or loggia, its perfectly proportioned double arches separated by a fluted pillar. Here, as a child, William Croft may well have gained inspiration for his later works of church music. He was born in 1677 and brought up in the Shirley household. Near the house is the old church with a partly Norman tower. The bell openings date from about 1200. The south wall of the chancel still stands and the ruins are dramatically continued by a splendid avenue of tall trees. In 1825 a south transept was built to contain the mortuary monuments of the Shirley family. There is a very good example of the work of the Irish stained-glass artist, Evie Hone, set into the east light between 1948 and 1949.

A short walk leads to one of the earliest Friends meeting houses in the county. Stone built in severe Quaker style, it is only 18 ft by 24 ft in area and has a typical Warwickshire mullioned window. It is one of the few meeting houses to possess all its original furniture.

EVESHAM, *Worcestershire* (8–SP0344), is an important market town and the centre of the fruit-growing area of the VALE OF EVESHAM. Its tree-lined walks and lawns along the Avon give it both distinction and charm. The precincts of its ancient ruined Benedictine abbey founded in 714 run right down to the river bank. Its two splendid churches share the same churchyard with Clement Lichfield's beautiful 110-ft-high bell-tower built in 1539 between them. Abbot Lichfield was the last of a succession of 55 abbots; for the Dissolution occurred in the same year that work was completed on his tower. Its superb panelled faces, ogee arches and elaborate decoration of its buttresses, together with its delicate pierced parapet and finely ornamental pinnacles, place it among the treasures of English architecture. The oldest part of All Saints' Church dates from the 12th cent., although it gives a general impression of being Perpendicular. It has an embattled tower with an octagonal spire. The porch has some intricate heraldic carving made up of the Tudor rose, the fleur de lis, the three ostrich feathers of the Prince of Wales, a rose

Eardisland: Staick House, a 14th-cent. yeoman's hall on the River Arrow

Evesham: the bell tower is a superb example of Perpendicular architecture

halved with a pomegranate and a crowned rose. The most rewarding part of this church is the Lady Chapel, built when Clement Lichfield was still Prior and therefore dating from before 1513. Coming through the panelled four-centred arch, the visitor can only be amazed at the richly carved fan vaulting of the roof, springing from shafts at four angles and from the centre of the south wall. The band of quatrefoils beneath the windows is particularly handsome. The Abbot is buried in a marble tomb which lost its brass inscriptions during the Puritan regime. The church has suffered much from Victorian restoration.

On the other side of the bell-tower is the Church of St Laurence, rebuilt on the site of an ancient chapel in the 16th cent. It has suffered badly over the centuries from both neglect and poor restoration work. However, the east end of the chancel has some good Perpendicular panelling and the chantry chapel of Abbot Lichfield has a fan tracery roof with a pendant boss. There is some good modern glass by the late Geoffrey Webb. The very fine exterior of the east end is worth close examination.

Evesham has many fine houses and old inns, notably the late 15th-cent. Booth Hall or Round House. It has been dramatically but beautifully restored with all its close timberwork seen to good advantage. On the south side of Bridge Street is the old Crown Hotel built round a courtyard. At the end of this street is part of the town's original medieval wall. Dresden House is perhaps the

finest building in the town. Of mellowed brickwork, it has a richly carved cornice and a doorway with enormous iron brackets dated 1692. About 1 m. NW. on the Worcester Road is the Abbey Manor, probably built around 1840. It stands in pleasantly wooded gardens where an obelisk commemorates the terrible Battle of Evesham. Here on 4 August 1265 in the fury of a thunderstorm Henry III's son, Edward, by cunning strategy, defeated Simon de Montfort who was slain while leading the forces of the rebel barons. De Montfort's son Henry, some 18 barons, 160 knights and 4,000 men-at-arms perished in a battle lasting three hours.

FAIRFORD, *Gloucestershire* (5–SP1501), on the A417 from LECHLADE to CIRENCESTER is best seen from the parapet of the little bridge crossing over to Fairford Mill and looking across the stone roofs and curving grey walls to the Perpendicular Parish Church of St Mary. This wool church is one of the best surviving examples. Built in the latter part of the 15th cent. by John Tame, a wealthy cloth merchant, it has notable uniformity of design and construction. The parapeted central tower with well-proportioned pinnacles and quatrefoil piercing, the clerestoried nave, porch and the chancel with the original priest's door into the sacristy are all well-preserved. The carvings in wood and stone, particularly the amusing carved misericords, are worth close examination. The Founder's Tomb lies under the screen separating the church from the Lady Chapel where there is a good 16th-cent. tomb of a member of the Lygon family. There are stone angels supporting the timber roof and the remains of the original wall paintings. The church is most famous, however, for the 15th- to 16th-cent. painted glass windows, the finest in such quantity in England. There are in all 28, telling the Christian story from the Creation, with the stories of Moses, David, Solomon and the Queen of Sheba all vividly portrayed, right up to the Crucifixion and the early development of the Church. Finally, in the west window the Last Judgment is depicted in horrifying detail.

In a house in the tree-lined square John Keble, the poet and cleric, was born in 1792. His classic work *The Christian Year* did much to revive a liturgical renaissance in the Church of England, and Keble College, OXFORD, was founded in his memory. In and around the square are several old inns.

FOREST OF DEAN, *Gloucestershire* (4–SO 6209). Gloucestershire has within its borders one of the greatest primeval forests in the kingdom. It is said that over 20 million trees go to make up the Royal Forest of Dean: oaks, ash-trees, hollies, birches and conifers. Forest wild life abounds and wild flowers, rare kinds among them, thrive. It is said that there are over 2,000 m. of woodland paths. The people who live in and around the Forest of Dean are known as Foresters. They preserve their ancient privileges and customs. Below the woodlands is a 22,000-acre coalfield and now abandoned iron-workings.

The Romans mined here and traces of these so-called scowles can often be discovered under small green mounds. Forest of Dean ironworks provided the material for most of the weapons used by the English soldiery during the later Crusading centuries. Part of the open land within the forest is used for grazing the Foresters' sheep and feeding the pigs when the acorns fall. A few charcoal-burners still practise their craft.

The forest is bounded on the E. and S. by the Severn, on the W. by the Wye and on the N. by the Herefordshire border. **Newnham** on the A48 makes an excellent gateway into the forest. This is a very pleasant little town right on the banks of the Severn. It was from here that Henry II set sail for Ireland to consolidate and control the conquests of his vassal Strongbow, Earl of Pembroke. It has some good 18th- and 19th-cent. houses. The good view from the churchyard can be best appreciated on a fine day. NW. of Newnham is the village of **Littledean** on the edge of the forest. Besides having one of the most splendid views of the Severn valley, there are many traces of Roman road pavings leading to their well-worked mines; the best are to the E. of the village. It has an interesting 13th-cent. church with some earlier Norman pillars with shamrock carving.

To the W. of the main road going S. are **Upper** and **Lower Soudley** with the magnificent Soudley Valley between. Little roads and criss-cross paths make this ideal forest country for the walker, but it is a good idea to have a compass handy. The A48 continues S. towards **Blakeney**, another natural gateway to the forest. It rises steeply from the distant Severn shore ½ m. away, its hillside is wooded and many of the stone houses are colour-washed. Thomas Sternhold, who with John Hopkins wrote the first vernacular metrical version of the Psalms, was born in a Blakeney house called Hawfield in the 16th cent. A walk out to nearby **Gatcombe** can be rewarding for the dedicated fisherman. The main road now follows the original Roman route a short distance to the rather uninspiring little town of **Lydney**. The park known as Camp Hill has the remains of a Roman temple dedicated to a Celtic god called Nodens. Several other considerable finds have been made, including a hoard of Roman coins. The market cross is 14th-cent. A visit to the little dock may be a reminder that many Elizabethan ships were built of timber hewn in the nearby forest.

Hewelsfield is a high village between two stretches of forest and between the Severn and Wye. It is a good centre for walks northwards into the forest and another road dips dramatically westwards to the Wye and Tintern Abbey. In the 17th cent. members of the famous Throgmorton family were buried in the mostly Norman village church. The B4234 running directly N. from Lydney leads to the heart of the forest. The first village reached on this road is **Bream's Eaves** adjoining the lower village of **Bream**. Here can be seen the Roman scowles. The huge caverns are mysterious and masked in the depth of a wood. The colliery village has the usual colour-washed stone houses. Unclassified roads to the W. are signposted to **St Briavels**, an understandably favourite halting place for visitors to the forest. It stands high above a wooded valley which drops steeply down to the Wye. There are remains of a fortified stronghold covering more than an acre, built in the 13th cent. as protection against Welsh marauders. The gatehouse has two round towers still standing. The Norman church with 13th-cent. additions has been much restored.

Continuing northwards from Bream's Eaves, **Parkend**, a colliery village, is reached. The miners are independent and their workings unnationalized. The village has a good Gothic Revival church built in 1822. A forestry school has also been established here. The mysterious Cannop Ponds on the road N. are well worth stopping at for a short halt.

Coleford, a scattered miners' village, claims the title of capital of the Forest of Dean. Its 17th-cent. Market Hall was restored in the 19th cent. Its charter derives from Charles II, since the manor had sheltered Charles I after the Battle of Edgehill. The B4226 runs diagonally across the heart of the forest through **West Dean**, a mining village of red-stone houses in the depth of the oak forest. In an old inn called the Speech House, the Foresters' Court is held 10 times a year. The ancient rights and privileges of the forest are upheld in the galleried court room with its open hearth and court officer's rostrum. Some of the hollies in Speech House Wood are said to be over 300 years old. Walks in the area are particularly good. The road continues to the northeast edge of the forest at **Cinderford**; its mining connections are as obvious as its name suggests, but it is edged by superb oak woodlands. It is a useful departure point for **Mitcheldean**, the northernmost tip of the forest. It has an interesting parish church with a tapering spire and a good Market Hall. Easily reached from here is the orchard village of **Blaisdon**, famous for its plums. So, too, is **Brierley** and not far distant **English Bicknor**, high up above the Wye with panoramic views across the forest. It has all the reticent attractiveness of the forest towns and villages. Its Norman Church of St Mary has some interesting early 14th-cent stone figures.

FOWNHOPE, *Herefordshire* (8–SO5734), lies 7 m. SE. of HEREFORD on the B4224 on the banks of the Wye. It has black-and-white cottages and an imposing Transitional parish church with a tall Norman tower carrying a 14th-cent. broach spire. The remarkably good Norman tympanum has been shifted from its doorway to the interior of the west wall for the sake of preservation. The Virgin is seated, raising her hand in blessing. The hand of the Infant Jesus catches the rhythm of the gesture. The flowing design is continued in the rich foliage work which enfolds a lion with extended claws and a bird, perhaps an eagle symbolizing St John the Evangelist. Some good and interesting houses to see, within walking distance of the village, are the Jacobean Fownhope Court, the Georgian Nash Farmhouse, and Capler Farm which has a good barn. A short distance NW. is **Holme Lacy**, another Wye village as rich in beauty as in history. It has a little church set in meadowland about 1 m. from the village. Dedicated to St Cuthbert, it has a low roof and a six-bayed 14th-cent. arcade of great merit. The Scudamore monuments, particularly those of the 16th and 17th cents., are noteworthy for Classical elegance. This was the family which built the Palladian Holme Lacy House towards the end of the 1670s. The house still contains much beautiful carving, though some of the best is now in the Metropolitan Museum, New York. The house was much modernized in 1910 when a new ballroom and an impressive main staircase were added. This is the house where Alexander Pope is reputed to have written his eulogy to the "Man of Ross". The park has some fine trees and the little orangery is attractive. The house is now used as a mental hospital.

GLOUCESTER, *Gloucestershire* (4–SO8318). Gloucester began with Glevum, a Roman fort which guarded the lowest Severn crossing and the legions' routes into Wales; it became one of the four *coloniae* of Roman Britain. Anglo-Saxon Gleawcester was a royal *burh* or fortified town in Alfred the Great's time and had its own mint. The Norman and Angevin kings often made it their residence and it was here that William the Conqueror decided on the Domesday survey.

The city has long been an inland port. It has its own harbour master and now stretches for miles along waterways handling an ever-growing outflow from local engineering industries. Industrial and commercial developments have kept the bulldozers busy in Gloucester. Much has been demolished but the opportunity has been taken for archaeological excavation. This has revealed the site of a complete Roman forum, which must have covered about 2 acres. The site of the basilica or administrative building has been discovered as well as the flanking colonnades on the east and south sides. Fragments of an equestrian statue of an emperor have been collected and identified, and also the bronze tassels of his saddle and the plinth of the statue. The excavation has apparently confirmed the hypothesis that there were two Roman occupations. The principal finds are in the City Museum.

The city's main thoroughfares still follow the Roman roads and meet at the Cross. In Eastgate Street stands the Guildhall. Nearby in Brunswick Street is a memorial to Robert Raikes, who founded the Sunday school movement in St Catherine Street. New Inn in Northgate Street was a timbered 15th-cent. pilgrims' hostelry; the interior has been modernized but it preserves its courtyard with surrounding balconies. Another ancient inn, the Raven Tavern in Hare Lane, has been saved from demolition by private subscription. It was once the home of the Hoares, who sailed in the *Mayflower* to New England. At the bottom of Westgate Street is an old 16th-cent. gabled house built by Thomas Payne, a mayor of Gloucester, and nearby are the 15th-cent. St Bartholomew's Almshouses much Gothicized in the 18th cent. Also in Westgate Street is a 16th-cent. timber-framed house reputed to have sheltered Bishop John Hooper on that February night before he was burnt at the stake in 1555 in the reign of Mary Tudor. It now houses one of the best folk museums in the country with comprehensive collections of everything to do with early trades, crafts and industry as well as exhibits of historical interest. Among these is a whole gallery entirely devoted to the story of the Civil War siege of Gloucester in 1643. Another section has the Port Book records showing Gloucester's maritime importance from 1580 onwards. The medieval Church of St Mary de Crypt in Southgate Street has been much restored. It has a peal of eight bells cast by Rudhall, the famous Gloucester bell founder. Inside the church is the font where George Whitefield, the preacher, was baptised. He was born in the city and attended the St Mary de Crypt Grammar School next to the church.

The cathedral is still the chief glory of Gloucester. Its Norman plan and structure were preserved as the body of this magnificent church, to which the work of later periods was added. It therefore affords an illustration of architectural development which can hardly be bettered anywhere in Europe. The Norman pillars of the 174-ft-long nave up to the stone screen remain as they were during the first building period of 1089 to 1100. Here the merging of Norman into

Transitional style can be seen. The vaulting above the nave dates from 1242. The south transept has the earliest Benedictine essays in Perpendicular style, following hard on the splendid Decorated work. The choir was built for the abbey (it did not become a cathedral until the reign of Henry VIII) in 40 years of fervour between 1337 and 1377. Even this fine choir really only masks the original Norman one with the Norman crypt beneath it. The beautiful Lady Chapel was built nearly a century later. The east window has some glass whose colour is unrivalled even at YORK; many of the heraldic devices are those of families who fought at Crécy in 1346. It is 78 ft high and has over 2,700 sq. ft of traceried stone and glass. Its theme culminates gloriously in the Coronation of the Virgin amid a host of saints, apostles, popes and kings. The 225-ft pinnacled tower, with its open parapets and flying buttresses at the corners of the church, is built of beautiful Pains-wick stone and took nearly 100 years to achieve, being completed during the troubled times of the Wars of the Roses. The Great Peter weighing 3 tons is reputed to be the oldest medieval bell of this size in the country. The cloisters have the earliest and most exquisite fan vaulting achieved by the abbot's stonemasons between 1351 and 1412. It was the inspiration for the roof of Henry VII's Chapel in WESTMINSTER ABBEY and the equally superb fan vaulting of St George's Chapel, WINDSOR. The cloister still encloses the monastic garden with its 14th-cent. well in the centre. On the south side of the cloisters are the arched recesses of the scriptorium; at the other end is the vaulted lavatorium with the original washing basins on recesses for holding towels. The glass is mostly modern, though there are roundels with 16th-cent. glass from Prinknash, country home of the later abbots of Gloucester. The Chapter House has the original Norman barrel roof. The change to cathedral at the Dissolution fortunately caused little iconoclastic damage, though some of the monuments suffered defacement. One of the loveliest examples of medieval funerary art remained unscathed: it portrays Edward II, whose remains were brought here by the monks after his brutal murder and interred in 1337. The library is well worth a visit and has some priceless 10th-cent. manuscripts. Gloucester, with HEREFORD and WORCESTER Cathedrals, is one of the centres of the Three Choirs Festival – the oldest festival of its kind in Europe, founded in the first years of the 18th cent.

GOLDEN VALLEY, *Herefordshire* (8–SO 3537), extends from **Pontrilas** in a WNW. direc-tion to **Dorstone** and offers some of the most tranquil and beautiful scenery in this part of England. It is backed to the W. by an undulation of hills rising to the 2,300-ft ridges of the Black Mountains and to the E. by gentle hills extending from the 376-ft Forty Acre Pitch to Green Hill rising to the 824-ft summit that looks down on MOCCAS COURT. Down this valley flows the Dore from its source in the hills above Dorstone.

Pontrilas is a convenient point to start a tour of the Golden Valley, but has little to interest the visitor other than the 17th-cent. stone mansion Pontrilas Court, from which it is believed the village took its present name: its original name seems to have been Elwistone. The next village along the B4347, **Ewyas Harold** has a great deal of charm and an interesting history. Osborn Pentecost was one of the early "Trojan Horse" Normans who infiltrated the country in the reign of Edward the Confessor and built a castle, at the same time ruthlessly terrorizing the countryside. The castle was destroyed by Earl Harold, claimant to the Confessor's throne, in 1052. Between then and 1066 another Norman, William FitzOsborn, built and fitted out some 60 ships in Normandy for the Conqueror's invasion. He was rewarded in part by the lands and castle of Ewyas. After a short period as joint regent of England in the king's absence, he returned to Normandy and was killed at Cassel. His eldest son Harold inherited his castle and it is from him the village derives its name. Only the conical mound and earthworks remain. The view is entrancing across the Dulas Brook which flows round the much-restored Early English church with its squat 13th-cent. tower. On the north side, recessed into the interior chancel wall, is a curious 14th-cent. effigy of a woman clasping a heart casket. She wears an unusual headdress which shows she had taken a vow of chastity. From here the valley becomes rich and green, with scattered orchards as the road follows the river upstream. On the east side stands **Abbey Dore**. Cistercians founded the church in 1147 – six years before the death of St Bernard, who revolted against the architectural extravagances of Cluny and restored simplicity to all his subsequent churches. The rebuilding of Dore Abbey between 1175 and 1220 reflects the dynamics of this discipline. Later, when the house had become wealthy, a more splendid retro-choir was built which throws the simplicity of the earlier building into greater relief. The way the red sandstone of the fabric contrasts with the rich green surroundings makes the interesting proportions of this unusual church vividly apparent. However, the 17th-cent. tower set between choir and transept rather disturbs the rhythm of line. It must be remembered that though the monastery was destroyed at the Dissolution, it is thanks to the good offices of Lord Scudamore, who in 1633 called in the gifted John Abel, later known as the "King's Carpenter", to restore the abbey as a parish church, that one of the finest examples of Cistercian-inspired Early English architecture in the country has been preserved. The cathedral-like grandeur of the presbytery with its 13th-cent. ambulatory and the three-bayed choir, lit by a clerestory pierced by lancets, never fail to impress. The choir has its original stone altar of remarkable size, re-discovered many years ago in a local dairy. The 17th-cent. glass floods the interior with colour. John Abel carved the oak screen and surmounted it with three armorial bearings: those of the Stuarts, Viscount Scudamore and Archbishop

Laud. He also did the ceiling. Besides two mutilated and worn effigies, one in each of the choir aisles, there is an interesting collection of fragments of sculpture left behind after the Dissolution. The 13th-cent. tiles in the chancel with heraldic devices are interesting. Those around the font are undecorated but of the same period.

The timber-framed 14th-cent. Grange Farm just outside the village makes a worthwhile short walk from the abbey church. It has a porch with good plasterwork and a ceiling dated 1603.

Bacton is one of the prettiest villages in the valley and has a 13th-cent. church on a hill with a 16th-cent. battlemented tower. It possesses an ancient rood-beam and staircase which connected with the rood-loft. This must have been demolished after the Reformation. Its main treasure consists of some exquisite embroidery worked on an early altar frontal with large formalized flowers, beasts and birds, tiny insects and a boat with two passengers. It is popularly believed to have been the work of Elizabeth Parry, maid of honour to Queen Elizabeth I. Her alabaster monument showing her curtseying to her queen has a lengthy inscription ending with the line "wythe maeden quene a maede dyd ende my lyffe." It is worth leaving the B4348 that runs through the upper half of the valley to visit the little village of **Vowchurch**, where a bridge crosses the Dore by the 16th-cent. Old Vicarage. The church, rebuilt in the 14th cent. and with 15th-cent. additions, has a profusion of woodwork and carving in its roof, screen and communion rails. All this makes an interior of splendid richness which stands out well against the plaster and scraped walls of the nave and chancel. The church owns a most unusual wooden chalice carved from beechwood and dating from the first years of the 17th cent. Poston Lodge, an Adamesque shooting box somewhat spoiled by later Victorian additions, lies about 1 m. N. in wooded country, high enough up to give lovely views of the valley. Nearby is a prehistoric hill-fort later used by the Romans. At **Peterchurch** the valley opens out into meadowland and cornfields. A little to the E. of the not particularly attractive village is Wellbrook Manor. Stone built, with its original interior timber-framing and its solar wing preserved, it is one of the best examples of a 14th-cent. hall in the county. The stone chimney-piece and shaft have withstood 600 years of use. Another heritage from feudal days is Urishay Castle, 1½ m. SW., once a medieval fortress house later domesticated into a Jacobean manor and now a ruin. However, the chapel, which had long served as a barn and was later restored to its original use, is almost certainly a Norman building. The village church is Norman and has a notable double chancel. On the south side is a door with excellently preserved zigzag moulding. Of the three round-headed archways spanning the church, the centre one also has fine zigzag ornamentation. Not least of its features are the good modern hand-beaten ironwork fittings for the electric lighting of the church.

From Peterchurch the more interesting route runs W. of the river through the hamlets of Hinton and Fine Street. One m. before Dorstone are the remains of **Snodhill Castle**, high on a mound whose earthworks cover about 10 acres. It existed when the Domesday Book was compiled and was rebuilt in the reign of King Stephen. There are remains of round towers and considerable parts of the 14th-cent. bailey. It was of importance to the defence of the border and was at one time a fief of Warwick the Kingmaker. The 17th-cent. stone-built Snodhill Court lies just S. of the castle; a farm-house now, it has a fine hall with an oak ceiling and a good Jacobean oak staircase. The road into Dorstone passes the ruins on the castle tump standing nearly 30 ft above the surrounding fosse. In the 13th and 14th cents. it belonged to the Sollers family who gave their name to a village on the outskirts of HEREFORD called Bridge Sollers. Hills rise all round the village, the highest being the 1,045-ft Merbach Hill. Climb to the Arthur's Stone long barrow for good views down the valley. Dorstone was the last refuge of Richard de Brito, one of the four knights who slew Thomas à Becket. The church, which has some 13th-cent. features left intact, was almost entirely restored in 1889. It possesses a 13th-cent. pewter chalice and paten, discovered in a tomb built into the wall beneath a recess on the south side. The church bells are very ancient.

GOODRICH, *Herefordshire* (8–SO5719), lies between the A40 and **Kerne Bridge**, 5 m. SSW. of ROSS. It is dominated by the splendid ruins of Goodrich Castle built high on a spur above the Wye. The name derives from Godric's Castle and is mentioned as such in an early 12th-cent. document. The lands and castle were bestowed on William Marshall by King John in the early 13th cent. Marshall considerably enlarged the castle and added many amenities. It was approached by a vast barbican which led to a bridge supported by arches crossing the exceptionally deep moat cut into solid red rock. The gatehouse has an enormous semi-circular tower which housed a chapel. It is vaulted and had portcullises on both sides. The most ancient part of the castle is the grey stone keep, a typical four-square Norman tower, three stories high. The castle is rectangular with angle towers in each corner of the courtyard. The great hall in the west range was 65 ft long with its trefoil-headed windows in good repair. In the west wall, the fire-place still stands with its corbelled hood. Beyond the hall is the huge south-west tower which housed the buttery and pantry.

In the 14th cent. Goodrich Castle passed to the Talbots, and in the 17th cent. by marriage to the de Grey family. It was the last Herefordshire defence to hold out for Charles I, under the leadership of Sir Henry Lingen. It finally fell under the assault of a locally-made cannon called Roaring Meg, the walls being breached on the south side by Parliamentarians under the command of Colonel Birch. Roaring Meg has been preserved and stands on Castle Green by HEREFORD Cathedral. Some of the cannon-balls weighing 200 lb can be seen in the castle grounds.

Great Malvern: the Malvern Hills provide fine walking country close to the town

The Parish Church of St Giles with its unusual unbuttressed tower carrying a 14th-cent. broach spire is closely associated with the Swift family. Dean Swift's grandfather, Thomas, was vicar here and his tombstone is under the high altar. The vicarage was attacked several times by Parliamentarians as Thomas Swift was known for his Royalist sympathies. He was to give proof of these by swimming the moat of Raglan Castle and handing to the Governor the remains of his fortune in gold sewn into his waistcoat pocket. St Giles's still possesses the chalice which had been looted from him. Dean Swift recovered the silver vessel and gave it back to the church in 1726.

Wordsworth loved all the Wye valley and was a frequent visitor to Goodrich, where he met the little girl who was the inspiration of the poem, "We are Seven". About ½ m. away from the castle, Blore built a fantastic mock castellated house in 1828 called Goodrich Court. It so infuriated Wordsworth by what he called its "impertinence" that he wished it could be blown up. The house has recently been demolished and shipped stone by stone to the United States. An inn called Ye Old Hostelrie built in 1830 has, however, survived. With all its pinnacles and Gothic windows it may well be true that it was copied from an ancient illumination. About ½ m. NE. of Goodrich is **Flanesford Priory**, the mellow ruin of an Augustinian priory built in 1346 and well worth the short walk. Some of the 14th-cent. windows remain in a barn belonging to the farm now built on the site.

GREAT BADMINTON, *Gloucestershire* (4–ST8082), 5 m. E. of CHIPPING SODBURY, owes its tidy stone cottages, its church and most of its living to the 52,000-acre estate of the Dukes of Beaufort. Badminton House was originally built for the 1st Duke of Beaufort in 1682. The present magnificent façade, seen in dramatic perspective

at the end of a 3-m. avenue of beech trees, was the result of a remodelling of the house undertaken by William Kent about 1740 for the 3rd Duke. Kent was also responsible for the superb Worcester Lodge which provides a grand approach. His whole Palladian concept was achieved with absolute integrity. He surrounded the spacious grounds with a wooded belt extending for 12 m. He preserved much of the early lay-out of the grounds, but his was an age of inventive variety and any possibility of monotony was broken by additional lodges and castellated follies, of which the keeper's lodge is perhaps most typical. Here is a small square "castle", with round tower and turreted stairway with window slits. These whimsical structures set off the natural grandeur of the deer park and the ancient oaks and elms. The house contains a wealth of Grinling Gibbons carving and is filled with priceless paintings, *objets d'art* and worthy ducal furnishings. It is open to the public for most of the summer months. The church, built in 1783 and reached through a rose arbour, within the precincts of the garden, is very much a mausoleum for the Beaufort family. It contains many fine tombs, notably that of Henry Somerset, the 1st Duke, his effigy robed in his Garter mantle. It was brought from the Beaufort chapel in WINDSOR. There are several Rysbrack monuments of interest and some impressive Italian paintings.

The present renown of Badminton derives from the most important annual equestrian event in the kingdom, the Three Day Horse Trials, usually attended by the Queen. The kennels of the famous Beaufort hounds can also be visited at certain times.

On the far edge of the park is the hamlet of **Little Badminton** with its Early English church, roofed with ancient Cotswold tiles, set in a peaceful meadow. Its turreted dovecot is very old, and local lore says it has as many nesting holes as days of the year. The cottages probably antedate the great mansion by at least two centuries. Out on the BATH road is an old inn, the Beaufort Arms, which readers of Jane Austen will remember from a description in her novel *Northanger Abbey*.

GREAT MALVERN, *Worcestershire* (8–SO 7845). Set in the 9 m. range of the Malvern Hills, Great Malvern has a Continental flavour, partly because of the way it is terraced on its hillside site. Its history as a settlement probably begins in the 11th cent. with the foundation of the Benedictine priory. Its modern history possibly owes its beginnings to a treatise by Dr Wall published in 1756 extolling the medicinal virtues of the waters of the **Malvern Wells**, which had in fact been discovered 100 years earlier. Within 30 years of Dr Wall's death, a pump room, baths, and residential terraces of houses and hotels were built on ground above the priory. One of these early hotels, the Foley Arms, has survived with its splendid cast-iron verandas intact and much of its original furnishings. From the time of Princess Victoria's visit here eight years before she became Queen to Princess Mary of Teck's visit with members of the German court in 1891, the town expanded continually. Malvern College for boys was founded in 1862 and Gothic Revival churches sprang up everywhere. Malvern could compete with BATH, BUXTON and CHELTENHAM and like them attracted the same element of retired colonial administrators and army officers. Few spas can match the beauty of its surroundings. Today, the spa no longer exerts its importance as such. It has become much more a popular resort and even a dormitory town for WORCESTER and BIRMINGHAM.

The Norman Priory Church of SS. Mary and Michael is still Malvern's most dominant feature and its most cherished possession. Built less than 20 years after the Conquest, it became almost immediately a dependency of WESTMINSTER ABBEY. Originally a great cruciform building with a central tower, considerable additions were made in the 13th and 14th cents. including a Lady Chapel in Decorated style which was destroyed after the Dissolution. It was mainly in the 15th cent. that a tremendous reconstruction of the Norman church was undertaken. The piers and arches of the early building were enclosed in the new style of architecture then prevailing. A lofty clerestory and roof were added filled with jewelled lights. A new tower rose on the foundations of the old. Its massive lines were decorated in the same manner as the tower of GLOUCESTER Cathedral, which it resembles. It seems likely that the same masons worked on both. Everything E. of the tower was rebuilt at the same time. The famous tiles were all handmade in the monastery, mostly between 1453 and 1456. About 1,000 were used in the decoration of the church, and over 100 different designs. Some can be seen in the outer wall of the apse. Occasionally it took four tiles to complete a small design. At the time of the reconstruction 40 vast windows were filled with stained glass, in colour and design rivalling even that at YORK Minster. The east window is filled with jewelled fragments, some almost pictorially complete. The later clerestory glass should be seen from the aisles of the choir. During the First World War, all the medieval glass was removed and stored in a place of safety. The releading and restoration after the war left the glass probably in better condition than it had been over two centuries. The other remarkable furnishings which have survived the years since the Dissolution are the two rows of original dark oak monastic choir stalls with finely carved misericords. They date mostly from the 15th cent., though some may be earlier. The carvings portray the seasons with vividness and often humour. St Anne's Chapel in the south choir aisle, much restored, has a stairway to the tower and belfry which has a bell dating from the 14th cent. Two of the early priors are buried here. In 1860 the whole church underwent a restoration by Sir Gilbert Scott. Thirty-four years later the north-west porch was rebuilt and a year after this the tower was repaired and strengthened. Of the monastery, only the gatehouse survives.

The town owns Priory Park with its fine trees and abundant flowers and, in keeping with Malvern's importance as an inland resort, an open-air heated swimming-pool. The fish pond, with huge golden carp, is the same pool used by the Benedictines more than 400 years ago. There is good walking to be had on the hills behind the town; the ascent of the **Worcestershire Beacon**, where William Langland is supposed to have composed *Piers Plowman*, is recommended.

Little Malvern, the smallest of the Malverns, has a wooded setting against a rising hill and St Giles's, a gem of a church which is all that remains of another great priory, founded in 1171. The tower and chancel survive from this period. Bishop Alcock of Worcester rebuilt the rest in the late 15th cent. He inserted a fine west window, now fragmented, that portrays Edward IV and Elizabeth Woodville, his queen. There is a 14th-cent. altar tomb with four figures carved in the panels. The floor has encaustic tiles from the priory kiln at Great Malvern. Almost adjoining is Little Malvern Court which incorporates part of the priory buildings. It is mostly 15th-cent., but the round tower is probably part of the original 12th-cent. edifice. It has been in the possession of the Roman Catholic Berrington family since the 17th cent. and can claim that through all the religious struggles the Mass has been said here during the last 800 years. Through a window in the roof can still be seen the priests' hiding hole used in the days of persecution. One treasured possession is a travelling trunk and a quilt owned by Catherine of Aragon. Two m. NE. is the moated **Madresfield Court**, owned by the Earls of Beauchamp since 1260. It is set in a magnificent park, with a mile-long avenue of trees making a majestic approach. Five m. SE., in fine pasture-land sheltered by the Malverns, is a timbered grange called **Birtsmorton Court**. It is still completely encircled by a watered moat. One of the bridges leads to a 14th-cent. embattled stone gateway with two round bastions. Four wings surround the courtyard built between the 13th and 20th cents. The earliest south wing contains the great hall. Here is a secret hiding place where Sir John Oldcastle, the Lollard leader, sheltered after his first escape from the TOWER OF LONDON. Here, too, during the Wars of the Roses, Queen Margaret of Anjou fled with her son Edward, Prince of Wales. The chamber in which they hid is still there. Thomas Wolsey, who was to become cardinal under Henry VIII, was once a simple house chaplain to Sir Richard Nanfan, who probably introduced him to the Court. The Queen Anne plaster ceiling in the great hall is most handsome and the earlier Elizabethan panelling is perfectly preserved. Originally built by the Birt family, it was bought back by one of their descendants in this century but has now passed out of the family again. It is open to the public at advertised times, particularly in the summer season; it can be reached most easily from the A438, midway between TEWKESBURY and LEDBURY. The little 14th-cent. church has a good marble tomb of Sir Richard Nanfan, who died in 1504.

GREAT MILTON, *Oxfordshire* (5–SP6302), lies just off the A40, 4 m. W. of Tetsworth, beyond flat cornfields in a wooded hollow. A largish stone-built village, it is renowned for the fine tomb with relief carving of Sir Ambrose Dormer who fought at Calais in 1347 and is buried in the church. The entrance to the Early English church is opposite the Red Lion Inn. The 14th-cent. tracery and windows are outstanding. The four-poster Dormer tombs of Sir Michael Dormer, who died in 1618, has rich allegorical sculpting, depicting Youth, Age and Immortality. Nothing remains of the original Dormer mansion other than a fine Renaissance gateway, set into a wall near the church, which frames a charming timbered country house. **Little Milton** nearby is the more beautiful village, with weathered and thatched stone cottages and a Manor House.

GREAT WITLEY, *Worcestershire* (8–SO75 66), lies 5 m. SW. of STOURPORT at the junction of the A451 and the A433. Woodbury Hill rises to the S. At this main junction is a pleasant red-brick Georgian inn called the Hundred House. From the road on the hillside the Classical lines of the Parish Church of St Michael with its burnished dome can be seen through the trees of the parkland of the once great estate of the Foley family. Witley Court at the bottom of the hill was practically burnt to the ground in 1937. It was originally built by the 1st Lord Foley in the early part of the 18th cent. and sold to the Earl of Dudley in 1838 to house Queen Adelaide in suitable state. It is, however, the church built by Lady Foley in 1735 which excites most interest and admiration. It was considerably embellished by the Earl of Dudley and presents a riot of colour and plasterwork in its interior. The superb ceiling and painted windows were brought from

the Duke of Chandos' demolished palace in Canons, Middlesex. They were re-erected in 1747. The white and gold plasterwork and scrolls by Pergotti show to great advantage the magnificent ceiling paintings by Laguerre from the original designs of Verrio. The elegant organ casing above the balustraded organ-loft once housed the instrument on which Handel played and composed at Canons. Even the 19th-cent. Gothic woodwork and carving fits into this glorious display of 18th-cent. elegance. The south transept is dominated by the massive monument of figures, draperies and Grecian urn set against a pyramidic background, which Rysbrack carved to the memory of the 1st Lord Foley. The motorist should not be deterred by the bad state of repair of the private yew-lined road leading to the church, for its rococo work can hardly be matched in England. It is sad that the magnificent Italian gardens are now overgrown and the fountains which jetted more than 90 ft into the air no longer play.

Little Witley to the SE. of the park has a Gothic chapel built very much as a labour of love in 1867 by A. E. Perkins at the inspiration of the rector, the Rev. C. Sale and his wife, who were both accomplished carvers. While the rector built the chancel of his church, Mrs Sale carved both the pulpit and font. To the N. of Great Witley rise the Abberley Hills with views across into Herefordshire. On the northern side of the hills is the village of **Abberley** with an attractive old country church which is partly in ruins and a somewhat grand Victorian church just outside the village, built in the mid-19th cent. in late 13th-cent. style. The rectory is pre-Reformation and mostly ruined, though its solar still has its timber-framing intact and the roof over the original hall. The mid-19th-cent. Abberley Hall, just outside the village, came into the Jones family from the Moilliets, who employed Dawkes to build the house in an Italianate style. It is now a school. Joseph Jones's son John built a fantastic Gothic clock tower in 1883 between the Abberley and Woodbury Hills to the memory of his father and, according to gossip, to impress his noble neighbour at Witley Court. It is very high and visible for miles around. Its 20 bells are so tuned that 42 different melodies can be rung out over the countryside. It was soon known as Jones's Folly.

GUY'S CLIFFE, *Warwickshire* (9–SP2866). Just outside WARWICK, on the main Warwick–KENILWORTH road, is a place of history and legend by the River Avon. Tall cliffs, caves, a ruined house, great cedars, oaks and fir trees all tend to give the legend the greater prominence. It is said that here in the 10th cent. Earl Guy, having slain the Danish giant Colbrand, strangled a wild boar and killed dragons, retired to live the life of a hermit in the cave that bears his name. There are many caves cut into the great cliff where later hermits sought shelter and escape from the world, and in due course it became a place of pilgrimage. Between 1422 and 1423 Richard Beauchamp rebuilt the chapel and endowed a chantry. One of the first of these chantry priests was the renowned antiquary John Rous who compiled the famous Rous Roll, chronicling the lives and events of the Earls of Warwick from the time of Guy to the holder of the title in his day. This can be seen in the BRITISH MUSEUM. Beside the cave in 1751 a beautiful Palladian house was built by Samuel Greatheed and much added to in 1818 by his son. An earlier Elizabethan mansion had stood on the site. That so splendid a house should in this century have been allowed to fall into ruin is a sad commentary on the age. The actress Sarah Siddons was once a ladies' maid in the house.

The chapel is cut into the rock and has an interesting doorway and good fan vaulting. On the right of the chapel is the 8-ft statue of Guy carved out of the rock some time in the late 14th cent.

Down at river level is the old Saxon Mill. A building with great charm, it belies its claim to a greater antiquity than the record which states that a mill, probably on this site, was given in the 12th cent. to Gilbert of Warwick and became the property of Kenilworth Priory. The present building with its 100-ft timbered balcony is now a restaurant and dates principally from 1822. An earlier part, however, is 17th-cent. It was much painted by David Cox and greatly admired by Ruskin.

HAGLEY HALL, *Worcestershire* (8–SO9181). This is one of the stateliest houses in the county, at the foot of the CLENT HILLS. The entrance to the park lies a little outside the village of Hagley, 2 m. S. of STOURBRIDGE. The great Palladian mansion was built by the 1st Lord Lyttelton between 1754 and 1760. The Lyttelton family still owns it. Sanderson Miller, who designed the building, built on the site of a much earlier Lyttelton home. Its rich brown stone contrasts well with the raised lawns with their low stone walls. Pedimented in pure Classical style, its roof balustrades run the length of the four square-towered wings in the tradition of Inigo Jones. A bad fire in the 1920s damaged part of the interior; it was skilfully restored. The entrance hall has charming stucco decoration. The dining-room has a magnificent rococo ceiling; this, too, was damaged but restored. The fine gallery also has a rococo ceiling and is rich in tapestries and pictures. The park is imaginatively landscaped with an Ionic temple, a rotunda, now rather weathered, and a folly in the form of a Gothic ruin. The house has entertained many great poets, architects, scientists and politicians; Gladstone was one of them. Hagley Hall has a fine collection of Chippendale furniture. It is open to the public in the summer season.

One m. NE. is Wychbury Hill Camp, a prehistoric fortification with splendid views over the Stour Valley.

HALESOWEN, *Worcestershire* (8–SO9683), lies 4½ m. E. of STOURBRIDGE and 9 m. from BIRMINGHAM. It is an industrial town: its products include electrical apparatus, agricultural implements and weldless tubing. It is undergoing a considerable rebuilding and modernization. The early 13th-cent. remains of its Premonstratensian abbey, founded in 1218, are incorporated into the 19th-cent. Manor Farm to the S. of Manor Lane. The long wall surrounding the farm-house originally enclosed the cloister garth and has a 13th-cent. coffin lid carved in relief with a Calvary. In a recess barely a foot and a half high is a 14th-cent. effigy of a knight with crossed legs, holding the hilt of his sword. The large and impressive Norman Church of St John the Baptist is masked by later Perpendicular work and has an outer aisle built in the 1880s. The 15th-cent. tower rises with its spire and three tiers of gabled lights from the centre of the nave, rather more to the west than the original Norman tower which collapsed. It rests on arches with huge piers, one of which contains a stairway. William Shenstone the poet is buried in the churchyard and has a monument dated 1763 in the north aisle of the church. The Leasowes was the home of the poet. He spent long years here and much money on beautifying the house. It is now pebble-dashed and serves as the club house of a golf course, where part of the old landscaping remains.

HALFORD, *Warwickshire* (9–SP2545), is set in wooded country 7 m. SE. of STRATFORD-UPON-AVON on the Roman Fosse Way. The name of the village is pronounced Hah-ford. Below the new bridge crossing the River Stour is a much older bridge considerably damaged in the Civil War. There are views of the weir and the old mill from here. The small Church of St Mary possesses what is perhaps one of the best preserved pieces of Romanesque sculpture in England in its Norman tympanum over the north door. A seated angel holds aloft a scroll; the wings are spread and delicate drapery flows over the protruded knees. Inside is a good Norman chancel arch with carved capitals in the restrained Transitional associated with early French Cistercian influence. A Norman niche was discovered high above the arch in 1960 with a much defaced seated figure, probably that of the Virgin Mary. Another empty niche on the opposite side seems likely to have held a statue of St John. A plain Norman doorway is set into the south wall. The rest of the church, other than its 13th-cent. tower, was badly restored towards the end of the 19th cent. The octagonal 16th-cent. font has a carved oak crocketed cover with five mitred heads upon it. The curious fire-hooks to be seen to one side were kept to draw off burning thatch from the nearby cottages. Outside the west end is a gargoyle in the form of a monkey, its arms clutched round its head. Just N. of the church is the Old Manor House with ancient woodwork and 16th-cent. Cotswold stone. It is well restored and blends perfectly with its setting.

HAMPTON-IN-ARDEN, *Warwickshire* (9–SP2081). An attractive village with steep streets and several 15th-, 16th- and 17th-cent. houses, many of the earlier ones with overhangs, stands in what remains of the Forest of Arden. This is said to have been Shakespeare's setting for his *As You Like It*, although claims have also been made for the Belgian Ardennes. The most interesting feature of all is Moat House, built in the 16th cent. It stands W. of the church. The uncommonly good 15th-cent. timbers are in perfect condition. The best can be seen at the rear of the house. The Church of SS. Mary and Bartholomew suffered somewhat from late 19th-cent. restoration, but it has a late Norman nave. In the south wall is a recess with a curious 13th-cent. column. The blue and white Calvary tiles are extremely rare and probably date back to the time of the Wars of the Roses.

About 1 m. SE. of the church flows the River Blythe, and near Bradnocks Marsh is one of the few packhorse bridges left in the county. This is 15th-cent. work. Five stone arches support the narrow parapet-less bridge. On one of its piers is the base of its original wayside cross.

HANBURY, *Worcestershire* (8–SO9663), is a long scattered village 2½ m. E. of DROITWICH. From its hill-top church, the landscape rises and falls with wooded hills stretching away to the Malvern Hills and Bredon Hill. The Church of St Mary's has a late 18th-cent. exterior and west tower. The piers of the nave are late Norman. The chancel was rebuilt by Street in 1860. It has some splendid monuments to the powerful Vernon family. Hanbury has three impressive country houses. **Hanbury Hall**, set in 13 acres of parkland, was built for Thomas Vernon in 1701. Red-brick and in the style of Wren, it has suffered little change with the passing of time. The staircase and hall were painted by Sir James Thornhill, illustrating the story of Achilles, in 1710. The Long Room had remarkably good plaster decoration. There is a distinctive Queen Anne orangery in the gardens. Acquired by the National Trust, it is open to the public. Some 1½ m. S. of the village is **Mere Hall**, the home of the Bearcroft family since the 14th cent. and one of the largest timbered houses in the county. It has an unusual ball-topped lantern above its four recessed gables and the windows in the supporting wings of the house are filled with delightful Gothic glazing bars making a pleasant curved contrast to the vertical, horizontal and diagonal beams. The Georgian forecourt has two pretty Queen Anne gazebos built of brick. Most of the present house dates from 1560; the date 1337 on a bracket refers to the earlier structure. Also nearby is the late 16th-cent. twin-gabled timber-framed Broughton Court, once the dower house to Mere Hall.

HENLEY-IN-ARDEN, *Warwickshire* (9–SP 1465), is a delightful old market town consisting of a High Street almost 1 m. long with nearly every type of English domestic architecture. It is situated where the WARWICK–Redditch road crosses the A34 9 m. NW. of STRATFORD-UPON-AVON. Once a stronghold of Plantagenet power, Henley belonged to the influential de Montfort family and after the death, at the Battle of EVESHAM, of Simon de Montfort it was pillaged

and burnt to the ground. Having risen from its ashes, it obtained a charter from Henry VI in 1449 and still has its High Bailiff elected annually by the Court Leet. Its 15th-cent. Guildhall was built by Sir Ralph Boteler. Henley has many ancient inns, among them the White Swan dating from the early 1600s. The most interesting buildings are on the north side of the main street, notably the Old George and the Blue Bell Inn, part of which is 15th-cent. The White House, now a restaurant, is a good example of a 16th-cent. dwelling.

Where the wide High Street narrows, rises the tower of the Church of St John the Baptist. It is purely 15th-cent. The roof has fine stone corbels, tie-beams and unusual queen-posts.

Just outside of Henley-in-Arden in **Beaudesert** is a good example of a Warwickshire Norman church built in the 11th cent. A little to the N. of the church lie earthworks protected by a deep entrenchment. The Mount, as it is called, is all that remains of the castle of the de Montforts.

HENLEY-ON-THAMES, *Oxfordshire* (5–SU7682), is a picturesque Thamesside town separated from the neighbouring county of Buckinghamshire by an elegant bridge spanning a wide stretch of the river. The bridge was designed by Salopian William Hayward in 1786 and he was aided by a remarkable woman sculptor, Anne Damer; she was a cousin of Horace Walpole and her friendship with the Emperor Napoleon caused much gossip. The bridge is decorated with keystone masks of Father Thames and the goddess Isis. The town, approached from OXFORD by the famous Fair Mile, has a great variety of buildings to offer the sightseer. The red-brick Red Lion Inn on the banks of the river, the Catherine Wheel in Regency white stucco and at least 20 other old inns indicate a town hospitable to visitors. It was at the Red Lion that Shenstone scratched a well-known quatrain on a pane of glass in the mid-18th cent.:

Whoe'er has travelled life's dull round
Where'er his stages may have been,
May sigh to think he still has found
The warmest welcome at an inn.

Among the many interesting houses is that of William Lenthall, who was Speaker of the House of Commons during the Long Parliament. The Victorian Town Hall tends to obstruct the pleasant vista of Market Street. In New Street are some bow-windowed houses, among them the Henley Brewery Office, a reminder of the days when Henley boasted a number of "gentlemen brewers". Chantrey House is a good timber-framed house with an overhang, built by a zealous priest in 1420 as a school for poor boys. It is now the Church House. In 1805 the people of Henley, who were very theatre conscious, built their own Kenton Theatre, with a charming curved gallery. Its round leaded windows still look out on to the street below. The flint- and chequer-work parish church, with its tall Perpendicular tower serving as a landmark, has some 14th-cent. features but is

Henley-on-Thames is linked to Buckinghamshire by an elegant 18th-cent. bridge

mostly 15th-cent. with later additions. It is rich in monuments to wealthy benefactors to the town. In the churchyard is the tomb of Richard Jennings, master builder of ST PAUL'S under Christopher Wren.

The Henley Regatta has brought more fame to the town than any other of its many activities. The first inter-university boat race was held here in 1829, and by 1839 it had become a recognized event and its reputation established by splendid prizes offered by patrons. Not least was the patronage afforded by the Prince Consort who bestowed the title of Royal Henley Regatta. By late Victorian and Edwardian days it had become one of the highlights of the English Season, with fashionable and pretty girls vying for attention with the athletic prowess on the river. It is held at the beginning of July and lasts for four days, usually ending with a splendid fireworks display on the Saturday.

Stonor Park is a beautiful old manor house of splendid proportions which lies 5 m. N. of Henley on the B480. It is open to the public for a considerable part of the year. Set in richly timbered parkland beneath a wood-crested hill, its mellow Tudor brickwork is unimpaired by time and weather. The Stonors have worshipped in the private chapel of the house for over 600 years. The original medieval buildings were made into one house in Tudor times, and the library and Great Hall date from this period. In 1760 a new roof and additional windows were incorporated, giving Stonor Park the appearance it has today.

In the Elizabethan religious unrest Edmund Campion was a constant visitor and had a secret printing press in a concealed room. The park is one of the most beautiful in southern England with paths winding under the shade of spreading nut trees. It is worth asking the way to the little hamlet of Maidensgrove and going on foot, since directions are too complicated to write down.

HEREFORD, *Herefordshire* (8–SO5040), is situated on a level plain bounded in the distance by low-lying hills. The southern area of the town is edged by the River Wye which flows under a medieval bridge, to the W. of which is a modern span of concrete and steel carrying the new ring road over the river from its route along the line of the medieval city wall. Hereford is a cathedral city, albeit of modest size, and also an important agricultural centre. It has a bustling cattle market where farmers from either side of the border mingle. Hereford's history is closely bound up with Wales. Great changes are taking place in the city at present, with much modern development.

The Cathedral Church dedicated in honour of SS. Mary and Ethelbert is likely to be the first monument to arouse the visitor's interest as he comes down Broad Street. That there was an ancient Celtic bishopric here before the arrival of St Augustine in England seems very likely. The cathedral owes its foundation to King Offa of Mercia, who built the famous dyke that runs 6 m. to the W. of the city and defined and defended English territory. Offa was responsible for the beheading of Ethelbert, King of East Anglia. In expiation he built a costly shrine to receive the body of the martyred king. In 825 a new stone church was built over the shrine and in 1030 this was replaced by a still larger church which was destroyed by Welsh marauders in 1056. The cathedral was probably begun by the Norman Bishop Robert Losinga in 1079, although documentary evidence credits Bishop Reynelm with founding the present church.

Besides the massive red sandstone tower built between 1300 and 1310 (the pinnacles were only added in the last century), the cathedral is notable for the superb Norman work which has survived in the great pillars of the nave arcade. What is seen today, however, is only a part of what the Norman builders achieved. In 1786 their lofty west tower collapsed and destroyed two bays of the nave and the greater part of the original triforium and clerestory. The efforts of famous architects throughout the last 200 years to try to restore the balance of the building have not always been successful. To the rest of the varied architecture, every age has added something of value. The beautiful Lady Chapel is Early English in style. It possesses some of the oldest

Hereford: a distant view of the cathedral across the River Wye

stained glass in the cathedral. To the south is a screen dividing it from Bishop Audley's magnificent two-storied chantry, with its stair-turret. The three original chantry chapel doors are particularly fine. The north transept is perhaps the most rewarding part of the cathedral. It was planned by Bishop Aquablanca in the reign of Henry III. He was the friend of Peter of Savoy who built the palace of that name in London. The bishop is buried here in a tomb which is a worthy tribute to his sensitivity and taste. The work is Early English at its purest, with tall slender windows rising to the full height of the transept. It was probably built about the mid-13th cent. as Aquablanca died in 1268. The work was completed by St Thomas Cantilupe who died in 1282 and was canonized in 1320. The rich pedestal of his shrine is still here, arcaded with Purbeck shafts and guarded by 15 carved effigies of Knights Templar, of whose order Bishop Cantilupe was Grand Master. In the south transept is a fine German 16th-cent. triptych of the Adoration of the Magi. Most unusual here is the ancient fire-place; one of only two of its kind to survive in England. Another rare treasure is the ancient Mappa Mundi; a map of a flat world, drawn and painted by a prebendary of Hereford, Richard of Haldingham, probably at LINCOLN in 1275. Measuring 65 in. by 53 in. it includes considerable, if curious detail. Jerusalem is shown as the centre of the world and England and Ireland on the very outside edge. Above the east aisle is the biggest chained library in the world. It consists of some 1,500 books, both printed and handwritten. Its most ancient treasure is a 7th-cent. commentary on the Gospel of St Matthew; the early centuries are spanned by a most unusual collection. Seventy printed books date from before 1500, including two by Caxton.

Much of the exterior of Hereford Cathedral has suffered from the ravages of time, battle and restorers. In the mid-19th cent. there was a general restoration by Sir G. Gilbert Scott whose work generally replaced the rebuilding undertaken by James Wyatt after the disaster of 1786. Wyatt's west front was rebuilt to Oldrid Scott's plans between 1904 and 1908.

The Bishop's Palace stands on the south side of the cathedral overlooking the river. It presents a fine Georgian façade which conceals a Norman hall with wooden columns and arcades. It was well restored in 1954. The Vicars College can be reached through a door in the south-east transept. It is connected to the cathedral by an oak-roofed gallery dating from the 15th cent.

Hereford Cathedral shares the Three Choirs Festival with WORCESTER and GLOUCESTER and this major musical event is held here every third year.

Hardly less important in Hereford's history is the 14th-cent. Church of All Saints. Most of the present church was built in the early 14th cent. and by the beginning of the 16th cent. it was more or less as it is seen today. An earlier church had close connections with Vienne, near Lyons. It was a *Commanderie* hospice of the Order of St Anthony the Hermit which was absorbed into the Order of St John of Jerusalem during the Crusades. In the south chapel is yet another chained library of considerable importance. It possesses a copy of a book on the seven Deadly Sins by an Englishman, Alexander Carpenter, but printed in Paris by Pierre Levet in 1497. The choir stalls are 14th-cent. and have misericords that include two mermaids, two mice and two bears. David Garrick was baptized here in 1717.

In the centre of the town stands an attractive timber-framed house which was built in 1621 and is known as the Old House. It houses an excellent collection of 17th-cent. furniture. Down a narrow passage near the Old House is the ancient Booth Hall, now a hotel. Its main restaurant is in the 14th-cent. panelled and timber-roofed hall on the first floor. It seems likely that this was the original Merchants' Guild Hall. The City Museum and Art Gallery in Broad Street, apart from contemporary watercolours, has a fine collection of Roman remains, including two tessellated pavements dug up from the nearby garrison centre of Kenchester (Magnis). The nearby Green Dragon Hotel has on its first floor a Jacobean room with some lovely plasterwork and a wooden frieze of dolphins. On the other side of the road what is now the City Arms Hotel was once the 18th-cent. residence of the Dukes of Norfolk.

In Gwynne Street, earlier known as Pipe Lane, down towards the river, is a tablet recording the site of the house where Nell Gwynn was born. Charles II made her son Duke of St Albans and his son became Bishop of Hereford. N. of the junction of High Street and High Town is Widemarsh Street, at the end of which stands the Coningsby Hospital founded in 1614. It retains parts of the 13th- and 14th-cent. Templar house of the Knights of St John. Just behind is the only surviving friars' preaching cross in England, a reminder that adjoining was a "Blackfriars" built in 1322 in spite of the opposition of the cathedral chapter to the coming of the Dominicans. One of the most pleasant places to stroll is Castle Green with its almost 30-ft-high ramparts, once the bailey of the castle. The Castle Pool Hotel stands approximately where the moat was. The Nelson Column on the Green reminds the visitor that Lord Nelson was a freeman of the City of Hereford.

A major contribution to modern Hereford's prosperity is its cider industry and it claims the world's biggest cider-making plant. The special bitter-sweet varieties of cider apples are grown all over the county and gathered towards the end of the autumn season. They are then delivered to the Hereford factory where the process of fermenting, filtering and blending can be viewed on a guided tour of the factory. Some 2½ m. SE. of the city is Dinedor Hill with splendid views across the FOREST OF DEAN. Its summit, sheltered by beeches, is said to have been the camp of the Roman general Ostorius Scapula when attacking the forces of Caractacus.

Much Dewchurch, 6 m. SSW. of the city on the B4348 linking the A465 and A49, is a charming old village with a timbered inn. The church, which has a Norman chancel arch, contains memorials to the Pye family who defended KILPECK Castle during the Civil War. **Lugwardine** is another typical little Herefordshire village just 2 m. E. of Hereford on the A438. The ending -wardine is also typical of the county. In Anglo-Saxon days it referred to an enclosed farmstead, like the names ending in -worth, of which it is a variant. Just above the banks of the River Lugg, which is crossed by two ancient bridges, one of them 14th-cent. or older, it has the usual trim black-and-white cottages far removed from the rather drab newer building at the other end of the village. The red-sandstone church appears to have had Norman origins though the tower is good 14th-cent. Its 17th-cent. monuments and brasses are interesting. There are two good country houses in the area. Longworth House about 1¼ m. to the SE. was built in 1788 by Anthony Keck. Almost opposite is New Court, an interesting Georgian house, much Gothicized with castellations and turrets at the beginning of the 19th cent. Its Georgian integrity is preserved inside where there is a fine rococo plaster ceiling completed in the early 1750s.

HOARWITHY, *Herefordshire* (8–SO5429), is a pleasant village about 6 m. NW. of ROSS,

crossed by a loop in the Wye, where the salmon fishing (privately owned) is particularly good. It can be reached by an unclassified road turning off the A49 about halfway between ROSS and HEREFORD. It possesses an extraordinary Italianate church, built in the 19th cent. complete with a good campanile. William Poole, a prebendary of Hereford and vicar here for nearly 50 years, spent a fortune on building and embellishing the church. A large team of Italian workmen was brought over to work with local craftsmen and a number settled in Herefordshire. The chancel is enriched with marbles brought from Ireland and the Continent, and the choir dome is supported by columns of pink-grey marble from Devon. Everywhere the glitter of gold mosaic and the lavish use of lapis lazuli catch the eye. Mosaic pavements and cosmati work such as may be seen in early Roman basilicas complete the Italian effect.

Little lanes lead through a countryside of great charm to **Kings Caple**, past the Aramstone estate where unhappily the 18th-cent. red-brick mansion has been torn down, though left with fine outhouses and stables. The village has a red-sandstone church with a good 14th-cent. tower and spire. It contains interesting monuments to the Scottish Ferguson family, who were connected by marriage with many of the neighbouring county families. Also a short drive away through unspoilt country is the little village of **Fawley** with its tiny Norman church and Fawley Court, a splendid timber-framed farm-house that stands by a pond and has beautiful black-and-white barns. The staircase with turned balusters points to a prosperous 18th-cent. period, as does much of the unimpaired panelling in the house.

HONINGTON, *Warwickshire* (9–SP2642), just off the A34 N. of SHIPSTON-ON-STOUR, is an agreeable parkland village set round a green with its main street tucked discreetly away. It seems to have come into being because a London merchant Sir Henry Parker built Honington Hall in 1682 as an expression of his prosperity. The Church of All Saints has only a 15th-cent. tower to justify its claim to antiquity; the rest of the building is purely late 17th-cent. Classical with some excellent English rococo work. The Stour flows close by and is crossed by a five-arched bridge with 22 stone balls on the parapet. Just by the gate piers stands a timber-framed building known as Magpie House, well worth the short walk to see it.

KELMSCOTT, *Oxfordshire* (5–SU2499), is a place of pilgrimage for devotees of the Pre-Raphaelite movement, founded by William Morris (who is buried with his wife in the churchyard) and his friend Burne-Jones. They were joined in a community venture by Rossetti, Ford Madox Brown and the architect George Edward Street, and revolutionized design in English interior decoration. Kelmscott enshrines their conception of beauty and their attempts to uphold the individuality and dignity of hand work against the uniformity of mass production. Morris moved here from Kent in 1871 and bought the

Elizabethan manor house, now owned by the Society of Antiquaries. He died in 1896. His grave is under the shade of an evergreen with a simple stone carved by Philip Webb with oak and vine leaves. The little 12th-cent. church has some wall paintings in the north transept and original scroll paintings in reds and golds on the inside of the rounded arches. The village with gabled stone houses remains well cared for. Its name gave Morris the imprint for his private printing press.

KENCOT, *Oxfordshire* (5–SP2504). About 2½ m. S. from BURFORD, on the A361, an unclassified road off to the left leads through meadows and orchards to the village of Kencot, with its ancient elm islanded on a small green. An interesting small Norman church makes the detour well worth while. The tower base was begun in the 13th cent. and completed 200 years later. The south door has an unusual Norman tympanum with a centaur shooting an arrow into the throat of a fearsome beast. The sculptor inscribed it with the word Sagittarius to show its astrological significance. Inside are good Norman pillars and a painted Jacobean pulpit.

The little by-road winds on to an adjoining village called **Broadwell** which has some fine weathered stone cottages. The tall Early English spire was built on to a late Norman church with good chevron and dogtooth carving.

Just beyond these two last villages on the same winding lane is another attractive stone village, **Langford**, which is set in the meadows of the upper reaches of the Thames. How such a splendid very early Norman church came to be built in this little backwater is something of a mystery. There was certainly an Anglo-Saxon church on which the Normans built. Carvings and grotesques round the gabled roof date from the time of King Stephen. The 12th-cent. doorway is set between two flying buttresses. The most interesting features are the Norman rood with later 14th-cent. carvings of SS. Mary and John; their heads turned away from the cross. On the other side on the east wall is a carving of Christ which may well be Anglo-Saxon. The chancel and west end are Early English and have unusual distinguishing features which add to the interest of this most unusual church. Within walking distance are two other villages with delightful English names, Filkins and Broughton Poggs.

KENILWORTH, *Warwickshire* (9–SP2872), lies between COVENTRY and WARWICK on the A46. It is rapidly becoming a dormitory for Coventry. Its rather pretentious Victorian residential area was given some of its impetus by the fame of Sir Walter Scott's historical novel. On the north side of the town several old houses of considerable charm survive from an earlier phase of building from the 15th cent. Kenilworth Castle remains the chief glory. This has been called the grandest fortress ruin in England. Norman, Plantagenet and finally Tudor monarchs all played a part in its development.

Starting as a wooden fortress built in A.D. 1112

by Geoffrey de Clinton, who was chamberlain and treasurer to Henry I, it rapidly gained in importance. The keep that still stands was built in 1162 by a son of the first de Clinton, with money provided by Henry II. King John paid several visits to Kenilworth and provided £2,000, a lot in those days, to be spent on its defences. In 1199 another de Clinton surrendered all his rights to the king. Henry III gave it to his sister who had married Simon de Montfort. By 1361 Kenilworth Castle came into the possession of Blanche, of the Lancastrian house, who married John of Gaunt. He was the first owner to transform it from a fortress into a grand castle.

He built the great hall and the long wing of private apartments. Much of this is still recognizable in the ruins. From John of Gaunt the castle went to his son Henry IV and remained a royal residence, until in 1563 Queen Elizabeth gave the castle to her favourite Robert Dudley. The queen conferred on Dudley the title of Earl of Leicester. Then began a new and magnificent period for Kenilworth. Costly entertainments such as had rarely been seen in England were provided for the pleasure of the queen. Leicester converted all the old apartments and erected a great range of new buildings to adjoin the chapel built by Henry VIII. Nothing remains of this chapel other than the foundations. The Long Barn and Great Gatehouse were all built by him at this period. It was only after his death that Kenilworth began its slow decline.

The end came with the Civil War when Cromwell ordered the castle to be dismantled. After the Restoration it passed into the hands of the Clarendon family, whose successors passed it over to the state shortly before the Second World War. The ruins are now in the care of the Ministry of Public Building and Works.

The Church of St Nicholas, though mainly Perpendicular in style, has a good Norman doorway. It is believed that it may have been an entrance to the old priory church of the Augustinians which like Kenilworth Castle was founded by Geoffrey de Clinton. It is situated in Abbey Fields where intelligent excavation has revealed practically the whole lay-out of this great abbey, dissolved by Henry VIII.

KIDDERMINSTER, *Worcestershire* (8–SO 8376). This great carpet-manufacturing centre on the River Stour lies on the north-west fringe of the county, 17 m. from BIRMINGHAM and 15 m. from WORCESTER. Flemish weavers gave Kidderminster a certain prosperity between the 13th and 14th cents. and in the 18th cent. the foundations of its carpet industry were laid. John Broom speculated three fortunes on improving his handloom and by 1735 Pearsall had built the first factory. There is a good museum in Exchange Street with a working model of the old carpet loom, complete with specimen carpet. It also has some fine examples of Japanese silk embroideries. There is little in the town to excite interest except its late medieval, red-sandstone church. The building is rich in fine monuments with an excep-

British Travel Association

Kilpeck church: the south doorway

tional brass dated 1415 to the memory of two warriors, the richer armour and scabbard denoting the knight, Sir John Phelip, and the plainer armour his wife's first husband, Walter Cookesey. The lady is in early 15th-cent. dress and stands between them with a little dog looking up at her. Tombs of Lady Joyce Beauchamp and Thomas Blount, the latter dated 1569, are worthy of note. A famous son of Kidderminster was Sir Rowland Hill who established the penny post. There is a statue of him in the centre of the town. Nearby is also a statue of Richard Baxter, the 17th-cent. Presbyterian divine, who attracted such vast crowds to the church to hear him preach that five galleries had to be built to hold them. He was imprisoned for nonconformism. He made the town his principal centre of evangelism.

One m. NW. of the city in pleasant wooded countryside is **Harvington Hall**, a 16th-cent. gabled brick house with stone and mullioned windows masking a late medieval building. It is surrounded by a moat crossed by two bridges and was the home of another man persecuted for his faith, John Wall, a Roman Catholic priest and one of the last men in England to be martyred for his faith, in 1679. The house originally belonged to the Pakington family and passed from them by marriage to the Throckmortons. That the house had long been used as a shelter for hunted priests is evidenced by the honeycomb of secret passages, trapdoors, sliding panels and the hidden rooms called priests' holes; one of them is secreted under a false stairway. The house now belongs to the Archdiocese of Birmingham. This house is open to the public at advertised times. There is a portrait of John Wall in the Roman Catholic church and a crucifix to his memory in the churchyard.

KILPECK, *Herefordshire* (8–SO4430), owes its fame to its small Norman church, the most perfectly preserved and architecturally the richest example of its kind in the British Isles. Kilpeck lies about 9 m. from HEREFORD, just S. of the A465. It had a long military and monastic history. Little remains of the castle other than the ruins of what must have been an important motte and bailey: the walled enclosure was of impressive size and included the church. Nothing remains of the priory. It seems that Hugh FitzNorman gave the land to the Benedictines of St Peter at GLOUCESTER, who founded the priory in 1135 and built the church within the next five years on the site of an earlier Anglo-Saxon structure, of which some stones remain in the north-east corner of the nave. The south doorway is sumptuously carved. In the tympanum is a formalized Tree of Life bearing thick grapes. The outer arch is rich in linked medallions of birds, mythical monsters, fish, a lion with a very human face, a phoenix in flames and dragons swallowing each other with such abandon that the final dragon is swallowing itself. A flying angel with a palm restores a sense of the triumph of order. The shafts are equally decorated with snake-like monsters entwining other figures. Two men wearing Phrygian caps and tight trews are intriguing. The stone to build this church must have been well chosen for it has weathered nearly 900 years, and the detail remains clear. The interior of the church, consisting of nave, chancel and apse diminishing in both height and width, gives a great sense of length. The two chancel arches demand particularly close attention as the carving is obviously by a different hand. The draping of the haloed apostles is most graceful. On the piers of one of the arches are three groups of male figures, one on top of the other. The top one carries a book and cross, the middle one, a book and key, and the lowest, a book and water sprinkler. On the exterior a corbel table embraces the whole church with such a wealth of carving that the visitor could spend hours on a summer afternoon and still not exhaust the humour of the figures. There are at least 80 figures left (when very careful Victorian restoration work was carried out, some of the figures were considered too erotic in detail and removed). The west window is quite unusual, nook-shafted with good interlacing. A holy-water stoup standing by a curious carved figure has an enormous bowl clasped by elongated arms and resting on a base carved with snakes' heads. Under the Jacobean gallery (which does not seem out of place) at the west end, is a huge Norman font carved out of breccia standing on five shafts, one of which has been restored. Coming out into the light of day the visitor may be surprised at the wealth of late Georgian tombstones in the churchyard.

Dippersmoor Manor nearby is 15th-cent.; its owners breed pedigree Jersey cattle.

KING'S PYON, *Herefordshire* (8–SO4350), lies 8 m. NW. of HEREFORD just W. of the A4110 in a beautifully wooded part of the countryside with views of the Malverns on one side and the distant Welsh hills on the other. The church in a lovely setting overlooking the village has a Norman south doorway with a Transitional chancel arch. Its chief glory, however, is its superb early 14th-cent. black-and-white roofs over the nave and over the south transept. In this transept under a Decorated canopy are two 14th-cent. alabaster effigies of a somewhat mutilated hip-belted knight and his lady wearing a curious square-topped headdress. One m. S. of the village is the Butthouse (pronounced Buttus locally), an unusual early 17th-cent. timber-framed house with an even more interesting ornamented gate-house dated 1632 incorporating a dovecot. The ancient Augustinian priory of Wormsley was near this site. A little to the SW. is a farm called Black Hall which has a medieval barn with cruck trusses. This is yet another Herefordshire village which invites the motorist to leave his car and wander off in almost any direction to enjoy an infinitely varied and tranquil countryside.

KINGTON, *Herefordshire* (8–SO2956), is a small and ancient market town sheltered by the 1,389-ft Hergest (pronounced Hargest, the "g" hard) Ridge. It is situated near the Welsh border on the A44, 14 m. W. of LEOMINSTER. The River Arrow flows through. It remains important for its sheep and cattle market. Its Norman church can be seen at the top of a steep hill from an old stone bridge crossing the river. Although it retains its Norman tower and doorway as well as an exquisite 13th-cent. chancel, most of the church was unfortunately restored in 1874. It has a fine tomb with the alabaster figures of Thomas Vaughan and his wife. He was killed at the Battle of BANBURY in 1469. Many of the more interesting buildings were either swept away or restored out of recognition in the mid-Victorian period. However, some good Georgian houses escaped. Just outside Kington is the Vaughans' mostly 15th-cent. Hergest Court, a farm-house since they departed. It was reputed to be haunted by the ghost of a black bloodhound and by Black Vaughan. On nearby Rushock Hill and Kennel Wood is a good stretch of **Offa's Dyke**. Like CHURCH STRETTON in Shropshire, Kington claims England's highest golf course.

KNOWLE, *Warwickshire* (9–SP1876). This village, where much new housing has been built, lies almost on the perimeter of **Solihull** on the main WARWICK road. The village centre remains remarkably unspoiled. Knowle has perhaps the best Perpendicular church in Warwickshire, built by Walter Cook and completed in 1402. Fourteen years later it became a collegiate church with 10 priests attached to it. This was due to the rapid rise of the guild which Cook had founded. The church has a handsome screen and carved choir-stalls all dating from the 15th cent. On the pulpit may be seen a curious 17th-cent. hourglass for timing sermons. Cook's beautiful guild house, with a timbered hall, stands just W. of the church-yard.

Chester House in the High Street is a fine twin-gabled, timber-framed house of the 15th cent.

A worthwhile ½-m. walk northwards out of Knowle leads to Grimshaw Hall, built about 1560. Its lovely leaded upper windows are set into overhanging gables with varied herringbone and lozenge timber designs. The house with its fine projecting porch has undergone little restoration and the oriel windows on brackets are just as they were when it was built.

The new shopping centre fits quite well into its village setting.

LAPWORTH, *Warwickshire* (9–SP1671). Just SSE. of Hockley Heath, on the WARWICK road, this scattered village has great charm and an interesting church. There is a small Norman north window, but most of the church dates from the 13th or 14th cent. An unusual feature is the partly detached tower which is connected by a passage with the north aisle. There is some good modern glass in the north window and a sensitive carving by Eric Gill of the *Mater Amabilis* on the west wall. It is well worth visiting the porch with an unusual room above it which was possibly used for the exposition of relics. A good walk 1½ m. E. to Kingswood leads to a cast-iron bridge at a junction of the Grand Union and STRATFORD-UPON-AVON Canals, with good views over the basin.

LEAMINGTON SPA, *Warwickshire* (9–SP 3166). This town of about 50,000 inhabitants owes its being to the passion for taking the waters which was at its fashionable height in the late 18th and early 19th cent. It followed in the wake of BATH and was contemporaneous with MAT-LOCK and BUXTON. Camden had in fact discovered the curative qualities of its waters in 1586 but it was only in 1786 that William Abbots built the first Spa Bath.

Dr Henry Jephson, a brilliant physician who received Queen Victoria in 1838, was really responsible for the planning of the town as it is today, and gained it its royal prefix. The Pump Room dates from 1814 but was rebuilt in 1925. All the lovely Georgian, Regency and early Victorian terraced houses are to be found on the north side of the River Leam crossed by the Victoria Bridge. Lansdowne Crescent, where Nathaniel Hawthorne lived at No. 10, and Newbold Terrace can compare with the Bath streets and crescents. Napoleon III lived at No. 4 Clarendon Square for a while after the débâcle of 1870. The Jephson Gardens were laid out as a memorial to the town's great benefactor, whose foresight had drawn to Leamington Spa not only the Queen but the Duke of Wellington, Longfellow and Sarah Bernhardt, and many more of the famous and the great, to take its waters. These gardens along the River Leam remain a popular place of promenade. The Church of All Saints was built in rather pretentious French Gothic style between 1843 and 1869, though it possesses, through benefactors, some good Tudor and 17th-cent. plate.

LECHLADE, *Gloucestershire* (5–SU2199). Almost on the borders of Oxfordshire, Berkshire and Wiltshire, where the tributaries Leach and Coln flow into the Thames, here called the Isis, is the unspoilt village of Lechlade. It has a good number of small brick and stone Georgian houses. The elegant spire of the 15th-cent. Perpendicular church dedicated to St Lawrence dominates the village. The panelled chancel roof is ornamented by some 40 exquisitely carved bosses and stone corbels, and the exterior is parapeted with two rich tiers of quatrefoils. Pinnacled buttresses bear the weight. Lechlade is naturally a favourite place for boating. It is interesting to remember that stone for Sir Christopher Wren's dome of ST PAUL'S was loaded into barges here.

LEDBURY, *Herefordshire* (8–SO7037). Almost on the borders of Herefordshire, Gloucestershire and Worcestershire, Ledbury stands on the lower slopes of a ridge running parallel to the nearby Malvern Hills which lie to the E. of the ancient town. It is situated on the A438, roughly midway between TEWKESBURY and HEREFORD and is a good centre for exploring an exceptionally beautiful part of England. Ledbury is traversed by a long street with its angled Market Place dominated by a delightful black-and-white Market House, timbered in herringbone pattern, raised on 16 columns of oak timber. The windows have leaded panes. It was built between 1617 and 1655. Cobbled Church Lane connects the Market Place and the church and epitomizes Tudor and Stuart streets. It has half-timbered houses with overhanging upper stories and a well-used and lived-in air that enhances its beauty. Almost opposite the Market House is St Katharine's Hospital founded in the 14th cent. by Bishop ffolliott. Only the red-stone chapel, with some stained glass and some tiles, belongs to this period; of the remainder some was rebuilt by Smirke in 1822 and the rest in 1866. The famous Feathers Hotel nearby is one of the best of the many good half-timbered buildings of which Ledbury is justly proud. First place of honour must, however, be given to the five-gabled Ledbury Park built by Lord Biddulph in 1590. Along the WORCESTER road is an early 19th-cent. extension and the garden wall skirts along Southend. From this house Prince Rupert directed a successful engagement with the Parliamentarians in 1646.

By New Street is another old inn, The Talbot, which possesses a beautiful panelled room with an overmantle, all of which dates from 1596. On the opposite side is The Steppes, equally old but partly restored. The mostly 14th-cent. Church of St Michael claims pre-eminence among all the parish churches of Herefordshire. It has an unusually wide nave and side aisles. The nucleus of the original church is Norman, as can be seen from the chancel arcade with its round pillars supported on sturdy square bases. The west door has a round arch and late Norman zigzag work. The north porch is Early English and a jamb of the door still bears the incision of a consecration

cross. The upper story of the porch seems to have been added in the 14th cent. The detached early 13th-cent. tower of the church has an 18th-cent. recessed spire 202 ft high built by Wilkinson of Worcester to replace an earlier timber spire. A great deal of the glass in the church is Victorian, by Kempe, though there are some very early fragments, particularly in the north chapel which also possesses a fine effigy of a 13th-cent. priest in full eucharistic vestments. The church is rich in monuments, especially of the Biddulph family. The Renaissance Skynner Tomb is a particularly interesting piece of humanized funerary sculpture. The five slightly bearded sons and five Stuart-capped daughters kneel beneath the canopied slab with the two beruffed parents kneeling with a plump baby in long clothes between them. At the east end of the north aisle is a monument to Edward Moulton Barrett who is buried here. He was the unbending father of Elizabeth Barrett Browning who was brought up at nearby Hope End, where at 15 she had the accident which was to aggravate her long illness. Three nearby houses are of considerable interest. The 15th-cent. Woodhouse Farm, gabled with tall chimneys, has a great hall and buttery. The five-bayed Dingwood Park, approximately 1¾ m. SSE. from the town centre, was built about 1700 and has elegant stucco ceilings with flower and vine designs. Poet Laureate John Masefield was born in a Ledbury house called the Knapp in 1878.

Eastnor, a village in lovely countryside, is just 2 m. E. of Ledbury on the A438 and has black-and-white cottages set against a tree-lined green. There is a pyramid-roofed well with interesting terracotta panels. In 1812 the 1st Earl Somers built a romantic baronial castle reminiscent of the Marcher days of Edward I. It was completed by the architect Smirke in 1814. He built a great hall 60 ft long and 65 ft high in the centre of the castle. The drawing-room was both designed and furnished by A. W. N. Pugin. The castle, which is open at advertised times to the public, is set in a fine deer park. This is beautifully wooded and has many rare trees. The collection of armour, paintings, tapestries and *objets d'art* is quite outstanding. The parish church, though a Norman foundation, is practically entirely the work of Sir G. Gilbert Scott who rebuilt the church and rectory between 1849 and 1852. The 14th-cent. tower was rebuilt but a late Norman south doorway was left intact. One of the church's acquired treasures is a superb embroidered Venetian red-velvet altar-frontal. A pleasant walk may be made 1 m. eastwards to **Bronsil Castle** which is a genuine but romantic ruin of the crenellated fortress of Richard Beauchamp, treasurer to King Henry VI. Little remains but the inner moat, which is still filled with water, and part of the gatehouse. The tall obelisk nearby was raised by Earl Somers to the memory of his son, who died in battle at Burgos the year building commenced on Eastnor Castle. Two m. to the E. lies the greater part of an Iron Age hill-fort marked by the twin summits of Midsummer Hill and Hollybush.

LEOMINSTER, *Herefordshire* (8–SO4959), pronounced "Lemster", was for 500 years one of the great wool markets of England and is now the centre of a thriving agricultural area. It is set among pastureland, hopfields and orchards in a countryside watered by three streams, the Lugg, the Pinsley and the Arrow. The narrow High Street runs N. and S. and is fronted by medieval timber-framed houses with overhanging gables. Drapers Row, behind High Street, and even narrower, has some good Tudor houses. Broad Street and Etnam Street by contrast are wide thoroughfares with Georgian brick houses telling of Leominster's 18th-cent. prosperity, when the fine wool known as Lemster Ore was renowned in all England. In Bridge Street is a house, No. 29, dating from 1400. The mid-Victorian Italianate Town Hall leaves something to be desired, the more so as comparison with the old Town Hall is inevitable. The latter, near the ancient priory church and now known as Grange Court, was built in 1633 by the remarkable John Abel, and originally stood at the crossroads in the town centre. Up to the time of its removal in 1855, its ground floor with its colonnade of oaken Ionic columns was used as the butter market. It was sold for the derisory sum (even for Victorian days) of £95. It was re-erected on its present site and the ground floor filled in with masonry. It is one of the loveliest timber-framed houses in the county, two-storied with fine bays and adorned with elegant carvings. The windows of the upper-story project and have unusual carvings of male and female busts. John Abel's original inscription can still be read on the frieze in which he says his columns support the fabric as "noble gentry . . . support the honour of a Kingdom".

Although Leominster is so rich in early English domestic architecture it is its reddish stone Priory Church set on open swards of green which can never fail to delight and impress the visitor. Its foundation is generally attributed to Earl Leofric, husband of Lady Godiva, who established a nunnery here. Nothing survives of the Anglo-Saxon church and in Norman times a Benedictine priory was founded from READING Abbey, which was already wealthy in the time of Henry I. The north aisle with its massive Norman columns gives a majestic sense of spaciousness while the triforium with interlaced arches and the rounded windows of the clerestory give an impression of height unequalled in any other Norman church in the country. This is the earliest part of the priory church which has no less than three naves. The central nave is enriched with a traceried 15th-cent. west window. The 14th-cent. aisle has superb Decorated windows. The west tower was built in the following century with fine Perpendicular panelling. In 1699 a disastrous fire destroyed the original chancel and damaged the arcade, necessitating the rebuilding of the columns supporting it. The more recent restoration work has been carried out with restraint and such skill that the church has probably not looked more beautiful during the last 250 years than it does today. It possesses one of the finest 15th-cent. chalices in England. A ducking stool is preserved in good working order in the church. Silver birches, limes and yews grow in the churchyard.

Leominster Out Parish, the area S. and W. of the town, has a number of interesting houses. There are timber-framed farm-houses, barns and hop-kilns as well as some fine Georgian brick mansions. Outstanding among these is Broadward Hall, 1½ m. S. of the town, a two-storied building with a good Venetian window and an earlier square dovecot bearing the date 1652. Wharton Court, a rather severe Jacobean house, should also be seen. It has not suffered from undue restoration. It is famous for its elaborate staircase, dating from the first year of James I's reign, which sweeps upwards to the third story of the house. About ½ m. beyond Wharton on Brierley Hill is an Iron Age hill-fort, one of the most interesting prehistoric camps in the county.

About 3 m. N. of Leominster, just W. of the A49, is **Berrington Hall**, a handsome red sandstone 18th-cent. house built by the younger Henry Holland between 1778 and 1781 for Thomas Harley. The house, owned now by the National Trust and open at advertised times during the summer season, is practically as Holland built and decorated it. The hall, library and drawing-room all have remarkable plaster ceilings and are splendidly furnished. The Classical staircase is most impressive. The house stands in 455 acres of parkland, with rare trees, shrubs and plants. This includes the famous pool of 14 acres laid out by Capability Brown in 1780. About 1¼ m. W. of the A49 Leominster–LUDLOW road, reached by an unclassified road, is **Eye Manor**, also open to the public at advertised times. The house, set in fine grounds, was built by a Barbados slave-trader Ferdinando Gorges in 1680. The beautiful interior, with splendid plasterwork and rich in furniture and paintings, is an abiding testimony to the profitability of that inhuman commerce. There is a collection of books and period costumes. The church has a fine porch of carved oak.

Some 7 m. WSW. of the town on the A4112 road to Brecon is the village of **Dilwyn**, with a number of half-timbered houses and a fine parish church, wide, with lofty 13th-cent. arcades and clerestory. It has its original medieval roof. It has three finely traceried screens, dating from the 15th cent.; that of the chancel is elegant, with fan vaulting springing from fluted columns. The massive tower belonged to an older church and dates from the late 12th and early 13th cent. The little spire was added 200 years ago. About 1½ m. WNW. of the church is a timber-framed manor house called Luntley Court. Not least of its charms are to be found in its outhouses and gabled dovecot with 500 nesting holes. Two m. in the opposite direction lies Swanston Court which had major additions in the 18th cent. but retains its 14th-cent. hall range in its cross-wings. One m. to the N. is yet another uncommon house, Bidney Farm with an early 17th-cent. black-and-white dovecot. All around is pleasant walking country.

MAPLEDURHAM, *Oxfordshire* (5 SU6776), is one of the villages in South Oxfordshire which lie on the banks of the River Thames. It is a short distance from PANGBOURNE and Caversham on a by-lane off the main Goring to READING road. Sheltered by wooded hills, it slopes down to the river, dotted with picturesque cottages, and boasts an ivy-clad mill and a row of early 17th-cent. almshouses. They were built by John Lister, a member of the ancient Blount family. Sir Michael Blount built the impressive pink-brick Tudor manor house, Mapledurham Court, where he entertained Queen Elizabeth I. Two of his descendants were the somewhat eccentric Martha and Teresa Blount, friends of the poet Alexander Pope. The lovely manor houses many art treasures and is still privately owned. It is open to the public at weekends during the summer and on weekdays by arrangement.

The church built between 1381 and 1397 has some fine monuments to the Bardolphs and the Blounts. At one time, the living of the church, which is still in the possession of ETON College, was regarded as one of the plum benefices of the Church of England and a stepping stone to a bishopric. The south aisle remains a Roman Catholic chapel owned by the Blounts, who adhered to this faith. The oak-timbered arcaded ceiling is particularly rare.

MARSHFIELD, *Gloucestershire* (4–ST7773), just off the A420 road into BRISTOL, is almost on the borders of Wiltshire and Somerset. It was once the last staging post for the coaches carrying nobility and gentry into the fashionable BATH of the late 18th cent. Most of the houses date from this period and the inns of the village still carry the stamp of their coaching past. Long before LUTON, Marshfield's fame for making sun bonnets was unrivalled. The long grey-stone street is dominated by the church tower with a graceful gold cock weathervane. The height of the village makes this a landmark for miles around. The church is spacious but not conspicuously interesting. Nicholas Crispe's Almshouses at the other end of the street were built in 1625 and are well worth visiting. So, too, is the great 15th-cent. tithe barn nearby with its 15 splendid bays. Just by the Three Shire Stone outside the village is the entrance to an imposing mansion called the Rock with its avenue of beeches; it was built on to a late Norman castle. There are good views down the valley.

MAXSTOKE CASTLE, *Warwickshire* (9–SP2386). Just off the A47, 1½ m. E. of Coleshill, and reached by a twisting road, stands a square red sandstone fortress, looking rather like a Crusaders' castle of Asia Minor, with turreted polygonal towers and battlemented curtain walls. Maxstoke Castle was built in about 1345 by William de Clinton, Earl of Huntingdon, and has been lived in continuously ever since. It was partially remodelled by Humphrey Stafford, 1st Duke of Buckingham, in 1440 and came into the Dilke family in the late 16th cent. Many of the

alterations which have remained to modern times were accomplished by Sir Thomas Dilke. A fine avenue of trees leads to great oak gates where a portcullis once hung. A stone bridge now crosses the perfect moat which is exceedingly deep in places. The great hall of 1345 survives and much history has been enacted within its walls. Many treasures from the time of Richard III to the late Stuarts are preserved here.

From the castle, country roads lead through an area of dairy farms to the village of Maxstoke, where to the W. of the Church of St Michael are the ruins of an Augustinian priory founded in 1336 by that same William de Clinton. The principal items of interest are the two sides of the central tower, the outer gatehouse (the inner gatehouse became an Elizabethan dwelling) and the west wall of the infirmary. The priory originally housed the prior and 12 canons.

MINSTER LOVELL, *Oxfordshire* (5–SP81 11), is one of the most attractive of all the Windrush villages and is famed in history and romantic verse as the home of the ill-fated Lovells. It is situated just off the A40 between WITNEY and BURFORD (5 m. away) across the ancient bridge and sheltered by a hillside. The home of the Lovells, now in ruins, is under the care of the Ministry of Public Building and Works. Francis Lovell, "Lovell the Dog", in the old rhyme, was implicated in the schemes of Richard III and fled after the defeat at Bosworth in 1485, returning in 1487 to champion the Pretender Lambert Simnel. After the débâcle of the Battle of Stoke it is said he returned to Minster Lovell and hid in a secret room. He was looked after by a single servant who died, and Lovell, locked in his concealed room, is said to have perished by starvation. When repairs to the house were being effected in 1718 a vaulted room was discovered with a skeleton seated at a table and the skeleton of a dog at its feet – whether it was Francis Lovell will never be known. The other well-known story connected with the house is that known as "The Mistletoe Bough": a bride of one of the Lovells playing hide-and-seek on her wedding night hid in an ancient chest which locked itself under the weight of its heavy lid. A skeleton was found in a chest many years later. The ruins of the house are open to the public.

The church is Perpendicular and has fine vaulting under the central tower. The church suffered from 19th-cent. restoration but still possesses some 15th-cent. glass.

MOCCAS COURT, *Hereford* (8–SO3542). On a curve of the River Wye, just S. of the little village of **Monnington-on-Wye** off the A438 HEREFORD to Hay road, a lane called Monnington Walk leads to an elegant lodge designed by G. S. Repton, who was working for John Nash at that time. The road leads through the park to Robert Adam's severely Classical brick house, Moccas Court, built between 1775 and 1780 by Anthony Keckby for the Cornewall family. The interior is extraordinarily rich. The Circular Room is exquisite with panelled Etruscan or Pompeian designs. The furnishings are all in keeping with the grand scale of this country house. The grounds were landscaped by Capability Brown. In the park stands a beautiful Norman church which has been carefully restored. It was built of tufa about 1130 and possesses some fine 14th-cent. stained glass with two tiny but interesting figures. The proportions of the round chancel arches are perhaps only second in the county to those at KILPECK.

MORETON-IN-MARSH, *Gloucestershire* (5–SP2032), is a pleasant, prosperous-looking small town with a wide grass-verged main street. The word marsh is a corruption of march, meaning a boundary. The broad street is actually built on the Roman Fosse Way and was originally the crossroads of four counties. It is only 8 m. from CHIPPING NORTON on the A44 Evesham road and 4 m. N. from STOW-ON-THE-WOLD. The old curfew bell still hangs in its tower overlooking the Fosse Way which has a 17th-cent. clock. The church is new but possesses some good Elizabethan plate. Most unusually in this part of the country, it is dedicated to St David. The town has some good 17th- and 18th-cent. houses and has had long connections with the Redesdale family. The Redesdale Arms is a famous old coaching inn and one of several interesting inns in the town. The railway station has long been popular with children for the topiary on its platform.

MORTIMER'S CROSS, *Herefordshire* (8–SO4263). Some 6 m. WNW. of LEOMINSTER on the A4110 is the approximate scene of one of the bloody battles of the Wars of the Roses. An obelisk was erected in 1799 to perpetuate "the memory of an obstinate, bloody and decisive battle fought near this spot in the civil wars between the ambitious houses of York and Lancaster on the second day of February 1460". All this part of Herefordshire was the feudal domain of the powerful Mortimer family. The leader of the Yorkist force on this occasion was Edward Mortimer, Earl of March. The Lancastrians supporting Henry VI were under the command of the Earl of Pembroke and the Earl of Wiltshire. Some 4,000 men were slain in that one day, one of the almost unknown warriors who was taken prisoner and who was later executed in HEREFORD was the Welshman Owen Tudor, whose grandson was to turn the tables and found the Tudor dynasty. With an army of 30,000 men, Edward Mortimer was on his way to London to avenge the murder of his father the Duke of York by Queen Margaret, when he received word of the Lancastrian force barring his way. His victory won him the crown of England to which he laid claim, through his descent from Philippa Plantagenet, grand-daughter of Edward III. One month later the 19-year-old Herefordshire warrior was crowned in London as Edward IV.

All around are delightful villages, many with black-and-white cottages. **Lucton** is nearby with its schoolhouse built by the London merchant John Pierrepont in 1708 and still a public school. **Aymestrey** is set in countryside which invites even the sluggard visitor to walk. Its church has an impressive tall rood-screen. Nearby Yatton Court is a Georgian country house with a very fine Venetian window.

MUCH MARCLE, *Herefordshire* (8–SO6533), is almost on the Gloucestershire border on the A449 ROSS–LEDBURY road and set among cider orchards. It has a beautiful 13th-cent. church, its spacious nave arcades lit by lofty clerestory lights. Its unusually long chancel holds an exquisite 14th-cent. effigy of Blanche, Lady Grandison, her splendidly fitted gown flowing away gracefully and her beautiful hands seeming barely to touch her rosary. The wooden effigy of a man on the window-sill, carved in oak with slender folds, is of one of the rarest types of effigy found in England. Sir John Kyrle is buried in the north chapel in an alabaster tomb. His feet rest on the hedgehog crest of the Kyrles while those of his wife rest on bear's paws, signifying that she was one of the great Scudamore family.

The Kyrles still own Homme House. The early part of the house dates to the beginning of the 16th cent. and the east front is purely Georgian. Above and behind the house is a delightful gazebo dated 1670. The other famous mansion in the neighbourhood is Hellens, a fine Jacobean brick house and once the seat of the Walwyns. There are several superb period rooms, some with very early plaster ceilings. The monogrammed dovecot in the grounds bears the date 1641.

About 1½ m. W. of the Much Marcle church, by the television mast, is an Iron Age hill-fort. Part of the original enclosure exists but the south side has been almost obliterated by cultivation.

NORTH CERNEY, *Gloucestershire* (5–SP 0208). A little to the E. of the CHELTENHAM–CIRENCESTER road, in the Churn valley, is the lovely village of North Cerney. It has some unusually good 18th-cent. houses, Cerney House and the Queen Anne rectory among them. No less attractive are the old farm-house, the mill and the weathered inn. The church is an example of Anglican liturgical taste at its best. The way in which colour has been used enlivens this Norman and Early English church and the whole suggests a continuing sturdy faith. The saddle-back west tower was started by the Normans and completed a century later. The south door has five rows of good zigzag Norman ornament. The door and the ironwork on it are at least 600 years old. The rood-loft is modern with an early 17th-cent. Italian Christus. The woodwork of the rood-screen is Jacobean. The church possesses its pre-Reformation altar stone, some good candelabra and altar candlesticks, as well as a 15th-cent. carved wooden statue of the Virgin. Three of the windows at least have 15th-cent. glass. Both pulpit and font are superb examples of the 15th-cent. stonemasons' art. There is a 14th-cent. cross in the churchyard.

Worcestershire: springtime in an orchard in the Teme valley   Kenneth Scowen

STOKE-HOLE

NORTHLEACH, *Gloucestershire* (5–SP1114), was one of the very prosperous wool towns of the Cotswolds, and its rich, lofty Perpendicular church is a worthy memorial of those days. There is a certain faded beauty about the twisting streets and green-swarded market place and a tranquil imperturbability that ignores the arterial traffic on the A40. There are some pleasant old houses which have also ignored the passing of time: 16th-cent. almshouses, timber-framed houses with overhangs, and a 17th-cent. manor house as well as a tall gabled grammar school.

Its main feature to encourage the motorist to stop is certainly its 15th-cent. parish church with its beautiful south porch. Here canopied niches shelter their ancient saints, centred by the Blessed Virgin Mary, while the upward thrust of the buttressed arch finds its apex in the carving of the Trinity. The vaulted roof rests on six rounded shafts with flowered capitals. The irrepressible humour of this robust period is caught in a grotesque of a cat fiddling to three rats. The nave with its tall clerestory was built by John Fortey. Near the chancel under the north arcade is a brass recording his death in 1458 showing him with his feet on a wool sack and sheep. There are many fine brasses worth close inspection. Nearly all show, by the richness of their clothing, the wealth of the burgher class of Northleach in the Middle Ages. To see the beauty of the battlemented tower and line of parapets and pinnacles at its best, the church should be seen from just outside the eastern boundaries of the town.

OTMOOR, *Oxfordshire* (5–SP5614). This curious area of almost wild fen-like desolation has been described by various writers as "bewitched Otmoor", the "forgotten land", and "sleeping Otmoor cast under a spell of ancient magic". Yet its mysterious centre is only about 5 m. from Headington. The B4207 leaves OXFORD by Magdalen Bridge and leads via Headington to **Stanton St John,** with its fine thatched farms, its stone mullioned houses, its ancient Manor House and lovely church. John White, chief founder of the State of Massachusetts, was born here. From this village it is possible to make a ring tour of the little villages that surround Otmoor. From nearby **Beckley** a sweeping vista of these 4,000 acres of almost roadless moors meets the eye. There are green tracks, however, one of which follows an ancient Roman road between DORCHESTER and Alchester near BICESTER. There are some interesting though much eroded wall paintings in the church. From Beckley the road runs to Studley, with timbered and thatched cottages and an Elizabethan house, Studley Priory, built on the site of an ancient Benedictine nunnery. From here the road winds up to wooded **Boarstall,** with its tower owned by the National Trust, once the gateway to a moated castle. The next village is **Murcott,** right on the edge of the moor, crisscrossed by tributaries of the Ray, once the scene of bloody disturbance during the riots following the 18th-cent. Enclosure Acts. Although very liable to flooding, all this forgotten territory is

still good grazing land. From Murcott the little road crosses humped stone bridges across the Ray and its many streams and comes into **Charlton-on-Otmoor.** The Perpendicular parish church has a fine rood-screen. Its high Early English tower can be seen for miles around. May Day is celebrated by the garlanding of the church by the village children and May Day dances. This area is a paradise of wild-fowl and rare wild flowers and in spring the blackthorn blossom and later the deep pink of the wild roses have to be seen to be believed. Here is the tiny village of **Oddington,** with an unusual if somewhat horrifying brass of a 16th-cent. parson in a state of decomposition. From Oddington the road twists down to the most important of the villages surrounding Otmoor. **Islip** once had the palace of the most important Anglo-Saxon kings and in 1004 St Edward the Confessor was born here. Nothing remains of this building. Three major battles were fought here during the Civil War. Swift once tried to get the living of this church but instead became Dean of Christ Church in Dublin. The little main street has picturesque cottages. A short drive on the B4027 leads you to another little lane, signposted **Noke,** the remotest village on Otmoor. On the other side of the road is perhaps the prettiest of all its villages, **Woodeaton,** with its woods, charming village green and Early English church which has an enormous 14th-cent. mural of St Christopher. The translation of the Norman-French scroll emerging from the Saint's mouth reads: "Whoever will see this image today will not die a violent death".

The country lane now leaves Otmoor to lead to **Marston,** headquarters of the Cromwellian troops during the siege of Oxford. This is all good walking country, but you should only attempt crossmoorland walks in dry weather. Providing attention is paid to this, the nature lover will find much satisfaction both here and in the distant WYCHWOOD FOREST country in the west of the county.

OXFORD, *Oxfordshire* (5–SP5305). This great university town is, for its history and associations and for its architecture, one of the most rewarding in England. In spite of recent industrialization, its beauty and dignity have emerged relatively unscathed. "That sweet city with her dreaming spires", as Arnold called Oxford, seen from the top of Boar's Hill 3 m. away is an evocative and unforgettable sight.

The university is the second oldest in Europe, acknowledging only the Sorbonne in Paris as its senior. One theory as to its origins attributes its foundation to the expulsion of foreign students from Paris in the 13th cent., but in fact evidence of organized teaching there can be traced to the 12th cent. A chancellor was appointed in 1214 and the collegiate system began in the latter part of the 13th cent. with the establishment in Oxford of various religious orders. There was much conflict between "town and gown" in the Middle Ages as charters from successive monarchs conveyed privileges upon the university which caused hardship to the city merchants. During the Civil War

Chedworth: a mosaic from the Roman villa   *Picturepoint*

Oxford was important as the Royalist head-quarters and the seat of Charles I's parliament.

The centre of the town is Carfax, where the main E. to W. and N. to S. roads converge. The four streets leading from it are the High Street (E.), Queen Street (W.), Cornmarket Street (N.) and St Aldate's (S.). The best way for a visitor with limited time to spend in Oxford to see the city is to obtain a guide and map from the information centre in St Aldate's, giving recommended walking tours of different lengths.

All Souls College was founded in 1437 by Henry Chichele to commemorate Henry V and those who fell at Agincourt. It has no undergraduate members, only graduate fellows elected for their academic distinction. Its architecture is among the finest in Oxford. The frontage on the High Street with the gateway over which a carving depicts souls in purgatory and the front quadrangle remain virtually unaltered since their foundation. The north quadrangle and the twin towers are by Hawksmoor, also the architect of the Italianate Codrington library. The chapel is remarkable for its reredos, which was uncovered and restored by Scott in the 19th cent., its oak stalls and misericords and the 15th-cent. glass in the ante-chapel.

Balliol College, originally founded in the 13th cent. by John de Baliol, has always enjoyed a high academic reputation, associated with Benjamin Jowett, the famous Master in the 19th cent. Most of the buildings, by Salvin and Butterfield, are 19th-cent. and two modern blocks have just been completed.

Brasenose College was founded in 1509 on the site of an earlier community. Its name is thought to be derived from an ancient brass knocker in the form of a nose brought to the college from a house in STAMFORD called Brasenose Hall to which some students retired in the 14th cent. from the unrest rife in Oxford. The front of the college, the first quadrangle and the gateway tower date from the foundation; the hall and chapel are attributed to Wren (1663 and 1666).

Christ Church occupies one of the finest positions in Oxford overlooking the beautiful meadows leading down to the Thames and the Cherwell. It was founded by Cardinal Wolsey and licensed by King Henry VIII under the name of Cardinal College in 1525, several religious foundations having been suppressed to make way for Wolsey's grandiose design. A new see was created in 1542 and the Church of St Frideswide became the college chapel and the cathedral of the diocese. The front quadrangle, known as Tom squad, from the great bell in the tower over the gateway which is dedicated to St Thomas of Canterbury, is the largest in Oxford. There is a magnificent hall, notable for its fine timbered roof and its collection of portraits, among them those of Henry VIII and Wolsey, traditionally by Holbein. The cathedral, the smallest in England, has many beautiful features from many centuries: Norman vaulted aisles, Perpendicular fan-tracery in the roof of the choir, the Decorated Latin Chapel and window in St Lucy's Chapel, a 15th-cent. shrine of St Frideswide and the fine Early English

chapter house, adjoining the cloisters on the south side.

Corpus Christi College, though small, has much rich, Perpendicular architecture dating from its foundation in 1516. Among its treasures are the altar-piece in the chapel, which has been ascribed to Rubens, its library of rare books and its fine collection of old plate.

Exeter College was founded by a Bishop of EXETER in 1314, but most of its buildings have been restored or rebuilt. The Victorian chapel is by Sir Gilbert Scott and contains tapestries by Burne-Jones and William Morris.

Hertford College occupies the site of several earlier halls but in its present form was incorporated in 1874. Its buildings are all 18th-, 19th- and 20th-cent.

Jesus College has always been associated with Wales since its foundation by Queen Elizabeth I in 1571 at the request of Hugh ap Rice who endowed it and provided scholarships for Welsh students. Its chapel and library date from the 17th cent.

Keble College was erected by subscription as a memorial to John Keble and aimed originally at providing an education based on the precepts of the Anglican Church. Its red-brick buildings designed by Butterfield can be regarded as hideous or as a fine example of high Victorian architecture, according to one's taste. The chapel is well worth visiting for its rich mosaic decoration and Holman Hunt's famous picture *The Light of the World*.

Lincoln College, founded in 1427 by Richard Flemyng, Bishop of LINCOLN, has an interesting chapel built in 1630, an example of very late Perpendicular architecture.

Magdalen College, founded by William of Wayn-flete in 1458, is one of the largest and most beautiful of all the Oxford colleges. Its most striking feature is the Perpendicular bell-tower, begun in 1492 and completed in 1509. Here the choristers sing their traditional Latin hymn at five o'clock on May-day morning. The main quadrangle is surrounded by cloisters and above the west walk is the library, which contains an exceptionally valuable collection. To the N. of the cloisters are the New Buildings, an 18th-cent. Classical range, overlooking the Grove, a deer-park where open-air plays are performed every summer.

Merton College, founded in 1264, is one of the three oldest colleges. Among its fine buildings the library and chapel are outstanding. The library, lying on two sides of the so-called mob quad, dates from the 14th cent.; the choir of the chapel is of pure Decorated workmanship and has exquisitely traceried windows. There is also a beautiful garden.

New College was founded by William of Wykeham, the founder of WINCHESTER School, in 1379, and the connection between the college and the school still survives today in the form of a number of closed scholarships. Many of the original buildings, in the Perpendicular style, survive as evidence of Wykeham's magnificent design. The cloisters and the chapel, the latter restored by

A. F. Kersting

Oxford: New College chapel

Oxford: the Radcliffe Camera

A. F. Kersting

James Wyatt and Sir Gilbert Scott, should be seen, as well as the pleasant garden enclosed by the remains of the ancient city walls.

Oriel College, though endowed by Edward II in 1326, has no buildings of this age, the oldest being 17th-cent. In the 19th cent. it became associated with the Oxford Movement, Keble, Thomas Arnold, Newman, Pusey and Froude all being elected fellows.

Queen's College is named in honour of Queen Philippa, wife of Edward III, and was founded in the 14th cent. by Robert de Eglesfield. The statue overlooking the High Street depicts Queen Caroline, wife of George II. The splendid Classical buildings are by Wren and Hawksmoor, and the library is of particular interest for its valuable collection and its carvings by Grinling Gibbons. There is some medieval stained glass in the chapel, preserved from the earlier chapel on the site.

St John's College, founded in 1555, has particularly fine gardens and an interesting back quadrangle with a south wing attributed to Inigo Jones in Classical style and cloisters of the same period on the north and west sides.

Trinity College, the traditional rival of Balliol next door, was founded in 1555. Its most interesting feature is the chapel, with a rich alabaster tomb of Sir Thomas Pope, the founder, and a carved screen and altar-piece by Grinling Gibbons.

University College is the oldest of all the colleges, although the exact date of its foundation is difficult to determine. Whether or not claims that Alfred the Great established it in the 9th cent. are justified, it is certain that a college in something like its present form was in existence in the mid-13th cent. The oldest part of the present buildings was begun in 1634 and the chapel, though redesigned by Sir Gilbert Scott, contains woodwork and windows of this period. There is a romantic statue in white marble of Shelley lying in the building to the right of the lodge.

Wadham College has some fine Classical buildings coeval with its foundation in 1612. In the quadrangle is a clock by Wren, an undergraduate of the college.

Worcester College also has a frontage in the Classical style dating from its foundation in its present form in 1714, but the buildings surrounding the quadrangle are of much earlier date. The beautiful gardens and lake are well worth visiting.

Among the colleges of comparatively recent foundation are the five women's colleges: Lady Margaret Hall, Somerville, St Hilda's, St Anne's and St Hugh's. Women account for about one-seventh of the undergraduate population. The newest male undergraduate college is St Catherine's, which should be seen as an example of how modern architectural design copes with the problems of providing residential quarters for students.

Among the graduate colleges are that of Lord Nuffield's foundation (1937) and St Antony's, which accepts both men and women students.

The widest street in Oxford is St Giles, with

colleges, ecclesiastical study houses and old inns on either side. Sir Gilbert Scott's Martyrs' Memorial, commemorating Ridley, Latimer and Cranmer, stands on an island with the Church of St Mary Magdalen. In St Giles Street on the first Monday and Tuesday following the Sunday after St Giles's Day the colourful St Giles Fair takes place.

The Ashmolean Museum built in the mid-19th cent. by C. R. Cockerell houses one of the oldest museum collections in the world, with fine displays of Greek, Roman, Egyptian and British antiquities, Chinese porcelain, Indian and Persian miniatures and a large and valuable collection of Old Master paintings and drawings, as well as a good collection of Pre-Raphaelite pictures. The Radcliffe Camera is one of the reading rooms for the Bodleian Library, its dome a landmark in Oxford's centre. The Bodleian Library is one of the oldest in the world, second only in importance to the Vatican Library in Rome; possessing as it does many of the rarest manuscripts extant. The visitors should see Duke Humphrey's Library and the old Divinity School with its exquisite groyned and traceried ceiling.

The Sheldonian Theatre at the west end of Broad Street was designed by Christopher Wren. Started in 1664, it was completed in 1669 and it is here, at the end of the summer term, that Commemorations or Encaenia are held and degrees are conferred. The busts of emperors, much eroded by time, are held in considerable affection. The interior with its gallery and tiered seats holds the chair of the Vice-Chancellor of the University and its Classical decoration is enhanced by a splendidly painted ceiling. From Wren's cupola can be seen practically all the colleges and important buildings of Oxford.

Just off the Cornmarket, through Frewin Court, is the building which houses the Oxford Union, the famous University Debating Society, founded in 1823.

The walks in little back streets, strolls along the banks of Christ Church Meadows where the River Isis becomes the Thames, or further down the Cherwell, all help to capture the atmosphere of Oxford, which is perhaps seen at its best during Eights Week, when everyone goes down to the river to watch the races. One of the most rewarding walks is to go through Port Meadow along the footpaths to the old Trout Inn at **Godstow**. In a meadow nearby are the ruins of the convent where Fair Rosamond, rival to Queen Eleanor of Aquitaine for the affection of Henry II, died in 1176.

Just opposite Magdalen College and close to the High Street are the earliest surviving Botanic Gardens in Britain. Laid out in 1621 on the instructions of Henry, Earl of Danby, as a Physic Garden, it retains something of the agreeable formality of that period. You enter through the beautiful Italianate Gateway designed by Nicholas Stone, to find open beds of flowers, trees and greenhouses full of rare plants which have been collected over the centuries from every part of the world.

The industrial centre of **Cowley** is $2\frac{1}{2}$ m. SE. of the city, off the ring road. It was here that William Morris, later Lord Nuffield, took over a building in 1912 to make bicycles and ended up as the Henry Ford of Britain. From the modest beginnings of Morris Garages has sprung one of the biggest motorcar industries in the world. The factories of what is now the British Leyland Motor Corporation employing vast numbers of workers has brought great prosperity to this little Oxford suburb and great philanthropic benefits to the university city itself. There is little left to suggest Cowley's great antiquity, but it was important even when the Domesday Book was compiled. Its parish church, though enlarged and restored, still possesses two Norman doorways and a Norman chancel with Early English developments.

About 2 m. away on the B480 is the village of **Littlemore**. It was in this village, where an important 12th-cent. nunnery was founded by Roger de Sandford, that Newman and his fellow Tractarians, particularly Dr Pusey, formed a community in a farm-house, from which the "Tracts for the Times" were issued. Newman was vicar in the Gothic Revival church in the village, until his secession from the Church of England.

Another suburb of the city 2 m. SE. of Oxford and on the banks of the river is the village of **Iffley**, with one of the richest Norman churches in the country. Built in 1170 on an earlier Anglo-Saxon church, its west front has one of the finest examples of beakhead and zigzag carving. Its splendidly proportioned tower has perfect Norman arcades. A later window was inserted into the base of the tower in the 15th cent. Inside the north door, a 12th-cent. black slate font is set on a central pillar supported by four corner columns. The Norman chancel has an excellent vaulted roof with a curious central boss of grotesque faces.

Just N. of the London Road out of Oxford is the suburb of **Headington** which also boasts a 12th-cent. church with a perfect Norman chancel arch. It was much restored in Victorian times. Headington was once famous for its stone quarries which supplied most of the stone for the colleges of Oxford from the 14th to the 18th cent.

PACKINGTON HALL, *Warwickshire* (9–SP2284). Just off the A45 about 7 m. W. of Meriden, set in 700 acres of woodland and reached only by lanes, are Great and Little Packington. Packington Hall, not open to the public, is one of the most remarkable Italianate houses in Warwickshire. It was built in 1693 but considerably enlarged in 1766 by the 3rd Earl of Aylesford. About 16 years later the 4th Earl employed Bonomi who produced a Pompeian scheme of décor unmatched in England.

The Old Hall, a much smaller brick house incorporating an even earlier timbered building, was where Charles I stayed on his way to Edge Hill. Later Charles II stayed in the house with Jane Lane who rescued him dramatically after the Battle of WORCESTER. She lies buried in the church which Bonomi built between the two

Halls in 1790 to look as if it had been lifted bodily from Italy. The interior has fine paintings by Rigaud. Capability Brown laid out the park.

PACKWOOD HOUSE, *Warwickshire* (9–SP1872), is a rewarding example of domestic Tudor architecture with later additions. It is situated 1½ m. E. of Hockley Heath, 11 m. SE. of BIRMINGHAM. The National Trust owns it and it is open to the public. From a side road, coming through an old gateway, this mellowed timber-framed house with its later 17th-cent. brickwork makes an almost theatrical impact. The restorations were undertaken with care for authenticity, how successful they were can be seen by the excellence of the renewed gabling. The National Trust has put much valuable and interesting period furniture into the house. The beautiful Jacobean panellings are original but only that in the Ireton Room, which also has a splendid overmantel, is in its original position. Lovers of needlework and tapestry will find here much to interest them. There is some unusual lead work which can be seen on the exterior of the house. The groupings of chimneys are visually most satisfying.

The stables, built before 1666 by John Fetherstone in his enlargement of the house, are perfectly proportioned. Fetherstone's greatest achievement is his celebrated Yew Garden, the glory of Packwood House. Clipped yews of a symmetry unexcelled in their period, they are generally held to represent the Sermon on the Mount. The garden leads to an avenue called Multitude Walk. There are twelve large Apostles; four even higher Evangelists and finally a huge yew, which represents Christ. The whole garden was planted about 1650 and has weathered walls with a particularly decorative gateway: 30 unusual bee boles are niched on either side of it.

The nearby Church of St Giles is 13th-cent. though it has been much, and badly, restored. Its register contains the record of the marriage of Michael Johnson of LICHFIELD to Sara Ford "of these parts". They were the parents of Samuel Johnson.

PAINSWICK, *Gloucestershire* (4–SO8609), high up on the Cotswolds, edged by a woodland valley sweeping down to GLOUCESTER, is one of the most interesting of all the many wool towns. Parking is something of a problem and the motorist is advised to pass the churchyard in the direction of STROUD for a few hundred yards to where the town has opened a "trust the motorist" parking area. Painswick has many houses and inns dating from the 14th to the 18th cents. Among these, the most important is Painswick House, built in 1737 with some later work by Basevi, who designed the Fitzwilliam Museum in CAMBRIDGE. It is open to the public on Sundays during the summer. Castle Godwyn; the Court House, gabled with tall chimneys and a fine terraced garden; Tocknells Court; Lovedays; the Yew Tree House and the ancient Little Fleece, owned by the National Trust, are a few of the buildings worth seeing. The Beacon opposite the churchyard has splendid interior stucco décor and may well have been the work of the younger Wood who designed many of the Georgian streets and houses in BATH.

The churchyard of St Mary's is famed for its 99 clipped yews, planted in 1792. The church with its high spire built in 1632 on to the square early 15th-cent. tower became a dangerous ranging mark during the Civil War when Charles I stayed in Painswick after a defeat inflicted on the Parliamentarians in 1643. The church has been much restored, though the nave dates from 1480. The 19th-cent. work was in no little measure due to a terrible thunderstorm in 1883 when lightning struck the spire, causing 40 ft of it to crash on to the nave roof and also to damage many of the tombstones. There are many good monuments within the church and an excellent example of modern glass, in a memorial window designed and executed by Payne, a local Minchinhampton artist.

The Painswick Feast Sunday with its Clipping Ceremony dates back to the early 14th cent. It is held on or near 19 September, the Feast of the Blessed Virgin according to the old calendar. "Clipping" in this case comes from an early English word meaning to enclose and has nothing to do with the clipping of yews.

A little to the N. of Painswick is delightful undulating country centred around the hamlet of **Sheepscombe**, rich in Cotswold stone cottages. Cranham Woods is a lovely beech forest. There is little of interest in the village itself. The 14th-cent. church was much restored in the last century but the Tudor rood-screen was left intact. The nearby hamlet of **Paradise** has appropriately an inn called the Adam and Eve. On the other side of the main CHELTENHAM road is the principal entry to the Benedictine abbey of **Prinknash** (pronounced Prinnage). The drive curves down the hillside to the 250 acres of Prinknash Park in the valley. Here in 1520 on a terraced shelf William Parker, the last Abbot of Gloucester, rebuilt the ancient hunting lodge, derived from a privilege granted by Edward III in 1355. The lovely Cotswold manor house was to see many changes. Shortly after being entertained here by the abbot, Henry VIII dissolved all the monasteries. By 1540 Prinknash ceased to be Benedictine property and passed through the centuries into the possession of many distinguished families. It is believed on good authority that Prince Rupert directed the siege of Gloucester from here. In the late 19th cent. it was sold to Thomas Dyer-Edwards who desired that if possible the property should return to Benedictine use. By a curious sequence of events, a remarkable man of vision, Abbot Aelred Carlyle, had attempted to restore Benedictine life within the Anglican communion by establishing a community on Caldy Island in Pembrokeshire. Its eventual reception into the Roman obedience left the community homeless in the second decade of this century. An offer by Dyer-Edwards was accepted and after many difficulties the Benedictines returned to Prinknash, where by diligent application they have made the name of this monastery world-famous. The pottery, which can be visited by the public, sells its wares right across the globe. Down in the valley a new monastery of concrete, steel and glass is fast rising as the modern designs of John Broadbent take shape. When this great new abbey and church are completed the old manor house will continue to dispense Benedictine hospitality in accordance with the Benedictine rule.

PAUNTLEY, *Gloucestershire* (4–SO7328). In a rather remote part of the beautiful valley of the Leadon, about 9 m. NW. of GLOUCESTER, and reached by unclassified roads, is the village of Pauntley. It is situated between Upleadon and Redmarley D'Abitot. Its renown derives from its having been the birthplace in the late 1350s of one of England's greatest merchant princes, Dick Whittington. Alas for the pantomime myth, he was born of a knightly family and married a woman of considerable estate. He was, however, four times Lord Mayor of London and he did achieve his great wealth by his own endeavours and left many great benefactions to the City of London. He died in 1423. Almost certainly he added the fine tower to Pauntley's 12th-cent. Norman church with its huge rounded chancel arch and splendid zigzagged doorway. Dick Whittington's coat of arms can be seen in the west window of the tower. The ancient moated Pauntley Court was long associated with the Whittingtons until they moved to Notgrove in the mid-16th cent.

PEMBRIDGE, *Herefordshire* (8–SO3858). This large village lies a short distance from EARDISLAND on the A44 to KINGTON. It has many lovely half-timbered houses, a number of them dating from the 14th cent. The 16th-cent. Market Place, diminished in importance now, is screened behind the main street. On the north side is an interesting hostelry called the New Inn, built in the early 1600s. Pembridge has a fine early Decorated church with a detached, 14th-cent. belfry that looks more Essex than Herefordshire. It is supported inside by a host of great timbers. There are two interesting almshouses in the town: one founded by Bryan Duppa, Bishop of Winchester, in 1661; the other by Dr Thomas Trafford in 1686.

PERSHORE, *Worcestershire* (8–SO9446), lies 9 m. from WORCESTER on the west side of the VALE OF EVESHAM. The River Avon flows to the S. of the town and from the modern bridge can be seen its six-arched, mostly medieval, bridge with its central larger arch restored after Civil War damage. It is a delightful, prosperous, Georgian town, situated in the heart of the fruit-growing country, in an area particularly renowned for its plums. It remains a country town with many impressive houses lining Bridge Street. Of these Barclays Bank and particularly Perrott House, built in 1760, still have their large gardens backing on to the Avon. This is equally true of the High

Street, where the Angel Hotel, restored in 1920, has some fascinating rooms; in one of them there is an inlaid overmantle with a painted figure and the date 1575. At the end of Broad Street known as the Square is an old house with beautifully proportioned bay windows. The Three Tuns Inn has a most elaborate ironwork veranda.

The history of the town seems to have begun with St Oswald's religious foundation in 689. With the coming of the Normans, the Benedictines built what was probably one of the greatest pre-Reformation abbeys in the country. It was certainly much larger than Worcester Cathedral and its destruction at the Dissolution must rank as one of the major disasters of that period. The beautiful surviving remnant was preserved because the people of Pershore bought the monastic part of the church for their own worship. This section has a splendid Transitional to Early English lantern tower of remarkable proportions, enhancing the strength of the curves of the Norman arches supporting it. The beautiful arcading of the presbytery is all 13th-cent. Inside the lantern is fine trefoiled arcading which screens a passage. From the exterior the corner turrets with spirelet pinnacles present a perfection matched perhaps only by those of LINCOLN Cathedral. The Church of St Andrew opposite came into being when Edward the Confessor seized the revenues of Pershore Abbey for the benefit of his royal foundation at WESTMINSTER. The church is mostly 15th-cent. and has little to attract attention other than a tympanum carved with a cross and shell-like bosses. Roman pottery has been discovered in this area as well as early Roman coins.

Overbury is an exceedingly pretty little village with BREDON Hill for a background. The church, greatly restored, has an Early English chancel with a much earlier Norman nave. All around are attractive timber-framed stone or brick houses of considerable merit. Overbury Court is early 18th-cent. with interesting upper window heads. The garden and park with many rare trees are beautifully kept.

RAGLEY HALL, *Warwickshire* (9–SP0755). Two m. SW. of ALCESTER on the A435 large, simple iron gates between two well-proportioned lodges open on to a driveway to Ragley Hall. This 15-bayed house is full of treasures and one of the stateliest homes of England, owned and occupied by the Marquess of Hertford. Built between 1680 and 1690 by Robert Hooke, it is one of the outstanding Warwickshire country houses. Many great artists and decorators have contributed to its magnificence over the centuries, yet it retains the atmosphere of a house lived in and loved by its owners.

James Gibbs designed the great hall for the 2nd Lord Conway, who became Earl of Hertford in 1750. The Baroque ceiling medallion is an arresting feature of this grand room, 70 ft long, 40 ft wide and 40 ft high, and is attributed to Vassali, who was working at Ragley about this time. From the library, with Reynolds's painting

A. F. Kersting

Ragley Hall: a fireplace in the great hall

of Horace Walpole, is a sweeping view of the lake, with the horizon bounded by the Cotswolds. The china room has a wonderful Worcester dessert set displayed to perfection. The Blue drawing-room has a much envied portrait of Marie Antoinette, and pale blue Sèvres china. The Red saloon has rich hangings, an Angelica Kauffmann ceiling and the Rubens painting of the Holy Family. In the Green drawing-room are some fine examples of chinoiserie. The fire-place came from an old family home in Lisburn in Ireland. The Prince Regent's bedroom is a perfect period piece. There is a portrait of Queen Victoria, and one of the Prince Consort by Winterhalter. Thirty guests can sit at table in the dining-room.

The original park was laid out by Capability Brown in the 1750s though the gardens were much altered towards the latter part of the 19th cent.

Ragley is by no means the largest stately home in England, but it comes near to epitomizing all the rest.

The house is open at advertised times in the summer months.

REDDITCH, *Worcestershire* (8–SP0467), 13 m. S. of BIRMINGHAM, is the centre of the needle-making industry. It was established here by the monks of the now-vanished Cistercian abbey of Bordesley. This abbey was built in the 12th cent. From the needle industry was developed the manufacture of kindred fish-hooks and tackle. Whole new industries have been set up in and around the town, which is undergoing a long-term modernization plan.

RICHARD'S CASTLE, *Herefordshire* (8–SO4969), is right on the Shropshire border, 3½ m. S. of LUDLOW on the B4361, with only the earthworks left of a Norman castle. A steep path has to be climbed to reach them on the flank of Vinnall's Hill. The castle was built by a Norman knight in the reign of Edward the Confessor and is one of the two pre-Conquest fortresses in the county. The old Parish Church of St Bartholomew retains its 17th-cent. bow pews. The tower is 14th-cent. and there remains some good stained glass of the same period. The hatchments on the walls are mostly memorials to the Salweys, one of the most ancient families listed in Debrett. The 17th-cent. Court House to the SE. of the village has an old cider mill in the grounds and a much earlier dovecot.

ROLLRIGHT STONES, *Oxfordshire* (5–SP3030). Third in importance only to STONEHENGE and AVEBURY, these Bronze Age monolithic circles are about 3 m. N. of CHIPPING NORTON just off the A34 and right on the Oxfordshire-Warwickshire boundaries on the edge of the Cotswolds. There is a circle, popularly called the King's Men, and a group of stones called the Whispering Knights. A third menhir enclosed by iron railings is called the King's Stone and actually stands in Warwickshire. Archaeologists agree that the stones pre-date 1500 B.C. and were probably used for funerary ceremonial purposes but certainly had nothing to do with the later Druids. The main circle is about 100 ft across and consists of stone varying from a few inches to some 7 ft in height.

Nearby is the village of **Great Rollright** with grey stone cottages overgrown with climbing roses, set on undulating breezy heights. It has a Norman church with a good Perpendicular tower and a 12th-cent. carving on the tympanum of a crocodile swallowing a man. It also has a 15th-cent. painted rood-screen.

Little Rollright seems almost forgotten, set down in meadow land and reached by a rough lane. As a result it is quite unspoilt, with little cottages supporting a once important manor farm-house. The old church has a narrow nave with two disproportionately large 17th-cent. monuments to the Blower and Dixon families in the chancel.

ROSS-ON-WYE, *Herefordshire* (8–SO6024), is a modest market town set on a red sandstone cliff above a lovely sweep of the River Wye, and a magnet for summer tourists. Although its origins may well go back to Roman times, the essential character of the town as it is seen today is due to the extraordinary efforts of one man, John Kyrle. He was born in Dymock, Gloucestershire, in 1637, studied at OXFORD and the Middle Temple and then resided in Ross until his death in 1724. He was wealthy yet his own tastes were simple, enabling him to become a great benefactor of the town he loved. Such was his modesty and unassuming nature that had it not been for Alexander Pope who, staying frequently at nearby

Ross-on-Wye owes much of its charm to the generosity of John Kyrle, a 17th-cent. resident

Holme Lacy, wrote his praises as the "Man of Ross" in his *Moral Essays*, posterity might have known little about John Kyrle. His house can still be seen at No. 34 in the triangular Market Place. It is possible to visit the little garden at the back; this must have been laid out some time before the end of the 17th cent., which makes its Gothic summer-house and grotesque ornamental arches all the more remarkable. The Market Place is dominated by the 14-arched, double-gabled, 17th-cent. Market Hall, of sandstone with medallioned upper windows and arched lights. Between the two gables is a carved medallion of Charles II. Parts of the timber balcony and balustrade of the older Booth Hall which stood on the same site are incorporated into the building.

Among the many aspects of early town planning initiated and financed by John Kyrle is the Prospect, a walled public garden, SW. and E. of the church. There are good views of the town, and not least of the elegant new bridge carrying the rebuilt A449 across the river. Kyrle's gates survive on the E. and S. with their Classical elegance unimpaired. They bear the cipher of his name and the date A.D. 1700. He also planted the famous elms in the churchyard and raised the causeway leading to the splendid 16th-cent. Wilton Bridge which was reinforced during the First World War and has since been considerably widened. It is a bridge to lean upon and watch the eddying river below; although an 18th-cent. sundial on the parapet has a moral verse inscribed against the vice of wasting time. Kyrle also gave the town its first water supply and repaired the upper part of the 208-ft, 14th-cent. spire of St Mary's and added pinnacles. From the early 13th cent., when it was begun, until the 15th cent. the church acquired much good stained glass (that in the east window is notable and dates from 1430) and new windows were inserted in the north aisle. The arcades were considerably raised in the mid-18th cent., greatly changing the

aspect of the church. Although still lofty and light, St Mary's suffered from the work of restorers between 1862 and 1878.

The church is rich in monuments, particularly those to the right of the chancel arch in the south aisle belonging to the Rudhall family. The alabaster tomb of William Rudhall, who was Attorney General to Arthur, the elder brother of Henry VIII, was carved by one of the last of the great medieval guilds in NOTTINGHAM and was brought to Ross by packhorses. Among the saints carved on the tomb is the unusual St Zita of Lucia, the patron saint of domestic servants. In the north wall of the sanctuary is the monument to the "Man of Ross". He is buried under the sanctuary floor. The churchyard contains a rare plague cross, restored, but its base still bears the inscription "Plague, Ano. Dom. 1637. Burials 315. Libera nos Domine." The picturesque almshouses with their gables and diamond-leaded dormer windows in Church Street were built by a member of the Rudhall family in the early 17th cent. Some good Georgian houses still stand on the north-west side of the Market Place. Walks N. and S. of the town along the river banks will give as much enjoyment today as they did to the young Victoria, who stayed at the Royal Hotel overlooking the river before her accession to the throne.

To the S. of the town are the lovely **Penyard Woods** and nearby is the site of the Roman settlement of Ariconium, then a great forge for the arms of the Roman legionaries stationed in Britain. Bearing a little to the W. through leafy lanes, the walker can reach **Kerne Bridge** with its fine vistas up and down stream. Nearby devoted anglers can be rewarded by visiting the site of the home of Robert Pashley, one of the most remarkable salmon fishermen who ever lived. The fame of the "Wizard of the Wye" extends across the English-speaking world. He died in 1956.

Brockhampton-by-Ross lies 5 m. to the N. of

Ross and just off the B4224. It has a remarkable concrete and stone church built by W. R. Lethaby in 1901–2. It has honest craftsmanship – Lethaby was a disciple of William Morris – and an integrity of structure which, although medieval in inspiration, looks forward to modern architecture. Burne-Jones designed the tapestry and Morris & Co. made it. Lethaby's design is in perfect harmony with its rural surroundings and is approached by a thatched lych-gate on massive semi-circular supports. The ruins of the old church stand in the grounds of what is now the Brockhampton Court Hotel which incorporates a gracious rectory of the late 18th cent.

ROUSHAM HOUSE, *Oxfordshire* (5–SP47 24). Twelve m. N. of OXFORD off the BANBURY road (A423) is the grey-stone walled village of **Steeple Aston** above the valley of the Cherwell. They say its ancient inn, the Hopcroft's Holt, still rings with the ghostly sounds of horse's hooves as Claude Duval rides by. He was a French highwayman who found the village well situated for his exploits, which led him eventually to Tyburn gallows.

The Early English church owns one of the finest examples of the *Opus Anglicanum* embroidery in the world. Originally a magnificent cope, it was cut up after the Reformation and framed as an altar-frontal and is often on loan to the VICTORIA AND ALBERT MUSEUM. Nearby is one of the great Jacobean mansions of England, Rousham House, built by Sir Robert Dormer in 1635. It was considerably improved in the following century by William Kent. Many of the rooms remain exactly as he left them with all their original furniture. One of these has a beautiful painted ceiling and remarkable plasterwork. The fire-places and door-cases are examples of the graceful proportions this English master of 18th-cent. domestic interiors invariably achieved. In 1764 Thomas Roberts, who had done the plasterwork of Christ Church library in Oxford, was called in to redesign the library at Rousham as a salon. This was accomplished with undeniable aesthetic success. There are over 150 magnificent portraits and other paintings to be seen. The house is open to the public through most of the spring and summer. Nowhere can William Kent's genius as a landscape gardener be better than here, where his work has remained completely unspoilt. It extends over 30 acres of ground with the River Cherwell flowing through, crossed by an ancient bridge. Kent used all the natural advantages he found, to achieve a visual effect epitomizing the civilized horticultural conceptions of his age. If he borrowed from Italy, he did so with an economy that could be adapted to the aristocratic taste of his English patrons. These were the Cotterell-Dormers, whose family still own the property. He used the Cherwell to provide attractive waterfalls. One of the many lovely vistas he created was the view from the statue of Hercules to the Praeneste which aroused the admiration of Horace Walpole. The sturdy walker should walk northwards up to an extraordinary structure (now a farm-house) with a pinnacled Gothic gable and supported by flying buttresses on each side. It was known as the Temple of the Mill. Above this on the hill, Kent built one of the outstanding follies in the county, appropriately called the Eye Catcher. It resembles a castle gateway with three narrow, round-topped arches and surmounted by small pinnacles like jagged teeth. The manner in which it is buttressed gives a different appearance from every angle of vision. It is hard to reach, but rewarding for the student or connoisseur of English follies.

RUGBY, *Warwickshire* (9–SP5075). The town of Rugby developed during the later stages of England's industrialization. There are railway engineering works and heavy electrical equipment and, more recently, radio components are manufactured. Its main claim to fame, however, lies in its public school. Rugby School is known all over the English-speaking world through Thomas Hughes' *Tom Brown's Schooldays*. Equally famous is the football game that bears its name. The school was founded in 1567 by a local grocer, Lawrence Sheriff who, having made his fortune in London, endowed a free grammar school for boys. The buildings were moved to the present site in the mid-18th cent. It was under Dr Thomas Arnold, headmaster from 1828 to 1842, that the school grew tremendously in importance and established the pattern of education followed by the greater number of public schools in the mid-Victorian era.

It was Dr William Temple, later Archbishop of Canterbury, who during his headmastership from 1857 to 1869 did most to expand the material resources of the school. He was responsible for a great deal of building, for which he commissioned the architect Butterfield. Victorian Gothic and Tudor can often be inventive and exciting but the general impression of the exterior of Rugby School is somewhat dismal. It boasts many great names on its rolls, among them Walter Savage Landor (expelled); Matthew Arnold, the poet son of the headmaster; C. L. Dodgson, better known as Lewis Carroll, who came here from RICHMOND in Yorkshire; Rupert Brooke, the poet; and Wyndham Lewis, writer and artist.

A granite tablet on Doctors' Wall tells briefly the origin of Rugby Football, "the exploit of William Webb Ellis, who with a fine disregard for the rules of football as played in his time, first took the ball in his arms and ran with it, thus originating the distinctive feature of this Rugby game A.D. 1823". It should be remembered that players at this time often numbered as many as 50 a side and by 1871 laws regarding the number of players and rules of play became necessary. The Rugby Union was thus formed.

SHIPSTON-ON-STOUR, *Warwickshire* (9–SP2540), is an old sheep-market town on the A34, 10 m. SSE. of STRATFORD-UPON-AVON. Its former wool-based wealth is expressed in its many Georgian houses. It has a number of interesting old inns, among them the Horseshoes in Church Street and the George Hotel in the High Street. Shipston's situation in the Vale of the Red Horse makes it an excellent base for exploring the northern spurs of the Cotswolds. Ilmington Down, at 854 ft the highest point in Warwickshire, can be reached by unclassified roads and Meon Hill gives a good view. **Upper Brailes**, reached by way of Fant Hill, stands 757 ft up with lovely views over the Stour and Avon valleys. **Lower Brailes** on the opposite side of the valley has a fine 14th-cent. church known locally as the "Cathedral of the Feldon". Another unclassified roads leads to Edgehill, an L-shaped ridge 4 m. long rimming the Civil War battlefield at **Radway**. On 23 October 1642, 14,000 men of the Royalist army under the command of Prince Rupert confronted 14,000 Parliamentary troops, led by the Earl of Essex. It was a confused, disorderly battle. King Charles claimed the victory and marched to London. However, a young captain called Oliver Cromwell from Huntingdon had been present among the Parliamentarians and he learnt several stern lessons to the advantage of his side.

At the time of the battle, Radway Grange in the village was owned by a John Washington, of the Washington family from Sulgrave, and an ancestral connection of the first President of the United States. In 1712 the house was acquired by Sanderson Miller, whose son was one of the great protagonists of the Gothic Revival in England. He was responsible for the delightful folly, a yellow freestone sham castle known as Radway Castle or Radway Tower.

SLIMBRIDGE, *Gloucestershire* (4–SO7303), 4 m. E. of Sharpness just off the A38 in the Vale of BERKELEY, has the biggest and most varied collection of waterfowl existing in the world, under the direction of the Severn Wildfowl Trust founded by artist and ornithologist Peter Scott in 1946. Here swans, flamingoes, geese and ducks can be seen in natural surroundings: as many as 5,000 wild geese winter in the Severn Estuary and visitors can observe them from towers. Slimbridge is open to the public and enjoys a deserved popularity.

The village Church of St John has late 12th-cent. nave arcades with particularly beautiful capitals, some of which have been described as exemplifying the best traditions of the medieval stonecarvers in England. The rest of the church suffered from poor restoration work in the mid-19th cent.

STANTON HARCOURT, *Oxfordshire* (5– SP4105), is set in gentle stream-crossed meadowlands and lies to the W. of OXFORD about 3 m. S. of Eynsham on the B4449. The square tower of the Early English cruciform church with its Norman windows, its pinnacled buttresses and late Norman doorways is mirrored perfectly in one of the nearby ponds. The partly painted screen is very old, at least 13th-cent. Among the many baronial tombs of the ancient Harcourt family is a particularly fine 17th-cent. example of

the Baroque. The Harcourt family lived here from the 12th to the 18th cent. when they moved to **Nuneham Courtenay**. The Manor was where Alexander Pope lived while translating Homer's *Iliad*. He left a record on a pane of glass, "In the year 1718 Alexander Pope finished here the fifth volume of Homer." The curious kitchen with its ingeniously conceived chimney with a pyramidal roof giving fool-proof ventilation and crowned with a griffin weathercock still stands in the private garden. The splendid three-storied tower where Pope had his study can also be seen reflected in the pools. Aerial photography has proved the existence of a Bronze Age settlement here and three prehistoric stones which are known locally as "The Devil's Quoits" can be easily seen in a nearby meadow.

STONELEIGH, *Warwickshire* (9–SP3272), is an interesting village situated near the confluence of the Rivers Sowe and Avon on the A444, 6½ m. S. of COVENTRY. There is a nine-arched bridge of considerable antiquity as well as a later 18th-cent. one. Some of the old houses are of brick and timber, others are in the local red sandstone. A chestnut tree actually shades a smithy by the village green. It is best, if possible, to drive to Stoneleigh Abbey from LEAMINGTON SPA, through Stoneleigh Park. Here, the River Avon flows by the original sandstone gatehouse of the abbey dating from the 14th cent. Stoneleigh Abbey has been described as the grandest, most dramatic Georgian mansion of Warwickshire. Originally a Cistercian abbey founded by Henry II in 1155, it was one of the smaller abbeys, having only 12 monks and an abbot at the Dissolution. Although the king's commissioners reported favourably, nothing could save it and it passed into the hands of the Duke of Suffolk. It was later sold in 1651 to Sir Thomas Leigh whose family have owned it ever since. Part of the original monastery still survives. The gabled Elizabethan part of the house, which is seen from the Park Drive, dates from this period. In 1710 Francis Smith created the present grand west range for the 3rd Lord Leigh. It might be described as a brilliant piece of Italian Baroque expressed in English understatement. It was completed in 1726. It remained almost unchanged until the Elizabethan long gallery was removed to make way for the fine north porch built in 1836 by C. S. Smith, who was responsible for much of the building in Leamington Spa. He also built the present long gallery into which he incorporated some good Elizabethan glass. There is a good description of the house before Smith made his alterations given in a letter of 1806 written by Jane Austen, whose mother was a Leigh.

The house has been closed to the public since a disastrous fire on the upper floors in 1960. It contains some of the finest furniture attributed to Grinling Gibbons and Chippendale, and superb paintings, tapestries and carvings as well as other great historical treasures.

The Parish Church of St Mary has a fine chancel arch with its Norman carvings still clearly defined. There are many other Norman features, particularly a north door with a weathered tympanum, sculpted with serpents and dragons. The tall sandstone Old Almshouses in the village with their strikingly beautiful chimney stacks date from 1594. They were built by Alice Leigh, whose father was Lord Mayor of London at the time of Queen Elizabeth I's coronation.

Stoneleigh Park is the permanent site of the Royal Agricultural Society's show.

STOURBRIDGE, *Worcestershire* (8–SO8984), is an industrial town on the south bank of the Stour, situated on the edge of the Black Country. This makes for a striking contrast between the conglomerate of industries on one side of the town with pleasant Midland scenery on the other. The town does not have a great deal to interest the tourist. Its early importance was due to its glass-making industry, introduced by refugees fleeing from 16th-cent. religious persecution in Hungary. Its modern rebuilt Edward VI Grammar School stands on the site of a stipendiary priests' school established in 1430. In the High Street is an old 17th-cent. inn, the Talbot, with some 18th-cent. additions. From Old Swinford, the oldest part of the town, a belt of fireclay runs generally north-eastwards. It is reputed to be the best fireclay in the world. The countryside around Stourbridge has much to recommend it. One m. SSW. of the town, **Kinver Edge** is easily reached by a winding uphill lane from Whittington. There are splendid views from the top and the site of a Danish camp. The Norman village church has a good late 16th-cent. tomb and brasses. About 1½ m. S. through Old Swinford is the little village of **Pedmore**, sheltered under Wychbury Hill, crowned with its pre-historic camp. The Norman Church of St Peter has a primitive tympanum with Christ in Glory, wearing a drooping moustache and with an over-emphasized hand raised in blessing. He is surrounded by symbols of the Evangelists. The church was much restored in the late 19th cent. Nearby Pedmore Hall is 17th-cent. with later additions that included huge pilasters.

Two m. WNW. of Stourbridge on the BRIDG-NORTH road is **Stourton Castle**, where in 1500 Reginald, Cardinal Pole and Archbishop of Canterbury was born. Further along the same road is Enville with its Tudor Hall which was much altered in 1760 by the poet Shenstone. It has a fine park with the splendid Shenstone Cascade, a water ornament in best Classical Italian style.

STOURPORT-ON-SEVERN, *Worcestershire* (8–SO8171). This town owes its prosperity to a number of industries, among them carpet manu-facture and the largest chain-works in Europe, and it is overshadowed by a huge power station. Nevertheless, it remains a place of pilgrimage for those who love canals. It stands where the River Stour meets the Severn, 4 m. SSW. of KIDDER-MINSTER. The town took on its importance from the realization of what seemed to be a dream of an illiterate farmer's son. Derbyshire-born James Brindley came to Worcestershire in 1756 with the idea of cutting a canal which would link up the navigable Rivers Trent and Severn. He proposed to end his canal at BEWDLEY. To their later regret, the people of Bewdley refused to cooperate. Brindley then explored this junction of the Severn and Stour. From that moment a new town came into being around the basin that linked the river with his canal. Today much of the Georgian charm of this waterway remains, with the original long red-brick warehouse with its spark-ling white wooden clock tower, and at its south end the Tontine Inn opened in 1788 by the canal company. The renewed interest in canals has led to an even greater interest in Stourport. The basin is always gay with every type of inland water craft taking advantage of the 46-m. stretch of the Staffordshire and Worcestershire Canal up to its junction with the Trent and Mersey Canal at Great Haywood.

Across the Severn is the scattered village of **Areley Kings**, reached by a fine cast-iron bridge. It is famous for having been the home of Layamon, the priest who in *c*. 1200 wrote *Brut*, a poem based on a Norman-French work but written in English, giving a somewhat mythical history of Britain.

At Hartlebury, 2 m. E., the heavily restored church has parts of its medieval chancel and a 16th-cent. tower. **Hartlebury Castle** is a red sand-stone 17th-cent. mansion on the site of a medieval castle, from which the moat remains. For cen-turies it has been the palace of the Bishops of WORCESTER; part of it is still so used. The north wing houses the Worcestershire County Museum. Its collection includes items illustrating the social and industrial history of the county.

S. of Stourport, towards **Astley**, are the Hermit-age or Redstone Caves. They are made up of a whole series of chambers and cells dug into the rock and are believed to have been used by hermit monks. Bishop Latimer said of them that they could house 500 men.

STOW-ON-THE-WOLD, *Gloucestershire* (5–SP1925). At an altitude of 800 ft, this is the highest town in the Cotswolds and is situated where eight roads meet. It is easy to understand that this was once the most thriving wool market in the kingdom. Daniel Defoe, long before he wrote *Robinson Crusoe*, records that the year he came to Stow Fair 20,000 sheep were sold. The large Market Place has an old Market Cross with a restored lantern head and some fine old gabled houses clustered around the square. Particularly notable is what was once the little Elizabethan Grammar School. The gabled and spired Town Hall has some good, and some not so good, paint-ings of outstanding figures of the Civil War and the Restoration. In a central niche is a statue of King Edward the Confessor looking across to another fine old house appropriately called St Edward's. Behind this stands the parish church, which is dedicated to St Edward. Each age from Norman times down to the present has added something of interest to this building. Norman walls were buttressed by the work of 13th-cent.

masons and 13th-cent. quatrefoil tracery and good windows grace the north porch. The canopied sedilia in the moderately restored 14th-cent. chancel are interesting. The south aisle has a 17th-cent. Flemish painting of the Crucifixion by de Craeyer, a pupil of Rubens. There is some good early glass, and some by the mid-19th-cent. stained-glass revivalist, William Wailes, whose output seems to have been enormous. The church has a sturdy 15th-cent. tower. Cromwell imprisoned 1,000 captured Royalists in the church after one of his victories.

STRATFORD-UPON-AVON, *Warwickshire* (9–SP2055), on the west bank of the River Avon, stands at the hub of many radiating trunk roads, the A34, A46, A422 and A439 among them. It is perhaps the least spoilt "cult town" in the world. It has kept its essential character of a thriving Midland market town. Not only does it possess fine 15th- and 16th-cent. timber-framed houses but has a good Georgian overlay. However, it cannot be denied that its later prosperity has derived considerably from the fact that on or about 23 April 1564 William Shakespeare was born here and a few days later baptized in the Parish Church of Holy Trinity. Yet it was through the enthusiasm of the actor David Garrick some 200 years later that a Shakespeare Festival was first held. The idea slowly began to attract visitors to the town over the next 100 years and that attraction has now grown and raised Stratford to become England's prime tourist centre outside London.

There was a Bronze Age settlement here and a Romano-British village. A monastery was founded in Anglo-Saxon days and by 1196 the Bishop of WORCESTER granted the town the right to hold a weekly market. Its growing prosperity led to independence and by the 13th cent. the great Church of Holy Trinity was being built, and at the same time the prosperous and powerful Guild of the Holy Cross built its chapel. The guild generally assumed the powers of municipal government. Henry VIII suppressed it in 1547. The guild was replaced by a bailiff, 14 aldermen and 14 burgesses. In 1568 the office of bailiff was held by John Shakespeare, William's father. Little is known of Shakespeare's boyhood other than that he went to school in Stratford. In 1582 he married Anne Hathaway, a women eight years his senior. In 1590 he had met William Alleyn, the actor who was to found DULWICH College. About this time Christopher Marlowe made a marked impression on him. By 1592 Queen Elizabeth, her court and the citizens of London had shown their approval of the playwright and in 1597 he was able to buy New Place, regarded as the finest house in Stratford. By 1603 he had been summoned to the court of James I as a member of the King's Players. Between 1610 and 1612 he often spoke of retiring permanently to his native town and possibly did so in the latter year. Four years later on 23 April 1616, his 52nd birthday, Shakespeare died. His tomb in Holy Trinity Church is incised with the following lines:

Kenneth Scowen

Stratford-upon-Avon: Halls Croft

> Good frend for Jesus sake forebeare
> To digg the dust encloased heare!
> Bleste be the man that spares the stones
> And curst be he that moves my bones.

Among the many buildings in Stratford that have direct association with Shakespeare are the reputed and likely birthplace in Henley Street; a glorious Tudor gabled house, Halls Croft, in the Old Town, where John Hall who married Shakespeare's daughter Susanna lived; Anne Hathaway's cottage at Shottery; New Place, the playwright's own home; and just outside of the town Clopton House which is well signposted. Much useful information may be had from the Shakespeare Birthplace Trust, which has its new centre comprising museum, library and records collection in a wholly modern building in Henley Street, opened in 1964. This was designed by Laurance Williams and has some fine engravings on the glass doors by John Hutton, who did similar work for COVENTRY Cathedral. The statue of Shakespeare inside the building was the work of Douglas Wain Hobson.

The existence of the Royal Shakespeare

Theatre was due to the enthusiasm and liberality of Charles Edward Flower, the brewer. He first established the Shakespeare Memorial Association. The first theatre was opened in 1879 and over the years demand rapidly outgrew availability of seats. In 1932 the present theatre, by Elizabeth Scott, a cousin of the architect Sir Giles Scott, was opened – fire destroyed the old one in 1926.

There is much to see in Stratford-upon-Avon quite apart from the Shakespearean connections. The 14-arched Clopton Bridge is most visitors' gateway into the town. It was built by Sir Hugh Clopton between 1480 and 1490. The Town Hall at the top of Sheep Street is a fine Palladian building erected in 1767 by Robert Newman. Harvard House on the High Street, between Ely Street and Wood Street, dates from 1596. Thomas Rogers built the house, and his initials and those of his wife, Anne, are carved on the front of the house. Their daughter Katherine married Robert Harvard of Southwark and it was their son, John, who founded Harvard University in the United States. The Falcon Hotel has some of the most attractive timberwork in the town and has not been marred by the modernization achieved at the rear of the building. Opposite the Falcon the Guild Chapel on the corner of Church Street and Chapel Lane has some remains of a remarkable medieval fresco of the Last Judgment. Next to it stands the ancient Guildhall and next to that the almshouses founded by the guild in the 15th cent. They still house 24 elderly townsfolk.

The Bancroft Gardens and walks are well laid out and by the Avon can be seen Holy Trinity with its Georgian pastiche steeple, which was erected in 1763.

The Canal Wharf on the BIRMINGHAM Canal is most attractive and the southern section of the Stratford-upon-Avon Canal has been completely restored by the National Trust. This canal was first opened in 1816 and was unusual interest because its sections were constructed at different periods with different engineers. Each stamped his own individuality in the bridges and lockhouses which were built.

Stratford-upon-Avon in its original rôle as a Warwickshire market town is best seen on market day. Around and in the town, brewing, fruit-canning and light metalwork are carried on. It is perhaps as well that Stratford's own unique celebration, the annual Mop Fair, is held out of the tourist season on 12 October. This was the day in pre-Tudor times when farmworkers and apprentices offered themselves for hire. The mayor, aldermen and macebearers preside at the Roasting of the Ox. Country-dancers compete with pop-singers. The scene cannot be much different from the days when wandering players and jugglers from Coventry set up their carts on this day to entertain the townsfolk.

Four m. E. of Stratford-upon-Avon is **Charlecote Hall**, home of the Lucy family since the 12th cent. A turning N. off the B4086 runs alongside Charlecote Park with views of an Elizabethan house, rebuilt in 1558. The octagonal towered gatehouse is completely unaltered since that time. The house, expanded in the 19th cent., is now owned by the National Trust, although the family still live here. It is open to the public at advertised times. It has much fine furniture and paintings acquired by the Lucys over the ages. It was in the Deer Park, with two rivers flowing through it which meet near the house, that Shakespeare is alleged to have been arrested for deer poaching. The fallow deer seen today have been bred from the same stock for the last 200 years.

STROUD, *Gloucestershire* (4–SO8504). A steep old town once famous as the country's most important centre for the manufacture of broadcloth. It still supplies most of the world's requirements for billiard-table cloth and has a flourishing dye trade. Its scarlet dyes are world renowned. Some of the 18th-cent. woollen mills witness to this important past. Piano manufacture is now included in the activities here. The museum at Lansdown under the Cowle Trust is one of the most interesting in the county. It illustrates old methods of cloth-weaving, local crafts and industries, and there is even a detailed collection of pin-makers' tools. The Archaeology Room has finds from prehistoric barrows at nearby Nymphsfield and Rodborough. There is a good geological section and a collection of local costumes.

All round Stroud is the most beautiful hill country. Four m. SE. is **Minchinhampton** with panoramic views. The village has ancient ties with Normandy. Matilda, wife of William the Conqueror, asked her husband to present the Manor of Hampton to the newly founded Abbaye-aux-Dames in Caen. It is well worth a ¼-m. walk to see the old church with its curious corona and pinnacled tower.

Amberley, S. of Stroud, is some 630 ft above sea-level with glorious scenery all round. Take a short walk across National Trust common land to Tom Long's Post. The view from here is breath-taking. Rose Cottage in the village was described in the Victorian novel *John Halifax, Gentleman*. A short distance from Amberley, still overlooking the valley across to Stroud, is Rodborough Hill, surmounted by an 18th-cent. castellated house called Rodborough Fort. It is a landmark for miles around. Between Stroud and Amberley is **Woodchester**, which has the foundations of one of the largest Roman villas ever excavated in England. The site is generally covered and only rarely can the magnificent mosaic paving depicting Orpheus be seen. The monastery and Dominican convent were designed by Hansom, who invented the cab of that name.

Further S. lies the Cotswold village of **Nymphsfield** at the top of the Stroudwater Hills. The poorly restored church retains its good 15th-cent. tower. It has a pleasant old inn with tall chimneys. The prehistoric Buckholt Barrow is nearby.

STUDLEY, *Warwickshire* (9–SP0763). This small town is probably the largest needle-manufacturing centre in Europe. It is set in pleasant Warwickshire countryside, just 5 m. N. of

ALCESTER. It has been making needles for more than 300 years, though it was in 1800 that Pardow first applied steam power to mass produce them in a factory. The town has old houses and inns dating from its handcraft days. The Barley Mow is a good example of the latter. A little way E. of the main road are the gabled Castle Cottages, near the church. In Elizabethan days it was one complete, rather grand house. The church, dedicated to the Nativity of Our Lady, has a Norman nave, a Jacobean pulpit and some good medieval roodstairs. The 13th-cent. coffin lid brought from the ruins of Studley Castle is a particularly beautiful example of the stonemason's art. The manor house on the main street is a good 17th-cent. domestic building with a fine doorway. The Old Castle just N. of the church dates from the early 1500s and was built on the site of the original Studley Castle.

The present Studley Castle, until recently an agricultural college, was built in 1834 by Beazeley who showed considerable inventiveness in its design. Three m. N. of Studley, walled in on a hill and a little off the A435, is Gorcott Hall. It seems to have been hodge-podged together since the 15th cent. and has recently been extremely well restored. Its timberwork, high gables, diamond-paned windows and high chimneys all make for a wonderful variety of line and texture. It is now privately owned.

SUTTON COLDFIELD, *Warwickshire* (9–SP1296). Although a municipal borough with a population of over 80,000, Sutton Coldfield is only 7 m. from BIRMINGHAM and has become mainly a residential area for that city. Its nucleus is the old market town, important in the Middle Ages, and it has its own modern shopping centre. The Parade reflects a continuity of spirit from its early days. The town owes much to a native son, John Veysey, who became Bishop of EXETER in 1519. He lived at Moor Hall, now in the park adjoining the golf links. Many of the buildings he erected still stand, notably Veysey Grange in Weeford Road, New Hall Mill, High Heath Cottage, and the Old Stone House. He not only founded the school here, but built the Moot Hall and completely paved the streets of Sutton. He is buried in the large Parish Church of Holy Trinity, with his brilliantly painted effigy lying upon his tomb.

Sutton Park is one of the largest and finest pleasure gardens in the county. Its 2,400 acres of woodlands and lakes has the ancient Roman Ryknild Street running through it. Presented to the Warden of the Royal Town by a Charter of Henry VIII, it is still administered by the Corporation of Sutton Coldfield. Just N. of the park is one of the main television transmitting stations with its 750-ft mast.

SWINBROOK, *Oxfordshire* (5–SP2812). Halfway between WITNEY and BURFORD, a signpost points northwards to **Asthall** and following this provides a pleasant country drive to Burford through the valley of the Windrush away from diesel fumes and traffic on the A40. Asthall is a charming village with little picture-calendar cottages, a manor house and an attractive Transitional church. Following the river, the road turns right across a new stone bridge into Swinbrook. It has the usual attractive stone cottages of the Windrush valley backed by meadows and little brooks sparkling their way into the river. The village is famous for the storied tombs in the Church of St Mary the Virgin of the Fettiplace family who flourished with great wealth and influence in Tudor and Stuart days. One of them married a Portuguese princess and brought her to the chillier climate of Oxfordshire. The family are reputed to have owned land in 15 counties. Nothing now remains of their great mansion except the terraced fields beyond the church. The number and size of their tombs make this little Oxfordshire church a rather crowded mausoleum. The best tomb is that designed by Annis of London in 1743 commemorating the 5th and last baronet – a delicate Italianate work.

SYMOND'S YAT, *Herefordshire* (8–SO5516). This famous beauty-spot lies 5½ m. SW. of ROSS-ON-WYE on the Gloucestershire border. The Wye in its narrow gorge flows in a 5-m. loop around Huntsham Hill to make a near-island only a few hundred yards across at the neck. "Yat" is an old form of the word gate and also meant "gap" or "pass".

Relics of cave-dwellers of 20,000 years ago were found in King Arthur's Cave in the Doward Hills some 3 m. downstream.

TEMPLE BALSALL, *Warwickshire* (9–SP 2076), was, as its name suggests, an important centre and Preceptory of the Knights Templars. Simon de Mowbray gave it to the Templars in the reign of Stephen. After the papal suppression in 1248 it passed to the order's successors, the Knights Hospitallers, who were finally established throughout Europe as the Knights of St John of Malta. The Hospitallers at Temple Balsall were suppressed by the Act of Dissolution under Henry VIII. The chapel fortunately remains and as it was not a parish church it has no division between nave and chancel; only gradations of floor levels to meet the knights' liturgical needs. That it all has the appearance of being too new is due to the fact that it was almost geometrically restored by Sir Gilbert Scott in 1849. Even so it remains an awe-inspiring building with a superb east light. After the Dissolution and several owners, Lady Katherine Leveson and her sister bequeathed part of the property as an almshouse for 20 impoverished women. This almshouse survives; its tenants still wear the grey gowns, shawls and headgear prescribed by Lady Katherine. There are many walks around Balsall; one leads nearly 3 m. to the Moat Farmhouse, built about 1500, which has all its original timbering.

TENBURY WELLS, *Worcestershire* (8–SO 5968), is a friendly little market town on the banks of the Teme in a countryside of orchards and hop-

Tewkesbury: the mill and the Abbey tower

fields, where Worcestershire, Herefordshire and Shropshire meet. In 1839 saline springs were discovered, a pump room was erected and for a time it enjoyed some popularity as a spa, particularly as the London to North Wales coaches stopped here. In Market Street the black-and-white Royal Oak is a reminder of these days; so, too, is the King's Head, which is a timber-framed building with an overhang on brackets. The bridge over the Teme takes the traveller into Shropshire. Its three arches are medieval. Almost any of the inns in the town will supply information about the excellent trout-fishing to be had. The chancel of the parish church is probably 14th-cent., but almost the entire fabric was rebuilt in 1865. The square tower is late Norman.

TETBURY, *Gloucestershire* (4–ST8993), lies almost on the Wiltshire borders between STROUD and MALMESBURY. A quiet little market town, it gains distinction from its mid-17th-cent. Town Hall, built up on three rows of pillars. It has a heritage of good 18th-cent. houses with its earlier Chipping Square reached by well-worn steps. In 1781 Francis Hiorne completed one of the best early Gothic Revival churches in the country. The interior is singular and rather Nonconformist in aspect with its typically 18th-cent. gallery and wooden supporting columns; box-pews, however, strike an Anglican note. The pinnacled tower with its lofty spire was rebuilt at the end of the last century. There are a number of interesting monuments from an earlier church.

Tetbury Upton, a village just to the N. of the town, has an elegant 18th-cent. house set in parkland and some good stone houses.

To the SW. on the A433 is **Westonbirt** with its 19th-cent. Italianate house built by Lewis Vulliamy, now a girls' school, but still set in its splendid park with beautiful gardens, terraces and fountains and an unrivalled collection of rare plants and shrubs. Beyond this on the west side of the road, partly in Wiltshire, is the Westonbirt

Arboretum covering 116 acres, managed by the Forestry Commission and open to the public. Started by Robert Slayner Holford in 1829, it is generally regarded as one of the finest collections of trees in the world. The seasonal colourings can be breathtaking, and azaleas, camellias and rhododendrons thrive.

TEWKESBURY, *Gloucestershire* (4–SO8933), is an attractive old town with a wealth of ancient houses and timbered inns. The Bell Inn, one of the best examples, was once a monastery guest-house and has some 13th-cent. wall paintings dating from that time. Like so many places in Tewkesbury, it has associations with Mrs Craik's *John Halifax, Gentleman*. The Hop Pole is yet another ancient inn with a good 14th-cent. fire-place before which, in Dickens's book, Mr Pickwick warmed his coat tails. The house of the Nodding Gables next to the rebuilt Swan Inn has an appearance consonant with its name. Warwick House is 16th-cent. The Cross House on Tolzey Lane has splendid Elizabethan panelled rooms and is believed to have been the Court House of the Lords of Tewkesbury. The Baptist Chapel is one of the oldest in England; the present building was put up in 1690 and has some good 17th- and 18th-cent. furnishings. The Tudor House, a hotel, dates from 1540 and has a priests' hiding hole in the chimney of what used to be the mayor's parlour and is now a coffee room. The Classical Town Hall has some fine portraits in the mayor's parlour. Among them is a good half-length portrait of James Martin, a late 18th-cent. M.P., painted by George Romney. The oldest inn of all claims to date from 1308. This is the Black Bear, a half-timbered building at the top of the High Street near King John's Bridge which crosses the River Avon and has incorporated into it part of the bridge built in 1200. The town stands by the confluence of the Severn and Avon and from the heights of Mythe Tute, between the two rivers, there is a view of the riverside country around, dominated by Thomas Telford's graceful iron bridge with its 176-ft span over the Severn.

Tewkesbury was the scene of one of the bloodiest last battles of the Wars of the Roses. After the death of Warwick the Kingmaker at Barnet, Margaret of Anjou, wife of Henry VI, determined to make a final desperate bid for the Lancastrian cause. On 4 May 1417 the Queen's forces took up their positions on what is now known as Queen Margaret's Camp, Gunhill Manor and Lincoln Green. The Yorkists led by Edward IV took advantage of the poor tactics of the Lancastrians under the Duke of Somerset and destroyed them. The site is still known as the Bloody Meadow and can be seen from Lincoln Lane off the A38.

There is evidence that monks were settled in Tewkesbury by 715 and built a church in these meadows by the river. The Norman nave and tower of the present Tewkesbury Abbey are comparable to the best found anywhere in southern England. The tower is 132 ft high and 46 ft square. The pinnacles added in the 17th cent. might be regretted, but even these cannot detract from this majestic tower. The top affords a panoramic view of the Avon and Severn valleys, the Malvern Hills and, on a fine day, the Welsh mountains. The west front has a recessed sixfold Norman arch, 65 ft high, the largest of its kind in the kingdom. The great window was inserted in 1686. The 14 Norman columns supporting the 14th-cent. vaulting of the roof are some 19 ft round and over 30 ft high. Six chapels radiate from the 14th-cent. apsidal choir. Monuments to the historic families of the De Clares and Despencers abound. The beautiful Warwick Chantry was endowed by the Beauchamps (the family to which Warwick the Kingmaker belonged) and many of them lie buried in the abbey. The choir windows have some of the best English 14th-cent. glass. The south transept has its original Norman apse built before 1178. It now serves as a side chapel and has a Raphael painting which once hung at Versailles. The abbey possesses three organs. One is known as the Milton Organ and was in fact built for Magdalen College, OXFORD. The organ case is a great deal older. Cromwell had it removed to HAMPTON COURT and it is from this time it derives its name, as it is believed that Milton played upon it while he was secretary to the Protector.

Some of the loveliest stretches of the Lower Avon can be navigated for some 32 m. from Tewkesbury to Offenham, 2 m. above EVESHAM.

THAME, *Oxfordshire* (5–SP7006), is an ancient, broad-streeted market town whose charter goes back to the days of Wulfhere, King of Mercia. Only 14 m. from OXFORD and less than 50 m. from London, its enormously wide High Street is packed once a year with all the colour of a medieval fairground at the time of the Thame Show.

The High Street is lined with every style of architecture, weathered and blended from the 15th cent. to the present day. It has many famous inns but none more famous than the Spread Eagle. This was due to John Fothergill, who between the two World Wars was responsible for the vast improvement in country-inn catering throughout Britain. Beyond the 16th-cent. almshouses at the north end of the High Street is a gabled stone building of 1569. This was the famous Thame Grammar School which numbered Milton, Speaker Lenthall and John Hampden among its pupils. In 1878 the school moved to less distinguished quarters. Nearby is the house where John Hampden died in 1643 after being wounded at the Battle of Chalgrove.

The cruciform Church of the Blessed Virgin stands down by the bridge which crosses the Thame on the north side of the town. The present church, possibly built on early Anglo-Saxon foundations, is mostly 13th-cent. This part comprises the chancel, the nave arcades and the lower part of the central tower which was raised nearly 100 ft in the 15th cent. There was considerable and intelligent restoration work carried out at the end of the last century. Particularly notable are the altar tombs of the Quatremain family, all 14th- and 15th-cent. work. The most magnificent is the tomb of Lord Williams who died in 1559 and who had acted as host to Princess Elizabeth as a prisoner and entertained her twice as Queen. Later adapting himself to the changes wrought by Mary Tudor, he supervised the burning of Archbishop Cranmer and his companions at Oxford.

Thame Park, just about 1½ m. S. of the town, stands on the site of Thame Abbey, listed as the third richest Cistercian house in England at the Dissolution of the Monasteries. Many features of the abbey are incorporated into the house, which is now a private residence.

THORNBURY, *Gloucestershire* (4–ST6590), is a quiet little town with good views across the Severn. It has many interesting houses which witness to its earlier importance and a broad street sweeping down to an early 16th-cent. church with an earlier buttressed and parapeted tower. This is a landmark for miles around. There has been a manor here since 925, in the reign of King Athelstan. At the time of the Norman Conquest William I bestowed the manor and all the lands on his wife Matilda. It later passed into the hands of 28 generations of the Stafford family, until it was sold to the Duke of Norfolk in the early 18th cent. and it remained in the Howard family until 1959. In 1508 Edward Stafford, 3rd Duke of Buckingham, started to rebuild the present castle on the site of the old manor. An indiscretion treated by Cardinal Wolsey as an insult led to the duke's impeachment and execution in 1521, before his castle was completed. Henry VIII and Anne Boleyn spent some time here, as did Mary Tudor. The castle had a long period of disuse though the south side of the gatehouse was re-roofed in 1720. A certain amount of restoration work was done by Salvin in 1850. The inner court has perhaps best preserved the atmosphere of the original castle. There is a huge double chimney even larger and more elaborate than those of HAMPTON COURT. Below the heraldic arms of the Staffords is the date "Anno Christi 1514". The castle now houses a restaurant. It is worth trying to see some of the extracts from the Duke of Buckingham's household book, when he fed 589 persons on Christmas Day, 1507.

TYSOE, *Warwickshire* (9–SP3344), lies on the Warwickshire-Oxfordshire border, 7 m. WNW. of BANBURY. It is divided into Lower Tysoe, somewhat sparsely populated; Middle Tysoe, with its splendid late 11th-cent. Church of the Assumption and charming cottages with Venetian windows and doors, and Upper Tysoe, which has a manor house dating from the 16th cent. The great house of COMPTON WYNYATES lies within the parish boundaries.

The district has long been famous for the enigmatic Great Red Horse of Tysoe cut into Sun Rising Hill (where the A422 rises in a 1 in 6 up-grade). It seems that there have been in all five Red Horses of Tysoe. Aerial photography in 1964 revealed that three horses had been cut on the hill called the Hangings between Lower and Middle Tysoe. One was nearly 300 ft long and 210 ft high and was probably the horse which gave its name to the Red Horse Vale – and to the stories of a horse of vast size that had been current for centuries. In 1965 the Institute of Archaeology officially undertook scientific investigation of the site.

Hill-walking in this area can be rewarding since much can still be learnt from the friendly people living hereabouts or in the inns about the ancient festivals of the Red Horse, including the famous Scouring of the Horse every year on Palm Sunday.

UPTON HOUSE, *Warwickshire* (9–SP3545), is an impressive late 17th-cent. mansion 1½ m. from Radway and 8 m. NW. of BANBURY on the A422. It stands high up to the S. of Edge Hill with fine views. It is owned by the National Trust, conveyed to them by the 2nd Viscount Bearsted, together with one of the finest collections of pictures and *objets d'art* in the country. It is open to the public at advertised times. Its interior setting is modern and adapted to its use as a museum. Practically every European school of art from Early Flemish onwards is represented. Rare Brussels tapestries, 18th-cent. furniture, porcelain and a collection of exquisite Chelsea figurines can all be seen under conditions it would be hard to better. The gardens also are open to the public and at the south end is Temple Pool, a charming Tuscan-columned edifice, believed to have been built by Sanderson Miller.

UPTON-ON-SEVERN, *Worcestershire* (8–SO8540), is a pleasing country town on the banks of the Severn 10 m. from WORCESTER and 7 m. from GREAT MALVERN. It is full of delightful houses from early Tudor to early Victorian. Two superb Georgian houses are Waterside House and the Malt House near the river. In the High Street is a very early 17th-cent. timber-framed hostelry, the Anchor Inn. This street also has the famous

three-storied stuccoed White Lion with its huge pilasters and porch surmounted by a lion. This was a setting used by Henry Fielding in his novel *Tom Jones*. All that remains of the old church is its red sandstone tower. The new church was built in 1879 by Blomfield. It does, however, possess a 14th-cent. effigy of a cross-legged knight grasping his sword, presumably saved from the earlier church. The graceful modern single-span bridge crossing the river was completed in 1940. Upton is ideal as a centre for some of the best river cruising in the county. It is possible to sail from here right into the centre of EVESHAM.

VALE OF EVESHAM, THE, *Worcestershire* (9–SP0943), is comprised of most of the county immediately to the S., the SE. and E. of EVESHAM. Like Kent, this lovely countryside is called the Garden of England, a title based on orchard blossoms, and massed fields of daffodils and narcissi. Market-gardening, too, has brought considerable prosperity; asparagus beds are particularly fine. **Wickhamford** lies 2 m. SE., off the A44. There is a modern highway growth of bungalows and market-gardeners' sheds but the heart of the old village is set among trees by Badsey Brook, with its waters rushing over a weir. Here are age-old cottages, a fine timber-framed farm-house, the gabled and timbered 16th-cent. manor house, shadowing with its authority, a perfect little village church. Built on the site of an earlier grange belonging to Evesham Abbey, it was owned by the Sandys family who were connected by marriage to George Washington's family. There are two particularly fine Sandys tombs, canopied and carved in alabaster, in the church. This has a good 13th-cent. chancel with a Decorated arch and east window. Its tower is 16th-cent. It still has the box-pews built for the gentry with linenfold embellishment and under the pulpit the lower tiers of the original three-decker. On the east wall is an ancient wall painting of the Virgin and Child.

E. of Evesham is **Badsey**, another village with a new and not particularly attractive fringe around its original core. The manor house, once an infirmary for the monks of Evesham, is of mellowed stonework and timber-framing. Much of this work was the result of the rebuilding when the property passed to Sir Philip Hoby in 1545. Since 1946 it has been much overgrown with its old carriageway blocked. Just by the church is the late 17th-cent. Stone House with twin gables, looking like a typical Cotswold manor. The church in its yew-shaded churchyard is mostly Norman and early 14th-cent., but suffered a rather ruthless restoration in 1885. The canopied wall monument to Richard Hoby (who died in 1617) and his wife Margaret is interesting because the sculptured children are made to kneel facing W. instead of E. to show that they were Margaret's children by a previous marriage.

A short distance away on the B4035 is the village of **Bretforton** watered by three tributaries of the Avon. The 600-year-old Fleece Inn is timbered and has a Cotswold stone roof. It houses a

The Vale of Evesham: the old Fleece Inn in the village of Bretforton

priceless collection of Stuart pewterware. The most interesting feature of St Leonard's Church is the fine range of 12th- and early 13th-cent. arcades. Carvings on the capitals include a terrifying dragon swallowing a saint who is obviously rescued at the last moment by the hand of God. The tower is 15th-cent. Perpendicular. The three-gabled manor house by the church was built in the early part of the 17th cent. and restored with additions in late Victorian times. Bretforton Hall is a perfect example of early 19th-cent. Gothic with its porch supported by pillars carrying narrow ogee arches which in turn support a semi-circular balcony with elegant ironwork. The Grange Farm is medieval, much rebuilt during Tudor and Jacobean days. Prince Rupert sheltered here in 1645. It has a beautiful 15th-cent. tithe barn. The village has what is probably the largest village collection of dovecots in the country; one at least was built by the monks of Evesham and at least two are early 17th- and 18th-cent. respectively.

N. of Bretforton are three villages, **South Littleton**, **Middle Littleton** and **North Littleton**. The first village consists of a red-brick manor house built on to a Tudor building in 1721; it has dormer windows, a splendid weathercock and a fine yew hedge in the gardens. The church has a 14th-cent. tower but much earlier Norman doors. Its chief treasure is a finely carved Norman bowl, on its font. It also has some of the oldest Decorated pews in the county. The chancel was over-restored in the last century. Middle Littleton has a pleasing group consisting of a three-gabled Elizabethan manor house, a tithe barn built by an Abbot of Evesham in 1376 of beautiful blue lias and Cotswold stone dressing. It looks like a largish church, being some 140 ft long and 40 ft wide

and is in fact not only the biggest but one of the finest in the county. This is followed by an impressive dovecot with some 750 holes. The parish church has good early lancet windows, some well-preserved medieval tiles and an excellent Norman font. The embattled chapel built over the porch was added by Thomas Smith in 1532. The last village has little to recommend it other than one Hans Andersen sort of cottage with a very early medieval window.

The road continues N. to nearby **Cleeve Prior** with its broad streets, its air of prosperity and its stone cottages set on rich green verges looking on to a triangular village green, dominated by an old elm. It derives its name from the priors of WORCESTER who were the lords of the manor. The tall-chimneyed manor house is seen through an avenue of 12 clipped yews leading up to its Jacobean doorway. There is a priests' hole in the house which secreted Thomas Bushell, who acted as banker to Charles I during the Civil War. The churchyard boasts a 600-year-old yew and some intriguing headstones. The Church of St Andrew has a Norman nave and doorway, Early English lancet windows and a 14th-cent. tower. The King's Arms probably dates from the 15th cent. The motorist with a little time to spare should ask the way to the footbridge across the river, where a beautiful stretch of the River Avon is enhanced by a weir and an old mill.

WARWICK, *Warwickshire* (9–SP2865). This is one of the least spoilt county towns in England, set at the hub of radiating roads: the A41, A46, A425 and A445. The town stands on a north rise from the River Avon which is crossed by two bridges, the Castle Bridge and the Old Bridge in the castle grounds. It was this dominant situation that accounted for its early importance. One of the daughters of Alfred the Great, Ethelfleda, raised a fortress on the mound here to ward off attacks from the Danelaw. By the time of the Norman Conquest, it became a royal borough, increasing considerably in size and importance. Shortly after the Conqueror's death it was given to Henry de Newburgh, who began the present castle and became the 1st Earl of Warwick. He was the predecessor of the Beauchamp family who held the title for the following 400 years. After this line became extinct, Queen Elizabeth revived the earldom, conferring it upon the Dudley family who still hold the title.

A small remainder of the medieval town encircles the present centre, the result of a terrible fire which broke out in the centre of old Warwick in 1694, burning down more than 250 dwellings and a very considerable part of the cathedral-like St Mary's Church. The damage was such that practically the entire town had to be rebuilt.

Some of the most delightful pre-1694 houses are to be found in Castle Street. Outstanding is the isolated timbered house of Thomas Oken which, carefully restored, is now a Doll Museum, with an interesting collection assembled by Mrs Joy Robinson.

Most famous of all the remaining medieval houses is Lord Leycester's Hospital by Warwick's West Gate. Originally the Guild House of St George, by the end of the 14th cent. it had become the home of the united and powerful Guilds of the Holy Trinity and Our Lady. Their powers were such that the affairs of Warwick were virtually governed from here. After Henry VIII's dissolution of the guilds, the buildings, considerably rebuilt, became the beautiful timbered, gabled, and terraced structure seen fronting the street today. It was transformed in 1571 by Robert Dudley, Earl of Leicester, into almshouses or a hospice for old and disabled "brethren", usually soldiers who had served with the fighting earls. Today 12 brethren and a master still occupy the building. Their quarters have been modernized in keeping with the structure. On special occasions they still wear their traditional Elizabethan dress. The chapel, somewhat restored, the courtyard with its oriel windows, the kitchen and the banqueting hall are perfectly preserved and used. Other famed houses of the period are Tinker's Hatch at No. 105 High Street and Tudor House in West Street. Out at Bridge End is Brome Place built in the mid-15th cent.

Of the post-conflagration period, the Court House in Jury Street shows that rebuilt Warwick reflected the power of the wealthy burgesses as well as the earls. Francis Smith built it between 1725 and 1728 with an Italianate Doric colonnaded façade of rusticated stone. The eye is held by a statue of Justice by Thomas Staynor. Among its treasures are the Great Mace of 1672 and Thomas Oken's painted chest. The one-storied, pedimented Shire Hall in Northgate Street built in 1753 has fine coffered and stucco ceilings and an original octagonal lantern. The Town Hall in the

Market Place is now a museum. Landor House (1692) has a doorway with a pediment on brackets. It is now part of a girls' school. Walter Savage Landor, poet and essayist, is one of Warwick's most distinguished sons. Other examples of this remarkable period are Eastgate House in Jury Street and the Pageant House which is late Georgian.

Apart from the castle, the dominant architectural feature of Warwick is the lovely Church of St Mary with its 174-ft tower and pinnacle. Situated on one of the highest points of Warwick, it is on the site of an early Norman church. The great fire destroyed the nave and aisles of the Norman and 14th-cent. building; only the crypt, the chancel and the south transept can really give a true idea of its collegiate splendour. The crypt has enormous Norman circular piers with four diagonal shafts and scalloped capitals. An impression of tremendous strength is gained, suggesting it must even then have supported an enormous building. The chancel's soaring roof is a perfect example of the vision of Perpendicular architecture. In the centre is the tomb of Richard Beauchamp, the Earl of Warwick who figures in the story of the burning of Joan of Arc. One of the great figures of the Middle Ages, he commanded Calais for Henry V. The tomb constructed by John Borde in Purbeck marble with the effigy cast by William Austen, a Londoner, is one of the most beautiful in Europe. The Beauchamp Chapel is incomparable. Other tombs of interest are built to the memory of the later Dudleys. Ambrose, who died in 1590, was given the vacant title by Queen Elizabeth. The tomb of Robert, his brother, is exuberantly heraldic. The Chapter House, which has been restored, contains a monument to Fulke Greville, the poet who was counsellor to Queen Elizabeth and James I, and yet another famous son of this city.

Another Warwick place of worship of contrasting interest is the old Friends' Meeting House built in 1695 with its original simple furnishings.

Warwick Castle must compare favourably with any of the great fortress houses of Europe, not even excluding WINDSOR. The outlines of the original motte or keep with its bailey which contained the domestic buildings are still visible. None of the present buildings date back before the 13th cent. It is still the home of the Earls of Warwick. The outstanding buildings are Caesar's Tower, the Gatehouse or Clock Tower, Guy's Tower, which is 128 ft high, and the south range housing the living quarters of the present earl, dramatically set above the winding river. The guides in Warwick Castle are expert and well worth listening to. The great hall must be seen, so, too, the state dining-room. The fine library was carefully restored after the fire in 1871.

In the conservatory is the famous Warwick Vase found by Sir William Hamilton in the grounds of Hadrian's villa at Tivoli. It is attributed by scholars to Lysippus.

The castle contains a fine collection of Classical paintings from all over Europe.

The magnificent gardens were laid out by

Capability Brown, who began his work here in 1753.

The Old Bridge across the Avon was built in the late 14th cent. and has romantically overgrown arches.

WATLINGTON, *Oxfordshire* (5–SU6994), is 7 m. S. of THAME and once owed its importance to its position on the **Icknield Way** following the foot of the main Chiltern Hills. Its narrow streets have many old half-timbered houses, some of stone and some in chequered brickwork. They are mostly 17th-cent. The gabled Town Hall built in 1664 on open arcaded work of brick stands prominently on the triangular market place. As late as the 19th cent. the "County" gave balls in an Assembly Room in the Hare and Hounds Hotel which was connected with the first floor of the Town Hall by a bridge.

The Church of St Leonard stands nearly a mile from the market place and is reached through tree-lined meadows. It was completely rebuilt in 1877 and only the tower is original, though it stands on the site of an ancient castle. It has a good painting by one of the pupils of Annibale Carracci who decorated the Farnese Palace in Rome, given by a benefactor.

WELFORD-ON-AVON, *Warwickshire* (9–SP1552). This is a pretty village with old timber-framed houses. It lies 4 m. SSW. from STRATFORD-UPON-AVON and has become a dormitory area for that town, but remains unspoilt. On the village green stands a tall striped maypole surmounted by a golden ball and a fox weathervane. On May Day there are genuine traditional revels on the green with all the fluttering ribbons, the clatter and red-streamered straw hats of Morris dancing in its most authentic form.

The lych-gate leading to the church is said to be one of the oldest in Warwickshire. Part of the church is Norman, and it has an interesting 15th-cent. sanctus bellcot. Just NE. of the church is a good Georgian brick house called Cleavers, well worth looking at. The village is situated on a loop of the Avon where there is an inn with a painted sign showing a king, a parson, a soldier and a farmer, with a quaint verse indicating that it is always the countryman who pays for all. The inn is called The Four Alls. Some say this is a corruption of Four Ales.

WELSH BICKNOR, *Herefordshire* (8–SO 5917), an isolated parish on the Gloucestershire border near the Wye, reached by a minor road from GOODRICH. Welsh Bicknor is where the boy grew into young manhood who became Henry V, hero of Agincourt. Courtfield Park became the country seat of the Herefordshire Vaughans, one of whose sons was the 3rd Cardinal Archbishop of Westminster. The house is now a home of retirement for Roman Catholic priests. The church, rebuilt in the mid-19th cent., retains the 14th-cent. tomb of Margaret Montacute with her recessed effigy above a 12th-cent. coffin lid.

WEOBLEY, *Herefordshire* (8–SO4051), pronounced without the "o", has a wealth of early timber-framed houses and lies to the E. of the A4112, about 9 m. NW. of HEREFORD. Mentioned in the Domesday Book, its later importance was such that before the 1832 Reform Bill it was a borough returning two Members of Parliament. After the Battle of NASEBY in 1645, King Charles stayed at a long, low timbered building then called the Crown Inn, later the Throne, and now a private house. The old Red Lion Inn was built in the 14th cent. but many additions were made in the 17th and 19th cents. The little cottage at the back is said to be the oldest house in the county.

In local lore Weobley has always been famed for its witches. Once there were said to be more than 50 sorceresses within a 2-m. radius of the village. Its early prosperity was based on the manufacture of gloves and ale. The church has a fine buttressed spire and some good monuments. In the sanctuary is a marble figure of Colonel John Birch who took Hereford for Parliament. He later quarrelled with Oliver Cromwell and is reported to have been imprisoned no less than 20 times. He afterwards played a leading part in the Restoration. He was Member of Parliament for Weobley from 1678 to his death in 1691. In the churchyard is a preaching cross on its original medieval base; local legend associates it with conjuring up the Devil. The house called the Ley, situated about ½ m. to the SW., is dated 1589 and has an attractive line of uneven gables.

WHICHFORD, *Warwickshire* (9–SP3135), is a charming village just far enough off the A34 OXFORD to STRATFORD-UPON-AVON road to have preserved its serenity. The old schoolhouse built 100 years ago stands at the top of the wide green which is flanked by some substantial, mullioned stone houses built by yeoman farmers. Some have been excellently restored to their original beauty, making amends for a Victorian phase of too much money and too little taste. All have thatched or stone roofs. The village pumps are 19th-cent. The old Church of St Michael, and a castle of which there are few traces, was built by a Norman knight De Mohun. The earliest part of the church is the south doorway which has a good Norman dogtoothed arch supported by two single piers, with one capital carved with a beast, the other an empearled pattern having a suspended cord, Byzantine in feeling. The tympanum is plain with a rim of geometric ornament. The northwest tower is well-proportioned and dates from the early 13th cent. The clerestory with five good square-headed windows was a 15th-cent. addition to give more light. The church contains two remarkable tombs and a south chantry chapel with the recessed 14th-cent. heraldic coffin lid of Sir John Mohun, the last male heir of the family, who died in battle. From the female side of this family were descended the Earls of Derby. The fine table tomb on the north side of the chancel has a superb alabaster slab incised with the effigy of John Merton, rector and chaplain to the Earl of Derby who died in 1537. On the south side of the chancel is the tomb of Nicholas Asheton, an early post-Reformation rector whose brass inlay shows him in Geneva gown and broad-scarf. At each corner of the tomb is a shield of lead portraying his arms.

Whichford House next to the church was once the rectory. Records at WORCESTER seem to suggest that the present house was built on to a much earlier rectory and the contrasting and unusual roof lines seen from the back of the house would seem to confirm this. The early 18th-cent. part of the building was planned ambitiously to have seven bays but the two left-hand ones were never built, giving a charming variety to a dignified pedimented façade with one dormer window high up in the roof looking like an afterthought. The house has been thoroughly restored by the present owners who have laid out a pleasant English country garden with loving care, to achieve variety of line with a blaze of colour. The clematis on one wing of the house sets off the weathered stonework. The gardens are occasionally open to the public. Beyond the grounds the wooded countryside rises to Great Rollright.

WIGMORE, *Herefordshire* (8–SO4169), is a village of history and beauty to the SE. of Leintwardine on the A4110. Wigmore Hall at the south end of the village is notable with its gabled two-storied porch. The church, at the top of the village street with its clustered half-timbered houses, has some good Norman herringbone masonry. To the W. of the church is the mound of Wigmore Castle built by the Norman William Fitz Osborn on the site of a fortress erected by the daughter of Alfred the Great. It passed into the hands of the great Mortimer family and it was from here Edward Mortimer set out on his journey which was to give him his victory at MORTIMER'S CROSS. Wigmore Abbey, about 2 m. to the N. of the village, was founded in 1179 by the Augustinian Canons of St Victor of Paris and became the last resting place of generations of Mortimers. The weathered stonework and ancient timbers are lovely in decay. Part of the western range of the abbey is preserved in Wigmore Grange in **Adforton**. The remains of the outer gatehouse, and the inner gatehouse with its stone arch surmounted by black-and-white work with braced timbered building on either side, are striking and open to the public.

A good walk is from Wigmore to **Lingen** through the ancient **Forest of Deerfold**. This wood was a sanctuary of the Lollards during their persecution period and Sir John Oldcastle hid in nearby Chapel Farm for four years before his capture and execution. A fine mistletoe oak still flourishes in the forest. From Lingen, a lane leads down to the banks of the River Lugg. Here may be discovered the ruins of the Augustinian nunnery, **Limebrook Abbey**, founded by Robert de Lingen in 1189. The woods above have ancient trees and wild flowers abound: the *Assarabacca*, purple iris, the cuckoo flower, the little alchemilla, columbines, the brilliant veronica and a particularly beautiful species of lungwort all thrive. The total walk is about 3 m.

WINCHCOMBE, *Gloucestershire* (5–SP0228), lies 7 m. NE. of CHELTENHAM in beautiful hill country by the River Isbourne. In Anglo-Saxon times this little town was the capital of the kingdom of Mercia and boasted a remarkable abbey founded in 797 which housed the shrine of the young King Kenelm, said to have been martyred. Destroyed by Henry VIII, its ruins are still being excavated. The Parish Church of St Peter was begun in Perpendicular style in the mid-15th cent. It has an embattled and pinnacled tower with a brilliant gilt weathercock. It has almost 40 remarkable grotesques carved on its walls. The 700-year-old pilgrims' inn, the George, with its galleried coachyard, still bears on the lintels of its lion-headed doorway the monogram of Richard Kidderminster, the last but one Abbot of Winchcombe.

On the heights above Winchcombe is a 178-ft-long Neolithic barrow called Belas Knap in which many prehistoric objects have been found. Just to the S. of the town is **Sudeley Park** with Sudeley Castle, once the home of Catherine Parr, the last wife of Henry VIII. Little remains of the old medieval castle, but parts of the 15th-cent. structure are incorporated into Sir Gilbert Scott's reconstruction of 1858. There are some fine pictures, priceless tapestries and good furniture to be seen. The castle is open to the public at advertised times in the summer season. Catherine Parr's tomb in the chapel was destroyed in the Civil War; the present ornate canopied tomb was designed by Sir Gilbert Scott. The formal gardens with trimmed yews screening the pinnacled chapel are particularly beautiful.

WITNEY, *Oxfordshire* (5–SP3509). Just 10 m. W. of OXFORD on the A40 is the prosperous little town of Witney. Its fame for blanket-making has made its name known all over the world. The Domesday Book mentions the existence of two mills established here in 1085 and it has derived its wealth from weaving for centuries, being situated on the Windrush, on the very edge of the rich Cotswold sheep-rearing area. It is a mellowed stone-built town with a wide street gradually narrowing and continuing for nearly a mile. This leads to a green, bordered by cool lime trees and interspersed with the Cotswold merchants' houses. Its Butter Cross was built in 1683 and is surmounted by a clock-turret and sundial. It rests on 13 stone pillars; the central one is thought to have been the column of the original Market Cross. The nearby arched Town Hall is almost Provençal in its appearance. The Grammar School, set in an avenue of elms, was built and endowed by a wealthy grocer, Henry Box, in 1663, and the Old Blanket Hall with its one-handed clock dates from about 1720. The library possesses an edition of Homer with an imprimatur of 1542. The architectural outlines of the church show various styles from Early English onwards. There is good evidence of all this having been built on to an even earlier Norman church. It has a good Transitional doorway and porch with a cornice above which are curious carvings of animals. All this, however, is dwarfed by the splendour of the 156-ft-high Early English spire which is visible for miles around the countryside. The soaring arches of the tower supporting the steeples are no less impressive. The church has some good 15th-cent. monuments to the Wenham family, who were making blankets in Witney 300 years ago.

Even the blanket factories do not spoil the beauty of the town. The most modern blanket factory blends serenely into the warm stone buildings adjoining. It is sited on the foundations of an earlier weaving mill founded by the present Early family some 300 years ago. In 1669 Thomas Early started making blankets, some of which he shipped out to the North American colonies. This connection with Canada and the United States has been maintained to the present day.

Just outside of Witney, towards Oxford, turning right at the Griffin Inn, a short walk leads to a little hamlet called **Cogges**. The fine Decorated church was built and owned by the Benedictine monks of Fécamp in Normandy, who also built and maintained the Manor House. The chantry chapel to the north of the chancel is particularly fine. The hamlet is full of strange little twists and turns and has some good old stone houses which partly obscure the church.

Another walk 1 m. NE. of Witney leads to the little village of **North Leigh** with a romantic disused windmill on its hill-top. The church has an Anglo-Saxon tower and Norman and later work. The Wilcoate Chapel has a Perpendicular fan tracery roof, while the north aisle is in 18th-cent. Classical style. It also possesses an unusual collection of coffin plates.

A short walk to the NE. leads to the remains of a Roman villa, with a tessellated pavement and a hypocaust or central-heating system. It is unwise to try to drive a car to the villa as it is at the bottom of a steep and narrow lane with no turning space.

WOODSTOCK, *Oxfordshire* (5–SP4416), is a fascinating old country town 8 m. N. of OXFORD, bisected by the handsome bridge over the River Glyme. It shares with WINCHESTER and WINDSOR the title of royal demesne, since from Anglo-Saxon to late Tudor days it saw a succession of monarchs in residence. The Black Prince, son of Edward III, was born here in 1331. His ancestor Henry I had not only a deer-park in Woodstock but, most unusually, a zoological collection of wild beasts. Another ancestor, Henry II, set up his mistress "The Fair Rosamund" in some state here. The royal country house was known as Woodstock Manor. Its site is roughly N. of the bridge which crosses the lake in the Duke of Marlborough's park. It was probably rebuilt several times and here as well as at HATFIELD the Princess Elizabeth was held as a prisoner by her sister Mary. The house was practically destroyed in the Civil War, but enough remained to shelter Vanbrugh when he was building BLENHEIM PALACE. A square well still fed by a spring is about all that remains of the old manor enclosure. Even Woodstock's market owes its origin to King John. By the time Elizabeth I came to the throne, and she returned in state to the scene of her imprisonment, the town had become one of the greatest glove-making centres in the country; the industry is still carried on today. There are many lovely old stone houses, and the famous Bear Inn was already old when the palace was being built. According to local lore it dates back to 1237. Much of the present structure is 16th-cent. The Town Hall was built by Sir William Chambers in Classical style in 1766 with funds provided by the Duke of Marlborough. Particularly fascinating are the shapes and sizes of some of the ancient chimney pots, one of which, a soaring medieval construction, was climbed by Sir Winston Churchill at the age of 12. The church has a Norman south door with arched bands of chevrons going right to the ground, dispensing with the usual Norman capitals, and in contrast to the Classical 18th-cent. tower. The 600-year-old octagonal font with its unusual traceried panels is noteworthy, and so is the 15th-cent. screen. The bosses on the roof are particularly fine. The church bells have a different chime for every day of the week. The pleasant streets lead inevitably to the great palace, since this is the magnet that brings thousands of visitors from all over the world.

Just outside Woodstock on the south side of Blenheim Park, is the little village of **Bladon**. The village pump, the Old Malthouse with its tall 15th-cent. chimneys and mullioned windows, and its quaint cottages all testify to its claim to be the mother parish of Woodstock. The present church is a dull Victorian reconstruction of 1894 on the site of an earlier church, itself rebuilt in 1801. In January 1965 Sir Winston Churchill was buried very simply in the churchyard at the head of the grave of Lady Randolph Churchill, his mother. She was the beautiful Jenny Jerome, daughter of an American newspaper magnate of the last century. His father, Lord Randolph Churchill, is buried alongside. The plain slab tomb bears the simple inscription "WINSTON LEONARD SPENCER CHURCHILL 1874–1965". Cars should be left in the official village car park and the short, steep climb to the church made on foot.

WOOLHOPE, *Herefordshire* (8–SO6135), on high ground between FOWNHOPE and LEDBURY and reached by twisting lanes, is of major interest to geologists all over the kingdom as the place of origin of the Woolhope Society of Naturalists and Archaeologists. A phenomenon here is the Silurian limestone protruding through the red sandstone of the hills. Woolhope is associated with Lady Godiva and her sister Wulviva who gave the manor to HEREFORD Cathedral in the 11th cent. The Norman church was much restored by the Victorians, some of it well done, some of it regrettable. A modern window portrays the traditional Lady Godiva.

WOOTTON WAWEN, *Warwickshire* (9–SP 1563), a village on the busy A34, 6 m. NW. of

A. F. Kersting

Worcester: the Guildhall was designed by a pupil of Sir Christopher Wren

STRATFORD-UPON-AVON, has the most ancient church in the county. Although no Anglo-Saxon traces are evident from the outside, the church, in fact, embodies work of this period, particularly the lower parts of the tower, resting on four arches, which date from about 1042. There was, however, a much earlier church dating back to 723 when an Anglo-Saxon nobleman named Ethelric received the land from Ethelbald, King of Mercia.

During the 13th cent. the church grew in importance and size and the three distinct periods of building give almost the impression of three churches joined together. There are some good brasses and monuments; particularly fine is the tomb of John Harewell who died in 1428. Wootton Hall just E. of the church is a dignified late 17th-cent. house with good Classical pediments, triangular and segmental in the accepted Italian tradition.

WORCESTER, *Worcestershire* (8–SO8555). The ancient cathedral city of Worcester lies in the centre of its county. Although built on both sides of the Severn the principal part of the city has grown over the centuries on the steeper eastern bank. This was in order to avoid the flooding which frequently was a greater menace

than the many marauding armies the district has known: Romans, Anglo-Saxons, Danes and the Welsh all contributed to a turbulent history. The fertility of the surrounding Severn valley was always sufficient to make Worcester a coveted prize. The Civil War inflicted terrible damage. Worcester was the first city to declare for the King and the last to surrender in 1646. In 1651 Cromwell's "crowning mercy" was the final battle at Worcester when Charles II was completely defeated and had to flee for his life. Modern Worcester is at the hub of radiating main roads and the M5 skirts it. Road-building has meant the loss of much that was old, beautiful and even great,

The first cathedral church at Worcester was built by St Oswald who later became Archbishop of York and a friend of St Dunstan, who considerably influenced him. He attached a community of Benedictine monks to the church in about 961. Some 80 years later the church was almost destroyed by the Danes. In 1062 Wulfstan, Prior of Worcester, was made bishop. This English prelate submitted to William after Harold's death and was not therefore replaced by a Norman. He started work on the present cathedral in the year 1084. The crypt, one of the most inspiring parts of this very beautiful cathedral, is to all practical purposes exactly as St Wulfstan (or

Wulstan) built it. The interior of the cathedral blends different styles harmoniously. The two west bays of the nave are fine Transitional work with both round and pointed arches. In the early part of the 13th cent. the master mason engaged on the building of LINCOLN Cathedral started work on his design for the choir. Building went on unabated for more than 100 years in the Early English style. The visitor today sees a forest of slender pillars supporting a high vaulted roof. In the centre of the exquisite chancel, in front of the high altar, is the tomb of King John. He was buried here in the cathedral between the shrines of St Wulfstan and St Oswald by his own wish, expressed in his will which has been preserved. On the south side of the chancel is the tomb of Henry VII's eldest son, Prince Arthur, who died at the age of 15 in 1502. The tomb is contained in a Perpendicular chantry chapel of delicate stonework. The arches of the Lady Chapel behind the high altar are perhaps among the most beautifully proportioned 13th-cent. work to be found in the country. The cathedral library above the south aisle of the nave contains some leaves of a copy of a Mercian Gospel written in the 8th cent.

The cathedral has suffered a great deal from restorers. Between 1857 and 1874 practically the whole of the surface of the exterior was completely restored including a number of windows.

A 13th-cent. gateway opens out on to College Green, virtually all that the cathedral has in the way of a precinct. It leads on to the cloisters, the King's School and the chapter house as well as the ruins of the old Guesten Hall – the guesthouse the monks built in 1320. The cloisters are mostly 14th-cent. but have Norman outer walls. East of the cloisters is a very early Norman passageway known as the Slype in which are a number of stones reputed to have formed part of Oswald's original Anglo-Saxon church. They are certainly the oldest stones in the cathedral. The Norman chapter house was built probably about the year 1120. It was the first to be built in this country with a single central pillar supporting a vaulted roof. More than any other, the view from College Green of the monastery ruins, the magnificent cathedral, the watergate and the ferryways all conveys an impression of monastic Worcester. Just to the W. of the gateway, which is also called the Edgar Tower, is the deanery, an early 18th-cent. house with a particularly beautiful pedimented doorway. Just outside St Peter's Gate is the 15th-cent. Commandery (now owned by the National Trust), on the site of the Hospital of St Wulfstan founded in 1085. It is timber-framed with a most impressive great hall which has a lofty open roof and is divided into five bays. It has some good 15th-cent. stained glass. The magnificent Elizabethan staircase leads to upper rooms, one of which has fine 16th-cent. wall paintings of various religious subjects.

The river below the cathedral is crossed by a fine stone bridge built by John Gwynn between 1771 and 1780. It was later enlarged.

Worcester's other great claim to fame is the Royal Worcester Porcelain Works, whose ware ranks with some of the world's greatest. It all started with a Worcester citizen, Dr Wall, anxious to restore the prosperity of the city after the decline of the cloth trade. He worked on a substitute for china clay which, up to that time, had not been found anywhere in these islands. By 1751 he was able to open a porcelain factory in the city which not only copied Chinese and Japanese porcelains, and Sèvres, Dresden and Meissen ware, but attracted gifted designers who achieved originality and attracted the patronage of the great. Dr Wall died in 1766 but the royal seal of approval was given by King George III some 12 years later. There were difficult days ahead but in the early 1860s the Worcester Royal Porcelain Co. was formed to maintain the exquisite craftsmanship which had been the hallmark of the 18th cent. The Works and Dyson Perrins Museum in Severn Street may be visited by appointment.

Worcester's other still flourishing industry is that of glove-making. Worcester Sauce really is made in Worcester, from the receipe of an early Governor of Bengal, Sir Marcus Sandys, who lived in the county.

Worcester retains a number of interesting old houses. The Guildhall is one of the most gracious Queen Anne buildings in the county. Of brick with stone dressing, it has a great pediment carved by its probable architect, Thomas White, who was a pupil of Sir Christopher Wren. Two niches each contain statues of Charles I and Charles II; Queen Anne looks down from a central niche over the doorway. On the top floor is the splendid Assembly Room in which hangs a Reynolds portrait of George III presented to the town by that monarch. The painted ceiling has a light-heartedness in keeping with its period. The old timbered Queen Elizabeth House has been moved back a few yards to Trinity and is now called Trinity House. King Charles's House in New Street is now a shop but has an interesting inscription over its 1577 doorway. Next to No. 32 Friar Street is what was once the guest-house of the Franciscan friary established in 1239. The present building dates from about 1480 and is now owned by the National Trust. It is one of the most beautiful timber-framed and tiled houses in Worcestershire. Additions were made in the 17th and 18th cents. The National Trust also owns Nos 14, 16 and 18 in the same street. These are also timber-framed and tiled and were built between the 15th and 16th cents. Some are now partially converted to shops, but with no diminishment of their beauty. Other fascinating old houses can still be discovered in Fish Street and New Street where Nos 5 to 7 form Nash's House, a typical important town house of the 16th cent. It has unfortunately had to be considerably restored with the loss of buildings at the rear. Opposite is an ancient inn, the Old Pheasant. The Berkeley Hospital on the corner of Shaw Street is one of the best early 18th-cent. buildings in the city. It was actually founded six years before its completion in 1703. Nearby Foregate Street has a wealth of Georgian houses, significant of that period of prosperity.

Bromyard: the 15th-cent. manor house at Lower Brockhampton   Picturepoint

Further on in Upper Tything is St Oswald's Hospital, founded in 990 and rebuilt in 1873 to house 37 elderly people. Also close by is the remains of White Ladies, a convent founded in 1250. The east wall of their chapel is still preserved. Near to this is Britannia Square with a spacious green, setting off to advantage Britannia House which dates from the Queen Anne period. It was probably the work of the same architect as the Guildhall.

Outstanding among the many important parish churches of the city is St Helen's, built on the site of an early church in honour of the mother of Constantine and considered the mother church of the city. It is now used as the County Record Office. The 245-ft spire of St Andrew's still stands, though the church has been demolished. Across the river is St John's in Bedwardine with a beautiful late 12th-cent. north arcade. Built of red sandstone and set among trees, it is one of the most attractive churches in the city.

The Roman Catholic church in Sansome Place was built in 1829 on the site of an earlier chapel used by James II. It was much embellished in the 1880s and is a place of musical pilgrimage: Sir Edward Elgar was organist here like his father before him. Elgar's birthplace at **Lower Broadheath** is open to the public. Every three years in late summer the city is packed for the famous Three Choirs Festival.

The terminus of the Worcester and Birmingham Canal is a reminder that in the 18th cent. the junction at Diglis Lock led to a network of canals linking every part of the country.

WROXTON ABBEY, *Oxfordshire* (5–SP41 41), 3 m. NW. of BANBURY on the A422 is Wroxton Abbey, a fine early 17th-cent. gabled house which was built on the site of an Augustinian priory founded in 1207. There are traces of this original building built into the basement foundations. There are three Holbeins to be seen and a superb Zucchero. Among its other many treasures and mementoes of the numerous royal personages entertained in the house is a quilt embroidered by Mary Queen of Scots, and the bedroom where George IV as Prince Regent slept can be seen. Sir William Pope built the house and was host to King James I. It later passed to the North family, one of whose ancestors was Lord North, who as Prime Minister was responsible for losing those North American Colonies which became the United States. His tomb lies in the 14th-cent. parish church and is remarkable for its sculpture of Britannia by Flaxman. There are many other important tombs and memorials in the church, including that of Thomas Coutts, the Edinburgh merchant's son, who founded the banking house. The church has a good example of a Georgian Gothic tower built by Sanderson Miller. The village is attractive with mullioned cottages of brown stone, many of them still thatched.

WYCHWOOD FOREST, *Oxfordshire* (5–SP3418). An entry to some of the loveliest scenery in Oxfordshire lies about 4 m. N. of BURFORD in what remains of the ancient Forest of Wychwood. Passing through **Fulbrook**, which has an interesting Transitional church with sturdy Norman pillars and grotesque roof bosses, the CHIPPING NORTON road climbs Fulbrook Hill from the Windrush valley to a high plateau, descending to the Evenlode valley. The bright little Evenlode river winds its way through the valley against the dark woodlands of Wychwood. This was once a favourite hunting ground of the Plantagenet kings.

The village names are delightful: **Milton-under-Wychwood** follows **Shipton-under-Wychwood** to nearby **Ascott-under-Wychwood**. A little to the NW. of this region and reached by twisting by-lanes is the long ridge of Daylesford leading to the village of **Kingham**. The whole of this area with streams and watermeadows banked by the woods is a delight to ornithologists because of the many varieties of rare birds which seem to flock to this completely unspoilt beauty spot. Perhaps no one expressed the quiet beauty of the Evenlode River better than Belloc, who wrote "A lovely river, all alone . . . Forgotten in the western wolds."

Shipton-under-Wychwood has many fine old houses, among them the 1603 Shipton Court. An old inn called the Shaven Crown was originally a hospice run by the monks from Bruern Abbey, which is now a private house. The Great Hall, now the lounge of the hotel, was the monks' refectory, while a bedroom (number 11), was the original hospice chapel. The parish church is a fine example of the Early English style. Particularly interesting is the font with a panel carved with the Bear and Ragged Staff, device of the Earls of Warwick. Note the 18th-cent. double tomb in the churchyard. In a wooded setting nearby is the ancient Prebendal House with its 15th-cent. chapel, reminder of the days when the church was a prebend of SALISBURY Cathedral. Turning right in the centre of the village, a road leads to Ascott-under-Wychwood which has an interesting partly Norman church surrounded by weathered stone houses. Continuing on the road to the right of the village green, following a signpost to Leafield a turning to the left leads to the larger **Charlbury** which lacks the character of the smaller villages. Just beyond Charlbury the road opens up views of some of the loveliest vistas of the Evenlode valley and leads to the boundary of Wychwood Forest.

Nearby is **Shorthampton**, whose basically Norman church contains box-pews, a three-decker 18th-cent. pulpit and some good medieval frescoes. Almost every winding lane will take the traveller to surprisingly little-known places like Hawkstone, a prehistoric monolith, or Knoll Bury on Chadlington Downs, an encampment whose origin is unknown. Nearby is Cornbury Park which gives some idea of the former density of the ancient forest. Further to the E. lie the little hamlets of **Finstock** and **Fawler**, originally built by the Romans. This area and that surrounding OTMOOR is the most unspoilt in the whole county.

Symond's Yat is a famous beauty spot on the River Wye   Kenneth Scowen

The North Midlands

*Shropshire   Staffordshire   Derbyshire   Nottinghamshire
Leicestershire   Rutland   Lincolnshire*

PHIL DRABBLE

The region here described as the North Midlands includes Rutland, the smallest county in England, and Lincolnshire, the largest but one. Industries range from the mass production of cigarettes in Nottinghamshire, manufactured by sophisticated methods of automation, to fishing off the Lincolnshire coast, which is among mān's most primitive trades. You can enjoy timeless solitude on the barren Derbyshire Pennines, or watch rare birds on Shropshire meres. If you appreciate the individual qualities of real craftsmanship you will find glass being made today, in Staffordshire, as good as the best on show in antique shops. The chains forged for ships' anchors are still so much better than any in the land that it is worth transporting them all the way from the heart of the Midlands to the sea. Whatever your tastes you will find something to admire – and probably something to dislike – in the North Midlands.

On the western borders of Shropshire it is impossible to tell without the map where England ends and Wales begins. Old battle scars have healed along Offa's Dyke, yet there is still an indefinable air of strife, so that neither Welsh nor English appreciate being confused with the other.

At the top of Hope Valley, on the way from Shrewsbury to Bishop's Castle, are the scars of industry instead of battle. Large areas of sterile grey waste still obtrude where vegetation refuses to cloak the dross left by old-time lead miners. Beneath your feet are shafts and crumbling buildings, but if you look backwards to Wales from the hilltops, or forward to England, the views are superb and the air crystal clear and free from industrial haze.

Gliders find the Long Mynd, at Church Stretton, the perfect place to soar upwards on the eddies, as the west wind buffets skyward from the steep escarpment; and they can spiral like buzzards on the thermals. The wind hums round them so that, at close quarters, they are not nearly as silent as they seem. The whole midland plain rolls out below Ketley, stretching eastwards, apparently flat and featureless. But when you climb down it isn't flat at all. It is richly wooded, with unexpected hills and delightful tree-strewn parks, like Aqualate, near Newport, which has a herd of fallow deer that can wander down to the mere to drink.

Staffordshire is not really one county but two, with little in common between the north and south. Both have industry, of course, and it is so famous that strangers believe that the Black Country, in the south, stretches unbroken to the Potteries in the north. But there is wonderful country between. Cannock Chase covers some sixteen square miles, about half of which is still indigenous heather and birch and oak, though the other half has been planted with softwoods by the Forestry Commission. There is a large motorless zone, where the public can wander, with nothing to distract them but a sweet wilderness, which seems as remote as the centre of Dartmoor. There are grouse in the heather and green woodpeckers in the trees. In the centre is a hut built on stilts from which it is possible to watch foxes and wild deer and badgers and red squirrels and rare birds. This hut can be hired by the day from the Forestry Commission offices at Lady Hill, near Rugeley. It is an unexpectedly wild spot for central England, but further east the landscape mellows into fertile farms, with some of the best dairying land in the country around Uttoxeter. The water meadows of the Dove are unsurpassable for beef, and a local saying proclaims that "in April, Dove's flood is worth a King's good [ransom]".

The north of the county, past the Potteries, merges into the moorlands of Derbyshire and the craggy hills of the Pennine chain. It is bleak, stone-wall country, with rocks so near the surface that the soil has never been defiled by ploughs or other tools of man. This is a sparsely populated area for the reason that the land here is miserly with her gifts. Cattle drink from ancient dew ponds, and the milk churns are returned to isolated farms filled with drinking water, because pure water is so scarce on these wild hills. The air is fresh and you hear the limpid cries of curlew and sighing winds in bended trees, which were planted in clumps as some protection for the lonely farmsteads. The primitive vigour of these Derbyshire hills was once emphasized for me by the unexpected music of a pack of blood-hounds in full cry. They were streaming over the stone walls, hot on the scent of their quarry, which was not deer or fox but an athletic man.

Nothing could contrast more with this than the neighbouring county of Notting-ham. It is well wooded, with scores of small villages but few big towns. Its coal-fields still thrive, when others are spent; but do not run away with the idea that it is a county of dereliction, for it is not. There is gypsum in the Newark area, a central clay plateau, round Ollerton, and limestone east of Trent.

But the charm and individuality of Nottingham are in Sherwood Forest and the Dukeries. Neither are what they were. Once the great monastic houses of Welbeck and Newstead and Rufford Abbey stood proudly on the sandy soil. When the monasteries were dissolved, the nobles built great houses there instead. There were Welbeck and Thoresby and Clumber and Worksop Manor. The Dukes of Portland and Newcastle and Norfolk and Earl Manvers had their seats here. Sherwood Forest has few of the fine oaks and beeches left, which made it once so famous. The Forestry Commission has planted part with firs and pines. As compensation, large tracts are now free for the public to roam in and dream of Robin Hood and other robbers like him who made sport with the purses and the wenches of the rich from here to Needwood Forest in Staffordshire.

To the east of Nottingham, Lincolnshire is one county by name but three by nature. Almost a million acres of the northern part is Lindsey, which was once a Saxon kingdom on its own. Kesteven is about half the size, and Holland a little over a quarter of a million acres. They are separate administrative areas and of different character,

The chalk uplands, running towards the Humber, were once rounded tree-clad hills, but now have been tamed into superb farmland. The marshes between the wolds and the sea are famous for their Lincoln red cattle, but the most famous part of all is the Fens. Drainage was started here by the Romans, who cut dykes which were continued by the monks. Land left by the waters dried out into rich, black peat, the most fertile soil in England. Now it is a wasting asset, shrinking year by year, some carried on crops and some being lost by windblow. Gigantic farm machines need huge fields, with room to gambol and cavort about. But the ferocious east wind whips up the dry dust from these great fields into a vortex which drops out on another farm. We may live to see this rich ground wither into infertility.

Such flat land reveals enormous skies. Views are spacious and enlivened by

Sport and General

Hunting country. The Quorn Hunt moves off from a meet in Leicestershire

photogenic windmills. The bulb-fields and Lincoln red cattle paint kaleidoscopic mosaics, and it always comes as a delightful surprise to find sea-going trawlers moored in the heart of towns like Boston, apparently land-locked and marooned.

Turning back to the west, little Rutland, only sixty square miles in area, lies uneasily between Lincolnshire and Leicester. Opencast iron workings tear at her vitals, water undertakings covet her rich farmlands for reservoirs, and neighbours have tried to carve her up to make Big Brother administrations even bigger. But Rutland still remains prosperous, still independent, and still beautiful. Along the Welland valley, which divides her from Northamptonshire, cattle graze on pastures as lush as the Dove valley in Staffordshire or the marshes of Lincolnshire. Apart from the belt of ironstone, the rest is predominantly fertile plough, with no major industries to clog the roads with commuters or lorries. The limestone belt running through the county has produced villages of dignity and charm, with two major schools, at Uppingham and Oakham, a generous allowance for a county of less than twenty thousand souls.

Leicestershire, between Staffordshire and Rutland, has extremes of scenery. Charnwood Forest, a tumbling mass of crags and boulders, is as untamed now as

Noel Habgood

Tulip fields near Spalding in Lincolnshire

in prehistoric times. In summer, when green leaves clothe its vigour, it might be any lovely wooded spot in England. But when leaves are off, in winter, it has a strangely rugged grandeur of its own. At the other extreme, Leicestershire can be unutterably drab and depressing. Anyone who is unmoved by the murk of Coalville or the dull brick-and-slate hosiery villages must be immune to squalor.

The most typical scenery of Leicestershire, however, is neither industrial villages nor untamed woods. Much of the county is gently rolling clay, with villages widely dispersed. It is well-clothed clay, with sweet green grazing, shadowed by noble trees. By no means all are hedgerow or parkland trees. Many have been set in clumps or little woods, which give a delightful variety to the landscape. Although the views they give are so superb, they were not put there by aesthetes; they were planted strategically as fox coverts designed to give the finest hunting in the land as hounds pushed their fox from one covert to the next. The fields are divided by thorn hedges which, as well as keeping cattle in their place, test the courage of the highest jumping horse and the most unimaginative rider. Even the roads seem to have been made with one eye on the hunting field. The hedges are so wide that foxes lie hid in their immensely thick bottoms, and horses have a soft green verge to tread. The Quorn and the Belvoir are among the fox-hound packs which have made Leicestershire famous throughout the sporting world.

Windblow from the rich peat in the Lincolnshire fens is but one of the factors which are changing the industries in this region more, perhaps, than in any other generation. The face of the land has been lined by more roads since the last war than at any time since the Romans came. And modern roads have an insatiable appetite for concrete. In consequence, machines are gulping gravel, undisturbed since the Ice Age, from the whole valley of the Trent. Land there is being replaced by huge lagoons which flood the worked-out gravel pits outside Nottingham. Sails now appear by the sides of Midland roads as dramatically as along the lanes near Norfolk broads.

Easy transport and modern industry are depopulating the wilder parts of western Shropshire, and there is a real danger that numbers will shrink until there are not enough ratepayers to pay for essential services. Yet a century and a half ago the Ironbridge gorge throbbed with trade. When the raw materials petered out the whole area was discarded as a derelict memorial. Even the churchyard at Jackfield was not immune from subsidence, and the graves split open to gape at man's misdeeds. Now efforts are being made to reintroduce more industry, to encourage folk to stay in the remoter areas. The most ambitious scheme is Telford New Town which, if it is successful, will breathe new life into bones which have rotted since the last Industrial Revolution.

The whole region provides raw materials to ensure our industrial future. The coalfields of Nottingham and Derbyshire and Staffordshire are still productive. There is ironstone at Scunthorpe, gravel in the basin of the Trent. These may well mar the beauty of the North Midlands, but you couldn't have some of the pleasanter things without them. There would be no sweet-toned bells from Loughborough, chiming their message across quiet countrysides, without the coal to cast them. There would be no delicate glass from the Black Country, nor fragile china from Stoke-on-Trent, nor motor-cars nor kitchen goods, if we didn't tear the heart from the earth for raw materials. And sheep on the Shropshire hills, cattle by the Dove, and the seas of waving corn in Lincolnshire far outweigh the industrial eyesores.

The famous people of the region are as varied as the scenery. You can take your choice from men of letters, like Dr Johnson, from Lichfield, or Byron and D. H. Lawrence, who added immortality to the county of Nottingham. Or you may prefer to remember the engineers, like Boulton and Watt, who worked at Smethwick and laid the foundation stone for the civilization we are accustomed to. Charles II played hide-and-seek with the soldiers of Cromwell in the oak at Boscobel, and those who are tired of oppression by bureaucracy may have a sneaking regard for Hereward the Wake, Robin Hood or Guy Fawkes, whose gunpowder plot was hatched at Holbeach House, in Staffordshire.

I think my own choice of North Midland people falls on Bess of Hardwick. Not that she was comely or had an attractive personality. I admire Bess because of the great houses she left as the result of her scheming.

The whole of the North Midlands is architecturally rich. This richness ranges from the restrained delicacy of little Lichfield Cathedral to the magnificence of Lincoln. Crowland Abbey in the same county, or Chartley Castle in Staffordshire, or Ludlow Castle in Shropshire are comforting links with the past, and the Derbyshire villages, in the Peak district, are surely as unspoilt as villages can be. But Bess of Hardwick at various times owned or built some of the most remarkable houses in England. She had a flair for marrying people who left her their estates. When fourteen years old and almost penniless she married Robert Barlow, who died and left her his Derbyshire estate next year. She didn't remarry until she was over thirty, when she became the wife of Sir William Cavendish. Later she married Sir William St Loe, who left her his West Country estates, and lastly she married the Earl of Shrewsbury. During this time, she built Hardwick Hall, in Derbyshire, and was connected with fine houses at Rufford Abbey and Bolsover Hall and Welbeck Abbey. Her most magnificent memorial is Chatsworth.

Quite the most bizarre building associated with Bess, though she did not make it so, is Welbeck Abbey. She started the house, which went to her grandson and, by marriage, to the Duke of Portland. Bess was said to have been such a compulsive builder because she was told by a gypsy that she would only escape death as long as she was building. Similar blood must have coursed through the veins of the 5th Duke of Portland. Ancient aristocracy was traditionally addicted to follies, and the life-sized weeping willow in the garden of Chatsworth, which deluges visitors with sprays of water from its hollow branches, would win awards for practical jokes in almost any age. But the 5th Duke of Portland had a horror of ostentation. So he built a tunnel at Welbeck, a mile and a quarter long, big enough to take a horse and carriage, simply so that he could enter or leave his estate unseen. For eighteen years he employed around fifteen thousand men, mainly building underground. He built a riding school, and a complete suite of subterranean rooms, including a ballroom and three libraries. These were prodigious feats for unmechanized days, when every ton of soil had to be shifted by a shovel and barrow and sweat.

We take our pleasures now more simply. Whether we ride or walk, there are wild deer to watch on Cannock Chase in Staffordshire or in Bradgate Park, now owned jointly by the town and county of Leicester. On every reservoir there are sailing boats or birds to be seen; there are seals in the Wash. Local authorities are wisely siphoning off hordes of people with no specialized tastes to organized amusement parks, like Alton Towers or Trentham Gardens, in Staffordshire.

The most outstanding area of unspoilt natural beauty in the North Midlands is the Peak District National Park. It was the first of our national parks so to be designated, in 1951. The southern part, known as the White Peak, is rolling lime-stone uplands and wooded dales. The Dark Peak, north of Hope Valley, is equally beautiful, though more exposed, moorland. To the south-west, over the border of Staffordshire, a few wallabies, whose ancestors escaped years ago, still roam wild on the moors above Leek, and the Roaches there are cascading crags which seem to threaten the road below.

The Peak Planning Board, based at Bakewell in Derbyshire, issues a whole range of excellent leaflets; and of interest to motorists and walkers alike will be *The Shell Guide to the Pennine Way*. You can start from the park, along the Pennine Way, which is the first and longest national footpath. If you are stout enough, you can walk two hundred and fifty miles along the Pennines and over the Cheviots to the Scottish border. There is pony trekking and youth hostelling, rock climbing above ground or pot-holing below. There is skiing and gliding for the adventurous, and motoring through the finest scenery in the land for the less energetic. You can watch sheepdog trials on the hillsides, or the ancient folk customs of well-dressing in villages like Eyam or Tissington or Wormhill. You can eat roast venison from a deer on the spit at Whitworth Show, and if it is the climax to a hard day's walking on the hills, it will taste as sweet as any shot by Robin Hood in Sherwood Forest in days gone by.

The North Midlands: Gazetteer

NIGEL BATLEY AND BETTY JAMES

ABBOTS BROMLEY, *Staffordshire* (9–SK 0824). Five inns, a cluster of old black-and-white cottages, a church with 14th-cent. arcades and an old butter cross make this one of the most charming villages in the county. But Abbots Bromley, 5 m. S. of UTTOXETER, owes its fame not to its buildings but to its annual Horn Dance, normally performed on the Monday after the Sunday following 4 September. The dance, which is believed to have religious, or at least ritualistic connections – the dancers' gear is stored in the church – probably dates from before the Normans came to England. Twelve people take part in the dance: a man on a hobby horse, a maid, a jester, a boy with a bow and arrow, six men wearing reindeer antlers and two musicians on accordion and triangle.

Abbots Bromley once had strong connections with the Bagot family. They lived at a moated manor house at Bagots Bromley, 1 m. NW., from the time of the Conquest until the 14th cent., when they moved to nearby BLITHFIELD. The old house was used as a farm until it was demolished in 1811. A stone in Monument Field marks the site.

ABDON, *Shropshire* (8–SO5786). A small, scattered village, 8 m. NE. of LUDLOW. It lies in the lee of Shropshire's highest hill, the 1,792-ft Brown Clee. There are three Iron Age forts on Brown Clee, the most important being Abdon Burf. The others are Clee Burf and Nordy Bank – but little remains of any of them. However, those who tackle the climb are rewarded by magnificent views of the Shropshire countryside.

ACTON BURNELL, *Shropshire* (8–SJ5301). Tucked away in a corner of this pretty village, so that it has to be looked for, stands the ruin of one of the oldest fortified houses in England. Acton Burnell Castle was built for Robert Burnell, chaplain and secretary to Edward Longshanks, later Edward I, between 1284 and 1293 at the time that Burnell was Lord Chancellor and Bishop of Bath and Wells. Built of warm red sandstone, the castle is more like a small country house with a fortified tower at each corner and, apart from its roof, is almost intact. The setting in smooth lawns, and the giant cedar which overtops one of the 40-ft towers, emphasize the manor house aspect. Today the castle is in the care of the Ministry of Public Building and Works and can be viewed.

The beautiful Church of St Mary is the same age as the castle. Built of grey stone, with a squat tower added in the 19th cent., the church is plain from the outside but inside offers much to please the eye. The font is 13th-cent., the pulpit Jacobean. There are medieval tiles on the floor of the north transept and strangely carved heads everywhere. Among the monuments is the tomb of Sir Nicholas Burnell (1382) bearing a fine brass likeness of him; and in a recess the full-length figures, in alabaster, of Sir Richard Lee and his wife, dated 1591.

Looking E. from the castle stand the remains – two large, near-triangular stone gables – of what was believed to have been the castle barn, a building more than 150 ft long. Some say that it was in this barn that England's first properly constituted parliament, including commoners, was held here during a visit of Edward I to Bishop Burnell.

The village of Acton Burnell is an English blend of black-and-white cottages and larger Georgian houses. One of the roads approaching it from the S. is arrow-straight, part of the Roman Watling Street; and near it, excavations have revealed part of a Roman bridge.

ALBERBURY, *Shropshire* (8–SJ3514). Situated about 8 m. W. of SHREWSBURY on the B4393, Alberbury once had a castle, part of the stone curtain built to keep back the marauding Welsh; all that remains is an ivy-clad tower, which is almost linked to the Church of St Michael by a flying buttress. The church, surprisingly large for such a village, has a massive, 14th-cent. saddleback tower and contains interesting memorials, including seven embossed brasses, to the local landowning family, the Leightons. About 1 m. NE. of the village are the remains of Alberbury Priory, founded about 1225 and now part of a farm-house. **Loton Park,** still in the ownership of the Leightons, is now used for motor sport: the Severn Valley Motor Club promote National Hill Climb meetings there on the last Sunday in April, and in the autumn, when ancient Alberbury resounds to 20th-cent. noise.

ALDRIDGE, *Staffordshire* (9–SK0500), is chiefly famous for Barr Beacon, about 2 m. SW. of the town, which, with the adjoining 150 acres, is preserved as a natural park. The land was bought by a Colonel Wilkinson as a memorial to the Warwickshire and Staffordshire men who died in the First World War. Rising to about 750 ft, the Beacon offers wide views over the surrounding countryside which can be viewed through a mounted telescope.

The town of Aldridge was mentioned in the Domesday Book but the only remaining bits of its

Abbots Bromley: the traditional Horn Dance is held annually

early history are in the square-towered medieval church. There are two 14th-cent. effigies: in a recess in the south wall of the chancel is one of a priest, and at the eastern side of the south aisle is Sir Robert Stapleton (d. 1333) in full armour.

ALFRETON, *Derbyshire* (13–SK4155). Although this was originally a mining area, Alfreton is more attractive than many such small industrial towns and boasts a fine church, a pleasing main street, several attractive old houses and one of the most modern lidos in the county. The latter is its most recent acquisition, built for £85,000 in the grounds of the park. It was opened by the Duke of Edinburgh in 1964, contains a championship-size swimming-pool, a separate diving pool and a children's pool, and is open daily throughout the summer.

Alfreton Hall, built in 1730 but added to during the 19th cent., is an imposing mansion which is now an Adult Education Centre. St Martin's, standing at the entrance to the Hall grounds, is a large church founded in the 13th cent. and added to and altered over the following 200 years.

ALKBOROUGH, *Lincolnshire* (13–SE8721). The village is bleak, but views from the 11th-cent. church are splendid, since it stands on a high ridge overlooking the Falls where the Trent and the Ouse join to form the Humber. From the tower can be seen LINCOLN Cathedral, BEVERLEY Minster and YORK Minster. Nearby are the remains of a Roman camp now known as

Countess Close, named after the Countess Lucy, wife of Ivo Tailbois, who owned the Manor in Norman times. At Julian Bower, through a five-barred gate, is a maze cut in the ground, believed to have been made by monks in the 12th cent. A replica of the maze is cut into the floor of the church porch and a picture of it is incorporated in the rebuilt Victorian triple-lancet east window of the chancel. A pretty cliff walk leads southwards from here above the Trent to **Burton-upon-Stather.** In this parish is Normanby Park, former home of the Sheffields.

ALREWAS, *Staffordshire* (8–SK1715), is one of the prettiest black-and-white villages in the county; the wide main street contains many Tudor thatched cottages. A settlement already existed when the Romans came and for many centuries the village was famous for its eel fishery and for the basket-weaving of its inhabitants, who used the osiers which then grew thickly along the banks of the River Trent. There was probably a church here in the 9th cent.; the present building is mainly 13th- and 14th-cent. It contains much that is worth a second look, especially the 14th-cent. font, embellished with four grotesque heads.

Alrewas keeps its ancient tranquillity and there are pleasant walks by the winding Trent and the Trent and Mersey canal. At Wychnor, close by, the fine gardens of the park, containing a remarkable yew hedge, are occasionally open to the public. The Wychnor Flitch, still hanging in the Hall, performed a similar function to that of

DUNMOW, in Essex, which is presented to any couple who can prove that they have never regretted their marriage.

ALTON, *Staffordshire* (9–SK0742), is one half of "The Rhineland of Staffordshire"; the other half is ALTON TOWERS. The stone-built village of Alton lies E. of CHEADLE, on the rocky, wooded slopes of the Churnet valley, all towers, turrets and spires. Every road and lane is a hill; every bend or gap in the trees or houses offers the kind of view more usually associated with central Europe than with the English Midlands. Above the village, on the edge of a sheer cliff high above the river, are Alton Castle, now a Roman Catholic boys' preparatory school, and Alton Hospital: impressive and picturesque buildings designed by A. W. N. Pugin for the 16th Earl of Shrewsbury and built between 1840 and 1852. In the gardens of the school stand the remains of the medieval castle – a ruined round tower and a part of the wall – the last link with Alton's Norman beginnings. The castle was built about 1175 by Bertram de Verdun, a Crusader with Richard Lionheart, and an arcade in the nearby church dates from about the same time. Alton itself contains some interesting old houses but the most unusual building is the sinister-looking tower in the centre of the village. Circular, built of heavy, dark-grey stone, with a small door and no windows, this was the village lock-up.

ALTON TOWERS, *Staffordshire* (9–SK0742), is the other, and more exciting half of Staffordshire's "Rhineland". Once the home of the Talbot family, the Earls of Shrewsbury, Alton Towers, about 1 m. from ALTON along the CHEADLE road, is now one of North Staffordshire's two famous playgrounds and pleasure gardens. The other is TRENTHAM.

The mansion, an array of towers, battlements, turrets and spires, is now virtually a shell. During the Second World War, it was requisitioned and used by an officer-cadet training unit. For six years afterwards it stood untouched and the combined effects of neglect and rough treatment made restoration impossible. Now only a small part of it is in use, housing a model railway, gift shops, a bar and a cafeteria. But, shell though it may be, Alton Towers is still a magnificent if slightly incredible sight, especially appealing to the romantic imagination in misty or lowering weather.

Nowadays it is the grounds, and especially the gardens, of Alton Towers which are the focus of attention: justifiably, because, to a large extent, the grounds pre-date the house. Hundreds of acres of North Staffordshire came into the hands of the Talbots in the mid-15th cent., but it was not until early in the 19th cent. that Charles, the 15th Earl, visited Alton, then known as Alveton, and dreamt of creating a heaven on earth from the 600 acres of wild countryside in the Churnet valley. On the site where the Towers now stands was Alveton Lodge, the house of the earl's bailiff; all around, where the woods now shelter the gardens

and grounds, was farmland, and an enormous rabbit warren in the slope of the valley.

Charles, nearing 60, had no intention of building a great mansion; his aim was to give rein to his considerable talent for landscape design. In 1812, the hill and parks were planted with their sheltering screen of trees and two years later the earl moved into Alveton Lodge to supervise the transformation of the wilderness. Money was not spared. Builders, masons, carpenters and other skilled craftsmen, and a multitude of labourers, began the work of laying out the gardens and terraces which are there now. Thousands of tons of soil were excavated to make the lakes and pools; water was channelled from a spring 2 m. away in the hills to the N. Walls and staircases were built. Paths were laid out apparently at random, but in fact the line of each was meticulously worked out so that at each twist and turn a new view could be obtained. The buildings were put up which are still features of the gardens today: the various fountains, the most impressive of which is the Chinese pagoda fountain at the bottom of the gardens; the Gothic-style Chinese temple; the conservatories; and the Swiss cottage, built as a home for a blind Welsh harpist so that he could play, often unseen, for strollers in the gardens. Finally came the trees and plants themselves which, saplings and seedlings then, can now be seen in their mature beauty: thousands of rhododendrons; azaleas; roses; heathers; Japanese maples; dwarf conifers; giant Wellingtonias; gracious cedars; Judas and tulip trees; hemlocks; and many other rarities.

During the 12 years he was creating his garden, Charles also took over Alveton Lodge as his summer residence and enlarged it in Gothic style, renaming it Alton Abbey – despite its lack of any religious connection. The only other person who played a major part was John, the 16th Earl, who succeeded to the title on the death of Charles, his uncle, in 1827. John inherited not only the Talbot title and lands but also his Uncle Charles's determination to make Alton one of the wonders of England. In 1831 he made Alton his permanent home and it was he who enlarged Alton Abbey with towers, turrets and galleries and called it Alton Towers.

He also completed the gardens with the classically beautiful "Her Ladyship's garden" beside the chapel, the terraced gardens near the conservatory, and the Dutch gardens. He also erected in memory of his uncle the copy of the Choragic monument to Lysicrates in Athens, which bears the inscription "He made the desert smile" and has pride of place at the head of the gardens.

In 1924 the Shrewsbury family sold the estate to a private company who opened it to the public. Today Alton Towers can accommodate both the lover of beauty and the seeker of fun. The visitor can row on the large lake, take an aerial cable car at tree-top height over the gardens, marvel at the £5,000 model railway, travel on the miniature railway, watch the trio of sea-lions disporting in their pool, or enjoy all the fun of the fair. Alton

Towers can now boast truly of offering something for every taste – which was possibly not quite the 15th Earl's intention.

ALVELEY, *Shropshire* (8–SO7584), is a pleasing stone-built village with a part-Norman church whose most treasured possession is an altar frontal first used 500 years ago. The original colours, vertical stripes in what might have been cream or yellow and green or red, are now much faded but the embroidered figures of Abraham and the cherubs can still be easily made out. At a crossroads about 1 m. NNW. stands an old butter cross with a solid circular head which probably marked the site of a medieval open-air market.

ANCASTER, *Lincolnshire* (13–SK9843). Lying in a natural break in the limestone hills of Lincoln Edge, Ancaster is famous for its local stone, which hardens rapidly after quarrying. The 9-acre site of Causennae, a Roman camp and posting station, is situated on Ermine Street. Coins, pottery, an altar, a milestone, kilns and mosaic flooring of the 3rd cent. found here are in GRANTHAM Museum. The Romans are supposed to have raced chariots in the long valley nearby. The church is built of local stone and retains some Norman work. Two massive coffins in the churchyard are reputed to be Roman.

Ashbourne church, "the cathedral of the Peak"

Kenneth Scowen

ANNESLEY, *Nottinghamshire* (13–SK5052). Near this vanished village with its forest background is Annesley Hall, once the home of Mary Chaworth, the subject of Byron's first unrequited boyhood love – his "bright morning star of Annesley". They used to meet in the home park, on Diadem Hill, 578 ft above sea-level and a landmark for miles. In the ruined church lies William Chaworth, Mary's father, who was killed in a duel with his cousin, Byron's great-uncle, the 5th Lord Byron. Up the hill is the new village of Annesley where the church, built in 1874, houses a beautiful Norman font and the alabaster figure of a man.

ARBOR LOW, *Derbyshire* (12–SK1662), is Derbyshire's most ancient monument, a prehistoric "henge" ranking in importance with STONEHENGE and AVEBURY. Situated just off the A515 about 8 m. SE. of BUXTON, Arbor Low is open to the public. At a height of more than 1,200 ft above sea-level on Middleton Moor, the monument consists of a plateau about 50 yds across on which more than 40 huge slabs of limestone lie in a circle. None of the stones is still standing and all are irregular in size, shape and thickness. There are also several similar slabs lying in the centre of the circle, one of them 14 ft long and another more than 8 ft wide. Outside the plateau is a circular bank, 15 ft high in places; and inside that a ditch about 5 ft deep. Close by Arbor Low is the largest round barrow in the county, Gibb Hill.

Arbor Low was constructed during the Late Stone Age or Early Bronze Age (2000–1600 B.C.) but the significance of its name, which is Anglo-Saxon, is unknown. Certainly the monument must have been there about 2,500 years when the Anglo-Saxons first came to Derbyshire.

ASHBOURNE, *Derbyshire* (12–SK1846), is the gateway to the Izaak Walton country of DOVEDALE. It lies at the southern end of the Peak District. A small market town, its main street, Church Street, still looks much as it did when Charles I attended a service in St Oswald's Church after his defeat at NASEBY in 1645.

The church, with its 215-ft spire, has been called "The Cathedral of the Peak". George Eliot, who set her novel *Adam Bede* in Ellastone, 4 m. SW. of Ashbourne on the Staffordshire bank of the Dove, described Ashbourne church as "the finest mere parish church in the kingdom". Consecrated in 1241, it has been weathered and scarred: marks made by the Parliamentary artillery in 1644 can still be seen on the outside west wall of the nave, near the figure of St Oswald. That the damage was so slight was due to the courage and indignation of the townspeople of Ashbourne who sent out a deputation to remonstrate with the Parliamentary forces – and made their point.

The pillars of the main wrought-iron gates bear an unusual decoration of skulls and flames. The inside of the church is impressive, with its 176-ft nave and chancel and spectacular crossing-tower. There is some of the original glazing in the great 14th-cent. east window; the font is 13th-cent.;

and both pulpit and lectern are ornamented with Derbyshire's famous Blue John stone. Monuments abound. That to Sir Thomas Cockayne bears what is believed to be the earliest rhyming epitaph in existence ("And did his house and name restore, Which others had decayed before"). His son's tomb has a good brass of 1538. But the most famous monument is that to five-year-old Penelope Boothby, a life-size figure in white Carrara marble, carved by Thomas Banks in 1791. Penelope, who lies asleep, is said to have been able to speak in the four languages inscribed on her tomb: Italian, French, Latin and English. The English inscription reads: "She was in form and intellect most exquisite. The unfortunate Parents ventured their all on this frail Bark, And the wreck was total."

If spring is early, the churchyard will be full of daffodils when one of Ashbourne's major annual events takes place on Shrove Tuesday and Ash Wednesday. This is the ancient and robust football game between the inhabitants of two banks of the Henmore Brook. The goals are 3 m. apart, at Sturston Mill and Clifton Mill, the rules are few, and any number can play.

Ashbourne, like BAKEWELL, can claim fame for a foodstuff. Ashbourne Gingerbread, a ginger shortbread biscuit with an unusual flavour, came to the town from France with the 300 French prisoners from the Napoleonic Wars who were billeted here. The recipe has been passed from baker to baker down the years.

Many reckon Church Street the finest street in Derbyshire. Its varied parts have mellowed into a harmonious whole. A number of the buildings are worth more than a casual glance: the Elizabethan Grammar School; two sets of almshouses, Owlfield and Pegg's; the Mansion House where Dr Samuel Johnson was once a regular visitor; and the curiously named Green Man & Black's Head with its inn sign right across the street and a tiny courtyard.

Within easy reach of Ashbourne are some of the prettiest villages in Derbyshire: HARTINGTON, 9 m. N., just off the BUXTON road, in a beautiful setting; **Osmaston**, 2 m. S. off the DERBY road, with its thatched cottages; **Parwich**, 5 m. N., with ancient earthworks nearby; and **Fenny Bentley**, 3 m. N., where there is a most curious monument in St Edward's Church, the shrouded figures of Thomas Beresford, his wife and 21 children, carved in alabaster.

ASHBY-DE-LA-ZOUCH, *Leicestershire* (10–SK3516). One of the few towns in Leicestershire, Ashby (deriving from the Old English *æsc* for ash and the Scandinavian *byr* for a habitation) received its distinguishing nomenclature from the Breton nobleman, Alain de Parrhoet la Souche, who acquired the manor by marriage in about 1160. The town is pleasant. Market Street is long and wide and often perfumed by the soap factory nearby. This specialized industry supplies the most expensive brands. S. of the west end of the street is the Grecian, or Spa, quarter which contains Gilbert Scott's 70-ft cross to the memory of

Lady Loudoun, who died in 1879 gratefully remembered by the people of Ashby for her goodness. Her house, built in the 19th cent., is now part of the Boys' Grammar School.

Lady Loudoun was a member of the famous Hastings family so closely associated with the impressive ruin, Ashby-de-la-Zouch Castle, which stands to the E. of the town. Originally a Norman manor house, it was granted to the first Baron Hastings by a grateful Edward IV in 1461. Towards the end of the Wars of the Roses in which Lord Hastings and his private army played a leading part on the Yorkist side, the magnificent tower was added, designed as a self-contained fortress. In 1569 and 1586 Mary Queen of Scots stayed in Ashby Castle as the prisoner of Lord Hastings's grandson, who had been created 1st Earl of Huntingdon by Henry VIII. She occupied the mainly 15th-cent. solar, a long, narrow room with a beautiful fireplace and great twelve-light mullioned windows. James I visited the castle with his entire following in 1617, almost impoverishing the earl. Charles I and Henrietta Maria stayed there in 1634, but when Charles returned 11 years later it was only to rest for a few days before and after the Battle of NASEBY. By then Henry Hastings, Lord Loughborough, brother of the earl, was holding the castle for the king. He held out against the Commonwealth troops for more than a year. After his final surrender the castle was slighted – disarmed and demolished – by Lord Grey. The remains comprise the tower, parts of the walls and solar, and various domestic buildings including the huge kitchen dating from about 1350. Sir Walter Scott laid the scene of the famous pageant and tournament in *Ivanhoe* in the fields nearby.

Not far from the castle is St Helen's Parish Church where the east window contains some ancient heraldic glass taken from the ruined castle chapel. There are various Hastings monuments, including one to Lady Selina, who joined Wesley and formed Lady Huntingdon's Connexion of Nonconformist chapels. There is also the only known survival of a finger pillory, consisting of two beams with 13 grooves each, which were fastened with a lock on the hands of those who were absent from, or misbehaved in church.

ASHFORD-IN-THE-WATER, *Derbyshire* (12–SK1969). There are three bridges across the River Wye in this small village 2 m. NW. of BAKEWELL. The oldest is the Sheepwash bridge, as narrow today as it was the day it was built, and one of the others dates from 1664. Close by the village are the quarries from which the famous Ashford marble came. The Church of the Holy Trinity was rebuilt about 100 years ago but the fine Norman tympanum, showing a tree of life, was incorporated over the south doorway. Inside hang four paper garlands, rare and ancient, of the kind which were carried at funerals. At Fin Cop, 1½ m. NW. of the village, are the remains of an Iron Age fort.

ASHOVER, *Derbyshire* (13–SK3463). One of the few Norman lead fonts remaining in England is in the church of this unspoilt village in the valley of the Amber, about 3 m. NE. of MAT-LOCK. The church, 600 years old, has a slender spire 128 ft high, a landmark for miles around, and contains an early 16th-cent. rood-screen and an alabaster tomb of the same date. It still uses a bell which cracked while ringing out the news of Napoleon's fall in 1814. Not far from the village stand the ruins of the Elizabethan Eastwood Hall, a once-fortified manor house destroyed by the Parliamentarians in 1646.

ASLOCKTON, *Nottinghamshire* (13–SK7440). In this tiny village just E. of BINGHAM Thomas Cranmer, first Protestant archbishop, was born and lived for 14 years in an old manor house which no longer exists. It is thought to have been in the fields by the path now called Cranmer's Walk. On this path towards Orston, past the ugly 19th-cent. church, there is a castle of motte and bailey type with a moated mound about 16 ft high, said to be part of an ancient earthwork. This is Cranmer's Mound, where he sat as a boy and "surveyed the face of the country and listened to the tunable bells of Whatton", the church across the River Smite. He returned infrequently for short periods only after going to CAMBRIDGE. In the village mission room are the remains of the walls of an ancient chapel he must have known before it was desecrated in the Reformation, in which he was martyred.

The village also contains the only three mud cottages in the county.

ASTON-ON-CLUN, *Shropshire* (8–SO3981). A huge oak tree draped with flags of all nations is the first sight which has greeted visitors to this tiny village, about 2½ m. W. of Craven Arms on the B4368 to CLUN, for almost 200 years. Tradition has it that the flags were first hung on the Arbor Tree on 29 May 1786, to celebrate the marriage of local landowner John Marston to Mary Carter, and the custom has continued ever since. If you want the full story you will almost certainly get it from one of the customers at the village's oddly named Kangaroo Inn. The village has a third curiosity: a tiny round stone house, one of the few remaining in the country.

ATCHAM, *Shropshire* (8–SJ5409), is a place whose name can confuse the visitor because here is **Attingham Park** which some people refer to as Atcham Park. The explanation is that Atcham is a corruption of Attingham, the village having settled for the shorter form while the park, with its fine Hall, retains the longer name. The village lies beside the wide, fast-flowing Severn, and is distinguished by having two bridges, side by side, over it. The original bridge, with its seven grace-ful arches, was built by John Gwynne of SHREWS-BURY, a founder-member of the Royal Academy, 200 years ago; the new concrete one was erected in 1929.

Near the river are two of Atcham's three most important buildings: the church, with its unique dedication to St Eata; and the imposing red-brick Georgian hotel, curiously named the Mytton and Mermaid. The red sandstone church, a little of it Norman, but mainly 13th- and 16th-cent. contains what are probably Roman stones brought from nearby WROXETER. There is some interesting 15th-cent. glass in the windows. Opposite the Mytton and Mermaid stands the classically-simple lodge to Attingham Park. The Hall, now a National Trust property, is used as Shropshire's Adult Education College. Designed by George Steuart in 1785 for Lord Berwick, the Hall is famous for its interior decoration; the drawing-room is especially worth seeing, and the Picture Gallery is interesting as the earliest roof-lit picture gallery to have survived.

ATTENBOROUGH, *Nottinghamshire* (13–SK5134). Oliver Cromwell once stabled his horses in the nave of the lovely church lying in broad Trent fields between the main road and the river. A farm-house with its garden adjoining the churchyard still bears traces of the Ireton brothers, who were born there and whose names appear in the register in 1611 and 1615. Henry, the eldest, married Cromwell's daughter, Bridget, and became Cromwell's right-hand man. He signed the death-warrant of Charles I, died of overwork and the plague, lay in state at SOMERSET HOUSE and was buried in WESTMINSTER ABBEY. At the Restoration he was taken from his grave and hanged from Tyburn Tree for a day. He was then buried again, under what is now MARBLE ARCH. His younger brother, John, also a loyal Cromwellian, became Lord Mayor of London, was imprisoned and then released and transported to the Scilly Isles.

The Church of St Mary Magdalene has a tower 500 years old and the interior is also much as the Iretons must have known it. The doorway is 14th-cent. and the door itself is said to be one of the oldest in the country, possibly 13th-cent. Under the tower are two 700-year-old arcades which were each halved when it was built. The altar table is Jacobean but the font is 13th-cent. There is some lovely stained glass, and four Jacobean panels preserved in the modern choir stalls are carved with mermaids, mermen, a sea-monster and a dragon. A 14th-cent. craftsman has carved the capitals around a mitred bishop's head with grotesques, some pig-faced others puny-headed, with wings, huge hands, claws and limbs but no bodies.

AXE EDGE, *Derbyshire* (12–SK0370), is one of the county's finest viewpoints. Standing about 1,600 ft above sea-level, Axe Edge is crossed by the A53 some 2 m. S. of BUXTON. There are good walks around here and panoramic views in all directions, especially W. into Cheshire. Just over the border stands the Cat and Fiddle Inn, the second highest inn in the country. Here at the southern end of the Edge is the source of the River Dove.

AYSTON, *Rutland* (10–SK8601). This is one of the prettiest villages in this loveliest of English counties, with cottages built of the ubiquitous local ironstone and roofed with thatch or Colly-weston slates. In a small, well-timbered park and beautiful garden stands Ayston Hall, a handsome late-Georgian mansion. Neatly adjoining is the Church of St Mary, with work of all centuries from the 12th to the 16th. The windows contain some glass 500 years old showing the crucifixion, and there is a curious fragment of ancient sculpture in which the figures of two sisters, one-armed twins, are just recognizable. In spite of their affliction they made enough money by spinning to buy a field, which they left as a legacy to the poor of UPPINGHAM. The craftsman carving the memorial was moved to give one of the cripples two hands, that they might be represented clasped in prayer.

Well kept and on high ground about a mile from Uppingham, Ayston is worth a small detour.

Take the secondary road due N. and then E. at the T-junction from here to **Preston** on the A6003 to visit this attractive village of stone-built houses, constructed for the most part in the Stuart period; it includes a particularly fine gabled manor house of about 1600. Although there was almost certainly a church here in Anglo-Saxon times, as is suggested by the name "priest's village" in translation, the present building is basically Norman. The chancel, the south arcade and the font are all 14th-cent. and the handsome, canopied sedilia have been in place for 600 years. It is interesting to see that much of the church furniture is of eastern origin. Two pieces of marble

floor mosaic on either side of the chancel step were brought from Constantinople after its destruction by the Turks; an almsbox comes from a church in Asia Minor; and some of the lamps and candlesticks once officiated in Damascus. The yew trees in the churchyard, traditionally planted to make supple bows for England's defence, were brought from the Garden of Gethsemane.

BAKEWELL, *Derbyshire* (12–SK2168), has a beautiful setting and contains much of interest. The small market town is built almost entirely in warm, brownish stone and lies in a sheltered valley of the Derbyshire Wye with rolling wooded hills to the N., W., and E. which make fine walking country. Bakewell's most impressive building is the large Parish Church of All Saints, standing halfway up the hill on the west side of the town, its spire a landmark. Parts of the present buildings date from the 12th cent. but there is evidence of a church here in Anglo-Saxon times; and in the churchyard stands an 8th-cent. sculptured cross, much worn but with many of the symbols carved on it still recognizable. Many other stone fragments dating from Anglo-Saxon times are on view in the church porch. Among the monuments in the church is an imposing table tomb to Sir George Vernon, the last of his line, known as the "King of the Peak" because of the lavish hospitality he provided at nearby HADDON HALL.

Bakewell's name has nothing to do with baking or its renowned pudding. The first part comes

Bakewell: the medieval bridge was originally built for packhorses

Kenneth Scowen

from an Anglo-Saxon personal name and "well" refers to the warm springs which come to the surface here – you can swim today at the 17th-cent. Bath House in water which remains at a natural 15 °C. winter and summer. Other buildings of interest are the 13th-cent. bridge over the Wye, one of the oldest in England; the old Town Hall, dating from 1709; the Old House, just above the church, the oldest house in the town and now a museum; and the Rutland Arms Hotel where the Jane Austen Room is still preserved. It was here that the famous novelist stayed in the early 19th cent. while working on *Pride and Prejudice* and it is believed that the Lambton in the novel is, in fact, Bakewell, and that two of the novel's romantic scenes are set in the room at the hotel.

The hotel is also connected with the "discovery" of the famous pudding, the result of a misunder-standing between a Mrs Greaves, then mistress of the hotel, and her cook. Instead of stirring the egg mixture into the pastry and then filling the tart with jam, the cook put the jam into the tart and then poured the egg mixture over it. So successful was the outcome that the recipe was preserved and Bakewell puddings have been made to the original formula ever since 1859 at the pudding shop in The Square.

Bakewell is a convenient centre from which to explore much of central and western Derbyshire. DOVEDALE, DARLEY DALE, **Monsal Dale** and **Lathkill Dale** are within easy distance; HADDON HALL and CHATSWORTH are not far away; ARBOR LOW, a prehistoric monument, is only 7 m. SW.; and EYAM, the plague village, only 6 m. N. At **Flagg**, about 6 m. W., are held each April the exciting High Peak point-to-point races; near BIRCHOVER, 4 m. S., are strange rock formations; and a number of the local villages engage in the Derbyshire custom of well-dressing.

BAMFORD, *Derbyshire* (12–SK2083). Set in the hills about 11 m. NE. of BUXTON, this small village boasts a church tower as tall and slim as any in the county, surmounted by a sharp spire. The countryside around adds to Bamford's attraction. To the N. lies the chain of three huge reservoirs, Ladybower, Derwent and Howden, separated by massive dams, under whose waters lie two villages. An exciting scenic drive is along the shore of the Ladybower and on over the famous Snake Pass to Glossop. Each year sheep-dog trials are held at Bamford.

BARDNEY, *Lincolnshire* (13–TF1169). A rather plain little Fen town with a long high street lead-ing down to the River Witham where a large sugar-beet factory stands next to the bridge. Bardney was once famed for the great Benedictine abbey traditionally founded in the 7th cent. by Ethelred, king of Mercia, and his queen, Ostryth, niece of Oswald, king of Northumbria. Many years after Oswald was slain in battle in A.D. 642, Queen Ostryth brought his remains to Bardney Abbey and buried them within the walls; these still remain, covering 25 acres and mostly over-grown. Pilgrims flocked to the shrine until the

abbey was destroyed by the Danes in 870. In Norman times it was sumptuously rebuilt by the Earl of Lincoln, and its abbots sat in Parliament as Lords of Lindsey. In the Domesday Book it was valued at £429 a year.

In 1912 the abbey ruins were excavated and many relics and interesting bits of stonework are now preserved in the Parish Church of St Law-rence. The church is mainly 15th-cent. with a later medieval brick chancel, and one of the finest of the monuments unearthed from the abbey is that of Abbot Richard Hornastel, who died in 1508. The high altar is said to be the body-stone of King Oswald. Many of the other relics discovered, including a Roman lock 2,000 years old, are in LINCOLN Museum.

BARDON HILL, *Leicestershire* (10–SK4513), just beyond the west edge of CHARNWOOD FOREST, is the highest point in Leicestershire, rising 912 ft above sea-level. One can certainly imagine it as an ancient stronghold hidden in moor and primeval forest, through which it is said a man could walk to Beaumanor without once seeing the sky. A Bronze Age axe, 3,000 years old, was found here when the present huge granite scars were being quarried from the sides of the hill.

Though it is necessary to leave the car and climb on foot, the glorious views over the hills of Derbyshire and Shropshire are worth the effort. On a clear day can be seen the Malvern Hills, the Wrekin, the Sugar Loaf and Black Mountains of Wales, Dunstable Downs, and the Wash. LINCOLN Cathedral rises gracefully amid factory and colliery chimneys 60 m. away.

BASWICH, *Staffordshire* (8–SJ9422). N. of this village about 3 m. ESE. of STAFFORD are the ruins of an Augustinian priory dedicated to St Thomas of Canterbury. It was founded about 1174 by Gerard Fitz Brien of Stafford; his work was completed by Bishop Richard Peche, who was buried there in 1182. In the village is a church with a medieval tower and chancel arch, a three-decker pulpit and a large galleried pew.

BEESTON, *Nottinghamshire* (13–SK5336), is mainly remarkable as a monument to the 1st Lord Trent, who started work in his mother's herbal shop in Nottingham at the age of 14 and opened Jesse Boot's in Goosegate as his own business when he was 27 in 1877. His drug factories now cover over 1¼ million square feet and into them have gone 20 acres of glass, enough cement in bags to reach from Beeston to Paris, and steel bars from Beeston to Constantinople.

The Trent is pretty at Beeston Weir.

BELTON PARK, *Lincolnshire* (13–SK9239). Three m. from GRANTHAM is Belton House, the ancestral William and Mary period home of Lord Brownlow. The house and main drive of the park are open to the public. It was built in 1689 from designs by Christopher Wren, altered about 80 years later by James Wyatt, and has some superb

Belvoir Castle has been rebuilt many times; the present building is largely 19th-cent.

Grinling Gibbons's wood-carvings, especially in the cedar-wood chapel. There is also a fine collection of paintings and porcelain, tapestries and antique silver, and the fabulous "blue bed" of William III. Of more recent interest are some personal souvenirs of King Edward VIII (now the Duke of Windsor), to whom Lord Brownlow was Lord-in-Waiting. The car park is free and refreshments are available in the Camellia Café in the gardens.

The Church of SS. Peter and Paul contains a Norman font, and the villages of **Belton** and neighbouring **Manthorpe** are two of the loveliest in Lincolnshire.

BELVOIR CASTLE, *Leicestershire* (10–SK 8133). When William the Conqueror gave the Mound and all the land visible therefrom to his standard-bearer, Robert de Todeni, he built a castle there and named it Belvedere (now pronounced "Beever").

Most of the imposing, castellated pile dominating the valley is now a mixture of medieval and 19th-cent. It has passed in almost direct descent to the present incumbent, the 19th Earl and 10th Duke of Rutland. In the years between the castle has been destroyed, rebuilt, and improved countless times. In 1461 Thomas Lord de Ros, who had inherited the property via the de Todeni female line and fought on the wrong side in the Wars of

the Roses, was beheaded. The castle was given to Lord Hastings, who removed part of it to build ASHBY and let the rest fall into decay. Twenty-four years later Henry VIII restored the castle to a de Ros, who died childless. Belvoir passed to his sister, who married Sir Robert de Manners, thus introducing the Manners's ownership. The first Earl of Rutland was created in 1525 and he rebuilt a great portion of the castle.

In 1603 James I visited the castle and it is recorded that "before he went to break his fast, he made forty-six knights; among them were Sir George and Sir Oliver Manners".

By the second marriage of the 6th Earl there were two boys, who both died young of "wicked practice and sorcery". The accounts of the trial and confessions of the alleged witches are hair-raising, culminating in one of them calling for bread and wishing it might choke her if she lied. Taking a piece in her mouth, she immediately fell dead.

Belvoir was again destroyed during the Civil War and rebuilt in 1668, with gardens and plantations added. In 1703 the 9th Earl was created Marquis of Granby. It is his great-grandson – a very extravagant fellow, who was moved at one time to write to his wife: "It is impossible we can continue our present mode of living long . . . you must not purchase everything your eye is attached to. . . ." – whose bald-headed likeness is suspended from so many public houses. His son, the 5th Duke, decided to re-model his home into a semblance of a medieval castle and obtained the services of James Wyatt, much of whose work was destroyed by fire in 1816. The Duchess, who fancied herself as an architect, then decided to take over, aided by the Duke's cousin the Rev. Sir John Thoroton. The results of many of their efforts are unfortunate.

The interior, much of which is by Wyatt's sons, Benjamin and Matthew, contains magnificent Gobelin tapestries, paintings by Van Dyck, Reynolds, Hogarth, Murillo, and one of the finest portraits of Henry VIII by Holbein. The gardens, particularly the azaleas and rhododen-drons in the Water Garden, are splendid. Outside the Mausoleum is a monument to the first Vis-count Norwich (Duff Cooper), husband of Lady Diana Manners, daughter of the 8th Duke. The altar within the mausoleum consists of a white marble memorial to the 5th Duchess, whose rise to heaven amid eerie lighting is welcomed by her four dead children offering her a crown of glory.

Belvoir is open to the public and refreshments are served inside.

For those who are wondering about the famous Belvoir Hunt, which sports the best-looking pack in the country, it should be added that, though Leicestershire is a huntsman's paradise, the Belvoir actually meets in Lincolnshire. The Fernie alone hunts in Leicestershire exclusively.

BERESFORD DALE, *Derbyshire* (12–SK 1359). Although the scenery is not as dramatic as that in DOVEDALE, Beresford Dale is the genuine Izaak Walton stretch of the River Dove. It was here that he and his friend Charles Cotton spent many hours fishing. Beresford Hall, Cotton's birthplace which looked down on the Dale, is now in ruins; but the famous Fishing Temple still stands, a stone-built, single-roomed structure with a pyramid roof, erected by Cotton in 1674. It is now in private hands but can be seen from the footpath on the other bank. Halfway along the dale is the Pike Pool, so named by Cotton because of the "pike", a tall, narrow grey rock which sticks up out of the waters like a giant fish.

BETLEY, *Staffordshire* (8–SJ7548), is a serene village about 5 m. W. of NEWCASTLE-UNDER-LYME, with a wide street and half-timbered houses. There is a 13th-cent. church, which was restored during the 17th cent. and contains a remarkable amount of timber; the splendid roof, nave arcades and clerestory are all of oak and the eight nave pillars have been carved from fully grown oaks. In the late summer a flower show with a high local reputation is held at Betley Court.

BIDDULPH, *Staffordshire* (8–SJ8857). Not far from this small town, which almost touches the Cheshire border, rises the River Trent, one of England's longest rivers, which then flows for 170 m. through the Midlands. The river rises on Biddulph Moor, 1,100 ft above sea-level. Not far

away are the BRIDESTONES, a Neolithic burial chamber to which a later legend became attached: a Viking and his English bride were said to be buried here. There is a Norman-based font in the church, and some glowing Flemish glass. Of the two big houses here one, the 16th-cent. Old Hall, is a ruin. It was destroyed by Cromwell's men during the Civil War, for the Biddulphs were Royalists; the other, the Grange, is now a chil-dren's hospital and is set among magnificent gardens laid out by the famous 19th-cent. horticulturist, James Bateman.

BINGHAM, *Nottinghamshire* (13–SK7039), is a rapidly growing village, with a sports centre which is a prototype for the whole country.

Its other main interest is the Early English Perpendicular-style steeple of All Saints'. It has one of the finest broach spires in the country, broad and strong with corner buttresses and an additional buttress in the middle of each side. Notable lancet windows set into the thickness of the wall support two-light lancets higher up.

A wooden floorstone commemorates one of the most famous of Nottinghamshire warriors. Sir Thomas Rempstone – rechristened by Shakes-peare, probably for reasons of metre, John Ramston – appears in *Richard II* as of the company listening to John of Gaunt declaiming: "This royal throne of Kings, this sceptred Isle". Sir Thomas helped Henry defeat Richard and claim the crown.

At the west end of the church there is a carving of the Seven Deadly Sins, and a sequence of memorials culminates in the figure of Ann Har-rison, who worshipped at this place for all of her 99 years. A fish-seller, she put every other half-crown she earned into the collection. Her photo-graph is displayed at the beginning of the Book of Honour to the Fallen for which she paid with her contributions. It is laid on a splendid lectern given to the church by the men who came back.

BIRCHOVER, *Derbyshire* (12–SK2462), is a small village 5 m. S. of BAKEWELL. Many of the strange rocks in the area are believed to have connections with the Druids, a belief reflected in the name of the village pub – Druid Inn. Behind the inn are the Row Tor Rocks, a pile of gritstone about 80 yds long by 50 ft high which includes two "rocking stones", one estimated to weigh 60 tons. The Rev. Thomas Eyre, vicar here in the late 17th cent., had seats carved in some of the rocks and he also built the Church of the Holy Name of Jesus to which the chancel was added in the mid-19th cent. Along the road to Winster can be seen Robin Hood's Stride, two pinnacles of rock which are occasionally tackled by climbers.

On nearby Stanton Moor, which reaches more than 900 ft in parts, are many Bronze Age remains including numerous barrows and several stone circles, the largest of which is known as the Nine Ladies. Many of the finds made in excavations on the moor can be seen in the Heathcote Museum in the village. The old stocks have been restored to their original position at Upper Town.

BISHOP'S CASTLE, *Shropshire* (8–SO3288). Bishop's Castle was the smallest borough in England until 1967, when it lost that distinction, but none of its quaintness. Situated off the A488 from SHREWSBURY to Knighton, it clings to a steep little hillside, 500 ft up – yet overtopped by the hills which surround it. Its Town Hall, one of the smallest in England, stands at the top of the High Street, forcing the road to bend to pass it, with a clock-tower above and an old stone lock-up in its basement. Included in the town's insignia are two fine silver maces, hallmarked 1697.

Administratively linked with CLUN, 5 m. to the S., Bishop's Castle is in the centre of sheep country. There are several fine Tudor houses: the Old Hall, believed to be the birthplace of Edmund Plowden, the builder of Plowden Hall (*see* LYDBURY NORTH), the Old Porch House; and the aptly named House on Crutches. There are also several Georgian houses. Of the original castle, now only part of a wall remains, flanking a bowling green which is the highest point in the town.

The little town had an unusual origin. An Anglo-Saxon landowner, Egwin Shakehead, was cured of his palsy at the shrine of St Ethelbert in HEREFORD and in gratitude bequeathed his manor of Lydbury North to the Bishops of Hereford. They built a castle on the land and in the 13th cent. the little settlement which had sprung up around it became a separate parish, with its own church. Of that first church, very little remains for it was fired and ruined during the Civil War when Bishop's Castle was loyal to the King.

The oldest inn in the town is probably The Three Tuns whose history has been traced back to 1642, but may well go beyond that. The inn is distinguished today by being one of the few left where the landlord still brews his own ale. The brewhouse stands beside the inn.

BLEAKLOW, *Derbyshire* (12–SK1096), is one of the largest areas of England still uncrossed by a road. It is an almost completely unpopulated area of the High Peak in the NW. of the county running up to the Yorkshire border. It lies between the A628 and the A57 and is, as its name suggests, a grim, bleak stretch of high, bare country best avoided in winter; but in summer it is a place for those with an eye for wide skies and an ear for silence, a strange but beautiful area. Bleaklow Hill is over 2,000 ft and to the S. Alport Moor is only a little lower. Several rivers rise in Bleaklow, including the Derwent and the Alport.

BLIDWORTH, *Nottinghamshire* (13–SK5855). In what remains of SHERWOOD FOREST, with good views, is the Church of St Mary where, so it is said, Will Scarlet is buried. It is also said that Maid Marian left her home at Blidworth to marry Robin, and that on the hill on which this pic-,turesque colliery village stands is a cave where the outlaws stored their food. Even if the stories are apocryphal they are nevertheless charming.

It is possibly the same ability for telling a fine tale with conviction which accounts for local assurances that a natural boulder at the foot of the hill – 90 ft in circumference, 15 ft high and with a passage through the middle – is part of Druid remains.

BLITHFIELD HALL, *Staffordshire* (8–SK 0423), has been the home of the Bagot family and their ancestors, the de Blithfields, for almost 900 years. N. of RUGELEY on the UTTOXETER road, the present Hall, mainly Elizabethan with Georgian and Regency additions, is open to the public. The wooded parkland of the Blythe valley makes a gracious setting for the house which is built round a central courtyard and contains much fine woodwork, notably the magnificent carved oak staircase. There is a unique collection of relics from the Stuart period, a children's toy museum, and an exhibition of needlework figures. Georgian costumes are displayed on life-size figures and the old family coaches can be seen in the stables. Outside, views of Blithfield Reservoir can be obtained from the landscaped gardens which contain an 18th-cent. orangery. The Bagot family's link with ABBOTS BROMLEY is maintained by a performance of the ancient Abbots Bromley Horn Dance at the Hall each September.

BLYTH, *Nottinghamshire* (13–SK6287). An old village of great architectural merit on the ancient highway from London to YORK. In the centre of the wide main street there is a long, elm-shaded island on which stands a building with mullioned windows, stone walls, and a 700-year-old doorway still preserved. This building, now serving as a school, was once the property of the Hospital of St John, founded for the care of lepers in the 12th cent. The parish church is developed from the original nave and aisles of a priory built by Roger de Busli in 1088 as a cell of the Abbey of St Catherine at Rouen, and contains the oldest example of Norman architecture in England in its style, if not in date. The south aisle was enlarged to its present size in 1290, with five windows and seven grotesque gargoyles, and the beautiful west tower, 100 ft high, was added in the 14th cent.

BOLSOVER, *Derbyshire* (13–SK4770). This small industrial town, 5 m. E. of CHESTERFIELD, offers a striking visual contrast between what was and what is: down in the valley is all the evidence of the mining industry and its offshoots which make the town important today, while perched on a wooded eminence above the town stands the castle. The original castle was built in Norman times by William Peveril, but the building which occupies the site today, in the care of the Ministry of Public Building and Works and open to the public, was built in the early 17th cent. by Sir Charles Cavendish. The date of its building makes this one of England's most curious castles, for this was not a time when men felt the need, as they had done 500 years earlier, to build fortresses for themselves. It is thought, indeed, that Sir Charles's main intention must have been to re-create the atmosphere of times gone by. That he succeeded is there for all to see today, for although his

G. Douglas Bolton

Boston Stump

castle has battlements and turrets, it also has two pretty cupolas, picturesque riding stables and rooms with names like the Star Chamber and the Heaven Room.

Also worth a visit in Bolsover is the Parish Church of St Mary. It was gutted by fire towards the end of the last century and much reconstruction work had to be done, but the 13th-cent. greystone tower escaped the flames, and inside is a large relief sculpture of the Nativity, also 13th-cent.

BOSCOBEL, *Shropshire* (8–SJ8308). Here, among leafy lanes about 5 m. E. of SHIFNAL, stands the house where Charles II hid from the Parliamentary troops seeking him, after his defeat at WORCESTER on 3 September 1651. Boscobel House was put up about 1600 by John Giffard, a Catholic, and therefore included a number of built-in hiding places. In one of these, which is shown to visitors, the king spent one night. And nearby stands a majestic oak tree, successor of the one in which Charles remained concealed during the day while Cromwell's men searched Boscobel House and its grounds – but never, apparently, lifting their eyes.

About 1 m. away stands another building which has associations with Charles II and which, like Boscobel House, is now in the care of the Ministry of Public Building and Works and can be viewed. This is **Whiteladies** where the king was also briefly sheltered in a house near the ruins of the 12th-cent. nunnery.

BOSTON, *Lincolnshire* (13–TF3244). The name Boston is thought to be a corruption of "St Botolph's Town" and its earliest associations are with this Anglo-Saxon monk whose history is shadowy but whose relics are spread as far as Denmark and Norway. There are 80 churches dedicated to him in England, but Boston is the most famous with its Boston Stump rising to 272½ ft, said to be the second highest church tower in Great Britain.

By 1204, when King John granted a charter to Boston, its fame as a port was second only to that of London, and by the end of the 13th cent. it was paying more than London in customs duties. The great church, whose beacon-light shining from the octagon guided travellers over land and sea for centuries, was rebuilt on the foundations of the St Botolph's mentioned in the Domesday Book. The merchants, growing rich in the wooltrade with Flanders, fashioned it somewhat in the manner of Antwerp or Bruges. It was started in 1309, though the tower was not added until 1460, and for those with energy enough to climb 365 steps there is a splendid view of ships going down the River Witham to the sea. The interior, the oldest part, is magnificent with its high embossed roof. The elaborately carved and brightly coloured stalls with hinged *miserere* seats, all but two of the original 14th-cent. ones surviving, are among the finest in the land.

Plagues, floods, and the turning of trade towards new lands across the Atlantic with the subsequent super-importance of western ports like BRISTOL, turned Boston into a distressed area by the end of the 16th cent. But in the years between, the nucleus of the first Pilgrim Fathers was arrested while trying to escape religious persecution and imprisoned in the Guildhall, where their cells can still be seen. In the following year, 1608, they finally sailed to Holland, reaching the shores of New England some 12 years later, 10 years after others had landed in Plymouth, Massachusetts, and founding the town of Boston. In 1633 John Cotton, Boston's famous Puritan vicar, sailed to America with Richard Bellingham, who became the first of five subsequent Lincoln-Boston Governors of Massachusetts. To this day the whole town flies the Stars and Stripes on 4 July, and Fydell House, built in 1726 and now housing the Pilgrim College, still keeps one room dedicated to the use of visiting American Bostonians.

Other famous Boston men are remembered by the Australians: Sir Joseph Banks, who sailed with Captain Cook in the *Endeavour*, and George Bass, who sailed right round Tasmania and discovered the Strait which still bears his name. The town is proud of Jean Ingelow whose poem, "High Tide on the Coast of Lincolnshire", written in the 19th cent., describes the devastation of the floods of 1571 when the water reached halfway up the church. A remnant of her house still stands opposite the Guildhall, and the tune played on the church chimes was composed in honour of her poem. In the Market Place is a statue of Herbert Ingram, who founded the *Illustrated London News*, the first publication of its kind, in 1842.

There are many fascinating streets, ancient houses and old warehouses in Boston. Those who drive through too fast might later be sorry to have missed a significant part of our history.

BOTHAMSALL, *Nottinghamshire* (13–SK67 73). A neat, quiet village on the slopes of the valley where the Meden and the Maun flow together to become the River Idle. At the join of the rivers is Conjure Alders. Ash and alder trees grow here by the place the Anglo-Saxons used as a ford called Coningswath.

Bothamsall Castle, W. of the village, is probably the earthwork of a Norman castle. A climb up through the sycamores, beeches and elms growing over it to the old oak rising from the top of the hill is well worth the effort for the fine views over SHERWOOD FOREST.

BOTTESFORD, *Leicestershire* (10–SK8038). Here again we pick up the history of BELVOIR CASTLE, for this village church with a lovely spire is where the lords of Rutland have brought eight of their earls to lie in great splendour, together with the monuments of ancestors originally buried in the priory at Belvoir. The first to be buried in the Church of St Mary was Sir Thomas Manners, Lord de Ros, and 1st Earl of Rutland, favourite of Henry VIII. His tomb cost £20 and is surrounded by mourners in the shape of his nine daughters and six sons, one of whom, John, made

a romantic match with Dorothy Vernon of HADDON HALL. The 5th Earl, who endowed the white almshouse opposite the church in 1612, has the richest tomb, with a peacock at his feet. His wife's effigy is also on the tomb though she, the only child of Sir Philip Sidney, was buried at Shoreditch. Francis, the 6th Earl, lies between his first and second wives – the second one, Cecilia, being the mother of the "two sonnes, both of which died in their infancy by wicked Practice and Sorcerye" as is recorded on the monument. This tomb reaches up to the chancel ceiling and was the cause of shocked consternation when it was erected since it hides the altar from the nave and leaves very little room for the choir and clergy to pass. The Marquis of Granby is also buried here, but has no monument.

All these memorials afford a splendid study in changing aristocratic tastes. In the market place, by the stump of the ancient cross, stand the stocks and whipping post to remind us of what happened occasionally to those who could not afford monuments.

BOURNE, *Lincolnshire* (13–TF0920). Mainly famous now for the B.R.M. works, this market town was certainly the birthplace of Robert Mannyng in about 1264 and is reputed, since Charles Kingsley made it so, also to have been the birthplace of Hereward the Wake.

An abbey for Augustinian canons was founded here in 1138 in which Robert Mannyng, whose work was so important to the development of English, inscribed his translations from the French. The only Norman remains of the abbey are incorporated in the nave of the church, four round arches on massive piers supporting scalloped capitals.

The four main streets converge on the Market Place where in 1520 Lord Burghley, statesman and founder of the Cecil fortunes, was born in which is now the Burghley Arms Hotel. Near the disused railway station is Red Hall, an Elizabethan brick building, the home of the Digby family in the 18th cent.

One of the best sports grounds in Lincolnshire, with a splendid swimming-pool, is endowed by an ancient charity at Abbey Lawn. Ever since 1770 another charity has bought bread for the poor after a race by schoolboys over a measured distance at White Bread Meadow. Bidding for the field continues until the boys finish the race and the highest bidder holds the land for a year, giving his rent to the charity.

BRADGATE PARK, *Leicestershire* (10–SK 5908). One of the earliest of the fine Leicestershire houses built for pleasure rather than fortification, Bradgate in its 1,000-acre park 6 m. from the centre of LEICESTER was started by Thomas Grey, Earl of Huntingdon and 1st Marquis of Dorset, in about 1490 and finished by his son, grandfather of Lady Jane Grey. Born in 1537, she spent the only happy part of her life here with her tutor, Aylmer, later Bishop of London, before her scheming father married her at the age of 16 to

Lord Dudley with whom she was beheaded in the Tower not long afterwards.

The house is now a ruin, but the park, which is open only on Thursdays during the summer to motorists, incorporates much of CHARNWOOD FOREST where the woods, bracken-covered hills, striking granite outcrops and charming by-ways make delightful walks. Bradgate Park is also a reserve for Leicestershire Trust for Nature Conservation. Take the path from the main gate, turning left uphill past the war memorial to Old John, the highest point. There is a folly tower there with an adjoining arch and a direction indicator from which to choose a number of walks, all of them equally lovely.

BRADWELL, *Derbyshire* (12–SK1781). Situated in the beautiful Hope Valley about 2 m. S. of HOPE, this small village has not only a rocky dale of its own, but also its own cave. The well-known Bagshawe's Cavern, approached by more than 100 descending steps, contains some weirdly beautiful stalactites and other crystallized formations. This is also another of Derbyshire's well-dressing villages, two being dressed each August.

BRAMCOTE, *Nottinghamshire* (13–SK5037), is worth finding for its beautiful views over five counties and the Trent valley, and because it is one of the prettiest villages hereabouts. The Manor House, one of the finest brick buildings in Nottinghamshire, was in existence in 1564 and has been turned into charming dwellings set about a rockery with pools.

The famous Hemlock Stone, 30 ft high, of red sandstone, which has resisted the action of the elements longer than man can tell, also belongs to Bramcote. It is about 70 ft in circumference and probably weighs over 200 tons. It is popularly connected with Druid rituals and has been declared an Area of Special Scientific Interest.

BRAUNSTON, *Rutland* (10–SK8306). Amid beautiful hilly country, Braunston lies on the side of a hill rising from the valley of the little River Gwash. The farm-houses, cottages and church are built of the charming, dark-brown local ironstone. The church is externally 15th-cent. Perpendicular but there is evidence inside of an originally Norman building of the 12th and 13th cents. in the responds of the chancel arch and the doorway from chancel to vestry. There are also still some traces of medieval wall paintings.

The name was Danish, meaning "Brand's village". About one mile NW. of the village are sunken roads and ancient earthworks where pottery has been found.

Leave by the road to Tilton and LEICESTER which affords fine views over the wooded hills. One m. SE. of Braunston is **Brooke**, only 2 m. from OAKHAM, yet pleasingly remote. In particular, Brooke's charming little Church of St Peter is worth a detour to visit. The tower is 13th-cent. and there are traces of Norman work, but it is the Elizabethan craftsmanship which is the

most interesting. In 1577 the "archdeacon's visitations" described the church as ruinous and the curate often "marvellously overcome with drink". But it was rebuilt in 1579, a most unusual time for church building, and retains an impression of the worshippers of the time still being there, surrounded by the screen, benches, box pews, family pews, pulpit, reading desk and communion rail of the period.

Stones on the chancel floor record the depressing life of one Henry Rawlins, and his four wives, who all died within 13 years. His fifth wife, however, managed to break the curse, and buried *him* in 1742. There is also a lovely Renaissance alabaster monument to Charles Noel, which was erected in 1619 and still retains its original colours. In 1549 the Noels bought the site of Brooke Priory, founded before 1153, the only monastic house in Rutland. They built a large mansion on it of which only the ruined gateway and porter's lodge are left. The present house, called The Priory, is late 17th-cent. and the porter's lodge became an 18th-cent. dovecot.

BREEDON-ON-THE-HILL, *Leicestershire* (10–SK4022). The village is uninteresting, but people who climb the rocky road up to the Iron Age encampment still known as "The Bulwarks" on the top of the hill find the place weird and uncanny.

As early as the 8th cent. there was an Anglo-Saxon monastery here of which some sculpture still survives in the present church. There are 30 fragments built into the structure, Mercian work which, fitted together, would cover 60 ft. The strips of frieze are about 9 in. high, the longest one is behind the altar and the most beautiful one, an angel, is 3 ft long. The Danes obliterated this monastery and only ruins were left until the early 12th cent., when the foundations were used to build an Augustinian priory, traces of which still remain in the west end of the tower. In the 13th cent. a new chancel was added, constituting the present building.

BRIDGNORTH, *Shropshire* (8–SO7193), is really two towns, High Town and Low Town, connected by many flights of steps and a railway with the steepest gradient in Britain. The setting, part spread across the red sandstone ridge, part at its foot, is unique in England; and the buildings in the town live up to it. The oddest is undoubtedly the remains of the 12th-cent. castle which was destroyed by the Parliamentarians in 1646. They left about 30 ft of the tower of the keep and this still stands – or leans – unbelievably at 17 degrees from the perpendicular, more than three times the lean of the tower at Pisa. The castle grounds are now a public park and a fascinating view of the Low Town can be had from Castle Walk, a promenade running 100 ft above the River Severn.

The next most conspicuous building is the Town Hall; half-timbered and set on arches, it straddles the High Street, traffic passing beneath it. There are many half-timbered and 18th-cent. houses in the High Street, which is one of the most pleasing thoroughfares in the county, straight, wide and gracious.

One of the best vistas in the town is to be had in East Castle Street which vies with High Street with its many fine, well-proportioned houses. The street is a cul-de-sac, sealed off by Bridgnorth's most striking church, St Mary Magdalene's. Built in white stone with Tuscan columns, a square, pillared tower surmounted by a lead dome, the church looks as if it would be more at home in a Mediterranean town than in its English setting. Its designer was the engineer Thomas Telford.

The Parish Church of St Leonard, badly damaged during the Civil War, was almost entirely rebuilt about 100 years ago in its 15th-cent. style. In red sandstone, the church is remarkably wide. It has an impressive tower and a stair turret topped with a miniature spire.

Climbing up steeply from Low Town to High Town is the Cartway. Here are caves, hewn out of the sandstone, where people lived until little more than 100 years ago. Here, too, is the town's oldest house, a near-perfect example of Elizabethan black-and-white building which was the birthplace of Bishop Thomas Percy. The bishop is mainly remembered for his collection of old English poetry, *Reliques of Ancient English Poetry* (1765).

There are some interesting houses in Low Town: Cann Hall where Prince Rupert lodged in 1642; Diamond Hall, built by Colonel Roger Pope in the late 17th cent. with the winnings of his horse, Diamond; and the 17th-cent. Vine Inn by the river.

BRIERLEY HILL, *Staffordshire* (8–SO9187). Fine glass has been made here since French glassmakers came to the town at the beginning of the 17th cent. and many examples, including historical pieces, can be seen in a collection at the Central Library in Moor Street. On Ashwood Heath are the remains of a 1st-cent. Roman camp.

BROCKLESBY, *Lincolnshire* (13–TA1311). The 1,000-acre park of this, the still almost feudal family seat of the Earls of Yarborough, was laid out by Capability Brown. The house is of red brick, set amid lily-ponds and dating originally from 1730. It contains beautiful works of art, magnificent furniture, and paintings by Lely, Romney and Reynolds. The family, who are descended from Elizabeth I's eminent military commander, Sir William Pelham, are famous for the trees they have planted in the park. They began with 40,000 saplings two years before the French Revolution and the 1st Baron is recorded as having planted 12,552,700 trees between 1787 and 1823. His wife, Sophia, is buried at Limber Magna in the Brocklesby Mausoleum, built by James Wyatt, with a statue by Nollekens, amongst cedars on what was once a tumulus. Roman combs, rings, urns, beads, bones and ashes have been found there.

Some of the Pelham ancestors are buried in the

Barnaby/Mustograph

Bridgnorth: a view from the High Town

13th-cent. church in the Park in tombs ornamented with the Buckle badge which can also be seen in many Sussex churches. This badge was granted to Sir John Pelham for his courtesy on the field of battle at Poitiers, where he captured King John of France.

BROWNHILLS, *Staffordshire* (8–SK0405). Close to this town on the edge of the Black Country is one of the country's largest watersports centres, Chasewater. The 260-acre lake is used by the Cannock Sailing Club, and the South Staffordshire Hydroplane and Speedboat Club and in summer there is always something for the visitor to see. There are also gardens, an amusement park and a paddling pool. In Brownhills, at a junction on Watling Street (A5) near the railway station, stands what is believed to be one of the oldest signposts in England, dated 1777. Three m. to the E. is the ancient Roman site of WALL; and at Ogley Hay is a relic of Roman earthworks.

BUILDWAS ABBEY, *Shropshire* (8–SJ6304), is reckoned one of the three finest ruined abbeys in England. In a meadow beside the Severn on the road from MUCH WENLOCK to IRONBRIDGE, its Norman ruins contrast with a six-chimneyed modern power station. More surprising than its location, perhaps, is the fact that after 800 years so much of the abbey should still be standing; this is largely due to the rescue operation carried out by the Ministry of Public Building and Works.

The abbey was founded in 1135 by Roger de Clinton, Bishop of Coventry and Lichfield, and the present buildings are believed to date from about 15 years later. Impressive but not over-poweringly so, the abbey is about 180 ft long. The nave, with its huge round pillars and Norman arches, is almost intact save for the roof: and parts of the chapter house, the sacristy, the crypt and tower still stand. The piscina, the stone seats for the priests and other pieces of carved stone from the time of Henry II and Becket also remain for the visitor to see.

BUNNY, *Nottinghamshire* (13–SK5829). Much of this pretty village was designed by the eccentric but kindly "Wrestling Baron", Thomas Parkyns. Encouraged by his mother in ideas which were then almost revolutionary, Sir Thomas did all he could to improve the lot of his tenants, rebuilding farm-houses and dwellings, many of which still bear his initials, and designing four charming 17th-cent. almshouses and a school (now used as a village room) near the church gate. They still have mullioned windows and on the division between the first and second floors Sir Thomas, who had compiled a Latin Grammar and dis-played tags wherever he could, has had inscribed: *Scientia non habet inimicum nisi ignorantem* – "Learning has no enemy except the ignorant man".

In designing his own home, Bunny Hall, Sir Thomas showed his eccentricities to the full. His greatest interest, however, was in wrestling and he wrote a book about it called *The Cornish Hugg* which he dedicated to George I. When he died in 1741 he was buried in the 14th-cent. church in one of the stone coffins he used to collect and give away to anybody who asked for one. He designed his own monument which depicts him standing aggressively, waiting to start a wrestling bout. By his side is a tiny little figure lying flat on a pallet with Father Time by his side. Part of the epitaph reads: "That Time at length did throw him it is plain".

BURFORD, *Shropshire* (8–SO5868), is a small village, 1 m. from Tenbury Wells and separated from Worcestershire by the River Teme. Tucked away down a quiet lane off the A465, the red sandstone Church of St Mary bears traces of its Norman origins but much of the present building, including its imposing tower and battlements, dates from the late 19th cent. The most striking of the many church monuments for which Burford is famed is a triptych, 11 ft tall, signed by the Italian painter Melchior Salaboss and dated 1588. The two panelled doors are painted with the figures of the Twelve Apostles and these open to reveal life-size paintings of three of the Cornwalls, lords of Burford for 400 years until the family sold their lands in 1721.

A more recent source of fame are the Burford House clematis. Burford House, which stands on the site of the original Cornwall castle, is a typical early Georgian (1726) mansion, part of which can be looked over. In 1954 the gardens round the house were completely re-designed and re-claimed from nature, and were opened to the public for the summer months four years later. Many unusual shrubs and plants from all over the world are on show and scattered among them, mostly informally, are more than 120 species of clematis. But it is the clematis in the glasshouses, with flowers the size of plates, which remain most strongly in the memory.

BURLEY, *Rutland* (10–SK8710). The village is chiefly famed for the most beautiful country house in the county. Burley-on-the-Hill. It is best ad-mired from the S. on the OAKHAM–STAMFORD road, looking up the great avenue of trees to the top of what must once have been an ancient earth-work 500 ft above sea-level, the highest point in Rutland, overlooking the Vale of Catmose.

The first house was built in the 16th cent. by Sir John Harington, who entertained James I there on his way to be crowned. By the time he revisited it in 1620 it had been bought and rebuilt by his favourite, the Duke of Buckingham. Before that building was destroyed by Crom-well's armies, Charles I and Henrietta Maria had also paid it a visit, and it was on this occasion that the famous Oakham Dwarf, Jeffery Hudson, jumped out of a pie as it was cut at the dinner-table. Henrietta Maria was so enchanted with the dwarf that the Duchess gave him to her, and Van Dyck painted the two together in a picture now hanging at PETWORTH in Sussex.

The present house, with its beautifully re-strained detail, was designed by John Lumley for David Finch, Earl of Nottingham, in 1694–1705. In 1815 the Duke of Wellington thought of buying and rebuilding it, but was most fortunately directed elsewhere. The church, almost ruined by the Victorian "restorer" Pearson, still bears Norman and 13th-cent. traces inside. There is a lovely, very pathetic, marble monument to Lady Charlotte Finch, governess to the children of George III, but, oddly enough, no other mem-orials to the family.

In the woods behind the house is a circular hermit's sanctuary, built of rustic-work in 1807.

BURTON-UPON-TRENT, *Staffordshire* (9–SK2423). On a warm day the rich, "home-cook-ing" smell of beer being brewed hangs in every street of this important brewing town. Here, too, are the huge buildings bearing the names familiar to everyone who takes a glass of ale. Yet Burton was not always a brewing town; once its pros-perity was geared to the clothing industry, although story has it that a 13th-cent. abbot of Burton used the water from the local wells for brewing. Of his abbey only fragments remain and the man most remembered here in stone and brick is Michael Bass, a member of the famous brewing firm who became Lord Burton during Mr Gladstone's premiership. To Lord Burton the town owes its fine Town Hall, the beautiful St Paul's Church, St Margaret's Church and a number of other public buildings.

The parish church is St Modwen's, dedicated to the founder of the first Christian settlement at Burton in the 7th cent. The church, standing near

Burton-upon-Trent: a bridge across the river

the Trent, was built in the early 18th cent. and contains a 15th-cent. font, probably a relic from an earlier church.

Fine views of the river can be had from the three bridges – the main Burton bridge, the iron Anglesey Bridge, and the long footbridge, known as the Stapenhill Viaduct.

BUXTON, *Derbyshire* (12–SK0673). Buxton's fame rests on both its air and its water. This is the highest town in England – just over 1,000 ft above sea-level; it is also one of the oldest spas in the country. The Romans were the first to appreciate the value of the waters which come to the surface here but it was the efforts of the 5th Duke of Devonshire from 1780 onwards – and those of his two successors to the title – which established Buxton as a second BATH. The 5th Duke had the sweeping Crescent, still the finest sight in the town, built close to the original St Ann's Well which is open daily throughout the season. In the Crescent, too, are the Natural Baths which stand upon the site of a Roman Bath. Today the nine springs, which are estimated to be between 3,500 and 5,000 ft below ground, produce about a quarter of a million gallons of warm water each

day. It gushes into a beautiful white Italian marble basin which emphasizes the colour of the pale blue water. It is also Buxton's claim that this natural mineral water is without the unpleasant smell and taste usually associated with spa waters.

Buxton sets out with firm purpose to entertain the visitor and nowhere more so than in the Pavilion Gardens, 23 acres of lovely grounds surrounding the Pavilion itself, which contains a large concert hall and a ballroom. In the grounds are putting and bowling greens and tennis courts; there is boating on the lake; and there is a children's play area which includes both model and miniature railways. There are other pleasing open spaces, such as the Serpentine Walks by the Wye and the walk to Grinlow Woods and the strange tower known as Solomon's Temple on the south side of the town. Corbar Woods are another worthwhile goal for the walker and there are paths to the top of Corbar Crags with their fine views.

In Buxton Museum in Terrace Road can be seen collections of local rocks and fossils, and ornaments made of Blue John stone and Ashford marble. There is another museum at Poole's

Cavern housing ancient British, Roman and animal remains found in the Cavern; the cave itself is also open to the public.

Derbyshire play county cricket at the charming ground just off the town centre; and there are two 18-hole golf courses, one high above the town on the road to Glossop which is reckoned one of the driest courses in the country.

Buxton is in the heart of impressive scenery, some of the best being seen by taking the minor road to the small villages of **Peak Dale** and **Peak Forest** to the NE. Here you cross the roof of England, a wide, almost prehistoric landscape, criss-crossed with grey, drystone walls, here and there a hill rearing up, and the bareness relieved only by the occasional cluster of trees in a sheltered hollow, rarely enough to make a wood.

CAISTOR, *Lincolnshire* (13–TA1101). High on a western spur of the Wolds, with views of LINCOLN Cathedral, Caistor, in the county division of Lindsey, is now a quiet little market town serving the rich farming country surrounding it.

It was once a walled Roman camp, succeeding a British hill-fort called Caer-Egarry, and the Roman Ermine Street passed near it. Fragments of the Roman wall can be seen in the garden of the headmaster of the Grammar School, a 17th-cent. building carefully restored in 1930, where once the poet, Sir Henry Newbolt, was a pupil.

The Venerable Bede mentions Caistor as an Anglo-Saxon place of importance called Tunne-Ceaster and some mounds just outside the town are supposed to mark the site of the battle in A.D. 828 in which King Egbert of Wessex defeated the Mercians.

The Church of SS. Peter and Paul has early Anglo-Saxon and late Norman work in the lower part of the tower and there is a Roman well still in use nearby. At the east end of the north aisle is the Crusader tomb of Sir William de Hundon and the vestry contains an alabaster monument to Sir Edward Maddison, who died in 1553, aged 100. A "gad whip" – one of four still in existence – is preserved in the church.

The village of **Cabourne**, 1½ m. E. on the A46, has a church tower dating from before the Norman Conquest, and Pelham Column, 128 ft high, erected in 1840 to commemorate the planting of 12 million trees by Lord Yarborough of BROCKLESBY.

CALVERTON, *Nottinghamshire* (13–SK6149). Famous as the probable birthplace of the inventor of the stocking-frame, an Elizabethan parson called William Lee. It was due to Lee's invention that the hosiery industry flourishes today, though he made no money out of it and it was eventually developed in France. This frame, the most amazingly complete invention ever to be devised in a single operation, was the first machine to produce a looped or knitted fabric and was the beginning of the great hosiery and lace-making factories which abound in Nottinghamshire today. The more romantic story about the invention was that Lee nearly 400 years ago was courting a lady who infuriated him by continuing to knit while he paid his addresses. In exasperation he gave up the care of his parish to invent the knitting machine, taking it to Queen Elizabeth, who refused to grant him a patent because it only made wool stockings. Lee then made another frame to produce silk stockings, but the Queen again refused a patent in case it threw the hand-knitters out of work. There are still hand-knitters in the cottages of Calverton today, recognizable by the wide windows where globes of water hang to catch the light.

The Church of St Wilfrid has seven Norman stones carved into the belfry illustrating the "occupations of months".

CANNOCK, *Staffordshire* (8–SJ9710), now a thriving industrial town, owed its existence originally to CANNOCK CHASE, lying to the N. It is more than likely that there was a small settlement of some kind 1,000 years and more ago; and to the NE. of the town is an area of about 18 acres known as Castle Ring which was an Iron Age encampment.

There was a church on the site of the present St Luke's Parish Church in the 12th cent., and a few traces of that original building remain. The church was rebuilt in the 14th cent., and has several times been altered and restored since. A more curious and unusual building is the Tank House. Built of brick, hexagonal and with a pyramid roof, this was where the pipe bringing Cannock's first secure water supply, in 1736, came out.

One of the most attractive buildings is the white 18th-cent. former mansion which houses the Council offices – and next to it is one of the most perfect bowling greens in the Midlands, which has been in constant use for more than 170 years. Within easy reach of the town, on the edge of Cannock Chase, is the famous Beaudesert Golf Club; and the nearby Hednesford Hills are good for walks.

CANNOCK CHASE, *Staffordshire* (8–SJ 9816). Once, 1,000 years and more ago, there were so many trees, many of them giant oaks, on Cannock Chase that a stranger could lose himself in half an hour. Today, crossed by one good road, bordered by others and networked with tracks and forest rides, the Chase consists of some of the most beautiful country in the Midlands, easily accessible to motorist, rambler and walker. Where once the kings and nobles of England hunted for sport, keeping the Chase as their own private preserve, the visitor today can wander freely in countryside that looks well in all seasons, but is perhaps loveliest in spring and autumn.

Today there are fewer trees but the Forestry Commission have established many plantations. Some of the majestic oaks remain in Brocton Coppice; this is where, with luck, wild deer may be glimpsed.

The forest rides between South Street and Abraham's Valley offer pleasant walks through the orderly pine and spruce plantations. Many areas in high summer are seas of waist-high bracken; but to the W. of Sherbrook Valley heather and gorse take over the hillside. There is a large variety of bog-plants to be seen in Sherbrook Valley or down Oldacre, including the rare fly-catching sundew – and the even rarer long-leaved sundew. Beetles abound near the streams. Birch trees grow on the Black Hills and from any of the hilltops near Seven Springs can be had magnificent views over large areas of the Chase. Besides trees, gorse and heather there is the Trent flowing beneath the fine bridge at Colwich. Low, narrow and with 14 grey-stone arches – once it had 43 – the Essex Bridge, as it is now called, was perhaps built by the Elizabethan Earls of Essex as a short cut to the Chase.

CANWICK, *Lincolnshire* (13–SK9869). One m. SE. of LINCOLN, off the B1188, Canwick offers such world-famous views of the cathedral that it is worth visiting if for nothing else. It can also be reached on foot by taking the charming path down the cliff by the edge of South Common and up the tree-lined ridge.

But the church is also interesting, built by the Normans on the tessellated floors of a Roman villa. No Roman traces remain, but there is a Norman chancel still standing amid the many alterations which continued until the 19th cent.

Canwick is in the North Kesteven district of Lincolnshire and the Hall is the ancestral home of the Sibthorps. John Sibthorp was a famous 18th-cent. botanist; the Rev. Richard scandalized the early Victorians by dithering for years between the Church of England and the Roman Catholic faiths, finally dying a Catholic and insisting on being buried with the English rites; and politician Charles sold his land to the railway for the GRANTHAM–Lincoln line on the condition that it never ran on a Sunday; this it never did. The line is now closed to passengers.

CASTLE BYTHAM, *Lincolnshire* (13–SK 9818). Cottages cluster up the hill towards the church in this very charming village in the South Kesteven district of Lincolnshire. On the other side of the stream flowing down to the River Glen are the great earthworks mentioned in the Domesday Book as held by Earl Morcar, brother of King Harold. Morkery Wood, W. of the village, still bears his name.

Finished by the Conqueror's half-brother, Odo, the castle stood here until it was besieged and razed to the ground by Henry III in 1221. A second castle was built by William de Colville which was burned in the Wars of the Roses.

The Church of St James is 12th-cent. though it has a Norman nave. It is cruciform and on the south of the tower is an 18th-cent. sundial inscribed with the pun, "Bee in Thyme". The brass candelabra was made just after Waterloo. In a corner of the nave stands a ladder inscribed, "This ware the May Poul 1660" – the village maypole later used as steps to the belfry.

CASTLE DONINGTON, *Leicestershire* (10–SK4427). Castle Donington is the administrative centre of a rural district covering 37 sq. m. and including East Midlands Airport. It was once the site of the first Norman castle, built by Henry de Lacy, Earl of Lincoln, whose London home was LINCOLN'S INN. In 1595 Sir George Hastings, 4th Earl of Huntingdon, "ruined the castle" and built a house in the park 2 m. away. The Hall, designed by Wilkins, architect of the NATIONAL GALLERY, is now a hotel. A castellated building close by called the Kings' Mill overlooks the Trent at a popular boating and picnic spot with a weir, many small islands, and a row of white cottages.

The town itself still has some lovely houses, in particular the Old Key House, a timber-framed building halfway up the hill to the SW. of the church. Houses and cottages incorporating the original stone now stand on the site of the castle with their gardens in part of the old moat.

The Church of St Edward is essentially 13th- and 14th-cent. Brass-rubbing enthusiasts should visit the fine memorial to Robert de Staunton and his wife. The oldest tomb is that of a tonsured monk sculptured in about 1320. The inside of the pulpit is constructed of memorial slabs to children, taken from the floor.

Castle Donington has a fine power station, a lesson to those who think these must always be monstrosities.

CASTLETON, *Derbyshire* (12–SK1582). This is the country of the caverns. Four of the most famous in the country are to be found in and around this large village in the northern Peak District, about 8 m. NE. of BUXTON. But the first thing the visitor sees are not the caverns but the ruined Norman Peveril Castle, immortalized in Sir Walter Scott's *Peveril of the Peak*, which stands high above the village. Now in the care of the Ministry of Public Building and Works, much of the castle has been fittingly restored to its former grandeur. It is well worth the climb to see it.

William Peveril was given the land for the castle by William the Conqueror and immediately set about the building. The site was well chosen: terrain offered natural protection on three sides and only the N. called for serious fortification. It was here that Peveril threw up the curtain wall which survives almost in its entirety – although much repaired over the years, the typical Norman herringbone masonry can easily be detected. Traces of other Norman parts of the castle can also be seen. The imposing keep came almost 100 years later, erected by Henry II in 1176.

The nearest cavern to the village and the castle is the Peak Cavern and indeed a passage has been discovered connecting one of the branches of the Peak, Devil's Cavern, to the castle. Peak Cavern always comes as a surprise to the first-time visitor to Castleton: there is a little street with a stream running beside it, and there in this rural and domestic scene the huge mouth of the cavern gapes. Centuries ago, in dangerous times when raiders from the north swept down into Derbyshire, the whole population of the village used to seek refuge in this cave, living here for considerable periods. The smoke from their fires produced the blackened ceiling seen today. From the Peak Cavern, passages lead into others with names like Roger's Rain House, where water trickles continuously down the walls; the Bell House; Devil's Cavern; and the Orchestral Chamber where, from time to time, choral concerts are held.

W. of Castleton, just off the A625 to CHAPEL-EN-LE-FRITH, is a spectacular ravine called The Winnats, and Speedwell Cavern lies beneath it. The approach to this cavern has to be made by boat along an old channel, about 750 yds long, made by 18th-cent. lead-miners. The guide propels the boat along by pushing against the walls of the passage leading to the cavern. Here the visitor can look down into the Bottomless Pit and watch – and hear – the water disappearing into the darkness.

The other two sets of caverns are both in Treak Cliff, the Treak Cliff Caverns at its foot, the Blue John Caverns at its summit. These are beautiful. Flood-lighting has been installed in the Treak Cliff Caverns to illuminate the strange rock formations, the stalagmites, stalactites and anemolites and the arch of Blue John stone. Easy paths lead to a grotto.

Similar underground scenery characterizes the Blue John Caverns, where spacious chambers and connecting passages are believed to run for two miles into the hills. Here the unusual Blue John stone, found nowhere else in the world, can be seen in its natural setting. Some of the finest specimens of it are at CHATSWORTH, KEDLESTON HALL and in ASHBOURNE parish church, all in Derbyshire, and in the Vatican Library in Rome. Trinkets and other articles made from the stone are sold at the caverns and in the villages. Many interesting finds from the caverns can be inspected in the Douglas Museum.

St Edmund's Church in Castleton was of Norman foundation, but only the fine chancel arch remained after rebuilding in 1837. The church possesses an unusually large library, including works on divinity, biography and history, and a rare "breeches Bible" of 1611. It is also the scene of the climax of an unusual custom that commemorates the restoration of Charles II. On 29 May each year, known locally as Garland Day, a group of Morris Dancers, led by the "King" and his "Consort" and accompanied by a band, goes in procession through the village to the Market Place, when the maypole is plaited and a garland of flowers from the shoulders of the "King" is hoisted to the top of the church tower.

CHAPEL-EN-LE-FRITH, *Derbyshire* (12–SK0580). The church here has an unusual dedication – to St Thomas à Becket – which points to the age of the place and explains its puzzling name. It is known that the first church here was a chapel built in the early 13th cent. – not many years after Becket's murder – by the men who worked in the Peak Forest; and the little settlement at that time would quite likely have been in the edges of the forest – "en le frith". Today's church dates from the early 14th cent. and the tower was brought up to date about 1733. The small market town, itself set on a high ridge in the north-west corner of the Peak District – the market place is 776 ft above sea-level – is ringed by even loftier hills and is one of the gateways to the famous walking and climbing country in this part of Derbyshire, and to the caverns at CASTLETON. Chapel-en-le-Frith is sturdy rather than picturesque but several of its old inns are still in business. It has a 17th-cent. market cross and the old town stocks are still there.

CHARNWOOD FOREST, *Leicestershire* (10–SK4914). The Forest covers an area of about 15,000 acres NW. of LEICESTER but many of the large private estates have been sold for building, quarrying, or coal-mining, and the trees have been felled. It can be motored through on the A50 to ASHBY-DE-LA-ZOUCH in 10 minutes but it is a pity to rush through this Triassic landscape, which had a large active volcano in one corner when mammals were beginning to appear on the face of the earth. There are still some 212 acres of forest and moorland (with Nature Reserves at BRADGATE PARK and **Swithland Wood**) preserved around **Beacon Hill**, the **Hangingstone Rocks**, and **Windmill Hill** at **Woodhouse Eaves**.

Leicestershire footpaths are not often very clearly defined but a lovely, quiet walk through the Forest starts from **Groby**, leaving the A50 just N. of the church and going down to Groby Pool. Walk back between Groby and **Newtown Linford** to the footpath on the far side of the quarry which leads into Newtown Linford and the entrance to Bradgate Park. Walk past the ruins of Lady Jane Grey's home to the top of Old John, where there is a direction indicator and extensive views. Continue in the same direction to the park boundary, turn left and follow the wall back to the village. An alternative route starts almost opposite the main entrance to the park, crosses the Newtown–Groby road and leads by the edge of Old Wood and Lady Hay Wood to the A50 a third of a mile NW. of the starting point. This is a walk of approximately 7 m.

CHATSWORTH, *Derbyshire* (12–SK2670). Everything about Chatsworth – house, furnishings, pictures and gardens – invites the superlative. Here, in a lovely park about 2½ m. E. of BAKEWELL, is one of England's great houses, the Derbyshire home of the Dukes of Devonshire, open to the public for the summer months.

The first house at Chatsworth was set, like the present one, on ground overlooking the River Derwent, and its designers were Sir William Cavendish and his wife, the famous Bess of Hardwick. Bess, who later became the Countess of Shrewsbury, was said to be "building-mad" and although nothing of her building at Chatsworth, except the Hunting Tower, among the woods above the present house, remains, she was to leave a more durable memorial in HARDWICK HALL. The present Chatsworth was begun by her great-great-grandson, the 1st Duke of Devon-

A. F. Kersting

Chatsworth House: the chapel

shire, and continued at intervals by his successors, notably the 4th and 6th Dukes. In the course of all this work the aspect of the house was changed from E. to W., a big bend in the Derwent was straightened, the gardens were created much in their present form, and the entire village of EDENSOR was moved to its present position out of sight of the house.

Chatsworth is a harmonious complex of stone buildings of palatial appearance, set against a wooded slope and with the drive curving over an old bridge across the Derwent. But if the house is imposing from the outside, inside there is beauty, elegance and splendour.

The architects involved were William Talman, Thomas Archer and Sir Jeffry Wyatville, all renowned in their day; three French masters are generously represented – Tijou, the smith, whose wrought-ironwork can be seen in the Painted Hall, and Laguerre and Verrio, responsible for much of the painting on ceilings and walls. There are several works by Van Dyck, notably the full-length portraits of Arthur Goodwin and Jeanne de Blois in the Dining Room, a Tintoretto (*Samson and Delilah*) and a Landseer (*Bolton Abbey*). Much of the fine carving both in wood and stone is the work of Samuel Watson of Heanor and there are a number of William Kent chairs. In the Entrance

Hall stands a 1st-cent. Roman sculpture of a mother and child. There are Mortlake tapestries and a fine collection of blue and white Delft tulip-vases. In face of the richness of all this workmanship and colour and texture it is easy to overlook the house itself, a perfect casket for the treasures it contains.

Outside there is a beauty of a different order. Little remains of Bess of Hardwick's Elizabethan garden apart from Queen Mary's Bower (where Mary Queen of Scots spent some time during her periods of imprisonment); there is evidence of the "loose landscape" style incorporated during the period about 1760 when Capability Brown was brought in as adviser; but today's gardens owe most to the ideas and skill of the 6th Duke's employee and friend, Joseph Paxton, later to design the Crystal Palace. Outstanding are the many waterworks: the Sea Horse and Cascade Fountains, the large Canal Pond and the spectacular Emperor Fountain which can throw its jet to a height of 290 ft and is operated solely by the natural pressure of the head of water from the large pond which Paxton constructed on top of the hill to the E. Recent additions include a yew maze planted in 1962 and the serpentine beech hedge near the Ring Pond. Paxton's "Conservative Wall" has been restored.

CHEADLE, *Staffordshire* (8–SK0043). The outstanding building in this old market town is the red stone Roman Catholic church with its 200-ft spire, a landmark for miles. The church, built in 1846, was designed by A. W. N. Pugin, and is regarded as one of his masterpieces. Brass lions rampant guard the west door and inside all is rich colour. Cheadle's parish church, only eight years older, retains the communion rails and an oak chest from an earlier church.

About 3 m. E. of Cheadle lies the village of Oakamoor and between the two are the 250 acres of the **Hawksmoor Nature Reserve** which is also a bird sanctuary. Hawksmoor was bought by public subscription and presented to the National Trust by its founder, Mr J. R. B. Masefield, a well-known Staffordshire naturalist. The Reserve was opened to the public in 1927 and six years later the gates at the entrance were erected and opened by the founder's cousin, the late John Masefield. There are nature trails through the Reserve, which rises to 750 ft in one part. Birds of all kinds, including curlew and pheasant, can be seen; and unusual trees such as lodge pole pine and red oak have been planted.

CHECKLEY, *Staffordshire* (8–SK0237). Much that is ancient can be seen in and around this small village in the Tean valley about 5 m. NW. of UTTOXETER. There are ancient earthworks at Toothill; in the churchyard are the shafts of three Anglo-Saxon crosses, 1,000 years old; and there is the church itself built 900 years ago, with an old sundial on its outside wall and a Norman font inside. The lofty chancel dates from the 14th cent. and some of the traceried windows are filled with glass of the same date.

Kenneth Scowen

Church Stretton: the view towards Caer Caradoc

CHESTERFIELD, *Derbyshire* (13–SK3871). Well known for its strange landmark, the crooked spire of its parish church, Chesterfield is also worth a visit for some of its fine, modern buildings. The new courthouse, circular and with a many-gabled roof, is a striking building in the modern idiom, while a new but more conventional structure is the glass and concrete block which houses the Accountant General's Department of the Post Office. The Town Hall, a gracious, long-fronted building with an impressive pillared entrance, built just before the Second World War, is set among wide lawns. The new College of Technology is another building which catches the eye. The footbridge linking Queen's Park and the piazza of the Accountant General's Department building, a graceful arch of pre-stressed concrete, is a beautiful design.

Although its spire is what has made the Church of St Mary and All Saints famous, the building itself is a fine example of 14th-cent. church architecture. Cruciform and 173 ft long by 110 ft wide, the church is beautifully proportioned. The font is Anglo-Saxon, there is an unusual hagioscope and three medieval screens, and a collection of perfectly preserved monuments to the Foljambe family, covering the latter half of the 16th cent. The octagonal spire, 228 ft high, leans 7 ft 6 in. to the S., 7 ft 10 in. to the SW., and 3 ft 2 in. to the W. and its odd twist is believed to have been caused by the changing temperatures reacting on the lead covering of the wooden frame. Although it appears in imminent danger of toppling over, it has a very low centre of gravity and is quite stable.

The Anglo-Saxons called the place Cestrefeld, the first part of the name showing that the Romans had preceded them on the site. Some of the street-names are ancient: The Shambles, Glumangate, Packer's Row and Knifesmithgate among others. In The Shambles stands the only remaining Tudor building in the town, the attractive Royal Oak. At Old Whittington is the Revolution House, then known as the Cock and Pynot (magpie) Inn, where the Earl of Devonshire and his fellow-conspirators in 1688 plotted to overthrow James II and put William of Orange on the throne. The house is now a museum.

Chesterfield has strong links with George Stephenson. He surpervised the building of the railway through the town and spent the last years of his life at Tapton House. He is buried in Holy Trinity Church. The glorious window in the church, and the Stephenson Hall which now houses the Civic Theatre, the Library and Information Centre, are memorials to him.

The town has a growing reputation in the sporting world. The main soccer club plays in the Football League; Derbyshire County Cricket Club play matches on the pleasant Queen's Park; and, in an annexe to the Park, in May 1962, was opened a sports stadium with a running track of championship standard, to which a new indoor swimming-pool has been added.

CHURCH STRETTON, *Shropshire* (8–SO 4593). It is the surrounding hills and the famous golf course, rather than the little town itself, which draw visitors to Church Stretton, 13 m. S. of SHREWSBURY. This is Mary Webb country: she spent her honeymoon here and the Shepwardine of her novels is Church Stretton.

The bleak, heathery Long Mynd to the W. is 10 m. long, from 2 to 4 m. wide, and reaches almost 1,700 ft. Some of it is accessible to cars, but most of it demands that the visitor walks. The views reward the effort. One of the most noted beauty-spots is the **Carding Mill valley**. Further S. are the less well-known valleys of Ashes Hollow and Callow Hollow, each with its stream, and the latter with a small waterfall, too.

The 18-hole golf course, set among some of the Long Mynd hills, contests with KINGTON, in Herefordshire, the claim to be England's highest. Much of it is around or above 1,200 ft and few courses can offer such views: from the 3rd tee the town itself; from the 11th the steep-sided Carding Mill valley that leads up to Robin Hood's Butts; and on the 14th green, on Bodbury Hill near the site of a clearly marked Iron Age camp, the golfer reaches the highest point of the course. Besides the Bodbury Ring camp, there are many ancient barrows hereabouts and along the whole length of the Long Mynd runs the Portway, a track which must be centuries old. All of this makes good walking across sheep pasture, some-times with sailplanes from the Midland Gliding Club overhead.

Fine walks are also to be had among the seven hills of the Caradoc range. Caer Caradoc, the highest, rises to 1,500 ft. Some say Caractacus (an earlier form of Caradoc Latinized) fortified this hill and the cave below bears his name.

Church Stretton became a fashionable resort towards the end of the 19th cent. and much of its architecture, including the half-timbered build-ings, dates from then. The Parish Church of St Lawrence is the outstanding exception, a fine building with much of its Norman work remain-ing. The nave is pure Norman, with the carving peculiar to that period, and the crossing-tower dates from the 12th cent. There is a Sheila-na-gig, a fertility figure, over the north doorway and the raftered roof of the nave is believed to be 700 years old.

N. and S. of the town lie the adjoining villages of **All Stretton** and **Little Stretton**. The latter boasts one of the few thatched churches in England, but the black-and-white building, though pretty, is not old, dating from 1903. About 2 m. SW. of Church Stretton, still in the lee of the Mynd, is the tiny village of Minton: cottages clustered round a small green, with a manor house beside a large Anglo-Saxon mound.

CLEETHORPES, *Lincolnshire* (13–TA3008). A hundred years ago Cleethorpes was a little fishing village. Now it has a permanent popula-tion of 33,970 and a million visitors a year during its short season. Its attractions include some 3 m. of sands, a boating-lake in half a mile of beautiful park, a scenic railway, the largest open-air swimming-pool on any part of the coast and a magnificent zoo complete with its Marineland full of performing dolphins. There are also a winter garden, paddling pools, children's entertain-ments and an 18-hole golf course.

The view of the Yorkshire coast with Spurn Head's light revolving 6 m. away is attractive. And it is interesting to park on Marine Walk and watch the ships bound for HULL or GRIMSBY at the mouth of the Humber.

CLEOBURY MORTIMER, *Shropshire* (8–SO6775), is 12 m. from LUDLOW on the A4117, the other side of the Clee Hills. Although some have doubts about it, the inhabitants claim it as the birthplace of William Langland, author of the 14th-cent. *Piers Plowman*. A beautiful east win-dow in the green sandstone Parish Church of St Mary is dedicated to the poet, showing Piers "dreaming his dreams". The church is also not-able for its wooden spire which, despite efforts to straighten it, still has a distinct twist. The main street has a quiet charm with its pavements at different heights, its row of pollarded trees and its mixture of mellowed timbered and Georgian houses. The most striking building, apart from the church, is the Talbot Hotel, built about 1560, once a coaching inn, with an old stone mounting block on its forecourt.

CLIFTON CAMPVILLE, *Staffordshire* (9–SK2510), is renowned for the beautiful, slender, 189-ft spire of the 14th-cent. Church of St Andrew. The church itself is regarded as the best example of medieval church architecture in the county. It contains much fine carving, some unusual monuments and an ancient chest carved from a solid tree-trunk. The unspoilt village, clustered round a hill, takes its name from the family of Camville, lords of the manor from 1200, one of whom married an heiress to the manor of Clifton.

CLIPSTONE, *Nottinghamshire* (13–SK6064). One of the gateways into the Dukeries – the land taken back by the dukes when the monasteries disappeared in 1536–40. Roads through SHER-WOOD FOREST became private drives entered by impressive gateways. Streams were dammed to make lakes, forests replanted for hunting. Now most of the peers have gone.

In Clipstone are the remains of what is now known as King John's Palace, built before the time of King John and the favourite Royal Hunt-ing Lodge until the end of the Tudor reign.

Two m. away on the EDWINSTOWE road is a Gothic arch built by the eccentric 4th Duke of Portland in 1844. It has buttressed walls and it is known as Archway Lodge, or Duke's Folly. On its north and south sides are niched figures of Richard Lionheart, who is supposed to have stayed hereabouts on his return from the Crus-ades in 1194, Robin Hood, Friar Tuck, Maid Marian, Little John and Allan-a-Dale.

CLUMBER PARK, *Nottinghamshire* (13–SK 6274). Until 1938, when the land was sold and the house pulled down, this was one of the only three remaining rich estates of the old Dukeries. In 1707 a licence was given to John Holles, Duke of New-castle, who lived at WELBECK ABBEY, to enclose a park "for the Queen's use". Nothing was done until 1770, when a house was built, followed in 1774–89 by the enclosing of the still beautiful lake. In Victorian days the house was grandly rebuilt and improved with princely gardens for the incumbent Duke of Newcastle by Sir Charles Barry, architect of the House of Commons. After a fire in 1879 it was refurbished by his son, another Charles, who designed BURLINGTON HOUSE. The lovely church which still stands was built at a cost of £30,000 in 1886 of red Runcorn sandstone and white Steetley stone. It is 107 ft long with a spire 180 ft tall and contains Belgian wood-carvings and stained glass by Kempe. It belongs to the National Trust and services are held there during the summer. It stands reflected in the lake, a lovely memorial to the passing of an age.

The park of over 3,400 acres is open to the public and offers many lovely walks amid SHER-WOOD FOREST country. Some of the grounds were ruined during the war when they were used as an ammunition dump, which caught fire. Roads are excellent, particularly Duke's Drive, a famous avenue 3 m. long bordered with limes.

CLUN, *Shropshire* (8–SO3081), is one of A. E. Housman's "four quietest places under the sun" (see *A Shropshire Lad*); the others are the nearby Clun valley villages of **Clunton, Clunbury** and **Clungunford**. This small town was not always peaceful and evidence of its stormy history is all around. Caractacus, the Ancient British chief, resisted the Romans hereabouts: Gaer Ditches is thought to have been one of his camps. A few miles W. is **Offa's Dyke**, the 8th-cent. earthwork which runs 81 m. through the border country and was part boundary mark, part Mercian fortification against the Welsh. It was around Clun that Edric the Wild, the English earl, harried the Normans whose castle keep stands high in a bend of the River Clun. For centuries, Clun was disputed between the English and the Welsh: four times between 1195 and 1400 the Welsh attacked the castle and burned the town.

Clun was a settlement before recorded time. In the museum – once the town gaol – in the Georgian Town Hall are flint and stone tools, weapons and the partial cremation of a Bronze Age inhabitant. At Pen y Wern, a little to the SW., stand the ruins of a stone circle.

CODNOR, *Derbyshire* (13–SK4149). The ruins of what was once one of Derbyshire's most important castles are to be found near this village, about 2 m. N. of Heanor. Preservation work is now being carried out to prevent further deterioration, but parts of the high outer wall and of the circular towers, an unusual stone dovecot, and other fragments can be seen. The castle, built on the site of an original Peveril fortress, dates from the early 13th cent.

CONDOVER, *Shropshire* (8–SJ4906). The Hall in this quiet village in Mary Webb country is one of the most handsome 16th-cent. houses in the county. Built of creamy-pink stone, the wide-fronted house, with its gables and chimney-stacks, makes an impressive picture at the end of its short, yew-lined drive, especially when seen framed in the arch of the entrance gates. For some years the Hall has been a school for deaf and blind children but it is open for viewing in August each year.

Nearby, again built in creamy sandstone, is the Parish Church of St Mary and St Andrew. Little remains today of the original Norman building, the church having been substantially rebuilt in the mid-1600s. More remarkable than the building itself are the monuments inside it which include, most unusually, two babies and their mothers. There is a bust of Martha Owen, with her baby lying in front of her, dated 1641; and the even more touching sculpture of Alice Cholmondeley, carved by her husband Reginald in the mid-19th cent. She lies asleep, a wife for only a year, her baby in her arm, its empty cradle at her feet. The inscription on the white marble reads: "Reginald, always standing by, carved me with his own hand".

Less moving but even more striking is the life-size sculpture of another Cholmondeley, Sir Thomas, who died in 1864. The kneeling, bearded figure in the uniform of a soldier of the Crimean War, looking heavenwards, his hands clasped on his sword, was carved by the famous Victorian artist, George Frederick Watts.

CONINGSBY, *Lincolnshire* (13–TF2258). A Fenland village near TATTERSHALL, notable for its church of St Michael and All Angels which has a handsome 15th-cent. tower with a pathway through it. Its unique feature is a one-handed clock, $16\frac{1}{2}$ ft in diameter, the largest in the world.

Laurence Eusdon, an 18th-cent. rector of Coningsby, was said to have been made Poet Laureate because he flattered the Lord Chamberlain. According to Thomas Gray, Eusdon was "a drunken parson" and certainly his lines dedicated to George II on his coronation have nothing to recommend them. "They virtues shine peculiarly nice," he carolled, "Ungloomed with a confinity to vice".

About a mile N. up the A153 is the pretty village of **Tumby**, E. of which is a 100-acre wood full of oak and larch and wild lilies of the valley in season.

CORBY, *Lincolnshire* (13–SK9925), is remarkable mainly for the lovely medieval wall paintings discovered under nearly 1,200 sq. ft of plaster when the church was being restored in 1939. These paintings are among the most significant medieval remains in the country.

There is an ancient market cross, erected in the reign of Edward III, and an annual October Sheep Fair to which sheep are brought from England, Scotland and Wales.

COTTESMORE, *Rutland* (10–SK9013). About 4 m. NE. of OAKHAM on the B668, Cottesmore was made famous by the hunt, one of the most famous in this pre-eminently fox-hunting part of England. The Cottesmore Hounds were established in **Exton** in 1732 but moved here in 1788. They are now kennelled about halfway along the road from Oakham to Ashwell.

The airfield and quarries spoil the village but there are some charming stone-built and thatched houses and good trees. The Church of St Nicholas has a complicated history, with a font probably of *c.* 1200, a 14th-cent. spire and 17th-cent. pulpit. Anglo-Saxon finds have been excavated in the neighbourhood.

Up a small lane $1\frac{1}{2}$ m. to the NW. **Barrow** stands high and commands fine views to Leicestershire.

From here take the road due E. crossing the A1 past **Stretton** to **Clipsham**, a journey of about 4 m. to see this pretty show village on the borders of one of our loveliest yet most unsung counties. There are many fine 16th- to 19th-cent. buildings of the famous honey-coloured Clipsham limestone, particularly Clipsham Hall, which is 18th-cent. and has a splendid yew hedge and a bird and fish topiary avenue.

The Church of St Mary has a 14th-cent. broach spire of unusual design and an originally Norman interior. In the north chapel is some heraldic glass, once part of the ancient church at Pickworth, which was shattered in the Wars of the Roses.

Try to visit the quarries, which have been worked since the mid-13th cent. and have supplied stone to PETERBOROUGH and ELY cathedrals, many OXFORD colleges and the house at BURLEY. It was also chosen for the rebuilding of the bombed House of Commons. There is no blasting. The stone is excavated with drills and wedges.

At **Greetham**, 3 m. away on the B668 to Oakham, is the well-known Ram Jam Inn.

CRESWELL CRAGS, *Derbyshire* (13–SK 5274). Here, in a narrow gorge between cliffs of grey limestone are the caves where men of the Early Stone Age lived and rested between their hunting forays. In these caves, situated almost on the Nottinghamshire border about 9 m. E. of CHESTERFIELD, and given such names as Mother Grundy's Parlour, Robin Hood's Cave and the Pinhole, have been found remains from this prehistoric culture, including bones of the mammoth and primitive tools and weapons, some of which are now in the BRITISH MUSEUM.

CRICH, *Derbyshire* (13–SK3554). One of the most unusual museums in the country is situated in this hill village 5 m. SE. of MATLOCK. It is devoted entirely to tramcars. The unique collection of trams of all kinds – there are 40 in all – has been gathered from all parts of the country, and abroad, by the Tramway Museum Society. Visitors are welcome at weekends and Bank Holidays and no charge is made except during the annual Grand Transport Extravanganza each September. The museum is a "live" one for it is housed in the disused Cliff Quarry, and a number of lines have been laid so that the trams can still run.

The visitor can ride in Sheffield 15, a single-deck horse-car built in 1874, drawn by Bonny, the museum's resident mare; or in Blackpool 59, one of the two-deck, open-top trams which used to carry holidaymakers along the promenade at the Lancashire resort; or in Glasgow 1297, a sleek modern tram, built as recently as 1948 and in service until the 1950s; or in a number of other trams. One of the museum's prized possessions is a steam tram, built for the New South Wales government in 1885.

Standing on the edge of Cliff Quarry, on a site known locally as Crich Stand, is another of Crich's sights – the tower with a beacon light, standing 950 ft above sea-level, which is the war memorial of the Sherwood Foresters. The regiment's annual pilgrimage is made here every July.

Crich is also known for the views from the surrounding hills; and for its Norman church, in which can be seen one of the rare stone Bible rests.

CROMFORD, *Derbyshire* (12–SK2956), is where the first rumblings of the Industrial Revolution were heard. In this sturdy-looking, stone-built village S. of THE MATLOCKS, in 1771, Sir Richard Arkwright built the first mechanized textile factory in the world, equipping it with the cotton-spinning machinery he had recently invented. The original mill still stands by the road, dour, forbidding, intended to be stout enough to withstand any attacks by the frightened weavers, bent on smashing Arkwright's machines. Two more of Arkwright's important buildings still stand in Cromford: the Church of St Mary and Willersley Castle. Many of the old cottages are those he built for his workpeople.

Not far from Cromford are the famous **Black Rocks**, a rugged mass of gritstone on the hills on the WIRKSWORTH road. The rocks are about 80 ft high and erosion has left them with a face which makes particular appeal to rock-climbers from all parts of the country. They also offer a fine viewing point, the panorama stretching across the valley in which The Matlocks lie to Riber Castle on its peak.

Also from Cromford runs a beautiful stretch of road with a Latin name. But the **Via Gellia** owes nothing to the Romans; it was constructed during the 19th cent. by Philip Gell of Hopton Hall, Wirksworth, along a wooded ravine between Cromford and Grangemill. It is particularly colourful in bluebell time and is famous for its lilies of the valley.

CROWLAND, *Lincolnshire* (13–TF2310). Three-quarters of a mile from the ruins of the Benedictine abbey raised by his relative, King Ethelbald of Mercia, to his memory, St Guthlac landed his boat in the swamps at a place still called Anchor Church Field. Born in A.D. 673, he had had a wild youth until he decided to become a hermit, building a cell to which people came for help and advice. He died in 714 and the abbey, partly destroyed and rebuilt many times, was at one time the wealthiest mitred abbey in the county. The ruins still have great magnificence, the north aisle now being used as the Parish Church of St Mary with SS. Guthlac and Bartholomew. A tower at the west end survives, and the west front with five tiers of sculptures representing personages associated with the history of the abbey, and saints and apostles.

A fascinating triangular bridge of three semi-circles meeting at an apex, built in the 13th cent. when the streets were waterways, still stands in the village. Henry VI and Edward IV landed here – Edward on his way to FOTHERINGHAY Castle. For about 200 years a seated figure of Our Lord holding the world has adorned the bridge.

CROXDEN ABBEY, *Staffordshire* (9–SK 0639), is where it was thought for many years that the heart of the little-loved King John was buried. But this has now been disproved: the mistake arose because of confusion with Croxton Abbey in Leicestershire. Croxden was founded by the man responsible for ALTON Castle, Bertram de Verdun. Enough of it still stands to show how noble it must have been: the remains of the west front, the south transept and parts of the sacristy, chapter-house, parlour and abbot's house. The ruins are now partly incorporated into a farm-house.

DALE ABBEY, *Derbyshire* (13–SK4338). There is an interesting legend concerning the foundation of this abbey. A DERBY baker saw a vision of the Virgin Mary which led him to renounce the world and live as a hermit. He crossed the River Derwent and made himself a hermitage in the sandstone cliffs of Deepdale. Later the abbey was raised on the same site. Today the hermitage in the rocks can still be seen but all that remains of the once splendid abbey is the superb arch of the east window. It gives a clear indication of the fine proportions of the abbey – and emphasizes strongly the difference between that building and the present village church, surely one of the smallest and most curious churches in England. The chancel and nave measure a mere 25 ft by 25 ft – and the whole church is under the same roof as a farm-house. It has Norman masonry in the walls, and wall paintings dating from the 13th cent. The building is full of box-pews and there is a gallery; the raised altar has drawers and cupboards underneath it.

DARLEY DALE, *Derbyshire* (12–SK2762), is part of the lovely valley of the Derwent running N. from THE MATLOCKS and offers pleasant walking country for the visitor. Here is a fine 13th-cent. church with part of the shaft of a carved Anglo-Saxon cross, two fonts – one

Norman, one Jacobean – some fine stained glass believed to be by Burne-Jones and, in the church-yard, perhaps the oldest tree in Britain, a yew reputed to be 2,000 years old.

Sir Joseph Whitworth, the engineer and inventor, lived part of his life in Darley Dale and the extensive park is a memorial to him. There is an annual show at **Whitworth**. Wild rhododendrons grow profusely in Darley Dale. There is a fine walk along a footpath known as Lady Grove which offers a view across the valley to Knab Rocks, the dramatic, sheer gritstone cliffs on the other side. On another wooded hill can be seen the square stone tower commemorating the passing of the Reform Bill in 1832.

DERBY, *Derbyshire* (12–SK3435). Despite its rapid expansion over the last 100 years to a thriving industrial town of more than 200,000 people, Derby, county town and cathedral city, has retained much from its past. It has Roman roots; the legions had a camp near the east bank of the Derwent. The town was named by the Danes, who made it one of their Five Boroughs, the key points of the Danelaw. By the time the Domesday Book was published in 1086, Derby was a town of 2,000 inhabitants with six churches and 14 mills. It received its first market charter from Henry II in 1154 but by the time, 600 years later, that it gave a cool reception to Bonnie Prince Charlie, the town had grown but little. Not until the Industrial Revolution and the eventful establishment of the Midland Railway's

Crowland: the triangular bridge; the carved figure is believed to have come from the abbey

Kenneth Scowen

great works in the town, did it begin to grow apace.

The links with the Midland Railway are underlined by a scale working lay-out in the museum in the Strand, which also includes a large technical and industrial section; archaeological exhibits; local porcelain; and paintings by Derby's own Joseph Wright.

The most striking building is the cathedral with its pinnacled, 178-ft tower, built during the reign of Henry VIII and second only to BOSTON Stump as the tallest parish church tower in England. Apart from the tower, the Parish Church of All Saints as it then was – it was elevated to cathedral rank in 1927 – was rebuilt by James Gibbs in the early 18th cent. It contains the large, carved alabaster tomb of the much-married, "building-mad" Bess of Hardwick, Countess of Shrewsbury. There are other interesting tombs and a bishop's chair which came from Asia Minor. But the cathedral's great treasure is the superbly fashioned wrought-iron screen, the work of Robert Bakewell. More of Bakewell's brilliant craftsmanship can be seen in the entrance gates to the cathedral which once stood in front of a private house, but were given to the cathedral and dedicated in 1958.

Derby's oldest church is St Peter's, largely 14th-cent. but with some Norman work. There are also several other interesting churches, notably St Werburgh's, which has a wrought-iron font-cover by Bakewell and parish registers dating back to 1583 – they contain the entry of Dr Samuel Johnson's marriage to Tetty Porter; St Mary's Roman Catholic church with its 117-ft tower topped by a figure of the Virgin Mary, designed by Pugin; and St Mary's Chapel, Bridge Gate, one of the few surviving chapels built on bridges.

There are also a considerable number of interesting old houses, some Georgian, some earlier: among these the oldest are the black-and-white Dolphin Inn in Queen Street, and the 17th-cent. gabled building in Wardwick. Modern developments include a well-designed bus station, a huge modern hotel, and an open-air market.

Derby is well-blessed with open spaces. There are almost a score of parks, the oldest of which, the Arboretum, was given to the town by Joseph Strutt and contains a monument to the eminent car-maker, Sir Henry Royce; the firm of Rolls-Royce has been associated with Derby since 1908.

DONINGTON, *Lincolnshire* (13–TF2135). An ancient little town, once the most important flax and hemp centre, and still a flourishing twice-yearly venue for horse and cattle fairs. The earliest attempts at reclamation were made here in the Fenland by the Romans at Carr Dyke and the Roman Bank. Traces remain of Salters Way, built by them from the Midlands to the coast. Subsequent silting up of the Wash has recovered a 10-m. stretch for cultivation.

The market place is still cobbled and has Georgian and earlier houses and a delightful grammar school founded in the 18th cent. by Thomas Cowley "for twenty poor children to be taught to read English and write". Over the old portico is a sundial dated 1719.

The church has a fine Decorated tower and spire rising to 200 ft, built in the 14th cent. and surmounted by a golden ball and weathercock.

Donington was the birthplace of Matthew Flinders in 1774. He went to sea after reading *Robinson Crusoe*, and travelled with Bligh, after the *Bounty* mutiny, and with Bass of BOSTON. He was the first to discover the error of compasses due to iron in ships, and he died in Donington on the day of the publication of a book on his voyages, in 1814.

DOVEDALE, *Derbyshire/Staffordshire* (12–SK 1452). This famous dale forms the boundary between Staffordshire and Derbyshire. It has connections with Izaak Walton and his companion angler Charles Cotton, and other literary figures, and its magnificent scenery has earned it the name of "Little Switzerland". The first-time visitor may be surprised how short it seems on a map – it stretches little more than 2 m. But he will be delighted by the constantly changing views and many unusual features it has to offer. Some of the dale can be seen by car, but to explore its beauty in full the visitor needs to walk.

Dovedale is part of the Peak District National Park and its southern entrance is near the village of ILAM, guarded by two hills, Thorpe Cloud (900 ft) and Bunster Hill (1,000 ft). It is here that the narrow, twisting limestone gorge begins, its steep wooded banks rising high above the river. Many of its rocks and rock formations have been weathered into strange shapes and colourfully named: Dovedale Castle, the Twelve Apostles, Lover's Leap, the Tissington Spires, the Lion's Head and the Ilam Rock, slightly on the tilt. There are, too, the caves like the Dove Holes and Reynard's Cavern with its arched entrance 30 ft high and 15 ft wide.

The Dove, of course, is not just a river to look at but also one to fish – for the descendants of the trout which old Izaak and his friend cast for and caught there. Many of the hotels in the area offer angling facilities in the Dove to their guests. Dovedale, too, is famous for its sheepdog trials held near the Izaak Walton Hotel at the southern end of the dale each August. And it offers access to other dales including **Milldale**, **Wolfscote Dale**, **Hall Dale**, **Narrowdale** and BERESFORD DALE; and to the beautiful MANIFOLD VALLEY.

DRAYTON BASSETT, *Staffordshire* (9–SK 1900). This village, 4 m. S. of TAMWORTH, was where Sir Robert Peel, Prime Minister, father of our police force and Corn Law repealer, was born. His house, Drayton Manor, is no more – but in the park which was once part of the grounds is now a golf course and the Drayton Manor Park and Zoo. The zoo occupies 15 acres of the 160-acre park and contains a wide selection of animals. There is a large amusement park and a lake. Aerial cars run above it all at 60 ft for a distance of $\frac{1}{3}$ m.

Kenneth Scowen

Dovedale: stepping-stones over the River Dove

DUNSTON, *Lincolnshire* (13–TF0663). Still a lonely village on the enormous Heath, Dunston used to be lit by the famous "Dunston Pillar", a "land lighthouse" 92 ft high, with a lantern 15 ft high, placed there by the otherwise infamous Sir Francis Dashwood of the Hellfire Club to guide travellers to LINCOLN and protect them from highwaymen. Sir Francis lived at Nocton Hall, which came to him through his wife. Twenty years later, in 1810, his successor removed the light and raised in its stead a huge statue of George III to celebrate his jubilee. This statue proved a danger to aircraft during the last war, and so was removed and the pillar shortened.

EAST STOKE, *Nottinghamshire* (13–SK7549). Half a mile N. of the village is the site of Ad Pontem, a Roman fort built on a crossroads at Fosse Way, which led to a crossing close by over the River Trent. Round the small, mainly 17th-cent. church amid the trees of the park of Stoke Hall are mounds marking the site of a medieval village.

East Stoke was the scene of a spectacular and bloody battle in 1487. In 1486 Henry VII had tried to end the Wars of the Roses by marrying Elizabeth of York, but there was still unrest, particularly in the breast of the one-time heir apparent, the Earl of Lincoln. With the help of a priest named Richard Simon, the earl found Lambert Simnel, the son of an OXFORD joiner, who resembled the Earl of Warwick (also a claimant to the throne) and took him to Dublin

where he was "crowned" king of England. Then he crossed with an army of some 6,000 and landed on the Lancashire coast to march against the king. On 16 June the armies met at East Stoke and Lincoln's force was cut to pieces. The Yorkists were driven from Fosse Way down to the road to Fiskerton Ferry, which is still called Red Gutter, and their dead were buried in what are known as Dead Man's Fields. Lambert Simnel was contemptuously pardoned and allowed to work as a scullion in the royal kitchens.

Lord Pauncefote, the first British ambassador to the United States, had his home at Stoke Hall and is buried in the churchyard.

EASTWOOD, *Nottinghamshire* (13–SK4646). "The scene of my Nottinghamshire-Derby novels all centres round Eastwood, where I was born: and whoever stands on Walker Street will see the whole landscape of *Sons and Lovers* before him." Admirers of D. H. Lawrence should visit this place, still peaceful and rural in the midst of the colliery area. Here he lived with his parents, described in the first section of *Sons and Lovers* – his mother, whose maiden name was Lydia Beardsall, feeling so superior to her miner husband. Yet it was from his father who "loved the countryside, just the indiscriminating feel of it", that Lawrence inherited his imagination.

ECCLESHALL, *Staffordshire* (8–SJ8329). This typical small market town, 6 m. SW. of STONE, has long associations with the bishops of

Lichfield: six of them are buried in the large, 12th-cent. parish church and its churchyard. For 700 years the bishops of Lichfield lived at Eccleshall Castle, of which one of the towers, the moat and the bridge over it are preserved. The square, pinnacled tower of the church, which is almost 100 ft high, contains some carved Anglo-Saxon stones, a rare possession.

EDALE, *Derbyshire* (12–SK1285). Immediately S. of the Peak District's highest area, the Kinder Hills, the village and dale which give their name to this area are quiet and unspoilt. The valley offers delightful walking country with the rugged hills all around. Crowden Head at 2,070 ft is the highest point visible, but Win Hill, with its Roman road, Lose Hill, **Mam Tor**, Mount Famine and Rushup Edge are almost as high. Mam Tor, more than 1,700 ft high, is known as the "Shivering Mountain" because of the landslides which regularly occur, caused by the unusual composition of alternate layers of grit and shale. Near the top is an Iron Age camp covering 16 acres within a circumference of 1,200 yds. The Kinder Hills can be reached by the path called Jacob's Ladder which climbs over a shoulder in the hills, past a cross dated 1610. During the winter months the famous white, or mountain hares of Kinder can be seen zig-zagging across the faces of the slopes. The village of Edale has a gentler appearance than many of the Derbyshire hill villages. In the church, the third on the site, is a Bible in English printed in 1541 by Edward Whitchurch. The parish registers date from 1633.

EDENHAM, *Lincolnshire* (13–TF0621). The whole village is extremely impressive, as befits the setting for **Grimsthorpe Castle**, the home of the Earls of Ancaster and the grandest house in Lincolnshire. The cottages are of stone and the church is large, shaded by 100-year-old cedars and containing the shaft of a medieval cross in the churchyard. Nearby is the vicarage where Charles Kingsley is supposed to have written *Hereward the Wake*.

Vestiges of architecture from Anglo-Saxon times remain inside the church and it is full of valuable possessions. But it is the grandiose monuments to the Willoughby de Eresby family, Dukes and Earls of Ancaster, which catch the eye: the one to the 12th Baron, who died at Edgehill in the arms of his son; another to that son, Montague, who fought at NASEBY and was one of the few people courageous enough to attend Charles I's funeral at WINDSOR. The huge monument to Robert Bertie, 4th Earl of Lindsey and 1st Duke of Ancaster, was sculptured by Scheemakers, and the pretentious tomb opposite for the 3rd and 4th Dukes is by Charles Harris. This noble structure informs us that the 3rd Duke lived "with Magnificence and Liberality" but died of a "lingering bilious disorder". A charming bust of Lord Gwydyr, who married the sister of the 4th Duke, is by Nollekens.

Grimsthorpe Castle stands palatially in its 2,000-acre park, some 16 m. round, easily seen just over a mile from the road. It has a magnificent chestnut avenue and is famed for its herds of fallow and red deer. Most of the original quadrangular building was erected by Charles Brandon, Duke of Suffolk, in Tudor times, but a bastion in the south-east corner dates from the 13th cent.

The 1st Duke of Ancaster commissioned Vanbrugh to rebuild the north side in 1722 in stone quarried from the park. Vanbrugh died four years after finishing this, the last of his castles. His magnificent 110-ft hall houses paintings of seven kings to whom the Willoughby de Eresby family owe a great deal of their wealth, they having been successive Lord Great Chamberlains of England.

The castle contains Brussels tapestries, paintings by famous masters such as Lawrence and Reynolds, a Van Dyck of Charles I and his family, and the actual dress worn by Charles when he sat for the portrait. There are coronation chairs, and robes worn by sovereigns since James II. There is the House of Lords clock, which stopped the minute George III died, and the table on which Queen Victoria signed her oath of accession.

EDENSOR, *Derbyshire* (12–SK2469), must be one of the few villages in England set in what was a private park, and still to be entered through a white gate. It is probably the only one which was moved from its original site to satisfy the aesthetic whim of an aristocrat. Originally Edensor could be seen from the great mansion of CHATSWORTH, on the further bank of the Derwent. The 6th Duke of Devonshire, deciding that it spoiled the view, had it demolished in 1839 and the present model village built about a mile away. The result, to a large extent, reflects the eccentricity that was present at its birth. Only the fact that all the houses, many of them detached, are built in the same local stone gives the village any unity. Otherwise everything is a jumble of gables, porches and odd windows. The entrance lodge looks like a small fort; in another corner stands a mock Swiss chalet in brown stone; one house has Tudor chimneys, another Italian-style windows. The setting is charming with the road winding round the church and up a small hill which is a cul-de-sac. It is worth the short climb to the top of the hill not so much to see the octagonal-shaped house there as to obtain the view over the village, across the wide Derwent valley to the Hunting Tower of Chatsworth high in the woods on the far bank. And from here, too, the large village church with its tall slender spire does not seem as out of place as it does from the entrance gate. The church was built in 1867 to the design of Sir Gilbert Scott, but a few fragments of the original Norman building can still be seen.

EDWINSTOWE, *Nottinghamshire* (13–SK 6266). Near Warsop on the River Maun, Edwinstowe lies at the edge of the spacious common leading to Birklands and Bilhagh, two of the most beautiful parts of SHERWOOD FOREST, with a good road between them. Bilhagh has the grandest remains of the old forest and Birklands has a wealth of beech and silver birch and – within a mile of the Church of St Mary – the Major Oak, reputed to be over 1,000 years old, probably the biggest oak in Britain. It has a hollow trunk 30 ft round, inside which it is reported that seven people once ate breakfast. A mile and a half W. of here is another oak called Robin Hood's Larder in which Robin is said to have hung his game. Those who believe in Robin Hood will believe that he married Maid Marian in the 12th- to 13th-cent. church at Edwinstowe.

ELFORD, *Staffordshire* (9–SK1810). The church in this village about 5 m. ENE. of LICHFIELD is well known to heraldry enthusiasts for it contains a remarkable collection of shields, all in excellent condition. Here, too, is a monument commemorating the death of a child at play: the grandson of Sir John Stanley holds the tennis ball which is reputed to have struck him on the temple and caused his death in 1460. Nearby are two Anglo-Saxon barrows which are said to have been used as shooting butts by Robin Hood. The paper mill by the bridge was owned for about 50 years until his death in 1801 by Robert Bage who wrote the novel *Hermsprong, or Man as he is Not*.

ELLESMERE, *Shropshire* (8–SJ3934), is 30 m. from the sea, but has many boats. This small market town, set among nine meres, is the capital of Shropshire's Lake District. The scenery, pretty rather than impressive, is in marked contrast to that in the S. of the county. All the meres are accessible to the visitor: Blake Mere and tiny Kettle Mere, joined to it, are set in woodland, as is Cole Mere; White Mere is the headquarters of the Shropshire Sailing Club; Hanmer Mere is 5 m. away but is usually included in the group; Crose Mere and Sweat (Sweet) Mere are haunts for birds; while The Mere, the largest and covering 116 acres, has been developed as a pleasure resort. Fishing and boating are available on some of the meres.

The town itself has strong nautical associations, and an arm of the Shropshire Union Canal ran into it. Although nothing now remains of the castle, and little of the Norman church, Ellesmere still has attractive old streets and houses, and the roof of the chancel chapel in St Mary's Church is reckoned one of the finest in Shropshire.

EMPINGHAM, *Rutland* (10–SK9408). Rutland is at its loveliest in this large, attractive village with a splendid church on the road from OAKHAM to STAMFORD. The three churches of Empingham, **Exton** and KETTON, which all lie near to one another, would be hard to match for beauty and interest.

It is worth stopping at Empingham to study St Peter's: well proportioned, with a handsome tower, spire and west front, largely 13th-cent. with 14th- and 15th-cent. alterations. Considerable

traces of medieval colour remain, and some fragments of ancient glass. The chancel has such a beautiful double piscina and triple sedilia that even those who usually look away at the mention of such details should try to find somebody knowledgeable enough to point them out.

Nobody should leave Rutland without making time to stay at Exton, about 3 m. NW., since this thatch and limestone village and the fascinating monuments in the Church of SS. Peter and Paul cannot be appreciated in a hurry. The best approach, particularly lovely when the may blossom is out, is N. from Empingham along a small secondary road, which gives a splendid view from the S. of Burley-on-the-Hill, and thence along Barnsdale Avenue, thickly lined with chestnuts, limes, ash, birch, beeches and sycamores, to 1,000-acre Exton Park. The Old Hall, now in ruins, was probably built by Sir James Harington in the time of Elizabeth I, and was destroyed by fire in 1810. It was the home of the Noels, Viscounts Campden, Earls of Gainsborough. The New Hall was completed in 1852. The church, accessible to the public, was struck by lightning in 1843 and was somewhat drastically rebuilt in 1850.

It is not, however, the building, but the monuments inside which will attract the visitor – marvellous English sculpture from the 14th to the 18th cents.: Nicholas Grene, *c*. 1379, John and Alice Harington, 1524; the splendid tomb of Robert Kelway, 1580, erected by his daughter and her husband, the first Lord Harington, who are depicted kneeling with their daughter, Lucy; the tomb of their son, Kelway Harington, aged 21 weeks; the appealing epitaph to Sir James and Lady Lucy Harington, 1591; the exceptionally beautiful tomb of Anne, grand-daughter of the first Lady Harington, 1627; the monument to 18-year-old James Noel, "grave, discreet, and wise" and his two baby brothers; Grinling Gibbons's colossal statue to the 3rd Viscount Campden, for which he charged £1,000, 1683; the Nollekens to the Countess of Gainsborough, 1771, and Lt-Gen. Bennett Noel, 1766.

Do not miss the angel seated at the organ on the tower screen and the helmets, sword, gauntlets and spurs in the nave arcade.

You should also walk round the village on the east side of the park to see the excellent buildings dating from the 16th cent., beautifully grouped on all sides, the well with its stone roof and eight brick pillars, the 14 sycamore trees on the green, and the glimpses of old-world gardens and green hills behind.

EPWORTH, *Lincolnshire* (13–SE7803). Now the administrative centre for the Isle of Axholme, Epworth was the birthplace in 1703 of John Wesley. His brother Charles, who wrote over 6,000 hymns, was born four years later. John was the fifteenth of the nineteen children of Samuel Wesley, who arrived here as rector in 1696 and is buried in the churchyard of St Andrews – the tomb on which John stood to preach night after night in 1742 when he was denied access to the church itself.

The old rectory belongs to the Methodist church and is open to the public, but it is not the famous one which was burned down in 1709 by a furious mob who objected to Samuel Wesley's political sympathies, and from which John was only rescued a moment before the roof fell in.

In the district there survive remnants of the open-field system of medieval agriculture.

EYAM, *Derbyshire* (12–SK2176). A chair in the 13th-cent. church in this small village 6 m. N. of BAKEWELL and a gravestone in the churchyard tell the story of tragedy and courage which put Eyam into the history books. The chair is inscribed MON 1665 EYAM and it commemorates William Mompesson, the rector of Eyam at the time the Great Plague of 1665–6 descended on the village. The infection was brought to the village in a box of clothes and within a matter of months had claimed more than 80 per cent of the inhabitants as victims. By example and character the rector persuaded the people not to flee from the stricken village – and thus the plague was prevented from spreading into Derbyshire and further afield. Among the victims was Mompesson's wife and it is her grave you can see in the churchyard. During the plague the rector preached in the open air, from a rock in a dell which has since become known as Cucklet Church. It is here that an annual commemoration service is held on the last Sunday in August. The Sunday before, a well-dressing festival is held. Mompesson's Well can also be seen. It was there that the villagers dropped the money for goods which were delivered to them during their grim siege.

In the churchyard is an Anglo-Saxon cross, dating from early in the 9th cent., which is remarkable because the cross-head is still there, and an unusual 18th-cent. sundial which tells the time throughout the world by a curved graph. Near the village are several spots worth a visit: Sir William's Road, a hill-track almost 1,200 ft up from which much of the Peak District can be seen; the so-called Rock Garden with its strange echo; and Wet Withens, on Eyam Moor, a Bronze Age circle of 16 stones.

FOREMARK, *Derbyshire* (12–SK3326). Not far from this small village which lies near the River Trent about 5 m. S. of DERBY is what is known as an "anchor church" – caves in a cliff once occupied by an anchorite. Nearby, too, at **Ingleby,** is an unusually large collection of Danish burial mounds. There are 60 in all, the biggest 15 yds across and several feet high; they are believed to date from the late 9th cent. In the church dedicated to St Saviour in Foremark itself are wrought-iron communion rails thought to be work of Robert Bakewell – one of whose major pieces, the "Birdcage", can be seen at nearby MELBOURNE Hall. There are also a three-decker pulpit and original box-pews in the church, which was entirely built in 1662.

GAINSBOROUGH, *Lincolnshire* (13–SK81 89). King Alfred married Ealswith here in 868,

E. Preston

Eyam: the sundial telling world-time

and Cnut's father, Sweyn, King of the Danes, died at his camp at Thonock Park in 1014. Gainsborough was a frequent battleground between Royalist and Parliamentarian troops. George Eliot used it as the prototype of St Ogg's in *The Mill on the Floss*, describing the curious tidal wave known as the Bore, or the Aegir, which rushes up the Trent to a height of several feet during the spring tides. There are some interesting 18th-cent. warehouses on the quayside, but otherwise Gainsborough only retains one outstanding example of its past history, the Old Hall in Parnell Street, one of the largest and most important of the surviving late medieval houses in the country open to the public.

It was built by Lord de Burgh in 1484 after the Lancastrians had wrecked his former home, and here he received Richard III. Henry VIII visited the house in 1509, and in 1540 was introduced there to his last wife, Katharine Parr, widow of Lord de Burgh's eldest son. Thomas, the last de Burgh to live here, was Queen Elizabeth's ambassador in Scotland and Lord Deputy in Ireland, but so extravagant that the year before he died in 1597 he had to sell his property in Gainsborough to William Hickman of London. Several generations of Hickmans lived here until 1720 when they moved their family seat out to the "sylvan pleasaunces" of Thonock. Thereafter the Old Hall became in turn a parish church, a linen factory, a corn exchange, a mechanics' institute, a Congregational church, a selection of tenements and shops, a theatre, a soup kitchen after the Napoleonic Wars, a 19th-cent. public house, an auction sale-room, a public ballroom, and a Masonic temple. Perhaps this is something to be grateful for. The resulting lack of desire to improve and modernize, as in the case of most private dwellings, has left it with the best surviving example of a medieval kitchen in the country, a magnificent timbered great hall containing the finest remaining single-arch braced roof, and a very lovely stone oriel window.

GOTHAM, *Nottinghamshire* (13–SK5330), is a very ordinary village of mines and plaster works, but who has not heard of the 16th-cent. *Merrie Tales of the Mad Men of Gotham*? The men who sent cheeses rolling downhill to NOTTINGHAM, dragged a cart to the top of a barn to shade the roof from the sun, burned a forge to get rid of a wasps' nest, tried to drown an eel in a pond, and built a hedge round a cuckoo so that it might stay and sing for them all the year round. Cuckoo Bush Hill, Cuckoo Bush Mound, and the Cuckoo Bush Inn are here still to remind us; though many think that the men of Gotham only pretended to be mad in order to deter King John, who was threatening to build a hunting lodge in the middle of their village.

If Gotham does not please you, drive to the wooded hills behind it, where there are masses of bluebells in the spring.

GRANTHAM, *Lincolnshire* (13–SK9335). The best preliminary view of the 281-ft spire of St Wulfram's Church, a landmark for miles around, is obtained by leaving LINCOLN along The Cliff to the A607, passing two other notable spires on the way: the impressive one at **Leadenham**, and the apparently crooked one at **Caythorpe**.

Grantham, centre of fine coaching inns serving the old road to the North, once belonged to Edith, queen of Edward the Confessor. It was the second place in which an Eleanor Cross was erected, as Edward I directed they should be wherever his wife's body rested on its way back to London from HARBY, where she died. The cross

was destroyed in the Civil War and now a statue of Sir Isaac Newton, unveiled in 1858, stands in its place opposite the Victorian guildhall.

St Wulfram's magnificent, cathedral-like church is in Swinegate. There are six pillars left of the Norman church which it replaced, but its greatest beauties are its 14th-cent. additions: the lady chapel with a lovely six-light traceried window, the north porch, the double-vaulted crypt, and the splendid steeple. Above the south porch, in what was once a priests' recess and washroom, is the chained library left to the church in 1598. The oldest book was printed in Venice in 1472, and 83 of the 150 are still attached to their original chains.

Immediately E. of the church is Grantham House in 25 acres of land, making an open space in the middle of the town. It is now the property of the National Trust, open to the public at certain times. The central hall is late 14th-cent. and once housed Princess Margaret Tudor, daughter of Henry VII, on her way to marry James IV of Scotland.

Separated from the churchyard by a narrow lane is the 15th-cent. grammar school, now known as King's School. The building with its high-pitched stone roof and mullioned windows is little changed. Among the hundreds of signatures on the sills are those of Isaac Newton, who arrived here in 1654, aged 12, Colley Cibber, and Queen Elizabeth's great treasurer, Lord Burghley.

In the Market Place is the stone conduit built in 1597 to protect the water brought by the Grey Friars from the springs at Gonerby. The two most important coaching inns are the 18th-cent. George Hotel, and the Angel & Royal Trust House Hotel, one of the very few medieval hostelries left in the country, established by the Knights Templar. The gatehouse dates from the 15th cent. and King John held court in 1213 in a room still known as the King's Chamber.

The fine 20th-cent. museum and library is interesting for, among other things, some charming valentines and other bygones. And, in spite of the 40 shillings left by Michael Solomon, the 18th-cent. landlord of the Angel & Royal, for a sermon to be preached against drunkenness in the parish church, nobody should leave without visiting the Beehive Inn in Castlegate. It has a living sign – a real beehive perched in a lime-tree outside.

GREAT CASTERTON, *Rutland* (10–SK99 09). The town was named after the *castrum*, or Roman fort, always known to have lain NE. of the church where Ermine Street crossed the River Gwash into Rutland. However after the abnormally dry summer of 1959 cropmarks appeared and the remains of a 2nd- to 5th-cent. town and a late-4th-cent. villa were discovered. With the 1st-cent. fort and defences, best seen from the little secondary road to RYHALL, this epitomizes the history of Roman Britain. In 1966 a road-widening scheme revealed a Romano-Saxon burial site, a stone coffin from which is now in the County Museum at OAKHAM. Other relics have also been excavated, among them some Romano-Saxon pottery and a hoard of coins from the 4th and 5th cents. buried under a joist beneath the floor of the villa.

Those who like beautifully plain, white-washed, and almost completely unrestored churches should visit that of SS. Peter and Paul to admire especially the early-13th-cent. foliaded capitals. The square Norman font is also exceptional. The tower is 15th-cent. and the pulpit Georgian, and the churchyard contains some good examples of carved and winged Ketton headstones.

The poet John Clare, peasant son of an inarticulate labourer, worked on a farm in Great Casterton and met there his wife – "Sweet Patty of the Vale".

GRIMSBY, *Lincolnshire* (13–TA2810). This old, world-famous fishing port is operated as a twin to **Immingham** about 5 m. N. up the coast (though by road it may only be approached on the tortuous A1136 skirting both towns). Whereas Immingham owes its fame to the 20th cent., when modern, deep-water docks were constructed to accommodate ocean-going vessels from Oslo, Lisbon, Istanbul and Africa, the history of Grimsby was written during the Danish invasions of Britain, even though it comes down to us only in the 14th-cent. *Lay of Havelock the Dane.* This tells how Havlok, son of a Danish king, was pushed out to sea in a boat after his father was murdered. He was rescued and brought up by a Lincolnshire fisherman named Grim. When Havlok grew up he regained his kingdom and richly rewarded his rescuer, who used this wealth to found the port of Grimsby.

Little ships from the North Sea ports sail into Grimsby, the oldest chartered town in England (1202), and 56 per cent of all plaice and 40 per cent of all turbot for England and Wales are landed here. The Fish Dock is the largest fish market in the world, and is in the biggest town of Lincolnshire.

The Pilgrim Fathers sailed from Immingham Creek to Holland in 1608 before crossing the Atlantic in 1620. Street names, and a monument at South Killingholms Haven tipped with a fragment of Plymouth Rock, celebrate this historic occasion.

Four miles N. of Grimsby, where the Humber meets the North Sea, is the seaside resort of **Humberston Fitties**. Those tiring of too much industry might like to drive S. of Grimsby down the B1431, W. of which they will find **Hatcliffe**, tiny, loftily sited above the wooded Ravendale valley, and one of the show-pieces of Lincolnshire. Almost opposite, on the other side of the same road, is **Ashby-cum-Fenby**, where the church has a particularly beautiful medieval oak screen, and almshouses built by Lady Wray during the reign of Elizabeth I. A little further S., down a secondary road off the B1203 is **Wold Newton**, which is noted for the modern figures of the saints in its church.

HADDON HALL, *Derbyshire* (12–SK2366), embodies many of the romantic writer's ideas of an English castle: grey-stone walls and battlemented towers and turrets, a heavily wooded slope as its backdrop, an ancient bridge over the River Wye at its feet and the general air not of a grim fortress but of a gracious, rambling house.

The fine, stone-built Hall, regularly open to the public, has changed little over the past 300 or more years. There are traces of the original building which William Peveril, illegitimate son of William the Conqueror, built in the 11th cent., notably parts of the Peveril Tower and the chapel. The house then was probably no more than a modest hall of its period, but under the later Peverils and the three families who succeeded them as owners – the Avenels, the Vernons, here from 1170 to 1567, and the Manners, from 1567 to the present day – Haddon Hall grew to its present delightful form.

Visitors can look over most of the house, much of it still furnished as it was. In the huge kitchens are the ancient water storage troughs and a dresser worn through with long use; and the bench, salting trough and chopping block can be seen in the butcher's shop. In the fine banqueting hall is a tapestry from the 15th cent. and the antlers on the wall have been there since Charles II's day. There is much heraldic panelling and carving in the dining-room, and a magnificent ceiling; on the staircase landing are three of the set of five Mortlake "Senses" tapestries, probably made originally for Charles I.

There is a small museum at the hall containing many items recovered from behind wainscoting and from under floors during restoration work – coins, dice, knives, pipes, keys, rings etc.; and there is also a rare type of short-pendulum clock, dating from about 1670, and the death-mask of Lady Grace Manners.

The gardens at Haddon are also open to the public. Lying mainly on the south side, they are laid out in a series of stone-walled terraces, with lawns, clipped yews and flower-beds. The rose is the flower of Haddon; there are masses of them everywhere, in formal beds and climbing against the stone walls. These serene gardens make an altogether English setting for this great house.

HAMBLETON, *Rutland* (10–SK9008). Start at Upper Hambleton on its sharp 417-ft hill with fine views over the Vale of Catmose. Upper Hambleton also has a church with a 13th-cent. tower and stumpy spire so characteristic of Rutland. It is essentially 12th-cent., particularly in the south doorway and north and south arcades, but much Victorian rebuilding and decoration has been added. Near the church is the 16th-cent. Priest's House, and there is a 17th-cent. manor house near the modern Hall.

Middle Hambleton is of little account, but tucked below is Nether Hambleton with a delightful Jacobean house of 1610, now a farmhouse but still retaining its gables, colonnades and balustraded balconies.

Leaving Hambleton due S. along the village street brings you to **Egleton** where there is an exceptionally interesting church with rich Norman work, dating from about 1160, in the chancel arch, font and south doorway. Leaving E. along the hilltop you will find the little white Church of St Matthew standing lonely in the now denuded park of the old estate of **Normanton**, which once belonged to the vastly rich Sir Gilbert Heathcote, one of the original founders of the Bank of England in 1694, and Lord Mayor of London in 1711. The village which once stood near the church was pulled down in 1764 by Sir Gilbert in order to enlarge the park. The villagers were transferred to EMPINGHAM.

HARBY, *Nottinghamshire* (13–SK8770). An unremarkable village but historically interesting because the gentle Queen Eleanor of Castile died here on 27 November 1290 in the manor home of Richard de Weston. She had come with Edward I to spend some weeks in SHERWOOD FOREST. He wrote of her: "I loved her tenderly in her lifetime, and I do not cease to love her now she is dead". She was embalmed at LINCOLN and taken to be buried in WESTMINSTER ABBEY, each resting place on the way being marked by a cross – the last and most famous at CHARING CROSS in London. The only original crosses remaining, however, are at GEDDINGTON in Northamptonshire and at WALTHAM CROSS in Hertfordshire.

The old manor house has gone, apart from a small section of its moat next to the churchyard. The chapel Edward I built to her memory has also gone but two relics are preserved in the rather ugly Victorian St Helen's Church built in 1882: the plain Norman doorway to the vestry and the 14th-cent. font. A brass plate on the altar step records her death, and a statuette in a niche above the tower doorway is flanked by shields of Castile and Leon, England and Ponthieu, as on her tomb in the Abbey.

HARDWICK HALL, *Derbyshire* (13–SK46 63). It is impossible not to be impressed, even if not wholly favourably, by Hardwick Hall, one of the trio of great Derbyshire houses – the others being HADDON HALL and CHATSWORTH. Hardwick, 6 m. SE. of CHESTERFIELD, is the monument to Bess of Hardwick who, to make sure no one forgot that this house was her creation, indeed her *chef d'œuvre*, had her initials, writ large, set on top of the four massive, square towers of the west front.

The present building, now in the keeping of the National Trust and open to visitors, is in fact the new hall. The ruined shell of Hardwick Old Hall, where Bess was born in 1520, stands a little distance away. Bess was married four times, the last time to the Earl of Shrewsbury, and with each marriage she became richer, more powerful and more of a character. She became a widow for the fourth time in 1590, at the age of 70, and the following year began her most ambitious undertaking, the creation of a new Hardwick Hall. The building took six years to complete and is distinguished for its symmetry – a rare architectural attribute in Tudor England – and for the fact that there is more glass than stone in the walls. There

are no fewer than 50 windows, some of them enormous, in the imposing west front.

The exterior of the Hall is plain, not to say severe; but inside much of the furnishing and decoration is lavish. To a large degree the interior is much as it must have been in Bess's day and some of the elaborate plasterwork, the exquisite needlework and tapestry is as fine as any in the country. Of the latter, some of the most valuable are the pieces of needlework representing the Virtues; the Mortlake tapestries telling the story of Hero and Leander, on the main stairs; and the 13 pieces of Flemish tapestry hanging in the gallery telling the story of Gideon and which Bess herself bought in 1592 for £326, a prince's ransom then.

HARTINGTON, *Derbyshire* (12–SK1360), is unusual for the county in that the small town is built round a very large, spacious square of a kind more often found much further S. in the country. This, together with the mellow, fawn stone buildings, lends Hartington a Georgian grace not often seen in Derbyshire's hill country. On the River Dove equidistant from BUXTON and ASHBOURNE, some 2 m. W. of the A515, Hartington is famous for its scenery. The road to the A515 winds its way through a narrow valley with limestone crags often rising sheer on either side. BERESFORD DALE can be reached by a footpath from the village. Overlooking the town stands the Church of St Giles, built in red sandstone and with a sturdy tower, battlements and a curious collection of gargoyles. Just off the square stands the old Town Hall, a pretty, arched building dating from 1836 which is now a shop.

HATHERSAGE, *Derbyshire* (12–SK2381). There is a fine open-air swimming-pool in this small hill town, about 8 m. N. of BAKEWELL. It is said that Little John, Robin Hood's henchman, was born here; and that from a cottage here he shot the arrow to mark the spot where he wished to be buried. The Church of St Michael occupies a commanding position on the highest point of the town, and accentuates it by its spire. Built towards the end of the 14th cent., but restored by Butterfield in 1862, it is highly thought of by authorities on church architecture; and is renowned for its wealth of good brasses, memorials to the Eyre family dating back to 1459.

HAUGHMOND ABBEY, *Shropshire* (8–SJ 5415). Built in the lee of a hill, about 5 m. NE. of SHREWSBURY, the abbey was founded about 1135 by William Fitzalan as a house for Augustinian canons. It was rebuilt about 50 years later when the church was considerably enlarged, and had an uneventful history until the Dissolution. Then it passed into private hands and at times was used as a dwelling house.

Apart from the church, much of the abbey still stands substantially as it has done for 800 years. The first impression of the grey-stone front of the abbot's lodging, with its large bay window and oriel window, is of a gracious country house.

The impression is heightened by the spacious hall, the kitchen with its large chimneys, and the doorways which led into the buttery and pantry. Perhaps the most impressive building in the abbey is the 12th-cent. chapter house with its finely carved Norman doorway. Here a small museum of architectural fragments has been established, including an ancient font and a 13th-cent. sculpture of the Virgin and Child. At the north end of the abbey the foundations indicate that a noble church once stood there; in front of the high altar are two Fitzalan gravestones.

HAYFIELD, *Derbyshire* (12–SK0386), is a village in the highest ground of the Peak District and offers the best approach to **Kinder Scout** which reaches 2,088 ft. On the journey there can be seen the Kinder Waterfall with the Mermaid's Pool at its foot. Much of the high plateau is a private grouse moor, but large areas are open for walkers, climbers and ramblers by access agreements which have been made with the landowners. Further E. is the area known as Derbyshire's Lake District, the string of three reservoirs, Howden, Derwent and Ladybower, which run through **Derwent Dale.** The scenery of the whole area is never less than magnificent and occasionally awe-inspiring.

HECKINGTON, *Lincolnshire* (13–TF1444). The village is not exciting and the landscape is flat. Nevertheless there are two things which make Heckington worth visiting: its well-preserved eight-sail windmill, the only one in England still operating, and one of the finest Decorated cruciform churches in the country.

The church, St Andrew's, was built in the 14th cent. by the rich abbots of BARDNEY, and is an enduring and unaltered monument to English architecture at its best. It is the third church on the site but embodies none of the features of the others. The outside is richly carved, buttressed, canopied, turreted, and pinnacled. The inside is disappointing apart from a wonderful Easter sepulchre built by Richard de Potesgrave, vicar of the church and chaplain to Edward III. His tomb and stone effigy are in the chancel next to the sepulchre. Two other features of note are the beautifully carved sedilia and the tracery in the east window.

HOAR CROSS, *Staffordshire* (9–SK1223). Many aver that the church in this small, pretty village about 8 m. W. of BURTON-UPON-TRENT is the most beautiful built in England during the 19th cent. – and some would include the 20th. The architect was George Frederick Bodley, and he chose red sandstone which comes wonderfully alive in evening sunlight. He gave it a strong, embattled central tower more than 100 ft tall to catch those slanting rays. The church, built in 1876, was the inspiration of a young widow, Emily Meynell Ingram, daughter of Viscount Halifax. In 1863 she came to the village as the bride of Hugo Meynell Ingram, of Hoar Cross Hall, and it was his early death, eight years

later, which prompted his widow to build the church.

The desire to make this a beautiful building is reflected inside as well as out: in the magnificent stained glass, again the work of Bodley; in the lofty pillars and soaring arcades; in the black-and-white marble floor with the Meynell Ingram arms set at the foot of the altar steps; in the exquisitely carved woodwork, especially the spire-shaped oak canopy to the font. Here, too, are the monuments to the widow and her husband, both recumbent figures in alabaster: he, in the uniform of the Staffordshire Yeomanry with a favourite hound at his feet; she, head on a cushion, hands raised in prayer with her pet dog at her feet. Some of the painting is so close to the medieval style that a couple of genuine old Italian paintings were for a long time thought to be 19th-cent. work.

HODNET, *Shropshire* (8–SJ6128). The beautiful Hall gardens, which are open to the public, and an old church are the chief attractions of this predominantly black-and-white town about 5 m. SW. of MARKET DRAYTON. Hodnet Hall, a large attractive red-brick house, Elizabethan-looking but built only about 100 years ago on the site of an older house, is not open to the public but good views of it can be obtained from the gardens. Thoughtfully landscaped and covering more than 60 acres, the gardens were created from a wilderness of shrubs covering a narrow, marshy valley by the late Brigadier A. G. W. Heber-Percy, whose son and family still live at the Hall. The work was begun in 1922 and took 30 years and today the gardens, which contain many unusual plants and shrubs, offer interest and beauty at all seasons. The gardens are laid out to incorporate a necklace of pools of various shapes and sizes and these, together with the forest trees and sweeping lawns, form a perfect setting for the great splashes of daffodils, rhododendrons, azaleas and lilacs, the peonies, roses and primulas of summer and the foliage and berries of the autumn shrubs. There is a fine cedar tree planted in memory of the founder and a garden built round a glacial boulder of granite. The visitor can take tea in a pretty half-timbered building which contains an unusual collection of big-game trophies; and a little way from the house stands a timber-framed barn dating from 1619.

The Church of St Luke crowns the hill round which the small town clusters and has a christening gate in the churchyard and wedding steps leading to the drive to the Hall. There is Norman work in the church, the octagonal tower of which is unique in Shropshire. One of its treasures is a small chained library which contains a Latin Bible printed in Nuremberg in 1479, only 10 years after the first printed book. The church's most famous rector, from 1807 to 1823, was Reginald Heber who later became Bishop of Calcutta. The coloured tile paving in the chancel is in memory of this man who wrote many famous hymns, among them "From Greenland's icy mountains" and "Brightest and best of the sons of the morning"

HOLBEACH, *Lincolnshire* (13–TF3925). Holbeach, in the midst of the aptly named "Parts of Holland" bulb-growing district of Lincolnshire, was mentioned in the Domesday Book. The Church of All Saints is a little later than the one at HECKINGTON and a good example of the transition from Decorated to Perpendicular. The tower and spire are magnificent and there is typical flamboyant tracery in some of the windows. On a large tomb inside, the effigy head of Sir Humphrey Littlebury, killed during the Wars of the Roses, rests mysteriously on the head of another man, caught in a net.

William Stukeley, one of the founders of the Society of Antiquaries in 1718, was born in Holbeach in 1687. Another native of this market town was Susannah Centlivre, born about 1667. Six years before her marriage at 29 to Joseph Centlivre, chef to Queen Anne and George I, she had written her first play. Until she died in 1723 she wrote one play a year, all full of rich comedy and invention and in one of them David Garrick played the lead.

HOLME, *Nottinghamshire* (13–SK8059). Rather inaccessible between the Trent, Slough Dike and the Fleet, Holme once stood on the west bank of the Trent, but is now on the east due to one of the river's medieval changes of course.

Small St Giles' Church is one of the most remarkable in the county, for nearly everything about it is early Tudor. It was rebuilt in the late 15th cent. by John Barton, who made a fortune out of the wool trade with Calais and had, so it is said, an inscription in the window of his house which read: "I thanke God, and ever shall. It is the shepe hath payed for all." His monument in two tiers, with a rotting corpse in the lower one, lies between the chancel and the chapel. It is thanks to the sensitive restoration begun in 1932 by Mr Nevil Truman that this little church is still so attractive with its leaning walls, original screens, and benches carved with poppy-heads. Also due to Mr Truman is the east window, a medieval medley of pieces including John Barton's memorial glass. A room above the porch is known as Nanny Scott's Chamber, after an old woman who took refuge here with plenty of food when the plague struck Holme in 1666. From the small window she watched the funeral cortèges of her friends until, forced down to get more food, she found only one person still left alive. Horror-stricken, she returned to her chamber to die; the coffin-shaped chest in which she kept all her possessions is still there.

You will be told that Dick Turpin stopped at a cottage here to give Black Bess a drink on his famous ride to YORK.

HOPE, *Derbyshire* (12–SK 1783). Two m. E. of CASTLETON and in the centre of the Hope Valley, this rather plain village is known for the fishing and rough shooting available here. On the nearest Saturday to St Peter's Day (29 June), a well is dressed in the village; and in late summer, the Hope Valley Agricultural Show with its well-known sheepdog trials is a major attraction. The parish church has a 14th-cent. tower with a broach spire, and a number of remarkable gargoyles, large and crude. In the churchyard is a 9th-cent. Anglo-Saxon cross shaft. Near the village – and looking rather like a miniature Cape Kennedy – are the works of a famous cement company.

HOPTON CASTLE, *Shropshire* (8–SO3678). The most striking thing about Hopton Castle is the unexpectedness with which the traveller comes upon it. There are several approaches, but the easiest to find is the turning off the B4367 at Hopton Heath. About 1 m. down this country lane you turn a corner and there in a field stand the ruins of the castle. The lovely setting makes it seem incredible that this was the scene of one of the most brutal minor encounters of the Civil War. Colonel Samuel More held the castle for three weeks for the Parliamentarians against the Royalists; 31 defenders against 500 besiegers the records say. When the garrison eventually was forced into surrender, the Royalists shot everyone except the colonel and threw the bodies into a nearby pool. The castle can be viewed.

HORNCASTLE, *Lincolnshire* (13–TF2669). Situated at the south-west foot of the Wolds where they come down to the Fens, at the confluence of the Rivers Bain and Waring, was the Roman fort of Banovallum – the walled place on the River Bain – which forms the central part of this little market town. The walls of the fort are still visible, though the town was largely rebuilt in the middle of the 19th cent. A well-preserved portion of the Roman wall was incorporated in the structure of a library built in 1969.

Horncastle's ten-day August Horse Fair was once famed throughout Europe and is described by George Borrow in *The Romany Rye*. The frequently restored Church of St Mary has many relics of the Battle of **Winceby**, which was fought nearby in 1643 with Cromwell and his Roundheads. Cromwell's horse was shot dead beneath him and as he scrambled to his feet he was charged by Sir Ingram Hopton. Seizing another horse, Cromwell charged again and won the battle which sealed his fame; Sir Ingram Hopton was killed in the second charge. Next day Cromwell rode into Horncastle and arranged for Sir Ingram to be buried in the church, so it seems ungrateful that Cromwell should be described on Sir Ingram's elaborately painted canvas memorial as an "arch-rebel". In the church are also pikes from the battle and 13 scythes, used either at Winceby or in the Lincolnshire Rising in defence of the monasteries. On the north wall is a brass of Sir Lionel Dymoke of SCRIVELSBY wearing the armour of the King's Champion, and on the floor below a worn brass depicting him in his shroud, 1519.

In a corner of the market place once stood Sellwood House from which Louisa and Emily, daughters of Henry Sellwood, a Horncastle solicitor, married Charles and Alfred Tennyson.

E. Preston

Ironbridge is the site of the first cast-iron bridge ever erected

HUCKNALL, *Nottinghamshire* (13–SK 5349). The village of Hucknall is remarkable only for its church, and the Church of St Mary Magdalen is remarkable only for two things. It was here that Lord Byron's body was brought to be buried with his ancestors when his family discovered that permission for him to be interred in WESTMINSTER ABBEY was unlikely to be granted. It is a place of pilgrimage for Greeks into whose War of Independence Byron had thrown himself too wholeheartedly for his already weakened constitution, and for whose cause he died. His bust is on the chancel wall with a lamp of brass burning continually, and in the floor is set a stone sent by the King of Greece and decorated with a brass laurel wreath. His mother had been brought to be buried here from the family home at NEWSTEAD ABBEY 13 years before. His one child, Augusta Ada, was buried by his side in 1852. It was only in 1968 that a memorial of Lord Byron – "mad, bad, and dangerous to know" – was allowed in Poets' Corner at the Abbey. The other remarkable thing about the church is the set of 25 stained-glass windows by Kempe. This is Victorian stained glass at its best. It begins with the east window of 1883; the others are mainly 1888 to 1890.

At Broomhill Park is Sherwood Zoo, covering 17 acres. It has polar bears and parrots, falconry displays and large picnic areas.

ILAM, *Staffordshire* (8–SK 1351), is where the empirical Dr Samuel Johnson carried out his experiment with marked corks to satisfy himself that the stream which emerges from the cliffs in the grounds of Ilam Hall was indeed the River Manifold which disappears underground about 4 m. N. Ilam village is another of the model villages which were rebuilt during the last century, this one by Jesse Watts-Russell, who also built the stately Hall on the site of an earlier house. The Hall and its 50 acres of wooded grounds are now owned by the National Trust and are always open to the public; the Hall itself is, in part, a youth hostel. Watts-Russell's wife is also remembered in Ilam in an unusual monument. Close by the bridge over the Manifold he had erected to her memory a Gothic cross as tall as a house.

The village church, in the Hall grounds, dates from the 13th cent. but it was much restored in 1856. The oldest relics are three Anglo-Saxon crosses: two in the churchyard and one in the grounds of the Hall. The church has a Norman font; and a 13th-cent. shrine to St Bertram who is believed to have been the man who brought Christianity to the area. There are a number of fine monuments in the church, the most impressive of which is that depicting the deathbed scene of David Watts, the work of Sir Francis Chantrey (1781–1842), sculptor of the "Sleeping Children" tomb in LICHFIELD Cathedral. The sculpture shows the dying man raising himself from his couch to lay his hand on the head of his daughter (the woman commemorated by the cross in the village) with her three tiny children clustered around.

Ilam has a link with the English stage; it was here in 1693 that William Congreve, the Restoration dramatist, wrote his comedy, *The Old Bachelor*, while recovering from an illness. Here also is the spot which Dr Johnson is said to have used as his model for the Happy Valley in *Rasselas*.

Ilam is the gateway to the MANIFOLD VALLEY and gives access to DOVEDALE. Here, too, the Dovedale Sheepdog Trials are held each August.

ILKESTON, *Derbyshire* (13–SK4642), on high ground above the Erewash Valley, is the third largest town in the county and is only just inside the county boundary. There was an Anglo-Saxon settlement here before the Danes came in the 9th cent., but not until the late 19th cent. did the small village begin to develop into today's industrial town. The oldest building in the town is the Parish Church of St Mary. Although much restored about 100 years ago, parts of the original Norman building can still be seen and there is an unusual 14th-cent. stone screen and a Crusader's tomb. The county cricket club play a number of matches each season in the Rutland Recreation Ground; and Ilkeston retains its links with its past in the annual three-day fair held in the Market Place in October.

INGESTRE, *Staffordshire* (8–SJ9724), on the River Trent about 4 m. NE. of STAFFORD, has a rare possession – a Wren church. St Mary's was built in 1676 by Walter Chetwynd to the designs of Sir Christopher. The documents relating to its building have been lost but architectural authorities are convinced from its style that it is indeed one of the master's works. Fruit and flowers are the dominant motifs inside – on the plasterwork ceiling, the oak panelling in the chancel, the oak chancel screen and the pulpit. The Hall, a Jacobean building and home first of the Chetwynd family and then of the Earls of Shrewsbury, was burnt down in 1882 and the present building, now an Arts Centre, is a skilful reconstruction of the first Hall. Part of Capability Brown's landscaping for Ingestre – his first Staffordshire commission – survives.

On the road from Stafford stands the shell of Tixall gatehouse, one of the most important remaining examples of early Elizabethan architecture, and all that remains of a large mansion.

NW. of Ingestre lies **Hopton Heath**, where in 1643 a Parliamentary army defeated the Royalists under the Earl of Northampton.

IRONBRIDGE, *Shropshire* (8–SJ6703), must have been an attractive spot before the Industrial Revolution, for the little town is set on steep limestone slopes above a narrow gorge through which the River Severn flows. Ironbridge has become famous because the world's first iron bridge was built here. It was designed by Abraham Darby II and cast, in 1778, at his foundry in nearby Coalbrookdale. Today the bridge is restricted to foot traffic but it is well worth walking across it, and along the bank to get a distant view of it. Then, for all its size (it is 196 ft long, with one major span of 100 ft and two smaller ones at one end, and weighs 380 tons) the bridge looks insubstantial.

KEDLESTON HALL, *Derbyshire* (12–SK 3140), is reckoned by many to be the finest Robert Adam house in England. Kedleston, 4½ m. NW. of DERBY, has been the Derbyshire home of the Curzon family for 850 years, but of the original house nothing remains. It was pulled down in the last years of the 17th cent. and then began a period of building, alteration and rebuilding which went on until late in the 18th cent. The first architect employed was Matthew Brettingham, and his basic plan for a main block with two projecting wings linked to it by corridors is what gives the house its present-day form. At a later stage, another architect, James Paine, at that time more famous than Robert Adam, was called in and to him goes the credit for the imposing north front with its giant columns and triumphal arch. Adam came on the scene in 1760 and he was the designer of the more unusual south front and of much of the interior, his masterpiece being the Marble Hall with its 20 huge columns of pink, veined alabaster, its floor of Derbyshire stone and Italian marble, its alcoves containing statues and its monochrome panels round the walls depicting scenes from Homer. This is considered one of the most splendid rooms in Europe.

Many of the other rooms in the Hall are of a piece with this famous room. In the Music Room is a gilded organ designed by Adam and the chimney-piece is inlaid with Derbyshire's own stone, the Blue John. The outstanding feature of the State Drawing Room is a beautifully proportioned Venetian window. The Saloon is a rotunda with a dome 62 ft high, and the State Dining Room, a symphony of browns, buffs and whites, is distinguished by a semi-domed alcove for the better display of the table silver. Pictures by such artists as Reynolds, Reni, Van Dyck and Veronese adorn the walls; there are magnificent marble fireplaces, furniture designed by Chippendale and Adam, a plaque made by Josiah Wedgwood, and much early Crown Derby china dating from 1760. Visitors may also see Adam's original drawings for the work, outside and in, which he did at Kedleston; and the Indian Museum containing the collection of silver, ivories, ancient weapons, including poisoned arrows, and Oriental

A. F. Kersting

Kedleston Hall: the Marble Hall was designed by Robert Adam

works of art made by Lord Curzon while he was Viceroy of India from 1898 to 1905.

In the grounds can be seen the Boathouse and graceful bridge, both designed by Adam; and the 13th- and 14th-cent. Church of All Saints which contains a remarkable collection of Curzon monuments.

KEGWORTH, *Leicestershire* (10–SK4826). Kegworth is saved from being commonplace by its Church of St Andrew, which stands on a hill above the water-meadows of the Soar, stately and cohesive in its architecture. It is late Decorated with an extra aisle on each side taking the place of transepts, and every window, with the exception of the large east window, is of the same size and pattern. The nave roof has a medieval choir of men and women playing musical instruments, and the chantry roof is supported by ten stone angels.

Thomas Moore brought his young wife, Bessie, to live in Kegworth in 1812 where, he wrote, "she runs wild about the large garden". His house, The Cedars, stands on the LOUGHBOROUGH road. Here he composed some of his *Irish Melodies* and here his favourite daughter, Anastasia, who died of consumption when she was 16, was born.

There are some houses worth noting in the main street running S. from the church. The first, dated 1698, is the best. Behind the Britannia Inn is an old stockinger's cottage which was used for the purpose until 1956.

KELHAM, *Nottinghamshire* (13–SK7755). Kelham Hall casts its spiky reflection on the waters

of the River Trent. It was built by Sir Gilbert Scott after the first Kelham Hall, said to be the house in which Charles I finally surrendered to the Scots, was destroyed by fire in 1857. Now a theological college, Kelham Hall was once described by the Archbishop of Canterbury as "extraordinarily like St Pancras station". The chapel, built in 1928, has a plain but inspiring interior with a beautiful modern crucifixion scene by Charles Sargeant Jagger. The Church of St Wilfrid contains a monument to Lord and Lady Lexington and their son who died aged 15. The inscription telling of Lord Lexington's career is long, ponderous and not very pious. There is also a monument to a daughter of the 7th Earl of Scarborough by the then very fashionable Gaffin of REGENT STREET.

Leave the village by Kelham Bridge, which was snapped in two by a small iceberg in the terrible winter of 1854–5, and stop in **Averham** to look at the Robin Hood Theatre. It was built in 1914 by a rector of St Michael, a smaller replica of a West End theatre. The late Sir Donald Wolfit made his first stage appearance there in 1917. Later rectors found it embarrassing to have a theatre in their garden, and it was bought by a private enthusiast who puts on all types of amateur and professional shows.

KETTON, *Rutland* (10–SK9704). A large and most attractive village full of excellent building in the famous butter-coloured local stone, which has been quarried from here since the Roman era. The Parish Church of St Mary, with its exquisite tower and spire, rises amid trees above the sepia Collyweston slate roofs of the village. This church is one of the finest in the North Midlands, large for a village. The west front is an excellent example of 12th-cent. work and the rest of the church is almost entirely 13th-cent. apart from the chancel rebuilt by Sir Gilbert Scott, but good nevertheless. The east window and altar are by Sir Ninian Comper (1907). The church is of stone from BARNACK, a village SE. of STAMFORD, but there are some beautiful Ketton headstones in the churchyard, in particular one near the lychgate depicting masons' tools. It was carved by William Hibbins (1717), whose family still flourish in Ketton as stone masons. Some of their tools can be seen at the County Museum at OAKHAM, along with a fine specimen of their work.

From Ketton drive due W. past Normanton Park about 3 m. to **Edith Weston**, charming, like nearly all Rutland villages. Edward the Confessor gave his wife, Queen Edith, this western part of the county, hence the name. It remained a royal manor until Henry I gave it to his chamberlain, William de Tankerville, who in turn gave it to the Norman abbey of St George de Boscherville. The abbey established a cell at Edith Weston where there were never more than two or three monks, and only one in 1357.

The village is built round a green, surrounded by thatched cottages, and it stands on a limestone plateau between the valleys of the Chater and the Gwash. The old rectory, W. of the church, is dated 1626 and the hall is 1830-Tudor.

The church has an original late-Norman nave, with a north aisle added around 1190, and a south aisle added immediately afterwards. Changes were made in the 14th cent. and the tower was added in 1380. The chancel was rebuilt in 1865. The church possesses one of the oldest positively dated timepieces in England, known as the Commonwealth Clock. It is 300 years old and has recently been restored.

KINGERBY, *Lincolnshire* (13–TF0392). The 19th-cent. Hall stands on the elevated site of a Roman camp, but the mound itself was occupied by Ancient Britons, whose skeletons have been found buried in sawdust with mosaic bracelets on their arms. The Church of St Peter, opposite a wood full of flowers in spring, is especially interesting. The Young family, who owned the Hall for many years, were Catholics and so this Anglican church escaped too much restoration. The tower and south door are both 12th-cent. and there are a lead roof and Georgian lead windows. Two stone effigies of knights rest on the floor and against the chancel wall is a 600-year-old coffin-shaped monument to a member of the Disney family. It shows the bust of a man under a canopy, his feet in another niche below resting on a dog. The space between is occupied by a cross and two shields.

KINGSTON-ON-SOAR, *Nottinghamshire* (13–SK5127). Kingston Hall, built by the first Lord Belper, the son of Jedediah Strutt of hosiery fame, is not particularly exciting except for the lovely fir, pine and cedar panelling lining its walls.

The church is ugly, but contains one of the most important and fascinating church monuments in the county – the Babington chantry. When the church was rebuilt in 1900 the monument, dating from about 1550, was moved to its present position intact. The columns are covered in tracery, shields, small figures and trailing vines; there are coffins giving up their dead with some climbing to heaven and others falling into the jaws of a monster. The main capitals are carved with what is a pun on the Babington name – about 200 babes in tuns. A Sir Anthony Babington is said to have erected the chantry. Another Anthony Babington, a Roman Catholic, is said to have hidden on its canopy after his share in the conspiracy to put Mary Queen of Scots on the throne. He was beheaded in 1586, aged only 25, for his part in the plot.

As you move S. out of the village notice the fine buildings of the NOTTINGHAM University School of Agriculture. These were used as German prison camps during the War.

KINOULTON, *Nottinghamshire* (13–SK6730). Stop here, if only for the glorious view over the Vale of Belvoir with the cattle on the horizon, and the woodlands known as the Borders. The Grantham Canal runs under the road. Opposite the forge is the bright red brick church built by the Earl of Gainsborough in 1793. Close to Fosse Way is the site of the old church with slate headstones including one of the finest in the county. Kinoulton has one of the best village cricket grounds in Nottinghamshire, and the Neville Arms is the rendezvous of the Nottingham Old Crocks Car Club.

KINVER, *Staffordshire* (8–SO8483). One of the finest Staffordshire views is to be had from the famous Kinver Edge, below which this small town clusters, in the south-west corner of the county. On top of the Edge, National Trust property, is an early Iron Age hill-fort; and there are also the strange "rock houses" at Holy Austin Rock, rooms carved out of the solid sandstone, their "chimneys" holes in the hillside. Two m. away stand the remains of Stourton Castle, birthplace of Reginald Pole, Archbishop of Canterbury during the reign of Mary Tudor.

KIRKSTEAD, *Lincolnshire* (13–TF1762). Here by the Witham in 1139, Hugo Brito, son of a Lord of TATTERSHALL, founded the Cistercian abbey of which all that remains is a corner of the transept and the now solitary little Church of St Leonard – the Cistercians' "church outside the gates" for lay worshippers. Standing on bumpy pastoral land described in a charter of the time as, "a horrible and vaste solitude surrounded by swamp and bramble bushes on all sides", this church should not be left out of the sightseers' itinerary since it is an unspoilt example of 13th-cent. architecture and contains what is thought to be the second-oldest timber screenwork in England. It has a charming arcade of three arches with a window in the centre and is still lit by candles in two fine candelabra. The triple lancets in the east wall are enriched with dogtooth carving, foliage, and clustered and banded shafts. The altar stone from the abbey is now on the floor. A figure of a knight in a flat-topped helmet with a long slit for the eyes is thought to be the 2nd Lord Tattershall, who died in 1212. The abbey was dissolved in 1537 on the "confession" of the abbot that his monks had "vainly, detestably, and ungodly devoured their yearly revenues in continual ingurgitations of their carrion bodies, with vain and unholy expenses, enormities and abuses".

The Abbey Lodge Inn near the ruins is 18th-cent. There is good fishing in the River Witham at this point.

LAMBLEY, *Nottinghamshire* (13–SK6245), has beautiful scenery in a deep sheltered vale with the Lambley Dumble running through the village. The excellently proportioned Perpendicular Church of the Holy Trinity was built for Ralph de Cromwell, Lord High Treasurer of about 1450, who is credited with having produced the first budget. One of the wealthiest nobles of his time, he was born at Lambley in 1394 and though his body lies at the church in TATTERSHALL, his badge of office, a purse, is carved on the outside of the east window here. Originally there was a two-storied chantry on the north wall built by the sixth Ralph Cromwell. The "squint" from its upper room is still visible in the stones of the wall.

LANGAR, *Nottinghamshire* (13–SK7235). The large church with a tower over the central crossing is often called the Cathedral of the Vale of Belvoir. It is badly restored outside but is nevertheless mentioned in a number of reference books because of its monuments. The one of Lord Thomas Scroope (1609) and his wife, Philadelphia, is a splendid, free-standing alabaster, which has been described as "almost the finest effigy in England". Details of the robes are worth close study, though this is not easy since the doors of the chapel are locked and the visitor has to look down from a stone balcony. This monument was erected by their son, Emanuel, who is represented as a curious, small bearded figure kneeling at their feet and holding a book. In the north transept are the Chaworths of whom Mary of ANNESLEY, Byron's first love, was the last of the line, dying at Langar in 1832. Admiral Earl Howe (of the Glorious 1st of June) – whose family lived in the Hall before it was rebuilt – is buried in the south transept, though his main monument is at WESTMINSTER ABBEY. The 16th-cent. altar cloth is made from Italian material he brought back to England from one of the seven ships he captured on the day of his famous battle. You will note that the other two Howe monuments have the Christian name Scroope, the Scroopes and Howes having been linked by marriage in the early 18th cent.

Just near the church is the Georgian rectory where Samuel Butler was born. He used Langar

as the prototype for Battersby in *The Way of all Flesh* after his harsh and embittering childhood behind those too-narrow windows.

LAXTON, *Nottinghamshire* (13–SK7266). This village is famous for preserving the old agricultural system of open-field farming. This was Saxon in origin, consisting of hedgeless, one-acre, co-operatively farmed strips; after the Norman Conquest the method was adapted to the manorial system, with one field for the bread crop, one for the drink crop, and one fallow. The strips were a furlong (furrow-long) in length and a chain (the length of a cricket pitch) in width; an individual's holding was scattered to ensure a fair share of good and bad land. The open-field system at Laxton is registered as an Ancient Monument.

LEEK, *Staffordshire* (8–SJ9856). Leek stands at the southern end of some of the most impressive scenery in the county. N. of the town, the road to BUXTON climbs over a stretch of wild moorland, patterned by black, drystone walls and dominated by the fortress-like hills known as The Roaches. The highest is Five Clouds, 1,500 ft high; but perhaps the best-known is the solitary, grim-looking Hen Cloud. Here occurs at midsummer a remarkable phenomenon, the so-called double sunset: the sun, having dipped behind one of the hills, re-appears and then slowly slips out of sight again.

Leek was settled before the Romans came. Roman remains have been found at Abbey Green, and at Cock Low, a mound which stood near the present Spring Gardens, was found a funeral urn believed to be pre-Saxon. This can now be seen at the town's Arts Centre in the Nicholson Institute. In the churchyard of St Edward's, the parish church, is the shaft of a cross which may be Danish, and another which may be Anglo-Saxon.

Of the Abbey of Dieulacres, founded in 1214 by Ranulph, 7th Earl of Chester, only traces remain, but there are a number of interesting old buildings in the town. The church, with its eight-pinnacled tower, dates mainly from the 14th cent. although the chancel was almost wholly rebuilt about 100 years ago. Prince Charlie's House commemorates the fact that the Pretender stayed in Leek in 1745 on his way to DERBY. There are a number of old inns, notably the Red Lion, dating from 1626, the 17th-cent. Swan, and the Bowling Green and the George which were built in the 18th cent. That part of the town near the church known as Petty France is a reminder that French prisoners-of-war were brought to Leek during the Napoleonic Wars.

Leek has long been known as a silk and textile town and it was a group of women from the town who in 1885–6 spent 12 months making a copy of the famous Bayeux Tapestry. The copy was purchased in 1895 and presented to READING Museum.

LEICESTER, *Leicestershire* (10–SK5904). The history of this thriving and largely modern city, the centre of the Heart of England, goes back over 2,000 years. Long before the first wave of Romans established their township of Ratae in the lush meadows beside the River Soar the Celtic peoples were here. Traces of roads they built are still to be found, but the Romans, in their 400 years of more or less benign occupation, constructed the highways that inspired the building of today's fine network across the county.

The most impressive surviving memorial of these ancient times is the Jewry Wall, believed to date from A.D. 130, a massive fragment 73 ft long and 20 ft high, in alternate courses of brick and stone. Until recently the deep arched recesses, edged with tiles, on the east face of the wall were thought to be openings in the western gateway of the city. Excavation has now shown them to be windows of a vast basilica. Behind the wall a courtyard 175 ft wide has been opened up, revealing porticos leading into shops, the whole area having once been the forum from which the governor administered justice and laws were passed on to the British people. It is here that the largest Roman bath in England was found. Nearby are tessellated pavements with intricate designs in colour, and coins, pottery and other relics are housed in the new museum.

The hub of the city is the clock tower, a Gothic structure erected in 1868 to commemorate four benefactors of Leicester since the Norman Conquest. The most famous of these was Simon de Montfort, Earl of Leicester, the powerful baron whose hatred of tyranny eventually forced Henry III, his brother-in-law, to grant the first English parliament in 1275. The other three were William Wyggleston, Sir Thomas White and Gabriel Newton, all of them founders of schools or charitable institutions.

Leicester Castle in its original form dates from 1088, but the red-brick frontage added in about 1690 has sadly diminished the grandeur of the earlier concept. Behind it is the great hall which was once part of John of Gaunt's country residence and is now the assize court. The architecture of the stone hall places it almost certainly between 1140 and 1160. The roof of braced beams which span the whole of the building is particularly imposing. An outside flight of steps leads down to what may have been cellars or dungeons. A few yards away is the new work, or Newarke as it is known today, a walled enclosure of about four acres, outside the castle boundaries, in which stood the noble Collegiate Church of St Mary, founded by Henry, Earl of Leicester and Lancaster in the 14th cent. The finest monument of the Newarke is the high stone gateway at the east side, with three arches, a vaulted canopy and ornamented square-topped windows.

The beautiful Church of St Mary de Castro, the church of the castle, is a direct link with the Norman ascendancy. From having been completely Anglo-Saxon it was rebuilt by succeeding Earls of Leicester. The pinnacled tower and the belfry were begun in the 13th cent. and the slender spire was added a hundred or so years later. Of especial antiquarian interest are the five sedilia, or priests' seats, and the magnificent 700-year-old font.

Older still is the Church of St Nicholas, whose history goes back through Saxon times to obscurity in the Roman basilica; but the natural choice for the cathedral of the diocese of Leicester on its re-establishment in 1926 was the civic church of St Martin. Although this noble edifice has been much restored in recent times, not always in harmonious accord with the styles of earlier reconstructions, the graceful old arches and rich decoration of the interior remain unchanged. The bishop's throne is unsurpassed in splendour, standing about 16 ft high and reaching almost to the roof in declining tiers adorned with tracery. Adjacent to the cathedral is the 14th-cent. guildhall, now a repository for books and other exhibits connected with the past. Two m. from the city centre, Belgrave Hall, a small Queen Anne house and garden, is worth a visit.

Leicester today combines the charm of its ancient foundations with the forward march of industry. Two hundred years ago only hosiery was produced here. The bulk manufacture of boots and shoes emerged in the 1850s. In the present century the majority of its people are employed in engineering.

LICHFIELD, *Staffordshire* (9–SK1209). Although Lichfield is a thriving centre of light engineering, it is not industrial installations but the "Ladies of the Vale", the three spires of the cathedral, that the visitor first sees, from whatever direction he approaches the city.

The present red sandstone cathedral, begun in the 1190s and completed about 150 years later, shows splendid Early English and Decorated work. Although this is one of the smallest and most heavily restored cathedrals in the country, the west front has an indisputable grandeur. The twin spires flanking the doorway are almost 200 ft high; the central tower is 60 ft taller. Within the arcades and panels of the front are 113 statues: figures from the Old Testament, the Holy Family, the Apostles, saints, bishops, 24 kings of England, including William the Conqueror and Edward the Confessor, and two genealogies of Christ. Much of this carving dates from the 19th cent.

The most prized treasure is the early 7th-cent. manuscript book known as the St Chad Gospels – the complete gospels of St Matthew and St Mark, and part of the gospel of St Luke – which can be seen after application in writing to the Cathedral Librarian. The name of the manuscript commemorates the first bishop to have his cathedral at Lichfield, in 669, though the gospels themselves did not come to Lichfield until many years after his death. (Lichfield was made an archbishopric in about 787, in mighty Offa's reign, but was a bishopric again by 803.) Another priceless possession are the Herckenrode Windows in the Lady Chapel, among the most beautiful glass in England. The glass was originally in a Cistercian abbey at Herckenrode, near Liège in Belgium, and was brought to

England by Sir Brooke Boothby in 1802. He presented it to the cathedral for just £200, the price he had paid for it. At the east end of the south aisle is the famous "Sleeping Children" monument by Sir Francis Chantrey.

Lichfield has a pleasant cathedral close, a cobbled market square, narrow streets, and many links with Dr Johnson. A statue of the great man sits at one end of the Market Square, facing – but not looking at – his birthplace on the corner of Breadmarket Street. This house, where Samuel's father Michael had his bookshop, is now a museum of Johnsonian relics: it has his favourite armchair, his walking stick, his silver teapot, and many of his manuscripts and letters. Johnson's birthday, 18 September, is celebrated on the Saturday nearest to it with an official gathering round his statue and a candle-lit supper in the Guildhall.

At the other end of the Market Square, looking in the direction of the cathedral, is a statue of Johnson's biographer, James Boswell. At this end, too, is a memorial to Edward Wightman of BURTON-UPON-TRENT, who was burnt at the stake there for heresy on 11 April 1612, the last person so to die in England.

Further along Breadmarket Street is the birthplace of the antiquary and herald Elias Ashmole, who presented his unique collection of antiquities and documents to OXFORD University. In Beacon Street is the house where Dr Erasmus Darwin, grandfather of Charles, lived and the site of one where David Garrick, the actor, often stayed.

Lichfield also has long military associations. At Whittington Barracks, home of the Staffordshire Regiment, a little way out on the TAMWORTH road, the Regimental Museum is open to visitors.

Masons, carvers and joiners can be seen working in wood and stone on the premises of a local firm in Dam Street – appropriately near the cathedral, that treasure-house of their forerunners' skills.

LILLESHALL, *Shropshire* (8–SJ7315). This village is now famous because of the national athletics centre which has been established in the Hall. This is not open to the public, but Lilleshall Abbey, in the grounds of the Hall, is. The ruins are among the most impressive in Shropshire, a group of roofless walls in a lovely setting. The abbey is Norman, founded in 1148. The high west front is particularly grand and through it you can look down the whole length of the 228-ft abbey and through the graceful arch of the empty east window to the trees beyond.

The Church of St Michael is also Norman in part, with a simple Norman font and an unusual monument to two members of the Leveson family, who were given Lilleshall by Henry VIII on the Dissolution of the Monasteries. Sir Richard Leveson and his wife rest on shelves, he above in robes, she below in a shroud. He died in 1661 and she lived on for another 13 years.

The village also has a 70-ft obelisk, commemorating George Greville, Duke of Sutherland – for whom the Hall was built – who died in 1833.

Kenneth Scowen

Lichfield Cathedral with its three spires

LINBY, *Nottinghamshire* (13–SK5350). This is one of the prettiest villages in Nottinghamshire: stone cottages, red roofs, two village crosses, and a little stream flowing on each side of the road.

There is Norman masonry in the north wall and the south side of the chancel in the Church of St Michael, which was mentioned in the Domesday Book. The door is also Norman. But it is Castle Mill, E. of the village and halfway to **Papplewick,** which is of the greatest interest. It was rebuilt and castellated by the Hon. Frederick Montague, 18th-cent. Lord Treasurer, as part of his Papplewick Improvements. Here in 1785 James Watt put up his first steam-engine for cotton-spinning and the 163 graves in the churchyard tell of the pitiful little children who were imported from London to work in it and died under the forced labour conditions of the Industrial Revolution. Castle Mill is now converted into flats but the water wheel, 100 ft round and one of the biggest in England, is still there.

At Papplewick, E. along the B6011, is Papplewick Hall, built in 1787 for the Hon. Frederick Montague by the Adam brothers. In the grounds are an urn to the memory of his friend, Thomas Gray, the poet, and a little temple to William Mason, who wrote part of his *English Garden* here. Frederick Montague also rebuilt the little church in 1795 and his grave is in the churchyard under a sort of stone table on six legs. Part of the legend of Robin Hood still exists here in a cave cut in the rock and guarded by an old oak, where the outlaw is said to have stabled his horses.

LINCOLN, *Lincolnshire* (13–SK9771). The ancient part of this historic city occupies a rugged hill-top rising 200 ft above the River Witham. In earliest times the Celtic tribesmen called their settlement Lindon, "the hill-fort by a pool", until with the coming of the Roman IXth Legion in A.D. 47 the name was latinized to Lindum and later Lindum Colonia, from which the name Lincoln was derived. The subsequent history of this turbulent place was always determined by its geographical position. The elevated limestone plateau provided a natural strategic command of the valley below, and the river served as an extra wall to slow the advance of the enemy. Excavations show that the first Romans maintained a garrison here from which to pivot their forces for the control of eastern England. The river also functioned as a main artery through which flowed the trade that brought prosperity to the whole community.

Roman Lincoln had fine colonnaded streets, and elaborate public baths which are only slowly being revealed through careful archaeological digging. It has been found that drinking water was supplied in earthenware pipes, under pressure, from a source a mile and a half away from the hill. The dominant industry of this important region was agriculture, the successful development of which resulted in a major extension of the town walls to encompass a well-planned suburb. The present Stonebow stands on the site of the Roman south gate here, and beyond this, where Newport Arch still bestrides the ancient Ermine Street, the advanced settlements of the 3rd cent. A.D. started a trend towards civilized living that was to continue in later periods of Lincoln's history.

With the ending of the Roman occupation the Middle Ages inherited road and canal systems, a labyrinth of sewers, working farms, and a wealth of tile and stone. In Anglo-Saxon times Lincoln became part of the kingdom of Mercia, and after Paulinus had introduced the Christian faith a stone church is said to have been built within the old Roman walls. The Danes made Lincoln the chief of the Five Boroughs of their Danelaw, as street names like Saltergate, Danesgate and Hungate bear witness, but it was to be the Norman invaders whose influence made Lincoln one of the most important cities in the realm.

Lincoln Castle was founded by William the Conqueror in 1068. His purpose, like that of his predecessors, was to create an invulnerable stronghold. Even today the battlemented castle walls inspire awe in the beholder. The building encloses a roughly quadrangular area of more than six acres, with lawns and trees. The walls vary from 8 to 10 ft in thickness and double this in height. At the north-east corner there is a low tower known as Cobb Hall and on two great detached mounds on the south side are the Observatory Tower and the uprights of the Norman keep.

Cobb Hall was added in the 14th cent., to be used as a place of punishment. The iron rings to which prisoners were fastened are still to be seen in the walls, and the roof of the tower remained a place of public execution until 1868. Within the passage of the castle gateway is all that is left of the Eleanor Cross, which was set up close to the Gilbertine priory of St Catherine, where the body of Eleanor of Castile, the wife of Edward I, was embalmed. This was the first of the famous crosses erected to mark the halting places of the queen's funeral procession from HARBY in Nottinghamshire to WESTMINSTER ABBEY.

The domestic architecture of the period is splendidly represented by a building put up in about 1170 and known as the Jew's House. This fine example of Norman house construction, serving today as an antique dealer's shop, is at 15 The Strait and is notable for its superb decorated doorway and chimney above. Close by on the east side of Steep Hill is Aaron's House, a well-preserved building dating from the period when Lincoln was at the height of its wool-based prosperity. It is said to be the oldest inhabited house in England.

In Castle Square there is a faithfully restored timbered building of the 16th cent. which is now the premises of the Westminster and National Provincial Bank.

The Cardinal's Hat, probably named in compliment to Cardinal Wolsey, who was Bishop of Lincoln in 1514, is another attractive, timber-framed building leading off The Strait in company with others similarly restored. Some 300 yds from here stands the imposing 15th- and 16th-cent. Stonebow Gateway of which the upper story accommodates the city Guildhall. The wide central archway in massive stonework carries on the south face canopied statues of St Mary and the Archangel Gabriel. Over the arch are the arms of James I. On the battlemented roof the mote bell, dated 1387, is still rung to summon council meetings. It is believed to be the oldest mote bell in Britain. In the Guildhall itself is Lincoln's magnificent collection of civic insignia, which includes the sword given by Richard II in 1387, Henry VII's sword, believed to have been presented after a victory over the Earl of Lincoln in 1487, and the blade of a sword presented by Charles I in 1642.

Other monuments to Lincoln's ancient story include Greyfriars, a fine medieval building now altered for use as the City and County Museum. This was originally a two-story church, dating from the 13th cent., which in 1574, some 40 years after the suppression of the monasteries, became a free school. The building is the earliest church of the Franciscan order now surviving in England. A further continuous link across the years is provided by the Newport Arch, already mentioned here, which exists as the only Roman gateway in Britain still used by traffic. There is also evidence in the prison chapel of the castle that man's inhumanity to man persisted well into the 19th cent. This is part of the debtors' prison built by John Carr of YORK, where the worshippers were ordered in one at a time and compelled to occupy narrow enclosed pews, which prevented them from seeing their companions, made standing impossible, and afforded only a view of the preacher in his pulpit high above the floor. A more pleasing reminder of the last century is the great bronze statue of the Lincolnshire poet, Alfred, Lord Tennyson, sculptured by his friend G. F. Watts and set in the lawns of Minster Green in 1905.

The most modern repository for Lincoln's treasures is the Usher Art Gallery, on the Lindum Road, which was given to the city by James Ward Usher in the fulfilment of his promise, made in 1916, that a gallery to house his gift of precious jewels, watches and miniatures would belong to his birthplace for ever.

Lincoln Cathedral is the third largest in England, exceeded only by York Minster and ST PAUL'S. Its area is about 57,000 sq. ft. In 1072 William the Conqueror appointed Bishop Remigius to the vast diocese sweeping from the Humber in the north to the Thames, and directed him to build a new cathedral commensurate with the importance of the area. By 1092 the work was done, and a great church some 325 ft long dominated the crown of Lincoln hill. A disastrous fire in 1141 resulted in major restorations being carried out by the third bishop, Alexander the Magnificent, who greatly enriched the stonework and added to the height of the existing west towers. More changes were to follow, for in 1185 an earthquake devastated the structural bulk of the cathedral. A year later a Carthusian monk, Hugh of Avalon, became bishop and it was he who in 1192 began the immense task of rebuilding in Early English style the noble edifice which has endured to this day as the glorious, triple-towered Cathedral Church of St Mary.

The nave, choir and retro-choir are all aisled, each having a triforium and clerestory. The nave belongs to the first half of the 13th cent. and contains a rare black mid-12th-cent. font in Tournai marble. St Hugh's Choir, named after the founder, is remarkable for the profusion of pinnacles and wealth of carved misericords in its 14th-cent. choir stalls. The shrine of St Hugh is housed in the retro-choir, or Angel Choir, which is a supremely beautiful monument of English Geometrical Decorated work. The splendid east window, judged the finest of its period, is filled now with 19th-cent. glass, but the windows east of the aisles delight with a medley of brilliant 13th-cent. figure glass. Shining into the great transept are the two Eyes of the cathedral, the Dean's Eye at the north end, a rose window containing vividly coloured glass made for it between 1200 and 1220, and the Bishop's Eye at the south end, containing a mosaic of ancient fragments assembled in the 18th cent. Another important feature of Lincoln Cathedral is the arcade designed by Sir Christopher Wren in 1674, the year in which he began the rebuilding of St Paul's in London. Above this is Wren's library, in which are kept first editions of *Paradise Lost*, *Don Quixote* and part of Spenser's *Faerie Queene*. Two more valuable possessions, now removed from the library to one of the cathedral chapels in the north choir aisle, are William of Normandy's charter for the transfer of the see from DORCHESTER in Oxfordshire to Lincoln and the finest of four contemporary copies of the Magna Carta still extant. This is the only part of the cathedral for which an admission charge is made.

Modern Lincoln owes its prosperity to the many technological advancements of the engineering industry. A consequence of the great agricultural wealth of the countryside was the mechanization of farm implements in the middle of the last century. This was followed by a diversification into engineering manufacture for general use. Today the city of Lincoln provides employment for some thousands of people in heavy industry while still retaining the character and tone of a long and noble past.

LITTLEBOROUGH, *Nottinghamshire* (13–SK8282). In this tiny village looking across the Trent to Lincolnshire is one of the smallest Norman churches in the county. It is aisleless, with large areas of herringbone masonry, a nave 24 ft long and a chancel barely 13 ft. A few Roman tiles appear in the stonework, and in the drought of 1933 when the river was very low the stone-paved ford made in Hadrian's time was revealed. Harold crossed here with his army on their way to HASTINGS. The ford is said to be the oldest in England, used since Roman days without a break, now almost abandoned. Roman finds have been made at various times, including the perfectly preserved body of a young woman wearing a garment fastened with a Roman brooch. It was dug up in the graveyard and crumbled to dust immediately. It is assumed from these finds that this was the site of the Roman station known as Segelocum, through which ran their road, still known as Tillbridge Lane.

LLANYBLODWEL, *Shropshire* (8–SJ2322). This tiny village, with a Welsh name and within hailing distance of Wales, is wholly English in appearance: a handful of old cottages scattered on the hillside above a swift-running river, a hump-backed stone bridge, a 16th-cent. black-and-white inn and, among the trees, one of the strangest churches in the country.

The early history of the Church of St Michael the Archangel is obscure, although there are traces of its Norman origins. But the present building, inside and out, is largely the work of one of its vicars, the remarkable Rev. John Parker, incumbent from 1845 to 1860, who, had he not gone into the Church, would undoubtedly have made his name as architect, church furnisher or artist. During his years at Llanyblodwel he transformed the church, drawing up the plans, carrying out some of the work himself, and footing a substantial part of the bill. His great work may appal some and amuse others. Certainly his church is unique, especially its strange tower and spire, looking like a moon-rocket ready on its pad. Almost detached from the rest of the church, the structure is 104 ft high with a slightly swelling outline to midway and no break at all between tower and spire. Octagonal in shape, it cost £1,529 13s. 10d. – and much anxiety to the masons – to build.

There is plenty of evidence inside the church of the vicar's eccentric approach to his self-imposed task: the most obvious are the meticulously painted texts which cover almost every available blank piece of wall. One thing he left was the battered south door dated 1713; and another is the portion of a 14th-cent. tombstone, in the porch, on which is carved the figure of a running hare being chased by a greyhound (only the head of the latter is there).

LLANYMYNECH, *Shropshire* (8–SJ2620). Half in England, half in Wales – the border runs through the Lion Hotel – this large village, 6 m. S. of OSWESTRY, lies beneath the cliffs of Llanymynech Hill. The hill is honeycombed with the shafts and galleries of the Roman mine workings which once produced copper, silver, zinc, lead and limestone. In 1965 a party of schoolboys exploring one of the shafts known as Ogof's Hole found a hoard of 33 silver Roman denarii which are now on display in Oswestry Library.

From the top of the cliffs, which from a distance look like castle walls, there are magnificent views in all directions. The 8th-cent **Offa's Dyke** and the subsidiary and less well-known **Wat's Dyke** can be seen, and to the S. a wide view across the lovely Vyrnwy valley to the Breidden Hills where Caractacus is said to have gathered his tribesmen for the last stand against the Romans. On the hills, too, can be seen the monument the farmers of Shropshire and Montgomeryshire erected to Admiral Rodney, said to be a tribute to the famous admiral for buying timber from the area.

LONGDON-UPON-TERN, *Shropshire* (8–SJ6215). It was in this small village in 1794 that Thomas Telford built the first cast-iron aqueduct, to carry the Shropshire Union Canal over the River Tern. Like a long, narrow, straight-sided iron bath, raised on four arches, the aqueduct is still in use today.

LOPPINGTON, *Shropshire* (8–SJ4629). This small village 3 m. W. of WEM has one most unusual claim to fame: in front of the Dickin Arms is preserved the only bull ring still in existence in Shropshire.

LOUGHBOROUGH, *Leicestershire* (10–SK 5319). The second largest town in the county, which became the only borough in 1888, Loughborough was an ancient hamlet long before the Romans came, or the Danes sailed up the River Soar to plunder, burn, and then to settle. A tour should start in the Market Place, the centre of the town's life and of its street system. The Thursday market has been in existence since the right was granted in 1206 by Hugh Despenser, who had inherited the hamlet by marriage from Hugh Lopes, Earl of Chester, who in turn had been given it by William I. The town hall is the only building of interest here, built in 1855, with a kind of double bellcot.

From the Market Place go by Church Gate, past the Baptist Chapel, to the large and prosperous Parish Church of All Saints. Very much restored by Scott in a manner almost obliterating its 14th-cent. origins, the church contains in its 100-ft, 500-year-old bell-tower some of the bells the famous John Taylor came from OXFORD to recast. He liked Loughborough so much that he stayed to set up in 1840 the foundry in Cherry Orchard now renowned all over the world. This foundry also cast Great Paul of ST PAUL'S CATHEDRAL, the biggest bell that rings in England. The Taylor memorials are in the lower chamber of All Saints', and the *Book of the Taylor Foundry* is preserved in a glass case on the south wall. On Easter morning in 1909 ten ringers took part in a feat of pealing, starting at 8 a.m. and, not stopping to eat, ringing 18,027 "Stedman Caters" in just over 12 hours.

The organ case was carved by a Belgian refugee who received hospitality in Loughborough during the First World War, and in the outer south aisle is the Burton Chapel, the memorial to Thomas Burton, the town's most notable benefactor. In this chapel is also a splendid alabaster altar table with early-18th-cent. wrought-iron legs. Thomas Burton, a prosperous wool-merchant, died in 1496, the money he left being used to found a grammar school. A new school has risen on the foundations of the old one just W. of the Leicester Road but the leafy Burton Walks are still there.

From All Saints' return to the Market Place and take the stretch called Devonshire Square to little Queen's Park where the war memorial contains one of the finest carillons in the country, set up in a tower 151 ft high, from which was made the first broadcast of bell music. The climb to the top is by 138 steps, past a small museum. Forty-seven bells hang in the chamber, the heaviest weighing over 4 tons and the smallest 20 lb., made at the Taylor foundry.

Along the Ashby Road S. out of Loughborough are the colleges that arose over the last generation: the University of Technology, given its charter in 1966; the largest training colleges in the country; a college of art and a technical college; a students' village; a campus with an all-weather recreation area; and the modern Loughborough College Grammar School.

From 1400 to 1600 the town was an important centre of the wool trade. In the 1700s it was famous for its maltings. 1800 introduced the worsted hosiery trade with some 6,000 persons clattering away on their stocking frames and, the legs of both sexes being worthy of adornment, seldom working (according to a writer of the time) less than three days a week and earning the princely sum of 15s. doing it. In 1809 Mr John Heathcote brought the lace bobbin here but the Luddites, led by the half-witted Ned Lud, stormed and burned his factory in 1816, destroying 53 bobbin-net machines worth £6,000 in half an hour. So disgusted was Mr Heathcote that he moved his works to TIVERTON in Devon. Now Loughborough is a thriving industrial town full of young and enterprising firms with famous names.

We must not leave without mentioning one of the sons of which it is most proud, the Cavalier poet, John Cleveland, son of a Loughborough schoolmaster, scholarly, witty, one of the most ardent and outspoken supporters of the Royalist cause. In those days his name would sell almost anything, but his writings are too topical to be appreciated nowadays except by keen students of his time. He died in 1658 almost on the eve of the Restoration.

LOUTH, *Lincolnshire* (13–TF3287). Louth is an old market town, deriving its name from the River Lud, near the wooded gorge of Hubbards Hill. Although Roman and Anglo-Saxon remains have been found in the area the main interest concentrates on the spacious Perpendicular Church of St James, a splendid example of late Gothic design, rising to the height of 300 ft. The building was completed in 1441 and the spire added between 1501 and 1515. Twenty-one years later the sermon which incited the Pilgrimage of Grace, in which 20,000 Lincolnshire men took up arms in defence of the monasteries, was preached from the pulpit. Henry VIII was quick to suppress this well-meaning rebellion, describing the townsfolk in his reply to their petitions as the "rude commons of one shire, and that, one of the most brutal and beestlie of the whole realm". The vicar and more than 60 other men from Louth, and as many more from surrounding parts of the country were hanged at Tyburn. The fine Cistercian abbey which inspired the Lincolnshire rising was built by the monks at the instigation of Bishop Alexander of Lincoln in 1139. It flourished until the Black Death almost wiped out the inmates, and was finally destroyed shortly after the Dissolution. All that may be seen today are two gaunt fragments of chancel wall and a maze of mounds and dykes.

The exterior of St James's Church is impressive for its lofty windows, its brave array of battlements, and the east gable with a pierced parapet surmounted by a cross. The tower and crocketed spire are almost equal in height and completely in harmony. Inside there is an interesting modern font in alabaster, and in the north aisle an early-15th-cent. font with a buttressed stem enriched with traceried panels.

Louth is and has been for centuries the busiest cattle market in Lincolnshire, but now in addition to local industries, which include the manufacture of farm implements, plastic sheeting, and packaging materials, a huge malt-silo has been constructed at Newbridge Hill.

LUDLOW, *Shropshire* (8–SO5175). Few towns in England have more to show for their history than Ludlow. The most spectacular approach to the town is from the W., along the small road from Wigmore, over Mary Knoll which rises to about 900 ft. For the last mile or so the road drops sharply to show Ludlow spread over its own hill below, a view that is beautiful in clear weather and magical in the mist.

Anglo-Saxon coins unearthed here indicate that the defensive assets of the rising ground partly circled by the Rivers Teme and Corve had been recognized long before Roger Montgomery, Earl of Shrewsbury and Arundel, arrived here in 1085 and built his massive castle. Some authorities attribute its building to Roger de Lacy, one of Montgomery's chief henchmen, but whoever occupied it during its early years was as likely to have had to contend with fellow-Normans as with the marauding Welsh against whom it was built. Today much of it still stands and the visitor tours a fortress seen by Edward IV; the so-called Princes in the Tower; Catherine of Aragon, when a young bride; Henry VIII's brother, Prince Arthur, who died here; Sir Philip Sidney; John Milton, whose *Comus* was first performed here in 1634; and a host of other great figures.

The castle is .impressively large. The outer bailey is as big as a cricket ground. The inner bailey is large enough to house actors and audience for the performance of a Shakespeare play during the annual Ludlow Summer Festival.

Ludlow: a misericord in the church choir

Within the inner bailey is the most unusual part of the castle: the circular nave of the Norman chapel.

The tower of the Parish Church of St Laurence at 135 ft stands higher than the castle. This is one of the largest parish churches in England with almost cathedral-like proportions. There are earlier fragments but substantially the church is 15th-cent. Interesting and historic features abound, notably the misericords in the choir. The east window in the chancel, 30 ft high by 18 ft wide, depicts the life, history and miracles of the patron saint in 27 separate scenes containing about 300 figures.

The finest thoroughfare in Ludlow is Broad Street where every building dates from the 14th or 15th cents. It climbs from the sturdy, hump-backed stone Ludford Bridge, through Broad Gate, the only remaining gateway in the original town walls, past the black-and-white timbered front of the Angel Hotel, where Nelson was once a guest, to end at the Butter Cross.

Near the church are two buildings of unusual interest. In the churchyard itself is the Reader's House – formerly the Church House. It is part-medieval, part-Tudor and has a very fine three-story Jacobean porch. It is believed that Mary Tudor was imprisoned here for some time. The plaster ceilings are adorned with floral emblems.

Tucked into a courtyard off Church Street is the Rose and Crown, first licensed in the 16th cent. Another hostelry, known to travellers from many parts of the world, is the Feathers Hotel in the Bull Ring, one of the best examples of 17th-cent. half-timbered work in England – and standing now firmly, but far from straight and true. It is believed the entrance door is the original one – more than 300 years old; in the centre of the dining-room ceiling is an embossed copy of the arms of James I, surrounded by thistles, acorns and grapes.

Ludlow is an admirable centre from which to explore south Shropshire: the Clee Hills are only a short journey to the E., Wenlock Edge and the Corve valley to the N., and the Long Mynd country to the NW.

LUTTERWORTH, *Leicestershire* (10–SP54 84). This large village rises steeply from the foot of its pretty 18th-cent. bridge. On the horizon is the church made famous by Canon John Wycliffe, the 14th-cent. religious reformer.

Here Wycliffe lived in semi-retirement for 20 years while he was translating the Bible from Latin into English. Thirty years after his death his writings were condemned and his body was disinterred, burned, and thrown into the River Swift.

The Parish Church of St Mary, towering over grazing land, was ancient even before Wycliffe arrived. There are traces of 13th-cent. work in the chancel and tower; the clerestory and nave roof festooned with coloured, shield-bearing figures are 500 years old. In 1712 the tower crashed down in a storm and one of the stones which fell is preserved in the church; a rather insipid Wycliffe memorial in white marble dated 1837 hangs under the east window of the south aisle; some brasses to John Fielding, 1403, and his wife, 1418, are in the north-east corner, and, due to the fame John Wycliffe finally achieved many years after his death, St Mary's also contains a number of alleged but spurious "relics", which one feels are hardly in keeping with his teachings against the usury of monies from pilgrims. Amid Gilbert Scott's ubiquitous restorations two other things of interest have also been left. Above the chancel arch is a 14th-cent. doom-painting of agitated white figures rising from their tombs and trying to make their way up to Christ, who is seated on a rainbow resting on the sun and the moon, and attended by trumpet-blowing angels. In the north aisle is another painting of the same period which, it is suggested, represents Richard II with his queen and John of Gaunt. It is more likely, according to experts, to picture a favourite 14th-cent. subject of three dead and three living kings – a representation of a royal hunting party faced with three crowned skeletons urging them to repent.

There are some pretty, timber-framed, thatched cottages, in particular a 17th-cent. one in Bell Street, and The Terrace contains a dignified building, c. 1840, which marks the end of good construction in Leicestershire for some considerable time thereafter.

LYDBURY NORTH, *Shropshire* (8–SO3486), lies almost in the centre of a wide, flat-bottomed valley 4 m. SE. of BISHOP'S CASTLE. The square tower of the Norman church, large for a village of this size, dominates the village. The heavy door, in an impressive porch, swings on strap hinges 500 years old, and is bullet-scarred. Inside, there is much rich wood-carving: the pulpit is dated 1624; the screen to the north chapel, the Plowden Chapel, is a century older; the altar rails are 17th-cent.; and the rare wooden, baluster-shaped candlesticks are dated 1640. Above the rood-screen are painted the Creed and the Commandments and the date, 1615.

Lydbury North has long connections with its two famous houses, Walcot 1 m. to the S. and Plowden Hall 2 m. to the E. A fine view of the timber-framed Plowden Hall, built in the days of Elizabeth I for the notable lawyer, Edmund Plowden, and still in the same family, can be had from the road to Plowden village. Walcot, occasionally open to view, is a large brick mansion, built for Clive of India in the latter half of the 18th cent. It looks down over fine grounds to a large lake where Canada geese can sometimes be seen.

Snowdrops grow thickly around Lydbury North, especially in the lane which climbs N. out of the village to join the curiously named Stank Lane, more than 900 ft up. From here the view stretches W. to the Welsh hills, S. to Clunton Hill and SW. to Bury Ditches, an ancient British camp.

LYDDINGTON, *Rutland* (10–SP8797), lying entirely along one street, is a place to be explored in leisurely fashion on foot if one wants to see what English builders at their best could do in the days from Elizabeth I onwards. Several cottages carry date-stones and it is possible to study the change from Jacobean mullioned windows and straight hoods to the classical style.

The bishops of Lincoln had a stopping-place here in the time of King John, since it lay on the lines of travel over their vast diocese which stretched from the Humber to the Thames. The present Bede House was built by Bishop Russell as an episcopal residence in the late 15th cent. and is a good example of its period. The great hall, with its carved cornice, oriel window, and open fireplace, is particularly worth seeing. In 1547 the bishop was forced to surrender the manor to Henry VIII. It then passed in Elizabeth's time to Lord Burleigh. In 1602 Thomas Cecil, Earl of Exeter, converted it into an almshouse. Hence its name, since Bede derives from "biddan" – to pray; for people receiving charity were bound to pray for those who advanced it to them. At the south-west angle of the precinct is a watch-tower built over the village street, known as The Bishop's Eye, and in a field NE. of the church are trenches which were once the bishops' fish-ponds.

The parish church is mainly Perpendicular of the late 15th cent., though the tower and chancel are part of an older building erected about 1320–40. Particularly interesting are the earthenware jars built into the walls, with their openings towards the chancel – a primitive type of acoustic.

MABLETHORPE, *Lincolnshire* (13–TF5085). The principal attraction of this small holiday resort a few miles N. of SKEGNESS is the invigorating sea air sweeping in from the E. For this reason, and because the new groynes costing nearly £2 million have provided a splendid beach of firm, golden sand, the combined watering-places of Mablethorpe and **Sutton on Sea** are especially good for children throughout the season. In addition the 11-acre Queens Park offers facilities for bowling, tennis, putting, a second boating lake, a children's pool and an adequate car park.

Like many other little townships of Lincolnshire its roots go back to medieval times. The only church surviving the onslaught of the sea is St Mary's, a rather squat building with a steep pitched roof which is higher than the tower. The south doorway and the nave arcades are 13th-cent., but the main fabric dates chiefly from 1714. Among other medieval relics is a 14th-cent. tomb with a broken helmet hanging above it, said to be that of a knight slain in a duel at Earl's Bridge 2 m. away. His opponent also died in the encounter and is similarly represented by a stone figure in the church at **Maltby-le-Marsh** nearby.

MANIFOLD VALLEY, THE, *Staffordshire* (12–SK1154). This valley, which starts near ILAM, is for its first few miles an area of gentle countryside with sloping fields on either bank. But from about halfway up the valley its scenery becomes almost as impressive and dramatic as that of its neighbour the Dove. Beeston Tor, a forbidding precipice, is the equal of any rock formation in DOVEDALE; the caves in the Tor have yielded interesting Roman pottery and Anglo-Saxon coins. Animal remains found there, including the teeth of a brown bear and of a hyena, are now in BUXTON museum. Further up the Manifold is Thor's Cave which is entered through an arch almost 40 ft high. The River Manifold, and the River Hamps which flows into it a little below Thor's Cave, disappear underground in dry weather. Their waters fall away through a stretch where the bed is porous to flow underground before re-appearing on the surface in the grounds of Ilam Hall – a phenomenon which the ever-sceptical Dr Samuel Johnson refused to believe until he had tested it with marked corks.

MANSFIELD, *Nottinghamshire* (13–SK5361). Now one of the most important industrial centres in the North Midlands, Mansfield was once a place of only a few thousand inhabitants in the heart of SHERWOOD FOREST. It was the home of a community from earliest times, however, as is proved by the number of remarkable cliff dwellings hewn out of the sandstone in Southwell Road. These are known as the Rock Houses and were fully inhabited in the 1860s, the last tenant leaving in the early years of the present century. Coins found dating from the times of Vespasian, Constantine, Marcus Aurelius and later emperors and the remains of a villa in the adjoining mining village of **Mansfield Woodhouse**, pinpoint the area as a Roman settlement. During the Anglo-Saxon heptarchy the city was a temporary residence for the Mercian kings. In the time of Edward the Confessor it was a royal manor, and remained one until Stephen de Blois granted it to the Earl of Chester. Henry VIII gave it to the Duke of Norfolk as a reward for his gallantry at Flodden Field. It then reverted to the crown until the reign of Elizabeth, when it was held by the Earl of Shrewsbury. In 1631 it was owned by William Cavendish, Earl of Newcastle, from whose family it passed to the Dukes of Portland.

One of the earliest of Mansfield notables was John Cockle, known as the Miller of Mansfield, who entertained Henry II after finding him lost in the woods, and, not realizing who his guest was, served him a great pasty stuffed with venison poached from the king's own forests. Mansfield was also the birthplace of Archbishop Sterne, who was present at the scaffold when William Laud was executed and was the grandfather of Laurence Sterne, author of *Tristram Shandy*. Another famous man born in Mansfield, in 1704, was Robert Dodsley, who ran away to London to become a footman. In 1732 he produced a book of poems called *A Muse In Livery*, which brought him to the notice of Alexander Pope. Pope helped him to produce a play, *The Toy Shop*, a great success at COVENT GARDEN. With his profits Dodsley opened a bookshop, and in 1738 he published *London*, which he had bought for

£10 from an unknown author called Samuel Johnson. The two became great friends and it was Dodsley who suggested to Johnson the scheme of the English Dictionary. Finally Dodsley became one of the greatest of the 18th-cent. publishers, bringing out works by Pope, Goldsmith, Horace Walpole, and Sterne.

The prosperity of modern Mansfield, standing amid the remains of the Dukeries, rests principally on the coal lying under its surface. No collieries are in the town itself, but many of the 55,000 inhabitants are employed in the ones nearby. Mansfield is famous, too, for its hosiery manufacture, footwear and "cotton doubling" – a twisting together of several threads of cotton yarn to make lace, net and quality cloths.

In the middle of the town rise the high arches of the railway viaduct, cutting off the market place from the Parish Church of St Peter. This church has an exceptional Norman steeple but the main impression is 14th-cent. The Church of St Mark in Nottingham Road is worth a visit, since it is one of the best Victorian churches, built in 1897 by Temple Moore. The market place Moot Hall was given to Mansfield by the lady of the manor, the Countess of Oxford of WELBECK ABBEY, in 1752. In 1836 a neo-Classical town hall was added and later still a huge memorial was erected to Lord George Frederick Cavendish Bentinck, son of the 4th Duke of Portland, whose biography was written by Disraeli.

About 1 m. away, on the secondary road to SOUTHWELL, is the enclosure containing the grave of Charles Thompson, who endowed Brunt's School in Mansfield. He became rich in Europe and the East, but after the shock of seeing Lisbon destroyed in the earthquake of 1755 he returned and settled in his home town. He was buried in 1784 in the grave he had chosen because the place reminded him of the spot where he had been standing when he witnessed the appalling spectacle in Portugal.

MARKET BOSWORTH, *Leicestershire* (10–SK4003), was an important market town in the Middle Ages but is now a quiet place, more village than town. It is well worth exploring since it has some pretty thatched cottages and a famous Hall and school. For about 300 years Market Bosworth was associated with the Dixie family, the first of whom, Sir Wolstan Dixie, bought the Hall with the fortune he had inherited from his namesake who was Lord Mayor of London in the time of Elizabeth I. In 1601 he refounded the Tudor grammar school in the market place. There young Samuel Johnson – uncouth, shabby and sullen – taught as second master, or usher, and officiated as a kind of domestic chaplain to Sir Wolstan and said grace at his table. Boswell says of him at this time: "the dull sameness of his existance . . . was as unvaried as the note of a cuckow: and he did not know whether it was more disagreeable for him to teach, or the boys to learn, the grammar rules." The Hall is a fine piece of English Renaissance of the time of Queen Anne, very much like HAMPTON

COURT, in red brick and white stone. The mainly 14th- and 15th-cent. Church of St Peter is set amid trees and has many memorials to the Dixie family and a lovely peal of bells.

Market Bosworth is associated with the Battle of Bosworth, which ended the Wars of the Roses on 22 August 1485, but the battle actually took place on Redmoor Plain between **Shenton**, SUTTON CHENEY and STOKE GOLDING. Alongside Shenton station is a farm-house, behind which is King Dick's Well on Ambien Hill protected by a little wall. Here it is said King Richard took his last drink before going into battle with his crown over his visor, crying "I live a king: if I die, I die a king." At the Sutton Cheney end of Bosworth Park is a spinney called King Dick's Clump where Richard is supposed to have raised his standard for the last time. Near it is the site of the Duke of Norfolk's camp, still known as Dickon's Nook after the note the duke found affixed to his tent, warning him: "Jack of Norfolk, be not too bold! For Dickon, thy master, is bought and sold!" And near Stoke Golding is Crown Hill, the traditional site of the "coronation" of Henry Tudor, when Sir Reginald Bray is said to have found the crown fallen from the dead Richard's head in a thorn bush and to have placed it over the helmet of the new king.

About 2 m. S. on the A447 is the little village of **Cadeby**, once considered to be the perfect village and easily passed unseen amid its trees. On the secondary road N. from the centre of Market Bosworth is the oddly named **Barton-in-the-Beans**, a reminder of Roman times when the land was cultivated exclusively for beans, a staple food. And about 8 m. E. on the B582 is the castle of **Kirby Muxloe**, which was built by Lord Hastings, who obtained "licence to crenellate" in 1472. The building of the moated "fortified home" was begun in 1480 but was brought rapidly to a close in 1484 following the execution of Lord Hastings in London the previous summer. It is open to the public all the year round.

MARKET DRAYTON, *Shropshire* (8–SJ67 34), is an attractive old town, famous as the birthplace of Robert Clive – Clive of India. He was a pupil at the Grammar School, founded in 1558, and his desk bearing the carved initials R.C. is still preserved. Clive, so the story goes, also has a connection with the fine parish church, St Mary's: he is reputed to have climbed the lofty tower and perched on one of the gargoyles. The church is mainly of 14th-cent. origin but has a Norman doorway.

A market has been held in the High Street every Wednesday since Edward I granted the charter to hold one almost 700 years ago. There are many black-and-white buildings and others dating from the 17th and 18th cents., including the Butter Market, the Crown Hotel, Sandbrook's Vaults, the Red House and the Star Hotel.

Market Drayton also possesses a fine modern amenity, the Shropshire Lido which contains a swimming-bath 165 ft long and 50 ft wide.

MARKET HARBOROUGH, *Leicestershire* (10–SP7387). Market Harborough was first mentioned as a place of commerce in 1203, but was created by Henry II long before especially to be a market. Visitors should make straight for the Square, a most pleasing triangular piece of townscape with the steeple of the fine church – a rare dedication to St Dionysius – forming the focal point. This church started as a "chapel of ease" to **Great Bowden**, about 4 m. N., which originally owned Market Harborough, so it has no protecting churchyard and looks almost Continental. The steeple is one of the finest in England, Decorated, with a tower of singular beauty covered with a broach spire and in contrast the building and interior are a little disappointing. Local tradition ascribes St Dionysius, of early-13th-cent. origin, to John of Gaunt, but the Decorated work is earlier and the Perpendicular later than his time. The church bells are rung every November to commemorate the rescue of a merchant lost on the Welland marshes in 1500 and the ringers receive "one shilling for beer".

Just S. of the church is the charming half-timbered and gabled old grammar school founded by Robert Smythe in 1613, which is supported on wooden pillars with a freeway beneath. Under these cool arches was once the butter market, but now both the school-children and the market women have gone. Many of the lovely old houses around the market and the High Street are now shops, but none the worse for that.

Market Harborough is famous now for its Fernie Hunt and owes much of its present prosperity to the Symington family and their red-brick Victorian factory behind the church – where liberty bodices were founded, but now concentrating on soups and groceries. It was historically important, however, as the headquarters of the Royalist army on the eve of their defeat at the Battle of NASEBY in 1645. Charles I returned here twice, once in disguise to join the Scots, and again when they had failed and he was a prisoner on his way back to London.

The largest inn here, the Three Swans, was immortalized in Whyte-Melville's great Victorian hunting novel, *Market Harborough*, and it still has one of the most beautiful and famous wrought-iron signs in England, dating from the 18th cent.

About 4 m. N. of Market Harborough on the A6 and 1 m. W. up the secondary road is tiny **Foxton** where an impressive system of ten locks conveys gaily-painted narrow boats, small barges and motor craft uphill from the Grand Junction Canal to the Market Harborough Basin. At weekends in the summer these locks are crowded with spectators helping to man the gates or just watching other people at work.

MARKET OVERTON, *Rutland* (10–SK8816). Situated high on a limestone plateau and commanding extensive views, Overton is a place of great antiquity, which had a market as early as 1200. The Church of SS. Peter and Paul stands within the remains of Roman earthworks, and

some remarkable finds of the early Anglo-Saxon period have also been made since the beginning of ironstone working here in 1906. Gold, bronze and silver ornaments from A.D. 600 are now in the County Museum at OAKHAM, proving that there was a flourishing community here in the late pagan period maintaining contacts, probably along Ermine Street, with the rest of England and thence with the Continent, mainly south Germany.

The church is mainly 14th-cent. but the tower-arch is pre-Conquest – 10th-cent., the only work in Rutland of this date. A stile in the churchyard is set between two Anglo-Saxon baluster shafts, once part of the ancient belfry. Under a group of trees on the village green are the stocks and whipping post still in use when Sir Isaac Newton, whose mother came from Market Overton, was a little boy living in the village with his grandmother, after his mother had married again.

On a corner of the church tower is a sundial said to have been presented by the family of Sir Isaac, who was born six months after his father died and was so small his mother used to say that she could have cradled him in a quart mug.

Market Overton Hall is Early Georgian and there are many attractive houses and cottages surrounding it.

There is a delightful rural walk SW. to **Ashwell**, which takes its name from the ash-lined stream nearby, and then W. to WHISSENDINE.

MATLOCKS, THE, *Derbyshire* (12–SK3060). The Matlocks are usually taken to include Matlock Bath and Matlock itself, which consist of the chain of small towns running N. to S. down the lovely, wooded Derwent valley. Known as the area of a thousand views, and one of the gateways to the Derbyshire Dales, the Matlocks typify Derbyshire scenery at its best: a combination of river valley, steep-sided, wooded hills, and the occasional dramatic limestone crag and peak. Happily, there is a network of paths which enable the visitor to explore this countryside and to find his own favourite views.

Matlock Bath became renowned during the 19th cent. for its thermal waters which maintain a constant temperature all the year round. At the Grand Pavilion a music festival is held each year in June; motor-boat trips start from the landing-stage alongside it, and rowing boats can be hired. Between the Pavilion and the river lie the charming Derwent Gardens and opposite them, on the other bank, the so-called Lovers' Walks. Coloured lights illuminate the gardens and the walks during September. The thermal waters here are the cause of several unusual features: in the Fish Pond adjoining the Grand Pavilion can be seen rare and many-coloured fish; the growth in the pools and grottoes in Derwent Gardens contain particularly lush vegetation; there are the famous Petrifying Wells, one of Nature's curiosities; and the thermal springs also produce a material known as tufa which looks like a rocky sponge.

Opposite the Pavilion are the famous Heights

of Abraham, given their name by an officer who fought with General Wolfe at Quebec and likened Matlock Bath's eminence to the plateau on which the battle took place. On the Heights stands the Victoria Prospect Tower, right on the crest, offering views over the whole area. In the grounds, too, are two caverns, Rutland and Masson, which can be explored; both were once worked by the Romans for lead and offer the newcomer an easy initiation into caving. In Matlock Dale, just N. of Matlock Bath, rises the impressive peak of High Tor. Paths provide an easy climb to the top of the Tor which gives views of the 1,100 ft Masson Hill and the gorge below.

Further up the valley, Matlock Dale gives way to Matlock town itself and here are the Hall Leys, pleasure gardens where there are facilities for many outdoor sports and a recreation ground for children. Here, too, is Riber Castle, the most famous landmark in the Matlocks. This, despite its battlements and turrets, is not truly a castle. It was built in the mid-19th cent. for Mr John Smedley, a local textile manufacturer who was the man who developed Matlock as a spa. For a number of years the castle, perched 800 ft up, was a school but between 1930 and 1950 it fell into ruins. In 1962, however, a group of zoologists acquired the ruin and its grounds and established there a zoo for British and European animals which is open to the public. Smedley's former Hydro now houses the County Council offices.

In the northern end of Matlock is the Lido with two pools, one covered and one open-air, and only a walk away is the famous Wishing Stone in Lumsdale. You may not get your wish granted but you will have the pleasure of one of the best of Matlock's thousand views.

MAYFIELD, *Staffordshire* (9–SK1545). This old village hugs the western bank of the Dove and is linked to Derbyshire by the Hanging Bridge. It is said that on this bridge, in 1745, a number of Scottish rebels were hanged after the Jacobite rebellion of that year, but the name of the bridge is known to date from much earlier times. Charles Edward Stuart, the Young Pretender, had reached DERBY by December 1745 when he was turned back by the superior forces of the Duke of Cumberland. Evidence of the skirmish that must have taken place in Mayfield in that winter of 1745 can still be seen in the bullet-scarred door of the parish church.

Moore Cottage, now a farm-house, at Upper Mayfield is where Thomas Moore lived for four years in the early part of the 19th cent. and wrote his most famous work, *Lalla Rookh*. Buried in Mayfield churchyard is Moore's baby daughter, Olivia. It is believed that her tragic death was in his mind when he wrote the second verse of his famous poem, "Those Evening Bells":

Those joyous hours are passed away
And many a heart that then was gay
Within the tomb now darkly dwells
And hears no more those evening bells.

The bells are undoubtedly those of St Oswald's Church, ASHBOURNE, only a mile or so across the river.

The Hanging Bridge itself is a bridge within a bridge: the original 14th-cent. arches, grey stone and pointed, can still be seen inset into the wider bridge which was rebuilt in 1936.

MELANDRA CASTLE, *Derbyshire* (12–SK 0394). This was the most northerly of the three Roman forts in Derbyshire – and lying as it does about 1 m. WNW. of Glossop, it is only just inside the county boundary. The fort measures 130 yds long by 120 yds wide and covers an area of 2 acres. Excavations by members of the Derbyshire Archaeological Society have revealed the foundations of the corner towers and the guardrooms. Some finds, including Roman bricks and sherds, can be seen in BUXTON Museum.

MELBOURNE, *Derbyshire* (13–SK3825), which takes its name from the mill stream running through it, is a small town about 8 m. S. of DERBY with a direct link with its Australian namesake: Lord Melbourne, Queen Victoria's famous Prime Minister, was born at the Hall in this Derbyshire townlet and the Australian city, then a small settlement, was named after him.

Melbourne Hall, the most charming and homely-looking of Derbyshire's great houses, is as famous for its large, formal gardens as for the house itself. These were thought for some years to have been the work of André Lenôtre, who laid out the gardens at Versailles, but it is now known that they were designed by Henry Wise who was much influenced by Lenôtre. The terraced, sweeping lawns, the lake, the yew hedges and the avenues of limes form a gracious

Melbourne Hall: the "Birdcage" of wrought iron

Country Life

setting for the occasional discreetly placed feature such as the two embracing cherubs, the little lead cupids and the Four Seasons monument. Perhaps the two features which most readily catch the eye are the long yew tunnel, and the so-called Birdcage, a masterpiece in wrought iron, as delicate as a piece of jewellery, made by Robert Bakewell.

The house itself, which is still lived in, can be visited, as can the gardens, during the summer months. There are many delightful rooms, charmingly furnished, and a particularly fine collection of portraits by such artists as Cornelius Janssens, John Hoppner, Sir Peter Lely and Michael Dahl.

St Michael's Church is one of the most impressive Norman churches in the country, with a fine crossing tower and two unusual pyramid-roofed towers at the west end. The inside is dominated by the huge Norman pillars of the nave.

There was an important castle here in the 14th cent., but now only a part of one wall remains.

Melbourne was the birthplace of another well-known Englishman, Thomas Cook of travel-agency fame.

MELTON MOWBRAY, *Leicestershire* (10–SK7518). This world-famous home of pork pies, Stilton cheeses and the Quorn Hunt, where once to be rated a "Tip Top Meltonian" was to rank as a buck of the first water, has the stateliest and most impressive church in all Leicestershire. It is 154 ft long with a tower 100 ft high and is one of only four English parish churches with transepts flanked by aisles. It represents Early English, Decorated and Perpendicular, the last outstandingly evidenced by an amazing clerestory with 48 windows, the tower and bell-story, pinnacles, battlements and quatrefoil frieze. It is cruciform with eight pinnacles, the bulk of it built between *c.* 1280 and *c.* 1330. There is a beautiful Early English door leading into the nave, with canopied niches on either side. The best view is from the south-west Galilee porch at the west end; very white and clean, it rises over the market town whose buildings are not generally of great consequence.

The one house of distinction is Egerton Lodge, 1829, once the hunting lodge of the Earl of Wilton with lawns sloping down to the river by the bridge, and now the offices of the Urban District Council. There is also a house *c.* 1700 in the Market Place with the upper floor supported and projected over the pavement. Next to the church is the house which it is said Henry VIII gave to Anne of Cleves, together with the manor and parsonage, for as long as she lived in England; but there is no evidence that she ever occupied it. It has a lovely old roof and a three-light window overlooking the churchyard. In the street opposite is the charming Bede House, or Maison Dieu, founded in 1640 by Robert Hudson, who was later created a baronet by Charles II. He endowed it for six old men to whom he left 1*s.* 6*d.* a week. A hundred years ago this was increased to 4*s.* by the Rev. H. Storer, who also provided for six old women.

Those who want to know what Melton was like in its 19th-cent. heyday of "larking", "ragging" and midnight steeplechases, when to be "in the swim" meant at least £1,000 a year spent on hunters alone, and the Quality came from all over the world for the hunting season, should search diligently for the paintings of John Ferneley. A poor Leicester lad born in **Thrussington** nearby, he was charging, and getting, at least £2,000 for his pictures around 1823.

MELVERLEY, *Shropshire* (8–SJ3316), is only just in England, almost where the Rivers Vyrnwy and Severn join, and is chiefly remarkable for its black-and-white church. This is one of only two timber-framed churches in the county: the other is at Halston but has a brick tower. Melverley's church is wood throughout and black and white inside as well as out.

MEOLE BRACE, *Shropshire* (8–SJ4811). The big, sandstone Church of Holy Trinity, with its bold square tower, is imposing enough to catch the eye from the outside. But its real glory is inside. Here is what is reckoned to be some of the finest stained glass in the county, if not further afield, almost all of it made by William Morris and his friend Burne-Jones. Dating from the year after the church itself was built in 1868, many rate it the best example of Morris glass. The three windows glow like jewels and depict the Crucifixion and other biblical scenes including the Garden of Eden, the building of the Temple, the wedding at Cana, the miracle of the loaves and fishes, and the raising of Jairus's daughter.

MORETON CORBET, *Shropshire* (8–SJ55 23), is a quiet village now, about 5 m. SW. of HODNET; but when the famous Shropshire family, the Corbets, lived here, it must have throbbed with life. The village's history is that of the family. In the Church of St Bartholomew, with its Norman chancel, are many memorials to past Corbets including the fine, coloured tomb of Sir Robert and his wife (1513) and, in contrast, a graceful monument to four young Corbet boys, all in different-coloured marbles. Outside, in the churchyard, is a bronze sculpture in memory of 13-year-old Vincent Corbet who died at ETON in 1904.

But perhaps the most striking memorial to the Corbets is the shell of their 17th-cent. castellated mansion which stands near the church, gaunt but still impressive. Begun in 1606 but never finished, it is open to view.

MORLEY, *Derbyshire* (13–SK3941). There is some excellent stained glass in the parish church of this small village about 5 m. NE. of DERBY. Much of it came from Darley Abbey at the time of the Dissolution and can now be seen in the north windows in the chancel of St Matthew's Church, a rich reminder of the skill of the medieval craftsmen. The church possesses Norman arcades, a 13th-cent. tower and spire, and much 14th-cent. work.

MOSELEY OLD HALL, *Staffordshire* (8–SJ9304), is where Charles II lay in hiding for two days after his defeat at the Battle of WORCESTER on 3 September 1651, while Parliamentary troops scoured the countryside seeking him. Now in the care of the National Trust, the house, on the edge of CANNOCK CHASE about 4 m. N. of WOLVERHAMPTON, is open to the public.

The king, who had spent the previous night in hiding at BOSCOBEL, came to Moseley Old Hall in the early hours of 8 September. The house was then owned by the Whitgreave family – and it continued in their possession until 1925. Today the visitor can enter the house through the "orchard door" which the king used that night, and retrace his steps up the twisting back staircase to his room. There can still be seen the four-poster bed in which he slept and, leading from this room, the secret hiding place – a cramped recess beside the chimney, only 5 ft long – where the king crouched during the following day when Cromwell's men visited the Hall. The soldiers came to accuse, without justification and, as it turned out, unsuccessfully, the son of the house, Thomas Whitgreave, of fighting with the king at Worcester. They were unaware that the man they really sought lay only yards from them.

At a casual glance the Hall does not appear old enough to have been the scene of this dramatic piece of English history. Originally it was a typical black-and-white, half-timbered Elizabethan building – it was built in 1600. But in 1870, because of its poor state of repair, the whole house was encased in brick and, from the outside, only the gables and the heavy chimneys declare its age. Inside all is still much as it must have been during the king's stay and the garden, too, has been laid out in the style of the 17th cent., using only those plants which were then in cultivation.

MUCH WENLOCK, *Shropshire* (8–SO6199). The changes of the last few centuries have been superficial in this small market town, so it has kept a great deal of its medieval character. The two most scenic approaches are the roads running either side of Wenlock Edge: the B4371 from CHURCH STRETTON along the northern escarpment of the Edge, and the B4368 from Craven Arms up through the lovely Corvedale. There are splendid views from the B4371 where the ground falls away sharply from Wenlock Edge; and a few miles short of Much Wenlock are a string of sizable limestone quarries, still being worked.

Much Wenlock's most famous attraction is its ruined priory. Originally founded as a convent by St Mildburga in the 7th cent., the Danes destroyed it in the late 9th cent. It was rebuilt about 100 years later at the instigation of Lady Godiva, but was razed again by the Normans. The final restoration was begun in 1080 by Roger de Montgomery when it became a Cluniac priory, and it is the remains of this, with subsequent additions, which the visitor can see today. There remain considerable parts of the west front; the walls of the chapter house, one of them with a

Edwin Smith

Much Wenlock: a carving in the priory

remarkable pattern of interlaced Norman arches; the 13th-cent. south transept; parts of the broken columns; a fragment of the monks' lavatory; and pieces of sculpture.

Not far from the priory stands the old Guildhall, black and white, built on the sturdy oak arches of the butter market. It is still in use as a court and also houses the Council Chamber. In the courtroom, over the presiding magistrate's chair, is a curious inscription, dated 1589, in which the nouns in the top line have to be associated with the verbs immediately below them in the bottom line to make sense. The old stocks, on wheels, are preserved.

Parts of the Parish Church of Holy Trinity are Norman but the best of this work is hidden: the Normans added a tower to the west front after the church had been built. There is a 14th-cent. porch with a room built over it which is kept as it was in the days when it served as the deacon's living quarters.

Picturesque houses abound in Much Wenlock. Those in the Bull Ring are notable; also the 15th-cent. house near St Owen's Well which has an archway made of three pairs of oak boughs.

Within striking distance of the town are two more historic houses which are open to the public: the romantic-looking, 16th-cent. stone house, **Benthall Hall,** 4 m. NE., with its fine, original plaster ceiling and unusual carved oak staircase; and **Shipton Hall,** 6 m. SW., an Elizabethan manor house with a beautiful garden. In the district is **Coalbrookdale,** the site of the ironworks where iron was first successfully smelted with coke and a place of great importance in the Industrial Revolution of the late 18th cent.

MUGGINTON, *Derbyshire* (12–SK2843). Here, 7 m. NNW. of DERBY, is a village with a Norman church – and a tiny chapel founded in a manner which must be unique. The story has it that one Francis Brown, a farmer, decided on a moonless night early in the 18th cent. to ride into Derby. He had been drinking and when he finally tracked down his horse in a field and tried to halter it he discovered it had horns. Brown thought that he was trying to halter the Devil and fainted with shock. On recovering – and sobering up – Brown was convinced that the only way he could send the Devil finally packing was to build a chapel – and the present building, enlarged in 1890 and now attached to a farm-house, was the result. It is known as the Halter Devil Chapel. The Parish Church of All Saints had a more orthodox foundation in the early 13th cent. and contains much interesting work from the two following centuries.

NEWARK, *Nottinghamshire* (13–SK7953). The name "The Key to the North" was given in late Anglo-Saxon times, for Newark, or New Work, lay between the River Trent and the River Devon and was also a point of vantage on the Roman Fosse Way. There is no evidence that the Romans built fortifications here; the first recorded owner of the town was Lady Godiva, the famous wife of Earl Leofric, ruler of Mercia. In 1055 Lady Godiva presented the small township as her gift to the monastery of STOW, further down the Trent. In Stephen's reign it was held by Bishop Alexander of LINCOLN, who in 1125 entirely reconstructed the existing timber castle in stone. The north gateway, the largest and most elaborate of the sort in the country, and the chapel on the first floor, still surviving, date from the brief period after 1139 during which it was surrendered to the Crown. Other 12th-cent. remains are the tower at the south-west corner of the building and the eight-bayed crypt, which lies below ground level under part of the west wing. King John frequently stayed at the castle both before and after he came to the throne. During the struggle which ended with the granting of Magna Carta the castle was seized by the barons. It became the king's again in the following year, and here he died in 1216 from overeating, but some say from poison.

The greatest days in the history of Newark Castle came with the Civil War. The people of Newark rallied to the side of Charles I and the castle proved impregnable. Only at the king's express command did Lord Bellasis surrender, and then to march out with all the honours of war, but the castle itself was again reduced to ruin. All that is left is a mere shell. The west wall remains intact, with a tower at each end. The three large windows in the west front mark the great hall, which was much altered when the castle was used as a residence in the 15th cent. To this period belongs the beautiful oriel window, which still retains the arms of Thomas Scot, Bishop of Lincoln, and far below are the infamous dungeons to which King John once sent men to die.

The heart of Newark is the old, cobblestoned market place surrounded by many buildings of great beauty. The White Hart Inn, next to a draper's shop, is 14th-cent., one of the oldest domestic buildings in the Midlands; nearby is the Saracen's Head, where an inn of this name has existed since 1341; the hotel next door is called the Clinton Arms, formerly the Kingston Arms. In 1800 it was important enough to have stables for 90 horses. Lord Byron stayed there when he was supervising the publication of his first book of poems, and Mr Gladstone made his first public political speech from one of the windows.

The Church of St Mary Magdalen stands close to the market place and is remarkable for having a spire 30 ft greater than the length of the ground-plan. The lower part of the tower is Early English of the 13th cent. and the upper part and the needle-sharp spire with its four tiers of dormer windows are 14th-cent.

Newark is now the permanent site of the county agricultural show.

NEWCASTLE-UNDER-LYME, *Staffordshire* (8–SJ8445). This thriving industrial town, the western neighbour of the Potteries, has little to show of the castle – new in the 12th cent. – which gave it the first part of its name; no one is sure how the "under Lyme" part came into being. The most straightforward explanation offered is that it refers to the Lyme brook. King Stephen gave the "new castle" to Ranulf de Gernon, Earl of Chester, in 1149. It later reverted to the Crown, but its low-lying position led to a decline in its importance in the 15th cent., and by about 1541 it was in ruins. Only a length of its original wall, excavated in 1934, remains to be seen in what is now Queen Elizabeth Park.

Most of the town's history is to be found in the museum and art gallery in Brampton Park where seven ancient charters, dating from 1281 to 1685, are on view. The oldest public building is the Guildhall which dates from 1713 but was restored in the mid-19th cent. The Church of St Giles was founded in the 12th cent. but the present building dates from 1876, only the refaced square tower remaining of the original building. A more interesting church is that at **Whitmore,** about 5 m. SW., which is one of the few half-timbered churches in the county and has a unique timbered bell-turret dating from 1632. **Keele Hall,** 3 m. W. of Newcastle, is a happy marriage of the old and the modern for in 1949 it was converted into a university college and has now become the University of Keele.

Newcastle can claim a number of famous sons, among them Thomas Harrison, who was executed in 1660 as one of the Regicides, and Philip Astley who, in the 18th cent., gave England its first circus.

NEWPORT, *Shropshire* (8–SJ7419). This small, old market town, 13 m. W. of STAFFORD on the A518, is really one long, wide and pleasant High Street. The town is far from the sea and the "port" in the name probably has its old sense of borough or market town. At the northern end of the High Street the road divides so that the imposing Parish Church of St Nicholas, with its red sandstone tower, stands on an island site. The church contains interesting monuments, and a list of rectors back to 1100. Near the church is the Royal Victoria Hotel with its pillared entrance. Inside the foyer is displayed the shell of a large turtle, 2 ft across, which was served to celebrate the opening of the hotel, then known as the Union Hotel, in October 1830. Two years later, the then Princess Victoria visited Newport and its new hotel and, in recognition of the loyalty and warmth of her reception, she allowed the hotel to change its name.

Aqualate Park, nearby, is attractive with its herd of deer.

NEWSTEAD ABBEY, *Nottinghamshire* (13–SK5454). The famous ancestral home of Lord Byron, in a beautifully wooded park 9 m. from NOTTINGHAM. The building was founded by Henry II in 1170 as a priory of Black Canons of the Augustinian order. After the Dissolution it passed into the hands of Sir John Byron of Colwick, "little Sir John of the great beard", who at once set about converting the structure into a magnificent residence. In 1643 the family was raised to the peerage for services to the Royalist cause. The 5th Lord Byron, known as the Wicked Lord, became a recluse after killing his cousin, William Chaworth of ANNESLEY, in a duel, and allowed Newstead to fall into disrepair. He died in the scullery, the only place where the roof was watertight. He was succeeded by his great-nephew, George Gordon Noel Byron, the poet. The young Lord Byron and his mother, widow of Mad Jack Byron, were too poor to live in the abbey, but the poet was a frequent visitor and wrote *Hours of Idleness* here in 1806. He at last came to live in the home of his forebears in 1808, but after a period of acute financial distress and a disastrous marriage, resulting from his well-known eccentricity of behaviour, he left Newstead and England for ever. The property was sold a few years later to Colonel Wildman, Byron's schoolfellow at Harrow, for £100,000 and a further £¼ million was spent on restoration. Now owned by the Nottingham Corporation, it is one of the noblest houses in the county open to the public.

A long rhododendron drive leads to the dignified 13th-cent. west front, set off by a lawn and a lake with waterfalls. The monk's parlour leads directly from the entrance, the chapter house survives as a private chapel, and Byron's bedroom forms part of the prior's lodging. The grand saloon is 75 ft long, with a roof of plaster and oak of the time of Charles II. Among the pictures in this room is a portrait of Lord Byron, painted by Phillips. The bedroom and dressing-room are much as the poet left them: the original paper is on the walls, the four-poster remains where it was, and the table on which he wrote part of *Childe Harold* is still among the furnishings.

The house is also famous for its connection with David Livingstone, who wrote his journals here.

In the garden, at the extremity of the ruins of the old church, there is a monument on an octagonal pedestal panelled with white marble and surmounted by an ornately carved urn, on which is written a long epitaph to Byron's Newfoundland dog, Boatswain. In his will of 1811 Byron directed that he should be buried in the vault below the monument, near his dog; but his wish was not fulfilled.

NORTH LUFFENHAM, *Rutland* (10–SK 9303). A place of delightful views, fine limestone buildings and Collyweston slates. The 6th- and 7th-cent. finds, now in the County Museum at OAKHAM, from the excavation of an Anglo-Saxon burial ground just N. of the church, prove that North Luffenham was one of the earliest and most prosperous villages to be settled.

Luffenham Hall, E. of the church, was built by John Harington in 1538–53 and his son built the large barn, still standing and dated 1555. The Hall was greatly altered in the 17th, 18th and 20th cents., but there is still a hole in the wall flanking the church path, through which the owners used to pass food to the poor. A dry ditch also remains, part of the siege works against 200 Royalists surrounded in the Hall during the Civil War.

The founder of UPPINGHAM and Oakham schools, Archdeacon Johnson, has a brass plate to his memory on the wall of the sedilia of the late 13th- to early 14th-cent. Church of St John Baptist where he was rector. There is still ancient heraldic glass in some of the windows, which dates from the 14th cent. Especially notable is the 15th-cent. nave roof.

In Clay Lane at the west end of the village is Manor Farm, built in 1640, and there is an early 18th-cent. house opposite. Just S. of this is The Pastures, an excellent house built by C. F. A. Voysey in 1901, with a large walnut tree in the garden.

North Luffenham has a fine golf course, where leading amateur competitions are held.

NORTON DISNEY, *Lincolnshire* (13–SK 8859). A timeless village on the wooded banks of the River Witham. Nothing remains of its ancient castle nor of the manor house built from its ruins in the 17th cent., but the monuments in the wonderful old Church of St Peter continue to keep alive the name of the Disney family. From the 13th cent. until the time of James II the d'Isigny lords of the manor influenced the cultural and religious character of the small farming community here. The name changed from the Norman form to Disney, and lives in our memory of Walt Disney, who was a descendant of the junior branch. In its early days the church belonged to Sempringham Priory. It has an Early English nave of three bays, a Decorated chancel with north chapel, a Perpendicular tower, a Jacobean pulpit with canopy, and an Elizabethan screen. In the chancel is a beautiful recumbent effigy of a lady, said to be Joan d'Isigny, c. 1350. An exceptional late palimpsest brass set in a hinged

frame on the north side of the chapel bears a
Dutch inscription of 1518 about the founding of a
chantry in the Netherlands. The glass of the east
window commemorates the Lord St Vincent
whose title came down to him from John Jervis,
the admiral who was raised to the peerage after his
great victory over the Spaniards in 1797 near
Cape St Vincent.

NOTTINGHAM, *Nottinghamshire* (13–SK54
40). This is a largely modern city which has
triumphed over many troubled periods in its
history to become "The Queen of the Midlands",
a prosperous centre for the manufacture of
cigarettes and tobacco, pharmaceutics, leather,
textiles, bicycles and electronic equipment, as
well as its traditional Nottingham lace. The
change from an agrarian to an industrial centre
came with the Industrial Revolution of the early
19th cent. Nottingham had long been a hosiery
town, but it was not until the power-loom and
the flying shuttle that it was truly identified with
cotton-spinning. An adaptation of the stocking-
frame quickly brought to the area the mechanized
craft of lace-making, a thriving trade which
benefited even local architecture, as may be seen
in the unique lace market occupying a large part
of the site of the medieval town.

The tempestuous story of Nottingham Castle
covers nine centuries. Edward the Elder built
fortifications on the south bank of the Trent in
920 in an attempt to prevent the Danes from
infiltrating along the waterway. To the conquering Normans the tall bluff of sandstone to the N.,
with its sheer cliff providing natural defence, was
the obvious site for a permanent fortress. William
of Normandy reached the Trent crossing in 1068
and directed William Peveril to build the first
castle on the hill. During the reign of Stephen it
was destroyed twice in internecine struggles and
rebuilt in 1154 by Henry II, who presented it
20 years later to his son John. When Richard
Lionheart became king and departed on his
crusades he left his brother John in command of
Nottingham Castle and seven others. At about
this time the legend of Robin Hood and his Merrie
Men of SHERWOOD FOREST gained its place in
local folklore: the cruelties inflicted on the
people of the Trent valley warranted opposition
and it may well have happened that supporters of
the absent king took armed refuge in the greenwood. To this day there is an inn with the crusading name of the Trip to Jerusalem built into the
cliffside, with cellars forming a labyrinth of caves
and passages in the great rock on which the castle
stands.

It is recorded that after John became king and
tried to enforce his authority on the landowners
he on one occasion held 28 Welsh boys hostage in
the castle as security against rebellion by their
chieftain fathers. When there were signs of a
rebellion he ordered all the 28 boys to be dragged
from their play and hanged from the castle walls.
Throughout the turmoil of the Wars of the Roses
the castle remained a Yorkist stronghold, until
with the coming of the Tudors it fell into disrepair;

Kenneth Scowen

Nottingham University

but it was still from here that Charles I raised
his standard and plunged the country into
Civil War in 1642. By 1651 the once proud
fortress was an uninhabitable devastation. The
ruins were bought by the Duke of Newcastle
and converted into a house for his own use, but
after many more years of political involvement the
castle was gutted by the mob during the Reform
Bill riots of 1831. Nottingham Castle is now the
property of the Corporation and is used as the
city's main museum and art gallery. It is still
possible to tour the many caves and tunnels
leading into the Castle Rock. One of the most
famous there is Mortimer's Hole, a passage

through which, it is believed, Edward III and his companions entered the castle to arrest Roger Mortimer, the adventurer who because of his influence with the Queen Mother, Isabella of France, almost became ruler of England.

The city centre is dominated by the Council House, a vast building overtopped by a dome which reaches 200 ft from the ground and is modelled on that of ST PAUL'S in London. The construction of this worthy addition to the modern development of Nottingham was completed in 1928. It contains the Lord Mayor's Parlour, the council chamber, numbers of reception rooms, and a clock with a bell named Little John after Robin Hood's outlaw companion, because of its great size. Before the Council House was built the site had for at least 400 years been the place where Nottingham's annual Goose Fair was held, an event which now takes place on the first Thursday, Friday and Saturday of October at the Forest Recreation Ground.

The University of Nottingham was established by Royal Charter in 1948, after 67 years as the University College. The University is situated in a park some 3 m. from the city centre, with the main buildings looking out across sloping lawns to a broad lake. Altogether the needs of 6,000 students are catered for. The existence of today's superb seat of learning is mainly due to the generosity of the 1st Lord Trent, earlier Sir Jesse Boot, who presented the original building. The huge firm of Boots began as a one-man business in Goose Gate, Nottingham and now employs over 1,100 men and women on research, manufacturing and administration in the Nottingham area alone. John Player & Sons, now a branch of the Imperial Tobacco Company Ltd, is another giant concern which began as a small local factory. In ironic contrast to the days when the early cotton workers had a life expectation of 20 years, the denizens of this modern city enjoy working conditions not bettered anywhere in the country. Raleigh Industries Ltd is the largest cycle factory in the world; its products are exported to over 140 countries. Output is in the region of 1,250,000 bicycles and 2,000,000 three-speed units a year.

To all this may be added up-to-date parking and garaging facilities. Trent Bridge, the ground of the Nottinghamshire County Cricket Club, is terraced on every side to accommodate as many as 40,000 spectators. The ancient inns, besides the Trip to Jerusalem, include the Salutation Inn in Hounds Gate, dating back to 1240; the Flying Horse on the site of a medieval hostelry; and The George, which shows in one of its bars the cheque with which Charles Dickens paid his bill.

The stately Church of St Mary's, which is the principal of the many fine places of worship within the civic boundaries, rises 126 ft from the heart of the Lace Market. It is a splendid example of 15th-cent. work and is richly adorned with the buttresses and panelled battlements of the period. The interior is lit by 12 great windows on each side and treasures a glorious Madonna and Child painted by Fra Bartolomeo, the pupil of Raphael. The Roman Catholic cathedral designed in Gothic Revival style by Pugin, lies near the centre of the city; and opposite it is the Playhouse, one of the best modern theatres in England with a lively repertory company.

In the fields around Nottingham there flourishes another great industry, which is the growing of tens of millions of roses. **Wollaton Hall**, a fine example of Elizabethan Renaissance architecture, on the outskirts of the city, now houses the Natural History Museum.

O A K H A M, *Rutland* (10–SK8509). The origin of the name of this pleasant county town remains obscure, but local belief maintains that there is a connection between the name Oakham and Occa, an influential Anglo-Saxon landowner of whom nothing more is known. Most certainly the manor later became the property of the Anglo-Saxon queens, and on the death of Edward the Confessor's wife, Edith, in 1075, the town, with its castle and church, as recorded in Domesday Book, was taken over by William of Normandy. By 1130 it was held by the powerful Ferrers family who built the castle, strictly speaking a fortified house, of which the surviving great hall is the finest of its kind in England. The hall, open to the public, is 60 ft long and 40 ft wide, a fascinating structure with handsome aisles and decorated doorways dating from *c.* 1180. The interior is filled from floor to roof with a remarkable collection of horse-shoes, following a centuries-old custom, perhaps starting from the time when the Conqueror's farrier lived here, of taking a token horse-shoe from every peer passing through the town. The highest ranks are represented here, including those of royalty, in a bewildering variety of horse-shoes ranging from some measuring only a few inches across to others of more than a yard. One of the shoes is said to have been given by Queen Elizabeth I. More recently, one was presented by Queen Elizabeth II on her visit to the county in May 1967.

Oakham was the birthplace, in 1619, of Jeffery Hudson, the dwarf presented in a pie to Charles I at BURLEY. Also born here, in 1649, was the infamous Titus Oates.

Oakham School was founded in 1584 by Archdeacon Robert Johnson. The original schoolhouse was restored in 1723 and is still used as a class-room. It also housed a museum of Anglo-Saxon antiquities, until the exhibits were moved into the new Rutland County Museum, which was opened in 1969 in a building originally used as an indoor riding school. Also displayed in the new museum are items showing different aspects of daily life in the county from prehistoric times to the present day.

The parish church, All Saints, has a 14th-cent. spire and south porch dating from about 1190. The font has a 12th-cent. circular bowl, and a square base which apparently belongs to the 14th cent. In the market place stands the picturesque old Butter Cross with its eight oak posts and a massive central shaft and steps. Here too are the well-worn stocks, a chilling reminder of village justice administered in a bygone age.

On the A606, 3½ m. NW. of Oakham, is **Cold Overton Hall**, an early-17th-cent. manor house open to the public. It is now National Trust property, well worth visiting for its fine Gothic, Elizabethan and Jacobean furniture, needlework and adjoining 13th-cent. church.

From Oakham to **Langham** is only 3 m. along the A606. There was probably an Iron Age settlement on Ranksborough Hill, at the east foot of which this straggling village lies. A Roman bronze statue was found there, now in the BRITISH MUSEUM.

Langham is proud of its 17th-cent. Hall and manor, but the church is the principal feature of the village. Its noble tower and spire are seen to advantage from lanes on the south side, the tower being 13th-cent. with a Decorated 14th-cent. spire added. It is spacious, with lovely windows in the chancel and the south transept by Comper. The pinnacled porch has a stone platform above, once part of an upper chamber.

OLD BOLINGBROKE, *Lincolnshire* (13–TF 3564). In the already ancient Norman castle of this historic village in the rolling foot-hills of the Wolds Henry IV · was born in 1367, son of John of Gaunt and Blanche, heiress of the Earl of Lancaster, Lord of Bolingbroke. In 1643 the castle was captured by the Parliamentarians, and was reduced to ruin in the years that followed. The Church of SS. Peter and Paul stands to the N. of the castle site. It consists of the old south aisle from the 14th cent. turned into nave and chancel, a sturdy, battlemented tower, and a north aisle added in 1890. Of special interest are the two worn heads by the old doorway, believed to be John of Gaunt's parents, Edward III and Queen Philippa.

OLLERTON, *Nottinghamshire* (13–SK6567). The small mining town at the junctions of the Rivers Rainworth Water and Maun is one of the best centres from which to visit THORESBY Park and walk among the rhododendrons and stately beeches of CLUMBER PARK and the Dukeries. Ollerton Hall is built on the site of an Elizabethan mansion belonging to the Markham family, the last of whom died following the Civil War. It is a handsome, red-brick house in the late Restoration manner with projecting wings and a doorway made prominent by large stone pilasters and pediment.

OSWESTRY, *Shropshire* (8–SJ2829). Not surprisingly in view of its violent history, little remains to show that this market town on the Welsh border existed, in some form, before the Romans came to Britain. Man has lived here, in fact, for 2,500 years at least – but rarely in peace. The remains of an Iron Age Fort, dating from about 550 B.C., can be seen to the N. of the town, the earliest evidence of the need to seek security behind fortifications. The field where the Roman Catholic church now stands is believed to be the site of the Battle of Maserfield in A.D. 642, when the pagan King Penda of Mercia defeated

and killed Oswald, the Christian King of Northumbria: this was the origin of the name Oswestry. The town was a frequent bone of contention between the Normans and the Welsh tribes. King John burnt it down in 1215 – and 18 years later Llewellyn of Wales did the same. Owen Glendower sacked the town and almost demolished the church in 1400; and there were three accidental but disastrous fires between 1542 and 1567.

The result of all this destruction and pillage is that Oswestry is now largely a product of the 19th cent. But odd traces remain: in the Norman foundations of the tower of St Oswald's Church; in the original buildings of the Grammar School, dating from 1407, now divided into three cottages; and in the early 17th-cent. Llwyd Mansion in the centre of the town, a well-preserved black-and-white building bearing, strangely, on its wall the double-headed eagle of the Holy Roman Empire, arms granted to a member of the Llwyd family, owners of the mansion, for distinguished service during the Crusades.

Oswestry Castle, built originally by the Normans, was destroyed on Cromwell's orders after the Civil War and today only fragments of the walls remain. But the site has been made into a public park which offers fine views from the top. King Oswald's Well, which is still in existence, is fed by a spring which, according to legend, sprang from the spot where an eagle dropped one of Oswald's limbs after the Battle of Maserfield. The Croeswylan Stone – the Cross of Weeping – can be seen in Morda Road, near the boys' secondary modern school. The stone marks the spot, then outside the town walls, where the markets were held in 1559 when the plague struck the town. Some say the hollowed-out stone was the base of a cross; others that money was washed in the "bowl" to avoid contamination.

Oswestry is a natural centre for visiting North and Central Wales as well as Shropshire.

Two famous men are natives of Oswestry. In Willow Street a plaque marks the house where Sir Walford Davies, the organist, composer and, for some years, Master of the King's Musick, was born. And Plas Wilmot is similarly commemorated in Weston Lane as the birthplace of Wilfred Owen, one of the Great War's finest poets.

OWTHORPE, *Nottinghamshire* (13–SK6733). A remote little village in a hollow of the Wolds, hard by the beautiful Vale of Belvoir. This is where Colonel Hutchinson, the Puritan governor of NOTTINGHAM, "rob'd of every thing which the neighbouring garrisons of Shelford and Wiverton could carrie . . ." paid the penalty of taking sides against his king in the Civil War. Owthorpe Hall was destroyed by the avenging Cavaliers and although rebuilt shortly afterwards is now represented only by the trees and gardens laid out by the regicide prior to his own death while imprisoned in 1664. He is buried in the Church of St Margaret, which was largely restored in 1705 and has an 18th-cent. clock which is kept going for the benefit of workers in the nearby fields.

PITCHFORD, *Shropshire* (8–SJ5303), is reckoned by experts to be the finest Elizabethan building in Shropshire. The massive black-and-white timbered Pitchford Hall is not open to the public but splendid views of it can be obtained from the road from ACTON BURNELL which runs beside the park. A closer view can be had from the Churchyard of St Michael's which stands near the house, at the end of a long drive leading off the road. From there the elaborate diagonal strutting and the star-shaped chimneys can be seen. The Hall was built by Adam Otley, a wool merchant from SHREWSBURY, between 1560 and 1570. In the grounds, in the branches of a lime tree, can be glimpsed a 200-year-old summer-house.

The church, although outshone by the Hall, is 300 years older and contains one of the most unusual church monuments in the county, an effigy in oak of Sir John de Pitchford who died towards the end of the 13th cent. The figure is 7 ft long, a knight in armour, his feet resting on a lion, his hand drawing his sword.

QUATFORD, *Shropshire* (8–SO7390). The remains of what are probably Danish earthworks, two follies and an ancient church are what this small village, 2 m. SE. of BRIDGNORTH, offers the visitor. The red-brick Watch Tower, perched on a crag to the N. of the church is one folly – but this is much overshadowed by the other, Quatford Castle. This was put up by John Smalman, a builder, for himself in 1830, complete with sham battlements. The Church of St Mary Magdalene has an impressive position, standing on a sandstone cliff approached by steps cut in the rock. The story goes that the church was built by Roger de Montgomery, the Norman Earl of Shrewsbury, to fulfil a vow made by his wife-to-be – that if she reached him safely on her journey from France a church should be built on the spot where they met. True or not the church still bears traces of its Norman foundation; and there is good reason to believe that there was a crossing of the Severn at Quatford years before Bridgnorth came into being.

QUORN, *Leicestershire* (10–SK5616). This rather industrialized village, part of what is sometimes called "the cream of the Shires", owes its fame to the non-industrial blood sport of fox-hunting. The pleasures of the chase are becoming less popular in Leicestershire, partly because of the encroachment of motor-roads across the hallowed fields, partly perhaps because the need for this sort of recreation is less urgently felt. A more placid connection with the past is the fine granite church, with its massive 15th-cent. tower and Norman doorway embellished with a double row of chevrons. It also possesses the 14th-cent. Farnham Chapel, with valuable Tudor relics which have belonged to the Farnham family for 700 years.

REDBOURNE, *Lincolnshire* (13–SK9699). The parish, lying off the continuation of Ermine Street, N. of LINCOLN, is entered by a fine stone gateway, with a lion crest and characteristic rural carvings, leading into the 300 acres of Redbourne Park. The old Hall, of which this is the setting, passed from the Carter family in the 18th cent. to the Dukes of St Albans, the lineal descendants of Charles II and Nell Gwynn. The Church of St Andrew has a lofty Perpendicular unbuttressed tower of the 15th cent., rising in four diminishing stages. Against the south wall of the chancel is an incised slab bearing the effigy of Sir Gerard Sothill, which dates from 1401 and marks the last link with Redbourne Castle. Of especial interest is the 19th-cent. east window of the church, which depicts the Last Judgment in vivid colour.

REPTON, *Derbyshire* (12–SK3026). There are few more ancient places in the county than this small town, once the capital of Mercia and now famous as the home of one of England's oldest public schools. The first monastery was founded here in A.D. 653. This was overrun by the invading Danes two centuries later but some 100 years after that, about 975, a new church was built, St Wystan's. This is the church that can be seen today, much enlarged in the 13th–15th cents. when it was given its 212-ft spire, but which still includes part of the original building. The tiny crypt, about the size of an average living-room, is among the limited number of survivals of Anglo-Saxon architecture, a priceless heritage almost 1,000 years old.

Near the church, in the 12th cent., was founded the priory which fell into ruin after the Dissolution. These ruins were eventually, in 1556, incorporated into Repton School by its founder, Sir John Port. Today the original arched gateway stands intact and parts of the priory buildings can also be seen. There is a museum in the cellars of the school, showing the history of both the village and the school, which can be viewed by appointment.

RETFORD, *Nottinghamshire* (13–SK7080), is the main market town in the N. of the county and one of the oldest chartered boroughs in the country. It is divided into two parts – East and West Retford – which are joined by a bridge across the River Idle. Its public buildings are mainly 19th-cent., though the grammar school was founded in 1552. The Church of St Swithun dates from the 13th cent., but was largely rebuilt in the 1650s. It contains Victorian stained glass.

ROTHLEY, *Leicestershire* (10–SK5812). For many centuries Rothley Temple, founded as a preceptory for the Knights Templar in the reign of Henry III, was the home of the Babington family; but it is as the birthplace of Lord Thomas Babington Macaulay, poet, historian and dramatist, that the name is best remembered. The 13th-cent. chapel, with the worn figure of a Knight Templar at the entrance, still stands at the side of the Elizabethan house, which is not, however, open to the public. The old granite church, dating from Norman times, has a massive 15th-cent.

Rudyard Lake provided the inspiration for Kipling's Christian name

tower, with nave and aisles added at a later period. In the churchyard is a weather-worn Anglo-Saxon cross, some 12 ft high, believed to be over 1,000 years old.

RUDYARD, *Staffordshire* (8–SJ9557), is a village whose name has gone round the world because Mr and Mrs Lockwood Kipling chose it for their son, later to become one of the most famous English writers of the early part of this century. The story has it that young Lockwood Kipling and Alice Macdonald frequently came to this village, about 3 m. NW. of LEEK, to walk in the woods and along the edge of Rudyard Lake – and that it was here that he asked her to marry him.

In the village itself there are some pretty houses and some prettier gardens; but the real beauty is to be found along the lake, really a reservoir constructed originally to supply the Trent and Mersey Canal. Two m. long and several hundred yards wide, the lake is now managed by the British Waterways Board and offers facilities for boating and fishing. In some places the surrounding woods come right to the edge of the lake, in others there are small cliffs of red earth; but there are also plenty of places on the lake shore for strolling and picnics.

RUFFORD ABBEY, *Nottinghamshire* (13–SK6464), 2 m. from OLLERTON, is approached by an avenue of lime trees and is set in a deer park of over 500 acres. The abbey was founded by Gilbert de Gaunt in the 12th cent. but almost all that remained after the Dissolution was the vaulted refectory which is now a hall. In the chapel in 1574 the Earl of Lennox married Elizabeth Cavendish. Rufford Abbey became the home of their daughter, Arabella Stuart, who,

because she was the niece of Lord Darnley, brother of the Earl of Lennox and close in succession to James I, died tragically in THE TOWER of London. The house now belongs to the Nottinghamshire County Council.

RUGELEY, *Staffordshire* (8–SK0418). In the churchyard of St Augustine's Church in this pleasant little town, to the NE. of CANNOCK CHASE, is a tombstone to John Parsons Cook. The simple inscription gives a date, 1855, and the statement "His life was taken away". The facts behind that relate to one of the most sensational murder trials of the mid-19th cent. when William Palmer, a Rugeley doctor born in 1824 and educated at the local grammar school, was found guilty, after a 12-day hearing, of poisoning Cook, a bookmaker to whom he owed money. Palmer was executed in public at STAFFORD, taking with him the secret of the poison he had used.

RUSHTON SPENCER, *Staffordshire* (8–SJ 9362), a small village with an unusual church, is tucked away in the north-western corner of the county, about 6 m. NW of LEEK. The Church of St Laurence the Martyr, once known as the "Chapel in the Wilderness", was originally built entirely of wood in the 14th cent. Over the years stone has replaced much of the timber but parts of the original can still be seen, including some remarkable dogtooth carving in oak, dating from the reign of Henry III, over the piers on the north side of the nave. The name of the hill near the village is The Cloud. Rising to almost 1,200 ft, it offers wide views over Cheshire and Staffordshire.

RUYTON-OF-THE-ELEVEN-TOWNS, *Shropshire* (8–SJ3922), must have one of the longest village names in England, and almost one of the longest village streets. Once, in the 14th cent., this was important enough to be a borough and the vicar still has the evidence of this, a fine silver mace more than 300 years old. The unusual name came into being in 1301 when 11 of the neighbouring townships were united into the one manor, but now even Ruyton itself is no more than a townlet.

The long street winds up from the narrow stone bridge over the River Perry at one end, along the side of a red sandstone hill. Many of the small houses and cottages are built of large slabs of the red stone. Ruyton is mentioned in the Domesday Book and its church, with its battlemented tower, dates from that time. In the churchyard are the last traces of the castle built in the early 14th cent., three fragments of the greyish-white, 8-ft-thick walls of the keep. Where the village street touches the overlooking hill at its steepest is an unusual war memorial: an alcove has been hewn out of the rock and in it stands a simple, 10-ft-tall cross, made of the local red stone, commemorating the 22 local men who died in the two World Wars.

RYHALL, *Rutland* (10–TF0311). The Church of St John the Evangelist here is traditionally associated with the legend of St Tibba, the patron saint of falconers. She was the niece of King Penda of Mercia, and is said to have lived, about 1,300 years ago, in a cell where the church now stands. In the 9th cent. her remains were transferred to the great abbey of Medeshamstede, later called PETERBOROUGH, but there is still a St Tibba's Well to be seen near the church today. The 13th-cent. tower and spire of St John's are particularly beautiful; the sedilia are 14th-cent.; in the north arcade is a crouching stone figure of St Christopher, wearing a coronet of fleurs-de-lis; the south doorway, with its border of floral moulding, is surmounted by a priest's chamber, which was once a school.

From here drive 1 m. N. up the B1174 to **Essendine**, so tucked away off the busy A-roads that you are likely to see a golden pheasant crossing unhurriedly in front of the car.

Surrounded by a moat in which water still lies are the small remains of the old home of the Cecils, a 12th-cent. castle given by Queen Elizabeth to Lord Burghley. The Church of St Mary, said to have been the castle chapel, is still substantially a Norman building, remodelled in the 13th cent. and with an especially remarkable door (*c.* 1140), which is often photographed. Note especially the tympanum decorated with a figure of Christ and two angels – more usually found in French churches. The double bellcots are typical of Rutland. SE. of the church is a 17th-cent. bridge with massive cutwaters.

Do not miss the chance of driving 1 m. N. along the B1174 to **Carlby** to see the enchanting little church with its 700-year-old spire, rescued from decay in the 1930s.

SANDON, *Staffordshire* (8–SJ9429). There are two unusual monuments to former prime ministers in this small village, 6 m. NE of STAFFORD. Both are in the grounds of Sandon Hall, the 19th-cent. home of the Earl of Harrowby: one is a 75-ft column, modelled on the Trajan Column, and set up by the 1st Earl of Harrowby in memory of William Pitt; the other is a Gothic shrine, dedicated to Spencer Perceval who was assassinated in the House of Commons. Sandon Hall itself, and its 50 acres of magnificent gardens, are open to the public on certain days. The 13th-cent. parish church contains much that is old and also something which is probably unique: on the walls are painted the family pedigree of the Erdeswicke family, long connected with Sandon. The genealogical trees, painted in 1603 and rediscovered in 1929, grow out of the family tombs below them, the trunks encircled with vine and honeysuckle.

SCRIVELSBY, *Lincolnshire* (13–TF2665). The historic importance of Scrivelsby is at once identifiable with the crowned heraldic lion surmounting the gateway to the 360-acre park, which contains the home of the Hereditary Grand Champion of England. The office of King's Champion was first conferred by William the Conqueror and together with Scrivelsby Court and the accompanying manor became the inheritance of the Dymoke family in 1350. In former times it was the duty of the King's Champion to ride, clad in full armour, into WESTMINSTER HALL during the coronation ceremony and challenge to single combat any person who dared to deny the new king's right to the throne. The privilege is now represented by the carrying of the Royal Standard. The little 13th-cent. church, with modern windows and a tower and spire dating from 1861, is filled with monuments of the Dymokes and includes two figures, of a knight in chain mail and his wife on a separate great stone in the aisle, which date from 1292.

SCROOBY, *Nottinghamshire* (13–SK6590), is a small village, which declined from some eminence in the 13th cent., but has acquired renown as the birthplace of William Brewster, one of the two leaders of the Pilgrim Fathers, who in 1620 were to sail for New England in the *Mayflower*. It is thought that he lived in what is now the manor farm-house; a tablet states that this was his home from 1588 until 1608 and was where he became Ruling Elder of the Pilgrim Church he originated. A similar claim is made for an old inn in the village street, and a cottage near the churchyard bears an inscription stating that he lived there for a time. It is certain that he and others of the Pilgrim Fathers worshipped at Scrooby church, and many of the furnishings, including Brewster's Pew, attract a large number of visitors from America every year.

SCUNTHORPE, *Lincolnshire* (13–SE8910). This large industrial town with a population of over 70,000 has evolved within a single century from a group of small villages including **Frodingham**, **Brumby**, **Crosby** and **Ashby**. This rapid growth was due to the ironstone beds discovered in about 1864 around the area, which are believed to be the most extensive in Europe. In 1967 they produced 11·8 per cent of all the ingot steel and 16·5 per cent of all the pig iron manufactured in Britain.

The centre of Scunthorpe is rather drab and uninteresting, but to the S. near the railway there has been some excellent town planning and modern building. Outstanding are the Civic Centre built in 1962 in Central Park, the Civic Theatre, and the interesting museum and art gallery in Oswald Road. The 13th-cent. Church of St Lawrence has extensive 20th-cent. additions, though the new Church of St Hugh, built in 1939 in Brumby just S. of here, is perhaps more interesting to students of architecture. Brumby Hall has a three-storied, 17th-cent. porch with a sundial dated 1637. Now a students' hostel, it was in turn the property of the Bellinghams, Fiennes and Pinders.

Two m. N. of the borough is **Normanby Hall**, built in 1825–9 by the famous Sir Robert Smirk for Sir Robert Sheffield. The reception rooms and double staircase form a setting for Regency furniture and works of art, and the house, with 40 acres of lawns and gardens, is open to the public.

SERLBY HALL, *Nottinghamshire* (13–SK 6488). In the pleasant little red-roofed village of **Harworth** Serlby Park and Hall is the residence of the Dowager Viscountess Galway. Somewhat gaunt and barrack-like, it is said to have been built by James Paine in 1760, and was considerably enlarged in the early 19th cent. It contains paintings of Henry VIII by Holbein and Charles Stuart by Van Dyck. At one end of one room, almost covering an entire wall, is a picture by Daniel Mytens depicting Charles and Henrietta Maria with two horses and dogs, and the dwarf, Jeffery Hudson, of BURLEY fame trying to quieten the dogs.

SHAWELL, *Leicestershire* (10–SP5480). A small village in a pretty valley formed by a tributary to the Avon. The chief interest of Shawell lies in the fact that Tennyson wrote much of his *In Memoriam* there after the death of his friend, Arthur Hallam. Mrs Elmhirst, wife of the rector of Shawell, had been a ward of Tennyson's father at SOMERSBY as a child, and Alfred Tennyson occasionally visited her, doing his writing in the garden summerhouse since smoking was forbidden in the rectory. The rectory had been burnt down after the Battle of NASEBY because of the strong Royalist sympathies of the rector.

From here take the secondary road which crosses the A427 going SE. to **Stanford** where the Hall built by Sir Roger Cave between 1697 and 1700 is the finest house of its date in the county and is open to the public. It stands on the Leicestershire bank of the Avon; Stanford church is on the other bank and is therefore in Northamptonshire. The house contains furniture, pictures and antique family costumes; the saloon is remarkable for its decoration, in particular the chimney-

piece put in by William Smith the Younger.

A pillar set up in the meadow commemorates P. S. Pilcher who carried out flying experiments in the 1890s and was killed during an exhibition flight in Stanford Park in 1899 after rising 50 ft and travelling 150 yds. A flying machine of 1898 is exhibited among the vintage vehicles in the museum attached to the house. Traction-engine rallies take place at Stanford Hall on spring Bank Holidays. There is a pretty walled rose garden, an old forge, amusements for children and fishing.

SHELVE, *Shropshire* (8–SO3399). Looking at the scattering of cottages and the tiny church, perched more than 1,000 ft up, it is difficult to appreciate that Shelve was once a place of some importance – sufficiently so in the 12th cent. for it to be granted a royal charter to hold a market. That was in the days when the lead mines in the ridge of surrounding hills, the Stiperstones, were being worked. The derelict buildings of one of the old mines, with its ruined engine house, can be seen from the A488. The Stiperstones themselves, rising to 1,647 ft, are wild in places but offer magnificent views to those who climb them.

SHERWOOD FOREST, *Nottinghamshire* (13–SK6660). In the early 13th cent. some 100,000 acres of woodland and pasture on the outskirts of NOTTINGHAM carried stalwart oaks which were in constant demand for ship-building. Today few of these remain, although at **Bilhagh** on an open space just N. of EDWINSTOWE the Major Oak, or Queen Oak, measuring 30 ft around the trunk with an overall circumference of nearly 270 yds, is still alive and growing. Between Edwinstowe and MANSFIELD is the husk of the Parliament Oak, under which Edward I is said to have gathered his ministers in 1290. The largest tree of all is the Green Dale Oak, ½ m. S. of WELBECK ABBEY, which is at least 800 years old and perhaps as much as 1,500. In 1724 a coach road was driven through the trunk, leaving an aperture 10 ft 3 in. high and 6 ft 3 in. wide. A piece of furniture was made from part of the wood removed in the cutting and is now known as the Green Dale Cabinet. Still within the forest boundary there is another famous oak known as Robin Hood's Larder. It is believed, against all the evidence to the contrary, that Robin Hood was born in Locksley in Nottinghamshire in about 1160, and that he was in truth the Earl of Huntingdon.

Sherwood Zoo is at HUCKNALL on the A611.

SHIFNAL, *Shropshire* (8–SJ7407). This small town, mentioned by Charles Dickens in *The Old Curiosity Shop*, was once an important stopping place for coaches on the Holyhead road. A casual glance suggests the town is Georgian for there are quite a number of fine examples here of architecture of that period. But Shifnal is much older than that as the timber-framed Old Idsall House and the largely Norman Church of St Andrew prove. The explanation is that Shifnal was largely destroyed by fire in 1591 and those two buildings are the only ones of note which survived.

Shrewsbury with its two church spires piercing the skyline

The church is unusual in having in effect two chancels, one behind the other, the original Norman and the lofty 14th-cent. one. There is also a dog – a stone one lying under the feet of the stone figure of Thomas Forster, a priest who died in 1526.

In St Mary's Roman Catholic Church is a beaten silver chalice, almost 500 years old, with a curious story. It disappeared after the Reformation, was lost for hundreds of years, turned up in a Yorkshire curio shop and was returned to the church, the finder taking to heart the injunction engraved around it: "Return Mee to Sheafnall in Shropshire"

SHREWSBURY, *Shropshire* (8–SJ4912), is one of the best-preserved medieval towns in the country with much for the visitor to see.

It came into being when the inhabitants of WROXETER – the Roman town of Viroconium – were seeking a more easily defended place to live during the uneasy years which followed the departure of the Roman legions in the 5th cent. Five m. W. of Wroxeter they chose a near-island of rising ground in a loop of the Severn which met their needs; there is no doubt that they carried some of the stone from their former home to help to build the new settlement. The name Shrewsbury is believed to have come into use during the 8th cent. when the town became part of the kingdom of Mercia – and has nothing to do with the tiny mammal or a scolding woman. Scropesbyrig, or Scrobbesbyrig, the Anglo-Saxon name, probably meant the borough or fortified place of a man called Scrobb. The county name Shropshire comes from this old form.

When the Normans arrived, Roger de Montgomery was quick to appreciate that the narrow neck of land in the NE. corner, where the Severn almost knots its loop, was a natural site for a castle and there he built one. The castle remains which can be viewed today, however, date more probably from the time of Henry II, about 100 years after the Conquest; and the building was further enlarged another 100 years later by Edward I. It had fallen into grave disrepair when, in 1790, the engineer and architect, Thomas Telford, refurbished it as a private house for Sir William Pulteney. Laura's Tower, named after Sir William's wife, commemorates Telford's work; the gateway, the postern gate and the main hall pay tribute to the earlier builders.

The largest church of the Shrewsbury skyline is St Mary's and its fine stone spire is one of the three tallest in England. Built about 1200, the nave arcades, of noble proportions, the south porch and the south transept are all of that date. The beautifully carved nave roof is 15th-cent. The plentiful stained glass is reckoned the finest in Shropshire; the Jesse window in the chancel is especially rich in colour. The other major spire belongs to St Alkmund's, built in the late 18th cent. on the site of a medieval church. This, too, has good stained glass: an east window which is an adaptation by Francis Egginton of BIRMINGHAM of Reni's Assumption of the Virgin. The most unusual-looking of the town's churches is St Chad's which stands in a commanding position above the river. It has an oddly shaped tower, its top half a kind of minaret crowned with a dome; the nave is circular – one of the very few round churches in the country.

Many of Shrewsbury's old buildings have been pulled down over the years to make way for new: the railway station is a notable example of Victorian Gothic while the new Shirehall and Law Courts, opened in 1967, and the Mardol Block, housing the market hall, are interesting examples of post-war architecture. But much that is old still remains. Gullet Passage and Grope Lane exemplify the bizarre alley and street-names hereabouts and have changed little from the days of Elizabeth I: quaint, narrow passage-ways over which the leaning upper stories almost meet.

There are many fine timber-framed houses to be seen. Wyle Cop is especially rich in them – Owen's Mansion, the Plough Inn, the Cross Keys Inn and Ireland's Mansion. Another notable black-and-white structure is the Abbot's House at the top of Butcher Row, which dates from about 1450; the shops at ground level are original and retain the wide oak sills on which the medieval shopkeepers displayed their wares. Yet another is Rowley's House, situated in the centre of the bus station; it is now a museum, open to the public, housing finds from Wroxeter. Here can be seen the silver mirror once used by a Roman officer's wife, and her toilet requisites, trinkets and ornaments together with scores of other objects from the excavations at Wroxeter. The town's main museum and art gallery occupy what were the original buildings of Shrewsbury School, opposite the entrance to the castle. These buildings with an embattled tower look rather like a three-story church and date from 1598; in the garden in front is a bronze statue of one of the school's most famous old boys, the great 19th-cent. naturalist Charles Darwin. In the art gallery is a permanent exhibition of Shropshire landscapes. There is a military museum at Sir John Moore Barracks, home of the Light Infantry Brigade, which includes the county regiment, the King's Shropshire Light Infantry. Exhibits covering 200 years of military history are on view and the museum is regarded as one of the best of its kind in the country. It can be visited by appointment.

Shrewsbury School is now on the other side of the Severn in Kingsland, a residential district approached by a toll-bridge. On the town side of the river lies a park with an unusual name, The Quarry, which bears witness to the talents of that famous gardener, Percy Thrower. The splendid formal gardens of The Dingle, near the middle of the park, are Mr Thrower's great work. The Quarry is the setting for the Shrewsbury Flower Show every August.

Boats may be hired for rowing or paddling along the river to see aspects of Shrewsbury denied to the viewer on foot. Certainly the river offers the best views of the two main bridges, the English and the Welsh.

Shrewsbury in fact has a bookful of sights, and mention must also be made of the Lion Hotel, with associations with Dickens, Jenny Lind and Paganini; Pugin's fine Roman Catholic cathedral; the Lord Hill Column, just shorter than Nelson's in TRAFALGAR SQUARE; the Guildhall; the Watch Tower; and the Whitehall. From our times there is the castle footbridge of 1951, the first of its kind, concrete and cantilever, to be built in this country. Finally there is an old malting house in the suburb of Ditherington, built in 1796 and the oldest surviving iron-framed building in the world.

SHUGBOROUGH, *Staffordshire* (8–SJ9821), has been the home of the Anson family for about 350 years, has strong associations with Admiral Lord Anson, contains an important collection of 18th-cent. French furniture, and, in its grounds, has a remarkable collection of garden monuments. The mansion, near the village of Great Haywood 5½ m. SE. of STAFFORD, is now a National Trust property but is administered by Staffordshire County Council who have established the County Museum in the mid-18th-cent. stable block.

The present house was begun in 1693 by William Anson, on a small scale, and it was largely due to the efforts of Thomas Anson, his more famous brother George, the admiral, and their great-nephew Thomas William Anson, that the house was enlarged during the 18th and early 19th cents. to its present size. Samuel Wyatt was one of the architects responsible for the house as it stands today. Inside, the house is decorated and furnished in magnificent style: there is much elegant Louis XV and Louis XVI furniture, fine silver and glassware dating from the 18th and 19th cents., and pictures by such artists as Reni, Sir George Hayter, Reynolds and Nicholas Dall.

There are seven unusual monuments in the garden and grounds. The Chinese House, which was completed in 1747, doubtless owes much to the influence of Admiral Anson whose round-the-world voyage had included a prolonged call at Canton. Then there is the so-called Cat's Monument, thought for some time to commemorate the cat which accompanied the Admiral on his voyage but now believed to be in memory of one of Thomas Anson's cats. The Shepherd's Monument, erected before 1758, is something of a mystery: the name is derived from the marble relief on the monument but the inscription on the base has never been deciphered and the architect is unknown.

The other four are all the work of James Stuart who had been in Greece studying classical buildings: these structures at Shugborough are among the first in the Greek Revival style to be found in England. They are: a Doric Temple; the Tower of the Winds, a reproduction of the Horologium of Andronikos Cyrrhestes in Athens; the Lanthorn of Demosthenes, a copy of the Choragic Monument of Lysicrates in Athens; and – probably the most imposing – the Triumphal Arch, a copy of Hadrian's Arch in Athens.

The River Wye at Monsal Dale, near Bakewell   Pix Photos

SIBTHORPE, *Nottinghamshire* (13–SK 7645), is a bare little village centred around the Church of St Peter, which has a splendid 14th-cent. chancel of the type for which Nottinghamshire is famous, and 20 1,000-year-old Irish yew trees in the churchyard. Against the north wall is one of the renowned Lincolnshire/Nottinghamshire Easter sepulchres. These are the remains of the elaborate and dramatic service which used to be performed in these churches on Easter morning. The sepulchres provided the setting for a commemoration of the Resurrection, when on Good Friday the crucifix was removed from the high altar and placed within the niche provided. From that time until Easter morning the sepulchre was attended by watchers, sometimes dressed to look like Pilate's soldiers. After the third lesson on Easter morning three priests approached the sepulchre swinging censers and wearing square pieces of white linen on their heads, to make them look like women. They then intoned the scriptural dialogue between the three women and the angel. In the Sibthorpe sepulchre the soldiers guarding the tomb are represented as sleeping while the Resurrection takes place. In later Easter sepulchres they are sometimes seen starting up in surprise as the figure of Christ leaves the tomb. Also worth looking at in the church is the excellent alabaster tomb of Edward Burnell dated "made anno domini 1590". It was erected by his widow, Barbara, who is also the third of three wives represented on the tomb of Richard Whalley at **Screveton**, just up the road, whose tomb she was also responsible for erecting.

Near the church stands a fine stone circular dovecot, 98 ft in circumference, of the early 13th cent. It contains 1,260 nesting places in 28 tiers and probably belonged to Thomas Magnus, who owned the former manor house of which only the 620-ft-long moat remains. There is a letter from Magnus to his patron, Cardinal Wolsey, who apparently asked if he could stay at Sibthorpe after his downfall, replying that his house had "but poor accommodation".

SKEGNESS, *Lincolnshire* (13–TF5663). Renowned for its bracing air, this once tiny fishing village, loved by Lord Tennyson and his brothers, is now one of the largest and best-equipped seaside resorts in Britain. There is an iron pier 1,843 ft long; one of the largest swimming-pools on the East Coast; a very popular sun castle with palm court lounge, balconies, and a Continental courtyard overlooking bowling greens; a mile-long waterway threading through the sea-front gardens planted with 100,000 flowering plants including 40,000 wallflowers in an annual spring display; a boating lake, roller-skating rink, paddling pools; a tropical plant-house, vivarium, aquarium, and jungle pavilion known as Natureland; outdoor pools accommodating sea-lions, seals and penguins; two golf courses; and entertainments including weekly bathing-beauty contests, fireworks, treasure hunts and donkey races.

The sandy beach is some 6 m. long, reaching from the holiday camp at **Ingoldmells** to Gibraltar

Point where the Lincolnshire Trust for Nature Conservation have established a reserve and bird sanctuary covering an area of over 1,200 acres of sandhills, rough grazing, fresh and salt-water marshes, beach and foreshore. There is also a bird observatory at this key migration point.

Seven m. W. of Skegness on the A158 is **Gunby Hall**, a deep-plum-coloured house belonging to the National Trust and open to the public. Referred to by Tennyson as "a haunt of ancient peace", it is a William III house built by Sir William Massingberd in 1700, showing the influence of Sir Christopher Wren. There is a contemporary oak staircase and nearly every room is wainscoted. The contents include furniture, portraits by Reynolds and numerous deeds and papers. There are kitchen and formal gardens and herbaceous borders; 1,406 acres of grounds include 15 farms.

Almost next door is the little village of **Burgh le Marsh** with its five-sailed tower mill in working order and impressive church built in Perpendicular style of Portland stone. It consists of a chancel, a clerestoried nave, two fine porches and a tower surmounted by 16 iron crosses.

SLEAFORD, *Lincolnshire* (13–TF0645), is a small market town where the quiet River Slea divides into two channels. Little is known of the town itself until its emergence in the Domesday Book, but after that it became a place closely associated with the bishops of LINCOLN. The Church of St Denis, dominating the market place, has the nobility of a cathedral in the richness of its fabric, particularly on first sight of its grand west front surmounted by the sturdy tower which supports one of England's earliest stone spires; but the outstanding feature of Sleaford church is the wealth of flowing tracery that beautifies the windows beyond comparison with those of almost any parish church in the country.

Another building for which Sleaford is notable is the Carre Hospital opposite, a fine group of grey-stone almshouses founded in 1636 by Sir Robert Carre, whose family is remembered in this and the fine Sleaford Grammar School for its many works of charity in the past.

SOMERSBY, *Lincolnshire* (13–TF3472). This tiny, unremarkable village, typical of many in the wooded hollows of the Wolds, is famous as the birthplace of Alfred, Lord Tennyson. The house where he was born exists as a rambling cottage, enlarged from the original by the poet's father, the Rev. George Tennyson, to serve as a rectory. The later additions, completed early in the 19th cent., include a large dining-room with high Gothic windows and gables. The house is, however, not open to the public. The 15th-cent. Church of St Margaret safeguards a number of Tennyson memorials; many of the fine views from nearby Warden Hill are unchanged since his day.

SOUTH SCARLE, *Nottinghamshire* (13–SK 8463). This village NE. from NEWARK on the county boundary draws attention to itself

Lincoln Cathedral   Kenneth Scowen

because of the magnificent proportions of its Church of St Helen with eight-pinnacled west tower. This, the battlemented nave, aisles and south porch are late medieval, but inside the church is a splendid Norman arcade, very rich and with two bays only. A massive ladder leads to the belfry and a figure of St Helena sits in a niche over the 15th-cent. porch entrance.

From the edge of the village there is a fine view of LINCOLN Cathedral. There are several brick houses, one dated 1700 and another 1739, and a stone dovecot with pyramidal red roof.

SOUTHWELL MINSTER, *Nottinghamshire* (13–SK7053). Visible across 20 m. of the Trent Valley, dominating and dwarfing a small town of some 3,000 inhabitants (called by Byron, "a detestable residence" and by John Byng in 1789, "A well-built clean town such a one as a quiet distressed family ought to retire to"), this little-known mother church of Nottinghamshire is worth a wide detour to visit if only for the incredible beauty of the foliage carvings in its chapter house. It is one of our more recent sees, created in 1884, and its early history is mainly based on legend.

Work on the present church began in about 1108 under Thomas, Archbishop of York, and the minster is almost unique in this country for retaining all three of its Norman towers, the pyramidal roofs of two of them having been rebuilt to the original design after a fire in 1711. The façade, nave, crossing, crossing tower and transepts date also from early Norman days. The capitals of the east crossing piers have roughly carved stories on them, Anglo-Saxon rather than Norman. The nave has very short, thick, circular piers, saved from being overpowering by the elastic design of the tribune arches above, and lit by a huge seven-light Perpendicular window at the west end, which was unfortunately added in the 15th cent. and necessitated the destruction of almost the entire Norman west front. The choir was added in about 1234 and is approached through a marvellously sculptured screen carved with 289 small figures, dated about 1340. But it is the chapter house most people come to see. This was begun in 1292, built without a centrally supporting pier, and decorated in a manner so felicitous by an unknown artist that it is probably the finest example of 13th-cent. stone-carving in Britain. It is approached by a doorway carved with oak, mulberry and maple leaves and buttercups. Inside are more leaves, no two alike, chief among them oak, maple, vine, hop, ivy, rose, whitethorn, hawthorn, ranunculus and potentilla, copied from SHERWOOD FOREST's foliage, or from sketches made on a possible apprenticeship in France. The artist has managed to impart to his work such delicacy and joy that the effect is light rather than overwhelming. Among the leaves are little people and animals.

The glass in the east window of the minster was brought from the chapel of the Knights Templar in Paris where Marie Antoinette was imprisoned. The brass lectern was found in the pond at NEW-

National Monuments Record

Southwell: carved leaves in the minster

STEAD ABBEY – now known as the Eagle Pond – where the monks had hidden it 300 years before on the Dissolution. They had secreted their ancient deeds and charters in the ball on which the eagle stands in the hope of returning to the monastery and recovering them. Four pieces of sculpture are of special interest. The east end of the choir contains the kneeling effigy in bronze of the first Bishop of Southwell, the Right Rev. George Ridding, who was also headmaster of WINCHESTER College for nearly 20 years. Over the door leading to the belfry is one of the oldest sculptures in the Midlands, a late Anglo-Saxon representation of St Michael with a lion, a lamb and a very scaly and well-coiled dragon. In the body of the church is the well-executed Elizabethan alabaster tomb of Archbishop Sandys, who died in 1588, with richly carved figures of his wife and eight children on the front panel. And in the corridor between chancel and chapter house is a carving of a "secular" cleric pulling both the ears of a "regular" monk, a reminder that Southwell was founded as a collegiate church for secular clergy. These clergy did not live inside a monastery but outside with their families. In a chapel off the north transept is a more modern memorial made of parts of aeroplanes which crashed in the First World War. The minster itself must be the only place of worship in which there is a notice saying "Dogs Welcome"!

At the crossing of the main street of Southwell is the 17th-cent. Saracen's Head where Charles I stayed on his way to raise his standard at NOT-

TINGHAM in 1646, and again on his way back in the same year to surrender to the Scots at KELHAM. He spent his last night of freedom here before the long imprisonment which ended with his execution, and ate the last meal before his arrest in the coffee room.

On the south side of the minster is the Bishop's Palace built by Caroe in 1907–9. It borders on the remains of the Archbishop of York's monumental palace covering 1½ acres, started by Thoresby in 1360 and finished by Kemp in 1430. Wolsey, whose seat is in the choir at the minster, came here in 1530 when the clouds had already gathered about him and did not leave until he went to LEICESTER to his death. While he was there he built a unique tower still known as Wolsey's Lavatories.

On Burgage Green is Burgage Manor, where Lord Byron lived with his mother in about 1810, when he was still at Harrow. His autograph is preserved on a wall in the hall. Nearby lived his friend, Miss Elizabeth Bridge Pigot, with her mother and brother, John. Not far from the house is a rustic gate dated 1807 which led to the ill-reputed House of Correction where inmates slept in chains in a dank dungeon beneath the floors. Vicars' Close is worth inspection since it consists of the houses of the vicars choral, who did the work of non-resident canons. It was rebuilt in 1780 and makes a delightful group, with the provost's house in the middle, embellished with a porch.

At the **Easthorpe** end of Southwell, in a small garden, is a famous apple tree which began its life in about 1805 as a pip planted in a pot. By 1857 Mr Bramley, the owner of that tree, was allowing grafts to be taken on condition that his name was included in the title. Patched-up and supported, it is still on view at Bramley Tree Cottage, and is the parent of thousands of descendants in this country and overseas.

SOUTH WINGFIELD, Derbyshire (13–SK 3755).

Just outside this village, which is about 12 m. N. of DERBY, stand the picturesque ruins of Wingfield Manor House now in the course of preservation by the Ministry of Public Building and Works with the aim of opening the manor again to the public. The tall ruins, with the main tower more than 70 ft high, stand on a small hill and can easily be seen from a considerable distance. They make a striking sight. Built by Ralph, Lord Cromwell in 1440, the manor house was once larger than HADDON HALL. It eventually passed into the hands of the Earls of Shrewsbury and one of its most famous guests was Mary Queen of Scots, imprisoned there four times between 1569 and 1584. It was the scene of much fighting during the Civil War, changing hands twice, and in 1646 the Parliamentarians made it unhabitable – and so it has remained. It is, in fact, surprising how much of it still stands – the gatehouse and barn, the banqueting hall and the crypt, and the remains of many of the ancillary buildings, including the apartments in which Queen Mary was held.

SPALDING, Lincolnshire (13–TF2422).

More than half the acreage of bulbs grown in England, often surpassing the famous fields of Holland in a blaze of extraordinary beauty, is concentrated on an area of the Lincolnshire Fens around Spalding. The Dutch character of this important agricultural town is enhanced by the River Welland flowing through its centre like a highway. The seven bridges, principal of which is the High Bridge, rebuilt in 1838, invite pleasant walks among the many historic buildings along the river bank. One of these, Ayscoughfee Hall, dates from the early 15th cent. and now serves as a museum and recreation centre for the public. The Hall was once the home of Maurice Johnson, who in 1710 founded the Gentlemen's Society of Spalding, a social club designed to encourage the study of scientific and literary subjects and the forerunner of the Society of Antiquaries. The Spalding Gentlemen's Society, with its library and museum of antiquities, is now housed in a building in Broad Street. It also owns the Bird Museum in Red Lion Street from which many hundreds of specimens have now been transferred to the Hall. Superbly tended grounds present fine views of the Hall itself, with its long galleried porch in mellow stone and two-storied bay windows surmounted by Dutch gables. Fresh green lawns, tennis courts, aviaries and a small aquarium merge peacefully into a landscape dignified by yew hedges and a yew tunnel.

Near are several ancient inns, of which the White Horse with its bold frontage and thatched roof is the most attractive architecturally, and the White Hart the oldest, tracing its origin back to 1377. The 13th-cent. Church of SS. Mary and Nicholas is impressive and owes much to the painstaking restoration carried out by Sir Gilbert Scott. The district of which Spalding is the centre is the most fertile in England, renowned for its output of sugar beet and potatoes; above all the tulips, daffodils, narcissi and hyacinths in a vast carpet of breathtaking colour attract visitors from all parts of the world. The culminating glory is the Spalding Flower Parade, held each year at the beginning of May, when over 6 million tulip blooms are used to decorate floats.

SPILSBY, Lincolnshire (13–TF4066).

A pleasant little market town on the edge of the Wolds and overlooking an expanse of marsh and fens towards the North Sea. The graceful market cross, with its restored centre part and 600-year-old base, denotes the town's receipt of its charter through Sir William de Willoughby in the 14th cent. With the merging of the Willoughby and d'Eresby families the parish church became for many centuries the repository of their memorials, the oldest of these being the stone tomb of John, 2nd Baron Willoughby d'Eresby, who died in 1349, three years after he had fought at Crécy. Also in the church is a tablet in remembrance of Sir John Franklin, the Spilsby-born explorer, who met his death in 1847 in the Arctic while in command of the expedition which first discovered the North West Passage. A statue of him stands in the Market Place. Much of the old church has been lost in renovations, but the unusual 15th-cent. tower in green sandstone remains.

STAFFORD, *Staffordshire* (8–SJ9223). The county town, Stafford has a history going back 1,200 years. It is mentioned in the Domesday Book of 1086 as a borough; it had a market in 1230; and it has been represented in Parliament since 1295. But its fame in the wider world rests on its being the birthplace of the world's most renowned angler, Izaak Walton. He was born here in 1593 and although he left for London to become an apprentice, he always remembered his native town. At **Shallowford**, 5 m. NE. of the town, the Borough Council have taken over the trusteeship of the Izaak Walton Cottage which was opened as a museum in 1924. This was the farm Walton left to Stafford with the stipulation that the rent should be used each year to apprentice two poor boys, provide a marriage portion for a servant girl, and pay for coal for the needy. The small black-and-white cottage has been burnt down twice since 1924, but it has been carefully restored to as near the original as possible.

Stafford has connections with another famous Englishman: playwright Richard Brinsley Sheridan was its M.P. from 1790 to 1806.

There are a number of buildings in the town which are worth a visit. The Church of St Mary in a garden of remembrance just behind the main shopping street, is striking for its unusual octagonal tower in dark grey stone. In the curiously shaped Norman font, Izaak Walton was baptized. A white bust in the north aisle is inscribed "Izaak Walton, Piscator". It was around this site, at a crossing place over the River Sow, that the town began to grow. Stafford is a contraction of Staith-ford – a ford by a landing place. The story is a shadowy one of a prince of Mercia, Bertelin, repenting of his sins and building a hermitage about A.D. 700; of a church being eventually built on the same spot, to be followed by the building of the present church late in the 12th cent.

Close by St Mary's is Stafford's oldest house, the handsome, four-story, timbered High House, where Charles I and Prince Rupert stayed for three nights in September 1642 while recruiting. The house, which is excellently preserved, probably dates from the mid-16th cent., and the beams were shaped from locally grown trees.

Stafford once had two castles. William the Conqueror built one in the north-west part of the town. One of his barons, Robert de Stafford, built his on a hill to the W. of the town, overlooking the present M6 and the A518 from NEWPORT. William's disappeared centuries ago; Robert's was rebuilt in the mid-14th cent., stood until its demolition by the Parliamentary forces when they captured it in 1643, was rebuilt once more early in the 19th cent. – and is again a ruin, its gaunt remains approachable only on foot.

Another building certain to catch the eye is the Royal Brine Baths, black-and-white but dating only from 1892. Stafford has large salt deposits,

at a depth of 400 ft, found by accident during the 19th cent. when the council was searching for new sources of drinking water. The salt is extracted as brine – and the unusual amenity of brine swimming is available at these baths.

Two more of Stafford's buildings should be mentioned: the small Church of St Chad, tucked between the shops in Greengate Street, and possessing a fine Norman chancel arch; and the 17th-cent. Noel Almshouses in Mill Street. Several factories continue to make shoes, for centuries the town's staple manufacture; they have today been joined by other types of industry, such as English Electric's concrete and glass complex on the LICHFIELD road, on the outskirts of the town.

STAMFORD, *Lincolnshire* (13–TF0207). This quiet grey town, richly fashioned from mellowed local stone, is one of the finest examples of sustained architectural dignity in England. In Danish times it was selected capital of the Fens and one of the Five Boroughs of the Danelaw. Its charter was granted by Henry III in 1254, with the start of ecclesiastical building. Much damage was done during the Wars of the Roses in the 15th cent., but gradually present-day Stamford began to emerge. It has many ancient churches, Queen Anne houses and Georgian mansions, with vaulted crypts and stone-tiled roofs to mark the ages in between. Groups of almshouses, known as "callises", were founded all about the town by rich wool merchants, who traded with France through Calais. One of these old people's hospitals is the almshouse near the bridge over the River Welland, which was built by Lord Burghley in 1597; the best preserved is Browne's Hospital in Broad Street, a superb foundation endowed by William Browne in the reign of Henry VII and called the Hospital of All Saints. In the little chapel here there are a Tudor screen in excellent condition and much stained glass of considerable beauty. The audit room of the hospital contains a magnificent 16th-cent. refectory table and distinguished carved bench-ends. The oldest building in Stamford is the ruined chapel of St Leonard's Priory, founded in the 7th cent. by Wilfrid, Bishop of York.

In the 14th cent. some students quarrelled with the authorities at OXFORD and established alternative colleges at NORTHAMPTON and Stamford. When, in 1336, their differences were made up and the students returned to Oxford, they left behind them the association of names in Brasenose Hall and the impressive gateway, a pointed arch in the wall of the ancient grammar school, which still survives.

The Church of St Mary is built around a 13th-cent. tower, with a 163-ft spire added a century later. Most of the nave was rebuilt in the 15th cent. as was the notable chapel of the golden choir, so called because of the stars of gold studding the beautiful painted roof, where each star frames a laughing or grotesque face. The golden choir is completed by a modern east window ascribed to Christopher Whall and portrays the Madonna with an archangel. The two lesser lights show Adam carrying a spade and Eve a distaff. Among other churches of architectural interest is All Saints, dominating Red Lion Square, of which the great tower and spire are Perpendicular and most of the work inside is 13th-cent. The impressive timbered chancel roof is adorned with painted angels with outspread golden wings.

Daniel Lambert, the biggest Englishman ever, lies buried in the churchyard of St Martin's, near the gateway to Burghley Park. When he died in 1809, aged 39 and 5 ft 11 in. tall, he weighed nearly 53 stone. Some of his clothing may be seen by arrangement with Stamford Corporation. Sir Malcolm Sargent is also buried at Stamford.

For Burghley House *see* STAMFORD BARON, Huntingdonshire.

STANTON-ON-THE-WOLDS, *Nottinghamshire* (13–SK6330). Nearly deserted since the depopulation of the windswept Wolds, the tiny Church of All Saints stands alone and lost in the trees. The Norman masonry of the west side can still be seen though it is much overgrown, and there is a badly preserved Norman font.

There are grand views of the Trent Valley from the 18-hole golf course. From a house that then stood close to the church Colonel Hutchinson made a spectacular escape when surprised by a party of Royalists during the Civil War. The house belonged to William Needham, governor of LEICESTER and a colonel in the Parliamentary forces.

STAUNTON HAROLD, *Leicestershire* (10–SK3721). Approach Staunton Harold along the road giving a view from due E. The group comprising the house, chapel and lakes seen from this angle is unsurpassed anywhere else in England. The Harold in its name derives from an owner in Anglo-Saxon times and it was given by William the Conqueror to Henry de Ferrariis. It passed by the marriage of Margaret de Staunton to Ralph Shirley in 1423 into the Shirley family, but the Ferrers title was called out of abeyance by Charles II in gratitude for the family's loyalty during the Civil War. The Ferrers family have thus been the owners since the time of the Conqueror. It is one of the most beautiful country houses in Leicestershire, now a Cheshire Home for the Disabled.

The 1st Earl had 27 children, and was the patron of Robert Bakewell, who fashioned for him the magnificent wrought-iron screen at the chancel entrance to the church. The same earl also laid out magnificent formal gardens, swept away 70 years later by the 5th Earl who transformed the canal into a lake. It was also Washington, 5th Earl Ferrers, who built the present large and beautifully proportioned house. It dates from 1770 but incorporates part of the older house, a Palladian north-east front designed by Inigo Jones, probably dating from the second quarter of the 17th cent.

The church is unique and one of the most perfect things in the county. It is now the property of the National Trust and a place of pilgrimage, architecturally one of the most unspoilt buildings in Leicestershire. It was founded by Robert Shirley as an act of defiance against the Commonwealth at a time when new churches in England were rare. Over the doorway, guarded by two angels, an inscription tells the story: "In the year 1653 When all things Sacred were throughout ye nation Either demolisht or profaned Sir Robert Shirley, Barronet, Founded this church; Whose singular praise it is To have done the best things in ye worst times, and hoped them in the most callamitous." Built in the best Perpendicular style of two centuries earlier it has been little altered and retains its contemporary fittings. Since the church was not meant to be a showpiece, these are endearingly humble. Sir Robert Shirley was imprisoned in THE TOWER many times for plotting against the Commonwealth and finally died there aged only 28. He was brought back from London to be buried in the church he had built. Along the chancel is an inscription: "Sir Robert Shirley Baronet Founder of this church anno domini 1653 on whose soul God hath mercy." The church and fittings were finished nine years after his death.

STEETLEY, *Derbyshire* (13–SK5377), is a small, seemingly unremarkable village on Derbyshire's north-east boundary, almost in Yorkshire. Yet here is to be found what Sir Nikolaus Pevsner describes as "the richest example of Norman architecture in Derbyshire". Steetley Chapel is tiny, only 52 ft long by 15 ft wide, yet the quality of the 12th-cent. decoration of the interior stonework, and its lavishness, is of a kind rarely found in Norman churches in England.

STOKE DRY, *Rutland* (10–SP8597), is a hamlet with a small church set on a steep hillside. It looks over the 400-acre sheet of water opened in 1940 to make the Eye Brook Reservoir, a fine unofficial wildfowl refuge with many rare ducks and waders on passage, and in winter the heron and the Canada goose.

The Church of St Andrew is of the simple country type, but full of curious features and furnishings. Externally it is mainly 15th-cent. Perpendicular except for a 13th-cent. west tower. The interior has an early-14th-cent. arcade on the north side and an early-13th-cent. one on the south side. The mural paintings should not be overlooked and the barbaric Norman decoration on the responds of the chancel arch are worth a close examination. From the middle of the 15th cent., when Everard Digby of Tilton married the heiress to Stoke Dry, the Digby family made it their principal seat until the early 17th cent. There is a splendid alabaster table-tomb in the chancel bearing the recumbent figures of Sir Kenelm Digby (d. 1590) and his wife Anne (d. 1602). Standing against the sides of the tomb are the figures of their children, delightfully carved.

The Digby home is now no more, but it was the house of the infamous Sir Everard Digby who financed Guy Fawkes and the Gunpowder Plot. He was hanged for his part in the conspiracy and there is no memorial to him in the church.

STOKE GOLDING, *Leicestershire* (10–SP 3997). One of the villages on the edge of the famous Bosworth Field, near Crown Hill, Stoke Golding contains a very small church, with the most beautiful detail of any in the county. It is a noble edifice, with two naves of equal width, length and height, and a fine west tower and spire. Its arcade and windows are unrestored, and the clustered pillars have elaborately carved capitals thick with foliage and the heads of knights and ladies supporting the finely moulded arches. In the chancel is possibly the most beautiful of any five-light geometric window.

The fabric of the church is mainly 13th-cent. with earlier and later work. It is certainly worth a visit.

STOKE-ON-TRENT, *Staffordshire* (8–SJ 8747). The present Stoke-on-Trent came into being in 1910 when the then Stoke-upon-Trent was combined with five adjoining towns: **Tunstall, Burslem, Hanley, Fenton** and **Longton**. But long before then the area was collectively "The Potteries". Excavations in the city have established that pottery was made here during the Roman occupation: flagons, vases and platters of remarkable quality, dating from the 1st cent., can be seen in the new museum in Hanley, which also possesses one of the world's finest collections of pottery and porcelain. However, even earlier pottery has been found within the city boundary, including an Early Bronze Age (1700 B.C.) beaker and an incense-cup from roughly the same period.

Most of the great names in pottery which are famous today – Wedgwood, Minton, Spode, Coalport (originally a Shropshire firm) – date from the late 18th cent. The present factories can be visited if application is made direct to the firm concerned.

Stoke-upon-Trent was only a village round a church with 11th-cent. origins until the Industrial Revolution. The present church of St Peter ad Vincula was built between 1826 and 1830 but there is part of an Anglo-Saxon cross in the churchyard; and in the chancel a memorial tablet to Josiah Wedgwood, with a portrait medallion in high relief by Flaxman. Wedgwood is also the subject for the best known statue in the Potteries; the bronze figure of the master potter, appraising one of his own vases, greets the visitor at the railway station.

In Tunstall, most northerly of the six towns, the Primitive Methodist movement was founded by Hugh Bourne and William Clowes and the first chapel was built there in 1811, next to the present site. Bourne's home, Ford Hayes Farm, Bucknall, still stands.

Burslem was Wedgwood's birthplace, in 1730, and his association with the town is commemorated by the Wedgwood Memorial Institute, built on the site of his first factory. Burslem has had three town halls, the most interesting of which is the slightly oriental-looking second, now a public library, with its gilded angel surmounting the clock tower.

Hanley's most famous son, Arnold Bennett,

Josiah Wedgwood & Sons

Stoke-on-Trent: a statue of Josiah Wedgwood stands outside the modern factory at Barlaston

was born in Hope Street in 1867 and later lived for brief periods in Dain Street and Newport Lane in Burslem, before the family finally settled in 1880 in a house in Waterloo Road, Cobridge, the suburb which links Burslem and Hanley. The house is now the Bennett Museum, containing drawings and other personal relics. The museum supplies a leaflet which matches the fictitious names Bennett gave to the towns, villages, streets and buildings mentioned in his novels with their originals. Hanley was the birthplace of another famous Englishman, Reginald Mitchell, the designer of the Spitfire fighter, and his association with the town is commemorated by the Mitchell Memorial Youth Centre in Broad Street.

Stoke is not renowned for ancient buildings but it has one small gem: Ford Green Hall in Smallthorne, a 16th-cent. timber-framed manor house which has been restored with period furniture and domestic utensils and is open to the public.

STOKESAY, *Shropshire* (8–SO4381). The castle and the church stand side by side, separated only by the moat; at a distance the visitor could take the squat, embattled church tower for the castle. A little way off the A49, about 1 m. S. of Craven Arms, Stokesay Castle is one of the earliest fortified manor houses in England and is in a remarkable state of preservation. It can be freely visited.

The castle is approached through a black-and-white gatehouse, with gabled stone roof and overhanging story. The contrast with the main castle buildings across the courtyard, two stone towers joined by a long, gabled banqueting hall, is marked. The great hall was built towards the end of the 13th cent. and is remarkable for the size of its windows; few families risked having windows so large in those times. Also unlike most unhomely castle chambers is the gracious, oak-panelled drawing-room approached by an outside staircase. Happily the castle avoided damage in the Civil War when those garrisoning it for Charles I surrendered after brief resistance.

The church, which, with the castle, is set beside a small lake, has a Norman doorway but was largely rebuilt in the mid-17th cent. Nearby is the cast-iron bridge over the River Onny, one of Thomas Telford's minor works.

STONE, *Staffordshire* (8–SJ9034), a pleasant old town beside the River Trent, is the birthplace of one of England's most famous admirals, John Jervis, who, after helping to win the battle off the Cape St Vincent in 1797, became the Earl St Vincent. His imposing mausoleum is in the parish churchyard. Tradition has it that the town took its name from the cairn of stones erected over the bodies of two Mercian princes who were killed by their pagan father, King Wulf here, in the 7th cent., for embracing Christianity. They are commemorated in a window in the 18th-cent. parish church.

There was an Augustinian priory at Stone in the 12th cent. and fragments of the cloisters and an arch can be seen in Abbey Street, near the churchyard. This and the pleasing long High Street apart, Stone's main interest for the visitor lies in the country on its doorstep, which includes Tittensor Chase, a stretch of heath and woodland well served with footpaths. Here, too, are the "Petrifactions"; the water of a stream which runs through a wooded hollow has a strange petrifying effect on plant life.

This is also a nursery area. One, which covers 513 acres, including 100 acres of nursery stock, is one of the largest in England. Millions of forest trees, ornamental trees, roses and shrubs are grown there – but one tree is not for sale, a huge weeping birch reputed to be more than 120 years old

STONEY MIDDLETON, *Derbyshire* (12–SK2275). One of the few completely octagonal churches in the country stands in this small village, whose other remarkable feature is its setting among the often towering limestone crags and cliffs about 4 m. N. of BAKEWELL. There are quarries here – and every tree for miles around is coated with white dust so that at night the effect is of a ghostly forest. There are two wells in the square in front of the church which are blessed and dressed each year in August in accordance with the custom peculiar to Derbyshire. The dressing, as in other villages, takes the form of an intricate reproduction in thousands of flower petals, leaves, mosses, fir cones and tiny pieces of bark of a biblical scene. Many of the pictures are as much as 8 to 10 ft tall and are the product of hours of painstaking work on the part of the villagers.

STOTTESDON, *Shropshire* (8–SO6782). Men have worshipped in the Church of St Mary in this tiny village, hidden in the lanes about 4 m. N. of CLEOBURY MORTIMER, for perhaps 900 years. And for all that time they must have gazed up at the tympanum and wondered why two of the crudely carved animals on it stand on their heads while the third stands normally. Only the Anglo-Saxon mason – or it may have been a Norman – could give the answer. The animals are actually on the stone lintel, the tympanum proper being carved with a haphazard group of saltire crosses, a bearded Norman head being at the top of the arch.

The tympanum, which is over the west doorway, now an inner doorway inside the tower, the tower itself, the arcaded nave and the font, all Norman, make this one of the most interesting churches in the county.

STOW, *Lincolnshire* (13–SK8981). An obscure, straggling village between LINCOLN and GAINSBOROUGH, occupying what is believed to be the site of the Roman station of Sidnacester. The earliest church here is said to have been built by King Ecgfrith of Northumbria in A.D. 678 to commemorate a miracle. While his wife, St Ethelreda, foundress of ELY, was in flight from him following a quarrel she stopped at this place and drove her staff into the ground, whereupon it took root and became an ash tree. King Ecgfrith on learning of this commanded that a church should be built here in respectful recognition of the event. This church was destroyed by the Danes in about 870 and remained a ruin until *c.* 1040 when it was rebuilt by Eadnoth, Bishop of Dorchester, with monetary help from Leofric, Earl of Mercia, and another determined woman, known to us as Lady Godiva, his wife. The church has been beautifully restored and is especially notable for its central tower, which springs directly from the ground to accord with the original 11th-cent. piers. The interior is a vista of great arches, the round-headed Norman alternating with the 15th-cent. pointed arches framing the original masonry.

Stow church was once the cathedral of the diocese of Lindsey, and is still known as the Dowager Minster of Lincoln.

STOWE-BY-CHARTLEY, *Staffordshire* (8–SK0027). Here, 7 m. NE. of STAFFORD, are the

Tamworth Castle stands at the junction of two rivers

ruined towers of the original Chartley Castle, now much overgrown, built in 1220 by the Crusader, Ranulf de Blundeville, Earl of Chester. A second castle here was visited by Queen Elizabeth in 1575 and was one of the places in which some years later Mary Queen of Scots was kept prisoner. This castle, and its successor, the third, was destroyed by fire. In the village of Stowe is the 12th-cent. Church of St John the Baptist, reckoned by some to be one of the best examples of the combination of ancient and Victorian architecture to be found in Staffordshire. Here, all in the one building, are a Norman chancel arch, an Early English window, a tower part 14th-, part 15th-cent. and a north aisle built less than 100 years ago.

SUDBURY, *Derbyshire* (12–SK1631), is another of Derbyshire's model villages – brick, pretty and built largely in the 17th cent. It is about 6 m. E. of UTTOXETER and here, too, is Sudbury Hall, the seat of the Vernon family which is now in the care of the National Trust. Begun by Mary Vernon in 1613, the Hall was left unfinished at her death but was eventually completed by George Vernon between 1670 and 1695. The Long Gallery is aptly named, being 138 ft long; there is much fine work to be seen including ceiling paintings by Laguerre, a staircase carved by Pierce and overmantel carvings of exceptional quality by Grinling Gibbons. Not far from the house is a strange brick structure with turrets known as "The Eye-catcher". The village church, All Saints, dating from the 14th cent., contains many monuments to the Vernon family and a stained-glass window given by Queen Victoria.

SUTTON BRIDGE, *Lincolnshire* (13–TF 4821), is a town of diminished importance which was the point of embarkation across the Cross Keys Wash where King John lost his treasure and all his baggage in 1216. It is now an occasional port on the reclaimed marshland served by the River Nene. In 1831 a wooden bridge was built here which, with the coming of improved lines of communication, was replaced by an iron swing-bridge designed by Robert Stephenson. This gave way to the present road and railway bridge built in 1894, operated by hydraulic power. Since the collapse of faultily constructed new docks in 1881 no new plans have been adopted, so the area is largely derelict; but visitors to the scene of King John's misfortune will find an excellent nine-hole golf course on the site.

SUTTON CHENEY, *Leicestershire* (10–SK 4100), is a small village overlooking Bosworth Field. The Royal army encamped near here before the battle. The Church of St James is 13th-cent. with a 14th-cent. chancel arch, priest's doorway, east window and south aisle doorway and windows. There is an effigy of Geoffrey May, who was lord of the manor in the 17th cent. The manor has now disappeared but an Elizabethan farm-house with a stone dated 1601 set in the wall remains. Another effigy is that of Sir William Roberts (1633) with his two wives. The almshouses E. of the church were founded by Sir William in 1612. The end one of these has holes honeycombed in the gables as if the builder wished to encourage birds to nest in the roof. The third monument of note in the church is a plaque to Thomas Simpson, a local boy who became interested in astrology. Soon he became famous locally and people started to consult him, but fees were small and to keep going he married his landlady, who was 50 years old and had a son two years older than

Simpson. Finally he frightened one of his clients almost to death and had to flee to London, where he edited the first "glossy", *The Ladies' Diary*. In his spare time he studied mathematics and became a Fellow of the Royal Society and professor of mathematics at the Royal Military Academy. He was highly regarded and when he died George III awarded a large pension to his widow, who had been almost permanently drunk, and was a slut and scold into the bargain.

SWARKESTONE, *Derbyshire* (13–SK3728). The graceful bridge over the River Trent is the chief attraction for the sightseer in this small village about 4 m. SE. of DERBY. Built in the 13th and 14th cents. and much restored about 1800, its 17 sturdy old arches and the causeways stretch for three-quarters of a mile. There is also an architectural curiosity here, the so-called Summer House – also known as the Grandstand. With its two square corner towers and battlemented centre it looks like a small fort, but may well have been the grandstand in a bull-baiting arena. The enclosed area around it is known as the Cuttle.

SWINESHEAD, *Lincolnshire* (13–TF2340). The worn remains of the market cross preserved with another relic of bygone times, the old broken stocks, in the War Memorial garden here indicate that this large village was formerly a market town. It is one of the few places in England where, from October until March, the curfew still tolls at dusk. The medieval Church of St Mary, with its massive and very tall tower, is an outstanding landmark for many miles. The lower portion of this tower is 14th-cent., and the superstructure, comprising a pinnacled belfry and embattled octagon from which the spire rises a further 160 ft, dates from a century later. The interior is almost cathedral-like in its grandeur, with fine timbering and stonework providing a dignified setting for the many ancient memorials relating to the long history of the parish. A mile NW. of the village is the site of a small Cistercian abbey founded in 1148, where King John and his retinue lodged for a few days after losing their equipment at SUTTON BRIDGE while attempting to traverse the treacherous waters of the Wash. There is no foundation to the tradition, the plot of Shakespeare's tragic play, that the king was poisoned by the monks of Swineshead Abbey before meeting his end at NEWARK Castle.

SWYNNERTON, *Staffordshire* (8–SJ8435). This village, 3 m. NW. of STONE, is thought by some to be the inspiration for Longfellow's poem "Under the Spreading Chestnut Tree". Certainly there is such a tree opposite the 17th-cent. village inn, the FitzHerbert Arms; and an old smithy near at hand. Here there are thatched cottages and a fine early-18th-cent. Hall, but the oldest building is the church, which has Norman arcades and much else that is almost as old. The most striking feature in the church is the huge medieval statue of Christ.

TAMWORTH, *Staffordshire* (9–SK2004), possesses one of the two finest castles in Staffordshire – the other is at TUTBURY. Owned now by the Corporation – it was bought for £3,000 in 1897 as a memorial of Queen Victoria's Diamond Jubilee – the castle was lived in for 700 years from its erection in Norman times. But Tamworth's history goes back further than that: as long ago as 757 Offa, the Anglo-Saxon King of Mercia, had a royal palace at Tamworth but no trace of it remains. In 913, Ethelfleda, daughter of Alfred the Great, won a great battle against the Danes at Tamworth and to thwart a counter-attack built a stockade on a huge mound at the junction of the Rivers Tame and Anker. It was around this mound that Robert de Marmion, one of William the Conqueror's barons, began to build the fortress, much of which still stands today.

The Castle is, in fact, a mixture of Norman, Gothic, Tudor, Jacobean and early-19th-cent. architecture. The walls of the keep, 10 ft thick at their base, and the solid Norman tower with its dungeon, were the work of the Marmions. To the Tudor period belongs the more domestic warden's lodge and the splendid banqueting hall with its great oak-mullioned window. In the state dining-room, in the north wing – which also houses the royal bed-chamber – is a frieze of 55 oak panels painted with the arms of the lords of the castle up to 1787. There is a haunted staircase and a long gallery which is now the main museum area, where a collection of coins from Offa's Tamworth mint can be seen.

The parish church, with the rare dedication to St Editha, has one unique feature. The square tower is topped by a spire on each corner and in the south-west corner is a double-spiral staircase. There are 101 steps in the one spiral, 106 in the other, so arranged that the floor of one is the roof of the other. Climbers of one spiral do not see climbers of the other until they both reach the top. One spiral ascends from an entrance in the churchyard, the other from inside the tower.

Tamworth Town Hall is one of the prettiest in the country, built in mellow red brick with arcades at ground level, large Jacobean windows and a high-pitched roof, the whole topped with a cupola. It was built in 1701 by Thomas Guy, then M.P. for the town, whose name lives on in Guy's Hospital, in Southwark.

TATTERSHALL, *Lincolnshire* (13–TF2157). The feature of this otherwise undistinguished township is the immense castle keep built by Ralph, Lord Cromwell, in c. 1455, on the remains of a fortress raised by Robert de Tateshall in 1240 and acquired by the Cromwells through marriage. The building of castles solely for military purposes had reached its climax in the reign of Edward I. By the 15th cent. gunpowder superseded the old method of attack with cumbrous siege-machines, and warfare had taken to the open fields. The fortified mansion serving as stronghold and home resulted. Even so, Ralph Cromwell, Lord Treasurer to Henry VI from 1433–43, provided the castle with imposing defences of very great strength and saw to it that the basic structure was proof against the ravages of time. How well he and those who completed the work succeeded is shown in the massive remnant, now the property of the National Trust. The great quadrangled tower is one of the best examples of medieval brickwork in England, with windows, battlements and fireplaces of Ancaster stone. There are four stories, each of which has a large central room containing a fine heraldic chimney-piece and other emblems of Lord Cromwell's official standing. From the parapet wall above the gallery, and also from the top of the south-west turret, reached by a winding stairway of 181 steps, it is possible to see LINCOLN Cathedral in one direction and the BOSTON Stump in another. The guard house, set well within the periphery of the double moat, is now a museum.

Although little remains of the collegiate buildings also founded by Cromwell, the striking cruciform Church of the Holy Trinity, which he began in 1440, exists as a continuing memorial to his energy and vision. It is a remarkably beautiful edifice in durable Ancaster stone with insignia commemorating both Ralph Cromwell and William of Waynflete, Bishop of Winchester, who continued the work so ably begun.

TEALBY, *Lincolnshire* (13–TF1590). A beautiful village on the slopes of the Wolds, with the River Rase running down from Bully Hill. Across the valley once stood Bayons Manor, the house of the grandfather of Tennyson, which once belonged to William the Conqueror's half-brother, Bishop Odo of Bayeux; Bayons is an anglicized version of the title. A walk in the steps of Alfred, Lord Tennyson, is accomplished by starting in Tealby itself and setting off in a SE. direction downhill past the church to meet the bridge over the River Rase at the entrance of Bayons Park. Continue through the recently cultivated park until the track sweeps to the left. By bearing right after this, through fields and on to High Street Farm, and again at **Hainton**, with its 145-acre parkland landscaped by Capability Brown, the walk leads back through delightful scenery to cross the River Rase again and ends at Tealby. Tealby Church is an imposing building dating back in part to Norman times.

TELFORD, *Shropshire* (*see* Madeley, 8–SJ 6904). Although much work is already under way at this new town, much is still only in the planners' minds. This exciting concept for Britain's first new major city for centuries began in 1963 with a plan to develop Dawley by marrying it into one unit with **Madeley**, IRONBRIDGE and Coalbrookdale. But in 1968 the decision was made to broaden the concept and take in Wellington and Oakengates. At the same time it was decided to give the new city – for city rather than town it will be – a new name. Telford was chosen to commemorate a man whose bridges, viaducts, canals and churches can still be seen in all parts of Shropshire: Thomas Telford, 1757–1834, the

Scottish-born stone-mason, who became one of the world's most famous engineers. It is fitting that two of his major works, the Holyhead Road and the unusual octagonal church in Madeley, should be within the area of the new city which bears his name.

The plan visualizes the welding of the scattered towns of East Shropshire, with a present combined population of about 70,000, into a new, integrated city which, by the late 1980s, will be home for 220,000 people. The new city will be almost in the shadow of Shropshire's most famous hill, the 1,300-ft WREKIN, and will be flanked by the River Severn.

Building and rebuilding is going on on a vast scale. New houses by the thousand, shops, churches, factories, schools, roads and roundabouts the size of tumuli are emerging everywhere. The new city will first of all get its main artery and then its new heart. The aim of the proposed urban motorway is to join Dawley, Madeley and Stirchley in the S. with Oakengates, Trench and Wellington in the N. Then in the Malins Lee area will be built a new city centre, incorporating every modern facility and feature.

Already a new district shopping centre is under construction in Madeley and domestic building is going on apace in the Woodside area between Madeley and Coalbrookdale. But it is at Sutton Hill that the visitor can best see the physical surroundings in which people will live in the 21st cent. Here is the first completed Local Centre – scores of short terraces of modern houses grouped round a large, traffic-free precinct with lawns, shrubs and flowers. In the centre are a supermarket, other shops, the Red Admiral public house, a health clinic and surgeries, a library and church centre, and a community centre containing an assembly hall, coffee bar and children's play centre. The church, with plate-glass windows to ground level and tall, metal cross set in a courtyard, is particularly interesting.

A few miles away, just below the old village of Madeley, a huge educational and recreational centre is under construction. It is planned to include not only assembly halls but also a swimming-pool and a bowling rink. On the edge of this development stands Madeley's oldest building, Madeley Court. The Elizabethan building has lost much of its original splendour but its strange sundial, a large stone ball with holes through which could be assessed the positions of the planets and the moon, can still be seen in the garden. So future generations will be able, by a mere turn of the head, to see the buildings of the first and second Elizabethan eras.

THORESBY HALL, *Nottinghamshire* (13–SK6371). This impressive Victorian mansion near OLLERTON, 180 ft square with a great hall 61 ft long, 31 ft broad and 48 ft high, is the home of Countess Manvers and open to the public. It is the third house on the site, one of the most thickly wooded in SHERWOOD FOREST. The building, begun in 1864, was finished in 1874. The first Thoresby was enclosed out of the forest by the Duke of Kingston in 1683 and was the home of his famous daughter, Lady Mary Wortley Montagu, the greatest of English women letter writers, whose first volume of *Complete Letters* was published in 1966. In 1745 this building was destroyed by fire and replaced by a small brick mansion, the residence of the celebrated Duchess of Kingston, who was tried for bigamy in 1776. This house was described by Horace Walpole in 1772 as a place in which there was "no temptation to stop".

The present house, built when the Dukeries were fashionable, was designed by Anthony Salvin and is set in 12,000 acres. There are many magnificently furnished rooms, including the blue drawing-room and the Victoria bedroom. The principal floor contains 29 rooms and there are 78 bedrooms. The fireplace in the great hall is carved with a history of the Manvers family and there is a picture here of Lady Mary Wortley Montagu. In the library are statues of Robin Hood and Little John. Exhibitions of topical interest are held and cars may drive through the superb chestnut avenues in the park, and round the beautiful ornamental waters made by damming the River Meden. On the western extremity of the lake is a model village built in 1807 and a charming castellated folly called Budby Castle. About 1 m. E. is the village of **Perlethorpe** where Salvin built a Victorian Decorated parish church with a spire of about 130 ft.

THRUMPTON HALL, *Nottinghamshire* (13–SK 5131). Built in about 1608 by the Pigots, who also gave it its massively carved wide staircase at the time of the Restoration, Thrumpton Hall is now owned by the Seymours. It is of brick with stone dressings in an H-type plan with a contemporary loggia on the garden side which was balanced with a similar loggia on the opposite side, facing a backwater of the Trent, in 1830–40.

The Church of All Saints is remarkable since it embodies the only work of restoration in the county carried out by the famous Victorian architect, G. E. Street, who designed the ROYAL COURTS OF JUSTICE in London. His work is particularly recognizable in the chancel rails and seating. Memorials to the Pigots and Emmertons are in the tower. When the pulpit was removed during the restoration it was found that a carpenter from the village had placed a board beneath it bearing the inscription: "A proud parson and a simple squire Bade me build this pulpit higher".

Thrumpton Hall, with its lovely staircase, priest's hole, carvings, paintings and gardens, may be viewed by the public at certain times.

TICKENCOTE, *Rutland* (10–SK 9809). A magnet for photographers and students of architecture, Tickencote's Church of St Peter is famous for its amazing late Norman chancel arch of five orders, each carved with a different design in about 1160–70. The outer line has a unique pattern of foliage; the next a double zigzag; the third has grotesques

and foliage among which may be seen a muzzled bear, a fox's head with a monk, a green man, and two crowned heads looking opposite ways, thought to represent Stephen and Maud, rivals for the English throne; the fourth order has embattled moulding and zigzag on the soffit; and the last plain, round, stepped moulding. The sexpartite vaulting of the chancel is also late Norman; the only other occurrence of this type of vaulting is at CANTERBURY Cathedral. There is a font of 1200 and an oak effigy of a knight, possibly Sir Roland de Daneys, who died in 1363.

In 1792 the church was restored and partly rebuilt in a somewhat unattractive fashion by S. P. Cockerell.

Due N. on the A1 from here is **Stretton**, where there is another little church worth stopping to see. It has a very simple Norman south doorway and an early-13th-cent. arcade of fine design. The south transept was added in the beginning of the 17th cent., an unusual time for church building in England. Stocken Hall, about 1½ m. E., is an early-17th-cent. house with a good Georgian façade.

Continue along the A1 due N. for 1½ m. then turn right past the site of the Battle of Losecoat Field to **Pickworth**, one of the 14 Lost Villages of local lore, so called in this case because of the ravages of the plague from 1349 to the end of the 17th cent. and the disastrous event of the Battle of Losecoat Field in 1470. All that is left is one gaunt arch of the parish church standing alone in a field, a desolate monument with a beauty of its own. It was this and a few then-remaining fragments that inspired the rustic poet, John Clare, who worked as a lime-burner in Pickworth, to write the melancholy verse which made him famous.

TIDESWELL, *Derbyshire* (12–SK 1575), is famous for its fine, big church, known as the "Cathedral of the Peak". This small, stone-built town lies 6 m. ENE. of BUXTON among the limestone hills of the High Peak and is dominated by its parish church, St John the Baptist, with its tall, heavy, eight-pinnacled tower, one of the earliest Perpendicular towers in England. The church was built during the 14th cent. and contains a fine collection of pre-Reformation monuments, including the best single brass in Derbyshire, that to John Foljambe who died in 1383.

About 2 m. from the town to the N. are three ancient barrows, and 3 m. to the NW. the remains of a Roman road, Batham Gate. Tideswell holds an annual Wakes Week towards the end of June and during it the well-dressing ceremony is held, and there is Morris dancing in the main street. At **Great Hucklow**, a hamlet in the hills to the N. of Tideswell, are the headquarters of the Derbyshire and Lancashire Gliding Club where instruction is given to beginners; and most surprisingly, a splendid small theatre in a barn, home of the Village Drama Players.

TISSINGTON, *Derbyshire* (12–SK 1752). This exceptionally beautiful old village 3 m. N. of

ASHBOURNE is believed to have been where the Derbyshire custom of well-dressing began, as long ago as 1350. There are no fewer than five wells here and they are dressed in an interesting ceremony on Ascension Day each year. The village is a delightful ensemble with its triangular green surrounded by mellow stone houses, the church and Jacobean hall in the background. The church shows traces of its Norman origin and contains a most unusual Norman tub font carved with animals and a snake.

TITTERSTONE CLEE HILL, *Shropshire* (8–SO5878), is one of Shropshire's highest hills, 1,749 ft above sea-level. On the flat crown, an area of about 70 acres, was an Iron Age camp. Parts of the original earth and timber rampart and the rough-hewn basalt blocks used to strengthen it can still be seen.

TONG, *Shropshire* (8–SJ7907), which lies just off the A41 to WOLVERHAMPTON, about 8 m. S. of NEWPORT, has a church with one of the largest and most remarkable collections of monuments in the Midlands. The church itself, built on the foundations of an earlier one, was founded in the early 15th cent. by Lady Elizabeth Pembruge, in memory of her husband Sir Fulke, and alabaster effigies of them are among the earliest of the monuments. Many of the others are of members of the Vernon family and among the most interesting are those to Sir Richard, Speaker of the House of Commons in 1426, whose armoured figure in alabaster lies beside that of his wife; a particularly fine brass to Sir William, High Constable to Henry V; and, in an alcove, the bust of Arthur Vernon, a 15th-cent. CAMBRIDGE don. The red sandstone church itself, with its tower which starts square and then becomes octagonal, its battlements and unusual miniature stone spire, and its position on top of a small mound, cannot fail to catch the eye of anyone passing along the main road below.

In the 18th cent. George Durant bought the Vernons' castle and rebuilt it. His son, also George, put up several follies in the grounds, of which the Convent Lodge and the Egyptian Aviary remain.

TRENTHAM, *Staffordshire* (8–SJ8640), has been famous for 40 years as the site of Trentham Gardens, one of the Midlands' chief pleasure parks. But the village itself is of ancient foundation; a burial mound in Northwood Lane, excavated in 1859, is believed to date from about 1000 B.C. And as early as A.D. 660 King Wulf here, first Christian king of Mercia, had a palace near here and his daughter founded the nunnery which stood on the site of the present parish church. Trentham is mentioned in the Domesday Book and for 400 years up to the Reformation there was an Augustinian priory here. The Norman pillars of that building were incorporated into the present church which was erected in 1844.

Trentham Hall, eventually to become of palace proportions, was built in the early 17th cent. by Sir Richard Leveson whose successors the

G. Douglas Bolton

Tissington: a traditional well-dressing

Leveson-Gowers, later to become the Dukes of Sutherland, enlarged it and landscaped the estate around it so that by the mid-19th cent. Trentham was a vast Italianate mansion surrounded by formal gardens of a size and intricacy rarely found in England. Today only the ballroom and one hall of the original building remain, but the Italian garden, with its main parterre (geometric design area), can still be seen by the visitor, albeit in a simpler, less formal style.

In the grounds there is a beautiful lake, now used for boating; and on a hill-top a reminder of the former owners of Trentham – a tall, stone column on which stands a statue by Chantrey of the 1st Duke of Sutherland. Trentham can claim to have been in the "stately home" business 50 years before it became a commonplace. In the early years of this century local people were allowed to stroll through the grounds on public holidays and brass bands would play during the wakes weeks. The house has twice been described in novels: the Brentham in Disraeli's *Lothair* is Trentham, as is Sneyd Hall in Arnold Bennett's *The Card*; and in the latter, the Countess of Chell is thought to be a comic portrait of the 4th Duchess.

TUTBURY, *Staffordshire* (9–SK2129). This small, attractive old town beside the River Dove claims to have the finest Norman church in the county and, indeed, in the Midlands. The west end of the 11th-cent. building, with its doorway of seven receding Norman arches, all full of intricate and delicate carving, has a dignity which belongs to a much larger, more imposing building;

Kenneth Scowen

Uppingham: the ancient turf maze at Wing resembles certain pavement mazes in France

and inside, the thick Norman pillars frame an impressive nave. There are other treasures, too: an ancient parish chest; another Norman doorway with an Anglo-Saxon tympanum; a 13th-cent. head of Christ behind the pulpit; and the old village stocks.

Tutbury has the remains of an imposing castle; like so many in this part of the country, it was despoiled by the Parliamentarians after twice being besieged by them. Dramatically sited on an isolated rock, the castle was the final successor of a number of forts dating back to the Iron Age. Today the visitor can see John of Gaunt's gateway, built in the 14th cent.; the south tower with a winding staircase leading to an ante-chamber and the presence chamber; and the high tower where Mary Queen of Scots spent many years of her captivity. This tower has a winding staircase of 67 steps which is well worth climbing for the view it affords over Needwood Forest and into Derbyshire.

The main street of the little town is another of its charms; it is wide and gracious with Tudor, Georgian and Regency houses. Perhaps the most striking building is the black-and-white Dog and Partridge Inn, once the home of the Curzon family and later a coaching inn.

The ancient ceremony of bull running at Tutbury dates from the time of John of Gaunt, when a bull was mutilated and let loose. If the townsfolk caught him before he crossed the river he was theirs; if not he belonged to the abbot.

UPPINGHAM, *Rutland* (10–SP8699). An unhurried little town of old-fashioned, bow-fronted shops, quiet streets and sombre ironstone houses, many of them unchanged since the 18th cent. The market here was first authorized by Edward I in 1281. and a fair was granted at the same time. Great prosperity followed, reaching its height in the Elizabethan era, but today it is evident that times have changed, for little business is transacted in the market place. The prime importance of Uppingham lies in its great public school, the magnificent buildings of which occupy by far the larger part of the south-west quarter of the town. The original building, founded in 1584, accommodated no more than two dozen boarders and rated as a grammar school. In the 19th cent., under the headmastership of the Rev. Edward Thring, its increase in both size and standing can only be described as tremendous. Uppingham now has probably the biggest school playing-fields in England, a superb block of buildings, a museum, a chapel and a memorial hall in which is preserved the original charter of the school with the seal of Elizabeth I.

About 3 m. to the NE. of Uppingham is the village of **Wing**, of which the Church of SS. Peter and Paul has a Norman arcade rich with carving, and many surviving traces of 13th- and 14th-cent. stonework. Of especial interest here is the ancient turf maze, some 40 ft across, which is believed to have served as a means of doing penance.

UPTON, *Nottinghamshire* (13–SK7354). There are many fine views from this pleasant halting-place, taking in much of the countryside down to where the River Greet joins the Trent and affording a clear sight of the cathedral at LINCOLN in the distance. St Peter's Church here has an Early English arcade, a Decorated chancel and an unusual Perpendicular tower with nine instead of eight pinnacles. Also in the tower is a priest's room with a fireplace, and high in the walls are holes which show that doves were once encouraged, as was then usual, to build their nests in the stonework. Upton is the village where James Tennant was born in the 19th cent. From the humblest beginnings he went out into the world to become Professor of Mineralogy at King's College, CAMBRIDGE, and in that capacity was given the task of cutting the Koh-i-Noor diamond for Queen Victoria's crown.

UTTOXETER, *Staffordshire* (9–SK0933). The strangest thing about this small market town is its name. Today it is often called "Ucheter" or "Uxeter" and in the past it has been spelt in a variety of ways: Wotocheshede (Domesday Book, 1086), Uttokishedere (1175), Wittokeshather (1242), Uittokesather and Huttokesather (1251). It is believed to derive from a form of Witta, a man's name, and an old word for heath.

Today Uttoxeter is known mainly for its racecourse, reckoned the finest National Hunt Steeplechase course in the Midlands; and for a visit paid it about 1780 by Dr Samuel Johnson. Johnson's father was a bookseller in LICHFIELD and used to have a stall in Uttoxeter market. On one occasion, the young Samuel, too proud to stand at a market stall, refused to go with his father to Uttoxeter. Many years later, an old man near the end of his life, Dr Johnson returned – to do penance for his act of disobedience. For several hours he stood bareheaded, in the rain, on the spot in the Market Place where his father's stall used to stand: "In contrition I stood, and I hope the penance was expiatory." Today there is a substantial stone conduit here with a carving depicting the scene.

About 3 m. N. of Uttoxeter, among meadows between the Rivers Dove and Churnet, lies the village of **Rocester**. Once a Roman station, Rocester has seen much history. In the churchyard is the shaft of a 700-year-old cross, with interlaced work, said to be the best preserved example in the country; nearby are the remains of an Augustinian abbey. The visitor must look for these. He will have no need to look for Rocester's present claim to fame: the huge works of a famous firm of excavator manufacturers whose grounds are full of the "diesel dinosaurs" which have carved out the motorways.

WAINFLEET ALL SAINTS, *Lincolnshire* (13–TF4959). This small market town on the River Steeping was once a port. It is famous as the birthplace of William of Waynflete, Bishop of WINCHESTER and founder of Magdalen College, OXFORD. He founded the turreted Magdalen College School in Wainfleet in 1484.

WALL, *Staffordshire* (9–SK0906). The most complete Roman bath-house found to date in Britain was unearthed near this small village, 2 m.

S. of LICHFIELD. Wall was originally the Roman fort of Letocetum, built where Ryknild Street crossed Watling Street, and was a military centre of some importance for about three decades from A.D. 50. Excavations which eventually revealed the three baths – cold, tepid and hot – the furnace room with its floor of Roman cement and the exercise hall, were not begun until the 19th cent. The site is now in the care of the Ministry of Public Building and Works and is open to the public. A small museum has been established there containing finds made in the area, including cremation vessels.

WALSALL, *Staffordshire* (8–SP0198), is now an industrial town of a hundred trades but was once famous for only one – the working of leather. The nickname of the town's football team, the Saddlers, commemorates this connection. Today only the records remain of the town's long history: the first charter dated 1159; the Roll of Mayors back to 1377; the links with Warwick the Kingmaker, whose crest of bear and ragged staff appear in the Walsall coat of arms. The crypt of the Parish Church of St Matthew, dating from the early 13th cent., is probably the oldest building. An unusual feature of the church is the evidence in the vaulted archway beneath the high altar that a road once ran under the chancel.

Walsall's most famous son is Jerome K. Jerome, author of *Three Men in a Boat*, whose birthplace in Bradford Street is marked by a plaque. In the town centre, on The Bridge, is a bronze statue to Dorothy Pattison, known as Sister Dora, who spent 12 memorable years between 1865 and 1877 caring for Walsall's sick in an age when industrial accidents were common and smallpox epidemics not unknown.

The town, now including Willenhall, Darlaston and parts of WEDNESBURY and Bilston, has an impressive number of parks, playing fields and open spaces. The finest is undoubtedly the Arboretum, 80 acres set among trees and lakes, within two minutes' walk of the town centre. For a fortnight each September the park becomes a Chinese garden of coloured lights and lanterns and rainbow fountains.

Willenhall has been turning out locks and keys for 400 years and most of those manufactured in England still originate here. Exhibits in the Lock Museum attached to the Public Library tell of the history and technical development of the lock and key.

WALTHAM-ON-THE-WOLDS, *Leicestershire* (10–SK8025). A large and pretty village, standing high in the heart of the Wolds and a good place from which to explore them, Waltham-on-the-Wolds has one of the more important black smock windmills of Leicestershire, now unfortunately sailless. Most of the buildings are of the attractive, silver-grey oolitic limestone, and Roman pavements and Anglo-Saxon stone coffins have been found in its soil. Most of the Church of St Mary Magdalene is very fine, early 14th-cent. with many grave, gay and grotesque carvings on the nave arcade, and ten angels supporting the chancel roof, but two Norman doorways have survived – one plain and one zigzagged – and the semi-Norman font is one of the best in the county. There is a font at **Stonesby**, on the secondary road to the E., by the same artist.

WANLIP, *Leicestershire* (10–SK5910). The little church on the banks of the River Soar was entirely rebuilt in the last quarter of the 14th cent. by Sir Thomas Walsh, and Wanlip is thus worth visiting for the comparative rarity of its style in Leicestershire. The brass to its founder has the earliest prose inscription in English on any brass in the country. It tells how his wife, portrayed by his side, "in her tyme made the Kirke of Anlep and Halud the Kirkeyard". There are also some old heraldic glass shields and three medieval bells.

A legend hereabouts is that a giant named Bel vowed to reach LEICESTER from **Mountsorrel** in three leaps. He mounted his giant horse and their first jump landed them in Wanlip (One Leap). The second leap ended at **Burstall**. But the third leap was too much for them. They both fell dead a mile and a half short of Leicester and were buried in one grave – at **Bel-grave**. Possibly by the time they got to Burstall they were bursting all to get to their avowed destination.

WEDNESBURY, *Staffordshire* (8–SP0095). On its hill-top dominating this large town stands the Parish Church of St Bartholomew, reckoned one of the most beautiful Perpendicular churches in the Midlands. Parts of it date from the 12th cent.; there is some richly-coloured stained glass from the 15th cent.; a carved oak pulpit from the early 17th cent.; and a wooden lectern in the shape of a cock which is 600 years old. The town was named after Woden, the Anglo-Saxon god.

WELBECK ABBEY, *Nottinghamshire* (13–SK5674). This vast and extraordinary complex of 12th- to 19th-cent. building and subterranean labyrinth began in 1153, with the foundation of a monastic house of the order of Premonstratensian canons by Thomas de Cuckney. After the Dissolution the abbey was granted by Henry VIII to Richard Whalley, and through his heirs it eventually came into the possession of the redoubtable Bess of Hardwick. This ambitious and immensely able woman acquired incalculable wealth through successive marriages and the application of astute business acumen. Having bought Welbeck Abbey from the Whalley family she bequeathed the estate to Charles, her son by Sir William Cavendish. The son became father of another Sir William Cavendish who, because of his services to the king, was created the 1st Duke of Newcastle.

The south wing of Welbeck, built by the Duke of Newcastle in about 1630, was rebuilt in 1751 after the estate had, by several marriages, passed into the possession of the 2nd Duke of Portland, in whose family it was to remain until the 20th cent., when the greater part was put to use as an Army boarding school.

It was during the 19th cent. that the already magnificent and treasure-filled house was extended and literally undermined by the eccentric 5th Duke. This strange man was a recluse, whose morbid fear of being seen impelled him to build mile upon mile of underground tunnels and even entire suites beneath the surface. One of these consisted of three library rooms nearly 250 ft long followed by a ballroom and picture gallery measuring 174 ft by 64 ft and 22 ft high, which is described as the largest private apartment in England. After that came the Rose Corridor, a long underground conservatory with a glass roof. At the time of the 5th Duke's death in 1879 15,000 men were permanently employed on 36 different building projects in the grounds.

A disastrous fire in 1900 gutted the Oxford wing, following which considerable restoration and modernization was affected by the 6th Duke, but the great days of Welbeck Abbey were nearly over. The Army College is not open to the public.

WELL VALE, *Lincolnshire* (13–TF4574). This delightful beauty-spot on the eastern slope of the Wolds provides a perfect setting for one of the most beautiful country houses in Lincolnshire. Well Vale Hall is a fine example of early Georgian architecture, in red brick with a central pediment and an austerity of ornamentation characteristic of the period. Surrounding the house is a noble park of 170 acres, with two broad lakes fed by a chalk spring which together with the closely wooded valley gives the place its name. A few cottages, a school and a little church resembling a Grecian temple face the entrance to the Hall amid cedars, oaks and pines.

WEM, *Shropshire* (8–SJ5129), was once owned by Judge Jeffreys who was created Baron of Wem in 1685, the year he held his Bloody Assizes at which he dealt ruthlessly with those who took part in Monmouth's rebellion. This small market town 10 m. N. of SHREWSBURY was almost destroyed by a great fire in 1667, which explains why there is little pre-17th-cent. building to be seen. Today only the church and a few houses are worth a second glance. The parish church has a strong, 14th-cent. tower and inside a huge brass chandelier. The Old Hall has a pleasing black-and-white, gabled exterior. Lowe Hall, once the home of Judge Jeffreys, has a fine Jacobean interior behind a 19th-cent. façade. A little white house in Noble Street is one with interesting literary connections: it was the boyhood home of William Hazlitt, the essayist and critic. Wem gets its water from a 70-ft-deep well at nearby Preston Brockhurst; Wem ales are famous throughout the county. There could be a connection.

WEST BROMWICH, *Staffordshire* (8–SP 0091), contains four buildings which speak of its earlier history. The Manor House, now a restaurant, is regarded as a perfect example of a timber-framed manor of the late 13th and early 14th cents. Those interested can look over the great hall, the chapel, gatehouse and kitchens. A fine half-timbered building of a later period is Oak House. Built in 1450, it was given to the town by its first Mayor, Alderman Reuben Farley, and is now furnished in the style of the period and contains much handsome moulded panelling. Its tall Tudor chimneys and black-and-white "turret" give the house a striking appearance. Oak House can be viewed, as can be Asbury Cottage in Newton Road, also owned by the Corporation. This was the boyhood home of Bishop Francis Asbury, the founder of the Methodist Church in America; it has been tastefully restored.

The Parish Church of All Saints was rebuilt in the 19th cent. but the tower is 600 years old. There is a Norman oak chest, a medieval font and an oak altar dating from 1626.

WESTON UNDER REDCASTLE, Shropshire (8–SJ5628), is a charming, black-and-white

village about 4 m. E. of WEM which gets the colourful part of its name from the adjoining **Hawkstone Park**. The Hall, in the grounds, was built in the early 18th cent. for Sir Richard Hill and later added to by his nephew Sir Rowland Hill; today it is the home of a religious foundation but can be visited occasionally on application. The park itself, once one of the wonders of Shropshire, was the brain-child of Sir Rowland and his successor, another Sir Richard Hill. It covers a long, rocky ridge with sheer red sand-stone cliffs falling away along one side and isolated crags scattered here and there along it. It is a spectacular stretch of country which can be seen from the road to HODNET. Once it contained, among other oddities, a menagerie, a "Scene in Switzerland", a vineyard laid out to look like a fortress and a hermitage complete with resident hermit. Today the most obvious sights are the 112-ft obelisk, with a look-out on top, which was erected in 1795, and the Red Castle itself, built in the early 13th cent. but now a ruin strange only in its colouring.

The castle and other features of the park can be well seen from the fairways and greens of a golf course which has been laid out in part of the grounds of the park, owned by the hotel which was once the stable block for the Hall. There is a swimming-pool at the hotel and there is fishing in the nearby Hawk Lake.

A mile or two along the road towards Hodnet is what appears to be another red castle, perched on a small hill – but this is only a folly.

WHISSENDINE, Rutland (10–SK8214). A

large, strung-out village with too many red-brick houses in it to be pretty. It is set in the middle of magnificent open hunting country with good views over Leicestershire, but its greatest attraction is the Church of St Andrew, the 14th-cent. west tower of which is one of the finest in Rutland. The exterior of the church was very badly designed at the same period on the west and south sides to accommodate a staircase, and there are also a clumsy parapet and turret pinnacles. The beauti-ful capitals and delicate carving in the two nave arcades are evidences of earlier building. Par-ticularly notable, too, are the traceries of the windows, and the fine 15th-cent. nave roof and clerestory are admirable specimens of that period.

Between the transept and the aisle is the church's greatest possession, a 16th-cent. screen from St John's College, CAMBRIDGE, given by Margaret Beaufort, mother of Henry VII. When the college chapel was demolished Sir Gilbert Scott could find no place for the screen in his rebuilding, and it was acquired for Whissendine.

A walk starts from the village via Thomas Hill to **Ashwell**, NE. to MARKET OVERTON, then W. to **Edmondthorpe**, through the grounds of the Hall to **Wymondham**, and over Cord Hill back to Whissendine. Altogether about 12 m. and with the possibility of meeting a hunt in full cry along the way.

WHITCHURCH, Shropshire (8–SJ5441).

Roman coins, pottery and burial urns, which can be seen in the local museum, indicate that there was a settlement at Whitchurch at least 1,800 years ago. Today this is a pleasant, mellow market town, buildings from the 16th and 17th cents. blending happily with those of more recent vintage. The original church was built here early in the 10th cent. by King Alfred's daughter, Queen Ethelfleda, who dedicated it to an early Christian martyr – and her great-great-grand-father – St Alkmund. This was replaced in the 14th cent. by another building in white stone from which the town derives its present name. This building completely collapsed on the evening of 31 July 1711, just after the congregation at Evensong had departed, and the present church, still dedicated to St Alkmund, was built im-mediately afterwards. A painting of the famous "White church" can be seen in the vestry of the present church whose tall tower is a landmark. Here, too, is a surprising treasure, the silken arms which formerly hung behind the Speaker's Chair in the House of Commons. Under a stone slab in the church porch, in a silver urn, lies the heart of the famous John Talbot, 1st Earl of Shrewsbury, who was killed in 1453 at the age of 80 while fighting with the English army against Joan of Arc, and whose dying wish was that his heart should be buried in the church of his native town. Another famous son of Whitchurch was the composer Sir Edward German, born in St Mary's Street in 1862.

WIDMERPOOL, Nottinghamshire (13–SK63

27). Some of the loveliest woodland scenery in the county provides the setting for this little village in the Wolds. A leisurely walk takes the visitor to the Hall, a neo-Elizabethan house with tower and terraces, close to the Church of SS. Peter and Paul. Almost all that remains of the old church building is the 14th-cent. tower with its corner buttresses and diagonally projecting corner pinnacles; the rest was built between 1888 and 1895. Inside there is an exquisite sculpture of Harriet Anne Robert-son, fashioned in white marble by an Italian artist whose work details every fold of her gown with painstaking skill.

Barnaby/Mustograph

Wirksworth: the lid of an Anglo-Saxon coffin in the parish church

WIGHTWICK MANOR, *Staffordshire* (8–SO8597), is that rarity, a house which is not yet 100 years old but which is nevertheless of great interest both for its architecture and its interior decoration and furnishings. The Manor, 3 m. W. of WOLVERHAMPTON, at a casual glance might appear to belong to the Elizabethan or Jacobean age but it was, in fact, erected in two stages, in 1887 and 1893, for Mr S. T. Mander who employed as architect the half-timber expert, Edward Ould, and for the interior used the materials of William Morris and his contemporaries in the Arts and Crafts Movement. The house and its 17 acres of grounds were presented to the National Trust in 1937 and are regularly open to the public.

Black-and-white on a red sandstone base, the house is many-gabled and has the traditional imposing Elizabethan chimneys. Inside are many fine examples of Morris wallpapers, hangings and tapestry, notable among them being his "Diagonal Trail" tapestry in the Great Parlour, the house's principal room, the "Willowbough" paper on its pale green background on the Visitors' Staircase, and the "Dove and Rose" silk and wool tapestry in the Drawing Room.

There is much else to delight the eye, including tiles designed by William de Morgan, stained glass by C. E. Kempe, drawings by Burne-Jones and pictures by such artists as Ford Madox Brown, D. G. Rossetti, Ruskin, Millais, Turner and G. F. Watts. There are also exquisite carpets and rugs, much fine furniture and china.

The gardens are a pleasing composition of the formal and the "loose landscape" with fine lawns, paths running between yew hedges, a wood and two pools. In the beds and borders are shrubs and plants from the gardens of Morris, Tennyson, Kempe, Burne-Jones and Ruskin. Among the famous people who have planted trees at Wightwick are the Duke of York, later King George V (a purple lime), Earl Attlee (a hornbeam) and Lord Samuel (an oak).

WILLOUGHBRIDGE, *Staffordshire* (8–SJ 7440). Here, in a small hamlet about 3 m. SE. of Woore, is a unique woodland garden. Set in a disused, 200-year-old gravel quarry at the top of a small hill, the garden is a fine example of marrying the natural with the cultivated. Within the framework of tall oak trees are masses of rhododendrons and azaleas of all colours, at best in May and early June; and a little earlier there is as much colour, but from banks of daffodils.

WILLOUGHBY-WITH-SLOOTHBY, *Lincolnshire* (13–TF4772). An attractive village of tree-lined roads, small cottages and flower-clustered gardens on the edge of the Lincolnshire marshland. The site was originally a Roman settlement, the mounds of what is believed to have been a Danish encampment are nearby, and traces of Anglo-Saxon masonry are to be found in the church. The village is notable for having been the birthplace of John Smith, the intrepid explorer whose discoveries established Virginia as the colony from which sprang the United States of America. It was he whose life was saved by Pocohontas, daughter of Powhattan, paramount chief of the Indians, but all that is recorded in the Church of St Helen's is the entry in the register stating that John Smith was baptized there on the 9th day of January, 1579.

WIRKSWORTH, *Derbyshire* (12–SK2854), is an attractive small old town among the hills 5 m. S. of MATLOCK. It was once the centre of the Derbyshire lead-mining industry. At the Moot

Hall can still be seen the oblong dish which was used for measuring the lead; and pigs of the mineral dating from Roman times have been found in the neighbourhood. This was the town which George Eliot used as a background for much of her novel, *Adam Bede*, and those familiar with the novel will find it an interesting exercise to try to match the places in the novel with their real-life counterparts. Other scenes in the novel were set in the village of **Roston**, about 5 m. SW. of ASHBOURNE (about 13 m. in all from Wirksworth).

There are many old buildings in Wirksworth, none older than the imposing Church of St Mary. In the church can be seen an Anglo-Saxon coffin lid, believed to have come from the stone coffin of a saint who was buried here almost 1,200 years ago. The carving on the lid is crude but quite clear and obviously depicts scenes from the life of Christ, including the washing of the disciples' feet, the raising of Jairus's daughter, and the descent into hell, as well as the symbols of the four gospel-writers. Other ancient sculpture, mainly Norman work, can be seen in the walls of the church.

Other interesting buildings include the old hospital, now a guest-house, which dates from 1588; Dale End, a gabled 17th-cent. house; Gell's Bedehouses, dating from 1584; and a number of attractive Georgian houses.

Along the road from Wirksworth to **Middleton** is some of the most spectacular scenery in the county. Here are the extensive Hopton Wood quarries with sheer walls of rock often towering impressively above the road.

WOLVERHAMPTON, *Staffordshire* (8–SO 9198). A flaming brazier and a padlock are included in the coat of arms of Wolverhampton. Today these are more obviously symbolic of this "Capital of the Black Country" than the cross, ascribed to the Anglo-Saxon King Edgar, and the woolpack, which are also in the arms and hint at Wolverhampton's beginnings. The town was first referred to as Heantun in a royal charter of 985. The name later became Wulfrunishamtun, after Wulfrun, a Mercian lady.

Most of the striking buildings to be seen here – the tower blocks of flats, the award-winning housing estates, the Mander Centre and Wulfrun Shopping Precinct – are all post-war. The outstanding exception is the Church of St Peter, in red stone, approached by a flight of wide steps, standing near the heart of the town with something of the grandeur of a small cathedral. The oldest parts are the arches under the square, 15th-cent. tower, which date from 1205. There was an earlier monastery on the site, refounded in 994 by the Lady Wulfrun, a translation of whose charter hangs in the vestry. The south chapel dates from 1350 and the nave, with its unusual double clerestory windows, from about 100 years later. The 15th-cent. carved stone pulpit, with its staircase winding round one of the nave pillars, is very rare. In the north chapel are monuments to members of the Lane family, one of whom helped Charles II escape from BOSCOBEL

House after the Battle of WORCESTER in 1651. Another monument worth seeing is the strong, bronze statue of Admiral Sir Richard Leveson, carved by Hubert Le Sueur in the early years of the 17th cent. Outside the south door of the church stands an ancient carved pillar, believed to be the remains of a column dragged from one of the nearby Roman sites by 9th-cent. Anglo-Saxons.

There are two unusual features about Wolverhampton's other town church, St John's. Built in 1760 it could be mistaken at first for ST MARTIN-IN-THE-FIELDS in London; and it has one of the most famous organs in England, built by Renatus Harris about 1683. The instrument came to St John's by accident. After being for many years in Christ Church Cathedral in Dublin, it was replaced by a new instrument. The maker of this took the old organ in part exchange and it had reached Wolverhampton on its way to London when its owner died. His widow sold it to St John's for £500.

Wolverhampton possesses a fine municipal art gallery and museum in Lichfield Street, with a good collection of English enamels and early Staffordshire pottery, and pictures by Romney, Turner and Gainsborough, among others. At Bantock House, in 43 acres of grounds 1 m. from the town centre, there are exhibits illustrating the town's industrial history: japanning, cut steel and locksmiths' work; also a collection of beautiful English porcelain.

Within reach of the town are a number of historic houses including MOSELEY OLD HALL, WIGHTWICK MANOR, **Chillington Hall** and **Himley Hall.** Chillington Hall, 8 m. N., is a fine Georgian house with gardens landscaped by Capability Brown and a magnificent avenue of trees; it is occasionally open to view. Himley Hall, owned by the Wolverhampton and Dudley Councils, is not open to the public but the extensive grounds are, including the Great Pool, in which fishing is available. Not far from Himley Hall is the village of **Wombourne;** the spired church, with a unique dedication to St Benedict Biscop, overlooks one of the few remaining walled-in cricket grounds in England.

WOODBOROUGH, *Nottinghamshire* (13–SK 6347). A village of terraced cottages, built for the 18th-cent. stocking knitters, each with its broad upper window behind which stood the frame. In 1769 a son was born to one of these hard-working families, who because of his knowledge of the Bible was later to be affectionately known as the Walking Concordance. He was George Brown, the Nottinghamshire evangelist, who devoted 50 years to preaching the gospel from house to house. This was also the home of Richard Strelley, builder of Woodborough church, with its fine windows, gabled buttresses and beautiful sedilia. Much has been added to his 14th-cent. work, particularly in sculpture and wood-carving, the latter having been executed by Mansfield Parkyns, a distinguished explorer, geographer and linguist who was also a highly talented craftsman.

WOOLSTHORPE, *Lincolnshire* (13–SK 9224). This tiny hamlet in the south-west corner of the county is famous for containing within its narrow boundaries the birthplace of Sir Isaac Newton, the supreme mathematical genius whose theory of gravitational pull revolutionized man's knowledge of astronomy. Woolsthorpe Manor, where he was born in 1642, is a small but attractive house of the 17th cent., with mullioned windows, beamed ceilings and tall, square chimneys set off by mellowing grey-stone walls. The apple orchard in the front contains a descendant of the tree which so momentously affected Sir Isaac Newton's studies. Today the whole property is in the hands of the National Trust and is open to visitors.

WOOLSTON, *Shropshire* (8–SJ3224). This hamlet is about 5 m. SE. of OSWESTRY, just off the main road to SHREWSBURY. It is unremarkable save for one building, the smallest there. At the end of a short, grassy path, set between high hedges, stands a tiny, black-and-white cottage, with musk and pink honeysuckle on the walls. This is the site of one of England's holy wells, that of St Winifred. The legend says that this is the place where a well gushed forth from the ground when the body of the saint rested there on its way from Holywell to Shrewsbury.

The cottage is built into the side of a small hill so that on its lower side there is an extra story at ground level. This looks like a large, open-fronted porch and it is here that the well emerges, bubbling up into a large, shallow stone bath with steps leading down into it. The rust-coloured water then runs down into a second, lower bath in the open air, and thence on to a small stream. Here pilgrims came to immerse themselves in the holy water. Today visitors are welcome but must not bathe. Happily the shrine is kept in good repair.

WREKIN, THE, *Shropshire* (8–SJ6208). At 1,334 ft, the Wrekin is not Shropshire's highest hill; both the Clees, Brown and Titterstone, are more than 400 ft higher. Yet on a clear day the view from the top of the Wrekin, a couple of miles S. of Wellington, is as panoramic as any in England, embracing 17 counties. This was the site of an Iron Age fort, begun about 200 B.C. Almost 1,800 years later a beacon fire blazed on its crown to give warning of the Spanish Armada. Today the visitor can climb its grassy slopes, peer into its rocky clefts, find the Gates of Heaven and Hell, the Needle's Eye, and, on the very summit, the Raven's Bowl.

WROXETER, *Shropshire* (8–SJ5608). Here, 5 m. SE. of SHREWSBURY, are the remains of what was the fourth largest town in Britain in Roman times. Wroxeter, or Viroconium, was the Roman capital of a large area of central Britain

and covered an area of 180 acres, compared with Roman London's 325 acres.

Wroxeter had a chequered history. Begun *c.* A.D. 60, it flourished for about 30 years, then relapsed until the visit to Britain of the Emperor Hadrian in 121, when it was rebuilt. For almost 150 years the city prospered and grew but with the gradual withdrawal of the Romans from Britain, Wroxeter slipped gradually into decay. By early in the 5th cent. the site was deserted and eventually was plundered for its stone by Anglo-Saxons building Shrewsbury.

Excavation was begun in 1863 and went on at intervals until the work was taken over, in 1948, by the Ministry of Public Building and Works. The results of all that work are now there for all to see, although much is still not known. However, the visitor can walk in the forum where Roman legionaries walked 1,900 years ago, see the small market stalls where they shopped, look down into the pool where they swam, and stroll through the inter-connecting areas of the bath-house. Here were the hot, tepid and cool rooms, the furnace and the cold plunges and, all down one long side, the exercise hall, separated from the bath-house by the largest remaining fragment of the original building, part of the Roman wall, the rough stone levelled off at intervals with a course of red tiles.

At the site, too, is an excellent museum containing many of the finds made here (there are others in Rowley's House Museum in Shrewsbury). Among the exhibits are fragments of architecture and sculpture from the temple; mosaics and tiles – one bearing the clear imprint of a cat's paws; many pottery bowls and vases; bottles, flagons and perfume flasks in blue, amber and green glass; writing implements; bronze brooches, bracelets and keys; dice and counters in bone; coins; and primitive surgical instruments. But perhaps the most important exhibit is the stone inscription which was set up over the entrance to the forum on its completion in A.D. 130. Its five lines of finely chiselled lettering were cut in slabs of fine-grained sandstone almost 12 ft long and dedicate the building to the Emperor Hadrian. It must have impressed the Cornovii, the Ancient British tribe who were rulers of this area until the Romans came.

YOULGREAVE, *Derbyshire* (12–SK2164). The small, hill-top town, about 4 m. S. of BAKEWELL, is remarkable for the size of its church with its tall, imposing square tower, topped by eight pinnacles. Much of the building is Norman and the unusual, two-basin font and a sculpture of a man in a long frock also date from this period; there are also a number of interesting monuments dating from the 14th, 15th and 16th cents. The stained glass in the east window is a good example of the work of William Morris. About 3 m. W. of Youlgreave is ARBOR LOW.

Yorkshire

PHYLLIS BENTLEY

Yorkshire, 3,735,322 acres (about 6,100 square miles) in extent, is the largest county in England. It contains approximately one-eighth of the area of England, and with its four and a quarter million people, about one-tenth of England's population.

Its shape is simple: roughly a square, pulled down a little in its lower left-hand corner. Its west boundary is formed by the line north and south of the mountains of the Pennine Chain, and it stretches right across England eastwards to a slightly north-west south-east coast on the North Sea. Its northern boundary is the east-running River Tees; the southern is partly the estuary of the Humber, but further west it makes a protrusion, once very marshy, south of this line.

If its shape is simple, however, in all other respects Yorkshire is highly diversified. Geologically it is amazingly various, and this has given it not only a most delightful and refreshing variety of landscape but certain contrasts in history and economics, in dialect and ways of life, sometimes even, within a strong native similarity, in types of character.

In the north-west of the county the Pennine mountains are composed of the beautiful grey-white limestone. No heather grows on limestone; these hills are covered with short, very bright green grass, very agreeable food for sheep. Then the character of the rocks changes; south of a geological disarrangement known as the "Craven fault", which makes a gap in the chain through which the River Aire flows, the rock is millstone grit, a hard, dark, gritty rock on which grow heather and long, tough, pale grass of no great pastoral value, though even on this sheep will feed. The millstone grit is fringed, to the south-east, with coal measures, part of one of the greatest coalfields in Britain, and in these measures lie also some precious nodules of iron ore. The large central plain of the county is rich alluvial soil, which grows abundant crops and vegetables, besides providing dairy pasture. To the north-east of this the land climbs into the Hambleton Hills by the severe gradient of Sutton Bank, and from thence into the North Yorkshire Moors, composed of the considerable Cleveland Hills. North of these we find a mixture of rocks, sloping down to the valley of the Tees, amongst which is found, again, a considerable deposit of ironstone.

The county of Yorkshire is extremely well watered. Its main river system is best understood by thinking of the Humber as the wrist of a hand, the Ouse as the palm into which the tributary rivers, like fingers only more numerous, flow. From north to south these tributaries are Swale, Ure, Nidd, Wharfe, Aire, Calder, Derwent, Don. (The word *Sunwacdd* is a useful aid here to memory.) All these rivers except the last two rise in the west, in the Pennines, flow through beautiful dales, join the Ouse before or after York, and reach the North Sea through the Humber. Thus the county can show all kinds of river scenery, from the tumbling rocky mountain "beck", as Yorkshire people call their streams, to the broad smooth navigable river. Outside of this system flow the northern Tees, which directs itself due east into the North Sea, and the Ribble, which after flowing down the west side of the county has the audacity to enter Lancashire and pour itself into the Irish Sea.

Hundreds of minor tributaries in Yorkshire play a part, not only in beautifying the landscape, but in enriching, as we shall see, the economic life of the county.

There are quite a few prehistorical habitation remains to be found in Yorkshire; these will be noted as they occur, in the gazetteer. When the region emerges from the veil of prehistory we find British tribes in occupation, rebelling against Roman legions sent to keep order in this far-flung outpost of the Roman Empire. The great legacy of the Romans, here as elsewhere, was their fine road network. One great road leads north from Doncaster to Isurium (Boroughbridge) and Richmond, with branches off west and east to various camps in the Pennine Hills and signal stations on the coast. Another Roman road, Ermine Street, leads presumably to a ferry crossing the Humber to Brough, and thence proceeds along a limestone ridge which rose above the marsh, to York.

By the fifth century A.D., however, the Romans grew tired of wasting men and money on such a distant and unrewarding land as Britain. The Picts and Scots they had more or less succeeded in temporarily keeping out by building walls across the narrow neck of land between Clyde and Forth, and from Tynemouth to Solway, but the invasions of Angles and Saxons, marauding tribes from across the North Sea, had recently become a perpetual nuisance. After the Roman legions departed (c. A.D. 410) the Angles overran England and it became their country, even adopting, as we see, their name. During this period Christianity came to England, and to the North from Kent and Cornwall and from the island of Iona.

The Angles did not rule long in peace, for in the eighth and ninth centuries a fresh set of invaders poured into England – Danes and Norwegians. Vikings in their beaked ships, tall, fierce, ruthless men who, coming first to plunder and murder, presently settled in the rich lands of England and made the country into a kingdom of their own. Some sailed up the Humber; others approached by way of the west coast of Scotland, coming south thence and through the Aire gap into Yorkshire. There are many traces left in Yorkshire of our Angle and Danish conquerors. Especially is this the case with our language; innumerable dialect words today are really relics of the speech of these invaders. Place-names ending in *ham* are of Saxon origin, while *by*, *kirk*, *thorp* are Danish terminations. It was the Danes who first divided York into Ridings; the word comes from the Danish *treding*, a third part. Thus there are North, West and East Ridings, but no fourth division. (The use of "South Riding" by that fine novelist Winifred Holtby is a brilliant invention to give locality without the embarrassment of real names.) The name of York itself, after Eburach, Eboracum, and Eoforwic, gained its final form from the Danish Jorvik.

The story of the coming of our final conquerors, the Normans, is well known; it has its beginning in our county. Harold, King of England after the death of the childless Edward the Confessor, had banished his brother Tostig for ill-treatment of his northern earldom. Tostig sought help from the Norse king Hardrada, and they invaded Yorkshire. Harold marched against them, and after a brisk exchange of insults defeated them, killing both. But while still celebrating this victory he heard that William of Normandy had invaded Sussex. Marching his tired and reluctant army south through the length of the English counties, Harold met William near Hastings, and was defeated and killed there. The whole of England fell into William's hands, and he gave it away piecemeal under feudal tenancy, as rewards to his supporters and relations.

Yorkshire owes much of both good and evil to the Normans.

The evil was a massacre, outrageous even for the fierce eleventh century. The northern region rebelled three times against William the Conqueror. After the third of these rebellions William's patience was exhausted, and he harried the North with fire and sword so terribly that there was scarcely a town inhabited, a building standing, a being, animal or human, left alive in the whole stretch of land. The description of the state of Yorkshire after this harrying, by contemporary writers, is awful – corpses rotting by the wayside because there was nobody to bury them – and it was many years before the county recovered. The effects show only too clearly in the entries in Domesday Book, the account compiled twenty years later (1089) by William's orders, of every piece of land in England. After recording the size of the land in question, entry after entry in the North reads like this: *Grim* (Saxon) *held it, Ranulf* (Norman) *holds it now; T.R.E.* (in the time of King Edward) *it was worth 20 shillings, now worth five shillings and fourpence. It is waste.*

On the other hand, the Normans gave us relief from Danish invasions, increasing law and order, and many buildings of great beauty. The Norman barons built castles (twenty-two in Yorkshire before 1216) to defend themselves and their lands. Some of these have decayed, some have been destroyed, by battle or by order, but impressive remains still exist of these massive and often magnificent constructions, e.g. Scarborough, Skipton, Conisbrough, Pontefract, Richmond. The Normans also built cathedrals (such as York, Beverley) churches, abbeys, monasteries. Before Henry VIII's dissolution there were more monasteries in Yorkshire than in any other county of England, and Fountains and Rievaulx, only partly ruined, remain to show their greatness and beauty. As to parish churches, it has been said that out of eleven hundred parish churches in England, more than four hundred are in Yorkshire. They do not all exist in their entirety; but arches, doorways, pillars, remain to delight us.

England accepted, if somewhat sullenly, the Norman rule, and Yorkshire thenceforward became part of the kingdom of England and participated in the general course of English history. Its chief trouble was the Scots, who all too frequently still charged down the west side of the Pennines and crossed into Yorkshire through the Aire gap, or raided down the less hilly east coast.

A good many of the battles in the Wars of the Roses (1455–85) were fought in Yorkshire. But these did not really concern the territories of Yorkshire and Lancashire; the nobles who contested the crown chanced to hold these titles, and their men fought, not from conviction, but as their feudal allegiance required. Far different was the case during the Civil War between King and Parliament in the seventeenth century. The allegiance of Yorkshire was divided. The towns of the West Riding, and Hull on the Humber on the other side of the county, were strongly for Puritanism and Parliament; the rich central plain was for the Church of England and King Charles I. Thus already the contrasts between the Ridings show themselves.

Speaking in general terms, it may be said that the North Riding, stretching in a broad riband across the county from the Pennines to the North Sea, is pastoral and agricultural; the West Riding, shaped like a leg of mutton, nestling against the Pennines at its narrow end and spreading towards the south-east, is industrial; the East Riding, tucked between them, has a long sea coast, rich arable land, and the third port of the kingdom, Hull, on the broad estuary of the Humber.

The North Riding, including the north corner of the West, is the most strikingly beautiful stretch of the county. Fine Pennine heights – among them Ingleborough, Whernside, Pen-y-Ghent – make a superb backcloth to the landscape, and the lovely northern dales of Swaledale and Wensleydale roll away in beauty to the east. Swaledale is steep and rocky, with the marvellous castle at Richmond sitting high on its cliff; Wensleydale is serene and grassy, with Bolton Castle, where Mary Queen of Scots was imprisoned, gazing in grim strength across the broad valley. Nor must the northern Teesdale, perhaps the most rich and least bleak of Yorkshire scenery, be omitted. As the North Riding stretches east, it rises into the Cleveland Hills, which offer heather-covered slopes and some beautiful if less well known dales: Farndale, noted for its daffodils, Rosedale, Bilsdale. On the coast, at the mouth of the Tees, lies that remarkable phenomenon, the town of Middlesbrough. In 1801 only twenty people were living on the spot where the town now stands. Now, thanks to the discovery of iron ore nearby and its exploitation, Middlesbrough makes millions of tons of steel, exports it (for example, the girders for the bridge across Sydney harbour) and has a population of some 200,000.

The coast of the North Riding holds fishing villages such as Staithes and Robin Hood's Bay, and celebrated seaside resorts: Whitby, once famous for its jet, always famous for its ruined abbey and for Captain Cook; Scarborough, "queen of watering places", with its large castle and the grave of Anne Brontë on the cliff.

The West Riding has been industrial for a long time, for Sheffield discovered its iron ore and the "Little Masters" smelted it by charcoal and made steel of it in their homes as far back as the fourteenth century. We know this for certain because the Miller in Chaucer's *Canterbury Tales*, written about 1387, carried "a Sheffield thwytel in his hose". Pronounce *thwytel* as Chaucer pronounced it and you hear the origin of the word *cutlery*. Today Sheffield melts its ore, largely imported from Sweden, by coal, and though still world-famous for its cutlery, produces enormous quantities of high-quality steel in larger shapes.

The other great industry of the West Riding is the wool textile trade. Sheep and streams had always existed abundantly in the county, and from these essentials woollen cloth was made by hand in the workers' homes for many centuries, and possibly was even exported as early as A.D. 796. Edward III helped to improve this manufacture in the fourteenth century by inviting to England skilled Flemings, who taught Yorkshire folk how to spin more (and finer) yarn than previously from a pound of wool. Towards the end of the eighteenth and beginning of the nineteenth centuries it was discovered that some textile processes could be performed by simple machines run by water power. This gave the West Riding, with its abundant wealth of tumbling water, a great impetus, and the textile trade, which in its early days had flourished chiefly in a Weavers' Guild in York, gradually became the pre-eminence of the West Riding. In a few years steam was harnessed to power, and again the West Riding profited, for it had coal to raise steam, and iron to make machines, only a few miles away to the south. As a consequence of this Industrial Revolution, from hand-power to steam, the West Riding became a vast conurbation, where today thirty thousand looms continually weave cloth and 150 million pounds worth of cloth is exported yearly. Its towns are, however, agreeably separated by Pennine hills, grass or heather-covered.

May I mention that the tall mill chimneys which characterize the textile West Riding are most unjustly disliked? The smoke which they poured out (now greatly diminished) was certainly odious, but the slender circular chimneys themselves are skilful and beautiful structures.

Another beauty which the West Riding owes to the textile industry is its domestic architecture, Elizabethan and Jacobean. Sir Nikolaus Pevsner calls them "Halifax houses", these long low yeomen clothiers' houses of local stone, with their long rows of mullioned windows, and the weavers' cottages with the row of windows in the second story to lighten the loom-chamber. These houses and cottages are tucked into the hillsides, beside a stream, just below the brow. Here the textile trade began; in the valleys below, tower the huge mills of the nineteenth century.

The West Riding is not without its scenic beauty, too, for it contains the whole of lovely Wharfedale, whose mingled beauties, wood and fell and river, are a great attraction to visitors. Bolton Abbey, more correctly Bolton Priory, has an unrivalled situation on the Wharfe banks, and the rocky Strid gorge of the river is well worth visiting – but please do *not* try to jump this, it has been regularly fatal for some eight centuries. Nidderdale, another West Riding dale, is, too, very beautiful and has a unique gorge, How Stean, and a superb view down the whole dale from the upland village of Middlesmoor.

A great factor in the making of Yorkshire has been religion. Puritans in the days of Charles I, many Yorkshire people welcomed Quaker teachings in the seventeenth century, and in the eighteenth century the West Riding was strongly affected by the preaching of John Wesley, who made more than forty visits to Yorkshire. All over the Riding can be seen the chapels – some small, early, humble, some huge and proud, all without the ornament they despised – of the various nonconformist religious sects which helped to give the nineteenth century its staunch moral background.

The East Riding of Yorkshire, with the exception of its popular seaside resorts Bridlington and Filey, is perhaps insufficiently appreciated by tourists. Many fine churches enrich this flat, rich, once marshy now richly arable land. The Minster at Beverley is, by reason of the unique height and slenderness of its towers, particularly beautiful. Hull, besides being the third port of England – with vast docks, grain silos, piles of merchandise for export and import – and the centre of a large fishing fleet, holds much of interest of a historical kind. The house of William Wilberforce, the school he attended, the old fast-vanishing streets, recall days when Hull played a striking part in English history, and the branch headquarters of the Trinity Brothers, who manage our coastwise lights, is a fine building.

The striking fact about the East Riding is that its long coastline in Bridlington Bay is continually in process of erosion. Churches, houses, villages, even towns, a few hundred years ago thriving and important, now lie beneath the North Sea waves. On the other hand, the long thin sandy headland which curves round to end in Spurn Head to the south has often changed its shape by addition as well as by erosion, and there is a piece of land within its curve, Sunk Island, which has emerged from the sea, so to speak, of its own accord.

North of Holderness, as this part of Yorkshire is called, the land rises into grassy chalk wolds, which presently surge out to sea as the huge white Flamborough Head.

York, the capital city of the county, which stands at the junction of all three Ridings, belongs to none. A fortress since A.D. 71, since 1389 it has been a city with a Lord Mayor, since 1396 a county to itself, with its own Sheriff. It is, of course, a centre of government of the northern province of the Church of England, the headquarters of the Archbishop of York. With its superb Minster – the glorious elegance of the Five Sisters window must on no account be missed – its twelfth-century city walls, its innumerable old churches and streets, its ancient remains, the broad sweep of the River Ouse, the wonderful City Museum, it seems full to the brim of picturesque testimonies to English history.

The Yorkshire dialect varies between the Ridings. In the East their speech is warmer and slower than in the West. Between North and West Riding speech the

Guisborough Priory. Watercolour drawing by   Edinburgh, National Gallery of Scotland
Thomas Girtin, 1801

River Wharfe forms a boundary; for example, to the north *she* is *hoo*, to the south *she* is *sha*, and there are other such differences.

Yorkshire people are often vexed by the attitude of more southern counties, who seem to regard us as uncultured barbarians, as if we had not yet recovered from William's fire and sword. Let us note, then, that William Wilberforce, M.P. for Hull, initiated and saw through Parliament the Act which in 1834 terminated slavery in British possessions. Richard Oastler of the West Riding initiated the movement which forbade children to work long hours in mills. We were the first to give protection to seabirds. The first great Education Act, passed in 1870, which began to give free education to all British children, was initiated and seen through Parliament by W. E. Forster, the M.P. for Bradford (West Riding) at that time. We have today five universities: Leeds, Sheffield, Hull, York, Bradford. We are devoted to music – not, perhaps, in so poetical and inspired a style as our Welsh colleagues, but in a serious and knowledgeable fashion; music societies abound in all our towns, and the Huddersfield Choral Society is famous all over the world for its admirable performances of Handel. We love cricket, and if I may be allowed to say so, are proficient in this beautiful game. Nor are we backward in football, particularly in the game of our own invention. We play to win, but lose with stoicism. Racehorses flourish in the North Riding.

In literature we have a decidedly interesting record. We have not produced a poet of the highest class, but from the Brontës onwards clusters of novelists have recorded and enriched our scene, and today some of these have ventured into new forms of drama, both on the stage and television. In drama we have experienced with others the decay of the professional theatre, the dauntless activities of serious amateur players, and the revival of the arts under regional Art Councils.

Yorkshire is a county rich in amateur societies. There are gliding clubs, sailing clubs, literary clubs, gardening clubs, tennis clubs, science clubs and the usual Young Farmers, Women's Institutes and Townswomen's Guilds in great abundance, all democratically run by properly elected committees.

The Yorkshire people are by reputation robust in physique though not especially handsome, efficient and vigorous in their undertakings, blunt in speech and rather well satisfied with themselves. They dislike excessive expressions of emotion and are cautious with strangers, but once they accept you they are staunchly if soberly faithful. They prefer practice to theory. Above all, they are extremely independent. An Abbot of York wrote to Henry VIII: "there be such a company of wilful gentlemen within Yorkshire as there be not in all England besides". In Queen Elizabeth's days the men of Halifax were spoken of as behaving "after the rude and arrogant manner of their wilde country". It would be rash to suggest that Yorkshire folk have changed much since those days, and this applies to the women as well as to the men. A Yorkshire person has a strong backbone; lean on it but do not try to bend it.

The Strid, near Bolton Abbey. Painting by James Stark (1794–1859)   Norwich, Castle Museum

Yorkshire: Gazetteer

ELLEN WILSON

ADEL, *West Riding* (12–SE2740). Here on the NW. outskirts of LEEDS is one of the county's gems, a small Norman church dedicated to St John and built in the mid-12th cent., with few alterations imposed since. It consists of a nave and lower chancel. The two features which draw admirers are the south doorway and the chancel arch, both beautiful in design. The doorway stands under a gabled portal and is richly carved with four orders of zigzag, roll moulding, flowers and beakheads. The chancel arch is sculptured with zigzag, ladder-like moulding and picturesque heads. The capitals show the baptism of Christ on the north, and the Crucifixion on the south responds. The original bronze door ring shows a monster devouring a man, whose head alone is still visible. A memorial window and heraldic glass are by Henry Gyles, and date from 1681 and 1701.

ALDBOROUGH, *West Riding* (13–SE4065). The pretty village with a maypole on the green drowses on the site of the ancient capital of the Brigantes, largest Celtic tribe in Britain, who called it Iseur. It consisted of huts behind an earth and wood stockade when the conquering Romans came. They made it an important camp and a civilian suburb of YORK. It was known as Isurium Brigantum. It was favourably situated at the highest point for navigation up the River Ure and at the junction of important roads. The Romans circled it with a 9-ft-thick wall 20 ft high and built houses, courts, a forum and a temple here. Corn shipments were transported overland from here to the northern troops. With the withdrawal of the Romans, Aldborough fell victim to successive Angles, Scots, Danes and Normans. Under the Normans, a new bridge was built across the Ure at BOROUGHBRIDGE, less than 1 m. away, dealing the village a final blow. Part of the Roman wall, two pavements, and the museum founded in 1864 and filled with excavated objects recalling the days of Roman gracious living are in the care of the Ministry of Public Building and Works. At least 12 fine pavements were saved here, the best known being in Kirkstall Museum, LEEDS. Roman wall stone found its way into St Andrew's Church. A badly worn stone panel of Mercury is in the north aisle. The church has good woodwork and a fine brass monument of William de Aldeburgh of about 1360, the figure life-size.

AMPLEFORTH, *North Riding* (13–SE5878), is famous for its abbey and college, a Roman

Catholic public school founded in 1802 by English Benedictine monks who had settled in France in 1607, then returned as refugees from the Revolution in 1793. Most of the stone-built village lies along one street on a shelf of the Hambleton Hills with the Abbey of St Lawrence and college at the east end. The view across a beautiful valley toward GILLING CASTLE is grand. The college church, designed by Sir Giles Gilbert Scott, is of greenish stone and was completed in 1961, in Romanesque style. The parish church, St Hilda's, has Norman north and south doorways and a curious stone effigy of a bearded, praying man with a woman looking over his shoulder, from about 1330. The Ampleforth sword dance has been revived by students.

AUSTERFIELD, *West Riding* (12–SK6594). William Bradford, one of America's Pilgrim Fathers, was born here in 1590 and baptized in the simple Norman Church of St Helen's. He was a member of the Brownists, an extreme separatist Puritan group, who sailed on the *Mayflower* in 1620. He was the second governor chosen in the New England colony of Massachusetts and wrote a history of it before his death in 1657. Austerfield Manor where he was born is a Tudor yeoman's house, two stories with pantile roof. The most prominent village building is the church. It has a new bellcot and windows were inserted in the 13th and 14th cents. The north aisle arcade was rebuilt in 1897 by the Society of Mayflower Descendants in honour of "the first American citizen of the English race who bore rule by the free choice of his brethren". The Norman doorway in the porch has an interesting carved arch and tympanum with a strange dragon or sea monster in relief.

AYSGARTH, *North Riding* (12–SE0088). The beautiful falls – a series of three cascades – extend for ½ m. on the River Ure in Wensleydale. The foaming waters rush over great ledges or steps between limestone walls overhung with trees and bushes, where violets and primroses thrive in season. For the Upper Falls, the approach is down a road near the youth hostel to a single-arch 16th-cent. bridge, widened in recent times, where the view is enthralling. From the next bend in the road, a footpath leads to the Middle and Lower Falls. Cars can be left in the former station yard. Aysgarth's parish church, St Andrew's, is nearly 1 m. W. of the village. It overlooks the bridge. Except for the west tower, which is medieval in its lower stages, the church is a product of 19th-

T. Parker

Aysgarth Falls on the River Ure in Wensleydale

cent. rebuilding. Two finely carved screens and a reading desk are believed to have come from JERVAULX ABBEY.

BARNSLEY, *West Riding* (12–SE3406). Few buildings here are much more than a century old and new public works are replacing some of those. Barnsley is the exact centre of the Yorkshire coalfield, the biggest in Britain, and its older streets wear the grime to prove it. There are reminders, too, of the price of coal. Silkstone church has a memorial which records that women and children were among 26 mineworkers drowned when a pit flooded in 1838. A monument on Kendray Hill commemorates the deaths of 361 men and boys in an explosion and its aftermath in the Old Oaks colliery in 1866. In the 18th cent. it was a major centre for linen weaving. The glass industry, still the second largest employer, started even earlier. The huge market, which began in 1249, is still held thrice weekly on the original town centre site and it is a major regional attraction. St Mary's Parish Church has a 15th-cent. embattled tower but the rest of the building is early 19th-cent. The 1933 Town Hall is heavily Classical. The old grammar school building in Church Street, founded in 1660, houses the free Cooper Art Gallery with its good collection of paintings and English drawings. In Cannon Hall, at Cawthorne village W. of Barnsley, the town keeps a country-house museum of decorative arts, featuring glass, period rooms and furnishings. The house is 17th-cent. with 18th-cent.

additions by John Carr. The park is a popular picnic spot. Locke Park on the south side of town was given in 1861 by the widow of Joseph Locke, an apprentice of George Stephenson, who became a famous railway builder. Near the tower, a memorial to Mrs Locke by her sister, is a view over Barnsley. On the north-eastern outskirts are the excavated ruins of MONK BRETTON PRIORY. Wentworth Castle, to the S., is a College of Education now.

BARTON-LE-STREET, *North Riding* (13–SE7274). St Michael's Church contains an astonishing amount of stone carving in the Norman style. Some of it is original and the rest was produced for an elaborate rebuilding in 1871. The quality of the Victorian contribution is outstanding and a great deal of the original fabric was re-used or reproduced. Thus this fine village church makes a fascinating study of high Norman work. The building may date from about 1160 and it shows the influence of Norman work in the area of Poitiers, although reasons for the similarity are not clear. The north porch with its handsome entrance arch of old with new work shelters a second splendid doorway, the original south doorway, moved here in the 19th-cent. rebuilding. In addition to intricate but conventional bands of ornamentation, there are studies of St Michael and the dragon on the entry arch, Samson and the lion on the doorway and numerous bizarre figures and animals. Above the doorway are scenes of shepherds in bed being visited by angels (sometimes described as a nativity with Mary in bed), the Wise Men and labours of the month. Inside the porch also, parts of the beautiful Norman corbel table are preserved, with delightful small heads in the arches linking the corbels. A Victorian Norman corbel table runs around the outside wall now. The church interior exhibits fine Norman-style carving in its chancel arch. Original work is retained in the capitals of the arch, in the corbel table in the chancel, the unusual wall frieze in the nave and in the piscina shaft.

BEDALE, *North Riding* (12–SE2688). The main street widens where the market is held then narrows at the top of the slope where the Church of St Gregory and Bedale Hall occupy opposite and commanding positions overlooking the agreeable townscape. The church tower is 14th- and 15th-cent. work and has a porch on the south side. A room on the first floor was reached by a stair guarded by a portcullis, a defensive measure in case of Scottish raids. Walls in the nave may be Anglo-Saxon in origin; the east window was possibly brought from JERVAULX ABBEY. The alabaster effigy of Sir Brian Fitzalan who died in 1306 is one of the earliest of its kind. The rear of Bedale Hall is brick and matches the rest of the Georgian-style houses in the market place, but its front faces the country and is formal, in stone, dating from about 1730. It houses the Rural District Council offices, a library and a museum. The great ballroom has a marvellous coved stucco ceiling with chubby figures fairly leaping over the cornice. The flying staircase has a bulb and umbrella balustrade. The house was built for Henry Peirse. This is splendid hunting country.

Snape Castle is 3 m. S., part ruin and part residence. The old chapel is preserved, a single room with Perpendicular windows and lively Dutch carvings of the life of Christ. Catherine Parr, sixth and last wife of Henry VIII, lived here.

BENINGBROUGH HALL, *North Riding* (13–SE5158). This early Georgian country house, 8 m. NW. of YORK at Newton-upon-Ouse, was built by an unknown architect for John Bourchier and completed in 1716. Two hundred years later it was bought by the Earl and Countess of Chesterfield and in 1959 it came from the Treasury to the National Trust in payment of death duties. On the outside, it is a simple and dignified building of small red bricks ornamented sparingly with stone quoins and sculptured pediments. The two main stories and attic are 11 bays wide. Inside, the rooms are attractive and even grand, but it is the wood-carving which will arouse the most admiration; the Hall is a storehouse of the splendid work of the York craftsmen of the day. The oak staircase, for example, has parqueted treads and a baluster so light that it seems at first glance made of wrought-iron. The stairs are supported only by fastenings in the wall. Throughout the rooms, chimney-pieces, door surrounds and friezes exhibit the artistry and tireless imagination of the wood-carvers. The Hall is open to visitors at advertised times in the summer months.

BEVERLEY, *East Riding* (13–TA0339). The capital of the East Riding is dominated by two churches, almost equally splendid. The minster is the one with two towers. There is no disputing the claim that it is one of the most beautiful churches in Europe. The Early English east end was begun in 1220 and the magnificent Perpendicular west front with its richly pinnacled towers was completed in 1420. John of Beverley built a church here in the 7th cent. and the town really grew up around the monastery that accompanied it. He became Bishop of HEXHAM and later Bishop of YORK and ended his days back here. A slab in the centre of the church marks his vault. He was canonized in 1037 and his burial place was a shrine for pilgrims. The later church erected on the site burnt down and the new minster was begun. It is in the unusual form of a double cross. Inside, amid the immense display of ornament and sculpture, the visitor may note in particular the glorious Percy Shrine – the canopy is regarded as the finest 14th-cent. work of its kind – which can be viewed best from the reredos gallery; the Frith Stool, or stone sanctuary chair; the biggest collection of misericords in England (68); and the 12th-cent. font of Frosterley marble. Nothing is left of the old monastery but a brick wall E. of the minster. St Mary's Church, hardly ½ m. away, was begun in the 12th cent. as a chapel to the minster. In rebuilding the nave in the 13th cent., the walls were so weakened that the central tower finally collapsed in 1520, killing several worshippers. In restoration, the roofs were repainted in lively medieval fashion. Also noteworthy is the minstrels' pillar in the north arcade.

Beverley is linked by river to HULL, builds trawlers, tans leather and serves as a market centre for the area. In the Saturday Market is a market cross of 1714, an open octagon on steps with pillars supporting the domed roof which displays the arms of England, France, the town and the two Members of Parliament who donated it. The Guildhall is 17th-cent. with a portico added in 1832. Beverley was protected by a ditch and five drawbridges defended by gates. Only one survives, the North Bar, brick-built in the 15th cent.

BIRKIN, *West Riding* (13–SE5226). In two directions from St Mary's churchyard on the edge of this obscure hamlet the view is now blocked by ranks of steaming cooling towers. But the church seems sublimely indifferent to change. It has been here since about 1100, looking much as it does today. Grey stone, with a plain stout tower decorated in the 15th cent. with parapet, pinnacles and gargoyles, the building invites close study. It has a rare vaulted Norman apse, a beautiful climax to the aisleless nave. A south aisle was added in the 14th cent. The south doorway, protected by a decaying wooden porch, is enriched with three orders carved with medallions, zigzag and beakheads, and faces. The tall inner arches, serving the tower and the chancel, also bear zigzag carving. A 14th-cent. stone effigy of an unknown civilian lies in a niche of the north wall of the nave. He carries his heart in his hands, his

A. F. Kersting

Beverley Minster: a detail of the Percy Shrine

hair is carefully curled and his feet rest on a dog. An 18th-cent. wall monument records the misfortunes of one of the Thorntons who served as rectors here for 106 years. This one, Robert, came in 1612 but in 1649 he was arrested as a Royalist "tied to a horse rail and dragged to Cawood Castle" but he returned to his post 15 years later. The 18th-cent. pulpit has a finely carved tester or sounding board.

BIRSTALL, *West Riding* (12–SE2226). Oakwell Hall, now owned by the Batley Corporation, was visited by Charlotte Brontë, who thereupon used it under the name of "Fieldhead" in her novel *Shirley*. It was built by John Batt in 1583, and although later somewhat altered, retains the character of an Elizabethan house. It is surrounded by fine gardens. The house has been used as a young ladies' academy in the past and now serves as a museum, with a permanent collection of English chairs. Plays, recitals and art exhibitions are held here. Birstall is the birthplace of Joseph Priestley (1733–1804) the dissenting theologian who was also a chemist and discovered nine gases, including oxygen. The town was "Briarfield" in *Shirley*.

BISHOP BURTON, *East Riding* (13–SE 9839), is an unforgettable village, cupped in a hollow with a large wayside pond reflecting the scene. It is a place of white-walled, red-roofed houses, trees and a grey stone village church. The village belonged for a long time to the Archbishops of YORK and one of their palaces is said to have stood in a field named Knight Garth SW. of the village. Rebuilding has left little of the original medieval All Saints Church. In the chancel is a chalice brass to Vicar Johnson, 1460, one of the earliest known examples of this kind of brass, which originated in Yorkshire. There is a bust of John Wesley carved from an elm on the green where he preached and a peace memorial cross on an island in the pond.

BOLTON ABBEY, *West Riding* (12–SE0753). The nave built by the Augustinian canons is now the parish church while the east end of the monastic house of worship is a ruined skeleton. The site is alluring near a sweeping bend of the Wharfe bordered by green pastures with wooded slopes beyond. Stepping stones cross the river. The priory was founded here in 1151 by Alicia de Romilly whose family had been granted these lands by William the Conqueror. Before that, this was the site of an Anglo-Saxon manor. With the advent of the Romillys, the centre moved to SKIPTON where the castle was built. The church is 13th-cent. with an elaborate west front and west tower unfinished by the time of the Dissolution. The ruined chancel had been built in the 14th cent. Painters have loved this scene, and Landseer made it famous with his early-19th-cent. *Bolton Abbey in Olden Time.* The rectory nearby was a free school until the later 19th cent. The priory's gatehouse is in Bolton Hall, a residence of the Dukes of Devonshire. The hamlet is known erroneously, but by long usage, as Bolton Abbey. Three m. upstream where the Wharfe narrows is the small, humped Barden Bridge and above it the ruined Barden Tower built in 1485 by Henry Lord Clifford.

BOLTON CASTLE, *North Riding* (14–SE 0391), is in the village called Castle Bolton and dominates not only the village but a lot of Wensleydale as well. The first Lord Scrope built it and Mary Queen of Scots was held prisoner here for six months in 1568–9. The Scropes had a manor house here in the 13th cent., but when given licence to crenellate in 1379, Lord Scrope put up a completely new castle. It is unusual for the size of the living-rooms, their fireplaces and privies. It suggests that some comfort was possible in a building concerned firstly with protection. It was one of the first to employ chimneys. The domestic quarters were scattered against the walls around the courtyard and in the towers. The castle was dismantled after the Civil War and lost one of its four corner towers in a storm in 1761. The Great Chamber is a Wensleydale folk museum now. The castle, village and dale were made familiar to many through the watercolours of the late Fred Dawson who came here on holiday in 1910 and stayed until his death at 80 in 1968.

BOLTON PERCY, *West Riding* (13–SE5341). This secluded village SE. of TADCASTER has an exceptional parish church, All Saints, which someone has gone so far as to call the "cathedral of the Ainsty". It was designed by Rector Thomas Parker during his incumbency here from 1411 to 1423 and completed shortly after his death. All of the details are finely attended to and the east window still has about one-half of its original glass. Two medieval altar stones and a 12th-cent. font are among the relics, and the woodwork, ranging from 15th-cent. roofs to a Georgian pulpit, is excellent. Monuments to Fairfaxes, including Ferdinando Lord Fairfax, a commander at MARSTON MOOR, are here. The shady village also has a former rectory built in 1698 and a 15th-cent. gatehouse, known locally as a tithe barn, with a good deal of carved timber work in it.

BOROUGHBRIDGE, *West Riding* (13–SE 3966). A bridge over the Ure in Norman times gave the town its start and it became an important road centre with 22 inns at one time. An impressive number of inns remain. In the 18th cent. it was a port for KNARESBOROUGH's linens. Here in 1322, Edward II defeated Thomas, Earl of Lancaster, who was followed into the church where he had taken refuge, carried a prisoner to his own castle at PONTEFRACT and beheaded. That church is no more, having been pulled down in 1851. St James's was built the next year with a few relics incorporated, including a late Norman doorway. The town's attractions include fine old houses, many trees, a cobbled square with a fanciful 1875 market cross, fishing and boating.

To the SW., behind a housing estate and on the road to Roecliffe, stand the mysterious **Devil's Arrows,** three huge weather-worn standing stones, the most famous prehistoric monuments in Yorkshire. They are probably 3,000 years old and could have been important to the Brigantes as late as Roman times. The folk story was that they were bolts shot by the Devil at ancient cities to destroy them. They stand on beds of clay and coarse stone 6 ft deep and weigh 36 tons each. They would have been quarried near Knaresborough, 7 m. away. A fourth stone was taken down and cut up for building the bridge on the small Tut long ago.

BOWES, *North Riding* (14–NY9913), gained some dubious publicity as the site of Dickens's Dotheboys Hall. He stayed at the Unicorn Inn at whose door in that day boys attending one of the several boarding schools, or "boy farms", in the vicinity were dropped by stagecoaches. Dickens's school was probably a composite of places he had visited or heard of, but by popular consent the Bowes school run by William Shaw is taken for the model, with Shaw the real-life Wackford Squeers. It is doubtful whether he merited this savage portrait, but the school had to close after the publication of *Nicholas Nickleby*. The building known as Dotheboys Hall is now a café. The Shaw family as well as the 19-year-old youth, George Arthur Taylor, whose gravestone so moved the novelist, are all buried in the churchyard of St Giles, a restored medieval building with two ancient fonts, one Norman and one early 13th-cent. The church also contains a Roman dedication stone of about A.D. 204. To the Romans, Bowes was Lavatrae: it may have been a place where baths were provided for legionaries travelling the Stainmore Road (Watling or Dere Street). Like the church, Bowes Castle used Roman stone for building. The Norman keep was the only stone building of the castle, completed in 1187, and now in the hands of the Ministry of Public Building and Works. The thick walls are still 50 ft high. It was built for Henry II by Alan Niger, Earl of Richmond.

Bowes, high on a hillside site, is 4 m. SW. of BARNARD CASTLE. The stump of the Rey Cross stands near the road, 5¾ m. W., supposedly the boundary mark in the 10th cent. between English and Danish territory and the old kingdom of Strathclyde to the NW. It is a perfect spot for moorland views. NW. looms **Mickle Fell,** at 2,591 ft, Yorkshire's highest mountain; sometimes there is snow on the top from autumn to early summer.

BRADFORD, *West Riding* (12–SE1633). The great wool town has other admirable claims to fame. It was first with a school board, school medical and dental services, school baths, school meals, a nursery school, municipal hospital, electricity department and railway – and it must be one of the first to make money extracting wool grease from its sewage and selling it in the form of lanolin and other useful products around the world.

Much of Bradford looks confidently Victorian but new building is rapidly altering the old business centre and eliminating the back-to-back housing. The residents look cosmopolitan. The city over a century has accommodated Irish, German, Eastern European, Italian and, most recently, West Indian and Asian immigrants. Their biggest employer is the wool trade, which was firmly established here in the 18th cent. Large numbers also work in engineering, chemicals and the mail-order clothing business.

Those who have not seen Bradford lately have surprises coming. Smokeless zoning already affects more than 80 per cent of the houses. The massive Gothic-style Town Hall with its illuminated campanile tower has been scrubbed and is now buff instead of black. Next to it is a new park with rose gardens, part of the city centre building and landscaping programme. There is a new entertainment centre, a new £800,000 Central Library (claimed to be the finest in Europe) and a new university, chartered in 1966, which grew out of the College of Advanced Technology. St George's Hall, highly praised for its acoustics, is once more resounding to orchestras and choirs after a bad patch as a cinema. But the house where Frederick Delius was born in 1863 has been replaced by a garage.

A few things do not change. The patron saint of woolcombers, St Blaise, still overlooks Market Street from the tower of the Wool Exchange where traders from the world market still gather. The cathedral is one link to the remoter past. It is late-15th- to early-16th-cent. Perpendicular with modern additions and was a parish church until 1919. The chancel contains excellent Victorian stained glass. The cathedral stands on a hillside and Church Bank runs down it into the square named after the Bradford M.P., W. E. Forster, who sponsored the compulsory education act of 1870. Another local hero is Richard Oastler, who fought the use of child labour in the mills. His statue stands in Darley Street.

Two Bradford parks of special interest are Lister and Bowling, respectively NW. and SE. of the centre. Lister Park is named after the 1st Lord Masham who invented a woolcombing machine and founded a silk mill. It has a scented garden for the blind, a boating lake and a pleasant 1½-m. walk. In Cartwright Memorial Hall, built in 1904 on the site of Lord Masham's old home and named after the inventor of the power loom, is the City Art Gallery and Museum. At the park entrance is an elaborate memorial to Sir Titus Salt, who moved his alpaca and mohair mills in the 1850s to a healthier situation and built **Saltaire** near Shipley, a model village in its day.

Bowling Park spreads out opposite **Bolling Hall**, now a museum. The house includes a peel tower built in about 1400, a 17th-cent. addition and finally a wing by John Carr in 1779. The Hall was the home of Bollings, Tempests and Saviles.

A short excursion E. and S. from Bradford will take in **Fulneck**, where a Moravian settlement was established in the 18th cent.; **Tong**, for a look at an almost untouched 18th-cent. village group of hall (now a Bradford University residence), church and cottages; and finally **Wyke**, a smaller Moravian settlement.

BRAMHAM PARK, *West Riding* (13–SE 4041). The small village of Bramham, S. of pleasant-looking Boston Spa, has a number of fine houses in its vicinity but easily the grandest is Bramham Park. At one time the gardens, too, were among the most remarkable in England, a rare surviving example of French-style land-scaping of the days of Louis XIV. The grounds were notable for long avenues lined with towering beech hedges, with calculated vistas and orna-mental buildings and ponds. A gale in 1962 destroyed 490 of the trees, including the oldest. Although the temples and obelisk were spared and the grounds have been replanted, a generation or

more must pass before they acquire their former magnificence. The gardens, however, are still unusually fine and, like the house, are open to view at advertised times. The Hon. Mrs M. A. Lane Fox is the owner today. Both house and gardens were the work of Robert Benson, the 1st Lord Bingley, who lived at YORK where he, like his father before him, was Lord Mayor and M.P. He was at one time the Ambassador to Spain and on the Continent developed a taste for the gardens of André Le Nôtre, his inspiration in planning his own park. The house and park were designed and built from about 1700 to 1710. It is believed that Benson was his own architect for the Classical buff sandstone building with its two-story centre block balanced at each side with an open colon-nade and pavilion. A fire in 1828 devastated the house, and although a temporary roof was put over it, restoration did not take place until 1907. A new addition then was the horseshoe-shaped staircase copied from one at Fontainebleau. A little summer-house by James Paine (1760) at the end of the terrace was converted to a chapel. In it stands a figure of Lord Bingley. The stable block is also believed to be by Paine.

BRANDESBURTON, *East Riding* (13–TA 1147). The church, St Mary's, in an otherwise unremarkable village, is built of cobbles with a brick clerestory and south porch, and it exhibits work from the Normans to the 15th cent., when the tower was built. There is a very large piscina in the east wall of the chancel and a niche built aslant in the north. In the chancel floor is the only example of a bracket brass in the riding, a now headless memorial to Rector William Darell who died in 1364. Opposite are two brasses to Sir John de St Quintin, who died in 1397, and Lora, his wife, who died two years later. The knight has lost his head but his heart is in his hands. A grey-hound lies under his feet. His wife wears a flowing tunic and the little dog at her hem has bells on his collar.

BRANDSBY, *North Riding* (13–SE5872). Here the road from YORK to HELMSLEY climbs into the wooded Howardian Hills and back over your shoulder you can see the Plain of York with the minster towers in the far-off haze. Thomas Atkinson designed both All Saints Church, com-pleted in 1770, and the Hall, finished three years earlier. Harmonious short terraces of cottages are placed here and there on the slopes. A 16th-cent. rectory with 19th-cent. additions and a wood-carver's shop are the other village features. The church has a stone cupola on its hipped roof and this is supported inside by a pleasing arrangement of four Doric columns with cross vaults. A local man made the wrought-iron gate leading into the nave. A small crucifix is thought to be Norman.

BRIDLINGTON, *East Riding* (13–TA1766). This used to be the most "genteel" of the York-shire seaside resorts; it is simply one of the most popular now. Protected on the NE. by the great headland of FLAMBOROUGH, it lies near the top

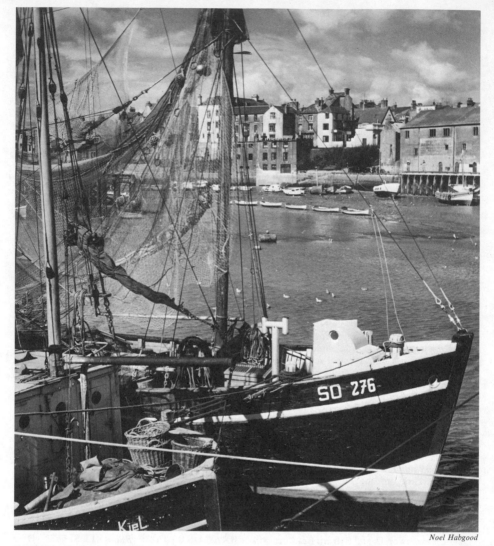

Bridlington harbour

of Bridlington Bay with long stretches of fine sand both N. and S. of the harbour. A small fishing fleet still sails from here. Stones from the old priory were used to build the two harbour piers and there is some fishing-village atmosphere in the houses that cluster near the waterside. It figured dramatically in history on 22 February 1643 when Queen Henrietta Maria landed from Holland with arms for Charles I. The vessels were bombarded by Parliamentary ships. As the cannon-balls "sang merrily" around her, the Queen took refuge in a ditch, later moving on to Boynton Hall.

The great attraction of old Bridlington, 1 m. inland, is the Church of St Mary. It includes the nave of the Augustinian priory founded here in about 1119 by Walter de Gant and was saved from destruction at the Dissolution because it was already in use as a parish church. Next to BEVERLEY Minster, it is considered the finest ecclesiastical building in the East Riding. It was restored in the mid-19th cent. Portions to linger over are the richly decorated north porch, the beautiful west doorway beneath a huge window, and the 14th-cent. south aisle. The north-west tower has a plain Early English parapet but the rebuilt south-west tower has crocketed pinnacles in 15th-cent. style. Inside is a black grave slab on two low pedestals which may belong to William de Gant. It is carved with two dragons, a cat, and a fox and crane drinking from a jug. It has been used as a bread table for distributing food to the poor.

The priory's Bayle Gate across the green was built in 1388 and was, at various times, the prior's courtroom, a sailors' prison, a barracks and a school. Now it is a museum. This priory was wealthy and had several important figures, including John who worked miracles before and after his death in 1379. The last prior was hanged at Tyburn for his part in the Pilgrimage of Grace.

William Kent, the first English architect to design furniture, was born here in 1685. The 18th-cent. **Sewerby Hall**, on the cliffs NE. of the town centre, is a Corporation art gallery with interesting gardens.

Boynton, a neighbour to the NW., has pretty cottages and a Tudor hall, altered in the 18th cent. and open by appointment. The church close to the hall gates is medieval with nave and chancel rebuilt in brick in 1768 by John Carr. One Strickland family monument is attributed to William Kent. There is a choice turkey lectern.

BRIMHAM ROCKS, *West Riding* (12–SE 2165), are a collection of grotesque rock formations scattered over a 50-acre site on a heathery moor 950 ft above the Nidd valley. Found E. of PATELEY BRIDGE, they are a popular picnic spot and an endless marvel to children. The rocks are millstone grit roughly carved over thousands of years by sheets of ice, winds and frosts. The names which have been given to individuals among the weird assortment suggest their shapes: Yoke of Oxen, Pivot Rock, Chimney Rock, Baboon, Dancing Bear and Druid's Skull. An 18th-cent. visitor discovered that the stones, in some cases standing on a sort of pedestal, would rock. The 200-ton Idol Rock rests on a stem only 12 in. thick.

BROMPTON-IN-ALLERTONSHIRE, *North Riding* (15–SE3796). There are many Bromptons, but this one is near NORTHALLERTON. Here in 1867, a restoration of St Thomas's Church uncovered the best collection of Anglo-Danish hogback tombstones in the country. Six were taken to DURHAM Cathedral Library but four whole and fragments of two others are here. They are characterized by carvings of bears hugging the slabs, with strapwork in their mouths. They are probably 1,000 years old. They may have bordered a grave with crosses standing at head and foot. Portions of several fine Anglo-Saxon crosses and shafts can also be seen here.

BROUGH, *East Riding* (13–SE9326). A ferry on the YORK to LINCOLN route carried Roman soldiers across the Humber here in the days of the Roman station of Petuaria. The location was established firmly with the discovery in 1937 of an inscribed stone of A.D. 160 recording the gift of a theatre by Marcus Ulpius Ianuarius. The station covered about 12 acres and was stone-walled. The village is now an appendage of HULL.

BROWSHOLME HALL, *West Riding* (12–SD6845). A landscaped garden and lake were created here by Thomas Lister Parker as a tribute to his good friends, the Prince Regent and Mrs Fitzherbert, and a bedroom suite with an exclusive view of his charming idea was arranged in the Hall. Parkers have been at home here since 1380.

The present Hall, near Waddington and just over the Yorkshire border from CLITHEROE in Lancashire, dates from 1507 with a new front put on in 1604 by Thomas Holt of YORK and alterations again made in 1711 and 1800. The house is of red sandstone. The oak panelling is admired.

BURNSALL, *West Riding* (12–SE0361), presents a charming picture from the grassy fells above. Its grey-stone buildings lie low amid trees and a five-arched bridge crosses the Wharfe. This is a favourite centre for Wharfedale excursions. Diversions offered include fishing for trout or grayling, boating and walking. A maypole stands on the village green where the annual feast-day games in August draw crowds to watch the amateurs compete at canoeing, tug of war, fell races, pillow fights and sprints. St Wilfrid's Church is almost entirely Perpendicular. It was "butified" in 1612, according to a plaque, at the expense of Sir William Craven. He also founded the grammar school in 1602. The building, which resembles a manor house, is now the primary school. The church treasures include an 11th-cent. font crudely carved with birds and beasts; two hogback tombstones, one showing monster heads and scales; 12 Anglo-Saxon sculpture fragments; and a lovely alabaster panel of the mid-14th cent. showing the Adoration of the Magi. To the list could be added the pretty lych-gate with its stone weights. In the churchyard are kept the village stocks. A Dawson family tombstone was designed by Eric Gill.

BURTON AGNES, *East Riding* (13–TA1063). A captivating Elizabethan great house which contains modern French paintings and a ghost is the magnet at this village. It is of mellow red brick with stone trim. The exterior is distinguished by semi-octagonal bays on the east and west sides and semi-circular bays on the south front. A gatehouse with octagonal towers, built a little later but in the same style, leads to the house, elegantly set off by the velvet lawns and almost 100 clipped yews. The house has been in the hands of the family that built it for 350 years. Sir Henry Griffith was the builder, and it was constructed between 1598 and 1610 to replace the Manor House of 1170, much of which still stands (though in an Elizabethan brick casing) under the care of the Ministry of Public Building and Works. Visitors will be hard pressed to absorb all the splendid architectural detail of the richly furnished rooms, but especially memorable are the stone and alabaster chimney-piece and oak and plaster screen of the great hall, the gilded oak panelling of the drawing-room, the massive staircase, the honeysuckle ceiling of the queen's bedroom and the beautifully restored Long Gallery. The ceiling of the gallery collapsed in 1810, and two-thirds of the room, which ran the length of the house, was converted to staff bedrooms. In 1951, the present owner, Marcus William Wickham-Boynton, began the restoration. It was a tribute to modern craftsmen that from a scrap of surviving plaster-work they could re-create the Elizabethan original.

Burton Agnes House contains a fine collection of modern French paintings

The house contains a fascinating collection of paintings which is still growing. The impressive array of French work includes Cézanne, Pisarro, Gauguin, Matisse, Vuillard, Dufy, Vlaminck and many more. The ghost is of Anne, youngest daughter of the builder, whose portrait hangs in the inner hall. She died after being attacked by ruffians at **Harpham**, and her dying wish was that her skull should remain forever in the house she loved. But her sisters buried her in the churchyard, and the place was racked with ghostly disturbance. The coffin was opened and the head found severed from her body. It was reburied in the house and each attempt to get rid of it has been followed by trouble. It is thought now to be built into a wall of the great hall. The village church, St Martin's, late Norman to Perpendicular, is found through an archway of yews and contains family tombs. At St John's Church in Harpham, ¼ m. SW., there are fine 15th-cent. brasses of the St Quintin family and a rare incised alabaster slab. Harpham was the birthplace of St John of BEVERLEY.

BURTON CONSTABLE, *East Riding* (13–TA1836), the home of the Constables, whose landholdings in the East Riding go back to the 11th cent., is open to visitors daily during the summer season. The great house is set in a 200-acre park filled by Capability Brown with oaks, chestnuts and elms, a lake with an arched bridge, an island and a bird sanctuary, and a pretty French garden. The central block and two projecting wings of the house were built in 1570, but most of the rooms were redone in the 18th cent. by such Georgian craftsmen as Robert Adam and James Wyatt. The remodelling was the work of William Constable, who collected many of the pictures which make

up the excellent collection. The house interiors run the gamut from a Georgian dining-room to a Tudor Long Gallery with pendant ceiling. The east front of Burton Constable is known for its domed bays and gabled flanking ranges. The west front, where columns support the pediment and a tower stands guard at each end, measures more than 200 ft. In the stately homes competition, this one offers a zoo, model railway, collection of carriages, children's playground, camping and caravan sites. You can even tour the grounds by stagecoach.

BUTTERTUBS PASS, *North Riding* (14–SD 8795). High, wide views greet the motorist taking the road from **Hawes** N. to Thwaite over the Buttertubs Pass. It is the justly famous link between Wensleydale and Swaledale, and one of the highest sections of road in the country; like all Pennine roads, it can be made hazardous by snow and ice at any time during the long winter season. It gets its name from a series of deep limestone shafts which might be said to look like buttertubs (or pots or churns, as fancy dictates). Motorists will not see them unless they get out of their cars. They are 4½ m. from Hawes and 50 to 100 ft from the side of the road on the right.

BYLAND ABBEY, *North Riding* (13–SE5478). After several unhappy moves, a Cistercian colony settled in this broad valley 2 m. NE. of COXWOLD in 1177. Here they drained the marshes, built their quarters and their church and led an uneventful life until the Dissolution. Byland is a haunting ruin now, on a bend in the road, confronting a small inn in a region that seems otherwise uninhabited. The tall west front with its vast broken circle of a rose window and a single turret beside it

Castle Howard is one of the most palatial country houses in England

is a telling reminder of the magnificent church that once stood here. The plan of the church and monastic buildings is easily followed on the excavated site, now in the care of the Ministry of Public Building and Works. Here you can see the green and yellow glazed tiles in geometric patterns which used to cover the nave and transept floors.

CAMPSALL, *West Riding* (13–SE5313), is known for the architectural interest of its Church of St Mary Magdalene and for Robin Hood: the legendary outlaw is supposed to have preyed on travellers passing through the Barnsdale forest which once surrounded the village. Modern housing estates are crowding the old village centre with its core of church, vicarage and hall, but the church is least affected. The Norman west tower, called by Pevsner "the most ambitious . . . in the Riding", was given battlements and pinnacles somewhat later. The west door is framed in zig-zag moulding. Over the west bay of the south aisle is a priest's room. A new south chapel uses a carved and colourfully painted stone altar by A. W. N. Pugin from the abandoned Ackworth Grange Chapel. The treasured 15th-cent. rood-screen bears a rhymed inscription. The vivid Te Deum east window was completed in 1964 by H. W. Harvey of YORK.

CARLTON-IN-CLEVELAND, *North Riding* (15–NZ5005). Under the moors S. of STOKESLEY is a village of great charm, the one-time parish of a splendid sporting parson. He was the Rev. J. L. Kyle, who came here in 1894 when the parish was under a cloud. His predecessor, George Sangar, had toiled mightily to build a new church. It was completed in 1879, and burnt in

1881. The vicar was charged with arson, but later cleared. Canon Kyle remained until his death in 1943, a hearty man who farmed, rode to hounds, kept a pub (the Fox and Hounds next to the vicarage, "to reform it"), and raised the money for the present St Botolph's Church. Both church and lych-gate were designed by Temple Moore and completed in 1897. They fit well into the village. On the main street are gracious cottages and a manor house, built after 1740, a small-scale Palladian villa with a five-bay centre block and flanking pavilions. On Carlton Bank are the remains of an alum works, which closed in 1771, and a hangar of the NEWCASTLE Gliding Club. There are two lovely runs from Carlton, SE. over the hills to Chop Gate in Bilsdale, with marvellous views all the way, or SW. to Faceby beneath Whorl Hill, a conical mound and the reputed lair of a dragon.

CASTLE HOWARD, *North Riding* (13–SE 7170). Seen against the orthodox prettiness of the Howardian Hills, the splendour of Castle Howard is all the more astonishing. This palace 6 m. W. of MALTON, the largest house in Yorkshire, has no counterpart among English country houses. It is Sir John Vanbrugh's first; his second was BLENHEIM. Castle Howard was built to replace Henderskelfe Castle which burnt down in 1693. The 3rd Earl of Carlisle chose Vanbrugh to design it, a surprise since at that time (1699) Vanbrugh was a captain of marines and successful playwright, but a complete amateur in architecture. But he in turn chose Nicholas Hawksmoor, Wren's clerk, to be his clerk of works, a partnership of brilliance and experience. The building and grounds took from 1700 to 1737 to complete at a cost of more than £78,000. By then, the earl, Vanbrugh and Hawksmoor were dead.

The west wing was added by the 4th Earl's son-in-law, Sir Thomas Robinson. The stables were designed by John Carr in 1781. With its long arched windows, pilasters, frieze, balustrade and bristling urns and statues, the great house spreads from a central block into wings, with a cupola, unheard of for houses at this date, forming a magnificent central climax. Indoors the grandeur continues with the great marble entrance hall, lit by the dome, a suitable introduction. The house has a vast treasure of statuary, furniture, china, miniatures and paintings by masters such as Rubens, Tintoretto, Van Dyke, Canaletto, and Reynolds. Perhaps its most famous picture is Holbein's Henry VIII. The house is the home of George and Lady Cecilia Howard. It has been open to the public throughout its existence. The 1,000-acre park has two lakes and many notable ornaments, including Vanbrugh's Temple of the Four Winds and Hawksmoor's Mausoleum, the size of a Wren church. The house itself is commemorated in a 100-ft obelisk on the road through the park, erected in 1714.

CATTERICK, *North Riding* (15–SE2497). The military connection goes back a long way here. The Romans had a camp they called Cataractonium to the NW. of the present village. This was probably the Catraeth that appears in an early Welsh poem telling of a doomed counter-attack by Celtic Britons against the incoming English, after the legions had gone. Catterick Camp with its monotonous buildings lies $3\frac{1}{2}$ m. W. of the village and is the overwhelming presence now. According to tradition, **Hipswell** close by was the birthplace of John Wycliffe.

Catterick village used to be a major coaching stop on the Great North Road. The Perpendicular Church of St Anne is interesting partly because a contract describing the plans in detail exists for its building. A north chapel was added in 1491 and a south chapel in 1505. There are a 14th-cent. effigy of a knight and two 15th-cent. brasses among the monuments. A contract also survives to document the building of the low bridge over the Swale in 1422, 1 m. N. of the village. There has been an inn there ever since the bridge went up. Big crowds used to gather for the cockfighting. Today they come for the horse-racing.

CAWOOD, *West Riding* (13–SE5737). A tall white stone gatehouse dating from the 15th cent., and incongruously linking a brick house and a barn now, is the only physical reminder of the great palace of the archbishops of YORK which once stood here. It is an ancient site, having been used by Romans, Angles and Vikings. King Athelstan built the castle which in the 14th cent. became the palace. Seven archbishops died here and in 1465 George Neville celebrated his appointment with a gigantic feast employing 2,000 cooks for untold guests. Cardinal Wolsey had hoped to make this palace a rival to HAMPTON COURT, which he had given to Henry VIII. Wolsey was arrested here while he was ill. Cawood was taken in the Civil War and nearly demolished. With its

clustering cottages and narrow winding streets it is a pretty sight from the swing-bridge or from the churchyard. All Saints stands near the muddy banks of the Ouse. It is mainly late Norman, with a Perpendicular tower reinforced with buttresses, battlements and pinnacles. It contains a dignified monument to Archbishop Mountain who died in 1623.

About 2 m. SW. on the B1222 is the newly opened **Bishop Wood** park, part of the Forestry Commission's Selby Forest. The area is low-lying and paths may be muddy. Unlike most of the Plain of York, Bishop Wood was never reclaimed for farming so it stands as an ancient example of woodland. Poplars are a special feature and there are 300 kinds of plants and ferns, 70 species of birds, and mammals from hedgehogs to badgers to look for.

CLAPHAM, *West Riding* (12–SD7469), is the centre for potholing. Upstream a short distance is Ingleborough Cave, 900 yds into the great hill of **Ingleborough**, which was made accessible in 1857. It is a place of many eerie chambers and imaginatively named rock formations and it is open to the public. A mile further on is Gaping Gill. You can earn the freedom of Craven by descending its 378 ft, but it is necessary to go with a potholing club. A winch will lower the venturesome in 90 seconds. Gaping Gill has an underground chamber large enough to accommodate a small cathedral. The summit of Ingleborough provides far-ranging views on a good day.

Clapham itself is a tidy village of grey-stone houses and whitewashed cottages along a beck. Pretty gardens and fine trees add to the village scene. St James's Church, happily sited, was completely rebuilt in 1814 except for the Perpendicular west tower. Ingleborough Hall, developed out of a shooting lodge, is used by the West Riding County Council as a special school. The beck was dammed to create an 8-acre lake in the grounds and a waterfall spills into the ravine from it. Reginald Farrer, the botanist who introduced a hundred plants to Europe and wrote extensively on rock gardens, lived here, and the monthly magazine, *The Dalesman*, devoted to all aspects of Yorkshire country life, has been published in Clapham since 1939.

CONISBROUGH, *West Riding* (13–SK5198). The great white circular keep of the Norman castle rises dramatically above surrounding greenery high over the River Don, with a little town at its feet. The keep is 90 ft high, 52 ft in diameter and has six massive buttresses 9 ft thick. It is the oldest and best of its kind in the country and is in the care of the Ministry of Public Building and Works. The castle was founded by the de Warennes and the surviving work was by Hameline Plantagenet, who married the last of the Warenne family and took his wife's name. He built an identical keep in Normandy. This one probably dates from 1185. A narrow barbican with two turns leads inside. The tiny chapel on the third floor, built into the buttress, was the setting for a scene in Sir Walter Scott's *Ivanhoe*. From the roof is a wide view of the coalfield.

On a lesser height in the hilly town is St Peter's Church which dates from Anglo-Saxon times, with substantial parts of it constructed at the same time as the castle. The chancel arch, west tower, aisle arcades (with deeply carved capitals) and south doorway are all 12th-cent. The most important church treasure is the extraordinary Norman tomb-chest or gravestone. It is decorated all over in patterns and figures, with remarkable scenes of a man battling a dragon, two mounted knights jousting, and Adam with Eve.

COVERHAM ABBEY, *North Riding* (12–SE 1186).

Coverdale is one of the smallest and quietest of the Yorkshire dales. The stream has only a short run before it empties into the Ure below MIDDLEHAM. In the valley are the slight remains of Coverham Abbey, now in the grounds of a private home. The abbey was founded by Helewisia de Glanville, wife of Robert Fitzralf of Middleham Castle, at Swainby. Her son, Ralf Fitzrobert, had many quarrels with the Premonstratensian canons and for some reason moved them to Coverdale about 1212. Relics of the abbey include portions of the arcade and transept and coffin lids, including late-13th-cent. effigies of cross-legged knights who may have been Helewisia's son and grandson. The humpbacked Coverham Bridge, the restored country church on the steep bank, the abbey mill and miller's house complete the picture in the secluded dale. Here was born Miles Coverdale who produced the translation known as the Great Bible for the common people in 1538.

COXWOLD, *North Riding* (13–SE5377),

a dream of a village: a wide sloping street with broad verges, rows of honey-coloured cottages, spreading trees, and at the top a 15th-cent. church with an unusual octagonal tower. It is in the area of the gentle Howardian Hills with lovely countryside and neighbouring villages to enjoy. Despite its fame as a beauty-spot, Coxwold has managed to stay unspoilt and serene, a tribute to residents as well as the landowners, the Wombwell family.

Laurence Sterne came to Coxwold in 1760, just after he had published his first novel, *The Life and Opinions of Tristram Shandy* ("shandy" is Yorkshire for wild or eccentric). The obscure country clergyman was just becoming a social lion. He rented a rambling house N. of town, because the church had no vicarage, and named it Shandy Hall. Here he wrote at least two more volumes during a seven years' residence. He died in 1768 in London and his remains were returned to Coxwold churchyard in 1969 from a Bayswater burial ground. The Sterne Trust now owns Shandy Hall and is restoring it as a museum. The old brick farm-house has medieval timber framing, a bulky chimney and a warren of rooms.

Another notable Coxwold building is the Fauconberg Arms, 17th-cent. in its origins and restored in the 18th cent., with the family crest on the front. Under the old manorial system, the inn is allowed the right to graze four cows on a large meadow shared by the villagers and to cut hay from two strips of the town pasture.

The church is chiefly Perpendicular but the chancel was rebuilt in the 18th cent. Pulpit, communion rail and box pews also are Georgian. There are a number of monuments of the Bellasis family, one of whom became the Earl of Fauconberg. Behind the church is Colville Hall, the former Manor House, an early 17th-cent. gabled building. Across the street is the Old Hall, formerly a grammar school and also 17th-cent.

S. of the village is **Newburgh Priory**; the pond and ornamental hedges are eye-catching features on the road. A private residence of the Wombwells, it is essentially an 18th-cent. hall. Its predecessor on the site was a house of Augustinian canons who settled here about 1150. With the Dissolution the property went to Anthony Bellasis, Henry VIII's chaplain. A Fauconberg married the daughter of Oliver Cromwell who is supposed to have brought her father's body – perhaps only the heart – back here for burial. It is thought the pitiful remains are in a bricked-up end of a small attic room.

CRAVEN, *West Riding* (12–SD9070 *around*).

The district known as Craven, in the western Dales, consists of fells and peaks, nine of them more than 2,000 feet high. The best known and grandest are Whernside, Ingleborough and Pen-y-Ghent. The rivers Wharfe and Ribble, among other streams, rise in these hills. The landscape is distinguished by limestone scars and cliffs (notably MALHAM Cove, Gordale Scar and KILNSEY CRAG), underground streams, caves and potholes. Climbing and caving are naturally enough favourite pastimes in Craven. A fine example of the caverns carved by subterranean rivers is Stump Cross near PATELEY BRIDGE. Potholing requires both skill and good equipment here. Among the most explored potholes are Gaping Gill on Ingleborough and the Hunt and Hull Pots on Pen-y-Ghent. The scenery owes its dramatic appearance to the Craven Faults, giant dislocations of the Pennine rock, worked upon over the ages by wind and water. The vantage point for seeing the line of the faults is Buckhaw Brow out of GIGGLESWICK. Ingleborough was a walled stronghold of the Brigantes who resisted the Roman occupation. Collections from caves used in earlier periods can be examined at the Craven Museum, SKIPTON, and the Pig Yard Museum, SETTLE.

CRAYKE, *North Riding* (13–SE5670).

You cannot miss this tiny village for it sits on a small hill on the Plain of York. On top are a church and a battlemented residence made out of the tower house of the 15th-cent. castle, and at the bottom a green and old cottages. The castle at one time was a house of the Bishops of DURHAM. Nothing remains of either the presumed Anglo-Saxon fortress or the Norman castle which came after it. St Cuthbert's Church is Perpendicular with some very good furnishings.

CROFT, *North Riding* (15–NZ2909). The village bestriding the Tees had a brief fling as a spa and even sold its bottled waters in London in the early 18th cent. But the rise of HARROGATE was the downfall of Croft. The red sandstone church at the end of the 15th-cent. bridge (widened, of course), the rambling Croft Spa Hotel and some pleasant Queen Anne and Georgian houses remind the visitor of the more important village of the past. Lewis Carroll's father, the Rev. Charles Dodgson, was vicar here for 25 years. The boy, Charles, was 12 when the big family settled into the rectory (now flats) in 1843. The long, low-lying Church of St Peter should be visited to see the 17th-cent. Milbanke pew, erected an arrogant 6 ft above the floor near the chancel. Attained by a staircase and resting upon Tuscan columns, the pew is 15 ft long. Lord Byron and his bride probably sat in it when visiting at Halnaby Hall, once the home of the Milbankes, Lady Byron's family, but now demolished.

DANBY-IN-CLEVELAND, *North Riding* (15–NZ7007). The classic account of moorland life is still *Forty Years in a Moorland Parish* by Canon John Christopher Atkinson, who spent 53 of his 86 years at St Hilda's Church here and was buried in the churchyard in 1900. The village, also called Dale End, is at the head of Danby Dale which runs S. into the moors. The church is 2 m. from the village, with the rectory halfway between. The church has a Perpendicular south porch and a fragment or so of other old stone, but is chiefly an 18th-cent. nave on a 19th-cent. chancel. One m. SE. of the village is the ruin of 14th-cent. Danby Castle, now built into a farmhouse. Catherine Parr's second husband, Lord Latimer, owned it in those days. After his death she married, and survived, Henry VIII. Near the castle is the packhorse Duck Bridge, built around 1386. On the 1,000-ft Danby Beacon, $1\frac{1}{2}$ m. NE. of the village, stands a radar station. Danby Dale is a beautiful broad valley of the Esk, with many ancient cairns. Much scenic beauty awaits you if you cannot resist the names of Little Fryup and Great Fryup.

DENT, *West Riding* (12–SD7087). The only town in Dentdale has a narrow cobbled main street which no one who has driven or walked over will soon forget. Dent is picturesque in a wholly natural, effortless way. It lies deep in the valley cut by the Dee, unspoilt, unimportant, unhurried. Grey-stone cottages, many now painted white, are what the visitor remembers of the town. Against one rests a slab of Shap granite that forms a drinking fountain memorial to a famous 19th-cent. local man, Adam Sedgwick, the vicar's son who became a pioneer geologist. There was a move in his day to change the name of a Dentdale hamlet from Cowgill to Kirkthwaite, because it was thought seemlier. Sedgwick is remembered locally for his *Memorial* in defence of the homely old name which was confirmed by Act of Parliament.

Dent has lost many of its old activities, such as making cheese, or hay rakes and butter boxes. In the 18th cent. people here turned out hand-knitted garments so rapidly that they were known as the "terrible knitters of Dent". Marble quarried in the upper valley for more than a century was made into countless tombs, fonts, tables and stairs. It is almost entirely a farming economy now, with an inflow of townsfolk and holiday-makers partly offsetting the loss of other vocations. The steep slopes of Whernside, Great Coum, Middleton Fell and Rise Hill which form the dale walls tempt walkers.

DONCASTER, *West Riding* (13–SE5803). The classic St Leger has been run since 1776, although it was not given the name of its founder until two years later. Thus it is four years older than the Derby. The grandstand designed by John Carr in 1776 and enlarged in the early 19th cent. is an attractive component of the Doncaster racing scene which goes back 400 years. Dickens came to the races in 1857, stayed at the then relatively new New Angel Hotel and commented acidly on the "horse-mad, betting-mad, drunken-mad, vice-mad" crowds. Doncaster was the site of a Roman station, Danum, with extensive iron and pottery works. It was also known to Anglo-Saxons and Normans. Although the charters date back to 1194, it is a modern town, transformed from an agricultural to an industrial centre by the arrival of the railway in 1848 and a carriage works in 1853. The surrounding coalfield is today the basis of the economy: Doncaster is ringed by mining villages. The National Coal Board's 10-story office block is one of the buildings in the new Civic Centre, Glasgow Paddocks.

The Museum and Art Gallery, completed in 1964, is in Chequer Road and contains relics from the Roman station, fossils from mines, and British birds. Paintings and sculpture are mainly by British artists. Fabio Barraclough and Frantz Belsky did the sculptures on the exterior.

Among older buildings, two churches and the Mansion House stand out. The Mansion House, the pretty pride of Doncaster, is in the High Street and was completed in 1748. James Paine's plan included two supporting wings but these were never built. A third story was added in 1801, in place of the original pediment, for the mayor's use but the building has not been a mayoral residence for 140 years. It is used for civic and social occasions. The façade has first-floor Corinthian columns and a lovely Venetian window which lights a handsome ballroom with stucco work by Joseph Rose and two fireplaces probably by Robert Adam.

St George's Parish Church is on almost cathedral scale and it replaced a medieval church burnt in 1833. It was designed by Sir George Gilbert Scott and completed in 1858. It is 170 ft long and its massive tower stands 170 ft high. The exterior bristles with pinnacles. Scott also designed the Doncaster Grammar School for Boys, 1864. Christ Church in Thorne Road was designed by William Hurst and completed in 1829. It has a steeple and octagonal lantern.

Dent: the Adam Sedgwick memorial in the village street

On Hall Cross Hill is the monument rebuilt by the corporation in 1793 to replace a cross originally in Hall Gate which commemorated Ote de Tilli about 1182.

Doncaster manufactures wire and wire rope, brass fittings, nylon yarn, agricultural equipment and the famous butterscotch.

At the South Yorkshire Industrial Museum in Cusworth Hall on the outskirts, an absorbing hour or two can be spent among exhibits tracing the social history of mining and manufacturing in this area.

EASBY, *North Riding* (15–NZ1800). An ancient church and picturesque monastery ruins await the traveller who takes the footpath from RICH-MOND station along the River Swale or turns his car off the B6271 SE. of Richmond. St Agatha's Church is much older than the religious house, though mainly 13th- and 14th-cent. as it now stands. Rather plain and low, the church contains three features of special interest: a Norman font; a cast of the very early-9th-cent. Easby Cross (the original is in the VICTORIA AND ALBERT MUSEUM); and wall paintings of the mid-13th cent. The cross is the best Anglo-Saxon sculpture in Yorkshire and depicts birds and beasts on the back with Christ and the Apostles on the front. Scrolls and foliage are carved on the sides and borders. The wall paintings in the chancel are fairly well preserved and tell the story of man from the creation of Eve through the expulsion from Eden, the Annunciation, Nativity and Entombment. In the splays of the windows are the homely labours of the months: hawking, digging, pruning and sowing, all delightfully drawn. Portraits of archbishops are visible on the sedilia.

The extensive remains of the monastery are crowded on the bank of the Swale on the strip of land which rises towards Easby Hall, a Georgian mansion. The abbey was founded for Premonstratensian canons about 1155 by Roald, Constable of Richmond Castle. It suffered at the hands of both English and Scots and was greatly damaged in 1346 when the English army was billeted here. It was acquired by the Scrope family in the same cent. The Ministry of Public Building and Works is the guardian now. The highlight of a tour in the ruins probably will be the splendid windows of the great refectory, where the walls still stand almost to their full height. There is a fine east window here and windows along the south wall, with beautiful tracery. The 14th-cent. gatehouse remains but there is little left of the church, though enough to recapture the sense of this medieval community.

ECCLESFIELD, *West Riding* (12–SK3393). This steel town has a large and handsome parish church, St Mary's, which is chiefly Perpendicular in style with traces of earlier work. An unusual feature are the small flying buttresses which link the buttresses and pinnacles to the church body. The windows contain an assortment of 19th-cent. stained glass and there is good 16th-cent. woodwork. The parish was once exceptionally large and the church was known as the "Minster of the Moors". It had one vicar for 63 years, Alfred Gatty, who served here until the age of 90. His wife wrote children's books, as did their daughter, Juliana Heratia Ewing. The Rev. Joseph Hunter, the 19th-cent. Yorkshire historian who traced the names and towns of the people who sailed for America on the *Mayflower*, is buried in the churchyard. A cell of the Benedictines was established here and some remains of their priory are now in the house called The Priory, N. of the church. Whiteley Hall, in the valley ¾ m. NW., was built in 1584 with a wing added in 1683. Later alterations were made to front and rear. It is a horticultural centre now.

EGGLESTONE ABBEY, *North Riding* (14–NZ0615). A pastoral setting on a knoll beside the Tees 1½ m. S. of BARNARD CASTLE gives the abbey ruins their quiet charm. The river is crossed here by a single-arch stone bridge with a battlemented parapet, built in 1773. This is the place to enjoy the river view. Over Thorsgill Beck, which the monks employed in their drainage system, stands an old packhorse bridge. Woods and running waters combine here to create a memorable scene. The abbey was founded for Premonstratensian canons from EASBY by Robert de Malton in about 1196. It was neither large nor important when it surrendered in 1540. Robert Strelley acquired it in 1548 and converted a range of buildings on the east side into a house. The ruins are chiefly of the cruciform church. The Ministry of Public Building and Works is in charge. There are pleasant walks to and from Barnard Castle.

EGTON, *North Riding* (15–NZ8006). High in the moors, this village overlooks the Esk and is noted for salmon fishing and a Gooseberry Fair in August. Bronze and jet ornaments have been found in ancient graves in the vicinity. St Hilda's, the parish church, was rebuilt in the 1870s in the Norman style. Below at leafy Egton Bridge is St Hedda's Roman Catholic Church built a decade earlier. This was a Catholic stronghold and near here lived the last of the English martyrs, Father Nicholas Postgate. He was finally arrested after baptizing a child, tried at YORK, and hanged at the age of 83 in 1679.

ESCRICK, *East Riding* (13–SE6243). A substantial village near enough to YORK for its residents to work there, Escrick has a lovely Victorian church, St Helen's, built in 1857 and designed by F. C. Penrose in 14th-cent. style. It makes colourful use of marble in the semi-circular west-end baptistry where the vaulted brick roof is supported by red and black marble pillars. The font is the work of Giovanni Tognoli of Rome and consists of a translucent white marble basin upheld on the heads of two standing cherubs. Pink stone is used in the body of the church which has a fine barrel-vaulted roof. A legless effigy by York craftsmen is of Sir Thomas de Lascelles who died in 1324. An 1868 marble effigy of the 1st Lady Wenlock by Count Gleichen shows her as an old lady in a lace shawl. Escrick Park was the home of Sir Thomas Kynvet who discovered the gunpowder hidden by Guy Fawkes (a York lad) in the HOUSES OF PARLIAMENT. The hall has been converted to flats.

FILEY, *East Riding* (13–TA1180). Filey Brigg is a mile-long rocky reef jutting out from the Carr Naze headland at the top of Filey Bay. Half of the brigg is under water and the rest gives anglers, picnickers and geologists endless happy hours. It is a coralline oolite ridge topped with boulder clay. Weather and erosion have carved it into ledges, coves, caves, cliffs and pools. The waves hammer it mercilessly in stormy weather, sending up seething clouds of spray. The Romans left traces and it may have provided them with an anchorage. From it you can look S. to FLAMBOROUGH Head and N. to SCARBOROUGH Castle. It forms a natural pier and breakwater for Filey, part old-world fishing village and part modern holiday resort with promenade, gardens and long sandy beach. Most of the town stands on the cliff top with a fine outlook over the crescent bay. Wooded Church Ravine runs up from the sea and above it stands St Oswald's Church which belonged until 1537 to the Augustinian canons of BRIDLINGTON. Its oldest parts date to the late 12th cent. There is a fishermen's memorial window to those lost at sea and a "weatherfish" on the heavy square tower. The Roman Catholic Church of St Mary is in the form of an ancient basilica with an altar in 6th-cent. Italian style and a mosaic on the east end. Charlotte Brontë often stayed at Cliff House, now a café.

FLAMBOROUGH, *East Riding* (13–TA2570). The chalky cliffs of Flamborough Head jut out of the Yorkshire coast where the wolds plunge into the sea. The promontory forms the "nose" on the bearded profile of the Yorkshire map. Ships have often foundered here and in 1779 people watched John Paul Jones win a sea fight with two English men-of-war. The area was taken by Vikings 1,000 years ago and is still sometimes called "Little Denmark". The South Landing offers a view of BRIDLINGTON while on the North Landing you can watch the cobles hauled up by engine and the crab pots unloaded on a beach embraced by cliffs. Flamborough village is 2 m. inland from the lighthouse, a straggling place with a much restored church, St Oswald's. It has a fine 16th-cent. rood-screen and a rare loft, monuments to Constables and Stricklands, and a pair of white paper gloves such as were worn at a maiden's funeral. The monument to Sir Marmaduke Constable who died in 1520 shows him with bared heart, a reference to the gruesome story that his heart was eaten by a toad he had swallowed.

The wind- and wave-sculptured cliffs, 300 to 400 ft high, between Flamborough and **Bempton** are the best and largest mainland breeding ground for sea birds in England, with numbers at their peak in the first half of July. The only mainland gannet colony in Britain is slowly increasing here and there are numbers of kittiwakes, herring gulls, guillemots, razorbills and some puffins. At times in the past the birds have been shot for food or feathers and crowds used to come to watch the climmers, as they are called here, risk their necks to plunder nests for eggs to sell the spectators. That trade was stopped by Act of Parliament in 1954.

J. K. St Joseph, Cambridge University Collection

Fountains Abbey preserves the plan of a medieval monastery almost intact

FOSTON, *North Riding* (13–SE6965). In Sydney Smith's church here a bronze wall tablet pays tribute to him as "the faithful friend and counsellor of his parishioners; a fearless advocate of civil and religious freedom; a seeker and ensuer of peace; a wit who used his powers to delight and not to wound. One of the founders and first editor of *The Edinburgh Review.*" The great cleric and reformer served this parish as rector, doctor and magistrate from 1809 to 1829. St Paul's Church, up a cobblestone path lined with yews, was consecrated in 1290, the church notes tell us, but it must be even older in light of the sumptuous Norman south doorway. Sheltered by a timber-framed porch, it has a series of medallions on the hood mould with such scenes as the Last Supper, St George and the Dragon, David with a harp, and various angels, beasts and humans. There is a lesser Norman doorway on the north wall, reset in the aisle added in 1911, and a Norman pillar piscina. Pink roses nod over the wall of the churchyard in this hamlet. A friendly note pinned to the visitors' book in the church invites all callers to a cup of tea at the rectory in Flaxton. The rectory that Sydney Smith built, a long pink-brick classically Georgian house, is about 1 m. away near Thornton-le-Clay and open to visitors on summer Sundays.

FOUNTAINS ABBEY, *West Riding* (12–SE 2768). The incomparable ruins of the greatest abbey in England stand in the lovely valley of the River Skell 4 m. SW. of RIPON. The amazing thing is how much is left. Partly this is due to William Aislabie, owner of adjoining STUDLEY ROYAL, who acquired Fountains in 1768 and, continuing the landscaping hobby of his father, "gardened" the ruins. The story of the abbey is one of humble beginnings, a rise to power, and eclipse. The prior and several monks at St Mary's Abbey, YORK, disapproved of the laxity which had overtaken their house and with the help of Archbishop Thurstan left to make a new beginning. They adopted the Cistercian rule and began building. They grew in property and recruits but unfortunately the estates outstripped the number of lay brothers and the monks had to let their farms and employ workers. Their huge wool clips paid for the building programme. Power and the display of wealth had replaced the reformist zeal by the time of the Dissolution. Fountains was a great prize, and Henry VIII sold it to Sir Richard Gresham in 1540.

The ruins give a comprehensive picture of life in a medieval monastery. The church extended 360 ft with a 168-ft tower added just before the end. The east window and Chapel of the Nine

G. Douglas Bolton

Fylingdales: the radomes of the Early Warning Station are designed to detect ballistic missiles

Altars are special points of interest. The cellarium with its double row of arches is outstanding among the features of the monastic quarters. Near the West Gate, Fountains Hall was built in 1610 by Sir Stephen Proctor who helped himself to abbey stone for the purpose. The house is a Jacobean triumph, built on a hillside and five stories tall. It is furnished in the style of the period. The banqueting hall has a minstrel gallery and an oriel window contains fine heraldic glass. Among the many treasures kept here is the foundation charter for Fountains. Today the abbey, Hall and grounds are owned by the West Riding County Council and cared for by the Ministry of Public Building and Works.

FYLINGDALES, *North Riding* (15–SE9199). Since 1961, the empty moor inland from ROBIN HOOD'S BAY has had a focal point – the radomes of the Air Ministry's Ballistic Missile Early Warning Station. Visible for miles, the three giant white globes have an unearthly look. Their intrusion into the NORTH YORK MOORS NATIONAL PARK was much regretted by many people but to Pevsner they represent "the geometry of the space age at its most alluring and most frightening".

GIGGLESWICK, *West Riding* (12–SD8163). The village with the infectious name enjoys spectacular upland scenery in its nearby Giggleswick Scar and the heights of Ingleborough and Pen-y-Ghent (2,273 ft) to the N. The well-known public school occupies grey-stone 19th-cent. buildings to the W. of the village, with its chapel under a copper dome, now turned green, standing conspicuously above. The school was founded here in 1553. The parish church is dedicated to St Alkelda, an obscure Anglo-Saxon saint said to have been martyred by the Danes, and is wholly Perpendicular. It contains excellent 17th-cent. furnishings including a pulpit, reading desk, communion rail and poor box. It also has a battered effigy of a knight, Sir Richard Tempest, who was buried in 1488 with the head of his favourite horse. The village itself is pleasantly old-fashioned

with market cross, stocks and tithe barn near the church and period cottages. Near the foot of the Scar is the Ebbing and Flowing Well, an oddity which behaves as its name suggests. It is beside the steep Buckhaw Brow road to CLAPHAM.

GILLING CASTLE, *North Riding* (13–SE 6277), at Gilling East between the Hambleton and Howardian Hills, was built on a steep rise above the village. The house is a fascinating study for its mixture of building styles, its beautiful chimney-pieces, panelling and heraldry, and for its gardens. It stands on three sides of a courtyard. The central block is Tudor and was built on medieval foundations of a 14th-cent. tower house of Thomas of Etton. The wings are 18th-cent. for the most part. Vanbrugh, Wakefield and Gibbs have all been mentioned as possible architects. The castle was occupied by Fairfaxes and their successors from 1492 until 1930. Precious parts were sold in 1929. The wall panelling and heraldic glass of the Great Chamber, for example, were bought by William Randolph Hearst, the American publisher. After Hearst's death in 1951, these were found still in packing cases and re-purchased for the castle. The Long Gallery sold at the same time is at the Bowes Museum, BARNARD CASTLE. AMPLEFORTH College bought the castle as a preparatory school in 1930, preserving the rest. It is open to visitors. The Great Chamber is a stunning room built in 1575–85 with its restored stained-glass windows and painted frieze above the panelling showing family trees bearing 370 coats of arms. The ceiling has a pattern of ribs and pendants. The lofty entrance hall has Corinthian columns and stucco work by Cortese.

GOATHLAND, *North Riding* (15–NZ8301). Tourists and sheep occupy the residents of this big, breezy village, an ideal centre for the North York Moors. It spreads around a very large green. Among the mixed old and new inns and houses, St Mary's Church, built in the 1890s to a plan of W. H. Brierley, fits pleasantly. It has a stone roof and a low oblong tower between the chancel and the nave. An early stone altar and font link it to the past. A path leads off the green to Mallyan Spout, a 70-ft waterfall, one of several in the neighbourhood (Nellie Ayre, Thomason and Water Ark being among the better known). A waterfall is known as a foss in these parts; the word is one of many reminders of Danish settlement. Two m. S. of Goathland station is a mile-long section of the Roman road, kept by the Ministry of Public Building and Works. The road probably dates from the 1st cent. and crosses Wheeldale Moor, part of Wade's Way from MALTON to WHITBY. On special occasions, men and boys perform the ancient longsword and plough stots dances here. Stots is the name for bullocks and here applies to the men who drag the plough around to collect donations for a merry celebration on Plough Monday. Goathland's famous hunt dates from 1750.

GOODMANHAM, East Riding (13–SE8842).
The village NE. of Market Weighton in the good farmland of the East Riding is one of the oldest as well as most evocative religious sites in the county. Bede's History of the English Church and Nation relates the conversion of King Edwin to Christianity in 627 and tells how the high priest, Coifi, also renounced his pagan beliefs. But not content with words, Coifi borrowed arms and a horse from the king and smashed and burnt his own temple, where Goodmanham church now stands. This church is All Saints, commendable for its simplicity and its age. Parts are Norman – the lower part of the stubby tower and the nave – while the north aisle was added and the chancel rebuilt in the 13th cent. In the 15th cent., the tower was given a belfry and battlements. Two unusual fonts are owned by the church. A 15th-cent. octagonal one 5 ft tall is heavily sculptured. The other, well worn from use as a horse trough, could be Anglo-Saxon.

GOOLE, West Riding (13–SE7423).
Fifty miles from the sea is this busy port, established as the terminus of the Aire and Calder canal from Knottingley in 1826. The canal company sought to improve navigation to the Ouse to speed the export of Yorkshire coal and textiles. At this point, the Don and Ouse rivers meet by way of the "Dutch River", so named because it was cut by Cornelius Vermuyden, a Dutch engineer, in the days of Charles I to drain the Hatfield Chase marshes. The area around Goole, low and watery, does have a Netherlandish feeling. The red-brick town is visible for some distance across the flat land, its high points being two water towers, the church steeple and the dockside cranes. Town life centres around the busy docks, with municipal and harbour offices sharing the Bank Chambers, built in 1892. The port handles two million tons of cargo a year, its inland position making it handy for the coalfields and industrial areas. Nearly all of Goole was built after 1820. The Lowther Hotel, Georgian, is the oldest standing building. The larger water tower was once

reckoned to be the biggest in England, able to hold 750,000 gallons. St John's Church, completed in 1838 by the navigation company, is Perpendicular in style. It is close to the dock sheds and contains memorials to ships as well as seamen. The Garside local history collection is in the new Public Library and museum building in Carlisle Street.

GRASSINGTON, West Riding (12–SE0064).
This Wharfedale village is one of the most appealing in the dales; its buildings crowd around a small market place paved with cobblestones and along irregular passages. The river is crossed by a stone bridge placed there in 1603 and widened in the late 18th cent. One of the houses, the Old Hall, dates in part from the 13th cent., and 17th-cent. cottages are fairly common. It has been a centre for lead-mining but today is largely dependent upon the visitors' trade. Fishing and walking are two popular diversions. River paths lead to BURNSALL and BOLTON ABBEY or up into the moors. Grassington has always appealed to people, it seems, for the area has numerous prehistoric sites. An especially good one is Lea Green, a pasture reached from Chapel Street, where an Iron Age village stood. Grass Woods nearby is a nature reserve.

GREAT AYTON, North Riding (15–NZ5510).
Approaching from the SW., the visitor first sees the obelisk to Captain James Cook, famed navigator and explorer, standing boldly on Easby Moor. To this village he was brought at the age of eight from his birthplace at Marton-in-Cleveland NW. of here. His baptism is entered in the parish register at Marton and a granite vase marks the site of his birth in 1728. A piece of sandstone with dogtooth carvings, saved from the rebuilding of Marton's church, is cherished in the church at Gisborne, New Zealand, near the spot where the captain landed. At Great Ayton, the boy studied his lessons in the Old School, 18th-cent. and of course new in his time. The red-brick Cook cottage was taken down in 1934 and re-erected in Australia, but a marker records its site. In the upper room of the school is a museum of Cook mementoes. At 13, the boy was apprenticed from here to a grocer at STAITHES.

Outstanding in the great range of the Cleveland Hills hereabouts is cone-shaped Roseberry Topping, a pinnacle preserved from erosion by its sandstone cap. It makes a delightful landmark. There are grand views from the Cook monument, at 1,064 ft, and better ones from Roseberry Topping, 1,057 ft. Revealed from here are the North Sea, the industrial area of Teesside and the hill country. It is an ancient beacon site and Bronze Age implements were found here.

GREAT DRIFFIELD, East Riding (13–TA0257).
This brisk market town on the edge of the Yorkshire Wolds was more important perhaps a century ago than it is today, but it still serves as the focal point for its area. One of its most admired possessions is the tower of the pre-

dominantly Early English All Saints Church. The tower is a remarkably handsome 15th-cent. conception with panelled and graduated buttresses, parapet and eight crocketed pinnacles combining to suggest grace and nobility. The tower has been credited to human frailty: a Hotham, whose family arms share a place on the western face of the tower with those of six other important families, is by tradition believed to have paid for the tower to absolve himself from a vow, made during a serious illness, to undertake a pilgrimage to the Holy Land. (Another version has him paying the price for absolution of immoral conduct.) Driffield is known to anglers for its trout streams, which pour out of the Wolds to form the River Hull. Barges and houseboats moor along its 18th-cent. canal. It is 1 m. from Little Driffield where King Aldred of Northumbria is said to be buried under the chancel. At **Kirkburn**, 4 m. SW., the church vies with NORTH NEWBALD as the best of the Norman style in the East Riding. The font is of Conquest date with animal motifs carved in the lower tier and scenes from the life of Christ above.

GRETA BRIDGE, *North Riding* (14–NZ0813). In spite of some ravages of time, this is still a lovely and romantic spot where the bridge built in 1776 crosses the Greta, a tributary of the Tees. The view painted by John Cotman of the bridge has been spoilt by a new steel span to the N. Nevertheless, this gateway to Teesdale deserves a second glance. The Morritt Arms on the site of a Roman fort is at one side of the bridge and opposite is the entrance to Rokeby Park. It is privately owned but permission can be obtained to follow the Greta through the estate to the Meeting of the Waters which J. M. W. Turner painted. Sir Walter Scott was a frequent guest at Rokeby Hall and wrote his poem of the same name there. His host arranged a writing desk for him in a cave in the secluded woods overlooking the river.

GUISBOROUGH, *North Riding* (15–NZ61 15). One of the last quiet spots before the northbound traveller plunges into the industrial turmoil of Teesside, Guisborough is a busy market town with a motley collection of buildings. It is distinguished by its ancient priory which lifts its broken east end most evocatively above the trees and roofs now crowding in upon it. It is owned by Lord Gisborough and is in the grounds of Gisborough Hall though it lies close to the parish church. The Ministry of Public Building and Works cares for it. The priory belonged to the Augustinian canons and was founded by Robert de Brus (Bruce) about 1120. It became very rich. The great east end, late 13th-cent., and the 12th-cent. gatehouse and dovecot are, however, the only standing remains. St Nicholas's Church is strikingly low, about 1500 in date, and in it is the Brus cenotaph, a good 16th-cent. work, formerly in the priory. Carved upon it are 10 knights from the English and Scottish branches of the family. The town itself looks friendly and well-used. It accommodates Teesside workers now and has a

quarry and tailoring factory among its own industries. There is a very long main street, with a widened market place where cars can be parked on the cobbles.

GUISELEY, *West Riding* (12–SE1941). St Oswald's Church is an interesting building with Norman features (the south doorway and south arcade), fine 13th-cent. south transept and a splendid 15th-cent. tower. In the 20th cent., there was extensive rebuilding of the nave and chancel in Perpendicular style under the direction of Sir Charles Nicholson. Near the church is the charming rectory, dated 1601, with mullioned windows and a three-story porch. It stands in park-like ground and was built on the site of a medieval moated house. The market place has a village cross and stocks but the village has changed into a lively market and manufacturing town. It clings to tradition, however, with an annual Pageant of St Oswald in the rectory grounds in August. Patrick Brontë, a poor curate at Hartshead at the time, and Maria Branwell were married here on 29 December 1812, and founded the most remarkable literary family in English history. The grandfather of the American poet Henry Wadsworth Longfellow emigrated from Guiseley and Longfellows are buried in the churchyard.

HALIFAX, *West Riding* (12–SE0825). Motorists have good reason to know Halifax for here Percy Shaw in 1934 produced the first of the reflecting roadstuds (cats' eyes) that now guide them through fog or darkness. English toffee also was invented in Halifax, which further claims to be the home of the world's largest building society. Other important products are carpets and yarns. But Halifax was built on the cloth trade as far back as the 13th cent., and it is still a major producer of cloth. The Piece Hall, an Ancient Monument, was completed in 1779 with 315 rooms around a quadrangle for cloth traders' displays. It has three stories and is used now for a vegetable market. Until the mid-17th cent. there was a gibbet law under which a theft of cloth valued at $13\frac{1}{2}d$. or more was punishable by beheading, hence the Beggar's or Vagrant's Litany: "From Hull, Hell and Halifax, good Lord deliver us." The 50th and last victim of the guillotine-like gibbet was executed in 1650. The site of the gibbet is still visible in Gibbet Street.

The town in the Pennine foothills has a spectacular setting. It rises on steep hills from Hebble Brook. Like other West Riding industrial centres it is largely 19th-cent. in appearance. The Town Hall of 1863 was designed by Sir Charles Barry in more or less Italian style with a tall clock tower. Wainhouse Tower is the most familiar landmark, an octagonal stone 270-ft chimney built in 1871 to serve a dye-works but never used. Up 400 winding steps there is a panoramic view. Another fine viewpoint is Beacon Hill, 850 ft high.

St John's blackened parish church, once the centre of the old town, now has factories, the railway station and a viaduct for company. It dates from the 12th cent. but is mainly, in its present form, of the 15th and 16th cents. It has excellent woodwork, including ceilings, font cover, stalls, communion rail and pews, also fine windows of Commonwealth glass. Beside the poor box is a life-size figure known as Old Tristram, supposed to have been modelled on a local beggar, dated 1701. All Souls Church, Haley Hill, built to serve the model suburb of Akroydon, was completed in 1859 and Sir George Gilbert Scott called it "on the whole, my best church".

The Old Cock Hotel in South Gate has a handsome 16th- or 17th-cent. oak-panelled room. Shibden Hall, a splendid 15th-cent. timbered house with 17th- and 19th-cent. additions, belongs to the corporation and contains period furnishings. Its outbuildings house an unusual folk museum. The Bankfield Museum occupies the Italian-style mansion of the Akroyd family. The major historical collection here is of textile machinery, fabrics and costume, including Balkan peasant dress. The museum has the *Young Actress* by Halifax's famous artist-son, Sir Matthew Smith. Mendelssohn in 1842 and John Joubert in 1968 composed for the Halifax Choral Society. Halifax is the birthplace and home of the novelist Phyllis Bentley.

Luddenden, in a glen 2 m. NW. of Halifax, recalls the atmosphere of an upland weaving hamlet with its 17th-cent. buildings and tricky steep and narrow streets.

HARDRAW SCAUR, *North Riding* (14–SD 8891). Fossdale Beck, a tributary of the Ure, rises on Great Shunner Fell and drops over a limestone scar or cliff 2 m. N. of **Hawes** as a force nearly 100 ft high. The cliff projects so that you can walk behind the waterfall. Hardraw Force as it is called is reached through the grounds of the Green Dragon Inn. The glen used to be a popular place for brass band contests because of its splendid acoustics. Some of the thinnest and smoothest stone slates for traditional Dales roofs have come from here for centuries. Fell-climbing is popular around Hawes, the last town as you travel westwards up the dale; Wensleydale cheese is made at factories here. Great Shunner is the highest of the nearby fells, at 2,340 ft, with Dodd Fell and Lovely Seat not far short of this. To the SE. over Wether Fell lies a lonely tarn, **Semer Water**, approachable by a steep narrow road from **Bainbridge**, E. of Hawes. There are two Roman camp sites near this epitome of a Dales village.

HAREWOOD HOUSE, *West Riding* (12–SE3144). This opulent 18th-cent. mansion, planned by John Carr and largely decorated by Robert Adam, is beautifully sited for views over the rolling countryside. Capability Brown landscaped the grounds in 1772 and his achievement survives despite a 1962 storm that destroyed thousands of trees. The house was built by Edwin Lascelles in 1759 with stone quarried on the grounds. It succeeded Gawthorpe Hall, the Gascoigne mansion demolished in 1771, and the even earlier

Harewood Castle of the 12th and 13th cents., the ruins of which can be seen from the road. Lascelles' father, Henry, having made his fortune in the West Indies, had bought the estate in 1738. The new house cost, reportedly, £100,000. In the 1840s, a third story was added and Sir Charles Barry redesigned the south front and added the grandiose terraces.

Room after room reflects the exquisite crafts-manship of the 18th cent., with Adam-designed stucco work carried out by Joseph Rose and William Collins and decorative painting by Bagio Rebecca, Angelica Kaufmann and her husband, Antonio Zucchi. Harewood offers many examples of Adam's passion for designing rooms as a whole, including ceilings, chimney-pieces, mirrors and carpets. He even designed fur-niture for the master, Thomas Chippendale, to make.

Harewood also has a notable collection of paintings with works by El Greco, Tintoretto, Veronese, Titian, Bellini, Turner, Sargent and Munnings, among others.

Edwin Lascelles also had Harewood village moved out of the grounds and replanned by John Carr in long terraces extending from the main gates. All Saints Church was left behind in the park, in a clump of trees. Of 15th-cent. origin, with alterations in the 18th and mid-19th cents., it has six impressive 15th-cent. monuments of the Redmans, Rythers, Gascoignes and Nevils.

HARROGATE, *West Riding* (12–SE3055). The demand for spa cures may be dwindling but the appetite for conferences is not, and Harrogate adapts to modern ways more easily than some towns. Attractive in itself and handy for some of the best scenery of Yorkshire and the North, Harrogate is becoming Britain's convention centre. It is a stately place, with numerous dig-nified hotels and houses built of dark stone in the late 19th cent. when respectability was taken seriously. But the effect is softened by the high, airy location, spacious parks, great abundance of trees and lavish flower-beds, especially in Harlow Car Gardens. Famous for its toffee, it is a town for fine shopping and rich teas, and is also a dormi-tory town for LEEDS and BRADFORD.

Harrogate's mineral springs were discovered by William Slingsby in 1571. He was a travelled man and he knew the water from Tewit (local name for lapwing) Well tasted like waters he had drunk abroad. A temple has since been erected over this well on the wide Stray.

In the early spa days, people bathed in or drank waters brought to their lodgings in barrels. The first public baths went up in 1842, the Royal Pump Room, now a museum. The town became very popular in the 18th and especially the 19th cent. when London society came for relaxation and treatment for gout, rheumatism, lumbago, the liver or jangled nerves. In 1840, the Duchy of Lancaster began to develop the town in earnest. In 1949, the cure was nationalized and patients were treated under the National Health Service.

In 1969, however, the Royal Municipal Baths were closed.

Harrogate features French and Italian weeks and puts on an annual festival of arts and sciences. To look at all of it properly, you should climb the observatory tower, built in 1829 on Harlow Hill in Otley Road. The tower overlooks Harlow Moor and a lot of Yorkshire.

Three m. SE. of Harrogate is **Rudding Park**, open to the public at advertised times in the summer seasons. A fine example of Regency building, it was designed by James Wyatt.

HAWNBY, *North Riding* (13–SE5389). The road to this Hambleton Hills village from RIEVAULX is crowded with choice views; another beautiful run through sheep and heather carries you on over the moors towards Osmotherley. The small grey-stone village clings to a hillside above the Rye, with All Saints Church below near the stream. Originally a Norman church, it has been considerably refashioned, with nave, chancel and bell-turret added in the 14th and 15th cents.

HAWORTH, *West Riding* (12–SE0337), thrills some visitors and depresses others. It was, of course, the home of the amazing Brontë family. Not everyone is prepared to find it a small manufacturing town in a Pennine area of industrial valleys separated by brief stretches of sombre moor on which people still can get lost. The village is all grey-stone houses, slate roofs and smoking chimneypots. It still carries on the spinning and weaving tradition and is about the same size as it was when the Brontës lived here from 1820 to 1861. But there is a whole new industry in tourism. Haworth, 4 m. SW. of **Keighley**, is outranked in pilgrims only by STRATFORD-UPON-AVON as an English literary shrine.

The main street paved with stones struggles up an incredibly steep bank. Near the top the street widens into a little square with the Black Bull Hotel, where Branwell Brontë drank away the hours, on the left. A winding lane leads higher to the Church of St Michael and All Angels and finally, past a gloomy graveyard, to the parsonage, now the Brontë Museum. Behind the parsonage lies moorland and a hint of that windswept isolation which so vividly recalls the writings of the talented sisters, Charlotte, Emily and Anne.

The Brontë Society was founded in 1893 and for some time operated from rooms above the Yorkshire Penny Bank. Then in 1926, Henry Houston Bonnell, an American publisher, bequeathed his extensive collection to the Society. Sir James Roberts bought the parsonage for it. Like much of the town it overlooks, the parsonage is a grim, blackened and plain 18th-cent. sandstone building. Inside, the rooms are furnished with family articles restored to the house over the years, including the sofa on which Emily died in 1848; Mr. Brontë's Bible and spectacles; the children's pencil drawings; some of the tiny home-made books of their childhood writings; Branwell's portraits of his sisters; and Charlotte's work-box. The Bonnell collection of letters, manu-

G. Douglas Bolton

Haworth: a corner of the moorland village

scripts and first editions is available to scholars.

The church has nothing but the west tower remaining of the building the Brontës knew, having been rebuilt in 1880. It contains a brass plaque and chapel in memory of the family and a 19th-cent. stained-glass window given "in pleasant memory of Charlotte Brontë by an American citizen" (Thomas Hockley of Philadelphia).

Keighley, to which the girls used to walk to shop and borrow books, is a pleasant, open 19th-cent. town with a variety of local industries. In the museum at Cliffe Castle there is a large collection of Victorian bygones and the loom of the last weaver to work at a handloom in England. One m. E. is **East Riddlesden Hall**, a National Trust property consisting of a 1692 manor house with 17th-cent. furnishings and one of the finest medieval barns in the North.

The Keighley and Worth Valley Light Railway has been preserved by enthusiasts and offers trips up and down its line from Keighley to Oxenhope. Its workshops and museum at Haworth station are open to visitors.

HEBDEN BRIDGE, *West Riding* (12–SD 9927). Together with its higher neighbour, **Heptonstall**, Hebden Bridge illustrates the story of the Industrial Revolution in the narrow West Riding valleys. And the illustration in this case is exceedingly picturesque. First there was Heptonstall, a village of stone weavers' cottages and crooked streets that grew up on a moorland ridge. There was a 15th-cent. church, dismantled in 1854

Noel Habgood

Helmsley is an attractive market town

with the ruins of the tower, porch and double nave left standing in the churchyard next to its successor. An octagonal Wesleyan chapel was built in Northgate in 1764 and the 17th-cent. grammar school, lately an old people's club, was nearby. When the village was young, the weavers worked in their homes. With the coming of steam power, mills were set up lower down the valley and this was Hebden Bridge. Terraces of workers' cottages with a boss's house at the end of each row crowded on to the hillsides. These are often of several stories, the top ones entered from the upper level of the hill, the lower ones from below. A modern road, painfully steep, connects the two communities; the old packhorse track called the Buttress, was even steeper. The pine-clad **Hardcastle Crags** in a glen 3 m. NW. provide a fine bit of rocky scenery and are sometimes known as "Little Switzerland". A reservoir is to be constructed in the upper glen.

HEDON, *East Riding* (13–TA1828). The "King of Holderness" is St Augustine's Church here (the "Queen" is in PATRINGTON), with its 129-ft pinnacled central tower which calls attention boldly to an otherwise dowdy town. The church building began in the mid-12th cent. when Hedon was at its peak as a trading centre. Although 2 m. inland from the Humber, it had, through Hedon Haven and a system of canals, become a major port. By the time the church was finished (it took over 300 years to complete) HULL had created port facilities that far outstripped its small neigh-

bour. The church has a particularly striking original north front with lancet windows and doorway ornamented with well-carved dogtooth design. Church Lane leads into a small green beside the church which gives something of the old atmosphere of the early village in the shadow of the great church. Some interesting-looking houses are, however, going to ruin hereabouts. In the Town Hall is a mace said to be the oldest in England. It dates from Henry V.

HELMSLEY, *North Riding* (13–SE6183). One of the North Riding's prettiest market towns, Helmsley lies in a hollow of the River Rye, an excellent entrance to Ryedale and the Yorkshire Moors. The view, dropping into it from the S., takes in the red-roofed houses, the spacious market square, the pinnacled church tower and the gaunt bones of Helmsley Castle. The square has a stately Victorian monument to the second Lord Feversham, a modest early-20th-cent. Town Hall and several inns, one of which, the Black Swan, spreads over two Georgian houses and an adjoining 16th-cent. timber-framed house. Off one corner is All Saints Church, rebuilt in the 1860s. It keeps some features of its predecessors, including the Norman south doorway and chancel arch. Murals in the north aisle were completed in 1909 to picture the development of Christianity in the area with Helmsley as the tree from which branches grew. Canon's Garth nearby was built originally for priests of KIRKHAM appointed vicars here.

Helmsley Castle, just off the town centre, had a rather pacific history. It was started by Walter L'Espec in the 12th cent. but the oldest part of the ruins date from 1200 or later. The castle surrendered after a three-month siege in the Civil War in 1644, and was partly repaired. But when Sir Charles Duncombe, a London banker, bought Helmsley in 1689 he had Duncombe Park built by Sir John Vanbrugh and the castle fell into disuse. Duncombe Park is now a school and the castle is in the care of the Ministry of Public Building and Works. It is remarkable for its earthworks, the deep double ditch which surrounds the curtain wall, towers and keep. A domestic range of the 16th cent. has some oak panelling and plaster frieze work.

HEMINGBROUGH, *East Riding* (13–SE67 30). The grandeur of St Mary's Church contrasts sharply with the simplicity of the village. The great cruciform church was built of white Tadcaster stone chiefly in the 13th and 15th cents. The feature that draws the traveller to it across the Plain of York is the 120-ft needle-sharp spire set on a squat 60-ft tower. A close look can just make out the worn row of washing tuns or tubs carved in the tower moulding: a pun on Prior Washington who built the tower. This church was made collegiate with the founding by the Prior of DURHAM in 1426 of the College of the Blessed Mary, the last church in the North to which the system was applied. Very interesting woodwork here: the fine Perpendicular screens and surviving stalls of that date; the restored bench-ends in the nave (note the carvings of a jester in belled cap with a dragon underneath on one, the bust of a young man and grotesque mask on another); and a four-panel carving carelessly hung in the south transept showing a monkey or dog with its paw in a dragon's mouth, two beasts in combat, a two-headed dragon, and a female figure crouching under a man in a tree (an Adam and Eve perhaps?). A painted panel hung in the south aisle describes the church's famous peals of bells and the bell-ringers who performed them on special occasions from 1909 to 1919.

HOLME-UPON-SPALDING-MOOR, *East Riding* (13–SE8138). A memorable sight in the Vale of York is All Saints Church crowning this island hill (the meaning of holme) in the flat former marshland. The stiff climb or easy drive up is worth it for the expansive view. The steadily growing town is some distance W. and the church site encourages a sense of rural detachment. Trees and gravestones crowd the churchyard. The building itself is a time-worn patchwork of 15th- and 16th-cent. stone with 17th-cent. brick parapets and porch. The walls inside are plastered now, and their white sets off the good woodwork: medieval screen, Jacobean pulpit, 18th-cent. gallery and dark roof. Holme Hall, of late a convent, stands out in the view from the hill-top.

HORNSEA, *East Riding* (13–TA2047). The largest freshwater lake in Yorkshire – a placid 467 acres – is only ¾ m. from the North Sea and the wonder of this small town in Holderness. The lake was formed by glacial deposits and it has wooded banks, two small islands and wildfowl sanctuary. Herons, geese, swans, grebes, cormorants, teal, and goldeneye are seen here. There are also rare plants. The lake has a sailing club. Boating and angling can be arranged for visitors. The mere belongs to a descendant of the Constable family who lives at Wassand Hall. For about 20 years in the 13th cent. it was the object of bitter dispute over fishing rights between the abbots of St Mary's, YORK, and Meaux. They decided to settle it with a duel and engaged champions. The contest lasted all day and, apparently without bloodshed, St Mary's knight won. A public footpath allows you to make the 5-m. walk around the lake. Building hides the mere from the main street which winds through the holiday town, but it is found easily enough by a lane. The old village has extended itself to the sea, where there are boarding houses, sandy beaches and bracing views. A small museum of Roman and Anglo-Saxon relics can be visited in the Town Hall. St Nicholas's Church was built of cobbles in the 14th and 15th cent. The spire fell from its battlemented tower in 1733.

HOVINGHAM, *North Riding* (13–SE6675). This restful village of substantial stone cottages clusters around Hovingham Hall, designed and built around 1760 by Sir Thomas Worsley, Surveyor-General under George III. It is of local yellow limestone and is entered in an unusual manner through the vaulted archway of a gatehouse which is really a riding school – a place to exercise the horses under cover. In latter years, the riding school has been the scene of music festivals. On the west lawn of the Hall is the village cricket ground. Cricket festivals have brought in many notable players. The Hall is the home of Sir William Worsley, father of the Duchess of Kent. It is close to the village green on which stands the Georgian Worsley Arms. All Saints Church has a late Anglo-Saxon west tower and west doorway with thick roll moulding, but basically the present building dates from 1860. In it is a carved Anglo-Saxon slab, possibly from an altar, a cross head and several other early fragments. When the grounds of the hall were landscaped, relics of a Roman villa were found, including part of a bath-house and two tessellated pavements.

HOWDEN, *East Riding* (13–SE7428). Written descriptions do not prepare the visitor for the startling sight of this magnificent church framed in its own ruins just off a small market place. Lordly St Peter's today consists of a living part – the nave and transepts with tower between them; and an empty shell – the ruined east end, chancel and chapter house. The tower rises in splendour over the little town and makes the church seem very close to all that goes on. A walk through the churchyard is the quickest way to get from the market place on the E. to a similar centre on the W. Terraces of pleasingly proportioned but now deteriorating houses of the last two centuries surround the church closely. All that is needed is some active restoration to transform Howden into a charming place. Perhaps the people now moving in from GOOLE will make the "discovery".

The church has ancient roots. It was raised by the Prior of DURHAM to collegiate status in 1267. Most of the present church is of late 13th- to early 14th-cent. construction. As the work progressed westwards from the tower, the 107-ft-long nave beautifully illustrates the change from Early English to Decorated styles, with the crowning touch on the west end where the great window is set off by four octagonal turrets, pierced and pinnacled with crocketed spires. The chancel, 110 ft long, continued this style and was finished in 1335. Towards the end of the 14th cent., the beautiful octagonal chapter house was built by Bishop Walter Skirlaw in Perpendicular style with 30 seats, each backed by a carved panel in deep relief quatrefoil design. To keep up this magnificence after the Dissolution was a great burden and by 1609 the parishioners were using only the nave, as now. The lead was taken from the chancel roof to repair the nave and in 1696 the chancel collapsed in a thunderstorm. The chapter house, similarly neglected, fell in 1750.

The church contains a wealth of interesting detail and fine objects, such as the 1480 brass portrait of a knight in the Lady Chapel near a 1340 stone statue of the Annunciation showing a dove on the shoulder of the Virgin; the tomb effigies of the 14th cent. in the Saltmarshe Chapel; and the three heavy churchwardens' chests, one roughed out of a single tree trunk.

A path beside the church leads to the playing fields past the old bishop's palace, now a private residence.

HOWSHAM, *East Riding* (13–SE7362). George Hudson, the YORK draper who became a great railway tycoon of the 19th cent., was born in this tiny village in 1800. He was a yeoman farmer's son and was apprenticed after his father's death. He made good as a draper and then, with an inheritance, plunged into railway promotions. By 1848, he controlled nearly one-third of all the lines in the kingdom. He was thrice Lord Mayor of York and M.P. for SUNDERLAND. Then the boom ended amid charges of financial wrongdoing. Broken, he ended his days on the charity of friends. His village, 7 m. SW. of MALTON, is tucked away on a wooded bank of the River Derwent. The toffee-coloured stone cottages run down the slope towards Howsham Hall. Halfway down is St John's Church, designed by G. E. Street and built in neo-Gothic style in 1860. A tall bell-turret on one side and the steep roof blend with the hilly surroundings. The Hall, an elegant grey stone Elizabethan manor with Georgian interiors, is a preparatory school and open to visitors in May and June.

HUDDERSFIELD, *West Riding* (12–SE1416), means music and worsted. The town sponsors several concert series in the Town Hall, featuring visiting artists as well as local choirs and soloists. The hall is packed out, as a rule, except for the occasional jazz concert. Choir and organ programmes in the municipal series are inexpensive and lunchtime concerts are free. The Huddersfield Choral Society's performance of Handel's *Messiah* is an institution rooted in the tradition of choral singing in the Pennine valleys and Nonconformist churches.

As for cloth, Huddersfield has been the centre of textile production for centuries and its special reputation was built on fine wool worsted. At first the cloth was woven in homes, and houses with many mullioned windows are still to be seen in the villages at the edge of the Pennine moors which have gradually been absorbed into the town. The first market was **Almondbury**, in the 13th cent., the oldest and still the prettiest of these villages. Until the Huddersfield market was established in 1672, cloth was traded there in the parish churchyard with gravestones for tables. The mills grew up along the river and introduction of machinery brought violent Luddite protest in the early 19th cent. Today the major textile industry relies heavily on women workers brought in daily by coach from surrounding areas. Huddersfield makes, among other things, dyestuffs, detergents, pickles and footballs.

The town is extremely hilly and it covers a spectacular site in the Colne valley on the edge of the Pennines. It climbs 1,000 ft from the east to the west sides of town. Since 1920, it has owned all of its centre and it is carrying out what is regarded by experts as an enlightened plan for redevelopment and rebuilding. Older buildings are chiefly 19th-cent., including the Italianate Town Hall and Gothic Revival Market Hall of the 1870s. The parish church, St Peter's, was rebuilt in 1834–6 by J. S. Pritchett of YORK on the Norman foundations. The huge block of the modern public library houses a periodicals room stocked with the European and Indian languages press, a local history room, and an art gallery which has a good permanent collection (Henry Moore, L. S. Lowry, Stanley Spencer, Ben Nicholson, Ruskin, Turner, Constable, Gainsborough etc.) and 15 exhibitions a year. The noted College of Technology has added virtually a new plant, two seven-story blocks and a single-story workshop for textile and chemistry laboratories, and is scheduled to become a polytechnic. The Huddersfield College of Education is one of four in Britain that trains teachers in technical education.

Ravensknowle Park and Hall, 1½ m. from the centre, were given to the town by Leigh Tolson in memory of two nephews lost in the First World War. The Hall, an 1860 residence, is now the Tolson Memorial Museum, with interesting collections, among them the Foggitt herbarium of British plants, restorations of early Christian monuments, dolls and doll furniture, the kitchen of a weaver's cottage, and early weaving machines and relics of the Luddite riots.

Huddersfield's railway station, completed in 1848, has an impressive portico with Corinthian columns and long colonnaded wings.

At Almondbury, All Hallows Church is chiefly Perpendicular, with an Early English chancel and battlements and pinnacles added in the 19th cent. The ceilings are particularly handsome and the 15th-cent. font cover one of the county's best. Wormall's Hall nearby is dated 1631 and consists of a stone ground floor with black-and-white timbered overhanging upper story. It is now a clubhouse. Weavers' cottages with the long upper windows for lighting the work are in Lumb Lane.

On Castle Hill are the remains of an important Iron Age camp, later partly obscured by a stone keep. The hill-top is crowned by the 1897 landmark of Victoria Tower with a heady view.

Prime Minister Harold Wilson was born here.

HULL, *East Riding* (13–TA0929). Almost a new town since the Second World War, when Hull was the hardest hit of any place in the North. Modern, if unexciting, new buildings have sprung up in the centre where the lawns, flower-beds and pools of Queen's Gardens cover the site of the first (1778) dock. The city is very proud of its tidy flower-beds. The third largest port in the kingdom, it has docks running for 7 m. on the north bank of the Humber and the country's largest fishing operation. It handles cargoes valued at more than £600 million a year and 160,000 passengers annually travel to and from Rotterdam and Gothenburg. Hull also manufactures oilcake, metal boxes, plastic bags, excavators and caravans. The growing University of Hull and the Colleges of Technology are part of a lively scene.

There was a small settlement at this junction of the Hull and Humber rivers in the 12th cent., acquired from the Abbot of Meaux by King Edward I in 1293, when it took the name of Kingston-upon-Hull. (Today it is officially acceptable to call it simply Hull.) The port began to flourish when the patronage of William de la Pole, the biggest merchant of the day, was switched from HEDON. He became the first mayor.

What is now called the Old Town is the section which was bounded by the Hull on the E., the Humber on the S., and a moat on the W. and N. Docks were built in the moat later. Surviving in the area today are Holy Trinity Church, of the 13th to 15th cents. with an unusual early brick chancel and seats for 2,000 in the nave alone; a lane called Land of Green Ginger; and Ye Old White Harte Inn, the house where the Governor and others decided not to let King Charles into the city in 1642.

The poet Andrew Marvell was brought to Hull from nearby Winestead at the age of three. Later he represented Hull in Parliament for 18 years. In a town of museums, one of the most interesting is in the old High Street, where William Wilberforce was born in 1759. A wealthy young man about town, he was elected to Parliament at 21 and his monument was the 1833 Act abolishing slavery throughout the Empire. He was known as "the nightingale of the House of Commons". His home now contains relics of the slave trade, the appro-

priately furnished room of his birth and other historical mementoes. The Maister's House across the street is another Georgian dwelling, with a splendid staircase. It is used for offices but owned by the National Trust. At the Transport Museum in High Street you can see the excellent archaeological collection, including mosaic paving from a Roman villa at RUDSTON. A Maritime Museum of Shipping and Fisheries is in Pickering Park. The Hull Trinity House was built in 1753, the headquarters of the guild which in early days controlled pilotage in the Humber and in later times supported a navigational school and welfare services for seamen and their dependants.

Do not look for red telephone kiosks in Hull. Since 1904, it has owned its own telephone system and is the only municipality in Britain to do so. You can dial for recipes, pop record releases, bedtime stories and Santa Claus at Christmas time.

HUTTON-LE-HOLE, *North Riding* (15–SE 7090). The red-roofed stone houses are widely dispersed around an irregular green which is divided by Hutton Beck, with small white bridges crossing the stream. Weekenders and retired people make up much of the resident population of this best-known Yorkshire Moors beauty-spot. Here is the peace of bright gardens and browsing sheep, but it is a peace shattered all summer by streams of motorists. Hutton-le-Hole does not have a long history. Quakers settled here in the 17th cent. In the 18th cent., its people worked in small-scale coal-mining on the moors and in the 19th cent. they worked in local ironstone mines and wove linen. The earliest building is the 1695 Quaker Cottage, associated with John Richardson, a missionary to America, who became a friend of William Penn, founder of the State of Pennsylvania. Brookside Cottage is on the site of the Quaker Meeting House which had a stable below and the meeting room above it. The Hammer and Hand, so named for the motto carved on the lintel ("By Hammer and Hand All Arts Do Stand"), was built in 1784 and once served as an inn. The school went up in 1875, the church in 1935 and the village hall in 1939. The Ryedale Folk Museum near the Crown Inn is worth a visit. It occupies a range of farm buildings and is filled with local farming and household bygones. The idea, the nucleus of the collection and the building came from the late R. W. Crosland and the plan was carried out by his friend Bertram Frank.

The road to **Gillamoor** brings sweeping views across the moors, superb when the heather is in bloom. Both villages are to the S. of **Farndale**, the beautiful valley cut by the River Dove, famous for its profusion of wild daffodils and now a nature reserve.

ILKLEY, *West Riding* (12–SE1147). This spa in the moors gave Yorkshire its national anthem, "On Ilkla Moor baht 'at", a ballad about the uselessness of it all, set to a hymn tune. The town is not like that, however. It is a lively tourist

T. Parker

Ingleton: the summit of Ingleborough seen from the pavement of limestone on Twisserton Scar

and shopping centre as well as a health resort. Situated on the Wharfe, a safe distance from the industrial grime of the LEEDS–BRADFORD area, Ilkley is a favoured place of residence. On first glance it is thoroughly modern, its chief public buildings and hotels having been put up in the late 19th or early 20th cent. There are some houses of earlier date, for example, the 16th-cent. Manor House, now a museum, or the 18th-cent. Box Tree Cottage, now a restaurant. The spring waters here were found to have medicinal value in the 1840s and hydrotherapy was introduced. The older part of town is near the parish church, All Saints, which is Ilkley's most obvious link with the past. The south doorway here is 13th-cent., enriched with mouldings and dog-tooth carving. The tower is of the 15th cent. and much of the rest reflects the 19th-cent. restorations and alterations. There are three Anglo-Saxon cross shafts in the churchyard. Bronze Age carvings in considerable number have been found in the area and some cup-and-ring examples are exhibited in the gardens opposite the church. The Manor House Museum, too, displays pre-historic and Roman relics from the locality. A popular walk from Ilkley leads west up the valley and up Heber's Ghyll to the Swastika Stone on the moor. It is the only one in Britain, and like other ancient markings, full of mystery. It may have been used in fire worship.

INGLEBY GREENHOW, *North Riding* (13–NZ5806). Set beautifully on the edge of the Cleveland Hills, the village boasts a Norman church "barbarized and rebuilt" (says Morris) in 1741. The barbarians, however, left the chancel and tower arches and north arcade at St Andrew's for antiquarians to puzzle over the carvings on the capitals – foliage, heads, dragons, pigs and other grotesques included. Two good but not well preserved effigies show a 13th-cent. priest and a 15th-cent. knight. Ingleby Moor rises nearly 1,300 ft above, and across it to the SE. is Burton Howe with four large Bronze Age cairns, one 50 ft in diameter and 8 ft high.

INGLETON, *West Riding* (12–SD6972). This is a one-industry town and the industry is tourism. The main street is solidly lined with shops and cafés and the pavements thronged with fell-walkers, climbers and potholers. Signs of Ingleton's small-scale industrial past are blurring. Coal workings established it in the first place, and cotton mills and lime kilns kept it going. But the railway from SKIPTON in 1849 made Ingleton a tourist centre for the ruggedly beautiful terrain of the far West Riding. The little town clings to the hillside above the junction of the Twiss and Doe rivers which thereafter become the Greta. There is a beautiful 4-m. walk up the Twiss valley, across the moors and down the Doe with views of the renowned waterfalls. For climbers, **Ingleborough** summit at 2,373 ft is less than 4 m. by a good path. A long ridge walk (some 7 m.) leads to the top of **Whernside**, 2,414 ft above sea-level. For those fascinated by caves, there are the popular **White Scar Caves**, open to the public, with their intricate rock formations, stalagmites and stalactites, underground river and lake, and Skirwith Cave with its waterfall.

JERVAULX ABBEY, *North Riding* (12–SE 1785). The Cistercian abbey ruins SE. of MIDDLE-HAM are privately owned, but open to the public on an honour system of admission. Although the remains are rather sparse, the site is charming. It has not been tidied up completely, and shrubs and trees are allowed to grow among the ancient stones in a romantic fashion. The ground plan can be seen very well and the best feature is the wall of the monks' dormitory with a fine row of lancet windows high up. The monastery was founded in 1156 and 15 different mason's marks are still discernible on the building fragments. The order was not supposed to eat meat except in illness, but lots of bones were found here. The last abbot was executed in 1537 for taking part, albeit unwillingly, in the Pilgrimage of Grace, and the abbey was destroyed.

KILBURN, *North Riding* (13–SE5179). When Yorkshire people see hand-made oak furnishings, they search for the mouse, the signature of Robert Thompson of Kilburn. He was born here in 1876, son of the local joiner, and here he realized his dream of carving in oak. One of his first assignments was furniture for AMPLEFORTH College, 7 m. away. The mouse adorns pieces in more than 700 churches as well as homes, schools and offices in Britain and abroad. Thompson said he got the idea for the mouse when, as he carved a beam on a church roof, a companion muttered something about their being poor as church mice. "On the spur of the moment I carved one. Afterwards I decided to adopt the mouse as a trade mark, because I thought how a mouse manages to scrape and chew away the hardest wood with his chisel-like teeth, and it works quietly; nobody takes much notice. I thought that was maybe like this workshop hidden away in the Hambleton Hills." Since Thompson's death in 1955, his workshop has carried on with his grandsons and some 30 craftsmen. It is the major industry in this village of snug stone houses strung out along a beck. The Mouseman's Cottage is a rambling brick and timbered building near the centre. An annual quoits competition is held on the green. Six hundred ft above the village rises Roulston Scar with its familiar white-horse landmark. It was dug out in 1857 and covered in white stone by the village schoolmaster, Thomas Hodgson, and a swarm of boys. The horse is 180 ft long and 80 ft high.

KILNSEY CRAG, *West Riding* (12–SD9767). This famous limestone scar juts out in Wharfedale, dwarfing the village near it and providing an imposing landmark for travellers. On the meadow between the precipice and the river, the annual Upper Wharfedale show is held and young men who are fit enough compete in the Crag Race to the top of the hill and back. The village is of ancient origin and was given to FOUNTAINS ABBEY in 1156. It became the monks' headquarters for manor courts and sheep-shearing. Mastiles Lane, an old drovers' road, gives walkers a good route to MALHAM.

KIRBY MISPERTON, *North Riding* (13–SE7779). **Flamingo Park Zoo** has taken over the park and 18th-cent. Hall here in the heart of the Vale of Pickering.

KIRKBYMOORSIDE, *North Riding* (13–SE6986). An unexciting small market town but an agreeable starting point for explorations of the moors. It is just off the PICKERING–HELMSLEY road and the main street climbs steeply towards the hills. On Vivers Hill behind the church are the sketchy remains of a Norman castle. The Black Swan Inn has a timber porch from 1634. In the building called Buckingham House near the top of the street, George Villiers, 2nd Duke of Buckingham, a great wit and friend of Charles II who had fallen from favour, died after a fall while hunting. The town has an unusual number of blacksmiths.

KIRKDALE, *North Riding* (13–SE6885). The little church 1½ m. W. of KIRKBYMOORSIDE, once the minster church of St Gregory, has an Anglo-Saxon sundial over its south doorway with an Old English inscription which translated says "Orm, the son of Gamal, bought St Gregorious' Minster when it was all broken and fallen and he let it be made new from the ground in Edward's days the King, and Tosti's days the Earl", which puts its date of rebuilding at 1060. Of the same period is the chancel arch but the church was largely rebuilt again in the 19th cent. There are two Anglo-Saxon coffin lids, one 11th- and the other 7th-cent., it is believed. Kirkdale Cave, discovered in quarrying operations in 1821, held the bones and teeth of hundreds of hyenas and their victims – rhinoceros, mammoth, tiger, bear, bison and others – and the pygmy flints of the Mesolithic hunters.

KIRKHAM PRIORY, *North Riding* (13–SE 7565). Secluded in an entrancing site on the River Derwent 5 m. SW. of MALTON are the ruins of this priory. The lawns stretch gently to the river and thick woods cover the opposite bank. This was a house of the Augustinian canons, founded about 1125 by Walter L'Espec, according to legend in memory of an only son killed in a riding accident near the fragment of a cross at the entrance to the monastery. Visitors will want to study at least two features: the 13th-cent. gatehouse and the handsome lavatorium. The gatehouse has a good deal of fine sculpture, including figures (from the top down) of Christ seated, St Philip and St Bartholomew in niches and St George and the Dragon opposite David and Goliath. There are also 10 carved heraldic shields. In a corner of the cloister, near the fine Norman doorway leading into the refectory, is the lavatorium where before meals the monks washed in leaded troughs under a beautiful late-13th-cent. arcade. The priory was working in the 13th cent. on a great enlargement of its Norman church but apparently ran out of money after the presbytery and choir were built, so the nave and transepts are on the smaller earlier scale.

KIRKLEATHAM, *North Riding* (15–NZ5921). S. of REDCAR is this astonishing piece of 17th-cent. philanthropy, Sir William Turner's Hospital, possibly England's most impressive almshouse. The U-shaped range of buildings has for its showpiece a chapel, flanked by what were two charity schools. The wings extending forward to the road contained the apartments of the deserving 10 men and 10 women. The place had markedly declined by the time of the death of the last owner in 1948. There were only eight residents and almost no modern conveniences. A kind of revival followed the 1951 Act of Parliament permitting the institution to continue under the Charity Commissioners after the sale of the Kirkleatham estate. It is fully occupied now. School rooms were converted into flats to help support the place and the chapel is open to the public. Briefly, the hospital was founded in 1668 and built in 1676 by Sir William, a self-made and wealthy woollen draper and twice Lord Mayor of London, who lived by the rule that if you kept to your shop your shop would keep you. He was a friend and financial resource of Charles II who gave him his knighthood. He was also a friend of Sir Christopher Wren and the elegant chapel, a miniature Wren church, was designed in Wren's workshop although the master himself did not come here. Nicholas Hawksmoor did visit the work and James Gibbs,

another pupil, arranged for the beautiful Venetian-style window by Sebastiano Ricci behind the altar. The right-hand window is of Turner (and an extraordinary death mask of him stares from a glass case at the rear). The chapel was completed in 1742 with heavy exterior additions in 1820. Noteworthy among so many fine features are the fluted Ionic columns, decorated arches, wrought-iron railings by John Tijou who worked for Wren, mahogany pews facing the centre, baroque gilt chandelier and two gilt chairs probably made by William Kent.

Kirkleatham Hall stood a short distance away. It is gone and a modern school occupies the site. The old stables and fine gateposts remain. Across the road is St Cuthbert's Church, 18th-cent., and thought to be designed by John Carr. Its distinguishing feature, and jarring note, is the octagonal baroque mausoleum to Turner, who died in 1692, designed by James Gibbs. It has heavy rusticated foundations and odd pyramid top. A prettily garlanded doorway leads into its stern interior from the chancel and it holds the Classical Turner family monuments. In the chancel are two interesting brasses to a four-year-old girl, Dorothy, who died in 1628 and Robert Coulthirst buried in 1631 aged 90. At the back is a large iron-bound 14th-cent. chest carved with monsters and tracery.

KNARESBOROUGH, *West Riding* (13–SE 3557). The most picturesque town of the Riding covers a bluff on the Nidd with a pleasant jumble of buildings that lie in irregular tiers above the riverside. The town has England's oldest linen mill and once employed weavers in cottages for miles around. Today it is chiefly a market town.

Knaresborough is picturesquely situated on the River Nidd

Kenneth Scowen

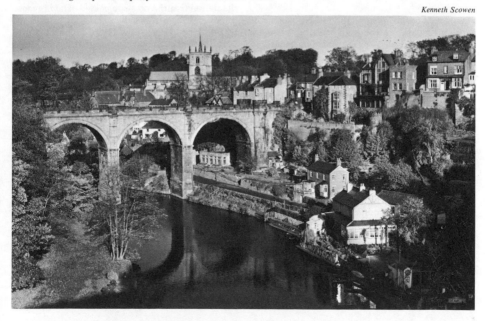

The ruins of the castle stand on a strategic height and from them you can get a heady view of the town and the river gorge. A Norman castle was built here by Baron Serlo de Burg but the existing remains date from 1310 to 1340. They include some curtain wall with towers, the rectangular keep of three floors and a basement, and a 14th-cent. gatehouse. Near the entrance is the old Court of Knaresborough with a 14th-cent. lower story and 17th-cent. upper. The ground floor of the castle keep is a museum, among its items being armour worn at MARSTON MOOR. History did not pass Knaresborough by. The murderers of Thomas à Becket hid out for three years and Richard II was imprisoned here on his way to death at PONTEFRACT. The castle was sacked by the Scots and thoroughly "slighted" by Parliament after the Civil War.

Halfway up the hillside between Waterside and High Street is St John's Parish Church whose central tower is crowned with a little spirelet. The church is mainly of 13th- and 14th-cent. date with some rebuilding in the 15th. Furnishings include a poor-box of about 1600 shaped like a clock. There are three noteworthy 17th-cent. monuments to Slingsbys, including a standing figure of Sir William Slingsby in an arched niche. He died in 1634 and is partly remembered for discovering the mineral springs at HARROGATE.

St Robert's Chapel in Abbey Road is named after Robert Flower (1160–1218), its fanatical founder. It is tiny but ornamented with primitive colonettes, a vaulted roof and carved faces. At the entrance stands the 16th-cent. larger-than-life figure of the hermit saint, drawing his sword. Dropping Well is a petrifying spring whose limestone content solidifies objects which fall into it. It is near Low Bridge and not far off in a cave once lived Mother Shipton, a prophetess of the 1500s who forecast motorcars, aircraft and other strange things.

Knaresborough boasts the oldest chemist's shop in England, in the Market Place. The Old Manor House, now a restaurant, is a medieval building with chequerboard walls, built originally around an oak tree. It was a royal fishing lodge given by James I to his son, and Cromwell slept here. Among other buildings of special interest are Knaresborough House, a Georgian mansion now used for council offices; Conyngham Hall, another 18th-cent. house whose grounds are a public park and zoo; and Fort Montague built into the cliff above the cave chapel. Knaresborough is a good starting point for Dales tours. Boats and punts can be hired on the river, which is spanned by High and Low bridges on either side of the towering railway viaduct.

Schoolchildren know all about Blind Jack Metcalf of Knaresborough, born in 1717, who in 93 years of vigorous living was a violinist, soldier, forest guide, and major roadbuilder.

LASTINGHAM, *North Riding* (15–SE7290). The precious 11th-cent. crypt beneath St Mary's Church is a complete little church in itself, with a vaulted roof borne on thick low columns, a chancel, nave and aisles. It was built between 1078 and 1085 as a shrine for St Cedd. According to Bede's history, Bishop Cedd came to this remote edge of the moors to found a monastery for King Ethelwald. He died of the plague in 664. In the 9th cent. the monastery was destroyed by the Danes. In 1078 Abbot Stephen of WHITBY began the restoration by building the crypt for the remains of the founder. In 1086, Stephen moved on to YORK to establish St Mary's Abbey. The church contains some 11th-cent. work with later work concluding in the 15th-cent. tower. From the unusual size of an Anglo-Saxon cross head here, the original cross must have been more than 24 ft high. There are other early carved stones, including a hogback tombstone with a bear on it. The village is comfortably sheltered in a dip of the ridge between Rosedale and Farndale.

LEEDS, *West Riding* (12–SE3034). When Dickens visited Leeds he decided "you must like it very much or not at all". If you like it very much you will be attracted by a town that is big (over 500,000), bold in replacing old buildings with brash new ones, and brisk. Leeds works at an enormous variety of manufacturing activities, is the ready-to-wear capital of the country, and a centre of coal and iron industries. Iron forging began with the monks of **Kirkstall Abbey** in 1200. The cloth trade was firmly established by the 17th cent., and the first wholesale clothier began in 1856.

Leeds spreads over a large and hilly area with a town centre on Victoria Square. Here the Town Hall, a famous and architecturally successful example of Classic revival, was built in a great burst of civic confidence in the 1850s and opened by Queen Victoria. On that occasion, the streets were lined with palm trees and triumphal arches. Eighteen thousand Sunday-school children sang the national anthem as she passed. The immense building, brown stone then and soot-black now, was designed by a young HULL architect, Cuthbert Broderick. Giant columns line the façade and the 225-ft clock tower is the symbol of Leeds. The building is guarded by white lions, cut out of Portland stone which is more resistant to grime. Its ornate Victoria Hall is the scene of the famed triennial music festival.

Broderick planned some other major buildings which give Leeds a strong Victorian flavour: the public baths and Civic Theatre in Cookridge Street and the oval Corn Exchange in Duncan Street, for example. One of the newer streets, Headrow, opened the centre considerably. A principal shopping street is Briggate, off which are examples of the typically Leeds arcades, delightful glass-roofed passages lined with shops. One has a clock with revolving figures from Scott's *Ivanhoe*. The City Market was enclosed in 1904 giving the city a dashing new roofline of towers and spires.

Leeds is one of the few places where it is worth noting the warehouses, although the bulldozers are moving in fast. Eighteenth-cent. gentlemen designed their country houses after the Classical themes they admired on the Grand Tour; 19th-cent. industrialists put these ideas into their mills. One Leeds chimney was a brick version of Giotto's campanile in Florence, and an Egyptian temple was the model for a mill.

City offices now occupy the Civic Hall opened in 1933 in Calverley Street, a noteworthy building with columned portico, pediment and slender towers. New buildings have gone up for the Central Colleges (of education, technology, art, commerce and home economics) and the University, which covers a hill-top overlooking the centre. The university began in 1904, growing out of the Yorkshire College of Science. Its old buildings are red-brick, its more recent ones ponderous stone. The blocky tower of the Parkinson administration building, opened in 1950, is a landmark.

There are no medieval churches in central Leeds. One that is architecturally important is St John the Evangelist in New Briggate, completed in 1634 and a rare example of early-17th-cent. ecclesiastical work. It has twin naves, a plaster-work ceiling and an excellent Jacobean screen across the whole width. Another is Holy Trinity, Boar Lane, completed in 1727, whose charming spire ornaments the commonplace shopping area.

The Yorkshire County Cricket Club grounds at Headingley need no introduction. The largest park is Roundhay, an open space of lake and woodland bought in 1872. The City Art Gallery near the Town Hall has a good permanent collection of painting and sculpture and a print room and library for scholars. The gallery was a first patron of Castleford-born Henry Moore, who, like Barbara Hepworth, born at WAKEFIELD, trained at Leeds School of Art.

Visible efforts are being made to clear slum housing and derelict factory areas. When the Quarry Hill estate flats were built in 1935, they were the largest public housing project in England.

The corporation owns two remarkable places of special historical interest: **Temple Newsam**, a great country house, and Kirkstall Abbey, both in easy reach of the centre. Temple Newsam was started by Thomas Lord Darcy before 1521. It was modernized and enlarged in the early 17th and late 18th cents. A splendid mansion, it contains a superb collection of furniture, paintings, ceramics and porcelain. The original park has suffered from opencast mining, but the grounds contain two golf courses and the gardens are noted for roses, azaleas and rhododendrons.

Kirkstall Abbey was founded in 1152 as a daughter house of FOUNTAINS and much of the building was completed by 1175. The chapter house, cloisters and abbot's lodging are outstanding.

The Abbey House Museum in the 12th-cent. gatehouse has re-created three streets of Victorian shops.

LEVISHAM, *North Riding* (15–SE8390). The isolated moorland village overlooks Newton Dale ½ m. off the WHITBY–PICKERING route. The road plunges downhill to the station, a watermill and a church on Levisham Beck. St Mary's has the marks of antiquity in its Anglo-Saxon chancel arch and a fragment of an Anglo-Danish gravestone, carved with a dragon. A 19th-cent. church, St John's, stands in the village above. Interesting explorations include the **Hole of Horcum**, at the head of the beck, the largest hollow in Yorkshire. It is a natural amphitheatre carved by glaciers and springs. It is carpeted with meadow and once supported a small settlement. Only one family still lives there. There is a good footpath over the moor. A 5½-m. Newton Dale drive was opened in 1969 by the Forestry Commission. It starts at Levisham station and carries on to the Mauley Cross and Stape village. There are picnic spots, views, and you might see deer. The **Bridestones** to the E. are strange rock formations and they, together with 870 acres, belong to the National Trust.

LEYBURN, *North Riding* (15–SE1190). Take the corner near the Bolton Arms to get on to the Shawl, a broad mile-long terrace shaded with evergreens, oaks and sycamores which allows entrancing views over Wensleydale. Among other landmarks will be two castles, BOLTON and MIDDLEHAM. Tradition says that this was where Mary Queen of Scots was recaptured after an escape from Bolton Castle which lasted a brief two hours. Leyburn's wide sloping market place is filled on Fridays with traders and shoppers from up the dale.

For a higher vantage point, take the steep road up to Preston Scar.

LINTON-IN-CRAVEN, *West Riding* (13–SD9962). Linton Beck which divides the village green can be crossed in a number of ways: by clapper bridge, packhorse bridge, ordinary road bridge, stepping stones or ford. At one end of the green stands the little community's largest gift, the Georgian hospital – seven almshouses endowed by Richard Fountaine in 1721 for poor women. It is still in use, but by both sexes. Beside the green, the old rectory is now a youth hostel. Linton has been called the prettiest village in the North. It is nearly hidden in trees. A mile away on the Wharfe is St Michael's Church which serves four parishes. It is charming in both its structure and its setting. There are some Norman features but chiefly it is a 14th-cent. building with later restorations.

LITTLEBECK, *North Riding* (15–NZ8707). This hamlet may be found S. of WHITBY and W. of the SCARBOROUGH or E. of the PICKERING roads, if you are willing to risk the descent of the twisting road leading into the narrow valley. The approach is slightly easier from the Scarborough road side. You will find a few cottages, farms, a chapel, village hall and the workshop of woodcarver Thomas E. Whittaker, who signs his oak pieces with a gnome. Nearby are a hermit's cave, a small waterfall called Falling Foss and a number of wooded walks and picnic spots.

LONDESBOROUGH, *East Riding* (13–SE 8645), is a placid Yorkshire Wolds village now but it has seen some stirring days in the past. By tradition this was the site of the summer palace of King Edwin of Northumbria and the place where he was converted to Christianity. From here the Anglo-Saxon priest, Coifi, rode forth to destroy his own temple at GOODMANHAM in that same year, 627. Londesborough is thought to have been on the Roman map of Britain (a bit of a Roman road was seen when the lake in Londesborough Park was drained in 1895). Here the boy Henry Lord Clifford was hidden for a time among the shepherds to evade the Yorkists. Later he went to Cumberland, staying in hiding until 1485 when, aged 30 and illiterate, he returned to his station in life and became an astronomer. All Saints Church at the park gates has an ancient sundial above the Norman doorway, a brass inscription to the Shepherd Lord's mother and four funeral banners of the Earls of Burlington. The 3rd Earl laid out the park with an avenue of elms planted in memory of his friend, David Garrick, who on one visit coached the local parson in effective reading of the Bible. This earl also planted the circle of trees known as Londesborough Clump and visible for miles. The 6th Duke of Devonshire pulled down the old hall in 1812, and regretted it later. However, he managed to sell the property to the railway king, George Hudson, for £470,000. Hudson routed the YORK – Market Weighton line past his gates where he had a private station.

MALHAM, *West Riding* (12–SD8963). The hamlet of stone cottages and a humped bridge is surrounded by moorland, high and wild, and some spectacular limestone scenery is within easy reach. Malham Cove is ¾ m. N., a curving sheer white cliff about 240 ft high of the Great Scar Limestone created by the Craven Fault. The River Aire steals out from its base. Above the rock stretches the dry valley along which, before the Ice Age, the Aire used to flow, plunging over the Cove in a great waterfall. It is a 2-m. walk up the valley to Malham Tarn (also accessible by road from Malham), a 150-acre natural lake formed by a dam of glacial moraine, on which there is skating in winter. Tarn House, the lake and 2,000 acres between Ribblesdale and Wharfedale now belong to the National Trust. The house is used by the Field Studies Council. It is said that Charles Kingsley, while staying at Tarn House, humorously explained the dark marks on the Cove as made by a chimney sweep falling over, and from this was born *The Water Babies*. Two m. NE. of Malham is **Gordale Scar**, also part of the CRAVEN Fault. It is possible to drive to within a quarter of a mile of this winding gorge with its splendid series of cascades.

MALTON, *North Riding* (13–SE7871). Too many remember Malton as a traffic bottle-neck on the way to or from SCARBOROUGH, but there is more to it than that. It is in fact two places, Old Malton and New, with the site of a Roman station between them. New Malton was built after the old

Malham Cove was the site of a great waterfall before the Ice Age

T. Parker

village was burnt down in 1138 to drive out the Scots. It is a teeming market town for a large farming district and its big irregular square is full of activity. St Michael's Church competes for attention in the middle of things. It is a sturdy-looking Norman church with a 15th-cent. tower and not too successful 19th-cent. additions. The spire on Church Hill belongs to St Leonard's Church, now redundant, and the subject of proposals for transfer to the Roman Catholics. It is Norman in character with a Perpendicular tower and 19th-cent. spire. It contains an amusing monument to an iron-founder, Arthur Gibson, who died in 1837. Of metal entirely, it carries a brass plate showing the deceased in prayer and at drink. He designed it himself. The Town Hall around the corner from the square is 18th-cent. and a plaque on it records that Edmund Burke was Malton's M.P. from 1780 to 1794. Among buildings of interest in the centre is the Cross Keys Inn in Wheelgate which has a medieval crypt, possibly from the former Hospital of St Mary Magdalene here.

Old Malton is on the road to PICKERING, with old-fashioned cottages and inns. Its Church of St Mary is built in part from the church of the Gilbertine priory founded in c. 1150.

There is little to see on the site of the Roman station in a pasture called Orchard Field but finds from excavations can be examined in the Roman Malton Museum in the market place.

MARKENFIELD HALL, *West Riding* (12–SE3066). This is one for collectors of out-of-the-way places. It is a remarkable example of a fortified manor house and, given persistence, you will find it at the end of a long lane which leaves the HARROGATE road about 3 m. S. of RIPON. The owners do not believe in signs although visitors are welcome at advertised times during the summer season. The lane is surfaced and there are plain stone gate piers where it begins on the right-hand side of the main road, if approached from Ripon. After a mile and two gates, the visitor will be in a farmyard staring in amazement across a moat at the protective grey walls of the manor house.

The Hall was built by John de Markenfield in 1310 and except for the addition of domestic ranges in the 17th cent., it has suffered little change. The original Hall is L-shaped and it faces the gateway across the courtyard. The moat is crossed now by a small stone bridge to the 16th-cent. gatehouse. The Hall has battlements and an outside turreted staircase. In its first days, it had a hall on the upper floor with kitchens and cellars below and a chapel in the wing.

The Markenfields forfeited the Hall after supporting Mary Stuart's claim to the throne and Queen Elizabeth gave it to Lord Chancellor Ellesmere. It has not apparently been used as a home since, although the outbuildings are occupied.

MARSTON MOOR, *West Riding* (13–SE 4853). The battle of 2 July 1644 was fought N. of the road that connects the villages of **Long Marston** and Tockwith. It was the turning point in the Civil War, a clear victory for the Parliamentary forces under the Yorkshire Fairfaxes and Cromwell over those of Charles I. The field today is marked by an obelisk near the intersection of the road with a track. Royalist YORK was under siege 7 m. W. when word came that Prince Rupert, nephew of the king, was coming from Lancashire with 20,000 Royalist troops. The Parliamentary force moved out to Marston Moor to prevent the prince joining forces with the Marquess of Newcastle in the city. The tactic failed and Rupert entered York on 1 July. But the next day he and Newcastle left York for Marston Moor. The Parliamentary army had started to retreat to better ground at TADCASTER, but turned and the two armies lined up on opposite sides of a ditch running parallel to the present road. After a fierce battle of varying fortunes, in which Sir Thomas Fairfax showed great valour, Cromwell charged at 7 p.m., when the opposing commanders, by some accounts, were at supper. He was wounded and at one point appeared to have lost the battle, but recovered the initiative and by 10 o'clock had won. In this three-hour engagement of 40,000 troops, 4,000 Royalists and 300 Parliamentarians died. It was another four years before the war was over.

The parents of General James Wolfe, who defeated Montcalm on the Plains of Abraham before Quebec and won Canada for England, were married in All Saints Church at Long Marston.

MASHAM, *North Riding* (12–SE2280). Just off the main road is the shady market square with a maypole and cross, but the market for which the village was chartered in 1250 has long since ceased to be held. Here the River Ure has left Wensleydale and is crossed by a four-arched bridge built in 1754. St Mary's Church at the corner of the square has a Norman tower on which a 15th-cent. spire was raised. In the churchyard is the treasured circular shaft of an Anglo-Saxon cross, probably 9th-cent. work. It shows four tiers of figures. Across the river in Swinton Park, part of the castle is used for a Conservative College.

METHLEY, *West Riding* (13–SE3826). Monuments in St Oswald's Church impressed the young Henry Moore, born at Castleford not far away to the E. The church does contain a rich collection of sculpture. The oldest is the tomb-chest with alabaster effigies of Sir Robert Waterton (who died in 1424) and his wife, elaborately and delicately carved. Another alabaster tomb-chest bears the effigies of Lionel Lord Welles (who fell at Towton in 1461) and his first wife. Two stone figures, originally part of this monument, now occupy recesses in the aisles. A tall black-and-white marble tomb-chest of the early 17th cent. honours Sir John Savile, his son, Sir Henry, and Henry's wife, whose son sits at her feet. The figure of Charles Savile (who died in 1741) reclines on another monument with his bereaved wife shown at his feet. A later 18th-cent. monument to John Savile, 1st Earl of Mexborough, who died in 1778, and a 19th-cent. tablet with draped figures and a relief of the resurrection of Lazarus, erected to Sarah Dowager Countess of Mexborough who died in 1821, complete the array of major memorials. The church was rebuilt in the 12th cent., but the oldest visible work now dates to the 14th and 15th cents. The excellent woodwork includes an Elizabethan font cover, a pulpit of 1708, 17th-cent. screen and an ornate 16th-cent. eagle lectern, probably Dutch, with niches and statues in the pedestal.

MIDDLEHAM, *North Riding* (12–SE1287). The monks of JERVAULX ABBEY probably started the horse-breeding and training that made this a racing centre before NEWMARKET. The former capital of Wensleydale is only a village now, but a pretty one. The castle that led to the settlement is now a ruin in the care of the Ministry of Public Building and Works. The Nevilles got it through marriage in the 13th cent. and made it the "Windsor of the North". Richard III acquired it in 1471. His son was born here. The castle was dismantled in 1646. The keep, built in the 1170s by Robert Fitzralf, survives nearly to its full height. The 13th-cent. chapel and 14th-cent. gatehouse are still to be seen. The Church of SS. Mary and Alkelda is mainly 14th-cent. It contains a 10-ft-high Perpendicular font cover.

MIDDLESBROUGH, *North Riding* (15–NZ 4920). Since 1968 this has been the administrative centre of **Teesside**, the county borough with a population of nearly 400,000, created in the great and growing complex of industrial towns and villages on the Durham and Yorkshire banks of the Tees. Middlesbrough is a latecomer among them. It was a dying village in 1831 when the backers of the STOCKTON and DARLINGTON railway bought land here to augment facilities for coal export at Stockton. Ten years later the first ironworks were started. The phenomenal growth came with the discovery in 1850 of iron ore in the Cleveland Hills. In 1875 came the move to steel. Teesside now has Europe's largest petro-chemical industry and is a leading contender in steel, iron and engineering. It is an area of hard work, strong beer and sport. The shopping centres, especially Middlesbrough's, are rebuilding at a great rate and housing estates multiply as fast as factory chimneys. Just about all that is left of Middlesbrough in ancient times is a Norman font, recovered from a farmyard, and placed in the new (1840) St Hilda's Church. The town has a large Roman Catholic population and a Catholic cathedral, red-brick St Mary's, was built in 1872. Still the most fascinating structure in Middlesbrough is the gaunt iron Transporter Bridge, built in 1911 and a wonder of its time. It was designed by the Cleveland Bridge & Engineering Co. of Darlington to replace a ferry. It is the largest of its kind in the world. It carries 10 vehicles and 600 passengers in the travelling cable car.

The 18th-cent. **Ormesby Hall**, 3 m. SE. of Middlesbrough and a National Trust property, has exceptionally fine interior work, including stucco, chimney-pieces and staircase. It was built by the Pennymans, whose village of Ormesby is nearly swallowed now by urban development.

MONK BRETTON PRIORY, *West Riding* (13–SE3607). With the coalfield in the distance and a modern housing estate at its gates, Monk Bretton comes as a surprise 2 m. NE. of BARNSLEY, just off the junction of the A633 and A628. Here are the ruins of an important Cluniac house, much admired for its well-preserved drains. The monastery was founded about 1154 by Adam Fitzwane whose father had been a benefactor of the Cluniac priory at PONTEFRACT. There were vigorous – even violent – disputes over supervision and appointments between the two houses and in 1281 it was agreed that Monk Bretton should be an independent Benedictine priory visited by the Archbishop of YORK.

At the Dissolution, the prior and some half a dozen monks here decided to continue as a community so they bought the monastery library (148 books) and went to live at Worsborough. In 1589 after the lead had been stripped from the church, the bells sent to London and parts of the stone sold, the property was purchased by the Earl of Shrewsbury who gave it to his son Henry Talbot. The prior's house was converted to a residence. The site was excavated after it was bought by Henry Horne in the 1920s and later acquired by the Borough of Barnsley which put it in the care of the Ministry of Public Building and Works. Visitors will be interested in the 15th-cent. gatehouse, the 13th-cent. guest-house or administrative building in the outer courtyard, and the remains of the late-12th-cent. church. The drainage system devised for kitchens and dormitories is particularly easy to see here.

MOUNT GRACE PRIORY, *North Riding* (15–SE4498). In spring, the lawns around the ruins of the country's finest example of a Carthusian monastery are strewn with daffodils. It is a lovely site, tucked under the protective moors N. of **Osmotherley** and just off the A19 below its junction with the A172. Mount Grace was established in 1398 by Thomas Holland, Duke of Surrey, the last monastery founded in Yorkshire. He lost his dukedom when Richard II (son of his grandmother, the Fair Maid of Kent, by a second marriage) was deposed and the priory had a great deal of trouble holding on to its endowments. Thomas later rebelled against King Henry IV and was beheaded and buried here. With the Dissolution, the last prior, John Wilson, was granted the Chapel of Our Lady and a dwelling house on the steep bank above the priory. Called the Lady's Chapel, it is still in use, and the view from it is extensive.

The Carthusians, a contemplative order reacting against the laxity of many monasteries, lived as hermits within their communities and the remains at Mount Grace give a vivid picture of

Newby Hall: the Tapestry Room

their establishment and rule. Each monk had a little house or cell, 27 ft square, consisting of a bedroom, living-room, study and lobby on the ground floor and a workshop above. Each house opened into a walled garden with a lavatory at the bottom of it. There was a dog-leg hatch in the front wall through which food was passed. The monks ate together only on Saturdays. The cells surrounded a large cloister and the plain, rather small church. One cell has been restored. Cookhouse, granaries, guest-house and stables were built on the outer courtyard. In 1654, Thomas Lascelles, then the owner, converted the buildings to the left of the gate into a private residence, still lived in. The property belongs to the National Trust and is cared for by the Ministry of Public Building and Works.

Near the market cross at Osmotherley, there is a heavy stone table which John Wesley used as a pulpit. One of the first Methodist chapels was built here in 1754.

NEWBY HALL, *West Riding* (12–SE3467), illustrates the finest work of Robert Adam. Located between RIPON and BOROUGHBRIDGE at the hamlet of Skelton, Newby Hall was started in 1705 for Sir Edward Blackett, whose wealth came from the mines. In the mid-18th cent. the new owner, William Weddell, made the Grand Tour and in Italy acquired a splendid collection of sculpture. He employed Adam to redesign and enlarge his home especially to house his new

treasures. The work was under way from 1765 to 1783. The house and gardens – 25 acres of beautifully laid out shrubberies, flower-beds and rock gardens sloping down to the River Ure – are now held by R. E. J. Compton. The house is open four days a week and the gardens daily. The house is, of course, famous for its Roman sculpture galleries, which Adam created as two rectangular rooms linked by a rotunda with a Roman bath of white and purple marble as a final touch. The most notable piece of statuary displayed is the Venus from the Barberini Palace. Hardly less renowned is the Tapestry Room hung with a complete set of Gobelin tapestries designed by Neilson and Boucher. The room as planned by Adam has harmonizing carpet and furnishings and the plasterwork ceiling has inset paintings by Antonio Zucchi. The Adam entrance hall has a particularly rich ceiling reflected in the design of the Sicilian marble floor, again the Adam method. Adam and Thomas Chippendale made much of the furniture.

The ornate village church of Christ the Consoler in the grounds was completed in 1872 as a memorial of Lady Mary Vyner to her son. It has, in Pevsner's view, "uncommonly excellent" Victorian stained glass designed by F. Weeks and made by Saunders & Co.

NORTHALLERTON, *North Riding* (15–SE 3793), is another of those old posting towns still generously endowed with inns. Strong ale and dear prices seem to be the thing travellers of old remembered to jot down about it. There is a long, curving street to which most of the town is attached. This street broadens near the centre for a busy market place and narrows at the north end near the Parish Church of All Saints. This is the capital of the North Riding and county offices are housed in a dignified but ornamental building of brick and stone which went up in 1906. The Town Hall is older, 1873, and on an island site in the centre. There is a good deal of Georgian work about. Imposing All Saints overlooks a triangular green with several old houses grouped around it. Its Perpendicular, pinnacled tower is set off by trees. Much of the structure is earlier, the nave dating to before 1200. The chancel was rebuilt in Perpendicular style in 1885. There are some Anglo-Saxon and Danish carved stone fragments inside.

NORTH NEWBALD, *East Riding* (13–SE 9136). There are no less than four Norman doorways to examine in St Nicholas's Church, often thought of as the best Norman church in the Riding. The most elaborate of the quartet is the south entrance with four orders of arches beautifully enriched with zigzag and cable, and foliage embellishing the capitals. An oval niche above the door houses Christ in Majesty. The other Norman doors lead into the transepts and vestry. The central tower is Norman in its lower parts, with an Early English belfry. The battlements and rebuilt chancel are 15th-cent. The church dates from 1151 but is so well kept that it defies its age. Other points of interest: the medieval iron handle on the priest's door and the consecration cross and mason's mark on the right-hand jamb; the font carved in bands of leafy scroll in the late 12th or early 13th cent.; the four fine round arches in the crossing with their chevron markings. The town around is as neat as its parish church and stone-built, with a small sloping green.

NORTH YORK MOORS NATIONAL PARK, *North Riding* (15–NZ7010). A great area of heather-covered moorland is included in the 550 sq. m. of the park designated in 1952 in the North Riding. In August, the moors are purple. In October, the bracken turns dark gold. The park includes Pickering Forest District along the southern border, where tree planting began in 1921. Several drives and nature trails are available now to visitors. The **Cleveland Hills** form the highest range in the park, rising to 1,400 ft. The series of four heights, Hasty Bank, Cold Moor, Cringle Moor and Carlton Bank, is a familiar landmark. Deep valleys break into the uplands. The park reaches from the **Hambleton Hills** to the North Sea coast above SCARBOROUGH and includes moorland villages, old fishing ports, abbeys, prehistoric and Roman remains, early Christian crosses and some of the loneliest countryside in this crowded island.

NOSTELL PRIORY, *West Riding* (13–SE 4117). Nothing remains of the Augustinian priory founded in the 12th cent., but the Georgian mansion on its site, 6 m. SE. of WAKEFIELD, exhibits side by side the work of James Paine and Robert Adam. Paine was only 19 when Sir Rowland Winn commissioned him to build this house in 1733. He planned the stone structure in the Palladian style and intended four pavilions to be built, but only one was completed. The house was redesigned 30 years later by Robert Adam, who also planned the stable block. Rooms on the south side are mainly as Paine would have them while those in the north range are in Adam style. Adam engaged such masters of interior decoration as Joseph Rose for stucco work and Antonio Zucchi and Angelica Kaufmann for painted murals. The house contains a good deal of furniture made to order by Thomas Chippendale whose accounts are also on view. In the park are a lake, a bridge, a herd of deer and the parish church of **Wragby**, St Michael's, a large Perpendicular building. The windows contain hundreds of panels of Swiss glass collected by one of the family and ranging from the early 16th to the mid-18th cent. Nostell Priory is the home of the present Rowland Winn (Lord St Oswald) who gave it to the National Trust in 1953. A vintage motorcycle museum is on the premises.

NUN MONKTON, *West Riding* (13–SE5057). The tranquil village at the end of Pool Lane near the meeting of the Rivers Nidd and Ouse, has all the charm of a rural retreat and with it the hint of a greater past. There is a large green, bordered by brick cottages, with a maypole. An avenue leads to the Church of St Mary which is partly obscured by an old weeping beech. Nearby is the Hall, built in 1690. This house is believed to stand on the site of the Benedictine nunnery which was founded here by William de Arches in about 1150. A prioress and 12 nuns inhabited it, but nothing remains save the late-12th- or early-13th-cent. nave of the nuns' chapel which is now the parish church. Worthy of special note are the fine west doorway and front and the handling of the lancet windows with tall arcades in the upper nave. The east end was redone in the 1873 restoration and in the three lancet windows of the east wall is what has been called the finest stained glass in the West Riding, by William Morris.

OTLEY, *West Riding* (12–SE2045). This Wharfedale town lies at the foot of the Chevin, a 900-fthigh hill with a superb view at the end of the path leading from the station. It serves the agricultural area as a market town and manufactures printing machines. Thomas Chippendale was born here in 1718 but his birthplace has been supplanted by the building bearing a memorial plaque. J. M. W. Turner painted many scenes in the area when he was a guest at nearby Farnley Hall. The town has a maypole, old inns, a rebuilt medieval bridge and a bevy of antique shops. The Museum of the Liberty of Otley, in Queen's Place, has a local history collection. All Saints Parish Church has a Norman north doorway and long chancel windows, while the rest of the building is of 14th- and 15th-cent. work. It contains 17 sculptured fragments of four Anglo-Saxon crosses from the 9th to 11th cents. There is also part of a grave-slab with Viking ornament. The Lyndley and Palmes, Fairfax and Fawkes families are remembered in monuments. The Otley agricultural show each May is claimed to be the oldest of its kind.

Bramhope Chapel, in the grounds of Bramhope Hall SE. of Otley, is Puritan, of 1649 date, with box pews grouped around a three-decker pulpit. It was recently restored by the Wharfedale Rural District Council and is frequently open to visitors.

PATELEY BRIDGE, *West Riding* (12–SE 1565). Upper Nidderdale, which contains the noted How Stean gorge, is easily explored from Pateley Bridge, the ancient centre of the dale. It has a narrow, plunging High Street. Well above the town are the ruins of the medieval St Mary's Church with distant views of the moors from the churchyard. This has been a market town since the 14th cent. The Romans worked the lead deposits in the vicinity. Flax and linen industries once flourished in this remote and beautiful setting. In steep Greenhow Hill are the **Stump Cross Caverns** with a quarter mile of strange rock formations.

PATRINGTON, *East Riding* (13–TA3122). The "Queen of Holderness" (the "King" is at HEDON) is St Patrick's here, and it is an incomparable parish church. It is well worth a detour to this flat peninsula close to the mouth of the Humber. A cathedral in miniature, it is utterly beautiful in a pale, serene way, a masterpiece of the Decorated. The building seems all of a piece with restrained use of exquisite but imaginative carving for decoration. The church has been associated with Robert of Patrington, who became master mason at YORK Minster in the later 14th cent. St Patrick's was built rather quickly, most of it done between 1310 and 1349, although parts were not finished until 1410 because of the blow to all activity dealt by the Black Death. The later – and lesser – work includes the chancel and Perpendicular tracery in the east window and west windows of the nave aisles.

In the north wall of the sanctuary is a splendid Easter sepulchre showing at the bottom, in deep relief, three nodding soldiers, and above the chamber for the host and cross, the Lord rising from his coffin with angels swinging censers on either side.

The spire which soars 189 ft serves as a beacon to Holderness and Lincolnshire as well. It is set in a corona which rests on the central tower. The gargoyles at Patrington are unusually fierce but four on the south transept are not of traditional subjects. Instead they represent two musicians and two saints.

The village that produced this magnificent building was once a fairly important market town. The archbishops of York were lords of the manor. They liked to leave the doldrums of York for the bracing air of the Holderness. Shipping in the Humber estuary can be watched from the churchyard.

PICKERING, *North Riding* (13–SE7983). Neat terraces of stone cottages lead into a town which is visually far more rewarding than it may at first appear to a traveller hurrying between SCARBOROUGH and HELMSLEY. Narrow up-and-down streets lead off in all directions and above the piles of red-tiled roofs there are glimpses of the spire of the Church of SS. Peter and Paul. At one end of the town lies a ruined castle. The market place straggles along the hilly main street. This is both a trading and a tourist centre for the Vale of Pickering and the North York Moors. Visitors short of time will concentrate on the church and castle. The former, medieval and much restored, has one of the most complete series of early wall paintings in England and present-day visitors are lucky to be seeing them. They were discovered under whitewash in 1851 by a vicar who regarded them as "purely ridiculous" with a "tendency to excite feelings of curiosity and distract the attention of the congregation". He ordered them whitewashed once more. But 25 years later they were restored under a more appreciative incumbent. Although considerably touched up, the paintings show how a medieval church must have looked. The basic colours are black and reddish. Crude and compelling, the murals are thought to have been done by a travelling artist in the late 15th cent. They cover the walls of the nave with imaginative recollections of the lives of saints.

The castle ruins peer above the treetops on a hill near the stream which runs through town. A castle was founded here by William the Conqueror but the standing buildings date from a later period. Some of the curtain wall with towers, the shell keep on a 43-ft-high motte, two halls and a chapel survive. The castle was badly damaged in the Civil War. It belongs to the Duchy of Lancaster and is in the care of the Ministry of Public Building and Works.

At the end of the low partly medieval bridge, tall trees shade Beck Isle, an interesting Georgian house which now contains a voluntarily assembled and staffed local folk museum. The house belonged to William Marshall, an 18th-cent. pioneer of modern farming who in 1818 altered the house (the long Gothic windows left of the porch were added) to use it as a college of agriculture. It is not certain whether it was actually used as a teaching centre for he died that year. Marshall travelled the country to collect the best information on farming practice and his dream was to disseminate this knowledge. He introduced the idea of a ministry of agriculture.

Beyond Beck Isle, on Potter Hill, is the newest of the three influential Primitive Methodist chapels Pickering has had. Further on, St Joseph's Roman Catholic Church and hall form an attractive composition designed by Leonard Stokes in 1911. The church contains a sculptured font by Eric Gill, made in 1910.

POCKLINGTON, *East Riding* (13–SE8048). Beyond the red roofs of this homely market town lie the Yorkshire Wolds. All Saints Church is the chief legacy from the Middle Ages, a large cruciform structure of the 13th and 15th cents. which replaced a Norman one. Among many interesting details are the grotesque carvings on the 13th-cent. north arcade, a beautifully sculptured cross head (on modern base) with Crucifixion scenes on both north and south sides and a stone credence table or gospel lectern in the sanctuary. William Wilberforce, the abolitionist, went to the grammar school here. It was founded in 1514 by Archdeacon John Dolman.

One of the finest collections of water lilies in Europe (more than 50 varieties) is in bloom from May to October in the gardens of **Burnby Hall** on the outskirts of the town. The gardens and an astonishing array of souvenirs housed in a new exhibition hall were given to Pocklington by the late Major P. M. Stewart. The gardens and collection are open at advertised times in the summer. Burnby Hall now houses local council offices. The water gardens were started by the Major, an ardent angler, as trout ponds. The water-lily beds were planted in 1935. The Stewart collection reflects the donor's favourite pastimes – hunting and fishing – with trophies brought back from frequent expeditions around the world. He also acquired objects of art and household use and weapons, all of which are also on view. Major Stewart was a Cambridge tutor before he settled down on estates near Pocklington in 1904. He died in 1962.

PONTEFRACT, *West Riding* (13–SE4522). The liquorice for the famous Pontefract cakes is no longer grown here though once a field of it filled the ruined castle precincts. The Romans chewed the sweet roots, and cakes of liquorice were made for medicinal purposes early on. But not until 1760 did George Dunhill, a local chemist, add sugar and start the production of the sweets known today. Five firms now make them here. The best viewpoint for a survey of the town and collieries is the castle keep, part of the sparse ruins which stand in a public park on a rocky hill. Pontefract Castle, built by Ilbert de Lacy in the late 12th cent. and later strengthened, figured largely in history. One owner, Thomas Earl of Lancaster, was brought home in chains after the Battle of BOROUGHBRIDGE in 1322, found guilty of treason and beheaded. Richard II was a prisoner here in cold and misery until his murder. The castle also imprisoned James I of Scotland. Charles Duke of Orleans was held here for many years; he was captured at Agincourt. It was a place of execution in the War of the Roses. No wonder Shakespeare called it "bloody Pomfret". A Royalist stronghold in the Civil War, it was surrendered in 1648. The townspeople petitioned that it be pulled down and in 10 weeks it was in ruins.

The castle stood just above All Saints Church which was damaged in the Civil War and only repaired in 1838 when the crossing and transepts were restored to use. The nave was extended recently. The revived church is within its ruins, a curious sight.

There are some good 18th- and 19th-cent. buildings here. The Town Hall of 1785 faces the Market Place where there also is a 1734 butter cross, a round-arched, hipped-roof arcaded stone shelter. The red-brick Red Lion Hotel was remodelled in 1776 by Robert Adam. St Giles's Church, which originated in the 14th cent., became the parish church in 1789.

Below the hospital in Southgate is the 14th-cent. Hermitage carved out of stone by Brother Adam de Laythorpe. It has two chambers and an underground spring.

RALPH CROSS, *North Riding* (15–NZ6802). This is one of the more noticeable of about 30 surviving wayside crosses that dot the North York Moors and which, like the occasional line of shooting butts, provide small points of interest in the vast rolling sweep of heather and bracken. Not much is known about them but they are usually on some ancient track or crossroads and may have been set out by monasteries to guide pilgrims. Sometimes they were boundary posts. Ralph Cross is about 9 ft high, an 18th-cent. replacement of the original, with a hollow on top for coins for poor passers-by. It is on Castleton Rigg in Westerdale Moor at a spot where many tracks meet at 1,409 ft. A few hundred yards W. is Young Ralph and down the ROSEDALE road is Fat Betty (White Cross). Lilla Cross on FYLINGDALES moor may be the oldest. It is a memorial to a thane of King Edwin of Northumbria who died saving the king from assassination in about 626.

REDCAR, *North Riding* (15–NZ6024). The "poor fysher-toune" of the 16th cent. has turned into a holiday resort for Teesside. Coatham, now part of Redcar, was the more significant port in medieval times, manufacturing salt by boiling sea water and later turning to alum burning. Redcar has three beaches and three long rocky reefs, called scars, running out to sea which are left bare, but for seaweed, in low tides. These form a breakwater which has also been a hazard to shipping throughout history.

REETH, *North Riding* (14–SE0499). This was a market town in the 17th and 18th cents., a lively centre for lead-miners in the 19th (the area once produced a large percentage of the national tonnage). Reeth today serves the holidaymakers in Swaledale. It is on the hillside where Arkengarthdale and Swaledale join. Beside Arkle Beck is a miller's house with small millstones set over the windows. High Row, the western border of what is perhaps the best green in this part of Yorkshire, is lined with 18th-cent. inns and shops. Walkers and motorists have many scenic routes to choose from. The road to RICHMOND has been described as the most beautiful in England. The road W. from Reeth leads to some of the wildest country in the Dales. To the NW. beyond Arkengarthdale is **Tan Hill** and England's highest inn.

The parish church stands across the valley at Grinton. People used to bear their dead on wicker biers over rough tracks to its churchyard

Richmond is dominated by the keep of the Norman castle

from the far-flung corners of the parish, which before its subdivision stretched some 20 m. to the Westmorland border.

RICHMOND, *North Riding* (15–NZ1701). An early visitor, given to understatement, observed, "This towne standeth on unequal grounde": Richmond's setting at the entrance to steep-sided Swaledale can hardly be matched, even in a region of dramatic sites. Looking at the town across the river, the viewer is first struck by the strength of the ruined Norman fortress on its sheer rock. The castle was begun by Alan Rufus in 1071, when the border of newly conquered England ran not far to the NW. It is distinctive for having its keep at the gate, a handsome 100-ft tower built in the 12th cent. From its top is the best viewpoint, over the market place, the old town about it, the Swale – the fastest-flowing English river – and the moors. The castle still has two of its towers on the curtain wall and, in Scollard's Hall, built in 1080, it has perhaps the oldest domestic building in Britain. Splendid as it is, the castle was never completed and had little part in history, but it claims one of those unlikely legends of Arthur and his knights asleep until the country needs them. Another story tells of an underground passage to EASBY Abbey, down which a ghostly drummer boy can be heard. The castle is in the hands of the Ministry of Public Building and Works now and is open to the public.

The market place is large, sloping and cobbled. An easy blend of Georgian and Victorian stone buildings surrounds it. The Town Hall on the south side was built in 1756. The obelisk near Holy Trinity Church was put up in 1771. The medieval church itself is a curious assemblage of the ecclesiastical and secular, shops and offices having been built into it; this undermining by commerce at one time threatened the tower.

Friars Wynd leads off to the perfect Georgian Theatre Royal. It was built in 1788 and is one of only two theatres of the period left, the other being at BRISTOL. It closed in 1848. After a long interval as an auction room, corn-chandler's shop, furniture warehouse and salvage depot, it was restored and reopened in 1962. The audience crowds close to the little stage, watching the action from the original pit, boxes and gallery.

Across Queen's Road is Greyfriars Tower, 15th-cent. relic of the Franciscan church. A walk along Frenchgate, leading NE. off the market place, passes some of the finest early residences.

I'Anson Road commemorates Frances I'Anson, the "Lass of Richmond Hill" to whom the famous song was dedicated in 1785. LEYBURN-born, she spent her girlhood here at Hill House.

St Mary's, the parish church on steep ground overlooking the Swale, was extensively restored by Gilbert Scott in 1859–60. In the chancel are 12 medieval canopied stalls from Easby, with some fascinating carvings under the seats. The church contains the memorial chapel of the Green Howards, whose regimental museum in Gallowgate is open to the public.

Lewis Carroll attended for a time the Grammar School opposite, a foundation much older than its Elizabethan charter, when his father was vicar of CROFT.

RIEVAULX ABBEY, *North Riding* (13–SE 5785). Walter L'Espec, the founder of KIRKHAM PRIORY, granted this site in the wilderness to a band of 12 Cistercians in 1131, and thus began an exceptionally prosperous house. Its grandeur is indicated by the ruins here of buildings mostly completed before the end of the 12th cent. Under the third abbot, the great Aelred (1147 to 1167) there were 140 monks and more than 500 lay brothers. The abbey was too large by the 15th cent., however, and parts of the chapter house, warming house and dormitory were taken down. By the Dissolution in 1539 there were only 22 monks. The site, now tended by the Ministry of Public Building and Works, is one of the loveliest in England. It is in the Rye valley 3 m. NW. of HELMSLEY, marvellously secluded, sheltered from the moors which rise above it, and filled with beautiful trees. Rievaulx was the first Cistercian abbey in Yorkshire. There are considerable remains of the lofty church and the extensive monastic quarters. The church nave dates from about 1135. The choir is a particularly fine example of 13th-cent. work.

The long curving terrace which overlooks Rievaulx affords the most satisfying vantage point. This gem of 18th-cent. landscaping belongs to Duncombe Park. When it was laid out, the gentry would drive over to enjoy the views of the desolate abbey and the wide sweep of Yorkshire beyond the valley. At one end was built an oblong Ionic temple, richly decorated and furnished, for hunting parties. At the other end there is a small round Doric temple for solitude. Along the easy stroll between them are openings in the forested slope, cleverly cut to show Rievaulx from interesting angles. These are the views that held Dorothy Wordsworth spellbound, that Turner painted and that made Cowper wish to stay forever. The terrace is reached by a side lane from the Helmsley road.

RIPLEY, *West Riding* (12–SE2860). One wide street and a small cobbled square make up the village remodelled by one of the Ingilbys of Ripley Castle in 1827 to resemble an Alsatian community. Bypassed by the RIPON-HARROGATE road, Ripley offers motorists who stray from the main route an old church and a weeping cross, claimed to be the only one in the county, as well as the castle. All Saints had to be rebuilt after the River Nidd undercut its site in about 1395. A clerestory and upper part of the tower were added in the 16th cent. and there have been 19th-cent. restorations, with much Victorian glass put in. Its oldest monument is a 14th-cent. effigy of Sir Thomas de Ingilby and wife with their children lining the sides of the chest. A stair turret climbs the tower and there is a priest's room above the south chapel. The weeping cross is in the churchyard, with shaft and head missing. What remains is the base with eight niches in which to kneel and repent. It may be 2nd-cent. There are stocks in the square and the village cross. The castle is open on Sundays throughout the summer and the landscaped grounds with lake and walled garden are open on Saturdays as well. The 15th-cent. gatehouse leads into a courtyard where a tower from the original castle now joins a late-18th-cent. hall. Both James I and Cromwell stayed here, the latter, it is said, watched throughout the night by Lady Ingilby armed with pistols. In the library you can see the foundation charter for MOUNT GRACE PRIORY.

RIPON, *West Riding* (12–SE3171), is a small market town with a great cathedral and a Hornblower in three-corner hat who nightly sounds a horn at the market cross and in front of the Mayor's house, carrying out a tradition said to be 1,000 years old.

An Anglo-Saxon church destroyed in 950 stood where the relatively small but impressive cathedral now stands. Building took place mainly in the 12th and 13th cents. but important changes were made in later centuries, including a 19th-cent. restoration. The oldest part, and one of the oldest Christian shrines in England, is the crypt, all that remains of the original Church of St Wilfrid and very like the crypt from his church of the same period at HEXHAM. It lies below the central tower. The west front is exceptionally beautiful Early English work. Among notable furnishings are a late 15th-cent. screen and misericords of the same period by the local carvers' guild, among them delightful versions of Samson, Jonah, a pelican, fox and geese, pigs, an owl and an angel.

The heart of the town is the rectangular market place with its dominating 90-ft obelisk raised in 1781 to William Aislabie of STUDLEY ROYAL, the M.P. for 60 years. The Town Hall, designed by James Wyatt in 1801, faces the square, and the medieval Wakeman's House is near one corner. The house was built in the 13th cent. and the Wakeman, or night watchman, lived there. If householders who had paid for his services were robbed, the Wakeman paid the loss. Under a 1604 charter, Wakemen were replaced by mayors. Hugh Ripley was last Wakeman and first Mayor. The house is now a café and a museum.

The town museum is in Thorpe Prebend House in St Agnesgate, rebuilt in the 17th cent. Ripon was a clothmaking centre in the Middle Ages, but by the 16th cent. the trade was moving to towns in the W. of Yorkshire. This also was a lacemaking centre, the only one in the county. Probably the craft was started by refugee monks or nuns. By 1862, only one lacemaker was left. Ripon was also famous for its spurs.

The city motto is inscribed on the Town Hall in glittering letters: "Except ye Lord keep ye cittie, ye Wakeman waketh in vain."

ROBIN HOOD'S BAY, *North Riding* (15–NZ9505). On the top of the cliffs are run-of-the-mill houses but down the ravine towards the shore is an old fishing village. There is a tangle of houses, cafés, shops and inns, many all too precariously perched on their rocky ledges and often connected by narrow passages or a flight of steps. The village is sought out by artists as well as holidaymakers. Many of the red-roofed cottages are done up in bright paint and flowers. The village is near the north end of a sweeping bay which extends from the cliffs of Ravenscar on the S. to the jutting headland of Ness Point on the N.

Inland stretches FYLINGDALES Moor. Strange things happen here. Every house used to have a hiding place for contraband in the 18th cent. The bowsprit of a stranded ship once pierced the window of an inn. Rocks frequently, but cottages rarely, fall into the bay, yet erosion has claimed at least two rows of houses and a road in the last 200 years. It is not clear why it was named after the legendary outlaw, but it adds to the romance of the place. One story is that Robin Hood came here to get boats ready for an escape to the Continent. The old Fylingdales parish church, St Stephen's, rebuilt in 1822, is interesting for its box pews and three-decker pulpit.

ROCHE ABBEY, *West Riding* (13–SK5489).
This Cistercian house founded in 1147 lies in ruins 1½ m. SE. of Maltby. Its founders were Richard de Bully, Lord of TICKHILL, and Richard son of Turgis, owners of the land on either side of the stream. The monastery here was colonized by Newminster near MORPETH. It got its name from a rock formation which bore some likeness to a cross and was an object of pilgrimage. When the property was surrendered in 1538 it was plundered by the neighbourhood. The site was granted to Thomas Vavasour and William Ramsden in 1554. Eventually it came into the hands of the 10th Earl of Scarbrough who put the ruins in the care of the Ministry of Public Building and Works.

The great charm of Roche today is its position, sheltered by cliffs overgrown by trees and shrubs and standing on a grassy valley bottom landscaped by Capability Brown. The buildings were constructed on both sides of the stream which formed a natural drain, with the water supply controlled by a dam. The area is entered by a fine vaulted gatehouse, partly rebuilt in the 14th cent. The east walls of the transepts of the church still stand, and the outlines of the rest of the buildings are substantial.

ROMALDKIRK, *North Riding* (14–NY9921).
The village takes its name from the Church of St Romald, which is derived from the name of St Rumwald and is perhaps the only dedication to this prodigious infant saint. The church is cruciform and the fabric spans the ages from the late-12th-cent. arcades and south doorway to the 15th-cent. tower. It contains a Norman font carved with rows of foliage in circles and a 14th-cent. effigy of Sir Hugh Fitzhenry in the act of drawing his sword. The church, the irregular green, the scattered houses, a stream, almshouses and the fragments of stocks and a pound for stray cattle all give the village a beguiling air: most visitors find it one of the prettiest in Teesdale.

ROSEDALE ABBEY, *North Riding* (15–SE 7296), is a sturdy hamlet in the middle of Rosedale, largest of the moorland valleys. There is a steep drop down to it on the W., past the landmark chimney of the old ironworks, and a nearly equally steep climb out. A Cistercian nunnery was established here in the mid-12th cent., but it was demolished by the Scots in 1322. Much of the stone went into various village buildings. A few carved stones and fragment of a turret stair survive in the new (1839) Church of SS. Mary and Lawrence. The church has an interesting angel lectern, probably 17th-cent. Dutch. The Milburn Arms Hotel has been the social centre for over 500 years. BYLAND ABBEY made iron here from the mid-13th to the 16th cent.

ROTHERHAM, *West Riding* (13–SK4492).
A close neighbour to SHEFFIELD, Rotherham, too, is chiefly a child of the Industrial Revolution. Its coal-mines, iron, steel, brass and glass works dominate its situation in the Don valley. Like other towns of its generation, Rotherham has been rebuilding in recent years, but some of the medieval street plan remains. With the founding of the College of Jesus in 1482 by Archbishop Thomas Rotherham of YORK, the town became an important centre of learning. The college ended with the Dissolution.

The town's showpiece, All Saints Church, succeeded Anglo-Saxon and Norman churches on its site. Its pinnacled tower, 1409, is the earliest part and the remainder is almost entirely 15th-cent. There are some finely carved bench ends and stalls. It was restored in 1875.

The other medieval survivals in the town are the Chapel of Our Lady and the four-arched bridge at which it stands. The only other bridge chantry in the county is at WAKEFIELD. This one was built in 1482 and after the Dissolution served successively as an almshouse, a prison and a tobacconist's shop. It was restored in 1924. The old bridge, returned to its 15-ft width, was scheduled as an Ancient Monument when the new Chantry Bridge was completed in 1930.

Modern growth began with the establishment of the first ironworks in 1746 by Samuel Walker, a former schoolmaster. John Wesley often visited Rotherham and Nonconformity became firmly established, especially after Walker built the Independent Chapel in 1763. He died 20 years later and his mausoleum is in the chapel graveyard. His son, Joshua, was at the time of his father's death building Clifton House, with John Carr of York as his architect. The house is now the local museum, notable for remains from the excavated site of the Roman fort of Templeborough, 1½ m. SW., and for a remarkable collection of Rockingham china, including tea services and ornamental ware. The china used to be made at nearby Swinton.

A favourite outing is to ROCHE ABBEY, 8 m. E. **Wentworth Woodhouse**, which is really two 18th-cent. houses facing in opposite directions, is 4 m. from the town centre and home of the West Riding County Council's Lady Mabel Training College. It has the longest frontage (600 ft) of any country residence in England. The park is open to the public. In the grounds are three follies: Hoober Stand, built in 1748 by the Marquess of Rockingham; Keppel's Pillar, a huge Doric column erected in honour of Admiral Keppel; and the Needle's Eye, a pyramid pierced by an arch, built in 1780.

Scarborough: the harbour

RUDSTON, *East Riding* (13–TA0967). Another uncanny monolith, but larger than the Devil's Arrows at BOROUGHBRIDGE, stands in the churchyard. It measures 25 ft 4 in. high, 6 ft wide and 2 ft 3 in. thick at the base. It may be as deep into the ground as it is high, but this is a guess. Since the nearest quarry would be 40 m. away, it is believed that the stone was deposited here by glacial action and then erected on this hill by prehistoric men for reasons not now discoverable. The circular churchyard encloses All Saints, which surveys the Yorkshire Wolds 5 m. W. of BRIDLINGTON. It has a thick west Norman tower with most of the fabric Decorated, and restored in 1861. The Norman font is circular with diaper pattern carving. SW. towards Kilham, the site of a Roman villa was uncovered by a ploughman in 1933. Three fine tessellated pavements from here are now in the HULL Transport Museum. The largest is 13 ft by 10 ft 6 in. and shows a bulging Venus with flying hair holding an apple and a mirror, the artist's conception of Venus at her bath. Leopards, hunters and birds are arranged around her. The stone, the pavements and the church speak of occupation stretching over thousands of years. Winifred Holtby, the novelist and journalist, was buried here in 1935. Her *South Riding* was the East Riding.

SCARBOROUGH, *North Riding* (13–TA03 88). It is easy to enjoy this big breezy North Sea resort which combines castle ruins, a fishing village, a working port, luxury hotels, boarding houses, sands, terraced gardens, long wave-swept promenades, views, walks, and carnival-style amusements of all descriptions. Scarborough holds an annual cricket festival. It also puts on an annual Continental festival in a bid to attract visitors from those parts. According to the sagas, the town was founded by a Norseman. It cele-

brated the 900th anniversary of its burning by another one, Harald Hardrada, in 1066 with the friendly co-operation of modern Norsemen. This was a stylish spa in the 17th and 18th cents. and it is still a popular place for retirement or a second home or flat.

Scarborough is built below and on top of a cliff, with steep streets, footpaths and lifts connecting the parts. To the W. stretch new suburbs. The interest for the visitor is concentrated near the sea. The castle ruins stand on a narrow headland which was earlier an ancient British camp and a Roman signal station. The approach is by a 13th-cent. barbican which leads to the shell of the square keep, built about 1160. The curtain wall was the first feature of the castle, probably built 30 years earlier. Remnants of three medieval chapels and a house survive. The site is 300 ft above the sea and covers 19 acres. The castle looks down upon the medieval red-roofed town around the harbour. Here stand the 18th-cent. Customs House, King Richard III House (now a café), old pubs, gaudy arcades and souvenir shops. Hotels, including the monumental Grand, and terraces of houses line the banks. The valley separating the southern parts of town is crossed by high bridges and was landscaped in the 19th cent. Villas were built along its steep sides, for the Victorians did not wish to face the sea. Three of these houses, all in The Crescent, are now the Natural History Museum, Art Gallery and Medical Baths. The museum occupies Woodend, the 1840 seaside home of the Sitwells.

The splendid Marine Drive and promenade, completed in 1908 after repeated delays due to gales, follows the base of the castle promontory and the wide curve of North Bay. Some fine walks run along the cliffs above South Bay. There is a matchless view from Oliver's Mount, the 500-ft-high hill with a war memorial obelisk.

Anne Brontë is buried in the hillside churchyard of St Mary's below the castle. St Mary's was built in the early 12th cent. but rebuilt into the 15th, by which time it was a large cruciform building with three towers. It was severely damaged in the Civil War and the central tower rebuilt at the east end, with the chancel abandoned. There is an interesting row of 14th-cent. chapels on the south aisle.

SEDBERGH, *West Riding* (14–SD6592). There are two points of interest in this hill town in a north-west corner of Yorkshire. The noted boys' school was founded by Roger Lupton, a canon of WINDSOR and provost of ETON, in 1525. A new school built in 1716 is now the library and museum and most of the present buildings, extending to the S., are late 19th-cent. An early and successful headmaster had the unlikely name of Posthumous Wharton. The Quaker meeting house was built in Brigflatts, just over 1 m. SW., in 1675. Whitewalled and furnished in utter simplicity, it keeps a fragment of a yew tree under which George Fox preached. The parish church, St Andrew's, is chiefly 13th-cent. work with some 18th-cent. furnishings. Sedbergh's setting, below the slate Howgill Fells, is more like the Lake District just over the border than the Yorkshire Dales to the S. and E. These are huge smooth hills with rich grass cover. A busy market town, Sedbergh has to handle heavy traffic on its narrow main street.

SELBY, *West Riding* (13–SE6132). The abbey in 1969 celebrated its 900th anniversary. It was founded by Benedict of Auxerre who was directed in a vision to go to "Selebaie" in England. Discouraged by his superiors, he fled, taking St Germain's finger with him. As he sailed up the River Ouse, three swans settled in the water where Selby now stands. This he took as a sign of the place in his dream. He planted a cross and built a hut. He had trespassed on royal property, but with the approval of the Norman governor and the assent of King William, Benedict was made an abbot and given the land.

The present abbey was begun in about 1100. The nave took 100 years and with its absorbing development from Norman to Early English styles as building progressed from east to west it is, perhaps, the greatest attraction of this noble building. The chancel was built between 1280 and 1340 and includes an east Jesse window of about 1330 with roughly one-fourth of its original glass. Worshippers enter the nave through two magnificent doorways: the Norman west doorway with its beautifully carved five recessed arches or the equally handsome north doorway within a 13th-to 15th-cent. porch. The abbey has withstood several disasters, but rebuilding and restoration have left an unusually complete abbey church. In the Dissolution, it became the parish church. In 1690 the central tower fell and in 1906 a great fire swept the building. The last work was completed in 1935.

Selby is believed to be the birthplace of Henry I, only son of William the Conqueror to be born in England. Small boats still come up the Ouse to unload and load at the modest dock and motor traffic crosses by an 18th-cent. wooden toll-bridge. The abbey, in its railed lawn, faces the most attractive part of the town, the broad Market Place. Outer Selby is dominated by flour and cattle-feed mills but fortunately none is so close to the heart of the town as to lessen the joy of seeing the beautiful white towers of the abbey rising from their surrounding trees.

SETTLE, *West Riding* (12–SD8263). A picturesque centre for touring in an area of great limestone hills and crags, across the Ribble from GIGGLESWICK. Narrow streets, tiny courtyards, and good Georgian houses contribute to an interesting townscape. In the Market Square are the Elizabethan-style Town Hall built in 1832 and the 17th-cent. Shambles, with living-quarters opening on to a gallery above the filled-in arcade. The large stone town house built in 1679 by Thomas Preston is known as The Folly because he lacked the money to finish it. Lovers of panoramas will toil up Castleberg Crag that stands 300 ft above the town. The Pig Yard Club Museum has many of the weapons, bones, tools, ornaments and coins found in Victoria Cave, discovered in 1838 at Langcliffe, NE. of Settle. The cave is 1,450 ft above sea-level, and it had through the ages been a hyena den, a hunters' refuge and a place of concealment during the troubled days of the later Roman occupation. Benjamin Waugh, the founder of the National Society for the Prevention of Cruelty to Children, was born in Settle. So, too, was Dr George Birkbeck who founded the mechanics' institutes and whose name is remembered in Birkbeck College, London.

SHEFFIELD, *West Riding* (13–SK3587). The steel capital of Britain has the best of two worlds. It is a thriving industrial centre but it is not stifled by its factories. It holds a happy situation on three hills at the meeting of two rivers, the Don and Sheaf. The Pennines, castles, priories and abbeys are only a short distance away. Civic planning by a forward-looking authority, smokeless zoning, and outstanding modern architecture have improved appearances in recent years. Sheffield was famous for cutlery as early as the 14th cent. (there is a famous reference in Chaucer's *Canterbury Tales*) and it began to specialize in such tools with the arrival of Flemish immigrants in the 16th cent. Steel products followed the invention of the crucible process by Benjamin Huntsman in 1740. At about the same time Thomas Boulsover found out how to fuse silver to copper ingots and roll the silver plate by which Sheffield is known the world over.

It was not always such a stimulating place to visit, but damage suffered in the Second World War forced rebuilding of the grimy centre, and under the guidance of City Architects J. L. Womersley and L. L. Clunie, buildings worthy of their sites began to rise. There is little building older than Victorian left, except for part of the

Henk Snoek

Sheffield University Library

cathedral and a handful of houses. The Town Hall, opened in 1897, towers over the city centre with a statue of Vulcan, appropriately, on the very top. The Cutlers' Hall of 1832 stands nearby. The Master Cutler is second only to the Lord Mayor in Sheffield. The hall contains a fine collection of silver from 1773 to the present. The city's major social event, the Cutlers' Feast, is held annually in the banqueting hall, a 350-year-old tradition.

The City Museum near the University in Weston Park has an unmatched collection of cutlery from the 16th cent. and the world's largest array of Sheffield plate. The University of Sheffield, chartered in 1905, specializes in applied sciences. It has a red-brick core and some striking new buildings, including a library rated the best 20th-cent. building in town. A low, square structure with bands of glass and stone, it is connected by a bridge to the 19-story glass Arts Tower. Another institution, Sheffield Polytechnic in Pond Street, occupies a 12-story slab-like building with two low wings close to the railway and bus stations and car parks.

Sheffield has been daring in its treatment of both shopping and housing. The Castle Market, on the site of vanished Sheffield Castle, opened in 1959 as a roofed shopping centre. There is street access from three floors because of the hilly terrain. Multiple stores and shops are connected to the market by covered galleries.

Housing here became famous with the Park Hill development on a derelict area above the Sheaf. Huge blocks of flats, 4 to 14 stories high, were built in polygonal shapes so that there would be a variety of views. The units open on to wide decks that serve as internal streets and are reported to be socially successful. This is part of an even larger scheme, Hyde Park, to the E. The largest Sheffield housing estate is at Gleadless Valley where three neighbourhoods with 17,000 people were established.

The Cathedral Church of SS. Peter and Paul, across from Cutlers' Hall in Church Street, dates

from about 1435, and is Perpendicular in style with a crocketed spire. The building has been extensively altered and enlarged with, among other changes, a new glass and steel entrance, modern tower and lantern. Visitors will want to look at the Shrewsbury Chapel monuments and the stained-glass windows by Christopher Webb relating local history, and to linger over his Chaucer window in the chapter house.

There are two art galleries, the Graves on the top floor of the Central Library with a fine collection of Chinese ivories, and the Mappin Art Gallery in Weston Park, featuring English art. Persons interested in industrial antiquities should contact the City Museum for permission to visit the Shepherd Wheel in Whiteley Woods, the only known working water-powered grinding wheel and, at the new Abbeydale Industrial Hamlet, a scythe-works of the 18th and 19th cents.

Sheffield and its neighbours strongly back the Sheffield Repertory Company and a £900,000 theatre is opening in 1971 to replace the present Playhouse.

Sheffield relishes its reputation as a city without rigid class barriers, of friendly and city-proud residents.

A round walk of 10 m. will take visitors around the town on public parks property through shady suburbs, woods and fields. The Civic Information Service in the Central Library can provide details. The walk passes **Beauchief Abbey**, founded in 1175, of which only the west tower stands. The Church of St Thomas in this former village was built with abbey stones in the 17th cent. and has fine contemporary furnishings, including box pews. The walk also leads through Graves Park from which there is an overall view of this surprising city.

SHERIFF HUTTON, *North Riding* (13–SE 6566). The village is easily spotted by the broken towers of Sheriff Hutton Castle, the backdrop for a farmyard today, but at one time the centre for great intrigues and deeds of violence in the Wars of the Roses. The village stands on a rise above the Plain of York and you can see YORK Minster's towers from it. The once-mighty fortress was built in the 14th cent. replacing an earlier 12th-cent. castle put up by Bertram de Bulmer, Sheriff of Yorkshire, after whom the village took its name. In the medieval Church of St Helen and Holy Cross with its low Norman west tower are several interesting monuments. The worn alabaster effigy of a boy is supposed to represent Edward Prince of Wales, the son of Richard III, who died in 1484 at the age of 11 at MIDDLEHAM Castle. A cross-legged knight effigy with two angels near the pillow is of Sir Edmund Thweng who died in 1344. There is also a brass memorial to two babies, Dorothy and John Fenys, who died in 1491 and are shown in swaddling clothes. The church is furnished with box pews and a Jacobean communion rail.

SKIPSEA, *East Riding* (13–TA1655). The earthworks of a Norman castle outside the old village constitute the best feudal relic in the Riding. The large circular motte or mound is separated from the bailey by an area once covered with water known as Skipsea Mere. A causeway crossed it. This part of the lowland of Holderness was granted by William the Conqueror to Drogo de Brevere, a "Flemish adventurer", who had married a relative of the king. According to a medieval historian, Drogo killed his wife and obtained by a ruse enough money from the king to finance an escape to the Continent. His lands and Skipsea Castle were of course seized. Later a centre for rebels, the castle was demolished by Henry III about 1220. From the top of the motte there is a view of the sea N. to FLAMBOROUGH. The unpretentious parish church, All Saints, was built, mainly in the 13th cent., of cobbles in a lively zigzag pattern.

SKIPTON, *West Riding* (12–SD9851), has its mills (it makes among other things mercerized thread), but it still has the feel of a country town in a green setting and this contributes to its popularity as a good gateway to the Dales. It is easily accessible today, even by canal, although in 1747 John Wesley complained that it was so "pent up" in its valley that "you can expect little company from without". Skipton contains charming old houses, courtyards, an old toll-booth and stocks in Sheep Street, a 16th-cent. grammar school, a Palladian (1862 vintage) Town Hall, and a simple 1693 Friends Meeting House. But its focal points are the castle and the church, both located where the High Street fans out at the top. The first castle was built by Robert de Romille, but only one gateway of this Norman fortress survives. The present castle dates from the time the Cliffords took possession in the 14th cent. The last Clifford to own it was Lady Anne, who died in 1676. The castle had been partly demolished in 1649 and she reconstructed it. One of her additions was the balustrade over the gatehouse incorporating the family motto "Desormais"

(henceforth). On either side of the gatehouse are massive round towers. Lawns and cobbles inside the walls set off the main buildings and towers. Conduit Court is particularly lovely, shaded as it is by an ancient yew. Among parts of the castle open to the public are an 18th-cent. room lined with pearly shells and the dungeon. This castle is one of the most complete and well preserved in the country.

Holy Trinity Church was extensively restored also by Lady Anne. Among its older parts are the 12th-cent. font, with a superb spire-like Jacobean font cover; the 14th-cent. sedilia with four seats; and the early-16th-cent. screen. There are several impressive Clifford tombs. Skipton was the sheep town (Sceptun) of the Angles and it still has a sheep and cattle auction.

SLEDMERE, *East Riding* (13–SE9364). The house is interesting but the family a Yorkshire institution. Much of what attracts the traveller in the Yorkshire Wolds is their doing. Sir Christopher Sykes transformed the open fields of the area into the splendid agricultural area it still is. Before his death in 1801 he had planted trees and hedgerows, built new roads with wide verges for ordinary folk to graze their cattle on, and pioneered in growing grain for the newly popular wheaten bread. In 1823, the title went to his second son, Sir Tatton, a legend in his own time. He was famous for farming, hunting, racing, boxing, building schools, breeding sheep and establishing the Sledmere stud. He married at 50 and died at 91. His son, also Sir Tatton, was a shy man who spent £2 million rebuilding and restoring churches between the 1860s and his death in 1913. He passed his summers here, taking daily walks for which he would start swaddled in waistcoats. As the day advanced he would peel them off, to be collected by a footman in the rear. His son, Col. Mark, was a soldier and scholar who raised the Yorkshire Waggoners in 1912 and died in 1919. Today Sledmere House is the seat of Sir Richard Sykes and is open daily in summer except Mondays and Fridays. The 1787 mansion was burnt in 1911 and was rebuilt in the same handsome style. It is beautifully set in a park arranged by Capability Brown. Sir Richard, when at home, plays the organ during the Sunday afternoon "viewings".

The church within the park is counted among the loveliest modern parish churches in England. The tower is old, the rest rebuilt by Temple Moore in 1898, one of that Sir Tatton's works. A staircase leads to a small study furnished with the favourite books of the late Col. Mark Sykes. There are far more noticeable monuments in the almost-too-tidy village. A fascinating one was designed by Col. Mark and built after his death to the Waggoners. The panels of low relief carvings on it show these Yorkshire farm boys in driving competitions, at work, joining up, saying good-bye, on the sea, disembarking, and putting the Germans to flight. A canopied well was erected to Sir Christopher by his son and a 60-ft-high cross is the local war memorial. It would be quite at home in a city. On Garton Hill just outside the village is a great spire honouring the most celebrated Sir Tatton. He is pictured on horseback in a carving on the front. The view from here displays the full glory of the Wolds.

SPOFFORTH CASTLE, *West Riding* (13–SE3650). The castle, a 14th-cent. fortified manor house, is a ruin but with hall and solar wing standing. Its licence to crenellate was granted Sir Henry Percy and the house was wrecked by his enemies after his death at Towton in 1461. It was dismantled almost completely in 1650. Built against the natural rock, the house had an outside door leading directly into the upper floor with its great hall and other main rooms. The vaulted basement and kitchen were below. The Ministry of Public Building and Works maintains the site. All Saints Church here has a 15th-cent. tower and the rest of the building is Norman revival of 1855. Some traces of original work survive, including beakhead and zigzag ornament and 12th-cent. capitals. There is a fragment of an Anglo-Saxon cross shaft and a badly worn 14th-cent. figure of a cross-legged knight, Sir Robert de Plumpton III. The rectory stands behind a medieval gateway.

STAITHES, *North Riding* (15–NZ7818). As many as 400 fishermen sailed from this small harbour in the old days, and even in the early 19th cent. it was a principal centre for cod, haddock and mackerel. WHITBY nearby was specializing in whaling and the coastal trade. Three fish trains a week left Staithes when the railway came. But with the growth of Whitby and the arrival of steam trawlers, Staithes fell into decline. The village is said to have begun when a shipwreck cast many Frenchmen ashore and they remained. Smuggling was a local industry in the 18th cent. and alum and jet were mined in the area. As at Whitby, the women then – and some now – wore frilled cotton bonnets and the men navy blue granzies (jerseys). The only road into the village is extraordinarily steep, even by North Riding standards, and the houses in every shape and size cling to the slope at all levels. At the bottom is the Cod and Lobster Inn. It does not look very picturesque, but then it has been washed away three times, and each time rebuilt. It is the village social centre and here the menfolk still sing hymns over their pints. Two famous names: Dame Laura Knight lived and painted here for 18 years, and James Cook, born at Marton-in-Cleveland, was apprenticed to a grocer around the corner from the inn. Fishermen's tales or the stern treatment of his master encouraged the boy to run away to Whitby and sign on as a cabin boy. He is supposed to have taken a shilling from the till to finance the flight which was to lead him to fame as a navigator. Two m. N. is **Boulby Cliff** which, at 666 ft, is the highest coastal point in England.

STAMFORD BRIDGE, *East Riding* (13–SE7155). This was a famous victory in 1066, but this is England and so it is not as well known as the defeat at HASTINGS. Here on the Derwent 8 m.

E. of YORK Harold of England decisively defeated Harald of Norway and saved his kingdom for a while. The invaders, after harrying the coast, had sailed up the Humber and Ouse, landed at Riccall and taken York. King Harold hastened north with what forces he could muster. The Norse king went to Stamford Bridge, a road centre from Roman times, to receive tribute and hostages from local leaders, but the English king pounced and the unprepared Norsemen, many of whom had shed their armour in the heat, were slaughtered. Two tales emerge: of the Norse warrior who held the wooden bridge for hours until he was speared from beneath by an Englishman floating downstream in a tub; and of a parley in which King Harold, asked what terms he would offer his enemy, replied, "Six feet of English earth – or say he is a giant, seven". This was all on 25 September. On 14 October, a weary King Harold met the Norman invaders at Hastings with dire results. The present (1727) narrow arched bridge is of stone and it stands above the flats where the battle was fought. The women here occasionally bake the spear pies that used to be a traditional September dish, recalling how the bridge was taken. There is a stone marker on a weedy green. The village is something of a dormitory for York now, with little of the picturesque about it.

STANWICK FORTIFICATIONS, *North Riding* (15–NZ1813). From these impressive earthworks, King Venutius of the Brigantes led the last serious battle against the conquering Romans in A.D. 74, and was defeated. The defences are reached from Forcett village 6½ m. N. of RICHMOND. Venutius was the great organizer of resistance to the Romans, while his wife, Cartimandua, sided with the invaders and, with their protection, sought to stop the guerilla attacks. These defences were built from about A.D. 69 to 72, first as a bank and ditch surrounding a 17-acre site and then expanded to enclose 850 acres in all. The place chosen to make the stand was a prominent point, Toft Hill, on a crossroads. The excavated section is carefully preserved.

STILLINGFLEET, *East Riding* (13–SE5940). The Norman south doorway of St Helen's Church makes this insignificant hamlet a place of pilgrimage. There are five orders arching over the entry, a geometrical design, beakheads, two rows of zigzag, and a combination of beasts, medallions and heads. The oak doorway itself may be original and the ironwork is a delight. There are two C-hinges, a small pair of gesturing figures at the top left and, near the centre, a (possibly Viking) ship. These could be the fragments of a larger design which related a story. The churchyard is entered through a fine lych-gate and a gravel walk leads through aged holly, yew and conifers. The Moreby Chapel, founded about 1336, has its old piscina, two Jacobean screens and the 14th-cent. figure of a knight. There is a second Norman doorway in the north wall of the nave, with zigzag and ball moulding.

STOKESLEY, *North Riding* (15–NZ5208). The immediate charm of this market town at the foot of the Cleveland Hills arises from its wealth of early houses, mainly brick, around an irregular and spacious centre. The scale is small and harmonious. The River Leven runs along one side with many little footbridges across it. There are frequent narrow cobbled passages between houses. At either end of the long market place are the East and West Greens. On an island in the middle, more or less, stands the straightforward 1853 stone Town Hall. Many buildings – both houses and commercial places – have been lovingly kept or restored, but others, regretfully, are in danger of being lost altogether or brutally altered, which will be a great loss. Facing the Town Hall across the market place is the former Manor House, now the Rural District Council offices. It is a simple, three-story stone composition of the 19th cent. with a wing to the right.

Nearby is the Church of SS. Peter and Paul with its low battlemented tower and small chancel, both Perpendicular, connected by a broad nave of 1771. The path through the churchyard leads across the Leven into a lovely tree-shaded walk which follows the stream as it skirts the town centre, passing modest but interesting houses of the last three centuries. A plaque commemorates Miss Jane Page, a Stokesley native who in 1836 became the first white woman to settle in Victoria, Australia, and in whose memory the trees on Levenside were planted 100 years later. The packhorse bridge is locally thought to be either of 1640 or an 1850 imitation. Near the iron bridge further on, Levenside widens with pretty cottages on either side of the stream. Behind is the well-kept 19th-cent. Union Mill and a former home of a candle factory. West Green has many pleasant houses with bay windows and also the imposing Handyside, red brick trimmed with stone, now the home of the Bishop of WHITBY. Behind the neglected Stone Hall, with its Classical 18th-cent. façade, is the old Wesley Chapel of 1812, now a brewery. A major agricultural show and fair fills the town centre each September.

STUDLEY ROYAL, *West Riding* (12–SE 2768). The beautiful parkland adjoins, and provides a superb entrance to, FOUNTAINS ABBEY. The entrance gates stand near a group of pretty cottages known as Studley Roger. Inside the park is the Church of St Mary, a William Burges creation of the 1870s, very rich, with good Victorian glass and much use of marble from faraway places: Purbeck, Sicilian, Belgian, Tennesseean and Californian. The house burnt down here in 1945 and the owner lived in the High Stables, built about 1720, until the property was sold to the West Riding County Council. The fine stone buildings enclose a courtyard. A large herd of deer shares the park with various livestock and is usually visible from the drive. The grounds were laid out by John Aislabie in the leisure following his forced retirement as Chancellor of the Exchequer. William Fisher was his landscape gardener and the work was spread over

Staithes was an important harbour in the 18th cent.

Noel Habgood

Thornton Dale is one of the prettiest villages in the North Riding

the years 1720 to 1740. The climax was the "pleasure grounds" which begin at the lake (the weir end) and lead on a half-mile or so through the valley to the abbey. This is a pure 18th-cent. conception, making delightful scenic use of woods, walks, towers, temples, ponds, a canal, statuary and "surprise" views. Truly a setting to dawdle in.

SUTTON BANK, *North Riding* (13–SE5383), is one of the most famous viewpoints and one of the toughest road ascents in the county. From Sutton-under-Whitestone Cliffe, the road twists and climbs 500 ft in half a mile. It is 960 ft high at the top. An escarpment of the Hambleton Hills E. of THIRSK, the great Sutton Bank is a landmark for miles across the level plain below it. To the right of the sheer cliff is Roulston Scar on which the white horse of KILBURN was cut in 1857. There is space to park for viewing across the Vale of York to the Pennines. Below to the NW. is Gormire, a natural lake where a landslip formed a kind of dam. Roulston Scar is headquarters of the Yorkshire Gliding Club.

TADCASTER, *West Riding* (13–SE4843), has been brewing beer since the 18th cent. and the breweries are the most conspicuous objects on its landscape today. St Mary's Church has traces of

Norman work inside, but it is mainly Perpendicular, a fine white stone building which was taken down between 1875 and 1877 and reconstructed 5 ft higher up to protect it from River Wharfe floods. Its exterior is livened with pinnacles and gargoyles. It has fine modern woodwork. The Wharfe bridge is early 18th-cent., later widened, with seven arches. Above it stands the "virgin viaduct", built in 1849, but the railway that should have used it was never built. Tadcaster was a Roman outpost for YORK and known then as Calcaria. The Ark Museum, built near the church in the 15th cent. and used as a meeting place by Dissenters in the 17th, is maintained by a brewery and open at advertised times. Tadcaster is 2 m. N. of **Towton,** a hamlet near which a bloody battle of the Wars of the Roses was fought in a snowstorm on 29 March 1461. A cross near the road to Saxton marks the field where 50,000 men fought, said to be the largest number ever engaged on English soil, and thousands died.

THIRSK, *North Riding* (13–SE4282), is a thriving market town and convenient stop at a major crossroads. You can hurry through the newer part of town on one main road or crawl through the crowded market square on another. The square, still cobbled, is surrounded by old shops and inns. This was an important posting station in the 18th and 19th cents. The Three Tuns is the oldest inn, an 18th-cent. front with a fine staircase inside. The Fleece, also Georgian, was once the main coaching inn. It has horse paintings and a coaching clock by Palliser. The Crown Inn dates from 1682. St Mary's Church may well be the best example of Perpendicular work in the county, a notable dark stone building with fanciful openwork parapet outlining walls, tower and porch. The tower is braced by stepped buttresses; 15th-cent. details include the door in the porch, the barrel roof of the nave and some glass. The church was begun in 1430 and completed in the early 16th cent., with 19th-cent. restoration. It was based on a chantry founded by Robert Thirsk who died in 1419. His small brass memorial is inside. Thirsk Hall, a handsome 18th-cent. brick house, stands across from the church.

THORNTON DALE, *North Riding* (13–SE 8383), often earns plaudits as prettiest or tidiest village. On the main PICKERING–SCARBOROUGH road, it is strung out along a stream crossed by little bridges. At the central crossroads are a market cross and stocks. Stone cottages and houses all seem to have pretty gardens. Almshouses and a grammar school were 17th-cent. benefactions. Thornton Hall, with parts dating to Tudor times behind an 18th-cent. façade, is now a hotel. All Saints Church was rebuilt in the 14th cent. and has a large chancel from 1866. A stone effigy of a woman has been dated to the early 14th cent. and the font assigned to 1200. At Low Dalby, 1 m. N., you can now stretch your legs on the **Sneverdale Nature Trail** in Allerston State Forest. A mile's walk from the car park will take you to the forest nursery. A 3-m. hike will reveal the whole story of how the forest grows.

TICKHILL, *West Riding* (13–SK5892). A pleasant change in a colliery area, this was never more than a village although it had one of the most important castles in the North, now in very sketchy ruins, and a splendid parish church. Richard Lionheart licensed the castle for tourneys, and it was demolished by Cromwell's men. The remains, in the grounds of a modern house at the edge of the village, include the 75-ft mound on which the keep stood, some curtain wall and the roofless 12th- and 15th-cent. gatehouse. St Mary's Church, considered one of the finest in the West Riding, has a 124-ft tower notable for its graceful arcades and pinnacles. The church is of the 13th to 15th cents. with many beautiful details and furnishings. A tomb-chest with effigies of Thomas Fitzwilliam, who died in 1478, and his first wife is dated about 1530 and follows the Italian Renaissance style. It was formerly in the Friary, at the west end of town, once part of the Austin Friars house founded in the 13th cent. St Leonard's Hospital, a fine 1470 timbered house, is now the parish room. The Maison Dieu almshouses were believed founded by John of Gaunt. In the market place is a 1766 cross consisting of a dome over eight columns on steps.

WAKEFIELD, *West Riding* (12–SE3320). An important weaving and dyeing centre as far back as the 13th cent., Wakefield did not grow quite so highly industrialized as other south Yorkshire towns. In the mid-19th cent. it was the chief grain market (the Corn Exchange, built in 1838, was reckoned the best building in town, but was demolished in 1963 just the same) and it also became the administrative headquarters of the West Riding. Wakefield builders have been fond of towers and turrets, which give the place an interesting skyline as it spreads up the hillsides from the River Calder. The Cathedral Church of All Saints, completed in 1329, then pulled down and rebuilt in the 15th cent. (and altered again in the 19th and 20th), added its 247-ft spire, the highest in Yorkshire, in 1861. The clock tower on the 1880 Town Hall on Wood Street rises 200 ft and the County Hall, opened in 1898, has a 130-ft dome. The city centre is the Bull Ring, redeveloped with modern shops and flower-beds. The cathedral towers overhead. Kirkgate leads to the Old Bridge, a nine-arch stone structure with a tiny chantry chapel, St Mary's, the best example in England. Traffic now flows over the New Bridge of 1933. The chapel is 14th-cent. and was heavily restored by Sir George Gilbert Scott. The original west front was removed and now stands in the Kettlethorpe Hall grounds. The chapel has lovely traceried windows, pinnacled buttresses and an embattled turret.

Some good Georgian houses remain, for example those on South and West Parades behind Kirkgate on a green square and in the northern parts of the city. In 1954, the city bought Newmillerdam, a suburb to the S. with a lake noted for bird life. The grassy mounds marking the site of the castle at Sandal are now part of the city, too. St Helen's Church nearby is chiefly 14th-cent.

Three estates have been combined to give Wakefield a central 130-acre park with a chestnut-lined drive, 6,000 roses and an alpine garden near Holmefield House which now includes a licensed café. The Art Gallery in Westworth Terrace has a large collection of drawings of Yorkshire and fine modern sculpture.

Only a mile from the city centre is Heath Common, a rough open space around which were loosely gathered three houses of major architectural importance, one Elizabethan and two Georgian. **Heath Hall**, however, is the only one to get needed attention. It was rescued after 50 years of neglect by Mr and Mrs Muir M. Oddie and is open to visitors at intervals. The central part of the handsome grey stone block was built in the early 18th cent. and then incorporated into a much grander design of John Carr in the 1750s. As completed, it is 11 bays wide with detached pavilions on either side. Among the finely restored rooms, the drawing-room is the most elaborate with its dashing stucco work. The Hall was once the home of the eccentric Charles Waterton.

John Carr, the son of a mason, was born in 1723 at **Horbury**, SW. of Wakefield. He designed and built the church there, and paid for it, in 1794. He died in 1807 and is buried in the churchyard.

Noel Habgood

Whitby is still an active fishing port

WENSLEY, *North Riding* (12–SE0989), has given its name to a dale (the other Yorkshire dales are named after their rivers) and a cheese. Wensleydale is a large and fertile valley drained by the River Ure, and Wensley, now a small village, was once its market town. It has a gentle valley site. Houses, church and the gates to Bolton Hall, a mile away through the park, all face the sloping green. Holy Trinity Church has been called the best in the dales. It is chiefly 13th- and 14th-cent. Among its possessions is an old chest, possibly a reliquary from EASBY Abbey which may have held the bones of St Agatha; a finely carved rood-screen, quite likely from the same source, which is now situated behind the Bolton box pew; and a late 14th-cent. brass to a priest, Sir Simon de Wenslaw.

WHITBY, *North Riding* (15–NZ8911). The sound of gulls, the smell of fish, the sight of red roofs up the steep banks from the quay and above the ruin of the abbey on the cliff – this is Whitby. The River Esk, emptying here into the North Sea, divides the town. The older part is on the East Cliff, under the abbey. The West Cliff is a 19th-

cent. development along the sands, and connected to the harbour by the romantically named Khyber Pass cut through solid rock. Whitby is still a port and fishing town – fishermen still mend their nets by the harbour – but it reached its seafaring peak with the whaling in the 18th cent. Although it is increasingly a holiday town, it still has little of the artificial feeling of resorts with no other industry and little history; there is character here and an exhilarating sense of place. Whitby's story probably goes back to a Roman signal station and certainly dates to 657 when St Hilda founded the abbey for King Oswy of Northumbria in thanks for his victory over the heathen Penda of Mercia. The Synod of Whitby of 664 committed the English Church to the Roman instead of the Celtic rite. Both men and women lived in the early monastery, a renowned centre of learning. This is where the herdsman Caedmon was inspired to sing of Creation. The abbey was destroyed by the Danes in 867 and not refounded until 1078 by the Benedictines. It flourished then until its surrender in 1539. The property went to the Cholmley family. The Ministry of Public Building and Works has had custody since 1921. The monastic buildings have virtually disappeared but the church was not so much pulled down as blown away. The lead was taken from the roof but the building left as a seamark, familiar to sailors. In its cruelly exposed position, it could not last. Nave, south transept, west front and central tower had collapsed by 1830, and in 1914 came a final indignity – shelling by the German fleet.

St Mary's Parish Church is at the top of 199 steps near the ruins. It is a large medieval church with a low Norman tower, but drastically altered by the Georgians. It is full of galleries and box pews, with a three-decker pulpit presiding.

The 1788 Town Hall, off Church Street, has its ground floor open for traders, behind Tuscan columns. The home of the great navigator, Captain James Cook, is marked by a plaque in Grape Lane. The handsome Georgian Mission to Seamen is in Haggersgate and the Museum and Art Gallery in Pannett Park contains one of the country's finest fossil collections. More jet, or fossilised wood, is found in the Whitby area than anywhere else in Britain. It was especially popular with Victorians and in 1873, 200 workshops were kept going here. A few craftsmen still work in jet.

YARM, *North Riding* (15–NZ4112), has a strong 18th-cent. feel, perhaps rightly so since that was its greatest period. Today's small market town and gateway to the North Riding on the River Tees was up until two centuries ago the main port of Teesside, busily exporting corn and lead. It was displaced by STOCKTON in the 18th cent. Granaries close to the river are one of the few reminders of this past. It was also prominent as a coaching stop and in 1848 it had 16 inns and public houses. There are still eight in the High Street. The oldest is the Ketton Ox, possibly 400 years old, and named after a shorthorn reared near DARLING-TON which weighed 220 stone when it was slaughtered in 1801. This inn was known for cockfighting. The cockpit was in a second-floor room. When the sport was made illegal in 1849, another room was used with a trap door to permit escape if the place was raided. At another inn, the George and Dragon, the first meeting of promoters for the Stockton and Darlington railway was held in 1820.

The bridge which links Yarm and County Durham was built in 1400 by Bishop Walter Skirlaw and quite naturally has been much repaired. Another connection is the 43-arch railway viaduct designed by Thomas Grainger in 1849. Yarm's High Street is wide and cobbled, with tall terraces of brick houses bordering it. The Town Hall was built in 1710 and two of the churches date from that building period. St Mary Magdalene was rebuilt in 1730 and still has a Norman west front and tower. Its interior is Victorian except for a stained-glass window by William Peckett and the Venetian east window. The octagonal Wesleyan Chapel in Capel Wynd was built in 1763, and Wesley himself pronounced it very elegant.

YORK (13–SE6052). The fascinating townscape of this walled city illustrates much of its nearly 2,000 years of history. Although York possesses in its minster the largest medieval church in northern Europe, the general scale of its buildings is small and human. York lies at the juncture of the three Ridings but belongs administratively to none. Historically it has been similarly independent, acting as a regional capital more often than as a county one and bypassed almost entirely by the Industrial Revolution. Even today York seems more medieval than almost any other English town. The compact core is a treasure-house for anyone interested in history, architecture or ancient crafts, and it is best seen on foot. For a good introduction, join one of the 1½-hour walks, led by a voluntary guide, which start twice a day in summer from the City Library.

The Romans, who called the place Eboracum, built a fort in A.D. 71, the headquarters for their campaigns in the unruly North for three centuries. Constantine the Great was proclaimed emperor here in 306. York has been a garrison town ever since – it is now the headquarters of Northern Command. For the sightseer, a multi-angular tower remains from Roman York, the west corner of the Roman fortress. The inside of this fine ruin can be seen beside the City Library (and Information Centre) in Museum Street and the outside from Museum Gardens. The Museum of Natural History at the top of the gardens and the Hospitium down the slope contain important relics of Roman occupation, including a superior statue of a legionary and the hair of a Roman lady.

Under the Angles, York was capital of their Kingdom of Deira; King Edwin was baptized here by Paulinus, who became the first Archbishop of York in 634; and a grammar school was founded by the great Alcuin. The Danes captured and burnt York in 867 and it was their capital in England for nearly 100 years; they called it Jorvik and it is from this that the present name derives. Anglo-Saxon and Danish York left nothing to see, but the use of "gate" for street is a reminder that the Danes settled here; Goodram-gate has been said, but not proved, to be named after Guthrum, the Danish leader defeated by Alfred. The Normans found a thriving little trading centre and burnt it in 1069, during their frightful ravaging of the North, and then rebuilt the walls, expanding them to take in the present 263 acres. They erected two castles. The Norman period saw the founding of most of the institutions which flourished through the Middle Ages, but the existing remains of them are chiefly of later date. There is a partial Norman house off Stone-gate, however, newly restored. In Gray's Court, now part of St John's College, the original Treasurer's House was built.

Medieval York is everywhere, not least in the web of narrow streets. The Shambles and Stone-gate are two of the best preserved examples. But the minster is the city's chief glory, appropriate to the dignity of an archbishopric. Built between 1220 and 1470, at least the fourth church on that site, it is a textbook of Early English, Decorated and Perpendicular styles. Since 1967, it has been

J. Allan Cash

York: (above) *a view of the minster from the city walls;* (below) *the Merchant Adventurers' Hall*

G. Douglas Bolton

the object of a £2 million rescue operation to strengthen the foundations and prepare it for another few centuries. It contains England's greatest concentration of medieval stained glass, principally from the 13th and 14th cents. The two most famous windows are the Five Sisters and the magnificent 15th-cent. east window, largest in the world. The minster's length is 518 ft and it is 241 ft wide at the transept. The central tower rises 198 ft and is the largest lantern tower in Britain. The 14th-cent. chapter house, with seven lovely window walls, has no central support for its conical roof, just the great buttresses on the eight sides. Rebuilding the present minster, around its Norman predecessor, began with Archbishop Walter de Gray, who was responsible for construction of the transept in the new Early English style in the mid-13th cent. It was so vast that the nave was enlarged by the mid-14th cent. This was followed by the chapter house around 1340. The choir was completed by 1400 and its great climax, the east window, with 2,000 sq. ft of ancient glass by John Thornton of COVENTRY, was finished in 1408. The massive towers came last.

To the E. of the minister is the half-timbered St William's College, the 15th-cent. home of the chantry priests, now the headquarters of the Northern Convocation. In the Civil War, it was the location of a Royalist printing press. From the 11th cent. onwards, some 40 parish churches sprang up in York. An embarrassing number (considering the upkeep problems) survive. Each has a particular interest but the visitor unfortunately short of time might well choose 15th-cent. All Saints, North Street, and its unique windows and medieval woodwork. Three of the nine guildhalls survive, and the Merchant Adventurers' in Fossgate, dating from the 14th cent., gives perhaps the clearest picture of how powerful these institutions were.

The scant 13th-cent. remains of St Mary's Abbey form a backdrop in Museum Gardens for the triennal performance of the York Mystery Plays, and the abbot's house is the nucleus of the rambling King's Manor facing Exhibition Square. This is one of York's most fascinating buildings, restored now by the university, after many years as a school for the blind. It was the seat of the Council of the North after the Dissolution and in its patchwork fabric records many chapters of civic history. Above all, the city walls are medieval, rebuilt on the old Roman and Norman foundations in the 13th cent. A 2½-m. footpath on the walls gives a circular tour (with a few gaps) of the city, passing the four remaining "bars", Micklegate, Bootham, Monk and Walmgate.

In the Middle Ages, York was England's second city, a great religious and commercial centre, fattening on the wool trade. The economic impact of the Dissolution was cushioned by the establishment here of the Council of the North. When this was abolished in the 17th cent., York declined. It revived in the 18th cent. as a social centre for county families. The race-course on the Knavesmire and the Theatre Royal both opened in the 18th cent., and continue to be magnets

today. York saw a great burst of new building in the 1700s, and a whole school of craftsmen made the city known.

Georgians left a pronounced impression on York, particularly in the former town houses along such streets as Micklegate and Bootham. Notable public buildings of the 18th cent. include the Mansion House, Assembly Rooms, Judge's Lodgings, and Assize Courts. The early 18th-cent. Debtors' Prison and the later Female Prison, almost equally grand, now house the justly famous Castle Museum with its period rooms and streets. The Mansion House is the official residence of the Lord Mayor, but can be seen (along with the exceptionally large collection of civic plate) by arrangement. Just behind it is the 15th-cent. Guildhall, bombed in 1942 but restored in 1960.

Victorian York saw the start of the confectionery industry, now the biggest employer, and the establishment of the railway centre here thanks to its enterprising citizen, George Hudson. The station is a superb example of graceful iron construction and the Railway Museum nearby has 12 famous locomotives that children can clamber on.

The City Art Gallery in Exhibition Square, of 1878 vintage, contains a good collection of old masters and work by William Etty, a York man, famous for his nudes in the 19th cent.

The University of York opened in 1963, taking over an Elizabethan manor house and estate at Heslington village where a completely modern complex has grown up around an artificial lake. The university is a collection (five at present) of colleges each with teaching and residence facilities. Economics, English, history and education are major departments. The music department with its own fine concert hall offers an extensive public programme.

At **Bishopthorpe**, 2½ m. S. of York, is the Archbishops' palace, which includes traces of an Early English structure. Excursion boats from York's Lendal Bridge take visitors past the palace on the River Ouse.

YORKSHIRE DALES NATIONAL PARK, *North and West Ridings* (12–SD9080). Some 680 sq. m. of the two Ridings were set aside in 1954 as a National Park. High fells, moors of heather and bracken, limestone screes, scars and outcrops, richly wooded dales, swift becks, tumbling forces and unpretentious grey-stone villages all combine to produce truly refreshing landscapes. First-time visitors will be nervous about the drystone walls that so closely border the twisting roads in many places. There are steep gradients and upland sheep abound. It is not much use planning for average speeds above 20 to 25 m.p.h. The park takes in much of the central Pennines and the **Pennine Way** from Derbyshire to Scotland passes through it. Fishing, nature and archaeological studies, potholing, walking, ponytrekking and just plain viewing are the natural activities for the Dales. There is an information centre at the Reading Room in CLAPHAM.

The North-East

Durham   Northumberland

THOMAS SHARP

Northumberland and Durham are more than merely two neighbouring counties. Physically they are a kind of north-eastern "peninsula" of England. Some hundred miles of sea constitute their eastern boundary. On the north the broad Tweed and the mass of the Cheviot Hills cut them off from Scotland in a fifty-mile stretch crossed by only half a dozen roads. Down the west, forty miles of Pennines crossed by five mountain roads and one valley road separate them from the similar "peninsula" containing the two neighbouring north-western counties. Only at the southern boundary, where the lowland country of south Durham shades into the North Riding of Yorkshire, is the physical form of the "peninsula" open enough to give it a firm regional attachment to the rest of England.

Physically isolated in this way, the two counties have had close historical associations. From Roman times onward Northumberland was the frontier land of England's northern boundary, defended first by the legionaries of the Roman Wall and then later, through medieval times, by the Prince Bishops of Durham, whose jurisdiction extended, indeed, to detached pockets of Northumberland itself in the palatinate areas around Norham and Bedlington. Then, later, the winning of coal and the industrial development subsequently associated with it brought something like economic and social unification to at least their adjoining lowland areas. So today the close past and present relationship is expressed, among other ways, in the existence of such bodies as the Durham and Northumberland Miners Association, the Northumberland and Durham Association, the Northumberland and Durham Travel Association, and so on.

Yet, associated though they are in these many ways, the two counties have their marked individual characteristics and qualities. Even their historical development, though related, differed markedly – and indeed inevitably – because of the relationship itself. County Durham, secure behind the defensive works and the frontier lands of its northern neighbour, and under the control of its Prince Bishops, was settled and peaceful centuries before Northumberland achieved that condition. It was the need for peace and security that drove the early saints and scholars down to Durham from that great cradle of early Christianity in England at Holy Island. And it was the combination of the affairs of church and state-defence that established the Prince Bishops in the Durham palatinate after the Norman Conquest. Here they ruled like the kings themselves, and in their name. They had their own parliament, their own coinage. They gave licences to crenellate castles. They bade their subjects to military service, levied taxes, administered their own laws. So they continued all down the medieval centuries; the palatinate, with its powers slowly reduced over the years, continuing, indeed, until comparatively recent times, and not being finally abolished until 1836, with vestiges of it continuing even today.

Under the comparative peace of this protected part of the frontier, agriculture developed, inclosure proceeded; and County Durham got the landscape pattern it shows today in its small-to-medium-sized fields, hedged in its lowland parts, stonewalled in its hill country, together with the frequent villages and the small market-towns of a settled moderately-populated countryside – to which, of course, over the last century, has been added, in the coalfield which occupies much of its lowland area, the thickly scattered villages and half-towns, and the other physical appurtenances, of mining.

Northumberland was still wild and unsettled hundreds of years after County Durham was more or less secure. The raiding, pillaging and murder that for centuries had ravaged the county as far down as the Tyne valley, officially ended with the Act of Union between England and Scotland in 1707: but, even for some time following that, raiding by the county's own moss-troopers and rival families was not unknown. Against this war and raiding the powerful families lived in great castles and the lesser gentry in peel-towers, where the humbler folk took refuge, if they could, while their huts were being burned and their cattle and horses carried off. A catalogue of 1541, covering only part of the county, listed no less than 120 castles of various types. Under conditions of that kind there could be little agricultural development. It was not until well into the eighteenth century that Northumberland was brought into settled agricultural use. Then the making of roads, the draining of moorland farms, the planting of woods and the inclosure of the waste lands began to bring the countryside towards the appearance that it is seen in today. Late though the beginning of that transformation was, it was long in completion. Even as late as the 1770s, at least half the county was still in a waste state: and it was not until well into the nineteenth century that the transformation of all the cultivable lands from waste to cultivation was accomplished. So it is probably true to say that in large part the agricultural landscape of Northumberland is the newest (or the least old) of any in England. And, even so, transformation in some parts goes on again today, in the ecological-economic revolution that the Forestry Commission is making in the planting of its great new hill-country forests – the most extensive in the country.

This fashioning of the Northumberland landscape did not come about solely out of the opportunity afforded by settled conditions. The manner in which the opportunity was taken had a decisive effect on the special scenic character that the landscape developed. Its character over large areas even today is of landowners' landscape. Many of the old landowners of the great castles played their part in its creation. But newcomers also moved in to take over some of the old estates, particularly those which were confiscated from supporters of the Stuart cause. These newcomers were people who had made their fortunes in the coal and shipping trades of Tyneside and the developing industries associated with them. So the improvement of the rest of the Northumbrian countryside was largely created out of the spoliation of one small corner of it.

The landscape that resulted from these changes is very different from the landscape of the neighbouring county. Whereas the feeling of the Durham countryside, even in the mining areas, is of medium-sized hedged fields with hedgerow trees (small and stunted as they often are), or of stone-walled fields in the hill country, that of Northumberland is much more open – often, indeed, wide-open – with large fields and relatively fewer trees, except in the river valleys or in the parklands of the mansions and castles. There is still a strong feeling of feudalism in the Northumbrian countryside – not of feudal landscape, of course, but a sense and an evidence of large estates seen not only in the parklands and in glimpses of castles and large country houses, but in the number of hamlets at or near park-gates – tidy groups of estate-cottages that have a character of their own. And the sense of quiet and remoteness which still characterizes the county (away, at least, from the main roads) must arise out of this combination of conditions that brought it into being in its present form – the sparseness of its population in the lawless times and the manner of its establishment through the agency of large estates. For Northumberland, outside the industrialized corner of Tyneside, is still the quietest and most sparsely populated county in England. In all that wide area there are only five or six small towns and less than a dozen substantial villages. For the rest, such population as there is is either gathered into insignificant hamlets or thinly scattered in isolated cottages and farm-houses.

This past history has been described at some length because here, more than in most parts of England, it illuminates the striking differences of the effect of human exploitation in two neighbouring counties that are historically closely associated. The combination of this human exploitation and the physical terrain upon which it has been imposed creates the individual kinds of countryside in which the counties show their differences.

Leaving aside the industrial areas for the moment, it can be said that there are some six or seven distinctive kinds of scenery here. The two coasts themselves differ. Between the level lands and the wide sandy beaches at the estuaries of the Tees, the Wear and the Tyne, the 25-mile-long Durham coastline is of low cliffs with few appreciable bays. It is not naturally very interesting, and the industrial additions to it have not made it more attractive. The Northumberland coastline is generally lower, except at the one or two places where the Whin Sill that slashes across the county ends in iron-hard dolerite cliffs, as at Cullernose, Dunstanburgh and Bamburgh. Most of it is pitched up into sandhills; there are miles of splendid accessible sands running down to the sea; and the succession of large and small bays, headlands with castles, and offshore islands with lighthouses on them, makes it a coast that has a good deal of incident and variety.

Back from the sea, right up from Tyne to Tweed and almost as far west as the Great North Road, there is a low-lying coastal plain. It is bleakly industrialized for the first dozen miles from Tynemouth; with, further on, scattered collieries and (in the late 1960s) occasional heavy disturbances by open-cast coal-workings – which will no doubt be restored when the available coal has been won. But beyond Warkworth it is land of a very special quality, land which is considered by many people to be the richest fattening ground in England. Here, and back some way towards the hills, in the cattle-sheep-and-barley country of highly-mechanized mixed farming, farms are large (750 acres not being considered a particularly big farm there), and the countryside tends to be wide and somewhat open, though well hedged and diversified with hedgerow trees and patches of woodland.

Back from the coastal plain, between Alnwick and Chollerford, is a large triangle of upland-feeling country, rather bare-seeming for much of the year, with fewer trees, and those mostly late-leafing ash. And then, for the rest of this part of Northumberland (by far the greater part), as far down as where the South Tyne valley constitutes the Tyne Gap, there are the hills – the wide rolling lonely range of the Cheviots.

Something like two-thirds and more of the two counties is hill country – hill country of two distinct kinds. These Cheviots are not moorlands in the ordinary sense, nor whale-backed hills. They are more bumpy, with individual summits; and there is not much heather on them. More generally (except now in the large areas of Forestry Commission plantations) they are covered with the fine bent grass that takes changing colour from varying wind, sun and cloud. The highest

Barnaby/Mustograph

The Cheviot Hills

of them, Cheviot itself, though impressive with its 2,678 feet of height, is perhaps lumpish rather than of fine outline. But others have more peak-like outlines among the general wave-like crests, like Yeavering Bell, Hedgehope and Peel Fell. And the subsidiary range of the Simonsides especially has a pronounced wave-like character.

The lesser rivers of the northern Cheviots, College Burn, Harthope Burn, the Breamish and others, run in narrow dales. And so does the Coquet in its upper reaches. But the more substantial rivers, the Rede, the North Tyne, and the South Tyne as far up as Haltwhistle where it turns in from the south, run in wider more open-sided valleys rather than true dales. The true dales belong to the other type of hill country, where again a difference in the two counties is shown.

Not that Northumberland has no Pennine country. As has been indicated, it has a very substantial knob of it southwards of the main South Tyne valley. There, and over the whole of the western half of County Durham, the whale-backed Pennine moors are for the most part heather-covered, and are deeply indented by narrower dales. The Northumberland dales of this part, those of the South Tyne, the West Allen and the East Allen, are richly wooded in their lower reaches towards the main Tyne valley, and bare in their upper miles. The Durham dales of the Wear and

Crown Copyright

Hadrian's Wall at Housesteads in Northumberland

the Tees are rather more open and have more of the typical patterns of stone-walled fields which give such individuality to Pennine country.

Those are the main types of landscape in the two counties. There remains a smaller lowland countryside of mixed farming in south Durham between the mining area and the lower Tees valley. And, as well as that, the mining and industrial areas themselves.

These, too, differ between the two counties. In Northumberland the nearly-twenty-mile stretch along the Tyne from Heddon-on-the-Wall to Tynemouth constitutes a practically continuous urban sprawl. And it is much the same on the Durham side of the valley from Blaydon to South Shields. But the mining areas behind these show some differences in kind. On the level Northumberland land the pit villages seem to stretch out and run together more than those south of the river. The Durham coalfield extends further back into the county (though in the south-western part mining is now almost completely dead). Its surface, right back from the coast, is more broken, has a more upland feeling. Its pit villages are somewhat less contiguous, and many of them are centred on the older villages and hamlets of the earlier-settled countryside. But in both counties these industrial districts have the sad and forlorn ugliness that characterizes all the older industrialized areas of England, though perhaps here it is less oppressive than in most.

Except for some most notable examples, as in a few still comparatively uncorrupted old towns, building in the two counties is not of any very high quality. Durham city, Berwick, Alnwick, Hexham still have an attractive general character; and the Grainger-built section of Newcastle is an example of central city planning and building that is unique in Britain. But most of the older places are sadly corrupted – Stockton, whose wide High Street must once have been especially pleasant; Sunderland become nondescript; Darlington ditto; Old Hartlepool a ruin; North Shields almost derelict; Morpeth vulgarized. Few even of the small towns and older villages off the coalfield have kept their character unblemished – industrial corruption spreads all too easily beyond its own boundaries. In Northumberland, in any case, because of its late settlement, some of the few villages and most of the scattered hamlets have little obvious historical character. They are apt to be somewhat dour and hard-faced. Many, perhaps most, even of the churches – country as well as town churches – are late and austere; nineteenth-century-new in Northumberland because of the late settlement; nineteenth-century-restored-and-rebuilt or newly built in County Durham because of the rapidity of the industrial expansion of that time. Perhaps the most consistently attractive district of buildings in relation to landscape is the Teesdale area of County Durham – and that due to a policy of estate management rather than architectural quality. There, on the Raby estates and in their neighbourhood, running up from east of Staindrop to the hill country of the county boundary, groups of white- or cream-washed farm-houses and farm buildings delightfully enliven and humanize the landscape – an effect charmingly seen in small unfrequented Langleydale immediately west of Staindrop, as well as in Teesdale itself.

In spite of the moderate quality of most of its ordinary buildings, the genius of the county seems to lie in the invention and making of things rather than in the pursuit of any of the creative arts. Invention in building, too, at an earlier time: for it was in Durham Cathedral that the first developments were made towards the Gothic style of architecture which came to characterize so many of the cathedrals and churches of western Europe. But mainly it has been in machines and utilities – for the winning of coal to begin with, and its transport by sea and land. Colliers for bearing the sea-coal down to London; and, from that, ship-building, with the invention of the first steam turbine. Railways, first for getting the coal to the sea-ports; then, in the Darlington and Stockton railway (the first of its kind in the world), for the carrying of passengers. And, along with these, other engineering inventions: the first large-scale cast-iron bridge (the High Level) at Newcastle; Armstrong's hydraulic engines and armaments; Swan's electric bulb; the first dynamo; and so on through things like the first self-righting lifeboat at South Shields and the first friction matches at Stockton. And invention has lain not only in inanimate things but in living ones, too: the famous Durham Ox, bred by Charles Colling at his farm near Darlington, the father of the whole short-horn breed throughout the world; the dairying rather than the beef-producing type of that animal developed by Thomas Bates at Halton in the Tyne valley; the Cheviot sheep (the unconscious instrument of the Highland clearances) developed in the hills by a farmer called Robson; and, more domestically, that canine curiosity, the woolly-coated terrier named after Bedlington.

They are mixed counties, these. Town building at its best (in Newcastle) and near its worst in scores of industrial places concentrated in a comparatively small fraction of the whole. History visible everywhere, even in the industrial areas themselves: but especially in the wide countrysides; in the different agricultural landscapes there as well as in the castles and the battlefields. And, after the stormy history, a peace and a calm now such perhaps as cannot be got in any other part of this country. Here, away from the industrial areas, in these lowlands, these dales, on these remote far-ranging hills and moors, is the widest and least populated, and one of the quietest (as well as one of the most individual) regions in the whole of England.

The North-East: Gazetteer

ELLEN WILSON

ALLENDALE, *Northumberland* (14–NY8455), claims to be the geographical centre of Great Britain. True or false, this is a splendid centre for getting to know the beautiful scenery of the moorland district watered by the East and West Allen Rivers and Allendale to the N. where the two streams meet. Allendale once was the market town for an important lead-mining area. Today it lives on hill farming and holiday-resort business. It is 1,400 ft above sea-level and offers a variety of sport including trout fishing and skiing. Allendale keeps a pagan New Year's Eve custom, well attended by outsiders. Twenty-four masked men, or guisers, march behind a band round the town, carrying barrels of blazing tar on their heads. A fire is lit in the large market place and the tar barrels are thrown upon it. Then the marchers and townspeople dance until midnight, when "first footing" begins. Described in the late 19th cent. as "straggling, dreary looking place", Allendale in recent years has spruced itself up and repeatedly won county contests for the best-kept village.

ALNHAM, *Northumberland* (14–NT9910). A few scattered houses, a castle site, a fortified former vicarage and an appealing little church make up the hamlet of Alnham today. Three hundred years ago it was an important place at the crossroads of many packhorse and drovers' tracks and at the south end of Salter's Road from Scotland. The vicarage, which dates from 1541 and incorporates the old peel-tower, has been converted into a handsome residence. The grassed-over remains of Alnham Castle, demolished or burnt in 1532, are opposite the church. In the hills round about are several Ancient British camps and earthworks. St Michael and All Angels, standing in a tree-bordered churchyard, has a snug and earthy quality and it retains a sense of age despite several restorations which rescued it from ruin as late as the mid-1960s. A broad (12th-cent.) round arch leads into the chancel, where a fine oak-timbered ceiling adds to the feeling of strength. Four medieval tomb lids have been set in the chancel floor. Near the 1664 font is an unfinished monument. The mason, in 1611, must have grown weary, or bored, when filling the slab with the history and virtues of one George Adder for, about three-quarters of the way down, he decided he had done enough and ended abruptly "and so forth". The River Aln rises near here.

ALNMOUTH, *Northumberland* (15–NU2410). From the WARKWORTH road, there is a striking view of this small red-roofed town piled beside the estuary where the Aln flows into the North Sea. Once an important grain-shipping port (and smugglers' haven, reputedly) it is now a holiday resort with yachting, good sands both N. and S., and one of the oldest golf courses in England. A pleasant walk on the sands leads 3 m. S. to Warkworth past a pile of rocks called Birling Carrs. Alnmouth was the port for ALNWICK in the late 12th cent., and in the early 19th cent. it was still exporting considerable amounts of corn and importing Norway timber. Ships were built here. Some of the granaries were later converted to houses. In a terrible storm on Christmas Day, 1806, the crashing seas broke through the northeast bank of the river and the Aln changed course, pouring into the sea through the new opening on the north side of Church Hill. The harbour was left on the south side where it gradually silted up. Church Hill is the site of an Anglo-Saxon church and the ruins of the later Norman church were finally destroyed by the 1806 gale. Alnmouth is the probable site of the great synod of 684 in which Cuthbert was chosen Bishop of Lindisfarne. The little town witnessed several naval encounters in the 18th-cent. war with France and in 1779 it was itself bombarded. The American John Paul Jones, who had been cruising along the coast, fired a cannon at the old church. He missed, and the cannon-ball, weighing 68 lb, hit the ground, bounced three times and crashed into the end of a farm-house. Beacon Hill N. of the town is an Ancient British camp.

ALNWICK, *Northumberland* (15–NU1912), still looks like a stronghold of the Earls and Dukes of Northumberland. You may enter from the S. through a narrow medieval arch of Hotspur Tower and within moments confront the great barbican guarding the gateway to Alnwick Castle. From the Lion Bridge on the N. the castle appears all-powerful and brooding. Within the town, age speaks from the narrow streets, cobblestones, passageways, sturdy grey buildings and monuments. Alnwick is 4 m. from the coast and on the A1 almost exactly halfway between NEWCASTLE-UPON-TYNE and BERWICK-UPON-TWEED, a convenient centre for touring and a destination in its own right. It grew up on the River Aln beside the great border castle whose walls enclose 7 acres. Below and around the castle are grounds landscaped in 1765 by Capability Brown, forming a beautiful park. The Pastures, the riverside section of the castle grounds, has a footpath

Noel Habgood

Alnwick Castle has hardly changed outwardly since the 14th cent.

leading from the 18th-cent. Lion Bridge to the CRASTER road, with views of the castle along the way.

The castle was begun by the de Vesci family in the early 12th cent. The last of the legitimate line died in 1297 leaving the castle in trust for a natural son. The trustee was the Bishop of DURHAM, who sold the castle to Henry Percy in 1309 and, it is said, pocketed the money. The castle was elaborated and strengthened during the years of border warfare, then stood a ruin for nearly 200 years. The 1st Duke of Northumberland restored it in the 18th cent. with James Paine and Robert Adam. In the mid-19th cent., the 4th Duke employed Anthony Salvin to make extensive changes in the interior. Most of the Adam work was removed and an Italian Renaissance style adopted. Outwardly, however, the castle has not altered much since the 14th cent. The great walls, huge keep and flanking towers make it one of the more spectacular sights in the country. The exceptionally fine barbican, topped with figures which look as if they had just raced there to take up their guard duties, now leads into the present ducal residence and a teachers' training college. Visitors are admitted at advertised times to such apartments as the armoury in Constable's Tower, the museum of British and Roman antiquities in Postern Tower, the keep, and many splendidly furnished rooms including the library, largest room in the castle, and grand staircase.

In the town, a broad main street, with sloping, tree-shaded cobblestone parking space alongside,

passes near a market square. A free-standing 18th-cent. hall has an arcade for shops in the ground floor and assembly rooms upstairs.

The first object to greet the traveller arriving from the S. is the Percy Tenantry Column, an 83-ft fluted monument erected in 1816 by grateful tenants because their rents had been reduced during a period of agricultural depression. A Percy lion with straight, stiff tail stands majestically on the top. The column is sometimes known as "The Farmers' Folly" because, so the story goes, the duke was surprised to find his tenants were rich enough to afford such a tribute and raised their rents again.

On the other side of Alnwick is St Michael's Church, said to be the most important 15th-cent. work in Northumberland. It stands on a hillside overlooking the river. The battlemented tower is stoutly buttressed in steps and the church is wide, with aisles running the full length of nave and chancel. Among the interesting contents are two 14th-cent. tombs with figures of a man in a tunic and a lady, a third medieval figure which appears to be a cleric, and a handsome 14th-cent. Flemish carved chest.

In a town so dominated by its castle, two well-known schools are named, appropriately, the Duke's School and the Duchess's School. An Old Ragged or Industrial School Foundation still educates needy boys and girls. The Bondgate Gallery regularly exhibits the work of living artists. Fishing tackle is manufactured here.

The remains of HULNE PRIORY are $3\frac{1}{2}$ m. NW.

ALWINTON, *Northumberland* (15–NT9206). An unusual split-level church with a tall west end and pointed bell turret stands on a hillside S. of this hamlet tucked into a hollow of the CHEVIOT HILLS where the Alwin and the Coquet rivers meet. The Church of St Michael has remnants of its original fabric dating from the late 11th cent., but most of it is 13th-cent., considerably restored in the 19th. The chancel is 10 steps above the nave, and a crypt housing Selby family tombs is under the elevated portion. Clennell table tombs are in the north aisle. The path leading to the church door is paved with interesting gravestones and it leads through a well-kept churchyard with a good view of the gently rounded hills. Near the gate is a little stone-roofed stable where the parish hearse is stored. It was bought in 1840 for £9 and is rarely used today for lack of horses strong enough to pull it. The handsome wooden body surmounted by an urn stands on wheels large enough to pass through fords or deep snows. There is good angling and walking in the vicinity, and the Coquet river-bed has been known to yield agates, cornelians and pebble crystals. One walk follows old Clennell Street, the drovers' road, to the Scottish border at Russell's Cairn on top of Windy Gyle, 2,034 ft high. The cairn is named after Lord Francis Russell who was murdered by Scots at a border meeting in 1585. Sir Walter Scott stayed at the Rose and Thistle in Alwinton when he was working on *Rob Roy*. Alwinton has a famous sheep show and hound trials each October. There are remains of prehistoric camps and earthworks in the area.

AYCLIFFE, *Durham* (15–NZ2822). An ancient church is the chief reminder of the long history of this limestone village N. of DARLINGTON. The future doubtless will centre at Newton Aycliffe nearby, a new town for workers from a trading estate which was developed out of a wartime munitions works. St Andrew's Church has interesting relics of its Anglo-Saxon foundation, although most of the present structure is 12th- and 13th-cent., partly rebuilt in 1882. There are remains of two Anglo-Saxon cross shafts, one with crucifixion scenes, which probably were gravestones in the 10th cent. An early 14th-cent. tomb lid with birds and oak leaves is in the north aisle floor and there are attractive 17th-cent. furnishings.

BAMBURGH, *Northumberland* (15–NU1834). No castle could look more imposing than Bamburgh, a magnificent red sandstone mass which presents a startling sight whether approached from N. or S. The road takes the motorist directly under its walls on its land side, while on the other it towers over the sea from a 150-ft precipice. Bamburgh was founded in 547 by King Ida who built a wooden fortification here. It was given by his grandson, Ethelfrith, to his wife Bebba and became known as Bebbanburgh, from which the modern name derives. Although the seat of the government of Northumbria moved in the mid-8th cent. to CORBRIDGE, Bamburgh remained a royal residence. It was rebuilt in Norman times and by then included a keep, chapel, living quarters and enclosures for the garrison and for prisoners. Much of the castle was restored and altered in the 18th cent. by trustees of Lord Crewe, Bishop of DURHAM, who had acquired the property after marrying into the Forster family. They added a long range of domestic buildings. During the late 18th cent., out of Lord Crewe's beneficence, the castle was used as a boarding school to train servant girls, as a surgery and dispensary for the poor, as the site of a windmill to grind corn for those in need and as a haven for shipwrecked sailors. In 1894, the 1st Lord Armstrong bought the castle and it was again extensively restored. It is open daily and from the upper terraces where the guns still point out to sea, there is a celebrated view of the FARNE ISLANDS.

The castle rises boldly at the apex of a triangular wooded green which is the centre of a still unspoilt and – despite the endless streams of Sunday motorists – peaceful village of soft grey stone. St Aidan's Church is mainly 13th-cent. with a fine and large chancel. During work in 1837, an unusual 13th-cent. crypt was discovered. In it were coffins of the Forster family, who owned Bamburgh and BLANCHLAND. The crypt may have been built originally for relics of St Aidan.

In the churchyard is an over-elaborate monument to the 19th-cent. heroine of the village (and the country) Grace Darling. She was born here in 1815 in the house which is now the post office and she died at the early age of 27, but not before she had engraved her name in the hearts of her own and later generations. She was the daughter of the lighthouse keeper on Longstone Light. On 7 September 1838, the *Forfarshire* was wrecked in a gale. Grace and her father rowed out in the storm to rescue nine survivors. The coble they used and other souvenirs of the heroic event are in the Grace Darling Museum of the Royal National Lifeboat Institution which stands opposite the church.

BARNARD CASTLE, *Durham* (14–NZ0516). Here, on a cliff above the Tees, is a picturesque centre for discovering the delights of Teesdale. The castle was founded by Guy de Bailleul and rebuilt by his nephew, Bernard Balliol, after about 1150. Its ruins cover 6½ acres. The chief survival is the Round Tower, mostly 14th-cent., offering a splendid view which inspired Sir Walter Scott when he was writing *Rokeby*.

The town which grew up outside the castle has two broad main thoroughfares today: Galgate, leading up to the Methodist church and castle entrance, and Market Place, at a right angle to it, with a cobblestone car park and, at the bottom, an octagonal, two-tiered Market Hall or Cross built in 1747. There used to be a lock-up in the centre, shelter for butter-sellers in the colonnaded veranda and an administrative hall upstairs. Charles Dickens stayed at the King's Head Hotel in 1838 while writing *Nicholas Nickleby*. At a corner of the Market Place is St Mary's Church, largely

Norman and Transitional. The west tower is a replacement of 1874. Inside, the 15th-cent. chancel arch, leading into the raised chancel, rests on the head of Edward IV on the left pillar and that of Richard III, who obtained Barnard Castle by marriage, on the right.

Descending The Bank from the Market Cross, the visitor comes to Blagraves House, now a café, a narrow, four-story gabled Tudor house in which Oliver Cromwell may have been entertained with mulled wine and shortcake in 1648. Thorngate still has some interesting 18th-cent. houses. Their long top-floor windows used to light weaving lofts. On the riverside are disused sandstone factories which recall the days when the town was important as a textile and carpet manufacturing centre. It lives now on the work provided by a penicillin factory, on tourism and as a shopping centre. There are lovely riverside walks here, especially to EGGLESTONE ABBEY on the Yorkshire side.

The **Bowes Museum** W. of the town is a surprise however many times you see it. It is a massive 19th-cent. French château designed by Jules Pellechet for John Bowes, son of the Earl of Strathmore, and his wife, a French actress and artist. The couple collected paintings, furniture and ceramics. Both had died by the time their dream of a museum was realized in 1892. The museum was run by trustees until the Durham County Council acquired it in 1956. It stands in a 21-acre park with gardens, bowling green and tennis courts. It claims to house 10,000 beautiful things in 22 exhibition rooms. Notable are paint-ings by El Greco, Goya, Boucher, Courbet, Sassetta and Tiepolo; French 18th-cent. furniture, tapestries, period rooms and a children's room with dolls and doll's houses.

BEADNELL, *Northumberland* (15–NU2329). The harbour walls were built in the drystone wall way, probably in the 1790s when the lime kilns which stand nearby were also constructed. The kilns, a relic of the days when Beadnell shipped coal and lime, belong to the National Trust. There is some crab and lobster fishing and a good holiday trade here. The sandy beaches are excellent and there is safe yachting in the wide Beadnell Bay. A large caravan park shelters behind the dunes. The Craster Arms is built round a 1460 defensive peel-tower. The 1740 church was restored in pseudo-Gothic fashion with an odd pierced octagonal stone screen placed round its short spire in 1860.

BEDLINGTON, *Northumberland* (15–NZ 2581). The Northumberland miners' picnic is held here annually in June in Attlee Park, with marching bands, juvenile jazz bands, a beauty contest and an array of politicians. Bedlington was the capital of a shire attached to the Palatinate of DURHAM until 1844. The church's dedication to St Cuthbert refers to the night in 1069 when the Durham monks, carrying the saint's coffin and in flight from the Normans, stopped on their way to Lindisfarne. In 1669 a resident named Cuthbert Watson, locally renowned as a sleepwalker,

Barnard Castle: the Bowes Museum houses a magnificent collection of paintings and works of art

Barnaby/Mustograph

Bellingham stands on the edge of the moors

climbed a buttress, was awakened by a passer-by and fell to his death. A stone inscribed "Watson's Wake" was placed in the north aisle to mark the event. A plaque on the King's Arms hotel marks the birthplace of Sir Daniel Gooch, born in 1816, who laid the Atlantic cables in 1865 and 1866. The extinct Bedlington Iron Works produced the first rolled iron rails, used by George Stephenson's locomotives. Bedlington terriers were bred here for badger baiting. The broad Front Street leads downhill to the River Blyth.

BELFORD, *Northumberland* (15–NU1033). This small town on the A1 has long been a coaching stop for travellers. The centre of Belford climbs a long southward-looking slope off which run streets of stone houses and cottages with a good deal of modern housing growing up around the edges. Entering from the S., the visitor sees on the E. the large park and honey-coloured façade of Belford Hall, designed by James Paine in 1756 for Abraham Dixon, manufacturer and merchant. It was partly remodelled by John Dobson in 1818. Further on, the long, low ivy-covered brick front of the old Blue Bell Inn encloses the view. Belford had a difficult history. It suffered repeated border raids, which accounts for the fact that most of its buildings are relatively modern. As late as 1639 it was described as "the most miserable, beggarly town, or town of sods, that ever was made in an afternoon of loam and sticks". The houses were described as hovels with roofs of heather or sod. Later it became a fox-hunting centre and now it is a market town. To the SW., Belford Moor on the way to WOOLER provides splendid views towards the CHEVIOT HILLS on one side, and the coast on the other.

BELLINGHAM, *Northumberland* (14–NY 8383). People here still like to draw water from St Cuthbert's Well which is supposed to have healing powers (and which is reached by a winding path behind the churchyard towards the North Tyne). The big attraction for many visitors, however, is the curious pack-shaped tombstone in the churchyard, associated with the Legend of the Long Pack. It is told that a pedlar called one day at Lee Hall, the Georgian riverside mansion of a Col. Ridley who had made his fortune in India, and asked for a night's lodging. The colonel was not at home and the maid, Alice, refused the request. But she allowed the man to leave his heavy pack in the kitchen. Some time later she saw the pack move and called for help. A ploughboy fired a shot into the pack and blood poured out. Inside was the body of a young man. The servants realized that a raid was imminent, mustered help and then blew the silver horn found on the body. When the robbers came they were met with force, and fled. The man in the pack was buried, unidentified, in the churchyard.

Bellingham may be plain, as many a border town preferred to be in the days of marauding neighbours, but it is a friendly and accommodating spot and a gateway to the great moors and forests of this area. A special point of interest is St Cuthbert's Church which has a weighty and unique stone roof, well restored in recent years. It is barrel-vaulted with hexagonal stone ribs about a yard apart. The building had to be buttressed in the 18th cent. to counteract the thrust of the roof. The stone slabs were laid after two fires had destroyed wooden roofs. The church has whitewashed walls, narrow deep-splayed windows, a chastely restored and furnished chancel and an air of fortitude. The churchyard overlooks the river and here you can rest in view of the 1835 stone bridge and in sound of the running waters.

The market place is ornamented with a dainty Boer War memorial and handily situated just behind the village hall with its wooden cupola and clock. Next to the hall is a Chinese gingall (a mounted musket) taken in 1900 and presented by Cdr E. Charlton of H.M.S. *Orlando*. The name recalls the town's long prominence as a haunt and target of such rival graynes or clans as the Charltons, Armstrongs, Dodds, Milburns and Robsons in the days when the frontier was in turmoil.

A popular agricultural show is held in September.

BELSAY, *Northumberland* (15–NZ1078). Travellers on the A696 must often wonder about the unusual and attractive sandstone arcade of shops that sets Belsay apart from other villages along the busy NEWCASTLE to Carter Bar route. These Italianate buildings were designed by Sir Charles Monck, assisted by the architect John Dobson, when the village was re-created in the early 19th cent. Nearby, but no longer open to the public, is Belsay Hall, built by Monck in the style of a Grecian temple. The beautiful park includes the ruins of the 14th-cent. Belsay Castle, said to have been the finest English tower house in the North. Stone for the hall was quarried on the grounds and the quarries were later transformed into gardens.

BERWICK-UPON-TWEED, *Northumberland* (14–NT9953). Somewhat seedy, but highly picturesque, Berwick is the northernmost town in England, steeped in history, and fascinating to explore on foot. It is built mainly of stone in grey or pinkish-brown. The roofs are mostly red-tiled and many a street is cobbled. The harbour has swans. The town is piled upon a peninsula at the mouth of the Tweed and it faces the river, rather than the sea. Three great bridges connect it with Tweedmouth on the south side of the estuary: the low stone bridge with 15 arches of varying height and width, completed in 1634; the 1928 concrete span known as the Royal Tweed which carries the heavy vehicular traffic now; and the railway's Royal Border with its 28 soaring arches, completed in 1850. The town is an entrancing sight from the Tweedmouth bank or the railway bridge.

Berwick's well-worn appearance seems to suit its historical rôle as a buffer town. It was an important trading centre and international port and was captured or sacked 13 times before 1482 when it was finally made English. But almost until the Union of the Crowns in 1603, it was regarded on both sides of the border as an English outpost. Until 1746, Berwick had a special status as a free borough and was mentioned separately in Acts of Parliament. (So far as records show, it is still at war with Russia in the Crimea, having been specifically listed as declaring hostilities in 1854 and having been left out of the 1856 peace treaty.) Berwick was part of the ransom paid by the

captured William the Lion of Scotland to Henry II in 1147. It was sold to the Scots by Richard I to get money for his Crusade. It was destroyed in 1216 by King John in person. When William Wallace was executed in 1305 in London, one quarter of him was displayed here as a warning to other rebels. The Countess of Buchan, who had crowned Robert Bruce King of Scotland, was caged for six years in the castle yard from 1306.

Berwick has had two sets of protecting walls and the remains of the later ones give visitors their most interesting circuit of the town. The first walls were completed in the reign of Edward II and little is left of them. The town was then fortified by Elizabeth, starting in 1558, on the new Italian design with great emphasis on effective use of artillery. The Berwick walls are the only example of this style in Britain and among the earliest of the type in Europe. Three of the projecting bastions, shaped like flat arrowheads, remain. Cowport is the only surviving original gate. The high ramparts of earth and stone include Meg's Mount with its superb view of the town, the river and the sea.

In the late 18th cent., the medieval riverside walls were rebuilt with gun emplacements overlooking the river mouth. Most of the old guns were turned into scrap for the Second World War. A pleasant walk along the Quay Walls passes a number of interesting looking buildings, including the Customs House.

The Town Hall, built in the 1750s, is possibly the handsomest building, facing and dominating broad Marygate. Of rich brown stone in a Classical design, it has a grand portico with giant Tuscan columns and a tall spire. The bells of the Town Hall ring for Holy Trinity Church as well as the town curfew. The top floor used to be a gaol and prisoners were aired on the balcony around the roof. The restoration of the hall, which reinstated the butter market in the colonnaded rear ground floor and brought in a coffee bar and small shop, won a Civic Trust award in 1969.

Holy Trinity Parish Church in Wallace Green, which has no bell-tower, was completed in 1652 under Colonel George Fenwick, the Puritan governor, and is one of the few examples of its period. The Barracks were built between 1717 and 1721 in response to town objections to billeting soldiers in public houses. Their design is attributed to Vanbrugh. They contain the museum of the King's Own Scottish Borderers, open to the public.

Little is left of the ancient castle, except for a small ruin of the watch-tower on the riverside near the railway bridge and a length of wall which guarded a flight of steps up the steep bank. Much of the castle stone went into the railway bridge and the station occupies the castle site.

Berwick cockles are an old-fashioned peppermint sweet. Modern industries include the manufacture of puff pastry and components (such as doors and windows) for houses.

BILLINGHAM, *Durham* (15–NZ4624), was transformed from a sleepy village into a thriving industrial complex on Teesside when the chemicals industry, dominated now by Imperial Chemical Industries, developed here after the First World War. The need to produce home-made explosives and fertilizers had been underlined by the German blockade and this location was conveniently near a coalfield and the sea. Looking at the practically all new town, it is hard to think of it as 1,000 years old, but it was founded in the 10th cent. by Edgar, father of Ethelred II. In 1801, its population was only 335; today it is 35,000. The chemicals industry employs some 15,000 highly skilled workers and it has been said that Billingham has a record number of graduates per acre. There is almost an industrial forest of plant, pipe and retort here. The showpiece is the new town centre, with its hotel, shops, offices, library, car park and £1 million Forum, said to be unique in Europe, which provides indoor ice-skating, swimming, squash, badminton and a theatre. St Cuthbert's Church symbolizes the marriage of old and new. It was founded in 860 and has a tall, square Anglo-Saxon tower, a long, narrow Anglo-Saxon nave, altered in the 12th cent., and a broad, light chancel completed in 1939.

Billingham was incorporated in the county borough of Teesside in 1968.

BISHOP AUCKLAND, Durham (15–NZ 2029). Although the busy commercial and social centre of the south-west Durham coalfield, Bishop Auckland is much older than the Industrial Revolution and has not lost all of its country charm. It is fortunate in having a beautiful open space on its edge. This is Bishop's Park, which surrounds the castle, official residence of the Bishops of DURHAM for more than a century. The bishops had a country residence here from the 12th cent. onwards, and the town grew up round a market at its gates. The 800-acre park, entered through an imposing 1760 gatehouse off the market place, has winding walks, lovely trees and lawns and two small streams, the Gaunless and Coundon Burn. It is open to the public as is the 18th-cent. deer shelter within it. The castle and its splendid chapel, however, are open to visitors only about once a year. Inside the gate, a screen wall designed by James Wyatt about 1800 divides the public park from castle and gardens. The residence began as a Norman manor house and was castellated about 1300. Extensive alterations were made in the 18th cent. The chapel of St Peter is considered an architectural treasure and should not be missed. This was the former banqueting hall. Bishop Cosin converted it into a chapel after 1660 because the original chapel was pulled down by a previous occupant to erect a new mansion on the site. The chapel is late 12th-cent., with tall, wide arcades, shafts of Frosterley marble and limestone, handsome marble arches and mouldings. The elaborate roof and screens are 17th cent. Bishop Cosin died in 1672 and is buried here as he wished under a marble slab in the nave.

St Andrew's Church, well out of the town itself, at South Church, is a choice example of Early English architecture and the largest parish church in the county. It has an Anglo-Saxon cross relic from about 800 with interesting eastern motifs, a holy-water stoup made from a Roman altar, and effigies and a brass of the 14th cent.

Bishop Auckland is seeking new industries to provide alternative employment for displaced miners, and industrial and housing estates are rising everywhere. The urban district includes St Helen's and West Auckland, which are today mainly continuations of the mother town, strung out along a busy road. The largest new trading estate is at **St Helen's Auckland**, a former mining village. It is worth pausing here to visit the church. Small, grimy and yet appealing, it squats beside the road in an overgrown churchyard with a sprawl of commercial development and council houses nearby. It is almost entirely late 12th- or early 13th-cent. with simple round-arched arcades in the nave and small round-headed clerestory windows. St Helen Hall, beside the main road, is an interesting house of the 17th and 18th cents. The one or two other interesting-looking old houses in the neighbourhood seem neglected and doomed.

West Auckland is an old spoiled village round a large green.

BISHOP MIDDLEHAM, Durham (15–NZ 3231), was the site of a favourite manor house of the Bishops of DURHAM, and two of them died in it in 1283 and 1316. But by the end of the 14th cent. they preferred BISHOP AUCKLAND. All that is left of the former residence are the grassy mounds S. of the church, St Michael's, which itself is nearly all 13th-cent. It has a large original font of Frosterley marble and an inscription to Robert Surtees, the county historian, who lived at Mainsforth Hall nearby. Surtees' grave is in the churchyard. He died in 1834 and his massive *History and Antiquities of the County Palatine of Durham* was published between 1816 and 1840. Shortly after his death, the Surtees Society for publishing historical works of the North of England was founded as a memorial. Surtees, a kindly country gentleman, was a talented antiquary and scholar. He also had lighter moments. A friend and correspondent of Sir Walter Scott, he once sent the latter a ballad which he claimed to have heard from an old countrywoman. Scott printed it, quite unaware that it was Surtees' own invention. The village today is a centre for farming and quarrying. Outside the Dun Cow Inn at the bottom of Church Street hangs a stone sign, an interesting piece of 18th-cent. folk art.

BLANCHLAND, Northumberland (14–NY 9650), has been called one of the most perfect villages of England, and few travellers who drop from the wild moorland around it down into this wooded glen of the Derwent would dispute the label. A medieval gatehouse bars the HEXHAM road and a 19th-cent. stone bridge carries the road out on the opposite side of the village. Charming houses of warm stone surround the L-shaped centre, probably once the outer yard of the old monastery. The Lord Crewe Arms includes parts of what was the abbey guest-house and the later residence of the Forster family. Blanchland, named for the Premonstratensian white canons, dates to the founding of the monastery by Walter de Bolbec in 1165. After the Dissolution, Blanchland fell into decline. The estate was owned first by the Radcliffes and then bought in 1623 by the Forsters of BAMBURGH. It probably was used as a hunting box. A Dorothy Forster in 1699 married Lord Crewe, Bishop of DURHAM, who bought the debt-ridden estate here in 1704. Lady Crewe's niece, the second Dorothy Forster, helped her brother, Thomas, escape from Newgate after he was taken in the Jacobite rising of 1715. She became the heroine of Sir Walter Besant's novel, *Dorothy Forster*, and many of the scenes were laid here and in Bamburgh.

When Lord Crewe died, he left his estates to trustees with the income to go to OXFORD and various schools and almshouses. The Crewe trustees are still in charge. It was they who in the mid-18th cent. used the abbey ruins to rebuild the houses and create the model village seen today. Most of the inhabitants in those days worked in the nearby lead mines. The trustees also rebuilt the abbey church chancel of the 13th cent. as a parish church. This was restored later, in the 19th cent. Three medieval coffin lids in the transept floor are interesting. Two are of abbots and are marked by a pastoral staff and a host and chalice, and the third is of an abbey huntsman, Robert de Eglyston, who was buried under a slab carved with a horn, sword and arrow.

BLYTH, *Northumberland* (15–NZ3181). One of the oddities here is an 18th-cent. lighthouse, once on the shore, and now stranded in the rear of a terrace of houses. Blyth rose to prominence as a coal-shipping port and ship-building centre in the late 19th cent. It never became a seaside resort like some of its northern neighbours, although it has developed a 3-m. stretch of sands which, in 1795, accommodated 7,000 horse and foot soldiers in a fine parade inspected by the Dukes of York and Gloucester under the eyes of 30,000 spectators. With collieries closing down, Blyth of late has sought new industries, and residents are now engaged in manufacturing ladies' underwear, cosmetics, tractors and electronic equipment. They also, of course, work on the docks, and in the remaining pit. Ship-building ended but the production of bridges and industrialized housing began. Two power stations are located here. Blyth got additional encouragement when Alcan Aluminium (U.K.) Ltd began to build its £60 million smelter and power station at **Lynemouth** to the N. and to improve harbour facilities at Blyth for handling alumina cargoes: Lynemouth, with Ellington colliery 6 m. N., forms the largest undersea mine in the world. The Royal Earsdon Sword Dancers of Blyth perform the "rapper" or short sword dance adapted from a Viking rite. Rappers were used in the early coal-mines and the five dancers, fiddler and two clowns dress somewhat like pitmen of 150 years ago.

BOLAM, *Northumberland* (15–NZ0982). It is hard to believe that this was once a village of 200 houses with a market, a fair, a school and an inn. Now there are only a church, a rectory, a few cottages and Bolam House. But Bolam Lake, designed by John Dobson, remains a beauty-spot, with a great variety of flowering shrubs, trees, birds and waterfowl to be enjoyed on a walk round it. St Andrew's Church is mainly Norman, but it has a late Anglo-Saxon tower with triangular-headed belfry windows. It was bombed by a German aircraft during the Second World War. From the churchyard there is a good view of the SIMONSIDE HILLS. Bolam took its name from the Baron de Bolam, the first owner of record in the 13th cent. Stone from the original tower house went into Bolam House. Within walking distance W. are the **Shaftoe Crags,** with a remarkable punch-bowl hollowed out of the flat sandstone rock. Legend describes the Romans making celebratory drinks in it.

BOTHAL, *Northumberland* (15–NZ2386). This pretty Wansbeck hamlet has two points of special interest: the castle and the Church of St Andrew. The small castle is now owned by a BEDLINGTON manufacturer of electrical components and used for entertaining business guests. It was built in 1343 by Robert Bertram. It is the surviving gatehouse, with its twin towers facing the hamlet, which was converted into a residence. Below the castle is the 13th-cent. church which was altered and enlarged in the 14th cent. It has a notable bell turret with three oblong openings. Inside is an angel roof and the worn but impressive alabaster tomb of Ralph Lord Ogle, who died in 1516, and his wife.

BRANCEPETH, *Durham* (15–NZ2238). St Brandon's Church is the place to see "Cosin style" woodwork at its finest. John Cosin, later Bishop of DURHAM, was the rector from 1626 to 1644. He was responsible for the restoration of many parish churches after the Commonwealth, and the carving here, by Robert Barker, is outstanding in the pews, pulpit, screen, choir stalls, font cover and roof. Pevsner calls the Cosin style with its "fully conscious Gothic revival" plus contemporary 17th-cent. elements "one of the most remarkable contributions" of County Durham to English architecture. The church stands in the grounds of Brancepeth Castle and both date from the late 12th cent. The village consists of a few Georgian and later houses at the gates of the castle. From the S., especially, the castle provides a splendid view. Close up, it turns out to be mainly 19th-cent. work, some of it "remarkably incorrect" in the expert view. The castle passed through several families including the Nevilles before it was bought in 1796 by William Russell, a wealthy Sunderland banker who made a fortune from mines. He and his son, Matthew, started rebuilding in 1817 at vast expense. The castle ceased to be a residence in 1922 and today it is a research centre for the Pyrex company in SUNDERLAND.

BRANXTON, *Northumberland* (14–NT8937). S. of St Paul's Church is the historic battleground of Flodden. There on a small knoll in a field stands a plain granite cross erected in 1910 to honour "the brave of both nations". The battle occurred on 9 September 1513, between Scottish and English armies. It was a fierce engagement, and it settled nothing. The Scots were defeated and the losses, by various estimates, were from 9,000 to 16,000 men. Among the slain was James IV of Scotland who had led his troops here to help create a diversion for the French who were under attack at home by Henry VIII and the bulk of the English army. A northern army led by the ailing Earl of Surrey was hastily recruited to meet him. The cross is supposed to mark the spot where James fell. A line of pylons marching in the distance mars the scene today, but inside the small church, the past can be summoned. With its blue painted walls and lino down the aisle it is a homely enough place, but in it one can still imagine the refuge it must have seemed the night James's body was carried in. The corpse next morning was borne to BERWICK to be embalmed, encased in lead and taken finally to London. The slightly pointed arch is the only survival of the original 12th-cent. church structure. The building was virtually re-created in 1849, in a heavy Norman style. The altar rails are of oak taken from a ship which foundered off the FARNE ISLANDS.

BRINKBURN, *Northumberland* (15–NZ1198). One of the loveliest spots in the county is the site of Brinkburn Priory church which, since its 19th-cent. restoration by Thomas Austin of DURHAM, has been called probably Northumberland's best Gothic church. Found SE. of ROTHBURY in a loop of the River Coquet, it is now in the care of the Ministry of Public Building and Works. The church is all that is left of the Augustinian priory founded about 1135 by William de Bertram. It is noteworthy for its spaciousness, lancet windows, stone-vaulted roof and numerous splendid details. During the days of the border troubles, the priory often was disturbed by raids, and on one occasion the monks, believing they had escaped the Scots, rang the bells in jubilation. The joyful peal guided the raiders to the densely wooded and secluded spot which they had inadvertently missed. They threw the bells into a deep pool of the Coquet where they are supposed to lie to this day. A ruined watermill is just E. of the church. There is a tradition that a shady green spot nearby is the burial place of Northumbrian fairies, among the foxglove, woodruff, figwort and other flowers they loved. The Hall, near the church, is in a ruinous state.

BYWELL, *Northumberland* (14–NZ0461), on an enchanting site on the River Tyne, is a village no longer. But here, in witness to a livelier past, are two fine churches, a vicarage, an empty castle, a hall, a medieval market cross and a farm – all framed in trees and meadowland. The story goes that two quarrelling sisters, owners of adjacent manors, founded rival churches within a few yards of each other. But there is nothing to substantiate this account and it is more likely that the manors built neighbouring churches to give the clergy companionship. St Andrew's Church, the "white" church, belonged to Premonstratensian canons of BLANCHLAND. It has the county's best Anglo-Saxon tower, according to Pevsner. It is tall, unbuttressed and has round-headed windows. The body of the church dates from the 13th cent. and the chancel is longer than the nave. Medieval tombstones have been built into the north wall exterior. The larger St Peter's Church has Anglo-Saxon and Norman traces with 13th- and 19th-cent. changes. It is the "black" church because it was served by Benedictine monks of DURHAM. The vicarage is a late 17th-cent. building. The Hall is dated 1760 and was designed by James Paine. The castle is a fine tower house with four turrets from the 15th cent. Bywell in 1570 had 15 shops and was a centre of ironwork, particularly famous for making harness and other gear for the border horsemen. A hundred years later, a visitor reported that the inhabitants rode small horses, wore long beards and dressed with cloaks and swords. By the 19th cent. hardly a handful of houses remained.

CALLALY CASTLE, *Northumberland* (14–NU0509). The present mansion, representing Classical styles from about 1675 to 1835, incorporates a 15th-cent. peel-tower and can be visited on weekends and Bank Holidays. Only three families – Callalys, Claverings and Brownes – have owned the estate 2 m. from WHITTINGHAM since Anglo-Saxon times. The south-west corner includes the medieval tower but it is thoroughly disguised by later building work. According to legend, the Lord of Callaly wanted to build his tower on Castle Hill ½ m. SE. but his wife preferred the sheltered valley. As work began at his choice of site, the determined spouse engaged the steward to pull down every night what the masons had put up by day. Her lord finally decided to sit up all night to find out what or who was responsible. His wife dressed the steward as a wild boar and instructed him to dance wildly around, pulling down the stones and singing a ditty to the effect that only a tower erected where she had wished it would ever stand. The thoroughly frightened lord gave in. Italian stucco artists from WALLINGTON HALL did the plasterwork in the showpiece drawing-room, possibly to the design of James Paine. The first hall was built just E. of the tower in 1619. Robert Trollope of NEWCASTLE designed the late-17th-cent. changes. There were other alterations and additions in Georgian and Victorian times. A false flue in the drawing-room chimney was prepared by the Catholic Claverings for use as a priest's hiding hole.

CAPHEATON, *Northumberland* (14–NZ0380). The road leading off the A696 to the village is lined with magnificent trees and known as Silver Lane. In its vicinity in 1747, a group of workmen found a hoard of Roman coins and silver dishes.

Chillingham church: the Grey monument

Capheaton Hall, which is not open to visitors, was designed by Robert Trollope of NEWCASTLE and built in 1668; it is historically a building of architectural importance. The village, consisting chiefly of a row of low cottages with overhanging front eaves, has a good view over the park with its shallow lake. Swinburnes have lived at Capheaton since the 14th cent. The present hall was built by Sir John Swinburne, whose grandson Algernon Charles spent his holidays here. At WALLINGTON HALL, the future poet met John Ruskin and Dante Gabriel Rossetti and other literary lights.

CHESTER-LE-STREET, *Durham* (15–NZ 2751).

Very old, and not much to show for it. This was the site of an important Roman military station on the River Wear. The church stands where the remains of St Cuthbert rested in a little wooden Anglo-Saxon church from 882 to 995, before they were taken by the monks from Lindisfarne first to RIPON and finally to DURHAM. For these 113 years, the town was the centre of a large diocese. The present church, St Mary and St Cuthbert, was begun in the early 11th cent. and rebuilt in the 13th and 14th. The octagonal tower dates from about 1400. A small stone cell for an anchorite huddles against the north wall of the tower, with a narrow squint into the church. It became an almshouse after the Reformation. Inside on a stone bench along the wall of the north aisle are squeezed 14 effigies of members of the Lumley family, put there in 1594 by John Lord

Lumley. LUMLEY CASTLE is 1 m. E. The town is now a market place for the area. **Lambton Castle**, 1½ m. NE., is a romantic reproduction of a medieval castle, turrets, curtain wall and all. The original was dismantled in 1797 and replaced by a hall which in 1833 was enlarged and castellated. Almost wrecked in 1854 by mining subsidence, it was altered again in 1875. It is now the County Council's adult residential college.

CHEVIOT HILLS, *Northumberland* (14–NT 81).

The great bald domes of the Cheviots are among the most pronounced and the most memorable landmarks in the county. They lie in the north-west corner and form a barrier to Scotland. They offer some of the grandest scenery to be found anywhere. The hills cover 200 sq. m. of Northumberland and spill over another 100 sq. m. into Roxburghshire. The chain extends 35 m. in length. The Cheviots make up the northern third of the NORTHUMBERLAND NATIONAL PARK. The highest among them is Cheviot itself, 2,676 ft above sea-level. The summit here is level and some 50 acres in extent, most of it peat bog. It can be climbed in 1½ hours from Langleeford SW. of WOOLER. But many prefer Hedgehope, 2,348 ft high, which can be climbed in about an hour from Langleeford and rewards the visitor with marvellous views in all directions. Other main hills are Comb Fell, Bloodybush Edge, Windy Gyle, the Schil and Black Hag. The Cheviots look gentle because of their rounded shapes and seemingly smooth, grassy surfaces and they do in fact provide unrivalled walking. But ramblers are warned not to attempt long outings in bad weather and to wear brightly coloured garments to aid searchers, if a search proves necessary. The range is thinly populated, mainly with hill farmers, and there is only about one person to each 350 acres around Cheviot. This is sheep country with a distinctive breed of white-faced sheep. The Cheviots were carved out of one huge mountain by the streams that rise on Cheviot and radiate from it – the Rivers Breamish and Coquet, and the Harthope and College Burns. The waters attract many anglers, and archaeologists are drawn by numerous ancient remains.

CHILLINGHAM, *Northumberland* (14–NU 0625).

A small herd of white cattle, descendants of prehistoric wild oxen, inhabit the wooded park of Chillingham Castle. They are under the watchful care of the Chillingham Wild Cattle Association and can be visited by the public. There were 34 in 1969, surprisingly near the 28 in the herd in 1692 when records began. It is believed that the herd was trapped here when the 600-acre park was walled in 1220. The cattle are small and creamy white. Their crescent-shaped horns are tipped in black and they have black muzzles. They are fleet and shy (but they sent Thomas Bewick, the engraver, up a tree when he was sketching for his Chillingham Bull study).

The castle, home of the Earl of Tankerville, is not open to the public. It was fortified in 1344 and consists of four square angle towers linked by a curtain wall, with domestic buildings added at various later dates. The grand entrance was built in the 17th cent. The grounds were laid out by Sir Jeffry Wyatville, who did WINDSOR Castle, in the early 19th cent.

Chillingham church is a much restored building of 12th-cent. origin with an exceptionally interesting monument. On a sandstone altar tomb lie alabaster figures of Sir Ralph Grey, who died in 1443, and his wife Elizabeth. The sides are richly carved with niches and canopies and contain 14 figures of saints alternating with angels bearing shields. Unlike many others, this tomb escaped injury in the 16th and 17th cents. and Pevsner regards it as an important example of dated sculpture of about 1450.

CHOLLERFORD, *Northumberland* (14–NY 9372). One of the most interesting and accessible forts of HADRIAN'S WALL stood on the bank of the North Tyne in this wooded valley. It was **Chesters (Cilurnum)**. It housed 500 troops and guarded the west side of a bridge. It covered 5¾ acres, which made it the largest fort in Northumberland. It is now in the custody of the Ministry of Public Building and Works. Excavation on the beautiful site has revealed a great deal about the life of the fort. Its rectangular wall was 5 ft thick with an earth bank behind and a ditch in front. There were six gatehouses with guard chambers. Spring water was brought in to a settling tank by aqueduct. Refuse reveals that the soldiers managed to get quantities of oysters, mussels, cockles and limpets though 30 m. from the sea. Layers of debris pointed to three destructions of the fort, which was each time rebuilt. The visitor can marvel here at the "modern" conveniences the Roman forces provided. A commandant's house has underfloor heating. The regimental bathhouse, between the fort and the river, is a most imposing ruin, with round-headed niches or cupboards, latrines, and provision for hot or cold, dry or steam baths.

An abutment of the Roman bridge is reached by crossing the present bridge near the George Inn and taking a footpath along the former railway line on the east bank of the river.

The fort site was in the park of Chesters, an 18th-cent. mansion, whose owner, John Clayton, a Classical scholar, was the first to examine the Roman remains systematically. He died in 1890, and the preservation of the surviving Wall owes much to his work and concern. The museum at Chesters was built in his memory.

CONSETT, *Durham* (15–NZ1150). The steaming chimneys, furnaces and roofs of the giant Consett Iron Co. fill the horizon on the high ground between the Derwent and Wear rivers. This great complex of quarries and brickworks, engineering shops and slag-heaps seems all the more overpowering to the traveller for looming on its own in a rural landscape. The company dates from 1840, but iron was being produced as far back as Roman times at **Ebchester**, 3 m.

away. The limestone and coal needed to manufacture steel still come from local sources, but all of the iron ore is now imported. Consett has some other industries, including a new man-made fibres plant. The first Salvation Army band in the world was organized here in 1879. Anyone can buy a meal at the Trade Union Memorial Hall.

CORBRIDGE, *Northumberland* (14–NY9964), with its lofty trees and charming stone-built houses, is steadily becoming more attractive the more it is "discovered" by Tynesiders. It is on the River Tyne, 16 m. W. of NEWCASTLE, and at many times in its long history has been of considerable importance. The town probably grew out of its proximity to the Roman camp at **Corstopitum** and the later presence of an Anglo-Saxon monastery. In its medieval heyday, Corbridge had four churches, two peel-towers, a mint and two burgesses in the first English parliament. It was burnt three times in the period of border clashes. In the 18th-cent., travellers reported that it was filthy and populated by half-fed, sallow people. But by the 19th cent. it had recovered enough to be considered a bracing health resort.

St Andrew's Church is the most important Anglo-Saxon survival in the county after the crypt at HEXHAM across the river. Lower parts of the slender tower are dated before 786 and there are two Anglo-Saxon windowheads in the nave. A few Norman features are evident, but most of the present building dates to the 13th cent. An interior tower arch is a Roman gateway, transported intact.

Low Hall at the east end of the main street has a peel-tower of about 1500 in a later house. Opposite is Monks Holme, a former inn said to be on the monastery site. The fortified vicarage near the churchyard dates to 1318. Other interesting domestic buildings are the 17th- to 18th-cent. Angel Inn and the 1700 Heron House, now an art gallery.

The seven-arch bridge was built in 1674. It was the only bridge to withstand the great Tyne flood of 1771. The good footing on this stretch of the river probably accounts for the location of Corstopitum here.

A walk 1½ m. NE. takes the visitor to **Aydon Castle**, a choice example of a medieval fortified manor house now belonging to the Ministry of Public Building and Works. **Dilston Castle** is 1¼ m. to the SW., a ruin in a delightful wood.

Corstopitum, ½ m. to the W., was at the junction of the Roman roads Dere Street, running N. from YORK, and Stanegate, joining with CARLISLE. It was 2½ m. S. of HADRIAN'S WALL. The site was first excavated in 1201 by King John's men, searching for treasure. The first systematic examination of the site was in 1906–14 and work resumed in 1934. The Ministry now has custody.

The camp served successively as a fort, supply base for actions against the Picts, and an arsenal with a large civilian settlement. The excavated portion discloses the foundations of the headquarters building, two military compounds, two temples, granaries, a spring-fed fountain, and an imposing storehouse. A museum contains many post-1906 finds, including inscriptions. The most famous of the objects is the Corbridge Lion, shown by the sculptor feeding on a stag.

CRAGSIDE, *Northumberland* (15–NU0702). The grounds of the Armstrong estate just outside ROTHBURY are open to the public for walks or drives, and they are famous for rhododendrons, azaleas and rock gardens. Lord Armstrong, the great inventor (of the hydraulic crane and first rifled gun) was regarded also as the "great magician" when he transformed a barren hillside on the River Coquet into a magnificent setting for his Wagnerian mansion by Norman Shaw, begun in 1863. The house is set in an estate of 14,000 acres. Here Lord Armstrong planted 7 million trees, diverted streams and created lakes, a waterfall, terraces, winding paths, gardens and orchards. Lord Armstrong's was the first house in England completely fitted out with electric light in 1880. The power came from a stream on the grounds. He also introduced "communication by means of the telephone" to his shooting box on the moors.

CRASTER, *Northumberland* (15–NU2519). This tiny fishing village is still famous for its oak-smoked kippers but the fish nowadays are imported from North Shields. Crab and lobster are still caught by local boats. Until the nearby quarry closed in 1939, Craster shipped whinstone. The harbour was built in 1906 by the Craster family as a memorial for a brother who died in Tibet. Craster Tower, the family home, is an 18th-cent. residence incorporating a 15th-cent. tower. There is an easy walk by path along the sea 1½ m. N. to DUNSTANBURGH CASTLE.

CULLERCOATS, *Northumberland* (15–NZ 3571), is a suburb of TYNEMOUTH, and still a fishing village. Its red-roofed houses cluster on a cliff with a fine sandy beach around the bay. In the last century, Cullercoats attracted many artists, including Winslow Homer. The village once exported salt, grindstones and coal, but the last ship to clear the harbour was the *Fortune of Whitby*, loaded with 21 tons of salt, in 1726. St George's Church, a large Early English, stone-vaulted edifice, was built in 1882–4. It has been described as a 13th-cent. ideal rarely achieved in the 13th cent. In the days when some 50 fishing cobles worked out of Cullercoats, the women played a key rôle in the local industry. They prepared bait, carried gear to the boats and hawked the catch on Tyneside. The fishwives' distinctive costume of blue serge jacket, full skirt, large apron and black straw bonnet is a museum piece now. The Dove Marine Laboratory, part of the University of NEWCASTLE, has an aquarium open to the public. The Watch House on the Bank Top is a good place to meet the locals.

DARLINGTON, *Durham* (15–NZ2914), the "cradle of railways". In Bank Top station are *Locomotion Number One*, George Stephenson's

early engine, standing on two original rails, and the 1845 model locomotive, *Derwent*. John Dobbin's painting of the opening of the first public railway, the Darlington and STOCKTON-ON-TEES, on 27 September 1825 hangs in the Art Gallery. Stephenson's genius and the financial backing of Edward Pease, a public-spirited Quaker businessman, made Darlington the important rail centre that it was. British Rail closed the locomotive engineering shops in 1966, thus ending a historic chapter in the town's life. Originally an Anglo-Saxon settlement on the River Skerne, it became a lively market town with a textile industry even before the railway age dawned. Today, its diversified industries range from iron-founding, heavy engineering, spinning, wire rolling and the manufacture of agricultural implements to the production of knitting wools. Darlington pioneered nursery education and double the national average of pupils leave its secondary schools each year for universities.

Darlington's skyline is now dominated by bulky cooling towers but it presents an attractive and busy face to visitors. The Town Hall clock tower, given by Edward Pease, rises over the sloping market place. On the opposite side is the spire of St Cuthbert's, sharp as a needle. This is one of the most important Early English churches in the North. It was built by Bishop Pudsey about 1192 and, except for the early 14th-cent. aisle windows and crossing tower, exhibits little of a style later than 1250. The woodwork includes medieval stalls with misericords alive with heads, angels, monsters and branches. This is the home of the *Northern Echo*, the first halfpenny paper in England when it began publication in 1869. Its most famous editor was W. T. Stead, who was in charge from 1871 until 1880.

DODDINGTON, *Northumberland* (14–NU00 32). The peel-tower here was built in 1584 and is one of the last to be constructed for defence before the union of England and Scotland. A ruin, it is now enclosed in a farmyard in the village. The Church of SS. Mary and Michael is 13th-cent., restored and rearranged in the late 19th cent. Its Norman font has a massive carved round bowl. The watch-house was built in the churchyard in 1826 to guard against body-snatchers. Dod Law, which rises 654 ft on the S., has two early British forts, hut circles and rocks with cup and ring markings. Within a 5-m. radius of Doddington are said to be more of these mysterious markings than in any comparable area in Britain. Typically they consist of a cup-shaped design surrounded by one or more concentric rings. They are found in high places but their purpose is obscure. Dod Law provides wide views of the CHEVIOT HILLS. On the south side of the hill is a cave known as Cuddy's Cove where St Cuthbert is supposed to have sheltered when he was a shepherd. Above it is a stone block on which the devil is supposed to have hanged his grandmother. Rowting Linn camp, 3½ m. N., is another earthwork. It is near pretty falls and has unusual cup and ring markings above it.

DUDDO, *Northumberland* (14–NT9342). On a knoll in a field 1 m. NW. of this hamlet stand the remains of a red sandstone circle which may have marked an Ancient British burial place. There are five stones, 5 to 10 ft high, with worn channels on their tops. They form the best megalithic monument in Northumberland.

DUNSTANBURGH CASTLE, *Northumberland* (15–NU2523). The eerie skeleton of Dunstanburgh Castle seen through a sea fret is one of the spectacular sights of the Northumberland coast. It is the county's largest castle site, its walls having enclosed some 9 acres on the outcrop of the Great Whin Sill. There is little left, but the jagged remains of curtain wall, towers and gatehouse have not undergone modernization or restoration (beyond strengthening) and they furnish plentiful inspiration for a romantic imagination. Turner painted the castle three times. It is reached by footpath from EMBLETON or CRASTER. Since it was given to the nation by Sir Arthur Sutherland, the shipowner, in 1929 it has been in the care of the Ministry of Public Building and Works.

Dunstanburgh seems to hold an invincible site on the basalt crag rearing up more than 100 ft from the sea. It is believed to have been a site for Roman and British strongholds but the existing castle was built in the 14th cent. by Thomas Earl of Lancaster who was executed for treason in 1322, nine years after he started the castle. It may have been intended originally as a fortified port. The castle then went to John of Gaunt who added the surviving gateway. During the Wars of the Roses, the castle changed hands five times, suffering great damage from bombardment. By 1538 it was in ruins. Crops of hay and corn were harvested inside the walls.

Tomlinson notes that the castle had no significant rôle in history but that four persons connected with it were canonized or revered as saints: Queen Margaret, Simon de Montfort, Thomas of Lancaster and Henry VI.

Dunstanburgh diamonds, little coloured quartz crystals, are found in the cracks of the crag here. A fascinating feature on the shore is the "Rumbling Churn", a cavern in the rocks into which waves rush causing a great noise, by rolling stones about, and sending up sprays of water.

DURHAM, *Durham* (15–NZ2742). It is not necessary to be a student of architecture or a lover of history to be thrilled by Durham. It is one of the most visually exciting cities in Britain. The magnificent Norman cathedral and the castle which form the centrepiece stand proudly on a sandstone bluff almost enclosed, as by a moat, in a steep-banked, wooded bend of the River Wear. It is a scene worth gazing upon from every vantage point. The best views are obtained from the railway station, Prebends' Bridge, South Street, Gilesgate, the south end of Church Street and finally at Palace Green, close up.

The Green, in fact, is a logical place from which to start an exploratory walk along the streets, footpaths and alleys of the ancient town.

The castle was built in 1069 after the North had rebelled against the Norman conquerors. It was sited at the top of Palace Green where it could guard the northern neck of the peninsula. The curfew instituted then still rings on weekdays at 9 o'clock. A small town grew up under the

Durham University: the bridge and Dunelm House

RIBA Photo Library

castle walls between two river crossings, Elvet and Framwellgate bridges.

The cathedral was founded as a shrine for the body of St Cuthbert. When Viking raids forced the monks on Lindisfarne to flee in 875, they carried with them the body of the saint. They first found their way to CHESTER-LE-STREET and then to RIPON before they reached Durham in 995. Here the coffin became rooted to the ground and the spot for the new shrine was revealed in a vision. This must have seemed a safe place to the wanderers, almost a natural fortress. By 998 they had built their church, of which no trace is left. It quickly became, and long continued to be, a place of pilgrimage. Pilgrims' offerings made the town prosper and enabled the bishops to build on a far grander scale.

Durham's prince bishops had unique powers. They were lay rulers as well as religious leaders. As a palatinate, Durham could have its own army, nobility, coinage and courts. These privileges ended in 1836, though vestiges remain. Around Palace Green are various 15th- to 20th-cent. buildings which originally housed courts, hospitals, almshouses or residences and most of which are now used by the university.

The present Cathedral Church of Christ and Blessed Mary the Virgin was built between 1093 and 1133 to a plan of Bishop William of Calais. He died and was succeeded in the course of the building by Bishop Flambard, who saw the work completed. This is undoubtedly the finest Norman building in Europe. Only two significant additions were made, both highly successful. Bishop Pudsey built the Galilee Chapel (the Lady Chapel oddly placed at the west end of the nave), between 1170 and 1175. Its roof is supported by slim clusters of Purbeck marble and stone and with its remarkable light, airy feeling gives a quite different impression from the rest of the church. At the opposite end, the Chapel of the Nine Altars, or eastern transept, was added between 1242 and 1280. Here are the pointed arches and richly carved capitals of the Early English style. St Cuthbert's body was brought to his shrine behind the high altar in 1104.

Almost no amount of time is too long to spend in Durham Cathedral and visitors probably will want to provide themselves with a detailed guide, but some of the other features to look for on a first visit may be mentioned here. The impression of strength and antiquity begins with the bronze knocker on the broad Norman north door. The ferocious beast's head has lost its enamel eyes but it still clenches the great ring which gave sanctuary to anyone who grasped it in the Middle Ages. A sanctuary book records that 331 criminals sought refuge here between 1464 and 1524, most of them murderers.

The cathedral was the first in northern Europe to be covered with stone-ribbed vaulting and it has the earliest pointed transverse arches in England. It was also the first European church to decorate the aisle walls with an arcade of arches. The nave is lined with massive compound piers alternating with circular ones which are deeply carved in geometric designs. The round pillars have an equal height and circumference – 22 ft.

There are few monuments because of a long-held rule that no one should be buried in the shrine of St Cuthbert. The first layman to lie here was Ralph Lord Neville, commander of the English army which defeated the Scots at Neville's Cross at the edge of the city in 1346. There is also the tomb of his son, John, who gave the cathedral the splendid stone screen behind the high altar. The 107 statues that once adorned it and all the stained glass were destroyed either in the Dissolution or during the Commonwealth. The cathedral was used by Puritan soldiers to hold Scots prisoners.

The choir stalls are fine 17th-cent. work as is the font at the west end of the nave. In front of the font is a line of Frosterley marble, the nearest women were allowed to get to the altar. Bishop Hatfield's throne of the 14th cent. is the highest known. He prepared his own tomb under it.

From the south aisle a door leads to the cloisters and the monks' dormitory, a great timbered hall 194 ft by 39 ft where some of the cathedral's prized possessions can be seen. They include relics of St Cuthbert, illuminated manuscripts and a collection of crosses.

The keep of the Norman castle was rebuilt in 1840 to house students and the moat has been filled in. Here the visitor can see the tiny Norman crypt chapel, Bishop Cosin's black staircase of 1662, the great hall of 1284 and the 15th-cent. kitchens. The castle was the bishop's official residence and the key to the town's early defences. Durham University was created as the third university in England by Act of Parliament in 1832, and the castle was turned over to University College by Bishop van Mildert in 1836. He was the last count palatine. New university colleges, now totalling 14, have grown up E. and S. of the peninsula. The expansion of the university in this historical setting has been a challenge to architects and one of their most successful creations is the bridge (by Ove Arup) from the Palace Green across the river to Dunelm House, on the far bank. The university uses the Victorian Shire Hall in Old Elvet for administrative headquarters.

Durham is still small (just over 24,000 population); it is a centre for local government and education and its chief industrial concerns are a carpet factory and two organ-building firms. The generally admired new county buildings on the north part of the city form a complex which includes an open-air museum, police headquarters, council chambers and school.

The old city centre is now the traffic-choked market place where municipal offices and banks predominate. In Saddler Street leading out of the market place, the world's first ground mustard was prepared. Production of Durham mustard has now ended. The North and South Bailey which run from the market place along the east side of the cathedral still have many 18th-cent. town houses now used by the university. There are good 18th-cent. houses in Old Elvet and South Street.

Boating is a popular recreation here, and a regatta, claimed to be the oldest in Britain, is held in June. The Durham miners' gala on the third Saturday of July still fills the streets with bands and marchers.

The Gulbenkian Museum of Oriental Art and Archaeology in Elvet Hill Road is unique in Britain. Its collections include Egyptian art and tomb furnishings, Chinese and Japanese jades, ceramics, sculptures and bronzes, and Chinese and Tibetan paintings. A museum of relics and trophies of the disbanded Durham Light Infantry opened in the County Hall grounds in 1969. The jutting concrete building includes an art gallery.

From the village of **Shincliffe**, 1 m. SE. of the city, a beautiful view of the cathedral and castle can be had from the bank top across the Wear valley. The walk to the village passes an old gravel working where in 1940 remains of a Roman farm were found, confirming for the first time the activities of Roman civilians in the county. The village itself is pleasant, with trees and a roadside green.

EASTGATE, *Durham* (14–NY9538), and **Westgate**, 3 m. W., were entrances to the Old Park, hunting grounds of the Bishops of DURHAM. Today Eastgate is a hamlet near Low Linn Falls, where Rookhope Burn tumbles over a horseshoe of rocks. The stream attracts geologists and botanists alike. There is a large new cement works in the valley, but this will not deter holiday visitors in search of fine moorland scenery. The large All Saints Church, an 1887 gift to the community, has a massive font of Frosterley marble. Westgate also has a 19th-cent. church and an old watermill. It was once a cockfighting centre. The site of the bishops' hunting lodge has been excavated and the only medieval thimble ever found was brought to light.

EDLINGHAM, *Northumberland* (15–NU11 08). Little St John's Church is so plain and sturdy that it is easy to mistake it for a farm building when it is viewed across the valley from the scenic ALNWICK road. It stands in trees on the hillside just above the ruins of a 14th-cent. castle, and both stand apart from the small village further up the slope. The church is mainly Norman, with a square tower and slit windows. It must have afforded protection in the days of border raiding. The first church on the site was probably wooden and built in the 8th cent. The stone building began in about 1050 and the west wall of the nave dates to this time. The wide round chancel arch, the chancel itself and the beautiful north aisle arcade are 12th-cent. Fragments from earlier times include part of a sculptured cross in a recess below the pulpit and the base of the font.

Edlingham was the home of an alleged witch, Margaret Stothard, in the 17th cent. She was never punished, perhaps because the charges against her were so flimsy. In 1879 the vicarage burglary brought other notoriety to the village. Two men were wrongly convicted and served 10 years in prison before the real culprits were brought to justice. The case inspired the novel, *The Massingham Affair*, by John Grierson.

EDMONDBYERS, *Durham* (14–NZ0149). Isolated high in the moors, this is a popular centre for hiking and bicycling holidays. The village has an appealing little church founded in 1150 and a youth hostel. With its neighbour, **Muggleswick**, it lies just N. of Muggleswick Common where Hise Hope, Smithyshaw and Waskerley reservoirs attract fishermen and picnickers. A giant reservoir has been built on the River Derwent on the Northumberland border N. of both villages. It covers 1,000 acres.

EGGLESCLIFFE, *Durham* (15–NZ4213), faces the town of YARM in Yorkshire across the River Tees. The towns are connected by a stone bridge that dates from 1400 (the medieval work is still visible on the Yorkshire side) but has since been widened and mended. A 43-arch brick railway viaduct of 1849 marches majestically across the river nearby. The village, expanding now with modern houses along the riverside, was built originally around a sloping green. At St Mary's Church, a Norman south doorway is the oldest important feature. The building also has a 15th-cent. battlemented tower, a 13th-cent. chancel arch built of alternating red and white stone, an oaken barrel roof, fine 17th-cent. furnishings, and two well-worn 13th-cent. sandstone cross-legged knights. The church has two chained books, Bishop Jewell's *Apology* and *Eikon Basilike*.

ELSDON, *Northumberland* (14–NY9393). There is still a gibbet 2 m. SE. of Elsdon and the official guidebook to the area begs that "overseas visitors should note that gibbets in Britain are long since disused". But it fits in with the atmosphere of this isolated – and captivating – moorland village. This was a lawless area not so very long ago, the gathering place and market centre for the Redesdale clans. The wide-open village green, ringed with houses, covers 7 acres. During times of danger or in severe weather the cattle were herded here. The stone-walled pound for strays is still in use. In the last century, Elsdon folk often took their herds to the upland pastures and lived in huts through the summer. Those were also the days when cattle were driven through a midsummer bonfire in a rite passed down from pagan times.

An unsightly coalyard spoils the entrance from the W. to the village but at the NE., across the pretty burn, are two interesting mounds, sometimes called mote hills, 70 and 63 ft high. They were some sort of fortification, and probably an 11th-cent. motte and bailey castle.

St Cuthbert's Church lies low among the trees in a walled yard. As it stands now, it is mainly a 14th-cent. building with an odd heavy bell-turret decorated with stone knobs. Three horse skulls were found there in 1877, thought to be protection against lightning or an aid to acoustics, but one historian at least has hinted they might

G. Douglas Bolton

Escomb has one of the most complete Anglo-Saxon churches in England

have come from victims of some ancient sacrificial rite performed when the church was built. Worse, a mass grave was found in 1810 under the north wall of the church. More than 100 human skulls were found, probably English soldiers killed at OTTERBURN. In the church is a Roman tombstone erected to a commandant by his wife. It was found at High Rochester.

The 14th-cent. vicar's peel is part of a handsome residence on high ground behind the church.

A former café, marked by a sculpture of Bacchus over the door, now houses a crafts studio.

EMBLETON, *Northumberland* (15–NU2322). The village consists of unpretentious old cottages and streets of new houses on the outskirts. It lies 1 m. inland from the sea with a striking view across the meadow to DUNSTANBURGH CASTLE on the southern tip of Embleton Bay. There is an 18-hole golf course between the village and the shore. Holy Trinity Church is medieval but considerably altered in the 19th cent. The ground floor of the 12th-cent. tower is tunnel-vaulted with stone arches. The vicarage includes the typical Northumberland peel-tower dated about 1415. One notable Embleton vicar was the Rev. Mandell Creighton, later Bishop of Peterborough and London, who wrote *History of the Papacy*. Memorials to the Greys of Falloden are contained in the church. Embleton in 1849 was the birthplace of W. T. Stead, the doughty editor. On the $1\frac{1}{2}$-m. walk to Dunstanburgh Castle you can see Saddle Rock, a strange limestone outcrop.

ESCOMB, *Durham* (15–NZ2029). One of the most complete small Anglo-Saxon churches in England is found here at the bottom of a steep road leading through a former pit village about $2\frac{1}{2}$ m. from BISHOP AUCKLAND. It has probably survived because it was so obscure and unimportant. For a short period in the mid-19th cent., St John's was unused and partly roofless. It was only in 1875 that its true character was recognized and reported by the Rev. R. E. Hooppell and a public appeal launched to repair it. The building, its stone now blackened, stands rather sternly in a leafy churchyard enclosed by a circular wall. The key can be had from the house facing the entrance. No one knows exactly when the church was built but it is contemporary with those of the 7th cent. at JARROW and MONKWEARMOUTH, and may even be older. The porch was added in the 12th cent. and five larger windows inserted in the 13th and 19th cents., but these alterations do not detract from the church's appearance of great antiquity. Above the porch and to the right is a sundial, part of the original fabric, and probably the oldest in the country. The dial is a raised semi-circle with a serpentine border. All but the upper parts of the walls are built of stones from the former Roman fort at Binchester and the Roman tool-marks are easily seen. On the north wall is embedded a small raised rosette which may have been a sacrificial stone and, under a projection, there is an upside-down inscribed stone marked LEG VI, for the 6th Roman Legion. The serenity of the interior is a tribute to the care with which the recent

G. Douglas Bolton

The Farne Islands are an important bird sanctuary

restoration was done. The walls are white. Both the new and the old windows are of clear glass through which the branches of the trees outside wave a pattern. The modern oak furnishings are simple and unobtrusive. The long, narrow nave culminates in a small square chancel. There are two small round-headed windows and two square-headed ones with another tiny original window high in the gable end. But the most striking feature is the slim, round-headed chancel arch. It has the remains of a 12th-cent. painting on the underside of the curve. The arch is believed to have been taken intact from Roman Binchester and put here. A patch of the original cobble-stone floor is preserved near the font. Behind the altar table is a pre-Norman carved stone cross.

The village of Escomb is being attractively rebuilt.

ETAL, *Northumberland* (14–NT9339). A street of thatched cottages with a manor house at one end and a crumbling castle ruin at the other gives Etal its own distinctive aspect among the county's villages. New slate roofs over new stone houses are appearing, but efforts are clearly made to keep the additions in harmony with the past legacy. The cottages are set behind flower gardens and trees shelter the site on the River Till. The manor house is not open to the public. It was built for Sir William Carr in 1748 and enlarged a few years later. In its grounds stands the Church of the Blessed Virgin Mary, designed by William Butterfield in 1850 for Lady Augusta FitzClarence in memory of her husband and child. All that remains of the castle is the south-east gate-tower and a portion of curtain wall with parts of two other towers. It was built about 1342 for Sir Robert de Manners and destroyed in 1496 by James IV of Scotland. The village's most charming building is the thatched and white-washed Black Bull Inn.

FARNE ISLANDS, *Northumberland* (15–NU 2337). Best known as a bird sanctuary, the Farne Islands number about 25, are of basaltic rock and lie from 2 to 5 m. off the Northumberland coast. They are visited by boat from BAMBURGH or SEAHOUSES. The favoured time (for bird-watching) is late May or early June. The islands, virtually uninhabited, are the property of the National Trust and administered by a joint committee of the Trust and the Farne Islands Association. The largest and nearest is the Inner Farne (or House Island) which covers 16 acres and has cliffs 80 ft high. A peel-tower built in 1500 by Prior Thomas Castell of DURHAM has been converted into the headquarters of the Farne Islands bird observatory. During migration seasons, it is manned around the clock. The tower was used for warning lights to mariners until a lighthouse was established on Longstone Island. It was from the latter that Grace Darling and her father set forth in a gale in 1838 to rescue survivors of the *Forfarshire* which had run aground on Big Harcar Rock. On these bleak outcrops is seen a great variety of bird life: eider ducks, cormorants, shags, fulmars, oystercatchers, ringed plovers, guillemots, razor-bills and puffins, four species of terns, herring gulls and kittiwakes. The islands are the only east-coast breeding place of the grey seal.

The first recorded visitor to the Farnes was St Aidan, Bishop of Lindisfarne (HOLY ISLAND), who came here to meditate in 635. St Cuthbert in 676 built a hermitage on Inner Farne. It had no window openings save a hole in the roof through which he could see heaven. He lived here till 684 when he was persuaded to become bishop. Two years later he resigned his high office to return to the hermitage, but he died only three months afterwards. His cell and well may have been on the site of the later tower, where there is the only well now. A chapel to St Cuthbert was built in 1370 and in an 1848 restoration it was fitted out with 17th-cent. panelling and pews from Durham Cathedral.

FELTON, *Northumberland* (15–NU1800). The barons of Northumberland met at Felton Park on 22 October 1215 to transfer their allegiance from the English King John to Alexander of Scotland. The following year King John burnt down the village. Few other historic events disturbed the village. Thomas Forster managed to raise 70 horsemen here in the 1715 Jacobite uprising. The Duke of Cumberland stopped in 1745 on his way to victory at Culloden. In 1766, John Wesley preached but "very few seemed to understand anything of the matter". N. of the village and away from the road is a Nelson monument erected in 1806 by a friend, Alexander Davison, an army clothing contractor. Two bridges, medieval and modern, span the Coquet River here. St Michael's Church, W. of the village, has been altered so often that it is difficult even for experts to work out its dates. It probably is a 13th-cent. heritage, with aisles added in the 14th.

FINCHALE PRIORY, *Durham* (15–NZ29 47). Set in a loop of the Wear NE. of DURHAM are the ruins of the 13th-cent. Finchale Priory, now an Ancient Monument. Their story begins with St Godric, a pedlar and shipowner who later became a hermit. He built a hut a short distance upstream in about 1110 in response to a vision. Later a stone chapel and living quarters were constructed on the priory site. St Godric lived here until he died in 1170 at the age of 105. Durham Priory took over the chapel and in the 13th cent. it was considerably enlarged. Later it became a kind of holiday resort for monks from Durham. Traces of the first chapel can be detected in the chancel wall, and a cross marks St Godric's grave. The ruins include four piers of the central tower of the church, most of the transept walls and a little of the cloister, chapter house, refectory and prior's house.

FORD, *Northumberland* (14–NT9437). A ponderous model village of the mid-19th cent., Ford could be a prosperous suburb instead of the adjunct to an ancient castle. Ford Castle, owned by Lord Joicey and used as an educational and cultural centre by the Northumberland County Council, was started in 1287 by Odenel de Forde and crenellated in 1338. It was demolished by the Scots in 1385 and attacked again in 1549. It was in the style of four corner towers with a curtain wall, and three of the original towers survive. The castle was extensively restored and altered in both the 18th and 19th cents. St Michael's Church in the castle grounds dates from the early 13th cent. with a thorough 19th-cent. restoration.

Ford village as seen today is the work of Louisa, Marchioness of Waterford, who did it over as a memorial to her husband who suffered a fatal fall from a horse in 1859. Tastes may differ about the result (to the 19th-cent. historian Tomlinson there was "no sweeter village outside Arcadia") but her Biblical paintings in the former village school are a memorial that requires no defence. Lady Waterford was a talented artist in the pre-Raphaelite style. She spent 22 years (from 1860 to 1882) on this series of watercolours on paper which was applied to canvas and then fitted into the walls and gables of the long school hall. Residents who attended classes there tell how the Bible lessons were drawn from Lady Waterford's pictures. She used villagers for models and paid the children sixpence and a "gilly piece" (bread and jelly) for their sittings. A surprising number of descendants of those models visit Ford to see the paintings.

FROSTERLEY, *Durham* (14–NZ0237). Churches throughout County Durham exhibit fonts, pillars and memorials in Frosterley marble, actually a grey limestone full of fossils which becomes black when polished. In the 13th cent. it was as greatly prized here as Purbeck marble in the South. The Weardale village, originally Forest Lea, has working quarries still but Frosterley marble, which occurs in thin bands between courses of limestone, is now only produced for special orders. In St Michael's Church, built in 1866, a beautiful sample of the marble is mounted near the door with the tribute: "This Frosterley marble and limestone, quarried for centuries in this parish, adorns cathedrals and churches throughout the world."

GAINFORD, *Durham* (15–NZ1716). One of the loveliest villages in southern County Durham, Gainford lies round a large and tranquil green between the A67 and the Tees. The Georgian flavour predominates, but the houses fronting the green or crowded into the narrow streets round it offer a variety of style and colour. Probably the most striking domestic building is the Hall, built in 1603 by Vicar John Cradock and now a farmhouse. It has 11 chimneys rising from the middle of the three-story stone structure. A big circular stone dovecot stands nearby. St Mary's Church at a corner of the green is almost all excellent 13th-cent. work with a west stair and turret added in 1786. Within the porch is a collection of tomb lids and carved stones. According to Sir Timothy Eden this is the church where, on three successive days, the vicar married a Pigg, christened a Lamb, and buried a Hogg.

GATESHEAD, *Durham* (15–NZ2562). Fine views from here of the five famous Tyne bridges linking Gateshead to NEWCASTLE-UPON-TYNE. Dr Johnson once referred to this place as "a dirty lane leading to Newcastle", but in its own right Gateshead is a major town, third largest in County Durham. The name means "goat's headland". At the start of the 19th cent. it was still little more than a village with numerous oak trees and 11 windmills, now all gone. In the beginning, the protection of the Bishops of DURHAM, and later the grit of the citizens kept

Gateshead from becoming a suburb of bigger, richer Newcastle. Today it is nearly all modern; a great fire in 1854 took most of the historical buildings. Its famous residents have included Sir Joseph Swan, inventor of the incandescent lamp in 1878, Thomas Bewick, the great engraver, and in modern times, Alex Glasgow, the composer, singer and writer. Daniel Defoe is said to have written *Robinson Crusoe* here. New houses and blocks of flats are replacing rows of 19th-cent. workers' dwellings. The Team Valley Trading Estate, begun in 1936 to relieve unemployment, is considered a model of industrial planning. Salt-well Park, high on the bluffs, provides the town with a central recreation ground, gardens and lake. Its large pavilion café is owned by the Corporation. Near it are the Shipley Art Gallery, the library and an industrial museum. The gallery has a varied permanent collection and loan exhibitions nearly every three weeks. St Mary's Church near Tyne Bridge is the oldest ecclesiastical building. It dates from the 12th cent. but was almost completely rebuilt in 1855. The earliest feature is the south doorway. The body of the church is mainly 14th-cent. and it has an 18th-cent. tower. An anchorage rebuilt in the 18th cent. is attached to the north aisle and serves as a vestry. Gateshead workers are engaged in engineering, brass and iron-founding, and the manufacture of paper, glass, hawsers, hemp, oils, paints and enamels.

GIBSIDE CHAPEL, *Durham* (15–NZ1758). The 18th-cent. estate SW. of GATESHEAD is in ruins, but the classical chapel, originally a mausoleum and designed by James Paine about 1760, is exquisite and open to visitors since the National Trust restored it. It stands on a terrace at the end of an avenue of trees. The grounds were landscaped by Capability Brown. The chapel takes the shape of a Greek cross with a shallow dome over the centre. Four Ionic columns guard the portico. Inside, the altar is placed under the central dome. The furnishings, including a three-decker pulpit and box pews, are all in cherrywood and mahogany. On a 140-ft Tuscan column NE. stands a British Liberty statue, 12 ft high, erected by George Bowes in about 1750.

GREATHAM, *Durham* (15–NZ4927). Brine pumped from salt beds 1,000 ft below ground at Greatham yields the greater part of the salt for British tables. "Salt de Gretham" has been known from the 15th cent. The industry grew out of the early custom of slaughtering and salting meat in early November for a winter-long supply. Most of the town will not long delay visitors but the Hospital of God, the Blessed Mary and St Cuthbert, N. of the churchyard, is well worth a second glance. Founded in 1272 by Bishop Robert de Stitchill, it was re-established in 1610 and rebuilt in part in the late 18th and early 19th cents. It is single storied with an octagonal bell-turret above the clock tower. Almshouses for 13 men and six women were provided in the wings. The much grander master's house, Greatham Hall, was built in 1725. The Church of St John the Baptist dates

from the 12th cent. but was rebuilt and enlarged in the 18th, 19th and even 20th cents. It has its original round Norman nave arcades, a Norman font and a medieval altar of Frosterley marble.

HADRIAN'S WALL, *Northumberland* (14–NY6367 to 15–NZ1366). An amazing fortification, 73½ m. long, in Roman days divided the difficult province of Britain from unoccupied Caledonia, from Wallsend on the E. to Bowness on the W. The finest stretch of the surviving wall is in the NORTHUMBERLAND NATIONAL PARK between the North Tyne River and GILSLAND. The ruins constitute a unique monument of the Roman Empire and they are found, in places, among some of the most dramatic scenery in Britain.

The wall was built after a visit to Britain by the Emperor Hadrian in A.D. 122. He decided a permanent barrier was required for defence against the unsubdued Caledonian tribes. It was planned first as a series of signal stations but in the end it consisted of 17 forts (permanent quarters for garrisons) with mile castles every Roman mile for patrols, and turrets or signal towers between, all linked by a curtain wall. There was a ditch on the N. as added protection against the Picts, and a broad vallum, or flat-bottomed trench, at the southern boundary of the military zone. The giant project was probably finished by A.D. 138. Legionary soldiers were responsible for the building and the wall was garrisoned by some 5,500 cavalry and 13,000 infantry. The wall stood perhaps 20 ft high, to the top of the parapet, and 8 to 10 ft broad, but the highest remaining portion is about 9 ft. The work consumed one million cubic feet of stone.

The wall suffered destruction during three periods of civil disorders and in each case was rebuilt by the Romans. Uprisings in continental Europe caused the reduction of Roman forces in Britain in the 4th cent., and by the early 5th cent. the remaining token force of troops, or farmer-soldiers as many were by now, merged with the native tribes, allies of Rome. The wall became a vast quarry for building stone. Its greatest destruction occurred in 1751 when Parliament ordered a new road between NEWCASTLE and CARLISLE. For much of the way this was built on and with material from the Wall.

It is thanks to scholars and antiquaries that anything is left to see today. The Wall was described as early as 1599 and the first accounts of the whole line came in the early 18th cent., notably by the Rev. John Horsley of MORPETH. William Hutton of BIRMINGHAM, at 78, walked it from end to end in 1801 and wrote a history. Near Planetrees Farm, the old man's tears persuaded one Henry Tulip, then building a house, not to tear down a fine section of wall. The Rev. John Hodgson's *History of Northumberland* was the first to date the vallum with the Wall. Since 1851, J. Collingwood Bruce's *Handbook to the Roman Wall* has been the standard guide. The first accurate survey was made in the 1850s and a special Ordnance Survey map came out in 1964.

A special debt is owed to John Clayton (1792–1890) of Chesters (site of Cilurnum) who inherited or acquired five wall forts and did the first systematic excavations.

For non-specialist visitors, the best sense of the original Wall will come with time spent at such sites as those at CHOLLERFORD, HOUSESTEADS and CORBRIDGE and from a walk along some of the line, perhaps the superb and wild stretch between Housesteads and the Once Brewed youth hostel and Park Information Centre.

HALTWHISTLE, *Northumberland* (14–NY 7064). A small market town for a large rural district, Haltwhistle makes a good jumping-off point for visits to HADRIAN'S WALL which lies to the N. The town is tucked into the juncture of Haltwhistle Burn and the South Tyne. Its area has turned from coal-mining to light industry, including paint manufacturing, and quarrying. Holy Cross Church, towerless and almost hidden in trees, is regarded as an unusually good example of Early English architecture. On the north bank of the river about 3 m. away is **Featherstone Castle**, a 14th-cent. peel-tower to which a Jacobean mansion was attached. Part of it is now in use as a young people's holiday centre. Another peel-tower forms part of the Red Lion Hotel. Haltwhistle Castle, a fortified house, has been demolished.

HAMSTERLEY, *Durham* (15–NZ1131). A thousand acres of Hamsterley Forest have been opened as a park, giving additional access to the most beautiful woodland in the county. The new road, which is open to motorists but not to heavy coaches, crosses streams and is crowded with beauty-spots. There is a forest trail for children with a printed guide available to help them identify plants and animals. This State Forest contains conifers and broad-leaved trees and already has a popular picnic area at **Bedburn**. The village of Hamsterley overlooks Bedburn Beck. There is a restored 13th-cent. church to one side. Some carved medieval monuments have been built into the church walls. One m. N. of Bedburn are **The Castles**, remains of a stone-walled British camp built after the Roman occupation. On the other side of the road by the church is a series of Anglo-Saxon or medieval fields stepping down the hillside.

HARBOTTLE, *Northumberland* (14–NT9304). This ancient village, deep in Coquetdale, used to be known for its good health, having one of the lowest death rates known. The fragmentary remains of Harbottle castle are on a hill at the north-eastern outskirts of the village. It was the second castle on the site, built about 1160, but by 1541 it was a ruin. Here in 1515 Queen Margaret of Scotland gave birth to a daughter who was to become mother-in-law of Mary Queen of Scots and grandmother of James I. Further along the road, a footpath on the left leads up to the dramatic rock formation known as the Drake (or Dragon) Stone. It is 30 ft high, rising above Har-

bottle Crag. It was the scene of Druidic rites, and well into the 19th cent. sick children were passed over it to be cured. In a lonely lake near it, black-headed gulls breed. The modern Harbottle Castle was designed by Dobson in 1829 and includes 17th-cent. work. A private residence, it also houses a crafts centre.

HART, *Durham* (15–NZ4735). Here, NW. of HARTLEPOOL, is the town's mother church. It stands on a slanting street from which the North Sea can be seen. St Mary Magdalene is built of grey stone rubble with larger stones for quoins. Its aisle-less nave suggests its Anglo-Saxon origins which were confirmed during a restoration in 1885. Several carved stones were found in the walls, notably a semi-circular sundial now built into the west wall of the south aisle. The low tower is Norman. Most of the windows were replaced in the 17th and 18th cents. and the chancel was rebuilt and restored in the 19th. There are two fonts, one simple, square and Norman, and the other 15th-cent. and richly carved all over the eight-sided bowl and shaft. The village once was owned by the Bruce family and by tradition this is the birthplace of Robert the Bruce.

HARTBURN, *Northumberland* (15–NZ0886). The Church of St Andrew probably began with a free-standing tower built or taken over by monks from TYNEMOUTH Priory in the 11th or 12th cent. But most of what stands today dates from the 13th cent., with many repairs and alterations in all the centuries since. The small, heavily buttressed tower is attached to a square nave with aisles which, in turn, leads into a long narrow chancel. Among many interesting furnishings are four wooden collection boxes. Two are plain and crude, dated 1721 and 1725, and the two others are elegantly carved at a later date. Also on view is a Cromwellian money box and a carved oak plaque of Adam and Eve. Florentine brass lamps hang in the chancel. The Rev. John Hodgson, the county historian, was vicar here when he died in 1845. A crenellated school was built in Hartburn by Dr John Sharp when he was vicar from 1749 to 1796.

HARTLEPOOL, *Durham* (15–NZ5032), is an ancient seaport and county borough which merged with its Victorian neighbour, West Hartlepool, in 1967. It was really a reconciliation, since West Hartlepool was built by Ralph Ward Jackson in the 1830s partly in protest against coal shipment charges at the senior port. Recorded history begins in the early 7th cent. when the Bishop of Lindisfarne authorized a religious house on the Heugh, the headland N. of the harbour. Its second abbess was St Hilda who later founded WHITBY Abbey. The establishment was completely destroyed by the Danes. The harbour had seen the assembly of a Crusader fleet before King John gave the town a charter in 1201. The town was walled in the Middle Ages, and a 600-yd relic can be seen on the south side of the headland. In the Napoleonic wars, says a legend, a French ship was wrecked offshore and the loyal Hartlepool fishermen hanged its only survivor, a monkey. This is commemorated in the emblem of the local Rugby Union football club tie. The town was shelled by German warships in 1914, 128 people being killed and 400 wounded.

Such rapid development has taken place that half the buildings in Hartlepool are new. It is still a major port, but its last shipyard closed in 1962. Since then, the town has concentrated on diversified industry, and among its products are telecommunications equipment, vacuum flasks, knitwear, crankshafts, anchor chains and marine engine controls. It makes refractory magnesia from sea-water and salvages pure tin from waste. Its port operates two systems: tidal, for the coastal coal trade and for handling iron ore, other ocean cargoes and liquefied chemicals; and enclosed, where the large timber import trade is centred. There is a modern fish quay and a marina for pleasure sailors. Although coal exports have declined here as elsewhere, the port still handles close to two million tons a year. Construction has begun on a £125 million nuclear power station S. of **Seaton Carew**, within the county borough.

The College of Art, for years the only separate art college in the North-East, is putting up a new building which will include a theatre workshop, cinema and exhibition hall. The most important historic building is St Hilda's Church, founded in 1129 on the site of the much older monastery, and now in a rundown neighbourhood on the headland. Its architecture is early Early English, later restored, with exceptionally large buttresses supporting a massive tower. "Pillow stones" from the Anglo-Saxon burial-ground discovered in 1833 can be seen inside. Christ Church, near the railway station, with its strange tower and spire, was built in 1854 from limestone quarried by Jackson for West Hartlepool docks. For fun, the people of Hartlepool have, among many choices, the seaside resort of Seaton Carew with some of the most golden sands in Britain, a week-long August fair on the Town Moor, and a "floral mile" in Burn Valley Gardens. Sir Compton Mackenzie was born here.

HAUGHTON-LE-SKERNE, *Durham* (15–NZ3015). Now a suburb of DARLINGTON, this village has the visual attractions of fine 18th-cent. houses, a principally Norman church, and the long green typical of County Durham. The furnishings of St Andrew's Church are in the late 17th-cent. style identified with Bishop Cosin's restoration work. Here they are unusually complete, and include box pews, panelled walls, pulpit, lectern, font cover and two armchairs. The village can claim an important rôle in the Industrial Revolution in that flax was first spun by machinery here, by John Kendrew at his mill.

HAYDON BRIDGE, *Northumberland* (14–NY8464). The South Tyne divides this quiet stonebuilt village. The bridge, rebuilt in 1773, had to be chained and barred in the more turbulent days of Scottish raiding parties. Of special interest is the

Reece Winstone

Hexham: the Frith Stool

Old Church, standing apart from the village on a hillside. Its nave was pulled down in the late 18th cent. to build the new church in the centre. But in the late 19th cent. it was repaired. Much of the Old Church was of stone from nearby Roman sites. In its abbreviated form today, it consists of a Norman chancel and a 14th-cent. chapel. The east window is a triplet of lancets only 7 in. wide. The font was once a Roman altar.

About 1½ m. SW. is **Langley Castle**, a fine example of a 14th-cent. battlemented tower house, restored in 1900. Its walls are 6 ft thick. Now it is used by a girls' school. **Staward Pele** is 4 m. SW., a ruin on a steep and rocky bank of the Allen River. The tower is at least 14th-cent., and its occupants have included an 18th-cent. outlaw, Dicky of Greenwood. The **Allen Banks**, 3 m. W. of Haydon Bridge where the Allen joins the Tyne, are National Trust property. Here are 185 acres of hill and river scenery to walk in.

HEDDON-ON-THE-WALL, *Northumberland* (15–NZ1366). A splendid fragment of HADRIAN'S WALL can be seen alongside the road 7 m. from NEWCASTLE and just below this hilltop village. The visible portion, 100 yds long and from four to seven courses high, is more than 10 ft wide. From high ground above the wall it is possible to see the defensive ditch and vallum which completed the wall complex. The village is where a mile-castle stood. In 1796 the government allotted cottages built for the miners of Heddon colliery, but never used by them, to refugee French royalist priests; this was the origin of their name, Frenchman's Row. The priests left in 1802. Crowning the hill is St Andrew's Church with several traces of its Anglo-Saxon origins in the fabric. That first church was rebuilt in early Norman times and altered again in subsequent centuries. A good deal of the Roman wall went into the church building.

HEIGHINGTON, *Durham* (15–NZ2522). This hillside village in the form of an irregular square has a particularly large and spacious green in a county noted for long greens. On its north side stands the important St Michael's Church, Norman except for the 13th-cent. south aisle, 19th-cent. north aisle and 15th-cent. tower. The singular chancel arch is Norman. The church's rarest article is said to be its pre-Reformation oak pulpit with six traceried linenfold panels and an inscription beseeching prayers for the donor, Alexander Flettcher and his wife Agnes. Beside the B6275, 2½ m. W., stands a railed-in piece of stone shaft known as **Legs Cross**. It affords a panoramic view of the Tees valley. Its origin and purpose are obscure: suggestions include a Roman milestone, a marker for the 10th Roman Legion (LEG X), an Anglo-Saxon cross or a reminder of a stop made by James I, on his way to London for his coronation, who sat cross-legged on a stone here to admire this "bonny, bonny land".

HEXHAM, *Northumberland* (14–NY9364). Hexham is endowed with a beautiful setting on the Tyne. It is convenient for exploration of HADRIAN'S WALL and a major social and shopping centre (even drawing housewives from NEWCASTLE). It has three steeplechase meetings a year. Hexham's historical associations have left some delightful street names, for example, Priestpopple, Hencotes, Quatre Bras and St Mary's Chare. Modern developments (the cinema being one of the most obvious) have spoilt some of the visual charms of the town but it remains a very attractive and lively place. The abbey church makes Hexham an important place, but it also has other rewards: the market square beside the church has a small colonnaded shelter put up in 1766; the Moot Hall, or council chamber, was the 12th-cent. gatehouse of a castle; the 14th-cent. Manor Office was the gaol until 1824; the grammar school was founded in 1599; and a pretty park crossed by a burn lies next to the abbey church. Another park is laid out on The Seal, a hill which affords an excellent view of the town.

The first church in Hexham was founded by St Wilfrid on land given him by Queen Etheldreda. It was completed in 678. St Wilfrid was the queen's spiritual adviser and such an influential one that he persuaded her to leave her husband and became a nun.

Stone for that first church came from the Roman camp of Corstopitum near CORBRIDGE.

It was said to have been a magnificent building for its day, but only the crypt now remains – the finest Anglo-Saxon crypt in England. It may have housed relics of St Andrew to whom the church was dedicated. Two stones in the crypt have Roman inscriptions.

The Anglo-Saxon Frith Stool (St Wilfrid's chair) in the chancel marks the site beneath of the Anglo-Saxon apse. The stone chair, believed used for Northumbrian coronations, in later days gave sanctuary to anyone who sat in it, as its name implies. The font bowl, also Anglo-Saxon, was carved from a Roman stone.

The church standing now was begun by the Augustinians in the 12th cent. The beautiful choir is 13th-cent. with a 15th-cent. roof. The transepts, also 13th-cent., include on the west wall the strikingly broad and worn Night Stair which once led from the monks' dormitory. The nave was partly in ruins before its rebuilding in the early 20th cent. by Temple Moore in 14th-cent. style.

Hexham's church is especially rich in furnishings. A notable ornament is the Anglo-Saxon Acca cross, set up in 740 at the grave of Bishop Acca. Another is the Roman monument to Flavinus, showing the Roman standardbearer riding over a crouched Briton who is armed with a dagger. There are three other Roman altars in the church and many carved Roman and Anglo-Saxon stones in the rebuilt wall of the nave.

There are 38 splendid medieval misericords, screens and rare painted panels. Benches and bench-ends were sold in 1858 for firewood. Prior Rowland Leschman's 15th-cent. chantry includes intriguing stone caricatures by local masons of St Christopher, St George and dragon, musicians, a fox preaching to geese, a jester and representations of vanity, piety, purity, gluttony and other human attributes.

HIGH FORCE, *Durham* (14–NY8828). During or just after a rainy period is the best time to see England's highest waterfall in all its fury. Here the Tees drops 70 ft over a huge black cliff of the Great Whin Sill. There is a second channel on the Yorkshire side, and in flood times even the central rock between the two may be briefly covered with water. The Force freezes in hard winters. The falls plunge into a deep pool which is enclosed by rocks and shrubs. A wooded path leads down the bank to the falls from an entrance opposite the High Force Hotel on B6277, which winds past many beauty-spots and whitewashed stone cottages. High Force is 5 m. NW. of MIDDLETON-IN-TEESDALE. The Tees has another spectacular offering, and one even preferred by some, about 6 m. upstream. This is **Caldron Snout**. It is a little harder to reach. The visitor turns off B6277 at Langdon Beck, drives about 2½ m. and then walks along a track for another mile. Caldron Snout is a great cascade where the river tumbles some 200 ft down a dolerite staircase. The water feeding the falls comes out of a deep winding pool known as the Weel. This is to become a reservoir behind the new Cow Green dam. Between High Force and

Barnaby/Mustograph

High Force on the River Tees is England's highest waterfall

Caldron Snout there is a small area of slate with the ruins of a mill where slate pencils were made for much of the 19th cent. Good walking here-abouts: this is where the famous walk to Dufton begins.

HOLY ISLAND (LINDISFARNE), *Northumberland* (15–NU1342), is famed as the birthplace of English Christianity. It is reached from **Beal** on the A1. A 3-m. causeway connects the island to the shore at low tide and can be travelled during six-hour periods between tides. Despite a rather dull appearance from afar, Holy Island makes a fascinating place to visit, with an invincible atmosphere of age and the lure of all island communities. It has a population of some 250 mostly engaged in fishing or tourism. The island even produces souvenirs in the form of mead, honey and liqueur.

In A.D. 635, St Aidan came on the invitation of

King Oswald from Iona on the west coast of Scotland to teach Christianity to the Angles of Northumbria. Lindisfarne monastery was estab-lished and the first English diocese founded. The sixth bishop was St Cuthbert, who came to the island in 664 and was buried here until the monks of the time fled with his coffin ahead of the invading Danes in 875. The Danes destroyed the abbey and the island lay deserted until a priory was founded by Benedictines from DURHAM in the early 11th cent. The picturesque remains of this red sand-stone building are now in the care of the Ministry of Public Building and Works. They exhibit some of the same Norman features as Durham Cathedral, including carved pillars and zigzag ornament. There is a museum here. Near to the priory ruins are those of the old parish church, built about 1140 but with the surviving fabric mainly of late-12th- and early-13th-cent. date.

On a small pyramid of rock overlooking the

tiny harbour is the castle, built about 1500 and restored as a private dwelling for Edward Hudson by Sir Edwin Lutyens in 1902; it now belongs to the National Trust. Stone from the monastery went into the castle.

HOLYSTONE, *Northumberland* (14–NT9502). A path behind the Salmon Inn leads to the spring-fed Lady's Well which dates at least to Anglo-Saxon times. Now a National Trust property, it feeds a railed-in pool in the shadow of tall beech trees. Here Paulinus is supposed to have baptized 3,000 persons at Easter in 627, but historians have no evidence to support the tale. Missionaries of those days may, however, have preached at a "holy stone" here. There was an Augustinian nunnery here before 1124 and the village church probably was built out of its chancel.

HORNCLIFFE, *Northumberland* (14–NT92 49). A shallow crossing of the River Tweed is spanned by the Union Bridge, the first important suspension bridge in Britain. It is 432 ft long and 69 ft above the water, and links Northumberland to Scotland. Sir Samuel Brown designed it – and later the chain pier at BRIGHTON. The village of red sandstone houses is on the cliff to the S.

HOUGHTON-LE-SPRING, *Durham* (15–NZ3450). Historical interest is concentrated around the church in this bustling mining town. St Michael and All Angels is large, impressive and, as it stands today, largely 13th-cent. with traces of earlier work. The south chancel wall with eight lancet windows is noteworthy. A small detached two-story building in the corner between the chancel and south transept was put up in the 15th cent. for the Guild of Holy Trinity. A chantry priest lived upstairs. A passage leads into the church. Monuments include the great tomb chest of Bernard Gilpin, the kindly, generous evangelist known as the "Apostle of the North". Gilpin was rector here from 1556 until his death in 1583. It was the richest living in England in those days, and he shared it widely. He fed two dozen poor men every week and held open house for all comers on Sundays. He completely supported and educated 24 boys. It was said that if a horse were turned loose anywhere in the county, it would make its way to the rectory stables. Gilpin refused a bishopric to carry on his ministry here, among a notoriously wild and lawless people. He died at 66 after being knocked down by an ox in DURHAM market. His tomb is decorated with panels carved in circles and squares. Buildings of the Kepier Grammar School which he founded with John Heath, a wealthy Londoner and Durham landowner, in 1574 are at the north-east corner of the churchyard, with 18th-cent. additions. The Davenport almshouses, founded in 1668 by Rector George Davenport, are at the south-east corner. The rectory, a stone battlemented house, medieval in origin but rebuilt later, now contains council offices. The garden is a public park. Houghton Hall, the manor house of the old village, was built about 1600 and is now a YMCA centre.

The town was popular with wealthy Georgians, drawn by the pure spring waters, and many of their pleasant houses remain. The market place is surrounded by new council houses. The shopping centre has been redeveloped and major road re-alignments have altered the face of the town. A noticeable secular building is the old four-story brewery, not now in use.

HOUSESTEADS, *Northumberland* (15–NY 7868). The Roman fort here is considered the finest on HADRIAN'S WALL and it occupies the highest ground, on a ridge N. of the military road 8 m. W. of CHOLLERFORD. The Roman name of the fort is not known, but **Borcovicium** has been suggested. A footpath over hilly pastures leads to it from the roadside car park. The site was bought by the late Professor G. M. Trevelyan in 1930 and given to the National Trust; the Ministry of Public Building and Works cares for it. Housesteads has the typical Roman rectangular walls with rounded corners and it accommodated 1,000 infantrymen in its 5 acres. It guarded the gap where Knag Burn runs through the Wall by means of a Roman culvert. The fort stands on a cliff with a superb view of the Wall snaking over the hills. There is a museum here and a good deal to see on the actual site: walls 12 courses high, gateways, the foundations of the headquarters, commandant's house, hospital, granaries, barracks and officers' baths (supplied by rainwater). Outside the south gate, by which visitors usually enter, are the unusual indications of a large civil settlement, including an inn, a shop and the "murder house", where skeletons of a woman and a man with a sword in his ribs were found.

A short distance W. of the fort, the visitor can see a substantial ruin of a mile-castle. In this direction, too, is a thrilling walk along or on top of the Wall which follows the crags, overlooking Greenlee Lough and beautiful Crag Lough.

HOWICK, *Northumberland* (15–NU2517). Howick Hall gardens and woods about ½ m. from the tiny village are open to the public each afternoon during the summer. From the park immediately around the house, the visitor can walk along a little burn 1½ m. to Howick Haven cove on the North Sea shore. The variety of plantings is great, from the kitchen and flower gardens to the Silver Wood (planted on a silver wedding anniversary). Howick Hall has been the home of the Grey family since 1319. The house was built for Sir Henry Grey in 1782 and rebuilt in 1926 after a fire. St Michael's Church in the grounds was rebuilt in Norman style in 1849. It contains many Grey monuments including one to the 2nd Earl Grey, who died in 1845 and who pushed through the Reform Bill, and another to the 4th Earl, a Governor-General of Canada.

HULNE PRIORY, *Northumberland* (15–NU 1615). The ruins of what may be the earliest Carmelite establishment in Britain are 3 m. NW. of ALNWICK, in the park of Alnwick Castle. The priory was founded about 1240 by William de Vesci. It is said that a de Vesci Crusader found a Northumbrian knight, Ralph Fresborn, living in a monastery on Mount Carmel and encouraged him to return home and found the priory here. Other accounts say that Fresborn was so impressed with the monks of Mount Carmel when he visited them that he brought them here and made himself their first abbot. These white friars kept a severe discipline. Each had a coffin in his cell and every morning each dug a shovelful of earth for his grave. They slept on straw and ate sparsely of vegetable foods but their services were unusually splendid. The ruins, including part of their church, are in a lovely setting on a hill above the River Aln. The best of the remains is the tower built in 1488 to protect the friars when beset by Scottish raiders. The only other English monastery which had such a refuge was HOLY ISLAND (LINDISFARNE). In the 18th cent., the Duke of Northumberland did quite a lot of building on this romantic site, adding a Gothic-style summer-house on the west side of the cloister and a house, now in ruins, to the tower. Two 18th-cent. cottages are still used. The priory is enclosed by its original 12-ft-high wall. The walk along the river to the priory takes the visitor past the lesser remains of Alnwick Abbey, founded in 1147 by the de Vesci family for the Premonstratensian canons. A 14th-cent. gatehouse with four square towers and battlements marks the site. **Brizlee Hill**, 2 m. NW. of Alnwick, reminded the friars of Mount Carmel. On its top is the 1781 tower designed by Robert Adam, circular and 78 ft high – a matchless viewpoint.

HURWORTH, *Durham* (15–NZ3010). Off the beaten track, and lying along a green, is this brick-built village with several fine Georgian houses. It was the birthplace and lifelong home of William Emerson, an 18th-cent. mathematical genius and eccentric, whose tomb is in the churchyard. Emerson, the son of the local schoolmaster, was a rough, unkempt character with an encyclopedic knowledge. His odd ways and talents made the villagers think him a kind of wizard and it enraged him when they sought his advice. He liked his ale and it seems fitting that his birthplace is now a pub, the Emerson Arms. All Saints Church has a 15th-cent. tower but the rest was thoroughly restored and rebuilt twice in the 19th cent. Two mutilated cross-legged knight effigies in Frosterley marble lie in niches at the end of the nave. Both are 14th-cent. and may have come from Neasham Priory.

HYLTON CASTLE, *Durham* (15–NZ3558). Experts disagree as to whether this ancient monument just outside SUNDERLAND is a gatehouse, a castle or a keep, and the Ministry of Public Building and Works resolves the dispute by calling it a "keep gatehouse". It was built by William de Hylton in the early 15th cent. and wings were added in the 18th and 19th cents. It guarded a ford on the Wear against the Scots. Pevsner believes it was built about 1400 and is a complete

castle of the tower-house type. There is a curious detached chapel of the 15th cent., which may have been used for domestic purposes at a later date.

INGRAM, *Northumberland* (14–NU0116). A NORTHUMBERLAND NATIONAL PARK information centre and the park's only camping site, 400 acres in extent, are on the outskirts of this village in the broad Breamish valley where the river flows over a stony bed. It is a popular weekend destination for the citizens of NEWCASTLE. St Michael's Church which stands opposite the information centre, has parts dating from the 11th to the 19th cent. The oldest survival may be the plain and heavy tower arch and the tower itself is of Norman date, later restored. The church was burnt by Scots raiders in the late 13th cent. and the lead roof stripped off by another party in 1578. By the mid-17th cent. the church was in ruinous condition, and little wonder. In Ingram church, the relics include tombstones in the chancel floor and a carved fragment, the feet, of an effigy of a cleric. Upstream the Breamish valley narrows and fills with heather, bracken, birch and hawthorn trees. Many prehistoric earthworks can be found hereabout. The prehistoric village of **Greaves Ash** is near **Linhope Spout**, a 56-ft waterfall $1\frac{1}{2}$ m. uphill from the hamlet of Linhope, which is $3\frac{1}{2}$ m. upstream from Ingram. The falls are on private land but may be visited.

JARROW, *Durham* (15–NZ3265). Modern Jarrow is known as "the town that was murdered" by readers of Ellen Wilkinson's 1939 book which described the intense poverty that followed the closing in 1933 of the Charles Palmer shipyards. The desperate hunger march warned the rest of Britain of the dangers of depending upon a single industry within one area. Jarrow is still part of the teeming industrial Tyneside. It lies at the Durham end of the Tyne tunnel. New houses and blocks of flats are replacing some of the rough slums and a traffic-free shopping centre has been built, which has a C. M. Davidson sculpture of two spindly-legged Vikings. Many small factories, turning out metal goods, furniture and pharmaceuticals, have been introduced to prevent another civic murder. But visitors will be more interested, probably, in St Paul's Church, one of the most important of Christian shrines and the "cradle of English learning".

It was part of the monastery where the Venerable Bede passed almost all of his productive and scholarly life. The church where he worshipped is next to the very few remains of the religious establishment where he came at the age of about seven and remained until his death in 735. The church's site seems incongruous today, with a new trading estate in one direction, the mudflats of the estuary (Jarrow Slake) in another and the busy Tyne beyond. It probably was built within an earlier Roman fort. It was founded by Benedict Biscop in 681, seven years after MONKWEARMOUTH. It was twice sacked by the Danes in their attacks on the Northumbrian kingdom and razed by William the Conqueror only to be rebuilt in

1074. But not long afterwards, the monks of Jarrow moved to DURHAM. The original Anglo-Saxon church nave is now the chancel, with a Victorian nave added. The fine masonry is believed to be the work of stonemasons imported from France by Biscop. Original round-headed windows and doorways exist along with window additions of the late 13th and 14th cents. The tower may date from the 11th-cent. rebuilding. The original dedication stone of 685 has been set above the chancel arch. The modern east window by L. C. Evetts shows Bede in a blue robe with a book in his hand, together with the crucifixion and St Peter with a sword. "Bede's chair", a battered relic, probably dates from the 14th cent. The church is still in use and an annual Bede lecture has been instituted there. Looking at the modest remnant, it is hard to imagine Jarrow's importance in Bede's time. There were 600 monks here and at Monkwearmouth. The 79 books Bede wrote for his students represented the collected knowledge of his time in science, literature, philosophy and the arts. His most famous book is the *Ecclesiastical History of the English People*. He made the first translation of St John's Gospel into English.

KIELDER, *Northumberland* (14–NY6293). The Border Forest National Park, largest forest area in Britain, covers some 200 sq. m. and has significantly altered the look of the countryside since planting of spruce, pine and larch began in 1926 in a previously nearly treeless area. In recent years, the Forestry Commission has developed public access to many sections of the forest, thus creating a new and delightful recreation ground. The **Pennine Way** crosses the forest and camping, caravan and picnic sites have been established. Permits can be obtained for deer stalking and trout fishing. There are a few observation points from which visitors can watch or photograph wild life, including the increasing number of roe deer. The country's first trailside museum is situated near the Lewisburn camp site. Kielder Castle and Lewisburn forest trails have been laid out and helpful printed guides for them make it easier to enjoy the outings and to identify the trees, plants and bird or animal life encountered along the route. (Information on public facilities is available from the Forestry Commission headquarters at Kielder Castle, BELLINGHAM, or H.M.S.O. shops and other booksellers.) Kielder (from the Old Norse *kelda* or spring) is one of the forest villages built to house the workers in this new industry. The castle, standing above the meeting of the North Tyne River and Kielder Burn, is the administrative headquarters for one forest area and a social club for the workers. It was built in 1775 as a shooting box by the Duke of Northumberland. Early visitors told of the inhabitants indulging in a riotous folk dance in which the men drew their dirks and appeared, all things considered, "scarcely less savage than the Indians of California". Kielder viaduct was purchased in 1969 by the Northumberland and Newcastle Society to preserve "the finest example of Victorian railway architecture in Britain".

KIRKHARLE, *Northumberland* (14–NZ0182). Capability Brown was born in this hamlet in 1716, and it has been suggested that the place deserves more visits. But finding it in this county, where off-the-beaten-track signposting is fairly whimsical, is the problem. After leaving the A696, you pass through an unmarked white farm gate, across a pasture and through another gate to reach the church in the farmyard. St Wilfrid's Church has no memorial to Brown but many to the Loraine family who were here for about 400 years. The church was rebuilt in 1336 and has a fine triple sedilia and a pretty fluted piscina. The font, which seems too monumental for the little parish, dates from 1500 and came out of All Saints Church in NEWCASTLE. Carved around the bowl are the arms of various Northumberland families and these are repeated in brass at the base. A reminder of turbulent days comes from a stone erected by a descendant in 1728 to Robert Loraine who died in 1483 at the hands of a party of Scots raiders.

KIRKNEWTON, *Northumberland* (14–NT91 30). The panorama of hills, the presence of ancient ruins or the Church of St Gregory might cause visitors to call at this remote village in the Cheviot foothills. The highest point in the vicinity is **Yeavering Bell**, 1,182 ft high, 2 m. to the SE., which provides a viewpoint near the traces of a large ancient camp. At the nearby place called Yeavering, a mile or so E. of the church, it is believed that King Edwin of Northumbria had a palace. He married the Christian Ethelburga here. Beside a particularly beautiful stretch of the B6351 stands a cairn, erected in 1964, marking the royal township known of old as Gefrin. "Here the missionary Paulinus in A.D. 627 instructed the people in Christianity for thirty-six days and baptized them in the River Glen close by", the plaque records. The church has been rebuilt several times and probably dates to the late 12th or early 13th cent. The present comfortable structure reflects the work of John Dobson in the 19th cent. for the most part, but remnants of earlier times provoke considerable curiosity. Both the chancel and the south transept are tunnel-vaulted. In the chancel the side walls are less than 3 ft high and extremely thick. In the transept there is no vertical wall, the vaulting starting from floor level. Both could have been part of a defensive building or one used for refuge, during the border troubles. Behind the lectern is a primitive carving of the Adoration of the Magi. It shows a stiff-armed Virgin greeting the three Wise Men. Each of the bearers of gifts seems to be dressed in a kilt and each has both knees bent to the mother and child. Experts differ on its date, but the charming though primitive work may have survived from a previous Anglo-Saxon church here. Some believe it to be 12th-cent. Josephine Butler, the great social reformer, is buried here. She died in 1906.

KIRKWHELPINGTON, *Northumberland* (14–NY9984). This pastoral village near the

River Wansbeck has cottages of a tawny stone around a small, low-walled meadow opposite the church. Rolling farmlands seem to seal the village off from the bustle of the nearby road to Carter Bar. An early 19th-cent. bridge spans the Wansbeck. One of the vicars at St Bartholomew's Church was the Rev. John Hodgson who wrote most of his *County History of Northumberland* while he was here. The church has a generally make-do-and-mend air (for example, a plain Georgian window is stuck into the chancel wall). It is a puzzle as to dates but is basically 13th-cent. in style with later alterations. A monument to Gawen Aynsley, who died in 1750, and his wife should give pause to all who take the trouble to read it. They were, it reports: "Kind to their children. Humane to their servants. Obliging to their neighbours. Friendly, just, and courteous to all. Religious without superstition. Charitable without ostentation. Lovers and practisers of virtue." The churchyard contains the grave of Sir Charles Algernon Parsons, inventor of the steam turbine, who died in 1931.

LANCHESTER, *Durham* (15–NZ1647). The Roman fort of Longovicium was ½ m. SW. of Lanchester but it is now grassed over. The most the visitor will see here of that period in history now is the assortment of Roman relics incorporated in the church. The fort, 560 by 485 ft, was built about A.D. 122, destroyed in 197 and restored about 240. It then remained in use by some 1,000 men until the end of the 4th cent. It guarded the route from YORK to HADRIAN'S WALL. All Saints Church has a Roman altar, dated 244, in its south porch. The 15th-cent. tower has Roman stones, and Roman pillars are used in the north aisle arcade. The rest is Norman or Early English. The sculpture is of particular interest, and it includes head corbels used as candle brackets. Recesses in the side walls of the chancel were made to allow room for stalls for vicars choral when the church was made collegiate in 1283.

LUMLEY CASTLE, *Durham* (15–NZ2851). This splendid castle E. of CHESTER-LE-STREET now belongs to University College, DURHAM, but it was for generations the seat of the Lumleys, Earls of Scarbrough. It is built on four sides of a courtyard with bold buttressed and crenellated towers in the angles. It appears now much as it did when new, in the late 14th cent. John Lord Lumley, who was responsible for the row of family effigies in the church at Chester-le-Street, began his genealogical hobby here by adding a display of shields in the courtyard about 1580. He also contributed a huge fireplace with classical columns to the hall. In the early 18th cent., Sir John Vanbrugh designed a library and made other alterations.

MARSDEN ROCK, *Durham* (15–NZ4064). On the coast S. of SOUTH SHIELDS is this offshore mass of weathered limestone rock pierced by an arch through which boats may pass at high tide. It is a haunt of kittiwakes, fulmar petrels and

cormorants. Let into Marsden Cliff is a lift which will take visitors down to the beach and to Marsden Grotto, an inn in a cave, from which they can watch the birds outside and fish in glass tanks inside. Further S. is Souter Point lighthouse.

MIDDLETON-IN-TEESDALE, *Durham* (14–NY9425). The Quaker-run London Lead Co., which developed the lead-mines in Teesdale in the mid-18th cent., continued until it closed in the early 20th cent. to be a strong influence in this area. Its imprint, and its concern for the well-being of its workers, is clearly seen in the substantial stone buildings in Middleton, in the snug miners' cottages in the villages throughout the valley, and even in the road system. Its headquarters here at Middleton House on Hude Hill is used today for private shooting parties and Middleton itself is a convenient centre for upper Teesdale holidays. The town is built in terraces along the road as it climbs up from the river. Outside the churchyard is a spot where the visitor can join the locals, sitting and watching the traffic, or examine the old cross which also once marked the village stocks. Inside the churchyard railings, a 13th-cent. window has been planted in the grass. This, the piscina in the vestry and the font pedestal are nearly the only reminders of the church which preceded the present St Mary's, built in 1876. A dozen interesting fragments of medieval grave covers, mouldings and other stone carvings have been mounted attractively in the white wall of the north aisle. The tomb lids have such symbols as spades, hoes, crosses and swords to indicate the life's work of the deceased. A feature of this church is the stubby stone bell-tower, completely detached, which dates from the 16th cent. One of its three bells is dated 1558. In the town centre further up the hill is a Victorian cast-iron fountain, painted in cheerful blue and white, with a cherub.

MITFORD, *Northumberland* (15–NZ1685). The Wansbeck valley is at its most charming around Mitford, 2 m. W. of MORPETH. The village once was more important than Morpeth and numbered among its attractions a snuff factory. Today it is an insignificant hamlet except for its proximity to the castle, manor house and St Mary Magdalene Church. The castle, long in ruins on the rocky river bank, was built in the 12th cent. by William Bertram. By 1323 it was useless, the victim of repeated assaults and seizures. Mitford Hall was designed in 1828 by John Dobson to replace the 17th-cent. manor house of which only a battle-mented gatehouse survives. It is a private residence. The church was extensively restored and rebuilt in 1875, when the steeple and spire were added, but it has a splendid Norman south arcade and 13th-cent. chancel.

MONKWEARMOUTH, *Durham* (15–NZ39 58). This is the old portion of SUNDERLAND (originally known as Wearmouth), lying N. of the River Wear. Like the church at JARROW, St Peter's here is a cherished link with early Christianity, and it, too, must now be sought in an unlovely industrial scene. This church was part of a monastery established shortly before Jarrow (in 674) by Benedict Biscop, the Anglian nobleman educated in France, who had returned to his native Northumbria. His two establishments had 600 monks at one time. Only the west wall and the tower remain here of the original church, and the tower has been heightened. Anglo-Saxon baluster shafts in their original position can be seen in the doorway of the vaulted porch. Above, over a window, there are traces of a large sculptured figure, the earliest major sculpture in England. A collection of important Anglo-Saxon carvings is exhibited in the church, including two stones with lions. Biscop is believed to have imported craftsmen from France for his building, and excavations here have indicated that these buildings had windows of glass made on the site. This makes St Peter's the first English church to use glass.

MORPETH, *Northumberland* (15–NZ2085), is a very old place with little visible history but travellers find it useful as a shopping centre and a gateway to the moors, hills and coast of Northumberland. It is an attractive town in a U-shaped bend of the River Wansbeck with plentiful trees and parks, including the 400-acre Common with its golf course. In Carlisle Park are formal flower-beds, tennis courts and bowling greens. It is the scene of the annual miners' gala. On quaintly-named Ha' Hill overlooking the park were found early remains of a fortification. The remnants of Morpeth Castle are on a steep bank S. of this hill. A restored 15th-cent. gatehouse is the chief survival. A good view of the town can be had from the path E. of the castle.

The Parish Church of St Mary is on the southern edge of the town, a 14th-cent. building with later restoration. The east Jesse window contains the most important 14th-cent. glass in the county. An 1831 watch-house guards the churchyard against body-snatchers. In the Presbyterian Church of St George near the Telford Bridge (1861) is a memorial to Dr John Horsley, "father of British archaeology", who died here in 1732, the year his *Britannia Romana* was published. Opposite this church is the former All Saints chantry chapel, which marked the river crossing in the 13th cent. and in the 16th cent. became part of a grammar school. The west porch and the north wall are all that remain of the original and the building is now a soft drinks factory.

The south entrance to Morpeth passes a huge battlemented tower which turns out to be the courthouse and police station (1822, by Dobson) with the gatehouse for a gaol. In the Market Place stands the Town Hall, designed in 1714 by Sir John Vanbrugh and rebuilt in 1870. The hall opening into the street was the butter and egg market. The 15th-cent. clock tower with later additions is planted sturdily in the middle of Oldgate. It was the house of correction at one time and its bells still ring a curfew. Further along the street on the north side is the late Georgian Collingwood House, which once belonged to Admiral Collingwood.

Until the railway made it unnecessary, there was a weekly market in the Market Place, Bridge and Newgate Streets for cattle and sheep from the whole of the North of England and Scotland, with buyers from as far away as the North Riding of Yorkshire. There is still a weekly mart.

A walk 1½ m. W. brings you to Newminster Abbey, a 12th-cent. Cistercian monastery site. It was the daughter of FOUNTAINS ABBEY and the mother of ROCHE.

NEWBIGGIN-BY-THE-SEA, *Northumberland* (14–NZ3188). Just a few of the many brightly coloured cobles, the characteristic inshore fishing-boats of the North-East, that used to cover the shore of Newbiggin bay still fish off here today. The old Herring House, where the daily catch was washed and sold, is gone, too. The men of the sea now work in the neighbouring mines or new industries, or cater for the visitors who seek sea air here. The sands have suffered from wave action and industrial pollution at Lynemouth and BLYTH above and below on the coast. But Newbiggin offers a promenade, a golf course and a caravan site near the Town Moor. St Bartholomew's Church, with its landmark of a 14th-cent. stone spire, stands dangerously close to the cliffs on the north-eastern tip of the bay. It goes back to the 13th cent. At some later date both aisles were removed. The north aisle was restored about 1910. Several medieval tombstones have been set in the north wall. In the Second World War, mines exploding on the rocks below damaged the roof and windows, since repaired.

NEWCASTLE-UPON-TYNE, *Northumberland* (15–NZ2464). Approach this impressive regional capital, if you can, from the S. for a quick survey, from one of the five bridges that reach across the Tyne, of the city packed on the steep north bank. It is a complex scene of blackened masses of old building, tall new blocks, the ornamental crown of St Nicholas Cathedral, the pretty spire of All Saints, the square-shouldered castle keep, the quays, warehouses and industry. The city holds up, upon scrutiny, to the first impression of a rather special place, particularly in the area of most concern to visitors, the square mile between the riverside and the Town Moor.

Newcastle began as a minor fort and bridge on HADRIAN'S WALL, which started from neighbouring Wallsend, the ship-building town on the E. Westgate Road now follows the line of the wall and vestiges can be seen along it. A causeway crossing the vallum and relics of a temple can be found in residential Benwell, rather comically surrounded by tidy brick houses. After the Romans came an obscure religious colony known as Monkchester and then the Normans, who in 1080 established the "new castle" on the Roman site. A stone castle replaced the wooden one from 1172 onwards. Of this, the very complete keep and 13th-cent. fortified Black Gate survive as museums now hemmed in by railway lines and the High Level Bridge. The restored battlemented roof of the keep is a good place from which to look at the Tyne.

Medieval Newcastle was a base for the continuous warfare with the Scots. It lay inside 2 m. of city wall begun in 1280. A part of the restored West Wall can be seen in Bath Lane. The Plummer Tower in Croft Street now houses 18th-cent. furnishings from the Laing Art Gallery; the Sallyport or Wall Knoll tower at the top of Causey Bank Steps, off City Road, has been restored by the Corporation for meeting rooms.

Newcastle established itself as a market town and seaport because of the surrounding coalfield, one of the first to be worked in England and the first to export coal. But the 19th cent. brought the greatest growth and firmly established the city as a major heavy engineering centre. The key industries continue to be ship-building and repair and the manufacture of marine engines, ship fittings, generators and transformers, but the city also now makes scores of other products including detergents and flour. Most of the city seen today dates from this expansive period. One way to explore it is from the riverside up the hill, roughly the way it grew.

Of the great bridges that overshadow the waterfront, the High Level for rail and road traffic was earliest, flung across the Tyne gorge by Robert Stephenson in 1849. The Swing Bridge designed by the inventive Lord Armstrong replaced a medieval span in 1876. The King Edward, now the main railway bridge, opened in 1906 and the Redheugh and Tyne road bridges are 20th-cent. Near the Swing Bridge is the 17th-cent. Guildhall with a 1796 façade, that has been renovated. The centre of local affairs until the 19th cent., it is still used by the freemen. Merchants lived in timbered houses in Sandhill and from No. 41, Bessie Surtees in 1772 eloped with the man who became Lord Eldon and Chancellor of England. A popular Sunday morning market is held on Quayside where an obelisk marks the spot on which John Wesley first preached in 1742. Trinity House in Broad Chare is the ancient headquarters of the mariners. St Nicholas's Church became a cathedral in 1882. A mainly 14th-cent. building with rare 15th-cent. crown and spire supported by delicate arches, it is richly endowed with monuments, fine woodwork and a charnel chapel or crypt discovered in 1824. All Saints was designed in 1788 by David Stephenson and survives as a beautiful example of a rare elliptical style. It contains the largest memorial brass in England, to Roger Thornton who died in 1429. Redundant, but with prospect of becoming a concert hall, the church is the focal point of a Quayside redevelopment plan. Keelmen's Hospital, built in 1701, is off City Road not far from Holy Jesus, the important 17th-cent. hospital for aged and impoverished freemen which is being restored as a museum after years of neglect.

Richard Grainger, with John Dobson as his architect, and John Clayton, the Town Clerk as his supporter, were the courageous planners responsible for the sense of order and space in the present commercial centre which they thoroughly reconstructed between 1835 and 1840. Grey Street is their masterpiece, with its curve of gracious façades culminating in the stately Theatre Royal, by Benjamin Green, sweeping uphill to Grey's Monument. Their Grainger Street leads into broad Neville Street with Central Station, also by Dobson, behind a grand-scale portico. Covered markets are a city centre feature.

The sparkling new Civic Centre at Barras Bridge dominates an interesting precinct of the city which was rural land when the 19th-cent. planners were at work. Cool white office blocks and a mushroom-capped round chamber bring Newcastle well into the 20th cent. The centre was designed by City Architect George Kenyon. The main 12-story block is capped by a copper lantern and beacon with three gold castles from the coat of arms 250 ft above the street. A carillon in the tower plays Tyneside tunes four times a day. Impressive use is made of modern sculpture with, most noticeably, a 16-ft-long River God Tyne by David Wynne.

In the neighbourhood are the proliferating buildings of the University of Newcastle; the Hancock Natural History Museum famous for amphibian fossils; and three other museums connected with the university: the Greek Museum, the Hatton Art Gallery, and the Museum of Antiquities with one of the most important collections of Roman inscriptions and sculpture in the country and a reconstructed Temple of Mithras. The Laing Art Gallery, with a fine permanent collection of British art, is near the new Central Library in New Bridge Street and the Municipal Museum of Science and Industry is in Exhibition Park.

Foremost of Newcastle parks is the vast Town Moor which gives this highly industrial city its unique breathing space in 927 windswept acres on which freemen can – and do – pasture cows. The country's biggest fair or "hoppings" is held there in June.

NORHAM, *Northumberland* (14–NT9047). The pinkish castle rises high on rocks above the River Tweed and the view of it from the riverside near the bridge was the one chosen by Turner to paint. The ruin, in the care of the Ministry of Public Building and Works, is what remains of a major border stronghold. It was built about 1160 by Bishop Pudsey of DURHAM as the capital of Norhamshire, part of the Durham palatine. Its keep was one of the best of its period in Britain. Alterations were made into the 16th cent. and the ruins were partially restored in 1900. The road from BERWICK now runs through what was the castle moat. The village with its large triangular green is one of the oldest on the border and it suffered all of the usual vicissitudes. St Cuthbert's, a plain church which faces the castle across the green, once was held as a fortress for a year by the Scots. It is early Norman in its foundation although Christianity was practised here in the 7th cent. around a preaching cross. At midnight on 14 February each year the vicar blesses the nets to open the salmon fishing.

Newcastle-upon-Tyne: a view of the bridges over the river

NORTHUMBERLAND NATIONAL PARK, *Northumberland* (14–NY8595). Most of the county's fine wild uplands are within the 398 sq. m. of the park, designated in 1956. It runs from the CHEVIOT HILLS in the N. to HADRIAN'S WALL in the S. and forms an eastern boundary to the Border Forest National Park. It takes in the SIMONSIDE HILLS. The variety of landscape is wide, with mountains, moors, forests and river valleys. The park is dotted with the sites of Ancient British tribes and evidences of Roman occupation, as well as with survivals of border defences. Many places are associated with early Christianity. The **Pennine Way** enters the park near Greenhead and leaves some 60 m. further N. near the Roman camps of Chew Green on the Scottish border. Information centres with exhibits of the geology, history, flora and fauna of the park area are maintained at INGRAM and near the Once Brewed youth hostel. A 40-m. stretch of the coast, from WARKWORTH to near BERWICK was in 1958 declared an area of outstanding natural beauty.

NORTON, *Durham* (15–NZ4421), is a Georgian suburb which first catered for merchants from STOCKTON-ON-TEES and now is taking the well-off overflow from the newer BILLINGHAM chemical industry as well. Yet it has managed to main-tain its village tranquillity. The tree-shaded High Street leads to a green bordered with numerous fine houses, including a handsome 1762 vicarage. Once Norton eclipsed Stockton in importance. The Norton Iron Co. in 1856 made the first bell for Big Ben. But it cracked when tested, and the contract went to another firm. The ironworks closed in 1916. St Mary's Church is the only cruciform Anglo-Saxon church in the North. The crossing tower, with eight triangular-headed windows, has a battlemented top of later date. The rest of the church has been altered at various times. There is an excellent 14th-cent. effigy of a knight in chain mail, bare-headed and cross-legged. At his feet are a lion and a dog, and a small figure reading prayers. A comical head peers over his shield. In the churchyard is the grave of John Walker who invented matches (or friction lights as he called them).

With Stockton and Billingham, Norton was incorporated in the county borough of Teesside in 1968.

OTTERBURN, *Northumberland* (14–NY8893). The battle of Otterburn (better known in song as Chevy Chase) was fought in August 1388. Historically it may have settled nothing but it achieved fame through the best known of border ballads. It was fought between soldiers led by the

Earl of Douglas and Sir Henry Percy. The Scots won the moonlight affray but Douglas was killed on the battlefield about 1½ m. NW. There is a memorial at Bennetsfield. Otterburn is a sleepy kind of place on the River Rede on the NEW-CASTLE–Carter Bar road. This route, which crosses the CHEVIOT HILLS, offers immense blue vistas. The Otterburn Towers Hotel occupies the battlemented mansion which was built on to a medieval peel-tower. The Otterburn Mill, still using an old water-wheel, produces widely known tweeds and rugs, and visitors may see them made.

OVINGHAM, *Northumberland* (14–NZ0863), and **Prudhoe** occupy opposite banks of the River Tyne, with a narrow iron bridge connecting them across the wide river bottom. Ovingham is known for Thomas Bewick who was born at Cherryburn House across the river in 1753. He taught himself to draw and when every inch of his books was filled, he drew on the church floor and grave-stones. The only paintings he knew were the pub signs. He was apprenticed to Ralph Beilby, a NEWCASTLE engraver, and went on to become one of the great artists of that and later days. His best works were a history of quadrupeds and British birds. He died in 1828 and a monument in the chancel here pays tribute to the local boy "whose genius restored the art of engraving on wood". The church has a large late Anglo-Saxon west tower, dated 1050, probably originally defensive. Roman stone went into the church building; most of the present fabric is 13th-cent. in origin. The vicarage is partly 14th-cent.

Prudhoe is the bigger and more industrial community. It consists mostly of long terraces of houses on the steep river bank as well as much new housing. But on a wooded spur overlooking the Tyne, is Prudhoe Castle. It has been taken over from the Duke of Northumberland by the Ministry of Public Building and Works and is to be opened to the public. Prudhoe (proud hill) was built by the d'Umfravilles as an earthwork defence about 1150, with a stone curtain wall and keep added in the late 12th cent. It was strengthened further in the 13th cent. and came into the hands of the Percys in 1381. Its substantial remains include an almost perfect 14th-cent. barbican, a long stretch of curtain wall and a splendid gatehouse. Above the latter is a chapel with the oldest oriel window in England, it is believed. A second-story chamber has its original chimney and battlements. The castle never fell until Oliver Cromwell knocked down the tower with cannon fire.

A Georgian house was built in the inner courtyard. There is a legend that a lady walks in the corridors, but the caretaker has never seen her. There is another that Prudhoe is connected to BYWELL Castle, miles away, by a secret underground passage.

PENSHAW MONUMENT, *Durham* (15–NZ 3253). This notable landmark on the A183 SW. of SUNDERLAND was erected to honour the Earl of Durham, first to bear that title and first High Commissioner for Canada, in 1844. It stands on Penshaw Hill in the form of a roofless Doric temple. The National Trust owns it now. Visitors will be rewarded with a splendid view of north Durham, collieries, quarries and all.

PETERLEE, *Durham* (15–NZ4440). The most distinctive of Durham's new towns, Peterlee was established near Easington to accommodate some 30,000 people, to provide a shopping and recreational centre for many more, and to attract industry employing women into the south-eastern part of the county. The last objective had to be revised to give priority to jobs for displaced colliers as pits in the area closed down. The Victor Pasmore houses of timber panels and brick in a white and dark grey-blue colour scheme surround a modern centre with two-tier shops, car parks, blocks of flats, civic offices and places of entertainment. So far, the new town has acquired firms producing such things as clothing, potato crisps, zip fasteners, wall coverings, fire surrounds, lingerie, kitchen units and machine tools. International Business Machines is setting up a centre for research into management science and computer application which, the developers hope, will bring other laboratories and institutes here and make Peterlee the "intellectual powerhouse" of its region.

Peterlee has what most new towns can only dream about – a nature reserve of its own. **Castle Eden Dene,** now owned by the development corporation, is one of the last unspoilt woodlands in eastern Durham. It runs about 3 m. to the North Sea. Hundreds of species of flowers, grasses, ferns, trees and shrubs as well as bird, animal and insect life have been identified here. In the tiny village at the head of the dene is Castle Eden Castle, an 18th-cent. mansion now the property of the National Coal Board. In the 1764 church, a rich stained-glass window by L. C. Evetts commemorates the last survivor of the Burdon family which held the manor from 1758.

Peterlee is named after Peter Lee who died in 1935. He started work in the pits at 10 and rose to become president of the Miners' Federation and first chairman of a Labour county council. He was also a Methodist preacher.

PIERCEBRIDGE, *Durham* (15–NZ2115), was built inside the nearly 11-acre area of a Roman fort which guarded Dere Street where it crossed the Tees. It was the largest fort in the county, and could have accommodated 1,000 cavalry. The fort was constructed about A.D. 297 and the only remaining evidence of it is some turf-covered mounds and part of the drainage system in the north-east corner. The most picturesque part of the village is the rectangle of white-washed and red-roofed cottages round the broad green. The village museum has some of the relics excavated on the fort site. A three-arched, 18th-cent. bridge, recently widened, now spans the river. On the Yorkshire side is the old George Inn where the clock that inspired the song "My grandfather's clock" stands in a passage.

PITTINGTON CHURCH, *Durham* (15–NZ 3245), is originally Anglo-Saxon, was dedicated to St Lawrence, and worth seeing for the 12th-cent. north arcade, consisting of six round arches with bold zigzag carving. The eight-sided pillars have alternating square and round reeding and the circular ones a dashing spiral motif, both in high relief, and similar to, though livelier than, those in DURHAM Cathedral. Many other features will repay close study. In the jambs of the Anglo-Saxon windows are traces of 12th-cent. red paintings, depicting the consecration of St Cuthbert and his vision in WHITBY Abbey. There is a Norman font, a 13th-cent. cross-legged knight in Frosterley marble and a 13th-cent. foot-long monument to two boys, with two toy swords carved on it. An 1183 tombstone to "Christian" may mark the grave of Bishop Pudsey's master mason during the great period of church building in Pudsey's long reign from 1153 to 1195 as bishop.

ROKER, *Durham* (15–NZ4059). With **Seaburn,** Roker is the pleasure ground of SUNDERLAND. Within 10 minutes of the city centre on the north shore, tired workers can find every sort of recreation from angling and archery to tenpin bowling and tennis. There are parks, a 1½-m. promenade, sandy beaches, car parks and picnic areas. In Roker Cliff Park, a memorial cross to the Venerable Bede was erected in 1904. St Andrew's Church (1906) is a successful example of neo-Gothic architecture. Its modern fittings, including tapestry, carpets, furniture and glass, also are admired. On the sea-front can be seen the unique "cannon-ball" rocks, formed from the underlying limestone bed.

ROMAN WALL, *see* HADRIAN'S WALL.

ROS CASTLE, *Northumberland* (14–NU0725). Many a native Northumbrian will insist that the view from Ros Castle surpasses all others in this county of splendid views. This is a 1,000-ft height overlooking CHILLINGHAM. It has easy access, for the motorist can drive from the A1 to within a 10-minute climb to the top. The outlines of an ancient fort can be traced on the summit. But visitors are chiefly rewarded with a sweeping picture which embraces to the E. the FARNE ISLANDS, BAMBURGH and DUNSTANBURGH castles on the shore and to the W. the CHEVIOT HILLS. Just below lies Chillingham Park with an occasional glimpse of its herd of wild white cattle. This was a favourite spot for Viscount Grey of Falloden and 7½ acres on the crest were given to the National Trust in his memory. Ros Castle was doubtless a beacon hill in prehistoric times and in the days of border fighting, too.

ROTHBURY, *Northumberland* (14–NU0601). Few villages in the county have a longer history than Rothbury, which can trace its origins to long before the Norman Conquest. It spreads over the banks along the narrowing Coquet valley and makes an ideal centre for touring, walking, or

fishing for trout and salmon. It is convenient for visits to the CRAGSIDE gardens and BRINKBURN PRIORY. The SIMONSIDE HILLS stretch to the S. The ruins of Cartington Castle stand 3½ m. to the NW. Across the river is Whitton where a peel-tower has been converted into a children's convalescent home. Other such fortifications stand at Tosson and Hepple. Lordenshaws Camp, a well-preserved hill-fort, is also nearby. Rothbury has a cheerful atmosphere suitable to its reputation as a healthful summer resort. The main street, lined with sycamores, cuts through a sloping green with shops and houses above and below it. Visitors are welcomed at all local dances, concerts, matches, and sports clubs, although officials admit most of those who come are apt to be solitary anglers or walkers. To the W. of town, a row of benches beside the road encourages travellers to linger over the view across the Coquet to the Simonsides. Lord Armstrong, the inventor and engineer who died at Cragside in 1900, is commemorated in the chancel screen of the parish church.

RYTON, *Durham* (15–NZ1564). This former colliery village, always one of Tyneside's attractions, made such a good readjustment after its five famous pits closed that it won a Britain in Bloom trophy in 1968. After the first mine opened in 1800, the industry grew rapidly here. Then 10 years ago, the pits were shut down. Ryton's determined citizens removed the pit-heads and heaps and introduced modern light industries on landscaped sites. The fine 18th-cent. buildings on the wooded, sloping green are now shown to even better advantage. Many residents work in NEWCASTLE-UPON-TYNE. The 13th-cent. broach spire of Holy Cross Church rises 120 ft. Among its possessions is a 13th-cent. Frosterley marble effigy of a deacon holding a book, resting his head upon a cushion.

SEAHAM, *Durham* (15–NZ4250). Lord Londonderry hired John Dobson of NEWCASTLE-UPON-TYNE to design a port to ship his coal. Operations began in 1828 amid the firing of cannon and the cheers of 5,000 people. There is nothing picturesque about it; it is just a workaday outlet for colliery wastes and a declining coal trade. The promenade on the sea-front to the N., however, is good for views. On the limestone cliffs above is St Mary's Church, in the old village, an interesting small and low building with aisle-less nave and chancel, dating from Anglo-Saxon times. Some Roman stones were used in the walls. Over the double piscina, a carved hand seems to be raised in blessing. There is an early 13th-cent. font and a 16th-cent. pulpit.

Seaham Hall was the scene of the unfortunate marriage of Lord Byron and Anne Isabella Milbanke in 1815. Byron, we are told, loathed Seaham and wrote to a friend, "Upon this dreary coast we have nothing but county meetings and shipwrecks; and I have this day dined upon fish, which probably dined upon the crews of several colliers lost in the late gales."

A. F. Kersting

Seaton Delaval is a masterpiece in the Palladian style by Sir John Vanbrugh

SEAHOUSES, *Northumberland* (15–NU2232). Boat trips to the FARNE ISLANDS start from this busy little port. The village grew up in the late 19th cent. when the harbour here was built to serve North Sunderland inland. A small fleet of fishing-boats still works out of Seahouses but the chief reason for existence now seems to be summer visitors. The village centre is a car park and new houses fill the perimeter. Excellent sandy beaches stretch S. towards BEADNELL and EMBLETON bay.

SEATON DELAVAL HALL, *Northumberland* (15–NZ3075), is held by many to be Vanbrugh's masterpiece. No other work of the architect is so "mature, so compact and so powerful", Pevsner says. No expense was spared when Admiral George Delaval commissioned a new mansion that would compare with CASTLE HOWARD or any other great house. It took 10 years and was finished in 1728, five years after the admiral's death from a fall from his horse. His nephew, Captain Francis Blake-Delaval, inherited. He had a family of eight sons and five daughters and they led a gay and spendthrift life.

The house, said a visitor, was "an Italian palace, and the grounds were a perfect fairyland". The Delavals loved entertainments and on one occasion borrowed Drury Lane Theatre for their own production of *Othello*. The House of Commons adjourned two hours early to attend. The captain's son, Sir Francis, was fond of practical jokes, such as suddenly lowering the beds of guests into cold baths in the middle of the night. He was also, it should be added, an M.P. of talent.

Built in the Palladian style, Seaton Delaval consists of a central block with a great entrance flanked by huge Tuscan pillars and dominated by a lofty portico. On either side are long wings. Visitors can tour the uninhabited main block with its statuary, spiral staircases and room of historic documents; the modernized west wing, now the family residence of the owner, Lord Hastings; and the stables in the east wing. The 18th-cent. gardens have been restored.

The hall was burnt twice, stood without a roof for 50 years and was used by the military in both World Wars. It was nearly derelict when the restoration work began more than 20 years ago. Medieval banquets with traditional entertainments, costume and pageantry are held here for the public most evenings.

In the grounds is the tiny Norman church, consecrated in 1102 as a family chapel, and made into a parish church in 1891. The nave has its original west door and broad arch with zigzag ornament leading into the chancel. There are two 13th-cent. effigies of a knight and a lady.

Seaton Sluice is the harbour built by Sir Ralph Delaval in the early 17th cent. at the outlet of Seaton Burn. It was a flourishing port for two centuries.

SEDGEFIELD, *Durham* (15–NZ3528), has been an active market town since the 14th cent. St Edmund's Church has 17th-cent. carved oak woodwork in the style of Cosin comparable with that at BRANCEPETH. It is by the same craftsman, Robert Barker, who lived here. The church building is mainly 13th-cent., with a particularly beautiful nave and a 15th-cent. tower rising 90 ft and topped with battlements and pinnacles. The Cooper almshouses date from 1703 and the rectory from 1792. The spacious Georgian manor house is now the headquarters of the Rural District Council. A Shrove Tuesday football match has been played on the green here since the 12th cent. This old game of "pila" originated in CHESTER-LE-STREET and is played between tradesmen and countrymen. The game can last for hours and get rather rowdy. The object is to "alley" the ball – get it into the part of the village defended by the other side. It is said to have started from a quarrel between Chester-le-Street apprentices and a retainer at LUMLEY CASTLE, and the first football used was the latter's head. Sedgefield is a centre for fox hunting and its racecourse has six steeplechase meetings yearly. Hardwick Hall, 1 m. W., is a fine 18th-cent. mansion which in recent years has been a workers' training centre and a maternity hospital. Now it is a hotel. Several ornamental but deteriorating outbuildings are attributed to James Paine. They are an octagonal temple, a banqueting house and a sham gatehouse.

SIMONBURN, *Northumberland* (14–NY 8773). A green surrounded by low cottages, many of them white-washed, friendly gardens, and tall trees: that is all there is to Simonburn, but it is enough to make it lovely. There is a fragmentary ruin of Simonburn Castle within short walking distance. The last attack on it is said to have been by villagers searching for a hidden treasure which reputedly was so great it could buy all of Northumberland. On the crags nearby is a circle of four standing stones known as the Goat Stones. St Mungo's Church is a handsome buff stone building of 13th-cent. origin with rebuildings in 1762 and 1863. The floor slopes from W. to E., in harmony with the site, or perhaps because the chancel was once a few steps down from the nave. Portions of ancient carved stones are attractively set in a niche in the porch. An original double piscina is in the sanctuary wall. Near the wooded churchyard stands the 18th-cent. rectory.

SIMONSIDE HILLS, *Northumberland* (ROTHBURY: 14–NU0601). The sharp outline of this range of hills in the centre of Northumberland suggests a series of steps or breaking waves, and offers a notable contrast to the great domes of the CHEVIOTS to the N. The Simonsides are rocky and heather-clad, good to look at and to climb for justly famous views. The centre for the sandstone range is ROTHBURY. The highest peak is Simonside, 1,409 ft, which can be climbed from Great Tosson, a hillside village SW. of Rothbury. The view from this summit encompasses the whole Northumberland coast, in fine weather. Access to the Simonsides is somewhat restricted by forestry plantations and the Redesdale All Arms Range. The Grasslees Valley divides the Harbottle from the Simonside hills.

SOUTH SHIELDS, *Durham* (15–NZ3667), was established by the Romans about A.D. 80 but their real interests lay up the Tyne at NEWCASTLE, and South Shields never caught up with its neighbour. Nevertheless, through the centuries, it has been important for saltworks, glass-making, coal-mining, shipping, ship-building, engineering, electronics and the manufacture of such items as cigarette filters, women's clothes, meat pies and metal tanks. Recently a large chain of northern night clubs was launched here. The port runs from Jarrow Quay to Souter Point 3 m. S. and the great Tyne Dock handles iron ore for the works at CONSETT, as well as other cargoes. The town gives a strong impression of pulling down and putting up as dreary terraces yield to modern housing. Like several other Durham industrial areas, South Shields has its breezy escape, in this case to a variety of sea-front parks, long sandy beaches and a broad grassland known as the Leas along the Coast Road. There is a thoughtfully planned garden for the blind with flowers chosen for their scent and shrubs labelled in Braille. The Marine and Technical College is a notable centre for the study of marine engineering and navigation. The Museum exhibits the original model of the first self-righting lifeboat, invented by William Wouldhave in 1789. A memorial to him and Henry Greathead, the shipbuilder, stands at the sea end of Ocean Road. The world's first lifeboat service began here in 1790. Ocean Road-King Street cuts through the northern tip of the town. At the Tyne end is the small square 1768 Town Hall, with an arcade round the ground floor and an upper room ornamented by Venetian windows. Twice-weekly markets are held in the large Market Place outside, near the rail, bus and North Shields ferry terminals. Also nearby is a late-18th-cent. church, St Hilda's. The 20th-cent. Baroque municipal buildings in Westoe Road have been called "the most convincing expression in the county of Edwardian prosperity". An island of good Georgian and Victorian houses survives in Westoe Village, on either side of a long green. No visit is complete without a call at the Roman fort, Arbeia, on the Lawe at the north end of Baring Street. Although surrounded by houses and a

school, it is quite possible to imagine from the excavated evidence the great supply base this was in the early 3rd cent. There were nine large well-ventilated graneries, an imposing headquarters, barracks and offices. In the 4th cent., four granaries were converted to quarters for the garrison which now included experienced Tigris lightermen. They took ship cargoes by boat upriver to Wallsend and beyond. In the museum on the site, see the two famous tombstones. One commemorates Victor, a 20-year-old Moor and ex-slave of a Roman trooper, pictured in paradise being handed a cup of wine. The other depicts Regina, a native Briton who was enslaved then freed and married by a Syrian soldier. She is shown in a wicker chair with her jewel box and sewing basket to hand. For a good view of water-front activity, take the River Drive curving NE. from the Market Place.

STAINDROP, *Durham* (15–NZ1220). St Mary's is an exceptionally interesting church and not solely because of the many monuments to the Neville family of nearby **Raby Castle**. The blocked round-headed windows in the upper nave walls indicate an earlier Anglo-Saxon church. The west tower is Norman and the aisles and arcades were added in about 1170. A century later, the north transept was added, with a two-story priest's dwelling, now the vestry, and the east chancel. The south aisle and porch were built in 1343. In the 15th cent. the tower was heightened and clerestory and flat nave roof added. It is an architectural text spanning some six centuries. The church has the only pre-Reformation screen in the county. Among the numerous effigies is a battered alabaster tomb-chest of 1425 bearing the figures of Ralph Neville and two wives. Other monuments, which overflow into a mausoleum, date from the 13th to 19th cents. The village grew up beside the castle and has a single street with a very long green between two lines of houses, some 18th-cent. and earlier.

The full splendour of a medieval stronghold can be seen in the castle, the seat of the Nevilles for two centuries and in the hands of the Vanes since the early 17th cent. It is open two afternoons a week. It stands superbly in a great park of 270 acres with gardens, deer and two lakes. The fortress is built round a courtyard and encircled by a moat. Its notable features include the Neville gateway, which allowed carriages to drive inside and stop near an inner stair, and the nine distinctive towers. The highest of these is the Clifford, 80 ft high, and the others are known as Joan, Kitchen, Bulmer, Watch, Chapel, Raskelf, Keep and Neville. Although it existed as early as 1016, and has been altered in later years, the castle looks essentially 14th-cent. Much history was made here. In the vast Baron's Hall, the Rising of the North, intended to put Mary on the throne in place of Queen Elizabeth, was planned on 13 November 1569. It failed, and the castle was forfeited to the Crown. In addition to portraits by Lely, Reynolds, Kneller and others, the castle contains interesting furniture and ceramics. The octagonal drawing-room is said to be the finest Victorian drawing-room in the country. The kitchen has a smoke-driven spit and the stables house a fine array of carriages.

STAMFORDHAM, *Northumberland* (14–NZ 0772). Recent additions do not detract from the 18th-cent. feeling of the village with its rows of houses confronting each other across a long, bare village green. Between them is the plain little 1736 market cross. St Mary's Church, the oldest structure here, has a tower, chancel and priest effigy (possibly the oldest in Northumberland) all dating from the 13th cent. Interesting parts of medieval coffin covers are inserted in the porch. The church had extensive work done on it in 1848.

STANHOPE, *Durham* (14–NY9939), the "capital" of Weardale, lies high in the moorland with fells reaching more than 2,000 ft towards the SW. Weardale is a quiet holiday haven, an old lead-mining centre which is now more concerned with farming, quarrying and visitors. The area, still rich in beauty-spots, walks and drives, once provided good hunting for medieval knights and princes of the Church. There are plentiful caravan and camping sites. Stanhope itself is memorable for its lime trees, the Old Rectory, which was built in 1697 and rebuilt as it was in 1821, the 18th-cent. castle, and St Thomas's Church, with the market cross at its gate. The church dates from 1200. In the sanctuary hang two interesting Flemish carved oak plaques (one showing Adam and Eve and the other Christ baptizing St Peter) and a painting, probably also Flemish. The old stone font is thought to be Anglo-Saxon. The Victorian font is of Frosterley marble and local marble also borders the altar dais. Stanhope Castle, fronting the market place, was rebuilt in 1798 on a medieval foundation. It is now an approved school for boys. A Roman altar discovered in the 18th cent. on Bollihope Common is in the choir vestry. The giant stump of a fossilized tree can be seen through a gap in the churchyard wall. At the west side of town, a path up Stanhope Dene leads through a wooded gorge to **Heathery Burn Cave**, where in 1843 men building a tramway for a limestone quarry broke into a cave from which a remarkable collection of Bronze Age tools and weapons was taken in the next few years. The finds are now in the British Museum. They are believed to be relics of a wealthy family which took refuge in the cave and was drowned when the waters rose rapidly. Among the articles found were spearheads, axes, a gold bracelet, a bronze bucket, and cheek pieces and a bit which pointed to the first use of domesticated horses and wheeled vehicles in Britain.

STOCKTON-ON-TEES, *Durham* (15–NZ 4419), since 1968 administratively part of Teesside, is famous for an open-air market which started in 1310. It is still held on Wednesdays and Saturdays in the broadest High Street in England. There are some 175 open-air stalls and 75 more in a covered market building called the Shambles.

Stanhope: lies in the high moorland country of Weardale   Kenneth Scowen

On an island in the street is the 18th-cent. red-brick Town Hall. History was made in Stockton when the world's first railway passenger train steamed in on the afternoon of 27 September 1825. The same century saw its development as a ship-building and engineering centre. Its factories have diversified in the 20th cent. St Thomas's Church, a spacious red-brick edifice built in 1710–12, is supposed to have had the benefit of Sir Christopher Wren's advice. It was here that John Walker, a chemist, invented the friction match in 1827. He made and sold them at his shop for a couple of years and then left the exploitation of his idea to others. Thomas Sheraton was born here in 1731, but he made his name after he moved to London.

SUNDERLAND, *Durham* (15–NZ3957). The county's largest town (pop. 220,000) grew out of three settlements at Wearmouth: MONKWEAR-MOUTH, N. of the river under the monks of DURHAM; Bishopwearmouth on the south bank, which belonged to the Bishop of Durham; and Sunderland to the E., which had been "sundered" from the monastery founded in 674. Although its origins are ancient, the town achieved size only with the Industrial Revolution and it is today undergoing another kind of renewal. It claims, for example, to have built more new houses per head of population than any county borough in Britain since the Second World War. The visitor can read the story in the new estates forming a wide outer fringe and the belt of dingy commercial and domestic building surrounding the old centre. This has been a ship-building and coal-exporting town since the 14th cent. Glass-making became the first other industry in the 17th cent. The 18th cent. brought potteries, a theatre and the Wear-mouth Bridge (replaced in 1929). This was one of the first cast-iron bridges, and the biggest, with a span of 236 ft. It was originally designed by Thomas Paine, author of *The Rights of Man*, for Philadelphia, Pa. The 19th cent. was one of rapid growth and booming trade with new docks, the railway, the development of marine engines, and the erection of numerous undistinguished public buildings. It is famous today for a first division football team, but it lives on its ship-building, marine engineering and great variety of new manufacturing. It still makes traditional stained glass but also modern ovenproof glassware. It has created a new shopping centre with a hotel, walkways, car parks, offices and flats. Sir Basil Spence designed the £3 million new civic centre near Mowbray Park.

Sunderland prides itself on a reputation for friendly, civic-minded and forward-looking people. It pioneered in developing the Empire Theatre (now leased to a private operator) as a social service to bring the arts to the people, with opera, films, ballet and drama, drawing large audiences. Its technical college was the first in the country to offer sandwich courses. The Museum contains an important collection of local pottery and glass, including the Rowland Burdon collection of Sunderland lustre ware. There is also the James Wilson Collection of English silver from the 15th to the 19th cent. Models, paintings and prints of locally built ships are also on display. Other exhibits call attention to the inventions of native sons: Dr William Reid Clanny's miners' safety lamp and Sir Joseph Wilson Swan's electric lamp. To see Sunderland as a whole, go to Mow-bray Park in the centre where, near the bronze statue of General Sir Henry Havelock, hero of the Indian Mutiny (who was born at Ford Hall nearby), there is a panoramic view of town, docks and sea. ROKER and Seaburn on the northern edge of modern Sunderland give the populace its own seaside resort area.

TWIZEL, *Northumberland* (14–NT8743). Some 5 m. S. of NORHAM, a historic bridge in a wooded setting marks the confluence of the Rivers Till and Tweed. The bridge is thought to be 15th-cent. It is narrow and unusually high (46 ft) with a 90-ft span. High up on the bank are the pathetic ruins of an 18th-cent. folly, Twizel Castle, with its back in a ploughed field. Sir Francis Blake began to build his medieval fortress about 1770. In 1812 it was five stories high but never finished. Much of its stone has gone into another house.

TYNEMOUTH, *Northumberland* (15–NZ 3468). A walk along the ¾-m. North Tyne Pier has been called a trip to sea without leaving land. It is an excellent vantage point for ship-watching or for viewing the priory ruins and the coastline. Tynemouth occupies the cliffs on the north side of the river mouth and it has been known as a seaside resort for at least 200 years. It had a rapid growth in the 19th cent. The haunting intermingled ruins of Tynemouth Priory and Castle stand on the crag above the North Tyne Pier. The surviving parts date from the 11th and 14th cents. and are in the custody of the Ministry of Public Building and Works. The priory succeeded an earlier 7th-cent. Anglo-Saxon monastery which was destroyed by the Danes in 865. Benedictines founded the later house. Visitors pass through the ruined gateway at the end of Front Street to reach the site where there are parts of the curtain wall, church nave and chancel.

Sheltered by the pier and the headland where the priory stands is Prior's Haven, a sandy cove used for sailing, boating and fishing. On the road above is the Tynemouth Volunteer Life Brigade headquarters and Watch House, containing a collection of relics from 19th-cent. wrecks. The country's first volunteer life brigade was established here in 1869. Near the Watch House is the huge Collingwood Monument, with a highly rewarding view from the top. It was erected in 1845 to Admiral Lord Collingwood who led the British fleet into battle at Trafalgar.

Tynemouth boasts that its Long Sands are one of the finest stretches of beach in the country. They are overlooked by a well-developed amusement centre and park.

Harriet Martineau lived at 57 Front Street from 1840 to 1845 and entertained there the literary lights of her day.

Durham Cathedral   Pix Photos

Industrial Tynemouth is concentrated in **North Shields**, and the two towns are visually almost inseparable. North Shields has a very long history of trades connected with the sea. The port activities of today include ship repairing, coal bunkering, and passenger services to the Scandinavian countries. The fish quay and market attract many visitors. In Northumberland Square is a life-size figure of a CULLERCOATS fishwife known as Wooden Dolly. John Dobson, the NEWCASTLE architect, was born at North Shields in 1787.

USHAW, *Durham* (15–NZ2143). The Roman Catholic St Cuthbert's College stands on a 600-ft hill W. of DURHAM. It was opened here in 1808 by refugees from the seminary founded in Douai in 1568 and destroyed in the French Revolution. Most of the 400 students in residence are training for the priesthood. Francis Thompson, the poet, attended the college. The first buildings were classical in design. Numerous changes and additions in the later 19th cent. were in the neo-Gothic style. The chief architects were A. W. N. Pugin and his son, and Joseph and Charles Hansom. The main buildings surround a quadrangle and include the elaborate and colourful Chapel of St Cuthbert. There is a large library and cloisters and several smaller chapels are also provided. The community is virtually self-sufficient, supplying much of its own food, quarrying its own stone and making its own furniture. Visitors may see it by arrangement.

WALLINGTON HALL, *Northumberland* (14–NZ0384). In the Wansbeck valley, about 1 m. below the pretty village of **Cambo**, stands Wallington Hall, a late 17th-cent. mansion. Together with 13,000 acres and most of the village it was given to the National Trust in 1941 by Sir Charles Trevelyan. It is one of the most distinguished and probably the most popular of the Northumberland stately homes open to the public. The hall was preceded by a border castle and then a 15th-cent. house which was pulled down by Sir William Blackett, a NEWCASTLE merchant, when he built the present elegant buff sandstone residence in 1688. Forty years later, Sir Walter Blackett devoted himself to improving the house and its unprepossessing and largely treeless neighbourhood. He planted woods and hedges and built roads and bridges. He enhanced the hall with staircases and beautiful plasterwork, done by a resident team of Italian *stuccatori* whose masterpiece is the great saloon with its deep coved ceiling. He added stables, cottages and the clock tower to the estate. The gardens were designed by Capability Brown, who began his professional career as a gardener here. Sir Walter died in 1777 and the hall went to his sister, a Trevelyan by marriage.

The next great changes came in 1855 when Pauline Lady Trevelyan, who had made the hall a gathering place for the literary and artistic figures of the day, was persuaded by John Ruskin to cover the central court for a picture gallery, lighted through a glass roof. The arcading formed recesses in which William Bell Scott, a Newcastle pre-Raphaelite, painted the story of Northumberland: the building of the Roman wall; St Cuthbert; the death of Bede; the invasion of the Danes; the legend of the spur in the dish; Gilpin as the North's apostle; the heroism of Grace Darling; and the final (1861) entrance of the coal and iron age. The hall contains a number of important paintings, including one of Luther by Cranach, and family portraits by Sir Joshua Reynolds and Gainsborough; a collection of Chinese porcelain and a fine library collected by Sir George Otto Trevelyan, the statesman and historian. Also here are books of his uncle, Lord Macaulay, and the latter's writing table. Macaulay wrote much of his *History of the American Revolution* at Wallington.

Appropriately for a seat of a family with a long tradition of public service and learning, the hall has been used for many weekend schools and had the county's first youth hostel.

Cambo on the ridge-top was created as model village in 1740 and is almost unchanged. Its oldest building is the post office-general store which includes a medieval fortified vicarage. Capability Brown, born at KIRKHARLE, went to school here. The church was built in 1842. It has a slender spire and several window memorials to Macaulays and Trevelyans.

A charming arched bridge across the Wansbeck beyond the hall was designed by James Paine about 1760.

WARK-ON-TYNE, *Northumberland* (14–NY 8576). A great horse chestnut tree stands in the centre of the green in this pleasant village on the North Tyne. It was a larger place at one time and can trace its history at least to 788 when it is believed to have been the scene of the murder of the "just and pious" King Alfwald of Northumbria. The Normans had a castle here but only a turf-covered earthwork remains on the river bank. The village itself is particularly charming when seen as a huddle of roofs from the narrow iron bridge that crosses the stream. On the east side of the river, 1½ m. from the village, Chipchase Castle can be seen from the road. The present mansion consists of a 1621 building added to a medieval tower. When it was the capital of Tynedale, Wark (meaning work or earthwork) was the scene of courts held by Scottish kings.

WARKWORTH, *Northumberland* (15–NU 2306). The castle dominates the town from a hill up which the main road angles and climbs. When traffic entered from the N. through a narrow medieval bridge and gatehouse arch, the effect was even more dramatic than today when a new bridge over the Coquet sweeps motorists easily into the centre. The 14th-cent. bridge is now for pedestrians only. The village itself is of interest with terraces of 18th- and 19th-cent. houses built in grey stone with red roofs. It still looks as if it were clinging to the protection of the great stronghold. It is, in fact, tightly packed on a

Seahouses: the harbour   Kenneth Scowen

A. F. Kersting

Warkworth Castle was one of the most important in the north of England

peninsula of the river, with the castle guarding the neck and the sea within earshot. St Laurence's Church is the only fairly complete Norman church in the county. It has five Norman windows in the nave, a highly decorated chancel arch and vaulted chancel ceiling, and a rare 14th-cent. stone spire. There is a 15th-cent. priest's room over the porch. The church has a well-preserved effigy of a cross-legged knight of about 1330.

Warkworth, near the mouth of the Coquet, has a sandy beach only 1 m. away and fishing and boating in the river. You can travel by boat from the castle (or follow a shady path) upstream to the

Hermitage, an unusual refuge dug into the face of the bluff by some hermit in the 14th cent. Not much is known about him, but he hollowed out a chapel and two living chambers on two floors connected by steps. Hermits lived here into the 16th cent. The hermitage belongs to the Ministry of Public Building and Works as does the castle. Coquet Island offshore was also supposed to be the retreat of solitary monks.

The castle is the most splendid ruin of its type in Northumberland. It has not been extensively restored as were the castles at BAMBURGH and ALNWICK. The first fortification on the site was probably in 1139, with a curtain wall added in the early 13th cent. The chief building period came in the late 14th and early 15th cent. and a good deal remains from this, including the highly impressive keep. The castle came into the hands of the Percys in the 14th cent. and remained theirs for some 600 years.

WASHINGTON, *Durham* (15–NZ3056). A new town is rising upon this former colliery village. Streets of old miners' houses have been demolished, pit-head buildings converted to a museum, and the pit heap moved away. The population eventually will be 80,000. All this is taking place round the original town centre where stands the Old Hall, a medieval building greatly altered in the 17th cent. It housed the ancestors of George Washington, first president of the United States. The Washingtons, under many spellings of the name, were lords of the manor here from 1183 to 1376, when they moved to Sulgrave in Northamptonshire. Their arms, three stars and two stripes, provided the inspiration for the American flag. Gifts from America helped restore the hall, a National Trust property, which is open daily and also serves as a centre for local social events.

WHALTON, *Northumberland* (15–NZ1281). This is the only community in the county known to keep the ancient rite of the bale fire on 4 July, the old Midsummer Eve. The tradition has been observed here for probably 1,400 years, since the Angles originated it. "Bale" is from an Anglo-Saxon word for great fire. It is thought to have been the custom to drive cattle through the fire to purify them or rid them of vermin and at one time the villagers themselves used to jump into the flames. Within living memory, people carried burning branches from the fire around the fields to protect against blight and around houses to fend off witches. Some took home the ashes from the fire for good luck.

Whalton is an exceptionally pretty and well-kept village, laid out along a broad street with stone houses and bright gardens on either side. At the east end is the Manor House, which was four village houses until they were combined and converted by Sir Edwin Lutyens in 1909. The gardens there are sometimes open to visitors.

St Mary Magdalene Church, S. of the main street, although much restored in modern times, retains some interesting early-13th-cent. features. One is a square pier in the north chancel arcade which is made up of four shafts with huge segments of dogtooth carving running vertically between them.

WHITBURN, *Durham* (15–NZ4061). An old custom here, but reported, alas, to be dying out, was the offering of a "hot pot" composed of mulled ale and spirits to newly married couples as they left the parish church. The church itself, a coastal landmark, is early 13th-cent., but with heavy-handed Victorian restoration. The village lies between SUNDERLAND and SOUTH SHIELDS, and has a pleasant sycamore-shaded green. Whit-

burn Hall is a rambling building with parts attributed to the 17th and 19th cents. Whitburn House, 19th cent., has a Perpendicular window from St John's Church, NEWCASTLE-UPON-TYNE, in the garden.

WHITLEY BAY, *Northumberland* (15–NZ 3572). Most of the beaches on Northumberland's lovely coast are lightly used and stretches often lie empty, but not so at Whitley Bay, the most popular of the resorts. It is too close to industrial Tyneside, in easy reach for a day's outing. The beach with its grassy banks runs the length of the town. Among the entertainments provided for holidaymakers are one of the North East's biggest amusement parks, a children's sandpit and pool, an ice-skating rink, a bowling club and two miniature golf courses. A full-size golf course has been built over the site of an opencast working. The sea-angling festival here each autumn is the largest in Europe. St Mary's Island lying off the north end of the bay can be reached by foot at low tide or by boat otherwise. Its white lighthouse is a seamark.

WHITTINGHAM, *Northumberland* (14–NU 0611). This inviting village is divided by the River Aln and connected by a fine stone arch for motorists and a pretty footbridge for pedestrians. It was, in olden times, the location of a famous fair (and still holds a games day near 24 August, St Bartholomew's day). On one side of the village is St Bartholomew's Church, where in 1840 an Anglo-Saxon tower was destroyed to make way for one in the Gothic fashion. It has some surviving interior Norman and 13th-cent. features. On the opposite side of the Aln is a peel-tower dating from the 15th cent. Its battlemented top overlooks a new housing estate. Unused now, the tower belonged to Lord Ravensworth of Eslington and existed as early as 1415. In 1845 the tower long used by villagers for refuge "in times of rapine and insecurity" was converted by Lady Ravensworth into an almshouse. There Henry Ogle, inventor of the reaping machine, was born in 1765. He died in ALNWICK workhouse in 1848. Attractive stone houses and shops enclose a small tree-shaded green. CALLALY CASTLE is only 2 m. away.

WINSTON, *Durham* (15–NZ1416). To walk into the shady churchyard of St Andrew's standing on an airy height above the Tees, is to enter an earlier, more peaceful world. The church is a little apart from the village proper. It dates from 1254, with changes made in 1848. There is a small bell-turret, but no tower. Inside is a wide, light chancel with lancet windows, and a trefoiled piscina with nutmeg ornament. Two other interesting windows also light this area, one round-headed and the other slightly pointed, both narrow and both with mouldings around them. The 13th-cent circular stone font deserves a close look. The date of the carving puzzles experts. The subjects shown are two Celtic-headed dragons biting each other, a flower and oak leaves.

WITTON-LE-WEAR, Durham (15–NZ1431). Witton Castle outside the village is almost best known as the home of Sir Thomas Lawrence's painting of Master Lambton, *The Red Boy*. The castle was erected by Ralph de Eure in the 15th cent. and although much altered by rebuilding in the 18th and 19th cents., still presents a romantic front from its valley site, well framed in trees. The castle grounds have become probably one of the county's prettiest caravan and camping places, with woods and stream to give a sense of solitude. The castle was crenellated in 1410. In 1689 it was partially dismantled and the material auctioned. In the early 18th cent. it was rebuilt only to suffer some time afterwards a disastrous fire that took all but the outer walls, tower house and turrets. The living quarters were rebuilt once more.

There is a good view of the castle from the triangular village green which occupies a hillside above the River Wear. Here the Church of SS. Philip and James, of Norman foundation, was rebuilt in 1902. On the north side of town is Witton Tower, a private residence, which incorporates a medieval tower house and even older chapel.

WOLSINGHAM, Durham (14–NZ0737). To travellers approaching from the E., Wolsingham is the entrance to some of the finest Weardale scenery. It is sturdily built of stone with a rather prim town hall standing on its own in a small market place. Its chief industry is the large steelworks on the outskirts. This is a good walking centre and Tunstall Reservoir on Waskerley Beck to the N. is a good hunting-ground for birds and flowers. The Parish Church of SS. Mary and Stephen has a late-12th-cent. west tower with the rest 19th cent., in pseudo-Early English style. The sanctuary and chancel are marble-floored, partly in the Frosterley marble of Weardale. The church owns three chained books (not on display). The Grammar School on the west side of town opened in 1911. In Chapel Garth are the bare remains of a moated residence, Chapel Walls.

WOOLER, Northumberland (14–NT9928), is a workaday town, but a welcome sight to travellers in the thinly populated Glendale district it serves. It has an unusual number of shops, some 50 for a population of 2,000, since it is the market place for a large sheep-farming and forestry area around. The natural centre for exploring or angling in the CHEVIOT HILLS, it is a breezy place, nicely set above the Milfield plain with the great Cheviot in its background. The town suffered frequent raids in the Middle Ages and destructive fires in 1722 and again in 1862, so there are few buildings of much age. The oldest church building is Presbyterian, founded in 1700. At one time there were three Presbyterian churches at Wooler. It has always been a grey-stone town and it must be said that newer buildings of pantile roofs, stucco and smooth red brick strike a jarring note.

There are many fine walks from Wooler. One of 2½ m. leads to the prehistoric Kettle's Camp and the wishing well, Pin Well, S. of it. The Happy Valley along Colegate Burn involves a 6-m. return walk. Many visitors like to climb Humbleton Hill, just 1 m. away, to see the terrace fortifications, cairn and fine view.

A plaque on Victoria Villas in Queen's Road records the death here in 1906 of Josephine Butler, fighter for women's education and legal rights, who is buried at KIRKNEWTON.

WORM HILL, Durham (15–NZ3053). Near Fatfield, just off the A182 S. of WASHINGTON, is a small mound near a bridge, associated with the most famous of the many "loathly worm" legends in County Durham. There is a little war memorial there now, but the mound recalls, for those who enjoy folk tales, the story of the heir of the Lambtons who, while fishing in the Wear, hooked a small worm and threw it into a nearby well. There it grew to enormous proportions, and then spent part of its time coiled (nine times) round Worm Hill and part of the time wound round a crag in the river. Unless it were daily fed the milk of nine cows, it would devour any living creature it could find. The young Lambton returned from the Crusades to find the countryside terrified. He tried to kill the worm by cutting through it, but the worm had the knack of joining its parts as new. Finally, the young man decided to consult a wise woman who told him to don a coat of mail covered with razors and await the worm on its river crag. The worm soon wrapped itself round Lambton and was cut to bits, which drifted away in the water before they could be reunited. In return for the advice, Lambton had promised to kill the first thing he saw after the slaying. He had arranged with his father to send a dog out to meet him at his signal. But the father, happy at his son's success, rushed out himself. Lambton did not carry out his pledge, and the wise woman decreed that for nine generations no Lambton would die in his bed. And none did. "Worm" here seems to have its old meaning of serpent or dragon. The tale may hark back to pagan Anglo-Saxon or Norse dragon-slaying legends which later become localized and acquired Christian elements.

WYLAM-ON-TYNE, Northumberland (15–NZ1164). New housing for the workers of NEWCASTLE 8 m. away is filling the outskirts of this village on the last rural stretch of the River Tyne. It goes into history because it is the birthplace of the famous engineer and railwayman, George Stephenson. The 18th-cent. miner's cottage in which he was born in 1781 (and where he lived as a child) was given to the National Trust by the North-East Coast Institution of Engineers and Shipbuilders, but it is not open to the public. The house, known as High Street House, stands beside a line which, in Stephenson's time, was a waggon-way carrying coal waggons on wooden rails from the local colliery. In 1813 on this line William Hedley tried out his pioneer locomotive and namesake, Puffing Billy.

Barnaby

Witton-le-Wear: a view of the river

The North-West

Cheshire   Lancashire   Westmorland   Cumberland

PETER FLEETWOOD-HESKETH

England's North-West comprises the counties of Cheshire, Lancashire, West-morland and Cumberland. Each has its history and individuality, upon which rests the loyalty of its people. Those who would arbitrarily redraw the boundaries of these ancient territories may not realize what they would be destroying or how bitterly such tampering would be resented and resisted.

The entire region is bounded on the east by the Pennine Chain and on the west by the hills of North Wales and the Irish Sea. Between these are smaller ranges of hills in central Cheshire and Lancashire, and the larger Cumbrian group in the north, which includes Sca Fell Pike (3,210 feet), the highest point in England. The rest is relatively low-lying country, mostly in the south, becoming extremely flat along the Lancashire coast.

The principal rivers of the North-West, from south to north, are the Dee, Mersey, Ribble, Lune and Eden. The Mersey separates Cheshire from Lancashire, but through both now passes the M6 motorway, revealing their landscape to great advantage and leading northwards to the mountainous Lake District which is shared between Lancashire, Westmorland and Cumberland. Of the many lakes in this region Ullswater is the most spectacular, Derwentwater the most picturesque, Wastwater the most sombre, and Windermere the most frequented.

Agriculturally, Cheshire is both pastoral and arable, Lancashire mainly arable in the south, becoming more pastoral towards the north, where it meets West-morland and Cumberland, which are both predominantly pastoral. Forestry on a large scale is now an important industry in all four counties.

Throughout the North-West stone is the traditional building material in the hilly country – red sandstone in the south and north, millstone grit in the east, and limestone in the centre. In the flat country timber was the basic building material until the introduction of brick in the sixteenth century.

Of the ancient capitals and county towns, Chester and Carlisle retain their cathedrals (the latter much reduced in the Civil War), while Lancaster and Appleby are still dominated by their somewhat remodelled medieval castles.

Modern industry is mainly concentrated in the southern part of the region, where coal has been mined in Lancashire from very early times and salt in Cheshire. Among the Pennine Hills the cotton industry developed logically from the wool trade. Some of the earliest developments of the Industrial Revolution were born north and south of the Mersey, eventually to form an industrial band from York-shire to the Irish Sea, with the great cities of Manchester in the east and Liverpool in the west. The Weaver Navigation scheme was undertaken in the eighteenth century to provide an outlet to the Mersey for the salt, mined in central Cheshire, while soon afterwards the Sankey (1755–60) and Bridgewater (1759–65) Canals, the earliest of modern canals, were constructed to serve a similar purpose for the Lancashire coalfields. Here, too, we find the world's first great railway, from Manchester to Liverpool, opened in 1830.

Yet this industrialized region possesses numerous examples of the finer arts: two fine monuments by the younger John Bacon in the parish church of Runcorn, signed and dated 1792 and 1796; and, at Widnes, others by Chantrey and Tenerani in Farnworth church; or Alkrington Hall, four miles north of the centre of Manchester, recently identified as an authentic work of the Venetian architect, Giacomo Leoni.

Cheshire is a county of prosperous farms and large estates. Its roads are good, but inadequately signposted. Chester, of ancient origin, is the capital. It stands on the Dee, near the Welsh border, and its buildings range from the medieval city walls and cathedral, timber-framed Tudor houses and those of Georgian brick, to the great sandstone castle, rebuilt about 1800 in Classic style by Thomas Harrison, who later bridged the Dee here with a single arch of 200-foot span; the handsome Italianate railway station; a fine Gothic town hall of 1869 and the later Victorian work of John Douglas. Threading through the two main streets are the "Rows" – covered footways at first-floor level.

Birkenhead is a modern seaport (though it has an ancient priory) on the flat Wirral peninsula separating the Dee from the Mersey, on whose opposite bank is Liverpool. Crewe, in the south, is also modern, an important railway and industrial town. Among the older, smaller towns, Frodsham, Tarporley and Malpas are as well endowed as any with their legacy of inherited charm.

Cheshire is remarkable for its handsome churches, of which there are many, its ancient castles such as Beeston and Halton – both of them spectacular ruins perched high above the surrounding country – and some great houses. Dunham Massey, near Altrincham, and Lyme, high up on the edge of the Derbyshire moors, are quadrangular Elizabethan houses remodelled (the former almost rebuilt) early in the eighteenth century. Adlington, near Macclesfield, is also an ancient quadrangle with a fifteenth-century timber hall and brick Georgian additions. Doddington, Tabley and Tatton are later Georgian, and there are similar and smaller houses of that era. Peckforton and Cholmondeley are grand nineteenth-century castles; Hawarden Castle is of various dates, while Capesthorne is an early Victorian-Jacobean rebuilding of a burnt Georgian house. Grandest of all, but now largely demolished, is Eaton Hall, built in 1870–82 for the 1st Duke of Westminster by Alfred Waterhouse in robust Victorian Gothic.

In north-east Cheshire there are prosperous suburbs of Manchester at Altrincham and Hale, and beyond Stockport a tongue of hilly, romantic and half-industrial country forming a wedge between Lancashire, Derbyshire and the West Riding of Yorkshire. Lower down the Mersey, at Runcorn, is some of Cheshire's finest scenery. Resembling a miniature Mont Saint Michel, the village of Halton clusters round its lofty ruined castle, its high-roofed Victorian church and eighteenth-century court house. The noble water-tower at Norton stands like a temple on the skyline; and in the west the rugged escarpments of Frodsham and Helsby Crag stand out against the western sky. But at the moment of writing this landscape is being bulldozed out of existence to make way for Runcorn New Town. Twenty-seven good Cheshire farms are disappearing in the process.

At this point we may pass from Cheshire into Lancashire by crossing the magnificent new bridge which brings us over the Mersey into Widnes. North-east from the bridge can be seen the immense new power station at Fiddler's Ferry – an industrial building of vast dimensions, symmetrical in design and perfectly composed from every angle, which retains its elemental beauty through every change of light and shadow.

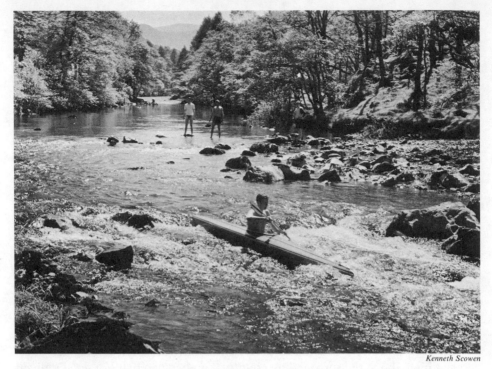

Kenneth Scowen

The Lake District: the River Derwent in Borrowdale

Lancashire has upwards of a hundred miles of coastline, of which at least thirty have been developed as holiday resorts – Southport, Blackpool, Fleetwood, Morecambe and Grange, to name only the chief ones. A further seven miles comprise the Liverpool docks.

Industry and commerce are mainly in the south of Lancashire, with Liverpool and Manchester as the principal centres. The latter is virtually joined to the East Lancashire manufacturing towns of Oldham, Rochdale, Bury, Bolton and Salford, which are interspersed with innumerable smaller ones. Blackburn, Accrington, Burnley, Nelson and Colne form the northern fringe of industrial Lancashire. Liverpool is almost joined to St Helen's, the seat of the glass-making industry.

The development of the Lancashire coast for recreation began in the eighteenth century, Southport and Blackpool being among the earliest places of resort. The latter was already popular locally in 1730. By 1788 it had fifty houses and four hundred visitors from Manchester at the height of the season. In Southport the first house was built in 1792 but the place did not receive its name till six years later, from Dr Barton of Hoole at a public dinner held there.

These remain the largest of the Lancashire coastal resorts, but many others have since grown up and indeed joined up, all providing for the recreational needs not only of Lancastrians from the more industrial districts but for visitors from elsewhere. To Southport, the first "Garden City", soon was added Birkdale and then Ainsdale, to form a quiet, dignified and rather opulent town largely used by commuters with business in Manchester and Liverpool. Its wide streets are well laid out as tree-lined avenues. The sea, however, has tended to withdraw from this part of the coast as much as it has tried to erode further north.

Blackpool fulfils a rather different rôle, and though it has its permanent popula-

G. Douglas Bolton

A great house in Cheshire: Lyme Hall was remodelled in the 18th century

tion, its prosperity depends largely upon its enormous holiday trade, as well as great political conferences. The sea air at Blackpool is strong and invigorating – somewhat flavoured with fish and chips – in marked contrast to the more relaxing air and genteel atmosphere of Southport.

Now practically joining Blackpool southwards are St Anne's, Fairhaven, Ansdell (named after the Lancashire painter who lived there) and Lytham, an older place, more dignified and less pretentious than some of its neighbours. North of Blackpool is Fleetwood, founded in 1836 to provide a rail and sea link with Ireland and Scotland, and a seaside resort for industrial East Lancashire. It is now chiefly known for its fishing fleets, and might be called the Grimsby of the West Coast. Further north still is Morecambe, whose chief asset is its magnificent view over the Bay to the fells of Cartmel and Furness. On the other side is Grange-over-Sands, a pleasant place of Victorian retirement.

From south to north through Lancashire, along the old Roman road, stand the ancient towns of Warrington, Wigan, Preston (the capital) and Lancaster (the county town). M6 runs close to this route to a point north of Carnforth where it rejoins the old road to Kendal. West of the motorway the land flattens out towards the sea, while to the east it rises gently to the Pennine Chain which forms the frontier with Yorkshire.

North-west, over Morecambe Bay, is the detached part of Lancashire comprising Cartmel and Furness, formerly connected by the coach route over Cartmel Sands. This is the most picturesque part of the county and forms a large part of the Lake District, including the lake of Coniston and its fell, called the "Old Man" – the highest point in the county (2,633 feet) – and more than two-thirds of the shores of Lake Windermere. In the Furness peninsula are the old towns of Ulverston,

The River Mersey at Liverpool

Dalton and Broughton, and the modern ship-building port of Barrow.

Of Lancashire's ancient towns, Lancaster, with its castle, priory church and Georgian streets, is the only one that can claim consistent over-all beauty, though Clitheroe and Broughton-in-Furness have the same quality in a lesser degree. Other towns, however, have buildings or groups of buildings of very high quality that make some compensation for their shortcomings. Liverpool possesses two buildings – the town hall and St George's Hall – which rank among the most beautiful in the world in the Classic tradition, which is magnificently continued in Preston's Harris Library, Museum and Gallery (1882–93). The town halls of Manchester and Rochdale represent the height of Victorian Gothic, while that of Warrington is a perfect Georgian house designed by James Gibbs.

The most important monastic remains in Lancashire are the abbeys of Furness and Whalley, and the priory church of Cartmel, its greatest parish church. Great houses include Towneley Hall, now a museum, Stonyhurst, a public school since 1794, and Hoghton Tower. These are mainly pre-1600. Later in their present form are Croxteth and Knowsley. The castles of Thurland and Hornby are of ancient foundation, though both considerably rebuilt. Among Victorian houses the most important architecturally is Scarisbrick, remodelled in the Gothic style by the Pugins for Charles and Anne Scarisbrick between 1836 and 1870; and Holker is perhaps the most charmingly situated. Both incorporate parts of earlier houses, while Leighton Hall, near Carnforth, a house of many dates, with its "Gothick" front of white stone and mountainous background, provides a piece of breath-taking scenery that has no rival in the county.

Besides these, Lancashire still has a number of lesser country houses – "semistatelies" and even the occasional "mini-stately" – but their number has diminished as the families which were their *raison d'être* have died or departed. Like Cheshire, Lancashire has some important timber-framed houses, of which Speke Hall (1500–98), near Liverpool, is one of the most complete, while Rufford Old Hall has the finest fifteenth-century open-roofed great hall.

Westmorland embodies both banks of the Leven estuary, thereby separating Cartmel and Furness from the rest of Lancashire. It includes a large part of the Lake District, with all the mountains and fells from Windermere to Ullswater, while high rolling country stretches away eastwards to make a long frontier with Yorkshire and a short one with Durham. Appleby, in the north-east, is the county town. It has a pleasant wide main street leading up to the gates of the castle, which retains its Norman keep but was otherwise rebuilt in the seventeenth century. It was one of several owned by Lady Anne Clifford (1590–1676), whose tomb and that of her mother are in the church. Kendal (the capital) is a much larger place – the metropolis of the Lake District. It is ancient but has a strongly Georgian flavour, and the ruins of a castle that was probably the birthplace of Catherine Parr. Here the country of Wordsworth and George Romney is entered, through Windermere and Ambleside to Grasmere. As everywhere in this northern region, the farm-houses are low and long and cling to the hillsides.

South of Kendal are the ancient houses of Levens Hall and Sizergh Castle. Near Milnthorpe is Dallam Tower, which is early Georgian. At Shap are the ruins of a medieval abbey and at Lowther the shell of an early nineteenth-century castle that remains a picturesque and commanding feature in a noble landscape. To the south is the eighteenth-century "model" village, well laid out but unfinished. A little to the north is the county boundary.

In Cumberland the first town reached by this route is Penrith, in open rolling country with views of the fells west and south, flattening out northwards to Carlisle, the capital. Westwards from here is the coast on the Solway Firth, and further south the coastal towns of Maryport, Workington and Whitehaven – the chief port in the north-west until overtaken by Liverpool, and an early coal-mining centre where some of the mines ran several miles under the sea. The north of Cumberland is relatively flat, but the south includes some of the most spectacular and magical scenery in the mountain group it shares with Westmorland and Lancashire.

Cumberland's greatest legacy from antiquity is, perhaps, the remains of the Roman Wall which was built in the second century A.D. and restored in the third. It crosses from west to east a little to the north of Carlisle. Next in antiquarian interest are the peel-towers, of which a number survive. Of the ancient religious establishments, Lanercost Priory and the ruins of Calder Abbey are the most important.

Naworth, near Brampton, is possibly the best-preserved ancient castle, and Muncaster, largely rebuilt by Salvin in the nineteenth century, the best situated. Among other castles, Dacre comprises an ancient keep; Greystoke near Penrith is chiefly remarkable for the follies that were built to enliven the views from its windows; Highhead was rebuilt in Georgian days and has recently been burnt; while Dalemain is a fine early Georgian house. Hutton-in-the-Forest is a highly romantic house of three main periods, romantically situated as its name suggests. And among the more picturesque smaller houses are Moresby Hall, north of Whitehaven, and Dalegarth, with its waterfall, in Eskdale. Irton Hall is built round a peel-tower in some of the loveliest country in West Cumberland.

The North-West: Gazetteer

J. B. WILLAN AND BETTY JAMES

ACTON, *Cheshire* (12–SJ6253), is in the neighbourhood of NANTWICH and has fine views over the countryside. St Mary's Church is mainly 13th- and 14th-cent., and its tower, rebuilt in the 18th cent., dominates the village. There are several monuments, including a knight in armour, and a beautiful 17th-cent. screen with rich gates.

ADLINGTON HALL, *Cheshire* (12–SJ8880). This magnificent old house, part Elizabethan timber-and-plaster and part brick from its restoration and enlargement in 1757, is sited on a pre-Norman hunting lodge built between two giant oak trees, the roots of which still support the east end of the 15th-cent. great hall. For 600 years the house has been in the hands of the Legh family, one of the oldest in Cheshire. Sir Uryan Legh, whose smiling portrait may be seen with others of the family collection, was knighted for his services under the Earl of Essex during the siege of Cadiz in 1596. A ballad of the time records that he captured a Spanish lady while he was there and treated her with such courtesy that she declined to be released and insisted on returning to England with him. How Sir Uryan resolved this difficulty is not known, but the gold chain she gave him as a memento of the encounter is included in the portrait. During the Civil War the Hall was strongly besieged for a fortnight and eventually taken by the Roundheads, leaving scars on the exterior apparent to this day. The older part of the house is beautiful for its black-and-white timbering. The gables and porch, the latter dating from 1581, face a wide courtyard and the open roof is mounted on hammer-beams decorated with angels. The Hall is still partly surrounded by an old moat, the whole structure standing in a fine park with one of Cheshire's noblest chestnut avenues. It is believed that Handel once played the organ which stands in the great hall and composed his *Harmonious Blacksmith* when a guest at the house. The organ was the work of Bernard Smith, or Schmidt, in *c.* 1670. Enlarged in the 18th cent., it was put out of action by children about 1800 and restored in the 1950s. Adlington Hall is open to the public.

ALSTON, *Cumberland* (14–NY7146). At Townfoot in Alston the milestone shows a height of 921 ft above sea-level, and not far up the main road it is 1,000 ft. This is the highest market town in England, and although Alston stands in the valley of the South Tyne it is almost surrounded by the highest fells of the Pennine Chain. Five roads converge: NEWCASTLE (A686), CARLISLE, PENRITH, the B6277 from Scotch Corner, and the B6293 from Weardale. Alston is a holiday centre, offering numerous walks in the sweeping moorland scenery. Variations of hardness in the limestone layers produce several waterfalls, such as Ashgill Force.

This was one of the richest mineral areas in Britain until the early 19th cent., with lead and silver, iron, zinc and copper ores and fluorspar. The only workings now are small anthracite drifts. Two Middle or Late Bronze Age barrows were found at Ayle; N., and near it the Roman mounds and ditches of Whitley Castle can be clearly seen. Some old buildings date from the late 17th and early 18th cents., when there was a renewal of mining operations, such as Church Gaytes House (1681) and the Quaker Meeting House (1732–59). The parish church, St Augustine's, built in 1869, is the third on the site and has records from 1154. The 1765 Market Cross, replacing an earlier one, has been knocked down by a lorry. Also of architectural interest are Kirkhaugh Church near Alston, and the Old Manor House on the HEXHAM road. Just W. of Alston runs the **Pennine Way**. It passes through Garrigill (to the SE. near the B6277), which may pre-date the earliest settlement in Alston. Eastward on the B6293 is Nenthead, 1,415 ft, the highest village in England. The Penrith road climbs SW. from Alston on **Hartside Height** to 1,903 ft, offering a panoramic view over the Eden valley: it ranges from Lakeland fells to Scottish hills, with the Solway Firth like a golden ribbon at sunset. Cross Fell, to the SSE., at 2,930 ft is the highest point of the Pennines. The road drops down Hartside with awe-inspiring zigzags to Melmerby.

The Hartside route is not one to choose in ice or snow. Winter is a time when the tourist may be unable to see Alston. He may reach only the north or east edges of the great white waste, since the famous Helm Wind from Cross Fell may have piled snow 15 ft or higher round the isolated town.

ALTRINCHAM, *Cheshire* (12–SJ7687). An industrial and residential centre close to MANCHESTER, but still retaining its own individuality. The town was first granted borough status by Hamon de Massey, Lord of Dunham, in 1290, implying partial relinquishment of the traditional powers of the lord of the manor. It is recorded that since 1452 more than 500 mayors have been elected to office here. Today Altrincham is often

Kenneth Scowen

Ambleside: the Bridge House

chosen as the starting-point for visits to the many beauty-spots in the neighbourhood. Within walking distance of the town, towards the SW., are picturesque villages, ancient churches, and broad stretches of placid water reaching for miles across the countryside. In the environs is Dunham Massey park, where some of the trees in the beech avenue are said to be over 250 years old and a herd of deer roams as it has for centuries past. Dunham Massey Hall, seat of the Earls of Stamford and their ancestors the Booths, is a fine, mainly 18th-cent. quadrangular house of brick and stone.

At **Ringway**, about 4 m. SE. of Altrincham, is Manchester Airport.

AMBLESIDE, *Westmorland* (14–NY3704), is, like KESWICK, a principal tourist centre in Lakeland, particularly for the more southerly areas. The town lies on the main north and south through route, the A591, close to WINDERMERE. Being protected by mountain groups from north and east winds, and open to warmer air from the S., Ambleside claims an equable temperature and, for the Lakes, a comparatively low rainfall, probably due to the fact that the nearest peaks to the SW., the CONISTON fells, are about 3 m. away. The town has many hotels and guest-houses, especially in the newer part, W. of the division made by the main road. Shops offer a variety of holiday equipment, gifts and souvenirs. A pottery shop is called Ruskin House; Ruskin

had close associations with the Lakes, especially Coniston.

In Borrans Park and owned by the National Trust, where the River Brathay enters Windermere, are remains of the Roman fort of Galava, probably built between the 2nd and 4th cents., and of an earlier one believed to be of about A.D. 79 during Agricola's campaign. The Roman road from Ravenglass on the west coast, via HARD-KNOTT, passed near Borrans Field and then over the ridge of High Street mountain range to BROUGHAM. Discoveries in the 21-acre field (open to the public) are in the museum at the Armitt Library. The library itself was endowed by Miss Mary Louisa Armitt, who left her books to it, and opened in 1912. It received the balance of funds of the old Ambleside Book Society (founded in 1828) to which Wordsworth belonged. There are now over 6,000 books and pamphlets in the library, many from donors, of literary, scientific and antiquarian value. The Ambleside Ruskin Library is also housed here.

The former parish church, now used as a parish hall, is of a typically primitive Lakeland type. Attractive old houses are perched around it on the hillside. The present parish church, St Mary the Virgin, on the W., was erected in 1854 to the design of Sir Gilbert Scott. He gave it a steeple – unusual in the Lakes – a handsome feature to be seen across the old roofs of the houses. There is a fine marble reredos. Memorial windows to

Wordsworth and his family are in the Wordsworth Chapel. The Bible on the lectern was given by Mrs Wordsworth. On the west wall a mural (1944) by Gordon Ransom depicts the ancient rush-bearing ceremony. The bearings are now crosses and designs in flowers and rushes, carried by children in a procession to St Mary's in late July. Owen Lloyd, a friend of Hartley Coleridge who was the son of Samuel Taylor Coleridge, composed the rush-bearing hymn which is sung in the Market Place. This ceremony, which has continued for centuries, is believed to derive from the annual renewal of rushes on the church floor in the Middle Ages, or to be a mixture of something like the Roman *floralia* and of a thanksgiving and merry-making to mark the safe gathering of the hay. At GRASMERE there is a similar ceremony, and both have been recorded by Wordsworth.

The tiny Bridge House is a curiosity, only a few yards long, which in the 18th cent. was probably a summer-house for Ambleside Hall. There are two rooms, and the house is now an information centre for the National Trust which bought it by subscription in 1928. The story is told that a Scotsman built this rough stone structure on its arch over the little river so that he could avoid paying ground rent!

Ambleside has many literary associations. The Wordsworths lived at nearby Grasmere and RYDAL, and besides Ruskin and the Coleridges, authors who visited or stayed in the area include Keats, Southey, De Quincey, and Mrs Humphrey Ward. Harriet Martineau, who died in Ambleside in 1876, lived at the Knoll, which is outside the town on the Keswick road. She was visited there by Charlotte Brontë and George Eliot. Along the River Rothay is Fox Howe, the summer residence of Dr Thomas Arnold, the headmaster of RUGBY School and father of Matthew Arnold. Nearby are the much photographed stepping stones across the river. Loughrigg Holme was the house of Wordsworth's daughter, Dora.

The town has sporting facilities, and in August the Ambleside Sports and the internationally famous sheepdog trials are held in Rydal Park. At Waterhead on the N. of Windermere is one of the great boating centres of Lakeland, with a car park. Other lakes within walking distance are ELTERWATER, RYDAL WATER, and Grasmere. There is a variety of routes to explore on foot. STOCK GHYLL is in the park, to the E. Signs from Waterhead lead to Jenkin's Crag with excellent views of Windermere and the mountains. For Loughrigg, *see* Grasmere. Sweden Bridge and Skelwith Force are other walks, as are Nab Scar and Fairfield (2,863 ft), both on the N. Besides the north and south roads for Keswick and WINDERMERE TOWN, other motoring routes are to the NE. for ULLSWATER (the direct route from Ambleside to the KIRKSTONE PASS is not advised for towing caravans), or W. for the LANGDALE PIKES, WRYNOSE PASS, or Coniston.

APPLEBY, *Westmorland* (14–NY6820), is the county town. It is set in the pleasant Eden valley, sheltered from much of the western rains by the LAKE DISTRICT mountains, on a well-drained site in a loop of the river by the A66. To the NE. the Pennines run like a wall for about 30 m. The area is rich in flora and fauna, and geological formations are diverse. Appleby has been an inhabited site for over 1,000 years but has none of the more ancient British remains whose builders, unlike the Anglo-Saxons and Vikings, seemed to prefer the higher land, such as around CROSBY RAVENSWORTH. Traces of the Roman road (BROUGH to KIRKBY THORE) can be seen on the E. but the first evidence of settlers is that of Norsemen in the 10th cent. The town was transferred from Scotland to England only in 1092; but suffered Scottish attacks later, culminating in that of 1388, which laid it waste.

The castle is a motte-and-bailey type of the 12th cent., the main eastern part having been rebuilt by Lord Clifford in 1454. A later member of his family, Lady Anne Clifford, dismantled and restored the castle (now a private residence) in the mid-17th cent. She became an important figure in the history of this part of Westmorland, and rebuilt her family's castles at Brough, BROUGHAM, and Pendragon (KIRKBY STEPHEN), as well as restoring churches in these places and in Appleby, building bridges and endowing almshouses.

Lady Anne's tomb is in St Lawrence's Church. This, the parish church, was rebuilt in the late 12th cent. after the Scots had burnt the earlier one. From that rebuilding there remains the tower's lower story, with its small original window, and the base of the chancel's east wall. There was more rebuilding in the 13th cent., the 15th, and by Lady Anne in the 17th. Most of the clerestory and upper walls are 15th-cent. The organ, formerly in CARLISLE Cathedral, is one of the three oldest in the country. St Michael's has Appleby's oldest stone monument, a Scandinavian hog-back gravestone, built into its north wall. Lady Anne also did much to restore this church.

The main street, Boroughgate, has old houses, mainly Georgian in the upper part. The hospital has old carvings. The grammar school succeeds an earlier building on another site, which has a record of a headmaster as far back as 1478. The school had a number of famous men as pupils, including the Dean of Lichfield (1632–1703), who was the father of Joseph Addison the essayist (1672–1719), and John Langhorne, the translator of Plutarch's *Lives*, published in 1770. The Moot Hall, with one stone dated 1596, is another historic building. The annual fair, traditionally the horse fair, is in June.

There are various pleasant country walks in the neighbourhood, including that to High Cup Nick where a beck flows in unusual Pennine formations.

ARLEY HALL GARDENS, *Cheshire* (12–SJ6565). Arley Hall gardens (open to the public) lie 6 m. from KNUTSFORD on the west side of the M6. These large and old-established gardens are in the estate of Arley Hall (not open), the private residence of Viscount and Viscountess Ashbrook.

The hall has been well known as the seat of the Warburtons since the period of Henry VIII. Teas are provided in the 16th-cent. barn, which is of historic and architectural interest. The gardens have a topiary with roses, rhododendrons, azaleas and a herbaceous border.

ARMATHWAITE, *Cumberland* (14–NY 5046), lies about 2 m. E. of the A6 and SE. of CARLISLE. An old bridge crosses the River Eden and beside the river stands the small Chapel of Christ and St Mary, set in pleasant scenery. The chapel consists of a chancel, a nave, a wooden roof and a small bell-turret. The original 12th-cent. building fell into ruins and was used to house cattle, but was rebuilt in the 17th cent. In 1914 Morris and Co. made the east window.

ASHTON-UNDER-LYNE, *Lancashire* (12–SJ9399). The Church of St Michael, though completely restored, is on a site that has held a church since the 13th cent. St Michael's is noteworthy for its stained glass of about 1500 portraying the Assheton family, and there are also five windows depicting the history of St Helena and her discovery of the True Cross. Sir Ralph Assheton was known as the Black Knight from the colour of his armour and Sir Thomas fought at the battle of Nevilles Cross, DURHAM.

Medlock Vale, 1½ m. NE. of the town, is on the banks of the Medlock with Hen Cote Cottage at Daisy Nook. It is a rural refuge in an industrial area, and comprises 15½ acres of National Trust property, bought in 1944 and 1951.

ASTBURY, *Cheshire* (12–SJ8461). The old church here is mainly of the 14th and 15th cents. and those parts of it still identifiable with that era are excellently preserved. There are two towers, the more ancient, of Norman foundation, being linked on to another built 300 years later and carrying an imposing spire dating from 1823. Several stones from the original structure were employed in the walling of the chancel, some showing fragments of Norman and Anglo-Saxon carving. Grotesque faces peer down from the stonework, and over the door of the west tower porch is a weathered figure with four stone minstrels, one with bagpipes. The south porch has a priest's room and some fine windows, while the church interior has a Jacobean nave roof and massive clustered pillars lending great dignity to the whole structure. During the Civil War Sir William Brereton and his followers made Astbury their headquarters in the siege of BIDDULPH Hall and stabled their horses in the pews, damaging the woodwork and many of the windows and screens. They also dismantled the church organ and buried it in a field which was afterwards known locally as Organ Close. Astbury church contains memorials connected with many of the powerful Cheshire landowning families, the Moretons, Davenports, Venables, Mainwarings, Shakerleys, Breretons, and Wilbrahams, from whom any account of the history of the county is inseparable.

AUGHTON, *Lancashire* (12–SD3905). At Aughton, SW. of ORMSKIRK, is the garden of Cranford (open to the public). It covers half an acre and is of unusual design, with shrubs, roses and rare trees. St Michael's Church is a mixture of styles. The tower has a square base and an octagonal upper part below the Decorated spire. The north aisle is 16th- or 17th-cent., and a north window is dated 1623. There is a Westmacott memorial to a rector. In 1829 the low church building was repaired and pointed.

BACUP, *Lancashire* (12–SD8622), is a town in the Irwell valley, surrounded by stretches of moorland close to the Yorkshire border, with a textile manufacturing background. The Natural History Society Museum has collections of natural history, geology and old household items.

Rawtenstall, on the W., also has moorland scenery. The Museum and Art Gallery is in Whitaker Park. There is a fine art collection, and the museum, although small, has interesting displays of natural history and curiosities and crafts of the area.

BADDILEY, *Cheshire* (12–SJ6049), is a quiet village with the small Church of St Michael, reached by a winding route. The nave lacks aisles and the chancel is built of brick and timber. There is painted work dated 1663 of the Creed, the Commandments, the Lord's Prayer and a coat of arms. There are also box pews and a large monument.

BAMPTON, *Westmorland* (14–NY5118), is a village about 2 m. NE. of the foot of HAWES WATER, in an agricultural area. The Church of St Patrick was founded in 1726 and has timber arcades. There are remains of ancient British settlements in the neighbourhood. In this quiet village the grammar school was founded in 1623 and a number of its pupils reached distinguished positions in various parts of the country. The free library, founded by Lord Lonsdale in 1710, was one of the first in Britain.

BARROW-IN-FURNESS, *Lancashire* (12–SD1969). Although this county borough is better known as an industrial and ship-building town, with acres of docks and quays, there are beaches here. The long stretch of Walney Island shuts off the Irish Sea to enclose the dockyards. On Piel Island the rebuilt castle is a link with the monks of FURNESS ABBEY. The Council runs the town's museum in Ramsden Square. This includes some discoveries from prehistoric sites, mainly Bronze Age, and models and exhibits relating to the area.

BASSENTHWAITE *Cumberland* (14–NY2332). This village lies near the north end of the lake of the same name; to the east side of the A591, and somewhat remote from the Lakes area generally. Its people must have been remote, too, for centuries. There were Norse settlers here: "thwaite", so common in Lakeland and Yorkshire Dales place-names, is from the Norse word for cleared land. In the Middle Ages a church was built beside the village, and in the 19th cent. the Church of St John. During the coaching era Bassenthwaite was on the route to CARLISLE. Armathwaite Hall, before it became a hotel, included among its owners the Speddings (*see* BASSENTHWAITE LAKE), the Vanes, and a family of ironmasters from BECKERMET. The folk hereabouts are said to live long.

BASSENTHWAITE LAKE, *Cumberland*
(14–NY2332). Bassenthwaite is a beautiful lake, lying between the smaller peak of Lord's Seat on the W., and the bulk of SKIDDAW on the E. Everyone sees it from the busy route that runs along its west shore between KESWICK and COCKERMOUTH and the Cumberland coast, from which Skiddaw is also prominent, but it is worth going round the N. of the lake and coming S. on the A591 past the wooded reaches of Dodd Fell for the view of the DERWENTWATER valley opening out with Keswick nestling at the head of its lake. It is perhaps passed by more often than visited, because considerable stretches of the lakeside are private property, and so not easy for the tourist to reach. As the most northerly of the Lakes, Bassenthwaite lies in a direct line between breeding grounds of wildfowl at MORECAMBE Bay and the Solway Firth, and is visited by many varieties of migrating birds. Bassenthwaite is usually called a lake, not a "water" or "mere" like the others, and has the largest catchment area of any of them. Counting the stretch from BORROWDALE, it also has the longest valley. Boats can be hired near Piel Wyke.

A mile or so before the south end of Bassenthwaite is the small Church of SS. Bridget and Bega between A591 and the lake. The church is late 12th- to 13th-cent., restored in the 19th cent., and has a Norman chancel arch and Early English features. It is one of two dedicated to St Bega, the other being at ST BEES. Wordsworth and other Lake Poets knew this lakeside church, and Mire House nearby, owned by the Spedding family, also has literary associations. James Spedding, the biographer of Francis Bacon, was visited there by Tennyson, Edward FitzGerald and Carlyle.

Above the main road, near the south end of the lake's 4-m. stretch, is the white rock called the Bishop; there are various stories about its name, some saying a bishop rode up to it. Castle How at the N. (near Piel Wyke) has some traces of an ancient fort, and the early British Embleton Sword was found and sent to the BRITISH MUSEUM.

BECKERMET, *Cumberland* (14–NY0207), is
a village S. of EGREMONT, between the A595 and the coast. It has two parts – St John and St Bridget Beckermet – in an old iron-ore producing area. St John's Church has a good site near where two becks meet (hence the village name) and was rebuilt during the 19th cent. It is small but well-designed, with a bell and clock tower. The interesting collection of carved stones dates from before the Norman Conquest. St Bridget's has two shafts of ancient crosses.

BEETHAM, *Westmorland* (14–SD4979). This
village lies off the A6, with two old mills, a waterfall, and a riverside mansion. Beetham Hall was originally a peel-tower and in the Middle Ages became a castle; but it is now a farm-house and the 14th-cent. great hall is a barn. The original Church of St Michael was early Norman, but the present structure shows a mixture of Gothic styles. It is approached under a pergola of rambler roses.

BILLINGE, *Lancashire* (12–SD5300). St
Aidan's Church stands on fairly high ground near the south end of the straggling village, and its 18th-cent. structure is in a curious mixture of Classical and medieval styles. It has a clock-turret over the west door and a bell in a cupola above. The small transepts are modern, built in the Gothic style, and the nave arcades have Doric columns. There is a fine two-tier chandelier. The chancel apse has black-and-white marble paving and a domed roof. There are no pews. The old west gallery has extensive panelling.

On Billinge Hill a square stone beacon was put up in 1780 and this site gives a view over the countryside towards the Irish Sea.

BIRKENHEAD, *Cheshire* (12–SJ3188).
Birkenhead Priory existed before there was any town of Birkenhead as such. It was founded in the mid-12th cent. when land was granted to a Benedictine order, the Black Monks, who may have come from CHESTER. They favoured this secluded spot near the head of the Wirral peninsula where their priory was screened by forests on the landward side. There was a ferry-boat point nearby over which the monks later gained rights, granted by a charter from Edward III. The remains of the priory were acquired by Birkenhead Corporation in 1896. The Wirral area was less troubled by the strife of the post-Dissolution period than places further inland, and even up to the 19th cent. Birkenhead remained a quiet hamlet. St Mary's was built from 1819 to 1821 as the parish church, in Victorian Gothic style on a cruciform plan. In 1817 the steam ferry began to operate and this encouraged people from the north side of the Mersey to settle in Birkenhead. From 1824 William Laird began to buy land, and established a boiler works and then ship-building yards. The first docks opened in 1847, and from then on the two major industries of ship-building and docks were the decisive influences in the steady growth of the town. Its links with the north side of the Mersey were further improved by the opening of the Mersey rail tunnel in 1886, and the **Mersey Tunnel** in 1934 for road traffic.

In 1826 Hamilton Square was laid out by Gillespie Graham like an Edinburgh square, with the support of William Laird. Originally residential, it is now mainly business premises, and has a public garden. The handsome town hall was built in 1887. Several sites have been used for the Central Library, and the present building was opened in 1934. The large entrance portico is in a dignified Classical style, decorated with marble: grey travertine with a black inlay for the floors, door architraves and wall pilasters and golden travertine marble for the columns. The imposing Williamson Art Gallery was specially designed for its purpose and opened in 1928. English water-colours are a special feature, and there are many English oils of the late 18th and early 19th cents. and some of the 20th cent. The Knowles Boney Collection of Liverpool porcelain may be the largest of its kind in the country. Other ceramics include Japanese, Persian, early Viennese, Venetian, Dresden and French pottery, and examples of Crown Derby and Staffordshire work. In 1962 the Shipping Gallery was added which, with models and other material, it illustrates the work of the town and its port. Considerable residential and shopping development has taken place in recent years in Birkenhead and in the outlying districts of Oxton, Claughton and Prenton.

Arrowe Park, which the corporation acquired in 1927, contains 425 acres of fine woodland and a bird sanctuary. There is also a golf course and various playing fields. Arrowe Hall is an 1835 building in Elizabethan style.

Men associated with the town include Lord Birkenhead, better known there as F. E. Smith, who was born at 8 Pilgrim Street; J. L. Garvin of the *Observer* who was born at 117 Anne Street; and Wilfred Owen, the poet, who was born at OSWESTRY, went to Birkenhead in 1900 and died in France a week before the 1918 armistice. At the Y.M.C.A. hall in Whetstone Lane is a tablet that commemorates the inauguration of the Boy Scout movement in Grange Road Hall by Baden-Powell in 1908. Nathaniel Hawthorne lived at Rock Ferry and became American consul at Liverpool in 1853.

Bidston Hill on the NW. is the oldest of the town's open spaces, and the old windmill is a well-known landmark. There is a direction indicator for the extensive views from the top of the hill. Liverpool University has an observatory and Tidal Institute on the hill, which provides meteorological information and makes tidal predictions for some 160 ports throughout the world. Bidston Old Hall, which became a farm-house, is believed to have been rebuilt in 1620 by William, 6th Earl of Derby, and looks down on Leasowe Castle (WALLASEY), another residence of the Stanleys, the Earls of Derby (*see* KNOWSLEY HALL and CHESTER).

BIRTLES, *Cheshire* (12–SJ8574). This is fine walking country, with miles of lanes and tracks inviting exploration of the undulating heights and woodland glades. The hamlet of Birtles, too small to appear on all but the most detailed of maps, offers access to Alderley Park, a beautiful stretch of the central Cheshire uplands containing all that remains of the ancestral home of a junior branch of the Stanley family. The 19th-cent. church, with its octagonal tower and unusual porch, has many attractive roundels in its 16th- and 17th-cent. windows, the dominant colours

employed by the Flemish craftsmen being blue and red.

Birtles Hall is a handsome Georgian house.

BLACKBURN, *Lancashire* (12–SD6827). The town's museum has collections of local geology, mineralogy and natural history, with a small archaeological and Egyptian section, some medieval manuscripts and early printed books, coins (including Roman), porcelain, pottery and glass. The art gallery has oil paintings, 18th- to 20th-cent. English watercolours, Japanese prints and examples of industrial art.

An aspect of the town's industrial background is shown in the Lewis Textile Museum which traces the development of the spinning and weaving industries and contains early examples of machinery. James Hargreaves, who was born near Blackburn about 1720, invented a carding machine in 1760 and the spinning-jenny about 1764. These were among the developments which led to the Industrial Revolution. They came at a time when labourers' living standards were affected by bad harvests and the Corn Laws, and there were riots in Lancashire by those who saw their livelihoods further threatened by the introduction of machines. Hargreaves' inventions were smashed more than once, and in 1768 he moved to NOTTINGHAM. Richard Arkwright of PRESTON also removed to avoid such attacks. Later these inventions, as at BOLTON, led to enormous expansion of the Lancashire cotton industry.

Blackburn has in recent years seen considerable development and re-planning. Modern industries now range from valve-making to heavy engineering. The town has six parks, and is also within reach of the Ribble and Hodder Valley moorlands.

BLACKPOOL, *Lancashire* (12–SD3035). If there is a form of holiday entertainment that Blackpool cannot provide it is difficult to think of. The town stretches along the Lancashire coast with a resident population of some 152,000, annually swollen by the hordes of people lured to this metropolis of pleasure packed with all the elements of a vast fun-fair. Yet beside the strident and overcrowded entertainments, there is another and a quieter Blackpool – a resort of spacious parks and bowling greens for those who prefer their recreation in a more individual form. The town claims to have everything for holidays, from old-style tram rides along the sea-front to remedial and sauna baths. It also has the Grundy Art Gallery, in Queen Street, with a permanent collection of 19th- and 20th-cent. British artists.

The tower is Blackpool's great landmark. This showpiece and engineering feat is well worth inspection. Except in windy weather, the lift carries passengers to a height of 518 ft for the breathtaking view from the top. Housed in the tower is a fine aquarium, a zoo, a circus, a ballroom and the well-known organ. The promenade runs for 7 m. and most of it is traversed by the trams. Stanley Park has Italian-style gardens, a huge boating lake, and bowls, tennis and golf.

Blackpool: the Tower and the beach

Its rose garden displays some 30,000 blooms, and in the conservatories is a "living museum" of 700 species of chrysanthemum. Blackpool has 26 municipal bowling greens, two 18-hole golf courses, 16 children's playgrounds, three piers, a winter garden and a waxworks. Among its annual events are the Lancashire Agricultural Society show, the veteran car run from MANCHESTER, and the "milk race" (the cycling tour of Britain). The famous illuminations are a great attraction from early September to late October, when 6 m. of promenade, the tower and the pleasure beach are lit up. Spectators can also travel in the illuminated trams.

BLACKSTONE EDGE, *Lancashire* (12–SD 9717). E. of Littleborough the route of the old Roman road goes steeply up to the borders of Yorkshire. It ran originally all the way from MANCHESTER to ILKLEY, it is believed, but much of it has been obliterated. At Blackstone Edge, however, a lengthy stretch, probably the best surviving section of Roman road in the country, demonstrates an engineering feat of nearly 2,000 years ago; the solid foundations have kept the paving in place against all the moorland storm and frost. Some difference of opinion exists about the depression in the middle, as to whether it held turf for the horses to get a grip or was worn down by the chariots.

BOLTON, *Lancashire* (12–SD7108). Bolton is a busy Lancashire industrial town. There is an imposing town hall in Classical style by William Hill, 1873, and the civic centre houses an aquarium, the museum and the art gallery. Museum collections include geology, botany, zoology, ornithology, archaeology and an Egyptian collection. The art gallery has English paintings, English 18th-cent. pottery, and English and European sculpture with an Epstein collection.

Bolton's history goes back to before the Conquest but the town became prominent with the development of the cotton industry. It has grown into one of the largest boroughs in Lancashire, although many old mills are now devoted to other manufactures. During the Civil War the town was the scene of a massacre committed by Royalists, and James Stanley, Earl of Derby (*see* ORMSKIRK) was beheaded in retaliation by Cromwell. In one of the ancient streets, Churchgate, is Ye Old Man and Scythe, dated 1251, with a statement that in this hostelry Stanley passed his last few hours before execution. At a cottage in Firwood Fold, off Crompton Way on the north-east edge of Bolton, is the birthplace of Samuel Crompton, the inventor of the spinning-mule (*see* HALL I' TH' WOOD, his residence). Crompton's tomb is in the parish churchyard. The town was also the birthplace of William Hesketh Lever (1851–1925), who became the 1st Viscount Leverhulme. Lever, whose father was a Bolton grocer, began to make soap at WIGAN in 1886. He founded Lever Brothers (which became Unilever Ltd after his death) and his Sunlight Soap became well known. Lever bought and restored Hall i' th' Wood; and then, in 1902, presented it to the town, of which he was mayor in 1918. He was Liberal M.P. for the Wirral Division (1906–10), and he built the model village and fine art gallery of PORT SUNLIGHT. Bolton also has one of Lancashire's oldest manor houses, SMITHILLS HALL. The arts are well represented by a variety of cultural organizations, using lecture rooms at the Central Library; and by the highly successful Octagon Theatre. Built only a few years ago, it is a source of civic pride to the inhabitants of Bolton, and has become a theatrical centre for the North West.

Besides St Saviour's in Bolton, there is St Mary's Church at **Deane**, nearby. It is in the Perpendicular style with a Decorated west tower. The nave and chancel have a continuous roof dated 1570.

BOLTON, *Westmorland* (14–NY6323), is a village on the west side of the River Eden. Its small church, All Saints', has ancient stonework. There is a Norman nave and two Norman doorways. Above the north doorway is an interesting small medieval carving of knights jousting. The west turret, built in 1693, has two bells. The chancel screen with open tracery is probably late 18th-cent.

E., beyond the main road, are the Pennine villages of Dufton and Knock, an area of narrow roads leading past Milburn's medieval streets to Skirwith and **Kirkland**, which lies below the 2,930 ft of **Cross Fell**, the highest point of the Pennines. At Kirkland is the curious formation of ground called the Hanging Walls of Mark Anthony.

BOOT, *Cumberland* (14–NY1700). You can drive to this village from either direction on the road through ESKDALE; or, in the summer at least, you can travel there on the miniature railway from **Ravenglass** on the coast. The line was laid in the last century to carry ore from the mines at Boot, and soon carried passengers, too, later adding other freight when the mines closed, and stone from a quarry. Dalegarth Force and Birker Force are high waterfalls near Boot. Dalegarth Hall, which became a farm-house, is an old seat of the Stanley family, dating from the 16th cent.

"Owd Ratty" is the nickname for the miniature railway, so called after the original contractor, Ratcliffe. Its popularity increases, and it is one of the institutions of Lakeland. There is nothing "owd" (old) about the equipment which is specially built. The latest diesel locomotive, with a rare drive system, can haul 21 coaches up to **Dalegarth** (the actual terminus) on the 7 m. of 15-in. gauge. A private company runs the system and has even made innovations which have been adopted on full-scale railways. Saloon coaches are available in case of wet weather. The company also operates cafés, shops and car parks, with a games and picnic field at Dalegarth.

BOOTLE, *Lancashire* (12–SJ3394), is a thickly populated industrial town at the mouth of the River Mersey. It adjoins LIVERPOOL and is very much a continuation northwards of its larger neighbour's dockland. The Bootle Museum and Art Gallery in Oriel Road is administered by the Corporation and contains the Lancaster collection of English figure pottery and the Bishop collection of Liverpool pottery. Various art exhibitions are held there.

BORROWDALE, *Cumberland* (14–NY2514), is often described as the most beautiful valley in the Lakes, and is one of the great centres of attraction for climbers. It is the southward continuation of the valley where DERWENTWATER lies and the River Derwent flows down the **Seathwaite** branch of Borrowdale; various parts of it are owned by the National Trust. At **Grange**, S. of Derwentwater, the roads round each side of the lake join to enter the well-known Jaws of Borrowdale. This entry is formed by Grange Fell on the E. and Scawdel close by on the W. The village of Grange is in a beautiful spot beside the old bridge over the river and backed by mountain views. Although so well known because of its site, Grange is a tiny place. It once had connections with FURNESS ABBEY.

The Bowder Stone is below Grange Fell. This huge boulder (National Trust) is metamorphic rock, estimated to weigh about 2,000 tons, and can be ascended by ladder despite its apparently precarious balance. Castle Crag is further in through the Jaws, W. of the river. It gives a view of Derwentwater, and on its summit is the site of an ancient British fort. Further up the valley, and 6 m. from KESWICK, is ROSTHWAITE. Like Borrowdale village a little to the S., it is beloved of walkers and climbers. The Borrowdale Yews are higher up the Derwent valley, near Seathwaite, and were celebrated by Wordsworth before a storm destroyed most of them. Seathwaite (not the one in DUDDON VALLEY) is situated just off the B5289. It has the highest average rainfall in England. The road peters out beyond this village, one track going over Sty Head Pass beside GREAT GABLE (2,949 ft) on the SW., and another to Esk Hause, high in the knot of peaks of the SCA FELL and BOW FELL group. These wild and lofty regions offer magnificent views but are only for experienced climbers, and even they should avoid them if the weather is not clear. Glaramara (2,560 ft) divides Seathwaite from Stonethwaite, the east valley of Borrowdale, where Stake Pass leads to the LANGDALE valleys.

An industrial footnote: Seathwaite once mined the graphite for Keswick pencils.

BOSLEY RESERVOIR, *Cheshire* (12–SJ 9365). A beautiful sheet of water, of about 120 acres, with an island on which grows a clump of Scots firs. It is backed by high hills on the N. and E. and may best be viewed from the heights of Bosley Cloud, at the far end of which are the remains of an ancient Roman fort. The village and reservoir are close beside the River Dane, which here forms the boundary between Cheshire and Staffordshire, flowing under Hug Bridge, the

Bramall Hall

scene of an early battle between the men of the district and the invading Danish forces. The church nestling among the trees was restored towards the end of the 18th cent. but still has its early 16th-cent. tower with strange figure carvings weathered by time. It is said that Bosley was the birthplace of Raphael Holinshed, upon whose *Chronicles* Shakespeare drew heavily for his historical plays.

BOW FELL, *Cumberland* (14–NY2406). Bow Fell towers over Great Langdale in the wild region that lies in the heart of the Lake District. It is at 2,960 ft the highest point in the eastern range of the central knot of peaks. Between Bow Fell and the western part of this group lies the head of Eskdale and Esk Hause, the highest pass for climbers and fell-walkers where tracks from Wasdale, Borrowdale, and Langdale meet. Bow Fell is often climbed, along with Crinkle Crags to the S.

BOWNESS, *Westmorland* (14–SD4097), is on the shore of Windermere and virtually a continuation of Windermere Town, but its centre is off the main (A591) road. It lies roughly midway on the E. of the lake, and its proximity to the Windermere railhead has established it as the vital link in the lake's transport system, both between the north end at Waterhead (for Ambleside and centres northward) and the south end at Lake Side (for Ulverston and the western areas); also for the west shore of the lake by the car ferry service, which runs just S. of Bowness and cuts out a long drive round the 10½-m. lake to reach Hawkshead and Coniston. In the season, Bowness pier is busy with passengers using the summer service of British Rail motor vessels to travel to either end of the lake, and with those using them for pleasure trips throughout its length. Besides this steamer pier are other, public, piers, and facilities for hiring all manner of craft, from rowing boats to high-powered launches and cruising

vessels with sleeping accommodation. The lake has been a water highway for centuries, and it is now the greatest centre in the Lakes for cruising and for every kind of water sport: water-skiing, underwater swimming, or yachting. It is well provided with boat builders, boat repairers and equipment suppliers. It is also the headquarters of the Royal Windermere Yacht Club and their sails are a familiar sight on the water. A favourite excursion is by the ferry to see Beatrix Potter's house at Sawrey (Esthwaite Water).

Users of the lake must remember that the rules of conduct are mandatory, and that the lake patrol, there to help in emergencies, will also enforce the rules (*see* Windermere).

St Martin's Church at Bowness is the parish church of Windermere. It has been the site of a religious foundation for over 1,000 years; the old structure was burnt and was rebuilt in 1484, with restoration in 1870. Its east window contains 14th- or 15th-cent glass from Cartmel Priory. There are mural inscriptions, some chained books, a "Breeches" Bible, an ancient font and a monument by Flaxman.

BRAITHWAITE, *Cumberland* (14–NY2323), is about 2½ m. W. of Keswick at the entry to Whinlatter Pass. From it several roads lead S. along the west side of Derwentwater. The village is the starting point for climbing Grisedale Pike, one of the northern peaks in the Grasmoor group of mountains. It lies near the edge of the plain N. of Derwentwater, and from here you can drive along a beautiful alternative route on the west side of Bassenthwaite Lake.

BRAMALL HALL, *Cheshire* (12–SJ8984). This may well be the finest surviving black-and-white house in England. It dates from the 15th cent., the manor having passed by marriage from the ancient Bramhale family to the Davenports, who held it for 500 years. Considerable rebuilding was carried out by Sir William and Dame

Dorothy Davenport in about 1600, but in 1819 the whole of the west side of the structure was taken down and the remainder shaped into its present form. The Hall has now been acquired by the local Urban District Council and is open to the public all through the year at advertised times. A spiral stairway of solid oak leads from the ground floor to a beautiful Elizabethan drawing-room, notable for its superb ceiling, oriel window and vast fire-place. The banqueting hall has a roof of great arched timbers believed to have been set in position in an even earlier building of the 14th cent., but the outstanding feature of the house is a tapestry representing the Fall of Man. This magnificent example of 17th-cent. craftsmanship was the work of Dame Dorothy Davenport and took 36 years to complete.

BRIDESTONES, *Cheshire* (12–SJ9164). This is the principal megalithic monument in the county, lying just within the boundary line that divides Cheshire from Staffordshire, and must in some way be connected with the adjacent earthworks believed to be of Roman or even much earlier origin. The Bridestones consist of a number of rough-hewn blocks arranged in the semblance of an uncompleted box, with two tall uprights standing at the open end. The whole is believed to be the remains of a prehistoric burial chamber and was formerly covered with a mound of earth. The indication is that the sepulchre may have been raised by people who were contemporaries of the builders of STONEHENGE, as a last resting-place for some important tribal chieftain; but local legend holds to the more romantic theory that a Viking nobleman married an Anglo-Saxon girl from BIDDULPH and that both are buried here.

BROTHERS' WATER, *Westmorland* (14–NY4012), is a lonely place, set below the north end of the KIRKSTONE PASS and its sweeping sides, with the hard volcanic crags and black fissures of the HELVELLYN range high up to the W. Dove-dale, on this side, is one of the steepest valleys, with an overhanging crag. On the east side, next to ULLSWATER, is Place Fell, 2,154 ft, and lesser slopes S. of it. But the lake itself lies in a pleasant pastoral plain. The water is only about ¼ m. wide. It is alleged that the reason for changing its name from Broadwater was because two brothers were drowned there. Although it is so quiet now, the valley must have been busier once, for there are remains of lead-mines, of old habitations and of a cornmill. A farm, Hartsop Hall, is included in land given by the Treasury, which had accepted these properties in lieu of death duties, to the National Trust – the first property so acquired. This land includes the lake itself.

BROUGH, *Westmorland* (14–NY7914). The history of this small town goes back almost 2,000 years. It was a coaching town in the last century and still holds a horse fair at the end of September. Brough is at the foot of the long ascent (difficult in winter) over Stainmore where the A66 follows the route of the old Roman road most of the way across the moors to the E. The castle probably dates from the 11th cent. but the keep was added between 1175 and 1200. The south-east round tower, gatehouse and curtain are probably of the early 13th cent. Lady Anne Clifford (*see* APPLEBY and BROUGHAM) repaired the castle in the late 17th cent. It is an Ancient Monument (open to the public), and lies in the northern part of the Roman fort of Verterae, where the Roman road continued to KIRKBY THORE. St Michael's Church is mainly Early English and Perpendicular, with a 17th-cent. stone pulpit. Musgrave Fell, to the N., a limestone pavement area for plants, is protected by the National Trust.

BROUGHAM, *Westmorland* (14–NY5228). Brougham Castle (open to the public) is an extensive and important military survival. This ruined but imposing building is on the banks of the River Eamont near where it joins the River Lowther, about 1 m. S. of PENRITH on the APPLEBY road. The earliest part, the keep, was built *c.* 1170–80 and much of the curtain wall in the 13th cent. In 1202 it passed from Gospatrick to the Viponts, and later by marriage to the Cliffords, who made additions. It was here that Thomas, Lord Dacre, carried off the heiress, Elizabeth, from the care of the Cliffords.

Against the castle the outlines of the Roman fort of Brocavum are to be seen. This was an important site where two Roman roads joined, from Ravenglass via HARDKNOTT and from the S., as well as from KIRKBY THORE on the E.

The Church of St Ninian, in a dale by the River Eamont, is known as "Nine Kirks", and an Anglo-Saxon church once stood on the site of the present Norman one. This remains as it was rebuilt by Lady Anne Clifford of Brougham Castle in 1660, with its contemporary furnishings. St Wilfrid's Chapel nearby was restored, by Lady Anne Clifford in the 17th cent., and again in the 19th cent. The plain building belies the rich interior which is full of finely carved oak, a 15th-cent. altar-piece and carved scenes on the church walls.

BROUGHTON-IN-FURNESS, *Lancashire* (12–SD2087). In this old market town, less than 1 m. E. of the River Duddon, the historic charter is still proclaimed each August in the market square. The DUDDON VALLEY, on which Words-worth wrote a series of poems, can be explored from here, and for climbing there is Black Combe (1,969 ft) on the W. The Church of St Mary, in the Early English style, was largely rebuilt in 1873, but parts may date from the 12th cent. and a fine Norman south doorway remains. Of the old castle of the Broughton family the tower and the dungeons are all that remain. A modern mansion built round the tower is a school for delicate children. **Swinside Stone Circle** is 5 m. W. and 20 minutes' walk from the road. Over 50 stones, many fallen, make a circle roughly 100 ft across. It is 2,000 to 3,000 years old, and called Sunken-kirk but its purpose is unknown.

BUDWORTH, *Cheshire* (12–SJ6677). At **Great Budworth** is the Church of St Mary and All Saints which, with its imposing tower, dates from the 14th and 15th cents. The interior has some of the original roofing, and there are medieval stalls, which may be 14th-cent., a 15th-cent. font and many monuments, including those of the Leycester and Warburton families.

Budworth Mere is one of a number of meres in this part of the country. The village of **Nether Tabley**, which is 2½ m. from KNUTSFORD, and W. of the M6, has the fine estate of the Leycester-Warrens. The ruined Old Hall stands on an island in the lake. It was built originally by Sir John Leycester; the new frontage is of 1671. Tabley House (open to the public occasionally), standing in an estate of 800 acres, dates from 1760 and was built by Carr of YORK.

BUNBURY, *Cheshire* (12–SJ5658). This village with its old cottages and pleasant lanes has the interesting Church of St Boniface, a large collegiate church of the 14th cent. with additions in the 15th. It has 16th-cent. oak doors, and memorials of Sir George Beeston, who fought against the Armada, and Sir R. Egerton, standard-bearer to Henry VIII. Bunbury has a strong Methodist tradition, and John Wesley preached here.

Peckforton village, to the W. of Bunbury, has some half-timbered cottages. N. of the village is the imposing castle, the seat of the Tollemache family, set on a lofty site. It is 19th-cent. and designed by Salvin, one of his best works.

BURNLEY, *Lancashire* (12–SD8332). The name of Burnley can be traced back two centuries before the Norman Conquest, and the history of St Peter's Church is believed to go back to the 12th cent. The history of the Towneley family, conspicuous in Burnley, started about the beginning of the 13th cent. when land was granted by the Normans. The woollen industry began in the late 13th cent., and Burnley grew as a market town; the Industrial Revolution brought great expansion due to the cotton-spinning industry which preceded the present emphasis on engineering.

Towneley Hall (open to the public) is to the SE. of Burnley. Its 6-ft-thick walls have undergone so many alterations that it is difficult to decide on the hall's original character. The south-east wing was probably begun in the mid-14th cent. as a two-story building. The central part and the north-west wing were probably built about a century later on three sides of a square, as they stand today. The square was completed later, but a variety of alterations followed, including removal of this fourth side; and in the 19th cent., with the additions to the north-west wing, and the castellations and turrets, the hall's exterior assumed its present form. In 1725 Richard Towneley began alterations to the central hall, then decorated in neo-Classical style by Vassali, the Italian plaster sculptor. Other rooms contain an Adam-style fireplace and a hiding place for priests. Old

English vestments of cloth of gold, 17th-cent. panelling and a Spode dinner service are on display. Paintings include oils by Constable, Peter Lely and Fantin Latour, and watercolours by Gainsborough, Prout, de Wint, Turner and Cox. The John Zoffany oil of *Charles Towneley and his friends* has been widely exhibited and reproduced. Notable rooms are the bedrooms off the 85-ft Long Gallery, the dining-room, servants' dining-room and the chapel. A triumph of the Libraries and Arts Committee of Burnley Corporation, which bought the Hall in 1901, was to buy back the altar-piece. This has fine Netherlandish wood sculpture, probably early 16th-cent., in the oak reredos with scenes of the life of Christ. The altar itself is of later production, possibly late 17th cent., with three panel scenes. It was retrieved from the Convent of Notre Dame in Sussex, and in 1969 was replaced in the chapel where Charles Towneley (1737–1805), the art collector, had placed it. He brought to England a collection of Greek and Roman art, later bought by the BRITISH MUSEUM. Other Towneleys include Christopher (b. 1603), the Lancashire antiquary, and John (b. 1697), the translator into French of *Hudibras*. Besides being the town's art gallery, the hall is also a museum of geology, archaeology and natural history.

On the road to Padiham is **Gawthorpe Hall** (open to the public after restoration) the home of the Shuttleworth family since 1330. The present mansion was built round an earlier house about the beginning of the 17th cent., and elaborated by Sir Charles Barry in 1850. It is a fine specimen of the architecture of its period. It has many displays of textiles and other crafts in a collection established by the late Hon. Rachel Kay Shuttleworth.

BURTON, *Cheshire* (12–SJ3174). Charles Kingsley's poem beginning "Mary go and call the cattle home . . . Across the sands of Dee", refers to the wide stretches of tidal sand which grew over the centuries as the Dee became silted up. As a result, the village of Burton lost its status as a port for Ireland. It is one of the most charming villages in the Wirral. Bulley's Gardens, originally belonging to A. K. Bulley, a LIVERPOOL cotton merchant, were handed on for public use by his daughter. Mr Bulley himself gave to the National Trust the area of Burton Wood, 20 acres of Scots pines above the village. The cottage where Bishop Thomas Wilson was born in 1663 is preserved by the council. He was famous in the locality as a writer and benefactor, and became Bishop of Sodor and Man. The Parish Church of St Nicholas, on a fine site, was rebuilt in 1721 and has 17th-cent. altar rails, and old relics. There is evidence of a church on the site in Norman times.

Ness, to the N., is where Nelson's Lady Hamilton was born. She was much painted by Romney (*see* DALTON-IN-FURNESS) and others.

BUTTERMERE, *Cumberland* (14–NY1815), is a lake set among some of the most beautiful scenery in the LAKE DISTRICT. It is an ideal centre for climbing the peaks. Sour Milk Gill

Carlisle: a misericord in the cathedral showing a man in a kilt being swallowed by a dragon

originates in Bleaberry Tarn, set 1,600 ft up among the slopes of Red Pike and High Stile on the W. and comes rushing down in milk-like spray to Buttermere. Walkers and climbers may come in from various directions. The motorist can choose only from three, for the High Stile range blocks his access on the W.: he can enter from the N. beside CRUMMOCK WATER, from the E. by **Newlands Pass** (with care down the last mile), or from the S. by HONISTER PASS. Crummock Water is often considered the most pleasant approach, with the magnificent Fleetwith Pike S. of Buttermere.

The latter is hemmed in by mountains, those of Robinson and Hindscarth on the E. being lower than High Stile (2,644 ft), Red Pike and High Crag opposite. There is pleasant pastureland N. and S. of the lake, joined by an attractive path along the west side. Buttermere is noted for its fishing, and rods and boats are let by the National Trust which owns the whole lake and 94 acres of plantations on the south shore.

BUTTERMERE (VILLAGE), *Cumberland* (14–NY1717). This is a small village and is roughly halfway between the north end of Buttermere itself and CRUMMOCK WATER. The road from **Newlands Pass** descends steeply to the village, joining the one that runs from HONISTER PASS N. to Crummock Water. The village is popular with walkers and climbers as a centre for excursions in the Cumbrian mountains, and has hotels, guest-houses and an old church.

Wordsworth includes the local tale of the Maid of Buttermere in Book VII of *The Prelude*. She was the daughter of the landlord of the Fish Inn and had the misfortune to marry a man who proved to be a forger and bigamist and was later hanged. She later moved to CALDBECK.

CALDBECK, *Cumberland* (14–NY3239). Caldbeck lies at the northern edge of the LAKE DISTRICT National Park. The Church of St Kentigern is 12th- to early 16th-cent., but mostly of the latter period, when it was partly rebuilt. Various windows are later still: one has unusual columns below the wooden lintel.

In the churchyard the Maid of BUTTERMERE was buried. Better known is that tireless pursuer of foxes, John Peel, born at Greenrigg nearby, whose 1854 gravestone is decorated with a horn. His friend, J. W. Graves, wrote the song during the huntsman's lifetime.

CALDER ABBEY, *Cumberland* (14–NY0307), is E. of Calder Bridge (A595) in a fine situation beside the River Calder. The site, open to the public at advertised times, is administered by the Ministry of Public Building and Works. The ruins that remain include the nave, the church aisles and parts of the cloister. The abbey was founded in 1135 by the Savignac Order from FURNESS ABBEY, which later became Cistercian. The earliest parts of the ruins are 12th-cent., and the latest part, the chapter house, is late 13th- or early 14th-cent.

Ponsonby Hall is a fine 18th-cent. house built by the Stanleys.

CAPESTHORNE, *Cheshire* (12–SJ8372). This is the seat of the Bromley-Davenport family, who for many centuries have exerted their influence in Cheshire affairs. The old hall was burned down in 1861 and a large, impressive Victorian building by Anthony Salvin took its place, incorporating parts of the earlier house in the wings. The chapel adjacent to the new hall was built in 1722 in the Classic style and restored in 1888. The most attractive feature of the area is Redes Mere, a beautiful sheet of placid water over 60 acres in extent. Many of these lakes to the W. of MACCLESFIELD were formed from the marl-pits dug in the meadows during the 13th cent. The one here came more recently as the result of silica sand excavations and has become the haunt of waterfowl. There are many delightful walks for nature-lovers among the giant oaks and beeches with which the estate abounds.

CARLISLE, *Cumberland* (14–NY3955), is the county and principal town of Cumberland. Its previous Celtic settlement is undated. The Roman period began under Agricola about A.D. 80. The Romans called it Luguvallium. Later HADRIAN'S

WALL was built, passing just N., and when Stanwix fort was placed there it left Carlisle as a civic centre for administering the whole western area of the Roman frontier. The town held this role for 250 years, benefiting from Roman civil organization. But the apparent security was breached by raids, and Picts and other tribes over-ran the Roman sites in 181, and again in 367. The Vikings sacked the town in 875. It was added to England after the Norman Conquest; William Rufus claimed it in 1092 and it was then that the city walls, castle and priory were begun. But for nearly seven centuries after that Carlisle could change little in size and shape owing to its un-certain position: there were frequent border raids, and the town became a shuttlecock passed be-tween England and Scotland. The longest siege was in 1644–5 when Royalist Carlisle fell to the Scots. It fell to them again when it surrendered to Bonnie Prince Charlie in 1745 as he set out on his march into England that was only halted at DERBY. In the last two centuries, the city has had a chance to settle down, after 1,700 years of warfare, struggle or family feuds – probably the longest period of strife known by any English town.

The first Town Hall, apparently built in Eliza-bethan days, was succeeded by another in 1717, partly on the same site; with the 14th-cent. Guild Hall nearby, it was the town's governmental centre for nearly six centuries. Much plate from the eight trade guilds is in the City Museum. The Town Hall had two bells: the one that, from 1584 until the mid-19th cent., announced the opening of the market, and the "muckle town bell", whose alarm warning could be heard for 11 m. Both are in the museum. The two round towers that are so prominent at the city centre, above the railway station, represent the citadel, and are a recon-struction (1807) of the original citadel built in 1541–3, which was a second defence in case the castle fell. The present citadel was built in 1807 by Sir Robert Smirke, who designed the BRITISH MUSEUM. At the west tower of the original was English Gate (or Botchergate), and the other two gates in the city walls were Scotch Gate on the E. and Irish Gate on the W. They were slammed at dusk: after that, let no Scot dare to move about inside. Carlisle Cross (1682) stands in English Street on the site of the traditional town centre where Bonnie Prince Charlie made his proclama-tion in 1745. The old town hall faces it but is dominated by the 1964 civic centre to the N., with an elaborate octagonal council chamber. Beyond it is a modern square office block, incongruous in the old city.

The small cathedral was finished in 1123 as the Church of the Blessed Virgin Mary and became an Augustinian priory. The priory church became the cathedral when the diocese of Carlisle was founded in 1133. The nave then became the parish church. A larger choir was made but was destroyed by fire in 1292. The monks did more building later, including the magnificent Decor-ated east window, 58 ft high and 32½ ft wide, which has original 14th-cent. glass at the top. The tower

was added about 1401. After the 1644–5 siege General Leslie tore down about two-thirds of the nave (in ruins since the Dissolution) and much of the cloisters and other buildings to obtain stone for repairing city walls and castle. Only about 1853 was serious restoration work begun. There is a fine 15th-cent. fratery and traces of other monastic buildings. About 39 ft of the original 140 ft of the Norman nave remain. Sir Walter Scott was married in it in 1797; he had many associa-tions with the Border country. There are 15th-cent. paintings on the backs of the choir stalls in the north aisle and interesting misericords, a Renaissance screen and a carved head, probably of Edward I.

Tullie House Museum was originally a Jaco-bean mansion and the southern façade has orna-mented fall pipes dated 1689. The original staircase with oak banisters remains. Various public rooms were added after the building was acquired in 1893 as a cultural centre, and it now houses an art gallery, a library and a museum. There is a gallery containing geological specimens, a Roman gallery with material from Hadrian's wall, and a natural history section.

The bluff where the castle was built N. of the medieval city was probably the site of an ancient British camp or *caer*, a term preserved in the name Carlisle. The castle, which is open to the public, was founded in 1092 and enlarged later. The existing keep, built at some time in the 12th cent., has been considerably altered. It is now a museum of the history of the Border Regiment. The castle was badly damaged when taken by the Scots in 1216, and fell into disrepair, subsequently to be rebuilt and strengthened at various periods. The badge of Richard III can be seen on the Tile Tower and the arms of Elizabeth I near the keep. The apartments where Mary Queen of Scots was imprisoned have gone, but Queen Mary's Tower remains, as does the 14th-cent. main gate.

At **Burgh-by-Sands**, 6 m. NW. of Carlisle, St Michael's is a strongly fortified church, built almost entirely from Roman stones. Edward I, who died on his way to attack the Scots, lay in state there and a monument to him stands near the village.

CARNFORTH, *Lancashire* (12–SD4970). Nearby are two old houses of interest, open to the public: **Borwick Hall** and **Leighton Hall**, Borwick, about 2 m. NE., stands among fine gardens. It is an Elizabethan manor house, and has not been altered since it was built round an earlier structure in 1595. Leighton Hall occupies a fine site in extensive grounds about 3 m. N. of Carnforth via Yealand Conyers. It has belonged to the Gillow family for many generations and has good early furniture and pictures. The façade of the hall is Gothic, of *c.* 1800–20, superimposed on a Classical building.

S. of Carnforth is **Halton** village on the River Lune, E. of the M6. The churchyard cross is 11th-cent. and its original shaft carved by Norsemen shows a combination of Christian and pagan symbolism. The cross head was added in 1890.

CARROCK FELL, *Cumberland* (14–NY3334), is not easily accessible to the motorist, although a road N. from the A66 to the E. of KESWICK runs below the fell. Thereafter a steep climb leads to the remains of a hill fort. Its unknown builders added to the deterrent of the steep slopes a stone wall surrounding five acres of land. It is possible that it dates from the Early Iron Age, although the fort-dwellers could have been following the earlier Bronze Age mode of life. To the N. are various cairns, similar to one in the enclosure, which may be of the Bronze Age. Do not try the ascent in bad weather, as Dickens and Wilkie Collins are said to have done.

CARTMEL, *Lancashire* (12–SD3778). The village is 2 m. W. of GRANGE-OVER-SANDS, below the high limestone ridge of Hampsfell. The gatehouse and the church are the only two remaining parts of Cartmel Priory. The gatehouse, overlooking the village market cross, is a picturesque building over the street, dating from about 1330. From 1624 to 1790 it was used as a grammar school and is now an artist's studio. It is National Trust property. The Priory Church of St Mary the Virgin, in Transitional style, was founded in 1188. Its square central tower, 15th-cent. in the upper part, is set diagonally on its base. By 1618 the roof had gone, the priory having apparently decayed since the Dissolution, although not destroyed then. George Preston of Holker carried out restoration from 1618, erecting the stall canopies and the superb Renaissance screens. Notable are the stained glass and the carved misericords on the choir stalls. The chancel arcades are round, but the central arches and those in the aisles and the triforium are pointed. The east window is Perpendicular. There are many memorials, including the 14th-cent. Harrington monument with recumbent effigies, and brass chandeliers. Among the many treasures of the priory is a first edition of Spenser's *Faerie Queen*.

The Church of St Andrew at Cartmel Fell, to the N., built about 1503, has roughcast walls and a low tower. It contains screened pews, a three-decker pulpit, good medieval stained glass, and a carved pre-Reformation figure of Christ, a rare specimen, although much damaged.

CASTLE ROCK, *Cumberland* (14–NY3121). Castle Rock is in St John's Vale, and the latter runs N. after the junction of the B5322 and A591 near the north end of THIRLMERE. St John's Beck flows out of Thirlmere, through the vale, and down to the River Greta near THRELKELD. E. is Great Dodd (2,807 ft) and just S. of this is Watson's Dodd, a lower peak which has, jutting up below it, Castle Rock. This is Sir Walter Scott's rock in his poem, *The Bridal of Triermain*, and it is also called the Rock of Triermain. This crag has climbing routes and some are classed as very severe.

Further N., on the west side of the vale, is High Rigg with the Church of St John's-in-the-Vale on its northern slopes. The church was built there in the 19th cent. It seems an unusually high position for a church, but it is believed there was a hermitage of St John there in the 13th cent.

CATON, *Lancashire* (12–SD5365). Caton is famous because of its association with Turner who painted its celebrated Crook O' Lune. This beautiful curve of the Lune's course is best seen in spring, when it is covered with bluebells. St Paul's Church in the hamlet of **Brookhouse** has been entirely rebuilt apart from its 500-year-old tower. The Norman doorway has fragments of an Adam and Eve carving.

Claughton, about 5 m. E. on the A683, has a Tudor house, Claughton Hall, most of which has been moved uphill from its old site. The church, renewed in the last century, has a bell marked 1296, one of the oldest dated English bells.

St John the Baptist's Church (formerly St Michael's), Perpendicular with large buttresses, is at **Tunstall**, further NE. on the A683. When the Brontë sisters were at **Casterton** (*see* KIRKBY LONSDALE, Westmorland) they had to attend this church – the Brocklebridge of *Jane Eyre*. Since then the 500-year-old glass of the east window has been brought from Belgium and a Roman altar stone found.

Thurland Castle nearby has been rebuilt since the destruction of the interior in the Civil War.

CHEADLE, *Cheshire* (12–SJ8788). A pleasant residential area some 7 m. SE. of MANCHESTER but with little left to show of its early history. There is evidence that the Romans maintained a fortification here and that the Anglo-Saxons set up a stone cross on the south bank of the Mersey dedicated to St Chad, from whose name Cheadle is derived. With the coming of the Normans the place had identity enough to be listed in the Domesday Book. The first church at Cheadle was built about 1200 but burnt down in 1520. Only a few fragments of glass and two old monuments remained for incorporation in the 16th-cent. rebuilding, but the 16-windowed clerestory lighting the nave, with its two chapels, and the three stone monuments of knights in armour, together with the many sculptured figures projecting from the exterior are points of unusual interest.

Moseley Old Hall, at the end of Cuthbert Road off Stockport Road, is a half-timbered building bearing the date 1666. It has been much restored in recent times, although a large fire-place and part of a staircase remain unchanged.

CHESTER, *Cheshire* (12–SJ4066). A combination of Roman and medieval relics, as well as many fine timber-framed buildings, makes Chester, the city of Deva, one of England's most interesting old cities. It also contains the architecturally important work of Thomas Harrison, who rebuilt the castle and constructed a single-span bridge here in the early 19th cent., as well as some excellent examples of Victorian black-and-white buildings. It has been chosen for government conservation studies, which will perhaps ensure the survival of its historic monuments.

Little Moreton Hall is an outstanding example of black-and-white architecture   G. Douglas Bolton

Roman occupation in the later 1st cent. made Chester an important military point, with a fortress on a sandstone hill at the head of the estuary. During most of the Roman occupation it was the headquarters of one of the three Roman legions of Britain. The first defences were turf ramparts with wooden gates. After the 1st cent. there was a stone wall with four stone gates and 26 stone towers, and on the north and east sides of the city, from St Martin's Gate to Newgate, the present city wall follows the line of the Roman wall, incorporating parts of it. The west and south sides of the old stone wall were later destroyed and the walls extended over a wider area, including that of the castle. It is not certain whether the extension was made by Romans or Anglo-Saxons, and it could even have been as late as the 12th or early 13th cent. Roman remains were found in the Eastgate when it was rebuilt in 1769. Near steps leading down to Frodsham Street are the lower parts of the Roman wall and the foundation of a 13th-cent. drum tower. Between King Charles' Tower and Northgate are two stretches of Roman wall as much as 17 ft high. The foundations of the Roman gate were found when Northgate was rebuilt in 1808. The open space of the Roodee is where the Romans had a harbour and a large section of their quay wall stands on the race-course below the city walls. The south-east angle of the Roman wall meets the medieval wall near the Wolfe Gate with the lower Roman courses visible. The most important Roman area is the amphitheatre, E. of Newgate. It is the largest Roman amphitheatre so far discovered in Britain, built of stone, covering an area of 314 ft by 286 ft, with an arena 190 ft by 162 ft. The street plan of the city originated with the Romans, and inside the walls the four main streets today follow their plan: Eastgate Street, Watergate Street, Bridge Street and upper Northgate Street. There were Roman roads to London and YORK below Lower Bridge Street and Foregate Street. A Roman hypocaust is in the basement of Quaintways Café, Northgate Street, and on the opposite side, in the cellars of No. 23, are bases, shafts and a capital from the Roman headquarters.

The Roman legion probably abandoned Chester before the early 5th cent. and the fortress was then deserted for hundreds of years. By late Anglo-Saxon times the city was important enough to produce coins at its own mint, and it was four years after the Conquest before the city gave way to Norman rule. The 13th and early 14th cents. were a period of great importance, when the port had become prominent and traded with Ireland, Scotland and parts of the Continent. Like York, Chester had medieval mystery plays, presented at Abbey Square, then the outer court of the Abbey of St Werburgh, and in the streets. In the 15th cent. the city had a military quarrel with the Welsh, but a greater problem was the silting-up of the River Dee, which choked the trade of the port, whereas in Roman times the tower at the northwest corner had stood in the water. This impoverished the city as did the siege in the Civil War which interrupted commerce on land that was never subsequently regained.

The remarkably well-preserved walls, with their medieval reconstruction, provide an interesting walk and cover a circuit of 2 m. There was further re-fortification of the walls in the Tudor and Civil War periods, from which some of the present towers date. The Eastgate with a large 1897 clock is the main entrance. King Charles' Tower (NE.) is said to be where Charles I watched the defeat of his forces by the Parliamentarians after the city had been more or less besieged for two years. The tower has a Civil War exhibition. West of Northgate tower is Morgan's Mount, which was violently bombarded during the Civil War. St Martin's Gate, further W., was built in 1966 to allow the ring road to breach the walls. The Goblin Tower dates from 1702 and 1894. Bonewaldsthorne's Tower is at the northwest corner, connected to the Water Tower which the recession of the Dee left high and dry. The Water Tower built in 1322 is substantially unaltered and contains an exhibition of medieval Chester with dioramas. Watergate, on the west side, was once controlled by the Earls of Derby who charged a toll on goods taken through. Their kinsmen, the Alderley Stanleys, owned Stanley Palace (1591), a fine half-timbered building. By the 16th cent. the city was a well-known centre of drama with Whitsuntide and midsummer festivals; some researchers have suggested that Shakespeare lived in Chester, or even that the author of his plays was not Shakespeare but William Stanley, 6th Earl of Derby. William was brother to the 5th Earl, Ferdinando, who was a patron of actors, including Shakespeare. Bridgegate (S.) is 18th-cent. and replaces a medieval gate. Newgate is modern (1938), built to give more space than the old Wolfe Gate nearby.

The Rows, a unique feature of the city, can be found in Watergate Street, Eastgate Street and Bridge Street. You can inspect modern shops in the appropriate stretches of these streets, take the first flight of steps you find between shops and find yourself walking on the roofs of the shops beside another row of shops set further back; an interesting form of "pedestrian precinct" that surpasses the modern type.

The Cathedral was designed as an abbey church and the buildings round the cloisters were the monks' living-quarters. On this site there was a church or minster founded in the 10th cent. to hold the body of St Werburgh. In 1092, Hugh Lupus, the Norman Earl of Chester, made it an abbey of Benedictine monks, and for five centuries this monastery was powerful and owned much land. After the Dissolution the abbey became a cathedral and bishopric. The consistory court has woodwork and a screen of the 17th cent. The nave was begun in the 14th cent. but not completed until the 16th. In the north aisle of the choir parts of the 12th-cent. abbey church were incorporated in the foundations built some two centuries later. There are remarkable late 14th-cent. carvings on the choir stalls, including a Tree of Jesse with the genealogy of Christ. The

Kenneth Scowen

Chester has many good examples of black-and-white buildings, both medieval and Victorian

south transept is 14th-cent. and was once the Parish Church of St Oswald. There is a fine stone pulpit in the refectory, and the chapter house has early MSS. and printed books.

The Grosvenor Museum has two important Roman galleries, the Newstead and another with an unrivalled collection of inscribed material. A third gallery has coins from Chester mint. An early 18th-cent. house attached to the museum holds costumes, a Victorian room, period furniture, natural history, and watercolours and drawings of the locality.

Chester Zoo, to the N., is famous. Its aim is to show animals, birds, reptiles and fish in conditions as much like their natural environment as possible, and bars and cages are minimized. Gardens are an integral part of it, and there is a special tropical house.

CHIPPING, *Lancashire* (12–SD6243). This charming village has beautiful scenery around, with moorland on the N. It lies in an agricultural area with some old industry. The Church of St Bartholomew is mainly early 16th-cent. with 19th-cent. restoration, but traces survive of all periods from the 12th cent. onward. There is a 12th-cent. piscina.

At **Bleasdale**, NW. of the village, an important discovery was made of wooden posts in a circular area similar to Woodhenge, and relics of human occupation were also found. The posts were intact at a certain distance below ground level but threatened to decay after exposure to the air. They were removed to PRESTON Museum and concrete posts substituted to mark the site.

CHOLMONDELEY, *Cheshire* (12–SJ5351). The large early-19th-cent. castle lies in a 500-acre deer park, between MALPAS and NANTWICH, and is the private residence of the Marquess of Cholmondeley. On the estate, which has close historical connections with Malpas, is a 13th-cent. chapel, rebuilt in the 18th cent. It contains 17th-cent. box pews, a large family pew, altar rails and a fine screen.

CHORLEY, *Lancashire* (12–SD5817). Chorley, with its grim industrial atmosphere, is the indirect source of a great art collection: Henry Tate, founder of the sugar firm, was born here in 1819, and with the fortune he made, he endowed London's TATE GALLERY.

After five minutes' walk from Union Street car park you escape through the big gates of Astley Hall into spacious and peaceful parkland. It takes three or four times as long to stroll across to the Hall (open to the public). This Renaissance structure is superbly set beside placid water. The oldest part dates back to the 16th cent., the main front having been rebuilt in the 17th. The entrance leads into the great hall with its wooden panel portraits, including those of Drake and Columbus. The drawing-room has a fantastically decorated ceiling and tapestries with scenes from the story of the Golden Fleece. Astley Hall's many interesting features and fine furniture include the long gallery's shovel-table, $23\frac{1}{2}$ ft long. In one bedchamber is a bed Cromwell is said to have slept in after the battle of PRESTON. An upper room has been converted into a modern art gallery.

Miles Standish of the *Mayflower* was born at

Duxbury Hall, now demolished, $1\frac{1}{2}$ m. S. of Chorley.

CLIFTON, *Westmorland* (14–NY5326). This was the scene of the last battle on English soil (between English forces and the Jacobites): in 1745, on his retreat from DERBY. Bonnie Prince Charlie had a minor success here before Butcher Cumberland ended his hopes at Culloden. The dead were buried in Clifton churchyard; it was in a sense the last chapter in the long border warfare that had plagued this part of the country (formerly the old Celtic kingdom of Strathclyde), and which is indicated by all the fortified houses and churches and peel-towers, such as those at DACRE, GREY-STOKE or GREAT SALKELD

Clifton is on the A6, like **Eamont Bridge** whose triple-arched medieval bridge has for long carried trunk road traffic into PENRITH. Just S. of Eamont Bridge is **King Arthur's Round Table**. This prehistoric earthwork about 300 ft across is roughly circular and surrounded by a ditch. **Mayburgh** is nearby to the W., another circular structure, wider than the table and with a single standing stone remaining in the centre. Bronze and stone axes were found at Mayburgh.

CLITHEROE, *Lancashire* (12–SD7441), is a very old Ribble Valley town, now an industrial centre but with a pleasant country atmosphere and delightful walks in the locality. The town is the second oldest borough in Lancashire (WIGAN is the oldest) and gained its charter in 1147. Traces of the Roman road from RIBCHESTER to Yorkshire can be seen. Pendle, the 1,831-ft hill on the E. is the reputed old haunt of witches (*see* WHALLEY). The castle on its limestone crag in the town is a dominant landmark. It was built in the 12th cent. before LANCASTER castle; held first by Roger de Poitou, then the de Lacys until 1311, it was a Royalist stronghold in the Civil War and then had various owners. In 1920 it was bought for the town and now much of the 16-acre grounds is a recreational area. Little remains apart from the keep with its 9-ft walls, of interest as one of the oldest stone structures in Lancashire and as the smallest keep in England. St Mary Magdalene Church, on a lesser knoll, has been the site of a church for more than 800 years. In the early 19th cent. the church was dismantled and rebuilt, a twisted spire being added later. The bells were recast in 1658. The Town Hall has the sculpted arms of the de Lacys (the Lords of Lancaster), and carving by a local craftsman inside. An attractive building is the Royal Grammar School; it was founded in 1554, but there is evidence that a school existed as far back as the 13th cent. A notable headmaster was the Rev. T. Wilson, who in the 18th cent. compiled the *Archaeological Dictionary* and dedicated it to Dr Johnson, receiving a flattering acknowledgment. Low Moor, now closed, was a large Lancashire mill built by the Garnett family of Waddow Hall. They built a little self-contained township round the mill, and were connected with the foundation of the *Manchester Guardian*.

Stonyhurst, to the SW., formerly the seat of the Shireburne family, has since 1794 been a Roman Catholic public school, with a library of over 40,000 books. Among its treasures are works printed by Caxton, a copy of the Gospel of St John with a 7th-cent. binding judged to be the oldest in England, and what is believed to be the Book of Hours owned by Mary Stuart at her death. There are paintings attributed to Rubens and Murillo. Arthur Conan Doyle was a pupil here.

Browsholme Hall, NW. of Clitheroe and reached by minor roads, actually stands in beautiful surroundings in Yorkshire. It contains considerable art treasures, and house and gardens are open to the public at advertised times.

COCKERMOUTH, *Cumberland* (14–NY 1230), can be used as a base for motoring tours into the LAKE DISTRICT. It is among the 51 towns recommended by the Council for British Archaeology for preservation. This confluence of the Rivers Cocker and Derwent was a strategic point for the Romans, and stone from their fort at Papcastle was used in 1134 by Waltheof of Dunbar to build a castle. It was partly destroyed by Robert the Bruce, and after various other attacks and sieges was partly dismantled after the Civil War. The present ruins (open to the public) are said to be 13th- and 14th-cent. Cockermouth was a busy market town in the 16th cent., and the county's commercial centre by the mid-17th. It was one of the oldest parliamentary boroughs in the country. The statue in the pleasant wide main street is of Earl Mayo, one of its Members of Parliament. In 1568 Mary Queen of Scots was received at Cockermouth Hall after her flight from the Battle of Langside via WORKINGTON.

Cockermouth was the birthplace of several famous people, including John Dalton, formulator of the atomic theory, and Fletcher Christian, leader of the mutiny on the *Bounty*. The house where Dalton was born is at Eaglesfield, 3 m. SW., and bears a commemorative plaque. Christian was born in 1764 at Moorland Close, a farmhouse near the southern boundary of the town beside the A5086.

But the great figures of Cockermouth, of course, are the Wordsworths, and Wordsworth House (open to the public) is internationally known as one of the two principal residences of the poet to visit in the Lake District, the other being Dove Cottage at GRASMERE. That at Cockermouth is on the north side of Main Street, near the west end, and was acquired by the National Trust in 1938 after a public appeal. It is a handsome house built in 1745 and became the home of William's father in 1766 when he was made steward to Sir James Lowther. William was born here in 1770, and Dorothy in 1771. It is a house with many windows, and the original staircase, fire-places and panelling are to be seen. A reception book holds the names of famous visitors from many parts of the world. William spent some time at a PENRITH school, but when he was only eight, his mother died and he went to HAWKSHEAD. In *The*

Prelude he recalls the garden behind the house, and Dorothy mentions the house in her Journals.

The 19th-cent. Church of All Saints, S. of the market place, has a memorial stained-glass window to Wordsworth, and his father's grave near the east end. He and Fletcher Christian also attended the grammar school, formerly on the site in the churchyard where the church rooms now stand. At Pardshaw the Society of Friends has one of its oldest meeting houses. George Fox preached at Pardshaw Crags in 1657 and 1663.

COLNE, *Lancashire* (12–SD8839), is an old market town, with mixed industries. Beyond it is the moorland country of the Brontës. The Romans had a chain of forts in Lancashire, linked by military roads, and their road from MANCHESTER ran through Colne and on to Yorkshire. The roads in this area, as in other parts of England, were used for centuries after the Romans left; they later carried the produce of hand-loom weaving. The Church of St Bartholomew has Perpendicular features (but was probably begun in an earlier period) and a 16th-cent. roof. There are monuments by Sir Robert Taylor. The town's museum includes collections of geographical, historical, geological and natural history material. Wycoller Hall, E. of Colne and now in ruins, is the house that Charlotte Brontë made into Ferndean Manor in *Jane Eyre*.

CONGLETON, *Cheshire* (12–SJ8562). An important cattle market and Cheshire's second silk town, more concerned today with manufacturing for the general textile trade. At one time there was a minor Roman settlement at the crossing-point on the River Dane where the town now stands, but most signs of early habitation have been swept away in the waves of prosperity that followed. In 1035 it was part of the extensive possessions of Earl Godwin, Harold's father, and was recorded in the Domesday Book of 1086, by which date it had become one of the properties of the great Norman family of de Lacy. In 1272 Henry de Lacy procured a charter freeing Congleton from feudal tolls and conferring the right to hold fairs and a weekly market. During the 13th cent., various trade guilds were formed. It was during this period that Congleton's long association with the production of leather gloves and laces began. After a calamitous flooding of the River Dane in the reign of Henry VI, the king gave permission for the course of the river to be diverted and in addition granted the town a royal mill. The latter events made for a long run of prosperity, lasting until the terrible plague epidemics of 1603 and 1641 wiped out almost the entire local population.

The most prominent citizen in the history of Congleton was the Cromwellian fanatic John Bradshaw, a native of STOCKPORT, in his capacity as Mayor. Bradshaw later became High Steward, Lord Chancellor, and finally Lord President of the High Court when he was to be a key figure in the trial and execution of Charles I. The seals of office he used are kept with other relics of Congleton's past in the present Town Hall, a fine Victorian building, in the Venetian Gothic style, conspicuous by its 110-ft clock tower. Also to be seen here are records of the appointment and activities of various town officers, with the intriguing titles of ale taster, swine catcher, and chimney looker. An interesting oddity is a leather belt, fitted with three bells called St Peter's chains, which was used to proclaim the chimney sweep's holiday in the days when most of this dangerous work was carried out by boys small enough to clamber up the inside of the stack. It was the custom for three priests or acolytes to dance with these belts on the Eve of St Peter's Day, a link with pagan times when it was believed that the ceremony would drive away evil spirits. Another item in the collection is one of the old branks, or scold's bridles, with a chain by which nagging wives could be attached to a wall in the market place.

St Peter's Church is a plain 18th-cent. structure, unremarkable except for its profusion of massive woodwork in the interior, which includes a Jacobean pulpit and a fine lectern decorated with four apostles and an angel. On one of the walls is a memorial to Sir Thomas Reade, who was a member of the Governor's entourage at St Helena when Napoleon was a captive there and in another connection became famous for having persuaded the Bey of Tunis to abolish slavery as long ago as 1849. Of the few half-timbered houses still standing in Congleton, three are inns: the curiously-fronted White Lion Hotel; the Swan and Lion, which dates from the 15th cent.; and the Bear's Head Hotel, named after the medieval sport of bear-baiting which flourished longer in Congleton than anywhere else in the country.

CONISTON, *Lancashire* (14–SD3097). This village lies on the west side of CONISTON WATER, and is accessible from AMBLESIDE, N., from BROUGHTON or Lowick Bridge, S., or from BOWNESS ferry, E. Along the NW. of the village run the Coniston Fells, dominated by Coniston Old Man, with the DUDDON VALLEY behind them. Coniston is the centre for ascents of this range. In the churchyard is the cross commemorating Ruskin (*see* CONISTON WATER). Of hard green local stone, the cross is carved on four sides, one of them showing an artist drawing with the sun rising above pine trees. The small Ruskin Museum in Yewdale Road illustrates the life and work of the critic and writer, together with material relating to the locality. On view are handbells with which he made musical experiments, specimens of his mineral collection (he presented the Edwardes Ruby to the NATURAL HISTORY MUSEUM, London), his paintbox and sketch books, and drawings and books.

Tarn Hows, celebrated for its beauty, is NE. of the village and near the road, surrounded by areas of National Trust property. It is a favourite place for excursions, and from the slopes above there are magnificent views of mountains that include Red Screes, Fairfield, the HELVELLYN range and

LANGDALE PIKES. Yewdale Tarn is near, and W. lies the Tilberthwaite valley with a series of waterfalls.

CONISTON WATER, *Lancashire* (14–SD 3094),

is about 5½ m. long, with tree-lined bays, and its background of wooded hills and mountains on the W. make a striking picture. The Coniston Fells run along the north-west side of the lake, rising to 2,633 ft at the summit of Coniston Old Man. Beyond them Grey Friar and Dow Crag look down on the DUDDON VALLEY. There are continuous ridges leading to several connected heights on the Coniston range. Old Man is a well-known peak for climbers and walkers, but its east side particularly, and other parts of the range, have been defaced by old quarries and copper mines; these should be avoided for safety reasons. Around the lake most place-names have Norse origins, as elsewhere in Lakeland. There is fishing, boating and swimming on the lake. It was here that Donald Campbell died in 1967 in an attempt to break the water speed record.

Brantwood (open to the public) is on the east side. John Ruskin bought this house in 1871, and died there in 1900. Ruskin insisted on the value of hand-made as against machine-made goods, and preached the gospel of beauty. He could read and write at the age of four, at six began trying to write books and at seven poetry. Volume I of his *Modern Painters* (arising from his spirited defence of Turner) made him famous as an art critic at 24. He championed the Pre-Raphaelites, and opened a window on the beauty of Italian art. A passionate campaigner, he spent most of his father's legacy of £157,000 on educational work, gifts and attempts to improve working-class conditions. While at Brantwood Ruskin attempted one of his industrial experiments, a revival of the old hand-made linen industry at ELTERWATER; and at KESWICK his work is also remembered. In CONISTON village the museum and churchyard cross are a reminder of the man who believed that the gentleman should labour and the labourer should exercise mind and soul. Brantwood is kept by the Education Trust as a memorial. It contains some 250 paintings by Ruskin.

Another old building is Tent Lodge, where Tennyson once stayed. Monk Coniston Hall is a National Trust property that is let to the Holiday Fellowship. Among various routes for walks are those towards Walna Scar, Broughton Mills, the Grizedale Forest (*see* HAWKSHEAD, nature trail), and W. of Water Yeat and Blawith. **Tarn Hows** to the N. gives good views along Coniston Water.

CROSBY GARRETT, *Westmorland* (14–NY 7309),

near KIRKBY STEPHEN, has a group of ancient village settlement sites. They comprise three lying roughly in line over about 1,000 yds, the south-west one being largest. It has remains of a large rectangular hut and smaller ones. The other two sites are similar but smaller. Around them are the traces of boundaries and pathways.

The Church of St Andrew at Crosby Garrett village is mainly Norman.

CROSBY RAVENSWORTH, *Westmorland* (14–NY6214),

E. of SHAP, is a village in an area of great antiquity. On a 2- or 3-m. stretch of moorland about 1 m. SW. are some 90 sites of prehistoric village settlements. One of them, Ewe Close, has walls about 6 ft high, and covers more than an acre roughly square in shape where there are also traces of banks and ditches. It is believed to date from the Iron Age and also to have been occupied in Roman times. Another, Burwens, has the remains of a hut, 25 ft across, inside an enclosure of about 1 acre with a causeway outside it. The picturesque village has the Church of St Lawrence, of the 15th cent. or earlier, the origins of which were 11th-cent.

CROSSCANONBY, *Cumberland* (14–NY 0739),

lies N. of the A596 about 3 m. from MARYPORT. The Church of St John the Evangelist is a 12th-cent. structure with later additions, but it made use of Roman stones in its early stages. There is a carved hog-back tomb, some interesting Anglo-Saxon and early Norman carving, and some early 18th-cent. woodwork. In 1880 C. J. Ferguson of CARLISLE made a conscientious restoration.

CROSTON, *Lancashire* (12–SD4818),

stands in the valley of the twisting River Yarrow. The Royal Umpire Museum and Carriage Exhibition (open to the public) is on the CHORLEY to SOUTHPORT road. This is one of the country's best collections of old carriages and coaches, and it includes vintage cars. Other attractions of the museum are relics from old Croston Hall, a replica of an 18th-cent. village, and a monk's cell. There is also an aviary, a children's playground and a lake and waterfall.

A church was on the site of St Michael's in the reign of the Conqueror; it is supposed to have been rebuilt in 1577 and was restored in 1866–7.

CRUMMOCK WATER, *Cumberland* (14–NY1519).

Like BUTTERMERE to the S., Crummock Water has the road (B5289) along its east side. It must be approached (by road) from either the north or south end, and lies in the same valley as Buttermere, to which it was probably joined once. Crummock is a fairly large lake, 2½ m. long, and has Grasmoor, 2,791 ft, E. of its northern end and S. of it is Whiteless Pike. An impressive sight on the W. of the lake is Mellbreak; it is only 1,668 ft high but below its top lie the screes. A path lies along the lake below Mellbreak, between the Buttermere end and a subsidiary road from the village of LOWESWATER at the N. On the W. of the main road and just N. of the lake is Lanthwaite Hill. It is only 674 ft high and well worth climbing for a fine view along the lake towards GREAT GABLE beyond Buttermere. Coming down to Crummock Water S. of Mellbreak is Scale Force, the highest waterfall in the Lakes. It drops more than 100 ft, and after rain

Noel Habgood

Coniston Water lies in an area of fine wooded country: a view of Tarn Hows

is even more striking. Crummock Water, owned by the National Trust, is a good area for walking, climbing and fishing.

DACRE, *Cumberland* (14–NY4526). A few miles W. and N. of PENRITH a number of fortifications, such as peel-towers, were built against Scottish raiders who, in the 14th and 15th cents., often came south through what was then the Royal Forest of Inglewood. *See* GREYSTOKE (church and castle).

Dacre Castle, 14th-cent., was one stronghold which later became a farm-house. Hutton-in-the-Forest is a romantic house consisting of a 14th-cent. peel-tower with 17th-cent. and later additions. The house and gardens, laid out in the 17th cent., are open by appointment. Hutton John is a peel-tower near Dacre (open by appointment), where a manor house was added later.

Dacre's church, St Andrew's, has 9th- or 10th-cent. cross shafts and an Early English chancel. Bede's ecclesiastical history mentions a monastery at Dacre in the 7th cent. It was here, according to tradition, that the Scots met King Athelstan of England to sign a treaty in the 10th cent. Dacre Castle may be on the site of this meeting.

DALTON, *Lancashire* (12–SD4907), is a small village about 5½ m. NW. of WIGAN, where the River Douglas winds along on the N. In this stretch of fertile farmland, which contrasts with the busy towns it supplies with its crops, is Ashurst Hill. The old beacon on top of the hill is a prominent landmark with its pointed top which from a distance looks like a church steeple. It was built of strong masonry, with nothing inflam-

mable, in the Napoleonic war, and was intended as one of that chain of beacons right across England which would blaze to raise the alarm when invasion was imminent. In this neighbourhood was built a curious structure called Parbold Bottle, looking like a large beehive, which is said to commemorate the Reform Act of 1832.

DALTON-IN-FURNESS, *Lancashire* (12–SD2374), was the old capital of the Furness district. Its castle, of which the 14th-cent. tower remains in the main street, was the Court House of the Abbot of St Mary, but after the Dissolution the district's trade gradually passed to ULVERSTON. During the 19th cent. Dalton became important again while its iron-ore mines were busy, but did not regain its position as the market town of Furness. George Romney, the portrait painter, was born in a house called Beckside nearby in 1734, and worked with his father, a cabinet-maker, at a house at High Cocken. He was apprenticed to Steele, an artist, at KENDAL, before achieving fame in London, particularly with portraits of Emma Hart, later Lady Hamilton. The NATIONAL and TATE galleries have works by Romney. He died at Kendal in 1802 and was buried at Dalton, in the parish churchyard.

Urswick, to the E., has the Church of St Mary where a rush-bearing ceremony is still performed. Three dolorosas on the west wall were almost completely destroyed by Cromwellians. There is an organ-grinder and monkey carved in wood, a well-carved font top, a three-decker pulpit, fragments of a 9th-cent. Anglo-Saxon cross, and a Viking cross with runic inscriptions. The church has a massive tower as well as box pews.

DARESBURY, *Cheshire* (12–SJ5782). The parsonage, now demolished, in this village was the birthplace, in 1832, of the Rev. Charles Lutwidge Dodgson, poet, mathematician and author. He took deacon's orders in 1861. He became famous under his pen-name of Lewis Carroll when he published *Alice's Adventures in Wonderland* in 1865. He also wrote on mathematics, and lectured for 20 years on the subject at OXFORD. The Daresbury church is the delight of all children (and not a few adults) for its memorial window depicting the Cheshire Cat, White Rabbit and other characters. Daresbury Hall is a fine brick Georgian house.

DERWENTWATER, *Cumberland* (14–NY26 21). The lake is oval in shape, 3 m. long and $\frac{1}{2}$ m. to $1\frac{1}{4}$ m. wide. Round most of the lake the rounded forms of the mountains are due to the effect of weathering on the SKIDDAW slate. The grass-covered slopes are broken here and there by sharper screes where the brittle rock has fallen away. But the eastern crags, and especially the heights piled beyond the south end of Derwentwater, through BORROWDALE up to SCA FELL, are composed of hard volcanic blocks. The only break in the encircling slopes is to the NW., where the longest Lakeland valley, beginning in Borrowdale below the central cluster of peaks, carries the River Derwent out through BASSENTHWAITE LAKE. The vast bulks of Skiddaw (3,054 ft), fourth highest of the LAKE DISTRICT mountains, and SADDLEBACK, lie across the north, sheltering KESWICK. The roads to PENRITH and GRASMERE climb out of Keswick at the lake's northeast corner. Contours rise to Bleaberry Fell and High Seat (1,996 ft) to shut in the lake along the east side. Across the S. is the glorious sight of the opening of Borrowdale beyond the lakeside road, through the Jaws of Borrowdale, beyond which Castle Crag stands, with the rugged Glaramara, and BOW FELL and Sca Fell, further S. The Dale Head group of peaks come down the west of Borrowdale to the south-west corner of Derwentwater at Manesty Park, and near here is Brackenburn, the house where Hugh Walpole lived. His *Rogue Herries* series of novels covers various Lakeland scenes, as at WATENDLATH. This valley, an offshoot to the E. of Borrowdale, is approached by a road leaving the lakeside route and crossing **Ashness Bridge,** a noted beauty-spot overlooking Derwentwater. Just W. of this area and behind the Lodore Hotel are the well-known Lodore Falls, cascades in Watendlath Beck. To complete the scene on the lake's west shore is the lower but graceful shape of Cat Bells, followed by Swinside.

Below Cat Bells are the 108 acres of Brandelhow, the first property acquired by the National Trust in the Lake District. The Trust protects for the public many acres of beauty around the Derwentwater area. Among them are Castle Head, which gives a good view of the lake on the NE.; and below this Friar's Crag, another famous vantage point, notable for the Ruskin memorial; as well as St Herbert's, Lord's, and Derwent islands. On St Herbert's Island are traces of the home of St Herbert, a disciple of St Cuthbert in the 7th cent., although these traces could be of a later structure. Lord's Island was the residence of the Earls of Derwentwater.

As well as fishing and swimming facilities there is a motor launch service and motor boats and rowing boats can be hired. You can also drive all the way round this, the widest of the Lakes.

DORFOLD HALL, *Cheshire* (12–SJ6352). This handsome Jacobean country house (open to the public) is 1 m. W. of NANTWICH on the road to TARPORLEY. The hall dates from about 1616, and is noted for the fine plasterwork decoration of its ceilings and its panelling. It was for long the home of the Wilbraham family, well known in Cheshire. During the Civil War Dorfold Hall was captured by the Royalists who used it as a site from which to attack Nantwich. The hall stands in a large park with fine gates and is approached along an avenue of trees.

DUDDON VALLEY, *Cumberland* (14–SD 1988). The River Duddon rises near Three Shires Stone at the top of WRYNOSE PASS. At the stone you can step through Cumberland, Westmorland and Lancashire within a few seconds. The river descends through Wrynose Bottom, dividing Cumberland on the W. from Lancashire on the E. And from here, where it leaves the road that begins (at Cockley Beck Bridge) to climb HARDKNOTT PASS, the river is the county boundary to the sea. A road follows the Duddon's east side through Seathwaite (not the BORROWDALE one) and Dunnerdale villages, crosses to Ulpha in Cumberland, and returns to the east side to join the A595 at Duddon Bridge. The CONISTON range is on the E. At Ulpha you can turn NW. to reach ESKDALE without surmounting Hardknott Pass. The lower area of Duddon is also called Dunnerdale.

The river inspired 35 of Wordsworth's sonnets; his Notes on the Duddon series commemorate the Rev. Robert Walker–"Wonderful Walker"– of the now rebuilt Seathwaite church. The poet's "Kirk of Ulpha", built in local stone, is still there.

EASEDALE, *Westmorland* (14–NY3110). This is a small dale on the north-west side of GRASMERE. The walk up and down it from Read's bookshop in the town covers 4 m. and includes a rise of about 700 ft. It is approached by crossing the KESWICK road and entering Easedale Tarn Road. After passing through several gates, you begin to climb more steeply, beside Sour Milk Ghyll (the same name as the one in BUTTERMERE), which forms some fine waterfalls. At the top of the rise you turn left on to a level stretch and then climb to the ruins of a refreshment hut and to the tarn. W. are High Raise and Sergeant Man peaks, both over 2,000 ft. The dale is rocky in places.

ECCLES, *Lancashire* (12–SJ7798), is 4 m. W. of MANCHESTER, and its south boundary lies along

T. Parker

The Duddon divides Cumberland from Lancashire

Eccles is famous for its cakes

British Travel Association

the Ship Canal with which the town's more modern growth has been associated. On the River Irwell medieval villages developed into towns, including Patricroft and Ellesmere Park, which eventually became part of the borough of Eccles. This is in a busy part of Lancashire, with the M62 motorway at the west side, but nevertheless has some pleasant countryside beyond the motorway. The central library contains microfilm records of local history and special collections dealing with Harold Brighouse, the dramatist, Lettice Cooper, novelist, and James Nasmyth, the inventor of the steam hammer. Monk's Hall is the oldest secular building; it dates from the Tudor period, with early 19th-cent. additions. The hall was a farmhouse during the 17th, 18th and early 19th cents., then became a residence; it was bought by the corporation, and opened as a museum and art gallery in 1961. Machine tools made by Nasmyth at his Bridgewater foundry are on show, as well as monthly night sky charts; there are permanent collections of art and pottery, as well as temporary exhibitions. In the 1862 restoration of St Mary's, the parish church, Norman masonry was found, but it is thought that there was an earlier Christian church on the site in Anglo-Saxon times. In the 13th cent. there was a church comprising a chancel, a nave without aisles, and a tower. Various alterations and additions were made during the next two centuries. The Boothe chantry chapel is 14th-cent. and in the 15th a clerestory and the handsome panelling were added. Until 1939 curfew was rung by St Mary's. Near the pulpit is part of the shaft of a pre-Conquest cross. The oak south door is 14th-cent. and there is some 16th-cent. Flemish glass.

Having inspected ancient and modern features, and noted that the aeronautical pioneer Sir Alliot Verdon-Roe was born at the house named The Poplars, visitors may recall another tradition: Eccles cakes. A shop in Church Street still makes them from the original recipe, and was rebuilt in the 19th cent. on the site of their first production.

ECCLESTON, *Lancashire* (12–SJ4895), a village on the western boundary of ST HELENS, that was the birthplace of Richard Seddon, who became Prime Minister of New Zealand. Christ Church is a massive 19th-cent. building in red sandstone with a spire and high pinnacles. It was designed by Samuel Taylor. Inside are an oak gallery and hammer-beam roof. There are lavish carvings of fruit, flowers and foliage. Panels from New Zealand include a memorial to Seddon.

EGREMONT, *Cumberland* (14–NY0110), on the A595, near the more pleasant area of ST BEES, is an industrial town producing plastic and leather goods, and with a grimy air due to the reddish iron ore with which it has been particularly associated. But even here Wordsworth found inspiration. In 1806 he wrote "The Horn of Egremont Castle", ". . . which none could sound . . . Save He who came as rightful Heir". This castle, of the House of Lucie, was built about 1140 to uphold Norman rule, but was destroyed in the

16th cent. and is now a ruin. St Mary's is on the site of a church believed to date from the 12th cent. It is late 19th-cent. but includes early features.

ELTERWATER, *Westmorland* (14–NY3204). This small lake, not easy of access on its shores, is at the entrance to the LANGDALE valleys. There was formerly much slate production in the area, and some is still carried on today. Varied species of bird frequent this lake. On the River Brathay, which flows from the SE. of Elterwater, there is the charming waterfall of Skelwith Force before the river reaches Skelwith Bridge. A path leads to the fall from near this bridge. At Neaum Crag is the caravan, chalet and camping site run by the Lake District Planning Board. The site covers 18 acres of fell and woodland, with good views from the higher part. White Craggs Rock Garden (open to the public), at the junction of the A593 and B5343, has a colourful display of rare shrubs, azaleas and rhododendrons; it also has parking space. Near Elterwater village, at the late 17th-cent. St Martin's Farm, John Ruskin (*see* CONISTON WATER) established a centre for the revival of the hand-made linen industry.

ENNERDALE WATER, *Cumberland* (14–NY1015). It is impossible to approach this lake by road except from the W., and it is the most westerly of all the lakes. Near the west end of the lake the track becomes very rough and you must proceed on foot or not at all. From there the dale stretches SE. for about 8 m. and near its head Black Sail Pass leads to the SW. into WASDALE for WASTWATER. The pass is only a track, of course, 1,800 ft up in the wild and very isolated region of Ennerdale that is a favourite with rock-climbers. The High Stile range lies along the north-east side of the dale with BUTTERMERE beyond. On the south-west side is the Pillar group of peaks with the formidable-looking Pillar Rock dominating the view of precipices; Pillar itself is higher (2,927 ft) and further back. Then beyond Black Sail Pass and Kirk Fell the dale is closed by the majestic GREAT GABLE.

The National Trust owns many acres of land stretching over into Stockdale and Wasdale. But the approach to Ennerdale by road has less in common with the peaceful solitude of these acres encompassing or adjoining the mighty peaks; it is more akin to the Cumberland coastal stretch and the decayed industrial atmosphere of Cleator Moor. There are various old iron mines, and the iron ore was known in Roman times. A mile or so W. of the lake is the small village of Ennerdale Bridge. Its churchyard was the setting for Wordsworth's poem, "The Brothers".

ESKDALE, *Cumberland* (14–SD1599), can be reached either up the extremely steep HARDKNOTT PASS from the E., or from the W. The west end is reached by various roads from the coastal area, and one crossing over the Esk from further down the DUDDON VALLEY. In summer, as a change from driving, you can take the miniature railway from **Ravenglass** as far as BOOT. The lower reaches, green with farmland, have occasional houses dotted about and footpaths near the River Esk. Beyond the villages of Eskdale Green and Boot the valley turns towards the N., leaving the road before Hardknott, and rises into the wild regions between the two SCA FELL peaks (both over 3,000 ft) and BOW FELL (nearly 3,000 ft). At the end is Esk Hause, where the Sca Fell and Bow Fell tracks join at the watershed above BORROWDALE. Around the hause is a conjunction of tracks well known to climbers – those from WASDALE, from Borrowdale and from LANGDALE. At 2,490 ft, this is the highest pass in Lakeland.

ESTHWAITE WATER, *Lancashire* (14–SD 3596), is a beautiful small lake only about 1½ m. long. Small roads surround the lake, there are fells in the distance, and nearby are the wooded areas that lie between CONISTON WATER and WINDERMERE. Historic HAWKSHEAD is close to the N. of the lake and Ruskin's home, Brantwood, is beside Coniston Water. Rowing boats can be hired on Esthwaite, which has trout and perch, and birdlife around its quiet recesses.

Wray Castle is NE., near Windermere. It is a mansion built in early Victorian times in the medieval style. It is National Trust property and the grounds are open to the public. Esthwaite Hall, on the west side of its own lake, is a historic house which became the home of the Sandys family. Edwin Sandys was Archbishop of YORK in the 16th cent.

Hill Top, a house popular with visitors, is E. of Esthwaite Water, in Near Sawrey, a village which, like Hawkshead, can be reached by the ferry from BOWNESS across Windermere. In 1944, under the will of Beatrix Potter, the National Trust acquired about half the village, including Hill Top and Castle Farm, cottages, Town Bank estate and a field. The 17th-cent. house (open to the public) contains Beatrix Potter's furniture, china, pictures and some of her drawings and is full of the atmosphere of characters from her books such as Jemima Puddleduck and Tom Kitten. She invented the Peter Rabbit character earlier, and was able to buy Hill Top, and there continued her series of children's books.

EUXTON, *Lancashire* (12–SD5518). With the River Yarrow nearby on the S., and on a site some 2 m. W. of CHORLEY, Euxton has a little church that seems to have lost the record of its dedication. It consists of a 14th-cent. nave without aisles, and has the date of 1513 on the south wall. Rebuilt about 1724, and enlarged in the 19th cent., the church has a good roof, which has been reinforced, and an old sundial.

FARNWORTH, *Lancashire* (12–SJ5187). This village adjoins Widnes, the industrial port on the Mersey. The Church of St Luke, of 12th-cent. origin, retains its 14th-cent. tower and south arcade. It was restored later. It has Tudor wood ceilings in the south transept and the chancel. The chapel of the Bold family was rebuilt about 1855. There are interesting monuments.

FLEETWOOD, *Lancashire* (12–SD3247), faces into MORECAMBE Bay at the mouth of the River Wyre. On a clear day you can see from the Mount Pavilion, above the Marine Hall and gardens, across the bay to the LAKE DISTRICT fells and inland to the Lune valley and the Pennines.

Fleetwood was originally the northern terminus of the railway from Euston, with connections by sea to Scotland and Ireland. In 1847 Queen Victoria first set foot in Lancashire at Fleetwood on her return from Scotland.

Fleetwood is a fishing port and a resort, bounded by the sea on three sides. It has a fine promenade and spacious sea-front gardens, a marine pool and an amusement park. Pleasure cruises cross Morecambe Bay and there is a hovercraft service.

The town was founded in 1836 by Sir Peter Hesketh-Fleetwood of Rossall Hall, 2 m. to the S., which became a public school in 1844. Decimus Burton laid out the town, but did not complete the plan. His buildings include the North Euston Hotel, Queen's Terrace, both lighthouses and the lodge to the Mount Pavilion.

FORMBY, *Lancashire* (12–SD2907). The sea was here once and there was a fishing village on the shore, but the sea has receded as on various parts of the west coast. At Formby it is a mile or so away, beyond extensive sandhills. The National Trust control 400 acres of sand dunes and foreshore W. of the town. These were bought by public subscription in 1967 as part of Enterprise Neptune, and constitute the nearest unspoilt coastline to the centre of LIVERPOOL. The Church of St Peter of brick and stone was built in 1736. It has a bell-turret, large windows with round tops and clear glass. A chancel and side chapel were built in Gothic style in 1873.

FOXDENTON HALL, *Lancashire* (12–SD 9005), is in Foxdenton Park, Chadderton, about 4 m. NE. of MANCHESTER, and owned by the Chadderton Urban Council. This Stuart mansion (open to the public) was restored in 1965. The present structure dates from the beginning of the 18th cent., when it was erected on the base of the 1620 hall which was partly demolished. There had been an earlier hall owned by the de Trafford family.

FURNESS ABBEY, *Lancashire* (12–SD2271), lies NE. of BARROW-IN-FURNESS in a narrow, thickly-wooded valley. Its red sandstone ruins are an Ancient Monument, open to the public, and show the great size of this rich and powerful religious house. Savignac monks founded the abbey in 1127. When the parent house at Savigny in Normandy adopted the Cistercian rule about 1147, the Furness monks followed suit. King Stephen endowed the abbey with nearly all the Furness area, later kings adding large estates in other parts of Lancashire and in Yorkshire. The Abbot of Furness ruled the district as a feudal lord from an abbey that was richly decorated and had well-equipped domestic buildings. The monks

administered the area until the Dissolution, and built a castle on Piel Island as a refuge from Scottish raids.

The parts of the church nave and transepts that remain date from the 12th to 13th cents. Notable features include the late Norman arches of the cloisters; three fine Transitional arches on the east of the north transept; the Early English chapter house, an extension of the south transept; and the good carved work of the sedilia and piscina. Among other remains are the infirmary and the abbot's lodging.

GAWSWORTH, *Cheshire* (12–SJ8869). An enchanting village, set among forest, parkland and ornamental ponds. The beautiful timber-framed Gawsworth Old Hall was the seat of the Fytton family from the time of building in the 16th cent. until it was taken over by the Mainwarings. The house is notable for its black-and-white gable and great windows overlooking spacious lawns and gardens embellished with five lakes. In the grounds are the traces of one of the finest tilting arenas in England, 200 yds long and over 60 yds wide. That it should have been here was fully in character with the reputation for aggressiveness which caused the Fytton family to be known as "The Fighting Fyttons" among the chroniclers.

At the end of an avenue of elms is the Old Rectory, with its black-and-white medieval walls dating from 1470. The building encompasses a gracious central hall with an open roof and carved timbers, the whole fronted by a window made up of scores of diamond panes. The church is mainly a 15th-cent. Perpendicular structure, on Norman foundations, and stands near two of the Gawsworth lakes in company with yews which may well have supplied the Cheshire archers with bows in the 12th cent. Gargoyles and other carvings enrich the tower, matching their oddity with heraldic shields and canopied niches ornamenting the buttresses. A Tudor doorway leads from the neat stone porch to the nave, with its 400-year-old font bowl and delightful painted roof. In the chancel are the tombs of the Fytton family, one of whom, Sir Edward Fytton, married Anne Warburton when he was only 12 years of age and she a month younger. They lived together for 34 years in uninterrupted harmony and had 15 children. A son, also Sir Edward, born in 1550, became Lord President of Munster and died in London in 1606. His monument is at Gawsworth church without his effigy, but his wife and children are represented in stone at the side of the space it should have occupied. One of the daughters in the group attained the distinction of being accepted as a favourite maid of honour by Elizabeth I, but was soon in disgrace following an affair with the Earl of Pembroke. It is of particular interest that she is now thought to have been the Dark Lady of Shakespeare's sonnets.

Near the church is a wood in which may be seen the tomb of "Maggotty Johnson", sometimes called "Lord Flame" after the leading character in one of his operas. He was by profession a fiddle-player and stilt-walker, who had begun life as a dancing-master, and is remembered more for his eccentricity as a person than as a playwright. The opera was called *Hurlothrumbo* and ran for a month, encouraging Johnson to write three more plays in expectation of a London production, but this time he failed to arouse any interest and returned, chastened, to the village. He died in 1773, aged 82, and was buried in the place of his own choosing.

The new Hall, much larger than the old one, was built early in the 18th cent. by Lord Mohun, whose duel with the Duke of Hamilton in KENSINGTON GARDENS resulted in both their deaths. The duel, which arose from differences connected with the disposal of the estate, became the subject of a chapter in Thackeray's *Henry Esmond*. The new Hall is now a home for the aged, but Gawsworth Old Hall is open to visitors.

GILSLAND, *Cumberland* (14–NY6366), is about 1 m. N. of the A69 from CARLISLE and is a small village at the edge of the county where the River Irthing flows down from almost deserted land stretching to the Scottish border. A good section of HADRIAN'S WALL extends to Gilsland from the E. Part of Poltross Burn milecastle is in the railway embankment, and a stretch of wall is in a garden E. of the school. There are Roman inscriptions on two altars. The Wall continues W. It was in Gilsland that Sir Walter Scott met Charlotte Carpenter, and they were married in Carlisle. Several years after their marriage, they revisited the wells of Gilsland, to spend a few days among the scenes where they had first met. Whilst they were at the spa, the invasion was signalled by beacon-flares on hill-tops and Martello towers spread across England. Scott immediately set off on horseback to volunteer to fight Napoleon, and rode a hundred miles into Scotland in twenty-four hours; only to find that it was a false alarm.

Birdoswald, close to Gilsland, has the remains of a 5-acre Roman fort, comprising walls and east gateway.

Brampton, W., is a pleasant market town. The Written Rock of Gelt, a rock inscribed by a Roman standard bearer, is on the River Gelt $1\frac{1}{2}$ m. S. of Brampton.

Bewcastle, a Roman site, is 11 m. N. of Brampton and has some remains of a castle. The famous Bewcastle Cross, the only one of its kind in England, is in the churchyard. It is a shaft, dating from the late 7th cent., classed as an Ancient Monument. St John the Baptist, Christ, and a "falconer" (St John the Evangelist? or Alcfrith?) are shown, with Runic inscriptions and decorations.

GRANGE-OVER-SANDS, *Lancashire* (12–SD4178). Backed by wooded fells, Grange is a fine seaside resort, sheltered and with a mild climate, overlooking MORECAMBE Bay. It has a promenade free of traffic, good sands, a bathing pool and tennis and golf. There is pony-trekking to CARTMEL (2 m.). The Lakeland Rose Show is held annually at the beginning of July. The town's parks are noted for flowering shrubs, alpine and rock plants and herbaceous plants. Many species of bird have been noted, and sometimes the rare golden eagle at WITHERSLACK. The Nature Conservancy has a research station at Merlewood. Nearby Hampsfell (750 ft) has an indicator and view of LAKE DISTRICT mountains.

Lindale, 2 m. N., has a monument to John Wilkinson, the 18th-cent. ironmaster, who launched the first iron ship, on the River Winster.

GRASMERE, *Westmorland* (14–NY3307). This tranquil little lake is famous above all as Wordsworth's home from 1799 until he moved to RYDAL in 1813. Dove Cottage, where he lived for nine years, is open to the public. The site of his Wishing Gate is on the old road, which gives fine views of the lake running behind the main road along the east shore. There is a little island of which Coleridge wrote, "We drank tea the night before I left Grasmere, on the island in that lovely lake, our kettle swung over the fire, hanging from the branch of a Fir-tree". Rowing boats can be hired.

The area around village and lake is notable for the scenery along various walking routes. The strikingly shaped Helm Crag lies NW., Rydal Fell and Nab Scar lie E., and Yew Crag and Silver Howe W. Apart from the main road, the only motoring exit is SW. past the lake to Red Bank where the road forks right for ELTERWATER and the LANGDALE PIKES, and left to pass Loughrigg. From the top of the steep bank the path of Loughrigg Terrace on the left gives fine views of the lake. There is little parking space at Red Bank, and cars are better left at the village or White Moss Common in order to cross the Rothay footbridge and come up at the middle of the Terrace. This continues E. above RYDAL WATER, and past a huge cave left from an old quarry which can be penetrated by the light from the entrance. Other walks are to Helm Crag, to Grey Crag and Alcock Tarn, to Silver Howe, to Dow Bank, and to Swinescar Hause. To reach the tops of Helm Crag, the Howe and Swinescar, however, you must climb over 1,000 ft.

GRASMERE (VILLAGE), *Westmorland* (14–NY3307). Placed just W. of the main road to the N. of GRASMERE (LAKE), the village can be missed by the motorist. Grasmere village and its offshoot to the S., the tiny group of houses of Town End, are not particularly notable in themselves; it is their setting below Helm Crag and Nab Scar, above the lake, which provides the attraction. Wordsworth pronounced it "the loveliest spot that man hath ever found", and Thomas Gray called it "this little unsuspected paradise".

At Town End is Dove Cottage (open to the public), the home of Wordsworth where he lived with his sister, Dorothy, from 1799 to 1808. He brought his bride, Mary, to Dove Cottage in 1802. What is often regarded as his best work was written at this small house, a former inn, and probably built in the 17th cent.; and it was a meeting point for famous literary figures – Coleridge, Southey, de Quincey and others. It is preserved almost as it was when Wordsworth lived there, by the Dove Cottage Trust, and holds many relics. Coleridge followed Wordsworth to the Lakes in 1800 and lived at Greta Hall, KESWICK, until 1804. He returned to the Lakes in 1808 and lived for two years at Wordsworth's next home, Allan Bank. Later, de Quincey lived in Dove Cottage for 26 years from 1809. The Wordsworth Museum nearby contains MSS. and other important items.

Allan Bank, Wordsworth's next home, is just NW. of the village. Owned by the National Trust, it is private, but visitors may view it from the drive. While there from 1808 to 1811, the poet wrote most of *The Excursion*. He then lived at the old rectory, opposite St Oswald's Church, before moving to RYDAL in 1813.

In *The Excursion* he gives a description of St Oswald's, which he attended during his life at Grasmere. In the churchyard are the graves of Wordsworth and his wife, his sister, his daughter Dora and her husband, and of Hartley Coleridge. It is believed that there was a 12th-cent. church on the site, of which parts may be incorporated in the present one. It contains the 17th-cent. manor pew of the Le Fleming family, with other monuments. A Wordsworth plaque, a pitch pipe, old chairs and alms box can be seen. An annual rush-bearing festival is held, similar to the one at AMBLESIDE.

The Grasmere Sports is famous and traditionally is held on the Thursday nearest to 20 August. Up to 20,000 spectators gather in a large field to watch the Cumberland and Westmorland wrestlers, the hound trail, the athletes who race to the top of Butter Crag, and other events.

The Swan Hotel, an old coaching inn, appears in Wordsworth's poem *The Waggoner*. At the bottom of the south slope of Helm Crag is Lancrigg, the house where Wordsworth composed much of *The Prelude*, walking to and fro on a garden terrace as his sister took it down.

The 1970 Wordsworth Bi-Centenary Celebrations, supported by Mr Richard Wordsworth, great-great-grandson of the poet, and Cecil Day-Lewis, the Poet Laureate – with the inclusion of the world première of Wordsworth's only play, "The Borderers" – underline the importance of his Grasmere period. It was appropriate to arrange these events in the village, a place Wordsworth always valued for the inspiration such an environment gave "to see into the heart of things".

GREAT GABLE, *Cumberland* (14–NY2110). This is the seventh highest Lake peak and is 2,949 ft high. Its majestic bulk makes it a favourite subject for photographs. Although the north and south sides are very precipitous, the stony wilderness at the top is reached frequently by climbers, who have given various names to its features, such as Moses' Sledgate or Moses' Trod. This is a route made by quarrymen and supposed to have been used by Moses the smug-

gler; it comes from HONISTER PASS quarries. Great Gable is the highest of a group of peaks, among which are Kirk Fell, above ENNERDALE, to the W., and Fleetwith to the N. SW. is WASTWATER and S. is SCA FELL.

GREAT SALKELD, *Cumberland* (14–NY55 36), is NE. of PENRITH. The massive fortified tower of St Cuthbert's Church is a reminder of the many Scottish raids into Cumberland. It was added to the Norman nave in the 14th cent. The south doorway is notable. **Long Meg and her Daughters,** near Little Salkeld, are standing stones in a ring about 350 yds in circumference, with resemblances to STONEHENGE. Long Meg is a stone about 18 ft high. The Little Meg circle is nearby at Maughanby. Both may date from the Bronze Age.

GREAT SANKEY, *Lancashire* (12–SJ5688). This small village and church lies W. of WARRINGTON in an old agricultural area. St Mary's was said to have been built by subscription in the reign of Charles I, but little used. After the Restoration it continued in use as a Presbyterian chapel until, in 1728, it was handed to the Church of England by the Atherton family. It was rebuilt in the later 18th cent. and consecrated in 1769. The brick building contains marble tablets.

GREYSTOKE, *Cumberland* (14–NY4330). On the A66, about 5 m. W. of PENRITH, Greystroke has the interesting Church of St Andrew, one of the largest in the diocese. The earliest part is 13th-cent. and later the church became collegiate. Most of the structure is 15th-cent., when it was considerably rebuilt. The tower and the sacristy have battlements. Notable is the east window with very fine stained glass of the 15th cent. or earlier, inscribed brass, two effigies (probably 14th- and 15th-cent.), stalls with misericords, and a chancel screen with a carved rood-loft.

The castle is the residence of the descendants of Thomas Howard, Duke of Norfolk in the reign of Elizabeth I, and was restored in the 19th cent. by Anthony Salvin. It is remarkable for the follies built to enhance the view from the windows.

GRISEDALE, *Westmorland* (14–NY3715). The lovely valley of Grisedale descends from the SW. to the upper end of ULLSWATER, following the course of Grisedale Beck, and is a magnificent area for walking. The A592 crosses the beck near the lake, just N. of PATTERDALE. And from this end you can mount towards impressive views on the eastern slopes of the HELVELLYN range, from which the famous Striding Edge juts out to the N. of Grisedale. The path rises between the Edge and St Sunday Crag (2,756 ft) to the S., leading to Grisedale Tarn, 1,768 ft above sea-level and S. of Dollywagon Pike (2,810 ft), ascended by a path. From the tarn a path covers 6 m. to GRASMERE, first surmounting Grisedale Pass at 1,929 ft between Sea Sandal on the W. (2,415 ft) and Fairfield on the E. (2,863 ft). Not

Hardknott Pass, with a flock of the tough Herdwick sheep

far from the tarn the path passes Brothers' Rock, sad memorial of the last time that Wordsworth saw his brother John, who was drowned at sea in 1805.

HADRIAN'S WALL, *Cumberland* (14–NY 2363–14–NY6366). The Emperor Hadrian, on a visit to Britain in A.D. 122, decided to build a wall as a permanent defence against Pictish invaders, and to mark the northern limit of the Roman Empire. Aulus Platorius Nepos supervised the building from 122 until at least 126, but final completion was not until after 130. It ran for 73 m. from Wallsend to the Solway Firth.

The Wall was more than a wall: it was more elaborate than Roman demarcations of the same nature on the Continent. In front, on the northern side, ran a ditch, averaging about 27 ft wide and 9 ft deep, except where the wall was above the sea or some steep edge. The wall itself was about 7½ ft thick, and the part to walk on is supposed to have been about 15 ft above ground with the breastwork above that. The military way was behind, and the vallum behind that again, the latter having subsequent alterations, but being originally about 20 ft wide and 10 ft deep. Forts adjoined the south side of the wall at intervals, the smaller type holding 500 infantry and the larger having 1,000 infantry or 500 cavalry. There were milecastles, usually at a Roman mile apart, and two turrets between each pair of milecastles. One theory advanced for the vallum was that it was a defence against attack from the rear by the Brigantes, whose territory ranged over the whole north from what is now Lancashire and Yorkshire into the area beyond the wall. They never became so reconciled to Roman rule as tribes further south. About 140 the Romans built another wall between Forth and Clyde – probably this was stretching their lines of communication too far, and after the troubles they had from 155 to 181 it was abandoned.

The Romans held Hadrian's Wall through various disasters, but after 383 it lost its importance for them.

A good section of wall extends into Cumberland from the E. at GILSLAND, where part of Poltross Burn milecastle is in the railway embankment, and a stretch of it is in a garden E. of Gilsland school. Willowford is the east abutment where the Roman bridge crossed the River Irthing, and 1,000 yds of wall run W. to the abutment. Across the river the wall continues W. from Harrow's Scar milecastle. This is where the original turf wall, on a slightly different route, began – replaced with a stone one which goes W. to **Birdoswald**. Here the east gateway and walls of a 5-acre fort are preserved. The wall can be followed for some distance W. to LANERCOST. Stanwix, just N. of CARLISLE, was the largest and most important fort. Rich Roman discoveries have been made in these two areas: *see* Tullie House Museum, Carlisle. The wall ended at Bowness-on-Solway. But to prevent its end being turned, there were Roman defences S. along the West coast including Beckfoot, MARYPORT, Burrow Walls and Moresby. Cumberland S. of the wall was linked by various forts (and roads) such as **Ravenglass** (under MUNCASTER), HARDKNOTT and BROUGHAM.

HALL I' TH' WOOD, *Lancashire* (12–SD 7512). The Hall (open to the public) is on the Breightmet–Astley Bridge Road, N. of BOLTON. It is a half-timbered manor house, built in 1483, with a stone wing of 1591 and alterations of 1648. Mr W. H. Lever, later 1st Viscount Leverhulme (*see* Bolton) bought and restored the Hall, and presented it to the Corporation in 1902. Between 1758 and 1782 part of it was inhabited by Samuel Crompton, who invented the spinning-mule in one of the rooms. The Hall is now a folk museum.

At Tonge Moor Road, Bolton, is the Tonge Museum, where a collection of historic textile machinery can be seen, including Hargreaves' spinning-jenny (about 1764), Arkwright's spinning-frame (1769) and Crompton's spinning-mule (1779). Crompton (1753–1827) was born in a house to be seen at Firwood Fold, off Crompton Way, and his tomb is in the parish churchyard. The "mule" he invented was an improved version of Hargreaves' spinning-jenny for fine cottons, and a cross between that and the Arkwright frame. The Lancashire cotton industry had formerly been limited to hand-production, and the advent of machinery was to have widespread repercussions. The Industrial Revolution increased cotton production fourfold, but brought with it "dark Satanic mills" and appalling working conditions. In a sense, the whole technological evolution of the present era can be traced back to these primitive looms.

HALSALL, *Lancashire* (12–SD3713). This West Lancashire village has a very fine church. The tower is 15th-cent., an octagonal shape on a square base. Nave and chancel have steep and beautiful roofs. In the north wall is a Decorated doorway with the original oak door. Inside, this wall has a finely ornamented tomb recess, probably of the 14th cent. The chancel is notable for rich carvings in wood and stone and sculptured figures. Effigies of the Halsall family are in the church.

HARDKNOTT PASS, *Cumberland* (14–NY 2101), is well named. Whether it is approached from the E., from the GRASMERE, AMBLESIDE or CONISTON areas, or from the W. up ESKDALE, matters little, except that from the E. the WRYNOSE PASS will provide a foretaste of what is to come. The Hardknott is nearly the highest – 1,291 ft at the summit – and certainly the most difficult motoring road in Lakeland. It is surfaced but narrow, and there are gradients of 1 in 3 with bends. The vehicle should be in first-class condition – and the driver, too. It would be wise to avoid being on the pass after dark.

Hardknott Castle is N. of the road at the west end of the pass, where you can stop to inspect this fort the Romans used in the 2nd cent. A.D. It covers more than 2 acres, has ramparts 20 ft thick, walls and gateways. It was on the route of the Roman road from Ravenglass on the coast, through Ambleside, and over High Street mountain to PENRITH.

HAWES WATER, *Westmorland* (14–NY4713), is no longer a lake but a reservoir like THIRLMERE, and is not only the most easterly of Lakeland waters, but is also one of the most difficult to reach from the central areas. The widespread High Street group of peaks prevents all access for vehicles from the W., as do continuations of this group into the SHAP fells across the S. This combined knot of mountains in the western part of Westmorland leaves only the KIRKSTONE PASS and Shap Fell roads as north and south routes on each side of it. Hawes Water, lying inside the angle of this L-shaped knot, can be reached by car only from its east end. The Romans, however, had a road right along the High Street ridge, close

to its 2,718-ft summit, which came up from AMBLESIDE and went down to the PENRITH area. There are plenty of tracks for climbing up to this ridge, and cars can get below it by the road along the south-east side of Hawes Water that begins at BAMPTON. The road ends in the Mardale area, where Mardale village was submerged by the MANCHESTER waterworks scheme that raised the level by some 90 ft. The road along the other side of the lake was submerged, but a footpath remains. High up in a recess on the slopes of High Street the tarn of Blea Water stands at over 1,500 ft; it is more than 200 ft deep – the deepest tarn in Lakeland. Some unsightly concrete was laid to link it with waterworks schemes. At the north-west corner of Hawes Water, above the footpath, are the Standing Stones, one of several groups of remains of ancient communities in the area.

HAWKSHEAD, *Lancashire* (14–SD3597), lies near ESTHWAITE WATER and was formerly a market centre. It is one of the most delightful villages in Lakeland, with old cottages and narrow alleyways and courtyards. It was here that Wordsworth went to school when he was sent from COCKERMOUTH at the age of eight after his mother died.

The Grammar School is at the south end of the village. It was built in 1585, and is an interesting structure with old mullioned windows, and a door with large corbels supporting a pediment over which is a big sundial. The school is now a museum and library (open to the public), and many people go to see the desk on which Wordsworth carved his name. He attended from 1778 until shortly before he went to CAMBRIDGE in 1787. "And has the sun his flaming chariot driven", is among the early verse he wrote at this period. Wordsworth lodged at Anne Tyson's Cottage while at the school.

The Courthouse (open to the public) stands at the north end. This pre-Reformation building is historically connected with the monks of FURNESS ABBEY and in 1932 was given to the National Trust. It is now a folk museum, housing a collection from Abbott Hall, KENDAL, arranged by the Lake District Museum Trust. The National Trust also has four cottages in Vicarage Lane near Wordsworth's lodging, and 10 other properties around the village.

St Michael's Church was built in the late 15th cent. on the site of a 12th-cent. or earlier church or chapel. The modest tower is in rough stonework. In Wordsworth's time the exterior was whitewashed. The arcades inside have short, thick pillars that lack both base and capital and there are restored mural paintings. There are wall monuments to Thomas Bowman and Daniel Rawlinson, both connected with the grammar school, and to Edwin Sandys who became Archbishop of YORK. The ancient Quaker Meeting House is at Town End nearby. The medieval gatehouse and part of one wing, now a farm-house, survive of Hawkshead Hall, an old manor house. At Hawkshead Hill is the Baptist chapel (1678).

There is a 4-m. walk, as an alternative to

driving, between Hawkshead and the ferry at WINDERMERE. A Nature Trail can be followed for an hour, starting at the car park 1 m. from Satterthwaite. This is arranged by the Forestry Commission (at Grizedale) which has an information room, a wildlife centre and a forest nursery. There are photographic facilities on the trail. Another trail runs from the Claife shore of Windermere.

HESWALL, *Cheshire* (12–SJ2682), is a residential area on the main road running along the W. of the Wirral peninsula. It stands on the highest part of the peninsula and there are good views across the Dee estuary to the Welsh hills. Reaching from WEST KIRBY almost to Heswall is a line of cliff, interesting geologically as it is believed to be a relic of the Ice Age.

At **Bebington**, E. across the peninsula, the Mayer Free Public Library was founded by Joseph Mayer, the Liverpool goldsmith who helped to found the City Museum, LIVERPOOL.

Parkgate, S. of Heswall, was once a busy port, but the water has receded with the silting-up of the Dee, as at CHESTER. Handel stayed at the George Inn (Mostyn House school) when waiting to sail to Ireland in 1741 for the great Dublin performance of the *Messiah* that made London reverse its attitude to the composition. John Wesley sailed many times from Parkgate.

HEVERSHAM, *Westmorland* (14–SD4983), is an attractive village on a hill with an old hall, and a grammar school founded in 1613. The church was originally Norman but was altered in the 14th and 15th cents. and considerably rebuilt in the later 19th. There are fragments of an Anglian cross.

HOLKER HALL, *Lancashire* (12–SD3677), is 4 m. W. of GRANGE-OVER-SANDS. This former home of the Dukes of Devonshire is still owned by the Cavendish family. The house, open to the public at advertised times, is famous for the local craftsmanship shown in the interior woodcarving. A 17th-cent. structure, it was partly rebuilt in 1873, after a fire, with additions from local material and timber on the estate. The collection includes period furniture and paintings. It was the favourite seat of William Cavendish, the 19th-cent. 7th Duke, the agriculturalist and patron of science and industry. The grounds, on the edge of MORECAMBE Bay, have a 200-acre deer park with one of the oldest and largest herds of fallow deer in the country, and extensive gardens.

HOLME CULTRAM ABBEY, *Cumberland* (14–NY1750), in Abbey Town, is the remains of a Cistercian abbey founded about 1150. The 12th-cent. nave survives, used as the Parish Church of St Mary, with the west porch built by Abbot Chamber in the early 16th cent. The abbey underwent many restorations in the 17th and 18th cents. The fine arches of the nave were filled in to make the outer walls.

Silloth, to the NW., is a small port and coastal resort on the Solway Firth.

HONISTER PASS, *Cumberland* (14–NY 2214). This famous pass is not the steepest road in the Lakes, but it is probably the most dramatic pass for the motorist. To obtain the striking view of Honister Crag, with the valley of BUTTER-MERE opening far beyond the tiny ribbons of road and beck that fall towards it, you should enter Honister from the BORROWDALE end. There is a 5-m. drive to Buttermere, from Seatoller where the pass begins suddenly, on a twist to the right with an unexpectedly steep gradient of 1 in 4. At the hause, or summit (1,190 ft), there are youth hostel and quarry buildings. Behind is a fine view over Borrowdale with HELVELLYN in the far distance. To the right is Dale Head (2,473 ft) whose ridge is joined by that of Grey Knotts (2,287 ft on the S.) where the hause lies. Hindscarth and Robinson peaks extend NW. from Dale Head. And dominating the view down the pass ahead is the mighty sweep of Honister Crag on the left of the road, jutting out from Fleetwith. These gigantic slopes were carved millions of years ago by the grinding might of natural forces, volcanic eruptions followed by the tremendous weight of the Ice Age glaciers. Many ages later came the men who opened the quarries to extract the slate of the Honister area that became noted as Buttermere green slate.

From its top, the pass falls about 500 ft in the first ½ m., and then becomes a steadier descent below the towering mountain walls as it emerges into the rich beauty of Buttermere valley.

HOOLE, *Lancashire* (12–SD4623), near the Ribble estuary, was the home of a pioneer English astronomer, Jeremiah Horrocks, the curate of Hoole church, who is reputed to have lived at the 17th-cent. Carr House. He studied Kepler's works and in 1639 caught the silhouette of Venus on the sun's disc which he projected through his telescope on to a piece of paper – the first time the transit had been observed. St Michael's Church, Toxteth, LIVERPOOL, has a monument to him. The Church of St Michael at Hoole was rebuilt in 1628. In 1720 the stone tower with battlements was added, and the chancel in the 19th cent. There are box pews and a two-decker pulpit of 1695. Horrocks's observation of Venus is commemorated in a window.

HORNBY, *Lancashire* (12–SD5868). There is a striking view of Hornby Castle and its tower on the road NE. from CATON and Scott paints a romantic portrait in *Marmion* of Sir Edward Stanley (1460–1523), the knight who built this keep. As a thank-offering for his safe return from Flodden Field, Stanley built the octagonal tower of St Margaret's Church. There is a new nave and a modern reredos. Dr John Lingard (d. 1851), the Roman Catholic historian, is commemorated by a memorial on the wall. The base of an Anglo-Saxon cross is in the churchyard.

Also in this area is **Castle Stede**, a Norman

and contains Wordsworth's epitaph to him in brass. The church is in Renaissance style with a marble floor.

JODRELL BANK, *Cheshire* (12–SJ8071). This tiny spot just off the A535, between Holmes Chapel and Alderley Edge, is internationally famous as the site of the giant steerable radio telescope, built by MANCHESTER University and put into service in 1957. It has a 250-ft reflector with a beam width of 12 minutes of arc. Radio waves of much longer wavelength than light are constantly being detected by this sensitive receiver, with its special aerial systems, and the information used to record the movement of extra-terrestrial bodies.

A settlement on Tunstead Hill, near the village of **Withington**, is known to have existed in pre-Anglo-Saxon times. Old Withington Hall is a large mansion situated in a fine open park of 112 acres with a lake; and Welltrough Hall, a farm-house in what was formerly called Lower Withington and is now part of Chelford parish, was at one time a seat of the Davenport family.

KENDAL, *Westmorland* (14–SD5192), is an ancient town: there is some evidence of early British settlement on the site of Castle How, and there was a Roman camp at Watercrook which was part of the road system connected with HADRIAN'S WALL. Later there was the Anglo-Saxon occupation. But most of Kendal's recorded history dates from the time of the Conqueror, who gave land to his Norman henchmen. Richard I made the town a barony in 1189, and Richard II made divisions in this barony, of which one passed to Sir William Parr, an ancestor of Catherine Parr. There were Scottish raids – even as far south of CARLISLE as this – particularly in 1210; and fires and floods. Later came the Black Death, but by 1331 the woollen industry had begun. Edward III authorized John Kemp of Flanders to establish Flemish weavers in the town, and the woollen industry flourished for six centuries. Hence the Latin motto on the town's coat of arms, *Pannus mihi panis* (Wool is my bread). The town was noted for the production of "Kendal Green", a green woollen cloth, mentioned as the clothing of archers by Shakespeare in *Henry IV* and Scott in *The Lay of the Last Minstrel*. Since then other industries have superseded woollen manufacture, such as footwear, hosiery, carpets, engineering and insurance.

"The Auld Grey Town", so called because of its many grey limestone buildings, is the largest and most important in Westmorland. It lies in the valley of the River Kent, with six bridges (three of them good stonework), the A6 road and the main railway for Scotland; it is the centre of communications and the market town for the surrounding agricultural area. Market days have been held since the market charter of 1189. Off the main streets are the old yards with narrow pavements, probably designed for easy access to the main streets and the river for handling the wool. Kendal lies just outside the Lakeland

Camera Press

Jodrell Bank radio telescope

earthwork, and **Melling-with-Wrayton** church, a medieval structure on a steep site above the River Lune.

HOYLAKE, *Cheshire* (12–SJ2189). This is a combination of residential and seaside resort with good beaches, a 4-m. promenade and the links of the Royal Liverpool Golf Club at the corner of the Dee estuary. Once it was a hamlet used as a port of embarkation for Ireland, and then became a fishing village. The small **Hilbre Islands** lie off this coast and at one time were used by Benedictine monks. The islands have a considerable variety of bird-life.

HUXLEY, *Cheshire* (12–SJ5061). Huxley Lower Hall, W. of TARPORLEY and near the village of Huxley, is a 17th-cent. manor house (open to the public) with richly decorated plaster ceilings and a moat. In the Civil War the hall was involved on the Parliamentarian side. It was the home of ancestors of Professor Thomas Henry Huxley, the famous scientist.

INGS, *Westmorland* (14–SD4498), is a place little known to the average tourist, by the main road between WINDERMERE TOWN and KENTMERE valley. The Church of St Anne was built in the 18th cent. by Robert Bateman, a local man,

National Park, the Lake District proper. But it is the gateway to the Lakes from the SE., by way of the A591, the through road that leads first to WINDERMERE TOWN, only 8 m. away, and the M6 extension is not far E. of Kendal. The town's own surroundings are attractive, however, with a backcloth of Westmorland fells on three sides. The approach from Sedbergh on the E. is over a switchback moorland road offering glimpses of groups of Lakeland peaks. Kendal is well enough equipped with hotels to make it a centre from which to visit the Lakes, or the local countryside, and GRANGE and MORECAMBE are not far off.

Abbot Hall Art Gallery was opened in 1962 in a country mansion built in the town in 1759 by John Carr of YORK, adjoining the parish church and surrounded by gardens. The original carving and panelling on the ground floor has been restored. The gallery has permanent and changing displays of 18th-cent. furniture, paintings, silver, porcelain and glasswork. Other cultural activities are pursued at this centre. The Borough Museum has collections dealing with natural history and the history of the area as well as items of general interest.

The Parish Church of the Holy Trinity, in Kirkland, is one of the largest churches in England, a Gothic structure of the 13th cent. It is built on the site of an earlier church, and is unusual in having four aisles. The interior is a complicated arrangement of pillars and arches within the building's wide rectangle. Above the rather squat roofs is the square tower, 80 ft high. Some parts of the church date from about 1200, and there were 19th-cent. restorations. Chapels of the Parr, Bellingham and Strickland families of Kendal have various arms and monuments. A sword and helmet are traditionally associated with "Robin the Devil", Major Robert Philipson, the Royalist, who was besieged on Belle Isle, WINDERMERE, by Colonel Briggs, the Roundhead. After the siege Philipson is said to have ridden into Kendal church on horseback in a vain attempt at revenge on Briggs who was attending a service. Scott made this exploit one of the adventures of the hero in the poem *Rokeby*.

The ruined Norman castle apparently decayed some time after 1586, when it was pronounced by Camden, the historian, as being ready to drop with age. Catherine Parr, the last, and surviving, wife of Henry VIII was born there; she was the daughter of Thomas Parr, the lord of the castle. Her prayer book is on show in the Town Hall; it is bound in solid silver, has fine lettering, and cost £500 when it was bought by public subscription in 1936. The castle dairy (open to the public) in Wildman Street is a well-preserved example of Tudor domestic architecture with richly carved oak beams. It was rebuilt in 1564 by Anthony Garnet. The Town Hall is comparatively modern. Its tall clock tower has a carillon of bells which, on different days of the week, chooses in turn one of seven tunes, from English, Scottish, Welsh and Irish sources, to be played six times in the day. Seven paintings by George Romney adorn the Town Hall. Romney, associated with DALTON-

IN-FURNESS, served his apprenticeship in Kendal, left in 1762 to achieve fame in London, but returned to Kendal and died at Romney House in Kirkland in 1802. The house where he was an apprentice was in a yard W. of Stricklandgate. Sandes Hospital, near the Town Hall in Highgate, was built in 1659 by the Sandes, cotton manufacturers. The Call Stone, formerly in the Market Place, is before the Town Hall and is the traditional stone for proclaiming English monarchs. Near the G.P.O. in the house now occupied by the Y.W.C.A. Prince Charlie stayed on his march to DERBY and again on his retreat; two nights after that his pursuer, "Butcher" Cumberland, slept at the same house in the same bed. The Old Grammar School was founded in 1525.

There are several parks and open spaces, such as Castle Hill and Serpentine Woods, and sports facilities, including golf. The town also holds music festivals. Joan Littlewood's Theatre Workshop became noted while it was in Kendal. Many areas exist for excursions beyond the town, including Skelsmergh, Longsleddale and Bannisdale.

KENTMERE, *Westmorland* (14–NY4504), is entered by the road turning N. from the KENDAL to WINDERMERE route. But this dale is not enhanced by its industrial developments. The lake was drained in the 19th cent., disclosing deposits of diatomaceous earth for insulating material. Since then a Viking spearhead and a medieval canoe have been found. Near the village of Kentmere is Kentmere Hall where in 1517 Bernard Gilpin was born; he became Archdeacon of DURHAM and was known as the Apostle of the North. The road ends above the village; there is water beyond but it is a reservoir. Higher still, the foot-track goes over Nan Bield Pass, one of the wildest in Lakeland, and over 2,000 ft high. Harter Fell and Ill Bell that enclose this way to HAWES WATER rise about 500 ft above the pass.

KESWICK, *Cumberland* (14–NY2723). Keswick, the northern centre of the Lakes, lies in a beautiful position below the towering bulks of SKIDDAW and SADDLEBACK. It has a remote and almost magical quality.

Its beauty has made the town a mecca for poets, artists and visitors from all over the world. The town is attractive in itself, with intriguing narrow streets and buildings of old grey stone; a natural convergence of roads makes it an excellent centre for tours to other parts of Lakeland. Every type of accommodation can be found, from luxury hotels to guest-houses and private homes, but in the busy season the tourist who has no reservation may have difficulty in finding a room. At such times driving cars is a problem and the town is best seen on foot. A short walk takes one down the pleasant road below The Heads to the edge of DERWENTWATER, where the landing stages cater for cruises, motor boats and rowing boats on this, the "queen of the English lakes" (*see* Derwentwater).

Kirkby Lonsdale: the Devil's Bridge

T. Parker

Coleridge came to live at Greta Hall, behind the school, in 1800, pursuing his friendship with William and Dorothy Wordsworth who were already settled at GRASMERE village. Southey followed Coleridge in 1803. Charles Lamb came to Keswick for holidays, and Shelley resided there for a time after his marriage. Southey lived at Greta Hall for many years after Coleridge left Keswick in 1804. The Royal Oak Hotel was patronized by Scott, Tennyson, R. L. Stevenson and Wordsworth, and visited by the Southeys and Coleridge.

The Fitz Park Museum and Art Gallery has a large and famous collection of MSS. by Robert Southey, as well as those of Wordsworth, Coleridge's son, Hartley, and Hugh Walpole, six MSS. of whose novels it contains. There is a small collection of letters by John Ruskin. One of his paintings, together with works by Turner and others, is in the art gallery. Tunes can be played on the "musical stones" in the museum. There is a scale model of the Lake District, and a large collection of mineral and rock specimens of the geology of the area, as well as specimens of birds, butterflies and fossils. Fitz Park itself includes a recreational area and a children's playground.

The School of Industrial Arts was founded in 1883 by Canon H. D. Rawnsley, the friend and disciple of Ruskin, and Vicar of Crosthwaite, who was also one of the founders of the National Trust (*see* THIRLMERE). John Ruskin (*see* CONISTON WATER) once had a branch of his hand-made linen industry at Keswick, as he had at ELTERWATER.

Crosthwaite church, on the north-west side, is dedicated to St Kentigern. In this saint's time Cumberland was in the Kingdom of Strathclyde, ruled by the pagan Morken, from whom Kentigern fled to erect his cross in this "thwaite". The church is said to have been founded in the 12th cent. Its present form, which makes it the oldest structure in the valley, is a rebuilding, probably of 1553. It has a rare set of old consecration crosses and a 14th-cent. font and 15th-cent. effigies. In 1844 the church was restored by Gilbert Scott. It has a memorial effigy to Southey.

The tiny moot hall with its one-handed clock dates from 1813.

Special facilities are offered to visitors by the Public Library (St John's Street), which has a large collection of material on Keswick and the Lake District. Sporting facilities include golf, and there are numerous well-known walks to be taken. One is to **Friar's Crag** on the lakeside, the scene of much photographed views across the water, described by Ruskin as one of the earliest memories of his life. It is National Trust property, bought as a memorial to Canon Rawnsley, and also has a stone memorial to Ruskin. Inland beyond the lakeside road is **Castle Head**, 20 acres of National Trust woodland, where a point over 500 ft high gives a panorama of peaks identified on the indicator.

Castlerigg Stone Circle is an Ancient Monument (National Trust), 2 m. E. of Keswick. It is also called the Carles and the Druids' Circle, and is about 100 ft in diameter, formed of 38 megalithic stones. Inside this oval ring there is an oblong space of 10 more stones. From this prehistoric site there are excellent views.

KIRKBY LONSDALE, *Westmorland* (14–SD 6178), is easily missed from the E., being hidden behind the junction of the A65 and the A683. The Devil's Bridge over the River Lune, an Ancient Monument of obscure origin, is probably 13th-cent. and considered one of the finest ancient English bridges. Turn N. from the main road to enter this charming old town of narrow streets and Georgian buildings.

A good centre for visiting the unspoilt Lune valley, the town is a market and social centre for the surrounding agricultural area which, like much of the north-west region, has relics of the long Roman occupation. There are some good, small shops, particularly the bookshop. Restaurants are few, but there are several residential hotels and guest-houses. The motorist can park in the little Market Square (with the still smaller Horsemarket beyond), or in car parks uphill from it, and walk N. along the main street and then left, past old inns like the Sun, with its stone columns. At the church gates is the notice pointing to the place, the view from which Ruskin described as "one of the loveliest in England and therefore in the world". A plaque on the wall at Church Brow, quotes "Fors Clavigera", his monthly letter to "the workmen and labourers of Great Britain", and marks the spot where Turner (whom Ruskin so strongly championed) painted a picture of the Lune.

St Mary's Church is Norman, built on an Anglo-Saxon site, and the earliest of the churches in the valley. It has been developed and added to rather haphazardly, the remaining parts of the Norman period being the three westernmost arches and piers of the nave's north arcade, and the south and west doorways. The mosaic reredos, iron screen, attractive stained glass, choir seats and encaustic floor tiles are all Victorian. The six-sided pulpit is 17th-cent. There are various 18th-cent. mural tablets, and a font that came from the 14th-cent. Killington chapel.

Casterton, about 1½ m. N., is on the route of a Roman road. The well-known Casterton Girls' School (the Clergy Daughters' School) was formerly at Cowan Bridge, where four Brontë sisters were pupils, and may be the original of "Lowood" in *Jane Eyre*.

KIRKBY STEPHEN, *Westmorland* (14–NY 7708). Largely consisting of its main street, this old picturesque market town lies among the moors. The Church of St Stephen dates from Anglo-Saxon times and parts, including the impressive nave, are in the Early English style. The west tower has battlements. Carvings and memorials commemorate the Musgrave and Wharton families. One of the old buildings, now called the Fountain Café, dates from about 1650, and is listed as a building of historical interest. It has provided hospitality in some form for travellers during most of its 300 years' existence.

Wharton Hall, an Ancient Monument which is now a farm-house, is about 1¾ m. S. of the town, and the name of this family has a long association with Kirkby Stephen. It is a hall with two cross wings, built in the late 14th or early 15th cent. A new great hall was added by Thomas, Lord Wharton, in 1540; he founded a grammar school in Kirkby Stephen in 1566, and the 4th Lord Wharton a Bible Trust. The gatehouse and north-west part of the hall were added about 1559, and the original block was restored in 1785.

Further S. is Mallerstang Common, a fertile valley where the River Eden begins, with Wild Boar Fell on the W. This valley has been occupied from the Bronze Age onward. Part way up is **Pendragon Castle**, and to the E. Mallerstang Edge marks the Yorkshire border. There is a tradition that Pendragon was built by the father of King Arthur. It is certainly one of those castles that later belonged to the Clifford family and which were rebuilt by the energetic Lady Anne Clifford of APPLEBY and BROUGHAM. Recent excavations have yielded pottery in the ruins.

KIRKBY THORE, *Westmorland* (14–NY 6325). This was the site of the Roman fort and settlement of Bravoniacum, and the junction of

Roman roads. One came from E. over the moors via BROUGH on the way to BROUGHAM, and another came from Whitley Castle near ALSTON to the N. of Kirkby Thore. Roman relics have been found during building operations. The church, St Michael's, is 12th- to 14th-cent., with 17th-cent. altar rails and pulpit.

KIRKOSWALD, *Cumberland* (14–NY5541). This small village is up the Eden valley above ARMATHWAITE. The Church of St Oswald, from which the village derives its name, has a 19th-cent. tower standing apart 200 yds away uphill. The chancel is 16th-cent., and other parts range from the 12th to 14th cents. A spring flows below the nave and emerges at the west.

Kirkoswald also has a ruined castle, of which dungeons and one turret remain, and a private house, the College, with 16th- and 17th-cent. features.

KIRKSTONE PASS, *Westmorland* (14–NY 4008). This is the longest and the highest of all the LAKE DISTRICT motor passes, and its summit is 1,476 ft above sea-level. It is part of the A592 linking ULLSWATER and PENRITH in the N. and WINDERMERE (and AMBLESIDE) to the S. It is the only motor route between the Fairfield and HELVELLYN range on the W. and the High Street group of peaks on the E. Beyond High Street the mountain area reaches to SHAP Fell, making this part of Westmorland impassable for drivers just as the SCA FELL group does in Cumberland. The pass has gradients of up to 1 in 4, and needs much care and patience; it "lengthens" the 12 m. between Windermere and PATTERDALE. The Kirkstone Pass Inn is at the top, commanding good views; there is a parking space. At this area a branch of the pass comes twisting up from the SW. on the slopes of Snarker Pike (2,096 ft) – a direct route from Ambleside (instead of the main road from Windermere via TROUTBECK) but not practicable for caravans. Red Screes (2,541 ft) lies to the W., Caudale Moor to the E., and BROTHERS' WATER to the N.

KNOWSLEY HALL, *Lancashire* (12–SJ4493). In a park of some 2,000 acres W. of ST HELENS, surrounded by a wall about 12 m. long is Knowsley Hall, the private residence of the Stanley family, the Earls of Derby. The Stanleys are prominent in Lancashire and their history is interwoven with that of England. This site has been theirs for some six centuries, and the oldest part of the present mansion dates from the 15th cent. It contains old masters and family portraits. The park is one of the largest in the county. A portion of the Hall that was prepared for the reception of Henry VII was rebuilt in 1820. On the gateway to the deer park are carved the words: "Bring good news and knock boldly". Thomas, 1st Earl of Derby, married Margaret Beaufort, Countess of Richmond and mother of Henry VII. Sir Edward Stanley, of HORNBY Castle, was the fifth son of the 1st Earl. Henry, the 4th Earl, was one of the commissioners who tried Mary Queen of Scots in 1586. One member of the family, Ferdinando, Lord Derby, better known as Lord Strange, appears in our literary history. He was a patron of players, including Shakespeare, and had a book dedicated to him by Robert Greene, the poet, and panegyric by Spenser. The wife of the 7th Earl, Charlotte Stanley, held Lathom House near ORMSKIRK against the Parliamentarians in 1644. In 1780 the 12th Earl instigated the Derby horse-race. The 14th Earl, Edward Stanley, was a Classical scholar and statesman. As colonial secretary he carried out the emancipation of the West Indian slaves. He was three times Prime Minister. He published a translation of the Iliad into blank verse in 1864. The 15th Earl was also a distinguished Liberal politician. He was offered the crown of Greece in 1863, but he declined it.

Rainford, a village NE. of Knowsley Hall, is in pleasant farming country, much of it owned by the Stanleys and Pilkingtons. Between Rainford and BILLINGE is **Crank**, on a ridge of higher land with some interesting caves where it is believed that Roman Catholic priests hid from persecution.

KNUTSFORD, *Cheshire* (12–SJ7578). Knutsford is a pleasant town with an old-world atmosphere and with good hotels and guest-houses from which to explore the countryside or the great TATTON HALL estate to the N. MANCHESTER is accessible by road or a quick rail service. Knutsford is essentially residential and has interesting associations and buildings. It makes a special event of May Day celebrations, which are among the oldest in the country and on two occasions have had Royal patronage. A procession precedes the crowning ceremony, with such characters as "Highwayman Higgins" and "Jack-in-the-Green". Carriages carry the May Queen, with the Lord Chamberlain, judge and courtiers. A sedan chair is carried by chairmen in livery. The queen is crowned on the heath, where there is dancing round the may-pole.

Tradition links Knutsford with King Cnut, or more strictly with Knut, another Dane said to have forded the stream. It has had a charter since 1292 and was once the capital of mid-Cheshire. For the last two centuries it has had associations with many interesting people. Edward Penny, R.A., a founder member of the Royal Academy and its first professor of painting, was born in Silkmill Street in 1714. In about 1760, Thomas Gaskell, maker of the famous long-case clocks, had premises in King Street. Sir Henry Holland (1788–1873), physician to William IV and Queen Victoria and also a writer, was born in the house that is now a stationer's shop, opposite the Royal George Hotel. His sisters, the Misses Mary and Lucy Holland, were the originals of Miss Deborah and Miss Matty Jenkyns, the heroines of *Cranford*, written by Knutsford's greatest figure, Mrs Gaskell. Sir Henry's son, Henry Thurston, became the 1st Lord Knutsford, and later Secretary of State for the colonies. Frank Boyd Merriman, who became Solicitor-General, was born in Knutsford in 1880 and it was his father who bought from the Hollands Church House, associated with Mrs Gaskell's book, *Wives and Daughters*. It was while Sir Henry Royce was living in Legh Road in 1904 that he met Charles Stewart Rolls, a meeting which led to the great Rolls-Royce partnership.

Knutsford is very proud of Mrs Gaskell (1810–65), *née* Elizabeth Cleghorn Stevenson. Her mother, one of the Hollands, died a few months after Elizabeth was born and the girl lived with an aunt in what is now 17 Gaskell Avenue, Knutsford. In 1832 she married William Gaskell at the parish church, and they lived in Manchester. But the names of Mrs Gaskell and Knutsford became inseparable, and *Cranford* is considered a portrayal of the town and its personalities. Mrs Gaskell was a close friend of Charlotte Brontë, whose biography she wrote. The Unitarian chapel in Knutsford is where Mrs Gaskell taught in the Sunday School, and she and her husband were buried in the chapelyard. Edward Higgins, the highwayman, lived at 19 Gaskell Avenue; he appears in Mrs Gaskell's *Squire's Tale* and in De Quincey's *Reminiscences*. In Mrs Gaskell's *Wives and Daughters* Tatton Hall appears as Cumnor Towers, and in *Cranford* she mentions the Royal George Hotel. This is the town's chief hotel, an ancient hostelry that was once the White Swan.

Drury Lane, Legh Road and the King's Coffee House were designed by Richard Harding Watt. He was influenced by continental travels and his Ruskin Rooms show Italian influences in the tiled roofs and little tower. The Coffee House is a striking building with a principal tower and a subsidiary tower. Round a pillar are inscribed names and dates of English monarchs. The parish church, 1744, is early Georgian and replaced earlier chapels of ease. Parochial registers go back to 1581. Princess Street runs parallel with the trunk road on the edge of the town, and is interesting architecturally. King Street has a number of timbered buildings of historic interest, some well-preserved, and in parts of this narrow street old porches and steps cover the pavement.

LAKE DISTRICT, THE, *Cumberland* (14–NY1740), is a heading that applies equally to Westmorland and northern Lancashire from a descriptive point of view. But if the Lake District National Park is taken as the area that defines the District, Cumberland contains rather more of it than the other two counties. The Lake District is quite small and compact: some 30 m. across. The only way really to absorb the beauty of this unique area is to go on foot. The views from a moving vehicle are no substitute and however busy the main traffic routes may be, the walker can, in many parts of Lakeland, soon reach areas remote from crowds and the hum of modern life.

For motorists, gradients on the main routes present no great difficulty. But roads squeezed between mountain bases in remote areas demand constant alertness for abrupt corners, bridges and similar hazards, not to mention sudden confrontations with large motor coaches, for which such conditions were never designed. The wise driver ensures that his vehicle is in good order before approaching the mountain passes. Those who tow caravans are advised to verify that their proposed routes are suitable. The western road passes, except possibly the WHINLATTER, are not suitable for caravans, nor is the direct route between AMBLESIDE and the KIRKSTONE PASS (well named The Struggle). For the more difficult passes, *see* WRYNOSE and HARDKNOTT. About caravan sites, as well as general information on walking routes, historic sites, buildings and gardens, literary associations, advice for fell-walkers, exploring North-West England by car, nature trails, riding, books and maps, consult The Lake District National Park Information Service, District Bank House, High Street, WINDERMERE, Westmorland. The Lake District has been a National Park since 1951, administered by the Lake District Planning Board. In 1966 the Board bought Brockhole, a country house halfway between Windermere and Ambleside on the main road, and established the Lake District National Park Centre, the first of its kind. The centre (open to the public) has information rooms, educational facilities including a lecture room, a unique exhibition tracing the physical and human development of the District, and a tea-room. The 32 acres of grounds have a car park, refreshment and picnic areas, formal gardens, a putting green and a jetty. Other important organizations for information are The English Lakes Counties Travel Association, Ellerthwaite, Windermere, Westmorland, for general and local brochures, and the area office of The National Trust, Broadlands, Borrans Road, Ambleside, Westmorland. The Trust has done much to protect amenities (*see* THIRLMERE).

No single area of natural beauty in England has such a wealth of literary associations as the Lake District. It was visited at various times by Sir Walter Scott, Tennyson, Hazlitt, Shelley, Charles Lamb and Carlyle; and John Ruskin (*see* CONISTON WATER), De Quincey and Hugh Walpole lived there. It is, of course, particularly associated with the Lake Poets – William Wordsworth, the Coleridges, and Robert Southey, who were connected with KESWICK among other places. Wordsworth (*see* particularly COCKERMOUTH, PENRITH, HAWKSHEAD, GRASMERE (village), and RYDAL) made an important contribution to the national idea of the Lake District. Topographical references are scattered through numerous poems, and he wrote a whole series on the DUDDON VALLEY. From his peaceful contemplation of the peaks and lakes he derived his idea that Nature is our great source of solace and strength, from the spirit that lies behind its outward manifestation. "I sit upon this old grey stone, And dream my time away", he said, and the visitor who spends his limited time at a single lake will better appreciate the atmosphere than those who try to cover the whole area in a single visit.

LANCASTER, *Lancashire* (12–SD4761). The history of this town goes back more than seven and a half centuries. There were various early occupations of Castle Hill, where prehistoric flint implements were found, and its vicinity. There was a Roman camp by the River Lune (or Loyne). It is supposed that before the Romans came the river flowed on the S. of Castle Hill instead of the N. as now, and attempts have been made to establish its exact course. Little is known of the Anglo-Saxon period: some survivals of this are in St Mary's Church. William I bestowed Halton Manor, which included Lancaster, on Roger de Poitou. The latter built the first fortifications of the Norman castle on Castle Hill, the site of a Roman military station, in the 11th cent. The great square Norman keep was built about 1170, and this, still to be seen, is 78 ft high with walls 10 ft thick. King John built a curtain wall with round towers, and a massive gateway, round the keep, enclosing a roughly circular area 380 ft by 350 ft; and also built Hadrian's Tower, which still remains (it was drastically restored in the 18th and 19th cents.). In 1322 Robert Bruce burnt most of the town but made no impression on the castle. Edward III's son, John of Gaunt, was much associated with the castle; he is "Time-honour'd Lancaster" in Shakespeare's depiction. But John of Gaunt paid only brief visits to his castle. On the keep a turret named after him was used as a beacon to signal the approach of the Armada. The lower parts of the gateway were added to in the 15th cent.; begun by King John, this, like his Well Tower, is still to be seen. There was repair work by Elizabeth I, shown by her initials on the castle. It was a Parliamentary stronghold in the Civil War, and later George Fox, founder of the Society of Friends, was twice imprisoned there. The castle is used as the gaol and for assize and other courts (it is open to the public subject to court requirements).

The Shire Hall is within the castle and has an impressive display of heraldry with the coats of arms of all sovereigns from Richard I.

Lancaster is the county town and has many fine buildings. The Priory and Parish Church of St Mary is particularly interesting. There was first a church on this site built by the Romans, probably before the end of the 2nd cent. Part of its east end was discovered in 1912, and Roman lamps with Christian marking were found in the vicarage garden. The converted Anglo-Saxons built a church on the site, and its remains are a small square-topped doorway and part of the west wall. A rare type of early Anglian cross with runic inscriptions was found in the churchyard and sent to the BRITISH MUSEUM. Roger de Poitou gave St Mary's to a Benedictine abbey of Normandy, which founded a small monastery at the end of the 11th cent. There is no record of a Norman church, but, E. of the Roman section choir walls in the Transitional style came to light. The south-west doorway is in the same style, so there may have been a 12th-cent. church almost as large as the present one. It was probably destroyed when the town was twice burnt by the Scots or during the Black Death of 1349. Rebuilding began before the end of the 14th cent. In the 1414 suppression of foreign priories the Lancaster one was given to the

Noel Habgood

The Lake District: a view of Derwentwater

Brigitine Convent of SYON (Middlesex). In 1430 St Mary's became the parish church of Lancaster, but its fabric is largely that built by the nuns of Syon, including its main features: the great east window, the windows of the north and south walls, and the clerestory. The church contains outstanding Decorated choir stalls of about 1340, possibly brought from FURNESS ABBEY. John Ruskin considered the carved work of their canopies to be the finest in England. The carved oak two-decker pulpit is early 17th-cent., as is the font cover; the font itself is early 19th-cent. The colourful stained glass is mid-19th-cent. One of many wall tablets is by Fisher of YORK, and another by L. F. Roubiliac. The previous Gothic tower was replaced by the present one, built in 1759 to the design of Henry Sephton.

The handsome old Custom House has graceful Ionic columns at its front, each carved from a single block. It was built in 1764 to the design of Richard Gillow, of the family whose Lancaster furniture factory became famous for nearly three centuries. The Friends' Meeting House, founded in 1690, is associated with their leaders, including George Fox. It is now a modern school, of high educational standards. The old Town Hall has fine proportions and dates from 1781–3. It houses the Regimental museum and the Lancaster museum, the latter illustrating the history of Lancaster from the Stone Age to modern times. The Storey Institute holds the art gallery. The new Town Hall, by E. W. Mountford, who also designed THE OLD BAILEY, was given by Lord Ashton in 1909. It is a dignified Classical building, with a marble staircase and two stained-glass windows, containing handsome plate and historic charters. There is a domed council chamber, and seating for 1,300 in a large concert hall. Lord Ashton also gave the town its dominant

landmark, the Ashton Memorial which, with its green dome, overlooks the city from Williamson Park. The memorial's higher galleries give a panorama of BLACKPOOL, MORECAMBE Bay, the LAKE DISTRICT hills, the Lune Valley and Ingleborough in the West Riding.

The Roman Catholic cathedral was erected in 1859. It has a chancel with a gilded roof, and brilliant frescoes of saints, kings and angels. The Last Supper is carved in relief. The reredos has gilded canopies and the windows stained glass. There is a prominent statue of St Peter. Each chapel has a well-decorated altar, and the Hardman baptistry has fine stone vaulting.

In St Leonardgate is the Grand Theatre, listed as a building of architectural and historic interest. On its site was the old Athenaeum where Mrs Siddons acted. The city has some fine Georgian mansions with good hooded doorways. The Royal King's Arms, where Dickens stayed, replaced in Victorian times the original inn of 1625. Prince Charlie, on his southward march in 1745, stayed in the house which is now the Conservative Club. Skerton Bridge, crossing the Lune, was built in 1783–8 by Thomas Harrison. Modern buildings include the new Lancaster University, developing on a campus basis to the S.

Lancaster is a good tourist centre for the Lake District some 35 m. N. and for some of the loveliest moorland, where Lancashire and Yorkshire meet across the **Trough of Bowland**. Most north-west coastal resorts are easily reached, and HEYSHAM is a port for Northern Ireland.

LANERCOST PRIORY, *Cumberland* (14–NY5563), was founded about 1144 as an Augustinian priory by William de Vaux. The buildings date from the 12th to 13th cents. There is a gatehouse in which Edward I was received by the monks. Queen Eleanor, the Scottish King David, and Robert Bruce are others associated with the priory's history. The nave and north aisle were restored in the last century and subsequently used as the parish church. There are fine clerestory arches, the Lanercost Cross of 1214, a bold recessed doorway in the west front, the old monastic building called Dacre Hall, cloisters and interesting memorials and tombs.

LANGDALE PIKES, *Westmorland* (14–NY 2707).

Here is scenic splendour on a grand scale, ranging from the two rugged pikes piled up like gigantic sculpture in rock to the green dales with their tarns. You can approach from GRASMERE, AMBLESIDE or CONISTON. Beyond ELTERWATER there are the two Langdale valleys: Great Langdale on the N. and Little Langdale on the S.

Along the north side of Great Langdale the land rises from Silver Howe and Yew Crag past Stickle Tarn to the two pikes. First is Harrison Stickle, 2,403 ft, and then Pike o' Stickle, 2,323 ft, both rising steeply from the valley; Dungeon Ghyll begins in their cleft and flows SE., with the celebrated Dungeon Ghyll Force within walking distance of the road where it passes the New Hotel. The Force was depicted by Wordsworth and Coleridge. The Old Dungeon Ghyll Hotel is National Trust property and beyond it are the roadless Mickleden and Oxendale branches of the valley. Mickleden leads NW. to Stake Head Pass, for the Stonethwaite branch of BORROWDALE, and Rossett Gill Pass, for the SCA FELL group. Across the ends of both Langdale valleys are BOW FELL on the N., nearly 3,000 ft, and Crinkle Crags S. of it.

The WRYNOSE PASS rises steeply out of the west end of Little Langdale, for the DUDDON VALLEY or HARDKNOTT PASS. The road from Wrynose descends Little Langdale beside the River Brathay (which is the North Lancashire boundary), and this was the route of the Roman road from Hardknott and the west coast. E. of the Pike of Blisco, which is below Crinkle Crags, is the pleasant dale with Blea Tarn where a steep road joins the two Langdale valleys. This dale is the scene of The Solitary in Book II of Wordsworth's *The Excursion*, and the poet also knew Blea Tarn House, a farm N. of the tarn. The Little Langdale road passes Little Langdale Tarn, Birk Howe (a 17th-cent. farm-house bought by the National Trust) and Colwith Force, another waterfall accessible on foot.

Both Langdale valleys are well worth exploring on foot, and are also favoured by rock-climbers.

LEVENS HALL, *Westmorland* (14–SD4886),

is a beautiful Elizabethan mansion (open to the public at advertised times in the summer), at Levens Bridge on the River Kent. Among its important features are the plasterwork ceilings, fine oak chimney-pieces, Spanish leather panelling and – outside the house – the particular attraction of the topiary gardens. These were designed by Monsieur Beaumont, the man who remodelled the gardens of HAMPTON COURT for

James II. They retain their original plan of 1689. This estate was occupied by the Redmans in 1188, the Bellinghams in 1489, the Grahames and Howards from 1688 to 1885, and the Bagots from 1885. In the 14th cent. the Redman family built a peel-tower; portions of it are incorporated in the present house, which is mainly of about 1585. Up the river there is a well-wooded park. Downstream is Nether Levens Hall, a 14th-cent. peel-tower developed into a 16th-cent. farm-house.

LITTLE MORETON HALL, *Cheshire* (12–SJ8558).

This magnificent 16th-cent. moated manor house, 2 m. S. of CONGLETON, on the A34, is unquestionably one of the finest specimens of black-and-white architecture in England. It is approached on the south side by way of an arched stone bridge and high timbered gatehouse, with rooms above the entrance, leading into a cobbled courtyard of great beauty. The house itself is built on three sides of the quadrangle, the fourth side having been cleared at one period of restoration to provide a vista of perfectly kept gardens sweeping down to the tall green mound where once the watch-tower stood.

At Little Moreton Hall the upper story is reached by three or four narrow stairways emerging from the gatehouse, and the stately rooms in the body of the house are entered after passing through a series of small panelled apart-

Langdale: the Little Langdale valley

T. Parker

ments. One of them contains a sliding panel giving access to a secret room behind the chimney-breast. This secret chamber may have been designed to be discovered without much difficulty, because far below the moat, at the end of a tortuous underground passage, there is a tiny cell which in time of danger served as the real hiding-place. The wainscoted long gallery, 68 ft by 12 ft, is superbly representative of Elizabethan England. Its immense fire-places are decorated with the Royal Arms of England and France, the roof is splendidly beamed in oak, and the fine leaded windows are excellent examples of the glazier's art. The retiring room of the long gallery has a fire-place with a carved stone coat of arms of the Moreton family. The exact date of construction is not known, although an inscription on one of the window beams states that "Richard Dale, Carpeder", made them in 1559. The entire building is very slightly tilted, and has, in fact, been discreetly strengthened by steel and concrete supports behind the panelling. Many of the old furnishings remain in their original setting. The huge kitchen serving the banqueting hall contains 25 spice drawers in a chest, an oak table, quantities of pewterware, and a fire-place large enough to roast an ox.

Moreton Old Hall, as it is also known, is now the property of the National Trust and is open to the public.

Liverpool: the Roman Catholic cathedral

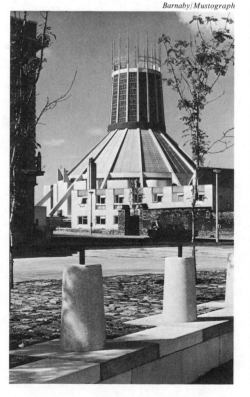

LIVERPOOL, *Lancashire* (12–SJ3591). The waterfront of Liverpool, dominated by the big buildings of Liver, Cunard and the Docks Board claims to be Europe's greatest Atlantic seaport. Seven m. of docks are packed along this waterfront; and it has the world's largest floating landing stage, about ½ m. long, and adjustable, to move up and down with the tide. Liverpool began as a fishing village in the 13th cent., and its present, comparatively modern, form derives from its rapid growth during the 18th cent. Now it concerns itself with many more industries than shipping, but in spite of its transformation the city retains distinctive landmarks, has many cultural features and a flourishing musical and artistic life.

Just above the waterfront stands the fine 18th-cent. *Town Hall* (normally open to the public for a week in August). It was designed by John Wood of BATH and completed in 1754. The interior was rebuilt (after a fire) between 1795 and 1802, by John Foster, under James Wyatt, who added the dome in 1802, with Felix Rossi's figure of Minerva, and the portico in 1811. The mirrors in the small ballroom came from Lathom House (ORMSKIRK) and are probably early 18th-cent. Italian. The Hall's furniture harmonizes with its architectural period. Then comes the entrance to the **Mersey Tunnel**, which traffic approaches through an elaborate central traffic scheme, and above this are St George's Hall, the City Museums, the Central Libraries, and Walker Art Gallery.

St George's Hall, with its 60-ft-high Corinthian columns, concert hall and law courts, was designed by Harvey Lonsdale Elmes. It was begun in 1838 and finished by C. R. Cockerell in 1854, seven years after Elmes's death. The Great Hall is 151 ft long, richly finished, and contains a magnificent organ which was rebuilt in 1957 after its war-time destruction.

The City Museums owe their foundation to the 13th Earl of Derby, who bequeathed his natural history collection, and Joseph Mayer, a Liverpool goldsmith, who gave his archaeological and ethnographical collections; Liverpool became famous for its ivories, gold and jewelry, plant collections, fossils, and the Derby collection of birds. The original museum building perished in flames in May 1941, with valuable material. Fortunately much had been sent for safe storage. The first part of the rebuilding plan has provided an aquarium, and galleries dealing with prehistoric life, shipping, local history and applied and decorative arts. The second stage aims to restore the main museum completely, and to include an astronomy gallery and planetarium.

The Central Libraries comprise the Picton, Horn and Brown buildings. Picton has the reference library, with some 92,000 books, and holds regular exhibitions of its treasures. On the ground floor is the international library (100,000 books), which also has regular exhibitions. Hornby has first editions, prints and fine bindings, permanently displayed. Brown has scientific and technical sections; visitors are welcome.

The Walker Art Gallery, endowed by Sir Andrew Barclay Walker, could well claim the best provincial collection in England. Its early Italian and Flemish works are especially notable. Simone Martini's *Christ Discovered in the Temple* (14th-cent. Sienese) is a work that influenced the "international Gothic" style, and a beautiful *Pietà* by Ercole de' Roberti represents the 15th-cent. school of Ferrara. There are the *Portrait of a Young Man* from the Giovanni Bellini studio, an attribution to Basaiti, and a Bonifazio Veronese (*Virgin and Child*). From Veronese's studio is *The Finding of Moses*. Besides one painting attributed to Francesco Bassano and another from his studio, there is a Jacopo Bassano work (*Country Scene*), and two Guardis. The *Portrait of a Young Man* by Jan Mostaert is noteworthy and there is an outstanding mature work by Rubens, the *Virgin and Child with St Elizabeth and the Child Baptist*. Among the Dutch paintings is a river scene by Ruysdael. The most famous picture here is Rembrandt's early work, *Portrait of the Artist as a Young Man*. From Germany there is a Cranach the Elder, and from Spain a Murillo. British portraits include Kneller and Hogarth, and British landscape is well represented by works by Richard Wilson, Cox, Turner, Constable and Stubbs. There are Pre-Raphaelite works by Millais, Rossetti and Burne-Jones. French paintings include a Poussin, a Fragonard, an early Cézanne, a Monet, a small Seurat and a Matisse. Henry Moore and Victor Pasmore are among the gallery's increasing number of 20th-cent. acquisitions. The Sudley Gallery, in a 19th-cent. house in Mossley Hill Road, has a large British collection including two Turners. The house and its contents were bequeathed by Miss Holt.

Liverpool (Anglican) Cathedral soars superbly on its lofty site. It was the life work of Sir Giles Gilbert Scott who died in 1960 in his 80th year, still supervising it. When complete (1975?) it will be second in size only to St Peter's in Rome. Sir Giles's conception is generally Gothic but not really classifiable. The decoration in red sandstone is an integral part of the fabric. A special feature is that the aisles are built as tunnels in the walls. The nave, not yet completed, and the choir lie at opposite ends of what, with the under-tower and transept crossings, is called the central space. The central tower, across the full width of the nave, rises 331 ft above floor level. The vast scale creates an atmosphere of peace and grandeur. Notable are the font, the stained glass in all windows, and the sandstone reredos and sculptured panels.

The Roman Catholic Cathedral is completely different. The foundation stone was laid in 1933 but the design has been completely changed, and its final form, designed by Sir Frederick Gibberd, is a total departure from the original plan by Sir Edwin Lutyens. The building is circular, round the focal point of the high altar; this circle is surmounted by a conical roof capped with a tower of coloured glass by John Piper and Patrick Reyntiens, which throws a pool of light on the altar. The cathedral itself is raised on an upper level, on a concrete base above the crypt completed by Lutyens. Below, the approach road runs right through, with a car park under the nave.

The Philharmonic Hall, home of Liverpool's great orchestra, is on the site of the "Old Phil", which fire destroyed in 1933. Its acoustics are among the best in Britain. A financial arrangement with the corporation gives the orchestra security. About 75 public concerts are given annually in the hall, and the orchestra appears about 55 times outside Liverpool and gives about 60 concerts to schools. The Royal Liverpool Philharmonic Society is at the head of the city's musical fame.

Bluecoat Chambers, originally the Bluecoat School, in the shopping centre is a Queen Anne building, which is now a centre for the arts, and open to visitors.

Liverpool has many and varied churches. St Agnes, Sefton Park, is by J. L. Pearson, 1883–5, with a reredos in cream, red and gold. All Hallows, Allerton (1872–6, by Grayson and Ould), has a fine set of Burne-Jones glass made by William Morris. All Saints, Childwall, is medieval with a tower erected in 1810 and an ancient font. The 19th-cent. St Bridget at Wavertree is graceful and has a Last Supper in mosaic. Also at Wavertree, Holy Trinity is good Georgian, its classic steeple a landmark, at present awaiting rebuilding. St Mary's, Edge Hill, is neo-Gothic, with clustered columns and handsome doors. St Michael, Toxteth, is also 19th-cent., and has a monument to Horrocks, the HOOLE astronomer.

Theatres include the well-known Playhouse, and the Everyman. Besides having so many cultural amenities, Liverpool has a large, steadily developing civic university. There are ample facilities for entertainment and sport, and **Aintree** is 6 m. N. The city is ringed by parks and open spaces, led by Sefton, its "HYDE PARK".

The shopping centre represents a commercial aspect as important, or more so, as the industrial one. Well defined and compact, the main shopping area is Castle Street, Dale Street, Lord Street, Church Street with offshoots, and Bold Street. It has customers as far as the Lakes, the Isle of Man and Ireland, and Liverpool is called the shopping capital of North Wales. The city's airport is Speke, 6 m. SE., which claims to be the most modern in the country. Also there is SPEKE HALL, run by Liverpool Corporation for the National Trust.

Within reach of the city are golf courses, the Lancashire coastal resorts, the Wirral Peninsula and historic CHESTER. Liverpool calls itself the gateway to the world, with its passenger liners and some 30 million tons of cargo handled annually. And it looks to the future: to an underground railway linking the main city stations and to an internal motorway, among many other plans for development.

LOWER PEOVER, *Cheshire* (12–SJ7474). A tiny village of thatched and timbered cottages, an old water-mill, an inn and a 17th-cent. schoolhouse, surrounded by quiet fields and woodlands of the fertile Cheshire Plain. The outstanding feature is the richly handsome church, with its overhanging eaves and startling black-and-white gables. Some of the great oak beams are believed to date back to 1296, when the church was a chapel of ease to Great BUDWORTH 5 m. to the NW. The stone tower is 16th-cent., but the nave and chancel are of 14th-cent. timber and plaster-work in the prevalent style of the period. Inside are massive pillars with plain capitals supporting a raftered roof of singular beauty, and the splendid woodwork is continued throughout the composition of the church. Of special note are the strange old box pews with narrow doors raised high above the floor to keep out draughts. Wooden shelves on one of the pillars were meant to carry charity loaves to be given to the poor every Sunday. In the chapel hangs a curious wooden hand, thought to have been exhibited outside the church in medieval times to show that buying and selling might be carried out at fair-time. Here, too, is a vast oaken chest, of which local legend has it that unless a girl could lift the lid with one hand she was not fit to be a farmer's wife. In the side chapels are monuments to generations of the Cholmondeley, de Tabley and Shakerley families, one of which commemorates Sir Geoffrey Shakerley who fought for Charles I and distinguished himself at the battle of Rowton Heath.

At the side of the church stands the ancient and famous Warren de Tabley Arms Hotel, a fine hostelry more generally known as the Bells of Peover.

LOWESWATER, *Cumberland* (14–NY1421). This is the last lake in the NW. of the Lake District. Beyond it Lakeland proper ends towards the A5086 connecting COCKERMOUTH and Cleator Moor. But it is precisely from this end that the approach to the small lake is more interesting, showing how the character of the countryside changes from the coastal plain to the grandeur of the mountain groups. Thus beyond and to the E. of Loweswater the great peak of Grasmoor can be seen, followed by Whiteless Pike. Further S. are Robinson, Dale Head and Fleetwith. Opposite Grasmoor is Mellbreak, with its impressive screes, on the west side of CRUMMOCK WATER. The road is narrow and leads to the village of Loweswater, which lies halfway across the plain towards Crummock Water. After the village the main road turns NE. towards the Vale of Lorton to skirt the end of Crummock Water, but there are some smaller roads between the two lakes, and a footpath goes along the south-west side of Loweswater. This lake, with Holme Wood where the footpath runs, is National Trust Property.

LOWTHER, *Westmorland* (14–NY5223). Lowther Castle was one of the great baronial houses of England which once entertained royal and foreign guests, including Mary Queen of Scots, and was the home of the Earls of Lonsdale until 1936. It stands in a 3,000-acre park just W. of the A6. It had magnificent proportions, of which the preserved frontage gives some idea, although it was rebuilt at various times in its history. The huge park contains beautiful countryside and also Lowther church, dedicated to St Michael. The church pillars and arches date from the 12th or 13th cents. but the walls were rebuilt in 1686. Outside it is the mausoleum of the Lowthers, the Earls of Lonsdale. The home of the present Earl is **Askham Hall,** a 14th-cent. fortified tower. It is to the W. across the River Lowther, at the entrance to the picturesque village of Askham. The name of Lowther figures in Wordsworth's history. His grandfather, Richard Wordsworth, became superintendent to the Lowther estates about 1725, and lived at Sockbridge near PENRITH. The poet's father, John, became chief law-agent to Sir James Lowther, later the 1st Earl of Lonsdale. Wordsworth's poem, "To the Earl of Lonsdale", welcomes a legal vindication of the character of William Lowther, Sir James's successor, who discharged to Wordsworth the debt which the late earl had owed John Wordsworth but had refused to pay.

The village of Lowther lies on the east side of the park, with interesting old cottages. At nearby Hackthorpe, Lowther Wildlife Park is an interesting experiment in presenting in a natural setting various species of deer, cranes and other animals and birds. They are free to wander in more than 100 acres of parkland (open to the public). Visitors are encouraged to establish friendly relations with the animals.

LYME PARK, *Cheshire* (12–SJ9784). The house is of Elizabethan origin, but was provided with an impressive Palladian exterior in the 18th cent. It was the home of the Legh family for 600 years and is now owned by the National Trust. It contains some elaborate Jacobean rooms and carvings by a student of Grinling Gibbons. The extensive park contains a herd of red deer. The entrance to the park is on the western outskirts of Disley, through which the **Peak Forest Canal** runs through beautiful country to its terminus at Whaley Bridge.

LYTHAM AND ST ANNE'S, *Lancashire* (12–SD3328). Of quite a different character from its larger neighbour BLACKPOOL on the N., Lytham and St Anne's has a charm of its own. Some half-timbered buildings mingle pleasantly with a scene of peaceful parks and gardens, with their floral displays. A promenade borders $1\frac{1}{2}$ m. of coast along part of the town, and in one area encloses Lytham Green, with its old windmill on the lawns and the church steeple and houses behind. In all there are $6\frac{1}{2}$ m. of sandy beaches and dunes. Ashton Gardens are a minute's walk from the busy little shopping centre, with tree-lined paths, rose garden, water-course and bowling green. Lowther Garden has sweeping lawns and trees, with areas for bowls, tennis, putting and crazy golf. The Alpine Gardens with their little bridges are pleasant for gentle strolls. Fairhaven Lake offers sailing dinghies, rowing boats, motor boats and water skiing. There is also a separate boating lake, and a pool for children to paddle and sail model yachts. The Ribble Cruising Club has its headquarters on the promenade and organizes regattas and weekend races. Beach chalets, and both open-air and indoor swimming-pools are available, as is horse-riding in the country lanes. The combined borough of St Anne's with Lytham has excellent golf links. The visitor can use four championship courses: the Royal Lytham and St Anne's, St Anne's Old Links, Fairhaven and Lytham Green Drive.

John Carr of YORK built Lytham Hall in *c.* 1760, incorporating part of an earlier house.

MACCLESFIELD, *Cheshire* (12–SJ9173). The emergence of Macclesfield as one of the leading silk manufacturing towns in England has given it an interesting architectural legacy of good 18th- and early 19th-cent. mills. They contribute to the town's character. Macclesfield is mentioned in the Domesday Book as having formed part of the demesne of Edwin, Earl of Chester, before the Norman Conquest. In 1261 a charter granted by Edward, Prince of Wales and Earl of Chester, constituted Macclesfield a free borough. In 1278 Edward I and Queen Eleanor founded the Parochial Chapel of Macclesfield, dedicated to All Saints. At some unknown date in the 18th cent. the church was re-dedicated to St Michael and All Angels. Very little remains of Queen Eleanor's chapel, the church having been rebuilt twice, in 1739 in the Classical style and again between 1898 and 1901. St Michael's may either be entered from the level of the wide market place or by climbing 108 steps from below. The newly pinnacled west tower rises high and contains in its walling many carved fragments from the medieval foundation. Over the south door is a stone anointed by the bishop conducting the first service 700 years ago. There is a fine hammer-beam roof to the chancel, a superb clerestory, and among the multitude of scenes depicted in the windows is a glorious Ascension designed by Burne-Jones and made by his friend William Morris. On the east wall of the Legh Chapel, which survives from the earlier building, there is a tablet to the memory of John Brownsword, a grammarian and poet who is believed to have been a master at STRATFORD-UPON-AVON at a time when William Shakespeare could have been one of the pupils. The epitaph of another master of the school, William Legh, is inscribed on brass in the church and dated 1630. The Savage Chapel was built by Thomas Savage, who became Archbishop of York in 1501, with the intention that it should serve as a college, but instead it became the mortuary chapel of his family. Of special interest here is the Legh Pardon Brass of 1506, encased in a wooden frame. It shows Roger Legh kneeling with his six sons below the vision of Pope St Gregory, the inscription recording that, as a reward for good works and prayers, pardon had been offered to him and his family for 26,000 years and 26 days. The Savage Chapel is reached from the south aisle through a doorway guarded by two unicorns and an angel, and from the south

tower below a delicate oriel window. Marble tombs and effigies fill the church.

Macclesfield's Town Hall is a good Georgian building. The market cross, now removed to the West Park, once stood in the centre of the market square, and it was from here that proclamations were read out to the townspeople, as when the yeomen and archers of the borough mustered to march to Bosworth Field and again to Flodden Field in 1513. In West Park can also be seen some old iron stocks in an excellent state of preserva-tion and a 30-ton boulder believed to have been brought from Cumberland by Ice Age glaciers. Here, too, is one of the largest bowling greens in the North of England (crowned, as is usual in the North), covering approximately 1 acre, and at the gates of the park itself is a museum and art gallery.

Macclesfield Forest, 5 m. E. of Macclesfield, on the A537, is a tiny village on the edge of a wide stretch of wild country presenting magnifi-cent views across crags and narrow valleys to-wards the Peak District. The Forest Chapel here, originally built in 1673, was largely rebuilt in 1834. The ancient ceremony of the rush-bearing service, at which the floor is covered with rushes as of old, is held every August and attended by large numbers of people from all over the county. Two m. further along the road is Cheshire's most famous inn, the Cat and Fiddle, 1,600 ft up and one of the highest licensed houses in England. From this remote point close to the county boundary the vista is remarkable. Whetstone Ridge, 1,795 ft high, rises to the S. directly in front of the inn, with many other summits of over 1,000 ft on every side. In the past this was a region of turbulence to match the rugged grandeur of its scenery. The Davenports of CAPESTHORNE were the hereditary sergeants of the forest, whose duty to the king was to keep the 4,000 acres in readiness for hunting parties and prevent bands of outlaws from killing for the pot deer that were meant to provide royal sport. Lawlessness thrived until well beyond medieval times. Gangs of robbers, poachers and cut-throats made travel so hazardous that merchants dared only cross the area in the often questionable protection of professional guards. The wildness of Macclesfield Forest is reflected today in some of its names: Cat's Tor, Wolf's Edge, Dane's Moss, and Wildboarclough.

MAIDEN CASTLE, *Cheshire* (12–SJ5053), an ancient earthwork on the east side of the A41, is thought to date from the Iron Age. It lies on top of a small hill and on the south-east side, where it joins the main hill, there is a shallow ditch between two banks. The other sides face out above the slopes of the hill. The earthwork has stone and timber banking up the interior.

MALPAS, *Cheshire* (12–SJ4847), is one of the pleasantest old towns in Cheshire, with rows of timbered houses and cottages, some of which are good examples of medieval brickwork. There is a block of old almshouses, and many old inns, one of which has an oak chair said to have been used by James I. Visitors can regale themselves with the famous Cheshire cheeses – red Cheshire, white Cheshire and the coveted "Old Blue" – for Malpas is set in rich farming land where dairy farms are a speciality. The farming community is very strong in the town and has its own club and social centre. Formerly Malpas was a market town but now it is mainly a shopping centre for the surrounding villages. It is set on a hill-top, 2 m. from the road between CHESTER and the West Midlands, and is a junction for various local routes. This makes it an excellent centre from which to tour south-west Cheshire, the Dee valley, northern Shropshire and the Wrexham area of Wales.

Although it is an old town not much of its early history is recorded. A mound on the Bickerton Hills indicates a castle, possibly Norman, which served to repel Welsh invaders from the other side of the River Dee which winds only 4 m. away. In the 14th cent., it is said, Malpas people hardly dared to go out to church for fear of being attacked by Welshmen. There was an attempt to get the chapel on the estate at CHOLMONDELEY, 4 m. NE., raised to church status as it would have been a safer place for worship. The Civil War caused much damage and the beautiful church was used as sleeping quarters for Parliamentarian troops. A battle was fought at Oldcastle Heath nearby in 1643. Today, Malpas, which is well equipped with shops, is developing as a residential area for business people of Merseyside.

The town's treasure is the spacious and well-proportioned Church of St Oswald. It was built mainly in the 14th and 15th cents., and by the late 15th was practically complete in its present form. It is built of red sandstone and the external walls of the aisles with the clerestory above have good examples of medieval work: windows with rich tracery, castellations and pinnacles. Above each buttress is a set of gargoyles of various creatures. The tower is in keeping with the craftsmanship of the rest. Inside, a high tower arch and a broad, low chancel arch set off the nave, which has slender, clustered columns. Panelled roofs complete the nave and chancel. The long chest in the south aisle, companion to another in the crypt, has ironwork dating from the 13th cent. There are four sedilias, one of which, carved with grinning faces, is 600 years old. Two windows are of Flemish medieval glass. The east window commemorates Bishop Heber, a friend of Tennyson, who became Bishop of Calcutta, and wrote many hymns that are used today, including *Greenland's Icy Mountains* and *Holy, holy, holy.* There are monuments to the Cholmondeley family, of the nearby estate, and the finely sculpted tomb of Randolphus Brereton dressed in the armour of a Tudor knight. The Breretons, one of the great Cheshire families, were prominent in Malpas, and their seat, the 16th-cent. Brereton Hall, is one of the county's finest mansions. Sir Randle Brereton was a patron of Malpas, and founded a grammar school in 1528, endowed a hospital, presented a bell in the church tower and founded a chantry of St George.

Around Malpas are several interesting places to visit, such as Peckforton Hills, TARPORLEY, the Delamere Forest, Shocklach, Tilston and Tushingham.

MANCHESTER, *Lancashire* (12–SJ8397), may claim to be the country's second city, but the radical innovations for which its history has been notable have often placed the city not second, but first. It is also the capital of the North: far enough south of the bulk of the western Pennines that compress Lancashire's northern area and far enough into their recess where the county widens to be a natural centre of communications. There Manchester sprawls across an area that is about 12 m. from N. to S. and between 3 and 5 m. from E. to W., the great hub in a conglomeration of other towns whose divisions are difficult to distinguish. Within a ring 5 m. from Manchester's centre, one million people live, and within 10 m. there are two and a half million. It is one of the most thickly populated areas of England. Among the traffic noise below Manchester's vast buildings, the constant millions of transactions and the daily hordes of people, in the air that is Mersey-grey or humidly tinted by the sun, there hang memories of causes lost or won beyond counting. Much redevelopment is foreseen, with planning schemes that seem designed to sweep away many of the present central buildings and leave the cathedral dwarfed among square blocks. As part of these developments the Mancunian Way swings across the city – a modernistic road on stilts. Piccadilly, the large square which forms the centre of Manchester, has also been extensively redeveloped, with new parades of shops and the towering Piccadilly Hotel, designed to equal the large London hotels with facilities for an international clientele.

Manchester's site has been important since Roman times, with several river crossings and easy access from other parts of the country. Later came the exploitation of the coal supplies, and the water power and the humid air helped the development of the textile industries. The fairly flat land favoured transport by railways and canals. Thus circumstances combined to encourage the rapid development of commerce and industry in the 19th cent. The social and political struggles this engendered was the background for the radical ideas for which Manchester became prominent. In the earlier part of that century there was appalling squalor, moral degradation and poverty among people living under vile conditions in congested districts of the city, described by James P. Kay, the physician (later Sir James Kay-Shuttleworth). Workers, a third of them women, worked for 12 hours a day in mills. There were many strikes, food riots and machine smashing. Eventually discontent brought the notorious mass meeting, nicknamed Peterloo, when troops rode into the crowd with slashing sabres; there were 11 deaths and hundreds of injuries. This was a set-back for the working-class part of the Radical movement, but it strengthened the hands of middle-class Radicals,

Manchester: the John Rylands Library

who finally achieved a measure of reform in the
Factory Acts.

The Peterloo Chartists also wanted parliamentary reform, and a middle-class Radical, John
Edward Taylor, founded the *Manchester Guardian*
in 1821, two years after Peterloo, to support constitutional reform. The *Guardian* became outstanding under the driving force of great editors
and its influence for reform was felt on a national
scale. The greatest of these editors was C. P.
Scott, LL.D., and the art gallery has a bust of him
by Epstein. Leading Manchester men founded
the Anti-Corn Law League, which from 1838 had
its headquarters in the city, with John Bright and
Richard Cobden among its leaders. The Free
Trade Hall was built as the League's headquarters in 1840. A great engineering feat was the
building of the Ship Canal, which opened in 1894.
Industry had tended to move to the ports, so the
great spinners and merchants solved the problem
by making Manchester an inland port. This
helped to obviate dependence on the cotton trade,
by bringing in raw materials for other industries.
Thus Manchester is the third port of England. It
is also the second most important commercial,
financial and banking centre. It is still the country's second centre for newspapers, having not
only its own newspapers but being the northern
centre for editions of national papers. The Manchester Press Club is the oldest in the country.

The Cathedral stands on what was the old
centre of the town. Largely a 15th-cent. structure,
it was the parish church, and became the cathedral
when the Manchester diocese was created in 1847.
Chapels added to the outer north and south
aisles make it one of the widest churches in the
country. Cleaning has revealed the original sandstone. A special feature is the 30 choir stalls with
canopies, all in intricately carved wood.

The galleries and museums comprise the *City
Art Gallery* and six branches. As they hold some
23,000 items, not all collections can be shown at
once and what is currently on view is indicated on
the City Gallery notice boards. The best of the
foreign collection is permanently shown at the
City Art Gallery, designed by Sir Charles Barry,
where Italian works include a Piero di Cosimo,
four works of the Lo Spagna school and a
Matteo di Giovanni. North European works include an early Flemish *Madonna and Child*, a
Holy Family by Van Dyck, a seascape by Ruysdael, and landscapes of Teniers the Younger and
Cuyp. Later European exhibits are mainly 19th-
cent. French from the Barbizon and Impressionist
schools including works by Corot, Millet and
Fantin Latour; and Pissarro, Gauguin, Sisley,
Renoir and Vlaminck, among others. British
works form the largest part of the collection,
covering the better known artists mainly from the
mid-18th cent. onward. There are works by
Hogarth, Gainsborough and Reynolds and a
unique set of 18 idealized portraits by Blake.
Notable are Turner's *Heidelberg Sunset* and
Constable's *Hampstead*. Important Pre-Raphaelite works include *Autumn Leaves* by Millais,
Hireling Shepherd by Holman Hunt, and several
by D. G. Rossetti. Their associates are well
represented by numerous works by Ford Madox
Brown and Burne-Jones. Later British painters
displayed include Sargent, Sickert, John, Orpen,
Nevinson, Paul and John Nash, the Spencers,
Lowry, Piper, Sutherland and Pasmore. The
Athenaeum Annexe, adjacent to the City Gallery,
has pottery and porcelain from early times to the
19th cent.

Queen's Park Art Gallery has important sculptures by Rodin in bronze, and by Epstein, whose
large male figure, *Youth Advances*, was made for

the Festival of Britain exhibition. It also displays Victorian painting and sculpture.

Heaton Hall, like the other outlying galleries, stands in its own grounds. The former home of the Earls of Wilton, it was built in 1772 to the design of James Wyatt, and has period collections of paintings, watercolours, furniture, ceramics, silver and glass.

The Gallery of English Costume, in the fine Georgian mansion of Platt Hall, Rusholme, former seat of the Worsley family, has one of the most comprehensive collections in the country.

The Fletcher Moss Museum is housed in the Old Parsonage at Didsbury. This has the best of the watercolour collections, including works by Turner, David Cox and Paul Sandby, with early 19th-cent. silver and porcelain.

Wythenshawe Hall is a half-timbered house built in the 16th cent. with later additions. It is devoted to collections of Elizabethan furniture, Staffordshire ware, English delft pottery and English and European paintings. There are also displays illustrating various aspects of daily life in the past and of Chinese porcelain of the 17th and 18th cents.

Whitworth Art Gallery, run by the University in Oxford Road, displays English watercolours, European prints and engravings from the 15th cent. to the present and textiles and embroideries.

Manchester Museum, also in Oxford Road, has a large collection of geology, botany, zoology, archaeology and anthropology. There is also the famous Lloyd Japanese collection and an aquarium.

The John Rylands Library holds a multitude of treasures, and is of world importance for its collection of medieval jewelled bindings. As a whole, this library (open to the public) is the most notable of English provincial endowed libraries. It is remarkable that it arose from the industry of one man, Rylands, who was a weaver in WIGAN. From his legacies, his widow founded the library as a memorial and bought many rare books and manuscripts for it; two such purchases alone (Earl Spencer's Althorp collection and the famous Crawford MSS.) cost half a million pounds. The library opened in 1900 in a fine neo-Gothic building by Basil Champneys. The Printed Book Department has the earliest dated Western print (St Christopher, 1423), the Gutenberg Bible, valuable editions of English and foreign classics, works of art from 16th-cent. scholar printers and from de-luxe printers of the 17th and 18th cents. – in all over 3,000 incunabula from the leading English and Continental presses. The department has exceptional facilities for specialists in fields such as Egyptology, archaeology, French Revolution broadsides, select editions and foreign periodicals. The Manuscript Department has records on clay, bark, bamboo, papyrus and parchment, representing over 50 cultures and languages from the 3rd millennium B.C. onward, with some 250,000 documents from the 11th to the 20th cent. Its treasures include the earliest known manuscript of a New Testament book (a fragment of St John's Gospel, written before A.D. 150).

The Chetham Library (open by arrangement) was founded in 1653 and was the first free public library in Europe. Its founder, Humphrey Chetham, provided parish libraries in Manchester and BOLTON and was a merchant, who at one time owned TURTON TOWER. Chetham's is still housed in its old collegiate building, and has 100,000 books and MSS.

The Central Library has, in its fine circular building by Vincent Harris, 1930–4, a Shakespeare hall and a huge window that depicts the playwright surrounded by many of his famous characters. The building contains one of the greatest reference libraries in England. It is also unusual in that the basement houses a fully equipped theatre, naturally called the Library Theatre.

Other theatres of note include The Opera House, which receives such distinguished visiting companies as the London Festival Ballet and GLYNDEBOURNE Opera Company, the Stables Theatre Club, a platform for prospective television drama, and the University Theatre which provides a mixture of professional and student productions.

Anyone approaching the centre of Manchester along Oxford Road will see the large number of university buildings on either side, and there are many more situated off the main roads. Redevelopment on this long road is extensive and many new university buildings are rising from the stretches of waste ground.

The Hallé arose from the Art Treasures Exhibition of 1857; Charles Hallé founded the concerts as a private venture in the following year, and Manchester's love of music developed along with this famous orchestra. After Hallé's death the Hallé Concerts Society was founded in 1898, and a series of distinguished conductors followed. Prominent among them was Sir John Barbirolli, who, during his leadership of the orchestra in the last two decades, was largely responsible for establishing the international reputation which the orchestra today enjoys.

The Free Trade Hall was first a wooden building built in 1840 as the headquarters of the Anti-Corn Law League, followed by the brick one of 1843, which served the League until the repeal of the Corn Laws in 1849. Later users of the hall included the Athenaeum Society, of which Dickens was chairman at the first meeting, and later chairmen included Disraeli and Ralph Waldo Emerson. The third hall, built in 1856, was the best known building in Manchester, and the Hallé concerts started there. The hall was destroyed by fire bombs in 1940, but the Peter Street and South Street façades survived with damage. It was the Palladian style of these façades that Professor Reilly described as the greatest architecture in Manchester. The reconstruction (completed in 1951) by Mr Leonard C. Howitt, architect to the corporation, which became owners of the hall in 1921, preserved them and completely restored the vaulted arcade adjoining Peter Street, although the Windmill Street façade is in a simplified modern style. The hall is still the home of the Hallé and also provides some of the finest Folk and Jazz concerts in the country. It stands on part of the site of the Battle of Peterloo, which is depicted in a mural. (Open to the public at times.)

The Town Hall (open to the public) is a Gothic-style building completed in 1876, one of the most important works of Alfred Waterhouse. It has statues of various historic figures outside. Inside are those of John Bright and Richard Cobden, John Dalton, Gladstone, Sir Charles Hallé and others. The large hall has Ford Madox Brown's 12 mural paintings depicting scenes of local history. Notable are the fire-place in the reception room, the conference hall, the valuable collection of civic plate and the insignia.

Belle Vue is the great entertainment, concert and exhibition centre, along with one of Britain's largest zoos. There is a vast amusement park, a boating lake and a model village. The stadium can hold 25,000 spectators for speedway and sports events. Hallé concerts take place in Kings Hall, as well as sports events and ice shows. Among other features are three halls for trade fairs and exhibitions, and extensive catering facilities.

MARYPORT, *Cumberland* (14–NY0336). The shipping of coal and the iron industry were once the most important activities of Maryport. Now the harbour is closed to shipping and other industries have been developed, including plastics, clothing, engineering and chemicals. But Maryport is also a coastal resort with a good stretch of sands. Mote Hill is a vantage point from which to watch the blaze of colour made by the sunset across the Solway. **Allonby,** further N. on the coast, is an old and pretty little resort with good sands. Romans built a fort at Maryport, one of their chain of defensive points along the coast as a precaution against northern tribes turning the flank of HADRIAN'S WALL, which ended at Bowness on the Solway. The Maryport fort was called *Alauna,* and important discoveries of Roman altars and other relics have been made. The town has a golf course and fishing facilities.

MIDDLETON, *Lancashire* (12–SD8606), is about 6 m. from MANCHESTER's centre and near OLDHAM. Silk and cotton were its staple products, but the emphasis now is also on things like chemicals, plastics and engineering. St Leonard's Church was rebuilt in the 16th cent. and the tower has a curious wooden belfry cap with gables, added later. There is a Tudor screen, and brasses to the Assheton family. The stained glass is interesting, and a window depicts Sir Ralph Assheton's archers who fought at Flodden Field. The Boar's Head Inn is a 17th-cent. black-and-white building.

MIDDLETON, *Westmorland* (14–SD6286). Middleton Hall (a farm) is N. of KIRKBY LONS-DALE. The hall was the home of an important family through several centuries from Edward III to Charles I. With its walled courtyards it is a good example of 15th-cent. manor house domestic architecture. A Roman milestone, erected in recent times on a nearby field, indicates the 53rd

Roman mile from CARLISLE along an old Roman road which ran in this area. The Standing Stone of Whelprigg, an ancient cross, is in the vicinity.

At Firbank Fell to the N., the founder of the Society of Friends, George Fox, preached to a large crowd on Trinity Sunday, 1652.

MIDDLEWICH, *Cheshire* (12–SJ7066). The second oldest of the Cheshire salt towns, thriving today on an industry having its beginnings in Roman times. A collection of Stone Age tools and weapons and fragments of Roman pottery recently found in the area is on display in the town. One of the many encounters between Royalists and Parliamentarians took place here in 1642, resulting in the total defeat of a party of Royalist troops attacked while plundering the town. There are associations with violence of another sort: Middlewich was one of the last outposts of bear-baiting in the country.

The parish church here is mainly Perpendicular in style and contains some interesting old chairs and settles in wood together with memorials of the Venables family that date from the 17th cent.

MILLOM, *Cumberland* (14–SD1780), is in the south-west tip of the county, not far from the DUDDON VALLEY. It has the remains of a 14th-to 15th-cent. castle that became a farm, and the Church of the Holy Trinity near it. The church has Norman work: a doorway and piers in the nave. There is a beach at nearby **Haverigg.**

MOBBERLEY, *Cheshire* (12–SJ8081), has some half-timbered houses. The National Trust owns 20 acres to the N. of Mobberley, given to it by the Cheshire County Council and local residents to protect the church, St Wilfrid's. A public footpath leads from the S. of the church, which is mostly late medieval, with a good rood screen of *c.* 1500, a tower screen dated 1683, and some old stained glass. There are some wall paintings, one of them of St Christopher. A modern window commemorates George Mallory, born here in 1886, who was last seen when he and Irvine began the final stage of the climb to the top of Mount Everest in 1924.

MORECAMBE AND HEYSHAM, *Lancashire* (12–SD4364). Morecambe was originally Poulton-le-Sands, an ancient fishing village mentioned in the Domesday Book, and became popular as a holiday resort about half a century ago, following the construction of the railway. In the Town Hall grounds is a gateway from Old Poulton Hall, which was on the site of the present open-air market and which belonged to the paternal ancestors of George Washington. Growth of the town as a resort necessitated the building of a new port at Heysham between 1900 and 1904. Now the M6 which passes only 4 m. to the E. makes access still easier. Morecambe Bay is vast, and it is possible to walk across the sands to GRANGE-OVER-SANDS, but *not*, the council rightly insists, without the safety of an official

British Travel Association

Nantwich: a bedroom in Churche's Mansion

guide. These official walks take three hours and may be cancelled if rainfall has endangered the channels. Moored off the central promenade is *Moby Dick*, the famous sailing ship.

New Heysham Head Entertainments Centre is a major attraction which cost almost £500,000. Its Bird House has some rare species. The centre has tea-gardens, a children's zoo, an Old World Village and go-kart racing. The other major feature is Marineland – the first oceanarium built in Europe, the town claims. Its special event is the summer circus, in which dolphins perform. There are also sea-lions, chimpanzees and a well-stocked aquarium. Other attractions include the swimming stadium, the ballroom, variety shows, ice-skating, a model railway, a yachting slipway, boating pools, water-ski facilities and the notable autumn illuminations.

Heysham is a very old village. There is evidence that its church was built by the Angles in the 7th cent. Dedicated to St Peter, the church is modelled on the ruins of St Patrick's Chapel which a previous generation of Angles destroyed. The chancel was added in the 14th cent., making the original church into the present nave. The south aisle was built on in the 15th cent., and lengthened in the 17th. The north aisle was added in 1864.

Several of Peter Scott's books on wild birds deal partly with Morecambe Bay, which has various winter migrant flocks, and breeding grounds in the area. The eider and sheld-duck are notable.

MOW COP, *Cheshire* (12–SJ8557). A stark limestone ridge rising well over 1,000 ft above the Cheshire Plain and the lowland towns of CONGLE-TON and ASTBURY, it is in fact the last escarpment of the Pennines in their southward sweep from the Peak District. The climb to the top provides a rewarding view in all directions, of undulating hills and contrasting sweeps of broad fertile valley. It was here at the summit that a beacon tower was raised in the days of the Armada to signal news of invasion. The beacon is gone, but in its place stands a sham ruin, built in 1750 by Randle Wilbraham on a rock called "The Old Man of Mow" and known as Mow Cop Castle to hosts of summer picnickers. On this site, too, in 1807, the Primitive Methodists held their first meeting. Mow Cop covers six acres of country and is owned by the National Trust.

MUNCASTER, *Cumberland* (14–SD1096). Muncaster Castle (A595) is near **Ravenglass** and the Esk estuary. The castle (open to the public) is the seat of the Pennington family and this site has been theirs since the 13th cent. The original castle was built then or earlier, and the later 19th-cent. reconstruction by Anthony Salvin incorporates an ancient tower. The valuable collection of furniture and other items includes the "Luck of Muncaster", a bowl presented by Henry VI, who took refuge there after his defeat at Hexham in 1464, to ensure prosperity for the family. The flowering gardens and views from the castle terrace are famous. The church in the grounds contains Pennington family monuments and ancient stones.

At Ravenglass are the important Roman ruins known as Walls Castle (Clanoventa), remarkable in being one of the best preserved Roman sites in the N. From here the Roman road ran over HARDKNOTT PASS to PENRITH. In summer at least, the miniature railway train (*see* ESKDALE) carries passengers for some 7 m. from Ravenglass to BOOT, a pleasant way to see the countryside.

NANTWICH, *Cheshire* (12–SJ6552). This is a pleasant old market town on the River Weaver. It was once a busy salt-producing town and still has facilities for brine-bathing, the brine springs having been noted in Roman times. Nantwich is surrounded by a rich agricultural area that produces Cheshire cheese. The town suffered a disastrous fire in 1583 when most of the buildings were destroyed. Rebuilding gave it a wealth of Elizabethan structures, and the Crown Hotel is an example of that period. There are at least a hundred buildings of architectural interest, including some of the Georgian period. There were about 400 salt works in the town in the reign of Henry VIII, but the industry had dwindled by the mid-19th cent. Nantwich was harassed by Welsh raids in earlier days, and during its Parliamentary allegiance in the Civil War was severely besieged by the Royalists. There is a group of almshouses built in the 17th cent. The stone bridge over the Weaver was built in 1803, replacing one of 1663.

Churche's Mansion is a fine half-timbered Elizabethan merchant's house built in 1577 that survived the fire. The fine oak panelling was revealed during restoration. The large grammar school is also a 16th-cent. foundation.

St Mary's Church, one of the best in Cheshire, is a handsome structure in red sandstone with Decorated and Perpendicular work and a central octagonal tower. The church had considerable restoration in 1885, but there is a fine vaulted chancel of the 14th cent. with magnificent carved choir stalls. The font, the stone pulpit and the stone chancel screen are of note. Among the old window glass decoration is a Tree of Jesse.

The large industrial town of **Crewe** is close to Nantwich and a great contrast to it. Crewe, of course, is always associated with its great railway junction, and it was from its importance in this connection, and its spread of railway workshops in the 19th cent., that Crewe developed out of a combination of two villages. Railway engineering is still important among the town's industries, but other factories now employ a similar number of people and include the production of Rolls-Royce and Bentley cars. Crewe has seen considerable housing developments and has a modern town centre. Its theatre was saved from closure by being administered as a trust. There are golf and fishing facilities, and motor racing at **Oulton Park** 10 m. to the NW.

NAWORTH CASTLE, *Cumberland* (14–NY 5662), is just N. of the A69 about 3 m. E. of **Brampton**. It is owned by the Earl of Carlisle and parts of it are open by arrangement. The castle is 14th-cent. (1335), with alterations in the early 16th and 17th cents. It was restored by Anthony Salvin after a fire in 1844. It is built round a central courtyard and has a great hall, oratory and rich tapestry furnishings. In the park is a ruined 16th-cent. house with cattle sheds on the ground floor and living quarters above.

NEW BRIGHTON, *Cheshire* (12–SJ3093), is only 15 minutes by ferry from LIVERPOOL. Sea trips are a feature of this resort in summer. There are two-hour pleasure cruises, giving fine views of the ever-changing shipping scene along the Mersey waterfronts to the entrance of the MANCHESTER Ship Canal. The resort also has sea trips to Ireland and Llandudno. There are 7 m. of coastline and ample parking facilities on its King's Parade promenade. The town has good sports facilities, with a sports festival in June that covers some 20 different activities, numerous public tennis courts and bowling greens and three first-class 18-hole golf courses run by the WALLASEY, Leasowe and Bidston clubs. Vale Park near the New Brighton seafront has a bandstand, and other attractions are Tower Grounds, the Floral Pavilion and Marine Park. The extensive Marine Lake offers boating, and the bathing pool can accommodate 4,000 bathers and 10,000 spectators. There is also the indoor New Palace amusement park. Three m. of the promenade from New Brighton to Seacombe are prohibited to vehicles and children can roam freely.

NEWBY BRIDGE, *Lancashire* (12–SD3685), is a charming village on the River Leven where it leaves WINDERMERE. There is an unusual stone bridge with arches of unequal size and the pretty Swan Hotel. This is a convenient centre from which to explore the Furness district, Windermere, or CONISTON WATER, and with walking routes along the Leven, in Grizedale or in the CARTMEL area. Lake Side is the pier for the motor vessel service on Windermere, with a park for 350 vehicles. British Rail closed the passenger line from Lake Side to ULVERSTON in spite of this being a much-used connection with the lake vessels. The alternative motor-coach service adds to road congestion.

NORTHWICH, *Cheshire* (12–SJ6573). For centuries the chief concern of Northwich was getting salt. There was formerly a museum of the history of the salt industry, but it was closed several years ago. Ludwig Mond with J. T. Brunner founded an alkali works at Winnington nearby, which was eventually to grow into the vast I.C.I. There has been some replanning in the town and a modern shopping precinct has been built. Subsidence caused by old salt workings can still take place today; its occurrence in the past has left some walls out of true. A number of the black-and-white buildings here are modern. VALE ROYAL is a few miles SW.

OLDHAM, *Lancashire* (12–SD9305), is a big and important town in Merseyside's northern area. Arkwright's spinning-frame and James Watt's steam engine boosted the town's cotton industry in the early 19th cent., work which continues with the addition of textile engineering today. The Town Hall is in Classical style. Early English watercolours are a notable feature of the art gallery, which also exhibits British paintings of the 19th and 20th cents. The watercolours include works by Sandby, Cozens, Girtin, Turner, Constable, Prout and Cox. The Werneth Park Study Centre has a natural history collection.

ORMSIDE, *Westmorland* (14–NY7017). In an area of country roads and wild flowers W. of the A66 is the little village of Ormside where St James's Church overlooks the River Eden. The Black Prince made a will here, which the vicar witnessed, perhaps on his way to the Border. In 1823 the churchyard yielded the Ormside Cup, of Anglo-Saxon workmanship in gold and enamel, now at YORK. The church is mainly Norman, with an Anglo-Saxon tower that was probably used for defence. The chancel roof is 16th-cent.

ORMSKIRK, *Lancashire* (12–SD4107). The Church of SS. Peter and Paul has both a tower and a separate spire, the tower of about 1540 and the spire being earlier. The church, partly rebuilt in 1729, is largely Perpendicular; the tower was probably added to house bells brought from Burscough Priory after the Dissolution. The church also has effigies of the 1st Earl of Derby and his wife, also from the priory, the ruins of which are nearby, and early memorials of the Scarisbrick family.

The Stanley family, the Earls of Derby from KNOWSLEY HALL, were long associated with the Ormskirk area, and were also the ancient kings of the Isle of Man. The 7th Earl, James Stanley, was a rich landowner and raised a Royalist army in the Civil War. His French wife, Charlotte, held out for months (in Stanley's absence) against Cromwell's forces at Lathom House, until the besiegers retreated before the approach of Prince Rupert. Stanley was later beheaded at BOLTON by Cromwell.

ORTON, *Westmorland* (14–NY6208), is a small village N. of TEBAY with some old buildings and, on its N., Orton Scar. From this, just above the road, there is a good view over the village towards the upper reaches of the River Lune and Tebay Gorge. All Saints' Church at Orton is mostly late medieval with a nave roof of the 15th cent. In many areas of north-western England the Society of Friends has always been strong. In this peaceful village George Whitehead, a man who influenced the Society's growth, was born in 1636. He joined the Society at the age of 14, became an itinerant Quaker preacher in many parts of the country and suffered imprisonment, but improved the legal status of the Friends by interviews with successive sovereigns.

OVER DENTON, *Cumberland* (14–NY6065), near GILSLAND, is an interesting small church of an early type, thought to have been built by Anglo-Saxons using stone from HADRIAN'S WALL. There are new windows from 1881 restorations but a small Anglo-Saxon window remains. An unusual feature is the arch in the chancel, which is believed to be a rebuilt Roman arch, with stones possibly brought from **Birdoswald**.

PATTERDALE, *Westmorland* (14–NY3915). This small village is a well-known vantage point at the head of ULLSWATER. The visitor who comes here over the great height of the KIRKSTONE PASS on the S. finds Patterdale superbly placed among fields beside the lake and hemmed in by mountains on all sides except the north. To the E. the High Street group continues northward to Place Fell (2,154 ft), which rises steeply above the village and the lake. On the other side of the descent from Kirkstone are the slopes below St Sunday Crag; and beyond these the great eastern bulks of the HELVELLYN range stretch away to the N. Only a mile or so along the west shore of Ullswater is Glenridding, from which motor-vessel services traverse the lake to the other end, at POOLEY BRIDGE. According to tradition, St Patrick, patron saint of Ireland, preached at Patterdale; the church is dedicated to him. This village is a good centre for exploring the Ullswater area. The A592 runs northward along the whole length of the lake, but only beyond Glencoyne Park do any other roads lead away from it.

PENRITH, *Cumberland* (14–NY5130), is an ancient and historic town. There are indications of Celtic occupation in about 500 B.C. First the Romans, who built a road through it, and then Norsemen and Angles came to the area. In the 9th and 10th cents. the town was the capital of Cumbria, a semi-independent state in the Kingdom of Strathclyde. For nearly three centuries up to 1603 Penrith was plagued by Scottish raids and was sacked twice. Penrith Castle, now in ruins (open to the public), was built as a defence against the Scots, the original tower being erected in 1397–9. Later owners included the Earl of Warwick, the "King-Maker". The castle was enlarged by the Duke of Gloucester, who became Richard III.

St Andrew's, the parish church, in the town centre stands on a site that is believed to have been a place of worship for more than 1,500 years; the present church was established before 1133, although there has been rebuilding since, including that of the nave in 1719 and 1722. Parts of the church are Norman: the strong tower with 6-ft-thick walls built by the Nevilles which bears the arms of the Earls of Warwick. It contrasts with the classical Georgian architecture which is seen to advantage since the 1951 interior re-decoration which restored the chancel and the sanctuary to their original style. There are two Hutton family effigies, and in the chancel arch a wall painting by Jacob Thomson frames the east window. This has some interesting 15th-cent. stained glass: a portrait said to be of Richard II or III, and two others formerly believed to be of Richard, Duke of York, and Cecily Neville, the parents of Edward IV and Richard III, but now thought to be of Cecily Neville's parents, Ralf Neville, 1st Earl of Westmorland, and his wife Joan, daughter of John of Gaunt.

The Giant's Grave is a popular sight in the churchyard, and is supposed to be of Owen, or Owen Caesarius, King of Cumbria in 920–37. But the two stone crosses and the four hogs-back stones are probably separate memorials from different periods of the 10th cent. Nearby is the "Giant's Thumb", possibly dated as early as 920, also connected with Owen Caesarius. It was once surmounted by a wheel cross but the upper arms are missing. A number of interesting gravestones have regrettably been removed in recent years, including that of "a straw-bonnet maker". By the church is a 16th-cent. building which was formerly the Queen Elizabeth Grammar School, believed to be founded in 1340 and re-established in 1564.

Wordsworth had connections with Penrith. His paternal grandfather lived at Sockbridge nearby. William's father, after moving to COCKERMOUTH, was married in Penrith to Ann Cookson, the daughter of William Cookson, a Penrith mercer, shown in the parochial register of 1766. William and Dorothy paid visits from Cockermouth to their grandfather Cookson. At one period, 1776–7, they attended Dame Birkett's infant school, which was possibly in the building overlooking St Andrew's churchyard. At the same time Mary Hutchinson, daughter of a prominent Penrith tobacconist, and William's future wife, attended the same school. The Cookson house was on the site of Messrs. Arnison, drapers. About 2 m. S. of Penrith at Yanwath on the A592 is to be seen the house, The Grotto, where Wordsworth often visited Thomas Wilkinson, his Quaker friend, as did Clarkson, who worked with Wilberforce against the slave trade, and Charles Lloyd, the friend of Lamb and Coleridge. The house was also known to De Quincey, Scott and Coleridge. The Penrith Town Hall is formed of two houses built in 1791 and designed by Robert Adam. One was the residence of Wordsworth's cousin John.

The Gloucester Arms hotel, one of the oldest inns in England, dating from 1477, is said to have been the residence of Richard III and bears his coat of arms. The Two Lions hotel building dates from 1584. The mansion of Carleton Hill was built by Mrs Frances Trollope, mother of Anthony, the novelist. Up the hill on the NE. is the famous Penrith Beacon. This was built in 1719, but the site was used long before that to flash warnings. Sir Walter Scott was in Cumberland in 1805 when it flashed the warning of Napoleon's expected invasion, and he dashed back to Scotland. The Luck of Edenhall, a medieval glass goblet in the VICTORIA AND ALBERT MUSEUM, came from the now demolished Eden Hall near Penrith. The goblet may date from about 1240 and was possibly brought back by one of the Musgrave family from the Crusades. The clock tower in the centre of Penrith is a Musgrave monument.

The town has golf and many other sports facilities. It is a touring centre for the pleasant Eden Valley, for ULLSWATER and for the Pennines.

PEOVER HALL, *Cheshire* (12–SJ7674). The hamlet of Over Peover, sometimes called Peover Superior, or Higher Peover, and recorded as Pevre in the Domesday Book, is historically important only because it contains within its manorial boundaries the great house which was for many generations the property of the Mainwaring family. Peover Hall, originally a timber building, was rebuilt by Sir Randle Mainwaring in 1585, largely in brick, and restored many times in later centuries. Above the main door appears the date 1654, the year in which Ellen, the wife of one of Sir Randle's sons, built the remarkably fine stables of which the carved Jacobean woodwork and ornamental plaster ceilings survive. The Hall has several tall gables and delightful mullioned stone window frames, the whole being surrounded by a moat. The Tudor part retains a long dining-room above the huge kitchen with its complicated timber roof.

Through the stableyard leading from the back of the building is the church with its two chapels dedicated almost solely to the Mainwarings. The church itself was originally built in the reign of Edward III, in the style of the period, and rebuilt in brick in 1811, while still retaining its old font, its perfect Jacobean pulpit and a chair said to have been made from a still earlier pulpit of some 400 years ago by one of the Mainwaring family.

The two chapels contain splendid tombs and are well preserved. An American flag and plaque have been placed in the church to commemorate the fact that General George S. Patton and his staff of the American Third Army worshipped here while occupying Peover Hall during the Second World War.

POOLEY BRIDGE, *Westmorland* (14–NY 4724), is on the A592 beside the River Eamont where it flows out of the east end of ULLSWATER. This small village is a good starting point from which to see this fine lake; the scenery becomes more impressive as you go W. along the lakeside road, passing the area of Wordsworth's daffodils (*see* Ullswater) and reaching the far end where PATTERDALE is hemmed in by high fells. A pleasant alternative is to take one of the passenger vessels which sail regularly in summer. There are boats for hire at Pooley Bridge. The village is also a good centre on this eastern fringe of Lakeland for exploring the Eden Valley or PENRITH. Near the village, at Eusemere, lived Thomas Clarkson, the abolitionist, who was visited by Wordsworth and other men of letters; and it was along the Pooley road that Coleridge walked from GRASMERE to find the Penrith printer, Brown, who afterwards printed "The Friend" for him.

There is a road part way along the south-east side of Ullswater and into **Martindale**. Here the 19th-cent. Church of St Peter, built in the Early English style, stands on a steep and isolated slope. It has 17th-cent. woodwork and occupies the site of 11th- and 17th-cent. churches. Also in Martindale is the deer forest, the home of wild red deer.

PORT SUNLIGHT, *Cheshire* (12–SJ3483). It is well worth turning W. from the main road S. of BIRKENHEAD to visit Port Sunlight. This is the model village built for his employees by the 1st Viscount Leverhulme, the great benefactor. He was William Hesketh Lever, born in BOLTON in 1851, who began to make soap at WIGAN in 1886 and whose Sunlight Soap became famous. The centre-piece of the village is the Lady Lever Art Gallery and Museum. Its 31 rooms contain a magnificent collection of works of art collected by its founder over half a century. The gallery was designed as a memorial to Lady Lever and was opened in 1922.

British painters are strongly represented. There are many Pre-Raphaelite works, including Holman Hunt's *The Scapegoat* and *May Morning on Magdalen Tower*, Ford Madox Brown's *Cromwell on his Farm* and Rossetti's *Blessed Damozel* (1879). There are various works by Millais, including *Sir Isumbras at the Ford*. Mostly they are of the period of this and later pictures, when he was moving away from Pre-Raphaelite principles. Works by the Victorians Lord Leighton and Alma-Tadema are included: two small works by the latter, and *Garden of the Hesperides* and *Daphne-phoria*, a large-scale representation of a Greek procession at Thebes, finished to the last detail, by the former. The portraitists shown include Hoppner, Reynolds, with several works including *Elizabeth Gunning*, Gainsborough, with *Mrs Charlotte Freer*, and Romney. Burne-Jones's *Beguiling of Merlin* is included. There are landscapes by Richard Wilson, Constable's *Gamekeeper's Cottage* and Turner's *Falls of Clyde*. As well as a set of Turner drawings there are English watercolours of the late 18th and 19th cents. In the north Sculpture Hall the marble *Antinoüs* is shown to advantage in the centre; it was found in the ruins of Hadrian's Tivoli villa. The so-called Gladiator in polished black marble, probably of the 2nd cent., is a Roman copy of an earlier Greek bronze.

The gallery also has Epstein's *Deirdre* in bronze and works by Nollekens and Flaxman. The bust of Ferdinando de' Medici is by Giovacchino Fortini of Florence. It contains one of the best English collections of furniture, mostly of the second and third quarters of the 18th cent. A rosewood dressing table and a mahogany bookcase may have come from the workshop of Thomas Chippendale the Elder. Various period rooms show work from Tudor and Stuart times up to Wedgwood. There are important collections of Wedgwood pottery, Carrara marble mantlepieces and interesting old clocks. Chinese pottery and porcelain are a special feature, including Han, T'ang, Sung and Ming works.

POULTON-LE-FYLDE, *Lancashire* (12–SD 3439), is an old market town. Its Church of St Chad has an early 17th-cent. tower in the Perpendicular style. The rest of the church was rebuilt in stone in 1752–3. The Romanesque chancel was added in 1868. There are Doric doorways with pediments, and a Georgian interior. A staircase leads to the galleries, which have square pews with the original candle sockets. There are wall monuments to Fleetwoods and Heskeths and a vault dated 1699. The baptistry has a 17th-cent. screen, and there is a carved Jacobean pulpit.

PRESTBURY, *Cheshire* (12–SJ8976). Lying 2½ m. NW. of MACCLESFIELD, Prestbury has a strong claim to being the prettiest and most visited town in Cheshire. The attractive appearance of so many timbered cottages, each differently presented in a frame of trees and flowered gardens, might well be qualification enough; but to this is added a wealth of ancient buildings of great interest.

The earliest relic is an Anglo-Saxon cross, about 4 ft in height, which is made up of fragmented carvings at least 1,200 years old. It stands, encased in glass, in the churchyard of the beautifully restored and enlarged 13th-cent. church adjacent to a Norman chapel and in company with two fine yew trees planted here 600 years ago. The church, dedicated to St Peter, is in styles of architecture from Early English to Perpendicular. The oldest part is the chancel, dating from *c.* 1220. The pillars on the north side of the nave are 13th-cent. and those on the

south side probably a century later. Among the memorials on the north wall of the chancel is a monument to Reginald Legh, of 1482, who was concerned in the building of the tower. This tower, with its rows of faces and grotesques, still stands, the massive base forming a porch. Also in the chancel is the armoured figure of Sir Edward Warren and on the south side are the figures of Robert Downes and his wife. Another elaborate sculpture, of Jasper Worth with his wife and three children, is affixed to the wall of the Tytherington Chapel, and at the east end of the north aisle is the Legh Chapel where several members of this family are buried. Great antiquarian interest will attach to the sanctuary chair, the oak screens and the two old chests, one of which is 8 ft long, all originals of the Jacobean period. The churchyard, already mentioned, contains several other curiosities. One is the grave of Paul Mason of Rainow, who, when he died in 1752 at the age of 95, was the father or grandfather of 94 children. Another is that of Sarah Peckford "who died a bachelor in the 48th year of her life". The third is a 19th-cent. inscription to Maria Rathbone, a child who lost her way home and whose body was found 25 days later as the result of a dream by a complete stranger.

The Norman chapel next door is kept bare and plainly furnished in simulation of its appearance when its first worshippers attended here more than 750 years ago. The doorway is the oldest in a neighbourhood famous for ancient buildings. The arch above it is carved with zigzags and strange beaked heads, opening into a further Norman arch leading to the chancel. Only the roof had to be made new in the restoration work carried out two centuries ago.

Opposite the churchyard is the handsome black-and-white Priest's House, probably 14th-cent., with gables and diamond-paned windows. During the days of the Commonwealth a parson ejected from the church used to preach from a gallery over the door. This superbly maintained and rare building is now the property of the District Bank. At the far end of the town is a Reading Room, built in 1720 and endowed by Anne Whittaker for "promotion of a schoolmaster to teach ten of the poorest children in the township of Prestbury from the Primer to the Bible". Today this is used as a branch of Williams Deacons Bank, with other sections appropriately housing a library and the parish council chamber. Still another link with the past has been effected by restoring the old village stocks to their original site after they were found to have been serving as a farmyard gate in 1934.

The amenities of Prestbury include one of the best golf courses in the county, several restaurants, and three fine inns in late Tudor style: the Unicorn, the Admiral Rodney and the Legh Arms.

PRESTON, *Lancashire* (12–SD5329). It was at the Battle of Preston in 1648 that Cromwell inflicted a decisive defeat on the Royalist forces. Milton, devout propagandist of the Lord Protector, mentions the event at the River Darwen, "with blood of Scots imbrued". In the 18th cent. Preston was associated with another kind of battle – the Industrial Revolution's consequences. The introduction of machinery lessened the demand for hand-labour and, combined with bad harvests and the Corn Laws, brought riots and demands for the destruction of machinery. Richard Arkwright, who was born at Preston in 1732, invented the spinning-frame (1769) to cheapen cotton production but had to remove to NOTTINGHAM first to avoid the attacks that drove Hargreaves out of Lancashire. Another northerner, John Horrocks, set up the first cotton mill in Preston, and the town became an important centre of the industry. Local history is told in the exhibits of the Harris Museum, which also has burial urns and wood timbers from **Bleasdale**, a unique wood circle (*see* CHIPPING), as well as other archaeological relics, pottery, porcelain, glass and costumes. There is material relating to Francis Thompson, the poet, who was born at Preston in 1859; his birthplace is 7 Winckley Street. The art gallery is in the same building as the Harris museum, a fine late Classical building, built 1882–93, to the design of James Hibbert, architect and alderman of Preston. The gallery has a special collection of works and relics of the Devis family, and works by 19th- and 20th-cent. painters and sculptors. St George's Church is early 19th-cent. and was rebuilt in 1884. St Peter's was designed by Rickman in 1832–5 in Gothic style, with the spire added later. It has flying buttresses outside and many cusps in the interior design.

Hoghton Tower is about 5 m. SE. of Preston, but is a private residence. For long the home of the de Hoghton family, the tower has mementoes of a visit by James I; he is said to have "knighted" a piece of beef as "Sir Loin", creating the word sirloin, but the veracity of this episode is dubious.

PUDDINGTON OLD HALL, *Cheshire* (12–SJ3273), is above the Dee between BURTON and SHOTWICK. Now privately owned, it has been involved in much of Cheshire's history as the home for seven centuries of the de Masseys, a family known all over the county. The Hall was also called The Priest's House because of the Catholic faith of its owners, and was suspected of being the centre of plots and conspiracies. In the hysteria of Titus Oates' "popish plot", Father Plessington of Burton, the chaplain of the Masseys, was seized, and slaughtered at CHESTER, in 1679. The last of the Masseys, William, fought in the battle of PRESTON as a Jacobite in 1715. He escaped after the battle but was caught at Puddington and died in Chester Castle dungeon. The great Cheshire families were seriously perplexed over their loyalties in the Jacobite uprising; the meeting of the Ten Cheshire Gentlemen after the battle of Preston finally decided to cast their lot with the King and not the Old Pretender. Their portraits can be seen at TATTON HALL.

RAVENSTONEDALE, *Westmorland* (14–NY7203), is a village set below Ash Fell, SW. of

KIRKBY STEPHEN, in pleasant moorland. St Oswald's Church is 18th-cent. but includes portions of an older structure. Sections of the congregation sit facing each other and the pulpit is on three levels. Ash Fell rises to 1,185 ft and gives a good view of the dale, in which rises the River Lune.

RIBCHESTER, *Lancashire* (12–SD6435), is a village with an ancient history 10 m. NE. of PRESTON; the Romans were followed there by Anglo-Saxon settlers and then by Norman conquerors. It was listed in the Domesday Book. A Royalist outpost, it was the site of several battles in the Civil War. It has pleasant houses, and an old bridge over the Ribble where there was a Roman ford; this area was the scene of some most important Roman discoveries. The Church of St Wilfrid is probably 13th- or 14th-cent. Two pillars fitted to hold the organ loft are believed to come from the Roman site.

The Ribchester Museum of Roman Antiquities has remains from Bremetennacum, the great Roman fort covering about six acres. An excavated area adjoining the museum shows the foundations of two granaries built by Agricola about A.D. 80. Among objects found were Samian pottery, coins and inscribed stones. A Roman helmet with a visor was sent to the BRITISH MUSEUM. Even wheat from the granaries was found, which crumbled when exposed to the air. The museum was bought by the National Trust in 1912, and the foundations were given to the Trust in 1922. The site is scheduled as an Ancient Monument and is of great archaeological importance. Roman roads led from here to MANCHESTER and E. through the Pennines, others to the Lune valley, LANCASTER and Preston.

Stydd church, near Ribchester, is believed to have been built in the reign of Stephen and to be the oldest church in the Ribble valley. It has neither tower, turret nor belfry. Many original features remain, and an old gritstone font with crude carvings.

The White Bull Inn, Ribchester, has Doric pillars supposed to be of Roman origin. There are pleasant picnic spots on the river banks, and the area has a number of old manor houses.

RIVINGTON, *Lancashire* (12–SD6214), lies to the SE. of CHORLEY, between a reservoir and the moorland where Rivington Pike rises to 1,190 ft. The Pike is the site of an old tower, dated 1733, said to be used as a beacon, and from here there are extensive views. The Lever Park at Rivington of about 400 acres was presented to the public by the 1st Lord Leverhulme, who was born at BOLTON (*see also* HALL I' TH' WOOD). The Hall in the park, rebuilt in 1744, is now a museum. The small Church of Holy Trinity was built about 1540 by the Pilkington family, of whom there is a genealogical picture. The church was re-modelled later and has an unusual belfry standing apart from the church. The pulpit has linenfold panels. See also the Unitarian chapel, scarcely altered since its erection in 1703.

Rosthwaite lies in the valley of Borrowdale

ROCHDALE, *Lancashire* (12–SD8913). This old mill town, 400 ft up near the Pennine moors, evokes memories of women spinning cotton, of John Bright, of Gracie Fields, of 19th-cent. economic struggles and of the little co-operative store opening in Toad Lane. Rochdale became so well known as a cotton town that people forget its original source of industrial prosperity, which was based on wool, for woollen textiles were the main local industry until the end of the 18th cent. The town's history can be traced back for very many centuries before that. A considerable collection of flints and Bronze Age implements were gathered for the Rochdale Museum, showing that the area was inhabited since prehistoric times. A Roman road is believed to have run to the town from MANCHESTER, and a remarkably well-preserved stretch of it can be seen up in the moors at BLACKSTONE EDGE where it crosses into Yorkshire. Rochdale was in King Athelstan's West Saxon kingdom, was listed in the Domesday Book, and was one of the largest manors in medieval times in the Hundred of Salford. It has had a weekly market charter from 1251, and since that time the wool industry developed from the moorland sheep. But by the end of the 18th cent. cotton was beginning to replace wool, and many mills sprang up. The industry suffered depression at various times, and severe conditions led a little band of Rochdale men to make a co-operative effort by establishing their own shop and dividing the surplus for mutual benefit. They met with hostility and suspicion, but finally set up their shop in 1844 as the Rochdale Society of Equitable Pioneers. The co-operative movement was developing simultaneously elsewhere, but Rochdale is generally regarded as the first; and its old "co-op" store is still there as a museum for visitors. Varied new industries now supplement textiles, and square blocks of flats are dominant.

The borough has a handsome town hall, completed in 1871, in Gothic style by W. H. Crossland, with a frontage of 264 ft. There is a hammer-beam roof of a single span over its Great Hall of 90 ft by 58 ft. *The Signing of Magna Carta,* a fresco by Henry Holiday, covers the east wall. The exterior of the Parish Church of St Chad is in Perpendicular style, and in the 19th cent. much of the interior was restored, but there are 13th-cent. arcades, and carved 16th-cent. screens. The art gallery contains works in oils and watercolour. Archaeological and geological material is stored in the museum, with new premises under development. Among special sections in the central library are the Ember Collection dealing with cricket, works on the co-operative movement, and the John Collier Collection. Collier, the painter and earliest of the Lancashire dialect poets, wrote as Tim Bobbin. The most famous 19th-cent. citizen of Rochdale, John Bright, was born here in 1811; he is best known as an opponent of the Corn Laws, and a bronze statue of him stands in Hillside Gardens. Gracie Fields was also born in Rochdale, and was made a Freeman.

The art gallery at **Bury,** W., contains the Wrigley Collection which includes works by Constable, Turner, Crome, Cox, de Wint, Canova and Epstein. Thomas Wrigley (portrayed by G. F. Watts), a 19th-cent. paper-maker and pamphleteer, formed the collection. Bury was the birthplace of Sir Robert Peel, whose statue is in the market place. Kay Gardens commemorates John Kay, inventor of the flying shuttle.

Radcliffe, SW. of Bury, has a local history museum, covering the district from prehistoric times, and the remains of Radcliffe Tower (*c.* 1403).

ROSTHWAITE, *Cumberland* (14–NY2514). This is a small village, but it lies in a setting that amply repays the visitor's journey. It is surrounded in almost every direction by the magnificent peaks and fells of BORROWDALE. It is 6 m.

Rydal church from Dora's Field

Kenneth Scowen

S. of KESWICK, centrally placed in the valley, and is a good departure point for walking or climbing in such areas as Dale Head, Langstrath, Sty Head or GREAT GABLE, Greenup and WATENDLATH. Seatoller and HONISTER PASS are SW., and the Seathwaite and Stonethwaite areas lie to the SW. and SE.

RUFFORD, *Lancashire* (12–SD4515), NE. of ORMSKIRK on the main road, has Rufford Old Hall (open to the public) on a site of 14½ acres owned by the National Trust. The building is one of the best remaining examples of a late medieval timber-framed hall with plaster panels. It was built by the Hesketh family in the 15th cent., with wings added in 1662 and 1821. The great hall is notable for its ornate hammer-beam roof, and for a rare type of 15th-cent. movable screen with rich panels. The property was given to the Trust in 1936 by the 1st Baron Hesketh with an endowment; one wing, containing the Philip Ashcroft folk museum, with collections from surrounding areas, was given in 1946. The hall has fine displays of 17th-cent. furniture, 16th-cent. arms and armour, old English coins and tapestry, and Roman relics.

Rufford's church, St Mary's, is an 1869 building with a spire and succeeds an earlier church on the site. There is interesting window glass and carving on the capitals of pillars. A chapel is devoted to the Hesketh family of Rufford. The memorials (some of them from the older church) include a marble carving by Flaxman, and a wall tablet to Sir Thomas Hesketh with a verse by William Cowper.

RYDAL AND RYDAL WATER, *Westmorland* (14–NY3606). On 23 April 1850 William Wordsworth died at Rydal. He was born on 7 April 1770 at COCKERMOUTH. In a life of 80 years Wordsworth changed in his outlook from youthful ardour for the French Revolution ("Bliss was it in that dawn to be alive") to conservatism; his work at Rydal, during which he became Poet Laureate, shows a corresponding change of emphasis from that of the great periods of the "Lyrical Ballads" and GRASMERE. Nevertheless, he continued to work unceasingly in his last 37 years, which he spent at Rydal Mount after moving there in 1813. The house is up the hill, on the left, on the road for Rydal Hall.

Below Nab Scar is Nab Cottage, off the main road by Rydal Water, where De Quincey lived and later Hartley Coleridge, when De Quincey moved to Dove Cottage, Wordsworth's former home, in 1809. Behind Nab Cottage runs a path, one of Wordsworth's routes between Rydal Mount and Grasmere. Dora's Field is also on the north side of the main road opposite the lake. Wordsworth bought the field in 1826, and his grandson, Mr Gordon Wordsworth, gave it to the National Trust in 1935. St Mary's Church, 19th-cent., has a memorial window to Dr Thomas Arnold, his wife, and their son Matthew, the poet. Dr Arnold lived at AMBLESIDE.

Rydal Water is a small but beautiful lake, sheltered by Rydal Fell, 2,000 ft high on the north side. Round either end of the lake you can walk to Loughrigg Terrace (*see* Grasmere) on the S. Rydal Water is one of the first lakes to freeze in winter and then becomes a popular skating resort.

SADDLEBACK (BLENCATHRA), *Cumberland* (14–NY3227). The name derives from the saddle-shaped hollow between Foule Crag and the main summit. The alternative name of Blencathra is a reminder that this was Celtic territory before the English inroads from the E. and Norse settlement from overseas. THRELKELD, about 4 m. E. of KESWICK, is below Saddleback, and the climb from here is more severe than by routes from Scales, further E. A series of peaks joined by hollows form a ridge in which Saddleback itself is 2,847 ft high. Along the top from E. to W. there is more than a mile of good views. To the S. is the HELVELLYN range, SE. the High Street group above HAWES WATER, and more to the W. are GREAT GABLE and SCA FELL. To the W. of DERWENTWATER lie the beautiful smaller peaks of the Catbells, and to the N. is a wild region similar to that beyond SKIDDAW.

ST BEES, *Cumberland* (14–NX9611), is a small coastal resort, about 4 m. S. of WHITE-HAVEN. The town lies mainly inland but has a good beach. Nearby is St Bees Head in fine red sandstone – the most westerly point of Cumberland.

The Church of SS. Mary and Bega belonged to a Benedictine priory of the 12th cent. and is one of the most outstanding in Cumberland. St Bega is believed to have come from Ireland in about A.D. 650 to found a nunnery that preceded the priory, and the other church dedicated to her is at BASSENTHWAITE LAKE. St Bees Church has work of Norman and later periods; there has been much restoration and the central tower was altered in the 19th cent. by Butterfield. The fine Norman doorway should be noted. An impressive carved stone in the churchyard wall shows St Michael fighting a dragon. It is thought to be 8th-cent. and may have survived from the nunnery.

St Bees grammar school was founded in the 16th cent. and is now a public school.

ST HELEN'S, *Lancashire* (12–SJ5094). This industrial centre has since the 18th cent. gained a world-wide reputation for its production of glass. In Prescot Road is the Pilkington Glass Museum (open to the public), displaying English and Continental examples of the craft. There is also a tiny figure from Egypt of the god Bes, and a George IV glass decanter. Ample supplies of almost uniform sand grains has helped glass-making at St Helen's.

The Gamble Institute houses the library, the art gallery, with periodic exhibitions, and a museum dealing with natural history, glass and folklore.

Prescot, to the SW., has the Church of Our Lady, with the tower and spire added by Henry Sephton in 1729, above a notable black-and-white Jacobean roof. The spire was later rebuilt after lightning had struck it.

Rainhill, to the S., has an ancient stone cross, a 19th-cent. church with a hollow spire, and a Grecian-style Roman Catholic church.

SALFORD, *Lancashire* (12–SJ7796), is more or less joined to MANCHESTER and its docks. Salford developed as a cotton-spinning town, and the industry continues today, together with important rubber and waterproofing industries; there has been considerable re-planning. The

museum and art gallery is at Peel Park. A feature of the museum is Lark Hill Place, a reconstruction of a street in a 19th-cent. northern industrial town. The art gallery is notable for its L. S. Lowry collection. At Buile Hill Park is the science museum, containing exhibits of mammals, local natural history, coal-mining and general science. Ordsall Hall is a medieval manor house, formerly the home of the Radcliffe family.

Sir Charles Hallé, the conductor, is buried at Salford.

SAMLESBURY, *Lancashire* (12–SD6231), in the Ribble valley has the Church of St Leonard standing on a low site near the river. A stone church, it was rebuilt in the 16th cent., of which period is the nave with its clerestory and aisles. The tower is of about 1900. There are 17th- and 18th-cent. box pews, a two-decker pulpit, a plain Norman font, and Jacobean altar rails. Memorials and relics include those of the Southworth family.

Samlesbury Hall (open to the public on Sundays in summer) is on the PRESTON to BLACKBURN road within five minutes of the M6, and has an ample car park. The building dates mainly from the 15th and 16th cents., but was considerably altered in the 19th. Some of the windows in the later parts of the Hall were acquired from nearby WHALLEY Abbey after the Dissolution. There are nearly 100 pictures on view, including a collection of watercolours, specially painted for the Hall by Sir Charles Holmes, showing local Lancashire scenes. There are also 50 European and oriental casks and cabinets of various ages on display. A previous fortified house was destroyed by the Scots after Bannockburn, and the present mansion was owned by the Southworth family, to which John Southworth, the Jesuit martyr, belonged. The Hall is now in charge of the Samlesbury Hall Trust.

SANDBACH, *Cheshire* (12–SJ7560). A small town of considerable industrial importance, which still preserves many interesting features connected with its long history. The winding streets, the cobbled market place and the rows of old timbered houses show connections with past ages of prosperity, but the outstanding historical possession of Sandbach is the pair of Anglo-Saxon crosses on a stone platform in the square. The taller of these is over 16 ft high and the shorter nearly 12 ft. It is believed that they were put here some 1,300 years ago to commemorate the conversion to Christianity of Paeda, the son of Penda, King of Mercia. After the Reformation the crosses were broken up and the pieces distributed about the area for use in building. In 1816 Dr Ormerod, the Cheshire historian, collected most of the fragments and had them restored to their original position. The weathered carvings are in rough bas-relief and depict Biblical scenes. These monuments are certainly among the earliest of their kind left in England.

Sandbach was once a salt town and later became the centre of the silk trade. Both of these industries

Southport: one of the handsome shopping boulevards

continue to flourish under modern conditions, in the company, since 1901, of the giant Foden's Motor Works, whose prizewinning band is well known to brass bandsmen everywhere.

SCA FELL, *Cumberland* (14–NY2006), is described as the highest mountain in England, and it is in the sense of giving its name to the group which includes the real summit, Sca Fell Pike, 3,210 ft, Sca Fell itself being 3,162 ft high. This dominating group is like a giant knot near the geographical centre of Lakeland, as if a mighty convulsion had thrust it up and thrown the main lakes outward from it. Sca Fell, Glaramara and Bow Fell, with the flanking groups of Great Gable and the Pillar group on the NW., and the Langdale Pikes on the E., force motoring routes to keep to the N. and S.; even the road via Wastwater near Sca Fell can be reached only from the W. The stony crags of this volcanic range are a scene of grandeur, but they are no place for inexperienced climbers.

SCARISBRICK HALL, *Lancashire* (12–SD 3713). This attractive building is worthy of inspection by those interested in architecture. It stands 3 m. SE. of Southport, on the site of a 13th-cent. dwelling, and has 150 rooms. The fine setting is in a private estate protected by a preservation order, for the hall is officially listed as a building of special architectural interest. The wide expanse of woodland and pasture, with pleasant gardens, orchard and lake, create an atmosphere of peaceful grandeur. The present hall was remodelled by John Foster in 1814 and by Augustus Welby Northmore Pugin in 1836–45; it was added to (including the tower, now minus its wrought-iron cresting) by Edward Welby Pugin in 1860–70. It is a handsome example of neo-Gothic residential architecture. Inside are elaborate oak carvings, panelling and finely decorated ceilings. A fine collection of 17th-cent. oak carvings of Flemish craftsmanship, in the oak room, provide a wealth of pictorial scenes and decoration. The Kings' Room has 27 oil paintings of royal personages set in panelled walls, and a finely carved ceiling.

In 1946 the Scarisbrick family left the hall and the estate was bought by the Church of England Commissioners. With Ministry of Education aid, the building was equipped as a modern teachers' training college at a cost of £250,000, which included making it structurally sound and adding central heating and hot-water systems, laboratories, an art room and playing fields. New buildings were added to provide a chapel, a sanatorium, dormitory wings, a dining hall, kitchen and gymnasium. In 1963, the hall and 38 acres of the estate were bought by Mr Charles A. Oxley, sometime housemaster in Alexandria, Egypt, and principal of Tower College, Liverpool. He has established an independent school for boys, Christian but inter-denominational, run as a non-profit-making company with strong emphasis on academic attainment along with outdoor and voluntary activities. The owner welcomes visits – in the summer vacation – from those interested in the building. Guided tours are provided; so are a cafeteria and outdoor café, boats on the lake, tennis, badminton, putting and croquet.

SEASCALE, *Cumberland* (14–NY0301). This small resort stands on a pleasant stretch of coast with good sands and a golf course. S. is Ravenglass Gullery Nature Reserve (entry by permit) at Drigg Point with the largest colony of black-headed gulls in Europe. Seascale is convenient for reaching Wastwater. About 2 m. N. are Windscale and Calder Hall atomic stations. It was Windscale, in 1957, that had the leakage into the atmosphere of radioactive iodine which necessitated the banning of milk sales over 200 sq. m. for six weeks.

Forces of a different kind contended 1,000 years ago at **Gosforth**, 3 m. to the E. The famous 14½-ft Gosforth Cross combines Christian and pagan symbols. The representation on this cross of the Norse god Loki and his wife Sigun, and other figures who may be Baldur and his unwitting slayer, or Heimdal, or Odin who gave an eye for wisdom, shows how shallow-rooted the new faith then was among these early settlers and how they preferred to take no spiritual chances. St Mary's Church, rebuilt in the 19th cent., is probably on the site of a Norman, or earlier, structure. There are several ancient relics besides the Gosforth Cross, including two hog-back carved tombstones and cross shaft.

SEFTON, *Lancashire* (12–SD3500), is a little village on the coastal plain, N. of LIVERPOOL, and its Church of St Helen has been called the queen of Lancashire churches. An outstanding feature is the 16th-cent. carved woodwork of the rood-screen with its canopy (restored in the 19th cent.), the screens north and south of the chancel, and the screens in two chapels. The fine carved pulpit and its canopy (1635) and the screen of Lord Sefton's pew should be seen. The church has a lofty 14th-cent. spire but the rest of the building dates from the early 16th cent. There is also a notable series of monuments and brasses to the Molyneux family, including a knight in armour.

SHAP, *Westmorland* (14–NY5615). Shap Summit is, at over 1,300 ft, the highest point of the A6. One of the wildest-looking English main roads, it is often blocked when snow falls. The northward continuation of the M6 route approaches further E., avoiding the KENDAL route. Shap village, N. of the summit, is nearly 1,000 ft above sea-level. The parish church was restored in the 19th cent. but may have origins older than Shap Abbey. The Shap granite works are near the summit, but the abbey is hidden in a valley W. of the village. The Ministry of Public Building and Works has charge of the abbey (open to the public), which was founded about 1191 by Premonstratensian canons. Most of the ruins date from the early 13th cent. when the church was begun, but the tower is early 16th-cent. Keld Chapel nearby, administered by the National Trust, is a small pre-Reformation building.

SHOTWICK, *Cheshire* (12–SJ3371), is a very quiet village, although not far from an ironworks and an atomic factory. The River Dee, which once washed the edge of Shotwick, is now nearly 2 m. away. There was a ford here as a route to Wales, no doubt much used by armies to attack the Welsh. The battlements of St Michael's Church are a reminder of troubled times at this strategic point. The old church retains a Norman doorway and some interesting stained glass which may be 14th-cent. There is a three-decker pulpit, box pews, a churchwarden's seat with a canopy and a low arcade. The Elizabethan Shotwick Hall became a farm-house. To the S. is the site of the former castle, supposed to have been built by Hugh Lupus, Earl of Chester.

SIZERGH CASTLE, *Westmorland* (14–SD 4988), is 3 m. S. of KENDAL on the road to LANCASTER. This site has been the home of the Strickland family for 700 years, whose chapel is in the parish church of Kendal. The castle (open to the public at advertised times) is a peel-tower, built about 1340; additions – including that of the Tudor great hall – and alterations were made in the 15th, 16th and 18th cents. There is some fine Tudor panelling, furniture, 17th-cent. Flemish tapestry, and Stuart and Jacobite relics, as well as decorated plasterwork on ceilings and a portrait collection. A bell beaker was found in a cairn on Sizergh Fell and preserved. The castle stands in 1,556 acres and, with the estate, was given by the Stricklands with an endowment to the National Trust in 1950. E. of the castle is a panorama of countryside rising to the Pennines.

SKIDDAW, *Cumberland* (14–NY2629), dominates the Skiddaw group of fells, and at 3,054 ft is overtopped in the Lakes only by the two SCA FELL peaks and HELVELLYN. But Skiddaw is a favourite because it is what climbers call an easy ascent; however, those unaccustomed to the lengthy exercise involved should allow most of the day for the task so as to have intervals for rest. The north side slopes down through the wilds of Uldale Fells. Eastward is SADDLEBACK; and to the S. are magnificent views over DERWENT-WATER and KESWICK, with Helvellyn and BORROWDALE. W. of Derwentwater are Causey Pike, Grisedale Pike, Lord's Seat and BASSENTHWAITE. Occasionally Ireland can be seen.

SMITHILLS HALL, *Lancashire* (12–SD70 12). This Hall (open to the public) is one of the oldest manor houses in Lancashire, and is a good specimen of English domestic architecture. It lies in parkland 2 m. NW. of BOLTON on the slopes of the moors overlooking the town. Various parts of the Hall are of the 14th and 15th cents. Certain rooms were added in Tudor times. The great hall is timbered, and there is a withdrawing room with fine panelling. The house has had restorations and additions, and has been the home of such families as the Radcliffes, Bartons, Byrons, Shuttleworths, Belasyses and Ainsworths, until acquired by Bolton Corporation in 1938. Smithills is scheduled as an Ancient Monument, and contains furniture mainly of the Stuart period.

SOUTHPORT, *Lancashire* (12–SD3316). Southport is a pleasant resort most notable for Lord Street, a handsome boulevard, lined with trees and elegant shops which runs parallel to the coast for 1½ m. with its continuation, Albert Road. Marine Lake and Princes Park lie outside the promenade. Beyond, Marine Drive runs right along the seafront, passing the municipal golf links on the N. and Victoria Park and its esplanade on the S.

Southport Flower Show is a famous annual event, with horse-jumping trials as an added attraction. Other special events include county cricket, lawn tennis, golf tournaments, a music festival and a stage dancing festival. The Royal Birkdale Golf Club is well known, and the Ryder Cup Competition has been held there more than once. Marine Lake has 91 acres of water for sailing yachts and other boats. Besides its 6 m. of sandy beach, Southport also has a miniature model village. Conferences are catered for in two halls. In Lord Street the art gallery has a permanent collection of British art over the last 300 years. The museum, in the botanic gardens, includes a Victorian period room and a display of 18th-cent. Liverpool porcelain.

St Cuthbert's is the parish church of **North Meols**. It was rebuilt in 1730 and the spire is dated 1739. Enlargements and additions were made by Isaac Taylor in 1908. There is a Nolle-kens monument, and carving by Richard Prescot of about 1704. Holy Trinity Church is 19th-cent., rebuilt by Huon Matear, 1903–14. Its high tower is a landmark in the town; its pinnacles were restored with fibreglass. The interior has a ribbed barrel vault, and flamboyant stone tracery in the chancel roof.

SPEKE HALL, *Lancashire* (12–SJ4383), is one of the best half-timbered houses in the county. In a rural setting in 35 acres of land near the Mersey sheltered by trees, it would be peaceful indeed but for the roar from LIVERPOOL airport close by. The Norris family built Speke Hall round a square courtyard during the 16th cent. Sir Edward Norreys completed it in 1598 and an inscription on the north front records that this was his work. The hall was for long the ancestral home of the family. There is a wainscot which was said to have been brought from Holyrood Palace, Edinburgh, by Sir William Norreys (who fought at Flodden Field), and which Sir Edward inherited. A red sandstone bridge crosses the hollow that was formerly the moat, and leads to a series of small rooms, some of which conceal secret chambers. The interior has rich decoration and furnishings, including Mortlake tapestries, and other fine antiques. There is elaborate 16th- and 17th-cent. plasterwork in the great hall, and a fine plastered ceiling and carved chimney-piece in the great parlour. The kitchen has stone mullioned windows and a display of polished brass and copper.

Hale, about 3 m. E., was called by Jane Carlyle, wife of Thomas Carlyle, the "beautifullest village in all England". It has old cottages and flowers, and an 18th-cent. church with a 500-year-old tower. In the churchyard was buried the Childe of Hale, John Middleton, said to have been over 9 ft tall. There are many tales of this giant who visited the court of James I and defeated his wrestler. S. of the village is the southernmost tip of Lancashire, and E. of it a ford where Prince Rupert is said to have escaped into Cheshire after the Battle of MARSTON MOOR.

STALYBRIDGE, *Cheshire* (12–SJ9698). The name of this small manufacturing town on the River Tame probably derives from that of the Stayley or Stavelegh family, who were prominent landowners in the district from the 14th cent. The present Stayley Hall was constructed in 1580 on the site of an earlier building of 1343. It is said that

The British Tourist Authority

Speke Hall

John Wesley preached here in 1745. Stalybridge reached its full stature early in the 19th cent. as a cotton town, having been one of the first to employ steam power in the mills, but with the decline of cotton local enterprise was largely deflected into light industry. The amenities of the borough include Cheetham Park, with its colourful bird sanctuary, and the beautiful Stamford Park of 60 acres surrounding a large boating lake.

STAND, *Lancashire* (12–SD8007). The lofty Church of All Saints with its tower and pinnacles was built between 1822 and 1826 to a neo-Gothic design by Sir Charles Barry.

STANDISH, *Lancashire* (12–SD5609). The church has an imposing steeple rebuilt in 1867, which is a landmark for miles. In the churchyard to the left of the main entrance lies a boulder about 4 ft high, found buried 11 ft deep in 1895 according to its inscription, and presumably from the Ice Age. The Church of St Wilfred is a curi-osity: late Gothic (1582–4) in general form – it has Classical details. Where the nave and chancel meet are two domed turrets with stairs inside them. Of note are the roofs, font, pulpit, tombs and monuments. The rich stained glass is Victorian, and a modern vestry was added in 1913.

STOCK GHYLL, *Westmorland* (14–NY3804). Stock Ghyll Force is about 1 m. from the centre of AMBLESIDE. You leave by Stock Ghyll Road (E.) beside the River Stock and enter Stock Ghyll Park, where there is an old bobbin mill and its dam which interested Dickens. The mill obtained its timber from ample woodland in the neighbourhood. The way to the Force, which becomes audible as you approach, is along the path by the stream. Set among trees, the torrent leaps down some 75 ft. It rises in Red Screes 4 m. above the Rothay.

STOCKPORT, *Cheshire* (12–SJ8989). This county town was a market centre with its own bridge across the Mersey in the 13th cent. In the street called Great Underbank stands a timber-framed hall, believed to have been built in the late 15th cent., which was occupied for three centuries by the Arderne family who claimed kinship with Shakespeare through Mary Arden. It contains an 18th-cent. oak staircase. The house, excellently preserved, is now a branch of the District Bank. A few doors away is the White Lion, the town's oldest hostelry.

Stockport, however, is largely the product of the Industrial Revolution and the railway age. There are mills and great chimneys, and a fine 19th-cent. railway viaduct, over 100 ft high, dominates the town. The parish church, dedicated to St Mary the Virgin, is also 19th-cent., having been rebuilt in the Perpendicular and Decorated styles between 1810 and 1817, but some 14th-cent. fragments remain in the finely restored chancel. There is a modern brass here to the memory of John Wainwright, who composed the hymn "Christians Awake". The church stands at one end of the market place, believed to be the site of a 12th-cent. Norman castle built over a Roman fortification of A.D. 79. A Victorian iron-framed covered market occupies a large part of the area. On market days the stalls spread colourfully into the surrounding streets.

The town has an interesting piece of early 20th-cent. civil engineering: the Mersey is covered over here by a road built along its course.

About ½ m. from the market place, in the direction of the river, is Vernon Park Museum, beautifully situated on a high point affording fine views of the hills in the background and the river far below. In addition to its comprehensive coverage of local fauna, flora and geology, the museum is notable for an unusual window made up of some 250 pieces of fluor-spar from the Blue John Mine at CASTLETON. One room is set aside for an impressive bird collection, and another for items connected with local history, of which a particularly barbarous scold's bridle is a disconcerting example.

STYAL, *Cheshire* (12–SJ8383). A picturesque little village of Cheshire "magpie" inns, white cottages, a valley and an old mill, all now administered by the National Trust. The 18th-cent. cotton mill still stands, where the River Bollin flows swiftly through a deep wooded glen. The great mill-wheel has gone, but the original sluice and tunnel remain, with the rest of the structure, much as they would have appeared in the days when the employment of child labour was accepted as normal practice. Below the mill is Norcliffe Hall, a modern mansion built in Elizabethan style, where Audubon, the famous American naturalist, used to stay as a guest of the Greg family. He says in his reminiscences that

about here he saw the finest cattle in England. In the woods of the ravine are some very tall trees planted by Robert Hyde Greg in 1838 from cuttings taken from Wellingtonias (*Sequoiadendron giganteum*) in California. These parent trees are 3,500 years old and have attained a height of 350 ft, as one day may their offspring.

SWINTON AND PENDLEBURY, *Lancashire* (12–SD7802). These two towns have become a joint modern borough lying about 5 m. NW. of MANCHESTER. With a coal-mining background, it is an industrial area for textiles and engineering products, but the borough is also a residential district. Replanning has provided a modern town hall combined with a recently developed civic centre which includes a library and civic hall, and also shopping precincts. Pendlebury's Church of St Augustine is in brick, a Gothic masterpiece by Bodley and Garner. Nearby is Warke Dam, shared with WORSLEY.

TARLETON, *Lancashire* (12–SD4420), is a village by the River Douglas. St Mary's is an early 18th-cent. brick church; a stone turret and a cupola were added in the 19th cent. It has the square pews, original benches and clear glass windows. Carr House to the NE. near Bretherton is a 17th-cent. house formerly containing Barry Elder's Doll Museum, a collection of dolls and tapestries.

TARPORLEY, *Cheshire* (12–SJ5562). This old town with gabled houses stretches along the A51 (A49). The Church of St Helen is medieval in origin, but considerably restored so that most of it is now 19th-cent. work. It has a handsome tower, long gables and great width. Notable are the monuments to the Done family, a historic name in these parts. A large marble monument depicts Jane Done (died 1662) and her sister, Mary Crewe. Another is the tomb of Sir John Crewe. There is some colourful stained glass.

The 13th-cent. **Beeston Castle** is about 3 m. S., ruins on a steep rock that gives a magnificent view. The castle was destroyed after the Civil War. It stands in the park of Peckforton Castle, one of Salvin's best works (*see* BUNBURY).

TARVIN, *Cheshire* (12–SJ4867), is beside the A51, the Roman Watling Street, and 5½ m. E. of CHESTER. It is a small, old village that was of strategic importance in the Civil War when it was a garrison for the Parliamentary side. Where the A51 leaves for TARPORLEY stands the 14th-cent. Perpendicular Church of St Andrew. It has a square tower and the doorway is decorated with angels and the parapet with gargoyles. There are grotesque figures on the north wall. Six dormer windows light the nave and chancel, and the south aisle has a fine roof. The screen is massive.

Duddon, 2½ m. to the SE., is a tiny village, with old farm-houses and black-and-white cottages.

TATTON HALL, *Cheshire* (12–SJ7582). Although Tatton Park abuts on the north side of

KNUTSFORD, the entrance for motorists is further round the estate, by the Rostherne gates. It claims to be the most visited house owned by the National Trust. The building is of excellent proportions, exquisitely furnished and in perfect order; it also has a wide range of pictures. Tatton was built soon after the end of the 18th cent. but the architect, Samuel Wyatt, elder brother of James, died in 1807 before it was complete, and his nephew, Lewis Wyatt, took over the design. Likewise the owner, William Egerton, died before completion, and his son Wilbraham worked with the new architect. A former hall stood on the estate held by the Egertons since 1598, when Sir Thomas was prominent at the court of Elizabeth I. A later relative, Samuel Hill, an art collector, secured the apprenticeship of his nephew, Samuel Egerton, to Joseph Smith, later the consul at Venice who patronized Canaletto and shipped art works for young Englishmen making the Grand Tour. Thus it was probably Samuel Hill who commissioned the two works by Canaletto now in the drawing-room, and other Italian works no doubt arrived by arrangement with Consul Smith. One of Canaletto's two Venice scenes includes the Doge's Palace and the other the Grand Canal. The third most important painting is Van Dyck's *Martyrdom of St Stephen*, painted in Rome about 1623. Other works include those by followers or imitators of Titian, Rubens, Poussin and Jacopo Bassano, a Veronese studio work, an attribution to Domenico Tintoretto, a portrait begun by Lawrence, a Murillo and a Chardin.

There are Italian Renaissance chests, a Boulle bookcase, Chippendale ladder-back chairs, a French Boulle clock (Louis XV), Adam-style chairs, and a fine collection of china, silver and glass. The library has an impressive collection, begun in the 18th cent. on foundations laid in the 16th and 17th cents. There are important works on architecture with collections of engravings, and on travel, husbandry, horticulture and estate management, and also atlases. A table is set with fine silver and glass in the dining-room, below the large 18th-cent. cut-glass chandelier. Upstairs are the portraits of the Ten Cheshire Gentlemen (*see* PUDDINGTON). After the sumptuous bedrooms and the 17th-cent. oak staircase, the kitchens and the Tenants' Hall laid out as a museum by Maurice, the last Lord Egerton, should be seen. The last Egerton was a many-sided character, a big-game hunter, a pioneer in motor travel with his Benz of 1900 (on view), a pioneer aviator and a friend of Orville Wright. As a young man he disappeared, and was found living with a tribe in the Gobi desert; he even tried to stake gold in the Yukon.

Humphry Repton laid out the 54 acres of formal gardens and woodland. Oranges and lemons grow in the orangery and there are exotic plants. A classical temple is based on the Choragic Monument of Lysicrates in Athens. Nearby is the Japanese Garden where a Shinto temple stands on an islet in the Golden Brook. The temple is said to have come from Japan and

to have been erected by Japanese workmen. The mere, in the park of over 1,000 acres, is about a mile long and the home of many wildfowl. The grounds can accommodate huge numbers of visitors, but, if necessary, entrance to the building is regulated so that visitors can proceed at leisure. There are some catering facilities. The hall and grounds were both opened to the public only in 1962, and by 1967 the millionth visitor had passed through.

About $\frac{1}{2}$ m. N. is **Rostherne**, an attractive village which has a large mere and a church with monuments.

TEBAY, *Westmorland* (14–NY6104), is a village among high fells at the north end of the Lune Gorge, which has traces of Roman occupation. Down the gorge the River Lune flows S. on its way to the Irish Sea past CATON and LANCASTER. The impressive landscape of the gorge has been long known to travellers on the main-line railway, but now it is also the route of the M6 extension. The fells stretch E. to RAVENSTONEDALE and NW. to the SHAP Fell area.

TEMPLE SOWERBY, *Westmorland* (14–NY6127), a pleasant village SE. of PENRITH, has a village green, an old church and a four-arch bridge, and prides itself on being Queen of the Westmorland Villages. To the N. is Acorn Bank, or Temple Sowerby Manor, a red-sandstone house, mainly 18th-cent., but with some 16th-cent. work. It is National Trust property; its famous rose gardens are open to the public, but not the house.

THIRLMERE and HELVELLYN, *Cumberland* (14–NY3116). The Thirlmere of today is not the one Wordsworth knew. In the days of the Lake Poets it was a smaller area, comprising two natural lakes which were almost joined. There were about 14 farms around the Dalehead and Armboth end of the valley, often on the sites of earlier, Norse dwellings. Along the west shore was the main coach road from GRASMERE to KESWICK, and at the south end the community's centre, Wythburn. The Wordsworths often rested or met Coleridge at the village's oldest inn, the Cherry Tree, and it appears in Wordsworth's Poem, "The Waggoner". In the later 19th cent. MANCHESTER secured the water for its growing population, but only in the teeth of a raging controversy over industrial progress versus conservation. Thirlmere became a reservoir, with a dam at the N. raising the level 50 ft; Hawes How and Deergarth How became islands; all farms in the valley itself were submerged or demolished except two; and the remainder of Wythburn was cut off from the burn. The 17th-cent. church mentioned by Wordsworth survives, but not the Cherry Tree. At Thirlspot, about 3 m. N. of Wythburn and also on the east side, the Wordsworths sometimes visited the King's Head Inn, which is still there.

It was out of such controversy as that over Thirlmere that the National Trust was born. In

1895 it was founded by Miss Octavia Hill, Sir Robert Hunter, and Canon H. D. Rawnsley, the vicar of Crosthwaite (*see* Keswick) and a writer and poet. In the Trust's words: "Each had realised that the growth of population, the spread of industrialisation and a lack of planning were rapidly spoiling much of the beauty of England. To halt this uncontrolled destruction, to educate public opinion and to give people access to the countryside, they agreed to set up a body of responsible private citizens who would act as trustees for the nation in the acquisition and ownership of land and buildings worthy of permanent preservation." The Trust's first acquisition in the Lakes was Brandelhow (DERWENTWATER) in 1902; now it owns 72,884 acres in the district, 14,188 of them protected, and 14,710 sheep, all these properties being in the National Park.

Helvellyn is 3,118 ft high and the third highest Lakeland peak. It stands towards the southern end of a long series of fells that reach about 9 m. from Dollywaggon Pike on the S. to Clough Head on the N., and measure about 5 m. across their widest part. Slopes are steeper on the W. and often have spectacular crags and valleys on the E. Until the 18th cent. Helvellyn itself was believed to be the highest peak in England, but SCA FELL PIKE and Sca Fell precede it by a few score feet. Helvellyn is probably the most popular mountain for ascents in the Lakes, being within reach of various main resorts and with the A591 along its base. Two favourite routes are from Wythburn and Thirlspot; they are shorter than those from PATTERDALE or Grasmere but are fairly steep. There is some parking space at Wythburn and Thirlspot. Those climbing from the former place follow the footsteps of Wordsworth, Sir Walter Scott and Humphry Davy who went up together.

There are extensive views from various points on the top of this range, such as over Red Tarn, the famous Striding Edge, Swirrel Edge, and, in clear weather, as far as Scotland.

Dunmail Raise is on the A591, a pass just S. of Thirlmere where the road climbs up from Grasmere. It is not very steep. A cairn on the west side of the summit is alleged by tradition to be the burial place of Dunmail, King of Cumbria, who was killed here in a 10th-cent. battle with Edmund, King of the English, who gave Cumbria to Malcolm of Scotland.

THRELKELD, *Cumberland* (14–NY3225), is a small village about 4 m. to the E. of KESWICK. SADDLEBACK (Blencathra) towers above Threlkeld to the N. and the village is a centre for climbing this range. St John's Vale is S. (*see* CASTLE ROCK) and the slopes of Great Dodd, beginning of the HELVELLYN range.

TORPENHOW, *Cumberland* (14–NY2039), is E. of the A595, about 8 m. from COCKERMOUTH. St Michael's Church was built about 1170. Its Norman door, arches, chancel arch and font still remain. There is a painted deal ceiling with flowers and gilding, added in the late 17th cent. The church is unspoilt, without restorations. The site gives good views towards the Solway Firth and the beginnings of the Lake District hills.

TORVER, *Lancashire* (14–SD2894), lies on the main road, about 1 m. W. of CONISTON WATER. As it lies close to the Coniston range of peaks, the village affords excellent views of them. Walna Scar and Dow Crag are nearer summits, and further N. is the 2,633-ft Coniston Old Man. Ascents of the Old Man often start from the village. The church is 19th-cent., but one of its records, a paper of consecration signed by Cranmer in 1538, showed that there was an earlier church on the site. A curiosity is a chest made from a hollowed-out single log, and there is an ancient font. On the slopes of Bleaberry Haws, to the W., are lines of ancient fortifications. At **Lowick Bridge**, S. beyond the lake, Arthur Ransome lived at Lowick Hall; some think that the setting of his children's book *Swallows and Amazons* was based on WINDERMERE.

TROUTBECK, *Westmorland* (14–NY4103). This is a wild and beautiful valley, with a stream and a village of the same name. The beck flows down from the mountainous area E. of the KIRKSTONE PASS into WINDERMERE, and the main road for ULLSWATER climbs up to the pass from the A591, N. of WINDERMERE TOWN. A tradition of the ancient village is that it once had a race of giants or strong men. Townend is National Trust property and open to the public. Its house, built about 1626, was the home of a yeoman family, the Brownes, who lived there for three centuries. Their furniture and possessions, and carved woodwork, are preserved. The house stands in 776 acres of farmland, at the south end of the village.

TURTON TOWER, *Lancashire* (12–SD7315). The house is 4½ m. N. of BOLTON, near Turton village, and its history goes back some 800 years. There are three sections of the building: the peel-tower itself, the east wing (with the present entrance hall and flanking rooms), and the north-east wing. The tower itself was probably begun in the 12th cent. as a simple defensive structure, with a vault below to house cattle. In the 15th cent., windows, instead of mere slits, were made in the three lower stories, and the present top story was added in the late 16th cent. The east wing was built in the early 16th cent., two stories high; another story, with heavy mullioned windows, the entrance hall and the adjoining rooms were added to it in about 1596. The north-east wing is also early 16th-cent., but its north and east sides, and third story were built in 1844 in the Jacobean style. Much of the gabling is also 19th-cent.

The manor of Turton belonged in the 12th cent. to Roger Fitz-Robert and to Henry, Duke of Lancaster. The Orrell family had the house in the 16th cent., and in the 17th cent. it was acquired by Humphrey Chetham (founder of the Chetham Library, MANCHESTER). In the 19th cent. it passed to James Kay who saved the building by carrying out restoration work, though not always in keeping with its character. Until this time, it was probably the north-east wing, and not the tower itself, that was used as a residence. Turton Tower was sold in 1903 to the Knowles family, who gave it to Turton Urban District Council in 1930.

The stone walls behind the panels in the dining-room are probably original 12th-cent., and the upper lights of the large window have early 17th-cent. Swiss glass. The morning-room is mainly early 16th-cent. The drawing-room of 1596 is now the council chamber of Turton Council. The grandfather clock may have been made by Samuel Crompton (*see* HALL I' TH' WOOD). Among the interesting items to be seen are the arms and armour in the entrance hall, cradles, old furniture (including Early English inlaid work) and paintings in the Ashworth Room, and a carved oak tester bed in the Bradshaw Room. The Chetham Room (1596) has old furnishings, arms, fire-place and kitchen implements, and a candelabra made from stags' horns. The house, which is unusually well documented and has housed a folk museum in the upper story since 1952, is well worth visiting. It is open to the public at advertised times.

ULLSWATER, *Cumberland* (14–NY4220). There are four main routes to this lake: from the S. via the KIRKSTONE PASS, from the N. by leaving the A66 at TROUTBECK station, and from the E. either from PENRITH or via POOLEY BRIDGE. Between the Troutbeck and Penrith routes are several smaller roads; but the north and south approaches are the only roads in their areas. The Kirkstone road is the A592, a main north and south through road for the Lakes. It gives magnificent views over PATTERDALE, but probably the best way to see the lake itself is to approach from its lower, Pooley Bridge and Penrith end, where the River Eamont runs out. The Cumberland and Westmorland border runs through Ullswater, but the A592 goes along the Cumberland side, the NW. There is a road from Pooley Bridge part way along the other side but it ends in the Martindale area, and the circuit of the lake can be completed only on foot. Ullswater is over 7 m. long and second in size only to WINDERMERE.

Gowbarrow Park, 4 or 5 m. from the east end of the lake and beside the A592, should be seen in spring for its daffodils immortalized by Wordsworth. He knew this area well: "List, ye who pass by Lyulph's Tower", he wrote at the beginning of *The Somnambulist*, and also refers to Aira Force, the fine waterfall away from the road, on Aira Beck. Lyulph, or L'Ulf, is said to have been the baron or chieftain who built a tower on this site (the present tower is modern), and Ullswater may be derived from his name. The National Trust owns most of this area, as well as some land at the head of the lake on the east side of Stybarrow Dodd, one of the peaks of the range of HELVELLYN mountains. Wordsworth climbed Helvellyn from the west side with Scott and Humphry Davy in 1805. There are paths up this range from the

Ullswater side, including Striding Edge, which juts out towards the lake. GRISEDALE comes down between this range and St Sunday Crag, 2,756 ft, which is SW. of the lake; a path goes up Grisedale to Dollywaggon Pike. **Glenridding** is a hamlet by the lake, N. of Grisedale. Opposite across the head of the lake is Place Fell, over 2,000 ft.

This stretch of the water is one of three which mark Ullswater's length, and their changes of direction alter the view considerably as you proceed. E. of Place Fell and the Martindale area the High Street range, with its highest peak well to the S., slants northward towards the Pooley Bridge end of the lake. All these lofty peaks ranging round the south, west, and east areas of Ullswater make an impressive background to the quiet lake scene. In summer there is a regular service of motor vessels along the lake between Pooley Bridge and Glenridding, passing, towards the south end, the island of House Holme that is associated with legends of King Arthur. The full trip, either way, takes about an hour, and is, especially for drivers, a relaxing means of seeing the lake. Boats can also be hired.

ULVERSTON, *Lancashire* (12–SD2878), is a market town for the district, and lies between green fells and the sea. The lighthouse on The Hoad is a monument to Sir John Barrow (1764–1848, founder of the Royal Geographical Society), and Barrow Sound is named after him. Swarthmoor Hall was the home of Margaret Fell. She was the wife of Judge Fell (died 1658) and was converted to the Quaker faith by George Fox, its founder. Margaret Fell opened her house to the Society of Friends' preachers, became one of their leaders, and was imprisoned after her husband's death. She married George Fox in 1669 and died in 1702. She is buried nearby at **Sunbrick**, together with some 200 other Friends. The Quaker Meeting House at Rake Head was given by George Fox. St Mary's Church is supposed to have been founded in 1111 but has been much rebuilt since. The Norman doorway is the oldest part, but has a modern porch. The tower was built in Tudor times. **Bardsea** is a village on the coast road 3 m. from Ulverston; a lane leads up to the Stone Circle on Birkrigg Common, where Bronze Age implements were found. **Colton** is a tiny village N. of Ulverston. Its church has a bell more than 500 years old and a silver paten dated 1671. Below the church is the holy well of St Cuthbert where this 7th-cent. missionary is said to have won converts and baptized children.

UPHOLLAND, *Lancashire* (12–SD5105). The Church of St Thomas in this small town occupies a high site at the top of a curve of the main road. The tower is square and squat, but the 14th-cent. church is fairly massive as it incorporates the remains of an earlier Benedictine priory. The priory chancel, with soaring arcades and arch, became the nave. The colourful stained glass came from the priory.

UTKINTON, *Cheshire* (12–SJ5564). This small

Noel Habgood

The Vale of Newlands

village is near the road that rises through a cut in the rock NE. of TARPORLEY. Utkinton Hall, now a farm-house, was formerly the seat of the Dones, a family that had branches in other parts of Cheshire – the Dones of Flaxyards, of Crowton, of Duddon and of Oulton. The Utkinton Dones were Chief Foresters for the king at Delamere Forest in the days when the sovereign visited VALE ROYAL for hunting. The last of the male line was Sir John Done who was knighted by James I. Family monuments can be seen in St Helen's Church, Tarporley.

VALE OF NEWLANDS, *Cumberland* (14–NY2422). From the KESWICK side the approach is via Portinscale or BRAITHWAITE up to the tiny village of Stair. This faces S. up Newlands Valley proper, down which the Newlands Beck runs from Dale Head, a peak 2,473 ft high. The valley is roughly parallel with DERWENTWATER but ends a good deal further S. For motorists, however, the route runs SW. from Stair over the 5-m.-long **Newlands Pass** (1,096 ft) leading via Keskadale to BUTTERMERE VILLAGE. For about 4 m. the pass is a reasonably steady ascent to its top, with craggy heights all around, but once beyond that the driver faces a descent of about 700 ft in 1 m. to Buttermere.

VALE ROYAL, *Cheshire* (12–SJ6369). Vale Royal of England was the old name for the area,

and Vale Royal is the great hall that stands there in the heart of Cheshire, not far from the Delamere Forest. The estate is SW. of NORTHWICH, and the easiest way to reach it is to turn S. from the A533 near its junction with the A556. The drive from the road leads under a lofty archway of trees through beautiful parkland to the hall which stands near the River Weaver. It is strange to think that in this quiet spot there was once a huge Cistercian abbey, of which Edward I laid the foundation stone in 1277. The traces of the foundations remaining after its destruction in the Dissolution indicate a larger size even than FOUNTAINS ABBEY. The hall stands on the site. Its old wing was built by the Holcrofts in the 16th cent. and the Cholmondeleys of CHOLMONDELEY made alterations at various times. James I stayed at Vale Royal to hunt in Delamere Forest with John Done of UTKINTON, whom he knighted. The hall has had various owners in recent years.

WALLASEY, *Cheshire* (12–SJ2992), is a county borough in the north-east corner of the Wirral peninsula, of which NEW BRIGHTON forms a part. The ferry crosses from LIVERPOOL to Wallasey in 7 minutes. As well as being a holiday resort Wallasey is a residential area. Wallasey beach overlooks the Irish Sea and from New Brighton along the King's Parade promenade is a pleasant walk. Wide stretches of sand continue to the borough boundary at HOYLAKE. These are used for motor-cycle races in spring and autumn. Wallasey offers yacht sailing, the Derby and Guinea Gap bathing pools and an 18-hole miniature golf course. With the sandhills and Moreton Common, the beach provides nearly 3 m. of unspoilt coastline.

Leasowe is an area of natural sandhills W. along the coast. The castle here was built in 1593 by Ferdinando, 5th Earl of Derby, a member of the Stanley family of KNOWSLEY HALL and patron of Shakespeare and actors. The castle was apparently a summer residence, and probably it was also a convenient spot on the way to the Stanley family estates in the Isle of Man. The castle became known as Mockbeggar Hall when it fell into ruin during the vicissitudes of the Stanleys after the Civil War (the 7th Earl was executed by Cromwell and the family lost much of its estates). More recently it became a convalescent home.

WARBURTON, *Cheshire* (12–SJ7089). The main attraction of this 700-year-old village on the banks of the MANCHESTER Ship Canal is the old church built on the site of an earlier one founded by the daughter of Alfred the Great. The timber-framed structure, common to many churches in 14th-cent. Cheshire, was considerably renovated with brick and stone some 300 years later and remains today a building of oddity and charm. The beams and rafters of the roof interior are said to be secured with deer horns and the pillars of the nave are of time-hardened oak as enduring as stone. The brick tower is curiously placed in the E., and the north wall is wooden with wattle-and-daub plasterwork. In the village a fine yew tree and the old stocks lend extra interest to the medieval character of the area.

WARRINGTON, *Lancashire* (12–SJ6088), is a town with locks on the MANCHESTER Ship Canal. It is an industrial town, in which clock-making has played a part, and is a gateway to Cheshire. Nearby, the Romans had a ford across the Mersey at Latchford. Warrington was the scene of many battles from Roman times until 1648, when Cromwell entered after his victory at PRESTON. His statue stands near the bridge. The town was the first in the country to have a public library supported from the rates (1848). St Elphin's Church has a large 19th-cent. spire and a 14th-cent. chancel. Memorials include those of the Botelers and the Pattens. Holy Trinity is a fine church of the 18th cent. probably built to the designs of James Gibbs, the architect of Bank Hall (1750), the seat of the Patten family and since 1872 the Town Hall. The municipal museum and art gallery is in Bold Street. Museum collections include natural history and anthropology. The gallery has English watercolours and glass.

To the SW., across the border into Cheshire, towns such as **Runcorn, Halton** and **Frodsham** are not without their own charm and are situated in attractive landscape, though the New Town at Runcorn is destroying some pleasant scenery.

WARTON, *Lancashire* (12–SD4972). The Church of St Oswald or Holy Trinity is 15th-cent. and has been restored. On the tower are the arms of the Washington family (ancestors of George Washington) who lived in the area for many generations. Thomas, last of the Washingtons of Warton, was parson at the church, 1799–1823. To the NW. is **Silverdale**, where the National Trust owns many acres that give a panorama of MORECAMBE Bay. This village has associations with Mrs Gaskell, who lived at a house where she was often visited by Charlotte Brontë. W. Riley, author of the *Windyridge* novels, also lived in the village.

WASTWATER and WASDALE, *Cumberland* (14–NY1505). Wastwater is the deepest English lake, reaching nearly 260 ft in places, and is also the most rugged and spectacular in setting. It is about 3 m. long, but narrow. The Screes, a forbidding wall of rubble, line the steep drop along most of its south-east side. Motorists can reach the lake only from the W., and can follow the north-west side as far as a parking place in Wasdale (or Wastdale), the nearest point accessible by car to the majestic SCA FELL peaks which, at over 3,000 ft, wall in the Sty Head Pass against GREAT GABLE on the N. The pass winds at 1,600 ft like a rock ladder between the eastern ramparts of Wasdale. SE. is Esk Hause, the great crossroads for climbers from Wasdale, from BORROWDALE, from ESKDALE and from LANGDALE. Motorists should follow at least part of the lakeside road on foot fully to appreciate the stern beauty of the scenery. The north-west wall of the valley begins with smaller hills but mounts to Yewbarrow and Kirk Fell, both over 2,000 ft, before Great Gable.

Wasdale Head is a hamlet where many climbers stay; some of the graves in its churchyard are those of climbers who have died in the fells.

WATENDLATH, *Cumberland* (14–NY2716), is sometimes grouped with BORROWDALE, but is more an offshoot to the E., quiet, remote, and one that has been called a secret valley. It is a place of great charm, deserving the regard in which it is held, and is easily reached from DERWENTWATER. The route leaves the road going S. on the east side of the lake and goes uphill to **Ashness Bridge**, also a notable Lakeland scene. There is a narrow old packhorse bridge over the beck, where the bend and the width can easily be miscalculated. Higher up a good view of the lake can be had, and from High Crag, higher still, an impressive sight of the lake landing stage far below. Next is Shepherd's Crag, but this has to be climbed on foot to see the view.

Watendlath itself is a hamlet, its houses built and roofed with stone. The entire hamlet, except for one dwelling house, is fortunately protected by the National Trust which also owns the tarn and the surrounding land. Thus the character of the place is preserved as it ought to be. This is *Rogue Herries* country, for Hugh Walpole laid the scenes of these novels in the countryside round Borrowdale and KESWICK. Watendlath

T. Parker

Wastwater and Wasdale seen from Great Gable

itself is introduced into *Judith Paris*.

The tarn is fed from Blea Tarn higher up, in the slopes of Ullscarf. Where the Watendlath tarn flows out, it forms the curious Churn, or the Devil's Punch Bowl. The peak on the E. of the valley is High Seat, 1,996 ft high.

WEST KIRBY, *Cheshire* (12–SJ2181). This residential and seaside resort adjoins HOYLAKE to the N., but enjoys a more sheltered climate because of its site just inside the Dee estuary, with the ridge of the Grange and Caldy hills behind it on the E. It was one of the oldest places of settlement in the Wirral peninsula, and was granted a charter by the Conqueror although its history pre-dates his period. There is a marine lake of over 30 acres, and pleasant beaches.

There are three areas of National Trust property in the vicinity: Caldy Hill, 1 m. SE., Harrock Wood, E. of Irby, and Thurstaston Common, 2 m. SE. of West Kirby. Caldy and Thurstaston give fine views over the Dee estuary. The road from West Kirby climbs steadily up to the plateau of Thurstaston Common, where you can park in pleasant picnic areas.

WETHERAL, *Cumberland* (14–NY4654). A Benedictine priory was founded in Wetheral, which is about 5 m. E. of CARLISLE, but only the 15th-cent. gatehouse remains. Near the river are caves said to have been the cell of St Constantine.

The Gothic Church of the Holy Trinity is 15th-cent., but has undergone considerable alteration. Apart from the stained glass, the most interesting feature is a large monument by Joseph Nollekens, 1789, to Lady Maria Howard of Corby. The figure of Religion points to heaven beside a young woman with a baby.

Corby Castle, built mainly in the 17th cent., stands by the River Eden. The grounds (open to the public) were laid out by Thomas Howard before 1740.

WHALLEY, *Lancashire* (12–SD7335). Whalley is an interesting village on the River Calder, about 12 m. ENE. of PRESTON on the A59. The Ancient Monument of Whalley Abbey (open to the public) is the ruin of a Cistercian house that was partly rebuilt. The monks who founded it came from Cheshire in the 13th cent. Among notable features of the remains are the north-east and north-west gateways, the chapter house, the abbot's lodging and the kitchen. Parts of the structure were made into a residence for the Assheton family in the late 17th cent.

The parish church, St Mary's, is mainly 13th-cent., with a 15th-cent. tower and clerestory. There are very fine wood carvings, including the stalls. The screened pews are 17th- and 18th-cent. work. An organ of 1729 came from LANCASTER parish church.

The village is associated with the witches of Pendle, whose misfortunes are described in Harrison Ainsworth's *Lancashire Witches*. Roger Nowell, a magistrate, and member of the Read Hall family, began enquiries into witchcraft that

Barnaby/Mustograph

Wigan pier

led to a group of unfortunate women being tried at Lancaster in 1612; most were executed. Nowell quarrelled with the Whalley church authorities over a specially large pew he wanted to install to emphasize his importance. There was a comic impasse when the church would not admit it and Nowell would not withdraw it; the pew ended in a barn and it was 70 years before it was finally put into the church.

WHINLATTER PASS, *Cumberland* (14–NY 1924), is, at its highest point, 1,043 ft high. It is the best road for driving over any of the Lakeland passes as its bends are not excessively sharp. From KESWICK you take the road round the north end of the lake through the little village of Portinscale, and then the B5292 through BRAITH-WAITE. The road climbs soon after that affording views of SKIDDAW and BASSENTHWAITE below. The peak of Whinlatter lies N. (1,696 ft) and Grisedale Pike to the S. (2,593 ft). At the other end of the steep-sided pass the road descends into the Vale of Lorton and goes NW. to COCKERMOUTH. After High Lorton one can turn S. and return to Keswick via CRUMMOCK WATER, BUTTERMERE, HONISTER PASS and BORROWDALE.

WHITEHAVEN, *Cumberland* (14–NX9718). This was previously a hamlet, but in 1690 Sir John Lowther began the work that eventually transformed it into a seaport and coal-mining town. Its development was fostered by Sir James Lowther (1736–1802), the 1st Earl of Lonsdale, who built Whitehaven Castle (now a hospital) in 1769. The Friends' Meeting House, the lighthouse, the new quay, and St James's Church were built in the 18th cent. There are also Georgian houses in Lowther Street. Whitehaven is now an industrial area but can be used as a centre for visiting the western lakes and is the nearest important town to ENNERDALE.

Paul Jones attacked Whitehaven in 1788 and a German U-boat shelled it in 1915.

WIGAN, *Lancashire* (12–SD5805), is sometimes dismissed as an industrial town of little interest, with memories of *The Road to Wigan Pier*. The pier was so named from the wharf made on the canal cut in the 18th cent., one of many linking Lancashire towns for the transport of goods. The first industries were pewter, brass, bell-founding, clock-making, cotton, coal-mining, iron and clothing; now Wigan relies more on things like light engineering, plastics, coach-building and container-making. But Wigan is also a historic town, with names of Norse, Celtic and Saxon origin, and relics of Roman occupation. It had a charter as far back as 1246 and its coat of arms is unusual for the privilege of bearing royal symbols. Wigan was Royalist in the Civil War and James Stanley, 7th Earl of Derby, was routed there (*see* ORMSKIRK and KNOWSLEY HALL). He was later executed at BOLTON. In Wigan Lane is the monument marking the spot where the earl's general, Tyldesley, was killed.

Haigh Hall (open to the public), about 1½ m. NE. of Wigan, is the former house of the Earls of Crawford, a family who collected thousands of books and manuscripts. With the plantations of over 200 acres, the hall and grounds were acquired from the Earl of Crawford by the corporation in 1947 at a generously low price. It houses a local history museum, containing archaeological and industrial exhibits, and certain rooms are used for exhibitions. Wigan's library has a Public Record Office with 60,000 MSS. of archives for the area. There is also a Little Theatre, a Historic and Antiquarian Society and several organizations catering for music and drama. The Parish Church of All Saints is Gothic in style, largely rebuilt. An inscription on the churchyard wall is dated 1683. Among monuments is that to Sir William Bradshaigh and his wife. According to legend she believed her husband dead after several years of his absence, and married a Welsh knight; on his return she walked barefoot in penance once weekly for a year from Haigh to Mab's Cross (in Standishgate). It was in Wigan that William Hesketh Lever (of Bolton and PORT SUNLIGHT) began making soap in 1886.

WILMSLOW, *Cheshire* (12–SJ8580). Here is a small town which is outwardly a modern shopping-centre and also a dormitory area for MANCHESTER, but behind the appearance of modernity there is much that connects Wilmslow with the past. Intolerance of one kind or another was a characteristic of Cheshire people for centuries and the Quaker Meeting House in the town was often the scene in the 17th cent. of cruel persecutions against a sect which refused to conform to the established church. Wilmslow is also the town of Samuel Finney, the portrait painter who became a special favourite of Queen Caroline. In his *Historical Survey of the Parish of Wilmslow* he railed against the drunkenness and disorder which was prevalent there in the 18th cent. Later, when he became a magistrate, he put down hooliganism with such firmness that Wilmslow has wryly claimed a reputation for respectability ever since.

An object of really unusual interest to visitors is the green-and-white gypsy caravan at Parkway, which is carefully preserved as a memorial to the celebrated naturalist and broadcaster "Romany of the B.B.C.", in private life the Rev. G. Bramwell Evans, who spent the last years of his life here.

Wilmslow lies in a deep valley of the Bollin river which has its source near Shuttlings Low and flows through some 20 m. of extremely beautiful country before eventually finding its way into the Mersey near Heatley. On the banks of the river is Wilmslow church with its fine tower and sombre walls dating mainly from the 16th cent., as does the splendid oak roof of the chancel. Under two arches are monuments to Humphrey Newton and his wife, which have been here for 400 years, and the brass in front of the altar, a memorial to Robert Booth of Dunham and his lady, is the oldest in Cheshire.

WINDERMERE, *Westmorland* (14–SD3995). This is the largest lake in England. It covers 10½ m. from N. to S., and in that distance its surroundings change in character from the milder countryside at the south end, to the mountainous scenery at the north where the lake reaches almost to AMBLESIDE. But it is not really a mountain lake, having no high peaks rising beside it. The shores are thickly wooded, so that when driving round Windermere, you often have only restricted views of the water from the road.

Ambleside was on the route of the Roman road from Ravenglass and HARDKNOTT to PENRITH, and the Roman fort of Galava stood between Ambleside and the lake. Roman remains have also been found on Belle Isle. Norsemen settled here in the 10th cent. Windermere was a forest belonging to the lords of KENDAL in the 11th cent. and was included in the manor of Strickland Ketel, which changed hands at various times: like other parts of the North of England, it was held by the Scots at one period. In the reign of Henry II it passed to the Lancasters, and in the 13th cent. a Lancaster nephew founded a hermitage on the island of Ladyholme. Belle Isle became the home of the Philipson family and one of them was besieged there by the Roundheads. From far back in history Windermere has been constantly used by boats of various kinds, serving as a water highway for the transport of goods to the lakeside communities.

Since the 19th cent. Windermere has become noted for its sailing clubs and its yacht racing; it is the country's greatest inland water centre for sailing and boating. A wide variety of craft can be hired, from rowing boats to cabin cruisers with sleeping accommodation. The lake has the headquarters of the Royal Windermere Yacht Club at BOWNESS Bay, the South Windermere Sailing Club at Fell Foot, and the Windermere Motor Boat Club at Broad Leys. In summer the passenger vessels ply from end to end of the lake. There is a public pier for visiting vessels at

Louis and Daphne Peel

Windermere from Ambleside at sunset

Bowness Bay and similar ones at Parsonage Bay and Waterhead. At the height of the season there can be as many as 1,500 boats using the lake, besides the increasing number of underwater swimmers. It became necessary to make a code of conduct if all users of the lake were to enjoy its facilities with safety, and a Collision Rules Order was established. This is outlined in the Council's booklet, *Chart of Lake Windermere*, containing information for all who use the lake. A chart shows the position of rocks and shallow areas, fairway markers, submarine contours and so on. The booklet gives information on angling, swimming and yachting. Lake Wardens patrol the lake during the season in a motor launch, specially equipped for emergencies, which keeps in touch with a police patrol boat by radio. Observance of the lake rules is compulsory.

The passenger vessels are a traditional means of transport for holidaymakers arriving from WINDERMERE TOWN railway station: the boats take them either to the Ambleside end of the lake for bus services to KESWICK, or to Lake Side for services to ULVERSTON. But a trip on one of these boats – or a craft from the various boating companies – is an admirable way of seeing the lake. The passenger boats take 1¼ hours to cover the length of the lake, including the busy stop at Bowness; S. of here there is also a ferry across the lake, for HAWKSHEAD and CONISTON.

Pony-trekking is an enjoyable activity in the countryside, and at Windermere it is organized by the Central Council of Physical Recreation (Storrs Hall).

The widest view around the lake is from Orrest Head, on the N. of Windermere town, where there is a chart to indicate the peaks. Across the lake, beyond the woods of Claife Heights, is Coniston Old Man, and N. of it are Carrs and Wetherlam with the DUDDON VALLEY hidden behind them.

Then there are Crinkle Crags with Pike of Blisco in front and SCA FELL behind, BOW FELL, GREAT GABLE, and the LANGDALE PIKES. The view N. shows the TROUTBECK valley and High Street, and SE. are the Ingleborough moors in Yorkshire. The National Trust owns various properties around the lake, including Claife, Cockshott Point, Ladyholme island, and Queen Adelaide's Hill. Cockshott and Adelaide are among vantage points for views.

WINDERMERE (TOWN), *Westmorland* (14–SD4198). The town's rise to importance dates from the introduction of the railway in 1847; before that it was merely a village called Birthwaite. The town is now administered jointly with BOWNESS, which is on the lakeside. The word Windermere used alone really denotes the lake. The railway meant an influx of holidaymakers to one of the few points in the LAKE DISTRICT that could be reached by rail. The station is linked to Bowness by a bus service so that passengers can use the summer motor-vessel services to both ends of the lake, and from these travel to other parts of Lakeland. Thus the town is largely a modern development in its present form; but various old Westmorland families have been prominent in the area for centuries, and as far back as the 11th cent. the lake was part of a manor called Strickland Ketel, which later passed through various hands in the barony of KENDAL or Kentdale.

The town is one of England's most important holiday centres and is easily accessible from the M6. It lies on the A591, between Kendal to the SE. and AMBLESIDE, GRASMERE and KESWICK to the N. It offers a wide range of accommodation, from first-class hotels to quiet guest-houses and caravan sites; it has garages and boat-builders. In or near the town are ample facilities for golf, tennis, fishing, water-skiing, pony-trekking, and every form of water sport. Sheepdog trials are held on Applethwaite Common, to the N., in August.

Orrest Head is a well-known vantage point on the north side with an extensive view of Lakeland peaks (*see* previous entry). Other views can be had from Queen Adelaide's Hill, National Trust property, 1 m. W. of Windermere station.

WINSFORD, *Cheshire* (12–SJ6565). This is a small industrial region comprising the townships of Over, Swanlow, and Wharton, all of which are linked by a modern bridge across the River Weaver. The whole of the area is utilized for the production of salt and chemicals and this largely determines its appearance. Winsford has a fine grammar school, founded in the last century by Sir Joseph Verdin, but its main function, apart from industry, is as a dormitory for LIVERPOOL and MANCHESTER. The urban district of Over is the reputed birthplace of Robert Nixon, "the Cheshire Prophet", an illiterate ploughboy whose predictions were to earn him a place in Cheshire folklore. The square-towered Church of St Chad, about 1 m. from the town, was rebuilt in 1543, restored in 1870, and considerably altered since.

WINWICK, *Lancashire* (12–SJ6094). This little village with the Church of St Oswald lies between WARRINGTON and M6. As evidence of a long history it contains an inscription which records the attachment to this church of Oswald, King of Northumbria, who died fighting against the pagan King Penda of Mercia. Centuries later the Royalists were defeated here in two engagements of the Civil War in 1643 and 1648. Presumably there was an earlier church on this site as St Oswald's is partly 14th-cent. Two chantry chapels have memorials to the Legh and Gerard families. A. W. N. Pugin designed the chancel, 1847–8. The churchyard has part of a fine large wheel cross, possibly of Anglo-Saxon workmanship.

WITHERSLACK, *Westmorland* (14–SD4384). St Paul's Church, NW. of the A590, has a restrained Classical interior with four pillars and 17th-cent. woodwork. It was endowed and built by John Barwick, who became Dean of ST PAUL'S, in 1664–9. There were alterations in the 18th cent.

WOODPLUMPTON, *Lancashire* (12–SD 4934), is the birthplace of Henry Foster, the 19th-cent. navigator, who was drowned in the Gulf of Mexico in 1831. The Church of St Anne has a memorial to him. A low building in warm-coloured stone, St Anne's has a belfry with an octagonal dome. It is 15th-cent., apparently re-erected in 1630, and with further rebuilding work in 1748. There are three aisles under separate roofs, and interesting stained glass.

WORKINGTON, *Cumberland* (14–NX9928), was Gabrosentum in Roman times and the site of a fort. Anglian invaders settled at some stage of the Anglo-Saxon conquest. In the 9th cent. the Lindisfarne monks, fleeing from the Danes on the north-east coast of England tried to sail for Ireland from Workington, and the Lindisfarne Gospels (BRITISH MUSEUM) were washed overboard. The Curwen family, claiming descent from Malcolm II of Scotland and Ethelred the Unready, built Workington Hall (not in use now) in the 14th cent. Mary Queen of Scots spent a night there in 1568 after fleeing from the battle of Langside. The Helena Thompson Museum exhibits costumes, ceramics, glass and local objects. There is a civic theatre. St Michael's Church, largely rebuilt in 1887 after a fire, is late Decorated Gothic. Cross fragments indicate use of the site from the 8th cent. St John's (1823) has a Classical exterior, a replica of St Paul's, COVENT GARDEN. Sir Ninian Comper designed the painted interior with its golden columns in 1931. The town's main industry is steel.

WORSLEY, *Lancashire* (12–SD7400), lies between the MANCHESTER Ship Canal and BOLTON. Several old houses have been demolished but Worsley Old Hall, former seat of the Earl of Ellesmere which is now offices, and the 16th-cent. Wardley Hall remain. Sir Geoffrey de Massey of Worsley was the founder of the Trinity Chapel in St Mary's Church at ECCLES in 1454. Worsley was a centre for coal-mining in the time of the ironworks of James Nasmyth of Eccles, and the Duke of Bridgewater built the canal in 1759–65 to take coal from his mines at Worsley to Manchester. A Tudor-style building, the Aviary, is modern. The golf club at Monton Green has an 18-hole course of 6,429 yds founded in 1894. A pleasant spot is Warke Dam, shared with SWINTON AND PENDLEBURY.

WRENBURY, *Cheshire* (12–SJ5947). St Margaret's Church is early 16th-cent. Its pleasant renovated interior has a west gallery and box pews, and monuments include one to Sir Stapleton Cotton, one of Wellington's generals. **Combermere Abbey**, S. of Wrenbury, stands in a large park with a mere and was the former home of the Cotton family. **Audlem**, SE. of Wrenbury, has a number of timbered buildings. The Gothic church has a handsome oak ceiling.

WRYNOSE PASS, *Westmorland* (14–NY 2602–3105). Its eastern ascent is in Westmorland, but the descent at the south-west end is just on the Lancashire side of the River Duddon, which to the SW. marks the border with Cumberland (*see* DUDDON VALLEY). Near the top of the pass Three Shires Stone marks the junction of the three counties. The pass reaches 1,270 ft, and can be approached only from the E. (GRASMERE or AMBLESIDE areas) or from the W. (up the Duddon valley or the notorious HARDKNOTT PASS). Wrynose has gradients of up to 1 in 4 on its narrow road, which, though surfaced, must be treated with caution. There are wide sweeps of moorland on each side, with the Pike of Blisco (2,304 ft) to the N. and the beginning of the CONISTON range to the S. – a wild, lonely area.

A Brief Bibliography

GUIDE BOOKS

In the space available it is impossible to list under each area the many admirable local guide books or studies of special areas that are available. Booksellers mostly stock such standard series as Methuen's Little Guides, Benn's Blue Guides, Robert Hale's County Books, and Arthur Mee's The King's England (Hodder & Stoughton). A series of great value and authority as regards architecture, listing as it does the more important buildings of each parish, is Sir Nikolaus Pevsner's *Buildings of England*, of which some 36 volumes have been published so far by Penguin. The Shell County Guides so far published (Faber) are:

Cornwall: *John Betjeman*   Derbyshire: *Christopher Hobhouse*
Devon: *Brian Watson*   Dorset: *Michael Pitt-Rivers*
Essex: *Norman Scarfe*   Gloucestershire: *Anthony West, David Verey*
Herefordshire: *David Verey*   Isle of Wight: *J. Pennethorne Hughes*
Leicestershire: *W. G. Hoskins*   Lincolnshire: *Henry Thorold, Jack Yates*
Norfolk: *Wilhelmine Harrod, The Rev. C. L. S. Linnell*
Northamptonshire: *J. Smith*   Northumberland: *Thomas Sharp*
Oxfordshire: *John Piper*   Rutland: *W. G. Hoskins*
Shropshire: *John Piper, John Betjeman*
Somerset: *C. H. B. & Peter Quennell*   Suffolk: *Norman Scarfe*
Wiltshire: *David Verey*   Worcestershire: *J. Lees-Milne*

The following is a short list of books for further reading on the subjects of the introductory chapters.

THE BEGINNINGS

ATKINSON, R. J. C. *Stonehenge*. Hamish Hamilton, 1956
CLARK, Grahame. *Prehistoric England*. Batsford, 1962
CLARKE, Rainbird. *East Anglia*. Ancient People and Places Series, Thames & Hudson, 1960
FOX, Aileen. *South-West England*. Ancient People and Places Series, Thames & Hudson, 1964
GRINSELL, L. V. *Ancient Burial Mounds of England*. Methuen, 1956
HAWKES, Jacquetta. *Guide to the Prehistoric and Roman Monuments of England and Wales*. Chatto & Windus, revised edition, 1954
HAWKES, Jacquetta. *A Land*. Chatto & Windus, 1951
STONE, J. F. S. *Wessex*. Ancient People and Places Series, Thames & Hudson, 1958
THOMAS, Nicolas. *A Guide to Prehistoric England*. Batsford, 1960

THE AGRICULTURAL HERITAGE

ERNLE, Lord. *English Farming, Past and Present* (ed. Fussell and
O. R. Macgregor). Cassell, 6th edition, 1961
FUSSELL, G. E. *Farming Technique from prehistoric to modern times.*
Commonwealth Library, Pergamon Press, 1966
HARTLEY, Dorothy. *The Countryman's England.* Batsford, 1935
HOSKINS, W. G. *The Making of the English Landscape.* Hodder &
Stoughton, 1955
STAMP, L. Dudley. *Britain's Structure and Scenery.* Collins, 1946
STAMP, L. Dudley. *Types of Farming Map of England and Wales.*
Ministry of Agriculture, 1941 etc.

TREES AND WOODLANDS

BRIMBLE, L. J. F. *Trees in Britain.* Macmillan, 1946
EDLIN, H. L. *Know Your Broadleaves.* Forestry Commission, 1968
EDLIN, H. L. *Know Your Conifers.* Forestry Commission, 1966
EVELYN, John. *Sylva.* Various publishers
HADFIELD, Miles. *British Trees.* A Guide for Everyman, Dent, 1957
HADFIELD, Miles. *Landscape with Trees.* Country Life, 1967
MAKINS, F. K. *The Identification of Trees and Shrubs.* Dent, 1948
RODGERS, J. *The English Woodland.* Batsford, 1942
STROUD, Dorothy. *Capability Brown.* Country Life, 1950
TANSLEY, A. F. revised by M. C. F. Porter. *Britain's Green Mantle.*
Allen & Unwin, 1968
WOOD, R. F. and ANDERSON, I.A. *Forestry and the British Scene.*
Forestry Commission, 1968

THE VILLAGE

FINBERG, J. *Exploring Villages.* Routledge, 1958
HOSKINS, W. G. *The Making of the English Landscape.* Hodder &
Stoughton, 1955
MUNRO CANTLEY, H. *Suffolk Churches and their Treasure.* Batsford, 1937
'MISS READ'. *Village School.* Michael Joseph, 1955
The Legacy of England (anthology). Batsford, 1935

THE TOWN

DALE, A. *The History and Architecture of Brighton.* Bredon &
Heginbotham, 1950
DYOS, H. J. *Victorian Suburb.* Leicester University Press, 1961
ISON, W. *The Georgian Buildings of Bath.* Faber, 1948
ISON, W. *The Georgian Buildings of Bristol.* Faber, 1952
LITTLE, B. *The Buildings of Bath.* Collins, 1947
SUMMERSON, Sir John. *Georgian London.* Pelican, revised edition, 1962

THE COUNTRY HOUSE

DUTTON, Ralph. *The English Country House*. Batsford, 1950
HILL, Oliver, and CORNFORTH, John. *The English Country House: Caroline, 1625–85*. Country Life, 1966
HUSSEY, Christopher. *The English Country House: Early Georgian, 1715–60*. Country Life, 1955
HUSSEY, Christopher. *The English Country House: Mid-Georgian, 1760–1800*. Country Life, 1956
HUSSEY, Christopher. *The English Country House: Late Georgian, 1800–40*. Country Life, 1958
LEES-MILNE, James. *The English Country House: Baroque, 1685–1714*. Country Life, 1970
LLOYD, Nathaniel. *A History of the English House*. Architectural Press, 1949
SUMMERSON, Sir John. *Architecture in Britain, 1530–1830*. Penguin, 1953
WOOD, Margaret. *The English Mediaeval House*. Phoenix House, 1965
Historic Houses, Castles and Gardens in Great Britain and Ireland: Published annually by Index Publishers, giving days and times of opening throughout the year
The National Trust's List of Properties. Published biennially, free to members

CATHEDRALS AND CHURCHES

BATSFORD, H. and FRY, T. *The Cathedrals of England*. Batsford, 1936
BATSFORD, H. and FRY, T. *The Greater English Church*. Batsford, 1940
BETJEMAN, John (editor). *Guide to English Parish Churches* (2 vols). Collins, 1958
BETJEMAN, John and CLARKE, B. *English Churches*. Studio Vista, 1964
BOND, F. *Introduction to English Church Architecture* (2 vols). Humphrey Milford, 1913
COOK, G. H. *The English Cathedral through the Centuries*. Phoenix House, 1957
COOK, G. H. *English Collegiate Churches of the Middle Ages*. Phoenix House, 1959
COOK, G. H. *The English Medieval Parish Church*. Phoenix House, 1954
COX, J. C. and FORD, C. B. *Parish Churches*. Batsford, 1961
CROSSLEY, F. *English Church Craftsmanship*. Batsford, 1941
CROSSLEY, F. *English Church Monuments*. Batsford, 1920
ESDAILE, Katherine. *English Church Monuments, 1510–1840*. Batsford, 1946
HARVEY, John. *The English Cathedral*. Batsford, new edition, 1961
HUTTON, Graham and SMITH, Edwin. *English Parish Churches*. Thames & Hudson, 1952
PEVSNER, N. *Buildings of England series*. Penguin Books, 1951–
WHIFFEN, Marcus. *Stuart and Georgian Churches*. Batsford, 1947–8

FOLLIES

JONES, Barbara. *Follies and Grottoes*. Constable, 1953
MACAULAY, Rose. *Pleasure of Ruins*. Weidenfeld & Nicolson, 1953

THE INDUSTRIAL HERITAGE

BARTON, D. B. *The Cornish Beam Engine.* D. Bradford Barton, 1965
HADFIELD, E. C. R. *British Canals.* David & Charles, 1962
KLINGENDER, F. D. *Art and the Industrial Revolution,* second edition
edited by Sir Arthur Elton. Evelyn, Adams & Mackay, 1968
RICHARDS, J. M. and DE MARE, Eric. *The Functional Tradition.*
Architectural Press, 1958
ROLT, L. T. C. *Victorian Engineering.* Allen Lane, the Penguin Press,
1970
SIMMONS, Jack. *The Railways of Britain.* Routledge, 1965
There are also two series of books on Britain's Industrial Archaeology.
One is published by David & Charles and volumes covering the
following districts are currently available: Bristol Region, Dartmoor,
Derbyshire, East Midlands, Hertfordshire, Lake Counties, Lancashire,
Scotland, Southern England, The Tamar Valley. The series published
by the Longman Group is on a subject basis and the four following
titles have been published so far: *Navigable Waterways, Roads and
Vehicles, Iron and Steel, The Textile Industry.*

MOUNTAIN, HILL AND MOORLAND

BLACKSHAW, A. *Mountaineering.* Kaye & Ward, 1968
BYNE, Eric and SUTTON, G. *High Peak: the story of walking and
climbing in the Peak.* Secker & Warburg, 1966
CLARK, R. C. and PYATT, E. C. *Mountaineering in Britain: a history from
earliest times to the present day.* Phoenix House, 1957
CROSSING, W. *Guide to Dartmoor.* Macdonald, 1965
EDWARDS, K. C. *The Peak District.* Collins, 1962
HARVEY, L. A. and ST LEGER GORDON, D. *Dartmoor.* Collins, 1953
MARRIOTT, M. *The Shell Book of the Pennine Way.* Queen Anne Press,
1968
NATIONAL PARKS COMMISSION and DARTMOOR NATIONAL PARK
COMMITTEE. *Dartmoor.* H.M.S.O., 1957
NATIONAL PARKS COMMISSION. *North York Moors.* H.M.S.O., 1966
P.P.P.B. *Peak District.* Bakewell P.P.P.B., 1960
PEARSALL, W. H. *Mountains and Moorlands.* Collins, 1950
PEEL, J. H. B. *Along the Pennine Way.* Cassell, 1969
POUCHER, W. A. *The Lakeland Peaks.* Constable, 2nd edition, 1962
PYATT, E. C. *A Climber in the West Country.* David & Charles, 1968
PYATT, E. C. *Mountains of Britain.* Batsford, 1966
PYATT, E. C. *Where to Climb in the British Isles.* Faber, 1960
UNSWORTH, W. *The English Outcrops.* Gollancz, 1964
WAINWRIGHT, A. *Pennine Way Companion.* Kendal, Westmorland
Gazette

SEASCAPE

ADDISON, W. *Thames Estuary.* Hale, 1954
ADLARD COLES, K. *Creeks and Harbours of the Solent.* E. Arnold, 1959
ADMIRALTY, Hydrographic Department. *North Sea Pilot, Channel Pilot,
Bristol Channel Pilot, Northern Irish Sea Pilot.* H.M.S.O.

ARNOTT, W. G. *Alde Estuary*. Norman Adlard, 1954. Also *Suffolk Estuary* and *Orwell-Estuary*

BELLOC, Hilaire. *The Cruise of the Nona*. Constable, 1925

BENHAM, Hervey. *The Last Stronghold of Sail*. Harrap, 1949

DAVIES, G. M. *The Dorset Coast*. Black, 1956

JESSUP, R. F. and F. W. *The Cinque Ports*. Batsford, new edition, 1956

PHILLIPS-BIRT, Douglas. *Waters of Wight*. Cassell, 1967

POOLEY, D. J. *West Country Rivers*. Yachting Monthly, 1957

WENTWORTH DAY, James. *Coastal Adventure*. Harrap, 1949

STEERS, J. A. *The Coastline of England and Wales*. Cambridge University Press, 1946

RIVERS

CHALMERS, Patrick R. *The Angler's England*. Seeley Service, 1938

COOTE, J. H. *East Coast Rivers*. Yachting Monthly, 1956

GIBBINGS, Robert. *Sweet Thames Run Softly*. Dent, 1940

GIBBINGS, Robert. *Coming Down the Wye*. Dent, 1942

GIBBINGS, Robert. *Till I End my Song*. (The Thames) Dent, 1957

GOODSALL, R. H. *The Medway and its Tributaries*. Constable, 1955

HILLS, J. W. *A Summer on the Test*. Bles, 1946

WATERS, Brian. *Severn Tide*. Dent, new edition, 1963

WENTWORTH DAY, James. *A History of the Fens*. Harrap, 1954

PLUNKET-GREENE, H. *Where the Bright Waters Meet*. Witherby, new edition, 1969

WILLIAMSON, Henry. *A Clear Water Stream*. Faber, 1958

THE ENGLISH GARDEN

CLARK, H. F. *The English Landscape Garden*. Cresset, 1949

FAIRBROTHER, Nan. *Men and Gardens*. Hogarth Press, 1956

HADFIELD, Miles. *A History of British Gardening*. Revised edition, Spring Books, 1969

HUNT, Peter (editor). *The Shell Garden Book*. Phoenix House and Rainbird, 1964

HYAMS, Edward. *The English Garden*. Thames & Hudson, 1964

TAYLOR, Geoffrey. *The Victorian Flower Garden*. Skeffington, 1952

An essential guide to the larger gardens, including many National Trust properties, is *Historic Houses, Castles and Gardens in Great Britain and Ireland*. For gardens open for charity, see *Gardens of England and Wales Open to the Public Under the National Gardens Scheme*, obtainable from 57 Lower Belgrave Street, London S.W.1, and *Gardens to Visit*, from Mrs K. Collett, White Witches, Claygate Road, Dorking, Surrey.

Index

This provides an index to all the places mentioned in the Gazetteers, either as main entries or as sub-entries. In cases where these places are also referred to in the Introductory Essays, these page references are printed in italic type. When more than one place of the same name is referred to, the names of the counties in which the places lie have been added.

Maps

Legend

═══	Motorways	Buxton	Gazetteer entry
▭▭▭▭	(Under construction)	●	Place of interest
━━━	Trunk roads	■	Building of interest
───	Main roads	○	Town or Village
───	Selected 'B' roads	– – –	County Boundaries

Scale

```
0        10        20        30        40        50 Miles
0    10    20    30    40    50    60    70    80 Kilometres
```

Map Pages

Key to Counties and sections

South-East
1 Kent
2 Sussex
3 Surrey

South Country
4 Berkshire
5 Hampshire
6 Wiltshire
7 Dorset

West Country
8 Somerset
9 Devon
10 Cornwall

East Anglia
11 Essex
12 Suffolk
13 Norfolk
14 Cambridgeshire

South-East Midlands
15 Hertfordshire
16 Buckinghamshire
17 Bedfordshire
18 Huntingdonshire
19 Northamptonshire

West Midlands
20 Oxfordshire
21 Warwickshire
22 Gloucestershire
23 Herefordshire
24 Worcestershire

North Midlands
25 Shropshire
26 Staffordshire
27 Derbyshire
28 Leicestershire
29 Rutland
30 Nottinghamshire
31 Lincolnshire

Yorkshire
32a North Riding
32b East Riding
32c West Riding

North-East
33 Durham
34 Northumberland

North-West
35 Cheshire
36 Lancashire
37 Westmorland
38 Cumberland

2

SR

SR

SW

SR
SW

SW

LUNDY

BARNSTAPLE

HARTLAND POINT

Hartland
Morwenstowe
Kilkhampton
Stratton
Holsworthy

Penfound
Manor

Boscastle
Tintagel
Delabole
St Clether
Launceston
Port Isaac
Altarnun
St Endellion
St Kew
Padstow
BODMIN MOOR
St Merryn
Wadebridge
Blisland
BEDRUTHAN STEPS
St Mawgan-in-Pydar
Bodmin
St Neot
St Cleer
St Columb
Major
Landydrock
House
Liskeard
Newquay
C O R N W A L L
St Cubert
Roche
Lostwithiel
St Keyne
St Germans
LUXULYAN
VALLEY
Lerryn
Perranporth
Lanteglos-
by-Fowey
TREVAUNANCE
COVE
St Austell
Looe
Fowey
Polperro
Probus
Truro
St Michael
Penkevil
Mevagissey
Redruth
Veryan
St Ives
Camborne
ROSELAND
Zennor
St Just-in-Roseland
Chysauster
St Mawes
St Just
in Penwith
Lanyon Quoit
Penzance
Godolphin House
Falmouth
Newlyn
ST
MICHAELS
MOUNT
Breage
Glendurgan
Gardens
Mousehole
Helston
St Antony in Meneage
Helford
LAND'S END
Porthcurno
Gunwalloe
GOONHILLY
DOWNS
Mullion
Coverack
KYNANCE COVE
LIZARD POINT

Clovell